The People's Chronology

The People's Chronology

A Year-by-Year Record of Human Events from Prehistory to the Present

edited by

James Trager

Holt, Rinehart and Winston
New York

Copyright © 1979 by James Trager

Published by Holt, Rinehart and Winston, 383 Madison Avenue, New York, New York 10017.

Published simultaneously in Canada by Holt, Rinehart and Winston of Canada, Limited.

Library of Congress Cataloging in Publication Data

Trager, James.
The people's chronology.

Includes index.
1. Chronology, Historical. I. Title.
D11.T83   902'.02   78-23808
ISBN 0-03-017811-8

First Edition

Editorial and Production Services: Cobb/Dunlop Publisher Services, Inc.

Printed in the United States of America

10 9 8 7 6 5 4 3 2 1

Text Credits

Excerpts from *Rudyard Kipling's Verse,* copyright 1940, Doubleday & Co. Reprinted by permission of Doubleday & Co., Inc. Excerpt from *Salt Water Ballads* by John Masefield, copyright 1913, The Macmillan Co. Reprinted by permission of Macmillan Publishing Co., Inc. Lines from "When I Was One-and-Twenty" from "A Shropshire Lad" —Authorised Edition—excerpted from *The Collected Poems of A. E. Housman.* Copyright 1939, 1940, © 1965 by Holt, Rinehart and Winston. Copyright © 1967, 1968 by Robert E. Symons. Reprinted by permission of Holt, Rinehart and Winston, Publishers. Excerpts from *Collected Poems* by Edna St. Vincent Millay, Harper & Row. Copyright 1922, 1923, 1950, 1951 by Edna St. Vincent Millay and Norma Millay Ellis. Reprinted by permission of Mrs. Ellis. Excerpt from *Poems* by Alan Seeger, copyright 1917. Reprinted by permission of Charles Scribner's Sons. Lines from "The Soldier" excerpted from *The Collected Poems of Rupert Brooke,* copyright 1941. Reprinted by permission of Dodd, Mead & Co. Excerpt from *Chicago Poems* by Carl Sandburg reprinted by permission of Harcourt Brace Jovanovich, Inc. Excerpts from *The Poetry of Robert Frost* edited by Edward Connery Lathem. Copyright 1923, 1930, 1939, © 1969 by Holt, Rinehart and Winston. Copyright 1951, © 1958 by Robert Frost. Copyright © 1967 by Lesley Frost Ballantine. Reprinted by permission of Holt, Rinehart and Winston, Publishers. Excerpts from *The Portable Dorothy Parker,* copyright 1973. Reprinted by permission of Viking Penguin, Inc. Excerpt from *Animal Farm* by George Orwell, copyright 1946. Reprinted by permission of Harcourt Brace Jovanovich, Inc. Excerpt from *1984* by George Orwell, copyright 1949. Reprinted by permission of Harcourt Brace Jovanovich, Inc. Lines from "The Hollow Men" excerpted from *Collected Poems 1909–1962* by T. S. Eliot, and excerpts from *Murder in the Cathedral* by T. S. Eliot reprinted by permission of Harcourt Brace Jovanovich, Inc. Excerpt from *The Poems of Dylan Thomas.* Copyright 1952 by Dylan Thomas. Reprinted by permission of New Directions. Excerpt from "Letter from Paris" by Janet Flanner in the February 4, 1950 issue of *The New Yorker.* Reprinted by permission of *The New Yorker.* Excerpt from *Catch 22,* copyright 1955, 1961 by Joseph Heller. Reprinted by permission of Simon & Schuster, a Division of Gulf & Western Corporation. Excerpt from *On the Road* by Jack Kerouac, copyright 1957. Reprinted by permission of Viking Penguin, Inc.

Picture Credits

Acknowledgments

The editor would like to express his gratitude to Chie Nishio, Jay J. Smith, and Sally Smith for their help in developing the graphic symbols, to Marie Claire Ged and George M. Overholser for computerizing the index, to Jerome D. Greene for his supportive kindnesses, to Lila Gardner of Cobb/Dunlop Publisher Services, Inc. for her many helpful suggestions and to Ellyn Polshek of Holt, Rinehart and Winston for her courage, her patience, and her encouragement.

Preface

A newspaper editor surveys the events of a single day, headlining the events that seem most important. This book examines the years of our past, taking each year as the newsman takes a single day but viewing it with the benefit of hindsight.

Hindsight makes it clear that some events which never made the front page proved more significant than those which did.

History is too often written by ground rules similar to those that bound Greek drama, highlighting only what affected the rich and well-born, treating as comic relief what befell the common man. Social studies have tended, as a result, to be anti-social studies. Of swords instead of plowshares. Yet no strategem of a Metternich, no ploy of a Clemenceau ever touched the lives of so many people as did, say, the discovery of the potato by an obscure conquistador in South America.

The People's Chronology does include major happenings of national and international political history, but it also attempts to give appropriate prominence to such historic developments as canned food, the steam engine, smallpox vaccine, the railroad, the sewing machine, electric lighting, x-rays, the motorcar, Einstein's theory of relativity, the airplane, antibiotics, television, and the Pill.

The religious-philosophical ethic of more than two milennia have discouraged interest in the mundane matters of farming, food, disease, commerce, and population growth, yet these are what often have shaped the events emphasized in conventional history books. The world's population has quadrupled within the lifespan of many who are still alive. Humanity's continuation as steward of the earth now depends in large measure on our ability to restrain the human capacity for violence and to control human proliferation. The mushrooming of population is tracked as a continuing leitmotif in *The People's Chronology*.

The purpose and ambition of *The People's Chronology* is to make the past more accessible, to bring some sense of progress, some order of events to the very human milestones of human experience. And to let the achievements of farmers, scientists, explorers, architects, and composers interact contrapuntally with those of industrialists, poets, economists, artists, novelists, athletes, and statesmen. With some room for what the newspaper editor calls "human interest."

Presenting the material chronologically has certain advantages. It helps demonstrate that knowledge grows incrementally, that one advance leads to another, that most innovations of value come from people who have built on work done by people of years or generations past. A chronology also helps to show interrelationships (often obscured in conventional histories) between political, economic, scientific, and social facets of life.

The obvious hazard of a chronology is that it may dissolve into a welter of unrelated facts and events. *The People's Chronology* has an alphabetical index and it employs two devices to avoid chaos. One, referent dates help the reader or researcher relate a given event to a preceding or subsequent event. The parenthetical reference alerts the reader to a related entry. Two, appropriate graphic symbols aid the reader in following a subject or in retrieving a piece of information. Entries are grouped by category instead of being organized vertically according to national or geographic locus, and the graphic symbols serve as guideposts to the categories. A key to the symbols may be found on page ix.

Any work of this scope is certain to contain some errors. Space limitations account for most of the sins of omission. As for the other kind, the editor of these annals has taken infinite pains to avoid them but accepts sole responsibility for any that may occur. He will make every effort to correct them in future editions.

George Santayana's timeworn remark, "Those who cannot remember the past are condemned to repeat it," is in many ways more appropriate to the history of science, medicine, technology, and human rights than to the passing military and political struggles that generally dominate history books. Political history is important, but it has often been merely incidental to the flow of events that have given the modern world its shape and its problems, events logged in the pages that follow.

James Trager

Key to Symbols

political events

exploration, colonization

economics, finance, retailing

human rights, social justice

science

technology

energy

transportation

medicine

religion

education

communications, media

literature, publishing

art

photography

theater

music

sports

everyday life

tobacco

crime

architecture

environment

agriculture

marine resources

food availability

nutrition

consumer protection

food and drink

population

PREHISTORY

3 million B.C. An upright-walking australopithecine ape-man appears on the earth in the late Pliocene period and has thumb-opposed hands in place of forefeet, permitting him and his female counterpart to use tools. (Fossil remains found by Carl Johanson in Ethiopia's Awash Valley, A.D. 1974; further finds in A.D. 1975.)

1.75 million B.C. Anthropoids use patterned tools (Oldowan choppers) (*see* Leakey, A.D. 1959).

1 million B.C. Australopithecine ape-man becomes extinct as the human species becomes more developed. *Homo erectus erectus* is unique among primates in having a high proportion of meat relative to plant foods in his diet, but like other primates he is omnivorous, a scavenger who competes with hyenas and other scavengers while eluding leopards (*see* 1959).

400,000 to 360,000 B.C. *Homo erectus hominid* of the Middle Pleistocene period (Peking man) may use fire to cook venison, which supplements his diet of berries, roots, nuts, acorns, legumes, and grains. By conserving his energies, he can track down swifter but less intelligent animals (but he still splits bones to get at the marrow because he does not use fire effectively to make the marrow easily available) (*see* Black, A.D. 1927).

120,000 to 75,000 B.C. Neanderthal man of the Upper Pleistocene period has large front teeth, which he may use as tools. Less than half of his surviving infants reach age 20, 9 out of 10 of these die before age 40 (*see* A.D. 1856).

75,000 B.C. Neanderthal man has become a skilled hunter, able to bring down large, hairy elephantlike mammals (*Mammuthus primiginius*), saber-toothed tigers, and other creatures that will become extinct.

Neanderthal man cares for his sick and aged but engages in cannibalism when necessary.

50,000 B.C. Date palms flourish in parts of Africa and Asia where they will become an important food source.

Neanderthal man may be on the west coast of the Western Hemisphere and may even have reached the continent 20,000 years earlier (as determined by racemization tests that record the extent to which molecules of aspartic acid in a specimen have altered in their fifiguration from the form that occurs in living bone to its mirror image; such tests will be conducted in the A.D. 1970s on bones found between A.D. 1920 and A.D. 1935, but the rate of change is affected by such factors as temperature, so the tests will not be conclusive).

42,000 B.C. The continent that will be called Australia is populated by the earth's first seafaring people. Colonists arrive from the Asian mainland.

38,000 B.C. *Homo sapiens* emerges from Neanderthal man and, while physically less powerful, has a more prominent chin, a much larger brain volume, and superior intelligence. *Homo sapiens* will split into six major divisions, or stocks—Negroids, Mongoloids, Caucasoids, Australoids, Amerindians, and Polynesians, and some of these will have subdivisions (Caucasoids, for example, will include Alpine, Mediterranean, and Nordic stocks).

His control of fire, his development of new, lightweight bone and horn tools, weapons, and fishhooks, and his superior intelligence permit man to obtain food more easily and to preserve it longer. Hunters provide early tribes with meat from bison and tigers, while other tribespeople fish and collect honey, fruits, and nuts (as shown by cave paintings near Aurignac in southern France).

Increased availability of food will lead to an increase in human populations.

36,000 B.C. *Homo sapiens* reaches the northern continent of the Western Hemisphere, where Neanderthal man has probably preceded him.

33,000 B.C. *Homo sapiens* becomes the dominant species on earth with no serious rivals to his supremacy.

28,500 B.C. The island that will be called New Guinea is populated by colonists who arrive either from Australia or from the Asian mainland (*see* 42,000 B.C.).

27,000 B.C. The islands that will be called Japan are reached by *Homo sapiens* who may have arrived in the islands as much as 5,000 years ago over ice sheets or land bridges (*see* 660 B.C.).

25,000 B.C. Fishermen in Europe's Dordogne Valley have developed short baited toggles that become wedged at an angle in fishes' jaws when the line, made of plant fibers, is pulled taut.

Small pits lined with hot embers or pebbles preheated in fires are used by *Homo sapiens* for cooking food that may be covered with layers of leaves or wrapped in seaweed to prevent scorching.

13,600 B.C. A Great Flood inundates much of the world following a sudden 130-foot rise in sea levels as a result of runoff from a rapid melting of a glacial ice sheet covering much of the northern continent of the Western Hemisphere (time is approximate and somewhat conjectural).

12,000 B.C. The dog is domesticated from the Asian wolf and is used for tracking game. (Fossil remains found in a cave near Kirkuk in Iraq in the A.D. 1950s will be dated in the 1970s by fluorine analysis.)

11,000 B.C. Vast fields of wild grain appear in parts of the Near East as the glaciers begin to retreat.

10,500 B.C. Human habitations appear even at the southernmost parts of the Western Hemisphere, where cavemen pursue guanaco and hunt a horse species that will become extinct. (Fossil evidence found 1,200 miles south of Buenos Aires in the A.D. 1970s.)

10,000 B.C. Goats are domesticated by Near Eastern hunter-gatherer tribespeople who have earlier domesticated the dog.

Homo sapiens increases in number to roughly 3 million.

9000 B.C. The New Stone Age begins in Egypt and Mesopotamia.

8500 B.C. Goats milk becomes a food source in the Near East, where goats have been domesticated for the past 1,500 years (as determined by carbon 14 radioactivity decay studies on fossil evidence found at Asiab, Iran) (*see* Libby, A.D. 1947).

8000 B.C. Agriculture begins at the end of the Pleistocene era in the Near East. Women use digging sticks to plant the seeds of wild grasses.

Europe's final postglacial climatic improvements begin. They will produce a movement of people to the north of the continent, where the settlers will eat fish caught in nets of hair, thongs, and twisted fiber, along with shellfish, goose, and honey.

Earth's human population soars to 5.3 million, up from 3 million in 10,000 B.C., as agriculture provides a more reliable food source. Where it has taken 5,000 acres to support each member of a hunter-forager society, the same amount of land can feed 5,000 to 6,000 people in an agricultural society.

7700 B.C. Desert predominates over fertile lands in the arc extending from the head of the Persian Gulf through the Tigris-Euphrates Basin to the eastern Mediterranean and then south to the Nile Valley. Men and animals are crowded in oases in the region that will be called the "Fertile Crescent" by U.S. archaeologist James Henry Breasted (A.D. 1865–1935).

Ewes' milk becomes a food source and supplements goats' milk and mothers' milk as lamb and mutton begin to play a large role in human diets in the Near East, where sheep are domesticated. (Sheep remains that vastly outnumber goat remains will be found at Asiab in Iran, and a large majority of the sheep remains will be from yearlings, good archaeological evidence that sheep have been domesticated.)

7300 B.C. Dogs are domesticated by tribes in the British Isles. (Evidence from carbon 14 bone studies of fossil remains found at Star Carr in Yorkshire).

7200 B.C. Sheep are domesticated in Greece (Argissa-Magula) (*see* 7700 B.C.).

Populations in the Middle East will increase in the next two millennia, and more permanent camps will be established by people who have lived until now in small groups that shifted camps every 3 or 4 months. Seed collecting will become more important to the food supply.

7000 B.C. Emmer wheat (*Triticum dicoccum*), domesticated from the wild *Triticum dicoccoides,* grows in the Kurdistan area lying between what will be southeastern Turkey and northwestern Iran.

Barley (*Hordeum spontaneum*), millet (*Panicum miliaceum*), and certain legumes, including lentils, are cultivated in Thessaly, where the Greeks may also have domesticated dogs and pigs (based on evidence found in excavations at Argissa-Magula). (Domestication of swine has been delayed by the need of pigs for shade from the sun and by the fact that they cannot be milked, cannot digest grass, leaves, or straw, and must therefore be given food that man himself can eat—acorns, nuts, cooked grain, or meat scraps.)

Glaciers recede in the northern continent of the Western Hemisphere.

Greek seafarers sail to the Aegean island of Milos, 75 miles from the mainland, to obtain obsidian.

Fish too large to be caught from shore are caught at sea by Greek fishermen.

The Jordanian town of Jericho, 840 feet above sea level, has a population of some 2,500, attracted by the area's perennial spring. The city will soon be walled to protect it from attack.

6800 B.C. The Kurdistan village of Jarmo is founded with some 30 dwellings that cover 3 acres and house 200 people. It is one of the first permanent agricultural settlements (*see* A.D. 1948).

6500 B.C. The wheel will be invented sometime in the next two centuries by Sumerians in the Tigris-Euphrates Basin and will radically change transportation, travel, warfare, and industry. Other parts of the world, including the Western Hemisphere, will never develop the wheel on their own and will not enjoy its benefits until it is introduced by foreigners.

The wheel (above) will not only speed transportation but will also facilitate construction and will lead to many technological advances.

The aurochs, ancestor of domestic cattle, will be domesticated in the next two centuries if it has not been domesticated earlier (Obre I, Yugoslavia). The fierce beast will be the last major food animal to be tamed for use as a source of milk, meat, power, and leather.

6000 B.C. Village farmers begin to replace food-gathering tribespeople in much of Greece (*see* 7000 B.C.).

Inhabitants of the Swiss lake regions have domesticated dogs and plow oxen.

Swiss lake dwellers (above) collect wild flax (*Linum usitatissimum*) or cultivate it and use its strong fibers to make lines and nets for fishing (and for animal traps and ropes and cords for building construction and navigational purposes).

 Swiss lake dwellers (above) make bread of crushed cereal grains and keep dried apples and legumes (including peas) in the houses they build on stilts. (Evidence from excavated remains of the houses and their contents.)

The first true pottery evolves and makes possible new forms of cookery (although food has earlier been boiled in gourds, shells, and skin-lined pits into which hot stones were dropped).

5508 B.C. Year of Creation that will be adopted in 7th century A.D. Constantinople and that will be used in the Eastern Orthodox Church and used secularly in Russia until early in the 18th century A.D.

5500 B.C. Copper smelted from malachite (copper carbonate) by artisans in Persia produces the first metal that can be drawn, molded, and shaped, but the metal is too soft to hold an edge (*see* bronze, 3600 B.C.).

5490 B.C. Year of Creation as it will be reckoned by early Syrian Christians.

5000 B.C. Villages begin to cluster together in the Fertile Crescent, but a common need for water sometimes leads to savage warfare.

Domesticated cattle are common in the valleys of the Tigris and Euphrates Rivers, and villagers often cooperate to build primitive irrigation canals and ditches.

Lands bordering the Nile River begin to dry out. The Egyptians build dikes and canals for irrigation and start to develop a civilization in North Africa.

Agricultural peoples inhabit the plains of southeastern Europe.

Corn (maize) and common beans grow under cultivation in the Western Hemisphere.

4350 B.C. Domesticated horses provide parts of Europe with a new source of power for transportation and agriculture. (Evidence from Derivka in the Ukraine) (*see* 3400 B.C.; work collar, 10th century A.D.).

4004 B.C. October 23: date of Creation as it will be reckoned by Irish theologian James Ussher in A.D. 1650.

4000 B.C. Peoples of the Indus Valley raise wheat, barley, peas, sesame seeds, mangoes, and dates on irrigated fields, but the large fields of grain encourage a multiplication of insects, and the stores of dry grain bring an explosion in rodent populations. Asses, horses, buffalo, camels, and cattle are bred for meat and for use as draft animals. Bananas, lemons, limes, and oranges are cultivated as are grapes for wine, which

The wheel devised by the Sumerians was slow to reach Egypt. Meanwhile, rich Egyptians rode in slave-borne palanquins.

is also made from flowers. (Evidence from excavations at Mohenjo-Daro beginning in A.D. 1922 and at Harappa 300 miles away beginning in A.D. 1945.)

The world's population reaches roughly 85 million.

3760 B.C. Year of Creation as it will be reckoned in the Hebrew calendar that will be used from the 15th century A.D. (*see* Judaism, 1700 B.C.).

3641 B.C. February 10: date of Creation as it will be reckoned by Mayan calendars in the Western Hemisphere.

3600 B.C. Bronze made by southwest Asian artisans is the first metal hard enough to hold an edge. Copper is alloyed with tin, which is even softer than copper, but the combination (5 to 20 percent tin) creates a metal with many more practical uses than copper (*see* 5500 B.C.; iron, 2500 B.C.).

3500 B.C. The Sumerian society that marks the beginning of human civilization develops in the valleys of the Tigris and Euphrates Rivers, where annual floods deposit fresh layers of fertile silt. Agricultural tribespeople settle in communities and evolve an administrative system governed by priests.

Animal-drawn wheeled vehicles and oar-powered ships are developed by the Sumerians (above; *also see* 2500 B.C.; wheel, 6500 B.C.).

Bronze enables the Sumerians (above) to make objects that were impossible to make with softer, less fusible copper (*see* 3600 B.C.; iron, 2500 B.C.).

A written cuneiform alphabet developed by the Sumerians (above) facilitates communication (*see* 2500 B.C.).

The Sumerians (above) harness domestic animals to plows, drain marshlands, irrigate desert lands, and extend areas of permanent cultivation. By reducing slightly the number of people required to raise food, they permit a few people to become priests, artisans, scholars, and merchants.

ANTIQUITY

3400 B.C. Egypt's 1st Dynasty (Thinite dynasty) unites northern and southern kingdoms under the pharoah Menes, who has founded a city that will be called Memphis.

3000 B.C. *Gilgamesh* in Sumerian cuneiform is the first known written legend and tells of a great flood in which man was saved by building an ark (*see* 13,600 B.C.; Smith, A.D. 1872).

Cotton fabric is woven in the Indus Valley (*see* 4000 B.C.; A.D. 1225).

The Sahara Desert has its beginnings in North Africa, where overworking of the soil and overgrazing are in some places exhausting the land in a region that is largely green with crops and trees (*see* Lhote, A.D. 1956).

Potatoes are cultivated in the Andes Mountains of the Western Hemisphere (*see* A.D. 1530).

Dolphins are killed in the Euxine Sea (Black Sea), but in some parts of the world the dolphin is considered sacred and is left unmolested.

Sumerian foods mentioned in *Gilgamesh* (above) include caper buds, wild cucumbers, ripe figs, grapes, several edible leaves and stems, honey, meat seasoned with herbs, and bread—a kind of pancake made of barley flour mixed with sesame seed flour and onions.

The world's population reaches 100 million.

2980 B.C. Egypt's 3rd Dynasty is founded by the pharoah Zoser (Tosorthros), who will rule for 30 years with help from his counselor-physician Imhotep.

Imhotep (above) will make the first efforts to find medical as well as religious methods for treating disease.

The pyramid of Zoser that Imhotep will erect at Sakkara (Step Pyramid) will be the world's first large stone structure, a tomb copied in stonework from earlier brickwork piles.

2920 B.C. The Egyptian pharaoh Snefru (or Snofru) develops copper mines in Sinai, increases sea trade by using large ships, and raises his country to new heights of prosperity. He is the last pharaoh of the Memphite 3rd Dynasty.

The two pyramids of Dahshur that will memorialize the pharaoh Snefru (above) will each rise more than 310 feet and will commemorate a reign that has vanquished the Nubians and Libyans and has seen the development of a sea trade in cedar with Byblos.

2900 B.C. Egypt's 4th Dynasty is founded by the pharoah Cheops (Khufu), who will reign for 23 years. (Dates for all early pharaohs are approximate and controversial.)

The Great Pyramid of Cheops at Giza will by some accounts be the work of 4,000 stonemasons and as many as 100,000 laborers working under conditions of forced servitude and given rations consisting in large part of onions and garlic. Rising to a height of 481.14 feet and covering upwards of 13 acres, the Great Pyramid will contain stones weighing as much as 5 tons, each of which will be moved into place with primitive equipment and put together with virtually no space between them. (Variance from absolute accuracy of the work is so small that the four sides of the base have a mean error of only 0.6 inches in length and 12 inches in angle from a perfect square.)

2850 B.C. The Egyptian pharaoh Khafra (Khafre, or Chephren) rules as the third king of the 4th Dynasty.

The Great Sphinx carved from rock at Giza by order of the pharaoh Khafre (above) is a wingless symbol of the god Harmachis in whose image the 189-foot-long monument is fashioned.

The pharaoh Khafre (above) erects a second pyramid at Giza.

2800 B.C. The yang and yin philosophy of nature originated by the legendary Chinese emperor Fu Hsi says that health and tranquility require perfect equilibrium—a harmonious relationship among the five elements (wood, fire, earth, metal, and water), which correspond to the five planets, the five seasons, and the five colors, sounds, senses, viscera, and tastes. The yang (male element) is always dominant, says Fu Hsi.

A third pyramid erected at Giza by Egypt's 4th Dynasty (Memphite) pharaoh Menkure is the smallest but most perfect of the pyramids at Giza. Menkure's reign marks the beginning of his dynasty's decline.

The sickle invented by Sumerian farmers of the Tigris and Euphrates Valleys is a curved instrument of wood or horn fitted with flint teeth. It will remain the predominant tool for harvesting grain until it is superseded by tools with tempered metal blades.

2750 B.C. Tyre is founded by mariners on the east coast of the Mediterranean and begins its rise as a great Phoenician seapower. (The Greek historian Herodotus will say in 450 B.C. that Tyre was founded "2,300 years ago.")

2700 B.C. Principles of herbal medicine and acupuncture originated by the legendary Chinese emperor Shen Nung are based, in part, on the basic principles of yang and yin proposed a century ago by Fu Hsi. The body has 12 canals related to vital organs, says Shen Nung. They circulate the two principles of yang and yin; puncturing the canals with small needles permits the escape of bad secretions or obstructions and restores the body's overall equilibrium.

The "Divine Husbandman" Shen Nung (above) orders Chinese government clerks to classify plants in terms of both food and medicinal value. The clerks list barley, millet, rice, soybeans, and wheat as the five principal and sacred crops.

2600 B.C. Oxen harnessed to plows in the Near East make it possible to plow deeper and to keep the soil productive longer.

Annual Nile floods permit the Egyptian peasant to produce enough barley and Emmer wheat to feed three with the surplus going to the builders of flood control projects, public buildings, and pyramid tombs.

The Egyptians preserve fish and poultry by sun-drying.

2595 B.C. *Nei Ching* by the legendary Chinese emperor Huang Ti is the most ancient of medical texts. Chinese medicine will contribute to the pharmacopoeia such substances as camphor, chaumoogra, ephedrine, opium, and sodium sulfate.

2500 B.C. The Iron Age dawns in the Middle East where artisans produce a new metal much harder than the bronze used since 3600 B.C. The men use temperatures of 1500°C, much higher than the heats needed to smelt copper, but the new metal will not come into wide use for another 1,000 years.

Egypt and Mesopotamia are well into the Bronze Age that began in 3600 B.C., but central Europe and the British Isles are only entering the Stone Age that began in 9000 B.C.

The Sumerians develop a cuneiform script alphabet of some 600 simplified signs. They have earlier developed a written language using thousands of picture-signs, or ideograms, as in the Gilgamesh legend of 3000 B.C., and the new alphabet is based on those ideograms (*see* 1300 B.C.; Grotefend, A.D. 1837).

2475 B.C. Maize is domesticated in primitive form in the isthmus that links the two continents of the Western Hemisphere, while potatoes and sweet potatoes are cultivated in the southern continent.

Olive trees are cultivated in Crete which grows rich by exporting olive oil and timber.

2350 B.C. The Akkadian Empire that will rule Mesopotamia for the next two centuries is founded by Sumer's Sargon I. The Sumerian city-state civilization reaches its zenith, and the Akkadian Empire will incorporate the advances made by the Sumerians, giving them wide currency.

2300 B.C. Rice (*Oryza sativa*) from the Indus Valley is introduced in northern China where a civilization flourishes on a level comparable to any at Mohenjo-Daro or Harappa.

2205 B.C. The Hsia dynasty that will rule much of China for roughly 700 years is inaugurated.

The Chinese domesticate dogs, goats, pigs, oxen, and sheep.

The Chinese demonstrate the first knowledge of milling grain.

2000 B.C. Decimal notation appears in Babylonia which has replaced Sumer as the dominant power in the Middle East.

Europe remains in the Stone Age as the Bronze Age proceeds in the Near East.

Square sails on two and even three masts assist Phoenician and Cretan oarsmen.

Byblos, on the Levant Coast, has grown into a port for the export of Lebanese timber to Egypt.

Phylakopi, on the Aegean island of Milos, has become a center of trade in the volcanic glass obsidian found on the island for at least 5,000 years.

Some cattle is used for meat and some for milk by farmers in the Near East.

The Egyptians abandon efforts to domesticate antelope, gazelle, and oryx. They devote more effort instead to hunting, fowling, fishing, and gathering wild celery, papyrus stalks, lotus roots, and other plant foods to supplement the grain and vegetables they grow on their Nile flood plains.

Watermelon is cultivated in Africa, figs in Arabia, tea and bananas in India, apples in the Indus Valley, and agriculture is well established in most of the central isthmus of the Western Hemisphere.

1970 B.C. Egypt's Amenemhet I dies after a 30-year reign that has founded the 12th Dynasty. He is succeeded by his son who has served as coregent since 1980 B.C. and who will reign alone until 1935 B.C. as Sesostris I. The new ruler will complete the conquest of Nubia.

1950 B.C. Babylon's sixth king, Hammurabi, conquers all of Mesopotamia, carries out extensive public works, and imposes an exemplary code of laws: "If a man put out the eye of another man, his eye shall be put out."

1935 B.C. Egypt's Sesostris I dies and is succeeded by his son who has served as coregent since 1938 B.C. and who will reign alone until 1903 B.C. as Amenemhet II. The new king will increase trade with Punt.

1913 B.C. Babylon's Hammurabi dies after a 42-year reign.

1903 B.C. Egypt's Amenemhet II dies after a 32-year reign. He is succeeded by his son who has served as coregent since 1906 B.C. and who will reign until 1887 B.C. as Sesostris II.

1900 B.C. Stonehenge will be erected sometime in the next three centuries by Bronze Age Britons as a monumental calculator to chart the movements of the sun, the moon, and the planets.

1887 B.C. Egypt's Sesostris II dies after a 16-year reign. He is succeeded by his son who will reign until 1849 B.C. as Sesostris III and who will make Egypt a great power holding sway over 1,000 miles along the Nile.

A canal through the Nile's first cataract will be dug during the reign of Sesostris II (above).

1849 B.C. Egypt's Sesostris III dies after a 38-year reign in which he has invaded Palestine and Syria to maintain Egyptian trade routes. He is succeeded by his son who will reign until 1801 B.C. as Amenemhet III and who will develop mines in the Sinai region to keep the nation prosperous.

A vast irrigation system will be developed in the reign of Amenemhet III (above).

1801 B.C. Egypts's Amenemhet III dies and is succeeded by his son, who will reign until 1792 B.C. as Amenemhet IV.

1800 B.C. Taboos against eating pork appear among some peoples of the Near East, possibly because they are sheepherding peoples and the pig is the domesticated animal of their farmer enemies (*see* 621 B.C.; Shariah, A.D.; 629; Cook, A.D. 1779).

1792 B.C. Egypt's 12th (Theban) Dynasty ends with the death of Amenemhet IV after 208 years, and the power of the Egyptian king declines.

1750 B.C. The great Indus Valley cities of Mohenjo-Daro and Harappa collapse as the soil of the region becomes too saline to support extensive crop growth after centuries of unscientific irrigation (*see* 4000 B.C.).

1700 B.C. Judaism is founded by Abraham, a prince of Ur in Mesopotamia, who moves to Canaan, replaces human sacrifice with the sacrifice of rams, and begins a religion that will attract many followers in the Middle East (*see* Jacob, 1650 B.C.).

An Egyptian papyrus written during the reign of Re-Ser-Ka shows that Egyptians suffer from tooth decay and from ophthalmic troubles. A German Egyptologist will discover the document in A.D. 1872 and it will be called the Ebers papyrus.

Smallpox or a similar disease occurs among the Chinese.

Babylonians employ windmills to pump water for irrigation.

Knossus, on the island of Crete, is destroyed either by earthquake or by troops from the rival city of Phaistos, but the Minoans (who take their name from the legendary king Minos) will rebuild the city (*see* 1600 B.C.).

Eastern Europeans cultivate rye (*secale cereale*). It will soon become the major bread grain of the Slavs, the Celts, and the Teutones in northern areas where the growing season is too short for dependable wheat production (*see* ergotism, A.D. 857).

1680 B.C. Egypt is invaded by Hyksos tribesmen from Palestine, Syria, and farther north. They introduce horses that will help them dominate the Egyptians for the next century.

Leavened (raised) bread is invented in Egypt (time approximate).

1650 B.C. The Jewish religion begun half a century ago by Abraham and carried on by his son Isaac is propagated by his grandson Jacob whose 12 sons will come to head 12 tribes of Israel (*see* 933 B.C.).

1600 B.C. Knossus, on the island of Crete, is rebuilt within a century after its destruction in 1700 B.C. A brilliant civilization flourishes at Knossus and at Phaistos, Tylissos, Hagia, Triada, and Gornia (but *see* 1470 B.C.).

1570 B.C. The New Kingdom that will rule Egypt until 332 B.C. is inaugurated at Thebes by the Diospolite (18th Dynasty) pharaoh Amasis who begins to drive out the Hyksos who invaded Egypt in 1680 B.C. and to reunite Upper and Lower Egypt.

1557 B.C. Egypt's Amasis I dies after a 23-year reign and is succeeded by his son who will reign as Amenhotep I until 1540 B.C. The new pharaoh will invade Nubia and will war with the Libyans and Syrians.

1540 B.C. Egypt's Amenhotep I dies after a 17-year reign. He is succeeded by Thutmose I who is not of royal blood but who is proclaimed king. His reign will continue until 1501 B.C. and will be marked by the Egyptian conquest of Nubia.

Egypt's Thutmose I (above) will restore the temple of Osiris at Abydos and will build hypostyle halls at Karnak. He will also erect two pylons and two obelisks and will have a record of his deeds preserved in an inscription on rocks near the third cataract of the Nile.

1520 B.C. A volcanic eruption on the Greek island of Thera (Santorini) destroys all life on the island (*see* 1470 B.C.).

1501 B.C. Egypt's Thutmose I is deposed after a 39-year reign in which he has led successful expeditions into Asia as far as the Euphrates. He is succeeded by his bastard son who will rule with his wife and half- sister Hatshepsut until 1496 B.C.

1500 B.C. Geometry helps the Egyptians survey boundaries of fields whose dividing lines are effaced by the annual floods of the Nile (*see* Euclid, 300 B.C.).

Aryan nomads from the Eurasian steppes push into the Indian subcontinent, bringing with them flocks of sheep and herds of cattle.

Horse-drawn vehicles are used by the Chinese (*see* Sumerians, 3500 B.C.).

Silk is woven by the Chinese who also use potters' wheels.

Water buffalo are domesticated, along with several species of fowl, by China's Shang dynasty which rules at Anyang on the Yellow River.

All major food plants that will be used in the 20th century, with the exception of the sugar beet, are being cultivated somewhere in the world.

A diet heavily dependent on dairy products is introduced into India by Aryan invaders (above) who use *ghee* (clarified butter) rather than whole butter which is too perishable for the hot climate of India.

1496 B.C. Egypt's Thutmose III is deposed by his father Thutmose I and his half-brother Thutmose II who will reign jointly until 1493 B.C.

1493 B.C. Egypt's Thutmose I dies after a brief second reign, his weak son Thutmose II is deposed, and Thutmose III regains the throne he occupied from 1501 until 1496 B.C. and will retain until 1447 B.C.. He will reign jointly with his wife and half-sister until her death in 1481 B.C.

1485 B.C. Two obelisks at Karnak are erected by the Egyptian queen Hatshepsut who has built a magnificent temple on the west side of the Nile near Thebes and has had its walls decorated with pictorial representations of an expedition to the land of Punt.

1470 B.C. A volcanic eruption on the Greek island of Thera that is far more violent than the eruption of 1520 B.C. deposits ashes on Crete and emits poisonous vapors that destroy the Minoan civilization of 1600 B.C. Seismic waves 100 to 160 feet high, created by the eruption, rush in to fill the void created at Thera, temporarily dropping water levels on the eastern shores of the Mediterranean.

Egyptian croplands are engulfed by seawater from seismic waves (above), the land is made uncultivable, and famine ensues.

Mycenae is established as a new cultural center in the Greek Peloponnesus by survivors of the Minoan civilization destroyed in Crete (above).

1447 B.C. Egypt's Thutmose III dies after 34 years of reigning alone and is succeeded by his son who will reign until 1420 B.C. as Amenhotep II. The new king has ruled jointly with his father for the past year, and he begins his reign with successful campaigns in Judea and on the Euphrates.

1420 B.C. Egypt's Amenhotep II dies after a 27-year reign and is succeeded by his son who will reign until 1411 B.C. as Thutmose III. The new king will marry a Mitannian princess, he will form alliances with Babylonia and with the Mitanni, he will lead military expeditions into Phoenicia and Nubia, and he will complete the last obelisk of his grandfather Thutmose II.

1411 B.C. Egypt's Thutmose III dies after a 9-year reign and is succeeded by his son who will reign until 1375 B.C. as Amenhotep III, the last great ruler of the Middle Kingdom.

1400 B.C. The Iron Age begins in Asia Minor as an economical method is found for smelting iron on an industrial scale (*see* 2500 B.C.).

The first domestic poultry is introduced into China from the Malayan Peninsula, where the jungle fowl *Gallus bankiva* has been domesticated.

1380 B.C. A canal to connect the Nile with the Red Sea is constructed by the slaves of Egypt's Amenhotep III. The new canal will remain in use for some centuries (*see* 609 B.C.).

1375 B.C. Egypt's Amenhotep III dies after a 36-year reign in which Egyptian supremacy in Asia has been recognized by Babylonia. The king has led a successful expedition into Upper Nubia above the second cataract of the Nile, he has developed his capital at Thebes into a monumental city of great temples, pylons, and colossi, he has erected hypostyle halls at Karnak, and he has reigned in an era of prosperity and magnificence. Amenhotep is succeeded by his son who will reign until 1358 B.C. as Amenhotep IV (Ikhnaton), but the Hittite king Suppiluliumas will take advantage of Egypt's weakness in the next 35 years to build an empire that will extend south from Anatolia to the borders of Lebanon.

1374 B.C. Monotheism is introduced by the Egyptian king Amenhotep IV, who will be called Ikhnaton (Akhenaten or Akhnaton), meaning "Aten is satisfied." The pharaoh establishes a new cult that worships the sun god (or solar disk) Aten, and he opposes the priests of Amen as he bows to the influence of his beautiful Hittite wife Nefertiti.

Stonehenge, built by Indo-Europeans who invaded the British Isles, served as a Bronze Age astronomical observatory.

1358 B.C. Egypt's Ikhnaton dies after a 17-year reign and is succeeded by his 9-year-old son-in-law who will rule until 1350 B.C.. The new pharaoh Tutankhamen has accepted the sun worship faith of his wife and her father, but he will return to the religion of the priests of Amen and will move Egypt's capital back to Thebes from the new city of Akhetaton.

1350 B.C. The Egyptian throne is seized by the soldier Harmhab who will reorganize the country's administration, will reign until 1315 B.C., and will found Egypt's 19th Dynasty.

1344 B.C. Egypt's late Tutunkhamen is buried at Thebes in a magnificent pyramid erected in his honor (*see* Carter, A.D. 1922).

Worship according to the traditional tenets of the Amen priests has been restored by the Egyptian king Harmhab.

1315 B.C. Egypt's Harmhab dies and is succeeded by the aged Ramses I who will reign only briefly but who will plan and begin a great hypostyle hall at Karnak.

1313 B.C. Egypt's Ramses I dies and is succeeded by his son who has served since last year as coregent. He will reign until 1292 B.C. as Seti I.

1300 B.C. Alphabetic script developed in Mesopotamia is a refinement of the simplified cuneiform alphabet of 2500 B.C..

1292 B.C. Egypt's Seti I dies after a 21-year reign in which he has defeated the Libyans west of the Nile Delta and has made peace with the Hittites in Syria. Seti is succeeded by his son who will reign until 1225 B.C. as Ramses II.

A colonnaded hall at Karnak begun by his father Ramses I has been completed by Seti I (above) who has also built a magnificent sanctuary at Abydos dedicated to the great Egyptian gods.

1275 B.C. A 40-year Israelite migration begins after three centuries of Egyptian oppression. The prophet Moses and his brother Aaron lead tribesmen and their flocks of sheep out of Egypt toward the Dead Sea in Canaan on a roundabout journey that will take them through the Sinai Peninsula, Kadesh, Aelana, and Petra.

The wandering Jews (above) will survive starvation at one point by eating "manna," possibly a kind of mushroom.

1272 B.C. A permanent peace with the Hittites is arranged by Egypt's Ramses II who marries the daughter of the Hittite king.

Ramses will devote the rest of his long, peaceful reign to such projects as the completion of Seti's temple at Abydos, additions to the temples at Karnak and Luxor, construction of a great mortuary temple at Thebes with colossal statues of himself, and construction of a rock-cut temple at Abu-Simbel in Nubia.

1225 B.C. Egypt's Ramses II dies after a 67-year reign in which he has used forced Israelite labor to build the treasure cities of Pithom and Ramses. He is succeeded by his son Merneptah who will reign until 1215 B.C..

1221 B.C. Egypt is invaded by Libyans who are defeated by the pharaoh Merneptah.

1215 B.C. Egypt's Merneptah dies after a 10-year reign and is succeeded by a series of pharaohs who will rule briefly to end the 19th Dynasty founded by Harmhab in 1350 B.C. They will be followed by an interregnum that will continue until 1198.

1200 B.C. Lower Egypt's remaining Jews are expelled in the confusion following the end of the 19th Dynasty. The Jews have been active in the country's administration, arts, and trade.

The Egyptians have learned to make fine linen from flax stalks, and their high priests wear only linen, which is used also to wrap embalmed bodies (*see* flax 6000 B.C.).

1198 B.C. Egypt's 20th Dynasty entrenches itself as its second king begins a 31-year reign as Ramses III. He will rally the Egyptians against a confederation of Philistines, Sardinians, Greek Danaoi, and other sea peoples.

1184 B.C. King Priam's city of Troy at the gateway to the Hellespont in Asia Minor falls to the Greeks after a 10-year siege in the Trojan War that represents Greece's last effort at expansion. The Greek army has been led by Agamemnon (*see* Homer, 850 B.C.; Byzantium, 658 B.C.).

1170 B.C. The first recorded strike by laboring men occurs at the Egyptian necropolis of Thebes, where acute inflation brings an organized protest by men working on a new pyramid. When the payroll is delayed, the men refuse to work.

1160 B.C. Egypt's Ramses V dies. His mummified remains will show that the pharaoh had smallpox.

1150 B.C. Egyptian medicine splits into two basic schools. Empirico-rational medicine rests on the premise that fever, pain, or tumor is a disease rather than a symptom, but practitioners of this school charge such high fees that only the very rich can afford them. The magico-religious school of medicine relies basically on expelling demons or spirits and is popular because it is inexpensive. Physicians and priests both prescribe enemas, purgatives, special diets, herbs gathered from the patients' own gardens, and external applications of animal fat, especially oxen fat.

Egyptian aristocrats enjoy leavened bread and drink some wine (but mostly beer) as they dine at tables and sit on chairs which they have developed, but in the bread stalls of village streets, only flat breads are commonly available.

1146 B.C. Nebuchadnezzer I begins a 23-year reign as king of Babylon.

1141 B.C. Israelite forces lose 4,000 in a battle against the Philistines and then lose another 30,000.

The Israelites' sacred Ark of the Covenant is carried off to Ashdod by the Philistines, and a plague breaks out among the Philistines, spreading with the Ark to Gathen and then to Ekron. The Philistines return the Ark to Joshua the Bethshemite in order to end the plague, but 70 Bethshemite men who peer into the Ark die of plague, which then spreads throughout Israel, killing some 50,000.

1122 B.C. The Chou dynasty that will rule China until 255 B.C. is founded by Wu Wang, son of Wen Wang. He overthrows the emperor Chou Hsin, who burns himself to death.

1100 B.C. Assyrian forces under Tiglath-Pileser I reach the Mediterranean after having conquered the Hittites. The Assyrians encounter the seafaring Phoenicians, who hunt sperm whales and conduct a farflung sea trade (see 2750 B.C.; 878 B.C.).

1025 B.C. The prophet Samuel anoints Saul who begins a 13-year reign as king of Hebron.

1012 B.C. The Battle of Mount Gilboa ends in defeat and death for Hebron's Saul and his eldest son Jonathan at the hands of the Philistines. Jonathan's friend David succeeds Saul to begin a 7-year reign as king of Hebron.

1005 B.C. Jerusalem falls to David of Hebron who is anointed king of Judea by the prophet Samuel and begins a reign of 33 years in which he will break the power of the Philistines and defeat the Moabites, the Ammonites, and the Edomites.

1000 B.C. The Iron Age that began 400 years ago in the Near East moves to Europe in the Hallstatt region of what will become Austria. Iron tools and weapons begin to spread throughout Europe.

The Chinese cut down forests to create more farmland. The deforestation will lead to soil erosion, floods, and drought in millennia to come.

Land sown with grain in Egypt yields crops as bountiful as any the Egyptians will reap in the 20th century A.D.

The Chinese cut ice and store it for refrigeration.

990 B.C. The king of Judea's third (and favorite) son Absalom kills his half-brother—David's eldest son Amnon—in revenge for the rape of his full sister Tamar. David banishes Absalom from Judea (date approximate).

978 B.C. The king of Judea's son Absalom regains David's favor through the offices of David's nephew Joab, but Absalom leads a rebellion against David on the ad-

vice of David's counselor Ahithophel. Joab will suppress the rebellion, will kill the fleeing Absalom and his captain Amasa (Joab's cousin), and the counselor Ahithophel will commit suicide.

973 B.C. Judea's King David dies and is succeeded by his son Solomon who begins a 40-year reign by making alliances with Egypt's ruling priests and with the Phoenician king Hiram of Tyre. Solomon is David's son by his second wife Bathsheba, whose first husband David murdered in order to marry her.

Solomon executes David's former army commander Joab for having killed David's son Absalom in violation of David's orders and for having killed his rival Amasa.

Solomon's fleet sails the Red Sea, trading products of Judea at Tyre and Sidon and in Africa and Arabia, where Solomon begins mining gold.

The Great Temple of Jerusalem goes up in the one-time Jebusite stronghold captured by David to house the sacred ark of Yahweh (see 1141 B.C.). Construction of the temple had been proposed by David but had been prevented by the prophet Nathan (see 586 B.C.).

A new royal palace and a city wall at Jerusalem will be built by Solomon who will use forced labor to erect buildings throughout his realm, introducing taxation to finance his projects.

950 B.C. The household of Judea's King Solomon includes 700 wives and 300 concubines and consumes 10 oxen on an ordinary day, along with the meat of harts, gazelles, and hartebeests. The Book of Deuteronomy in 621 B.C. will say that the king had 12,000 horsemen scouring the countryside in search of "victual for all who came to Solomon's table" and that for feast days he sacrificed 22,000 oxen and any number of fattened fowl.

945 B.C. Egypt's throne is usurped by the Libyan Sheshonk, who founds the 22nd (Bubastite) Dynasty that will rule Egypt for 200 years.

933 B.C. Judea's King Solomon dies and is succeeded by his son Rehoboam in Jerusalem, but 10 northern tribes secede when Rehoboam refuses their demand for relief from taxation. They establish the kingdom of Israel with Rehoboam's brother Jeroboam as king.

926 B.C. Palestine is invaded by Egypt's pharaoh Sheshonk, who plunders Jerusalem and many other Judean cities.

900 B.C. The first Italian towns are established by Etruscans who have emigrated from Lydia after an 18-year famine. Lydia's King Atys, who rules the Asian country opposite the Greek islands of Chios and Samos, has commanded half his subjects to emigrate. They have journeyed to Smyrna under the leadership of Atys's son Tyrsanus, they have loaded their belongings onto ships, and they have come to the Italian peninsula, where their towns are built mostly

900 B.C. (cont.) on hillside terraces and are enclosed with massive timbered walls (*see* 396 B.C.; Rome, 753 B.C.).

878 B.C. The Assyrian king Assur-Nacir-Pal annexes Phoenicia as he takes over the entire eastern Mediterranean coast. The Phoenicians pay Assur-Nacir-Pal tribute that includes ivory from the teeth of whales and dolphins.

Carthage is founded in North Africa by refugee Phoenician colonists (or "Punians" from the adjective *punicus*) (*see* 300 B.C.).

850 B.C. The *Iliad* and the *Odyssey* are inscribed by the blind Greek poet Homer, so the historian Herodotus will write some four centuries hence, but the date may be as much as a century earlier, and while references to "the deathless laughter of the blessed gods" appear in both works, they may have been written by different people employing earlier lays handed down orally before articulation in the "winged words" of Homer.

The *Iliad* is an epic poem of Ilium (Troy) and its siege by the Greeks from 1194 to 1184 B.C., a poem mixing gods and mortals in its history of Priam, Helen, Paris, Menelaus, Hector, Achilles, Aphrodite, Agamemnon, and Odysseus (Ulysses). "I shall go out with the chariots to counsel and command, for that is the privilege of the old; the young must fight in the ranks" (IV); "Our business in the field of fight/ Is not to question but to prove our might"; "Men grow tired of sleep, love, singing and dancing sooner than of war" (XII); "A glorious death is his/ Who for his country falls" (XV); "After the event even a fool is wise" (XVII); "The issue is in the laps of the gods" (XVII).

The *Odyssey* is an epic poem about the wanderings of Odysseus (Ulysses) who is kept as a lover for nearly 8 years by the goddess Calypso while his wife Penelope home at Ithaca is besieged by suitors and unwanted guests and while his son Telemachus is growing to manhood. "And what he greatly thought, he nobly dared" (II); "There is no part of man more like a dog than brazen Belly, crying to be remembered" (VII); "How prone to doubt, how cautious are the wise" (XIII); "There is nothing worse for mortals than a wandering life" (XV); "True friendship's laws are by this rule express'd,/ Welcome the coming, speed the parting guest" (XV); "Day-long she wove at the web but by night she would unravel what she had done" (XXIV, a reference to wife Penelope, who has vowed to accept no second husband until she has completed a winding-sheet for her aged father-in-law, a ruse she continues until she is betrayed after 3 years by one of her serving maids).

Fish cultivation is discussed in a voluminous treatise by the Chinese author Fan-Li (manuscript in British Museum, London) (*see* oyster cultivation, 110 B.C.).

801 B.C. Egypt and Greece will begin regular trade relations in the next 100 years

Aryan religious epics, or Vedas, will lead in the next 200 years to a veneration of the cow in much of India and to a sanctification of dairy products.

800 B.C. Rice becomes an important part of Chinese diets (*see* 2300 B.C.).

776 B.C. Greece's first recorded Olympic (or Olympian) games are held where the Alpheus and Cladeus Rivers converge at Olympus, although many of the great buildings within the enclosure for the games and associated religious celebrations date back as much as 500 years. Only pure Greeks may compete and only Greeks who have no police records or even any relatives with police records. The competition in the first 13 of the quadrennial Olympiads will be limited to a footrace of some 200 yards (*see* 724 B.C.).

772 B.C. Construction begins at Ephesus on the Mediterranean coast of Asia Minor on the Temple of Artemis that will be one of the wonders of the ancient world (*see* 356 B.C.).

771 B.C. China's Chou capital at Hao on the Wei River is destroyed by barbarians from the north. The capital will be moved in the next year to Loyang near the Yellow River.

753 B.C. Rome is founded, according to legend, on a wooded Italian hilltop overlooking the Tiber. The founders are infant brothers Romulus and Remus who are suckled by a she-wolf.

724 B.C. Greece's 14th Olympiad is held at Olympus, and a second footrace is added in which competitors run twice around the stadium to cover a distance of nearly half a mile (*see* 776 B.C.; 720 B.C.).

721 B.C. The kingdom of Israel, founded in 933 B.C., is conquered by Assyria's Sargon II who deports 27,000 people of Israel's 10 northern tribes to Central Asia where they will disappear from history (the "lost tribes of Israel").

720 B.C. Greece's 15th Olympiad is held at Olympus, and the Olympic games are extended to include a long-distance race of some 2.5 miles that requires contestants to run 12 times round the stadium.

710 B.C. Egypt is conquered by Ethiopian invaders.

708 B.C. Greece's 18th Olympiad is held at Olympus, and the Olympic games are enlarged by the addition of a pentathlon event in which contestants must compete in broad jumping, javelin throwing, a 200-yard dash, discus throwing, and wrestling. The javelin is a bronze-tipped elderwood spear and the discus is a heavy bronze disk (*see* 720 B.C.; 696 B.C.).

7th CENTURY B.C.

Olive trees are planted on the Iberian Peninsula by Phoenician colonists.

Crop rotation is taught to Chinese peasants by the minister of agriculture under the emperor Kuan Chung. He also teaches them to dig drainage ditches, he rents them farm equipment, and he stores grain surpluses to provide free food in time of famine.

700 B.C. Aqueducts are built to carry water to the cities developing in the Near East.

Laws against animal slaughter are relaxed in India.

698 B.C. Greek colonization of the Mediterranean in the next two centuries will be motivated primarily by a need to find new food sources as Greece's population expands.

696 B.C. Greece's 23rd Olympiad is held at Olympus and boxing is added to the Olympic games which are more and more intended as preparation for war.

693 B.C. Babylon is destroyed by the Assyrian king Sennacherib, but the city will be rebuilt in even greater splendor and luxury (see 597 B.C.).

682 B.C. Greece's 25th Olympiad is held at Olympus with the first equestrian event. A four-horse chariot race is run at the nearby Hippodrome.

660 B.C. Japan's main island of Honshu is invaded, according to legend, by Jimmu Tenno (Kami Yamato Ihare-Biko) who crosses from the island of Kyushu to establish himself as the country's first emperor (the invasion will actually occur at least 600 years hence).

658 B.C. Byzantium is founded by Greek colonists from Megara who establish a settlement to the east (see 340 B.C.; Constantinople, A.D. 330).

650 B.C. Greek hillsides are bare of trees which have been cut down to provide wood for houses, for ships, and for the charcoal used by metalworkers. Loss of the trees leads in many areas to soil erosion and to a loss of fertile land (see Solon, 594 B.C.).

Greece's 33rd Olympiad is held at Olympus with a new event: the pancratium is a no-holds-barred contest that combines boxing and wrestling.

626 B.C. Assyria's King Ashurbanipal dies after a 43-year reign that has brought great prosperity to the country. He is the last major ruler of the Sargonid dynasty that has ruled for nearly a century, and the empire will crumble in the next 20 years.

625 B.C. Metal coins are introduced into Greece. Stamped with the likeness of an ear of wheat, the coins are a reminder that grain, usually barley, has previously served as a medium of exchange, but the new coins are lighter and easier to transport than grain and do not get moldy (see Croesus, 560 B.C.).

624 B.C. Corinth's tyrant Periander invites the city-state's nobility to a party and has his soldiers strip the women of their gold jewelry and of gowns adorned with golden thread. The gold will finance Periander's government for decades to come.

621 B.C. The Athenian lawgiver Draco issues a code of laws that makes nearly every offense punishable by death. Barbarously cruel or harsh punishment will forever be called "Draconian."

The Book of Deuteronomy, compiled by Israelite scribes, is among the five books of Moses containing what purports to be the dying testament of Moses to his people (see 1275 B.C.).

The Law of Moses in Deuteronomy (above) imposes dietary restrictions:

> You shall not eat any abominable thing. These are the animals you may eat: the ox, the sheep, the goat, the hart, the gazelle, the roebuck, the wild goat, the ibex, the antelope, and the mountain-sheep. Every animal that parts the hoof and has the hoof cloven in two, and chews the cud, among the animals, you may eat. Yet of those that chew the cud or have the hoof cloven you shall not eat these: the camel, the hare, and the rock badger, because they chew the cud but do not part the hoof, are unclean for you. And the swine, because it parts the hoof but does not chew the cud, is unclean for you. Their flesh you shall not eat, and their carcasses you shall not touch.
>
> Of all that are in the waters you may eat these: whatever has fins and scales you may eat. And whatever does not have fins and scales you shall not eat; it is unclean for you.
>
> You may eat all clean birds. But these are the ones which you shall not eat: the eagle, the vulture, the osprey, the buzzard, the kite, after their kinds; every raven after its kind; the ostrich, the nighthawk, the sea gull, the hawk, after their kinds; the little owl and the great owl, the water hen and the pelican, the carrion vulture and the cormorant, the stork, the heron, after their kinds; the hoopoe and the bat. And all the winged insects are unclean for you; they shall not be eaten. All clean winged things you may eat.

Greece's Olympic Games, inaugurated in 776 B.C., started to become war games beginning with a boxing event in 696 B.C.

621 B.C. **(cont.)** You shall not eat anything that dies of itself; you may give it to the alien who is within your towns, that he may eat it, or you may sell it to a foreigner. . . .

You shall not boil a kid in its mother's milk. (*see* Sharia, A.D. 629; Maimonides, A.D. 1163).

612 B.C. Nineveh falls to the Medes and the Chaldeans. The fall of the Assyrian capital will soon be followed by the disappearance of the Assyrian Empire.

609 B.C. A new canal to link the Nile with the Red Sea is begun by the Egyptian pharaoh Necho, but while the Greek historian Herodotus will write that Necho completed a channel "four days' journey in length and wide enough for two armies abreast," the canal will not be completed. More than 120,000 men will die in the effort to build it (*see* 1380 B.C.; 520 B.C.).

Necho's ships in the next 14 years will circumnavigate Africa, proceeding from east to west and taking 3 years (including a stop to plant and harvest a grain crop on the North African coast).

605 B.C. Necho is defeated at Carchemish by the Chaldean son of Nabopolassar who begins a 43-year reign at Babylon as Nebuchadnezzar II.

6th CENTURY B.C.

The Persian religious leader Zoroaster in this century will found a faith whose sacred literature will be the Zend-Avesta. The teachings of Zoroaster (Zarathustra) will dominate Persian religious thought for centuries.

Rome's Cloaca Maxima will be built in this century. The giant drainage system will drain the marshy area that will become the site of the Roman Forum.

Rome remains a small town but begins to experience food shortages. It will have occasional serious famines in this century.

Humped cattle from India become widespread in the Mediterranean countries.

600 B.C. Marseilles is founded by Greek colonists, who establish the settlement of Lacydon (see 330 B.C.).

597 B.C. Jerusalem falls to Babylonia's Nebuchadnezzar II. The last great Chaldean king has invaded Judah, and he returns to Babylon with many Jews as prisoners (see 587 B.C.).

Wheeled carts drawn by onagers (small Asiatic asses) bring food into Babylon, while riverboats powered by scores of oarsmen bring copper, silver, gold, and vegetable oils from fields north of the Tigris. Camels in long caravans enter the city with dyestuffs, glassware, precious stones, and textiles.

Plagues are occasionally brought to Babylon by the camel caravans (above), while malaria, dysentery, and eye diseases are carried by flies and mosquitoes that breed in polluted irrigation canals. Priest-physicians treat chest diseases by fumigation, letting smoke from a fire of thorns spread with tar powder enter the patient's anus, mouth, and nose (the fire may also be fueled by dog, fox, gazelle, jackal, or pig dung or by bitumen, hartshorn, human bones, or sulfur).

Babylon is a magnificent city of public buildings faced with blue, yellow, and white enameled tiles that face on broad avenues crossed by canals and winding streets.

The Hanging Gardens of Babylon are one of the seven wonders of the ancient world, with exotic shrubs and flowers irrigated by water pumped from the Euphrates.

594 B.C. The Athenian statesman Solon, 42, who has regained Salamis from the Megarians establishes a timocracy (government by the richest) and begins constitutional reforms at Athens.

Solon (above) forbids export of any Athenian agricultural produce: his well-intentioned edict will lead to more planting of olive trees. Their roots soak up deep moisture but do not hold soil together, so while olive oil and silver mines will bring riches to Athens, Solon's edict will hasten the erosion of Greek hillsides (see Plato, 347 B.C.).

590 B.C. The Greek poet Sappho flourishes on the island of Lesbos as priestess of a feminine love cult and celebrates the love of women for other women in poems that will survive in papyrus fragments and in quotations by later critics. The geographer Strabo will write some 600 years hence that "Sappho was something to be wondered at. Never within human memory has there been a woman to compare with her as a poet."

587 B.C. Jerusalem falls to Babylon's Nebuchadnezzar after a 16-month siege. He carries the Jews off to exile in a "Babylonian captivity" that will continue until 538 B.C..

586 B.C. Jerusalem's Great Temple is destroyed by the forces of Nebuchadnezzar.

573 B.C. The Phoenician city of Tyre falls to Nebuchadnezzar after a 13-year siege.

568 B.C. Nebuchadnezzar invades Egypt.

565 B.C. Taoism is founded by the Chinese philosopher Lao-tse, 39, in Honan province. He sets down principles of conduct in *Tao Te Ching* ("teaching of Tao"). The liberal religion teaches that forms and ceremonies are useless; it advocates a spirit of righteousness, but it will degenerate in future centuries into a system of magic.

Athenian forces from Megara conquer Salamis under the command of their general Peisistratus. He organizes the diakrioi, a new political party of small farmers, artisans, shepherds, and other poor people.

562 B.C. Nebuchadnezzar II of Babylon dies after a reign of 43 years. He is succeeded by his son Evil-Merodach.

561 B.C. The Athenian general Peisistratus makes himself tyrant but is driven out almost immediately by Lycurgus, who leads the city's nobility, and by Megacles the Alcmaeonid, who leads the middle class.

560 B.C. Babylon's Evil-Merodach is deposed by conspirators who kill him. He has released Jehoiachin, king of Judah, who had been imprisoned for 36 years.

559 B.C. Athens restores Peisistratus, who has won the support of Megacles.

559 B.C. (cont.) Metal coinage is invented by Croesus, king of Lydia, to replace commodities as a medium of exchange (year approximate) (*see* 900 B.C.; 625 B.C.).

556 B.C. Athens expels Peisistratus again after he has broken with Megacles. He will spend some years amassing a fortune from his mines in Thrace and will make Lygdamis tyrant of Naxos.

Babylon's last king, Nabonidus, begins a 17-year reign.

550 B.C. The king of Anshan Cambyses I dies after a long reign and is succeeded by his 50-year-old son Cyrus. The new king will create a Persian empire in his 21-year reign by uniting the Medes, the Persians, and other tribes.

546 B.C. Lydia's rich king Croesus is surprised at Sardis by Persians under the command of Cyrus the Great. Croesus has ruled for 14 years but Cyrus kills him and conquers his country.

Athens restores Peisistratus to power (he has obtained support from Thessaly and from Lygdamis of Naxos). He exiles his opponents, confiscates their lands, and uses them to benefit the poor, making the *hectemoroi* (sharecroppers) landowners and encouraging industry and trade.

Peisistratus introduces the cult of Dionysius to break down the power of the Athenian nobility through its hereditary priesthoods.

539 B.C. Persia's Cyrus the Great defeats the Babylonian king Nabonidus, who has alienated the priesthood and has built temples at the expense of the country's defenses. Cyrus enters the city of Babylon October 20 amidst wild rejoicing by the populace and either has Nabonidus killed or banishes him to Carmania.

538 B.C. The Babylonian prince Belshazzar (Bel-shar-usur), son of Nabonidus, tries to expel the forces of Cyrus the Great but suffers a crushing defeat. Cyrus destroys the city of Babylon and permits its Jews to return from their 49-year exile to Jerusalem, where they will rebuild the Great Temple built by Solomon in 973 B.C.

The first known Jewish dietary and sanitary laws appear in the Hebrew Book of Leviticus (*see* Deuteronomy, 621 B.C.).

528 B.C. Buddhism has its beginnings in India where Siddhartha Gautama, 35, has found enlightenment after a long and severe penance at Buddh Gaya, near Benares. A prince who renounced the luxury of palace life 5 years ago, Siddhartha went into the wilderness wearing sackcloth, but he found the ascetic life futile. In the next 45 years he will travel up and down the Ganges River; he will be called the Buddha (Enlightened One); and he will found monastic orders of a religion that will become dominant in China, Japan, and some other Asian countries (*see* 260 B.C.).

Vegetarianism will be an essential part of the Buddhist religion (above), although Siddhartha himself will abandon strict vegetarianism and will die at age 84 after feasting on pork.

527 B.C. The Athenian tyrant Peisistratus dies and is succeeded by his sons Hippias and Hipparchus.

525 B.C. The Persian prince Darius, son-in-law of the late Cyrus the Great, conquers Egypt.

521 B.C. Persian noblemen choose Darius Hystaspis, now 37, to succeed his late father-in-law Cyrus. He begins a 35-year reign as Darius I.

520 B.C. A Carthaginian fleet of 60 vessels under the command of Admiral Hanno lands some 30,000 settlers at the mouth of the Rio de Oro on Africa's west coast. The colony will survive for half a century.

The Persian emperor Darius digs a canal to connect the Nile with the Red Sea, continuing work begun nearly a century ago by the pharaoh Necho (*see* 609 B.C.; Suez, A.D. 1853).

Phoenicia continues to grow rich on trade in grain, cloth, wine, and the purple-black dye obtained from a gland of the rare purple sea snail, or murex. Long shallow-draft Phoenician galleys powered by oarsmen slaves and large square sails may long since have circumnavigated Africa (*see* Necho, 609 B.C.). They supply Phoenicia with African gold and ivory, Spanish silver, tin from the "Tin Isles" (probably Cornwall), gold, iron, and lead from the southern shore of the Euxine (Black) Sea, copper, grain, and cypress from Cyprus, wine from southern France, slaves from everywhere.

Reliefs and inscriptions in Persian, Elamitic, and Babylonian chronicle the achievements of Darius (above) on a steep cliff near Behistun.

Phoenicia's island city of Tyre has a population of 25,000; Old Tyre on the mainland is even larger.

516 B.C. Jerusalem's Great Temple is rebuilt 70 years after its destruction by the Babylonian troops of Nebuchadnezzar II (*see* 165 B.C.).

509 B.C. Rome overthrows her Tarquin (Etruscan) king, becomes a republic, and begins her struggle to dominate Italy and the world. Legend will relate the uprising to the rape of Lucretia, beautiful and virtuous wife of the Roman general Lucius Tarquinius Collatinus, by Sextus Tarquinius, a son of the king Tarquinius Superbus. Lucretia tells her father and husband about the rape, makes them swear vengeance, and stabs herself to death. Her husband's cousin Lucius Junius Brutus agitates against the Tarquins, raises a people's army, and drives out the Tarquins.

5th CENTURY B.C.

The Greek historian Herodotus will write in this century that "India is the farthest known region of the inhabited world to the East," but while natives of the Caucasus Mountains practice cannibalism, a great civilization is developing in China.

500 B.C. "In ancient times, people were few but wealthy and without strife," writes the Chinese philosopher Han Fei-Tzu. "People at present think that five sons are not too many, and each son has five sons also and before the death of the grandfather there are already 25 descendants. Therefore people are more and wealth is less; they work hard and receive little. The life of a nation depends on having enough food, not upon the number of people."

495 B.C. The Chinese philosopher Confucius (K'ung Fu-tzu) resigns as prime minister of Lu at age 56 when the ruler gives himself up to pleasure. In the next 12 years, Confucius will wander from state to state teaching precepts dealing with morals, the family system, and statecraft, with maxims that comprise a utilitarian philosophy. A brief record of Confucian teachings will be embodied in the *Analects,* one of the Four Books of Chinese classics, and his Golden Rule will be honored (often in the breach) throughout the world: "What you do not like when done to yourself, do not do unto others."

490 B.C. The Battle of Marathon gives Athens her first great military triumph but begins a long period of conflict with Persia. A Persian army of 15,000 sent by Darius is repulsed by 11,000 Greeks under the leadership of Miltiades 40 kilometers northeast of Athens between Mount Pentelikon and the Gulf of Marathon.

News of the victory at Marathon (above) is carried more than 26 miles to Athens by the runner Pheidippides, who falls dead after delivering the message, an event that will be commemorated in Olympic games footraces (*see* 776 B.C.; A.D. 1896).

Persia's Darius I has a thousand animals slaughtered each day for the royal table at his capital of Persepolis (or so the historian Xenophon will record: *see* 401 B.C.).

480 B.C. The Battle of Thermopylae August 19 is won by the Persians under Xerxes, son of Darius, whose army of nearly 200,000 engulfs the force of 300 Spartans and 700 Thespians under Leonidas, who enable the main Greek force to escape but who are destroyed after holding the Persians at bay. Breaking through the pass at Thermopylae from Macedonia into Greece, the Persians occupy Attica and sack Athens, whose citizens flee to Salamis and the Peloponnese.

The Battle of Salamis September 23 brings victory to the Greeks, whose Athenian general Themistocles lures the Persians into the Bay of Salamis, between Athens and the island of Salamis. More than 1,000 Persian vessels are rammed and sunk by fewer than 400 Greek ships. Xerxes is sent packing back to Persia, but he leaves behind an army under Mardonius.

479 B.C. The Battle of Plataea August 27 ends the Persian invasions of Greece as the Persian commander Mardonius is routed by the Greeks under Pausanius.

475 B.C. Iron comes into use in China nearly 1,000 years after its use became common in the Near East and half a century after its introduction into Europe (*see* 1000 B.C.).

474 B.C. The Greek poet Pindar moves to Thebes at age 44 after 2 years at the Sicilian court of Hieron at Syracuse. "Hopes are but the dreams of those who are awake," writes Pindar, who composes great lyric odes (epinicia) to celebrate triumphs in the Olympian games and other athletic events, and he quotes the maxim, "The issue is in God's hands."

472 B.C. Theater *The Persians* (*Persae*) by Athenian playwright Aeschylus, 53, who gained his first prize for drama in 484 B.C. and who has founded classical Greek tragedy by taking a relatively simple form and infusing it with heroic and unsophisticated magnificence.

470 B.C. Alfalfa is grown by the Greeks who have been introduced to the plant by the Persians and who use it as fodder for their horses.

468 B.C. The Athenian prize for drama is won by the Greek playwright Sophocles, 28, who defeats Aeschylus in the annual contest. Sophocles will be remembered for ages to come for his *Ajax* and other tragedies.

467 B.C. Theater *Seven Against Thebes* by Aeschylus.

466 B.C. Benghazi is founded on the North African coast by citizens of Cyrenaica, who will make it their capital.

458 B.C. The Roman general Lucius Quinctius Cincinnatus is summoned from his small farm by a delegation from the Senate to defend the city from attack by the approaching Aequians. Cincinnatus is named dictator of Rome, he gathers troops, he attacks and defeats the Aequians, he resigns his dictatorship, and he returns to his farm, all within 16 days (*see* Cincinnati, A.D. 1791).

458 B.C. (cont.) Theater The *Oresteian* trilogy by Aeschylus includes the plays *Agamemnon, The Libation Bearers* (*Choephoroi*), and *The Eumenides,* and its story of the blood feud in the house of Atreus will have a powerful influence on future writers and thinkers. Clytemnestra is murdered by her son Orestes for her murder of his father Agamemnon, and although he has been urged to commit the act by the god Apollo, he is pursued by the Furies. Orestes flees to Athens, where the goddess Athena establishes the court of Areopagus, grants forgiveness to Orestes, and changes the name of the Furies to "the kindly ones." Aeschylus will die in 2 years at age 69, but he will be survived through the ages by tragedies that include *Prometheus Bound* and *The Suppliants.*

457 B.C. A 28-year Golden Age begins in Athens as the statesman Pericles makes the city preeminent in the world in architecture and the arts while preparing for the inevitable conflict with Sparta.

Pericles (above) studies with the philosopher Anaxagoras, 43, who has been teaching at Athens for the past 5 years and who introduces a dualistic explanation of the universe: all natural objects are composed of infinitesimally small particles, or atoms, containing mixtures of all qualities, and the human mind acts upon masses of these particles to produce visible objects.

Athens has between 75,000 and 150,000 slaves, who represent 25 to 35 percent of the population. Some 20,000 work in the mines at Laureion producing silver which Athens trades for foodstuffs and other imports.

450 B.C. The British Isles are overrun by the Celts, an Indo-European people that has crossed the channel separating the islands from the European mainland.

The Temple of Theseus is completed at Athens.

449 B.C. *History* by the Greek historian Herodotus, 36, gives an account of the Graeco-Persian War that lasted from 490 to 479 B.C. along with lengthy digressions giving geographical descriptions of the eastern Mediterranean, relating anecdotes, making anthropological observations, and reporting legends. Herodotus will be called the "father of history" (date approximate).

448 B.C. Rebuilding of the Acropolis at Athens begins under the direction of architects Ictinus and Callicrates whose work will continue over the next 15 years as Pericles rebuilds what the Persians destroyed in 480 B.C. to make Athens a brilliant city.

445 B.C. The Temple of Poseidon is completed south of Athens at Cape Sunion.

441 B.C. Theater The Athenian prize for drama is won by the playwright Euripides, 43, who made first effort to win the prize 14 years ago but whose sensational plays have won him more notoriety than approval.

440 B.C. The Greek philosopher Heracleitus at Ephesus in Asia Minor teaches that everything is mutable, "all is flux." Principles are constantly modified through an incontrovertible law of nature that governs the universe in which worlds are alternately being created and destroyed.

Heracleitus (above) is the first man to declare that dreams are not a journey into the supernatural but are rather a retreat into a personal world (*see* Freud, A.D. 1900).

Theater *Antigone* by Sophocles is a tragedy whose heroine defies Creon, king of Thebes, and buries a declared traitor, claiming authority higher than the king's. She is condemned to death and kills herself before Creon, who has changed his mind, can save her or save his son (who has been betrothed to Antigone and who also commits suicide).

438 B.C. The Parthenon on the Acropolis at Athens is completed by Ictinus and Callicrates and is consecrated after 9 years of construction.

435 B.C. A gold and ivory statue of Zeus, king of the gods, is completed at Elis by the Athenian sculptor Phidia. The statue will be called one of the seven wonders of the ancient world.

433 B.C. Pericles concludes a defensive alliance with Corcyra (Corfu), the strong naval power in the Ionian Sea which is the bitter enemy of Corinth. Pericles also renews alliances with the Rhegium and Leontini in the west, threatening Sparta's food supply route from Sicily. Corinth appeals to Sparta to take arms against Athens, and the appeal is backed by Megara (which has been ruined by Pericles's economic sanctions) and by Aegina (which is heavily taxed by Pericles and which has been refused home rule).

432 B.C. The Peloponnesian Wars that will occupy 20 of the next 27 years begin in Greece following a revolt in the spring by the Potidaea in Chalcidice against their Athenian masters. Pericles blockades the Potideae; they refuse to arbitrate. The naval and military demands of the blockade drain Athens; Sparta seizes the opportunity to declare war on Athens; and Corfu declares war on Corinth.

The philosopher Socrates saves Alcibiades, 18-year-old nephew of Pericles, at Potidaea.

Spartan troops will lay waste the countryside round Athens in the Peloponnesian Wars (above), destroying not only grain fields but also olive trees, vineyards, and orchards that will not recover for decades.

431 B.C. Sparta's Archidamus II gains support by calling for the liberation of the Hellenes from Athenian despotism, and he sets out to annihilate Athens. Pericles works to make Athens-Piraeus an impregnable fortress, planning to lay waste the Megarid each spring and autumn while the Spartans are occupied with sowing and reaping their own crops.

The idea that the body has four "humors"—blood, bile, black bile, and phlegm—is propounded by the

Greek physician Empedocles, whose concept will dominate medical thinking for centuries to come.

Pepper from India is fairly common in Greece, but *Piper nigrum* is used as medicine, not as a food seasoning.

🎭 Theater   *Medea* by Euripides depicts the reactions of a wife discarded in favor of a younger rival. The fiery barbarian princess destroys her rival and kills her own children by the faithless Jason.

430 B.C. Athens sends a peace mission to Sparta in August but has no success. Potidaea capitulates to Athenian siege forces in the winter, but by that time the Athenian port of Piraeus is in the grip of plague.

An epidemic of blinding, paralytic deadly fever strikes Piraeus. Possibly a malignant form of scarlet fever that originated in Ethiopia, the plague has symptoms that begin with headache and progress to redness of the eyes, inflammation of the tongue and pharynx, sneezing, coughing, hoarseness, vomiting, diarrhea, and delirium. The plague does not affect the Peloponnese, but the Spartans kill everyone who falls into their hands lest they catch the disease, which rages also in the little Italian town of Rome.

Every natural event has a natural cause, says the Greek philosopher Leucippus.

429 B.C. The Athenian admiral Phormio wins naval victories at Chalcis and Naupactus at the mouth of the Corinthian Gulf, but in Athens thousands die of the plague.

Pericles dies of the plague in September, and the Golden Age of Greece is ended as at least one-third the population (and possibly two-thirds) are killed by the epidemic. The entire city indulges in drunkenness, gluttony, and licentiousness as the citizens lose their fear of the gods and their respect for law. "As for the first," the historian Thucydides will write, "they judged it to be just the same whether they worshipped them or not, as they saw all alike perishing; and as for the latter, no one expected to live to be brought to trial for his offenses."

Spared by the plague is the physician Hippocrates the Great (as distinguished from one previous and five future Greek physicians named Hippocrates). He is the first to say that no disease is entirely miraculous or adventitious in origin and that disease is not sent as punishment by the gods. He uses dissection and vivisection of animals to study anatomy and physiology, but he often applies the results of his experiments to human bodies without further evidence. Hippocrates adds to medical terminology such words as chronic, crisis, convalescence, exacerbate, paroxysm, relapse, and resolution. Fever, he says, expresses the struggle of the body to cure itself; health results from the harmony and mutual sympathy of the humors (*see* Empedocles, 431 B.C.; Fu Hsi, 2800 B.C.). Hippocrates' cult of Aesculapius is named after a physician who may have lived about 1250 B.C., and it marks the beginning of scientific medicine.

The Hippocratic Oath

I swear by Apollo Physician, by Aesculapius, by Health, by Heal-all, and by all the gods and goddesses, making them witnesses, that I will carry out, according to my ability and judgment, this oath and this indenture: To regard my teacher in this art as equal to my parents; to make him partner in my livelihood, and when he is in need of money to share mine with him; to consider his offspring equal to my brothers; to teach them this art, if they require to learn it, without fee or indenture; and to impart precept, oral instruction, and all the other learning, to my sons, to the sons of my teacher, and to pupils who have signed the indenture and sworn obedience to the physicians' Law, but to none other. I will use treatment to help the sick according to my ability and judgment, but I will never use it to injure or wrong them. I will not give poison to anyone though asked to do so, nor will I suggest such a plan. Similarly I will not give a pessary to a woman to cause abortion. But in purity and in holiness I will guard my life and my art. I will not use the knife on sufferers from stone, but I will give place to such as are craftsmen therein. Into whatsoever houses I enter, I will do so to help the sick, keeping myself free from all intentional wrong-doing and harm, especially from fornication with woman or man, bond or free. Whatsoever in the course of practice I see or hear (or even outside my practice in social intercourse) that ought never to be published abroad, I will not divulge, but consider such things to be holy secrets. Now if I keep this oath, and break it not, may I enjoy honor, in my life and art, among all men for all time; but if I transgress and forswear myself, may the opposite befall me.

428 B.C. The revolt of Mitylene in June opens to question the impregnability of the Athenian maritime empire. Mitylene is the chief city of Lesbos.

🎭 Theater   *Hippolytus* by Euripides shows the irreconcilable conflict between sexual passion and asceticism.

427 B.C. Sparta's Archidamus II dies after a 49-year reign. The Spartan admiral Alcidas, sent to help the rebels on Lesbos, makes a hurried raid on Ionia and flees home after seeing two Athenian warships.

Mitylene surrenders to Athens in July, and the Athenians punish the city with cruel severity.

Plataea surrenders in August after its garrison has come close to death from starvation. The Athenians slaughter the Plataeans in cold blood and completely destroy the city at the insistence of Thebes.

426 B.C. Corfu's democratic faction kills supporters of Sparta in a savage massacre and secures the island for Athens.

426 B.C. (cont.) The Athenian general Demosthenes and the demagogue Cleon revitalize the city's military and naval forces despite opposition from Nicias, a rich merchant who represents the Athenian middle class. Demosthenes outlines a vigorous strategy of offense designed to make Sicily, Boeotia, and the Peloponnese itself spheres of Athenian influence.

Demosthenes proceeds in June to Acarnania with a handful of troops. He raises a large army of local levies with the hope of invading Boeotia by way of Phocis while Nicias (above) invades by way of Tanagra to threaten Thebes from the southeast, but natives in the Aetolian forests trap his army and cut it to pieces. Demosthenes barely escapes with his life; he reaches the Athenian base at Naupactus, and secures it just in time to defend it against a large Spartan army from Delphi under Eyrylochus.

Victories by Demosthenes at Olpae and Idomene destroy Peloponnesian and Ambraciot influence on the Ambraciot Gulf. Demosthenes shatters Spartan prestige and returns in triumph to Athens.

425 B.C. An Athenian fleet summoned by Demosthenes bottles up the Spartan navy in Navarino Bay. Demosthenes has built and garrisoned a fort on Pylos promontory and has defended it against the attacking Spartans. A Spartan force landed on the island of Sphacteria is cut off from rescue, the Spartan naval commander surrenders under a temporary armistice, but peace talks break off when Athens refuses to surrender the Spartan ships.

Nicias resigns his generalship, his successor Cleon increases by 50 percent and more the tribute demanded from most members of the Athenian Empire, and Cleon lands reinforcements on Sphacteria (above) to overwhelm the Spartans. He brings 292 heroic Spartan defenders back to Athens and places them in dungeons to safeguard Attica from invasion, Sparta sues for peace, but Cleon refuses.

Theater *Hecuba* by Euripides; *The Acharnians* by Aristophanes, a 25-year-old comic playwright whose first play won a second prize 2 years ago and whose new comedy is an attack on war.

424 B.C. A congress at Gela in the spring hears the statesman Hermocrates of Syracuse urge the exclusion of foreign powers. The Sicilians send home an Athenian naval force.

Pagondas of Thebes crushes an Athenian army at Delium, making skillful use of cavalrymen. The Spartan general Brasidas thwarts Athenian efforts to take Megara; he then marches rapidly through Boeotia and Thessaly to Chalcidice, where he offers liberty and protection to cities rebelling against Athens. The city of Amphipolus surrenders, and a naval force from Thasos in the north arrives under the command of Thucydides in time only to save Eion at the mouth of the Strymon (the vengeful Cleon exiles Thucydides for 20 years).

Theater *Oedipus Rex* (or *Oedipus Tyrannus*) by Sophocles (date approximate). Oedipus, king of Thebes, has left his native Corinth to escape fulfillment of a prophecy that he would kill his father and marry his mother, but Oedipus investigates the murder of his predecessor, Laius of Thebes, and discovers that he himself killed Laius, that Laius rather than the king of Corinth was his father, and that his wife Jocasta is also his mother. Jocasta kills herself, and Oedipus blinds himself (the tragedy will deeply affect future generations). *The Knights* by Aristophanes.

423 B.C. The Truce of Laches in April is concluded by Athens to check the progress of Sparta's Brasidas who ignores the truce and proceeds to take Scione and Mende in hopes of reaching Athens and freeing the prisoners taken 2 years ago at Sphacteria. Athens sends reinforcements under Nicias, who retakes Mende.

Theater *Maidens of Trachi* by Sophocles (date approximate); *The Clouds* by Aristophanes.

422 B.C. Cleon of Athens meets Brasidas outside the city of Amphipolis, and both men are killed.

Theater *The Wasps* by Aristophanes.

421 B.C. The Peace of Nicias April 11 brings a temporary end to the Peloponnesian War, but Alcibiades, nephew of the late Pericles, engineers an anti-Spartan alliance between Athens and the democracies of Argos, Mantinea, and Elis.

Theater *The Peace* by Aristophanes.

420 B.C. Corinth and Boeotia refuse to support last year's Peace of Nicias, and although Athens has released her Spartan prisoners, she has retained Pylos and Nisaea because Sparta has claimed that she is unable to turn over Amphipolus. A new Quadruple Alliance of Athens, Argus, Mantinea, and Elis, organized by Alcibiades, confronts a Spartan-Boeotian alliance in July, but the middle classes of Athens do not support Alcibiades who nevertheless dominates Athenian life and politics.

Theater *The Suppliant Women* by Euripides.

419 B.C. Sparta's King Agis gathers a strong army at Philus and descends upon Argos by marching at night from the north. His Boeotian forces fail him in the clutch, but he is able to conclude a treaty with Argos.

Theater *Andromache* by Euripides (not produced at Athens). *Electra* by Sophocles, who takes his theme from *The Libation Bearers* by Aeschylus, but whose play is more melodramatic than tragic (date approximate).

418 B.C. The Battle of Mantinea in August is the greatest land battle of the Peloponnesian War and gives Sparta a stunning victory over Argos, which has broken its treaty with Sparta's Agis at the insistence of Alcibiades and has threatened Tegea. Alcibiades has not been re-elected general, and Sparta breaks up the Athenian confederation with the unwitting help of Alcibiades's political enemies in Athens.

417 B.C. Athenian forces are turned back in Chalcidice.

416 B.C. Alcibiades urges the Athenians to conquer Syracuse, subdue Sicily, crush Carthage, and thus gain added forces that will enable them to finish the war against Sparta. His bold offensive plan wins the support of the Athenians.

415 B.C. Athens prepares an armada to attack Sicily, but on the eve of its departure the Athenians are given a bad omen: the Hermae busts in the streets of Athens are mysteriously mutilated May 22. Alcibiades is accused of having originated the crime and also of having profaned the Eleusinian mysteries. He demands an immediate inquiry, but he is ordered to set sail. When he reaches Sicily, Alcibiades is recalled to Athens to stand trial. He escapes to Sparta on the return voyage, learns that he has been condemned to death in absentia, openly joins with the Spartans, and persuades them to send Gylippus to assist Syracuse and to fortify Decelea in Attica.

Athenian forces land at Dascon in Syracuse Great Harbor in November, but their victory is of little use.

Theater   *The Trojan Women* by Euripides is presented shortly after the massacre by Athenians of the male population of Melos, which has tried to remain neutral in the Peloponnesian War.

414 B.C. The Athenian fleet and army moves on Syracuse from Catana in April and begins a wall to block Syracuse's land approaches while the fleet blocks approach to the city from the sea, but the Athenian commander Lamachus is killed, the fleet is defeated, and supplies run short. Sparta's Gylippus arrives to strengthen the Syracusans, and Athens responds to appeals from Nicias by sending out 73 vessels in a second armada under the command of Demosthenes.

Theater   *The Birds* by Aristophanes is presented as Athens awaits the outcome of its military expedition in Sicily.

413 B.C. Demosthenes arrives at Syracuse in July but is defeated in a nocturnal attack and sustains heavy losses. He urges Nicias to leave, Nicias delays and finally consents, but his soothsayers persuade him to remain after a lunar eclipse August 27 has aroused superstitious fears among the men. The Athenian fleet is bottled up in the harbor and is destroyed in the Battle of Syracuse in September. Demosthenes and Nicias are captured and executed in cold blood after taking to the hills with an army of foot soldiers.

Survivors of the massacre mostly die in the quarries at Syracuse.

Theater   *Electra* by Euripides, who puts the legend of Orestes' revenge in modern dress and depicts the ancient matricide as a contemporary crime.

412 B.C. Alcibiades loses the confidence of the Spartans, antagonizes their king Agis, and retires to the court of the Persian satrap Tissaphernes. He advises Tissaphernes to withdraw his support from Sparta while conspiring with the oligarchic party at Athens as Sparta's allied cities break away in a series of revolts.

411 B.C. The discredited democracy of Athens is overthrown in July by the oligarchic extremists Antiphon, Peisander, and Phrynichus, who open secret and treasonable negotiations with Sparta. They are overthrown by the moderate Theramenes, who establishes the "Constitution of the Five Thousand." The Athenian navy recalls Alcibiades from Sardis, his election is confirmed by the Athenians at the persuasion of Theramenes, and a Spartan fleet in the Hellespont at Cynossema is defeated in September by an Athenian fleet.

Theater   *Iphigenia in Tauris* by Euripides, whose heroine priestess of Artemis finds that the intended victims of human sacrifice are her brother Orestes and his friend. She outwits the barbarian king and organizes an escape. *Lysistrata* and *The Women at the Thesmophoria* (*Thesmophoriazusae*) by Aristophanes. The women in *Lysistrata* revolt against war by denying their sexual favors to their husbands.

410 B.C. Alcibiades crushes the Spartan navy and its supporting Persian land army in March at Cyzicus in the Sea of Marmora. Sparta makes peace overtures but the new Athenian demagogue Cleophon lets the opportunity escape.

409 B.C. Alcibiades recaptures Byzantium, ends the city's rebellion from Athens, clears the Bosporous, and secures the Athenian supply route for grain from the Euxine (Black) Sea region.

Theater   *Philoctetes* by Sophocles who returns for his theme to the Trojan War of the 12th century B.C.

408 B.C. Alcibiades enters Athens in triumph June 16 after an absence of 7 years. He is appointed general with autocratic powers and leaves for Samos to rejoin his fleet. The Spartan admiral Lysander arrives at Ephesus in the fall and builds up a great fleet with help from the new Persian satrap, Cyrus.

Theater   *Orestes* by Euripides who continues the theme of his 413 B.C. tragedy *Electra. The Phoenician Women* by Euripides and other playwrights who have helped to complete the work. Euripides leaves Athens in dissatisfaction and travels to the court of Archelaus in Macedonia, where he will die in the winter of 407–406 B.C. at age 77, leaving incomplete his *Iphigenia at Aulis* but leaving behind

408 B.C. (cont.) his masterpiece *The Bacchants*, which will be produced at Athens by his son and will be the last great Greek tragedy.

"The beauty of Helen was a pretext for the gods to send the Greeks against the Phrygians" (in the Trojan War), says Euripides in *Orestes* (above), "and to kill many men so as to purge the earth of an insolent abundance of people." Greek city-states have few resources and are not organized to support many people.

407 B.C. Sparta's Admiral Lysander refuses to be lured out of Ephesus to do battle with Alcibiades who runs out of supplies and is forced to sail north and plunder some enemy coastal towns. Alcibiades leaves behind a squadron under the command of his boyhood friend Antiochus who violates orders and taunts Lysander. The Spartan fleet responds to the challenge, sallies forth from Ephesus, and routs the Athenians at Notium, administering a defeat that gives the enemies of Alcibiades at Athens an excuse to strip him of his command.

406 B.C. Alcibiades is replaced with a new board of generals, one of whom is blockaded in Mitylene harbor by the Spartan Callicratidas who gains prominence despite hindrances by Lysander and his Persian ally Cyrus. Athens raises a huge fleet to relieve the siege of Mitylene. Callicratidas is defeated and drowned in August at the Battle of Arginusae. Sparta sues for peace but is again rejected by the drunken demagogue Cleophon.

405 B.C. The Spartan admiral Lysander captures the Athenian fleet without resistance in September, only 20 ships escape under the command of Conon, and the Spartan king Pausanius lays siege to Athens while Lysander's fleet blockades Piraeus. Athens executes the demagogue Cleophon and begins 6 months of slow starvation as Corinth and Thebes demand the destruction of the city.

Theater *The Frogs* by Aristophanes: "Alone among the gods, Death loves not gifts." (The Greeks believe the god of the underworld to be implacable and make no efforts to propitiate him.)

The Erectheum is completed in Ionian style on the Acropolis after 16 years of construction. The female figues that support its roof are called Caryatids because they are modeled after girls from the town of Caryae.

404 B.C. Athens capitulates April 25, and the Peloponnesian War is ended as Theramenes secures terms from the Spartans and saves the city from destruction. Athens has been starved into submission, her long walls are torn down to the sound of flutes, and her empire is dissolved. The oligarchy of the "Thirty Tyrants" takes power under Critias who has Theramenes forced to drink poison hemlock on charges of treason. Alcibiades is murdered in Phrygia at the behest of Sparta.

Plague sweeps Athens as the city is weakened by starvation. Foreign merchants may number half the city's citizenry, and the total population of 60,000 to 70,000 includes slaves who may number half the total.

401 B.C. Persia's Cyrus the Younger leads a revolt against his brother Artaxerxes II but is defeated and killed by Artaxerxes at Cunaxa. Greek commanders in the rebel army are killed, but the Greek essayist Xenophon, 33, takes command of 10,000 Greek soldiers and leads them back to the Euxine (Black) Sea in a journey that he will describe in his *Anabasis*.

The Greek historian Thucydides dies at age 60, leaving behind an account of the Golden Age of Pericles and of the Peloponnesian War up to 404 B.C.. He has attempted to be objective and will be called "the father of scientific history."

Theater *Oedipus at Colonus* by the late Sophocles is presented at Athens and is the greatest tragedy of the playwright, who died 5 years ago at age 90. His life spanned the ascendance and decline of the Athenian Empire.

Athens and Sparta joined in resisting the Persians but fell to fighting each other in the Peloponnesian Wars.

4th CENTURY B.C.

400 B.C. London has its origins on a rise above marshy wastes at the point where the Walbrook joins the Thames River. The Celtic king Belin rebuilds an earth wall surrounding a few dozen huts and orders a small landing place to be cut into the south side of the wall, along the river front, where a wooden quay is built. The watergate cut in the wall to permit entry to the settlement from quayside will be called Belinsgate, a name that will be corrupted to "Billingsgate" (*see* A.D. 43).

399 B.C. The Greek philosopher Socrates is condemned for flouting conventional ideas and for allegedly corrupting the youth with his impiety. While his disciples, including Plato, look on at the prison where he is confined, Socrates drinks a potion made from poison hemlock (*Conium maculatum*) (*see* Plato, 347 B.C.).

396 B.C. The Etruscan city of Veii in southern Etruria falls to Roman forces after a 10-year siege as the Romans begin to end the Etruscan civilization in Italy (*see* 900 B.C.; 509 B.C.).

A Carthaginian army besieging Syracuse is stricken with smallpox.

393 B.C. Theater *The Ecclesiazusae* is a bawdy new comedy by Aristophanes.

388 B.C. Theater *Plutus* is a new comedy by Aristophanes.

356 B.C. The Temple of Artemis built at Ephesus beginning in 772 B.C. is burned down by a certain Herostratus, who destroys one of the seven wonders of the ancient world in a perverted bid for immortality.

354 B.C. A tomb enclosed by Ionic columns that will be called one of the seven wonders of the world is built at Halicarnassus in Caria for King Mausolus from whose name the word "mausoleum" will derive.

350 B.C. References to wheat first appear in Greek writings as wheat suitable for bread is introduced from Egypt.

The Greek poet Archestratus in Sicily writes a book called *Gastrology*.

347 B.C. The academy founded by the Athenian philosopher Plato will continue for 876 years. Plato's friends have purchased a suburban grove for the school dedicated to the god Academus. Philanthropists bear all costs; students pay no fees.

Plato's *Republic* will quote Socrates as saying,

Until all philosophers are kings, or the kings and princes of this world have the spirit and power of philosophy, and political greatness and wisdom meet in one, and those commoner natures who pursue either to the exclusion of the other are compelled to stand aside, cities [states] will never have rest from their evils—no, nor the human race.

Plato (above) will express certain medical beliefs along with his political philosophies. The heart is the fountainhead of the blood, says Plato, the liver mirrors the soul, the spleen cleanses the liver, and he introduces the word *anaisthesia* (*see* A.D. 1846).

Plato urges temperance and bewails the changes in the Attic landscape since his youth. Green meadows, woods, and springs have given way to bare limestone partly because the planting of olive trees has led to the ruin of the land (*see* Solon, 594 B.C.).

344 B.C. Aristotle travels from Athens to the Aegean island of Lesbos where he will spend 2 years studying natural history, especially marine biology. Now 40, Aristotle is a follower of Plato, and his father is a physician to the king of Macedon.

342 B.C. Aristotle returns to Macedon at the invitation of her king Philip and begins 7 years of teaching. His pupils will include Philip's son Alexander, now 14.

340 B.C. Philip of Macedon fails in a siege of Byzantium, whose sentries may have seen Philip's advance by the light of a crescent moon and thus have been able to save the city. The Byzantines will adopt the crescent symbol of their goddess Hecate as the symbol of Byzantium (*see* Viennese bakers, A.D. 1217).

338 B.C. Philip of Macedon defeats the Athenians and Thebans in the last struggle for Greek independence August 2 at the Battle of Chaeronea in western Boeotia (*see* Thessalonica, 315 B.C.).

336 B.C. Philip of Macedon is assassinated at Aeges during the wedding feast of his daughter. He is succeeded by his son Alexander, now 20, who will carry out Philip's planned expedition against the Persians.

335 B.C. Aristotle returns to Athens from Macedon and opens a lyceum in an elegant gymnasium dedicated to Apollo Lyceus, god of shepherds. The lyceum contains a museum of natural history, zoological gardens, and a library.

Aristotle (above) attempts to develop a deductive system as comprehensive as is possible with the scientific materials available. He concerns himself chiefly with the anatomical structures of animals, their re-

335 B.C. (cont.) production, and their evolution, and he founds the study of comparative anatomy in an effort to categorize animal life into biological groups.

Aristotle describes various parts of the digestive canal in some detail, but his ideas of physiology are primitive in the absence of any chemical knowledge. Everything in life is subject to basic law, says Aristotle, but he believes that food is "cooked" in the intestinal tube, and he praises garlic for its medicinal qualities.

Aristotle (above) advises abortion for parents with too many children, and he writes in *Politics* that "... neglect of an effective birth control policy is a never failing source of poverty which in turn is the parent of revolution and crime." But the Greeks (and later the Romans) will encourage large families lest they have a dearth of recruits for their armies.

334 B.C. Alexander of Macedon invades Asia with an army that includes 5,000 mercenaries. The Persian army that opposes him includes 10,000 Greek mercenaries.

333 B.C. The Battle of Issus in October gives Alexander of Macedon a great victory over the Persians but the emperor Darius III escapes.

332 B.C. Alexander the Great of Macedon conquers Egypt and founds a city that will be called Alexandria.

331 B.C. The Battle of Arbela (or Gaugamela) October 1 in northern Mesopotamia gives Alexander the Great another victory over Darius III. Alexander becomes master of the Persian Empire, ending the Achaemenid dynasty founded in 550 B.C.

Wheat is grown extensively in southeastern parts of the British Isles and is threshed under great barns, reports a traveler from the Greek colony at Marsilea that will later be called Marseilles (*see* Lacydon, 600 B.C.).

330 B.C. The Persian king Darius III is murdered by his satrap Bessus after a 6-year reign. Alexander the Great sacks the Persian capital of Persepolis. It takes 20,000 mules and 5,000 camels to carry off the loot.

The atomic theory developed by the Greek philosopher Democritus says that all matter is composed of tiny atomic particles, the word "atom" meaning unbreakable or indivisible (*see* Thomson, A.D. 1897). Nothing happens through chance or intention, says Democritus; everything happens through cause and of necessity. All change is merely an aggregation or separation of parts, nothing which exists can be reduced to nothing, and nothing can come out of nothing. Democritus distinguishes between vertebrate and invertebrate animals, both of which he dissects.

329 B.C. Alexander the Great conquers Samarkand (Maracanda), capital of Sogdiana, in central Asia.

327 B.C. Alexander the Great invades northern India after having gained ascendancy over all of Greece, occupied Egypt, and destroyed the power of Persia. But Alexander is persuaded to abandon his plans for invading the Ganges Valley by his army, which is tired of campaigning.

Alexander appoints Nearchus as admiral and places under his command all in the ranks with any knowledge of seafaring. Nearchus has Indian shipwrights build 800 vessels, some as large as 300 tons, and uses Indian pilots to guide his fleet through Persian Gulf waters to Babylonia.

Bananas (*Musa sapientum*) are found growing in the Indus Valley by Alexander the Great (*see* A.D. 1482).

325 B.C. *The Persae* by Timotheus of Miletus is the earliest papyrus written in Greek that will survive.

The first known reference to sugar cane (*Saccharum officinarum*) appears in writings by Alexander's admiral Nearchus who writes of Indian reeds "that produce honey, although there are no bees." The word "sugar" (adapted from the Arabic *sukhar,* which derives from the Sanskrit *sarkara,* meaning gravel or pebble) begins to appear frequently in Indian literature (*see* 300 B.C.).

The poor of Athens exist mainly on beans, greens, beechnuts, turnips, wild pears, dried figs, barley paste, and occasional grasshoppers, with only sporadic welfare assistance.

324 B.C. Theater A "New Comedy" pioneered by the Athenian playwright Menander, 19, employs lighthearted humor rather than the virulent personal and political satire of the late Aristophanes and has realistic plots and characters based on the domestic life of ordinary citizens. Son of the rich Diopeithes of Cephisia, Menander will win his first dramatic prize in 316 B.C. but will win no more than eight prizes in all.

323 B.C. Alexander the Great dies at Babylon at age 32, and a 42-year struggle begins that will be called the Wars of the Diadochi (successors). Alexander's generals, Antigonus, Antipater, Seleucus, Ptolemy, Eumenes, and Lysimachus, contest control of the Macedonian Empire.

The Museum of Alexandria is founded by Ptolemy (above), who takes over Egypt. Like Alexander, he has studied under Aristotle, and he will staff the museum with some 100 professors paid by the state.

322 B.C. *Politics IV* by Aristotle says, "When there are too many farmers the excess will be of the better kind; when there are too many mechanics and laborers, of the worst."

321 B.C. The Battle of the Caudine Forks (Caudium) brings defeat to a Roman army trapped by the Samnites in a pass near Beneventum. The Romans are forced to pass under the yolk (a horizontal spear placed atop two upright spears) as a symbol of submission.

The assassination of Philip of Macedon began the reign of his son Alexander, later called Alexander the Great.

319 B.C. Alexander's general Antipater falls fatally ill and names as his successor the aged regent Polysperchon, whose authority is challenged by Antipater's son Cassander, 31.

316 B.C. Macedonia's regent Polysperchon is defeated and overthrown by Cassander, who seizes Olympias, mother of the late Alexander the Great, has her put to death, and marries Thessaloniki, half-sister of Alexander, with whom he will rule until 297 B.C.

Eumenes and Antigonus, rivals to Cassander for control of Macedonia, meet in battle in Media, with Eumenes commanding a force of 36,700 foot soldiers, 6,050 cavalrymen, and 114 elephants against 22,000 foot soldiers, 900 horsemen, and 65 elephants for Antigonus. But cavalrymen sent out by Antigonus take advantage of cover provided by dust raised by the elephants and seize the baggage camp of Eumenes, whose cavalrymen desert. Antigonus offers to return the baggage camp and the wives he has captured if the enemy will desert and hand over Eumenes, who is put to death by his guard after a week's captivity.

315 B.C. The Macedonian port city of Thessalonica is founded by Cassander whose wife Thessaloniki was named by her father Philip II of Macedon to commemorate his victory (Niki) over Thessaly in 338 B.C.

314 B.C. Antigonus promises freedom to the Greek cities in a bid to gain support against Cassander. The Aetolians enter into an alliance with Antigonus; Cassander marches against them with his allies Lysimachus, Ptolemy, and Seleucus.

312 B.C. The Battle of Gaza brings triumph to Ptolemy and Seleucus over the one-eyed Antigonus (called Antigonus Cyclops, or Monophthalmos) who is captured but is immediately released.

The Roman censor Appius Claudius Caecus begins construction of the Appian Way.

Rome gets its first pure drinking water as engineers complete an aqueduct into the city.

308 B.C. Egypt's Ptolemy is defeated in a naval battle off Cyprus by Demetrius Poliorcetes, 29, son of Antigonus Cyclops, who was defeated with his father at Gaza in 312 B.C.

307 B.C. Rhodes is besieged by Demetrius Poliocertes, who employs 30,000 workmen to build siege towers and engines, including the tower Helepolis that requires 3,400 men to move and a 180-foot ram that is moved on wheels by 1,000 men. But the siege will fail.

305 B.C. The Seleucid Empire that will rule Babylonia and Syria until 64 B.C. is established by Seleucus, now 53, who takes the title Nicator and continues conquests that will extend the empire to the Indus River.

301 B.C. The Battle of Ipsus in Phrygia ends the ambitions of Antigonus, who assumed the title of king 5 years ago, has invaded Egypt, but is slain at age 81 by the forces of Lysimachus and Seleucus, who defeat his son Demetrius.

3rd CENTURY B.C.

Nomad tribes begin to occupy parts of northern China.

On Stones by the Greek philosopher Theophrastus mentions fossil substances "that are called coals, . . . found in Liguria and in Elis, on the way of Olympias, over the mountains . . . which kindle and burn like woodcoals . . . ; they are used by smiths" (*see* A.D. 852).

History of Plants and *Theoretical Botany* by Theophrastus (above) mention plant diseases such as rusts and mildews and describe "caprification" of figs (*see* A.D. 1885).

The Chinese build a vast irrigation system to reduce the flooding of Szechwan's Red Basin.

Indigenous Chinese regard the dairy products of the nomad tribes (above) as unhygienic.

The Athenian philosopher Epicurus extols luxury and indulgence in eating and drinking. Pleasure is the only good and the end of all morality, says Epicurus, but a genuine life of pleasure must be a life of prudence, honor, and justice.

300 B.C. *Elements* by the Greek mathematician Euclid is a 13-volume work that states the principles of geometry for the first time in formal style (*see* 1500 B.C.). Euclid has founded a school at Alexandria.

Carthage in North Africa gains economic ascendancy in the Mediterranean by trading in slaves, Egyptian linen, products of the African interior that include ivory and animal skins (lion and leopard), Greek pottery and wine, iron from Elba, copper from Cyprus, silver from Spain, tin from the British Isles, incense from Arabia, and purple-black dyestuffs from Tyre.

Carthaginians are the world's greatest shipbuilders and sail the seas in quinquiremes—ships with five banks of oars manned by well-drilled government-owned galley slaves.

Carthaginian planters own fertile lands in Libya and in some cases have as many as 20,000 slaves.

Sugar from India is introduced to the Middle East, where it is planted in areas wet enough to support its growth (*see* 325 B.C.; A.D. 1099).

297 B.C. Macedonia's Cassander dies at age 53, and Demetrius Poliocertes returns to Greece with the aim of becoming master of Macedonia and Asia.

295 B.C. Athens falls to Demetrius after a bitter siege, and its tyrant Lachares is destroyed.

288 B.C. Demetrius is driven out of Macedonia by Lysimachus and Pyrrhus, king of Epirus, after Seleucus, Ptolemy, and Lysimachus have formed a coalition to block plans by Demetrius to invade Asia.

285 B.C. Egypt's Ptolemy Soter abdicates at age 82 after a 38-year reign that has founded a dynasty which will rule until 30 B.C. He is succeeded by his 24-year-old son, who will rule as Ptolemy II Philadelphus until 246 B.C., first with the daughter of Lysimachus as his wife and thereafter (from 276 B.C.) with his own sister as his wife.

Demetrius Poliocertes is deserted by his troops and surrenders to Seleucus, who will keep him prisoner until his death in 283 B.C.

280 B.C. A Roman army is defeated at Asculum by King Pyrrhus of Epirus who says, "Another such victory and we are ruined." A triumph that has cost the victor more than the vanquished will be called a pyrrhic victory for millennia to come.

The Colossus of Rhodes is completed by the sculptor Chares of Lindus after 12 years of work and will stand as one of the seven wonders of the ancient world until it is shattered by an earthquake in 224 B.C. Made from the spoils left by Demetrius Poliocertes when he raised the seige he began in 307 B.C., the Colossus is a bronze statue of the sun god Helios. It is so large that a ship can pass between its legs and it rises to a height of perhaps 120 feet above the harbor that has grown rich in the slave trade.

275 B.C. The Museum of Alexandria founded by Ptolemy II maintains and supports scholars from all countries and encourages them in their research into all branches of known science. The museum will be the leading Greek university.

The Museum of Alexandria employs knowledge gained by the Egyptians in the practice of embalming to expand knowledge of anatomy and physiology. The museum's leading medical professor is the Greek Hippocratist Herophilus of Chalcedon, who scorns the traditional fear of dissecting human bodies and who conducts postmortem examinations that enable him to describe the alimentary canal (he gives the duodenum its name), the liver, the spleen, the circulatory system, the eye, the brain tissues, and the genital organs. Herophilus is the first to make a distinction between sensory nerves and motor nerves, and he founds the first school of anatomy.

272 B.C. Egypt's Ptolemy annexes Miletus, Phoenicia, and western Cilicia after defeating his rebellious half-brother Magas and the Seleucid emperor Antiochus I Soter in the First Syrian War.

Rome's war with Pyrrhus of Epirus ends after 10 years as Tarentum is surrendered to the Romans.

270 B.C. Rome's subjugation of Italy is completed by the recapture of Rhegium from the Mamertines and the defeat of the Brutians, the Lucanians, the Calabrians, and the Samnites.

268 B.C. The Roman denarius is minted for the first time. The silver coin will become familiar throughout the Western world. (*see* A.D. 81).

265 B.C. The Archimedian screw for raising water is devised by the Greek mathematician Archimedes who is studying at Alexandria. A native of Syracuse, Archimedes says that he could move the earth if he had a lever long enough and a fulcrum strong enough ("Give me where to stand and I will move the earth").

Archimedes (above) has discovered ("Eureka!") the law of specific gravity while sitting in his bathtub: a body dropped into a liquid will displace an amount of liquid equal to its own weight.

264 B.C. A Punic War embroils Rome in a conflict with Carthage that will continue for 23 years (*see* 878 B.C.; 260 B.C.).

260 B.C. The Battle of Mylae off the north coast of Sicily gives Rome her first naval victory over Carthage. The Roman admiral Gaius Duilius Nepos commands quinqueremes modeled after a Carthaginian ship found stranded on the Italian coast, and he uses grappling irons and boarding bridges to revolutionize naval warfare and to defeat a larger, more maneuverable Carthaginian flotilla.

Buddhism is adopted by the third emperor of India's Mauyra Dynasty, which arose following the confusion of Alexander the Great's invasions in the last century. The emperor Asoka establishes India's first hospitals and herbal gardens and places them under Buddhist control in opposition to the Hindu Brahmins (*see* 528 B.C.; China, A.D. 517).

250 B.C. Alexandria's Pharos lighthouse is completed on the small island of Pharos by the engineer Sostratus of Cnidus. Funded by Ptolemy II, the 600-foot tower will be called one of the seven wonders of the ancient world.

The Pharos lighthouse (above) beams the light of a fire that will remain burning for 1,500 years to guide mariners who can see it from nearly 100 miles at sea.

246 B.C. Egypt's Ptolemy II dies at age 63 and is succeeded after a peaceful reign of 39 years by his 36-year-old son who will reign less peacefully until 221 B.C. as Ptolemy III.

Syria is invaded by Egypt's Ptolemy III who seeks vengeance for the death of his murdered sister Berenice. He throws his armies against those of Seleucus II.

245 B.C. Babylon and Susa fall to the Egyptian armies of Ptolemy III.

243 B.C. Ptolemy III is recalled from Syria by a revolt in Egypt and ceases his martial interests and his support of the Egyptian army.

237 B.C. The Iberian Peninsula is invaded by a Carthaginian army under Hamilcar Barca, 33.

228 B.C. Carthage's General Hamilcar Barca falls in battle. Command of his army in the Iberian Peninsula passes to his son-in-law Hasdrubal.

222 B.C. Mediolanum (Milan) falls to Roman legions in Lombardy. The town has been occupied successively by Ligurians, Etruscans, and Celts.

221 B.C. The Carthaginian general Hasdrubal is assassinated. Command of the troops is assumed by Hannibal, 26-year-old son of the late Hamilcar Barca, and his brother Hasdrubal.

Egypt's Ptolemy III dies at age 61 after a 25-year reign. He is succeeded by his 23-year-old son who will rule with his sister-wife Arsinoe III, but the 18-year reign of Ptolemy IV will be dominated by court favorites.

Modern China has her beginnings in the Ch'in dynasty founded by Shih Huang-ti who makes himself "first" emperor of a country whose name will derive from the dynastic name Ch'in. The short-lived Ch'in dynasty will extend the country's waterworks, build a network of roads, and raise a great defensive wall (*see* 214 B.C.).

The Ch'in emperor Shih Huang-ti (above) burns books to eliminate the stultifying classicism of earlier dynasties, saving only works on medicine, agriculture, and astrology (but other books are hidden by priests and scholars and will survive).

Egyptian medical studies at Alexandria are supported by Ptolemy IV (above), who is weaker than his predecessors but who is devoted to the pursuit of science.

Alexandrian medical science is headed by Herophilus and his rival Erasistratus, formerly court physician to the Seleucides of Syria. Erasistratus gives heart valves the names they will henceforth carry, he establishes the connection between arteries and veins, he investigates the lymphatic ducts, he expands knowledge of the nervous system (distinguishing between motor nerves and sensory nerves), and he describes in detail the convolutions of the brain.

220 B.C. The Flaminian Way is completed between Rome and Rimini.

Armored elephants helped Hannibal's Carthaginians defeat superior Roman numbers in the Second Punic War.

218 B.C. A Second Punic War begins as Rome's Hispanic allies are attacked by a Carthaginian army under Hannibal. He besieges the town of Sagunto, whose inhabitants eat their own dead rather than surrender but are eventually forced to yield. He crosses the Alps and defeats Roman forces at the Ticino River and again at the Trebbia River.

217 B.C. Roman forces are defeated by Carthage's Hannibal at Lago di Trasimeno, 10 miles west of Perusia June 24. A large army under Gaius Flaminius is almost completely destroyed by Carthaginians and Gauls, some 16,000 Romans including Flaminius himself are killed, and the lake is turned red with blood.

216 B.C. The Battle of Cannae in early summer is won by Hannibal, whose army of 40,000 defeats a heavily armored and unmaneuverable Roman force of 70,000. Some 50,000 Roman and allied troops are butchered, 10,000 are taken prisoner, but Hannibal lacks the catapults and battering rams needed to besiege Rome and contents himself with laying waste the fields of Italy, forcing Rome to import grain at war-inflated prices.

Rome has been deserted by her allies and starves out Capua and loots Syracuse as an object lesson to other allies.

215 B.C. Theater *The Menaechmi* by Roman playwright Titus Maccius Plautus, 39 (dates of all Plautus's plays are conjectural).

214 B.C. Construction begins on a great Chinese defensive wall to keep out the Mongol tribesmen who menace the territories of Ch'in emperor Shih Huang-ti. Extending 2,500 miles from Mongolia to the sea, the Great Wall is made initially of earthwork but will later be of brick.

Theater *The Merchant* (*Mercator*) by Titus Maccius Plautus.

213 B.C. Theater *The Comedy of Asses* (*Asinaria*) by Titus Maccius Plautus: "Such things are easier said than done" (I, iii); "Man is a wolf to man" (*Homo homini lupus*," II, iv).

207 B.C. The Battle of Metaurus in Umbria ends Hannibal's hopes of success in Italy. A Carthaginian army under Hannibal's brother Hasdrubal is defeated by the Romans under the consuls Claudius Nero and Livius Salinator. Hasdrubal is killed in the battle.

204 B.C. Carthage is besieged by the Romans under P. Cornelius Scipio (Scipio Africanus). One hundred boys of noble birth are immolated by the Carthaginians in an effort to propitiate the god Moloch to raise the Roman siege.

202 B.C. The Han dynasty that will rule China for more than four centuries is inaugurated as the last Ch'in emperor dies and one of his minor officials assumes power.

The Second Punic War is ended and the power of Carthage largely destroyed by the Battle of Sama October 19. Scipio Africanus defeats a combined army of Carthaginians and Numidians under the command of Hannibal and forces Carthage to capitulate.

Theater *The Casket* (*Cistellaria*) by Titus Maccius Plautus.

201 B.C. Carthage surrenders all her Mediterranean possessions to Rome, her Iberian territories included. The Carthaginians agree to pay Rome 200 talents per year for 50 years to make no war without Rome's permission and to destroy all but 10 Carthaginian warships (*see* 150 B.C.).

2nd CENTURY B.C.

200 B.C. Theater *Stichus* by Titus Maccius Plautus: "An unwilling woman given to a man in marriage is not his wife but an enemy."

197 B.C. The Battle of Cynoscephalae in Thessaly gives a Roman army under T. Quinctius Flaminius victory over Philip V of Macedon. The Romans will force Philip to surrender Greece, reduce his army to 5,000 and his navy to five ships, promise not to declare war without Rome's permission, and pay Rome 1,000 talents in 10 years.

196 B.C. Theater *The Haunted House* (*Mostellaria*) by Titus Maccius Plautus: "Things which you don't hope happen more frequently than things which you do hope" (I, iii); "A woman smells well when she smells of nothing." Plautus's play *The Persian* (*Persa*) will appear next year.

194 B.C. Theater *The Pot of Gold* (*Aulularia*) and *The Rope* (*Rudens*) by Titus Maccius Plautus, whose play *The Weevil* (*Curculio*) will appear next year.

192 B.C. Syrian forces under Antiochus III invade Greece at the invitation of the Aetolians.

191 B.C. Roman forces at Thermopylae rout Antiochus III, repeating the maneuver executed by Xerxes in 480 B.C.

Cisalpine Gaul becomes a Roman province.

Theater *Pseudolus* by Titus Maccius Plautus: "If you utter insults you will also hear them" (IV); *Epidicus* by Plautus.

190 B.C. The Battle of Magnesia near Smyrna gives the Romans another victory over Antiochus III. L. Cornelius Scipio (soon to be called Scipio Asiaticus) and his brother Scipio Africanus have crossed the Hellespont to pursue Antiochus. They force the Syrian to surrender all his European and Asiatic possessions as far as the Taurus Mountains, to pay 15,000 talents over a period of 12 years, and to surrender Hannibal (who will escape).

189 B.C. Theater *The Two Bacchaides* by Titus Maccius Plautus: "He whom the gods love dies young, while he is in health, has his senses and his judgment sound" (IV, vii).

188 B.C. Theater *The Captives* (*Captivi*) by Titus Maccius Plautus: "It is the nature of the poor to hate and envy men of property" (III); "All men love themselves" (III).

187 B.C. Theater *Three-Penny Day* (*Trinummus*) by Titus Maccius Plautus: "Keep what you have; the known evil is best" (I, iii); "What you lend is lost; when you ask for it back, you may find a friend made an enemy by your kindness" (IV, iii).

186 B.C. Theater *Amphitryon* (*Amphitruo*) by Titus Maccius Plautus: "If anything is spoken in jest, it is not fair to turn it to earnest" (III), *Truculentus* by Plautus.

185 B.C. Theater *Casina* by Titus Maccius Plautus, who will die in 184 B.C. at age 60.

Eastern indulgence is introduced into Rome by troops returning from the war with Syria's Antiochus III. Titus Livy will write nearly 200 years hence that "the Army of Asia introduced foreign luxury to Rome. It was then that meals began to demand more preparation and expense.... The cook, considered and employed until then as a slave at the lowest cost, became extremely expensive. What had been only a job became an art."

183 B.C. Hannibal poisons himself at the court of Bithynia's Prusia I, who was about to betray him to the Romans.

Pisa and Parma become Roman colonies.

179 B.C. Rome's Pons Aemilius, completed across the Tiber, is the world's first stone bridge.

172 B.C. A Roman army is defeated by the Macedonian king Perseus, who succeeds his father Philip V and is attacked by the Romans, beginning a war that will continue until 168 B.C.

170 B.C. The world's first paved streets are laid out in Rome. The new streets are passable in all weather and easier to keep clean, but they add to the din of traffic.

Rome's first professional cooks appear in the form of commercial bakers, but most Roman households continue to grind their own flour and bake their own bread.

168 B.C. The Battle of Pydna gives Roman forces a victory over the Macedonian king Perseus who has succeeded Philip V. The Roman general Lucius Aemilius Paulus, 51, returns with Perseus in his triumphal procession.

Huge amounts of booty brought home by Paulus after the Battle of Pydna (above) enrich the Roman treasury. Rome relieves her citizens of direct taxation (the *tributum*).

168 B.C. (cont.) Macedonians captured by Pydna (above) are sold into slavery at Rome. Females fetch as much as 50 times the price of a male.

Syria's Seleucid king Antiochus IV Ephiphanes outlaws Judaism, lays waste the Great Temple at Jerusalem, and tries to Hellenize the Jews by erecting idols to be worshipped by the people of Judea.

167 B.C. The Jewish priest Mattathias of Modin defies Syria's Antiochus IV Ephiphanes who has outlawed Judaism. Mattathias escapes into the mountains outside Lydda with his five sons and begins a revolt. He will die in 166 B.C., but his sons will continue the revolt, and his third son Judah will receive the surname Maccabaeus—the Hammerer.

166 B.C. Theater *The Women of Andros* (*Andria*) by Roman playwright Terence (Publius Terentius Afer), 24, with flute music by his fellow-slave Flaccus at the Megaleusian games in April. "Obsequiousness makes friends; truth breeds hate" (I, i); "Lovers' quarrels are the renewal of love"; "There is such malice in men as to rejoice in misfortunes and from another's woe to draw delight" (IV, i).

165 B.C. Judah Maccabee (Maccabaeus) and his brothers retake Jerusalem from the Syrians.

The Maccabees (above) cleanse the Great Temple, destroy the idols erected by Antiochus IV, and restore the monotheistic religion of Judaism. It will later be said that the Maccabees found only enough oil in the temple to keep a light burning for 1 day, but that somehow the oil lasted for 8 days, and Jews will commemorate the event in the annual Feast of Dedication called Hanukkah.

Theater *The Mother-in-Law* (*Hecyra*) by Terence, who has adopted a play by Apollodorus.

163 B.C. Antiochus IV of Syria dies after a 12-year reign and is succeeded by his 10-year-old son, who will reign briefly as Antiochus V under the regency of Lysias who will make peace with the Jews.

Theater *The Self-Avenger* (*Heautontimorumenos*) by Terence: "I am a man; and nothing human is foreign to me" (*Homo sum; humani nihil a me alienum puto*, I, i).

162 B.C. Syria's Antiochus V is overthrown and killed by his cousin Demetrius I Soter, who will reign until 150 B.C.

161 B.C. Theater *The Eunuch* (*Eunuchus*) by Terence: "I know the nature of women;/ When you want to, they don't want to;/ And when you don't want to, they desire exceedingly" (IV, vii), *Phormio* by Terence: "So many men, so many opinions" (II, iv); "A work to the wise is sufficient" (*Dictum sapienti sat est*, III, iii).

160 B.C. The newly appointed governor of Judea is killed in battle by the Maccabees whose leader Judah Maccabee is killed soon after at the Battle of Elasa. Judah

is survived by his older brother Simon and by his youngest brother Jonathan who succeeds as leader and will make Judea a nearly independent principality by the time of his death in 143 B.C.

Theater *Brothers* (*Adelphoe*) by Terence: "It is better to bind your children to you by a feeling of respect, and by gentleness, than by fear" (I, i). A Carthaginian who was brought to Rome as a slave for a senator, Terence will die next year.

153 B.C. January 1 becomes the first day of the civil year in Rome. An uprising in Rome's Spanish provinces obliges Roman consuls to take office earlier than the traditional date of March 15.

150 B.C. "Carthage must be destroyed" (*Delenda est Carthago*), says the Roman censor Marcus Porcius Cato, 84, who has been urging destruction of the prosperous Punic city since 157 B.C., when he helped arbitrate a truce between Carthage and her former ally Masinna, 88-year-old king of Numidia. Masinna is now Rome's ally, Carthage has attacked Numidia, and Cato demands that a Roman army be sent against Carthage.

The Syrian usurper Alexander Balas, who claims to be a son of the late Antiochus IV Epiphanes, defeats Demetrius I Soter in battle and kills him. The Romans support him, and he will rule Syria until 145 B.C.

149 B.C. A Roman army invades North Africa and lays siege to Carthage. The Carthaginians offer to submit but refuse to vacate their city.

Cato the Elder dies at age 85, leaving as his legacy some commentaries on agriculture. *De Agricultura* (or *De Re Rustica*) says that farming has become more amusement than a source of income and that pasturage is far more profitable than tilling the soil; it urges farmers to plant grapes and olives that draw moisture and nutrients from the subsoil rather than grain, which is more subject to drought.

146 B.C. Carthage is destroyed. Romans under Scipio Aemilianus end the Third Punic War and create a new Roman province in the environs of Carthage.

Rome adds Macedonia and Achaea to her list of provinces.

145 B.C. Syria's Alexander Balas falls in battle near Antioch, his forces flee from Demetrius II and Ptolemy VI Philometor, and his son by Cleopatra Thea succeeds to the throne. The boy will rule under a regent as Antiochus VI until 142 B.C.

143 B.C. The Syrian usurper Tryphon traps Judea's Jonathan Maccabee and kills him at Bethshean. Jonathan's older brother Simon succeeds him and will drive all the Syrians out of the citadel at Jerusalem.

142 B.C. Syria's boy king Antiochus VI dies and is succeeded by the son of Demetrius I Soter who will reign as Demetrius II Nicator.

Judea gains independence from Syria under the leadership of Simon Maccabee. He sends an embassy to Rome and begins coinage of money.

141 B.C. Jerusalem is liberated from the Seleucid emperor Demetrius II Nicator by Jewish forces under Simon Maccabee while Demetrius is occupied with conquering Babylon.

Agriculture in the region of Jerusalem has been improved by the Maccabaeus brothers and their followers, who have gained an independence in Judea that will last until 63 B.C.

140 B.C. China's Han dynasty emperor Wu Ti begins a 53-year reign in which he will extend the empire to the south, annex parts of Korea and Tonkin, and send his emissary Chang Ch'ien halfway round the world to Bactria and Sogdiana to seek an east-west alliance against the Huns, or Hsiung Nu.

News of Chang Ch'ien (above) and of Serica, "land of silk," will reach Rome, and caravans will begin to carry the first apricots and peaches (the "Chinese fruit") to Europe while Chang Ch'ien introduces grapes, pomegranates, and walnuts to China.

135 B.C. Rome's first Servile War begins as slaves on the large Sicilian estates revolt under the Syrian Eunus, who calls himself King Antiochus and holds Henna and Tauromenium against Roman armies sent to subdue the insurrection.

134 B.C. Judea's Simon Maccabee is treacherously murdered by his son-in-law, governor of Jericho. Simon's sons Mattathias and Judah are also killed, but he is succeeded by his surviving son John Hyrcanus, who will rule Judea until 104 B.C. and will extend the kingdom to include Samaria, Idumaea, and lands east of the Jordan.

133 B.C. Tiberius Sempronius Gracchus, 30, is elected Roman tribune on a platform of social reform. He proposes an agrarian law that would limit holdings of public land to 312 acres per person, with an additional 250 acres for each of two sons, but large landholders in Etruria and Campania block efforts to recover lands held in violation of the new law, and Gracchus is murdered. The great estates (*latifundia*) are not distributed among new settlers but grow at the expense of the small peasants and to some extent of Rome's urban proletariat.

132 B.C. Rome's Servile War is ended as Roman forces capture the Syrian Eunus and savagely execute him and his supporters.

129 B.C. Pergamum becomes the Roman province of Asia.

Rome's Scipio Aemilianus is found dead with suspicions of murder after favoring some concessions to the Italian peasants who have grown increasingly bitter at their treatment by Roman landowners.

123 B.C. Gaius Sempronius Gracchus, 30, is elected Roman tribune on a platform similar to that of his late brother Tiberius. A more forceful man, Gaius puts through a far more extreme program, which includes a law obliging the government to provide grain to Rome's citizens at a price below the market average. The law protects the poor against famine and against speculators and establishes a precedent. State control of the grain supply will permit demagogues to gain popular support by distributing free grain.

110 B.C. Oysters are cultivated in the first Western efforts to domesticate marine wildlife. Cultured oyster beds are operated in the vicinity of Baia near the town that will become Naples, where local oysterman Sergius Orata makes a fortune selling his bivalves to the luxury trade (*see* 850 B.C.; A.D. 407).

105 B.C. Two Roman armies are defeated at Arausio, on the Rhône, by the Cimbri, a Celtic or Germanic people from east of the Rhine who have moved into the Alpine regions and across the Rhône.

104 B.C. Judea's John Hyrcanus dies after a 30-year reign and is succeeded by his 37-year-old son who will rule briefly as Aristobulus I. He will complete the conquest of Galilee, and will force the people of Hurae to embrace Judaism.

103 B.C. Judea's Aristobulus I dies at age 38 and is succeeded by his brother Alexander Jannaeus, who will extend the boundaries of the kingdom in a selfish and savage reign that will continue until 76 B.C.

A second Servile War erupts in Sicily as slaves rebel under the leadership of Tryphon and Athenion. Slaves from lands conquered by Rome's legions provide much of the power for Roman agriculture, being able to follow verbal orders even though they are less powerful and less docile than horses, whose efficiency is limited also by lack of metal horseshoes and lack of proper harnesses.

102 B.C. The Battle of Aix-en-Provence gives the Roman consul Gaius Marius, 53, a victory over the Teutones and Sciri. Marius has been re-elected consul repeatedly since 107 B.C. in violation of the law of 151 B.C. The people of Provence hail his triumph, and they will name one of their sons Marius by tradition for more than 2,000 years.

101 B.C. The Battle of Campi Raudii near Vercellae gives the Roman consuls Gaius Marius and Quintus Lutatius Catulus, 51, a victory over the Cimbri. Marius becomes a national hero.

The Romans apply waterpower to milling flour and are the first people to do so.

Chinese ships reach the east coast of India for the first time with help from the navigational compass pioneered by the Chinese. They have discovered the orientating effect of magnetite, or lodestone (*see* A.D. 1086).

1st CENTURY B.C.

Sulla, Lepidus, Crassus, Pompey, Julius Caesar, Marc Antony, and Octavian (Augustus) will rule Rome in this century.

99 B.C. Rome's second Servile War ends after 4 years as the consul M. Aquillius subdues an army of slaves that has put up a stubborn resistance.

96 B.C. The Seleucid king Antiochus VIII is murdered by his court favorite Heracleon after a 29-year reign in which he has been forced to divide the realm with his half-brother Antiochus IX, who will reign alone until 95 B.C.

95 B.C. The Seleucid king Antiochus IX is defeated in battle and killed by the son of his late half-brother who will reign briefly as Seleucus VI.

Armenia's Artavazd I dies and is succeeded by his son Tigranes, who has been held hostage for several years by some powerful Parthians. The 45-year-old Tigranes is ransomed for "70 valleys" and begins a 40-year reign that will make Armenia the most powerful nation in western Asia.

93 B.C. Armenia's Tigranes II seals an alliance with the Parthian king Mithridates by marrying his daughter Cleopatra. Tigranes has murdered a neighboring Armenian prince and has taken over his territory. He invades the kingdom of Cappadocia in the name of his new father-in-law, but the Roman general L. Cornelius Sulla comes to the aid of Cappadocia and forces Tigranes to retire.

92 B.C. Parthia's Mithridates II makes an alliance with Rome and prepares to invade Mesopotamia.

91 B.C. The Republic of Italia is set up by Italian insurrectionists, who establish a capital at Corfinium and begin a 3-year war against Rome.

88 B.C. Parthia's Mithridates the Great dies after a 36-year reign in the closing years of which he has conquered Mesopotamia. His son-in-law Tigranes II of Armenia invades Parthia and begins a war in which he will recover the 70 valleys paid for his ransom in 95 B.C. and will overrun four Parthian vassal states, reducing the size of Parthia and extending the borders of Armenia.

The king of Pontus Mithradates VI Eupator begins the first of three wars that he will wage against Rome. The 44-year-old Mithradates has made himself master of Cappadocia, Paphlagonia, Bithynia, and all of the Black Sea's southern and eastern coasts.

Civil war breaks out in Rome as the legions suppress the insurrection of 3 years ago and as fresh legions are raised to fight the king of Pontus.

87 B.C. The Roman general L. Cornelius Sulla marches on Rome. He kills the demagogue P. Sulpicius Ruffus and other rebels, and he leaves for Asia as proconsul after having instituted reforms that will be short-lived.

A new Roman demagogue appears in the person of L. Cornelius Cinna who begins a reign of terror against the reactionary Roman nobility.

86 B.C. Athens falls to Rome's General Sulla who defeats the forces of Mithradates and his allies.

84 B.C. Sulla forces Mithradates to make peace, to evacuate all the territories he has conquered, to surrender 80 warships, and to pay an indemnity of 3,000 talents. Sulla sails for Brundisium, leaving two legions to police Rome's Asiatic territories and to help L. Licinius Lucullus collect a fine of 20,000 talents from the Asiatic cities.

The Seleucid king Antiochus XII who has seized Damascus is killed on an expedition against the Nabataeans.

82 B.C. Sulla repels rebellious Samnites from Rome in the Battle of the Colline Gate in November. Sulla appoints himself dictator, he moves to punish cities that have sided with Rome's enemies, and he begins a tyranny that will continue until 79 B.C.

81 B.C. The Japanese emperor Sujin begins a great shipbuilding effort in a move to provide his people with more of the seafood on which so many depend for sustenance.

80 B.C. The Roman dictator Sulla halts public distribution of free grain (*see* 123 B.C.; 71 B.C.).

79 B.C. Sulla retires voluntarily from public life after completing substantial reforms in Rome's legal and judiciary system.

78 B.C. Sulla dies at age 60 and efforts to undo his work begin under the democratic consul M. Aemilius Lepidus who tries to abrogate the constitution passed by Sulla. Lepidus is thwarted; he raises an army of malcontents in Etruria, but his colleague Q. Lutatius Catulus defeats him in battle outside Rome.

77 B.C. M. Aemilius Lepidus suffers total defeat at the hands of a protegé of Sulla. The 29-year-old Gnaeus Pompeius (Pompey) forces Lepidus to flee to the Hispanic provinces where he soon dies.

75 B.C. The Greek physician Asclepiades of Bithynia opposes Hippocratic medicine of 429 B.C., insisting that disease is a result of an inharmonious motion of the corpuscles that compose all bodily tissue. But Asclepiades is the first to distinguish between acute and chronic disease, and many are helped by his recommendations with regard to diet, bathing, and exercise (his patients will include Cicero, Crassus, and Marc Antony).

74 B.C. Cyrene becomes a province of Rome.

73 B.C. A third Servile War begins under the leadership of the Thracian slave Spartacus, a gladiator who seizes Mount Vesuvius on the Bay of Naples with the help of other gladiators and who rallies fugitive slaves to the insurrection.

72 B.C. Roman armies sent against Spartacus defeat his force of fugitive slaves.

71 B.C. The king of Pontus Mithradates VI is driven out of his country by the Roman legions of L. Licinius Lucullus and takes refuge at the court of Armenia's Tigranes II.

Spartacus is defeated by the Roman praetor M. Licinius Crassus, 41, who has enriched himself in the service of the late dictator Sulla by buying up properties of proscribed Romans. Pompey returns from the Hispanic provinces and destroys the remnants of the servile army.

70 B.C. Crassus and Pompey break with the Roman nobility and use their troops to gain the consulship. They restore the privileges of the tribunate which were removed by Sulla.

Armenia's Tigranes II completes conquests that extend his empire from the Ararat Valley in the north to the ancient Phoenician city of Tyre on the Mediterranean coast. Calling himself "king of kings," Tigranes begins construction of a new capital to be called Tigranocerta at the headwaters of the river Tigris.

The Seleucid king Phraates III begins to restore order in Parthia but will not be able to repel the Roman legions of Lucullus and Pompey.

Crassus and Pompey resume distribution of free grain. Some 40,000 adult male citizens of Rome receive grain dispensations, and the number will rise rapidly (see 58 B.C.).

69 B.C. The Roman general and epicure Lucius Licinius Lucullus defeats Armenia's Tigranes II who has seized Syria and begins a push into the mountains of Armenia and Parthia toward Pontus.

Cherries from the Black Sea kingdom of Pontus sent back to Rome by Lucullus (above) introduce a new fruit tree to Europe.

68 B.C. Roman troops in Armenia mutiny, Lucullus is forced to retreat to the south, and the king of Pontus begins a campaign to regain his realm. Many of the Roman legions have been on campaign for 20 years.

Crete falls to the Roman legions.

67 B.C. Mediterranean pirates who have been interfering with Rome's grain imports from Egypt and North Africa are defeated by Quintus Caecilius Metellus.

The Seleucid king Antiochus XIII, who was installed last year at Antioch, is treacherously killed by the Arabian prince of Emesa.

66 B.C. Armenia's Tigranes II falls into the hands of Pompey who has driven the king of Pontus Mithradates VI to the eastern edge of the Black Sea and who imposes a fine of 6,000 talents on Tigranes. The Armenian king will rule henceforth as a vassal of Rome, Mithradates will flee next year to the Crimea, (see 63 B.C.).

Lucullus returns to Rome and begins entertaining on a lavish scale at feasts so extravagant that the word "Lucullan" will be used for millennia to denote flamboyant sumptuousness.

65 B.C. Rome's Asian and Syrian territories are reorganized by Pompey who establishes four new Roman provinces. He leaves as client kingdoms Cappadocia, Eastern Pontus, Galatia, Judea, and Lycia.

Apricots from Armenia, peaches from Persia, plums from Damascus, raspberries from Mount Ida (southeast of the old city of Troy), and quinces from Sidon are introduced to Rome's orchards and cuisine by Pompey.

64 B.C. Jerusalem falls to Pompey after a siege as the Romans move to subdue Judea.

The Catiline conspiracy rallies Rome's discontented debtors, veterans, ruined nobility, and others under the leadership of L. Sergius Catilina, 44. A former governor of Africa, Catiline tried 2 years ago to run for consul on a radical program, but he was unable to get his name presented to the Comitia Centuriata as a result of his alleged extortions in Africa. He runs again, but he is defeated by the orator M. Tullius Cicero, 42.

63 B.C. Pompey completes his conquest of Palestine and makes it part of the Roman province of Syria.

Roman authorities arrest Lucius Sergius Catiline and his fellow conspirators, the Roman consul Cicero makes orations against Catiline in the Senate, and the conspirators are put to death as *hostes* without appeal.

Mithradates learns of a revolt by his son in Pontus and commits suicide in the Crimea (see 66 B.C.).

A system of shorthand notation is invented by Marcus Tullius Tiro, formerly a slave of Cicero (above).

62 B.C. Florence is founded on the Arno River in Tuscany (*see* florins, A.D. 1189).

60 B.C. A triumvirate to rule Rome is formed by Gaius Julius Caesar, 42, a son-in-law of the late Cinna and an agent of Crassus. Caesar returns from his governorship of Rome's Hispanic provinces and forges an alliance with Pompey and Crassus.

59 B.C. Campanian lands are distributed among Pompey's veterans by the new Roman triumvirate, which is solidified by the marriage of Caesar's daughter Julia to Pompey. The eastern settlements of Pompey are confirmed after years of opposition to such confirmation by the Senate, and Julius Caesar is granted Cisalpine Gaul and Illyria for a 5-year period.

58 B.C. Julius Caesar invades Gaul with the aim of enriching himself and creating a military establishment that will rival the forces of Pompey. He defeats the Helvetii at Bibracte (Autun) and triumphs over the German Ariovistus near Vesontio (Besançon).

The Roman demagogue Appius Claudius Pulcher distributes free grain to as many as 300,000 in a bid for the consulship.

57 B.C. Julius Caesar's legions defeat the Belgae in northwestern Gaul while the demagogue Appius Claudius Pulcher back at Rome becomes praetor.

Philosophy *De Rerum Natura* by the Roman poet-philosopher Titus Lucretius Caro, 39, is a six-volume didactic poem of Epicurean philosophy dealing with ethics, physics, psychology, and the materialistic atoms suggested by the Greek Democritus in 330 B.C. *"Quod ali cibus est aliis fiat acre veneum,"* says Lucretius ("What is food to one man may be a fierce poison to another").

The Roman Senate gives Pompey power to supervise the city's grain supply as a grain shortage looms.

56 B.C. Julius Caesar defeats the Veneti on the southern coast of Brittany, he defeats the Aquitani in southwestern Gaul, and he meets with Pompey and Crassus at Luca to make plans for subduing the opposition against the triumvirate that has arisen at Rome.

55 B.C. Rome makes Pompey and Crassus consuls. The Senate extends Caesar's command in Gaul another 5 years, and it gives Crassus command of Syria and Pompey command of two Hispanic provinces. Crassus leaves for the east; Pompey remains at Rome.

54 B.C. Julius Caesar invades Britain. He fails to conquer the islands, but he does open them to Roman trade and influence (*see* A.D. 43).

Caesar's daughter Julia, who is married to Pompey, dies. The triumvirate that rules Rome begins to break up.

Appius Claudius Pulcher becomes consul at Rome.

Crassus plunders Jerusalem's Great Temple.

Julius Caesar (above) finds the Britons making Cheshire cheese.

52 B.C. The Gallic leader Vercingetorix, chief of the Averni, surrenders to Julius Caesar after a siege by the Roman legions.

51 B.C. Julius Caesar completes his conquest of Gaul.

49 B.C. Julius Caesar leads his forces across the Rubicon River into Italy to begin a civil war. "The die is cast (*alea iacta est*)," says Caesar.

48 B.C. Julius Caesar defeats Gnaeus Pompey June 29 at Pharsalus in southern Thessaly and becomes absolute ruler of Rome. Pompey flees to Egypt where he is slain.

Some 500 bargeloads of foodstuffs and other imports for Rome are pulled up the Tiber by oxen each month from the port of Ostia.

The Gallic art of making pork sausage is introduced into Rome by Julius Caesar.

47 B.C. Julius Caesar defeats the king of Pontus Pharnaces III August 2 in a battle near Zela. Pharnaces has been an ally of the late Gnaeus Pompey, and Caesar announces his victory with the brief dispatch, "I came, I saw, I conquered (Veni, vedi, Vici)."

46 B.C. Julius Caesar returns in triumph to Rome with prisoners who include Vercingetorix, chief of the Averni, who is executed.

Julius Caesar grants Roman citizenship to Greek physicians whose status has until now been that of slave or freedman.

45 B.C. A new "Julian" calendar of 365.25 days is introduced by Julius Caesar, who has commissioned the Greek astronomer-mathematician Sosigenes of Alexandria to reform the calendar. The first day of the year falls on January 1 under the new calendar (*see* 153 B.C.; A.D. 1582).

Julius Caesar adopts his great-nephew Gaius Octavius (Octavian) as his son (*see* 43 B.C.).

44 B.C. Julius Caesar is made dictator for life. He reduces the number of Romans receiving free grain from 320,000 to 150,000.

Julius Caesar is assassinated at the Senate March 15 by conspirators who include Decimus Junius Brutus and Marcus Junius Brutus, both former governors of Gaul, and Gaius Cassius Longinus, who had been pardoned by Caesar for fighting alongside Pompey at Pharsalus in 48 B.C.

Caesar's mistress Cleopatra returns to Egypt with her son Caesarion and murders her brother (and former husband) Ptolemy IV to make room for Caesarion as ruler of Egypt.

Roman orator Marcus Antonius (Marc Antony), 39, persuades the Romans to expel Caesar's assassins.

43 B.C. Marc Antony marches north to dislodge Decimus Brutus from Mutina (Modena), but he is defeated in two battles and forced to retire westward toward Gaul by Gaius Octavius, 19-year-old great-nephew of the late Julius Caesar. Octavius calls himself Gaius Julius Caesar Octavianus, he forces the Senate to elect him consul, and he joins with Marc Antony and Marcus Lepidus in November to form a second triumvirate.

Cicero is executed December 7 by agents of Marc Antony with the acquiescence of Octavian.

42 B.C. Julius Caesar is deified by the Roman triumvirate, which erects a temple to Caesar in the Forum and obliges Roman magistrates to take an oath to support the arrangements of the late Caesar.

Cassius is defeated by Marc Antony and Octavian at Philippi and commits suicide after hearing a false report that M. Junius Brutus has also been defeated. Brutus has, in fact, won a victory over Octavian, but he is finally defeated 20 days later and also commits suicide.

41 B.C. Egypt's Cleopatra meets Marc Antony at Tarsus, and the 42-year-old Antony succumbs to the 28-year-old Cleopatra just as Julius Caesar, at 51, succumbed to a younger Cleopatra 8 years ago. Antony had planned to punish Cleopatra, but he follows her to Egypt.

Poetry *Eclogues* by the Roman poet Virgil, 29, are pastoral poems expressing emotion at having his lands confiscated (*see* below). Virgil will obtain restitution of his lands by personal appeal to Octavian.

Farmland in the Campania is confiscated by Rome's triumvirate for distribution among returning legionnaires.

40 B.C. Marc Antony's wife Fulvia and his brother Lucius Antoninus make war against the faithless Antony but are defeated at Perusia (Perugia). Fulvia dies, and Marc Antony is left free to remarry. He marries the sister of Octavian (Octavia), and Octavian takes Gaul from Lepidus, leaving him only Africa.

Banquets of Marc Antony and Cleopatra at Alexandria have been described to Fulvia at Rome in letters from Antony's aide-de-camp:

> We have five or six courses of fish, oysters, mussels, sea-hogs with asparagus; then we have capons, pies, and patties of fish and venison, many kinds of sea fruits and lobsters and polypuses cooked in spicy sauces, and partridges, cutlets of deer and gazelles, pheasants inside sweet crusts, big game, piglets stuffed with becassins and quails, ducks and turkeys and peacocks roasted and served with all their wonderful feathers, woodcocks in all kinds of sauces, tunny fish of Calchedony, sturgeons of Rhodes, lampreys, and patisserie of many kinds that I had never tasted before, and wonderful fruit from the East.

(The reference to "turkeys" will mislead future food historians; *see* A.D. 1523).

39 B.C. Rome's triumvirate signs the Pact of Mycaenum recognizing the Mediterranean pirate Sextus Pompey as ruler of Sicily, Sardinia, Corsica, and the Peloponnese. Pompey's fleet can interrupt Rome's grain supply and this puts him in a position to dictate terms.

Octavian divorces his second wife and marries Livia, previously the wife of Tiberius Claudius Nero.

38 B.C. Iberia is conquered for Rome by Octavian who at age 25 begins to gain ascendancy in the triumvirate that rules Rome. Mark Antony returns to Egypt.

Sculpture *The Laocoön* by Rhodian sculptors Agesander, Polydorus, and Athenodorus (*see* A.D. 1506).

37 B.C. Judea's Herod the Great begins a 33-year reign at age 36 2 years after his confirmation as king by Marc Antony, Octavian, and the Roman Senate.

36 B.C. Octavian's general Marcus Vipsanius Agrippa makes the Mediterranean safe for Roman shipping by defeating the pirate Sextus Pompey with a fleet that includes ships supplied by Marc Antony. Sextus Pompey flees to Miletus where he dies. Lepidus occupies Sicily but his troops desert to Octavian who ends the ambitions of Lepidus. Octavian places Lepidus in captivity at Circeii where he will live until his death in 13 B.C.

Parthian forces defeat Marc Antony, he retreats to Armenia, and he openly marries his mistress Cleopatra despite his existing marriage to Octavia.

35 B.C. Octavian consolidates Roman power in the Alps and in Illyria.

The assassination of the dictator Julius Caesar in the Roman Senate began 13 years of civil war.

34 B.C. Dalmatia becomes a Roman province.

32 B.C. Octavian arouses fears in Rome that Egypt's Cleopatra will dominate the Empire. He publishes what he purports to be the will of Marc Antony, a will in which Antony bequeaths Rome's eastern possessions to Cleopatra. Marc Antony divorces Octavia, and her brother has the comitia annul Antony's imperium.

31 B.C. The Battle of Actium September 2 ends in a naval victory for Octavian who becomes ruler of the entire Roman world. Cleopatra flees to Egypt and is followed by Antony, whose army then surrenders to Octavian.

30 B.C. Marc Antony commits suicide after hearing a false report that Cleopatra has killed herself—which she does after failing to seduce Octavian upon his arrival at Alexandria. Egypt becomes a Roman province.

Poetry *Georgics* is completed after 7 years' work by Virgil, whose didactic four-volume work ennobles the Italian land, its trees, its grapevines and olive groves, its herds and flocks, and its beehives.

The sundial invented by the Chinese serves as a primitive clock.

29 B.C. Greek mariners employed by Rome's Octavian open the ancient trade routes from Egypt to India as peace returns to the Roman world.

27 B.C. The Roman Empire that will rule most of the Western world until A.D. 476 is founded January 23 by Octavian who 1 week earlier received the name Augustus Caesar from the Senate in gratitude for his achievements. Helped by the rich Roman merchant Mycenas, Octavian makes himself emperor at age 35 with the title Imperator Caesar Octavianus, a title he will soon change to Augustus Caesar as he begins a 41-year reign.

The number of poor Romans receiving free grain is increased by Augustus from 150,000 to 200,000.

24 B.C. The emperor Augustus acts to reduce the exorbitant price of spices in Rome. He appoints the prefect of Egypt Aeilius Gallus to lead a campaign that incorporates the south Arabian spice kingdom into the Roman Empire, but the expedition will fail as a result of bad roads, poor navigation, hunger, disease, and fatigue.

20 B.C. Rebuilding of Jerusalem's Great Temple is begun by Herod the Great, a convert to Judaism in his youth who has been building theaters, hippodromes, and other public buildings (*see* A.D. 64).

19 B.C. Poetry *The Aeneid* by Virgil is a great epic about the role of Rome in world history: "I sing of arms and of the man . . ." (*Arma virumque cano . . .*). Virgil sets off for Athens to spend 3 years in the east, but he meets the emperor Augustus. The emperor persuades the poet to return with him to Italy, and Virgil dies September 21 at age 50, a few days after landing at Brundisium.

The Pont du Gard, completed by Roman engineers across the Gard River 19 kilometers northeast of Nimes, is an aqueduct bridge 600 yards long with three tiers of arches rising 160 feet above the river.

18 B.C. Poetry *Amores* by the Roman poet Ovid (Publius Ovidius Naso), 25, who has been educated for a career in law but who has devoted himself instead to writing love poems.

17 B.C. Ode *Carmen Saeculare* by the Roman poet-critic Horace (Quintus Horatius Flaccus), 47, is sung by a chorus of youths and maidens at a great festival of games put on by the emperor Augustus. Horace is well known for his *Odes* ["Seize the day," *carpe diem* (I, ix)], his *Satires* ["There is a certain method in his madness" (II, iii)], and his *Epistles* ["Well begun is half done" (I, ii)].

16 B.C. A vertical waterwheel is described by the Roman engineer Marcus Vetruvius Pollio.

15 B.C. Rome extends her frontier to the upper Danube by annexations following an uprising by Germanic tribesmen.

Poetry *Heroides* by Ovid: "Where belief is painful, we are slow to believe" (II, ix).

14 B.C. Augsburg has its beginnings in the Gallic colony Augusta Vindelicorum founded by the Roman emperor Augustus on a 1,500-acre plateau between the rivers Lerch and Wertach, which meet in the plain below (*see* A.D. 1276).

7 B.C. The infant Jesus, who will become an important religious leader, is born at Bethlehem near Jerusalem to a Jewish carpenter's wife who professes to have been a virgin at the time of her child's conception. Mary's first-born will be baptized at age 30 by her cousin John the Baptist after working as a carpenter and rabbi at Nazareth. (Year of the nativity determined by modern astronomers on the basis of a conjunction of the planets Saturn and Jupiter within the constellation Pisces, a conjunction that gives the appearance of a great new star and the fulfillment of a prophecy by Jewish astrologers at Sippar in Babylon, who have predicted the arrival of a long-awaited Messiah at some time when the two planets would meet. Some astronomers, however, will cite Chinese and Korean annals referring to a stellar flare-up, or nova, that blazed in the skies for 70 days in the spring of 5 B.C.).

The population of the world reaches roughly 250 million, up from 100 million in 3000 B.C. (*see* A.D. 1650).

4 B.C. Judea's Herod the Great dies at age 69 after a 33-year reign in which he has secured many benefits for the Jews and has begun the rebuilding of the Great Temple at Jerusalem. Herod is succeeded by his son Archelaus, who begins a 10-year reign.

1st CENTURY A.D.

Augustus, Tiberius, Caligula, Claudius, Nero, Vespasian, Titus, Domitian, and Trajan will be the major Roman emperors of this century.

Poetry *The Art of Love* (*Ars Amatoria*) by Ovid scandalizes Rome: "It is expedient that there should be gods, and since it is expedient let us believe that gods exist" (I); "A woman is always buying something" (I); "Nothing is stronger than habit" (II); "When the rose dies, the thorn is left behind" (II, cxvi); "Delay is a great procuress" (III).

De Re Rustica by Lucius Iunius Moderatus Columella is a didactic poem that advises switching from grain to vines, ". . . for none in Italy can remember when seeds increased fourfold." The common yield for a bushel of seed is only 2 or 3 bushels of grain, and while an acre of land may, at best, yield 4 to 6 bushels of wheat or barley the more usual yield is 2 to 3 bushels, and most of Rome's grain comes from Egypt and North Africa (*see* A.D. 6).

"The Earth neither grows old, nor wears out, if it be dunged," writes Columella (above), who urges crop rotation that alternates grain with legumes.

Romans use blood and bones as fertilizer. They grow clover and will later grow alfalfa, but they disdain to use human excrement for fertilizer.

5 Lombard tribes that have established themselves on the lower Elbe River are defeated by Roman legions.

6 The number of Romans receiving free grain rises to 320,000, up from 150,000 in 44 B.C. Close to one-third the city is on the dole.

Rome imports some 14 million bushels of grain per year to supply the city alone—an amount that requires several hundred square miles of croplands to produce. One-third comes from Egypt and the rest largely from North African territories west of Egypt.

Chinese candidates for political office are required to take civil service examinations.

7 Poetry *Metamorphoses* by Ovid, whose works have been banned and who will be exiled next year by Augustus to the Roman outpost of Tomis (Constanza) on the Black Sea in part for his elegiac poem instructing a man in the art of winning and keeping a mistress and instructing a woman on now to win and hold a lover. Ovid will destroy his new masterpiece at news of his banishment, but copies made by his friends will survive with such lines as "Love and dignity cannot share the same abode" (II); "You will go most safely in the middle" (II); "None must be

counted happy till his last funeral rites are paid" (III); "The cause is hidden, but the result is known" (IV); "I see the better course and I approve of it,/ But I follow the worse" (VII); "There is no such thing as pure pleasure: some anxiety always goes with it" (VII); "A pious fraud" (IX); "All things change; nothing perishes" (XV); and "Time that devours all things" (XV), a reference to the Titan Kronos in Greek mythology who devoured his own children.

9 The Battle of Teutoburger Wald (Forest) permanently secures the independence of the Teutonic tribes and establishes the Rhine as the boundary between Latin and German territories. Germanic tribes under Arminius annihilate three Roman legions under the command of the legate P. Quinctilius Varus.

The Hsin dynasty emperor Wang Mang nationalizes Chinese land, dividing the country's large estates and establishing state granaries.

Wang Mang (above) grants manumission to China's slaves.

12 The Chinese repeal the radical land reforms made by the emperor Wang Mang 3 years ago. The reforms have met with widespread protests.

14 The Roman emperor Augustus dies at Nola August 19 at age 76 after a 41-year reign. He is succeeded despite legal obstacles to dynastic succession by his stepson Tiberius Claudius Nero, 55, who will rule as the emperor Tiberius until his death in 37. Son of the late emperor's widow Livia by her first marriage, Tiberius will carry on the imperial regime inaugurated by Augustus in 27 B.C.

De Re Coquinaria (or *De Re Culinaria*) by the Roman gastronome M. Gabius Apicius is the world's first known book of recipes. Apicius prepares broiled broccoli that is much enjoyed by the son of the new emperor Tiberius (above) and prepares eggs with honey and pepper, a dish he calls *ovemele* egg honey), possibly the origin of the English word "omelette."

16 The Germanic kingdom of Arminius is broken up by the Roman emperor's son Drusus, 31, who defeats Arminius, recovers the eagles of the legions lost at the Battle of Teutoburger Wald 7 years ago, and avenges the defeat of Varus.

17 Rome's Emperor Tiberius sends his nephew Germanicus to install a new king in Armenia.

Cappadocia and Commagene become a Roman province following the death of their king.

17 (cont.) A tax on slaveholding is enacted in China, where slaves do most of the menial work as they do in Rome.

Seven regional Chinese commissions are directed to establish annual high, low, and mean price levels for staples and to buy surplus goods at cost, but merchants and capitalists employed by the emperor Wang Mang as administrators will provoke revolts.

19 Germanicus is poisoned in Syria, the Syrian legate Piso is charged with the murder by enemies of the emperor Tiberius, and Piso commits suicide.

23 Drusus, son of the emperor Tiberius, is poisoned by Lucius Aelius Sejanus, ambitious equestrian prefect of the guard, who has designs on the imperial throne and who begins an 8-year domination of the emperor.

China's Emperor Wang Mang is killed in a revolt after a 14-year reign in which he has attempted to curb usury and advance the welfare of the masses.

25 The eastern Han dynasty that will rule at Loyang until A.D. 220 is founded by a collateral imperial scion, who will reign until A.D. 57 as Kuang Wu Ti.

Rome's Emperor Tiberius is persuaded by the prefect Sejanus to retire from the hostile political climate of Rome and to settle on the island of Caprae (Capri) in the Bay of Naples.

29 Jesus of Nazareth leaves Galilee after a brief ministry and travels to Jerusalem to observe Passover at a ritual Seder meal that will be depicted by future painters as *The Last Supper*. Jesus has antagonized the priestly class by driving the money changers out of the Great Temple at Jerusalem and attacking the hypocrisy of the privileged classes. With a price on his head, he is betrayed by his disciple Judas Iscariot and seized by Roman soldiers who deliver him to the high priest and the Sanhedrin (great council and tribunal of the Jewish nation). He is condemned as a blasphemer and sent to the Roman procurator Pontius Pilate who sends him to the ruler of Galilee Herod Antipas who sends him back to Pilate. He is finally turned over to Jewish authorities, and he is crucified on Golgotha, a knoll to the north of Jerusalem near the Damascus Gate.

Disciples of Jesus (above) will profess to have seen him resurrected after his burial in the tomb of Joseph of Arimathea. They will proclaim him Messiah and Savior, and they will found the Christian faith that will grow to dominate much of the world.

30 *De Res Medicas* is compiled as a collection of Greek medical writings by Roman physician Aulus Cornelius Celsus, who also published *De Artibus*. Tracing medical history from simple remedies through Hippocratic and Alexandrian contributions, Celsus describes in careful detail the surgical instruments of his own day after witnessing many operations and dissections. "I am of the opinion that the art of medi-

cine ought to be rational," writes Celsus. "To open the bodies of the dead is necessary for learners" (*see* Galen, A.D. 180; "Paracelsus," A.D. 1530).

31 Rome's Lucius Aelius Sejanus is executed by order of the emperor Tiberius, who has discovered the intrigues of his former favorite (*see* A.D. 23).

A horizontal waterwheel is described in Chinese writings, which discuss a mechanism in which the wheel employs a series of belts and pulleys to drive a bellows that works an iron furnace for the casting of agricultural implements.

37 Rome's Emperor Tiberius dies at age 78 and is succeeded by Gaius Caesar, 25, youngest son of the late Germanicus Caesar and nephew of Tiberius, who is called Caligula because of the *caligae*, or soldiers' boots, he has worn. The new emperor Caligula introduces cruel oriental excesses in a monarchy that will rule Rome for more than 3 years.

40 The Greek merchant Hippalus voyages in 1 year from Berenice, on Egypt's Red Sea coast, to India's Madras coast and back, a journey that has previously required 2 years. Hippalus has discovered that the monsoon winds (the word derives from *mawsim*, Arabic for seasons) reverse direction twice a year, a fact the Arabs may have known for centuries. The southwest wind, favorable for voyages from Egypt to India, prevails from April to October, and the northwest wind for the return trip prevails from October to April (*see* A.D. 90).

A power shortage halts Rome's flour mills, and the emperor Caligula commandeers all draft animals to keep the mills in operation.

41 The Roman emperor Caligula is murdered January 24 by a tribune of the guard after a megalomaniacal reign of savage tyranny. He is succeeded by a 50-year-old nephew of the late emperor Tiberius, a crippled man with a speech defect whose name is Tiberius Claudius Drusus Nero Germanicus and who will rule until 54 as the emperor Claudius.

43 The Roman emperor Claudius leads a personal expedition to conquer Britain and Romanize her people (*see* 54 B.C.; A.D. 48).

London (Londinium) is founded by the Romans (*see* 400 B.C.; A.D. 61).

44 The apostle James who has preached the divinity of Jesus becomes the first Christian martyr. He is executed on orders from the Judean king Herod Agrippa.

Judea's Herod Agrippa dies at age 54 after a 3-year reign and Judea becomes a procuratorial province of Rome once again. Agrippa's 17-year-old son is studying at the court of the emperor Claudius in Rome and beginning in A.D. 48 will reign for 5 years as Herod Agrippa II.

The capon is created by Romans who geld cocks to make them grow larger.

Vomitoriums gain popularity in Rome. The emperor Claudius and others employ slaves to tickle their throats after they have eaten their fill in order that they may return to the banquet tables and begin again. Most Romans live on bread, olives, wine, and some fish, but little meat.

46 The apostle Paul journeys to Cyprus and Galatea with the Cypriot Barnabas and with Mark, a young cousin of Barnabas.

48 Roman legions invade Wales. They will conquer the country in the next 30 years while Roman engineers construct a great network of British roads.

49 The emperor Claudius expels Jewish-Christians from Rome.

50 Cologne has its beginnings in the town of Colonia Agrippina built on the left bank of the Rhine at the site of Oppidum Ubiorum, chief town of the Ubii. The Roman emperor Claudius fortifies the town at the request of his niece and bride Agrippina, 35, who was born in the place.

The apostle Paul travels to Greece on a journey that will take 3 years.

54 The Roman emperor Claudius dies October 13 at age 63 after eating poisonous mushrooms given him by the physician Stertinius Xenophon as part of a plot inspired by the empress Agrippina. She will seek to rule Rome through her 16-year-old son Nero Claudius Augustus Germanicus, who will reign as the emperor Nero until A.D. 68.

Epistles to the Corinthians by the apostle Paul deal with a variety of moral and ethical questions.

55 *De Materia Medica* by Greek botanist Pedanios Dioscorides details the properties of some 600 medicinal plants. Dioscorides has served as a military surgeon in Nero's army, he describes animal products for which he claims dietetic or medicinal value, and his text will remain an authoritative guide for 1,500 years.

58 The apostle Paul arrives at Jerusalem but authorities at Caesarea arrest him and hold him for trial before the procurator of Judea.

59 The Roman emperor Nero has his mother Agrippina put to death at the urging of his councilor Lucius Annaeus Seneca, 61.

60 Festus succeeds Felix as procurator of Judea and holds a new trial for the apostle Paul who makes an "appeal unto Caesar" in the presence of Herod Agrippa II.

61 London is sacked by the Trinovantes of Essex and Suffolk and by the Iceni of Norfolk and Suffolk whose queen Boudica (Boadicia) revolts upon the retirement of the Roman governor Seutonius Paulinus.

Rome's legions crush the Britons and restore the Roman authority that will continue until A.D. 407.

Roman engineers surround London with a wall 8 feet thick.

62 Roman authorities permit the apostle Paul to live in Rome but keep him under house arrest. Albinus succeeds Festus as procurator of Judea and the Romans permit Paul to resume his travels.

63 *Epistilae Morales* by the Roman philosopher Seneca says, "All art is but imitation of nature."

64 Rome has a fire that begins the night of July 18 in some wooden booths at one end of the Circus Maximus, spreads in one direction over the Palatine and Velia hills and up to the low cliffs of the Esquiline, spreads in another direction through the Aventine, the Forus Boarium, and the Velabrum until it reaches the Tiber and the Servian Wall, and destroys nearly two-thirds of the city. The emperor Nero has fretted (not "fiddled") while Rome burned and begins rebuilding to a master plan that will give the city straight, broad streets and wide squares whose cleanliness will be supervised by the *aediles*.

Persecution of Christians begins at Rome.

Jerusalem's Third Temple is completed after 84 years of construction (but *see* A.D. 70).

Vast quantities of grain are stored at Rome under the supervision of the *aediles* who control the food supply. They introduce regulations to ensure the freshness of meat, fish, and produce sold in the city.

65 A plot to murder the Roman emperor Nero comes to light. The conspirators are executed or are forced to take their own lives.

The Gospel according to St. Mark.

67 Roman armies under Titus Flavius Sabinus Vespasianus, 58, and his 27-year-old son Titus enter Galilee to put down a revolt by Jews who have massacred a body of Roman soldiers in protest against their sacrileges and extortions. All the Jews of Caesarea have been slaughtered by the town's gentile citizens. The Jews are furious, but the Roman army is overwhelming. Jewish general Joseph ben Matthias, 30, holds out in a siege of the fortress Jotapata, but he yields after 47 days to Vespasian and gains the favor of the Roman general.

The Christian apostle Paul is executed June 29 on the Via Ostia 3 miles from Rome. The first great Christian missionary and theologian, Paul will hold a position in the faith second only to that of Jesus.

68 Rome's Emperor Nero is sentenced to death by the Senate under pressure from the praetorian guard which has recognized the legate Servius Sulpicius Galba, 65, as emperor. Nero commits suicide June 9 at age 30. His death ends the Julio-Claudian line of Caesars that has ruled Rome for 128 years, and he

68 (cont.) is succeeded by Galba, who will rule for less than 6 months before being challenged.

History of the Jewish People is compiled by the Jewish general Joseph ben Matthias, who has taken the Roman name Flavius Josephus (*see* A.D. 67).

69 Eight legions on the Rhine refuse allegiance to the Roman emperor Galba and salute as emperor their legate Aulus Vitellius, 54. Galba is murdered January 15 along with his newly adopted successor, Piso Licinianus, the murderer is Marcus Salvius Otho, 36, a dissolute friend of the late emperor Nero, and the Senate recognizes Otho as emperor.

Aulus Vitellius (above) sends two legions to the Po Valley. They defeat the emperor Otho April 19 in the Battle of Bedriacum near Cremona, and Otho commits suicide, leaving Vitellius to face a challenge from Titus Flavius Sabinus Vespasianus, 59, legate of Judea. The prefect of Egypt proclaims Vespasianus emperor July 1, the legate of Syria and all the Danubian legions rally to his support, and the emperor Vitellius mobilizes forces to oppose them. Antonius Primus, commander of the Seventh Legion in Pannonia, leads other Danubian legions against Vitellius and defeats him in late October in the second Battle of Bedriacum. He sacks Cremona and forces the Senate to recognize Vespasianus as the emperor Vespasian.

The Roman emperor Vitellius dies in a street battle December 20, leaving Vespasian to begin a reign that will continue until 79.

The emperor Vespasian lays siege to Jerusalem as the Jewish Zealot leader John of Giscala continues resistance after having eliminated his rival Eleazar.

70 The emperor Vespasian returns to Rome, leaving his son Titus to continue the siege of Jerusalem. He turns his energies to repairing the ravages of civil war. He suppresses an insurrection in Gaul, restores discipline to the demoralized Roman army, renews old taxes and institutes new ones, and rebuilds the Capitol which was burned in the fighting that raged in the city last autumn.

Jerusalem falls September 7. The Romans sack the city and destroy most of the Third Temple, which was completed only 6 years ago. The one wall left standing will become famous as the "Wailing Wall."

Titus gives some of Judea to Marcus Julius "Herod" Agrippa II but retains most as an imperial domain. Rome quarters a legion in Jerusalem under a senatorial legate whose position is higher than that of the procurator. The Romans abolish the Jewish high priesthood and Sanhedrin (Jewish national council), and they divert the 2-drachma tax paid by Jews for support of the Great Temple to a special account in the imperial treasury (*fiscus Iudaicus*).

The Jewish teacher Johanen ben Zakkai saves Judaism. A disciple of the late Babylonian Jew Hillel, who died some 60 years ago, Johanen has had himself carried out of Jerusalem during the siege. He has asked Vespasian to grant him a boon, and he opens a school at Jabneh with Roman permission.

Panic strikes Rome as adverse winds delay grain shipments from Egypt and North Africa, producing a bread shortage. Ships laden with wheat from North Africa sail 300 miles to Rome's port of Ostia in 3 days given good winds, and the 1,000-mile voyage from Alexandria averages 13 days. The ships often carry 1,000 tons. Shipping adds little to the price (which may double if hauled overland); wheat is a cheap commodity, but the supply depends on favorable winds.

71 The Arch of Titus erected at Rome by the emperor Vespasian celebrates the triumph of the emperor's son last year at Jerusalem.

A palatial public lavatory built by the emperor Vespasian opens in Rome which now has an extensive system of waterworks with flush toilets and urinals.

77 The Roman governor Gnaeus Julius Agricola arrives in Britain to continue the conquest begun by the emperor Claudius 34 years ago. He finds "a fierce and savage people running through the woods."

79 The Roman emperor Vespasian dies June 23 at age 69 after a 10-year reign. He is succeeded by his 38-year-old son Flavius Sabinus Vespasianus Titus who will rule as the emperor Titus until A.D. 81.

Mount Vesuvius on the Bay of Naples erupts August 24 after 16 years of increasingly violent earthquakes that have seriously damaged towns in the Campania. Tons of lava, mud, and ashes bury the cities of Herculaneum and Pompeii, killing thousands. The Roman scholar Pliny the Elder (Plinius Secundus), 56, witnesses the eruption from a ship in the bay. He takes refuge with a friend at Stabiae, and he dies of suffocation from poisonous fumes (*see* A.D. 513).

Historia Naturalis by Pliny (above) survives as his legacy. The 37-volume encyclopedia of natural history says of agriculture, "The farmer's eye is the best fertilizer."

Liquamen has been a leading product of Pompeii (above). It is a seasoning made from fermented fish.

80 Anthrax sweeps the Roman Empire in epidemic form, killing thousands of humans and animals (*see* below).

Book on Spectacles (*Liber de Spectaculis*) by the Roman epigrammatic poet Martial (Marcus Valerius Martialis), 40, commemorates the dedication of the Colosseum (*see* below).

The Colosseum dedicated at Rome by the emperor Titus is a great Flavian amphitheater with solid masonry walls rising 160 feet above the ground and with 50,000 marble seats around the 617- by 513-foot oval arena built above its basements and subbasements.

Three months of celebration mark the opening of the Colosseum (above). The emperor has 500 wild beasts and many gladiators slain to amuse the populace.

Bread and circuses, including games at the great new Colosseum, kept the Roman populace in line.

Anthrax (above) strikes the cattle and horses of tribespeople on the borders of China, where an extended drought withers the grasslands. The tribespeople begin moving westward to seek new pastures.

The tribespeople moving westward from Mongolia avoid scurvy by consuming large quantities of mares' milk. The milk contains four times as much of the accessory food factor ascorbic acid as does cows' milk (no milk is notably rich in ascorbic acid but little is needed to avoid scurvy).

Some 30,000 Asian tribespeople migrate to the west with 40,000 horses and 100,000 head of cattle, joining with Iranian tribespeople and with Mongols from the Siberian forests to form a group that will be known in Europe as the Huns (*see* 140 B.C.; A.D. 451).

81 The Roman emperor Titus dies September 13 at age 40 after a 2-year reign. He is succeeded by his 29-year-old brother Titus Flavius Domitianus who will reign until A.D. 96 as the emperor Domitian.

The silver content of the Roman denarius will rise in the reign of Domitian to 92 percent, up from 81 percent in the reign of Vitellus.

The Arch of Titus raised by the emperor Domitian at Rome has bas-reliefs that commemorate the military triumphs of Titus and Vespasian.

83 Roman forces under Gnaeus Julius Agricola in Britain defeat the Caledonians and reach the northernmost point that they will attain in the British Isles (possibly near what will later be Aberdeen, Scotland).

84 The Roman emperor Domitian recalls Gnaeus Julius Agricola from Britain to help repel barbarian invaders near the Rhine and the Danube.

The Gospel according to St. John and the Gospel according to St. Matthew are transcribed.

90 *The Periplus of the Erythraean Sea (Sailing Round the Indian Ocean)* by a Greek sea captain gives instructions on how to use the monsoon winds to advantage (*see* Hippalus, A.D. 40).

Roman ships break the Arab monopoly in the spice trade. The ships are large enough to sail without difficulty from Egyptian Red Sea ports to India, but while spices become more plentiful, they drain Rome of her gold reserves.

Use of spices is one of the excesses that will bring about the fall of Rome, says the Christian prophet John of Ephesus in his *Revelations* (18:11–13). John writes metaphorically of Babylon, but he means Rome.

95 A severe form of malaria appears in the farm districts outside Rome and will continue for the next 500 years, taking out of cultivation the fertile land of the Campagna whose market gardens supply the city with fresh produce. The fever drives small farmers into the crowded city, they bring the malaria with them, and it lowers Rome's live-birth rate while rates elsewhere in the empire are rising.

At least 10 aqueducts supply Rome with 250 million gallons of water per day, some 50 gallons per person, even after the public baths have used half the supply.

Iron plows with wheels help some of Rome's barbarian neighbors to control the depth of plowing (and to save the plowmen's energies). The barbarians use coulters to cut the soil and moldboards to turn it over. While Roman farmers practice cross-plowing, the barbarians plow deep, regular furrows that will lead to the cultivation of long strips of land rather than square blocks.

96 The Roman emperor Domitian is stabbed to death by a freedman September 18 at age 44 after a 15-year reign. The empress Domitia and officers of the court have conspired against Domitian, he is succeeded by the former Roman consul Marcus Cocceius Nerva, 60, and the new emperor Nerva recalls citizens exiled by Domitian, restoring to them what remains of their confiscated property.

97 The Roman emperor Nerva recalls the general Marcus Ulpius Trajanus, 44, from the Rhine and formally adopts him in October at ceremonies in the temple of Jupiter on the Capitol.

98 The Roman emperor Nerva dies suddenly January 25 at age 63. He is succeeded by his adopted son who will reign as the emperor Trajan until A.D. 117.

The silver content of the Roman denarius will rise slightly to 93 percent under the emperor Trajan, up from the 92 percent level that prevailed under Domitian.

2nd CENTURY

Gladiators who died for the public's entertainment in the Roman Colosseum were generally slaves captured in battle.

✗ Trajan, Hadrian, Marcus Aurelius, and Commodus will be the major Roman emperors of this century.

105 Paper is invented by Chinese eunuch Ts'hai Lun, 55, to replace the bamboo slips and silk on which Han scholars have written until now (*see 1150*).

106 Dacia (Romania) becomes a Roman province following the defeat of her king Decebalus by the emperor Trajan.

110 Caravans make regular departures from Lo-yang with Chinese ginger, cassia (a type of cinnamon), and silk to be bartered in Central Asia for gold, silver, grape wine, glassware, pottery, asbestos cloth, coral beads, and intaglio gems from Rome.

♟ Biography   *On Illustrious Men* (*De Viris Illustribus*) by the Roman biographer Suetonius (Gaius Suetonius Tranquillis), 44.

114 Armenia is annexed to the Roman Empire by the emperor Trajan.

115 Roman legions occupy Mesopotamia up to the river Tigris.

116 The Roman emperor Trajan makes Assyria a province of Rome and crosses the Tigris to annex Adiabene. He proceeds to the Persian Gulf and conquers territory that becomes the province of Parthia.

117 The emperor Trajan dies August 8 at Selinus in Cilicia at age 63 while en route from Mesopotamia to Italy. His kinsman Publius Aelius Hadrianus, 41, is advised August 9 at Antioch that he has been adopted by Trajan. He learns of Trajan's death August 11, and he begins a 21-year reign as the emperor Hadrian.

Jews throughout the East rise to massacre Greeks and Romans at news of Trajan's death (above).

$ The silver content of the Roman denarius will fall to 87 percent in the reign of Hadrian, down from 93 percent in the reign of Trajan.

♟ History   *Historia* by the Roman historian Cornelius Tacitus, who dies at age 60. His work covers the years 69 to 96, and his *Annals* cover the preceding period from 14 to 69.

121 Biography   *The Lives of the Caesars* (*De Vita Caesarium*) by Suetonius is spiced with anecdotes gathered from private sources as well as from public records.

122 Hadrian's Wall goes up in Britain following the arrival in the spring of the emperor Hadrian on a tour of military inspection. The 72-mile wall from the Tyne to the Solvay is built mostly of stone with at least 16 forts and will provide a defensive barrier against the Picts and other tribesmen to the north (*see 333*).

123 The emperor Hadrian averts a war with the Parthians by meeting in person with the king of Parthia.

125 "Bread and circuses" (*panem et circensis*) keep the Roman citizenry pacified, writes Roman lawyer-satirist Decimus Junius Juvenalis (Juvenal), 65, in his *Satires.*

♆ Plague sweeps North Africa in the wake of a locust invasion that destroys large areas of cropland. The plague kills as many as 500,000 in Numidia and possibly 150,000 on the coast before moving to Italy, where it takes so many lives that villages and towns are abandoned.

♟ Famine contributes to the death toll produced by the plague in North Africa and Italy (above).

128 Roman agriculture declines as imports from Egypt and North Africa depress wheat prices, making it unprofitable to farm and forcing many farmers off the land.

✗ "Acorns were good enough until bread was invented," writes Juvenal in his *Satires XIV*. Roman bakeries produce dozens of different bread varieties, and the Romans distribute free bread to the poor in times of need.

130 The Temple of Olympian Zeus, begun at Athens in 530 B.C., is completed by the Roman emperor Hadrian. It is 354 feet long, 135 feet wide, and 90 feet in height and is the largest temple in Greece.

132 A Jewish insurrection against Rome begins under the leadership of Simon Bar Kokhba (or Bar Cochebe), who enjoys initial success against the legions of Hadrian.

135 The Romans kill Simon Bar Kokhba at the village of Bethar near Caesarea and crush his Jewish rebellion.

Roman legionnaires sack Jerusalem following the end of the Jewish War of Freedom (above). The emperor Hadrian orders that the site of the city be plowed over and that a new city be constructed with the name Aelia Capitolina (Hadrian has returned to Rome but spends much of his time at his villa at Tibur).

Hadrian orders that Jews be excluded from the new city to be built on the site of Jerusalem (above) but permits Christians to enter if they have not sided with the Jews in the rebellion.

138 The Roman emperor Hadrian dies at Baiae July 10 at age 62 after a 21-year reign. He has adopted Titus Aurelius Fulvius Boionus Arrius Antoninus, 52, in February on condition that Antoninus adopt the 17-year-old nephew of his bride Faustina and that in addition to adopting Marcus Annius Verus he adopt the 8-year-old Lucius Celonius Commodus, adopted 2 years ago by Hadrian himself. The new emperor Antoninus, who will reign until 161, goes to the Senate and asks in person that the senators confer divine honors on the late Hadrian, an act for which he will be called Antoninus Pius.

The silver content of the Roman denarius will fall to 75 percent in the reign of Antoninus Pius, down from 87 percent in the reign of Hadrian.

139 Rome's Castel Sant' Angelo is completed as a mausoleum for the late emperor Hadrian and his successors (*see* 590).

140 The Antonine Wall goes up in Britain from the Firth of Forth to the Firth of Clyde. Built on turf on a stone foundation as a barrier against the Picts and Caledonians, the wall is 10 feet high, 14 to 16 feet wide, and will have 13 to 19 forts along its 37-mile length.

161 Rome's Emperor Antoninus Pius dies of fever at Lorium in Etruria March 7 at age 75 after a reign marked by prosperity in the provinces, liberal relief to cities in distress, construction of aqueducts and baths, progress in art and science, increased importance of the Roman Senate, and construction of the wall of Antoninus from the Forth to the Clyde in Britain. Antoninus is succeeded by his adopted son

Marcus Annius Verus, 40, who will reign as Marcus Aurelius until 180.

The silver content of the Roman denarius will fall in the 19-year reign of Marcus Aurelius to 68 percent, down from 75 percent in the reign of Antoninus Pius.

165 Roman legions returning from the east spread a plague that may be smallpox, and it moves through much of Europe and the Near East, seriously depopulating the empire.

166 Rome expropriates peasant lands and awards them to returning legionnaires, few of whom will make good farmers.

167 The first full-scale barbarian attack on Rome destroys aqueducts and irrigation conduits, but the emperor Marcus Aurelius repels the invaders.

168 Marcus Aurelius and his coemperor Lucius Verus subdue the Marcommani, a barbarian tribe from north of the Danube that has been in northwestern Italy for 7 years.

169 The Roman coemperor Lucius Verus dies early in the year at age 39, leaving Marcus Aurelius to reign alone.

A full Roman army moves out in the fall to repel the Marcommani who have broken the peace concluded last year. The Romans will drive off the Marcommani in the next 3 years, and the tribe will be virtually annihilated—as much by plague (which also infects the Roman army) as by force of arms.

174 The Roman legions of Marcus Aurelius defeat the Quadi in a victory that will be commemorated by a great column at Rome.

175 Roman legions in Asia revolt under the leadership of Avidus Cassius, following rumors that the emperor Marcus Aurelius has died. Cassius had defeated the Parthians 10 years ago. He proclaims himself emperor with the encouragement of his officers, but they assassinate him and send his head to Marcus Aurelius, who persuades the Senate to pardon Cassius's family.

176 Marcus Aurelius and his son Commodus enter Rome after a campaign north of the Alps and receive a triumph for their victories over the barbarians.

177 Marcus Aurelius begins a systematic persecution of the Christians at Rome who oppose emperor-worship and thus pose a danger to the established order. The persecution forces adherents to the new religion to practice in secret. Many take refuge in the catacombs—the underground cemetery outside the city hewn out of solid rock since Etruscan times, and the fish becomes a symbol of Christianity (the initial letters of Iesous Christos Theou Uios Soter spell *ichthus*, the Greek word for fish).

180 Rome's Emperor Marcus Aurelius dies March 17 at age 58 after a week's illness either at his camp on the Save in Lower Pannonia or at Vindobona (Vienna).

180 (cont.) He is succeeded by his 18-year-old son Lucius Aelius Aurelius Commodus, who will rule tyrannically and recklessly until his murder in 192.

Methodus Medendo by the 52-year-old Greek physician Galen of Rome correlates extant knowledge of medicine into a system that will influence medical thinking for 15 centuries, but his hundreds of treatises based on empirical therapy are speculative in terms of physiology and pathology, and they will mislead future generations. Galen has fled the city's plague after 16 years of practice in which he has treated Roman gladiators, merchants, and emperors. He has dissected two human corpses in defiance of a Roman law forbidding dissection, and he has dissected Barbary apes to develop a view of anatomy that is basically correct. But he credits the longevity of his centenarian father to a diet that never included fruit and warns that eating fruit can cause fevers. He mistakenly attributes gout to overindulgence (*see* Garrod, 1859), and he asserts that the inner walls of the heart contain invisible pores (*see* Andrea Columbus, 1559; Harvey, 1628).

Reflections, or *Meditations* left behind by the emperor Marcus Aurelius is a compendium of his Stoic philosophy: "Nothing can come out of nothing any more than a thing can go back to nothing"; "Observe constantly that all things take place by change, and accustom thyself to consider that the nature of the Universe loves nothing so much as to change the things which are, and to make new things like them"; "What is good for the swarm is good for the bee"; "A man's happiness is to do a man's work"; "The act of dying is also one of the acts of life."

183 The emperor Commodus escapes death at the hands of assassins who have attacked him at the instigation of his sister Lucilla and a large group of senators. He puts many distinguished Romans to death on charges of being implicated in the conspiracy, and he puts others to death for no reason at all.

185 Rome's capable praetorian prefect Perennis is put to death at the request of a deputation from Britain who represents mutinous legionnaires.

The Roman emperor Commodus drains the treasury to put on gladiatorial spectacles and confiscates the property of the rich to support his pleasures and his soldiery.

189 The Roman mob blames a grain shortage on the mercenary freedman Cleander, who succeeded Perennis as prefect 4 years ago. Cleander is sacrificed to the mob.

Plague, possibly smallpox, kills as many as 2,000 per day in Rome. Dying farmers are unable to harvest their crops, dying carters are not able to deliver what grain there is, and food shortages bring riots in the city (above).

The column of Marcus Aurelius is completed at Rome.

192 The Roman emperor Commodus is murdered December 31, and his death ends the Antonine line that has reigned since 138. The emperor's mistress Marcia, his chamberlain Eclectus, and the prefect of praetorians Laetus have found their names on the imperial execution list and have hired the wrestler Narcissus to strangle Commodus.

193 Publius Helfius Pertinax, 67, is chosen by the Roman Senate against his will to succeed the late Commodus as emperor, but his strict and economical rule arouses quick opposition and he is murdered March 28 by members of the Praetorian Guard who invade the imperial palace. The empire is auctioned off to the highest bidder and goes to Rome's wealthiest senator, Didius Julianus, 61, who has made a fortune in shipping and who outbids the father-in-law of the late Pertinax by offering 300 million sesterces. Didius Julianus is challenged by legates in Britain, Syria, and Pannonia, and the Pannonian legate Lucius Septimius Severus, 47, offers his troops on the Danube huge bonuses if they will leave immediately for Rome. He marches them 800 miles in 40 days, enters the capital June 1 in full battle dress, has Didius Julianus put to death in the palace baths, and begins a reign that will continue until 211.

The silver content of the Roman denarius will fall in the 18-year reign of Septimius Severus to 50 percent, down from 68 percent in the reign of Marcus Aurelius.

194 The Syrian legate C. Pescennius Niger Justus is defeated by the emperor Septimius Severus and is put to death near Antioch.

195 "Scourges, pestilence, famine, earthquakes, and wars are to be regarded as blessings to crowded nations since they serve to prune away the luxuriant growth of the human race," writes Carthage's ecclesiastical author Tertullian (Quintus Septimius Florens Tertullianus), 35. Tertullian was converted to Christianity 5 years ago.

196 Byzantium is sacked by the emperor Septimius Severus and is reduced to the status of a village.

197 Rome's British legate D. Clodius Septimius Albinus is defeated by Septimius Severus and is slain February 19 at Lugdunum (Lyons). The town is sacked by the legionnaires and will never regain its prosperity.

200 The Japanese empress Jingu sends a vast fleet to invade Korea. The Koreans capitulate at sight of the huge multioared ships, and they offer tribute.

Afghanistan is invaded by the Huns.

3rd CENTURY

✗ Septimus Severus, Caracalla, Heliogabalus, Decius, Valerian, Aurelian, and Diocletian will rule the Roman Empire in this century.

✊ Some 400,000 slaves perform the menial work of Rome, with middle-class citizens owning about 8, the rich owning from 500 to 1,000, while an emperor may own as many as 20,000. Free urban workers enjoy 17 to 18 hours of leisure each day, with free admission to baths, sports events, and gladiatorial contests.

☤ Rome establishes medical licenses, awarded only to trained physicians who have passed examinations. Medical societies and civic hospitals are set up, and laws are passed to govern the behavior of medical students. They are prohibited from visiting brothels.

⚡ Roman public roads are so good that travelers can average 100 miles per day.

🌐 Rome is a city of about 1.5 million, its people housed mostly in 46,600 *insulae*, or apartment blocks, each three to eight stories high, flimsily made of wood, brick, or rubble, with shutters and hangings to deaden the nightly din of iron-rimmed cartwheels in the streets.

✗ The average Roman breakfasts on bean meal mash and unleavened breadcakes cooked on cinders and dipped in milk or honey. Midday meals, often eaten standing up in a public place, consist generally of fruit, a sweetmeat, cheese, and watered wine (the *prandium*). The evening meal, or *convivium*, may include meat, fish, cereals, a porridge of breadcrumbs and onions fried in oil and seasoned with vinegar and chick-peas.

204 A trade recession in North Africa's Leptis Magna region is alleviated by Rome's Emperor Septimius Severus, a native of Leptus, who buys up the country's olive oil for free distribution in Rome.

211 Rome's Septimius Severus dies in Britain at Eboracum (York) February 4 at age 64 and is succeeded by his eldest son Augustus, who is called Caracalla (or Caracallus) after the long-hooded tunic he introduces from Gaul.

212 The Edict of Caracalla (*Constitutio Antoniniana*) extends Roman citizenship to all free inhabitants of the empire with the exception of a limited group that may include Egyptians.

213 The Baths of Caracalla, completed by the Roman emperor, have public baths (*Thermae*), reading rooms, auditoriums, running tracks, and public gardens that cover 20 acres. The main building alone

covers 6 acres and can accommodate as many as 1,600 at one time. The poor of Rome are obliged to bathe in the Tiber, and while Rome has sewers and public health inspectors (who enforce hygiene in brothels and markets), the streets are filthy, and in small towns and villages outside the capital the streets stream with excrement.

217 The emperor Caracalla is murdered April 8 by a group of his officers as he prepares to invade Parthia. He is succeeded briefly by the Mauretanian M. Opellius (Severus) Macrinus, 53.

218 Rome's Emperor Macrinus tries to reduce the pay of Roman troops, is defeated and slain near Antioch June 8, and is succeeded by the Syrian Varius Avitus Bassianus, 14, a grandnephew by marriage of the late Septimius Severus, who claims to be a son of Caracalla and calls himself Heliogabalus, or Elagabalus, taking the name of the Syrian sun king.

💲 The silver content of the Roman denarius will fall to 43 percent under Heliogabalus, down from 50 percent under Septimius Severus.

✗ Rome's new emperor maintains a fleet of fishing boats to catch eels, prized for their roe. He has conger eels kept in tubs and fattened on the flesh of Christian slaves killed in the Colosseum. He has 600 ostriches killed to make ostrich brain pies for one meal. Serving banquets that cost the equivalent of $10,000 each, Heliogabalus empties the treasury of Rome with his excesses while his mother Julia Maesa runs the empire.

222 Rome's Emperor Heliogabalus is murdered March 11 by the praetorians and is succeeded by his 14-year-old cousin and adopted son (Gessius) Bassianus, who takes the name Marcus Aurelius Severus Alexander and begins a 12-year reign that will be dominated by his mother Mamaea.

💲 The silver content of the Roman denarius will fall to 35 percent under Severus Alexander, down from 43 percent under Heliogabalus.

Government control of Rome's trade guilds will be extended under Severus Alexander.

❀ Gunpowder will be invented in the next half century by Chinese alchemists of the Wu dynasty who will mix sulfur and saltpeter in the correct proportions and at the correct temperature to produce the explosive (*see* 1235).

✗ Tea will be mentioned as a substitute for wine for the first time in Chinese writings of the next half century.

226 The Sassanian dynasty that will rule Persia until 642 is begun by the rebel prince Ardashir, grandson of Sassan, who 12 years ago gained control of the region surrounding Persepolis and who defeats Artabanus at Hormuz. Artabanus is killed and the Parthian Arsacid dynasty ends after roughly 500 years.

234 Ready-made bread rather than grain is issued to the poor of Rome by decree of the 26-year-old Emperor Severus Alexander.

235 Rome's Severus Alexander is killed March 18 by his troops on the Rhine after he has bought peace from the Alamanni who have invaded Gaul. The Thracian Gaius Julius Verus Maximinus, 62, is proclaimed emperor by the troops, and he begins a 3-year reign.

238 Roman subjects in Africa revolt against the emperor Maximinus and elect as emperor their 80-year-old proconsul Marcus Antonius Gordianus Africanus. A rich descendant of the Gracchi and of the emperor Trajan, Gordianus yields to public demand that he succeed Maximinus. The Senate and most of the provinces support him, but a supporter of Maximinus besieges Gordianus for 36 days at Carthage. Gordianus commits suicide at news that his 46-year-old son and namesake is dead, and the Roman populace proclaims his 14-year-old grandson Marcus Antonius Gordianus III emperor. The praetorians conspire to murder the emperor Maximinus in mid-June, the Praetorian Guard names young Gordianus sole emperor, and he begins a 6-year reign.

The silver content of the Roman denarius will fall to 28 percent under the emperor Gordianus III, down from 35 percent under Severus Alexander.

244 The Roman emperor Gordianus III drives a Persian army back across the Euphrates and defeats the Persians in the Battle of Resaena. Mutinous soldiers murder the emperor at the urging of the Arabian Marcus Julius Philippus. They proclaim Philippus emperor, and he makes a disgraceful peace with the Persians.

The silver content of the Roman denarius will fall to 0.5 percent under the emperor Philippus, down from 28 percent under Gordianus III.

248 The Roman emperor Philippus holds a great exhibition of games to celebrate the 1,000 anniversary of the founding of Rome in 753 B.C.

249 The Pannonian-born Roman commander Gaius Messius Quintus Traianus Decius, 48, puts down a revolt of troops in Moesia and Pannonia. Loyal troops proclaim Decius emperor, and he kills the emperor Philippus, who has advanced to oppose him at Verona.

250 The Roman emperor Decius institutes the first wholesale persecution of Christians in an attempt to restore the religion and institutions of ancient Rome. The persecution produces martyrs who will be revered as saints.

Arithmetica by the Greek mathematician Diophantus at Alexandria includes the first book on algebra.

251 The Roman emperor Decius and his son die fighting the Goths on swampy ground in the Dobrudja. His treacherous general Gaius Vibius Trebonianus Gallus, 46, succeeds as emperor, he makes peace with the Goths, he permits them to keep their plunder, and he offers them a bribe not to return.

253 Roman soldiers who have campaigned against the barbarians on the Danube elect the governor of Pannonia and Moesia as emperor. The emperor Gallus marches out to meet his rival. The new emperor Aemilianus defeats Gallus and kills him but dies himself soon after, and a supporter of Gallus who has arrived too late to save him wins the support of the legions, who elect him emperor. Publius Licinius Valerianus, 60, begins a 7-year reign as the emperor Valerian.

A 15-year plague begins in the Roman Empire.

255 *De Mortalitate* by Thascius Caecilius Cyprianus, bishop of Carthage, describes a pandemic said to have started in Ethiopia. Symptoms include diarrhea and vomiting, an ulcerated sore throat, high fever, and gangrenous hands and feet. The pandemic will pass through Egypt and will extend through Europe to the northernmost reaches of the British Isles.

"The world itself now bears witness to its failing powers," writes Carthage's Bishop Cyprian (above) to the Roman proconsul of Africa. "There is not so much rain in the winter for fertilizing the seeds, nor in the summer is there so much warmth for ripening them. The springtime is no longer mild, nor the autumn so rich in fruit."

256 The great pandemic of the Roman world strikes violently in Pontus on the Black Sea and causes enormous loss of life in Alexandria, encouraging thousands to embrace Christianity.

258 Carthage's Bishop Thascius Caecilius Cyprianus is beheaded (*see* 255).

260 Rome's Emperor Valerian is defeated by Persia's Shapur I at Edessa and is taken prisoner after being seized treacherously at a parley. His son Publius Licinius Egnatius Gallienus, 42, who has reigned with him, continues to reign alone as pretenders appear throughout the empire.

268 Rome's Emperor Gallienus is killed by his own soldiers at Mediolanum (Milan) while besieging the pretender Aureolus, who is slain in turn by the pretender Marcus Aurelius Claudius, who will reign until 270.

269 A Gothic invasion of the Balkans is repelled by Rome's Emperor Claudius II, who is given the title Gothicus for his victory.

270 Rome's Illyrian Emperor Claudius Gothicus dies of plague and is succeeded by his brother Quintillus, who is proclaimed as Marcus Aurelius Claudius Quin-

Barbarian prisoners taken by the victorious legions often ended up working in Roman mines, galleys, and bathhouses.

tillus but is deserted by his troops. He commits suicide and is succeeded by an associate of his brother who will reign until 275 as Lucius Domitius Aurelianus.

💲 The silver content of the denarius has fallen to 0.02 percent, down from 0.5 percent under the emperor Philippus.

271 The Alamanni are expelled from Italy by the Roman emperor Aurelianus, who has abandoned transDanubian Dacia, settled its Roman inhabitants in a new Dacia carved out of Moesia, begun new walls to protect Rome, and is called *restitutor orbis* (restorer of the world).

272 Three Christians are beheaded on the road to the Temple of Mercury that stands atop a hill that will be named Montmartre (Mountain of Martyrs) in Lutetia, later to be called Paris.

273 Palmyra is sacked by Rome's Emperor Aurelianus to put down a revolt.

Rome's daily bread ration is increased to nearly 1.5 pounds per capita by the emperor Aurelianus, who adds pork fat to the list of foods distributed free to the populace.

274 Gaul is recovered from insurgent forces by Rome's Emperor Aurelianus in a battle at Chalons and returns to Rome in triumph.

A 100-foot oar-powered ship is built for Japan's Emperor Ojin. The Japanese will not use sails for another seven centuries.

275 Rome's legions retreat from Transylvania and the Black Forest and fall back to the Rhine and the Danube. The situation has become so perilous that the emperor Aurelianus pushes construction of fortifications for Rome begun 4 years ago.

Aurelianus is slain by some of his officers as he prepares to invade Persia and is succeeded by an elderly senator, who is appointed against his will and who will rule briefly as Marcus Claudius Tacitus.

A plague so severe that many wonder whether mankind can survive weakens the Roman legions in Gaul and in Mesopotamia.

276 Rome's Emperor Tacitus is killed by his troops after having defeated the Goths and Alans who have invaded Asia Minor. He is succeeded by his brother Marcus Annius Florianus, who is soon killed and is succeeded by the Illyrian Marcus Aurelius Probus, who will reign until 282.

The Persian sage Mani is executed at age 60 after 30 years of preaching his "heresy" at the court of the late Sassanian king Shapur I and on long journeys to Turkestan, India, and China. Mani has claimed that he received divine revelations and was the final prophet of God in the world; his system combines Zoroastrian dualism with Christian salvation. He has incurred the hostility of the Zoroastrian priests at Ctesiphon, but his disciples will gain wide support for Manichaeism despite opposition from Byzantine and Roman emperors.

282 Rome's Emperor Probus tries to employ his troops in such peaceful projects as clearing the canals of Egypt after having driven the Franks and Alamanni out of Gaul, suppressed pretenders in Gaul, quieted Asia Minor, and strengthened defenses on the Danube. Probus is murdered by his troops in the autumn and is succeeded by an Illyrian who has served as praetorian prefect to the late Aurelianus and who conducts a successful campaign against the Persians to begin a brief reign as M. Aurelius Carus.

283 Rome's Emperor Marcus Aurelius Carus dies and is succeeded by his son and coemperor Marcus Aurelius Numerius Numerianus.

284 The Roman emperor Marcus Aurelius Numerius Numerianus is assassinated in late summer and is succeeded by the 39-year-old Illyrian general Gaius Aurelius Valerius Diocletianus Jovius. He is proclaimed emperor at Chelcedon August 29 and begins a 21-year reign of oriental despotism at Nicomedia in Bithynia while his colleague Marcus Aurelius Valerius Maximianus Herculius will control the west from Mediolanum (Milan).

August 29, 284 will be the first day of the calendar used by Egyptian Coptics and Abyssynians.

4th CENTURY

Diocletian, Constantine, Licinius, Julian, Valens, and Theodosius will be the major emperors in this century but will be challenged in Rome's outlying provinces and territories by Persians and barbarians. Most of Rome's rulers will be of peasant or barbarian origin themselves, the hereditary upper classes having become effete.

301 Rome's Emperor Diocletian limits prices of goods and services in an effort to end the economic distress caused by the collapse of Roman currency, but no attempt is made to enforce his edict in the west, and in the east it soon proves impracticable.

The kingdom of Armenia makes Christianity an official state religion and becomes the first nation to do so.

302 The public baths of the emperor Diocletian at Rome open with 3,000 rooms. They are even larger and more elaborate than the Baths of Caracalla completed in 211.

303 A general prosecution of Christians in the Roman Empire begins February 24 by edict of the emperor Diocletian who has been persuaded to revive the old religion in a move to strengthen the empire.

305 The Roman emperor Diocletian abdicates May 1 at age 60 and retires to Salona after a reign of nearly 21 years in which the last vestiges of republican government have disappeared. Diocletian is succeeded by the Thracian Galerius Valerius Maximanus, who persuaded Diocletian to persecute the Christians in 303. He assumes the title Augustus and begins an 8-year reign with his Illyrian colleague Flavius Valerius Constantius.

Rich landowners dominate the Roman Empire and enjoy the title of senator, which makes them exempt from the crushing taxes imposed on the rest of the population. The Senate has lost all its power and the landowners almost never attend Senate sessions. Labor and property is evaluated in terms of a unit of wheat-producing land (*iugum*), members of municipal senates (*curiales* or *decuriones*) are charged with the responsibility of collecting taxes and paying arrears; smaller landowners are held responsible for providing recruits for the legions and with keeping wastelands under cultivation.

306 The Roman coemperor Constantius dies July 25 at age 56 outside Eboracum (York) during a campaign against the Picts and Scots. Roman troops in Britain salute his 18-year-old bastard son Flavius Valerius Constantinus as emperor, but the emperor Galerius in Rome elevates Flavius Valerius Severus to the rank of coemperor. The Roman despot Marcus Aurelius Valerius Maxentius leads an uprising, and the praetorians proclaim him Caesar.

307 The Roman coemperor Severus dies November 11. The emperor Galerius replaces him with the Illyrian Flavius Galerius Valerius Licinianus, who will rule as the emperor Licinius until 324. Flavius Valerius Constantinus in Britain proclaims himself emperor, but he rules only in Britain and Gaul (*see* 306; 312).

308 The Roman despot Marcus Aurelius Valerius Maxentius banishes his father Maximian to Gaul.

309 Anthrax or a similar plague begins to spread across the Roman Empire. The disease will sharply reduce the empire's population in the next 5 years.

311 The Roman emperor Galerius dies in May after the despot Marcus Aurelius Valerius Maxentius has driven him out of Italy. The despot's father Maximian committed suicide in Gaul last year when authorities discovered his conspiracy against the emperor Constantine, who begins to march on Rome.

312 The Battle of Milvian Bridge (or *Saxa Rubra*) 4 miles north of Rome October 28 gives the emperor Constantine a victory over the despot Maxentius. He kills Maxentius and becomes absolute master of the western Roman Empire.

Constantine (above) will claim to have seen a vision in the sky of a luminous cross bearing the words "*In hoc signo vinces*" (By this sign thou shalt conquer). He will adopt the words as a motto.

313 The Roman emperor Constantine and his coemperor Licinius accept Christianity. They return property confiscated from Christians under terms of the Edict of Milan.

314 The Battle of Cibalae October 8 gives the Roman emperor Constantine a victory over his coemperor Licinius, who loses all of the Balkans except for Thrace.

315 The Arch of Constantine completed by the Roman emperor commemorates his victory at the Milvian Bridge in 312.

317 Northern and southern dynasties will divide China over the next 272 years.

320 The Gupta dynasty begins to unify northern India after five centuries of division.

321 The Roman emperor Constantine forbids work on the Sabbath and endorses Sunday (*see* "blue laws," 1781).

The emperor Constantine assigns convicts to grind Rome's flour in a move to hold back the rising price of food in an empire whose population has shrunk as a result of plague (*see* 309). Barbarian peoples have used waterpower for years and pressure mounts to use such power in Rome, where rulers have opposed it in the past lest it cause unemployment.

323 The Battle of Adrianople July 3 gives the Roman emperor Constantine's son Flavius Julius Crispus a triumph over the naval forces of Licinius. The co-emperor has angered Constantine with his anti-Christian policy, and he loses again September 18 at Chrysopolis in Anatolia.

324 The Roman emperor Constantine has his coemperor Licinius executed. He reunites the empire, and he rules singlehanded from the Clyde River to the Euphrates.

The empire will recover from the chaos of the 3rd century under Constantine. External peace, internal unity, a new coinage supported by confiscated treasure, and state revenues supported by a new, simplified taxation system will bring prosperity to the great cities of the empire. Jobs will become hereditary, even in the female line (if one marries a baker's daughter, one must become a baker).

325 The Council of Nicaea summoned by the Roman emperor Constantine is the first ecumenical council of the Church. It supports the doctrine that God and Christ are of the same substance. The priest Arius has maintained the opposite view, he will be tortured to death in 336, but Constantine and his successors will move the Church increasingly toward Arianism. Athanasianism will not become the dominant view until after 379.

330 Constantinople is dedicated May 11 and becomes the new capital of the Roman Empire. The emperor Constantine has spent 4 years building the new city on the site of ancient Byzantium (*see* 658 B.C.).

333 The Romans begin pulling troops out of Britain and abandon work on the 72-mile Hadrian's Wall begun in 122. The wall includes at least 16 forts.

337 The Roman emperor Constantine dies May 22 at age 49. His wife Fausta persuaded him 11 years ago to execute Flavius Julius Crispus, his son by his first wife, and he is succeeded by three sons born to Fausta.

Rome will war indecisively with Persia for the next 24 years.

360 Japan begins a 30-year period of great influence in Korea.

The Huns invade Europe.

Picts and Scots cross Hadrian's Wall and attack Roman forces in Britain.

Roman authorities in Britain have encouraged production of wheat, which they export to supply the legions on the Rhine.

361 The Roman emperor Constantius dies November 3 near Tarsus in Cilicia at age 44 as he marches to join his 30-year-old cousin Flavius Claudius Julianus. Constantinople acknowledges Julianus as sole head of the empire, he enters the city December 11, and he begins an 18-month reign as the emperor Julian.

The new Roman emperor Julian (above) tries to organize a pagan church and substitute it for Christianity.

Constantinople enforces a strict licensing system for physicians. The royal physician Oribasius, who is reputed to have discovered the salivary glands, writes works on diet in pregnancy, children's diseases, and contraception.

363 The Roman emperor Julian sustains a mortal wound June 26 in a battle with the Persians. The last champion of polytheism, he is succeeded by the captain of his imperial bodyguard, Flavius Iovianus, 32, who will reign for 7 months as the emperor Jovian.

364 The Roman emperor Jovian signs a humiliating treaty with the Persian shah Shapur II, he yields the kingdom of Armenia and most Roman holdings in Persia, and he is found dead in February at Dadastana en route back to Constantinople. He is succeeded by the Pannonian general Valentinian, 42, who appoints his 36-year-old brother Valens coemperor. Valentinian I rules from Caledonia to northwestern Africa, Valens rules from the Danube east to the Persian border.

371 The neo-Persian Empire reaches the height of its power under Shapur II as the Romans and Persians renew their wars. Hostilities will continue for the next 5 years.

Imperious Roman legions raped and pillaged until the "barbarians" turned the tables on them.

372
The Huns begin new incursions into the West. They defeat the Alens and the Heruls, they destroy the Ostrogothic Empire of Hermanric, they absorb the Ostrogoths for a time, and they rout the Visigoths from the Dneister River.

375
The Roman emperor Valentinian dies November 17 at age 53 in a fit of apoplexy while attending a meeting on the Danube. Extreme cruelty has marked his 11-year reign but he has founded schools and has provided physicians to serve the poor of Constantinople. Valentinian I is succeeded nominally by his 4-year-old son who is hailed as Valentinian II, but the boy's half-brother Flavius Gratianus, 17, assumes the real power. He will rule from Milan until his death in 383 as the emperor Gratian.

Epitoma Rei Militaris by the Roman military surgeon Flavius Vetetius declares, "An army must not use bad or marshy water; for the drinking of bad water is like poison and causes plagues among those who drink it. . . . If a large group stays too long during the summer or autumn in one place, the water becomes corrupt, and because of the corruption, drinking is unhealthy, the air is corrupt, and so malignant disease arises which cannot be checked except by frequent change of camp."

376
Roman authorities order Visigoths who have taken refuge in the empire to disarm and settle across the Danube in Lower Moesia. The Romans fail to disarm the Visigoths, they bungle administration of the refugees, and are obliged to fight with the barbarians.

378
The Roman emperor Gratian completely defeats the southernmost branch of the Alamanni at Argenatria, but the Battle of Adrianople August 9 ends in disaster for the Romans. Mounted Visigoths kill the emperor Valens and rout his foot soldiers in a victory that presages a revolution in the art of war. The power of cavalry will determine European military, social, and political development for the next 1,000 years.

The Roman emperor Gratian summons his general Flavius Theodosius, 32, to replace Valens as emperor in the East. A veteran of many campaigns with his late father, who was executed at Carthage 2 years ago on charges of conspiring against Valens, the new coemperor has fought the Picts in Britain and has defeated the Sarmatians in Moesia.

379
The Roman coemperor Theodosius assumes office at Sirmius January 19 with power over all the eastern provinces, he comes to terms with the Visigoths, and he settles them in the Balkans as military allies (*foederati*).

The Persian shah Shapur II dies at age 70 after a lifetime reign in which he has humbled the Romans, has conquered Armenia, has transferred multitudes of people from western lands to Susiana (Khuzistan), has rebuilt Susa, and has founded Nishapur.

383
Roman legions desert the emperor Gratian at Lutetia (Paris), he flees to Lyons, and he is delivered over to one of the generals who have risen in revolt against Rome. The emperor is assassinated August 25 at age 25 after an 8-year reign in which Christianity has become the dominant religion in the empire.

The Roman general Magnus Clemens Maximus has led the insurrection in Britain and Gaul, Gratian's younger brother Valentinian II and his coemperor Theodosius recognize Magnus Maximus as Augustus, he receives recognition in Britain, Gaul, and the Hispanic provinces, and he begins a 5-year reign as coemperor.

388
The Roman emperor Magnus Maximus crosses into Italy but the emperor Theodosius defeats him July 28 at Aquileia. He is subsequently murdered while Theodosius devotes himself to gluttony and voluptuous living.

390
An insurrection in Macedonia arouses the anger of the emperor Theodosius who has 3,000 Macedonians and Greeks massacred at Thessalonica.

392
The Roman emperor Valentinian II is murdered May 15 at Vienne in Gaul at the instigation of his Frankish general Arbogast who sets up the grammarian and rhetorician Eugenius as emperor. The death of Valentinian at age 21 enrages the emperor Theodosius who marches against Eugenius.

394
Eugenius is killed in battle September 6 by the barbarian legions of the emperor Theodosius. The Frankish general Arbogast escapes into the mountains but commits suicide 2 days later.

395
The Roman Empire splits into eastern and western empires following the death at Milan January 17 of the emperor Theodosius at age 49. His 17-year-old son Arcadius has married Eudoxia, daughter of the Frankish leader Bauto, and will rule from Constantinople while his 10-year-old son Honorius rules from Milan under the dominance of his Vandal master of troops Stilicho, whose daughter Maria will be married to Honorius in 398.

The split in the Roman Empire (above) is considered temporary but will prove permanent.

An estimated 330,000 acres of farmland lie abandoned in Rome's Campania, partly as a consequence of malaria from mosquitoes bred in swampy areas, but mostly because imprudent agriculture has ruined the land.

397
The Roman master of troops Stilicho drives Alaric and his Visigoths out of Greece after a 2-year campaign.

The Scottish apostle Ninian establishes a church at Whithorn to help him in evangelizing the southern Picts. A British chieftain's son, Ninian has made a pilgrimage to Rome and has been consecrated a bishop after 15 years of study.

399
Confessions by the North African cleric-philosopher Augustine, 44, says, "How small are grains of sand! Yet if enough are placed in a ship they sink it." Converted to Christianity by Bishop Ambrose of Milan, Augustine has served for the past 3 years as Bishop of Hippo and will continue in that position for the next 31 years (see 426).

48

5th CENTURY

401 Visigoths penetrate the northern defenses of Italy and begin to ravage the countryside.

402 The Battle of Pollentia April 6 ends in victory for the Roman legions of Stilicho who stymies the Visigoths in their efforts to move south.

405 Rome's Colosseum is closed by the emperor Honorius in an austerity move that abolishes amusements.

406 Barbarian forces led by Radagaisus into Italy meet defeat at Florence August 23 as Roman legions under Stilicho break up the invading army.

Hordes of Vandals cross the Rhine under their new king, Gunderic, who will reign until 428. Allied with the Alans and the Sciri, they follow the Moselle and the Aisne and proceed to sack Rheims, Amiens, Arras, and Tournai, and turn south into Aquitaine.

Cultivation of rye, oats, hops, and spelt (a wheat used for livestock feed) is introduced into Europe by the invading Vandals, Alans, and Sciri (above), who also introduce a heavy wheeled plow that enables farmers to plow deeper, straighter furrows (see 90).

Butter is introduced by the invading Vandals, Alans, and Sciri (above) to replace olive oil.

407 Britain is evacuated by Roman legions who are needed closer to home. The British Isles return to Saxon rule after 360 years of Roman control.

Oyster cultivation has been introduced into Britain by the Romans (above; see 110 B.C.).

408 Rome is besieged by the Visigoths under Alaric, and the Roman master of troops Stilicho is murdered August 22 on orders from the emperor Honorius.

The eastern emperor Arcadius, whose eunuch general Eutropius has been unable to thwart barbarian invasions, dies at age 31 after a 13-year reign. He is succeeded by his 7-year-old son who will reign until 450 as Theodosius II but who will be dominated by his sister Pulcheria.

The Visigoth king Alaric (above) exacts a tribute from Rome that includes 3,000 pounds of pepper (5,000 pounds by some accounts). The spice is valued for alleged medicinal virtues and for disguising spoilage in meat that is past its prime.

409 Alaric's Visigoths invade Italy again, and Alaric sets up a pagan emperor whom he soon deposes.

Vandals cross the Pyrenees into the Iberian Peninsula but find food supplies short as a Roman fleet blockades imports from the North African granary.

410 Invading Huns ravage the Roman Empire and extort tribute. They introduce trousers, which replace togas, and stirrups (a Chinese or Korean invention), which make it easier to ride horses.

Rome is sacked August 14 (or 25) after a third siege by Alaric, who dies soon afterward in southern Italy.

411 The self-proclaimed Roman emperor Constantine (Flavius Claudius Constantinus), who has gained control of Britain, Gaul, and Spain in the past 4 years, is defeated near Arles by the Roman general Constantius in the service of the emperor Honorius. Constantine is taken prisoner and put to death at Ravenna.

412 Visigoth forces move into Gaul under the leadership of Ataulf, brother of the late Alaric.

415 Visigoths invade the Iberian Peninsula and begin to conquer territory taken earlier by the Vandals.

422 The walls of Rome's Colosseum crack during an earthquake.

423 A farmer's strike is organized by Visigoths who have been settled south of the Danube by Theodosius (see 379). The Visigoths are prevented from occupying Rome only by payment of what amounts to a huge farm loan.

425 The Huns are halted in their unopposed advance on Constantinople by a plague that decimates their hordes.

426 *The City of God (De Civitate Dei)* by the Christian philosopher Augustine, now 72, declares that empires like Rome are merely temporary (temporal) and that the only permanent community is the Church—visible and invisible—the city of God.

The purpose of marriage is procreation, says Constantine (above), and his view will dominate Church thinking for at least 12 centuries.

427 Korea's King Changsu moves his capital from the banks of the Yalu River to Pyongyang.

429 North Africa is invaded by 80,000 Vandals under their king, Gaeseric, who leads his forces from the Iberian Peninsula across the narrow Straits of Gibraltar (see 415; 430).

430 The Vandals who have invaded North Africa extend their power along the Mediterranean coast and lay siege to Hippo.

Bishop Augustine dies in the siege of Hippo (above) at age 76, leaving behind his monumental work *The*

430 (cont.) *City of God* and other works that will have more influence on Christianity than those of anyone else except for the apostle Paul.

Britain's Bishop Patrick is sent as a missionary to Ireland. A native of the Severn Valley, he will labor for 30 years to convert the Irish to Christianity.

431 The patriarch of Constantinople Nestorius is deposed for heresy by the Council of Ephesus for preaching the doctrine that in Jesus Christ there was joined in perfect harmony a divine person (the *Logos*) and a human person but that the harmony was of action, not of a single individual. Nestorius is banished to the Libyan desert, but his followers will spread Nestorianism widely through Persia, India, Mongolia, and China (*see* 781).

The cult of the Virgin begins to spread westward from Byzantium following a decree of the Council of Ephesus (above) recognizing Mary as the Mother of God.

433 Attila becomes leader of the Huns, whom he will rule until his death in 453.

436 The Burgundian kingdom of Worms established in 406 is destroyed by Attila's Huns.

The last Roman legions leave Britain.

439 The Codex Theodosianus drawn up by appointees of the Roman emperor Valentinian III is a summary of Roman law.

Carthage falls to the Vandals who have been led since 428 by Genseric (Gaiseric). He makes Carthage his capital.

The Vandals establish a North African granary that will enable them to enforce their will on other nations as they become dependent on North Africa for food staples.

441 German Saxons establish themselves at the mouth of the Thames River.

443 The Alamanni settle in Alsace.

444 A "pestilence" that is probably bubonic plague strikes the British Isles and makes the country vulnerable to conquest (*see* 449).

The wheelbarrow is invented by the Chinese.

446 Chinese Buddhists are persecuted by the northern Wei, who have heretofore encouraged the Buddhists but whose secular government is threatened by the drain of manpower and tax money to the temples and monasteries. Monks and nuns are murdered, temples and icons destroyed, and all men under age 50 prohibited from joining any monastic order in a program that will continue until 450 and will aid the Confucianism of the Han Chinese to gain dominance over Buddhism.

449 Britain is conquered by Angles and Saxons who have been invited to the British Isles to fight against Pict (Caledonian) and Scottish foes of the Britons' King Vortigern, but who have wound up fighting the Britons as well. The conquest has been facilitated by an epidemic that weakened the country 5 years ago.

450 The Hawaiian Islands are discovered by Polynesian chief Hawaii-Loa, who has sailed across 2,400 miles of open water from the island of Raiatea, near Tahiti (date is approximate) (*see* Cook, 1778).

Metal horseshoes come into more common use in the Near East and in Europe, increasing the efficiency of horsepower in agriculture and transportation (*see* 770).

451 The Battle of Chalons ends in defeat for Attila's Huns at the hands of a Roman force under Flavius Aetius with help from the Visigoths. The Huns have triumphed over the Alans, the Heruls, the Ostrogoths, and the Visigoths, they have ravaged much of the Italian countryside, and they have forced people to settle on marshy islands that will become the city of Venice (*see* 687).

452 The Japanese crown prince Karu is killed by his brother Anko who becomes emperor following the death of his father Ingyo and who will reign for 3 years and 8 months. Anko kills his uncle Okusaka and marries his uncle's wife Nakatarashi.

Attila's surviving Huns in Europe are reduced in numbers by plague and food shortages.

453 Attila of the Huns dies, and his followers are driven out of Italy by Roman troops with barbarian reinforcements.

455 Rome is sacked by the Vandals whose pillage is so thorough that the name "Vandal" will become a generic word for a wanton destroyer.

Barter economy replaces organized trade as Romans and other city dwellers desert their towns for the countryside where they will be less visible targets of barbarian attack (*see* 350).

Orae Favianae (Vienna) is struck by an epidemic that spreads through the Roman provinces. The disease is probably streptococcus or a form of scarlet fever with streptococci pneumonia.

Chichen-Itza is founded by Mayans on the Yucatan Peninsula of the Western Hemisphere. Chichen will spread to cover 6 square miles of pyramids, temples, an observatory, ceremonial ball courts, and dwellings.

456 The Japanese emperor Anko is killed by the 10-year-old son of his late uncle Okusaka. Young Mayuwa strikes while Anko is asleep with his head on the lap of Nakatarashi, but he himself is killed with other princes by Anko's 38-year-old brother, who begins a 23-year reign as the emperor Yuryaku.

460 A famine that will last for several years begins in the neo-Persian Empire.

466 The Huns invade Dacia but are repelled by the eastern emperor Leo I with the help of his generals Anthemius and Anagastus.

467 The eastern emperor Leo I has his general Anthemius elected emperor of the west, and together they mount a fleet of more than 1,100 ships with an army of 100,000 to attack the pirate empire of the Vandals in North Africa.

Rome has an epidemic that takes many lives.

468 The Imperial Fleet commanded by Basiliscus, brother-in-law of the eastern emperor Leo I, is surprised by the Vandal king Genseric, and half the vessels in the fleet are sunk or burned.

Another invasion of Dacia by the Huns is repelled by Leo I.

471 The failure of the Imperial Fleet against the Vandals in 468, for which he himself was responsible, is used by the emperor's brother-in-law Basiliscus as an excuse to murder the Goth Aspar. The murder is used by the Goths as an excuse to attack the approaches to Constantinople, but the threat is ended when the emperor's son-in-law Zeno has the Gothic leader Ardaburius assassinated.

474 The eastern emperor Leo I dies at age 74 after a 17-year reign. He is succeeded by his 48-year-old Isaurian son-in-law who will reign for all but 2 of the next 17 years as the emperor Zeno.

476 The western Roman Empire founded by Augustus in 27 B.C. ends August 28 at Ravenna, where the emperor Augustulus (Romulus Augustus) is deposed by the Herulian (Saxon) leader Odovacar (Odoacer). Because he is a mere boy, Augustulus is sent off to Naples with an annual pension of 6,000 pieces of gold.

The eastern emperor Zeno is forced to abdicate by his wife's uncle Basiliscus who usurps the throne to begin a 2-year reign.

477 The eastern emperor Basiliscus is deposed by the ex-emperor Zeno who regains the throne he will hold until 491.

480 The Visigoths extend their rule from the Loire to Gibraltar and from the Bay of Biscay to the Rhine. Their seat of empire is Toulouse.

481 The king of the Salian Franks Childeric I dies at age 44 after a 24-year reign. He is succeeded by his 15-year-old son who will reign until 511 as Clovis I.

482 The eastern emperor Zeno issues a letter ("Henoticon") in an unsuccessful effort to resolve differences between the eastern and western churches, but the Menophysite controversy continues to divide the churches.

488 Italy is invaded by an army of Ostrogoths commanded by Theodoric who has been persuaded to make the invasion by the eastern emperor Zeno.

490 Ravenna is besieged by Theodoric and his Ostrogoths.

491 The eastern emperor Zeno dies at age 65 after a 17-year reign and is succeeded by a 61-year-old palace official who is elevated to the throne, marries Zeno's widow Ariadne, and begins a 27-year reign as Anastasius I.

493 The Herulian leader Odovacar surrenders Ravenna after a 3-year siege to Theodoric who invites Odovacar to dinner and has him murdered. Theodoric will unite Italy as an Ostrogoth kingdom that will control the peninsula until 554.

495 The Wei dynasty in China moves its capital to Loyang.

496 Clovis of the Salian Franks defeats the Alamanni near Strasbourg.

Clovis (above) is converted to Christianity and is baptized by his friend Remy, bishop of Rheims.

500 Bavaria is invaded by the Marcomanni from Bohemia whose lands are taken up by the Czechs.

Incense is introduced in Christian church services.

6th CENTURY

Disease, war, famine, and natural disasters will take a heavy toll of the decayed Roman Empire in this century.

501 The Susruta medical book that will become a classic of medicine in India is compiled (date approximate).

502 The Chinese emperor Wu-Ti begins a 47-year reign.

507 The Visigoths are defeated in the Battle of the Campus Vogladensis by a Frankish army under the command of Clovis. Alaric II is killed, and Clovis annexes the Visigoth kingdom of Toulouse, but the Visigoths will remain in control of the Iberian Peninsula for the next two centuries, even though they are outnumbered 30 to 1 by the native population of 6 million.

508 Paris (Lutetia) is established as the Frankish capital by Clovis. He has triumphed over the Visigoths, and he wants to be close to the lands he has conquered.

Rome's Colosseum suffers further damage from an earthquake (*see* 442; 851).

510 Provence is overrun by the Italian Ostrogoths.

Roman philosopher Anicius Manlius Severinus Boethius, 30, is appointed consul by his friend Theodoric who rules the Ostrogoths from his capital at Ravenna (*see* 522).

511 Clovis of the Salian Franks dies at age 45, and his Merovingian dynasty is continued by his four sons, Theodoric, Chlodomer, Childebert, and Lothair, who divide the Frankish kingdom and rule from capitals at Metz, Orléans, Paris (Lutetia), and Soissons, respectively.

513 Mount Vesuvius erupts as it did in 79 A.D., and Pompeii is buried once more under lava, mud, and ashes.

517 Buddhism is introduced to central China by the emperor Wu-Ti who has ruled since 502 and who is converted to the Buddhist faith (*see* 260 B.C.).

518 The Byzantine emperor Anastasius I dies July 9 at age 88 after a 27-year reign and is succeeded by his 68-year-old uneducated Illyrian bodyguard who will reign until 527 as Justinus I. The new emperor is counseled by his able nephew Justinian, 35.

519 The eastern and western Catholic churches are reconciled to end the schism that began in 484.

520 *Institutionis Grammaticae* by Constantinople's Latin grammarian Priscian (Priscianus Caesariensis) codifies Latin grammar in 18 volumes that will be widely used through the Middle Ages. Violating rules of grammar will be called "breaking Priscian's head."

522 Rome's consul Boethius is arrested on charges of having conspired against Theodoric the Great. He admits that he would like the integrity of the Roman Senate restored, but he insists that all hope for that is gone and that the letters from him addressed to Justinus at Constantinople are forgeries. He is imprisoned at Pavia (*see* 524).

524 Boethius is executed without trial after a prison term during which he has written *The Consolation of Philosophy* (*see* below).

Burgundy's King Sigismund is killed by Chlodomer after an 8-year reign and is succeeded by Godomar.

Rome and Persia renew hostilities to begin a war that will last for 7 years.

The Consolation of Philosophy (*De Consolatione Philosophiae*) by Boethius (above) alternates between poetry and prose in an exposition of neo-Platonism and stoicism: "For in all adversity of fortune the worst sort of misery is to have been happy" (II, iv).

525 The birth date of Jesus is incorrectly given as December 25, 753 years after the founding of Rome, in "Easter Tables" issued by Roman theologian-mathematician Dionysius Exiguus, 25, whose error will be standardized in all Christian calendars.

The Yemen is conquered by Ethiopian forces.

Alexandrian explorer-geographer Cosmas Indicopleustes travels up the Nile. He will venture as far to the east as Ceylon, he will become a monk, and he will write *Topographia Christiana* to vindicate the biblical account of the world.

526 Theodoric the Great dies August 30 at age 72 and is succeeded as king of the Ostrogoths by his 10-year-old grandson Athalaric who will rule until 534 with his mother Amalasuntha as regent.

A Roman army is defeated by Persian forces.

An earthquake shatters Antioch and kills between 200,000 and 300,000 people.

A magnificent tomb is erected at Ravenna for the late Theodoric the Great (above).

527 Constantinople's Justinus I takes his nephew Justinian as coemperor April 1 as an incurable wound weakens him. He dies August 1 at age 77, and Justinian (Flavius Anicius Justinianus, or Flavius Petrus Sabbatius Justinianus) begins a 38-year reign that will be strongly influenced by his 19-year-old wife Theodora until her death in 545.

528 Persian forces are defeated in the Battle of Daras by Justinian's 23-year-old commander Belisarius, who begins an outstanding military career.

529 The Benedictine order of monks is established at Monte Cassino near Naples by Benedict of Nursia, 49, who founds a monastery and formulates strict rules in his *Regula Monachorum*. Benedict inaugurates monasticism in western Europe (*see* 1080; Franciscans, 1209).

The academy founded at Athens by Plato in 347 B.C. is closed by the emperor Justinian on charges of un-Christian activity. Many of the school's professors emigrate to Persia and Syria.

The Codex Vitus (Code of Civil Laws) is issued by Justinian.

Ratisbon is made the capital of Bavaria.

530 Justinian's commander Belisarius gains another victory over the Persians but is defeated at Callinicum.

532 A Perpetual Peace with Persia is signed by Justinian to free his Byzantine armies for operations in the west.

The Nika insurrection destroys large areas of Constantinople as crowds shouting "Nika!" (Victory!) set fires that destroy the city. Justinian panics but is persuaded by his wife Theodora to remain. Between 30,000 and 500,000 are put to the sword by the troops of Belisarius, and the young military commander helps Justinian begin an era of absolutism.

The kingdom of Burgundy is overthrown by the Franks.

533 Belisarius invades North Africa with a relatively small force. He defeats the Vandals and regains the region as a Byzantine province for Justinian.

534 Malta becomes a Byzantine province.

Toledo becomes the capital of the Visigoth kingdom that controls the Iberian Peninsula and will remain the capital until 711.

535 Belisarius invades Sicily and moves north to conquer the Ostrogoth kingdom of Italy.

A Christian basilica is completed at Leptis Magna in North Africa.

536 Rome falls to Belisarius December 9 as Byzantine forces recover the peninsula from the Ostrogoths.

Provence becomes part of the Frankish kingdom.

537 Rome resists a year-long siege by the Ostrogoth king Witiges, who fails to force the city's surrender.

King Arthur of the Britons is killed in the Battle of Camlan according to legend. Later evidence will suggest that the king was not a Celtic or Welsh monarch but perhaps rather the leader of a Sarmatian kingdom whose ancestors came to England as mercenaries for the Romans.

Constantinople's Cathedral of St. Sophia is completed after 14 years of construction with a large dome, colored mosaics, lacelike carving, and lavish use of gold.

538 Buddhism is introduced to the Japanese court of the emperor Senka, who receives a Korean delegation that includes some Buddhists (*see* 517; 586).

539 Ravenna falls to Belisarius who captures the Ostrogoth king Witiges. But Belisarius is recalled to Constantinople, Milan is starved into submission by the Ostrogoths under their new chief Totila, 300,000 Milanese are put to the sword, and the Ostrogoths begin to reconquer the peninsula.

A Byzantine–Persian war begins that will last for 23 years.

The Japanese emperor Senka dies at age 72 and is succeeded by his 30-year-old half-brother Kinmei who will reign until 571.

540 Persian forces invade Syria and take Antioch from the Byzantines.

Byzantine rule in Italy is ended by Totila the Ostrogoth.

The Monastery of Vivarium near Squillace is founded by the Roman statesman Flavius Magnus Aurelius Cassiodorus, who retires from public life to devote himself to study and writing. He directs his fellow monastics in copying and translating Greek works.

541 The Great Plague of Justinian (bubonic plague) spreads from Egypt to Palestine and thence to Constantinople and throughout the Roman–Byzantine world, bringing agriculture to a standstill and causing widespread famine. As many as 5,000 to 10,000 die each day for a period in Constantinople, and the plague will continue with resulting famine for the next 60 to 70 years in Europe, the Near East, and Asia.

Justinian himself contracts the plague, and although he recovers after a few months, he is obliged to abandon plans to invade Gaul and the British Isles.

The Ostrogoth king Hildebad dies and is succeeded by his nephew Totila who will rule until 552.

Constantinople mills and bakeries are forced to cease operations because of the Great Plague (above).

The Great Plague of Justinian (bubonic plague) killed hundreds of thousands in Europe, the Near East, and Asia.

542 The Great Plague of Justinian that came into Constantinople last year by way of rats imported from Egypt and Syria fans out through Europe.

De Excidio et Conquestu Britanniae by the British monk Gildas, 26, is a history of early Britain.

543 Belisarius completes his reconquest of North Africa from the Vandals.

Disastrous earthquakes shake much of the world.

545 Justinian attempts to impose the Roman date for Easter on Constantinople in place of the Alexandrian date. The people protest by refusing to patronize butcher shops.

546 Rome falls to Totila and his Ostrogoths after a decade of rule by the Byzantine forces of Belisarius. The city's aqueducts have been cut, its aristocracy has long since fled, its population has been reduced from 500,000 to little more than 500 civilians, and these few are starved into submission by Totila.

A monastery is founded at Beneventum by Cassiodorus (*see* 540).

547 The Great Plague of Justinian reaches the British Isles, where King Ida accedes to the throne of Bernicia, the more northerly of the two Anglo-Saxon kingdoms.

Bamburgh Castle is built by Ida (above).

Ravenna's Church of St. Vitale is completed in double octagonal shape with mosaic portraits of Justinian and his wife Theodora, who has introduced long white dresses, purple cloaks, gold embroidery, tiaras, and pointed shoes into Byzantine fashion.

548 The Byzantine empress Theodora dies at age 40, leaving Justinian to rule alone.

Topographia Christiana by the Alexandrian explorer-monk Cosmas Indicopleustes describes the importance of the spice trade (especially in cloves and sweet aloes) in Ceylon and the harvesting of pepper in the hills of India (*see* 525).

549 Petra falls to the Persians, who will hold the eastern outpost of Byzantium for 2 years.

The Church of St. Apollinare is completed outside Ravenna at Classe after 14 years of construction.

550 The Teotihuacan civilization in the Western Hemisphere is conquered by the Toltecs, who overrun the Yucatán Peninsula.

Rome is conquered for a second time by Totila the Ostrogoth.

East Anglia and Northumbria are founded as new kingdoms in the British Isles.

Wales is converted to Christianity by David (Dewi) who will be canonized in 1120 and will be the patron saint of Wales.

De Bellis is completed by the Byzantine historian Procopius, 60, who has served as private secretary to Belisarius and who described the Persian, Vandal, and Gothic wars.

Poetry *Hero and Leander* by the Greek poet Musaeus Grammaticus.

Mosaics installed in the new Church of St. Apollinare at Classe near Ravenna include a representation of *The Last Supper*.

551 The Ostrogoth navy is defeated by a Byzantine fleet.

552 The Italian Ostrogoths are decisively defeated and their king Totila killed in the Battle of Tagina, which is won by a Byzantine army of barbarian mercenaries led by the eunuch general Narses, 74, who has replaced Belisarius and who has taken his forces overland to invade from the north.

The European silk industry is begun by the emperor Justinian who sends missionaries to China and Ceylon to smuggle silkworms out of the Orient.

553 Rome and Naples are annexed to Byzantium by General Narses.

Justinian makes the silk industry a Byzantine imperial monopoly.

Anecdota by the Byzantine historian Procopius is full of scandalous gossip about Justinian, Belisarius, and the late empress Theodora, but its veracity will be challenged by later historians.

554 Narses is made prefect (exarch) of Italy and completes his reconquest of the peninsula for Justinian.

Italian lands taken from the Ostrogoths are restored to their original owners by Justinian's Pragmatic Sanction, but the landowners have sunk into serfdom, and the depopulated farmlands have returned to wilderness.

558 The Frankish kingdom is reunited by Clotaire I, king of Soissons, who becomes king of all the Franks following the death of Childebert, king of Paris.

Plague takes a heavy toll throughout the Byzantine Empire.

559 An army of Huns and Slavs advances to the gates of Constantinople but is repelled by Belisarius who comes out of retirement to drive off the barbarian invaders.

560 The Kentish king Eormenric dies and is succeeded by his son who will reign until 616 as Ethelbert I.

The Abbey of Bangor is founded in Caernarvonshire, Wales, by Deniol.

561 The Frankish king Clotaire I dies after a 3-year reign, and his sons divide the kingdom once again. Sigibert will rule Austrasia until 575, Charibert will rule Paris until 567, Guntram will rule Burgundy until 592, and Chilperic will rule Soissons until 584.

563 The Irish missionary Columba (Colum), 42, founds a monastery on the island of Iona in the Hebrides and begins to convert the Picts with 12 of his disciples.

565 The Byzantine emperor Justinian dies November 14 at age 83 after a 38-year reign. His nephew succeeds to the throne as Justin II and begins a 13-year reign by paying Justinian's debts and declaring religious toleration.

Lombards in the north of Italy drive the Byzantines south but permit them to retain Ravenna.

568 A Lombard kingdom that will rule northern and central Italy until 774 is founded by the Lombard ruler Alboin, who lays siege to Pavia. Alboin destroyed the Gepidae 2 years ago with help from the Avars; he killed the Gepidae king Cunimund and married his daughter Rosamund. The Gothic wars—accompanied by famine and disease—have exhausted the Italian countryside.

571 The Japanese emperor Kinmei dies at age 62 after a 32-year reign. He is succeeded by his 33-year old son Bintas who will reign until 585.

572 Pavia falls to the Lombard king Alboin, who takes over almost the entire Italian peninsula.

A new Persian-Byzantine war begins. It will continue until 591.

573 Sigibert of Austrasia (France) goes to war against his brother Chilperic of Soissons at the urging of his wife Brunhilda. Chilperic has murdered his wife Galswintha, sister of Brunhilda (both are daughters of the Visigoth king Athanagild), in order to marry his mistress Fredegund. Sigibert appeals to the Germans on the right bank of the Rhine for help, and they obligingly attack the environs of Paris and Chartres, committing atrocities of all sorts.

575 Sigibert of Austrasia pursues his brother Chilperic as far as Tournai. As the nobles of Neustria are raising Sigibert in triumph on the shield in the villa at Vitry near Arras, he is assassinated by hirelings of his brother's mistress Fredegund. Sigibert is succeeded by his young son Childebert II, with Brunhilda as regent.

The Slovenes move into Carnelia.

De Re Medica is compiled by Alexander of Tralles.

577 English forces from Wessex defeat the Welsh at Deorham.

578 The Byzantine emperor Justin II dies after several periods of insanity. On the advice of his wife Sophia he has raised his general Tiberius to the rank of co-emperor, Tiberius has ruled jointly with Sophia since December 574, and he now begins a 4-year reign as Tiberius II Constantinus.

580 The last of Italy's Ostrogoths are driven across the Alps by the Lombards, who will rule the peninsula until 744. The Lombards are few in number, they will never take Rome or Naples, they are bitterly opposed by the natives, but they will Italianize their names.

581 The Sui dynasty that will rule China until 618 is founded at Ch'ang-an by Yang Ch'ien, chief minister of the northern Chou who have ruled since 557.

582 The Byzantine emperor Tiberius II Constantinus dies after a 4-year reign during which Thrace and Greece have been inundated by Slavs. He is succeeded by his 43-year-old son-in-law who will reign until 602 as Flavius Tiberius Mauricius (Maurikios).

History The *Ostographia* by Flavius Magnus Aurelius Cassiodorus who dies at age 92 leaving behind an account of the Ostrogothic rule of Italy.

584 Chilperic of Neustria dies and is succeeded by his son who will make himself king of all the Franks and who will reign until 628 as Clotaire II.

Mercia is founded in the British Isles and becomes a new Anglo-Saxon kingdom.

585 The Visigoth king Leovigild puts down a revolt by his son Hermenegild who has married a Catholic princess and has been converted from his father's Arian faith. Leovigild imprisons his son, has him killed, and proceeds to conquer the entire Iberian Peninsula.

585 (cont.) The Japanese emperor Bintas dies at age 47 after a 14-year reign and is succeeded by his 45-year-old brother Yomei who will reign for 2 years.

∞ Buddhist temples in Japan are burned by Moriya Mononobe who opposes the imperial rule and the Buddhist faith.

586 The Visigoth king Leovigild dies and is succeeded by Recared who will rule until 601.

∞ Japanese Buddhism is called a "foreign" religion by Moriyo Mononbe and Okoshi Mononbe, who say it conflicts with the native Shintoism, but the new emperor Yomei and his grandfather Iname Soga support Buddhism. The agrarian-naturist Shinto religion will adopt Buddhist imagery to embody its gods with a Buddhist counterpart to every *kami* (deity) in the Shinto iconography.

587 The Japanese emperor Yomei dies at age 47 and is succeeded by the 66-year-old nephew of strongman Iname Soga. The new emperor Sushun will rule until 592.

Agents of Iname Soga (above) kill the anti-Buddhist Morio Nomomobe.

∞ The first Japanese Buddhist monastery is founded.

The Visigoths ruled by Recared are converted to Christianity.

589 The Chinese Empire is reunited by the Sui emperor, who conquers the south to end the Ch'en dynasty that has ruled since 557.

The Sassanid Persian emperor Hormizd is deposed and assassinated after suffering military reverses at the hands of the Byzantines. He is succeeded by his son who is helped by the Byzantine emperor Maurikios to gain the throne and who begins a 39-year reign as Khusru Parviz (Chosroes III) that will see the Persian Empire reach its zenith and suffer its downfall.

Arab, Khazar, and Turkish forces invade Persia but are repelled.

∞ The Lombards are converted to Roman Catholicism under their king and queen, Authari and Theodelinda.

590 Gregory I becomes the 64th pope—the first monk to be elected to the papacy—and at age 50 begins a
∞ 14-year administration of rigorous discipline during which Rome's aqueducts will be repaired, her courts reformed, and her people fed with doles of grain as they were under the old imperial rule.

Claims to papal absolutism are established by Pope Gregory (above), who leads Italian opposition to Lombard rule.

The Lombard king Authari dies after a 6-year reign and is succeeded by Turin's Thuringian Duke Agilulf, who marries the widow of the late king Alboin's grandson, founds a Roman Catholic Lombard state, and begins a 25-year reign.

A plague strikes Rome but subsides, allegedly after Pope Gregory (above) has received a vision of the Destroying Angel sheathing his sword atop the mausoleum of Hadrian which is renamed the Castel Sant' Angelo (*see* 139).

592 The Japanese emperor Sushun is murdered after 5 years on the throne by agents of his uncle Umako Soga who is jealous of the emperor's power. Sushun is succeeded by the 38-year-old widow of the late emperor Bintas who will reign for 35 years beginning next year as the empress Suiko.

593 The Japanese empress Suiko is the first to receive official recognition from China and begins a long reign during a pivotal period in which Buddhism will take firm root and Japanese culture will be Sinoized. Suiko's 19-year-old son, Crown Prince Shotoku, is made prime minister and with strongman Umako Soga, will hold power for 30 years.

∞ Japan's Shitenno-ji monastery is founded at Osaka by the Crown Prince Shotoku.

Construction begins at Osaka of the Temple of Four Heavenly Kings (Shitenno-ji).

Hoko Temple is built.

594 The Japanese empress Suiko announces that she will
∞ support Buddhism.

595 A 25-year-old Arab camel driver and caravan leader of the Koreish tribe marries his wealthy 40-year-old
∞ employer the widow Khadija. Mohammed will start a new religion that will embrace much of the world (*see* 610).

597 Conversion of Jutes in the British Isles to Christianity is begun by the monk Augustine who has been sent
∞ by Pope Gregory with 40 other monks. Augustine lands in Thanet, baptizes Ethelbert of Kent, and founds a Benedictine monastery at Canterbury.

598 The first English school is founded at Canterbury.

Food production increases in northern and western Europe as a result of agricultural technology introduced by the Slavs who have made it possible to farm virgin lands whose heavy clay has discouraged agriculture. The Slavs employ a new, lightweight plow with a knife blade (coulter) that cuts vertically, deep into the soil, and a plowshare that cuts horizontally at grassroots level, together with a shaped board, or moldboard, that moves the cut soil or turf neatly to one side.

A population explosion begins in northern and western Europe as the new agriculture (above) increases the availability of food.

7th CENTURY

The Franks, Merovingians, and Carolingians will successively control most of Europe in this century as royal power declines and strong feudal lords rise in power to gain the allegiance of the people and replace state governments.

A Japanese feudal nobility will also rise in this century.

601 The *Vaghbata* is compiled by Indian physicians. At least one Indian medicinal herb mentioned in the classic work—*Rauwolfia serpentina*—will be employed in Western medicine (*see* 1949).

602 The Byzantine emperor Maurikios (Maurice) is executed at Chalcedon after being forced to witness the slaughter of his five sons and all his supporters by the centurion Phocas, who has been proclaimed emperor by legions fighting the Avars on the Danube.

The archepiscopal see of Canterbury is established by Augustine of Canterbury, who is made archbishop of Canterbury.

603 England's bishopric of Rochester is founded, St. Andrew's Church of Rochester is built, and London's first St. Paul's Church is built.

604 Pope Gregory the Great dies March 12 at age 64 after a 14-year papacy that has laid the foundations for claims to papal absolutism, pioneered the conversion of Britain to Roman Catholicism, and led the war against the Lombards.

A Japanese constitution is issued by Crown Prince Shotoku, whose Shotoku Taishi code demands veneration of Buddha, Buddhist priests, and Buddhist laws.

605 A Chinese Grand Canal is completed by a million laborers who link existing waterways to connect the new Chinese capital, established last year at Loyang, to the Long River. The canal will be extended to Hangchow by 610.

606 A northern India empire is established by Harsha of Thanesar, who will reign until 647.

607 The first Japanese envoy to China's Sui Court is sent by the empress Suiko, who begins a long interchange that will lead to the Sinoization of Japan.

Japan's Horyuji Temple and hospital are constructed of wood by the Crown Prince Shotoku.

608 Syria and Mesopotamia are overrun by Persian forces, who have recaptured Dara in a renewal of war with Constantinople.

Japan's Hokoji Temple is completed after 20 years of construction.

609 The Pantheon at Rome is consecrated as the Church of Santa Maria Rotonda.

610 A new religion, to be called Mohammedanism, is preached in secret by the prophet Mohammed (*see* 595) who has become a merchant, has meditated for years on the ignorance and superstition of his fellow Arabs, and has felt called upon to teach a new faith that will grow to embrace a major part of mankind in the milennium ahead (*see* 613).

The Byzantine emperor Phocas is challenged by his African governor Heraclius, 35. He surrenders with little resistance, is sent to the scaffold by the mob at Constantinople, and is replaced as emperor by Heraclius, who is helped by his father to establish a new dynasty that will rule for 31 years.

611 Antioch is sacked by Persian forces of the last Sassanian king Khusru Parvis (Chosroes II) who is creating a neo-Persian empire to rival that of more than eight centuries ago.

612 Harsha of Thesar takes the title "Emperor of the Five Indies" (*see* 606; 635).

Arnulf, counselor to the Frankish king Clotaire II, becomes bishop of Metz, his wife enters a convent, and his son marries the daughter of Clotaire's mayor of the palace Pepin of Landen.

The Monastery of St. Gallen is founded by Gallus, a disciple of Columban.

613 Mohammed begins to teach openly. He attracts followers who are persecuted by the leaders of Mecca who oppose any change in the traditional tribal and religious customs (*see* 610; 622).

Austrasia and Burgundy are united by Clotaire II of the Franks who captures the 80-year-old queen mother Brunhilda, widow of the late Sigibert, who was his uncle, and has her executed by being dragged to death behind a wild horse.

Britons are defeated near Chester by Northumbrians under Ethelfrit.

614 Damascus is sacked by the advancing Persian armies of Khusru Parviz.

The *Edictum Chlotachariii,* issued by the Frankish king Clotaire, defines the rights of king, nobles, and the church.

614 (cont.) The Italian Monastery of Bobbio is founded by Columban.

615 Jerusalem is sacked by the Persians, who take the "True Cross" as part of their booty.

The Irish missionary Columban dies at age 72 a year after founding a monastery in the Appenines.

616 Egypt is overrun and subjugated by the Persians.

Ethelbert of Kent dies, Kent passes to Wessex, and Northumberland becomes the leading Anglo-Saxon state of the British Isles.

618 The T'ang dynasty that will rule China until 907 is founded by an official of the Sui regime who was helped last year to seize the key city of Ch'ang-sen and who now establishes himself as the emperor Kao Tsu, meaning High Progenitor. The T'ang dynasty will bring a golden era to Chinese culture.

619 Jerusalem is sacked by Sassanid Persian forces.

620 The Persian Empire as it existed in 495 B.C. under Darius I is restored by Khusru Parvis whose forces capture Rhodes.

621 An imperial bureau for the manfacture of porcelain is established by the Chinese whose technology will be further advanced under the T'ang dynasty (*see* 1708).

622 A civil war is begun by the prophet Mohammed who has been forced to flee Mecca by city leaders opposed to his teachings (his flight will be called the Hegira). Mohammed has taken refuge in the town of Yathrib, which will be called Medina (*see* 613; 629).

The Persian forces of Shar-Baraz are defeated by the western Roman emperor Heraclius who has landed at Issus.

623 Armenia is invaded by the Byzantine emperor Heraclius.

624 Shar-Baraz is surprised by Heraclius and is defeated once again as he was in 622.

625 Constantinople is attacked by Avars and Persians who are repelled by the emperor Heraclius.

626 Edinburgh is founded by Edwin of Northumbria, who begins Christianizing his subjects.

627 The Chinese emperor Kao Tsu abdicates after a 9-year reign that has inaugurated the T'ang dynasty. He is succeeded by his son who will reign until 649 as T'ai-Tsung.

Medina is besieged by enemies of the prophet Mohammed from Mecca who slaughter 700 Jews.

Assyria and Mesopotamia are invaded by the Byzantine emperor Heraclius with an army aroused by religious enthusiasm. Refusing to be distracted by the Avars who are constantly attacking his Balkan territories, Heraclius gains a decisive victory December 12 in the Battle of Nineveh and saves Constantinople from the Persians.

628 The Persian king Chosroes II, who has reigned since 590, is imprisoned after a mutiny by the military following last year's disastrous Battle of Nineveh. He is murdered by his son who takes power as Kavadh II and makes peace with the Byzantine emperor Heraclius. Prisoners are exchanged, conquered lands are mutually restored, and the "True Cross" carried off by the Persians is returned to Jerusalem.

Mecca falls to the forces of Mohammed who writes letters to all the world's rulers explaining the principles of the Moslem faith.

The Japanese empress Suiko dies at age 74 after a 35-year reign and is succeeded by a grandson of her late husband Bintas. The 35-year-old grandson will reign until 641 as the emperor Jomei.

Sugar from India is brought to Constantinople by Byzantine soldiers who found it last year upon capturing the Persian castle at Dastagerd.

629 Mohammed returns to Mecca as master with the *Koran* (*see* below) in which he has established the monotheistic principles of Islam. The Koran's Arabic name, *Qur'an*, means "recitation," and it says, "There is no god but Allah and Mohammed is His messenger."

Moslems (Mohammedans) will recognize the authority of the Sharia, a complex legal system much like that of the Jewish Talmud, which will forbid gambling, public entertainment, and art that portrays the human figure. The Sharia will require women to remain veiled and segregated, and it will order severe punishments for crimes—murderers to have their hearts cut out, thieves to have a hand severed, adulterers to be tied in a sack and stoned to death.

The Byzantine emperor Heraclius recovers Jerusalem from the Persians, who have held it since 619, and restores it to Byzantine suzerainty.

The Frankish kingdom gets its last strong Merovingian ruler as Clotaire II dies and his son Dagobert succeeds to the throne (*see* 613). Counseled by the bishop of Metz Arnulf and by Pepin the Elder (Pippin of Landen), Dagobert will make wide dynastic alliances, but his firm rule will lead to revolt (*see* 639).

The Koran (above) depicts the joys of heaven and the pains of hell in vivid imagery while warning that the last day is approaching. Written largely in the first person as if voiced by God, it requires Moslems to offer prayers five times a day according to an elaborate ritual, to fast during daylight hours in the lunar month of Ramadan, to give one-fortieth of their income in alms, and to make a pilgrimage to Mecca once during their lives if such a pilgrimage is not physically or financially impossible.

✗ The Sharia (above) forbids eating of pork and thus follows the Mosaic law of Deuteronomy in 621 B.C., but it permits camel meat. The Sharia prohibits consumption of alcohol, but Mohammed's followers circumvent his prohibition against wine by boiling it down to a concentrate and sweetening it with honey and spices, and even Mohammed himself drinks *nabidh*, a mildly alcoholic ferment of raisins or dates mixed with water and aged for 2 days in earthenware jugs (but not aged longer lest it become too strong).

630 ✗ The Chinese T'ang court established 12 years ago receives its first Japanese ambassadors.

⚙ Norway has its beginnings in a colony founded in Vermeland by Olaf Tratelia, who has been expelled from his native Sweden.

632 ∞ The prophet Mohammed dies June 7 at age 63 (or 65) and leaves behind an Islamic monotheism whose believers will soon conquer the Near East and North Africa.

✗ Mohammed's youngest daughter Fatima (accent on first syllable) dies at age 26, leaving two sons—Hassan and Hussein—who will found the Fatimid dynasty that will rule Egypt and North Africa from 909 to 1171.

Mohammed's father-in-law Abu Bekr establishes himself as the first caliph, with Medina as his seat of power.

633 ✗ The Arabs attack Persia and begin the conquests that will give them power over much of the world.

Edwin of Northumbria is defeated and killed by the Mercians, who overwhelm the Roman Catholic forces in the north of England and begin a period of anarchy. The Roman Church is replaced in many places by Celtic Christianity championed by Oswald of Northumbria (Aidan from Iona).

∞ Christian churches at Alexandria, Antioch, and Jerusalem are turned into Mohammedan mosques.

634 ✗ The first caliph, Abu Bekr, dies at age 61 and is succeeded by Mohammed's adviser Omar who will reign until 644 and conquer Syria, Persia, and Egypt in a "holy war".

635 ✗ Damascus falls to Mohammedan forces under the "Sword of Allah," Khalid ibn-al-Walid, who defeats the Byzantines at nearby Marj al-Saffar. Damascus is made the seat of the caliphate and will remain so until 750.

Gaza falls to the Mohammedans.

Chalukyas in India repel an invasion by Harsha.

The Byzantine emperor Heraclius makes an alliance with Kuvrat, king of the Bulgars, to break the power of the Avars.

⚙ Basra is established as a port at the head of the Persian Gulf where the Tigris and Euphrates Rivers converge. The port will become a major trading center for commodities from Arabia, India, Persia, and Turkey.

636 ✗ Syria is conquered by Islamic forces after a decisive defeat of the Byzantines at Yarmuk south of the Lake of Tiberias.

∞ Churches are built at Glastonbury, St. Albans, and Winchester, and Christians in southern Ireland submit to Roman Catholicism.

▮▮ French and German language differences appear in the Frankish Empire.

637 ✗ Persian forces are decisively beaten by the Arabs at Quadisiya (Tunis) and at Ualula. The Moslems loot Ctesiphon; they proceed to invade Mesopotamia and then conquer Jerusalem.

∞ The Arabs do not force their conquered subjects to embrace Islam, but they do require acceptance of the Koran as the doctrine of divine teaching, and they will oblige their subjects to learn Arabic, thus building an empire united by a common tongue.

638 ✗ Iraq is invaded by Moslem forces who also invade central Persia. The Persians appeal to the Chinese for help in resisting the Arabs.

639 ✗ The Merovingian Frankish king Dagobert I dies January 9 after a 10-year reign as king of all the Franks. His 6-year-old son succeeds him as Clovis II of Neustria and Burgundy.

Armenia is invaded by the Arabs.

Egypt is invaded by the Arabs.

640 ✗ Byzantine forces are defeated by the Arabs at Heliopolis as the Islamic conquest of Egypt continues.

A Welsh army defeats a Saxon army in the British Isles, where the Roman Church has lost power and where anarchy reigns. The Welsh victory is credited partly to the fact that each Welsh soldier has affixed a leek to his helmet so that Welshmen will not accidentally kill Welshmen, and the leek will become the national emblem of Wales.

✗ Indian techniques of sugar manufacturing that date to 100 B.C. are studied at Behar in the Ganges Valley by a Chinese mission sent by the T'ang emperor T'ai-Tsung. Extensive cultivation and manufacture of sugar in China will begin within a few years.

641 ✗ The Japanese emperor Jomei dies at age 48 and is succeeded by his 47-year-old widow who will reign until 645 as the empress Kogyoku.

642 ✗ The Battle of Nehawand gives the Arabs a final victory over the Persians and ends the Sassanian dynasty that has ruled Persia for four centuries. The Persian king Yezdigird III is a grandson of the late Khusru Parviz (Chosroes II). He appeals to the Chinese emperor for help, but his provinces are incorporated into the Arabian caliphate, and he will be murdered in a miller's hut near Merv in 651.

642 (cont.) Alexandria capitulates to the Arabs who complete their conquest of Egypt. The city's patriarch Cyrus has arranged the capitulation on condition that the Moslems guarantee security of persons and property and free exercise of religion in return for a payment of tribute.

The Arabs begin construction of the Amr Mosque at Cairo.

644 Japan has a terrible famine, thousands die, and a new religion springs up (Tokoyonomushi). Devotees worship a large worm, they get drunk on sake, they dance in the streets, and they give away all their money.

645 Japan has a coup d'etat in June. Iruka, grandson of the late Umako Soga, is killed at the imperial palace by Nakanō-ōenō-ōji, a cousin of the late Shotoku, and by Nakatomi Kumatari, who founds the Fujiwara (Kumatari) clan that will later control the Japanese throne. The empress Kogyoku is removed, the 49-year-old grandson of the emperor Bintas is made emperor to begin a 9-year reign as Kotoku, Nakanō-ōenō-ōji becomes crown prince and prime minister, and the Taika period begins as the Japanese adopt the Chinese custom of giving names to periods.

Alexandria revolts from Arab rule at the appearance of a Byzantine fleet, and the city is recaptured by Byzantine forces, but Egypt's Arab governor Abdalla ibn Sa'd mounts an assault that retakes the city, and he begins building an Arab fleet.

648 Cyprus is taken by Arab forces that have invaded the island from North Africa.

653 Armenia is conquered by the spreading forces of Islam.

654 Rhodes is plundered by Arab invaders.

The Japanese emperor Kotoku dies at age 58, and the empress Kogyoku, who was removed in 645, is restored. Now 60, she begins a 7-year reign under the name Saimei.

655 A Byzantine fleet under the personal command of the emperor Constans II is defeated off the Lycian coast by an Arab fleet, but disaffection grows among Arab forces in Iraq and Egypt as a result of blatant nepotism on the part of Othman, who has ruled the Islamic Empire since 644.

656 The Arab caliph Othman is assassinated at Medina at age 80, and civil war breaks out in the Islamic Empire.

661 The Omayyad caliphate that will rule the Islamic Empire until 750 is founded by a relative of the late Othman. The caliph Muawiya takes power following the murder of Othman's successor by a Kharijite.

The Japanese empress Saimei dies at age 67 and is succeeded by a 35-year-old son of the late emperor Jomei. He will reign until 671 as the emperor Tenji.

663 The Byzantine court moves from Constantinople to Italy as the emperor Constans II tries to stop the Arab conquest of Sicily and to restore Rome as the seat of empire. The Lombards resist Constans, and no Byzantine emperor will hereafter visit Rome.

664 Kabul falls to Arab forces that have invaded eastern Afghanistan.

The Synod of Whitby, which founded a monastery 7 years ago, returns the British Isles to the orbit of the Roman Church. It adopts the Roman Catholic faith, and the Northumbrian king Oswiu accepts the Roman ritual (*see* Theodore of Tarsus, 669).

The English public school St. Peter's is founded at York.

668 The Byzantine emperor Constans II dies under mysterious circumstances in his bath at Syracuse July 15 at age 37 during a mutiny. The Byzantine court returns to Constantinople after an absence of 5 years in which the Arabs have made annual invasions and devastations of Anatolia. Constans is succeeded by his sons Pogonatus, Heraclius, and Tiberius, but Pogonatus (the "Bearded") will reign alone beginning in 680 as Constantine IV.

669 Theodore of Tarsus becomes archbishop of Canterbury at age 67 and introduces a strict Roman parochial system and a centralized episcopal system.

The system introduced by the archbishop of Canterbury (above) will become the model for the secular state and will create a new concept of kingship. Rival kingdoms will come together in the British Isles in the next 30 years, and an evolutionary process will begin that will create an English nationality and English national institutions destined to spread throughout much of the civilized world.

Constantinople is besieged by Arab forces that have taken Chalcedon.

670 The conquest of North Africa (Ifrikquiya) by the Arabs is consolidated by the founding of Quairawan (Tunis).

671 The Japanese emperor Tenji dies at age 45 after a 10-year reign in which he has given the Fujiwara family its name. He is succeeded by his 23-year-old son Kobun, but the new emperor is opposed by Tenji's brother Ooama who objects that Kobun's mother was a commoner, the mistress of Tenji, and insists that the emperor must be entirely of royal blood.

672 The Japanese emperor Kobun is deposed after 8 months by his uncle Ooama. He commits suicide, and Ooama makes himself emperor with support from the Fujiwara family. He takes the name Tenmu and begins a reign that will continue until 686.

675 Childeric of the Franks is murdered while hunting, and his death leads to civil war and anarchy in the Frankish kingdom.

The first Bulgarian (Eastern) Empire is founded by Bulgarians who settle in districts south of the Danube.

677 The Arab fleet is destroyed by a Byzantine fleet at Syllaeum, and the Arab menace to Europe is ended.

678 Arab forces end a 5-year blockade of Constantinople and conclude a peace that will last for 30 years.

680 A Byzantine army is defeated by Bulgarian forces that have occupied the territory between the Danube and the Balkan Mountains while other Bulgars control Wallachia, Moldavia, and Bessarabia (*see* 675).

The Battle of Kerbela October 10 ends the life of Husain, 51-year-old son of a cousin of the Prophet. Husain was invited by the Kufans in Iraq to assume the caliphate following the death of Muawiyah, but he has been deserted by the Kufans while advancing from Mecca. The martyrdom of Husain will be celebrated annually in the month of Muharram by the Shi'ite sect, descendants of Mohammed's daughter Fatima and mother of the martyr al-Husain.

685 Justinian II assumes the Byzantine throne at age 16 following the death of his father Constantine IV and begins a 10-year reign.

Northumbrians are defeated by Picts in the Battle of Nechtansmere and are thwarted in their efforts to gain control of Scotland.

686 Sussex is converted to Christianity, and pagan resistance to the faith is ended in England.

The Japanese emperor Tenmu dies after a 14-year reign and is succeeded by his 21-year-old widow (and niece) who has her late husband's son executed for alleged treason in order that she may be succeeded by her own son by Tenmu, but the boy soon takes ill. His mother will reign as the empress Jito until 697.

Yakushi Temple is completed before his death by the Japanese emperor Tenmu.

687 The city of Venice elects its first doge and begins its rise as a major power in the Mediterranean (*see* below).

The Frankish kingdom is united by Pepin the Younger who gains a victory at Testry.

Venice (above) has been built up from fishing villages settled by fugitives from the Huns. The city occupies some 60 marshy islands near the head of the Adriatic Sea, and its citizens have grown prosperous in the fish trade, in their salt monopoly, and by virtue of their central location (*see* 1071).

688 The Wessex king Ine subdues Essex and parts of Kent.

689 Justinian II defeats the Slavs in Thrace and transfers many of them to Anatolia.

690 Wintred becomes king of Kent to begin a 35-year reign in which he will draw up a code of laws.

692 The Battle of Sevastopol in Cilicia ends in a bad defeat for Justinian II at the hands of the Arabs.

695 The Byzantine emperor Justinian II is deposed by army officers who cut off his nose and exile him to the Crimea (Cherson). One officer assumes the throne to begin a 3-year reign as the emperor Leontius.

The first Arab coins are minted.

697 Carthage is destroyed by the Arabs, and Byzantine rule in North Africa is ended forever.

The Japanese empress Jito abdicates at age 32 after an 11-year reign and is succeeded by the 14-year-old grandson of the late emperor Tenmu. He will reign until 707 as the emperor Momu.

698 The Byzantine emperor Leontius is deposed by the commander of the fleet, who begins a 7-year reign as the emperor Tiberius III Apsimar. The new emperor will gain military triumphs over the Saracens.

The island of Heligoland is discovered by the bishop of Utrecht Willibrord.

699 *Beowulf* has probably been completed by this time. The heroic epic of more than 3,000 lines in Old English poetry chronicles the deeds of the Geatish (southern Swedish) hero Beowulf who freed the court of the Danish king Hrothgar from the ravages of the monster Grendel and Grendel's mother, became king of the Geats, and ruled for 50 years until called upon to rescue the country from a fire-breathing dragon. Mortally wounded while slaying the dragon, Beowulf was cremated on a giant funeral pyre.

700 Thuringia becomes part of the Frankish Empire ruled by Childebert III.

Algiers falls to the Arabs.

Fiction *The Adventures of the Ten Princes* (*Dasakumaracharita*) by the Indian Sanskrit poet-novelist Dandin.

8th CENTURY

Bubonic plague will appear in Sicily and southern Italy in this century.

The Arabs in this century will lay waste the farmlands of Palestine, undoing the work of the Maccabees in the 2nd century B.C. and creating agricultural havoc that will not be repaired for 12 centuries.

701 The Japanese emperor Momu becomes sole proprietor of all the nation's land through a codification of political law.

Arab and Persian mariners visit the Spice Islands (the Moluccas) for the first time.

Arab merchants will introduce Oriental spices into Mediterranean markets in this century.

705 Justinian II Rhinotmetus regains the Byzantine throne that he lost in 695. He will rule until 711.

The Omayyad Mosque is erected at Damascus.

The circular church at Marienberg is erected near Würzburg by the duke Hetan II.

707 The Japanese emperor Momu dies at age 24 after a 10-year reign and is succeeded by his 46-year-old aunt who will reign until 715 as the empress Gemmei.

708 Tea drinking gains popularity among the Chinese in part because a hot drink is far safer than water that may be contaminated and may produce intestinal disease if not heated. Tea is also valued for its alleged medicinal values (*see* Japan, 805).

709 Mont Saint-Michel has its beginnings in an oratory on Mont Tombe in the Bay of St. Michael on the coast of Normandy built by the bishop of Arrandes Aubert. Additions to the oratory will make Mont Saint-Michel an architectural masterpiece.

710 Nara (Heijo) becomes the capital of Japan, which until now has had a new capital with each new emperor or empress (*see* Kyoto, 794).

The Japanese empress Gemmei completes a palace at Nara that is a copy of the Chinese imperial palace.

Sugar is planted in Egypt (*see* 300 B.C.; A.D. 711; 1279).

711 Moors (Arabs and Berbers) from North Africa invade the Iberian Peninsula under the command of the freed slave Tariq and defeat the Visigoth king Roderick, who dies fighting in July at the Battle of Wadi Bekka near Rio Barbate. Cordova and the capital at Toledo fall to Tariq, who becomes master of half the peninsula and moves on toward Seville.

The Byzantine emperor Justinian II Rhinotmetus sallies forth from Constantinople to oppose insurgent troops who have revolted in the Crimea and have marched on the capital under the leadership of a soldier named Bardanes. The troops defeat Justinian in northern Anatolia. They put him to death in December, thus ending the house of Heraclius that has ruled since 610, and proclaim the incompetent Bardanes emperor under the name Philippicus. The empire will have two other short-lived rulers in the next 6 years.

Moors invading the Iberian Peninsula (above) introduce rice, saffron, and sugar.

The Moors (above) also introduce barberry bushes (*Berberis vulgaris*) whose berries are used for a conserve and whose stems yield a juice valued for its alleged curative powers, but barberry bushes harbor black stem rust, which can be communicated to wheat crops under conditions of fog, dew, and warm rain.

712 Seville falls to the Moors, who invaded the Iberian Peninsula last year.

Samarkand is occupied by the Arabs who will make it a center of Islamic culture.

The first Arab conquests in India are made by the Moslem general Mohammed ibn-Kasim, who crosses Makran (Baluchistan), invades the Indus Valley, and conquers Sind.

Nonfiction *Kojiki* is the first history of Japan.

713 The Chinese emperor Ming Huang ascends the throne to begin a reign that will continue until 756. His court will be a center of art and learning.

The Byzantine emperor Philippicus is deposed after a 2-year reign in which he has been defeated by the Arabs. He is succeeded by the conspirator Anastasius II who will organize a strong army and navy and reign until 716.

715 The Japanese empress Gemmei abdicates at age 54 after an 8-year reign and is succeeded by her 35-year-old daughter, who will reign until 724 as the empress Gensho.

716 The Byzantine emperor Anastasius is deposed in an army mutiny and is succeeded by an obscure and incapable tax official who is raised to the throne and who begins a brief reign as the emperor Theodosius.

Lisbon falls to the Moors.

Chinese landscape painter Li Ssu-Hsun dies at age 65.

A shipment of spices from Fos is authorized for delivery to the monastery of Corbie in Normandy by the new king of Neustria, Chilperic II who will become king of all the Franks in 719. The spices include 1 pound of cinnamon, 2 pounds of cloves, and 30 pounds of pepper.

717 Constantinople is besieged by the Arabs, and the Byzantine emperor Theodosius is deposed. He is succeeded by the 37-year-old Leo III who will reign until 741, frustrate the Arabs in their efforts to take the city, and inaugurate the Isaurian dynasty, which will control the throne until 802.

A new Arab caliph takes power in the person of Omar II (Omar ibn-al-'Aziz) who grants tax exemption to all true believers and makes an unsuccessful effort to reorganize the finances of the empire.

Sculpture Japan's *Buddha with the Gods of the Sun and the Moon* is completed in bronze at Nara.

718 The Arab fleet at Constantinople is destroyed by the Byzantine emperor Leo III, and the siege of the city is lifted after 13 months.

The Spanish kingdom of the Asturias is founded by Pelagius.

719 The Moors reach the Pyrenees.

720 The Moors cross the Pyrenees and capture Narbonne.

Sardinia is invaded by Moslem forces.

Nihonshoki is compiled as a chronology of Japanese history and marks the first use of the word *Nihon* (Nippon) to designate Japan.

724 The Japanese empress Gensho abdicates and is succeeded by her 23-year-old nephew Shomu, son of Momu, who will reign until 749. Shomu orders that houses of the Japanese nobility be roofed with green tiles as in China and have white walls with red roof poles.

726 Greece revolts from the Byzantine rule of Leo III who has forbidden the worship of icons (images) in a move to check superstition, miracle-mongering, and the spread of monasticism which is draining thousands of men from active economic activity and is concentrating great wealth in the tax-exempt cloisters. A Greek fleet sets out for Constantinople with an antiemperor but is destroyed by the Byzantine imperial fleet with an incendiary mixture called Greek fire.

The iconoclasm of the Byzantine emperor is attacked by Pope Gregory II at Rome.

730 The Alamanni are joined to the Frankish Empire as a dukedom.

The Byzantine emperor Leo III is excommunicated by Pope Gregory II for his iconoclasm.

731 The Mayan Empire in the central Western Hemisphere begins its greatest period (*see* 1027).

An ecclesiastical history of England is completed by the English scholar Bede, 58, of the monastery at Jarrow whose *Historia Ecclesiastica Gentis Anglorum* marks the beginning of English literature. Bede will be known as "the venerable Bede" beginning in the next century.

732 The Battle of Tours near Poitiers October 11 ends the menace of a 90,000-man Moorish army that has invaded southern France under the Yemenite Abd-ar-Rahman, who has crossed the Pyrenees, captured and burned Bordeaux, defeated an army under Eudo, duke of Aquitaine, and destroyed the basilica of St. Hilary at Poitiers. The Moors march on Tours, attracted by the riches of its famous church of St. Martin, but they are routed in battle by the 44-year-old Frankish leader Charles Martel (Charles the Hammer), whose men kill Abd-ar-Rahman. The Moors retreat to the Pyrenees, and their advance into Europe is terminated, partly by their loss to Charles Martel and partly by a revolt of the Berbers in North Africa.

The Moors continue to harry the coasts of Europe with help from the Venetians and take slaves that are sold in the markets of Venice.

Bubonic plague again strikes Constantinople as it did in 541. The plague will kill as many as 200,000 in the next 4 years.

Pope Gregory II orders the Benedictine missionary Wynfrith Boniface, archbishop of Hesse, to forbid consumption of horseflesh by his Christian converts in order that they may be seen to differ from the surrounding pagan tribes and Vandals who eat wild horses and make the eating of horsemeat part of their pagan rites.

735 Burgundy is conquered by the mayor of Austrasia and Neustria, Charles Martel.

England's archbishopric of York is founded with Egbert as archbishop.

737 The Merovingian king of all the Franks Theodoric IV dies after a 16-year reign. He will be succeeded after a 6-year interregnum by his cousin Childeric.

739 Charles Martel is asked by Pope Gregory III to help fight the Lombards, Greeks, and Arabs.

The bishoprics of Passau, Ratisbon, and Salzburg are founded by Wynfrith Boniface.

741 The Byzantine emperor Leo III dies at age 61 after a 24-year reign that has saved the empire and has delivered eastern Europe from the threat of Arab conquest. He is succeeded by his 22-year-old son,

741 (cont.) who will reign until 775 as Constantine V (Copronymus).

Charles Martel dies October 22 at age 53 after dividing his realms between his elder son Carloman and his younger son Pepin (or Pippin), although the country has had no true king since the death of Theodoric in 737. Lands to the east, including Austrasia, Alemannia, and Thuringia, have gone to Carloman along with suzerainty over Bavaria, while Pepin has received Neustria, Burgundy, and Provence.

742 The Byzantine emperor Constantine V defeats his brother-in-law Artavasdus who has tried to usurp the throne and has led a 2-year insurrection.

743 The last Merovingian king of the Franks begins an 8-year reign as Childeric III succeeds to the throne left vacant by Theodoric IV in 737.

744 Swabia becomes part of the Frankish Empire of Childeric III.

Lombard rule ends in Italy as the Lombard king Liutprand dies at age 54 after a 32-year reign in which he has defeated the dukes of Spoleto and Beneventum and has brought Lombardy to the height of her power. Liutprand's policies will be continued by Aistulf, who will become king of the Lombards in 749 to begin a 7-year reign.

745 Syria is invaded by the Byzantine emperor Constantine V, who carries the war to the Arabs.

A gift of pepper is sent to Wynfrith Boniface, now archbishop of Mainz, by the Roman deacon Gemmulus.

746 Cyprus is retaken from the Arabs by the Byzantine emperor Constantine V, who destroys a great Arab fleet.

Constantinople is struck by the worst plague since the 6th century Plague of Justinian (*see* 732).

747 Pepin's brother Carloman unexpectedly abdicates, becomes a monk, retires to a monastery near Rome, and leaves Pepin as sole master of the Frankish realm.

748 Todai Temple is completed at Nara after 5 years of construction.

749 The Japanese emperor Shomu abdicates at age 48 after a 25-year reign and is succeeded by his 31-year-old daughter Koken who will reign until 758.

750 The kingdom of Galacia, conforming roughly to the Roman province of that name, is established by the duke of Cantabria Alphonso I.

The Abbasid caliphate that will rule most of the Islamic empire for 350 years is inaugurated by Abu-I-Abbas al-Saffah (*see* 754).

Plague follows a famine in the Iberian Peninsula and takes a heavy toll.

751 Charles Martel's son Pepin (the Short) has himself crowned at Soissons by the archbishop of Mainz Wynfrith Boniface and becomes Pepin III in a ceremony new to the Franks but one that gives the sovereign great prestige.

The first paper mill in the Moslem world is established.

752 Japan's 55-foot Buddha statue *Rushanabutsu* is completed at Nara after 9 years of work.

754 Pepin III is crowned at Saint-Denis by Pope Stephen II, and the new Frankish dynasty is proclaimed holy and its title indisputable (*see* 756).

The Abbasid caliphate begun in 750 is firmly established by al-Mansur, 42, who succeeds his brother Abu-I-Abbas to begin a 21-year reign that will see the new caliphate recognized everywhere except in the Iberian Peninsula and Morocco. A revolt by al-Mansur's uncle Abdallah, governor of Syria, is crushed, and Abdallah is murdered on orders from al-Mansur.

A T'ang census shows that 75 percent of Chinese live north of the Yangtse River. Ch'ang-en has a population of 2 million and more than 25 other cities have well over 500,000.

756 The donation of Pepin establishes the papal states and begins the temporal power of the papacy. The Frankish king Pepin III has taken lands that legally belong to the eastern empire, and he gives them to Pope Stephen II, thus tacitly recognizing claims of the popes to be heirs to the empire in Italy.

Cordova is made capital of Moorish Spain by Ab-ar-Rahman I and begins a great period of prosperity.

Japan's Shosoin treasure collection of the late emperor Shomu is placed in the 8-year-old Todai Temple at Nara.

758 The Japanese empress Koken abdicates after a 9-year reign and is succeeded by her 25-year-old cousin Junin who will reign until 764, but Koken and the Fujiwara family retain power.

759 Poetry *Manyoshu* by Japanese poets, including the emperor, noblemen, and commoners, contains some 500 poems.

761 The Japanese empress mother Koken is "cured" of a disease by the priest Dokyo, who has used prayers and potions and who becomes Koken's court favorite, arousing the jealousy of the emperor Junin.

762 The Arab seat of empire is moved to Baghdad by the Abbasid caliph al-Mansur who starts building a new capital in the still fertile Tigris Valley (*see* 766).

764 A revolt against the Japanese empress mother Koken and her favorite Dokyo is led by Nakamaro Fujiwara, but the revolt is suppressed, the emperor Junin is forced into exile, and Koken reassumes the imperial throne. She takes the name Shotoku, and she makes Dokyo her prime minister, beginning a reign that will continue until 770.

765

A three-field crop rotation system is mentioned for the first time in European writings which describe a northern system in which some spring plantings supplement the traditional winter plantings of the south. The system makes a given section of land productive 2 years out of 3, instead of every other year, as one field is sown with wheat or rye at the end of the year, a second is sown in the spring, and a third is left fallow. The second field is sown with barley, broad beans, chick-peas, lentils, oats, or peas, and the land thus produces food with more protein value.

766

Baghdad nears completion as 100,000 laborers create a circular city 1.5 miles in diameter with a palace at its center for the caliph al-Mansur (*see* 762). The city is ringed by three lines of walls, some containing bricks that weigh 200 pounds.

768

Pepin the Short dies at age 54 and is succeeded as Frankish king by his 26-year-old son Charles, who will be known as Charles the Great, or Charlemagne. Pepin's son Carloman becomes king of Austrasia.

770

The Japanese empress Shotoku (Koken) dies at age 52 and is succeeded by the 62-year-old grandson of the late emperor Tenji, who will reign until 781 as the emperor Konin. The accession is engineered by Nakamaro Fujiwara who prevents the accession of the crown prince Ochi.

Horseshoes come into common use in Europe and make horses more efficient for pulling farm implements on stony ground (*see* 450).

771

Charlemagne becomes king of all the Franks upon the death of his brother Carloman, king of Austrasia, and he marries Hildegarde of Swabia.

772

Charlemagne begins a 13-year war with the Saxons that will end with their subjugation on the Continent.

773

Charlemagne is crowned king of Lombardy after invading the country and subduing the Lombards.

774

Charlemagne becomes the first Frankish king to visit Rome, and he confirms the Donation of Pepin granted in 756 while making it clear that he is sovereign even in papal lands. Well over 6 feet tall, Charles the Great is a superb athlete. He is a merry man who can speak Latin and understand Greek even though he cannot learn to write, and he has repudiated his 771 marriage to Hildegarde, daughter of the Swabian king Desiderius.

Charlemagne absorbs Lombardy into his Frankish Empire and establishes his rule in Venetia, Istria, Dalmatia, and Corsica.

The Mercian king Offa subdues Kent and Wessex.

775

The Byzantine emperor Constantine V Copronymus dies at age 56 after a 34-year reign in which he has suppressed monasticism and image worship, restored aqueducts, revived commerce, and repopulated Constantinople. He is succeeded by his

25-year-old son Leo the Khazar who will reign as Leo IV for 5 years and will continue Constantine's energetic campaigns against the Arabs and Bulgars. Byzantine forces defeat the Bulgars at Lithosaria.

The Abbasid caliph al-Mansur dies at age 63 after a 21-year reign in which he has made Baghdad the seat of a powerful empire. He is succeeded by his son who will reign for 10 years as al-Mahdi.

Tibet subdues her Himalayan neighbors and concludes a boundary agreement with the Chinese.

777

Charlemagne gains a victory over the Saxons and invades Moorish Spain, but his advance is checked at Saragossa where he encounters a heroic defense.

778

Charlemagne's rear guard is annihilated by Basques at Roncesvalles in the Pyrenees.

Byzantine forces defeat the Arabs at Germanikeia and expel them from Anatolia.

Charlemagne's paladin Roland is killed at Roncesvalles (above), and his death gives rise to the epic *Chanson de Roland* (*Song of Roland*), the beginning of a great body of medieval French literature.

779

The Mercian king Offa makes himself king of all England.

780

The Byzantine emperor Leo IV dies at age 30 after a 5-year reign in which he has been dominated by his beautiful Athenian wife Irene, now 28. He is succeeded by his 10-year-old son who will reign until 797 as Constantine VI, with Irene as regent until 790.

Image worship is restored by the queen mother Irene (above).

Charlemagne encourages the three-field system of crop rotation in his realms (*see* 765).

781

The Japanese emperor Konin dies at age 73 after an 11-year reign and is succeeded by his 44-year-old half-Korean son who will reign until 806 as the emperor Kanmu.

Chinese Christian monasteries are built by Nestorians who have been in China since 645 and who proselytize among the Chinese (*see* 431).

The bishopric of Bremen is established.

782

Arab forces advance to the Bosporus, but agents of the Byzantine child-emperor Constantine VI and his mother Irene will buy the Arabs off.

Charlemagne executes 4,500 Saxon hostages at Verdun and issues the "*Capitulatio de partibus Saxoniae.*"

The Mercian king Offa builds Offa's Dyke to protect his realm against Welsh attacks.

783

The Byzantine general Staurakios wages a successful campaign against the Greek and Macedonian Slavs.

Charlemagne, the Frankish king who made himself the first of 29 Holy Roman Emperors to be crowned at Rome.

785 The Abbasid caliph al-Mahdi dies after a 10-year reign and is succeeded by his son, who will reign for 1 year as al-Hadi.

The Japanese strongman Tanetsugu Fujiwara has his granddaughter married to the 11-year-old son of the emperor Kanmu in anticipation of young Heizei's ascension to the imperial throne (*see* 806).

786 Harun al-Rashid becomes the fifth Abbasid caliph at age 22, succeeding his brother to begin a 23-year reign that will make Baghdad the center of Arabic culture. Al-Rashid will extend the power of the eastern caliphate over all of southwestern Asia and northern Africa. He will have diplomatic relations with China and will exchange gifts with Charlemagne (*see* 809).

787 Iconoclasm is abandoned by the Council of Nicaea, which orders the worship of icon images, a major victory for the monks who will advance extensive claims to complete freedom for the Church in religious matters.

788 A Moroccan empire that will last for more than 1,000 years is started by a local governor who rebels from the caliphate that rules Islam from Baghdad to Cordova.

790 Constantine VI is placed in command of the Byzantine Empire at age 19 by the army, which mutinies against Constantine's unscrupulous mother Irene and against the monkish party.

Irish monks reach Iceland in hide-covered curraghs to begin settlement of that island (*see* 874).

792 Constantine VI recalls his mother Irene and makes her coruler of the Byzantine Empire.

794 Japan's seat of government is transferred to Heian (Kyoto), where it will remain until 1868 (*see* 710). A golden age of Japanese culture begins and will endure for four centuries under the domination of the Fujiwara, Minamoto, and Taira families (*see* 1190).

Scotland has her first Norse invasion.

795 Ireland has her first Norse invasion 8 years after the first recorded raid of the Danes on England. The Danes have begun to pour into Ireland.

Charlemagne bans the export of grain from his dominions in order to avoid food shortages.

The Fighting Cock is founded at St. Albans as an English pub (public house) that will survive for more than 1,180 years.

796 The Avars on the lower Danube are reduced by the forces of Charlemagne.

797 Constantine VI is seized and blinded by orders of his mother Irene, who has been placed in control of the Byzantine Empire by a new army uprising. She begins a 5-year reign as first Byzantine empress at age 45.

800 Charlemagne is crowned head of the western Roman Empire at Rome on Christmas Day but is not recognized by Irene, empress of the eastern Roman Empire.

An improved still is invented by the Arab scholar Jabir ibn Hayyan, but distillers are still able to do little more than separate liquids (like rosewater) from solids (*see* brandy, 1300).

9th CENTURY

Alfred the Great divided parts of Mercia into shires, consolidated England, and drove off the Danes.

Scandinavian invaders in this century will overrun France, sack and burn Aachen and Cologne, and take London, Cadiz, and Pisa.

From the semibarbaric kingdoms of eastern and central Europe, and even from Europe's western edges, the Vikings will take slaves (the word comes from the same root as "Slav") and will sell them to rich Moslems in the eastern Mediterranean.

Europe's peasantry is, in effect, enslaved to large landowners, who defend them in frequent wars, feed them in times of famine from stores held in reserve against such times, but generally exploit them.

Agronomic science is now in a decline, despite the growing use of the three-field system (see 780), and while the Scandinavians will improve agriculture, which has been unprofitable since the 4th century, Europe will experience famines from now to the 12th century.

Famines will be less severe in this century than they have been in the past and will be in future, since almost everybody now lives on the land. Towns have practically disappeared, and since farm surpluses have no market, the farmers raise only enough for their own needs plus small quantities for barter.

Chinese aristocrats eat from translucent porcelain plates that Europe will not be able to duplicate for more than 900 years (see 621; 1708).

802 The Byzantine empress Irene is deposed by a conspiracy of patricians upon whom she has lavished honors and favors in a 5-year reign of prosperity. They exile her to Lesbos and oblige her to support herself by spinning (she will die there next year), and they replace her with the minister of finance, who will reign until 811 as Nicephorus I.

805 Tea is introduced to Japan as a medicine. The Buddhist bonze (priest) Saicho, 38, has spent 3 years visiting Chinese Buddhist temples on orders from the emperor and he returns with tea (see 708; 1191).

806 The Japanese emperor Kanmu dies at age 69 after a 24-year reign that has seen Korean culture and technology introduced into Japan. Kanmu is succeeded by his manic-depressive 32-year-old son Heizei who becomes hysterical at news of his father's death but who will reign until 809.

Fez becomes the capital of a new Moroccan Empire (see 788).

Norsemen sack the monastery of Iona founded in 563.

Famine strikes Japan.

807 An Arab fleet ravages Rhodes.

808 The Byzantine emperor Nicephorus invades Arab territory.

809 The Abbasid caliph Harun al-Rashid dies in March at age 46 on an expedition to put down an uprising in Khurasan, one of many that have plagued his 23-year reign. The caliph will be glorified in Arabic legend and in the *Arabian Nights*, which will be published in English in 1888. One of his sons will reign until 813 as al-Amin, but his son Mamun is accepted as caliph in Persia and begins a revolt against al-Amin.

The Japanese emperor Heizei abdicates after a 3-year reign. His 23-year-old brother Saga succeeds to the imperial throne and will reign until 823.

Famine sweeps the empire of Charlemagne.

811 The Byzantine emperor Nicephorus invades Bulgaria, whose King Krum took Sofia in 809. He forces Krum to ask for terms, but the Bulgarians surprise the Byzantines and kill the emperor along with much of his army. Nicephorus has reformed Constantinople's finances in his 9-year reign, and his son Staurakios succeeds him for a few months. Staurakios is

811 (cont.) succeeded in turn by his brother-in-law who will reign incompetently until 813 as Michael I Rhangabe.

812 Charlemagne orders that anise, coriander, fennel, flax, fenugreek, sage, and other plants be planted on German imperial farms.

813 The Byzantine army deposes the emperor Michael I Rhangabe and replaces him with the Armenian who will reign until 820 as Leo V.

The Abbasid caliph al-Amin surrenders Baghdad after his brother's general Tahir has granted peace terms, but he is treacherously murdered, and his brother begins a glorious 20-year reign as al-Mamun (Mamun the Great) in which he will encourage Arabian science and literature.

814 Charlemagne dies of pleurisy January 28 at age 71. The Carolingian Empire begins as Charlemagne's 36-year-old son becomes Holy Roman Emperor to begin a 26-year reign as Louis I (the Pious), a name derived from Clovis (see 508).

Japan's Minamoto (Genji) family has its beginnings as 32 of Emperor Saga's 50 children are made either commoners or Buddhist priests to reduce the imperial budget. The commoners will be called "Genji."

817 The Holy Roman Emperor Louis the Pious partitions the Carolingian Empire for the first time. His son Lothair receives most of Burgundy plus the German and Gallic parts of Francia, his son Louis the German receives Bavaria and the marches to the east, and his son Pepin (Pippin) receives Aquitaine and parts of Septimiania and Burgundy (see Treaty of Verdun, 843).

820 The Byzantine emperor Leo V is murdered by supporters of his Phrygian general Michael, who has been sentenced to die for conspiring against Leo. The general begins a 9-year reign as Michael II Psellus (the Stammerer).

823 The Japanese emperor Saga abdicates at age 37 after a 14-year reign. He is succeeded by his 31-year-old brother who will reign until 833 as the emperor Junna.

825 Japan's Taira family has its beginnings as children of the late emperor Kenmu are made commoners to reduce the imperial budget. They are given the name Taira (see Minamoto family, 814; power struggle, 1156).

826 Crete is conquered by Moslem pirates from Spain who will use the island as their base until 961.

827 Sicily is invaded by Saracens from North Africa who begin a 51-year war of conquest.

Spinach is introduced into Sicily by the Saracens (above) who found the plant originally in Persia.

829 The Byzantine emperor Michael II dies. The arrogant religious fanatic Theophilus succeeds to the throne and will reign until 842.

832 The Byzantine emperor Theophilus promulgates a new edict against idolators and persecutes violators with great cruelty.

833 The Japanese emperor Junna abdicates at age 47. His 23-year-old nephew succeeds and will reign until 850 as the emperor Ninmio.

837 Naples beats off a Saracen attack (see 827).

840 The Holy Roman Emperor Louis the Pious dies June 20 at age 62 on an island in the Rhine after suppressing a revolt by his son Louis the German. His 45-year-old son Lothair succeeds as emperor and tries to seize all the domains of the late Charlemagne. His 17-year-old son Charles succeeds as king of France and joins with Louis the German in resisting Lothair.

841 The Battle of Fontenoy ends in defeat for the Holy Roman Emperor Lothair, but while his brothers Charles and Louis triumph, Lothair will remain emperor until his death in 855.

842 The Byzantine emperor Theophilus dies in January after a 14-year reign devoted chiefly to warring against the caliphs of Baghdad, who have taken the city of Amorium, cradle of the Phrygian dynasty, slaughtered its 30,000 inhabitants, and razed it. Theophilus is succeeded by his 3-year-old son who will reign until 867 as Michael III (the Drunkard), his mother Theodora will serve as regent in his minority and will neglect his education. He will war with the Saracens, the Bulgarians, and the Russians.

843 The Treaty of Verdun, executed between the sons of France's late Louis the Pious, gives his son Lothair the title of emperor together with Italy, the valley of the Rhône, the valleys of the Saone and the Meuse, and the capital cities of Rome and Aix-la-Chapelle. France's Charles the Bald receives the rest of Gaul, Louis the German receives lands to the east, and the treaty breaks the unity of the Carolingian Empire.

844 The Holy Roman Emperor Lothair has his 19-year-old son Louis crowned king of Italy at Rome June 15 by Pope Leo IV. Louis soon marries a daughter of his uncle Louis the German.

France's Charles the Bald decrees that a traveling bishop may requisition at each halt in his journey 50 loaves of bread, 50 eggs, 10 chickens, and 5 suckling pigs.

847 Pope Leo IV builds the Leonine Wall to protect St. Peter's at Rome from Moslem invaders.

850 The Norseman Rurik makes himself ruler of Kiev. The house of Rurik will be an important Russian royal family until the end of the 16th century.

The Japanese emperor Ninmio dies at age 40 and, after a struggle over the succession, is succeeded by his 23-year-old son who will reign until 858 as Montoku.

The astrolabe is perfected by Arab scientists as a navigational aid. The compact instrument facilitates observation of the celestial bodies.

Salerno University has its beginnings.

Yiddish has its beginnings as groups of Jews settle in some of the German states and develop their own language, mixing German, Hebrew, and other languages.

Coffee is discovered, according to legend, by the Arab goatherd Kaldi in east Africa who notices that his goats become frisky after chewing the berries from certain wild bushes (see 1453).

851 Canterbury Cathedral is sacked by Danish forces that enter the Thames estuary, but they are defeated at Ockley by the king of the Kentishmen and West Saxons, Ethelwulf.

Pope Leo's 4-year-old Leonine Wall is damaged by a violent earthquake that further destroys the Colosseum at Rome (see 508).

852 The Bulgarian czar Malamir dies after a 23-year reign in which the Bulgarians have gradually expanded into upper Macedonia and Serbia. He is succeeded by Boris I who will reign until 889 (see 864).

The Omayyad emir of Cordova Abd-ar-Rahman II dies after a 30-year reign and is succeeded by Mohammad I who will put down a Christian uprising and reign until 886.

Coal is mentioned for the first time in English chronicles, although the fossil fuel has been used to some extent for centuries to supplement the solar energy obtained from wood (see Theophrastus, 3rd century B.C.). The Saxon Chronicle of the Abbey of Peterborough states that the abbot of Ceobred has rented the land of Sempringham to one Wilfred, who is to send to the monastery each year "60 loads of wood, 12 loads of coal, 6 loads of peat, etc . . ." (see 1285).

853 The king of the West Franks Charles the Bald goes to war with his half-brother Louis the German.

The first important Japanese painter, Kudawara Kuwanari, dies.

855 The Holy Roman Emperor Lothair dies September 29 at age 60 after dividing his lands between his three sons and is succeeded as emperor by his 33-year-old son who will reign until 875 as Louis II. He has been king of Italy since 844 and receives Italy along with the imperial crown while his brother Lothair II receives part of Austrasia, which is renamed Lotharingia (kingdom of Lothair), or Lorraine. A third son, Charles, receives Provence and southern Burgundy.

The king of the Kentishmen Ethelwulf makes a pilgrimage to Rome with his 6-year-old son Alfred.

856 The Kentish prince Ethelbald leads a rebellion against his father Ethelwulf.

An earthquake at Corinth kills an estimated 45,000 Greeks.

857 The first recorded major outbreak of ergotism occurs in the Rhine Valley, where thousands die after eating bread made from rye infected with the ergot fungus parasite *Claviceps* (clubheaded) *purpura* (purple). The fungus contains several alkaloid drugs including ergotamine, which is transformed in baking into an hallucinogen (see 943ff.).

858 The Kentish king Ethelwulf dies after having given up the kingdom of the West Saxons to his rebellious son Ethelbald and is succeeded by his son Ethelbert who will reign until 866.

Algeciras is sacked by Vikings who are driven off by the Arabs.

The Japanese emperor Montoku dies at age 31 and is succeeded by his 8-year-old son Seiwa who will reign until 876.

860 The simplified Japanese alphabet Hiragana, with far fewer characters than the Konji (Chinese) alphabet, becomes popular among Japanese women. The phonetic alphabet will be further simplified and reduced to 51 basic characters that will be used to supplement the Konji alphabet, which contains thousands of characters.

861 Paris, Cologne, Aix-la-Chapelle, Worms, and Toulouse are sacked by marauding Norsemen.

862 Novgorod is founded by the Scandinavian chief Rurik who makes himself grand prince and establishes the Russian royal family that will rule until 1598.

863 The Cyrillic alphabet that will be used by Russians, Bulgarians, and other peoples is invented by the Macedonian missionary Cyril, 36, and his brother Methodius, 35, who have preached the gospel to the Khazar and who begin preaching in Moravia, where they have been sent by the Byzantine emperor Michael at the request of Moravia's ruler Rostislav.

864 The Bulgarian czar Boris I accepts Christianity.

865 Constantinople is attacked by Russian Norsemen.

866 Byzantine strongman Caesar Bardas is murdered in April with the consent of his nephew, the emperor Michael III. The assassin is Michael's Armenian chamberlain Basil, who has divorced his own wife to marry a mistress of the emperor in order to please Michael, who rewards him by making him coemperor.

867 The Macedonian dynasty that will rule the Byzantine Empire until 1054 is founded by the coemperor Basil, who has Michael III murdered in September and begins a 19-year reign as Basil I. Raised in Macedonia, the new emperor will rebuild the Byzantine army and navy in an effort to restore the empire.

A schism with the Roman Church that will become final in 1054 is begun by the patriarch of Constantinople Photius, 47, who was excommunicated by Pope Nicholas I 4 years ago and who issues an encyclical against the pope, who is anathametized by the Council of Constantinople.

Pope Nicholas dies November 13 at age 67.

868 The *Diamond Sutra*, produced in China, is the world's first printed book (it will be found by archaeologists in the Caves of the Thousand Buddhas at Kansu).

869 Malta is taken by Arab invaders.

870 Lorraine is partitioned under terms of the Treaty of Mersen forced upon the king of Lorraine Charles the Bald by the Holy Roman Emperor Louis II who gains territory west of the Rhine. The realm is divided equally on the basis of revenue.

England's Ethelred I defeats the Danes December 31 in a skirmish at Englefield in Berkshire.

871 England's Ethelred I is defeated by the Danes January 4 at Reading, he gains a brilliant victory January 8 at Ashdown, he is defeated January 22 at Basing, he triumphs again March 22 at Marton in Wiltshire, but he dies in April. Ethelred is succeeded by his 22-year-old brother Alfred who will reign for 28 years and who will be called Alfred the Great.

874 Iceland is discovered by Viking Norsemen who begin almost immediately to colonize the country (*see* 790).

875 The Holy Roman Emperor Louis II dies August 12 in Brescia at age 50 after having named his cousin Carloman as his successor, but Carloman, son of Louis the German, is persuaded to go home by Charles the Bald who beats Louis the German to Rome and makes himself emperor.

876 Louis the German dies at Frankfort September 8 at age 72 while preparing for war with the Holy Roman Emperor Charles the Bald. Most competent of Charlemagne's descendants, he is succeeded by his son Carloman.

The Japanese emperor Saiwa abdicates at age 26 and is succeeded by his mentally and physically weak 8-year-old son Yozei, who will reign until 884.

877 Exeter is seized by Danish forces while their leaders are deceptively negotiating with Alfred. He blockades the town, a relief fleet is scattered by a storm, and the Danes are forced to surrender and to withdraw to Mercia.

Charles the Bald dies October 5 at age 54 while crossing the pass of the Mont Cenis en route back to Gaul. He is succeeded as king of France (but not as emperor) by his 30-year-old son Louis le Begue (the Stammerer), king of Aquitaine, who will reign briefly as France's Louis II.

878 The English king Alfred is surprised by the Danes in January at Chippenham where he has been celebrating Christmas. Most of his men are killed, but he escapes through woods and swamps with a small band of survivors and prepares a counteroffensive from Athelney. Troops from Somersetshire, Wiltshire, and Hampshire join Alfred in mid-May, he meets the Danes at Edington in Wiltshire, and he gains a great victory.

The Danish king Guthrum, who submits to Alfred (above), accepts baptism to Christianity along with 29 of his chief officers.

879 France's Louis II (the Stammerer) dies at Compiegne April 10 at age 32 after an ineffectual reign of 18 months. He is succeeded by his teenage sons, who assume the throne jointly as Louis III and Carloman. They are crowned at Ferrière in September and divide the kingdom between them a few months later.

England's Alfred the Great clears the Danes out of Wessex and most of Mercia, but London remains in Danish hands.

881 The throne of the Holy Roman Empire, vacant since 877, is filled in February. Pope John VIII crowns the 48-year-old third son of the late Louis the German at Rome, and the stout king of Swabia begins a 6-year reign as Charles III.

882 France's Louis III dies at St. Denis August 5 at age 19, and his brother Carloman becomes sole king.

884 The Japanese emperor Jozei, who has devoted himself mainly to his horses, is forced to abdicate at age 16 after an 8-year reign and is succeeded by the 54-year-old half-brother of his grandfather, who will reign until 887 as Koko.

France's Carloman dies December 12 while out hunting and is succeeded as king of the West Franks by the Holy Roman Emperor Charles III (the Fat), son of the late Louis the German.

885 The Holy Roman Emperor Charles III disposes of his rival Hugh of Alsace, illegitimate son of the late Lothair II.

London is retaken from the Danes by England's Alfred the Great, who suppresses a revolt by the East Anglian Danes.

886 Paris is besieged by Norsemen. The Holy Roman Emperor Charles III arrives with a large army in October, but he agrees to let the invaders withdraw, paying them a heavy ransom and permitting them to ravage Burgundy without interference on his part.

The Byzantine emperor Basil I dies August 29 after a 19-year reign that has been marked by rare wisdom despite its treacherous beginnings and despite Basil's lack of education. He is succeeded by a son of the late emperor Michael by Basil's widow Eudocia who will reign until 912 as Leo VI (the Wise).

887 The Holy Roman Emperor Charles III (the Fat) is deposed in November by an assembly meeting at Tribur. There will be no emperor until 891.

The Japanese emperor Koko abdicates and soon dies at age 57. He is succeeded by his 20-year-old son who will reign as Uda until 897.

888 Odo, count of Paris, is elected king of the West Franks by one faction to succeed the emperor Charles the Fat. He will be opposed by Charles the Simple, 10-year-old son of the late Louis the Stammerer, who will rule from Laon until 923 as the last Carolingian king but who will have no real authority.

890 England's Alfred the Great extends the power of the king's courts and establishes a regular English militia and navy.

Fiction *Taketori Monogatari* (the story of a bamboo gatherer) by a Japanese writer.

891 The king of Italy Guy (Guido) of Spoleto is crowned Holy Roman emperor by Pope Stephen V.

892 England is invaded in the autumn by Danish forces who arrive from the mainland in 330 ships and are accompanied by their wives and children.

893 Danish forces in England are defeated by Alfred the Great's 23-year-old son Edward at Farnham and are forced to take refuge on Thorney Island. Another force of Danes besieges Essex, but the siege is raised by Alfred and the Danes receive other setbacks.

Nonfiction *The Life of Alfred the Great* by the Welsh monk Asser, bishop of Sherborne, who studies for 6 months each year in Alfred's household.

894 The Holy Roman Emperor Guy of Spoleto dies after a 3-year reign and is succeeded by the coemperor Lambert with whom he has reigned since 892 and who will continue as emperor until 898 (but *see* Arnulf, 896).

Moravia's Svatopluk dies after a 34-year reign in which he has united Moravia, Slovakia, and Bohemia under the name Great Moravia to oppose the Germans but who has himself been overcome by the Magyars and their leader Arpad.

Danish forces in England retire to Essex after being deprived of food by Alfred the Great. They draw their ships up the Thames and the Lea and entrench themselves 20 miles above London.

895 England's Alfred the Great blocks the Lea River, captures the Danish fleet, and forces the Danes to move off to the northwest.

The Magyars are expelled from southern Russia and are led into Hungary by Arpad.

896 The Bavarian king Arnulf has himself crowned Holy Roman emperor by Pope Formosus at Rome in February. He sets out to establish his authority in Spoleto but is seized en route by paralysis.

England's Alfred the Great ends the Danish threat to his country. The Danes abandon the struggle, and some return to the mainland, while others retire to Northumbria and East Anglia.

897 The Japanese emperor Uda abdicates at age 30 after a 10-year reign and is succeeded by his 12-year-old son who will reign until 930 as the emperor Daigo.

899 England's Alfred the Great dies after a 28-year reign in which he has forced invading Danes to withdraw, consolidated England round his kingdom, divided parts of Mercia into shires, compiled the best laws of earlier kings, and encouraged learning by bringing famous scholars to Wessex and by making his own translations of Latin works. Alfred is succeeded by his 29-year-old son Edward who will reign until 924.

The Holy Roman Emperor Arnulf dies in December at age 49 and is succeeded as German king by his 6-year-old son Louis, who will reign until 911 as Louis III (the Child), the last of the German Carolingian kings.

900 Greenland is discovered by the Norseman Gunbjorn, who is blown off course while sailing from Norway to Iceland and who comes upon the large ice-capped island (*see* 874; Eric the Red, 981).

Breslau has its beginnings in the Bohemian fortress of Wrotizlav built on the banks of the Oder River.

The Czechs assert their authority over all Bohemian tribes.

The first distinction between measles and smallpox is made by Rhazes (Abu-Bakr Muhammed ibn-Zakariya' al-Razi), chief physician of a busy Bagdhad hospital, who gives the first description of smallpox and establishes criteria for diagnosing the disease that will be used until the 18th century (*see* inoculation, 1718).

England receives her first shipments of East Indian spices, used chiefly for their alleged medical benefits.

10th CENTURY

The century will be marked by struggles between Moslems and Christians, Greeks and Russians, and Lombards, Bulgarians, Arabs, and Byzantines.

The work collar, or broad-breast collar, for draft animals will come into general use in this century, allowing a horse to draw from its shoulders without pressing upon its windpipe and quadrupling a horse's efficiency as compared with horsepower derived from animals harnessed with neck yokes of the kind employed on oxen.

Horses will come into wider use in those parts of Europe where the three-field system produces grain surpluses for feed, but hay-fed oxen will be more economical, if less efficient, in terms of time and labor and will remain almost the sole source of animal power in southern Europe, where most farmers will continue to use the two-field system.

Europe will suffer 20 severe famines in this century, some of them lasting for 3 to 4 years. An alimentary crisis will occur every few years for the next three centuries, in fact, and as populations grow and become more urbanized, the famines will strike more cruelly, although they may be fewer in number than in some earlier centuries.

901 The 21-year-old son of the late king of Provence (or Lower Burgundy) Boso is chosen king of the Lombards at Pavia and is crowned at Rome in February by Pope Benedict IV to begin a 27-year reign as the Holy Roman Emperor Louis III.

England's Edward the Elder takes the title "King of the Angles and Saxons."

904 Thessalonica is stormed by the Saracen corsair Leo of Tripoli, who plunders the town and carries off some 20,000 of its inhabitants as slaves.

Constantinople is attacked by Russians.

905 The Holy Roman Emperor Louis III is surprised July 21 after having subdued the Lombards. He is blinded and sent back to Arles.

Navarre is made a kingdom as the Christian reconquest of Spain begins under the 57-year-old Alfonso III of Leon and the Asturias.

906 Annam in Southeast Asia obtains independence after more than 1,000 years of Chinese domination.

907 China's T'ang dynasty comes to an end after 289 years as the Khitan Mongols under Ye-lu A-pao-chi begin to conquer much of the country. Five different dynasties will assert imperial authority in the next 52 years, but none will exercise much power beyond the Yellow River Basin (*see* Sung, 960).

Hungary's Magyar chief Arpad dies after having founded a dynasty that will reign until 1301 (although its first king will not be crowned as such until 997). The Magyars destroy the Moravian Empire and make raids into German and Italian territory.

Russian forces under Prince Oleg appear at Constantinople and secure trading rights from the world's leading commercial and cultural city.

909 England's Edward the Elder defeats an army of invading Danes.

910 England's Edward the Elder gains fresh victories over the Danes, and he takes possession of London and Oxford on the death of his brother-in-law Ethelred of Mercia.

The kingdom of Asturias is renamed the kingdom of Leon with Alfonso III as its king.

The Byzantine emperor Leo VI (the Wise) is forced to pay tribute to the Magyars.

The Benedictine Abbey of Cluny is founded.

911 The dukedom of Normandy is established by the Treaty of St. Clair-sur-Epte and Rollo the Viking (Hrolf the Ganger) becomes France's first duc d'Orléans as the Scandinavian Norsemen extend their domination over the Franks. Rollo will be baptized next year, he will take the name Robert, and he will acquire large parts of what will later be called Normandy.

The German king Louis the Child dies at age 18, and the son of Conrad, count of Lahngau, is chosen German king November 8 at Forchheim. Lorraine transfers her allegiance to France.

912 The Byzantine emperor Leo VI dies after a 26-year reign in which he has completed the Basilian code of laws begun by his predecessor. He is succeeded by his brother who will reign for less than a year.

913 The Byzantine emperor Alexander II dies and is succeeded by his 8-year-old nephew, son of the late Leo VI, who will reign until 959 as Constantine VII Porphyrogenitus ("born to the purple"). The government is administered by a regency composed of Constantine's mother Zoë Carbonopsina, the patriarch Nikolas, and John Eladas.

Constantinople is menaced by Bulgarian forces under the czar Symeon who calls himself emperor of the Romans.

914 Adrianople falls to the Bulgarian czar Symeon but is soon retaken by Byzantine forces.

England's Warwick Castle near Stratford-upon-Avon is fortified by a daughter of the late Alfred the Great.

915 Famine strikes the Iberian Peninsula, possibly as a result of a wheat crop failure due to rust.

918 The German king Conrad I dies September 23 after a 7-year reign in which he has warred with the Danes, the Slavs, the Magyars, and the 42-year-old duke of Saxony. The Lombard king Berengar, a grandson of Louis the Pious, was crowned Holy Roman Emperor in 915 and will continue as such until his death in 924, but Conrad I has advised his nobles to make the duke of Saxony the next German king. They will elect the duke king at Fritzlar next May, and he will reign until 936 as Henry the Fowler.

919 Famine returns to the Iberian Peninsula, which is ruled in the south by the Omayyad caliph Abd ar-Rahman III and in the Christian north by princes who are establishing the beginnings of Leon, Castile, and Navarre.

922 France's Charles III (the Simple) is deposed by rebellious barons and replaced with Robert, brother of King Odo, who is crowned king of the Franks at Reims June 29 while Charles gathers an army to march against the usurper.

923 The Battle of Soissons June 15 ends with the death of Robert at the hands of Charles III, but Charles is defeated and the barons elect Rudolf, duke of Burgundy, to succeed Robert. They imprison Charles, who will die at Peronne in 929.

924 England's Edward, son of Alfred the Great, dies and is succeeded by his son Athelstan, who begins a 16-year reign in which he will continue his father's conquest of the Danelaw north of the Thames-Lea line from the Vikings who have been in Britain since 787.

927 Famine devastates the Byzantine Empire. Constantinople's Constantine VII and his coemperor father-in-law Romanus Lecapenus push through stringent laws to prevent great landed magnates from buying up the small holdings of poor farmers.

928 France's Louis III (the Blind) dies at Arles in September at age 48 after a 27-year reign, of which 23 were sightless. His son Charles Constantine succeeds only to the county of Vienne.

930 The Japanese emperor Daigo dies at age 45 after a 33-year reign and is succeeded by his 7-year-old son, who will reign until 946 as the emperor Suzaku. The boy was kept indoors until age 3 by his mother, who will dominate him, but the ex-emperor Uda remains the power behind the throne and will retain power until his death next year at age 65.

936 The duke of Burgundy Rudolph dies and is succeeded as king of France by the 15-year-old son of the late Charles III. His mother is the sister of England's Athelstan and had fled with him to England after the imprisonment of Charles in 922. The boy is chosen king by the count of Paris, Hugh the Great, whose father Robert was killed at Soissons in 923. The new king is consecrated at Laon June 19 and begins an 18-year reign as Louis IV d'Outremer.

The German king Henry the Fowler dies at Memleben July 2 at age 60 after a 17-year reign in which he has created the Saxon army and founded Saxon town life. He is succeeded by his 23-year-old son who will be crowned Holy Roman Emperor in 962 and who will reign until 973 as Otto I.

Peking is attacked by Tartars who capture the city (see 1151).

943 Ergotism strikes Limoges in France, killing an estimated 40,000 who have eaten bread made from diseased rye (see 857; 1039).

945 Kyoto is invaded by several thousand farmers who demonstrate against requisition of their rice and other crops.

946 The Japanese emperor Suzaku dies at age 23 after a 16-year reign and is succeeded by his 2-year-old brother Murakami who will reign until 967.

950 Europe's intellectual center is Cordova in Moslem Spain. The city of 500,000 is served by libraries, medical schools, and a large paper trade.

954 France's Louis IV dies September 10 at age 33 and is succeeded by his 13-year-old son Lothair who will reign until 986, initially under the guardianship of Hugh the Great, count of Paris, and later under his maternal uncle Bruno, archbishop of Cologne.

955 The Battle of the Lechfeld August 10 ends the threat of Magyar invasion of the West. Otto the Great defeats the Magyars with an army recruited from all the duchies. He will go on to defeat the Wends on the Recknitz, and he will re-establish Charlemagne's East Mark (Austria) with Bavarian colonists.

956 Hugh the Great dies June 17, 2 months after becoming effective master of Burgundy. He is succeeded by his 18-year-old son Hugh Capet who is recognized with some reluctance as duke of the Franks by his cousin Lothair, king of the Franks.

959 The first king of England is recognized as such in the person of Edgar, who ascends the throne at age 15 following the death of his elder brother Eadwig in October. The king is the great-grandson of Edward and great-great-grandson of Alfred the Great.

The Byzantine emperor Constantine VII dies after a reign of 47 years and is succeeded by his young son Romanus II, who begins a 4-year reign of dissipation.

The English monk Dunstan, 50, is recalled from exile in Flanders by Edgar (above) who makes him first bishop of Worcester and then bishop of London.

960 The Sung dynasty that will rule China until 1279 is established by Chao K'uang-yin who begins to restore China's unity. He will rule until 976 as (Sung) T'ai Tsu to begin the dynasty that will overlap the Mongol Yuan dynasty, which will begin in 1260 (*see* 618).

The first ruler of Poland establishes himself in the person of Mieszko, who has conquered territory between the Oder and the Warthe Rivers. He will be converted to Christianity in 966, he will rule until his death in 992, but he will be defeated by the margrave Gero and forced to recognize German suzerainty.

961 Crete is reconquered from Saracen pirates by a great Byzantine armada commanded by Nicephorus Phocas who storms Candia, expels the Moslems, and converts the people to Christianity.

England's Bishop Dunstan is made archbishop of Canterbury by Edgar whose coronation will not take place until 973 but whose chief adviser will be the archbishop.

962 Rome's feudal anarchy is ended by the Saxon Otto I who is crowned Holy Roman Emperor February 2 by Pope John XII. The Western Empire is revived by Otto, who begins a period of friction with Constantinople.

963 The dissolute Byzantine emperor Romanus II dies at age 25, probably of poison administered by his wife Theophano. He is succeeded by his infant son who will reign until 1025 as Basil II with help from the great general Nicephorus Phocas, now 41, who will be coemperor until 969, and John Tzimisces, now 39, who will assassinate Nichephorus II Phocas in 969 and will serve as coemperor until his own sudden death early in 976.

967 The Japanese emperor Murakami dies at age 41 after a 21-year reign and is succeeded by his 17-year-old son, who is insane but who will reign until 969 as the emperor Reizei.

969 The mad Japanese emperor Reizei is removed by the Fujiwara family after a reign of nearly 2 years and is replaced by his 10-year-old brother who will reign as the emperor Enyu until 984.

970 A great hospital is founded at Baghdad by the Vizier Abud al-Daula. Physicians are divided into the equivalent of interns and externs, a primitive nursing system is developed, and the hospital's pharmacy is stocked with drugs from all parts of the known world, including spices thought to have medicinal value.

973 The Holy Roman Emperor Otto I dies May 7 at age 60 after an 11-year reign. He is succeeded by his 18-year-old son who has been joint emperor since Christmas of 967 and who last year took as his wife the Byzantine princess Theophano, daughter of Romanus II. The new emperor will reign until late in 983 as Otto II.

Cloves, ginger, pepper, and other Eastern spices are reported available for purchase in the marketplace at Mainz by the Moorish physician-merchant Ibrahim ibn Yaacub who has visited Mainz. The spices have been brought to the city by Jewish traveling merchants known as "Radanites" who have kept some international trade channels open in the three centuries of conflict between the Christian and Islamic worlds. In addition to spices, the Radanites have traded in numerous other commodities, transporting furs, woolen cloth, Frankish swords, eunuchs, and white female slaves to the Orient, while returning to Christian Europe with musk, pearls, precious stones, aloes, and spices that include cinnamon.

Direct trade between Egypt and Italy begins.

975 The king of the English Edgar the Peaceful dies at age 31 after a 16-year reign in which he has ceded Lothian (northern Bernicia) to Scotland's Kenneth for the sake of good will and has organized a fleet to defend the English against northern pirates. He is succeeded by his 12-year-old son Edward, who will reign until 978.

Garde-Freinet is taken from the Arabs by William, count of Arles.

Modern arithmetical notation is introduced into Europe by the Arabs.

976 The Byzantine coemperor John I Tzimisces dies January 10 at age 51 after returning from a second campaign against the Saracens. The emperor Basil II, now 20, will reign alone until 1025.

The Bulgarian Samuel sets himself up as czar to begin a 38-year reign in which he will challenge the power of the Byzantine emperor Basil II (above; *see* 996).

Modern Austria has her beginnings in a margraviate on the Danube granted by the Holy Roman Emperor Otto II to the Franconian count Leopold (Luitpold), whose family will rule the country until 1246 (*see* 1156).

Cordova's caliph Hakam II dies at age 63 after a 15-year reign in which he has ended the Fatimid dynasty in Morocco and has made the University of Cordova the greatest institution of learning in the world. He is succeeded by his 12-year-old son Hisham who will be caliph until 1009 and then again from 1010 to 1013 but who will never have any real power (*see* 978).

978 The king of the English Edward is assassinated March 18 at Corfe Castle in Dorsetshire at age 15 in a conspiracy engineered by his stepmother Elfthryth, who wants the crown for her 10-year-old son Ethelred, who succeeds Edward the Martyr and who will reign until 1016 as Ethelred the Unready.

Aix-la-Chapelle is sacked by the Holy Roman Emperor Otto II who is at war with the French king Lothair.

Cordova's regent al-Mansur (Mohammad ibn-abi-'Amir), 39, seizes power from the 14-year-old caliph Hisham II. Finance minister under Hashim's late father, Hakam II, al-Mansur will wage successful campaigns against the Christian kingdoms to the north, he will check separatist religious movements, and he will extend the power of the Omayyad caliphate in the next 24 years.

980 Kiev falls to Viking warriors called in by the 24-year-old Vladimir of Great Novgorod who makes himself grand duke of Kiev and begins a 25-year reign that will extend Russian dominions (*see* 987).

England's ports of Chester, Southampton, and Thanet are attacked in a renewal of Danish raids.

981 Norse Icelanders sail for Greenland in 25 ships that carry 700 people with cattle, horses, and other necessities for starting a colony (*see* 900). The expedition is led by Eric the Red, an exiled murderer whose family came to Iceland more than 20 years ago from Jaeder. Only 14 of the 25 ships will reach their destination (*see* 982).

The Holy Roman Emperor Otto II marches into Apulia to punish the Saracens who have invaded the Italian mainland.

982 Last year's invasion of Apulia by the Holy Roman Emperor Otto II provokes the Byzantine emperor Basil II who sends troops to support the Arabs. Otto sustains a devastating defeat in July and escapes on a Greek vessel to Rossano without revealing his identity.

Dorset, Portland, and South Wales are raided by Vikings.

The first Viking colonies in Greenland are established by Eric the Red (*see* 981; 985).

983 The Holy Roman Emperor Otto II raises German and Italian princes for a new campaign against the Saracens, but he hears of a general rising by the Slavs east of the Elbe River, and he dies in his palace at Rome December 7 at age 28. He is succeeded by his 3-year-old son who is crowned German king Christmas Day at Aix-la-Chapelle by Germans unaware of the emperor's death.

984 The German king Otto III is seized early in the year by the deposed duke of Bavaria, Henry the Quarrelsome, who was defeated and dethroned by Otto II in 976 and forced to give up Carinthia and Verona. The 33-year-old Henry (Heinrich der Zanker) has recovered his duchy and claims the regency as a member of the reigning house, but he is forced to hand over the boy to his mother Theophano who arrives with the boy's grandmother Adelaide.

The Japanese emperor Enyu abdicates in favor of his 16-year-old son, who will reign until 986 as Kazan.

985 The Danish king Harald II (Bluetooth) dies after a 35-year reign and is succeeded by his son Sweyn (Forkbeard), who will defeat the Norwegians, Swedes, and Wends, conquer England, and reign until 1014.

986 Lothair of the Franks dies March 2 at age 44 and is succeeded by his 19-year-old son, who will reign briefly as Louis V (le Faineant) and who will embroil the Carolingians with Adalberon, archbishop of Reims, and with Hugh Capet.

India is invaded by the Moslem sultan of Ghazni Subuktigin, a former Turkish slave who has obtained the sultanate by marriage and who founds the Ghaznevid dynasty that will rule Afghanistan and much of India.

The Japanese emperor Kazan is tricked into abdicating at age 18 and becomes a Buddhist priest 1 year after the death of his wife in childbirth. He is succeeded by his 6-year-old half-brother, who will reign until 1011 as Ichijo.

al-Tasrif is compiled at Cordova and will serve for centuries as a manual of surgery. The surgeon Albucasis (Abul Kasim), who served as court physician to the late caliph Hakam II, illustrates the resumé of Arabian medical knowledge in which he describes the position for lithotomy (cutting a stone out of the urinary bladder), differentiates between goiter and cancer of the thyroid gland, and instructs surgeons in the delivery of infants in abnormal positions, use of iron cautery, amputation of limbs, transverse tracheotomies, removal of goiters, tying of arteries, repair of fistulas, healing of aneurisms and arrow wounds, and other matters.

987 Louis V of the Franks dies in May, and it is alleged that his mother Emma poisoned him. His death at age 20 ends the Carolingian dynasty founded by Charlemagne in 800, and the Capetian dynasty that will rule until 1328 comes to power in the person of Hugh Capet. The archbishop of Reims declares that the Frankish monarchy is elective rather than hereditary, he denies the claims of the late king's uncle Charles, duke of Lower Lorraine, and he engineers the election of his 49-year-old friend Hugh Capet who is crowned in July and who will reign until 996.

Anatolia is overrun by the great feudal barons Bardas Phocas and Bardas Skleros who rise against the Byzantine emperor Basil.

Kiev's Grand Duke Vladimir acts after long consultations with the boyars and sends out envoys to study the religions of Kiev's neighbors. They report that "there is no gladness" among the Moslem Bulgarians on the Volga but "only sorrow and a great stench; their religion is not a good one." They find "no beauty" in the temples of the Germans, but they report back from Constantinople that the ritual of the Orthodox Church is so awesome that "we no longer knew whether we were in heaven or on earth, nor such beauty, and we know not how to tell it." They also return with an offer from the Byzantine emperor Basil of his sister Anna in marriage.

988 Kiev's Grand Duke Vladimir has himself baptized at Cherson in the Crimea, and takes the Christian name Basil in honor of the emperor at Constantinople. He marries the emperor's sister Anna, returns in triumph to Kiev, and begins a general conversion of Russians to Eastern Orthodoxy (*see* 1054).

Constantinople is threatened by the insurgents Bardas Phocas and Bardas Skleros.

989 Bardas Phocas is defeated at Abydos and soon after dies, thus ending the threat to Constantinople. Bardas Skleros submits to the forces of the emperor Basil.

992 Poland's first recorded ruler, Mieszko I of the house of Piast, dies after a reign of more than 30 years and is succeeded by the 25-year-old Boleslav the Brave (Chrobry), who will reign until 1025. Boleslav begins an invasion of eastern Pomerania to gain access to the Baltic.

Venice is granted extensive trade privileges in the Byzantine Empire.

993 Sweden's first Christian ruler comes to power in the person of Olaf Skutkonung, son of Eric the Conqueror, who will reign until 1024.

994 Poland's Boleslav completes his conquest of eastern Pomerania.

995 Syria is incorporated into the Byzantine Empire by Basil II, whose forces take Aleppo and Homs.

996 Otto III invades the Italian peninsula and replaces the Crescentine pope with his cousin Bruno, who is elected Pope Gregory V, but the new papacy will be short-lived.

Greece is reconquered for Byzantium by Basil II, who defeats the Bulgarian king Samuel on the Sperchelos River and bribes supporters of Samuel to defect as he proceeds to reduce Bulgarian strongholds in a campaign that will continue until 1014 and will cause him to be known as Basil Bulgaroktonos (Slayer of the Bulgarians).

Hugh Capet dies at Paris October 14 at age 58 and is succeeded by his 26-year-old son who will reign as Robert II until 1031.

997 The first Christian Magyar duke Geza dies and is succeeded by his 20-year-old son, who will rule as Stephen I until 1038. Married last year to the daughter of Bavaria's Duke Henry II, Stephen has chosen St. Martin of Tours as his patron saint and is engaged in putting down a pagan uprising between the Drave and Lake Balaton.

1000 Norseman Lief Ericsson discovers the Western Hemisphere when storms drive him westward while he is attempting to return to Norway from Greenland. Landing on the coast of what later will be either Newfoundland or Nova Scotia, Ericsson makes his way back to Greenland with descriptions of Vinland (Wineland) where grapes and wild wheat grow.

Saxons settle at Bristol, England.

Norway's Olaf I Tryggvesson falls in battle with the kings of Denmark and Sweden after a 5-year reign in which English clergymen have helped him convert Norway, Iceland, and Greenland to Christianity. The Danes take over Norway.

Poland's Boleslav the Brave unites Bohemia and Moravia and persuades the Holy Roman Emperor Otto III to create the independent archbishopric of Gnesen.

Ceylon (Sri Lanka) is invaded by the Chola king Rajaraja the Great.

The Japanese emperor Ichijo, now 20, makes his 25-year-old wife Sadako (Teishi) empress, but she dies after 10 months, and the 12-year-old Akiko becomes empress.

The Danegeld imposed by England's Ethelred II is a general tax levied to support the king's forces as he ravages Cumberland and Anglesey. In addition, Ethelred demands that merchants wishing to trade in London pay a tax in peppercorns for the privilege (*see* 900).

The Milennium of the supposed birth of Christ brings fear of the Last Judgment and the end of mankind throughout the Christian world.

Hungary's Arpad king Stephen I founds the monastery of Gran.

The Indian mathematician Sridhara recognizes the importance of the zero.

The Chinese Bridge of the Ten Thousand Ages is completed at Foochow.

The Pillow-Book of Sei Shonagon will be compiled in the next 15 years by a lady-in-waiting to the late Japanese empress Sadako (above). Daughter of the wit Mutosuke Kiyowara, the 37-year-old Sei Shonagon will fill her notes and comments with scathing criticisms and polished indelicacies that will make her diaries popular for centuries.

The "grapes" found by Lief Ericsson (above) are either mountain cranberries, wild currants, or gooseberries, and his wild "wheat" is Lyme grass (Elymus arenarius, var. villosus), a tall wild grass with a wheatlike head whose seeds are used to make flour for bread in Iceland.

11th CENTURY

1002 The Holy Roman Emperor Otto III dies January 23 at age 21 while conducting a campaign against the Romans. He is succeeded as king of the Franks and Bavarians June 7 by his 28-year-old cousin Henry, duke of Bavaria, who will become emperor in 1014.

The Omayyad vizier al-Mansur of Cordova dies at age 63 after 21 years in power, and the caliphate begins to decline under Hisham II.

The Byzantine armies of Basil II overrun Macedonia and defeat the Bulgarians at Vidin.

Danish settlers in England are massacred on St. Brice's Day by order of Ethelred II.

Iron plows with wheels will replace wooden plows in much of northern Europe in this century. Food will become more abundant as a result of such agricultural improvements, but France will nevertheless have 26 famines and England will average one famine every 14 years.

1003 Norse mariner Thorfinn Karlsefni leaves Greenland with three ships for a 3-year visit to the northern continent of the Western Hemisphere. His attempts at settlement will not be successful, nor will any other attempt for nearly 600 years (*see* Ericsson, 1000; Corte Real, 1500).

The Viking king Sweyn Forkbeard plunders the English coast and exacts tribute in retaliation for last year's massacre of Danish settlers by Ethelred II. The raids will continue almost annually until 1014.

1004 The Lombard king Ardoin is defeated by Henry of Bavaria, who has himself crowned king of Lombardy at Pavia, but Ardoin continues to make war on Henry.

1005 Scotland's Kenneth III dies after an 8-year reign and is succeeded by Malcolm II who will rule until 1034.

1006 Burgundy's last independent king Rudolph II makes Henry of Bavaria his heir. Henry makes an alliance with France's Robert II against Baldwin of Flanders.

Mohammedans settle in northwest India.

The Chinese Sung emperor established granaries for emergency famine relief in every prefecture.

1007 England's Ethelred II pays the Danes £40,000 to gain 2 years' freedom from the attacks of the Viking Sweyn.

1008 Mahmud of Ghazni defeats Hindu forces at Peshawar as he works to extend his Afghan kingdom from the Tigris to the Ganges.

1010 Poetry *The Book of the Kings* (*The Shah-nama*) by the 75-year-old Persian poet Mansur Abu'l-Quasim Firdawsi is presented by its author to the Sultan Mahmud of Ghazni. It will survive as the great epic poem of Persia.

1011 The Japanese emperor Ichijo dies at age 31 after a 15-year reign and is succeeded by his 35-year-old cousin who will reign until 1016 as Sanjo but who begins to lose his eyesight almost immediately.

South Wales is invaded by Ethelred II, and Canterbury is taken by the Danes in his absence.

1012 England's Ethelred II pays the Danes another £48,000 to cease their raids.

"Heretics" are persecuted for the first time in the German states.

1013 The Danes conquer England. Ethelred II takes refuge in Normandy.

Cordova's Hisham II dies after a caliphate that began in 976 but was interrupted between 1009 and 1010 as Omayyad power declined in Spain. He is succeeded by Sulaiman al-Mustain, who was installed as caliph by the Berbers from 1009 to 1010 and who will reign until 1016, but civil war is precipitated by the death of Hisham II.

1014 The German king Henry of Bavaria recognizes Benedict VIII as the rightful pope and is crowned at Rome February 14 to begin a 10-year reign as the Holy Roman Emperor Henry II.

The Viking king Sweyn Forkbeard dies suddenly at Gainsborough in February and is succeeded by his 20-year-old son Canute, who flees to Denmark as Ethelred returns from Normandy.

Norse rule of Ireland is ended by the Irish king Brian Born at the Battle of Cloutarf.

The Bulgarian army is blinded on orders from Basil II, whose Byzantine armies annex the western part of Bulgaria.

1015 Norwegian independence is restored by Olaf II who reinstates Christianity in Norway.

Wessex yields to Canute who has returned to England to wage war against Edmund Ironside.

Sardinia is conquered by the Arabs.

Leipzig is settled by Slavs on a plain just above the junction of three small rivers.

1015 (cont.) Fiction *The Tale of Genji* (*Genji Monogatari*) by Japanese baroness Shikibu Murasaki, 35, whose work will be a classic of world literature. Widowed at age 21, the baroness has become a lady-in-waiting to the empress Akiko and has probably written her long novel to be read as entertainment for the empress.

1016 The blind Japanese emperor Sanjo abdicates at age 40 and is succeeded by the 8-year-old son of the late Ichijo who will reign until 1036 as Goichijo.

England's Ethelred II dies at age 48 after a 38-year reign and is succeeded by his son Edmund Ironside, who is chosen king by Londoners, while Canute is chosen by the witan at Southampton. Edmund's brother-in-law Edric deserted him last year in anger at Edmund's marriage to the widow of a Danish earl, and while Edric now rejoins the new king, his treachery causes a rout of the English at Assundum (Ashingdon) in Essex. Canute defeats Edmund but permits him to reign in the south until his death later in the year at age 26, whereupon Canute proceeds to conquer all of England.

1017 King Canute divides England into four earldoms, and while Edric is restored to an earldom, he is found untrustworthy and is executed.

1018 Byzantine forces defeat an army of Lombards and Normans at Cannae in a great victory that assures continued domination of southern Italy by the Greeks.

The Bulgarians submit to Constantinople, which regains Macedonia.

The Treaty of Bautzen ends a 15-year German-Polish war. Poland's Boleslav the Brave is given Lusatia as an imperial fief.

1019 Russia's Prince of Kiev Jaroslav the Wise begins a 35-year reign in which he will codify Russian law and build cities, churches, and schools.

1020 Norway's Olaf II gains recognition as king from Faroes, Orkney, and Shetland islanders.

Pisa annexes Corfu.

Bemberg Cathedral is consecrated by Pope Benedict VIII.

1021 Armenia is invaded by the Byzantine army of Basil II.

Epidemics of St. Vitus's dance sweep Europe. The disease is a chorea whose victims invoke the name of a Christian child martyr of the 3rd century.

1022 Byzantine forces in southern Italy are defeated by the Holy Roman Emperor Henry II.

The Synod of Pavia orders celibacy among the higher clergy.

The Japanese Buddhist Hōjō Temple is completed by the prime minister Michinaga Fujiwara, 57.

1024 The Holy Roman Emperor Henry II dies July 13 at age 51 after a 10-year reign. He is succeeded as king of the Germans and as Roman emperor by his 34-year-old son who will reign as Conrad II until 1039 and who founds the Franconian (or Salic) dynasty that will rule until 1125.

Sweden's first Christian king Olaf Skutkonung dies after a reign of 31 years, and the Goths and Swedes begin 110 years of religious wars.

1025 Poland's Boleslav the Brave makes himself king but soon dies at age 33, leaving a nation that is one of Europe's most powerful, extending from the Elbe to the Bug and from the Danube to the Baltic, with Russia as her vassal. Boleslav is succeeded by his son, who will reign until 1034 as Mieszko II, but other sons take parts of the country, and dynastic conflicts begin that will lose most of Boleslav's territorial gains to neighboring countries.

1026 King Canute fights off the kings of Norway and Sweden in their attempt to conquer Denmark. He begins a pilgrimage to Rome.

Solmization in music (do, re, mi, fa, sol, la . . .) is introduced by the Benedictine monk Guido d'Arezzo, 31.

1027 Normandy's Duke Richard the Good dies after a 31-year reign in which he has defeated English and Swedish forces and has brought Normandy to the height of her power. He is succeeded by his son, who will reign boldly but unscrupulously as Robert I (Robert le Diable) until 1035.

The Mayan Empire in the Western Hemisphere suffers an epidemic that weakens her people and begins her decline (*see* 731).

1028 King Canute conquers Norway. He will rule that country along with Denmark and England until his death in 1035.

The Byzantine emperor Constantine VIII dies at age 68 and is succeeded by his 48-year-old daughter Zoë. She marries the 60-year-old Romanus III Argyrolpolus and makes him coemperor.

Castile is conquered by Navarre's Sancho III (Sancho Garces el Mayor), who has also conquered Leon and proclaims himself "king of Spain."

Nonfiction *Eiga* is a Japanese history covering two centuries and 15 emperors from Uda to Horikawa, but it embellishes on true history.

1030 Norway's Olaf Haraldsson is defeated at the Battle of Stikelstad and is killed by King Canute.

The Byzantine emperor Romanus III is defeated in a battle with the Moslem emirs who have attacked Syria.

Canon of Medicine by the Arab physician Avicenna (Abu Sina) follows the thinking of Aristotle and of Galen, but his work is so well written and organized that it will be a major influence on medical thinking for centuries.

1031 France's Capetian king Robert the Pious dies July 10 at age 61 after a short war in which he has been defeated by his younger sons. He is succeeded by his 23-year-old son by Constance of Aquitaine who has ruled with his father since 1027 and who will reign until 1060 as Henri I.

The Omayyad caliph Hisham III dies after a 4-year reign, and his death ends the caliphate of Cordova that has ruled since 756.

1032 France's Henri I is helped by the duke of Normandy Robert II to defeat his mother Constance and his younger brother Robert and to end civil war in France.

Burgundy's Rudolph III dies after a 39-year reign and his kingdom is inherited by the Holy Roman Emperor Conrad II, who unites it with the empire.

1033 Poland's Mieszko II is defeated by German and Russian forces 1 year after the division of his realm with two relatives by order of the emperor Conrad II.

Castile regains her independence from Navarre.

1034 The Byzantine empress Zoë poisons her husband Romanus III and marries the epileptic weakling Michael IV Paphlagonian with whom she will reign until 1041.

Poland's Mieszko II dies and his death begins a 6-year period of dynastic warfare and insurrection during which peasants will rise against landlords, churches will be burned, and clergymen will be massacred.

Silesia is overrun by Bretislav the Restorer, who will rule Bohemia and Moravia until 1055 and will for a period rule Poland as well.

Scotland's Malcolm II dies and is succeeded by his grandson Duncan, who will reign for 6 years.

1035 Castile's Sancho the Great (Sancho III of Navarre) dies at age 65 after ruling Navarre for 35 years, Castile for 8. The kingdom of Sancho Garces el Mayor is divided among his four sons, and he is succeeded in Castile by his second son who will reign until 1065 as Ferdinand I.

King Canute dies at Shaftesbury November 12 at age 39. His four sons are unable to control England, and Norway breaks away from Denmark.

1036 The Japanese emperor Goichijo dies at age 28 after a 20-year reign and is succeeded by his 27-year-old brother who will reign until 1045 as the emperor Gosuzaku.

Modern musical notation is pioneered by Guido d'Arezzo, who also invents the "great scale," or gamut, the hexachord, and hexachord solmization (*see* 1026).

1037 Castile's Ferdinand I conquers the Spanish kingdom of Leon and makes himself king.

The *Constitutio de Feudis*, issued by the Holy Roman Emperor Conrad II, makes Italian fiefs of small landholders hereditary.

1038 Hungary's Stephen I dies at age 61 after a 40-year reign. He is succeeded by his 27-year-old nephew Peter Orseolo whose father is doge of Venice (but *see* 1041).

1039 The Holy Roman Emperor Conrad II dies at Utrecht June 4 at age 49 and is buried in the cathedral he has started at Spires. Conrad's 21-year-old son Henry succeeds as German king.

The Welsh prince Gruffydd of Gwynedd and Powys defeats English forces.

Ergotism breaks out in parts of France (*see* 943; 1089).

1040 Scotland's Duncan Canmore is slain by Macbeth (or Maelbaethe), Mormaor of Moray, who seizes Duncan's kingdom and begins a reign of 17 years (*see* 1054).

England's Harold Harefoot dies, and his half-brother Hardicanute arrives from Denmark with a large fleet. He is crowned king in June to begin a 2-year reign that will antagonize his English subjects.

Lady Godiva rides naked through the streets of Coventry to persuade her husband Leofric, earl of Mercia, to remit the heavy taxes that oppress the citizens (year approximate). The earl has said that he would grant his wife's request if she would ride naked through the streets, Lady Godiva (Godgifu) has issued a proclamation asking all citizens to remain indoors with their windows shut, she has only her long hair to cover her on the ride, her husband keeps his word and abolishes the taxes, but a local tailor is reputedly struck blind because he peeped.

Increased planting of oats in the three-crop system of the past three centuries has led to an expanded use of horses in Europe and thus to increased trade, larger towns, and more people who do not raise their own food.

The Weihenstepan brewery is founded in Freising near Munich.

1041 Hungary's Peter Orseolo is driven out by the usurper Samuel Aba, brother-in-law of his late uncle Stephen, and takes refuge with the German king Henry.

Bohemia's Bretislav is defeated by the German king Henry and is forced to pay homage.

Northumberland's Eardwulf is murdered by the Danish husband of his niece, who makes himself earl of Northumberland and begins a 14-year rule as Siward the Strong.

The Byzantine emperor Michael IV Paphlagonian dies in the autumn and is succeeded by his nephew who will reign for 4 months as Michael V Kalaphates (the caulker).

Movable type for printing will be used in the next 8 years by the Chinese printer Pi Sheng, who will use hundreds of clay blocks bearing Chinese ideograms (*see* 1381).

The Bayeux tapestry recorded the Norman conquest of England, a triumph of Norsemen over Saxons.

1042 England's Hardicanute dies at age 23, and the 42-year-old son of the late Ethelred the Unready is recognized as king. He will reign until 1066 as Edward the Confessor, last of the Anglo-Saxon kings.

The German king Henry receives the homage of Burgundy.

The Byzantine emperor Michael V Kalaphates shuts the empress Zoë up in a cloister, but the Constantinople nobility rises against him, locks him up in a monastery, and releases Zoë. She marries the scholarly 42-year-old Constantine IX Monomachus with whom she will reign until 1055.

The Seljuk Turks rise against their Byzantine overlords.

1043 England's Edward the Confessor is crowned at Easter. He has been helped to gain the throne by the powerful earl of Wessex, Godwin whose daughter Edith will be married to the king in 1045.

The German king Henry III moves against Hungary's Samuel Aba, who has attacked eastern Bavaria.

1044 Hungary's Peter Orseolo is restored by the German king Henry III, who brings Hungary under German control after gaining a great victory in July at Menfo (but *see* 1047).

The kingdom of Pagan, which will later become Burma, is founded in Southeast Asia. The Mons and the Burmese end their rivalry and join together after generations of vying for control of the region.

Korea completes a defense system that consists largely of a great wall across the northern part of the peninsula to keep out Mongol and Turkish raiders.

1045 The Japanese emperor Gozaku dies at age 36 after a 9-year reign and is succeeded by his 16-year-old son who will reign until 1069 as the emperor Goreizei.

1046 The German king is crowned Holy Roman Emperor Henry III Christmas Day at Rome by the bishop of Bemberg who he has installed as Pope Clement II.

1047 Magnus I dies after 12 years as king of Norway and 5 as king of Denmark. He is succeeded in Norway by Harald Haardraade, 32, who will reign until 1066 as Harald III, and he is succeeded in Denmark by Sweyn Estrithson, grandson of Sweyn Forkbeard, who will reign until 1075 as Sweyn II but who will be at war with Norway's Harald III until 1064.

The duchies of Carinthia, Bavaria, and Swabia are restored by the Holy Roman Emperor Henry III.

Hungary's Peter Orseolo is overthrown by his cousin Andras, who will reign until 1060 as Andras I.

1050 The Byzantine empress Zoë dies at age 70, and her older sister Theodora, who has shared the throne since 1042, is left to rule with Constantine IX. He has spent huge sums of money on luxuries and on public buildings, but his profligacy has weakened the empire.

Oslo is founded by Norway's Harald III who has visited Novgorod, Kiev, and Constantinople.

1052 Sardinia is conquered by Pisa from the Arabs, who have held the island since 720.

1053 The Norman Empire in southern Italy is founded by the Norseman Robert Guiscard, 38, who takes Benevento from the Byzantines.

England's earl of Wessex dies and is succeeded by his 31-year-old son who becomes chief minister to his brother-in-law Edward the Confessor.

The Danegeld is abolished in England after 53 years.

1054 Scotland's Macbeth is defeated at Dunsinane by Malcolm Canmore, whose father Duncan was slain by Macbeth in 1040. Malcolm is aided by the Dane Siward, earl of Northumberland, who has invaded Scotland to support his kinsman (*see* 1057).

Normandy is invaded by France's Henri I, who is defeated at Mortemer.

The Eastern (Orthodox) and Western (Roman) Churches break irreparably apart as Pope Leo IX (the antipope Bruno) excommunicates Michael Cerularius and his followers. Leo declared war last year against the Normans in southern Italy, but his army of Italian and German volunteers was defeated at Astagnum near Civitella. He was captured, and he dies April 19 at age 51.

A minor star in the constellation Taurus explodes July 5 in a supernova that is visible by daylight for 23 days and remains visible at night for another 633 days, an event recorded by pictographs in China and in the Western Hemisphere. The irregular gas cloud created by the supernova will be called by astronomers the crab nebula.

1055 Northumberland's Siward the Strong dies after having helped to rout Scotland's Macbeth and to make Malcolm III king of Cumbria. He is succeeded by Tostig, a son of the late Godwin of Wessex and a brother-in-law of Edward the Confessor.

The Byzantine emperor Constantine IX dies at age 55, leaving his sister-in-law Theodora to rule alone.

1056 The Holy Roman Emperor Henry III dies October 5 at age 38 and is succeeded as German king by his 5-year-old son, who will reign as Henry IV until 1106, with his mother Agnes as regent until 1065.

The Byzantine empress Theodora dies at age 76 to end the Macedonian dynasty that has ruled the empire since Justinian the Great took power in 527. Theodora's successor Michael VI (Stratioticus) will be overthrown early next year by a revolt of the feudal barons of Anatolia.

1057 The Comnenus dynasty that will rule the Byzantine Empire until 1185 is founded by Isaac I Comnenus, a military leader who is proclaimed emperor by the insurgents who have overthrown Michael VI. The new emperor eliminates many sinecures and reforms Byzantine finances.

Macbeth is murdered by Malcolm Canmore and is succeeded by his stepson Lulach (*see* 1054; 1058).

1058 Scotland's Lulach is slain by Malcolm Canmore who makes himself king of Scotland to begin a 35-year reign as Malcolm III MacDuncan.

Geoffrey of Anjou is defeated by William of Normandy at the Battle of Varaville.

Poland's Grand Duke Casimir I dies at age 43 after having regained much of Poland's lost territory with the help of the late Henry III and restoring Christianity. Casimir is succeeded by his 19-year-old son who will rule until 1079 as Boleslav II (the Bold).

1059 The Byzantine emperor Isaac I Comnenus abdicates in favor of a high financial officer who begins an 8-year reign as Constantine X (Dukas). The new emperor will neglect and antagonize the army by giving more authority to the civil service, the church, and the scholars.

Papal election by cardinals only is decreed by the new pope Nicholas II.

1060 France's Henri I dies August 4 at age 52 and is succeeded by his 8-year-old son who will reign until 1108 as Philip I.

Hungary's Andras I is driven from the throne by his brother and dies after a 14-year reign in which he has gained imperial recognition of Hungarian independence. The brother will reign until 1063 as Bela I.

West Africa is conquered from the kingdom of Ghana by Arabs who are supported by Berbers greedy for the salt mines of Ankar. Founded in the 4th century, the kingdom of Ghana has ruled from near the Atlantic Coast almost to Timbuctu.

Byzantine mosaic *Christ as Ruler of the World* at Daphni, Greece.

1061 Scotland's Malcolm III MacDuncan invades Northumbria.

Bohemia's Spytihnev dies after an uneventful 6-year reign and is succeeded by Vratislav II, who will reign until 1092.

1062 The archbishop of Cologne Anno II seizes the 11-year-old German king Henry IV in the coup d'etat of Kaiserswerth. Henry is forced to yield control to Anno and to the archbishop of Bremen Adalbert.

Marrakech is founded by sultans of the Almoravide dynasty who start a tent settlement on the West Tensift River, northwest of the High Atlas range.

1063 Harold of Wessex subdues Wales with help from his brother Tostig of Northumbria.

1064 Belgrade is taken from the Byzantines by Hungarian forces led by the new king Solomon.

Armenia is conquered by the Seljuk Turks.

"Regulative granaries" are established by Chinese emperor Ying-tsung to buy up surplus grain when harvests are good, to release stocks in times of shortage when prices are too high for ordinary citizens, and thus to discourage speculation (*see* 1006); but a large investment by the state is required to make the new system work.

1065 Castile's Ferdinand I dies after a 32-year reign in which he has made himself king of Leon by defeating his brother-in-law Bermudo II and has begun the reconquest of Spain from the Moors. Fernando el Magno is succeeded by his son who will reign until 1072 as Sancho II (el Fuerte).

The University of Parma has its beginnings.

Westminster Abbey is consecrated after 13 years of construction.

1066 The Battle of Hastings October 14 seals the Norman conquest of England by Norsemen under William, 39-year-old duke of Normandy who will be called William the Conqueror and who will rule England as William I until his death in 1087. Edward the Confessor has died January 5 and has been succeeded by Harold of Wessex, who secured his election as king January 6 and has ruled as Harold II.

Norway's Harald III Haardraade has been invited by Tostig of Northumbria to aid in the conquest of England from Harold II. He has sailed with a large fleet, but he has been killed September 25 at the Battle of Stamford Bridge. William the Conqueror has landed September 28 at Pevensey, Harold II is killed in the Battle of Hastings, and William is crowned December 25.

A comet appears in the skies that will later be called "Halley's Comet" (*see* 1705).

1066 (cont.) No written account of the Battle of Hastings will appear until that of the chronicler Guillaume de Poitiers, whose *Gesta Willelmi* will appear late in the century, but events of the savage battle will be depicted in the Bayeux Tapestry.

Many French words will be introduced into the language of England by the Normans from across the Channel (*see* 1100).

The French words *boeuf, mouton, veau, porc,* and *poularde* introduced by the Normans (above), will be the basis of the English words "beef," "mutton," "veal," "pork," and "poultry."

1067 Scotland's Malcolm III MacDuncan marries Margaret, 22-year-old sister of the Saxon Edgar the Aetheling, and she brings the Black Rood to Scotland, thus beginning the country's transition from Celtic culture and Columban religious rites to the Anglicized feudal system and Roman Catholic ritual.

Kiev is taken by Poland's Boleslav II.

The Byzantine emperor Constantine X Dukas dies at age 60, and his widow Eudoxia Macrembolitissa marries a general who will reign jointly with her until 1071 as Romanus IV Diogenes.

The world's first leprosarium is founded by the Castilian Ruy Diaz de Bivar, a 27-year-old soldier who is known as El Cid.

Export of sulfur or saltpeter is prohibited by a Chinese edict aimed at keeping gunpowder a Chinese monopoly (*see* 222; 1234).

1068 Saxon nationalists in the north and west of England rise to challenge William the Conqueror and his Norman barons.

The Chinese Sung emperor Shen Tsung begins a 17-year reign that will see radical reforms put through over bitter opposition from conservatives.

The Japanese emperor Goreizei dies at age 39 after a 23-year reign and is succeeded by his 34-year-old brother Gosanjo, who will reign until 1072. Goreizei had married a daughter of Yorimichi Fujiwara, son of the late strongman Michinagi Fujiwara, but she has not borne a child and has thus frustrated her father's ambition to be the grandfather of an emperor.

1069 England's William I puts down a great rising of Saxons in the north who have won Danish support. The Normans confiscate Saxon lands and establish their feudal superiority in the "harrying of the north" that devastates and depopulates a strip of territory from York to Durham.

The Chinese prime minister Wang An-Shih, 48, reforms his government by cutting the budget 40 percent and raising salaries to make it possible for ordinary government officials to afford to be honest.

Wang An-Shih (above) empowers China's chief transport officer to accept taxes in cash or in kind in order to avoid excessive transport costs and to control prices.

Wang An-Shih (above) begins a radical program to reform Chinese agriculture after finding the nation's granaries stocked with emergency stocks of relief grain valued at 15 million strings of cash. He offers poor farmers loans at 2 percent interest per month in cash or grain to free them from usurers and monopolists who charge higher rates. He gives his chief transport officer power to sell from state granaries when prices are high and to buy when prices are low.

1070 The order of the Knights of St. John is founded at Jerusalem by merchants from Amalfi to care for the hospital of St. John. The Hospitalers will be militarized in 60 years along lines that will be established by the Knights Templar in 1120 (*see* 1113).

Roquefort cheese is discovered in France.

1071 The Battle of Manzikert (Malaz Kard) virtually ends Byzantine power in Asia Minor. The emperor Romanus IV Diogenes has led a Christian army of 60,000 to recover some fortresses from the Seljuk Turks in the spring, but he has encountered a 100,000-man army commanded by the sultan Alp Arslan. Byzantine noblemen, including Andronicus Dukas, desert Romanus, who falls into enemy hands. He gains release, but when he tries to regain his throne, his enemies put out his eyes, and he soon dies. The bureaucrats at Constantinople elevate the son of the late Constantine X to the throne, and he begins a 7-year reign as Michael VII Parapinakes, with the scholar Michael Psellus as his chief adviser.

Byzantine rule in Italy ends as the Norman Robert Guiscard takes Bari.

Venice completes the Cathedral of San Marco after 95 years of construction on the Piazza San Marco (the chapel will be consecrated in 1094). An annex to the Doge's Palace, the cathedral will be used for the civil and religious ceremonies that will be important to the political life of the republic.

A two-pronged fork is introduced to Venice by a Greek princess who marries the doge. Rich Venetians adopt a new fashion in eating (*see* 1518; 1570).

1072 Castile's Sancho el Fuerte is assassinated at the siege of Zamora while warring with Sancho IV of Navarre. He is succeeded by his brother, who begins a 37-year reign as Alfonso VI and who will resume the Christian reconquest of Castile with help from El Cid (Ruy Diaz de Bivar).

The Norman Robert Guiscard takes Palermo and begins to conquer all of Sicily.

The Japanese emperor Gosanjo abdicates at age 38 (he is ill and will die next year). He is succeeded by his son Shirakawa, 19, who will reign until 1086.

Parma Cathedral is completed after 16 years of construction.

1073 Pope Alexander II dies after a 12-year papacy in which the archdeacon Hildebrand, now 50, has played a major role. Hildebrand is elected to succeed

Alexander and will hold the chair until his death in 1086, attacking simony, upholding celibacy among the clergy, and fighting for papal omnipotence.

A reorganization of the English Church makes York subordinate to Canterbury.

1074 The Norman Robert Guiscard is excommunicated by Pope Gregory VII (Hildebrand) who also excommunicates all married priests.

The Peace of Gerstungen ends conflicts between the Saxons and Henry IV. Hungary's Solomon is defeated by his cousin who succeeds him and begins a brief reign as Geza I.

1075 The Synod of Rome called by Pope Gregory VII passes strict decrees against simony (purchase or sale of church offices; the name is derived from that of Simon Magus, a Samaritan sorcerer mentioned in the Bible). A 47-year struggle against the papacy begins as German bishops oppose Hildebrand's confirmation as pope and a papal letter of rebuke is ignored by Henry VI.

Syria and Palestine are subdued by the Seljuk Turk Malik Shah.

Acoma (the Sky City) in the Western Hemisphere is founded by tribespeople who have moved 3 miles from the "Enchanted Mesa" following an earthquake that has destroyed trails to the top of the mesa and has left those at the top to starve to death. Acoma will grow to have a population of 5,000 and will be the oldest continuously inhabited town in the northern continent of the hemisphere.

1076 The Synod of Worms is called by Henry IV under pressure from the German bishops, who repudiate their allegiance to Pope Gregory VII and declare him deposed. Henry demands Gregory's abdication and is supported by north Italian bishops at Piacenza. But Gregory assembles a Lenten Synod at Rome, suspends and excommunicates the rebellious German and Lombard prelates, deposes and excommunicates Henry, and creates political and ecclesiastical chaos in the German states and Lombardy. The Diet of Tribur in October orders Henry to humble himself, to stand trial, and to clear himself of Gregory's charges before February 22, 1077.

The duke of Lower Lorraine is assassinated.

The Ghana capital Kumbi is plundered by the Almoravids, who are conquering West Africa. Ghana will never recover, and her decline will be hastened by the growing barrenness of the region as a result of overgrazing.

1077 The penance at Canossa January 21 wins absolution for Henry IV, but civil war begins in the German states. The king presents himself as a penitent at Canossa after a midwinter dash across the Alps with his wife Bertha to avoid public trial at home, but while Hildebrand grudgingly accepts Henry's promises and his solemn oaths of contrition, the German nobility elects Rudolf of Swabia as anti-king with approval of the pope's legates.

The first English Cluniac monastery opens at Lewes.

Hungary's Geza I dies after a 3-year reign and is succeeded by the 37-year-old son of the late Bela I, who will reign until 1095. Ladislas I will support the pope in his conflicts with Henry IV (above), and he will restore order and prosperity at home in the greatest reign since that of Stephen I.

1078 England's William I is defeated in battle by France's Philip I, who supports William's son Robert Curthose against Anglo-Norman pressure.

The Byzantine emperor Michael VII abdicates and is succeeded by a soldier chosen by the Asiatic troops. The new emperor begins a 3-year reign as Nicephorus III Botaniates, and while some of the army mutinies the insurrections are put down by General Alexius Comnenus.

1079 The bishop of Cracow excommunicates Poland's Boleslav II (the Bold) after denouncing his excesses. Bishop Stanislas joins a conspiracy of nobles against the king. Boleslav has the 49-year-old prelate murdered while he is saying mass in his cathedral, Pope Gregory VII excommunicates Boleslav, and Polish rebels chase him out of the country. He flees with his son to Hungary, where he will die in 2 years at age 42, and is succeeded by his lazy brother who will reign until 1102 as Ladislas I Hermann.

Bishop Stanislas (above) will be canonized in 1253 and will be the patron saint of Poland.

Newcastle-on-Tyne is founded in England by William the Conqueror to resist the incursions of Scotland's Malcolm III MacDuncan (see coal, 1233).

1080 Rudolf of Swabia is defeated and killed to end civil war in the German states. Henry IV has steadily gained strength, and while he is once again deposed and excommunicated by Pope Gregory, the pope himself is deposed by a synod of German and Lombard prelates who attempt to install a new pope.

Medical research is advanced at the Benedictine school associated with the monastery established at Monte Cassino in 529. Arabian, Jewish, and Greco-Roman medical works are translated into Latin by Constantine the African, a physician who has studied medicine and magic at Babylon and who is now disguised as a monk. His translations of Galen and Avicenna help to emancipate medicine from the religious bonds that have held it.

Greek, Latin, Jewish, and Arabic medical teachings are employed at Salerno, some 125 miles from Monte Cassino (above), where neighboring Benedictine monasteries support a medical school whose teachers are mostly clerics but include some women physicians. Christian dogma is not strictly observed, pigs are dissected, Arabic dietetic ideas are followed,

1080 (cont.) bleeding is regarded as a panacea, but the first medieval pharmacopoeia is begun (*see* 1231).

1081 The Byzantine emperor Nicephorus III abdicates under pressure from his 33-year-old general Alexius Comnenus, who assumes the throne to begin a 37-year reign as Alexius I Comnenus. He signs a commercial treaty with Venice.

The Norman Robert Guiscard invades the Balkans, landing in Epirus and laying siege to the Byzantine city of Durazzo.

The German king Henry IV invades Italy and places Matilda, marchioness of Tuscany, under the imperial ban for supporting Pope Gregory VII. Henry accepts the Lombard crown at Pavia and forces a council to recognize the archbishop of Ravenna as Pope Clement III.

1082 The German king Henry IV lays siege to Rome and finally gains entrance after two futile attempts. He fails in his efforts at reconciliation with Pope Gregory VII, who calls on the Norman Robert Guiscard to support him, and he makes a treaty with the Romans, who agree to call a synod that will rule on the dispute between crown and papacy.

Robert Guiscard (above) defeats the Byzantine forces of Alexius I Comnenus and takes Durazzo, occupying Corfu as well.

1083 A synod meets at Rome to resolve the quarrel between Pope Gregory VII and the German king Henry, but the synod has secretly bound itself either to crown Henry emperor or to select a new pope.

1084 The Synod of Rome declares Pope Gregory deposed in March and recognizes the antipope Clement, who crowns Henry March 31. The emperor attacks fortresses still in Gregory's hands but retreats back across the Alps as Norman forces under Robert Guiscard advance from the south. The Normans sack Rome, Pope Gregory is unable to remain in the ravaged city, and his supporters take him to Salerno where he will die next spring.

Defensio Henrici IV by Peter Crassus (who teaches Roman law at Ravenna) takes the position that neither the pope nor Henry's rebellious subjects have any more right to interfere with the emperor's hereditary territorial possessions than they have to take away any person's private property.

1085 Toledo is taken by Castile's Alfonso VI, and the Arab center of science falls into Christian hands.

The "Peace of God" is extended over the entire Holy Roman Empire by Henry IV as Pope Gregory VII dies May 25 at Salerno.

The Norman Robert Guiscard dies July 15 at age 60 of fever after regaining Corfu and Kephalonia, which his son Bohemund had lost. The duke is succeeded by his 54-year-old brother Roger Guiscard who has conquered Sicily and who will rule until 1101.

1086 The Oath of Salisbury makes English vassals responsible directly to the crown. Some 170 great tenants-in-chief and numerous lesser tenants have emerged to replace England's earls, and the oath is exacted from all such vassals, prohibiting them from making private wars.

Castile's Alfonso VI is defeated at Zallaka by a Moslem army from Africa under Yusuf ibn Tashfin, leader of the fanatic Berber sect (the Almoravids) that has gained dominance in North Africa.

The Japanese emperor Shirakawa abdicates at age 33 and makes his 7-year-old son Horikawa emperor. Japan's emperor is not permitted to have private property, and Shirakawa's move begins a long era of voluntary abdications in which the ex-emperor will retain power.

The magnetic compass is pioneered by Chinese waterworks director Shen Kua, who writes that magicians can find directions by rubbing a needle on a lodestone and hanging the magnetized needle by a thread. The needle, he says, will usually point south but sometimes will point north.

The Domesday Book compiled on orders from England's William I lists the assets of landowners to provide a basis for taxation and administration. The royal commissioners oblige the landowners to give information under oath as to the size of every piece of land, its resources, and its ownership—past and present.

The Domesday Book (above) lists more than 25,000 slaves and 110,000 villeins (serfs) among the properties and assets of English landowners.

The Domesday Book (above) lists some 5,000 English flour mills—one for every 400 inhabitants.

1087 William the Conqueror invades the French Vexin to retaliate for raids on his territory. He sacks and burns the town of Mantes, but when he rides out to view the ruins, his horse plunges on the burning cinders. William sustains internal injuries, he is carried in great pain to Rouen, and he dies there September 9 at age 59 or 60, leaving his third son, William Rufus, 31, to rule England until 1100 and his eldest son, Robert Curthose, 33, to succeed him as duke of Normandy until 1106.

The Byzantine emperor Alexius I Comnenus is defeated with a large army at the Battle of Drystra by heretic Bogomils in Thrace and Bulgaria who have revolted against Constantinople.

Control of the western Mediterranean is wrested from the Arabs by Genoa and Pisa, whose forces capture Mahdiyah in Africa.

1089 Ergotism strikes a French village, whose inhabitants run through the streets in fits of madness (*see* 1039; 1581).

1091 The Treaty of Caen ends hostilities between England's William II and Normandy's Robert Curthose.

Sicily is freed of the last of the Moslems who have held the island for 130 years. Noto yields to Roger in February, and the count completes his conquest.

1092 Cumberland is conquered by England's William II.

✗ Bohemia's Vratislav II dies after a 31-year reign, but the crown given him by Henry IV in 1086 is not inherited by his successor who will rule until 1110 as Bretislav II.

1093 Scotland's Malcolm III MacDuncan and his eldest son Edward are entrapped and killed November 13 at a place that will be called Malcolm's Cross. Malcolm has been laying siege to Alnwick in an invasion of England, his wife Margaret dies 4 days later, and he is succeeded by his brother Donald Bane who will reign until 1097.

1094 Valencia falls to El Cid June 15 after a siege of 9 months by an army of 7,000 men, most of them Moslems. El Cid violates all the conditions of surrender. He has the cadi ibn Djahhaff burned alive, he slaughters many of the citizens, and he rules a kingdom that extends over nearly all of Valencia and Murcia.

1095 Pope Urban II preaches a Crusade against the infidel and gains support from Peter the Hermit and others for his holy war. A learned French nobleman, the pope points out that vast areas of land are available to knights (many of whom are landless younger sons) who will join the crusade.

Pope Urban II receives an appeal from the Byzantine emperor Alexius Comnenus for aid against the Seljuk Turks. He proclaims the Crusade at the Synod of Clermont, and he excommunicates France's Philip I for adultery.

✗ Hungary's Ladislas I conquers Croatia and Dalmatia, where he introduces Catholicism, founds the bishopric of Zagreb (Agram), and persecutes the heathen, but he dies suddenly July 29 at age 55 just as he is about to join the Crusade (above). Ladislas is succeeded by his nephew Coloman, son of his late brother Geza, who will reign until 1116.

1096 The First Crusade raises more than 30,000 men and converges on Constantinople in three groups as Norman-French barons rush to take the cross. Godfrey of Bouillon and his brother Baldwin lead an army from Lorraine via Hungary, Count Raymond of Toulouse and the papal legate Adhemar of Puy lead an army from Provence via Illyria, and Bohemund of Otranto leads an army from Normandy via Durazzo, traveling both by sea and land. A leading figure is the 18-year-old Norman knight Tancred, a nephew of Sicily's Roger Guiscard.

✗ The Byzantine emperor Alexius Comnenus provides food and escort for the Crusaders. He exacts an oath of fealty from the leaders in an effort to protect his title to any recovered "lost provinces" of the Greek Empire, but Count Raymond of Toulouse refuses to take any such oath.

Anti-Semitic outbreaks occur in France as the Crusade against the infidel empties whole villages.

1097 The Battle of Nicaea ends in defeat for a Moslem army by a combined force of Crusaders and Byzantine Greeks who take the Seljuk Turks' capital. The French knight Walter the Penniless (*Gautier sans avoir*) is killed after having led hordes through Europe and Asia in what will be called the Peasants' Crusade.

Scotland's Edgar is proclaimed king and begins a 10-year reign. Son of the late Malcolm III MacDuncan, Edgar has a 47-year-old uncle, also named Edgar, who leads an expedition to Scotland but who will soon join the First Crusade (above).

Half the knights of France will set off in the next 30 years either for the Levant or for Islamic lands in northern Spain, but the First Crusade has been inspired as much by population pressures (a product of the new agriculture) as by religious zeal or desire for plunder.

1098 Antioch falls after a 9-month siege by Bohemund of Otranto who has lost 5,000 of his 7,000 horses to hunger and disease. So many of his men have sickened and died so quickly that it has not been possible to bury all the corpses, and there has been a falling out between Norman and Provençal Crusaders.

The Orkneys, the Hebrides, and the Isle of Man are seized by Norway's Magnus III.

France's Philip I makes his 17-year-old son Louis coregent and charges him with resisting the intermittent attacks by England's William II Rufus and Normandy's William III.

∞ The Cistercian order of monks has its beginnings in the monastery of Cîteaux founded by French ecclesiastic Robert de Molesmes, 69, and English ecclesiastic Stephen Harding, 50.

1099 Jerusalem falls to the Crusaders July 15 after a siege of just over 1 month. The streets of the city run with blood as the Crusaders slaughter 40,000 and set fire to mosques and synagogues, and the First Crusade comes to an end.

A kingdom of Jerusalem is established under the Norman Godfrey of Bouillon who is elected king and who assumes the title Defender of the Holy Sepulcher. He defeats an Egyptian force at Askalon August 12, but disease and starvation have reduced the Crusaders to a force of 60,000, down from an original strength of 300,000, and most of the survivors head for home.

El Cid dies in July at age 59 after being defeated by the Almoravids at Cuenca. His widow will hold Valencia against the Moors until 1102.

Sugar is planted in canefields planted by the Crusaders in the Holy Land (*see* 300 B.C.; A.D. 1104).

1100 Jerusalem's Godfrey of Bouillon dies in July at age 39 after successful forays against the Seljuk Turks that have taken him as far as Damascus. He is suc-

1100 (cont.) ceeded by his older brother Baldwin, count of Flanders, who will rule until 1118 with help from Tancred, the Sicilian Norman who is now prince of Galilee.

England's William II Rufus dies August 2 at age 44 after being struck by an arrow while hunting in the New Forest. Sir Walter Tyrel is accused of having shot the arrow but flees the country to avoid a trial and then protests his innocence (Ralph of Aix is also accused). Also in the royal hunting train is William's 32-year-old brother who assumes the throne as Henry I to begin a 35-year reign.

Middle English begins to supersede Old English, and the dialect of the Ile-de-France begins to prevail over other French dialects.

12th CENTURY

1101 England is invaded by Normandy's Robert Curthose, who has returned from the First Crusade and who tries to take the English throne from his younger brother Henry. He is bought off in the Treaty of Alton.

Sicily's Roger I Guiscard dies June 22 at age 70 and is succeeded by his 8-year-old son who will reign as Roger II beginning in 1112.

China's Sung emperor Hui Tsung ascends the throne at age 19 to begin a 24-year reign.

China's Imperial Academy of Painting will be founded by Hui Tsung (above), who is himself an able painter.

Gothic architecture will appear in Europe beginning in this century (*see* 1136; 1184; 1550; Chartres, 1260).

The Castle Chillon is built near Geneva.

Florence's baptistry is erected.

1102 Poland's Ladislas I Hermann resigns the royal title after a 23-year reign in an effort to secure peace by supporting the Holy Roman Emperor Henry IV. He is succeeded by his 16-year-old son who gains the throne after a violent struggle with another son and who will reign until 1138 as Boleslav III (Wrymouth).

Hungarian conquest of Dalmatia from the Venetians is completed by Coloman I.

1103 Ireland is invaded by Norway's Magnus III who is killed in battle.

1104 Acre surrenders to Jerusalem's Baldwin I, a Norman army is badly beaten on the River Balikh near Rakka while trying to take Harran, but Byblus falls to Raymond of Toulouse who lays siege to Tripoli.

Bohemund of Otranto appears at Epirus with a huge army that he has raised in Italy to challenge the Byzantine emperor Alexius Comnenus, who conquers the towns of Cilicia.

Iceland's Mount Hekla volcano erupts and devastates farms for 45 miles around. The volcano will have 14 eruptions in the next 850 years (*see* 1154).

Sugar serves as an emergency ration for Crusaders laying siege to Acre (above) (*see* 1099; 1148).

1105 The Holy Roman Emperor Henry IV is captured by his 24-year-old son Henry, who last year announced that he owed no allegiance to his excommunicated father and who has been supported by the emperor's enemies, especially in Saxony and Thuringia. The emperor is compelled to abdicate in December by a diet at Mainz, but the conditions of his abdication are violated, and he is held prisoner at Ingelheim.

Angoulême Cathedral is erected.

1106 Henry IV escapes his captors at Ingelheim, enters into negotiations at Cologne with English, French, and Danish supporters, begins to collect an army to oppose his treacherous son, but dies August 7 at age 54. His son Henry has received homage from some princes at Mainz in January, and he begins a 19-year reign as Henry V, last of the Salic emperors (he will be crowned in 1111) who have ruled since 1024.

The Battle of Tinchebrai September 28 ends in defeat for Normandy's Robert Curthose at the hands of England's Henry I who has crossed the Channel and who takes his brother home in chains. Robert will be imprisoned first in the 28-year-old Tower of London, later in the castles of Devizes and Cardiff, and will remain a prisoner until his death early in 1134.

1107 Scotland's Edgar dies after a 10-year reign. His 29-year-old brother succeeds him to begin a 17-year reign as Alexander I during which he will put down an insurrection of northern clans.

The Sicilian Norman Tancred recovers the Cilician towns conquered by Alexius Comnenus 3 years ago.

Crusaders built imposing castles in the Holy Land as they advanced against the Saracen "infidels."

1107 (cont.) The Japanese emperor Horikawa dies at age 28 after a 21-year reign. He is succeeded by his 4-year-old son Toba who will reign until 1123, but his father Shirakawa remains the country's strongman (*see* 1118).

1108 France's Philip I dies at the end of July at age 56 after a reign of nearly 48 years. He is succeeded by his 27-year-old son, who will reign as Louis VI until 1137, but the new king faces insurrections from feudal brigands and rebellious barons, and it will take him 24 years to root out the robber barons who depend for their livelihood on plundering travelers en route to and from Paris.

The Byzantine emperor Alexius Comnenus defeats Bohemund of Otranto at Durazzo and makes him a vassal.

1109 Poland's Boleslav III defeats the Pomeranians at the Battle of Naklo and defeats the German king Henry V at the Battle of Hundsfeld near Breslau.

France's Louis VI goes to war with England.

1110 The dukedom of Bohemia is secured for Ladislas I following the death of Bretislav II. Ladislas is helped by the German king Henry V and will rule until 1125.

Henry V invades Italy with a large army and concludes an agreement with Pope Paschal II at Sutri. Henry renounces the right of investiture, and the pope promises to crown him emperor and to restore to the empire all lands given by kings or emperors to the German church since the time of Charlemagne.

An English miracle play presented at Dunstable is the earliest of positive record. Priests have celebrated great ecclesiastical festivals since the 9th century with presentations of the Easter story, but the new miracle plays are based on legends of the saints.

1111 Henry V presents himself at St. Peter's February 12 for his coronation, but when Pope Paschal II reads the treaty terms commanding the clergy to restore the fiefs of the crown to Henry, there is a storm of indignation. The pope thereupon refuses to crown the king, Henry refuses to renounce the right of investiture, and he leaves Rome, taking the pope with him. When Paschal is unable to obtain help, he confirm's Henry's right of investiture and crowns him emperor.

1112 The Portuguese monarchy and the Burgundian dynasty that will control the monarchy until 1385 are founded on the death of Henry of Burgundy, count of Portugal. Henry's 3-year-old son succeeds him, with the boy's mother Teresa as regent, but the new king will assume authority in 1128 and will reign until 1185 as Afonso Henriques.

The Holy Roman Emperor Henry V is excommunicated by the Synod of Vienna, but an uprising led by Lothair, duke of Saxony, is easily quelled.

1113 The Balearic Islands (Majorca, Minorca, Ibiza, and others) are conquered by Pisa.

The great-grandson of Vladimir the Great becomes grand duke of Kiev at age 60 and begins a 12-year reign in which he will campaign against the Cumans on the steppes. Vladimir Monomakh will also write works depicting conditions of Russian life.

Novgorod's Church of St. Nicholas pioneers the onion-domed style of Greek Orthodox church architecture.

1116 Hungary's Coloman I dies at age 44 and is succeeded by Stephen II who will reign until 1131.

1118 The Byzantine emperor Alexius I Comnenus dies at age 70 after having the heretic Bogomilian leader Basilius burned to death. He is succeeded after a 37-year reign by his 30-year-old son who will reign until 1143 as John II Comnenus.

Japan's 15-year-old emperor Toba takes as his wife the pretty 17-year-old mistress of his grandfather, the ex-emperor Shirakawa. Shoshi is a daughter of Kimizane Fujiwara and is pregnant with Shirakawa's son Sutoku (*see* 1123).

1119 Charles le Bon becomes count of Flanders at age 36. A son of Denmark's late Canute IV and a grandson of Robert I the Frisian, Charles tries to promote the welfare of the Flemish and will rule until 1127.

England's Henry I defeats his Norman foes in a skirmish at Bremule. He dissuades Pope Calixtus II from supporting the French rebels who have rallied behind William the Clito, son of his imprisoned brother Robert (Henry released Clito after the victory at Tinchebrai in 1106).

1120 England's Henry I makes peace with France's Louis VI, but his only legitimate son is drowned in the disaster of the White Ship off Harfleur.

The order of the Knights of the Temple is founded in a house near Jerusalem by Hugh of Pajens to guide and protect pilgrims. Knights Templar will be organized among noblemen of several countries and, with their men-at-arms and chaplains, will take monastic vows of poverty, chastity, and obedience to an order that will survive until 1312 (*see* 1070).

Measurement of latitude and longitude in degrees, minutes, and seconds is pioneered by the Anglo-Saxon scientist Walcher of Malvern, who in 1092 observed the solar eclipse and tried to calculate the difference in time between England and Italy.

1121 Southwestern Anatolia is recovered from the Seljuk Turks by the Byzantine emperor John II Comnenus, who abandons further action against the Seljuks and hastens to the Balkans, where the Patzinaks are continuing their incursions.

French theologian-philosopher Pierre Abelard, 42, is condemned by the Concordat of Worms for his teachings of the Trinity, and he is castrated by the hirelings of one Fulbert, whose niece Héloïse he has secretly married. Abelard withdraws to a monastery pursued by his former student Héloïse, and he begins a persecuted life of wandering from one monastery to another, founding the priory of the Paraclete at which Héloïse will be prioress (see 1140).

1122 The Holy Roman Emperor Henry V renounces the right of investiture with ring and crozier in the September Concordat of Worms, he recognizes freedom of election of the clergy, and he promises to restore all church property.

The Patzinak Turks in the Balkans are exterminated by the emperor John II Comnenus and his Byzantine hordes, but a 4-year war with Venice is precipitated by John's refusal to renew exclusive trading privileges granted to Venice by the late Alexius Comnenus in 1082.

1123 The Japanese emperor Toba abdicates at age 20 in favor of his 4-year-old uncle and stepson Sutoku, son of the ex-emperor Shirakawa, who will reign until 1141.

Serbian forces in the Balkans are defeated by John II Comnenus.

Marriage of priests and the practice of simony are forbidden by the First Lateran Council.

A strict Buddhist law against killing any living thing (including fish, poultry, livestock, game and game birds) is imposed by Japan's ex-emperor Shirakawa (see 1126).

St. Bartholomew's Hospital of London has its beginnings in the Augustine priory of St. Bartholomew founded by a canon of St. Paul's Cathedral.

Persian poet-astronomer Omar Khayyam dies at age 96, leaving works that include the *Rubaiyat* (see 1859).

London's Smithfield meat market has its origin in the priory (above) founded beside the "Smooth" field just outside the city's walls. The field will soon be the scene of St. Bartholomew's Fair, where drapers and clothiers will exchange goods and where a weekly horsemarket will be held (see 1639).

1124 Hungary's Stephen II is defeated in battle by the Byzantine emperor John II Comnenus, who supports claims to the throne by Bela, blinded by the late Hungarian king Coloman. John acts to keep the Hungarians from gaining control of Dalmatia, Croatia, and Serbia.

Scotland's Alexander I dies April 27 at age 46 after a 17-year reign and is succeeded by his 40-year-old brother David, who has ruled in the south since the death of their father Edgar in 1107. The new king will reign until 1153 as David I and will be called "the Scotch Justinian."

The first Scottish coins are struck.

Rochester Cathedral is completed.

1125 The Holy Roman Emperor Henry V dies at Utrecht May 23 at age 44 after having led an expedition against France's Louis VI and then against the citizens of Worms. He is succeeded by the 55-year-old Lothair who is crowned at Aix-la-Chapelle September 13, 2 weeks after being chosen king at Mainz with support from the papal party.

Frederick of Hohenstaufen is asked by the new emperor to restore to the crown the estates he has inherited from the late Henry V (above). He refuses and is placed under the ban.

Morocco is conquered by the Almohades.

1126 Lothair III makes his son-in-law Henry the Proud (Heinrich der Stolze) duke of Bavaria at age 18 (see 1138).

The Peace of 1126 ends hostilities between John II Comnenus and the Hungarians and Venetians. The emperor secures Branicova on the Danube but is forced by Venice to renew the republic's exclusive commercial privileges.

Japanese fishing nets are collected by order of the ex-emperor Shirakawa and are burned in front of the imperial palace to assure compliance with Buddhist law. Cormorants (used for fishing), hunting dogs, and falcons are ordered to be released (see 1123; 1129).

1127 Sicily's Roger II claims the Hauteville possessions in Italy and also claims overlordship of Capua, but subjects of Apulia resist union with Sicily. They are supported by Pope Honorius II, and Roger II of Capua and Roger's brother-in-law Ranulf of Alife (Avellino) are set against Roger by the pope who preaches a crusade, excommunicates Roger, and lays claim himself as feudal overlord to Norman possessions in southern Italy.

1128 Sicily's Roger II is invested as duke of Apulia by Pope Honorius II at Benevento in August after failure of the pope's coalition against Roger.

Portugal's Afonso Henriques assumes authority at age 19, repudiates his mother Teresa's agreement to accept Castilian domination, defeats Castile's Alfonso VII, and drives his mother into exile (see 1112; 1139).

The Abbey of Holyrood is founded by Scotland's David I.

The order of the Knights Templar, founded in 1120, is recognized and confirmed by Pope Honorius II.

Cistercian monks from Normandy settle in England and begin an extensive program of swamp reclamation, agricultural improvement, and stock breeding (see 1098). The Cistercians live austerely, they depend for their income entirely on the land, and they will have a salutary effect in improving English and European horse and cattle breeds and in raising the standards of agriculture.

1129 Sicily's Roger II is recognized as duke at Melfi in September by the barons of Naples, Bari, Capua, Salerno, and the other cities that have resisted him.

1129 (cont.) A Japanese fisherman caught violating the Buddhist law of the ex-emperor Shirakawa is dragged on the ground before Shirakawa as punishment. Shirakawa dies 3 months later (July 7) at age 76, and his grandson Toba takes over as the power behind the emperor.

1130 Pope Honorius II dies February 13. Gregorio Papareschi is elected to succeed him as Innocent II, but Cardinal Pierleone is elected as an antipope, and Innocent flees to France. The antipope is supported by Sicily's Roger II, who is crowned at Palermo December 25 by Anacletus II, beginning a 10-year war with Pope Innocent's champion, Bernard of Clairvaux, who calls Roger a "half-heathen king" and enlists the support of France's Louis VI, England's Henry I, and the German king Lothair.

The antipope Anacletus II (above) is more acceptable canonically than is Innocent II, but his father is a rich converted Jew and anti-Semitism prevents him from gaining secular support.

1131 Tintern Abbey is founded in Wales by Cistercian monks in the Wye Valley. A larger structure will be erected in the 13th and 14th centuries (*see* Wordsworth, 1798).

1133 The German king Lothair II arrives at Rome in March with Pope Innocent II and a small army after a 6-month journey across the Alps. He finds St. Peter's in the hands of the antipope Anacletus II. He is crowned emperor by Innocent II at the Church of the Lateran June 4, and he receives as papal fiefs the vast estates of Matilda, marchioness of Tuscany, which he secures for his daughter Gertrude and her husband Henry the Proud of Bavaria.

England's Durham Cathedral is completed after 37 years of construction.

1134 The German House of Brandenburg has its beginnings as the emperor Lothair II makes Albrecht the Bear, 34, head of the Nordmark, and Albrecht founds the ruling house of Anhalt (*see* 1150).

The Pontifical University of Salamanca has its beginnings in Castile.

1135 The Holy Roman Emperor Lothair II receives homage from Denmark's Eric II, he is promised tribute by Poland's Prince Boleslav III, he receives Pomerania and Rugen as German fiefs, and he is implored by the Byzantine emperor John II Comnenus to help oust Roger II of Sicily.

The Hohenstaufen king Conrad III submits to Lothair, he is pardoned, and he recovers his estates in October.

England's Henry I dies December 1 at age 67 after a 35-year reign (his brother Curthose has died earlier as a prisoner at Cardiff). He is succeeded by his nephew Stephen of Blois, 38, who asserts his claim to the throne in opposition to claims by Henry's 33-year-old daughter Matilda, widow of the late emperor Henry V, whose successsion was accepted by England's barons in 1126 and who was married 2 years later to Geoffrey Plantagenet of Anjou.

1136 Apulia is conquered from Sicily's Roger II by the emperor Lothair II, who has invaded southern Italy in response to last year's appeal from John II Comnenus.

England's Matilda asserts her right to the throne of her late father.

Historia Calamitatus Mearum by Pierre Abelard describes his love affair with Héloïse (*see* 1121; 1140).

The French church of St. Dénis, completed by the 45-year-old abbé Suger, is a romanesque structure but it includes some pointed arches and high clerestory windows that mark the beginning of Gothic architecture. "Bright is the noble edifice that is pervaded by new light," says Suger, who initiates the idea of the rose window and argues that people can only come to understand absolute beauty, which is God, through the effect of precious and beautiful things on the senses. "The dull mind rises to truth through that which is material."

1137 France's Louis VI dies August 1 at age 56 after a 29-year reign. He is succeeded by his 16-year-old son who assumes the throne as Louis VII, marries the heiress to the duke of Aquitaine at Bordeaux, and with his bride, Eleanor of Aquitaine, begins a 43-year reign.

The prince of North Wales Gruffydd ap Cynan dies at age 56 after having rebuilt Welsh power overturned earlier by England's late Henry I. Gruffydd's sons Owain and Cadwaladr work to revive the power of the principality of Gwynedd behind the Snowdonian range.

The Holy Roman Emperor Lothair II dies December 4 in the Tyrolean village of Breitenwag at age 67 while retreating from Italy after a mutiny among his troops and a breach with Pope Innocent II as to who shall have overlordship in Apulia.

Antioch is forced to pay homage to the Byzantine emperor John II Comnenus, who has conquered Cilician (Little) Armenia.

Les Halles is established before his death by France's Louis VI (the Fat). Les Halles will be the central food market of Paris (and of France) until 1969.

1138 Swabia's House of Hohenstaufen begins a 130-year domination of the German states as Conrad is chosen German king for a second time March 7 by princes meeting at Coblenz in the presence of the papal legate. Now 45, Conrad is crowned March 13 at Aixla-Chapelle. Bavaria's Henry the Proud refuses his allegiance and loses Bavaria to the Franconian margrave of Austria Leopold IV, and a long struggle begins between the "Ghibellines" and the "Guelphs" (the Hohenstaufens take their name from their Swabian castle Staufen on their estates of Waiblingen, whose name will be corrupted by their Italian supporters into "Ghibelline," while the family name Welf of Bavaria's Henry will be corrupted into "Guelph").

Poland's Boleslav III (Wry-mouth) dies at age 62 after a 36-year reign. He has divided his realm among his five sons.

The Battle of the Standard fought in August near Northallerton ends in defeat for Scotland's David I who has invaded England in support of Matilda against Stephen, but David does take possession of Northumberland.

1139 Civil war begins in England as Matilda lands at Arundel with an army to support her claims to the throne.

Portugal gains her independence from the Moors and begins to achieve identity as a sovereign nation. Portuguese forces under Afonso Henriques defeat the Moors July 25 in the Battle of Ourique in Allentejo (*see* 1128; 1143).

1140 Bohemia's Sobeslav I dies after a 15-year reign and is succeeded by Ladislas II who will reign until 1173 (*see* 1156).

The fortress of Weinsberg is captured from the Welf in December by Conrad III who permits the women of the town to leave. Each is permitted to take with her as much property as she can carry on her back and each comes out bearing on her back a husband, father, or son who thus escapes.

Pierre Abelard is condemned for his "heresies" by the Council of Sens and sets out for Rome to present his defense.

Spanish rabbi Judah ben Samuel ha-Levi (Abu'l Hasan) dies at age 55, leaving as his chief philosophical work *Sefer ha-Kusari*, which categorizes revealed religion as superior to philosophic and rational belief.

1141 England's King Stephen is surprised and captured while laying siege to Lincoln Castle. Matilda reigns for 6 months as "Domina of the English," but Stephen's supporters secure his release in exchange for the earl of Gloucester, Matilda's half-brother Robert, bastard son of the late Henry I.

Hungary's blind king Bela II dies after a 10-year reign in which he has taken terrible revenge on his opponents: he is succeeded by Geza II who will reign until 1161.

The Japanese emperor Sutoku abdicates at age 22 after an 18-year reign and is succeeded by his 2-year-old half-brother Konoe who will reign until 1155.

1142 The German king Conrad III makes peace in May at Frankfort with the duke of Saxony, Henry the Lion (Heinrich der Lowe), 13-year-old son of the late Henry the Proud of Bavaria. Young Henry is confirmed in his duchy, while Bavaria is given to Conrad's stepbrother Henry Jasomirgott, margrave of Austria, who marries Henry the Proud's widow Gertrude.

England's Matilda is expelled from Oxford after a long siege by Stephen, who forces her to take refuge in the western part of the country. A 5-year period of anarchy begins.

Pierre Abelard dies at age 63 while en route to Rome. His body will be given to his widow, Héloïse, who will be buried beside him in 1164 (both will be re-entombed at Paris in 1817).

1143 Portuguese independence is recognized by Castile in the Treaty of Zamora arranged by the Vatican. Afonso Henriques, now 31, is proclaimed king by the cortes and begins a 42-year reign that founds the Portuguese monarchy and the Burgundian dynasty (*see* 1139; 1185).

The Byzantine emperor John II Comnenus (Kalojoannes) dies at age 55 after a 25-year reign. He is succeeded by his 23-year old son, who will reign until 1180 as Manuel I Comnenus.

1144 Geoffrey of Anjou, son-in-law of England's late Henry I, becomes duke of Normandy upon news of the death last year of his father Foulkes le Jeune who was king of Jerusalem from 1131 until his death at age 51.

1145 A Second Crusade is preached by the Cistercian French ecclesiastic Bernard of Clairvaux, 54, whose resistance to the idea has been overcome by the new pope Eugene III.

Pope Eugene III is forced into exile by Arnold of Brescia, 45, a student of the late Abelard who has fought corruption in the clergy, was condemned along with Abelard in 1140 by the Council of Sens, and turns Rome into a republic with a government patterned on that of ancient Rome.

"Prester John" is described in a chronicle by Otto, bishop of Freising, as a Christian king or priest (presbyter) living in the Orient beyond Persia and Armenia (*see* 1459).

The Danube is bridged at Ratisbon by a span begun 10 years ago.

1147 A Second Crusade assembles some 500,000 men under the leadership of France's Louis VII and the German Conrad III, who take separate routes but who give the Crusade no coherent command, achieve nothing, and lose most of their Crusaders to starvation, disease, and battle wounds.

Sicily's Roger II is enabled by the distraction of the Second Crusade (above) to seize the Greek islands and to attack Athens, Thebes, and Corinth. An 11-year war begins between Sicily and the Byzantine Empire.

1148 The Byzantine emperor Manuel I Comnenus purchases Venetian aid to help him resist the Norman fleets of Sicily's Roger II, who has plundered Thebes and Corinth.

1148 (cont.) An Italian silk industry is started at Palermo by Roger II (above) who takes numbers of silk workers back from Greece.

Sugar is taken back to Europe from the Middle East by returning Crusaders (*see* 1104). The sweetener is virtually unknown in Europe, even in the greatest castles, but it will soon be prized above honey (*see* 1226).

1149 Corfu is regained for the Byzantines by their Venetian mercenaries.

Theisir (*al-Taysir*) by the Arab physician Avenzoar (Abu Mervan ibn Zuh) describes otitis media, paralysis of the pharnyx, and pericarditis in a work based on personal experience, independent observation, and sound judgment. Opposing purgatives, Avenzoar strongly advocates venesection (phlebotomy) but expresses firm belief in the powers of bezoar, allegedly produced by the eyes of a deer.

1150 Sweden's Sverker is deposed after a 16-year reign that has amalgamated the Swedes and the Goths. He is succeeded by Eric IX, who will reign until 1160.

Brandenburg is inherited by Albrecht the Bear (*see* 1134).

Magnetic compasses are used in crude form by Chinese sea masters and caravan leaders to guide them in their journeys (*see* 1086).

The University of Paris has its beginnings (*see* Sorbonne, 1253).

The Black Book of Carmarthen is compiled in Wales.

Troubadour music is organized in the south of France.

1151 Peking is retaken from the Tartars by the Chinese (*see* 936).

Ghazni is burned by the Shansabani Persian princes of Ghur (Ghor) who will drive the Yamini to the Punjab and will depose them in 1186.

Geoffrey of Anjou dies September 7 at age 38. He has been called "Plantagenet" for his habit of wearing a sprig of broom (genet) in his cap, and he is succeeded as count of Anjou by his 18-year-old son Henry to whom he gave the duchy of Normandy last year.

The first fire and plague insurance is issued in Iceland.

1152 The German Hohenstaufen king Conrad III dies at Bemberg February 15 at age 58 after a 14-year reign. He is succeeded by his 29-year-old red-bearded nephew Frederick, duke of Swabia, who is chosen king at Frankfurt March 5 partly because he is of both Welf and Waiblingen blood. It is hoped that he will end the rivalry that has divided the German states since 1138, and he is crowned at Aix-la-Chapelle March 9 to begin a 38-year reign as Frederick III (Frederick Barbarossa).

The 15-year marriage of France's Louis VII and Eleanor of Aquitaine is annulled, and the 30-year-old Eleanor, who has produced no male heir, marries the 19-year-old Henry Plantagenet, count of Anjou, Maine, and Touraine and duke of Normandy, who gains by marriage domains that make him master of more than half of France (*see* 1154).

1153 Scotland's David I dies at Carlisle May 24 at age 69 and is succeeded by his 12-year-old grandson who will never marry but who will reign until late in 1165 as Malcolm IV.

1154 Roger II of Sicily dies at Palermo February 26 at age 60 and is succeeded by his fourth son William who begins a 12-year reign.

England's King Stephen dies October 25 at age 54 and is succeeded by his adopted son Henry Plantagenet who is crowned at age 21 to begin a 35-year reign as Henry II that inaugurates a Plantagenet dynasty that will rule England until 1399.

The first and only English pope begins a 5-year reign as Nicholas Breakspear is elected to the papacy. Adrian IV tries to end the anarchy that has persisted in Rome.

Iceland's Mount Hekla erupts as it did 50 years ago, and word spreads through the Catholic world that Hekla's craters are the entrance to Hell.

England's domestic wine industry begins to decline as cheap French wines are introduced by Eleanor of Aquitaine, wife of the new king Henry II (above).

1155 The Japanese emperor Konoe dies at age 16 after a 14-year reign, and a fight begins over the succession. The emperor's half brother Sutoku wants to place his own son on the throne but is thwarted by his stepfather (and nephew) the ex-emperor Toba, who makes Sutoku's 28-year-old brother Goshirakawa emperor (*see* 1156).

Rome's Arnold of Brescia is interdicted by the new English pope Adrian IV. He is forced to flee, he is betrayed by Frederick Barbarossa, and he is hanged at Rome.

Ireland is given to England's Henry II by Pope Adrian IV.

English fiscal earldoms are abolished by Henry II who restores the royal demesne.

The Carmelite order of mendicant monks is founded by the Crusader Berthold from Calabria and 10 companions who establish themselves as hermits on Mount Carmel in the kingdom of Jerusalem.

1156 William of Sicily destroys the Byzantine fleet May 28 at Brindisi and recovers Bari from Greek barons who have been encouraged by Pope Adrian IV to revolt. William and Adrian come to terms at Benevento June 18, and William is confirmed as king.

Frederick Barbarossa is married June 9 at Wurzburg to Beatrix, daughter of the late count of Upper Burgundy, Renaud III, and he adds Upper Burgundy (Franche Comte) to his domain.

The margraviate of Austria is made a duchy after 180 years of rule by the Babenberg family and is given special privileges (*see* 1246).

The former Japanese emperor Toba dies at age 53 in the midst of a struggle over the succession. His son Sutoku obtains help from Tameyoshi Minamoto and Tadamasa Taira, and they rise against Sotoku's half-brother Goshirakawa, who is in turn supported by Minamoto's son Yoshitomo Minamoto and by Taira's nephew Kiyomori Taira. Tameyoshi Minamoto is killed by his son and by Kiyomori Taira. Minamoto's father is exiled to the island of Izo-no-Oshima, south of Edo. Sutoku fails in his attempt to take over and is exiled to Sanuko on the island of Shikoku in the Inland Sea, and Goshirakawa remains as emperor.

1157 Frederick Barbarossa invades Poland, forces the submission of Duke Boleslav IV, and in October receives the homage of Burgundian noblemen at Besançon.

Finland is conquered by Sweden's Eric IX who forces the vanquished Finns to be baptized.

Frederick Barbarossa's army at Rome is destroyed by typhus or some other plague.

Ye Olde Bell opens at Harley outside London. The public house (pub) will survive for more than 800 years.

1158 The Japanese emperor Goshirakawa abdicates after a 3-year reign, and his 15-year-old son Nijo begins a 7-year reign that will be interrupted briefly next year. Goshirakawa retains power and gives strongman Kiyomori Taira a higher position than Yoshitomo Minamoto, antagonizing Minamoto (*see* 1159).

Castile's Alfonso VII dies at age 32 in the Sierra Moreno while returning to Toledo after a campaign against the Almohades, whose power is increasing. "The Emperor" had held Leon through most of his 23-year reign, but Leon breaks away as Alfonso's infant son ascends the throne to begin a 56-year reign as Alfonso VIII.

Frederick Barbarossa leaves in June for a second Italian expedition, Milan is taken from its insurgents by Frederick's imperial officers (podestas) in northern Italy, and a long struggle begins between Frederick and the pope.

Lübeck is founded on the Baltic by a consortium of families who deal in grain, timber, fish, and other commodities. Each family takes a large block of land, builds a house on the best corner lot, and rents the balance to newcomers, while the consortium runs bakeries and operates the town's marketplace (*see* Hanseatic League, 1241).

1159 An English army led by Henry II's chancellor Thomas à Becket, 41, invades Toulouse to assert the rights of Henry's wife, Eleanor of Aquitaine, but the English are driven off by France's Louis VII.

The Japanese emperor Nijo and his father Goshirakawa are dethroned and imprisoned by Noboyori Fujiwara and Yoshitomo Minamoto who stage a palace revolution while Kiyomori Taira is away from Kyoto visiting the Kumano shrine. Kiyomori returns quickly at news of the coup, he kills both Fujiwara and Minamoto, he reinstates the emperor Nijo, and he becomes the new power behind the throne (*see* 1160).

Policratus by England's John of Salisbury is the first medieval attempt to formulate an extended and systematic treatment of political philosophy. John denounces Henry II for exacting funds from the church to support his invasion of Toulouse (above) and he presents the first explicit defense of tyrannicide.

1160 England's Henry II comes to terms with France's Louis VII after failing to enlist the aid of Frederick Barbarossa, but the peace is unstable. Desultory skirmishing continues between the French and English.

Norman forces are expelled from North Africa by the Arabs.

Kiyomori Taira is elevated to the nobility by the ex-emperor Goshirakawa.

Theater *Jeu de St. Nicholas* by French troubadour Jean Bodel, 12/6 at Arras.

1162 Milan is destroyed by Frederick Barbarossa in his continuing campaign against supporters of the pope (*see* 1158; 1167).

The archbishop of Canterbury Theobald dies, and England's Henry II has his chancellor Thomas à Becket elected to the primacy. Becket immediately becomes an ardent champion of Church rights.

1163 England's Henry II returns from the Continent and begins almost immediately to quarrel with the archbishop of Canterbury Thomas à Becket who defends clerical privileges. The king proposes that a land tax, which has been used to pay part of the sheriff's salary, shall henceforth be paid into the exchequer, but Becket opposes the move and defeats the proposal in July at the Council of Woodstock.

Dissection of human bodies is discouraged by a Church dictum promulgated by the Council of Tours in connection with the practice of dismembering dead Crusaders and boiling them down for transport back home: "The Church abhors the shedding of blood."

Spanish physician Moses Ben Maimon (Maimonides), 28, leaves his native Cordova and settles at Cairo, where he will become physician to Saladin, sultan of Egypt. Maimonides will write works on medicine, law, mathematics, logic, and theology.

The Mosaic law of 621 B.C. against mixing meat and dairy products ("You shall not boil a kid in its mother's milk") will be ascribed by Maimonides (above) to an aversion by ancient Jews to a fertility ritual practiced by pagan cults in Canaan.

Henry II of England submitted to whipping at Canterbury as penance for the murder of Thomas à Becket.

1164 England's Constitutions of Clarendon are an attempt by Henry II to delimit spiritual and temporal jurisdictions. The archbishop of Canterbury Thomas à Becket has excommunicated a tenant-in-chief who has encroached on Canterbury lands, he has protected a clerk charged with assaulting a royal officer, he renounces his promise to observe the constitutions, he flees to France in November, and he persuades Pope Alexander III to condemn the constitutions.

Poetry *Eracle* by French court poet Gautier d'Arras.

1165 The Byzantine emperor Manuel I Comnenus makes an alliance with Venice against Frederick Barbarossa who takes an oath at the Diet of Wurzburg in May to support the antipope Paschal III against Pope Alexander III.

Scotland's Malcolm IV dies December 9 at age 24 and is succeeded by his 22-year-old brother William the Lion who will reign until 1214.

The Japanese emperor Nijo abdicates and dies after a 7-year reign and is succeeded by his year-old infant son who will reign until 1168 as the emperor Rokujo.

1166 Sicily's William I dies May 7 after a 12-year reign. William the Bad is succeeded by his 13-year-old son who will reign until 1189 as William II, championing the papacy and joining the Lombard cities in a secret conspiracy against Frederick II Barbarossa.

Ballad *The Song of Canute* by an English monk of Ely.

The Cairo citadel is built by a 28-year-old city official named Saladin (Salah-al-Din Yusuf ibn-Ayyub).

1167 Frederick Barbarossa enters Rome by storm on a fourth expedition into Italy. He has the antipope Paschal III enthroned, he has his wife Beatrix crowned, but his army is destroyed by a sudden outbreak of pestilence, and he returns to Germany.

Copenhagen is founded by the Danish soldier Absalon (or Axel), 39, archbishop of Lund, who has delivered Denmark from Wendish pirates and has conquered much of slavonic Mecklenburg and Estonia for the late King Waldemar and for Canute VI.

Oxford University has its beginnings (*see* Balliol, 1261).

1168 The Japanese emperor Rokujo is removed at age 4 and is succeeded by his 7-year-old uncle who will reign until 1180 as the emperor Takakura.

1170 England's Henry II has himself crowned by Roger, archbishop of York, in violation of the rights of Thomas à Becket, who persuades Pope Alexander III to suspend Roger of York and other bishops who have supported Henry and have agreed to royal control of episcopal elections and other extensions of royal power (*see* below).

Henry II increases the crown's power by replacing England's baronial sheriffs with men of lower rank trained in the royal service, thus breaking the hold of the barons on the shrievalty. Pope Alexander III forces Henry to reconcile his quarrel with Thomas à Becket in July.

Brandenburg's Albrecht the Bear, who has founded the House of Anhalt, dies November 13 at age 70 after dividing his territories among his six sons.

Thomas à Becket returns to England in early December after more than 6 years in France. He refuses absolution to the country's bishops, and overzealous knights murder him in the cathedral at Canterbury December 29.

The "Inquest of Sheriffs" strengthens the English exchequer by its financial inquiry.

Poetry *Le Chevalier a la Charette* by French poet-troubadour Chrétien de Troyes introduces the Arthurian hero Lancelot du Lac.

Japan has her first recorded instance of ritual suicide: a feudal warrior slashes his own belly to commit *seppuku.*

1171 England's Henry II lands at Waterford in response to a request for aid from Ireland's deposed king Dermot MacMurrough (Diarmaid Macmurchada) who ruled Leinster from 1126 but who was banished 5 years ago by Irish chieftains and who dies at age 61. Henry is greeted as "lord of Ireland" and claims the country as his own (*see* 1155).

Egypt is subdued by Saladin of Damascus who suppresses the Fatamid dynasty that has ruled since 909.

1172 England's Henry II receives homage at Tipperary's 200-foot high Caskel Rock from Irish princes who include Donal O'Brien. Henry has gone to Ireland in part to avoid the attacks of Pope Alexander III for the assassination of Thomas à Becket.

Eleanor of Aquitaine raises Aquitaine against her faithless husband Henry II, and he is forced to reconcile his differences with the pope.

The powers of Venice's doges is restricted by the Venetian Grand Council.

Poetry *Roman de Rou* by Anglo-Norman poet Wace is a chronicle of the dukes of Normandy.

1173 England's Henry II has his wife Eleanor of Aquitaine held captive while he dallies in western Herefordshire with his mistress Rosamund Clifford, daughter of Walter de Clifford. Henry's sons Henry, Richard, and Geoffrey lead a rebellion against their father but the House of Commons gives hearty support to the king.

Hungary's Stephen III dies after a 12-year reign and is succeeded by Bela III, who has been educated at Constantinople. The new king will introduce Byzantine customs in a reign that will continue until 1196.

The Waldensian movement begins at Lyons, where local merchant Peter Waldo renounces the world, gives away all his goods and property to the poor, and devotes himself to preaching voluntary poverty (*see* 1179).

1174 Tuscany, Sardinia, Corsica, and Spoleto are purchased by Frederick Barbarossa from Henry the Lion's uncle, Welf VI.

England's Henry II does penance at Canterbury for the murder in 1170 of Thomas à Becket who was canonized last year as Saint Thomas Becket.

Woodblocks for printing elaborate capital letters in manuscripts are cut at Engelberg monastery.

The Leaning Tower of Pisa has its beginnings in a campanile (bell tower) built by architect Bonnano Pisano. The 177-foot tower will tilt until it is more than 18 feet off the perpendicular (*see* Galileo, 1592).

1175 India is invaded by Persia's Mu'izz-ad-din, Mohammed of Ghor.

1176 The Battle of Legnano May 29 gives the Lombard League a victory over Frederick Barbarossa, who sustains a wound so serious that he is thought for a while to be dead.

The Egyptian sultan Saladin conquers Syria and mounts a campaign to drive the Christians from the kingdom of Jerusalem.

The University of Modena has its beginnings.

Welsh ecclesiastic Walter Map, 36, organizes legends of King Arthur and his knights of the round table at Camelot (*see* 537). Map has traveled abroad on foreign missions.

The Eisteddfod festival of Welsh music, poetry, and drama at Cardigan Castle begins an annual competition by bards that will continue at various locations for more than 800 years.

Rabbits are introduced into England as domestic livestock.

1177 Frederick Barbarossa and Pope Alexander III sign the Treaty of Venice in August to begin a 6-year period of peace between the Lombard League and the Holy Roman Emperor.

England's Henry II and France's Louis VII sign the Treaty of Ivry as Pope Alexander III intervenes to bring the two monarchs to terms.

Cambodia's capital of Angkor is captured by Champa invaders who will hold the city for 4 years.

Belfast is founded in northern Ireland as a castle built by John de Courcy to command a ford near the mouth of the Lagan River.

1178 Frederick Barbarossa is crowned king of Burgundy at Arles July 30. He will repeat the ceremony in 1186.

A meteorite strikes the moon June 18. English monks at Canterbury record that "a flaming torch sprang up" from the crescent moon, "spewing out, over a considerable distance, fire, hot coals, and sparks."

1179 The Waldensians are prohibited by Pope Alexander III from preaching without permission of the bishops, but Peter Waldo replies that he must obey God, not man (*see* 1173; 1184).

1180 France's Louis VII dies September 18 at age 59 after a 43-year reign and is succeeded by his 15-year-old son who was crowned last year at Reims and who will rule until 1223 as Philip II Augustus.

The Byzantine emperor Manuel I Comnenus dies at age 60 after a 37-year reign of great splendor that has involved the empire in repeated conflicts with the Normans and has weakened it financially. Manuel is succeeded by his 12-year-old son who will reign briefly, with his mother Maria of Antioch as regent.

An uprising against Japan's ruling Taira family begins as Kiyomori Taira alienates the imperial family with his excesses following the death last year of his eldest son Shigemori at age 41. One revolt is led by an imperial prince and another by the 74-year-old Yorimasa Minamoto, who is supported by some of the monasteries but who is killed by the Taira. A general uprising is led August 17 by Yoritomo Minamoto, 33, who is helped by his father-in-law Tokimasa Hojo. The emperor Takukura abdicates at age 19 and is succeeded by his 2-year-old son Antoku, grandson of Kiyomori Taira, whose forces are opposed on the Fuji River in October by troops raised by the Minamoto family. A Minamoto detachment gets behind the Taira position, the Taira are alarmed in the night by a sudden flight of waterfowl, the Taira flee, and the Minamoto forces begin a series of victories.

Glass windows appear in private English houses (*see* tax, 1695).

1182 A Constantinople mob massacres the Latins who rule as agents of the regent Maria of Antioch. They kill city officials and traders, and they proclaim an uncle

1182 (cont.) of Alexius II Comnenus coemperor to rule as Andronicus I Comnenus together with his nephew.

Denmark's Waldemar the Great dies at age 51 after a 25-year reign. His 19-year-old son succeeds as Canute VI. He will reign until 1202, he will extend Danish dominion over Pomerania and Holstein, and he will call himself king of the Danes and Wends.

France banishes her Jews.

England's port of Bristol sends wooden vessels built "shipshape and Bristol fashion" out to Spain (Jerez) for sherry, to Portugal (Oporto) for port wine, to Iceland for stockfish (dried cod), and to Bordeaux and Bayonne in Gascony for woad from the plant *Isatis tinctoria* to make blue dye for Bristol's woolens.

1183 The Byzantine emperor Alexius II Comnenus is strangled to death by agents of his uncle and coemperor, who assumes sole power and begins a 2-year reign as Andronicus I Comnenus.

The Peace of Constance ends the conflict between the Lombard towns, the pope, and Frederick Barbarossa, but it also ends any remnant of unity in the Holy Roman Empire.

Aleppo is taken by Saladin.

Japan's Taira clan is driven out of Kyoto by Minamoto clansmen led by Yoshinaka, 29-year-old cousin of Yoritomo. The Minamoto family installs the 3-year-old half-brother of the emperor Antoku as the emperor Gotoba in rivalry with the Taira family's emperor (*see* 1185).

Poetry *Senzaishu* by Japanese poet Saigyo-hosi, 75, who at age 23 abandoned his wife and family to become a priest and who has spent his life wandering through Japan composing short poems of 31 syllables each, called tanka. These poems depart from the typical love poetry of the Heian court with expressions closer to nature that reflect Buddhist thinking and a sense of melancholy.

1184 The Great Diet of Mainz, held by Frederick Barbarossa, is a colossal medieval pageant at which his two sons are knighted in the presence of a multitude of princes and knights.

Cyprus gains her freedom from the Byzantines.

Georgians make the 25-year-old Tamara their queen, and she begins a 28-year reign that will raise Georgia to the peak of her political power.

Japan's Minamoto military leader Yoshinkaka is killed at age 30 as the Taira and their enemies battle in the Inland Sea region.

Peter Waldo is excommmunicated by Pope Lucius III (*see* 1179).

Modena Cathedral is consecrated after 85 years of construction.

Canterbury Cathedral is completed in Kent after 5 years of construction to replace the cathedral in which Thomas à Becket was murdered at the end of 1170. Architect for the great Gothic structure is William of Sens, who has built the French cathedral at Sens that has helped establish the Gothic style in which pillars supported by buttresses replace walls as the main support of vaulted roofs, making possible large stained-glass windows to permit the entrance of mysterious colored light. The cathedral will be given a nave in the late 14th century and a central tower in the 15th century.

1185 The Japanese emperor becomes the puppet that he will remain under 1868 as the shoguns (generals) assume power. The Minamoto family, led by Yoritomo's half-brother Yoshitsune, defeats the Taira clan at Danoura on the Inland Sea. The emperor Antoku is drowned, and the imperial sword is lost. The 5-year-old Gotoba reigns without the sword and with no real power, and Japan enters a centuries-long period of civil wars among the feudal lords (*daimyo*) who rule under the shoguns with support from retainer-knights (*samurai*).

Norman forces attack the Byzantine Empire. They take Durazzo, and storm Thessalonica with an army and navy and massacre the Greeks. The Greek nobility, led by Isaac Angelus, deposes the Byzantine emperor Andronicus I Comnenus who is tortured and executed. The Byzantine general Alexius Branas defeats the Normans at Demetritsa. Isaac begins a 10-year reign as Isaac II Angelus, but his regime will restore the corruption that Andronicus had begun to eliminate, and the empire will begin to disintegrate.

A great Bulgarian insurrection that will lead to the creation of an independent Bulgaria begins under the boyars Peter and John Asen, who gain support from the Cumans against the extortions of Byzantine revenue agents from Constantinople. Much of the Greek population of the Balkans will be annihilated in the revolt, and much of the region will be desolated.

Mosul is seized by the Egyptian sultan Saladin who begins to conquer Mesopotamia.

Portugal's Afonso Henriques dies at age 76 after a reign that has founded the Portuguese monarchy. He is succeeded by his 31-year-old son who will reign until 1211 as Sancho I in a reign that will be notable for the roads and cities that will be built in the realm.

The Knights Templar, founded at Jerusalem in 1120, is established at London.

Japan's Kyoto is a city of 500,000 and is larger than any city in the west with the possible exceptions of Cordova and Constantinople.

1186 The Kamakura period that will dominate Japan until 1333 is begun by the 39-year-old Minamoto leader Yoritomo, whose family is based in the village of Kamakura (*see* 1189).

A triple coronation occurs at Milan as Frederick Barbarossa is crowned king of Burgundy, his 21-year-old son Henry is crowned Caesar in a deliberate revival of the old Roman title, and Henry's bride Constance, daughter of Sicily's late Roger II, is crowned queen of the Germans.

∞ Frederick Barbarossa takes the cross and prepares for a Third Crusade.

1187 Jerusalem is retaken for Islam by Egypt's Saladin who defeats a Christian army at Hittin and thus inspires European enthusiasm for a Third Crusade.

The Punjab is conquered by Mohammed of Ghor who rules at Ghazni as governor for his brother Ghiyas-ud-Din Mohammed.

Verona Cathedral is completed after 48 years of construction.

1188 The Saladin tithe is imposed by France's Philip III to raise money for a Third Crusade. It is the first tax to be imposed in France.

England's Prince Richard Coeur de Lion does homage to Philip II for English possessions in France and does so in the presence of his father Henry II at the November 18 Conference of Bonmolins. A struggle follows in which Henry is overpowered. He is chased from Le Mans to Angers and is forced to buy peace by conceding to all demands, including the immediate recognition of Richard as his successor (*see* 1189).

The Rhône is bridged at Avignon for the first time. The Pont Saint Benezet is completed after 10 years of construction and will be made famous by a French folk song.

1189 The Third Crusade begins in May as Frederick Barbarossa leaves Regensburg at the head of a splendid army.

England's Henry II dies July 6 at Chinon at age 54 after doing homage to France's Philip II and surrendering the territories of Gracy and Issoudon. He is succeeded by his son Richard Coeur de Lion, who will spend only 1 year of his nearly 10-year reign in England and who will visit the British Isles only twice. The new English king quickly ends his friendship with France's Philip by continuing his father's policy of territorial aggrandizement and by refusing to honor his contract to marry Philip's sister Alais to whom he has been betrothed since age 3, but at year's end, Richard and Philip exchange pledges of mutual good faith and fellowship as they prepare to join the Third Crusade.

Sicily's William II makes peace with the Byzantine emperor Isaac II Angelus, abandons Thessalonica and his other conquests, and dies childless in November at age 36 as he prepares to join the Third Crusade. Tancred of Lecce, bastard son of the late Roger II, will succeed William next year and will reign until his death in 1194.

Japan's shogun Yoshitsume is killed by his older brother Yoritomo, who will crush the Fujiwara clan in the north (*see* 1186; 1192).

English Jews are massacred at the coronation of Richard I (above) (*see* 1290; France, 1182).

The first silver florins are minted at Florence (*see* 1252).

A commercial treaty is negotiated by German merchants with Novgorod.

The first paper mill in Christian Europe is established at Herault, in France, some 38 years after the opening of a paper mill in Moslem Spain but parchment remains almost the only writing material in Europe.

The Trip to Jerusalem is founded at Nottingham as a way station for Crusaders en route to the Holy Land. The English pub will survive for some 800 years.

1190 The Holy Roman Emperor Frederick I Barbarossa drowns June 10 at age 67 while crossing (or bathing in) the river Calycadnus (Geuksu) near Selucia (Selefke) in Cilicia. He is succeeded by his son who was crowned Caesar 4 years ago at Milan and who has been serving as regent, but while Henry will be crowned next year and will reign until 1197 as Henry VI, his father's death leaves the Third Crusade temporarily without a leader.

France's Philip II prepares to join the Third Crusade by making arrangements to rule France from the Holy Land.

England's Richard the Lion-Hearted takes desperate measures to raise and equip a force of 4,000 men-at-arms and 4,000 foot soldiers for the Third Crusade.

French poet Chrétien de Troyes dies at age 60 after having written works that include *Perceval, ou Le Conte du Graal*, earliest known version of the Holy Grail legend. His works have been translated into English and German and are highly popular.

1191 England's Richard the Lion-Hearted embarks on the Third Crusade with a fleet of 100 ships but spends the winter quarreling with France's Philip II in Sicily. He leaves Messina in March, conquers Cyprus, and sells it to the Knights Templar. He moves on to join the siege of Acre in June and takes a major role in reducing Acre, but he offends Leopold of Austria with his arrogance.

France's Philip II falls ill, leaves the crusade, and returns to Paris by Christmas after concluding an alliance en route with the new Holy Roman Emperor Henry VI against England's offensive Richard Coeur de Lion who meanwhile has gained a brilliant victory over the forces of Saladin at Arsuf and who has led the Christian host to within a few miles of Jerusalem.

∞ The Order of the Teutonic Knights has its beginnings in a hospital founded at Acre by merchants of Lübeck and Bremen. The hospital will soon become attached to the German church of Mary the Virgin at Jerusalem (*see* 1198).

Zen Buddhism is introduced to Japan by the 50-year-old priest Aeisai, who returns from a visit to China.

Tea seeds are planted in Japan by Aeisai (above) who makes medicinal claims for tea that will be published in 1214 (*see* 805; 1597; tea ceremony, 1484, 1591).

1192 The Third Crusade follows treacherous guides into the desert beyond Antioch, where its numbers are reduced by famine, plague, and desertions from

1192 (cont.) 100,000 to 5,000. Richard the Lion-Hearted makes a truce with Saladin under which the Christians are permitted to keep the coastal towns they have taken and receive free access to the Holy Sepulcher at Jerusalem. Richard leaves for home October 9, traveling in flimsy disguise. He is captured December 20 at Vienna, and he is imprisoned by Leopold of Austria in the duke's Durenstein castle on the Danube.

Japan's Yoritomo is appointed shogun by the emperor and continues his efforts to crush the Fujiwara clan in the north.

1193 England's Richard the Lion-Hearted is surrendered early in the year to the Holy Roman Emperor Henry VI, who resents the support that the Plantagenets have given to the family of his German rival Henry the Lion and the recognition that Richard has given to the Norman antiking Tancred of Sicily. Henry demands a ransom of 150,000 marks for the return of the English king.

Egypt's Ayyubite sultan Saladin dies at Damascus March 4 at age 52, and his empire is divided among his relatives. Saladin has briefly united the Moslem world and has stemmed the tide of Western conquest in the East.

Aztecs in the Western Hemisphere invade Chichemec territory and conquer the Chichemecs.

Indigo from India is imported to the British Isles for dyeing textiles.

The first known merchant guild is established at London.

1194 Richard the Lion-Hearted returns to England in March following payment of the first installment of the king's ransom to the Holy Roman Emperor Henry VI (who will never receive the full amount he demanded). England has levied the first secular taxation to be imposed on movable property, and her resources have been strained to the utmost to raise the ransom. Richard remains for only a few weeks before returning to the Continent. He leaves the administration of England in the capable hands of the archbishop of Canterbury Hubert Walter, who accompanied Richard on the Third Crusade, led his army back to England, levied the taxes to pay the king's ransom, and has put down a plot against Richard by the king's worthless brother John Lackland.

Norman rule in Italy ends after 91 years as the emperor Henry VI reduces Sicily with help from Pisa and Genoa to terminate the reign of the rich Tancred of Lecce, who has gained support from the pope and from England's Richard Coeur de Lion. Henry also reduces southern Italy and part of Tuscany. He is crowned king of Sicily, he retains the Matildine lands in central Italy, he organizes an imperial administration of his territories, and he begins to plan a great empire with its base in Italy.

Norsemen discover Spitzbergen far to the north of the Arctic Circle. The island will later be an important fishery and whaling center (*see* 1557).

The Elder Edda is a collection of Scandinavian mythology.

China's Yellow River begins flowing southward from the Shantung massif after repeated alterations of its streambed. The river will retain its new course until 1853.

1195 The Byzantine emperor Isaac II Angelus is dethroned by his brother Alexius while he is off on a hunting trip. Alexius is proclaimed emperor by the troops and begins a 9-year reign as Alexius III Angelus. He captures Isaac at Stagira in Macedonia, has his eyes put out, and takes him prisoner despite Isaac's having redeemed him from captivity at Antioch and having loaded him with honors.

The Holy Roman Emperor Henry VI marries his brother Philip of Swabia to Isaac's daughter Irene and thus tries to give the Hohenstaufen a new title and a valid claim against the usurper Alexius (above).

1196 Hungary's Bela III dies after a 23-year reign in which he has helped the Byzantine emperor Isaac II Angelus against the Bulgarians. Bela is succeeded by his son Emeric, who will reign until 1204 but whose position will be challenged by his brother Andras, 21.

The Holy Roman Emperor Henry VI persuades the diet, which meets at Wurzburg in April, to recognize his 2-year-old son Frederick as king of the Romans, but the will of the diet is thwarted by opposition from Adolph, archbishop of Cologne, and others.

1197 The Holy Roman Emperor Henry VI goes to Italy to persuade Pope Celestine III to crown his son Frederick, who has been chosen king of the Romans at Frankfort. The pope refuses. Henry takes cruel measures to put down an insurrection in the south that has been provoked by the oppression of his German officials, he prepares to embark on a crusade against the Byzantine usurper Alexius III Angelus, but he catches cold while hunting at Messina and dies September 28 at age 32.

A 15-year German civil war begins upon the sudden death of Henry VI (above), whose Waiblinger (Ghibelline) brother Philip of Swabia is supported by France's Philip II against the Welf (Guelph) Otto of Brunswick, son of Henry the Lion, who is supported by England's Richard the Lion-Hearted.

Bulgarian insurgent Peter Asen is assassinated by rival boyars and is succeeded by his younger brother Kaloyan (Joannitsa) who becomes czar of the Bulgarians and who will complete the conquest of northern Bulgaria from the Byzantines.

Bohemia ends 14 years of dynastic struggle during which the country has had some 10 different rulers. Duke Ottokar I, who was deposed in 1193, is restored to power and begins a 37-year reign in which he will strenghten Bohemia by taking advantage of German civil war to make Bohemia a decisive factor in German affairs.

Château Gaillard is completed on the Seine by England's Richard the Lion-Hearted as he fights a war of vengeance to restore Angevin power in northern France.

1198 *"Dieu et mon droit"* (God and my own right) is adopted as the motto of the royal arms of England by Richard the Lion-Hearted at the Battle of Gisors. Richard asserts that he is no vassal of France but royal by God's grace and his own, but he is forced to cede Gisors to France's Philip II, along with the fortresses of Neaufles and Dangu.

France's Philip II is excommunicated by the new pope, Innocent III, for repudiating his 1193 marriage to Ingeborg, 22-year-old sister of Denmark's Canute VI to whom he took an almost instant dislike, but public opinion forces Philip to effect a reconciliation with the pope.

The Teutonic Knights (Order of the Knights of the Hospital of St. Mary of the Teutons in Jerusalem) is established by Germans gathered for a new crusade (*see* 1191). Headquarters of the order will remain at Acre until 1291, membership will be open only to Germans, and knighthood will be reserved for noblemen (*see* 1226; Battle of Tannenberg, 1410).

1199 England's Richard the Lion-Hearted lays claim to a French treasure trove, he becomes embroiled in a dispute with the viscount of Limoges, and he harries Limousin and lays siege to the castle of Chalus. He is wounded in the shoulder by a crossbow bolt while directing an assault on the castle, the wound mortifies, and Richard dies April 6 at age 32. He is succeeded by his brother John Lackland (or Softsword), who is crowned with support of the Norman barons who reject claims of primogeniture advanced by supporters of John's nephew Arthur, 12-year-old posthumous son of the late Geoffrey, count of Brittany, who died in 1186.

The right of German princes to elect the German king is confirmed in the Declaration of Speyer.

Japan's shogun Yoritomo Minamoto dies at age 52 after a 7-year reign that has founded the Kamakura shogunate. A council of 13 takes power under the leadership of Yoritomo's widow Masako and her father Tokimasa Hojo, 62, who has supported Yoritomo against the Taira.

Liverpool is founded at the mouth of the Mersey River in the west of England (*see* 1207).

1200 The Peace of Le Goulet ends hostilities between England and France.

Anglesey is seized by the prince of North Wales, Llewelyn, who 6 years ago returned from exile and drove his uncle David I from his territory.

Poetry *Der Arme Heinrich* by German poet Hartmann von Aue is an epic poem.

13th CENTURY

1201 The St. Gotthard Pass opens through the Swiss Alps between the cantons of Uri and Ticino.

Europe's commercial capital is Venice, whose location is midway between the East and the cities of Europe. Venice's Lido and marshes protect it from invaders, and its position gives it natural access via the Adriatic to both the eastern and western Mediterranean, with direct connections via the Po and Adige Valleys to the rich north Italian cities of Brescia, Ferrara, Mantua, Milan, Padua, and Verona. The city has links via eastern Alpine passes to the cities of southern Germany and via western Alpine passes to Constance, Geneva, Lucerne, and Zurich, and while Genoa's commercial ventures receive little official encouragement, Venice's doge and senate are eager to support commercial interests.

1202 Pope Innocent III requests a Fourth Crusade in hopes of reuniting the Greek and Roman Churches, which have been split since 1054, but he lacks seapower for an invasion of Egypt and the Holy Land. The pope gives the count of Champagne, Thibaut III, command of the new Crusade, but Thibaut dies and is replaced by the count of Montferrat, Boniface III. Montferrat gains support from Venice's doge Enrico Dandolo, now 94, who has abstained from earlier Crusades because the Arabs are Venice's best customers but who now sees potential for profit. Dandolo agrees to provide ships for a maritime attack on Egypt provided that he be given 85,000 marks plus half of all the booty. The Crusaders gather at Venice in the autumn, but they cannot raise the 85,000 marks, and Dandolo finally agrees to transport the Crusaders on condition that they first sack the city of Zara on the Dalmatian coast.

The Crusaders sack Zara in November and are joined by Alexius, son of the deposed Byzantine emperor Isaac II Angelus. Alexius makes large promises and persuades many of the Crusaders to follow him to Constantinople and overthrow the usurper Alexius III.

Pope Innocent III excommunicates the Fourth Crusade following the sack of Zara (above).

The papal bull "Venerabilem" asserts the Vatican's right to pass upon the fitness of any candidate elected to rule the Holy Roman Empire and to review disputed or irregular elections (*see* 1338).

Court jesters make their first appearance in European courts.

1203 The Fourth Crusade reaches Constantinople in July, and the usurper Alexius III takes flight and dies in exile. The Crusaders retrieve the blind Isaac II Angelus from the dungeons and restore him to the Byzantine throne, but Isaac's mind has grown feeble after 8 years in prison, and his son Alexius rules as regent for the vicious Isaac.

Mohammed of Ghor completes his conquest of Upper India.

Arthur, count of Brittany, is murdered at Rouen by order of his uncle John Lackland of England, who removes any chance that the 16-year-old boy may challenge John's claim to the throne.

Siena University has its beginnings.

Poetry *Parzival* by German poet Wolfram von Eschenbach, 31, is an epic romance of the Holy Grail based on *Perceval* by the late Chrétien de Troyes.

Livestock breedings and vineculture increase in parts of France and the Lowlands as cheap grain from the new granary in the Baltic Sea region makes it less profitable to grow wheat, rye, barley, and oats.

Famine ravages England and Ireland as it will repeatedly throughout this century. Recurrent crop failures will bring hardship to the British Isles, the German states, and Poland, but cheap grain from the Balkans will lower food prices in much of the Continent.

A large brewing industry develops at Hamburg and in the Lowlands as barley malt from the Baltic becomes more readily available at lower prices.

1204 The blind Byzantine emperor Isaac II Angelus is deposed again after a 6-month reign with his son Alexius IV Angelus. The throne is usurped by Isaac's general Mourzouphles, who has the son put to death and who is proclaimed emperor with the title Alexius V Ducas. The new emperor tries to defend Constantinople against the Fourth Crusaders, but the city falls April 12 and is mercilessly sacked. Alexius is driven out of the city, arrested in Morea, and executed.

A Latin empire is established at Constantinople, and the 33-year-old count of Flanders Baldwin IX is elected first emperor. He begins a brief reign as Baldwin I.

The Venetian Thomas Morotinople is made patriarch of Constantinople, and Venice's Doge Enrico Dandolo receives "a quarter and a half" of the Eastern Empire, adding numerous islands and coastal ports to expand Venetian territory and influence.

The empire of Trebizond that will survive until 1461 is founded by Byzantine leaders who establish themselves under Alexius Comnenus on the northern coast of Anatolia at Trebizond. David Comnenus is at Sinope, Theodore Lascaris is in Bithynia, Theodore Mancaphas is at Philadelphia, Manual Maurozomes is in the Meander Valley, while Leo Gabalas takes over the island of Rhodes.

An independent Greek empire is founded by Michael Angelus Comnenus who makes himself despot of Epirus and begins a 10-year reign.

Thessalonica is sacked by the count of Montferrat Boniface III who has been chosen leader of the Fourth Crusade following the death of the count of Champagne Thibaut III. Boniface will rule Greece and Macedonia as king of Thessalonica until 1207.

Bubonic plague reduces the ranks of the Fourth Crusaders, prevents them from reaching Jerusalem, and ends the Crusade.

A hospital of the Holy Spirit is founded at Rome by Pope Innocent III.

The University of Vicenza has its beginnings.

Damson plum trees from Damascus are planted in France by returning knights who will hasten the spread to Europe of such Arabic products as rice, sugar, lemons, and cotton.

1205 Frankish Crusaders are defeated near Adrianople by the Bulgarian king Kaloyan, who is supported by the Cumans and by local Greeks in a battle at which the Venetian doge Enrico Dandolo and the emperor Baldwin I are defeated. Dandolo dies at age 97, Baldwin is captured, Baldwin's able 31-year-old brother is named regent, and when Baldwin dies in captivity the brother begins an 11-year reign as Henry I.

Hungary's Arpad dynasty begins its most disastrous reign. The king who succeeded Emeric I last year as Ladislas III is dethroned by Emeric's brother Andras who begins a profligate 30-year reign as Andras II.

1206 The Persian sultan Mohammed of Ghor, who has founded Moslem power in India, is assassinated, and Delhi is taken over by his former viceroy Kuth-ud-din-Aibak, first independent Mohammedan ruler of north India. A former slave from Turkestan who was named viceroy in 1192, Aibak will be killed playing polo in 1210, but the slave dynasty he founds will rule until 1266 and will be followed by five other slave dynasties, which will rule until 1526.

The Ulgurs on the Chinese border are overrun by Mongol forces led by their 44-year-old chief Temujin, who is proclaimed Genghis Khan ("Emperor Within the Seas") at Karakorum.

Block printing has been adopted by the Ulgurs (above), who use it to print Buddhist works in the Turkish language, using alphabet script derived from the Phoenician through Aramaic and other languages, with Sanskirt notes and Chinese page numbers. The Ulgur scholar Tatatonga is employed by Genghis Khan (above) and applies the Ulgur script to the Mongol language.

1207 Liverpool becomes chief English port for trade with Ireland following the silting up of the river Dee, which makes the approach to Chester unnavigable.

1208 The German king Philip of Swabia is murdered June 21 at Bamberg by the 26-year-old Otto of Wittelsbach, Bavaria's count palatine, to whom he has refused the hand of his 10-year old eldest daughter Beatrix. Otto has been at odds with Philip since 1198, he receives overtures from many former supporters of Philip, and he is chosen king November 11 at Frankfort. He is betrothed to Beatrix and receives large concessions from the pope who has earlier sided with Philip.

The Nicaean Empire is founded by Theodore Lascaris (see 1204).

An Albigensian Crusade against the heretic Catharists of Albi is called by Pope Innocent III, and a Waldensian Crusade is called against followers of Peter Waldo. Church lands in the south of France have been appropriated by noblemen who have espoused the movement of the lower classes against Church corruption.

England is placed under interdict by Pope Innocent III (see 1209).

A school of medicine is founded at Montpelier by students from Bologna (see Arnold of Villanova, 1300).

1209 Carcassonne surrenders after a siege by the Crusader Simon de Montfort, 49-year-old earl of Leicester and comte de Toulouse, who captures the Albigensian "heretics." But war continues between the French nobility of the north and the Provençal nobility which has protected the ascetic "bon hommes" and their antisacerdotal teachings.

Scotland is invaded by England's John Lackland.

The Magna Charta signed at Runnymede by John Lackland limited the power of the English monarchy.

1209 (cont.) Otto of Wittelsbach invades Italy, he meets with Pope Innocent III at Viterbo, he refuses papal demands that he yield to the Church all territories in dispute before 1197, but he agrees not to claim supremacy over Sicily and is crowned emperor at Rome October 4 to begin a reign of more than 8 years as the Holy Roman Emperor Otto IV.

The coronation of Otto IV (above) is followed by fighting between German and Roman soldiers. The pope asks the emperor to leave Roman territory, Otto refuses to leave until he receives satisfaction for losses suffered by his troops, and he then violates his treaty with the pope by taking property that Innocent has annexed to the Church and distributing disputed territories among his supporters, whom he rewards with large estates.

∞ England's John Lackland is excommunicated by the pope in November for opposing the election of Stephen Langton as archbishop of Canterbury, an election consecrated by Innocent III more than 2 years ago. John has banished the monks of Canterbury and has threatened to prevent any English appeals from being brought to Rome, an action which last year caused the pope to place England under the interdict.

The Franciscan order of monks has its origin at Assisi, where Italian friar Giovanni Francesco Bernardone, 27, obtains approval from Pope Innocent III for rules he has drawn up to administer the new order. The friar has consecrated himself to poverty and religion, he has gathered some like-minded companions at Assisi, and his order will be confirmed in 1223 by Pope Honorius III (see 1212; 1228).

England's Cambridge University has its beginnings (see 1217).

1210 The Holy Roman Emperor Otto IV is excommunicated by the pope November 18 but proceeds to complete his conquest of southern Italy. The emperor's excommunication coalesces German opposition by princes who are supported by France's Philip II Augustus.

Poetry *Tristan und Isolde* by German poet Gottfried von Strassburg, who will die with his epic incomplete.

1211 Portugal's Sancho I dies at age 57 after a 26-year reign and is succeeded by his stout 26-year-old son, who will reign until 1223 as Afonso II (Afonso o Gordo).

China is invaded by Genghis Khan who will withdraw his Mongol forces in a few years to seek opportunities for plunder in the West.

1212 German princes elect a 17-year-old grandson of the late Frederick Barbarossa to succeed Otto IV, whom they deposed late last year. Otto returns from Italy in March and makes some headway against his enemies, but his wife dies in August, and his hold on the southern duchies is thus weakened. Young Frederick

arrives from Sicily in the fall and is welcomed in Swabia, and he is crowned December 9 at Mainz.

The Moors are expelled from most of the Iberian Peninsula by Castile's Alphonso VIII, who breaks the power of the Almohades at the Battle of the Navas de Tolosa just south of the Sierra Morena.

Crete (Candia) is conquered by Venice.

∞ A Children's Crusade is led by a French shepherd boy known only as Stephen and by a child from Cologne named Nicholas. Stephen's army is kidnapped by slave dealers and sold into Egypt, Nicholas's crusade is aborted in Italy, and some 50,000 children are lost (many are sold into slavery at Marseilles).

The Order of the Poor Clares (Franciscan nuns) is founded by the 18-year-old Italian nun Clara of Assisi with help from Friar Giovanni Francesco Bernardone (see 1209).

1213 The English Parliament has its beginnings in the Council of St. Albans.

Aragon's Pedro II is killed September 12 at age 39 in the Battle of Muret where he has resisted the Crusaders of Simon de Montfort who have used religious zeal as a pretext for invasion. Pedro is succeeded by his 5-year-old son who 2 years ago was betrothed to the daughter of Simon de Montfort and was placed in de Montfort's hands. The young king will be put in the care of the Knights Templar at the insistence of Pope Innocent III, he will be brought to Saragossa in 1216, and he will begin a reign that will continue until 1276 as James I.

∞ England's archbishop of Canterbury Stephen Langton returns after years on the Continent and absolves John Lackland, who submits to Pope Innocent III. Both England and Ireland become papal fiefs.

The German king Frederick, whose rival Otto IV is supported by his uncle, England's John Lackland, gains papal support by a bull he promulgates July 12 at Eger renouncing all lands claimed by the pope since the death of the emperor Henry VI in 1197.

1214 The Battle of Bouvines July 27 establishes France as a major European military power, brings Flanders under French domination, gains the imperial crown for Frederick II, and ruins John Lackland of England. A great anti-Capetian alliance formed by John with the emperor Otto IV, the counts of Boulogne and Flanders, and most of the Flemish, Belgian, and Lorraine feudal nobility suffers defeat near Tournai at the hands of professional cavalry fighting for Philip II Augustus in alliance with young Frederick, who will be crowned emperor in 1220.

Scotland's William the Lion dies at age 71 after a 49-year reign in which he has established a Scottish Church independent of the English Church and subject only to the see of Rome. He is succeeded by his 16-year-old son who will reign until 1249 as Alexander II.

Genghis Khan captures the Chinese town that will become Peking (*see* 1211; 1216).

1215 The Magna Charta signed at Runnymede in mid-June limits the power of the English monarchy. Feudal barons supported by Scotland's new king Alexander II meet with England's John Lackland between Staines and Windsor and exact major concessions reaffirming traditional feudal privileges contained in the accession charter signed by Henry I a century ago. John immediately appeals to Pope Innocent III, who issues a bull annulling the charter. John imports foreign mercenaries to fight the barons, but the Magna Charta will remain the basis of English feudal justice.

German nobles crown the Hohenstaufen king Frederick II at Aix-la-Chapelle July 25. Now 20, Frederick has been king of Sicily since age 3; he was married at age 14 to the daughter of Aragon's Alfonso II (widow of Hungary's late king Emeric), and the victory of his ally Philip Augustus of France at the Battle of Bouvines last year has strengthened his hand. His rival Otto will die in 1218 leaving him undisputed ruler of the Germans.

The Magna Charta (above) reaffirms human rights. Chapter 39 of the document states, "No freeman shall be arrested and imprisoned, or dispossessed, or outlawed, or banished, or in any way molested; nor will be set forth against him, nor send against him, unless by the lawful judgment of his peers, and by the law of the land."

The Fourth Lateran Council prohibits trial by ordeal.

The Dominican order of monks (Fratres Praedicatores, or Preaching Friars) is founded by the Spanish-born priest Dominic, 45, who was made canon of the cathedral at Osma at age 24 and who 10 years later attacked the Albigenses in Languedoc.

1216 French mercenaries land in England in January to help John Lackland fight the barons, who last year forced him to sign the Magna Charta.

The French dauphin Louis Coeur de Lion, 28, lands in England in May. Some of the barons who had earlier supported John rally to Louis, and many of John's French mercenaries desert to Louis. Lincoln Castle is besieged by barons friendly to Louis, the castles of Nottingham and Newark are taken by rebel barons in Nottinghamshire, Louis takes Winchester in the south, but he is unable to take Windsor or Dover.

England's John Lackland comes down with dysentery in October after crushing resistance in the north. He crosses the Wash and reaches Newark Castle, but he dies there October 19 at age 38. The king is succeeded by his 9-year-old son, who will reign until 1272 as Henry III, the earl of Pembroke William Marshal serves as regent, and the moderate party

takes control, thus ending the need for opposition to royal authority.

Genghis Khan invades the Near East with 60,000 Mongol horsemen who destroy ancient centers of civilization, ruin irrigation works, and destroy every living thing in their path (*see* 1214; 1222).

1217 French forces leave England after being defeated at Lincoln and at Sandwich.

Norway's late Eric X Cnutsson, who died last year after an 8-year reign, is succeeded by the 13-year-old bastard son of the late Haakon III Sveresson who ruled briefly from 1202 to 1204. The new king begins a 46-year reign as Haakon IV Haakonsson, with Earl Skule as regent.

Castile's Ferdinand III is declared of age at 18 and begins a rule of 35 years in which he will end the dynastic wars that have plagued the country and achieve successes against the Moors. As peace returns, there will be a renewal of Spanish agriculture, which has been disrupted by the wars.

A Moorish army is defeated by Portugal's Afonso o Gordo at Alcacer do Sal.

Salamanca University has its beginnings in a school founded by Alphonso VIII of Leon.

England's Cambridge University is founded (*see* 1209).

Vienna's bakers pay homage to Duke Leopold VI, who is about to leave on a crusade against the Moors in Egypt and the Holy Land. They offer him rolls baked in the shape of crescents (*see* 340 B.C.; 1683).

1218 The Holy Roman Emperor Otto IV dies May 19 at age 36, leaving the German king Frederick II without opposition.

The Peace of Worcester ends hostilities between England's Henry III and the Welsh.

Persia is conquered by Genghis Khan.

A Fifth Crusade is preached by Pope Innocent III at the Fourth Lateran Council as the sultan Malik-al-Adil is succeeded by Malik-al-Kamil late in the year. The king of Jerusalem John of Brienne is displaced as leader of the crusade by the papal legate Pelagius.

The Danneborg is adopted as the Danish national flag and will survive as the world's oldest national flag.

London's Newgate Prison is built. It will be used for more than 560 years as a debtors' prison (*see* 1782).

1219 Minamoto family control of the Japanese shogunate ends in January with the assassination of the shogun Sanetomo Minamoto while he is returning from the shrine at Kamakura. His uncle Yoshitoke Hojo, 57, has encouraged the assassins. He installs Yoritsume Fujiwara as shogun, although the real power remains in his own hands and in those of his sister Masako, and the Hojo family will rule Japan until 1333.

1220 The German king Frederick sets out for Rome in August. He promises the new pope Honorius III that he will undertake a new crusade, and the pope crowns him Holy Roman Emperor November 22, but he becomes involved in restoring order in Sicily, using cruel measures to suppress the country's anarchy.

Dresden's Boys' Choir is founded at the Kreuz-Kirche.

Geneva's St. Peter's Cathedral is completed atop the city's highest hill after 60 years of construction in Roman and Gothic styles (*see* Calvin, 1541).

1221 The Hojo family, which seized power in Japan 2 years ago, exiles the ex-emperor Gotoba and three other ex-emperors to various small islands. It installs the 4-year-old son of the exiled Juntoka as emperor in April, and replaces him in June with the 9-year-old Gohorikawa. He will reign until 1232, but he will be confined to one-quarter of the imperial palace.

Genghis Khan plunders Samarkand in his march to the West.

1222 A Golden Bull, issued by Hungary's Andras II under pressure from his son Bela and other feudal lords, strengthens the monarchy but limits its functions. The bull exempts the clergy and the gentry from taxation, it orders periodic meetings of the diet, it guarantees the nobility against arbitrary imprisonment and confiscation, and it grants landowners the right to dispose of their domains as they see fit.

The Mongols make their first appearance in Europe as Genghis Khan invades Russian territories.

England's Council of Oxford establishes April 23 as St. George's Day to honor the Christian martyr who died early in the 4th century. The patron saint of England is said to have slain a dragon (representing the Devil) to rescue the king's daughter Sabra (representing the Church).

No lands or offices may be given to foreigners or Jews under terms of Hungary's Golden Bull (above).

The University of Padua has its beginnings.

1223 The Battle of the Kalka River shows Europe the power of the Mongols. Their leader Subutai defeats a Russian army supported by Cuman allies, but the Mongols do not press their victory and withdraw back into Asia (*see* 1235).

France's Philip II Augustus dies July 14 at age 57 after a reign of 43 years. His weak 36-year-old son will rule as Louis VIII, but only for 3 years.

Portugal's Afonso II dies at age 38 and is succeeded by his 15-year-old son who will reign as Sancho II until the pope deposes him in 1245.

1224 A new Anglo-French war begins and the French take English lands between the Loire and the Garonne.

Franciscan monks arrive in England (*see* 1209).

The True Pure Land sect (Jodo Shin) that will be Japan's most popular religious sect is founded by the theologian Shinran Shonin, 51, as an offshoot of his master's Pure Land sect. The Jodo Shin will be rivaled only by the Zen.

Naples University has its beginnings.

Geographical Dictionary is completed by the Greek Moslem geographer Yaqut ibn 'Abdullah (Abdullah ur-Ruml), 45, who was captured as a child in Asia Minor, sold as a slave at Baghdad to a merchant who had him educated, and was later sent as the merchant's agent to the Persian Gulf and to Syria. Freed in 1199, Abdullah became a scribe and bookseller, he traveled in 1213 to Syria, Egypt, Iraq, and Khurasan (northeastern Persia), spent 2 years working at libraries in Central Asia, but returned to Mosul and Aleppo to escape the Mongol invaders of Genghis Khan.

1225 English territory taken by the French last year is regained with the exception of Poitou, the Limousin, and Perigord.

Cotton is manufactured in Spain. The fabric will compete with linen and wool (*see* 3000 B.C.).

Poetry *Roman de la Rose* by French poet Guillaume de Lorris whose allegorical metrical romance of courtly wooing will be completed by Jean de Meung (Jehan Clopinel).

"Sumer is icumen in" is sung as a round in England.

1226 France's Louis VIII dies at Montpensier November 8 at age 39 after conquering the South in a renewal of the 1208–1213 crusade against the Albigensian heretics. Louis is succeeded by his 12-year-old son who assumes the throne November 29 at Reims to begin a 44-year reign as Louis IX.

Francis of Assisi (Giovanni Francesco Bernardone) dies October 3 at age 44, 2 years after allegedly having a vision of an angel.

The Teutonic Knights founded in 1198 are commissioned to conquer and convert Prussia.

"Kreuzlied" is sung by Middle High German lyric poet and minnesinger Walther von der Vogelweide, 56, whose religious songs follow love songs such as "Unter den Linden" and political songs ("Sprüche") that he has sung at the courts of Philip of Swabia, Hermann of Thuringia, Otto IV, Frederick II, and others since 1198. The political songs have urged German unity and independence and have opposed the more extreme claims of the popes.

England's 19-year-old Henry III asks the mayor of Winchester to obtain 3 pounds of sugar, a quantity considered enormous.

1227 Genghis Khan dies at age 65 and his vast empire is divided among his three sons.

England's Henry III declares himself of age and begins a personal rule that will continue for 45 years, but he remains under the influence of Hubert de Burgh.

The landgrave of Thuringia Louis IV dies, and his widow Elizabeth, 20-year-old daughter of Hungary's Andras II, is driven out along with her infant son Hermann by Henry Raspe, the 25-year-old brother of Louis, who makes himself landgrave.

Frederick II embarks September 8 from Brindisi on a new Crusade to the Holy Land, but his army is stricken with fever. He lands at Otranto 3 days later, is suspected of malingering by Pope Gregory IX, is excommunicated September 29, and he spends the rest of the year in violent quarrels with the pope.

Japanese porcelain production is pioneered by the potter Toshiro who returns after 4 years of travel in China.

Construction begins at Beauvais of Saint-Pierre Cathedral.

Construction of Toledo Cathedral begins.

1228 A Sixth Crusade embarks for the Holy Land in midsummer under the leadership of the excommunicated Holy Roman Emperor Frederick II who capitalizes on dissensions among descendants of the late Malik-al-Adil to achieve his ends through diplomacy (see 1229).

Francis of Assisi is canonized 2 years after his death by Pope Gregory IX. Franciscan monks will play a major role in history for the next four centuries.

Papal soldiers of Pope Gregory IX (above) invade the lands of Frederick II (above) in what the pope calls a crusade against the "non-Christian" king.

1229 Frederick II gains possession of Jerusalem, Bethlehem, Nazareth, the coastal towns that have been taken by his Crusaders, and a corridor from Jerusalem to the port of Acre for use by Christian pilgrims to the Holy Land. He signs a treaty February 18 with the Egyptian sultan Malik-al-Kamil, nephew of the late Saladin. He enters Jerusalem, and because his accession is opposed by the patriarch of the city, he is obliged to crown himself King of Jerusalem which he does March 18 in the Church of the Holy Sepulcher, assuming the monarchy by right of his marriage in November, 1225, to the late Iolande (Isabella) who was the daughter of Jerusalem's titular king John, count of Brienne. Frederick returns to Italy in June and drives out his enemies with little trouble.

The Balearic Islands are conquered by Aragon.

The Inquisition at Toulouse imposed by Albigensian Crusaders forbids laymen to read the bible.

The University of Toulouse has its beginnings.

First Legend by Franciscan monk Thomas of Celano, 29, is a biographical sketch of St. Francis of Assisi

whom Thomas joined at age 14. His *Second Legend* will appear in 1247.

1230 The Treaty of San Germano in July ends hostilities between Pope Gregory IX and Frederick II who is absolved from excommunication after promising to respect the papal territory and to allow freedom of election to the Sicilian clergy.

Bohemia's Ottokar I dies after a 33-year reign and is succeeded by his son who will rule until 1253 as Wenceslaus I.

Berlin is founded on the site of former Slavic settlements.

Leprosy is introduced into England by returning Crusaders who have accompanied Frederick II to the Holy Land.

1231 A medical school is founded at Salerno by Frederick II who decrees that the school's curriculum shall include 3 years of logic, 5 years of medicine, and 1 year of practice, with a diploma to be granted at the end of the 9 years. The school is directed by Nicolaus Praepositus, author of the first medieval pharmacopoeia the *Antidotorium* (see 1235).

The Japanese shogun orders his people not to sell their children into slavery.

Japan has a famine in the spring that will be followed by many similar famines in this century.

1232 The Nasrides dynasty that will rule Granada until 1492 comes to power in the person of Mohammed I, 29, who will rule until 1273. He stiffens Moslem resistance to Christian Spain.

Verona's Ezzelino IV da Romano succeeds to power at age 36. He will be a powerful opponent of the papacy and will lay waste northeastern Italy.

Antony of Padua is canonized by Pope Gregory IX. The Portuguese Franciscan teacher died last year at age 36.

1233 England's Henry III faces a rebellion of barons led by Richard Marshall, third earl of Pembroke, who gain support from the prince of North Wales Llewelyn the Great and demand that Henry dismiss the Poitevin foreigners with whom Peter des Roches has filled the royal administration. The king summons Pembroke to Gloucester in August, the earl fears treachery and does not go, Henry declares him a traitor, and Pembroke crosses to Ireland where Peter des Roches instigates his supporters against the earl.

Mongol forces under Souboutai capture a Chinese ammunition works at Pien Ching.

The "Great Hallelujah" penitential movement begins in the north of Italy.

Pope Gregory IX entrusts the Inquisition to the Dominicans.

England mines coal at Newcastle for the first time. The town will become so famous for its coal that "carrying coals to Newcastle " will become a common phrase to signify superfluous effort.

1233 (cont.) A Japanese royal family adopts the ancient practice of staining teeth black (*ohaguro*). The practice begins to gain wide acceptance as a sign of beauty.

1234 The earl of Pembroke falls into enemy hands in April after a treacherous betrayal, he is wounded and dies in captivity, the new archbishop of Canterbury Edmund Rich, 59, rebukes Henry III for following foreign counselors, he holds him responsible for Pembroke's murder and threatens him with excommunication, the king dismisses his Poitevin friends, but he replaces them with a new clique of servile and rapacious followers.

France annexes Navarre and will retain it for two centuries.

Pope Gregory IX who canonized St. Francis of Assisi in 1228 canonizes the Spaniard Dominic, who began the mendicant Dominican order that rivals the Franciscans.

1235 The Mongols annex the Chin empire despite Chin efforts to resist them with explosive bombs.

Hungary's Andras II dies after a 30-year reign in which he has lost vast territories. His son succeeds as Bela IV to begin a 35-year reign in which he will try to recoup the losses sustained by Andras.

Frederick II of Hohenstaufen marries Isabella, the sister of England's Henry III.

Surgeons at the school of medicine in Salerno supported by Frederick II (above) dissect human bodies for the first time since the Ptolemic enlightenment of Alexandria in the 3rd century B.C. (*see* 1163; 1231).

Frederick II (above) employs Michael Scot to translate the writings of Aristotle from Greek into Latin.

1236 Castile's Ferdinand III recovers Cordova from the Moors who have held it since the 8th century. He encounters little resistance.

The Delhi slave dynasty sultan Altamsh dies after a 25-year reign in which he has enlarged and strengthened the Moslem Empire of northern India, has conquered the governors of Bengal and Sind, has escaped destruction by the hordes of Genghis Khan (who stopped at the Indus), has destroyed the capital (Ujjain) of the ancient Hindu kingdom of Vikramaditya, and has built the Kutb Minar tower at Delhi. He is succeeded by his daughter Raziya (Raziy'yat-ud-din) who will rule until she is assassinated by her Hindu followers in 1240—the only Moslem woman to rule on Indian soil.

Anesthesia is pioneered by the Dominican friar Theodoric of Lucca who teaches at Bologna. Son of a surgeon to the Crusaders, Theodoric advocates the use of sponges soaked in a narcotic and applied to the nose in order to put patients to sleep before surgery, he favors use of the opiates mandragora and opium, and he recommends mercurial ointments for skin diseases.

Bavarian knight-poet Neidhardt von Reuenthal dies after a career in which he has founded the popular lyric poetry of the German courts. He has been nicknamed Neidhart Fuchs (the Fox) for his poems ridiculing the rude life and manners of rich German peasants.

1237 Mongol forces under Souboutai use gunpowder and possibly firearms to conquer much of Russia, Hungary, and other eastern European territories. They devastate Poland but will fail in their efforts at conquest (*see* 1241).

A second Lombard League is shattered by Frederick II who gains a great victory November 27 at Cortenuova. Frederick has secured the election of his 8-year-old son Conrad as king of the Germans to succeed the imprisoned Henry.

The Teutonic Knights merge with the Livonian Brothers and move to convert Russians from the Greek church to the Roman as Moscow falls to the Mongols (above).

Eyeglasses and distilled alcoholic beverages will be introduced to Asia from Europe by the Mongols (above).

1238 Novgorod elevates the 18-year-old Aleksandr Nevski to the rank of prince. (He will be called Nevski after his victory on the Neva River in 1240.)

The Holy Roman Emperor Frederick II fails in an attempt to take Brescia from the second Lombard League. Pope Gregory IX has taken alarm at a projected marriage between Frederick's bastard son Enzio and Adelasia, heiress to Sardinia, and has made an alliance with the Lombard League.

France's Louis IX rebuilds Foulque Castle at Angers in slate on a white stone foundation.

1239 Pope Gregory IX excommunicates the Holy Roman Emperor Frederick II for a second time March 20, calling him a rake, a heretic, and the anti-Christ.

1240 The prince of Novgorod Aleksandr Nevski wins the name Nevski July 15 by defeating Swedish forces under Birger Jarl on the banks of the Neva River.

Mongols of the Golden Horde conquer Kiev as they sweep through southern and central Russia.

England and Scotland fix the border between them.

A crusade to the Holy Land that violates a prohibition by Pope Gregory IX embarks under the leadership of Richard Cornwall, 31-year-old brother of England's Henry III, and Simon de Montfort, 32-year-old earl of Leicester, who has married Henry's sister Eleanor, widow of the late William Marshal, second earl of Pembroke.

The earl of Leicester (above) has expelled the Jews from Leicester.

Bolognese poet Guido Guinizelli founds the *dolce stil nuovo* school of Italian love poetry.

1241 The Battle of Liegnitz (Wahlstatt) in Silesia ends in victory for the Mongols of the Golden Horde who cut down the feudal nobility of eastern Europe, including the German Knights Templar, but the Mongols who have invaded Poland, Hungary, and much of Russia soon retire to Asia upon the death of their khan Ughetai.

Pope Gregory IX dies August 22 at age 94 while the Holy Roman Emperor Frederick II is advancing against him. The pope has called a synod at Rome to depose Frederick who ravages papal lands, nearly takes Rome, and captures a large delegation of French prelates off Genoa who are en route to the synod (he is induced to release the clergymen by France's Louis IX).

A Hanseatic League is formed by Baltic trading towns that will soon include Lübeck, Cologne, Breslau, and Danzig with concessions as far distant as London and Novgorod (see 1158; 1250).

Ships of the Hanseatic League (above) employ new navigational discoveries including the rudder and the bowsprit. The rudder is an improvement over the oar that has been used canoe-fashion at the side of the stern, and the bowsprit permits the lower forward corner of the mainsail to be hauled beyond the bows so that a ship may sail more closely into the wind.

1242 England's Henry III invades France to support feudal lords in the South who have rebelled against Louis IX, but Aquitaine and Toulouse will soon submit to the king, and the coalition of rebellious barons will collapse.

The Holy Roman Emperor Frederick II pays a short visit to his German realms which have been threatened earlier by the Mongols. He gains some support by granting extensive privileges to certain towns.

The Mongol Golden Horde regroups at Sarai on the lower Volga under the command of Batu, grandson of the late Genghis Khan.

The Battle on Lake Peipus April 5 ends in a victory for Aleksandr Nevski over the Teutonic Knights.

1243 A 5-year truce ends hostilities between France and England.

Famine sweeps the German states whose towns are infested like most in Europe by black rats that have come westward with the Mongols (see Black Death, 1340).

1244 Jerusalem is recaptured by the Moslem mercenaries of the Egyptian pasha Khwarazmi whose action will inspire a Seventh Crusade, but Jerusalem will remain in Egyptian hands until 1517 and in Moslem hands until 1918.

Rome University has its beginnings.

England holds her first Dunmore Flitch archery competition.

1245 A Seventh Crusade mobilizes forces under the leadership of France's Louis IX who takes the cross against his mother's advice. He will embark in 1248 on an expedition to regain Jerusalem from the Egyptians who took the city last year.

Pope Innocent IV flees to Lyons as Frederick II resumes his ravages of papal territories and summons a general council. Frederick sends his justiciar Thaddeus of Suessa to represent him, but a sentence of excommunication is pronounced on the emperor despite his open letter rebutting charges of persecuting the clergy, abetting heretics, breaking oaths, and violating treaties.

Frederick II is declared deposed by Pope Innocent IV, and war breaks out throughout the German and Italian states as the pope orders the Germans to elect a new king.

Portugal's Sancho II is deposed by Pope Innocent IV who offers the crown to Sancho's brother Afonso, count of Boulogne. Afonso will reign until 1279 as Afonso III despite efforts by Sancho to regain the throne through civil war.

1246 German electors choose the landgrave of Thuringia Henry Raspe as king in May to replace the deposed Frederick II. He defeats Frederick's 18-year-old son Conrad near Frankfurt in August, but Conrad obtains help from the towns and from his father-in-law Otto II, duke of Bavaria, and he drives Henry Raspe out of Thuringia.

The last Austrian Babenberg duke Frederick II has died after a 16-year reign to end the dynasty that began in 976. The deposed German king Frederick II seizes the vacant dukedom of Austria and Styria, and he uses ruthless measures to suppress a formidable conspiracy of discontented Apulian barons (see 1278).

Franciscan monk Bartholomaeus Anglicus recognizes the contagious nature of leprosy but he believes that it comes from eating hot food, pepper, garlic, and the meat of diseased dogs, and that it is hereditary (see Hansen, 1874).

Poetry Meier Helmbrecht by German aphoristic poet Wernher der Gertenaere is the earliest German peasant romance. Wernher is one of the 12 founders of the Meistersinger guild.

1247 Parma falls to Lombard Guelphs who surprise the city while its imperial garrison is off guard. Frederick II concentrates a large army outside Parma and lays siege to the town.

The city of Buda is founded by Hungary's Bela IV to replace the city of Pest destroyed 6 years ago by the Mongols. Bela repopulates the city with foreign colonists, mostly Germans.

England's St. Mary of Bethlehem hospital for the insane has its beginnings. The word "bedlam" will be derived from its name and will be applied to situations such as those that will prevail in the new hospital.

Awe-inspiring cathedrals helped to keep religion the dominant force in medieval Europe.

Siena University has its beginnings south of Florence in Tuscany.

A gravestone erected in Yorkshire bears the inscription, "Hear underneath dis laihl stean/ las Robert earl of Huntingtun/ neer arcir yer az hie sa geud/ And pipl kauld im Roben Heud/ sick utlawz as he an iz men/ il england nivr si agen/ Obiit 24 kal Decembris 1247."

1248 Lombards besieged at Parma break out in February while Frederick II is off on a hunting expedition, they storm the imperial wooden town which Frederick has built and has named Vittoria in accordance with a prediction by his astrologers. The emperor's forces are scattered or destroyed, his harem and some of his most trusted officers fall into Lombard hands along with the treasury and the imperial insignia. The Lombards hack Thaddeus of Seussa to pieces, and they place the imperial crown on the head of a hunch-backed beggar who they carry back to the city in mock triumph.

Genoese forces take Rhodes.

The Crusaders retake Seville from the Moors, and the Seventh Crusade embarks for Egypt in August under the leadership of France's Louis IX, who is accompanied by his three brothers and the 24-year-old chronicler Jean de Joinville.

The University of Piacenza has its beginnings on the Po River in northern Italy.

Spanish poet Gonzalo de Berceo dies at age 68 after writing some 13,000 verses dealing largely with the lives of the saints, miracles of the Virgin, and other devotional subjects.

1249 Scotland's Alexander II dies at Kerrera July 8 at age 51 while en route to subdue the Western Isles which are dependent on Norway. He is succeeded by his 8-year-old son who will reign until 1285 as Alexander III.

The Hague becomes the seat of Dutch government as Count Willem II of the Netherlands builds a castle in the town.

Bolognese forces defeat and capture Sardinia's 24-year-old titular king Enzio, bastard son of the Holy Roman Emperor Frederick II. They will hold him in a dungeon until his death in 1272.

The Seventh Crusade led by Louis IX invades Egypt in the spring, takes Damietta without a blow, marches on Cairo, but is halted before Mansura.

Roger Bacon makes the first known European reference to gun powder in a letter written at Oxford. The 35-year-old English Franciscan writes 12 years after the Mongol invasions.

Oxford's University College is founded.

1250 The Battle of Fariskur April 6 ends in a victory for Egyptian forces who route the scurvy-weakened Seventh Crusaders of Louis IX and massacre them. Louis himself falls into the hands of the new Egyptian sultan Turanshah who has arrived from Syria to claim the throne left vacant last year by the death of Malik al-Salih Najm al-din. Turanshah releases Louis after he agrees to evacuate Damietta and to pay a ransom of 800,000 gold pieces.

The new Egyptian sultan advances from Mansura to Fariskur. His conduct troubles the emirs who have raised him to the throne, and when he advances to Shajar al-durr, they overthrow him. The Mamelukes will rule Egypt until 1517 and thereafter under Ottoman suzerainty until 1805. (Originally purchased as slaves from the Georgian Caucasus, the Mamelukes have fought in the armies of the sultans.)

The Holy Roman Emperor Frederick II dies at Fierentino December 13 at age 55 after a 38-year reign. He is succeeded as German king by his 22-year-old son who narrowly escapes assassination at Regensburg and who will reign until 1254 as Conrad IV.

England's Henry III confirms letters of protection to the "merchants of Germany" whose London Steelyard is an outpost of the fledgling Hanseatic League (*see* 1241; 1252).

Cinnamon, cloves, coriander, cumin, cubebs, ginger, mace, and nutmegs carried back by returning Crusaders are now to be found in rich English and European houses but are in many cases valued more for supposed medical value than for culinary purposes.

Arabic numerals and the Arabic decimal system, both of Indian origin, have been introduced to Europe by the Crusaders.

Poetry *Heike* by Japanese poet Yukinaga Shinanozenji is a popular epic account of the Taira family (*see* 825).

1251 Portuguese forces seize the Algarve in the southwest corner of the Iberian Peninsula.

Shepherds and farm workers in northern France abandon flocks and fields in a widespread insurrection. The rebels assemble at Amiens and then at Paris, they spread out to England, and the revolt spreads as far as Syria with bloody demonstrations and riots that meet with ruthless suppression.

1252 Castile's Ferdinand III dies at age 53 after a 35-year reign in which he has regained Cordova from the Moors and has obtained permission to establish a Christian church at Marrakah. His death aborts plans to invade Africa, and he is succeeded by the learned 24-year-old Alfonso X who will reign until 1284.

Aleksandr Nevski becomes grand duke of Vladimir by order of the grand khan who replaces Nevski's elder brother Andrew. The new duke works to prevent any renewal of the Mongol invasion.

India's Ahom kingdom is founded in Assam.

France's Louis IX expels the country's Jews (*see* 1182; 1269).

The Inquisition uses instruments of torture for the first time.

A Hanseatic settlement in the Flemish harbor of Bruges is established by merchants from Lübeck and Hamburg who have earlier taken joint action in England and in the Netherlands. They obtain common rights at Bruges (*see* 1250; 1259).

Florence issues 54-grain gold "florins" in an assertion of independence (*see* 1189; 1257).

The Kamakura Daibutsu is cast by Japanese sculptor Ono Goroemon 32 miles from Edo. The 40-foot tall 100-ton statue of the Buddhist divinity Amida has a circumference of 96 feet at its base and portrays the divinity in the traditional meditative position with hands in lap, palms up, fingers touching.

The Church of St. Francis is completed at Assisi.

Sake (rice wine) production is halted by the Japanese shogun to conserve rice.

1253 Bohemia's Wenceslas I dies after a 23-year reign in which he has encouraged widescale German immigration and has antagonized the nobility by seeming to favor the Germans. He is succeeded by his 23-year-old son the duke of Babenberg who will reign until 1278 as Ottokar II and who will make Bohemia one of the richest countries in Europe by opening her silver mines.

Franciscan friar Guillaume de Roubrock arrives at Karakorum on a mission from France's Louis IX and finds a silver fountain built for the Mongol prince Mangu Khan by Frankish goldsmith Guillaume Boucher. The fountain's four spouts dispense wine, mead, rice wine, and kumyss (mead and kumyss are alcoholic beverages made, respectively, from honey and mare's milk).

Price controls are imposed by the Japanese shogun to halt inflation.

The Sorbonne founded for indigent theological students is the first college in the University of Paris. It opens under the name Community of Poor Masters and Scholars and has been started by Robert de Sorbon, 52, who is chaplain and confessor to Louis IX.

1254 The German king Conrad IV dies in Italy May 21 at age 26, and election of his 2-year-old son Conradin is barred by German and papal opponents of Conrad and of the late Frederick II. The death of the last Hohenstaufen king begins a 19-year Great Interregnum in the Holy Roman Empire (*see* 1273).

France's Louis IX returns after an absence of 6 years in Egypt and the Holy Land and by moral force ends the dissension that has engaged his nobles in petty civil wars since the death late in 1252 of his regent Blanche of Castile.

1255 England's Henry III accepts Sicily for his 10-year-old son Edmund (Crouchback), earl of Lancaster, who has been given the title King of Sicily by the new pope Alexander IV.

Poetry *Frauendienst* by German lyric poet Ulrich von Lichtenstein, 55, is an autobiographical novel in verse containing minnesongs about chivalry. Italian poet and Franciscan monk Thomas of Celano dies at age 55 leaving behind lyrics to the hymn "Dies Irae."

1256 Venice and Genoa go to war in a conflict that will last for a century.

Italian scholar-philosopher Thomas Aquinas, 31, is given papal dispensation to receive the master of theology degree at the University of Cologne which had required that a master of theology be at least 34. Aquinas is named to fill one of two chairs allotted to Dominicans at the university and begins writing scholastic disputations refuting accusations against the Dominicans and Franciscans.

The monastic order of Augustine Hermits is founded.

1257 England's 48-year-old Richard of Cornwall, brother of Henry III, is elected Holy Roman Emperor, defeating Castile's Alfonso X, and is crowned at Aix-la-Chapelle. He establishes his authority in the Rhine Valley but soon runs out of money, and when he asks England's great council to give the pope one-third of all English revenue, the request is refused.

A gold penny twice the weight of a silver penny and worth 20 times as much is coined in a time of great economic distress by England's Henry III (*see* Florence, 1252).

1258 The Provisions of Oxford establish the English House of Commons in a move by the barons to restore the Magna Charta of 1215. The commons is a council of 15 men, most of them barons, who have veto power over the king and who are to be superseded by a committee of 12 that will meet three times each year with the permanent council of 15. Henry III, his

1258 (cont.) 19-year-old son Edward, and all other officials take an oath of loyalty to the new Provisions.

A rumor that the 6-year-old king of Jerusalem and Sicily, Conradin, is dead reaches Palermo where Conradin's regent Manfred is crowned king August 10. Manfred is the 26-year-old bastard son of the late Holy Roman Emperor Frederick II (Sicily's Frederick I), he refuses to abdicate when the rumor about Conradin proves false, insisting that Sicily needs a strong, native ruler. Pope Alexander IV excommunicates the handsome Manfred but the new king rallies Ghibelline support (*see* 1260).

The eastern Abbasid caliphate that has ruled Baghdad since 762 and has made it one of the world's great centers of learning and culture ends in a terrible slaughter. Hulagu Khan, grandson of Genghis Khan, sacks Baghdad and massacres tens of thousands in a single week.

Mongol invaders pillage Hanoi.

∞ A flagellant movement arises in Europe following widespread famine and disease (*see* below). Organized under masters, the flagellants wear special uniforms, live under strict discipline, and conduct public and private self-flagellation, beating themselves according to a set ritual to divert divine punishment and forestall plagues thought to be sent by heaven as chastisement for sins (*see* 1349).

🏛 England's Salisbury Cathedral is completed after 38 years of construction.

La Sainte-Chapelle is completed at Paris after 12 years of construction.

👤 Famine and disease follow crop failures in the German and Italian states (*see* flagellant movement, above).

1259 France's Louis IX yields Perigord and the Limousin
✗ to England in exchange for renunciation of English claims to Normandy, Maine, and Poitou.

China's Sung armies make the first known use of firearms that propel bullets. They repel a Mongol invasion with bullets fired from bamboo tubes.

💲 The Hanseatic towns Lübeck, Rostock, and Wismar agree not to permit pirates or robbers to dispose of goods within their environs. Any city that violates the agreement is to be considered as guilty as the outlaw (*see* 1241; 1300).

England's Henry III grants commercial rights to merchants of Genoa.

1260 The Yuan dynasty that will rule China until 1368 is
✗ founded by a grandson of the late Genghis Khan. Kublai Khan, 44, has himself elected by his army at Shant-tu (*see* Khanbelig, 1267).

The Mamelukes who have ruled Egypt since 1250 save the country from the Mongols at Ain Jalut and preserve the last refuge of Moslem culture. The Mamelukes revive the caliphate by inviting to Cairo a scion of the Abbasid house and giving him the title Mustansir l'Jllah.

Sicily's Manfred defeats a Guelph army September 4 at Monte Aperto with Ghibelline support (*see* 1258; 1265).

∞ The papal bull *Clamat in suribus* issued by Alexander IV appeals for unity among the forces of Christendom against the common danger of the Mongols.

⊛ Venetian merchants Niccolo and Maffeo Polo sail from Constantinople for the Crimean port of Sudak where a third Polo brother, Marco the Elder, has a house (*see* 1271).

💲 England's Henry III extends to all north German cities the trading rights he granted in 1250 to the merchants of Cologne and Lübeck.

🎨 Painting *Madonna* by Italian painter-mosaicist Giovanni Cimabue (Cenni di Pepo), 20, for Florence's Trinita.

🏛 France's Chartres Cathedral is consecrated after 66 years of construction. Built largely between 1195 and 1228, the great Cathedral of Notre Dame in the Loire valley raises Gothic architecture to its greatest glory with a Vieux Clocher rising 351 feet in height (the Clocher Neuf will rise 377 feet when it is completed in the 16th century).

1261 The Latin empire founded in 1204 ends July 25 as
✗ Constantinople falls to a Greek army under Alexius Stragopulos who has taken advantage of the absence of the Venetian fleet to cross the Bosporus and drive out the emperor Baldwin II who has reigned since 1228. The Palaeologi family that will rule until 1453 takes power as Michael VIII Palaeologus, 27, begins a 21-year reign, restoring Byzantine control.

Bohemia's Ottokar the Great annexes Styria.

🎓 Balliol College is founded at Oxford, England, where a school has existed since the 9th century (*see* 1167; 1209; 1264).

1262 Pope Urban IV determines to end Hohenstaufen
✗ power in Italy and offers the kingdom of Naples and Sicily to Charles d'Anjou, 36-year-old brother of France's Louis IX. A veteran of the Seventh Crusade, Charles has forced several communes in the Piedmont to accept his suzerainty (*see* 1265).

Crusaders on the Iberian Peninsula recover Cadiz from the Moors who have held the city for more than 500 years.

Aleksandr Nevski persuades the Tartars to accept a smaller tribute and to drop their demand that Russians render military service.

Norway's Haakon IV unites Iceland and Greenland with Norway.

1263 A Venetian war fleet off the Greek island of Spet-
✗ sopoula pounces on a Genoese convoy of merchant carracks and fighting galleys in early summer and gains a victory that will bring a partitioning of naval control in the Eastern Mediterranean. Venice has learned of the convoy's departure from its Monemvasia refuge for a destination either in the Cyclades,

Constantinople, or the Black Sea where Genoa holds a dominant trade position.

Scotland's Alexander III defeats the Norwegian king Haakon IV to win the Hebrides. Alexander has laid formal claim to the islands on which Scandinavians have settled since the 9th century. Haakon has sailed round the west coast of Scotland to Arran; Alexander has prolonged negotiations there in anticipation of autumnal storms. Haakon finally attacks but encounters a terrible storm that severely damages his ships. The Battle of Largs October 12 is not decisive, but it leaves Haakon in a hopeless position. He turns for home but dies en route at age 59 after a 46-year reign.

The grand duke of Vladimir Aleksandr Nevski dies at age 43.

1264 England's Henry III wars with the country's barons and is captured by the earl of Leicester Simon de Montfort after an ignominious defeat at the Battle of Lewes. Leicester becomes virtual governor of England and 2 days after the battle receives the surrender of Henry's son Edward, now 25, who has contributed to his father's defeat by a rash pursuit of the Londoners and who is forced to give up his earldom of Chester.

Oxford's Merton College is founded by the former chancellor of England Walter de Merton whose new school begins Oxford's collegiate system (*see* Balliol, 1261; Queen's, 1340).

Nonfiction *Summa Contra Gentiles* by Thomas Aquinas; *De Computo Naturali* by Roger Bacon.

1265 England's Prince Edward escapes from his custodians at Whitsuntide. He gains support from lords of the Welsh march who are still at arms, and he kills the earl of Leicester Simon de Montfort August 4 at Evesham. Edward will dictate government policy for the remaining 7 years of his father's reign.

Pope Clement IV induces Charles d'Anjou to accept the Kingdom of the Two Sicilies as a papal fief, offering conditions even more favorable than those offered by Pope Urban IV in 1262. He grants Charles all the privileges of a crusade; Charles sails for Rome. He narrowly escapes capture by the fleet of the Sicilian king Manfred, but he reaches Rome safely and is crowned by the pope.

The motet musical form developed by Franco of Cologne and Pierre de la Croix will not reach mature form until the 16th century.

London's Covent Garden market has its beginnings in a fruit and vegetable stand set up on the north side of the highway between London and Westminster by monks of St. Peter's Abbey. They begin to sell surpluses from their garden that exceed the requirements of their Westminster Abbey (*see* 1552).

1266 The king of the Two Sicilies Charles d'Anjou defeats his rival Manfred in battle near Benevento February 26. Manfred is killed at age 33 after a reign of less than 8 years, and Italian Ghibellines send envoys to

Bavaria to request the help of the 13-year-old son of the late German king Conrad IV. Young Conradin crosses the Alps to Verona where he issues a manifesto setting forth his claim to the Sicilian crown, his partisans take up arms in the north and south of Italy, and he receives a tumultuous welcome at Pavia and at Pisa.

A new slave dynasty at Delhi succeeds the one founded in 1206. Purchased as a slave in 1233, the new sultan Balban was made chamberlain in 1242, and he married his daughter to the sultan Mahmud. The sultan dies after a 20-year reign, and Balban succeeds to the throne to begin a 21-year reign in which he will end highway robbery in the south and east and will repress the Indian nobility with help from an effective army and a corps of royal newswriters.

Kyoto's Sanjusangendo Temple is completed.

English bakers are ordered to mark each loaf of bread so that if a faulty one turns up "it will be knowne in whom the faulte lies." The bakers' marks will be among the first trademarks.

1267 Pope Clement IV excommunicates Conradin in November for claiming sovereignty over Sicily, but Conradin's fleet gains a victory over that of Charles of Anjou (*see* 1266; 1268).

Peking has its beginnings in the town of Khanbelig constructed by Kublai Khan (*see* 1260; 1271).

Cambridge, England, is chartered by Henry III.

Members of London's goldsmith and tailor guilds fight each other in fierce street battles.

England's Roger Bacon, the first truly modern scientist, describes the magnetic needle and reading glasses, he predicts radiology, and he predicts the discovery of the Western Hemisphere, the steamship, the airplane, and television (*see* 1249; 1277).

Roger Bacon (above) describes principles of a camera obscura that can project pictures (*see* Porta, 1553).

1268 Conradin receives an enthusiastic reception at Rome in July but his troops are defeated at Tagliacozzo in August by the king of the Two Sicilies Charles d'Anjou. Agents of Charles seize Conradin at Astura, he is tried as a traitor and condemned, he is beheaded at Naples with his friend Frederick of Baden, titular duke of Austria, and the house of Hohenstaufen becomes extinct. The execution of the 16-year-old Conradin has at least the tacit approval of Pope Clement IV, it shocks Europe, antagonizes England's Henry III and France's Louis IX, and begins a long-lasting alienation of Germans from the Roman Church.

Pope Clement IV dies at Viterbo November 29 and will not be replaced until 1276 except for the antipope Gregory X (Tebaldo Visconti) who will fill the vacancy from 1271 to 1276.

1268 (cont.) France's Cathedral of Notre Dame at Amiens is completed after 49 years of construction. The immense church is one of the country's finest Gothic structures.

An earthquake in Silicia, Asia Minor, kills an estimated 60,000.

1269 Bohemia's Ottokar the Great takes Carinthia and Carniola from Hungary.

Niccolo and Maffeo Polo reach Acre, eastern outpost of Roman Christendom (*see* 1260; 1271).

France's Louis IX orders French Jews to "wear the figure of a wheel cut out of purple Woolen Cloth, sewed on the upper Part of their Garments on the Breast, and between the Shoulders . . ." (*see* 1252; 1306).

The first toll roads appear in England.

1270 France's Louis IX leads an Eighth Crusade, he arrives at Carthage after a 17-day voyage, but he dies of plague August 25 as his army is cut down by heat and disease. Louis is succeeded after a reign of nearly 44 years by his 25-year-old son who will reign until 1285 as Philip III (his father will be canonized as St. Louis in 1297).

France's Carcassonne is walled with an outer ring of fortifications by Louis IX (above) before his departure. The city is considered impregnable and will not be attacked for centuries.

The German poet-minnesinger Tannhäuser dies at age 65.

1271 Kublai Khan assumes the dynastic title that he will hold until his death in 1294 and founds the Mongol dynasty that will rule China until 1368.

Marco Polo, 17, joins his father Niccolo and his uncle Maffeo as they travel once more to Acre and begin a journey to India and the Far East (*see* 1269; 1274).

1272 The king of the Romans Richard, earl of Cornwall, dies at age 62 of paralysis following the murder late last year of his eldest son Henry of Cornwall by the sons of the late Simon de Montfort.

England's Henry III dies at Westminster November 16 at age 65 after a reign of 56 years. His 33-year-old son Edward hears of the death late in the year while in Sicily on an Eighth Crusade. He will do homage in late July of next year to his cousin Philip III at Paris, and he will reign as Edward I (*see* 1274).

Languedoc comes under French control following the death of Philip III's uncle Alphonse of Poitiers.

A silk-reeling machine is invented and will spur the use of silk textiles.

Caephilly Castle is built in Wales by Gilbert de Clare, 29, earl of Gloucester and Hertford.

1273 The Great Interregnum that has left the Holy Roman Empire without a ruler since the death of the last Hohenstaufen king in 1254 ends September 29 with the election of the Count of Hapsburg as German king. The 55-year-old Rudolph has increased his estates at the expense of his uncle Hartmann of Kyburg and of the bishops of Strasbourg and Basel, he has gained election largely through the efforts of his brother-in-law Frederick III of Hohenzollern, burgrave of Nuremberg, he has purchased support from the duke of Saxe-Lauenburg and the duke of Upper Bavaria by betrothing two of his daughters to them. He promises to renounce imperial rights in Rome, in the papal territories, and in Sicily. He vows to lead a new crusade, and is thereupon recognized by Pope Gregory X who crowns him October 24 at Aix-la-Chapelle, and he begins an 18-year reign as the emperor Rudolph I.

Nonfiction *Summa Theologica* by Thomas Aquinas, now 48, who began the work in 1267 but who stops writing December 6 leaving it incomplete: "I can do no more; such things have been revealed to me that all I have written seems as straw, and I now await the end of my life" (Aquinas will die March 7 of next year) (*see* 1323).

The Persian poet Djeleddin Rumi dies. He has founded the Order of the Dancing Dervishes.

Painting Roman painter-mosaicist Pietro Cavallini, 23, completes mosaics for Rome's Church of Santa Maria Maggiore.

Peking's Drum Tower is erected at Khanbelig (*see* 1267).

1274 England's Edward I lands at Dover August 2, he is crowned at Westminster August 18, and he begins a reign of 33 years.

China's Kublai Khan sends an invasion fleet to conquer Japan whose emperor has refused dispatches calling on him to submit. 300 large vessels plus 400 to 500 smaller vessels manned by 8,000 Korean and 20,000 Mongol troops begin landing at Hakata Bay in Kyushu October 19. The invaders are equipped with iron cannons and cannonballs, they use poisoned arrows, and they violate traditional Japanese protocol, but a typhoon strikes November 20 sinking more than 200 Mongol ships along with 13,000 men sleeping aboard, and the survivors retreat to the mainland in terror (*see* 1281).

England's Edward I (above) takes over the Kentish castle of Leeds begun by a Saxon chief and rebuilt by the Norman baron Robert de Crevecoeur in 1119. Edward will make many improvements.

Marco Polo visits Yunnan and sees the "Tartars" eating raw beef, mutton, buffalo, poultry, and other flesh chopped and seasoned with garlic. Young Polo will enter the service of Kublai Khan next year and will continue until 1292.

1275 Amsterdam is chartered by the count of Holland Floris IV who exempts the new town from certain taxes.

Chirurgia by William of Saliceto contains the earliest record of human dissection, a practice discouraged by the Church since 1163.

Zohar by the Jewish theologian Moses de Leon will endure as the fundamental work on Jewish mysticism.

Lausanne's Cathedral of Notre-Dame is consecrated with great pomp and ceremony by Pope Gregory X.

1276 The prince of North Wales Llewelyn II ab Gruffyd, grandson of the late Llewelyn the Great, refuses to pay homage to England's Edward I. The English king prepares to invade North Wales.

The German king Rudolph outlaws Bohemia's Ottokar the Great, but Ottokar submits to Rudolph who permits him to retain Bohemia and Moravia.

Augsburg becomes a free city. Founded in 14 B.C., it is now a major textile-producing center.

Paper-making reaches Montefano in Italy (*see* 1189; 1293).

Theater *Le Jeu de la feuille* by French playwright Adam de la Halle, 26.

1277 England's Edward I invades North Wales, blocks all the avenues to Snowdon, and forces the surrender of Llewelyn ab Gruffyd for lack of supplies. Edward reduces the Welsh prince to the status of a petty chieftain and will devote the next 5 years to establishing English government in the districts ceded by Llewelyn (*see* 1282).

The Visconti family that will rule Milan for 170 years gains control in the person of the Ghibelline leader Matteo Visconti, 27, whose 70-year-old great uncle Ottone Visconti is Milan's archbishop (*see* 1351).

Bulgaria's Constantine Asen is killed by a peasant usurper after a 19-year reign as czar in which he has fought the Hungarians and the Byzantine emperor Michael VIII Palaeologus. The Asen dynasty that has ruled since late in the last century is extinguished and Bulgarians will be subject to Serbian, Greek, and Mongol overlords.

England's Roger Bacon is imprisoned for heresy. He will remain imprisoned until 2 years before his death at age 80 in 1294.

1278 The Hapsburg family gains sovereignty over Austria to begin a dynasty that will continue until 1918. The Bohemian king Ottokar the Great has renewed his claims to three Swiss and Austrian duchies, the new German king Rudolph of Hapsburg defeats Ottokar August 26 at Durnkrut in Marchfeld. Ottokar is killed at age 48, and he is succeeded by his 7-year-old son who will reign until 1305 as Wenceslaus II.

Andorra in the Pyrenees becomes an autonomous republic. The French counts of Foix have been contesting possession of the mountain stronghold but agree to let it be independent.

London cracks down on coin-clippers but with unequal punishment. 278 Jews are hanged while Christians convicted of the same crime are merely fined.

The glass mirror is invented.

1279 Portugal's Afonso III dies at age 69 after a 34-year reign and is succeeded by his 18-year-old son who has led a rebellion against him. The son will reign as Diniz (the Worker) until 1325.

Kublai Khan calls in Egyptian experts to improve Chinese techniques of refining sugar (*see* 100 B.C.). The Egyptians have acquired a reputation for making exceptionally white sugar.

1280 Marco Polo visits Hangchow and finds it an eastern Venice, a city of 900,000 that Marco will call "beyond dispute the greatest city which may be found in the world, where so many pleasures may be found that one fancies himself in Paradise." Having come from Europe's most sophisticated city, Marco is awed by the countless ships bringing spices from the Indies and embarking with silks for the Levant. The city bustles with Arab, Persian, and Chinese Christian merchants who patronize busy hotels, restaurants, taverns, and tea houses.

Paper money, unknown in Europe, is used by the merchants of Hangchow (above).

Flemish textile workers rebel against their exploiters.

Poetry *Oeuvres* by the French trouvère Rutebeuf is a collection of poems barbed with satire.

1281 Kublai Khan sends a second invasion fleet to conquer Japan. 42,000 Mongol troops from Korea arrive in Kyushu in May, they are joined in July by 100,000 more from southern China, but the Japanese are saved by the elements as they were in 1274. A typhoon destroys most of the Mongol invasion fleet July 29, more than 2,000 of the invaders are taken prisoner, scarcely one-fifth of the Mongols and Koreans survive, and the Japanese begin calling typhoons kamikaze (divine winds).

Kublai Khan employs imperial inspectors to examine the crops each year with a view to buying up surpluses for storage against possible famine.

1282 The prince of North Wales Llewelyn II ab Gruffyd leads a second rebellion against England's Edward I. He is killed in a skirmish near Builth in central Wales by Roger de Mortimer who is himself killed.

The Sicilian Vespers rebellion that begins in a church outside Palermo at the hour of vespers March 31 (Easter Tuesday) leads to a wholesale massacre of the French and triggers a war that will continue for years. A French soldier has allegedly insulted a Sicilian woman but the real basis of the rebellion is the heavy taxation imposed by Charles I (Charles d'Anjou) to equip an expedition against Constantinople.

1282 (cont.) Sicilian noblemen support the popular uprising against French insolence and cruelty, they persuade the king of Aragon Pedro III to assert claims to the Sicilian crown (Pedro's wife Constanza is the daughter of the late Sicilian king Manfred killed in 1266), and Pedro arrives at Palermo in September.

Florence's bourgeois merchants stage an armed rebellion against the nobility and set up a reformed government with the sanction of Pope Martin IV.

💲 Florence's upper classes are known as the *popolo grasso* (fat people), the poor are the *popolo minuto* (small, or lean people). Detached from the soil, the city's lower classes are dependent on their employers who often force them to labor at night by torchlight.

1284 Castile's Alfonso El Sabio (the Wise) dies at Seville at
✗ age 63 after a 32-year reign in which he is reputed to have said, "Had I been present at the Creation, I would have given some useful hints for the better ordering of the universe." He is succeeded by his second son Sancho whom he has tried to exclude from the succession but who will rule through violence and strife as Sancho IV (el Bravo) until his own death at age 37 in 1295.

💲 Silver ducats are coined for the first time at Venice which prospers in trade with the East while Florence thrives on trade with the North (*see* florins, 1242).

🌐 Rats are so prevalent in Europe that a story appears about a piper who leads children into a hollow because townspeople have refused to pay him for piping their rats into the river Weser. Rattenfanger von Hameln may also have reference to the Children's Crusade of 1212, but much distress is caused by rats which consume grain stores, seeds, poultry, and eggs and which also bite infants and spread disease (*see* 1483; Black Death, 1340).

✗ Ravioli is eaten at Rome where the people have been eating lagano cum caseo (fettucini) since early in the century.

1285 The king of the Two Sicilies Charles I (Charles d'An-
✗ jou) dies at Foggia January 7 at age 58 as he prepares to invade Sicily again with a new fleet from Provence. His 34-year-old son Charles the Lame remains a prisoner of the king of Aragon but beginning in 1289 will reign as Charles II until 1309.

France's Philip III (the Bold) dies of plague October 5 while retreating from Gerona. He is succeeded after a 15-year reign by his 17-year-old son who will rule until 1314 as Philip IV in one of France's most momentous reigns.

☤ The plague that kills Philip III (above) turns the French back from their march into Aragon and kills most of the army's officers and many of the men as well as the king.

🌐 Smog problems develop as Londoners burn soft coal for heat and cooking (*see* 1306).

1286 Scotland's Alexander III falls from his horse March 16
✗ while riding in the dark to visit his new queen at Kinghorn. He dies at age 43 after a 35-year reign, two

sons and a daughter have predeceased him, and his only living descendant is the infant daughter of his own late daughter by the Norwegian king Eric Magnusson. The Great Council of Scottish tenants in chief appoints guardians to govern in the name of Margaret of Norway, but some clans begin a rebellion (*see* 1290).

The king of Aragon Pedro the Great repels a French invasion of Catalonia but dies November 8 at age 50. He is succeeded by his weak son who will reign until 1291 as Alfonso III and who will recognize the right of his nobility to rebel, a move that will make anarchy permanent in Aragon.

🎭 **Theater** *Le Jeu de Robin et Marian* by Adam de la Halle is the first French pastoral drama. The playwright presents it at Naples where he has followed the late Charles d'Anjou, king of the Two Sicilies.

1288 The new king of Aragon Alfonso III releases Charles
✗ the Lame on condition that he is to retain Naples alone, that Sicily is to remain an Aragonese kingdom, and that Charles is to persuade his cousin Charles of Valois to renounce the kingdom of Aragon given him by Pope Martin IV.

1289 Pope Nicholas IV takes office February 22. Charles
✗ the Lame meets with him at Rieti. The new pope absolves Charles of the promises he made to the king of Aragon, crowns Charles king of the Two Sicilies, and excommunicates Alfonso III as Charles of Valois prepares to take possession of Aragon in alliance with Castile.

Tripoli on the coast of Asia Minor falls to the Ottoman Turks (*see* Acre, 1291).

🎓 France's University of Montpellier has its beginnings.

▌▌ Block printing is employed for the first time in Europe at Ravenna.

1290 The Ottoman Empire that will rule much of the
✗ Mediterranean for the next six centuries is founded by the Bithynian king Osman al-Ghazi, 31, who 2 years ago succeeded his father Ertogrul as leader of the Seljuk Turks. Osman establishes the Islamic principality of Osmanli (Ottoman) and begins a reign that will continue until 1326.

The Khalji dynasty that will rule Delhi until 1320 is founded by the Firuz shah Jalal-ud-din. A Moslem long resident among the Afghans, Jalal-ud-din overthrows the Moslem slave dynasty founded by Balban in 1266.

Cuman rebels assassinate Hungary's Ladislas IV July 10. Dead at age 28, he is succeeded by his senior kinsman who will rule as Andras III until his death in 1301, the last king of the Arpad dynasty founded in 907.

Sweden's Magnus Ladulos dies at age 50 after an 11-year reign. He is succeeded by his 10-year-old son who will be crowned Birger III in 1302 and who will reign until his exile in 1318.

Scotland's titular queen Margaret, the maid of Norway, reaches the Orkneys where she dies in September under mysterious circumstances at age 7. Margaret had been betrothed to Edward, 6-year-old son of England's Edward I, who intervened to secure her throne in 1286, and her death leaves Scotland without a monarch (see 1292).

England's Edward I exiles the country's Jews at the behest of Italians who seek to handle English banking and commerce (see 1259; 1306; France, 1252).

The University of Lisbon has its beginnings.

A Chinese earthquake at Chihli September 27 kills an estimated 100,000.

1291 The German Hapsburg king Rudolph I dies at Spires July 15 at age 73 after a reign of nearly 18 years. He has invested his 41-year-old son Albrecht with Austria but has been unable to obtain Albrecht's election as German king.

Switzerland has her beginnings in the League of the Three Forest Cantons formed by Uri, Schwyz, and Unterwalden. The league is for mutual defense, but the cantons do not claim independence from Austria (see 1315; Lucerne, 1332).

Acre falls to Mameluke forces who end Christian rule in the East as enthusiasm for the Crusades wanes in Europe (see 1271; Tripoli, 1289). The Knights of St. John of Jerusalem settle in Cyprus.

Venice moves its glass ovens to the island of Murano to remove the danger of fire. The city establishes draconian penalties for any glassmaker caught jeopardizing the Venetian monopoly in clear glass by taking production secrets abroad.

Painting   Mosaics by Pietro Cavallini for the apse of Rome's Santa Maria in Trastevere.

1292 Adolph of Nassau is elected German king May 5 to succeed the late Rudolph I, but he has only nominal allegiance from many princes, including Rudolph's son Albrecht of Austria (see 1298).

The Scottish succession is resolved by England's Edward I who selects John de Baliol, 43, to succeed the late Alexander III and Alexander's granddaughter, the maid of Norway. John de Baliol is crowned at Scone November 30 after swearing fealty to Edward, and he pays homage to Edward at Newcastle.

Venice in this decade will develop the "great galley" that will be capable of long voyages with large cargoes. The shallow-draft single-deck merchant vessels, 120 to 150 feet in length, will have one or two masts for sails but will be powered mostly by oarsmen. Crews of 100, 200, and more will man two or three banks of oars with 25 to 30 benches of oarsmen on each side (see 1317).

Some 20,000 gondoliers pole their slim craft through the more than 100 canals that link Venice's 112 islands. Rich families in the lagoon city of 200,000 own as many as five gondolas, some of them up to 33 feet in length (see 1881).

1293 England's Edward I surrenders Gascony temporarily as a pledge following a Gascon-Norman sea battle. France's Philip IV confiscates Gascony and summons Edward to his court, and Philip's treachery precipitates a war.

A Chinese naval expedition to Java is forced to return after some initial success.

Florence excludes from its guilds anyone not actively practicing his profession. The Law of 1282 permitted nobles to participate in government only if they joined a guild, the new ordinance effectively removes the nobility from all share in the city government, and it gives rise to two factions of Guelphs. One faction will favor repeal of the ordinance, the other (its members will be called Ghibellines) will favor its retention.

Paper is manufactured in the Italian province of Ancona at Fabriano (see 1276; 1320).

Painting   Mosaics by Pietro Cavallino for Rome's Santa Cecilia in Trastavere.

A Japanese earthquake at Kamakura May 20 kills an estimated 30,000.

1294 China's Kublai Khan dies at age 78 after a 35-year reign that has established the Mongol (Yuan) dynasty, has subdued Korea and Burma, and has founded the city that will become Peking. The great khan is succeeded by his grandson Timur Oljaitu who will rule until 1307 and who will be succeeded in turn by eight short-lived and ineffectual Yuan dynasty khans who will rule until 1368.

The Siamese kingdoms of Xieng-mai and Sukhotai are forced to pay tribute to Kublai Khan before his death (above).

Genghis Khan and his Mongols invaded Eastern Europe but failed to keep the territories they overran.

1294 (cont.) England's Edward I begins a series of futile expeditions against France's Philip the Fair in an effort to regain his Gascon fortresses. He is supported by an alliance with the count of Flanders.

 England's Devonshire mines in the next 7 years will provide the country's mint with an average of 500 pounds of silver per year, but most English coins will continue to be made from imported silver.

Paper money printed with both Chinese and Arabic characters is used at Tabriz in Azerbaidjan (*see* 1280).

Travel in England is easier than it will be at any time for the next 500 years.

English grain exports supply the Continent with wheat from the South and barley and oats from the North. Collected in manorial barns and in market towns for carriage by wagon to the ports, the corn is carried in heavy wagons on well-maintained roads.

Famine strikes England with special severity despite the fact that more English land is tilled than ever has been before and ever will be again.

1295 England's Model Parliament sits at London where it has been convened by a summons to bishops, abbots, earls, barons, knights, burgesses, and representatives of all the realm's chapters and parishes: "Quod omnes tangit ab omnibus approbetur," says the summons (let that which touches all be approved by all), but most of the clergy soon quits to form its own assembly, or convocation, and the only Church people left are the great prelates who attend in a feudal rather than ecclesiastical capacity.

Scotland's John de Baliol ignores a summons to attend England's Edward I and forms an alliance instead with France's Philip IV, thus provoking an invasion by English forces.

Castile's Sancho el Bravo dies at age 37 after an 11-year reign marked by continuous dispute and violence. He is succeeded by his 9-year-old son whose minority will be a period of anarchy but who will reign until 1312 as Ferdinand IV (el Emplazado, the Summoned).

Marco Polo returns to Venice after having traveled from 1275 to 1292 in the service of the late Kublai Khan. He brings home spices, oriental cooking ideas, descriptions of Brahma cattle, reports of cannibalism, and curious ideas of diet.

Painting *Madonna with St. Francis* by Giovanni Cimabue.

Theater *The Harrowing of Hell* is an English miracle play.

Construction begins at Florence on the Church of Santa Croce designed by Arnolfo di Cambio.

1296 The Battle of Curzola gives Genoa a victory over the Venetian fleet. The Genoese capture 7,000 Venetians including Marco Polo who has commanded a galley and is thrown into prison.

Sicily elects her 24-year-old governor king after he has refused to yield Sicily to the pope. He begins a 41-year reign as Frederick II, but Carlos II of Naples attacks him to begin a 6-year war.

The Marinids who will rule Morocco until 1470 capture the nation's capital from the Berber Almohades.

The senile Turkish ruler Firuz (Jalal-ud-din) at Delhi, who has ruled since 1290 to found the Khilji dynasty, is murdered by his nephew Ala-ud-din who buys support with booty acquired in a recent surprise attack on Maharashtra. Ala-ud-din begins a 20-year reign in which he will consolidate the empire.

Scotland's John de Baliol surrenders in July to a bishop representing England's Edward I who has invaded his realm. He appears before Edward at Montrose and abdicates his throne. The English take him home in chains with his son Edward, they move the Scottish coronation stone from Scone to Westminister, and Baliol will remain in captivity until 1299.

England's clergy refuses a grant to the crown in accordance with the bull "Clericis laicos" issued by Pope Boniface VIII. Edward I withdraws protection of the clergy by the royal courts, he is supported by the public, most of the clergy evades the papal bull by making "gifts" to the crown, recalcitrants have their lands confiscated, and the pope is forced to modify his stand.

Book of Various Experiences will be dictated by Marco Polo (above) in the next 3 years to his fellow prisoner Rusticiano of Pisa. The book will describe the Orient in which the Venetian traveler has spent one-third of his life.

Costard apples sold in English streets by costard mongers at 12 pennies per hundred are among the earliest cultivated varieties.

1297 The Confirmation of Charters reaffirms the Magna Charta of 1215. A coalition of English barons angered by the loss of Gascony to France and of middle-class groups angered by rising taxes forces Edward I to reaffirm the great charter and to agree that the crown may not levy a nonfeudal tax without a grant from Parliament.

England's Edward I invades northern France.

Scotland's 25-year-old "Hammer and Scourge of England" William Wallace ravages Northumberland, Westmoreland, and Cumberland after driving the English out of Perth, Stirling, and Lanark. Wallace routs an English army of more than 50,000 at Stirling Bridge in September.

The giant Moas giraffe bird becomes extinct in the South Pacific islands that will be called New Zealand.

1298 The Battle of Falkirk July 22 in Stirlingshire gives English archers a victory over Scotsmen led by William Wallace. The longbow scores its first great triumph in pitched battle, taking a heavy toll of clansmen armed with swords and spears.

The bold German king Adolf of Nassau alarms the electors with his imperialist advances in Meissen and Thuringia. They depose him and kill him at age 48 in the Battle of Gollheim. Adolf is replaced by Albrecht, 48-year-old son of the late Hapsburg king Rudolf, who will reign until 1308.

The invention of the spinning wheel revolutionizes textile production.

The archbishop of Genoa Jacobus de Varagine dies at age 68 after having written a chronicle of Genoa up to the year 1296. He is more celebrated as the author of *The Golden Legend*.

1299 The Scottish patriot William Wallace begins soliciting French, Norwegian, and papal intervention in behalf of his country against England. Pope Boniface VIII persuades England's Edward I to release John de Baliol and his son Edward from captivity and let them move to France.

Rotterdam begins its rise to a position of importance. Count John grants the people of the Dutch port town the same rights as those enjoyed by the burghers of Beverwijk and Haarlem. Rotterdam expands the English trade that will help it become the leading Dutch commercial center and the third largest port on the Continent (*see* 1632).

Construction begins at Florence on a palace designed by Arnolfo di Cambio (*see* 1295). The front section of the Palazzo Vecchio will be completed in 1315 (*see* 1592).

1300 The papacy at Rome reaches its zenith as Pope Boniface VIII (Gaetani) holds a Great Jubilee to mark the beginning of a century (which will not actually begin until 1301). Some 2 million Christians make pilgrimages to Rome, where huge donations intended for the subjection of Sicily and for a second Gaetani state in Tuscany are raked over public tables by papal "croupiers."

The Vatican's treasury has been drained as a result of resistance, led by France's Philip IV, to the 1296 papal bull "Clericis laicos" which forbade laymen to tax the clergy and made it an excommunicatory sin for any clergyman to pay taxes and for any layman to impose them. Philip has forbidden export of precious metals.

The Hanseatic League begun in 1241 is solidified by a network of agreements among towns on the Baltic and on north German rivers. Ships of the towns import salt from western Europe, wool and tin from England, and olives, wine, and other commodities from Lisbon, Oporto, Seville, and Cadiz, to which they carry dried and salted fish, hides, tallow, and other items of trade (*see* 1344).

Florentine poet-philosopher Guido Cavalcanti dies August 29 at age 45 of malaria, leaving behind love lyrics, sonnets, and ballads. Cavalcanti has been exiled to Saranza with other leading Guelphs and Ghibellines but has returned to Florence to die.

The Baltic Sea has been rich in fish through most of this century and will remain so in the century to come. The Hanseatic fisheries have developed an efficient system for salting the herring, a fat fish, within 24 hours after catching it, and Europe holds the Hanse herring in higher esteem than fish salted at sea by Norfolk doggers or by English fishermen out of Yarmouth or Scarborough.

The first brandy is distilled at the 92-year-old Montpellier medical school by French medical professor Arnaldus de Villa Nova (Arnaud de Villeneuve, or Arnoldus Villanovanus), 65 (*see* 800).

14th CENTURY

1301 The Arpad dynasty that has ruled Hungary since 907 ends with the death of Andras III after an 11-year reign. The nomadic Magyars have adopted Christianity and have accepted an absolute monarchy under the Arpad kings. Andras defeated the late Holy Roman Emperor Rudolph I who claimed Hungary for his son Albrecht, but the king has not been able to control the Hungarian magnates and his death begins a civil war that will continue for 7 years.

The Ottoman sultan Osman defeats Byzantine forces at Baphaion.

1302 The Battle of the Spurs at Courtrai in Flanders July 11 follows a massacre of the French (Matin de Brughes). The flower of French chivalry is defeated by Flemish burghers led by Count Guy de Dampierre who have been alienated by Philip IV.

France's Estates-General is convened for the first time with representatives of the towns in their feudal capacity. They meet to show support for Philip the Fair in his struggle with Pope Boniface whose bull "Unam sanctam" asserts papal supremacy, saying, "Men live on two levels, one spiritual, the other temporal. If the temporal power should go astray, it must be judged by the spiritual power."

The Black Guelphs (Neri) triumph in Florence and expel the White Guelphs (Bianchi), among them the poet Dante Alighieri.

De Potestate Regia et Papali by the Dominican friar John of Paris defends the authority of the king, denies the ownership of ecclesiastical property by the pope (whose control is that of an executive acting for the community and who can be held accountable for any misuse of church property), and denies the papal claim to a unique type of authority.

1303 France's Philip the Fair sends Guillaume de Nogaret to seize Pope Boniface and fetch him back to France to face trial by a general council. On the "Terrible Day at Anagni" September 8, Nogaret and Sciarra Colonna gain entrance to the papal apartment, find Boniface in bed, and take him prisoner after threatening to kill him. Nogaret and Colonna are forced to flee but Boniface is taken to Rome and confined by the Orsini family in the Vatican, where he dies humiliated in October.

France returns Gascony to England's Edward I.

The carte mercatoria, or merchant's charter, granted by England's Edward I, allows foreign merchants free entry with their goods and free departure with goods they have bought or have failed to sell (with the exception of wine, which is too much in demand to be allowed to leave the country). Edward's policy, with some modifications forced by English merchants and by certain towns, will endure for nearly two centuries.

The Universities of Avignon and Rome are founded.

1304 Franciscan missionary Oderico da Pordenone, 18, sets out to retrace Marco Polo's journey to China in the 1270s. His *Description of Eastern Regions* in 1330 will corroborate Polo's accounts and will say that Canton is "three times as large as Venice" and that Hangchow is "greater than any [other city] in the world."

Painting Florentine painter Giotto di Bondone, 38, decorates Padua's Arena Chapel and breaks away from the flowing linear style of Byzantine painting that has prevailed for 500 years. The money-lender Enrico Scrovegni wants to atone for the sins of his father (who has been imprisoned for usury) and has commissioned Giotto to create frescoes for the chapel. Giotto portrays a genuine likeness of Scrovegni presenting a model of his chapel to three angels, and he accompanies it with scenes from the lives of the Virgin and Christ, including *Wedding Procession, Noli Me Tangere,* and *Lamentations over Christ.*

1305 The Scottish patriot Sir William Wallace is betrayed, Sir John Mentaith captures him near Glasgow August 5 and takes him in fetters to London, an English court at Westminister Hall tries Wallace on charges of treason. Wallace protests that he cannot be a traitor since he has never been a subject, the court nevertheless finds him guilty, he is hanged the same day, and his body is drawn and quartered (see 1299; Bannockburn, 1314).

Poland's Wenceslas II abdicates and then dies at age 34 after a 5-year reign. He is succeeded as king of Poland and Bohemia by his 16-year-old son who will reign until his death next year as Wenceslas III. Otto of Bavaria assumes the Hungarian throne to begin a 2-year reign as Otto I.

The French prelate Raimond Bertrand de Got, 41, is elected to succeed the late Pope Boniface VIII who died a prisoner in the Vatican 2 years ago. He begins a 9-year reign as Clement V (but see 1309).

France's University of Orléans has its beginnings.

Painting *The Life of Christ, The Last Judgment, Pietà,* and other frescoes for Padua's Church of Santa

Maria dell' Arena are completed by Giotto di Bondone.

Sculpture *Madonna and Child* by Giovanni Pisano.

Opus Ruralium Commodorum by Bolognese agriculturist Pietro Crescenzi (Petrus de Crescentiis), 75, is the first book on agriculture to appear in Europe since the 2nd century.

1306 The Premyslid dynasty that has ruled Bohemia since 1198 ends with the death of Wenceslas III at age 17 after a 1-year reign. The Holy Roman Emperor Albrecht I gives the Bohemian crown to his son Rudolf, but the Bohemians will not accept Rudolf and an interregnum begins that will continue until 1310. Wenceslas is succeeded in Poland by the diminutive former king of Great Poland who has gained the support of Pope Boniface VIII. Now 46, he will unite the principalities of Little and Great Poland, will be crowned at Cracow early in 1320, and will reign until 1333 as Ladislas IV (or I) (Lokietek).

Rhodes is purchased by the military order of the Knights of St. John of Jerusalem founded in 1113. The knights will defend the island until 1522.

France arrests her Jews, strips them of their possessions, and expels them (*see* 1269).

England whips and expels some 100,000 Jews who have remained since Edward I's expulsion order of 1290 (*see* Cromwell, 1657).

Only the tiniest fraction of the world's energy comes from sources other than manpower, animal power, and solar sources which include wood and windmills, but use of coal is increasing (*see* below; 1615).

Painting *The Lamentation* by Giotto di Bondone for Padua's Arena Chapel.

A Londoner is tried and executed for burning coal in the city (*see* 1285).

1307 England's Edward I dies July 7 near Carlisle at age 68 while preparing to take the field against Scotland's Robert Bruce and is succeeded by his fourth and only surviving son who assumes the throne at age 23 to begin a reign of 20 years as Edward II. The new king immediately recalls his homosexual lover Piers Gaveston from exile, abandons the campaign against Robert Bruce, and devotes himself to frivolity.

France's Philip IV seizes the property of the Order of the Knights Templar. The rich but decadent order has become the king's creditor as well as the pope's and has made itself virtually a state within the state, but Philip launches a propaganda campaign to stir the people against the Knights (*see* 1308).

Constantinople turns back attacks by 6,000 Catalan mercenaries headed by German military adventurer Roger di Flor, 27, who is assassinated by order of Andronicus II and his coemperor son Michael IX. The Catalan Grand Company turns westward and lays waste Thrace and Macedonia (*see* 1311).

The *Commedia* that will become immortal as *The Divine Comedy (Divina Commedia)* is begun by Italian poet Dante Alighieri, 42, as a philosophical-political poem recounting an imaginary journey through Hell, Purgatory, and Paradise (Inferno, Purgatorio, Paradiso). Dante's work of 100 cantos begins with the "Inferno" whose first lines are, "In the middle of the road of life/ I found myself in a dark wood,/ Having strayed from the straight path . . ." and which includes the line, "Abandon hope, all ye who enter here." Immortalized in Dante's work are his Florentine friends and enemies including the late noblewoman Beatrice Portinari de' Bardi who died in 1290 when she was 24 and Dante 25.

1308 England's Edward II journeys to France and on January 25 marries Isabella, 15-year-old daughter of Philip IV, while his favorite Piers Gaveston rules as regent at home. Gaveston marries the king's niece Margaret of Gloucester and receives the earldom of Cornwall.

France steps up her attack on the Knights Templar with an appeal to the Estates-General. Pope Clement V is obliged to cooperate, and torture is used to force confessions that will result in the abolishment of the order in 1312.

Albrecht I of Austria refuses demands by his 18-year-old nephew John for John's hereditary domains and he is murdered May 1 by conspirators organized by John (the Parricide) who flees to the south (he will be arrested at Pisa in 1312 and will be executed the following year). The 58-year-old Albrecht has been German king since 1298 and is succeeded by the 39-year-old count of Luxembourg who is elected king November 27. He will be crowned emperor in 1311 and will reign until 1313 as Henry VII.

The universities of Perugia and Coimbra have their beginnings.

1309 The Babylonian Exile of the papacy that will last until 1377 begins at Avignon, an enclave in papal territory within France. Clement V moves the papal court to Avignon at the request of his friend Philip the Fair since Clement's predecessor has been exiled by the anarchy at Rome. The Avignonese papacy will embrace seven pontificates.

The king of Naples Charles II dies in August at age 59 after a 20-year reign in which he has been forced to give up all claims to Sicily. He is succeeded by his cultivated 34-year-old son Robert who will reign until 1343, fighting the Ghibellines in behalf of the popes and supporting writers such as Petrarch.

Venice begins construction of a doge's palace that will not be completed until 1483.

1310 Venice establishes a Council of Ten to rule the city.

England's barons force Edward II to appoint lords ordainers to help him rule.

1311 Notre Dame Cathedral at Reims is completed after 99 years of construction on the site at which Clovis

1311 (cont.) was reputedly baptized in 496. The cathedral is a masterpiece of Gothic architecture.

The pulpit of the Pisa Cathedral is completed after 11 years of work by sculptor-architect Giovanni Pisano, now 66.

1312 The Gascon knight Piers Gaveston, favorite of England's Edward II, is kidnapped by English barons and is treacherously executed. Edward is forced to stand aside and permit 21 lords ordainers to govern the country under a series of ordinances drawn up last year.

Lyons is incorporated into France under terms of the Treaty of Vienne.

The Canary Islands are rediscovered by Genoese mariners (*see* Portuguese conquest, 1425).

1313 The Holy Roman Emperor Henry VII of Luxembourg dies at Buonconvento near Siena August 24 at age 44. He has taken ill while en route with Venetian allies to attack Robert of Naples.

Austria's Duke Frederick the Fair is called in by the nobles of Lower Bavaria but is defeated at Gammelsdorf November 9 by the Bavarian duke Louis.

Nonfiction *De monarchia* by Dante Alighieri is a treatise on the need for the dominance of royal power in secular affairs.

1314 The Battle of Bannockburn June 24 assures the independence of Scotland. 30,000 Scotsmen under Robert Bruce VIII, 40, rout a force of 100,000 led by England's effeminate Edward II and take Stirling Castle, the last Scottish castle remaining in English hands.

Private wars break out in England as Thomas, earl of Lancaster, 37, takes advantage of Edward's defeat at Bannockburn (above) to wrest control of the government from Edward and his new favorite Hugh le Despenser, 52, but Lancaster is opposed by other barons who make it impossible for him to govern.

Louis of Bavaria is chosen king of the Germans October 20 at Frankfort and is crowned November 25 at Aix-la-Chapelle to begin a reign of nearly 33 years. The 27-year-old Louis is opposed by Austria's 28-year-old Duke Frederick the Handsome who was chosen by a minority of the electors and who begins an 11-year civil war with Louis IV.

France's Philip IV dies November 29 at age 69 after a momentous 29-year reign. He is succeeded by his 25-year-old son by Jeanne of Navarre who has been king of Navarre since his mother's death in 1305, but France's Louis X will rule for scarcely a year and a half before his untimely death.

The grand master of the French Knights Templar Jacques de Molay, 71, has been seized by order of France's Philip IV (above), taken before the French Inquisition at Paris, charged with heresy, found guilty, and burned at the stake.

St. Paul's Cathedral is completed at London (*see* 603; 1666).

1315 The Swiss infantry gains renown and begins a brilliant career by handing Leopold of Austria a thorough defeat November 15 at the Battle of Morgarten. Leopold had sought to crush the Swiss for supporting Louis of Bavaria as German king against the claims of his brother Frederick the Handsome (*see* 1314).

The first public systematic dissection of a human body is supervised by Italian surgeon Mondino de Luzzi, 40, who shows his students the abdominal organs, the thorax, the brain, and the external organs. His *Anatomia* will be the first manual based on practical dissection.

A silk industry is developed at Lyons by Italian immigrants.

Disastrous famine strikes large parts of western Europe and will continue for the next 3 years.

English wheat prices climb to 3 shillings 3 pence per bushel as a short crop combines with export demand to inflate price levels.

Sharp drops in population will occur in some parts of Europe in the next 3 years as a result of famine.

1316 France's Louis X dies suddenly June 5 at age 26 after an 18-month reign. His posthumous son John born November 15 briefly succeeds Louis "the Quarreler" (le Hutin) but he dies November 22. Louis's 22-year-old brother Philip proclaims himself king, and he begins a reign as Philip V that will continue until early in 1322.

Lithuania's prince Witen dies and is succeeded by his brother (or possibly his servant) Gedymin who inherits a domain that extends from the Baltic to Minsk but is controlled largely by the Teutonic Knights and by the Livonian Knights of the Sword. Gedymin will marry his daughter Anastasia to Muscovy's Grand Duke Simeon, he will marry another daughter to the son of Poland's Ladislas Lokietek, he will marry his son Lubart to the daughter of the prince of Halicz-Vladimir, and by thus gaining powerful allies he will assist the republic of Pskov to break away from Great Novgorod and join with Lithuania to create a vast country ruled from the capital that Gedymin will establish at Vilna in 1321.

Eight Dominicans sent to Ethiopia by the new Pope John XXII check on rumors of a Christian king named Prester John (*see* 1145; 1459).

1317 France adopts the Salic Law to exclude women from succeeding to the throne (*see* 1322; 1328).

A fleet of Venetian great galleys makes the longest voyage undertaken by European trading vessels since ancient times. A quarrel between Venice and France has made land travel difficult.

The Venetian galleys (above) carry sugar, spices, currants, dates, wine, paper, glass, cotton, silk, damask from Damascus, calico from Calicut, alum, dyes, draperies, books and armor. The great galleys return with hides, leather, tin, lead, iron, pewter, brass, cutlery, bowstrings, Cambrai cambric, Laon lawn, Ypres diapered cloth, Arras hangings, caps, and serges that include serge de Nimes (denim) used for sailcloth—all obtained at Bruges, Europe's most important commercial city outside the Mediterranean.

1318 Ireland's Edward Bruce is killed in October at Dundalk 3 years after being proclaimed king. Younger brother of Scotland's Robert the Bruce, Edward has failed to conquer the country south of Ulster.

German poet Heinrich Frauenlob von Meissen dies at age 68. Founder of a meistersinger school at Mainz, von Meissen has been called "Frauenlob," meaning "praise of women," because he has used the word "Frau" for woman rather than the word "Weib."

1320 The Declaration of Arbroath asserts Scottish independence from England. The Scottish Parliament meets April 6 at Arbroath and drafts the letter to Pope John XXII reciting in eloquent terms the services which their "lord and sovereign" Robert the Bruce has rendered to Scotland (see 1323).

The Peace of Paris ends hostilities between France and Flanders which retains her independence.

Poland's Ladislas IV Lokietek is finally crowned 14 years after ascending the throne.

The Moslem Tughlak dynasty that will rule western India until 1413 is founded by the elderly Turkish shah Ghiyas-ud-din Tughlak who has gained numerous victories over the Mongols and who will make Warangal and Bengal provincial states before his death in 1325. Tughlak leads a rebellion that overthrows the Khaljis who have ruled since 1290 and as Gharzi Khan he moves the capital 4 miles east from Delhi to the new city of Tughlakabad.

Paper is produced at Mainz and will soon be made at Cologne, Nuremberg, Ratisbon, and Augsburg. Invented by the Chinese in A.D. 105, paper replaces the vellum which has given monasteries a monopoly on manuscripts and on written communication.

Paper (above) will lead to paper currency in Europe. First used by the Chinese in 1236, paper money was discontinued in 1311 when treasury reserves failed to keep up with the flood of paper money, depreciating the value of money through inflation and diminishing the financial (and moral) credit of Kublai Khan's Yuan dynasty.

Poetry *Sir Gawain and the Green Knight* by the English "pearl poet" deals with the legendary King Arthur and his round table at Camelot (see 537; 1190; 1203).

Painting Frescoes by Pietro Cavallini for the Church of Santa Maria Donnaregina.

1321 Hugh le Despenser is exiled by England's Parliament at the behest of the earl of Lancaster who con-

tinues to dominate the country in opposition to Edward II.

The University of Florence has its beginnings.

Italian poet Dante Alighieri dies September 14 at age 56 while attending Guido da Polenta at Ravenna. Dante's treatise *Concerning Vernacular Eloquence (De Vulgari Eloquentia)* is left unfinished but is a pioneer philological study of literary use of the Italian vernacular.

1322 France's Philip V dies at Longchamp January 2 at age 28 after a 6-year rule in which he has ended a war with Flanders and has inflicted heavy taxes on French Jews, extorting 150,000 livres from the Jews of Paris alone. Philip is succeeded by his 27-year-old brother who will be the last of the direct line of Capetian kings and who begins a 6-year reign as Charles IV.

The Salic Law adopted 5 years ago that the French throne can pass only through males is established in principle by the accession of Charles IV (above) to the exclusion of England's 9-year-old prince Edward, grandson of France's late Philip IV.

England's Edward II recalls Hugh le Despenser from exile and makes war against the barons. He defeats the earl of Lancaster at Boroughbridge, 22 miles northwest of York, has him beheaded at Pontefract, restores Hugh le Despenser as his counselor, and makes him earl of Winchester.

The Battle of Muhldorf September 28 ends in victory for the German king Louis IV, largely through the timely aid of Frederick IV of Hohenzollern, burgrave of Nuremberg. Frederick of Austria is taken prisoner.

Use of counterpoint in church music is forbidden by Pope John XXII.

1323 The Treaty of Northampton between Scotland and England recognizes Robert the Bruce's title to the Scottish throne and provides for the marriage of Bruce's son David to Edward II's daughter Joanna.

Pope John XXII canonizes Thomas Aquinas 49 years after the death of Aquinas.

1324 The Japanese emperor Godaigo tries to regain power from the country's feeble-minded regent Tatatoki Hojo who occupies himself mainly with drinking and dogfights. Now 36, Godaigo is betrayed by an informer, but he denies everything (see 1331).

Defensor Pacis by the rector of the University of Paris Marsilius of Padua (Marsiglio dei Mainardini), 34, and John of Jandun is a juridical treatise against the temporal power of the pope. Addressed to Louis the Bavarian, the work is denounced by the Vatican, Marsilius will be forced to flee Paris in 1326, Pope John XXII will condemn him and excommunicate him in 1327, but Marsilius will help Louis of Bavaria conquer Rome in 1328 and will enjoy imperial protection until his death in 1343.

Marco Polo traveled to China, served Kublai Khan, and returned to Venice with wondrous tales of the Orient.

1325 England's Queen Isabelle travels to France and arranges the marriage of her 12-year-old son Edward to the 11-year-old Philippa of Hainault.

The German king Louis of Bavaria accepts Frederick of Austria as coregent, but attempts at joint rule will not succeed.

Portugal's Diniz dies at age 64 after a 46-year reign that has raised the cultural level of the Portuguese court and has brought prosperity through agricultural and economic development. Diniz is succeeded by his 35-year-old son who ascends the throne as Afonso IV to begin a 32-year reign that will be marked by civil war with his son Pedro.

Delhi's Ghiyas-ud-din Tughlak is murdered by his son after a vigorous 5-year rule. He is succeeded by the parricide who will reign until 1351 as Mohammed Tughlak.

Mexico City has its beginnings in the city of Tenochtitlan founded by Aztecs in Lake Texcoco. The Aztec empire that now begins to arise is the culmination of a history that has seen Olmec, Teotihuacan, and Toltec cultures come and go (*see* 1521).

1326 The French queen of England's Edward II invades her husband's realm, which is effectively ruled by the earl of Winchester Hugh le Despenser and his son Hugh. Isabelle vows revenge for the execution of the earl of Lancaster in 1322, she has the support of her paramour Roger de Mortimer, 39-year-old baron of Wigmore who has been outlawed by Edward at the urging of the earl of Winchester, and Edward's supporters desert him. The king flees London October 2, he takes refuge on the Glamorgan estates of the earl of Winchester. Isabelle's forces capture both Despensers and put them to death. Edward tries to escape by sea, Isabelle's men capture him November 16, and they imprison him at Kenilworth Castle.

The first Ottoman emperor (emir) Osman I dies at age 67 after a 36-year reign. He is succeeded by his 47-year-old son who will reign until 1359 as Orkhan and who begins to extend Ottoman domains from Angora in central Anatolia to Thrace in Europe, taking the title "sultan of the Gazis" (warriors of the faith).

Orkhan (above) strikes the first Ottoman coin.

The Florentine banking house of Scali fails, and its 200 creditors clamor for the 400,000 gold florins they are owed. The creditors include France's Charles IV.

Oxford University's Oriel College is founded.

Cambridge University's Clare College is founded.

1327 England's Edward II is in effect deposed by his wife Isabelle and her lover Mortimer who have the parliament of Westminster force the king's abdication and replace him with his 14-year-old son who will reign until 1377 as Edward III.

The deposed Edward II is imprisoned at Berkeley Castle in Gloucestershire and is mistreated in hopes that he will die of disease and malnutrition, but the 43-year-old king has a strong constitution so he is put to death with cruelty September 21, and it is announced that he has died of natural causes.

Munich has a great fire which destroys much of the city.

1328 The German king Louis of Bavaria is crowned Holy Roman Emperor January 17 at Rome after forcing the surrender of Pisa. The Roman nobleman Sciarra Colonna places the crown on Louis' head and the emperor replies to attacks by Pope John XXII by proclaiming the deposition of the pope and undertaking an expedition against the pope's ally, Robert of Naples.

France's Charles IV dies February 1 at age 33, and his death without an heir ends the direct line of Capetian kings descended from Charlemagne. An assembly of French barons confirms the Salic Law that "no woman nor her son may succeed to the monarchy" and Charles the Fair is succeeded by his 35-year-old cousin who will reign until 1350 as Philip IV. He establishes the Valois dynasty that will rule until 1589, but he regards the monarchy not as an obligation but merely as a possession, and he leaves the country's administration to a royal bureaucracy.

Scottish independence receives formal recognition in a final treaty signed at Northampton between England's young Edward III and Robert the Bruce who is now disfigured with leprosy. The treaty is ratified by the marriage July 12 of Bruce's young son David to Edward's sister Joanna.

1329 The king of the Scots Robert the Bruce dies of leprosy June 7 at age 54 and is succeeded by his 5-year-old son David who will reign as David II until 1371 (but *see* 1332).

England's Edward III pays homage to France's Philip VI for his French fiefs. Flanders, Guienne, and Burgundy remain outside Philip's control, but the thrones of Provence, Naples, and Hungary are occupied by rulers from the Capetian house of Anjou, the papacy at Avignon is under strong French influence, French culture is dominant in England and northern Spain, and French interests are well entrenched in the Near East.

1330 England's Edward III leads a baronial revolt against his regent Roger de Mortimer. He has Mortimer hanged, and at age 17 he begins a personal rule that will continue until his dotage in the late 1360s and nominally until his death in 1377.

The Hapsburgs recognize Louis IV of Bavaria as Holy Roman Emperor upon the death of Frederick of Austria.

Serbian forces defeat the Bulgars in a decisive battle to end the powers of the Bulgars.

1331 The Japanese emperor Godaigo renews his efforts to regain power from the Hojo regent, he is informed upon again as in 1324, he escapes to Nara, the Hojo capture him and exile him to Oki Island, and civil war begins against the Hojo (see 1333).

1332 England's Edward III and Edward de Baliol invade Scotland, Edward installs Baliol as the new king of Scotland, and they oblige David Bruce to flee to France.

Denmark's Christopher II abdicates under pressure from Gerhard, count of Holstein, who parcels out crown lands, establishes German noblemen in every major Danish fortress, gives German traders full reign, and begins an 8-year period of anarchy.

The Battle of Plowce September 27 gives the Teutonic Knights their first serious reverse. Forces of Poland's Ladislas IV Lokietek emerge triumphant.

Lucerne joins the three Swiss forest cantons of Uri, Schwyz, and Unterwalden in the Helvetic confederation (see 1291; Zurich, 1351).

Trading in bitter oranges begins at the French Mediterranean town of Nice. No other kind of orange is known in Europe (see 1529; 1635).

1333 Poland's Ladislas IV Lokietek dies in March at age 72 after a 13-year reign in which he has reunited the principalities of Little and Great Poland, has suppressed the magistrates of Cracow, has saved Danzig from the margraves of Brandenburg with help from the Teutonic Knights, and has given the knightly order its first major setback (1332) to lay the foundations for a strong Polish monarchy. The diminutive Ladislas (or Wladislaw) is succeeded by his 23-year-old son who assumes the throne as Casimir II to begin a 37-year reign.

The Battle of Halidon Hill July 19 gives England's Edward III revenge for his father's defeat at Bannockburn in 1314. A Scottish army marching to relieve Edward's siege of Berwick is dispersed by Edward's forces under Edward de Baliol and Henry Beaumont, constable of England.

The Japanese emperor Godaigo escapes from Oki Island with help from confederates, he gains support from Takauji Ashikaga, the regent Takatoki Hojo commits suicide at Kamakura, Godaigo regains power from the shogunate, and he starts to rebuild the imperial palaces, but Godaigo takes territory from the samurai and he levies high taxes.

The death of the Japanese regent Takatoki Hojo (above) ends the Kamakura period that began in 1185 and ushers in the Muromachi period that will continue until 1568. The new era will be marked by the disintegration of the shogun's effective control and the rise of independent feudal domains (hans) governed by local warlords (daimyos).

The Black Death begins in China as starvation weakens much of the population and makes it vulnerable to a form of bubonic plague (see 1340; 1343).

Famine grips China following a severe drought.

1334 The Mogul emperor Mohammed Tughlak welcomes the Moorish traveler Ibn Batuta with fabulous gifts in hope that the Moor may help Mohammed conquer the world.

Poland's new king Casimir II grants extensive privileges to encourage Jewish immigration (see 1348).

Pope John XXII dies December 4 at age 85 after an 18-year papacy at Avignon in which he has levied heavy taxes on Christian Europe in an effort to regain independence and prestige for the Church. He is succeeded by the Cistercian cardinal Jacques Fournier who will serve as Pope Benedict XII until his death in 1342.

Painting *Madonna and Child with Saints and Scenes* by Florentine painter Taddeo Gaddi, 34, whose teacher Giotto di Bondone is now 68.

Florence appoints Giotto di Bondone (above) official architect, and he begins work on a campanile for the city's cathedral.

1335 Japanese troops organized by the Hojo family try to depose the emperor Godaigo in July but the warlord Takauji Ashikaga supports Godaigo and defeats the Hojo forces in August (see 1333; 1336).

The Byzantine emperor Andronicus III conquers Thessaly and part of Epirus from the despot John II Orsini.

English grain harvests amount to only 15 bushels of wheat, barley, and oats per capita after setting aside seed for the year to come. Part of the harvest goes to sustain work animals, livestock, and the mounts of knights and barons, while nearly one-third goes into making beer and ale.

1336 The Japanese warlord (daimyo) Takauji Ashikaga overthrows the emperor Godaigo and his son Morinaga in January, he drives them out of Kyoto,

1336 (cont.) and he installs a new emperor to begin the Muromachi (or Ashikaga) period that will continue until 1568 (*see* 1333).

Aragon's Alfonso IV dies at age 37 after a 9-year reign. He is succeeded by his 17-year-old son who will reign until 1387 as Pedro IV (Pedro the Ceremonious).

France's Philip VI purchases the Dauphine, the first major imperial fief to be added to French territory.

Greek forces reconquer Lesbos from the Byzantines.

💲 France's walled town of Carcassonne permits the Florentine banking house of Peruzzi to collect its taxes, giving the bankers a percentage of the take.

England's Edward III embargoes export of wool to frustrate the French in Flanders.

Florence's baptistery has the bronze doors at its south end decorated with reliefs of scenes from the life of John the Baptist. Sculptor-architect Andrea Pisano (Andrea da Pontadera), 46, has been working on the reliefs for 7 years.

1337 A "Hundred Years' War" between England and France begins as Philip VI contests English claims to Normandy, Maine, Anjou, and other French territories while England's Edward III denies Philip's legitimacy, assumes the title King of France, and orders Philip to yield his throne. Edward gains support from the townspeople of Flanders who depend on English wool for their industry and from the City of London which is concerned about French influence in their Flemish market (*see* embargo of wool, 1336).

Nicomedia (Ismid) falls to the Ottoman Turks.

💲 English merchants contribute 20,000 sacks of wool as a gift to pay the expenses of Edward III. The merchants depend on receipts from the sale of their wool at Bruges and Ghent to pay for the casks of wine they import from Bordeaux.

Giotto di Bondone dies at Florence January 8 at age 69.

1338 France's Philip VI declares England's French territories forfeit, he besieges Guienne, and he burns Portsmouth as the Hundred Years' War grows more intense.

England's Edward III gains the support of the Holy Roman Emperor Louis IV. Louis recognizes Edward's title to the French crown in the Alliance of Coblenz, and he names Edward vicar of the Empire.

The "Licet Juris" issued by the diet of Frankfurt declares that the electors are capable of choosing an emperor without papal intervention. The declaration effectively divorces the Holy Roman Empire from the papacy (*see* 1202; 1356).

🎓 Pisa University has its beginnings.

1339 *Jinno-shotoki* by the Japanese historian Kitabatake Chikafusa is a history of Japan imbued with extreme patriotic sentiments that promote nationalism as

civil war continues between the southern and northern courts which will not be reunited until 1392.

Venice conquers Treviso and gains her first mainland possession.

🎓 Grenoble University has its beginnings.

1340 The Battle of Sluys June 24 gives England's Edward III victory over a French fleet after Philip VI has dismissed two squadrons of Levantine mercenary ships. Edward gains mastery of the Channel and free access to northern France (*see* Crecy, 1346).

The Battle of Rio Salado October 30 ends forever the Moorish threat to Spain. Castile's Alfonso XI aided by Portuguese troops gains a decisive victory over a combined force of Spanish and Moroccan Moslems.

Denmark's anarchy ends with the murder of Gerhard, count of Holstein. The youngest son of Christopher II ascends the throne and will rule until his death in 1375 as Waldemar IV Atterdag (*see* 1332).

England's Parliament increases its power by requiring parliamentary sanction for nonfeudal levies and changes in levies. Parliament will appoint auditors of expenditure in the next year and will make money grants conditional on redress.

💲 The Florentine bankers who are financing Edward III in his war with France demand and receive as collateral the person of the archbishop of Canterbury. Florence's Peruzzi banking house asks 120 percent interest and charges an additional 60 percent when payment is not prompt, taking a lien on state income and installing two merchants to supervise Edward's household accounts.

⚡ The road from the Black Sea to Cathay (China) is safe both by day and by night, reports *The Merchant's Handbook* by Pegolotti.

⚕ Travelers on the road from China (above) will return with rat-borne ticks or fleas that will bring the Black Death to Europe (*see* 1333; 1343).

🎓 Queen's College is founded at Oxford.

1341 Civil war begins in the Byzantine Empire as Andronicus III Palaeologus dies June 15 at age 45 after a 13-year reign in which he has annexed large parts of Thessaly and Epirus but has lost them to the growingly powerful Serbs. The emperor's 9-year-old son and successor is challenged by the boy's guardian John Cantacuzene, 49, who sets himself up as emperor in Thrace with support from aristocratic elements and from Greek religious zealots inspired by the mystic teachings of the Mt. Athos monasteries.

∞ The Greek zealots (above) range themselves against the rationalist Greek orthodox clergy and against Anna of Savoy who rules as regent for her son John V (*see* 1345).

💲 France imposes the first Gabelle (salt tax) to help defray the cost of war against England's Edward III.

1342 Thessalonica has a popular uprising against the Byzantine emperor John V and his regent mother. The religious zealots (Hesychasts) who support John Cantacuzene in the civil war establish a nearly independent state that will continue until 1347.

Louis of Bavaria acquires the Tyrol and Carinthia by marrying the "ugly duchess" Margaret of Tyrol.

Painting *Nativity of the Virgin* by Italian painter Pietro Lorenzetti, now 62, who has been helped by his younger brother Ambrogio to produce frescoes for churches at Assisi and Siena.

1343 Florence's Peruzzi banking house fails as England's Edward III repudiates his debts and the bankers are unable to collect despite measures they have taken to protect themselves from default (*see* 1340; 1344).

Smyrna falls to Venetian forces which take advantage of the civil war in the Byzantine Empire to capture the valuable commercial port of Ionia.

The Black Death that began in China 10 years ago strikes marauding Tartars who attack some Genoese merchants returning from Cathay with silks and furs. The plague, called bubonic because of its characteristic bubo, or enlarged lymph glands, is transmitted by fleas, carried by rats, and harbored perhaps in the merchants' baggage. The Tartars besiege the merchants at the Crimean trading post of Caffa and before they withdraw they catapult their corpses over the walls into Caffa, infecting the merchants, some of whom die on the road home while others carry the plague to Constantinople, Genoa, Venice, and other ports (*see* 1340; Cyprus, 1347).

Inventorius sive Collectorium Partis Chirurgicalis Medicinae by French surgeon Guy de Chauliac, 43, will serve physicians as a manual for three centuries. De Chauliac has developed the treatment of fractures by slings and extension weights, he operates on hernias and cataracts, exorcises superficial growths, and he believes that pus from wounds serves to release the *materia peccans*.

The University of Pisa is founded.

Dialogues by English scholastic philosopher William of Ockham (or Occam) lay the foundations of modern theory of independence of church and state. Ockham, 43, has been imprisoned after defending evangelical poverty against Pope John XXII in his *Opus Nonaginta Dierum* of 1330 but has escaped and is living in Munich, where he has sided with the Holy Roman Emperor Louis IV in contesting the temporal power of the pope.

1344 Florentine banking prestige plummets with the failure of the Bardi banking house that comes on the heels of last year's Peruzzi collapse as England's Edward III repudiates his debts (*see* 1340). Civil war begins in Florence, the commune is restored under the sway of a businessmen's oligarchy, the smaller guilds lose power, and workers who belong to no guild are further exploited as the Florentine oligarchy seeks access to the sea, expansion in Tuscany to dominate trade routes, and support of the popes in order to retain papal banking business.

England coins gold "florins" that are twice the weight of Florence's 1252 florins, but most commerce is transacted in silver coins. The gold florins will soon go out of use.

The term "Hanseatic League" is used for the first time to denote the confederation of Baltic traders now so prominent in fish export (*see* 1300; 1360).

Spanish olive oil, fruit, and fine manufactured goods are exported from the South, wool and hides from the North as Castile and Aragon increase their commerce.

The Spanish Moors lose the southern port of Algeciras to Castile's Alfonso XI.

1345 The Ottoman Turks make their first crossing into Europe in response to a call for support by John Cantacuzene as civil war continues in the Byzantine Empire.

Florence has her first social revolution as the rising industrial proletariat attempts to overthrow the ruling business oligarchy (*see* 1344; Strozzi, 1347).

A bridge that will be called the Ponte Vecchio is completed across the Arno at Florence to replace a 13th century bridge that was swept away by a flood in 1333.

Poetry *De Vita Solitaria* by Petrarch.

The Cathedral of Notre Dame on the Ile de la Cité in the Seine at Paris is completed in Gothic style after 182 years of construction.

1346 The Battle of Crécy August 26 establishes England as a great military power, reorients English social values by its joint participation of yeomanry and aristocracy, and begins the end of the era of feudal chivalry (cavalry) that has dominated warfare since the barbarian invasions of the Roman Empire. Europe's greatest army of horse soldiers is massacred near Abbeville by England's Edward III who has landed July 12 at La Hague near Cherbourg with 1,000 ships, 4,000 knights, and 10,000 English and Welsh longbowmen equipped with the weapons acquired in the Welsh wars.

France's Philip VI meets with disaster as his 12,000 men-at-arms, 6,000 mercenary Genoese crossbowmen, 20,000 milice des communes, and assorted feudal vassals prove easy targets for the quick-shooting English archers and spearmen who make short work of the heavily armored knights (who cannot remount once their horses go down). The French attack the English lines 16 times by midnight and are practically annihilated (Edward's heralds count 1,542 dead French knights on the battlefield while English casualties total little more than 50).

1346 (cont.) Scottish allies of Philip VI invade England but are stopped at Neville's Cross. Scotland's 22-year-old David II, son of Robert the Bruce, is captured and will not be ransomed for 11 years.

Bohemia's blind John of Luxembourg is killed at age 50 while fighting in support of Philip VI at Crécy (above) and is succeeded by his 30-year-old son, who assumes the throne as Charles I to begin a "golden age" of Bohemian history. Charles is crowned German king at Bonn November 26 and prepares to attack the Holy Roman Emperor Louis IV of Bavaria (*see* 1347).

Serbian king Stephen Dushan, 38, proclaims himself Emperor of the Serbs, Greeks, Bulgars, and Albanians, establishes a court of Skoplye with elaborate Byzantine titles and ceremonies, and prepares to seize Constantinople and replace the Greek dynasty.

A Moslem dynasty in Kashmir that will endure for 243 years is founded by Shah Mirza, who will substitute a land tax of one-sixth for the extortionate taxes imposed by Hindu kings.

France's Estates-General at Langue d'Oil openly refuses to continue war levies in support of Philip VI and demands reforms in the country's administration as French cloth, gold and silver table services, jewelry, and other treasure is pillaged by the invaders and shipped off to England.

1347 English forces under Edward III take the French port of Calais after a long siege and make it a military and commercial outpost that will be English for 211 years. Edward celebrates the end of the long siege by taking as servants six of the city's leading burghers, whose lives he has spared only at the request of his wife Philippa (*see* Rodin, 1895).

Florentine banker Andrea Strozzi buys up quantities of grain in the midst of a Tuscan famine and sells it at low prices to the popolo minuto in a bid for their allegiance, but the people see through Strozzi's scheme and refuse to follow him, following instead the cunning suggestions of the Medicis and the Capponi to attack the houses of prominent older bankers such as the Pazzi, the Bardi, and the Frescobaldi.

The 6-year civil war in the Byzantine Empire ends in victory for John Cantacuzene who begins an 8-year reign as John VI Cantacuzene, nominally as coemperor with his ward John V. Thrace and Macedonia have been ravaged by Serbs and Turks brought in to support the rival factions, and the new reign will be marked by attacks from these outsiders and also from the Genoese.

Rome's dissolute plutocracy is overthrown in a revolt led by papal courtier Cola di Rienzi (Niccolo Gabrini), 34, who heads a procession to the Capitol dressed in full armor and is given unlimited authority by the assembled multitude. Rome's nobles leave the city or go into hiding, Rienzi takes the title of tribune in late May, he begins a government of stern justice in contrast to the license that has prevailed, he is

encouraged by the poet Petrarch, he proclaims the sovereignty of the Roman people over the empire in July, he is installed as tribune with great pomp in mid-August, but he is obliged to impose heavy taxes in order to maintain his costly regime. Rienzi offends Pope Clement VI by proposing to set up a new Roman Empire based on the will of the people, he is ridiculed for his pretensions, the pope empowers a legate to depose Rienzi and bring him to trial, Rome's barons gather troops, but Louis of Hungary comes to Rienzi's aid, the barons are defeated November 20 outside the city gates, and Rienzi's noblest enemy Stephen Colonna is killed. Denounced by the pope as a criminal, pagan, and heretic, Rienzi devotes himself to feasts and pageants until mid-December when he panics at some disturbance, abdicates, and flees the city.

The Holy Roman Emperor Louis IV of Bavaria has died on a bear hunt outside Munich October 11 at age 60, leaving Charles of Luxembourg undisputed ruler of Germany. He will be crowned emperor in 1355 and will reign until 1378 as Charles IV.

The Black Death reaches Cyprus, whence it will spread to Florence and find thousands of victims weakened and made vulnerable by famine (*see* 1348).

Efforts to regulate prostitution and thus reduce venereal disease are undertaken at Avignon, where Jane I, queen of both the Sicilies and countess of Provence, establishes a house of prostitution. "The Queen commands that on every Saturday the Women in the House be singly examined by the Abbess and a Surgeon appointed by the Directors, and if any of them has contracted any Illness by their Whoring, that they be separated from the rest, and not suffered to prostitute themselves, for fear the Youth who have to do with them should catch their Distempers."

Jews are not permitted to enter the Avignon house of prostitution (above).

1348 The Black Death that will devastate Europe reaches Florence in April and spreads to France and England, which it reaches in July or August, although London is spared until November (*see* 1349).

French surgeon Guy de Chauliac remains at Auvergne after most physicians have fled and writes, "The visitation came in two forms. The first lasted two months, manifesting itself as an intermittent fever accompanied by spitting of blood from which people died usually in 3 days. The second type lasted the remainder of the time, manifesting itself in high fever, abscesses and carbuncles, chiefly in the axillae and groin. People died from this in 5 days. So contagious was the disease especially that with blood spitting [pneumonic] that no one could approach or even see a patient without taking the disease. The father did not visit the son nor the son the father. Charity was dead and hope abandoned."

Blood-letting is recommended by Guy de Chauliac (above) to those unable to flee, and he also favors cupping and scarifying carbuncles, soothing the humors with Armenian bole, comforting the heart with senna and good-smelling things, purging with aloes, resisting putrefaction with acid things, and purifying the air with fires.

Jews are blamed for spreading the Black Death by deliberately contaminating wells and by "anointing" people and houses with poison. The Jews are persecuted first at Chillon on Lake Geneva and then at Basel and Freiburg, where all known Jews are herded into wooden buildings and burned alive. At Strasbourg more than 2,000 Jewish scapegoats are hanged on a scaffold erected at the Jewish burying ground.

Pope Clement VI issues two bulls declaring the Jews to be innocent, but the persecution continues. Thousands of Jews flee to Poland, Russia, and other more tolerant parts of eastern Europe (see 1334).

The University of Prague is founded by Charles IV in Bohemia.

England has her third cold, wet summer in a row, and this one is the worst. Rain falls steadily from midsummer to Christmas, crops are poor, food is short, and the hunger makes the country vulnerable to disease (see 1349).

The Black Death will extinguish nearly two-thirds of the population in some parts of Europe. At Locarno on Lake Maggiore the population will fall from 4,800 to 700.

1349 The Black Death kills from one-third to one-half the population of England which calls a truce in hostilities with plague-stricken France (see 1347; 1454).

A Scottish army invades England in the autumn and is stricken with plague which the dispersing soldiers carry back to Scotland in pneumonic (man to man) form (see 1350).

The Black Death reaches Poland and moves on toward Russia, flourishing on poverty and malnutrition, especially in the larger cities.

Pope Clement VI issues a bull against flagellants who have reappeared in force as a result of the Black Death (see 1258). The flagellants take on the character of a revolutionary movement against the Jews, the rich, and the Church, and many are beheaded, burned alive, or hanged.

English landlords offer high wages to field hands. Reapers and mowers spared by the Black Death eat better than they ever have or ever will again.

The motto "honi soit qui mal y pense" (evil to him who evil thinks) is adopted by the Order of the Garter founded by England's Edward III.

1350 France's Philip VI dies at Nogent-le-Roi August 12 at age 57 after a 22-year reign. He is succeeded by his 31-year-old son who assumes the throne as John II to begin a 14-year reign that will be dominated largely by evil counselors.

Rome's Cola di Rienzi emerges from hiding, reaches Prague in July, denounces the temporal power of the pope, and asks Charles VI to deliver Italy from its oppressors, but the emperor imprisons Rienzi in the fortress at Raudnitz and will turn him over to the pope next year.

Castile's Alfonso XI dies of the plague at age 38 at the siege of Gibraltar. He is succeeded by his 16-year-old son whose 19-year reign will be marked by excesses that will cause him to be called Pedro the Cruel.

The Black Death reaches Scotland and Wales.

The Black Death reduces population pressure on food supplies, which has been growing in England and Europe in this century, and prices drop for lack of demand. Where a good horse brought 40 shillings in England 2 years ago it now brings only 16, while a fat ox fetches only 4 shillings, a cow 1 shilling, and fat sheep sixpence, but wheat fetches 1 shilling per quarter (8 bushels), up from as little as 16 pence in good crop years, as the dearth of field hands reduces the crop and forces many landlords to turn farmland into pasturage (see 1349).

Salt production takes a sharp drop in northern Europe as a result of economic conditions and of the Hundred Years' War. Poor-quality salt from Brittany's Bourgneuf Bay begins to dominate the salt fish trade as good white salt becomes too costly. Great salt deposits will soon be opened in Poland, with a Genoese firm headquartered at Cracow receiving a monopoly in Polish salt production.

A wire-pulling machine invented in Europe is an early step in the development of metallurgical technology.

1351 An English Statute of Labourers fixes wages at their 1346 levels and attempts to compel able-bodied men to accept work when it is offered. The shortage of workers resulting from the Black Death has combined with prosperity produced by the Hundred Years' War to create an economic and social crisis in England.

The Statute of Labourers (above) helps keep wages within bounds as England adjusts to the fact that she no longer has a glut of labor, but while Parliament also orders victualers and other tradesmen to sell their goods at reasonable prices, the Statute of Labourers destroys the country's social unity without resolving its problems.

English landholders enclose common lands for sheep raising and begin to develop great fortunes while unrest spreads through the English yeomanry, which has emerged from its traditional passivity as it has shared in the plunder of war and in the higher wages paid to survivors of the Black Death.

The Order of the Star that will be replaced by the Order of St. Michael in 1469 is founded in France.

Florence goes to war with Milan, whose archbishop Giovanni Visconti, 61, tries to gain control of Tus-

1351 (cont.) cany. Florence permits her citizens to buy commutation of military service and employs mercenary captains (condottieri) to resist the Milanese (*see* 1353).

Zurich joins the growing Swiss Confederation (*see* 1332; 1352).

1352 The Black Death reaches Moscow and spreads eastward back to India and China.

Rome's Cola di Rienzi is tried by three cardinals at Avignon in August and is sentenced to death. The sentence is not carried out, Pope Clement VI dies December 6, and Rienzi is pardoned and released from prison by the new pope Innocent VI who wants to reduce the power of the Roman barons (*see* 1350; 1354).

Glarus joins the growing Swiss Confederation (*see* 1351; 1353).

Corpus Christi College is founded at Oxford.

1353 Bern joins the growing Swiss Confederation which now embraces 7 cantons (*see* 1352; Battle of Sempach, 1386).

Milan's Giovanni Visconti annexes Genoa which goes to war with Venice.

The Arab traveler Ibn Batuta visits Africa's Mandingo Empire.

Fiction *The Decameron* by Italian humanist Giovanni Boccaccio, 40, is a love story full of vivid description of the Black Death that has killed three out of every five Florentines. Boccaccio's 10 protagonists have fled the city to the seclusion of a villa garden on the slopes of Fiesole (*see* 1419).

1354 England resumes the Hundred Years' War after an interruption by the Black Death. The English will ravage Languedoc in the next 2 years, they will meet little opposition, and they will reduce the prestige of the French crown.

Cola di Rienzi receives the title senator from Pope Innocent VI, the pope sends him to Rome with the papal legate Cardinal Albornoz and a few mercenaries, he enters the city to wild acclaim in August. The Romans restore him to his position as tribune, but rioting breaks out October 8, Rienzi tries to address the ugly mob, the crowd sets the building ablaze, and Rienzi is murdered while trying to escape in disguise.

The Battle of Sapienza gives Genoa a victory over Venice, the Venetians lose their fleet, but Milan's Giovanni Visconti dies at age 64. He is succeeded by his two nephews who will mediate the war between Venice and Genoa.

Ottoman forces take the Gallipoli peninsula and spread through Thrace.

Granada's Alhambra Palace is completed on a 35-acre plateau after 106 years of work begun in the reign of the Moor Al Ahmar. Enclosed by a fortified wall, the palace is flanked by 13 towers.

1355 Nanking falls to the 27-year-old patriot Chu Yuanchang who leads a revolt against Mongol domination of China (*see* Ming dynasty, 1368).

The Byzantine emperor John VI Cantacuzene is driven out of Constantinople and retires to a monastery after an 8-year reign in which he has imposed heavy taxes in a vain effort to pay his foreign mercenaries. His former ward John V Palaeologus entered the city late last year and will reign until his death in 1391, except for the years 1376 to 1379 when his rebellious son Andronicus will reign.

Milan's Matteo Visconti is assassinated by his brothers Bernabo and Galeazzo who rule, respectively, at Milan and at Pavia. Their harsh administrations will be marked by ostentatious patronage of the arts and of learning.

France's John II obtains a grant of funds to resist England's Black Prince Edward, 25-year-old son of Edward III, who is laying waste the country.

The French king encounters opposition led by Etienne Marcel, the richest man in Paris, who persuades the Estates-General of Languedoc and Langue d'Oil to compel John to consult with the Estates before imposing new tax levies and to let a commission from the Estates supervise collection and expenditure of the tax moneys. John induces the Estates-General to adjourn, he proceeds to debase the nation's coinage in the interests of his treasury, and he organizes opposition to the Estates-General.

Painting *Madonna and Child with Angels* by Taddeo Gaddi.

1356 The Battle of Poitiers (or Maupertuis) September 19 ends in defeat for France's John II whose army is cut to ribbons by the English under the Black Prince of Wales Edward, 26. The Black Prince takes John as a prisoner to England along with a crowd of French aristocrats, leaving France to the regency of John's 18-year-old son Charles who is unable to prevent civil chaos.

The Golden Bull issued by the Holy Roman Emperor Charles IV fixes the form and place of the imperial election and coronation of electors, it establishes the duties and privileges of electors, and it transforms the empire from a monarchy into an aristocratic federation that will endure for 450 years (*see* 1338). Charles makes no secret of his view that the empire is an anachronism, but he values the emperor's right to nominate vassals to vacant fiefs, and he makes sure that the king of Bohemia is given first place among the empire's secular electors.

Korea lapses into a 36-year period of disorder. The Koryo kings who dominated the country for 235 years until 1170 have intermarried with the Mongols and have become mere satellites of the Mongol imperial family, they stage a successful revolt against the Mongols, but they have depended for their authority on Mongol prestige and are unable to suppress their vassals who are helped by Japanese pirates to create chaos (*see* 1369).

1357 Paris merchants rebel against the dauphin and recall the Estates-General under the leadership of Etienne Marcel. The members make no effort to reduce the monarchy's traditional powers, but they order reforms that include relief for the poor and frequent meetings of the Estates on a regular basis. The Great Ordinance passed by the Estates provides for a standing committee to supervise tax levies and expenditures.

Etienne Marcel (above) makes an alliance with Charles the Bad of Navarre and thus discredits the Estates-General, which splits into many factions. The regent Charles opposes the alliance and flees Paris to form a powerful coalition against the Estates-General and their ally Charles the Bad.

An account of travels by a fictitious Sir John Mandeville will appear in the next 15 years written in French and probably authored by Liege physician Jehan de Bourgogne (Jehan a la Barbe), a former chamberlain to England's John, baron de Mowbray. Borrowed from works by Giovanni de Piano Carpini, who traveled east to Karakorum in 1245, and by friar Oderic of Pordenone, whose *Travels in Eastern Regions* appeared in 1330, the John Mandeville travel accounts will describe such fanciful marvels as men whose heads grow beneath their shoulders.

1358 France's Etienne Marcel forces his way into the Paris palace of the dauphin February 22, and the marshals of Champagne and Normandy are murdered in the presence of young Charles, who rules in the absence of his father. Charles the Bad of Navarre approaches Paris in league with the English and gains avowals of support from Marcel, who is assassinated July 31.

French peasants and Parisians join in a violent rising of the Jacquerie in May against oppressive taxes imposed to ransom John II and other captives taken by the English at Poitiers in 1356 and to carry on the war. The rising is ruthlessly repressed in June with the aid of the English, who pause in their war with the French to join in the wholesale slaughter of rebellious serfs: 300 peasants trapped in a monastery are burned to death.

1359 Edward III begins a final expedition to France and penetrates the walls of Paris, but the south of France has been so devastated by war that the English have trouble provisioning their forces.

France's John II makes a preliminary peace with the English, who maintain him in luxurious captivity, but his virtual restoration of the old Angevin lands in France to Edward is rejected by his son Charles (*see* Peace of Bretigny, 1360).

Revolutionists wearing red hats storm Bruges as the artisan guilds of the Flemish city try to overturn the patrician government.

The Ottoman sultan Orkhan dies at age 70 after a 23-year reign and is succeeded by the 40-year-old Murad I who will make the Ottoman Empire the leading power in Anatolia and the Balkans, using a Janissary corps composed of war prisoners and, later, of Christians taken captive as children.

The Campanile, or bell-tower, is completed at Florence. It has been designed by architects who included the late Giotto di Bondone (*see* 1334).

1360 The Peace of Bretigny signed at Calais brings a brief truce to the Hundred Years' War that has exhausted both England and France. Edward III virtually renounces his claim to the French crown and Charles, regent for France's John II, promises a huge ransom for his father's return and yields Calais, Guienne (southwestern France), Ponthieu, and their immediately surrounding territories to England.

The Hanseatic League grows to include 52 towns that number among them Bremen, Cologne, Danzig, Dortmund, Gronigen, Hamburg, and Hanover. The number will be enlarged to 70 or 80.

English laborers who ask wages above the legal minimum established by the 1351 Statute of Labourers are ordered to be imprisoned with bail.

1361 Denmark's Waldemar IV begins a 2-year war against the Hanseatic League that will end with a sharp, but brief, curtailment of the Hansa's power (*see* 1360; 1370).

The duchy of Burgundy comes into possession of France's John II, who will give it to his son Philip in 1363.

Buda is selected as the capital of Hungary (*see* 1247).

The Black Death strikes again in England, but less severely than in 1349, and rages also in France, Po-

The Black Death (bubonic plague), transmitted by rat-borne fleas, killed almost everybody in some European towns.

1361 (cont.) land, and elsewhere in Europe, especially among children (*see* 1371).

The University of Pavia has its beginnings.

1362 Norse king Magnus Ericson sends an ill-fated expedition to look for would-be colonists who have failed to reach Greenland (*see* 981). The expedition may enter what will later be called Hudson's Bay (*see* 1610).

English is made the language of pleading and judgment in England's courts of law but legal French continues to be used for documents.

The Vision of William concerning Piers the Plowman, commonly called *The Vision of Piers Plowman*, will be written in the next 30 years, probably by English poet William Langland (or Langley), who will speak of "Lombards of Lucques that liven by lone as Jews" (*see* 1290; 1306; 1373).

The Palace of the Popes at Avignon is completed after 28 years of construction.

1363 Denmark's Waldemar IV forces the Hanseatic League to accept peace and a curtailment of its privileges. Waldemar defeated the Hanse fleets last year at Helsingborg.

Sweden's Magnus II abdicates under pressure at age 47 after a weak 44-year reign. He is succeeded by Albert of Mecklenburg, a tool of the Swedish aristocracy which will permit him to rule until 1387.

A leg of roast mutton sells in a London cookshop for as much as a farm worker earns in a day, and a whole roast pig sells for more than three times that amount to Londoners prospering by the war with France.

1364 France's John II dies April 8 at age 45 in England where he has been a prisoner since his capture at the Battle of Poitiers in 1356. His body is sent back to France with royal honors and he is succeeded by his 27-year-old son who will reign until 1380 as Charles V.

The University of Cracow is founded by Poland's Casimir the Great.

The University of Vienna has its beginnings.

Famine strikes France following a bad harvest, and plague in epidemic form follows on the heels of hunger.

1365 Adrianople falls to the Ottoman Turks who have overrun Thrace and who make the city their capital.

1366 The English Parliament refuses to pay feudal dues to the pope.

Poetry *Canzoniere* by Petrarch.

Toledo's El Transito Synagogue is completed by Meier Abdeli.

Europeans commonly eat the main meal of the day at 9 o'clock in the morning.

1367 Portugal's Pedro I dies at age 47 after a 10-year reign marked by severity and is succeeded by his 22-year-old son who will reign until 1383 as Fernão I (the Handsome). The new king will repudiate his betrothal to a Castilian princess in order to marry Leonara Telles, and the repudiation will provoke Castile's Henrico II (Trastamera) to invade Portugal (*see* 1373).

The Confederation of Köln (Cologne) brings together 77 German towns whose representatives organize common Hanseatic finances, form Scandinavian alliances, and prepare naval forces to counter Denmark's Waldemar IV (*see* 1363; 1370).

1368 The Ming dynasty founded by Chinese monk Chu Yuan-chang, 40, will rule until 1644 and begins a resurgence of Chinese nationalism. Chu seized the city of Chiang-ning (later Nanking) in the anarchy of 1356, set up an orderly government, and annexed the holdings of neighboring southern war lords. He drives the Mongols out of Peking, he will drive them out of Shensi and Kansu next year and out of Szechuan in 1371, and he will rule for 30 years under the name Hung-wu.

The Ming emperor Hung-wu (above) begins restoring the Great Wall of China.

1369 Tamerlane (Timur the Lame, or Tamburlaine) makes himself master of Samarkand in Turkestan at age 33. A descendant of Genghis Khan who succeeded his father as chief of a Turkish tribe 9 years ago, the lame leader of the western house of Jagatai begins to develop an armed horde that will conquer much of the world (*see* Persia, 1380).

Korea's state of Koryo submits to the Chinese Ming forces after 13 years of rebellion, but disorder continues in the country (*see* 1392).

Castile's Pedro the Cruel antagonizes the Black Prince of Wales Edward who deserts him, he is besieged at La Mancha (Montiel) by French soldiers of fortune enlisted by his bastard half-brother the count of Trastamara, he is tempted out of La Mancha March 23 by the count, and he is murdered at age 34 after a reign of more than 18 years. Pedro is succeeded by the count who begins a 10-year reign as Enrique II Trastamara.

1370 The Hanseatic League reaches the height of its power after taking united—and successful—military action against Denmark's Waldemar IV. The Treaty of Stralsund gives the League a monopoly in the Baltic trade that will continue for 70 years, and the League gains control of Scandinavian politics (*see* 1360; 1375).

England's Exeter Cathedral is completed after 90 years of construction.

1371 The Black Death reappears in England, but the outbreak is milder than in 1361 (*see* 1382; 1406).

1372 Pope Sixtus IV asks an astronomer to correct the Julian calendar in use since 46 B.C. because it is too long by 11 minutes and 15 seconds each year, but the astronomer will die before he can reform the calendar (*see* Gregorian calendar, 1582).

France's Charles V regains Poitou and Brittany from the English and regains control of the Channel after 32 years by defeating the English at La Rochelle. Charles is helped by a Castilian fleet which blocks English transport in the North.

The Channel island of Guernsey is captured by the self-styled prince of Wales Owen-ap-Thomas.

1373 England's 33-year-old duke of Lancaster John of Gaunt invades France, fanning out from Calais to Bordeaux.

Lisbon is burned by Castilian forces sent by Enrique II who is at war with both Portugal and Aragon (*see* 1374).

Brandenburg is annexed to Bohemia by the Holy Roman Emperor Charles IV of Luxembourg.

1374 England's John of Gaunt, duke of Lancaster, returns from the war in France and becomes leader of the state, using anticlerical feeling and social unrest to pursue his ambitions to succeed his father Edward III.

London retains Oxford don John Wycliffe, 54, to conduct negotiations with Pope Gregory XI.

Castile makes peace with Aragon and Portugal at Almazan and continues to lead in the reconquest of Spain from the Moslems.

Plague precautions are instituted at Venice, where three officials are appointed to inspect vessels wishing to enter ports of the Venetian Republic and to exclude any found to be infected with the Black Death (*see* Ragusa, 1377; waiting period, 1403).

A dancing mania sweeps the Rhenish city of Aix-la-Chapelle in July and sends hordes of men and women into a pathological frenzy of dancing in the streets. The dancing continues for hours until the crowds are too exhausted or too injured to continue, and the phenomenon will never be fully explained.

1375 The Kingdom of Armenia founded by Tigranes I in 94 B.C. ends with the surrender of the new Armenian king Levon V to the governor of Aleppo who has besieged the Armenian capital of Sis with a force of nearly 30,000 Mamelukes. The victors slaughter many of the Armenians and convert many of the rest to Islam, they take Levon to Cairo, he will remain in a royal prison until his royal Aragon and Castile in-laws ransom him in 1382, and France's Charles VI will give him a pension and a house.

The Truce of Bruges brings a pause in the Hundred Years' War between France and England.

Denmark's Waldemar IV Atterdag dies at age 55 after having recovered nearly all of Schleswig. He is succeeded by his 5-year-old grandson who will reign

until 1387 as Olaf II with his mother Margaret as regent.

The Hanseatic League wins formal recognition from the Holy Roman Emperor Charles IV of Luxembourg who visits Lübeck (*see* 1370; 1377).

The Hanseatic League (above) establishes common weights, measures, and coinage, it arranges for the settlement of disputes at home and abroad, it secures new trading privileges for its member cities, it protects merchants and their goods on the road and at sea, it draws up a *Seebuch* to help navigators find lighthouses, harbors, and buoys from Riga to Lisbon, and it opens up new lines of trade to supplement its commerce in herring, cod, salt, leather, hides, wool, grain, beer, amber, timber, pitch, tar, turpentine, iron, copper, horses, and falcon hawks.

England forbids transportation of seed oysters during the month of May. The English continue the oyster cultivation begun by the Romans in 110 B.C.

Le Viander de Taillevent by Guillaume Tirel, 49, gives a detailed account of France's developing cuisine. Tirel has served as cook to Philip VI of Valois and then to Charles V. He explains ragouts, galimafrees, mortreux, and hochepots, he describes 17 sauces including sauce Robert and fameline (*see* 1359), and he recommends using plain and grilled bread as binders in making sauce since the use of flour as a binder is unknown. Tirel tells of having coaxed the king to eat his first cabbage.

1376 John Wycliffe and his Reform party win control of London and oppose ownership of property by clergymen.

England's Black Prince Edward of Wales dies at age 46 of a disease contracted while fighting in Spain, and his death leaves Edward III with no mature heir to the throne (*see* 1377).

England's Good Parliament appeals to Edward III for the exclusion of foreigners from London's retail trade and asks the king to banish the Lombard bankers, enforce the 1351 Statute of Labourers, regulate the fisheries, and ban the export of English grain and yarn.

John Wycliffe (above) revises ordinances governing the sale of food and encounters opposition from London fishmongers and other victualers who depend on wines from France, spices from the Orient, and air-cured stockfish from Iceland (*see* Walworth, 1377).

John Wycliffe (above) expounds the doctrine of "dominion as founded in grace" by which all authority, both secular and ecclesiastical, is derived from God and is forfeited when its possessor falls into mortal sin. He attacks the worldliness of the medieval church and presents logical grounds for the refusal by England of certain tribute demanded by Rome.

1377 England's Edward III dies June 21 at age 64 shortly after a new parliament has reversed the acts of last year's "Good Parliament." Edward is succeeded by his 10-year-old grandson Richard, son of the Black

1377 (cont.) Prince. The dukes of Gloucester and Lancaster will administer the government until Richard attains his majority, and he will reign until 1399.

Parliament levies a poll tax that will lead to widespread rioting in 1381.

The Babylonian Exile of the papacy that began in 1306 has ended January 17 with the entry into Rome of Pope Gregory XI who left Avignon in September of last year.

Bulls promulgated by Pope Gregory XI accuse England's John Wycliffe of heresy. He is summoned before the bishop of London at St. Paul's to answer the charge, but he escapes trial as general rioting in the streets of London ends the session of the ecclesiastical court.

John Wycliffe's Reform party loses control of London to victualers headed by William Walworth. They raise food prices in the city.

The Hanseatic League retains its privileges in England and will keep them for nearly two centuries despite growing resentment against the League.

Population estimates based on the English poll tax (above) suggest that the nation's population is little more than 2 million, down from at least 3.5 million and possibly 5 million before the Black Death (*see* 1546).

1378 A Great Schism that will divide the Catholic Church for 39 years and bring society's highest authority into disrepute begins as Bartolommeo Prignani, 60, is elected Pope Urban VI and announces that he will reform the Church beginning with the sacred college of cardinals. 13 cardinals meet at Anagni and elect Robert of Geneva, 36, as Pope Clement VII, and he is supported by France's Charles V. This "antipope" establishes himself at Avignon (the Babylonian Captivity), and each pope appoints his own college of cardinals, collects tithes and revenues, and excommunicates partisans of the other (*see* 1417).

The Holy Roman Emperor Charles IV divides his lands among his three sons and dies at Prague November 29 at age 62. He obtained the margravate of Brandenburg 5 years ago for his son Wenceslas, now 17, who turns Brandenburg over to his 10-year-old half-brother Sigismund and succeeds Charles, beginning a 22-year reign as the emperor Wenceslas.

1379 Castile's Enrique II Trastamara dies at age 46 after a 10-year reign in which he has made vast grants of land and concessions to noblemen and to cities in return for support against the claims of the daughters of the late Pedro the Cruel. He of the largesse (El de las Mercedes) is succeeded by his 21-year-old son who will reign until 1390 as Juan I but whose crown is claimed by England's John of Gaunt who has married Constance, daughter of the late Pedro the Cruel, and who is supported by Portugal.

England's Winchester College is founded by William of Wykeham whose school will become a model for the nation's great public schools (*see* New College, 1394; Eton, 1440).

1380 Tamerlane invades Persia and his Mongol-Turkish hordes begin to overrun Khorasan, Jurjan, Mazandaran, Sijistan, Afghanistan, Fars, Azerbaijan, and Kurdistan (*see* 1369). They will invade Russia next year.

The Battle of Kulikovo September 8 ends in victory for the prince of Moscow Dmitri Donskoi, 30, who turns back the Mongols and destroys the prestige of Mongol power (although the Mongols will reach the gates of Moscow several times in the next few years).

France's Charles V dies at Vincennes September 16 after having eaten poisonous mushrooms. The 43-year-old king has ruled since the capture of his father at the Battle of Poitiers in 1356. He is succeeded by his 12-year-old son who will reign as Charles VI (Charles le Bien-Aimé), four uncles will rule as guardians until 1388, and the new king will reign until 1422 despite bouts of insanity beginning in 1392.

The *Apocalypse Tapestry* completed at Paris after 5 years of work depicts the biblical allegory. French authorities will discover the 70-panel tapestry in the 1840s, the bishop of Angers will buy it for 300 francs, he will have it restored, and it will hang at Angers Château.

The Gothic cathedral of Saint Etienne at Metz in Lorraine is completed after 130 years of work.

1381 Wat Tyler's rebellion creates anarchy in England as farm workers, artisans, and city proletarians stage an uprising against the 1351 Statute of Labourers and the 1377 poll tax. Mobs assemble in Essex, Kent, and Norfolk, sack palaces and castles at Norwich and Canterbury, take hostages, choose Wat (Walter) Tyler as their leader in June, and converge on London.

Some 30,000 rioters enter London over a drawbridge, burn John of Gaunt's Savoy Palace, the Temple used by London's lawyers, and the building at Clerkenwell of the Knights Hospitallers. Simon Sadbury, archbishop of Canterbury, is beheaded by the mob at Tower Hill and Hanseatic traders are chased into their fortified Steelyard (*see* 1250).

Richard II, the 14-year-old king, is presented with a list of demands by Wat Tyler at Mile End and replies with empty promises to demands for abolition of serfdom, of the poll tax, of restrictions on labor and trade, and of game laws, with a fourpence per acre ceiling on land rents and a ceiling on road tolls.

Fresh demands are made at Smithfield next day (June 15) and Wat Tyler is betrayed and killed with a cutlass by William Walworth (*see* 1377), now lord mayor of London, during a conference with the young king.

Similar uprisings occur in Languedoc as France suffers economic distress and the Tuchins stage an uprising against the tax collectors.

✗ Venice gains supremacy over Genoa after the 3-year War of Chioggia in which Genoa's admiral Luciano Doria has seized Chioggia and blockaded Venice but has been forced to surrender after being starved out by Venetians under Vittorio Pisano, who has blocked the channel.

💲 Parliament passes the first English navigation act as England begins its rise as a commercial power.

🍴 Movable type is used by French printers at Limoges (see Antwerp, 1417).

1382 England repeals the reforms granted to Wat Tyler last year and reestablishes serfdom, but the people have lost confidence in the Crown. The balladeered idolatry of the outlaw Robin Hood expresses their bitterness (see 1247).

The archbishop of Canterbury William Courtenay, 40, purges Oxford of Lollardy. Courtenay was made archbishop last year following the murder of Simon Sadbury. John Wycliffe has been discredited by last year's peasant rebellion, he has been condemned by the Church, and he withdraws to Lutterworth (see 1409).

The archbishop of Canterbury destroys academic freedom, he separates the Lollard movement from the cultured elite, but Parliament refuses to permit persecution of Wycliffe's followers.

Florence has a revolution as wool combers led by Michele di Lando seize the palace, but the labor government fails when the bourgeoisie object of Michele's assignment to Salvestro de' Medici of rents from shops on the 37-year-old Ponte Vecchio. Rival merchants and industrialists exile Michele, they close their shops and factories, they persuade neighboring landowners to cut off the city's grain and food supply, and a half-century of oligarchy begins in Florence.

✗ Hungary's Louis the Great dies suddenly at Nagyszombat September 10 after a 56-year reign that also has included nearly 12 years as king of Poland. Louis has gained Dalmatia from Venice and an annual tribute of 7,000 ducats by the peace that last year ended the War of Chioggia. He is succeeded in Hungary by his daughter Maria of Anjou, whose husband Sigismund of Luxembourg will rule Hungary for 50 years beginning in 1387. He is succeeded in Poland by his daughter Jadwiga (Hedwig), who will be married in 1386 to Jagiello, grand duke of Lithuania, who will rule Poland for 48 years as Vladislov V.

⚕ The Black Death sweeps Europe in a weaker epidemic than that of more than 30 years ago. It will take an especially heavy toll in Ireland in the next few years, and by the end of the century it will have killed an estimated 75 million people, leaving some areas completely depopulated (see 1403).

1383 Portugal's Fernão I dies without male issue October
✗ 22 at age 38 after having antagonized Juan of Castile by canceling the betrothal of his daughter Beatrix to Juan who lays claim to the Portuguese throne. Fer-

não's widow Leonora reigns as regent for Beatrix who marries Juan (see 1384).

🎭 The Japanese nō drama is pioneered by actor-dramatist Motokiyo Zeami, 20, who began appearing with his father Kan-ami at age 7 and who will write some 240 nō plays before his death in 1443, all employing male actors who perform on a bare wooden stage and wear masks to portray women, supernatural beings, or old men. Some of Zeami's nō plays will remain in the repertoire for as long as 600 years (see 1418).

✗ Munich's Löwenbräu brewery has its beginnings in Bavaria (see 1552).

1384 Lisbon is besieged by forces sent by Castile's Juan
✗ who has married the Portuguese infanta Beatrix, but whose claims to the throne are resisted by the people of Portugal (see 1383; 1385).

Flanders passes to Burgundy upon the death of the count of Flanders whose rebellious followers will be pacified within a year through cruel measures of repression.

∞ John Wycliffe dies December 31 at age 64 following a paralytic stroke, but his work will be carried on by others (see 1382; 1388; 1515).

1385 Portugal gains independence August 14 by defeating
✗ Castile in the Battle of Aljubarrota. The 28-year-old bastard son of the late King Pedro has taken power with unanimous support from the cortes at Coimbra, disease forces the Castilians to withdraw, and João I begins a 48-year reign that establishes the Avis dynasty (see 1386).

Parliament blocks England's Richard II from setting up a personal government. Richard makes an unsuccessful expedition to Scotland.

Ottoman forces capture Sofia (see 1393; 1443).

🎓 Heidelberg University has its beginnings in Baden-Württemberg.

1386 The Treaty of Windsor May 9 allies England and
✗ Portugal by joining Portugal's João I in marriage with John of Gaunt's daugher Philippa.

The Battle of Sempach July 9 gives the Swiss a victory over an Austrian army whose commander Leopold III dies fighting at age 34 as the cantons struggle to gain independence from Vienna.

1387 Denmark's Olaf II dies at age 17 after a 12-year reign
✗ and is succeeded by his 34-year-old mother Margaret who will unite Scandinavia under her rule. Daughter of the late Waldemar IV and widow of Norway's late Haakon VI, Margaret has served as regent of Denmark since her father's death, the Norwegians will elect her queen next year, and the disaffected Swedish magnates will help her drive out their king Albert of Mecklenburg (see 1389).

✒ Poetry *Troilus and Criseyde* by English poet Geoffrey Chaucer, 47, whose patron, John of Gaunt, last year helped him secure election as one of the two knights of the shire of Kent. Chaucer's *The Book of*

1387 (cont.) *the Duchess* was an elegy to John of Gaunt's first wife, Blanche, who died in 1369. Chaucer's wife Philippa is a sister of Katherine Swynford, who has married John of Gaunt, but his connections have not sufficed to prevent him from losing his positions as controller of the customs for wool and controller of the petty custom on wines. Chaucer lost both posts last year, but he represents Kent in Parliament and he begins work on the prologue to his great work *The Canterbury Tales* (*see* 1400).

1388 The first complete English translation of the bible is completed by John Purcey on the basis of work begun by the late John Wycliffe in an effort to reach the people directly with a bible they can read for themselves (date approximate).

France's Charles VI begins his personal reign at age 19 following the death of the duke of Anjou which leaves Philip of Burgundy in a position of great power. Charles replaces Burgundy with his own brother Louis, duc d'Orléans, but Louis is an unpopular dandy and Burgundy gains the support of the king's wife Isabelle of Bavaria and poses as a reformer.

Venice signs a treaty with the Ottoman Turks in its first effort to assure trading privileges in the eastern Mediterranean in the face of rising Turkish power.

The University of Cologne has its beginnings.

1389 England's Richard II begins his personal rule at age 22 by dismissing from office supporters of the duke of Gloucester and concluding a truce with France's Charles VI.

Margaret of Denmark has her 7-year-old grand-nephew Eric of Pomerania proclaimed her successor, he begins a 50-year reign as king of Norway. She receives an offer of the Swedish throne, her forces defeat the Swedish king Albert of Mecklenburg at Falkoping, and they take Albert prisoner (*see* 1395).

The Battle of Kossovo June 15 ends the Serb Empire. A coalition of Serbs, Bosnians, Albanians, and Wallachians led by the Serbian prince Lazar tries to stop the advance of the Ottoman sultan Murad I. A Serbian noble posing as a traitorous deserter kills the 70-year-old sultan in the battle, Murad is succeeded by his 50-year-old son Bayazid (Bajazet). The new sultan has Lazar captured and put to death, he routs the Balkan troops, and he will reign until 1402 as Bayazid I.

The Serbian prince Lazar (above) is succeeded by his son Stephen Lazarevich but the Serbs become vassals of the Ottoman Turks.

1390 Scotland's first Stuart king Robert II dies May 13 at age 74. His legitimized 50-year-old son John changes his baptismal name and ascends the throne as Robert III to begin a reign that will continue until 1424.

Castile's Juan I dies October 9 at age 32 after an 11-year reign in which his claims to the Portuguese

throne have been thwarted. He is succeeded by his delicate son of 11 who will reign until 1406 as Enrique III.

The Byzantine emperor John V is desposed briefly by his grandson who assumes power as John VII but who is himself soon desposed as John V is restored to the throne by his second son Manuel.

The Forme of Cury is an illuminated cookbook manuscript containing recipes of dishes prepared for England's Richard II and his barons. Possibly prepared to guide the steward who superintends the king's illiterate cooks and to help him keep track of the costly spices used, the manuscript includes recipes for macaroni adopted from the Italians and for hash, but many of the recipes are merely rude instructions such as, "take chickens and ram them together, serve them broken . . . ;" "take rabbits and smite them to pieces; seethe them in grease. . . ."

1391 The Byzantine emperor John V Palaeologus dies at age 59 and is succeeded by his able 41-year-old son who will reign until 1425 as Manuel II Palaeologus.

The khan Toqtamish of the Golden Horde is defeated by Tamerlane who has overrun Khorasan, Jurjan, Mazandaran, Sijistan, Afghanistan, Fars, Azerbaijan, and Kurdistan (*see* 1380; 1393).

The University of Ferrara has its beginnings.

1392 Japan is reunited after 56 years of civil war between northern and southern dynasties. The southern emperor abdicates in favor of the northern emperor on the understanding that the throne will alternate between the imperial family's two branches, but the northern branch will in fact never relinquish the throne.

The Yi dynasty that will rule Korea until 1910 is founded by the warlord I Sŏnggye, who proclaims himself king after a series of coups d'etat and assassinations and makes Kyonsong (Seoul) the capital.

392 Hanse vessels embark for London from Danzig during the year with cargoes of grain, honey, salt, potash, furs, and beer.

Playing cards that will be employed for at least the next six centuries in various games are designed by Jacques Gringonneur, court painter to France's Charles VI. The 52 cards are divided into four suits, each representing one of the four classes of French society. The spades stand for pikemen or soldiery, the clubs for farmers and husbandmen, the diamonds evoke the diamond-shaped hats worn by artisans, and the hearts represent the clergy, the word "coeur" evolving from the word "chorur," meaning the clergy (*see* 1742).

1393 Baghdad falls to Tamerlane, who 2 years ago defeated the khan of the Golden Horde. His Tartar horsemen overrun Mesopotamia (*see* 1391; 1398).

The Ottoman sultan Bayazid subdues Bulgaria.

The Holy Roman Emperor Wenceslas of Bohemia has the 54-year-old ecclesiastic John of Nepomuk tortured and drowned in the Moldau at Prague for refusing to reveal the confessions of the empress. John will be canonized in 1729 and will be the patron saint of Bohemia.

A German price table lists a pound of nutmeg as being worth seven fat oxen. In Europe 1 pound of saffron is generally equal in value to a plowhorse, 1 pound of ginger will buy a sheep, and 2 pounds of mace will buy a cow.

1394 England's Richard II sets off for Ireland to put down a rebellion.

The Holy Roman Emperor Wenceslas of Bohemia is taken prisoner by his cousin Jobst of Moravia.

New College at Oxford is founded by William of Wykeham who 15 years ago founded Winchester College.

1395 England's Richard II forces the Irish barons to pay homage to him and grants them amnesty.

The Swedish king Albert of Mecklenburg renounces the throne and retires to Mecklenburg and Margaret of Denmark continues her conquest of his realm (*see* 1389; 1397).

Milan's tyrannical Gian Galaezzo Visconti, 44, assumes the title of duke. His 1387 marriage to Isabelle of Valois will be the basis of French territorial claims to Milan (*see* 1500).

1396 The Crusade of Nicopolis advances along the Danube pillaging and killing under the leadership of the Hungarian king Sigismund who is supported by both the Roman and Avignon popes and who has enlisted Balkan princes, French, German, and English knights. The 20,000 Crusaders encounter an equal number of Turks 4 miles south of Nicopolis, the Turks overwhelm the Crusaders in a battle September 25, and they take many of the survivors prisoner.

France's Charles VI makes a truce with England. It will last for nearly 20 years.

1397 Ottoman forces under Bayazid I lay siege to Constantinople, but the marshal of France Jean Bouciquaut, 31, defends the city. Tartars led by Tamerlane distract Bayazid from the siege (*see* 1398; Battle of Angora, 1402).

Visconti forces from Milan invade Tuscany but Florence resists the Visconti.

Margaret of Denmark completes her conquest of Sweden, she has her grandnephew Eric crowned king of a united Scandinavia. Her dynastic Union of Kalmar will continue at least nominally until 1523, but Margaret herself will rule as the "Semiramis of the North" until her death in 1412.

Parliament demands that England's Richard II submit a financial accounting. Richard has the parliamentary leader condemned for treason (*see* 1398).

Kyoto's Golden Pavilion (Kinkaku) is completed on the Kitayama estate on the outskirts of town for the retired Ashikaga shogun Yoshimitsu, who has passed his title on to his son in order that he may live as a monk in the Golden Pavilion.

1398 England's Richard II moves the country toward totalitarian government after executing three dissident lords for treason and packing the House of Commons with his adherents. Richard exiles his cousin Henry of Bolingbroke, 31, son of John of Gaunt, has himself voted a lifetime income by Parliament, delegates Parliament's powers to a committee friendly to his own interests, imposes heavy taxes, and pursues a reign of terror designed to make him absolute monarch (*see* 1399).

Tamerlane leads his Tartar hordes through the passes into northern India after having conquered Persia, Mesopotamia, and Afghanistan. Crossing the Indus September 24 he advances 160 miles in 2 days in early November, overtaking thousands who have fled his approach at Bhatnair. He massacres 100,000 Hindu prisoners at Delhi December 12, sacks Delhi December 17, and moves on to Meerut (*see* 1399).

Merchant Richard Whittington is made lord mayor of London, having grown rich by importing silks, damasks, velvets, and other goods.

1399 England's John of Gaunt dies at 59, his Lancaster estates are confiscated by Richard II, and his son Henry of Bolingbroke returns from exile, landing at Ravenspur in July while Richard is in Ireland. When Richard returns, he is defeated and captured by Bolingbroke and deposed by Parliament, which acclaims the usurper Bolingbroke as Henry IV to begin a 62-year reign by the house of Lancaster.

Richard is imprisoned in the Tower of London and signs a deed of abdication, but rebellions are launched by his supporters, notably the Welsh chieftain Owen Glendower (Owain ab Gruffydd), 40, who proclaims himself prince of Wales and begins a 16-year war.

Tamerlane storms Meerut January 9 and fights his way back along the Himalaya foothills to the Indus River, which he reaches March 19 after having desolated the kingdom of Delhi.

1400 England's Richard II dies at the Tower of London in February, possibly at the hands of a murderer but more probably of illness in the cold, damp tower. Rumors spread that Richard has escaped and that the body buried without ceremony is that of another man. Supporters of Richard rise in revolt against the Lancastrian Henry IV.

The Holy Roman Emperor Wenceslas of Bohemia is deposed for drunkenness and incompetence after a 22-year reign. Wenceslas refuses to accept the decision and will continue to hold the imperial crown for 10 years against the challenges of his rivals Sigismund and Jobst who will have the support of two

1400 (cont.) rival kings. But the 48-year-old elector palatine of the Rhine is elected German king August 21 at Rense, Pope Boniface IX will recognize him in 1403, and he will reign until 1410 as the emperor Rupert.

 Nonfiction *Chronique de France, d'Angleterre, d'Ecosse et d'Espagne* by French chronicler Jean Froissart, 67, who visited England in 1360, toured Scotland in 1365, traveled to Milan in 1368 with Petrarch and Geoffrey Chaucer, and entered the Church in 1372.

Poetry *The Canterbury Tales* by Geoffrey Chaucer who dies October 25 at age 60, leaving the work incomplete. The tales will make the poet's name immortal with such Chaucerian phrases as "bless this house," "every man for himself," "through thick and thin," "love is blind," "brown as a berry," "pretty is as pretty does," "it is no child's play," "murder will out," and "for in the stars is written the death of every man."

London's population reaches 50,000, but no other English city is as populous as Lübeck or Nuremberg, each of which has 20,000, much less as big as Cologne, which has 30,000.

15th CENTURY

1401 England increases the power of the Church over heresy, principally Lollardy, by the statute "de Heretico Comburendo," first law of its kind to be passed in England.

The rise of capitalism in the first half of this century will begin a three-century advance in Europe's agricultural technology.

Conditions of European farm labor will be powerfully affected by improvements in agricultural technology in this century (above). Labor will be emancipated in the economically advanced nations of Tuscany, Lombardy, and the Low Countries, further enslaved in the less advanced nations.

The incidence of famine will decline in Europe in this century.

The Hanseatic League will lose its trade to Dutch fishing interests in this century as copepod crops fail in the Baltic, diminishing fish populations that feed on these tiny crustaceans.

Inca terraces (andanes) in this century will turn steep slopes in the Andes of the Western Hemisphere into arable land. Soil and topsoil will be carried up from the valleys below.

1402 The Battle of Angora in Anatolia July 28 gains victory for Tamerlane over the Ottoman sultan Bayazid I, who is deserted by his Turkish vassals and captured. Many of the Turkish emirs are restored by Tamerlane, who advances to Smyrna and Bursa as the Ottoman Empire verges on a breakup with Bayazid's sons wrangling over the succession.

Milan's Gian Galeazzo Visconti dies of plague September 3 while besieging Florence. His death at age 51 saves Florence but plunges Milan into anarchy as his son Giovanni Maria, 13, is proclaimed duke while his 10-year-old son Filippo Maria is made nominal head of Pavia (see 1395; 1412).

A Scottish invasion of England is stopped at Homildon Hill in Northumberland by Sir Henry Percy, 60, and his brother Sir Thomas Percy, 58, who support England's Henry IV (see 1403).

1403 China's Ming emperor Ch'eng Tsu, 44, begins a 21-year reign with the dynastic title Yung Lo. His nephew disappeared in a palace fire last year, great violence marks the start of the new reign, uneasiness persists that the deposed nephew will reappear, but the Yung Lo reign will bring progress to China.

The Ottoman emperor Bayazid who was captured last year in the Battle of Angora dies in captivity and a 10-year civil war begins as his sons Suleiman in Edirne, Isa in Bursa, and Mehmed in Amasia vie for power.

England's Henry IV subdues Percy of Northumberland who has joined the Welsh revolt of Owen Glendower that began in 1399.

The Hanseatic League gains complete control of Bergen, Norway, and enjoys a virtual monopoly in most of the commodities produced by northern Europe including fish, the salt used for curing fish, whale oil, pitch and rosin employed in shipbuilding and maintenance, and eiderdown (see 1406).

The doge of Venice imposes the world's first quarantine as a safeguard against the Black Death. All who wish to enter the city must wait, and the waiting time will be standardized at 40 days in 1485 (see 1374).

1405 Tamerlane dies suddenly at Atrar February 17 at age 68 while planning a campaign against China. The Tartar emperor has conquered Persia, Mesopotamia, Afghanistan, and much of India, but his empire quickly begins to dissolve.

Venetian forces defeat an army mounted by the Carrara family and seize Padua, Verona, Vicenza, and other domains of the Carraras and the Viscontis whose leader Gian Galeazzo Visconti of Milan died in 1402.

Florence buys Pisa to get direct access to the sea.

French troops land in Wales to support the rebellion of Owen Glendower. The archbishop of York makes his own break with England's Henry IV.

The Chinese emperor Yung Lo orders the first Chinese sea expedition. A fleet of 63 junks carrying some 28,000 men sails for islands to the south under the

Chinese war junks commanded by the eunuch admiral Cheng Ho subdued countries as far away as the Persian Gulf.

command of the Moslem eunuch Ma who calls himself Cheng Ho (*see* 1407).

The University of Turin has its beginnings.

1406 Scotland's Robert III suspects complicity by the country's real ruler Robert, duke of Albany, in the mysterious death of the king's elder son David in 1402, he sends his 11-year-old son James to France for safety, English sailors capture James, news of the capture reaches Robert III, and he dies April 4 at age 65. James I will remain in English hands until 1424.

England's French territories are attacked by Louis, duc d'Orléans, who is married to Valentina Visconti of Milan.

Castile's Enrique III (el Doliente, the Sufferer) dies Christmas Day at age 27 after a despotic reign of 16 years in which he has resolved rivalries between descendants of Pedro the Cruel and of Enrique II Trastamara by marrying the granddaughter of Pedro.

London names Richard Whittington lord mayor again and he loans money to Henry IV as he previously loaned money to Richard II (*see* 1398). Whittington will be the subject of a Mother Goose rhyme (*see Contes de ma mère l'oie*, 1697).

Hanseatic fishermen catch some 96 English fishermen fishing off Bergen (*see* 1403). They bind the Englishmen hand and foot and throw them overboard to drown.

1407 France's duc d'Orléans is assassinated November 23 at age 35 by partisans of the Burgundian John the Fearless and civil war is precipitated between Burgundians and Armagnacs. The latter are named for the count of Armagnac, father-in-law of the new duc d'Orléans, and are a reactionary, anti-English war party supported in the South and Southeast, while the Burgundians are pro-English, favor peace, support Pope Clement VII and his papal successors, and are themselves supported by the people, by the University of Paris, and by the Wittelsbachs.

China's Cheng Ho returns with the prince of Palembang (Sumatra), who has been defeated in battle and placed in chains (*see* 1405; 1408).

The Bank of St. George is established in Genoa's Piazza Caricamento and begins its growth as an important financial power.

The Black Death kills thousands in London (*see* 1499).

1408 Bohemian preacher Jan Hus, 35, is denounced by other clergymen who complain to the archbishop of Prague about the strong language used by Hus in reference to the sale of indulgences and other clerical abuses. Hus is stripped of his appointment as synodal preacher and is forbidden to exercise priestly functions, but he is defended by the populace.

The Chinese admiral Cheng Ho embarks on a second great expedition from which he will return with the

king of Ceylon and the Sinhalese royal family which has dared to attack Ho's mission (*see* 1407; 1412).

1409 The Council of Pisa assembles 500 prelates and delegates from all over Europe to end the schism between Rome and Avignon that has persisted since 1378. The conclave hears charges against Pope Gregory XII at Rome and Pope Benedict XII at Avignon. It declares both of them deposed, it elects Peter Philarges pope June 26, and he begins a brief papacy as Alexander V.

Pope Alexander V (above) promulgates a bull ordering the surrender of all books by England's John Wycliffe (*see* 1382). Bohemia's archbishop publicly burns some 200 of Wycliffe's writings.

Bohemia's archbishop excommunicates Jan Hus along with several of his friends who will appeal to the successor of Pope Alexander V. Hus continues to preach at the Bethlehem chapel and begins to defend in public the so-called heresies of John Wycliffe (*see* 1408; 1411).

Venice recovers its territories on the Dalmatian coast.

Leipzig University has its beginnings in a college founded by émigrés from Prague.

Sculpture *David* (marble) by Florentine sculptor Donatello (Donato di Noccolo di Betto Bardi), 23.

1410 Pope Alexander V dies at Bologna sometime before dawn May 4, possibly the victim of poisoning. He is succeeded by the Neapolitan cardinal Baldassare Cossa who is elected May 17 at Bologna and begins a 5-year papacy as John XXIII.

The Holy Roman Emperor Rupert dies at Landskron near Oppenheim May 18 at age 58. He is succeeded by the 42-year-old Sigismund of Luxembourg, brother of the deposed emperor Wenceslas of Bohemia. Sigismund's rival Jobst of Moravia will die next year; Sigismund will be crowned at Aix-la-Chapelle late in 1414, and will reign until 1437.

The Battle of Tannenberg July 15 gives a huge army of Poles and Lithuanians victory over the Teutonic Knights, but the victors are unable to exploit their triumph.

The notion that the world is round is revived by a translation into Latin of the *Geography* by the 2nd century astronomer-mathematician-geographer Ptolemy (*see* Columbus, 1474).

1411 The Peace of Thorn signed February 1 ends the Slavic advance but fails to give Poland access to the Baltic and costs the Teutonic Knights only the Lithuanian territory of Samogitia and an indemnity, despite their crushing defeat last year at Tannenberg.

Portugal and Castile make peace after 26 years of hostilities, and Portugal begins her rise as a great world power.

A new ban is pronounced in March on Prague's Jan Hus but he continues to preach in defense of the treatises written by England's John Wycliffe (*see* 1409; 1414).

A Celestine monastery is founded at Vichy by France's Charles VI (*see* 1605).

The University of St. Andrews is founded in Scotland.

1412 Margaret of Denmark dies suddenly October 28 at age 59 aboard her ship in Flensborg harbor. Her grandnephew Eric of Pomerania continues his reign as Eric VII of Denmark and Norway, Eric XIII of Sweden, but the death of the "lady king" (as delegates from Lübeck have called her) begins a long period of dissension as Eric assumes personal power and begins an oppressive rule.

Milan's Gian Maria Visconti dies at the hands of an assassin. His brother Filippo Maria is left to rule alone and will rule the duchy until his death in 1447.

The Chinese admiral Cheng Ho leaves on a third expedition that will take him as far as the Hormuz Straits, gateway to the Persian Gulf (*see* 1408; 1416).

The University of Turin opens in Piedmont.

1413 England's Henry IV dies the evening of March 20 at age 45 and is succeeded by his 25-year-old son who assumes the throne as Henry V to begin a 9-year reign that will raise England to the rank of a major European power.

Paris is seized by insurgent butchers led by skinner Simon Caboche who attempt to make the government more efficient by imposing the Ordonnance Cabochienne, but the Armagnacs soon regain control and revert to feudal reaction that ends all hope for reform.

Sculpture *St. Mark* by Donatello.

1414 The Council of Constance is assembled by Pope John XXIII at the insistence of Hungary's King Sigismund, the Holy Roman Emperor who wants the Church's unity restored. The purpose of the council is also to reform the Church's leadership and its members and to extirpate heresy, especially that of Bohemia's Jan Hus (*see* 1411), who has arrived under an imperial safe conduct that permits his free return to Bohemia whatever judgment may be passed upon him.

The Jews are expelled from Cologne.

A Lollard plot against England's Henry V is uncovered, a group of Lollards is seized, and most are hanged.

1415 The Council of Constance unanimously condemns the writings of England's John Wycliffe May 5 and demands that Jan Hus recant in public his "heresy." Hus refuses and is burned at the stake July 6.

News that Jan Hus has been savaged in violation of his imperial safe conduct produces a surge of Bohemian nationalism combined with demands for religious reform that will split the Holy Roman Empire (*see* 1420).

The Battle of Agincourt October 25 ends in defeat for the French at the hands of English archers, the lowest caste in the military hierarchy. Commanded by Henry V who has been delayed by torrential rain in his march from Harfleur to Calais, 6,000 archers, 1,000 men-at-arms, and a few thousand foot soldiers encounter a French force of 25,000 under the command of Charles d'Albret, the constable of France whose knights have not learned the lessons of Crécy and Poitiers (*see* 1346; 1356).

Henry's archers plant long pointed stakes in their midst at Agincourt (above), the French cavalry is impaled or trapped in the mud wearing heavy armor, Henry orders that prisoners be killed since he does not have enough men both to guard the prisoners and attack the foe, and the slaughter ends only when the French withdraw.

The constable of France Charles d'Albret dies in battle at Agincourt (above) along with 3 dukes, 5 counts, 90 barons, and 5,000 knights of noble birth. 1,000 prisoners are taken including the 24-year-old Duke Charles d'Orléans who will not be ransomed until 1440. English casualties number only 13 men-at-arms (including the duke of York) and 100 or so foot soldiers. France's nobility is shattered, the feudal system is discredited, and Normandy lies open to reconquest by the English.

Welsh chieftain Owen Glendower is defeated by the English after 16 years of rebellion and is pardoned.

The Very Rich Book of Hours of the Duke of Berry is prepared for the 75-year-old first duc de Berry Jean de France with illustrations by Belgian painter Pol Limburg and his brothers Hermann and Jan.

Sculpture *St. John the Evangelist* by Donatello.

1416 England's Henry V begins a 3-year move across Normandy in which he will take Caen, Bayeux, Lisieux, Alençon, Falaise, and Cherbourg.

The first war between Venice and the Ottoman Empire is won by the doge Loredano who defeats the Turks at the Dardanelles and forces the sultan to conclude peace.

A Chinese fleet under Cheng Ho reaches Aden (*see* 1412; 1421).

Sculpture *St. George* by Donatello.

1417 The Great Schism of the Catholic Church that began in 1378 is ended by the Council of Constance which elects the 49-year-old Oddone (Otto) Colonna Pope Martin V after having deposed Benedict XIII, Gregory XII, and John XXIII.

Merchants of the Hanseatic League agree not to buy wheat before it is grown, herring before it is caught, or cloth before it is woven. The League regulates city tariffs and prices to keep supplies of grain and meat cheap for townspeople even at the expense of peasants.

1417 (cont.) Movable type is used by printers at Antwerp (*see* Limoges, 1381; Haarlem, 1435).

1418 Rouen falls to England's Henry V December 31 after a 2-month siege in which the English have starved out a town as large as London.

The Japanese nō drama pioneered in the last century is taken up by the upper classes with support from the Ashikaga shogun Yoshimitsu. Originally played by farmers in the 11th century, the symbolic drama has been formalized by Motokiyo Zeami, now 55 (*see* 1383; Kabuki, 1603).

1419 Portugese explorers land in the Madeira Islands in the Atlantic off North Africa (*see* Henry the Navigator, 1421).

The Decameron completed by Giovanni Boccaccio in 1353 is published for the first time at Venice.

The doge's palace at Venice that dates to the 9th century and was rebuilt in later centuries receives a new facade that will endure for more than 550 years. The palace will be extended toward the Piazetta in 1424 and the Foscari Arch will be completed in 1471 (*see* 1520).

Sugar cane from Sicily is planted in the Madeira Islands (above) (*see* 1456; Columbus, 1493).

1420 An army of knights, mercenaries, and adventurers summoned by Pope Martin V to a crusade against heretics is defeated at Prague by a small force of Bohemian peasants and laborers led by the blind veteran John Zizka, 60 (*see* 1415; 1431).

Florence makes vain attempts to put a 20 percent ceiling on interest rates charged by Florentine bankers, especially on loans to the *popolo minuto*.

Painting *The Crucifixion* and *The Last Judgment* by Flemish painter Jan van Eyck, 35, and his brother Hubert, 50.

1421 The Portuguese prince Henry the Navigator, 27, assembles Europe's leading pilots, map-makers, astronomers, scholars, and instrument makers at Sagres on the Cape St. Vincent where they will pioneer a new science of navigation. Son of João I and grandson of England's John of Gaunt, Henry has his shipwrights develop a lateen-rigged caravel with three masts—a highly maneuverable vessel able to stand up to the winds of the open sea (*see* Madeira Islands, 1419; Canary Islands, 1425).

Florence buys Livorno (Leghorn) and establishes the Consuls of the Sea.

The Ottoman sultan Mohammed I dies at age 34 after an 8-year reign in which he has consolidated the empire. He is succeeded by his 18-year-old son who will reign until 1451 as Murad II and who will extend the empire into southeastern Europe (*see* 1432).

The Chinese Ming emperor Yung Lo (Ch'eng Tsu) moves his capital from Nanking to Peking as he continues to reform local governments and attempts to establish trade with islands to the south.

The emperor Yung Lo (above) sends Cheng Ho on a fifth expedition abroad (*see* 1416; 1431).

The North Sea engulfs more than 70 Dutch villages. More than 100,000 die as the shallow Zuider Zee spreads over thousands of square miles.

1422 England's Henry V dies of dysentery in France August 3 at age 35 protesting that he wants to live so that he may rebuild the walls of Jerusalem. He is succeeded by his 8-month-old son whose reign as Henry VI will be cut short in 1461. The will of Henry V names his 31-year-old brother Humphrey, duke of Gloucester, protector of the young king and names Richard de Beauchamp, 40, earl of Warwick, as the boy's preceptor.

France's Charles VI dies at Paris October 1 at age 53 after a 42-year reign. The Treaty of Troyes signed in 1420 disinherited the dauphin, now 19, and he will not be crowned until 1429. England's Henry VI is proclaimed king of France.

England resumes war with France under the leadership of the king's uncle John of Lancaster, 33, duke of Bedford, who will rule much of France in the absence of the dauphin and who will rule England in the minority of Henry VI through his brother Humphrey, duke of Gloucester.

Lisbon becomes Portugal's seat of government.

France's University of Besançon has its beginnings.

1423 Venice buys Thessalonica from Constantinople under terms of an agreement with the Byzantine emperor Manuel II to keep the Ottoman Turks from taking the city (but *see* 1430).

Scottish leaders sign a treaty at York in September undertaking to pay 60,000 marks for the "maintenance in England" of their uncrowned 29-year-old King James I and agree to the marriage of James to Jane, daughter of John Beaufort, earl of Somerset.

Painting *The Adoration of the Magi* by Italian painter Gentile da Fabriano (Gentile di Niccolo di Giovanni Massi), 53, who settled last year at Florence after having worked at Venice.

Sculpture *St. Louis* by Donatello.

1424 Italian count Giacomuzzo Sforza drowns in the Pescara River January 4 at age 54 while engaged in a military expedition against the Spanish near Aquila. His bastard son Francesco, 23, will carry on the Sforza name adopted by his father in the field and will become duke of Milan in 1450.

Scotland's James I gains his freedom at age 29 after nearly 18 years in English hands. The earl of Somerset remits 10,000 marks of ransom money as a dowry for his daughter Jane, she and James are married at Southwark February 12. James is crowned at Scone May 21, and he will reign until 1437.

England's duke of Bedford soundly defeats a combined force of French and Scottish troops August 17 at Verneuil and his brother Gloucester invades Hainaut in October.

De Imitatione Christi (Imitation of Christ) by German ecclesiastic Thomas à Kempis, 44, says, "Man proposes, but God disposes." "And when a man is out of sight, quickly also is he out of mind." "Sic transit gloria mundi" (So passes away the glory of this world).

Bronze doors designed by Florentine painter-goldsmith Lorenzo Ghiberti (Lorenzo di Cione di Ser Buonaccorso), 46, with reliefs depicting scenes from the life of Christ are installed as the north portals of the baptistery of San Giovanni at Florence. Ghiberti has worked for 21 years on the doors and is commissioned to create the east portals that he will complete in 1447.

1425 The Canary Islands less than 70 miles off the northwest coast of Africa fall to Portugal's Henry the Navigator who wrests them from Castile. The Canaries are seven volcanic peaks that rise out of the Atlantic to snow-covered peaks as high as 12,250 feet (*see* 1496; Henry, 1421).

The Byzantine emperor Manuel II Palaeologus dies at age 75 after a 34-year reign. He has recently been forced to pay tribute to the Ottoman sultan Murad II and he is succeeded by his 35-year-old son who will reign until 1448 as John VII Palaeologus.

Poetry *La Belle Dame sans Merci* by French writer-diplomat Alain Chartier, 40.

Sculpture *Habbakuk (Zuccone)* by Donatello in gilt bronze for the campanile of the Florence cathedral.

1426 England's duke of Bedford returns from France, he reaches London in January. He concludes an alliance with his brother Gloucester, he effects a reconciliation between Gloucester and the bishop of Winchester Henry Beaufort who is chancellor of England, and he knights the infant king Henry VI.

Venice goes to war with Milan's Filippo Maria, beginning 3 years of hostilities that will end with Venice gaining control of Verona, Vicenza, Brescia, Bergamo, and Crema.

Louvain University has its beginnings in a school founded at the French city.

Painting *Virgin Enthroned* by Florentine painter Masaccio (Tomasso di Giovanni di Simoe Cassai), 24, whose work serves as the central panel of the altarpiece for Pisa's Church of the Carmine.

1427 England's duke of Bedford leaves in March to resume the war in France after promising to act in accord with the council. He has ordered his brother Gloucester to desist from further attacks on Hainaut and he tries to restore prosperity to the French districts under his rule by reforming the debased coinage, by removing various abuses, and by granting privileges to merchants and manufacturers.

Sculpture *The Feast of Herod* is completed as a relief for the baptistery of Siena by the Florentine sculptor Donatello.

1428 The Treaty of Delft ends hostilities between England and Flanders, but English forces besiege Orléans in central France beginning in October with the reluctant consent of the duke of Bedford.

Venetian forces under the condottiere Carmagnola conquer Brescia and Bergamo.

Vietnam regains her independence from China's Ming Empire.

Japanese transport workers strike in protest against high prices as famine cripples the country. The strikers are joined by farmers who riot in the streets and wreck warehouses, temples, private houses, and sake production facilities.

The bones of England's late John Wycliffe are disinterred 44 years after his death and are burned by order of the Council of Constance.

The University of Florence begins to teach Greek and Latin literature with special emphasis on history and its bearing on human behavior and moral values.

Painting The *Merode Altarpiece* by Flemish painter Robert Campin, 50, the Master of Flemalle.

Florence's Church of San Lorenzo is completed by Filippo Brunelleschi after 7 years of construction.

1429 Joan of Arc (Jeanne d'Arc) becomes the heroine of France and changes the course of history. A shepherd girl of 17 from Lorraine, La Pucelle d'Orléans has heard voices and has seen visions of the Archangel Michael, Saint Catherine, and Saint Margaret, who pledged her to seek out the dauphin and deliver Orléans from the English. She persuades a royal captain to equip her with armor and have her conducted to Chinon, she finds the dauphin there, he provides her with a small army, and she liberates Orléans in early May.

England's duke of Bedford sends to London for reinforcements, strengthens his hold on Paris, visits Rouen to bind the Normans closer to England, but resigns the French regency to Philip of Burgundy in compliance with the will of the Parisians.

Joan of Arc (above) persuades the dauphin that he is the legitimate son and heir of the late Charles VI despite the Treaty of Troyes that disinherited him in 1420. He is crowned at Reims July 17, and he begins a 32-year reign as Charles VII.

Joan of Arc has a standard embroidered for her bearing the fleur-de-lys and the words "Jesus Maria."

The Order of the Golden Fleece is founded in Burgundy. It will become a Hapsburg order beginning in 1477.

Cosimo de' Medici becomes head of the Florentine banking house at age 40 upon the death of its founding father Giovanni. "I leave you with a larger business than any other in the Tuscan land," writes

1429 (cont.) Giovanni, and he advises his son Cosimo the elder to "be charitable to the poor," to belong to the popular political party, to "speak not as though giving advice," to "avoid litigation," and to "be careful not to attract public attention."

The Grocers' Company is formed in London to succeed the spicers' guild of 1180. The company will be granted a charter by Henry VI to sell wholesale—*vendre en gros,* source of the word "grocer"—and to manage the trade in spices (now used widely in medicine), drugs, and dyestuffs.

1430 Joan of Arc enters Compiégne outside Paris May 23 and is taken prisoner along with her brothers. She is delivered to Jean de Luxembourg and thence to the English, who imprison her in a tower at Rouen with the intent of discrediting her. Charles VII makes no effort to save Joan, nor is any interference made by the duke of Bedford, who was joined in April by the 8-year-old Henry VI in a temporary suspension of the regency (*see* 1431).

Thessalonica is taken by the Ottoman Turks under Murad II and begins nearly 500 years of Turkish rule (*see* 1423; 1913; Sofia, 1385).

Sculpture *David* (bronze) by Donatello.

Painting Mosaics for Venice's Church of San Marco are completed by Italian painter Paolo Uccello (Paolo di Dono), 33, who has been a member of the painters' guild since age 18.

1431 Joan of Arc is handed over to the former bishop of Beauvais Pierre Cauchon by the English who vow to seize her again if she is not convicted of high treason against God. The maid of Orléans is duly condemned by an ecclesiastical court and she is burned at the stake in the Old Market Square of Rouen May 30.

England's Henry VI is crowned at Paris in December.

John Zizka defeats another army of knights and adventurers at the Bohemian town of Tabor (*see* 1420; 1434).

China's Cheng Ho leads a final expedition that will reach 20 states. He will exact tribute from 11, including Mecca (*see* 1421; 1433).

The French university of Poitiers has its beginnings.

1432 The Azores are discovered off the west coast of Portugal by Portuguese mariner Gonzalo Cabral.

The Italian condottiere Carmagnola, conte di Castelnuovo, is convicted of treason by Venice's Council of Ten after leading an unsuccessful campaign against the Visconti forces of Milan whose duke he served from 1416 to 1423. The doge intercedes in his behalf, but Carmagnola is beheaded April 5 at age 41.

Constantinople withstands a siege by the Ottoman sultan Murad II who withdraws after a stubborn defense by the Byzantine emperor John VII Palaeologus.

Painting Fresco *Reform of the Carmelite Rule* by Italian painter Fra Filippo Lippi, 26, who leaves the Florentine monastery in which he has lived since being orphaned in childhood and goes to Padua.

1433 Africa's Cape Bojador south of the Canary Islands is rounded for the first time by Portuguese navigator Gil Eames (or Gillianes, or Guillanes), a captain of Prince Henry who has sailed out of the port of Lagos, Portugal.

Portugal's Joao I dies August 14 at age 76 after a 40-year reign. He is succeeded by his 40-year-old son Duarte (Edward) who will reign until 1438.

Timbuktu falls to the Berbers.

Bohemia's Hussite wars end after 13 years of hostilities between peasant armies and papal "crusaders." Hussites called to the Council of Basel will accept a compromise, but Bohemian nationalism has been asserted and the country has broken forever from its German ties.

Florence is defeated after a 4-year war on Lucca, and Giovanni de' Medici's son Cosimo, imprisoned as a scapegoat, is sentenced to a 10-year exile (but *see* 1434).

China's Cheng Ho returns from a seventh and final expedition that has taken his fleet to 20 states. Mecca and 10 other states send tribute to the Ming Dynasty emperor, who is presented by Cheng Ho with giraffes, zebras, and other foreign curiosities, but China's brief show of interest in the outside world will now end.

"De Concordantia Catholica" by the German Roman Catholic priest Nikolaus von Cusa, 32, gives the Council of Basel (above) a carefully reasoned defense of its authority but leaves open the question of whether ultimate power vests in the pope or in the council which has cited Pope Eugenius IV for failing to appear but whose deposition of the pope will have no practical effect.

Painting *The Man in the Red Turban* by Jan van Eyck.

1434 African slaves introduced into Portugal by a caravel returning from the southern continent are the first of millions that will be exported in the next four centuries (*see* 1441; 1510).

Florence recalls Cosimo de' Medici from exile, he will rule the city until his death in 1464, and his family will continue to dominate the city for 30 years thereafter (*see* 1433; 1440).

Poland's Jagellon king Ladislas (Vladislav) V dies at age 84 after a 38-year reign that has seen his country become a great power. He is succeeded by his 10-year-old son who will reign until his death in 1444 as Ladislas VI.

The radical Bohemian priest Procop the Great leads his Taborites into battle at Lipan but meets defeat as civil war wracks the country.

The Swedish peasant leader Engelbrecht Engelbrechtsen marches through eastern and southern Sweden, seizing castles and driving out bailiffs in a revolt that spreads to Norway.

Painting *Giovanni Arnolfini and His Bride* by Jan van Eyck.

Florence's Duomo (Cathedral of Santa Maria del Fiore) is completed after 140 years of construction with the installation of a 350-foot high dome designed by Filippo Brunelleschi, now 57.

Venice's Ca' d'Oro is completed in a brilliant blend of Veneto-Byzantine and Gothic styles.

1435 France's Charles VII agrees to punish the murderers of Burgundy's duke John and to recognize Philip as a sovereign prince. Burgundy agrees to recognize Charles's title, but the English refuse to make peace on terms acceptable to the French.

Naples is conquered by Aragon's Alfonso V (the Magnanimous) who ends the 21-year reign of Joanna (Giovanna) II, reunites Naples and Sicily, and makes Naples the center of a Mediterranean Aragonese empire.

Sweden's diet recognizes the claims of Engelbrecht Engelbrechtsen and elects him regent for the weak King Eric who has lost Schleswig to the dukes of Holstein.

Movable type is employed by Dutch printers at Haarlem (*see* Antwerp, 1417; Mainz, 1454).

Painting *The Descent from the Cross* by Flemish painter Roger van der Weyden, 35, on commission from the Louvain archers' guild. He is appointed city painter at Brussels; Swiss painter Konrad Witz, 35, becomes a citizen of Basel and is commissioned to paint the *Mirror of Salvation* altar (Heilsspiegelaltar); *The Vision of St. Eustace* by Italian painter Pisanello (Antonio Pisano), 40; *The Adoration of the Child* by Fra Filippo Lippi.

1436 France's Charles VII recovers Paris from the English as Scottish forces defeat the English near Berwick.

The Compact of Iglau ends the Hussite Wars as all parties agree to accept the Holy Roman Emperor Sigismund as king of Bohemia.

Della Pittura by Italian architect-scholar Leon Battista Alberti, 32, is the first literary formulation of the aesthetic and scientific theories embodied in Renaissance paintings.

Sculpture *Jeremiah* by Donatello at Florence.

England permits the export of wheat and other corn without a state license when prices fall below certain levels.

1437 Scotland's James I remains at Perth for 6 weeks despite warnings of danger and is stabbed to death February 10 at age 42 by Sir Robert Graham, a man James had imprisoned and then banished. Walter Stewart, earl of Atholl, has instigated the attack and is tortured and executed along with Graham. The king's 5-year-old son is crowned at Holyrood in March and begins a 5-year reign as James II that will be marked by civil war.

Portuguese forces suffer a crushing defeat at Tangier at the hands of the Moors. The king's youngest brother Fernando, 35, has urged the crusade. The Moors make the Portuguese promise to return Ceuta, Fernando offers himself as a hostage, but Portugal will not return Ceuta and Fernando will die in the dungeons of Fez after 5 years of cruel punishment.

The Holy Roman Emperor Sigismund dies December 9 at age 69, the house of Luxembourg becomes extinct; Sigismund will be succeeded as German king by his son-in-law Albrecht of Hapsburg (*see* 1438).

The University of Caen has its beginnings in France.

1438 The Inca dynasty that will rule Peru in the Western Hemisphere until 1553 is founded by Pachacutec (*see* 1525).

The Austrian duke Albrecht V of Hapsburg is elected German king to succeed his late father-in-law Sigismund (*see* 1437). The 40-year-old Albrecht is also crowned king of Hungary and Bohemia but will not be able to obtain possession of Bohemia and will spend most of his brief reign defending Hungary against the Ottoman Turks.

Portugal's Duarte I (Edward) dies at age 47 after a 5-year reign marked by a terrible epidemic of the plague and by last year's disaster at Tangier. He is

The Battle of Agincourt gave England's Henry V a great triumph over the knights of France.

1438 (cont.) succeeded by his 6-year-old son who will reign until 1481 as Afonso V (Afonso o Africano) with his uncle Pedro as regent until 1449.

Scotland and England conclude a truce that will last until 1448.

1439 The Hapsburg German king Albrecht II, who also has been king of Bohemia and Hungary and who has ruled as the uncrowned Holy Roman Emperor, dies at Langendorf October 27 at age 42 after a reign of less than 2 years spent mainly in defending Hungary against the Ottoman Turks. Albrecht has led an army to the gates of Baghdad, but he has lost much of his force to dysentery which hastens his own end.

The death of Frederick of Tyrol, Hapsburg cousin of Albrecht II, leaves Frederick's 24-year-old ward and nephew the senior member of the Hapsburg family. He succeeds Albrecht and will reign as Frederick IV beginning early next year.

Albrecht II (above) will be succeeded as king of Hungary and Bohemia by his posthumous son who will be born February 22 of next year, will be crowned less than 3 months later, and will reign until 1457 under the guardianship of his uncle Frederick.

The Ottoman sultan Murad II annexes Serbia and forces the Serbian despot George Brankovich, now 72, to take refuge in Hungary.

The Pragmatic Sanction of Mainz leaves the German church under imperial and princely control and postpones any reform in the church (see 1440).

The Council of Florence reaffirms the union between Constantinople and Rome. The Byzantine emperor John VIII Palaeologus accepts papal primacy.

Painting *Margaret van Eyck* by Jan van Eyck.

Sculpture Marble reliefs for the altar of St. Peter in the great cathedral at Florence by Florentine sculptor Luca della Robbia, 39.

1440 German electors at Frankfurt choose the Hapsburg duke of Styria and Carinthia February 2 to succeed the late Albrecht II. He begins a 46-year reign as Frederick IV.

The elector of Brandenburg Frederick I who has brought the house of Hohenzollern to greatness dies at Kadolzburg September 21 at age 48 shortly after declining an offer to accept the Bohemian throne. The king of Poland Ladislas VI has accepted the Hungarian crown in March and has begun a 4-year reign in July as Ladislas VI while the posthumous son of the late Albrecht II remains under the protection of his uncle Frederick III.

The Battle of Anghiari gives the 65-year-old condottiere Niccolo Piccinino, overlord of Bologna, a victory over the forces of Milan's Filippo Maria Visconti. Florence's Cosimo de' Medici backs the claims of Francesco Sforza to the duchy of Milan and supports a coalition of Venetians and Florentines who defeat Piccinino.

Harfleur falls to English forces under the duke of Somerset John Beaufort, 37, and his brother Edward. A peace mission to France led by Cardinal Henry Beaufort, now 67, has no more success than did a similar mission led by the cardinal last year.

Cosimo de' Medici (above) institutes a progressive income tax to lighten the burden on the poor of Florence who support the Medici family.

Florence's Platonic Academy is founded.

England's Eton School is founded by Henry VI. The King's College of Our Lady of Eton beside Windsor will become the largest of the ancient English public schools (see Winchester, 1379; St. Paul's, 1510).

Painting *Christ Appearing to His Mother* by Roger van der Weyden; *The Last Judgment* by German painter Stefan Lochner, 30; Florentine painter Andrea del Castagno, 17, is commissioned to paint a fresco on the facade of the Palazzo del Podesta. The fresco shows men hanged as traitors and Andrea will be nicknamed "Andrew of the Hanged Men" (Andreino degl'impiccati).

1441 African slaves are sold in the markets of Lisbon and a trade begins that will see more than 20 million Africans transported in the next 460 years to Europe and—more especially—to the New World (see 1510).

The University of Bordeaux has its beginnings.

1442 Austria's Hapsburg archduke Frederick V is crowned German emperor July 17 at Aix-la-Chapelle more than 2 years after having been chosen at Frankfurt. Now 26, he will reign as Frederick IV until 1493 (see 1452).

England's Gascon territory is conquered by the French with the exceptions of Bordeaux and Bayonne.

1443 Nish and Sofia are taken from the Ottoman Turks by Christian forces under the leadership of Poland's 19-year-old Ladislas (Vladislav) VI who is also king of Hungary. His success is made possible by the 56-year-old governor of Transylvania János Hunyadi and by the Serbian George Brankovich, but the Ottoman sultan Murad stops the Christians in a Balkan pass at the Battle of Zlatica (Izladi).

Painting *Madonna with Violets* by Stefan Lochner.

1444 The Truce of Adrianople (Edirne) June 12 brings temporary peace between the Christians and the Ottoman Turks. George Brankovich is restored to his Serbian despotate at age 77.

The Ottoman sultan Murad II summons the Wallachian prince Dracul across the Danube and forces him to leave as hostages his son Radu and his 13-year-old son Dracula (see 1448).

A papal representative encourages the Hungarians to break the Truce of Adrianople (above). They resume hostilities in September, and they advance through Bulgaria toward the Black Sea.

The Battle of Varna November 10 ends in victory for the sultan Murad II who has been called back from retirement to head the Ottoman army. Murad has crossed the Bosporus in defiance of a Venetian fleet that has blocked the Dardanelles, he defeats a large force of Hungarians and Wallachians, he kills Ladislas (Vladislav) VI, and he takes many knights prisoner.

The Senegal River is reached by Portuguese explorer Nino Tristram.

Venetian efforts to find new spice routes are spurred by Niccolo de' Conti, a traveler who has returned to Venice after 25 years in Damascus, Baghdad, India, Sumatra, Java, Indo-China, Burma, Mecca, and Egypt. De' Conti is ordered by Pope Eugenius IV to relate the story of his travels to papal secretary Poggio Bracciolini as penance for his compulsory renunciation of Christianity.

Painting *St. Peter Altarpiece* by Konrad Witz who uses a landscape of Lake Geneva to depict *Christ Walking on the Water*.

1445 The first permanent French army is established by Charles VII who creates 20 companies of elite royal cavalry with 200 lances per company, 6 men per lance.

Copenhagen becomes the capital of Denmark.

Africa's Cape Verde is rounded for the first time in modern history by Portuguese explorer Dinis Diaz.

Some 25 caravels per year trade between Portugal and West Africa.

Painting *Santa Lucia Altarpiece* by Domenico Veneziano represents the Madonna and the saints in the same scale for the first time and reveals a new use of light and shadow; *The Adoration of the Magi* by Fra Angelico and Fra Filippo Lippi; *Giants* by Paolo Uccello; frescoes of Dante, Petrarch, Boccacio, and other eminent Italians by Andrea del Castagno for the refectory of Florence's Church of Santa Apollonia.

Sculpture *The Resurrection* by Luca della Robbia who has perfected a technique of creating figures of terracotta glazed like faience in white relief against blue grounds.

1446 The Ordenacoes Afonisans gives Portugal her first code of laws, an amalgam of Roman and Visigothic law mixed with local custom.

Corinth falls to the Turks who abort an effort by the Greeks to expand from the Peloponnesus (Morea) into central Greece.

A Korean alphabet devised by two research teams is proclaimed "the right language to teach the people" by the Korean king Sejong October 9. The 28-letter alphabet will be disdained by the educated elite who will retain the thousands of Chinese ideographs, the masses will be unable to use even the simple new alphabet, but a written Hangul combining ideographs and alphabet will evolve.

Painting *Edward Grymestone* and *Carthusian Monk* by Flemish painter Petrus Christus, 26; *The Patron Saints of Cologne* by Stefan Lochner.

Florentine architect Filippo Brunelleschi dies April 15 at age 69, leaving the cupola of the great Duomo incomplete (*see* 1434).

Ireland's Blarney Castle is completed by Cormac Laidhiv McCarthy, lord of Muskerry. Set in a turret below the battlements is a limestone rock that will be called the Blarney Stone and that will be reputed to confer eloquence on anyone who hangs head downward to kiss it.

1447 Milan establishes an Ambrosian republic upon the death of the last of the Visconti, Filippo Maria (*see* Sforza, 1450).

Poland's nobility chooses the 20-year-old grand duke of Lithuania to succeed the late Ladislas VI, his older brother. He begins a 45-year reign as Casimir IV, he unites Lithuania with Poland, and he will give Poland access to the Baltic (*see* 1466).

The Turkestani shah Rukh, fourth son of the great Tamerlane, dies at Samarkand after a 43-year reign of great splendor. He is succeeded by Tamerlane's 53-year-old grandson Ulugh-Beg who will reign until 1449.

Painting *Presentation in the Temple* by Stefan Lochner.

1448 The Byzantine emperor John VIII Palaeologus dies at age 57 after a 23-year reign. He is succeeded by his 44-year-old brother who will reign until 1453 as Constantine XI Palaeologus, the last of the Byzantine emperors.

The Ottoman sultan Murad II gains a victory over the Albanian chieftain Scanderberg (George Castriota), Hungary's János Hunyadi marches to oppose him, treacherous Hungarian noblemen desert Hunyadi, and Murad II defeats him at the Battle of Kossovo.

The prince of Wallachia Dracula escapes his Ottoman captors and assumes the throne of his father who was murdered last year. Fearing for his own life, Dracula vacates the throne after a few months and departs for Moldavia and Transylvania (*see* 1444; 1476).

The Union of Kalmar that has united the three Scandinavian kingdoms since 1387 begins to crumble as Christopher of Bavaria dies at age 30 after a reign of 9 years in which the Hansa towns have determined national policy. The Danish council elects Christian of Oldenburg king but retains all real power. The Swedish nobility elects Karl Knutsson king, and he begins a 9-year reign as Charles VIII, but Christian of Denmark resists Swedish efforts to secure the Norwegian throne.

France's Charles VII takes Maine in a renewal of the Hundred Years' War with England.

1448 (cont.) Charles VII (above) puts down an insurrection of French noblemen (the Praguerie) supported by his son the dauphin. He exiles the dauphin to the Dauphine where the son continues to intrigue against the king.

The Concordat of Vienna establishes the authority of German princes over the German church (*see 1439*). The Vatican strikes a cynical bargain with the new German king Frederick IV, it triumphs over the conciliar movement for reform by agreeing to divide its profits with the princes and with Frederick, and it agrees to give the princes a share in episcopal tax revenues.

Painting *Adoration of the Shepherds* by Italian painter Pietro di Giovanni d'Ambrogio.

1449 The Turkestan prince Ulugh-Beg is assassinated at age 55 by a Moslem religious fanatic who ends the 2-year reign of Tamerlane's grandson.

The chief of a new Mongol federation captures the Chinese emperor Ying Tsung in battle after a 13-year reign. The Mongols will hold Ying prisoner until 1450, he will not regain his throne from his brother Ching Ti until 1457, but he will then rule until 1464.

The Japanese shogun Yoshimasa assumes power at age 14 to usher in a second period of Ashikaga art that will rival that of his grandfather Yoshimitsu, but Yoshimasa's 25-year shogunate will be marked by uprisings, civil war, plague, and famine.

Court favorites of Portugal's Afonso V persuade him to make war against his uncle Pedro. The regent who has given the country able and enlightened rule since 1438 is killed with his son at the Battle of Alfarrobeira.

Ulugh-Beg (above) has been a scientist who used a curved device more than 130 feet long set on iron rails to catalog 1,018 stars in the constellations, making tables so precise that his calculations of the annual movements of Mars and Venus will differ from modern figures by only 5 and 7 seconds, respectively. The Moslems have feared his learning.

1450 England's William de la Pole, 53, first duke of Suffolk, is banished for 5 years by Henry VI following the murder January 9 of former parliamentary treasurer Adam Molyneux by sailors at Portsmouth. Suffolk is widely resented for having banished Richard of York to Ireland and is accused of having sold Anjou and Maine to France. Intercepted off Dover as he sails for France May 1, he is beheaded May 2.

Cade's rebellion demands English governmental reforms and restoration of power to Richard, duke of York (above), who returns from Ireland and forces his admission to the council. Kentish rebel John (Jack) Cade rallies 30,000 other small Kentish and Sussex landowners in May to protest oppressive taxation and the corruption of the court of Henry VI. Henry's forces are defeated by the rebels at Sevenoaks June 18, the rebels enter London July 3, they force the lord mayor and judges to condemn to death William Crowmer, sheriff of Kent and collector of taxes, along with Lord Saye-and-Sele. But the rebels grow violent, exact forced contributions to their cause, are refused readmission to the city, are repulsed at London Bridge, and are dispersed under amnesty. Cade is hunted down and killed at Heathfield July 12.

Francesco Sforza overthrows the Ambrosian republic established 3 years ago by the Milanese upon the death of his father-in-law Filippo Maria Visconti, duke of Milan, and makes a triumphal entry as duke of the city March 25. Sforza and his son Galeazzo Maria will make the Sforza court a rival to that of the Medicis at Florence by attracting Italian scholars and Greek exiles (*see 1424; 1476*).

A 14-year civil war ends in the Swiss confederacy which has been strengthened by the conflict.

England's nobility encloses more lands to raise sheep at the expense of the peasantry. The landowning class is enriched by the rapidly developing wool trade and by the continuing war with France (*see More, 1515*).

Pope Nicholas V authorizes the Portuguese to "attack, subject, and reduce to perpetual slavery the Saracens, pagans, and other enemies of Christ southward from Cape Bajador and Non, including all the coast of Guinea" (*see 1433; 1434; 1460*).

Glasgow University is founded by Bishop Turnbull under a bull of Pope Nicholas V.

The Universities of Barcelona and Trier have their beginnings.

Painting *The Flood* and *The Drunkenness of Noah* by Paolo Uccello.

The exterior of Rimini's Church of San Francesco is redesigned by Leon Battista Alberti.

The Porta Giova of Milan's Sforesco Castle is designed by Florentine architect Filarete (Antonio di Pietro Averlino), 50.

1451 The Ottoman sultan Murad II dies at Adrianople at age 48 and is succeeded after a 30-year reign by his 21-year-old son who begins a 30-year reign that will be notable for its conquests. The new sultan Mohammed II will effectively establish the Ottoman empire by driving the Venetians and Hungarians out of Rumelia and Anatolia and by reasserting Ottoman authority over rebellious Turkish emirs.

Sculpture *The Ascension* by Luca della Robbia is a glazed polychrome terra-cotta work above a portal of the cathedral at Florence.

Florence's Rucellai Palace is completed by Leon Battista Alberti.

1452 The German king Frederick IV of Hapsburg crowned Holy Roman Emperor March 19 by Pope Nicholas will be the last emperor to be crowned at Rome. The 36-year-old Frederick has married Leonora of Portugal 3 days earlier, he will reign as

Frederick III, but his countrymen are indignant at his capitulation to the pope and their indignation will grow as they witness his apathy toward Turkish aggression.

War begins between Constantinople's last Greek emperor Constantine and the new Ottoman sultan Mohammed II as the sultan completes fortifications that control the flow of supplies to Constantinople.

France's Louis the dauphin strengthens ties with the Swiss cantons and makes treaties also with the towns of Trier, Cologne, and others and with Saxony as part of an anti-Burgundian policy.

Scotland's James II subdues the earls of Douglas and confiscates their lands.

Painting The *Braque Triptych* by Roger van der Weyden.

Florence's Medici Palace is completed on the Via de Ginori by architect Michelozzi di Bartolommeo for Cosimo de' Medici whose family will occupy the palazzo for 100 years (the Riccardi family will later acquire it).

The Castle of Europe (Rumili Hisar) is completed by Mohammed II opposite the older Castle of Asia (Anadoli Hisar) at the narrowest point of the Bosporus. Completion of the fortress alarms the Byzantine emperor Constantine who begins a war in June (above) (*see* 1453).

1453 Constantinople falls to the Ottoman Turks who end the Byzantine Empire that has ruled since the fall of the Roman Empire in 476. An enormous iron chain has kept the fleet of Mohammed II out of the Golden Horn, but he has had some 70 small ships dragged overland from the Bosporus to support the 250,000 troops that have besieged the city since April 6. Beginning April 12 he pounds the city walls with 1,200-pound cannonballs fired from a 26-foot long cannon built by the Hungarian renegade Urban. Dragged by 60 oxen and 200 men, the cannon has an internal caliber of 42 inches, it breaches the walls, the Turks force an entry at the Romanos Gate May 29, the last Byzantine emperor Constantine XI Palaeologus is killed in the fighting, the Turks sack Constantinople, and they make it the Ottoman capital.

The Hundred Years' War that has continued off and on since 1377 ends in France with the expulsion of the English from every place except Calais which England will retain for more than a century. The earl of Shrewsbury John Talbot, 65, is the last surviving general of the late Henry V, he has come ashore in the Gironde with a force of 3,000, Bordeaux and the smaller towns have risen to his support and have driven out their French garrisons, but the French kill Shrewsbury in mid-July at Castillon with roundshot, they slaughter his army, and the Bordelais surrender October 19 when it becomes clear that they can expect no further English aid.

England's Henry VI has his first episode of insanity, inherited from his grandfather Charles VI of France. His cousin Richard of York serves as regent.

The fall of Constantinople (above) ends the Greek Empire of the East and leaves the Roman pope without any serious rival.

Mohammed II follows up his victory at Constantinople by advancing into Greece and Albania.

The White Sheep dynasty that will rule Persia until 1490 comes to power in the person of Uzun Hasan who will extend Turkoman authority over Armenia and Kurdistan and then over Azerbaijan and Iran.

The fall of Constantinople (above) increases the need for sea routes to the Orient. Moslem rulers have imposed stiff tariffs on caravan shipments with the highest duties being levied on spices, and the sultan of Egypt exacts a duty equal to one-third the value of every cargo entering his domain.

Venice continues to import spices at higher prices and maintains her monopoly in the spice trade (*see* Lisbon, 1501).

Greek scholars fleeing Constantinople are welcomed by Cosimo de' Medici to his palazzo at Florence (*see* 1429).

Coffee is introduced to Constantinople (above) by the Ottoman Turks (*see* 850; 1475).

1454 Printers at Mainz use movable metal type for the first time (traditional date) (*see* 1381ff; Gutenberg Bible, 1456).

The Peace of Lodi ends hostilities between Venice and Milan.

England's Henry VI recovers from a period of insanity, and the duke of Somerset returns to power.

Some 28 French musicians inside a huge pie perform at the Feast of the Pheasant for the last duke of Burgundy Charles le Téméraire), 21. A Mother Goose rhyme about "four and twenty blackbirds baked in a pie" will commemorate the event.

1455 England's Wars of the Roses erupt in a civil war that will continue until 1471 between the houses of York and Lancaster. Excluded from the Council, the duke of York defeats royal forces at St. Albans in May and the earl of Dorset Edmund Beaufort is killed (*see* 1460).

The Cape Verde Islands off the coast of Africa are discovered by Venetian navigator Alvise da Cadamosto, 23, who will explore the Senegal and Gambia rivers in the next 2 years in the service of Portugal's Prince Henry (*see* 1421).

Fra Angelico dies at Rome March 18 at age 55; Lorenzo Ghiberti dies at Florence December 1 at age 77.

1456 Athens falls to the Ottoman Turks who will rule Greece and the Balkans for most of the next four centuries. The Hungarian prince János Hunyadi destroys the Ottoman fleet July 14, he routs an Ottoman

1456 (cont.) army besieging Belgrade July 21 and 22, he forces Mohammed II to return to Constantinople, he dies of plague August 11 at age 69, his eldest son Laszló will be arrested at Buda in mid-March of next year and beheaded at age 23 by order of the Hungarian governor, but the victory of János Hunyadi will keep Hungary free of Ottoman rule for 70 years.

The Gutenberg Bible published at Mainz by local printer Johann Gutenberg, 56, is a Vulgate bible that marks one of the earliest examples of printing from movable type in Europe (*see* 1454). Gutenberg has taken 5 years to produce the bible, it is printed in two volumes, folio, with two columns of 42 lines each per page (*see* Tyndale Bible, 1526).

Poetry *Le Petit Testament* by French poet François Villon, 25, is published in 40 stanzas. Villon stabbed a priest to death last year and is involved this year in a robbery at the College de Navarre in Paris.

Painting *Niccola da Tolentino* by Andrea del Castagno.

Florence's Church of Santa Maria Novella receives a new facade designed by Leon Battista Alberti.

Sugar from Madeira reaches Bristol to give many Englishmen their first taste of the new sweetener.

1457 Sweden's Charles VIII (Knut Knutsson) is driven out of the country in a revolt inspired by the Church, and Denmark's Christian I of Oldenburg is crowned king of Sweden while the noblemen Sten Stures, Svante Stures, and Sten the Younger hold the real power.

The king of Hungary and Bohemia Ladislas V flees to Prague to escape the storm of criticism that follows the execution of the Hungarian hero Laszló Hunyadi March 16 (*see* 1456). Ladislas prepares to marry Magdalena, daughter of France's Charles VII, but he dies suddenly November 23 at age 17, possibly the victim of poisoning, and will be succeeded in Hungary by the second son of the late János Hunyadi.

The University of Freiburg has its beginnings.

Donatello moves to Florence at age 71 after years of work at Rome, Naples, Padua, and Siena; painter Andrea del Castagno loses his wife to plague August 8 and dies of plague himself at Florence 11 days later at age 34.

Painting *Madonna with Saints Francis and Jerome* by Petrus Christus; *The Rout of San Romano* by Paolo Uccello.

"Futeball and golfe" are forbidden by Scotland's Parliament because their popularity threatens the sport of archery which must be encouraged for reasons of national defense. The ban will continue until 1491 (*see* curling, 1465; cricket, 1477).

1458 Matthias Corvinus wins election to the Hungarian throne at age 18 to succeed the late Ladislas. He begins a 32-year reign that will be among the great-est in Hungary's history, but the throne of Bohemia remains in dispute (*see* 1457; 1459).

The archduke Albrecht storms Vienna twice during the year.

Ottoman forces invade Morea and annex the remainder of Serbia.

Aragon's Alfonso V (the Magnanimous) dies at age 73 after a 42-year reign. He is succeeded in Aragon by his son Juan and in Naples by his unscrupulous son Ferdinand (Ferrante), 35, who has a struggle to gain the succession but who enlists the support of Francesco Sforza, now 57, and Cosimo de' Medici, now 69, who are alarmed at the presence of the French at Genoa.

Delhi's Mahmud I begins a 53-year reign that will be marked by the conquests of Girnar and Champanir, the further extension of Islam in northern India, and the construction of magnificent mosques and a great palace at Sarkhej.

Work begins across the Arno River from Florence on a great palace for Luca Pitti, a rival of the Medici family.

1459 George of Podebrad, 39, is elected king of Bohemia after having served as regent during the reign of the late Ladislas who died in 1457. He begins a reign that will continue until 1471 despite challenges by Hungary's Matthias Corvinus. George is an avowed follower of the late Jan Hus and is hence technically a heretic.

The realm of an African king named Prester John appears on a map drawn by the Venetian monk Fra Mauro (*see* 1145; Covilhão, 1487).

Painting *The Crucifixion* by Italian painter Andrea Mantegna, 28, is completed as part of the main altarpiece triptych for Verona's Church of Saint Zeno. Mantegna becomes court painter to the Gonzaga family at Mantua where he will remain until his death in 1506.

1460 England's deranged Henry VI is taken prisoner July 10 at the Battle of Northampton 66 miles from London by Yorkists wearing white roses who defeat the royal Lancastrians wearing red roses. Richard Plantagenet, 49, third duke of York, asserts his hereditary claim to the throne, he marches on London, he is assured by the lords that he will succeed to the throne upon Henry's death, but he is killed at Wakefield in the West Riding where his forces are defeated by an army raised in the north by Henry's wife Margaret of Anjou. Southern England rallies behind Richard's son Edward (*see* 1461).

Scotland's James II is killed August 3 when a cannon bursts while he is besieging Roxburgh Castle in a show of sympathy for the Lancastrian cause. He is succeeded by his 9-year-old son who will reign until 1488 as James III.

A Portuguese squadron returns from the west coast of Africa with a cargo of slaves.

The University of Basel has its beginnings in a college founded in the Swiss city.

Painting *The Seven Sacraments* is completed as an altarpiece by Roger van der Weyden.

Venice's Arsenal is completed. Almost a town within a town, the heart of the republic's naval power includes a large shipyard for building the vessels that provide Venice with her wealth and power.

Mantua's Church of San Sebastian is completed by Leon Battista Alberti.

1461 England's house of Lancaster is defeated at Mortimer's Cross by Edward of York, 19, who avenges his father Richard's death last year but is defeated himself at the second battle of St. Albans in February. Edward loses possession of the deranged Henry VI but he proclaims himself king, he defeats the Lancastrians at Towton, and he is crowned in June as Edward IV after Parliament declares the Lancastrians to be usurpers.

France's Charles VII dies July 22 at age 58 and is succeeded by his 38-year-old son Louis who made unsuccessful attempts to take the throne in 1446 and 1456, was banished to the Dauphine in 1447, and has not seen his father for 14 years. Called the Spider, the new king is crowned at Reims August 15 as Louis XI and begins his reign by imposing restrictions on the French nobility, even forbidding them to hunt without his permission, and by forcing the clergy to pay long-neglected feudal dues.

France's Louis XI makes a rapprochement with the papacy by a formal revocation of his father's 1438 Pragmatic Sanction of Bourges, but he sacrifices little royal power and he keeps the national church under firm control of the Crown whose power he begins to increase at the expense of local and provincial independence and of urban liberties.

Trebizond falls to the Ottoman Turks who take over the last Greek state on the Black Sea and absorb the 257-year-old kingdom into their empire. They also take over the principality of Kastamonu.

Japan has plague and famine that bring an uprising against the Ashikaga shogun Yoshimasa.

Poetry *Le Grand Testament* by François Villon is a lyric poem of 173 stanzas containing many ballads, or rondeaux. French authorities will banish Villon from Paris next year after arresting him for theft and brawling and then commuting his death sentence, but he will be quoted for centuries, especially for his line, "where are the snows of yesteryear?" (ou sont les neiges d'antan) from the "Ballade des Dames du Temps Jadis."

Sculpture *Judith* and *Holofernes* by Donatello. Domenico Veneziano dies at Florence May 15 at 55.

1462 The grand duke of Muscovy Basil II dies at age 47 after a 37-year reign marked by anarchy and civil war. Called Temny (the blind), Basil is succeeded by his son Ivan III Vasilievich, 22, who will become the

first Russian national sovereign and who will enormously enlarge Muscovite territory in his 43-year reign (*see* Novgorod, 1471).

The Holy Roman Emperor Frederick III is besieged in the Hofburg at Vienna by radical opponents led by his brother Albrecht.

1463 Upper and Lower Austria are united by the Holy Roman Emperor Frederick III following the death of his brother Albrecht, but the territories are ravaged by Bohemia's George of Podebrad and by Hungary's Matthias Corvinus who has been elected king of Bohemia by the nation's Catholic nobility but who is suffering defeats in battle at the hands of George of Podebrad (*see* 1459; 1466).

A 16-year war begins between Venice and the Ottoman Turks following Turkish interference with Venetian privileges in the Levant trade.

English landowners gain a monopoly in the home grain market by a statute that prohibits imports of grain except when prices rise to levels at which the export of grain is prohibited. Food prices in England will rise in the next two centuries without compensating wage increases, but almost no grain will be imported (*see* 1436; 1773).

The University of Nantes has its beginnings.

1464 England and Scotland make peace, but civil war continues in England. The duke of Somerset Henry Beaufort is captured and beheaded at age 28.

Florence's Cosimo de' Medici dies August 1 at age 75 while listening to one of Plato's *Dialogues*. He is succeeded as head of the great Florentine banking house by his son Piero the Gouty.

The Poste Royale founded by France's Louis XI pioneers national postal service (*see* 1621).

Roger van der Weyden dies at Brussels June 16 at age 63.

1465 Yorkists capture England's Lancastrian king Henry VI and imprison him in the Tower of London as the Wars of the Roses continue.

The French dukes of Alençon, Burgundy, Berri, Bourbon, and Lorraine defeat Louis XI at Montl'hery and force him to sign the Treaty of Conflans that restores Normandy to the duc de Berri and restores towns on the Somme to Burgundy. Louis begins immediately to evade the treaty and to split the League of the Public Weal by means of diplomacy.

The University of Bruges has its beginnings.

Painting *Duke of Urbino* by Piero della Francesca.

England's Yorkist king Edward IV forbids the "hustling of stones" and other sports related to bowling and curling (*see* 1457; cricket, 1477).

The fall of Constantinople to the Ottoman Turks ended the Byzantine Empire with a terrible sack of the city.

1466 Poland gains an outlet to the Baltic October 19 under terms of the Second Peace of Thorn that ends a war against the Teutonic order. The order becomes a vassal of the Polish crown and half the Teutonic Knights become Poles.

Pope Paul II excommunicates Bohemia's George of Podebrad and inspires a Hungarian crusade against the king (*see* 1463; 1470).

Florence's Luca Pitti fails in an effort to assassinate Piero de' Medici. He is stripped of his powers and the Pitti Palace he began in 1458 on the left bank of the Arno remains unfinished (*see* 1549).

Florence's Medici family forms a cartel alliance with the Vatican to finance the mining of alum (aluminum potassium sulfate) deposits in the papal states (the material is used as a mordant to fix dyes in textiles). The Medicis persuade the pope to excommunicate anyone who imports alum from the infidel Turk in breach of the Vatican–Medici monopoly (*see* 1471).

Painting *Pietà* by Venetian painter Giovanni Bellini, 36, whose sister Nicolosia is married to Andrea Mantegna of Padua and whose work shows the influence of Mantegna. Donatello dies at Florence December 13 at age 80.

1467 The duke of Burgundy Philippe le Bon dies June 15 at age 71 after a 48-year reign in which Burgundy has become the richest state in Europe. He is succeeded by his 32-year-old son Charles the Bold (Charles le Téméraire) who defeats the Liégeois at St. Trond and makes a victorious entry into Liege to begin a 10-year struggle with Louis XI.

Turkish forces enter Herzogovina and begin to conquer the Balkan country for the Ottoman Empire.

The Japanese shogun Yoshimasa chooses his brother Yoshime to be his successor and is challenged by supporters of his son Yoshihisa. A 10-year civil war begins at Kyoto, which will be nearly destroyed as both factions permit their unpaid soldiers to loot and pillage.

The Japanese Zen priest and landscape painter Sesshu, 48, goes to Peking to study after having studied for years under Shubun, a Chinese painter who became a naturalized Japanese and brought Chinese and Japanese art closer together.

1468 The duke of Burgundy Charles the Bold effects an alliance against France's Louis XI by marrying Margaret, sister of England's Edward IV.

Painting *Donne Triptych* by Flemish painter Hans Memling, 38, who has moved to Bruges; altarpiece for the Municipio of Massa Fermana at Ascoli by Italian painter Carlo Crivelli, 33; *Pietà* by Italian painter Cosme (Cosimo) Tura, 38, who has been court painter since 1452 to Duke Boso d'Este.

The Spanish plant rice at Pisa on the Lombardy plain. It is the first European planting of rice outside Spain (*see* 711).

1469 The Spanish crowns of Aragon and Castile join in alliance October 19 at Valladolid where the 17-year-old prince Ferdinand of Aragon and Leon marries the 18-year-old infanta Isabella of Castile.

Fra Filippo Lippi dies at Spoleto October 9 at age 63.

Florence's Piero de' Medici dies December 3 after 5 gouty years in which he has maintained authority chiefly through the prestige of his late father Cosimo. His 20-year-old son Lorenzo and Lorenzo's 16-year-old brother Giuliano succeed to control the now mighty Florentine banking house (*see* 1478).

1470 England's Henry VI regains his throne briefly with support from the earl of Warwick, but the duke of Clarence disapproves of the restoration, he deserts Warwick, and defects to Edward IV. Edward uses artillery to help his forces defeat Warwick in a battle at Stamford. He forces Warwick to take refuge in France, but his enemies force him to flee to Holland while Clarence takes refuge in France.

Hungary's Matthias Corvinus is proclaimed king of Bohemia and margrave of Moravia, but Bohemia's George of Podebrad gains Polish support by promising the succession to the son of Poland's Casimir IV, and he forces Matthias to come to terms.

Venice loses Euboea (Negroponte) to Constantinople. An enormous Ottoman fleet lands an army that takes the Venetian territory in the continuing war between the Turks and Venetians.

Portuguese explorers reach Africa's Gold Coast. Fernão Gomes has sent João de Santarem and Pedro de Escolar to Africa in accordance with terms of a 5-year lease on the Guinea trade granted to Gomes last year on condition that he carry explorations forward by at least 100 leagues per year.

The first French printshop is set up at Paris by three German printers (*see* 1454). It will be followed in the next few years by printshops in the Lowlands, in the Swiss cantons, in Castile, and in Aragon (*see* Caxton, 1475).

French printer Nicolas Jensen, 50, sets up shop at Venice as a publisher and printer after having learned the art from Gutenberg at Mainz (*see* 1456). Jensen will be the first to use purely roman letters, and they will be perfected in the next century by the French publisher Garamond, but most printers will continue to use Gothic letters for years to come.

Theater *Maître Pathelin* is the first French farce.

England's York Minster Cathedral of Saint Peter is completed after 250 years of construction on the site of a chapel erected for the baptism of Edwin of Northumbria in the 7th century.

1471 England's Edward IV lands at Ravenspur in March, defeats Warwick at Barnet April 14 in a battle at which Warwick is killed, and Edward's final victory at Tewkesbury is followed May 21 by the death of Henry VI in the Tower of London. Henry is murdered, possibly by Richard of Gloucester.

Bohemia's George of Podebrad dies at age 51 and is succeeded by the Polish prince Ladislas (Vladislav), 15-year-old son of Casimir IV, who begins a weak 45-year reign that will be dominated by nobles. The ascension of Ladislas begins a 7-year Hungarian war.

The grand duke of Muscovy Ivan III forces Novgorod to renounce her ties with Lithuania and to pay tribute to Moscow. Novgorod is the center of a vast republic in northern Europe, and while Lithuania extends from the Baltic to the Black Sea, Ivan has made Muscovy a more powerful nation (*see* 1479).

Tangier falls to Portugal which has earlier taken Casablanca in a campaign against the North African kingdom of Fez.

Pope Paul II dies July 26 at age 54 and is succeeded by the della Rovere cardinal who is elevated to the papacy and who will reign for 13 years as Sixtus IV.

Pope Sixtus IV cancels the Vatican alliance made with the Medici family in 1466 to monopolize the alum trade, but the new pope is conciliated by Cosimo de' Medici's 22-year-old grandson Lorenzo who is appointed receiver of the papal revenues and banker to the Vatican (but *see* 1475).

San Jorge d'el Mina is founded by the Portuguese as a port to trade in gold on what will be called Africa's Gold Coast.

The University of Genoa has its beginnings.

Painting *Madonna in a Garden* by Cosme Tura.

1472 Muscovy returns to the Roman Church through the marriage of the grand duke Ivan III to Zoë (Sophia) Palaeologa, niece of Constantinople's last Greek emperor Constantine XI Palaeologus. Zoë's father Thomas is despot of the Morea, Pope Sixtus IV has arranged the marriage, later Russian rulers will use it as the basis of their claim to be the protectors of Orthodox Christianity, Ivan will establish a Byzantine autocracy in Russia, and he will take the title czar (caesar).

Scotland acquires the Orkney and Shetland Islands from Norway.

Portugal's Fernando Po discovers islands off the coast of Africa that will bear his name.

Portugal's Lopo Goncalves crosses the equator.

Portugal's Ruy de Sequeira reaches latitude 2° south.

The University of Munich has its beginnings in Bavaria.

Painting *The Annunciation* by Florentine painter Leonardo da Vinci born out of wedlock 20 years ago at Vinci to a peasant girl and fathered by a prominent local notary who has taken the youth to Florence and has apprenticed him to the master Andrea del Verrocchio.

Sculpture Tomb of Giovanni and Piero de' Medici by Florentine sculptor-painter Andrea del Verrocchio (Andrea di Michele di Francesco Cione), 37.

Mantua's Church of San Andrea is completed by Leon Battista Alberti who dies April 25 at age 68.

The grand duke of Muscovy Ivan III (above) will use Italian architects brought in by his wife Zoë to rebuild Moscow's grand ducal palace the Kremlin.

1473 The *Dispositio Achilles* signed by the elector of Brandenburg Albrecht III, 59, legalizes the custom of primogeniture that has existed for centuries and that helped motivate younger sons of Europe's nobility to join the Crusades in quest of lands. Albrecht is known as Achilles and his "Dispositio" makes the eldest surviving male in a family the heir to the power and fortune of his father.

Burgundy's Charles the Bold occupies Alsace and Lorraine.

Cyprus comes under Venetian rule (*see* 1573).

Japan's western warlord Yamana Mochitoyo dies at age 69, and his son-in-law Hosokawa Katsumoto dies at age 48 in the Onin War that has raged since 1467. Civil war will continue until 1477.

Painting *The Virgin of the Rose Garden* by German painter-engraver Martin Schongauer, 23.

The Sistine Chapel is added to the Vatican Palace by Pope Sixtus IV (*see* Michelangelo, 1512).

1474 Genoese seaman Christopher Columbus, 23, begins discussing the possibility of a westward passage to Cathay (China). Also called Cristobal Colon or Cristoforo Colombo, the young navigator uses projections made by German mathematicians and Italian mapmakers at Sangres (*see* 1421) to revive the an-

1474 (cont.) cient Greek knowledge that the earth is round. Columbus has the advantages of the compass invented in the 12th century and of the more recently invented mariner's astrolabe by which a navigator can calculate the altitude of the sun, the moon, or the stars above the horizon and thus determine his distance north or south of the equator (*see* 1477; quadrant, 1731).

Isabella succeeds to the throne of Castile and Leon December 13 upon the death of her half-brother who has ruled since 1454 as Enrique IV. But Isabella's succession 5 years after her marriage to Ferdinand of Aragon is challenged by the daughter of Enrique, and the challenge is supported by Portugal's Afonso V.

The Union of Constance is formed with subsidies from France's Louis XI, and the coalition begins war on Burgundy's Charles the Bold.

The Japanese shogun Yoshimasa abdicates at age 39 after a 25-year reign and is succeeded by his son Yoshihasa, but the civil war that began in 1467 continues (*see* 1477).

Antwerp Cathedral is completed except for its spire after 122 years of construction. The spire for the great Gothic structure will be completed in 1518.

1475 *The Recuyell of the Historyes of Troye* published at Bruges by English printer-translator-cloth dealer William Caxton, 53, is the first book to be printed in English. Caxton has learned the printing trade at Cologne after having dealt in hand-written manuscripts, and he has spent 2 years in translating the *Recuyell* (*Collection*) from French (*see* 1476).

England's Edward IV invades France in support of Burgundy's Charles the Bold, but he is bought off by Louis XI who meets with him at Piquigny.

Isabella's succession to the throne of Castile with her husband Ferdinand of Aragon is recognized by the cortes of Segovia.

Florence's Medici family is replaced as papal bankers by the Pazzi family following a rapprochement with Don Ferrante of Naples by the della Rovere pope Sixtus IV who tries to consolidate the papal states.

Painting *St. Justine* by Giovanni Bellini; *The Adoration of the Magi* by Florentine painter Perugino (Pietro di Cristoforo di Vannucci), 29; *Apollo and Daphne* and *The Martyrdom of St. Sebastian* by Italian painter Antonio Pollaiolo, 44, and his brother Piero, 31; Paolo Uccello dies at Florence December 10 at age 78.

England's Winchester Cathedral is completed after 425 years of construction.

St. George's Chapel for the Order of the Garter founded in 1349 goes up on the grounds of England's Windsor Castle and incorporates part of a chapel built more than 230 years ago.

Concerning Honest Pleasure and Well-being (De Honesta Voluptate ac Caletudine) by Vatican librarian Platina (Bartolomeo Sacchi) is the world's first printed cookbook. Platina's pen name is a latinization of his hometown Piadena, he gives recipes for larks' tongues, hummingbird livers, and pasta.

The world's first coffee house opens at Constantinople under the name Kiva Han (*see* 1453).

1476 Burgundy's Charles the Bold conquers Lorraine, he makes war on the Swiss cantons that have allied themselves with France's Louis XI, but he is defeated at Grandson and Morat (*see* 1474; 1477).

Transylvania's Vlad Dracula is killed in battle outside Bucharest at age 45 (*see* 1448; Bram Stoker novel, 1897).

Milan's tyrant Galeazzo Maria Sforza is assassinated December 26 at age 32 by three young noblemen on the porch of the city's cathedral. He is succeeded by his 7-year-old son Gian Galeazzo under the regency of the boy's mother Bona of Savoy (*see* 1450; 1481).

The first English printshop to employ movable type is started by printer William Caxton who sets up a press under the sign of the Red Pale near the court at Westminster under the patronage of Edward IV (*see* 1475). Caxton prints an indulgence which is sold to raise money for a Christian fleet against the Turks.

William Caxton (above) will print more than 90 books before his death in 1491 or 1492, and they will include Chaucer's *Canterbury Tales*.

Painting The Demidoff altarpiece by Carlo Crivelli.

Sculpture *David* (bronze) by Andrea del Verrocchio.

1477 The Battle of Nancy January 5 ends in a triumph for Swiss pikemen who prevail over the cavalry of the duke of Burgundy Charles the Bold and demonstrate a prowess that will make them widely sought after as mercenaries. The 43-year-old Charles fails in his siege of Nancy, he is killed in the battle, and his body is found half-eaten by wolves.

The Hapsburgs acquire the Netherlands August 18 through the marriage at Ghent of the 18-year-old Maximilian, son of the Holy Roman Emperor Frederick III, to Mary, daughter of the late Charles the Bold (above), who is 2 years older than Maximilian.

Ottoman raiders reach the outskirts of Venice as the 14-year-old war with Constantinople continues.

Japan's 10-year-old civil war at Kyoto ends indecisively, but a 100-year period of internal wars begins. The wars will make it impossible for the imperial family to collect rents on its lands and will impoverish the family.

Christopher Columbus visits England but is unable to obtain backing for his projected venture in quest of a new route to the Indies (*see* 1474; 1484).

Sweden's Uppsala University has its beginnings.

Württemberg's Tübingen University has its beginnings.

Hesse's Mainz University has its beginnings.

Cricket is banned in England by order of Edward IV who fixes a fine and 2 years in prison as punishment for anyone caught playing "hands in and hands out" as the game is called because it interferes with the compulsory practice of archery (*see* "futeball and golfe," 1457).

The diamond engagement ring is pioneered by the counsel to the court of the Holy Roman Emperor Frederick III who has the young archduke Maximilian (above) use the gold and silver pressed upon him by villagers as he sets out for Burgundy to have a jeweler create a gold ring set with diamonds that form the letter M. Maximilian's bride Mary will die at Bruges late in 1482 after falling from her horse, but the Hapsburgs will retain the Netherlands and the diamond engagement ring will become a tradition in much of the world.

1478 Lorenzo de' Medici and his brother Giuliano are attacked while attending high mass in the cathedral at Florence April 26 in a plot engineered by the Pazzi bank and Pope Sixtus IV to remove the Medicis from power in the city. Giuliano is stabbed to death at age 25, but Lorenzo beats back his assailants, takes refuge in the sacristy, and wreaks cruel vengeance on the Pazzi, hanging several from the palace windows, having others hacked to pieces, dragged through the streets, and thrown into the Arno, while still other supporters of the Pazzi are condemned to death or sent into exile.

Novgorod loses her independence after a second war with the grand duke of Muscovy Ivan III (*see* 1479).

An Inquisition against converted Jews who secretly practice their original faith is launched by Isabella of Castile who persecutes the so-called Marranos (the word originally meant pigs). The Inquisition will be broadened to include all "heretics" (*see* Torquemada, 1483).

Lorenzo the Magnificent (above) blandly withdraws 200,000 gold florins from the Florence city treasury to cover the default of the Medici branch at Bruges. He is excommunicated by the pope (*see* 1480).

Painting *Primavera (Spring)* by the Florentine painter Sandro (Alessandro di Mariano de Filipepi) Botticelli, 34, for the villa at Castello of Lorenzo Pierfrancesco de' Medici, a cousin of Lorenzo the Magnificent (above). Botticelli has also done work for the palazzo of the great Lorenzo on the Via Larga.

Brussels becomes the center of Europe's tapestry industry following the destruction of Arras.

1479 The Treaty of Constantinople January 25 ends a 15-year war between Venice and the Ottoman Empire, whose forces have reached the outskirts of Venice. The Venetians retain Dulcigno, Antivari, and Durazzo but are forced to yield Scutari and other points on the Albanian coast, to accept the loss of Negroponte (Euboea) and Lemnos, and to pay a trib-

ute of 10,000 ducats per year for the privilege of trading in the Black Sea.

Aragon's John II has died January 20 at age 81 and is succeeded by his son Ferdinand who at age 26 assumes the throne as Fernando II of Aragon and through his 1469 marriage to his cousin Isabella as Fernando V of Castile and Leon, uniting the major crowns of Spain to begin a 37-year reign (*see* Columbus, 1486).

Novgorod is annexed by the grand duke of Muscovy Ivan III, who deports her resisting aristocrats to central Russia (*see* 1478; 1494).

The University of Copenhagen has its beginnings.

The Game and Playe of Chesse, first book to be printed from metal type in England, is published by William Caxton (*see* 1476), who has translated a French version by Jehan De Vigny of a Latin treatise by Dominican friar Jacobus de Cassolis.

1480 The grand duke of Muscovy Ivan III takes advantage of disunity among the Tartars to stop their advance on Moscow and free the country of Tartar domination.

Anjou, Bar, Maine, and Provence fall to the French crown upon the extinction of the house of Anjou. René, count of Anjou, dies without an heir July 10 at age 71 and Louis XI annexes his realms.

Otranto in southern Italy falls to the Ottoman Turks August 11, but Mohammed II (the Conqueror) fails in a siege of Rhodes. The Knights of St. John of Jerusalem who purchased the island in 1306 successfully resist the sultan from May to August. The fall of Otranto ends an Italian civil war precipitated by the Pazzi plot of 1478 that destroyed the balance of power among Florence, Naples, and Milan.

Ferdinand of Aragon helps Florence's Lorenzo de' Medici make peace with Pope Sixtus IV.

Pestilence decimates the Mayan empire in the Western Hemisphere.

Painting *The Seven Joys of Mary* by Hans Memling is hung in the chapel of the tanners in Notre Dame at Bruges. A rich member of the tanners guild named Peter Bultinc has commissioned the work and Memling has portrayed him as the foremost of the two observers of the Nativity. The Venetian republic appoints Giovanni Bellini official painter at a salary.

1481 The Ottoman sultan Mohammed II dies May 3 at age 49 as he prepares to begin another campaign in Anatolia. Word goes out that "the eagle is dead" and his 34-year-old son Bajazet is raised to the throne with support from the Janissaries. The new sultan Bayazid II is challenged by his younger brother Jem (Djem) who has had himself proclaimed sultan and who has proposed a division of the empire. Bayazid's first act is to have his brother strangled, and he begins a 31-year reign that will strengthen Turkish power in

1481 (cont.) Europe through wars with Poland, Hungary, and Venice.

Milanese power changes hands as the uncle of Gian Galeazzo Sforza ousts the boy's mother from her regency and takes over as Lodovico il Moro (*see* 1476; 1494).

Portugal's Afonso V (the African) dies at age 49 in August after a 43-year reign. He is succeeded by his 26-year-old son who will reign as João II until 1495.

Portugal's new king spurs explorations which have given his nation dominance in trade with West Africa.

1482 The Peace of Arras ends hostilities between the Hapsburgs and France's Louis XI who has lived in isolation for the past 2 years in his spider's nest château of Plessis-les-Tours 2 miles southwest of Tours surrounded by astrologers and physicians.

The bishop of Liége is killed by "the Wild Boar of the Ardennes" Guillaume de la Marck, 36, a Belgian soldier for France's Louis XI (the Spider). La Marck will be captured in 1485 and beheaded.

Venice begins a 2-year war with Ferrara that will result in the Venetian acquisition of Rovigo, the last expansion of Venice on the mainland.

Luca della Robbia dies at Florence February 23 at age 82.

Portuguese explorers on Africa's west coast find bananas growing and adopt a version of the natives' name for the fruit *Musa sapientum* (*see* 327 B.C.; de Berlanga, 1516).

1483 England's Edward IV dies April 9 at age 40 after a tyrannical reign in which he has multiplied his wealth by confiscating the estates of his enemies and putting his money to work in partnership with London merchants. He is succeeded by his 12-year-old son, but Edward's 30-year-old brother Richard, duke of Gloucester sends the new king and his younger brother to the Tower of London, he assumes the throne himself June 26 as Richard III, he has gained the support of Sir James Tyrell, and agents of Sir James smother young Edward and his brother to death in the Tower.

The duke of Buckingham Henry Stafford, 29, leads a rebellion against Richard III (above), but supporters of Richard suppress the revolt, they capture Buckingham, and they execute him at Salisbury.

France's Louis XI (the Spider) dies August 10 at age 60 after a 22-year reign in which the nation's prosperity has revived despite oppressive taxes. The tyrannical Louis is succeeded by his 13-year-old son who will reign until 1498 as Charles VIII.

The Spanish Dominican monk Tomas de Torquemada, 63, takes command of the Inquisition in all Spanish possessions at the request of Ferdinand and Isabella. A nephew of Cardinal Juan de Torquemada, the first grand inquisitor will persecute "heretics" with unparalleled zeal (*see* 1478; 1487).

Painting *The Magnificat* by Sandro Botticelli who was summoned to Rome last year along with Ghirlandaio to help decorate the Vatican chapel of Pope Sixtus IV. Botticelli's round picture of the Madonna with singing angels will be his most copied work; *The Virgin and Child and Six Saints* by Giovanni Bellini for Venice's Church of San Job; *Coronation of the Virgin* by Piero Pollaiuolo for the church of San Agostino at San Gimignano.

1484 Pope Sixtus IV dies August 12 after a 13-year papacy marked by nepotism and political intrigue in which the pope has warred with Florence and has incited Venice to attack Ferrara. The Venetians have saved Sixtus from a Neapolitan invasion, but he has turned on Venice for not halting the hostilities which he himself instigated. Venice acquires Rovigo and reaches the height of its mainland expansion. Venetian territory will remain essentially unchanged for more than 300 years, but the city's wealth and power will soon begin to decline.

Pope Innocent VIII succeeds to the papacy and issues a bull against witchcraft and sorcery. The bull "Summis desiderantes" issued December 5 initiates harsh measures against German "witches" and magicians. "At Hammel in Saxony, on the 20th of June, 1484, the Devil, in the likeness of a pied piper, carried away 130 children, that were never after seen," English physician Robert Burton will write in his *Anatomy of Melancholy* (*see* 1284; 1621).

Christopher Columbus asks Portugal's João II to back him in a westward voyage to the Indies, but João rejects the request (*see* 1477; 1485).

Portuguese explorer Diogo Cao (Diego Cano) discovers the mouth of Africa's Congo River. He will explore the west coast of the continent south to the 22nd parallel (*see* 1487).

Painting *St. Anthony* by Cosime Tura; *Garden of Delights* and *Earthly Paradise* by Dutch painter Hieronymus Bosch (Hieronymus von Aeken), 34 (dates of all Bosch paintings are speculative).

Kyoto's Silver Pavilion is completed for Japan's eighth Ashikaga shogun Yoshimasa near the Gold Pavilion completed in 1397.

The tea ceremony has been introduced by Japan's Yoshimasa (above). Now 48, the shogun has encouraged painting and drama, his reign has otherwise been disastrous, but the tea ceremony will remain for centuries a cherished part of Japanese culture.

1485 The Battle of Bosworth August 22 ends England's Wars of the Roses that have continued since 1460. The 28-year-old Henry, earl of Richmond, has landed at Milford Haven with French support after a sojourn abroad to escape the cruelties of Richard III. His Welsh allies help him defeat the king who falls in the battle; Richard's crown is found hanging on a bush and passes to the earl. He is crowned at Westminster October 30 as the first Tudor king Henry VII, he restores peace to the realm, and he begins a 24-year reign that inaugurates a 117-year Tudor dynasty.

Hungary's Matthias Corvinus expels the Holy Roman Emperor Frederick III from Vienna and Frederick becomes an imperial mendicant.

Venice standardizes its quarantine of 1403 at 40 days.

The "sweating sickness" cuts down the army of England's Henry VII (above) and postpones the king's coronation. The mysterious malady closes down Oxford University for 6 weeks, it spreads quickly to London, and within a week has killed two lord mayors and six aldermen along with thousands of citizens. "Scarce one amongst an hundred that sickened did escape with life," chronicler Raphael Holinshed will write in 1578, "for all in maner as soone as the sweate tooke them or in a short time after yeelded up the ghost."

Christopher Columbus sends his brother Bartholomew to France and England in hopes that he may interest Charles VIII or Henry VII in outfitting an expedition to the Orient, but Bartholomew has no success (see 1477; 1486).

Le Morte d'Arthur by Sir Thomas Malory is published by the English printer William Caxton (see 1476). Malory is probably a knight-retainer to the late earl of Warwick, his abridged compilation of French Arthurian romance has probably been completed in prison, and it includes such lines as "there syr launcelot toke the fayrest lady by the hand, and she was naked as a nedel."

Painting *Pietà Panchiatichi* by Carlo Crivelli.

1486 The 26-year-old son of the Holy Roman Emperor Frederick III is chosen king of the Romans February 16 at Frankfurt despite opposition from his father who was driven out of Vienna last year. The son is crowned king of the Germans April 9 at Aix-la-Chapelle and begins a 33-year reign as Maximilian I.

Hungary's Matthias Corvinus lays down a code of laws as part of a program that is making his country for a brief period the dominant state in central Europe.

Christopher Columbus submits his project for a westward expedition to the Orient to Castile's Isabella and Aragon's Ferdinand (see 1485; 1492).

Africa's kingdom of Benin begins trade with Portugal.

African slaves in the kingdom of Gaur in India rebel and place their own leader on the throne.

Painting *The Birth of Venus* by Sandro Botticelli is completed for the villa at Castello of his patron Lorenzo Pierfrancesco de' Medici; *Annunciation* by Carlo Crivelli.

1487 Pope Innocent VIII names Tomas de Torquemada grand inquisitor and Torquemada's Inquisition introduces measures of cruelty that will make his name infamous (see 1483).

The Star Chamber introduced under another name by England's Henry VII gives defendants no right to know the names of their accusers. The king moves toward royal absolutism.

A pretender to the English throne gains support from Margaret, duchess of Burgundy and sister of the late Edward IV. The 10-year-old imposter Lambert Simnel impersonates the earl of Warwick, 10-year-old son of the duke of Clarence who is imprisoned in the Tower of London. His supporters crown him Edward VI in Dublin Cathedral, he lands in Lancaster with a force of poorly armed Irish levies and German mercenaries. The English defeat him at Stoke June 16, Henry VII pardons him, and he will become a falconer to the king after a period as scullery boy.

Portuguese navigator Bartholomeu Dias, 37, leaves Lisbon with two caravels and a storeship. A storm drives his fleet round Africa's southernmost tip, which he names the Cape of Storms (see Cape of Good Hope, 1488).

Portugal's João II sends explorer Pedro de Covilhão, 37, to the Levant in search of spices and of the land of the legendary Prester John mentioned by Fra Maruo in 1459. Covilhão will proceed from Lisbon through the Mediterranean, he will cross to the Red Sea, he will cross the Arabian Sea to India, and he will visit Madagascar. He will meet the king's messenger José de Lamego at Cairo and will send home word that if Portuguese pilots can round southern Africa they will find pilots on Africa's east coast who will lead them to India. The information will be tested by Vasco da Gama in 1497.

Venice's Palazzo Dario is completed on the Grand Canal for Giovanni Dario, Venetian secretary to Constantinople.

1488 Scotland's nobility rebels against the lavish spending and Anglophilic leanings of James III, the clan chieftains seize the king's eldest son, and they defeat him in battle at Sauchieburn near Bannockburn. The 36-year-old king is murdered June 11, possibly by a soldier disguised as a priest, and his 15-year-old son assumes the throne as James IV to begin a reign that will continue until 1513.

Bartholomeu Dias returns to Lisbon and reports to Joao II. The king sees hope of a sea route to India and suggests that Dias's Cape of Storms be called the Cape of Good Hope (see Vasco da Gama, 1497).

Andrea del Verrocchio dies at Venice October 7 at age 53 leaving unfinished his painting *Baptism of Christ* and his equestrian statue of Bartolommeo Colleoni for the Campo San Zanipolo (Alessandro Leopardi will complete the statue which will be unveiled in 1496).

Munich's Church of Our Lady (Frauenkirche) is completed off the Kaufingerstrasse.

1489 The first major European epidemic of typhus breaks out in Aragon where the disease is introduced

1489 (cont.) by Spanish soldiers returning from Cyprus after helping the Venetians fight the Moors.

Malleus Maleficarum by the inquisitors Kramer and Sprenger is a handbook on witch-hunting that will be used to justify the burning and shackling of countless mentally ill people (*see* Wier, 1563).

1490 Hungary's Matthias Corvinus dies suddenly April 4 at age 50 after an illustrious 32-year reign. He is succeeded by Bohemia's Ladislas II who will reign until 1516.

England's Henry VII takes control of the country's wool trade out of the hands of Florentine bankers and turns it over to Englishmen. The loss in trade brings a new crisis to Florence and opens the way to foes of big business in the city, foes led by the monk Girolamo Savonarola, prior of San Marco.

Portuguese explorers ascend the Congo for some 200 miles and convert the king of the Congo Empire to Christianity. They establish a post at São Salvador and begin a sphere of influence that will continue for more than a century.

Sugar cane is planted on the island of São Thome and slaves are transported from the kingdom of Benin and other African countries to work in the cane fields (*see* Cadbury, 1901).

Painting *The Annunciation* by Botticelli is completed as a large altar piece.

1491 Girolamo Savonarola begins denouncing the corruption at Florence and particularly that of Lorenzo de' Medici. The 39-year-old spiritual leader of the democratic party (the Piagnoni) preaches vehement sermons deploring the alleged licentiousness of the ruling class, the worldliness of the clergy, and the corruption of secular life (*see* 1496).

France's Charles VIII annexes Brittany by marrying Anne, duchess of Brittany. England's Henry VII goes to war to prevent the annexation, making peace with Scotland to release his troops for action.

The Bohemian-Hungarian king Ladislas II signs the Treaty of Pressburg acknowledging the Hapsburg right of succession.

Painting *The Nativity* by Perugino, a triptych for Rome's Villa Albani; *The Last Judgment* (frescoes) for Breisach Cathedral by Martin Schongauer who dies at Breisach February 2 at age 40.

Spanish colonists plant sugar cane in the Canary Islands where the cane flourishes.

1492 Christopher Columbus weighs anchor Friday, August 3, with 52 men aboard his flagship the 100-ton *Santa Maria*, 18 aboard the 50-ton *Pinta* commanded by Martin Alonso Pinzon, 52, and another 18 aboard the 40-ton *Niña* commanded by Vicente Yanez Pinzon, 32. The *Pinta* loses her rudder August 6, the fleet puts in at Tenerife for refitting, the three caravels put out to sea again September 6, and land is sighted October 12.

Financed by Castile's Isabella who has borrowed the wherewithal from Luis de Santangel by putting up her jewels as security, Columbus has crossed the Atlantic to make the first known European landing in the Western Hemisphere since early in the 11th century. He disembarks in the Bahamas on an island he names San Salvador under the impression that he has reached the East Indies.

Columbus proceeds to land on the island of Cuba and moves on to the island of Quisqueya which he renames Hispaniola, but his *Santa Maria* runs aground on Christmas Day and must be abandoned.

Castile's Isabella and Aragon's Ferdinand take Granada and most of the rest of the Iberian peninsula from the Moors (*see* 1467).

Florence's Lorenzo de' Medici dies April 18 at age 43. He has helped to make the Tuscan dialect the language of Italy in place of the classic Latin, and he has helped to make his city a center of European culture.

Poland's Casimir IV dies in June at age 65 after a 45-year reign and is succeeded by his 33-year-old son who will reign until 1501 as John Albert. The new king will reduce the power of the Polish burghers and peasants while extending the powers of the gentry (*see* 1496).

Lithuania is invaded following the death of Casimir (above) who was grand duke of Lithuania before becoming king of Poland in 1447.

Isabella and Ferdinand (above) extend throughout Granada the Inquisition begun by Isabella in 1478. They expel as many as 200,000 Jews.

Piero della Francesca dies at his native Borgo San Sepolcro near Arezzo October 12 at age 72.

The first known reference to smoking tobacco is made by Luis de Torres and Rodrigo de Jerez who have been sent ashore in the New World by Christopher Columbus (above). They report seeing natives who "drank smoke," and Rodrigo will later be imprisoned by the Spanish Inquisition (above) for his "devilish habit" of smoking (*see* 1518).

Sweet potatoes that came originally from the Western Hemisphere have long been grown in the mid-Pacific and for a century or two have been cultivated as far west as the islands that will be called New Zealand where the tuberous roots have been introduced by the Maori tribespeople.

Foods unknown in the Old World are discovered by Christopher Columbus (above): maize, sweet potatoes, capsicums (peppers), allspice (*Pimento officinalis*), plantain (*Musa paradisica*), pineapples, and turtle meat.

1493 Christopher Columbus builds a fort on the island of Hispaniola using wreckage from the *Santa Maria*, he leaves 44 men at Fort La Navidad, he sets sail for home January 4 in the *Niña*, he is joined 2 days later by Martin Pinzon in the *Pinta*, but is afterwards separated from Pinzon by a storm. He reaches Lisbon March 4 after having been delayed for 6 days by the

Portuguese governor of the Azores, and he reaches Palos March 15.

Columbus presents Isabella with "Indians," parrots, strange animals, and some gold, he demands and receives the reward that rightfully belongs to the sailor Rodrigo de Triana of the *Niña* who first sighted land, the queen grants Columbus enormous privileges in the territories he has claimed for the Spanish, and she sends him back as governor with 1,500 men in a fleet of 17 ships which weighs anchor September 24.

Columbus lands Sunday, November 3, on an island he calls Dominica, he sights Hispaniola November 22, and he sails westward to La Navidad only to find that the fort has burned down and the colony has been dispersed.

Peppers brought back from the "Indies" by Columbus are used as a medicinal preparation to treat the ailing Isabella.

A papal bull issued by Alexander VI (Borgia) May 4 establishes a line of demarcation between Spanish discoveries and Portuguese. The Spanish are to have dominion over any lands they discover west of the line, the Portuguese over lands east of the line.

The Treaty of Narbonne signed January 19 has ceded Roussillon and Cerdagne from France to Aragon. France's Charles VIII has agreed to the treaty in hopes of obtaining Ferdinand's support for an invasion of Italy, but Ferdinand has joined with the pope, with the German king Maximilian I, and with Milan and Venice to block the French plan.

The German king Maximilian I takes Artois and Franche-Comte from France under terms of the Peace of Senlis in May.

Painting *Madonna della Candeletta* and *Coronation of the Virgin* by Carlo Crivelli.

Sculpture *Adam and Eve* (limestone) by German sculptor Tilman Riemenschneider, 33, who last year completed an altarpiece for the parish church at Münnerstadt.

The horses and livestock landed by Christopher Columbus (above) at Santo Domingo (Hispaniola) are the first seen in the New World. Columbus left Palos with 34 stallions and mares, he has 20 left when he arrives, but his cattle weigh only 80 to 100 pounds when fully grown. (The horse originated in the Western Hemisphere and migrated to Asia before becoming extinct in its continent of origin at the close of the Ice Age.)

Sugar cane and cucumbers planted by Columbus at Santo Domingo have come from the Canary Islands. Columbus has a special interest in sugar since his father-in-law owns a Madeira sugar plantation (*see* 1419; 1506).

Pineapples brought back to Europe by Christopher Columbus give Europeans their first taste of the fruit.

1494 Christopher Columbus discovers the island of Jamaica May 14 and names it Santiago (St. James). He proceeds to land on islands that will be called Guade-

loupe, Montserrat, Antigua, St. Martin, Puerto Rico, and the Virgin Islands on a voyage in which he goes for 33 days with almost no sleep, loses his memory, and comes close to death.

The Treaty of Tordesillas divides the globe between Spain and Portugal along lines similar to those established last year by Pope Alexander VI.

The grand duke of Muscovy Ivan III gains his sobriquet Ivan the Great by driving out Novgorod's German merchants, closing the Hanseatic Kontor, and extending his realm eastward to the Urals by annexing the vast territories of Novgorod.

The Drogheda parliament summoned by the English governor of Ireland Sir Edward Poynings, 35, enacts Poyning's law which provides that every act of parliament must be approved by the English privy council to be valid.

Milan's Lodovico the Moor receives the ducal crown October 22 following the death of the rightful duke Gian Galeazzo Sforza, who has probably been poisoned by his uncle Lodovico. France's Charles VIII has helped the new duke, but he soon joins a league against Charles. He gives his niece Bianca in marriage to the German king Maximilian, and he receives in return imperial investiture of the duchy of Milan (*see* 1476; 1499).

Queen Isabella of Castile suspends a royal order for the sale of more than 500 Carib "Indians" into slavery. Christopher Columbus (above) has brought the Caribs home from the West Indies but the queen suggests in a letter to Bishop Fonseca that any sale await an inquiry into the causes for the imprisonment of the docile Indians and the lawfulness of their sale. When theologians differ on the lawfulness, Isabella orders the return of the Caribs to their Caribbean island.

The discovery of new land by Christopher Columbus opened the Western Hemisphere to European conquest.

1494 (cont.) Genoese merchant Hieronomo de Santo Stephano visits Calicut on the Indian Coast and observes trade in ginger and pepper (*see* da Gama, 1498).

The first English paper mill begins operation.

The University of Aberdeen has its beginnings in Scotland.

Painting *The Pietà* by Perugino; *Calumny* by Sandro Botticelli. Ghirlandajo dies at Florence January 11 at age 44; Hans Memling dies at Bruges August 11 at age 64.

Flemish composer Josquin des Pres, 49, receives an invitation to leave the papal chapel at Rome where he has been since 1486 and to become chief singer at the chapel of France's Charles VIII; Josquin has composed numerous masses, motets, psalms, and other sacred works, he accepts the French invitation, and he will also serve the Holy Roman Emperor Maximilian.

1495 Syphilis strikes Naples in history's first recorded outbreak of the disease that will appear throughout Europe in the next 25 years, but the disease may have existed for years and been confused with leprosy. A more violent form of syphilis than the disease of later centuries, the "new" malady infects the army of France's Charles VIII (who takes Naples in February), the French call it the Neapolitan disease, the Italians call it the French disease (*see* Fracastoro, 1530).

France's Charles VIII (above) is crowned king of Naples, whose King Alfonso has abdicated in favor of his 25-year-old son Ferrandino. Charles retreats to the north as Pope Alexander VI organizes a Holy League to drive out the French. The Battle of Fornovo July 6 is a near-disaster for Charles who escapes back to France. Ferrandino retakes Naples with help from the Spanish general Gonzalo de Cordova. The French fleet is captured at Rapallo, and a French army capitulates at Novara.

Portugal's Joao II dies in October at age 40 after a 14-year reign in which he has encouraged exploration and has overcome the feudal nobility, putting its leaders to death. Joao the Perfect (O principe perfecto) is succeeded by his 26-year-old brother-in-law who will reign until 1521 as Manoel I during a golden age of Portuguese exploration and discovery.

A new pretender to the English throne gains financial support from the German king Maximilian, makes an unsuccessful attempt to invade Kent, but receives a welcome from Scotland's James IV who gives him Lady Catherine Gordon in marriage. Perkin Warbeck, 21, is a Walloon who worked as a servant to a Breton silk merchant in Ireland, some people have mistaken him for the son of the duke of Clarence or of Richard III. He professes to be the second of Edward IV's sons murdered in the Tower of London in 1484. He has been acknowledged as her nephew by Margaret, dowager duchess of Burgundy. The earls of Desmond and Kildare have lent him

their support, and France's Charles VIII has entertained him as Richard IV (*see* 1496; 1497).

The diet of Worms attempts to modernize the Holy Roman Empire. The Imperial Diet proclaims Perpetual Peace, sets up an Imperial Chamber and Court of Appeal, and imposes a general tax.

Augsburg's Jakob Fugger II will earn more than 500,000 gulden in the next 15 years by selling copper and silver from mines he leases in Hungary plus 200,000 gulden per year from selling to the mints of Europe the silver he mines in the Tyrol and Carinthia. Water-driven machinery devised by his engineer associate Johann Thurzo facilitates mining the metals and refining them, enabling Fugger to supply customers at Antwerp, Danzig, Nuremberg, and Venice and in Poland, Prussia, and Russia. The Fuggers' control of mercury production in Spain, whose "quicksilver" mines are now its chief source of income, gives the family a grip on political power in Spain which it will maintain until 1634. As one of the leading European importers of Portugal's spices, the Fuggers will almost always earn a 20 percent return on their investment, and in most years their profit will exceed 50 percent (*see* 1546).

Painting *Vulcan and Aeolus* by Florentine painter Piero di Cosimo, 33.

Leonardo da Vinci submits plans to control the Arno River and avoid its disastrous flooding. The Florentine artist-scientist-engineer now serves Milan's Lodovico Sforza (*see* 1679).

1496 England's Henry VII refuses to recognize Spanish and Portuguese claims under the papal bull of 1493. He grants a patent to John Cabot, 46, to search for new lands and to rule any he may find. Born Giovanni Caboto, Cabot is a Venetian merchant who has settled in England with his sons (*see* 1497).

Portugal's Manoel I orders the expulsion of all Jews and has many Jews massacred. He takes the action to please Ferdinand of Aragon and Isabella of Castile whose daughter Isabella he will soon marry (*see* 1492).

Spanish forces complete their conquest of the Canary Islands from Portugal and from the indigenous fair-skinned Guanche who have fought off invaders for a century. Tenerife, largest of the seven volcanic islands, falls to the Spanish, who will rapidly assimilate the Guanche.

The new king of Naples Ferrandino dies September 7 at age 27, the last of the Anjou line in Italy. He is succeeded by his 44-year-old uncle Frederick who will reign as king of the Two Sicilies until his death in 1504 but who will be forced to yield Naples to France's Louis XII in 1501.

Poland's Statute of Piotkow restricts the burghers from buying land, deprives the peasants of freedom to move about, and gives the Polish gentry (szlachta) extensive privileges in what will be called the Magna Charta of Poland.

Scotland's James IV invades Northumberland to press the claims of Perkin Warbeck (*see* 1495; 1497).

The *Intercursus magnus* grants mutual privileges to English and Flemish merchants and provides for fixed duties in a commercial treaty between England and the Lowlands.

Painting *Procession of the True Cross in St. Mark's Square* by Gentile Bellini; *The Blood of the Redeemer* by Vittore Carpaccio; *The Crucifixion* by Perugino for Florence's Church of S. Maria Maddalena dei Pazzi.

The Spanish who take Tenerife find bananas growing under intense cultivation (*see* 1482; 1516).

1497 Portuguese explorer Vasco da Gama, 28, leaves Lisbon with four ships to investigate the possibility of a sea route to India as was suggested by the voyage of Bartholomeu Dias in 1487 and by the report of Pedro de Covilhao. Da Gama rounds the Cape of Good Hope November 22 (*see* 1498).

Natal on the west coast of Africa is given its name by Vasco da Gama (above) who sails along the coast on Christmas Day.

Florentine seaman Amerigo Vespucci, 46, advances the claim that he discovered the American mainland in 1491. A resident of Seville who sails in the service of Spanish interests, Vespucci is probably an agent of Florence's Medici family (*see* 1500; Waldseemüller, 1507).

John Cabot reaches Cape Breton Island and discovers what later will be called Nova Scotia and Newfoundland. Cabot is accompanied by 18 men aboard his single ship the *Matthew* (*see* 1496; 1498).

England's Henry VII puts down an insurrection in Cornwall where the people have risen to protest taxes imposed to support English defenses against Scottish invasion forces. The Cornishmen are defeated at Blackheath.

Cornwall is invaded with a small force by the pretender Perkin Warbeck who has found no support in Ireland (*see* 1495). He fails in a siege of Exeter, he advances to Taunton, he takes sanctuary at Beaulieu in Hampshire, but he is forced to surrender in September and is imprisoned in the Tower of London with the earl of Warwick (*see* 1499).

Denmark's John I defeats a Swedish army at Brunkeberg, he enters Stockholm, he revives the Scandinavian Union that ended in 1412, and he begins a 4-year reign as John II.

The 17-year-old duchess of Ferrara Lucrezia Borgia, who was married at age 13 to the lord of Pesaro Giovanni Sforza by her father Pope Alexander VI, has her marriage annulled by the pope who has become friendly with Naples. He has Lucrezia betrothed to Alfonso of Aragon, a nephew of the king of Naples.

Persia's Rustam Shah dies after a 5-year reign that ends the dynasty of the White Sheep which has ruled since 1453 (*see* 1502).

The Florentine prior-dictator Savonarola celebrates the annual carnival with a "burning of the vanities" in the Piazza della Signoria. Masks related to carnival festivities, indecent books and pictures, and other items are burned, the crowds attracted by Savonarola are too great for the cathedral, the prior attacks the alleged crimes of Pope Alexander VI and indignantly spurns the offer of a cardinal's hat, but the pope is determined to silence the daring friar and he issues a bull excommunicating Savonarola (*see* 1491; 1498).

Painting *The Last Supper* by Leonardo da Vinci is completed for Milan's Lodovico Sforza in the monastery refectory adjoining the Church of Santa Maria delle Grazie; *Apollo and Marsyas* by Perugino; *The Meeting of Joachim and Anne at the Golden Gate* by Florentine painter Filippino Lippi, 40-year-old son of the late Fra Filippo Lippi. Benozzo Gozzoli dies at Pistoia October 4 at age 77.

Sculpture *Bacchus* by Michelangelo.

Vast codfish banks off the coast of Newfoundland are noted by John Cabot (above). The fishing grounds have been visited in the past by Breton fishermen and will be called the Grand Banks (*see* 1504).

1498 Vasco da Gama frees Europe from dependence on Venetian middlemen in the spice trade. He lands at Calicut where Arab spice dealers fearful of losing their monopoly give him a rude reception, and he establishes a sea route between Portugal and India (*see* 1453; 1497; 1501).

Christopher Columbus makes a third voyage to the New World, this time with six ships. He sights St. Vincent January 22, he sights Grenada August 15, he discovers Trinidad, and he lands at the mouth of the Orinoco River on the South American mainland.

Portuguese explorer-scientist Duarte Pacheco Pareira touches the South American coast. He will write in 1505 of a vast continent extending south from 70 degrees north latitude.

John Cabot and his son Sebastian coast Newfoundland, Nova Scotia, and points south on a second voyage with a fleet of six ships (*see* 1497).

The Spanish settle some 200 colonists in Hispaniola.

The Spanish ship some 600 cannibal Caribs home to Spain to be sold into slavery (*see* 1494).

France's Charles VIII dies April 8 at age 27 as he prepares a new expedition to invade Italy. Having no male heir, Charles is succeeded by his 36-year-old Valois cousin the duc d'Orléans who will reign until 1515 as Louis XII. The new king led a revolt against Charles more than a decade ago, he was imprisoned by Charles from 1488 to 1491, and his accession unites the duchy of Orleans with the royal domain.

Savonarola is burned at the stake for heresy May 23 in Florence's Piazza della Signoria off the Via Condotta (*see* 1497).

1498 (cont.) Painting *The Discovery of Honey* by Piero di Cosimo; *Baptism of Christ* (triptych) and *Judgment of Cambyses* by Dutch painter Gerard David; *The Apocalypse* (woodcuts) by Nuremberg painter-engraver Albrecht Dürer, 27, is the first book published by an artist from his own designs.

1499 Vasco da Gama returns to Portugal from Mozambique with pepper, nutmeg, cinnamon, and cloves after having lost 100 of his 160 men to scurvy (*see* 1498). His success encourages others to attempt the sea voyage around Africa to India (*see* Cabral, 1500).

France's Louis XII obtains a divorce from Jeanne, daughter of Louis XI, and marries Anne of Brittany, widow of the late Charles VIII, to keep the duchy of Brittany in the French crown.

Louis XII gains Venetian support for his claims to Milan, he invades Italy once again, he forces Lodovico Sforza to flee Milan, and the city surrenders to the French September 14.

The Swiss receive French financial support in a war with the German king Maximilian I; the southern German cities support Maximilian, but the Swiss gain a series of victories and force Maximilian to sign the Treaty of Basel September 22 granting the Swiss independence (formal independence will not come until 1648).

Venice begins a 4-year war with the Ottoman empire. The Venetians will lose some territory and trading posts to the Turks.

The Ottoman Turks conquer Montenegro (Zeta).

Perkin Warbeck is hanged November 12 for conspiring to escape from the Tower of London with the imprisoned earl of Warwick (*see* 1497).

Granada's Moors stage a massive revolt as the Spanish Inquisitor-General Francisco Jimenez de Cisneros, 63, introduces forced conversion to Christianity on a wholesale basis.

London has another epidemic of the Black Death. It will kill thousands in the next 2 years (*see* 1407; 1603).

Nonfiction *Bellus Helveticum* by German humanist Willibald Pirkheimer, 29, is a history of the Swiss war (above) and includes his autobiography.

Poetry *The Bowge of Court* by English poet-translator John Skelton, 39, is an allegory satirizing the court of Henry VII.

Theater *La Celestina* (*Tragicomedia de Calisto y Melibea*) by Spanish playwright Fernando de Rojas, 24.

Venice's campanile (clock tower) is completed in the Piazza San Marco after 3 years of construction. Two side wings will be added in the next 7 years, and additional floors will be added in 1755 to the campanile just west of the 400-year-old San Marco Church. Carved Moorish figures ring the campanile's great bell to provide a spectacle for the people.

Oriental spices such as those brought back by Vasco da Gama (above) are widely used to preserve meat and to disguise the bad taste of spoiled meat which comprises the bulk of human diets in late winter and spring.

1500 Portuguese navigator Gaspar de Corte-Real (or Corterreal), 50, makes the first authenticated European landing on the Northern Continent of the Western Hemisphere since Leif Ericson in 1000 and Thorfinn Karlsefni a few years later. Corte-Real's father Joao Vaz Corte-Real received an Azore Island captaincy in 1474 as a reward for having made a voyage to the "Land of the Codfish" and the younger Corte-Real explores the coast of Labrador (*see* 1501).

Portuguese explorer Pedro Alvares Cabral, 40, claims Brazil for Manoel I. Cabral has left the Cape Verde Islands with a fleet of 13 caravels bound for India, but contrary winds have driven him westward, he lands on Good Friday, and he takes possession in the name of the king Easter Monday.

Brazil's shoreline has been explored a few weeks before the arrival of Cabral (above) by the Spanish navigator Alonzo de Ojeda who may have been accompanied by the Italian Amerigo Vespucci (*see* 1497, 1501).

Spanish navigator Vicente Yanez Pinzon touches Cape St. Roque at the eastern extremity of Brazil. Pinzon captained the *Niña* on the 1492–1493 Columbus voyage.

Pedro Alvares Cabral (above) proceeds with his fleet to India in the company of Bartholomeu Dias and Duarte Pereira (*see* 1488; 1498). He will return loaded with spices to begin regular spice trade round the Cape of Good Hope.

Portugal's influence in Africa reaches its height.

France's Louis XII annexes Milan on the basis of his being the great-grandson of Gian Galeazzo Visconti (*see* 1395; 1499). Lodovico Sforza is thrown into a French prison where he will die in 8 years (*see* 1512).

Adages (*Adagia*) by Dutch humanist Desiderius Erasmus (Herasmus Gerardus), 34, is published at Paris. The collection of sayings from classical authors will be published in a much enlarged edition at Venice in 1508.

Painting *Christ Crowned with Thorns* and *Ship of Fools* by Hieronymus Bosch; *Mystic Nativity* by Sandro Botticelli; *Self-portrait* by Albrecht Dürer.

16th CENTURY

1501 Vasco da Gama wins control of the spice trade for Lisbon. He sets out with a fleet of 20 caravels to close the Red Sea and he cuts off the trade route through Egypt to Alexandria where Venetian merchants have been buying spices (*see* 1499; 1504).

Amerigo Vespucci makes a second voyage to the New World, this time in the service of Portugal (*see* 1497). Vespucci's account of the Brazilian coast will express his conviction that it is not part of Asia but is indeed a New World (*see* 1502).

Portugal's Gaspar de Corte-Real makes a second voyage to the northern continent of the New World, he kidnaps 57 "Indians" to be sold as slaves, but he drowns along with his crewmen and the slaves chained in the ship's hold as his caravel sinks in a storm on the homeward voyage. A second vessel reaches Portugal with seven Indians left alive, but Corte-Real's brother Miguel will be lost next year on a voyage in search of his lost sibling.

Spanish settlers at Santo Domingo introduce African slaves into Hispaniola—the first importation of blacks to the New World (*see* 1503).

Ferdinand of Aragon declares Granada a Christian kingdom but encounters resistance from the Moors.

Ferdinand (above) helps France's Louis XII conquer the kingdom of Naples from Frederick, king of the Two Sicilies. French forces enter Rome and Pope Alexander VI declares Louis king of Naples (*see* 1504).

The German king Maximilian I recognizes French conquests in northern Italy in the Peace of Trent.

England's Henry VII declines a papal request to lead a crusade against the Ottoman Turks who take Durazzo from Venice.

The grand duke of Muscovy Ivan the Great invades Lithuania.

The Spanish universities of Valencia and Santiago have their beginnings.

Nonfiction *Speculum Principis* by John Skelton is a moral treatise for England's Prince Henry.

Poetry *The Palice of Honour* by Scottish poet Gawin Douglas, 26, who has taken holy orders and becomes provost of Edinburgh's St. Giles Cathedral.

Painting *Life of the Virgin* by Albrecht Dürer.

Sculpture *Pietà* and *Bacchus* by Florentine artist Michelangelo (Michelagniolo Buonarroti), 26, who has created the *Pietà* on a commission from the French cardinal Jean de Villiers de la Grolaie, abbot of St. Denis, and the *Bacchus* for Roman nobleman

Jacopo Galli. Michelangelo returns to his native Florence after a 5-year stay at Rome and begins work on a great statue of David.

Venetian printers use movable type to print music for the first time.

1502 Amerigo Vespucci returns in September from a voyage to the New World. An account of this voyage will be the basis of the name America (*see* Waldseemüller, 1507).

Christopher Columbus has embarked May 11 on a fourth voyage to the New World, this time with 150 men in four caravels that take 8 months to make the Atlantic crossing, forcing the crews to eat wormy biscuit (dried bread), sharkmeat, and ships' rats in order to survive. Columbus discovers St. Lucia, the island of Guanaja off Honduras, Honduras itself, Costa Rica, and the Isthmus of Panama (*see* 1503).

Some 2,500 new colonists arrive at Hispaniola as Nicholas de Ovando is installed as governor of the new colony by Ferdinand of Aragon.

The last of the Moors are expelled from Castile.

Montezuma II ascends the throne of the Aztec Empire at Tenochtitlan at age 22 (*see* 1325; Juan de Grijalva, 1518).

A Spanish fleet seizes Taranto in March as Ferdinand of Aragon supports the claims of Louis XII to Naples.

Cesare Borgia, 27, is given French aid in putting down a revolt of his captains at Sinigaglia in December. Borgia is the son of Pope Alexander VI.

The Safavid dynasty that will rule Persia until 1736 is founded by the 16-year-old shah Ismail who last year defeated Alwand of the White Sheep after having emerged from years of hiding to take advantage of the confusion following the death of Rustam Shah in 1497. Ismail will reign until 1524.

The University of Wittenberg has its beginnings.

Painting *St. Jerome* by German painter-engraver Lucas Cranach, 29.

The Tempietto at St. Pietro in Montorio is completed by the Vatican architect Bramante (Donato d'Agnolo), 58, with a sculptured chapel that interrelates convex and concave elements.

1503 Christopher Columbus observes rubber on his fourth voyage to the New World. The heavy black ball used in games played by the natives astonishes the Spaniards by bouncing as if it were alive. The Spaniards are the first Europeans to see the vegetable gum made from the latex either of the guayule shrub *Par-*

1503 (cont.) *thenium argentatus* or of *Hevea brasiliensis*, but rubber will not come into commercial use for another three centuries and then only to rub out pencil marks, whence it will derive its English name rubber, or india rubber (*see* solvent, 1762).

Another 1,000 to 2,000 Spanish colonists arrive at Hispaniola.

Christopher Columbus discovers Panama November 2 and finds the "beautiful port" that will be called Portobelo (*see* Darien, 1509).

The Spanish governor of Hispaniola Nicolas de Ovando writes Ferdinand the Catholic to request that he permit no more black slaves to be sent out to the colony (*see* 1501; 1512).

France's Louis XII abandons claims to Naples following the breakup of his alliance with Ferdinand of Aragon and defeat of French forces by Ferdinand's general Gonzalvo de Cordoba (*see* 1504).

Poetry *The Thissill and the Rois* by Scottish poet William Dunbar, 43, who has composed the political allegory to honor Margaret Tudor whose marriage to James IV he has helped to negotiate.

Painting *Crucifixion* by Lucas Cranach; Leonardo da Vinci begins his great mural *The Battle of Anghiari* for Florence's Palazzo della Signoria (*see* 1440), and he paints *Leda and the Swan*.

England's Canterbury Cathedral is completed in Norman-Gothic style after 436 years of construction.

Portuguese caravels return from the East Indies with 1,300 tons of pepper—a quantity six times the amount that Egypt's Mameluke regime has permitted to be shipped in any one year.

1504 Ferdinand of Aragon completes his conquest of Naples January 1 with the surrender of French forces at Gaeta. France's Louis XII cedes Naples to Ferdinand in the Treaty of Lyons, the French control northern Italy from Milan, the Spanish control Sicily and southern Italy and will hold Naples until 1707.

Albrecht of Bavaria defeats Rupert, son of the elector Palatine, in the Bavarian War. The German feudal knight Götz von Berlichingen, 24, loses his right hand at the siege of Landshut, he has the hand replaced with an iron hand, and he will be called "Götz of the Iron Hand."

The Treaty of Blois signed in September brings accord between France and the German king Maximilian I whose 4-year-old grandson Charles is betrothed to Claude, daughter of France's Louis XII. Maximilian invests Louis with the duchy of Milan (above), and Louis promises to help Maximilian gain the imperial crown.

Castile's Isabella the Catholic dies November 24 at age 53 after a 30-year reign in which she has financed the voyages of Christopher Columbus and has persecuted non-Catholics with the Inquisition. She is succeeded by her daughter Juana and Juana's husband Philip the Handsome (Felipe el Hermosa), but they remain in Flanders and Isabella's widower Ferdinand of Aragon will rule Castile until 1506.

Christopher Columbus returns from a final voyage to the Western Hemisphere, landing at Sanlucar November 7 too ill after a 9-week voyage from Hispaniola to pay his respects to the dying Isabella.

Spices in the Lisbon market drop to 20 percent of Venetian prices, breaking Venice's monopoly in the spice trade and making her vulnerable to attack (*see* League of Cambrai, 1508).

Painting *Rest on the Flight into Egypt* by Lucas Cranach; *Adam and Eve* (engraving) by Albrecht Dürer.

Breton fishermen begin making annual visits to the Grand Banks off Newfoundland which they have been visiting periodically since before 1497.

1505 The grand duke of Muscovy Ivan the Great dies at age 65. He is succeeded by his 26-year-old son who will reign as Basil III Ivanovich until 1533 and will incorporate the last remaining independent Russian principalities with Muscovy (*see* 1510).

Poland's Constitution of Radom makes the national diet the supreme legislative body: no laws are to be passed without its consent. The Diet of Piotrkow 12 years ago was the first *seym* to legislate for all Poland. The nobility, voting in provincial assemblies, elects the new diet; the statute *nihil novi* gives the *seym* and the senate a voice equal to that of the Crown in executive matters.

Portugal sends Francisco de Almeida to the Indies as her first governor. He takes Quiloa and Mombasa on the African coast enroute to his post, and he establishes forts at Calicut, Cananor, and Cochin on the Malabar coast (*see* 1509).

Sri Lanka (Ceylon) is discovered by the Portuguese off the southeast coast of India.

Seville University has its beginnings.

Painting *The Madonna and Child Enthroned with Saints* by Raphael; *Portrait of Bishop Bernardo de' Rossi* by Italian painter Lorenzo Lotto, 25; *The Combat Between Love and Chastity* by Perugino.

1506 Christopher Columbus dies in obscurity at Valladolid May 21 at age 55 still believing that he has found an outlying part of Asia. The bones of the great navigator will be removed to Santo Domingo on the island he discovered December 5, 1492, changing the course of history.

Castile's Philip I dies suddenly at Burgos September 25 at age 28 and his wife Juana loses her mind. Her father Ferdinand II of Aragon becomes regent of Castile, he marries Germaine de Foix, niece of France's Louis XII, and he will rule Castile as Ferdinand V until his death in 1516.

Poland's Alexander I dies after a 5-year reign in which he has lost the left bank of the Dnieper to the grand duke of Muscovy Ivan the Great. He is succeeded by his brother who will reign until 1548 as Sigismund I.

Korean rebels overthrow the cruel ruler Yonsangun and will place Chungjong on the throne next year.

A Florentine militia created by the city's vice-chancellor Niccolò Machiavelli, 37, is the first Italian national army.

Lisbon has a riot in which between 2,000 and 4,000 converted Jews are slaughtered.

Poetry *The Dance of the Sevin Deidly Synnis* by William Dunbar.

Painting *St. Jerome in the Wilderness* by Lorenzo Lotto; *Madonna di Casa* by Raphael; the *St. Catherine* altarpiece by Lucas Cranach.

The *Laocoön* sculpture is unearthed in Rome's Esquiline Hill (*see* 38 B.C.).

The Italian architect Bramante begins rebuilding St. Peter's at Rome in the form of a huge Greek cross with a central dome. Bramante's plan will be altered by his successors.

An English worker can earn enough to buy 8 bushels of wheat by working for 20 days, 8 bushels of rye by working for 12 days, 8 bushels of barley by working for 9 days (*see* 1599).

The Spanish make their first efforts to cultivate sugar cane in the Caribbean's Great Antilles.

1507 *Cosmographiae Introductio* by German geographer Martin Waldseemüller, 37, gives Amerigo (or Americus) Vespucci credit for discovering the New World and calls it America (*see* 1501). The name will be applied at first only to the southern continent, but by the end of the century it will be generally applied to the entire Western Hemisphere.

La Prima Navigazione per l'Oceano alle Terre de' Negri della Bassa Ethiopia by Alvise Cadamosto describes his explorations.

The Portuguese capture Zafi in Morocco and begin commerce in captive Moors, Berbers, and Jews. Many are women, all are called white slaves.

The German king Maximilian I appoints his 26-year-old daughter Margaret of Austria guardian of her 7-year-old nephew the archduke Charles who is betrothed by treaty to the daughter of England's Henry VII. Maximilian makes Margaret regent of the Netherlands to serve until Charles is of age.

The Diet of Constance recognizes the unity of the Holy Roman Empire and founds the Imperial Chamber.

The Italian adventurer Cesare Borgia is killed March 12 at age 30 while besieging the rebellious count of Lerin at his castle of Viana. Borgia has been fighting in the service of his brother-in-law the king of Navarre to whose court he fled late last year after making his escape from a Spanish prison where he had been held for 2 years.

The sweating sickness that struck London in 1485 strikes again (*see* 1518).

Painting *Mona Lisa* by Leonardo da Vinci who has been making sketches since 1505 of Lisa di Anton, Neapolitan wife of local businessman-politician Francesco del Giocando, 46. His model leaves in the spring for Calabria on a long business trip with her husband, and the portrait is left incomplete; *Madonna with Child and Four Saints* by Lorenzo Lotto; *St. Mark Preaching in Alexandria* by Gentile Bellini who dies February 23 at age 77 and whose work is completed by his brother Giovanni.

Florence's Palazzo Strozzi is completed after 18 years of construction.

Pope Julius II proclaims an indulgence to raise money for the rebuilding of St. Peter's.

1508 The German king Maximilian assumes the title of Roman Emperor Elect February 4 at Trent, and Pope Julius II confirms the fact that the German king shall hereafter automatically become Holy Roman Emperor. Maximilian has set out for Rome, the Venetians have refused to let him pass through their territories, he attacks the Venetians, but he makes a truce when he finds that the war is not popular with the southern German cities.

The League of Cambrai formed by Pope Julius, France's Louis XII, and Ferdinand of Aragon plots to despoil Venice of her possessions on the mainland and in Apulia. The Italian peninsula will be a battlefield for the next few years, new political alignments will be created, England's Henry VIII will become involved, and various territories will change hands.

Mozambique is colonized by the Portuguese.

Cuba is explored by Spanish navigator Sebastian de Ocampo with a view to settlement.

Puerto Rico is explored by Juan Ponce de Leon, 48, a Spaniard who accompanied Columbus on his second voyage to America and who plants a colony on the island (*see* Florida, 1513; San Juan, 1521).

Painting *The Chess Player* and *Self Portrait* by Dutch prodigy Lucas van Leyden (Lucas Hugensz), 14; *Madonna and Saints* by Lorenzo Lotto; Raphael enters the service of Pope Julius II.

Theater *Cassaria* by Italian playwright Lodovico Ariosto, 34.

The native population of Hispaniola in the Caribbean falls to 60,000, down from 200,000 to 300,000 in 1492 (*see* 1514).

1509 England's Henry VII dies April 22 at age 52 after a reign of nearly 24 years. He is succeeded by his athletic, well-educated 17-year-old son who ascends the throne as Henry VIII to begin a stormy reign of nearly 38 years.

The Battle of Diu February 2 in the Indian Ocean has brought victory to Portugal's Indian viceroy Francisco de Almeida who destroys the Moslem fleet to establish Portuguese control over the spice trade.

The caravels that carried bold Spanish conquistadors to the New World in search of fabled treasure were often tiny.

Spanish forces invade North Africa. Cardinal Jimenez de Cisneros, 73, and Pedro Navarro, 49, lead a crusade against the Moslem rulers of Oran, Bougie, and Tripoli.

The Holy Roman Emperor Maximilian I joins the League of Cambrai but fails in a siege of Padua.

Portuguese navigator Ruy de Sequeira visits Malacca following the defeat of the Moslem fleet at the Battle of Diu (above).

Spanish explorer Alonso de Ojeda leaves Hispaniola for South American territory that will be called Colombia.

Spanish conquistadors found a colony at Darien on the Isthmus of Panama (*see* Balboa, 1513).

Fiction *Praise of Folly (Encomium Moriae)* by Erasmus is a witty satire written in the Bucklersbury house of England's Thomas More, 31, a former attorney at law who has subjected himself to the discipline of a Carthusian monk and who has been a member of Parliament since 1504 (*see* 1515). Erasmus has been teaching in England at Cambridge University where he will remain until 1514.

Poetry *The Ship of Fools (The Shyp of Folys of the Worlde)* by English poet Alexander Barclay, 34, who has adapted the popular German satire *Das Narrenschiff* of 1494 by Sebastian Brant.

Engraving *The Temptation of St. Anthony* by Lucas van Leyden.

Painting *Madonna with Angels and Saints* by Gerard David; *St. Anne Altarpiece* by Flemish painter Quentin Massys, 43.

1510 Russia's last free republic loses her charter January 29. Basil III Ivanovich obliges Pskov to send her assembly bell to Moscow.

Hamburg becomes a free city of the Holy Roman Empire.

The Swiss join the 2-year-old Holy League of Cambrai against the French.

England's Parliament attaints former House of Commons speakers William Empson and Edmund Dudley who are beheaded in mid-August. Henry VIII has charged them with treason, but their real crime has been the extortionary measures they have used in administering Henry VII's arbitrary system of taxation—measures that fattened their own purses and provided them with vast estates.

The island of Goa off India's Malabar coast falls to Portuguese forces. It is western Europe's first toehold in India and will remain in Portuguese hands for more than four and a half centuries.

European explorers probe the east coast of North America to a point north of the Savannah River.

A consignment of African slaves crosses the Atlantic to work on Portuguese sugar plantations in Brazil. By some accounts it is the first such consignment (but *see* 1503; *see also* 1526; 1888).

A horizontal water wheel designed by Leonardo da Vinci pioneers the water turbine.

Anatomy by Leonardo da Vinci contains drawings from life based on cadavers that Leonardo has somehow obtained and dissected, but he does not permit his work to be published (*see* Vesalius, 1543).

The Venetian painter Giorgione (Giorgio da Castelfranco) dies of plague at age 32 after having caught the disease from "a certain lady." The artist is remembered for his landscape *Tempesta,* and his death brings a rush by Italian art patrons for this and for a handful of other known Giorgione canvases including *Laura, The Three Philosophers, Trial of Moses, Judgment of Solomon, Sleeping Venus,* and *The Virgin and St. Francis and St. Liberale.* Sandro Botticelli dies May 17 at age 65.

Engraving *Ecce Homo, The Milkmaid, The Return of the Prodigal Son* by Lucas van Leyden.

Painting *Presentation in the Temple* by Venetian painter Vittore Carpaccio, 45; *The Gypsy Madonna* by Venetian painter Titian (Tiziano Vecellio), 23, who has worked with the late Giorgione (above) and who is commissioned by Padua's confraternity of St. Anthony to fresco the interior of its meeting hall; *Salome* by Venetian painter Sebastiano del Piombo (Sebastiano Luciani), 25, who apprenticed under Giovanni Bellini and then under the late Giorgione (above); *The Triumph of Galatea* by Raphael.

Theater *Everyman* is an English morality play based on the Dutch morality play *Elckerlijk* first performed in 1495.

Sunflowers from the Americas are introduced to Europe by the Spanish. In many countries they will be a major oilseed crop (*see* 1698).

1511 The papal forces of Julius II take Modena and Mirandola from the French in January, the French take Bologna May 13, the pope renews the Holy League in alliance with Venice to drive the French out of Italy, and in October Ferdinand of Castile joins the Holy League which will be joined next year by England's Henry VIII and the following year by the Holy Roman Emperor Maximilian.

Portuguese forces under Affonso d'Albuquerque capture Malacca, center of the East Indian spice trade, to complete Portuguese control of Far Eastern spice sources (see 1509).

A Spanish ship bound from Darien in Panama to Santo Domingo strikes a reef and founders in the Caribbean. The survivors reach Yucatán where some are killed and eaten according to native ritual and the remainder enslaved. Only two will survive (see Cortez, 1519).

Poland establishes serfdom under laws passed by the diet.

Watches mentioned for the first time in print in the Nuremberg *Chronicles* have hour hands but no minute hands. "From day to day more ingenious discoveries are made," writes Johannes Cocleus; "for Petrus Hele, a young man, makes things which astonish the most learned mathematicians, for he makes out of a small quantity of iron horologia devised with very many wheels, and these horologia, in any position and without any weight, both indicate and strike for 40 hours, even when they are carried on the breast and in the purse." (see 1670).

Painting *St. Sebastian* and *Marriage of St. Catherine* by Italian painter Fra Bartolommeo (Bartolommeo di Pagolo del Fatorino, or Baccio della Porta), 36, who has learned perspective from Raphael and who in turn has influenced Raphael; *The Sistine Madonna* by Raphael; *Julius II* by Raphael; *Deposition* (triptych) by Quentin Massys.

Woodcut Engraving *The Triumph of Christ* (10 blocks) by Titian (the work is nearly 9 feet long).

1512 Pope Julius II convenes a council at the Lateran to counter a church council summoned at Pisa last year by France's Louis XII. The Lateran council will remain in session for several years and will undertake the first reforms of abuses in the Church of Rome (but see Luther, 1517).

Forces of the Holy League renewed last year by Julius II meet defeat in an Easter battle at Ravenna. French forces under Gaston de Foix have taken Brescia by storm with help from the 39-year-old knight Pierre Terrail, seigneur de Bayard (known as chevalier sans peur et sans reproche), but a coalition of Swiss, papal, and imperial forces drive the French and their 5,000 German mercenaries out of Milan in May and return the Sforzas to power in the duchy (see 1500; 1536).

The Swiss take Locarno, Lugano, and Ossola as their reward for helping to drive the French out of Milan.

Spanish troops conquer Navarre which is annexed to Castile.

England's Henry VIII has laid claim to the throne of France, he sends troops into Spain, but they have no success.

The Ottoman sultan Bayazid II is deposed by his 47-year-old son Selim (the Grim) who is engaged in civil war with his brothers Ahmed and Corcud. Bayazid had designated Ahmed to be his successor and has taken refuge from Selim at Adrianople, Selim wins over the Janissaries to his side, Bayazid dies under suspicious circumstances, and Selim begins an 8-year reign in which he will conquer Syria and Egypt and end the Abbasid caliphate.

Poland and Muscovy begin a 10-year war over the White Russian region.

Golconda gains independence in India and will remain independent for 175 years.

Spanish colonists import black slaves into Hispaniola's western settlement to replace Indian slaves who have died in great numbers from disease and from being worked to death in the Spaniards' quest for gold (see Ovando, 1503; Las Casas, 1516).

Painting *The Creation of Adam* by Michelangelo on the ceiling of the Sistine Chapel at Rome; *The Prophet Jerome* by Michelangelo for the Sistine Chapel; *Madonna and Saints* by Fra Bartolommeo.

The Newfoundland cod banks provide fish for English, French, Portuguese, and Dutch vessels which use the island as a base, drying the catch there for shipment back to Europe.

Portuguese explorers find nutmeg trees to be indigenous to the island of Banda in the Moluccas. The Portuguese will dominate the nutmeg and mace trade until 1602.

1513 French forces in Italy suffer a bad defeat June 6 at Novara and the battle at Guinegate August 17 will be called the Battle of the Spurs because of the hasty flight of the beaten French from England's Henry VIII and the Holy Roman Emperor Maximilian. The allies force Louis XII to give up Milan and to end his Italian invasion.

The Battle of Flodden Field September 9 just south of the Scottish border ends in victory for an English army sent by Henry VIII under the earl of Surrey. Scotland's James IV is killed at age 40 while fighting on foot, nearly all his nobles are killed, and the king's only legitimate son succeeds to the throne at age 15 months to begin a 29-year reign as James V.

The Scottish Navy on which James IV has lavished so much money is sold to France as Scotland ends a quarter-century that has unified the country, has seen a flourishing of literature, and has given the Scots a prosperity they will not enjoy again for more than a century.

Denmark's John I, who ruled Sweden as John II from 1497 to 1501, dies after a 32-year reign. Scandinavian

1513 (cont.) noblemen assemble in the Herredag at Constantinople to confirm his 32-year-old son as successor, the new king will reign until 1523 as Christian II of Denmark and Norway, but the Swedes refuse to accept him (*see* 1520).

The Prince (*Il Principe*) by Florentine public servant Niccolò Machiavelli, now 44, is an analysis of the means by which a man may rise to power. Machiavelli has served for 14 years as vice chancellor and secretary of Florence and has observed the intrigues and machinations of the late Cesare Borgia of Romana. "Men are always wicked at bottom, unless they are made good by some compulsion," writes the cynical Machiavelli. "It is much more secure to be feared than to be loved." "Only those means of security are good, are certain, are lasting, that depend on yourself and your own vigor." "Hate is gained through good deeds as well as bad ones." "One who deceives will always find those who allow themselves to be deceived." "It is not titles that honor men, but men that honor titles." "Success or failure lies in conformity to the times." "The first method for estimating the intelligence of a ruler is to look at the men he has around him."

Florida is sighted and named by Spanish explorer Juan Ponce de Leon, now 53, who has remained in the New World after arriving with Columbus in 1493 and has become governor of Puerto Rico. He sights land on Easter Sunday, calls it Florida after Pascua Florida (the Easter season), and goes ashore.

Spanish explorer Vasco Nunez Balboa sights the Pacific Ocean which he calls the South Sea and takes possession of El Mar de Sur September 29 in the name of Spain (*see* Magellan, 1520). Now 38, Balboa has joined an expedition from Santo Domingo as a stowaway, he has taken command of the 190-man force supported by 1,000 natives, he has crossed the 45-mile-wide thickly forested Isthmus of Darien (Panama) in 25 days to reach a peak overlooking the sea, and he has sent three men including Francisco Pizarro to reconnoiter (*see* 1514).

A Portuguese caravel reaches Canton. It is the first European ship to land in China.

Peasant and labor rebellions in Europe spread eastward from Switzerland. They will continue for the next four years.

Pinturicchio dies at Siena December 11 at age 59.

Theater *Cassandra the Sibyl* (*Auto de la Sibila Casandra*) by Portuguese poet-playwright Raymond Gil Vicente, 43, 12/25 at the Convent of Euxobregas.

Chartres Cathedral is completed 60 miles southwest of Paris after nearly 400 years of construction. The new north tower gives the Gothic cathedral a magnificence matched only by its blue stained glass windows (*see* 1260).

Ponce de Leon (above) plants orange and lemon trees in Florida.

1514 "Not only the Christian religion but nature cries out against slavery and the slave trade" says Pope Leo X in a bull against slavery, but the trade continues to grow (*see* 1450; 1526).

England's Henry VIII concludes peace with Scotland and with France which cedes Tournay to England but will later buy it back for 600,000 crowns.

Persia is invaded by the Ottoman sultan Selim the Grim who has slaughtered an estimated 40,000 of his heretic subjects. He is determined to enforce his Sunnite faith on the Persians, whose shah Ismail is defeated in the Battle of Chaldiran which begins a conflict that will not end until 1555.

Cuba is conquered from the "Indians" by the Spanish (*see* Havana, 1515).

Some 1,500 Spanish settlers arrive at Panama (*see* 1509; 1513; Pizarro, 1524).

Trinity House at Deptford in Kent is chartered by England's Henry VIII who has made Deptford a royal dockyard. The "guild or fraternity of the most glorious and undividable Trinity of St. Clement" is an association of mariners that will monopolize the training and licensing of pilots and masters, it will be given charge of directing the new naval dockyard, it will be given authority late in the century to erect beacons and other marks to guide England's coastal shipping, and it will grow in influence for centuries to come.

Green peas come into use in England to a limited extent, but dried peas are more commonly used and are consumed as "pease porridge"—hot, cold, and even 9 days old according to the nursery rhyme (*see* 1555).

Hispaniola has 17 chartered Spanish towns, and the island's native population falls to 14,000, down from 60,000 in 1508 (*see* 1548).

1515 France's Louis XII dies January 1 at age 52 after a 15-year reign and is succeeded by his robust 21-year-old son-in-law and cousin once removed. The new king François I begins a 32-year reign by conquering Lombardy in northern Italy.

French forces gain a decisive victory over the Swiss and Venetians at the Battle of Maiganano in mid-September and conclude peace November 12. The Swiss retain most of the Alpine passes and receive a French subsidy in return for French rights to enlist Swiss mercenaries.

The South American territory that will be called Argentina is discovered by Spanish explorer Juan Diaz de Solis, 45. Guarani tribesmen will ambush him and kill him next year when he lands near the mouth of the Parana River (*see* Buenos Aires, 1580).

Havana, Cuba, is founded by Spanish conquistadors.

Utopia by English envoy to Flanders Thomas More describes an imaginary island governed entirely by reason and offers solutions to the social ills that plague England in a time when landlords are driving the peasantry off farm lands in order to develop sheep pastures for the burgeoning wool industry (*see* Erasmus, 1509).

Education of a Christian Prince (Institutio Principis Christiani) by Erasmus is published.

Hampton Court Palace is completed in Middlesex for England's Cardinal Wolsey. The 40-year-old Thomas Wolsey was made archbiship of York last year and has just been elevated to cardinal.

The Vatican appoints the painter Raphael chief architect of St. Peter's. He succeeds the late Bramante who died last year at age 70 (*see* 1506).

1516 The Hapsburg dynasty that will rule Spain until 1700 is founded February 23 upon the death at age 63 of Ferdinand V of Castile and Leon (Ferdinand II of Aragon). Ferdinand's 16-year-old grandson, a student in Flanders, succeeds as Carlos I of Spain, uniting Catalonia and Valencia with the kingdoms of Ferdinand and beginning a 40-year reign.

The Concordat of Bologna between France's François I and Pope Leo X (Giovanni de' Medici) rescinds the Pragmatic Sanction of 1438 and strengthens French royal power. It gives the French king freedom to choose bishops and abbots, and it removes the principle of the 1431–1449 Council of Basel that made the pope subordinate to an ecumenical council.

Bohemia's Ladislas II dies at age 60 after a weak reign of 45 years as king of Bohemia and 26 as king of Hungary as well. He is succeeded by his 10-year-old son Louis who will reign for 10 years as king of both countries.

The Battle of Marjdabik north of Aleppo August 24 gives the Ottoman sultan Selim a victory over the Mamelukes who consider artillery a dishonorable weapon. Selim takes Aleppo with his cannon, he enters Damascus September 26, he conquers Persia, and he moves on to Cairo (*see* 1517).

De Rebus Oceanicus et Novo Orbe by Italian historian and royal chronicler Peter Martyr (Pietro Martire d'Anghiera), 59, is the first published account of the discovery of America in 1492.

The Castilian regent Jiminez forbids importation of slaves into Spanish colonies, but Carlos I in Flanders (above) grants his courtiers licenses to import slaves into Spanish colonial islands.

A smallpox epidemic sweeps across Yucatán.

Painting *Baldassare Castiglione* by Raphael (*see* 1528); *The Tribute Money* by Titian.

Theater *The Ship of Hell (Auto de la Barca do Inferno)* by Gil Vicente; *Magnyfycence* by John Skelton is an English morality play.

The first sugar grown in the New World to reach Europe is presented to Spain's Carlos I (above) by Hispaniola's inspector of gold mines who gives the king six loaves.

Wheat, oats, and bananas are introduced into the Santo Domingo colony on Hispaniola by Spanish missionary Fra Tomas de Berlanga.

Maize is planted in China by the Portuguese.

1517 Reformation of the Catholic Church begins October 31 at Wittenberg, 60 miles southwest of Berlin, on the Elbe. Augustinian monk Martin Luther, 34, nails 95 theses to the door of the Wittenberg Cathedral and challenges the excesses and abuses of the Roman Church, notably the sale of indulgences. Luther's action begins a long period of religious and civil unrest in Europe.

Middle German working people and small merchants rally to Luther's cause in protest against the monopolies of the Fuggers and other papal bankers who are raising prices and sending German gold to Rome.

The Church's age-old prohibition against usury has been overturned by the Fifth Lateran (18th ecumenical) Council which ends 5 years of deliberations. Need for the change has been demonstrated by the Franciscan order which has set up pawnshops for the poor and has discovered that the shops are not viable unless some charge can be made for the loans extended. The growth of commerce, with its need for capital, has been making the Church's opposition to charging interest on loans quite untenable, but the Church's new position hurts Europe's Jews and Italians who have had a monopoly on moneylending.

Cairo is sacked by the Ottoman Turks January 22, the sherif of Mecca surrenders to the conquering sultan Selim, and the caliph Mutawakkil is sent to Constantinople as Selim secures control of the holy places of Arabia. But Selim leaves Egypt under the rule of the Mameluke beys who have administered the country's government since 1250.

Evil May Day riots at London are suppressed and 60 rioters are hanged on orders from Cardinal Wolsey.

A monopoly in the African slave trade is granted to Florentine merchants by the archduke Charles.

Enslavement of Indians in the New World is protested by the Spanish priest Bartolomeo de Las Casas, 43. Originally a Spanish planter in Hispaniola, Las Casas has been the first man to be ordained in the Western Hemisphere, he has turned his efforts to serve the interests of the oppressed natives, and he has voyaged back to Spain to plead the case of the Indians to Carlos I (*see* 1542).

Traces of a Mayan civilization in Yucatán are found by Spanish explorer Francisco Fernandez de Cordoba who has sailed westward from Cuba (*see* 1480).

Poetry *The Tunnynge of Elynour Rummyng* by John Skelton is a comic poem about tavern life.

Painting *The Raising of Lazarus* by Sebastiano del Piombo; *Lo Spasimo* by Raphael; *Erasmus* by Quentin Massys; Fra Bartolommeo dies at Florence October 31 at age 42.

1517 (cont.) Seville Cathedral is completed after 115 years of construction.

1518 Martin Luther's Reformation gains the support of Swiss clergyman Huldreich Zwingli, 34, at Zurich who persuades the city council to forbid entrance to the Franciscan monk Bernardin Samson despite Samson's commission to sell indulgences. Zwingli becomes priest at the Great Minster of Zurich.

A third major epidemic of the sweating sickness spreads over England with more severity than the epidemic of 1507. The epidemic wipes out most of the population in some towns, many important figures succumb at Cambridge and Oxford, the disease reaches Calais, but it affects only the English there (*see* 1529).

A college of physicians is founded by Oxford physician-humanist Thomas Linacre, 58, with authority from Henry VIII.

Spanish colonists in Santo Domingo import more slave labor from Africa to perform the hard work of chopping cane in the colony's 28 sugar plantations (*see* 1501). The island's native population has dwindled as a result of disease and exploitation.

New Spain gets its name from Spanish explorer Juan de Grijalva, 29, who has been sent to follow up last year's discovery of Yucatán by the late Francisco de Cordoba.

Painting *The Assumption* by Titian whose first teacher Giovanni Bellini died 2 years ago at age 86; altarpiece for Florence's Church of San Michele Visdomini by Italian painter Jacopo da Pontormo (Jacopo Carrucci), 24.

Theater *The Ship of Purgatory* (*Auto de la Barca do Purgatorio*) by Gil Vicente.

Tobacco is introduced to Juan de Grijalva (above) by a native chief who (according to Spanish historian Fernandez de Oviedo) "gave the general and to each of the Spaniards . . . a little hollow tube, burning at one end, made in such a manner that after being lighted they burn themselves out without causing a flame, as do the incense sticks of Valencia. And they smelled a fragrant odor. . . . The Indians made signs to the Spaniards not to allow that smoke to be lost" (*see* 1492; 1531).

Forks are observed at a ducal banquet in Venice where French silk merchant Jacques Le Saige notes that "these seigneurs, when they want to eat, take the meat up with a silver fork" (*see* 1071; 1570).

New Spain (above) has an estimated 11 million inhabitants while old Spain has 4.5 million (*see* 1519; 1547).

1519 The Holy Roman Emperor Maximilian I dies January 12 at age 41 in Upper Austria, and Spain's Carlos I is elected emperor as Charles V after some electors are bribed by the Fuggers and by other merchants of Augsburg. The election plunges Europe into political turmoil that will culminate in war.

Spanish adventurer Hernando Cortez, 34, sails from Cuba to conquer New Spain (*see* 1518). The Cortez expedition includes 500 Spaniards, nearly 300 Indians, and 16 horses—10 stallions, five mares, and a foal.

Cortez (above) moves up from the coast at Veracruz. Helped by an Aztec legend that the bearded white god Quetzalcoatl will return, Cortez is joined by an allied army of Totonacs, he enlists another army of Tlaxcalans, he vanquishes the Cholulans, he takes Montezuma II prisoner, and by year's end he is ruling the country through Montezuma (*see* 1502).

Portuguese navigator Ferdinand Magellan leaves Seville August 10 with a fleet of five ships, he remains at the mouth of the Guadalquivir for more than 5 weeks, and he puts to sea September 20 in quest of spices from the Orient with financial support from an Antwerp banker.

The dollar has its origin in the "thaler" minted in Bohemia at Joachimsthal where the large coin is called the Joachimsthaler.

Painting *Christopher Columbus* by Sebastiano del Piombo. Leonardo da Vinci dies May 2 at age 67 in Amboise castle on the Loire.

Theater *The Ship of Heaven* (*Auto de la Barca de la Gloria*) by Gil Vicente.

Hernando Cortez (above) hears of bearded men in Mayan towns and pays a ransom to secure the release of Geronimo de Aguilar who was shipwrecked off the coast of Yucatán in 1511 and who describes the foods he has eaten as a slave to a Mayan chief. The foods include *cacao* (chocolate), *cacahuates* (peanuts), *camotes* (sweet potatoes), and *uahs* (tortillas). Cortez also discovers turkeys, tomatoes, vanilla, papaya, and beans which the Mayans call *avacotl*, a word the Spanish will turn into *habicuela* and the French into *haricot* (*see* 1528).

1520 Denmark's Christian II invades Sweden with a large army of French, German, and Scottish mercenaries. He has persuaded Pope Leo X to excommunicate Sten Sture the Younger and to place Sweden under an interdict, he defeats Sture at Bogesund, Sture sustains a mortal wound January 19 at the Battle of Tiveden, and Christian advances without opposition on Uppsala where the Swedish Riksraad has assembled. The Swedish senators agree to accept Christian as king provided that he rule according to Swedish laws and customs and that he rule without recriminations. The king signs a convention to this effect March 31, but Sture's widow, Dame Christina Gyllenstjerna, at Stockholm has rallied the peasantry to defeat the Danish invaders at Balundsas March 19. The bloody Battle of Uppsala April 6 (Good Friday) gives Christian a narrow victory over the Swedish patriots, the Danish fleet arrives in May, Christian lays siege to Stockholm, and Christina surrenders September 7 on the promise of a general amnesty. Christian is crowned hereditary king of Sweden at Stockholm's cathedral November 4, Danish soldiers seize some of the king's guests November 7. The archbishop Gustavus Trolle who crowned Christian charges the prisoners with heresy and violence against the church, and he presides over their trial. The bishops of Skara and Stragnas are beheaded in the public square at Stockholm at midnight, November 8, and the Danes kill 80 other Swedes in the ensuing bloodbath.

Christian II (above) has his men exhume the body of Sten Sture and burn it along with that of Sture's small child. He has Sten's widow Dame Christina and other Swedish noblewomen sent to Denmark as prisoners, and he suppresses opposition on the pretense of defending the church.

Victims of the massacre at Stockholm (above) have included the nobleman Erik Vasa, whose 24-year-old son Gustavus Eriksson hears about the massacre from a peasant while hunting near Lake Mälar. Gustavus escaped last year from the island fortress of Kalo on the east coast of Jutland where Christian II had treacherously held him hostage for 12 months. The peasant tells him that the king has put a price on his head, he rallies the yeomen of the vales, and he will begin next year to drive the Danes out of Sweden.

Last year's election of Spain's Carlos I as the Holy Roman Emperor Charles V provokes an uprising of the communeros, a group of cities led by Toledo's Juan Lopez de Padilla, 30. The communeros take exception to the king's leaving the country and using Spanish men and money for imperial purposes. They organize a Holy League (Santa Junta) at Avila in July but radical elements soon displace the aristocratic and bourgeois leadership (see 1521).

The Ottoman sultan Selim dies September 21 at age 53 after an 8-year reign in which he has annexed Syria and Egypt to augment his Persian conquests. His 24-year-old son begins a reign of 46 years in which he will add to his father's conquests and will be called Suleiman the Magnificent.

A new Spanish army of 1,400 men arrives in New Spain under the command of Panfilo de Narvaez to challenge Hernando Cortez, but Cortez surprises Narvaez near Veracruz and captures him. He will remain a prisoner for 2 years.

Ferdinand Magellan negotiates a stormy 38-day passage through the straits at the southernmost tip of South America, he sails into the South Sea, and renames it the Pacific Ocean (see 1513; 1519; 1521).

Smallpox takes a heavy toll at Veracruz (above). Introduced by a black seaman on a ship carrying the troops of Narvaez, the pox will spread until it kills half the population of New Spain.

England's Henry VIII and France's François I meet with 10,000 couriers for 3 weeks outside Calais on the Field of the Cloth of Gold. The banquets, tournaments, and spectacles of this vainglorious display will leave the French treasury crippled for 10 years.

German gunsmith August Kotter invents the rifle.

Appeal to the Christian Princes of the German Nation (An den Christlichen Adel deutscher Nation) by Martin Luther has a first printing of 4,000 copies and sells out in a week.

Painting *The Madonna with Saints Aloysius and Francis* by Titian. Raphael dies April 6 at age 36, leaving his *Transfiguration* incomplete.

Venice completes a new wing to the doge's palace to replace a structure destroyed by fire in 1483.

The Prospect of Whitby is mentioned for the first time in writing. The London pub will be the scene of cockfights, prize fights, and press gang recruitment for the Royal Navy.

1521 "Here I stand," says Martin Luther before the Diet of Worms April 18. "I can't do anything else. God help me! Amen." (Hier stehe ich! Ich kann nicht anders. Gott helfe mir! Amen). Luther has come to Worms under a safe-conduct pass after the ban of the empire has been pronounced against him, Charles V's Diet orders him to recant, he refuses, and the German princes back him in starting an evangelical movement that will bring turmoil to much of Europe (see 1517).

Frederick the Wise of Saxony takes Martin Luther to Wartburg and protects him as he translates the bible in defiance of the Edict of Worms which prohibits all new doctrines (see Peasants' War, 1524).

Assertion of the Seven Sacraments by England's young Henry VIII is a reply to Luther. Pope Leo X gives Henry the title Defender of the Faith.

Belgrade falls to the forces of the Ottoman sultan Suleiman who begins moving into Hungary (see Rhodes, 1522).

The Battle of Villalar April 23 gives the Holy Roman Emperor Charles V a victory over the insurgent communeros and ends the last Spanish resistance to absolutism.

French support of the communeros (above) and French designs on Navarre precipitate a war between France and Spain that will last for 8 years. The war begins with the French taking Pamplona and Fantarabia.

The colossal Central American city of Tenochtitlan (Mexico City) falls to Hernando Cortez August 13 after an 85-day battle in which the emperor Montezuma II has been killed (see 1519). Cortez sees bison in the menagerie of Montezuma.

Portugal's Manoel I dies in December at age 52 after a 26-year reign marked by great Portuguese explorations and discoveries. He is succeeded by his 19-year-old son who will reign until 1557 as João III.

San Juan, Puerto Rico, is founded by Spanish conquistadors who will pave the city's streets with stones brought as ballast in ships from Spain (see 1508).

1521 (cont.) Ferdinand Magellan in the Pacific claims islands that will be called the Marianas in 1668. Magellan calls them Islas de los Ladrones (Islands of Thieves) because the natives steal articles from his ships.

Ferdinand Magellan discovers the Philippine Islands March 15 but is killed April 25 in Cebu by the chief Lapu-lapu in a skirmish with the natives. Only three of Magellan's original five ships have made the Pacific crossing, the other two have been lost, his men have come close to starvation, but survivors of the Cebu encounter sail on in two remaining ships to the Moluccas, or Spice Islands (*see* 1522; 1564).

Painting *The Marriage of St. Catherine* by the Italian painter Il Parmigianino (Girolamo Francesco Maria Mazzola), 18, who has been raised by two painter uncles; mythological frescoes by Jacopo da Pontormo for the Medici villa at Poggio a Caiano.

France's Château de Chenonceaux is completed in the Loire valley after 8 years of construction for the royal tax collector Thomas Bohier whose handsome castle will soon be taken over by François I (*see* 1547).

1522 The Holy Roman Emperor Charles V expels French forces from Milan with help from Florence, Mantua, and the papacy. England's Henry VIII joins the war against France.

Vizirs of the Ottoman sultan Suleiman capture the island of Rhodes from the Knights of St. John who have held Rhodes since 1306 and who put up a valiant defense. Charles V will resettle the Knights on Malta (*see* 1530; Battle of Mohacs, 1526).

The Ming emperor Chia Ching who will reign until 1566 comes to power and expels the Portuguese for acts of piracy by Simão d'Andrade and others.

Ferdinand Magellan's lieutenant Sebastian del Cano returns to Seville aboard the *Vittoria* with 18 surviving sailors of the Magellan expedition and with a cargo of valuable spices that more than pays for the expedition that has accomplished the first circumnavigation of the world.

Hispaniola has a large-scale slave rebellion that will be followed in the next 31 years by at least 10 such uprisings in the Spanish possessions.

Martin Luther returns to Wittenberg and introduces public worship with the liturgy in German. The Holy Roman Emperor Charles V has been distracted by his war with France (above) and the German knights Franz von Sickingen, 41, and Ulrich von Hutten, 33, help spread the Reformation, but Sickingen fails in a siege of Trier, he falls in battle after being besieged at Landstuhl, Hutten is forced to flee to the island of Ufnau in the Zurichsee, and he will die there next year after a bitter dispute with Desiderius Erasmus.

Huldreich Zwingli at Zurich condemns celibacy and Lenten fasting. He condemned the hiring of mercenaries last year, he calls on the bishop of Constance to stop enduring the scandal of harlotry and to permit priests to marry (or at least to wink at their marriages), and he will himself marry in the cathedral at Zurich in 1524.

Poetry *Colin Clout* and *Why Come Ye Nat to Courte?* by John Skelton are clerical satires directed against the rising power of Cardinal Wolsey.

Painting *The Resurrection Altar* by Titian.

1523 England's Henry VIII tries to force a grant of funds from Parliament and provokes a rebellion that ends only when the king abandons his demand.

Denmark's Christian II is deposed by the nobility after a cruel 10-year reign. He is succeeded in January by the 52-year-old duke of Holstein who will reign until 1533 as Frederick I.

The house of Vasa that will rule Sweden until 1665 and will make it the strongest power in the Baltic comes to the throne in the person of Gustavus Eriksson Vasa, now 27, who has led Swedish resistance to the Danes. He is crowned June 6 and will reign until 1560 as Gustavus I.

Chinese authorities expel Portuguese settlers.

Mennonite religious views have their origin at Zurich where a small community leaves the state church to pursue a form of Christianity that emphasizes the sanctity of human life and of man's word, acknowledges no authority outside the bible and the enlightened conscience, limits baptism to true believers, and denies the Christian character of the state church and of civil authorities while recognizing a duty to obey civil laws (*see* Simons, 1536).

Pope Adrian VI dies September 14 at age 64 after 20 months as pope. He is succeeded by Giulio de' Medici, as Clement VII, who is the first of a line of Italian popes unbroken until 1978.

Painting *Erasmus* by German painter-engraver Hans Holbein the Younger, 25, who has delighted the Dutch humanist with marginal drawings for his *Praise of Folly* (*see* 1509). Gerard David dies at Bruges August 13; Lucca Signorelli dies at Cortina October 16.

Turkeys from New Spain are introduced into Spain and will soon appear in England where they will get their name from the "turkey merchants" of the eastern Mediterranean who cannot pronounce the Mayan name uexolotl any better than can the English (*see* Cortez, 1519).

Conquistadors in Cuba recognize the possibilities of cultivating sugar there for the first time.

Maize grows in Crete and in the Philippines where Magellan's men introduced the plant 2 years ago.

1524 A Peasant's War breaks out in the German states as followers of Martin Luther battle Catholics in a rising against the landed nobility. "Heretical" books are burned in the marketplace at Mainz, and the country is plunged into an irreligious orgy of pillaging and slaughter (*see* 1519; 1526).

Ferdinand of Austria makes an alliance with the two dukes of Bavaria and with the bishop of southern Germany in a move to check religious changes taken at the instigation of the papal legate Lorenzo Campeggio.

The Swiss cantons of Lucerne, Uri, Schwyz, Unterwalden, and Zug join against Zurich and against the Reformation movement.

French forces invade Italy and retake Milan October 29 (but see 1525).

Aden becomes a tributary of Portugal.

Vasco da Gama returns to India as Portuguese viceroy (see 1499; Mogul dynasty, 1526).

Spanish forces in New Spain disperse the main body of the Quiche army outside the city of Xelaju February 20. Chief Tecum Uman descends from his golden litter and kills the horse of Pedro de Alvarado, a lieutenant of Hernando Cortez, in the belief that man and horse are one, Alvarado runs the chief through with his sword, and panic spreads through the Quiche warriors.

Guatemala City is founded by Pedro de Alvarado (above).

Francisco Pizarro proposes an expedition to "Piru." A 54-year-old Spanish officer who crossed the Isthmus of Panama with Balboa in 1513, Pizarro tells the governor of Panama about a land to the South where the people drink from golden vessels and have animals (llamas) that are half sheep, half camel (see 1525).

Giovanni da Verrazano explores the North American coast. A 39-year-old Italian navigator sailing the 100-ton *Dauphine* for the French, Verrazano discovers a "beautiful" harbor in April and he gives the name Angoulême to the island that will later be called Manhattan (see Hudson, 1609).

A lunar observatory to produce a standard time that may aid navigators to determine longitude is proposed by Peter Bennewitz, professor of mathematics, at Ingolstadt and a friend of the emperor Charles V. Observation of the moon's position among the fixed stars may produce such a standard time, says Bennewitz (see Frisius, 1530).

Painting *Ascension of Christ* by the Italian painter Correggio (Antonio Allegri), 30, is completed as a fresco on the cupola of the Benedictine church of San Giovanni at Parma; Il Parmigianino moves to Rome and presents as his credentials to Pope Clement VII a self-portrait reflected in a convex mirror.

1525 The Battle of Pavia February 24 gives Spanish and German forces a victory over France's François I and his Swiss mercenaries. The Spanish take François back to Madrid as a prisoner and he writes to his mother (Anne of Brittany), "There is nothing left to me but honor, and my life, which is saved."

The Grand Master of the Teutonic Knights Albert, 35, makes Prussia a secular duchy of Brandenburg with himself as duke. Prussia remains a fief of Poland whose Sigismund I rules without interference from the Teutonic Order.

Peru's 11th Inca king Huayana Capac dies at Quito and is succeeded by his son Huascar who rules over a nation of 12 million which has no written language but which has developed a complex, orderly society. Each head of family is allowed enough land to grow food sufficient to his needs and must also help cultivate common lands to support the Inca Huascar, his court, his brother Atahualpa at Quito, the priesthood, the bureaucrats, and the engineers who build fiber suspension bridges, stone roads, and irrigation systems. Old people, the sick, and orphaned children receive shares of the common crop, and surpluses are stored in state warehouses against crop failures.

Francisco Pizarro sails from Panama November 1 in two caravels with 112 men and a few natives to explore "Piru" (above) whose natives call it Twwantinsuyu (The Four Corners of the World) (see 1526).

Santa Marta is founded by Spanish conquistador Rodrigo de Bastidas, 65. It is the first settlement in the territory that will become New Granada.

German Anabaptist Thomas Münzer, 35, overthrows the town government at Mühlhausen and sets up a communistic theocracy. He collects a peasant army and establishes a camp at Frankenhausen, but Philip, landgrave of Hesse, disperses Münzer's army May 15, seizes Münzer, and has him executed May 27 at Mühlhausen.

Jakob Fugger II dies at age 66 after a life that has seen the Fugger family become Europe's great financial power and has seen Antwerp become the world's leading port, profiting from the wealth of the Indies and of the New World. The merchants of Augsburg have rejected a scheme devised by Fugger to fix the price of bread at a permanently low level.

Theater *Don Duardas* by Gil Vicente.

The elector of Saxony, who supported Martin Luther, read a protest at the Diet of Speyer. Hence the word "Protestant."

1525 (cont.) The Fuggerei left by Jakob Fugger II at Augsburg consists of 106 dwellings which Jakob the Rich has built for rental at low rates to the poor of the city. He leaves it as a legacy to the people.

Chili (or chile) peppers and cayenne from the Americas are introduced by the Portuguese into India where they will become the ingredients of the hottest curries.

1526 Congolese king Mbemba Nzinga protests to Portugal's Joao III that Portuguese merchants are "taking every day our natives, sons of the land and sons of our noblemen and our vassals and our relatives" in exchange for goods from Europe and are selling his people as slaves to Brazilian sugar planters (*see* 1510). The king is a convert to Christianity and he says the kidnappers are depopulating his country.

The Mogul Empire that will rule India until 1761 is founded by the robber baron Babar, 43-year-old descendant of the 14th century Prince of Destruction Tamerlane who at age 11 succeeded his father as head of a small principality to the north but who 10 years later was forced to flee across the Hindu Kush to Kabul. Invited by a faction of warring Moslem rulers to help them, Babar proceeded to make himself master of Lahore as compensation for the loss of Ferghana and Samarkand, and his decisive victory April 19 at the Battle of Panipat over Ibrahim shah Lodi makes him master also of Delhi and Agra.

Hungary's Louis II is killed at age 20 in the Battle of Mohacs August 29 and 30, and his 20,000 poorly disciplined knights and peasants are defeated as the Turkish forces of Suleiman the Magnificent extend their European conquests from Belgrade.

Hungary's crown goes to Transylvanian governor John Zapolya, 39, who served as regent during the minority of the late Louis and who is elected king to begin a 13-year reign.

Bohemia's crown goes to Louis's brother-in-law Ferdinand, brother of the emperor Charles V, who is elected king at age 23 to begin a reign that will continue until his death in 1564.

The Peasants' War that began 2 years ago in the German states ends after the annihilation of some 150,000 peasants.

The Teutonic Knights founded in 1198 break with the Church of Rome and become Lutherans, beginning a long association between Lutheranism and the landholding aristocracy that controls the vast grain estates of East Prussia.

Francisco Pizarro encounters rough seas en route to Peru and makes a landing at what will be called Port of Famine (*see* 1525). Pizarro's freshwater barrels have breached, his food stores have spoiled, his party is reduced to a daily ration of two ears of maize per man, the only food ashore is shellfish, wild berries, and an occasional animal caught by a native servant with a snare, and 20 men die of hunger before a caravel sent back for food returns with flour and fresh meat.

Pizarro returns to Panama for reinforcements after being wounded in a skirmish with hostile natives, but on a second expedition he explores the Gulf of Guayaquil and secures some gold from natives who greet him as Viracocha. They believe him to be the fulfillment of a legend that the 14th century Inca king Viracocha Inca will return (*see* 1531).

The University of Granada has its beginnings in southern Spain.

The Tyndale Bible published in secret at Worms is an English translation of the New Testament by English clergyman William Tyndale, 34, who has visited Martin Luther at Wittenberg. Tyndale has fled Cologne after the dean of Frankfurt discovered printers at work on the bible, persuaded the senate of Cologne to forbid further printing, and warned Henry VIII and Cardinal Wolsey to watch English ports for Tyndale. The archbishop of Canterbury William Warham buys up copies of the Tyndale Bible on the Continent and burns them, but some copies are smuggled into England where bishops suppress most of them (*see* 1536).

Painting *Madonna of Burgomaster Meyer* by Hans Holbein who visits Sir Thomas More in England with a letter of introduction from Erasmus; *The Last Judgment* by Lucas van Leyden; *The Four Apostles* by Albrecht Dürer is Dürer's last great religious painting (Dürer gives it to the city of Nuremberg); *Pesaro Madonna* by Titian.

France's Château de Chantilly is completed in Renaissance style in Ile-de-France by the Montmorency family that will add a Petit Château in 1560.

1527 The Renaissance greatness of Rome ends May 6 in a terrible sack of the city by Spanish and German mercenaries in the pay of the Holy Roman Emperor Charles V. The invaders besiege Pope Clement VII in the Castel San Angelo and take him prisoner.

A second war between Charles V and France's François I begins after François declares that all the conditions of last year's Peace of Madrid were extorted and that the treaty is therefore void.

England's Henry VIII appeals to Rome for permission to divorce Catherine of Aragon so that he may marry his young mistress Anne Boleyn (*see* 1533).

The Moslem Somali chief Ahmed Gran invades Ethiopia with firearms that take a deadly toll. The negus appeals for Portuguese aid (*see* 1541).

Hernando Cortez completes his conquest of New Spain.

England's Sir Hugh Willoughby searches for a northeast passage to Cathay and the Spice Islands, but Henry VIII is more intent on building the English navy to protect his merchant trade with nearby coastal ports than with financing explorations.

English trade with Russia begins.

Chemotherapy and the modern school of medical thinking are founded at the University of Basel by physician Theophrastus von Hohenheim, 34, whose critics call him Theophrastus Bombastus. Salt, sulfur, and mercury are the three prime "elements" from which all things are made, says Theophrastus, and he burns Greek medical books to promote his "new medicine" (see Paracelsus, 1530).

Painting *The Vision of St. Jerome* by Parmigianino who escapes to Bologna after the sack of Rome (above); *The Worship of the Golden Calf* and *Moses Striking Water from the Rock* by Lucas van Leyden.

Avocados, papayas, tomatoes, chocolate, vanilla, and turkeys are carried back to Spain by the conquistadors who have found natives of New Spain eating such foods in addition to algae, agave worms (maguey slugs), winged ants, tadpoles, water flies, larvae of various insects, white worms, and iguana (see 1528; tomato, 1543).

1528 The Reformation gains acceptance in Bern and Basel whose lead is followed by three other cantons, but the rural cantons of Lucerne, Uri, Schwyz, Unterwalden, Fribourg, Solothurn, and Zug remain staunchly Catholic (see 1531).

Austrian evangelist Jacob Hutter founds a "community of love" whose Austrian, German, and Swiss members share everything communally, but the Hutterites will seek refuge in Russia (see 1536).

Augsburg banker Bartholomäus Welser obtains rights to conquer and colonize most of northeastern South America as an hereditary fief. Welser has made a fortune trading in sugar, spices, and African slaves, and he has helped the emperor Charles V finance some Spanish expeditions to the New World (see 1527; 1546).

Hernando Cortez is recalled to Spain and returns with foods never before seen in Europe (see below).

Haricot beans brought back to Spain by Hernando Cortez will quickly gain popularity as a substitute for peas and for fava beans (*Vicia faba*), the only beans known to Europe until now. Many dare not eat fava beans lest they be stricken with favism, an hereditary disease whose victims lack the red blood cell enzyme needed to break down the peptide glutathione in the beans into its usable amino acids (the peptide ruptures blood cells and produces hemolytic anemia).

A typhus epidemic sweeps the Italian states and kills an estimated 21,000 in July. A French army laying siege to Naples is felled by the disease and by late August only 4,000 of the original 25,000-man army remains (see below).

The prince of Orange Philibert de Chalon, 26, is besieged for 6 weeks in Naples and writes June 14 to Charles V, "For ten days we have been living on bread and water; meat and wine have failed us, and your troops have not been paid for a long time. . . . Neither they nor I can accomplish the impossible, and when another month has passed, we will be near

the end," but the typhus epidemic forces the French to lift the siege at the end of August and the prince of Orange leads his cavalry out of the city to cut down the retreating forces of François I and Clement VII.

The Courtier (*Il Cortegiano*) by Venetian diplomat Baldassare Castiglione, 50, bishop of Avila in Spain, is a dialogue on ideal courtly life and comprises a guide to polite manners in the Spanish court.

Painting *Nicholas Kratzer* by Hans Holbein who returns to Basel after his visit with Sir Thomas More in England (religious warfare will make Holbein's life in Basel so unpleasant that he will return to England in 1532 and will remain there for most of his life); *The Artist's Family* by Hans Holbein; *Madonna of St. Jerome* (*Il Giorno*) by Correggio; *The Visitation* by Jacopo da Pontormo. Albrecht Dürer dies at Nuremberg April 6 at age 56.

Wheat is introduced into New Spain by Spanish colonists (see Mexico, 1941).

Sweet potatoes, turkeys, cocoa, and vanilla as well as haricot beans (above) are introduced to Spain by Hernando Cortez who presents some of the beans to Pope Clement VII (Giulio de' Medici).

1529 Protestantism gets its name as followers of Martin Luther protest a ruling by the Diet of Speyer forbidding the teaching of Luther's ideas in Catholic states while letting Catholics teach in Lutheran states.

The Ottoman Empire reaches the height of its imperial expansion, but the Turks fail in their siege of Vienna and settle in Buda across from Pest on the left bank of the Danube (see 1526).

The Holy Roman Emperor Charles V cedes Spanish rights in the spice islands to Portugal for 250,000 ducats.

Francisco Pizarro returns to Spain to claim the territory he has explored in Peru (see 1526). Charles V names Pizarro governor for life and captain-general of New Castile with a salary of 725,000 maravedis and nearly all the prerogatives of a viceroy, and he sends Pizarro back to Peru with 200 men and 27 horses in a fleet of three ships (see 1531).

South American territories of New Granada that will later be called Venezuela and Colombia are colonized by the Welsers of Augsburg whose agents explore the Andes and the valley of the Orinoco River (see 1528; Felderman, 1539).

London has a severe epidemic of the sweating sickness (last epidemic in 1518) and the disease spreads within 2 months to Hamburg, Lübeck, and Bremen, it reaches Mecklenburg a month later in August, it reaches Königsberg and Danzig in September, and it then reaches Göttingen where it rages so fiercely that one grave is obliged to serve for eight corpses. The epidemic moves on to Marburg where it interrupts the Council of the Reformation, to Augsburg, to Vienna where it has some influence in raising the Turkish siege (above), and to Switzerland, but the

1529 (cont.) sweating sickness somehow spares the French (*see* 1551).

Painting *The Madonna with St. Margaret and Other Saints* by Parmigianino.

Hymns "A Mighty Fortress Is Our God!" by Martin Luther; "Away in a Manger" by Martin Luther.

Paprika (capsicums) from the New World are planted by the Turks at Buda (above) (*see* 1928).

Vast fields of maize from America are grown in Turkey whence the grain will come to England as "turkey corn."

Sweet oranges from the Orient are introduced into Europe by Portuguese caravels and will forever be called portugals in the Balkans, in parts of Italy, and in the Middle East (*see* Chinese orange, 1635).

1530 The potato that will provide Europe with a cheap source of food and will thus spur population growth is discovered in the South American Andes by Spanish conquistador Jiminez de Quesada, 30, who finds the natives eating only the largest of the tubers, which they call papas, and planting the smallest, thus steadily reducing the size of the tubers they harvest. Soaked in water, the potatoes are allowed to freeze in the cold air of the altiplano, are dried in the sun, and are walked over with bare feet until their skins come off, a process that turns the potatoes hard and black (they must be soaked again for a few days before they can be eaten). The Spanish mistake the tubers for a kind of truffle since they are only about the size and shape of peanuts, and call them tartuffo, which will persist with variations as the word for potato in parts of Europe (*see* 1539).

Huascar's half-brother Atahualpa moves south from Quito with an army of 30,000 and destroys the town of Tumebanba. Huascar's army of 10,000 falls back leaving suspension bridges over the Apurimac River intact and Atahualpa crosses the Apurimac, his generals take Huascar prisoner, and Atahualpa rests at Cajamarca (*see* 1525; 1531).

Cortez returns to New Spain.

Spain's Carlos I is crowned Charles V of the Holy Roman Empire and king of Italy February 23 at Bologna by Pope Clement VII (Giulio de' Medici). It is the last coronation of a German emperor by any pope.

The Sovereign Military Hospitaller Order of Saint John founded in 1113 settles in Malta and will hereafter be called the Knights of Malta (*see* 1522; 1565).

Martin Luther's collaborator Melanchthon (Philipp Schwarzert Melanchthon), 33, tries to reconcile the differences between Protestantism and the Roman church at the brilliant diet at Augsburg presided over by Charles V (above). The diet orders the abolition of all innovations.

Die Grosse Wundartznei is published by Swiss alchemist-physician Paracelsus who assumes that name to put himself above the Roman physician of just 1500 years ago (*see* 1527). The Paracelsus book is one of many works describing the doctrine of "signatures" and other specious medical ideas, but it does establish sound principles that the life processes are based on chemical processes, that different diseases demand different treatments (mercury is a specific for syphilis, for example).

Syphilis sive Morbus Gallicus by Italian physician Girolamo Fracastoro, 47, gives a name to the disease first observed in 1495.

German mathematician Gemma Frisius suggests that accurate mechanical clocks be set to the local time of a prime meridian to produce a standard time for the measurement of longitude as an aid to navigation. Frisius is professor of mathematics at Louvain and cosmographer royal to Charles V (above) (*see* Bennewitz, 1524; Greenwich Observatory, 1676).

Confessio Augustana by Philipp Melanchthon (above) is published at Wittenberg. A disciple of Desiderius Erasmus, Melanchthon 9 years ago gave Lutheranism a dogmatic basis in his *Loci Communes*.

Poetry *Das Schlaraffenland* by Nuremberg cobbler-poet-dramatist Hans Sachs, 36, whose humorous anecdotes told in doggerel verse are called Schwänke. Their satirical good humor does not obscure their purpose of making moral points.

Painting *Adoration of the Shepherd* by Correggio; *Assumption of the Virgin* (*La Notte*) by Correggio who began the nativity scene 8 years ago at Reggio for Alberto Pratoneris; *Man in a Red Cap* by Titian.

1531 The Schmalkaldic League organized February 6 allies the majority of Europe's Protestant princes and imperial cities against the Holy Roman Emperor Charles V who has had his 27-year-old brother Ferdinand elected king of the Romans (meaning German king) at Cologne in January. The elector of Saxony leads the opposition to Ferdinand.

The Catholic cantons attack Zurich and defeat the Protestants October 11 in the Battle of Kappel. Huldreich Zwingli is killed in the fighting.

Atahualpa in the South American altiplano has his half-brother Huascar put to death and becomes the Inca himself (*see* 1530; 1532).

Francisco Pizarro and his brothers Gonzalo and Hernando leave Panama for Peru with 300 men and 100 horses (*see* 1529). Reinforcements under the command of Hernando de Soto, 31, join the expeditionary force and it moves up into the Cordilleras with two artillery pieces, encountering virtually no opposition (*see* 1526; 1532).

Sao Vicente is founded in Brazil by Portuguese conquistador Martin Affonso de Souza. New settlers extend Portugal's Brazilian holdings.

Sugar becomes as important as gold in the Spanish and Portuguese colonial economies.

The bourse that opens at Antwerp is the forerunner of all mercantile exchanges (*see* Fugger, 1535).

German sculptor Tilman Riemenschneider dies at Wurzburg July 8 at age 71.

Spain's West Indian colonists cultivate tobacco on a commercial scale (*see* 1518; 1560).

An earthquake shatters Lisbon January 26 killing 30,000.

1532 The religious peace of Nuremberg permits Protestants free exercise of their religion until the meeting of a new council to be summoned within a year.

The Ottoman forces of Suleiman II invade Hungary but Carinthia and Croatia repel Ottoman attacks.

Brittany's Duchess Anne signs the Treaty of Plessis-Mace with France's François I who adds the duchy to his realm (final absorption of Brittany into France will come in 1547).

The Inca Atahualpa visits the Spanish camp of Francisco Pizarro who has ascended the Andes. Pizarro seizes the Inca November 16, he holds him for ransom, and the absence of Atahualpa paralyzes the machinery of Inca government (*see* 1533).

Cartagena is founded by Pedro Herdia who acts by authority of the Holy Roman Emperor Charles V (Spain's Carlos I).

Poetry *Orlando Furioso* by Lodovico Ariosto, 58.

Painting *Charles V* by Titian; *Madonna of St. George* (*Il Giorno*) by Correggio; *Martin Luther* and *Philipp Melanchthon* by Lucas Cranach the Elder.

Russia's Church of the Ascension is completed at Kolomenskoie.

The Holy Roman Emperor Charles V establishes residence at Madrid and pays for improvements to the imperial palace with taxes on Caribbean sugar.

Horses introduced into Peru by Francisco Pizarro (above) will be seen within 3 years running wild on the pampas of eastern South America. Within 70 years the horses will be running in herds of uncountable size and will be revolutionizing daily life.

The almond pastry that will be called frangipani is invented by Rome's Count Cesare Frangipani.

1533 England's Henry VIII secretly marries Anne Boleyn, 26, who has been his mistress for the past 6 years. Thomas Cranmer, 43, has advised Henry that his 1509 marriage to Catherine of Aragon is null and void because she was previously married to Henry's late brother Arthur, prince of Wales, even though that marriage was never consummated. Henry has made Cranmer archbishop of Canterbury, and the archbishop performs the January 25 ceremony (*see* 1536).

Catherine de' Medici of Florence marries Henri of Valois, the 14-year-old duc d'Orléans who will become France's Henri II in 1547. Catherine is also 14, and her family has grown rich in the spice trade and by supplying alum to the textile industry.

Denmark's Frederick I dies at age 62 and is succeeded as king of Denmark and Norway by his 30-year-old son who will reign until 1559 as Christian III. Danish Catholics oppose Christian and hope to make his younger brother Hans king. Peasants and burghers hope to restore the imprisoned ex-king Christian II. Count Christopher of Oldenburg leads Lübeck in support of Christian II, but most of the nobility supports Christian III. He will crush the rebellion, will make peace with Lübeck, and will establish Lutheranism as the state religion.

The grand duke of Muscovy Basil III Ivanovich dies at age 54 and is succeeded by his 3-year-old son who will make himself czar of Muscovy and will rule until 1584 as Ivan IV ("the Terrible").

The Peruvian Empire ends August 29 with the strangulation of the last Inca, Atahualpa, who has professed himself a Christian and has received baptism. The conquistadors have accused the Inca of plotting to overthrow them, Francisco Pizarro has brought him to trial on charges of murder, sedition, and idolatry, he has been condemned to death despite the payment of a huge ransom for his release. Pizarro's advisers (with the exception of the priest Valerde) have protested the sentence to death by fire, calling it treacherous, so the Inca has died at the hands of a strangler.

The ransom paid for Atahualpa (above) has included gold and silver chairs, fountains, statues, plates, and ornaments made by generations of craftsmen—literally tons of gold and silver. The Spaniards melt it into ingots worth $4 million and distribute the bullion; most goes to Pizarro and his brothers, a little to the Church, and one-fifth to the Holy Roman Emperor Charles V (*see* 1532; 1534).

Hispaniola's slaves stage another uprising which the conquistadors suppress with great bloodshed.

The Algerian corsair Khair ed-Din, 67, evacuates Moors driven from Spain by the Inquisition. A former Greek, Khair ed-Din has commanded the pirates since the death of his brother at Spanish hands in 1518.

A new method of surveying that will replace the laborious method of pacing out distances is announced by Gemma Frisius (*see* 1530).

Fiction *Pantagruel* by French satirist François Rabelais, 39, is published under the pen name Alcofribis Nasier, an anagram of his real name. The bawdy novel will be a classic of racy humor.

Catherine de' Medici (above) introduces to France such vegetables as broccoli, globe artichokes, savoy cabbage, and haricot beans—fagioli given her by her brother Alessandro (*see* 1528; 1749).

The double boiler called by Italians the bagno maria after a legendary alchemist named Maria de Cleofa is introduced to the French court by Catherine de' Medici (above). The French will call it a bain marie.

Stuffed guinea hen is introduced by Catherine (above) and the dish will be known to the French as pintade à la Medicis. Catherine also introduces

1533 (cont.) truffles and starts the French digging enthusiastically for truffles of their own.

Pastries such as frangipani, macaroons, and Milan cakes introduced only recently to Florence will be introduced to France by Catherine (above) (*see* frangipani, 1532).

1534 England's Henry VIII breaks with the Church of Rome which has voided the annullment of his marriage to Catherine and has excommunicated him. The Reformation is established in England by the Act of Supremacy which appoints the king and his successors Protector and only Supreme Head of the Church and Clergy of England, but English dogma and liturgy will remain for a time essentially unchanged from Roman Catholic dogma and liturgy (*see* 1551).

Pope Clement VII dies September 25 after eating poisonous mushrooms. He has evaded Henry VIII's demand for nullification of the king's 1509 marriage to Catherine of Aragon, and he has refused to sanction Henry's marriage to Anne Boleyn who last year bore Henry's daughter Elizabeth.

Pope Clement (above) is succeeded by Alessandro Farnese, 66, who assumes the papacy as Paul III.

The Society of Jesus (Jesuit order) is founded by Basque ecclesiastic Ignatius Loyola (Inigo de Onez y Loyola), 43, and five associates (*see* 1540; 1541).

The Dutch Anabaptist fanatic John of Leyden (Jan Beuckelszoon) establishes a theocratic kingdom of Zion at Münster, saying that the world will soon end but that his followers will be spared. The 27-year-old former tailor, merchant, and innkeeper introduces communization of property and polygamy, he shocks the Catholic world with his hedonistic orgies, and he discredits the Reformation as Catholics charge that the antinomian anarchism of the Anabaptists illustrate the evil consequences of Martin Luther's doctrine of justification by faith alone (*see* 1521; 1534).

Tunis falls to Turkish forces led by the corsair Khair ed-Din (*see* 1533; 1535).

England's Henry VIII (above) will break up the nation's Catholic monasteries and will thereby upset the nation's land system. A merchant class will arise, more land will be enclosed, landlords will prevent peasants from grazing their cows and sheep on common land, the need for rural labor will decline, the enclosure system will lead to increased poverty and hunger, and the breakup of the monasteries will have other effects (*see* honey shortage, 1536; Thomas More, 1515).

Francisco Pizarro returns to Spain with the royal share (one-fifth) of the huge ransom paid for the Inca Atahualpa who was executed last year at Cajamarca.

Santiago de la Vega (Spanish town) is founded on the West Indian island of Jamaica.

French explorer Jacques Cartier, 43, sets out for the New World with two small ships and 36 men on orders from François I. Cartier sails into the Gulf of St. Lawrence, he plants the cross at Gaspé Bay, and he finds les sauvages growing beans.

Michelangelo moves from Florence to Rome after completing a tomb for the Medici family; Correggio dies at his native Correggio in Emilia March 5 at 45.

Chambord is completed in France's Loire Valley for François I. Built over a period of 15 years by a crew of 1,800 men, the great château replaces a 50-room hunting lodge with a fantasy of steeples, turrets, bell towers, and cupolas, it will be enlarged by the king's successors, and it will eventually have 440 rooms, more than 350 chimneys, 75 staircases, and nearly 14,000 acres of gardens and game reserves surrounded by a continuous 20-mile wall.

The Farnese Palace designed by Antonio Sangallo the Younger goes up in Rome for the new pope.

English fish consumption begins to decline as the king's break with Rome (above) ends church rules against eating meat on Fridays and during Lent. England will enact new fish laws to revive her coastal towns and to encourage the fishing industry from which the English navy draws recruits.

The first written description of a tomato appears in an Italian chronicle that calls the cherry-sized yellow fruit *pomo d'oro* (golden apple) (*see* 1519; 1596).

1535 Münster's Anabaptist John of Leyden beheads one of his four wives with his own hand in the marketplace in a fit of frenzy and justifies all his arbitrary actions on the basis of having received visions from heaven (*see* 1534). After 12 months of profligacy the besieged city falls to Francis of Waldeck June 24, and the leading Anabaptists are imprisoned (*see* 1536).

Sir Thomas More is beheaded July 6 at age 57 by order of England's Henry VIII for refusing to swear an oath of supremacy as required by last year's Act of Supremacy.

The principality of Wales is joined to England by the Act of Union (*see* Scotland, 1707).

Milan's Francesco Sforza II dies October 24 at age 43. He dies without issue, the main line of the Sforza dynasty is ended, and Milan becomes a suzerainty of the Holy Roman Emperor Charles V (*see* 1536).

Tunis falls to the forces of Charles V who has sent a fleet commanded by the Genoese admiral Andrea Doria. The pirate leader Khair ed-Din is defeated and Tunis is sacked (*see* 1534).

The viceroyalty of New Spain is established with Mexico City (Tenochtitlan) as its capital.

Lima, Peru, is founded by Francisco Pizarro who returns to Peru and resumes his exploitation of the Inca empire (*see* 1534; 1551).

Jacques Cartier returns to North America with 110 men and sails up the St. Lawrence River to what will later be the site of Montreal (*see* 1534). In November

Cartier's fleet is frozen solid at the mouth of the St. Charles River under the Rock of Quebec.

Fiction *Gargantua* by François Rabelais who has studied medicine at Montpelier and has practiced at Lyons. The new bawdy Rabelaisian novel is again published under the pen name Alcofribis Nasier. "There are . . . more old drunkards than old physicians" (I, xli).

Painting *Madonna del Collo Lungo* by Parmigianino.

Scurvy breaks out among the Hurons and then among the French under Jacques Cartier (above).

"All our beverages froze in their casks," Cartier will write, "and on board our ships, below hatches as on deck, lay four fingers' breadth of ice."

1536 John of Leyden and some of his more prominent Anabaptist followers are tortured with exquisite cruelty and are then executed in January in the marketplace of of Münster (the zealot's remains will swing in a cage from a church rafter until the 20th century). The Anabaptists are butchered wholesale and will hereafter lose their identity, but they will be confused by many with the Mennonites—followers of Friesland clergyman Menno Simons, 43, who leaves the Roman communion January 12 after several years of questioning infant baptism and getting inconsistent answers to his questions from Martin Luther and other Protestant leaders. Menno and his followers repudiate the doctrines of the Münster Anabaptists (*see* 1523; 1537).

The Anabaptist Jacob Hutter is arrested and burned at the stake on orders from the German king Ferdinand. Hutter has taught that his followers were God's elect and could only expect hardship and suffering (*see* 1528; 1874).

English clergyman William Tyndale of 1526 bible fame is condemned for heresy at Vilvorde Castle outside Brussels. He is strangled at the stake October 6.

Portugal installs the Inquisition and invites the Society of Jesus to send Jesuits into the country (*see* 1506).

Geneva adopts the Reformation as her ally Bern subdues Vaud, Chablais, Lausanne, and other territories of the duke of Savoy. A long struggle begins between Bern and Savoy (*see* Calvin, 1541).

England's Henry VIII has his wife Anne Boleyn beheaded May 19 on charges of adultery. On May 20 he marries Ann's lady-in-waiting Jane Seymour, 27, whose brother is duke of Somerset.

A Catholic rebellion in England gains support from the prelate Reginald Pole, 36, son of the countess of Salisbury. The rebellion is crushed, but Pole is created a cardinal by Pope Paul III who will dispatch him as an emissary to incite France's François I and the Holy Roman Emperor Charles V to send an expedition to depose Henry VIII.

A third war begins between Charles V and François I who has renewed claims to Milan following the death last year of Francesco Sforza. François makes a formal alliance in March with Suleiman the Magnificent after more than a decade of discussions between French and Ottoman emissaries, Suleiman advances on Hungary, and he sends fleets to ravage the coasts of Italy while French forces take Turin.

Portuguese mathematician Pedro Nunes, 44, describes errors in the plain charts used by seamen. Nunes will invent the nonius for graduating instruments, and his nonius will be improved and developed into the vernier (*see* 1631).

Lower California is discovered by Hernando Cortez (*see* 1530; 1540).

Spanish explorer Álvar Núñez Cabeza de Vaca, 46, reaches Mexico City (Tenochtitlan) after having been wrecked on a Texas coastal island in 1528. Captured by the natives and held captive for 2 years, Cabeza de Vaca has escaped, has made a long overland journey through the Southwest, and sails for Spain (*see* 1542).

The Practyce of Prelates by William Tyndale (above) is published in England. Tyndale lost favor with Henry VIII by criticizing the king's divorce from Catherine of Aragon

Jacques Cartier loses 25 men to scurvy in New France (*see* 1535). By mid-February, "out of the 110 men that we were, not ten were well enough to help the others, a thing pitiful to see." But although 50 Hurons in the area also die of scurvy, a Huron chief shows Cartier how to grind the bark of the common arborvitae *Thuja occidentalis,* boil the ground bark in water, drink the infusion every other day, and apply the residue as a poultice to swollen, blackened legs. Cartier digs up arborvitae saplings and transplants them in the royal garden at Fountainebleau upon his return with the Huron chief, the chief's two sons, three adult Hurons, two little girls, and two little boys (all of whom soon die). The Huron chief swears to François I that Saguenay is rich in cloves, nutmegs, and peppers and grows oranges and pomegranates.

England begins to suffer shortages of honey as monasteries which raised honey bees as a source of wax for votive candles are dissolved pursuant to the 1534 Act of Supremacy.

1537 Menno Simons preaches the Mennonite views of 1523 with modifications to some Anabaptists who have left the Münster faction (*see* 1536). Set apart to the eldership at Groningen in January, Menno repudiates the formation of a new religious sect, but he begins actively to advocate a faith that absolutely forbids oaths and the taking of life (and thus makes it impossible for a believer to be a magistrate or to serve in the army). He rejects terms such as Trinity which cannot be found in the bible, prohibits marriage with outsiders, but insists that his followers

The death of the Inca Atahualpa was the most infamous act of treachery committed by the Spanish conquistadors.

obey the law in all things not prohibited by the bible (*see* 1568; Amish, 1693).

Henry VIII's queen Jane Seymour dies October 24 after having given birth a few days earlier to a son who will become England's Edward VI in 1547.

Suleiman the Magnificent goes to war with Venice. He lays siege to Corfu with French aid and with help from the Algerian corsair Khair ed-Din who controls much of the Mediterranean.

Sweden's Gustavus I Ericksson ends the monopoly of the Hanseatic League in the Baltic after a war with Lübeck.

Asunción is founded on the Paraguay River in South America.

"Sublimus Deus" is issued by Pope Paul III who has been persuaded by friar Bernardino de Minaya to issue the bull with various briefs making it unlawful to enslave Indians. The friar has been with Pizarro in Peru, but he is imprisoned after Charles V forces the pope to recall his briefs.

Slaves on the island of Hispaniola stage another revolt (*see* 1533).

Nova Scientia by Italian mathematician Niccolo Tartaglia, 37, discusses the motion of heavy bodies and the shape and trajectory of projectiles. Tartaglia will discover the solution to the cubic equation in 1541, but his findings will be appropriated by the mathematician Geronimo Cardano, now 36.

The University of Lausanne has its beginnings.

The University of Strasbourg has its beginnings.

1538 The third war between France's François I and the Holy Roman Emperor Charles V ends June 18 with each side retaining possession of its conquests, but the truce of Nice is inconclusive.

A Holy League against the Ottoman Turks allies Pope Paul III, Venice, and the Holy Roman Emperor Charles V. Charles tries to buy off the corsair Khair ed-Din.

An Ottoman naval expedition takes over Aden and Yemen on the east coast of the Red Sea and ventures as far as the northwest coast of India.

Painting *The Venus of Urbino* and *The Allegory of Marriage* by Titian; *Christina of Denmark* by Hans Holbein.

The first definite reference to Newfoundland fishing expeditions appears in Basque records, although Basque fishermen have been visiting the Grand Banks for some decades and possibly for a century (*see* 1497).

Poule d'Inde (chicken of the Indies, meaning turkey) is served in France (*see* 1523). The French will call hen turkey *dinde,* tom turkey *dindon.*

English parish records begin to indicate births, marriages, and deaths. The records will make future population estimates more accurate.

1539 Potatoes arrive in Spain with conquistadors returning from Quito (*see* 1530). Pedro de Cieza of the Pizarro expedition describes the tubers as something similar to chestnuts (*see* 1540).

Portugal's agrarian system declines as a result of dependence on slave labor introduced since 1441.

Nikolaus Felderman arrives at Bogotá as agent for the Welsers (*see* 1528). The city has been founded in the past 2 years under the name Santa Fe de Bogotá by Gonzalo Jiminez de Quesada.

Franciscan missionary Marcos de Niza explores territory that will become Arizona and New Mexico. He returns from the Zuni pueblos with glowing accounts of gold in the legendary "seven cities of Cibola," but he will be discredited when the claims prove false.

England's Statute of the Six Articles makes it heresy to deny any of six positions: transsubstantiation, communion in one kind for laymen, celibacy of the priesthood, inviolability of chastity vows, necessity of private masses, necessity of auricular confession.

The Bank of Naples is founded with a capital of 4,000 ducats by Neapolitans Aurelio Paparo and Leonardo di Palma to free the poor from the evils of usury by granting loans on pledges without interest or at very low rates of interest. The bank will grow to become the most powerful agricultural credit institution in the southern Italian provinces.

A fixed maximum on Spanish grain prices becomes a permanent facet of royal economic policy. Applied only sporadically until now, the tasa del trigo has the effect of favoring sheepraising over tillage, making Spain dependent on imports for her food, and making food prices so high that the Spanish worker can barely afford food, clothing, housing, and fuel.

Painting *King François I* by Titian.

Mantua's Palazzo Ducale is completed by architect-painter Romano Giulio, 40, who was an assistant to the late Raphael.

1540 England's Henry VIII marries Anne of Cleves at Greenwich January 6 less than a week after meeting her and 4 days after saying openly that she had no looks, spoke no English, and was "no better than a Flanders mare." Anne is the 25-year-old daughter of the German Protestant leader John, duke of Cleves, and the marriage has been arranged by the lord privy seal Baron Thomas Cromwell, 54, to give Henry an ally against the Holy Roman Emperor Charles V and France's François I, but Henry soon finds that he has no reason to fear an attack from either. The king says the marriage has not been (and cannot be) consummated, he makes Cromwell earl of Essex but has the duke of Norfolk charge him with treason June 10. Parliament sends Cromwell to the Tower of London and declares the king's marriage null and void July 9. Henry marries Norfolk's 25-year-old niece Catherine Howard, and Cromwell is beheaded on Tower Hill July 28.

Pope Paul III recognizes the Jesuit order founded in 1534. The pope will make the Jesuits his chief agents in spreading the Counter Reformation.

Dutch whaling captain Jon Greenlander lands in Greenland and finds the last Norse colonist lying dead outside his hut with an iron dagger in his hand (see 985).

Hernando Cortez, now 55, returns to Spain (see 1536; 1547).

Spanish explorer Francisco Vazquez Coronado, 30, arrives in the American southwest accompanied by Marcos de Niza and by the first horses, mules, cattle, sheep, and hogs to be seen in the region.

Spanish explorer Hernando de Alarcon discovers the Colorado River.

Hernando de Soto lands at Tampa Bay with more than 600 men, 200 horses, and 13 hogs. Rich with gold from Peru, de Soto moves west (see 1541).

United companies of barbers and surgeons are incorporated at London.

Painting *Henry VIII* by Hans Holbein; *Doge Andrea Gritti* by Titian; *Adoration of the Shepherd* by Venetian painter Jacopo (or Giacomo) da Bassano (né Ponte), 30.

A specimen potato from South America reaches Pope Paul III via Spain. The pope gives the tuber to a Frenchman who introduces it into France as an ornamental plant (see 1539; 1740).

1541 John Calvin (Jean Chauvin) establishes a theocratic government that will make Geneva a focal point for the defense of Protestantism throughout Europe. The 32-year-old French theologian was banished from Paris in 1533, his *Institution Chretienne* was published 3 years later, he tried to establish a theocracy at Geneva with Guillaume Farel, 52, 3 years ago,

a popular revolt drove him out of town, but the Swiss burghers have invited him to return.

Catholic missionary Francis Xavier, 35, sails for the Orient from Lisbon as Jesuit apostle to the Indies at the behest of Ignatius of Loyola, first superior (or general) of the Society of Jesus (see 1540; 1551).

Portugal sends troops to Ethiopia under Christopher da Gama, son of the late explorer Vasco da Gama. The Portuguese will expel the Somali chief Ahmed Gran who invaded Ethiopia in 1527.

Francisco Pizarro completes his conquest of Peru but is assassinated June 26 at age 69 or 70 by supporters of Diego de Almagro, 21, whose father and namesake Pizarro defeated and executed 3 years ago. Diego is made governor of Peru, but royalists will defeat him next year and put him to death.

The Mississippi River is discovered by Hernando de Soto (see 1540; Marquette and Joliet, 1673).

France's Jacques Cartier makes a third expedition to North America. Financed by François I, Cartier establishes a short-lived community at Quebec (see 1534; 1546).

Painting *The Last Judgment* is completed by Michelangelo on the altar wall of the Sistine Chapel at Rome. The work measures 60 feet in length, 33 feet in height, and is the largest, most comprehensive painting in the world.

1542 The Universal Inquisition established by Pope Paul III at Rome July 21 tries to stem the tide of the Reformation with cruel repression (see Jesuits, 1540). A council of Dominican cardinals conducts trials of alleged heretics and permits them no legal counsel.

Spain forbids her colonists in America to enslave Indians but does not abolish Indian slavery (see Las Casas, 1517).

England's Henry VIII has his fifth wife Catherine Howard beheaded February 13 on charges of adultery. She has admitted to having had premarital intimacies with her cousin Thomas Culpepper and with Francis Dereham; she has had clandestine meetings with both since her marriage to the king, and they have been beheaded earlier.

Henry VIII makes Ireland a kingdom. The Irish summon a parliament in June and six Gaelic chiefs approve the act that makes Henry king of Ireland.

The Battle of Solvay Moss November 25 gives Henry VIII a victory over Scotland's James V, James dies December 14 at age 30, and he is succeeded by his week-old daughter Mary Queen of Scots who is born to his second wife Mary of Guise as he lies dying.

Some 150 Spanish colonists led by Álvar Cabeza de Vaca travel 600 miles inland from the coast of southern Brazil and settle at Asunción (see 1536; 1537).

Spanish explorer Juan Rodriguez Cabrillo probes the coast of California. His pilot Bartolomeo Ferello nearly reaches the mouth of the Columbia River (see Drake, 1579; Gray, 1791).

1542 (cont.) Hernando de Soto dies at age 46 after having spent the winter on the Ouachita River and is buried in the Mississippi which he discovered last year. De Soto's men descend the Mississippi under the command of Luis Moscoso de Alvarado from a point near the junction of the Arkansas River, they reach the Gulf in 19 days, and they proceed back to Panuco.

The University of Zaragoza has its beginnings.

1543 *De Revolutionibus Orbium Coelestium* by Prussian-Polish astronomer Nikolaus Copernicus (Mikolaj Kopernik), 70, defies Church doctrine that the earth is the center of the universe and establishes the theory that the earth rotates daily on its axis and, with other planets, revolves in orbit round the sun. Copernicus has not permitted the work to be published earlier, he sees the first copy on his deathbed, he dies May 24 of apoplexy and paralysis, and his idea is as revolutionary as his title (the word "revolution" will derive from his *Revolutionibus*). (*see* Tycho Brahe, 1572, 1576; Kepler, 1609; Galileo, 1613).

De Corporis Humani Fabrica by Belgian anatomist Andreas Vesalius, 29, with anatomic drawings by the Venetian painter Titian is the first accurate book on human anatomy. Vesalius has defied Church opposition to human dissection (*see* 1564).

England's Henry VIII marries Catherine Parr, 31, July 12.

Spanish conquistador Ruy Lopez de Villalobos is driven out of the Phillippine Islands by the natives a year after discovering the islands and giving them their name. He is captured by the Portuguese.

Japan receives her first European visitors as some Portuguese from a Chinese ship land on the island of Taneko off Kyushu. Called Namban by the Japanese, they introduce the musket which will be employed in Japanese warfare and will be called a taneko, although muskets may have been introduced from China in 1510.

The Spanish Inquisition burns Protestants at the stake for the first time.

Pope Paul III issues an index librorum prohibitorum (*see* 1559).

Painting *Ecce Homo* by Titian; Hans Holbein dies in England at age 45.

Wheat, barley, broad beans, chickpeas, European vegetables, and cows are introduced into New Spain by a new viceroy sent out to replace Pedro de Alvarado who died 2 years ago at age 46. The grains, vegetables, and livestock introduced into North America in the next few decades by English explorers will have been obtained in many cases from the Spanish to the south.

Baked bread is introduced to the Japanese by the Portuguese (above).

1544 Parliament recognizes two daughters of Henry VIII as heirs to the English throne in the event that Henry's son Edward should die without issue. Mary is Henry's daughter by Catherine of Aragon and Elizabeth is his daughter by Anne Boleyn.

Edinburgh is sacked by English forces under Edward Seymour, 38, earl of Hertford.

The Treaty of Crespy-en-Valois September 18 ends a 2-year war in the Netherlands between Charles V and France's François I. France loses Artois and Flanders and abandons her claims to Naples, but the treaty provides that the duke of Orléans shall marry either the daughter or niece of Charles and shall receive either the Netherlands and Franche-Comte or Milan as a dowry, a provision that will become meaningless next year when the duke dies at age 23. Piedmont and Savoy are restored to their legitimate ruler by terms of the treaty, Charles renounces his claim to Burgundy, and Milan continues in the possession of Charles as Holy Roman Emperor.

English troops besiege Boulogne.

Painting *Portrait of an Old Man* by Lorenzo Lotto.

Northern Europe suffers a honey shortage as a result of the breakup of monasteries by the Reformation (*see* England, 1536). The decline in honeybee colonies creates a growing need for cheap sugar, but sugar will remain a luxury for more than a century.

1545 The Council of Trent convened by Pope Paul III under Jesuit guidance undertakes reform of the Church. No Protestants attend, but the Tridentine Decrees issued by the Council will effect some genuine internal reforms while formulating rigid doctrines in direct opposition to Protestant teaching.

The Tridentine Decrees (above) will establish the Latin liturgy that will be used in Roman Catholic church services for more than 400 years.

A silver mine discovered by the Spanish at Potosí in the altiplano of New Castile will yield much of the wealth to fuel the commercial activity of Europe in the next century and prepare the way for an industrial revolution. Reports of the silver have reached conquistador Juan de Villaroel through a llama herder who said that he had built a fire to keep warm while he slept and the next morning had found shining silvery threads melted out of the rocks by the heat of the fire. Accompanied by Diego and Francisco de Centeno, Juan de Villaroel has come to Potosí and has found deposits that will yield an estimated $2 billion in silver and will later produce bismuth, tin, and tungsten (*see* 1611; Drake, 1573).

A typhus epidemic in Cuba kills as many as 250,000, while a similar number die in New Spain, 150,000 in Tlascala, and 100,000 at Cholula according to the friar Geronimo de Mendieta.

Painting *Venus, Cupid, Folly, and Time* by Florentine painter Il Bronzino (Agnold di Cosimo di Mariano), 41, who has been court painter to Cosimo de'

Medici since 1539 and who has specialized in elegant portraits with artificially elongated figures.

Fishing grows poor in the Baltic Sea while becoming good in the North Sea, a development that will have important economic and political consequences.

1546 Martin Luther dies at his birthplace of Eisleben February 18 at age 63, and the emperor Charles V goes to war at the urging of Pope Paul III who wants to restore the unity of the Church.

Charles V begins the Schmalkaldic War to crush the rebellious German states after having placed the elector of Saxony and the landgrave under the ban because they are leaders of the League of Schmalkalden. Saxony's duke Maurice makes a secret alliance with Charles and conquers the electorate from its elector John Frederick, the elector then reconquers Saxony while the emperor is occupied with crushing the southern members of the Schmalkaldic League (*see* 1547).

Ottoman forces occupy Moldavia.

Mayans in New Spain stage a major uprising against the Spanish but are crushed by the conquistadors.

Charles V (above) revokes the South American charter granted in 1528 to the Welser family of Augsburg whose banking house suffers enormous losses.

Europe's Fugger family is estimated to have a fortune of 6 million gulden (*see* 1525; 1550).

De Contagione et Contagiosis Morbis et eorum Curatione by Girolamo Fracastoro gives the first description of typhus and suggests that infections are carried from one person to another by tiny bodies (seminaria contagionum) capable of multiplying themselves (*see* 1530; van Leeuwenhoek, 1683; Nicolle, 1903).

The health of England's Henry VIII fails rapidly. The king has grown so grossly overweight that he must be moved up and down stairs by special machinery.

Oxford's Christ Church is founded in a reorganization of Cardinal College.

The Proverbs of John Heywood by English epigrammatist John Heywood, 47, includes the proverb "No man ought to look a given horse in the mouth," which goes back in one form or another to St. Jerome of 400 A.D. Other proverbs cited by Heywood: "All is well that ends well"; "A penny for your thoughts"; "A man may well bring a horse to the water, but he cannot make him drink"; "Beggars shouldn't be choosers"; "Better late than never"; "Butter would not melt in her mouth"; "Every man as he loveth, quoth the good man as he kissed the cow"; "The fat is in the fire"; "Half a loaf is better than none"; "Haste makes waste"; "The green new broom sweepeth clean"; "It's an ill wind that blows no good"; "Look before you leap"; "Love me, love my dog"; "Many hands make light work"; "Two heads are better than one"; "When the iron is hot, strike"; "When the sun shineth, make hay"; "The tide tarrieth for no man"; "One good turn deserves an-other"; "One swallow maketh not a summer"; "Rome was not built in a day"; "Out of the frying pan into the fire"; "To tell tales out of school," and "More things belong to marriage than four bare legs in a bed."

Painting *Martin Luther* by Lucas Cranach.

Theater *Orazia* by Italian playwright-poet Pietro Aretino, 54.

England's population tops 4 million, with many of the people desperately short of food after a series of bad harvests.

1547 The grand duke of Muscovy Ivan IV has himself crowned czar (caesar) January 16, the first Russian ruler formally to assume that title. Now 16, Ivan has ruled personally since age 14. He has virgins brought from all over Russia for his inspection, on February 3 he selects as his wife Anastasia Zakharina-Koshkina of the ancient and noble family that will later take the name Romanov. He establishes a council of selected advisers to counter the power of the boyars in their duma.

England's Henry VIII dies January 28 at age 55 of syphilis and liver cirrhosis. News of the king's death is kept from his 10-year-old son by the boy's uncle Edward Seymour, earl of Hertford, until he has obtained the boy's consent to become protector of England with power to act with or without advice of counsel. Jane Seymour's son thereupon ascends the throne to begin a 6-year reign as Edward VI.

France's François I dies March 31 at age 52 and is succeeded by his 28-year-old son who ascends the throne as Henri II. Catherine de' Medici is queen of France, but the new king is dominated by his 48-year-old mistress Diane de Poitiers who will have great influence over him throughout his 12-year reign. Brittany is fully united with the French crown under Henri II (*see* 1532).

The Battle of Mühlberg April 24 ends in victory for the Holy Roman Emperor Charles V who captures the elector of Saxony and lays siege to the elector's capital of Wittenberg. But the brief Schmalkaldic War soon ends with the Protestant German states retaining some independence.

The Battle of Pinkie September 10 ends in victory for the earl of Hertford (above) who is king in all but name and who crushes Scottish resistance to the new boy king. Now baron Seymour and duke of Somerset, the protector routs a much larger force led by James Hamilton, 32, who is second earl of Arran, duke of Chatelherault, and regent to Mary Queen of Scots.

Although beaten at Pinkie (above), the Scots thwart a plan by Somerset to enforce a marriage treaty between young Edward and his 4-year-old half-sister. They hastily arrange a marriage between Mary Queen of Scots and the 2-year-old French dauphin.

1547 (cont.) Henry Howard, 29, earl of Surrey, has been beheaded January 19 on trumped up charges of treason. He had blocked the projected marriage of his sister, the duchess of Richmond, to Thomas Seymour, 39, the lord high admiral, who now plots to displace his older brother Edward as guardian of the king.

Parliament repeals the Statute of the Six Articles enacted in 1539 to define heresy.

England's late earl of Surrey Henry Howard (above) was a poet who translated the second and third books of Virgil's *Aeneid,* introduced into English the blank verse form of five iambic feet, and introduced from Italy the sonnet form of three quatrains and a couplet.

Sebastiano de Piombo dies at Rome June 21 at age 61.

France's new king Henri II (above) gives the Château de Chenonceaux in the Loire valley to his mistress Diane de Poitiers who will add an Italian garden and a bridge over the Cher River (*see* 1521; 1560).

The population of New Spain falls to 6 million, down from 11 million in 1518 before the arrival of Hernando Cortez (who dies outside Seville December 2 at age 63). Economic upheaval, exploitation, and new diseases have taken a heavy toll among the Mayans and other tribespeople (*see* 1605).

1548 Poland's Sigismund I dies April 1 at age 81 after a 42-year reign. He is succeeded by his only son who ascends the throne at age 28 to begin a 24-year reign as Sigismund II in which the Protestant Reformation will spread to Poland. The new king refuses the diet's demand that he repudiate his second wife, the beautiful Lithuanian Calvinist Barbara Radziwill, and she will die under mysterious circumstances 5 days after her coronation in early December 1550.

The Holy Roman Emperor Charles V annexes the 17 Lowland provinces to the empire's Burgundian Circle. Included are Artois, Flanders, Brabant, Limburg, Luxembourg, Gelderland, Hainault, Holland, Zeeland, Namur, Zutphen, East Friesland, West Friesland, Mechlin, Utrecht, Overyssel, and Groningen.

Ottoman forces occupy Tabriz, Persia.

The Battle of Xaquixaguane in Peru gives Pedro de la Gasca a victory over Gonzalo Pizarro, son of the late Francisco Pizarro. He has Gonzalo executed.

Hispaniola has another slave uprising.

Painting *The Miracle of St. Mark* by Venetian painter Tintoretto (Jacopo Robusti), 30, whose father is a dyer (tintore) and who begins four scenes from *The Legend of St. Mark* which he will not complete until 1586; *Equestrian Portrait of Charles V* by Titian; *The Imperial Chancellor Antoine Perrenot de Granvella* by Titian.

Hispaniola's native population falls to 500 or less, down from 14,000 in 1514.

1549 English authorities arrest the lord high admiral Thomas Seymour in January and send him to the Tower of London on charges of having schemed to marry Edward VI to Lady Jane Grey, 12-year-old daughter of the duke of Suffolk, and to gain as his own bride Henry VIII's 16-year-old daughter Elizabeth by Anne Boleyn. Seymour is baron Seymour of Sudeley and brother of the protector, but he is convicted of treason and is executed March 20.

The thirteenth Baron Grey de Wilton William Grey puts down a rebellion in Oxfordshire.

The czar of Muscovy Ivan IV summons the first Russian national assembly.

The Book of Common Prayer (first Prayer Book of Edward VI) by the archbishop of Canterbury Thomas Cranmer simplifies and condenses the Latin services of the medieval church into a single, convenient, comprehensive English volume that will serve as an authoritative guide for English priests and worshippers. Cranmer has become an influential counselor to the young king, he discussed a draft of the book last year in a conference of scholars, Parliament has commissioned its publication, and other prayer books are forbidden after May 20 (a revised version will be published in 1552).

Portugal's first governor of Brazil Thome de Souza founds the city of Sao Salvador that will later be called Bahia.

The Villa d'Este at Tivoli outside Rome is completed by Piero Ligorio for the cardinal d'Este Ippolito II.

The wife of Florence's Cosimo de' Medici Eleanoro Toledo pays 9,000 florins to buy the Pitti Palace from Buonaccorso Pitti, now 79, and completes it as the Grand Ducal Palace (*see* 1466).

1550 Augsburg banker Anton Fugger fails in an attempt to monopolize the tin production of Bohemia and Saxony. Fugger goes bankrupt after losing half a million gulden, and his failure precipitates bankruptcies throughout Europe, producing financial chaos at Augsburg and at Genoa where millions of gulden are lost.

Prices in Europe and England rise as coins minted from Mexican and Peruvian gold and silver ingots devalue the old currencies and as population growth booms demand for food, clothing, and shelter (*see* 1559; Gresham, 1562).

Helsinki is founded on the Gulf of Finland.

Trigonometry tables are published by German mathematician Rhaticus (Georg Joachim von Lauchen), 36, who has studied under the late Copernicus.

A concordance of the whole English Bible is published by English theologian-organist John Marbeck.

Fiction *Facetious Nights* (*Tradeci Piacevoli Notti*) by Italian writer Giovanni Francesco Straparola is the first European collection of fairy tales. A second volume will appear in 1553.

Poetry *Odes* by French poet Pierre de Ronsard, 26.

Painting *Presentation of the Virgin* by Tintoretto for Venice's Church of Santa Maria dell 'Orto; *Eleanora of Toledo and Her Son* by Il Bronzino; *A Nobleman in His Study* by Lorenzo Lotto; *Deposition from the Cross* by Michelangelo.

The Lives of the Most Eminent Italian Architects, Painters, and Sculptors (*Le Vite de' Piu Eccellenti Architetti, Pittori e Scultori Italiani*) by Italian architect-painter Giorgio Vasari, 39, is published at Florence.

Japanese *ukiyoe* painting has its beginnings.

The Booke of Common Praier Noted by John Marbeck (above) adapts the plain chant of earlier rituals to the liturgy of England's Edward VI.

Billiards is played for the first time in Italy.

Vicenza's Villa Rotunda and Palazzo Chiericati are designed by local architect Andrea Palladio (Andrea di Pietro della Gondola), 41, who completes the city's Palazzo Thiene.

Gothic architecture is given its name and is disparaged by Giorgio Vasari (above). A pupil of Michelangelo, Vasari says that medieval cathedrals were built in a style originated by the Goths ("those Germanic races untutored in the classics"), and he describes them as a "heap of spires, pinnacles, and grotesque decorations lacking in all the simple beauty of the classical orders" (*see* 1184).

Corn (maize), sweet potatoes, and peanuts will be introduced in much of China in the next half-century. All will produce large yields and will spur population growth by creating abundance with declining prices.

France's population reaches 15 million while Spain's is half that. 6.5 million of Spain's population is in Castile which has lost at least 150,000 to American emigration in the past half-century.

1551 Forty-two articles of religion that will be the basis of Anglican Protestantism are published by England's archbishop of Canterbury Thomas Cranmer (*see* Thirty-Nine Articles, 1563).

Francis Xavier leaves Japan after 2 years in which he has been well received but has had little success at proselytizing. He writes to the pope that he will save the souls of the Japanese and will make them loyal to Portugal, he gives advice on what trade goods should be brought to Japan, and he leaves behind two Jesuits and some Japanese converts (*see* 1578; 1579).

The Ottoman Turks take Tripoli after failing in an attempt to take Malta.

Prosperity fueled by wars and by precious metals from America will swell the coffers of European merchants in the next 6 years.

A law to encourage employment of the poor is enacted by England's Parliament.

A fifth (and final) epidemic of the sweating sickness strikes England in April in Shrewsbury (*see* 1529). Foreigners living in England are somehow spared, but the disease follows Englishmen who flee to France and the Lowlands and kills them there without affecting the French or the Lowlanders (*see* Kaye, 1552).

Prudentic Tables (*Tabulae Prudenticae*) by German astronomer Erasmus Reinhold, 40, contains astronomical tables based on numerical values provided by the late Nikolaus Copernicus. They represent an improvement on the widely used Alfonsine Tables.

Historia Animalium by Swiss naturalist Konrad von Gesner, 35, is published in its first volume. Gesner has collected animals from the New World and the Old, and his work pioneers modern zoology.

The University of San Marco is founded at Lima.

The National University of Mexico is founded at Mexico City in New Spain.

Painting *Prince Felipe of Spain* by Titian.

Hymn "Praise God from Whom All Blessings Flow" by French composer Louis Bourgeois.

Italian composer Giovanni Pierluigi da Palestrina, 25, is appointed magister capellae and magister puerorum at Rome's church of St. Giulia by Pope Julius III (Giovanni Maria del Monte) who succeeds the late Paul III but who will be pope only until 1555.

English and Welsh alehouses are licensed for the first time.

1552 Maurice of Saxony surprises the Holy Roman Emperor Charles V, forces him to release his father-in-law Philip of Hesse, and obliges him to conclude the convention of Passau permitting adherents of the 1530 confession of Augsburg free exercise of their religion at least until the next diet. Maurice's ally Henri II of France seizes the bishoprics of Toul, Metz, and Verdun, the emperor lays siege to Metz, which is defended by Francis of Guise, and a 4-year war begins between France and the emperor.

The czar of Muscovy Ivan IV begins the conquest of Kazan and Astrakhan. One of the factions of Kazan has offered him the entire khanate, he invades the khanate with 50 guns and an army of 150,000, he lays siege to the fortress August 20, the Tartar defenders resist heroically, but the Muscovites take the fortress by assault October 2, and the Volga becomes a Russian river for the first time.

The Portuguese ship *São João* goes aground June 24 on the Natal coast with 610 aboard. Only 25 of the 500 who get ashore survive the long walk to the nearest Portuguese settlement at Sofola. Half a dozen major shipwrecks will land 3,000 Portuguese on Africa's east coast in the next 100 years, but scarcely 500 will be rescued (*see* 1683).

1552 (cont.) The Holy Roman Emperor Charles V (above) lifts his siege of Metz and withdraws after having lost more than 12,000 men in a single month to typhus and scurvy.

"The Sweate" by English physician John Kaye is a pamphlet describing a mysterious epidemic that may be a severe form of influenza (*see 1551*).

Christ's Hospital at London is founded by England's Edward VI.

Tabulae Anatomicae by Italian anatomist Bartolommeo Eustachio, 28, describes what will be called the Eustachian tube in the ear and the Eustachian valve of the heart. Eustachio also describes the stapes, the thoracic duct, the uterus, the kidney, and the teeth (*see Vesalius, 1543*).

Rome's Collegium Germanicum is founded by Jesuits.

Books on geography and astronomy are destroyed in England because they are thought to be infected with magic.

Poetry *Centuries* by French physician-astrologer Nostradamus (Michel de Notredame, or Nostredame), 52, is a book of rhymed prophecies that foretells the manner of Henri II's death in 1559. The rhymes of Nostradamus will be interpreted centuries hence as prophesying such events as the World War beginning in 1914 and the atomic bomb of 1945; *Amours de Cassandre* by Pierre de Ronsard appears in its first volume.

Painting *Self-portrait* by Titian. He has begun sending religious and mythological paintings to the 25-year-old Spanish prince Felipe who receives them gratefully and confers rich rewards on Titian.

Theater *Cleopatre Captive* by French dramatic poet Etienne Jodelle, 20, Sieur de Lymodin, is the first classical French tragedy; *Ralph Roister Doister* by English cleric-playwright Nicholas Udall, 47, is the earliest English comedy that will survive (year of first performance approximate). Udall was headmaster of Eton from 1534 until his dismissal for misconduct in 1541, and he has modeled his play on a comedy by Plautus).

Palestrina wins appointment to the Sistine choir from Pope Julius who will soon die (*see 1551; 1555*).

Scotland's Royal and Ancient Golf Club of St. Andrews has its beginnings (*see 1754*).

London's Covent Garden is granted to Sir John Russell, first earl of Bedford, whose family will retain the property until 1914. The land of the convent garden owned by the abbey of Westminster, now part of London, was confiscated along with other church properties in 1534 and will serve as London's produce and flower market beginning in 1661.

Löwenbräu beer gets its name as a two-tailed heraldic lion is placed over the entrance to the brewhouse founded at Munich in 1383. The Bavarian brewery will become known as Löwenbräu, or Lion Brewer.

1553 England's Edward VI dies of tuberculosis at Greenwich July 6 at age 15 and is succeeded by his 37-year-old Catholic half-sister Mary who has been raised by her mother Catherine of Aragon. A treaty of marriage is arranged between Mary and Spain's Philip, 26-year-old son of Charles V, who is to be given the title King of England but is to have no hand in government and no right to succeed Mary.

England's new queen (above) faces an insurrection led by Henry Grey, duke of Suffolk, who has married his 16-year-old daughter Lady Jane Grey to Lord Guilford Dudley as part of a plot to alter the succession (Dudley has induced the late Edward VI to sign letters of patent making Lady Jane Grey heir to the crown). Suffolk is supported by Sir Thomas Wyatt, 32, son and namesake of the poet-statesman who died in 1542, Lady Jane Grey is proclaimed queen July 9, but forces loyal to Mary disperse Suffolk's troops and imprison Lady Jane Grey July 19 (*see 1554*).

English navigator Richard Chancellor reaches Moscow by way of the White Sea and Archangel. Commander of a ship in Sir Hugh Willoughby's expedition of 1527 in search of a northeast passage to Cathay, Chancellor has studied navigation under John Dee (*see 1558; Muscovy Company, 1555*).

Christianismi Restitutio by Spanish theologian Michael Servetus (Miguel Serveto), 42, is the first book to refute the Galen idea of 164 A.D. that the ventricular system is perforated. Servetus shows a familiarity with pulmonary circulation, he is arrested for his views and brought before the Inquisition at Vienne, he escapes to Geneva, he is imprisoned on orders from John Calvin, and he is burned at the stake for heresy October 27.

Painting *Landscape with Christ Appearing to the Apostles at the Sea of Tiberius* by Flemish painter Pieter Brueghel, 28; *The All-Saints Altar (La Gloria)* by Titian. Lucas Cranach (the Elder) dies at Weimar October 16 at age 81.

The camera obscura devised by Roger Bacon in 1267 is improved by Italian physicist Giambattista della Porta, 15, who introduces a convex lens.

Florence's Strozzi Palace is completed by the sons of the late banker Filippo Strozzi the Elder who began construction of the palazzo in 1489 but died 2 years later at age 65.

The first written reference to the potato appears in *Chronica del Peru* by Pedro de Leon (Pedro Creca) which is published at Seville. The author calls the tuber a battata or papa (*see 1540; 1573*).

1554 England's Queen Mary releases the duke of Suffolk from prison in a show of clemency toward those who took arms against her last year, but she hardens her position when Suffolk again proclaims his daughter Lady Jane Grey queen and tries to rally Leicestershire to her support.

Sir Thomas Wyatt summons his Kentish followers to the Wyatt castle of Allington January 22 and raises a new insurgent army that occupies Rochester January 26. Wyatt reaches Southwark February 3, but some of his men are cut off, others desert, and Wyatt is forced to surrender.

Lady Jane Grey and her husband Guilford Dudley are executed February 12, 5 months after the execution of Dudley's father the duke of Northumberland. Wyatt is brought to trial for treason March 15 and is executed April 11.

England's 20-year-old princess Elizabeth is sent to the Tower of London in March as the Spanish cry for her execution. Edward Courtenay, 28, earl of Devonshire, has been released from the Tower after 15 years of imprisonment in connection with his father's aspirations to the crown. He has been foiled in his effort to marry the new queen, and he has plotted to marry Elizabeth and join her on the throne. Elizabeth is released from the Tower in May, Mary and the Spanish infante Philip are married July 25.

Mehedia on the Tunisian coast falls to Algerians led by the corsair Dragut who succeeded to the leadership of the pirates after the death of Khair ed-Din at Constantinople in 1546. The Spanish will be driven from the North African coast in the next 2 years.

The practical and theoretical medicine of the Renaissance is codified by the French physician-astronomer-mathematician Fernelius (Jean Fernel), 57, who rejects astrology and magic but emphasizes the functions of the organs.

Painting *Danaë* and *Venus and Adonis* by Titian.

Cruydeboek by the Dutch botanist Dodonaeus (Rembert Dodoens), 37, makes the first mention of kohlrabi and Brussels sprouts, both varieties of cabbage. A new edition will be published in 1563 (*see* Gerard, 1597).

Flemish hop growers emigrate to England and start growing hops in Kent for the English brewery trade.

Parliament reenacts the Corn Law of 1436 and enacts other statutes to encourage farming in England. The Corn Law regulates the export and import of grain according to prices, other laws forbid the enlargement of farms and place restrictions on storing, buying, and selling grain, but none of the measures relieves England's food shortages or lowers food prices.

1555 Bloody Mary returns Catholicism to England and persecutes Protestants. Hugh Latimer, bishop of Worcester, and Nicholas Ridley, bishop of London, have been imprisoned for 2 years on charges of heresy and the queen has them burned at the stake October 16 at Oxford. Bishop Latimer, now 70, says to Bishop Ridley, 55, "Be of good comfort, Master Ridley, and play the man. We shall this day light such a candle by God's grace in England as I trust shall never be put out" (*see* Cranmer, 1556).

Pope Julius III has died March 23 at age 67, his successor Marcellus II has died April 30 at age 54, and *his* successor Paul IV extends the powers of the Universal Inquisition founded by Paul III in 1542. The new pope orders that Rome's Jewish quarter be surrounded by a wall and creates the ghetto of Rome. "God has imposed servitude until they should have recognized their errors," says the pope.

The Treaty of Augsburg signed September 25 ends a period of religious wars in the German states by compromising differences between Catholics and Protestants.

A long period of peace settles on Europe as the Holy Roman Emperor Charles V turns over full imperial authority to his 52-year-old brother Ferdinand and turns over his sovereignty in the Netherlands to his 28-year-old son Philip in formal ceremonies October 25 in the Hall of the Golden Fleece at Brussels. Now 55, Charles is dyspeptic, gouty, and uncontrollably gluttonous. Ferdinand asks that formal abdication be delayed until 1558, but he begins a reign that will continue until 1564.

Japanese pirates besiege Nanking.

Portuguese Jesuit missions to Ethiopia begin under the direction of Pedro Paez and will continue until 1603.

Rio de Janeiro Bay in Brazil is settled by French Huguenots under the leadership of Nicolas Durand de Villegagnon (but *see* 1567).

A translation of Peter Martyr's 1516 Italian work *De Rebus Oceanicis et Novo Orbe* by Richard Eden stimulates English interest in America.

The Muscovy Company (the Association of Merchant Adventurers) founded by Richard Chancellor and others to trade with Russia is the first of the great English trading companies (*see* 1553; 1561; East India Company, 1600).

Maize from the New World provided a cheap new way to fatten livestock for Europe's multiplying carnivores.

1555 (cont.) *L'Histoire de la nature des oyseaux* by Pierre Belon is a pioneer study of birds.

Poetry *Amours de Marie* by Pierre de Ronsard.

Painting *St. George and the Dragon* by Tintoretto.

Sculpture *Pietà* by Michelangelo who has spent 5 years creating the work for the Duomo at Florence.

Palestrina is pensioned off along with two other members of the Sistine choir by the successor to Pope Julius (above). He is appointed choir-master of the church of St. John Lateran but will give up the post in 1558 after composing a book of magnificats and lamentations—settings of the Holy Week lessons from the Lamentations of Jeremiah (*see* 1552; 1558).

Villa Giulia is completed for Pope Julius III (above) who dies before he can occupy the summer palace. It has been designed by architect Giacomo da Vignola (Giacomo Barozzi), 48, in collaboration with Giorgio Vasari and Bartolommeo Ammanati.

Rome's Palazzo Farnese is completed by Giacomo da Vignola (above) and Michelangelo.

Famine grips England, and peas are discovered by the peasantry to taste good green as well as dried, according to a contemporary account (*see* 1696).

1556 England's archbishop of Canterbury Thomas Cranmer is degraded from his office February 14 in humiliating ceremonies conducted by papal delegates at Christ Church, Oxford, and he is burned at the stake March 21 at age 66 after renouncing the Church of Rome and refusing all recantations. Cranmer holds his right hand to the flame saying that the hand has offended and should therefore be burned first.

Cranmer (above) has been succeeded as archbishop by Reginald Pole, now 56, whose criticism of Henry VIII's divorce was published abroad 20 years ago, provoked Henry to execute Pole's mother and brother in England, and encouraged Pope Paul III to create him a cardinal.

Charles V (Carlos I) resigns his Spanish kingdoms and that of Sicily to his inept son Philip January 16, he resigns his county of Burgundy soon after, and he sails from Flushing September 17 to settle as a guest at a monastery in Estremadura where he will die in 1558. He leaves Philip to rule Spain, the Netherlands, Milan, Naples, Franche-Comte, and the rich Spanish colonies.

The czar of Muscovy Ivan the Terrible completes his conquest of Kazan and Astrakhan from the Tartars. His triumph opens the way for Russian expansion to the east and southeast.

The Hindustan empire is regained from the Hindus November 5 at the Battle of Panipat in the Punjab by the 14-year-old Mogul emperor Akbar (Jalal-ud-Din Mohammad) who returns from exile, defeats the Af-

ghans with guidance from his regent Bairam Khan, and begins a 49-year reign whose first years will be spent in constant warfare.

De Re Metallica by Bohemian physician-mine owner Georgius Agricola (Georg Bauer), 62, is the world's first textbook on mining and metallurgy and will be the only such text for centuries. Agricola's book establishes the science of mineralogy.

Castle of Knowledge by English mathematician Robert Recorde, 46, is a navigational guide for voyagers to Cathay. Recorde has taught at both Oxford and Cambridge, he has served as physician to Edward VI and Mary, and he will be the first to use the sign = to denote equality.

Theater *Der Paur im Egfeur* by Nuremberg's Hans Sachs dramatizes anecdotes and incidents of everyday life in a *Fastnachtsspiel* that will be produced each year at Shrovetide.

A book of motets by Belgian composer Orlando Lasso (or Lassus, Roland Delattre), 26, published at Antwerp includes an adulatory motet to England's new archbishop of Canterbury Reginald Pole. Lasso will soon be invited to Munich by Albrecht IV, duke of Bavaria, and will enjoy the duke's patronage until the duke dies in 1579.

Tobacco seeds reach Europe with Franciscan monk André Thevet who returns from Rio de Janeiro with seeds of what the Brazilian natives call petun, or petum (*see* Grijalva, 1518; Nicot, 1561).

The Château d'Anet for Diane de Poitiers is completed by French architect Philibert Delorme, 46, after 9 years of construction.

The worst earthquake in history rocks China's Shansi province January 24 killing more than 830,000.

1557 Portugal's João III (the Pious) dies on his 55th birthday June 6 after having instituted the Inquisition. He is succeeded by his 3-year-old grandson Sebastian who will reign for 21 years, most of them under a regency.

French forces under the duke of Guise are defeated and driven from Italy following the Battle of St. Quentin August 10 as England is drawn into the Spanish war with France and helps the Spanish gain victory.

Siena loses her independence as Florence's Cosimo de' Medici becomes ruler of the former republic.

A 14-year Livonian War begins as Russian forces invade Poland, the Swedes take Estonia, and the Danes acquire part of Courland in a dispute over succession to the Baltic territories ruled by the Teutonic Knights (*see* 1525).

Macao off the Chinese coast near Canton is settled by Portuguese colonists who establish regular trade with the Chinese mainland.

São Paulo is founded by the Portuguese in Brazil.

Whetstone of Witte by England's Robert Recorde is dedicated to the governors of the Muscovy Company which Recorde serves as technical adviser on matters of navigation (*see* 1555).

Poetry *Songs and Sonettes Written by the Ryght honorable Lorde Henry Howard Late Earle of Surrey, and Other* (apud Richardum Tottel) (*see* 1547); *Hundredth Good Pointes of Husbandry* by English versifier Thomas Tusser. "The stone that is rolling can gather no moss./Who often removeth is sure of loss;" "At Christmas play, and make good cheer,/ For Christmas comes but once a year."

Painting *Landscape with the Parable of the Sower* by Pieter Brueghel.

Observations of whales by voyagers of the Muscovy Company lead to the opening by the English of a whale fishery at Spitzbergen (*see* 1555; 1608).

1558 England's glorious Elizabethan age begins November 17 as Mary Tudor dies at age 42 and is succeeded by her half-sister Elizabeth, 25-year-old daughter of Henry VIII by the late Anne Boleyn. Elizabeth begins a reign of more than 44 years that will see a great flourishing of English arts and letters.

England loses Calais to France's duke of Guise after having held the port for 211 years. The English give up hopes of conquering France (*see* 1564).

Spain's Carlos I has died at age 58 at the monastery of Yuste in Estremadura where he has lived since February of last year. The former Holy Roman Emperor Charles V has suffered from indigestion for 3 weeks after eating an eel pie, he is widely mourned, but his son Philip II has ruled since 1556 from the Netherlands and will return to Spain next year.

Two compasses for master pilots of the Muscovy Company are invented by mathematician John Dee who succeeds Robert Recorde as technical adviser to the company.

The University of Jena is founded.

First Blast of the Trumpet Against the Monstrous Regiment of Women by Scottish clergyman John Knox, now 53, says, "The nobility both of England and Scotland are inferior to brute beasts, for they do that to women which no male among the common sort of beasts can be proved to do with their females; that is, they reverence them, and quake at their presence; they obey their commandments, and that against God;" Knox was captured at St. Andrews 10 years ago for preaching reform in religion, he was sent to prison in France, he was appointed a royal chaplain in England 3 years later, but he fled to the Continent at Mary Tudor's accession in 1553 and has been at Geneva since 1556, meeting occasionally with John Calvin (*see* 1541).

Painting *The Fall of Icarus* by Pieter Brueghel.

London's population reaches 200,000, four times its 1400 level (*see* 1603).

1559 The Danish-Norwegian king Christian III dies January 1 at age 55 after a reign of nearly 24 years that has strenghtened and enriched the realm. His cousin

who reigned as Christian II until he was deposed in 1523 dies later in the month at age 79, still a prisoner as he has been since 1531, and his 24-year-old son ascends the throne to begin a 29-year reign as Frederick II.

The Treaty of Cateau-Cambresis April 3 ends the last war between the late Holy Roman Emperor Charles V and France. The treaty confirms Spanish possession of the Franche-Comte and the Italian states Milan, Naples and Sicily. Spain's Philip II marries Henri II's daughter Elizabeth, Henri's sister Margaret marries the count of Savoy and becomes regent of the Netherlands.

France's Henri II sustains a head wound in a tournament June 20. The lance of the count of Montgomery pierces Henri's temple, the king dies of the wound July 10 at age 40, fulfilling a prophecy by Nostradamus published 4 years ago, and he is succeeded by his 14-year-old son who will reign for less than 8 months as François II. The new king is married to Scotland's Mary Stuart; his uncles François, duke of Guise, and Charles, cardinal of Lorraine, serve as regents.

Mary Queen of Scots (above) assumes the title Queen of England. England's Elizabeth I raises her court favorite Robert Dudley to the privy council.

Pope Paul IV founds the Order of the Golden Spur as a military body, but the Hapsburg duke of Alba defeats the papal forces. The pope dies August 18 at age 83, and he is succeeded by the 60-year-old Giovanni Medici, no kin to the de' Medici family of Florence, who assumes the papacy as Pius IV.

Romans vent their anger at the late Pope Paul IV by demolishing his statue, liberating the prisoners of the Inquisition, and scattering the Inquisition's records.

Some 1,500 Spanish colonists land at Pensacola, Florida, but hostile natives force them to move to Port Royal Sound in what later will become the English colony of South Carolina (*see* 1561; Ribault, 1562, St. Augustine, 1565; Albemarle, 1653).

Italian anatomist Realdo Columbus at Padua advances knowledge of human blood circulation. A pupil of Andreas Vesalius, Columbus shows that the right and left ventricles of the heart are separated by an impenetrable wall, that blood is conveyed from the right side to the lungs where it is mixed with air, and that it returns in aerated form to the right side. But Columbus hews to the traditional view that the liver is the center of the venous system and is the organ that creates blood (*see* Servetus, 1553; Harvey, 1628).

The University of Geneva has its beginnings.

The "Index auctorum et librorum qui tanquam haeretici aut suspecti aut perversi ab Officio S. R. Inquisitionis reprobantur et in universa Christiana republica interdicuntur" published by Pope Paul IV condemns certain authors with all their writings, prohibits certain books whose authors are known, and prohibits pernicious books published anony-

1559 (cont.) mously. It is the first Roman Index in the modern ecclesiastical use of the term (*see* 1543).

Painting *The Fight Between Carnival and Lent* and *Netherlandish Proverbs* by Pieter Brueghel; *The Entombment, Diana and Actaem,* and *Diana and Callisto* by Titian.

English food prices soar to three times their 1501 levels largely because Henry VIII debased the coinage to raise quick money for his wars with Spain, France, and Scotland. The typical English wage is up only 69 percent above its 1501 level (*see* 1550).

Ice cream appears in Italy as ice and salt are discovered to make a freezing combination.

1560 French troops in Scotland attempt to assert the claims of Mary Stuart, the 17-year-old Catholic daughter of Scotland's late James V and his Guise wife Marie of Lorraine. Mary is queen to France's young François II and has the support of European Catholicism which regards England's Elizabeth as illegitimate, but English forces besiege the French at Leith, Marie of Lorraine dies in June, and the Treaty of Edinburgh July 6 puts an end to French interference in Scotland.

The Conspiracy of Amboise organized by the French Huguenot Condé de Bourbon tries to overthrow the Catholic Guises, but the queen mother Catherine de' Medici helps the Guises thwart the Huguenots. Some 1,200 Huguenots are hanged at Amboise. France's François II dies December 5 at age 16 and is succeeded by his 10-year-old brother who will reign as Charles IX until his death in 1574.

Sweden's Gustavus I Eriksson has died September 29 at age 64 after a 37-year reign. His 27-year-old son, who for the past 2 years has been writing love letters and marriage proposals to Elizabeth of England, succeeds to the throne and will reign until 1568 as Eric XIV.

The Auracanian Federation destroys Spanish settlements in the interior of Chile.

A smallpox epidemic decimates Portugal's Brazilian colony and increases the need for African slaves to cut sugar cane.

Antwerp reaches the height of its prosperity. The city has a thousand foreign merchants in residence with as many as 500 ships entering its harbor each day from Danish, English, Hanse, German, Italian, Portuguese, and Spanish ports.

The Geneva Bible published by followers of John Calvin is the first bible to have both chapter and verse numbers. The same numerical divisions will be used for more than 400 years.

Painting *Children's Games* by Pieter Brueghel.

Tobacco grows in Spain and Portugal where it is cultivated as an ornamental plant and for its alleged medicinal properties (*see* 1531; Nicot, 1561).

The Villa Foscari (Villa Malcontenta) is completed by Andrea Palladio overlooking the Brenta at Vicenza.

France's Château Chenonceaux passes into the hands of the queen mother Catherine de' Medici who forces out Diane de Poitiers who was the mistress of the late Henri II. Catherine employs the architect Philibert Delorem, 35, to build a two-story gallery on the bridge erected by Diane de Poitiers (*see* 1547).

Venice gets its first coffee house. The city is a major sugar-refining center, using raw sugar imported through Lisbon, but Europe's chief sugar refiner is Antwerp (above) which also gets its raw materials from Lisbon but refines as much sugar in a fortnight as Venice does in a year.

1561 Mary Queen of Scots returns to Scotland following the death late last year of her husband François II of France. Denied passage through England, she lands at Leith, and she becomes embroiled in argument with Calvinist John Knox, who draws up the Confessions of Faith with other ministers of the Scottish church (*see* 1558).

Spain abandons her 2-year-old American colony at Fort Royal Sound because it is too isolated. Spain remains Europe's leading power and holds dominion over much of the world.

The Edict of Orléans suspends persecution of France's Huguenots.

England receives her first Flemish Calvinist refugees.

The Order of the Teutonic Knights in the Baltic states is secularized.

Anthony Jenkinson of England's Muscovy Company reaches Isfahan through Russia and opens trade with Persia (*see* 1555). Anglo-Persian trade will continue until 1581.

Theater *Gorboduc, or Ferrex and Porrex* by English playwrights Thomas Norton, 29, and Thomas Sackville, 25, first earl of Dorset and grandmaster of England's Freemasons. The earliest known English tragedy, it marks the first use of blank verse in English drama (all action occurs offstage).

The French ambassador to Lisbon Jean Nicot, 31, sends seeds and powdered leaves of the tobacco plant home to the queen mother Catherine de' Medici (*see* 1560). French physicians consider tobacco a panacea for many ills, the botanical name for tobacco, *Nicotiana rustica,* will derive from Nicot's name, as will the word "nicotine" (*see* Hawkins, 1565; Thevet, 1567; Vanquelin, 1810).

Venice's Ca' Corner della Ca' Grande is completed by Florentine architect Sansovino (Jacopo Tatti), now 75, who has built the imposing palazzo on the Grand Canal for Jacopo Cornaro, a nephew of the queen of Corsica.

Moscow's basilica of St. Basil is completed after 27 years of construction.

1562 A massacre of Huguenots at Vassy March 1 begins a series of civil wars in France (*see* 1572; Amboise, 1560).

English financial agent Sir Thomas Gresham, 43, writes that the setbacks of the Huguenots (above) "hath made such alteracione of credit as this penn cannot write you," and he worries about what will happen to the English pound (*see* note on inflation, 1559). "Here ys soche great dowtes cast upon our Estate, as the creadyte of the Queen's Majestie and all the whole nacyon ys at a stay; and glad ys that man that maye be quit of an Englishman's bill." Gresham will note that when two coins are equal in debt-paying power but unequal in intrinsic value, the less valuable coin will have a tendency to remain in circulation while the more valuable one is hoarded (Gresham's law).

England acts to aid the employment of the poor as she did in 1551, but at the same time she raises the price level at which wheat, barley, and malt may be exported, thus making food and drink more costly at home and enriching the landed gentry at the expense of the lower classes.

English navigator John Hawkins, 30, hijacks a Portuguese ship carrying African slaves to Brazil, he trades 300 slaves at Hispaniola for ginger, pearls, and sugar, he makes a huge profit, and his enterprise marks the beginning of English participation in the slave trade (*see* 1563).

A French expedition under Jean Ribault, 42, reaches Port Royal (*see* 1559; 1561). Ribault leaves 30 men at Charlesfort, named in honor of France's 13-year-old Charles IX, but the men are without means of support and they soon set out in small boats they have built. They are picked up half dead by an English vessel (*see* Ribault, 1564).

The University of Lille has its beginnings.

Painting *Europa and the Bull* by Titian; *The Suicide of Saul, The Monkeys, The Fall of the Rebel Angels,* and *The Triumph of Death* by Pieter Brueghel.

1563 The Peace of Amboise brings a truce in the war that has pitted French Huguenots against French Catholics for the past year in a conflict that has social and political roots as well as religious. The Huguenots come largely from the nobility and from the new capitalist-artisan class, with some peasant support in the southwest, while Paris and the northeast remain Catholic and both sides seek to gain control of the government in the absence of a strong crown.

Mary Queen of Scots sends her secretary William Maitland of Lethington, 35, to England to claim the right of succession to Elizabeth, but she receives no declaration from her half-sister.

The Anglican Church (Church of England, or Episcopal Church) is established by the adoption of the Thirty-Nine Articles, a modification of the 42 articles published by Thomas Cranmer in 1551. The Church is largely Protestant in dogma but has a liturgy reminiscent of the Tridentine liturgy established by the Council of Trent convened in 1545 and has a hierarchy similar to that of the Roman Catholic Church.

English dissenters or nonconformists include the Puritans who seek to "purify" the Church by substituting a simple, early-Christian ritual for the more elaborate ritual that has developed, but some Puritans leave the Anglican Church and organize their own churches as Separatists, while others become Presbyterians and seek to substitute organization by presbyters and synods for the organization by bishops within the Anglican church.

Dissenters are tolerated by England's Elizabeth, but she persecutes Catholics, Unitarians (who deny the doctrine of the Trinity), and Brownists—Puritans of the extreme left who will form the nucleus of the Congregationalist Church.

Wednesdays are declared fast days in England which now has more meatless days than any other country in Europe. A London woman is pilloried for having meat in her tavern during Lent (*see* 1534).

A Statute of Apprentices is enacted by Parliament.

John Hawkins sells a cargo of 105 African slaves in Hispaniola (300 by some accounts) (*see* 1562).

"If any African were carried away without his free consent," says Queen Elizabeth, "it would be detestable and call down the vengeance of Heaven upon the undertaking" (but *see* 1564).

De Praestigiis Daemonum by Belgian physician Johann Wier maintains that witches are merely miserable people with distorted minds, but much of the world will for centuries remain under the influence of the 1489 handbook on witch-hunting *Malleus Maleficarum* (*see* Loudon, 1634; Salem, 1692).

Painting A personification of *Summer* that includes an ear of maize is painted at Milan by German-born artist Guiseppe Arcimboldo (the "turkey corn" is familiar throughout much of the Mediterranean); *Landscape with the Flight into Egypt* and *The Tower of Babel* by Pieter Brueghel.

The Tuileries Palace is built at Paris for the queen mother Catherine de' Medici (*see* 1792).

France has famine which will be exacerbated by the country's religious wars (above).

Japan has rice riots at Mikawa following requisition of crops by the Tokugawa family and imposition of heavy taxes. Buddhist temples of the Ikko sect are burned in retaliation by the daimyo Ieyasu.

The potato is brought to England by Sir John Hawkins (above), but Hawkins's potato from Bogota may be the sweet potato.

1564 The Peace of Troyes ends hostilities between France and England. Huguenots and Catholics have joined forces to drive the English out of Havre, and England renounces all claims to Calais in return for 222,000 crowns (*see* 1558).

The Holy Roman Emperor Ferdinand I dies at Vienna July 25 at age 61 after 8 years in power. He

1564 (cont.) is succeeded by his 36-year-old son who will reign until 1576 as Maximilian II.

The Council of Trent convened by Pope Paul III in 1545 is concluded by Pope Pius IV who issues the "Professio Fidei Tridentina."

John Calvin dies at Geneva May 27 at age 54.

England's Elizabeth takes shares in John Hawkins's second slave-running venture and loans him one of her ships as her avarice overcomes the humane antipathy to slavery she expressed last year.

Andreas Vesalius is forced by the Inquisition to make a pilgrimage to the Holy Land as a condition for the commutation of his death sentence for dissecting human bodies (see 1543). Vesalius will disappear on the pilgrimage.

The Aztecs of New Spain are decimated by a new disease epidemic.

Miguel Lopez de Legazpe, 54, leaves New Spain with four ships to colonize the Philippines (see 1521; 1565).

French Huguenot leader Gaspard de Coligny fits out a second expedition to the New World. The fleet commanded by René de Landonniére sails to Fort Carolina on the St. John's River of northern Florida.

Jean Ribault arrives at Fort Carolina (above) with seven ships, 600 men (see 1562).

Painting *The Death of the Virgin, The Adoration of the Kings,* and *The Slaughter of the Innocents* by Pieter Brueghel. Michelangelo dies at Rome February 18 at age 88.

The sweet potato reaches England aboard one of John Hawkins's slave ships returning from New Castile. The tubers are planted to end England's reliance on imports for her sweet potato pies.

Lime juice is recommended as an antiscorbutic by Boudewijn Rousse de Ghent.

1565 St. Augustine, Florida, is established as the first permanent European settlement in North America. Spanish forces under Pedro Menendez de Aviles have attacked Fort Carolina, have slaughtered all its male inhabitants, and Menendez de Aviles settles 600 colonists at St. Augustine (see 1564; 1600).

A colony at Cebu in the Philippines is established by Miguel Lopez de Legazpe, who has been sent out from New Spain by the viceroy Luis de Velasco on orders from Spain's Philip II, has conquered the islands for Philip, and heads for home with a cargo of cinnamon (see 1564; Manila, 1571).

Malta is besieged in May by Ottoman forces who are resisted by the Knights of St. John under the command of their grand master Jean Parisot de La Valette, 71. Spanish forces arrive in September to relieve the siege, and they drive 31,000 Turks into the sea.

The London Royal Exchange is founded by Sir Thomas Gresham (see 1562).

London's Royal College of Physicians receives authority to conduct dissections of human cadavers.

Painting *Haymaking, The Harvesters, The Return of the Herd, The Gloomy Day, The Hunters in the Snow,* and *Winter Landscape with a Bird Trap* by Pieter Brueghel; *The Death of Aetaeon* by Titian.

Mass "Missa Papae Marcelli" by Palestrina.

The Bourée introduced at the French court of Catherine de' Medici is an adaptation of a peasant clog dance traditional in the French mountains.

John Hawkins introduces tobacco into England from Florida and writes, "The Floridians when they travell have a kinde of herbe dried, who with a cane and an earthen cap in the end, with fire, and the dried herbs put together, doe sucke thorow the cane the smoke thereof, which smoke satisfieth their hunger, and therewith they live foure or five dayes without meat or drinke, and this all the Frenchmen used for this purpose" (see 1600).

Venice's San Giorgio Maggiore is completed by Andrea Palladio.

France has a poor harvest. Catherine de' Medici decrees that meals shall be limited to three courses.

1566 The Italian secretary to Mary Queen of Scots is seized on the evening of March 9 by the earls of Morton and Lindsay who invade Mary's supper chamber with armed men, hack David Rizzio, 33, to death with daggers, and throw his body into the courtyard at Holyrood. The noblemen act on orders from Mary's husband Lord Darnley who will himself be murdered next year.

A German army of 80,000 under Maximilian II prepares to fight the Turks under Suleiman the Magnificent at Komon in Hungary, but the army is stricken with typhus and the campaign is abandoned.

Suleiman the Magnificent dies September 5 at age 70 during the siege of Szigeth. He leaves an empire that is the greatest and the best organized in Europe, but that will now begin a long decline as Suleiman is succeeded by his indolent son of 42 who assumes the imperial throne as Selim II and makes a truce with Maximilian II under which both sides retain their possessions.

Painting *The Census at Bethlehem, The Sermon of Saint John the Baptist,* and *The Wedding Dance* by Pieter Brueghel.

Theater *Gammer Gurton's Nedle* performed at Christ's Church, Cambridge, has probably been written by clergyman-teacher William Stevenson, perhaps with help from John Bridges and/or John Still. "I cannot eat but little meat,/ My stomach is not good;/ But sure I think that I can drink/ With him that wears a hood./ That I go bare, take ye no care,/ I am nothing a-cold:/ I stuff my skin so full within/ Of jolly good ale and old./ Back and side go bare, go bare,/ Both foot and hand go cold;/ But belly, God send thee good ale enough,/ Whether it be new or old" (the play will be published in 1575, the year Stevenson dies).

1567 Lord Darnley, husband to Mary Queen of Scots, is found murdered February 10 at Kirk o'Field, Edinburgh, and the queen is suspected of having been an accomplice. She is kidnapped April 24 by James Hepburn, 31, fourth earl of Bothwell, who marries the queen in a Protestant church May 15. The marriage provokes a rebellion by Scottish noblemen who desert the queen at Carberry Hill in June, force her to dismiss Bothwell, and make her sign an abdication in favor of her 13-month-old son who is proclaimed James VI of Scotland July 24. The young king will be raised at Stirling Castle by the earl and countess of Mar.

Spain's Philip II sends 20,000 troops under the duke of Alva to the Lowlands where they capture Antwerp as the Lowlanders prepare for an 80-year struggle to gain independence from the Spanish (see 1560; 1568).

French colonists in Brazil are captured and put to the sword by the Portuguese (see 1555).

Rio de Janeiro is founded by the Portuguese who destroy the French colony under the leadership of Mem de Sa.

England's John Hawkins joins two African kings in besieging an inland African town, he takes 470 slaves as booty, and he sells them to Spanish colonists in America (see 1562; 1568).

Rugby School is founded in England's east Warwickshire (see game of rugby, 1823).

Painting *The Wedding Banquet* (*Peasant Wedding*), *The Land of Cockaigne, The Conversion of Saul, Adoration of the Kings in the Snow* by Pieter Brueghel; *The Martyrdom of St. Laurence* by Titian.

"I can boast of having been the first in France who brought the seed of this plant [tobacco], who sowed it, and named the plant in question herbe Angoulmoisine," writes André Thevet in *Les Singulariés de la France antartique, autrement nommée Amérique* (see 1556). "Since then a certain individual, who never made any voyage, has given it his name, some ten years after my return" (see Nicot, 1561).

The Rotonda (Villa Capra) outside Vicenza is completed by Andrea Palladio.

Antwerp's sugar refining industry moves to Amsterdam following the capture of Antwerp by the duke of Alva (above).

1568 Mary Queen of Scots escapes from captivity in May but is defeated at Langside May 13 and is placed in confinement after fleeing to England.

Leaders of the Flemish opposition to the Spanish Inquisition are beheaded as traitors at Brussels June 4, and the action precipitates a revolt of the Lowlands that will continue for 80 years. Lamoral, Comte d'Egmont, is executed at age 46, Philip de Montmorency, Comte d'Horn, is executed at age 50, other prominent figures are executed, and there is a general confiscation of the estates of those who have failed to appear before the Council of Blood, including Willem of Orange who has left Holland with thousands of Netherlanders (see Goethe, 1788).

Sweden's Eric XIV is deposed September 30 after several years of increasing insanity and is replaced by his 31-year-old brother who will reign until 1592 as John III.

England's Sir John Hawkins is defeated by the Spanish at Veracruz while on a third slaving expedition to the New World, but he survives (see 1567; 1588).

Japan's Azuchi-Momoyama period of unification begins following the seizure of Kyoto by the Taira clan general Nobunaga Oda, 34, who begins subjugating feudal lords (daimyo), humbling Buddhist priests, destroying the political power of Buddhism, establishing order in many provinces, and making a start toward the unification of the empire.

The Solomon Islands of the Pacific are explored by Spanish mariner Albaro de Mendana de Neyra, 27, who discovered the islands last year and who will find the Marquesas just before he dies in 1595.

English explorer David Ingram travels from the Gulf of Mexico north to Canada and finds "vines which beare grapes as big as a mans thumbe."

Mennonites fleeing Spanish persecution in the Lowlands (above) move east. The pacifist Protestant sect will settle in the German states, Switzerland, and eastern Russia (see 1523; 1536; Catharine, 1783).

Abridgement of the Chronicles of England is published by English printer Richard Grafton who first records the mnemonic rhyme "Thirty days hath September,/ April, June and November;/ All the rest have thirty-one,/ Excepting February alone,/ And that has twenty-eight days clear/ And twenty-nine in each leap year."

Painting *Imperial Art Dealer Jacopo della Strada* by Titian; *The Peasant Dance, The Peasant and the Bird-Nester, The Cripples, Landscape with the Magpie in the Gallows, The Misanthrope,* and *The Parable of the Blood* by Pieter Brueghel.

1569 The Mercator projection map of the world published by Flemish instrument maker Gerhardus Mercator (Gerhard Kremer), 57, represents the meridians of longitude by equally spaced parallel lines and gradually spaces out latitude lines toward the polar regions to exaggerate degrees of latitude in exactly the same proportion as degrees of longitude. Mercator has studied under the late Gemma Frisius (see 1530; 1533), his map enormously simplifies the job of charting a course (the course of a ship on a constant compass bearing always appears as a straight line), and the map will contribute to the accuracy of navigation charts everywhere.

The Union of Lublin July 1 merges Lithuania with Poland over the objections of Lithuania.

The Massacre of St. Bartholomew in 1572 was a shocking new low in the history of French religious intolerance.

English earls to the north rebel against Elizabeth and sack Durham Cathedral, but the rebellion is easily suppressed.

Hunger and plague kill 500 people a day at Lisbon through much of the summer.

Painting *The Storm at Sea* by Pieter Brueghel who dies at Brussels September 5 at age 44.

1570 The czar of Muscovy Ivan the Terrible enters the city of Great Novgorod January 8 and begins a 5-week reign of terror. A man of dubious character has accused the Novgorodians of being sympathetic to Poland in the ongoing Livonian War, Ivan has ravaged the approaches to the second richest city in the czardom, and he has batches of Novgorodians from all classes of society massacred each day. Ivan has his men plunder every church, monastery, manor house, warehouse, and farm within a radius of 100 miles, leaving every structure roofless, destroying all cattle. Not until February 13 does he permit the survivors to begin rebuilding.

The Ottoman sultan Selim II declares war on Venice at the persuasion of the Sephardic Jew Don Joseph Nasi who has planned to make Cyprus a refuge for Jews. Venice has refused to cede Cyprus, Spain has come to Venice's support, but the Spanish and Venetian fleets are delayed and Cyprus falls to the Turks.

The Peace of Stettin in December ends a 7-year war between Sweden and Denmark, which recognizes Swedish independence. French and Polish diplomats have mediated to negotiate the peace, and the two Scandinavian powers will remain at peace with each other until 1611.

Five North American tribes confederate under the name Iroquois. The Mohawk brave Hiawatha and the brave Dekanawida, originally a Huron, have persuaded the Mohawk, the Oneida, the Onondaga, the Cayuga, and the Seneca to form a league with a common council, each tribe having a fixed number of chiefly delegates.

Tribesmen in the region that will be called Virginia kill Juan Bautista Seguar and other Jesuits, thus ending Spanish efforts to colonize the region (*see* 1584).

Large-scale traffic in black slaves begins between the African coast of Sierra Leone and the Brazilian bulge 1,807 miles away (*see* 1510; 1581).

Nagasaki begins its role as Japan's major port for foreign commerce. A local lord in Kyushu opens the fishing village to foreign trade (*see* 1638).

Leipzig banker Hermann Rott signs a contract with the Portuguese government giving him control of pepper imported from the Orient.

The Schoolmaster by the late English scholar Roger Ascham is a treatise on education: "It is costly wisdom that is bought by experience.... Learning teacheth more in one year than experience in twenty." Ascham died 2 years ago at age 53.

Painting *Moses Striking the Rock* by Tintoretto.

The Royal Exchange opened at London is a prototype department store that rents stalls to retail merchants.

I Quattro Libri dell'Architettura by Andrea Palladio is published at Venice.

Slave ships returning from Brazil (above) bring maize, manioc, sweet potatoes, peanuts, and beans to supplement Africa's few subsistence crops. Manioc (cassava) will prove highly resistant to locusts and to deterioration when left in the field, and it will serve as a reserve against famine.

Cooking Secrets of Pope Pius V (*Cuoco Secreto di Papa Pio Quinto*) by Bartolomeo Scappi is published at Venice with 28 pages of copperplate illustrations that include the first picture of a fork (*see* 1518).

Only two native villages remain in Hispaniola (*see* 1548).

Maize from Brazil (above) will fuel the population growth that will provide a steady supply of African slaves for the new trade.

1571 The Battle of Lepanto October 7 gives Spanish and Venetian galleys a stunning victory over a great Ottoman fleet. The Christian galleys number at least 200, with long sweeping oars in single banks, but the merchants of Venice are eager for peace, they do not follow up on their triumph, and Constantinople will regain its strength within a year.

Crimean Tartars sack Moscow.

The Japanese strongman Nobunaga Oda destroys the Enryakuji Buddhist monastery on Mt. Hiei and eliminates the most militarily powerful of his enemies.

Manila is founded May 19 by Miguel Lopez de Legazpe. He has subjugated the Philippine natives and moves his capital from Cebu to the new city, using it as a base for colonization (*see* 1565).

Harrow School is founded by a charter granted to John Lyon, a yeoman of Preston, by England's Queen Elizabeth. Harrow will open its first building to scholars in 1611, and by 1660 the headmaster will be taking advantage of a concession in Lyon's charter to admit boys from other parishes beyond the London suburb of Harrow, boys who will pay tuition.

1572 Danish astronomer Tycho Brahe, 26, discovers a bright new star beyond the moon in Cassiopeia and thus destroys the Aristotelian idea that no change can occur in the celestial regions. Brahe has used instruments of his own design to see the super nova that will be called Tycho's star and to accumulate data on planetary and lunar positions (*see* 1576).

The Massacre of St. Bartholomew August 23 and 24 kills an estimated 50,000 French Huguenots at Paris and in the provinces. Henri of Navarre marries Margaret of Valois, sister of Charles IX, and saves his own life by feigning conversion to Catholicism (*see* Edict of Nantes, 1598).

Pope Gregory and all the Catholic powers congratulate the French queen mother Catherine de' Medici, and the pope commands that bonfires be lighted and a medal struck to celebrate the massacre which he calls better than 50 Battles of Lepanto.

The Ottoman sultan Selim II rebuilds his navy following last year's Battle of Lepanto. His naval forces reach such imposing strength that Don John of Austria refuses to attack.

Dutch insurgents capture Brill as insurrection against the Spanish spreads in the North. The Spanish lay siege to Haarlem.

England's duke of Norfolk Thomas Howard III, 36, is beheaded for having conspired with the Spanish to invade England and free Mary Queen of Scots.

France's Admiral Coligny dies in the Massacre of St. Bartholomew (above). Losses suffered in the massacre will halt French colonial expansion for decades.

English navigator Francis Drake, 32, leaves with two small ships carrying 73 men and boys on an expedition to capture the annual shipment of silver from Peru that mules carry across the Isthmus of Panama to be loaded aboard Spanish galleons (*see* 1573).

French surgeon Ambroise Pare, 55, wins fame by ending the brutal treatment of "infected" gunpowder wounds with boiling alder oil. Physician to Charles IX, Pare has run out of oil and has improvised a compound of egg yolks, oil of roses, and turpentine, he has introduced arterial ligature to replace cauterization, he will perform herniotomy without castration, he treats infected burns by applying onion poultices, and he will be famous for his line, "I dressed him and God healed him."

Vienna's Spanish Riding School is mentioned for the first time. The Holy Roman Emperor Maximilian II has visited a riding school in Castile, he has decided that his knights need a similar school, he has imported Iberian horses, and the riding hall's Lippizaner stallions foaled in the town of Lipizza, dark brown at birth, turn almost pure white within 5 years.

Dutch insurgents besieged at Haarlem (above) use pigeons to carry out messages.

Poetry *Os Lusiadas* by Portuguese poet Luiz Vaz de Camoes, 48, is an epic of 10 cantos modeled on Virgil's *Aeneid* of 19 B.C. and recounts in ottava rima Vasco da Gama's discovery of the sea route to the Indies.

French painter François Clouet dies at Paris at age 62; Il Bronzino dies at Florence November 23 at age 69.

1573 The Polish throne is obtained for France's Henri of Valois by his mother Catherine de' Medici who pays a heavy price. Henri signs the Pacta Conventa which places strict limits on royal power and which formally recognizes the right of the Polish nobility to elect kings (*see* 1574).

The Edict of Boulogne July 8 ends a fourth war between French Catholics and Huguenots on terms favorable to the Huguenots (but *see* 1574).

Venice breaks with Spain, abandons Cyprus, and agrees to pay the Turks an indemnity of 300,000 ducats. Only Candia (Crete), Paros, and the Ionian Islands remain under Venetian control.

Don John of Austria takes Tunis from the Turks who have held it since 1569 and who will regain it next year.

China's Wan Li assumes the imperial throne at age 10 and begins a 47-year reign as Shen Tsung. Ming dynasty culture will flourish in the new reign, but Manchu power will increase.

The Ashikaga shogunate that has ruled Japan since 1336 is ended as the shogun Yoshiake takes arms against the strongman Nobunaga Oda who took power 5 years ago. Yoshiake is defeated, he shaves his head, and becomes a Buddhist priest (*see* 1582).

Francis Drake makes the biggest haul in the history of piracy. With assistance from Indians and blacks, he captures a shipment of Spanish silver from the Potosí mines of New Castile while it is being transported across the Isthmus of Panama for shipment to Spain (*see* 1545; 1572; 1577).

A typhus epidemic strikes the area surrounding the city of Mexico (Tenochtitlan) in New Spain.

Theater *Amyntas* (*Aminta*) by Italian playwright Torquata Tasso, 29, 7/31 at a theater on Belvedere Island in the Po River.

1574 France's Charles IX dies May 30 at age 24 and is succeeded by his 23-year-old brother Henri of Valois who vacates the Polish throne, returns to France, and assumes the throne as Henri III to begin a 15-

1574 (cont.) year reign that will be dominated by his mother Catherine de' Medici.

The departure of Henri (above) leaves Poland without a king (*see* 1575).

A new religious war begins between French Catholics and Huguenots (*see* 1573; 1576).

Spanish forces in the Lowlands lay siege to Leyden under the command of Luis de Requesens y Zuniga who has succeeded the duke of Alva and who gains a victory at Mookerheide. But Willem the Silent cuts the dikes in several places to flood the land and permit his ships to sail up to Leyden's city wall, he relieves the siege, and the Spanish are unable to suppress the Dutch revolt (*see* 1568; 1576).

The Ottoman sultan Selim II dies December 12 at age 50 after a drunken 8-year reign. He is succeeded by his 28-year-old son who begins a 20-year reign as Murad III.

Islands discovered November 22 some 365 miles off the west coast of South America will be named the Juan Fernández Islands after the 38-year-old Spanish navigator who has found them (*see* Defoe, 1720).

Poetry *La Franciade* by Pierre de Ronsard who has been court poet to Charles IX (above) since 1560 but whose national epic will remain unfinished.

Florence's Uffizi Palaces are completed after 14 years of construction by painter-architect Giorgio Vasari who dies June 27 at age 62. The two matching palaces frame a narrow piazza and serve as government offices for the grand duke of Tuscany Cosimo de' Medici.

Some 5,000 of Leyden's 15,000 people die of hunger in the 6-week siege by the Spanish (above), but burgomaster van der Werff cries defiance. He draws his sword and says, "You may eat me first; I will not surrender to the Spanish."

Leyden hutspot originated by besieged burghers in the Dutch city (above) is by some accounts a stew left behind by the departing Spanish and discovered by orphan boy Cornelis Joppensz who has been given 6 guilders to venture through the lines to see if the city is still surrounded. The stew is made from stale beef and long-lasting vegetables such as onions and carrots. Ships bearing white bread and herring relieve the city's hunger, and those foods along with hutspot will be served October 3 each year after 1648 to celebrate the liberation of the Netherlands.

An estimated 152,500 Spanish settlers are now in the Americas.

1575 Poland's nobility elects as king the Transylvanian prince Stephen Bathory, 42, who will reign until his death in 1586. The nobility has been influenced by the grand chamberlain Jan Zamojski, 34, who is made grand chancellor, and the election ends the period of confusion that has existed since last year.

Luanda is founded by Portuguese colonists in West Africa.

The University of Leyden has its beginnings in a college founded at the Dutch town that withstood a Spanish siege last year.

Poetry *Jerusalem Delivered* (*Gerusalemme Liberata*) by Torquato Tasso is an epic of the First Crusade.

Painting El Greco arrives in Spain at age 34 after having left his native Crete to study in Italy. Kyriakos Theotokopoulos has studied under Titian, he will settle at Toledo, and he will remain in Spain.

Sculpture *Mercury* (bronze) by Flemish-born Italian sculptor Giovanni Bologna (Jean Bologne), 46, who has been attached to the Florentine court of the Medici family since 1558.

England's royal organist Thomas Tallis, 60, and his fellow organist-composer William Byrd, 33, receive a 21-year license January 22 from Elizabeth to print and sell music and music paper. They issue their joint work *Cantiones quae ab argumento Sacrae vocantur, quinque et sex partium* containing 16 motets by Tallis and 18 by Byrd, some of which will be given English translations and will be sung for centuries as Anglican cathedral anthems.

The first European porcelain, created by Tuscany's Grand Duke Francesco Maria de' Medici, 34, is far inferior to the Chinese porcelain imported by Portuguese caravels. Almost all Europeans eat off earthenware plates or wooden trenchers (*see* Père d'Entrecolles, 1712).

1576 "The Spanish fury" erupts at Antwerp where Spanish troops massacre 6,000 citizens, burn 800 houses, and wreak costly damage to the city's commerce. The Lowland provinces unite by treaty in the Pacification of Ghent without regard to national or religious differences in a joint effort to drive out the Spaniards.

The Peace of Chastenoy May 6 ends France's fifth civil war since 1562, but the Paix de Monsieur concedes so much to the Huguenots that Catholics form a Holy League and make an alliance with Spain's Philip II to annihilate the reformed party and bring the Guises to the throne.

France's Henri III takes alarm at the ambitions of the Holy League, proclaims himself head of the League, and forbids the exercise of the Protestant religion in his realm.

The Holy Roman Emperor Maximilian II dies October 12 at age 49 and is succeeded by his eldest surviving son Rudolf, 24, who will reside mostly at Prague and will reign until his death in 1612.

An astronomical observatory on the island of Hven in the Sound is established with royal aid by Danish astronomer Tycho Brahe of 1572 super nova discovery fame, but Brahe will reject the Copernican system of 1543 and will hold that the five planets revolve about the sun which in turn revolves about an immobile earth (*see* Kepler, 1609; Galileo, 1613).

Baffin's Land and a bay that will be called Frobisher's Bay are discovered by English explorer Sir Martin Frobisher, 41, who commands an expedition in search of a northwest passage to Cathay and who returns with an Eskimo. Frobisher has studied navigation under John Dee (see 1558; Ross, 1818).

A typhus epidemic ravages New Spain as in 1551.

Warsaw University has its beginnings in a new Polish academy.

Six Livres de la République by French political economist Jean Bodin, 66, attempts to revive the system of Aristotle and apply it to modern politics. Bodin defines the powers of a sovereign, but his theory of sovereignty is full of discrepancies.

Titian dies at Venice August 27 in his late 80s.

Hans Sachs dies January 19 at age 81 after a career as *Meistersinger* in which he has composed innumerable *Fastnachtsspiele*—the popular plays that have emerged as drama have become more secular.

England's first playhouse opens at Shoreditch under the direction of actor-manager James Burbage who has been one of the earl of Leicester's players (see Blackfriar's, 1596; Globe, 1599).

Japan's Azuchi Castle goes up on the shores of Lake Biwa where the Taira strongman Nobunaga Oda builds the country's first great castle.

1577 French Catholics and Huguenots wage a brief sixth war. The Catholics triumph in mid-September but the Huguenots obtain favorable terms because Henri III is reluctant to let the Holy League become too powerful.

The Black Assize at Oxford, England, ends with the judges, the jury, witnesses, everyone in the court except the prisoners dying of "gaol fever," a pestilence believed to have arisen out of the bowels of the earth but actually typhus carried by the prisoners who live in filth.

England's Francis Drake embarks December 13 with a fleet of ships and sails down the African coast en route for South America. His flagship the *Pelican* is 102 feet in length overall and carries nine "gentlemen" in addition to a crew of 80 (which includes 40 men-at-arms, a tailor, a shoemaker, an apothecary, and Drake's personal trumpeter) (see 1578).

Venice's Church of the Redeemer (Il Redentore) designed by Andrea Palladio goes up with funds voted by the Venetian Senate at the height of a plague.

Martin Frobisher's men exploring the Atlantic coast of North America receive 1 pound of biscuit and 1 gallon of beer each per day, 1 pound of salt beef or pork on flesh days and one dried codfish for every four men on fast days, with oatmeal and rice when the fish gives out (see 1576). Each man also receives a quarter-pound of butter per day and a half-pound of cheese, with honey for sweetening and "sallet oyle" and vinegar, plus wild game, wild fowl, salmon, and fresh cod when it is available.

1578 Don John of Austria receives reinforcements in the Lowlands as Spain's Philip II sends an army under his Italian cousin Alessandro Farnese, 32. A patriot army is attacked and defeated at Gemblours January 31, Don John dies of fever October 1, and Farnese takes command of Spanish and Austrian forces in the Lowlands.

Portugal's Sebastian I is killed August 4 and his army annihilated at Al Kasr al Kebir in Northwest Africa where he has led a crusade in defiance of warnings by Spain's Philip II and Pope Gregory XIII. The king of Fez and the Moorish pretender are also slain in the battle, but the Portuguese people refuse to believe that the 24-year-old Sebastian is dead. "Sebastianism" develops as a religion whose votaries believe that the king is either away on a pilgrimage or is waiting on some enchanted island for an appropriate time to return. Four pretenders will successively impersonate Sebastian and will successively be executed, the last one being an Italian who speaks no Portuguese (see 1580).

Francis Drake navigates the Strait of Magellan in a 16-day passage after having lost four of his ships, he renames his flagship the *Golden Hinde*, he ravages the coasts of Chile and Peru, and he continues up the coast (see 1577; New Albion, 1579).

Queen Elizabeth grants a patent to Sir Humphrey Gilbert, 39, to "inhabit and possess at his choice all remote and heathen lands not in the actual possession of any Christian prince." Gilbert crosses the Atlantic in search of a northwest passage to the Indies (see 1583).

Chronicles of English History to 1575 by English historian-printer Raphael Holinshed continues work begun by his late employer Reginald Wolfe. Holinshed's *Chronicles* will be the source of plot material for historical dramas by William Shakespeare and other playwrights.

Fiction *Euphues, The Anatomy of Wit* by English author John Lyly, 24.

Poetry *Sonnets pour Hélène* by Pierre de Ronsard whose lyrical lines include "Quand vous serrez vielle, au soir à la chandelle. . . ."

China's population reaches 60 million.

1579 The Union of Utrecht joins Dutch patriots in opposition to the Spanish who occupy the Lowlands. It marks the foundation of the Dutch Republic.

The Dutch sign a military alliance with England.

The Irish rebel from England with support from Spanish troops.

Francis Drake lands in North America at a point north of what will be called San Francisco and claims possession of New Albion for Elizabeth (see 1578; 1769; Cook, 1778).

1579 (cont.) Russian pioneers move into Siberia. In the next 60 years a few thousand people will gain control of a vast region extending to the Pacific (see 1637; 1741).

Scotland enacts a law "for Punishment of the Strong and Idle Beggars, and Relief of the Poor and Impotent" (see 1551; 1601).

"Vindiciae contra Tyrannos" is published anonymously (probably by John Calvin's friend Theodore de Beze, 60, who succeeded to the leadership of French Protestantism after Calvin's death in 1564). The pamphlet attacks absolutism, declares that rulers must be accountable to the people, but insists that only magistrates may resist the king.

De Juri Regni apud Scotos by Scottish humanist George Buchanan, now 73, confutes absolutism with the argument that kings exist only by the will of the people. Written for the instruction of his royal pupil who will become England's James I, Buchanan's work justifies tyrannicide and states that the obligation of subjects to their king is conditioned on the performance of that king in the duties of his office.

Lives of the Noble Grecians and Romans by the Greek biographer Plutarch of the 1st to 2nd century A.D. is published in an English translation from the French of Jacques Amyot, 66, by English translator Sir Thomas North, 44, who will add additional *Lives* in 1595. North's work will influence Elizabethan poets and will provide material for playwrights.

Poetry   *The Shepheardes Calender* by English poet Edmund Spenser, 27, who secures a place in the earl of Leicester's household and dedicates the work to Leicester's nephew Philip Sidney.

Painting   *Trinity* and *Assumption* by El Greco who has been commissioned to decorate the high altar and two transept altars at Toledo's Church of S. Domingo el Antiguo.

1580 Spain and Portugal unite under one crown following the death of Portugal's Cardinal Henri after a 2-year reign as king. Spaniards under the aging duke of Alva invade the country, they defeat the Portuguese August 25 at the Battle of Alcantara near Lisbon, and Spain's Philip II is proclaimed Philip I of Portugal (see 1581; 1640).

An Irish rebellion supported by the Spanish is suppressed by the English who pacify the rebels by starving them.

A seventh French civil war between Catholics and Huguenots breaks out but is ended November 26 by the Treaty of Fleix which confirms earlier treaties granted to the Huguenots (see 1585).

The Moroccan port of Ceuta opposite Gibraltar is occupied by the Spanish who will hold it until 1688.

England's Francis Drake enters Plymouth harbor September 26 after having made the first circumnavigation of the world by an Englishman. He has left Java March 26, has rounded the Cape of Good Hope June 15 with only three casks of water for his 57 men aboard the *Golden Hinde,* he watered on the Guinea coast a month later, and he has completed his round-the-world voyage in roughly 34 months.

Buenos Aires is founded June 11 by Spanish conquistador Juan de Garay, captain-general of the La Plata territory, who will be killed in a massacre by natives in 1583 (see 1515).

Nonfiction   *Essais* by French writer Michel Eyquem de Montaigne is published in its first two volumes. Now 47, Montaigne served as a judge at Bordeaux from 1555 to 1570, he retired to Montaigne in 1570 and began work on his essays 2 years later, and while he will insist that "I do not teach, I recount," his pursuit of truth expressed in vernacular style reveals extraordinary insight into the human condition.

Fiction   *Euphues and His England* by John Lyly is a continuation of his 1578 book and is dedicated to his patron the earl of Oxford. A narrative centered on love, Lyly's didactic romance is marked by a pervading effort to achieve elegance by affectations that include alliteration and simile, but his intent is to reform education and manners.

Cocoa gains widespread use as a beverage in Spain (see 1527; 1615).

1581 Scholars attending commencement exercises at St. Mary's, Oxford, June 27 find on their benches 400 copies of the privately printed pamphlet "Decem Rationes" by English Jesuit Edmund Campion, 41, who has written an attack on the Anglican church. Authorities seize Campion July 14 as he preaches at Lyford in Berkshire, he is committed to the Tower of London and examined in the presence of the queen, he is placed on the rack three times in efforts to shake his faith in Roman Catholicism, he is indicted for having conspired to dethrone Elizabeth, and he is found guilty November 20. "If our religion do make traitors we are worthy to be condemned; but otherwise are and have been true subjects as ever the queen had," says Campion, but he is hanged December 1 and drawn and quartered.

Spain's Philip II sends some of his black slaves to his Florida colony of St. Augustine. They are the first blacks to be landed in North America (see 1565; Drake, 1586).

Poland's Stephen Bathory invades Russia, he gains a victory over Ivan the Terrible, and he advances on Pskov (see 1582). Stephen's brother Christoph dies and is succeeded as prince of Transylvania by his 9-year-old son Sigismund who will try to unite with the Hapsburgs for a grand assault on the Ottoman Turks, but who will be opposed by the Transylvanian nobility.

Spain's Philip II (above) unifies control of the Oriental spice trade, eliminating the competition in the sugar, spice, and slave trade that existed before the Spanish takeover of Portugal last year.

England's Francis Drake captures the richest prize ever taken on the high seas. He returns with Spanish gold, silver, and gemstones worth as much as the Crown's total revenue for a year, the Spanish ambassador demands restitution, but Elizabeth knights Drake after a 9-month delay.

"The Newe Attractive" by London compass-maker Robert Norman is a pamphlet describing Norman's discovery of the dip in the magnetic needle.

Ergotism kills thousands in the German duchy of Luxembourg and in Spain where the disease is endemic (see 1039; 1587).

Ballet *Ballet Comique de la Reyne* at Paris with music by the Italian composer Baltasarini who is known in Paris as Beaujoyeulx. Presented for the queen mother Catherine de' Medici, the ballet represents the first use of dance and music to convey a coherent dramatic idea (see first grand opera, 1600).

Andrea Palladio dies at Venice August 19 at age 71, but his books will spread his influence throughout the world.

The first potato recipes are published in a German cookbook, but few Europeans eat potatoes even in the German states.

1582 A new Gregorian calendar devised by the late Neapolitan astronomer-physician Aloysius Lilius (Luigi Lilio Ghiraldi) is instituted by Pope Gregory who abolishes the ancient Julian calendar because its error of one day in every 128 years has moved the vernal equinox to March 11. Gregory restores the vernal equinox to March 21, but while Europe's Roman Catholic countries adopt the new style calendar, the Protestant countries will adhere to the old style Julian calendar of 45 B.C. until 1700 or later, and the Russians will retain the Julian calendar until 1918 (see Britain, 1752).

Muscovy makes peace with Poland and Sweden but is obliged to accept most of the recent losses suffered by Ivan the Terrible. Differences among the warring powers have been mediated by the Jesuit Antonio Possevino who has been sent by Pope Gregory XIII in hopes of affecting a union of the Orthodox and Roman churches which have been split since 1054.

Japan's Taira strongman Nobunaga Oda travels to join his general Hashiba Hideyoshi, 46, who has conquered much of western Honshu from the Mori family. His enemy General Akechi Mitsuhido, 56, sets fire to a monastery where Oda has halted for the night. Oda dies in the flames or commits *seppuku* June 21 at age 48 after having destroyed the political power of the Buddhist priests. Hideyoshi kills Mitsuhido and gains support from Oda's Tokugawa daimyo Ieyasu, 39, at Edo. He begins to eliminate the Oda family in a great struggle for power (see 1573; 1584).

A delegation of Japanese Christian boys goes to Rome. The youths will return in April of 1586 after having visited Pope Gregory XIII.

Divers Voyages Touching the Discovery of America by Oxford clergyman-geographer Richard Hakluyt, 30, is published in England (see 1584).

The University of Edinburgh has its beginnings in Scotland.

The University of Würzburg has its beginnings.

Coffee (kahveh) is mentioned for the first time in print by Augsburg merchant Leonhard Rauwolf who left Marseilles for Arabia in 1576, has returned, and begins publications of his *Travels* at Frankfurt (see 1601).

The Paris restaurant La Tour d'Argent opens now by some accounts (see Boulanger, 1765).

1583 England's Humphrey Gilbert sails to Newfoundland, takes possession in the name of Elizabeth, and attempts to make the first English settlement in the New World (see 1578). Gilbert is lost on the return voyage, and the colonists he left behind in Newfoundland will disappear (see Virginia, 1584).

England's minister to Turkey William Harborne trades English woolens, tin, mercury, and amber for spices, cotton goods, silks, and dyes.

Portugal dominates the world sugar trade and sells Brazilian sugar at high prices for use by European aristocrats and capitalists (see below).

The first life insurance policy of record is issued on the life of "William Gybbons, citizen and salter of London." The annual premium is £32, and when Gybbons dies within the year his beneficiaries will collect £400 (see Tontine, 1653).

De Plantis by Italian physician-botanist Andre Cesalpino contains the first modern classification of plants based on a comparative study of forms. Cesalpino's work will be acknowledged by Linnaeus in 1737.

Nonfiction *The Names of Christ* (*De los Nombres de Cristo*) by Spanish poet-theologian Fray Louis (Ponce) de Leon, 56, who was imprisoned by the Inquisition in 1572 but was absolved in 1576. Leon's work is a Platonic discussion of the nature of Christ; *The Perfect Wife* (*La Perfecta Casada*) by Fray Leon is a handbook on the duties of a wife (Leon's poetry will not be published until 1631).

Sculpture *Rape of the Sabine Women* by Giovanni da Bologna for the court of the Medicis at Florence. The marble work stands 13 feet 6 inches high.

1584 The Virginia colony planted on Roanoke Island by English navigator-courtier Walter Raleigh, 32, is named for England's virgin queen who knights Raleigh for his services. Raleigh has secured the renewal of the patent on colonization granted in 1578 to his late half-brother Humphrey Gilbert, he has sent out an expedition in April under the command of captains Phillip Amadas and Arthur Barlow, both 34, they have sailed by way of the Canary Islands to Florida and thence up the coast in search of a suitable site for an English plantation in the New World,

1584 (cont.) and they have come to an inlet between Albemarle and Pamlico sounds.

A pamphlet by Phillip Amadas and Arthur Barlow (above) describes the soil of the New World as "sweet smelling" and speaks of vines "bowed down with grapes, the woods abounded with game, the waters with fish" in "the goodliest land under the cope of heaven."

"Discourse Concerning Western Planting" by geographer Richard Hakluyt is an essay addressed to Elizabeth encouraging colonization.

The czar of Muscovy Ivan the Terrible dies March 18 at age 53 after a 37-year reign and is succeeded by his somewhat feeble-minded 27-year-old son Fedor Ivanovich who will reign until 1598. Ivan struck his eldest surviving son 3 years ago in a momentary fit of fury, the blow proved fatal, the czar has been inconsolable ever since, the boyars have refused to let him abdicate, but he has joined the strictest order of monks. Boris Federovich Godunov, 33, a son-in-law and court favorite of the late czar, will dominate the 14-year reign of Fedor I and will try to conciliate the boyars by regularizing the conditions of serfdom.

Willem of Orange is murdered at Delft July 10 at age 51. Spain's Philip II has for 3 years offered a large reward to anyone who would rid the world of the man he calls a traitor, the Burgundian Balthazar Gerard has shot the stadtholder of Holland and Zeeland, and Willem is succeeded by his 17-year-old son Maurice of Nassau who has been studying at the University of Leyden.

Bern, Geneva, and Zurich form an alliance against Savoy and the Catholic cantons. The Catholic cantons will form an alliance with Spain in 1587.

Hashiba Hideyoshi gains hegemony over central Japan and on August 8 moves into Hideyoshi Castle at Osaka. Begun in September of last year, the castle has been built by 30,000 workers using stones brought to the site by 1,000 boats per day (see 1582; 1587).

"Drink wine, and have the gout; drink none, and have the gout," writes English physician Thomas Cogan in *The Haven of Health* (see Galen, 164; Garrod, 1859).

1585 France's War of the Three Henrys begins following the death last year of Henri III's brother François, duke of Anjou. Henri III's house of Valois is left without an heir, the Holy League is determined to bar Henri of Navarre from the French throne, and a 4-year war begins between Henri of Guise (who is supported by the Holy League and by Spain's Philip II), Henri III of Valois, and Henri of Navarre (see Coutras, 1587).

Antwerp surrenders after a long siege by the duke of Parma whose Spanish forces sack Europe's chief commercial center and exile its Protestants.

England's Elizabeth breaks with Spain, Philip II seizes all English ships in Spanish ports, and Elizabeth sends troops under the command of Robert Dudley, 53, first earl of Leicester, to aid the Lowlanders in their struggle against the Spanish.

Sir Francis Drake sails for the West Indies with 2,300 men in a fleet of 30 ships to attack the Spanish.

Sir Walter Raleigh sends a new expedition to Virginia under the command of his cousin Sir Richard Grenville, 44, and Sir Ralph Lane, 55.

Chesapeake Bay is discovered by Sir Ralph Lane (above) who remains in the New World as governor of Raleigh's Roanoke Island colony (see 1584; 1586).

Davis Strait is discovered by English explorer John Davis (Davys), 35 on the first of three voyages he will make with Adrian Gilbert in search of a northwest passage through North America to the Pacific.

La disme by Dutch mathematician Simon Stevin, 37, introduces decimal fractions (see 1586).

A code of etiquette is promulgated by France's Henri III for his courtiers.

Kronborg Castle is completed at Elsinore (Helsingör) for Denmark's Frederick II on the site of an earlier castle built early in the last century by Eric of Pomerania to enforce the collection of tolls on foreign ships passing through the Oresund.

Jamaican ginger reaches Europe on a ship from the West Indies. It is the first Oriental spice to have been grown successfully in the New World.

Deep-fried cookery (tempura) is introduced into Japan by Jesuit missionaries (see 1551).

1586 A plot to assassinate the English queen is discovered by the spies of Elizabeth's secretary of state Francis Walsingham. Anthony Babbington, 25, is a page to Mary Queen of Scots, he has conspired with Jesuit priest John Ballard, Mary is convicted October 25 of involvement in the plot. Babbington, Ballard, and a dozen others are executed while Mary's own life hangs in the balance (see 1587).

England's earl of Leicester gains a victory for the Dutch States-General over the Spanish at Zutphen September 22, but his nephew Sir Philip Sidney, son-in-law of Walsingham (above), is wounded in the thigh and dies 26 days later at Arnhem.

Sir Francis Drake takes the Spanish colonial cities of San Domingo and Cartagena, he attacks the Spanish colony established 21 years ago at St. Augustine, Florida, he puts the settlement to the torch, and he moves up the coast to Roanoke Island.

Poland's Stephen Bathory dies suddenly of apoplexy December 12 at age 53 after an 11-year reign. His death ends Polish plans to unite Poland, Muscovy, and Transylvania into one great state, and he will be succeeded in mid-August of next year by the 21-year old son of Sweden's John III who will rule until 1632 as Sigismund III in a reign dominated by the Jesuits.

Sir Richard Grenville arrives at Roanoke following the departure of Sir Francis Drake (above) and lands new settlers at Sir Walter Raleigh's colony before returning to England (see White, 1587). He captures a Spanish ship on his return voyage and stops to pillage in the Azores before setting to work at organizing English defenses against a Spanish invasion.

English navigator Thomas Cavendish, 31, sails for Brazil with three ships, he discovers Port Desire (Puerto Deseado) in Patagonia, he passes through the Strait of Magellan, he plunders a Spanish galleon captured in South American waters, and he proceeds westward. Cavendish will arrive home by way of the Philippines with Spanish gold but with only one ship, the *Desire,* and his voyage of 2 years and 50 days will make him the third man to circumnavigate the world (see del Cano, 1522; Drake, 1580).

Treatises on statics and hydrostatics by Simon Stevin give mathematical proof of the law of the level, prove the law of the inclined plane, and show that two unequal weights fall through the same distance in the same time (see 1585; Galileo, 1592). A military and civil engineer under Maurice of Nassau, Stevin has invented a system of sluices as a means of defense. He will enunciate the theorem of the triangle of forces, and he will discover that downward pressure of a liquid is independent of the shape of its container.

Painting *The Burial of Count Orgaz* by El Greco.

The 75-ton obelisk erected in Rome's St. Peter's Square in September after 17 months of work has required 907 men and 75 horses to move 800 feet from the Circus of Nero. Pope Sixtus V (Felice Peretti) works to suppress the powerful nobility of the Papal States, to rid the territory of bandits, to encourage silk culture, to put the finances of the papal states on a sound basis, and to beautify Rome. He will superintend construction of a Vatican Palace and Library, the Lateran Palace, the Santa Scala, and the completion of the dome of St. Peter's designed by Michelangelo before his death in 1564.

Potatoes picked up with other supplies at Cartagena are brought home by Sir Francis Drake (above) who returns also with Virginia tobacco and with starving and disheartened Roanoke colonists. The potatoes are planted on Raleigh's Irish estate near Cork.

1587 Mary Queen of Scots is beheaded February 8 by order of her cousin Elizabeth who has been persuaded that Mary Stuart's existence poses a continuing threat to the Protestant crown of England.

Spain's Philip II prepares an invasion fleet to take the English throne but is delayed by Sir Francis Drake who sails into the Bay of Cadiz April 19 and burns upwards of 10,000 tons of Spanish shipping, a feat he will later call "singeing the king's beard" (see 1588).

Henri of Navarre wins a victory over the Catholic League October 20 at Coutras, but the Catholic party is set back only temporarily (see 1588).

Persia's half-blind Shah Mohammed Khudabanda dies after a 9-year reign. He is succeeded by his 30-year-old son who assumes the throne as Abbas I to begin a 42-year reign that will see great expansion of Persian territory.

Subjugation of Japan's feudal barons (daimyo) is completed by the civil dictator (Kampaku) Hashiba Hideyoshi who was made prime minister (Dajodaijin) late last year and given the name Toyotomi (rich citizen) by the emperor Goyozei (see 1592).

Toyotomi Hideyoshi discovers the strength of Christianity in Japan and issues an edict in June prohibiting foreign missionaries. He has invaded Kyushu to subjugate the Shimazu family, and his request for a beautiful woman to sleep with has been refused because all the women have embraced the Christian faith (see 1593; 1597).

Sir Francis Drake captures the Spanish treasure ship *Sao Felipe* with her rich cargo of bullion, silks, spices, Chinese porcelains, pearls, and gemstones.

Virginia Dare is born August 18 on Roanoke Island to the daughter of John White and is the first English child to be born in North America. White lands 150 new settlers including 17 women in the Virginia colony on orders from Sir Walter Raleigh, but the new arrivals land too late to plant crops for fall and winter, so White returns to England for supplies to see them through (see 1586; 1591).

Ergotism reaches endemic levels in the German states, bringing insanity and death to thousands who eat bread made from infected rye (see 1581, 1595).

An Epistle of Comfort to the Reverend Priests by English Jesuit poet-priest Robert Southwell, 26, is a letter of encouragement to fellow Catholics including Philip Howard, 30, earl of Arundel, who became

The defeat of the Spanish Armada in 1588 gave Elizabethan England her most glorious military triumph.

1587 (cont.) a Catholic 3 years ago through the influence of his wife, but who has been imprisoned for trying to escape from England and will die in prison in 1594.

Theater *Tamburlaine the Great* by English playwright-poet Christopher Marlowe, 23, is presented in both its parts at London by the Admiral's Men, a theatrical company sponsored by the earl of Nottingham. *The Spanish Tragedie, Containing the lamentable end of Don Horatio,* and *Bel-imperia: with the pittifull death of olde Hieronimo* by English playwright Thomas Kyd, 29, whose aged Hieronomo is played by actor Edward Alleyn, the same man who plays Marlowe's Tamburlaine. Both plays are swashbuckling dramas that gratify the Elizabethan taste for bloody death, murder, and suicide.

Isfahan becomes capital of Persia by order of the shah Abbas (above) who undertakes to make the city a showplace of the world. Abbas will give Isfahan so many palaces, mosques, gardens, bridges, and caravansaries that its 600,000 inhabitants will say, "Isfahan is half the world" (Isfahan nesfe Jahan).

Pope Sixtus V writes that Rome is swarming with vagabonds in search of food as work goes forward to make the city a showplace of baroque palaces and cathedrals (*see* 1586).

Eggplant is introduced into England. The variety introduced is small, light brown in color, and egg-shaped.

1588 An "invincible" Spanish Armada of 132 vessels sails against England under the command of Spain's "admiral of the ocean," the untrained nobleman Alonso Perez de Guzman, 38, seventh duke of Medina-Sidonia. His largest ship is a 1,300-ton vessel but more than 30 are below 100 tons. The Royal Navy commanded by Lord High Admiral William Howard has only 34 ships, of which the largest is the 1,000-ton *Triumph*. Admiral Howard on his 800-ton flagship *Ark Royal* has the support of 163 armed merchant vessels, including the *Buonaventure*, first English vessel to round the Cape of Good Hope and sail on to India, and he has the help of Sir Francis Drake and Sir John Hawkins. The two fleets engage forces July 31, a great storm blows up in the following week, and the elements help the English defeat the Armada by August 8, scoring a victory that opens the world to English trade and colonization.

The Danish-Norwegian king Frederick II has died April 4 at age 53 after a 29-year reign. The beloved Frederick is succeeded by his 10-year-old son who will reign until 1648 as Christian IV.

Henri of Guise has entered Paris and has been acclaimed king of France to the delight of the Holy League and of Spain's Philip II. A popular insurrection May 12 (the Day of the Barricades) forces Henri III to take refuge at Blois, he receives no support from the Estates-General against the Catholic League and he has Henri of Guise and his brother Louis the Cardinal murdered December 23.

English merchants found the Guinea Company to traffic in slaves from Africa's Guinea coast.

A Briefe & True Report of the New Found Land in Virginia by English mathematician Thomas Hariot, 28, is based on a visit to Sir Walter Raleigh's Roanoke colony (*see* below; 1587; 1591).

Paolo Veronese dies at Venice April 19 at age 59.

Theater *The Tragedy of Dr. Faustus* by Christopher Marlowe at London with the Admiral's Men. "Was this the face that launched a thousand ships,/ And burnt the topless towers of Ilium?" (XVIII, i, 99).

Lamentations by Giovanni Pierluigi da Palestrina is published at Rome. Now 72, Palestrina complains in his introduction to Pope Sixtus V that he has been compelled by poverty to publish the book of sacred music in small format and to omit much that he has written, but Palestrina's music will be sung for centuries in the Sistine Chapel.

Venice's library is completed on the Piazza San Marco with a Doric arcade on its ground floor and Ionic columns on its second floor after more than a century of construction following a plan by the late Jacopo Sansovino (*see* 1561).

Potatoes are introduced into the Lowlands by Flemish botanist-physician Carolus Clusius (Charles de Lecluse), 62, who may have received the tubers from English herbalist John Gerard (*see* 1597; 1601).

Virginia fields planted Indian fashion with corn, beans, squash, melons, and sunflowers yield "at the least two hundred London bushelles" per acre, whereas in England "fourtie bushelles of wheat [per acre] ... is thought to be much," writes Thomas Hariot (above).

Maize "is a graine of marvelous great increase," writes Thomas Hariot (above). "Pagatowr, a kinde of graine so called by the inhabitants, the same in the West Indies is called mayze. English men call it Guinney wheate or Turkie wheate. [Its kernels are] of divers colours: some white, some red, some yellow, and some blew. All of them yeelde a very white and sweete flowre ... [which] maketh a very good bread."

1589 The Bourbon dynasty that will rule France until 1792 is founded by Henri of Navarre who is converted to Catholicism and who forces the Catholic party to recognize his claim to the throne following the death of Henri III, murdered by the monk Jacques Clement at St. Cloud outside Paris July 31. Henri III had fled to the Huguenot camp of Henri of Navarre when the Catholic party revolted at news that the king had had Henri of Guise and his brother murdered. Henri of Navarre begins a 21-year reign as Henri IV.

Portuguese pretender Antonio of Crato obtains support from the English and marches on Lisbon, but he is defeated by the Spanish who struggle to regain their national confidence after the defeat last year of their great armada.

The Russian Orthodox Church gains independence from Constantinople by the establishment of a separate Russian patriarchate in a move dictated by the swift decline of the Ottoman Empire through the degeneracy of its sultan Murad III and the corruption of its officials.

The first knitting machine is invented by English clergyman William Lee who will be refused a patent for his stocking frame first by Queen Elizabeth and then by James I, but who will set up his frames at Rouen (see 1603).

Theater *The Famous Tragedy of the Rich Jew of Malta* by Christopher Marlowe: "Thou has committed—/ Fornication—but that was in another country./ And besides, the wench is dead."

Kamurzell House is completed at Strasbourg.

England imports timber from western Norway because the British Isles have been so deforested by the national effort to build ships for defense against the Spanish Armada of 1588 (see 1605).

Destruction of forests by the Spanish in New Spain will lead to a water crisis in that country.

1590 The Battle of Ivry March 14 secures the French throne of Henri IV as the king defeats the Catholic League under the duc de Mayenne. Henri's 15,000-man royalist army besieges Paris in mid-May, the siege is raised after several months by the duke of Parma Alessandro Farnese who arrives with 14,000 men, but starvation produced by the siege kills thousands (see below).

Japan is unified by the dictator Toyotomi Hideyoshi whose vassal Ieyasu moves his headquarters to Edo to dominate the great plain of eastern Japan (see 1582; 1598).

Viaggio all' India Orientali by Venetian merchant-traveler Gasparo Balbi is the first European account of India beyond the Ganges.

Venice's Rialto Bridge is completed to join the island of Rialto, financial center of the city, with the island of San Marco.

Baltic trade with the rest of Europe will reach its peak in the next 3 decades as measured by shipping tolls exacted in the sound (see Kronberg, 1585).

The compound microscope is invented by Dutch optician Zacharias Janssen (see 1675).

The Black Death reaches Rome and other Italian cities.

Ergotism remains endemic in Spain.

Poetry *The Faerie Queene* by Edmund Spenser is published in its first three books with a letter to Sir Walter Raleigh explaining the purpose and structure of the work. "And all for love, and nothing for reward."

Painting *The Cardsharp* by Italian painter Michelangelo Merisi de Caravaggio, 17, who travels to Rome where he will paint from life, rejecting the current taste for the classics.

Theater *King Henry VI* by English playwright-poet William Shakespeare, 26, of Stratford-upon-Avon. An actor who married Anne Hathaway in 1582, Shakespeare will move to London in 1592 (dates for all Shakespearean plays are largely conjectural).

Palazzo Balbi is completed for Venetian merchant Nicolo Balbi after 8 years of construction on the bend of the Grand Canal.

The siege of Paris (above) brings hunger and malnutrition that kill 13,000 in the city. Food supplies are inadequate for the 30,000 inhabitants and the 8,000-man garrison, by mid-June the Spanish ambassador has proposed grinding the bones of the dead to make flour, by July 9 the poor are chasing dogs and eating grass that grows in the streets (from the diary of Paris lawyer Pierre de L'Estoile). A Fugger newsletter in August reports "great hunger in Paris; a pound of white bread costs half a crown . . . Rumor has it that people are eating mice, cats, and dogs." By the end of August "you could see the poor dying, eating dead dogs on the street; some ate garbage thrown into the river or rats or the flour made from bones [though most who did die did in agony]" and soon there is cannibalism as starving Parisians "began chasing children along the streets as well as dogs" (from L'Estoile's diary).

English vicar Edward Shawcross of Weaverham, Cheshire, is accused by the archbishop of York of being an "instructor of young folkes how to comyt the syn of adultrie or fornication and not to beget or bring forth children."

1591 England's earl of Essex Robert Devereux, 25, joins with French royalists to besiege Rouen, capital of Normandy and her richest city. The resulting starvation resembles that seen in Paris last year and may even be worse, albeit on a smaller scale.

North Africa's black culture is destroyed and the country made vulnerable to rival pashas as Spanish and Portuguese renegades in the service of Moroccans across the desert, use firearms to defeat the blacks, destroy Gao, and help the Moroccans establish themselves at Timbuktu. The pashas will gain independence from Morocco in 1612 and will rule Timbuktu until 1780.

Portugal closes Brazil to further immigration of anyone except Portuguese, but continues to import African slaves for the plantations of its Brazilian colony (see 1570).

John White returns to Roanoke after having been delayed by the war with Spain and finds the colony there has vanished, possibly victims of hostile Indians. The word "Croatan," never to be satisfactorily explained, is the only message left by the 117 lost colonists who include White's family (see 1589; Jamestown, 1607).

1591 (cont.) Plague and famine strike the Italian states. Nuremberg merchant Balthaszar Paumgartner writes home to his wife Magdalena, "It is reckoned that in one year here, one-third of the folk in all Italy has died, and a highly necessary thing, too. For were it not for the pest, they must die anyway, as there would not be enough for so many to eat."

Systematic use of letters in algebra to represent both coefficients and unknown quantities is introduced by French mathematician François Viete, 51, seigneur de la Bigotière, who will be called the "father of algebra." Viete has served as privy councilor to Henri IV, has discovered the key to coded messages from Spain to the Netherlands, and has decoded them. He will apply algebra to both geometry and trigonometry (*see* Descartes, 1619).

Dublin's Trinity College is founded by Queen Elizabeth.

Poetry *The Harmony of the Church* by English poet Michael Drayton, 28.

Theater *The Comedy of Errors* by William Shakespeare is derived from the Plautus comedy *The Menaechmi* of 215 B.C.: "They say every why has a wherefore" (II,ii); "There is something in the wind" (III, i); "Small cheer and great welcome makes a merry feast" (III, i).

Pamplona in northern Spain has a running of the bulls in which men run through the streets in front of the bulls being driven to the local bullring. The event will be repeated for centuries with occasional deaths and frequent injuries as men are gored or trampled.

Edinburgh's Canongate Tollbooth is erected.

Japanese teamaster Rikyu Sen commits ceremonial suicide (*seppuku*) on orders from Toyotomi Hideyoshi. Sen has formalized the tea ceremony (*see* 1484).

1592 University of Pisa mathematician Galileo Galilei, 28, quits under pressure and moves to the University of Padua after having defied the accepted belief that objects fall to the ground at speeds proportionate to their body weights. Galileo has purportedly climbed the spiral stairs to the top of the city's leaning tower, he has dropped cannonballs and bullets of various weights, one by one, and he has allegedly shown that except for fractional disparities caused by air resistance the objects all fall at the same rate of speed (*see* sector, 1597; Newton, 1666).

Rouen is relieved in April, the Duke of Parma receives a bullet in the arm soon thereafter, and he is dead by December.

Sweden's John III dies at age 55 after having failed to Romanize the country. He is succeeded by his 26-year-old son Sigismund who has been king of Poland since 1587 and who marries the Austrian archduchess Anne.

The Mogul emperor Akbar conquers Sind.

The Japanese dictator Toyotomi Hideyoshi invades Korea but is forced to return to Japan after having been refused passage to invade China.

The Malay Peninsula is rounded by English navigator Sir James Lancaster, a veteran of the 1588 battle with the Spanish Armada.

Mombasa on Africa's east coast is settled by Portuguese.

North America's Pacific coast is explored by Spanish navigator Juan de Fuca (*see* Vancouver, 1793).

A Russian census lists peasants under the names of landholders. The peasants will hereafter be considered the landlords' serfs (*see* 1597).

Jesuit Robert Southwell is apprehended while celebrating mass in a Catholic household. He is tortured severely and imprisoned in the Tower of London, but he refuses to reveal the names of fellow priests (*see* 1587; 1595).

Ergotism is endemic in many of the German states, as it was 5 years ago (*see* Marbourg, 1597).

Pamphlet "A Quip for an Upstart Courtier" by Robert Greene who dies September 3 at age 32 after having surfeited on pickled herring and Rhenish wine.

Painting *The Last Supper* by Tintoretto.

Theater *Two Gentlemen of Verona* by William Shakespeare: "Who is Sylvia? what is she?/ That all our swains commend her? Holy, fair, and wise is she;/ The heavens such grace did lend her" (IV, ii); *Titus Andronicus* by William Shakespeare: "And easy it is/ Of a cut loaf to steal a shive" (II, i, meaning that adultery is easily arranged and likely to go unnoticed); *King Richard III* by William Shakespeare: "Now is the winter of our discontent/ Made glorious summer by this sun of York" (I, i); "A horse! A horse! My kingdom for a horse!" (V, iv); "The early village cock/ Hath twice done salutation to the morn" (V, iii).

Florence's Palazza Vecchio is completed after 294 years of construction.

Heineken Beer has its beginnings in a Dutch brewery started under the name De Hooiberg (The Haystack) (*see* 1864).

1593 English admiral Sir Richard Hawkins begins an abortive voyage round the world after reporting that 10,000 men have died of scurvy under his command in the Royal Navy.

Spanish Franciscans arrive in Japan to begin proselytizing in competition with the Portuguese Jesuits who arrived in 1551 (*see* 1597).

English coal mining is given impetus by the shortage of wood which has become so costly that an Act of Parliament compels beer exporters either to fetch back their barrels or to return with foreign clapboard suitable for making the same number of barrels as was shipped (*see* 1589).

Poetry "Venus and Adonis" by William Shakespeare: "Love keeps his revels where there are but twain," "Love surfeits not, Lust like a glutton dies./ Love is all truth, Lust full of forgèd lies." Poet-playwright Christopher Marlowe is killed May 30 at age 29 in a tavern brawl at Deptford where his companion Ingram Frizer stabs him in the eye in self-defense. Marlowe is survived by lines of verse that include "Come live with me and be my Love/ And we will all the pleasures prove/ That hills and valleys, dale and field,/ And all the craggy mountains yield" (from "The Passionate Shepherd to His Love").

Theater *The Massacre at Paris* by Christopher Marlowe 1/26 at London's Rose Theatre (Lord Strange's Men); *The Troublesome Reign and Lamentable Death of Edward II* by Christopher Marlowe at London by Pembroke's Men.

Spain's Escorial Palace is completed near Madrid after 30 years of construction. Designed by architect Juan Bautista de Toledo, the palace includes a church, a monastery, and a mausoleum.

Potatoes are praised by Swiss botanist Gaspard Bauhin, 33, who engages some farmers in the Vosges region to plant the tubers (but *see* 1630).

Orange and lemon juice are recommended as antiscorbutics by Sir Richard Hawkins (above) (*see* 1564; Lind, 1747).

1594 France's Henri IV obtains the surrender of Paris March 22, is crowned at Chartres, and continues his campaign to win over each French province, either by negotiation or by force of arms.

England's Sir Richard Hawkins is defeated in Peru's San Mateo Bay and is taken prisoner after having rounded Cape Horn and plundered the Spanish port of Valparaiso. Hawkins will be sent back to Spain in 1597 and will not be ransomed until 1602.

Lisbon closes her spice market to the English and Dutch forcing formation of the Dutch East India Company to obtain spices directly from the Orient (*see* English East India Company, 1600).

The Central University of Ecuador has its beginnings in a school founded at Quito.

Fiction *The Unfortunate Traveller, or The Life of Jack Wilton*, by English novelist-playwright Thomas Nashe, 27, who pioneers the adventure novel.

Poetry "The Rape of Lucrece" by William Shakespeare: "Men's faults do seldom to themselves appear."

Painting *The Musical Party* by Michelangelo da Caravaggio. Tintoretto dies at Venice May 31 at 75.

Theater *Mother Bombie* by John Lyly: "There is no fool like an old fool;" *Dido, Queen of Carthage* by the late Christopher Marlowe, whose tragedy has been completed by Thomas Nashe (above); *King John* by William Shakespeare: "Well, whiles I am a beggar, I will rail/ And say there is no sin, but to be rich;/ And being rich, my virtue then shall be/ To say there is no vice but beggary" (II, i); "Bell, book, and candle shall not drive me back/ When gold and silver becks me to come on" (III, iii); "Life is as tedious as a twice-told tale/ Vexing the dull ear of a drowsy man" (III, iv); "And he that stands upon a slippery place/ Makes nice of no vile hold to stay him up" (III, iv); "To gild refinèd gold, to paint the lily,/ ... Is wasteful and ridiculous excess" (IV, ii); *Love's Labour's Lost* by William Shakespeare: "These earthly godfathers of heaven's lights/ That give a name to every fixèd star/ Have no more profit of their shining nights/ Than those that walk and wot not what they are" (I, i).

The sweet potato reaches China 30 years after being introduced by the Spanish into the Philippines.

Spain's Atlantic gateway port of Seville has a population of 90,000, up from 45,000 in 1530.

1595 Spanish forces land in Cornwall and burn the English towns of Penzance and Mousehole as hostilities continue between Elizabeth and Philip II.

The Ottoman sultan Murad III dies at age 49 after a 21-year reign of debauchery that has seen his empire begin a steep decline. He is succeeded by his 29-year-old son who begins an 8-year reign by having 19 of his brothers murdered and is proclaimed Mohammed III.

Transylvania's Sigismund Bathory has his opponents executed and subdues Wallachia by defeating Sinan Pasha October 28 at the Battle of Giurgevo.

English Jesuit poet Robert Southwell is tried for treason and is found guilty. He is executed February 21 at Tyburn.

Upper Austria has a peasant revolt.

The Dutch East India Company sends its first ships to the Orient, the Dutch make their first settlements on Africa's Guinea coast, Dutch ships arrive in the East Indies, and the Dutch begin colonization.

Sir Walter Raleigh sails with four ships and 100 men to explore the Orinoco River in South America, but he returns empty-handed (*see* 1589; 1618).

Measles, mumps, and typhus (*tabardillo*) are common among the Indians of New Spain, reports Friar Mendieta (*see* 1545).

Ergotism breaks out in epidemic form at Marbourg, France, and remains endemic in many of the German states (*see* 1592; 1597).

The University of Ljubljana is founded.

The University of San Carlos is founded at Cebu City in the Philippines.

Poetry by the late Robert Southwell (above) is published posthumously and includes *St. Peter's Complaint* and short devotional lyrics among which is "The Burning Babe." "An Apologia for Poetrie" by the late Sir Philip Sidney is also published.

1595 (cont.) Painting *Venus and Adonis* by Bolognese painter Annibale Caracci, 34, who has arrived at Rome to join his younger brother Agostino.

Theater *Romeo and Juliet* by William Shakespeare whose "star-cross'd lovers" belong to the rival Montague and Capulet families of Verona: "What's in a name? That which we call a rose/ By any other name would smell as sweet" (II, ii); "A plague o' both your houses!" (III, i); *Richard II* by William Shakespeare: "This royal throne of kings, this sceptered isle,/ This earth of majesty, this seat of Mars,/ This other Eden, demi-paradise,/ This fortress built by Nature for herself/ Against infection and the hand of war,/ This happy breed of men, this little world,/ This precious stone set in the silver sea,/ Which serves it in the office of a wall/ Or as a moat defensive to a house/ Against the envy of less happier lands—/ This blessed plot, this earth, this realm, this England,/ This nurse, this teeming womb of royal kings,/ Feared by their breed and famous by their birth (II, i); "For God's sake, let us sit upon the ground/ And tell sad stories of the death of kings—/ How some have been deposed, some slain in war,/ Some haunted by the ghosts they have deposed,/ Some poisoned by their wives, some sleeping killed,/ All murdered. For within the hollow crown/ That rounds the mortal temples of a king/ Keeps Death his Court, and there the antic sits,/ Scoffing his state and grinning at his pomp" (III, ii); *A Midsummer Night's Dream* by William Shakespeare: "The course of true love never did run smooth" (I, i); "What fools these mortals be!" (III, ii).

England's wheat crop fails and food prices rise sharply (*see* 1596).

1596 The Battle of Keresztes near Erlau in northern Hungary ends in victory for Ottoman forces over the Austrians as the Holy Roman Emperor Rudolf II occupies himself with wresting Transylvania from the Hungarians.

English forces sack Cadiz and Spanish forces take Calais in the continuing war between France and Spain.

France's War of the Catholic League ends with the decrees of Folembray.

China and Japan make peace following the failure of Japanese invasion forces in Korea.

Dutch navigator Willem Barents lands on the islands of Newland (Spitzbergen) which have been sighted earlier by mariners in the Arctic Ocean but which have never been explored (*see* 1557; Hudson, 1607).

Sir Francis Drake dies January 28 of the plague aboard his ship near the town of Nombre de Dios in the West Indies.

Nonfiction *The Triumphs over Death* by the late Robert Southwell is published posthumously.

Poetry *Metamorphosis of Ajax* by English poet Sir John Harington, 35, who is banished from the court for his satire: "I know that the wiser sort of men will consider, and I wish that the ignorant sort would learn, how it is not the baseness or homeliness, whether of words or matters, that makes them foul and obscene, but their base minds, filthy conceits, or lewd intents that handle them...." "From your confessor, lawyer and physician,/ Hide not your case on no condition."

Painting *View of Toledo* by El Greco.

Theater *The Taming of the Shrew* by William Shakespeare and collaborators: "There's small choice in rotten apples" (I, i); "Crowns in my purse I have and goods at home/ And so am come abroad to see the world" (I, ii); "Kiss me, Kate" (II, i); "Thereby hangs a tale" (IV, i); "Such duty as the subject owes the prince/ Even such a woman oweth to her husband" (V, ii); "Thy husband is thy lord, thy life, thy keeper,/ Thy head, thy sovereign, one that cares for thee,/ And for thy maintenance commits his body/ To painful labor both by sea and land,/ To watch the night in storms, the day in cold,/ While thou liest warm at home, secure and safe;/ And craves no other tribute at thy hands/ But love, fair looks and true obedience,/ Too little payment for so great a debt" (V, ii); *The Merchant of Venice* by William Shakespeare: "Hath not a Jew eyes? Hath not a Jew hands, organs, dimensions, senses, affections, passions? Fed with the same food, hurt with the same weapons, subject to the same diseases, healed by the same means, warmed and cooled by the same winter and summer as a Christian is?" (Shylock, III, i); "The quality of mercy is not strained,/ It droppeth as the gentle rain from heaven/ Upon the place beneath. It is twice blest;/ It blesseth him that gives and him that takes" (Portia, IV, i, but many playgoers come away remembering only the insistence of Jessica's father Shylock on "a pound of flesh").

Blackfriar's Theatre opens at London where actor-theatrical manager James Burbage has converted a private house into a playhouse (*see* 1576; 1599).

A practical water closet invented by English poet Sir John Harington (above) has little effect. The privy and chamber pot now in universal use will remain in common use for centuries (*see* Cummings, 1775).

Famine brings rural unrest to Austria (above), but food is plentiful—if costly—at Vienna. Food shortages create misery in much of Europe, in English cities, in Asia, in the Caribbean islands, and in Peru.

Basque whaling captain François Sopite Zaburu devises the world's first factory ship. Sailing out of a port that will later be called St. Jean de Luz, Zaburu builds a brick furnace on his deck and extracts whale oil from blubber which he has "tryed out" (boiled down) aboard ship, a procedure far more economical than dragging whale carcasses to shore factories.

The tomato is introduced into England as an ornamental plant (*see* 1534).

1597 The Irish rebel against England under the leadership of the baron of Dungannon and earl of Tyrone Hugh O'Neill, 57. Hugh Roe O'Donnell, 26, joins him in petitioning Spain's Philip II for aid in gaining religious and political liberty from the English.

England's Elizabeth I makes her court favorite the earl of Essex earl marshal of England. He embarks on an expedition to the Azores to capture the Spanish treasure fleet but the venture will fail.

The Japanese dictator Toyotomi Hideyoshi executes three Jesuits, six Franciscans, and 17 Japanese Christians, he orders all remaining missionaries to leave the country, but when most remain in defiance of his orders he refrains from pressing them lest he drive away Portuguese traders, especially now since direct commerce with China has ceased.

A Muscovite ukase requires the seizure of runaway serfs and their return to their masters (see 1592).

Akbar the Great orders that Indian peasants pay him one-third of the gross produce their fields are supposed to yield as determined by a detailed survey of the country's agricultural resources.

The sector is invented by Galileo Galilei. His draftsman's compass will, with refinements, serve for centuries as a calculating device capable of solving many algebraic problems mechanically (see 1592; telescope, 1608; Babbage, 1833).

Ergotism is caused by eating spurred rye, concludes the faculty of medicine at Marbourg, France (rye infected with ergot fungus appears to have spurred grain heads) (see 1595; 1674).

Nonfiction *Essays* by English barrister-scientist Francis Bacon, 36, who says in "Of Studies," "Some books are to be tasted, others to be swallowed, and some few to be chewed and digested: that is, some books are to be read only in parts, others to be read, but not curiously, and some few to be read wholly, and with diligence and attention"; *Herball* by English botanist John Gerard, 52, superintendent of the gardens of William Cecil, 77, 1st Baron Burghley and lord high treasurer of England. Gerard's *Herball* is largely a poor and thinly disguised translation of the 1554 *Cruydeboek* by Rembert Dodoens with most of its 1,800 illustrations lifted from a German work by Jacob Theodore of Bergzabern; *A Survey of London* by English historian John Stow, 72.

Theater *King Henry IV*, Part I, by William Shakespeare whose comic figure Falstaff says, "The better part of valour is discretion, in which better part I have saved my life" (V, iv).

Opera *Dafne* at carnival time in Florence's Palazzo Corsi with music by Italian composer Jacopo Peri, 36, who pioneers use of recitative in a reconstruction of musical forms used by the ancient Greeks in their tragedies; melodramatic libretto by Italian poet Ottavio Rinuccini, 35.

Iceland's Mount Hekla volcano erupts as it did in 1154 (see 1836).

Cauliflower (*chou de Chypre*) is first mentioned in French writings.

The blackness of Queen Elizabeth's teeth is noted by a German traveler visiting England. Paul Henter ascribes it to the Queen's excessive consumption of sugar, making the first recorded association between sugar and tooth decay.

The first English mention of tea appears in a translation of Dutch navigator Jan Hugo van Lin-Schooten's *Travels*. Van Lin-Schooten calls the beverage "chaa" (see 1609; coffee, 1582, 1601).

Potatoes are described by John Gerard (above) who has received some directly from Virginia and who mistakenly calls them "Batata virginian sive Virginianorum, et Pappus, Potatoes of Virginia": "These tubers are nourishing as well as a pleasant dish, equal in wholesomeness and salubrity to the batata [sweet potato], whether they be baked in hot ashes, or boiled and eaten with oyle, vinegar or pepper, or prepared in any other way by the hands of an able cook." The only potato common in England, however, is the batata, or sweet potato.

1598 The Edict of Nantes issued April 15 by France's Henri IV gives Protestant Huguenots equal political rights with Catholics, allows them to obtain some fortified towns, and opens political offices to them. The Edict does not establish complete freedom of worship, but it does permit Huguenots to practice their religion in a number of French cities and towns (see Revocation, 1685).

Muscovy's Fedor I dies January 7 at age 40 after a weak reign of more than 13 years. He is succeeded by his brother-in-law Boris Godunov, who has actually controlled the country since 1584 and who was probably responsible for the sudden death of the young czarevich Demetrius, at Uglich in mid-May of 1591. Godunov has recovered towns taken by the Swedes, has fought off a Tartar raid on Moscow, has built towns and fortresses to the northeast and southeast in order to keep the Tartar and Finn tribes in order, has recolonized Siberia, has supported the middle classes at the expense of the old nobility and peasantry, and has encouraged trade with English merchants by exempting them from tolls.

Spain's Philip II dies at the new Escorial palace September 13 at age 71 after a 42-year reign, leaving his country in dire financial straits. He is succeeded by his 20-year-old son who ascends the throne as Philip III to begin an indolent reign of nearly 23 years that will be controlled largely by the duque of Lerma.

Japan's dictator Toyotomi Hideyoshi dies September 18 at age 62. A power struggle among his former vassals plunges Japan into turmoil (see Ieyasu, 1600).

The murder of Henri III in 1589 ended the Valois dynasty that had ruled France since 1328.

The Japanese evacuate Korea after a disastrous campaign that has cost the lives of 260,000 men and has ruined the Japanese peasantry, whose crops have been commandeered to feed the troops.

The Island of Mauritius (Isle de France) is taken by the Dutch.

Some 14 Dutch ships have left early in the year for India following Lisbon's closing of trade with Holland. The Dutch set out to trade directly with the East and commence a gradual conquest of Portuguese possessions (*see* 1599).

Spain's new king Philip III offers a prize of 1,000 crowns for a method of ascertaining longitude. Holland's States-General offers a prize of 10,000 florins for a solution to the problem (*see* 1524; 1530; Greenwich Observatory, 1676).

A short-lived colony east of Nova Scotia is established on Sable Island by France's Marquis de la Roche who has obtained a patent from Henri IV and who lands two shiploads of vagabonds on the island (*see* Champlain, 1603, 1604).

Pueblo territory in the American Southwest is colonized by some 400 Spanish men, women, and children who arrive in more than 80 wagons with 7,000 head of livestock. Soldiers soon follow to subdue the Pueblo.

Fiction *Arcadia* by Spanish novelist-poet Lope de Vega, 36, who sailed with the Armada against England in 1588.

Poetry *La Dragontea* by Lope de Vega is an epic poem about Sir Francis Drake; "Address to the Nightingale" by English poet Richard Barnfield, 24, begins "As it fell upon a day/ In the merry month of May . . ."; "Hero and Leander" by the late Christo-pher Marlowe: "Who ever loved that loved not at first sight?"

Painting *St. Martin and the Beggar* by El Greco.

Theater *Every Man in His Humour* by English playwright-poet Ben Jonson, 26, in September at London with a cast (The Lord Chamberlain's Men) that includes William Shakespeare: "The rule, Get money, still get money, boy;/ No matter by what means"; "Odds me, I marvel what pleasure or felicity they have in taking this roguish tobacco! it's good for nothing but to choke a man and fill him full of smoke and embers" (III, ii); *King Henry IV*, Part II, by William Shakespeare: "Out of this nettle, danger, we pluck this flower, safety" (II, iii), "Uneasy lies the head that wears a crown" (III, i).

The Cuzco Cathedral in Peru is completed by Spanish architect Francisco Becerra, 53, who has been in Peru since 1573.

French tillage and pasturage are "the true mines and treasures of Peru," says the Duc de Sully Maximilien de Bethune, 38. One of Henri IV's highest officials, Sully calls le labourage et le pastourage the two breasts of France (*les deux mamelles dont la France*) from which the nation takes her nourishment (*see* Boisguilbert, 1695).

William Shakespeare relates overweight and life expectancy in *Henry IV*, Part II (above). The king warns a "surfeit-swell'd" Falstaff to "Leave gourmandizing; know the grave doth gape/ For thee thrice wider than for other men" (V, v). (Twentieth-century statistics correlating obesity with shorter life expectancy will bear out the 3-to-1 ratio cited).

1599 England's earl of Essex is sent by Elizabeth to subdue Ireland's rebellious earl of Tyrone but is defeated at Arklow, makes a truce with Tyrone, and leaves his post as governor general of Ireland to vindicate himself before the queen.

Four Dutch vessels return from India with cargoes of pepper, cloves, cinnamon, and nutmeg to establish Holland's control of the Oriental spice trade. The first Dutch trading posts are set up at Banda, Amboina, and Ternate, the Dutch raise the price of pepper from three shillings per pound to six or eight, and 80 London merchants are motivated to form their own East India Company (*see* 1598; 1600).

Prices in western Europe are generally at least six times what they were a century ago. The nobility is impoverished and in many cases is forced to sell its land to the despised middle class.

An English worker must work 48 days to buy 8 bushels of wheat, 32 days to buy 8 bushels of rye, 29 days to buy 8 bushels of barley (*see* 1506).

Spain grows increasingly dependent on northern and eastern Europe for grain staples. Her standard of living has declined markedly as prices have risen above those seen elsewhere in Europe, and her small landowners (*hidalgos*) are being forced off the land, which is falling into the hands of large absentee landlords. American colonial demand for Spanish cloth, wine, olive oil, and flour has slackened with the development of agriculture in Peru and New Spain, and as a result Spanish workers are increasingly idle or unproductively employed.

Essen merchant Arndt Krupp seizes the opportunity of plague in the Ruhr Valley to buy up extensive lands outside the city at giveaway prices. Krupp survives the plague to found a dynasty (see 1811).

The Black Death takes a heavy toll in the Hanseatic city of Essen (above) whose population of 5,000 makes it one of Europe's largest cities.

Plague and famine will decimate Andalusia and Castile in the next 2 years.

A recognizable map of North America is published by Richard Hakluyt in England (see 1584).

The New World has an estimated 900,000 black slaves, most of them engaged in producing sugar which is found to be effective in preserving fruit.

Theater *Much Ado about Nothing* by William Shakespeare: "Sigh no more, ladies, sigh no more,/ Men were deceivers ever,/ One foot in sea and one on shore,/ To one thing constant never" (II, iii); *The Life of King Henry the Fifth* by William Shakespeare: "Once more unto the breach, dear friends, once more,/ Or close the wall up with our English dead!/ In peace there's nothing so becomes a man/ As modest stillness and humility./ But when the blast of war blows in our ears,/ Then imitate the action of the tiger,/ Stiffen the sinews, summon up the blood,/ Disguise fair nature with hard-favored rage." (III, i); "This day is called the Feast of Crispian./ He that outlives this day and comes safe home/ Will stand a-tiptoe when this day is named/ And rouse him at the name of Crispin . . ./ We few, we happy few, we band of brothers . . . / And gentlemen in England now abed/ Shall think themselves accursed they were not here,/ And hold their manhoods cheap while any speaks/ That fought with us upon Saint Crispin's Day" (IV, iii).

The Globe Theatre is opened as a summer playhouse on London's Bankside by William Shakespeare and some partners who include the brother of the late actor James Burbage, who died last year after removing the fabric from his 1576 theater and taking it to Bankside. Burbage is survived by his son Richard, 33, who is England's most popular actor and who will help establish the roles that will make Shakespeare's great plays endure.

Hymn "Sleepers, Wake! The Watch-Cry Pealeth" by P. Nicolai, 43.

"It is unseasonable and unwholesome in all months that have not an R in their names to eat an oyster," writes London author Richard Buttes in *Dyet's Dry Dinner*. But while oysters spawn in such months in French and English waters, the concern of Buttes is not with any threat to their seeming inexhaustibility but rather with the difficulty of keeping oysters fresh in warm weather.

1600 The Honourable East India Company, the Governor and Merchants of London Trading into the East Indies is chartered to make annual voyages to the Indies via the Cape of Good Hope to challenge Dutch control of the spice trade (see 1599). Sir Thomas Smith is the first governor of the company which has an initial capital of £70,000 (see 1601).

A monopoly on fur trade in the New World is obtained by a commercial partnership formed in France.

Italian philosopher Giordano Bruno, 51, is burnt at the stake February 17 at Rome. The Inquisition has condemned him after 7 years of imprisonment for supporting Copernican astronomy and suggesting the possibility of more than one world and more than one absolute divinity (see 1543; Galileo, 1613).

The Battle of Sekugahara in September ends in a victory for the Japanese general Ieyasu over the other three regents for the 6-year-old son of the late dictator Toyotomi Hideyoshi. English navigator Will Adams reaches Kyushu and is summoned to Kyoto by Ieyasu, who retains Adams as adviser when the Englishman impresses him with his knowledge of shipbuilding and navigation. Ieyasu moves the capital from Kyoto to Edo (see 1603).

France's Henri IV marries his 27-year-old niece Marie de' Medici in October and gains control of Tuscany (see Opera, below).

The new French fur monopoly (above) establishes a colony on the St. Lawrence River at the mouth of the Saguenay (see Champlain, 1603).

A new French canal links the Rhône and the Seine Rivers (see 1603).

De Magnete, Magneticisique Corporibus by English physicist-physician William Gilbert, 60, is a pioneer work on electricity that introduces such terms as "electric attraction," "electric force," and "magnetic pole" (see Leyden jar, 1745).

Poetry "The Nymph's Reply to the Shepherd" by Sir Walter Raleigh whose ironic pastoral poem begins: "If all the world and love were young,/ And truth in every shepherd's tongue. . . ."

Painting *Flight into Egypt* by Annibale Caracci, who works with his younger brother Agostino on frescoes for the Farnese Gallery at Rome depicting scenes from classical mythology on great baroque ceilings.

Theater *The Shoemaker's Holiday, or The Gentle Craft*, by Thomas Dekker, 1/1 at the English court, by the Lord Admiral's Men; *As You Like It* by William Shakespeare: "Sweet are the uses of adversity,/ Which, like the toad, ugly and venomous,/ Wears yet a precious jewel in its head" (II, i); "All the world's a

The bard of Avon whose comedies and tragedies were the crowning triumph of the arts in Elizabethan England.

1600 (cont.) stage,/ And all the men and women merely players./ They have their exits and their entrances,/ And one man in his time plays many parts,/ His acts being seven ages./ At first the infant,/ Mewling and puking in the nurse's arms./ Then the whining schoolboy, with his satchel/ And shining morning face, creeping like a snail/ Unwillingly to school. And then the lover,/ Sighing like a furnace, with a woeful ballad/ Made to his mistress' eyebrow. Then a soldier, ..." (II, vii); *The Merry Wives of Windsor* by William Shakespeare: "We burn daylight" (II, i); "The world's mine oyster, which I with sword will open" (II, ii); "I cannot tell what the dickens his name is" (III, ii); *Julius Caesar* by William Shakespeare: "Let me have men about me that are fat,/ Sleek-headed men, and such as sleep o' nights./ Yond Cassius has a lean and hungry look./ He thinks too much: such men are dangerous" (I, ii); "Why, man, he doth bestride the narrow world/ Like a Colossus, and we petty men/ Walk under his huge legs, and peep about/ To find ourselves dishonourable graves./ Men at some time are masters of their fates./ The fault, dear Brutus, is not in our stars,/ But in ourselves, that we are underlings" (I, ii); "Upon what meat doth this our Caesar feed/ That he is grown so great?" (I, ii); "Cowards die many times before their deaths;/ The valiant never taste of death but once" (II, i); "Et tu, Brute?" (III, i); "Friends, Romans, countrymen, lend me your ears./ I come to bury Caesar, not to praise him./ The evil that men do lives after them,/ The good is oft interred with their bones" (III, ii); "If you have tears, prepare to shed them now" (III, ii); "This was the most unkindest cut of all" (III, ii); "There is a tide in the affairs of men,/ Which, taken at the flood, leads on to fortune;/ Omitted, all the voyage of their life/ Is bound in shallows and in miseries" (IV, iii).

Opera *Eurydice* 10/6 at Florence's Pitti Palace with music by Jacopo Peri: the world's first grand opera is presented on the occasion of the wedding of Marie de' Medici (above) to France's Henri IV who has made the match to the overweight Marie to satisfy his financial obligations to her father, the grand duke of Tuscany.

Tobacco sells at London for its weight in silver shillings and is a popular extravagance among the dandies. They dip snuff and blow smoke rings as they puff on clay pipes (*see* 1565; 1604).

Muscovy's Church of St. Nicholas is completed at Panilovo on the North Doina.

An estimated 350 mammal and bird species will become extinct in the next 370 years (*see* aurochs, 1627; dodo, 1681).

Théâtre d'agriculture des champs by French Huguenot squire Oliver de Serres is a revolutionary treatise on agriculture. The Languedoc landowner has imported maize from Italy, hops from England, he has introduced root crops for winter fodder, and he has sown grass on land normally left fallow. While the work impresses Henri IV who has parts of it read to him as he dines in public, only a few enthusiasts adopt the innovations of de Serres, the peasants being too conservative and the nobles too preoccupied with other matters.

The Arabian monopoly in coffee growing is broken by "seven seeds" of unroasted coffee beans that are smuggled from the Arabian port of Mocha to the western Ghats of southern India (*see* 1713; 1720).

"Let the sky rain potatoes," writes William Shakespeare in *The Merry Wives of Windsor* (above, V, ii), but the reference is evidently to the sweet potato (*see* Gerard, 1597).

Europe's most populous nation is France with 16 million as compared to 20 million in all the German-speaking nations, principalities, and city-states, 13 million in Italy, 10 in Spain and Portugal, and 4.5 to 5 in England. North America has roughly 1 million, but the New World will receive some 2.75 million slaves from Africa in the next century.

Some 54 million people will die in the world's wars over the next 345 years, but all the wars, famines, and disease epidemics will slow population growth only by some 10 years (according to a 1972 study).

17th CENTURY

1601 The first English spice fleet sails out of Woolwich in January under the command of James Lancaster, a veteran of Francis Drake's 1588 battle with the Spanish Armada. Lancaster's 600-ton *Red Dragon* flagship is twice the size of the *Hector* or of any of the other three vessels outfitted by the East India Company (*see* 1600; 1602).

A law corresponding to Scotland's 1579 Poor Law is enacted in England where an "Act for the relief of the poor" provides work for the able-bodied unemployed, assists those too old or too ill to work, provides for apprenticing children whose parents cannot maintain them, and specifies that support for the program must come from taxes levied in local parishes. Residence requirements prevent the needy from migrating to wealthier parishes.

England's earl of Essex is refused the renewal of his patent for sweet wines. He parades the streets of London February 7 with 300 retainers shouting, "For the queen, a plot is laid for my life!" Getting no support from the citizenry, he returns to Essex House, surrenders after a brief effort to defend himself from the queen's men, is brought to trial and attacked by his erstwhile friend Francis Bacon, and is executed February 25 at age 34.

English adventurer John Smith, 21, fights with Transylvania's Sigismund Bathory against the Turks, but is captured and sold into slavery (*see* 1603).

Japanese transportation is improved by an edict of the Tokugawa regent Ieyasu which orders that 53 stations be established between Edo and Osaka with ryokans (inns) at which travelers can stay overnight and obtain fresh horses (*see* paintings, 1833).

Theater *Twelfth Night, or What You Will* by William Shakespeare: "If music be the food of love, play on./ Give me excess of it, that, surfeiting,/ The appetite may sicken, and so die" (I, i); "I am a great eater of beef, and I believe that does harm to my wit" (I, iii); "Well, God give them wisdom that have it, and those that are fools, let them use their talents" (I, v); "Youth's a stuff will not endure" (II, iii); "O mistress mine! Where are thou roaming?/ Oh, stay and hear, your truelove's coming,/ That can sing both high and low./ Trip no further, pretty sweeting,/ Journeys end in lovers meeting,/ Every wise man's son doth know" (II, iii); "Dost thou think, because thou art virtuous, there shall be no more cakes and ale?" (II, iii); "She never told her love,/ But let concealment, like a worm 'i th' bud,/ Feed on her damask cheek" (II, iv); "But be not afraid of greatness: some are born great, some achieve greatness, and some have greatness thrust upon 'em" (II, v); "They that dally nicely with

words may quickly make them wanton" (III, i); "This is very midsummer madness" (III, iv); *Blurt, Master Constable* by Thomas Middleton.

The East India Company's James Lancaster (above) doses his crew with lemon juice while at the Cape of Good Hope, then heaves to off Madagascar to take on more lemons and oranges. His 200 men are the only crew not decimated by scurvy.

The word "coffee" appears in an English account by William Parry of the Persian expedition of adventurer Anthony Sherley who 2 years ago failed in an effort to make an alliance between Elizabeth and Persia's Shah Abbas. Sherley has also failed to make military alliances for the Shah against the Turks, but he has introduced coffee to London where it sells at £5 per ounce (*see* 1554; 1582; 1650).

1602 James Lancaster's English East India Company fleet arrives in June at Achin in northern Sumatra and is well received by the local ruler who has been antagonized by Portuguese traders and thus is delighted to meet the English who have defeated Portugal's allies in 1588. Finding no ready market for his wrought iron and clothing stores, Lancaster engages a large Portuguese galleon, defeats her, and loots her cargo of jewels, plate, and merchandise, some of which he trades for pepper at the Dutch port of Bantam in Java.

European pepper prices are doubled and even tripled by the Dutch East India Company.

The United East India Company is chartered by Holland's States-General.

"New England" is explored by English mariner Bartholomew Gosnold who has sailed from the Azores and is the first Englishman to set foot in the region. Sponsored by William Shakespeare's patron Henry Wriothesley, 29, third earl of Southampton, Gosnold sails from Maine to Cape Cod which he so names after "coming to anker" in the harbor of what will be called Provincetown. He names Martha's Vineyard after his eldest child, he builds a house on Cuttyhunk (which he calls Elizabeth's Island), he trades with the natives, and he returns with a valuable cargo of sassafras (believed to be a specific for syphilis), furs, and other commodities, leaving smallpox in his wake.

Santa Catalina Island gets its name November 25 as Basque navigator Sebastian Viscaino lands on the island off the west coast of North America on Santa Catalina's Day. Viscaino anchors a few days later some 325 miles up the coast in an "excellent harbor" which he names after the count of Monte Ray, viceroy of New Spain, who sent out the Viscaino expedi-

1602 (cont.) tion from Acapulco in April. Crews of the expedition's three ships are scurvy-ridden and 16 men have died (*see* Gaspar de Portola, 1769).

Nonfiction *A Defense of Rhyme* by English poet Samuel Daniel: "The wise are above books."

Theater *All's Well That Ends Well* by William Shakespeare: "Our remedies oft in ourselves do lie,/ Which we ascribe to heaven" (I, i); *Troilus and Cressida* by William Shakespeare: "One that loved not wisely but too well" (III, ii); *Hamlet, Prince of Denmark* by William Shakespeare, whose setting is the Kronborg Castle completed at Elsinore in 1585: "How weary, stale, flat and unprofitable,/ Seem to me all the uses of this world!" (I, ii); "Neither a borrower nor a lender be;/ For loan oft loses both itself and friend,/ And borrowing dulls the edge of husbandry" (I, iii); "There is nothing either good or bad, but thinking makes it so" (II, ii); "To be, or not to be —that is the question./ Whether 'tis nobler in the mind to suffer/ The slings and arrows of outrageous fortune,/ Or to take arms against a sea of troubles/ And by resisting, end them ... For who would bear the whips and scorns of time,/ The oppressor's wrong, the proud man's contumely,/ The pangs of dispriz'd love, the law's delay,/ The insolence of office, and the spurns/ That patient merit of the unworthy takes,/ When he himself might his quietus make/ With a bare bodkin?" (III, i).

1603 England's Elizabeth I dies March 24 at age 69, ending the reign of the Tudors after nearly 118 years. Elizabeth is succeeded after a 45-year reign by Scotland's James VI, the Stuart son of the late Mary Queen of Scots. He becomes James I of England and begins a 22-year reign over a united kingdom.

Sir Walter Raleigh is tried for high treason on charges of complicity in the "Main Plot" to dethrone James I (above). He is sentenced to prison.

John Smith kills his slave-master, escapes from captivity east of the Black Sea, and returns to England (*see* 1601; 1607).

The Ottoman sultan Mohammed III dies at age 37 and is succeeded by his 14-year-old son who will reign until 1617 as Ahmed I.

The Tokugawa shogunate that will rule Japan until 1867 is founded at Edo by Tokugawa Ieyasu who ushers in an era of domestic peace and prosperity (*see* 1600).

France's Henri IV names Samuel de Champlain, 36, pilot and geographer and sends him with fur trader François du Pontgrave to explore the Saguenay and St. Lawrence Rivers. Champlain and his companion learn from *les sauvages* of the Great Lakes and of Niagara Falls and they make an alliance with the Algonquins that will endure for 150 years (*see* 1604).

English merchant John Mildenhall reaches India via Isfahan, Kandahar, and Lahore and presents himself as self-appointed ambassador to the Great Mogul Ak-bar at Agra in hopes of obtaining commercial privileges for England (*see* 1608).

The English East India Company's James Lancaster returns with 278 of his original 460 men and sells a cargo of more than 1 million pounds of pepper at a good profit to the Company (*see* 1601; 1602). Lancaster is knighted and becomes a proprietor of the Company (*see* Bantam, 1605).

Japan's Tokugawa shogunate (above) will move the country from a rice economy to a money economy, and while Japan will have 125 crop failures in 265 years, with some degree of famine each time, her industry, commerce, and national wealth will increase. However, a rising living standard and a large population increase will produce economic troubles.

France begins a canal project to link the Atlantic with the Mediterranean (*see* 1681).

London has an epidemic of the Black Death that kills at least 33,000 (*see* 1625).

Painting *St. Bernardino* by El Greco.

Masque *The Magnificent Entertainment Given to King James* by Thomas Dekker 3/15.

Theater *Othello, the Moor of Venice* by William Shakespeare: "Who steals my purse steals trash: 'tis something, nothing;/ 'Twas mine, 'tis his, and has been slave to thousands;/ But he that filches from me my good name/ Robs me of that which not enriches him,/ And makes me poor indeed" (III, iii).

Japan's Kabuki theater has its beginnings in April at Kyoto where women led by Okuni Izumo dance at the Kitani shrine playing men's roles as well as women's (but *see* 1629).

Castelgondolfo is completed by Carlo Maderna who has built the papal summer residence 45 kilometers southeast of Rome at Castelli Romani in Latium.

Philip III sends food to starving Portuguese colonists in drought-stricken northeastern Brazil.

London's population reaches 210,000, up from 200,000 in 1583 (*see* 1692).

1604 The Dutch East India Company asks Dutch jurist Huigh de Groot, 21, to write a legal brief supporting the company's position in its quarrel with the Portuguese as to who has dominion over the oceans (*see* 1609).

Spanish forces capture Ostend from the Dutch after a 42-month siege.

England's James I makes peace with Spain and directs his efforts to American colonization (*see* 1606). James is proclaimed king of Great Britain, France, and Ireland on October 24.

Sweden's Charles IX has taken the title of king March 6 at age 53 after the 14-year-old Duke John has formally renounced his claim to the throne.

Samuel de Champlain explores the North American Atlantic Coast from Maine to what will be called Cape Cod. He plants a colony at what will be called Nova Scotia (see 1603; 1609).

England's James I presides over a Hampton Court Conference in January between Puritans and Anglican bishops, he issues a proclamation enforcing the Act of Uniformity, he banishes Jesuits and seminary priests, and he commissions Sir Henry Savile, William Bedwell, Lancelot Andrews, and nearly 450 other scholars to retranslate the Old and New Testaments (the king has been disturbed by marginal notes in many bibles questioning the divine right of kings) (see 1611; Wycliffe, 1376).

The Granth compiled in India will serve as the sacred scripture of the Sikhs.

The Pont Neuf completed across the Seine at Paris is the city's first paved bridge and the first to be lined with houses and shops.

The Triumphant Chariot of Antimony encourages European physicians to use antimony salts as a homeopathic remedy for fever. The work has probably been written by the monk-chemist Basil Valentine who has discovered that the salts improve the appetites of pigs when thrown into their feeding trough, and who has secretly added stibium salts to the food of fellow monks whose health and appetites were destroyed by excessive fasting. Valentine has changed the metal's name from stibium to antimony (antagonistic to monks) after some monks suffered intestinal upsets, profuse sweating, and in some cases death, but reputable physicians will prescribe "everlasting pellets" of antimony (swallowed, recovered from patients' stools, and used again) until the 19th century, and although it is toxic, antimony will later be found useful in treating snail fever, or schistosomiasis (see Louis XIV, 1657; Bilharz, 1856).

"Counterblaste to Tobacco" by England's James I is published anonymously and makes reference to two Indians brought to London from Virginia in 1584 to demonstrate smoking: "What honor or policie can move us to imitate the barbarous and beastly manners of the wilde, godlesse, and slavish Indian especially in so vile and stinking a custome?" The king points out that tobacco was first used as an antidote to the "Pockes" (see Nicot, 1561), but he observes that doctors now regard smoking as a dirty habit injurious to the health and he finds it on his own part "a custome lothsome to the eye, hatefull to the nose, harmefull to the braine, dangerous to the lungs and in the blacke stinking fume thereof, nearest resembling the horrible Stigian smoke of the pit that is bottomlesse" (but see 1612).

Poetry The Owl by Michael Drayton who has been rebuffed by James I (above).

Painting St. Ildefonso by El Greco; The Deposition by Caravaggio.

Theater Measure for Measure by William Shakespeare: "Our doubts are traitors,/ And make us lose the good we oft might win,/ By fearing to attempt" (I, iv); "Some rise by sin, and some by virture fall" (II, i); "But man, proud man, drest in a little brief authority,/ Most ignorant of what he's most assur'd,/ His glassy essence, like an angry ape,/ Plays such fantastic tricks before high heaven,/ As make the angels weep" (II, ii); Westward Hoe! by London playwrights John Webster, 24, and Thomas Dekker: "Is not old wine wholesomest, old pippins toothsomest? Does not old wood burn brightest, old linen wash whitest? Old soldiers, sweethearts, are surest, and old lovers are soundest" (II, ii); The Honest Whore, Part I, by Thomas Dekker and Thomas Middleton is presented by the Children of St. Paul's: "The calmest husbands make the stormiest wives" (V, i).

1605 A "Gunpowder Plot" to blow up the Houses of Parliament in revenge against harsh penal laws enacted against Roman Catholics comes to light when English Catholic Guy Fawkes, 35, is arrested the night of November 4 while entering the gunpowder-filled cellar under Parliament. Fawkes, a convert to Catholicism who has served with the Spanish in Flanders, has conspired with Robert Catesby, 32, and under torture he reveals the names of his co-conspirators who include also Thomas Percy, 45, and Thomas Winter, 33. Catesby is killed while resisting arrest; Percy is mortally wounded while fleeing arrest; Winter and his brother Robert will be hanged next year along with Fawkes.

The czar of Muscovy Boris Godunov has died April 13 at age 52. He is succeeded for a few months by his only son, but the new czar Fedor II is murdered by enemies of the Godunovs. The only legal heir of Fedor I was killed in exile at Uglich in 1591, but an imposter claiming to be that son Demetrius is supported by the boyars, the Cossacks, and Polish volunteers. The "false Demetrius" enters Moscow June 19, and he begins a reign of 11 months.

India's Mogul emperor Akbar dies at age 62 after a 49-year reign that has established the dynasty which will rule until 1858. Akbar is succeeded by his 36-year-old son who has been called Prince Selim. He will reign until 1627 as Jahangir ("Conqueror of the World"), but he is a drunk and will add little territory to the empire. When he marries in 1611, his empress Nur Jahan ("Light of the World") will control the realm.

Japan's Tokugawa shogun Ieyasu makes his 26-year-old son Hidetada coshogun.

English pilot Will Adams obtains an invitation to establish a Dutch trading post in Japan. Adams has been forced to remain in Japan since his shipwreck in 1600, he has become foreign adviser to the Tokugawa shogun, he has taken the Japanese name Anshin Miura, and he has taken a Japanese wife (see 1609; 1613).

English ships of the East India Company reach Bantam and load up with pepper.

1605 (cont.) Dye wood costs English dyers six times what it cost in 1550 (*see* 1589; 1593; 1615).

English explorer George Waymouth lands on an island off the North American coast and calls it Nanticut (*see* 1658).

Pope Clement VIII dies March 5 at age 70 and is succeeded by Leo XI who lives only until March 30. Camillo Borghese, 52, is elevated to the papacy May 16 and as Paul V he begins taking measures to improve the lot of Italian peasants.

The first great Paris salon is set up by Catherine de Vivionne de Savelli, 17, Marquise de Rambouillet, who finds herself annoyed by the coarseness of Parisian society under Henri IV. She packs her husband off to the country and she makes her home a center for refined and witty conversation.

The world's first newspaper begins publication at Antwerp under the direction of local printer Abraham Verkoeven, a notorious drunkard.

Poetry   *Poems Lyric and Pastoral* by Michael Drayton whose "Ballad of Agincourt" begins, "Fair stood the wind for France...."

Painting   *The Crucifixion, The Adoration of the Shepherds, The Resurrection, Pentecost, St. Peter,* and *St. John the Baptist and St. John the Evangelist* by El Greco; frescoes for Rome's Farnese Palace are created by Annibale Caracci.

Theater   *Volpone, or The Fox,* by Ben Jonson; *Eastward Ho!* by Ben Jonson; *The Honest Whore,* Part II, by Thomas Dekker and Thomas Middleton.

New Spain has a native population of 1,075,000, down from 6 million in 1547 and 11 million in 1518 as a result of disease and exploitation introduced by the conquistadors.

1606 A Virginia charter granted by England's James I establishes the Plymouth Company and the London Company made up respectively of men from those two English cities and their environs. The two companies are authorized to establish settlements at least 100 miles apart in North America, the Plymouth Company to settle somewhere on the coast between the 38th and 45th parallels, the London Company to settle between the 34th and 41st parallels.

A Plymouth Company ship sent out August 12 under Henry Challons is captured by the Spanish. A second vessel sent out in October under Thomas Hanham and Martin Pring reaches the coast of Maine and returns with glowing accounts (*see* 1620).

The London Company sends out 144 men under the command of Captain Christopher Newport in the *Sarah Constant,* the *Goodspeed,* and the *Discovery* (*see* 1607).

Sailors from the Dutch ship *Duyfken* (*Dove*) out of Java land at Cape Keerweer, Australia, and are driven off by natives after making the first landing by Europeans on the South Pacific continent (*see* 1699).

Portuguese forces in the Pacific drive off the Dutch after a 4-month siege of Malacca.

The Russian pretender is driven from the throne and is murdered May 17 by a faction of the boyars as the "time of the troubles" continues. The Muscovite boyar Basil Shuiski who has caused the death of the "false Demetrius" makes himself czar and begins a 4-year reign as Basil IV.

The Austro-Turkish Treaty of Zsitva-Torok recognizes the equality of the Austrians, relieves them of having to pay tribute for their part of Hungary, but gives Transylvania to Istvan Bocskay, the Transylvanian prince who has led Hungarian revolutionists against the Emperor Rudolf with Turkish support.

The Treaty of Vienna secured by Istvan Bocskay (above) gives Hungarian Protestants the same religious freedom as Catholics, but Bocskay dies at age 49, possibly a victim of poisoning by Counter-Reformationists.

Painting   *Fray Felix Hortensio Paravicino* by El Greco.

Theater   *King Lear* by William Shakespeare: "How sharper than a serpent's tooth it is/ To have a thankless child" (I, iv); *Macbeth* by William Shakespeare: "Tomorrow, and tomorrow, and tomorrow,/ Creeps in this petty pace from day to day,/ To the last syllable of recorded time;/ And all our yesterdays have lighted fools/ The way to dusty death. Out, out, brief candle!/ Life's but a walking shadow, a poor player/ That struts and frets his hour upon the stage/ And then is heard no more: it is a tale/ Told by an idiot, full of sound and fury,/ Signifying nothing" (V, v); *The Whore of Babylon* by Thomas Dekker is performed by Prince Henry's Servants; *A Trick to Catch the Old One* by Thomas Middleton is performed by the Children of St. Paul's.

France's Henri IV tells the king of Savoy that if he lives for another 10 years "there would not be a peasant so poor in all my realm who would not have a chicken in his pot every Sunday," but most French peasants live mainly on bread and gruel (*see* 1610; Hoover, 1928).

Australia (above) has an aborigine population that will be estimated to number 300,000.

1607 Jamestown, Virginia, is founded May 14 by Captain Christopher Newport of the London Company who sailed into Chesapeake Bay April 26 after losing 16 men on the voyage from England. Newport has come up a river he named the James, in honor of the English king, and he sails for home June 22 leaving behind colonists under Captain John Smith.

The Plymouth Company attempts a settlement at the mouth of the Kennebec River, but the colonists will abandon George Popham's settlement after a terrible winter (*see* 1620).

French colonists abandon the settlement founded by Samuel de Champlain in 1604.

The Muscovy Company employs English navigator Henry Hudson to find a passage to China (see 1555). Hudson coasts the eastern shore of Greenland with 10 men and a boy until he reaches "Newland," or Spitzbergen (see 1596; 1608).

A third English East India Company fleet sails in March for the Indies. The fleet includes the *Red Dragon* and the *Hector* as it did in 1601, and it will return with cloves and other cargo that will yield a profit of 234 percent (see 1621).

The English peasantry revolts against the enclosure of common lands and other abuses by the landed gentry, but the forces of James I subdue Captain Pouch's revolt.

Gascony becomes part of France.

Theater *The Knight of the Burning Pestle* by English playwrights Francis Beaumont, 23, and John Fletcher, 27, is the first of some 50 comedies and tragedies that Beaumont and Fletcher will write together before Beaumont's death in 1616; *Antony and Cleopatra* by William Shakespeare: "The barge she sat in, like a burnish'd throne,/ Burn'd on the water; the poop was beaten gold;/ Purple the sails, and so perfumed that/ The winds were love-sick with them; the oars were silver,/ Which to the tune of flutes kept stroke, and made/ The water which they beat to follow faster,/ As amorous of their strokes" (II, ii).

Opera *Orfeo* 2/24 at Mantua's Court Theater, with music by Italian composer Claudio Monteverdi, 29, who has studied with the late Giovanni Palestrina and who employs a new treatment of discords to provide emotional and dramatic values.

Jamestown's colonists (above) are sick and starving by autumn. Their Captain John Smith goes up the Chickahominy River in December to trade for corn with the Algonquins and is captured. By his own account his life is spared only by the intercession of the Powhatan chief's 12-year-old daughter Pocahontas who holds his head in her arms to prevent her father's warriors from clubbing Smith to death (see Rolfe, 1614).

1608 Captain Christopher Newport arrives at Jamestown in January with 110 new Virginia colony settlers. He finds that disease and malnutrition have reduced the original contingent to a group of 40. Jamestown's fort is destroyed by fire January 7.

Captain John Smith surveys Chesapeake Bay and the Potomac River through much of the summer, using an open boat to look for a passage to the South Sea.

Captain John Smith is elected president of the Jamestown Council September 10 and tries to cope with the disease and famine that have ravaged the colony since late summer.

Captain Newport arrives at Jamestown September 29 with a second supply ship and departs in December with Smith's map of Chesapeake Bay and its rivers. He carries back a cargo of pitch, tar, iron ore, soap ashes, and clapboards in place of the worthless mica he has twice carried home under the impression it was gold.

Henry Hudson searches the Barents Sea for a Northeast Passage on a second voyage for the Muscovy Company. His failure persuades the 51-year-old company to direct its future energies to developing its profitable Spitzbergen fishery (see 1611).

Paraguay is founded by Jesuits in South America (see Asunción, 1537; de Vaca, 1542).

France exports so much grain that "it robbeth all Spain of their silver and gold that is brought thither out of their Indies," says England's George Carew, 53, Baron of Clopton.

The English East India company ship *Hector* arrives at Surat after a 17-month voyage and becomes the first Company ship to reach India. William Hawkins disembarks with a letter from James I to the Mogul emperor Akbar asking for trade (see 1609).

The Mogul emperor Jahangir grants trading concessions to John Mildenhall (see 1603).

The Elector Palatine of the Rhine Frederick IV, 34, organizes a Protestant Union (see 1609).

The Holy Roman Emperor Rudolf II is compelled to cede the kingdom of Hungary and the government of Austria and Moravia to his brother Matthias in June.

Theater *Timon of Athens* by William Shakespeare: " 'Tis not enough to help the feeble up,/ But to support them after" (I, i); "Grant I may never prove so fond/ To trust a man on his oath or bond,/ Or a harlot for her weeping,/ Or a dog that seems a-sleeping,/

Henry Hudson and other English navigators tried to find the fabled Northwest Passage to China. Hudson came to grief.

213

1608 (cont.) Or a keeper with my freedom,/ Or my friends if I should need 'em" (I, ii); "Every man has his fault, and honesty is his" (III, i); "The learned pate ducks to the golden fool" (IV, iii); *Pericles, Prince of Tyre* by William Shakespeare and collaborators: "Few love to hear the sins they love to act" (I, i); *Philaster* by Beaumont and Fletcher; *The Revenger's Tragedy* by English playwright Cyril Tourneur, 33 (or by John Webster, Thomas Middleton, or John Marston).

Opera *L'Arianna* 5/28 at Mantua's Teatro della Arte, with music by Claudio Monteverdi.

1609 A Catholic League organized under the leadership of Bavaria's Duke Maximilian mobilizes its forces to oppose the Protestant Union organized last year by the Palatinate elector Frederick IV.

Spain's Philip III recognizes the independence of the northern provinces and signs a truce with the Dutch, but he does not seize the opportunity to reform Spanish society which is rapidly decaying through the extravagance of the court and nobility. Shipments of silver from America have diminished, sheepherding is replacing agriculture, and Spain is forced to import much of her food while exporting olive oil, wine, wool, and luxury goods, much of it to America.

Mare liberum by Hugo Grotius (Huigh de Groot) urges freedom of the seas to all nations. The work is premised on the assumption that the sea's major known resource—fish—exists in inexhaustible supply (*see* 1604; 1625).

A long period of hostility begins between America's Five Nations Iroquois and the French. Samuel de Champlain has precipitated the hostility by killing some Mohawks at the behest of the Hurons (*see* 1604).

Samuel de Champlain (above) has explored an area that will later be called Vermont as lieutenant to the owner of the French fur trade monopoly, and with a Huron and Algonquin war party he has discovered the lake that will later bear his name.

Henry Hudson makes a third voyage to America, this time in the employ of the 7-year-old United East India Company chartered by the Dutch, and he explores first the Barents Sea, then the New England coast and the bay that next year will be called Delaware Bay, and finally a river that will be called the Hudson which he ascends as far as what will one day be called Albany. Hudson's ship the *Half-Moon* carries a crew of 18 or 20 (*see* Fort Nassau, 1614).

The London Company chartered in 1606 obtains a new charter, receives additional land grants, and sends out a fleet of nine ships with 800 new settlers and supplies for the Virginia colony. Among the new colonists are John Rolfe, 24, and his young wife, but their ship the *Sea Venture* is wrecked with the rest of the fleet on reefs off one of the Bermuda islands whose beauty so delights George Somers, 54, one of the ship captains, that he will return to England and form a company to colonize Bermuda (*see* 1610).

Astronomia Nova . . . de Motibus Stellae Martis et Observationibus Tychonis Brahe by German astronomer Johannes Kepler, 38, establishes two of the cardinal principles of astronomy: planets travel round the sun in elliptical paths rather than in perfect circles, and they do not travel at uniform rates of speed. Kepler has headed the observatory at Prague since the death of his master Tycho Brahe in 1601 and has used data compiled by Brahe to arrive at the new astronomical laws (*see* 1619).

A *Majestatsbrief* (letter of majesty) from the Holy Roman Emperor Rudolf II permits free exercise of religion in Bohemia to the three estates—lords, knights, and royal cities.

Expulsion of the Morisco descendants of Spain's Moorish invaders of 711 and since begins as Philip III acts on the advice of the 57-year-old Duque de Lerma Francisco Gomez de Sandoval y Rojas. Some 275,000 Moriscos will leave the country in the next 5 years, disrupting the economic life of Valencia (which will lose one-fourth of her population) and creating problems in Castile, Aragon, and Andalusia as well.

England's William Hawkins defies Portuguese authorities at Surat and travels overland to Agra where he confers in Turkish with the emperor Jahangir (*see* 1608; 1612).

Dutch merchants establish a trading post at Hirado in western Japan at the invitation of the Tokugawa shogun Ieyasu who ends Portugal's monopoly in trade with Japan. The Dutch will operate the post until 1623 (*see* 1605; 1624).

The Bank of Amsterdam is founded with silver coined from South American ingots. Some 800 varieties of coins are in circulation, the new city-owned bank weighs coins to pioneer the principle of public regulation of money, and the bank soon finds that it can loan money at interest (*see* Bank of England, 1694).

Aviso Relation oder Zeitung begins weekly publication January 15 at Wolfenbuttel in Lower Saxony; *Relation* and *Aller Furnemmen und Gedenckwurdigen Historien* begins publication at Strasbourg. They are the world's first regular newspapers (*see* 1605).

Poetry *Sonnets* by William Shakespeare whose Sonnet 18 begins, "Shall I compare thee to a summer's day?" (The bard's inspiration has allegedly come from the "dark lady," Mary Fitton, a maid of honor at the court of Elizabeth who has been mistress to William Herbert, 29, earl of Pembroke, in an illicit affair that has caused Pembroke to be banished and briefly imprisoned.)

Painting *Flight into Egypt* by German painter Adam Elsheimer, 31, who has been at Rome since 1600; *Fra Paravicino* by El Greco; *Self-portrait with His Wife Isabella Brant* by Peter Paul Rubens. Annibale Carracci dies at Rome July 15 at age 48.

Theater *Epicoene, or The Silent Woman*, by Ben Jonson: "O revenge, how sweet thou art!" (IV, v);

Coriolanus by William Shakespeare, who relates hunger to political unrest: "They said they were anhungry; sigh'd forth proverbs,/ That hunger broke stone walls, that dogs must eat,/ That meat was made for mouths, that the gods send not/ Corn for rich men only: with these shreds/ They vented their complainings" (I, i).

"Three Blind Mice" ("A Round or Catch of Three Voices") is published in *Deuteromelia, or The Second Part of Music's Melodie, or Melodius Musicke.*

Venice's Palazzo Contarini degli Scrigni is completed on the Grand Canal.

The Virginia colony declines in population to 67 by January as food stocks run low despite the introduction of carrots, parsnips, and turnips. The colonists sustain themselves in the "starving times" until their crops ripen by gathering cattail roots, marsh marigolds, Jerusalem artichokes, and other wild plant foods. Still many die of hunger.

1610 France's Henri IV is assassinated at Paris May 14 by the fanatic François Ravaillac, 31. Dead at age 56 after a momentous reign of nearly 21 years, Henri is succeeded by his 9-year-old son who will reign until 1643 as Louis XIII. The boy's mother Marie de' Medici will act as regent until he is of age and will exercise power for long after.

The grand duke of Muscovy Basil IV Shuiski is deposed in July by the boyars and by the rising "men of service" (landlords). They carry him off to Warsaw and offer the ducal throne to Vasa, son of Poland's Sigismund III. The Cossacks and peasants oppose the Polish prince and support a second "false Demetrius" who has established a camp outside Moscow at Tushino. A Tartar in his retinue kills the false Demetrius in December, his supporters blockade Moscow, and a popular uprising forces the Poles inside Moscow to take refuge in the Kremlin.

The Virginia colonists are attacked by Powhatan chief Wahunsonacook, who may have been inspired by Spaniards to the south. A few colonists are killed.

Siderius Nuncius by Galileo Galilei creates a sensation with talk of the unevenness of the moon's surface as observed by Galileo through his spyglass. The three moons of Jupiter have been observed by Galileo on January 7. He calls them the Medicean stars, dedicates his treatise to Cosimo II de' Medici, and moves to Florence (*see* 1597; 1613).

Henry Hudson makes another attempt to find a Northwest Passage. Backed by Sir Thomas Smith, Sir Dudley Digges, John Wolstenholme, and other English investors, Hudson crosses the Atlantic in his 55-ton ship *Discovery*, but succeeds only in entering the strait which will later bear his name and in exploring the shallow bay which will be called first Hudson's Bay and then Hudson Bay (*see* 1611; 1668).

Jamestown colonists in Virginia prepare to abandon the colony and move to Newfoundland after having buried some 500 of their men, women, and children. En route down the James River, however, they encounter the *Virginia* commanded by Thomas West, 33, the Baron De La Warr, with 150 new settlers and fresh supplies. The outward bound vessels come about and return to Jamestown to try again with De La Warr as their first governor (*see* Cole, 1611).

Survivors of last year's Bermuda shipwreck build two new ships from timbers and planks salvaged from their wrecks and arrive at Jamestown May 24. Among the arrivals are John Rolfe and his wife (*see* 1612).

Delaware Bay is named in honor of Governor De La Warr by Virginia colonist Sir Samuel Argall.

The French queen mother Marie de' Medici removes Sully from office and installs her favorite, Concino Concini, in a position of power, ushering in an era of cruelty and oppression for the peasantry.

The duque de Lerma steps up the expulsion of Spain's Moriscos (Moors), who have contributed much to the country's culture and economy. Spain will never recover from the loss.

The Dutch East India Company introduces the term "share."

Wadham College is founded at Oxford by Nicholas and Dorothy Wadham.

Painting *Laocoön* and *The Opening of the Fifth Seal* by El Greco; *Raising of the Cross* by Peter Paul Rubens. Michelangelo Caravaggio dies at Port 'Ercole while en route to Rome July 18 at age 36 (he fled Rome after a fatal brawl in 1606 and has worked at Naples, Malta, and in Sicily); Adam Elsheimer dies at Rome in December at age 32.

Theater *Peribanez* by Lope de Vega who shows 15th century peasants driven to murder their tyrannical lord in defense of their honor; *The Alchemist* by Ben Jonson who refers in his prologue to "Fortune, that favors fools"; *The Roaring Girl, or Moll Cutpurse* by Thomas Dekker and Thomas Middleton at London's Fortune Theatre, with the Prince's Men; *Cymbeline* by William Shakespeare: "Hark, hark! the lark at heaven's gate sing" (II, iii); "Fear no more the heat 'o the sun,/ Nor the furious winter's rages;/ Thou thy worldly task hast done, Home art gone, and ta'en thy wages./ Golden lads and girls all must/ As chimney-sweepers come to dust" (IV, ii).

"Vespers" by Claudio Monteverdi are published at Mantua.

Only 150 of the 900 colonists landed in Virginia in the last 3 years have survived, the others having succumbed to starvation and disease. The colonists are primarily English but include some French, German, Irish, and Polish artisans.

1611 England's James I dissolves Parliament for the first time. His troops in Ireland force the earl of Tyrone Hugh O'Neill, now 71, to take refuge at Rome and the Plantation of Ulster is forfeited to the crown.

Denmark declares war on Sweden after more than 40 years of peace. Hostilities will continue until 1613.

215

1611 (cont.) Sweden's Charles IX dies October 30 at age 61 after a 7-year reign. His 16-year-old son has mastered Latin, Italian, and Dutch in addition to his mother tongues of Swedish and German, he has served as his father's coregent for the past year, and he begins a 21-year reign as Gustavus II Adolphus. The new king signs a royal charter giving the Swedish council and the estates a voice in all questions of legislation and a power of veto in matters of war and peace.

English mutineers maroon Henry Hudson on the shore of James Bay (see 1610). The expedition has been ice-bound through the winter, Eskimos kill some of the mutineers, others starve to death, Hudson and eight others will never be heard of again, and English authorities will imprison the surviving mutineers upon their return.

The new governor of the Jamestown colony in Virginia introduces private enterprise. The colony's agriculture has been a socialized venture until now, but Sir Thomas Cole assigns 3 acres to each man and gives him the right to keep or sell most of what he raises (see 1616).

Institutiones Anatomicae by Danish physician Kaspar Bartholin, 26, is published by the University of Copenhagen (see 1653).

The University of Rome is founded.

The University of Santo Tomas is founded at Manila in the Philippines.

The Authorized (King James) version of the bible is published for the Church of England after 7 years of effort by English scholars.

Poetry Homer's *Iliad* in a translation by English poet George Chapman, 52, whose first part appeared in 1598; *The Anatomy of the World* by English poet John Donne, 38, is published anonymously. Sir Robert Drury of Hawsted has permitted Donne and his young wife Anne to occupy an apartment in his large house in London's Drury Lane and Donne has written an extravagant elegy to his patron's late daughter.

Painting *Descent from the Cross* by Peter Paul Rubens.

Theater *The Atheist's Tragedy, or The Honest Man's Revenge* by Cyril Tourneur; *The Maid's Tragedy* by Beaumont and Fletcher; *A Chaste Maid in Cheapside* by Thomas Middleton at London's Swan Theatre, with Lady Elizabeth's Men; *The Winter's Tale* by William Shakespeare: "Should all despair/ That have revolted wives, the tenth of mankind/ Would hang themselves (I, ii); "A sad tale's best for winter" (II, i); "When daffodils begin to peer,/ With heigh! the doxy over the dale,/ Why, then comes in the sweet o' the year;/ For the red blood reigns in the winter's pale (IV, iii); "Let me have no lying; it becomes none but tradesmen" (IV, iii); "There was speech in their dumbness, language in their very gesture" (V, ii); *The Tempest* by William Shakespeare 11/1 at Whitehall, with the King's Men:

"Full fathom five thy father lies;/ Of his bones are coral made;/ Those are pearls that were his eyes:/ Nothing of him that doth fade/ But doth suffer a sea change/ Into something rich and strange . . ." (Ariel's song, I, ii); "Our revels now are ended. These our actors,/ As I foretold you, were all spirits and/ Are melted into air, into thin air;/ . . . We are such stuff/ As dreams are made on, and our little life/ Is rounded with a sleep" (Prospero's farewell, IV, i, is also Shakespeare's farewell as he prepares to leave London and return to his native Stratford-upon-Avon); *Catiline, His Conspiracy* by Ben Jonson; *A King and No King* by Beaumont and Fletcher 12/26 at the court.

The Muscovy Company sends out the first English ship to be fitted out for whaling (see 1557). The 150-ton *Mary Margaret* skippered by Steven Benet kills a small whale and 500 walrus in Spitzbergen's Thomas Smyth's Bay, but the ship is lost with all hands on her return voyage (see 1608; 1612).

Potosi in the South American Andes reaches its population peak of 160,000 as the Spanish employ Indian labor to produce tons of silver for shipment back to Spain (see 1545; Cerro de Pasco mine, 1630).

1612 The Holy Roman Emperor Rudolf II dies January 20 at Prague at age 59 after a reign of more than 35 years. He is succeeded by his brother Matthias, 54, who obtains the remaining Hapsburg dominions and is crowned in June to begin a reign of nearly 7 years.

Japanese persecution of Christians begins as a definite policy following a series of anti-Christian edicts that began in 1606. The retired shogun Ieyasu abandons his original friendly attitude toward missionaries after realizing that trade with Europe can be continued without their presence, which presents potential political dangers.

Two English East India Company ships defeat a Portuguese fleet of four galleons off the coast of India. The emperor Jahangir is so impressed that he grants trading rights to the English at Surat.

Tobacco cultivation gives Virginia colony settlers an export commodity that will provide a solid economic base for the colony. John Rolfe has obtained *Nicotiana tabacum* seed from the Caribbean islands and after two years in Virginia has learned from local Indians how to raise tobacco and cure the leaf that he ships to London. The James River Valley produces 1,600 pounds of leaf per acre, Jamestown becomes a boom town, the Virginia (London) Company grows prosperous, and James I is enriched by import duties that make him look more tolerantly on tobacco (see 1604; Rolfe, 1614).

A Bermuda colony is established by a shipload of men, women, and sailors who arrive on the islands that were claimed for England 3 years ago by the late Sir George Somers, who died in 1610. The colony will have 600 settlers by 1614.

A Map of Virginia by Captain John Smith describes the physical features of the country, its climate, its plants and animals, and its inhabitants.

Theater *The White Devil* by John Webster is performed by the Queen's Men: "Call for the robin redbreast and the wren,/ Since o'er shady groves they hover,/ And with leaves and flowers do cover/ The friendless bodies of unburied men" (V, iv); "Prosperity doth bewitch men, seeming clear;/ As seas do laugh, show white, when rocks are near" (V, vi); *Cupid's Revenge* by Beaumont and Fletcher in January at the court; *The Coxcomb* by Beaumont and Fletcher with the Children of the Queen's Revels; *King Henry VIII* by William Shakespeare: "Heat not a furnace for your foe so hot/ That it do singe yourself" (I, i); "No man's pie is freed/ From his ambitious finger" (I, i); "I charge thee, fling away ambition./ By that sin fell the angels; how can man then,/ The image of his Maker, hope to win by it?" (III, ii); "Had I but served my God with half the zeal/ I served my king, he would not in mine age/ Have left me naked to mine enemies" (III, ii); "From that full meridian of my glory/ I haste now to my setting: I shall fall/ Like a bright exhalation in the evening,/ And no man shall see me more" (III, ii); "Farewell! a long farewell, to all my greatness!/ This is the state of man: today he puts forth/ The tender leaves of hopes; tomorrow blossoms,/ And bears his blushing honors thick upon him;/ The third day comes a frost, a killing frost;/ And, when he thinks, good easy man, full surely/ His greatness is aripening, nips his root,/ And then he falls, as I do. I have ventured,/ Like little wanton boys that swim on bladders,/ This many summers in a sea of glory,/ But far beyond my depth: my highblown pride/ At length broke under me, and now has left me,/ Weary and old with service, to the mercy/ Of a rude stream, that must forever hide me" (III, ii); "Men's evil manners live in brass: their virtues/ We write in water" (IV, ii).

The Muscovy Company sends out four whaling ships, takes 17 whales, and pays its shareholders a 90 percent dividend. However, the company's whaling ventures will have only occasional success in the next dozen years and the English will virtually abandon whaling and will not resume for another 150 years.

1613 The Romanov dynasty that will rule Russia until 1917 is inaugurated July 22 with the crowning of Michael Romanov, 17-year-old son of the Patriach Philaret and grandnephew of Ivan IV. He has been elected czar by the boyars and he begins a weak reign that ends the "time of troubles" which has persisted since the death of Boris Godunov in 1605.

Bethlen Gabor (Gabriel Bethlen von Iktar), 33, overthrows Gabriel Bathory and becomes prince of Transylvania, ending the cruel Catholic reign of Bathory who is murdered at age 24. Bethlen establishes Protestantism in Transylvania and imprisons Bathory's cousin Elizabeth who is said to have killed more than 600 maidens and bathed in their blood (she will herself die in prison next year).

A Japanese embassy to Spain and the pope is dispatched by the daimyo Date Masamune, 48.

The first Japanese-built Western-style ship leaves October 28 for a 90-day voyage to Acapulco in New Spain. Built with technical advice from a Spaniard, the ship is commanded by the samurai Tsunenaga Hasekura.

An English factory (trading post) is established at Hirado and Will Adams attempts to establish trade between Japan and England through Captain John Saris at Bantam (*see* 1605; 1616).

The English East India Company establishes its first factory in India (*see* 1608; 1616).

English merchant John Jourdain buys pepper in Sumatra and cloves at Amboyana and Ceram in the Spice Islands.

Dutch merchants establish a fur trading post at the foot of Manhattan Island (*see* 1623).

Letters on the Solar Spots by Galileo Galilei advocates the Copernican system proposed in 1543. Galileo is admonished by the Church (*see* 1610; 1616).

Typhus strikes Württemberg and the Tyrol and appears in Magdeburg.

Plague appears at Regensburg and Leipzig and spreads through Bohemia, Austria, and eastward.

Painting *The Aurora* fresco in Rome's Raspigliosi Palace by Italian painter Guido Reni, 38, who has been influenced by the late Caravaggio.

Theater *The Masque of the Inner Temple and Gray's Inn* by Francis Beaumont 2/20 at Whitehall, on the marriage of the Prince and Princess Palatine; *The Two Noble Kinsmen* by William Shakespeare and John Fletcher. London's Globe Theatre burns down June 29 following a performance of Shakespeare's *Henry VIII*.

Spain's population falls as a consequence of wars and emigration to overseas colonies. The country becomes largely a wool-growing nation in a period of decadence and agricultural decline (*see* 1561).

1614 *Mirifici Logarithmorum Canonis Descriptio* by Scottish mathematician John Napier, 64, Laird of Merchiston, describes the most powerful method of arithmetical calculation. Napier has discovered logarithms that make it possible to multiply 7- and 8-digit numbers by simple addition and to raise numbers to the 15th or 16th power by simple multiplication, permitting calculations heretofore almost impossible and providing the basis of the slide rule.

French prelate Armand Jean du Plessis, 29, duc de Richelieu and bishop of Lucon, gains election to the Estates-General, representatives of the French people. Richelieu engineers the dismissal of the Estates-General which will not reconvene until 1789 (*see* 1624; Harrington, 1656).

England's "Addled Parliament" meets, refuses to discuss finance, and dissolves.

Sweden's Gustavus II Adolphus conquers Novgorod from the Russians.

1614 (cont.) Virginia colonists block French settlements in Maine and Nova Scotia.

Dutch navigator Adriaen Block explores the New England coast and sails up the Connecticut River. Block's name will survive in Block Island.

Dutch traders found Albany under the name Fort Nassau on the Hudson River (*see* 1609; 1624).

Virginia colony widower John Rolfe marries Pocahontas, favorite daughter of the Powhatan chief Wahunsonacook. Seized last year by the colonists and held for ransom, the 18-year-old Pocahontas has become Europeanized—she has changed her name to Rebecca and has adopted Christianity, and she will never see her father again (*see* 1607; 1617).

The Japanese shogun Tokugawa Ieyasu bans Christian missionaries from the country (*see* 1612; 1639).

England's Levant Company brings home pepper and other spices aboard its big Indiamen from Java and Sumatra for export to Turkey.

Painting *Descent from the Cross* by Peter Paul Rubens; *The Last Communion of St. Jerome* by Italian painter Il Domenichino (Domenico Zampieri), 32. El Greco dies at Toledo the night of April 6 at age 72.

Theater *The Duchess of Malfi* by John Webster: "He hath put a girdle 'bout the world/ And sounded all her quicksands" (III, i); "Glories, like glow-worms, afar off shine bright,/ But, looked at near, have neither heat nor light" (IV, ii); *Bartholomew Fair* by Ben Jonson; *St. Joan*, Part II (*La Santa Juana*) by Spanish playwright Tirso de Molina, 30, 6/24 in the orchard of the duque de Lerma in honor of Philip III's eldest son.

Venice's Church of San Giorgio Maggiore is completed after 55 years of work according to plans by the late architect Andrea Palladio.

Venice's prisons and their connecting Bridge of Sighs are completed after 41 years of work to enlarge the state prison in the doge's palace.

1615 Dutch forces seize the Moluccas from the Portuguese, an English fleet defeats a Portuguese armada off the coast of Bombay.

Captain John Smith of the Virginia colony surveys the New England coast from Maine to the cape that will be called Cape Cod. Commissioned by the Plymouth Company, Smith renames the native village of Patuxet, calling it Plymouth (Plimoth) (*see* 1606; 1620).

English slaver Thomas Hunt kidnaps a Wampanoag from Patuxet (above). He sells Tisquantum (Squanto) into slavery at Malaga, Spain (*see* 1621).

Rubber from South America reaches Europe but is little more than a curiosity (*see* 1503; solvent, 1762).

England turns increasingly to cheap coal as timber grows scarce and firewood becomes costly (*see* 1658).

Fiction *Don Quijote de la Mancha* by Spanish novelist Miguel de Saavedra Cervantes, 68, who completed the first part of the work 10 years ago. Cervantes's left hand was maimed at the Battle of Lepanto in 1571, Algerian pirates captured him in 1575 and held him for ransom until 1580. His writing has been published since 1585, and his burlesque of romantic chivalry contains phrases that will become part of the English language: "Not to mince words" (I, preface); "Give the devil his due" (I, III, 3); "Paid him in his own coin" (I, III, 4); "A finger in every pie" (I, III, 6); "Every dog has his day" (I, III, 6); "Give up the ghost" (I, III, 7); "Venture all his eggs in one basket" (I, III, 9); "Cry my eyes out" (I, III, 11); "A bird in the hand is worth two in the bush" (I, IV, 3); "The proof of the pudding is in the eating" (I, IV, 10); "All that glitters is not gold" (II, III, 3); "Honesty is the best policy" (II, III, 33); "A word to the wise is enough" (II, IV, 30); "A blot on thy escutcheon" (II, IV, 35); "Pot calls the kettle blackarse" (II, IV, 43); "Mum's the word" (II, IV, 44); "When thou art in Rome, do as they do at Rome" (II, IV, 54); "Born with a silver spoon in his mouth" (II, IV, 73); and "There are only two families in the world . . . the Haves and the Have-nots."

Poetry *The Odyssey* by Homer translated by George Chapman (*see* 1611); "Shepherd's Hunting" by English Cavalier poet George Wither, 27, who wrote the pastoral while imprisoned in Marshalsea for his libelous satire "Abuses Stript and Whipt" ("Little said is soonest mended," writes Wither); *The Author's Resolution* by George Wither contains the sonnet "Fidelia": "Shall I wasting in despair/ Die because a woman's fair?/ Or make pale my cheeks with care/ 'Cause another's rosy are?/ Be she fairer than the day,/ Or the flowery meads in May,/ If she think not well of me,/ What care I how fair she be?"

Painting *Scenes from the Life of St. Cecilia* by Il Domenichino for Rome's S. Luigi dei Francesi.

Recercari et Canzoni Francese with music by Italian composer Girolamo Frescobaldi, 32, is published at Rome. Frescobaldi is organist at St. Peter's.

Chocolate paste from the Spanish New World is introduced into Spain, Italy, and Flanders for drinking chocolate (*see* 1580; 1659).

1616 Belief in the revolutionary ideas of the late Polish astronomer Nikolaus Copernicus is a violation of holy scripture, says Jesuit prelate Cardinal Bellarmine (Roberto Francesco Romolo Bellarmino), 74, who has received secret reports about Galileo Galilei. The Vatican orders Galileo to stop defending Copernican "heresy" (*see* 1613; 1632; Copernicus, 1543).

Dutch astronomer-mathematician Willebrod Snellius, 25, discovers the law of refraction.

Dutch East India Company mariner Willem Cornelis Schouten, 49, who was born at Hoorn rounds Cape Horn for the first time and gives the cape its name. Navigator Jakob Le Maire, 31, accompanies Schouten and will help him explore the South Seas.

English navigator William Baffin, 32, discovers Baffin Bay on an expedition in search of a Northwest Passage. He sails to a latitude of 77°45'—farther to the north than any other explorer will venture for 236 years (*see* Frobisher, 1576).

A Description of New England by Captain John Smith is published in London with a map of the region (*see* 1615; 1620).

Jamestown, Virginia, colonists each receive 100 acres of land after having worked until now for the London Company. Each colonist will soon be given an additional 50 acres for each new settler he brings to Virginia (*see* 1611).

England's East India Company begins trading with Persia from its Indian base at Surat.

England's James I begins selling peerages to replenish the seriously depleted royal treasury.

Mitsui begins its rise toward becoming the world's largest business organization. Japanese samurai Mitsui Sokubei Takatoshi rebels against his noble caste; he opens a sake and soy sauce establishment, and his wife Shuho finds that patrons will pawn their valuables for a drink of sake (*see* 1683).

Japan's Tokugawa shogun Ieyasu dies June 1 at age 74 after a 13-year reign that has established the shogunate that will rule Japan until 1867. He is succeeded by his 38-year-old son Hidetada who will marry a daughter of the emperor Gomizno (all her siblings will be killed or aborted). He will reign until 1623.

China is invaded by Manchus.

English mariner Will Adams (Anshin Miura) embarks with Japanese vessels that will take him to Siam and Cochin China in the next 2 years (*see* 1613). Adams has built the ships to expand Japanese trade in silks and other valuable commodities from the mainland.

Persecution of Catholics intensifies in Bohemia.

The secret Rosicrucian Society said to have been started in the 15th century by Christian Rosenkreutz (Frater Rosae Crucis) is described in the anonymous pamphlet "Chymische Hochzeit Christiani Rosenkreutz" that will be ascribed to German Protestant theologian-satirist Johann Valentin Andrea, 30.

Poetry "A Select Second Husband for Sir Thomas Overburies' Wife" by English poet John Davies, 51, of Hereford: "Beauty's but skin deep"; *Poems* by Ben Jonson include "Drink to me only with thine eyes. . . ."

Painting *Banquet of the Officers of the Guild of Archers of St. George* by Dutch Painter Franz Hals, 36; *The Lion Hunt* by Peter Paul Rubens.

Theater *The Scornful Lady* by Beaumont and Fletcher; Francis Beaumont dies March 6 at age 34 and his last play contains the line derived from a proverb recorded by John Heywood in 1546—"Beggars must be no choosers" (V, iii). William Shakespeare dies at Stratford-upon-Avon April 23 at age 52.

Antwerp's Notre Dame Cathedral is completed after 264 years of construction.

1617 The Ottoman sultan Ahmed I dies at age 28 after a 14-year reign. His 16-year-old kinsman succeeds him as Mustafa I, but is so imbecilic that he will be deposed next year.

Sweden's Gustavus II Adolphus cuts Russia off from the Baltic, he restores Novgorod in the Treaty of Stolbovo, but he retains Carelia and Ingria.

France's prime minister Concino Concini is arrested and assassinated, the queen mother Marie de' Medici is banished to Blois, and the Duc de Luynes Charles d'Albert gains power over the 16-year-old Louis XIII.

England's James I releases Sir Walter Raleigh from prison in order that he may seek gold along the Orinoco River. The Spanish ambassador warns that Spain has settlements on the coast, but Raleigh promises to find a gold mine for James I without entrenching on any Spanish possession. He sails March 17 with his young son in an ill-equipped expeditionary fleet, and he reaches the mouth of the Orinoco December 31 (*see* 1603; 1618).

A smallpox epidemic in England kills Rebecca Rolfe, née Pocahontas, who is survived by a son.

An epidemic of what is probably smallpox sweeps the New England region and reduces the native population by some estimates from 10,000 to 1,000. A member of Thomas Hunt's 1615 slaving expedition has probably communicated the disease which leaves relatively few survivors (*see* Mayflower, 1620).

Bubonic plague becomes epidemic in India a year after being identified as such.

Japan's Yoshiwara prostitute section is established at Edo. It will flourish for 328 years (*see* 1789).

An itinerary written by Fynes Moryson, Gent. is published in England: "The English have an abundance of white meats, of all kinds of flesh, fowl, and fish and of things good for food. In the seasons of the year the English eat fallow deer plentifully, as bucks in summer and does in winter, which they bake in pasties, and this venison pasty is a dainty, rarely found in any other kingdom. England yea perhaps one County thereof, hath more fallow deer than all Europe that I have seen. No kingdom in the world hath so many dove-houses. Likewise brawn [boiled and pickled pork] is a proper meat to the English, not known to others. English cooks, in comparison with other nations, are most commended for roasted meats" (*compare* Kalm, 1748).

1618 The Defenestration of Prague May 23 precipitates a Thirty Years' War that will devastate Europe. Bohemian Catholics close a Protestant church and destroy another. Protestants are further embittered by the transfer of Bohemia's administration to 10 governors, of whom seven are Catholics. Two governors are thrown from a window in the palace of Prague, and although their 50-foot fall into a ditch

Virginia colonists found the natives less friendly than the ones who helped the Pilgrims in New England.

does not kill them, their "defenestration" begins a revolt headed by Protestant leader Count Heinrich Matthias von Thurn, 51, who gave the order for the defenestration and who takes command of rebel troops to march on Austria (see 1619).

France's Duc de Richelieu negotiates a treaty between Marie de' Medici and the duc de Luynes. The queen mother returns from exile.

The Ottoman sultan Mustafa I is declared incompetent to rule and his 14-year-old brother succeeds him to begin a 4-year reign as Osman II. The Ottoman Turks give up Georgia and Azerbaijan by treaty with Persia's Abbas the Great.

The Virginia House of Burgesses convenes at Jamestown. It is the first legislative body in the New World.

Sir Walter Raleigh sends five small ships up the Orinoco with his son and a nephew while remaining himself at Trinidad, ill with fever. The expedition under Lawrence Keymis encounters a Spanish settlement, Raleigh's son and several Spaniards are killed in the fight that ensues. Keymis returns to Trinidad with the bad news and kills himself after being reproached by Raleigh who returns to England, is arrested, and is executed October 29 at age 66 to fulfill the king's promise to the Spanish that any piracy on Raleigh's part would be punishable by death.

💲 French adventurer Etienne Brulé begins to assemble furs for sale to French traders. Brulé arrived at Quebec with Champlain in 1608 and has gone into the western wilderness where he lives with the Hurons who will kill him and eat him in 1633.

⚕ An epidemic of measles introduced by European explorers and colonists strikes native Americans and reduces their numbers.

A diphtheria epidemic kills up to 8,000 at Naples.

The London Pharmacopoeia is published in its first edition and contains some 1,960 remedies including worms, dried vipers, foxes' lungs, oil of ants and wolves, and 1,028 simples (see 1677).

🎨 Painting Crucifixion by Spanish painter Jusepe (José) de Ribera, 27, who has settled at Naples.

🎭 Theater King Torrismond (Il rey Torrismondo) by the late Torquato Tasso at Vicenza's Teatro Olympia (Tasso died in 1595 at age 51).

🌾 English gardeners are warned not to plant apricots or peaches in the cold climate of the British Isles.

👪 The population of the German states will decline by at least 7.5 million from its present level of 21 million as a result of the Thirty Years' War (above; see 1648).

1619 The basics of modern mathematics are established by French mathematician-philosopher René Descartes, 22, who applies algebra to geometry and formulates analytic geometry. Serving as a soldier to the Elector of Bavaria in his war against the Bohemian Protestants (below), Descartes makes the breakthrough November 19 that will provide the basis for exploring natural phenomena by mathematics, but his work will not be published until 1637.

The Harmony of the World (Harmonice Mundi) by Johannes Kepler at Linz shows that the planets move not in circles but in ellipses, traveling faster when they are close to the sun. Kepler writes out musical notations suggesting that the planets have "songs" which reach higher keys as they near the sun, his work is called heretical because only circular paths and constant speeds are considered perfect, but the celestial imperfection, Kepler explains, is to enable God to make better music.

⚔ The Holy Roman Emperor Matthias dies March 20 at age 62 at Vienna after a reign of less than seven years. He is succeeded by Bohemia's Ferdinand, 40, who has just been deposed as king of Bohemia but who is elected emperor at Frankfurt August 28 and begins a reign of more than 17 years as Ferdinand II.

Protestant forces under Count von Thurn besiege Vienna in November but cold, hunger, and the Catholic forces of the Bavarian elector Maximilian soon force them to withdraw (see 1618; 1620).

⚙ Batavia is founded by Dutch colonists in Java which will remain a valuable colony for 326 years.

✊ The first black slaves to arrive in the Virginia colony come ashore from a Dutch privateer whose booty includes Spanish plate and "twenty negars" (see 1649).

Most African slaves come to the West Indies and to Brazil where the sugar industry kills them faster than natural breeding can replace them. However, slaves will now begin to play a role in the North American economy.

Some 90 young women arrive at Jamestown from England to marry settlers who pay 120 pounds of tobacco each for the cost of transporting their brides.

The first American day of thanksgiving is celebrated November 30 by 30 Englishmen aboard the ship *Margaret* which touches land at what will be Hampton, Virginia. The new arrivals proceed up the James River and arrive December 4 at Berkeley Grant (*see* 1621).

The slaves landed at Jamestown (above) introduce to North America such African diseases as yellow fever, virulent forms of malaria, and hookworm (*see* 1647; Laveran, 1880; Ashford, 1899).

Burgundy bans the planting of potatoes on charges that the tuber produces leprosy (*see* 1630).

Painting *Adoration of the Magi* by Spanish painter Diego Rodriguez de Silva y Velázquez, 20; *Diana at the Chase* by Il Domenichino; *The Rape of the Daughters of Leucippus* by Peter Paul Rubens.

Jamestown produces a large enough crop to end the threat of starvation in the Virginia colony.

1620 The 180-ton vessel *Mayflower* out of Southampton arrives off Cape Cod November 11 with 100 Pilgrims plus two more born at sea during the 66-day voyage. The Pilgrims are English separatists who have emigrated from Scrooby to Amsterdam and thence to Leyden but who decided 3 years ago to seek a new home in order to preserve their English identity. They have obtained a patent from the London Company to settle in America (*see* 1606).

The Mayflower Compact drawn up by the Pilgrims (above) establishes a form of government based on the will of the colonists rather than on that of the crown. The Pilgrims have found that Cape Cod is outside the jurisdiction of the London Company, and they select Plymouth as the site of a settlement (*see* 1621; John Smith, 1615).

Spanish forces seize the vital Valtelline Pass communications link between Hapsburg Austria and the Spanish Hapsburg Italian possessions. The Spanish action against the Grisons League precipitates a 19-year conflict between Catholic and Protestant factions in Switzerland.

A Catholic League army commanded by Flemish field marshal John Tsaerclaes Count von Tilly, 61, defeats Bohemia's "Winter King" Frederick V November 8 in the Battle of the White Mountain as the Thirty Years' War ends its third year. Bohemia loses her independence and the lands of her native nobility are confiscated wholesale by von Tilly, by Maximilian of Bavaria, and by the Holy Roman Emperor Ferdinand II.

Baltic trade will collapse in the next decade as export staples from the region shift from foodstuffs to timber, metals, and naval stores while imports of western woollens diminish. French trade with the Levant will fall by half in the next 15 years, and Dutch Levantine trade will also languish as the Thirty

Years' War (above) reduces supplies of linen from Silesia and Lusatia and generally stifles commerce.

Novum Organum by England's Sir Francis Bacon, the first Baron Verulam, proposes an inductive method of interpreting nature as opposed to the deductive logic of Aristotle. Bacon insists on observation and experience as the sole source of knowledge (now 59, he advanced his career at age 45 by marrying a 14-year-old heiress).

Painting *The Water Carrier of Seville* by Diego Velázquez.

Pilgrims from the *Mayflower* (above) are aided by the Pemaquid Samoset and the Wampanoags Hobomah and Massasoit who have learned some English from earlier visitors and who share tribal stores of maize with the new colonists to get them through the winter. But, roughly half will die within 3 months of starvation, scurvy, and disease (*see* 1621).

1621 Spain's Philip III dies March 31 at age 42 after a 23-year reign. He is succeeded by his 15-year-old son who will reign until 1665 as Philip IV, but who will leave affairs of state to his prime minister Gaspar de Gusman, 34, El Conde-Duque de Olivares. The duque de Olivares breaks the truce of 1609 with Holland and resumes war, levying new taxes as he struggles to modernize the government and centralize power in the royalty.

Parliament impeaches the English lord chancellor Sir Francis Bacon on charges of having taken bribes in connection with the granting of monopoly patents that have enriched the brothers of the duke of Buckingham. Bacon confesses but protests that the presents he received from parties in chancery suits never affected his judgment. He is fined £40,000, is banished from the court and from Parliament, and is declared incapable of holding future office, but James I pardons Bacon and remits his fine.

The House of Commons petitions James I against popery and the marriage of his son Charles to the Spanish infanta; James angrily rebukes the Commons for meddling in foreign affairs; and the Commons declares in a Great Protestation December 18 "That the liberties, franchises, privileges, and jurisdictions of parliament are the ancient and undoubted birthright and inheritance of the subjects of England, and that the arduous and urgent affairs concerning the king, state, and defense of the realm . . . are proper subjects and matter of council and debate in parliament" (*see* 1622).

Another 35 English colonists arrive at Plymouth.

The Dutch West Indies Company is chartered by Holland which has been making inroads into Spain's overseas empire. The new company receives a monopoly in trade with Africa and America (*see* 1628).

The English East India Company has completed 12 voyages to the Indies and has earned an average profit of 138 percent on each voyage.

1621 (cont.) An Englishman calculates that 3,000 tons of spices bought in the Indies for £91,041 will fetch £789,168 at Aleppo, the trading center at the eastern end of the Mediterranean.

The Anatomy of Melancholy by English clergyman Robert Burton, 44, is a medical treatise on the causes, symptoms, and cure of melancholy that will be widely read for its wisdom and beauty of language. Says the vicar of St. Thomas's at Oxford: "Who cannot give good counsel? 'Tis cheap, it costs them nothing"; "Comparisons are odious"; "A good conscience is a continual feast"; "Desire hath no rest"; "Despair makes the monk"; "Like . . . a dog in the manger, he doth only keep it because it shall do nobody else good, hurting himself and others"; "Every other sin hath some pleasure annexed to it, or will admit of an excuse; envy alone wants both"; "Make not a fool of thyself, to make others merry"; "Man's best possession is a loving wife"; "When they are at Rome, they do there as they see done"; "Every man for himself, the Devil for all"; "A loose, plain, rude writer, I call a spade a spade"; "If there be a hell upon the earth it is to be found in a melancholy heart"; "Aristotle said . . . melancholy men of all others are most witty."

Pembroke College is founded at Oxford.

Heidelberg's University Library is sacked by the troops of Count von Tilly.

A national postoffice department is established by the French Estates-General at the urging of Armand Jean du Plessie, duc de Richelieu (*see* 1464).

Painting *Rape of the Sabine Women* by French painter Nicolas Poussin, 27; *Family Group* and *Rest on the Flight into Egypt* by Flemish painter Anthony van Dyck, 22; *Hercules* by Guido Reni.

Sculpture *Rape of Prospero* by Italian sculptor-painter Gian (or Giovanni) Lorenzo Bernini, 22.

Theater *A New Way to Pay Old Bills* by English playwright Philip Massinger, 38, who has drawn his central situation from Thomas Middleton's play *A Trick to Catch the Old One* of 1607; *The Witch of Edmonton* by Thomas Dekker, John Ford, and William Rowley at London's Phoenix Theatre.

Potatoes are planted for the first time in the German states.

Plymouth colonists have difficulty growing wheat and barley in fields poorly cleared of stumps and rocks but they are aided by the Wampanoag Indian kidnapped by slaver Thomas Hunt in 1615. Tisquantum (or Squanto) has made his way back from Spain, he presents himself at the Pilgrim settlement on Cape Cod Bay March 16, he speaks some English, and he shows the Pilgrims how to catch eels, and how to plant maize and beans using alewives, shad, or menhaden as fertilizer, a European idea he has learned either from French colonists in Maine and Canada or from English colonists in Newfoundland who have acquired the knowledge from the French.

Jamestown colonists build the first American grist mill to produce flour from their wheat.

A Thanksgiving dinner-breakfast is given by New England's Pilgrim colonists to entertain 92 Indian guests including Chief Massasoit. The meal includes wild turkeys shot by the colonists and popcorn which is introduced to the Pilgrims by the chief's brother (*see* 1863).

1622 England's James I tears out the page in the journal of the Commons bearing the Great Protestation of last December, he dissolves Parliament February 8, and he imprisons Sir Edward Coke, now 69, for 9 months along with the earl of Southampton John Selden, 38, and John Pym, 38.

The Battle of Wiesloch in April gives Protestant forces under Count Peter Ernst Mansfeld II, 42, a victory over Count von Tilly's Catholics. Mansfeld plunders Hesse and the Alsace, but Tilly triumphs a few weeks later over the margrave of Baden-Durlach and he defeats Christian of Brunswick in June as the Thirty Years' War continues.

The Ottoman sultan Osman II, determined to reform Constantinople's degenerate Janissaries, pretends to go on a pilgrimage to Mecca intending to march back with a loyal army he hopes to raise in Syria and Arabia. The Janissaries hear of his plan and revolt—they march Osman through the streets hurling insults at him, then they kill him, and restore the imbecilic Mustafa I.

Execution of Christian missionaries in Japan will reach its height in the next 3 years.

The Council for New England which has succeeded the Plymouth Company grants territory between the Kennebec and Merrimack Rivers to former Newfoundland governor John Mason, 36, and his rich English associate Sir Ferdinando Gorges, 56 (*see* 1629).

The Plymouth Plantation receives 67 new arrivals and earlier colonists are forced to go on short rations.

Indian attacks March 22 destroy a number of Virginia settlements within a few hours, killing 347 colonists and destroying the first American ironworks.

Disease takes a heavy toll among Virginia colonists and among their Indian neighbors.

London's Banqueting House at Whitehall is completed by English architect Inigo Jones, 49, who has studied in Italy.

Virginia colonists who pick corn prematurely are subjected to public whipping.

Population of the Virginia colony has quadrupled to some 1,400 in the last 5 years, but is reduced this year by disease and Indian massacres (above).

1623 England's 22-year-old Prince of Wales travels in secret to Spain with the duke of Buckingham who has persuaded him to seek the hand of the infanta Maria, sister of Philip IV. "Mr. Smith" and "Mr. Brown" arrive at Madrid March 7, they find the infanta and the Spanish court unenthusiastic and distrustful of young Charles's promise to change English penal laws against Catholics. Charles returns October 5, and he will be betrothed instead to the sister of France's Louis XIII.

The Holy Roman Emperor Ferdinand II gives the Upper Palatine to the duke of Bavaria Maximilian as the Thirty Years' War continues. Papal troops occupy the Valtelline and Count von Tilly advances to Westphalia after defeating Christian of Brunswick at Stadtlohn.

The Ottoman sultan Mustafa I abdicates in favor of his 14-year-old nephew who will reign as Murad IV until 1640. His mother Kussem Sultana will serve as regent until his majority.

Persia's Shah Abbas I takes Baghdad.

The Massacre of Amboyana by the Dutch drives colonists of the English East India Company out of the Spice Islands.

Dutch forces seize the Brazilian port of Pernambuco that will later be called Recife.

The Japanese Tokugawa shogun Hidetada abdicates at age 45 and is succeeded by his 19-year-old son Iemitsu who will raise the shogunate to its greatest glory in the next 28 years.

$ English traders in Japan abandon their commercial station at Hirado (see 1613).

A new English patents law protects inventors.

Another large group of English colonists arrives at Plymouth.

The port of Gloucester is founded.

The Dutch make New Netherlands a formally organized province and some 30 Dutch families land on Manhattan Island (see 1614). Some move upriver to Fort Nassau, some to the Connecticut River Valley (see 1624).

"Chyle" (lacteal) vessels are discovered by Italian anatomist Gasparo Aselli, 42, who performs a vivisection operation on a dog which has just eaten a substantial meal. Aselli finds that the dog's peritoneum and intestine are covered with a mass of white threads (see Pecquet, 1643).

The University of Salzburg has its beginnings.

Painting *Cardinal Bentivoglio* by Anthony Van Dyck; *Baptism of Christ* by Guido Reni; Diego Velásquez gains appointment as court painter at Madrid where he will be famous for his naturalistic portraits of Philip IV, the Infanta Maria, Marianna of Austria, Olivarez, court jesters, dwarfs, idiots, and beggars in addition to his religious paintings.

Sculpture *David* by Gian Lorenzo Bernini.

Theater *Love, Honor and Power* (*Amor, Honor y Poder*) by Spanish playwright Pedro Calderon de la Barca, 23; *The Duke of Milan* by Philip Massinger.

Mr. William Shakespeares Comedies, Histories and Tragedies According to the True Originall Copies (First Folio) is published at London.

The Paris Church of St. Marie de la Visitation is completed by François Mansart.

Brazil has 350 sugar plantations, up from five in 1550.

A Spanish edict offers rewards and special privileges to encourage large families but the offer has little effect on birth rates.

1624 France's Louis XIII makes Cardinal Richelieu his chief minister. Known as "the red eminence," Richelieu has been a cardinal since 1622 and he begins a domination of the government that will continue until his death in 1642.

France and England sign a treaty providing for the marriage of Charles, prince of Wales, to Henrietta Maria, daughter of Henri IV and Marie de' Medici.

England declares war on Spain.

$ Spain's Philip IV publishes sumptuary laws in response to popular criticism of his court's extravagance, he reduces his household staff, and he bans wearing of the ruff, a sartorial symbol of profligacy that will soon go out of style everywhere in Europe as luxury gives way to austerity.

Japan expels all Spanish traders and puts an end to trade with the Philippines (see 1609; 1634).

Eight men from the Dutch West Indies Company ship *Nieuw Nederland* land on Manhattan Island in May and move up the Hudson River to Fort Nassau, later to be called Albany. The men are Walloons led by Jesse De Forest of Avesnes, Hainaut (see 1623; 1626).

Italian medical professor Santorio Santorius, 63, resigns from the University of Padua where his students have included Englishman William Harvey (see 1628). Santorius has invented an apparatus for measuring the pulse, and a crude clinical thermometer, neither of which will be employed in medicine for centuries to come (see Floyer, 1707).

Poetry *Devotions upon Emergent Occasions* by John Donne, now dean of St. Paul's in London: "No man is an Iland, intire of it selfe; every man is a piece of the Continent . . . If a Clod bee washed away by the sea, Europe is the lesse . . . any man's death diminishes me, because I am involved in Mankinde; And therefore never seek to know for whom the bell tolls; it tolls for thee" (17th Meditation).

Painting *The Laughing Cavalier* by Franz Hals.

Snuff users are threatened with excommunication by Pope Urban VIII (Maffeo Barberini) as the use of tobacco from the New World gains in popularity.

The Louvre Palace at Paris is completed in part for Louis XIII by French architect Jacques Lemercier,

1624 (cont.) 39. The palace will be enlarged with additions over the next two centuries.

The Palais de Luxembourg at Paris is completed by Salomon de Brosse after nine years of construction on the left bank of the Seine. Queen mother Marie de' Medici takes up residence in the new palace.

1625 England's James I dies March 5 at age 58 and is succeeded by his 24-year-old son who ascends the throne March 27 to begin an ill-fated reign of 24 years as Charles I.

Charles I of England is married by proxy May 1 to France's Henrietta Maria, 16-year-old sister of Louis XIII, and receives her at Canterbury June 13.

France has a Huguenot revolt led by Henri, duc de Rohan, 46, and his brother Benjamin de Rohan, 42, seigneur de Soubise.

Parliament rebuffs England's new king in his demands for funds to carry on the war with Spain. Charles has lent ships to France's Louis XIII for use against the Huguenots at La Rochelle and Parliament's Protestant feelings have also been aroused by the king's support of Richard Montagu, 48, the royal chaplain who has repudiated Calvinist doctrine.

The Treaty of Southampton September 8 forms an Anglo-Dutch alliance against Spain. Charles sends an expedition to Cadiz under Sir Edward Cecil, 51, viscount Wimbledon, who bungles the mission and permits Spain's treasure ships to reach port. Charles tries to raise money on the crown jewels in Holland to make himself independent of the Commons.

De Jure Belli et Pacis by Hugo Grotius is an expansion of his 1609 *Mare librum* thesis and begins the science of international law. Grotius has been condemned to life imprisonment for leading a protest group called the Remonstrants but he has escaped and has emigrated to France (*see* 1702).

Dutch forces at Bahia yield to a Spanish fleet.

Fort Amsterdam is founded April 22 on the lower tip of Manhattan Island by the Dutch West India Co.

St. Christopher (St. Kitts) in the Caribbean is settled by French colonists.

The first English colony on Barbados is established under the leadership of Sir William Courteen.

A Colonial Office is established at London.

An epidemic of the Black Death kills 41,000 at London while 22,000 die of other causes (*see* 1603; 1665).

Glauber's salt (anhydrous sodium sulfate) is discovered by German physician-chemist Johann Rudolf Glauber, 21, whose salt will be used as a laxative and for dyeing textiles.

Painting *Marie de' Medici* by Peter Paul Rubens; *Job* by Guido Reni; *The Procuress* by Dutch painter Gerrit van Honthorst, 34.

Theater *Love Tricks* by English playwright James Shirley, 28.

Moscow's Gate of Salvation in the Kremlin gets a set of bells that will peal for centuries.

London's Covent Garden Church is completed by Inigo Jones.

Kyoto's Katsura Rikyu (detached palace) is completed for Toshihito, a prince of the Hachijo family.

The Plymouth colony for the first time has "corn sufficient, and some to spare for others"; Governor William Bradford writes home to England and credits part of the improvement to a revised plan of communal labor with equal rations, each family being assigned land according to its size: "This . . . made all hands very industrious. . . ."

Goiter is depicted by Peter Paul Rubens in his portrait of Marie de' Medici (above). The thyroid gland swelling is esteemed as a mark of beauty when only moderate in size (*see* Baumann, 1896).

1626 Manhattan Island is purchased from chiefs of the Wappinger Confederacy for fish hooks and trinkets valued at 60 guilders by Dutch colonists who call the natives Manhattes. Peter Minuit, Willem Verhulst, and the other Dutch leaders assign large tracts of Manhattan land to members of their company (patroons) on condition that they bring over stipulated numbers of settlers to the new town of Nieuw Amsterdam founded by Minuit.

Madagascar is settled by its first French colonists who seek to drive out the Hovas who have lived on the African island for 600 years.

Protestant forces under Count Mansfeld are defeated at the Bridge of Dessau by Catholics under the Austrian general Albrecht Eusebius Wenzel von Wallenstein, 43, who pursues the enemy through Silesia to Hungary where Mansfeld obtains support from the Transylvanian prince Bethlen Gabor. But Bethlen soon withdraws from the war and Count Mansfeld dies, as does Christian of Brunswick.

The 60 guilders paid for Manhattan (above) is by some accounts $24 and by others $39 (roughly 0.2 cents per acre), but a 20th century economist will reckon the purchasing power of 60 guilders at several thousand dollars in modern terms (and the recipients have sold land that does not belong to them).

Rome's Irish College is founded.

Fiction *La Historia de la vide del Buscon* by Spanish picaresque novelist Francisco Gomez de Quevedo y Villegas, 46, is full of grotesque atmosphere and Machiavellian characters.

Painting *The Baptism of the Moor* by Dutch painter Rembrandt van Rijn, 19; *The Clemency of Titus* by Rembrandt van Rijn; *Isaac Abrahamsz Massa* by Franz Hals; *Assumption of the Virgin* by Peter Paul Rubens (altarpiece at Antwerp).

Dutch whalers establish the port of Smeerenberg in Spitzbergen to process right whales, so called by the English to distinguish them from "wrong" whales which sink when dead. The whales are prized not as food but for their oil and whalebone, used respectively for illumination and lubrication and as stays.

Sir Francis Bacon experiments with the idea of freezing chickens by stuffing them with snow. He catches pneumonia and dies April 9 at age 65.

1627 The Catholic forces of Albrecht von Wallenstein and the baron von Tilly conquer Holstein, Wallenstein subdues Schleswig and Jutland, he drives the dukes of Mecklenburg out of that duchy, and he forces the duke of Pomerania to submit as Denmark's Christian IV withdraws temporarily from the Thirty Years' War.

A new Bohemian constitution confirms the hereditary rule of the Hapsburgs and strengthens royal power.

Manchu forces invade Korea. The Manchus will make Korea a vassal state in 10 years but Korea's court and people will remain loyal to the Ming.

The Mogul emperor Jahangir who has ruled tyrannically from Delhi since 1605 dies in October at age 58 while returning from Kashmir. His 35-year-old son has effected a reconciliation following an abortive rebellion, he has all his male collateral relatives murdered to remove any challenges to his succession, he orders construction of an extravagant Peacock Throne made of emeralds, diamonds, and rubies (it will take 7 years to complete), and he will reign as the emperor Shah Jahan until 1658.

France's Cardinal Richelieu founds the Company of the Hundred Associates to colonize New France. He gives the company all lands between Florida and the Arctic Circle with a monopoly in trade except in the cod and whale fisheries.

Barbados in the West Indies is colonized by some 80 English settlers who arrive aboard the *William and John* captained by John Powell but owned by a Dutch merchant in England. Captain Powell captures a Portuguese ship bound for Lisbon with Brazilian sugar, he delivers her cargo to the *William and John*'s Dutch owner, the Dutchman sells the sugar for nearly £10,000, and he devotes the windfall to developing the new colony at Barbados, an island never seen by Christopher Columbus (*see* 1636).

The English East India Company will omit dividends to its stockholders in 16 of the next 50 years, but they will be the only dividendless years in the 180 years between 1602 and 1780 (*see* 1708).

Fiction *Las Suenos* by Francisco de Quevedo y Villegas; *Le Berger extravagant* by French satirist Charles Sorel, 25.

Poetry *Nymphidia* by Michael Drayton.

Painting *The Jolly Toper* and *Banquet of the Civic Guard* by Franz Hals; *The Money-Changer* by Rembrandt van Rijn; *The Mystic Marriage of St. Catherine* by Peter Paul Rubens; *Crucifixion* by Spanish painter Francisco de Zurbaran, 28.

Opera *Dafne* 4/23 at Torgau with music by German composer Heinrich Schütz, 41, libretto by German poet-critic Martin Opitz, 30, who has adapted a 1594 melodrama by Ottavio Rinuccini to write the first German opera. Schütz will move to Venice next year to study under Claudio Monteverdi.

Queen's Chapel in St. James's Palace, Westminster, is completed by Inigo Jones after 4 years of work.

France's Louis XIII entrusts the planning of a great château at Versailles to Jacques Lemercier (*see* 1682; Louvre, 1624).

Peking's Pao Ho Tien is completed. It will be one of the Three Great Halls of the Purple Forbidden City.

The last aurochs dies in captivity in Poland. The prehistoric prototype of modern cattle becomes extinct.

Shad ascend the Hudson River with such regularity each March 11th that Dutch colonists at Nieuw Amsterdam call the herring *elft* (the eleven fish).

Dutch colonists at Nieuw Amsterdam will enrich the American cuisine in the next 37 years with cookies (*koekjes*), coleslaw, and waffles (*see* Irving, 1820).

1628 "Essay on the Motion of the Heart and Blood" ("Exercitatio de Motu Cordis et Sanguinis") by English physician William Harvey, 50, is published at Frankfurt-am-Main. Harvey's 75-page treatise based on his Lumleian lecture of 1616 establishes that the human heart is muscular despite earlier theories to the contrary, and that its regular mechanical contractions drive the blood out into the blood vessels. Harvey acknowledges the 1559 work of Andrea Columbus who first used the term "circulation," and he destroys the old idea that the liver converts food into blood, but Harvey does not offer a satisfactory new explanation for the creation of blood.

William Harvey (above) follows Galileo's principle of measuring what can be measured and shows that the heart contains 2 ounces of blood and, at 65 heartbeats per minute, that it pumps 10 pounds of blood out into the body in less than 1 minute, an amount greater by far than can be sustained by production from food consumed. But while eminent physicians and philosophers from Denmark, England, France, and the German states rally to Harvey's thesis it is roundly attacked by Scottish physician James Primrose and by the Paris Faculty of Medicine whose dean Guy Patin calls Harvey's theory "paradoxical, useless, false, impossible, absurd, and harmful."

Bubonic plague kills half the population of Lyons. The Black Death will kill a million in the northern Italian states in the next 2 years (*see* 1630).

The Duke of Buckingham George Villiers is assassinated August 23 at age 36 as he prepares to lead a final expedition for the relief of La Rochelle, center of France's Huguenot power. La Rochelle surrenders after a 14-month siege that three English fleets have not been able to lift, the Huguenots cease to be an

1628 (cont.) armed political power in France, and Buckingham is succeeded by his 7-month-old son and namesake.

The Austrian duke Wallenstein obtains the duchy of Mecklenburg. He assumes the title admiral of the Baltic, but suffers his first reverse when his siege of Stralsund is raised.

Dutch forces occupy Java and the Moluccas.

The Dutch West India Company founded in 1621 declares a 50 percent dividend after its admiral Piet Heyn surrounds and captures the Spanish silver fleet August 8 off the Cuban coast.

The London Company sends ships directly to the Persian Gulf, antagonizing the Levant Company.

English engineer Edward Somerset invents the first crude steam engine (*see* Savery, 1698).

Salem is founded on Massachusetts Bay by some 50 colonists who arrived in September with John Endicott, 39, who with five other Englishmen has bought a patent to the territory from the Plymouth Council in England and who will serve as first governor of the Massachusetts Bay colony until 1630.

Painting *The Martyrdom of St. Erasmus* by Nicolas Poussin; *The Siege of Breda* by French painter-engraver-etcher Jacques Callot, 36; *Charles I and Henrietta Maria with the Liberal Arts* by Gerrit van Honthurst.

Masque *Britannia's Honour* by Thomas Dekker 10/29.

Theater *The Lover's Melancholy* by John Ford 11/24 at London's Blackfriars Theatre, with the King's Men; *The Witty Fair One* by James Shirley at London's Phoenix Theatre.

1629 England's Charles I encounters opposition in the House of Commons where resolutions by Sir John Eliot are read while the speaker is held in his chair. The resolutions declare that anyone who advises the levy of tonnage and poundage taxes without grant of Parliament is an enemy of the kingdom and so is anyone who introduces innovations in religion or expresses opinions that disagree with those of the true church. English authorities arrest Sir John Eliot and eight other members of Parliament March 5. Eliot will be fined £2,000 next year and will die in prison 2 years later.

The Edict of Restitution March 29 restores ecclesiastic estates in Europe taken since the 1552 convention of Passau and permits free exercise of religion only to adherents of the 1530 Confession of Augsburg. All other "sects" are to be broken up, troops of the Catholic League and of the Austrian duke Albrecht von Wallenstein begin enforcing the edict, and they show no mercy to "heretics."

England's Charles I dissolves Parliament in March (above). It will not meet again until 1640.

The Treaty of Lübeck May 22 ends hostilities between the Holy Roman Emperor Ferdinand II and Denmark's Christian IV who regains his lands on condition that he abandon his allies and cease his interference in German affairs. The dukes of Mecklenburg are placed under the ban and the Austrian Albrecht von Wallenstein (above) is confirmed as duke of Mecklenburg.

The Truce of Altmark ends hostilities between Sweden and Poland.

Transylvania's Bethlen Gabor dies November 15 at age 49 after marrying a sister-in-law of Sweden's Gustavus Adolphus in hopes that the Swedes would help him obtain the Polish crown.

John Mason and Sir Ferdinando Gorges obtain a new grant of land between Maine's Kennebec and Piscataqua Rivers and join with others to form the Laconia Company and establish a farming community on the Piscataqua in what will become New Hampshire (*see* 1622; 1630).

The Dutch West Indies Company chartered in 1621 has more than 100 full-rigged ships in commission, most of them fitted out to fight pirates or other merchantmen. The company employs 15,000 seamen and soldiers (*see* 1628).

"A fool and his money is soon parted," writes English author James Howell, 35, in a letter October 20.

Painting *Allegory of War and Peace* by Peter Paul Rubens; *Bacchus* by Diego Velázquez who is given permission by Philip IV to visit Italy: Velázquez sails in August from Barcelona with the Marquis de Spinola who is en route to Milan where he will take command of Spanish troops.

Japan's Kabuki Theater becomes an all-male affair in October by order of the Tokugawa shogun Iemitsu who has decided that it is immoral for women to dance in public (*see* 1603). Women's roles are performed by men as in Elizabethan England, but the Japanese will take extraordinary measures to make the men playing female roles appear as women even to other Kabuki players; *The Grateful Servant* by James Shirley, in November at London's Phoenix Theatre, with the Queen's Men.

Giovanni Lorenzo Bernini is appointed by the Barberini Pope Urban VIII to finish St. Peter's at Rome. Bernini will design the Scala Regia in the Vatican, he will complete the Barberini Palace, he will redecorate the Lateran and the Bridge of Sant' Angelo, and he will construct fountains for Rome's Piazza Navona, Piazza Trevi, and Piazza Barberini.

"The aboundance of sea fish are almost beyond believing," writes Salem Puritan minister Francis Higginson, 42, of the Massachusetts Bay colony. "And sure I should scarse have believed it, except I had seen it with my own eyes. I saw great store of whales and crampusse [grampus, or dolphins] and such aboundance of mackerils that it would astonish one to behold, likewise cod-fish in abundance on the coast, and in their season are plentifully taken. There is a fish called a basse, a most sweet and wholesome fish as ever I did eat, it is altogether as good as our fresh sammon...."

The joint-stock company of Massachusetts Bay organized by Anglican Puritans will bring more than 17,000 settlers to America in the next 13 years.

1630 England makes peace with France in April and with Spain in November.

Sweden's Gustavus II Adolphus lands on the Pomeranian Coast in July to aid the oppressed Protestants, restore the dukes of Mecklenburg to whom he is related, and resist the extortion and cruelty of Wallenstein's army (see 1629; 1631).

Hungary's Bethlen Gabor (Gabriel Bethlen) is succeeded by George Rakoczi I who is elected prince of Transylvania at age 39 by the diet of Segesovar November 26. He begins a reign of nearly 18 years.

Bubonic plague kills 500,000 Venetians and hastens the decline of Venice.

Repeated epidemics in the decade ahead will reduce America's Huron tribe to a third of its estimated 30,000 population.

Boston, Dorchester, Roxbury, Watertown, Mystic, and Lynn are established as the Massachusetts Bay Colony receives 2,000 new settlers.

Portsmouth is established by John Mason in what will be the New Hampshire colony (see 1629; 1635).

Agents of Amsterdam pearl merchant Kiliaen van Rensselaer buy a tract of land for him on the west bank of the Hudson river. They give the Indians "certain quantities of duffels, axes, knives and wampum" for a territory 24 miles in length, 48 in breadth.

Peru's Cerro de Pasco mine opens 14,000 feet high in the Andes. The mine will yield gold, silver, copper, zinc, and antimony, it will become South America's largest lead producer, and it will be the world's largest producer of bismuth.

Painting *The Triumphs of Flora* by Nicolas Poussin for his patron Cardinal Omodei; *The Vision of Blessed Alonso Rodriguez* by Francisco de Zurburan.

Theater *Melite, or The False Letters* (*Melite, ou les fausses lettres*) by French playwright Pierre Corneille, 23, in January or February at the Berthault Tennis Court, Paris.

Cultivation of potatoes is forbidden by France's Parlement of Besançon. Some people who eat the tubers raw have contracted eczema, as have some cattle, and the tubers are suspected of causing leprosy (see Burgundy, 1619).

Lemonade is invented at Paris as sugar imported from the French West Indies drops in price.

Kikkoman soy sauce is originated at Noda, 25 miles upriver from Edo, by Japan's Mogi and Takanashi families who also develop miso (bean paste) to serve the growing community of Edo (see 1590). A refined version of an ancient sauce is brewed by the families whose descendants will control the firm for centuries. The name Kikko (tortoise shell) Man (10,000) is adopted because the tortoise is thought to live for 10,000 years, and the hexagon found in the pattern of many tortoise shells is adopted as the Kikkoman trademark.

A "Great Migration" begins that will bring 16,000 people to the Massachusetts Bay Colony in the next 10 years (above).

1631 Magdeburg falls to the forces of Count von Tilly May 20. The German cavalry general Count Gottfried Heinrich zu Pappenheim, 37, takes the city by storm; he massacres the citizenry and sacks the city; fires break out at scattered locations simultaneously, and the entire city burns with the exception of the cathedral as the Catholic soldiery commits terrible atrocities.

The Battle of Breitenfeld (or Leipzig) September 17 breaks the strength of revived Catholicism in central Europe. Tilly has burned Halle, Eisleben, Merseburg, and other cities, but the elector of Saxony John George has formed an alliance with Sweden's Gustavus II Adolphus, an army of Swedish Lutherans has crossed the Elbe at Wittenberg to challenge Tilly who has occupied Leipzig, and the Saxon-Swedish army of 40,000 defeats Tilly's army of equal size.

France's Cardinal Richelieu brings his country into the Thirty Years' War by subsidizing Sweden's Gustavus II Adolphus (above) and the 27-year-old Bernhard, duke of Saxe-Weimar.

Peter Minuit is recalled from Nieuw Amsterdam for granting undue privileges to patroons (landowners) and for concentrating economic and political power

The Thirty Years' War, a conflict between Catholics and Protestants, brought devastation to much of Europe.

227

1631 (cont.) in the hands of an elite few (*see* 1626). Minuit will enter the service of Sweden (*see* 1638).

Shipyards start up at Boston and other Massachusetts colony seaports as cheap American lumber makes an American-built ship only half as expensive as one built in England. The 30-ton sloop *Blessing of the Bay* is launched in August for Governor John Winthrop.

The vernier scale for making accurate measurements of linear or angular magnitudes for navigation is described by French mathematician Pierre Vernier, 51, in *Construction, Usage et Proprieties du Quadrant Nouveau de Mathematiques* (*see* Nunes, 1536; Greenwich observatory, 1676).

Cautio criminalis by German Jesuit poet Friedrich von Spee, 40, is published anonymously. Von Spee has often ministered to condemned witches and he attacks the mentality behind witch-hunts and the legal use of torture to extract confessions (*see* Wier, 1563; Loudon, 1634; Salem, 1692).

Theater *The Traitor* by James Shirley, in May at London's Phoenix Theatre; *The Humourous Courtier* by James Shirley, in November at London's Phoenix Theatre; *Love's Cruelty* by James Shirley, in November at the Phoenix Theatre.

Potatoes are cultivated in so much of Europe, yield so much food per unit of land, and grow so well even in years when grain crops are at famine level that the tubers have encouraged the start of a population explosion in those parts of the continent where the new food is accepted and where the ravages of the Thirty Years' War (above) have not totally disrupted society.

1632 Galileo Galilei repeats his advocacy of the Copernican system of astronomy in *Dialogo de Massimi Sistemi del Mondo*. He is summoned to Rome (*see* 1613; 1633).

Poland's Sigismund III Vasa dies suddenly at age 65 after a reign of 44 years—Moscow immediately declares war. Sigismund's son Ladislas IV, 37, begins a 16-year reign, he engages the Muscovites in a series of bloody battles in August, and he will pursue a course opposite from that of his father.

Sweden's Gustavus II Adolphus defeats the Catholic general von Tilly at the confluence of the Lenz and the Danube as the Thirty Years' War continues. Von Tilly is mortally wounded and dies April 30 at age 72 at Ingelstodt; Munich surrenders to Gustavus II Adolphus; and the Austrian duke Albrecht von Wallenstein tries to keep him from taking Nuremberg. Both sides withdraw from the city after 18,000 have died of scurvy and typhus.

The Battle of Lutzen November 16 pits 20,000 Swedes against 18,000 Catholics. The Swedes win, but Gustavus II Adolphus is killed at age 38. The German Gottfried Heinrich, count of Pappenheim is mortally wounded and dies the next day at Leipzig, at age 38.

Sweden's Gustavus II Adolphus (above) is succeeded by his 6-year-old daughter Christina and she will ascend the throne on her 18th birthday December 8, 1644 after a chancellorship administered by Count Axel Gustafsson Oxenstierna, 49.

Maryland is chartered as the first of the English proprietary colonies in the New World. A grant of land from the Potomac River north to the 40th parallel is granted by Charles I to Cecilius (Cecil) Calvert, 27, whose father George, Lord Baltimore, has just died at age 52 after having rejected a grant of Newfoundland on account of its harsh climate (*see* 1633).

Nova Scotia is founded as the French colony of Acadia by settlers who will cut farms out of the region's dense forests (*see* 1710).

Poetry "On His Having Arrived at the Age of Twenty-Three" by English poet John Milton, 23: "How soon hath Time, the subtle thief of youth,/ Stol'n on his wing my three-and-twentieth year."

Painting *De Tulp's Anatomy* by Rembrandt van Rijn who depicts members of Amsterdam's Guild of Surgeons; *The Garden of Love* by Peter Paul Rubens.

Theater *Hyde Park* by James Shirley, in April at London's Phoenix Theatre.

English Puritan William Prynne, 32, attacks the London theater in his pamphlet "Histriomatix": "It hath evermore been the notorious badge of prostituted Strumpets and the lewdest Harlots, to ramble abroad to plays, to Playhouses; whither no honest, chaste or sober Girls or Women, but only branded Whores and infamous Adulteresses, did usually resort in ancient times."

The English queen Henrietta Maria has taken part in a performance of a play at the court. William Prynne's lines (above) are construed as an aspersion on the queen; Prynne will be branded, his ears will be cut off, he will be heavily fined, and he will be imprisoned for 8 years of a life sentence beginning in 1634 (*see* theater closings, 1642).

The Palais-Royal is completed at Paris to provide a residence for Cardinal Richelieu.

Apple trees are planted by English colonists in territory that will become the New Jersey colony in 1665.

Rotterdam's population reaches 20,000. The city will become the world's largest port (*see* 1299).

1633 Galileo goes on trial at Rome April 12 and is threatened by the Inquisition with torture on the rack if he does not retract his defense of the Copernican idea that the sun is the center of the universe and the Earth a movable planet. Galileo yields and is sent to his villa outside Florence where he will be confined for the remaining nine years of his life (*see* 1632).

René Descartes takes warning from the trial of Galileo (above). Now living in Holland, Descartes stops publishing in France (*see* 1619; 1637).

An expedition to start the first Roman Catholic colony in North America leaves England in November as Cecil Calvert's younger brother Leonard embarks with the vessels *Ark* and *Dove* (see 1632; 1634).

Some 30 Dutch colonists settle in Delaware.

Dutch colonists from Nieuw Amsterdam establish a trading post on the Connecticut River at what later will be called Hartford (see 1636; Connecticut colony, 1635).

Poetry *The Temple* by the late English poet George Herbert who has died March 1 of tuberculosis at age 39.

Theater *A Match at Midnight* by William Rowley contains the line, "He's a chip o' the old block"; *'Tis Pity She's a Whore* by John Ford at London's Phoenix Theatre; *The Maidservant* (*La suivante*) by Pierre Corneille at the Fontaine Tennis Court, Paris; *Place Royale, or The Extravagant Lover* (*La place royale, ou L'amoureux extravagant*) by Pierre Corneille, in December, at the Fontaine Tennis Court.

1634 An imperial proclamation issued January 24 accuses the Catholic general von Wallenstein of involvement in a conspiracy to "rob the emperor of his crown," chief army officers are commanded to cease their obedience to Wallenstein, he is formally deposed as duke of Friedland by proclamation February 18, and he is assassinated a week later by English and Irish officers.

The Treaty of Polianov ends a 2-year Russian-Polish war. Poland's Ladislas IV renounces his claim to the Russian crown, but Russia's Michael Romanov gives up Smolensk and surrounding territories in return for recognition of his title (see 1613).

Curaçao and St. Eustatius in the West Indies are seized by Dutch forces (see 1779).

 French explorer Jean Nicolet, 36, makes an expedition to Lake Michigan and the Wisconsin region, the first white venture into that area. Brought to Canada by Champlain in 1618, Nicolet has lived among the Huron of the upper Ottawa River and he now travels west in search of furs and of a Northwest Passage. Nicolet lands at what will later be Green Bay where the Menominees have a settlement at a time when most indigenous tribes are being pushed westward by the Ottawa, Huron, and other eastern tribes.

Lord Calvert arrives in America late in March and establishes a Maryland settlement that will welcome Protestants as well as Roman Catholics (see 1633; 1688).

Permanent settlements are made in Connecticut by Massachusetts Puritans whose towns will later be called Windsor and Wethersfield (see 1635).

A ship-money tax formerly levied only on English coastal towns is extended to the whole country by Charles I and is defied by Buckinghamshire squire John Hampden, 40. Hampden will lose his case in court but he will have popular support in his cause against the king.

Speculation in tulip bulbs reaches new heights in the Netherlands where one collector pays 1,000 pounds of cheese, four oxen, eight pigs, 12 sheep, a bed, and a suit of clothes for a single bulb of the Viceroy tulip. Tulip bulbs have been imported from Turkey since the last century but the tulip's attribute of variation has been discovered only recently by a professor of botany at the 59-year-old University of Leyden whose botanical garden is the first in the north (see 1637).

 French witch-hunters at Loudon crush the legs of local curate Urbain Grandier, 44, and burn him alive August 18. The vain and handsome priest of the Huguenot St. Pierre-du-March church is a notorious seducer of virgins and widows in the prosperous walled city of 20,000, he has insulted Cardinal Richelieu in a matter of church protocol, and he has been accused and found guilty of bewitching the convent of Ursuline nuns whose hysterical, blasphemous fits have for years attracted morbid sightseers from all over Europe. Grandier protests his innocence to the end, the nuns are exorcised, Richelieu razes the fortified castle of Loudon to prevent its use by the Huguenots, but the descendants of the judges who sent Grandier to the stake will lead tormented lives and it will be said that Grandier put a curse on them.

 The University of Utrecht has its beginnings in a college that will become a leading Dutch center of learning.

Poetry *Epigrammatum Sacrorum Liber* by English poet Richard Crashaw, 21, is published anonymously.

 Painting *The Surrender of Breda* by Diego Velázquez; *The Judgment of Paris* by Peter Paul Rubens.

 Masque *Comus* by John Milton 9/29 at Ludlow Castle, celebrates the inauguration of John Egerton, the 55-year-old first earl of Bridgewater, as Lord President of Wales (see 1637).

1635 The Peace of Prague May 30 resolves differences between the Holy Roman Emperor Ferdinand II and the elector of Saxony John George; France's Cardinal Richelieu makes an alliance with Sweden's Count Axel Gustafsson Oxenstjerna; and the Thirty Years' War becomes a conflict between the Franco-Swedish alliance and the Hapsburgs. France agrees to regular subsidization of Bernhard, duke of Saxe-Weimar.

The Japanese Tokugawa shogun Iemitsu acts to prevent any feudal lord from becoming too rich and powerful. He orders that each *daimyo* must visit Edo every other year, must leave his wife and children at Edo for the year he is absent, and must pay all the expenses of maintaining two places of residence.

Dutch forces invade and occupy northern Brazil where Dutch planters will enter the lucrative sugar industry (see 1623; 1654).

The Connecticut colony is created by a union of the "River Towns" Windsor and Wethersfield with En-

1635 (cont.) glish settlements at Hartford and Saybrook (*see* 1634; Hooker, 1636).

Directors of the Plymouth colony prepare to surrender their charter and draw lots for apportioning the colony's territory. Captain James Mason who helped found the town of Portsmouth in 1630 has obtained a patent to the New Hampshire area from the London Company and he receives the entire area (*see* 1680).

The General Court of Massachusetts authorizes settlement of Concord and several families move inland to obtain more pasturage on the new frontier.

Indians destroy Dutch settlements founded in Delaware 2 years ago (*see* New Sweden Company, 1638).

Yellow fever breaks out in Guadeloupe and St. Kitts in the West Indies. The French physician Duterte gives the first reliable account of the disease in western medical literature.

The world's first free medical clinic for the poor opens at Paris under the direction of physician-journalist Theophraste Renaudot, 49.

The Académie Française is founded to establish rules of grammar and correct usage and to cleanse the French language of "impurities."

Boston Public Latin School opens. It is the first secondary school in the American colonies.

Budapest University has its beginnings.

England gets her first inland postal service as mail coach service begins between London and Edinburgh.

Painting *Self-portrait with Saskia* by Rembrandt van Rijn; *Charles I in Hunting Dress* by Sir Anthony Van Dyck; *The Immaculate Conception* by Jusepe de Ribera; *Prometheus* by Italian painter Salvator Rosa, 20, who has arrived at Rome from his native Naples. Jacques Callot dies at Nancy March 24 at age 42.

Theater *Medea* (*Medée*) by Pierre Corneille, in January at Paris; *The Comedy of the Tuileries* (*La comedie des Tuileries*) by Pierre Corneille, François Le Metel de Boisrobert, 42, Guillaume Colletel, and Claude de L'Estville, in February at the Louvre Palace, Paris; *The Challenge of Charles V* (*El desafio de Carlos V*) by Mexican born Spanish playwright Francisco de Rojas Zorrilla, 26, 5/28 at Madrid; *The Lady of Pleasure* by James Shirley.

A new French law restricts sale of tobacco to apothecaries on prescription from a physician.

The Mauritzhus at the Hague is completed by Dutch architect Jacob van Campen, 40.

The Chinese orange *citrus sinensis* reaches Lisbon and is even sweeter than the "Portugals" introduced to Europe by the Portuguese in 1529.

Thomas Parr dies shortly after having been exhibited at the English court by the earl of Arundel. Parr is said to be 152 years old and to have done penance for incontinence at age 105, but the longevity claims of "Old Parr" will be found to rest on a confusion of a

father's records with those of his son (*see* Joubert, 1814).

1636 Spain's Conde-Duque de Olivares invades northwestern France in a desperate gamble to defeat the French and restore Spanish power. Spanish soldiers burn villages in Beauvaise and Picardy, plunder crops, and force peasants to flee with food, livestock, and belongings. Basque seaports are ravaged, but the French win a narrow victory at Corbie, and Spain is forced into a war of attrition that will drain her for 23 years.

The Manchus at Mukden set up a civilian administration modeled on that of their Chinese neighbors to the south and proclaim an imperial Ta Ch'ing dynasty (*see* 1644).

Japan's shogun Iemitsu forbids his people to travel abroad (*see* 1623; 1638).

Providence is founded as a Rhode Island settlement by English clergyman Roger Williams, 33, who has been banished by the Massachusetts Great and General Court for his outspoken criticism of what he calls the "abuse of power" and who has sought a place where "persons" of distressed conscience" could go. Williams selects the name in gratitude for "God's merciful providence" that the Narragansett have granted him title to the site.

Springfield, Massachusetts, is founded by colonists who follow William Pynchon west to take advantage of the abundant pasturage in the area. Springfield will become an important meat-packing center.

Hartford, Connecticut, is founded by New Towne, Massachusetts, colonists who have traveled overland with clergyman Thomas Hooker (*see* 1635).

The town of Haarlem is founded by Dutch colonists on Manhattan Island.

Another epidemic of the Black Death strikes London (*see* 1625; 1665).

Harvard College has its beginnings in a seminary founded by the Great and General Court of Massachusetts at New Towne (*see* 1638).

Painting *The Blinding of Samson* by Rembrandt van Rijn; *The Triumph of Neptune* and *Amphitrite* by Nicolas Poussin. Dutch still-life painter Jan Davidsz de Heem, 30, moves to Antwerp because "there one could have rare fruits of all kinds, large plums, peaches, cherries, oranges, lemons, grapes and others, in finer condition and state of ripeness to draw from life."

Theater *The Comic Illusion* (*L'illusion comique*) by Pierre Corneille in January at the Théâtre du Marais, Paris.

Requiem *Musikalische Exequien* by Heinrich Schütz is the first German requiem.

A Dutch planter introduces sugar cane from Brazil into the West Indian island of Barbados whose English settlers have been cultivating cotton, ginger, indigo, and tobacco for export while growing beans, plantains, and other food for their own consumption. Sugar will become the chief crop of Barbados and of all the Caribbean islands (see 1627; 1641).

1637 *Discours de la Methode* by René Descartes establishes the "Cartesian" principle of basing metaphysical demonstrations on mathematical certitude rather than on scholastic subtleties (see 1613). The proper guide to reason, says Descartes, is to doubt everything systematically until one arrives at clear, simple ideas that are beyond doubt. He rejects any doubt of his own existence by saying, "I think, therefore I am" (*Cogito ergo sum*).

The Holy Roman Emperor Ferdinand II dies at Vienna February 15 at age 57. He is succeeded by his 28-year-old son who will reign until 1657 as Ferdinand III.

Korea becomes a vassal state of the Chinese Manchus after an invasion led by T'ai-tsung, but the Korean court and people remain loyal to the Ming.

Japanese peasants on Kyushu's Shimabara peninsula rise against the Tokugawa shogun Iemitsu. Their daimyo (feudal lord) Arima has been baptized, many of them have embraced Christianity, but the shogun begins a siege in December to force their submission (see 1638).

Massachusetts colonists have their first hostile encounter with the Pequot. A force of 240 militiamen, 1,000 Narragansetts, and 70 Mohegans destroy a stockaded fort at Mystic, they burn the town, and they slaughter 600 inhabitants (see 1675).

Edinburgh has riots June 23 when clergymen at St. Giles's Cathedral attempt to read the Anglican liturgy on orders from Charles I. Many Scottish Presbyterians regard episcopacy as popery and they organize to resist it (see 1638).

The Dutch move to assure themselves of African slaves for their sugar estates in the New World. Dutch forces take Elmina from the Portuguese and build forts along the Gold Coast.

A French expedition ascends the Senegal River for 100 miles and establishes posts.

The Swedish queen Christine charters the New Sweden Company to colonize the New World. Dutch colonists Peter Minuit and Samuel Blommaert have encouraged the queen's advisers (see 1638).

Russian pioneers reach the Pacific after a quick journey across all of Siberia (see 1579; 1689).

Dutch tulip prices collapse after years of speculation. Hundreds are ruined as the bottom falls out of the market (see 1634).

Poetry *Comus* by John Milton (quarto of 35 pages); "Lycidas" by John Milton who memorializes his friend Edward King, lost with all hands when his ship bound for Ireland out of Chester struck a rock in clear weather August 10 and foundered: "Fame is the spur that the clear spirit doth raise/ (That last

infirmity of noble mind)," lines 70, 71; "Aglaura" by English Cavalier poet John Suckling, 28, who has invented the game of cribbage, has served under Sweden's Gustavus Adolphus, and retired 2 years ago to the large Norfolk estates he inherited from his father at age 18: "Why so pale and wan, fond lover," writes Suckling whose poem "A Session of the Poets" describes his contemporaries.

Painting *Five Children of Charles I* by Sir Anthony Van Dyck; *The Triumph of Neptune and Amphitre* by Nicolas Poussin; Japanese calligrapher and lacquerware potter Koetsu Honami dies at age 59 after a brilliant career in which he has been supported by the Tokugawa shogun Iemitsu.

Theater *No Jealousy Without Cause, or The Servant Master* (*Donde hay agravios ho hay celos, o El amo criado*) by Francisco de Rojas Zorilla 1/29 at Madrid's El Pardo; *The Most Proper Execution for the Most Just Vengeance* (*El mas impropio verdugo para la mas justa verganza*) by Francisco de Rojas Zorilla 2/2 at Madrid's Coliseo de Buen Retiro; *Le Cid* by Pierre Corneille.

1638 Japanese peasants who have occupied Hara Castle near Nagasaki for nearly 3 months yield February 28 for lack of food and musket ammunition. Most of the 37,000 have accepted Christianity and the 124,000-man siege force of the Tokugawa shogun Iemitsu annihilates most of them. Iemitsu expels Portuguese traders from Japan on suspicion of complicity in the Shimabara uprising (which has actually been supported by a Dutch vessel), he presses Japanese isolation by prohibiting construction of large ships which might carry people abroad, and he orders any farmer who does not pay his taxes to be hanged as if he were a Christian (many cannot pay because of poor crops which have produced famine).

The Ottoman sultan Murad IV retakes Baghdad from the Persians.

Scottish Presbyterians circulate a National Covenant for signature throughout the country following a threat by England's Charles I to impose the Anglican liturgy. Charles offers to withdraw the new prayer book and to permit the meeting of a free assembly and a free parliament, but Scottish opposition mounts. The assembly that meets at Glasgow in December admits only Covenanters. Presbyterian extremists defy the royal commissioner, the assembly deposes Anglican bishops, repeals all the legislation by which James VI and Charles I have established episcopacy, and its actions precipitate civil war (see 1639).

Dutch colonists in the Indian Ocean settle on the island of Mauritius, named after the late Prince Maurice of Nassau, and begin clubbing to death the island's indigenous bird, the dodo (see 1598; 1681).

Wilmington, Delaware, has its beginnings in Port Christina on the Delaware River where Peter Minuit of the New Sweden Company lands two shiploads of

1638 (cont.) Swedish and Finnish colonists and builds a fort. Minuit is soon afterward lost at sea (*see* 1637; Stuyvesant, 1655).

The New Haven colony is founded on the southern New England coast by English colonists who name the colony after Newhaven in southern England and who follow a more rigid Puritanism than that observed in the Connecticut colony (*see* 1635).

English clergyman John Harvard, 31, dies of tuberculosis September 14 after 1 year in the Massachusetts Bay colony and leaves his library and half his estate of £800 to the "seminary" established at New Towne in 1636.

Because John Harvard (above) is a Cambridge University graduate, New Towne will be renamed Cambridge, the Great and General Court of Massachusetts next year will order that "the colledge agreed upon formerly to bee built at Cambridge shalbee called Harvard College," colonist Ann Radcliffe will contribute funds to the school, and by 1650 Harvard will have established the 4-year program that will become standard for U.S. colleges (*see* 1642).

Painting *Christ on the Cross* by Velázquez; *Et in Arcadia ego* by Nicolas Poussin; *Lords John and Bernard Stuart* by Sir Anthony Van Dyck. Adriaen Brouwer dies at Antwerp in January at age 31.

Boston gets its first brick house. Brick has been used until now only for chimneys, fireplaces, and backyard baking ovens.

Honeybees will be introduced into the American colonies in the next few years, will soon escape from their domestic hives, and will establish wild colonies. Indians will call honeybees "the white man's fly," and as the bees move westward many pioneers will be led to believe that the bees are indigenous (*see* Irving, 1835).

1639 The Scots seize Edinburgh Castle and raise an army, but they make peace June 18 with England's Charles I who has marched to meet them near Berwick. No military engagement takes place but a new Scottish parliament assembled after the armies have disbanded is intractable in its Presbyterian opposition to English episcopacy (*see* 1640).

Swiss alpine passes are left open for use by Spanish troops under terms of a September 3 treaty.

Japan's Tokugawa shogun Iemitsu finds that some Christian missionaries have remained despite his 1638 expulsion order. Iemitsu orders the massacre of any Portuguese who have not fled and he closes Japanese ports to all foreigners except for some Chinese and Dutch (*see* 1641).

France's Loire and Seine Rivers are linked by a canal (*see* 1603; 1681).

The Whole Book of Psalms Faithfully Translated Into English Metre (*The Bay Psalm Book*) published by English-American printer Stephen Day, 47, is the first book to be printed and bound in New England. Day has set up a printshop at Cambridge with encouragement from the Massachusetts Bay Colony government and his book will be republished in frequent editions until late in the 18th century.

Paroemiologia by English-American Baptist clergyman-physician John Clarke, 30, contains the verse, "Early to bed and early to rise, makes a man healthy, wealthy and wise." Clarke helped to found the Rhode Island colony last year and his verse will be widely credited a century hence to Benjamin Franklin, as will his line, "He that will not be counseled cannot be helped."

Painting The ceiling of Rome's Barberini Palace is covered with a gigantic fresco of clouds and swirling figures by Italian painter-architect Pietro da Cortona (Pietro Berretini), 42, who has been working on the project for six years; *The Martyrdom of St. Bartholomew* by Jusepe de Ribera.

Madrid's 353-acre Parque del Retiro is completed by Spain's Philip IV.

"Smithfield" hams shipped to England from the Virginia colony are sold at London's Smithfield Market which is taken over by the city after 516 years and is organized as a market for live cattle. The market area is paved and enclosed with railings.

1640 England's Charles I appoints the earl of Strafford Thomas Wentworth, 47, his chief adviser and makes him Baron Raby, lord lieutenant of Ireland. Strafford urges an invasion of Scotland to crush the Presbyterians and impose the English liturgy, he obtains £180,000 from the Irish Parliament, and he prepares to lead Irish troops against the Scots (*see* 1641).

Scottish forces cross the Tweed August 20 to begin the second Bishops' War; they defeat the English at Newburn August 28 and occupy Newcastle and Durham; the Treaty of Ripon October 21 ends hostilities; the English agree to pay the Scots £850 per day to maintain their army. Charles convenes the Long Parliament November 5; he sets free the members of Parliament he imprisoned earlier for refusing to loan him money; and he has the earl of Strafford (above) impeached and thrown into the Tower of London.

Catalonia obtains French support to begin a 19-year revolt against Spain in protest against Barcelona's taxes, quartering of troops, military recruitment, and general denial of Catalonian rights.

Portugal seizes the opportunity of the Catalonian revolt (above) to regain her independence after 60 years of Spanish rule. The Portuguese elect Joao da Braganza king to begin the dynasty that will reign until 1910, but Spain will not recognize Portugal's independence until 1668.

The Ottoman sultan Murad IV dies at age 31 after a 17-year reign in which he has restored order with a bloody reign of terror. Murad has retaken Baghdad and Ecrivan from the Persians. He has had all his brothers murdered except for Ibrahim, 25, who has feigned insanity and who begins an 8-year reign as Ibrahim I that will be dominated by his mother Kussem Sultana and his story-teller Sheker-Pare.

Dutch forces take Saba in the West Indies.

England's Puritan movement spreads to her lower classes.

Inflation in England reduces the value of money to one-third its value in 1540 and food prices outpace wage increases.

Copenhagen opens a stock exchange.

France enjoys power and prosperity under Cardinal Richelieu, but the mass of Frenchmen live on the edge of starvation.

A Portuguese delegation sent to reopen trade with Japan is summarily executed, leaving Japan with no means of contact with the outside world except via some Dutch traders at Hirado and some Chinese at Nagasaki (see 1623; 1641).

British coal mining gains impetus from the high cost of firewood whose price has risen to nearly eight times 1540 levels while most other prices have merely tripled (see 1615; 1658).

The first English stagecoach lines begin as roads and coaching houses are built to accomodate coaches and travelers.

Gardiner's Island at the eastern end of Long Island Sound gets its name as English colonist Lion Gardiner, 41, buys Manchouake Island from the Shinnecock a year after being given the property in a land grant from Charles I. Seven miles from the nearest point of land, the island is 7 miles long and up to 3 miles wide, it has been the scene of some major Indian battles (Manchouake means "the place where many have died"), and Gardiner calls it "The Isle of Wight" because it reminds him of the English Channel island. A military engineer standing well over 6 feet tall, Gardiner arrived at Boston in 1635; he was commissioned to help fortify Boston against the Dutch and to build a fort at the mouth of the Connecticut River; he has befriended the natives and learned their language; he will ingratiate himself with the most powerful of the chiefs by ransoming the kidnapped daughter of Wyandach and returning her to the chief on her wedding day; he will acquire 78,000 acres on Long Island that will permit him to walk on his own land from Montauk to Flushing; and although he will move in 1653 to what will become East Hampton, Gardiner's Island will remain in the Gardiner family for well over three centuries.

Painting *The Peasant Supper* by French painter Louis Le Nain, 52; *The Inspiration of the Poet* by Nicolas Poussin; *Self-Portrait* by Rembrandt van Rijn; *The Barrel Organ Player* by Dutch painter Adriaen van Ostade, 29; *Three Graces* by Peter Paul Rubens who dies at Antwerp May 30 at age 62.

Theater *The Two Households of Verona* by Francisco de Rojas Zorilla 2/4 at Madrid's Coliseo de

Buen Retiro; *Horatio* (*Horace*) by Pierre Corneille 3/9 at the Hôtel de Bourgogne, Paris; *Keep Your Eyes Open* (*Abire el ojo*) by Francisco de Rojas Zorilla 8/3 at Toledo; *Cinna, or The Clemency of Augustus* (*Cinna, ou Le clemence d'Auguste*) by Pierre Corneille in December at the Hôtel de Bourgogne, Paris.

The Massachusetts Bay Colony sends 300,000 codfish to market and some colonists begin to grow rich in the cod fishery (see 1512; 1700).

The British West Indies have a population of 20,000, most of it employed in growing sugar cane.

1641 The Archbishop of Canterbury William Laud, 68, goes to the Tower of London where the earl of Strafford is executed May 12 (see 1640). The archbishop has sought absolutism in church and state and has used the Court of High Commission and the Star Chamber to root out Calvinism and Presbyterianism.

The Long Parliament abolishes the Star Chamber and the Court of High Commission in July as it shows its determination to effect a revolution against the excesses of the English constitution.

Irish peasants begin a revolt against their landlords (who are mostly English) and Catholics massacre Protestants in Ulster (see 1642).

Louis XIII's brother Jean Baptiste d'Orleans exposes a conspiracy against France's Cardinal Richelieu. He reveals that the 21-year-old Marquise de Cinq-Mars Henri Coiffier de Ruze has taken advantage of his position as protegé of Richelieu and king's favorite to make a secret treaty with Spain (Cinq-Mars will be executed in mid-September of next year).

Dutch forces take Malacca and begin their domination of the East Indies (see 1623).

The Japanese remove Dutch East India Company traders at Hirado to Deshima, an islet in Nagasaki Harbor, and since the Dutch have no missionaries the Japanese permit them to remain on condition that Company officers visit Edo once a year, turn somersaults in the street, spit on the Cross, and pay a rent in peppercorns. They may bring in three ships per year, the number will be reduced to two in 1715, and although one ship in five will be lost in the heavy Japanese seas, the surviving ships will make vast profits for the Dutch.

The Massachusetts Bay Colony lowers to 8 percent the rate of interest any lender may charge to prevent "usury amongst us contrary to the law of God" (see 1693).

Painting *Manoah* by Rembrandt van Rijn; *Embarkation of St. Ursula* by Claude Lorraine; *The Cart* by Louis Le Nain; *The Seven Sacraments* by Nicolas Poussin; *Regents of the Hospital of St. Elizabeth* by Franz Hals; *Country Fair* by Flemish painter David Teniers, 30; *Scenes from the Life of St. Januarius* by Il Domenichino who dies at Naples April 6 at age 59; *Prince Willem of Orange* by Sir Anthony Van Dyck who dies at London December 9 at age 42.

Cardinal Richelieu ruled France with an iron hand for nearly two decades, but he encouraged playwrights.

Theater *The Cardinal* by James Shirley; *Polyentes* (*Polyente*) by Pierre Corneille, in December at the Théâtre du Marais, Paris.

Russia's Michael Romanov forbids sale and use of tobacco in a decree that mentions exile as a possible punishment. Users as well as sellers are to be flogged, but the crown will violate its own law and will make the "impious herb" a state monopoly, selling tobacco at high prices to produce revenue (*see* 1648).

The first sugar factory in the English New World goes up in Barbados using equipment supplied on credit by Dutch investors against the value of the sugar to be produced. A Colonel Holdip shows the colonists "the manner of planting, the time of gathering, and the right placing of their coppers in their furnaces . . . and the true way of covering their rollers, with plates or bars of iron" (*see* 1636; 1685).

1642 Civil war begins in England as Charles I sends his Cavaliers against the Puritan parliament at York. Supported by the gentry, the Anglican clergy, and the peasantry (especially in northern and west-central England), the king is opposed by the middle classes, the great merchants, and much of the nobility (*see* 1643).

France's Cardinal Richelieu dies December 4 at age 57 after 18 years in power.

Montreal is founded as Ville Marie by French colonist Paul de Chomedey, 30, Sieur de Maisonneuve, on the island in the St. Lawrence River first visited by Jacques Cartier in 1535 at the point where the Ottawa and Richelieu Rivers flow into the St. Lawrence.

Tasmania is discovered and named Van Diemen's Land by Dutch mariner Abel Janszoon Tasman, 39, who has been sent on an exploring expedition by Anton Van Diemen, 49, governor general of the Dutch East Indies.

New Zealand is discovered by Tasman (above) in December, 4 months after discovering Van Diemen's Land.

The first printed mention in Europe of cinchona bark, or Peruvian bark, is made by Seville physician Pedro Barba, who has relieved the Countess of Chinchon of her malaria by treating her with *polvos de la condesa*. The alkaloid drug quinine will be obtained from the bark.

German Jesuit scholar Athanasius Kircher uses a microscope to investigate the causes of disease and is the first to propound the doctrine of *cantagium animatum* (*see* Janssen, 1590). Kircher teaches mathematics and Hebrew at the College of Rome (*see* van Leeuwenhoek, 1675).

An adding machine invented by French mathematical prodigy Blaise Pascal, 19, adds and subtracts using wheels numbered from 0 to 9 with an ingenious ratchet mechanism to carry the 1 of a number greater than 9. Pascal has made the machine to help his father compute taxes at Rouen (*see* 1692).

Harvard College awards its first baccalaureate degrees (*see* 1638; William and Mary, 1693).

Nonfiction *Religio Medici* by English physician Thomas Browne, 37, appears in a pirated edition after 7 years of unauthorized circulation in manuscript (an authorized edition will be published next year): "I believe that our estranged and divided ashes shall unite again; that our separated dust, after so many pilgrimages and transformations into the parts of minerals, plants, animals, elements, shall, at the voice of God, return to their primitive shapes, and join again to make up their primary and predestinate forms" (I); "All things are artificial, for nature is the art of God" (I, xvi); "I fear God, yet am not afraid of him" (I, iii); "It is the common wonder of all men, how among so many millions of faces, there should be none alike" (II, ii); "But how should we expect charity towards others, when we are uncharitable to our selves? Charity begins at home, is the voice of the world; yet is every man his greatest enemy, and, as it were, his own executioner" (II, iv).

Poetry "To Althea, from Prison" by English poet Richard Lovelace, 24, who has been locked in the Gatehouse for seven weeks after presenting to Parliament in April the Kentish petition for retention of bishops and the Prayer Book, a petition Parliament had earlier ruled seditious: "Stone walls do not a prison make,/ Nor iron bars a cage;/ Minds innocent and quiet take/ That for an hermitage."

Painting *Night Watch* by Rembrandt van Rijn, a large canvas that will later be called *Sortie of the Banning Cock Company* (Rembrandt's wife Saskia dies, leaving him as trustee for his son Titus, the only one of their four children to survive infancy). *The*

Guard Room by David Teniers the Younger. Guido Reni dies at his native Bologna August 18 at age 66.

England's great Elizabethan and Jacobean theater is ended by a September 2 Ordinance of Parliament which says, "Whereas . . . the distracted state of England calls[s] for all possible means to appease and avert the wrath of God . . . it is thought fit and ordered by the Lords and Commons in this Parliament assembled, that . . . public stage-plays shall cease and be forborne" (*see* Prynne, 1632).

Opera *The Coronation of Poppy* (*L'Incoronozione di Poppea*) in the autumn at Venice's Teatro S. S. Giovanni e Paolo with music by Claudio Monteverdi is probably the first historical opera.

Beriberi is observed in Java. The disease is marked by debility, nervous disturbances, paralysis, heart weakness, swollen liver, weak and sore calf muscles, plugged hair follicles, and weight loss. It gets its name from the Singhalese word *beri* for weakness.

Some 600 Jews sail in various vessels from Holland to Brazil. They will be expelled in 12 years when the Portuguese take Pernambuco from the Dutch (*see* Nieuw Amsterdam, 1655).

New England has some 16,000 colonists whose transatlantic passage averaged 3 months' time.

1643 France's Louis XIII dies in May at age 43 after a reign of 33 years dominated by his mother Marie de' Medici and Cardinal Richelieu. He is succeeded by his 4-year-old son who ascends the throne as Louis XIV to begin a 72-year reign, longest in European history, that begins under the aegis of Giulio Mazarin, 41, a Sicilian who was naturalized as a Frenchman 4 years ago, was made cardinal 2 years ago, succeeded Cardinal Richelieu as prime minister, and has been retained by the queen regent Anne of Austria.

France's nobility will rise against Cardinal Mazarin (above) in the next 5 years in a final attempt to oppose the court by armed resistance and to substitute rule of law for rule by royal whim. The struggle will cause difficulties in transportation that will raise the price of flour and of bread.

Spain's Gaspar de Guzman, count of Olivares, is driven from office and sent into exile.

The New England Confederation (United Colonies of New England) is formed by Massachusetts, Plymouth, Connecticut, and New Haven colonists as the first union of English colonies in America.

Nieuw Amsterdam's Dutch governor orders a massacre of the Wappinger Indians who have sought Dutch protection from attacks by raiding Mohawks. Some 1,500 of the 15,000 Wappingers are treacherously wiped out.

The first permanent settlement in what will be Pennsylvania is made at Tinicum Island in the Schuylkill River where Swedish colonists build some log cabins

as an extension of New Sweden (*see* 1638; Penn, 1681).

English-American religious enthusiast Anne Marbury Hutchinson is killed by Indians in August at age 43 in the Long Island Sound settlement that will later be New Rochelle. Banished from the Massachusetts colony for her opposition to Puritan theocracy, Hutchinson is scorned by the Puritans and her death is viewed as a manifestation of divine providence.

The world's first barometer is devised by Italian mathematician Evangelista Torricelli, 35, who served as amanuensis to the late Galileo when the latter lost his eyesight. Torricelli has succeeded Galileo as mathematician to the duke of Tuscany Ferdinand II de' Medici, 33.

The ductus thoracicus that is the common trunk of the human lacteal and lymphatic systems is discovered by French medical student Jean Pecquet, 21, while performing a dissection (*see* 1623; 1653).

Typhus ravages an English Cavalier army of 20,000 and a Parliamentary army of the same size at Oxford. Charles I is forced to abandon plans to take London.

Painting *Village Fête* by David Teniers the Younger; *Three Trees* (etching) by Rembrandt van Rijn.

Theater *The Death of Pompey* (*La mort de Pompée*) by Pierre Corneille in January at the Théâtre du Marais, Paris; *The Liar* (*Le menteur*) by Pierre Corneille, in February at Paris; *Sly Gomez* (*Bellaco sois, Gomez*) by Tirso de Molina 4/27 at Madrid.

Würzberger Beer has its beginnings in a beer brewed at Bavaria's Würzburg Castle.

1644 The Ming dynasty that has dominated China since the 1380s ends with the suicide of the last Ming emperor. He hangs himself as Peking falls to the bandit and rebel leader Li Tzu-ch'eng, 39, who has overrun parts of Hopeh and Honan, has conquered all of Shensi, and has proclaimed himself emperor. The Manchu regent Dorgun helps the Ming general Wu San-kuei drive Li into Hopeh (where he will be killed) and the Manchus begin the Ch'ing dynasty that will rule China until 1912, imposing on the natives the shaven head with queue (pigtail).

The Battle of Marston Moor July 2 ends in victory for Oliver Cromwell's English Roundheads over the Cavaliers of Charles I and wins the north country for the Puritan parliamentary forces that oppose the Royalist elements of gentry, peasantry, and Anglican clergy (*see* Naseby, 1645).

French forces occupy the Rhineland.

Essay "Aereopagatica" by John Milton is a defense of the freedom of the press: "Truth never comes into the world but like a bastard, to the ignominy of him that brought her forth"; "As good almost kill a man as kill a good book: who kills a man kills a reasonable creature, God's image; but he who destroys a good

1644 (cont.) book, kills reason itself, kills the image of God, as it were, in the eye." (Milton has antagonized England's Presbyterians with pamphlets relating to divorce.)

Painting *Woman Taken in Adultery* by Rembrandt van Rijn; *The Kitchen of the Archduke Leopold Wilhelm* by David Teniers the Younger; *The Rest on the Flight into Egypt* and *The Three Marys at the Tomb of Christ* by Dutch painter Ferdinand Bol, 28; *Helena Van der Schalke as a Child* by Dutch painter Geraert Terborch, 27; *St. Paul the Hermit* by Jusepe de Ribera.

Rome's Church of S. Carlo alle Quattro Fontane is completed by architect Francesco Borromini (Francesco Castelli), 44, who assisted his kinsman Carlo Maderno until Maderno's death in 1629 and who worked under Gian Bernini until 1633 in executing commissions from the Barberini Pope Urban VIII (who dies July 29 at age 76).

1645 The Battle of Naseby June 14 ends in a defeat of Charles I's English Cavaliers at the hands of Oliver Cromwell's Ironsides in a triumph for the English middle class and merchants who are supported by many of the country's great noblemen in the continuing civil war.

Europe's Thirty Years' War nears its end. An imperial army under Count Matthias Gallas, 61, is repulsed in January by Sweden's Lennart Torstenson and Count Hans Christoph Konigsmark who block efforts by the army to relieve the hard-pressed Danes. They pursue the enemy into Germany, and nearly annihilate Gallas's army at Magdeburg. Torstenson gains a victory over the imperialists at Jankau in Bohemia in March, conquers Moravia with support from the Transylvanian prince George Rakoczi, and advances on Vienna while Turenne is defeated in Franconia but raises a French and Hessian army that defeats the Bavarians at Allersheim in August.

The Russian czar Michael Romanov dies July 12 at age 49 and is succeeded by his 16-year-old son Alexis Mikhailovich who will reign until 1676.

The Turks begin a 19-year war to wrest Crete from Venice which has lost most of its commercial power.

Plague breaks out in the army of Sweden's Count Torstenson as he lays siege to Brunn and he returns to Bohemia.

Portuguese colonists in Brazil begin a popular rising against the Dutch following the return of Prince Maurice to Holland.

Some 10,000 slaves per year will be imported into the Americas in this decade, most of them for the Brazilian sugar plantations.

Barbados has 6,000 slaves (*see* 1641; 1685).

Poetry *Poems* by English poet Edmund Waller, 39, who was banished to France 2 years ago for leading a Royalist plot to seize London for Charles I.

Poems of Mr. John Milton, both English and Latin . . . includes "Il Penseroso" and "L'Allegro": "Hence, vain deluding Joys,/ The brood of Folly without father bred" ("Il Penseroso"); "Where glowing embers through the room/ Teach light to counterfeit a gloom,/ Far from all resort of mirth,/ Save for the cricket on the hearth" ("Il Penseroso"); "Hence, loathed Melancholy,/ Of Cerberus and blackest Midnight born" ("L'Allegro"); "Come, and trip it as we go,/ On the light fantastic toe" ("L'Allegro").

Painting *Flight into Egypt* by Spanish painter Bartolomé Esteban Murillo, 28; *The Dance in Front of the Castle* and *Tavern Scene* by David Teniers the Younger; *The Rabbi* by Rembrandt van Rijn; *King Philip IV on a Boar Hunt* by Diego Velázquez; *Wife of Candaules* by Flemish painter Jacob Jordaens, 52.

The book of *Poems* by Edmund Waller (above) contains many lyrics to songs by English composer Henry Lawes, 49, whose composer-brother William is killed fighting for the Royalist cause.

1646 England's 4-year civil war ends as Lord Ashley is beaten and captured by Oliver Cromwell's Roundheads March 26 at Stowe-on-the Wold. Charles surrenders himself to the Scots May 5, but in July he rejects Parliament's Newcastle proposals that the king take the Covenant and support the Protestant establishment, and that he let Parliament control the militia for 20 years. A breach between the Presbyterians in Parliament and the Independents in the army is clearly imminent and Charles hopes to take advantage of differences between his opponents.

Sweden's Count Torstenson resigns his command on account of illness and is succeeded by Karl Gustav Wrangel, 33, Count of Salmis and Solvesborg who join forces with Konigsmark in Westphalia, links up with Turenne at Giessen, and helps lead a Franco-Swedish army into Bavaria.

Nonfiction *Pseudoxia Epidemica (Vulgar Errors)* by Sir Thomas Browne gives careful scrutiny to a number of superstitions and popular delusions.

Poetry *Steps to the Temple* and *The Delights of the Muses* by Richard Crashaw who has gone to France during the English civil war. Crashaw has been converted to Roman Catholicism and he expresses religious ecstasy in his *Steps; Poems, with the Tenth Satire of Juvenal Englished* by Welsh poet Henry Vaughan, 24, who includes "The Vanity of Human Wishes," a satire.

Painting *Count Peneranda* by Geraert Terborch who is attending the peace conference at Münster and is painting portraits of the delegates.

England has no hayfields. Grass seed has not been introduced to permit efficient raising of hay for the maintenance of livestock other than sheep.

1647 England's Charles I is surrendered by the Scots to Parliament January 30 in return for £400,000 in back pay and the king is brought to Holmby House in Northamptonshire as Parliament and the army become openly hostile. The army refuses to accept a

Parliamentary act disbanding all soldiers not needed for garrison duty or for service in Ireland, Charles is seized at Holmby House June 4 and taken prisoner by the army, Oliver Cromwell flees Parliament to join the army at Triptow Heath June 4, the army is joined in July by the two speakers of Parliament, 14 lords, and 100 members of the House of Commons, the army enters London August 6 and forces Parliament to take back Cromwell and the others, and Charles is removed to Hampton Court.

Charles I flees to the Isle of Wight November 11 and is detained by the governor of Carisbrooke Castle. The king signs a secret treaty with the Scots December 26 two days after receiving four bills from Parliament that would give Parliament more power, bills rejected by Charles December 28 after receiving Scottish promises to restore him by force upon his agreement to abolish Episcopacy and restore Presbyterianism to Scotland.

The Truce of Ulm in the Thirty Years' War is forced upon Bavaria's Elector Maximilian by France's Marshal Turenne and Sweden's Admiral Wrangel, but Turenne is recalled, Wrangel goes to Bohemia, and Maximilian breaks the truce.

Peter Stuyvesant is named governor of New Netherlands. The 55-year-old former governor of Curaçao lost his right leg 3 years ago in a campaign against the island of St. Martin (see 1625; 1655; New York, 1664).

An epidemic of yellow fever sweeps the West Indies.

The Black Death strikes Spain in an epidemic that will last for 4 years, the worst since 1599.

A handbook of anatomy with a detailed account of the lacteal vessels is published at Pavia by German anatomist Johann Vesling (see Aselli, 1623).

The Society of Friends (Quakers) has its beginnings in the "Friends of Truth" established in Leicestershire by English clergyman George Fox, 23, who begins preaching the need for inward spiritual experience. Troubled by the deadly formalism of Puritan Christianity, Fox extends the philosophy of the Anabaptists, making conscience and self-examination supreme, and he draws recruits from the lower middle classes who heed his protest against the Presbyterian system. The Friends will be called Quakers in 1650 by Justice Gervase Bennet either because of the Friends' vehemence in appealing to conscience, which makes them shake with emotion, or because they assert that those who do not know quaking and trembling are strangers to the experience of Moses, David, and other saints. Fox will make a missionary journey to Scotland in 1657, the first annual meeting of the Society will be held in 1669, and Fox will preach in Ireland, North America, the West Indies, and Holland until his death in 1691 despite persecution and imprisonment (see 1689; Penn, 1681).

English nonconformist Sarah Wright reportedly fasts for 53 days (see Gandhi, 1914).

1648 Europe's Thirty Years' War ends October 24 in the Peace of Westphalia whose treaties are guaranteed by France and Sweden. The long war leaves the German states destitute.

The Treaty of Münster recognizes the independence of the Dutch Republic of the United Provinces.

Poland's Ladislas IV has died May 20 at age 55 after a 16-year reign and has been succeeded by his 39-year-old Jesuit brother who will reign until 1668 as John II Casimir.

A second English civil war has begun along with an Anglo-Scottish war as Royalists battle Roundheads and Presbyterians battle Independents. A Scottish army invades England under the command of the 32-year-old William, Duke of Hamilton, who meets with defeat at the hands of Oliver Cromwell in the Battle of Preston that rages from August 17 to 20.

Parliament has renounced its allegiance to Charles I January 15 following revelations of a secret treaty signed by Charles with the Scots 20 days earlier promising to abolish Episcopacy and restore Presbyterianism. The army seizes Charles December 1, Parliament forcibly excludes 96 Presbyterian members December 6 and 7, and the remaining "Rump" Parliament of some 60 members votes December 13 that Charles be brought to trial.

A French parliamentary uprising to defend the independence of magistrates is called the Fronde (French for "sling") because stones are shot into the windows of Cardinal Mazarin in protest against the arrest of the aged magistrate Pierre Broussel. The bishop coadjutor Jean François Paul de Gondi, 35, sides with the insurgents in hopes of becoming prime minister. Broussel is released, he suggests a proclamation urging Parisians to lay down their arms, but the mob wants to get rid of Mazarin. The court takes refuge at Rueil, the Great Condé who has just gained a great victory over the Spanish at Lens is recalled to put down the Fronde, and the peace of Rueil permits the court to return to Paris (but see 1649).

The Ottoman sultan Ibrahim fails in an attack on Crete and is deposed and murdered by his Janissaries at age 33 after an 8-year reign. He is succeeded by his 7-year-old son who will reign until 1687 as Mohammed IV.

St. Maarten in the West Indies is taken by Dutch forces (see Stuyvesant, 1647).

The Dutch ship *Haarlem* breaks up at Table Bay, South Africa. Ship officers Leendert Jansz and Nicholas Proot survive the wreck, they are picked up 5 months later and returned to Holland where they urge authorities to establish a settlement at Table Bay for provisioning East India fleets with fresh fruit, vegetables, and other stores (see Capetown, 1652).

The Treaty of Münster closes the River Scheldt to navigation and Amsterdam begins to replace Antwerp as Europe's major commercial city (see 1567; 1815).

1648 (cont.) Swedish Army officers back from the war receive land grants from Christina. The grants will double the land held by the nobility as of 1611 and freehold peasants will face eviction as the expanding nobility applies German customs and attitudes toward the peasantry (*see* 1650).

Ukrainian serfs rise in a revolution that will continue for 6 years.

A pogrom against Ukrainian Jews by Greek Orthodox peasants destroys hundreds of Jewish communities and exterminates all Jews who will not embrace Christianity. Cossack Bogdan Chmielnicki, 55, leads the pogrom in quest of Ukrainian independence from the Polish nobility which owns lands along the Dnieper and which employs Jews to collect its taxes.

Ortus Mediciniae, vel Opera et Opuscula Omnia by the late Flemish physician-chemist Jan-Baptista van Helmont makes the first distinction between gases and air (*see* Boyle, 1662).

Nitric acid that will be used chiefly in explosives is invented by Johann Glauber of 1625 Glauber's salt fame (*see* Cavendish, 1766).

Digestion is the work of fermentation that converts food into living flesh, J.-B. van Helmont (above) has written. He says that a different ferment causes each physiologic process and that central control is vested in the solar plexus, and at a time when most physicians are prescribing enormous (and often lethal) doses, van Helmont advocates only small doses of chemicals with mild therapy consisting of diet and simples (medicinal herbs and plants) (*see* 1661).

A yellow fever epidemic sweeps the Yucatán Peninsula. It is by some accounts the first definitely identifiable outbreak (*see* Duterte, 1635).

Poetry *Hesperides, or The Works Both Human and Divine of Robert Herrick, Esq.,* by English poet Robert Herrick, 57, whose Royalist sympathies cause him to be evicted from his post as vicar of Dean Prior in Devonshire: "Gather ye rosebuds while ye may,/ Old Times is still a-flying:/ And this same flower that smiles today,/ Tomorrow will be dying" (from "To the Virgins, to Make Much of Time").

Painting *The Peace of Münster* by Geraert Torborch (*see* 1646); *Seven Sacraments* (second series) and *Diogenes Throwing Away His Scoop* by Nicolas Poussin; *The Holy Family with St. Catherine* by Jusepe de Ribera. Louis Le Nain dies at Paris May 25 at age 60.

Russia's 19-year-old Czar Alexis Mikhailovich abolishes the state monopoly in tobacco established by Michael Romanov in 1641 and reimposes the ban on smoking (*see* 1613; 1697).

The Taj Mahal completed outside Agra in India is a red and white sandstone and marble mosque, meeting hall, and mausoleum built by the Mogul emperor Shah Jahan, now 56, for his favorite wife Mumtaz Mahal (Jewel of the Palace) who died in childbirth some 17 years ago at age 34 after bearing him 14 children.

Pilgrim colonists in the Massachusetts colony have poor crops and avoid starvation only by eating passenger pigeons, still abundant in the colony despite efforts to eradicate them (*see* Josselyn, 1672).

The end of the Thirty Years' War (above) leaves the German states with a population of less than 13.5 million and possibly a good deal less. Mercenary troops from Bohemia, Denmark, France, Spain, Sweden, and the German states themselves have destroyed roughly 18,000 villages, 1,500 towns, and 2,000 castles.

1649 England's Charles I blandly denies the jurisdiction of a high court that sentences him to death, but he is beheaded January 30 at Whitehall. His 18-year-old son is proclaimed Charles II at Edinburgh, in parts of Ireland, and in the Channel Islands, but England becomes a republic headed by the Lord Protector Oliver Cromwell whose Commonwealth will rule until 1660.

Oliver Cromwell (above) suppresses an Irish uprising led by the marquis of Ormonde James Butler, 39. He storms Drogheda September 12, he sacks the town, he massacres its garrison, and the garrison at Wexford meets a similar fate.

France has a new Fronde uprising as the Great Condé turns against the court because he thinks Cardinal Mazarin does not accord him proper respect. Mazarin pretends to a reconciliation with the bishop coadjutant (*see* 1648; 1650).

Japanese farmers are saddled with a new tax which permits them barely enough for their basic needs and forces them to put their wives to work weaving cloth and to send surplus children to work in the city. All rice is requisitioned by the Tokugawa shogun and the farmers are left with little to eat but millet.

Black laborers in the Virginia colony still number only 300 (*see* 1619; 1671).

Massachusetts entrepreneur John Winthrop, Jr., 43, produces more than 8 tons of iron per week at the Saugus works he has built in back of Lynn with blast furnaces and a refinery forge manned by workers obtained in England. Son of the Bay Colony's first governor, Winthrop has raised £1,000 in England to purchase his equipment.

Tobacco exports bring prosperity to the Virginia colony.

Nonfiction *The Passions of the Soul* (*Les passions de l'âme*) by René Descartes.

Poetry "To Lucasta, on Going to the Wars" by Richard Lovelace, who has devoted his fortune to the Royalist cause, was wounded at Dunkirk while serving in the French army, and was imprisoned again upon his return to England: "I could not love thee, dear, so much/ Loved I not honour more."

Painting *The Four Regents of the Leper Hospital* by Ferdinand Bol; *The Vision of St. Paul* by Nicolas Poussin; *Juan de Pereta* and *Pope Innocent X* by Diego Velázquez; *Philip IV of Spain* by Geraert Terborch; *Christ Healing the Sick* (etching) by Rembrandt van Rijn.

Opera *Giasone* 1/5 at Venice's San Cassiano, with music by Italian composer Francesco Cavalli, 46, a pupil of the late Claudio Monteverdi who has changed his name from Pietro Francesco Caletti-Bruni in honor of his patron Federigi Cavalli, a Venetian nobleman.

The Virginia colony receives an influx of Cavalier (Royalist) refugees from England.

1650 Scotland's earl of Montrose returns from the continent to avenge last year's execution of Charles I but he loses part of his army in a shipwreck and he fails to rouse the clans. Surprised and routed at Carbiesdale in Ross-shire, Montrose is betrayed by Neil McLeod of Assynt, he is sentenced to death by Parliament, and he is hanged May 21 at Edinburgh.

England's Charles II returns from the continent, landing in Scotland June 24. He signs the National Covenant and is proclaimed king, but he is defeated September 3 at the Battle of Dunbar by Oliver Cromwell who just 1 month earlier wrote to the General Assembly of the Church of Scotland, "I beseech you, in the bowels of Christ, think it possible you may be mistaken."

Charles II is crowned at Scone despite his defeat at Dunbar and prepares to march on England.

France's Cardinal Mazarin has the Great Condé and his leading associates arrested January 14, Marshal Turenne is persuaded to lead an armed rebellion, French peasants rise against an army sent by the Archduke Leopold from the Spanish Netherlands to aid Turenne, Leopold withdraws, and Turenne's Frondeurs give way December 15 at the Battle of Blanc-Champ (or Rethel).

Britain has a typhus epidemic that by one account converts "the whole island into one vast hospital."

Ireland's Archbishop James Ussher, 69, calculates from biblical references that all life was created Sunday, October 23, 4004 B.C.

Nonfiction *Medulla Theologiae Moralis* by German Jesuit theologian Hermann Busembaum, 50, preaches the philosophy that "the end justifies the means." Busembaum's work will be condemned for its sections on regicide and copies will be publicly burned in 1757 by the Parlement of Toulouse.

Poetry *Silex Scintillans* by Henry Vaughan includes his poem "They are all gone into the world of light"; *The Tenth Muse Lately Sprung Up in America* by English colonist Anne Bradstreet, 38, is published at London and contains metaphysical Puritan poems that include "To My Dear and Loving Husband" and "Upon the Burning of Our House."

Painting *Woman With an Ostrich Fan* by Rembrandt van Rijn; *Jewish Merchant* by Rembrandt van Rijn; *Arcadian Shepherds* by Nicolas Poussin; *Self-Portrait* by Poussin; *View of Dordrecht* by Jan van Goyen; *The Holy Family with the Little Bird* by Bartolomé Murillo.

Theater *Andromeda* (*Andromède*) by Pierre Corneille at the Théâtre Royal de Bourbon, Paris; *Nicomedes* (*Nicomède*) by Pierre Corneille at the Théâtre du Marais, Paris.

The minuet is introduced at the French court where its tempo is slowed somewhat and its gaiety modified.

Sweden suffers a food crisis after the worst harvest she will have in this century. By March the bakers of Stockholm are fighting at the town gates for flour, but while the nation's sociopolitical balance is jeopardized as the clergy and burghers side with the peasants, a threatened revolution does not materialize.

Maize is eaten for the first time in Italy where "turkey corn" (*mais*) will be popular in *polenta,* in cornmeal mush, and hardened as a cake (*see* pellagra, 1749).

England's first coffeehouse opens at Oxford (*see* London, 1652).

London's population reaches 350,000, up from 200,000 in 1603, and the city contains 7 percent of the English population (*see* 1660).

Denmark will lose more than a fifth of its population in the next decade to disease and starvation.

Ireland will lose close to a quarter of its population in the next decade, declining from 1.3 million to less than 1 million as a result of ruinous wars, anti-Catholic penal laws, and laws that destroy the security of land-tenure and put Irishmen at the mercy of absentee landlords.

Africa occupies just over 20 percent of the earth's land surface and has roughly 20 percent of the world's population, but European slave traders in this century and the next will decimate the continent by exporting human chattels and introducing new diseases.

The world's population is roughly 500 million, twice what it was 1,650 years ago.

1651 *Leviathan,* or "The Matter, Form and Power of a Commonwealth, Ecclesiastical and Civil," by English philosopher Thomas Hobbes, 63, says that people to survive must surrender their individual rights and submit to an absolute sovereign whose duty is to protect them from outside enemies much as a feudal lord protected his vassals.

> Of the Naturall Condition of Mankind, As Concerning Their Felicity, and Misery, [writes Hobbes (above),] Whatsoever therefore is consequent to a time of Warre, where every man is Enemy to every man; the same is consequent to the time, wherein men live without other security, than what their own

1651 (cont.) strength, and their own invention shall furnish them withall. In such condition there is no place for Industry; because the fruit thereof is uncertain; and consequently no Culture of the Earth, no Navigation, nor use of the commodious Building; no Instruments of moving, and removing such things as require much force; no Knowledge of the face of the Earth; no account of Time; no Arts; no Letters; no Society; and which is worst of all, continuall feare, and danger of violent death; And the life of man, solitary, poore, nasty, brutish, and short.

French troops loyal to Louis XIV subdue minor Fronde uprisings, the court returns to Paris, Parlement releases the Great Condé, it gains the reluctant support of the queen mother Anne of Austria, it forces Cardinal Mazarin to leave Paris, and Pope Innocent X creates Mazarin's opponent Jean François Paul de Gondi Cardinal de Retz.

England's Charles II is crowned king of the Scots but Oliver Cromwell takes Perth in early August, he defeats the royal forces September 3 at the Battle of Worcester, and Charles escapes to France after traveling through a countryside alive with Roundheads, disguised as a servant to the daughter of a Royalist squire (*see* 1649; 1660).

The Japanese shogun Iemitsu dies at age 47 after a 28-year reign that has consolidated Tokugawa rule through national isolationism, oppression of the people, and suppression of Christianity. His 10-year-old son Itsuna begins a 29-year shogunate that will exhaust the treasury and debase the nation's coinage.

Parliament passes England's first Navigation Act to help the nation's merchant marine gain supremacy over the Dutch. The legislation forbids importation of goods into England or her colonies except by English vessels or by vessels of the countries producing the goods (*see* 1660).

Nonfiction *Jacula Prudentum* by the late George Herbert contains translations of proverbs that include "The eye is bigger than the belly"; "His bark is worse than his bite"; "Whose house is of glass, must not throw stones at another"; "God's mill grinds slow, but sure"; "For want of a nail, the shoe is lost, for want of a shoe the horse is lost, for want of a horse the rider is lost"; "One half the world knows not how the other half lives"; "He that lies with the dogs, riseth with fleas"; and "One hour's sleep before midnight is worth three after."

Painting *The Holy Family* by Nicolas Poussin; *Girl with a Broom* by Rembrandt van Rijn; *The Marriage of the Artist* by David Teniers the Younger who moves to Brussels and becomes court painter to Archduke Leopold Wilhelm; *The Institution of the Eucharist* and *The Last Supper* by Jusepe de Ribera.

Opera *Calisto* at Venice with a libretto about love among the gods and with music by Italian composer Francesco Cavalli.

"Rumbullion, alias Kill-Devill" is the "chief fudling they make in the Island" of Barbados, writes Richard Ligon. He calls rum "a hot, hellish and terrible liquor" made of "suggar canes, distilled" (*see* 1641; 1655).

Exercitationes de generations animalium by William Harvey of 1628 blood circulation theory fame is published at London. Now 73, Harvey was physician to Charles I until 1648 and he says, "All animals, even those that produce their young alive, including man himself, are evolved out of the egg," but he thinks that lower forms of life are capable of primal generation and he believes the pupa to be an insect egg (*see* Redi, 1668).

1652 The Battle of Bleneau April 7 brings victory to a new Fronde army commanded by the Great Condé, Marshal Turenne has switched back to the king's side and forces Condé to break off the engagement, both armies march to Paris to negotiate while more Flemish fortresses fall to the archduke Leopold and while the duc de Lorraine marches through Champagne with plundering mercenaries en route to join Condé. Turenne intercepts Lorraine and buys him off, he hems in the Frondeurs July 2 in the Faubourg St. Antoine outside Paris, the 25-year-old duchesse de Montpensier Anne Marie Louise d'Orléans persuades the Parisians to open the city gates and admit the Condé's army (which is supported by her father), she turns the guns of the Bastille on the royal forces of Turenne, an insurrectionist government is proclaimed, Cardinal Mazarin flees France, but the Parisian bourgeoisie quarrels with the Fronde and permits the king to enter the city October 21 (*see* 1651; 1653).

An Anglo-Dutch War precipitated by last year's English Navigation Act is proclaimed July 8 after the English have gained an initial victory in May off the Downs.

England's Rump Parliament antagonizes the army with an Act of Indemnity and Oblivion. The army charges members of Parliament with having received bribes from royalists whose estates were confiscated.

The new Japanese shogun Ietsuna survives the second of two attempted coups at Edo in the last challenge to its sovereignty that the Tokugawa family will face until the 19th century.

Capetown, South Africa, is founded by Dutch ship's surgeon Jan van Riebeck who goes ashore at Table Bay with 70 men carrying seeds, agricultural implements, and building materials (*see* 1648).

The General Court of Massachusetts makes a 35-year contract with Boston silversmith John Hull to produce silver coins with silver to be supplied by him. Hull is appointed mint master of the colony and strikes the Pine Tree shilling, receiving 15 pence for every 20 shillings he coins.

Nonfiction *O-Dai-Ichi-Ran* by Japanese historian Shunsai Hayashi, 34, is a history of Japan; *The Mount of Olives,* or *Solitary Devotions,* by Henry Vaughan.

Poetry *Deo Nostro Te Decet Hymnus* by the late English poet Richard Crashaw who died 3 years ago at age 36 after being named canon of a church at Loreto. Crashaw's posthumously published work includes the hymn to St. Theresa "The Flaming Heart" and is illustrated with 12 engravings by the baroque poet.

Painting *Portrait of Hendrickje* by Rembrandt van Rijn; *A View of Delft* by Dutch painter Carel Fabritius (Carel Pietersz.), 30. Georges de La Tour dies at his native Vic-sur-Seille January 30 at age 58; Jusepe de Ribera dies at Naples September 2 at age 61.

Theater Regents of the Japanese shogun Ietsuna prohibit young boys from taking roles in the Kabuki theater. Mature men will hereafter play all roles (*see* 1629; 1673).

Peking's Great White Dagoba is completed in the shape of a Buddhist reliquary. The structure's base, spire, crown, and gilded ball represent the five elements earth, water, fire, air, and ether.

Massachusetts colonist Joseph Russell starts an offshore whaling enterprise. Russell has founded New Bedford (*see* 1775; Nantucket, 1690).

London's first coffeehouse opens in St. Michael's Alley, Cornhill, under Armenian management.

The population of the Virginia colony reaches 20,000 including white settlers and black slaves.

1653 Amoy falls to the 30-year-old Chinese pirate-patriot Cheng Ch'eng-kung (the Portuguese call him Koxinga) who has ravaged the Chinese coast with a fleet of 3,000 junks in a continuing fight against the Manchus who have come to power with the end of the Ming dynasty (*see* 1644; 1661).

France's Cardinal Mazarin returns to Paris unopposed, the Fronde is ended, and the suppression of the rebellion begins a golden age and a period of absolutism.

Oliver Cromwell is proclaimed Lord Protector of the Commonwealth of England, Scotland, and Ireland December 15. *The Instrument of Government* drawn up for the Commonwealth is a written constitution that calls for a standing army of 30,000, a cooperative council of 21 to help the Lord Protector administer the Commonwealth, and a triennial Parliament of 460 members with sole power to levy taxes and grant funds and a guarantee against dissolution for 5 months once it has been summoned.

Nieuw Amsterdam colonists build a wall across Manhattan from the North River to the East River for protection against English attacks. Wall Street will get its name from the defensive wall.

Virginia settlers enter the region north of the Roanoke River and found the Albemarle settlement in what will be called North Carolina (*see* 1663).

The tontine system of life insurance is originated at Paris by Neapolitan banker Lorenzo Tonti who devises a scheme whereby a group of investors buys shares in a fund whose proceeds go to the shareholder who survives the others (*see* 1583).

The lymphatic system is described by Danish physician Thomas Bartholin, 37, who enlarges on his father's 1611 *Institutiones Anatomicae* and defends William Harvey's 1628 theory of blood circulation. Observations on the lymphatic system are published by Swedish scientist Olof Rudbeck, 23, who has discovered the system independently of Bartholin.

Painting *Aristotle Contemplating the Bust of Homer* by Rembrandt van Rijn; *The Picture Gallery of Archduke Leopold Wilhelm* by David Teniers, the Younger; *The Village Wedding (The Jewish Bride)* by Dutch painter Jan Havicksz Steen, 27.

The Compleat Angler, or The Contemplative Man's Recreation by English biographer Izaak Walton, 60, is "a Discourse on Fish and Fishing, Not Unworth the Perusal of Most Anglers." A former ironmonger, Walton writes of trout, "if he is not eaten within four or five hours after he is taken [he] is worth nothing."

1654 The Treaty of Westminster April 6 ends the Anglo-Dutch War that started in 1652. The Dutch agree to recognize the English Navigation Act of 1651 and to pay an indemnity, they agree to join England in a defensive league, and the province of Holland agrees secretly to exclude members of the house of Orange from the stadtholdership in deference to Oliver Cromwell's anxieties over the marriage of Mary, daughter of England's late Charles I, to Willem II of Orange.

England's Charles I went to the block, ushering in more than 11 years of stern Puritan Commonwealth rule.

1654 (cont.) The Swedish queen Christina abdicates June 6 after a 22-year reign in which she has sold or mortgaged vast amounts of crown property to support the 17 counts, 46 barons, and 428 lesser nobles that she has created. Christina leaves dressed in male attire under the name Count Dohna, she joins the Catholic Church, she settles at Rome, and she is succeeded by her 32-year-old cousin who will reign until 1660 as Charles X Gustavus.

The Ukrainian cossack Bogdan Chmielnicki swears allegiance to Russia's Alexis I Mikhailovich and gives up the Ukraine's aspirations to independence (*see* 1648). Russian troops seize Smolensk, beginning a 13-year war over the Ukraine between Russia and Poland. The war will bring the Russians into contact for the first time with the Turks in the Balkans.

Oliver Cromwell quarrels with Parliament September 3 and 9 days later orders the exclusion of hostile members of Parliament.

Portugal recovers the Brazilian territory taken by the Dutch in 1635.

Jesuit missionary Simon LeMoyne visits the area in upper New Netherlands that will later be the site of Syracuse (*see* Webster, 1786). He finds salt deposits that will later be important to the development of the area.

The Black Death strikes eastern Europe.

Painting *Jan Stix* by Rembrandt van Rijn; *Parental Admonition* by Geraert Terborch who settles at Deventer after having lived in Amsterdam, The Hague, and Kampen.

Sugar cane is planted by the French in Martinique which will become a major Caribbean sugar producer.

Béchamelle (or Béchamel) cream sauce is named in honor of French financier Louis de Béchameil, Marquis de Nointel, who serves Louis XIV in the honorary post of Lord Steward of the Royal Household.

1655 Swedish forces invade Poland as Charles X Gustavus takes advantage of Poland's struggle to save her Ukrainian territories from Russia. Charles launches the first Northern War that will take away Poland's last Baltic territories (*see* 1660).

English forces under the command of Vice Admiral William Penn, 34, take Jamaica in the West Indies from the Spanish who have called the sugar-rich island San Iago. Penn's action precipitates a 3-year war with Spain.

Dutch colonists occupy New Sweden on orders from Peter Stuyvesant, governor of New Netherlands (*see* 1638).

Sephardic Jews from Pernambuco, Brazil, establish a congregation at Nieuw Amsterdam despite efforts by Peter Stuyvesant (above) to exclude them (*see* 1642).

Oliver Cromwell suppresses an uprising against the Puritan government at Salisbury and divides England into 12 military districts, each controlled by a force that is financed by a 10 percent tax on royalist estates. The Puritans order Catholic priests to leave the realm, they forbid Anglican clergymen to teach or preach, they censor the press, and they impose rigid puritanical rules.

Nonfiction *The History of Scotland 1423–1542* by the late Scottish poet-historian William Drummond who died in 1649 at age 64.

Poetry "A Panegyric to My Lord Protector" by Edmund Waller who has made amends to Oliver Cromwell and has returned from France.

Painting *Woman Bathing in a Stream* and *The Rabbi* by Rembrandt van Rijn.

French society uses a clean plate for each new dish but Englishmen continue to dine off trenchers—wooden platters that give hearty eaters the name "trenchermen."

Beasts killed for food "eate much sweeter, kindlier and tenderer" if they are killed slowly and painfully, writes English physician Thomas Muffet in his *Health's Improvement*. A student of spiders whose daughter will be celebrated in a Mother Goose rhyme, Muffet says that meat is improved if an animal is destroyed "with fear dissolving his hardest parts and making his very heart become pulpy" rather than "if they be killed suddenly. . . ."

Rum from Jamaica (above) is introduced into the English Royal Navy to replace beer which goes sour after a few weeks at sea (*see* 1731).

The first known reference to the use of a sheath for contraception is made in an anonymous Parisian publication. *L'Ecole Des Filles* recommends a linen sheath to prevent passage of semen into the uterus, but while contraception will be widely employed among the upper-class French by the end of the century intra-uterine sponges will be favored over condoms (*see* Mme. de Sévigné, 1671).

1656 *The Commonwealth of Oceana* by English political theorist James Harrington, 45, takes the form of a political romance but is intended as a reply to Thomas Hobbes's *Leviathan* of 1651. The government, says Harrington, is certain to reflect a social system in which the bulk of the land is owned by the gentry rather than by the king and the Church as in ages past: "The law is but words and paper without the hands and swords of men."

England and Spain go to war. The English capture some Spanish treasure ships off Cadiz September 9 (*see* 1657; Jamaica, 1655).

Oliver Cromwell's Third Parliament convenes September 17. England has had no Parliament since January of last year.

Swedish forces invade Poland in the First Northern War. The army of Charles X Gustavus defeats the Poles at the Battle of Warsaw whereupon Russia, Denmark, and the Holy Roman Empire declare war on Sweden which is deserted by her ally Brandenburg. Poland recognizes the sovereignty of the Elector of Brandenburg over East Prussia.

Portugal's João IV dies November 6 at age 53 after a reign of nearly 16 years. He is succeeded by his 13-year-old son who has been paralyzed since the age of three but who will reign until 1667 as Afonso VI, the second Braganza king.

Dutch forces take Colombo from the Portuguese.

The Amsterdam synagogue excommunicates rabbinical student Baruch Spinoza, 24, in July for views the elders consider heretical. Spinoza turns to grinding lenses in order to support himself (see 1670).

Dutch East India Company shares plummet on the Amsterdam Exchange and many investors are ruined. Among them is painter Rembrandt van Rijn, now 50, who is declared bankrupt and whose possessions are put up for sale.

The Dutch in Ceylon make cinnamon a state monopoly.

Clock-making is revolutionized by Dutch mathematician-physicist-astronomer Christian Huygens, 27, who invents a clock regulated by a pendulum. He applies a concept that occurred to Galileo in 1583 while watching a lamp swinging from a long chain in Pisa Cathedral (see Clement, 1670).

Sweden's Olof Rudbeck returns to Uppsala after studying at Leyden, he is appointed professor of anatomy, he builds an anatomical theater in which he performs dissections on human bodies, and he scorns criticism of the practice which is new to Uppsala (see 1653).

English physician Thomas Wharton, 42, describes the anatomy of glands. He has discovered the duct (Wharton's duct) from the submaxillary gland to the mouth.

The Hôpital General opens at Paris. It is a combination hospital, poorhouse, and factory.

Painting *The Maids of Honor* (*Las Meninas*) and *The Spinners* (*Las Hilanderos*) by Diego Velázquez (the first depicts the family of Spain's Philip IV); *The Procuress* by Dutch painter Jan Vermeer, 23. Gerrit van Honthorst dies at Utrecht April 27 at age 65.

The Corsa al Palio held at the Italian town of Siena begins a July-August horse race event that will annually pit competitors from each of the city's contrades against each other.

1657 The Holy Roman Emperor Ferdinand III concludes an alliance with Poland to check the aggressions of Sweden's Charles X Gustavus who is driven out of Poland. However, the emperor dies April 2 at age 48 and is succeeded by his 16-year-old son who will reign for 47 years as Leopold I.

Sweden and Denmark go to war as Charles X Gustavus tries to extend his holdings on the southern coast of the Baltic. The Dutch intervene to prevent the Swedes from gaining exclusive control of the Baltic fishery.

The Ottoman Turks retake Lemnos and Tenedos.

A 4-year Dutch-Portuguese war begins over conflicting interests in Brazil.

An English naval force commanded by Admiral Robert Blake, 58, destroys the Spanish West Indian fleet April 20 off Santa Cruz.

Oliver Cromwell tacitly permits Jews to return to England (see 1306; Bevis Marks synagogue, 1701).

The Flushing Remonstrance written to Nieuw Amsterdam's Peter Stuyvesant December 27 is probably the first declaration of religious tolerance by any group of ordinary citizens in America. Townsmen of the Long Island settlement of Flushing tell Stuyvesant they will not accept his command that they "not receive any of those people called Quakers because they are supposed to be, by some, seducers of the people." Say the Flushing burghers, "We desire in this case not to judge lest we be condemned, but rather to let every man stand and fall to his own Master." However, five Quakers who have arrived at Nieuw Amsterdam are shipped off to Rhode Island.

France's Louis XIV recovers from typhoid fever. Antimony is falsely credited with having saved the king (see 1604).

Coffee advertisements at London claim the beverage is a panacea for scurvy, gout, and other ills.

Public sale of tea begins at London as the East India Company undercuts Dutch prices and advertises tea as a panacea for apoplexy, catarrh, colic, consumption, drowsiness, epilepsy, gallstones, lethargy, migraine, paralysis, and vertigo (see Garraway, below).

England's Durham University has its beginnings (see 1833).

Painting *The Birth of Bacchus* by Nicolas Poussin; *L'Umana Fragilita* by Salvator Rosa.

Fire destroys most of Edo and its castle buildings January 18 to 19 and kills more than 100,000 Japanese (see 1601; 1772).

The first London chocolate shop opens to sell a drink known until now only to the nobility. The June 16 London *Public Advertiser* carries a notice reading, "In Bishopsgate Street, in the Queen's Head Alley, at a Frenchman's house is an excellent West India drink called chocolate—where you may have it ready at any time, and also unmade, at reasonable rates" (see 1656; 1659).

Tea is offered to Londoners at Thomas Garraway's coffee house in Exchange Alley between Cornhill and Lombard Street.

1658 Sweden's Charles X Gustavus makes two invasions of Denmark but fails to take Copenhagen whose garrison puts up a valiant defense.

The Battle of the Dunes June 4 gives English and French troops a victory over a Spanish relief force and Dunkirk surrenders to the English after a siege.

1658 (cont.) Oliver Cromwell dies September 3 at age 58 after nearly 5 years as Lord Protector of the Commonwealth of England, Scotland, and Ireland. His son Richard, 31, succeeds to power and will retain the protectorship for nearly 9 months.

The Mogul emperor Shah Jahangir falls ill at age 66 after a 31-year reign that has raised the power of the empire to its zenith and has seen the founding of Delhi. The emperor's son Aurangzeb, 40, imprisons his father and will make himself emperor next year to begin a 49-year reign of bigotry that will alienate both Moslems and Hindus.

Salisbury, Massachusetts colonist Thomas Macy receives sanctuary from Puritan religious intolerance on the offshore island of Nanticut (Nantucket). Algonquins on the island welcome Macy, his family, and his friend Edward Starbuck (*see* 1605; 1659).

French fur trader Pierre Esprit Radisson, 22, explores the western end of Lake Superior and trades with *les sauvages* in company with Medard Chouart, 33, Sieur de Groseillers (*see* Rupert House, 1668). Radisson came to New France 7 years ago, he was captured and adopted by the Iroquois, but he escaped in 1654 (*see* 1659).

Dutch naturalist Jan Swammerdam, 21, gives the first description of red blood cells.

English coal production at Newcastle reaches 529,032 tons, up from 32,951 in 1564, as the deforestation of England and the continent spurs use of coal for fuel (*see* 1640; Newcomen, 1705).

Essays "Urne-Buriall" by Thomas Browne: "There is nothing strictly immortal, but immortality; whatever hath no beginning may be confident of no end" (V); "The Long habit of living indisposeth us for dying" (V); "Hydriotaphia" by Thomas Browne; "The Garden of Cyprus" by Thomas Browne, whose mystical treatise shows how the universe is pervaded by the "quincunx," an arrangement of five objects such as trees or buildings with one at each corner and one in the middle (*see* witches, 1664).

Painting *Courtyard of a House in Delft* by Dutch painter Pieter de Hooch, 29; *Farm with a Dead Tree* by Dutch painter Adriaen van de Velde, 27.

The London periodical *Mercurious Politicus* carries an advertisement: "That excellent and by all Physitians approved China Drink called by the Chineans Tcha, by other nations Tay, alias Tea, is sold at the Sultaness Head, a cophee-house in Sweetings Rents, by the Royal Exchange, London."

An English cookbook sanctions use of veal as food in defiance of an old Saxon tradition that had considered the killing of a veal calf a wanton act of the Norman invaders of 1066.

1659 A new English Parliament meets January 27 but soon bogs down in a dispute with the army. The new lord protector Richard Cromwell dissolves Parliament April 22 at the behest of the army, a Rump Parliament meets May 7 with William Lenthall as speaker and induces Cromwell to resign, the New Royalists led by George Booth, 37, join with the Cavaliers in August to restore the monarchy, the army commanded by John Lambert, 40, suppresses the insurrection in Cheshire and appoints a military committee of safety to replace the Rump Parliament in October, but the Rump Parliament is restored December 26 (*see* 1660).

The Treaty of the Pyrenées November 7 ends the ascendancy of Spain which has been exhausted by war and by domestic misgovernment that has produced the revolt in Catalonia which ends this year. Under terms of the treaty signed on the Isle of Pheasants in the Bidassoa River France's Louis XIV receives the Spanish frontier fortresses in Flanders and Artois, Spain's Philip IV cedes part of Rousillon, Conflans, and Cerdagne along with some towns in Hainault and Luxembourg, he makes other concessions, and the Spanish infanta Maria Theresa, 21, is betrothed to Louis XIV with a dowry of 500,000 crowns (she renounces her claims upon her inheritance for herself or for any issue she may have by Louis).

French fur trader Pierre Radisson travels through the upper Mississippi Valley.

Thomas Macy dispatches Edward Starbuck to the mainland to recruit new settlers for Nantucket Island (*see* 1658). Starbuck returns with nine, the settlers and Macy each take partners, and together they buy 90 percent of the island—including its Indian inhabitants—from owner Thomas Mayew in the Massachusetts colony (*see* whaling, 1690).

English physician Thomas Willis, 38, gives the first description of typhoid fever.

Painting *Infanta Maria Theresa* (above) and *Infante Philip Prosper* by Diego Velázquez; *Young Girl with Flute* by Jan Vermeer; *The Letter* by Geraert Terborch.

Theater *Oedipus* (*Oedipe*) by Pierre Corneille 1/24 at the Hôtel de Bourgogne, Paris; *The Amorous Quarrel* (*Le depit concoureux*) by the French actor-playwright Molière (Jean Baptiste Poquelin), 37, 4/16 at the Théâtre du Petit-Bourbon, Paris; *The Affected Ladies* (*Les precieuses ridicules*) by Molière 11/18 at the Théâtre du Petit-Bourbon: manager of a troupe known as the King's Comedians, Molière formed his own acting company at age 21 and last year gained the patronage of the court at Paris for his comedies.

Paris police raid a monastery and send 12 monks to jail for eating meat and drinking wine during Lent.

The Spanish infanta Maria Theresa (above) brings cocoa to France where it will be endorsed by the Paris faculty of medicine and will be received with enthusiasm until it becomes surrounded with suspicion as an aphrodisiac in some circles and as a mysterious potion in others. (Mme. de Sévigné will write to her daughter that "the marquise de Coetlogon took so much chocolate, being pregnant last year, that she was brought to bed of a little boy who was as black as the devil.")

1660 Sweden's Charles X Gustavus dies the night of February 12 at age 37 and is succeeded by his 4-year-old son who will take over from a corrupt regency in 1672 and will reign until 1697 as Charles XI. The Treaty of Copenhagen brings peace between Sweden and Denmark which gives up the southern part of the Scandinavian peninsula but retains Bornholm and Trondheim, the Treaty of Oliva May 3 ends the 5-year-old Northern War, Poland's John II Casimir abandons his claims to the Swedish throne, he cedes Livonia to Sweden, and Poland loses her last Baltic territories.

The Transylvanian prince George II Rákóczy who tried to depose Poland's John II Casimir 3 years ago dies in May at age 38 from wounds sustained while fighting the Ottoman Turks in the Battle of Gyula.

England's civil war ends May 8 after 11 years as the son of the late Charles I is proclaimed king. Now 29, Charles II lands at Dover May 26, he arrives at Whitehall May 29 amidst universal rejoicing, and he begins a reign of nearly 25 years.

Africa's Bambara kingdoms of Segu and Kaarta on the upper Niger begin their rise against the Mandingo Empire which they will replace in 1670.

A Second Navigation Act passed by Parliament declares that certain "enumerated articles" from England's American colonies may be exported only to the British Isles. Included are tobacco, sugar, wool, indigo, and apples. The list will be amended to include rice, molasses, and other articles, and Virginia tobacco prices take a precipitous drop as transport bottlenecks delay shipments, producing widespread economic distress and political unrest in the colony.

New Experiments Physico-Mechanical Touching the Spring of the Air and its Effects by Oxford chemist Robert Boyle, 33, is published (*see* 1661).

German woodcarvers in the Black Forest town of Fürtwangen create clockworks made entirely of wood. They have invented clocks from which wooden cuckoos appear periodically to sound the hours, half-hours, and quarter-hours.

Poetry *Satires* by French poet Nicolas Boileau-Despreaux, 23, who antagonizes many bad writers by naming them.

Painting *Maidservant Pouring Milk* and *View of Delft* by Jan Vermeer; *The Morass* by Dutch painter Jacob van Ruysdael, 32; *St. Peter Denying Christ* by Rembrandt van Rijn. Diego Rodriguez de Silva y Velázquez dies at Madrid August 6 at age 61.

Theater *The Golden Fleece* (*La toison d'or*) by Pierre Corneille in January at the Théâtre du Marais, Paris.

Rome's Church of S. Ivo della Sapienza is completed by Francesco Borromini.

London Royal Navy official Samuel Pepys, 27, notes in his secret diary that he has drunk a "cup of tee (a China drink) of which I never had drank before."

London's population rises to roughly 450,000, up from 350,000 in 1650 (*see* 1700).

China's population reaches 100 million, up from 60 million in 1578 (*see* 1700).

1661 China's Manchu regime decrees that populations within 10 miles of the coast be evacuated to points inland. The regime struggles to repel incursions by the pirate Cheng Ch'eng-kung who is besieging the Dutch settlement at Fort Zelandia on Formosa (Taiwan) where he will establish a Chinese government next year that will resist the Manchus until Cheng's son Cheng K'O-shuang surrenders in 1683.

The Manchu emperor Shun Chih dies after a 16-year reign that has launched the Ch'ing dynasty (*see* 1662).

The Sceptical Chymist by English chemist Robert Boyle discards the Aristotelian theory that there are only four basic elements (earth, air, fire, and water) and proposes an experimental theory of the elements (*see* 1660). Boyle will be called the "father of chemistry" but he holds views that encounter skepticism from later chemists, e.g., that plant life grows by transmutation of water, as do worms and insects since they are produced from the decay of plants (*see* Redi, 1668; Ingenhousz, 1779; Boyle's law, 1662).

Iatrochemical medical theories are consolidated as a systematic school by Prussian-born medical professor Franz de la Boe, 47, who calls himself Sylvius and teaches at Leyden. Sylvius propounds original ideas on the ductless glands, on the tactile senses, on acidosis, and he says digestion is a chemical fermentation (*see* Van Helmont, 1648; Prout, 1824).

Theater *The School for Husbands* (*L'école des maris*) by Molière 6/24 at the Palais-Royal, Paris; *The Bores* (*Les facheux*) by Molière 11/4 at the Palais-Royal.

London's Covent Garden becomes a market for fruit, vegetables, and flowers (*see* 1552).

Ices are sold for the first time at Paris by a Sicilian shopkeeper (*see* Café Procope, 1670).

1662 England's Charles II marries the Portuguese princess Catherine da Braganza, 23, who provides Charles with £300,000 in sugar, cash, and Brazilian mahogany plus the port of Tangier, the island of Bombay, and valuable trading privileges for English mariners in the New World. The May 20 marriage begins a lasting alliance between Portugal and England.

Dunkirk is sold by England to France for £400,000.

Holland and France form an alliance against possible attack by England.

Connecticut colonies are granted an unusually democratic charter by England's Charles II (*see* 1689).

Wampanoag Indian chief Massasoit dies and is succeeded by his son Metacum (*see* 1621; 1675).

1662 (cont.) China's Manchu emperor Shun Chih who died last year is succeeded by his son Hsuan Yeh who assumes the imperial throne as K'ang Hsi to begin a reign of 60 years. A boy of 8, the new emperor will begin his personal rule in 1667 and will usher in a period of cultural achievement under the Ch'ing dynasty that will surpass the greatest achievements of earlier dynasties. Jesuit scholar-missionaries will be encouraged to bring their scientific knowledge to China.

The Royal Society for the Improvement of Natural Knowledge is chartered at London.

Boyle's Law (the volume of a gas varies inversely as the pressure varies) is enunciated by Robert Boyle who has helped found the Royal Society (above; *see* 1661; van Helmont, 1648).

An Act of Uniformity passed by Parliament requires that England's college fellows, schoolfellows, schoolmasters, and clergymen accept everything in a newly published *Book of Common Prayer.* Those who refuse will hereafter be called "Nonconformists."

The Book of Common Prayer contains "A General Confession": "We have left undone those things which we ought to have done;/ And we have done those things which we ought not to have done."

The Day of Doom, or A Poetical Description of the Great and Last Judgement, by Malden, Massachusetts, clergyman Michael Wigglesworth, 31, contains a lurid exposition of Calvinist theology that children of the Massachusetts colony will be required to memorize.

Painting *The Syndics of the Cloth Guild* by Rembrandt van Rijn.

Theater *Sertorius* by Pierre Corneille in February at the Théâtre du Marais, Paris; *The School for Wives* (*L'école des femmes*) by Molière 12/26 at the Palais-Royal, Paris.

The Lisbon fashion of drinking tea is introduced to the London court by Catherine da Braganza (above) who also introduces the Chinese orange (*see* 1635).

1663 Louis XIV renews French rights to enlist Swiss mercenaries through an alliance obtained over the objection of Zurich and some of the Protestant cantons. The 25-year-old Louis rules without the help of Cardinal Mazarin, now 2 years dead, but Jean Baptiste Colbert, 44, is reforming the finances of the world's leading nation and will be named controller general of finance in 1665.

England's Charles II grants the Charter of Rhode Island and Providence Plantations that will remain the constitution until 1842.

England's Charles II grants Carolina territory from Virginia south to Florida as a reward to eight courtiers who have aided him in his restoration. The grant includes land between 31° and 36° North latitude, the grantees include the lord chancellor Edward Hyde, 54, first earl of Clarendon (*see* Sayle, 1670).

Parliament forbids English colonies to trade with other European countries and requires that European goods bound for America be unloaded at English ports and then reshipped even though English export duties and profits to English middlemen may make prices prohibitive in America (*see* 1672).

Parliament reduces duties on English grain imports but also reduces duties on imports. The domestic price level at which exports may be halted is increased in a move that serves the interest of landowners but not that of townspeople.

An epidemic of the Black Death kills 10,000 at Amsterdam out of the city's 200,000 people (*see* 1664).

Painting *Artist and Model* by Jan Vermeer; *Young Woman with a Water Jug* by Jan Vermeer; *Jacob and Laban* by Adriaen van de Velde.

Theater *Sophonisbe* by Pierre Corneille in January at the Hôtel de Bourgogne, Paris; *The Wild Gallant* by English playwright-poet John Dryden, 32, in February at London's Theatre Royal in Vere Street. Dryden marries the sister of Sir Robert Howard.

England's Royal Society urges that potatoes be planted to provide food in case of famine.

1664 Nieuw Amsterdam becomes New York August 27 as 300 English soldiers under Colonel Mathias Nicolls take the town from the Dutch under orders from Charles II (*see* 1626). The town is renamed after the king's brother James, duke of York, who is granted the territory of New Netherland, including eastern Maine and islands to the south and west of Cape Cod, which England claims on the basis of John Cabot's explorations in the late 1490s. Land between the Hudson and Delaware Rivers is granted by the duke of York to John Berkeley, first baron Berkeley of Stratton, and Sir George Carteret, 54, treasurer of the Royal Navy (*see* 1665).

Africa's Cape Verde Islands are taken by English seamen from Dutch forces in Guinea although no war has been declared.

Two English women are condemned as witches after professional evidence is given by Norwich physician-author Thomas Browne of 1658 *Urne-Buriall* fame.

Traité de l'homme et de la formation du foetus by René Descartes states unequivocally that blood in the body is in a state of perpetual circulation (*see* 1619; Harvey, 1628).

The valves of the lymph vessels are discovered by Jan Swammerdam (*see* 1658; 1669; Bartholin, Rudbeck, 1653).

The Black Death kills 24,000 in old Amsterdam while the English are taking Nieuw Amsterdam (above). The plague spreads to Brussels and throughout much of Flanders, and in December it kills two Frenchmen in London's Drury Lane (*see* 1663; 1665). Men who put the dead into the deadcarts keep their pipes lit in the belief, now widespread, that tobacco smokers will be spared.

Express mail service is established by Japanese merchants between Edo and Osaka. The three-times-per-month service takes 6 days as compared with 30 days for ordinary mail.

The Compleat Gamester by English poet Charles Cotten, 34, is more popular than his burlesque of Virgil which is also published (*see* Hoyle, 1742).

Painting *The Travellers* by Dutch landscape painter Meyndert Hobbema, 25; *Young Woman Weighing Gold* by Pieter de Hooch; *The Christening Feast* by Jan Steen; *The Lacemaker* by Jan Vermeer; *Apollo and Daphne* by Nicolas Poussin, now over 70. Francisco de Zurbaran dies at Madrid August 27 at age 65.

Theater *The Indian Queen* by John Dryden and Sir Robert Howard in January at London's Theatre Royal in Bridges Street; *The Forced Marriage* (*Le mariage force*) by Molière 1/29 at the Palais-Royal, Paris; *The Comical Revenge, or Love in a Tub* by English playwright George Etherege, 29, in March at the Lincoln's Inn Fields Theatre, London; *The Royal Ladies* by John Dryden in June at London's Royal Theatre in Bridges Street; *The Thebans, or The Enemy Brothers* (*La Thebaide, ou les frères ennemis*) by French playwright Jean Baptiste Racine, 25, 6/20 at the Palais-Royal, Paris, with Jean Baptiste Molière's company; *Othon* by Pierre Corneille 7/31 at the Hôtel de Bourgogne, Paris.

The French horn becomes an orchestral instrument.

Oratorio *Christmas Oratorio* by Heinrich Schütz at Dresden.

1665 London has its last large outbreak of the Black Death which is introduced either by Dutch prisoners of war or in bales of merchandise from Holland that originated in the Levant. Some two-thirds of London's 460,000 inhabitants leave town to avoid contagion but at least 68,596 die plus a few thousand at Norwich, Newcastle, Portsmouth, Southampton, and Sunderland, most of them poor people who are imprisoned in their houses (which are marked by large red crosses) and given food handed in by constables.

"Lord! how sad a sight it is to see the streets empty of people," writes Samuel Pepys in his *Diary*, "and very few upon the 'Change. Jealous of every door that one sees shut up, lest it should be the plague; and about us two shops in three, if not more, generally shut up."

Many physicians flee England and the court of Charles II moves first to Salisbury, then to Exeter.

A pamphlet published at London blames the plague on "eating radishes, a cat catter wouling, . . . immoderate eating of caviare and anchovies, tame pigeons that flew up and down an alley, [and] drinking strong heady beer."

A rumor that contracting syphilis will serve to ward off the more deadly plague drives the men of London to storm the city's brothels.

Dutch naval forces are defeated by an English fleet off Lowestoft June 3 as a second Anglo-Dutch war begins.

Spain's Philip IV dies September 17 at age 60 after a weak reign and is succeeded by his 4-year-old son Don Carlos, nearly crippled with rickets, who will be king for the next 35 years, the last of the Spanish Hapsburgs.

The New Haven colony accedes reluctantly to join the Connecticut colony rather than be taken over by New York (*see* 1638; 1662).

The New Jersey colony is founded by a group of English colonists brought across the ocean by Philip Carteret (*see* 1664). The group settles at Elizabethtown, which is made capital of the colony under the governorship of Carteret (*see* Newark, 1666).

Reflexions ou Sentences et Maximes Morales by French writer François de La Rochefoucauld, 52, is published anonymously. The wise and witty La Rochefoucauld will be quoted for centuries: "The surest way to be deceived is to think oneself more clever than the others." "Gravity is a mysterious carriage of the body invented to cover the defects of the mind." "When we think we hate flattery we only hate the manner of the flatterer." "The head is always the dupe of the heart." "We would rather speak ill of ourselves than not talk of ourselves at all." "The reason why so few people are agreeable in conversation is that each is thinking more about what he intends to say than about what others are saying, and we never listen when we are eager to speak." "There are few chaste women who are not tired of their trade." "Few people know how to be old."

Painting *Juno* by Rembrandt van Rijn who has used his common-law wife Henrickje Stoffels as his model; *The Jewish Bride* by Rembrandt; *The Artist's Studio* by Jan Vermeer; *The Physician in His Study* by Adriaen van Ostade. Nicolas Poussin dies at Rome November 19 at age 71 (or 72) after a career in which he has founded French classical art.

Theater *The Indian Emperor, or The Conquest of Mexico by the Spaniards* by John Dryden in April at London's Theatre Royal in Bridges Street; *Love Is the Best Doctor* (*L'amour médecin*) by Molière 9/22 at the Palais-Royal, Paris; *Alexander the Great* (*Alexandre Le Grand*) by Jean Racine 12/4 at the Palais-Royal, Paris.

Rome's Church of San Andrea delle Fratte is completed by Francesco Borromini.

Bucharest's Church of the Patriarchy is completed on a three-lobed plan with an icon dating from 1463.

Potatoes are planted on a limited basis in Lorraine (*see* 1663; 1683; 1744; 1757; 1770; Parmentier, 1771).

England imports less than 88 tons of sugar, a figure that will grow to 10,000 tons by the end of the century as tea consumption (encouraged by cheap sugar) increases in popularity.

Charles II restored the English monarchy and reigned for nearly 25 years through war, plague, and fire.

1666 The calculus discovered (or invented) by Cambridge University mathematics professor Isaac Newton, 23, provides rules for dealing with rates of change. The numbers in any given algebraic problem remain constant while a calculation is being made but problems that arise in engineering and in natural phenomena such as astronomy involve constant change which have made accurate mathematical calculation impossible without Newton's calculus.

Laws of gravity established by Isaac Newton (above) state that the attraction exerted by gravity between any two bodies is directly proportional to their masses, and inversely proportional to the square of the distance between them. Newton has returned to his native Woolsthorpe because the plague at Cambridge has closed Trinity College where he is a fellow, he has observed the fall of an apple in an orchard at Woolsthorpe, and he calculates that at a distance of one foot the attraction between two objects is 100 times stronger than at 10 feet (see Galileo, 1592).

A French Academy of Sciences founded by Louis XIV at Paris seeks to rival London's 4-year-old Royal Society. Jean Baptiste Colbert has persuaded the king to begin patronizing scientists.

The French queen mother Anne of Austria has died of breast cancer at Paris January 20 at age 64.

France and Holland declare war on England, French forces take Antigua, Montserrat, and St. Kitts (St. Christopher) in the Greater Antilles, an English privateer takes Tobago. The Dutch sign a treaty of alliance with the elector of Brandenburg Friedrich Wilhelm, and they sign a quadruple alliance with Brunswick, Brandenburg, and Denmark.

Hungarian noblemen revolt against the Holy Roman Emperor Leopold I.

French explorer René Robert Cavelier, 23, sieur de La Salle, voyages to the New World to occupy a grant of land he has received on the St. Lawrence River (see 1669).

Newark is founded on the Passaic River in the New Jersey colony by Connecticut Puritans who have arrived under the leadership of Robert Treat.

The Great Fire of London that begins early in the morning of Sunday, September 2, in Pudding Lane near London Bridge, spreads through the crowded wooden houses to the Thames wharf warehouses and continues for 4 days and nights until the flames have consumed four-fifths of the walled city plus another 63 acres of property outside the city walls. London's Guildhall, 44 of the city's rich livery company halls, the Custom House, the Royal Exchange, the great Gothic cathedral of St. Paul's, 86 other churches, and some 13,200 houses are destroyed, but a new city will spring up to make London the world's most modern metropolis (see Wren, 1667).

Destroyed in London's Great Fire (above) are thousands of old dwellings that have harbored lice-bearing rats which spread plague (see 1665). Some 2,000 Londoners nevertheless die of the plague, which rages also at Cologne and in the Rhine district where it will continue for the next 5 years (see 1673).

Sweden's University of Lund has its beginnings.

Poetry *Instructions to a Painter* by Edmund Waller.

Franz Hals dies at Haarlem August 26 at age 86; Guercino dies at Bologna December 22 at age 75.

Theater *The Misanthrope* by Molière 6/4 at the Palais-Royal, Paris: ". . . my mind is no more shocked at seeing a man a rogue unjust, or selfish, than at seeing vultures eager for prey, mischievous apes, or fury-lashed wolves (I, i); "Good sense avoids all extremes, and requires us to be soberly rational: (I, i); ". . . twenty, as everyone well knows, is not an age to play the prude" (III, v); *The Doctor in Spite of Himself* (*Le médecin malgré lui*) by Molière 8/6 at the Palais-Royal.

The Newton pippin will be so named to commemorate the apple that inspired Newton's law of gravity (above).

Louis XIV issues an edict encouraging large families. Designed by Jean Baptiste Colbert, the edict will prove ineffectual.

1667 The Treaty of Andrussovo January 20 ends a 13-year war between Russia and Poland which cedes Kiev, Smolensk, and the eastern Ukraine to Russia.

The Persian shah Abbas II dies at age 35 after a weak 25-year reign. He is succeeded by his dissolute son who will reign until 1694 as Shah Suleiman.

The Treaties of Breda signed July 21 end the second Anglo-Dutch war after a Dutch fleet has broken the chain in England's Medway River, has reached Chatham, and has captured the flagship *Royal Charles*.

England receives New Netherlands in return for sugar-rich Surinam in South America under terms reached at Breda (above). Acadia is restored to Holland's ally France, England receives Antigua, Montserrat, and St. Kitts from France, and England's Charles II makes a secret treaty with France's Louis XIV against Spain.

French troops invade Flanders and Hainault with grenades to begin the War of Devolution. Louis XIV, now 28, takes as his mistress the marquise of Montespan Françoise Atenais Rochechouart, 26, who proceeds to bear the first of several children she will have by the king.

Brooklyn is chartered under the name Brueckelen October 18 by the governor of New Netherlands Mathias Nicolls. The new town includes "all the lots and plantations lying and being at the Gowanus, Bedford, Walle Bocht and Ferry."

Blood alteration in the lungs is shown to be the essential feature of respiration. English experimental chemist-philosopher Robert Hooke, 32, has assisted Robert Boyle in showing that air is essential to life and he uses bellows in a dog's trachea to prove his point.

The first recorded blood transfusion is performed by Jean Baptiste Denis who transfers blood from a lamb into the vein of a boy (*see* Lower, 1677).

Poetry   *Paradise Lost* by John Milton who has been blind since 1652 but who has dictated the 10-volume work on the fall of man to his daughters. It enjoys sales of 1,300 copies in 18 months and will be enlarged to 12 volumes in 1684, the year of Milton's death; *Annus Mirabilis* by John Dryden is about the Dutch War (above) and the Great Fire of last year.

Painting   *Girl With a Red Hat* by Jan Vermeer.

Theater   *Secret Love, or The Maiden Queen* by John Dryden in March at London's Theatre Royal in Bridges Street which has escaped the Great Fire; *Sir Martin Mar-All, or The Feign'd Innocence* by John Dryden who has adapted Molière's *L'etourdo* as translated by William Cavendish, Duke of Newcastle, in August at the Lincoln's Inn Fields Theatre, London; *Andromache* (*Andromaque*) by Jean Racine 11/7 at the Hôtel de Bourgogne, in a performance by the group that rivals Molière's company whose work has not satisfied Racine.

Architect Christopher Wren, 35, is assigned the task of rebuilding London which in January is still smoldering after the Great Fire of 4 months earlier. An Oxford mathematician and astronomer as well as an architect, Wren has earlier been commissioned by Charles II to restore St. Paul's Cathedral which has been completely gutted by the Great Fire.

Rome's Piazza San Pietro (Saint Peter's Square) is completed after 11 years of work by Giovanni Lorenzo Bernini, now 68, who has designed the great square in monumental baroque style with a semicircular colonnade ringing the 83-foot Egyptian obelisk erected by Pope Sixtus V in 1586.

Rome's great baroque architect Francesco Boromini commits suicide August 3 at age 66 in a fit of depression.

The Mexico Cathedral is completed after 94 years of construction.

1668 A Triple Alliance negotiated January 23 joins England, Holland, and Sweden in resistance to France's Louis XIV in the Spanish Netherlands, but Louis will soon buy off the English and Swedes.

The Treaty of Aix-la-Chapelle May 2 ends a brief War of Devolution waged over Louis XIV's claim to the Spanish possessions in the Belgian provinces following the death of his father-in-law Philip IV of Spain in 1665. Spain regains Franche-Comte in return for Lille, Tournay, Oudenarde, and nine other fortified towns on the border between France and the Spanish Netherlands.

Poland's John II Casimir abdicates at age 58 and retires to France as the abbe de Saint-Germain. The Lithuanian Michael Wisniowiecki, 30, succeeds to the throne and will reign until 1673 (*see* 1670).

Sault-Sainte-Marie is founded between Lake Superior and Lake Huron—the first permanent white settlement in the Michigan region (*see* 1701; 1855).

Rupert House opens in the Canadian northwest—the first European trading settlement in the region. England's "Mad Cavalier" Prince Rupert, 49, a cousin of Charles II, has backed Pierre Radisson and his brother-in-law Medart Chourt, sieur de Groseilliers, in a venture to trade with *les sauvages* in the area of Hudson's Bay. Their 50-ton ketch *Nonsuch* skippered by Groseilliers sails into Hudson's Bay after a voyage of 118 days, and she anchors at the mouth of what will be called Rupert's River (*see* 1610; 1659; Hudson's Bay Company, 1670).

Spanish conquistadors in the Pacific rename the Islas de los Ladrones found by Magellan in 1521. They call them Las Marianas to honor Maria Anna of Austria, widow of Spain's Philip IV (*see* 1899).

The notion of spontaneous generation is not supportable, says Italian physician-naturalist Francesco Redi, 42. He shows that no maggots will develop in meat, no matter how putrified it may be, if it is covered with a thin cloth to protect it from flies that will lay eggs, but most people will continue for centuries to believe that maggots are products of spontaneous generation rather than of fly larva (*see* Needham, 1748; Pasteur, 1861).

The Black Death reaches Austria after having traveled from Flanders to Westphalia and into Normandy and Switzerland (*see* 1666; 1672).

Merck & Co. has its beginnings at Darmstadt in Hesse where German chemist Friedrich Jacob

1668 (cont.) Merck takes over a pharmacy "At the Sign of the Angel." The Engelapotheke will be the basis of the firm E. Merck (*see* 1827).

Fiction *Fables* by French fabulist Jean de La Fontaine, 47, who will follow his six-volume work with five more between 1678 and 1679 and with a twelfth in 1694.

John Dryden is named England's first Poet Laureate and renews a loan of £500 which he made last year to Charles II.

Theater *She Would If She Could* by George Etherege 2/26 at the Lincoln's Inn Fields Theatre, London; *The Sullen Lovers* (*or, The Impertinents*) by English playwright Thomas Shadwell, 26, 5/2 at the Lincoln's Inn Fields Theatre: Shadwell has adapted the Molière play *Les facheux* of 1661; *George Daudin, or The Abused Husband* (*Georges Daudin, ou Le mari confondu*) by Molière 11/19 at the Palais-Royal, Paris.

Swedish organist Dietrich Buxtehude, 31, is named organist at the Marienkirche in Lübeck where his sacred concerto *Abendmusiken* will be presented each year during Advent.

1669 *History of the Insects* by Jan Swammerdam presents a preexistence theory of genetics that the seed of every living creature was formed at the creation of the world and that each generation is contained in the generation that preceded it (*see* Maupertuis, 1745).

A substance that will be called phosphorus from the Latin word for morning star is discovered by England's Robert Boyle and, independently, by Hamburg merchant-alchemist Hennig Brand who distills urine and notices a white, translucent waxy substance that glows in the dark and has an unpleasant odor.

Crete falls to the Turks after a 24-year siege and the Venetians lose their last colonial possession. The Turks will rule the island until late in 1898.

The Mogul emperor Aurangzeb destroys Hindu temples and forbids practice of the Hindu religion. Hindus begin rebellions against the autocratic Aurangzeb.

The first French trading station in India opens.

The Hanseatic League begun in 1241 holds its last meeting.

The sieur de La Salle explores the region south of Lake Erie and Lake Ontario (*see* 1666; Louisiana, 1682).

German-American physician John Lederer leads an expedition across the Piedmont to ascend the Blue Ridge Mountains (*see* 1670).

Nonfiction "Meat out of the eater" by Massachusetts colony clergyman Michael Wigglesworth discusses the necessity of the afflictions that God visits upon His children.

Fiction *Der Abenteuerliche Simplicissimus Teutsch das ist; Beschreibung des Lebens eines Seltzamen Vagantens Genanni Melchior Sternfels von Fuchshaim* by German magistrate Hans Jakob Christoffel von Grimmelshausen, 49, is the first great German novel. The picaresque novel about the havoc of the Thirty Years' War relates the adventures of a youth who becomes successively a soldier, a jester, a bourgeois, a robber, a pilgrim, a slave, and a hermit.

Painting *Self-Portrait* by Rembrandt van Rijn who dies at Amsterdam October 4 at age 63 impoverished and alone; *Girl at the Spinet* by Jan Vermeer.

Theater *Tartuffe, or L'imposteur* by Molière 2/5 at the Palais-Royal, Paris; *Tyrannic Love, or The Royal Martyr* by John Dryden in June at London's Theatre Royal; *Britannicus* by Jean Racine 12/13 at the Hôtel de Bourgogne, Paris.

The Paris Opéra has its beginnings June 28 in letters of patent granted by Louis XIV "to establish an academy to present and have sung in public operas and spectacles with music and in French verse," the Academie de Royale Musique (*see* 1671).

The Stradivarius violin is created by Italian violinmaker Antonio Stradivari, 25, who has served an apprenticeship in his home town of Cremona in Lombardy to Nicola Amati, now 73, whose grandfather Andrea Amati designed the modern violin. The younger Amati has improved on his grandfather's design and has taught not only Stradivari but also Andrea Guarnieri, 43, who also makes violins at Cremona.

Famine in Bengal kills 3 million.

London's Yeomen of the Guard at the Tower of London get the name "Beefeaters" from the grand duke of Tuscany Cosimo de' Medici. Established in 1485 to guard the tower, the warders draw large daily rations of beef, says the grand duke.

The Turkish ambassador to the court of Louis XIV popularizes coffee among the *haut monde* of Paris. Suleiman Aga offers it to all his visitors, but Mme. de Sévigné writes to her daughter the Comtesse de Grignan, "There are two things Frenchmen will never swallow—the poetry of Racine [above] and coffee" (*see* 1699).

1670 Denmark's Frederick III dies at Copenhagen February 6 at age 60 after a 22-year reign in which he has used his personal popularity to make Denmark an absolute monarchy. His 23-year-old son begins a 29-year reign as Christian V in which he will put the interests of the upper middle class and of state officials ahead of those of the old nobility.

France's Louis XIV makes a defensive alliance with Bavaria and with England's Charles II whose sister Henrietta, duchesse d'Orléans, obtains the signatures of the English ministers to the Treaty of Dover in May. She returns to France and dies at St. Cloud June 30 at age 26, allegedly the victim of poison administered by order of her estranged husband Philip, duc d'Orléans, brother of the Grand Monarch.

French troops occupy Lorraine.

Ukrainian Cossacks rise against their Polish overlords but General John Sobieski, 46, puts down the rebellion (*see* 1648; 1671).

"The Governor and Company of Adventurers of England Trading Into Hudson's Bay" is chartered by Charles II (*see* Prince Rupert, 1668).

Two more expeditions venture into the Blue Ridge Mountains under the command of John Lederer.

France's Louis XIV founds Les Invalides at Paris to house up to 7,000 disabled soldiers (*see* below).

French clergyman Gabriel Mouton proposes a uniform and accurate decimalized system of measurements to replace the variously defined leagues, acres, pounds, and other units now in use (*see* 1790).

London clockmaker William Clement improves the accuracy of clocks by inventing anchor-shaped gadgets (escapements) that control the escape of a clock's driving force (*see* Huygens, 1656).

Minute hands appear on watches for the first time (*see* 1511).

Tractatus Theologico-Politicus by Dutch philosopher Benedictus (Baruch) Spinoza is published anonymously (*see* 1656). Spinoza shows that the bible, if properly understood, gives no support to the intolerance of religious authorities and their interference in civil and political affairs. The book creates a furor, it will provoke widespread denunciations as it goes through five editions in the next 5 years, and Spinoza, now 37 and consumptive after years of inhaling glass dust produced by his lens-grinding, moves to The Hague to gain the protection of influential friends.

Nonfiction *Pensées* by the late French philosopher-mathematician Blaise Pascal who died in August of 1662 at age 39 (the book is garbled and no clearly edited version of Pascal's jaundiced thoughts will appear for 175 years): "All men naturally hate each other"; "If men knew what others say of them, there would not be four friends in the world"; "Men never do evil so completely as when they do it from religious conviction"; "Cleopatra's nose: had it been shorter, the whole aspect of the world would have been changed"; "The heart has its reasons which reason cannot know"; "It [the universe] is an infinite sphere whose center is everywhere, its circumference nowhere"; "Man is but a reed, the most feeble thing in nature, but he is a thinking reed. The entire universe need not arm itself to crush him. A vapor, a drop of water suffices to kill him. But if the universe were to crush him, man would still be more noble than that which killed him, because he knows that he dies, and the advantage which the universe has over him: the universe knows nothing of this"; "What a chimera, then, is man! what a novelty! what a monster, what a chaos, what a contradiction, what a

prodigy! Judge of all things, feeble worm of the earth, depository of truth, a sink of uncertainty and error, the glory and the shame of the universe."

English Proverbs by naturalist John Ray, 43, includes "Misery loves company," "Blood is thicker than water," "I'll trust him no further than I can fling him," "Haste makes waste, and waste makes want, and want makes strife between goodman and his wife," "He that hath many irons in the fire, some will cool," "The misery is wide that the sheets will not decide," and "The last straw breaks the camel's back."

Painting *View of Haarlem* by Jacob van Ruysdael; *The Pearl Necklace* by Jan Vermeer; *Girl and Her Duenna* by Bartolomé Murillo.

Theater *Berenice* by Jean Racine 11/21 at the Hôtel de Bourgogne, Paris; *The Bourgeois Gentleman* (*Le Bourgeois Gentilhomme*) by Molière 11/23 at the Palais-Royal, Paris (*see* below); *Titus and Berenice* (*Tite et Berenice*) by Pierre Corneille 11/28 at the Palais-Royal, Paris; *The Conquest of Granada by the Spaniards* (Part I) by John Dryden, in December at London's Theatre Royal; *The Humorists* by Thomas Shadwell, in December at the Lincoln's Inn Fields Theatre, London.

Molière's *Le Bourgeois Gentilhomme* (above) includes a ballet with music by court composer Jean Baptiste Lully, 38, who has come to France from his native Florence and has changed his name from Giovanni Battista Lulli. The ballet is so popular that four performances are requested in the space of 8 days.

French court architect Jules Hardouin-Mansart, 24, designs a masterpiece of classical architecture for Les Invalides (above) and will complete the Church of the Doves for Les Invalides in 1706.

Landscape architect André Lenôtre lays out the Champs-Elysées at Paris.

Widehall mansion in the Maryland colony is completed for shipowner Thomas Smythe.

"Orange Girls" in English theaters sell Spanish Seville oranges which are popular despite their sourness. One Orange Girl, Eleanor "Nell" Gwyn, 20, has become an actress—and mistress to Charles II.

Café Procope opens in the Rue de l'ancienne Comédie on the Left Bank at Paris. Sicilian *limonadier* Francesco Procopio dei Coltelli serves not only lemonade but also coffee, "cremes glacées," sherbets, and Italian pastries and sweetmeats (*see* 1630; 1750).

Population in the Massachusetts colony reaches roughly 25,000.

1671 Welsh buccaneer Henry Morgan, 36, captures Panama City in violation of last year's Anglo-Spanish treaty. Morgan stands trial but Charles II forgives him, knights him, will make him lieutenant-governor of Jamaica in 1674, and will charge him with the task of putting an end to piracy.

The Turks declare war on Poland.

1671 (cont.) Russia's Czar Alexis suppresses a great peasant revolt in the southeast led by the Don Cossacks whose leader Stenka Razin is executed.

The Virginia colony's governor estimates that blacks comprise less than 5 percent of the population (see 1649; 1652; 1715).

A small English party penetrates the Ohio River watershed beyond the Blue Ridge mountains.

Poetry *Paradise Regained* and *Samson Agonistes* by John Milton who has written *Paradise Regained* at the suggestion of Quaker Thomas Ellwood, 32, who comes to his house each day to read to him in Latin. *Samson Agonistes* is a powerful drama based on Greek tragedy and comprises among other things the autobiography and epitaph of its author who will die of gout at age 65 in 1674.

Theater *Psyche* by Pierre Corneille, Molière, and Philippe Quinault 1/17 at the Salle des Machines, Paris, with music by Jean Baptiste Lully; *Love in a Wood* by English playwright William Wycherley, 31, who acts in his coarse comedy at London's Theatre Royal in Bridges Street and gains the patronage of the duchess of Cleveland and the duke of Buckingham; *Almanzor and Almahide, or The Conquest of Granada* (Part II) by John Dryden.

The French Academie de Royale Musique opens March 3 in the Salle du Jeu de Paume de la Bouteille. The Paris Opéra will be taken over beginning next year by Jean Baptiste Lully who will run it until 1687, rebuilding the house after fires that will burn it out of existence in 1678 and 1681 (see 1669; 1875).

Rice is introduced into the South Carolina colony by physician Henry Woodward who helped found the colony in 1663 and who has received some Madagascar rice from a visiting sea captain. The grain will for years be merely a garden curiosity since nobody knows how to husk it and use it for food.

French police receive the right to search houses during Lent and to give any forbidden items of food they may find to the hospitals.

France's Mme. de Sévigné writes to her daughter the Comtesse de Grignan, "Vatel, the great Vatel, maitre d'hotel to M. Fouquet and of late maître d'hotel to M. le Prince, has stabbed himself." Later chroniclers will speculate that Vatel was a great chef who committed suicide over the failure of a dish or of a dinner.

Use of the condom as a means of contraception is disparaged by Mme. de Sévigné (above) who describes it to her daughter as "an armor against enjoyment and a spider web against danger" (see 1655; Kennett, 1723).

1672 A French army of 100,000 crosses the Rhine without warning and invades the Dutch Republic as Louis XIV acts to punish the Dutch who have given refuge to his political critics. England's Charles II supports Louis under secret provisions in the Treaty of Dover of May 1670, the Royal Navy scores a victory at Southwold Bay May 28, the Dutch turn for

help to the prince of Orange, the states general revive the stadtholderate July 8, they make the 21-year-old Willem III of Orange stadtholder, captain-general, and admiral for life, a mob at The Hague brutally murders the grand pensionary Jan De Witt, 47, and his brother Cornelius, 49, and Willem rewards the instigators of the riot as he summons aid from the elector of Brandenburg to resist the French.

Ottoman forces invade Poland following a series of border raids by Tartars and Cossacks. A 4-year war begins over control of the Ukraine.

Russian serfs rise in revolt.

English merchants form the Royal Company to exploit the African slave trade.

The Dutch organize a system of relief for the poor who have been provided for up to now by prosperous merchants. With Dutch trade declining and the country at war, the merchants can no longer afford to be so generous.

The Black Death flares up again in Europe, killing 60,000 at Lyons and hundreds of thousands at Naples in just 6 months.

Charleston is founded in the Carolina colony by Puritans from the Bermudas, led by William Sayle, who arrived 2 years ago at Albemarle Point on the Ashley River and have moved to the peninsula between the Ashley and Cooper Rivers. Sayle has named the town after England's Charles II (see 1679).

England imposes customs duties on goods carried from one of her American colonies to another.

Boston-born English merchant Elihu Yale, 23, reaches India and enters the spice trade in the employ of the East India Company (see 1718).

New York merchant Frederick Philipse begins acquiring a manorial estate of 205,000 acres in upper Yonkers (some say by altering a phrase in a contract with the Indians).

The New York to Boston Post Road is laid out to speed coach travel between the second and third largest American cities.

Painting *Virgin and Child* by Bartolome Murillo; Adriaen van de Velde dies at Amsterdam January 21 at age 41.

Theater *Bajazet* by Jean Racine 1/1 at the Hôtel de Bourgogne, Paris; *The Learned Ladies* (*Les femmes savantes*) by Molière 3/11 at the Palais-Royal, Paris; *Marriage a la Mode* by John Dryden, in April at the Lincoln's Inn Fields Theatre, London; *The Gentleman Dancing Master* by William Wycherley, in August at London's Dorset Garden Theatre; *Pulcheria* (*Pulcherie*) by Pierre Corneille 11/14 at the Théâtre du Marais, Paris; *Epsom Wells* by Thomas Shadwell in December at London's Dorset Garden Theatre.

New England Rarities by English-American merchant John Josselyn says of passenger pigeons, "of late they are much diminished, the English taking them with nets" (*see* 1648; 1800).

The first Paris coffeehouse opens at the Saint-Germain Fair. An Armenian known only as Pascal does well at the fair, but he fails in the coffee house he opens thereafter in the Quai de l'École and moves to London (*see* 1652; Vienna, 1683; Paris, 1754).

1673 Willem III of Orange saves Amsterdam and the province of Holland from France's Louis XIV by opening the sluice gates and flooding the country. He is supported by Frederick William, elector of Brandenburg, who concludes a separate peace with Louis and retains most of his possessions in Cleves.

England's duke of York marries the Catholic Maria d'Este of Modena. Parliament passes the Test Act compelling all English officeholders to take oaths of allegiance and of supremacy, to adjure transubstantiation, and to take the sacraments of the Church of England. The Test Act will not be repealed until 1828 but it will be nullified after 1689 by bills of indemnity to legalize the acts of magistrates who have not taken communion in the Church of England (*see* Papist's Disability Act, 1678).

Dutch forces retake New York and Delaware (*see* 1655; 1664; 1674).

The American Northwest is explored by Jesuit Jacques Marquette, 36, and trader Louis Joliet, 28, who ascend the Fox River from Green Bay, make a short portage to the Wisconsin River, descend the Wisconsin to the Mississippi, paddle their canoes to the mouth of the Arkansas, return to the Illinois, ascend that river, make a portage to the Chicago River, and ascend to Lake Michigan. Joliet sees the possibility of a lakes-to-gulf ship waterway (*see* 1900).

Incidence of the Black Death begins to decline in Europe and England as the brown rat replaces the medieval black rat which is more inclined to carry plague-fleas (but *see* 1675; 1679 to 1682; 1707; 1720).

The first metal dental fillings are installed by English surgeons.

Poetry "On His Blindness" (Sonnet XIX) by John Milton who probably wrote the lines in 1655 and who begins, "When I consider how my light is spent . . ." and ends, ". . . They also serve who only stand and wait."

Painting *Madonna and Child* by Bartolomé Murillo.

Theater *Mithridates* (*Mithridate*) by Jean Racine 1/13 at the Hôtel de Bourgogne, Paris; *The Hypochondriac* (*Le Malade imaginaire*) by Molière 2/10 at the Palais-Royal, Paris (Molière's own illness is not imaginary and he dies a week later at age 51); *Amboyana, or The Cruelties of the Dutch to the English Merchants* by John Dryden in May at the Lincoln's Inn Fields Theatre, London.

1674 The Treaty of Westminster February 9 ends the 2-year war between England and the Dutch. The treaty returns New York and Delaware to England (*see* 1673) and frees the English to expand their trade and grow prosperous while Europe becomes embroiled in depleting warfare.

French troops devastate the Palatinate. Spain and the Holy Roman Empire join with the Dutch in a coalition to frustrate the ambitions of Louis XIV.

Poland elects General Sobieski king and he begins a 22-year reign as John III Sobieski. He has intimidated other contenders by arriving with 6,000 veterans of his triumph against the Turks November 10 of last year, the same day on which former king Michael Wisniowiecki died after a brief 4-year reign.

English Quakers purchase the New Jersey colony interests of Lord John Berkeley (*see* 1665).

English Puritan scholar Richard Baxter, 59, denounces slave hunters as "enemies of mankind" but he does not object to plantation slavery itself so long as the slaves are well treated.

Diabetes research is advanced by Oxford's Thomas Willis, now 53, physician to England's Charles II and a founder of the Royal Society in 1662. Willis establishes that the urine of diabetics is "wonderfully sweet as it were imbued with Honey or Sugar," but while he distinguishes diabetes mellitus from other forms of the disease Willis suggests that it is a disease of the blood (*see* 1788; Brunner, 1683).

The influence of the vagus nerve on the lungs and heart is established by Thomas Willis (above) who blocks the nerve in a live dog. Willis publishes works on the brain and nervous system (*see* Cannon, 1912).

Ergotism strikes French peasants at Gatinais in a severe outbreak (*see* 1597; 1777).

Poetry "L'Art poétique" by Nicolas Boileau-Despreaux is a treatise in verse expounding classical standards. The work establishes Boileau as the leading neo-classical critic of his time and his mock epic "Le Latrin" popularizes that genre.

Theater *Iphegenia* (*Iphegenie*) by Jean Racine 8/18 at Versailles and late in the year at the Hôtel de Bourgogne, Paris; *Surenas* (*Surena*) by Pierre Corneille 10/11 at the Hôtel de Bourgogne.

Japan has a great famine.

1675 Dutch naturalist Anton van Leeuwenhoek, 43, gives the first accurate description of red corpuscles. Van Leeuwenhoek has developed the first of more than 400 simple microscopes that he will produce (*see* 1677; Kircher, 1642).

The Black Death kills 11,000 in Malta.

France's Marshal Turenne inflicts a heavy defeat on the Dutch at Turkheim January 5, he recovers all of Alsace within a few weeks, but he is killed July 27 at age 63 by almost the first shot fired in a battle at Sassbach in Baden. The French retreat across the Rhine.

1675 (cont.) Swedish allies of France's Louis XIV invade Brandenburg but are defeated June 28 by the elector of Brandenburg in the Battle of Fehrbellin: the elector retaliates by invading Pomerania (*see* 1679).

King Philip's War devastates New England as Chief Metacum rebels against a 1671 order requiring his people to pay an annual tribute of £100. Called King Philip of Potanoket by the colonists, Metacum leads the Narragansett and Wampanoag in attacks on 52 American settlements, destroying 12 or 13 of them and killing 600 of New England's finest men (*see* 1662; 1676).

Père Marquette founds a mission at the Indian town of Kaskaskia in the Illinois wilderness (*see* 1673; 1699).

Boston has 30 merchants worth from £10,000 to £20,000 each and has 430 large vessels at sea "so that there is little left for the merchants residing in England to import into any of the plantations."

Painting *The Music Lesson* and *The Concert* by Geraert Torborch. Jan Vermeer dies at Delft December 15 at age 43.

Theater *The Country Wife* by William Wycherley in January at London's Theatre Royal in Drury Lane: "Good wives and private soldiers should be kept ignorant" (I); *The Mistaken Husband* by John Dryden in September at London's Drury Lane Theatre; *Aureng-Zebe* by John Dryden in November at the Drury Lane Theatre.

Construction of a new St. Paul's Cathedral begins at London June 21. Architect Christopher Wren lays the first stone of the cathedral that will replace an old Gothic church that was gutted in the fire of 1666, the choir of the new cathedral will open December 2, 1697, and the last stone will be set in place in 1710.

England tries to suppress the coffeehouses that have become gathering places for men who neglect their families to discuss business and politics over coffee.

New England has 50,000 colonists, up from 16,000 in 1642, while its native American population has been reduced to no more than 20,000.

1676 Russia's Czar Alexis Mikhailovich dies February 8 at age 47 after a reign of 31 years and is succeeded by his eldest surviving son who assumes the throne at age 15 as Fedor III. Disfigured and half paralyzed by disease since birth, Fedor is well educated and will rule effectively until his death in 1682.

The Treaty of Zuravno October 16 ends a 4-year war between Poland's John III Sobieski and the Ottoman Empire, which acquires most of Podolia and the Polish Ukraine, thus coming into contact with Russia.

King Philip's War in New England has ended in August with the killing in battle of Chief Metacum by colonial militiamen who break up Metacum's confederacy and take his head to Plymouth where it will be exhibited for the next 20 years. Fifty-two of New England's 90 towns have been attacked, 600 men have been killed, and at least 12 towns have been completely destroyed.

"King Philip's" widow and children are sold as slaves to the West Indies despite Increase Mather's vote that they be executed, and militiamen hunt down other survivors of the war to sell into slavery. Five hundred are shipped out of Plymouth alone.

Bacon's Rebellion stirs the Virginia colony but frontiersmen fail in their struggle against the tidewater aristocracy. The colony's slave trade increases.

Dutch traders buy black slaves at 30 florins each in Angola and sell 15,000 per year in the Americas at 300 to 500 florins each.

New Jersey's western part is conveyed to English Quakers who have entered into an agreement with Philip Carteret (*see* 1665; 1702).

Morrisania has its origin in a tract of land north of Manhattan Island granted by New York's colonial governor Edmund Andros to Colonel Lewis Morris.

England's Greenwich Observatory is established to study the position of the moon among the fixed stars and to establish a standard time that will help navigators fix their longitude, but determining accurate position remains a problem (*see* Bennewitz, 1524; Frisius, 1530; Board of Longitude, 1714).

"If I have seen further, it is by standing on the shoulders of giants," writes England's Isaac Newton February 18. Some of Newton's ideas on optics have been challenged by Robert Hooke and he replies by pointing out that every contributor to knowledge or learning builds on the contributions of predecessors. Newton has doubtless read Robert Burton's 1621 chrestomathy *The Anatomy of Melancholy* with its aphorism, "Pygmies placed on the shoulders of giants see more than the giants themselves," an apothegm derived from the writings of the 12th century scholastic Bernard of Chartres who said, "In comparison with the ancients we stand like dwarfs on the shoulders of giants" (a stained glass window at the Cathedral of Chartres depicts Matthew sitting astride the shoulders of Isaiah), but Newton gives the phrase new meaning and it will be called Newton's Other Law (*see* 1666).

The University of San Carlos of Guatemala is founded at Guatemala City.

Theater *The Man of Mode, or Sir Fopling Flutter* by George Etherege 3/11 at London's Dorset Garden Theatre: "Next to coming to a good understanding with a new mistress, I love a quarrel with an old one" (I, i); *The Plain Dealer* by William Wycherley 12/11 at London's Theatre Royal in Drury Lane.

A Philosophical Discourse of Earth . . . by English diarist John Evelyn, 46, is a translation from the French work by J. de la Quintinie.

1677 England and France sign a maritime agreement that permits English ships to carry Dutch cargoes without fear of French interference.

France's duc d'Orléans defeats the Dutch at Cassel.

A Dutch-Danish fleet defeats a Swedish fleet at Oland.

French forces in Africa take Dutch ports on the Senegal River and capture Gorée near Cape Verde. Gorée will be a major port for the slave trade (*see* 1698).

Culpeper's Rebellion in the 14-year-old Carolina colony protests enforcement of English trade laws by the colony's proprietors. Rebellious colonists install surveyor John Culpeper as governor but the proprietors will remove him in 1679.

Spain's territorial empire covers much of the known world but her soil is barely cultivated, her food is costly, her population is dwindling, and she has become a third-rate power (*see* 1613).

Willem of Orange turns 27 on November 4 and is married that day at London to the 15-year-old Mary, niece of England's Charles II (*see* "Glorious Revolution," 1688).

English physician Richard Lower, 46, introduces direct blood transfusion from one animal into the veins of another. Lower has injected dark venous blood into the lungs and has deduced that air turns blood red (*see* 1667; 1818).

The London Pharmacopeia of 1618 is published in a third edition which includes steel tonics, digitalis, benzoin, jalap, ipecacuanha, cinchona bark (*see* Barba, 1642), and Irish whisky (*acqua vitae Hibernoroium sive usquebaugh*).

Painting *Musical Party in a Courtyard* by Pieter de Hooch.

Theater *Phaedra* (*Phèdre*) by Jean Racine 1/1 at the Hôtel de Bourgogne, Paris (in the long absence of her husband Theseus Phaedra falls in love with her stepson Hippolytus, who has fallen in love with the captive princess Aricie. Theseus returns, he hears the stepson falsely accused of leading Phaedra into infidelity, he calls upon the god Neptune to destroy Hippolytus, but Phaedra is consumed with shame and remorse and kills herself); *All for Love, or The World Well Lost* by John Dryden in December at London's Drury Lane Theatre.

Microscopic spermatozoa in human semen are found by Anton van Leeuwenhoek and L. Hamm at Delft (*see* 1675).

1678 Reports of a "Popish Plot" rock England. Titus Oates, 29, is expelled from a Jesuit seminary when it is discovered that the Anabaptist preacher's son has been employed by English prelate Israel Tonge to feign conversion to Catholicism. Oates "uncovers" a plot whereby Roman Catholics are supposedly pledged to massacre Protestants, burn London, and assassinate Charles II. Oates swears before magistrate Sir Edmund Berry Godfrey that he is telling the truth, Sir Edmund is soon after found murdered, five Catholic lords are sent to the Tower of London, dozens of Catholics are executed, and Parliament passes the Papists' Disabling Act that excludes Roman Catholics from Parliament, an act that will stand until 1829 (*see* Test Act, 1673).

The Treaty of Nimwegen signed August 10 returns to Holland the territories she has lost to France and Spain on condition that she maintain neutrality. A second treaty signed at Nimwegen September 17 returns territories that France and Spain have taken from each other, but the peace will be short-lived.

Niagara Falls is discovered by French Franciscan missionary-explorer Louis Hennepin, 38, who has been in Canada since 1675 and who is so moved by the sight that he falls upon his knees. "The universe does not afford its parallel," Hennepin will write (*see* St. Anthony's Falls, 1680).

The excretory ducts of the kidneys (Bellini's ducts) are discovered by Italian anatomist-physician Lorenzo Bellini, 35, who has taught medicine at Pisa since at least 1664 and who publishes a book on the physiology of taste organs. Bellini also discovers the action of nerves on muscles.

Fiction *Pilgrim's Progress* by English preacher John Bunyan, 49, whose illustrated work inspires religious reverance while entertaining readers and achieves enormous popularity which it will continue to enjoy for two centuries. To Puritans kept ignorant of Homer, Shakespeare, and Cervantes the Bunyan book comes as a brilliant revelation that is enhanced by its engravings. *La Princesse de Cleves* by French novelist Marie Madeleine Pioche de La Vergne, 44, Comtesse de La Fayette.

Poetry English poet Andrew Marvell dies August 16 at age 57 after taking an overdose of an opiate for his ague. Marvell leaves behind verses that include the lines "To His Coy Mistress": "Had we but world

Père Marquette and Louis Joliet discovered the Mississippi as they explored the waterways of the American heartland.

1678 (cont.) enough, and time,/ This coyness, lady, were no crime …"; "At my back I always hear Time's winged chariot hurrying near."

Painting *Charles II* by German-born English painter Godfrey Kneller (né Gottfried Kniller).

Theater *The Kind Keeper, or Mr. Limberham* by John Dryden in March at London's Dorset Garden Theatre.

Opera The Hamburg Staatsoper opens January 2 with 1,675 seats. Johan Theile has composed the music for the opening opera *Adam and Eve*.

1679 The Habeas Corpus Act passed by Parliament in May obliges English judges to issue upon request a writ of habeas corpus directing a jailer to produce the body of any prisoner and to show cause for his imprisonment. A prisoner shall be indicted in the first term of his commitment, says Parliament, he shall be tried no later than the second term, and once set free by order of the court he shall not be imprisoned again for the same offense.

The Peace of St. Germain-en-Laye forced upon the elector of Brandenburg June 29 by France's Louis XIV obliges the elector to surrender to Sweden practically all of Brandenburg's conquests in Pomerania. The elector receives almost nothing in return.

Four new treaties signed at Nijmegen, Fontainebleau, and Lund settle disputes among France, Holland, Sweden, Denmark, and the Holy Roman Empire.

French explorer Daniel Greysolon, sieur Du Lhut (or Duluth) reaches the great inland sea that will be called Lake Superior and claims the region for Louis XIV (*see* La Salle, 1682).

Charleston in the Carolina colony receives a group of French Huguenots who have been given permission by the English to start a silk manufacturing industry. The industry will later be suppressed and families that include the Hugers, the Legares, the Legendres, the Manigaults, the Mazycks, and the Mottes will become Charleston's leading moneylenders, planters' agents, and shippers.

Scots-American Robert Livingston, 25, marries Alida Schuyler Van Rensselaer, widow of the late Nicholas Van Rensselaer, and extends his landholdings in the Albany, New York, area where he has made his home for the past 5 years (*see* 1630; 1686).

The constant relation between the pressure and volume of an enclosed quantity of air is announced by French physicist Edmé Mariotte, 59, who has made his discovery independently of work by Robert Boyle (*see* 1662).

The boiling point of water is shown to depend on atmospheric pressure by French Huguenot physicist Denis Papin, 32, who has worked since 1675 with Robert Boyle at London after working previously with Christian Huygens at Paris.

The Black Death takes at least 76,000 lives at Vienna.

Theater *Troilus and Croilus, or Truth Found Too Late* by John Dryden, in April at London's Dorset Garden Theatre.

Opera *Gli Quivoco nell'amore* in February at Rome's Teatro Capranica with music by Italian composer Alessandro Scarlatti, 20, who gains the protection of Sweden's former Queen Christina and begins a career that will produce important musical works for 44 years. Scarlatti's operas, church music, and chamber music will virtually create the language of classical music.

Sweden's Skokloster Castle is completed south of Uppsala.

Tuscany's Arno River is brought under control by Italian engineer Vincenzo Viviani who uses a modification of a plan devised by Leonardo da Vinci in 1495. The Arno will nevertheless continue to flood periodically and to inundate Florence.

1680 Europe enters a 40-year period of economic troubles that will be accompanied by wild price fluctuations, revolts, famines, and disease epidemics.

Bohemian peasants stage a major revolt to begin an era of endemic unrest among the serfs following a shift from soil tillage to dairy farming encouraged by the Thirty Years' War that ended in 1648.

Sweden's aristocrats are dealt a severe blow by Charles XI who brings pressures on the estates to pass a law requiring all earldoms, baronies, and other large fiefs to revert to the crown and legalizing wholesale confiscation of properties.

Japan's Tokugawa shogun Itsuna dies at age 39 after a 29-year reign and is succeeded by his 34-year-old brother who will reign until 1709 as Sunayoshi.

New Hampshire is separated by royal charter from Massachusetts whose Bay Colony governors have bought most of Maine from the heirs of Fernando Gorges.

Pueblo tribesmen at Taos and Santa Fe rise against the Spaniards August 11, destroy most of the Spanish churches, and drive the 2,500 Spanish colonists from their territory.

Minneapolis has its beginnings in St. Anthony's Falls named by Father Hennepin who has accompanied the sieur de La Salle through the Great Lakes to the upper Mississippi Valley (*see* 1678; 1819).

The Black Death strikes Dresden in epidemic proportions.

De Motu Animalium by the late Italian mathematician-astronomer Giovanni Alphonso Borelli expresses the view that digestion is a mechanical process with blood pressure inducing gastric secretion. Fevers, pains, and convulsions are the result of defective movements of the "nervous juices," says Borelli who died last year at age 71 after having founded the iatrophysical school of medicine by applying mechanical principles for the first time to the study of human muscular movement (see hydrochloric acid, 1824; pepsin, 1835).

Ferdinand Bol dies at Amsterdam July 24 at age 64; Gian Lorenzo Bernini dies at Rome November 28 at age 81.

Theater *The Spanish Friar, or The Double Discovery* by John Dryden in March at London's Dorset Garden Theatre.

Maryland colonists complain that "their supply of provisions becoming exhausted, it was necessary for them, in order to keep from starvation, to eat the oysters taken from along their shores" (see 1634).

1681 Pennsylvania has its beginnings in a land grant of 48,000 square miles in the New World given by England's Charles II to religious nonconformist William Penn, 37, whose late father has bequeathed him an immense claim of £15,000 against the king (see Jamaica, 1655). Penn has been the first person of means to join the Society of Friends founded by George Fox in 1647, he has served time in prison for writing and distributing pamphlets espousing the Quaker cause, and the king's generosity is motivated in part by a desire to rid England of nonconformists, but Charles honors the late admiral by prefixing "Penn" to the name "Sylvania" that William Penn gives to the new territory (see 1682).

England begins a period of prosperity that will be shared by the New England Confederation formed in 1643. Merchants become rich as the demand for ships and shipping increases.

The first bank checks are issued in England (see Bank of England, 1694; London Stock Exchange, 1698).

London's Chelsea Hospital is founded for wounded and discharged soldiers.

The Black Death takes 83,000 lives at Prague.

France's Languedoc Canal is completed to link the Atlantic with the Mediterranean. The late engineer Pierre Paul de Riquet who planned the canal and has spent most of his own personal fortune to pursue the project in the last 18 years had died at age 76, 6 months too soon to see his work complete (see 1603).

Poetry *Absalom and Achitophel* by John Dryden who satirizes the second duke of Buckingham George Villiers, 53. Buckingham was dismissed from his offices in 1674 for his personal immorality and for promoting popery and arbitrary government.

Geraert Terborch dies at Deventer December 8 at age 64.

Oxford's Tom Tower is designed by Christopher Wren for Christ Church.

Venice's Church of the Salute is completed after 50 years of interrupted activity. Ordered by a decree of the Senate in 1630 as a thanksgiving for delivering the city from the plague, the baroque church has been designed by Baldassare Longhena, now 83, who will die within a year.

The dodo becomes extinct as the last of the species dies on the Indian Ocean island of Mauritius. A flightless bird related to the pigeon but as large as a turkey, the dodo has been killed off by Europeans for food.

France's Louis XIV restricts fishing for mussels but places no restraint on dragging for oysters whose natural banks are called "inexhaustible" (see 1786).

1682 Russia's Fedor III dies April 27 at age 21, his 9-year-old half-brother Peter succeeds to the throne in preference to Fedor's mentally and physically defective brother Ivan, 15, Ivan's sister Sophia Alekseevna, 25, instigates the musketeers (Strelitzi) to invade the Kremlin and murder Peter's supporters, Ivan is proclaimed czar with Peter as his associate, and he begins a nominal 7-year reign in which Sophia will serve as regent and will exercise the power.

Austrian and Polish forces begin a 17-year war to liberate Hungary from the Ottoman Turks.

A Frame of Government drawn up by William Penn for the Pennsylvania colony contains an explicit clause permitting amendments, an innovation that makes it a self-adjusting constitution.

William Penn (above) lands at New Castle on the Delaware River late in the year after a voyage from Deal in the ship *Welcome*. A third of his 100 Friends have succumbed to smallpox on the voyage which has lasted nearly 2 months.

Philadelphia—a city "of brotherly love"—is founded by William Penn.

Louisiana Territory is so named by the sieur de La Salle who reaches the mouth of the Mississippi April 9 with a party of 50 men after having descended the great river from the Illinois River. La Salle has built Fort Prudhomme at the mouth of the Hatchie River in what later will be called Tennessee and he claims the Mississippi Valley for Louis XIV (see 1669; 1763).

Norfolk, Virginia, is founded on the site of an Indian village by colonist Nicholas Wise who will buy the land for $400 in tobacco from the government at Williamsburg.

Mennonites begin leaving the German states to settle at Philadelphia and on fertile lands that will extend from Easton through Allentown, Reading, and Lebanon to the Cumberland Valley (see 1586; Germantown, 1683).

The Black Death kills nearly half the 10,000 inhabitants of Halle and wipes out much of Magdeburg.

Methodus Plantarum Nova by English naturalist John Ray, now 55, first demonstrates the nature of buds and divides flowering plants into dicotyledons and monocotyledons (see Linnaeus, 1737).

"Thoughts on the Comet of 1680" by French philosopher Pierre Bayle, 35, uses rationalism to oppose superstitions about comets.

Fiction *The Life of an Amorous Man* (*Koshoku Ichidai Otoko*) by Japanese novelist Saikaku Ihara,

1682 (cont.) 40, who has confined himself until now to poetry but who reveals his talents as a novelist.

Poetry *The Medall; a Satyre against Sedition* by John Dryden is an even more direct attack on the earl of Shaftesbury: "Successful crimes alone are justified," writes Dryden, and his barbs force Shaftesbury to flee to Holland where he will die next year; *Mac Flecknoe* by John Dryden "All human things are subject to decay."

Jacob van Ruysdael dies at Amsterdam March 14 at age 53; Bartolomé Murillo dies at Seville April 3 at age 64; Claude Lorrain dies at Rome November 21 at age 82.

Theater *Venice Preserved, or A Plot Discovered* by English playwright Thomas Otway, 30, 2/9 at London's Dorset Garden Theatre.

Versailles becomes the seat of French government as Louis XIV moves his court into a palatial château built outside Paris at a cost of $325 million and some 227 lives. Waterworks constructed at Marly-le-Roi by the royal engineer Rannequin supply water from the Seine for the Versailles gardens and another château for the royal family goes up at Marly-le-Roi (*see* 1627; Hall of Mirrors, 1684).

The pressure cooker invented by French physicist Denis Papin employs a safety valve Papin has devised. He calls the cooker a "digester" (*see* 1679).

French chefs prepare foods en gelée using tasteless, odorless gelatin derived from animal bones by Denis Papin (above; *see* Peter Cooper, 1845).

Food served at Versailles (above) is generally cold because the kitchens are so far from the dining rooms.

The Mennonites (above) will introduce Pennsylvania "Dutch" (Deutsch) cooking and will contribute dishes such as scrapple to the American cuisine.

1683 England's Charles II compels the City of London to surrender its charter under a writ of quo warranto, various aldermen and officers are ejected and replaced by royal nominees, municipal charters throughout England are revoked to give the Tories control over appointment of municipal officers, and some of the defeated Whigs conspire to assassinate the king. The Rye House plot is uncovered in June along with a similar conspiracy, Lord William Russell, 43, is sent to the Tower June 26 along with Arthur Capel, 51, first earl of Essex, and Algernon Sidney, 51. Russell is executed July 21 at Lincoln's Inn Fields after trial and conviction on the testimony of a perjured witness, Essex is discovered in his chamber July 30 with his throat slit, probably by his own hand, and Sidney is beheaded December 7.

The king's bastard son James Scott, 34, duke of Monmouth, is subpoenaed to give evidence at the trial of John Hampden, 27, who has been arrested for alleged complicity in the Rye House plot (above), parti-

sans of the duke advance his claims to the crown, their hopes are dampened by the execution of Sidney (above), and the duke flees to Holland.

France's Jean Baptiste Colbert dies at age 64 leaving fine estates throughout the country but leaving the French navy without a champion at court. The navy will soon begin to decline.

Spain declares war on France, and Spain's Carlos II is joined by the Emperor Leopold in the League of The Hague which joins the Dutch-Swedish alliance against Louis XIV.

Portugal's dissolute Afonso VI dies at age 40 and is succeeded by his 35-year-old brother who has served as regent since 1667 and who will reign as Pedro II until his death in 1706.

Formosa is conquered by the Chinese who will hold the island (Taiwan) until 1895.

The Great Treaty of Shackamaxon is signed with the Delaware Indians by William Penn who buys territories that will become southeastern Pennsylvania.

A 58-day siege of Vienna by Ottoman troops under the grand vizir Kara Mustafa is relieved September 12 by a German-Polish army under Charles of Lorraine, 40, and John III Sobieski.

The germ theory of disease is pioneered by Anton von Leeuwenhoek who invents an improved microscope and finds living organisms in the calculus scraped off his teeth (*see* 1675; Fracostoro, 1546).

Knowledge of diabetes is pioneered by Swiss anatomist Johann Conrad Brunner, 30, who removes the pancreas from a dog and notes that the animal develops an inordinate thirst (*see* Cawley, 1788).

An accurate description of gout is given by English physician Thomas Sydenham, 59, who has suffered from the disease himself for 34 years (*see* Garrod, 1859).

The collected works of Thomas Sydenham (above) are published at Amsterdam and include writings that have been published since 1666. "Among the remedies which it has pleased Almighty God to give man to relieve his sufferings, none is so universal and so efficacious as opium," Sydenham has written in 1680. Opiates will remain the mainstay of treating severe pain from many illnesses for more than three centuries and one popular opiate will be Sydenham's drops (*see* morphine, 1803).

Iron deficiency anemia (chlorosis) is relieved by iron fillings steeped in Rhenish wine, Sydenham has written. Returning to the 5th century B.C. principles of Hippocrates, Sydenham has built a large and lucrative practice on the premise that the cause of all diseases resides in nature and that diseases tend to cure themselves. He uses diet, discreet blood-letting, Sydenham's drops (above), cinchona bark (*see* 1642), and vegetable simples; he gives clear clinical descriptions of malaria, hysteria, scarlatina, smallpox, and St. Vitus's dance (Sydenham's chorea); and he advises horseback riding for tuberculosis, cooling measures for smallpox, fresh air for sickrooms.

The first English shipwreck on Africa's East Coast strands sailors in Natal. Two more English wrecks and one Dutch wreck in the next few years will contribute to exploration of the region, at least one man will be trampled to death by an elephant, and some will report having met the survivor of a Portuguese wreck 42 years earlier who has married an amaMpondo woman.

Japan's Mitsui bank is opened in Edo's Surugacho district by merchant Mitsui Hachirobei Takatoshi, youngest son of Mitsui Sokuebei (see 1616). The Edo store Mitsukosho founded by the Mitsui family 10 years ago will become the Ginza's largest department store, it will introduce fixed prices (*Kanane-Nashi*) and cash-down installment buying (*Gen-Gin*) while the Mitsui bank founded with money made by selling brocades, silks, and cottons at low prices will grow into a major international trading company.

Nonfiction *Dialogues des Morts* by French man of letters Bernard Le Bovier de Fontenelle, 26, is an attack on authoritarianism; *The Growth of the City of London* by Sir William Petty; *A General Description of Pennsylvania* by William Penn.

Painting *Sir Charles Cotterell* by Godfrey Kneller.

Philadelphia is laid out by colonist Thomas Holme and other members of the Society of Friends with a grid pattern employed earlier by some Spanish colonial towns.

The Parson Cape House is completed at Topsfield in the Massachusetts Bay Colony.

Copenhagen's Charlottenborg Palace is completed in Dutch baroque style for Count Ulrik F. Byldenlove, illegitimate son of Frederick III. Eleven years in the building, it will be taken over by the dowager queen Charlotte Amalie in 1700 and 54 years later will become the Danish Royal Academy of Arts.

London's Piccadilly Circus and St. James's Place are designed by Christopher Wren.

Wild boars become extinct in Britain.

France's Louis XIV hears cries of hungry beggars outside the palace at Versailles and sends an order to his aged controller of finance Jean Baptiste Colbert (above): "The suffering troubles me greatly. We must do everything we can to relieve the people. I wish this to be done at once." But little in fact is done.

The Viennese have lost thousands to starvation in the 58-day siege by the Ottoman Turks (above). Survivors have sustained themselves by eating cats, donkeys, and everything else edible.

The *kipfel* is created as a crescent-shaped roll by Viennese bakers either to celebrate the lifting of the city's siege (above) or in anticipation of a Turkish victory, but the roll that will become the French *croissant* may date back to 1217 (see 340 B.C.; Marie Antoinette, 1770).

The first coffeehouse in central Europe is opened by a spy for the Viennese who has tasted coffee in his sallies among the 300,000-man Ottoman siege force and who obtains some bags of coffee after the Turks retreat. His coffeehouse Zum Roten Kreuz (At the Red Cross) is near St. Stephen's Cathedral (see 1700).

German Mennonites settle at "Germantown" near Philadelphia in America's first settlement of Germans. More Germans will emigrate to America than any other nationality group with the exception of the Anglo-Scots-Irish (see 1682; 1710; 1882).

1684 Venice joins Austria and Poland in the Holy League against the Ottoman Turks but Poland soon withdraws from the league sponsored by Pope Innocent XI at the insistence of France's Louis XIV.

French troops occupy Lorraine and Louis XIV signs a 20-year truce at Regensburg with the Holy Roman Emperor Leopold. Louis retains all the territory he has obtained up to August 1, 1681, including Strasbourg, and he retains Lorraine as well.

The Japanese prime minister Hotta Masatoshi is assassinated at age 50 and the shogun Sunayoshi is left with no able counselors. He will issue edicts inspired by Buddhism that will prohibit the killing of any living creature, he will extend special protection and privileges to dogs, he will wreck the finances of Edo, and he will bring hardship to the Japanese.

Parliament annuls the Massachusetts Charter of 1629 following charges that colonists have usurped the rights of Mason and Gorges and their heirs in New Hampshire, have evaded the Navigation Acts by sending tobacco and sugar directly to Europe, have exercised power not warranted by the charter, and have shown disrespect for the king's authority.

The word "American" appears for the first time in writings by Puritan minister Cotton Mather, 21, who entered Harvard College at age 12 and who will become assistant next year to his father Increase Mather at Boston's North Church (see 1693).

The sieur de La Salle returns to America with a force of more than 400 men but he lands in error on the Texas Gulf Coast where he gets lost and loses most of his men to fever and desertion (see 1682; 1687).

England has an outbreak of smallpox that adds to the misery of the cold (see below).

England's East India Company gains Chinese permission to build a trading station at Canton after years of having imported Chinese silks, porcelain, and tea by way of Java.

The Japanese poet Saikaku composes 23,500 verses in a single day and night at the Sumiyoshi Shrine in Osaka. The scribes cannot keep up with him and can only tally the number.

The Hall of Mirrors at Versailles is completed by the French architect Jules Hardouin-Mansart whose

259

1684 (cont.) uncle François brought the mansard roof into use. As building superintendent to Louis XIV, Hardouin-Mansart will create the Grand Trianon, the Place Vendôme, the Place des Victoires, and the dome of the Hôtel des Invalides (*see* 1682).

England emerges from her coldest winter in memory. The Thames has frozen over and even the sea has frozen for 2 miles from land.

England's Charles II roasts oxen and feeds the poor at his own expense as bitter cold grips the country.

Tea sells on the Continent for less than 1 shilling per pound but an import duty of 5 shillings per pound makes tea too costly for most Englishmen and encourages widespread smuggling. The English consume more smuggled tea than tea brought in by orthodox routes (*see* 1784).

1685 England's Charles II dies February 6 at age 54 saying, "Let not poor Nelly starve," a reference to actress Nell Gwyn, now 34, who made her last stage appearance in 1682, has borne the king two sons, but will die in 2 years. Charles has made a profession of the Catholic faith on his deathbed, his Catholic brother James, 51, succeeds him to begin a brief reign as James II, but his nephew James, duke of Monmouth, claims "legitimate and legal" right to the throne.

Monmouth (above) is the acknowledged son of Charles, he has taken the surname Scott of his wife Anne, countess of Buccleuch, and his mistress Henrietta Maria Wentworth, 28, baroness Wentworth, has supplied him with funds. He has the support of Archibald Campbell, Scotland's 56-year-old earl of Argyll, and he lands at Lyme Regis, Dorsetshire, with 82 supporters.

English troops loyal to James II capture the earl of Argyll (above) and he is executed June 30. The Battle of Sedgemoor July 6 is the last formal battle on English soil, James's troops easily defeat the duke of Monmouth, he is captured, and executed.

Titus Oates of 1678 "Popish Plot" notoriety is found guilty of perjury and is sentenced to be pilloried and imprisoned for life. Oates will be pardoned in 1689 and allowed a pension of £300 per year following the accession of William of Orange to the English throne.

The revocation of France's Edict of Nantes October 18 forbids the practice of any religion but Catholicism and forbids Huguenots to emigrate after 87 years of religious toleration (but *see* below).

A *Code Noir* issued at Paris establishes humane relations with respect to treatment of slaves on French colonial plantations but planters will generally disregard the Code.

French entrepreneurs establish the Guinea Company to engage in the slave trade which has become increasingly popular (*see* Senegal Company, 1673).

Barbados has 46,000 slaves, up from 6,000 in 1645. Blacks on the island outnumber Europeans 2 to 1.

Poetry *Of Divine Love* by Edmund Waller, now 79.

Painting *Philip, Earl of Leicester* by Godfrey Kneller; Adriaen van Ostade dies at Haarlem May 2 at age 74.

More than 50,000 Huguenot families begin leaving France following the revocation of the Edict of Nantes (above). Half a million people will leave for England (Spitalfields), Holland, Denmark, Sweden, the Protestant German states, South Africa, and North America, many countries will attract the emigrants by offering tax exemptions and transportation subsidies, the emigrants will include so many seamen that French shipping will be hurt for generations to come, and France will be crippled by the loss of so many craftsmen and intellectuals.

1686 The League of Augsburg created by treaty July 9 allies a formidable array of European powers against France's Louis XIV. The Holy Roman Emperor Leopold I, Spain's Carlos II, Sweden's Charles XI, and the electors of Bavaria, Saxony, and the Palatine all join the league.

Austrian troops liberate Buda from the Ottoman Turks who have controlled the city since 1541, but the Austrians find that the pashas have left Buda a ruin, its treasures destroyed or stolen.

Russia declares war on Constantinople.

France's Louis XIV annexes Madagascar.

The English East India Company begins to impose its will by force after 80 years of trying to cement relations with the rulers of India. Company official Job Charnock moves his factory from the besieged town of Hooghly to an island at the mouth of the Ganges and begins a pattern of company rule that will continue until 1858 (*see* Calcutta, 1690).

The Dominion of New England is created by the consolidation of English colonies under the administration of New York governor Sir Edmund Andros, now 49. He arrives at Boston December 20 and assumes control of the government of Plymouth and Rhode Island (*see* King William's War, 1689).

Robert Livingston creates a manor out of his American landholdings which ultimately will embrace 160,000 acres (*see* 1679; Louisiana Purchase, 1803).

England readmits Roman Catholics to the army.

Nonfiction *Entretiens sur la pluralité des mondes* by Bernard de Fontenelle popularizes Cartesian cosmology (*see* 1637); *L'Histoire des oracles* by Bernard de Fontenelle attacks credulity and superstition.

Fiction *Five Women Who Chose Love* (*Koshoku Gonin Onna*) and *A Woman Who Devoted Her Entire Life to Lovemaking* (*Koshoku Ichidai Onna*) by Saikaku Ihara, a widower whose realistic fiction reflects the sentiments and manners of Japan's masses.

Theater *Successful Kagekiyo* (*Shusse Kagekiyo*) by Japanese playwright Monzaemon Chikamatsu (Sugimori Nobumori), 33, who has become associated in the puppet theater at Osaka with the chanter Takemoto Gidayu. Together they have developed an advanced style and Chikamatsu has adapted a Japanese army play to the puppet theater.

The first Swedish theater opens at Stockholm.

Opera *Armide* 2/15 at Paris with music by Jean Baptiste Lully.

"Cordon Bleu" cookery has its origin in the Institut de Saint-Louis founded by Mme. de Maintenon for 250 daughters of the impoverished nobility, especially of titled army officers. Cookery is among the subjects taught and the school will become known for its cooking lessons and for the cordon bleu (blue ribbon) which the girls wear as part of their graduation costumes (*see* 1692; 1895).

Rum is deplored by Boston clergyman Increase Mather, 47, who has been president of Harvard College since last year and who writes, "It is an unhappy thing that in later years a Kind of Drink called Rum has been common among us. They that are poor, and sicked too, can for a penny or twopence make themselves drunk" (*see* 1655; 1688).

1687 *Philosophia naturalis principia mathematica* by Isaac Newton establishes laws of gravity and universal laws of motion. The *Principia* is published at his own expense by Edmund Halley who has inspired Newton to write the work (*see* Halley, 1705).

The Declaration of Liberty of Conscience issued by England's James II in April grants liberty of worship to all denominations in England and Scotland.

Ukrainian cossack Ivan Stepanovich Mazepa-Koledinsky, 43, visits Moscow, wins the favor of the prime minister Vasili Vasilievich Golitsyn, 44, and virtually purchases the hetmanship of the Cossacks July 25. Educated at the court of the late Polish king John II Casimir, Mazepa was caught in bed with a married Polish woman, her husband tied him naked to the back of a wild horse, Dnieperian Cossacks rescued him on the steppe, and he has risen to leadership among them (*see* 1704).

The Second Battle of Mohacs August 12 gives Charles of Lorraine a victory over the Ottoman Turks. The diet of Pressburg confers hereditary succession to the Hungarian throne upon the male line of Austria.

The Ottoman sultan Mohammed IV is deposed at age 46 after 43 years of at least nominal power. He is succeeded by his 45-year-old brother who will reign until 1691 as Suleiman III and whose minister Mustafa Kuprill will introduce many liberal reforms.

The Venetian general Francesco Morosini reconquers the Greek Peloponessus from the Ottoman Turks and even captures Athens.

The La Salle expedition on America's Gulf Coast is reduced to a band of 20 (*see* 1684). La Salle's men kill their leader and leave his body to the buzzards.

A Japanese law imposed January 28 by the shogun Sunayoshi forbids the killing of animals. Sunayoshi's only son has died, he has become a devout Buddhist, and beginning February 27 he forbids his people to eat fish, shellfish, or birds.

The University of Bologna is founded.

Traité de l'education des filles by French clergyman François de Salignac de la Mothe-Fénelon, 36, shows a rare insight into psychology. Fénelon was appointed at age 27 to head a Paris institution for women converts.

Poetry *The Hind and the Panther* by John Dryden: "By education most have been misled;/ So they believe, because they so were bred./ The priest continues what the nurse began,/ And thus the child imposes on the man"; *The Country Mouse and the City Mouse* by English poet Matthew Prior, 23, burlesques Dryden's *The Hind and the Panther* (above). Prior has written the poem in collaboration with Charles Montagu, 26.

Painting *The Chinese Convent* by Godfrey Kneller.

Paris Opéra director Jean Baptiste Lully dies March 22 at age 54 of blood poisoning after having stabbed himself in the foot with his long baton while conducting a "Te Deum" of thanksgiving for the king's recovery from an illness. Louis XIV has given Lully an unlimited budget and has at times appeared on stage himself to dance as Jupiter or Apollo with some of his top lords in operatic spectacles produced by Lully, spectacles that have included floating clouds, fireworks, volcanoes, and waterfalls.

The Temple of Athena on the Acropolis at Athens sustains severe damage as a Venetian shell scores a direct hit and explodes gunpowder stored in the temple by the Turks (*see* above).

1688 A "Glorious Revolution" ends nearly 4 years of Roman Catholic rule in England (*see* below) and the War of the League of Augsburg pits Protestant Europe and much of Catholic Europe against France's Louis XIV.

England's James II issues a proclamation in April ordering clergymen to read from their pulpits the king's Declaration of Indulgence of last year exempting Catholics and Dissenters from penal statutes. The birth of a son to James's queen Mary June 10 suggests the likelihood of a Catholic succession. England's Whig leaders send an invitation to the king's son-in-law William of Orange June 30, William issues a declaration to the English people September 21, he lands at Tor Bay November 5, and he moves to assume the throne with his wife Mary.

James II escapes to France December 23 and begins efforts to regain the throne (*see* Battle of the Boyne, 1690).

A French army invades the Palatinate and lays waste the countryside on orders from the minister of war François Michel Le Tellier, 47, marquis de Louvois.

William Penn bought vast territories from the Delaware Indians in the Great Treaty of Shackamaxon.

The revocation of the Edict of Nantes in 1685 has aroused Protestants against the French, the revocation has contributed to the success of William of Orange (above), and it has led to the formation of the League of Augsburg last year.

Lord Baltimore loses control of the Maryland colony as a result of the Glorious Revolution in England (above; see 1632; 1715).

French Huguenot refugees arrive in South Africa where they will strengthen the Dutch settlement founded in 1652.

English landowners seize the opportunity of the Revolution (above) to enact a bounty on the export of grain, an act that will increase domestic prices of grain (and of food) for the next few years.

Lloyds of London has its beginnings in a society to write marine insurance formed by merchants and sea captains who gather at Edward Lloyds's coffeehouse near the Thames. Lloyds encourages the underwriters by providing quill pens, ink, paper, and shipping information and the term "underwriting" will derive from his patrons' practice of writing their names, one beneath the other, at the bottom of each policy, with each man writing the amount he will insure until the full amount is subscribed (see 1870).

Venice's Ponte de tre Archi is completed across the Cannaregio Canal.

Nonfiction *Les Caractères de Théophraste, traduits du grec, avec les caractères et les Moeurs de ce Siècle* by French moralist-satirist Jean de La Bruyère, 43, whose portraits and aphorisms point out the arrogance and immorality of France's stupid ruling class. La Bruyère cries out against the social injustice that prevails; Bernard de Fontenelle defends evolution in the arts in *Digression sur les anciens et les modernes*.

Fiction *Oroonoko* by English novelist Aphra Behn, 48, who traveled to Surinam as a child, returned in 1658, married a London merchant named Behn, was sent to the Netherlands as an English spy, was never paid for her services, and served time in debtors' prison before starting a writing career which began with ribald stage comedies. Her novel introduces the figure of the noble savage.

Theater *The Squire of Alsatia* by Thomas Shadwell in May at London's Drury Lane Theatre. Shadwell has adopted the Terence comedy *Adelphi* of 160 B.C. and his play gives actress Anne Bracegirdle, 25, her stage debut.

Breadfruit (*Artocarpus communis*) is found growing on the Pacific island of Guam by English navigator-privateer-explorer William Dampier (see 1697; Bligh, 1787).

1689 The War of the League of Augsburg against France's Louis XIV widens as England's new king William III forms a Grand Alliance May 12 with the Dutch and with the League that Savoy joined 2 years ago.

The War of the League of Augsburg (above) begins the involvement of the Dutch Republic in a series of land wars that will cause the Dutch to neglect their naval strength and thus facilitate English domination of the high seas.

Scotland's Convention of Estates meets in April at the summoning of the prince of Orange, it declares that James VII has forfeited the Scottish Crown and offers it to William and Mary who accept, and the convention is converted into a parliament in June. Scottish Episcopalians form a Jacobite party to prevent the threatened abolition of episcopacy, they hold out at Edinburgh Castle until forced to surrender June 13, the 40-year-old Viscount Dundee John Graham of Claverhouse collects 3,000 men to oppose William and Mary, the Whig general Hugh Mackay is swept back into Killiecrankie Pass July 27 and loses nearly half his men, the Bonny Dundee gains a victory, but he is killed later in the day and the danger of a Jacobite restoration is ended (see 1707).

Russia's Regent and Czarina Sophia Alekseevna, 32, is deposed following exposure of a conspiracy to seize her 17-year-old half-brother Peter who is crowned czar in September and begins a reign of more than 35 years. The new czar was forced into a marriage January 27 with the beautiful but stupid Eudoxia Lopukhina but the marriage collapses by year's end as Peter devotes himself to sailing, shipbuilding, drilling, and mock battles while leaving administrative duties to others (see 1697).

The Treaty of Nerchinsk ends the first conflict between Russia and China. The Russians accept the advice of Jesuit negotiator Jean-François Gerbillon and they withdraw from territories their pioneers have occupied in the Amur region (see 1637).

King William's War begins in North America as an outgrowth of the War of the League of Augsburg (above).

Bostonians revolt at news of James II's flight from England, they restore charter government after imprisoning Sir Edmund Andros, but New York proclaims William and Mary the rightful monarchs of England and her colonies.

Connecticut's Charter Oak gets its name as representatives of William III try to take back the colonial charter granted by Charles II in 1662. Colonists hide the charter at Hartford in a centuries-old oak that will have a circumference of 33 feet when it is blown down in 1856.

France's Louis XIV has silver furniture at Versailles melted down to pay the cost of his war with the League of Augsburg (above).

Indians wipe out the colony at the mouth of the Mississippi River founded by the late sieur de La Salle (*see* 1687).

A smallpox epidemic in the Massachusetts colony kills more than a thousand in 12 months.

A Toleration Act excuses England's Nonconformists from church attendance but Dissenters continue to be persecuted for such reasons as non-payment of tithes (*see* 1662).

An Irish peasants' revolt is suppressed by William and Mary.

Nonfiction *Table-Talk*, a compilation of statements recorded by the secretary of the late English jurist-antiquary John Selden who died in 1654 at age 70: "Preachers say, 'Do as I say, not as I do.' But if a physician had the same disease upon him that I have, and he should bid me do one thing and he do quite another, could I believe him?" "While you are upon earth, enjoy the good things that are here"; "Old friends are best. King James used to call for his old shoes; they were easiest for his feet"; "No man is the wiser for his learning."

Painting *The Avenue, Middelharnis* by Meyndert Hobbema.

Theater *Esther* by Jean Racine 1/26 at Madame de Maintenon's School for Young Ladies at Saint-Cyr; *Bury Fair* by Thomas Shadwell in April at London's Drury Lane Theatre; *Don Sebastian, King of Portugal* by John Dryden in October at London's Drury Lane Theatre.

Opera *Dido and Aeneas* 12/30 at the Chelsea boarding school for girls operated by English dancing master Joseph Priest, with music by English composer Henry Purcell, 30, libretto by Irish-born poet Nahum Tate, 37.

1690 The Battle of Beachy Head June 30 gives the French a triumph over an English fleet commanded by Admiral Arthur Herbert, 43, earl of Torrington, who will be acquitted by a court martial of charges that he held back.

The Battle of Fleurus gives Louis XIV's marshal François Henri de Montmorency-Bouteville, 62, duc de Luxembourg, a victory over the prince of Waldeck.

The Battle of the Boyne July 1 completes the Protestant conquest of Ireland as England's William III defeats the Catholic pretender James II and his French supporters. James flees back to France, Dublin and Waterford fall to the Protestant English, but Limerick resists and the Irish Jacobite Patrick Sarsfield, earl of Lucan, forces William to lift his siege of Limerick.

Spain and Savoy (Sardinia) join the League of Augsburg against France's Louis XIV.

Ottoman forces drive the Austrians out of Bulgaria, Serbia, and Transylvania, they retake Belgrade, and they force the Serbs to flee into southern Hungary.

Two Treatises of Civil Government by English philosopher John Locke, 57, present a theory of limited monarchy, a social contract that will greatly influence the future course of monarchical government: "The liberty of man in society is to be under no other legislative power but that established by consent in the commonwealth, nor under the domination of any will, or restraint of any law, but what that legislative shall enact according to the trust put in it."

Slaves on Jamaican sugar estates reach an estimated total of 40,000 (*see* 1789; 1820).

The city of Calcutta is founded by the East India Company's Job Charnock (*see* 1686; 1756; earthquake, 1737).

Commodity futures trading has its beginnings in Japan where merchants trade rice receipts.

The paper mill put up at Germantown in the Pennsylvania colony is the first in America. Mennonite clergyman William Rittenhouse, 46, has been in Pennsylvania for 2 years and has organized a paper manufacturing company (*see* Robert, 1798).

Public Occurrences Both Foreign and Domestick begins publication at Boston but British authorities have forbidden publication of anything without authority from the Crown, they suppress local printer Benjamin Harris's newspaper after one day, and they destroy all undistributed copies (*see* 1704).

"An Essay Concerning Human Understanding" by John Locke (above) tries to resolve the question of what human understanding is and is not capable of dealing with. Locke returned to England early last year after a self-imposed exile of nearly 6 years in Holland, he has become commissioner of appeal following the Glorious Revolution of 1688, and his essay is the fruit of 17 years' effort.

Painting *The Mill* by Meindert Hobbema; David Teniers the Younger dies at Brussels April 25 at 79.

Theater *Amphitryon, or The Two Socia's* by John Dryden in October at London's Drury Lane Theatre.

Nantucket colonists launch an offshore whaling industry. They have sent to the mainland for Cape Cod shipwright-whaler Ichabod Paddock who has set up watch towers and has instructed the islanders (*see* 1659; 1712).

1690 (cont.) Dutch mariners smuggle coffee plants out of the Arab port of Mocha. They plant some in their Java colony and send others to the botanical gardens at Amsterdam (see 1713).

1691 The Battle of Aughrim July 12 gives William and Mary's Dutch-born general Godert de Ginkel, 47, a victory over Ireland's earl of Lucan Patrick Sarsfield and his French allies. General de Ginkel lays siege once again to Limerick which surrenders October 3. The Treaty of Limerick which ends the Irish rebellion grants free transportation to France for all Irish officers and men who wish it (the Irish Brigade will play a prominent role in French military history), and it promises religious freedom to Irish Catholics (but see 1695).

The Battle of Szcelankemen August 19 gives Louis of Baden a great victory over the Ottoman Turks. Louis has continued the fight abandoned by the Austrians, who have been sidetracked by their war with France as members of the League of Augsburg. The grand vizier Zade Mustafa Kuprili, 54, dies in the battle that will lead to the expulsion of the Turks from Hungary.

The Ottoman sultan Suleiman III dies at age 50 as his troops suffer reverses in the Morea (above). Suleiman has entrusted the government to his minister Mustafa Kuprili (above) and is succeeded after a 4-year reign by his 49-year-old brother who will reign until 1695 as Ahmed II.

The Massachusetts colony receives a new charter that gives it all North American territories north to the St. Lawrence River including the Plymouth colony, Maine, and Nova Scotia. The new governor Sir William Phips, 40, is vested with power to summon and dissolve the general court, to appoint military and judicial officers, and to veto acts of the legislature.

The Massachusetts colony (above) extends religious liberty to all except Catholics.

Japanese prospectors discover a copper and silver mine that will make Osaka's Sumitomo family one of the country's dominant financial powers.

Aelbert Jacobsz Cuyp dies at his native Dordrecht in November at age 71.

Theater *Athaliah* (*Athalie*) by Jean Racine in February at Mme. de Maintenon's School for Young Ladies at Saint-Cyr, with students playing the roles.

Opera *King Arthur, or The British Worthy* in March at London's Dorset Garden Theatre, with a libretto by John Dryden, music by Henry Purcell.

German immigrant farmers in the Pennsylvania colony choose heavily wooded lands with clay loams in preference to the light, sandy uplands favored by the English. While the English girdle trees to kill them, and then farm among the stumps, the Germans clear their land completely and plow deeply. Instead of planting tobacco, the Germans will stick to wheat, and instead of letting their stock roam freely they

will build barns before building houses as they populate Maryland, Virginia, and other colonies (see 1683; 1707; 1729; 1734).

1692 The Massacre of Glencoe February 13 enrages Scotland with its treachery and will lead to years of feuding in the highlands. Ian MacDonald, chieftain of the MacDonald clan at Glencoe, has taken an oath of allegiance January 6 to England's William III but William's agent John Dalrymple, 44, earl of Stair, has suppressed news of the oath and has conspired against MacDonald with Archibald Argyll, 41, and with John Campbell, 57, first earl of Breadalbane. A troop of soldiers whose ranks include many members of the rival Campbell clan has accepted the hospitality of the MacDonald clan at Glencoe, the Campbells have risen at a signal early in the morning, and they kill some 36 of the MacDonalds including MacIan.

The Battle of La Hogue May 29 costs France 15 ships and Louis XIV's military advisers persuade him that great fleets are a waste of money. France will avenge her loss next year but will leave England and the Dutch to dispute supremacy of the seas.

The Battle of Steinkirk (Steenkirken) July 24 gives France's duc de Luxembourg a victory over England's William III.

William Penn is deprived of his proprietorship by England's William and Mary. New York Governor Benjamin Fletcher is commissioned governor of Pennsylvania.

New Hampshire is made a royal colony once again.

Accusations of witchcraft by English-American clergyman Samuel Parris, 39, result in dozens of alleged witches being brought to trial at Salem in the Massachusetts colony. Nineteen will be hanged and one pressed to death in the next 2 years, many of them on the testimony of 12-year-old Anne Putnam (see 1664; 1700).

Scots-American sea captain William Kidd, 38, marries New York widow Sara Oart and increases his holdings by £155 14s (see 1698; 1701).

Jamaica in the West Indies has a violent earthquake. Port Royal, stronghold of Spanish Main buccaneers, is shattered and two-thirds of the pirate city falls into the sea with fortunes in booty.

A calculating machine invented by German philosopher-mathematician Gottfried Wilhelm von Leibniz, 45, multiplies by repeated addition and divides as well as doing the adding and subtracting performed by the 1642 Blaise Pascal machine. Leibniz employs a stepped drum to mechanize the calculation of trigonometric and astronomical tables (see Babbage, 1833).

The French school established by Mme. de Maintenon in 1686 becomes a convent and will remain such until 1789 (see Cordon Bleu Cooking School, 1895).

Aesop's Fables is published at London. English journalist Sir Roger L'Estrange, 76, has translated stories said to have originated with an ugly, deformed

Greek slave of the 6th century B.C. although some of the fables will be traced to earlier literature.

"Adeste Fidelis" is composed as a Christmas carol by English clergyman John Reading. An English version beginning "Oh Come All Ye Faithful" will be published in 1841 with lyrics by another clergyman.

England's two leading provincial towns of Bristol and Norwich have some 30,000 inhabitants each. York and Exeter are the only other towns with as many as 10,000, but London has close to 550,000 and rivals Paris as a center of population.

England's total population approaches 6 million of which half are farm workers in a country that is still half fen, heath, and forest.

1693 French naval forces defeat an Anglo-Dutch fleet off Cape St. Vincent May 26 to 27. The French commander Anne Hilarion de Cotentin, 50, Comte de Tourville, avenges the defeat he suffered last year in the Battle of La Hogue and gains another victory June 30 at the Battle of Lagos off Portugal.

The Battle of Neerwinden July 29 gives the duc de Luxembourg another victory over the English, but William III remains in the field as the French sack Heidelberg for a second time.

Swiss Protestant cantons agree to supply mercenary troops to the Dutch after Catholic cantons have supplied mercenaries for Louis XIV to throw against the Dutch. The Catholic cantons respond by supplying mercenaries to the Spanish, a move the Protestant cantons will counter by supplying mercenaries to the English as well as to the Dutch.

Scotland's clan Macgregor mourns the death of its chief Gregor Macgregor and acknowledges his 22-year-old son-in-law Rob Roy (so called because of his red hair) as the new chief. Rob Roy obtains control of lands from Loch Lomond to the Braes of Balquihidder (*see* 1712).

William III initiates England's national debt by borrowing £1 million on annuities at an interest rate of 10 percent (*see* Bank of England, 1694).

The Massachusetts colony reduces maximum legal interest rates to 6 percent, down from 8 in 1641.

English naturalist John Ray tries to classify different animal species into groups largely according to their toes and teeth (*see* Linnaeus, 1737).

The College of William and Mary is founded by royal charter in the Virginia colony at Middle Plantation, later to be called Williamsburg (*see* 1699). The college will award its first baccalaureates in 1770 (*see* Phi Beta Kappa, 1776).

The Wonders of the Invisible World by Boston Congregationalist minister Cotton Mather analyzes with scientific detachment the work of devils among the Salem witches (*see* 1684; 1692; 1702).

Theater *The Old Batchelour* by English playwright William Congreve, 23, in March at London's Drury

Lane Theatre: "Oh thou delicious, damned, dear, destructive Woman!" (III, ii); "Thus grief still treads upon the heels of pleasure,/ Marry'd in haste, we may repent at leisure" (V, iii); "Courtship [is] to marriage, as a very witty prologue to a very dull play" (V, x); *The Double Dealer* by William Congreve in October at London's Drury Lane Theatre: "There is nothing more unbecoming a man of quality than to laugh; Jesu, 'tis such a vulgar expression of the passion" (I, iv); "Why should I disparage my parts by thinking what to say? None but dull rogues think" (IV, ii).

French composer François Couperin, 25, is named organist du roi and begins a notable career of producing clavecin works and chamber music.

The Amish (or Amish Mennonite) sect has its beginnings in a schism from the Mennonite church in Switzerland led by Swiss Mennonite bishop Jacob Amman whose followers observe strict discipline marked by opposition to change in dress or way of life (*see* 1537).

Russia's Church of the Intercession of the Holy Virgin is completed at Fili near Moscow.

A November earthquake in the Italian province of Catania kills 60,000.

1694 The Bank of England chartered July 27 opens in London's Threadneedle Street to compete with small private banks that have grown out of the city's widely distrusted goldsmiths. A company of merchants headed by Scots financier William Paterson, 36, has received the charter in return for loaning the hard-pressed government £1.2 million, the government agrees to accept Bank of England notes in payment of taxes, and the new joint stock company will soon control the nation's money supply by setting the bank rate (discount rate) for commercial banks (*see* 1708; Bank of Amsterdam, 1609).

Parliament doubles the English salt tax to raise money for the continuing war with France.

The Royal Navy bombards Dieppe, Le Havre, and Dunkirk but the French turn back an attack on Brest despite having been weakened by hunger and disease (*see* below).

The Triennial Bill passed by Parliament provides for new English Parliamentary elections to be held every third year. The Place Bill prevents officers of the Crown from sitting in the House of Commons.

Persia's Shah Suleiman dies after a dissolute reign of 27 years. His 19-year-old son Husein succeeds to the throne and will reign until 1722.

Disease epidemics sweep through France's lower classes and take a heavy toll among people weakened by hunger and exhaustion.

England's press censorship ends with the expiration of the Licensing Act which is not renewed for 1695.

Painting *Hampton Court Beauties* by Sir Godfrey Kneller. Japanese *ukiyo-e* painter Morinobu Hishikawa dies at age 76 after a career in which he

1694 (cont.) has pioneered the art of making prints that depict the everyday life of the people.

Moravia's Frain Castle is completed with an oval Hall of the Ancestors after 6 years of construction by Austrian architect Johann Bernhard Fischer von Erlach, 38.

"All France is nothing more than a vast poorhouse, desolate and without food," writes François de Salignac de La Mothe-Fénelon, tutor of the grandson of Louis XIV.

French government economic controls prevent the free flow of food into famine districts, and speculators corner grain supplies, adding artificial scarcity to the natural famine that grips the country.

1695 The Royal Bank of Scotland is founded.

The Company of Scotland trading to Africa and the Indies is created by an act of the Scottish Parliament. Bank of England founder William Paterson has had a falling out with his colleagues and has returned to Edinburgh, he has proposed a scheme to establish a settlement on the Isthmus of Darien (Panama) and "thus hold the key of the commerce of the world," but the project will end in disaster (*see* 1698; Paterson, 1694).

A nation's wealth depends not on how much money she possesses but on what she produces and exchanges, writes French economist Pierre Le Pesant, 49, Sieur de Boisguilbert, in *Le Detail de la France, la cause de la diminution de ses biens, et la facilité du remede....* Boisguilbert describes the ruin that the burdensome taxes of the late Jean Baptiste Colbert have brought to all classes of society and says France could regain her prosperity by abandoning war and switching from a policy of mercantilist protection to one of free enterprise based on agriculture (*see* Sully, 1598; Smith, 1776).

France's Marshal Luxembourg dies January 4 at age 66 as the War of the League of Augsburg continues. The duc de Villeroi François de Neufville, 51, succeeds to the command of French forces in the Low Countries but will prove far less capable.

England's William III recaptures Namur from the French in September.

Epsom salts (magnesium sulfate) are isolated from springs in the North Downs by English botanist Nehemiah Grew, 54, whose four-volume *The Anatomy of Plants* in 1682 made the first observations of sex in plants.

The University of Berlin is founded.

England ends press censorship.

Fiction *Den Vermakelyken Avanturier* by Dutch physician-novelist Nicolaas Heinsius, 39, is a picaresque novel modeled on a Spanish novel.

Theater *Love for Love* by William Congreve 4/30 at the Lincoln's Inn Fields Theatre, London: "You must not kiss and tell" (II).

England imposes a window tax that will influence residential architecture until 1851.

France's duc de Montaussier invents the soup ladle but guests at most tables continue to dip into a common tureen with their own wooden or pewter spoons, an advance over the two-handled porringer passed round the table to be sipped from in turn.

1696 Parliament suspends the Habeas Corpus Act of 1679 following discovery of Sir George Barclay's plot to assassinate William III. Barclay is hanged along with Roman Catholic Jacobite priest Robert Charnock, 33, and the authorities also arrest Sir John Fenwick, 51, who will be hanged early next year, the last Englishman to be condemned by a bill of attainder. The Trials for Treason Act passed by Parliament requires two witnesses to prove an act of treason.

Poland's John III Sobieski dies June 17 at age 72 after a 20-year reign with the last 12 years full of disaster and humiliation.

Russian forces sent by Peter I defeat Ottoman defenders July 28 to capture the fortress that commands the Sea of Azov and the Black Sea. Other Russian troops conquer Kamchatka.

Spain establishes a Florida colony at Pensacola as a defense against the French.

The Navigation Act passed by Parliament April 10 forbids England's American colonists to export directly to Scotland or Ireland (*see* 1663; 1699).

Parliament reforms English coinage at the instigation of John Locke and Isaac Newton.

The first English property insurance company is founded.

England's Board of Trade and Plantations is founded.

English journeymen hatters strike for higher wages and better working conditions.

Lloyd's News begins publication three times a week at London under the direction of coffeehouse keeper Edward Lloyd (*see* 1688).

Theater *Love's Last Shift, or The Fool in Fashion* by English playwright Colley Cibber, 24, in January at London's Royal Theatre in Drury Lane: "One had as good be out of the world as out of the fashion"; *The Relapse, or Virtue in Danger* by English playwright John Vanbrugh, 32, 11/21 at London's Drury Lane Theatre; *The Gambler* (*Le joueur*) by French playwright Jean-François Regnard, 41, 12/19 at the Comédie-Française, Paris; *Woman's Wit, or The Lady in Fashion* by Colley Cibber in December at London's Drury Lane Theatre.

Hymn "While Shepherds Watched Their Flocks by Night" by Nahum Tate and his collaborator Nicholas Brady, 37, is published in their *New Version of the Psalms of David*.

Grapefruit cultivation in America has its origin in seeds from the Polynesian pomelo tree (*Citrus grandis*) introduced into Barbados by an English sea captain named Shaddock. A sweeter and thinner mutation of the fruit, or a botanist's development of the "shaddock," will be called grapefruit (*see* Lunan, 1814).

Green peas create a sensation at the French court (*see* 1555). Françoise d'Aubigne, Madame Maintenon, writes from Marly that "impatience to eat [peas], the pleasure of having eaten them, and the anticipation of eating them again are the three subjects I have heard very thoroughly dealt with. . . . Some women, having supped, and supped well at the King's table, have peas waiting for them in their rooms to eat before going to bed" (now 61, the king's former mistress has been secretly married to Louis since 1685).

A pioneer English statistician calculates that England's population will reach a high of 22 million in 3500 A.D. "in case the world should last so long."

1697 Sweden's Charles XI dies April 5 at age 40 after a brilliant 37-year reign. He is succeeded by his 14-year old son who will reign as Charles XII until 1718 and whose deeds will eclipse those of his father.

The Russian czar Peter visits Holland, France, and England incognito, the first Russian sovereign to venture abroad. A hulking giant of 25 who towers well over 6 feet in an age when few men approach that height, Peter tastes the fruits of Western civilization and determines to Westernize Russia.

Poland elects the elector of Saxony Frederick Augustus I, 27, to succeed the late John III Sobieski, he is crowned in September, and he begins a reign as Augustus II that will continue until his death in 1733.

The Battle of Zenta September 11 gives Eugene of Savoy a victory over the Ottoman Turks.

The Treaty of Ryswick September 30 ends the 11-year-old War of the League of Augsburg. France restores to Spain all conquests made since the Treaty of Nijmegen in 1679, the French East India Company regains the Indian pepper port of Pondichery on condition that the Dutch retain commercial privileges.

France recognizes William III as king of England in the treaty of Ryswick (above) with William's sister-in-law Anne as heiress presumptive.

Spain cedes the western third of Hispaniola (Haiti) to France under terms of the Treaty of Ryswick (above) (*see* slave revolt, 1794).

Chinese forces conquer western Mongolia.

Voyage Round the World, published from the journals of William Dampier, is the first general survey of the Pacific by an Englishman in a century (*see* breadfruit, 1688; Cavendish, 1586).

France attempts to colonize West Africa.

Gold is discovered in Portugal's Brazilian colony. The extensive deposits bring thousands of prospectors from coastal towns into the Minas Gerais (General Mines) area and attract immigrants from Portugal, many of whom will die of disease, hardship, and starvation (*see* diamonds, 1729).

New York colonist Stephen (Stephanus) Van Cortlandt receives the grant of a manor north of the city (*see* Fraunce's Tavern, 1730).

Nonfiction "An Essay upon Projects" by English journalist Daniel Defoe, 38, who suggests such innovations as an income tax, insurance, road improvements, and an insane asylum.

Poetry *Mother Goose Tales (Contes de ma mère l'oie)* by French author Charles Perrault, 69, whose tales are in many cases based on actual events. Perrault was secretary to France's finance minister Jean Baptiste Colbert from 1664 until 1683.

Theater *The Mourning Bride* by William Congreve 2/20 at the Lincoln's Inn Fields Theatre, London, with Anne Bracegirdle, now 34, creating the role of Almeria: "Music hath charms to soothe a savage breast,/ To soften rocks, or bend a knotted oak" (I, i); "Heav'n has no rage, like love to hatred turn'd,/ Nor hell a fury like a woman scorn'd" (III, viii); *The Provoked Wife* by John Vanbrugh in May at the Lincoln's Inn Fields Theatre, London.

Anthem "I Was Glad When They Said" by John Blow for the opening of Christopher Wren's Choir of St. Paul's Cathedral, London.

The Russian czar Peter (above) permits open sale and use of tobacco and imposes taxes to give the state a share in the profits from the lucrative trade (*see* Alexis, 1648).

Vienna's Palace of Prince Eugene is completed by J. B. Fischer von Erlach who will enlarge it between 1707 and 1710.

1698 A crude steam-powered "miner's friend" devised by English engineer Thomas Savery, 48, to pump water out of coal mines pioneers the steam engine (*see* Newcomen, 1705; Watt, 1765).

Parliament opens the slave trade to British merchants who will in some cases carry on a triangular trade from New England to Africa to the Caribbean Islands to New England. The merchant vessels will carry New England rum to African slavers, African slaves on "the middle passage" to the West Indies, and West Indian sugar and molasses to New England for the rum distilleries.

Arab forces expel the Portuguese from Africa's East Coast.

A Treaty of Partition signed by the European powers October 11 attempts to deal with the question of the Spanish succession. Spain's Carlos II is childless and the Spanish house of Hapsburg is doomed (*see* 1700).

Discourses Concerning Government by the late English republican leader Algernon Sidney will be influential in encouraging liberal provisions in various constitutions (*see* 1683).

1698 (cont.) The London Stock Exchange is founded. It is the world's first true stock exchange (*see* New York, 1792; 1825).

The General Society (New East India Trading Company) is founded at London.

The first ships of the Company of Scotland trading to Africa and the Indies sail from Leith July 26 with 1,200 pioneers who include William Paterson and his wife and child (*see* 1695). They arrive November 4 at Darien having lost only 15 men en route, they call the country New Caledonia, they choose a well-defended spot with a good harbor midway between the Spanish strongholds Porto Bello and Cartagena, but lack of provisions, sickness, and anarchy will soon reduce the settlers to misery (*see* 1699).

Captain Kidd seizes the Armenian vessel *Auedagh Merchant*, he captures other prizes, and he sails for the West Indies where he will find that he has been proclaimed a pirate (*see* 1692). Commissioned in 1696 to head an expedition against pirates in the Indian Ocean, Kidd took his first prizes off Madagascar last year, he will surrender to New England authorities next year on the promise of a pardon (but *see* 1701).

Architect Jules Hardouin-Mansart lays out the Place Vendôme at Paris with a statue of Louis XIV in the center (*see* 1810).

London's Whitehall Palace burns down except for the Banqueting Hall built by Inigo Jones in 1622.

Sunflowers introduced by the Russian czar Peter on his return from the West will be the leading source of oilseeds in Russia and Eastern Europe (*see* 1510).

Two-thirds of the New York colony's population remains on Long Island and near the mouth of the Hudson as the Iroquois and other hostile tribes block expansion to the north and west.

1699 William Dampier sails to the Pacific in the superannuated 290-ton ship *Roebuck* on the first Pacific expedition to be fitted out by the Admiralty, he explores the west coast of Australia and finds it disappointing, and he rounds the northern coast of New Guinea to discover a large island which he names New Britain (it will later prove to be three adjoining islands; *see* 1697; Cook, 1770).

French-Canadian explorer Pierre Lemoyne, 38, Sieur d'Iberville, pioneers settlement of the North American Gulf Coast with his brother Jean Baptiste Lemoyne, 19, Sieur de Bienville. They land on Dauphin Island at the mouth of Mobile Bay on their way to establish French colonies for Louis XIV in the Mississippi Delta (*see* Mobile, 1702).

Cahokia is founded by French priests of the Seminary of Foreign Missions. It is the first permanent settlement in the Illinois wilderness (*see* 1717).

The Virginia colony moves its capital to Middle Plantation (Williamsburg). A fire last year drove the colonists out of Jamestown and the 66-year-old settlement at Middle Plantation will remain the Virginia capital of Williamsburg until 1779 (*see* College of William and Mary, 1693).

Disease ravages the Darien colony of the Company of Scotland trading to Africa and the Indies, William Paterson loses his wife and child, he is reduced by illness to looking "more like a skeleton than a man," he is carried weak and protesting aboard ship in June, the hapless survivors embark in three ships for home, they reach England after a stormy passage in December, two shiploads of reinforcements that left England in May and four that left in August come to grief when they encounter superior Spanish forces at Darien, the Spanish force them to capitulate, and few of the Scotsmen will ever reach home (*see* 1698).

The Treaty of Karlowitz January 26 ends a 17-year struggle against the Turks who are obliged to give up all of Hungary except for the Banat of Temesvar to Austria which also obtains Transylvania, Croatia, and Slavonia. Poland regains Podolia and the Turkish part of the Ukraine, Venice receives the Morea and most of Dalmatia.

Denmark and Russia sign a mutual defense pact.

The Treaty of Preobrazhenskoe provides for the partition of the Swedish Empire among Denmark, Russia, Poland, and Saxony.

Denmark's Christian V dies in a hunting accident August 25 at age 53. He is succeeded by his 28-year-old son who will reign until 1730 as Frederick IV.

The Woolens Act passed by Parliament under pressure from the English wool lobby forbids any American colony to export wool, wool yarn, or wool cloth "to any place whatsoever." The act works a certain hardship on rural New Englanders but while nearly every New England family keeps sheep and has a spinning wheel, few Americans are eager to enter the woolen manufacturing industry.

Yellow fever epidemics kill 150 at Charleston and 220 at Philadelphia.

The Massachusetts colony passes a law designed to prevent the spread of infectious diseases.

Theater *Xerxes* by Colley Cibber in February at London's Drury Lane Theatre; *The Tragical History of King Richard III* by Colley Cibber in December at London's Drury Lane Theatre, an adaptation of the Shakespeare play of 1592.

Stockholm's Drottningholm Palace is completed in French Renaissance style to provide a summer residence for the royal family on the island of Lovo in Lake Malar.

1700 The Gregorian calendar of 1582 is adopted by the German Protestant states by order of the Diet of Regensburg but England and her colonies continue to use the Old Style Julian calendar as do many other countries (*see* 1752).

The Great Northern War begins in Europe as Russia, Poland, and Denmark join forces to oppose Swedish

Witch trials at Salem in the Massachusetts colony exposed the superstition and intolerance of the Puritans.

supremacy in the Baltic. Danish troops invade Schleswig and Saxon troops invade Livonia, but Sweden's 18-year-old Charles XII surprises the Danes by landing troops in Zeeland. Threatening Copenhagen, he forces Denmark to sign the Treaty of Travendal August 18 and to remove herself from the alliance against Sweden.

Charles lands 8,000 Swedish troops at Narva in Ingermanland November 30 and decisively defeats a Russian force that had been besieging that town.

Spain's Carlos II dies November 1 at age 39 after naming as his heir Philip of Anjou, 17, grandson of France's Louis XIV. The first Bourbon king of Spain ascends the throne as Philip V to begin a 46-year

reign—and to begin a War of the Spanish Succession (see 1701).

Smallpox will kill an estimated 60 million Europeans in the century ahead.

The Selling of Joseph by Boston jurist Samuel Sewall, 48, condemns the selling of slaves. Sewell 3 years ago made public confession of error and guilt for his part in condemning to execution 19 alleged witches at Salem in 1692.

Poetry "Annie Laurie" by Scottish poet William Douglas, 28, whose song is addressed to Anne, daughter of Sir Robert Laurie of the Maxwellton family: "Maxwellton's braes are bonnie/ . . . and for bonnie Annie Laurie/ I'd lay me down an' dee"; (see 1838); *Hans Carvel* by Matthew Prior who writes, "What if to Spells I had Resource?/ 'Tis but to hinder something Worse./ The End justifies the Means."

Theater *The Way of the World* by William Congreve in March at the Lincoln's Inn Fields Theatre, London: "I like her with all her faults; nay, like her for her faults" (I, iii); "'Tis better to be left/ Than never to have loved" (II); *The Ambitious Stepmother* by English playwright Nicholas Rowe, 27 in December at the Lincoln's Inn Fields Theatre; *Love Makes a Man, or The Fop's Fortune* by Colley Cibber 12/13 at London's Drury Lane Theatre.

Boston ships 50,000 quintals of dried codfish to market, the best of it to Bilbao, Lisbon, and Oporto. The refuse is shipped to the West Indies for sale to slaveowners.

London's population reaches 550,000, up from 450,000 in 1660. Despite the heavy losses to plague in 1665 and the destruction by fire of much of the city in 1666, London is the largest city in Europe.

England's American colonies have an estimated population of 262,000 with 12,000 each in Boston and Philadelphia, 5,000 in New York (see 1765).

18th CENTURY

Piracy on the high seas brought infamy to Kidd, Teach, and others but was the basis of some great family fortunes.

1701 The first Prussian king crowns himself at Königsberg January 18 and begins a 12-year reign as Frederick I. The Holy Roman Emperor Leopold I has given the 42-year-old elector of Brandenburg Frederick III sanction to assume the monarchy in return for a promise of military aid.

The Great Northern War continues with a Saxon siege of Riga. Sweden's Charles XII relieves the city June 10 and proceeds to invade Poland, beginning a 6-year string of victories over Poland and Saxony.

The War of the Spanish Succession begins in Europe as Philip of Anjou gains recognition as king of Spain, especially in Castile, and the Holy Roman Emperor Leopold I moves to take over Spain's Dutch and Italian possessions (see 1700). Britain and Holland, fearful of having the France of Louis XIV joined with Spain, form a Grand Alliance with the emperor, and Eugene, prince of Savoy, joins the alliance September 7.

Louisiana becomes a province of France covering most of the area drained by the Mississippi, Missouri, and Ohio River (see 1763).

The Charter of Privileges gives Pennsylvania the most liberal government of all English colonies in America (see Penn, 1682).

Detroit has its origin in the French settlement of Fort Ponchartrain established on the strait between Lake Erie and Lake St. Clair by Sieur Antoine de la Mothe Cadillac, 43, who needs a fort to control the entrance to Lake Huron from Lake Erie and thus control trade with the Illinois country of Louisiana (above). The name Detroit will be based on the French word for strait.

Yale University has its beginnings in the Collegiate School established at Saybrook in the Connecticut colony (see Elihu Yale, 1718).

The University of Venice is founded.

Nonfiction *Hankampu* by Japanese historian Arai Hakuseki, 27, is a history of Japan's *daimyo* (feudal lords); *The Great Historical, Geographical, Genealogical, and Political Dictionary* by English clergyman Jeremy Collier is published in its first volumes.

Theater *Tamerlane* by Nicholas Rowe, in December at the Lincoln's Inn Fields Theatre, London; *The Funeral, or Grief A-la-mode* by English playwright-essayist Richard Steele, 27, in December at London's Drury Lane Theatre.

London Jews build a synagogue in Bevis Marks that will stand for more than two centuries (see 1657). The congregation consists entirely of Sephardic (Spanish and Portuguese) Jews (see 1723).

Pirate William Kidd goes to the gallows July 6. Seized at Boston in 1699, Kidd has been sent to England for trial, but the rope breaks twice before he is dispatched (see 1698).

A seed-planting drill invented by Berkshire farmer Jethro Tull, 27, sows three parallel rows of seeds at once and will increase crop yields by reducing seed waste (see 1782; Swift, 1726).

1702 England's William III dies March 8 at age 51 after falling from his horse and suffering a chill. He is succeeded by his sister-in-law Anne, 37, who will reign until 1714 as the last monarch of the House of Stuart.

The War of the Spanish Succession widens in Europe as the Grand Alliance declares war on France May 14. Queen Anne (above) names John Churchill, 52, husband of her court favorite Sarah, as captain-general of England's land forces and raises him from earl of Marlborough to duke of Marlborough December 14 after he has forced the surrender of Kaiserswerth on the Rhine in June, of Venlo on the Meuse in September, and of Liege October 29.

England's Sir George Rooke, 52, captures part of the Spanish treasure fleet at Vigo Bay in October after failing to take Cadiz. Rooke destroys the warships of France and Spain.

Warsaw and Cracow fall to Sweden's Charles XII who has invaded Poland in the Great Northern War that will be fought largely on Polish soil.

The 3-mile territorial sea zone is established by Dutch jurist Cornelius van Bynkershoek, 29, who rules that a nation's territory extends 3 miles offshore (*see* Grotius, 1609). Van Bynkershoek will be made a member of the Supreme Council of Holland, Zeeland, and West Friesland next year (*see* 1793).

East and West Jersey combine to form the English colony New Jersey (*see* 1665; 1676).

The Chusingura "Forty-Seven Ronin" incident December 14 stirs Japan as retainers of the late lord of Ako Asano Naganori kill Kira Yoshinaka. The 47 ronin (unemployed samurai) have followed Confucian ethic in avenging the death of their 62-year-old lord who was ordered to commit *seppuku* (ritual suicide) last year for fighting at Edo Castle but they have broken the law in killing the kinsman of the shogun and they will be ordered to commit *seppuku*.

Mobile, Alabama, has its beginnings in the Fort Louis settlement founded by the Lemoyne brothers (*see* 1699). First French settlement on the Gulf Coast, Mobile will take its name from that of the Mauvilla Indians who inhabit the region (*see* 1704).

A yellow fever epidemic kills 570 New Yorkers.

London's *Daily Courant* begins publication. It is the city's first daily newspaper but by the end of the century London will have 21 dailies.

Fire destroys important scientific papers at Sweden's great center of learning at Uppsala.

Magnalia Christi Americana by Cotton Mather is a well documented history of New England compiled to show that God is at work in the new land (*see* 1693; smallpox inoculation, 1721).

Japanese painter Korin Ogota, 41, unites the two imperial schools of Japanese painting, the Kano and the Yamato.

Theater *She Wou'd and She Wou'd Not, or The King Imposter* by Colley Cibber 11/26 at London's Drury Lane Theatre.

England's Queen Anne gives royal approval to horseracing and originates the sweepstakes idea of racing for cash prizes (*see* Ascot, 1711).

Salzburg's Church of the Holy Trinity is completed by J. B. Fischer von Erlach after 8 years of work.

1703 The Grand Alliance proclaims Austria's 18-year-old Archduke Charles king of Spain and he prepares to invade Catalonia as the War of the Spanish Succession continues. England's duke of Marlborough invades the Spanish Netherlands and takes Bonn, Huy, Limburg, and Guelders.

Bavarian forces invade the Tyrol but are repulsed.

Sweden's Charles XII defeats a Russian force at Pultusk April 21 and lays siege to Thorn as the Great Northern War continues.

St. Petersburg is founded May 1 by Russia's Peter I on reclaimed marshlands at the mouth of the Gulf of Finland. Peter makes the new city Russia's capital and will make it the nation's seat of power, turning Russia's focus to the West.

The Methuen Treaty between England and Portugal December 27 facilitates trade in English woolens and Portuguese wines, which come from vineyards in the Oporto area. English families own many of the vineyards and England will admit the wine at duties one-third lower than those demanded of French wines in return for Portugal's agreement to import all her woolens from England.

Daniel Defoe is pilloried and serves a brief prison term for last year's ironic pamphlet "The Shortest Way with Dissenters," which has outraged both Whigs and Tories.

Theater *The Fair Penitent* by Nicholas Rowe, in May at the Lincoln's Inn Fields Theatre, London, introduces Rowe's rakish seducer the "gay Lothario"; *The Lying Lover, or The Ladies' Friendship* by Richard Steele 12/2 at London's Drury Lane Theatre is based on the Corneille play *Le menteur* of 1643; *Sonezakishinju* by Monzaemon Chikamatsu at Osaka's Takemoto Theater (puppet show).

The great storm that strikes England November 26 to 27 destroys the Eddystone Lighthouse and kills thousands.

A Japanese earthquake and fire December 30 destroys Edo and kills an estimated 200,000. The country will have further catastrophes soon (*see* 1707).

1704 Thorn falls to Sweden's Charles XII after an 8-month siege in which he has lost only 50 men. Charles has his ambassador at Warsaw use bribery and intimidation to secure the election July 2 of Stanislas Leszczynski, 37, to replace the elector of Saxony Augustus II as king of Poland.

The Cossack hetman Mazepa helps Russia's Peter I in the Volhynian campaign as the Great Northern War continues.

Gibraltar (Jebel-al-Tarik) falls to English forces August 4 (*see* 1702); Admiral George Rooke wrests the rocky fortress from the Spanish, and the English will hold the entrance to the Mediterranean for more than 270 years.

The Battle of Blenheim (Blindheim, or Hochstadt) August 13 gives England's duke of Marlborough a stunning victory over the French-Bavarian-Prussian coalition. Supported by Eugene, prince of Savoy (whose realm is overrun in his absence by French forces under the duc de Vendôme), Marlborough himself leads the cavalry charge that breaks the enemy's resistance. He drives his foes into the Danube, hundreds drown, the allies sustain 4,500 casualties plus 7,500 wounded, the English lose 670 plus 1,500 wounded. Marlborough and Eugene take 11,000 prisoners including the French general Camille de Tallard, 52, with 24 battalions of infantry and 4 regiments of dragoons that include the

1704 (cont.) finest in the French army. The French and Bavarians lose 100 guns, and the French survivors retreat first to the Rhine, then to the Moselle.

Canadian Indians and French forces attack Deerfield in the Massachusetts colony February 29, killing 49, carrying off 112 captives, 40 of them under age 12.

The "Casette girls" arrive at Mobile on the Gulf Coast in quest of husbands. The 25 young French women carry small trunks (casettes) filled with dowry gifts from Louis XIV (*see* 1702).

America's first regular newspaper begins publication at Boston. The weekly *News-Letter* published by local postmaster John Campbell, 51, consists of a single 7 by 11½ inch sheet covered on both sides with news and rumors received from post riders, sea captains, and sailors (*see* 1690; Zenger, 1735).

Fiction *The Arabian Nights' Entertainment* translated from a 10th century work is published in Europe with tales of Sinbad and his search for spices (*see* Burton, 1888); *The Battle of the Books* by English satirist Jonathan Swift, 37, is a travesty on the controversy over ancient and modern learning; *A Tale of a Tub* by Jonathan Swift satirizes corruption in religion and learning.

London's Christ Church is completed by Sir Christopher Wren who has designed 52 London churches.

The "Casette girls" (above) will obtain seeds and will cultivate figs, garlic, herbs, lemons, mustard, olives, onions, oranges, peaches, pears, and strawberries on the Gulf Coast.

The "Casette girls" (above) will use okra obtained from African slaves to develop a cuisine that will expand the local fare of maize products, beans, sweet potatoes, and local game and seafood (*see* 1784).

1705 The Newcomen steam engine invented by English blacksmith Thomas Newcomen, 42, at Dartmouth will pave the way for an Industrial Revolution. Helped by John Calley (or Cawley), Newcomen uses a jet of cold water to condense steam entering a cylinder. He thus creates atmospheric pressure which drives a piston to produce power that will be used beginning in 1712 to pump water out of coal mines (*see* Savery, 1698; Darby, 1709; Watt, 1765).

England's Queen Anne confers knighthood on Isaac Newton, now 62.

Halley's Comet will receive that name on the basis of studies reported by English astronomer Edmund Halley, 49, who notes that comets observed in 1531, 1607, and 1682 followed roughly the same paths. Halley suggests that they were all the same comet and that it will reappear in 1758 (*see* 1066).

The Holy Roman Emperor Leopold I dies May 5 at age 54 after a 47-year reign. He is succeeded by his 26-year-old son who will reign until 1711 as Josef I.

Stanislas Leszczynski is crowned king of Poland September 24 to replace the deposed Augustus II, he concludes an alliance with Sweden's Charles XII, and he supplies Charles with some help against Russia's Peter I in the continuing Great Northern War.

The Austrian archduke Charles lands in Catalonia and English forces help him take Barcelona October 14 in the continuing War of the Spanish Succession. Sentiment against the French has been strong in Catalonia and Valencia; both support Charles's claim to the Spanish throne.

Factum de la France by the sieur de Boisguilbert proposes a single capitation tax—10 percent of the revenues on all property to be paid to the state (*see* 1695). The farmers oppose the idea of taxes and it finds little support from anyone (*see* George, 1879).

Theater *The Tender Husband, or The Accomplished Fool* by Richard Steele 4/23 at London's Drury Lane Theatre, is an adaptation of the 1667 Molière comedy *Le sicilian*; *The Mistake* by John Vanbrugh 10/27 at London's Haymarket Theatre; *The Confederacy* by John Vanbrugh 10/30 at London's Haymarket Theatre; *Ulysses* by Nicholas Rowe 11/23 at London's Haymarket Theatre; *Idomeneus* (Idomenee) by French playwright Prosper Jolyot, 31, sieur de Crebillion 12/29 at the Comédie Française, Paris.

Opera *Almira* 1/8 at Hamburg, with music by German composer George Frideric Handel, 20.

First performances *St. John Passion* by George Frideric Handel.

Blenheim Palace goes up at Woodstock in Oxfordshire for the duke of Marlborough. Queen Anne has commissioned London playwright John Vanbrugh (above) to design the palace as a tribute to the victor of last year's great battle; Vanbrugh turns from drama to architecture. He gets a hand from architect Nicholas Hawksmoor, 44, who has been an aide to Christopher Wren.

Famine strikes France causing widespread distress that will continue for years.

1706 The Battle of Ramillies May 23 gives England's duke of Marlborough a victory over a French army commanded by the duc de Villeroi. Marlborough's triumph is followed by the submission of Brussels, Antwerp, Ghent, Ostend, and other major cities in the continuing War of the Spanish Succession.

Portuguese forces invade Spain in June, they install the Austrian Archduke Charles as king at Madrid, but Philip V drives them out in October.

Savoy's Prince Eugene vanquishes a French army at Turin September 7 with help from Prussian forces under Leopold of Dessau. Lombardy submits to Eugene, Charles III is proclaimed king at Milan, and the French are driven out of Italy.

Saxony's Elector Augustus II abdicates the Polish crown September 24 in the Treaty of Altranstadt, he recognizes Stanislas Lesczynski as king of Poland, and he breaks his alliance with Russia's Czar Peter.

Portugal's Pedro II dies December 9 at age 58 after a 23-year reign. He is succeeded by his 17-year-old son who will reign until 1750 as João V.

Albuquerque, New Mexico, has its origin in the town of Alburquerque founded in the northern part of New Spain. The town is named in honor of New Spain's new viceroy the duke of Alburquerque (the first "r" will be dropped in years to come).

Crosse & Blackwell is founded at London to supply produce to the English colonies.

Tom's Coffee House opened by London merchant Thomas Twining at 216 the Strand will become a major tea importing business.

1707 The Mogul emperor Aurangzeb dies March 3 at age 88 while campaigning against the Mahrattas after a 49-year reign in which he has annexed Bijapur and Golconda to extend his autocratic sway over all of northern and central India up to the Himalayas. The empire will quickly disintegrate as provincial governors gain virtual independence amidst wars of succession and foreign invasions.

The Battle of Almanza April 25 ends in defeat for Portuguese forces at the hands of a French army commanded by James Fitzjames, 37, duke of Berwick. Spain's Philip V has engaged the bastard son of England's late James II to head a mercenary army against the Portuguese.

The United Kingdom of Great Britain created May 1 unites England and Scotland under the Union Jack which combines the cross of St. George and the cross of St. Andrew. Scottish law and legal administration are to remain unchanged but the Scottish Parliament is to be abolished, Scotland is to send 16 elective peers and 45 members of the Commons to the British Parliament at London, no further Scottish peers are to be created.

Geneva suppresses a popular uprising with help from the oligarchies of Bern and Zurich.

Philadelphia mechanics demonstrate to protest competition from Indian slaves.

A "pulse watch" invented by English provincial physician John Floyer, 58, is the first efficient clinical precision instrument for medical diagnosis. A great believer in cold baths, Floyer has designed the watch to run for exactly one minute (*see* Santorius, 1624).

Willem van de Velde the Younger dies at Greenwich, London, April 8 at age 73.

Theater *The Comical Lovers* by Colley Cibber 2/4 at London's Haymarket Theatre, a comedy made up of scenes from two of John Dryden's plays; *The Beaux' Stratagem* by English playwright George Farquhar 3/8 at London's Haymarket Theatre: "How a little love and conversation improve a woman!" (IV, ii) (paid in advance, Farquhar was stricken with a mortal illness before completing Act II, but he has finished the play, an extra benefit performance is given 4/29, and Farquhar dies that day); *Crispin, Rival of His Master (Crispin, rival de son maitre)* by French playwright Alain-René Lesage, 34, 3/15 at the Comédie Française, Paris; *Atreus and Thyseus (Atree et Tysee)* by Prosper Jolyot sieur de Crebillon at the Comédie Française, Paris; *The*

Royal Convert by Nicholas Rowe 11/25 at London's Haymarket Theatre; *The Lady's Last Stake, or The Wife's Revenge* by Colley Cibber 12/13 at the Haymarket Theatre: "Tea! thou soft, thou sober, sage, and venerable liquid" (I, i).

Salzburg's Kollegienkirche is completed by J. B. Fischer von Erlach after 13 years of construction.

Japan's Fujiyama volcano erupts for the last time.

Fortnum & Mason's is opened in Piccadilly by London entrepreneurs William Fortnum, a former footman to Queen Anne, and Hugh Mason. Delicacies from Fortnum & Mason's will be a tradition in better English households for more than 270 years.

An emigration begins from the Rhineland Palatinate that will bring thousands of Calvinists, Lutherans, and even some Roman Catholics to England and thence in many cases to America, where the emigrants will settle in New York's Hudson and Mohawk Valleys and in Virginia (*see* 1710).

1708 Ghent and Bruges resume their allegiance to France in July, the duke of Marlborough fears that other cities will follow suit, he defeats the French July 11 at the Battle of Oudenarde with the help of Eugene of Savoy, he lays siege to Lille for nearly 4 months, and the citadel surrenders in December after 30,000 combatants have lost their lives in the continuing War of the Spanish Succession.

Sweden's Charles XII invades the Ukraine and lays siege to the Russian fortress of Poltava but the Russians intercept an auxiliary army carrying supplies to Charles, his own army is stricken with plague, and he is forced to yield his conquests.

The United East India Company created by a merger of Britain's two rival East India Companies is the strongest European power on the coasts of India. The company ships Indian silks, cottons, indigo (for blue dye), coffee, and saltpetre (for gunpowder) as well as China tea, and it will pay regular dividends of 8 to 10 percent (*see* 1627).

The Bank of England Act prohibits any other bank with more than six partners from issuing banknotes (*see* 1694; clearing house, 1775).

Canadian Indians and French colonists massacre settlers at Haverhill in the Massachusetts colony.

The 2,400 adult whites in the 45-year-old Carolina colony are outnumbered by 2,900 black slaves and 1,100 Indian slaves (*see* 1775).

The Sot Weed Factor, or A Voyage to Maryland by English satirist Ebenezer Cook, 36, expresses disgust at the greedy colonials. Cook has gone to America to buy tobacco.

Painting *The Departing Regiment* by French painter (Jean) Antoine Watteau, 23.

Theater *Electra (Electre)* by Prosper Jolyot, sieur de Crebillon 12/14 at the Comédie Française, Paris.

German organist-composer Johann Sebastian Bach, 23, becomes court organist at Weimar where he will

1708 (cont.) become court concertmeister in 1714. Bach has frequently walked 50 miles to Lübeck to attend the annual performance of the Abendmusiken concerto by the late Swedish organist-composer Dietrich Buxtehude who died 2 years ago at age 70 and who has had great influence on young Bach.

An alchemist trying to make gold at Meissen 14 miles northwest of Dresden in Saxony discovers a formula for making white porcelain (*see* Entrecolles, 1712).

Red porcelain equal in quality to Chinese "china" is produced at Meissen by Ehrenfried Walther von Tschirnhausen and Johann Friedrich Bottger who open a Meissenware factory at Dresden.

1709 An industrial revolution begins in England with the discovery that coke, made from coal, may be substituted for charcoal, made from wood, in blast furnaces used to make pig iron and cast iron. Growth of iron smelting has been limited by the fact that it takes 200 acres of forest to supply one smelting furnace with a year's supply of charcoal, but Quaker ironmaster Abraham Darby, 31, finds that coke serves just as well for his furnaces at Coalbrookdale, Shropshire, where he makes iron boilers for the Newcomen engine invented in 1705. Regular use of coke will not come for 50 years and will await improvements by Darby's son and namesake but Darby's breakthrough brings an immediate surge in the demand for coal and for the Newcomen engine whose energy will be used increasingly to permit production of coal from flooded colliery galleries.

The Battle of Poltava July 8 makes Russia the dominant power in northern Europe as Peter the Great breaks the power of Sweden and forces Charles XII to take refuge in Anatolia.

The elector of Saxony Frederick Augustus I renews his claims to the Polish crown following the defeat of Sweden's Charles XII at Poltova (above). He calls the 1706 Treaty of Altranstadt void, he renews his alliance with Russia and Denmark, and he deposes Stanislas Lesczynski, resuming the throne that he will try without success to make hereditary but holding it himself until his death early in 1733.

The Battle of Malplaquet September 11 is the bloodiest of the War of the Spanish Succession and takes 20,000 allied lives. The French retire in good order from the triumphant Prince of Savoy and from England's duke of Marlborough whose Tory opponents call him a butcher and use his excesses to attack the power of the Whigs (*see* 1710).

The Japanese Tokugawa shogun Sunayoshi has died in January at age 62 after nearly 29 years in power. He is succeeded by his 47-year-old cousin who will rule until 1712 as Ienobu (*see* below).

Portugal creates the Brazilian captaincies of Sao Paulo and Minas Gerais as Portuguese colonists settle in the interior of Brazil.

Britain's Caribbean colonies import 20,000 slaves per year by official estimates but many are for re-export to North and South America.

Close to 7 million Africans will come across the Atlantic in chains in this century—as many as 100,000 in a single year.

The new Japanese shogun Ienobu (above) releases nearly 9,000 prisoners, most of them victims of Sunayoshi's laws against killing animals or eating fish or birds.

France has food riots as frost creates famine in much of Europe (*see* below).

The Black Death kills 300,000 in Prussia.

The Fahrenheit alcohol thermometer introduced by German physicist Gabriel Daniel Fahrenheit, 23, has a scale on which "normal" human body temperature is in the neighborhood of 98.6°. The freezing point at standard atmospheric pressure (sea level) is +32° Fahrenheit (F) on Fahrenheit's scale; 212°F is the point at which water boils.

Aphorismi de Cognoscendis et Curandis Morbis by University of Leyden medicine and botany professor Hermann Boerhaave, 41, revives the Hippocratic method of the 5th century B.C. and emphasizes that medicine's principal aim is to cure the patient. Boerhaave is the leading medical technician and clinician of his day, he makes observations from the bedside rather than from textbooks, his slim but encyclopaedic medical text will be translated into many European languages as will his *Institutiones medicae in usus annuae exercitationis domesticos digestae* of last year, but like most others he has erroneous ideas about diseases of the solid parts as opposed to diseases of the so-called "humors."

The Tatler begins publication at London. Editor of the new triweekly journal of politics and society is playwright Richard Steele, who inserts essays under the name Isaac Bickerstaff and publishes numerous essays submitted by Joseph Addison, 37 (*see* 1711).

Meindert Hobbema dies at Amsterdam December 7 at age 71.

Theater *The Rival Fools* by Colley Cibber 1/11 at London's Drury Lane Theatre.

The Gravicembalo col piano e forte (pianoforte) built by the Florentine inventor Bartolommeo Cristofori, 54, is the first keyboard instrument with a successful hammer action. Cristofori is curator of a collection of musical instruments at the Medici court; his pianoforte has leather-covered poplar hammers that replace the jacks of the harpsichord and permit the player to produce gradations of tone by changing the force and manner in which the keys are struck.

Famine ravages Europe as frost kills crops, fruit trees, and domestic fowl as far south as the Mediterranean Coast.

French officials set up grain depots in an effort to make food distribution more equitable but they continue to export grain reserves. Restrictions on internal trade strangle shipments of food stores, keep food prices high, and contribute to the starvation.

"The fear of having no bread has agitated the people to the point of fury," writes French controller general of finances Nicolas Des Marets, 61, the Seigneur de Maillebois: "They have taken up arms for the purpose of seizing grain by force; there have been riots at Rouen, at Paris, and in nearly all the provinces; they are carrying on a kind of war that never ceases except when they are occupied with the harvest."

"The winter was terrible," writes the duc de Saint-Simon Louis de Rouvroy, 34, in his journal: "The memory of man could find no parallel to it. The frost came suddenly on Twelfth Night, and lasted nearly two months, beyond all recollection. In four days the Seine and all the other rivers were frozen, and what had never been seen before, the sea froze all along the coasts, so as to bear carts, even heavily laden, upon it [see England, 1684]. The violence of the cold was such that the strongest elixirs and the most spirituous liquors broke their bottles in cupboards of rooms with fires in them. There were no walnut trees, no olive trees, no apple trees, no vines left. The other trees died in great numbers; the gardens perished, and all the grain in the earth. It is impossible to imagine the desolation of this general ruin. . . ."

1710 ✗ England achieves her first clean-cut peaceful transfer of power. The Tory party wins a clear majority in the Commons in November and ousts the Whig government headed by the duke of Marlborough.

England's Tory cause has gained popular support as the result of the trial and conviction in March of political preacher Henry Sacheverell, 36, who has attacked the Whig ministry. Sacheverell had been impeached at the instigation of Sidney Godolphin, 65, lord high treasurer of England and an ally of Marlborough who has remained loyal to the Jacobite cause and who is dismissed by Queen Anne.

British forces occupy Acadia but leave the French Acadians in peace (see 1632; Nova Scotia, 1713).

Colonel Peter Schuyler of the New York colony takes five Iroquois chiefs to the court of Queen Anne to impress them with England's power.

Pennsylvania "Dutch" gunsmiths in the next decade will develop the Pennsylvania rifle with a spiral bore.

An English copyright law that will be the basis of all future copyright laws is established by Queen Anne.

Treatise concerning the Principles of Human Knowledge by Irish philosopher George Berkeley, 25, inaugurates the empiricist school of philosophy. Berkeley's system of subjective idealism (Berkeleianism) was first propounded by him last year in an "Essay Towards a New Theory of Vision" and will be popularized by him in 1713 with *Three Dialogues Between Hylas and Philonus.*

Poetry "England's Reformation: From the Time of Henry VIII, to the End of Oates' Plot" by English poet Thomas Ward, 58, is a satire which includes the lines, "A letter-missive is a writ/ That names the man the king thinks fit,/ And only he is chose by it./

Where to elect there is but one,/ 'Tis Hobson's choice: take that or none."

🎭 Theater *Tuscarot* by Alain-René Lesage 3/15 at the Comédie Française, Paris; *The Rival Queens,* with *The Humours of Alexander the Great* by Colley Cibber (burlesque), in June at London's Haymarket Theatre.

🏛 London's Marlborough House is completed in Westminster by Sir Christopher Wren, now 77.

Venice's baroque Palazzo Ca' Pesaro designed by the late Baldassare Longhena is completed for the powerful Pesaro family.

👫 A great German migration to America begins as Baron de Graffenreid brings 650 Swiss and German Palatines to North Carolina, where they will settle at New Bern on the Neuse River. New York governor Robert Hunter brings 3,000 Germans to settle on the Hudson River and produce naval stores.

1711 ✗ The Holy Roman Emperor Josef I dies of smallpox at age 32 April 17 at Vienna and is succeeded by his 26-year-old brother who assumes the throne as Charles VI, becomes heir to all the empire's Austrian territories, and fights to restore the empire of his Hapsburg ancestor Charles V in the continuing War of the Spanish Succession.

Hungarian followers of the patriot Francis II Rákóczi accept the peace of Szatmar May 1, the new emperor (above) agrees to redress Hungarian grievances and to respect the Hungarian constitution, Rákóczi takes refuge in Turkey after an 8-year revolt in which his forces have threatened Vienna.

Russia's Peter the Great advances with Moldavian and Wallachian allies on the Pruth River but he is surrounded there by superior Ottoman forces. Peter is forced to sign the Treaty of Pruth July 21, Azov is returned to the Turks, and Sweden's Charles XII is permitted safe return to Stockholm (but see 1713).

Afghanistan is established as an independent state by the Ghilzai chieftain Mir Vais, a Sunnite who defeats a Persian army sent to put down his uprising against Shah Hussein.

Britain undertakes an attack on French Canada with seven of the duke of Marlborough's best regiments augmented at Boston by 1,500 colonials, but French forces abort the invasion of Quebec by sea in August, the French sink 10 ships of the fleet as it enters the St. Lawrence River, and news of the naval disaster persuades Sir Francis Nicholson to give up a projected campaign against Montreal.

Rio de Janeiro is sacked by French forces under René Duguay-Trouin, 38, as Louis XIV fights the Portuguese allies of Britain in the War of the Spanish Succession.

The Landed Property Qualification Act passed by the landed gentry of Parliament excludes Britain's merchants, financiers, and industrialists from the House of Commons. The law will not be effectively enforced but it will not be repealed until 1866.

The roi de soleil Louis XIV reigned through 72 years of often stormy French history.

Queen Anne dismisses the duke of Marlborough at year's end as his enemies increase their influence on the queen. They have accused the duke of speculation and the queen makes James Butler, 46, duke of Ormonde, the commander in chief of British forces.

Tuscorora tribesmen massacre some 200 Carolina colonists, beginning a war that will not end until forces from Virginia move south to quell the revolt.

German scholar G. W. Leibniz denies spontaneous generation and attempts to reconcile natural science with divine will. Leibniz expounds his conclusion that all living matter is composed not of dead atoms but of living "monads," infinite in their variety.

The Black Death kills 300,000 in Austria, 215,000 in Brandenburg.

The Spectator begins publication March 1 at London under the direction of Richard Steele and Joseph Addison whose journal *The Tatler*, begun in 1709, appeared for the last time January 2. The new nonpolitical journal publishes Steele's *Roger de Coverley Papers* and will continue for 20 months.

Poetry "Essay on Criticism" by English poet Alexander Pope, 23: "A little learning is a dangerous thing;/ Drink deep, or taste not the Pierian spring" (II); "Be not the first by whom the new are tried,/ Nor yet the last to lay the old aside" (II); "To err is human, to forgive divine" (II); "Nay, fly to altars; there they'll talk you dead;/ For fools rush in where angels fear to tread" (III, lxvi).

Theater *Rhadamisthus and Zenobia (Rhadamiste et Zenobie)* by Prosper Jolyot de Crebillon 1/23 at the Comédie Française, Paris.

Opera *Rinaldo* 3/7 at London's Haymarket Theatre, with music by George Frideric Handel, libretto by Giacomo Rossi.

The Ascot races are established by England's Queen Anne (see 1702; 1807).

1712 French forces under Marshal Villars defeat British and Dutch forces commanded by the earl of Albemarle Arnold Joost van Keppel, 41, at Denain, the French recapture Douai, Le Quesnoy, and Bouchain, and the Congress of Utrecht opens to resolve the War of the Spanish Succession (see 1713).

Bernese forces triumph July 25 at Villmergen in a second Swiss war between Catholics and Protestants. The victory establishes the dominance of the Protestant cantons.

The Russian czarevich Alexius Petrovich infuriates his father Peter the Great by disabling his own right hand with a pistol shot. Peter has taken him on a tour of inspection in Finland, has sent him to see to the building of new ships at Staraya Rusya, and has ordered him to draw something of a technical nature to show his progress in mechanics and mathematics.

The Japanese Tokugawa shogun Ienobu dies at age 50 after a 3-year reign. He is succeeded by his 3-year-old son who will reign until 1716 as Ietsugu.

North Carolina and South Carolina are created by a division of the Carolina colony founded in 1663.

A slave revolt at New York ends with 20 blacks burned or hanged.

Pennsylvania forbids further importation of slaves.

French naturalist René Antoine Ferchault de Réaumur, 29, describes the ability of a crayfish to grow new claws (see steel, 1722; digestion, 1752).

Ferry service begins between New York's Manhattan and Staten Islands with a sailing vessel providing passage across the bay (see van Derbilt, 1810).

Fiction *The History of John Bull* by Scottish physician John Arbuthnot, 45, satirizes the duke of Marlborough and introduces the name "John Bull" as a symbol of England. Arbuthnot's character represents the English nation with characteristics considered typically English.

Poetry *The Rape of the Lock* by Alexander Pope is a mock-heroic poem describing a day at Hampton Court where Queen Anne does "sometimes counsel take—and sometimes tea."

Scotland's clan Macgregor chief Rob Roy fails to repay money he has borrowed from the duke of Montrose to carry on his business as cattle-dealer. The duke evicts him from his lands and declares him an outlaw, Rob Roy supports himself by depradations on the duke and his tenants, and he foils all efforts to capture him (see 1693; Sheriffmuir, 1715).

Vienna's Trautson Palace is completed by J. B. Fischer von Erlach after 3 years of construction.

Charleston's William Rhett house is completed in the South Carolina colony.

Nantucket whaling captain Christopher Hussey harpoons a sperm whale from an open boat and it is probably the first such whale to be killed by man since Phoenician times. *Physeter catodon* has an oil content averaging 65 to 80 barrels—far more than other whales—and Hussey's kill initiates a new era in whaling (*see* 1690). Spermaceti from the sperm whale will be used to make millions of wax candles, the whale's teeth are fine-grained ivory, the whale's skin is high in glycerin, and it is the only whale that produces ambergris, valuable as a perfume fixative.

French missionary Père d'Entrecolles sends home the first accurate description of how the Chinese make porcelain from kaolin (*see* 621; 1708; 1754).

1713 Ottoman forces attack Sweden's Charles XII in his camp at Bender in Moldavia February 1, they take him prisoner, and he will remain in Turkish hands for 15 months.

The first Prussian king Frederick I dies February 25 at age 55 after a 12-year reign in which he has welcomed and protected Protestant refugees from France and elsewhere, has founded the University of Halle and the Academy of Sciences at Berlin, and has lavished money on public buildings. He is succeeded by his 24-year-old son who will reign until 1740 as Friedrich Wilhelm I.

The Treaty of Utrecht April 11 ends the War of the Spanish Succession (called Queen Anne's War in North America). France's Louis XIV agrees not to unite France and Spain under one king, recognizes the Protestant succession in Britain, agrees to tear down French fortifications at Dunkirk and to fill up Dunkirk harbor, and gives up some North American territories to Britain.

Gibraltar and Minorca are ceded to Britain.

France cedes Newfoundland and Acadia to Britain, which cedes Cape Breton Island to France and changes the name of Acadia to Nova Scotia. France retains fish-drying rights on part of the Newfoundland coast and builds a fortress (Louisburg) on Cape Breton Island (*see* 1755; 1763).

France turns over her fur-trading posts on Hudson Bay to the Hudson's Bay Company, which gains control of the entire region.

The Caribbean island of St. Kitts is awarded to Britain, and the South Sea Company gains the right to send one ship per year to trade at Spain's isthmus city of Portobello (*see* 1716).

Spain cedes Sardinia and Naples to Austria and cedes Sicily to Savoy, which in 1720 will exchange Sicily for Sardinia (*see* 1735).

The South Sea Company receives *asientos* to import 4,800 African slaves per year into Spain's New World colonies for the next 30 years. Founded 2 years ago in anticipation of receiving the *asientos*, the company is essentially a British finance company, but it begins the most active period of British participation in the slave trade (*see* 1720).

Scots-American sea captain Andrew Robinson builds the first schooner at Gloucester in the Massachusetts colony. The ship's name derives from the Scottish dialect word "scoon," meaning to skip over the surface of water, other New Englanders quickly imitate the distinctively American vessel, and they create a fleet of schooners to fish the Grand Banks.

A privateer operated by Boston's Quincy family captures a Spanish treasure ship "worth the better part of an hundred thousand pounds sterling."

The French establish a trading post at the Great Village of Natchez (*see* 1729).

London physician John Woodward receives a letter from Greek physician Emanuel Timoni at Constantinople describing a method for preventing smallpox by immunization. Timoni reports that Greek physician Giacomo Pylarini at Smyrna removes some of the thick liquid from a smallpox pustule, rubs it into a small scratch made with a needle on the skin of a healthy person, and thus protects that person, who generally develops a mild case of smallpox but nothing worse (*see* 1714; Montagu, 1718).

First performances   A *Te Deum* and a *Jubilate* by George Frideric Handel 7/7 at St. Paul's Cathedral, London, to celebrate the Peace of Utrecht (above). Queen Anne has commissioned the works and five others, and she grants Handel a handsome lifetime pension of £200 per year.

Prague's Clam-Gallas Palace is completed by J. B. Fischer von Erlach after 6 years of construction.

France's Louis XIV receives a coffee bush whose descendants will produce a vast industry in the Western Hemisphere. The 5-foot bush from the Amsterdam greenhouses will be stolen and transported to Martinique (*see* 1690; 1723).

1714 The Treaty of Rastatt March 6 ends the war between Austria and Spain, the Spanish Netherlands become the Austrian Netherlands, and Spain gives up her possessions in Italy and Luxembourg along with those in Flanders.

The House of Hanover that will rule Great Britain for more than two and a half centuries comes to power August 1 upon the death of England's gouty Queen Anne at age 48 after a 12-year reign. Last monarch of the House of Stuart, Anne is succeeded under terms of the 1701 Act of Settlement by Hanover's Prince George Louis, 54, great-grandson of England's James I who speaks no English but who lands in England September 18 to assume the throne (the House of Hanover will be renamed the House of Windsor in 1917).

Sweden's Charles XII returns to Stockholm through Hungary but the Great Northern War continues.

A Turkish-Venetian war begins as the Turks capture Corinth and Venetian stations in Candia (Crete).

A Board of Longitude is established by the British government and offers a £20,000 prize to anyone who can devise a means of determining a ship's longi-

1714 (cont.) tude within 30 nautical miles at the end of a 6-weeks' voyage (*see* Greenwich, 1676; Harrison, 1728).

London physician John Woodward publishes Emanuel Timoni's account of smallpox variolation in the Royal Society's *Philosophical Transactions,* arousing interest in Britain and America (*see* 1713; 1718).

German physicist Daniel Fahrenheit devises a thermometer in which mercury replaces alcohol (*see* 1709).

The Virginia colony's lieutenant governor Alexander Spotswood, 38, establishes iron furnaces on the Rapidan River and imports German ironworkers to settle in the colony (*see* 1723).

Poetry *The Fable of the Bees: or, Private Vices, Public Benefit* by Dutch-born London philosopher-satirist Bernard Mandeville, 44, whose octosyllabic verse first appeared in 1705 in *The Grumbling Hive.* Every virtue is basically some form of selfishness, says Mandeville, human nature is essentially vile, and "it is requisite that great numbers be poor" in order that society may be happy (*see* Young, 1771).

Theater *The Tragedy of Jane Shore* by Nicholas Rowe 2/2 at London's Drury Lane Theatre.

Cantata "Ich hatte viel Bekummernis" by court concertmeister Johann Sebastian Bach 6/17 at Weimar's Schlosskirche.

Charleston's Mulberry Plantation house is completed for planter Thomas Broughton.

1715 France's Louis XIV dies September 1, 4 days short of his 77th birthday, after a 72-year reign. He is succeeded by his 5-year-old grandson who assumes the throne as Louis XV to begin a reign of almost 59 years. Philippe II Bourbon, 41, duc d'Orléans, is regent to the new king and has full governing powers.

French prelate André Hercule de Fleury, 62, is named tutor to the new king and will have great influence over Louis until his death in 1743.

France's middle class, established during the Sun King's long reign, holds a solid position which will become even stronger during the next two reigns.

The death of the French king weakens the position of the Jacobite pretender James Francis Edward Stuart who has challenged the House of Hanover's claim to the British throne (*see* 1708; 1714). The Scottish Jacobite John Erskine, 40, earl of Mar, raises a rebellion against the new British king George I, he proclaims the pretender James III and VIII at Aberdeen, and he gains support from Simon Fraser, 48, twelfth baron Lovat, from Henry St. John Viscount Bolingbroke, 37, from the 50-year-old James Butler, duke of Ormonde, from the 54-year-old Robert Harley, first earl of Oxford, and from much of the English and Scottish public, but most of the Lowlands remain loyal to George I. English authorities imprison Oxford in the Tower of London, and they force Bolingbroke and Ormonde to flee.

The Battle of Sheriffmuir November 13 halts the earl of Mar (above) in his march on Edinburgh. Some 4,000 Royalists under the 37-year-old John Campbell, second duke of Argyll, force Mar's 12,000 Jacobites to retreat to Perth after each side has lost 500 men (the outlaw Rob Roy plunders the dead of both sides). The Royalists defeat an uprising at Preston in the north of England November 14. The change in French policy has prevented the pretender James from joining his troops, but he lands near Peterhead December 22 and tries to rally support.

French forces in the Indian Ocean take Mauritius from the Dutch who have held it since 1638.

English colonial forces in America defeat Yamassee and allied tribes in the South Carolina colony and drive them across the Spanish border into Florida.

The Maryland colony is returned to the Calvert family, which lost it in 1688 (*see* 1729).

Black slaves comprise 24 percent of the Virginia colony's population, up from less than 5 percent in 1671.

The first treatise on finite differences is published by English mathematician Brook Taylor, 30, whose *Methodus Incrementorum Directa et Inversa* establishes the calculus of finite differences and sets forth Taylor's theorem, a fundamental theorem concerning functions. Taylor also publishes *Linear Perspective.*

Japan becomes alarmed at the amount of copper that has been exported by Dutch and Chinese traders and reduces the amount that it will permit to be exported. The number of Dutch vessels permitted to call annually at Nagasaki will be cut to two (*see* 1641).

Theater *The Tragedy of Lady Jane Gray* by Nicholas Rowe 4/20 at London's Drury Lane Theatre; *Kokusenya Gassen* by Monzaemon Chikamatsu at Osaka.

First performances Water Music Suite No. 1 in F major by George Frideric Handel 8/22 on the Thames at London.

French agriculture has declined in the long reign of Louis XIV (above), much of the peasantry has become impoverished, and great areas of land have gone out of cultivation (*see* Boisguilbert, 1695).

French distiller Jean Martell arrives in the Cognac region and begins distilling brandy from local wine. By 1728 J. & F. Martell and others will have exported 27,000 barrels of cognac brandy.

1716 Jacobite troops are dispersed by Scottish forces under the command of John Campbell, 37. The pretender flees to France February 5, and Jacobite leaders captured at Preston in November of last year are beheaded. Sir James Radcliffe, 27, third earl of Derwentwater, and William Gordon, sixth Viscount Kenmure, are both executed.

Simon Fraser, baron Lovat, receives a pardon and life rent on the Lovat estates as a reward for having brought in his clan on the side of George I, an action he has taken in order to obtain his cousin's estates.

Ottoman forces are defeated by Eugene of Savoy August 5 at Peterwardein and the Holy Roman Emperor Charles VI enters the war against the Turks.

Russia's Peter the Great receives a letter from his son Alexius Petrovich requesting permission to become a monk. Peter writes to Alexius from abroad August 26 urging him to join his father and the army without delay if he wishes to remain czarevich, but Alexius flees to Vienna, he places himself under the protection of his brother-in-law the emperor Charles VI, and he is sent first to the Tyrolean fortress of Ahrenberg and then to the castle of San Elmo at Naples in company with his Finnish mistress Afrosina.

Japan's Tokugawa shogun Ietsugu dies at age 7 after 4 years in power and is succeeded by the 39-year-old Yoshimune who will rule until 1745. Yoshimune will allow the Dutch at Deshima to bring Western books into Japan, he will help merchants establish a trade system, and he will build extensive irrigation projects to aid agriculture.

England's East India Company receives exemption from Indian customs duties and gains other concessions in return for gifts and medical services.

The East India Company (above) receives permission to bring a ship of 650 tons with trading goods into Portobello for the annual Spanish American trade fair (see 1713; Vernon, 1739).

"Wealth depends on commerce, and commerce depends on circulation [of money]," says Scottish promoter John Law, 45, and he persuades the French regent Philip d'Orléans to let him open the Banque Royale which pays Philip's debts and issues notes that the government accepts for taxes. Law has killed a man in a duel, he is wanted for murder, he has taken refuge in France, and while the banknotes of his private bank are backed in principle by gold and silver they are in fact based largely on the gold alleged to exist in France's Louisiana territory (see Boisguilbert, 1713; Louisiana, 1717).

A company of Virginia colonists crosses the Blue Ridge Mountains into the valley of the Shenandoah River under the leadership of Alexander Spotswood (see 1714; Iroquois treaty, 1722).

Christian religious teaching is outlawed in China.

Diario di Roma begins publication. It is the first Italian newspaper.

Painting *La Leçon d'amour* by Antoine Watteau. Japanese painter Korin Ogata dies at age 58. He has gained fame for his *Tale of Ise* and for his screens painted with iris and red and white plum trees.

Oratorio *Judithea* by Venetian violinist-composer Antonio Vivaldi, 41, who was ordained a priest at age 28, has taught violin since 1704 at the Conservatorio dell' Ospedale della Pieta, and is required to supply two concertos per month to the Conservatory.

1717 The triple alliance formed January 4 by Britain, France, and the Dutch Republic forces the Old Pretender James III to leave France. James has intrigued with the Swedish king Charles XII and with the Spanish prime minister Cardinal Giulio Alberoni, 53.

Cardinal Alberoni sends a secret Spanish expeditionary force to seize Sardinia and raid Sicily while Eugene of Savoy is engaged in fighting the Ottoman Turks (see 1718).

Eugene of Savoy takes Belgrade from the Turks.

Spain creates the viceroyalty of New Granada with its seat of power at Bogotá to reduce the viceroyalty of Peru to more manageable size (see 1529; 1539; 1776).

France gives Scotsman John Law a 25-year-monopoly on trade and government in Louisiana on condition that he send out at least 6,000 whites and 3,000 blacks to settle the vast territory that includes the Illinois country (see 1716; 1720).

The Lowlands begin a long period of commercial decline after more than a century of colonization and prosperity. The 2.5 million Dutch cannot support both a major army and a powerful fleet.

School attendance in Prussia is made compulsory.

Painting *Embarkation for the Isle of Cythera* by Antoine Watteau who is admitted at last to the French Academy at age 32.

Theater *Electra (Electre)* by Prosper Jolyot de Crebillon at the Comédie Française in Paris, with Adrienne Lecouvreur, 25, in her first appearance at the Comédie Française.

London's St. Mary-Le-Strand is completed by John Gibbs after 3 years of construction.

The Compagnie d'Occident is established by John Law (above) to encourage emigration to Louisiana (see 1719).

A great emigration to the Pennsylvania colony begins among German Dunkers, Mennonites, and Moravians (see Schwenkenfelders, 1734).

1718 "Innoculation Against Smallpox" by Lady Mary Wortley Montagu, 29, reports a workable method known in the East since ancient times. Wife of the English minister to Constantinople, Lady Mary describes inoculation parties she has witnessed at which a small wound is made in the arm, a few drops of smallpox pus inserted, and a walnut shell tied over the infected area, a procedure that produces a true case of smallpox but one so mild that 98 percent of those inoculated recover (see 1714; 1721).

A mysterious disease comparable in its effects to England's 1518 "sweating sickness" strikes Picardy in the first of a series of epidemics that will recur in France for more than a century. The "Suette des Picards" differs in its symptoms from the "sweating sickness" but is is no less deadly.

1718 (cont.) Russia's Czarevich Alexius Petrovich is brought back by his father's emissary Count Peter Tolstoi, he is forced to sign a "confession" February 18 implicating his friends, they are impaled or broken on the wheel or otherwise dispatched, the ex-czarevich Eudoxia is dragged from her monastery and publicly tried for alleged adultery, Alexius is given 25 strokes with the knout June 19 (nobody has ever survived 30), he is given 15 more June 24, and he dies June 26 at age 28 in the guardhouse of the citadel at St. Petersburg 2 days after being condemned by the senate for "imagining" rebellion against his father Peter the Great.

Spain's Philip V sends troops into Sicily in July and his seizure of the country raises fears of a new European war. Prussia, France, and Britain form an alliance August 2 that will be joined next year by the Republic of Holland as the major powers unite to prevent Philip from overturning the peace of 1714.

The Treaty of Passarowitz July 21 ends a 4-year war between Venice and Constantinople. The Ottoman Turks lose the Banat of Temesvar, Northern Serbia, and Little Wallachia but they retain the Morea while Venice retains only the Ionian Islands and the Dalmatian Coast.

Sweden's Charles XII is shot through the head December 11 as he peers over the parapet of the foremost trench 280 paces from the fortress of Fredriksten during a military expedition to Norway. Dead at age 36 after a momentous 21-year reign, Charles is succeeded by his sister Ulrika Eleanora, 30, who accepts the crown on condition that the riksdag be allowed to draft a new constitution, and who brings the Great Northern War to a close.

New Orleans is founded near the mouth of the Mississippi by the sieur de Bienville. A few Frenchmen emigrate to the Louisiana territory (see 1701; 1720).

San Antonio de Valero is founded in a Texas cottonwood grove by Franciscan monks who build a chapel they call the Alamo, meaning cottonwood (see 1836).

William Penn dies May 30 at age 73 leaving an estate of 21 million acres.

The first English bank notes are issued (see Bank of England, 1694).

The first table of chemical affinities is presented to the Academie by French chemist Etienne F. Geoffroy, 46, who shows how various chemicals react to each other.

Yale University renames itself as such to honor benefactor Elihu Yale who has become an official of the East India Company serving as governor of Fort St. George at Madras and who sends a cargo of books and East India goods to the Collegiate School founded at Saybrook in the Connecticut colony 17 years ago (see Yale, 1672). The school sells the cargo for £560 and uses the proceeds to move to New Haven (see 1861).

Poetry *Alma, or The Progress of the Mind* and *Solomon, or The Vanity of the World* by Matthew Prior, now 54, who played a leading role in negotiating the Peace of Utrecht 5 years ago.

Painting *Parc Fête* by Antoine Watteau; *The Duke of Norfolk* by Sir Godfrey Kneller.

Theater *The Non-Juror* by Colley Cibber; *Oedipe* by French playwright Voltaire (François Marie Arouet), 23, 11/18 at the Théâtre Français, Paris. Voltaire was released from the Bastille in April after serving nearly a year for libel.

The pirate Edward Teach known as Blackbeard is killed in a skirmish near Ocracoke Island in the North Carolina colony after having said, "I've buried my treasure where none but Satan and myself can find it."

Carolina coastal pirate Stede Bonnet dies on the gallows after having been seized with his crew.

Potatoes arrive at Boston with some Irish Presbyterian immigrants (see 1719).

A great Scots-Irish emigration to America begins.

1719 John Law renames his 3-year-old Compagnie d'Occident as reports circulate that Louisiana is rich in gold and diamonds. By midyear investors who paid 500 livres for shares in Law's Compagnie des Indes are reselling shares at 15,000 livres each in Paris's Rue de Quinquempoix, Parisians hear the word "millionaire" for the first time, and Law receives rights to collect all French government taxes and to issue paper currency (see 1720).

The Principality of Liechtenstein created by the Holy Roman Emperor Charles VI unites Vaduz and Schellenburg into a sovereign state of 61 square miles under the Austrian Count Hans Adam von Liechtenstein who has bought the territory and its 397-year-old Vaduz Castle from another count who is heavily in debt.

The Peace of Stockholm November 20 ends hostilities between Sweden and Britain's George I who gains Bremen and Verden for 1 million rix dollars as elector of Hanover (see Victoria, 1837).

The Mogul emperor Mohammed Shah assumes the throne at age 19 and begins a 29-year reign as the Great Mogul.

The French explorer Pierre François Xavier de Charlevoix, 37, sent to find a new route westward from Acadia, travels up the St. Lawrence River, through the Great Lakes, and down the Illinois and Mississippi Rivers to New Orleans (see 1682).

A British slaver anchors off Port Natal and buys 74 boys and girls for the Virginia colony's Rappahannock plantations. The Bantu are considered "better slaves for working than those of Madagascar, being stronger and blacker."

The science of pathological anatomy is initiated by Italian physician Giovanni Battista Morgagni, 37, who observes changes found in the bodies of disease victims (*see* 1760).

London's Westminster Hospital is founded.

Fiction *Robinson Crusoe* by Daniel Defoe whose novel is based roughly on fact. Defoe has read William Dampier's 1697 book *Voyage Round the World* and has heard accounts of Alexander Selkirk, now 43, a Scottish mariner who in October 1704 quarreled with Dampier while on a privateering expedition in the South Seas, was set ashore at his own request on Mas-a-Tierra in the Juan Fernández Isles off the coast of Chile, and remained there until picked up by another captain in February 1709 (*see* Rousseau, 1762).

Hymn "O God, Our Help in Ages Past" by English hymn writer Isaac Watts, 45, is published in *The Psalms of David*.

"Irish" potatoes are planted at Londonderry in the New Hampshire colony (*see* 1718) but will not gain wide acceptance in America for nearly a century.

1720 Spain's Philip V joins the Quadruple Alliance of Britain, France, Holland, and Austria in January, he signs the Treaty of the Hague February 17 giving up his Italian claims in return for an Austrian promise that his son Charles will succeed to Parma, Piacenza, and Tuscany. The Holy Roman Emperor Charles VI gives up his claims to Spain, and Savoy receives Sardinia from Austria in return for Sicily (*see* 1713).

Sweden's Ulrika Eleanora abdicates in favor of her husband Frederick of Hesse, 44, who will reign until 1751 as Frederick I, but a new constitution strips the new king of much of his power. Sweden's House of Nobles will largely control affairs of state through the 31-year reign of Frederick.

The British Parliament authorizes use of workhouses for confining petty offenders.

England's "South Sea Bubble" collapses in January producing widespread financial losses and a loss of confidence by investors in distant overseas enterprises. Parliament has given the South Sea Company permission to take over part of the British National Debt and to create £1 in new stock for every £1 of the National Debt it assumed. Share prices have soared to £1,050 each, but the *asiento* concession granted in 1713 has proved disappointing and so has the monopoly in British trade with Spanish America.

France names John Law Controller-General with power over the entire French economy but Law's so-called Mississippi Company has failed to attract reputable emigrants, New Orleans remains no more than a dismal collection of wooden shacks, Law's grandiose scheme turns out to be a speculative stock fraud much like the South Sea Company (above), and although the company has increased shipping between France and New Orleans and has brought some colonization of Louisiana, the collapse of the "Mississippi Bubble" ruins many French investors.

Marseilles has an epidemic of plague and more than 50,000 die in western Europe's last major epidemic of the Black Death.

A famine in Sicily weakens the population of Messina and thousands die in a typhus epidemic.

Japan's shogun Yoshimune removes the century-old ban on importing European books although he continues the prohibition against religious books. A small group of Japanese begins to study Dutch and begins through its studies to gain a knowledge of Western science, especially of medicine.

The nursery rhyme "Little Jack Horner" is published for the first time. Horner is believed to have been one Thomas Horner who was sent by the Abbott of Glastonbury to Henry VIII in 1543 with a placating gift of a pie containing deeds to valuable manors owned by the monastery (since Horner's family soon came into possession of a manor it is thought that Horner extracted one deed from the pie for himself).

Painting *Martyrdom of St. Bartholomew* by Venetian painter Giambattista (Giovanni Battista) Tiepolo, 24.

Theater *Robin, Bachelor of Love* (*Arlequin poli par l'amour*) by French essayist-playwright Pierre Carlet de Marivaux, 32, 10/17 at the Théâtre Italien, Paris. Marivaux has been ruined by the bankruptcy of John Law's Mississippi Company (above) but his comedy derived from the Italian *commedia dell'arte* launches him on a successful theatrical career; *The Love Suicides at Amijima* (*Shinju ten no Amijima*) by Monzaemon Chikamatsu at Osaka.

Divine and Moral Songs for Children by Isaac Watts includes the verse "How doth the little busy bee/ Improve each shining hour,/ And gather honey all the day/ From every opening flower."

London's Royal Academy of Music names George Frideric Handel as its director and presents Handel's oratorio *Esther.*

Belgian composer Jean Adam Joseph Faber uses the clarinet (*chalumeaux*) for the first time in a serious work.

1721 The Treaty of Nystadt August 30 gives Russia a "window" on the West and makes her a European power. Peter the Great obtains territories from Sweden that include Estonia, Ingermanland, Livonia, part of Carelia, and some Baltic islands and he is proclaimed Emperor of All the Russias.

China suppresses a revolt in Formosa.

England's Chancellor of the Exchequer John Aislabie, 51, goes to the Tower of London on charges of fraud in connection with last year's "South Sea Bubble." Sir Robert Walpole has profited with speculations in the South Sea scheme, he becomes prime minister and chancellor of the exchequer in April, he reduces import and export duties to encourage trade, and he averts financial panic by amalgamating South Sea Company stock with stock in the Bank of

1721 (cont.) England and the East India Company. Walpole's policy of "salutary neglect" of the American colonies will slacken enforcement of the navigation laws (*see* 1663; 1672; but *see* Molasses Act, 1733).

Philadelphia entrepreneur John Copson offers "Assurances from Losses Happening at Sea, &c." and pioneers marine insurance for American shipping.

The Japanese shogun Yoshimune bans expensive clothing, furniture, cakes, candies, and other extravagances in an austerity decree.

A London smallpox epidemic takes a heavy toll but Lady Mary Wortley Montagu has her 5-year-old daughter inoculated in the presence of some leading physicians (*see* 1718). The child has a mild case of smallpox that immunizes her, the physicians are impressed, and George I has two of his grandchildren inoculated—but only after the procedure has been tested on 11 charity school children and on 6 inmates of Newgate Prison who volunteered in return for having their death sentences commuted.

A smallpox epidemic introduced by ships from the West Indies strikes Boston in June. Local clergyman Cotton Mather, who belongs to the Royal Society and has read the account of variolation published in 1714, writes a treatise urging inoculation. The only Boston physician who acts on Mather's advice is Zabdiel Boylston, 42, who inoculates his 13-year-old son and two black slaves June 26. All three survive mild cases of the pox and Boylston then inoculates 247 colonists. Six die, many people accuse Boylston of spreading the pox and denounce him for interfering with nature, he narrowly escapes being hanged by a mob. But another epidemic strikes, 5,759 Bostonians—more than half the population—come down with the pox, and 844 die—more than 14 percent, as compared with 2.42 percent of Boylston's inoculated patients. Most of the survivors are left pockmarked (*see* Jenner, 1796; Waterhouse, 1800).

Regular postal service begins between London and New England.

Fiction *Lettres Persanes* by French lawyer-philosopher Charles de Secondat, 42, the Baron de la Brede et de Montesquieu, criticizes French society as seen through the eyes of two imaginary Persians traveling through the country.

Jean Antoine Watteau dies of tuberculosis at Nogent-sur-Marne July 18 at age 36.

Theater *The Refusal, or The Ladies' Philosophy* by Colley Cibber 2/4 at London's Drury Lane Theatre; *The Love Suicides at Sonezaki* (*Sonezaki shinju*) by Monzaemon Chikamatsu, now 68, at Osaka. The play is the first of several domestic pieces based on actual incidents that Chikamatsu will write about the love affairs of Japan's growingly important middle class.

First performances *The Brandenberg Concerti* by Johann Sebastian Bach.

Broccoli is introduced into England some 70 years after the "Italian asparagus" became popular in France (any dish "à Parisienne" includes broccoli).

Japan's city of Edo reaches a population level of more than a million despite the earthquake and fire that killed 200,000 in 1703.

1722 Persia is invaded by the Kandahar ruler Mir Mahmud who conquers Afghanistan, defeats the Persians at Gulnabad with an army of Afghans, takes Isfahan, and makes himself shah of Persia.

Russia's Peter the Great takes Derbent on the Caspian Sea and prepares to sweep through the Caucasus Mountains, hoping to distract the Turks with his cavalry while his navy captures the Bosporus and the Dardanelles from the grand vizier at Constantinople who is preoccupied with growing tulips (but *see* below).

China's Manchu emperor K'ang Hsi dies at age 68 after a personal reign of 53 years in which the provinces of Anhuei, Hunan, and Kansu have been added to 15 earlier Chinese provinces. The emperor will be succeeded beginning next year by Shih Tsung who will reign until 1735.

America's Iroquois tribes sign a treaty with Virginia governor Alexander Spotswood and agree not to cross the Potomac River or the Blue Ridge without the governor's permission.

Manchester, New Hampshire, has its beginnings in a settlement at Amoskeag on the Merrimack River established by Massachusetts colonists 55 miles northwest of Boston (*see* 1810).

New Orleans is made the capital of the Louisiana Territory by French authorities who have been persuaded by the sieur de Bienville (*see* 1718).

Easter Island is discovered Easter Sunday 2,000 miles off the coast of Chile by the Dutch explorer Roggeveen. The island has a Polynesian population of between 2,500 and 3,000 with artisans who have used easily-cut compressed volcanic ash to fashion monuments of from three to 36 feet in height, and up to 50 tons in weight. They have somehow moved the stone heads into position to stare vacantly out to sea, and they have developed a unique ideographic script, unparalleled in Polynesia, which will not be noted by archaeologists until 1864.

Ergotism aborts an attack by Russia's Peter the Great on the Ottoman Empire (*see* above). Peter marshals his Cossacks on the Volga delta at Astrakhan but his horses eat hay containing infected rye, his troops eat bread made from infected rye grain, hundreds of horses and men go mad, many die, and Peter has to abandon his plans.

Guy's Hospital at London is founded with a gift of £300,000 from local bookseller Thomas Guy, 77.

L'Art de convertier le fer forge en acier et l'art d'adoucir le fer fond by René A. F. de Réaumur is the first technical treatise on steelmaking (*see* 1712).

Réaumur will develop improvements in ironmaking and will work on improving steel and tinned steel.

Fiction *The Adventures and Misadventures of Moll Flanders* by Daniel Defoe.

Theater *Double Indemnity (La Double Inconstance)* by Pierre de Marivaux 5/3 at the Théâtre Italien, Paris; *The Conscious Lovers* by Richard Steele 11/7 at London's Drury Lane Theatre.

"Traité de l'harmonie" by French composer Jean Philippe Rameau, 39, calls attention for the first time to inverted chords but contains erroneous ideas about augmented sixths and the eleventh chord. Organist since 1715 at Clermont-Ferrand, Rameau has returned to Paris where he begins producing light dramatic pieces.

The Well-Tempered Clavier (Das wohltemperierte Klavier) by Johann Sebastian Bach is published in its first part.

Dresden's Zwinger is completed by German architect Matthaus Daniel Poppelmann, 60, who leaves its pavilion unfinished. He has spent 11 years building the Zwinger.

Durham mustard, produced at Durham, England, is the first commercial dry mustard. Mustard seeds have until now been brought to the table in their natural state and diners have crushed them with their knife handles on the sides of their plates, but a Mrs. Clements has conceived the idea of grinding mustard seeds in the same manner as wheat, she will win the patronage of George I which will make her product fashionable, and dry mustard powder will be used not only as a condiment but also in mustard baths and mustard poultices for cold symptoms, and in mustard emetics for stomach upsets.

Gruyère cheese is introduced into France, which will soon be its major producer. The most famous will be made at Jura in the Franche-Comté.

Boston's population reaches nearly 12,000 with one-third of the town's almost 3,000 houses made of brick (*see* 1638).

1723 The Treaty of Charlottenburg between Britain and Prussia provides that the grandson of George I shall marry a Prussian princess and that Prussia's Prince Frederick shall marry the daughter of the Prince of Wales.

Britain banishes the English bishop Francis Atterbury, 61, for complicity in a Jacobite conspiracy.

Britain permits Jews to take oaths without using the words, "On the true faith of a Christian" (*see* Jewish Naturalization Bill, 1753).

Yellow fever appears for the first time in Europe (*see* New York, 1702; Cadiz, 1741).

British industrial expansion proceeds at a growth rate of 1 percent per year (but *see* Kay, 1733).

An air furnace to smelt iron near Fredericksburg in the Virginia colony uses bituminous coal which is abundant in the region. Alexander Spotswood has

resigned as lieutenant governor to establish the furnace (*see* 1714; 1742).

Sir Godfrey Kneller dies at London November 7 at age 74–77.

Opera *Ottone* 1/23 at London's Haymarket Theatre, with music by George Frideric Handel.

First Performances *The St. John Passion* by Johann Sebastian Bach who is appointed Thomascantor at Leipzig after composer Georg Philipp Telemann, 42, has refused the post.

London architect Sir Christopher Wren dies February 25 at age 90 and is buried in his 13-year-old St. Paul's Cathedral while work proceeds on his Greenwich Hospital.

Austrian architect J. B. Fischer von Erlach dies April 5 at age 66 leaving his 30-year-old brother Joseph Emanuel to complete Vienna's Karlskirche (Church of San Carlo Borromeo), the Hofburg, and the Imperial Library.

Boston's Christ Church is completed 300 yards from the Old North Church completed in 1676.

An American coffee industry that will eventually produce 90 percent of the world's coffee has its beginnings in a seedling planted on the Caribbean island of Martinique by French naval officer Gabriel Mathieu de Clieu who has been helped by confederates to break into the French Jardin Royale at night and to make off with the seedling (*see* 1713; 1724).

The British prime minister Robert Walpole reduces duties on tea.

Simpson's Fish Dinner House opens in Bird-in-Hand Court, Cheapside, London and serves a 2-shilling "fish ordinary" of soup, three fish courses, haunch of

John Law, the Scottish financier. When his "Mississippi Bubble" burst, thousands of French investors were ruined.

1723 (cont.) mutton, and cheese as it will continue to do, at ascending prices, for more than 250 years.

The condom can emancipate young English wives from fear of "big belly, and the squalling brat," writes White Kennett, son of the Bishop of Peterborough, in his satirical poem "Armour" (*see* 1655; 1671; Julius Schmid, 1883).

1724 Russia and Turkey reach an agreement for the dismembering of Persia whose territory they have invaded and whose shah Mir Mahmud goes mad. The shah orders a wholesale massacre at Isfahan.

Rhode Island establishes property ownership qualifications for voters.

A craft guild along the lines of European guilds is established at Philadelphia.

Black slaves outnumber whites two to one in the South Carolina colony.

A Code Noir for regulating the blacks and expelling the Jews at New Orleans is proclaimed by Louisiana Governor de Bienville at New Orleans.

Longmans, Green & Co. publishers has its beginnings in a London publishing house founded by printer Thomas Longman, 25, whose nephew and namesake will carry on the firm after his death in 1755.

Nonfiction *The Origin of Myths (De l'Origine des fables)* by Bernard de Fontenelle explores the psychological and intellectual roots of mythology. Fontenelle refutes popular beliefs and superstitions.

Japanese *ukiyoe* painter Kiyonobu Torii dies at age 60. He has specialized in painting Kabuki actors and beautiful women.

Theater *Caesar in Aegypt* by Colley Cibber 12/9 at London's Drury Lane Theatre.

Vienna's Belvedere Palace is completed after 7 years of construction.

Bucharest's Stavropoleos Church is completed to complement the city's 2-year-old Cretulecu Church.

Carpenter's Hall is completed for Philadelphia's guild of carpenters.

Remy Martin Cognac is introduced by a French distiller.

1725 Russia's Peter the Great dies January 28 at age 52 after a 42-year reign and is succeeded by his 41-year-old consort who will reign until 1727 as Catharine I.

France's Louis XV marries the daughter of Poland's former king Stanislas Leszczynski who was deposed in 1709. The marriage of the 15-year-old king has been arranged by the inept duc de Bourbon (*see* 1733).

Persia's insane Mahmud Shah is succeeded after a reign of terror at Isfahan by Ashraf Shah who will defeat a Turkish army next year and who will reign until 1730.

The Russian Academy of Sciences is established on his deathbed by the czar Peter the Great (above). Since Russia has no scientists of her own, the Academy will be staffed by foreigners for years.

The New Science (Principi di Una Scienza Nuova d'intorno alla Comune Natura delle Nazioni) by Italian philosopher Giovanni Battista Vico, 57, attempts to discover and organize laws common to the evolution of all society.

The stereotype plaster of Paris impression invented by Edinburgh jeweler William Ged can be used to cast any number of metal printing plates and will lead to faster, cheaper letterpress printing. Papiermache versions will further reduce costs.

Opera *Giulio Cesare in Egitto* 3/2 at London's Haymarket Theatre, with music by George Frideric Handel; *Tamerlano* 11/11 at London's Haymarket Theatre, with music by George Frideric Handel.

Rome's "Spanish steps" are completed from the Piazza di Spagna up to the Church of Trinita dei Monti.

St. George's Church is completed by John James in London's Hanover Square after 13 years of work.

Trinity Church is completed at Newport, Rhode Island, with many design features developed by the late Christopher Wren.

France has famine. Paris workers riot when a baker raises the price of bread by 4 sous.

A Parisian craze for onion soup, tripe, and pigs' feet is created by the former Polish king Stanislas (above) who invents *baba au rhum*. The spongelike cake sometimes contains raisins and is soaked in a sauce of rum from the French West Indies.

London has nearly 2,000 coffeehouses, up from just one in 1652.

1726 France's Bishop André Hercule de Fleury is made a cardinal at age 73 and becomes virtual prime minister of the country following the dismissal of Louis Henry, duc de Bourbon. Fleury will continue in power until his death at age 89 in 1743 and his administration will be marked by peace, economic growth, and an upsurge of religious revivalism comparable to England's Methodism (*see* Wesley, 1729).

Montevideo is founded by Spanish conquistadors at the mouth of the Rio de la Plata.

Fiction *Gulliver's Travels* by Jonathan Swift is a satire on cant and sham in England's courts, in her political parties, and among her statesmen. Swift receives £200 for his story of Gulliver's adventures in Lilliput and Brobdingnag and it is the only payment he will ever receive for any of his writings.

England's Castle Howard is completed in Yorkshire by Sir John Vanbrugh who dies March 26 at age 62.

London's St. Martins in the Fields Church is completed by James Gibbs.

Virginia's Berkeley mansion is completed in Georgian style on the James River.

A character in *Gulliver's Travels* (above) "gave it for his opinion that whoever could make two ears of corn, or two blades of grass, to grow upon a spot of ground where only one grew before, would deserve better of mankind, and do more essential service to his country, than the whole race of politicians put together."

Japan's population reaches an estimated 26.5 million.

German settlers begin moving from the Pennsylvania colony into the valley of Virginia.

1727 Russia's extravagant, illiterate (but shrewd) Catharine I dies May 16 at age 44 after a brief reign and is succeeded by her 12-year-old son Peter who will reign until 1730.

Britain's George I dies of apoplexy at 67 the night of June 10 while en route by carriage to Hanover. He is succeeded by his 44-year-old son who begins a 33-year reign as George II, but the new monarchy will be guided by the king's wife Caroline and by his ministers.

The Russian-Chinese border is fixed by the Kiakhta treaty arranged by a mission to Peking headed by Sava Vladislavich.

Photography is pioneered by German chemist J. H. Schulze who uses a mixture of silver nitrate and chalk under stencilled letters and establishes that the darkening of silver salts is due to light, not heat (*see* Scheele, 1777).

Salzburg's Mirabell Palace is completed by Johann Lucas von Hildebrandt after 6 years of construction.

House rats overrun Astrakhan and appear within a few months in the German states. Originally from Eastern Siberia, the rats have not been seen in Europe until now (*see* England, 1728).

Vegetable Staticks by English physiologist-parson Stephen Hales founds the science of plant physiology with its studies of the rate of plant growth (*see* 1733).

Coffee is planted for the first time in Brazil.

1728 Yorkshire carpenter John Harrison, 35, completes plans for a practical spring-driven marine timekeeper that will advance navigation. Harrison obtains a £200 loan from clockmaker George Graham, 55, who has invented a mercurial pendulum and deadbeat escapement and he begins work to perfect his design and create a working model that will win the prize offered in 1714 by London's Board of Longitude (*see* 1736).

Danish explorer Vitus Bering, 47, discovers the Bering Strait between Asia and North America (*see* 1741).

The Spanish siege of Gibraltar is raised after 14 months (*see* 1704; 1779).

English astronomer James Bradley, 35, discovers the aberration of light from fixed stars.

The University of La Habana is founded in Cuba.

The Autobiography of Benvenuto Cellini is published for the first time and gives a vivid picture of 16th century Italian city life. Goldsmith-sculptor Cellini died early in 1571 at age 70.

Cyclopaedia, or An Universal Dictionary of Arts and Sciences by English encyclopaedist Ephraim Chambers is published in two volumes (*see* 1844; *Brittannica*, 1771).

Fiction *Memoires and Adventures of a Man of Quality* (*Memoires et adventures d'un homme de qualite*) by French novelist Abbé Prévost (Antoine François Prévost d'Exiles), 31, is published in the first four of seven volumes. The novelist became a Benedictine monk in 1721, he was ordained 2 years ago, but he has left the order and has traveled to Paris to have his work published.

Poetry *The Dunciad* by Alexander Pope satirizes dullness.

Painting *The Skate* and *The Rain* by French painter Jean Baptiste Simeon Chardin, 28.

Theater *Money Makes the World Go Round* (*Le Triomphe de Plutus*) by Pierre de Marivaux 4/22 at the Théâtre Italien, Paris; *Love in Several Masques* by English playwright-novelist Henry Fielding, 21.

Opera *The Beggar's Opera* 2/9 at the Lincoln's Inn Fields Theatre, London, with music by Berlin-born composer John Christopher Pepusch, 51, book and lyrics by English poet John Gay, 43 (the opera begins a 2-year run) (*see* 1928); *Siroe, Re di Persia* 2/28 at London's Haymarket Theatre, with music by George Frideric Handel; *Tolomeo, Re di Egitto* 5/4 at London's Haymarket Theatre, with music by George Frideric Handel who is named codirector of the King's Theatre in Covent Garden.

House rats reach England where they will be given the name *Rattus norvegicus* by naturalist John Berkenhout who hears a false rumor that the rats arrived with a shipment of Norwegian lumber (*see* 1727; Linnaeus, 1737; Boston, 1775).

1729 The Treaty of Seville November 9 ends a 2-year war between Spain and an Anglo-French alliance. The alliance agrees to the Spanish succession in the Italian duchies, Britain retains Gibraltar.

The town of Baltimore first settled more than a century ago is formally established in the Maryland colony by the purchase of land near deep tidal waters that extend deep into grain and tobacco fields at the head of Chesapeake Bay, land rapidly being developed by German immigrants.

Natchez Indians attack Louisiana's French colonists. More than 200 are killed, several hundred women, children, and black slaves are taken prisoner (*see* 1713).

Diamonds discovered at Tejuco, Brazil, in 1721 are confirmed as such by Portuguese-Brazilian Bernardo

1729 (cont.) da Fonseca Lobo who arrives at Lisbon with samples. A diamond rush begins to Tejuco, which will be renamed Diamintina.

A Modest Enquiry into the Nature and Necessity of a Paper-Currency is published by Philadelphia printer Benjamin Franklin, 23.

The Pennsylvania Gazette is purchased from his former employer Samuel Keimer by Benjamin Franklin (above) and his partner Hugh Meredith. Franklin began his career as apprentice to his half-brother James at Boston when James started the *New England Courant* in 1721, he took over when James was imprisoned briefly in 1722 for criticizing public officials, but he quarreled with James the following year, left for New York, moved on to Philadelphia, worked for Keimer, and in 1724 voyaged to London with the intent of buying equipment for a shop of his own. Not finding letters of credit promised by Pennsylvania Governor William Keith, Franklin worked for a London printshop until 1726 when he returned to Keimer's shop at Philadelphia, he went into partnership with Meredith last year, and he will buy out Meredith next year (*see* circulating library, 1730).

First performances *The St. Matthew Passion* (*Grosse Passionmusik nach dem Evangelium Matthaei*) by Johann Sebastian Bach 4/25 at Leipzig.

Methodism has its beginnings at Oxford University where fellow students call Charles Wesley, 22, a "methodist" because of his methodical study habits. Episcopal priest John Wesley, 26, comes into residence at Oxford in November and joins with his brother Charles and with James Hervey, 15, and George Whitefield, 15, in a Holy Club that meets at first each Sunday evening for strict observance of sacrament and then meets every evening, reading the classics and the Greek Testament, fasting on Wednesdays and Fridays (*see* 1735).

A Modest Proposal by Jonathan Swift is an ironical tract inspired by Irish population pressures: "I have been assured by a knowing American of my acquaintance that a young healthy child well nursed is at a year old a most delicious, nourishing and wholesome food, whether stewed, roasted, baked or boiled; and I make no doubt that it will equally serve in a fricasee or a ragout: I do therefore humbly offer it to public consideration that . . . 100,000 [infants] may, at a year old, be offered in sale to the persons of quality and fortune throughout the kingdom; always advising the mother to let them suck plentifully in the last month, so as to render them plump and fat for a good table."

England's death rate begins a sharp descent, producing population pressure on food supplies, but food remains more plentiful than in Ireland.

1730 The Russian czar Peter II dies of smallpox at age 14 January 30, the very day on which he was to have married Catharine, second daughter of Alexis Dolgoruki. Peter's 36-year-old cousin Anna Ivanovna enters Moscow February 26, her personal friends overthrow the supreme privy council in a coup d'etat March 8, and she summons her former lover Ernst Johann Biren, 39. Grandson of a groom to a former duke of Courland, Biren gained favor with Anna when she was duchess of Courland, she makes him grand-chamberlain and a count of the empire, he adopts the arms of the French ducal house of Biron. The new czarina gives him an estate at Wenden with 50,000 crowns a year, and he will dominate her 10-year reign, antagonizing most Russians with his rapacity and treachery.

Denmark's Frederick IV dies at Odense October 12, the day after his 59th birthday. He has been forced to give up some German territories in his 31-year reign and is succeeded by his narrow-minded 31-year-old son who will reign until 1746 as Christian VI. The new king will follow the whims of his wife Sophie Magdalene of Brandenburg-Kulmbach.

The Persian shah Ashraf who has ruled since 1725 is defeated with his Afghans near Shiraz, some of his followers murder him en route to Kandahar, and he is succeeded by Tahmasp II, a figurehead for the Afshar chief Nadir Kuli.

Thomas Godfrey in the Pennsylvania colony invents an improved mariner's quadrant (*see* Hadley, 1731).

The first American circulating library is established by Philadelphia's Benjamin Franklin who begins by having members of his club the Junto pool their books for borrowing. Franklin then obtains 50 subscribers at 40 shillings each and sends to England for 100 books.

Painting *The Symbolic Marriage of Venice to the Adriatic* by the Venetian painter Canaletto (Giovanni Antonio Canal), 33, who has formed a connection with English merchant–art collector Joseph Smith who will become British consul at Venice and who will serve as Canaletto's agent; *The Dancer LaCamargo* by French painter Nicolas Lancret, 40.

Theater *The Game of Love and Chance* (*Le Jeu de l'amour et du hasard*) by Pierre de Marivaux 1/23 at the Théâtre Italien, Paris; *The Tragedy of Tragedies, or The Life and Death of Tom Thumb the Great* by Henry Fielding, in April at London's Drury Lane Theatre; *Brutus* by Voltaire 12/11 at Paris.

"Gaudeamus Igitur" is published for the first time. The German drinking song may date to the 13th century.

Westover plantation house in the Virginia colony is completed for William Byrd in Charles City County; Stratford is completed in Westmoreland County (date approximate).

Carter's Grove plantation house is completed 6 miles below Williamsburg for planter Carter Burwell who has retained English architects Richard Bayliss and David Minitree.

The Serpentine in London's Hyde Park is created from the River Westbourne.

Scientific farming is introduced into England by Charles Townshend, Viscount Townshend of Raynham, who resigns from public life at age 56 to devote himself to his estates. Taking his cue from the Dutch, Townshend will find that he can keep livestock through the winter by feeding them turnips and by eliminating the need to slaughter most livestock in late September "Turnip Townshend" will reduce the need for costly spices, used for centuries to disguise the taste of spoiled meat. By making fresh meat available in all seasons and by paving the way for the development of larger cattle, Townshend will make an important contribution to the improvement of animal husbandry and of human diet (*see* 1732; Bakewell, 1755, 1760; Coke, 1772).

1731 The reflecting quadrant invented by English mathematician-mechanic John Hadley, 49, advances navigation by enabling a mariner to determine his latitude at noon or by night (*see* Godfrey, 1730). Hadley's instrument has an arc that measures one-fourth of a circle, a graduated scale is inscribed round its edge, its sliding vernier scale has minute subdivisions to facilitate measurement of the angle between the horizon and some fixed star at night, or between the horizon and the sun at noon, a Royal Navy vessel will test the quadrant next year by order of the Admiralty, and its readings will be so accurate that the Navy will adopt Hadley's device (*see* Campbell's sextant, 1757; Harrison's chronometer, 1736).

The Ostend East India Company set up to rival the Dutch and English companies comes to an end March 16 under terms of the Treaty of Vienna signed by the Holy Roman Emperor Charles VI with Britain. The Dutch sign the Pragmatic Sanction.

The Pragmatic Sanction of Charles VI decrees that lands of the Austrian Empire shall be indivisible, that they shall devolve upon his eldest daughter Maria Theresa if he should die without a male heir, and that the lands shall pass to the heirs of Maria Theresa or her sisters according to the law of primogeniture.

Parma and Piacenza pass to the son of Spain's Philip V as the head of the Farnese family Antonio Farnese dies at age 52 without male issue. Philip's son Carlos has taken Elizabeth Farnese as his second wife and Spain's recognition of the Pragmatic Sanction (above) aids the succession of Charles to the Italian duchies.

Persia's Shah Tahmasp II dies after a brief reign. He is succeeded by his 8-month-old son whose 5-year reign will end the Safavid dynasty that has ruled Persia since 1502.

Louisiana becomes a French royal province once again upon the surrender of the charter of John Law's Compagnie d'Occident (*see* 1716; 1720; 1763).

The Sieur de La Verendrye Pierre Gaultier de Varennes, 46, begins explorations of western Canada (*see* Lake of the Woods, 1732).

Welshman Morgan Morgan establishes the first permanent settlement in western Virginia on Mill Creek (*see* coal, 1742).

France forbids barbers to practice surgery but elsewhere barbers continue to double as surgeons.

A French Royal Academy of Surgery is founded under the direction of Jean-Louis Petit who will invent the screw tourniquet and will develop a procedure for mastoidectomy.

Fiction *Histoire des Grieux et de Manon Lescaut* by the Abbé Prévost whose work is condemned as immoral by French authorities. The story of an aristocrat who gives up everything in his passion for a demondaine will be the basis of romantic novels, plays, and operas in the next century.

Theater *The London Merchant, or The History of George Barnwell* by English playwright George Lillo, 38, 6/22 at London's Drury Lane Theatre. Lillo's play is the first serious prose drama whose chief figures are not of the nobility.

Opera *Poro* 2/2 at London's Haymarket Theatre, with music by George Frideric Handel.

London's No. 10 Downing Street is completed in Westminster to provide a residence for the British prime minister.

Porcelain factories multiply in Europe as demand grows for china plates and cups.

Half a pint of rum in two equal tots becomes the official ration for all hands in the British Royal Navy (*see* 1655; Vernon, 1740).

1732 The Holy Roman Emperor Charles VI obtains recognition of his Pragmatic Sanction order of succession (*see* 1731). The emperor is 46, has no male offspring, and has decreed that lands belonging to the Austrian Empire shall be indivisible, that if he should die without a male heir the empire shall devolve upon his daughters (the eldest, Maria Theresa, is now 15) and to their heirs by the law of primogeniture, and that if his daughters should die without heirs, the empire shall go to the heirs of his late brother Josef who died in 1711 (*see* 1740).

Genoa recovers Corsica from insurgent forces who revolted in 1730, but the Genoese will have to call on the French for help in controlling the island (*see* 1768).

America's Georgia colony has its beginnings in a charter granted by George II to English philanthropists who include James Edward Oglethorpe, 36, for lands between the Altamah and Savannah Rivers (*see* 1733).

The sieur de la Verendrye erects a fort on Lake of the Woods (*see* 1731; 1734).

Swedish botanist Carolus Linnaeus (Carl von Linne), 25, travels 4,600 miles through northern Scandinavia studying plant life (*see* 1737).

1732 (cont.) *Poor Richard's Almanack* is published at Philadelphia by Benjamin Franklin who will continue to publish new editions for 25 years and who will make his almanacs the most popular reading in the colonies next to the Bible. Primarily an agricultural handbook, the *Almanack* gives times for sunrises and sunsets, high and low tides, and the best dates for planting and harvesting. Along with weather predictions, the *Almanack* will be full of practical suggestions, recipes, advice on personal hygiene, and folksy urgings to be frugal, industrious, and orderly ("God helps those who help themselves," "Never leave till tomorrow that which you can do to-day") which are credited to a fictional "Richard Saunders."

Colonial postal service will be revolutionized by Franklin (above) to improve circulation of his *Almanack,* which will reach 10,000, and of his *Pennsylvania Gazette* (see 1729). Franklin will double and triple postal service in some areas, he will increase the speed of couriers, he will consolidate roads from Maine to Georgia into what will later be called Route No. 1, and he will produce for the English Crown three times the postal revenues obtained in Ireland.

Painting *Kitchen Table with Shoulder of Mutton* by Jean Chardin.

Sculpture Rome's Fontana di Trevi is completed by Italian sculptor Niccola Salvi.

Theater *Zara (Zaire)* by Voltaire 8/13 at Paris; London's Theatre Royal in Covent Garden opens 12/7 with the 1700 Congreve comedy *The Way of the World.*

Famine strikes western Japan as crops are ruined by an excess of rain and a plague of grasshoppers: 2.6 million go hungry, 12,400 die, more than 15,000 horses and work cattle starve to death in one of the worst of the 130 famines of the Tokugawa shogunate.

A threshing machine is invented by Scottish engineer-farmer Michael Menzies but it is not used to any extent.

The average bullocks sold at London's Smithfield cattle market weighs 550 pounds, up from 370 pounds in 1710 (see 1639; 1795).

London's beef, pork, lamb, and mutton for the next century and more will come largely from animals raised in Ireland, Scotland, and Wales, landed by ship at Holyhead, driven across the Isle of Anglesey, made to swim half a mile across the Menai Straits to the Welsh mainland, and then driven 200 miles to Barnet, a village on the outskirts of London, to be fattened for the Smithfield market. The meat will be generally tough and costly.

1733 The War of the Polish Succession begins in Europe following the death of Poland's Augustus II February 1 at age 62. Austria and Russia demand the election of the king's only legitimate son Frederick Augustus, 36, elector of Saxony, but France's Louis XV persuades the Polish nobility to restore his father-in-law

Stanislas Leszczynski to the throne (see 1725). A large Russian army invades Poland and obliges Stanislas to flee to Danzig, France declares war on the Holy Roman Empire and gains support from Spain and Sardinia, Russian forces lay siege to Danzig beginning in October, and Louis XV sends a French expeditionary force to relieve the Baltic city and to rescue Stanislas (see 1734).

French forces occupy Lorraine (see 1738).

A Molasses Act passed by Parliament to tax British colonists imposes heavy duties on the molasses, sugar, and rum imported from non-British West Indian islands and thus effectively raises the price of the rum that Americans consume at the rate of 3 Imperial gallons (3.75 American gallons) per year for every man, woman, and child.

Smugglers evade the Molasses Act (above) and in some cases carry African slaves to Spanish colonies, trade them for sugar and molasses, and sell the cargo to New England distillers for capital with which to buy more African slaves (see 1698).

Savannah, Georgia, is founded by James E. Oglethorpe who names the last of the 13 British colonies in America after George II and makes it an asylum for debtors. Oglethorpe settles at the mouth of the Savannah River with 120 men, women, and children (see 1732; 1742).

The Spanish Plate Fleet laden with silver and gold from South America founders in the shallow reefs of the Florida Keys and is wrecked.

The flying shuttle invented by English weaver John Kay revolutionizes the hand loom, cuts labor needs in half, and prepares the way for further developments that will speed the industrialization of Britain's cottage industry in textiles (see Arkwright, 1769).

Haemostaticks by Stephen Hales reveals his findings on blood circulation. Hales has tied tubes into the arteries and veins of living animals, he has measured blood pressure and circulation rates, and he has estimated the actual velocity of the blood in the veins, the arteries, and the capillary vessels. He shows that capillaries are capable of dilating and constricting (see 1727; Harvey, 1628).

Poetry *Essay on Man* by Alexander Pope contains lines and couplets that will become familiar in most English households: "Hope springs eternal in the human breast;/ Man never is, but always to be blest."

Painting *Southwark Fair* by English painter William Hogarth, 35.

Theater *The Death of Caesar (La mort de Cesar)* by Voltaire; *The Wiles of Love (L'Heureux stratageme)* by Pierre de Marivaux 6/6 at the Théâtre Italien, Paris.

Opera *The Servant Mistress (La Serva Padrone)* 8/28 at the Bartholomeo Opera House in Naples, with music by Italian composer Giovanni Battista Pergolesi, 23, who establishes the comic opera form that will continue for nearly a century; *Hippolyte et Aricie* at the Academie in Paris, with music by Jean Rameau to a libretto derived from the 1677 Racine tragedy *Phèdre; Achilles* at London's Covent Garden with a libretto by John Gay. *Rosamund* at London's Drury Lane Theatre with music by English composer Thomas Augustine Arne, 23.

The "Kyrie" and "Gloria" portions of his B Minor Mass are presented by Johann Sebastian Bach in July to the elector of Saxony whose accession to the Polish throne is being challenged (above).

The "Rode" violin is completed by Antonio Stradivari, now 89.

1734 Danzig falls to Russian forces June 2 after a siege of nearly 8 months. Poland's Stanislas Leszczynski eludes the Russians and escapes to Prussia (*see* 1735).

Spanish forces seize Naples and Sicily while Milan falls to another Spanish force that has invaded Lombardy as the War of the Polish Succession spreads through Europe (*see* 1735).

Schwenkenfelders from Silesia emigrate to America and drop anchor near New Castle, Delaware, where they obtain the first fresh water they have had in months.

German Protestants driven out of the principality of Salzburg settle some 25 miles above the mouth of Georgia's Savannah River at Ebenezer.

A French fort on Lake Winnipeg is erected by the sieur de La Verendrye (*see* 1731; 1738).

Caslon typefaces begin to supplant Dutch typefaces and earlier English typefaces. London type founder William Caslon, 42, started his career as an engraver of gun-locks and gun barrels, he opened a type foundry in 1720 with backing from two London printers who admired his silver-chasing and bookbinders' stamps, his son and namesake, now 14, will carry on his business after his death in 1766. Caslon type will enjoy a revival in 1843, and it will remain popular for well over a century.

Lettres anglaises ou philosophiques by Voltaire exalts the English constitution and makes special reference to representative government.

The autumn crocus (*Crocus sativa*) whose stamens yield the spice and dyestuff saffron will be introduced into America by the Schwenkenfelders (above) who will settle in the Pennsylvania colony.

An English seaman is afflicted with scurvy and is marooned on the coast of Greenland because the disease is thought to be contagious. The man cures himself by eating scurvy grass (*Cochlearia officinalis*) and is picked up by a passing ship. News of the incident will reach His Majesty's Hospital at Haslar, near Portsmouth, where navy surgeon James Lind will hear of it some years hence (*see* 1747).

Considerations sur les Causes de la Grandeur des Romains et de leur Decadence by Montesquieu

claims that the ancient Roman world had a population larger than that of 18th century Europe.

1735 The War of the Polish Succession ends October 5 in the Treaty of Vienna that will be ratified in 1738. The treaty legitimizes the Elector of Saxony as king of Poland and he will reign until 1763 as Frederick Augustus II, Austria cedes Naples and Sicily to the Spanish Bourbons on condition that they never be united with Spain under one crown, and the son of Spain's Philip V assumes the throne of Naples and Sicily as Charles III after giving up Parma and Piacenza to Austria (*see* 1738).

Russia gives up Peter the Great's last Persian acquisitions and joins in an alliance against the Ottoman Turks with Persia's Nadir Kuli who wins a great victory over the Turks at Baghavand and takes Tiflis.

Vincennes, Indiana, has its beginnings in a French settlement on the Wabash River.

French fur traders and lead miners found Ste. Genevieve, first permanent white settlement on the Missouri River.

Augusta, Georgia, is founded on the Savannah River by settlers in the new Georgia colony.

Trustees of the Georgia colony (above) prohibit slavery and the importation of rum.

Ergotism breaks out in Wurtemberg in a severe epidemic (*see* 1722; 1777).

Scarlet fever strikes New England in a devastating epidemic (*see* 1736).

John Peter Zenger, 38, gains a landmark victory for freedom of the press. New York Governor William Cosby has brought libel charges against the German-American printer for reporting that Cosby attempted to rig a 1733 election held at St. Paul's Church village green in the town of Eastchester, Philadelphia lawyer Andrew Hamilton admits that his client printed the report in his *New York Weekly Journal* as charged, but he persuades the jury that Zenger printed only the truth and wins acquittal.

Fiction *Gil Blas* (*L'Histoire de Gil Blas de Santillana*) by Alain René Lesage, now 67, whose four-volume pioneer picaresque novel appeared in its first volume 20 years ago.

Painting *The Pleasure Party* by Nicolas Lancret; *A Rake's Progress* by William Hogarth.

Opera *Olimpiade* 1/8 at Rome's Teatre Tordinona, with music by Giovanni Pergolesi; *Ariodante* 1/19 at London's Covent Garden Theatre, with music by George Frideric Handel; *Alcina* 4/27 at London's Covent Garden Theatre, with music by G. F. Handel; *Les Indes galantes* 8/23 at the Paris Opéra, with music by Jean Philippe Rameau.

John Wesley and his brother Charles lose their father April 25 and embark in October for the Georgia colony with two other Methodists and a party of Moravians (*see* 1729). The *Simmonds* encounters storms en

289

Philadelphia printer Benjamin Franklin worked to improve colonial transportation to help sales of his *Almanack*.

route, John Wesley finds his fears greater than his faith. He will provoke criticism at Savannah, but he will begin the first Methodist society (*see* 1738).

Pellagra is described for the first time by Don Gasper Casal, personal physician to Spain's Philip V (*see* Italy, 1749).

Botulism makes its first recorded appearance in one of the German states. An outbreak of the deadly food poisoning is traced to some sausage.

English distillers produce gin at a rate of 5.4 million gallons per year, nearly a gallon for every man, woman, and child (*see* 1740; American rum, 1733).

1736 The ship's chronometer presented to London's Board of Longitude by John Harrison is accurate to within one-tenth of a second per day (1.3 miles of longitude) and wins the prize offered by the Board in 1714 (*see* 1728). Harrison's chronometer is set to the time of 0° longitude (Greenwich time), a navigator can fix his longitudinal position by determining local time with the quadrant devised by John Hadley in 1731 and comparing it with Harrison's chronometer, the device weighs 66 pounds and is a complicated, costly, delicate affair, but it will soon be improved, reduced in size, and refined to keep it going through all weather aboard any sailing vessel (*see* 1761).

Mechanica sive motus analytice exposita by Swiss mathematician-physicist Leonard Euler, 29, is the first systematic textbook of mechanics. Euler has been at the Russian Academy of Sciences since 1727 (he arrived at St. Petersburg the day Catharine I died), he has been the Academy's leading mathematician since 1733, when his teacher Daniel Bernoulli returned to Switzerland, he has married, but he lost the sight of one eye last year (*see* 1748).

Chi'en Lung ascends the Chinese imperial throne at age 25 to begin a Ch'ing dynasty reign that will continue until 1796. He will extend Ch'ing control throughout central Asia.

The Safavid dynasty that has ruled Persia since 1502 ends with the death of the 6-year-old shah Abbas III. The Turk Nadir Kuli, 48, who has ruled the country effectively for the past decade succeeds to the throne and will rule as Nadir Shah until 1747.

Pope Clement XII condemns Freemasonry.

Britain repeals her statutes against witchcraft.

English surgeon Claudius Aymand, 56, performs the first successful appendix operation to be described in medical literature.

"The Practical History of a New Epidemical Eruptive Military Fever . . . in Boston . . . 1735 and 1736" by Boston physician William Douglass gives the first clinical description of scarlet fever.

Painting *The Good Samaritan* by William Hogarth.

Theater *Alzire* (*Les Americans*) by Voltaire 1/27 at the Comédie Française, Paris.

Opera *Atalanta* 5/23 at London's Royal Theatre in Covent Garden, with music by George Frideric Handel.

Passenger pigeons sell at six for a penny in Boston (*see* 1672; 1800).

1737 *Genera Plantarum* by Sweden's Carolus Linnaeus inaugurates modern botany's binomial system of taxonomy (*see* 1732). Basing his system on stamens and pistils, Linnaeus divides all vegetation into Phanerogams (seed plants) and Cryptogams (spore plants such as ferns). Phanerogams are in turn divided into Angiosperms (concealed seed plants such as flowering plants) and Gymnosperms (naked seed plants such as conifers). Angiosperms are further divided into Monocotolydons (narrow-leaved plants with parallel veins) and Dicotolydons (broad-leaved plants with net veins). Each of these is divided into Orders, Families, Genera, and Species (*see* 1738; 1789).

The last of the Medici family is driven out of Tuscany following the death of Giovan (or Gian) Gastone de' Medici at age 66 leaving vacant the ducal throne. Austria takes over and will give the ducal throne next year to Franz Stefan, duke of Lorraine.

The Philadelphia police force created by Benjamin Franklin is the first city-paid constabulary. Franklin has examined the "city watch" and has found it lacking. He will soon organize the first city bucket brigade (fire department).

Theater *False Secrets* (*Les Fausses Confidences*) by Pierre de Marivaux 3/16 at the Comédie Française, Paris.

An English Licensing Act restricts the number of London theaters and requires that all plays be subjected to the Lord Chamberlain for censorship before they may be presented (*see* 1968).

Opera *Castor and Pollux* 10/24 at the Paris Opéra, with music by Jean Philippe Rameau.

 Calcutta has an earthquake October 11 that kills an estimated 300,000, the second largest earthquake toll in world history.

 A group of 60 men building a new meeting house at Northampton in the Massachusetts colony consumes 69 gallons of rum, 36 pounds of sugar, and several barrels of beer and cider in 1 week.

1738 The Treaty of Vienna that ended the war of the Polish Succession in 1735 is ratified November 13. Stanislas Leszczynski receives Lorraine and Bar in compensation for renouncing the Polish throne but only on the condition that the duchies devolve upon France at his death; Spain receives Parma and Piacenza in exchange for Naples and Sicily.

 Sur la figure de la terre by French mathematician-astronomer Louis Moreau de Maupertuis, 40, is a report on an expedition to Lapland. Sent by Louis XV to measure a degree of longitude, Maupertuis confirms Isaac Newton's view that the earth is a spheroid flattened near the poles with a bulge near the equator.

Hydrodynamics by Swiss physicist-mathematician Daniel Bernoulli, 38, presents an early version of the kinetic theory of gases based on his investigations of the forces exerted by liquids (*see* d'Alembert, 1743).

Classes Plantarum by Linnaeus expands the system of taxonomy he introduced last year (*see* 1789).

Excavation begins in Naples to uncover the city of Herculaneum, buried under volcanic ash and lava by the eruption of Mount Vesuvius in 79 A.D. which killed far more people at Herculaneum than at Pompeii. The work will continue for more than 40 years.

 The sieur de La Verendrye builds a fort on the Assiniboine River (*see* 1734; 1742).

 Painting *La Gouvernante* by Jean Baptiste Chardin.

 John Wesley returns to England from the Georgia colony (his brother Charles returned in 1736 when his health failed), he starts a society that meets for the first time May 1, both brothers experience evangelical conversions, brother John will begin preaching in the fields at Bristol next year and will buy a deserted gun factory outside London for his prayer meetings (*see* 1735; 1744).

 More Frenchmen will die of hunger in the next 2 years than died in all the wars of Louis XIV, according to René Louis de Voyer, 44, the marquis d'Argenson, who will make the claim in later writings. Fragmentation of French land holdings to the point where a single fruit tree may constitute a "farm" has contributed to a decline in food production.

1739 Persian forces under Nadir Shah defeat a huge Mogul army at Karnal, they sack nearby Delhi, and they shatter the Mogul Empire. Afghan invaders sweep down from the northwest frontier, Marathas come east from the great central plateau of Daccan to threaten the fertile lands of Bengal, India's suahdars and nabobs establish independent states, some of these engage in wars, and the chaos opens the way to foreign domination of the subcontinent.

Ottoman forces approach Belgrade and the Holy Roman Emperor Charles VI signs the Treaty of Belgrade September 18, deserting his Russian ally and ending a 3-year war with Constantinople. Austria yields Belgrade and northern Serbia, Russia retains Azov but agrees to raze her forts and to build no fleet on the Black Sea.

The War of Jenkins's Ear between Britain and Spain begins in October as British naval squadrons receive orders to intercept Spanish galleons. The Spanish captain Fandino cut off the ear of English mariner Robert Jenkins at Havana in 1731, Parliament has decided to make an issue of Spain's alleged mistreatment of British smugglers and pirates, the Admiralty sends Admiral Edward Vernon to the Caribbean to harry Spanish shipping, and on November 22 Vernon captures Portobelo with a force of only six ships (*see* 1716).

 Treatise on Human Nature by Scottish philosopher David Hume, 28, challenges the prevailing monetary doctrines of mercantilism, notably the doctrine that a nation can continually increase her stock of gold and silver, and her prosperity, through surpluses in her balance of payments. Hume questions whether action by government is necessary or even helpful to the maintenance of a nation's money supply (*see* Adam Smith, 1776).

Persia's Nadir Shah seizes the Koh-i-noor diamond in the sack of Delhi (above). The 109 carat diamond has been a treasure of the Mogul emperors, the East India Company will acquire it when it conquers the Punjab, and the company will present it to Queen Victoria in 1850.

 English highwayman Richard "Dick" Turpin is convicted of horse-stealing at the York assizes and is hanged April 7 at age 33 after a notorious career that has made him a legend in his own time.

 The Cato Conspiracy at Stono, South Carolina, takes the lives of 44 blacks and 30 whites as slaves near Charleston arm themselves by robbing a store and set out for Florida, gathering recruits and murdering whites on the way. The rebellion is crushed by a hastily assembled force of whites.

 French explorers Pierre and Paul Mallet reach the headwaters of the Arkansas River and sight the Rocky Mountains for the first time.

 German-American glassmaker Caspar Wistar brings workers to the New Jersey colony and starts a factory.

 Treatise on Human Nature by David Hume (above) shatters the connection between reason and the empirical world, pioneering modern empiricism. If a

1739 (cont.) rock is dropped, says Hume, it is not reason that tells us the rock will fall but rather custom and experience, the truths of reason are true by definition, like mathematical axioms, but it is folly to think that any observed effect follows any cause by force of reason.

Joe Miller's Jests, or The Wits Vade-Mecum being a collection of the most brilliant jests, the polite repartees, the most elegant bon mots, the most pleasant short stories in the English language by the late English humorist Joseph Miller is a 72-page volume containing 247 original jokes. Miller died last year at age 54, he will be called the "father of modern humor," but he left his wife and children in poverty.

Painting *Le Déjeuner* by French painter François Boucher, 36, who has studied at Rome and has become the most fashionable painter of his day.

Theater *The Man of the World* (*L'uomo di mondo*) by Venetian playwright Carlo Goldoni, 32, in March at Venice's Teatro San Samuele.

Potato crops fail in Ireland. The effect is not calamitous since the tubers do not comprise the bulk of most people's diets as they will a century hence, but Irish cotters (tenant farmers) are becoming increasingly dependent on potatoes for food while raising cereal grains and cattle for the export market that provides them with rent money. The cotters are selecting potatoes for high-yield varieties and thus inadvertently narrowing the genetic base of their potato plants, breeding plants with little or no resistance to the fungus disease *Phytophthora infestans* (*see* 1822).

1740 Prussia's Friedrich Wilhelm I dies May 31 at age 51 after a 27-year reign in which he has made Prussia a formidable military power with a standing army of 83,000—enormous for a country of 2.5 million. His 28-year-old son succeeds to the throne as Frederick II, he will reign until 1786, he proceeds to occupy part of Silesia, and he thus precipitates a war with Austria that will continue for 15 of the next 23 years.

The Russian czarina Anna Ivanovna adopts her 8-week-old greatnephew October 5 and declares him her successor, she makes Count Biron regent for the infant czar Ivan VI, she dies October 17 at age 47, Field Marshal Burkhard Christoph von Münnich, 57, enters the regent's bedroom at midnight November 19 and seizes the hated Biron, and a commission is appointed to try the regent (*see* 1741).

The Holy Roman Emperor Charles VI dies October 20 at age 55, the last of the Hapsburg line that began in 1516. His daughter Maria Theresa is queen of Hungary and Bohemia, but the king of Saxony, the elector of Bavaria, and Spain's Philip V contest her right to succeed Charles. The War of the Austrian Succession will involve most of Europe's great powers in the next 8 years.

Typhus epidemics take thousands of lives in the central German states and in Ireland.

The Hydra discovered by Swiss naturalist Abraham Trembley, 40, in Holland is a freshwater polyp that combines both animal and plant characteristics. It can regenerate lost parts.

Crucible steel rediscovered by English clocksmith Benjamin Huntsman, 36, at Sheffield will make Sheffield steel as famous as was Damascus steel in antiquity, described by Aristotle in 334 B.C., used for centuries to make swordblades, employed in India, but lost over the ages. Huntsman heats metal in small, enclosed earthenware cupolas which he calls crucibles, he excludes air, and he produces a superior steel (*see* Krupp, 1811; Sheffield plate, 1742).

Connecticut colony tinsmiths Edward and William Pattison at Berlin begin manufacturing tinware and selling it from house to house—the first colonial tin peddlers, or tinkers.

A network of post roads connects the American colonies from Charleston to Portsmouth, New Hampshire. Packet boats operate on regular schedules to link the major colonial ports (*see* Franklin, 1732).

Bethlehem in the Pennsylvania colony is founded by Moravian emigrants who introduce the celebration of Christmas with such German customs as the visit from Saint Nicholas, or Santa Claus. In Puritan New England Christmas remains a working day.

Fiction *Pamela, or Virtue Rewarded* by English novelist Samuel Richardson, 51, who gains enormous popularity with his story in the form of correspondence of a servant who resists her master's seductions and winds up as his wife.

Theater *The Test* (*L'Epreuve*) by Pierre de Marivaux 11/19 at the Théâtre Italien, Paris.

Famine strikes Russia and France. French peasants are reduced to eating ferns and grassroots, but some survive by eating potatoes (*see* Parmentier, 1771).

The price of a 4-pound loaf of bread rises to 20 sous at Paris, and 50 die in a prison riot protesting a cut in bread rations.

British authorities exile Irish mercenary Richard Hennessy for agitating against the Crown, he settles at the French town of Cognac, and he begins exporting Cognac brandy to Ireland. The brandy finds favor among the local gentry who disdain the local whisky.

The unrestricted sale of gin and other cheap spirits reaches its peak in England. Some observers express fears that wholesale drunkenness is undermining the social fabric of the nation (*see* 1735; Hogarth, 1751).

Booth's distillery is founded at London. It will be famous for its House of Lords and High and Dry Gin.

The British navy's rum ration is diluted by Admiral Edward Vernon who is nicknamed "Old Grog" because he wears a grogram cloak in foul weather (*see* 1731). "Grog" will become a slang word for liquor, and groggy for drunken dizziness.

Berlin in Frederick II's Prussia has a population of nearly 70,000, up from 20,000 half a century ago.

1741 The British prime minister Sir Robert Walpole uses the phrase "balance of power" in a speech he delivers in the House of Commons February 13, giving expression to the principle that has long guided British foreign policy.

Prussia's Frederick II gains a victory April 10 at Mollwitz and later joins a secret alliance against Austria signed at Nymphenburg in May by France, Bavaria, and Spain who are soon joined by Saxony (see 1740). An allied French-Bavarian army invades Austria and Bohemia and seizes Prague with Saxon help after 30,000 Austrian defenders have died of typhus.

Frederick II (above) conquers Silesia and captures Brieg, Neisse, Glatz, and Olmutz before British diplomats mediate between Prussia and Austria.

Britain's Admiral Vernon leads a 100-ship, 27,000-man naval attack on the Spanish fortress San Felipe at Cartagena but abandons a proposed assault on the fortress after 2 months of dodging Spanish lead and slapping mosquitoes that carry malaria and yellow fever. The British retire to Jamaica after disease and battle wounds have reduced a force of 8,000 landed ashore near Cartagena to only 3,500 effectives.

Admiral Vernon (above) formally decorates colonial captain Lawrence Washington of the Virginia colony for having led three gallant charges against the walls of San Felipe. Washington returns to the Potomac River plantation he calls Green Mountain and renames it Mount Vernon (see 1751).

A Russian commission finds the regent Count Biron guilty of treason April 11 and sentences him to death by quartering (see 1740). The sentence is commuted to banishment for life to Siberia, the count's vast property is all confiscated, including diamonds worth £600,000. The French ambassador plots to destroy the Austrian influence dominant at St. Petersburg, he plays on fears of the 31-year-old daughter of Peter the Great that she will be confined to a convent for life, he supplies Elizabeth Petrovna with money. She drives with her supporters to the barracks of the Preobrazhensky Guards the night of December 6, she arouses their sympathies with a stirring speech, and she leads them to the Winter Palace for a coup d'etat. She seizes the new regent Anna Leopoldovna and her children, including the infant czar Ivan VI, she banishes Anna and her husband, she deposes the czar and has him imprisoned, and she ascends the imperial throne to begin a reign that will continue until her death early in 1762.

 New Yorkers charge a "Negro Conspiracy" with having started fires that break out through March and April. Roman Catholic priests, they say, are inciting black slaves to burn the town on orders from Spain; 4 whites and 18 blacks are hanged, 13 blacks are burned at the stake.

New York's journeymen bakers go out on strike.

 Essai de cosmologie by P. L. M. de Maupertuis suggests a survival of the fittest concept: "Could not one say that since, in the accidental combination of Nature's productions, only those could survive which found themselves provided with certain appropriate relationships, it is no wonder that these relationships are present in all the species that actually exist? These species which we see today are only the smallest part of those which a blind destiny produced." But few people read Maupertuis (see Darwin, 1840).

 An epidemic of exanthematous typhus kills 30,000 in France.

A typhus epidemic in Sweden comes on the heels of a poor harvest and takes a heavy toll.

A yellow fever epidemic at Cadiz kills 10,000.

 Russian pioneers in Siberia set out for North America in small boats from Kamchatka (see 1579). They have no navigational instruments but they have Danish navigator Vitus Bering, now 61, who will die of scurvy on the return voyage (see 1728).

 "Sinners in the Hands of an Angry God" by Calvinist clergyman Jonathan Edwards, 38, of Northampton in the Massachusetts colony graphically depicts the terrors of damnation. The sermon by the Connecticut-born Edwards at Enfield is published in pamphlet form and draws opposition from Boston clergyman Charles Chauncey, 36, and other rationalists.

Salem sea captain Richard Derby receives instructions from the owners of his schooner *Volante* to avoid the British Navigation Act of 1660 and subsequent acts by sailing under Dutch colors on his voyage to the Caribbean and to be prepared to bribe customs officials: ". . . If you should fall so low as Statia [the Dutch island of St. Eustatius, see 1634], and any Frenchman should make you a good offer with good security, or by making your vessel a Dutch bottom, or by any other means practicable in order to your getting among ye Frenchmen, embrace it. . . . Also secure a permit so as for you to trade there next voyage, which you may undoubtedly do through your factor or by a little greasing some others."

 Painting *Autumn* by François Boucher.

 Opera *Artaserse* 12/26 at Milan's Teatro Regio Ducal, with music by German composer Christoph Willibald Gluck, 27.

Ode "Rule, Britannia" by Thomas Arne, lyrics from the libretto of *Alfred: A Masque* by David Mallet or James Thomson presented last year.

 Some 70 fishing vessels put out from Gloucester in the Massachusetts colony, 60 from Marblehead.

 Indigo cultivation is introduced into the South Carolina colony by Elizabeth Lucas Pinckney.

1741 (cont.) British admiral George Anson, 44, arrives on the southwest coast of South America after a 7-month voyage from England during which he has lost three of his six ships and two-thirds of his crew to scurvy (*see* 1744).

China's population reaches 140 million (more than 220 million by some accounts), up from 100 million in 1660. The emperor Chi'en Lung restores the pao-chia system of local registration that will make population figures more reliable from now until 1851.

1742 Bavaria's Karl Albrecht is elected Holy Roman Emperor January 24 by opponents of Austria's Maria Theresa and her husband Franz Stefan, grand duke of Tuscany. The new emperor is crowned February 12 at Frankfurt-am-Main and begins a 3-year reign as Charles VII but while he is being crowned his hereditary domains are being overrun by Austrian troops in the continuing War of the Austrian Succession.

Prussia's Frederick the Great triumphs over the Austrians in May at Czaslau and Chotusitz but his troops are stricken with violent dysentery and he withdraws from the coalition against Austria.

The Silesian War is ended by the Treaty of Breslau in June and the Treaty of Berlin in July. Maria Theresa cedes to Prussia both upper and lower Silesia with their rich coal deposits, plus some other territory; Prussia assumes the Silesian debt of 1.7 million rix dollars held by English and Dutch creditors.

Maria Theresa makes an alliance with England, raises two armies, and drives her allied invaders out of Bohemia.

The Battle of Bloody Marsh gives Britain control of the Georgia colony. Troops under James E. Oglethorpe repel a Spanish attack against Fort Frederica on St. Simons Island and defeat the Spanish in battle.

The sieur de La Verendrye moves into the Black Hills region and adds the discovery of the Dakotas to his discoveries of Manitoba and western Minnesota.

Coal is found on the Coal River in western Virginia, the first of many deposits that will be found and exploited in the region over the next two centuries (*see* Morgan Morgan, 1731).

The Franklin stove invented by Philadelphia's Benjamin Franklin heats a room far more efficiently than does an open fireplace. Designed to be set inside a fireplace, Franklin's iron "Pennsylvania fireplace" represents the first application of the principle of heating by warmed air—it has a top, back, and sides with an air box inside joined to the sides but not reaching quite to the top. The fire built in front of its opening produces smoke that moves up the front of its air box, over its top, and down again behind it whence it enters the flue at floor level, thus heating the air in the air box which is released by shutters in the sides of the stove.

Sheffield silverplate invented by Thomas Boulsover at Sheffield, England, is a bond of heavy copper sheets fused between thin sheets of silver (*see* 1740).

Cotton mills open at Birmingham and Northampton. The Lancashire millowners will import East India yarns beginning next year to improve the quality of their textiles.

Fiction *The Adventures of Joseph Andrews and his Friend Abraham Adams* by playwright-novelist Henry Fielding ridicules Samuel Richardson's novel *Pamela* of 1740. Fielding makes his Andrews "a handsome model young man," the brother of Richardson's modest and prudent young woman.

Poetry *The Complaint: Or, Night Thoughts* by English poet Edward Young, 59, who writes, "Procrastination is the thief of time."

Theater *Mahomet the Prophet* (*Le fanatisme, ou Mahomet le prophete*) by Voltaire 8/9 at the Comédie Française, Paris.

Oratorio *The Messiah* by George Frideric Handel 4/13 at the Dublin Cathedral, with Mrs. Susannah Cibber singing the contralto part in a charity concert for the benefit of "the Prisoners in several Gaols, and for the support of Mercer's Hospital in Stephen Street, and of the Charitable Infirmary on the Inn's Quay." Mrs. Cibber was disgraced 3 years ago in a sex scandal that culminated in a trial which revealed the adulterous relationship forced upon her by her husband Theophilus Cibber (son of the playwright-theatrical manager). The chancellor of the cathedral rises after her aria describing Christ's suffering and cries out, "Woman, for this all thy sins be forgiven thee," the concert raises enough money to free 142 prisoners from debtors' prison, and performances of the oratorio will become an annual Christmas tradition.

Hymn "Joy to the World" by George Frideric Handel (*see* 1830).

Keyboard practice *Goldberg Variations* (*Aria mit verscheidenen Veraenderungen vors Clavicimbal mit 2 manualen*) by Johann Sebastian Bach.

Short Treatise on Whist by English card-player Edmond Hoyle, 70, gives the first systematization to a game that will develop first into auction bridge and then into contract bridge (*see* 1904; Vanderbilt, 1925). Hoyle's name will survive in the phrase "according to Hoyle."

Boston's Faneuil Hall is presented to the city by local merchant Peter Faneuil whose red brick meeting house will be enlarged by architect Charles Bulfinch and will be a Boston landmark for centuries.

1743 Austrian armies drive French and Bavarian troops out of Bavaria as the War of the Austrian Succession continues in Europe. An allied Pragmatic army of English, Hessian, and Hanoverian troops defeat the French June 27 in the Battle of Dettingen, the emperor Charles VII is forced to take refuge at Frankfurt, and the Dutch Republic takes sides with Britain in alliance with Austria's Maria Theresa who makes an alliance with Saxony.

War resumes between Persia and the Ottoman Empire.

Russia has pogroms that kill thousands of Jews.

The Dutch East India Company founded in 1594 remains richer and more powerful than its slightly younger British counterpart.

Traité de dynamique by French mathematician-philosopher Jean Le Rond d'Alembert, 25, announces d'Alembert's principle which will be applied by d'Alembert next year to the theory of the equilibrium and the motion of fluids. Internal forces constitute by themselves a system in equilibrium, hence the effective forces constitute a system which as a whole is statically equivalent to the system of external forces.

Theorie de la Figure de la Terre by French mathematician Alex Claude Clairaut, 30, reports the results of a mathematical investigation of the shape of the earth according to hydrostatic principles.

"Seasonable Thoughts on the State of Religion in New England" by Boston Congregationalist minister Charles Chauncey opposes the emotional revivalism of Jonathan Edwards at Northampton with theological liberalism (*see* 1741). The battle of pamphlets will continue until early in 1758 when Edwards will die shortly after assuming the presidency of the College of New Jersey at Princeton.

"Proposals for establishing an academy" by Benjamin Franklin is circulated in Philadelphia (*see* 1749).

The University of Delaware has its beginnings at Newark.

Fiction *The History of the Life of the Late Mr. Jonathan Wild the Great* by Henry Fielding.

Painting *Marriage a la Mode* by William Hogarth. Nicolas Lancret dies at Paris September 14 at age 53; Japanese potter Kenzan dies at age 81.

Theater *Merope* by Voltaire 2/20 at the Comédie Française, Paris.

Moët and Chandon has its beginnings in a champagne business founded by French entrepreneur Claude Moët whose firm will become France's largest champagne producer.

1744 Prussia's Frederick II starts a Second Silesian War by marching through Saxony with 80,000 troops. He invades Bohemia and takes Prague before the Hapsburg forces of Maria Theresa drive him back into Saxony.

The French desert Frederick II (above) and declare war both on Britain and on Maria Theresa.

King George's War breaks out in the Caribbean and in North America—an offshoot of the War of the Austrian Succession between Britain and France whose Western Hemisphere interests are now fiercely competitive. Britain has the advantage since her squadrons are permanently based in Jamaica and the Leeward Islands, with naval dockyards at Jamaica and Antigua, while the French have no dockyard facilities in the Caribbean, can rarely dispatch a ship from Europe for more than 6 months at a time, and must rely on convoys to protect their sugar shipments (French merchants pay for naval escorts).

Maria Theresa launches a pogrom to drive the Jews out of Bohemia and Moravia. Even where tolerated, Europe's Jews often live under degrading conditions with regulations designed to limit their expansion and keep their status at a low level (*see* Britain, 1753).

The gyroscope stabilizer for ships is pioneered by a Scotsman named Serson who persuades the British Admiralty to sea-test a spinning rotor that will indicate a stable reference for navigators. The rotor is supported on a pivot so that it will not be disturbed by the rocking or pitching of the ship.

London's Baltic Mercantile and Shipping Exchange has its beginnings in the Virginia and Baltic Coffee House, an outgrowth of the Virginia and Maryland Coffee House that will become the world's shipping exchange, a vast marble-floored room where shippers and their agents will match vessels and cargoes through deals ("fixtures") made in great secrecy—often "by the candle" with bids continuing until an inch of candle has burned itself out.

London publisher John Newbery, 31, sets up a bookshop and publishing house in St. Paul's Churchyard and starts putting out newspapers whose contributors will include Doctor Johnson and Oliver Goldsmith. The latter will portray Newbery in his 1766 novel *The Vicar of Wakefield.*

Tommy Thumb's Pretty Song Book is published at London with the earliest known versions of such nursery rhymes as "London bridge is falling down;" "Who killed Cock Robin?/ 'I,' said the Sparrow,/ With my bow and arrow, I killed Cock Robin;" "Hickory, dickory dock,/ The mouse ran up the clock;" "Ladybird, ladybird,/ Fly away home;" "Little Tommy Tucker/ Sings for his supper;" "Oranges and lemons./ Say the bells of St. Clements./ You owe me five farthings,/ Say the bells of St. Martin's;/" "Sing a song of sixpense/ A pocketful of rye."

Sotheby's art auction house has its beginnings January 7 as London bookseller Samuel Baker holds his first real auction, selling the library of a local physician for £826. Baker went into business early in 1733, he will take George Leigh into partnership in 1767 and will retire to his villa in Essex, Leigh will take Baker's nephew John Sotheby into partnership within a few weeks of Baker's retirement, John's nephew Samuel Sotheby will take over from John, Samuel's son Samuel Leigh Sotheby will head the firm until his death in 1861, and the auction house will grow to have auction rooms in 10 countries with annual sales of more than £125 million (*see* Christie's, 1766).

1744 (cont.) Anthem "God Save the King" is published at London with the opening words "God save our Lord the King." They will be changed next year to "God save great George our King" and will later be changed to "God save our gracious King" (see "America," 1831).

The Well-Tempered Clavier, Part II by Johann Sebastian Bach includes new preludes, toccatas, fugues, and other works.

The first recorded cricket match pits Kent against All England.

John Wesley holds love feasts modeled on rites of the primitive church (see 1738). He has held class meetings with admission by "society tickets" to exclude undesirables, he has journeyed on horseback through England to organize Methodist societies, and he holds the first conference of Methodists. Beginning in 1747, Wesley will make 42 trips to Ireland, beginning in 1751 he will make 22 trips to Scotland, and he will use his annual income of about £1,400 from his cheap books to help the needy and unemployed, in loans to debtors and businessmen, and to open dispensaries (see 1784).

Würzburg Residenz for the prince bishop is completed by German architect (Johann) Balthasar Neumann, 57, after 25 years of construction during which Neumann has worked on castles at Bruchsal and Werneck in addition to the baroque palace at Würzburg.

Philadelphia's Christ Church is completed minus a steeple which will be added by Robert Smith in 1755.

South America's Mount Cotopaxi erupts in the Spanish viceroyalty of Peru.

Free seed potatoes are distributed to reluctant Prussian peasants by Frederick II (above) who stations armed soldiers in the fields to enforce his edict that the peasants plant potatoes or suffer their ears and noses to be cut off.

Britain's Lord Anson returns with the last ship of his original six after having lost more than four-fifths of his crew to scurvy (see 1741; Lind, 1747).

The first known record of ice cream in America is made by a William Blake who visits Maryland: "You saw a plain proof of the Great Plenty of the Country, a table in the most splendid manner set out with Great Variety of Dishes, all serv'd up in the most elegant way, after which came a Dessert no less curious; among the Rareties of which it was Compos'ed was some fine Ice Cream which, with the Strawberries and Milk, eat most Deliciously."

1745 Scotland has an uprising of Highland peasants who have been driven off the land by "lairds" who want to break up the clans and use the Highlands for sheep-raising. The clansmen rally behind Charles Edward "Bonny Prince Charlie" Stuart, 25, who lands in the Hebrides July 25 and raises the Jacobite standard to proclaim his father James VIII of Scotland and James III of England. The Young Pretender leads some 2,000 men into Edinburgh September 11, the Jacobites win the Battle of Prestonpans September 21, and they follow Charles into England, reaching Derby December 4 (see Falkirk, Culloden, 1746).

The Second Silesian War ends in Europe as the Holy Roman Emperor Charles VII (Karl Albrecht of Bavaria) dies at Munich January 20 at age 47. His 17-year-old son Maximilian Joseph succeeds as elector of Bavaria, he concludes the Treaty of Fussen with Austria in April, and he regains the land conquered by Austria by surrendering any pretensions to the Austrian throne and by promising his vote at the imperial election to Maria Theresa's husband Franz Stefan.

A January alliance against Prussia has joined Austria, Saxony, Britain, and Holland. The Pragmatic army is defeated May 11 in the Battle of Fontenoy by the French under Marshal Maurice of Saxony who begins the conquest of the Austrian Netherlands.

Frederick the Great defeats Austrian and Saxon forces June 4 at the Battle of Hohenfriedberg in Silesia and he defeats Austrian forces September 30 at the Battle of Soor in northeastern Bohemia.

Maria Theresa's husband is elected Holy Roman Emperor and begins a 20-year reign as Francis I.

The Treaty of Dresden December 25 brings peace between Prussia, Austria, and Saxony, Prussia recognizes the Pragmatic Sanction of 1731 but retains Silesia, the British army is recalled to fight "Bonny Prince Charlie" (above), but the War of the Austrian Succession that began in 1740 continues.

The French fortress of Louisburg in Nova Scotia has been taken by British and New England forces June 16 after a 7-week siege by William Pepperell, 49, who is promoted to the rank of colonel and who next year will be created a baronet, the first American to be so honored.

Japan's Tokugawa shogun Yoshimune resigns and is succeeded after a 29-year shogunate by the far less competent Ieshige who will be shogun until 1760.

The Leyden jar (or Kleistian jar) discovered by Dutch mathematician-physicist Pieter van Musschenbroek, 53, at the University of Leyden and (independently) by Ewald Jurgen von Kleist, dean of the Cathedral of Kamin in Pomerania, is an electrical capacitor. The jar is partly filled with water, a nail projects from its cork, and it is accidentally found to retain charges of static electricity generated by a spark-making device that employs glass revolving between cloth rubbers (see Franklin, 1746).

Painting *The Marriage Contract* by William Hogarth; *Self-Portrait* by Hogarth; *Antony and Cleopatra* (frescoes) for Venice's Labia Palace by Giambattista Tiepolo.

Theater *Papal Tyranny in the Reign of King John* by Colley Cibber 2/15 at London's Covent Garden

Theatre; *Tancred and Sigismunda* by James Thomson.

🎼 Anthem "The Campbells Are Coming" is published in Scotland.

The quadrille becomes fashionable in France.

🏛 Vienna's Schönborn Palace is completed after half a century of construction by Johann Lucas von Hildebrandt, who dies November 16, 2 days after his 77th birthday. The palace will serve as a summer residence for the emperor.

Bohemia is completed on the eastern shore of the Maryland colony for Bohemian-American planter Augustine Herman.

👫 *Venus physique* by France's Pierre de Maupertuis challenges the preexistence theory of genetics advanced by Jan Swammerdam in 1699. Swammerdam's ovist theories, says Maupertuis, cannot explain congenital "monsters," nor the production of hybrids, nor even the fact that offspring usually have characteristics of both parents (*see* 1741; 1751).

1746 The Battle of Falkirk January 17 gives the Jacobite pretender Charles Edward Stuart and his Highlanders a victory over the British dragoons. Seven guns and 700 prisoners fall into Jacobite hands.

The Battle of Culloden Moor April 16 ends Stuart efforts to regain the British throne. The king's son William Augustus, Duke of Cumberland, has stopped at Nairn to celebrate his 25th birthday, "Bonnie Prince Charlie" has marched his 7,000 starving Highlanders across the moors by night to surprise the British, they have turned back exhausted, Cumberland's 9,000-man army arrives and opens fire with 10 guns to Stuart's nine, the Scots find themselves surrounded and flee leaving 1,000 dead on the battlefield, and the dragoons hunt down and massacre those who have survived the carnage.

"Bonnie Prince Charlie" escapes to the Isle of Skye June 29 disguised as Betty Burke, maid to Flora Macdonald, 24. The young pretender gets away to France September 20, the British imprison Macdonald briefly in the Tower of London, and they forbid anyone to wear the tartan, a ban that will continue until 1782.

The Battle of Rocoux gives France's Marshal Saxe a victory that frees the Netherlands from Austria.

Denmark's Christian VI dies at age 47 after a weak 16-year reign. His 23-year-old son has married the daughter of Britain's George II and will reign until 1766 as Frederick V.

Spain's first Bourbon king Philip V dies July 9 almost completely insane at age 62 after a 46-year reign that was interrupted in 1724 by his first son's brief reign. His 33-year-old second son by his first wife Maria Louisa of Savoy succeeds to the throne and will reign until 1759 as Ferdinand VI.

⚕ The duodenal ulcer described by German physician George Erhard Hamberger, 47, is the first description in medical literature of the ulcer that will plague modern society.

⚡ Benjamin Franklin begins experiments with electricity at Philadelphia. Franklin will improve the Leyden jar (or Kleistian jar) invented last year by replacing its water with pulverized lead and he will invent an adaptation of the Leyden jar—a foil-coated pane of glass that will be called the Franklin pane (*see* kite, 1751; Priestley, 1767).

🎓 Princeton University has its beginnings in the College of New Jersey founded at Newark by Presbyterian ministers who include Aaron Burr, 30. Classes open in a building that also houses the city courthouse and jail, Burr will be president of the college from 1748 to 1757, he will move it to Princeton in 1756, and it will adopt the name Princeton University in 1896 (*see* Nassau Hall, 1756).

🖋 Nonfiction *Pensées philosiphiques* by French man of letters Denis Diderot, 32.

🎨 Painting *Captain John Hamilton* and *The Eliot Family* by English painter Joshua Reynolds, 23; *The Vegetable Market at San Giacomo di Rialto* by Antonio Canaletto who moves to London where he will remain for 10 years except for two short visits home to Venice; *The Milliner* (*La Marchande de Modes*) by François Boucher.

🌾 English grain prices continue to fall as they have been doing for 30 years and will continue to do for another 10. Death rates will fall, too, as more people are able to afford better diets (*see* Burke's Act, 1773).

1747 The conquest of scurvy is pioneered by Scottish naval surgeon James Lind, 31, who conducts experiments with 12 scurvy victims aboard the Royal

Bonny Prince Charlie rallied the Scottish clans to restore the Stuarts to power, but he met with disaster at Culloden.

1747 (cont.) Navy's H.M.S. *Salisbury.* Lind finds that cider, nutmeg, seawater, vinegar, an elixir of vitriol (a sulfate), and a combination of garlic, mustard, myrrh, and balsam of Peru are all worthless as scurvy cures, but two scurvy seamen given two oranges and a lemon each day recover in short order, an indication that citrus fruits contain an antiscorbutic element (*see* 1734; 1753).

Scotland's Simon Fraser, Baron Lovat, is beheaded for his support last year of "Bonny Prince Charlie" at Culloden. He had protested his innocence but he had sent his clansmen to fight under the leadership of his son Simon, now 21, who will be pardoned in 1752 and who will command Highland troops in America.

The British admirals George Anson and Edward Hawke score smashing victories against the French in the West Indies. The Royal Navy dominates European waters and increases the peril to France's huge convoys of sugar from the Caribbean (*see* 1744).

Persia falls into anarchy following the assassination of Nadir Shah by one of his own tribesmen after an 11-year reign (*see* 1794).

The Barkzai dynasty that will rule Afghanistan until 1929 comes to power as one of Nadir Shah's generals assumes control of the Afghan provinces. He will reign until 1773 as Ahmad Shah.

Britain imposes a carriage tax.

Marine insurance companies in London charge rates as high as 11 percent on ship and cargo from New England to Madeira, 14 percent to Jamaica, and 23 percent to Santo Domingo as privateers and pirates menace shipping in the Atlantic and Caribbean but merchantmen out of Boston and Salem carry cod from the Newfoundland banks to the West Indies and southern Europe and they often make profits of 200 percent even after the high insurance rates.

Poetry "Ode on a Distant Prospect of Eton College" by English poet Thomas Gray, 31: "Where ignorance is bliss,/ 'Tis folly to be wise."

Oratorio *Judas Maccabeus* by George Frideric Handel at London's Covent Garden Theatre.

Potsdam's Sans-Souci Palace is completed by Georg Wenzeslaus von Knobelsdorff.

Use of beet sugar has its beginnings in the discovery by Prussian chemist Andreas Sigismund Marggraf, 38, that beets and carrots contain small amounts of sugar (*see* Achard, 1793).

1748 The War of the Austrian Succession ends after 8 years in the Treaty of Aix-la-Chapelle signed in October, but the peace is really no more than a truce (*see* 1755; 1756). The house of Hanover retains the succession in its German states and in Britain, the Pragmatic Sanction of 1720 is sustained in Austria, Silesia is given to Prussia which has become a great power, and there is a reciprocal restoration of conquests. France regains Novia Scotia's Louisburg from Britain

but gives up territory she has taken in the Lowlands and surrenders control of Madras in India (*see* 1754).

American colonists cross the Allegheny Divide and move into western lands (*see* George III, 1763).

The Spirit of the Laws (De l'esprit des lois) by France's Baron de Montesquieu pioneers sociology by showing the interrelation of economical, geographical, political, religious, and social forces in history, a revolutionary concept that makes Montesquieu's most important work a best seller.

Introductio in analysin ininitorum by the Swiss mathematician Leonhard Euler systematizes calculus, emphasizes the study of functions, classifies differential equations, and treats trigonometric functions and equations of curves without reference to diagrams.

Observations upon the Generation, Composition, and Decomposition of Animal and Vegetable Substances by English naturalist John Tuberville Needham, 35, gives "proof" of spontaneous generation. Needham says he has found flasks of broth teeming with "little animals" after having boiled them and sealed them but his experimental techniques have been faulty (*see* Redi, 1668; Maupertuis, 1751).

"Account of the Sore Throat Attended with Ulcers" by London physician John Fothergill, 36, gives the first description of diphtheria.

"The only principle of life propagated among the young people is to get money," writes Scots-American Cadwallader Colden, 60, "and men are only esteemed according to what they are worth—that is, the money they are possessed of."

Fiction *The Adventures of Roderick Random* by Scottish physician Tobias George Smollett, 27, enjoys such success that Smollett will give up his London practice and will devote himself to writing. "Some folks are wise and some otherwise," says Smollett in his anonymously-published picaresque novel (he sailed at age 20 as a surgeon's mate to Cartagena and last year married a Jamaican heiress); *Clarissa, or the History of a Young Lady* by Samuel Richardson whose seven-volume novel will establish his lasting reputation and that of his heroine Clarissa Harlowe.

Painting *Calais Gate* by William Hogarth.

Swedish botanist Peter Kalm, 33, describes English cooking (he has visited England en route to America). "Englishmen understand almost better than any other people the art of properly roasting a large cut of meat," writes Kalm, but he adds that "the art of cooking as practiced by most Englishmen does not extend much beyond roast beef and plum pudding."

1749 French troops move into the Ohio River Valley and claim it for Louis XV. Sent into the region by the Comte de Galissonière, they win over the Indian tribes, they force British traders to leave, and they proceed to build forts (*see* 1754).

The Ohio Company chartered by Britain's George II makes its first settlements in hilly Appalachian country along the Monongahela River. The king grants half a million acres to a group of London merchants and Virginia gentlemen who include the brothers of George Washington (*see* 1752).

Halifax, Nova Scotia, is founded to rival the French port of Louisburg. Edward Cornwallis names the town after the president of the London Board of Trade George Montagu Dunk, 32, earl of Halifax.

Histoire naturelle by French naturalist George Louis Leclerc, 42, comte de Buffon, is published in the first of its three volumes. Buffon rejects any preexistence theory of genetics such as that proposed by Jan Swammerdam in 1669, but he does not dispute the idea of spontaneous generation.

The University of Pennsylvania has its beginnings in the College of Philadelphia (*see* Franklin, 1743).

Letters on the Spirit of Patriotism: On the Idea of a Patriot King published anonymously at London advances the idea of an essential "harmony of interests" among different classes of society. Its author is former English politician Henry St. John, 71, first viscount Bolingbroke who retired 14 years ago to his wife's French estate near Touraine.

French philosopher Jean-Jacques Rousseau, 37, wins first prize at the Academy of Dijon for his essay "Discours dur les Arts et Sciences" glorifying the savage state and calling civilized society the inevitable source of moral corruption: "The man who first had the idea of enclosing a field and saying this is mine, and found people simple enough to believe him, was the real founder of society."

Painting *Mr. and Mrs. Robert Andrews* by English painter Thomas Gainsborough, 22. Allesandro Magnasco dies at Genoa March 12 at age 81.

Oxford's Radcliffe Camera is completed by James Gibbs after 12 years of construction.

London cabinetmaker Thomas Chippendale, 31, opens a factory that will be famous for its graceful, ornate furniture although many will prefer the work of his contemporary George Hepplewhite, 23, whose workshops are in the London parish of St. Giles, Cripplegate (*see* Sheraton, 1791).

New England suffers a drought so severe that farmers whose powder-dry pastures catch fire must send to Pennsylvania and even to England for hay.

Haricot beans are planted extensively for the first time in France. The flageolets planted near Soissons will soon replace fava beans in the area (*see* 1533).

Pellagra is described in Italy where polenta made of cornmeal is a dietary staple in some areas. The disease takes its name from the Italian words *pelle agra* (rough skin) and its further symptoms are diarrhea, dementia, and—ultimately—death (*see* 1735; 1915).

London's Justerini & Brooks has its origin in a wineshop opened at 2, The Colonnade by Italian wine merchant Giacomo Justerini who enjoys immediate success in partnership with George Johnson. When Justerini returns to Italy in 1760 Johnson will take his own son Augustus into the partnership, the younger Johnson will be killed in 1785 when a runaway horse overturns his sedan chair in Piccadilly, and when *his* son Augustus Johnson II sells the firm in 1831 to Alfred Brooks it will become Justerini & Brooks, a house at 2, Pall Mall that will be famous for its wines, cognac, and Scotch whisky.

China's population reaches 225 million.

1750 The Iron Act passed by Parliament prohibits Britain's American colonists from manufacturing iron products while permitting them to produce bar and pig iron from their ore deposits, using the fuel which they have in abundance, and permitting them to exchange the iron for manufactured articles. The act is an expression of classic mercantilism and embodies the chief principle of the British colonial system, namely to restrict the colonies to producing raw materials which the mother country can process or resell, and to use the colonies as a market for the mother country's manufactured goods. But the Iron Act will be generally ignored and by 1776 there will be as many iron mills in America as in England (*see* 1663; Woolens Act, 1699; Sugar Act, 1764).

Bituminous coal is mined for the first time in America at Richmond Basin in the Virginia colony (*see* Coal River, 1742).

Cumberland Gap through the Appalachians is found at an altitude of 1,665 feet by English physician Thomas Walker, agent for a Virginia land company. He names the gap for George II's third son William Augustus, duke of Cumberland.

Chippewa (Ojibway) Indians defeat Sioux tribesmen at the Battle of Kathio and gain undisputed possession of wild rice stands in the lakes of northern Minnesota.

Portugal's João V dies at age 61 after a 44-year reign and is succeeded by his 35-year-old son who will reign as José Manuel until his death in 1777.

London's Westminster Bridge is completed across the Thames. It is the first new bridge to span the river since London Bridge opened in the 10th century.

A flatboat for inland waterways is invented by Pennsylvania colonist Jacob Yoder.

Anti-Senèque, System d'Epicure by French philosopher-physician Julien Offroy de La Mettrie, 41, says that the only pleasures are those of the senses, that life should be spent in the enjoyment of pleasures as was advocated by the 3rd century B.C. Athenian philosopher Epicurus, and that the soul ceases to exist with the death of the body. La Mettrie has been attacked in France for his materialist teachings and he lives in Berlin.

1750 (cont.) Fiction *Fanny Hill, or the Memoires of a Woman of Pleasure* by English pornographic novelist John Cleland, 41, who worked at Bombay for the East India Company, lost his job after a quarrel with his employer, returned to London in poverty, wound up in debtors' prison, and wrote the book for a 28-year-old printer who offered to bail him out of Newgate Prison if he would write a licentious novel. Cleland receives 20 guineas for the work which earns the printer £10,000 and will be the underground classic of erotic literature for more than two centuries.

Theater *The Coffee House* (*La bottega del caffè*) by Carlo Goldoni 5/2 at Mantua; *The Liar* (*Il bugiardo*) by Carlo Goldoni 5/23 at Mantua; *The Comic Theatre* (*Il teatro comico*) by Carlo Goldoni 10/5 at Venice's Teatro Sant'Angelo.

Munich's Residenztheater is completed for the elector of Bavaria by his court dwarf and architect François de Cuvilles, 52.

The Art of the Fugue is completed by Johann Sebastian Bach who dies July 28 at age 65.

England raises the bounty on whales to 40 shillings per ton in a move that encourages Scotsmen to enter the whaling industry.

Famine ravages France.

Ices and ice cream are sold year round in Paris by Buisson, successor to Procope, whose competitors follow suit after having sold *glace* only in summer (*see* 1670).

Massachusetts has 63 distilleries producing rum made from molasses supplied in some cases by slave traders who sell it to the Puritan distillers for the capital needed to buy African natives that can be sold to West Indian sugar planters (*see* 1733).

Wild rice supplies some 25 percent of the caloric intake of the Chippewa (above) who call the rice from the plant *Zizania aquatica* by the name *manomin* (good berry). French voyageurs call it *folle avoine,* or wild oats.

France's population will increase from 22 million to 27 million in the next half century, Italy's from 15.5 million to 18 million, and Spain will have a similar increase, but the total population of Europe will grow from 140 million to 188 million as births consistently exceed deaths rather than alternately falling behind deaths as in previous centuries, and as more children survive beyond age 10.

London has 11 percent of England's population while Paris has only 2 percent of France's population.

The world's population reaches 750 million.

1751 Benjamin Franklin discovers the electrical nature of lightning by flying a kite in a thunderstorm. The kite has a wire conductor, a key at the end of its wet twine kite string, and a silk insulator which Franklin keeps dry by standing in a doorway. He sends his friends in England a paper entitled "Experiments and Observations on Electricity Made at Philadelphia," and he will follow it with other papers on the subject. He works to invent a lightning rod that will prevent the fires that so often begin in thunderstorms (*see* 1752).

Système de la Nature by France's Pierre de Maupertuis challenges the "proof" of spontaneous generation offered by John Needham in 1748. Maupertuis also challenges orthodox ovist genetic theories. He postulates a theory of *mostres par defaut et par exces,* which anticipates the later discovery of supernumerary or missing chromosomes, and he expands on his 1745 critique of ovist theories by observing that offspring reveal characteristics present in both parents, a fact well known to livestock breeders, and by pointing out that ovist theories cannot explain the periodic recurrence of six-fingered hands in members of a certain Berlin family nor explain albinism in blacks.

Nickel is isolated by German physicist A. Croustedt.

The study of reflexes as a distinct branch of physiology is pioneered by English physician Robert Whytt, 37, who shows that only a segment of the spinal cord is necessary for a reflex action and draws explicit distinction between voluntary and involuntary motion.

Pennsylvania Hospital is established at Philadelphia through the efforts of Benjamin Franklin (above) and local physician Thomas Bond.

Georgetown is founded as a port town on the Maryland shore of the Potomac River. The new port is named in honor of Britain's George II (*see* 1790).

Sweden's Frederick I of Hesse-Cassel dies at age 75 after a 31-year reign and is succeeded by the 41-year-old Adolphus Frederick of Oldenberg-Holstein-Gottorp, who has married the sister of Prussia's Frederick the Great and who will reign as Adolphus Frederick until 1771.

Dutch stadtholder Willem IV dies at age 40 after a 4-year reign and is succeeded by his 3-year-old son who will reign as Willem V until 1795.

The British consol is created by a consolidation of public securities, chiefly annuities, into a single debt issue—a consolidated annuity with no maturity (*see* Rothschild, 1815).

Fiction *The Adventures of Peregrine Pickle* by Tobias Smollett; *Amelia* by Henry Fielding, who calls gin "poison" (*see* Hogarth, below).

Poetry "Elegy Written in a Country Churchyard" by Thomas Gray: "The curfew tolls the knell of parting day,/ The lowing herd wind slowly o'er the lea,/ The ploughman plods his weary way,/ And leaves the world to darkness and to me. . . ." "Full many a gem of purest ray serene/ The dark unfathomed caves of ocean bear./ Full many a flower is born to blush unseen,/ And waste its sweetness on the desert air."

Painting *La Toilette de Venus* by François Boucher; *Gin Lane* (engraving) by William Hogarth, who satirizes the excesses of drinking among London's lower classes Japanese *ukiyoe* painter Sukenobu Nishikawa dies at age 80.

At least 60 New England vessels are engaged in whaling ventures (*see* 1712; 1775).

Virginia planter George Washington, 19, visits Barbados with his brother Lawrence, who requires a warm climate to recover from an illness (*see* 1741). Young George samples such tropical fruits as shaddock (*see* 1696) but writes in his diary that "none pleases my taste as do's the pine [pineapple]."

Pennsylvania farmer-naturalist John Bartram, 52, describes Indian cookery in *Observations . . . made by John Bartram in his travels from Pensilvania to . . . Lake Ontario*, which is published at London. Bartram has farmed for 13 years at Kingsessing outside Philadelphia.

England's Worcester Royal Porcelain Company has its beginnings in a crockery firm founded by potters John Wall and William Davis, whose china teapots, cups, and saucers are made from a paste containing soapstone (steatite) and whose designs are modeled on those of Meissen, Sèvres, and China.

"So vast is the Territory of North America that it will require many Ages to settle it fully," writes Benjamin Franklin (above), "and, till it is fully settled, Labour will never be cheap here, where no Man continues long a Labourer for others, but gets a Plantation of his own" (*see* 1755; Jefferson, 1782).

1752 Britain and her colonies adopt the Gregorian calendar of 1582 (the difference between the Old Style Julian calendar of 46 B.C. and the Gregorian calendar has grown to 11 days). Thursday, September 14, follows Wednesday, September 2, by decree of Parliament, the change confuses bill collectors, rumors spread that salaried employees are losing 11 days' pay and that everybody is losing 11 days of his life, Londoners cry, "Give us back our 11 days," and there are riots to protest the calendar change.

The Logstown Treaty June 13 has ceded Iroquois and Delaware lands south of the Ohio River to the Virginia colony and permits the 3-year-old Ohio Company to build a fort and to settle on lands west of the Alleghenies (*see* French, 1753).

The Philadelphia Contributionship for the Insurance of Homes from Loss by Fire is founded by Benjamin Franklin and a group of his friends for mutual protection (*see* lightning rod, below).

Public street lighting begins in Philadelphia. New York and Boston continue to light streets by placing a lamp in the window of every seventh house, but Philadelphia installs globe lamps imported from London.

Observations on the Diseases of the Army by British Army medical officer John Pringle, 45, will lead to some reforms and to rules of hygiene that will reduce the toll of typhus, a disease that Pringle identifies with "gaol fever" and "hospital fever."

The Manchester Royal Infirmary is founded.

French naturalist René de Réaumur proves that digestion is at least partially a chemical process (*see* 1712). He places food inside tiny perforated metal cylinders and feeds these to hawks; when he recovers the cylinders and finds that the food inside is partially digested he destroys the prevailing belief that the stomach digests food simply by grinding it physically (*see* Beaumont, 1822; hydrochloric acid, 1824).

Fiction *The Female Quixote, or The Adventures of Arabella* by English novelist-poet Charlotte Ramsay Lennox, 32.

Poetry "On the Prospects of Planting Arts and Learning In America" by Irish philosopher George Berkeley, now 68, who lived in the Rhode Island colony from 1728 to 1731: "Westward the course of empire takes its way . . ."; *Poems* by English poet Christopher Smart, 30.

London's Mansion House is completed by George Dance after 13 years of construction.

A French royal château at Choisy is completed by Jacques Ange Gabriel, 54, who succeeded his late father as first architect to Louis XV in 1742, completed enlargements of Fontainebleau in 1749, completed a château at Compiegne last year, and begins work on the Ecole Militaire at Paris.

Philadelphia's Liberty Bell cast by local foundrymen John Pass and John Stow for the belfry of the new Pennsylvania State House replaces a bell cast at London's Whitechapel Bell Foundry that has cracked soon after arrival. Made of a bronze alloy (77 percent copper/23 percent tin), the new 2,080-pound bell bears the same biblical inscription (from Leviticus 25:10) as the original. It cracks slightly while being tested, it will crack again in July, 1835, and will ring no more thereafter, but it has been cast to celebrate next year's fiftieth anniversary of Penn's Charter and it will serve its purpose: "PROCLAIM LIBERTY THROUGHOUT ALL THE LAND UNTO ALL THE INHABITANTS THEREOF LEV. XXV VSX / BY ORDER OF THE ASSEMBLY OF THE PROVINCE OF PENNSYLVANIA FOR THE STATE HOUSE IN PHILADA."

Moscow has a fire that destroys some 18,000 houses.

The lightning rod invented by Benjamin Franklin (above) is a metal conductor that will save houses from being set afire in electrical storms (*see* 1760).

George Washington inherits his brother's Mount Vernon plantation in the Virginia colony and works to improve its agricultural practices.

France's Louis XV orders that grain surpluses be stored as a reserve against famine, but government grain buying drives up bread prices. Thousands of Frenchmen are reduced to starvation and suspicions

1752 (cont.) arise that Louis is making millions of francs in profit from grain speculations (*see* 1768).

George Washington (above) builds a gristmill to produce flour from his own wheat that will be shipped in barrels from his own cooperage. Washington will build two more mills, and his "superfine flour" will go to markets as far distant as the West Indies. Washington will be the largest flour producer in the colonies, and he will have a large cash income that will enable him to buy good real estate and thus to hedge against inflation as colonial currencies depreciate (*see* 1781).

The first Irish whisky distillery is founded by distiller William Jameson.

The Gardener's Dictionary by Philip Miller, 61, "Gardener to the Worshipful Company of Apothecaries at their Botanick Garden in Chelsea," expresses doubts about eating tomatoes.

The Virginia colony has a population of nearly 250,000.

1753 Some 1,500 French troops from Canada sent by the Marquis Duquesne occupy the Ohio Valley and erect Fort Presqu'Isle and Fort Le Boeuf. The lieutenant governor of Virginia Robert Dinwiddie, 60, sends out surveyor George Washington to demand withdrawal of the French, Washington proceeds to Fort Le Boeuf, and he is told that Dinwiddie's letter will be forwarded to Duquesne (*see* 1754).

The Conestoga wagon introduced by Pennsylvania Dutch settlers in the town of Conestoga will come into wide use in the next 100 years. (Wagon drivers will smoke cheap cigars that will be called "stogies.") (*see* "The Flying Machine," 1818).

Parliament passes a Jewish Naturalization Bill but the measure arouses opposition. The bill will be repealed next year, and British Jews will not gain civic emancipation until 1860.

The British Museum has its beginnings January 11 as London physician Sir Hans Sloane dies at age 92, leaving the nation his library of 50,000 volumes, several thousand manuscripts, coins, curiosities, and pictures. The government buys the collection Sloane inherited in 1702 from the late naturalist William Courten and grants a royal foundation charter for a museum (*see* Royal Library, 1757).

Fiction *Ferdinand Count Fathom* by Tobias Smollett is a pioneer horror mystery story.

Poetry *Hilliad* by Christopher Smart satirizes critic John Hill.

Treatise on the Scurvy by James Lind is an account of his citrus cure (*see* 1747; 1757).

On the Numbers of Man by England's Robert Wallace echoes the view of Montesquieu in 1734 that the Greek and Roman world had a larger population than that of 18th-century Europe. Wallace argues against diverting capital and labor from basic commodities to the manufacture of luxury goods.

1754 French troops rout a force of Virginia frontiersmen building a fort at the confluence of the Allegheny and Monongahela Rivers and defeat a small British colonial expeditionary force led by George Washington.

Fort Duquesne is erected at the head of the Ohio River by the French, who hope to confine the British to the area east of the Appalachians while they build a French empire in the lands to the west.

The Albany Convention June 19 assembles representatives of New York, Pennsylvania, Maryland, and the New England colonies in a meeting with the Six Nations in order to work out a joint plan of defense by Indian and British colonial forces against the advances of the French.

A cartoon drawn by Benjamin Franklin shows a serpent divided into 10 pieces with its head labeled NE for New England and with its other segments labeled NY, NJ, P, M, V, NC, SC, and G. "Unite or Die," says Franklin's caption, but the plan of union drawn up by Franklin is rejected by the colonies.

French colonial administrator Joseph François Dupleix, 57, is recalled from India after a 12-year career as governor general of all French possessions in the subcontinent. The British are left in firm control.

Pittsburgh has its beginnings in Fort Duquesne built by the French (above).

The first iron-rolling mill is opened by English entrepreneurs at Fareham in Hampshire.

A Society for the Encouragement of Arts and Manufactures is founded in England.

Money from sugar, tobacco, sea-island cotton, and other commodities grown in the New World with slave labor rivals money from East India Company ventures to create a growing leisure class in England.

The Spanish church becomes practically independent of Rome under terms of a Concordat with the Vatican. The church is placed under Spanish government control.

Columbia University has its beginnings in the King's College founded at New York (*see* 1784).

Painting *The Election* by William Hogarth; *The Judgment of Paris* by François Boucher.

Scotland's Royal and Ancient Golf Club is founded at St. Andrews (*see* 1552).

St. Petersburg's Winter Palace is completed by the Italian architect Bartolomeo Rastrelli, 54, whose late father Carlo served as sculptor to Peter the Great.

Copenhagen's Amalienborg Palace is completed by Danish architect Nikolaj Eigtoed who dies at age 50.

Philadelphia's Christ Church is completed after 27 years of construction: the 200-foot steeple is the tallest structure in North America.

English porcelain production is pioneered by Quaker pharmacist William Cookworthy, 49, of Plymouth who finds a deposit of kaolin in Cornwall (*see* d'Entrecolles, 1712). In 1756 Cookworthy will find a deposit of petuntse, the feldsparlike material that is mixed with kaolin to produce fine porcelain (*see* 1751).

Paris has 56 coffeeshops, or cafés (*see* 1672).

1755 British General Edward Braddock lands at Hampton Roads, Virginia, February 20, with two regiments of regulars to assume command as commander in chief of British forces in America. He meets with colonial governors April 14 at Alexandria to plan a fourfold attack on French positions in Nova Scotia, at Fort Duquesne on the Monongahela River, at Crown Point on Lake George, and at Niagara.

Fort Beauséjour commanding the neck of the Acadian peninsula which links Louisburg with French Canada is besieged by British forces under Colonel Robert Monckton and surrenders June 16 after a fortnight of resistance. Some 6,000 Acadians who refuse to swear allegiance to George II are sent to Georgia and South Carolina with instructions from the British governor that they are to be "disposed of in such manner as may best answer our design of preventing their reunion." The property of the 9,000 remaining Acadians is for the most part confiscated.

A British force of 1,500 from Virginia is defeated July 9 by French and Indian forces on the Monongahela River, 7 miles from Fort Duquesne. Nearly 1,000 British colonials are killed or wounded, and General Braddock sustains mortal wounds.

The Battle of Lake George September 8 ends in defeat for the French, but the British under Sir William Johnson fail to reach Crown Point. Sir William erects Fort William Henry at the head of Lake George.

An expedition to Niagara under the governor of the Massachusetts colony William Shirley reaches Oswego, leaves a garrison of 700, but does not proceed.

Rangoon is founded by the Burmese king Aloung P'Houra, 44, who is fighting the French with help from the English East India Company.

"Experiments upon Magnesia, Quicklime, and other Alkaline Substances" by Scottish chemist-physician Joseph Black, 27, shows that magnesium is a distinct substance completely different from lime with which it has been confused. Black last year laid the foundations of quantitative analysis with a doctoral thesis on causticization.

Moscow State University is founded in Russia.

A Dictionary of the English Language by London lexicographer Samuel Johnson, 46, establishes the reputation of Doctor Johnson, whose work will be completed in 1773. "The chief glory of every people arises from its authors," says Doctor Johnson.

Painting *Milkmaid and Woodcutter* by Thomas Gainsborough, *A Father Explaining the Bible to His Children* by French painter Jean Baptiste Greuze, 30, who wins admission to the Paris Academy.

Theater *Miss Sara Sampson* by German playwright Gotthold Ephraim Lessing, 26, 7/10 at Frankfurt der Oder.

Venetian adventurer Giovanni Jacopo Casanova de Seingalt, 30, is imprisoned as a spy upon his return to Venice after 14 years of traveling from one European capital to another as preacher, alchemist, gambler, and violin player. Expelled from the Seminary of St. Cyprian at age 16 for scandalous behavior, Casanova has ventured as far as Constantinople. He will effect a daring escape from prison next year and will continue his roguish life, accumulating a fortune as director of state lotteries for France's Louis XV in Paris, receiving the papal order of the Golden Spur, and engaging in duels before accepting employment as librarian to Bohemia's Count von Waldstein at Dux Castle, where he will write his memoirs of amours and escapades (*see* 1838).

An earthquake rocks northern Persia June 7 killing 40,000.

The Lisbon earthquake November 1 is the worst in Europe since the Lisbon quake of 1531. It is followed by a seismic sea wave, by the flooding of the Tagus River, and by a great fire, from 10,000 to 30,000 (60,000 by some accounts) lose their lives in the All Souls' Day disaster, and the tragedy shakes the confidence of all Europe (*see* Voltaire, 1759).

Portugal's Marques de Pombal takes charge of rebuilding Lisbon (above) and seized the opportunity to create a great square at the edge of the Tagus. A huge bronze equestrian statue of the king will dominate the Praca do Comercio.

Williamsburg in the Virginia colony hails the new George Wythe House completed by Richard Taliafero for his daughter Elizabeth and her husband George, a professor of law at the College of William and Mary.

English agriculturist Robert Bakewell, 30, develops a new breed of sheep that will be called Leicester.

Gorton's fish factory is founded at Gloucester in the Massachusetts colony (*see* 1623; General Mills, 1968).

Dr. Johnson's *Dictionary* (above) defines oats as "a grain which is generally given to horses but in Scotland supports the people." Dr. Johnson's Scottish biographer James Boswell will say, "Yes, and that is why in England you have such fine horses and in Scotland we have such fine people" (*see* 1785).

Observations Concerning the Increase of Mankind by Benjamin Franklin expresses Franklin's faith in human progress. Born the twelfth of 14 children in an age of high infant mortality, Franklin attacks the idea of "inevitable" poverty and limited growth, voicing confidence that America's colonial population will double every 20 or 25 years.

1756 The Seven Years' War begins in Europe as Prussia's Frederick the Great invades Saxony after hearing that the Saxons have formed a coalition with Austria,

JOIN or DIE

Benjamin Franklin's cartoon of May 1754 was more than 20 years premature. Colonial governments spurned his advice.

France, Russia, and Sweden to destroy or cripple Prussian power.

The French and Indian War brings English and French forces into conflict in a North American offshoot of the European war (above).

The "Black Hole of Calcutta" incident enrages the British. The nabob of Bengal Suraj-ud-Dowlah sacks Calcutta, and forces 146 Englishmen who have not fled the city into the guard room of Fort William. The chamber measures only 18 feet by 14 feet 10 inches and has but two small windows for ventilation, and when the survivors are released next morning (June 21) only 23 of the 146 remain alive (see 1757).

Scottish chemist Joseph Black shows that fixed air (carbon dioxide) is consistently distinguishable from normal air.

Nassau Hall is completed at Princeton for the 10-year-old College of New Jersey, which moves to Princeton from Newark. Architects William Shippen and Robert Smith have designed the new building.

Philadelphia's Pennsylvania State House (Independence Hall) is completed by Edmond Wolley and Andrew Hamilton (see Liberty Bell, 1752).

Mayonnaise is invented by France's duc de Richelieu, a bon vivant who sometimes invites his guests to dine in the nude. His dressing is a mixture of egg yolks, vinegar or lemon juice, oil, and seasonings, and its name may come from that of a town in Minorca.

The Virginia colony's population reaches 250,000, of whom more than 40 percent are slaves, up from 24 percent in 1715.

1757 The Battle of Plassey June 23 establishes British sovereignty in India as Robert Clive, 32, wins a victory over a Bengalese nabob who has played him false. A British naval squadron supported by East India Company troops under Clive recovers Calcutta, avenges last year's "Black Hole" incident, and goes on to take the French settlement at Chandernagor. Clive installs a new nabob, he accepts a large gift plus the quitrent of the East India Company's territory, and he becomes virtual ruler of Bengal.

Prussia's Frederick the Great has invaded Bohemia and has defeated an Austrian army May 6 at Prague. The Battle of Kolin June 18 ends in defeat for Frederick despite his exhortations ("Schweinhunds, would you live forever?"), and he is forced to evacuate Bohemia.

The Battle of Rossbach November 5 gives Frederick the Great a crushing victory over the French. Louis XV (or his mistress Mme. de Pompadour) says, "Après moi le déluge" (After me, the flood), an expression that has long since become proverbial.

The Battle of Leuthen December 5 ends in victory for Frederick the Great over the Austrians.

Benjamin Franklin visits England and sends home advice as to how far American importers can safely go in flouting London's mercantilist acts (see 1750; Stamp Act, 1765).

British sea captain John Campbell creates the sextant by extending the arc of John Hadley's quadrant of 1731 to measure angles of up to 120 degrees rather than 90. Campbell's sextant has a triangular frame, with one side an arc, the arc has a scale of degrees, an index pointer pivots across the frame and the arc, and a system of reflecting mirrors brings together the two objects whose angle is to be observed by the navigator.

An essay "On the Most Efficient Means of Preserving the Health of Seamen" by James Lind establishes principles of hygiene to guard against typhus and other diseases (see below).

Only a few hundred Parisians concern themselves with "literature, the arts and healthy philosophy," writes journalist-critic Baron Melchior von Grimm, who has become a naturalized citizen noted for his letters about Paris. Not only are books expensive but publications banned because of salacious passages or anticlerical views are prohibitive in price.

London's Royal Library is transferred to the British Museum founded 4 years ago.

Painting The Artist's Daughter with a Cat by Thomas Gainsborough; The Fowler and La Paresseuse Italienne by Jean Baptiste Greuze.

Jacques Ange Gabriel completes enlargements to the Louvre Palace at Paris.

Potato planting increases rapidly in northern Europe as the famine that accompanies the Seven Years' War gives impetus to potato culture (see Frederick, 1744).

James Lind's 1747 experiment with scurvy patients is described by Lind in a second edition of his 1753 Treatise. He reports that he divided 12 patients into pairs and experimented with six different diets, trying such things as vinegar, cider, and elixir vitriol (sulfuric acid, alcohol, and an extract of ginger and cinnamon). The best results were obtained, Lind reports, when diets were supplemented with oranges and lemons. He proposes novel ways to keep fruit juices and greens from deterioration on long voyages, suggesting that juices be put up in pint bottles and covered with a layer of olive oil before being tightly corked and that leeks and other vegetables be cut into short lengths, sprinkled with a thin layer of bay salt, and then packed in salt, which will permit them to be prepared as fresh vegetables when the salt is washed away as much as 3 months later (*see* Cook, Pringle, 1775).

✗ George Washington seeks election to the Virginia House of Burgesses from Fairfax County, and he campaigns for votes with 28 gallons of rum, 50 gallons of rum punch, 34 gallons of wine, 46 of beer, and 2 of cider royal. The county has 391 voters.

1758 French forces suffer reverses in the continuing Seven
✗ Years' War. The duke of Brunswick's 37-year-old son Ferdinand drives the French back across the Rhine and defeats them June 23 in the Battle of Crefield, the French West African ports of Senegal and Gorée fall to the British, and the British score victories in America.

The French Canadian fortress of Louisburg falls July 26 to British forces under Generals Jeffrey Amherst, 41, and James Wolfe, 31, with support from Admiral Edward Boscawen as the French and Indian War continues in North America. The French have defeated a British force trying to take Fort Ticonderoga July 8, but the British take Fort Frontenac August 27 and Fort Duquesne November 25. They win control of Cape Breton Island, and they drive the French from other strongholds (*see* 1713; 1759).

The Battle of Zorndorff August 25 gives Frederick the Great a victory over Russian forces that have invaded Prussia, and while the Austrians defeat the Prussians October 14 at the Battle of Hochkirk, Frederick successfully resists efforts by Austria's Count Leopold von Daun, 53, to drive his forces out of Saxony and Silesia.

$ *Tableau Économique* by French surgeon-general François Quesnay, 64, propounds a system under which the products of agriculture will be distributed without government restraint among the productive classes of the community (landowners and land cultivators) and the unproductive classes (manufacturers and merchants). Agriculture is the only true source of wealth, says Quesnay, and his disciple the Marquis de Mirabeau will say that Quesnay's manifesto contributes as much to the stability of political societies as have the inventions of money and writing.

✒ *De l'esprit* by French philosopher Claude-Adrien Helvétius, 43, extends the sensationist psychology of England's John Locke to the ethical and social fields.

Helvétius produces a major scandal by propounding a utilitarianism with atheistic and materialistic implications (*see* Locke, 1690).

🎨 Painting *The Mill at Charenton* by François Boucher.

∞ *The New Jerusalem (De nova Hierosolyma)* by Swedish naturalist-scientist Emanuel Swedenborg, 70, is a religious treatise. Swedenborg distinguished himself at age 30 during a siege of Frederikshall by inventing machines for carrying boats overland from Stromstadt to Iddefjord, and Queen Ulrika Eleanora elevated him to the nobility the following year. He began having visions 15 years ago, and his followers have founded the Church of the New Jerusalem, or New Church.

🏛 Virginia's Gunston Hall is completed for George Mason by London architect William Buckland.

1759 French forces triumph over Ferdinand of Brunswick
✗ April 13 at Brunswick, but Ferdinand beats the French August 1 at the Battle of Minden. Russian forces defeat the Prussians July 23 at Kay, and Frederick the Great suffers a major defeat August 12 as a coalition of Austrian and Russian armies gain victory at the Battle of Kunersdorf.

Spain's Ferdinand VI dies August 10 at age 45 after a 13-year reign. Ferdinand had lived in a state of melancholy bordering on madness since the death last year of his Portuguese wife Barbara, and he is succeeded by his half-brother of 43, who will reign until 1788 as Carlos III.

French Canada falls to the British September 13 following James Wolfe's victory in the Battle of the Plains of Abraham outside Quebec City. Wolfe has scaled the heights on which the city stands and has come out of the darkness with an army of 5,000 men to surprise the French field marshal Louis Joseph, marquis de Montcalm de Saint-Veran, who falls mortally wounded at age 47 (Wolfe, too, is mortally wounded).

British forces under Brigadier General John Forbes, 49, occupy Fort Duquesne built by the French 5 years ago, but General Forbes dies along with many of his men. The British build a new, larger fortress that they call Fort Pitt after the prime minister Sir William Pitt.

Austria's Count Leopold von Daun surrounds a Prussian army commanded by Friedrich August von Finck, 41, at Maxen and takes some 13,000 prisoners. Finck is court-martialed, dismissed from the army, and imprisoned in a fortress.

$ "Silhouette" becomes a French word of derision meaning a figure reduced to its simplest form. The demands of war and the luxury of the court have drained the nation's treasury, Etienne de Silhouette, 50, has been named controller-general through the influence of the king's mistress Mme. de Pompadour, he has attempted reforms that have included a land tax on the estates of the nobility, a reduction of pen-

1759 (cont.) sions, and the melting down of table silver for use as money, but his efforts arouse a storm of opposition and ridicule.

Portugal expels her Jesuits (*see* France, 1762).

Voltaire reports in his novel *Candide* (*see* below) that heretics were publicly burned after the Lisbon earthquake of 1755 because the University of Coimbra declared "that the sight of several persons being slowly burned in great ceremony is an infallible secret for preventing earthquakes."

German anatomist Kaspar Friedrich Wolff, 26, observes the development of growing plants. Wolff will be a founder of modern embryology.

Tobias Smollett calls Doctor Johnson "that great Cham of literature" March 16 in a letter to John Wilkes, 32, a profligate member of Parliament who participates in the secret "Mad Monks of Medmenham" society founded by Francis Dashwood, 51, fifteenth baron le Despenser. The society conducts obscene parodies of Roman Catholic rituals at Medmenham Abbey.

Fiction *Rasselas* (*The Prince of Abyssynia: A Tale*) by Doctor Johnson (above) who wrote the two-volume novel in 8 days in January; *Candide* by Voltaire (above) whose best seller about Pangloss describes the Lisbon earthquake of 1755: the ultimate reason for things is unknown and unknowable, says Voltaire, who ridicules the optimism of the pope and his own earlier optimism: "All is for the best in the best of all possible worlds," but the predicament of man has become anything but "passable."

Painting *The 7th Earl of Louderdale* by Joshua Reynolds; *Sigismonda* by William Hogarth.

Theater *The Lovers* (*Gl'innamorati*) by Carlo Goldoni, in November at Venice's Teatro San Luca.

Porcelain teacups in Europe now generally have handles in a departure from Oriental design.

Irish brewer Arthur Guinness establishes a Dublin brewery that will become the world's largest. Guinness Stout will gain worldwide distribution.

1760 The Battle of Landshut June 23 in Bavaria ends with Austrian forces defeating and capturing a Prussian army, but Frederick the Great prevents a linkup of Russian and Austrian forces, and he defeats the Austrians August 15 at the Battle of Liegnitz.

A Russian army surprises Berlin October 9 and burns the city in 3 days before retreating at news that Frederick is rushing to relieve Berlin.

Britain's George II dies October 25 at age 77 after a 33-year reign in which he has lost favor by favoring Hanover's interests over those of Britain. His 22-year-old grandson George William Frederick assumes the throne as George III of Great Britain and Ireland and Elector of Hanover to begin a disastrous 60-year reign.

The Japanese Tokugawa shogun Ieshige abdicates at age 49, drunken and ill after 15 years in power. He is succeeded by the 23-year-old son of the late shogun Yoshimune, who will rule until 1786 as the shogun Ieharu despite his mental incompetence.

On the Seats and Causes of Disease by Padua physician Giovanni Morgagni, now 78, introduces the anatomical concept that will become the chief element in medical diagnosis. The founder of pathological anatomy, Morgagni has conducted hundreds of postmortem operations, and he shows the importance of recording a patient's life history, the history of his disease, the events connected with a final illness, and the manner of death (*see* 1719).

Some Account of the Success of Inoculation for the Smallpox in England and America by Benjamin Franklin is published at London (*see* Montagu, 1721; Jenner, 1796).

Nonfiction *The Sermons of Mr. Yorick* by English clergyman Laurence Sterne, 46, whose book is actually a collection of his own sermons as prebendary of York. Sterne's wife Elizabeth became disturbed by his "small quiet attentions" to other women and went insane 2 years ago.

Fiction *The Life and Opinions of Tristram Shandy, Gentleman* by Laurence Sterne (above) is published in its first two volumes and represents a bold and brilliant departure in the art of the novel. Says the *London Magazine*, "Oh rare Tristram Shandy!— Thou very sensible—humorous—pathetick—humane—unaccountable! What shall we call thee?— Rabelais, Cervantes, What?"

Poetry *Fragments of Ancient Poetry Collected in the Highlands of Scotland* by schoolmaster James Macpherson, 24, whose alleged translations from a 3rd century Gaelic poet will be much admired for their romantic rhythm and passages of beauty but will be exposed as fraudulent by Doctor Johnson.

Painting *Mrs. Philip Thicknesse* by Thomas Gainsborough; *Giorgiana* by Joshua Reynolds. London's Royal Society of Art holds its first exhibition of contemporary art.

Theater *The Boors* (*I rusteghi*) by Carlo Goldoni 2/16 at Venice's Teatro San Luca.

First performances Symphonies No. 2, 3, 4, and 5 by Viennese composer Franz Joseph Haydn, 28, who started as a choir boy at St. Stephen's Cathedral.

The first roller skates are introduced at London by Belgian musical instrument maker Joseph Merlin, who rolls into a masquerade party at Carlisle House in Soho Square playing a violin. Unable to stop or turn, Merlin crashes into a large mirror valued at more than £500, smashes it to pieces, breaks his fiddle, and severely injures himself (*see* 1863).

P. Lorillard Company has its origin in a tobacco manufactory opened on the High Road between New York and Boston at a point that will later be called Park Row. Huguenot French immigrant

Pierre Lorillard, 18, specializes in making snuff (*see* 1789).

 Christ Church at Cambridge in the Massachusetts Colony is completed by Peter Harrison.

Benjamin Franklin's lightning rod is praised by English traveler Andrew Burnaby, who is touring the American colonies (*see* 1752). "I believe no country has more certainly proved the efficacy of the electrical rods than this," writes Burnaby. "Before the discovery of them these gusts were frequently productive of melancholy consequences: but now it is rare to hear of such instances. It is observable that no house was ever struck, where they were fixed...."

London's Botanical Gardens open at Kew.

 British grain prices will rise higher in the next decade, and fewer Britons will grow their own food as public lands are enclosed and turned into pastures for sheep and as more of the peasantry are driven off the land (*see* 1755; 1769).

Robert Bakewell in Leicestershire begins experiments in the improvement of beef cattle (*see* 1755; 1769).

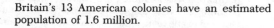 Large quantities of cloves and nutmegs are burned at Amsterdam to maintain high price levels.

Britain's 13 American colonies have an estimated population of 1.6 million.

1761 The Battle of Panipat in India January 14 ends in a crushing defeat of the Marathas at the hands of the Afghan chief Ahmad Shah Abdali, who withdraws soon afterward following a mutiny of his troops. The dissension left behind plays into the hands of the British, and while the Mogul Empire that began in 1526 will continue until 1857, it is the British who will henceforth rule India until 1947.

Portugal is invaded by French and Spanish forces, and the Portuguese summon British aid to help repel the invaders.

France, Spain, and the Bourbon states of Italy join in a pacte de famille against Britain August 15, Britain's Lord Pitt resigns October 5 when George III and Parliament refuse to declare war on Spain, and Britain's Tories come to power for the first time since 1714.

George III threatens to withdraw the subsidies that have enabled Prussia's Frederick the Great to withstand the combined forces of the coalition in the Seven Years' War that has exhausted all parties and cost hundreds of thousands of lives (*see* 1762).

A complete calculus of variations that incorporates both old and new results in a treatment that is both systematic and elegant is published by French mathematician Joseph-Louis Lagrange, 25, who has been a professor at an artillery school in Turin since age 19 and who has corresponded with the Swiss mathematician Leonhard Euler (*see* 1748).

The first association between tobacco and cancer is observed by London physician John Hill, who reports six cases of "polypusses" related to excessive use of snuff in his "Cautions Against the Immoderate Use of Snuff."

The percussion method of diagnosing lung disease is discovered by Viennese physician Leopold Auenbrugger von Auenbrügg, 39 (*see* Laënnec, 1819).

England's Bridgewater Canal is opened after 3 years' work to link Liverpool with Leeds.

The first test is made of John Harrison's 1736 chronometer which has been improved and which is essentially a watch 5 inches in diameter with a gridiron pendulum made of two metals that expand and contract in opposition. The chronometer is taken on a voyage to Jamaica aboard H.M.S. *Deptford* and is pronounced a success (*see* Leroy, 1765).

Britain takes £600,000 worth of exports from Guadeloupe, most of it in sugar, while Canada yields only £14,000 (*see* 1759; 1763).

The ruin of France's merchant marine and navy frees French mariners to become privateers. They seize as much as one tenth of all British merchant shipping, but France is no longer a major commercial rival to Britain.

Slave traders are excluded from the Society of Friends by American Quakers despite the fact that many Quakers own slaves.

Poetry *The Rosciad* by English poet Charles Churchill, 30, is published anonymously and cleverly satirizes London actors and actresses. An ordained priest, Churchill defends his dissipations in his poem "Night" and he attacks his critics in his poem "Apology."

Painting *L'Accorde de Village* by Jean Baptiste Greuze.

Theater *The Father of the Family* (*Le Père de Famille*) by Denis Diderot 2/18 at the Comédie Française, Paris; *The Rage for Country Life* (*Le Manie della Villeggiatura*) by Carlo Goldoni in October at Venice's Teatra San Luca.

First performances Symphony No. 7 in C minor (*Le Midi*) by Joseph Haydn who signs a contract in May to become vice-capellmeister to the court of Hungary's Prince Miklós József Esterházy at Eisenstadt.

St. Michael's Episcopal Church at Charleston in the South Carolina colony is completed by architect Samuel Cardy.

Philadelphia's Point Pleasant house is completed for John MacPherson.

1762 The Russian czarina Elizabeth Petrovna dies January 5 at age 52 after a 20-year reign and is succeeded by her 33-year-old son who ascends the throne as Peter III.

Russia withdraws from the Seven Years' War following the accession to power of Peter III (above) who

1762 (cont.) is an admirer of Prussia's Frederick the Great. Peter makes peace, he returns Pomerania to Prussia, and he offers his support against Sweden, which also withdraws from the war, and against France and Austria, which soon will make peace.

Russia's Peter III is deposed by a military coup in July, he is put to death July 18, and he is succeeded by his 33-year-old widow Sophia-Augusta of Anhalt Zerbst who has been converted to the Orthodox church, has changed her name to Catharine (Ekatarina Alekseevna), and begins a 34-year reign of "benevolent despotism" as "the Semiramis of the North," as Voltaire will call her.

British rear admiral George Brydges Rodney, 43, captures Martinique, Grenada, St. Lucia, and St. Vincent in the West Indies. Another British force takes Havana despite the loss of more than half its number to fever and dysentery, and British forces in the Pacific take Manila.

An epidemic of typhus that will continue through most of the decade sweeps across the Italian states, which are suffering famine (*see* 1764).

The Diseases of Children and Their Remedies by Swedish physician Nils von Rosenstein, 59, is the first systematic modern treatise on medical care of infants and children. The work establishes the science of pediatrics.

France expels her Jesuits who have been engaging in commerce and industry and who have made themselves unpopular by interfering in politics (*see* Portugal, 1759; Clement XIV, 1773).

George III appoints John Bartram Botanist Royal in America (*see* 1751). Now 66, Bartram journeys to Florida with his son William, who will remain in the south and who will compile notes on indigenous birds, fish, and plants (*see* Lewis and Clark, 1804).

French chemist François Fresnau discovers that raw rubber latex is soluble in turpentine, but no immediate commercial use follows (*see* 1503; Macintosh, 1823).

The Equitable Life Assurance Society is founded at London (*see* 1583). It will be the first company to grade premium rates according to age (*see* New York, 1859).

Nonfiction *The Social Contract* (*Le Contrat Social*) by Jean Jacques Rousseau expresses antimonarchist views that arouse such passions that Rousseau takes refuge in Switzerland to escape prosecution. "Man is born free yet everywhere is in chains"; "The body politic, like the human body, begins to die from its birth and bears in itself the causes of its destruction."

Fiction *Emile, ou Traité de l'education* by Jean Jacques Rousseau contains the line, "I hate books, for they only teach people to talk about what they do not understand" (I), but Rousseau goes on to say, "There exists one book, which, to my taste, furnishes the happiest treatise of natural education. What then is this marvelous book? Is it Aristotle? Is it Pliny, is it Bubbon? No—it is *Robinson Crusoe*" (III) (*see* 1719).

Painting Frescoes for Madrid's Royal Palace by Giambattista Tiepolo; *Garrick in 'The Farmer's Return'* by German-born painter Johann Zoffany, 29, who arrived in England last year after having studied in Italy; *Mares and Foals* by English painter George Stubbs, 38.

Theater *The Chioggian Brawls* (*La baruffe chiozzotte*) by Carlo Goldoni in January at Venice's Teatro San Luca.

Opera *Artaxerxes* 2/2 at London's Covent Garden, with music by Thomas Arne, arias that include "The Soldier Tired," "Water Parted from the Sea;" *Orfeo ed Euridice* 10/8 at Vienna's Hofburgtheater, with music by Christoph von Gluck whose expressive and dramatically forceful music will revolutionize opera, making music and drama interdependent; *Love in a Village* 12/8 at London's Covent Garden, with music by Thomas Arne, libretto by Irish playwright Isaac Bickerstaffe, 27, songs that include "There was a jolly miller once/ Lived on the River Dee."

New York's first St. Patrick's Day parade steps off March 17 to celebrate a man historians will agree was not named Patrick, was not Irish, did not drive the snakes from Ireland, did not bring Christianity to Ireland, and was not born March 17. Irish-Americans will grow in number until New York has a larger Irish population than Dublin, the parade will grow to become an event of paralyzing proportions, and it will never be canceled on account of inclement weather.

English dandy Richard "Beau" Nash has died at Bath February 3 at age 87 after a career in which he has made Bath a popular watering place, has abolished the habit of wearing swords in places of public amusement, has brought dueling into disrepute, and has induced gentlemen to wear shoes and stockings rather than boots in parades and assemblies. Nash has lived on a small pension and by selling snuff boxes and trinkets since 1745 when Parliament made gambling illegal.

France's Louis XV builds Le Petit Trianon for his mistress Madame DuBarry (*see* 1768).

A cook to France's Duc Louis George Erasmé de Contades reinvents pâté de foie gras. Known to the ancient Egyptians, pâté is made from the enlarged livers of force-fed geese (*see* Doyen, 1772).

Jean Jacques Rousseau blames English "barbarism" on high meat consumption in his novel *Emile* (above).

A French kaolin deposit is discovered that will lead to increased production of porcelain (*see* 1753; 1754).

English potter Josiah Wedgwood, 32, receives an appointment from George III who names him "Potter to the Queen" (Charlotte). Wedgwood will create superior tableware (*see* 1763).

The Mannheim Glassworks started in Lancaster County, Pennsylvania, by German immigrant Baron

Henry William Stiegel will be the first successful American producer of table and decorative glass.

Dutch ironworkers at Mary Ann Furnace, Pennsylvania, cast the first American iron cookstove.

Russia's population will increase in the next 34 years from 19 million to 29 million, partly because the potato has made food cheaper and more abundant and partly through annexation of new territory.

1763 The Treaty of Paris signed February 10 ends Europe's Seven Years' War.

France cedes to Britain her territories in Canada, Cape Breton Island, Grenada in the West Indies, and Senegal in Africa.

France regains Gorée in Africa, Pondichery and Chandernagor in India, and the sugar-rich island of Guadeloupe in the West Indies.

The treaty recognizes the Mississippi River as the boundary between the British colonies and the Louisiana territory that France has ceded to Spain (see 1800).

Spain cedes Florida to Britain and regains all of Britain's conquests in Cuba including Havana. Spain also recovers the Philippines but loses Minorca.

Poland's Augustus III dies at Dresden October 5 at age 66 after a 30-year reign. He has returned to Saxony following conclusion of the Treaty of Hubertsburg in February, and he will be succeeded next year by the 31-year-old Stanislaus Poniatowski, a favorite of the Russian czarina Catharine, whose influence will gain him election to the throne. He will reign until 1795 as Stanislaus II Augustus.

Ottawa chief Pontiac leads tribesmen of the American northwest in an uprising against Detroit and other British forts in an effort to drive the white settlers back east across the Alleghenies, but the Ottawa are deserted by their French allies in their siege of Detroit.

The door opened by the French and Indian War to westward movement of English colonists is closed October 7 by a decree of George III through House of Commons leader George Grenville. Sixty percent of American colonists are English, and the king decrees that they must remain east of the sources of rivers that flow into the Atlantic, but it is a decree that will be honored in the breach. Angry frontiersmen flout western land claims made by the seaboard colonies and the "sea to sea" grants of their original charters (see 1748; 1769).

St. Louis has its origin in a Mississippi trading post selected by French fur trader Pierre Laclede Liguest, who names the post after France's patron saint Louis IX. He will send his stepson René Auguste Chouteau to build St. Louis next year.

English philanthropist Granville Sharp, 28, finds a slave beaten and left to die in the streets of London by a Barbados lawyer. Sharp nurses the man back to health and protests when the lawyer then kidnaps the slave and ships him off to the West Indies to be sold. The case produces a public outcry (see 1772).

Treatise on Tolerance by Voltaire is published at Paris.

The British Mariner's Guide by English astronomer Nevil Maskelyne, 31, contains observations that will revolutionize navigation. Maskelyne's interest in the subject was aroused 2 years ago when he voyaged to the South Atlantic island of St. Helena in order to observe the transit of the planet Venus, and he has used lunar distances to calculate longitude at sea (see Harrison, 1760; Cook, 1768; Bowditch, 1802).

Of 14,000 hogsheads of molasses brought into New England this year, only 2,500 are from British sources; smugglers account for the remainder (see 1764; Molasses Act, 1733).

Poetry *Song to David* by Christopher Smart: "And now the matchless deed's achiev'd,/Determined, dared, and done."

Painting *The Election of the Doge of Venice* by Venetian painter Francesco Guardi, 49, who has evolved a style of his own after years of following the photographic style of Canaletto; *The Paralytic Cared for by His Children* by Jean Baptiste Greuze; *Death of Wolfe* by English painter George Romney, 28.

La Madeleine is completed at Paris.

Touro Synagogue is completed on Touro Street at Newport in the Rhode Island colony for the town's congregation of Sephardic Jews. Its sand floor commemorates the exodus of Jews from Egypt.

English potter Josiah Wedgwood perfects a vitrified "cream-color ware" that is not true porcelain but that will give Britain a hard tableware far more durable than earthenware (see 1762; 1769).

"Some people have a foolish way of not minding, or pretending not to mind, what they eat," says Doctor Johnson, who for the first time meets Scotsman James Boswell, 23. "For my part, I mind my belly very studiously and very carefully, for I look upon it that he who does not mind his belly will hardly mind anything else."

New York's Fraunces Tavern has its beginnings in the Queen's Head Tavern named in honor of George III's wife Charlotte. The tavern is opened at the corner of Broad Street and Pearl by West Indian immigrant Samuel Fraunces, a black man who last year took over the house built in 1719 by Stephen de Lancey (see 1905).

Prussia's Frederick the Great estimates that the Seven Years' War produced 853,000 casualties among his troops and that it directly killed 33,000 civilians, but war-related famine in 15 of the last 23 years has reduced the population of Europe far more drastically than has war itself.

1764 The Sugar Act passed by Parliament April 5 replaces the Molasses Act of 1733, but while it cuts in half the

1764 (cont.) sixpence per gallon duty on molasses imported into British colonies from non-British islands in the West Indies, the British send customs officials to America and order colonial governors to enforce the new law and apprehend smugglers (*see* 1763).

The British pay taxes at higher rates than any Europeans and have received little tax support from their colonists. They begin to take a harder line with the colonists (*see* Townshend Act, 1767; Hancock, 1768).

Pennsylvania colony mechanic James Davenport invents machinery to spin and card wool.

The Mohammedan soldier Haidar Ali, 39, usurps the throne of Mysore. He will assume the title maharaja in 1766. British forces under Sir Hector Munro defeat the Nabob of Dudh at Buxar in Bengal.

Russia confiscates Church lands.

Naples has a violent epidemic of typhus (*see* 1762).

Brown University has its beginnings in the Rhode Island College founded at Warren. The school will move to Providence in 1770, will maintain strict non-sectarian principles despite the fact that its founders are Baptists, and will adopt the name Brown in 1804 after receiving gifts from merchant Nicholas Brown, now 35, whose 2-year-old Nicholas Brown & Co. has been joined by brothers Joseph, 31, John, 28, and Moses, 26. The Browns are the leading colonial candlemakers and sell their candles at New York, Boston, Philadelphia, and the West Indian ports.

The Connecticut Courant begins weekly publication at Hartford October 29 (*see* 1866).

Manuel typographique by French engraver-type founder Pierre Simon Fournier, 52, is published in two volumes at Paris. Fournier has devised the first system for measuring and naming sizes of type.

Chinese novelist Ts'ao Chan (Hsüeh-ch'in) dies at age 48, leaving his novel *The Dream of the Red Chamber* incomplete. The only great novel of manners in Chinese literature, it describes in detail the glory and decline of the great Chia family with frequent references to a supernatural world, but novelist Kao Eh will write the final third of the work.

Poetry *The Traveler* by Irish poet Oliver Goldsmith, 35.

William Hogarth dies at London October 26 at age 66.

Sculpture *St. Bruno* by French sculptor Jean Antoine Houdon, 23. A servant's son who received the prix de Rome 3 years ago, Houdon continues his studies at Rome.

Theater *La Jeune Indienne* by French playwright Sebastien Roch Nicolas Chamfort, 23.

First performances Symphony No. 22 in E flat major (*The Philosopher*) by Joseph Haydn at the Esterházy court in Eisenstadt.

Madrid's Royal Palace is completed for Spain's Carlos III after 28 years of construction.

The Ruins of the Palace of the Emperor Diocletian at Spalato by Scottish architect Robert Adam, 36, establishes Adam's reputation. He designs Kenwood House in Middlesex.

London begins the practice of numbering houses.

Prussia's Frederick the Great moves to improve his country's agriculture after studying the intensive farming methods employed in the Lowlands. Frederick institutes a modified rotation system that employs clover to enrich the soil, turnips whose green tops help smother weeds, wheat, and barley (the turnips and clover both make good animal fodder; *see* Townshend, 1730). Frederick also drains the marshes along the Oder, Werthe, and Netze Rivers.

Wild orange groves 40 miles long are described in Spanish Florida (*see* 1513; 1519).

Baker Chocolate has its origin in a business set up by Irish-American chocolate maker John Hannon with help from Massachusetts Colony physician James Baker, who leases a small mill on the Neponset River at Dorchester, obtains millstones and kettles, and supplies Hannon with the necessary capital. Hannon will disappear at sea in 1779 after sailing for the West Indies to buy cocoa beans and Baker will take over the company (*see* 1824).

Baccarat glass has its origin in a petition to France's Louis XV from the monseigneur de Montmorency-Laval, bishop of Metz, who asks permission to establish a glassware factory across the Meurthe River from Baccarat, a town of 600. A nearby salt factory that has used the bishop's vast woodlands as a fuel source has closed, the bishop's Compagnie des Cristallieres de Baccarat will be established next year, and by 1789 it will have 400 employees.

1765 The Stamp Act passed by Parliament March 22 is the first measure to impose direct taxes on Britain's American colonists. Intended to raise £60,000 per year, the act requires revenue stamps on all newspapers, pamphlets, playing cards, dice, almanacs, and legal documents.

The Quartering Act passed by Parliament May 15 orders colonists to provide barracks and supplies for British troops.

Virginia patriot Patrick Henry, 29, protests the Stamp Act (above) in the House of Burgesses May 29: "Tarquin and Caesar each had his Brutus, Charles the First his Cromwell, and George the Third. . . ." The Speaker interrupts by crying, "Treason," but Henry resumes, ". . . may profit by their example. If *this* be treason, make the most of it."

Sons of Liberty Clubs formed at Boston and at other colonial towns resist the Stamp Act and a Stamp Act Congress convenes at New York in October with delegates from nine colonies to protest taxation without representation. The delegates resolve to import no goods that require payment of duty (*see* 1766).

The Holy Roman Emperor Francis I dies at Innsbruck August 18 at age 56 after a 20-year reign with his wife Maria Theresa. She succeeds as coregent with their 24-year-old son, who begins a 25-year reign as Josef II.

✊ Lisbon finally abolishes the auto-da-fé parade and ritual sentencing that for more than two centuries has been the occasion for violence against Jews and heretics, often with spectacular public burnings.

⚡ The steam engine invented by Scotsman James Watt, 29, produces power far more efficiently than the Newcomen engine of 1705. Mathematical instrument maker to the University of Glasgow, Watt employs a separate chamber, or condenser, to condense exhaust steam from the cylinder of his engine (*see* Boulton and Watt Foundry, 1769).

⚡ The steam-driven three-wheel gun tractor devised by French engineer Nicholas Joseph Cugnot, 40, pioneers development of the automobile. Cugnot's gun tractor can run at 2.5 miles per hour but must stop every 100 feet or so to make steam (*see* Trevithick, 1801; Benz, 1885).

The ship's chronometer invented at Paris by French horologer Pierre Leroy, 48, makes a major contribution to navigation. Leroy has discovered the isochronism of spiral springs, he has originated the detached escapement, and his instrument embodies all the essential features of the modern ship's chronometer (*see* Harrison, 1736; 1761).

A new canal links France's Loire and Rhône Rivers (*see* 1600; 1603).

Colonial American shipping interests have 28,000 tons of shipping and employ some 4,000 seamen. Exports of tobacco are nearly double in value the exports of bread and flour, with fish, rice, indigo, and wheat next in order of value. The major shippers are the Cabots and Thomas Russell of Boston, Thomas Francis Lewis of New York, and Samuel Butler of Providence.

💲 An economic depression begins at Boston that will stifle business, produce widespread unemployment, and throw many Bostonians into debtors' prisons. Workingmen and sailors average £15 to £20 per year when jobs are available, but it takes roughly £60 per year to support a family in the town, even when the wife makes all clothes except for hats, shoes, overcoats, and Sunday best.

The world's first savings bank opens in Brunswick. The German bank inspires other European entrepreneurs to open thrift institutions (*see* 1799).

⚕ The first American medical school opens at the College and Academy of Philadelphia. The school will become the College of Physicians and Surgeons.

✒ Fiction *The Castle of Otranto* by English man of letters Horace Walpole, 47, fourth earl of Orford, is the first Gothic horror novel and marks the beginning of the romantic school of English fiction. Walpole has written the book at his villa Strawberry Hill outside Twickenham, a property he purchased 7 years ago, converted into a gothic castle, and has equipped with a printing press.

🎨 Painting *The Gladiator* by English painter Joseph Wright, 31; *Corésus Sacrificing Himself to Save Callirhoé* and *The Swing* by French painter Jean Honoré Fragonard, 33. *Mme. Pompadour* by François Boucher, who is appointed court painter at Versailles; *Young Girl Weeping Over Her Dead Bird* by Jean Baptiste Greuze.

Japanese painter Harunobu Suzuki introduces color to *ukiyoe* painting and improves *ukiyoe* printmaking technique by assigning specific functions to specialized professionals. Suzuki specializes in painting beautiful women.

🏛 New York's Morris-Jumel mansion is completed for Colonel Roger Morris, whose Georgian frame-and-shingle house at the highest point in Manhattan (later 165th Street and Edgecombe Avenue) will be acquired in 1810 by French merchant Stephen Jumel. (Jumel's wife Betsy will bear an illegitimate son who will be named George Washington Bowen; her husband will leave her. After his death, she will marry Aaron Burr, who will die a few months later at age 79, and she will survive until 1865 before dying in the New York house that the city will buy in 1903.)

✗ The first true restaurant opens at Paris where a tavernkeeper named Boulanger defies the monopoly of the caterers (*traiteurs*) in the sale of cooked meat. Boulanger serves a "soup" made of sheep's meat in a white sauce, which he calls a "restorative" (*restorante*). The *traiteurs* sue, the case goes to the French parlement, Boulanger wins, and he gains the

James Watt's steam engine improved on the Newcomen engine and marked the real beginning of viable steam power.

1765 (cont.) right to serve *restorantes* at his all-night place in the rue Bailleul.

Philadelphia's population reaches 25,000 and becomes the second largest city in the British Empire after London. New York has 12,500, up from 5,000 in 1700 (*see* 1793).

1766 Denmark's Frederick V dies January 14 at age 42 after a 20-year reign. He is succeeded by his semi-idiot son of 16, who marries the 15-year-old daughter of the Prince of Wales Caroline Matilda and sinks into debauchery but who will reign at least nominally until 1808 as Christian VII.

Lorraine reverts to France upon the death of Stanislas Leszczynski in February at age 89.

Parliament repeals the Stamp Act passed last year to tax the American colonists, acting partly at the persuasion of Benjamin Franklin, but the Declaratory Act passed March 18 declares that the king—by and with the consent of Parliament—has authority to make laws and to bind the British colonies in all respects (*see* Townshend Acts, 1767).

The Treaty of Oswego in July ends Pontiac's War.

Virginia planter-miller George Washington ships an unruly slave off to the West Indies to be exchanged for a hogshead of rum and other commodities.

Russia's Catharine the Great grants freedom of worship (*see* 1783).

France abolishes internal free trade in grain (*see* 1774).

English engineer James Brindley begins construction of a Grand Trunk Canal to connect the Trent and Mersey Rivers. The 50-year-old Brindley works without drawings or written calculations, but his canal will open a water route from the Irish Sea to the North Sea.

Rutgers University has its beginnings at New Brunswick in the New Jersey colony, where members of the Dutch Reformed Church found Queen's College (*see* 1825).

Nonfiction *Confessions* by Jean Jacques Rousseau paraphrases Machiavelli with the line, "In the kingdom of the blind, the one-eyed are kings"; "It is not hard to confess our criminal acts, but our ridiculous and shameful acts," writes Rousseau.

Fiction *The Vicar of Wakefield* by poet-playwright Oliver Goldsmith (his only novel).

Painting *The Orrery* by Joseph Wright; *Queen Charlotte and the Two Eldest Princes* by Johann Zoffany.

Christie's art auction house opens at London to compete with the Sotheby firm founded in 1744. Auctioneer James Christie, 36, starts a business that will continue for centuries. His son James will carry on the business and will be an expert on Etruscan and Greek vases, his son Samuel Hunter Christie will be

a noted mathematician, and his grandson William Henry Mahoney will be a noted astronomer.

Theater *The Clandestine Marriage* by English actor-playwright David Garrick, 48, and playwright George Colman, 34, 2/20 At London's Drury Lane Theatre, which Garrick has comanaged since 1747.

Austrian composer Wolfgang Amadeus Mozart, 10, returns to his native Salzburg after having toured Paris and London with his father and sister. Young Wolfgang has performed on the harpsichord and has composed violin sonatas and improvisations, beginning a career that he continues by studying counterpoint under the direction of his father Leopold, 47, who is a violinist and composer in his own right.

London merchant Richard Tattersall, who has founded the Tattersall Horse Market, orders a special pattern for his horse blankets. The check pattern designed will be called the tattersall check.

Vienna's Prater Park opens with a 1,328-acre expanse of meadowland donated to the people by the young emperor Josef II, who serves as coregent of Austria with his mother Maria Theresa. The word "prater" comes from the Spanish *prado* for meadowland. The new park has bridle paths, a rowing lake, and other amenities, it lies on the island formed by the main stream of the Danube and its canal.

Rust ruins the Italian wheat crop, food prices rise, and widespread hunger ensues.

"Let them eat cake" [if there is no bread], writes Jean Jacques Rousseau (above) in his *Confessions*. Rousseau attributes the remark to "a great princess," but it will be widely ascribed in the 1780s and 1790s to Vienna's Marie Antoinette, now 11, who will become queen of France in 1774.

English chemist Henry Cavendish, 35, duplicates the process by which lightning in a thunderstorm produces nitrogen from the atmosphere to enrich soil. Cavendish passes electric sparks through a nitrogen-oxygen mixture, he produces nitrogen dioxide, and the NO_2 yields nitric acid when dissolved in water (*see* Glauber, 1648; Rutherford, 1772). The element nitrogen remains unknown, but the Cavendish experiment stimulates speculation on practical ways to enrich soils (*see* Wöhler, 1828; Humboldt, 1802; Haber, 1908).

1767 The Townshend Revenue Act passed by Parliament June 29 imposes duties on tea, glass, paint, oil, lead, and paper imported into Britain's American colonies in hopes of raising £40,000 per year. A town meeting held at Boston to protest the Townshend Act adopts a nonimportation agreement (*see* 1770).

Letters from a Farmer in Pennsylvania by Philadelphia lawyer John Dickinson, 34, are published in their first installments. Dickinson drafted the resolutions and grievances of the Stamp Act Congress 2 years ago as a member of that body, and his *Letters* on the nonimportation and nonexportation agreements (above) will continue to appear through much of 1768, winning him wide popularity in the colonies.

The Mason and Dixon line between the Pennsylvania and Maryland colonies is completed after a 4-year $75,000 survey by English surveyor-astronomers Charles Mason, 37, and Jeremiah Dixon who have been engaged to settle a century-old dispute as to ownership of lands which include the large fertile peninsula between Chesapeake Bay and Delaware Bay. Mason and Dixon's demarcation line is amazingly accurate and is marked by handsome boundary stones, with the Penn coat-of-arms on their north sides and the Calvert coat-of-arms on their south sides extending westward to the "top of the Great dividing Ridge of the Alleghaney Mountains" beyond which Mason and Dixon's Indian guides have refused to proceed out of fear of the Delaware and the Shawnee.

North Carolina woodsman Daniel Boone, 33, goes through the Cumberland Gap found in 1750 and reaches "Kentucke" in defiance of King George's 1763 decree. A veteran of the 1756 French and Indian War who has learned woodcraft from the Cherokees, Boone is reputed to be able to smell salt deposits 30 miles away, and in "Kentucke" he discovers a huge brine lake, a salt lick that attracts game and makes the region a hunting ground contested by various Indian tribes (*see* 1773).

The History and Present State of Electricity by English clergyman-chemist Joseph Priestley, 34, is published at Leeds and explains the rings, later to be called Priestley rings, that are formed by an electrical discharge on a metallic surface. Priestley proposes an explanation of the oscillatory character of the discharge from a Leyden jar (*see* 1745; 1746).

The study of "different kinds of airs" is begun by Joseph Priestley (above). Knowing that carbon dioxide, or "fixed air," is present above the open vats in which beer mash is fermenting at the Leeds brewery, Priestley holds two containers close to the surface of the fermenting mash and pours water back and forth between them; the water becomes charged with CO_2.

Fiction *The Life and Opinions of Tristram Shandy* by Laurence Sterne appears in its eighth and final volume after 7 years of earlier volumes; *l'Ingenu* by Voltaire criticizes French society from the viewpoint of an imaginary Huron *sauvage*.

Theater *Eugenie* by French playwright-watchmaker Pierre Augustin Caron de Beaumarchais, 35, 1/25 at the Comédie Française, Paris; *The Prince of Parthia* by American playwright Thomas Godfrey, 30, 3/24 at Philadelphia's Southwark Theatre (first play by an American dramatist to have a professional production); *The Free Thinker* (*Der Freigeist*) by Gotthold Ephraim Lessing at Frankfurt-am-Main; *Minna von Barnhelm, or The Soldier's Fortune* (*Minna von Barnhelm, oder Das Soldatenglück*) by G. E. Lessing 9/30 at Hamburg's Nationaltheater.

Opera *Apollo et Hyacinthus* 5/13 at Salzburg, with music by Wolfgang Amadeus Mozart; *Alceste*

12/16 at Vienna's Burgtheater, with music by C. W. Gluck.

Tryon Palace (Governor's Palace) at New Bern in the North Carolina colony is completed by architect John Hawks.

A fleet of 50 American whalers makes a foray into the Antarctic, the first whaling venture into that region.

French navigator Louis Antoine de Bougainville, 38, explores Oceania in hopes of expanding French whaling operations into the Pacific.

Carbonated water is pioneered by Joseph Priestley (above), who writes, "Sometimes in the space of two or three minutes [I have] made a glass of exceedingly pleasant sparkling water which could hardly be distinguished from very good Pyrmont." A more convenient way to make carbonated water will be devised by Priestley, and in 1772 he will publish a booklet dedicated to John Montague, fourth earl of Sandwich, with the title *Directions for Impregnating Water with Fixed Air* (*see* carbonic acid, 1770).

An English writer complains that "as much superfluous money is expended on tea and sugar as would maintain four millions more subjects on bread."

1768 British customs officials at Boston seize the sloop *Liberty* June 10, the action precipitates riots, and Boston merchants adopt a nonimportation agreement August 1. Owner of the sloop is John Hancock, 31, whose late uncle has left him a fortune gained by profiteering in food supplied to the British troops and who has enhanced that fortune by smuggling wine into Boston.

Delegates from 26 Massachusetts towns meet at Faneuil Hall September 22 in response to a call by Boston selectmen. They draw up a statement of grievances (*see* Boston Massacre, 1770).

The Treaty of Hard Labor signed in the South Carolina colony October 14 confirms cessions of Cherokee lands in the Virginia and Carolina colonies to the British Crown.

The Treaty of Fort Stanwix signed November 5 confirms the cession of Iroquois territories between the Ohio and Tennessee Rivers to the British Crown.

Genoa sells Corsica to France, whose Louis le bien-aimé is now widely hated. He has lost most of the French colonial empire and has taxed the people heavily to maintain his luxurious life-style.

Austria renounces all claims to Silesia.

British Royal Navy Lieutenant James Cook, 40, sails for the Pacific May 25 to establish an observatory at Tahiti. The admiralty has been persuaded by the Royal Society that an imminent passing of the planet Venus across the face of the sun should be observed from the South Pacific and the admiralty dispatches Cook who has helped to survey the St. Lawrence River with the late General Wolfe and who embarks in H.M.S. *Endeavour*, a slow 350-ton vessel built originally as a collier (*see* 1769).

1768 (cont.) Samuel Hearne, 23, of the Hudson's Bay Company begins a 2-year walk from Hudson Bay to the shore of the Arctic Ocean and back. He will encounter nothing that can be construed as a "Northwest Passage" from the Atlantic to the Pacific, and by scouting long-prevalent rumors, Hearne's findings will divert further explorations north to Baffin Bay (*see* Baffin, 1616).

Charlotte, North Carolina, is founded by colonists who name their settlement after George III's queen.

Italian naturalist Lazzaro Spallanzani, 39, disproves the universally believed notion of spontaneous generation of organisms (in mutton broth) (*see* Needham, 1748; Maupertuis, 1751).

Angina pectoris gets its first accurate description. London physician William Heberdeen describes chest pains caused by insufficient oxygenation of the heart muscle.

Nonfiction *A Sentimental Journey through France and Italy* by Laurence Sterne, who ridicules Tobias Smollett, calling him "Smelfungus" and, unlike Smollett, expresses delight in the French and Italian customs he has encountered between Calais and Lyons, but Sterne dies of pleurisy at London March 18 at age 54 leaving only two volumes of a projected four.

Fiction *Tales of the Rainy Moon* (*Ugetsu-monogatari*) by Japanese novelist Akinari Ueda, 34, who took up writing 2 years ago and who has collected stories from Japanese and Chinese tales. Born in an Osaka brothel district, Ueda was adopted at age 3 into a family of oil merchants and led a dissolute life until his marriage 3 years ago.

The Royal Academy of Art is founded at London, and its president Joshua Reynolds begins a series of 15 discourses on art. Reynolds is the city's most fashionable portrait painter and his canvases this year include *Garrick as Kitely*.

Other painting *Experiment with the Air Pump* by Joseph Wright. Antonio Canaletto dies at Venice April 20 age 70.

Theater *The Good Natured Man* by Oliver Goldsmith 1/29 at London's Royal Theatre in Covent Garden.

Opera *Lo speziale* (*The Apothecary*) in the autumn at Schloss Esterházy, with music by Joseph Haydn, libretto by Carlo Goldoni.

Italian composer-cellist Luigi Boccherini, 25, gains fame with a performance at the Concert Spirituel at Paris and receives an invitation to be composer to the court of the infante Don Luis at Madrid.

Le Petit Trianon is completed at Versailles for Mme. de Pompadour by Jacques Ange Gabriel.

London has bread riots. Government grain stores are pillaged by the mob.

The price of bread at Paris reaches 4 sous per pound and a placard appears in the city: "Under Henri IV bread was sometimes expensive because of war and France had a king; under Louis XIV it sometimes went up because of war and sometimes because of famine and France had a king; now there is no war and no famine and the cost of bread still goes up and France has no king because the king is a grain merchant."

French government regulations are said to discourage farmers from increasing their grain acreage. Critics demand free circulation of grain (*see* 1766; Turgot, 1774).

The East India Company imports 10 million pounds of tea per year into England (*see* 1773).

1769 The Great Famine of Bengal kills 10 million Indians, wiping out one-third of the population in the worst famine thus far in world history. Britain's East India Company increases its demands on Bengal's remaining 20 million people to insure "a reasonable profit," and the company opens stations in North Borneo.

The maharajah of Mysore, Haidar Ali forces the British to sign a treaty of mutual assistance.

Russian troops occupy Moldavia and enter Bucharest in the continuing war with the Ottoman Turks. Austrian forces occupy parts of Poland. Prussia's Frederick the Great and the Holy Roman Emperor Josef II meet in Silesia to discuss the partition of Poland.

James Watt patents his steam engine of 1765 with some improvements, he grants two-thirds of the profits to ironworks owner John Roebuck, who has financed Watt's experiments, and he goes into partnership with engineer Mathew Boulton, 41, to found the Boulton & Watt Foundry at Birmingham (*see* Wilkinson, 1774).

English inventor Richard Arkwright, 37, patents a spinning frame that can produce cotton thread hard and firm enough for the warp of woven fabric. Arkwright's invention will have a profound effect on Western society (*see* 1770; Luddites, 1811).

Benjamin Franklin charts the Gulf Stream whose force is understood by most American navigators but is a mystery to many English sea captains, who make slow progress trying to sail against the current.

Virginia colonists defy George III's 1763 decree and settle on the Watauga River in what will be Tennessee.

Daniel Boone leads an expedition to the Kentucke region (*see* 1767; 1775; Harrod, 1774).

San Diego, San Francisco, and Los Angeles have their origins.

Spanish Franciscans led by Father Junipero Serra, 56, come by ship from Mexico to found the Mission of San Diego de Alcala. A Spanish colony is established at San Diego by Gaspar de Portola, 46, governor of Baja California, who leads a party north and continues on to the Monterey Peninsula, where he establishes another colony (*see* 1536; 1602).

An Indian village visited by de Portola's company (above) is renamed Nuestra Senora la Reina de Los Angeles de Porciuncula by Mallorcan friar Juan Crespi, 47 (see 1781).

San Francisco Bay is named after St. Francis of Assisi by a Spanish scouting mission under Sergeant José Ortega which discovers the bay north of Monterey.

Spain's Carlos III has an empire that covers more than half the known world and authorizes the founding of 21 missions in California over the next 54 years along with four presidios (armed garrison forts) at San Diego, Santa Barbara, Monterey, and San Francisco (see Yerba Buena, 1776).

James Cook arrives at Tahiti and sets up an observatory (see 1768). He proceeds westward to chart the coasts of New Zealand, which he finds fertile and well suited to European colonization (see 1843; Australia, 1770).

Louis Antoine de Bougainville completes the first French expedition around the world.

$ Virginia's House of Burgesses issues resolutions May 16 rejecting Parliament's right to tax British colonists. The Virginia governor dissolves the House of Burgesses, but its members meet in private and agree not to import any dutiable goods.

Dartmouth College is founded by Congregationalists at Hanover in the New Hampshire colony (see 1819).

The *Morning Chronicle* begins publication at London.

Commentaries on the Laws of England by jurist Sir William Blackstone, 46, is published in its fourth and final volume. "It is better that ten guilty persons escape than that one innocent suffer," says Blackstone, and his *Commentaries* will be influential on lawmakers both in Britain and in America.

Debrett's Peerage and Baronetage by London publisher-genealogist John Debrett is published for the first time. Debrett will publish a *Peerage of England, Scotland, and Ireland* in 1802 and a *Baronetage of England* in 1808 (see Burke, 1826).

Painting *Offering to Love* by Jean Baptiste Greuze, who resigns from the Academy because it will not elevate him from genre painter to painter of history.

England's first Shakespeare Festival opens at Stratford-upon-Avon. David Garrick, now 52, begins an annual revival of the bard's immortal plays that will continue for more than two centuries.

Eloge de Molière by Sebastien Chamfort is given its first performance.

Opera *La finta Semplice* 5/1 at Salzburg, with music by Wolfgang Amadeus Mozart.

Monticello goes up in the Virginia colony for lawyer Thomas Jefferson, 26, who has designed a house inspired by the work of the 16th century Italian architect Andrea Palladio for a site 4 miles from his father's plantation at Shadwell. A member of the House of Burgesses (above), Jefferson gives his place the Italian name "little mountain" because it provides a 20-mile view of the Blue Ridge Mountains despite its modest elevation of just 600 feet.

Charleston's Colonel Isaac Motte house is completed.

The first wine grapes, oranges, figs, and olives to grow in California are planted by Father Junipero Serra at the Mission of San Diego de Alcala (above).

England's Robert Bakewell of 1755 Leicester sheep fame develops cattle with deeper, wider bodies, shorter and thicker necks, and with more flesh over their hind quarters, ribs, loins, and backs. Bakewell works on his premise that "like produces like" and often inbreeds stock selected for bulky bodies set low on short legs.

Josiah Wedgwood opens a pottery works at Etruria, near Burslem (see 1763).

Gordon's Gin is introduced by Scots-English distiller Alexander Gordon in the London suburb of Finsbury where he has taken a house near the Clerk's Well in Goswell Street behind Charter House Square and the Islington Road. Gordon's product will become the world's largest-selling brand of gin.

1770 New York's Battle of Golden Hill January 19 and 20 brings the first bloodshed between British troops and American colonists. The Sons of Liberty have put up a series of Liberty poles with pennants bearing slogans, the redcoats have torn them down, and when they tear down the fourth pole on the common west of Golden Hill two Sons of Liberty seize two soldiers. The soldiers resist, more citizens arrive with clubs, the officer in charge orders his men back to quarters, but a second skirmish occurs the following day.

The Boston Massacre March 5 leaves three dead, two mortally wounded, and six injured following a disturbance between colonists and British troops. Lawyers John Adams, 35, and Josiah Quincy, 26, defend the British captain and his men who fired on the Americans, a jury acquits them, but agitators use the incident to arouse colonial rancor against the British troops (see Boston Tea Party, 1773).

The Battle of Chesme July 6 ends in defeat for an Ottoman fleet. A Russian fleet that has come to the Anatolian coast from the Baltic under the command of British officers wins a clear victory (see Crimea, 1771).

$ Parliament repeals the Townshend Revenue Act of 1767 in a bill passed April 12. Prime Minister Frederick North, 38, has taken office January 31 after serving as first lord of the treasury and has used his influence to have the act repealed.

James Cook explores the eastern coast of New Holland (Australia), he makes a landing, and he takes possession of the island continent in the name of George III. Inhabited for more than 25,000 years, Australia has a population of more than 250,000 and

1770 (cont.) the great variety of plants obtained by his naturalists leads Cook to name his landfall Botany Bay (*see* 1788).

Zanesville, Ohio, has its beginnings in the first permanent settlement on the Ohio River. Pioneer Ebenezer Zane, 23, stakes a land claim at the river junction with Wheeling Creek and begins to acquire additional lands. Zanesville will be laid out in 1799, and it will become a major glass-making center.

Système de la nature by French philosopher Paul Henri Dietrich d'Holbach, 47, makes the first blunt denial of any divine purpose or master plan in nature.

"If God did not exist, it would be necessary to invent him," writes Voltaire, November 10.

A spinning jenny that automates part of the textile industry is patented by English weaver-mechanic James Hargreaves (*see* Arkwright, 1769; Crompton, 1779; Luddites, 1811).

The Black Death strikes Russia and the Balkans in epidemic form.

The *Massachusetts Spy* begins publication at Boston. Printer Isaiah Thomas, 21, soon buys out former master Zechariah Fowle and makes his Whig newspaper a voice for the colonists against the British.

Poetry *Faust* by German poet-playwright-law student Johann Wolfgang von Goethe, 21, is completed in its first part; *The Deserted Village* by Oliver Goldsmith is an outcry against the changes in England: "Sweet Auburn! loveliest village of the plain,/ Where health and plenty cheer'd the labouring swain,/ Where smiling spring its earliest visit paid,/ And parting summer's lingering blooms delay'd."

Painting *Paul Revere* by Boston portrait artist John Singleton Copley, 32, who depicts a local silversmith. Giambattista Tiepelo dies at Madrid March 17 at age 74; François Boucher dies at Paris May 30 at age 66; *ukiyoe* painter Harunobu Suzuki dies at age 52.

Theater *The Two Friends, or the Merchant of Lyons* (*Les Deux Amis, ou le Negociant de Lyons*) by Pierre Augustin Caron de Beaumarchais 1/13 at the Comédie Française, Paris.

Philadelphia's Lemon Hall is completed for local financier Robert Morris, 36, who arrived from his native Liverpool in 1747 and who grows lemons in hothouses on his 300-acre estate.

The Dutch monopoly in East Indies spice growing ends as Governor Poivre of Mauritius steals nutmeg seeds and starts new plantations on his French island.

England grows enough potatoes for public sale of the tubers for the first time.

The *kipfel* roll invented by Viennese bakers in 1683 arrives at Paris with Marie Antoinette, 14-year-old daughter of the Austrian empress Maria Theresa, who marries the 15-year-old French dauphin May 16 at Versailles. French bakers will turn the *kipfel* into the *croissant* pastry that will become a traditional French breakfast treat.

Swedish chemist Tobern Olof Bergman, 35, discovers a way to make carbonic acid gas in commercial quantities (*see* 1767; 1807).

Britain's 13 American colonies have an estimated population of 2.2 million, up from 1.6 million in 1760.

1771 Russian cossacks conquer the Crimean peninsula of the Ukraine for Catharine the Great in a triumph assisted indirectly by the British (*see* 1770). The Russian success alarms Prussia's Frederick the Great (*see* Poland, 1772; Crimean annexation, 1783).

Sweden's Adolphus Frederick dies at Stockholm February 12 at age 60 after a 20-year reign in which the riksdag has deprived him of all his powers of state. He is succeeded by his 25-year-old son, who will reign until 1792 as Gustavus III and who will regain absolute monarchical power next year by rousing fears of Russia and Prussia.

Damascus falls to the Egyptian Mameluke forces of Ali Bey.

The Battle of Alamance May 16 ends in a rout of back-country North Carolina colony farmers, known as Regulators, who have attacked the courts in a protest against taxes. British militiamen end their revolt.

Serfdom ends in Savoy (Sardinia) as Charles Emmanuel III nears the end of a 43-year reign.

English agriculturist Arthur Young writes, "Everyone but an idiot knows that the lower classes must be kept poor or they will never be industrious . . . they must like all mankind be in poverty or they will not work" (*see* Mandeville, 1714).

Voyage autour du monde by French explorer Louis Antoine de Bougainville suggests one concept of evolution (*see* 1767). Describing the Straits of Magellan, Bougainville says, "This cape, which rises to more than 150 feet above sea-level, is entirely composed of horizontal beds of petrified shellfish. I took soundings at the foot of this monument which testifies to the great changes that have happened to our globe" (*see* Maupertuis, 1741; Darwin, 1840).

Speeches made in Britain's House of Commons are ordered to be published despite protests by members of Parliament (*see* Hansard, 1774).

The Encyclopaedia Britannica, or a Dictionary of Arts and Sciences Compiled Upon a New Plan is published at Edinburgh by three men who call themselves "A Society of Gentlemen in Scotland" and whose chief compiler is printer-antiquary William Smellie, 26. The three-volume 2,659-page work whose first volume appeared in 1768 sells for £12, which is roughly what an Edinburgh artisan earns in a year, and is only casually researched and edited (California is described as "a large country of the West Indies" and "woman" is defined merely as "the female of man"), but the *Encyclopaedia* will be improved and expanded and will go into 14 new editions in the next 203 years (*see* 1784).

The French *Encyclopedie*, whose 28 volumes Denis Diderot is completing at Paris, has inaccuracies of its own despite contributory efforts to the *Dictionaire Raisonne des Sciences, des Arts et des Metier* by the Comte de Buffon, the baron de Montesquieu, François Quesnay, Jean Jacques Rousseau, A. J. J. Turgot, and Voltaire. Both encyclopaedias attempt to compile in alphabetical order what 18th-century man knows but has never had readily accessible in written form (*see* 1772).

Fiction *The Expedition of Humphry Clinker* by Tobias Smollett, whose poor health has obliged him to settle in Italy and who dies September 17 at Leghorn (Livorno) at age 50.

Painting *Penn's Treaty with the Indians* by American painter Benjamin West, 32, who has been the first American to study art in Italy and who breaks away from the standard portraiture that has characterized American painting until now. *Death of Wolfe* by Benjamin West shocks London's Royal Academy by placing the hero of the 1759 Battle of Quebec and other contemporary figures in a classical composition; the work gives impetus to the growing movement toward realism in art and wins West an appointment as painter to George III. *The Alchymist* by Joseph Wright.

Sculpture *Diderot* by Jean Antoine Houdon, now 30, who has been making portrait busts since his return from 8 years in Italy 2 years ago.

Theater *The Natural Son, or The Proofs of Virtue* (*Le Fils Naturel, ou les Epreuves de la Vertu*) by Denis Diderot 9/26 at the Comédie Française, Paris; *The Beneficent Bear* (*Le Bourru Bienfaisant*) by Carlo Goldoni 11/4 at the Comédie Française.

Potatoes are listed among vegetables that may be used in times of famine by French agriculturist-botanist Antoine-Auguste Parmentier in a thesis that is hailed by the Besançon Academy (Parmentier includes also acorns, horse-chestnuts, and the roots of bryony vine, couch-grass, gladioli, and iris).

Adulteration of British foods is described by Tobias Smollett in his novel *Humphry Clinker* (above). Matthew Bramble writes to a friend that "the bread I eat in London is a deleterious paste, mixed up with chalk, alum, and bone-ashes, insipid to the taste, and destructive to the constitution. The good people are not ignorant of this adulteration; but they prefer it to wholesome bread, because it is whiter than the meal of corn: thus they sacrifice their taste and their health, and the lives of their tender infants, to a most absurd gratification of a mis-judging eye ..." (*see* Accum, 1820).

1772 Poland loses one-third her territory and half her population as she is partitioned August 5 among Russia, Austria, and Prussia. Russia acquires White Russia and all the territory to the Dvina and the

Dnieper. Austria takes Red Russia, Galicia, and western Podolia with Lemberg and part of Cracow. Prussia takes Polish Prussia except for Danzig and Thorn.

Sweden's Gustavus III restores absolute monarchy by an August 19 coup d'etat that ends the power of the council and takes away the riksdag's power to initiate legislation. Gustavus will abolish torture, improve Sweden's poor laws, encourage trade, and proclaim religious toleration and liberty of the press, but his enlightened despotism will turn to reaction beginning in the summer of 1789.

Denmark's dictator Count Johann Friedrich von Struense, 35, is overthrown by a conspiracy of noblemen after being linked to a scandal concerning Queen Caroline Matilda. Struense has held absolute power for 10 months, but he is condemned to death, tortured, and beheaded.

Warren Hastings, 40, begins a 13-year term as governor of Bengal that will be marked by reforms which will include a simplification of Indian coinage and government control of salt and opium production.

A Committee of Correspondence is organized November 2 by Boston patriot Samuel Adams, 50, with local physician Joseph Warren, 31, and is soon followed by Committees of Correspondence throughout the colonies which relay the polemics of Adams and others against the British.

The Sommersett case marks a turning point in British toleration of slavery. England's Lord Chief Justice William Murray, 67, first earl of Mansfield, rules after some hesitation that "as soon as any slave sets foot in England he becomes free" (*see* 1763; 1787).

Explorer James Cook sails for the Pacific on a second expedition, this time as a captain with the ships *Resolution* and *Adventure* and with a copy of Harrison's 1761 chronometer (*see* 1770). Cook becomes the first to sail south of the Antarctic Circle, and he dispels rumors of a large southern continent.

Nitrogen is distinguished as a gas separate from carbon dioxide by Scottish physician Daniel Rutherford, 23, at Edinburgh (*see* Davy, 1800; Sassure, 1804; Wöhler, 1828).

Salem College is founded at Salem in the North Carolina colony.

Poetry *The Rising Glory of America* by College of New Jersey (Princeton) seniors Philip Morin Freneau, 20, and Hugh Henry Breckinridge whose work is published as a commencement poem; "The Progress of Dulness" by Yale graduate John Trumbull, 22, satirizes college education.

The *Encyclopedie* of Denis Diderot is published at Paris in its 28th and final volume after 21 years of effort. A six-volume supplement will appear in 1776 and 1777.

Painting *The Members of the Royal Academy* by Johann Zoffany.

Boston's "tea party" provoked London to impose harsh measures, provoking some colonists to demand independence.

🎭 Theater *Emilia Calotti* by Gotthold Ephraim Lessing 3/13 at Brunswick's Hoftheater.

🎼 First performances Symphony No. 48 in C major (*Maria Theresia*) by Joseph Haydn at Vienna; Symphony No. 21 by Wolfgang Amadeus Mozart at Salzburg; Divertimento for Strings in D major and two other divertimenti by W. A. Mozart at Salzburg.

🏛 Venice's Palazzo Grassi is completed for the Grassi family of Bologna. Designed by the late Giorgio Massari, who died 6 years ago at age 80, the trapeze-shaped palace was begun in 1748, it has an inner court, and it is the last of the great pieces of secular architecture in the Venetian Republic that is now approaching its end.

🌐 The Japanese city of Edo is destroyed by fire as it was in 1657 (*see* 1923).

🌾 A reform of animal husbandry is begun by English agriculturist Thomas W. Coke who will breed Southdown sheep, Devon cattle, and improved Suffolk pigs (*see* 1760; 1780).

🍴 Pâté de foie gras is improved by the French chef Doyen at Bordeaux. He flavors a loaf of pâté with wine and plants truffles down the middle to begin a lasting tradition (*see* 1762).

1773 The Virginia House of Burgesses appoints a Provincial Committee of Correspondence March 12 to keep Virginia in touch with the other colonies.

Parliament passes a Regulating Act in May in an effort to bring the East India Company under government control. The company has become far more than a commercial enterprise and according to Whig leader Edmund Burke, it is "in reality a delegation of the whole power and sovereignty of this nation sent into the East."

Denmark cedes the duchy of Oldenburg to Russia.

💲 Parliament lightens the duty on tea imported into the British Isles in order to give relief to the East India Company (above) which has 7 years' supply of tea in warehouses on the Thames and which is being strained by storage charges. But Parliament permits tea to be shipped at full duty to the American colonies and allows tea to be sold directly to retailers, eliminating colonial middlemen and undercutting their prices.

Two Letters on the Tea Tax by John Dickinson are published in November.

The Boston Tea Party December 16 demonstrates against the new English tea orders (above). Led by Lendall Pitts, scion of a Boston merchant family, a group of men, including silversmith Paul Revere, 38, disguise themselves as Mohawks, board East India Company ships at Griffen's Wharf, and throw 342 chests of tea from the London firm of Davison and Newman into Boston Harbor (the tea is valued at more than £9,650). The action has been organized by agitator Samuel Adams, and is supported by John Hancock, whose smuggling of contraband tea has been made unprofitable by the new measures that permit direct sale of East India Company tea to colonial retailers.

Tea is left to rot on the docks at Charleston. New York and Philadelphia send tea-laden ships back to England, but men of "sense and property" such as George Washington deplore the Boston Tea Party.

Burke's Act is passed by Parliament to permit the import of foreign wheat at a nominal duty when the home price reaches a certain level. The act will remain in effect long enough to establish regular imports of foreign grain, depending on the abundance of domestic harvests, and imports will for a short while exceed exports (*see* 1791).

⚕ Scottish physician John Hunter, 45, begins lectures in medicine at London where he has practiced since 1763. A brilliant surgeon and investigator, Hunter performs experiments in comparative physiology, morphology, and pathologic anatomy, he describes phlebitis, pyemia, and shock, and he saves thousands of limbs by establishing that aneurysms can be treated by a single proximal ligature (thread or wire) instead of by amputation. But like so many of his contemporaries, Hunter makes no distinction between the venereal diseases gonorrhea and syphilis.

Treatise on the Management of Pregnant Women and Lying-in Women by English surgeon Charles White devotes its first chapter to "The Causes and Symptoms of the Puerperal or Child-bed Fever" (*see* Gordon, 1795).

🌼 Daniel Boone leads a party of settlers to the western Virginia country that will be called Kentucky. Two youths including Boone's son are killed when Indians attack the company, and the frightened pioneers scurry back east of the Appalachians (*see* Harrod, 1774; Wilderness Road, 1775).

Louisville, Kentucky, has its beginnings in a town site laid out by Virginia surveyor George Rogers Clark, 21. The town will be settled in 1779, and it will be named Louisville the following year by the Virginia legislature in honor of France's Louis XVI.

Yale president Ezra Stiles, 46, and Congregational theologian Samuel Hopkins, 52, urge that freed blacks be resettled in West Africa.

The Holy Roman Emperor Josef II expels Jesuits from the empire and Pope Clement XIV dissolves the Society of Jesus founded in 1534.

Dissolution of the Jesuit order (above) disrupts education in Catholic Europe.

Painting *The Graces Decorating Hymen* by Sir Joshua Reynolds; *The Broken Pitcher* by Jean Baptiste Greuze.

Theater *She Stoops to Conquer* by Oliver Goldsmith 3/18 at London's Theatre Royal in Covent Garden: "This is Liberty-Hall, gentlemen. You may do just as you please here;" "Ask me no questions, and I'll tell you no fibs"; *Gotz von Berlichengen* by Johann Wolfgang von Goethe.

First performances Symphony No. 23 in D major, No. 24 in B flat major, No. 25 in G minor, No. 26 in E flat major, No. 28 in C major, and No. 29 in A major by Wolfgang Amadeus Mozart, concertmaster to the court of the archbishop Hieronymous von Colloredo at Salzburg.

Connecticut's Tapping Reeve House at Lichfield is completed for a local judge.

An earthquake destroys most of the Central American city that has been the capital of the Spanish captain-generalcy of Guatemala for more than 230 years. The Spanish abandon the ruins at Antigua and move the seat of power to Guatemala City.

1774 News of last year's Boston Tea Party reaches London January 19 via John Hancock's ship *Hayley*. Parliament passes the Boston Port Bill as the first of several coercive acts. The bill receives royal assent March 31, and Boston harbor is closed June 1 until the East India Company shall have been reimbursed for its tea and until British authorities feel that trade can be resumed and custom duties collected.

The American colonists thwart London's efforts to starve Boston into submission. Marblehead sends in codfish, Charleston sends rice, and Baltimore sends bread and rye whiskey. Colonel Israel Putnam, 56, of Connecticut joins with citizens of Windham to drive a flock of 258 sheep to Boston.

The British ship *London* docks at New York April 22, and the Sons of Liberty prepare to follow the example set at Boston 4 months earlier, but while they are making themselves up as Mohawks an impatient crowd on the pier boards the vessel and heaves the tea on board into the Hudson. Colonists at York, Maine, and at Annapolis, Maryland, conduct tea parties like the one at Boston.

France's Louis XV dies May 10 of smallpox at age 64 after a reign of nearly 59 years. He is succeeded by his 19-year-old grandson who assumes the throne as Louis XVI and begins a reign with his Austrian-born queen Marie Antoinette that will last until 1792.

The Virginia House of Burgesses is dissolved May 26 by Governor Dunmore 2 days after the House has set June 1 aside as a day of fasting and prayer in sympathy with Boston (above). The Burgesses meet May 27 at Williamsburg's Raleigh Tavern in an unofficial session that adopts a resolution calling for an annual intercolonial congress. Copies are sent to other colonial legislatures.

A new Quartering Act passed by Parliament June 2 updates the 1765 act. The new coercive law requires colonists to house British troops in their barns or public inns where barracks are not available.

The Quebec Act passed by Parliament June 22 extends the Province of Quebec south to the Ohio River and west to the Mississippi despite western land claims of Massachusetts, Connecticut, and Virginia.

The First Continental Congress assembles at Philadelphia September 5 with all colonies represented except Georgia.

The Suffolk Resolves protesting against Parliament's coercive acts are laid before the Continental Congress September 17 and approved. The resolves have been drawn up by Boston physicians Joseph Warren and adopted by a convention in Suffolk County, Massachusetts.

A Declaration of Rights and Grievances is adopted by the Continental Congress October 14, but George Washington writes that no thinking man in all of North America desires independence.

The Association adopted October 20 by the Continental Congress is an agreement to import nothing from Great Britain after December 1 and to export nothing to Great Britain, Ireland, or the British West Indies after September 10, 1775, unless the British redress grievances against the Crown. The Association will be ratified within 6 months by all colonies except Georgia and New York.

The Battle of Point Pleasant October 10 ends in defeat for Shawnee braves who have attacked frontiersmen at the juncture of the Ohio and Great Kanawha Rivers in western Virginia. The natives yield hunting rights in Kentucky under terms of the Treaty of Camp Charlotte and agree to permit transportation on the Ohio to go unmolested.

The first English settlement west of the Alleghenies is made by pioneer James Harrod from Pennsylvania, who leads 32 other men in canoes down the Ohio River, up the Kentucky River, and into the high fertile bluegrass country plateau on which they build Fort Harrod (*see* Boonesborough, 1775).

The Connecticut and Rhode Island colonies prohibit further importation of slaves.

1774 (cont.) Philadelphia physician Benjamin Rush, 29, joins with James Pemberton to form an antislavery society.

The Six Guilds of Paris are abolished by French controller-general Ann-Robert-Jacques Turgot, who tells labor it must not try to restrict jobs. The Six Guilds have maintained wage levels by limiting the number of artisans, but work, says Turgot, is the "inalienable right of humanity," and he forbids workers to "form any association or assembly among themselves under any pretext whatever."

Joseph Priestley discovers oxygen, a gas he calls "dephlogisticated air." He heats red oxide of mercury in a glass tube and obtains a gas in which a candle burns more brightly than in the air. Air "spoilt" by mice is refreshed by the presence of green plants, says Priestley (*see* 1767; 1779).

Chlorine and manganese are discovered by Swedish chemist Karl Wilhelm Scheele, 32.

English ironmaster John Wilkinson, 46, patents a precision cannon borer that will permit commercial development of the Watt steam engine of 1769. Wilkinson's borer permits accurate boring of cylinders (*see* steam flour mill, 1780).

Bridgewater, Massachusetts blacksmith John Ames uses bar iron to fabricate shovel blades that will replace the hand-hewn shovels and imported English shovels now used in America (*see* 1803).

London printer Luke Hansard, 22, begins printing the House of Commons journals (*see* 1771). Official reports of parliamentary proceedings will be called Hansards for more than two centuries.

Letters to His Son by England's late Philip Dormer Stanhope, fourth earl of Chesterfield, is published by his widow a year after the earl's death at age 79, which came 5 years after the death at age 36 of his son Philip, born of an intimacy with a Mlle. de Bouchet. The witty and cynical letters had helped the son fill diplomatic posts and a seat in Parliament obtained for him by Lord Chesterfield: "Whatever is worth doing at all, is worth doing well"; "Take care of the pence; for the pounds will take care of themselves"; "Advice is seldom welcome; and those who want it the most always like it the least"; "An injury is much sooner forgotten than an insult"; "A seeming ignorance is often a most necessary part of worldly knowledge"; "You had better refuse a favor gracefully than grant it clumsily"; "Wear your learning, like your watch, in a private pocket; and do not pull it out and strike it, merely to show that you have one ..."; "Women are all children of a larger growth"; "Let blockheads read what blockheads wrote"; "Young men are apt to think themselves wise enough, as drunken men are apt to think themselves sober enough."

The Journal of John Woolman is published 2 years after the death of American social reformer John Woolman, who took up the Quaker ministry in 1743 at age 23 and opened a Mount Holly, New Jersey, tailor shop to support himself. Woolman has traveled throughout the colonies, spreading the Quaker doctrine from North Carolina to New Hampshire and calling for the end of slavery as an institution incompatible with religion. He kept the journal beginning at age 35 in 1756, he worked to stop the sale of liquor to the Indians, he ate no sugar because it was produced by slave labor, and he wore clothing made from undyed materials because textile workers were sometimes injured by fabric dyes.

"On the Rise and Progress of the Differences between Great Britain and Her American Colonies" by Benjamin Franklin is published as a series of articles in the *London Public Advertiser*.

Observations on the Act of Parliament, Commonly Called the Boston Port Bill; with Thoughts on Civil Society and Standing Armies by Josiah Quincy, 30, is published as a pamphlet at Boston in May.

Considerations on the Nature and Extent of the Legislative Authority of the British Parliament by Philadelphia lawyer James Wilson, 32, is published following Quincy's pamphlet (above).

A Friendly Address to All Reasonable Americans is published anonymously at New York, where it has been written by King's College president Myles Cooper, a Loyalist.

Summary View of the Rights of Americans ... by Thomas Jefferson is published as a pamphlet at Williamsburg, Virginia, and at London.

Free Thoughts on the Proceedings of the Continental Congress by "Westchester farmer" Samuel Seabury, 45, is published as a pamphlet attacking the Congress. Loyalist Seabury is a Protestant Episcopal clergyman who was graduated from Yale in 1748.

Poetry *The Sorrows of Young Werther* (*Die Linden des Jungen Werthers*) by Johann Wolfgang von Goethe whose love story has been inspired by his affair with Charlotte Buff, 21.

Boston painter John Singleton Copley emigrates to Europe following a decline in his portrait commissions, partly for reasons of his Loyalist sympathies. Copley will settle permanently at London after a year's vacation in Italy.

Theater *Clavigo* by Johann Wolfgang von Goethe 8/23 at Hamburg; *Eloge de La Fontaine* by Sebastien Chamfort; *The Inflexible Captive* by English playwright Hannah More, 29.

Opera *Iphigenia in Aulis* 4/19 at the Paris Opéra, with music by C. W. Gluck.

English religious mystic Ann Lee, 38, settles on a tract of land northeast of Albany in the New York colony and introduces "Shakerism" into America. A member of the Shaking Quaker sect, Lee abandoned her Manchester blacksmith husband after losing four children in quick succession. She is given to hysterics, convulsions, and hallucinations, she denounces sex as a "filthy gratification," she calls a consummated marriage "a covenant with death and an agreement with hell," she preaches celibacy, and she establishes a following (*see* 1784).

 Kingsland House is completed at Flushing in the New York colony.

 A meager harvest in France increases the hunger that has oppressed the country since the poor harvest of last year.

French controller-general Ann-Robert-Jacques Turgot reintroduces the free trade in grain abolished in 1766, but the rivers freeze, grain cannot be moved by barge, and the price of a 4-pound loaf of bread rises in just a few months from 11 sous to 14 sous. A 4-pound loaf has sold for as much as 16 sous in earlier years, but where in the past high prices were blamed on the weather, now the government is blamed.

France has "flour wars" as rioters throw grain merchants into ponds, loot mills and bakeries, seize grain from barges, march on Versailles, and force Louis XVI to promise bread at 2 sous per pound. Some 400 rioters are arrested, and 2 are hanged for breaking into bakeries. No conspiracy to raise prices is uncovered, but such a conspiracy is almost universally suspected by the French public (*see* 1768; 1776).

1775 The American War of Independence begins April 19 at the Battles of Lexington and Concord. Boston silversmith Paul Revere has ridden to Lexington April 16 to warn patriots Samuel Adams and John Hancock of General Gage's intention to arrest them, and he has sent word to patriots at Concord that General Gage has found out about the war matériel they have accumulated. He has ridden out with compatriot William Dawes, 30, the night of April 18 to warn Adams and Hancock that 700 redcoats have been marching from Boston since midnight; local physician Samuel Prescott, 23, has joined Revere and Dawes in spreading the alarm. Revere is captured by the British, who force Dawes to flee, and it is Prescott who rouses Samuel Hartwell of the Lincoln minutemen and other patriots.

Redcoats under the command of Lieutenant Colonel Francis Smith, 51, and Marine Major John Pitcairn, 53, arrive at Lexington near dawn and encounter a force of minutemen under the command of John Parker, 45, who says to his men, "Stand your ground. Don't fire unless fired upon. But if they mean to have a war, let it begin here."

Eight minutemen fall to British musketfire at Lexington, and the rest retreat at bayonet point. The British cut down a Liberty pole at Concord, and they skirmish with the militia at a bridge.

British reinforcements arrive at Concord with two 6-pound cannon under the command of Brigadeer General Sir Hugh Percy, 33. Although outnumbered 4,000 to 1,800, the British are better organized than the militia. General Percy executes a skillful retreat, and the redcoats are back in Boston by nightfall after having lost only 65 dead, 173 wounded, 26 missing (American marksmen have picked off 15 British officers).

"Give me liberty or give me death," Virginia's Patrick Henry has said March 23 in an oration. Many patriots echo his sentiments (*see* 1765).

Captain Richard Derby at Salem assembles cannon and refuses to let British troops cross a drawbridge to seize the guns (*see* 1741). "Take them if you can," Derby shouts across the stream, "They will never be surrendered."

British naval forces begin an 11-month siege of Boston.

The first American victory comes May 10 as 83 Green Mountain Boys led by Ethan Allen, 37, and Benedict Arnold, 34, move on orders from Connecticut, cross Lake Champlain in the small hours of the morning, enter Fort Ticonderoga through a breach in the wall, and obtain surrender of the fort from its commandant Captain de la Place. An attempt to take Quebec fails, and the British capture Allen at Montreal, but Seth Warner takes Crown Point on Lake Champlain May 12.

The Second Continental Congress meets at Philadelphia May 10 and 2 weeks later chooses John Hancock of Boston as its president.

The Battle of Bunker Hill June 17 ends in victory for the British, but 1,150 redcoats fall in the battle, including Major Pitcairn (above), while the colonists lose only 411, including their leader General Joseph Warren, the Boston physician who was named general of militia June 14. Breed's Hill, lower than Bunker Hill and closer to the enemy, has been fortified by military engineer Colonel Richard Gridley, 64, whose men have been building breastworks since midnight and who is wounded in the battle that begins shortly after dawn. "You are all marksmen. Don't fire until you see the whites of their eyes," General Israel Putnam has ordered, and the militiamen have fired with deadly effect.

George Washington is appointed commander in chief of the Continental army June 17 and arrives at Cambridge, Massachusetts, July 3 to take command after a 12-day journey from Philadelphia.

An American navy is established October 13 by the Second Continental Congress, which authorizes construction of two "swift sailing vessels" (*see* 1779).

The British hire 29,000 German mercenaries from Hesse to fight the Americans.

 American imports from Great Britain decline by 95 percent as a result of efforts by the Association formed last year. English businessmen feel the loss of trade, they support the colonists, they ask Parliament to repeal the so-called Intolerable Acts, but while Edmund Burke makes a speech on conciliation with America (below), Lord North tells the House of Commons that Britons are paying 50 times more tax per capita than are the American colonists.

1775 (cont.) British banks organize their first clearing house in London's Lombard Street (*see* 1708; New York, 1853).

New York's Bowne & Co. is founded by local printer-stationer Robert Bowne, 31, whose firm will grow to become the largest American printer of bond and stock certificates and other financial instruments.

Philadelphia merchants form the United Company of Philadelphia for Promoting American Manufactures. The colonies have more iron furnaces and forges than England and Wales combined.

George III signs an order releasing from bondage the women and young children in British coal mines and salt mines. Many of the children are under 8 years of age, they work like the women for 10 to 12 hours per day, and they have been transferable with the collieries and salt works when the properties changed hands and when their masters had no further use for them (*see* Scottish coal miners, 1778).

Stop discrimination against women, says English-American pamphleteer Thomas Paine, 38, in his *Pennsylvania Magazine.* Paine has failed as a corsetmaker and tax collector in England, he has twice failed in marriage, and he arrived at Philadelphia late last year with letters of introduction from Benjamin Franklin and with encouragement to try his luck in America.

The first American abolition society is founded in Pennsylvania to free the slaves, whose population below the Mason-Dixon line now exceeds 450,000. Black slaves outnumber colonists two to one in South Carolina, while in Virginia the ratio is about equal.

The Transylvania Company employs Daniel Boone to lead a party of 30 North Carolina woodsmen westward (*see* 1773). The group sets out March 10 and breaks a Wilderness Road of nearly 300 miles that will be used in the next 15 years by more than 100,000 pioneers en route to the new territories of western Tennessee and Kentucky. Boone founds Boonesborough on the Kentucky River in April (*see* Harrod, 1774).

Captain Cook returns from a second voyage to the Pacific (*see* below).

News of the skirmish at Lexington, Massachusetts (above), is spread by post rider Israel Bissel, 23, who takes a note penned at ten in the morning of April 19, rides 36 miles to Worcester in 2 hours, alerts Israel Putnam at Brooklyn, Connecticut, during the night, and reaches Old Lyme at one in the morning of April 20. Bissel is ferried across the Connecticut River and reaches Saybrook by four in the afternoon and Guilford by seven. At noon on April 21 he arrived at Branford, and on the morning of April 22, he reaches New Haven, where local apothecary Benedict Arnold (above) calls out his company of militia and marches north. Bissel reaches New York City April 23, and the intelligence from Boston causes New Yorkers to close the port, distribute arms, and burn two sloops bound for the British garrison at Boston. Bissel is ferried across the Hudson, arrives at New Brunswick at two in the morning of April 24, reaches Princeton by dawn, and is in Trenton by six and in Philadelphia soon after, having traveled in 5 days a distance the fastest stage would have taken 8 days to cover.

Taxation No Tyranny by London's Doctor Johnson is published as a tract against the American colonies.

On Conciliation with the Colonies by Edmund Burke is published as a speech delivered by Burke in Parliament.

Nonfiction *A Journey to the Western Islands of Scotland* by Doctor Johnson (above), who toured Scotland in 1773 from August to November in the company of James Boswell.

Painting *Self-portrait* (pastel) by Jean Chardin, now 75; *Miss Bowles* by Sir Joshua Reynolds.

Theater *The Rivals* by Irish playwright Richard Brinsley Sheridan, 23, 1/17 at London's Royal Theatre in Covent Garden. Sheridan's Mrs. Malaprop delights audiences with "malapropisms" such as "headstrong as an allegory on the banks of the Nile" (III, iii). *The Barber of Seville, or The Useless Precaution* (*Le barbier de Seville, ou La precaution inutile*) by Pierre A. C. de Beaumarchais 2/23 at the Comédie Française; *St. Patrick's Day, or The Scheming Lieutenant* by Richard Brinsley Sheridan 5/2 at London's Royal Theatre in Covent Garden; *The Jews* (*Die Juden*) by Gotthold Ephraim Lessing 9/13 at Frankfurt-am-Main (one-act comedy).

English tragic actress Sara Kemble Siddon, 20, makes her debut at London's Drury Lane Theatre to begin a 32-year career that will make her the queen of the English stage.

Opera *La finta Giordiniera* 1/13 at Munich, with music by Wolfgang Amadeus Mozart; *Il Re Pastore* 4/23 at Salzburg, with music by W. A. Mozart, libretto by the Italian poet-playwright Metastasio; *The Duenna* 11/29 at London's Royal Theatre in Covent Garden, with music by English composer Thomas Linley, 42, libretto by Richard Brinsley Sheridan.

Stage musical *Maid of the Oaks* at London with music by London playwright-composer John Burgoyne, 53, songs that include "The World Turned Upside Down."

Wolfgang Amadeus Mozart at Salzburg writes five violin concerti between April 14 and December 20, each in one day except for the Concerto No. 4 in D major which he works on over the course of a month and completes in October.

First performances Concerto No. 5 in A major for Violin and Orchestra (*Turkish*) by Wolfgang Amadeus Mozart 12/20 at Salzburg.

Popular song "Yankee Doodle" with lyrics to an old English tune. American colonist Edward Barnes has written the words that will be popular in the Continental Army.

English inventor Alexander Cummings receives the first patent to be issued for a flush toilet, but such toilets will not come into common use for more than a century (see Harington, 1596; Bramah, 1778).

Bath's Royal Crescent is completed by English architect John Wood the Younger, 47.

Providence, Rhode Island, gets a new First Baptist Meeting House on North Main Street to replace the church built by Roger Williams in 1638. The new church is modeled on St. Martin's in the Fields at London.

The first house rats recorded in America appear at Boston (see 1728).

The New Bedford, Massachusetts, whaling fleet reaches 80 vessels. More than 280 whaling ships put out from American ports, 220 of them from Massachusetts (see 1751).

English mercantile interests re-enter the whaling industry largely abandoned by the British in 1612 as Dutch activity begins to wane (see 1789).

James Cook returns to England from the Pacific and is awarded the Royal Society's Gold Copley Medal for having conquered scurvy. Sir John Pringle, chief medical officer of the British army and physician to George III, hails Captain Cook's achievement in bringing 118 men through all climates for 3 years and 18 days "with the lofs of only one man by diftemper," and while Cook has succeeded with sauerkraut and may "entertaine no great opinion of [the] anti-scorbutic virtue" of concentrated citrus juices, Pringle suggests that he may be mistaken (see 1794; Lind, 1757).

Prussia's Frederick the Great moves to block imports of green coffee which are draining his country's gold as coffee becomes nearly a match for beer as the national beverage.

Denmark's Royal Copenhagen Porcelain Manufactory is founded by Queen Juliane Marie, who goes into partnership with some Copenhagen partners. Porcelain from the factory will be trademarked with three wavy blue lines and the queen will acquire full ownership in 1779.

1776 A Declaration of Independence drafted by Thomas Jefferson is edited to delete an attack on slavery and is signed July 4 at Philadelphia by Continental Congress president John Hancock, who writes his name in large letters and says, "There, I guess King George will be able to read that." The Declaration, which follows events detailed below, is set in type and printed in a shop at 48 High Street and is signed on and after August 2 by members of Congress including Benjamin Franklin, who says, "We must all hang together, else we shall all hang separately." The 56 signers have in many cases been persuaded by the pamphlet *Common Sense* written by Thomas Paine and published at Philadelphia January 10.

"We hold these Truths to be self-evident," says the Declaration, "that all Men are created equal, that they are endowed by their Creator with certain unalienable Rights, that among these are Life, Liberty, and the Pursuit of Happiness—That to secure these Rights, Governments are instituted among Men, deriving their just Powers from the Consent of the Governed, that whenever any Form of Government becomes destructive of these Ends, it is the Right of the People to alter or to abolish it, and to institute new Government. . . ."

Delaware forbids further importation of slaves as the slave population in the colonies reaches 500,000.

Britain's House of Commons hears the first motion to outlaw slavery in Britain and her colonies. David Hartley, 44, calls slavery "contrary to the laws of God and the rights of man," but his motion fails (see 1772; Wilberforce, 1787, 1789).

The Continental Congress starts a national lottery to raise money for the Continental army.

Inquiry into the Nature and Causes of the Wealth of Nations by Scottish philospher Adam Smith, 53, of Kircaldy, Fifeshire, proposes a system of natural liberty in trade and commerce (see Hume, 1739). "Consumption is the sole end and purpose of all production, and the interest of the producer ought to be attended to, only so far as it may be necessary for promoting that of the consumer," who in the long run has full control over what will and will not be produced, says Smith, who teaches at the University of Glasgow. His massive work establishes the classical school of political economy and will influence all future thinking on politics and economics, but it shows no awareness of the developing industrial revolution, and while it espouses free-market competition with limited government intervention it regards unemployment as a necessary evil to keep costs—and therefore prices—in check (see Ricardo, 1817).

"The discovery of America, and that of a passage to the East Indies by the Cape of Good Hope, are the two greatest and most important events recorded in the history of mankind," writes Adam Smith (above).

San Francisco has its beginnings in the settlement of Yerba Buena (good herb) established by Spanish monks in California (see 1769; 1846).

The Battle of Moore's Creek Bridge February 27 ends in defeat for Scottish Loyalists from upper North Carolina who lose 900 prisoners to Carolina patriots near Wilmington. The Americans discourage British General Henry Clinton, 38, from landing an expeditionary force.

British troops evacuate Boston March 17. General William Howe, 46, sails for Nova Scotia with 900 Loyalists; many will settle in New Brunswick.

Lee's Resolutions introduced into the Continental Congress at Philadelphia June 7 urge the colonies to make foreign alliances and urge a confederation of

1776 (cont.) the colonies under a constitution to be approved by each state. Virginia delegate Richard Henry Lee, 44, has been instructed by the Virginia Convention May 15 to propose independence, and his three resolutions include an announcement "That these United States are and of right ought to be free and independent states."

A British fleet under General Clinton (above) and Sir Peter Parker, 55, is repulsed June 28 by patriots at Sullivan's Island off Charleston, South Carolina (Fort Moultrie).

General Howe lands on Staten Island June 30.

Lee's Resolutions (above) are adopted by Congress July 2.

The Declaration of Independence is signed by John Hancock July 4 (above).

General Howe on Staten Island is joined July 12 by a British fleet under the command of his older brother Lord Richard Howe, 50, and on August 1 by General Clinton (above).

The Battle of Long Island August 27 ends in defeat for 8,000 patriots under General Israel Putnam at the hands of 20,000 British regulars led by General Howe.

General Howe and his secretary Sir Henry Starchey meet September 11 in a house on Staten Island with John Adams, Benjamin Franklin, and Edward Rutledge in an effort to end the war by negotiation. Howe learns for the first time that the Declaration of Independence (above) has been signed, the Americans refuse to retract the document, and negotiations break off.

General Howe lands at Kips Bay September 15, and he occupies New York City. He is by some accounts delayed in his pursuit of George Washington by Mrs. Robert Murray, who offers him tea at her farmhouse on what later will be called Murray Hill, and he narrowly misses catching Washington, who retreats to Harlem Heights and repulses a British attack September 16 with help from his sharpshooters. Armed with Pennsylvania long rifles, the sharpshooters can fire accurately at 200 to 400 yards, while musket balls can carry effectively only 80 to 100 yards (the British will complain that American sharpshooters are unsportsmanlike in concentrating their fire on officers).

Continental army captain Nathan Hale, 21, is captured by the British September 21 on his return to Manhattan from an espionage mission to gather intelligence on Long Island. Hale has set numerous fires to harry the British in New York, he has disguised himself as a Dutch schoolmaster to avoid arrest, and he is hanged September 22 by order of General Howe. His last words will be reported as, "I only regret that I have but one life to lose for my country."

Polish military tactician Tadeusz Andzej Bonawentura Kosciuszko, 30, enters the Continental army as a volunteer after having been wounded by the retainers of Sosnowski of Sownowicka, the Grand Hetman, with whose youngest daughter he had tried to elope. Kosciuszko has studied fortification and naval tactics at Polish government expense in Prussia, France, and Italy, he distinguishes himself in the American cause, and George Washington will make him his adjutant and will raise him to the rank of colonel of artillery (*see* 1794).

Benedict Arnold's fleet on Lake Champlain is defeated October 11 in the Battle of the Island of Valcour, but Arnold has delayed the southward advance of Sir Guy Carleton, who takes Crown Point but soon withdraws to Canada.

The Battle of White Plains October 28 gives General Howe a narrow victory over General Washington.

Fort Lee is surrendered to the British November 20 by General Nathanael Greene, and Washington begins a retreat across New Jersey the next day, with General Charles Cornwallis, 38, in hot pursuit.

General Washington crosses the Delaware Christmas night, surprises the Hessians at Trenton, and turns the tide of the war by taking more than 1,000 prisoners at the Battle of Trenton December 26.

Catharine the Great's court favorite Grigori Aleksandrovich Potemkin, 37, builds a Russian Black Sea fleet. Potemkin distinguished himself in 1769 fighting the Turks.

"Bushnell's Connecticut Turtle" pioneers the use of the submarine in warfare. Built by Yale graduate David Bushnell, 34, the pear-shaped 7-foot vessel is made of oak staves held together with pitch and iron hoops. It has ballast tanks operated by foot pumps, its conning tower has windows level with the head of the operator who uses two air tubes for intake and exhaustion of air (automatic valves close them for diving), it is propelled horizontally and vertically by hand-cranked propellers and is guided by a flexible rudder, it carries a powder magazine with a clock timer, and it goes into action the night of September 6 in New York Harbor. Bushnell's craft has an auger mounted on its top to bore a hole into the wooden hull of an enemy vessel so that it may plant its powder magazine, but many of the British vessels have copperclad bottoms to protect them against shipworms, and several attempts to plant charges prove fruitless (*see* Lake, 1897).

Uric acid is discovered in a kidney stone by Karl Wilhelm Scheele (*see* 1774; Garrod, 1859).

Smallpox decimates the Continental army in the north. By June some 5,500 of the 10,000-man force are incapacitated, largely by the dread pox to which the British are generally immune as a result of having had mild bouts with the disease in childhood or in some cases by inoculation (*see* 1747; 1777).

Hampden-Sydney College is founded at Hampden-Sydney, Virginia.

The Phi Beta Kappa Society is founded December 5 at Virginia's 83-year-old College of William and Mary in Williamsburg by five young men who have gathered at a local tavern for conviviality and to debate such subjects as "Whether French politics be more injurious than New England rum" or "Had William the Norman a right to invade England?" (Chapters of the new scholastic fraternity will be established at Harvard and Yale in 1779, Harvard men will debate the question of whether Adam had a navel, Yale men will debate the question of whether females have intellectual capacities equal to those of males, and election to $\phi\beta\kappa$ will carry great prestige in U.S. academic circles.)

"These are the times that try men's souls," writes Thomas Paine (above) in *The Crisis*, first in a series of 16 pamphlets that he will publish under that title in the next 7 years. Paine's *Common Sense* pamphlet in January marshalled arguments for the justice of the revolutionary cause, it sold half a million copies almost overnight, and it won its author a position as aide to General Nathanael Greene. His December pamphlet *The Crisis* has a similar electrifying effect.

The History of the Decline and Fall of the Roman Empire by English historian Edward Gibbon, 39, is published in its first volume and creates a controversy over the rise of Christianity (*see* 1781).

Painting   *The Washerwoman* by Jean Honoré Fragonard.

Sculpture   *Voltaire* by French sculptor Jean Baptiste Pigalle, 62.

Theater   *Stella* by Wolfgang von Goethe 2/8 at Hamburg; *The Twins* (*Die Zwillinge*) by German playwright Friedrich Maximilian von Klinger 24, 2/23 at Hamburg; *Storm and Stress* (Sturm und Drang) by Friedrich von Klinger 4/1 at Leipzig (von Klinger will move to St. Petersburg in 1780, he will enter the Russian army, he will be elevated to the nobility, and in 1790 he will marry an illegitimate daughter of Catharine the Great; the title of his new play will provide the name for a German literary movement headed by Goethe and Schiller); *The Soldiers* (*Die Soldaten*) by German playwright-poet Jakob Michael Reinhold Lenz, 25, who has followed Goethe to Weimar but is forced to leave because of his bad manners and tactlessness (Lenz will suffer a mental breakdown); *Mustapha et Zeangir* by Sebastien Chamfort, whose tragedy brings him a royal pension from the French royal family and confirms his success in society.

The Bolshoi Theater is founded at Moscow.

Vienna's Burgtheater opens to give the city a new opera house and concert hall. The Holy Roman Emperor Josef II has founded the theater and he forbids curtain calls, feeling that he is more worthy of applause than are his servants the actors.

First performances   Serenade No. 6 in D major for two Small Orchestras (*Serenata Notturna*) by Wolfgang Amadeus Mozart in January at Salzburg; Sere-nade No. 7 in D major (*Haffner*) by W. A. Mozart, 7/22 at Vienna, for the marriage of Elisabeth Haffner, daughter of the late Viennese burgomaster, to F. X. Spath.

Hymn   "Rock of Ages" verses by London editor Augustus Toplady are published in the February issue of *The Gospel Magazine*. They will be set to music in 1830.

England's St. Leger stakes race has its first running at Doncaster as its founder, Colonel Barry St. Leger, 39, prepares to leave for America to join General Burgoyne in the Hudson Valley.

Cattle ranches begin to flourish on the Argentine pampas as Spain creates the Viceroyalty of La Plata with its capital at Buenos Aires.

A good harvest in France reduces the price of bread, but the French again abolish internal free trade in grain (*see* 1774).

The cocktail is invented according to some accounts at an Elmsford, New York, tavern, where barmaid Betsy Flanagan decorates the bar she tends at Halls Corner with discarded tail feathers from poultry that has been roasted and served to patrons. An inebriated patron demands that she bring him "a glass of those cocktails," and Flanagan serves him a mixed drink garnished with one of the feathers.

Philadelphia's population reaches 40,000, making it larger than Boston and New York (24,000) combined.

1777   The Battle of Princeton January 3 gives George Washington a victory over three British regiments commanded by General Charles Cornwallis. General Benedict Arnold defeats the British April 27 at Ridgefield, Connecticut. The American garrison at Fort Ticonderoga abandons the fort at news that

Thomas Paine's fiery pamphlets *Common Sense* and *The Crisis* roused American sentiment against the British.

325

1777 (cont.) General John Burgoyne is approaching, Burgoyne defeats the retreating garrison force July 7 at Hubbarton, Vermont. General Philip Schuyler evacuates Fort Edward July 29 and the British take the fort, but Americans under the command of General Nicholas Herkimer check the British in their march down the Mohawk Valley, defeating them August 6 in the Battle of Oriskany despite the loss of General Herkimer in battle.

The Battle of Bennington August 16 ends in victory for the Americans under Captain John Stark who receives support from Colonel Seth Warner, but although the British abandon their siege of Fort Stanwix August 22 at the approach of Benedict Arnold, they defeat George Washington September 22 at the Battle of Brandywine.

The Continental Congress has voted July 31 to accept the services of French captain of dragoons Marie Joseph Paul Yves Roch Gilbert du Motier, 19, marquis de Lafayette, who was orphaned 6 years ago but was left with a princely fortune. Louis XVI had forbidden Lafayette to pursue his plan to support the American cause, but the young man escaped from custody, picked up a little English en route to America, landed in South Carolina, hurried to Philadelphia, and has been given the rank of major general. General Lafayette is wounded at Brandywine but soon secures the command of a division.

The First Battle of Saratoga (Bemis Heights) September 19 inflicts heavy losses on the British, but the redcoats hold their ground, and other British forces defeat Anthony Wayne at Paoli, Pennsylvania, September 20. General Howe occupies Philadelphia September 26, and he defeats General Washington at Germantown October 4.

The Second Battle of Saratoga October 7 gives General Horatio Gates a decisive victory over General Burgoyne, who surrenders with his entire force. Benedict Arnold has inspired Gates to defeat the British, General Burgoyne marches his troops to Boston, and he embarks for England, never to resume the war. The British gain control of the Delaware River in November, but when word of Burgoyne's surrender at Saratoga reaches Paris in early December, the American cause is assured of French support.

The Articles of Confederation adopted by the Continental Congress at York, Pennsylvania, November 15 provide that at least nine states consent to all important measures, requires unanimous consent for any changes in the Articles, provides no way for the central government to coerce recalcitrant states into compliance with congressional decisions, and denies Congress any power to tax or to regulate trade. Congress submits the Articles to the 13 states for ratification, it makes the first of several requisitions of funds, to be paid by the states in paper money, and it authorizes confiscation of Loyalists' estates.

Portugal's Brazil annexes Maranhão as the Spanish and Portuguese settle their differences over their South American colonies. The Portuguese move the capital of Brazil from Bahia to Rio de Janeiro.

Portugal's José Manuel dies at age 62 after a 17-year reign that has been left mainly in the hands of Sebastião José de Carvalho e Mello, now 78, who has been marques de Pombal since 1769. Pombal has broken the power of the nobility and of the church, he has reformed the Portuguese military, he has straightened out the country's finances, he has established trade companies with monopolistic powers to encourage industry, and he has attempted to improve education and revive industry. José Manuel has been insane since 1774, and he is succeeded by his feebleminded 43-year-old daughter Maria Francisca, who will reign as Maria I with her feeble-minded husband (and uncle) Pedro, brother of the late king, whom she married at age 26, but her mother Marianna Victoria will seize control and will dismiss the marques de Pombal (see 1786).

 General Washington obtains congressional approval in January to inoculate the entire Continental army against smallpox, which in some cases is further spread by inoculation (see 1776; vaccination, 1796).

Ergotism kills 8,000 in France's Sologne district (see 1720; 1816).

 Painting *The Watering Place* by Thomas Gainsborough.

 Rudimentary knowledge of photography is advanced by experiments with silver salts undertaken by Swedish chemist K. W. Scheele (see Schulze, 1727; Wedgwood, 1802).

 Theater *The School for Scandal* by Richard Brinsley Sheridan 5/1 at London's Theatre Royal in Drury Lane, which Sheridan has been managing for the past year: "Here's to the maiden of bashful fifteen;/ Here's to the widow of fifty;/ Here's to the flaunting, extravagant queen,/ And here's to the housewife that's thrifty;" *Percy* by Hannah More 10/12 at London's Covent Garden Theatre.

 First performances Concerto No. 9 for Pianoforte and Orchestra in E flat major by Wolfgang Amadeus Mozart, in January at Salzburg; Concerto for Three Pianofortes and Orchestra in F major by W. A. Mozart 10/22 at Augsburg.

 The Baldwin apple is discovered by Continental army officer Laomo Baldwin, 37, who had been invalided home to Wilmington, Massachusetts.

 George Washington retires with his hungry army to Valley Forge, Pennsylvania, to spend the winter. His salt stocks have been captured by General Howe. He leads his 11,000 ragged troops into Valley Forge December 14, at least 2,000 are barefoot, and food is scarce.

Bass Ale is introduced by English brewer William Bass, 57, who starts a brewery at Burton-upon-Trent that will be famous for its ale, beer, and other malt beverages.

1778 News of General Burgoyne's defeat last fall thrills Paris, which has been secretly supplying money and supplies to the American revolutionists for 2 years. The French recognize American independence and sign a treaty of commerce and alliance with Benjamin Franklin February 6. The Continental Congress ratifies the treaty May 4; the French alliance gives the Congress such assurance that it rejects British peace offers in mid-June.

The Battle of Monmouth June 28 ends in a victory for George Washington, whose army of 11,000 was reduced to 8,000 by hunger, illness, and exposure in winter quarters at Valley Forge. The troops have been drilled at Valley Forge by Friedrich Wilhelm von Steuben, 46, a Prussian general who performs valuable service.

General Charles Lee, 47, reluctantly agrees to lead the American attack in the Battle of Monmouth (above) but begins a retreat in the heat of battle. General Washington intervenes to save the day, General Lee is court-martialed July 4, and the court finds him guilty August 12 and suspends him for 12 months.

Kaskaskia falls to a troop of some 150 Virginia volunteers led by George Rogers Clark, who takes the chief British fort in the Illinois country July 4 and goes on to take Cahokia and Vincennes, but the British retake Vincennes December 17.

"Molly Pitcher" gains her soubriquet at the Battle of Monmouth (above) by carrying water to tired and wounded Continental army troops. When her husband George McCauley is overcome by the heat, Mary Ludwig "Molly Pitcher" McCauley, 23, takes over his cannon and uses it to good effect through the rest of the battle.

Colonial settlers are massacred in Pennsylvania's Wyoming Valley July 4 and in New York's Cherry Valley November 11 by British Loyalists (Tories) and their Indian allies.

Savannah is taken by the British December 29.

Bengal's Governor Warren Hastings takes Chandernagore, Pondichery, and Mahe in the continuing Anglo-Maratha War.

The War of the Bavarian Succession begins in Europe following the extinction of the electoral house of Bavaria with the death last year of Maximilian Joseph. The elector palatine, who is legal heir to the Bavarian lands, is persuaded to recognize some old Austrian claims to Lower Bavaria and part of the Upper Palatine, and Austrian troops occupy Lower Bavaria following the January Treaty of Vienna. The elector palatine is then persuaded by Prussia's Frederick the Great to renounce the Austrian claims, Saxony and Mecklenburg are persuaded by Frederick to oppose the Emperor Josef II, and Frederick invades Bohemia in July.

 The Sandwich Islands discovered by Hawaii-Loa in 450 A.D. are rediscovered in January by Captain Cook. He lands on the island of Kauai and names the islands after John Montagu, 60, fourth earl of Sandwich and first lord of the admiralty, who is said to have invented the "sandwich" (meat between two slices of bread) to eat at the gaming tables.

The Pacific coast of North America northward from Oregon is explored by Captain Cook (above), who lays the basis for future British claims to the region (see Drake, 1579; Gray, 1791; Columbia River Valley, 1843).

 Scottish coal miners gain freedom from the conditions of virtual slavery under which they have worked until now (see 1775), but they will not have complete freedom until 1799.

Parliament acts at the urging of English prison reformer John Howard, 52, and establishes the principle of separate confinement with labor and religious instruction (but see 1782).

The Virginia legislature forbids further importation of slaves at the persuasion of Thomas Jefferson (see manumission, 1782).

 Molybdenum is isolated by Sweden's Karl Wilhelm Scheele (see 1776).

France charters a Societé Royale de Medicine and charges it with the study of epidemics.

Mesmerism attracts the gullible elite of Paris. Viennese physician Franz (or Friedrich) Anton Mesmer believes he has occult powers to effect cures with animal magnetism. He founds a Magnetic Institute with support from Louis XVI and Marie Antoinette, he employs hypnotism, astrology, magic wands, and similar methods, but while he will "mesmerize" such eminent patrons as General Lafayette, the medical faculties will denounce him and will hound him out of France.

White Sulphur Springs health spa is founded in Virginia (see Greenbriar, 1913).

 Fiction *Evelina, or the History of a Young Lady's Entry into the World* by English novelist Fanny (Frances) Burney, 26, is published anonymously. Burney virtually invents the social novel of domestic life, and she introduces the phrase, "Before you could say Jack Robinson."

 Painting *Brook Watson and the Shark* by John Singleton Copley, who has been commissioned by the lord mayor of London to depict the grisly scene in which the lord mayor lost his legs at age 14 while swimming in Havana Harbor.

Milan's Teatro alla Scala opens August 3. The 2,135-seat opera house built by Giuseppe Piermarini, 44, takes its name from a nearby flight of stairs and will be the most famous opera house in the world.

Ballet *Les Petits Riens* 6/11 at the Paris Opéra, with music by Wolfgang Amadeus Mozart, choreography by Jean Noverre.

First performances Symphony No. 31 in D major (*Paris*) by Wolfgang Amadeus Mozart 6/18 at Paris.

1778 (cont.) A water closet whose valve-and-siphon flushing system will be the basis of all future toilet plumbing is patented by English engineer Joseph Brahma, 30, who will gain wealth and fame from this and future inventions. His factory at Pimlico will train other engineers and machine tool inventors, but his flush toilet will not come into wide use for more than a century (see 1775).

Philadelphia pepper pot soup is invented by some accounts at Valley Forge (above), where a cook in George Washington's army employs makeshift efforts to sustain the hungry troops wintering in Pennsylvania.

1779 British forces take Augusta, Georgia, January 29, they have mixed fortunes elsewhere in Georgia, they are repulsed February 3 by General William Moultrie at Fort Royal, South Carolina, and they surrender Vincennes to George Rogers Clark February 25.

Spain asks Britain to cease hostilities against the American colonies and to recognize their independence. The Spanish have loaned the colonists 219 bronze cannon, 200 gun carriages, 30,000 muskets, 55,000 rounds of ammunition, 12,000 bombs, 4,000 tents, and 30,000 uniforms and will give the colonists $5 million before the War of Independence is over.

Britain asks Spain to halt her aid and offers to give up Florida, Gibraltar, and codfishing rights off Newfoundland in exchange for withdrawal of Spanish support of the colonists, but Spain declares war on Britain June 21 and lays siege to Gibraltar.

The French West African port of Gorée falls to British forces, who attack the French in Senegal.

British troops take Stony Point and Verplanck, New York, May 31, but they lose Stony Point July 16 to Anthony Wayne, who has attacked "Little Gibraltar" at midnight and who is knocked unconscious by grapeshot. General Washington orders the post evacuated, and the Americans raze the fortifications.

The largest American naval armada to be assembled during the Revolution leaves Boston July 19 under the command of former privateer Dudley Saltonstall, 44, with orders to dislodge the British from a fort they are building at the head of Penobscot Bay. Saltonstall has 19 armed vessels with 344 guns and 24 transports with some 2,000 men, while the British have only 700 men under Brigadier General Francis McLean, but Saltonstall refuses to attack. His land force commander General Solomon Lovell and Lovell's second-in-command General Peleg Wadsworth of the Massachusetts militia put 200 men ashore but get little support from the expedition's artillery commander Paul Revere. British reinforcements arrive August 14 as seven ships from Halifax land 1,530 men and 204 guns. The Americans flee upriver toward Bangor, they run their ships ashore and destroy them, and they walk home to Boston through the woods. Saltonstall is cashiered for incompetence, and Revere is court-martialed for cowardly misconduct.

Continental army general John Sullivan marches against the Tories and their Iroquois allies in New York's Genessee Valley. He destroys Indian villages and goes on to defeat his foes in the Battle of Newtown near Elmira.

Continental navy captain John Paul Jones, 32, sails with a squadron of five ships in August with his flagship a refitted merchant vessel he renames the *Bonhomme Richard* in honor of Benjamin Franklin and his *Poor Richard's Almanack*. Sailing round the British Isles, Jones takes several prizes and on September 23 engages the British naval vessel *Serapis* which along with the *Countess of Scarborough* is escorting Britain's Baltic trading fleet. Heavily outgunned and outmanned, Jones moves in close, lashes his ship to the *Serapis*, and continues to grapple with the enemy even after the *Bonhomme Richard* begins to sink. Asked to surrender, Jones replies, "I have not yet begun to fight!" and it is the *Serapis* which surrenders after 3½ hours of bloody battle. Jones transfers his crew to the *Serapis*, and the *Bonhomme Richard* sinks 2 days later.

The Battle of Baton Rouge September 21 ends British hopes of controlling the Mississippi Basin. The Spanish governor of Louisiana Bernardo de Galvez has moved upriver from New Orleans with a force of Spaniards, Frenchmen, Germans, Acadians, free blacks, Indians, and Americans. He tricks British forces under the command of Lieutenant Colonel Dickson at Fort New Richmond into thinking that he is preparing an attack from the east, he opens fire at dawn with a roundshot volley from the south, and the British surrender within a few hours.

Natchez falls to Governor Galvez (above), and Spanish troops, landed last year in Florida, drive the British out of some Florida Gulf ports (see 1781).

The War of the Bavarian Succession in Europe has ended May 13 with the Peace of Teschen. Austria retains only the part of Lower Bavaria bounded by the Inn, the Salzach, and the Danube.

A British force sent from Calcutta by Warren Hastings reaches Surat and breaks the coalition between the Marathas, the Mysore rajah Haidar Ali, and the nizam.

St. Vincent and Grenada in the British West Indies fall to French forces.

British forces at Savannah come under siege by American forces commanded by General Benjamin Lincoln, 46, and the French naval commander Jean Baptiste Charles Henri Hector, 50, comte d'Estaing. They are joined October 9 by the Continental army's Polish military adviser Count Kazimierz Pulaski, who charges the British lines at the head of his cavalry. He sustains a mortal wound, he dies October 11 at age 32, and the Americans abandon the siege October 20 after 34 days.

British forces evacuate Rhode Island in October.

The capital of Virginia moves from Williamsburg to Richmond (*see* 1699; 1935).

England's Robert Walpole and scores of other British merchants smuggle arms and provisions to the American colonies through the West Indies, especially through the Dutch island of St. Eustatius (*see* 1634). The merchants are sympathetic to the American cause and eager for profit (*see* Rodney, 1781).

Experiments on Vegetables by Dutch plant pathologist Jan Ingenhousz, 49, establishes some of the principles of photosynthesis (which will get that name in 1862). Ingenhousz learned on a visit to England of Joseph Priestley's 1774 efforts to "improve" polluted air by introducing live plants, and he ascribes air purification to the action of sunlight on leaves to produce "dephlogisticated air" (to which French chemist Antoine Lavoisier will soon give the name "oxygen") (*see* 1784).

A muslin wheel, or spinning mule, which spins yarns suitable for muslin is devised by English millhand Samuel Crompton, 26, but he lacks the funds needed to obtain a patent for his improvement on the 1770 spinning jenny and is tricked into revealing his secret, a landmark in the Industrial Revolution.

Poetry "The House of Night" by Philip Freneau, who has returned after 3 years as secretary to a rich planter in the West Indies to serve in the militia against the British.

Painting *George Washington at Princeton* by Philadelphia painter Charles Willson Peale, 38, who returned to the colonies in 1769 after studying at London with Benjamin West; *Blue Boy* by Thomas Gainsborough. Jean Baptiste Chardin dies at Paris December 6 at age 80.

Theater *Iphegenia in Tauris* by Johann Wolfgang von Goethe 4/6 at Weimar; *The Fatal Falsehood* by Hannah More 6/5 at London's Covent Garden Theatre; *The Critic, or a Tragedy Rehearsal* by Richard Brinsley Sheridan 10/3 at London's Royal Theatre in Drury Lane, a revision of the 1671 burlesque of heroic tragedy by the late duke of Buckingham: "Nothing is unnatural that is not physically impossible" (II, i); "Well, if we must, we must" (II, ii); "An oyster may be crossed in love" (III, i).

Opera *Iphegenia in Tauris* (*Iphégenie en Tauride*), 5/18 at the Acadème de Musique, Paris, with music by Christoph Willibald Gluck, now 64.

First performances Concerto for Two Pianos and Orchestra in E flat major by Wolfgang Amadeus Mozart 1/15 or shortly thereafter at Salzburg, following Mozart's return after an 18-month absence in Munich, Augsburg, Mannheim, Paris, Strasbourg, and lesser towns; Symphony No. 32 in G major by W. A. Mozart; Symphony No. 33 in B flat major by W. A. Mozart, in July at Salzburg.

Olney Hymns is published with verses by English poet William Cowper, 47, and the Reverend John Newton, 54, who is evangelical curate at Olney in Buckinghamshire. Cowper's hymn "Light Shining Out of Darkness" contains the lines, "God moves in a mysterious way/ His wonders to perform;/ He plants his footsteps in the sea/ And rides upon the storm." Newton's hymns include "Glorious Things of Thee Are Spoken" and "One There Is Above All Others" (*see* Cowper, 1785).

The Derby is established at Epsom Downs in Surrey by the seventeenth earl of Derby.

The Oaks has its first running at Epsom Downs.

Sweet corn is found along the Susquehanna River by Richard Bagnal, an officer serving with John Sullivan (above) who makes the first written report of sweet corn. But although the Iroquois have been growing sweet corn for years and although Bagnal carries seeds back to Plymouth and plants them, sweet corn will be little used by Americans for another 70 years and will remain largely unknown in the rest of the world for more than a century after that.

"Taboo" is introduced to the English language by Britain's Captain Cook, who finds food taboos in Tahiti and in the Sandwich Islands (*see* 1778). Cook is killed early in the morning of February 14 by natives at Kealakekua Bay on the island of Hawaii.

Semen is proved necessary to fertilization by Italian naturalist Lazzaro Spallanzani (*see* 1768).

1780 Mobile falls to the Spanish governor Bernardo de Galvez March 14 as British forces under Sir Henry Clinton prepare to besiege Charleston. The South Carolina port city surrenders May 12 after a month's siege, the British take some 2,500 prisoners including General Benjamin Lincoln, and Clinton moves north to blockade the French fleet.

Some 6,000 French troops arrive at Newport, Rhode Island, July 10 under the command of Jean Baptiste Donation de Vimeur, 55, comte de Rochambeau, but the British have blockaded the French fleet in Narragansett Bay, Rochambeau is reluctant to abandon the fleet, and he will remain inactive for a year.

General Nathanael Greene defeats a British army June 23 at Springfield, New Jersey.

American forces under General Horatio Gates suffer a disastrous defeat August 16 at Camden, South Carolina, as redcoats under General Charles Cornwallis win the day.

The British spy Major John André, 29, falls into American hands September 23 with papers revealing a plot by Benedict Arnold to surrender West Point to Sir Henry Clinton (above). Arnold escapes to the British ship *Vulture*, and André is hanged October 2.

The Battle of Kings Mountain October 7 marks a turning point in the war in the south. Some 900 mounted North Carolina backwoodsmen defeat a

1780 (cont.) force of 900 Loyalist militiamen and kill Major Patrick Ferguson, 36, inventor of a breech-loading rifle and the best marksman in the British army.

George Washington meets with defeat at Germantown in October, he sustains nearly 700 casualties, the British take some 400 prisoners, and the Americans retreat to winter quarters at Valley Forge, Pennsylvania.

The Delaware River north to Philadelphia is safe to British shipping by late November.

In addition to their war with the Americans, the British go to war with the Dutch over the right to search ships at sea. The war soon ends with the Dutch losing some possessions in the East Indies and losing much of their power in that part of the world (*see* 1743).

A second Mysore War breaks out in India.

Maria Theresa of Austria, Hungary, and Bohemia dies November 28 at age 63, leaving her son Josef free to rule alone (he had visited Russia's Catharine the Great in April against his mother's wishes).

The Gordon "No Popery" Riots embroil London from July 2 to 8 as Lord George Gordon, 29, heads a mob of 50,000 that marches from St. George's Fields to the houses of Parliament with petitions to repeal a 1778 act relieving Roman Catholics of certain prejudicial disadvantages. The mob destroys Catholic chapels, breaks open prisons, and attacks the Bank of England. A court acquits Gordon of treason, but he will be excommunicated in 1787, and he will embrace Judaism before dying a debtor in Newgate prison in 1793.

The Holy Roman Emperor Josef II (above) abolishes serfdom in Bohemia and Hungary, completing work begun by his mother.

A Temple of Health opens at London with incense burners, flame-breathing dragons, lascivious paintings, and a Celestial Bed erected on 40 glass pillars with numerous electrical devices intended to rejuvenate the impotent and permit the childless to conceive. Edinburgh saddler's son James Graham has studied medicine but has no degree, he has visited Philadelphia and has heard about Benjamin Franklin's experiments with electricity, he has obtained backing from the duchess of Devonshire, and he has engaged dancer Emma Lyon, 19, as "goddess of health" to direct the sensuous revels at his new establishment. She will become mistress (beginning in 1786) to the diplomat-archaeologist Sir William Hamilton, now 50; she will become Lady Hamilton in 1791 and will accompany her husband and Admiral Horatio Nelson to Palermo in 1800, and in 1801 will give birth to a daughter, Horatio, who will be acknowledged by Admiral Nelson (*see* Battle of the Nile, 1798).

Nashville, Tennessee, has its beginnings in a fort that North Carolina pioneer James Robertson builds on the Cumberland River. The fort will take the name Nashville in 1784.

The American Academy of Arts and Sciences is founded at Boston.

London's first Sunday newspapers appear March 26 as the *British Gazette* and the *Sunday Monitor* begin publication.

Painting *Mary Robinson as Perdita* by Sir Joshua Reynolds; *Death of Chatham* by John Singleton Copley.

First performances Symphony No. 34 in C major by Wolfgang Amadeus Mozart, in July at Salzburg; Symphony No. 75 in D major by Joseph Haydn at Schloss Esterházy.

The first modern pianoforte is built at Paris by Sebasten Erard, 28 (*see* Cristofori, 1709).

Spanish dancer Sebastiano Carezo invents the bolero.

The Hudson River freezes over at New York, enabling British forces to cross on the ice with heavy gear that includes cannon. Blockhouses are erected on the ice to prevent Americans from crossing.

New England has a "dark day" May 19. Religious people believe the end of the world is at hand.

Congress appeals to the states November 4 to contribute quotas of flour, hay, and pork to support the Continental armies.

Britain enjoys something of an agrarian revolution as productivity is increased by more productive seed, more scientific crop rotation, more efficient tools, and improved livestock (*see* Bakewell, 1769; Coke, 1772). But the yield of European agriculture remains little more than five or six times the original seed, on average, and agricultural methods on the Continent are still largely medieval. A third or more of the land is left fallow (partly because of a manure shortage), the land is communally cultivated, and most livestock are still killed every fall (*see* 1730).

Artificial insemination is employed for the first time (in dogs) by Lazzaro Spallanzani, who publishes a *Dissertation on Animal and Vegetable Science* (*see* 1768; cattle, 1938).

A steam-operated flour mill is designed by England's James Watt (*see* 1769).

An automated flour mill is devised by Delaware storekeeper Oliver Evans, 25, who has seen millers toil up long flights of stairs with heavy bags of grain which they dump into chutes that flow into millstones. Evans invents a water-driven vertical conveyor belt that carries hoisting buckets, and he combines this with a horizontal conveyor that moves grain, meal, and flour from place to place on the ground (*see* 1787).

Irish distiller John Jameson starts making a whisky that will be popular for centuries.

English sugar consumption reaches 12 pounds per year per capita, up from 4 pounds in 1700, as Britons increase coffee and tea consumption (*see* 1872).

A chinoiserie "Willow"-patterned blue and white porcelain tableware designed by Thomas Minton, 27, is introduced at Caughley, Shropshire.

Of 21,000 children born in Paris, 17,000 are sent to the country to be wet-nursed, 3,000 are placed in nursery homes, 700 are wet-nursed at home, and only 700 are wet-nursed by their own mothers, who risk the scorn of society.

Urbanization advances in western Europe. France has more than a dozen towns of 30,000 or more, but 85 percent live in villages of 2,000 or less.

Italy and Spain each has nine cities of over 40,000, but no Bohemian town except Prague has more than 10,000. Warsaw has less than 30,000, and all the towns in Hungary put together have no more than 356,000, while Paris has nearly 700,000 and London well over 700,000.

1781 The American Revolution ends October 19 with the surrender of General Cornwallis, but the British will not evacuate Savannah until July of next year and Charleston until December, they will not evacuate New York until November 1783, and the Americans win their War of Independence only after some bloody encounters (below).

Spanish forces under Don Eugenio Pourre in Michigan take Fort St. Joseph from the British in January.

British forces plunder and burn Richmond, Virginia, January 5 with help from Benedict Arnold.

The Battle of the Cowpens in North Carolina January 17 ends in victory for 800 Continental infantrymen, dragoons, and militia commanded by Brigadier General Daniel Morgan. They defeat 1,000 British light cavalry dragoons and infantrymen under the command of Sir Banastre Tarleton, killing 110, wounding 200, and capturing 550, while losing only 12 killed, 60 wounded.

New Jersey troops mutiny January 20, but General Robert Howe soon arrives from West Point to quell the uprising. Pennsylvania troops at Morristown have broken camp with demands for back pay.

General Nathanael Greene reaches Virginia February 13 after a 2-week retreat from North Carolina in which he has eluded British pursuers.

Articles of Confederation and Perpetual Union are adopted by the colonies March 1 as delegates from Maryland add their signatures to the document after New York and Virginia have ceded their western land claims to the newly emerging republic (*see* 1777; Constitution, 1787).

Virginia's Thomas Jefferson has said in relinquishing his state's claims to western lands, "The lands . . . will remain to be occupied by Americans and whether these lands be counted in the members of this or that of the United States will be thought a matter of little moment."

The United States in Congress assembles March 2, but most Americans still call it the Continental Congress.

The Battle of Guilford Court House in North Carolina March 15 ends with the British proclaiming victory, but they are forced to leave North Carolina for Virginia. General Greene turns back and retakes South Carolina and Georgia, but he is defeated April 25 at Hobkirk's Hill, South Carolina.

Spanish forces take West Florida from the British, who surrender Pensacola to Governor Galvez May 9.

British Admiral George B. Rodney sails into the harbor of the St. Eustatius capital Oranjestad, sacks the town, and seizes 250 ships of all nationalities, taking arms and provisions intended for the American rebels. Rodney's action brings denunciations in Parliament from Edmund Burke and Charles James Fox, 32, who sympathize with the American cause, and angry British merchants strip Rodney in prize courts of much of the £4 million in loot that he has taken (*see* 1762; 1779).

French and Spanish naval forces take Tobago, St. Eustatius, Demerara, St. Kitts, Nevis, and Monserrat, but the British will restore their supremacy in the Caribbean next year.

The British at South Carolina's Fort Ninety-Six repulse General Greene June 19.

General Cornwallis repulses General Lafayette July 6 at Jamestown Ford, Virginia, but he is forced to retire August 1 to defensible positions on Virginia's York River at Yorktown and Gloucester Point.

A French fleet from the Caribbean arrives in Chesapeake Bay August 30 under Comte François Paul de Grasse-Tilly, 59. The British fleet is badly crippled September 5 by the Comte de Grasse and is unable to stop 16,000 Allied troops under Generals Washington, Lafayette, and Rochambeau from laying siege to Yorktown beginning September 28.

New London, Connecticut, is plundered and burned September 6 by British forces helped by Benedict Arnold.

The Battle of Eutaw Springs in South Carolina September 8 ends with General Greene retreating and with the British retiring to Charleston.

A new French squadron arrives in Chesapeake Bay September 10 under the 26-year-old Paul François Jean Nicolas de Barras.

General Cornwallis surrenders with 7,000 troops at Yorktown October 19.

Dutch settlements on the west coast of Sumatra are taken by the British.

A Moslem revolt in China's Kansu Province is suppressed by the imperial forces of Kao Tsung.

The surrender of General Cornwallis at Yorktown meant victory for the Americans in their War of Independence.

Russia's Catharine the Great signs a treaty with the Holy Roman Emperor Josef II promising Josef the entire western half of the Balkans. Catharine seeks to drive the Ottoman Turks out of Europe and to establish her 2-year-old grandson Constantine as head of a new Greek empire.

An Edict of Tolerance issued by the Holy Roman Emperor Josef II October 13 ends an 8-year period in which 700 monasteries have been closed and 36,000 members of religious orders released from their vows. The edict prescribes a new organization for the remaining 1,324 monasteries with their 27,000 monks and nuns, it weakens the link with Rome, it introduces innovations in the form of worship, and it establishes schools with church property (see abolition of serfdom, 1782).

Lynch law (or Lynch's law) punishes lawlessness that accompanies the American Revolution in Virginia (above). Planter Charles Lynch, 45, presides as justice of the peace at an extralegal court, the summary punishment that follows his frequent convictions generally consists of flogging, but the term "lynching" will usually mean hanging by an unlawful mob which takes the law into its own hands to seize a prisoner and execute him.

Los Angeles is founded in California by Spanish settlers who call the place El Pueblo de Nuestra Senora la Reina de los Angeles de Porciuncula (see 1763).

The world's first iron bridge opens to traffic January 1 across the River Severn in Shropshire to link Benthall and Madeley Wood, a town that will be renamed Ironbridge. The 100-foot, 378-ton span designed by John Wilkinson of 1774 cannon-borer fame has been cast at Coalbrookdale by Abraham Darby III, grandson of the coke smelter and iron pioneer (see 1709). It has taken 3 months to erect and has been built without nuts, bolts, or screws but only with dovetailed joints, pegs, and keys.

Uranus, first planet to be discovered since the Babylonian era of prehistory, is identified March 31 by German-born English music teacher William Herschel, 43, who moved to England at age 19 and changed his name from Friedrich Wilhelm Herschel. The amateur astronomer employs a homemade telescope in the rear garden of his house at 19 New King Street, Bath.

"Blue laws" get their name at New Haven, Connecticut, where a new town ordinance printed on blue paper prohibits work on Sunday and requires all shops to be closed on "the Lord's day."

The Bank of North America is chartered December 31 by Congress (above) meeting at Philadelphia. The first incorporated bank of the new American republic, it has been founded by superintendent of finance Robert Morris, now 48, who signed the Declaration of Independence in 1776 and who has served the Revolution by arranging for the financing of supplies for George Washington's armies. Morris has used his own personal credit to save the government from bankruptcy.

Nonfiction Critique of Pure Reason (Kritik der Reinen Vernunft) by German metaphysician and philosopher Immanuel Kant, 57, examines the limitations of human understanding and establishes the rationalism of pure experience with a scheme of transcendental philosophy; Decline and Fall of the Roman Empire (Volumes II and III) by Edward Gibbon, who presents Volume II on bended knee to the duke of Gloucester and is told, "Another damned thick book! Always scribble, scribble, scribble: Eh, Mr. Gibbon?" (see 1776; 1788).

Poetry "On the Memorable Victory of Paul Jones" by Philip Freneau.

Painting Belisarius by French painter Jacques Louis David, 33, who completes 6 years of study in Italy.

Opera Idomoneo King of Crete (Idomoneo re di Creta) 1/29 at Munich, with music by Wolfgang Amadeus Mozart.

First performances Concerto for Two Pianofortes and Orchestra in E flat major by Wolfgang Amadeus Mozart 11/24 at Vienna.

London's Asprey & Co. jewelers has its beginnings in a shop at Mitcham opened by metalworker William Asprey whose Huguenot ancestors arrived from France a century ago.

Some 3.5 million Americans live in the new nation, most of them on or near the Atlantic coast. Most of the country's 850,000 square miles of territory remain sparseley settled, and whites inhabit less than one third of the land claimed by the new republic

1782 Admiral Rodney restores British control of the Caribbean April 12 by defeating a French fleet under de Grasse in the Battle of the Saints fought in the strait between Guadeloupe and Dominica.

Admiral Rodney (above) forestalls a union between French and Spanish forces for an assault on Jamaica, but a new British government with a mandate to make peace comes to power under the second marquis of Rockingham, Charles Watson-Wentworth, 52.

Rockingham (above) sends English M.P. Thomas Grenville, 27, to Paris to open talks with Benjamin Franklin (see Treaty of Paris, 1783).

British forces evacuate Savannah in July and Charleston in December.

Spanish forces complete their conquest of Florida from the British.

Spanish forces in the viceroyalty of Peru suppress a 2-year revolt in the Audencia of Cuzco. Tupac Amaru, a descendant of Inca rulers, has made poorly armed attacks on Cuzco and has twice laid siege to La Paz, but the Spanish kill him and crush his native army (see San Martin, 1820).

Britain's *Royal George* sinks without warning August 29 while being repaired at Portsmouth. The flagship of Admiral Richard Kempenfeld goes down off Spithead with 800 men including the admiral.

India's Anglo-Maratha War is ended by the Treaty of Salbai after 7 years of conflict but the 2-year-old Mysore War continues. Mysore's Haidar Ali dies suddenly at age 60, but his 31-year-old son Tipu Sahib is crowned sultan and continues the war against the British, whose governor general Warren Hastings confiscates the treasure and part of the lands of the begum of Oudh, mother of the late Chait Singh, rajah of Benares.

A new dynasty that will rule Siam until 1932 is founded by Chao P'ya Chakri, who will reign until 1809 as Rama I; he will end Siam's long conflict with Burma in 1793, he will re-establish royal control over local potentates, and he will gain part of Cambodia through a division of that country with Annam.

Minorca is captured from British forces by the Spanish who are besieging Gibraltar.

 James Watt patents a double-acting rotary steam engine. He has improved on his engine of 1765 and employs the new engine to drive machinery of all kinds (see cotton mill, 1785).

 English prison reformer John Howard visits London's newly rebuilt Newgate Prison and finds inmates who have been locked up for 7 years awaiting trial. Jailers receive no formal salary, they charge fees before permitting debtors, felons, and others to be released, and Howard urges that jailers be paid salaries (see 1778; Newgate, below).

Serfdom is abolished in Austria and her dominions.

The Virginia legislature authorizes manumission of slaves as the "peculiar institution" begins to die out in some parts of the South (see 1778). Some 10,000 Virginia slaves will be freed in the next 8 years largely because they are too old, too ill, or too costly for their masters to maintain (but see 1803).

 German theologian-zoologist Johann Melchior Goeze finds a hair-like parasite in the intestine of a badger and calls it *der Haarrundworm* (hair-round worm). It will soon be called the hookworm (see Froelich, 1789).

 Nonfiction *Letters from an American Farmer* by French-American farmer-author J. Hector St. John de Crèvecoeur (Michel Guillaume Jean de Crèvecoeur), 47, who settled in New York's Orange County 13 years ago (see below); *Notes on Virginia* by former Virginia governor Thomas Jefferson (see below); *A History of the Corruptions of Christianity* by English clergyman-chemist Joseph Priestley.

Fiction *Les Liaisons dangereuses* by French novelist Pierre Ambroise François Choderlos de Laclos, 41; *Cecilia* by Fanny Burney.

Poetry *Poems* by William Cowper.

Painting *Fêtes for the Grand Duke Paul of Russia* by Francesco Guardi; *Colonel George K. C. Grenadier Guards* by Joshua Reynolds; *The Nightmare* by Swiss painter Henry Fuseli (Johann Heinrich Fussli), 41, who fuses Gothic elements of romanticism with classicism in his reclining figure with its supernatural presences and its mood of terror. Richard Wilson dies at Llanberis, Caernarvonshire, May 12 at age 67.

Sculpture *Monument to Pope Clement XIV* by Antonio Canova.

 Theater *The Robber* (*Die Rauber*) by German surgeon-playwright Johann Christoph Friedrich von Schiller, 22, 1/13 at Mannheim's Naturaltheater. Schiller had his play printed last year at his own expense, he has left his regiment at Stuttgart without leave to attend a performance at Mannheim, he is arrested by the Duke of Württemberg who appointed him physician to the regiment, he is condemned to write nothing but medical treatises, and he leaves Württemberg. Schiller will spend 9 years (the *Wanderjahre*) at Mannheim, Weimar, and Jena.

Opera *The Abduction From the Seraglio* (*Die Entführung aus dem Serail*) 7/16 at Vienna, with music by Wolfgang Amadeus Mozart; *Orlando Paladino*, in August at Vienna's Eszterháza Palace, with music by Joseph Haydn.

First performances Symphony No. 77 in B flat major by Joseph Haydn at Esterháza Castle; Serenade No. 10 in B flat major (*Gran Partita*) by Wolfgang Amadeus Mozart 8/4 for Mozart's wedding to soprano Constanze Weber, 19, at St. Stephen's Cathedral, Vienna.

 London's Newgate Prison is completed to replace an earlier prison burned down in the Gordon riots of 1780. Architect George Dance, 41, has made the

1782 (cont.) new prison almost windowless (windows are not his forte) and the structure is his masterpiece.

Salem's Pierce Nichols House is completed in Federal Street for East India merchant Jerathmeel Pierce by local architect Samuel McIntire, 25.

 Jethro Tull's seed-planting drill of 1701 is improved with gears for its distributing mechanism.

"The indifferent state of agriculture among us does not proceed from a want of knowledge merely," writes Thomas Jefferson in *Notes on Virginia* (above) which he has written at the request of the French government. "It is from our having such quantities of land to waste as we please. In Europe the object is to make the most of their land, labor being abundant; here it is to make the most of our labor, land being abundant."

"Our country teems with more destructive insects and animals than Europe," writes St. John de Crèvecoeur in *Letters from an American Farmer* (above).

Ice cream is served at a Philadelphia party given by the French envoy to honor the new American republic (*see* 1744; 1813).

"Here individuals of all nations are melted into a new race of men," writes St. John de Crèvecoeur (above; *see* Zangwill play, 1909).

1783 Congress proclaims victory in the American War of Independence April 19 but a mutiny of unpaid soldiers at Philadelphia has forced Congress to meet at Princeton, N.J. The North Carolina General Assembly recommends a Fourth of July Independence Day celebration April 19 but Moravians of the Wachovia settlement are the only citizens who respond to the governor's proclamation.

The Treaty of Paris September 3 recognizes the independence of the 13 American colonies, Britain cedes vast territories to the Americans, she grants them full rights to the Newfoundland fishery, she cedes Florida to Spain, she regains her West Indian possessions. France regains St. Lucia, Tobago, Senegal, Gorée, and her East Indian possessions, but the last British troops do not leave New York until November 25.

Congress meets November 26 at Annapolis, Maryland, the first U.S. peacetime capital. George Washington resigns as commander-in-chief of the Continental army December 23.

Sweden recognizes the new American republic; Denmark, Spain, and Russia soon follow suit, but Prussia's Frederick the Great says the United States is too large and will soon fall apart.

The Spanish siege of Gibraltar has ended February 6 after 3½ years of hostilities in which the British defenders have used red-hot lead to repel the battering ships of the enemy.

Russia's Catharine the Great annexes the Crimea that her favorite Grigori Aleksandrovich Potemkin, 44, has conquered from the Ottoman Turks, she expels the Turks, and she offers a large grant of land to the Mennonites, promising them religious freedom and exemption from military service (*see* 1568; 1771; 1784).

English Quakers form an association "for the relief and liberation of the negro slaves in the West Indies, and for the discouragement of the slave trade on the coast of Africa."

Maryland forbids further importation of slaves.

A crude electric cell constructed by Italian anatomist Luigi Galvani, 49, employs two different metals and the natural fluids from a dissected frog. Galvani decides that the electric current produced by the cell must derive from the frog fluids (*see* Volta, 1800).

Tungsten (wolfram) is produced in metallic form by Spanish chemists Juan and Fernando d'Elhuyer, who isolate an acid from wolframite and heat it with carbon.

Wrought iron production is revolutionized by English ironmaster Henry Cort, 43, who invents a process for puddling iron. Cort will patent the process next year, and he will also patent the reverberatory furnace that makes his purifying process possible.

English physician Thomas Cawley makes the first recorded diagnosis of diabetes mellitus. He shows the presence of sugar in a patient's urine (*see* 1788; Willis, 1674).

The Montgolfier brothers give the first public demonstration of an ascension balloon June 15 at Annoy, France. Joseph Michel Montgolfier, 43, and his brother Jacques Etienne, 38, have inflated their balloon with hot air and it makes a 10-minute ascent (*see* Jeffries, 1785; Charles, 1787).

The 600,000 tons of shipping employed in Anglo-American trade are almost entirely British, but Salem merchant Elias Hasket Derby, who has learned the value of fast ships in the Revolution, has improved the art of shipbuilding and outsails the Royal Navy in his 309-ton *Grand Turk*. He will soon send her to the East Indies and China (*see* 1784).

A postwar economic depression begins in the United States, which has foreign debts of $6.4 million to France, $1.3 million to Holland, and $174,000 to Spain.

British Orders in Council limit imports from America to naval stores and a few other commodities.

Revolutionary army soldiers and officers are issued script certificates entitling them to tracts of land west of the Appalachians, the acreages varying according to rank and length of service. Many sell the certificates to those who want land (and to land speculators).

The phrase "not worth a Continental" is heard as inflation reduces the value of paper currency issued by the Continental Congress to finance the Revolution. Corn sells for $80 per bushel, shoes for $100 per pair, and George Washington, richest man in America, says he needs a wagonload of money to buy a wagonload of supplies.

The $5 million William Penn estate in Pennsylvania is broken up, as are other large estates held by former Loyalists (Tories) including New York's 192,000-acre Philipse manor. New York's De Lancey manor is sold to 275 individuals, a 40,000-acre North Carolina estate is divided into farms averaging 200 acres each, but most of the land goes to speculators and to men who are already substantial property owners.

Philadelphia political leader William Bingham, a founder of the Bank of North America 2 years ago and a member of its board, will soon buy 2 million acres of Maine timberland on the upper Penobscot River for 12.5 cents per acre.

Webster's Spelling Book by Yale graduate Noah Webster, 25, is published under the title *Grammatical Institute of the English Language.* Webster standardizes American orthography and helps make pronunciation more uniform. His *Blue-Backed Speller* will have sales of more than 65 million copies in the next 34 years, and it will continue to sell through much of the next century (*see* dictionary, 1806; 1828).

Poetry *The Village* by English poet-curate George Crabbe, 28, employs heroic couplets in a reply to Oliver Goldsmith's sentimental *The Deserted Village* of 1770.

Painting *The Duchess of Devonshire* by Thomas Gainsborough; *Lady Hamilton as a Bacchante* by George Romney; *The Grief of Andromache* by Jacques Louis David, who gains admission to the Academy.

Theater *Nathan the Wise* (*Nathan der Weise*) by Gotthold Ephraim Lessing 4/14 at Berlin; *Fiesco, or The Conspiracy of Genoa* (*Die Verschwirung der Fiesko zu Genoa*) by Friedrich Schiller 7/20 at Bonn.

First performances Symphony No. 35 in D major (*Haffner*) by Wolfgang Amadeus Mozart 3/3 at Vienna's Burgtheater. The Holy Roman Emperor Josef II gives Mozart 25 ducats to show his appreciation; Concerto-Rondo for Pianoforte and Orchestra in D major by W. A. Mozart 3/11 at Vienna; Symphony No. 36 in C major (*Linz*) by W. A. Mozart 11/4 at the palace of Count Thun in Linz.

Iceland's Skaptar volcano erupts, killing 20 percent of the country's population.

Japan suffers her worst famine since 1732 following the eruption of Mount Asama (*see* 1787).

1784 The Ottoman Turks accept Russian annexation of the Crimea in the Treaty of Constantinople signed January 6 (*see* 1783; 1873).

The U.S. Congress meeting at Annapolis ratifies the Treaty of Paris January 14 to bring the War of Independence to a formal end. Congress remains in session until August 13.

The Holy Roman Emperor Josef II abrogates the Hungarian Constitution July 4 following a revolution in Transylvania. He removes the crown of Hungary to Vienna and suppresses Hungarian feudal courts.

The India Act that becomes law in Britain August 13 establishes a new constitution for the 184-year-old East India Company, it forbids company interference in India's native affairs, it forbids any declaration of war except in the event of aggression, and it makes the Company's directors answerable to a board appointed by the crown (*see* Sepoy Rebellion, 1857).

The India Act (above) has been put through by the new prime minister William Pitt ("the Younger Pitt") who at age 25 is also chancellor of the exchequer and first lord of the treasury. Pitt will rank as the greatest of all British prime ministers, he will retain the position until 1801, and he will serve again from 1804 until his death early in 1806.

British import duties on tea are further lowered (*see* 1773). The smuggling that has accounted for so much of the nation's tea imports and has hurt the East India Company is ended as the rewards become too small to justify the risks.

The first bale of American cotton reaches Britain as long-staple cotton comes into widescale production in the sea islands off the Carolina and Georgia coasts (*see* Whitney, 1792).

Economic depression begins in America.

The first American ship to reach China arrives at Canton. The 360-ton *Empress of China* out of New York has been financed by William Duer of New York, Robert Morris of Philadelphia, and Daniel Parker of Watertown, Massachusetts, and it carries a cargo of ginseng root, prized by Chinese physicians as a therapeutic drug and as an aphrodisiac. The cargo is bartered for $30,000 worth of tea and silk by Major Samuel Shaw, aide-de-camp in the Revolution to General Henry Knox. The investors receive a 25 percent return on their capital, Shaw becomes first U.S. consul at Canton, and more Americans are encouraged to enter the China trade, including Salem's Elias Derby (*see* 1783; Gray, 1790).

The Bank of New York has its beginnings at the Merchants' Coffee House, where merchants meet in response to an advertisement in the *New York Packet* placed by local attorney Alexander Hamilton, 27.

All Acadians who have remained in Nova Scotia and lower New Brunswick since the expulsion order of 1755 are transported to Maine and to Louisiana by the British (*see* Cajun cookery, below; Longfellow, 1847).

Serfdom is abolished in Denmark by Andreas Bernstorff, who was dismissed as prime minister in 1780 but who has been recalled to office.

1784 **(cont.)** Citric acid is discovered in certain plants by Sweden's Karl Wilhelm Scheele.

Quantitative chemistry is pioneered by French chemist Antoine Laurent Lavoisier, 41, who introduces modern names for chemical substances while retaining the old symbols of alchemy. Lavoisier relates respiration to combustion, and he demonstrates the indestructability of matter (*see* 1789; Ingenhousz, 1779).

Experiments on Air by English chemist-physicist Henry Cavendish, now 53, shows that water results from the union of hydrogen and oxygen. Cavendish has been the first to discover the true nature of hydrogen and to determine its specific gravity. He has determined the specific gravity of carbon dioxide, and he now shows that water is produced from an explosion of two volumes of hydrogen ("inflammable air") with one of oxygen ("dephlogisticated air").

The amount of oxygen ("dephlogisticated air") consumed in respiration and combustion and the amount of carbon dioxide and heat produced are measured by Antoine Lavoisier (above) and by French mathematician-astronomer Pierre Simon, 35, the marquis de Laplace.

Essai d'une theorie sur la structure des cristaux by French mineralogist-clergyman René Just Haüy, 41, enunciates the geometrical law of crystallization and founds the science of crystallography. Haüy has accidentally broken a crystal of calcareous spar and the accident has led him to make experiments.

John Wesley, now 81, charters Wesleyan Methodism February 28, signing a declaration that provides for the regulation of Methodist chapels and preachers. He ordains his clerical helper September 1 and instructs the new superintendent (bishop) to ordain two colleagues despite the disapproval of his brother Charles, who opposes ordination of presbyters (*see* 1744).

Shaker leader Mother Ann Lee dies at Watervliet, N.Y., September 8 at age 48, disappointing zealous followers who had believed her to be immortal. Shakerism will continue in America, setting an example with inventive, orderly methods of building, toolmaking, furniture making, animal husbandry, cooking, and the production of woodenware, yarns, textiles, and botanical herbs (*see* 1774; round barn, 1824).

U.S. Minister to France Benjamin Franklin invents bifocal spectacles. He will describe them for the first time in a letter from Passy May 23 of next year.

German poet-playwright Johann Wolfgang von Goethe discovers the human intermaxillary bone.

The first school for the blind opens at Paris. Valentin Haüy, 39, brother of the mineralogist (above) has invented a method for embossing characters on paper, and he will later open a school for the blind at St. Petersburg (*see* Braille, 1834).

New York's Columbia College opens after 6 years of wartime suspension of King's College, founded in 1754. The war has obliged King's College students including Alexander Hamilton (above) to educate themselves.

The Encyclopaedia Britannica first published from 1768 to 1771 appears in a new 10-volume edition (*see* 1797).

Nonfiction *Notion of a Universal History in a Cosmopolitan Sense* by Immanual Kant; "What is Enlightenment" by Immanuel Kant; *Ideas Toward a Philosophy of History* (*Ideen zur Philosophie der Geschichte der Menschheit*) by Johann Gottfried von Herder is published in the first of four volumes that will appear in the next 7 years.

Painting *The Oath of the Horatii* by Jacques Louis David; *Mrs. Siddons as The Tragic Muse* by Joshua Reynolds; *Don Manuel de Zuniga* by Spanish painter Francisco José de Goya y Lucientes, 38.

English portrait painter-cartoonist Thomas Rowlandson, 28, pioneers political caricature.

Theater *Cabal and Love* (*Kabale und Liebe*) by Friedrich von Schiller 4/13 at Frankfurt-am-Main. Schiller attacks the corruption of the petty German courts and their disregard of basic human values; *The Marriage of Figaro, or The Madness of a Day* (*La folle journee, ou Le mariage de Figaro*) by Pierre Augustin Caron de Beaumarchais 4/27 at the Comédie Française, Paris. Beaumarchais completed the work in 1778, but he has had difficulty in getting it staged because of its antiaristocratic implications.

First performances Concerto for Pianoforte and Orchestra in E flat major by Wolfgang Amadeus Mozart 2/9 at Vienna; Concerto for Pianoforte and Orchestra in B flat major by W. A. Mozart 3/17 at Salzburg; Concerto for Pianoforte and Orchestra in D major by W. A. Mozart in March at Salzburg; Concerto for Pianoforte and Orchestra in G major by W. A. Mozart 6/10 at a country house in Döbling outside Vienna; Sonata for Pianoforte in A major by W. A. Mozart.

The first Chinese "tree of heaven" (*Ailanthus altissima*) to grow in America is planted at Philadelphia. The fast-growing pollution-resistant tree will be brought to Long Island by a Flushing nurseryman in 1820, and by 1850 it will be common in the streets of New York, admired by some but scorned by others because of the unpleasant odor given off by its male flowers in the spring.

Famine continues in Japan; 300,000 die of starvation, and survivors in many cases eat corpses to stay alive.

English farmers show little interest in an iron plow developed by inventor James Small. They continue to use wooden plows (*see* Newbold, 1797).

Benjamin Franklin exhorts the French to set their clocks ahead 1 hour in spring and back 1 hour in fall to take advantage of daylight, but farmers resist the proposal. Franklin is widely credited with having originated the lines "Early to bed and early to rise . . ." first published in 1639, and he is well known for his aphorism "Time is money" (*see* Willet, 1907).

U.S. Shakers (above) will develop the Poland China hog by crossing backwoods hogs with white Big China hogs to produce the breed that will be the backbone of the U.S. pork industry for generations.

The Shakers (above) will innovate the practice of retailing garden seeds in small, labeled paper packets (*see* Burpee, 1876).

Shaker gravies are made from water in which vegetables have been cooked, and the Shakers will be famed for their breads, pies, and doughnuts.

Cajun cookery will be established in Louisiana by the Acadians (above), who will combine their Canadian recipes with those of the native "injuns."

Bushmill's distillery opens in the north of Ireland.

Abortion and infanticide become common among the poor of Japan as famine (above) discourages large families.

1785 The affair of the diamond necklace creates a sensation in France beginning August 15 when Cardinal de Rohan is arrested as he prepares to officiate at Assumption Day services for Louis XVI and Marie Antoinette. The 51-year-old cardinal has been led by his mistress the comtesse de La Motte to believe that the queen is enamored of him and that she has authorized him to buy a necklace of diamonds collected by the Paris jewelry firm of Boehmer and Bassenge originally for Mme. Du Barry. The comtesse de La Motte has presented the jewelers with notes signed by the cardinal, the jewelers have complained to the queen, she has told Boehmer that she never ordered the necklace and certainly never received it, the comtesse de La Motte is also arrested, and much of France chooses not to believe the queen. The case will be tried before the parlement next year.

The dollar is established as the official currency of the new United States. Congress employs a decimal system devised by Thomas Jefferson, who is named minister to France to succeed Benjamin Franklin.

U.S. economic troubles worsen as English goods undercut American manufactures. States erect tariffs to keep out goods from abroad and from other states, farmers are unable to sell their tobacco and surplus food crops because foreign markets have disappeared, and New Englanders can no longer find markets for the products of their shipyards.

A U.S. land ordinance provides for the sale of public lands at auction in tracts of 640 acres at a cash price of a least $1 per acre, but few would-be western settlers can put up $640 in cash (*see* 1800).

Steam is employed to power textile machinery for the first time. A Boulton and Watt rotative engine is installed in an English cotton factory at Papplewick, Nottinghamshire (*see* 1782).

Digitalis obtained from dried leaves of the foxglove plant *Digitalis purpurea* is introduced into medical treatment by English physician William Withering, 44, who publishes *An Account of the Foxglove*.

The gout remedy colchicine obtained from seeds of the same autumn crocus whose stamens yield saffron is introduced to America by Benjamin Franklin on his return from 9 years abroad as U.S. minister to France.

Boston-born English physician John Jeffries, 41, makes the first aerial crossing of the English Channel January 7. A Loyalist during the American Revolution, Jeffries has moved to England. He ascends in a hot air balloon from Dover with the French aeronaut François Blanchard and crosses to a forest at Guines (*see* Montgolfier brothers, 1783; Bleriot, 1909).

The University of Georgia is founded at Athens.

The University of New Brunswick is founded at Fredericton.

Nonfiction *The Journal of the Tour to the Hebrides* by Scottish lawyer James Boswell, now 46, describes a 1773 journey to his native Scotland and on to the isles of Skye and Raasay with the late Dr. Johnson, who died last year at age 75.

Poetry *The Task, a Poem in Six Books* by William Cowper who includes "Tirocinium, or a Review of Schools" to commemorate the tyranny he suffered as a schoolboy. Cowper also includes his ballad of 1782 "The History of John Gilpin:" "Variety's the spice of life,/ That gives it all its flavour . . ." (II, 606–607).

Painting *The Infant Hercules* by Sir Joshua Reynolds. Pietro Longhi dies at Venice May 8 at age 82.

Opera *The Marriage of Figaro* (*Le Nozze di Figaro*) 5/1 at Vienna's Burgtheater, with music by Wolfgang Amadeus Mozart, libretto by Lorenzo da Ponte from last year's Beaumarchais comedy.

First performances Concerto for Pianoforte and Orchestra in D minor by Wolfgang Amadeus Mozart 2/11 at Vienna's Cadisches Casino in the Mehlgrube; Concerto for Pianoforte and Orchestra in B flat major by W. A. Mozart 2/12 at Vienna; Concerto No. 21 for Pianoforte and Orchestra in C major by W. A. Mozart 3/12 at Vienna's Burgtheater (*see* Elvira Madigan, 1967); Concerto for Pianoforte and Orchestra in E flat major by W. A. Mozart 12/23 at Vienna.

Venice's Ca' Rezzonico palazzo is completed to celebrate Carlo Rezzonico's election to the papacy as Clement XIII. Begun in 1667 by Baldassare Longhena for the Priuli-Bon family, the palace had reached the first floor level by the time of Longhena's death in 1682.

Bangkok's Emerald Buddha Chapel is completed.

French explorer Jean François de Galaup, 44, comte de La Pérouse, looks for new whaling grounds in the Pacific. He embarks on an ill-fated voyage that will discover La Pérouse Strait between Sakhalin and Hokkaido.

1785 (cont.) France's Louis XVI is persuaded by Antoine-Auguste Parmentier to plant potatoes and to encourage their cultivation (*see* 1771; 1789).

Montreal's Molson brewery is founded by brewer John Molson, whose family will continue the enterprise for more than six generations.

Punta Mes Vermouth is introduced by Benedetto Carpano in Turin's Piazza Castello, the first vermouth to be sold commercially. While another winery that will be famous for its vermouth has been established earlier by Francesco Cinzano, it is Carpano who is first to put his vermouth on the market.

A Dissertation on the Poor Laws by England's Joseph Townsend suggests that hunger, "the stronger appetite," will provide a natural restraint on "the weaker" appetite and will thus "blunt the shafts of Cupid, or ... quench the torch of Hymen ..." to maintain a food–population equilibrium (*see* 1791; 1798).

1786 Prussia's Frederick the Great dies at Sans-Souci in Potsdam August 17 at age 72 after a 46-year reign. He is succeeded by his inept 41-year-old nephew, who assumes the throne as Friedrich Wilhelm II to begin an 11-year reign.

Portugal's feebleminded Pedro dies, his wife (and niece) becomes demented, and the government is taken over by their son João, 19, who will be named regent in 1792 and who will reign as João VI for 10 years after his mother's death in 1816.

Japan's feebleminded Tokugawa shogun Ieharu dies at age 49 after a 26-year reign and is succeeded by his 13-year-old kinsman Ienari, who will take power in 1793 after a 6-year regency. Ienari will rule until his abdication in 1837.

French manufacturers press for a measure of free trade that will give them a foreign market comparable to that of their envied British rivals. A commercial treaty is signed with London, English tariffs are lowered on French wheat, wine, and luxury goods, French tariffs are lowered on English textiles, but British imports flood the French market, undercut domestic prices, idle the looms at Troyes, and bring widespread unemployment, producing demands for renewal of tariff protection (*see* 1788).

France's diamond necklace affair ends in acquittal of Cardinal de Rohan May 31 (*see* 1785). The comte de La Motte is believed to have escaped to London with the necklace, and he is condemned in his absence to serve in the galleys for life. The comtesse de La Motte is condemned to be whipped, branded, and locked up in the Salpetrière. Cardinal de Rohan is exiled to the abbey of la Chaise-Dieu; Marie Antoinette is disappointed by his acquittal. It is widely believed that he was trapped by the queen, and when Mme. de La Motte escapes from the Salpetrière and takes refuge abroad, the court will be suspected of having connived in her escape.

Shays' Rebellion in Massachusetts is led by revolutionary war veteran Daniel Shays, 39, and others in a September uprising that aims to prevent further foreclosures of farms in the country's continuing economic depression. State militia prevent seizure of the Springfield arsenal in a confrontation with 800 armed farmers September 26, but the rebellion succeeds in having the state supreme court adjourn without returning indictments against the farmers. Scattered fighting will continue through the winter, but a party under the command of Shays will be defeated in early February of next year, Shays will escape to Vermont, most of the rebels will be pardoned later in the year, and Shays will be pardoned in 1788 as hard-money interests in maritime Boston win out over inflationary-minded farmers.

A convention that has assembled at Annapolis to remedy the weaknesses of the 1781 Articles of Confederation is encouraged by Shays' Rebellion (above) to create a Congress that will have exclusive powers to coin money, with the states forbidden such powers and forbidden to levy tariffs or embargoes against each other that would restrict internal free trade (*see* Constitution, 1787).

Rhode Island farmers burn their grain, dump their milk, and leave their apples to rot in the orchards in a farm strike directed against Providence and Newport merchants who have refused to sell for the paper money that has depreciated to the point of being virtually worthless. The strike has little effect, since 90 percent of Americans raise their own food, growing peas, beans, and corn in their gardens and letting their hogs forage in the woods for acorns.

Syracuse, New York, has its beginnings in a trading post established by Yankee trader Ephraim Webster (*see* 1654; 1825).

Penang on the Malayan Peninsula is founded by the British, who will make it a port for pepper exports.

The Pribilof Islands in the Bering Sea are discovered by Russian sea captain Gerasim Pribylov (*see* 1741).

Maryland agrees to let Delaware build a canal to connect the Delaware River with Chesapeake Bay.

Poetry *Poems, chiefly in the Scottish dialect* by Kilmarnock poet Robert Burns, 27, whose verse "To a Mouse" contains the line, "The best laid schemes o' mice an' men aft gang a-gley;" "To a Louse" contains the line, "Oh wad some Power the giftie gie us/ To see oursels as ithers see us!" and Burns includes also "The Cotter's Saturday Night," "Hallowe'en," "Scotch Drink," "The Vision," and "Epistle to Davie." His first edition brings in only £20 but its critical success dissuades Burns from emigrating to Jamaica, and an enlarged edition will be printed next year at Edinburgh; "The Wild Honey Suckle" by Philip Freneau.

Painting *The Duchess of Devonshire and Her Daughter* by Joshua Reynolds; *Colonel Mordaunt's Cock-Match* by Johann Zoffany who has lived in India since 1783 and will remain until 1789.

First performances   Concerto No. 24 for Pianoforte and Orchestra in C minor by Wolfgang Amadeus Mozart 4/7 at Vienna's Hoftheater; Symphony No. 38 in D major (*Prague*) by W. A. Mozart 5/1 at Vienna's Burgtheater; Concerto for Pianoforte and Orchestra in C major by W. A. Mozart in December at Vienna.

The first U.S. golf club is founded at Charleston's Green near Charleston, South Carolina, by local clergyman Henry Purcell, whose club will be rechartered in the Harbour Town clubhouse at Sea Pines Plantation, Hilton Head, South Carolina.

Americans mix woolen yarn with linen fibers to make rough "linsey-woolsey" cloth stained with sumac or with butternut dyes. They obtain the cash they need for salt, sewing needles, and land taxes by selling pot ashes (potash) produced by burning wood and leaching the ashes.

Providence, Rhode Island, hails a new brick house erected for local merchant John Brown. John Quincy Adams will call it "the most magnificent and elegant private mansion that I have seen in this continent."

Bridgewater, Massachusetts, inventor Ezekiel Reed patents a nail-making machine, but nails remain so costly that houses are put together in large part with wooden pegs (*see* Perkins, 1790).

London's Somerset House is completed by architect Sir William Chambers, 60, after 10 years of work.

The Pribilof Islands (above) have an estimated 5 million fur seals. Gerasim Pribylov founds a colony to harvest pelts (*see* 1867).

Paris sends the Abbé Dicquemare to report on the state of oyster beds in the gulf at the mouth of the Seine. The naturalist reports that the oysters have diminished by half "in the last forty years . . . The real causes of the deficit are the maneuvers of cupidity and the insufficiency of laws" (*see* 1681).

The first successful threshing machine is developed by Scottish millwright and agricultural engineer Andrew Meikle, 67, whose machine rubs the grain between a rotating drum and a concave metal sheet, employing a basic principle that will be used in future threshing machines.

1787 A Constitution for the new United States of America is drawn up by a convention that has been meeting at Philadelphia under the chairmanship of George Washington. Virginia's James Madison, 36, settles differences between proponents of a strong central government and proponents of absolute rights for the separate states, Washington resists efforts to make him king, and the Constitution establishes a balance of powers between the federal government and the state governments. It establishes a bicameral legislature rather than a parliament, and it provides for legislators and a chief executive to be elected for limited terms rather than for life. No provision is made for political parties or for a standing army.

"Federalist Papers" explaining the new Constitution appear under the name "Publius" in the *New York Independent Journal* beginning October 27 and will run for 7 months. The papers have been written by James Madison (above) and New York lawyer Alexander Hamilton, now 30.

Delaware ratifies the Constitution by unanimous vote December 7 to become the first state of the Union.

Pennsylvania votes 46 to 23 to ratify the Constitution December 12.

New Jersey ratifies the Constitution by unanimous vote December 18.

A Northwest Ordinance adopted by Congress sitting at New York provides for a government of the Northwest Territory. The region is to gain ultimate statehood, and no slavery is to be permitted.

South Carolina cedes its western lands to the federal government, and the Ohio Company signs a contract with the Treasury Board of Congress to buy lands on the Ohio River (*see* Losantiville, 1788).

Thomas Paine travels to Europe where he will remain for the next 15 years agitating for revolution.

Russia's Catharine the Great begins a second war with the Ottoman Empire, using Turkish intrigues with the Crimean Tartars as an excuse to pursue her objective of obtaining Georgia.

English cotton goods production is 10 times what it was in 1770, and iron production has quadrupled, but

The Montgolfier brothers freed man from earth's gravity with their pioneer ascension balloons.

1787 (cont.) cottage industry still prevails with few large power-operated mills. The Industrial Revolution is still in its early stages.

France's working class is ill-paid, the typical working day is 14 to 16 hours, workers are lucky to get 250 days of work per year. The basic food of the people is bread which takes 60 percent of the average man's wages.

Rice riots at Osaka climax years of Japanese peasant unrest. Rice warehouses are broken open May 11, the riots spread throughout the city May 12, by May 18 they have spread to Edo and 30 other cities, and by May 20 nearly every large rice merchant has seen his house destroyed as the rioters break into 8,000 establishments that include not only rice warehouses but also pawnshops, sake breweries, and shops dealing in textiles, dyes, drugs, and oils.

Britain begins clearing her prisons which are overcrowded with inmates who before the American Revolution would have been transported to the American colonies. The prisoners are transported to Britain's new Australian penal colony at Botany Bay (*see* Cook, 1770).

English philanthropist William Wilberforce, 28, begins agitating against slavery in the British colonies (*see* 1789).

"Essay on the Slavery and Commerce of the Human Species" by Cambridge University student Thomas Clarkson, 27, is an expanded version of an essay, originally in Latin, that won Clarkson a Latin prize.

The Free African Society is founded at Philadelphia by freedman Richard Allen, 27, and other blacks who were pulled off their knees in November at a "white" Methodist church. With Absalom Jones and others, Allen establishes the African Methodist Episcopal Church while working to improve the economic and social conditions of American blacks through the Free African Society.

A "three-fifths rule" is adopted at the Constitutional Convention (above) as a compromise to settle differences between Northern and Southern states over the counting of slaves for purposes of representation and taxation. Slaves are to be counted as three-fifths of a free man for both purposes.

A steamboat is launched on the Delaware River August 22 by U.S. inventor John Fitch, 44, who will build several steamboats in the next few years (*see* 1791; Symington, 1788).

A steamboat is demonstrated on the Potomac River in December by Maryland inventor James Rumsey, 44, whose craft is driven by streams of water forced through the stern by a steam pump.

The first hydrogen ascension balloon is launched by French physicist Jacques Charles, 41 (*see* Montgolfier, 1783).

Charles's law is enunciated in its first steps by physicist Charles (above), who calculates that for every degree Celsius rise in temperature, a gas expands proportionally to its volume at 0°C, an idea that he will develop into the law that will bear his name.

The University of Pittsburgh has its beginnings in a college founded at Fort Pitt (*see* 1759; 1816).

Painting *Lady Heathfield* by Sir Joshua Reynolds.

Theater *The Contrast* by U.S. playwright Royall Tyler, 29, 4/6 at New York's John Street Theater is the first comedy of any real merit by an American and one of the first to introduce the "stage Yankee," a shrewd and realistic rustic who will be a fixture in many plays; *Don Carlos, Infante of Spain (Don Carlos, Infante von Spanien)* by Friedrich von Schiller 8/29 at Hamburg's National Theater.

Opera *Don Giovanni* 10/29 at Prague's National Theater, with music by Wolfgang Amadeus Mozart, libretto by Lorenzo da Ponte based on a literary classic about the legendary Spanish lover Don Juan dating back to the Middle Ages.

First performances Eine Kleine Nachtmusik by Wolfgang Amadeus Mozart; Sextet for Strings and horns in F major [A Musical Joke *Ein musikalischer Spass*] by W. A. Mozart. Christoph Willibald Gluck dies November 15 at age 73, the Holy Roman Emperor Josef II appoints Mozart imperial composer to succeed Gluck, but he pays him only 800 florins per year whereas Gluck received 2,000.

The first English cricket match to be played at Lord's pits Essex against Middlesex May 31. The Marylebone Cricket Club plays its first match July 30 against the Islington Cricket Club (*see* 1788; Grace, 1860).

A French government edict intended to encourage agriculture removes the requirement that grain producers take their grain to market. The producers are permitted to sell directly to consumers or even to export their grain by land or sea with no restrictions whatever. French granaries are emptied in consequence, and the country is left unprepared for a bad harvest (*see* 1788).

English sea captain William Bligh, 33, sails for Tahiti on H.M.S. *Bounty* to obtain breadfruit plants for planting in the Caribbean islands as a new source of food for British colonists. As sailing master of Captain Cook's 1772–1775 voyage, Bligh developed an enthusiasm for breadfruit and has persuaded the admiralty that *Artocarpus communis* can be a boon to the Caribbean (*see* 1789; Dampier, 1688).

U.S. Minister to France Thomas Jefferson returns to his post from a visit to Italy with a rice-husking machine, Tuscan wine, Lombardy poplar saplings, and a spaghetti die which he uses to make pasta (*see* 1824; Agnesi, 1824; Buitoni, 1827).

Flour milling is further revolutionized by Delaware inventor Oliver Evans of 1780 conveyor belt fame who devises an automated process for grinding grain and bolting (sifting) flour. The process requires a certain capital investment, but it can be operated by just two men, it sharply lowers the cost of milling, it will make white bread widely available in America, and it marks the beginning of automation in U.S. industry (*see* 1791; "automation," 1946).

Stockholm's Operakallern opens in the cellar of the Swedish opera house as a new restaurant that will be world famous for its midday smorgasbord. The opera house will be demolished in 1892 and will be replaced 3 years later with a new house that will have the Operakallern as an adjunct.

1788 France's Louis XVI is presented by the Parlement of Paris with a list of grievances as the country suffers its worst economic chaos of the century. Louis recalls Jacques Necker as minister of finance and calls the Estates General to assemble in May of next year for the first time since 1614.

Sweden's Gustavus III invades Russian Finland to begin a 2-year war that will end with Finland and Karelia still in Russian hands.

Russia's war with the Ottoman Empire gains support from Austria, which joins with Catharine the Great under terms of a 1781 alliance treaty and declares war on the Turks.

Spain's Carlos III dies December 14 at age 72 after an enlightened reign of 29 years in which he has encouraged trade and industry, suppressed lawlessness, constructed roads and canals, and improved sanitation. Greatest of the Spanish Bourbons, he is succeeded, not by his firstborn son (an epileptic imbecile who is set aside), but by his slothful 40-year-old second son who will reign until 1808 as Carlos IV.

The United States Constitution becomes operative June 21 as New Hampshire ratifies the Constitution 57 to 47 and becomes the ninth state to ratify. Georgia, Connecticut, Massachusetts, Maryland, and South Carolina have ratified earlier in the year to become states of the Union, and Virginia and New York ratify June 25 and July 26, respectively, New York by a vote of 30 to 27.

The first permanent Ohio Valley settlement is established at Marietta by New Englanders under the leadership of General Rufus Putnam, 50.

Cincinnati has its beginnings in a few buildings erected on the Ohio River by settlers who call the place Losantiville (*see* 1790).

Dubuque has its beginnings in an Illinois country settlement established by French-Canadian entrepeneur Julien Dubuque, 26, who negotiates an agreement with Fox tribal leaders to mine lead.

Australia's Botany Bay, discovered by Captain Cook in 1770, becomes an English penal colony, and the first shipload of convicts is landed January 18. The 736 prisoners are soon augmented by new arrivals, and the penal colony is moved to a neighboring area that will be called Sydney after British Home Secretary Thomas Townshend, 55, first viscount Sydney.

The first practical steamboat is invented by Scottish engineer William Symington, 25, who installs a di-

rect-action steam engine in a paddle boat. His vessel attracts no commercial attention (*see* 1787; 1791).

A multitubular steam boiler for marine engines is invented by New Jersey lawyer-inventor John Stevens, 39 (*see* 1790; 1804).

Austrian Jews are ordered to adopt "proper recognizable surnames" by Josef II. The Jews have been known until now largely by biblical patronyms and when some object to changing their names, they are given such surnames as "Fresser," "Pferd," and "Weinglas" by the emperor's officials.

Traité des Affinities Chymiques, ou Attractions Electives by Swedish chemist-physicist Torbern Bergman includes affinity tables that summarize results of his studies of displacement reactions. The University of Uppsala scientist obtained nickel in its pure state for the first time 3 years ago (*see* 1770).

Mechanique Analitique by French mathematician Joseph-Louis Lagrange of 1761 calculus fame is a strictly analytical treatment of mechanics. Lagrange bases statics on the principle of virtual velocities and dynamics in a work that is based in turn on the 1743 d'Alembert's principle.

The Linnaean Society is founded at London.

English physician Thomas Cawley notes abnormalities of the pancreas in the autopsy of a diabetic patient (*see* 1783). Cawley believes diabetes to be a kidney disease, and he ignores his own observation, but it is the first known observation of any relationship between diabetes and the pancreas (*see* Lancereaux, 1860).

New York physicians go into hiding for 3 days in April as a mob riots in protest against grave robbers. Boys playing outside the Society of the Hospital of the City of New York on Broadway between Duane and Catherine Streets put a ladder against the hospital's wall Sunday afternoon, April 13. One boy climbs up, peers in the window, and discovers medical students and physicians dissecting a cadaver for study. He runs home and tells his father, the father and some of his friends visit the grave of his recently buried wife, and they find the casket open and the corpse gone. They rush to the hospital and seize four doctors, but the sheriff rescues the men and puts them in jail overnight to protect them. A mob of 5,000 storms the jail Monday afternoon and injures Alexander Hamilton, John Jay, Baron von Steuben, Mayor James Duane, and Governor George Clinton. The militia is ordered to fire into the mob, several citizens are killed or wounded, the riot continues through Tuesday, but the state will pass a law next year enabling physicians to obtain cadavers without robbing graves (*see* Bard, 1791; Burke, 1829).

The *Times* of London begins publication January 1. Former coal merchant John Walter, 49, was bankrupted 6 years ago by shipping losses after 27 years

1788 (cont.) in the coal business, he switched to publishing books, he went from that into newspaper publishing, and he changes the name of the *Daily Universal Register* that he has been publishing since 1785 (*see* 1908).

Nonfiction *Classical Dictionary (Bibliotheca Classica)* by English scholar John Lemprière, 23, whose work is a reference book in classic mythology and classical history; *Thoughts on the Importance of the Manners of the Great to General Society* by Hannah More; *Lettres sur le Caractère et les Ecrits de J. J. Rousseau* by French libertine Mme. de Staël (Anne Louise Germaine Necker, baronne de Staël-Holstein), 22, whose 2-year-old marriage to the Swedish ambassador has turned sour. Daughter of the finance minister Jacques Necker, Mme. de Staël is becoming notorious for her love affairs.

Poetry "The Indian Burying Ground" by Philip Freneau.

Painting *Antoine Lavoisier and his Wife* and *Love of Paris and Helena* by Jacques Louis David; *Tiger Hunt in the East Indies* by Johann Zoffany. Sir Thomas Gainsborough dies at London August 2 at age 61.

Wolfgang Amadeus Mozart at Salzburg composes his three greatest symphonies, but none is performed (*see* 1791).

England's Marylebone Cricket Club is founded and codifies the rules of a game played since the 16th century if not longer (*see* 1787; baseball, 1839).

French wheat prices soar as drought reduces the harvest. Grain reserves are depleted as a result of last year's edict permitting grain producers to sell without restriction, but grain exports are suspended by Jacques Necker (above), who is made secretary general and virtual premier. Necker requires that all grain be sold in the open market once again to allay suspicions that the endless line of heavy carts seen to be carrying grain and flour are bound for ports to be shipped abroad.

Most Frenchmen remain convinced that the king has an interest in the Malisset company he has entrusted with victualling Paris and that the king and the aristocracy are profiting at the people's expense. Wagons in transit are in many cases seized by hungry peasants and townspeople even when escorted in large convoys, and people starve as farmers resist bringing their grain to market lest it be commandeered.

1789 The French Revolution that begins with the tennis court oath June 20 follows widespread rioting triggered by rumors that the nobility and the clergy (the first and second estates) have plotted to collect all the nation's grain and ship it abroad. Jacques Necker has ordered requisitioning of all grain in April to assure fair distribution, he has convened the Estates-General for the first time since 1614, but there are rumors that the first and second estates intend to disrupt the Estates-General and to starve the people.

The Estates-General calls itself the National Assembly beginning June 17, its meetings are suspended June 20, and its members repair to a neighboring tennis court where they take an oath not to split up until they have given France a constitution. They elect Count Honoré de Mirabeau, 40, to head the assembly, and some members of the nobility and clergy join the bourgeois third estate in the assembly, but the king dismisses Jacques Necker July 11, he concentrates troops near Paris, and there are rumors that he will dissolve the assembly.

Members of the third estate attack the Bastille prison at Paris July 12, the Bastille falls July 14, and the revolutionists overthrow the regime of Louis XVI, maintaining the monarchy in name only.

The National Assembly recalls Jacques Necker, it names General Lafayette commander of the new National Guard, and it adopts the *tricoleur* as the flag of France.

The French nobility begins to emigrate as peasants rise against their feudal lords.

The guillotine proposed to the National Assembly by Paris physician Joseph Ignace Guillotin, 51, is a beheading machine originally called a louisette after Dr. Antoine Louis (who did not invent it any more than did Guillotin). A deputy of the Estates-General who was the first to demand a doubling of third estate representatives, Guillotin says, "My victim will feel nothing but a slight sense of refreshing coolness on the neck. We cannot make too much haste, gentlemen, to allow the nation to enjoy this advantage."

A Paris mob riots from October 5 to 6 and a revolutionary band, mostly women, marches to Versailles. General Lafayette rescues the royal family and moves it to Paris.

The price of bread reached 4.5 sous per pound at Paris in July, and in some places it is 6 sous per pound. Widespread unemployment has reduced the people's ability to avoid starvation, but the National Assembly permits duty-free grain imports to relieve the hunger.

The Austrian Netherlands (Belgian provinces) declare their independence from Vienna. The Holy Roman Emperor Josef II has ordered peasants to pay more than 12 percent of the value of their land in taxes to the state, plus nearly 18 percent to their feudal landlords.

North Carolina ratifies the Constitution to become the 12th state of the Union.

The House of Representatives holds its first meeting April 1.

George Washington takes office April 30 at New York's Federal Hall to begin the first of two terms as first president of the United States, taking care not to set any unfortunate precedents.

The Declaration of the Rights of Man adopted by the French assembly (above) declares that man has "natural and imprescribable rights. These rights are liberty, property, personal security, and resistance to oppression...." "No one may be accused, imprisoned, or held under arrest except in such cases and in such a way as is prescribed by law...." "Every man is presumed innocent until he is proved guilty...." "Free expression of thought and opinion is one of the most precious rights of mankind: every citizen may therefore speak, write, and publish freely...." "Since the ownership of property is a sacred and inviolable right, no person may be deprived of his property except with legal sanction and in the public interest, after a just indemnity has been paid...."

Planters in Saint Domingue on the Caribbean island of Hispaniola send delegates to the National Assembly in Paris demanding freedom to deal with the colony's affairs without interference. Saint Domingue has 480,000 slaves and is the envy of the Caribbean, but the revolutionists at Paris are not sympathetic to the slave-owning pressure group (see 1791).

Jamaica has 211,000 slaves, up from 40,000 a century ago. Britain's House of Commons hears from William Wilberforce that one third of the African slaves landed in the West Indies die within a few months of arrival, many of them by suicide (see 1787; 1791).

💲 Streetwalkers are banned in Japan and prostitutes at Edo are required to move into the Yoshiwara section established in 1617. Some 2,000 move into the area within a few days (mixed bathing is also prohibited, and public bath houses separate men from women).

A customs house opens at New York and levies duties of $145,329 its first year. The figure will grow to more than $0.3 billion in 165 years as New York becomes the major port of entry.

"Nothing is certain but death and taxes," writes Benjamin Franklin in a letter to a French acquaintance.

🧪 *Elements of Chemistry* (*Traité elementaire de chimi*) by Antoine Lavoisier is the first modern chemical textbook. Lavoisier lists 23 elements but includes as an inorganic element a substance he calls caloric (heat) (see 1784; 1794).

Zirconium is discovered by German chemist Martin Heinrich Klaproth, 46.

Genera Plantarum by French botanist Antoine Laurent de Jussieu, 41, improves on the Linnaean system of 1737 and begins the modern classification of plants.

⚕ Hookworm (*Haakenwurm*) gets its name in a report by a German zoologist named Froelich who has discovered a hairlike parasitic worm in the intestine of a fox (see Goeze, 1782). Froelich notes curious hooklike structures in the worm's tail, and he assigns it to a new genus which he establishes under the name *Uncinaria* (see Ashford, 1899).

🌸 England's textile technology is transplanted to the United States by Derbyshire technician Samuel Slater, 21, who has spent 6½ years as apprentice to a partner of Richard Arkwright and who is familiar also with the cotton-spinning inventions of James Hargreaves and Samuel Crompton (see 1769; 1770; 1779). Slater has posed as a common laborer to deceive English emigration inspectors, he arrives at Providence, Rhode Island, he contracts with the firm of Almy and Brown to construct machinery from plans he has committed to memory, and he will father the American factory system (see 1790).

☀ Rochester, N.Y., is founded by Yankee miller Ebenezer Allen, who settles in a swamp on the bank of the Genesee River at the point where it empties into Lake Ontario.

🎓 The University of North Carolina founded at Chapel Hill is the first U.S. state university.

Georgetown University has its beginnings in a Roman Catholic college founded by John Carroll, first archbishop of Baltimore. The Jesuit school will be prominent for its School of Foreign Service.

🖊 *An Introduction to the Principles of Morals and Legislation* by English barrister Jeremy Bentham, 41, expounds the basic ethical doctrine of "the greatest happiness of the greatest number" as the chief object of all conduct and legislation. Bentham returned last year from a visit to his younger brother Samuel, a naval architect in the service of Russia's Catharine the Great, and he suggests that the morality of actions is determined by utility, meaning the capacity for rendering pleasure or preventing pain. He takes his key phrase from clergyman-chemist Joseph Priestley, who used it in his 1768 "Essay on the First Principles of Government" (see 1774; Owen, 1809).

Poetry *Songs of Innocence* by English artist-poet William Blake, 32, includes "The Lamb" and is illustrated by Blake with water-colored etchings.

⏱ Pear's Soap is introduced by London soapmaker Pear.

🌿 The first known American advertisement for tobacco appears with a picture of an Indian smoking a long clay pipe while leaning against a hogshead marked "Best Virginia." The advertisement has been placed by Peter and George Lorillard whose father Pierre was killed by Hessian troops in the Revolution (see 1760; 1911).

▦ Sailors aboard H.M.S. *Bounty* bound for the West Indies with breadfruit plants mutiny April 28 in protest against being deprived of water that is being lavished on the plants (see 1787). Having spent 23 idyllic weeks on Tahiti, the mutineers, led by master's mate Fletcher Christian, cast Captain Bligh adrift in a 22-foot open boat with 18 men near the island of Tofau, they return to Tahiti for native brides, and Christian establishes a colony on the desolate 1.75-square-mile Pitcairn Island southeast of Tahiti where the group of 9 mutineers, 6 Tahitian men, and 13 women will remain undiscovered until

1789 (cont.) 1808. Bligh reaches Timor in the East Indies after a 45-day voyage across 3,600 miles of open sea in which he loses 7 of his 18 men (the mutineers will burn the *Bounty* January 23 of next year) (*see* 1791).

The Pantheon is completed in Paris as a monument to Saint Genevieve. Begun in 1764 by the late Louis XV, it was designed by the late architect Jacques Germain Soufflot who had seen the Pantheon of Agrippa in Rome.

The first movable-frame beehive is constructed by Swiss naturalist François Huber, 39, who has discovered the aerial impregnation of the queen bee and the killing of males by worker bees. Huber is nearly blind, but his wife, his son, and a servant have helped him to study the life and habits of honeybees (*see* Langstroth, 1851).

Traité sur la culture et les usages des pommes de terre by Antoine-August Parmentier at Paris instructs readers on how to cultivate potatoes and cook them (*see* 1785; Tuileries gardens, 1793).

"I am so antiquated as still to dine at four," writes English author Horace Walpole, now 72, but most English people are now dining at five or six o'clock (*see* Peel, 1829).

The first bourbon whiskey is distilled by Baptist minister Elijah Craig in the bluegrass country established as Kentucky County last year by the Virginia state assembly. The territory will become Bourbon County in the state of Kentucky, and Craig's corn whiskey is so refined that it will become more popular than rum or brandy in America (*see* tax, 1791; Whiskey Rebellion, 1794).

Nine out of 10 Americans are engaged in farming and food production (*see* 1820).

1790 The Holy Roman Emperor Josef II dies February 20 at age 48, 3 weeks after withdrawing all his reforms. He is succeeded by his 42-year-old brother, who will reign until 1792 as Leopold II.

France's Louis XVI accepts the constitution drafted by French revolutionists in the Festival of the Champs de Mars.

Belgians revolt against the new emperor Leopold (above), who threatens to cede the Austrian Lowlands to France if Britain supports the revolution. William Pitt yields to the pressure and refuses to recognize Belgian independence, and the Austrians suppress the revolt at Brussels.

The British make an alliance with the nizam of Hyderabad and a third Mysore War begins.

Benjamin Franklin dies at Philadelphia April 17 at age 84, and Philadelphia becomes the capital of the United States in August.

Rhode Island ratifies the Constitution May 29 and becomes the 13th state of the Union.

A new U.S. national capital site on the banks of the Potomac near the Maryland town of George Town is selected by Secretary of the Treasury Alexander Hamilton, who resolves a dispute between North and South. The Resident Act passed by Congress July 16 confirms Hamilton's choice and calls for a new federal city to be designed and laid out on the site. President Washington appoints French-American engineer Pierre Charles L'Enfant, 35, who has served in the Continental army, to design the city with a Capitol to be built on an 85-foot hill. Secretary of State Thomas Jefferson names as chief surveyor Andrew Ellicott, 36, of Maryland, who has helped continue the Mason and Dixon line of 1767, and Ellicott is helped in his task by astronomer-surveyor Benjamin Banneker.

Cincinnati gets its name as the 2-year-old town of Losantiville on the Ohio River is renamed by the Northwest Territory's first governor General Arthur St. Clair, who calls it Cincinnati after the Society of Cincinnati formed by officers of the Continental army at the end of the Revolution (*see* 458 B.C.).

The first successful U.S. cotton mill is established at the falls of the Blackstone River at what later will be called Pawtucket, R.I. Samuel Slater and ironmaster David Wilkinson set up a mill that operates satisfactorily after a correction is made in the slope of the carder teeth (*see* 1789; 1793; Whitney, 1792).

A patent office to protect inventors and give them an incentive to develop new machines and methods is established by Congress April 10. The legislation is enacted at the insistence of inventor James Stevens of 1788 steam boiler fame who wants protection.

The first U.S. patent is awarded July 1 to Vermont inventor Samuel Hopkins for an improved method of "making Pot-ash and Pearl-ash" (*see* 1792).

Newburyport, Mass. inventor Jacob Perkins, 24, invents a nail cutter and header that is effective in a single operation (*see* 1834). Nails are so costly that when a building burns down, the nails are carefully salvaged.

Some 200 English spinning mills now use the patented Arkwright frame of 1769, but France has at most only eight mills using the water frame, and the few steam engines being used in France are almost all of the crude Newcomen variety (*see* 1705).

France's revolutionary government acts to revive trade that has stagnated as a result of businessmen, capital, and gold fleeing the country. The government prints *assignats*—paper money issued against the security of public lands confiscated from noblemen who have emigrated—and the new paper money stimulates production for a while and revives employment (but *see* 1796).

A French committee to standardize measurements is established by the 124-year-old Paris Academy of Sciences at the request of Charles Maurice de Talleyrand-Perigord, 36, bishop of Autun and a member of the National Assembly. The committee includes the chemist Antoine Lavoisier and it works to institute a uniform system at a time when a meter measures 100 centimeters at Paris, 98 at Marseilles, 102 at Lille, and 96 at Bordeaux (*see* 1791).

Abolish slavery in the French colonies, English abolitionist Thomas Clarkson urges the revolutionists at Paris (*see* 1787; 1794).

French Jews gain a grant of civil liberties.

The Indian Nonintercourse Act passed by Congress forbids taking of lands from Indian tribes without congressional approval, but Maine, Massachusetts, and other states will continue to take Indian lands without such approval.

Virginia's slave population reaches 200,000, up from over 100,000 in 1756.

Boston sea captain Robert Gray brings his *Columbia* back to port after a 3-year voyage round the world and enriches the ship's seven stockholders, who include architect Charles Bulfinch and merchant John Derby. News that furs acquired for trinkets from Indians on the northwest American coast fetch high prices at the Chinese river marts of Canton begins a large triangular maritime trade. Boston merchants will ship cargoes of cloth, clothing, copper, and iron to the Columbia River to be bargained for furs and to the Sandwich Islands for sandalwood (*see* 1791). The sea captains will sell the cargoes at Canton and will return round the Cape of Good Hope with Chinese porcelains, teas, and textiles. In another triangular trade, the Bostonians will exchange West Indian sugar for Russian iron and linens.

Painting *Queen Charlotte* and *Miss Farren* (actress Elizabeth Farren, 29) by English painter Thomas Lawrence, 21, who has received almost no formal education or artistic training except for a few lessons with Joshua Reynolds; *Lady Raeburn* and *Sir John and Lady Clerk* by "the Scottish Reynolds" Henry Raeburn, 34.

First performances Concerto for Pianoforte and Orchestra in D major (*Coronation*) by Wolfgang Amadeus Mozart 10/9 at Frankfurt-am-Main for the coronation of Leopold II (above); Concerto No. 19 for Pianoforte and Orchestra in F major by W. A. Mozart 10/15 at Frankfurt-am-Main.

Pineapples are introduced into the Sandwich Islands (Hawaii; *see* 1778; first pineapple cannery, 1892).

The world's first carbonated beverage company is started at Geneva by Swiss entrepreneur Jacob Schweppe in partnership with Jacques and Nicholas Paul (*see* Priestley, 1767; Bergman, 1770). The partnership will dissolve within a few years, and Schweppe will move to London. He will open an establishment at 11 Margaret Street, Cavendish Square, to sell through chemists (pharmacists) his Schweppe's soda water in rounded-ended "drunken" bottles, so made in order to keep their corks damp and thus prevent the gas from escaping. Schweppe will take three Jerseymen into partnership and in 1799 will sell half his 25 percent interest to a jeweler and will retire to Geneva (*see* 1851).

England now eats off Wedgwood porcelain (*see* 1769), and the food eaten now includes cheddar cheese imported from the United States.

The population of the United States reaches 3,929,000; 95 percent of it is rural, and population density is between four and five people per square mile.

1791 The French National Assembly elects the comte de Mirabeau president but he dies April 2 at age 42. His death weakens support for the monarchy.

Louis XVI flees with his family to the northeast frontier to gain the protection of loyalist troops, but he is thinly disguised and is recognized June 22. Revolutionist Jean Baptiste Drouet, 28, sees the king at Sainte-Menehould in Lorraine, he crosses the Argonne Forest and alerts the townspeople of Verennes-en-Argonne, five National Guardsmen and a few townspeople arrest Louis June 25, and they return him to Paris with Marie Antoinette and his children.

British orator Edmund Burke criticizes the French Revolution and Thomas Paine answers him with the pamphlet *The Rights of Man.* Paine had returned to his native England 4 years ago to sell a pierless iron bridge he designed, he will enlarge upon his pamphlet next year to urge the overthrow of the British monarchy, British authorities will indict him for treason, he will escape to France, and the French will make him an honorary citizen.

Louis XVI accepts the constitution September 14, France annexes Avignon and Venaissin, and the National Assembly dissolves September 30 after voting that no member shall be eligible for election to the next assembly.

The Society of United Irishmen is founded to agitate for independence from Great Britain by revolutionists whose leadership includes Theobald Wolfe Tone, 28, Thomas Russell, 24, and James Napper Tandy, 51 (*see* 1796).

A new Polish constitution put through by patriots May 3 coverts Poland's elective monarchy into an hereditary monarchy. Frederick Augustus III of Saxony is offered the Polish throne but he declines, and the new constitution is resisted by Russia (*see* 1793).

The Canada Act passed by the British Parliament June 10 takes effect December 26 and divides Canada at the Ottawa River into Upper Canada (which is mainly English) and Lower Canada (mainly French) with two governors and two elected assemblies (*see* Act of Union, 1840).

Vermont is admitted to the Union as the 14th state. Created from parts of New Hampshire and New York, the new state will soon be the nation's leading sheep raiser.

Blacks born of free parents in the French West Indies gain voting rights and the same privileges as all French citizens. The National Assembly at Paris (above), rejects pleas from French Caribbean colo-

Eli Whitney's cotton gin made short-staple cotton profitable and increased demand for plantation slave labor.

nists, but Saint Domingue's 30,000 white colonists refuse to obey the assembly's decree and prepare to secede as the colony's 480,000 blacks and 24,000 mulattoes grow restless.

Free blacks and mulattoes at Saint Domingue revolt to obtain the rights they have been granted (above), and within a few months some 2,000 whites have been killed along with 10,000 blacks and mulattoes. Sugar plantations are burned but only after 70,000 tons of sugar have been produced (see 1792).

A motion by William Wilberforce to prevent further importation of slaves into the British West Indies fails by a 188 to 163 vote in the House of Commons, which has been prejudiced by the slave insurrection at Saint Domingue (above) and by similar revolts in Martinique and on the British island of Dominica (see 1823; 1833; Wilberforce, 1789).

More humane treatment of the insane is advocated by French physician Philippe Pinel, 46, in Traité Medico-Philosophique sur l'Alienation Mentale.

The Bill of Rights becomes U.S. law December 15 as Virginia ratifies the first 10 amendments to the Constitution drawn up in 1787. Freedom of religion, freedom of speech, freedom of the press, the right of peaceable assembly, and the right to petition the government for a redress of grievances are all guaranteed under the First Amendment; the right to keep and bear arms is guaranteed under the Second Amendment; quartering of soldiers without consent is forbidden by the Third Amendment; unreasonable searches and seizures are forbidden by the Fourth Amendment; legal rights of life, liberty, and property are established by the Fifth Amendment, which says that no person "shall be compelled in any criminal case to be a witness against himself"; rights of accused persons in criminal cases are protected by the

Sixth Amendment; trial by jury is guaranteed by the Seventh Amendment; excessive bail, excessive fines, and cruel and unusual punishment are prohibited by the Eighth Amendment; rights not enumerated in the Constitution are protected by the Ninth Amendment; "The powers not delegated to the United States by the Constitution, nor prohibited by it to the States, are reserved to the States respectively, or to the people," says the Tenth Amendment.

The Columbia River is discovered and is named after his ship *Columbia* by Boston shipmaster-explorer Robert Gray, who last year completed a round-the-world voyage and embarked a month later on a second such voyage. U.S. claims to Oregon territory will be based on Gray's discoveries (see Cook, 1778).

Odessa is founded by Russian pioneers on the Black Sea.

Captain William Bligh sails for Tahiti once again to obtain breadfruit (see 1789). Bligh has returned from the East Indies to England and he sails now on H.M.S. *Providence* to complete the mission he began in 1787 (see 1792; 1793).

U.S. privateer Joseph Peabody settles at Salem, Mass., after having amassed a fortune. Peabody starts a shipping business that will soon own 83 vessels, employ 7,000 sailors, and trade with Calcutta, Canton, St. Petersburg, and dozens of other world ports.

A steamboat patent is issued to John Fitch (see 1787), but the wreck of his fourth vessel in a storm next year will discourage financial backers, and Fitch will move to Kentucky (see Stevens, 1802; Fulton, 1807).

The first Bank of the United States receives a 20-year charter from Congress and succeeds the Bank of North America chartered at the end of 1781. The new bank has an initial capital of $10 million provided largely by private investors who buy stock with bonds they had acquired under a funding plan devised by Treasury Secretary Alexander Hamilton.

A "Report on Manufactures" prepared by Secretary Hamilton (above) with the help of Philadelphian Tenche Cox lists 17 viable industries in the new republic but makes no mention of milling, although flour has long been a major U.S. export.

The Leblanc process for making soda (sodium carbonate) for French glassmakers is perfected by French chemist Nicolas Leblanc, 49, in response to a 1784 prize offer of 12,000 francs by the French Academy for a substitute for the soda imported from Spain. Spanish soda is obtained from the ashes of burned seaweed, but Leblanc obtains it by treating salt (sodium chloride) with sulfuric acid to produce salt cake (sodium sulfate) which he roasts with charcoal and chalk to produce a black ash from which he dissolves out and crystallizes calcium carbonate (see Solvay process, 1863).

A General Commission of Weights and Measures is set up by the French National Assembly to "bring to an end the astounding and scandalous diversity in our measures." The Academy of Sciences committee established last year has advised the assembly to establish a natural standard for the *metre* (meter, from the Greek word for measure), making it one ten-millionth part of a quadrant of the earth's circumference, and the committee has urged that the gram be standardized at 1 cubic centimeter of water at 4° Centigrade (*see* 1799; 1801).

Titanium is discovered in the mineral ilmenite (or menaccanite) by English clergyman-chemist-mineralogist William Gregor, 30, at Manaccan in Cornwall and is isolated for the first time.

The shortage of trained French physicians that will result from the closing of the nation's universities (*see* below) will lead to a restructuring of a late 17th-century institution to create the modern medical clinic. The clinics will advance medical knowledge by applying observations gained in actual practice to modify dusty textbook theories.

New York Hospital is founded by a group whose leader is George Washington's personal physician Samuel Bard, 49, who helped establish the medical school at King's College (Columbia) in 1767. Bard was a Loyalist during the Revolution but he remained in New York after the British evacuated the city late in 1783, and he stood up to the mob in the riots of 1788, throwing open his windows, placing himself in full view of the crowd, and remaining unmolested while other physicians hid in fear for their lives.

France's revolutionaries close the nation's "Gothic universities and aristocratic academies" in order to open the learned professions to competition, experiment, and the unobstructed flow of ideas.

The University of Vermont is founded at Burlington.

The *Observer* begins publication at London December 5 with quotations from Doctor Johnson and with a motto promising that the paper will be "unbiased by prejudice, uninfluenced by party ... and delivered with the utmost dispatch." The weekly will gain wide readership with its accounts of sensational trials (*see* Astor, 1911).

Biography *The Life of Samuel Johnson* by James Boswell, who credits the late "Great Cham of Literature" with such lines as "No nation was ever hurt by luxury; for it can reach but to a very few" (4/13/73); "Patriotism is the last refuge of the scoundrel" (4/7/75); "Hell is paved with good intentions" (4/14/75); "When a man is tired of London he is tired of life; for there is in London all that life can afford" (9/20/77).

Fiction *Justine* by French pervert Donatien Alphonse François de Sade, 51, the marquis de Sade who has been confined for much of his life in prisons, partly for using Spanish fly made from the pulverized bodies of the blister beetle *Lytta vesicatoria* which irritates the bladder and urethra. Sexual gratification by inflicting pain on a loved one is described by the marquis in his obscene novel and will be called "sadism" (*see* "Masochisim," 1874).

Poetry "Tam O'Shanter" by Robert Burns appears in the March issue of the *Edinburgh Magazine;* "Lines Written for a School Declamation" by English schoolboy David Everett: "You'd scarce expect one of my age/ To speak in public on the stage;/ And if I chance to fall below/ Demosthenes or Cicero,/ Don't view me with a critic's eye,/ But pass my imperfections by./ Large streams from little fountains flow,/ Tall oaks from little acorns grow."

Opera *Cosi fan tutte (Women Are Like That)* 1/26 at Vienna's Burgtheater, with music by Wolfgang Amadeus Mozart; *La Clemenza di Tito* 9/6 at the Prague Theater, with music by W. A. Mozart, libretto from the Pierre Corneille play *Cinna* of 1640; *The Magic Flute (Die Zauberflöte)* 9/30 at Vienna's Theater auf der Wieden, with music by W. A. Mozart.

First performances Concerto No. 27 for Pianoforte and Orchestra in B flat major by Wolfgang Amadeus Mozart 3/4 at Vienna. Mozart completes the motet *Ave verum Corpus,* a Quintet for Strings in E flat major, and other works. He completes a Concerto for Clarinet and Orchestra in A major September 28, but he dies of typhoid fever December 5 at age 35 with his Requiem still incomplete. The three great Mozart symphonies No. 39 in E flat major, No. 40 in G minor, and No. 41 in C major *(Jupiter)*, all written in 1788 during a space of less than 2 months, remain unperformed (*see* Kochel listings, 1862). Symphony No. 93 in D minor and Symphony No. 96 in D major *(Miracle)* by Joseph Haydn 3/11 at London's Hanover Square Rooms, in a concert conducted by German-born London conductor Johann Peter Salomon, who has invited Haydn to England where the composer will write and conduct six new symphonies this year.

Berlin's Brandenburg Gate (Brandenburger Tör) is completed by Prussian architect Carl Gotthard Langhaus, 59, at the end of the Unter den Linden nearly a mile from the royal palace. Langhaus has copied the Propylaea at Athens.

The Dublin Customs House is completed on the north bank of the Liffey by Irish architect James Gandon, 48.

Venice's island of San Giorgio gets a new campanile (belltower) designed by Bologna architect Benedetto Buratti.

The Cabinet-Maker and Upholsterer's Drawing Book by London furniture maker Thomas Sheraton, 40, advocates a style more severe than those of Chippendale and Hepplewhite (*see* 1749).

France has famine which the Legislative Assembly has little power to relieve.

British landowners and farmers protest the low duty on grain imports which are depressing their prices.

1791 (cont.) Parliament responds by raising the domestic price level at which imports are permitted (*see* 1773; 1797).

The first U.S. crop report is prepared by President Washington in response to letters from England's *Annals of Agriculture* editor Arthur Young, 50, who has written to ask what crops are produced on American farms, what the crops are worth, and so forth. Washington has conducted a personal survey by mail and has compiled the results, giving all prices in English pounds but providing a conversion ratio (the dollar is worth 7 shillings 6 pence).

Congress imposes a 9 cent per gallon tax on whiskey to discourage frontier farmers, blacksmiths, and storekeepers from diverting grain needed for food to use as distillery mash (and from competing with rum made in New England distilleries) (*see* Craig, 1789; Whiskey Rebellion, 1794).

An "automated mill" in which power that turns the millstones also conveys wheat (grist) to the top of the mill is patented by Oliver Evans (*see* 1787; 1797).

Camembert cheese is invented, or reinvented, by French farmer's wife Marie Fontaine Harel at Vimoutiers in the Department of Orne. The cheese will be packed in light rounded wooden boxes invented by a M. Ridel whose boxes will permit the fragile cheese to be shipped abroad and to achieve worldwide fame.

"Increase the quantity of food, or where that is limited, prescribe bounds to population," writes Joseph Townsend in *A Journey Through Spain in the Years 1786 and 1787* (*see* 1785). "In a fully peopled country, to say, that no one shall suffer want is absurd. Could you supply their wants, you would soon double their numbers, and advance your population *ad infinitum.* . . . It is indeed possible to banish hunger, and to supply that want at the expense of another; but then you must determine the proportion that shall marry, because you will have no other way to limit the number of your people. No human efforts will get rid of this dilemma; nor will men ever find a method, either more natural, or better in any respect, than to leave one appetite to regulate another" (*see* 1798).

1792 Eli Whitney invents a cotton "gin" that will revolutionize the economies of the United States and Britain. Just out of Yale, the 27-year-old mechanical genius has been visiting at Mulberry Grove on the Savannah River, the Georgia plantation of Katherine Greene, widow of General Nathanael Greene who died 6 years ago at age 43. She met Whitney aboard ship while he was en route to the Carolinas for a tutoring position, she has invited him to Mulberry Grove, and he has observed that upland short-staple cotton has green seeds that are difficult to separate from the lint, quite unlike the long-staple sea-island cotton whose black seeds are easily separated and which has long been a staple of American commerce.

The simple cylinder produced by Eli Whitney (above) contains teeth made of bird cage wire bent and pointed into the shape of sawteeth, each circle of teeth moving in a slot slightly smaller than a cotton seed. When the cylinder is turned, the teeth carry the cotton through the slot, leaving the seeds behind, and a slave can clean 50 pounds of green-seed cotton per day instead of 1 pound—a great advance over the "churka" used in India since 300 B.C. to clean cotton at a rate of 5 pounds per day.

U.S. cotton production will rise from 140,000 pounds in 1791 to 35 million pounds in 1800 as the efficiency of the Whitney cotton gin leads to rapid growth of cotton planting in the South and to a boom in Northern and English cotton mills (*see* Lowell, 1812).

The increased planting of cotton (above) will bring an increased demand for slave labor (*see* 1782; 1803).

Denmark abandons the slave trade and becomes the first nation to do so (*see* Sweden, 1813).

English historian Edward Gibbon writes to Lord Sheffield to approve of the vote against slavery by the House of Commons, but he expresses a fear: "If it [the vote] proceeded only from an impulse of humanity, I cannot be displeased. . . . But in this rage against slavery, in the numerous petitions against the slave trade, was there no leaven of new democratical principles? No wild ideas of the rights and natural equality of man? It is these I fear" (*see* Paine, 1791).

Vindication of the Rights of Women by English feminist Mary Wollstonecraft, 33, is published at London. It is a blunt attack on conventions.

Paris sends an army to restore order in Saint Domingue, but the military commanders take the side of the slaves and support emancipation (*see* 1791; 1794).

The Holy Roman Emperor Leopold II dies suddenly March 1 at age 44 and is succeeded by his 24-year-old son, who will reign as the last Holy Roman Emperor Francis II until 1806 and then as the first Austrian emperor Francis I until 1835.

A Swedish assassin shoots Gustavus III in the back March 16 at a midnight masquerade at the Stockholm opera house, and the king dies March 29 at age 46 after a 21-year reign. His 13-year-old son succeeds to the throne and will reign as Gustavus IV until his forced abdication in 1809.

Austria and Prussia form an alliance against France, partly at the instigation of émigré French noblemen, and France declares war on Austria April 20.

Three French armies commanded by Lafayette, Rochambeau, and the 70-year-old Marshal Nicolas Luckner suffer reverses. The Legislative Assembly announces July 11 that the nation is in danger.

A Parisian mob storms the Tuileries Palace August 10 at the instigation of Georges Jacques Danton, 33, after Louis XVI orders his Swiss guard to stop firing on the people. The mob massacres some 600 guardsmen, the king is confined in the Temple, and the Paris commune takes power under Danton.

The French National Assembly declares General Lafayette a traitor August 19, he flees to Liége where the Austrians take him prisoner. The Prussians take Verdun August 20, but the revolutionary armies gain their first triumph a month later by defeating the Prussians at the Battle of Valmy, a fog-shrouded artillery duel that comes less than 2 weeks after the massacres at Paris.

The French National Convention meets September 21 and abolishes the monarchy, it decrees perpetual banishment for French émigrés, and it declares September 22 the first day of the Year One for the new French Republic.

French forces under Adam Philippe, 53, comte de Custine, rout the Prussians to take Mainz and Frankfurt-am-Main. Another French army takes Brussels and the Austrian Lowlands before the Prussians retake Frankfurt.

The French National Convention issues a proclamation November 19 offering assistance to peoples of all nations who want to overthrow their governments.

Kentucky is admitted to the Union as the 15th state. It incorporates territory ceded by Virginia in 1781, and its name is from the Wyandot word meaning "plain."

$ France's Girondist government issues more paper *assignats* as the war with Austria and Prussia creates irresistible demands for more paper currency (*see* 1790). The new *assignats* fuel the nation's inflation, diminish the people's traditional thrift, and encourage loose luxury as money declines in value and incentives to save disappear (*see* 1796).

The Mint of the United States established by Congress April 2 begins decimal coinage of silver, gold, and copper at Philadelphia (*see* 1873).

The New York Stock Exchange has its origin in an agreement signed by local brokers who have been buying and selling securities under an old buttonwood tree and who now formalize methods by which they will do business (*see* 1825).

U.S. money markets collapse following the failure of some land companies organized by New York speculator William Duer of 1784 *Empress of China* fame. A former assistant secretary of the treasury, Duer has sought European capital for the settlement of lands in the Ohio Valley, his scheme fails, and New York investors and speculators lose some $5 million, an amount equal to the value of all the buildings in the city (Boston and Philadelphia sustain losses of $1 million each).

The Secretary of the Treasury Alexander Hamilton averts a U.S. economic depression. He supports the government's 6 percent bonds at par value.

Boston's State Street Bank is founded. Governor John Hancock signs the bank's charter June 3.

The Lancaster Road has its beginnings at the Philadelphia State House where some 5,000 investors meet and subscribe $30 each to buy shares in the toll road that will be the first major publicly financed U.S. turnpike (*see* 1794; Cumberland Road, 1811).

The Western Inland Lock Navigation Company is incorporated through efforts by General Philip Schuyler and Pittsfield, Mass., businessman Elkanah Watson, 34. The new company improves the channel of the Mohawk River that will be the basis of a great inland waterway (*see* 1815).

 An epidemic of dysentery halts Prussia's Friederich Wilhelm II in his march against France's revolutionary armies (above). He retreats across the Rhine with only 30,000 effectives, down from an original force of 42,000 counting Austrian allies.

An epidemic of bubonic plague in Egypt takes as many as 800,000 lives.

Smallpox strikes Boston; 8,000 volunteer for inoculation (*see* 1721; Jenner, 1796).

Poetry "Afton Water" and "Ye Flowery Banks O' Bonnie Doon" by Robert Burns appear in the *Scots Musical Museum* IV: "Flow gently, sweet Afton, among thy green braes...."

Sir Joshua Reynolds dies at London February 23 at age 68.

Opera *The Secret Marriage (Il Matrimonio Secreto)* 2/7 at Vienna's Burgtheater, with music by Italian composer Domenico Cimarosa, 43.

Venice's Teatro de la Fenice opens with 1,500 seats between the Canal della Verona and the Campo San Fantin.

First performances Symphony No. 94 in G major *(The Surprise)* by Joseph Haydn 3/23 at Vienna.

Anthem "La Marseillaise" by French army officer Rouget de Lisle, 32, who composes the song the night of April 24 at Strasbourg not as a revolutionary anthem but as a royalist patriotic song in support of the government that 4 days earlier declared war against the Holy Roman Emperor Francis II and Prussia's Friedrich Wilhelm II.

Popular song "Oh! Dear, What Can the Matter Be?" is published at London.

Duncan Phyfe sets up a New York joiner's shop that he will continue until his retirement in 1847. The 25-year-old Scots-American cabinetmaker begins producing mahogany chairs, tables, and couches that will make the name Duncan Phyfe as famous as the names Hepplewhite, Sheraton, and Chippendale (*see* 1749; 1791).

Wholesale destruction of U.S. forests is spurred by demand for pearlash in the baking industry (below).

English country gentleman Sir John Byng visits the North Country and writes, "Sir Richard Arkwright may have introduced Much Wealth into his Family,

1792 (cont.) and into his Country, but, as a Tourist, I execrate his Schemes, which have crept into every Pastoral Vale, have destroy'd the course, and Beauty of Nature" (*see* Arkwright, 1769). Byng calls Manchester a "dog's hole" full of "gloom and dirt" and says he "wander'd about Town till Dinner Time, without seeing anything that I should ever wish to see again."

 Tahitian breadfruit is loaded aboard the decks of H.M.S. *Providence* for planting in the Caribbean islands by Captain William Bligh (*see* 1791; 1793).

The *Farmer's Almanac* is founded by U.S. printer Robert B. Thomas who establishes a format that will be continued for at least 185 years.

 Some 8,000 tons of U.S. pearlash (potassium carbonate) for use in baking are exported to Britain and Europe (*see* Hopkins, 1790). Produced by burning wood, pearlash releases carbon dioxide in the dough baking in an oven, it causes the bread to rise, and it revolutionizes the baking industry.

The first U.S. cracker bakery opens at Newburyport, Mass., where baker Theodore Pearson specializes in making pilot's bread (ship's biscuit) (*see* Bent, 1801).

1793 France's Louis XVI goes to the guillotine January 21 in the Place de la Revolution that will later be the Place de la Concorde. The king has been tried before the convention which has declared him guilty by a vote of 683 to 38 and has voted that he be executed rather than imprisoned or banished.

The French republic declares war February 1 against Britain, Holland, and Spain, and she annexes the Belgian provinces. Britain, Holland, Spain, and the Holy Roman Empire join in an alliance against France with Savoy (Sardinia) which has been at war with the French since July of last year.

President Washington meets with department heads at his house February 25 in the first U.S. cabinet meeting. The secretaries of state, treasury, and war, the attorney general, and the postmaster general comprise the first cabinet.

A French Committee of Public Safety organized at Paris April 6 has dictatorial powers. Leaders of the *Comité du salut public* include Georges Jacques Danton and Maximilien François Marie Isidore de Robespierre, 34.

President Washington issues a Proclamation of Neutrality in the European war (above) April 22. He has resisted pressure from Alexander Hamilton to support the British and from Thomas Jefferson to support the French.

French Girondists attack the radical Jacobin Jean Paul Marat and bring him to trial. Acquitted April 24, Marat joins with Danton and Robespierre of the *Comité de salut public* in overthrowing the power of the Girondists, 31 Girondist deputies are arrested June 2, but patriot Charlotte Corday, 25, is horrified by the excesses of the Jacobin terrorists and stabs Marat to death in his bath July 13.

Prussian forces recover Mainz from the French after a 3-month siege, and the Allies take Conde and the Valenciennes. The French general Adam Philippe, comte de Custine, is accused of treason, a revolutionary tribunal finds him guilty, and he goes to the guillotine at Paris August 28 at age 53.

France begins a levy of all men capable of bearing arms August 23 as the Allies drive republican troops back on all fronts and as the British lay siege to Toulon. Fourteen new French armies succeed in taking Caen, Bordeaux, and Marseilles.

Lyons falls to the French republicans in October after a 2-month siege, the city is partially destroyed, and much of the population is massacred.

The Reign of Terror gathers force at Paris and elsewhere. Marie Antoinette goes to the guillotine October 16, some 15,000 are guillotined in 3 months at Nantes, and the 21 Girondist deputies arrested June 2 are guillotined October 31.

Jeanne Manon Philipon Roland, 39, goes to the guillotine November 8 and her Girondist husband Jean Marie Roland de La Platiere, 59, commits suicide a week later in Normandy at news of Mme. Roland's death. Her last words are reported to have been, "O Liberty! Liberty! how many crimes are committed in thy name!"

Napoleon Bonaparte gains prominence for the first time as the French take Toulon from the British in December. The 24-year-old artillery officer from Corsica has won the favor of Robespierre's brother and is put in charge of directing siege operations to recover Toulon from the British squadron that has come to the aid of the city whose people have rebelled against the convention. Bonaparte is promoted to general of brigade for his success.

Poland has been partitioned for a second time January 23 with Russia taking most of Lithuania and most of the western Ukraine including Podolia, and with Prussia taking Danzig, Thorn, and Great Poland. Russia has been given free entry for her troops in Poland plus the right to control Poland's foreign relations (*see* first partition, 1772; Kosciuszko, 1794).

Japan's Tokugawa shogun Ienari begins a personal reign of 45 years after a 6-year regency during which Matsudaira Sadanobu, now 34, has put through a series of reforms. Ienari's reign begins with the failure by Russian lieutenant Adam Laxman to establish friendly relations with Japan and will be marked by the collapse of military rule and the growth of extravagance and inefficiency in the Tokugawa court.

U.S. Secretary of State Thomas Jefferson suggests that the nation's sovereignty should extend offshore as far as cannonball range (*see* van Bynkershoek, 1702; Santiago Convention, 1952).

 The French republic imposes anti-inflation measures to avoid a catastrophic fall in the value of the *assignats* that have been issued since 1790. The government fixes wages, it establishes maximum prices for many commodities, and while there are frequent violations of the maximums, the new laws permit a rationing of goods and make it possible to provision the French republican armies (but *see* 1796).

France's Charles Maurice de Talleyrand voyages to America in order to flee the Reign of Terror. He speculates in land and prospers (*see* 1790; 1796).

Worship of God is abolished in France November 10 and a cult of reason is founded by Commune of Paris leaders Jacques René Hébert, 38, Pierre Gaspard Chaumette, 30, and Jean Baptiste du Val-de-Grace, 38, baron de Cloots. All will be guillotined next year.

Scots fur trader Alexander Mackenzie, 29, reaches the Pacific after the first crossing of the North American continent by a European. Mackenzie has been employed by the Northwest Fur Company since age 15, he discovered the river that will be called the Mackenzie 4 years ago, he has set out from Fort Chippewa, and he has sustained himself on his journey by eating pemmican (dried lean meat from a large game animal pounded to shreds and mixed thoroughly half and half with melted fat, bone marrow, and wild berries or cherries; the word "pemmican" comes from the Cree word for fat).

English navigator George Vancouver, 36, explores an island off the west coast of Canada that will bear his name (*see* Juan da Fuca, 1592).

Toronto has its origin in the frontier hamlet of York founded by Canadian Governor John Graves Simcoe, 41. The settlement will be renamed Toronto in 1834, and it will become the financial capital of Canada.

An epidemic of yellow fever kills 4,044 at Philadelphia in the worst health disaster ever to befall an American city. Brought to the capital aboard a ship from the West Indies, the fever strikes nearly all of the 24,000 citizens who do not flee, and kills one in every six despite homemade preventives that include cloth masks soaked in garlic juice, vinegar, or camphor; the victims turn yellow, run high fevers, hiccup, and vomit blood.

"An Account of the Success of the Bark of the Willow in the Cure of Agues" marks the beginning of knowledge of salicylic acid. London clergyman Edward Stone reads his paper to the Royal Society (*see* 1835; Gerhardt, 1853; Bayer, 1899).

The Fugitive Slave Act voted by Congress at Philadelphia February 12 makes it illegal for anyone to help a slave escape to freedom or to give a runaway slave refuge (*see* "Underground Railway," 1838).

Child labor is introduced by Samuel Slater at the first U.S. cotton mill. Slater operates the mill under the name Almy, Brown and Slater and finds it advantageous to use children because they have small hands.

A cotton thread is perfected by the wife of Samuel Slater (above) (*see* 1790; Lowell, 1812).

Plymouth, Conn., clockmaker Eli Terry, 21, goes into business for himself after 7 years of apprenticeship (*see* 1803).

A Sunday school to teach factory children simple writing and arithmetic is started by Samuel Slater (above).

Williams College is founded at Williamstown, Massachusetts. French is accepted for entrance in lieu of the classics.

Hamilton College is founded near Utica, N.Y., under the name Hamilton Oneida Academy. The founder is Samuel Kirkland, 52, a missionary to the Iroquois who was influential in obtaining a declaration of neutrality from the Six Nations at the outbreak of the American Revolution in 1775 and who names Alexander Hamilton as first trustee. The college will take Hamilton's name when it receives a charter in 1812.

The semaphore is developed as a visual telegraph system by French engineer Claude Chappe, 30, and his brother Ignace Urbain Jean, 33, who achieve their first success transmitting messages between Paris and Lille and who see their system adopted rapidly throughout the country (*see* Henry, 1831).

Enquiry Concerning Political Justice by English philosopher William Godwin, 37, restates the political tenets of the Enlightenment and begins to develop a system of philosophical anarchy.

Advice to the Privileged Orders by Connecticut Wit Joel Barlow is published at London as a reply to Edmund Burke's tract on the French Revolution and wins Barlow citizenship in France.

Poetry *Geschichte des Dreissigjahrigen Kreiges* by Friedrich von Schiller is published at Jena, where Schiller has been professor of history since 1789.

Painting *The Death of Marat* by Jacques Louis David, who has become an associate of Robespierre (above) and who helps abolish the Academy. Francisco Guardi dies at Venice January 1 at age 80.

The Louvre Palace begun at Paris in 1564 and still incomplete is opened to the public as an art museum (*see* 1624).

The French republic proclaims a new Revolutionary Calendar with twelve 30-month days beginning with the Year One of the revolution (September 22, 1792). The new months are Vendemiaire, Brumaire, Frimaire, Nivose, Pluviose, Ventose, Germinal, Floreal, Prairial, Messidor, Thermidor, and Fructidor, every tenth day is a holiday, and there are five *sans culottides* (intercalary) days.

Lansdown Crescent is completed at Bath to create a spectacular new English townscape.

French revolutionists turn the Tuileries gardens at Paris into a potato field. A French ordinance forbids consumption of more than 1 pound of meat per week on pain of death.

1793 (cont.) Britain suffers from lack of French food exports and establishes a Board of Agriculture to make "the principles of agriculture better known" and to increase domestic food production.

U.S. farmers export grain and other foodstuffs to Britain and the Continent as the European war booms demand (*see* 1804; 1806).

Breadfruit is planted in St. Vincent and in Jamaica, British West Indies, by Captain Bligh who also plants seedlings of *Blighia sapida* whose fruit (ackee) will become a Jamaican food staple (*see* 1792).

A process for obtaining sugar from beets is revealed by Berlin chemist Franz Karl Achard, 40 (*see* 1799; Marggraf, 1747; Delessert, 1810).

1794 Robespierre crushes his rivals at Paris and has Danton and the others guillotined between late March and early April. He ends the cult of reason, he establishes himself June 8 as high priest of a new Festival of the Supreme Being, and the Reign of Terror reaches its height in June and July.

The Law of 22 Prairial passed June 10 allows juries to convict without hearing evidence or argument. As many as 354 per month go to the guillotine, and opposition to Robespierre mounts.

Lord Richard Howe has defeated a French fleet off Ushant June 1, capturing nine French ships in the Channel and sinking a tenth, but the Battle of Fleurus June 26 ends in victory for the French. They force the duke of Coburg to withdraw from Belgium.

The conspiracy of 9 Thermidor (July 27) topples Robespierre from power. Moderates arrest him, his brother, and his associates Georges Couthon, 39, and Louis Antoine Leon de Saint-Just, 27. Supporters of Robespierre release him and his companions but they are taken by surprise July 28 at the Hotel de Ville and sent to the guillotine with 18 others. More than 80 of Robespierre's sympathizers go to the guillotine July 29 as opponents resist efforts to make France "a republic of virtue," but public opinion forces Robespierre's successors to end the Reign of Terror.

The Thermidoreans (moderates) close Jacobin clubs but readmit to the convention those Girondists who have escaped with their lives.

Polish revolutionists rise in March under the leadership of American Revolution veteran Tadeusz Kosciuszko, but they are no match for the Russian and Prussian forces sent to suppress the uprising (*see* partitions, 1793; 1795).

The Kajar dynasty that will rule Persia until 1925 is founded by Aga Mohammed, a brutal chieftain who takes power following the defeat and death of Lutf Ali Khan who has reigned since 1789 and whose death ends the Zand dynasty founded in 1750. Aga Mohammed will be crowned in 1796 and will reign until his assassination the following year.

The Whiskey Rebellion by U.S. frontier farmers brings the first show of power by the new U.S. government. The farmers have converted their grain into whiskey in order to transport it more efficiently to market, but they have resisted a cash excise tax imposed on whiskey, which is itself a medium of exchange in western Pennsylvania. Federal militiamen put down the rebellion without bloodshed.

The Battle of Fallen Timbers August 20 ends the Indian menace to American settlers in the Ohio-Kentucky region. British provocateurs have encouraged the Indians to attack the whites but U.S. General Anthony Wayne defeats the tribesmen.

Jay's Treaty signed November 19 settles outstanding disputes that remain between the United States and Britain. President Washington has sent U.S. Supreme Court Chief Justice John Jay to London, the British agree to evacuate their posts in the U.S. Northwest between the Great Lakes and the Ohio River, and the treaty will spur settlement in the area.

A modification of Jay's Treaty (above) permits U.S. ships to carry cocoa, coffee, cotton, molasses, and sugar from the British West Indies to any part of the world.

Insurance Company of North America is chartered at Philadelphia. It is the first U.S. commercial firm to offer life insurance policies, but its chief business is in fire and marine insurance.

Eli Whitney patents his 1792 cotton gin and sets up a company with Mrs. Nathanael Greene's second husband Phineas Miller to establish gins at central points for processing planters' green-seed cotton. But the patent is infringed, Whitney earns nothing from his cotton gin, and Miller loses a fortune trying vainly to fight patent infringers (*see* 1798).

The first U.S. national arsenals are established at Springfield, Mass., whose citizens were asked in 1776 to produce firearms for the Massachusetts Committee of Public Safety, and at Harper's Ferry, Virginia. The 1795 Springfield flintlock musket will be the first official U.S. weapon, and Springfield will become the small arms center of the world (*see* Springfield rifle, 1903; Harper's Ferry, 1859).

The slide-rest that will be an essential part of the modern lathe is invented in England by Joseph Bramah, or by his employee Henry Maudslay, 23, or by the two working together. The slide-rest is a saddle which moves the cutting tool horizontally along the work being turned.

Radial ball bearings for the axle bearings of carriages are patented by Welsh ironmaster Philip Vaughan at Carmarthen, but full development of ball bearings will await the invention of precise grinding machines that can produce accurately spherical metal balls.

The Lancaster Road opens to link the "bonnyclabber" Pennsylvania Dutch country and Lancaster with Philadelphia and the Delaware River (*see* 1792). Stockholders have subscribed $465,000 to finance the road and will receive such handsome dividends

—as high as 15 percent in some years—that their success will inspire similar toll road projects (*see* Cumberland Road, 1811).

U.S. citizens are forbidden by Congress March 22 to participate in slave trade with foreign nations.

English abolitionist Thomas Clarkson issues a pamphlet urging suppression of slavery.

The French Legislative Assembly frees slaves in all French colonies. The action comes in the midst of the Reign of Terror (above) and makes France the first nation to free her slaves (but *see* Bonaparte, 1802).

Haitian slaves in the French colony of Saint Domingue on Hispaniola rise under the leadership of Pierre Dominque Toussaint L'Ouverture, 51, Jean-Jacques Dessalines, 36, and Henri Christophe, 27. They lead 500,000 blacks and mulattoes against the colony's 40,000 whites (*see* 1802).

New York's Bellevue Hospital has its beginnings in a pesthouse for plague victims founded on an East River site called Belle Vue.

The École Normale is founded at Paris.

The École Polytechnique is the world's first technical college. It is founded by the revolutionary government to provide training for scientists with special emphasis on mathematics and applied science.

A museum for the popularization of science is started by Philadelphia portrait painter Charles Willson Peale, a veteran of the War of Independence who is well known for his nearly 60 portraits of George Washington based on 7 he has painted from life.

Bowdoin College is founded at Bowdoin, Maine. It is named in honor of the late Boston merchant James Bowdoin, who served as governor of Massachusetts from 1785 to 1787 but who died in 1790 at age 64.

The University of Tennessee has its beginnings in a college founded at Knoxville in the North Carolina region that will become a state in 1796.

The Age of Reason, Being an Investigation of True and Fabulous Theology by Thomas Paine is published in the first of its three parts. It is perceived as an attack on religion and alienates Paine's friends both in Europe and America; *Foundation of the Whole Theory of Science (Grundage der gesammten Wissenschaftslehre)* by German philosopher Johann Gottlieb Fichte, 32, at Jena departs from Kantian transcendentalism by replacing God with an Absolute Mind *(Ur-Ich),* or Primeval Self (*see* Kant, 1781).

Poetry "Scots Wha Hae" by Robert Burns is published May 8 in the *Morning Chronicle:* "Scots, wha hae wi' Wallace bled,/ Scots, wham Bruce has often led,/ Welcome to your gory bed,/ Or to victorie . . .": French poet André Marie de Chènier is guillotined July 25 at age 31; *Songs of Experience* by William Blake indicates the poet's disillusion with France and describes with stark simplicity the shattering of inno-

cence by man and society: "Tiger! Tiger! burning bright/ In the forests of the night,/ What immortal hand or eye/ Could frame thy fearful symmetry?"

Painting *The Declaration of Independence* by U.S. painter John Trumbull, 38, who served as an aide to George Washington and then as adjutant to General Gates in the Revolution, attained a colonelcy before he was 21, sailed to England in 1780 to study with Benjamin West, was imprisoned on suspicion of treason, began his large canvas in London 8 years ago, and returned to the United States in 1789 to continue work on the painting, which includes 48 portraits, two thirds of them painted from life.

Japanese Kabuki players portrayed by *ukiyoe* painter Toshūsai Sharaku are exhibited for the first time. Possibly a Nō actor, Sharaku has been discovered by the publisher Tsu.

French playwright-aphorist Sebastien Chamfort dies in agony April 13 at age 53 from wounds self-inflicted late last year in a suicide attempt as he was about to be arrested for his outspoken opinions during the Reign of Terror. Chamfort's *Tableaux de la revolution française* will be published posthumously, as will his *Maximes et pensées, Caractères,* and *Anecdotes.*

First performances Symphony No. 99 in E flat major by Joseph Haydn 2/10 at London's Hanover Square Rooms; Symphony No. 100 in E major (*Military*) by Joseph Haydn at London; Symphony No. 101 in D major (*The Clock*) by Joseph Haydn 3/3 at the King's Concert Hall, a new addition to the King's Theatre, London. Haydn has come to England as he did in 1791 and once again writes six new symphonies for J. P. Salomon in little more than a year's time.

Popular songs "The March of the Men of Harlech" ("Gorhoffedd Gwyr Harlech") is published without

Louis XVI went to the guillotine in the French Revolution's bloody Reign of Terror. Marie Antoinette soon followed.

353

1794 (cont.) words at London. The song was allegedly composed during a siege of the Welsh castle in the 15th century Wars of the Roses.

Belle Grove south of Middletown in Virginia's Shenandoah Valley is completed for James Madison's brother-in-law Major Isaac Hite, a rich farmer and entrepreneur. Thomas Jefferson has contributed to the design of the house with a T-shaped hall, fanlights over interior doors, and a detailed false door in the parlor to balance a real door.

The founder of nutritional science and of modern chemistry Antoine Lavoisier goes to the guillotine May 8 at age 50 in retribution for his direction of *l'ancien régime's* tax organization the *Fèrme General:* "La république n'a pas besoin de savants," says the vice president of the tribunal Coffinhall, but mathematician Joseph-Louis Lagrange says, "It required but a moment to sever that head, and perhaps a century will not be sufficient to produce another like it."

A British naval squadron tests the scurvy-prevention theories of James Lind, who dies July 13 at age 78 (*see* 1747; 1753). The squadron sails for Madras with its hatches full of lemons and arrives 23 weeks later with only one seaman suffering from scurvy (*see* 1795).

Napoleon Bonaparte offers a prize of 12,000 francs to anyone who can invent a means of preserving food for long periods of time so that France's military and naval forces may be supplied on long campaigns (*see* Appert, 1795).

A Boston restorator is opened at the corner of Milk and Congress Streets by French refugee Julien (Jean Baptiste Gilbert Playen) who will introduce Bostonians to cheese fondue, truffles from Perigord, and a clear soup so delicious that news of it soon reaches another French refugee who is living at Hartford. Gastronome Jean Anthelme Brillat-Savarin, 39, fled the Terror in 1792, he is supporting himself by giving violin lessons, and he journeys to Boston to sample consommé Julien and other examples of Julien's cuisine (*see* Brillat-Savarin, 1825).

1795 The French capture the Dutch fleet lying frozen in the Texel, Willem V takes refuge in England, and the French establish a Batavian republic as the White Terror rules Paris. The Batavian republic will continue until 1806.

The British begin seizing Dutch colonies including the Cape of Good Hope and Ceylon.

The Treaty of Basel March 5 removes Prussia from the war against France. Saxony, Hanover, and Hesse-Cassel soon follow the Prussian example.

The second Treaty of Basel June 22 gives Santo Domingo (Saint Domingue) to France and returns territory in Catalonia and Guipuizcoa to Spain.

The French Convention, threatened by a royalist revolt, calls upon the dissolute rake Paul François Jean Nicolas, 40, comte de Barras, to defend it. Barras met the Corsican artillery officer Napoleon Bonaparte during the siege of Toulon in 1793, he has installed his creole mistress Josephine in Bonaparte's bed, he gives Bonaparte and other Jacobin officers command of forces defending the convention, and Bonaparte drives the Paris mob from the streets with a "whiff of grapeshot" on "The Day of the Sections" October 5 (13 Vendemiaire).

The French Convention names Napoleon Bonaparte commander of the Armée d'Interieur for saving the Tuileries Palace with his artillery cannonade from the Church of St. Rochelle and giving the convention a victory. The convention dissolves October 26 after voting that relatives of émigrés may not hold office.

The Directory that will govern France until 1799 takes power following the dissolution of the convention (above). Most prominent of the five directors is the comte de Barras (above).

The Treaty of San Lorenzo (Pinckney's treaty) signed by U.S. Minister to Great Britain Thomas Pinckney October 27 with Spain permits U.S. ships to store cargo at New Orleans. Spain grants free navigation of the Mississippi.

Poland's Stanislas II Augustus abdicates at age 63 after a 31-year reign as Russia, Prussia, and Austria partition his anarchic country for a third time October 24. Russia takes the remainder of Lithuania and the Ukraine, Prussia takes Mazovia and its city of Warsaw, Austria obtains the remainder of the Cracow region north of the Vistula and east to the Bug.

Britain's House of Lords acquits Warren Hastings of charges of "high crimes and misdemeanours" while governor general of India from 1773 to 1785. His trial has lasted for 7 years, during which he has been made the scapegoat for the offenses of the East India Company and the expenses of the trial have ruined him financially.

Theory of the Earth by Scottish geologist James Hutton, 69, appears 1 year after his *Investigations of Principles of Knowledge* and pioneers scientific geology. Hutton will be credited with originating the modern theory of the formation of the earth's crust and proposing the doctrine of uniformitarianism.

A Treatise on the Epidemic Puerperal Fever by Aberdeen surgeon Alexander Gordon suggests that the fever is contagious: "By observation, I plainly perceived the channel by which it was propagated, and I arrived at that certainty in the matter, that I could venture to foretell what women would be affected with the disease upon hearing by what midwife they were to be delivered, or by what nurse they were to be attended, during their lying in; and almost in every instance, my prediction was verified" (*see* White, 1773; Holmes, 1842).

Milwaukee has its beginnings in a trading post on Lake Michigan established by the North West Company (*see* Juneau, 1818).

Oak Island off the coast of Nova Scotia becomes the focus of a pirate treasure hunt after three boys digging in a hollow beneath a tree discover a clay-lined shaft and dig down to find two oak log floorings, one below the other. Two of the three will resume excavations in 1804 and will find another oak log platform every 10 feet down to a depth of 98 feet, where they will hit something solid. They will also find a mass of coconut fiber, some charcoal, ship's putty, and a stone chiseled with strange symbols, but the shaft will flood and the pirate treasure, if any, will elude searchers for more than 170 years.

 Vermont judge Nathaniel Chipman argues the value of history that emphasizes social forces rather than military encounters.

Union University has its beginnings at Schenectady, New York.

The Hasty Pudding Society is founded at Harvard (see 1844).

The Institut National is founded at Paris to replace the academies closed in 1791.

 Nonfiction *Tableau historique des progres de l'esprit humain* by the late marquis de Condorcet gives a classic exposition of the idea of human progress and suggests the ultimate perfectability of mankind. Marie Jean Antoine Nicolas de Caritat, marquis de Condorcet, was arrested with other Girondists in the Reign of Terror, he died in prison March 28 of last year at age 50, and his work is published posthumously.

Fiction *Wilhelm Meisters Lehrjahre* by Johann Wolfgang von Goethe.

Painting *The Duchess of Alba* by Francisco de Goya; *Isabey and His Daughter* by French painter François Pascal Simon Gerard, 25, who has studied with Jacques Louis David; *Madame Seriziat and Her Daughter* by Jacques Louis David.

First performances Symphony No. 102 in B flat major by Joseph Haydn 2/2 at London; Concerto No. 2 in B flat major for Pianoforte and Orchestra by German composer Ludwig van Beethoven, 24, 3/29 at Vienna's Burgtheater, in Beethoven's debut as composer and virtuose (he has studied piano and violin under Joseph Haydn and, briefly, with the late Wolfgang Amadeus Mozart); Symphony No. 103 in E major (*Drumroll*) and Symphony No. 104 in D major (*London*) by Joseph Haydn 5/12 at London.

The Paris Conservatoire de Musique is founded.

 Paris has bread riots April 1 (12 Germinal) as French food prices soar, but reactionary sentiment sweeps the peasantry which has grown rich supplying the black market and wants to maintain its position.

A poor English harvest drives up the price of bread, which now consists of 95 percent wheat flour.

English magistrates meeting at the Pelican Inn at Speenhamland, Berkshire, order a Poor Law giving bread to England's poor on a sliding scale based on the price of bread and the number of children in the family (see Malthus, 1798).

The average weight of cattle sold at London's Smithfield market is twice what it was in 1710 (see Bakewell, 1769; Coke, 1772).

Lime juice rations are ordered aboard all British naval vessels after the fifth or sixth week at sea following confirmation last year of James Lind's theory that citrus juice is an antiscorbutic (see 1794). The juice is usually combined with the rum ration (see 1740; 1805; 1884).

 Parisian confectioner Nicolas Appert, 43, begins work on a method for preserving food in response to last year's offer by Napoleon Bonaparte of a reward for an effective process. Appert will move in the next year from Lombard Street to Ivry-sur-Seine to devote all his efforts to the project (see 1804).

A stove that economizes on fuel is invented by American physicist Benjamin Thompson, 42, who in 1791 was given the title Count Rumford of the Holy Roman Empire by the elector of Bavaria. Rumford shows that 1,200 of the poor of Munich can be fed on barley soup thickened with potatoes and bread and seasoned with vinegar, at a cost of $3.44 per day, but the poor resist the idea of eating potatoes.

James B. Beam Distilling Company has its beginnings in a Kentucky territory distillery started by farmer Jacob Beam. The distillery will be carried on by his sons and grandsons at Clermont.

1796 English physician Edward Jenner, 47, pioneers the use of vaccination against smallpox. Testing the popular belief that a case of cowpox will avert smallpox, Jenner takes some of the lymph from cowpox pustules on the hands of dairymaid Sarah Nelmes at Berkeley in Gloucestershire. He scratches the lymph matter into the skin of 8-year-old schoolboy James Phipps, and a few weeks later he inoculates the boy with matter from a smallpox pustule. Young Phipps does not develop even a mild case of smallpox, encouraging Jenner, who will continue such experiments for 2 years (see 1798).

 French forces under Napoleon Bonaparte invade Italy and defeat the Austrians in April at Millesimo and the Piedmontese at Modovi. On March 9 Bonaparte has married Paris society leader Josephine de Beauharnais, the 33-year-old Martinique-born widow of the late vicomte de Beauharnais who was blamed for the fall of Mainz to the Prussians in 1793 and who went to the guillotine in July 1794.

Savoy and Nice are ceded to France, Bonaparte enters Milan May 15, he sets up the Lombard republic May 16, and he conquers all of Lombardy as far as Mantua, obtaining large sums of money and many art treasures from the pope, the king of Naples, and the dukes of Parma and Modena in return for truce agreements.

1796 (cont.) Babeuf's Conspiracy to overthrow the Directory that rules France is aborted May 10 by the arrest of socialist François Noel Babeuf, 35, whose song "Dying of Hunger, Dying of Cold" ("Mourant de jaim, mourant de froid") is popular in Parisian cafes. "Nature has given to every man the right to the enjoyment of an equal share in all property," Babeuf has said on posters headed "Analyse de la doctrine de Babeuf, tribun du peuple." He has tried to incite soldiers to revolt, he has attracted ex-Jacobins to his cause, but he will be executed next year along with an associate, and some of his followers will be exiled.

Baden, Württemberg, and Bavaria are forced to conclude truces in August with France's General Jourdan, but Jourdan is defeated at Amberg and at Würzburg by the archduke Charles, brother of the emperor Francis II, and he resigns his command. France's General Moreau is forced to retreat through the Black Forest to the upper Rhine.

The Treaty of San Ildefonso August 19 aligns Spain with France against the British (*see* 1800).

France's Charles Maurice de Talleyrand has arrived at Hamburg in January after 30 months in America. He travels to Paris in September and will become foreign minister next year (*see* 1793; 1803).

Ceylon falls to the British, who gain control of all the Dutch spice islands with the exception of Java.

China's Manchu emperor Ch'ien Lung (Kao Tsung) abdicates at age 85 after a 60-year reign in which he has enlarged the empire, established Chinese control over Tibet, sanctioned the establishment of trade relations with the United States at Canton, invaded Burma and Nepal, and encouraged literature and the arts, especially pottery. He is succeeded by his 36-year-old son Chia Ch'ing, who will reign until his death in 1820.

Russia's Catharine the Great dies of apoplexy November 10 at age 67 after a 34-year reign. She is succeeded by her mentally unbalanced son of 42, who will reign until 1801 as Paul I.

A French fleet of 43 ships and 15,000 men is assembled to invade Ireland in support of Irish rebels, and it leaves Brest December 15 under the command of General Louis Lazare Hoche, 28, and with "Adjutant-general Smith" (T. W. Tone) who has been allowed by the British to emigrate to America (*see* 1791). Tone has proceeded from America to Paris in quest of support from Napoleon, but while he has been successful in obtaining Napoleon's aid, the French ships are dispersed by a storm off the coast of Kerry and no invasion is made (*see* 1798).

"It is our true policy to steer clear of permanent alliance with any portion of the foreign world," President Washington has said in his Farewell Address September 17.

John Adams of Massachusetts is elected to succeed Washington as president after a bitter contest with Thomas Jefferson, who wins 68 electoral votes to 71 for Adams. Jefferson becomes vice president.

Tennessee is admitted to the Union as the 16th state. It has been part of North Carolina.

Cleveland has its beginnings in the town of Cleaveland founded at the mouth of the Cuyahoga River on Lake Erie by General Moses Cleaveland, 42, who has been sent out by the Connecticut Land Company to survey territory the company has purchased in the Western Reserve.

The first permanent white settlement in Oklahoma Territory is established at what later will be called Salina. The settlement is founded by French explorer Jean Pierre Laclede, 28, whose father founded St. Louis in 1763.

The first U.S. ship to enter California waters sails into Monterey Bay. The ship *Otter* is under the command of Yankee skipper Ebenezer Dorr.

France suffers ruinous inflation as her *assignats* of 1790 decline in value. A bushel of flour sells for the equivalent of $5, up from 40 cents in 1790; a cartload of wood sells for $250, up from $4; a pound of soap costs $8, up from 18 cents; a dozen eggs cost $5, up from 24 cents (*see* Bonaparte, 1800).

A Public Land Act passed by Congress May 18 authorizes the sale of U.S. government lands in minimum lots of 640 acres each at $2 per acre with payments to be made under a credit system (*see* 1820; Land Ordinance, 1785).

The Boston Dispensary is founded to provide medical care for the poor in their homes and in clinics.

Royal Technical College is founded at Glasgow.

France restores freedom of the press.

Nonfiction *The Influence of the Passions (De l'Influence des Passions)* by Mme. de Staël who fled to the Necker family estate at Coppet on Lake Geneva to escape the Reign of Terror, has borne two children by her lover Vicomte Louis de Narbonne, has begun an affair with the courtier Benjamin Constant, 28, who has left his wife to join her, and has returned to Paris to establish a salon.

Musenalmanach is founded by Friedrich von Schiller, whose contributions to the new literary journal will include "Das Ideal und des Leben," "Die Macht des Gesanges," "Wurde der Frauen," "Der Spaziergang," "Der Ring des Polykrates," "Der Handsuch," "Der Taucher," and "Das Lied von der Glocke."

Poetry "My love is like a red red rose" by Robert Burns; "Auld Lang Syne" by Robert Burns: "Should auld acquaintance be forgot,/ And never brought to mind?/ Should auld acquaintance be forgot,/ And auld lang syne?" *Joan of Arc* by English poet Robert Southey, 22.

Painting *George Washington* (the *Athenaeum Head*) by U.S. painter Gilbert Charles Stuart, 40, who studied at London during the American Revolution under the émigré master Benjamin West. Stuart returned to the United States 3 years ago, his *Athenaeum Head* will be the most popular of all Washington portraits, and he completes also his Lansdowne portrait of Washington. *The Victor of Arcole* by French painter Antoine Jean Gros, 25, who has studied with Jacques Louis David and has attracted the notice of Napoleon Bonaparte.

 Theater *Egmont* by Johann Wolfgang von Goethe 3/31 at Weimar's Hoftheater.

 Dublin's Four Courts are completed by James Gandon.

 American Cookery by Amelia Simmons ("an American orphan") is the first cookbook to contain native American specialties. Simmons includes Indian pudding, Indian slapjack (pancakes), jonnycake, pickled watermelon rind, Jerusalem artichokes, spruce beer, and a gingerbread that is much softer than the thin European gingerbread.

Bristol's John Harvey & Sons, Ltd. has its origin in a sherry importing establishment founded in Denmark Street by William Perry, who will be joined in 1816 by Thomas Urch, brother-in-law of Cornish sea captain Thomas Harvey. Urch will bring Harvey's son Thomas into the firm that will become John Harvey & Sons and will be famous for its "Bristol milk" and "Bristol cream" sherries from Jerez de la Frontera in Andalusia.

Veuve Clicquot Champagne is introduced by the widow (veuve) of a Reims champagne shipper who died 2 years after their marriage. Mme. Clicquot will make the brand an industry leader and will retire in 1820 at age 43 to live in her château until her death 46 years later (*see* Clicquot Club, 1901).

1797 The Battle of Rivoli January 14–15 on the river Adige
 gives Napoleon Bonaparte his first decisive victory. He separates the enemy infantry from its artillery and routs an Austrian army east of Lake Garda.

Mantua falls to Bonaparte February 2 after a siege of more than 6 months during which four Austrian attempts to relieve the fortress have been beaten back by the French. Romagna, Bologna, and Ferrara are ceded to France in the Treaty of Tolentino concluded by Pope Pius VI after Bonaparte has begun an advance on Rome.

Bonaparte crosses the Alps to challenge the archduke Charles at Vienna and is nearly cut off as the natives of Venetia and the Tyrol take arms against France.

A Cisalpine republic composed of Milan, Modena, Ferrara, Bologna, and Romagna is proclaimed by the French July 9, and the Republic of Genoa is turned into a Ligurian republic controlled by France.

A coup d'état at Paris September 4 (18 Fructidor) drives the party of reaction from power and gives the republican party control of the Council of 500.

The Treaty of Campo Formio October 17 obliges Austria to cede her Belgian provinces to France, to recognize the Cisalpine republic (above), to indemnify the duke of Modena with the Breisgau, and—under terms of secret articles—to cede the left bank of the Rhine to France and to make other concessions. Austria receives the territory of Venice as far as the Adige and obtains Dalmatia, Istria, and the city of Venice.

The XYZ affair brings France and the United States to the verge of war. France has regarded Jay's Treaty of 1794 as evidence of U.S. support for the British, President John Adams takes office March 4 and sends a conciliatory mission to Paris, three members of the French Directory known only as X, Y, and Z attempt to extort money from the Americans Charles Cotesworth Pinckney, 51, of South Carolina, John Marshall, 41, of Virginia, and Elbridge Gerry, 52, of Massachusetts, Pinckney and Marshall return home indignant, the American public and Congress is outraged, but President Adams resists Federalist pressure to declare war.

Prussia's Friedrich Wilhelm II dies November 16 at age 53, leaving his country bankrupt, the monarchy discredited, and the army weakened after an 11-year reign in which Prussia has been compelled to give up her territories west of the Rhine but has gained some Polish territory. He is succeeded by his 27-year-old grandson, who will reign until 1840 as Friedrich Wilhelm III but who will be little better.

Persia's Aga Mohammed is assassinated after a 3-year reign and is succeeded by his nephew, who will reign until 1835 as Fath Ali Shah.

 British sailors mutiny at Spithead April 15 demanding better treatment; the government meets their demands May 17, but a more serious mutiny breaks out at the Nore and is suppressed June 30 only by force.

 A poor wheat harvest forces Parliament to encourage imports, but grain prices shoot up as a result of the war with France, the breakdown in commerce, and the halt in specie payments by the Bank of England (*see* 1801).

Copper pennies and 1-pound notes are issued for the first time in England.

 Chromium is isolated by French chemist Louis Nicolas Vauquelin, 34.

Uranium oxide is produced from pitchblende by Berlin chemist Martin Klaproth, who has discovered and identified as separate elements cerium, titanium, and zirconium, although he does not obtain any of them in pure metallic form. A follower of France's late chemical pioneer Antoine Lavoisier, Klaproth improves and systematizes analytical chemistry and mineralogy (*see* Becquerel, 1896).

Theorie des Fonctions Analytiques by Joseph L. Lagrange of 1761 calculus fame improves upon the Taylor series of 1715.

1797 (cont.) The United States enters the world spice trade. Salem, Massachusetts, sea captain Jonathan Carnes returns to port with the first large cargo of Sumatra pepper (*see* 1805; 1818).

The first high-pressure steam engine is patented by Oliver Evans of 1791 "automatic mill" fame but he builds no practical engine (*see* Trevithick, 1802).

The Encyclopaedia Britannica is published in an 18-volume third edition (*see* 1784).

Fiction *Der blonde Eckbert* by German writer (Johann) Ludwig Tieck, 24.

Poetry *Hermann und Dorothea* by Johann Wolfgang von Goethe is an epic pastoral poem.

Painting *Millbank, Moon Light* by English painter J. M. W. (Joseph Mallord William) Turner, 22. Joseph Wright dies at Derby August 29 at age 62.

Anthem "Gott, Erhalte den Kaiser" is sung for the first time February 12 on the emperor's birthday. The "Emperor's Hymn" by Joseph Haydn with lyrics by Austrian poet Lorenz Leopold Hoschka, 48, will be Austria's national anthem.

First performances *The Emperor Quartet* by Joseph Haydn.

Opera *Medea* (*Medée*) 3/13 at the Théâtre Feydeau, Paris, with music by Italian composer Maria Luigi Carlo Zenobio Salvatore Cherubini, 36, who has lived at Paris since 1788. The libretto is adapted from the Pierre Corneille tragedy of 1635.

Cuban cigarmakers make "cigarettes" using paper wrappers derived from cotton to make the little cigars (*see* 1843).

Cuzco in Spain's Viceroyalty of Peru and Quito in the Viceroyalty of New Granada shudder in severe earthquakes that take up to 41,000 lives February 4.

English tea consumption reaches an annual rate of 2 pounds per capita, a figure that will increase fivefold in the next century (*see* 1840).

James Keiller starts packing orange marmalade at Dundee, Scotland. The Scots have been using home-made marmalades of quince and other fruits for more than a century, but Keiller's is the first commercial marmalade.

1798 *Inquiry into the Cause and Effects of the Variolae Vaccinae* by Edward Jenner announces his discovery of vaccination, a word that comes from the Latin *vacca* for cow and represents a much safer means of protection against smallpox than inoculation (*see* 1796). To counter widespread opposition to inoculation with an animal disease (Jenner gives cowpox the name *Variola vaccinae*), Jenner shows that lymph from cowpox pustules on human skin is just as effective as lymph from infected cattle (*see* Waterhouse, 1799).

"Right," "Center," and "Left" political designations have their origin as France's Council of 500 meets in the palace of Louis XIV's bastard daughter Louise-Françoise de Bourbon. The assembly hall in the palace's "grand apartments" is semicircular, and the representatives soon develop the habit of seating themselves with the most revolutionary at the left and the most conservative on the right.

Napoleon Bonaparte occupies Rome in February, proclaims a Roman republic, and takes Pope Pius VI off to Valence in southern France, where the pope will die next year.

Bonaparte assembles an army of England at Boulogne, but while the English await an invasion, Bonaparte sails from Toulon May 19 with 35,000 men and a corps of scientists. He takes Malta June 12, he lands in Egypt July 1, and he captures Alexandria July 2.

The Battle of the Pyramids outside Cairo July 21 gives the French an easy victory over the medieval cavalry force of the Mamelukes, armed only with lances. Cairo falls to Bonaparte July 22.

The Battle of the Nile August 1 destroys the French fleet in the harbor of Abukir east of Alexandria and cuts Bonaparte and his men off from their French homeland. News of Admiral Horatio Nelson's brilliant victory reaches Naples (which goes wild with joy), and swift couriers speed the news northward to the Papal States, Florence, Venice, and Vienna (*see* Haydn mass, below).

Irish resistance to British rule is broken June 21 by General Gerard Lake, 54, who savagely disarmed the north last year and who defeats the rebels in the Battle of Vinegar Hill and enters Wexford, which the United Irishmen have held for a month.

A French force sent to support the Irish rebels lands August 22 but is subdued in Connaught in October. The French have been sent by the Directory at the urging of T. W. Tone, whose brother is captured and hanged. Tone himself is taken in an October 12 naval encounter, he is sentenced to be hanged, and he dies November 19 after cutting his throat with his pen-knife. James Napper Tandy is taken by the British but is released upon the intercession of Napoleon and will be remembered as the hero in "The Wearing of the Green."

The Alien Acts that pass in Congress June 25 and July 6 empower President Adams to order any alien from the country and to imprison any alien in time of war. The acts force French aliens to flee the country at a time when war looms with France, Thomas Jefferson opposes the legislation and drafts Kentucky Resolutions that declare acts of Congress "void and of no force" when Congress "assumes undelegated powers," the governor of Kentucky approves Jefferson's resolutions November 16, James Madison drafts similar resolutions, and the governor of Virginia approves them December 24 (*see* Sedition Act, below).

Georgia forbids further importation of slaves (*see* 1808; South Carolina, 1803).

Tableau Elementaire de l'Histoire Naturelle des Animaux by French naturalist George Leopold Chrétien Frederic Dagobert, 29, the baron Cuvier, founds the science of comparative anatomy (*see* 1799).

Beryllium is isolated by Louis Nicolas Vauquelin.

A typhus epidemic kills thousands of Britons as starvation makes the country vulnerable to disease (*see* below).

A "pneumatic institution" for treating diseases by inhalation of gases opens at Clifton, England, under the direction of physician Thomas Beddoes, 38, who employs as his superintendent Humphry Davy, 20 (*see* "laughing gas," 1799).

M. M. Warburg & Co. is founded at Hamburg by German *Geldwechsler* Moses Marcus Warburg, 35, and his brother Gerson, whose banking house will become world famous.

A stirring process for making optical glass is patented by Swiss inventor P. L. Guinand, 50, whose process will be the basis of a great German optical industry.

Eli Whitney pioneers the "American system" of mass production with jigs—metal patterns that guide machine tools to make exact replicas of any part—that will doom the handicraft methods of cottage industry and will have an effect on American society as profound as that of the cotton gin (*see* 1792). Whitney has made little from his cotton gin, but he devises a method for producing firearms from interchangeable parts and obtains a $134,000 U.S. Army contract to deliver 10,000 muskets in 28 months (*see* 1801).

The Sedition Act passed by Congress July 14 suppresses editorial criticism of the U.S. president and his administration (*see* Alien Acts, above). Thomas Jefferson opposes the measure.

Paper making gains impetus with the invention of a machine that makes it possible to produce paper from wood pulp in continuous rolls. The inventor is Louis Robert, a clerk employed in France's Essonne paper mills, but the machine will be generally called the Fourdrinier machine after two English brothers who will introduce it in Britain (*see* 1807).

Lithography is invented by Bavarian printer Aloys Senefelder, 25, who has developed a technique based on the incompatibility of grease and water. The Senefelder process permits ink from a grease base to be deposited on grease-treated printing areas, while dampened areas that are not to be printed reject the ink. He produces words or pictures on a flat stone covered with a greasy substance from which ink impressions are taken (*see* color lithography, 1826).

Practical Education by English writer Maria Edgeworth, 32, and her father Richard, 54, is based on recorded conversations of children with their elders to illustrate a child's chain of reasoning.

Nonfiction *Alcuin: A Dialogue on the Rights of Women* by U.S. writer Charles Brockden Brown, 27.

The first American professional writer, Brown has been influenced by the ideas of England's William Godwin and Mary Wollstonecraft.

Fiction *Wieland, or The Transformation* by Charles Brown (above) is a Gothic novel that gains its author wide popularity.

Poetry *Lyrical Ballads* by English poets Samuel Taylor Coleridge, 26, and William Wordsworth, 28, whose distinctive blank verse rebels against artificial forms. Prevented by the Napoleonic wars from marrying a young woman of Blois who has born his child, Wordsworth lives with his sister Dorothy, 27, on a legacy of £900 received in 1795 and will spend the winter with her in Germany. "Lines Composed a Few Miles Above Tintern Abbey, on Revisiting the Banks of the Wye During a Tour, July 13, 1798" demonstrates Wordsworth's conviction that poetry should not be stylized or elaborate in language or content but should express rather the relation between man and nature. "The Rime of the Ancient Mariner" by Coleridge contains the lines, "Water, water everywhere,/ And all the boards did shrink;/ Water, water everywhere,/ Nor any drop to drink" (II, ix). "The Battle of Blenheim" by Robert Southey whose wife Edith is the sister of Coleridge's wife Sarah: " 'And everybody praised the Duke/ Who this great fight did win.'/ 'But what good came of it at last?'/ Quoth little Peterkin./ 'Why, that I cannot tell,' said he/ 'But 'twas a famous victory' " (*see* 1704).

Painting *Love and Psyche* by Baron Gerard; *Caspar Melchor de Jovellanos* by Francisco de Goya.

Theater *Speed the Plough* by English playwright Thomas Morton, 34: "Be quiet, wull ye [says farmer Ashfield]. Always ding, dinging Dame Grundy into my ears—What will Mrs. Grundy say? What will Mrs. Grundy think?" *Andre* by U.S. playwright William Dunlap, 31, 3/30 at New York; *Wallenstein's Camp (Wallensteins Lager)* by Friedrich von Schiller 10/12 at Weimar's Hoftheater.

Opera *Leonore, ou l'amour conjugal* 2/19 at the Théâtre Feydeau, Paris, with an overture by Ludwig van Beethoven (Leonore No. 2), other music by Pierre Gaveaux, libretto by Jean Nicolas Bouilly, 34.

First performances Concerto No. 1 in C major for Pianoforte and Orchestra by Ludwig van Beethoven at Prague; The Creation Mass by Joseph Haydn 4/29 at Vienna; Mass in D minor (*Nelson Mass*) by Joseph Haydn 9/15 at the court of Prince Nicolaus II Esterházy, with Haydn playing the organ solo. He has written the work without knowing of Nelson's victory at Abukir (above) but people will soon begin calling it the Nelson Missa.

London hatter John Hetherington makes the first top hat of silk shag, or plush, and thus reduces demand for American beaver pelts.

The replacement of beaver hats with silk hats in the next half century will produce a rise in the U.S. and Canadian beaver population (*see* Marsh, 1864).

Edward Jenner's vaccination helped end the horrors of small-pox after decades of chancy inoculations.

 Britain has a poor crop year. Wheat prices climb to £12 per ton and there is widespread hunger (*see* typhus, above; Malthus, below).

 Rule's Restaurant opens in London's Maiden Lane.

 Essay on the Principles of Population by English parson Thomas Robert Malthus, 32, expounds the thesis that population increases in geometrical, or exponential, progression (1, 2, 4, 8, 16, 32, etc), while food production ("subsistence") increases only in ar-ithmetical progression (1, 2, 3, 4, 5, 6, etc.). Resting his case on the history of the American colonies in this century, Malthus poses the inevitability of a world food crisis and attacks proposals to reform En-gland's Poor Law (*see* 1795). "A slight acquaintance with numbers will show the immensity of the first power in comparison with the second," says Malthus, but he opposes the use of "improper arts," meaning contraception (*see* 1805; Townsend, 1785, 1791).

1799 Napoleon Bonaparte invades Syria from Egypt in February following a declaration of war by Constan-tinople. The French storm Jaffa and massacre 1,200 Ottoman prisoners but are unable to take Acre. Plague breaks out among the French, and the army retreats to Egypt.

The Battle of Abukir July 25 ends in triumph for Bonaparte and his cavalry commander Joachim Murat, 32, over a Turkish force that has landed at Abukir with British support, but General Joubert is defeated and killed August 15 at the Battle of Novi, and Bonaparte embarks for France August 24 to stiffen the sagging French armies in Europe, leaving General Jean Baptiste Kleber in command of his Egyptian forces.

Russian forces are driven out of Zurich September 26 by the French commander who had been defeated in the Battle of Zurich June 4 to 7. The Russians have been reduced in number by starvation, and Moscow withdraws from the coalition October 22, complain-ing that Austria and the other allies have given her no support.

Bonaparte is elevated to first consul of France No-vember 19 (18 Brumaire) in a coup d'etat engineered by revolutionists who include the Abbé Sieyes (Em-manuel Joseph Sieyes), 51, and Pierre Roger Ducos, 52. The Constitution of the Year VIII receives over-whelming support from the public in a vote held December 24, the Directory that has ruled since 1795 is ended, and Bonaparte is established as dicta-tor of France.

George Washington dies at Mount Vernon Decem-ber 14 at age 67, and when the news reaches Phila-delphia 4 days later, Washington's wartime cavalry general Henry "Light-Horse Harry" Lee is chosen to deliver the funeral oration: "First in war, first in peace and first in the hearts of his countrymen, he was second to none in the humble and endearing scenes of private life. . . ."

 The first British income tax law passes Parliament January 9 and produces revenue of £6 million for the year. Introduced by the prime minister Sir William Pitt as a war measure, the law levies a standard rate of 10 percent on incomes over £200, it taxes incomes of £60 to £199 at reduced rates, and it allows deduc-tions for children, for life insurance premiums, for repairs to property, and for tithes (*see* 1802).

The first British savings bank opens at Wendover, Buckinghamshire, where clergyman Joseph Smith has acted on the suggestion of Jeremy Bentham (*see* 1765; first American savings bank, 1816).

French economist Pierre Samuel du Pont de Ne-mours, 60, emigrates to the United States after hav-ing been imprisoned for a time as a collaborator of the late A. R. Jacques Turgot (*see* 1774; 1776). Du Pont is a disciple of the late François Quesnay (*see* 1802).

Pennsylvania rebel John Fries, 48, leads an armed force of German-Americans against U.S. tax assessors in protest against a federal property tax levied in anticipation of a war with France. President Adams orders federal troops into the area, they arrest Fries, a court convicts him of treason and sentences him to death, but the president will pardon him next year.

The Dutch East India Company's charter expires af-ter 198 years in which stockholders have received annual dividends averaging 18 percent.

Welsh industrialist Robert Owen, 28, marries the daughter of Scottish industrialist David Dale, 60, and becomes manager and co-owner of Dale's cotton mill in England's Lancashire. He determines "to make arrangements to supersede the evil conditions [of the millhands] . . . by good conditions" (*see* 1806).

A letter announcing "the discovery at Rosetta of some inscriptions that may offer much interest" arrives at the Institute of Egypt founded by Napoleon Bonaparte at Paris to gather knowledge about the country he is conquering and colonizing. An Army Corps of Engineers captain named Boucard has found a large block of basalt whose polished surface has been chiseled with Greek characters, with hieroglyphs, and with characters that will later be called demotic. Boucard suspects that all three inscriptions may say the same thing and that this Rosetta stone may be the key to an understanding of the Egyptian language of antiquity and its hieroglyphic writings (*see* Champolion, 1831).

The term "phylum" to denote a category more general than "classes" in the Linnaean system is introduced by France's Baron Cuvier, who takes the word from the Greek for tribe (*see* 1798).

Prussian naturalist Friedrich Heinrich Alexander von Humboldt, 30, sails from Coruma, Spain, for Spanish America aboard the *Pizarro*. Accompanying him is French botanist Aimé Jacques Alexandre Bonpland (né Goujuad), 26, who will travel with von Humboldt in Cuba, Mexico, and the Andes, will be a professor of natural sciences at Buenos Aires from 1818 to 1821, and will be imprisoned by the dictator of Paraguay from 1821 to 1830 (*see* von Humboldt, 1800).

Values of meters and kilograms in the metric system are fixed by France's National Convention in the law of the 10th of December (*see* 1791; 1801).

 Digitalis is related to heart disease for the first time by physician John Ferriar, who notes the effect of dried foxglove leaves on heart action and relegates to secondary importance the use of foxglove as a diuretic (*see* Withering, 1785).

Nitrous oxide ("laughing gas") is produced by English chemist Humphry Davy who inhales 16 quarts of the gas and finds that it makes him "absolutely intoxicated" and immune to pain. Davy suggests that the gas may have use as an anesthetic in minor surgery (*see* 1798; 1800; Wells, 1844).

The first American vaccination against smallpox is administered by Harvard medical professor Benjamin Waterhouse, 35 (*see* 1800; Jenner, 1798).

 Gas lighting is pioneered by French chemist and civil engineer Philippe Lebon, 30, who develops methods for producing inflammable gas from wood. Lebon will make important contributions to the theory of gas lighting and will foresee most 19th-century uses of illuminating gas (*see* Winsor, 1801).

Methods for storing and purifying gas are developed by Scottish steam engineer William Murdock, 45, who has worked in Cornwall for Boulton and Watt since 1779 and who has carried out experiments in the distillation of coal, peat, and wood.

 Travels in the Interior of Africa by Scottish explorer Mungo Park, 28, is published at London. Park has returned from 19 months of travels that followed his escape from 4 months' imprisonment after being captured by an Arab chief. He will make a second expedition to the Niger in 1805 and will reach Bamako before perishing in the rapids during an attack by the natives in 1806.

 England's Royal Institution has its origin in an address by Count Rumford of 1795 cookstove fame who has formed a "Society for Encouraging Industry and Promoting the Welfare of the Poor." Rumford proposes to a committee of this society that a "Public Institution" be established "for diffusing the knowledge, and facilitating the general introduction, of useful mechanical inventions and improvements, and for teaching by courses of philosophical lectures and experiments the application of science to the common purposes of life."

 Crane Paper Mill is established at Dalton, Mass., as the first Massachusetts paper mill west of the Connecticut River. Entrepreneur Zenas Crane, 22, uses power from the swift Housatonic River to operate the machines that produce his rag paper.

 Fiction   *Ormond, or The Secret Witness* by Charles Brockden Brown.

Poetry   "The Pleasures of Hope" by Scottish poet Thomas Campbell, 21: "Tis distance lends enchantment to the view,/ And robes the mountain in its azure hue."

 Theater   *The Piccolominos* (*Die Piccolomini*) by Friedrich von Schiller 1/10 at Weimar's Hoftheater; *The Death of Wallenstein* (*Wallenstein's Tod*) by Friedrich von Schiller 4/20 at Weimar's Hoftheater (the plays complete the trilogy begun last year).

First performances   *The Creation (Die Schoepfung)* by Joseph Haydn 3/19 at Vienna under the direction of the composer; *Sonate Pathetique* by Ludwig van Beethoven.

The U.S. Executive Mansion at Washington, D.C., is completed after 7 years of construction by Irish-American architect James Hoban, 37, who won a $500 prize for his design in an open competition (*see* "White House," 1814).

New York's Gracie Mansion is completed at Horn's Hook on the East River for Archibald Gracie. The house will be enlarged in later years and will serve as the mayor's residence.

Prussia's Friedrich Wilhelm III receives a loaf of beet sugar from Berlin chemist Franz Karl Achard and is persuaded to give Achard some land at Cunern in Silesia and to give financial support to the cultivation of sugar beets (*see* 1793; 1801).

Cultivation of beets as a root vegetable gains importance in parts of Europe, but most farmers continue to cultivate the plant only for its greens.

1800 The Convention of El Arish concluded by Napoleon Bonaparte with the Ottoman Turks January 24 provides for French withdrawal from Egypt. Terms of

1800 (cont.) the treaty are rejected by Britain's Admiral George Keith Elphinstone, 54, Viscount Keith. France's General Kleber defeats the Turks at Heliopolis March 20 with a force of 10,000 men that is outnumbered six to one, but Kleber is assassinated by a fanatic at Cairo June 14 at age 47.

Austrian troops which starved Genoa into surrendering June 4 are attacked by Bonaparte, who crossed the St. Bernard Pass in May with 40,000 troops and wins a narrow victory June 14 at the Battle of Marengo over Baron Michael Friedrich Benedikt von Melas, 71. A truce signed by Melas with Bonaparte gives the French all Austrian fortresses west of the Mincio and south of the Po.

Munich is taken by French troops under General Moreau in July, and Moreau goes on to defeat the archduke John December 3 in the Battle of Hohenlinden.

A Jacobin conspiracy to assassinate the dictator Bonaparte is discovered at Paris.

West Africa's Ashanti throne is assumed by "the whale" Osei Bonshu who begins a reign as Asanthane. The gold-encrusted throne has been received "from heaven" by fetish prophet Okomfo Anokye to create the sacred empire of the Ashanti (*see* 1822).

The Indiana Territory is created out of the western part of the Northwest Territory by the Division Act of May 7.

The Louisiana Territory ceded to Spain by the Treaty of Paris in 1763 is returned to France October 1 by a secret agreement in the Treaty of San Ildefonso signed in 1796. France guarantees not to transfer the territory to any power other than Spain (but *see* Louisiana Purchase, 1803).

Thomas Jefferson wins election to the U.S. presidency by winning 73 electoral votes as compared with 65 for President Adams and 64 for Charles Pinckney of South Carolina. Aaron Burr of New York also wins 73 electoral votes, the Federalists force the election into the House of Representatives in an effort to make Burr president, and 35 ballots are taken before the firm opposition of Alexander Hamilton to Burr swings the decision to Jefferson.

Washington, D.C., replaces New York as the U.S. capital, 123 federal government clerks are moved to the new city during the summer, and Congress convenes at Washington for the first time November 17.

💲 The Banque de France is founded February 13 at the instigation of Napoleon Bonaparte "to counteract the displacement or dispersion of the funds serving to feed the trade of the nation, and all such influences as tended to impair the public credit and to clog the circulation of wealth in the country, influences arising from the French Revolution and expensive wars." The private bank has an initial capital reserve of 30 million francs (*see* 1848).

Napoleon Bonaparte acts to stop France's inflation and avert national bankruptcy (*see* 1796). Bonaparte raises 5 million francs from French and Italian bankers and 9 million from a national lottery, he introduces a new and tighter system of income tax collections, he reduces the budgets of all his ministries, he restores confidence among the bourgeoisie, and French government bonds that sold at 12 francs December 23 of last year reach 44 within the year and will advance in the next 7 years to 94.40.

Congress passes legislation to reduce the minimum amount of public land that may be sold at auction under the U.S. Land Ordinance of 1785. The bill introduced by Congressman William Henry Harrison, 27, of the Northwest Territory permits sale of 320-acre tracts at $2 per acre with a down payment of one fourth and the balance to be paid in three annual installments (*see* 1796; 1804).

⊛ Alexander von Humboldt explores the course of the Orinoco River in South America, covering 1,725 miles of jungle by foot and canoe in 4 months and establishing the water link between the Orinoco and the Amazon (*see* 1799; 1802).

Ottawa is founded on the Ottawa River in eastern Ontario.

✊ Gabriel's Insurrection inspires Virginians to support plans for black emigration to Africa. A conspiracy organized by the slave "General Gabriel" to attack Richmond comes to light, Governor James Monroe orders in federal militia, they suppress the insurrection, and the ringleaders are executed.

⚡ Pennsylvania engineer James Finley builds the first suspension bridge with iron chains (*see* 1825).

⚡ English engineer Richard Trevithick, 29, builds a high-pressure steam engine that will be used to power a road vehicle (*see* 1801; Watt, 1782; Evans, 1797).

The voltaic cell invented by Italian physicist Alessandro Volta, 55, pioneers the electric storage battery. Volta's cell consists of several metal disks, each made of one or the other of two dissimilar metals, in alternating series, and separated by pads moistened with an electrolyte. The word "volt" will be derived from Volta's name (*see* Daniell, 1836).

⧗ Infrared rays are discovered by Sir William Herschel, who discovered the planet Uranus in 1781. He uses a sensitive thermometer to show that the invisible rays beyond the red light of the sun's spectrum are essentially heat radiation.

Researches, Chemical and Philosophical, Chiefly Concerning Nitrous Oxide is published by Humphry Davy, who will soon be appointed lecturer in chemistry at the Royal Institution of Great Britain, set up this year pursuant to last year's proposal by Count Rumford (*see* Davy, 1799; 1807).

⚕ London's Royal College of Surgeons is founded.

A Prospect of Exterminating the Small Pox by Benjamin Waterhouse is published at Boston, but the disease will remain a leading cause of death throughout the world for well over a century.

Napoleon Bonaparte fought the monarchs of Europe who feared the spread of the French Revolution.

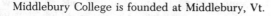 Middlebury College is founded at Middlebury, Vt.

The Library of Congress is established with a $5,000 appropriation to purchase some 900 books—including Adam Smith's 1776 *Wealth of Nations*—and maps that arrive from London in 11 trunks aboard a British cargo vessel, *The American* (*see* 1814).

"I have sworn upon the altar of God, eternal hostility against every form of tyranny over the mind of man," writes Thomas Jefferson in a September 23 letter to Dr. Benjamin Rush.

Fiction *The Life and Memorable Actions of George Washington* by Mason Locke Weems, 43, a Philadelphia clergyman turned book peddler. Weems has fabricated stories including one about young George chopping down his father's cherry tree. *Castle Rackrent* by English novelist Maria Edgeworth, who writes about Irish life.

Poetry *Lyrical Ballads* of 1798 by Samuel Taylor Coleridge and William Wordsworth is published in an expanded edition with a preface by Wordsworth who says, "Poetry is the breath and finer spirit of all knowledge; it is the impassioned expression which is in the countenance of all science." A poet is "a man speaking to men" but a man "endowed with more lively sensibility, more enthusiasm and tenderness, who has a greater knowledge of human nature, and a more comprehensive soul" than ordinary people, a man particularly "affected . . . by absent things as if they were present." He includes his poems "Lucy Gray," "She dwelt among the untrodden ways," and "Strange fits of passion have I known."

Painting *Portrait of Mme. Recamier* by Jacques Louis David; *Kirkstall Abbey* and *The White House at Chelsea* by English painter Thomas Girtin, 25.

Theater *Macbeth* by Friedrich von Schiller 5/14 at Weimar's Hoftheater, in a German version of the Shakespearean tragedy of 1606; *Maria Stuart* by Friedrich von Schiller 6/14 at Weimar's Hoftheater (Schiller settled at Weimar late last year to be near his friend Goethe).

First performances Symphony No. 1 in C major by Ludwig van Beethoven 4/2 at Vienna's Hofburg Theater, in a concert that includes also Beethoven's Septet in E flat major for Strings and Winds, Air and Duet from the Creation, and Improvisations on Haydn's Emperor Hymn; Concerto in C minor for Pianoforte and Orchestra by Ludwig van Beethoven 4/5 at Vienna's Theater-an-der-Wien.

An octagon house is completed at Washington, D.C. (above), by Colonel John Tayloe.

Passenger pigeons in America are estimated to number 5 billion and provide low-cost food in the Northwest Territory (*see* Josselyn, 1672; Wilson, 1810).

Sugar beets have a sugar content of roughly 6 percent, and efforts begin to raise the figure by selective breeding (*see* Achard, 1793; Delessert, 1810).

The Northern Spy apple is originated at East Bloomfield, New York. The new variety is good both raw and cooked.

Spode bone china is introduced by English potter Josiah Spode, 46, who uses hard feldspar paste to which he adds bone ashes.

The new U.S. capital at Washington, D.C. (above), has 2,464 residents, 623 slaves.

The world's population reaches 870 million (960 by some estimates) with some 188 million of the total in Europe (*see* 1901).

19th CENTURY

1801 The United Kingdom of Great Britain and Ireland is created by Parliament January 1 in an Act of Union that provides for one Parliament for both Britain and Ireland (*see* 1707; 1798; Home Rule Assn., 1870).

The Holy Roman Empire is practically destroyed by Napoleon Bonaparte February 9 in the Treaty of Luneville (*see* 1806).

Thomas Jefferson takes office as third president of the United States March 4, promising, "Peace, commerce, and honest friendship with all nations—entangling alliances with none" (*see* 1796).

Secretary of State John Marshall, 46, is named chief justice of the United States. In the next 34 years, Marshall's court will establish fundamental principles for interpreting the Constitution (*see* 1803; 1819; 1821; 1824).

Russia's Paul I is murdered in his bedroom at the St. Michael Palace in St. Petersburg the night of March 11 in a palace revolution that ends 4½ years of insane rule. Dead at age 46, the czar is succeeded by his 23-year-old son, who will rule until 1825 as Aleksandr I Pavlovich and who begins his reign by making peace with England and withdrawing from the Second Coalition against France.

Peace between Britain and France is concluded March 14, but the peace will not last.

The Battle of Copenhagen April 2 ends in defeat for a Danish fleet by a British armada of 18 ships commanded by Sir Hyde Parker, 62, whose second-in-command Horatio Nelson pretends he does not see Parker's signal to withdraw (he holds his telescope to his blind eye), an order that would have meant disaster. The Danes lose all but three of their ships, they sign an armistice, and Nelson, who has been vice admiral since January 1, assumes command of the fleet in May following the recall of Parker. He returns home in June and is given the title viscount.

Frankfurt-am-Main moneylender Meyer Amschel Rothschild, 58, becomes financial adviser to the landgrave of Hesse-Casal. Rothschild will serve as an agent of the British crown in subsidizing European opposition to Napoleon Bonaparte, and his sons will establish important banking houses at London, Vienna, Naples, and Paris (*see* Wellesley, 1812).

The metallic elements columbium and niobium are discovered by English chemist Charles Hatchett, 36.

The metric system fixed by France's National Convention late in 1799 is made compulsory by the convention in a move that will be followed by most of Europe but not by Britain or the United States.

The automatic Jacquard loom for weaving figured silk fabrics is developed by French inventor Joseph Marie Jacquard, 49, who employs punched cards to guide the movements of a loom that will later be used for making figured worsteds. The loom encounters initial resistance from weavers fearful of being displaced, but it will gain acceptance within the decade. France will have 11,000 Jacquard looms in operation by 1812.

Eli Whitney fails to meet his deadline for delivery of 10,000 muskets because he has taken so long to tool up a factory at the Lake Whitney fall line of the Mill River at Hamden, Conn. (*see* 1798). With only 500 muskets completed, Whitney puts on a show for President Adams and Vice President Jefferson in January, disassembling some guns, scrambling the parts, and then assembling new weapons to demonstrate the interchangeability of parts. The War Department is persuaded to give Whitney an extension and to advance him $134,000 so that he may fulfill his contract (*see* 1812).

The story of Whitney's demonstration (above) will be questioned by revisionist historians when ancient Whitney muskets are found to have parts that have been filed and drilled here and there to make them fit, raising doubts as to interchangeability of parts.

A gas-fueled thermolamp exhibited by Philippe Lebon in a Paris residence is successful both technically and aesthetically, but the French government is not forthcoming with funds to finance gas lighting on a large scale (*see* 1799; Winsor, 1804).

A British Health and Morals of Apprentices Act is passed by Parliament to supervise labor conditions. The act forbids hiring out of pauper children to work in the cotton mills until they are 9, it restricts their working day to 12 hours, and it prohibits their employment at night work (but *see* 1809).

The first steam vehicle to carry passengers is put on the road by England's Richard Trevithick, who employs his steam engine to power a road carriage (*see* 1800; locomotive, 1804).

The University of South Carolina is founded at Columbia.

How Gertrude Teaches Her Children (*Wie Gertrud ihre Kinder lehrt*) by Swiss educationalist Johann Heinrich Pestalozzi, 55, shows that to educate a woman is to educate a family community (*see* 1805).

The *New York Evening Post,* a new Federalist newspaper founded by Alexander Hamilton, begins publication November 16.

Painting *Napoleon au Grand Saint-Bernard* by Jacques Louis David; *Calais Pier* by J. M. W. Turner.

Theater *The Maid of Orleans* (*Die Jungfrau von Orleans*) by Johann von Schiller 4/11 at Leipzig.

Ballet *The Creatures of Prometheus* (*Die Geschöpfe des Prometheus*) 3/28 at Vienna's Royal and Imperial Theater, with music by Ludwig van Beethoven, choreography by Neapolitan ballet master Salvator Vizano, 31.

Oratorio *The Seasons* (*Die Jahreszeiten*) by Joseph Haydn 4/24 at the Vienna palace of Prince Schwarzenberg, text from the James Thomson poem.

Italian violin prodigy Nicolo Paganini, 17, completes a concert tour in which he has dazzled audiences with his virtuosity, using a violin made by Joseph Guarnerius given him by a French merchant after Paganini had pawned his own violin to pay gambling debts. Paganini will live for the next 3 years in Tuscany with a noblewoman who has fallen for him.

"Johnny Appleseed" arrives in the Ohio Valley with seeds from Philadelphia cider presses that will make the valley as rich a source of apples as Leominster, Mass.—home town of pioneer John Chapman, 26.

The world's first beet sugar factory opens in Silesia (*see* Achard, 1793, 1802).

U.S. salt prices fall to a new low of $2.50 per bushel as new sources come into production. Salt has been four times as costly as beef on the frontier but is essential to keep livestock (and people) healthy and to keep meat from spoiling.

A bakery to make ship's biscuit and hardtack opens at Milton, Mass., 6 miles south of Boston. Retired ship's captain Josiah Bent will introduce the first biscuits to be called "crackers"—water biscuits made of unsweetened, unleavened dough rolled many times to have a fine grain that will make them crisper than previous biscuits and will cause them to make a cracking noise when eaten.

The first accurate census shows that China has a population of 295 million, India 131 million, the Ottoman Empire 21, Japan 15, Russia 33, France 27.4, the German states and free cities 14.1, Britain 10.4, Ireland 5.2, Spain 10.5, Egypt 2.5, and the United States 5.3 million of whom 1 million live west of the Alleghenies.

Canton is the world's largest city with 1.5 million while Nanking, Hangchow, Kingtechchen, and the Japanese city of Edo each has 1 million.

London is by far the largest European city with a population of 864,000 as compared with 598,000 in Constantinople, 548,000 in Paris, 530,000 in the Japanese city of Kyoto, 300,000 each in Isfahan, Lucknow, and Madras, 183,000 in Berlin, 75,000 in Manchester, 10,000 in Dusseldorf, 6,000 in Stockholm, 60,500 in New York, 1,565 in Pittsburgh.

1802 The Italian republic created January 26 from the former Cisalpine republic with Napoleon Bonaparte as president annexes Piedmont September 21 and annexes Parma and Piacenza in October.

The Treaty of Amiens March 27 brings a temporary end to hostilities among Europe's warring powers. Spain yields Trinidad to Britain but secures Minorca, the Batavian republic cedes Ceylon to Britain, the British give up all their other conquests to France and her allies, but hostilities soon begin again.

The Legion of Honor (*Legion d'Honneur*) created by Bonaparte May 19 gives him a tool comparable to the orders of knighthood so that he may avoid criticism of his government by keeping his courtiers busy with matters of etiquette and protocol.

The French make Bonaparte first consul for life August 2 and give him the right to name his successor.

Bonaparte revokes the French assembly's emancipation decree of 1794, he reintroduces slavery in the colonies, and he sends an army of 25,000 under his brother-in-law Charles Victor Emmanuel Leclerc, 30, to put down the rebellion in Haiti. Leclerc sends Toussaint L'Ouverture to France, where the black general soon dies in prison, but Leclerc himself dies of yellow fever as do 22,000 of his men (*see* 1804).

Parliament repeals the British income tax of 1799 following the Peace of Amiens (above) and orders that all documents and records relating to the tax be destroyed in response to public outcry. Parliament will reimpose the income tax next year and will not remove it until 1815.

Biologie oder Philosophie der Lebenden Natur by German naturalist Gottfried Reinhold Treviranus, 26, introduces the word "biology." The six-volume work will be completed in 1822.

Boston's Board of Health orders vaccination against smallpox (*see* 1798; Waterhouse, 1800). The board begins to improve the city's hygiene, to regulate burials, and to impose quarantines.

The New American Practical Navigator by Salem, Mass., mathematician-astronomer Nathaniel Bowditch, 29, will soon be a second bible for sea captains. Bowditch has found 8,000 errors in the tables of the standard English work on navigation.

E. I. du Pont de Nemours and Company has its beginnings in a gunpowder plant built on the Brandywine River near Wilmington, Del., by Eleuthére Irénee du Pont, 31, whose father returns to France, where he will serve a dozen years hence as secretary to the provisional government (*see* 1799; 1803).

The Willard Patent Timepiece patented by Roxbury, Mass., clockmaker Simon Willard, 49, will become famous as the banjo clock.

Italian scientist Gian Domenico Romagnosi advances knowledge of electricity. He observes that an electric current flowing through a wire causes a magnetic needle to line up perpendicularly to the wire (*see* Oersted, 1819).

1802 (cont.) The United States Military Academy is founded at West Point, N.Y.

Fiction *Delphine* by Mme. de Staël, whose liberalism antagonizes Napoleon Bonaparte (he will exile her and her lover Benjamin Constant next year to the family estate at Coppet on Lake Geneva).

Poetry "Lochiel's Warning" by Thomas Campbell: "'Tis the sunset of life gives me mystical lore,/ And coming events cast their shadows before."

Painting *Madame Recamier* by François Gérard. Thomas Girtin dies at London, November 9 at age 27; George Romney dies at Kendal, Westmoreland, November 15 at age 67.

Sculpture *Napoleon Bonaparte* and *The Pugilists* by Antonio Canova.

The world's first photograph is produced by British physician Thomas Wedgwood, 31-year-old son of the late potter Josiah Wedgwood. He sensitizes paper with moist silver nitrate to retain an image projected on its surface but can find no way of fixing the image, which quickly fades (*see* Schulze, 1727; Scheele, 1777). Wedgwood reports to the Royal Society that silver chloride is more sensitive than silver nitrate (*see* Niepce, 1822).

Ludwig van Beethoven's *Sonata Quasi una Fantasia* is published in March at Vienna. It will be called the *Moonlight Sonata* in midcentury by the music critic Ludwig Rellstab.

English horse racing at Goodwood is introduced by Charles Lennox, 67, duke of Richmond.

Mme. Tussaud's wax museum is opened at London by Swiss wax modeler Marie Gresholtz Tussaud, 42, who was commissioned during the Reign of Terror at Paris 9 years ago to make death masks of famous guillotine victims. Mme. Tussaud will settle her collection in Baker Street in 1833 and will connect it with a chamber of horrors that will contain relics of criminals and instruments of torture.

Arlington House is completed on a Virginia hill across the Potomac from the U.S. capital to provide a residence for Martha Washington's grandson George Washington Parke Custis, 21. The house will later be the home of Custis's son-in-law Robert E. Lee.

The nitrogen potential of guano is studied by Alexander Humboldt, who has crossed the Cordilleras to Quito, has descended to Callao, and has found great deposits of guano concentrated on islands off the west coast of South America (*see* 1800). The guano represents droppings from seabirds over the course of thousands of years, nitrates from guano can be used both for fertilizer and for explosives, and Peru will export guano to Europe in large quantities primarily on the basis of Humboldt's reports (*see* 1809).

Soybeans are introduced into the United States via England.

The world's first beet sugar factory goes into production but soon runs deep in debt (*see* 1799; 1801). A disciple of Franz Karl Achard is no more successful with a factory he sets up at Krayn, also in Silesia, but he does succeed in growing the white Silesian beet that is higher in sugar content and that will be the basis of all future sugar beet strains (*see* 1808).

1803 The Louisiana Purchase doubles the size of the United States and extends her western border to the Rocky Mountains. French foreign minister Charles de Talleyrand is desperate for funds to finance Bonaparte's military adventures, he recognizes that France's hold on Saint Domingue is shaky, he ignores the terms of the 1800 Treaty of San Ildefonso with Spain, and he sells the 828,000-square-mile Louisiana Territory to the United States for 80 million francs ($15 million). U.S. Minister to France Robert R. Livingston negotiates the purchase, which is financed in part by the London banking firm Baring Brothers.

Chief Justice John Marshall of the U.S. Supreme Court rules that any act of Congress which conflicts with the Constitution is null and void. Marshall's decision in the case of *Marbury v. Madison* February 14 establishes the Court as the ultimate interpreter of the Constitution.

Massachusetts and New York threaten to secede from the Union in protest against the Louisiana Purchase (above) which has been made by Thomas Jefferson without consent of the Senate.

Ohio is admitted to the Union as the 17th state.

The eight major Sandwich Islands are united by Hawaiian chief Kamehameha, 66, who employs American, English, and Welsh governors (*see* Cook, 1778; Kamehameha II, 1819).

Britain and France renew war May 16, the French complete their occupation of Hanover, and they threaten to invade England from Boulogne, where they begin to assemble an invasion fleet.

Swiss cantons regain their independence under terms of the Act of Mediation.

An Irish rebellion against England is led by the 25-year-old nationalist Robert Emmet, who last year spoke with Bonaparte and Talleyrand in an effort to obtain French support. Emmet's small band of followers commits two murders and other acts of violence July 23 in a move to capture the viceroy, but the rioters are quickly dispersed. Emmet escapes into hiding but is captured August 25, tried by a special court, and hanged September 20.

The Battle of Assaye September 23 ends in victory for English forces under the 34-year-old Arthur Wellesley, brother of India's governor general Richard Colley the first Marquis Wellesley. The sindhia of Gwalior is defeated in the Second Mahratta War, but Wellesley is recalled as London becomes alarmed at his policies.

A table of atomic weights is arranged by English chemist-physicist John Dalton, 37, who gives the first clear statement of atomic theory. The Manchester scientist gave the first clear statement of color blindness when he was 28, and the defect will be called Daltonism (*see* Mendeléev, 1870).

Dalton's law of partial pressures is stated by John Dalton (above), in a paper on the "Absorption of Gases by Water and Other Liquids" (*see* 1808).

Cerium is discovered by Swedish chemist Jöns Jakob Berzelius, 24, at Uppsala, and Swedish mineralogist Wilhelm Hisinger, 37.

Osmium is discovered by English chemist Smithson Tennant, 42.

Essai de Statique Chemique by France's Claude Berthollet employs the system of chemical nomenclature that he devised with the late Antoine Lavoisier. It will serve as the basis for the modern system.

Edward Jenner is voted a grant of £10,000 by Parliament for his smallpox vaccination discovery of 1798. Jenner will be voted another £20,000 in 1806.

Morphine is isolated and is given its name by German pharmacist Friedrich Wilhelm Adam Seturner, 20, who uses the name of the Greek god of dreams Morpheus for his narcotic analgesic opium derivative (*see* Sydenham, 1683; codeine, 1832).

Chicago has its origin in Fort Dearborn, built by U.S. federal troops on Lake Michigan and named for President Jefferson's Secretary of War Henry Dearborn (*see* steamboat, 1832).

Buffalo, N.Y., is laid out at the mouth of the Niagara River on Lake Erie by the Holland Land Company's surveyor Joseph Ellicott (*see* Washington, 1790).

Harmony, Pa., is founded as a celibate religious communistic society by Harmonites led by German separatist George Rapp, 46, who emigrates to Pennsylvania's Butler County with a group of his followers. The group will move in 1814 to Indiana, where it will establish another Harmony in the Wabash Valley, but in 1825 it will move back to Pennsylvania to settle in a town below Pittsburgh that will be called Economy (*see* New Harmony, 1824).

South Carolina resumes importing slaves as Eli Whitney's 1792 cotton gin makes cotton growing profitable and boosts demand for field hands.

Cotton passes tobacco for the first time as the leading U.S. export crop.

Renewal of hostilities in Europe brings higher prices for American farm products and increases trade for U.S. shipping merchants such as Asa Clapp of Portland; George Cabot, Thomas Handasyd Perkins, and James Lloyd of Boston; and Cyrus Butler and Nicholas Brown of Providence.

E. I. du Pont de Nemours and Company is founded in Delaware with $36,000 (*see* 1802; 1814).

The Ames Shovel Company started by John Ames in 1774 is taken over by his son Oliver, who invests $1,600 to expand operations and moves the firm to Easton, Mass. Faced with little competition, Ames shovels will be the largest-selling U.S. shovels and will play a major role in digging the Erie Canal (*see* 1817) and other canals, in building U.S. railroads, in digging the trenches and foxholes that will be used by U.S. troops, and in digging the graves for America's dead (*see* Oakes Ames, 1862).

The Middlesex Canal opens December 21 to connect the Merrimack River with Boston Harbor. The canal has been dug with Ames shovels (above).

Construction begins in Scotland on a 60.5-mile Caledonian Canal to connect the Atlantic with the North Sea across northern Scotland.

A small ship propelled by steam power is developed by U.S. engineer Robert Fulton, 38, whose *Treatise on the Improvement of Canal Navigation* appeared in 1796 and who has been in Paris since 1797 working on his submarine *Nautilus* (*see* 1807; Symington, 1788; Fitch, 1791).

Connecticut clockmaker Eli Terry, 31, introduces wooden-wheeled clocks much like those produced in the Black Forest since 1660. Following the ideas of French watchmaker Frederic Japy and of Eli Whitney, Terry makes his clock parts interchangeable to permit mass production, and he will soon replace his wooden wheels with brass ones. When he encounters sales resistance to his clocks, Terry becomes the first U.S. merchant to offer merchandise on a free-trial, no-money-down basis, and he makes the discovery that farm families grow accustomed to having a clock and will sooner pay for the clock than give it up (*see* Seth Thomas, 1810).

U.S. political rivalry reached a low point when Aaron Burr killed Alexander Hamilton in a duel at Weehawken, N.J.

1803 (cont.)   An explosive shell that will be called the shrapnel shell is invented by English artillery officer Henry Shrapnel, 42.

Improvement in Education as it Respects the Industrious Classes by English Quaker schoolmaster Joseph Lancaster, 25, is based on his experience teaching a free school of 1,000 boys. Lancaster has organized a corps of elder boys as monitors to oversee and instruct and his Lancastrian system will be widely adopted in nonconformist schools.

Poetry   *Minstrelsy of the Scottish Border* compiled by Scottish poet Walter Scott, 32, is published as Scott works on his own first original poem (*see* 1805); "Misfortune and Pity" by French abbé Jacques Delille, 65; "Fate makes our relatives, choice makes our friends."

Painting   *The McNab* by Henry Raeburn; *Calais Pier* by J. M. W. Turner who last year made his first trip abroad and who has begun imitating the old masters: Titian, Poussin, and Claude Lorrain.

John James Audubon arrives at Philadelphia. Son of a Haitian Creole woman who has been legally adopted by his French father and raised at Nantes, the 18-year-old Audubon will move to Kentucky in 1808, he will open a general store at Louisville, and he will begin painting American birds from life (*see* 1813; 1830).

Theater   *The Bride of Messina* (*Die Braut von Messina*) by Johann von Schiller 3/19 at Weimar's Hoftheater.

First performances   Symphony No. 2 in D major by Ludwig van Beethoven 4/5 at Vienna's Theater-an-der-Wien, in a concert that includes also Beethoven's only oratorio *Christ on the Mount Olives* (*Christus am Oelberg*) and his Concerto No. 3 in C minor for Pianoforte and Orchestra with Beethoven as soloist.

The British Museum's "Elgin Marbles" have their beginning as Thomas Bruce, 37, seventh earl of Elgin, starts shipping home from Athens some portions of the sculptured frieze of the Parthenon completed on the Acropolis in 438 B.C. Elgin will ship large parts of the frieze to London in the next 9 years.

A Treatise on Practical Farming by Loudon County, Virginia, farmer John Alexander Binns, 42, originates what will be called the "Loudon system" of soil treatment. Binns has experimented with crop rotation, deep plowing, and the use of gypsum as fertilizer.

The first ice refrigerator (icebox) is patented by Maryland farmer Thomas Moore, who places one wooden box inside another, insulates the space in between with charcoal or ashes, and places a tin box container at the top of the inner box. Moore's icebox will be in common use by 1838 (*see* Perkins, 1834).

Abortion is made a statutory crime in England (*see* Pius XI, 1869).

1804   A royalist conspiracy against France's first consul Napoleon Bonaparte is discovered in February, and the 41-year-old conspirator General Jean Victor Mo-

reau escapes to America, but the 32-year-old duc d'Enghien Louis Antoine Henri de Bourbon Condé is seized in Baden, condemned by a commission acting under Bonaparte's orders without regard to law, and shot at Vincennes the night of March 20.

"It is worse than a crime; it is a blunder," says political leader Antoine Jacques Claude Joseph Boulay de la Meurthe, 42, at news of the duke's execution (above). General Charles Pichegru, 43, is imprisoned and is either murdered or takes his own life April 5, and Georges Cadoudal, 33, is guillotined June 5.

Napoleon is proclaimed emperor May 18 by the French senate and tribunate, his elevation is ratified in a national plebiscite by a vote of 3.6 million to 2,569, and the emperor Napoleon is consecrated December 2 by Pope Pius VII at Paris in a ceremony imitative of Pepin III's coronation in 754 and Charlemagne's in 800.

Austria's Francis II assumes the title Emperor Francis I of Austria, which he will hold until his death in 1835. The title gives some semblance of unity to the emperor's widely extended German, Hungarian, Bohemian, Austrian, and Italian dominions which he rules with his wife (and first cousin) Maria Theresa, daughter of Ferdinand, king of Naples.

The Code Napoleon (Code civil des Francaises) drafted by Boulay de la Meurthe (above) and others and promulgated March 21 (30 Ventose XII) goes into force immediately throughout France, Belgium, Luxembourg, the Palatinate, the parts of Rhenish Prussia and Hesse-Darmstadt situated on the left bank of the Rhine, the territory of Geneva, Savoy, Piedmont, and the duchies of Parma and Piacenza. It is a code of civil laws common to the whole realm as promised in the constitution of 1791 and will have great influence on the legal codes of most European countries and even of countries as far distant as Japan (after 1870). It combines Roman law with some of the radical reforms wrought by the French Revolution with respect to conditions affecting the individual, tenure of property, order of inheritance, mortgages, contracts, and the like, and it will make French law as much admired as French culture (but *see* below).

Spain declares war on Britain.

Haiti is established with a black republican government in the western part of Hispaniola following defeat of a 5,000-man army sent out by Napoleon to subdue the rebels (*see* 1794; 1802).

Former U.S. Treasury Secretary Alexander Hamilton is mortally wounded July 11 at age 49 in a duel at Weehawken, N.J., with Vice President Aaron Burr, who has been opposed in New York State politics by Hamilton, has heard of insults directed at him by Hamilton, and has demanded satisfaction (*see* 1800 election). Now 48, Burr is indicted in New York and New Jersey, he flees to Philadelphia, and he proceeds to the south where he will conspire in the next 3 years with General James Wilkinson, 44, who is secretly in the pay of Spain but who will soon be governor of the Louisiana Territory (*see* 1807).

The Twelfth Amendment to the Constitution is declared in force September 25. It requires separate electoral ballots for president and vice president to prevent a recurrence of the confusion 4 years ago when Aaron Burr was nearly elected president.

Thomas Jefferson is re-elected with an overwhelming plurality of 162 electoral votes versus 14 for Charles C. Pinckney.

Haiti's revolutionists (above) free all slaves and kill all whites who do not flee (many emigrate to Baltimore).

The Code Napoleon (above) regards an accused person as guilty until proven innocent. The tenet will be rejected in Britain and the United States.

Iridium is discovered by Smithson Tennant.

Palladium is discovered in platinum by English chemist-physicist William Hyde Wollaston, 38.

Gas lighting is demonstrated at London's Lyceum Theatre by a German promoter who has anglicized his name to Frederick Albert Winsor. A man of 41, Winsor has seen demonstrations by the French chemist Philippe Lebon, he has made his own thermolamp, and he has brought it to England (*see* Lebon, 1801; Pall Mall, 1807).

The first steam locomotive to be tried on rails hauls five wagons containing 10 tons of iron and 70 men some 9.5 miles at nearly 5 miles per hour. England's Richard Trevithick has built the locomotive and will be the first to apply high-pressure steampower to agriculture (*see* 1801; Blenkinsop, 1811).

The S.S. *Little Juliana* launched at Hoboken, N.J., by Colonel John Stevens and his two sons is a twin-screw steamship built with some parts brought from England. The vessel fails to achieve commercial success (*see* 1790; 1808; Fulton, 1807).

The Lewis and Clark expedition to explore the Louisiana Purchase territory begins its ascent of the Missouri River May 14 seeking to determine whether the Gulf of Mexico and the Pacific Ocean are linked by a river system, and in the absence of any such water connection, to pioneer an overland route across the Rocky Mountains. Funded by a congressional appropriation of $2,500, the 35-man expedition is headed by President Jefferson's personal secretary Captain Meriwether Lewis, 30, and William Clark, the 34-year-old brother of George Rogers Clark of 1778 Kaskaskia and Vincennes fame. Botanist William Bartram, now 65, declines an invitation from President Jefferson to join the party, which sights frequent herds of bison, estimated to number at least 10 million on the western plains and thought by some to number 5 or 10 times that many.

Congress permits 160-acre tracts of U.S. public lands to be sold at auction.

Ohio University is founded at Athens.

Painting *The Pesthouse at Jaffa* by Antoine Jean Gros.

Theater *Wilhelm Tell* by Johann von Schiller 3/17 at Weimar's Hoftheater is based on the 15th-century legend of a Swiss hero of the previous century who used his crossbow to shoot an apple placed on the head of his young son by the Austrian tyrant Gessler, bailiff of Uri (*see* Rossini opera, 1829); *Homage to the Arts* (*Die Huldigung der Kunste*) by Johann von Schiller 11/12 at Weimar's Hoftheater. Schiller has been in poor health and will die next year at age 45.

Ohio farmer George Rennic drives a corn-fed herd of cattle across the mountains to Baltimore, losing less than 100 pounds per head and making a sound profit. Many western farmers will be inspired to follow Rennic's example, but there are still food surpluses west of the Alleghenies and shortages on the seaboard.

Haitian sugar production falls to 27,000 tons, down from 70,000 in 1791, as agriculture is disrupted by the revolution against France (above) (*see* 1825).

Rust destroys part of England's wheat crop, bread prices rise, but Parliament imposes prohibitory duties that discourage imports of foreign grain. Customs and excise duties on food make up nearly half of Britain's total revenues (*see* Corn Law, 1815).

The world's first vacuum-bottling factory, or cannery, is opened at Massey (Seine-et-Oise) near Palaiseau and Paris by Nicolas Appert (*see* 1795). He has subjected his vacuum-packed foods to public tests at Brest, and he has been encouraged by the gastronome Grimod de la Reynière, who publicizes Appert's products in his *Almanach des Gourmands* (*see* 1808).

Almanach des Gourmands by Grimod de la Reynière (above) is the world's first restaurant guide. It lists some 500 Paris restaurants (*see* 1765; 1808).

The first shipment of bananas to arrive at New York is landed by Captain John Chester's schooner *Reynard* (*see* 1830; Baker, 1870).

1805 France's Emperor Napoleon crowns himself with the old iron crown of the Lombard kings May 26 in the cathedral at Milan, he appoints his stepson Eugene Beauharnais viceroy June 7, but a Third Coalition mobilizes against Napoleon as Austria, Russia, and Sweden make alliances with Britain, while Napoleon gains support from Spain, Bavaria, Württemberg, Baden, Hesse, and Nassau.

French troops mass at Boulogne to cross the Channel and invade the British Isles. Two squadrons of French ships are hastily put together under the command of Vice Admiral Pierre Charles Jean Baptiste Silvestre de Villeneuve, 42, to escort the landing barges, but the admiral and the minister of marine have no confidence in the ships, the officers, or the untrained crews. Villeneuve sails south rather than

1805 (cont.) enter the Channel, and he is blockaded in the harbor of Cadiz by Viscount Nelson.

Napoleon breaks camp at Boulogne, he proceeds by forced marches into Germany, he forces the surrender October 17 at Ulm of a 30,000-man Austrian army under Baron Karl Mack von Leiberich, 53, and he caps the victory by taking Vienna.

The Battle of Trafalgar October 21 ends French pretensions as a sea power as Admiral Villeneuve tries to escape the British blockade of Cadiz and a combined French and Spanish fleet is defeated off the Spanish coast near Gibraltar by the British Royal Navy commanded by Viscount Nelson. Signal Number 16 hoisted by Nelson before the battle says, "England expects every man to do his duty." Nelson takes 60 percent of the enemy fleet as prizes, but the great admiral is shot dead during the engagement by a French sharpshooter who picks him off from his command post on the flagship *Victory*.

The Battle of Austerlitz December 2 gives Napoleon a resounding victory over combined Austrian and Russian forces. The French success dissuades Prussia from joining the Third Coalition (above).

The Treaty of Pressburg December 26 ends hostilities between France and Austria. Piedmont, Parma, and Piacenza are ceded to France; the Tyrol, the free city of Augsburg, and other territory are ceded to Bavaria, which yields Würzburg to the elector of Salzburg, whose city is given to Austria along with Berchtesgaden and the estates of the Teutonic Order; Württemberg and Baden are recognized as kingdoms and are given what remain of the western lands of the Hapsburgs.

The Bourbons in Naples are dethroned in December by Napoleon in a proclamation issued at Schönbrunn.

Egypt gains independence from the Ottoman Turks, whose forces are driven out by the 36-year-old Mohammed Ali, a former tobacco merchant from Kavalla who came to Egypt in 1799 as commander of an Albanian contingent, was appointed governor by the Ottoman sultan, has intervened in political intrigues among Turkish officials and the Mamelukes, and is proclaimed pasha by Mameluke supporters.

A U.S. war with Tripoli is ended by a treaty signed June 4.

Michigan is made a territory separate from the Indiana Territory, and Detroit is made its capital (*see* 1701; Illinois Territory, 1809).

The District of Louisiana is made Louisiana Territory with its capital at St. Louis.

The Lewis and Clark expedition survives a bitter winter by eating wild roots which the men have been taught to find by Sacajawea, a teenaged Shoshone girl whose French-Canadian husband serves as the expedition's guide and interpreter. The expedition reaches the Pacific in November (*see* 1804; 1806).

U.S. Army lieutenant Zebulon Montgomery Pike, 26, ascends the Mississippi River in search of its source (*see* 1806; Marquette and Joliet, 1673).

The first American covered bridge is erected across the Schuylkill River. A Philadelphia judge has persuaded Timothy Palmer to cover the three-span structure to prevent snow from blocking it (*see* Vermont, 1824).

The Beaufort scale devised by British Royal Navy officer Francis Beaufort, 31, measures wind velocities and will be an aid to navigation.

Philadelphia merchant Stephen Girard, 55, builds ships to enter the lucrative China and West Indian trade. Frenchman Girard has made $50,000 selling the belongings of French planters killed in the insurrection last year at Saint Domingue (*see* 1812).

U.S. trade in Sumatra pepper reaches its peak. Re-exports alone total 7 million pounds (*see* 1797; 1873).

Boston entrepreneur Frederic Tudor, 21, pioneers export of U.S. ice. Tudor has declined to "waste his time" attending Harvard like his three brothers, he has heard that lumber shipped from New England ports in winter will sometimes still have ice on its plank-ends when unloaded weeks later at West Indian ports, and he engages men to chop ice from nearby lakes and ponds to be stored in icehouses. Tudor loads 130 tons aboard the brig *Favorite* bound for Martinique, but the voyage takes unusually long, most of the ice has melted by the time the ship arrives, most of the rest melts in port for lack of proper storage facilities, and Tudor loses $4,500. Undaunted, he will fit out the better-insulated ship *Trident*, will load her with ice 20 inches thick instead of the usual 9 or 10, will sail for Havana, and will obtain a virtual monopoly in ice trade to Cuba. He will build ice houses at Kingston, Port-au-Prince, Fort de France, Rio de Janeiro, and other ports, and will establish a large business (*see* 1833; Wyeth, 1825).

Prussia abolishes internal customs duties to improve her domestic economy.

Rhodium is discovered by England's William H. Wollaston.

England's Haileybury College is founded to train East India Company personnel.

Poetry *The Lay of the Last Minstrel* by Walter Scott is his first original poem: "Breathes there a man, with soul so dead,/ Who never to himself hath said,/ This is my own, my native land!"

Painting *Shipwreck* by J. M. W. Turner; *Greta Bridge* by English landscape watercolorist John Sell Cotman, 23; *Dona Isabel Cobos de Procal* by Francisco Goya.

Opera *Fidelio, oder Die eheliche Liebe* 11/20 at Vienna's Theater-an-der-Wien, with music by Ludwig van Beethoven who includes a second version of his *Leonore* Overture (*see* 1798; 1814).

First performances   Symphony No. 3 in E flat major (*Eroica*) by Ludwig van Beethoven 4/7 at Vienna's Theater-an-der-Wien. The composer dedicated the symphony last year to the French first consul Napoleon Bonaparte but has struck out the dedication upon learning that Bonaparte has accepted the title "Emperor of the French"; Sonata in A major for Violin or Piano (*Kreutzer*) by Ludwig van Beethoven 5/17 at Bonn, in a concert given at 8 in the morning. Beethoven has dedicated the work to violinist Rudolf Kreutzer who has called it "unintelligible" and has refused to play it.

Italian violinist Nicolo Paganini begins a second European tour.

The virtual abolition of scurvy from the Royal Navy has played a major role in the victory of the British at Trafalgar (above) (*see* 1794; 1884).

Tangerines from Tangier in Morocco reach Europe for the first time.

English population authority Thomas R. Malthus is named to a chair in political economy at the new Haileybury College (above) (*see* 1817).

1806 Napoleon places his older brother Joseph on the throne of Naples and his younger brother Louis on the throne of Holland, once the Batavian republic.

London announces a blockade of the European coast from Brest to the Elbe May 6 but permits ships from neutral nations to pass if they are not carrying goods to or from enemy ports.

The Holy Roman Empire that has existed since Christmas of 800 ends July 12 in the Confederation of the Rhine organized under French auspices. The confederation brings most of the German states under French domination and precipitates a war with Prussia, whose main armies are routed October 14 at the Battles of Jena and Auerstad.

Napoleon occupies Berlin October 27 and proclaims a paper blockade of Britain November 21 in the Berlin Decree that inaugurates the Continental system designed to deny the British food and supplies from the Continent.

British troops occupy the Cape of Good Hope.

Venezuelan Creole leader Francisco de Miranda, 50, fails in an effort to win freedom from Spain (*see* 1811).

The Lewis and Clark expedition returns to St. Louis September 3 after nearly 28 months of exploration. The expedition had been given up for lost, and its return is celebrated throughout the country. Only one man has been lost, and the maps, notes, and specimens brought back will be of immense value to scientists. Lewis is named governor of the Louisiana Territory and will hold the position until his mysterious death in October 1809 while traveling near Nashville, Tennessee, en route to Washington.

U.S. commerce falls to one-third its former value as a result of European trade restrictions. Thomas Jefferson introduces a bill to exclude such British goods as can be replaced by goods from other nations or can be produced domestically.

English textile mills shut down as supplies of raw cotton from the U.S. South run short.

Lancashire cotton mill owner Robert Owen continues to pay full wages to all workers at his New Lanark mill despite its shutdown for lack of raw cotton (above). Prejudice against Owen has been strong despite his closing of shops that cheat the people and his substitution of shops of his own that sell only pure food (and pure whiskey), but his maintenance of wages wins Owen the confidence and support of his workers (*see* 1799; 1809).

A cotton thread strong and smooth as silk is developed at Paisley, Scotland, by Patrick Clark, who has sold silk thread for the loops (heddles) that hold the lengthwise warp threads in place on a loom. The blockade (above) has cut Britain off from supplies of French and Oriental silk, but Clark's cotton heddles are so effective that silk heddles will no longer be used in Britain. The cotton thread will prove strong enough to replace the linen thread now in common use, and Clark with his brother James will open the first factory for making cotton sewing thread (*see* Coats, 1826).

Coal gas is used for lamps by David Melville at Newport, R.I., but candlewax and whale oil remain the chief sources of illumination (*see* 1804; 1807).

Construction of a road to connect Cumberland, Md., with the Ohio River is authorized by Congress (*see* Cumberland Road, 1811).

Construction of the Natchez Trace is authorized by Congress to follow the 500-mile Indian trail from Nashville to Natchez on the Mississippi River.

The Compendious Dictionary of the English Language by Noah Webster is published as the first Webster's dictionary (*see* 1783; 1828).

Poetry   *Simonidea* by English poet Walter Savage Landor, 31, contains his poem "Rose Aylmer" and gains him wide acclaim; *Original Poems for Infant Minds* by English poets Ann and Jane Taylor, 24 and 23, includes Jane's nursery rhyme "Twinkle, twinkle, little star,/ How I wonder what you are!/ Up above the world so high,/ Like a diamond in the sky."

Painting   *The Battle of Aboukir* by Antoine Jean Gros. George Stubbs dies at London July 10 at 81; J. H. Fragonard dies at Paris August 22 at 74; Japanese *ukioye* painter Utamaro Kitagawa dies at 53.

First performances   Concerto in D major for Violin and Orchestra by Ludwig van Beethoven 12/23 at Vienna's Theater-an-der-Wien.

Colgate-Palmolive-Peet Company has its beginnings in a New York tallow chandlery and soap manufactory opened at 6 Dutch Street by English-American candlemaker William Colgate, 23 (*see* 1928; Colgate University, 1890).

1806 (cont.) London architect John Nash, 54, begins work that will transform the city in the next few decades. Nash probably owes his new appointment as architect to the Chief Commissioner of Woods and Forests to the fact that his wife Mary Ann, 33, is the mistress of the Prince of Wales, who in 5 years will become Prince Regent. The prince has evidently given Nash the means to afford a handsome mansion in Dover Street and a large estate on the Isle of Wight (*see* Regent's Park, 1811).

Ireland suffers a partial failure of her potato crop (*see* 1822).

The western high plains of America are "incapable of cultivation," says Zebulon Pike, who leads an expedition to the Rocky Mountains (Pike's Peak) and compares the plains to the "sandy deserts of Africa" (*see* 1805; Long, 1820).

1807 A British Order in Council January 7 prohibits neutral nation ships from trading with France and her allies, but while Napoleon's ports are blockaded by the Royal Navy, the French are agriculturally self-sufficient and suffer less than do the British.

The Battle of Eylau February 7 to 8 pits Prussian and Russian forces against the French in a bloody slaughter that ends indecisively.

The Dardanelles are forced by a British squadron under Admiral Sir John Thomas Duckworth, 59, who appears before Constantinople. He is forced to retire with the loss of two ships to the Turks.

British forces occupy Alexandria March 18 but are able to hold it for only 6 months before the Turks force their evacuation.

French forces take Danzig May 26 and defeat the Russians June 14 in the Battle of Friedland. Napoleon occupies Königsberg, he concludes a truce after reaching the Niemen River, and he meets with Russia's Aleksandr I and Prussia's Friedrich Wilhelm III on a raft in the river to conclude the Treaties of Tilsit, July 7 to 9.

The Treaties of Tilsit (above) oblige Russia to recognize the grand duchy of Warsaw created from Polish territory acquired by Prussia, to recognize Jérôme Bonaparte as king of a new kingdom of Westphalia, to restore the position of Danzig as a free city, and to accept Napoleon's mediation in concluding peace with the Turks, while Napoleon accepts Aleksandr's mediation in concluding peace with Britain (a secret article provides for a Russo-French alliance against Britain should the British refuse to accept a peace offer). Bialystock in New East Prussia is ceded to Russia, while Prussia cedes to Napoleon all lands between the Rhine and the Elbe, makes other cessions, and recognizes the sovereignty of Napoleon's three brothers.

Copenhagen is bombarded by a British fleet in September for not joining the Continental system, the Danish fleet is carried off, Denmark makes an alliance with France, Russia declares war on Britain, and French troops occupy Stralsund and Rügen.

U.S. authorities arrest former Vice President Aaron Burr February 19 in Alabama and bring him to trial May 22 at Richmond, Va., in a circuit court presided over by Chief Justice John Marshall of the Supreme Court. Burr has evidently schemed to establish an independent nation comprised of Mexico and parts of the Louisiana Territory, but the court acquits him for lack of evidence. He will go to Britain and France next year in an effort to gain support for his various schemes, but he will return to New York in 1812, resume his law practice, and remain in obscurity until his death in 1836 (*see* Morris-Jumel mansion, 1765).

The British man-of-war *Leopard* fires on the U.S. frigate *Chesapeake* June 22 and removes four alleged British deserters. President Jefferson closes U.S. ports to all armed British vessels July 2 and tells France's Citizen E. C. E. Genêt that U. S. jurisdiction over territorial waters should extend to the Gulf Stream (*see* 1793).

Sierra Leone and Gambia become a British crown colony (*see* 1843).

The Ottoman sultan Selim III is deposed in July at age 46 after 18 years in power. The Janissaries revolt and put the 28-year-old Mustapha IV on the throne.

Portugal refuses to cooperate in Napoleon's Continental system and is invaded in November by a French army under Andoche Junot, 36, who captures Lisbon and is given the title duc d'Abrantès. Portugal's royal Braganza family flees November 29 to Brazil (*see* 1808; 1822).

The Milan Decree issued by Napoleon December 17 reiterates the paper blockade against British trade with the Continent.

An Embargo Act signed by President Jefferson December 22 prohibits all ships from leaving U.S. ports for foreign ports. The act is designed to force French and British withdrawal of restrictions on U.S. trade, but its effect will be to make overseas sales of U.S. farm surpluses impossible. New England shippers protest the embargo and are joined by southern cotton and tobacco planters (*see* 1809).

Prussian serfs are emancipated by the country's new prime minister Baron Heinrich Friedrich Karl vom und zum Stein, 60 (*see* 1810).

Britain's George III dissolves Parliament rather than grant emancipation to Catholics (*see* 1829).

A bill to forbid trade in slaves passed by Parliament before it dissolves (above) comes after great agitation by the humanitarian William Wilberforce (*see* 1789; antislavery society, 1823).

On Some Chemical Agencies of Electricity by Humphry Davy gives sodium and potassium their names. Davy has prepared the elements by electrolysis (*see* 1800; calcium, 1808).

Londoners see a demonstration of gas lighting on one side of Pall Mall in a display arranged by F. A. Winsor (*see* 1804; 1812).

The first commercially successful steamboat travels up the Hudson River August 17 and arrives in 32 hours at Albany to begin regular service between New York and Albany. Designed by Robert Fulton and backed by Robert Livingston of 1803 Louisiana Purchase fame, the *Clermont* has paddle wheels (suggested by inventor Nicholas Roosevelt, 40) that are powered by an English Boulton and Watt engine with a cylinder 24 inches in diameter and a 4-foot stroke. The *Clermont* is 133 feet long, 18 feet in the beam, with a 7-foot draft and a stack 30 feet high, and is the forerunner of steamboats that soon will be carrying western grain to Gulf Coast ports via the Ohio and Mississippi (*see* 1811; Stevens, 1803, 1808).

Phrenology arrives at Paris with German physician Franz Joseph Gall, 49, who introduced the pseudoscience in 1800. Gall claims that most emotional and intellectual functions are determined by specific areas of the brain that can be recognized by bumps in the skull.

The University of Maryland is founded outside Baltimore.

The Fourdrinier machine patented by English papermaker Henry Fourdrinier, 41, and his brother Sealy will spur the growth of newspapers (*see* Robert, 1798). Helped by civil engineer Bryan Donkin, 31, the Fourdrinier brothers have developed an improved machine that can produce a continuous sheet of paper in any desired size from wood pulp.

Poetry *Poems in Two Volumes* by William Wordsworth brings the poet to the height of his powers although his masterpiece *The Prelude* will not appear until after his death in 1850. Included are the sonnets "London, 1802" ("Milton! thou shouldst be living at this hour . . .") and "Composed Upon Westminster Bridge, September 3, 1802": "Earth has not anything to show more fair:/ Dull would he be of soul who could pass by/ A sight so touching in its majesty:/ This city now doth, like a garment, wear/ The beauty of the morning: silent, bare. . . ."

Other poems included by Wordsworth in his new books are "Ode to Duty," "Intimations of Immortality from Recollections of Early Childhood," "She Was a Phantom of Delight," "I Wandered Lonely as a Cloud" ("Daffodils"), all written in 1804, "My Heart Leaps Up" ("The Child is father of the man"), Wordsworth's 1806 sonnets "The World Is Too Much with Us" and "Thought of a Briton on the Subjugation of Switzerland," and his 1806 poem "Character of a Happy Warrior."

Juvenile *Tales From Shakespeare* by English essayist-critic Charles Lamb, 32, and his sister Mary Ann, 43. Lamb has been taking care of his sister since she killed their invalid mother in a fit of insanity 11 years ago and has given up a projected marriage to devote himself to that responsibility, although he himself has been mentally unbalanced and was confined to an asylum from age 20 to 21.

Painting *Coronation of Napoleon and Josephine* by Jacques Louis David.

First performances Symphony No. 1 in C minor and Symphony No. 2 in C major by German composer Carl Maria von Weber, 20, at Schloss Carlsruhe in Silesia where the sickly von Weber lives with his father and aunt at the invitation of Duke Eugen of Würtemberg; Symphony No. 4 in B flat major by Ludwig van Beethoven 3/5 at the Vienna palace of Prince Lobkowitz, in a program that includes Beethoven's three earlier symphonies, his *Coriolanus* Overture, and his Concerto in G major for Pianoforte and Orchestra; Mass in C major by Ludwig van Beethoven 9/13 at the palace of Nicholas Esterhazy; Sonata in F minor (*Appasionata*) by Beethoven.

England's Ascot Gold Cup horse race has its first running (*see* 1711; 1822).

English pugilist Thomas Cribb, 26, wins the title from Henry Pearce and offers to defend it "against any fighter in the world." The offer will have no takers after 1811 and Cribb will retire undefeated in 1822 (*see* first world championship, 1860).

Water carbonated with carbonic gas is bottled and sold in the New York City area by Yale's first chemistry professor Benjamin Silliman, 28 (*see* Bergman, 1770; Matthews, 1833).

1808 Napoleon announces that France must guard the coast of Spain against Britain, he orders upwards of 70,000 men to cross the Spanish frontier in January, French forces occupy the fortresses of San Sebastian, Pamplona, Figueras, and Barcelona by treachery in February, by mid-March there are nearly 100,000 French troops in Spain, and their commander in chief Joachim Murat occupies Madrid March 26. Carlos IV abdicates in favor of his 23-year-old son Ferdinand, Napoleon resolves to make his brother Joseph king of Spain, the Spaniards revolt May 2, Murat intimidates the Spanish council at Madrid May 13 into requesting Joseph as king, the Portuguese join in the insurrection, and they ask for British help.

Spanish forces at Bailen force a French army of 18,000 under General Pierre Antoine Dupont, 43, to surrender July 23.

British forces invade Portugal August 1 under Sir Arthur Wellesley, they defeat the French under General Dupont (above) August 21, but Wellesley's superiors prevent him from following up his victory.

The defeat of General Dupont at Bailen (above) forces Spain's new king Joseph Bonaparte to leave Madrid in August.

General Murat succeeds Joseph Bonaparte as king of Naples, he enters Naples in September as King Joachim Napoleon, and he wrests Capri from the British. Napoleon moves into Spain in the autumn with an army of 150,000, routs the Spanish in a series of

Robert Fulton's S.S. *Clermont* began a new era of steamboat travel, but sailing ships still ruled the waves.

engagements in November, takes Madrid December 4, and puts his brother Joseph back on the throne.

Denmark's demented Christian VII has died March 13 at age 59 after a 32-year reign. His 39-year-old son has ruled as regent since 1784, has become an ally of Napoleon, and begins a 31-year reign as Frederick VI.

The Ottoman grand vizier Mustafa Bairakdar, 33, marches on Constantinople to restore the sultan Selim III, the Janissaries strangle Selim to prevent his restoration, and Bairakdar has the new sultan Mustapha IV deposed and assassinated. He places Selim's 23-year-old nephew on the throne, sends his troops to the Danube, and commits suicide to avoid being captured by the Janissaries, but the new sultan begins a 31-year reign as Mahmud II.

A British mission to Japan arrives August 15, but the Tokugawa shogun Ienari rejects the emissaries.

Thomas Jefferson declines a third term, he supports his Secretary of State James Madison, and Madison's Jeffersonian Republican party wins the fall election with 122 electoral votes versus 47 for the Federalist Charles C. Pinckney.

Importation of slaves into the United States is banned as of January 1 by an act of Congress passed last year, but illegal imports continue (*see* 1814).

An Elizabethan statute making it a capital offense to steal from the person is repealed by Parliament following a campaign by London barrister Samuel Romilly, 51, who is reforming the English criminal laws and is agitating against slavery.

A New System of Chemical Philosophy by English chemist John Dalton establishes the quantitative theory of chemistry (*see* 1803).

Barium, boron, calcium, and strontium are isolated by Humphry Davy (*see* 1807; 1813; Choss, 1840).

The S.S. *Phoenix* launched by New Jersey engineer John Stevens is the first steamboat with an American-built engine (*see* 1790; Fulton, 1807). Stevens learns that his brother-in-law Robert R. Livingston and Robert Fulton have obtained a 20-year monopoly on steamboat operations in New York State waters and prepares to have his son take the new sidewheeler to Philadelphia (*see* 1809; 1824).

New York physician John Stearns describes amazing results in easing women's labor pains by administering a medication made according to an old midwife's instructions from diseased heads of rye (*see* ergonovine, 1935).

John Jacob Astor incorporates the American Fur Company with himself as sole stockholder. The German-American entrepreneur came to New York from his native Waldorf in 1783 at age 20, he apprenticed himself to baker George Dieterich, he soon quit to go into the fur trade, and he has bartered firearms, "firewater" (whiskey), and flannel with the Indians to obtain animal pelts, chiefly beaver for use in hats (*see* Hetherington, 1798; Pacific Fur Company, 1810).

The *Times* of London sends journalist-diarist Henry Crabb Robinson, 33, to report on the Peninsular War in Spain, and Robinson becomes the world's first war correspondent.

Poetry *Marmion* by Walter Scott, who introduces the romantic hero Young Lochinvar: "Oh, what a tangled web we weave/ When first we practice to deceive" (VI); *Lyudmila* by Russian poet Vasily Andryevich Zhukovsky, 25, who has adapted the 1773 poem *Lenore* by the late German poet Gottfried August Burger. Zhukofsky's ballad marks the start of modern Russian poetry.

Painting *The Battle of Eylau* by Antoine Jean Gros; *Execution of the Citizens of Madrid* by Francisco Goya y Lucientes, now 62, who records massacres by the French (above) that will be seen in his etchings *Disasters of the War.* Goya has been court painter to Carlos IV but becomes court painter to Joseph Bonaparte. Goya paintings owned by the Spanish prime minister Manuel de Godoy, 41, are inventoried and the list includes *The Naked Maja* and *The Maja Clothed,* painted nearly life-size and possibly showing the duchess of Alba who died in 1802. The word "Maja" is derived from "maya," title of the queen of the May; it means something between "wanton" and "wench," and the work is so scandalous that Godoy is able to keep it only by virtue of his position as prime minister and lover of the queen Maria Luisa. *La Grande Baigneuse* by French painter Jean Auguste Dominique Ingres, 28; *The Cross on the Mountains* by Dresden painter Kaspar David Friedrich, 34.

Theater *Faust* by Johann Wolfgang von Goethe is published in its first part. Goethe's drama of dissatisfaction, seduction, and infanticide is rooted in German legend, in the academic turmoil of his student days, and in the Christopher Marlowe drama of 1601 (*see* Gounod opera, 1859); *The Indian Princess, or La Belle Sauvage* by U.S. playwright James Nelson Baker, 24, 4/6 at Philadelphia's New Theater (a riot disrupts the performance).

First performances Symphony No. 5 in C minor and Symphony No. 6 in F major (*Pastoral*) by Ludwig van Beethoven 12/22 at Vienna's Theater-an-der-Wien, in a concert that also includes Beethoven's Concerto No. 4 in G minor for Pianoforte and Orchestra and Fantasy for Piano, Chorus, and Orchestra.

Irish Melodies is published with music by John Stevenson, lyrics by Irish poet Thomas Moore, 29. It includes "Believe Me, If All Those Endearing Young Charms" (Moore will gain fame also for "The Harp that Once Through Tara's Halls," "The Minstrel Boy," and "Oft in the Stilly Night").

Lectures on Animal Chemistry by Jöns Jakob Berzelius explores the composition of blood, gall, milk, bone, fat, and other elements. His studies will influence fundamental knowledge of life and bodily functions (*see* selenium, 1817).

French confectioner Nicolas Appert wins a prize of 12,000 francs (nearly $250,000) for his method of vacuum-packing food in jars (*see* 1804; Bonaparte, 1794). Appert's factory packs food for Napoleon's armies, and his method will remain briefly a French military secret (*see* Durand, 1810).

An article on beet sugar written by F. K. Achard in Berlin appears in France's *Moniteur* and arouses French interest in domestic sugar production, as the British Orders in Council issued last year cut France off from sugar imports (*see* 1810; Achard, 1802).

The first Parisian restaurant of any substance with fixed prices opens in the Palais Royal under the management of the restaurateur Very.

1809 French forces defeat Sir John Moore and kill him in the Battle of Corunna January 16. Sir Arthur Wellesley succeeds Moore as commander of British forces in the Peninsular War (*see* 1808; 1812).

Napoleon returns from Spain and finds that the Austrians have taken advantage of his absence to push preparations for war against the diminished French forces west of the Rhine. He orders the formation of new battalions to oppose the Austrians.

Seven Swedish army officers break into the royal apartments March 13, seize the insane Gustavus IV in a coup d'etat, and conduct him to the château of Gripsholm. A provisional government is proclaimed the same day under the 60-year-old duke of Sudermania. The king abdicates March 29 in hopes of saving the crown for his son, but the estates (dominated by the army) declare May 10 that the whole family has forfeited the throne. The duke is proclaimed king June 5 and will reign until 1818 as Charles XIII.

Austrian forces cross the Inn April 9, other Austrian regiments advance on Regensburg from Pilsen in Bohemia, while a French army advances on Regensburg under the command of the 39-year-old Louis Nicolas Davout, duc d'Auerstaedt.

Napoleon sustains a slight wound in late April while directing an assault on Regensburg but continues to direct French forces against the Austrians. Vienna falls to the French May 12, but the Battle of Aspern (Essling) May 21 to 22 brings Napoleon his first defeat.

The French retreat to the small (1 square mile) island of Lobau in the Danube, which they jam with upwards of 100,000 men plus 20,000 wounded but without medical supplies and with few provisions. Napoleon rejects his generals' advice to retreat and calls for reinforcements.

The Battle of Wagram July 5 to 6 ends in victory for the French but only at a terrible cost: 23,000 French soldiers are killed or wounded and 7,000 are missing out of a 181,700-man army that includes 29,000 cavalrymen, while the Austrian army of 181,700 (4,600 cavalrymen) is forced to retreat after having 19,110 killed or wounded and 6,740 missing.

Austria's 36-year-old statesman Clemens Wenzel Lothar Metternich-Winneburg has urged the war against Napoleon, he has been arrested at Paris in reprisal for Austria's action in interning two members of the French embassy in Hungary, he has been conducted to Vienna in June under military guard, he is exchanged in July for the two French diplomats, and he is present with the emperor at the Battle of Wagram (above).

Metternich (above) is made Austrian minister of state August 4, he leaves soon thereafter for a peace conference at Altenburg, and he is appointed minister of foreign affairs October 8 to begin a 40-year career in that post, but he has nothing to do with the peace treaty (below).

The Treaty of Schönbrunn signed October 14 ends hostilities between France and Austria, which joins Napoleon's Continental system.

Napoleon announces to his wife Josephine that he is compelled to divorce her for reasons of state, and his lawyers find a slight technical irregularity in the marriage ceremony of December 1, 1804, which they use to have the marriage declared null and void.

Britain's Sir Arthur Wellesley has defeated the Spanish king Joseph Bonaparte July 27 to 28 at Talavera de la Reina and has been made duke of Wellington after his triumph.

The papal states are annexed by Napoleon, and Pope Pius VII is taken prisoner July 5. He will remain in custody until 1814.

The Treaty of Amritsar in India checks the advance of a Sikh confederacy under Ranjit Singh, 29, and fixes the East India Company's northwest territorial border at the Sutlej River.

1809 (cont.) The territory of Illinois is cut from Indiana Territory and is established as a separate territory (*see* 1818; Michigan Territory, 1805).

The Treaty of Fort Wayne negotiated September 30 by General William Henry Harrison obtains 3 million acres of Indiana Territory Indian land on the Wabash River for the United States (*see* Tippecanoe, 1811).

Hudson's Bay Company fur trader David Thompson, 37, erects a trading post that is the first building in what will be Idaho Territory. Thompson will survey and map more than 1 million square miles of Canada between Lake Superior and the Pacific and will trace lakes and rivers that will include the Columbia, the Mississippi, and the Saskatchewan.

The British minister to Washington assures President Madison that Britain will repeal her 1807 Orders in Council, Madison withdraws the U.S. embargo on trade with Britain imposed late in 1807, 1,200 ships sail for British ports, but London says its ambassador has exceeded his authority and trade halts once again (*see* 1811).

A pamphlet on *The High Price of Bullion a Proof of the Depreciation of Bank-Notes* by London broker David Ricardo, 37, will be influential in determining British economic policy. It establishes Ricardo as a major economic theorist (*see* 1811; 1817).

Britain repeals her 1563 Statute of Apprentices in the name of "economic freedom." Parliament also repeals other measures that have protected British workers.

Robert Owen proposes to his partners that they stop employing children under age 10 in their cotton mills and that they build nurseries, schools, playgrounds, and lecture halls for the people of New Lanark (*see* 1806). The proposals are rejected, Owen finds new partners to buy out the old ones, but they "objected to the building of the schools, and said they were cotton-spinners and commercial men carrying on business for profit, and had nothing to do with educating children; nobody did it in the manufactories." Owen finds a London group that will go into business with him on the promise of a reasonable return on capital rather than of exorbitant profits, and the group includes Jeremy Bentham (*see* 1789), Quakers William Allen and James Walker, and the future lord mayor Michael Gibbs (*see* 1814).

The first ocean voyage by steamboat is made by U.S. mariner Moses Rogers, 30, in the *Phoenix,* launched last year by John Stevens. Rogers steams from New York round Sandy Hook and Cape May to the Delaware River (*see* 1819).

The reflecting goniometer for physics research is invented by England's William H. Wollaston.

Acquired characteristics can be inherited, says French naturalist Jean Baptiste Pierre Antoine de Monet, 65, the chevalier de Lamarck. The false ideas in his *Zoological Philosophy* (*Philosophie Zoologique*) will persist for more than a century.

The first recorded U.S. operation in ovarian surgery is performed by Danville, Ky., surgeon Ephraim McDowell, 38, who removes an ovarian tumor from Jane Todd Crawford at Greensburg and demonstrates that surgery of the abdominal cavity need not be fatal.

Miami University has its beginnings in a college founded on the Miami River at Oxford, Ohio.

The first U.S. parochial school is founded near Baltimore by English-American widow Elizabeth Ann Seton, 36, a recent convert to Roman Catholicism who is joined by other Catholic women in starting the Sisters of Charity, a religious order that will be allied in 1850 with France's Daughters of Charity of St. Vincent de Paul. Mother of five, "Mother Seton" will be credited with several "miracles" and will be canonized in 1975 as the first American saint.

Fiction *Coelebs in Search of a Wife* by Hannah More; *The Elective Affinities* (*Die Wahlverwandtschaften*) by Johann Wolfgang von Goethe.

Nonfiction *A History of New York from the Beginning of the World to the End of the Dutch Dynasty* by New York essayist Diedrich Knickerbocker (Washington Irving), 26, is published on St. Nicholas Day, December 6. Irving dedicates his comic history derisively to the 5-year-old New York Historical Society and makes 25 references to an impish, pipe-smoking St. Nicholas who brings gifts down chimneys, thus beginning a legend that will travel round the world (*see* Moravians, 1740; Moore, 1823).

Painting *Malvern Hill* by English painter John Constable, 33; *Mrs. Spiers* by Henry Raeburn; *Monch am Meer* by Kaspar Friedrich.

England's Two Thousand Guineas race has its first running at the Newmarket races.

Export of Chilean nitrates to Europe begins, but the nitrates are used less for fertilizer than for explosives (*see* Humboldt, 1804).

1810 Napoleon is married March 11 by proxy at Vienna to the 18-year-old Austrian archduchess Maria Luisa in a wedding arranged by Austrian foreign minister von Metternich. The "little corporal" hopes to father an heir to his vast empire.

Tyrolese patriot Andreas Hofer, 41, defeats a Bavarian army in a rebellion against Bavarian rule but is later defeated by combined French and Bavarian forces, forced into hiding, betrayed, and shot February 20 at Mantua.

Sweden's Prince Christian of Holstein-Augstenburg is elected heir to the throne but dies suddenly in May and is replaced as crown prince by Napoleonic general Jean Baptiste Jules Bernadotte, 47, who will succeed to the throne in 1818.

Holland is annexed to France July 9 following the abdication and flight of Napoleon's brother Louis Bonaparte, who has been king since 1806 but who has refused to join Napoleon's Continental system. The emperor annexes other lands along the Channel and North Sea coasts including Bremen, Lübeck, Lauenburg, Hamburg, and Hanover in an effort to discourage smuggling of British goods which continue nonetheless to enter European markets.

Prussia's Queen Louise dies July 19 at age 34. Napoleon has tried to destroy her reputation, but his charges have only endeared her to her people.

The British secretary of state for foreign affairs George Canning, 40, resigns September 9, saying that the War Office is hampering progress in the Peninsular War. The secretary for war and the colonies Robert Stewart, 41, marques of Londonderry and Viscount Castlereagh, thinks Canning has called him incompetent and challenges him to a duel. He wounds Canning in the thigh and disgraces him.

Spanish colonists in South America proclaim loyalty to Ferdinand VII who remains a French prisoner at the château of Valencay. A provisional government of the Rio de la Plata is established in Ferdinand's name May 25, a similar junta is established at Caracas, and another at Santiago.

Mexican rebels led by the Creole priest Miguel Hidalgo y Costilla, 57, capture Guanajuato, Guadalajara, and Valladolid. They approach the capital with an ill-equipped force of 80,000, but a small Spanish force under Felix Maria Calleja del Rey, 60, forces them to retreat November 6 (see 1811).

President Madison takes advantage of an insurrection in west Florida to seize Spanish territory whose ownership has not been clearly defined in the Louisiana Purchase of 1803 (see 1818).

$ U.S. Treasury Secretary Albert Gallatin, 49, estimates the total value of U.S. manufactured products at $120 million for the year. In some lines, says Gallatin, the nation is now self-sufficient.

The Pacific Fur Company is organized by John Jacob Astor (see 1808; Astoria, 1811).

Hartford Fire Insurance Company is organized by Jonathan G. W. Trumbull of Norwich, Conn.

❋ Amoskeag Manufacturing Company is founded on the Merrimack River in the New Hampshire town of Amoskeag that changes its name to Manchester, taking its name from the great English milltown. The new company will soon be operating the world's largest cotton mill.

Plymouth, Conn., clockmakers Seth Thomas, 25, and Silas Hoadley buy Eli Terry's clock business after fulfilling a 3-year contract to supply Terry with 4,000 clocks (see 1803). Thomas will sell his share in 1812 and go into business for himself at Plymouth Hollow (later Thomaston), he will organize the Seth Thomas Clock Company in 1853, and he will leave it to his son upon his death early in 1859.

Patents registered by the U.S. Patent Office begin a rapid rise after 20 years of averaging 77 per year.

U.S. cotton mills grow in number to 269, up from 62 last year (see Slater 1789; Lowell, 1812).

⚡ U.S. entrepreneur Cornelius van Derbilt, 16, establishes a ferry service between his native Staten Island and New York's Manhattan Island (see 1712; 1817; 1829).

The differential gear is invented by German art publisher Rudolph Ackerman, 46, to permit carriages to turn sharp corners. His steering mechanism will be used within the century on horseless carriages.

✊ Prussia abolishes serfdom and gives ex-serfs the lands they have cultivated for their landlord masters, allowing them to sell the lands if they choose, but Prussian peasants will live for nearly a century under conditions not far removed from serfdom (see 1807; Russia, 1858).

⚕ Barcelona and Cadiz lose as many as 25,000 to yellow fever.

Homeopathic medicine is founded by German physician Christian Friedrich Samuel Hahnemann, 55, with his *Organon of Therapeutics* (*Organon der Rationellen Heilkunde*). Hahnemann has noticed a similarity between the effects of Peruvian cinchona on a healthy person and the symptoms of the disease for which the bark is used. He has made further investigations, and he announced 14 years ago his principle that a patient can be cured if treated with a drug that produces in a healthy person symptoms similar to those seen in the patient.

🌿 The active principle in tobacco is identified by French chemist Louis Nicolas Vauquelin, who calls it *Nicotianine* after Jean Nicot (see 1561) and the plant *Nicotiana rustica*.

France makes tobacco a government monopoly.

✒ Nonfiction *De l'Allemagne* by Mme. de Staël is published in the first of its three volumes and introduces German romanticism to French literature.

Poetry *The Lady of the Lake* by Walter Scott: "Hail to the chief who in triumph advances."

🎨 Painting *Distribution of the Eagles* by Jacques Louis David; *The Battle of Austerlitz* by François Gerard; *Los Desastres de la Guerra* (engravings) by Francisco Goya. Johann Zoffany dies at Kew, Surrey, November 11 at age 77.

𝄞 First performances Music to Goethe's play *Egmont* of 1788 by Ludwig van Beethoven 6/15 at Vienna's Burgtheater.

🏛 Paris inaugurates a column in the Place Vendôme August 15 to commemorate Napoleon's victory at Austerlitz in December 1805. Modeled after Trajan's column of the 2nd century A.D. at Rome, the column is girdled with a spiral band of bronze made from 1,200 enemy cannon captured at Austerlitz, it is covered with bas reliefs depicting military scenes, and it is surmounted by a statue of Napoleon as Caesar.

Work continues at Paris on the Arc de Triomphe begun 4 years ago by French sculptor Clodion (Claude Michel), now 72 (see 1836).

1810 (cont.) A flock of passenger pigeons 250 miles long is sighted over Kentucky by Scots-American ornithologist Alexander Wilson, 44, who estimates the flock to contain 2 billion birds, nearly half of all the passenger pigeons in the country. Roughly one-third of America's avian population is comprised of passenger pigeons (*see* 1800; Audubon, 1813).

The U.S. cotton crop reaches 178,000 bales as Eli Whitney's cotton gin of 1792 encourages production.

The amino acid cystine is discovered in bladder stones by English chemist William H. Wollaston (*see* Braconnot, 1820).

Nicolas Appert announces his 1808 discovery of vacuum-packed food in *Le Livre de Tous Les Menages,* which is published in June. Subtitled *L'art de Conserver, Pendant Plusieurs Années, Toutes Les Substances Animales et Vegetables,* Appert's book will be revised by its author for 1811, 1813, and 1831 editions, it will be revised thereafter by his nephew Prieur Appert with a collaborator, and it will remain the bible of food preservation for most of the century.

Appert's conserves are studied by French chemist-physicist Joseph Louis Gay-Lussac, 32, who finds no oxygen inside Appert's jars and states in December that "animal and vegetable substances, through their contact with air, promptly become disposed to putrefaction and fermentation, but in exposing them at boiling water temperatures, in well-closed vessels, the absorbed oxygen produces a new combination which no longer is likely to produce fermentation or putrefaction. . . ." Appert has stated that "the subject of heat has the essential quality in itself not only of changing the combination of the constituent parts of animal and vegetable products, but also that, if not destroying it, at least of arresting for many years the natural tendency of these same products to decomposition." The view of the eminent Gay-Lussac that the food in Appert's jars is preserved because oxygen has been forced out of the jars will nevertheless prevail for more than half a century (*see* Pasteur, 1861).

The first English patent for a tin-plated steel container is issued to Peter Durand.

A London cannery that will soon be shipping thousands of cases of tinned foods for use by the Royal Navy is opened under the name Donkin and Hall by Bryan Donkin of 1807 Foudrinier machine fame who has interests in an ironworks (*see* 1812).

Beet sugar factories are set up at Passy by French banker Benjamin Delessert, 37, to supply France with sugar in the absence of imports blockaded by the British Royal Navy. The factories will produce more than 4 million kilos of high-cost sugar in the next 2 years (*see* 1811; 1814).

The Munich Oktoberfest has its beginnings in a festival staged to celebrate the marriage of Bavaria's 24-year-oid crown prince Ludwig (Louis) to the 18-year-old princess Therese of Saxe-Hildburghausen who will bear him seven children.

Old Overholt rye whiskey has its beginnings in a distillery opened by Pennsylvania farmer Abraham Overholt, 26 (*see* Frick, 1870).

New York passes Philadelphia in population to become the largest U.S. city.

New Orleans has a population of 24,562, while all of Louisiana has 70,000 and no other city in the West has more than a few thousand. Pittsburgh has 4,768, Lexington 4,326, Cincinnati 2,450, Louisville, Nashville, Natchez, and St. Louis about 1,000 each.

The U.S. population reaches 7,215,858 with nearly 4 million in the Northeast, 2.3 million in the South, and less than 1 million west of the Alleghenies.

France makes abortion a criminal offense (*see* 1814).

1811 "Luddites" riot against English textile manufacturers who have replaced craftsmen with machines at Nottingham. The organized bands who take their name from a real or imaginary "General Ludd" or "King Ludd" burn one of Richard Arkwright's factories and break into the house of James Hargreaves to smash his 1770 spinning jenny (*see* 1812; Arkwright, 1769).

A bullion report issued by British government economists establishes the intrinsic value theory of money. Banknotes may be a useful medium of exchange, but the notes must bear a definite ratio to the amount of coin and bullion in the vaults. Government cannot create money, which is rather a token of labor performed. Government can acquire money only through taxation or by borrowing, and for government to issue irredeemable paper money is to violate the sanctity of contracts, to cheat creditors, to increase prices, and to disrupt business (*see* Smith, 1776; Ricardo, 1809; Bank Charter Act, 1844).

U.S. customs duties fall to $6 million as loss of trade with Britain and France reduces duties to half their 1806 level. The Napoleonic wars and Britain's Orders in Council have reduced trade (*see* excise tax, 1813).

The charter of the Bank of the United States lapses (*see* 1791).

Britain's George III loses his favorite daughter Amelia and becomes permanently mad after having experienced periodic episodes of insanity beginning as early as 1765 and noted especially in late 1788. Blind as well as mad, the elderly king is replaced by his 49-year-old son under terms of a Regency Bill passed by Parliament.

The Ottoman viceroy Mohammed Ali invites Egypt's Mameluke leaders to a banquet at the citadel of Cairo March 1 and massacres them for having plotted against him. Only a few escape the slaughter, and Mohammed Ali will reign supreme until 1849.

British forces capture Batavia from the French in Java. English colonial officer Thomas Stafford Raffles, 30, has persuaded his superiors to take the island, he has accompanied the expedition, he will administer Java until 1816, and he will introduce a new system of land tenure and remove trade barriers.

British forces on the Iberian Peninsula triumph over the French May 5 at the Battle of Fuentes de Onoro and May 16 at the Battle of Albuera where General William Carr Beresford, 42, defeats the French marshal Nicolas Jean de Dieu Soult, 42.

Venezuelan independence is claimed by a junta formed by the captain general of Caracas, which disavows the Spanish regency created by Napoleon and which invites other Spanish colonies to follow its example. A commission is dispatched to enlist English support for the revolutionists of New Granada, Francisco de Miranda returns to Venezuela to assume leadership, Venezuelan independence is proclaimed by a general congress July 7, and Miranda is given command of the revolutionary forces; Simón Bolívar, 28, returns with the commission sent to London, becomes one of Miranda's lieutenants, and joins the fighting that begins against Spanish forces under Juan Domingo Monteverde (see 1812).

Paraguay declares her independence August 14.

Spanish control ends in the Banda Oriental, where Uruguayan revolutionist José Artigas, 65, has been active.

Chilean revolutionist José Miguel Carrera, 26, overthrows a conservative junta at Santiago (see 1813).

Cartagena in the Viceroyalty of New Granada declares its independence November 11.

Forces of the revolutionary Creole priest Miguel Hidalgo in New Spain are crushed by Spanish troops under Felix Calleja at the Bridge of Calderon near Guadalajara (see 1810). Hidalgo falls into Spanish hands and is tried and executed (see Mexican independence, 1821).

The Battle of Tippecanoe November 7 on the Wabash River ends in complete defeat for the Shawnee who have been drawn into battle by General Harrison in the absence of their chief Tecumseh (see 1809).

Fort Ross above San Francisco Bay is founded February 2 by Russians who land at Bodega Bay and build the fort as the center of a farming colony and as a trading post for sea otter skins (see 1769; Sutter, 1841).

Astoria at the mouth of the Columbia River is founded by the skipper of fur trader John Jacob Astor's ship *Tonquin* who establishes a trading post (see 1814; Pacific Fur Company, 1810).

The first crossing of the African continent is completed after a 9-year journey by two Portuguese half-caste explorers.

Construction begins on the Cumberland Road that extends westward from Cumberland, Md., but states' rights political forces will block congressional appropriations to continue the first national undertaking to improve U.S. internal transportation (see 1806; 1817; Lancaster Road, 1792; Jackson, 1830).

The S.S. *New Orleans* launched by Nicholas Roosevelt leaves Pittsburgh September 11 with Roosevelt and his wife among the passengers. First steamboat in the Mississippi Valley, the ship starts down the Ohio River for the Mississippi on a 14-day voyage to New Orleans (see Fulton, 1807; Shreve, 1817).

A two-cylinder steam locomotive patented by English engineer John Blenkinsop, 28, works by means of a racked rail and a toothed wheel. Blenkinsop will test his locomotive successfully next year and will see it used in collieries (see Trevithick, 1804; Stephenson, 1814).

Krupp *Gusstahlfabrik* (Cast Steel Works) "for the manufacture of English cast steel and all articles made thereof" is founded at Essen by German industrialist Friedrich Krupp, 24, a descendant of Arndt Krupp (see 1599; Huntsman, 1740). The emperor Napoleon has offered a 4,000 franc reward to the first steelmaker who can match the British process, and Krupp gives up his coffee and sugar wholesaling trade to try for the reward, opening a small steelworks in a shed adjoining his house (see 1816).

Iodine is isolated by French chemist Bernard Courtois, 34, who is studying products obtained by leaching the ashes of burnt seaweed. Iodine will be used in medicine as an antiseptic and will be used to purify drinking water.

Anatomy of the Brain by Scottish anatomist Charles Bell, 37, announces discovery of the distinct functions of sensory and motor nerves.

Fiction *Sense and Sensibility, A Novel by a Lady* is published anonymously at London. Its author is Jane Austen, 36, a spinster whose depiction of manners and mores in English country society will rank her as one of the world's great novelists.

London organist Vincent Novello, 30, arranges a collection of sacred music and establishes the publishing house Novello & Co. that will introduce to England works of Haydn, Mozart, and Palestrina hitherto unknown to the English. The firm will later introduce Felix Mendelssohn's works and will develop a system of printing cheap editions of standard musical works.

Opera *Abu Hassan* 6/4 at Munich's Court Theater, with music by Carl Maria von Weber, libretto by Franz Carl Hiemer.

First performances Concertina for B flat Clarinet and Orchestra by Carl Maria von Weber 4/5 at Munich; Concerto for Clarinet and Orchestra No. 1 in F minor and Concerto for Violincello and Orchestra in D major by Carl Maria von Weber 6/13 at Munich; Concerto for Pianoforte and Orchestra No. 2 in E flat

1811 (cont.) major by Carl Maria von Weber 11/9 at Munich; Concerto No. 5 in E flat major for Pianoforte and Orchestra (*Emperor*) by Ludwig van Beethoven 11/28 at Leipzig.

 John Nash designs Regent's Park and its terraces at London and will lay out Regent Street later in the decade (*see* 1806; Brighton Pavilion, 1815; Buckingham Palace, 1825).

Earthquakes beginning December 16 turn the Mississippi River to foam in places between Memphis and St. Louis, the current runs upstream for several hours, most of New Madrid, Mo., crumbles down the bluffs into the river, the sequence of shocks are felt as far away as Detroit, Baltimore, and Charleston, and the tremors continue for months.

 Napoleon awards Benjamin Delessert the medal of the Legion d'Honneur for his success with beet sugar, he orders the immediate allotment of 32,000 hectares to sugar beet cultivation, and he tells the Paris Chamber of Commerce that "the English can throw into the Thames the sugar and indigo which they formerly sold on the Continent with high profit to themselves" (*see* 1810; 1813).

 Iodine (above) will prove to be an essential nutrient in human diets (*see* Baumann, 1896).

 The Russian ambassador to Paris Prince Aleksandr Borosovich Kurakin, 35, introduces the practice of serving meals in courses (*a la Russe*) instead of placing many dishes on the table at once (*see* 1852).

 Napoleon decrees that foundling hospitals in France shall be provided with turntable devices so that parents can leave unwanted infants without being recognized or questioned. Millions of infants have been drowned, smothered, or abandoned, depriving the French army of potential recruits.

1812 Napoleon invades Russia in June as Britain and the United States go to war over the impressment of U.S. seamen (*see* below).

The Grande Armée of 600,000 that invades Russia includes Austrians, Dutch, Germans, Italians, Poles, Prussians, and Swiss as well as Frenchmen, but 80,000 are sick with dysentery, enteric fever, and typhus after the Battle of Ostrowo in July.

British troops under the duke of Wellington (Arthur Wellesley) defeat the French July 22 at Salamanca and enter Madrid in mid-August (*see* Rothschilds, below).

The Battle of Borodino, September 7, is a bloody encounter on the Moskova River. Russia's wily field marshal Mikhail Kutusov, now 66, retreats to save his army, Napoleon enters Moscow, but most of the 300,000 inhabitants have fled, and fires set by the Russians burn much of Moscow in the next 5 days.

Napoleon begins a retreat from Moscow October 19, and the retreat turns into a rout as Marshal Kutusov defeats Marshal Ney and Marshal Davout at Smolensk in November. Crippled by hunger, cold, and lack of salt, harrassed by Cossack troops and Russian irregulars, the invading force has dwindled to no more than 100,000 by mid-December, when the survivors finally straggle across the Nieman River.

The War of 1812 begins June 18 as Washington declares war without being aware that the British Orders in Council of 1807 were withdrawn June 16.

Canada is invaded by U.S. troops from Detroit in July under the command of General William Hull, 59, who is outmaneuvered and defeated by the British.

Fort Dearborn on Lake Michigan is evacuated by order of General Hull (above). Its inhabitants are massacred August 15 by Indians while being escorted to Fort Wayne, and all are killed including 12 children.

Fort Dearborn is sacked and burned August 16, and General Hull is forced to surrender. He will be court-martialed, convicted of cowardice and neglect of duty, and sentenced to be shot in 1814, but the sentence will not be carried out.

The British frigate *Guerrière* that has seized so many U.S. seamen is destroyed August 19 by the 15-year-old U.S. frigate *Constitution* under the command of Isaac Hull, 39. The *Constitution* has won the name "Old Ironsides" because enemy cannonballs appear to bounce off her tumble home, and her victory gives heart to the Americans.

The U.S. sloop *Wasp*, commanded by Jacob Jones, 44, captures the British frigate *Frolic* October 18, but Jones loses both his prize and his own ship when he encounters the 74-gun British vessel *Poictiers* while en route home.

The U.S. ship *United States* commanded by Stephen Decatur, 23, defeats the British frigate *Macedonian* October 25.

The British ship *Java* is defeated and destroyed December 20 by the *Constitution* (above) under the command of William Bainbridge, 38, but while the U.S. victories at sea win wide acclaim in America, the British actually enjoy more success in the sea war than do the Americans.

U.S. frontiersmen eager for lands that may be gained by war give James Madison his margin of victory over New York's DeWitt Clinton in the November elections (*see* below).

Louisiana is admitted to the Union as the 18th state.

Missouri Territory is established west of the Mississippi.

Eastern shipping interests support DeWitt Clinton and say President Madison's neutrality policy is helping the despot Napoleon, "war hawks" support Madison, Clinton carries every northern state except Pennsylvania and Vermont, but his 89 electoral votes are topped by Madison, who receives 128 and wins re-election.

"Gerrymander" is introduced as a term to describe the redrawing of election district boundaries for political purposes. Massachusetts senatorial districts are redrawn by the legislature to isolate Federalist strongholds and ensure Republican domination of future elections, and painter Gilbert Stuart of 1796 George Washington *Athenaeum Head* portrait fame adds a head, wings, and claws to a map of the districts, saying, "That will do for a salamander." Editor Benjamin Russell of the *Centinel* replies, "Better say a Gerrymander," but Massachusetts governor Elbridge Gerry, 68, who wins election as vice president under James Madison (above) has not been responsible for the redistricting.

A March 26 earthquake in Venezuela has spared territories held by the Spanish royalists but has wreaked havoc among Francisco de Miranda's revolutionists (*see* 1811). The clergy calls the catastrophe divine retribution for disloyalty, and the liberation forces are demoralized. Miranda is made dictator to reorganize the revolutionary elements, but he is forced to capitulate, he falls into Spanish hands, and he is sent as a prisoner to Cadiz, where he will die in 1816 (*see* Bolívar, 1813).

Mexican revolutionists led by José Maria Morelos take Oaxaca and move on to Acapulco (*see* 1811; 1813).

Revolutions are quickly suppressed by Spanish colonial troops in the captaincy general of Guatemala which includes territory that will become Guatemala, San Salvador, Honduras, Nicaragua, Costa Rica, and Chiapas.

Chilean revolutionist José Miguel Carrera finds his dictatorial rule opposed by patriot Bernardo O'Higgins, 34 (*see* 1811; 1817).

The duke of Wellington has been financed in his peninsular campaign (above) with gold, English guineas, Dutch gulden, and French Napoleon d'or smuggled south by the eight sons of Frankfurt's Meyer Rothschild, whose support has been obtained by the British government (*see* 1801). With no language other than Yiddish, the Rothschilds have used fake passports, false names, disguises, and bribes to elude the French and to organize what amounts to the world's first international bank clearing house (*see* Nathan Rothschild, 1815).

Philadelphia's Girard Bank is founded by merchant Stephen Girard with more than $1 million obtained in the shipping trade (*see* 1805).

New York's National City Bank has its beginnings in the City Bank of New York that opens June 16 at 52 Wall Street (*see* 1865).

The Luddite riots that began last year in England spread to Yorkshire, Lancashire, Derbyshire, and Leicestershire as wheat prices soar and inflate the price of bread. Public opinion supports the rioters especially after soldiers shoot down a band of Luddites at the request of a threatened employer who is subsequently murdered (*see* 1813).

New Englander Francis Cabot Lowell, 37, charters a cotton fabric company in association with his brother-in-law Patrick Tracey Jackson, 33. Lowell has memorized the designs and specifications of English textile machinery (*see* 1814; Slater, 1789).

Eli Whitney receives a second government contract, this one for 15,000 muskets (*see* 1801). Whitney will grow rich from his army supply business and will attract other gunmakers to his manufacturing ideas (*see* Colt, 1836).

Clockmakers from New Haven and the Naugatuck Valley come to observe Eli Whitney's methods and his crude milling machines for chipping and planing metals. A new machine tool industry begins to flourish in New England.

The 30-month War of 1812 (above) will encourage U.S. manufacturing (it will otherwise gain nothing for either side) and U.S. argriculture will begin its long, slow yielding of supremacy to industry.

The New England Journal of Medicine begins publication under the name *New England Journal of Medicine and Surgery.*

Napoleon's surgeon Baron Dominique Jean Larrey performs 200 amputations in 24 hours after the Battle of Borodino (above).

Recherches sur les ossemens fossiles by Baron Cuvier founds the science of paleontology (*see* 1798).

Swiss traveler-orientalist John Lewis Burckhardt, 27, rediscovers Petra in the Middle East August 22, finding ruins of a small fort built by Crusaders in the 12th century on ruins of the ancient Arab city 180 miles south of Aman. Local legend says that Moses brought forth water from a rock at Petra during the flight of the Israelites from Egypt but an earthquake leveled the city in 350 A.D.

Bonaparte's retreat. Russia's cold vastness and its wily Cossack leaders were too much for Napoleon.

1812 (cont.) Russian chemist Gottlieb Sigismund Iorchoff suggests the first understanding of catalytic processes. He shows that starch breaks down to the simple sugar glucose when boiled with dilute sulphuric acid.

A British National Light and Heat Company is chartered by the German promoter Frederick Albert Winsor, who lighted one side of London's Pall Mall with gas in 1807 and who has recognized the possibilities of piping gas from a central plant to consumers through a system of London gas mains. Winsor will be dismissed for incompetence this year by his German employers, but the German company will erect a London gasworks in 1814 and will supply gas to lamps in the parish of St. Margarets, Westminster. Other gas companies will be formed in other cities, and the age of gas lighting will arrive in Britain (see 1813; Welsbach, 1885).

European steam navigation is pioneered by Scottish engineer Henry Bell, 45, who for the next 8 years will operate his three-horsepower steamboat *Comet* on the Clyde River (see 1816; *New Orleans*, 1811).

Poetry *Childe Harold's Pilgrimmage* by English poet George Gordon, 24, Lord Byron, who traveled through Portugal and Spain 2 years ago despite the Peninsular War. Byron journeyed on to Greece and Turkey, he swam across the Hellespont May 3, 1810, and his first two cantos deal with his travels and love affairs of 1809 and 1810.

Painting *Mounted Officer of the Imperial Guard* by French painter Jean Louis André Théodore Géricault, 21, the first French romantic painter.

The camera lucida invented by William Hyde Wollaston uses mirrors to project the image of an external object on a plane surface so that its outline may be traced.

First performances Overture to *King Stephen* by Ludwig van Beethoven 2/9 at Budapest's Neues Deutsches Theater, for a new play by August Friedrich von Kotzebuhe.

France's Brigade de la Sureté is founded by detective François Eugène Vidocq, 37, who has been placed in charge of a plainclothes detail staffed entirely by ex-convicts. They prove far more efficient than the regular police force by infiltrating the underworld.

New York's City Hall is completed just north of the City Common at Broadway and Park Row. Designed in Federal style with French influence, its principal architect has been a Scotsman named Mangin who has helped design the Place de la Concorde in Paris.

British wheat prices soar to £30 per ton, the highest level thus far in history, and a level that will not be matched for another 160 years (see 1798; 1834).

An English canning factory at Bermondsey established by Bryan Donkin produces tinned foods for British naval and military forces, but such foods remain unavailable to the public which is hard-pressed by high food prices (see 1810; Donkin-Hall, 1814).

1813 Wars of liberation against the French begin in the wake of Napoleon's disastrous Russian expedition. Prussia's Friedrich Wilhelm III issues an appeal February 3 from Breslau calling for a volunteer corps, young men and students rally to the cause, the Treaty of Kalisch February 28 makes Russia a Prussian ally, and Friedrich Wilhelm establishes the Landwehr and the Landsturm Iron Cross March 17.

A Swedish army of 30,000 under the command of Crown Prince Bernadotte takes the field following a March 3 treaty with Britain. The British have paid a million rix dollars and have promised not to oppose the union of Norway with Sweden.

Russian troops occupy Hamburg in late March, and the dukes of Mecklenburg withdraw from the Confederation of the Rhine. Russian and Prussian troops occupy Dresden March 27 following the withdrawal of Marshal Davout, but Napoleon raises a new army of 500,000 to replace his Russian losses.

An Allied army of 85,000 attacks Napoleon on the Elbe but the emperor has a larger force and gains victory May 2 at the Battle of Lützen (Gross-Görschen) despite heavy losses. The Allies withdraw to Lusatia, the emperor enters Dresden, and the king of Saxony returns from Prague to form a close alliance with the French.

The Battles of Bautzen and Wurschen May 20 and 21 give Napoleon fresh victories, again at great cost in French lives (General Duroc is killed in action May 22). The emperor forces the Allies to fall back across the Spree into Silesia.

Marshal Davout retakes Hamburg May 30 following the withdrawal of Russian troops, and the Armistice of Poischwitz June 4 ends hostilities until August.

Britain agrees to subsidize Prussia and Russia under terms of a June 15 treaty signed at Reichenbach.

Austria declares war on France August 12 following the breakdown of negotiations at Prague in which von Metternich has tried to mediate with France's new minister of foreign affairs Marquis Armand Augustin Louis de Caulaincourt, 41, and with the Prussian envoy Baron Wilhelm von Humboldt, 46-year-old brother of the naturalist.

The 58-year-old Prussian general Baron Friedrich Wilhelm von Bülow saves Berlin August 23 by defeating the French at Grossbeeren. The crown prince of Saxony looks on, refusing to aid the French general Nicolas Charles Oudinot, 46.

The 71-year-old Prussian general Gebhard Leberecht von Blücher scores a victory August 26 at the Battle of Katzbach, defeating a French army under Jacques Etienne Joseph Alexandre Macdonald, 48. Friedrich Wilhelm III makes von Blücher prince of Wahlstatt.

The Battle of Dresden August 26 to 27 gives Napoleon his last major victory on German soil. He defeats an Allied army under the Austrian prince Karl Philipp von Schwarzenberg, 42, who served with Napoleon last year in Russia and who now commands a Bohemian army.

The Battle of Dennewitz September 6 results in victory for Baron von Bülow who prevents Marshal Ney from taking Berlin.

The Battle of Leipzig October 16 to 19 will be called the "Battle of the Nations," and it ends in defeat for the emperor Napoleon. He has lost 219,000 men to typhus and 105,000 in battle. He has left Dresden in order to avoid being cut off from France by the Allied armies, his Saxon and Württemberg contingents desert him October 18, the Allies storm Leipzig October 19, they capture the king of Saxony, and Napoleon begins a retreat after losing 30,000 men.

The Austrian emperor Francis I makes Metternich a hereditary prince of the empire October 20.

The kingdom of Westphalia comes to an end following the great French defeat at Leipzig (above). Napoleon's brother Jérôme flees from Cassel, and the old rulers are restored in Cassel, Brunswick, Hanover, and Oldenburg.

A Dutch revolt November 15 expels French officials, and an Allied army under General von Bülow enters Holland while Count Bernadotte invades Holstein with a Swedish army.

The duke of Wellington has advanced through northeast Spain following the recall of much of the French army to support Napoleon against the Prussians and Russians. He has triumphed over Marshal Jourdan June 21 at the Battle of Vittoria and sent Joseph Bonaparte scurrying back to Paris. Pamplona falls to British and Spanish forces October 31 after a long siege, and Wellington crosses the French frontier to defeat Marshal Soult November 10.

Dresden surrenders to Allied forces November 11; Stettin, November 21; Lübeck, December 5; Zamose, Modlin, and Torgau, December 26; and Danzig, December 30 as the Allies vow to invade France if Napoleon will not make peace.

The War of 1812 continues between British and U.S. forces. U.S. naval officer James Lawrence, 32, commands the *Chesapeake* in an engagement with the British frigate *Shannon* June 1. Lawrence has been transferred to the *Chesapeake* after defeating the British brig *Peacock* February 24, but the British defeat him, he is mortally wounded, and he is carried below decks crying, "Don't give up the ship!"

The Battle of Lake Erie September 10 ends in victory for an improvised U.S. squadron commanded by Captain Oliver Hazard Perry, 28, who sends a message to General Harrison of 1811 Tippecanoe fame: "We have met the enemy and they are ours: two ships, two brigs, one schooner, and one sloop."

General Andrew Jackson defeats Creek tribesmen in the Mississippi Territory November 9 at Talledega. The Creeks attacked Fort Mims in Alabama August 30, massacring more than 500 whites, Jackson retaliates, and he will defeat the Creeks again next year.

Simón Bolívar retakes Caracas (see 1811). Commissioned by the Congress of New Granada to fight the Spanish in Venezuela, Bolívar becomes virtual dictator (see 1815).

A Mexican Congress convened at Chilpancingo September 14 declares independence from Spain November 6. It makes José Maria Morelos head of the government and adopts reforms.

Leaders of England's Luddite movement are hanged or transported after a mass trial at York (see 1812; 1816).

Sweden abandons the slave trade.

English humanitarians organize a Society for the Prevention of Accidents in Coal Mines after a series of mine disasters (see Davy's safety lamp, 1815).

London's National Light and Heat Company has a violent explosion at its first gasworks in Peter Street (see Winsor, 1812). Royal Society president Sir Joseph Banks, now 70, leads a party to investigate and is reassured by the chief engineer of the gasworks, who takes a pickaxe, drives a hole into the side of a holder, uses a candle to ignite the escaping gas, and shows that it is not explosive (see 1819).

Theorie Elementaire de la Botanique by Swiss botanist Augustin Pyrame de Candolle, 35, advances the sciences of plant morphology, taxonomy, and physiology beyond the levels established by Linnaeus in his *Philosophia Botanica* of 1750.

The world's first power loom is produced by English inventor William Horrocks (see Bigelow, 1839).

J. P. Stevens & Co. has its beginnings in a North Andover, Mass., woolen broadcloth mill set up by Nathaniel Stevens, a captain in the state militia, who borrows money from his father to buy machines and start a textile factory with two partners in a converted gristmill. Stevens will be the first U.S. firm to produce flannels successfully (see 1837).

The British East India Company loses its monopoly in the India trade but continues its monopoly in the China trade (see 1833).

Britain issues her last gold guineas.

Colby College has its beginnings in the Waterville Literary College founded at Waterville, Me. The name will be changed to honor local benefactor Gardner Colby, now a child of 3, who will make a fortune in woolens and railroads.

"Uncle Sam" is used for the first time to mean the United States in an editorial published September 7 in the *Troy (New York) Post* (see 1852).

Fiction *Pride and Prejudice* by Jane Austen.

Juvenile *The Swiss Family Robinson* (*Der Schweizerische Robinson*) by Swiss writer-philosopher Johann Rudolf Wyss, 32, who has based the story on a tale his 70-year-old father Johann David

1813 (cont.) has told about a family shipwrecked on a tropical island. Young Wyss 2 years ago wrote the words to the Swiss national anthem.

Poetry "The Bride of Abydos" by Lord Byron; "Queen Mab" by English poet Percy Bysshe Shelley, 21, who was expelled from Oxford 2 years ago for circulating his pamphlet "The Necessity of Atheism." In addition to his antireligious poem, Shelley issues a treatise on vegetarianism.

Opera *Tancredi* 2/6 at Venice's Teatro de la Fenice, with music by Italian composer Gioacchino Antonio Rossini, 20; *L'Italiana in Algeri* 5/22 at Venice's San Benedetto, with music by Gioacchino Rossini.

First performances Symphony No. 1 in D major by Austrian composer Franz (Peter) Schubert, 16, in the autumn at Vienna's Stadtkonvikt (City Church School; private performance); Symphony No. 7 in A major by Ludwig van Beethoven 12/8 at the University of Vienna.

The London Philharmonic Society is founded.

The waltz gains widespread popularity in Europe.

A flight of passenger pigeons seen by painter John James Audubon takes 3 days to pass overhead and is described by Audubon as a "torrent of life" (*see* 1803; 1830; Wilson, 1810).

A vacuum pan that will spur the growth of the canning industry is developed by English inventor Edward Howard, who will obtain a patent in 1835 (*see* Borden, 1853).

Ice cream is served by Dolley Madison in March at the inauguration party of her husband James.

Commercial salt production begins at Syracuse, N.Y., to compensate for the cutoff of salt shipments from Bermuda and Europe (*see* 1786; 1863).

France has 334 sugar plantations by year's end and has produced 35,000 tons of beet sugar (*see* 1814; Delessert, 1811).

Noilly Prat Vermouth is introduced in France.

1814 Europe ends 22 years of war as America's 3-year War of 1812 draws to a close (below).

The Battle of La Rothière February 1 ends in defeat for Napoleon at the hands of the Prussian field marshal von Blücher, whose various corps are then defeated by Napoleon at Champaubert, Montmitrail, Chateau-Thierry, and Vauchamps. Napoleon beats the main Prussian army at Nangis and Montereau, and the emperor refuses an offer by the Allies to restore the French frontier of 1792.

The Battle of Laon March 9 to 10 begins a series of reverses for Napoleon by Allied armies. Bordeaux falls to the duke of Wellington March 12, Napoleon is defeated at the Battle of Arcis-sur-Aube March 20 to 21, the French are beaten March 25 at the Battle of La Fère-Champenoise, Allied troops storm Mont-

martre March 30, and the triumphant Allies enter Paris March 31.

Napoleon abdicates unconditionally April 11 and is granted sovereignty of the 95-square-mile Mediterranean island of Elba with an annual income of 2 million francs to be paid by the French. His wife Marie Louise receives the duchies of Parma, Piacenza, and Guastalla and retains her imperial title as does Napoleon. He arrives at Elba May 4.

The French monarchy is restored in the person of the comte de Provence, who assumes the throne at age 59 to begin a 10-year reign as Louis XVIII that will be interrupted for 100 days next year.

Charles Maurice de Talleyrand has been instrumental in restoring the Bourbon monarchy (above) and is named minister of foreign affairs to Louis XVIII.

Spain's Ferdinand VII is restored to the throne, which he will hold until 1833.

Sweden loses Finland to Russia but acquires Norway from Denmark when she agrees May 17 to a new constitution for Norway which provides for a single-chamber assembly (Storting) and denies the king his former right to dissolve the assembly or to exercise absolute veto power. The Norwegians try to elect the Danish prince Christian Frederick as their king but accept Sweden's Charles XIII after an invasion by the crown prince Jean-Baptiste Bernadotte.

The kingdom of the Netherlands is created by a union of the Austrian Netherlands (Belgium) and Holland under terms of the June 21 Protocol of the Eight Articles concluded between the prince of Orange and the Allied powers.

The Battle of Lundy's Lane near Niagara Falls in Canada July 25 ends with both British and U.S. forces claiming victory. Acclaimed as a hero is U.S. Brigadier General Winfield Scott, 28, who has been wounded twice in the fighting.

The Battle of Bladensburg 4 miles from Washington, D.C., August 24, ends in a rout of 7,000 U.S. militiamen by 3,000 British regulars who march into Washington, burn most of the city's public buildings (below) along with several private houses, and teach the U.S. government that green state militia cannot be relied upon for the nation's defense.

A U.S. naval force under Lieutenant Thomas Macdonough, 31, defeats and captures a British squadron on Lake Champlain September 11 in the Battle of Plattsburgh, 16,000 British troops that have launched an invasion from Canada are forced to retire, and the victory assures final success for the Americans.

Baltimore's Fort McHenry is bombarded by British ships September 14, and the bombardment is witnessed by Georgetown, Md., lawyer Francis Scott Key, 35, who has been sent on a mission to obtain the exchange of an American held on a British ship (*see* national anthem, below).

The Congress of Vienna convenes in September to work out the European peace settlement.

The Treaty of Ghent December 24 ends the War of 1812, but troops unaware of the peace treaty will fight the Battle of New Orleans 2 weeks after its signing (see 1815).

Britain and the United States agree to cooperate in suppressing the slave trade under terms of the Treaty of Ghent (above), but the trade actually expands as U.S. clipper ships built at Baltimore and Rhode Island ports outsail ponderous British man-of-wars to deliver cargoes of slaves.

Holland abandons the slave trade.

The duke of Sutherland George Granville Leveson-Gower, 56, destroys the homes of Highlanders on his Scottish estates to make way for sheep. The duke is married to the countess of Sutherlandshire, and by 1822 he will have driven 8,000 to 10,000 people off her lands, which comprise two-thirds of the county.

Lancashire mill-owner Robert Owen joins with Quaker philanthropist William Allen and with utilitarian philosopher Jeremy Bentham in a program to ameliorate living conditions of all millhands. Bentham is famous for his *Principles of Morals and Legislation* of 1789; Owen stated last year in *A New View of Society* that human character is determined entirely by environment (see 1809; 1824).

London banker Alexander Baring, 40, takes the position in a Parliamentary debate that the working classes have no interest at stake in the question of British wheat exports and that it is "altogether ridiculous" to argue otherwise: "whether wheat is 130s. or 80s., the labourer [can] only expect dry bread in the one case and dry bread in the other" (free export of British wheat has been permitted by Parliament and protests have come from manufacturing districts as food prices have risen) (see Corn Law, 1815).

The War of 1812 has inspired Americans to improve their roads, strengthen their national government, and support their toddling domestic industry.

The world's first steam locomotive goes into service on England's Killingworth colliery railway as English inventor George Stephenson, 34, applies Richard Trevithick's 1804 steam engine to railroad locomotion and replaces horses and mules for hauling coal (see Stockton-Darlington line, 1824).

Massachusetts becomes a cotton cloth producer to meet the pent-up demand for the cloth that came from England before the war. Francis Cabot Lowell raises $100,000 for the company he started with Patrick Jackson in 1812, he uses power from the Charles River to power machines he installs in an old paper-mill at Waltham, he employs farm girls to run the machines, and he houses them six to a room while they earn their dowry money. Lowell and Jackson card and spin cotton thread and weave cotton cloth in an enterprise that is soon producing some 30 miles of cloth per day and is paying dividends of 10 to 20 percent. After Lowell's death in 1817, Jackson will acquire mill sites on the Merrimack River, and two of these will become the cities of Lowell and Lawrence (see 1834).

E. I. du Pont de Nemours has supplied U.S. land and naval forces with 750,000 pounds of gunpowder and has been especially strengthened by the War of 1812 (see 1803; Henry du Pont, 1861).

John Jacob Astor loses his Astoria to the British, but he makes large and profitable loans to the U.S. government (see 1811; 1817).

The Library of Congress established in 1800 is largely destroyed by fire as British troops burn the Capitol. Only the most valuable records and papers are saved, but former president Thomas Jefferson offers his private library of some 6,500 volumes at cost, and Congress by a margin of 10 votes appropriates $23,700 to acquire Jefferson's collection as the nucleus of a new Library of Congress (see 1851).

Fiction *Waverley* by Walter Scott, who publishes a 19-volume *Life and Works of Swift* but turns his full energies to fiction; *Mansfield Park* by Jane Austen.

Poetry *The Corsair* by Lord Byron; *The Excursion* by William Wordsworth.

England's Dulwich Gallery opens to the public, the first public art gallery.

Painting *The Wounded Cuirassier* by Theodore Géricault; *2 May 1808* and *3 May 1808* by Francisco Goya; *King Ferdinand VII* by Francisco Goya.

Japanese *ukiyoe* painter Toyoharu Utagawu dies at age 79 after a career in which he has founded a new style by using Western perspective techniques.

Theater English actor Edmond Kean, 26, appears 1/26 at London's Drury Lane Theatre in the role of Shylock in *The Merchant of Venice*, he wins great acclaim, and he begins a 19-year career as England's greatest Shakespearean actor; *The Dog of Montargis, or The Forest of Bundy (Le chien de Montargis, ou La forét de Bundy)* by French playwright René-Charles Guilbert de Pixerecourt, 41, 6/18 at the Théâtre de la Gaité, Paris. Pixerecourt will be called "the father of melodrama."

Opera *Fidelio, oder Die eheliche Liebe* 5/26 at Vienna's Kartnertor-Theater, with music (including a new overture) by Ludwig van Beethoven (see 1805); *The Turk in Italy (Turco in Italia)* 8/14 at Milan's Teatro alla Scala, with music by Gioacchino Rossini.

First performances Symphony No. 8 in F major by Ludwig van Beethoven 2/27 at Vienna.

Anthem "The Star Spangled Banner" by Francis Scott Key (above) is published in the *Baltimore American* a week after the bombardment of Fort McHenry. The words are soon being sung to the tune

1814 (cont.) of "To Anacreon in Heaven," a song written by English composer John Stafford Smith (*see* 1931).

The Carabinieri founded by the restored king of Piedmont Victor Emmanuel I to restore law and order will grow to become an 83,000-member elite paramilitary police force with plumed cocked hats.

The White House at Washington gets its name as architect James Hoban works to rebuild the 15-year-old executive mansion and paints it white to conceal the marks of fire set by the British troops who have gutted the structure.

Hortus Jamaicensis by English botanist John Lunan uses the word "grapefruit" for the first time. The fact that the citrus fruit grows in grapelike clusters has evidently suggested the name (*see* Shaddock, 1696, 1751; Don Philippe, 1840).

England's Donkin-Hall factory introduces the first foods to be sold commercially in tins (*see* 1810; Dagett and Kensett, 1819).

French beet sugar production declines sharply as imports of cane sugar resume and undercut prices.

L'art du Cuisinier by Parisian restaurateur Beauvillier of the Grand Taverne de Londres extols such British dishes as "woiches rabettes," "plombpoutingue," and "machepotetesse."

Abortion in France is prohibited by a new law that will remain in force for more than 162 years. Abortion is permitted only "when it is required to preserve the life of the mother when that is gravely threatened."

Canadian bootmaker Pierre Joubert dies at age 113 years, 124 days. No greater human age will be authenticated for more than 163 years.

1815 The Battle of Waterloo that ends the career of the emperor Napoleon follows by more than 5 months the Battle of New Orleans fought by British and American troops unaware that the War of 1812 was ended 2 weeks earlier by the Treaty of Ghent.

The Battle of New Orleans gives the Americans their chief victory on land in the war that began in 1812. British forces attempt to seize New Orleans from the sea January 8, the city is defended by the 47-year-old U.S. major general Andrew Jackson with help from the French pirate-smuggler Jean Laffite, 34, whose aid has been sought by the British and who reveals British plans to the Americans. Many of Laffite's pirates serve on the American side in the battle which ends with 8 Americans killed and 13 wounded and 700 British killed and 1,400 wounded.

The emperor Napoleon hears of discontent under France's restored Bourbon monarchy, he returns from Elba and lands at Cannes with 1,500 men March 1, he attracts thousands to his cause as he marches on Paris, he reaches the city March 20, and he begins a new reign of 100 days as Louis XVIII flees to Ghent.

A new alliance mobilizes to oppose the Little Corporal's renewed threat to peace. Austria, Prussia, Russia, and Britain raise a million men.

The Battle of Quatre Bras June 16 pits France's Marshal Ney against the duke of Wellington, whose resistance (combined with a confusion over orders) prevents Ney from sending reinforcements to help Napoleon who is fighting the Prussians 8 miles away at Ligny. Napoleon wins his battle but not decisively.

The Battle of Waterloo June 18 near the Belgian town of that name is fought by opposing armies of 70,000 men each amidst blinding smoke and choking fumes, with the French facing an Allied army of British, Dutch, and German troops from Brunswick, Hanover, and Nassau under the command of the duke of Wellington. The French horses balk at charging the standing squares of British infantrymen, a Prussian army under General von Blücher (who was injured by his own cavalry at Ligny) arrives with vital reinforcements at evening and scatters the French.

Napoleon is forced to abdicate once more June 22. He is taken as a prisoner of war to the island of St. Helena in the South Atlantic, where he will live until his death in 1821.

The kingdom of the Netherlands is confirmed by the Congress of Vienna and is awarded the Spice Islands but not Ceylon or the Cape of Good Hope, which are awarded to Britain.

Lombardy and Venetia are awarded to Austria (*see* 1861).

Switzerland is established as an independent confederation of 22 cantons.

Legitimate dynasties are restored in Sardinia, Tuscany, Modena, and the Papal States, and the Bourbons are reinstated at Naples. The former king of Naples Joachim Murat sails for Calabria September 28 in a bid to recover the throne he held from 1808 to 1814, four of his six ships are scattered by a storm and one deserts, Murat lands at Pizzo with 30 men, he is captured soon after, he is court-martialed, and he is executed by a firing squad October 13 at age 48.

A Germanic confederation is created to replace the Holy Roman Empire that was ended in 1806.

Sweden retains Norway, which she received last year in the Treaty of Kiel. The Norwegians will not gain independence until 1905.

The kingdom of Poland is created from the grand duchy of Warsaw, but Russia's Aleksandr I is made king of Poland. The Poles will not gain independence until 1919 (*see* 1864).

Prussia obtains part of the grand duchy of Warsaw (above) not included in the new kingdom of Poland. Prussia also obtains Danzig and other territories.

Britain retains Malta, Heligoland, and some former French and Dutch colonies.

A force of 10,000 seasoned Spanish troops released by the peace in Europe lands in Venezuela. Led by Pablo Morillo, the Spanish defeat the revolutionary armies in New Granada, they restore royal authority, and they force Simón Bolívar to flee to Jamaica (*see* 1811; 1818).

U.S. Navy Commodore Stephen Decatur leaves New York May 20 with a fleet of 10 vessels bound for the Mediterranean. He signs a treaty June 30 with the Ottoman dey of Algiers, he follows it up with treaties with the sovereigns of Tunis and Tripoli, and all three agree to exact no further ransoms or tributes from U.S. merchant ships and to restrain their pirates from attacking U.S. vessels.

Decatur (above) proposes a toast at a banquet given to celebrate his return from the Mediterranean: "Our country! In her intercourse with foreign nations may she always be in the right; but our country, right or wrong!"

Zulus in Southeast Africa remain a clan of barely 1,500, but they will soon conquer their neighbors. Chief Senzangakona's 28-year-old son Shaka has devised a more effective *assegai* (spear), a shield that can serve as a weapon, and new military tactics. When his father dies next year, Shaka will begin a 12-year reign in which his army will increase from fewer than 400 men to more than 40,000, and he will rule with mercurial cruelty over the Zulu nation.

💲 London banker Nathan Meyer Rothschild, 38, receives carrier pigeon reports from Belgium advising him of Napoleon's defeat at Waterloo (above). Feigning gloom, Rothschild depresses the price of British consols by selling short, he then has his agents buy them up at distress prices, and when news of Wellington's victory sends prices sky-high, Rothschild sells, reaping a great fortune on the London Exchange (*see* consols, 1751; Rothschilds, 1812).

Britain suffers economic depression as demand for military supplies abruptly ceases and as Continental markets are unable to absorb backlogged inventories of English manufactured goods. Prices fall, thousands are thrown out of work, and 400,000 demobilized troops add to the problems of unemployment.

A Corn Law enacted by Parliament helps British landlords to maintain prices by restricting grain imports. The law permits wheat to enter the country duty-free only when the average domestic price exceeds a "famine" level of 80 shillings per bushel, but unemployment reduces demand, and the price of wheat falls to 9 shillings per bushel, down from a record 14 shillings 6 pence in 1812 (*see* 1838).

The British income tax ends and will not be resumed until 1842 (*see* 1802).

✊ England's Dartmoor Prison has a massacre of inmates April 6. A slight incident irritates the warden, he has his Somerset militiamen fire on the prisoners, and hundreds of men die—most of them American seamen convicted of privateering.

England's Humphry Davy invents a safety lamp for miners that will prevent colliery accidents (*see* 1813). A metal gauze surrounds the flame to prevent any inflammable gas from being ignited.

France promises to abolish her slave trade by 1819 and to limit the trade meanwhile to her own colonies.

⚡ The Congress of Vienna (above) relaxes the rule of 1648 against navigation on the Scheldt River.

Macadam road paving introduced by Scottish road surveyor John Loudon McAdam, 59, employs stone broken into pieces to create a hard, smooth, water-resistant roadway. McAdam has spent some years in America.

New Jersey grants the first state charter for an American railroad to John Stevens and his associates (*see* 1804; T-rail, 1830).

The New York State Legislature approves a plan to finance an Erie Canal with state bonds pursuant to a proposal by Governor De Witt Clinton (*see* 1817).

🎓 Allegheny College is founded at Meadville, Pa.

📰 London's 46-year-old *Morning Chronicle* scoops the competition June 22 with news of Napoleon's defeat at Waterloo 4 days earlier (*see* Rothschild, above).

The *North American Review* begins publication at Boston.

🖋 Fiction *Guy Mannering* and *The Antiquary* by Walter Scott; *Adolphe* by French novelist-statesman Henri Benjamin Constant de Rebecque, 47; *Grimm's Fairy Tales* (*Kinder- und Hausmarchen*) by German philologists Jacob and Wilhelm Grimm, 30 and 29, who include "The History of Tom Thumb," "Little Red Riding-Hood," "Bluebeard," "Puss in Boots," "Hop o' my Thumb," "Snow White and the Seven Dwarfs," "Goldilocks and the Three Bears," "The Princess and the Pea," "Thumberlina," "The Sleeping Beauty in the Wood," and "Cinderella" (which first appeared in a Chinese book nearly a thousand years earlier).

Poetry *Songs* (*Gedichte*) by German poet (Johann) Ludwig Uhland, 28, of Tübingen whose *Songs of the Fatherland* (*Vaterlandische Gedichte*) will appear next year. "Der Güter Kamerad" and other nationalist ballads by Uhland will become German folk songs.

🎨 Painting *Boulevard des Italiens* by English painter John Crome, 46, who visited Paris last year to see Napoleon's art collection; *Mrs. Wolf* by Thomas Lawrence, who is knighted by the prince regent. John Singleton Copley dies at London September 9 at age 77.

🎭 Theater France's Grand Guignol horror play theater has its beginnings in a puppetshow theater started at Lyons by puppetmaker Laurent Mourquet, 71, whose puppet hero Guignol is modeled on the popular Pierlichinelle (Punch) (*see* 1897).

Ludwig van Beethoven's musical imagination transcended his own inability to hear what he had composed.

🎼 Song "Eriking" by Franz Schubert who has been writing songs since age 14.

England dances the Quadrille for the first time.

🏛 Brighton Pavilion is completed by John Nash in a pseudo-Oriental redesign for the prince regent.

St. Petersburg's Admiralty is completed. Its architect Adrian Dmitrievich Zakharov died in 1811 at age 50.

Harvard's University Hall is completed in the Yard by architect Charles Bulfinch.

🌐 Thousands die in the East Indies as the volcano Tamboro erupts on Sumbawa Island, producing tidal waves and whirlwinds that raise enormous clouds of dust that will affect climatic conditions throughout the world (see 1816).

✗ France's economy is helped by German and British gastronomes and gourmands who flock to enjoy Gallic cuisine.

The word "bistro" for café is introduced by Russian soldiers who order Paris waiters to bring orders *"bistro, bistro"* (quickly, quickly).

A dinner at the Louvre Palace celebrates the restoration of the French monarchy. Chef Marie-Antoine (Antonin) Carême, 31, prepares food for 1,200 guests.

Royal Doulton Potteries is established in England.

Conrad J. Van Houten establishes a Dutch chocolate factory that begins the use of chocolate as a food in addition to its use as a beverage (see 1828).

👫 The population of the United States reaches 8.35 million, with 80 percent of it in New England and the Atlantic Coast states, the balance mostly in Ohio, Kentucky, and Tennessee, with scattered settlements in the Mississippi Valley.

Philadelphia is a city of 75,000 and is the social capital of America, while New York has 60,000, Baltimore nearly 30,000, and Boston 25,000.

1816 ✗ Brazil proclaims herself an empire January 16 with the Portuguese prince regent João as emperor.

Portugal's insane Queen Maria I dies March 20 at age 81 after a 39-year reign, the last 17 years of which have been controlled by her son. He succeeds to the throne to begin a 10-year reign as João VI but remains in Brazil (see 1820).

Argentina (United Provinces of La Plata) declares her independence from Spain July 29 in a proclamation issued by the Congress of Tucuman.

Britain returns Java to the Netherlands (see 1811).

A survey to establish the boundary between Canada and the United States begins under the supervision of David Thompson. The survey will take 10 years (see 1809; 1818).

Indiana is admitted to the Union as the 19th state.

President Madison's Secretary of State James Monroe, 58, wins election to the presidency, gaining 183 electoral votes as compared with 34 for Georgia states' rightist William H. Crawford, the last Federalist candidate for president.

✊ The Luddite movement that was suppressed in 1813 is revived as a dismal harvest produces economic depression throughout Britain. Well-organized efforts are made to smash machinery in riots at many industrial centers, a crowd gathers December 2 in London's Spa Fields and commits acts of violence, the rioters are vigorously prosecuted, but the Luddite movement will continue until it is ended by rising prosperity.

⚕ Ergotism strikes French peasants in Lorraine and Burgundy, where rural diets are comprised largely of rye bread (see 1777; Finland, 1862).

⚙ Pittsburgh is incorporated on the site of the Fort Pitt erected in 1759.

⚙ The first Krupp steel is produced at Essen by Friedrich Krupp (see 1811). It is not cast steel, which Sheffield has resumed exporting to Europe, but consists of tiny bars of low-grade steel marketed as files for tanners (see 1838).

💲 Congress imposes a 25 percent duty on all imports to protect America's infant industry from foreign competition and make the nation self-sufficient. Congressman Daniel Webster, 34, of New Hampshire has opposed the tariff as a representative of New England shipping interests, but British manufacturers will find ways to undersell the Americans despite their tariff wall.

The Bank for Savings founded at New York November 29 is the first American savings bank (see Britain, 1799). It will not open until July 3, 1819.

The Philadelphia Saving Fund Society opens December 2 in the office of its secretary-treasurer George

Billington in Sixth Street and is the first U.S. savings bank actually to accept deposits. It will receive a charter early in 1819 and will grow to become the largest U.S. thrift institution.

The Provident Institution for Savings in the town of Boston chartered December 13 is the first U.S. savings bank to receive a corporate charter. It will open February 17 of next year and will pay interest at the rate of 5 percent per annum.

The Black Ball Line begins regular Baltimore clipper ship service between New York and Liverpool, but the full flowering of the clipper ship will not come for three decades (see 1790; 1845).

The steamboat *Washington* launched June 4 at Wheeling, Va., sets a pattern for all future U.S. riverboats. Designed by steamboat captain Henry Miller Shreve, 31, the 148-foot 400-ton *Washington* has a shallow draft to clear the snags and sandbars of the Ohio and Mississippi, and her two decks rise high above the water with two chimneys on either side of her small, boxlike pilothouse, a design that inspires spectators to call her a "floating wedding cake." The ship has two high-pressure, 24-inch cylinder, 6-foot stroke engines placed horizontally on the deck instead of vertically in the hull. The engines each operate a side-wheel and are unconnected so that the pilot can reverse one engine to turn the ship in its own length. The second deck is for passengers who arrive at New Orleans on the ship's maiden voyage, October 7. By 1820, there will be more than 60 versions of Shreve's *Washington*, whose owner will be memorialized in the name Shreveport, La.

A French fleet of four naval vessels sets out in late June for Senegal in West Africa bearing the colony's new governor aboard the flagship *Medusa* with 240 passengers and a crew of 160. Navigated by a civilian friend of the governor who ignores the advice of seasoned naval officers, the *Medusa* founders on a sandbank off the African coast July 2. The captain refuses to jettison the ship's heavy guns or her cargo of flour, the governor orders a large raft built to accommodate all who cannot fit into the *Medusa*'s six boats, 89 of the 149 on the overcrowded raft are lost within 2 days, 12 more die the third night, but one body is saved from the sharks and is eaten by the survivors. Further acts of cannibalism ensue, only 15 survive after 13 days, and more than 16 die in the sands of the Sahara. The governor and his friend go free, and the captain is sent to prison for 3 years (see Géricault painting, 1819).

The United Kingdom has 2.5 million tons of merchant shipping; 1,000 tons are in steam (see 1826).

The celeripede invented by French physicist Joseph Nicephore Niepce, 51, is a primitive two-wheeled bicycle propelled by the action of the feet on the ground. A slightly more advanced version is developed by German inventor Karl D. Sauerbroun (see Macmillan, 1839; Niepce, 1822).

Hindu College is founded at Calcutta.

Nonfiction *Wissenschaft der Logik* by German philosopher Georg Wilhelm Friedrich Hegel, 46, whose third and final volume completes the "Hegelian" philosophy of the Absolute that will dominate metaphysics during the second quarter of the century (the first volume appeared in 1812).

Fiction *Emma* by Jane Austen, who will die next year at age 41, leaving her novels *Persuasion* and *Northanger Abbey* to be published posthumously; *The Black Dwarf* and *Old Mortality* by Walter Scott.

Poetry "The Story of Rimini" by English poet James Henry Leigh Hunt, 32, who since 1808 has been editor of the *Examiner*, a witty journal owned by his brother John, and who has been imprisoned with his brother for attacking the prince regent with the phrase "a fat Adonis of 50." "The two divinest things this world has got,/ A lovely woman in a rural spot!" writes Hunt, who returns to the rhythms of Chaucer and Spencer to pioneer a new romantic school. "The Siege of Corinth" by Lord Byron; "Kublai Khan" by Samuel Taylor Coleridge: "In Xanadu did Kublai Khan/ A stately pleasure-dome decree:/ Where Alph, the sacred river, ran/ Through caverns measureless to man/ Down to a sunless sea./ So twice five miles of fertile ground/ With walls and towers were girdled round"; English poet John Keats, 21, has his first sonnet published May 5 in Leigh Hunt's *Examiner* (above) and follows it in December with his sonnet "On First Looking into Chapman's Homer": "Then felt I like some watcher of the skies/ When a new planet swims into the ken;/ Or like stout Cortez, when with eagle eyes/ He stared at the Pacific—and all his men/ Looked at each other with a wild surmise—/Silent, upon a peak in Darien" (he means Balboa) (see 1513).

Opera *The Barber of Seville* (*Il Barbiere de Siviglia*) 2/5 at Rome's Teatro Argentina, with music by Gioacchino Rossini. Based on the Beaumarchais drama of 1775 and initially entitled *Almaviva*, Rossini's opera creates a furor. *Othello, or the Moor of Venice* (*Otello, o Il Moro di Venezia*) 12/4 at the Teatro Fondo, Naples, with music by Rossini.

The London music publishing firm Boosey & Hawkes has its beginnings in a shop opened at 28 Holles Street at Oxford Street by bookseller Thomas Boosey who has been at 4 Old Bond Street since 1792. Thomas Boosey, Jr., now 18, will begin manufacturing woodwind and brass instruments in the middle of the century, T. Boosey & Co. will add reed instruments beginning in 1879, and it will merge in 1930 with Hawkes & Son of Piccadilly.

English dandy George Bryan "Beau" Brummell, 38, flees to Calais in order to escape creditors hounding him for gambling debts. A friend of the prince regent, Brummell will be named British consul at Caen from 1832 to 1840 but will die in a French insane asylum in 1840.

1816 (cont.) Providence, R.I., gets a gray stone Unitarian church with the largest belfry ever cast by Boston's Paul Revere, now 81.

Pittsburgh (above) is known even now as a "smoky city" because of all its coal-burning houses and factories (see 1947).

Cold weather persists through summer in much of the world's temperate zones, apparently as a result of dust in the atmosphere following last year's volcanic eruption in the East Indies. Frost occurs from Canada to Virginia every night from June 6 to June 9, laundry laid out to dry on the grass at Plymouth, Conn., June 10 is found frozen stiff, heavy snows fall in the Northeast in June and July, and frost kills crops in what farmers will call "eighteen hundred and froze to death."

Cape Cod, Mass., cranberry production gets a boost from the discovery that cranberry vines grow more vigorously in places where the wind has blown sand over a mat of wild vines. The discovery by Henry Hall at Dennis will lead to the draining of swampy wastelands and to the development of commercial cranberry bogs (see 1912).

Port au Salut cheese is manufactured for the first time by French Trappist monks in northern Touraine, who use the milk of four cows to begin a major industry (see Port du Salut, 1878).

The French chef Antonin Carême is hired by the British prince regent, who has ruled since George III became mad in 1811. Carême has created beef Stroganov for the Russian czar Aleksandr I from whose palace he has sent home secret information to Talleyrand, and he continues to serve Talleyrand as he prepares food for the British (see 1815).

The Cook's Oracle (*Apicius Redivivus*) by English physician William Kitchiner gives exact measures of ingredients and their order of use in recipes (see Apicius, 14 B.C.; Mrs. Beeton, 1861). Meat, says Kitchiner, should always be hung for "such a time . . . as will render it tender, which the finest meat cannot be, unless hung . . . till it had made some advance towards putrefaction."

1817 Chile wins her liberation from Spain February 12 at the Battle of Chacabuco and will proclaim her independence early next year (see 1812). Bernardo O'Higgins has enlisted the support of Argentine military commander José de San Martín, 39, who has raised and trained a small army of Chilean and Argentinian volunteers, has crossed the high Andes with O'Higgins to surprise a royalist army, and helps make O'Higgins supreme dictator of Chile.

The Rush-Bagot Treaty signed April 28 limits U.S. and British naval forces on the Great Lakes. U.S. Secretary of State Richard Rush, 37, has negotiated the treaty with British minister to Washington Sir Charles Bagot, 36.

Mississippi is admitted to the Union as the 20th state.

Ohio Indians sign a treaty ceding their remaining 4 million acres of land to the United States.

The Seminole War begins as Georgia backwoodsmen attack Indians just north of the Florida border in retaliation for degradations by tribesmen (see 1819).

The Obrenović dynasty that will rule Serbia until 1842, and then again from 1858 until 1903, is founded by Miloš Obrenović, 37, who leads a second insurrection against the Ottoman Turks and gains recognition as prince of Serbia over the objections of the Karageorgevic family. The rival family's leader Kara George returns from exile in Austria but the Obrenovićs murder him, beginning a long blood feud between the two families.

Jena students organize the Wartburg festival to celebrate the Reformation and the Battle of Leipzig. They burn emblems of reaction October 18.

The British secretary for Ireland Robert Peel, 29, establishes a regular constabulary for Ireland, which is seething with discontent and on the verge of rebellion. The Irish will call the constables "Peelers" (see "Bobbies," 1829).

The Coercion Acts passed by Parliament in March extend the act of 1798 against seditious meetings, suspend temporarily the right of habeas corpus, renew an act punishing attempts to undermine the allegiance of soldiers and sailors, give the prince regent all the safeguards against treason as the king himself, and have the effect of stimulating activity by extremists in the radical movement (see 1819).

Principles of Political Economy by English economist David Ricardo contributes to Adam Smith's free trade theory of 1776 with a doctrine of "comparative costs" and a "labor theory of value." Ricardo postulates a basic antagonism between the landlords of England's "establishment" and the rising lords of English industry (see 1809).

John Jacob Astor gains a monopoly in the fur trade of the Mississippi Valley (see 1814; Juneau, 1818).

The Cumberland Road reaches west from Cumberland on the Potomac River to Wheeling, Va., on the Ohio. The road has a 30-foot wide gravel center on a stone base (see 1811; 1852).

The Conestoga wagon that covers the 90 miles between Philadelphia and New York in 3 days is called "the Flying Machine" (see 1753; 1840).

New York Governor DeWitt Clinton orders construction of a 363-mile Erie Canal that will connect Buffalo on Lake Erie with Troy on the Hudson River. The state legislature authorizes state funds for the canal and ground is broken July 4 (see 1815; 1819).

The first steam ferry between Manhattan and Staten Islands goes into service. The *Nautilus* is owned by U.S. Vice President Daniel D. Tompkins.

The stern paddle steamboat *Washington* leaves Louisville March 3 for a round-trip voyage to New Orleans and completes the first such voyage. By year's end, a dozen steamboats have gone up the Mississippi and penetrated the Ohio and other western rivers (*see* Lake Erie, 1818).

The first Waterloo Bridge is completed across the Thames at London by Scottish civil engineer John Rennie, 56, whose London Bridge will be completed by his son John in 1831.

A patent is filed in England for an engine that requires no boiler. The Stirling engine developed by Scottish engineer Robert Stirling, 27, employs a cylinder, a heat source, and reciprocating pistons. Gas inside the cylinder is continuously oscillated, its heat being raised at constant volume with each cycle while expanded at constant temperature (isothermally) to drive the output piston. The gas is then cooled at its now larger volume and compressed at a lower constant temperature (isothermally), but since the strong metal wall cannot be heated and cooled fast enough to drive an engine at a useful speed, Stirling's engine will not be practical for more than a century, and its potential will not be recognized for some 150 years.

A screw-cutting lathe and a machine for planing metal are devised by Welsh inventor Richard Roberts, 28, who will invent weaving improvements, advanced steam locomotives, railway cars, and steamships.

Cadmium is discovered as a new element by German chemist Friedrich Strohmeyer, 41.

Lithium is discovered as a new element by Swedish chemist A. Arfvedson.

Selenium is discovered as a new element by Jöns Jakob Berzelius.

The University of Michigan is founded at Ann Arbor.

Harvard Law School is established at Cambridge (*see* Eliot, Langdell, 1869).

The *Scotsman* begins publication as a weekly Edinburgh newspaper that will become a daily in 1855.

Blackwood's Magazine has its beginnings in the *Edinburgh Monthly Magazine* started by Scottish publisher William Blackwood, 41, who started the *Edinburgh Encyclopaedia* in 1810.

Harper and Brothers has its origin in a New York printing shop established in Dover Street by former printing apprentice James Harper, 22, with his younger brother John under the name J & J Harper. They will be joined by their brothers Wesley and Fletcher by 1825 and will revolutionize book publishing with the first books bound with cloth over boards and the first books to be published in series as "libraries." Harper and Brothers will be the first to make stereotyping a regular procedure and the first to employ editors (*see* 1850; Harper & Row, 1962).

Fiction *Rob Roy* by Walter Scott, whose novels will be published in America by Harper and Brothers.

Poetry *Poems* by John Keats, who has been helped by his friend Percy Shelley; "Beppo: A Venetian Story" by Lord Byron: "She was not old, not young, nor at the years/ Which certain people call a 'certain age,' which yet the most uncertain age appears" (stanza 22); *Lalla Rookh* by Thomas Moore: "Who finds not heavens to suit the tastes of all;/ Houris for boys, omniscience for sages,/ And wings and glories for all ranks and ages,/ Vain things!—as lust for vanity inspires,/ The heaven of each is but what each desires"; "Thanatopsis" by Great Barrington, Mass., lawyer-poet William Cullen Bryant, 23, whose "view of death" in the September issue of *North American Review* will be published in an expanded version in 1821.

Painting *Flatford Mill* by John Constable.

Opera *Cinderella* (*La Cenerentola*) 1/25 at Rome's Teatro Valle, with music by Gioacchino Rossini.

Haiti's Citadelle La Ferrière is completed for Henri I (Henri Christophe) atop a 3,100-foot peak outside Cap Haitien, where 200,000 former slaves have worked for 13 years at a cost of 2,000 lives to build the impregnable fortress that can hold 15,000 men with enough food and water for a 1-year siege.

U.S. farm prices fall as Europe's peace ends the foreign markets that have taken some of America's farm surpluses.

Hereford cattle are imported into the United States for the first time and raised in Virginia. The English breed will become the dominant cattle breed on the western plains (*see* Corning, Sotham, 1840).

"The hunter or savage state," writes President Monroe, "requires a greater extent of territory to sustain it than is compatible with progress and just claims of civilized life ... and must yield to it."

Artificial contraceptive devices are rejected by Thomas Malthus in a fifth edition of his 1798 *Essay*. The misery of overpopulation is necessary to "stimulate industry" and discourage "indolence," writes Malthus (*see* Place, 1822).

1818 Sweden's Charles XIII dies February 5 at age 69 after a 9-year reign and is succeeded by the 55-year-old crown prince Jean Baptiste Bernadotte, who founds a new Swedish dynasty and who will reign until 1844 as Charles XIV John.

Allied occupation troops leave France after 3 years of peace keeping in the wake of the Napoleonic wars.

India's Rajput states, Poona, and the Holkar of Indore come under British control.

The U.S.-Canadian border is established by a convention signed October 20, making the 49th parallel the boundary from Lake of the Woods to the Rocky Mountains as David Thompson continues his survey (*see* 1816). The two countries agree to a joint occupa-

1818 (cont.) tion of the Pacific Northwest territories for a 10-year period (see 1828; Drake, 1579; Cook, 1778; Gray, 1791).

Illinois is admitted to the Union as the 21st state.

Congress adopts a flag with 13 alternate red and white stripes and with a blue square containing a white star for each state of the union.

The Seminole War ends in Florida. Spain cedes Florida to the United States and agrees to relinquish all claims to Pacific Coast territory north of the 42nd parallel. The United States agrees to pay Floridians $5 million for their claims against Spain.

Simón Bolívar secures control of the lower Orinoco basin from the Spanish. Bolivar returned to the region in 1816 and has gained support from José Paez, 28 (see 1815; 1819).

Chile proclaims independence from Spain February 12, José San Martin defeats a royal army from Peru April 5 at Maipu, and he gains support from rebels at Buenos Aires and from former British naval commander Thomas Cochrane, now 43, who has been fined, imprisoned, and expelled from the Royal Navy on charges of having connived in a speculative fraud.

The Peul Diallo dynasty that has ruled on Africa's Niger River since the 15th century ends in a coup d'etat by the Moslem usurper Marabout Cheikou Ahmadou. He will organize the movement of nomads in the region and will establish patterns designed to conserve grass and water.

Scottish explorer John Ross, 41, searches for a Northwest Passage and discovers an 8-mile expanse of red-colored snow cliffs overlooking Baffin Bay. The cliffs will be called the Ross Ice Shelf (see 1576).

Guy's Hospital surgeon James Blundel at London performs the first successful human blood transfusion using a syringe for the purpose. Blundel will invent two special pieces of apparatus that will permit blood to be transferred from donor to patient with a minimum of physical interference (see 1677; 1909).

Failure of the Baltimore branch of the second Bank of the United States precipitates a U.S. financial crisis (see Supreme Court decision, 1819).

Brown Brothers & Co. is founded at Philadelphia by Baltimore merchant's son John A. Brown, 30, whose Irish-American father Alexander Brown has built up a mercantile and banking house with worldwide connections. John's older brother William has started the Liverpool firm Brown, Shipley & Co., and his younger brother James will open a New York Brown Brothers office in 1825 (see 1931).

John Jacob Astor's American Fur Company agent Solomon Laurent Juneau, 25, opens a trading post on Lake Michigan at a point that will later be the site of Milwaukee (see 1834; 1846; Astoria, 1811).

The U.S. steamboat *Walk-in-the-Water* leaves Buffalo for Detroit October 10 with 100 passengers.

The 388-ton 135-foot vessel is the first steamboat on Lake Erie and rivals the 2-year-old Canadian steamboat S.S. *Frontenac* which plies only Lake Ontario.

U.S. ships make 35 voyages to Sumatra for pepper (see 1805; 1873).

Dalhousie University is founded at Halifax, Nova Scotia. The ninth earl of Dalhousie George Ramsay, 48, will serve as governor in chief of the Canadian colonies from 1819 to 1828.

The *American Journal of Science and Arts* begins publication at New Haven. Yale professor Benjamin Silliman, 39, has founded the first U.S. scientific journal (see *Scientific American,* 1845).

Manuale Tipografico by the late Italian printer Giambattista Bodoni is published at Parma. Bodoni died in 1813 at age 73 after years of service as head of the duke of Parma's printing house, he designed the first Roman type that will be called "modern," and the book is a two-volume collection of his typefaces (see Jensen, 1470).

Fiction *Frankenstein, or The Modern Prometheus* by English novelist Mary Wollstonecraft Godwin Shelley, 21, gains instant success with its story about a scientist who takes parts of corpses to manufacture a living creature. Author Shelley is the wife of poet Percy Bysshe Shelley and daughter of women's rights champion Mary Wollstonecraft by the philosopher William Goodwin, now 62, who is supported by his son-in-law. The book will go through at least two printings per year for 40 years, it will be translated into 30 languages, millions of copies will be sold, and it will make the word "frankenstein" a common noun meaning any work that controls its originator. *The Heart of Midlothian* and *The Bride of Lammermoor* by Walter Scott.

Poetry "Ozymandias" by Percy Bysshe Shelley, whose sonnet has been inspired by a huge statue erected in the desert by the ancient Egyptian pharaoh Ramses II, a work that to Shelley symbolizes the futility of all human striving to achieve immortality through earthly glory: "And on the pedestal these words appear:/ 'My name is Ozymandias, king of kings:/ Look on my works, ye Mighty, and despair!'/ Nothing beside remains. Round the decay/ Of that colossal wreck, boundless and bare/ The lone and level sands stretch far away"; "Childe Harold" by Lord Byron, who says in his fourth and final canto, "Roll on, thou deep and dark blue ocean—roll!/ Ten thousand fleets sweep over thee in vain;/ Man marks the earth with ruin—his control/ Stops with the shore"; "Endymion" by John Keats contains the line, "A thing of beauty is a joy for ever;/ Its loveliness increases; it will never/ Pass into nothingness"; "The Old Oaken Bucket" by New York printer-poet Samuel Woodworth, 34, who begins, "How dear to this heart are the scenes of my childhood" (see 1822).

Painting *Archduke Charles* by Sir Thomas Lawrence, who has been sent to the Continent to paint the victors of the Napoleonic wars.

Family Shakespeare in 10 volumes by English editor Thomas Bowdler, 64, will go through four editions in 6 years and many subsequent editions "in which nothing is added to the original text; but those words and expressions are omitted which cannot with propriety be read aloud in a family." Bowdler will also edit a six-volume "bowdlerized" edition of Edward Gibbon's *Decline and Fall of the Roman Empire*.

Cantata "Jubel" ("Jubilee") by Carl Maria von Weber 9/20 at Dresden for the 50th anniversary of the accession of Saxony's Friedrich August I.

Ludwig van Beethoven becomes totally deaf after 20 years of defective hearing but continues to compose.

Hymn "Silent Night" ("Stille Nacht, Hellige Nacht") by Austrian theologian-poet Joseph Mohr, 26, will be set to music by composer Franz Gruber.

Brooks Brothers has its beginnings in a New York menswear shop at the corner of Catharine and Cherry Streets opened by merchant Henry Sands Brooks, 46, who invests $17,000 in a stock of imported British woolens and adopts as his symbol the golden fleece symbol of a dead lamb cradled by a ribbon, the symbol used in the 15th century for a knighthood established by the duke of Burgundy Philippe le Bon. Brooks Brothers will clothe bankers, lawyers, military officers, statesmen, and upwardly mobile Americans for generations (*see* 1833).

Angostura bitters are invented at Angostura, Venezuela, by German physician Johann Gottlieb Benjamin Siegert, who served as a surgeon under von Blücher 3 years ago at Waterloo and who has emigrated to South America. Siegert brews his elixir from gentian root, rum, and other ingredients as a stomach tonic to overcome debility and loss of appetite in the tropics, but it will gain wider use as a cocktail ingredient used by British colonials to make "pink gin." Siegert's son will take the formula to Trinidad and will produce angostura bitters in an abandoned monastery at Port of Spain long after Angostura has become Ciudad Bolívar (*see* 1821; 1878).

Cherry Heering is introduced at Copenhagen by Danish distiller Peter Heering.

Swiss chocolate maker Amedée Kohler founds a firm that will specialize in making confectioneries (*see* Peter, 1904; Cailler, 1819; van Houten, 1828).

London's Donkin, Hall & Gamble "Preservatory" in Blue Anchor Road, Bermondsey, turns out satisfactory canned soup, veal, mutton and vegetable stew, carrots, and beef (both boiled and corned, meaning salted), but the tinned foods will not be available in food stores until 1830.

The tin can is introduced to America by Peter Durant (*see* 1810; 1847).

Cincinnati begins packing pork in brine-filled barrels. Salt pork is a U.S. food staple, and Cincinnati will come to be called "Porkopolis."

1819 Reactionary German journalist August von Kotzebue, 58, is murdered March 23 at Mannheim by Jena University student Karl Ludwig Sand, 23, who calls Kotzebue a Russian spy and an enemy of liberty. Austria's Prince Metternich is alarmed, and he persuades Prussia's Friederich Wilhelm to issue the repressive Carlsbad Decrees that establish an inquisition at Mainz in July to look into secret societies, impose strict censorship on all publications, and place German universities under the control of commissioners appointed by German sovereigns.

The Peterloo Massacre August 16 at St. Peter's Fields, Manchester, kills several people and injures hundreds as English soldiers are ordered to arrest a speaker urging parliamentary reform and repeal of the Corn Laws. The incident is followed by the Six Acts passed by Parliament in December, a repressive code that curtails public meetings, forbids training in the use of firearms, empowers magistrates to search citizens for arms and to seize any that may be found, provides for speedy trial in "cases of misdemeanor," increases the penalties for seditious libel, and limits radical journalism by imposing the newspaper stamp duty on all periodicals containing news.

Alabama is admitted to the Union as the 22nd state.

Maine is separated from Massachusetts (*see* 1820).

Simón Bolívar moves up the Orinoco River, crosses the Andes, and with the help of British volunteers defeats a superior Spanish force under the command of Pablo Morillo, conde de Cartagena, August 7 at the Boyaca River. Bolívar occupies Bogotá August 10 and liberates New Granada from Spain. The Congress of Angostura, which includes representatives from New Granada, proclaims the independence of Great Colombia—comprised of New Granada, Venezuela, and Quito—and establishes Bolívar as president and military dictator (*see* 1818; 1820).

Hawaii's Kamehameha dies at age 82 after a 24-year reign that has consolidated the Sandwich Island kingdom (*see* 1803). He is succeeded by his 22-year-old son who will welcome Hawaii's first missionaries next year and who will overthrow the ancient Hawaiian taboo system and religion in his 5-year reign as Kamehameha II.

Singapore is founded under the direction of the East India Company's Thomas Stamford Raffles who persuades the sultan and tenggong of Johore (who has no authority to do so) to cede the fishing village to Britain. Raffles is governor of Benkuilen in Sumatra, he wants to check Dutch power in the East Indies, and he makes Singapore a British Crown colony.

Memphis is laid out on the Mississippi River at Fort Adams. It takes its name from the Egyptian city famous for its cotton.

Minneapolis has its beginnings in Fort Snelling, built by U.S. Army engineers some 900 miles up the Mississippi from Memphis (above) near St. Anthony's Falls (*see* Hennepin, 1680; Minneapolis, 1847).

1819 (cont.) The first stretch of the Erie Canal opens after 2 years of construction to connect Utica and Rome, N.Y. Yankee engineers have devised an endless screw linked to a roller, a cable, and a crank to pull down tall trees, they have improvised a horse-drawn crane to lift rock debris out of the cut, but most of the work is done by Irish immigrants who are paid 37.5 cents per day (plus as much as a quart of whiskey per day in periodic work breaks) and who die by the thousands of malaria, pneumonia, and snakebite (*see* 1825; White, 1820).

The first transatlantic crossing assisted by steam propulsion is made by the 350-ton U.S. ship *Savannah*, which sails from the Georgia port May 22 and arrives June 30 at Liverpool. Commanded by Moses Brown who piloted the *Phoenix* in 1809, the *Savannah* has one inclined direct-acting, low-pressure steam engine to power the side-wheels that supplement her sails, but she proceeds on steam for only 80 hours, and while she has 32 staterooms, the perils of her 90-horsepower engine have discouraged passengers and she carries none (*see* 1826).

French scientists make it possible to determine atomic weights. Chemist-physicist Pierre Louis Dulong, 34, who discovered nitrogen chloride 8 years ago, joins chemist-physicist Alexis Thérèse Petit, 30, in enunciating the rule that the product of the relative atomic weight and the specific heat of any element is constant.

Danish physicist Hans Christian Oersted, 42, advances knowledge of electromagnetic energy. He notices that a compass needle located close to a wire carrying an electric current will swing wildly but will finally settle at right angles to the wire. He suspects that the current in the wire must set up a magnetic field around it, and his observation will be the starting point for others (*see* Romagnosi, 1802; Ampère, 1820; Faraday, 1821; electromagnet, 1823).

London gas mains extend 288 miles, and some 51,000 houses in the city are equipped with gas burners. National Light and Heat Company has become the Gas Light and Coke Company, a firm that will continue for nearly 150 years.

No state may tax any instrumentality of the federal government, the Supreme Court rules March 6 in the case of *McCulloch v. Maryland*. The case specifically involves taxation of the Bank of the United States and its Baltimore branch by the state of Maryland (*see* 1818).

The U.S. economic depression that began last year brings appeals from manufacturers for higher protective tariffs (*see* 1816; 1820).

The New York Bank for Savings is founded.

The stethoscope invented by French physician René Théophile Hyacinthe Laënnec, 38, is a roll of paper that avoids the indelicacy of having to place the physician's ear to the heaving bosom of a female patient. Laënnec introduces the practice of auscultation (*see* Auenbrugg, 1761).

Cholera reaches Sumatra (*see* 1820).

Unitarianism is founded by Boston Congregationalist pastor William Ellery Channing, 30, who becomes the leader of a group that denies the holiness of the Trinity and believes in only one Divine Being. Channing will organize the American Unitarian Association in 1825.

The charter of a benevolent institution is a contract and is therefore inviolate, rules Chief Justice John Marshall February 2 in the case of *Dartmouth College v. Woodward.*

The University of Virginia is chartered at Charlottesville, 3 miles west of Thomas Jefferson's Monticello estate. The ex-president has been instrumental in obtaining the charter and is planning the grounds, buildings, and curriculum of the new university, whose students will begin classes March 27, 1825.

The University of Cincinnati is founded in Ohio.

Colgate University is founded as Madison College at Hamilton, N.Y. (*see* 1890).

Centre College is founded at Danville, Ky.

Norwich University is founded at Northfield, Vt.

Nonfiction *The World as Will and Idea* (*Die Welt als Wille und Vorstellung*) by German philosopher Arthur Schopenhauer, 30, who expounds a philosophy of pessimism that will be generally ignored for a generation but will have great influence in the latter part of the century.

Fiction *Ivanhoe* and *The Legend of Montrose* by Walter Scott.

Poetry "Ode to a Nightingale" by John Keats; "Mazeppa" by Lord Byron.

The Prado is completed at Madrid after 34 years of construction and is made the Spanish Royal Museum by Ferdinand VII, who brings together paintings and sculpture collected by Spanish kings since Carlos I.

Painting *The White Horse* by John Constable who is elected an associate of the Royal Academy; *George IV* and *Pope Pius VII* by Sir Thomas Lawrence; *The Raft of the 'Medusa'* by Théodore Géricault (*see* 1816).

First performances *Stabat Mater* by Franz Schubert in July at Steyr in Upper Austria.

Hymn "From Greenland's Icy Mountains" by English prelate Reginald Heber, 36, who will be bishop of Calcutta from 1822 to 1826: "What though the spicy breezes/ Blow soft o'er Ceylon's isle;/ Though every prospect pleases,/ And only man is vile. . . ."

The whaling industry expands to new grounds off Japan. Many whaling ships will obtain supplies from Japanese ports.

U.S. diplomats in foreign posts receive instructions to send home any valuable new seeds and plants.

An improved plow patented by Cayuga County, N.Y., farmer Jethro Wood, 45, is constructed in several major pieces so that a farmer who breaks one part can replace it without having to buy a whole new plow. Other plowmakers will infringe on Wood's patent, and many farmers will insist that cast-iron plows poison the soil and will refuse to give up their old wooden plows (*see* Lane, 1833; Deere, 1837).

Salmon, lobster meat, and oysters are packed in tin cans at New York by Ezra Dagett and Thomas Kensett (*see* Donkin-Hall, 1814; Kensett's patent, 1825).

An iron cooking stove is patented by Vermont inventor John Conant, but U.S. cooks and housewives spurn his invention, preferring the traditional practice of hearthside cooking (*see* 1795; 1850).

The world's first eating chocolate to be produced commercially is manufactured at Vevey, Switzerland, by François-Louis Cailler, 23, who introduces the first chocolate to be prepared and sold in blocks made by machine. Cailler starts a company that will specialize in fondants, but his chocolate is not candy (*see* Kohler, 1818; Peter and Kohler, 1911; van Houten, 1828).

The native population of the Hawaiian (Sandwich) Islands falls to 150,000 as a consequence of diseases introduced by Europeans and Americans since the landing of Captain Cook in 1778 and the arrival of occasional visitors in the past 41 years. Some 60 Caucasians live on the island of Oahu.

1820 Britain's George III dies January 29 at age 81 and is succeeded by the 57-year-old prince regent, who has ruled since 1811 and who will reign until 1830 as George IV. The king's 51-year-old wife Caroline demands recognition as queen, but the profligate George continues his efforts to obtain a divorce.

France's duc de Berry, heir presumptive to the throne, is assassinated February 13. The 41-year-old Charles Ferdinand de Bourbon is a nephew of Louis XVIII, and his posthumous son the comte de Chambord, born September 29, becomes heir to the throne.

The Cato Street Conspiracy to murder members of the British Cabinet is discovered February 23. Its ringleaders will be executed.

Maine is admitted to the Union as the 23rd state (*see* Missouri Compromise, below).

A Spanish revolution led by Colonel Rafael Riego forces Ferdinand VII to restore the constitution of 1812, which he does March 7.

The king of Naples Ferdinand IV promises a constitution July 7 following a revolt instigated by secret societies that include the Carbonari.

A Portuguese revolution begins August 24 at Oporto and reaches Lisbon 5 days later as discontent grows under the regency that rules with British influence while João VI lives in Brazil. Leaders of the revolution demand a constitution.

A bill of pains and penalties against Britain's Princess Caroline, wife of George IV, has been pending in Parliament since July 5 but is dropped November 10. Inquiry into Caroline's conduct and efforts to deprive her of her titles are also dropped as the public rallies to her cause.

President Monroe is re-elected with 231 electoral votes out of 232. One electoral vote is cast for John Quincy Adams by an elector who either opposes the Virginia dynasty of presidents or who holds the conviction that only George Washington should have the honor of unanimous election.

The Missouri Compromise accepted by Congress March 3 has permitted entry of Missouri into the Union as a slave state in exchange for Maine's entry as a free state (above) but only on condition that slavery be abolished in the rest of the Louisiana Purchase territory.

Liberia is founded by the Washington Colonization Society for the repatriation of U.S. blacks to Africa (*see* 1847).

English Quaker minister Elizabeth Gurney marries chocolate heir Joseph Fry at age 40 and works to improve English prison conditions. Elizabeth Fry will continue her philanthropic efforts until her death in 1845.

The Spanish Inquisition begun by Castile's Isabella in 1478 is ended by Ferdinand VII (above) as a result of the revolution that will have effects in Latin America (*see* 1821).

Indianapolis is founded on the White River in Indiana. Its name combines the Greek word for city (*polis*) with the name of the state.

England's Peterloo Massacre of 1819 reflected the almost universal political repression of the time.

1820 (cont.) Edward Bransfield of the Royal Navy surveys New South Shetland in Antarctica and proceeds as far south as 64 degrees 30 minutes.

U.S. sealer Nathaniel B. Palmer out of Stonington, Conn., discovers the mountainous archipelago south of 64 degrees 30 minutes that will be called Palmer Peninsula.

Regent's Canal is completed in London.

Connecticut architect Ithiel Town, 36, patents a truss bridge (*see* first Vermont covered bridge, 1824).

The first modern concrete to be produced in America advances construction of the Erie Canal. Engineer Canvass White patents the hydraulic use of cement made from "hydraulic lime" found in New York's Madison, Cayuga, and Onondaga Counties.

Russian prospectors discover rich deposits of platinum in the Ural Mountains.

French physicist André Marie Ampère, 45, discovers the left-hand and right-hand rules of the magnetic field surrounding a wire that carries electric current. Repeating last year's experiments by Hans Christian Oersted, Ampère reports that two current-carrying wires exercise a reciprocal action upon each other. (The unit of measurement of an electric current's intensity will be named the ampere.) (*see* Ohm, 1827).

A cholera epidemic begins to kill thousands in China and the Philippine Islands (*see* 1819; 1823).

The U.S. Pharmacopoeia established by New York physician Lyman Spalding, 45, is a government-approved list of medical drugs with their formulas, methods for preparing medicines, and requirements and tests for purity.

Quinine sulfate is discovered. The alkaloid drug is effective against malaria (*see* 1642).

Indiana University is founded at Bloomington.

Nonfiction *Lacon, or Many Things in Few Words Addressed to Those Who Think* by English clergyman-wine merchant-sportsman Charles Caleb Colton, 40, who writes, "Imitation is the sincerest form of flattery."

Fiction *The Monastery* and *The Abbott* by Walter Scott, who is made a baronet by Britain's new king George IV; *The Sketch Book* by Geoffrey Crayon (Washington Irving) contains "The Legend of Sleepy Hollow."

Poetry "The Eve of St. Agnes," "La Belle Dame Sans Merci," and "Ode on a Grecian Urn" by John Keats, who writes in his "Ode," "Beauty is truth, truth beauty—that is all/ Ye know on earth, and all ye need to know"; "Prometheus Unbound" by Percy Bysshe Shelley, whose "Ode" contains the line, "If Winter comes, can Spring be far behind?"; *Meditations Poétiques* by French poet Alphonse Marie Louis de Prat de Lamartine, 30, who celebrates his deceased love Mme. Julie Charles, marries Elizabeth Birch, and enters the diplomatic service to begin 10 years in Italy during which he will publish several other books of poetry.

Painting *Harwich Lighthouse* by John Constable; *The Book of Job* in the Old Testament is published with illustrations by William Blake. Benjamin West dies at London March 11 at age 81.

Sculpture *The Lion of Lucerne* by Danish sculptor Bertel Thorvaldsen, 52.

The *Venus de Milo* (Aphrodite of Melos) is discovered on the Aegean island of Melos by a Greek peasant named Yorgos, who dislodges a boulder and finds an underground chamber containing the armless marble figure of the 2nd century.

Theater *The Bear and the Pasha* (*L'ours et le Pacha*) by French vaudeville writer (Augustin) Eugène Scribe, 28, with Xavier Saintine, 2/10 at the Théâter des Varietés, Paris. Scribe has been writing vaudeville comedies since 1811 and will write more than 250 plays, opera librettos, and ballets.

Bristol's Royal York Crescent is completed.

U.S. farmers are encouraged by the land law enacted by Congress April 24 providing for the sale of 80 acres of public land at $1.25 per acre in cash, making it possible for a man to buy a farm for $100 with no need for further payments. Thousands of farmers are in debt to the government for public lands on which they have made down payments of only $80 each, and farmers who have paid in full are angry (*see* 1804; 1841).

Nebraska Territory is called "a great American desert" by U.S. Army officer Stephen Harriman Long, 36, who commands an exploring expedition into the Rocky Mountains (*see* Pike, 1806; Deere, 1837: irrigation, 1848).

The first amino acid (glycine) is isolated from gelatin by French chemist M. H. Braconnot, who then proceeds to isolate the amino acid leucine from muscle tissue. Amino acids will be found to combine in various ways to form protein, the basic substance of all living tissue (*see* Megendie, 1816; Mulder, 1838).

Adulteration of Foods and Culinary Poisons by English chemistry professor Frederick Accum enrages the vested interests, and Accum flees to Berlin in order to avoid public trial. A professor at the Surrey Institution, Accum has shown that pepper is almost invariably adulterated with mustard husks, pea flour, juniper berries, and sweepings from storeroom floors; counterfeit China tea is made from dried thorn leaves colored with poisonous verdigris; pickles are treated with copper to look green (*see* 1768; 1850).

"The ample charms of a genuine Dutch country tea table" are described by Washington Irving (above) in "The Legend of Sleepy Hollow": "Such heaped-up platters of cakes of various and almost indescribable kinds, known only to experienced Dutch housewives! There was the doughty doughnut, the tenderer oly koek, and the crisp and crumbling cruller ..." (*see* 1627; first ring doughnut, 1847).

Johnny Walker Scotch whiskey has its beginnings in a grocery, wine, and spirit business opened at Kilmarnock in Scotland by Ayrshireman John Walker, whose son Alexander will introduce the whisky that will become the world's largest-selling brand.

Beefeater Gin has its beginnings in a London distillery founded by James Burroughs.

Dutch-dominated South Africa gets its first large-scale British settlement in July. The Albany settlers, 4,000 strong, are settled by the British government at a place that will be called Grahamstown in the eastern coastal region where the colonists will be ruled by an autocratic British governor until 1825 (*see* 1826).

Jamaica in the West Indies has a slave population of 340,000. Some 800,000 have been imported since 1690, but adult males have far outnumbered adult females and infant mortality among slaves on the sugar estates has been 500 per 1,000 live births.

Great waves of immigration begin to the United States which will average 35,000 Irish immigrants per year for the next two decades (*see* 1846; 1851).

The U.S. population reaches 9.6 million, with some 83 percent of gainfully employed Americans engaged in agriculture. Between 2.5 million and 3 million live west of the Alleghenies, up from 1 million in 1801. Pittsburgh has a population of 7,248, while New York has nearly 124,000 and has passed Philadelphia to become the nation's largest city.

1821 A Greek War of Independence that will continue until 1831 begins following an insurrection in February against Ottoman-Greek rule in Wallachia. The Greek majority in the Morea slaughters the Ottoman Turks, who retaliate by hanging the Greek patriarch at Constantinople and massacring Greeks in the city. The Turks reject a Russian ultimatum delivered July 27 demanding restoration of Christian churches and protection of the Christian religion, and on October 5 the Greeks take Tripolitsa, the main Ottoman fortress in the Morea, and massacre some 10,000 Turks. Prince von Metternich of Austria and Viscount Castlereagh have averted Russian intervention by warning Czar Aleksandr against supporting the revolution.

Mexico declares her independence from Spain February 24 and claims freedom also for the provinces of California and Texas. Agustín de Iturbide, 38, becomes regent of Mexico pending selection of a new ruler (*see* 1822).

A junta convened by the captain general at Guatemala City declares independence September 14 and Iturbide (above) invites Guatemala to join Mexico (*see* 1822).

Simón Bolívar sends his lieutenant Antonio José de Sucre, 28, with an army to liberate Quito. Bolívar himself moves into Venezuela, joins with José Paez to defeat a royalist army at Carabob June 24, occupies Caracas 5 days later, and is named president of Venezuela August 30.

José de San Martin proclaims the independence of Peru July 22 and assumes supreme authority as protector of the new South American nation (*see* Chile, 1817). San Martin will resign in 14 months to permit Simón Bolívar to become dictator of Peru (*see* 1824).

Missouri is admitted to the Union as the 24th state under terms of last year's Missouri compromise that permits slavery in the new state (*see* Ashley, 1822).

The power of the U.S. Supreme Court is superior to that of any state court in matters involving federal rights, says Chief Justice John Marshall. He hands down the decision March 3 in *Cohens v. Virginia.*

Ohio Quaker saddlemaker Benjamin Lundy, 32, urges abolition of slavery and begins publication of his antislavery newspaper *Genius of Universal Emancipation.* He soon moves to Greenville, Tenn.; he will move to Baltimore in 1824. A slave trader will attack and severely injure him in 1828, but Lundy will enlist the support of William Lloyd Garrison, now 16, and Garrison will serve as associate editor for 6 months beginning in September 1829 (*see* 1831).

Austin, Tex., has its origin in San Felipe de Austin founded in Mexico's Texas territory (above) by Stephen Fuller Austin, 28, whose father has just died at age 60. Young Austin carries out his father's plans by obtaining a grant of land on condition that he settle a given number of families on the land, and he founds the first permanent Anglo-American Texas settlement. *Empresario* Austin will bring some 8,000 colonists to the region (*see* 1836).

Minneapolis has its beginnings in the town of St. Anthony founded on the east bank of the Upper Mississippi at St. Anthony's Falls (*see* Fort Snelling, 1819; Minneapolis, 1847).

The electric motor is pioneered by English chemist-physicist Michael Faraday, 29, who demonstrates electromagnetic rotation. Faraday has pondered on Oersted's 1819 discovery, and he conducts various experiments, including one that involves a 6-inch length of copper wire suspended from a hook with its lower end dipping into a bowl of mercury. A bar magnet is fixed vertically in the center of the mercury, and Faraday finds that when he passes a continuous electric current from a battery through the hook and down through the wire to the mercury, the wire begins to rotate and continues to do so for as long as the current flows (*see* Sturgeon, 1823).

The first U.S. natural gas well is tapped at Fredonia, N.Y.

McGill University is chartered at Montreal. Scots-Canadian businessman James McGill died in 1813 at age 69, leaving £10,000 to found a college.

The University of Buenos Aires is founded.

1821 (cont.) George Washington University is founded at Washington, D.C.

Boston's English High School opens with 102 students. The first tuition-free public high school teaches no language but English, it prepares students for the professions, both "mercantile and mechanical," with a curriculum that emphasizes science, mathematics, logic, and history, and by 1827 Massachusetts will require every town of 500 families or more to support a high school from public tax revenues, making secondary education a birthright rather than a privilege (*see* normal school, 1839).

The Emma Willard School has its beginnings in the Troy Female Seminary at Troy, N.Y. Educator Emma Hart Willard, 34, will prove that girls can master subjects such as mathematics and philosophy without losing their health or charm.

News of Napoleon's death at St. Helena May 5 reaches Britain only 7 weeks later.

The *Manchester Guardian* begins publication. The weekly founded by English Liberal John Edward Taylor, 30, will begin daily publication in 1855.

The *Saturday Evening Post* begins publication at Philadelphia. The weekly magazine founded by Samuel C. Atkinson and Charles Alexander will continue until 1969 (*see* Curtis, 1897).

Nonfiction "Confessions of an Opium Eater" by English author Thomas De Quincey, 36, appears in *London Magazine*. De Quincey began using opium in his second year at Oxford and dropped out in 1808.

Fiction *Kenilworth* and *The Pirate* by Sir Walter Scott; *The Spy* by U.S. novelist James Fenimore Cooper, 32, who has told his wife that he could write a better story than the popular English novel she was reading. Cooper's novel gains quick success.

The pornographic novel *Fanny Hill* of 1750 is the subject of a Massachusetts obscenity trial following passage of a state obscenity law.

Painting *The Hay Wain* by John Constable.

Opera *Der Freischutz* (*The Free-Shooter*) 6/18 at Berlin's Schauspielhaus, with music by Carl Maria von Weber.

First performances Konzertstück for Piano and Orchestra in F minor by Carl Maria von Weber 6/25 at Berlin; *Invitation to the Dance* (*Aufforderung zum Tanze*) by Carl Maria von Weber.

Cantata "Hinaus In's Frische Leben" by Carl Maria von Weber 11/16 at Dresden, for the birthday of the sister of Saxony's Friedrich August I.

March "Hail to the Chief" by Scottish composers James Sanderson and E. Rilley (who have adapted lines from Sir Walter Scott's *Lady of the Lake* poem of 1810) is played at the second inaugural of U.S. President James Monroe.

Poker has its beginnings in a card game played by sailors at New Orleans. They have combined the ancient Persian game *As Nas* with the French game *poque*, a descendent of the Italian game *Primiera*, and a cousin of the English game *Brag*. Played with three cards from a deck of 32, the new game contains combinations such as pairs and three of a kind, the draw and the full deck of 52 cards will soon be added, but the game of stud poker will not evolve for many years nor will straights or flushes (date approximate; *see* Schenck, 1871).

New York's Fulton Fish Market opens on the East River.

Game birds shot by market hunters are mainstays of the U.S. diet. A single market hunter kills 18,000 migrating golden plover within the year.

Britain's population reaches 20.8 million, with 6.8 million of it in Ireland. France has 30.4 million, the Italian states 18, Austria 12, the German states, duchies, free cities, and principalities 26.1.

1822 A Greek assembly at Epidauros proclaims independence from the Ottoman Empire January 13 (*see* 1456), an Ottoman fleet takes the island of Chios in April, massacres much of the island's population, and sells most of the rest into slavery. Greek patriots set the Ottoman admiral's flagship afire in reprisal, a Greek force under the 32-year-old Admiral Konstantinos Kanaris destroys the Ottoman fleet June 19, but an Ottoman army of 35,000 invades Greece in July, overruns the peninsula north of the Gulf of Corinth, and forces the new Greek government to take refuge in the islands.

Greek guerilla leaders including Demetrius Ypsilanti, 29, gain victories against the Turks.

Viscount Castlereagh slits his throat with a penknife August 12 and dies at age 53. He is replaced as foreign minister and leader of the Commons by George Canning, now 52. Robert Peel becomes secretary for home affairs at age 34, and a liberal wing of the Tory cabinet begins to make important reforms.

Orangemen at Dublin attack the British viceroy, and the city has bottle riots.

An Ashanti War that will continue for 9 years begins in West Africa following an exchange of insults between an Ashanti trader and a Fanti policeman. The tribesmen go into battle with one side blowing war horns, the other playing "God Save the King" (*see* 1824).

The Battle of Pichincha outside Quito May 24 gives José de Sucre a decisive victory over a Spanish royalist army. Sucre has moved up the Andes, José San Martin has sent forces to help him, he liberates Quito, and San Martin meets with Simón Bolívar at Guayaquil (*see* 1821; 1823).

Haiti conquers Santo Domingo from Spain and takes over the entire island of Hispaniola (*see* 1805; 1844).

Mexico crowns Agustín de Iturbide emperor July 25. Agustin I sends troops to force other Central American nations to join the new Mexican Empire (*see* 1821; 1823).

Brazil's Portuguese regent Dom Pedro, 24, proclaims independence from his father João VI, he is crowned emperor December 1, and he begins an 8-year reign as Pedro I over the country that occupies 47 percent of South America. Pedro took refuge in Brazil with his father 15 years ago when the French invaded Portugal, he has been prince regent since his father's return to Portugal last year, and he has sided with the Brazilians against the reactionary policies of Lisbon (*see* 1831).

Exploration of the upper Missouri River gains impetus from Missouri Lieutenant Governor William H. Ashley, 44, who places a notice in the newspaper at St. Louis: "To enterprising young men. The subscriber wishes to engage one hundred young men to ascend the Missouri River to its source, there to be employed for one, two, or three years." Within a week, Ashley and his associate Andrew Henry, 43, have the men they want to establish a permanent fur trade, and the men include keelboatman Mike Fink, 52, James Bridger, 18, Jedediah Strong Smith, 22, William L. Sublette, and Joseph Reddeford Walker, 23 (*see* South Pass, 1824).

Vesey's Rebellion fails in South Carolina June 16 when authorities at Charleston arrest 10 slaves who have heeded the urgings of local freedman Denmark Vesey, 55. Vesey himself is arrested, he defends himself eloquently in court, but he is hanged July 2 with four other blacks. Further arrests follow, more than 30 other executions will take place, and several southern states will tighten their slave codes.

The S.S. *Robert Fulton* completes the first steamboat voyage from New York to New Orleans and then proceeds to Havana. Scots-American shipbuilder Henry Heckford, 47, has built the vessel.

The S.S. *Aaron Manby* that slides down the ways at Rotherhithe, England, April 30 is the world's first iron steamship. Named for the proprietor of the Horsley Ironworks at Tipton, Staffordshire, she undergoes trials on the Thames and then goes into service across the Channel, arriving at Paris June 10 with a cargo of linseed oil and iron.

George Stephenson completes the world's first iron railroad bridge for the Stockton-Darlington line (*see* 1814; 1825).

French Egyptologist Jean François Champollion, 32, deciphers the Rosetta stone found in 1799 and thus makes it possible to read the papyri and stones that will expand knowledge of ancient Egyptian civilizations. Champollion has spent years studying the stone's hieroglyphics, he completes his translations, and he reports that the script contains both sound-signs (phonograms) and sense-signs (ideograms) that provide the necessary clues for deciphering all Egyptian inscriptions.

Histoire Naturelle des Animaux sans vertebres by the Chevalier de Lamarck proposes an erroneous theory of evolution that says environmental changes can produce structural changes in plants and animals (*see* 1809). Now 78, Lamarck contributes to science by introducing the classes Annelida, Arachnida, Crustacea, Infusoria, and Tunicata, but he claims that environmental changes can induce new or increased use of certain organs or parts and that these acquired characteristics can be transmitted to offspring.

U.S. Army physician William Beaumont, 37, begins pioneer observations on the action of human gastric juices. Serving on Michilmacinac (Mackinac) Island in the straits between Lake Michigan and Lake Huron, Beaumont has saved the life of a young French-American voyageur employed by John Jacob Astor's American Fur Company, but the shotgun blast wound in St. Martin's left side has not completely healed and the remaining fistula permits Beaumont to make his studies (*see* 1833).

Yellow fever strikes New York City and thousands flee to Greenwich Village whose growth is spurred by the influx of people.

The first typesetting machine is patented in England by Connecticut inventor William Church, whose machine casts letters in lead and composes words automatically. Spacing the words to desired line measurements must still be done by hand (*see* Mergenthaler, 1884; Lanston, 1897).

The *Sunday Times* begins publication at London (*see* 1788; Thomson, 1953).

Fiction   *The Fortunes of Nigel* by Sir Walter Scott.

Painting   *View on the Stour* by John Constable.

The first permanent photograph is made by French physicist J. N. Niepce of 1816 bicycle fame and his 17-year-old kinsman Claude Niepce. Seeking a compound that will stabilize a photographic image on paper, they follow Thomas Wedgwood's 1802 work and produce a heliograph, or heliotype, by using asphaltum, or bitumen of Judea, used for years in etching. The compound becomes insoluble in its usual solvents when exposed to light, they find, and in addition to giving a resist for the etching of metal, it produces transparent images on glass (*see* 1826).

Hungarian pianist Franz (Ferencz) Liszt makes his debut at Vienna December 1 at age 11 and meets composer Franz Schubert.

Popular songs   "The Old Oaken Bucket" ("Araby's Daughter") by English-American composer George Kiallmark, 41, with lyrics from the Samuel Woodworth poem of 1818.

Britain's George IV has the first Royal Enclosure erected at Ascot where horse races have been run since 1711.

Liggett & Myers Tobacco Company has its beginnings in a snuff factory started by Christopher Fouls at Belleville, Ill. (*see* 1847).

1822 (cont.) New York's Greenwich Village (above) is a rural Manhattan area whose streets will never conform to the grid pattern employed elsewhere in the city.

Potato crops fail in the west of Ireland as they will do again to some degree in 1831, 1835, 1836, and—most disastrously—in the mid-1840s (*see* 1739).

The name "chateaubriand" is given to the cut at the end of the beef tenderloin by the personal chef to diplomat-novelist Vicomte François René de Chateaubriand, now 54, who is serving as French minister to the Court of St. James at London.

The first U.S. spice-grinding company is established at Boston by English immigrant William Underwood, who from 1812 to 1817 was apprentice to the London shop of MacKey and Co., picklers and preservers. Underwood opens a shop on Boston's Russia Wharf, where he produces ground mustard from imported mustard seed. By employing English-style labels on the bottles and tin cannisters that contain his dry ground mustard and by selling his product at a price 25 percent below that of imported English mustards, Underwood will drive the English out of the Charleston and New Orleans markets in the next 4 years (*see* fish, shellfish, 1846).

New York City's population reaches 124,000. A family of 14 can live comfortably on $3,000 per year.

Contraception is recommended by English reformer Francis Place, 51, in his pamphlet *To the Married of Both Sexes of the Working People*. Place advises insertion of a soft sponge "as large as a green walnut, or a small apple" and "tied by a bobbin or penny ribbon."

1823 The Monroe Doctrine enunciated by President Monroe in his annual message to Congress December 2 states a nationalistic determination to oppose any European influence in the Western Hemisphere and to remain aloof from European conflicts: "The American continents . . . are henceforth not to be considered as subjects for future colonization by any European power."

U.S. forces have defeated the Sauk and Fox chief Black Hawk (Makataemishklakiak), 56, who has created an alliance with the Winnebagos, Pottawotamies, and Kickapoos to resist white incursions into the Illinois country (but *see* 1832).

Mexico's Emperor Agustín de Iturbide confirms the grant of land on the Rio Brazos River made by the Spanish viceroy to the late Moses Austin and now held by his son Stephen F. Austin.

An assembly at Guatemala City July 1 declares the sovereignty of the United Provinces of Central America and the independence of this confederation is recognized by Mexico August 20, but the confederation of Guatemala, Honduras, Costa Rica, Nicaragua, and San Salvador will dissolve by 1840 and further attempts at union will fail.

Spain is invaded by French troops, and the 3-year-old revolution is ended August 31 by the Battle of the Trocadero which restores Ferdinand VII to power. He ignores French advice to introduce a moderate constitutional regime and begins a repressive rule that will continue until his death in 1833.

Britain abolishes the death penalty for more than 100 crimes that have been capital offenses. The mitigation of capital punishment crowns efforts by the late Samuel Romilly (*see* 1808).

An antislavery society is established at London under the leadership of William Wilberforce and Thomas Fowell Buxton who has acquired a fortune as a brewer (*see* 1807; 1833).

The petroleum industry has its beginnings at the Caspian Sea port of Baku on Russia's Apsheron Peninsula where the "eternal fire" of natural gas holes has been known at least since the time of Alexander the Great in the 4th century B.C. Primitive drilling for oil begins at Baku, which will be yielding half the world's petroleum by 1900 (*see* 1296; 1859; 1871).

The first electromagnet is devised by English physicist William Sturgeon, 40, who varnishes an iron bar to insulate it, wraps the bar with copper wire, connects the wire to the terminals of a voltaic pile, and creates a crude device that can lift a few pounds of iron (*see* Volta, 1800; Faraday, 1821; Henry, 1827).

Asiatic cholera reaches the gateway to Russia at Astrakhan in an epidemic that will affect every nation of the Western world (*see* 1820; 1829).

The *Lancet* begins publication October 5 at London under the direction of local physician Thomas Wakley, 28, who has started the weekly medical journal to advance knowledge and to reform British medicine. Wakley will crusade against nepotism, the Royal College of Surgeons, and the adulteration of foods (*see* 1850).

Merck & Co. has its U.S. beginnings in the Philadelphia firm Zeitler & Rosengarten founded by German-American chemist George David Rosengarten who arrived in America 4 years ago. He buys a half-interest in the firm Zeitler & Seitler that has been making quinine sulfate since last year, the firm will add morphine, strychnine, and other pharmaceuticals, it will become Powers-Weightman-Rosengarten in 1905, and will become Merck & Co. in 1927 (*see* 1668; 1908).

Michael Faraday liquefies chlorine. The water-soluble poisonous gas will find wide use in water purification, in bleaches, and in warfare.

Trinity College is founded at Hartford, Conn.

An electric telegraph offered to the British admiralty by English inventor Francis Ronalds, 35, employs wires whose ends are attached to a battery at the sending point and to electrodes in acidified water at receiving stations, each electrode being marked with a letter or number. Ronalds has set up a complete telegraph system on his estate at Hammersmith using 8 miles of wire, but the admiralty rejects his offer, saying, "Telegraphs of any kind are wholly unnecessary and no other than the one in use (a semaphore installed in 1796) will be adopted" (*see* Chappe, 1793; Henry, 1831).

Fiction *The Pioneers* by James Fenimore Cooper begins Cooper's *Leatherstocking Tales*.

Poetry *Don Juan* by Lord Byron whose greatest work is based in part on the account of a 1741 shipwreck off the coast of Chile as described by his grandfather John "Foul-weather Jack" Byron, who made a round-the-world exploratory voyage from 1764 to 1766: "Man's love is of man's life a thing apart,/ 'Tis woman's whole existence." "A Visit from St. Nicholas" is published anonymously 12/23 in the *Troy (New York) Sentinel.* New York lexicographer Clement Clark Moore, 44, had his *Compendious Lexicon of the Hebrew Language* published in 1809 and he brings to life the figure depicted by Washington Irving in 1809: " 'Twas the night before Christmas . . . Now, Dasher! now, Dancer! now, Prancer and Vixen! On, Comet, on, Cupid! on, Donder and Blitzen!"

Theater *The Truthful Liar* (*Le Menteur Véridique*) by Eugène Scribe 4/24 at the Théâtre du Gymnase, Paris. 16 Scribe comedies are produced, up from 11 last year.

Opera *Semiramide* 2/3 at Venice's Teatro la Fenice, with a libretto based on a Voltaire tragedy of 1748, music by Gioacchino Rossini; *Clari, or the Maid of Milan* 5/8 at London's Covent Garden Theatre, with Charles Kemble, 48, music by English composer Henry Rowley Bishop, 37, libretto and lyrics by New York actor-playwright John Howard Payne, 37, arias that include "Home Sweet Home." The opera opens at New York's Park Theater 11/12, 100,000 copies of the song are sold in its first year, the London publishers net 2,000 guineas in profit, and Bishop will become the first musician to be granted knighthood (in 1842); *Euryanthe* 10/25 at Vienna's Kärntnerthor theater, with music by Carl Maria von Weber.

First performances Ballet-Musik aus Rosamunde by Franz Schubert 12/20 at Vienna.

Boston cabinetmaker Jonas Chickering starts a piano company that will become the largest in America. In 1843 Chickering will develop the first practical application of the one-piece solid casting for both grand and upright pianos, and in 1850 he will develop the first overstrung bass scale, features that will become standard with all pianos (*see* 1853; Steinway, 1859).

Rugby student William Webb Ellis, 17, inaugurates a new game whose rules will be codified in 1839. Playing soccer for the 256-year-old college in East Warwickshire, Ellis sees that the clock is running out with his team behind so he scoops up the ball and runs with it in defiance of the rules. Rugby College will adopt rugby football (or rugger) officially in 1841 (*see* 1839; Association soccer, 1863; football, 1869, 1873).

The Royal Thames Yacht Club is founded.

The Macintosh raincoat has its beginnings in a waterproof fabric of rubber bonded to cloth patented by Scottish chemist Charles Macintosh, 57, who applies his research on possible uses of the coal tar distillate naphtha. Macintosh's cloth will make the name Macintosh a British generic for the raincoat (*see* Goodyear, 1839; Aquascutum, 1851; Burberry, 1856).

New York's A. T. Stewart Department Store has its beginnings in a small dry goods shop opened by Irish-American merchant Alexander Turney Stewart, 20, who will open the world's first true department store (*see* 1846).

London's Sussex Place is completed by John Nash.

A new royal pavilion at Bath is completed by John Nash after 8 years of construction in a "Hindoo" Islamic style to replace a villa built for the prince regent in the late 1780s.

China's monopoly in the tea trade begins to fade as an indigenous tea bush is found growing in northern India's Upper Assam. Acting for the British government, Charles Bruce smuggles knowledgeable coolies out of China and puts them to work transplanting young tea bushes into nursery beds to begin tea plantations (*see* 1839).

Illinois is opened to U.S. corn farmers by the defeat of Black Hawk.

Mechanical refrigeration is pioneered by Michael Faraday (above) who finds that certain gases under constant pressure will condense until they cool (*see* Perkins, 1834; Gorrie, 1842).

Old Crow bourbon whiskey has its beginnings in a sour mash whiskey produced according to scientific principles by Kentucky distiller James C. Crow (*see* Craig, 1789). Aging in charred oak barrels will not begin until 1860, and whiskey will not take on color until then (the color will generally derive more from added caramel than from wood char).

1824 The landmark Supreme Court decision handed down March 2 in the case of *Gibbons v. Ogden* will free U.S. rivers from monopoly control. Steamboat operator Thomas Gibbons holds a monopoly originally granted by the New York State legislature to Robert Fulton and Robert Livingston, he has sued New Jersey steamboat operator Aaron Ogden, 68, who runs a ferry service between New York and Elizabethtown, Ogden has retained Daniel Webster to plead his case, Chief Justice John Marshall rules that the monopoly granted by New York violates the interstate commerce clause in the Constitution, and the ruling opens U.S. waterways to all steamships that can comply with regulations designed to keep boilers from exploding.

The U.S. Army Corps of Engineers embarks on a career of building harbors, damming and channeling rivers, and generally developing waterways and

Erie Canal barges brought grain from the Midwest to the Atlantic Seaboard, spurring the growth of New York.

his skull as a royal drinking cup at Coomassie, but their king Osai Tutu Kwadwo (Quamina) is killed.

The first Burmese War begins February 24 as the British governor general of India Lord Amherst declares war on Burma whose forces have captured the island of Shahpuri in violation of East India Company territorial rights. Rangoon falls to the British May 11.

South American liberation forces under Simón Bolívar and José de Sucre move into the Andean highlands of Charcas and defeat a Spanish force August 24 at Junin.

The Battle of Ayacucho December 9 gives José de Sucre and his 5,800 men a triumph over 9,300 Spanish royalists. The 23,000 royalists who remain in Peru are forced to withdraw (see 1825).

France's Louis XVIII dies September 16 at age 68 after a 10-year reign that was interrupted for 100 days in 1815. He is succeeded by his 66-year-old brother who will reign as Charles X until 1830.

Greek forces at Mitylene nearly annihilate an Ottoman army in October as the Greeks mourn the loss of Lord Byron, who died at Missolonghi April 19 at age 36 while helping the Greeks in their fight for independence.

The U.S. presidential election in November ends with no candidate having a majority in the Electoral College although John Calhoun is elected vice president. Andrew Jackson has 99 electoral votes, John Quincy Adams 84, William H. Crawford 41, Henry Clay 37 (see 1825).

South Pass through the Rocky Mountains into the Great Basin is discovered by Jedediah Strong Smith of the Rocky Mountain Fur Co. (see 1822; 1826).

New Harmony, Ind., is purchased from the German Lutheran Rappites who founded it 10 years ago by English reformer Robert Owen. Owen is starting communes in England, Ireland, Mexico, and the United States, all of them doomed to fail. New Harmony will be the first of many American communes.

 Robert Owen (above) promotes abolition of slavery, women's liberation, and free progressive education.

British workers gain the right to organize June 21 as Parliament repeals the Combination Acts at the urging of radical M. P. Joseph Hume, 47, who has been persuaded by reformer Francis Place, the contraception advocate (but see 1825).

Women's rights and free public schools are championed in America by Scottish social reformer Frances "Fanny" Wright, 29, who will settle in New York in 1829 and who will scandalize the nation by discussing contraception, a more equal distribution of wealth, an end to religion, and emancipation of the slaves with resettlement of Afro-Americans outside the United States.

Indiana settlers attack an Indian village and massacre two braves, three squaws, and four children. The

other civil projects under terms of a bill signed by President Monroe May 24 to establish the corps that had its real beginnings in 1775 when George Washington appointed Colonel Richard Gridley chief engineer to the Continental army just before the Battle of Bunker Hill. The primary mission of the corps will be one of providing support for military operations, but it will play a significant role in developing U.S. waterways and highways, often at the expense of the environment.

Vermont's first covered bridge spans the Missisquoi River at Highgate Falls (see Philadelphia, 1805). Scores of such bridges throughout the state will follow the arch truss bridge at Highgate Falls.

A Road Survey Act passed by Congress April 30 authorizes the Army Corps of Engineers (above) to survey possible road and canal routes.

Land grants to the Wabash and Erie Canal Company will total 826,300 acres in the next 10 years (work on the Wabash and Erie will start in 1832). Land grants to other private canal companies will total more than 4.2 million acres in the next 42 years (see Chesapeake and Ohio, 1828; Miami, 1829; Louisville and Portland, 1830; Cleveland to Portsmouth, 1832).

Portland cement is patented by English bricklayer Joseph Aspdin of Leeds who has mixed chalk and clay, has heated the mixture to a high temperature, and has created a cement impervious to water and as durable as the cement used by Roman aqueduct builders in ancient times (see White, 1820; reinforced concrete, 1849).

Ashanti tribesmen defeat a Fanti detachment January 21 at Essamako, outnumbering the Fanti 10,000 to 500. The Ashanti capture the British governor Sir Charles M'Carthy, they cut off his head, they will use settlers claim that "killing an Indian serves a better purpose than killing a deer," but the conscience of the white community is aroused, four of the killers are hanged, and tension grows between whites and Indians on the frontier.

The Royal Society for the Prevention of Cruelty to Animals (RSPCA) is founded at London (*see* 1866).

A principle that will be expressed as the second law of thermodynamics by England's William Thompson (Lord Kelvin) is stated by French physicist Nicolas Léonard Sadi Carnot, 28, in *Reflections on the Motive Power of Fire* (*Reflexions sur la puissance motrice du feu*), a major advance in the understanding of how heat can be used to drive engines. Carnot notes that steam engines are used to work mines, propel ships, excavate ports, forge iron, saw wood, grind grain, and spin and weave cloth, but he observes that "their theory is very little understood, and attempts to improve them are still directed almost by chance." Carnot states that "the production of motive power is then due in steam-engines not to an actual consumption of caloric, *but to its transportation from a warm body to a cold body* . . . [a principle that] is applicable to any machine set in motion by heat. According to this principle, the production of heat alone is not sufficient to give birth to the impelling power. It is necessary that there should also be cold; without it the heat would be useless" (*see* Clausius, 1850; Thompson, 1851).

In some engines, says Carnot (above), the cold element is provided by a water-cooled condenser, while others vent their steam into the atmosphere. For the latter the cooler element of the cycle is provided by the great volume of the atmosphere, and in the ideal "Carnot cycle" there is no heat loss through equipment, all of the heat being converted into motion. Heat used to produce motion can be regenerated by that same motion, making the cycle reversible.

Silicon is isolated by Jöns Jakob Berzelius.

Kenyon College is founded by Ohio's Episcopal bishop Philander Chase, 49.

Rensselaer Polytechnic Institute is founded at Troy, N.Y. It is the first U.S. engineering and technical school.

A Cherokee language alphabet with 85 letters is perfected by Cherokee scholar Sequoya, 54, who has taken the name George Guess from a U.S. trader he believes to be his father. The letters borrowed from the Roman alphabet bear no relation to their sounds in English but along with other letters they represent all the vowel and consonant sounds in the Cherokee language. Sequoya's "talking leaf" will make his people the first literate Indian tribe and literacy will spread so rapidly that the Cherokee *Phoenix* will begin publication in 1828, the first American Indian newspaper (*see* "Trail of Tears," 1838).

Fiction *Quentin Durward, Peveril of the Peak, Redgauntlet,* and *St. Ronan's Wall* by Sir Walter Scott who says in *Redgauntlet,* "Honour is sometimes found among thieves."

Painting *Massacre at Chios* by French painter-engraver (Ferdinand Victor) Eugène Delacroix, 26; Théodore Géricault dies at Paris January 26 at 32.

First performances Mass in D major (*Missa Solemnis*) by Ludwig van Beethoven 3/26 at St. Petersburg; Symphony No. 9 in D minor (*Choral*) by Ludwig van Beethoven 5/7 at Vienna. Now 53, Beethoven is so deaf that he must be turned round at the end to see that the audience is applauding.

Montreal's Gothic parish church of Notre Dame is completed south of the Place d'Armes to replace a structure dating back to 1672.

New York's Fifth Avenue has its beginnings as the city acquires title August 2 to seven blocks on the middle route between the Albany Post Road (Broadway) and the Boston Post Road (Third Avenue). Work begins in November on a 100-foot wide thoroughfare from Art Street (Waverley Place) north to 13th Street (*see* Brevoort, 1834).

The Rappites at New Harmony, Ind., (above) have built prefabricated houses and barns of poplar and walnut timbers fitted by mortise-and-tenon joints and sided with wood or bricks.

The first round barn is built by Shakers at their Hancock, N.Y., community (*see* 1784). Their barn has a silo at its center with stalls and stanchions radiating outward to save steps in feeding the livestock. In years to come the round barn will be widely adopted by Midwestern dairy farmers.

The Rhode Island red hen is produced at Little Compton, R.I., by a sea captain who has crossbred several domestic poultry breeds with an assortment of exotic fowl that he has brought from the Orient. The Rhode Island red will be famous for its brown eggs which New Englanders will prefer to white eggs that may not come from local hens and may therefore not be fresh.

Hydrochloric acid is isolated from stomach juices by London physician-chemist William Prout, 39, who establishes that HCl is the chief agent of human digestion (*see* Schwann's pepsin, 1835).

The daily rum ration in the British Royal Navy is reduced from half a pint to a quarter pint, and tea becomes part of the daily ration (*see* 1740; 1850).

The Glenlivet started at Glenlivet by Scottish entrepreneur George Smith, 32, is the first licensed Scotch whisky distillery. Smith will continue distilling his malt whisky until his death in 1871.

The first commercial Italian pasta factory is started at Imperia on the Italian Riviera by Paolo B. Agnese, whose family will continue the business for more than 150 years (*see* Buitoni, 1827).

1824 (cont.) Cadbury's Chocolate has its beginnings in a tea and coffee shop opened by Birmingham, England, Quaker John Cadbury, 23, who has served an apprenticeship at Leeds and for bonded tea houses in London. Given a sum of money by his father and told to sink or swim, Cadbury starts his business next door to his father's draper's shop, he will install Birmingham's first plate glass window, he will employ a Chinese to preside over his tea counter, and he will experiment with grinding cocoa beans, using a mortar and pestle (*see* Cadbury Brothers, 1847).

Baker Chocolate Company is adopted as the name of the 60-year-old Hannon Chocolate Company now operated by Walter Baker, grandson of James (*see* 1779; Postum Company, 1927).

Colby cheese has its beginnings in a Vermont cheese factory started at Healdville by local dairyman Alfred Crowley whose family will make the cheese for more than 150 years. A variation on cheddar cheese, Colby is softer and more openly textured than cheddar but is less long-lasting since it contains more moisture.

The Virginia Housewife by Mary Randolph is the first regional American cookbook. It contains recipes for such Southern specialties as Virginia ham, turtle soup, and gooseberry fool.

1825 England's Stockton and Darlington Railway opens September 27 with the world's first steam locomotive passenger service. Planned as a tramway by promoter Edward Pease, 58, the new 27-mile rail line has been built for steam traction with the help of engineer George Stephenson whose 15-ton locomotive *Active* pulls a tender, six freight cars, the directors' coach, six passenger coaches, and 14 wagons for workmen (*see* B&O, 1828).

The Erie Canal opens October 26 to link the Great Lakes with the Hudson River and the Atlantic. The $8 million state-owned canal is 363 miles long, 40 feet wide, and 4 feet deep, with tow paths for the mules that pull barges up and down its length. New York governor DeWitt Clinton greets the first canal boat. The time required to move freight from the Midwest to the Atlantic falls from 20 to 30 days down to 8 or 10, freight rates drop immediately from $100 per ton to $5, New York City becomes the Atlantic port for the Midwest, and the canal makes boom towns of Buffalo, Rochester, Cleveland, Columbus, Detroit, Chicago, and Syracuse (which is incorporated this year) (*see* 1819; 1836; 1917).

The Schuylkill Canal opens to connect Philadelphia with Reading, Pa.

The world's first wire suspension bridge opens near Lyons, France, where it has been built by engineer Marc Seguin, 39 (*see* Finley, 1800; Ellet, 1842).

The odious king of the Two Sicilies Ferdinand I dies January 4 at age 73 after a reign of suppression supported by spies and informers and by his wife Maria Carolina, daughter of the Austrian empress Maria Theresa. He is succeeded by his 47-year-old son who will reign until 1830 as Francesco I.

Greece's war of independence continues with a renewal of the siege of Missolonghi by Ottoman forces under Mustapha Mohammad Reshid Pasha, 23, who have invaded Greece from the North. Egyptian Ottoman forces land in the Morea and subdue the peninsula under the leadership of Mohammed Ali's son Ibrahim.

John Quincy Adams is elected U.S. president February 9 in the House of Representatives where Kentucky's Henry Clay controls the deciding block of votes. Clay chooses Adams over Andrew Jackson as the lesser of two evils and is named secretary of state.

The Hawaiian king Kamehameha III begins a 29-year reign at age 12 following news of his older brother's death last year in England.

Uruguayans revolt against Brazil with help from Argentina which hopes to annex the country and which begins a war with Brazil to acquire also the Banda Oriental.

Bolivia (the republic of Bolívar) is proclaimed an independent nation August 6 by a congress at Chuquisaca in upper Peru. The congress has been convened by the hero of last year's Battle of Ayacucho Antonio José de Sucre who will be Bolivia's first president from 1826 to 1828, but who will resign in the face of opposition from native Bolivians (*see* 1830).

Uruguay becomes independent of Brazil August 25, but Brazil goes to war with Argentina 3½ months later over the question of Uruguay.

Brazilian independence under Dom Pedro is recognized by Portugal August 29.

Russia's Aleksandr I dies in agony December 13 at age 47 after a 24-year reign. The czar has eaten poisonous mushrooms in the Crimea, and he is succeeded by his 29-year-old brother who begins an oppressive 30-year reign as Nicholas I.

A Decembrist uprising of young Russian aristocrat army officers tired of Romanov autocracy begins December 14, the new czar hopes to avoid violence, but when the rebel troops in St. Petersburg's Senate Square refuse to listen, he orders a cavalry charge to clear the square. Improperly shod, the horses of the cavalrymen slip and fall on the icy cobblestones, but the rising is ill-planned and is quickly suppressed.

A French law of indemnity enacted in April compensates the country's nobility for losses of lands during the French Revolution. Compensation is at the expense of government bondholders who are mostly members of the upper bourgeoisie.

Britain's Parliament enacts a law July 16 permitting workers to combine in order to secure regulation of wages and hours, but the law includes a provision that prohibits use of violence or threats of violence, it effectively denies the right to strike, and it introduces summary methods of conviction.

U.S. agitation for a 10-hour day begins with a great strike by 600 Boston carpenters. Master carpenters denounce the strike warning of the "unhappy influence" of change on apprentices "by seducing them from that course of industry" and warning of the "many temptations and improvident practices" from which journeymen are safe so long as they work from sunrise to dusk (see 1831).

Creek tribesmen in Georgia repudiate a February 12 treaty at Indian Springs in which their leaders have ceded all Creek lands in Georgia to the United States and have promised to leave for the West by September 1 of next year (see 1826).

France makes sacrilege a capital offense.

The New York Stock Exchange opens as such, but most of the securities traded are shares in canal, turnpike, mining, and gas lighting companies (see 1792). No shares in industrial corporations will appear on the exchange until 1831, and even on the Boston Exchange which is closer to the manufacturing center of the nation no industrial shares will be traded until 1827. Few will appear on either exchange for another 40 years.

U.S. gunsmith Henry Deringer, 39, designs the Deringer pistol—a short, single-shot percussion weapon deadly only at short range.

Omaha has its beginnings in a trading post established on the Missouri River. Fur trader Pierre Cabanne opens the post in Louisiana Territory that will later be called Nebraska.

Chicago (Fort Dearborn) begins to grow as the new Erie Canal (above) increases its importance. The fort has a garrison of 70 (see 1803; 1830).

Akron, Ohio, is founded by General Simon Perkins who served in the area during the War of 1812 and who has returned to the region south of Lake Erie to acquire vast tracts of wilderness land. Akron is Greek for high point, but the town site is only 395 feet above Lake Erie.

Scottish explorer Alexander Gordon Laing, 32, is sent to explore the Niger basin via Tripoli. He crosses the desert of Tuat and goes on to become the first European to visit Timbuktu.

Rutgers College gets its name. The 59-year-old Queen's College at New Brunswick, N.J., changes its name to honor local benefactor Henry Rutgers, 80.

Amherst College is chartered at Amherst, Mass., where Congregationalist clergyman-professor Zephaniah Swift Moore began giving lessons in 1821 and continued until his death 2 years ago at age 53. Moore had been president of Williams from 1815 to 1820 after 4 years as a professor at Dartmouth.

Nonfiction "Milton" by English essayist Thomas Babington Macaulay, 24, appears in the *Edinburgh Review; The Spirit of the Age, or Contemporary Portraits,* by English essayist William Hazlitt, 47; *The Norman Conquest of England (Conquête de l'Angleterre par les Normands)* by French historian Jacques Nicolas Augustin Thierry, 30.

Fiction *Tales of the Crusaders, The Betrothed,* and *The Talisman* by Sir Walter Scott.

Painting *The Leper's House* and *The Leaping Horse* by John Constable; *General Lafayette* by New York painter Samuel Finley Breeze Morse, 34; rural scenes by English-American artist-poet Thomas Cole, 24, who moves to Catskill, N.Y., and founds the Hudson River school of American painting; *The Peaceable Kingdom* by Pennsylvania Quaker preacher-carriagemaker-signpainter Edward Hicks, 45. Before his death in 1849 Hicks will have painted more than 60 variations on the theme taken from the Old Testament verse, "The wolf also shall dwell with the lamb, and the leopard shall lie down with the kid: and the calf and the young lion and the fatling together: and a little child shall lead them" (Isaiah 11:6). Henry Fuseli dies at London April 16 at age 84; Jacques Louis David dies at Brussels December 29 at age 77.

Opera *The Forest Rose, or, American Farmers* 10/7 at New York's Chatham Garden Theater, with music by John Davies, libretto by Samuel Woodworth.

London's Buckingham Palace is created out of Buckingham House by John Nash. The palace will be the residence of Britain's ruling family beginning in 1837.

London's Belgrave Square is laid out. Belgravia will become an exclusive residential area.

A coniferous evergreen that will be called the Douglas fir (*Pseudotsuga taxifolia* or *P. Douglasii*) is discovered in America's Pacific Northwest by Scottish botanist David Douglas, 27.

A Canadian forest fire burns over a tract of 4 million acres in New Brunswick extending more than 100 miles. The towns of Chatham, Douglas, and Newcastle are destroyed, 160 people are killed.

Coffee bushes are planted in Ceylon by English colonists (but see 1869).

Haitian sugar production falls to below 1 ton, down from 27,000 tons in 1804.

Avocados discovered by the Spanish conquistadors in Central America now grow in Africa, Polynesia, and the Sandwich Islands (Hawaii) (see Perrine, 1833).

The first U.S. patent for tin-plated cans is issued to Thomas Kensett (see 1819; 1847).

Buffalo, N.Y., becomes the meat-packing center of the United States as the Erie Canal (above) makes it a central shipping point.

An improved ice-harvesting method is patented in Massachusetts by Nathaniel Jarvis Wyeth, an associate of Fredric Tudor (see 1805). Tudor will use sawdust to insulate blocks of ice at the suggestion of Wyeth (see 1833).

1825 (cont.) *The Physiology of Taste (Physiologie du Goût), or Meditations on Transcendental Gastronomy*, by French lawyer-gastronome Jean-Anthèlme Brillat-Savarin is published at Paris. "Tell me what you eat and I will tell you what you are," says Brillat-Savarin who has long since returned from America (*see* Playen, 1794).

The first organized immigration of Norwegians to the United States arrives in October from Stavenger where 52 emigrants, many of them Quakers fleeing a hostile state church, boarded the sloop *Restauration* July 4. A baby has been born aboard ship and the 53 Norwegians who arrive at New York October 9 begin a movement that will take hundreds of thousands to New York, the Midwest, and the Northwest in the next 100 years.

1826 Portugal's Joao VI dies March 10 at age 56 after a 10-year reign of which half was spent in Brazil. His son Dom Pedro of Brazil succeeds to the throne as Pedro IV, draws up a charter giving Portugal a moderate British-style parliamentary government, but refuses to leave Brazil. He abdicates the Portuguese throne to his infant daughter Maria da Gloria, and she begins a 27-year reign with her 24-year-old uncle Dom Miguel as regent (*see* 1828).

Persian troops invade Russia's transcaucasian territories but Ivan Feodorovich Paskevich, 44, defeats the invaders at the Battle of Ganja. A 3-year war begins (*see* 1828).

Constantinople receives a Russian ultimatum April 5 to return to the status quo in the Danubian principalities. The sultan Mahmud II yields on the advice of Austria and France.

Ottoman Janissaries revolt in May following a decree by Mahmud II ordering formation of a new military corps to replace the inefficient Janissaries. A small corps of Janissaries loyal to the sultan bombards the barracks at Constantinople, the city's mob joins in the attack, and they massacre 6,000 to 10,000 Janissaries.

The Afghan capital Kabul falls to the 33-year-old ruler of Ghazni Dost Mohammed, who begins to extend his sphere of influence (*see* 1835).

The Treaty of Yandabu February 24 ends the 2-year Burmese War. Britain acquires Assam, Arakan, and Tenasserim.

British forces crush the Ashanti August 7 at Dodowa near Accra but hostilities will continue until 1831.

South Africa's Cape Colony extends her borders north to the Orange River (*see* 1820; 1834).

Peru recognizes Bolivian independence and Simón Bolívar organizes a government for the new mountain republic. He then departs for Colombia and the Pan American Congress at Panama in June. No U.S. representative attends (one delegate sent by Washington dies en route, the other arrives too late).

Former U.S. presidents John Adams and Thomas Jefferson die July 4, aged 90 and 83, respectively, on the fiftieth anniversary of the signing of the Declaration of Independence.

The Treaty of Washington January 24 abrogates last year's Treaty of Indian Springs with the Creek nation. The Creeks cede a smaller area to the United States and the treaty permits them to remain on their lands until January 1 of next year.

The Fugitive Slave Act of 1793 is effectively nullified by a Pennsylvania law which makes kidnapping a felony (but *see* 1842).

Batavia, N.Y., freemason William Morgan, 52, is arrested on trumped up charges of theft and indebtedness after conspiring with local printer David Miller to publish a book revealing the secrets of the Masonic order that has existed since ancient times. Morgan is committed to the Canandaigua jail in September, he is kidnapped from the jail and spirited off to Canada, he disappears, and the case brings accusations that the Masonic order has obstructed justice and has murdered Morgan, charges that begin press assaults on Freemasonry.

The first overland journey to Southern California begins August 22 as Jedediah Strong Smith leaves Great Salt Lake at the head of an expedition that reaches the lower Colorado River, crosses the Mohave Desert, and arrives November 27 at San Diego where a mission was established in 1769. Smith and two partners bought out William Ashley earlier in the year and have started a trading company at Great Salt Lake (*see* 1824; Vancouver, 1827).

Connecticut's 6-mile Windsor Locks Canal opens to provide safe passage round the Enfield Falls and rapids in the Connecticut River 12 miles upstream from Hartford.

The S.S. *Curaçao* crosses the Atlantic to pioneer use of steam power in oceanic transportation, but while the Dutch vessel has steam-driven paddle wheels to supplement her sails, the introduction of transatlantic steamers that operate entirely on steam power is delayed for lack of fresh water for steam boilers (*see* 1830; 1838).

Steam propulsion remains an auxiliary to sail. Of Britain's 2.3 million tons of merchant shipping only 24,000 are in steamships (*see* 1846).

Bromine is discovered by French chemist Antoine Jerome Balard, 24, who will devise a process for extracting sodium sulfate directly from seawater (*see* Dow, 1889).

Berlin's Unter den Linden is illuminated with gas lamps.

Electrodynamics by André Ampère expands knowledge of electricity (*see* 1820).

A galvanometer for measuring a small electric current is devised by Italian physicist Leopoldi Nobili, 42, whose astatic galvanometer minimizes the effect of the earth's magnetism.

U.S. silk production is advanced by Gideon B. Smith of Baltimore who plants the first of the new quick-growing Chinese mulberry trees (*morus multicaulis*) that will spur development of the infant silk industry (*see* Cheney brothers, 1838).

J. & P. Coats is founded at Paisley by Scottish weavers James and Peter Coats to make threads. By 1840 both Coats and the 20-year-old Clark firm will have New York agents for their sewing threads (*see* 1864).

Collins axes are introduced at Hartford, Conn., by local storekeepers Samuel and David Collins who start making their own axes after some years of buying British steel to supply blacksmiths for making axe blades. The Collins brothers buy up an old gristmill on the Farmington River, they rig up some machinery to blow air into the forges and to turn grindstones, they obtain dies and forging machinery devised by Elisha King Root, and they begin a business that will grow to turn out 40,000 axes per month. Standardized precision-made trademarked Collins axes will fell the trees of the American wilderness and Collins machetes (called cutlasses in the British West Indies) will clear tropical jungles for more than 150 years.

The lyceum movement in U.S. adult education is spurred by New Englander Josiah Holbrook who publishes recommendations that will be adopted by associations of villagers and urban workers who have had little formal education but who seek learning. The National American Lyceum will coordinate the activities of member groups beginning in 1831, by 1839 there will be 137 lyceums in Massachusetts alone, drawing 33,000 to lectures on the arts, sciences, and public issues, and by 1860 some 3,000 lyceums will be operating in New England, New York, and the upper Mississippi Valley.

Lafayette College is founded at Easton, Pa.

University College is founded at London.

Munich University is founded in Bavaria.

The French publishing house Hachette et Cie. is founded by Paris editor-publisher Louis Christophe François Hachette, 26, whose firm will become the nation's largest (*see* Gallimard, 1911).

Burke's Peerage by Irish genealogist John Burke, 39, is the first dictionary of British baronets and peers in alphabetic order (*see* Debrett's, 1769). Burke will later issue a dictionary of commoners under the title *Burke's Landed Gentry.*

Fiction *Woodstock* by Sir Walter Scott whose publisher partners James Ballantyne, 53, and Archibald Constable, 51, go bankrupt in January leaving Scott with £130,000 in liabilities. Scott's wife dies and he works feverishly despite his failing health to clear his debts (his efforts will produce £40,000 by January 1828); *The Betrothed* (*I Promessi Sposi*) by Italian novelist-poet Alessandro Manzoni, 41; James Fenimore Cooper continues the *Leatherstocking Tales*

that began with *The Pioneers* in 1823. Cooper travels to Europe where he will work for the next 7 years.

Poetry *Pictures of Travel* (*Reisebilder*) by German lyric poet Heinrich Heine, 29, who last year adopted the Christian faith and changed his name from Harry. Further volumes of Heine's travel sketches will appear in the next 5 years; "Past and Present" by English lyric poet Thomas Hood, 27: "I remember, I remember/ The house where I was born . . ."; *Silva a la Agricultura de la Zona Torrida* by South American poet Andres Bello, 44, who is serving at London as a diplomatic representative for Simón Bolívar.

Painting *Greece in the Ruins of Missolonghi* and *Execution of the Doge Marino Falieri* by Eugène Delacroix.

Photography is advanced by Parisian printer M. Lemaitre who has received etched metal plates from J. N. Niepce with instructions to print them (*see* Niepce, 1822). Lemaitre exposes the plates to iodine vapors in order to make the hardened bitumen highlights more distinct and the pictures sharper and he suggests using silvered copper plates.

Louis Jacques Mandé Daguerre, 39, approaches J. N. Niepce (above) and proposes a partnership. Daguerre paints scenery for the Paris Opéra but he has dabbled with silver salts in photography (*see* 1829).

A process for lithographing in color is invented by Aloys Senefelder of 1798 black-and-white lithography fame. Senefelder has been inspector of maps at the royal printing office in Munich for 20 years.

Opera *Oberon* 4/12 at London's Covent Garden Theatre, with music by Carl Maria von Weber, who dies of tuberculosis at London June 5 at age 39.

First performances String Quartet in B flat major by Ludwig van Beethoven 3/21 at Vienna, without the Grosse Fugue that Beethoven will write for the last movement; *Marche Militaire* by Franz Schubert.

Lord & Taylor opens in New York where English-American merchant Samuel Lord, 23, borrows $1,000 from his wife's uncle John Taylor to start a shop at 47 Catherine Street. By year's end Lord has taken into partnership his wife's cousin George Washington Taylor and by 1832 their business will have an annex in an adjoining building (*see* 1838).

London's Cumberland Terrace is completed by John Nash. The new royal palace overlooks Regent's Park which Nash will complete in 5 years.

The Zoological Gardens in Regent's Park (above) is founded by the Zoological Society of London which will open its "zoo" to the public for 2 days a week beginning April 27, 1828, with the first hippopotamus to be seen in Europe since the ancient Romans showed one at the Colosseum. The Society will help save some bird and animal species from extinction.

1826 (cont.) The world's first workable grain reaper is invented by Scotsman Patrick Bell who makes triangular knives which he joins to two horizontal bars at the front of a machine that is pushed by two horses through a field of ripe grain. The lower bar is fixed while the upper bar is geared to the ground wheels, giving it a reciprocating motion, and revolving sails hold the grain to the knives while a canvas drum lays aside the stalks in a neat swath, but horses resist pushing Bell's reaper, they cannot see ahead to move in a straight line, and the reaper is difficult to turn round at the end of a row. Bell obtains no patent, his reaper is poorly made for lack of money, and it will achieve only moderate success (*see* McCormick, 1831).

The first commercially practicable gas stove is designed by Northampton, England, gas company executive James Sharp and is installed in the kitchen of his home. Sharp will open a factory to produce the stoves in 1836 (*see* Reform Club, 1838).

An English biscuit company that will become Huntley & Palmers is established at Reading by Thomas Huntley (*see* 1851).

Boston's Quincy Market opens across the cobblestone square from Faneuil Hall in a handsome Greek revival building that will soon be surrounded by pushcarts.

Herkimer, N.Y., dairyman Sylvanus Ferris and cheese buyer Robert Nesbit develop a profitable scheme. Nesbit serves as advance man, turning down cheese offered for sale by farmers, hinting at a bad market, and deprecating the cheese. Ferris comes along later and buys the cheese at low prices for resale at high prices in the New York market.

The first tea to be retailed in sealed packages under a proprietary name is introduced by English Quaker John Horniman whose sealed, lead-lined packages have been designed in part to protect his tea from adulteration (*see* Accum, 1820). Horniman's tea will acquire an enviable reputation and will make his firm the largest in the business (*see* Tetley, 1837; Salada, 1886; Lipton, 1890; White Rose, 1901).

A sixth edition of the 1798 *Essay on Population* by Thomas R. Malthus expands the original pamphlet into a massive book which points out that in an industrialized society national income tends to outpace population growth. The size of the family becomes a function of choice through adequacy and prevalence of contraceptive measures. Poor laws, says Malthus, encourage large families with doles. He recommends late marriage and "moral restraint" to relieve mankind, at least briefly, of its inevitable fate (*see* 1834).

1827 Ohm's Law is discovered by German physicist Georg Simon Ohm, 38, who finds that the current flowing through an electrical conductor is proportional to the voltage across it and is inversely proportional to its resistance. The practical unit of electrical resistance will be called the ohm to honor Ohm's discovery of the relationship between the strength (or intensity) of an unvarying electrical current (the electromotive force) and the resistance of a circuit (*see* Ampère, 1820).

An electromagnet that can lift 14 pounds is built by U.S. physicist Joseph Henry, 30, who then uses a second layer of insulated wire overlapping the first layer to build an electromagnet that can lift 28 pounds. Henry will build an electromagnet for Yale's Benjamin Silliman that can lift 2,880 pounds (*see* 1831; Sturgeon, 1823; Faraday, 1831; telegraphy, 1831).

The world's first waterwheel turbine is devised by French engineer Benoit Fourneyron, 25, whose turbine is more powerful than a waterwheel alone and differs from a waterwheel in that the water flows under pressure from the hub toward the rim. More than 100 of Fourneyron's turbines will be built after he demonstrates an experimental 50-horsepower unit, but lack of adequate materials and technology will stymie Fourneyron's efforts to develop a steam turbine (*see* Parsons, 1884).

Peru secedes from Simón Bolívar's Colombia January 26, charging Bolívar with tyranny.

The Battle of Huzaingo February 20 gives the Brazilian forces of Pedro I a victory over Argentine and Uruguayan troops (*see* Uruguay, 1828).

Turkish forces enter Athens June 5 and the defenders on the Acropolis are forced to capitulate.

The Treaty of London July 6 allies Britain, France, and Russia in a pledge to support the Greeks against the Turks if the Ottoman sultan will not accept an armistice. The British prime minister George Canning who formed a government in April following the resignation of Lord Liverpool, who had suffered a stroke in February, dies August 8 at age 56, and the sultan Mahmud II rejects the allied demands for a truce August 16.

A large Egyptian fleet with transports lands at Navarino September 8, but the Egyptian and Turkish fleet is largely destroyed October 20 by British, French, and Russian squadrons in the Battle of Navarino (*see* 1828).

Persian forces have been defeated October 1 by Russian troops which take Erivan in Armenia.

Ottawa has its beginnings in the Bytown settlement founded at Chaudière Falls on Canada's Ottawa River (*see* 1857).

Jedediah Strong Smith blazes the first trail from southern California north to Fort Vancouver on the Columbia River, but Smith loses most of his men to Indian attackers (*see* 1826; 1830).

The Baltimore & Ohio Railroad has its beginning February 28 in a charter granted to Baltimore bankers George Brown, 40, and Philip Evan Thomas to build a 380-mile railway to the West that will compete with the 2-year-old Erie Canal which is diverting traffic from the port of Baltimore. The new railway is to be used for cars that will be drawn by horses or propelled by sails (*see* 1828).

Cincinnati gains new commercial importance with the completion of the Miami Canal (*see* 1790). By 1830 the city will have a population of 25,000 and the "Queen City of the West" will be second only to New Orleans.

The 11-mile Terneuzen-Ghent Canal opens to give the Belgian city of Ghent shipping access to the Dutch town of Terneuzen on the Scheldt Estuary.

The screw propeller for ships is invented by Austrian engineer Joseph Ressel, 34, and—independently— by Scottish engineer Robert Wilson, 24 (*see* 1832).

A sailing ship crosses from New Orleans to Liverpool in the record time of 26 days.

London's Hammersmith Bridge is completed and is the world's first suspension bridge of stone and metal. It will be replaced by a new bridge in 1887.

The first New York City public transit facility begins operations. Local entrepreneur Abraham Bower runs a horse-drawn bus with seats for 12 which he calls an "accommodation," but the city's population of 200,000 depends chiefly on private carts and carriages for transportation (*see* 1832).

Metallic aluminum is isolated from clay by German chemist Friedrich Wöhler, 27 (*see* 1855; Hall, 1886).

Bright's disease is described by London physician Richard Bright, 38, of Guy's Hospital in the first diagnosis of a kidney disease by the presence of albumin in the urine. The condition is also characterized by an elevated blood pressure and will be found to include a number of separate diseases including acute and chronic nephritis.

Heinrich Emanuel Merck at Darmstadt, Hesse, begins commercial production of morphine (*see* 1668; 1803). Merck will begin commercial production of codeine in 1836 and of cocaine in 1862 (*see* U.S. firm, 1823, 1908).

Disciples of Christ is founded by Irish-American evangelist Alexander Campbell, 39, who believes in the imminent Second Coming of Christ. Campbell practices baptism by immersion and crusades against the evils of drink.

Toronto University is founded in Ontario.

The *Evening Standard* begins publication at London (*see* Beaverbrook, 1916).

The *Freeman's Journal* published at 5 Varick Street, New York, beginning March 16 is the first U.S. black newspaper. The city's white press largely favors slavery, which is abolished in the state July 4, but the new black paper denounces slavery and urges free blacks to seek education and practice thrift. It has been started by local clergyman Samuel E. Cornish, who has founded the first U.S. black Presbyterian church, and by Jamaica-born college graduate John B. Russ-

worm, who will move to Liberia, will edit the *Liberia Herald* at Monrovia, and will serve as Liberia's superintendent of education (*see* Liberia, 1847).

The *Journal of Commerce* begins publication September 1 at New York. The semireligious publication has been started by silk and textile merchant Arthur Tappan and portrait artist Samuel F. B. Morse who last year helped to found the National Academy of Design and is its president (*see* telegraph, 1832).

The Youth's Companion begins publication at Boston under the direction of Nathaniel Parker Willis, 21. The new magazine will continue until 1929.

Fiction *The Prairie* by James Fenimore Cooper; *Cromwell* by French novelist-poet-playwright Victor Marie Hugo, 25, who was granted a royal annuity 5 years ago for his *Odes et poesies diverses* and married Adèle Foucher.

Poetry *Buch der Lieder* by Heinrich Heine contains poems that will serve as lyrics for numerous composers. Heine will be famous for such lines as, "The Romans would never have found time to conquer the world if they had been obliged first to learn Latin."

Painting *Death of Sardanapalus* by Eugène Delacroix; *The Cornfield* by John Constable. Charles Wilson Peale dies at Philadelphia February 22 at age 85; Thomas Rowlandson dies at London August 22 at 70.

Theater *Marriage for Money* (*Le mariage d'argent*) by Eugène Scribe 12/3 at the Théâtre Française, Paris.

First performances Overture to *A Midsummer Night's Dream* by German composer (Jakob Ludwig) Felix Mendelssohn (-Bartholdy), 18, 2/17 at Stettin. Ludwig van Beethoven dies of cirrhosis of the liver at Vienna March 26 at age 56.

"The Great Wave" by the Japanese *ukiyoe* painter Katsushika Hokusai reflected Japan's age-old insularity.

1827 (cont.) The "Lucifer" invented by English chemist (pharmacist) John Walker is the first friction match. Its head is made of potash, sugar, and gum arabic, and it must be drawn swiftly through a piece of folded sandpaper to ignite (*see* Phillips, 1836).

Sandwich glass is introduced at Sandwich, Mass., by Deming Jarves, 37, who has improved on a crude pressing machine recently invented by Cambridge, Mass., glassmaker Enoch Robinson. Jarves's 2-year-old Boston and Sandwich Glass Company has a monopoly on glass compounded with red lead.

The Paris Exchange is completed in the style of Rome's Temple of Vespasian after 19 years of construction.

A uniform standard for an acre of land is established by Britain's George IV who sets the measurement for an imperial (or statute) acre at 43,560 square feet (1/640th of a square mile). The standard is to apply throughout the United Kingdom, but parts of Scotland and Ireland will continue to use somewhat different measures. Most of Europe will measure land in hectares (1 hectare equals 2.47 acres).

The John Morrell meatpacking firm has its beginnings at Bradford in Yorkshire where local wool-comber George Morrell sees a bargeload of oranges in the local canal, buys the fruit with an £80 bequest left to his wife by an uncle, and sells the oranges at a profit in the streets of Bradford. Morrell starts a retail business in produce, butter, eggs, cheese, bacon, and hams (*see* 1842).

Ballantine's Scotch has its beginnings in a distillery started at Dumbarton by Scotsman George Ballantine.

Buitoni macaroni has its beginnings in the Italian hill town of San Sepolcro where Giulia Buitoni starts a family business with help from her husband Giovambattista. They are hampered initially by a lack of hard-grain semolina wheat (*see* 1842).

Boston's Union Oyster House opens in a Union Street house used as a home during his exile from France by the duc d'Orléans Philippe-Egalité who was guillotined in 1793.

New York's Delmonico Restaurant has its beginnings in a cafe and pastry shop opened in lower Manhattan by Swiss wine merchant Giovanni Del-Monico and his brother Pietro who has run a pastry shop at Bern (*see* 1831).

1828 The Tariff of Abominations is enacted by Congress May 19 with encouragement from Daniel Webster speaking for New England manufacturing interests and from Henry Clay speaking for western farmers. The new tariff bill which raises duties on imports has been framed by supporters of Andrew Jackson, hero of the 1815 Battle of New Orleans. They have intended to discredit President Adams and help Jackson gain the presidency, but they are surprised when the measure is enacted and signed into law.

Andrew Jackson is elected to the presidency in November with 178 electoral votes against 83 for Adams. Vice President Calhoun is reelected.

"South Carolina Exposition and Protest" drafted by Vice President John Caldwell Calhoun sets forth a theory that states may nullify within their borders any acts of Congress which their state conventions find unconstitutional. Calhoun is motivated by the Tariff of Abominations (above) which has created popular resentment by raising the price of both raw materials and manufactured goods, and his protest is reported December 19 to the South Carolina legislature which orders it printed.

Britain and the United States extend indefinitely their agreement of 1818 on joint occupation of the Pacific Northwest Territory (*see* 1845; 1846).

German foundling Kaspar Hauser is picked up by Nuremberg police and belief spreads that the 16-year-old boy is of noble birth, possibly the prince of Baden. Writer-professor Georg Friedrich Daumer, 28, is given custody of the boy, but he will later be adopted by England's earl of Stanhope Philip Henry, now 23, who will send him to Ansbach (*see* 1833).

The Treaty of Turkmanchai February 22 ends a 3-year Russo-Persian War that began with Russian seizure of disputed territory. Persia cedes two territories that include part of Armenia, she agrees to pay a huge indemnity, and the Russians obtain exclusive rights to maintain a navy on the Caspian Sea.

Russia declares war on the Ottoman Empire April 26 and sends troops across the Danube June 8, but the Russians are stopped by garrisons at the south bank fortresses of Shumla, Silistria, and Varna. Varna falls to the Russians October 12, and the invaders go into winter quarters.

Portugal's regent Dom Miguel stages a coup d'etat in May, he abolishes the constitution drafted by Pedro IV in 1826, and he has himself proclaimed king July 4. His 9-year-old niece Maria II is taken to England by her protectors, and a 6-year civil war begins.

Uruguay gains independence and is established as a buffer state between Brazil and Argentina on the Rio de la Plata. The Treaty of Rio de Janeiro resolves differences between the two larger countries after mediation by British diplomats.

Madagascar's Hova king Radama I dies after an 18-year reign that has encouraged the spread of British influence. He is succeeded by the Queen Ranavaloana I who will reign for 33 years and who will be hostile both to French and British influence and to the efforts of missionaries.

The Zulu king Shaka who has founded the Zulu nation is assassinated September 22 at age 41 after a 12-year reign that has ended the ancient pattern of Bantu society in South Africa (*see* 1879).

Synthetic urea (NH_2CONH_2) is produced by German chemist Friedrich Wöhler in the first laboratory synthesis of an organic compound. Wöhler heats ammonium cyanate and takes a pioneer step toward the production of artificial nitrogen fertilizer (*see* Cavendish, 1766; Haber, 1908).

Thorium is isolated by Jöns Jakob Berzelius.

The modern science of embryology is founded by Estonian naturalist Karl Ernst von Baer, who discovers the mammalian ovum.

A blast furnace to improve the manufacture of iron is devised by Scottish inventor James Beaumont Neilson, 26.

The British armament firm Vickers has its beginning in a tool and filemaking firm started by English steelmaker Edward Vickers, 24, with his father-in-law George Naylor. The firm will become Vickers' Sons & Co. in 1867 and will become an armaments producer beginning in 1888 (*see* 1847; Maxim, 1883).

Construction begins July 4 on the Baltimore & Ohio (B&O) Railroad chartered last year by the state of Maryland as the first U.S. railroad for the general transportation of freight and passengers (*see* 1815; 1825). Backed by the richest man in America Charles Carroll of Carrollton, now 90, who lays its cornerstone, the B&O has a narrow 4-foot 8.5-inch gauge that is based on the standard English track width for carriages (*see* Cooper, 1829).

Work begins July 4 on the Chesapeake & Ohio (C&O) Canal. President Adams turns the first spade of soil to start a race between the B&O and C&O across the Alleghenies (*see* 1839).

The Delaware and Hudson Canal opens between Kingston, N.Y., and Port Jervis on the Delaware River where the 59-mile canal connects with the 49-mile Lackawanna Canal to Honesdale, Pa.

English reformer Robert Owen breaks with his business partner William Allen saying, "All the world is queer save thee and me, and even thou art a little queer" (*see* 1814; 1824).

London University is founded by men who include Scottish jurist Henry Brougham, 50, Baron Brougham of Brougham, who tells the House of Commons, "Education makes a people easy to lead, but difficult to drive; easy to govern, but impossible to enslave."

An American Dictionary of the English Language is published after 28 years of work by Noah Webster, now 70, who has studied 26 languages in order to determine the origins of English words (*see* 1806). Webster defines nearly 70,000 words, he introduces such Americanisms as "revolutionary," "skunk," and "applesauce," and he gives words such as "colour" and "plough" American spellings (color, plow) (*see* Merriam, 1831).

Fiction *The Fair Maid of Perth* and *Tales of a Grandfather* by Sir Walter Scott.

Painting *Faust* (19 lithographs) by Eugène Delacroix. Francisco Goya dies at Bordeaux April 16 at age 82; Gilbert Stuart dies at Boston July 9 at age 52; Jean Antoine Houdon dies at Paris July 15 at age 87.

Opera *Count Ory* (*Le Comte Ory*) 9/20 at the Opéra-Comique in Paris, with music by Gioacchino Rossini.

First performances Fantasy in F minor for Piano Four Hands by Franz Schubert 5/9 at Vienna; Symphony No. 6 (or No. 7) in C minor by the late Franz Schubert 12/14 at Vienna. (Schubert has died of typhus November 19 at age 31 leaving his Symphony in B major unfinished.)

New York's Washington Square Park is created on the site of a potter's field cemetery that has been removed to a site on 42nd Street acquired by the city in 1823 (*see* Bryant, 1844).

A Japanese earthquake at Echigo December 28 kills 30,000.

A new British corn law introduced by the duke of Wellington gives consumers relief from the high food prices that have prevailed since the Corn Law of 1815. Wellington has been prime minister since January, and his law imposes duties on a sliding scale based on domestic prices but prices remain too low to permit grain imports.

Dutch chocolate-maker Conrad J. Van Houten patents an inexpensive method for pressing the fat from roasted cacao beans and produces the world's first chocolate candy (*see* 1815). Van Houten adds the fat that will be called cocoa butter to an experimental mixture of cocoa powder and sugar, and the resulting sticky substance cools into a solid form (*see* Cadbury, 1847; Nestle and Peter, 1875; Peter Paul, 1965).

America's Shakers change their permissive attitude toward alcohol (*see* 1774). They forbid the use of "beer, cider, wines, and all ardent liquors . . . on all occasions; at house-raisings, husking bees, harvestings, and all other gatherings."

Chili (or Chile) con carne is popular in Mexico's Texas Territory, writes a U.S. visitor to San Antonio. "When they have to pay for their meat in the market, a very little is made to suffice a family; it is generally cut into a kind of hash with nearly as many peppers as there are pieces of meat—this is all stewed together" (*see* chili powder, 1835).

1829 Greece gains her independence from the Ottoman Empire after four centuries of Ottoman rule, and Russia brings the empire to the verge of collapse. The London Protocol signed March 22 has made Greece an autonomous tributary state, Russia's German-born Count Ivan Ivanovich Dibich-Zabalanski, 44 (Hans Karl Friedrich Anton von Diebitsch) has won the Battle of Kulevcha June 11 and has crossed the Balkan mountains to take Adrianople. The Treaty of Adrianople is signed September 24 as disease makes the Russian army too weak to proceed.

1829 (cont.) Russia gains control of the mouth of the Danube and secures the eastern coast of the Black Sea, agreeing to pay an indemnity of 15 million ducats over the next 10 years for rights to occupy the Danubian principalities.

Romania gains autonomy from the Ottoman Empire under Russian occupation (*see* 1866).

Serbia gains autonomy with guarantees of religious liberty (*see* 1839).

The London Conference November 30 decides that Greece should have complete independence but her frontier is moved back almost to the Gulf of Corinth. Greek patriot Count Ioannes Antonios Kapodistrias, 53, rules as president-dictator.

Venezuela secedes from Simón Bolívar's Gran Colombia and will become an independent republic next year.

Tampico, Mexico, falls to Spanish forces from Cuba August 18, but the Mexicans retake the city September 11.

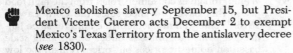 Mexico abolishes slavery September 15, but President Vicente Guerero acts December 2 to exempt Mexico's Texas Territory from the antislavery decree (*see* 1830).

"Slavery is not a national evil; on the contrary, it is a national benefit," says South Carolina governor Stephen D. Miller in a message to the state legislature.

Charleston women Sarah and Angelina Grimke leave for the North where they will become Quakers and will be active in the antislavery and women's rights movements.

The British Slave Trade Commission takes over the administration of the African island of Fernando Po with Spanish consent.

The Catholic Emancipation Bill pushed through Parliament by the duke of Wellington over Tory opposition gives British Catholics voting rights, the right to sit in Parliament, and the right to hold any public office except those of lord chancellor and lord lieutenant of Ireland. The right to hold office is granted only on condition that the officeholder swear an oath denying papal power to intervene in British domestic affairs, that he recognize the Protestant succession, and that he repudiate any intent to upset the established church.

At least 75,000 Americans go to prison for debt each year, says the U.S. Prison Discipline Society. More than half the debtors owe less than $20.

The *Stourbridge Lion* imported from England's Stephenson Engine Works goes into service between Carbondale and Honesdale, Pa. It is the first steam locomotive on any U.S. railroad.

The *Tom Thumb* produced by New York entrepreneur Peter Cooper, 28, is the first U.S.-built locomotive. Cooper has taken scraps of iron including pipes from musket barrels to build his steam locomotive in the shops of the Baltimore & Ohio Railroad (*see* 1828; 1830).

The *Rocket* built by England's George Stephenson and his son Robert wins a competition sponsored by the Liverpool and Manchester Railway. The tubular steam boiler locomotive sets a pattern for future railroad locomotive development.

The first French railway line opens to connect Lyons with St. Etienne using an English-built locomotive.

A horse-drawn omnibus goes into service at London to provide public transportation (*see* New York, 1827).

A steam-powered bus appears in Britain but draws bitter opposition from stagecoach interests (*see* Locomotives on Highways Act, 1865).

Cornelius van Derbilt begins building steamboats with the $30,000 he has amassed in coastal shipping by schooner and in working for Thomas Gibbons (*see* 1810; 1824; 1834).

The Welland Sea Canal opens to connect Lake Erie with Lake Ontario via a tortuous waterway that has 25 locks to permit ships to circumnavigate Niagara Falls (*see* 1932).

London's Baring Brothers finance the Planters Association in Louisiana—the first state loan in America to be underwritten by a London firm (*see* 1803; Trans-Siberian Railway, 1891).

Copenhagen's Joseph Hambro breeds pigs, he operates a flour mill, bakery, and salting house, he exports flour and bacon, and he lays the foundations of what will become a vast merchant banking house.

William Burke is hanged at Edinburgh at age 37 for having smothered victims whose bodies he has sold to physicians. The medical profession needs corpses for dissection but is unable to acquire them legally (*see* anatomy act, 1832).

Cholera breaks out at Astrachan in a more serious epidemic than one in 1823 (*see* 1830).

The world's first practical sewing machine is developed by French inventor Barthélemy Thimonnier, 36, who will obtain a contract to produce French army uniforms. 80 of Thimmonier's new machines will be destroyed by a mob that fears French tailors will be deprived of their livelihoods (*see* Luddites, 1811; Hunt, 1832).

The Perkins Institution for the Blind is founded at Boston under the name New England Asylum for the Blind. Its local benefactors include merchant Thomas Handasyd Perkins, 65, who will deed his home to the asylum in 1833 and its name will be changed subsequently to the Perkins Institution and Massachusetts School for the Blind (*see* Haüy, 1784; Braille, 1834; Helen Keller, 1887).

The first Baedeker travel handbook is issued as a guide to Coblenz by German publisher Karl Baedeker, 28, whose handbooks in German, French, and English will describe the sights, foods, and accommodations to be found in cities of Europe, North America, and the Orient which Baedeker will in many cases visit incognito.

The *Encyclopaedia Americana* is published in its first volumes. German-American scholar Francis Lieber, 29, fled to England after imprisonment as a radical, he has been in America for 2 years, and he will have 13 volumes in print by 1831 (*see* 1771).

Poetry *Al Aaraaf, Tamerlane, and Minor Poems* by Boston poet Edgar Allan Poe, 20, whose *Tamerlane* appeared in a 40-page book 2 years ago but gained little attention and left Poe in dire financial straits. Orphaned before the age of 3, Poe has been raised by John Allan of Richmond, Va., with whom he has had fallings out and reconciliations and whose wife has just died. Allan helps Poe secure a discharge from the army, in which he has enlisted under the name Edgar A. Perry, and to apply for an appointment to West Point; *Casablanca* by English poet Felicia Dorothea Hemans, 36, whose narrative poem based on the 1798 Battle of the Nile begins, "The boy stood on the burning deck/ Whence all but him had fled . . ."; *Joseph Delorme* by French poet-critic Charles Augustin Sainte-Beuve, 25, whose *Poesies et Pensées* purport to be the work of an imaginary poet who has died young.

Painting *Ulysses Deriding Polyphemus* by J. M. W. Turner.

Photographer Louis Daguerre goes into partnership with J. N. Niepce and accidentally discovers the light-sensitivity of silver-iodide (*see* 1826). Daguerre finds that an iodized silver plate exposed to light in a camera will produce an image if the plate is fumed with mercury vapor (*see* Talbot, 1839).

Theater *Faust* (Part I) by Johann Wolfgang von Goethe 1/19 at Brunswick (*see* 1854); *Metamora; or the Last of the Wampanoags* by U.S. playwright John Augustus Stone, 29, 12/15 at New York's Park Theater, with Edwin Forrest, 23, who last year offered a $500 prize for the best five-act tragedy whose "hero, or principal character, shall be an aboriginal of this country." (Stone will find that playwrights do not make much money and will commit suicide in 1834.)

Opera *William Tell* (*Guillaume Tell*) 8/3 at the Paris Opéra, with music by Gioacchino Rossini.

First performances Passion according to St. Matthew by Felix Mendelssohn 3/11 at Berlin; Symphony No. 1 in C minor by Felix Mendelssohn 5/25 at London's Argyll Rooms (with the scherzo from an octet Mendelssohn wrote in 1824 replacing the minuet); Variations on "La Co Darem La Mano" for Piano with Orchestral Accompaniment by Polish composer Frederic François Chopin, 19, 8/11 at Vienna.

The Henley Royal Regatta held in July pits amateur oarsmen from Cambridge and Oxford Universities who race over a 2-mile course to begin a sporting tradition. The crews compete 57.5 miles upriver from London at Henley-on-Thames, Oxfordshire (*see* 1876).

London "Bobbies" are introduced to safeguard citizens in a city that has one footpad, highwayman, or thief for every 22 inhabitants. The constables in London's first metropolitan police force are nicknamed after Home Secretary Robert Peel of 1817 "peelers" fame; their presence will permit late-hour dinner parties and will change London's dining habits by making the streets safe after dark.

The "Siamese twins" Chang and Eng arrive at Boston on the U.S. ship *Sachem* and sail in October for England where they attract wide attention among physicians and the general public. Joined at the chest since birth, the 18-year-old boys have been discovered by British merchant Robert Hunter, they will be exhibited by U.S. showman P. T. Barnum, now 19, they will marry two North Carolina women, they will sire 22 children between them, they will maintain two separate households, and they will amass a fortune of $60,000 (*see* Barnum, 1835).

Architecture is "frozen music," says Johann Wolfgang von Goethe, now 79, in a conversation March 23: "I have found a paper of mine in which I call architecture frozen music (erstarrte Musik). Really there is something in this; the tone of mind produced by architecture approaches the effect of music."

Boston's Tremont House opens in October with 170 rooms. It is the first modern hotel, and while lodgers at other hotels continue in many cases to sleep with strangers "spoon fashion," three and four to a bed, with women sometimes rooming with men, each guest or couple at the Tremont House receives a private room with a key. For $2 per day a guest receives four meals a day and is given a free cake of soap, but while the new gaslighted hotel has baths, they are all in the basement and must be entered from a separate street entrance. No hotel will have private baths until 1853.

The poinsettia is introduced into the United States from its native Mexico by Joel Roberts Poinsett, 40, first U.S. ambassador to Mexico. Poinsett has returned to his native South Carolina after a 4-year term at Mexico City and the winter-blooming subtropical plant of the genus *euphorbia* that he has discovered will be named after him and will become a traditional Christmas flower.

Massachusetts Presbyterian clergyman Sylvester W. Graham, 35, attacks meats, fats, mustard, catsup, pepper, and, most especially, white bread. He calls them injurious to the health or stimulating to carnal appetites (*see* 1839).

1830 "Liberty and Union, now and forever, one and inseparable!" declaims U.S. senator from Massachusetts Daniel Webster January 27 in his "Reply to Hayne" speech against Senator Robert Y. Hayne of South Carolina as the South threatens secession over the

1830 (cont.) issues of states' rights and high tariffs. Southern leaders demand low tariffs in the interest of their slave-owning planters, and Missouri's Thomas Hart Benton protests New England's attempts to limit the sale of western lands.

"Our federal union: It must and shall be preserved!" declaims President Jackson April 13 in a toast at a Jefferson Day dinner. The president thus signifies his determination to resist southern efforts to declare the 1828 Tariff of Abominations null and void.

"The Union, next to our liberty, most dear!" declaims Vice President Calhoun in a toast at the April 13 dinner. South Carolina's Calhoun signifies his determination to persist in his fight.

The Republic of Ecuador is created May 13 in a further breakup of Gran Colombia. The liberator Antonio José de Sucre has tried to maintain Colombian unity but is assassinated June 4 at age 35 in the forest of Berueros near Pasto, Colombia, while en route to Quito. The Great Liberator Simón Bolívar dies December 17 at age 47.

Britain's debauched George IV dies June 26 at age 67 and is succeeded by his 64-year-old brother William, duke of Clarence, who begins a 7-year reign as William IV. A general election turns out the Tories who have run Britain almost without interruption for nearly half a century and a Whig government takes power with Charles Grey, 66, as prime minister. Earl Grey's foreign minister is Henry John Temple, 46, Viscount Palmerston.

France's Charles X is deposed July 29 by Paris revolutionists and is succeeded after a 6-year reign by the 56-year-old Bourbon duc d'Orléans who is proclaimed "citizen king" by the journalist Louis Adolphe Thiers and is confirmed August 7 by the Liberals sitting as a rump chamber. Thiers, 33, has drawn up a protest against the five July ordinances of July 26 that established rigid governmental control of the press, dissolved the chamber, and changed the electoral system, but the radicals who have raised street barricades with the intent of making France a republic with the marquis de Lafayette as president are thwarted by Thiers and other Liberals. They make the duc d'Orléans king and he begins an 18-year reign as Louis Philippe.

Belgian revolutionists inspired by the July Revolution at Paris demand independence from the Netherlands and win support from workers and peasants, but moderate liberal elements protest that they merely want autonomous administration with the son of the Dutch king Willem I as viceroy.

Brussels workers force Dutch troops to evacuate the city in late September, an independent Belgium is proclaimed by a provisional government October 4, Antwerp is bombarded by the Dutch October 27, and dissolution of the Kingdom of the Netherlands is declared December 20 by an international conference that effectively recognizes the independence of Belgium (see 1831).

A Polish revolution against Russia begins as Polish nationalists form a union with Lithuania and declare the Romanov dynasty deposed (but see 1831).

The king of the Two Sicilies Francesco I dies at age 53 after a 5-year reign that was as reactionary as was that of his father. He has left the government to court favorites and to the police while he lives with his mistresses surrounded by soldiers to protect him from assassination, and he is succeeded by his 20-year-old son who will reign until 1859 as Ferdinand II and who will continue Francesco's despotic rule.

 Cholera spreads from Astrakhan throughout the interior of Russia (see 1829). In some areas there is widespread famine as quarantines and demoralization add to crop failures, and there are widespread riots against cholera controls as physicians, government officials, and quarantine guards are denounced by the clergy as Anti-Christ. The pandemic kills 900,000 this year and will kill several millions in Europe before it ends (see 1840).

The microscope invented by Anton van Leeuwenhoek in 1683 is improved by London wine merchant-optician Joseph Jackson Lister, 44, who discovers the law of the aplanatic foci, fundamental principle of the modern microscope. Lister will be the first to ascertain the true form of red corpuscles in mammalian blood (1834), and his son will be the founder of antiseptic surgery (see 1865).

 Chicago has its real beginnings as a town is laid out at Fort Dearborn on Lake Michigan (see 1825; steamboat, 1832).

The first covered wagon train from the Missouri River to the Rockies is led by William Sublette of the Rocky Mountain Fur Company and Jedediah Strong Smith. Smith and his partners sell their fur-trading interests to a new company organized by Jim Bridger and others (see 1827; 1831).

The Indian Removal Act signed by President Jackson May 28 provides for the general removal of Indians to lands west of the Mississippi (see 1832; 1834).

A commissioner of Indian affairs is named by President Jackson.

The Treaty of Dancing Rabbit Creek signed September 15 cedes Choctaw lands east of the Mississippi to the United States.

Mexico passes a law forbidding further colonization of its Texas Territory by U.S. citizens and prohibiting further importation of slaves into the Territory (see 1829; 1836).

Slaves from the schooner *Comet* wrecked on a voyage from Alexandria, Va., to New Orleans are declared free by British authorities in the Bahamas. The U.S. government registers a protest.

Service begins on England's Liverpool to Manchester Railway (see 1829).

A flanged T-rail that will be the basis of future railroad track development is invented by Robert Livingston Stevens, 43, son of steamboat pioneer John Stevens. Now the president and chief engineer of the Camden and Amboy Railroad and Transportation Company (see 1815), Stevens will also invent a hook-headed spike and a metal plate to cover the joint between rails.

The first division of the Baltimore & Ohio Railroad is completed May 24 to link Baltimore with Ellicott Mills, 13 miles away (see 1828). The first American-built locomotive is demonstrated August 28 by Peter Cooper who has named his steam locomotive *Tom Thumb* after the diminutive folktale hero (see 1829). Cooper's engine pulls a train in a race against a stagecoach, losing at the last minute when a pulley belt slips, but proving that a steam engine can pull a single car round a sharp curve.

The Boston & Maine Railroad has its beginnings June 5 in the Boston & Lowell, first steam railroad to be projected in New England (see 1833).

The locomotive *Best Friend of Charleston* built by New York's West Point Foundry pulls four loaded passenger cars over 6 miles of track on the Charleston & Hamburg Railroad, chartered by the South Carolina legislature as the first road intended from the start for use by steam cars.

A locomotive that can pull 15 tons at 15 miles per hour is developed by New York watchmaker Phineas Davis who wins a $4,000 prize from the Baltimore & Ohio. (The B&O will not reach Wheeling on the Ohio River until 1854, but it will eventually pay off handsomely for its investors.)

The Cumberland Road that reached Wheeling in 1817 is called a national project by President Jackson who approves an act of Congress appropriating $130,000 to survey and extend the road. Jackson signs the bill 4 days after vetoing the Maysville Road Bill that would have authorized federal aid to a Kentucky turnpike from Maysville to Lexington (federal expenditure for a local project is unconstitutional, says the president).

Louisville, Ky., begins its growth as a major river port with the opening of the Louisville and Portland Canal which allows riverboats to circumvent 26-foot falls in the Ohio River.

A surface condenser is invented that will solve the problem of providing fresh water for steam boilers and that will make oceangoing steamships economically viable (see 1826; 1838).

The Fairbanks scale devised by Vermont inventor Thaddeus Fairbanks, 34, is the world's first platform scale, using a system of multiplying levers to counterpoise a heavy object on the weighing platform by a light beam with a small sliding weight and slotted weights on an extension arm. A native of St. Johnsbury (named by Ethan Allen to honor St. John de Crèvecoeur) (see 1782), Fairbanks will go into business with his brother Erastus, and E. and T. Fairbanks & Company will become Fairbanks-Morse when it merges with a Chicago firm started by St. Johnsbury native Charles E. Morse.

The Church of Jesus Christ of Latter-Day Saints is founded April 6 at Fayette, N.Y., by local farmhand Joseph Smith, Jr., 25, who has *The Book of Mormon* published in 522 pages at Palmyra, N.Y. The book claims that the Indians of the New World were originally Jews who sailed from the Near East in the 6th century B.C. and who received a visit from Jesus Christ after his resurrection. Smith says he has translated the book with miraculous help from strange hieroglyphics on some golden tablets buried near Palmyra and revealed to him by an angel named Moroni, and the book sanctions polygamous marriage, a tenet that will make Smith and his followers unwelcome in many communities (see Nauvoo, 1839).

Randolph-Macon College is founded at Ashland, Va.

The *Boston Transcript* begins publication July 24. Henry W. Dutton and James Wentworth have started the paper at the suggestion of Lynde M. Walter, Dutton will be sole proprietor after Wentworth's death in 1847, and Dutton's descendants will run the paper for the city's Brahmins until 1940.

The *Philadelphia Inquirer* has its beginnings in the *Pennsylvania Inquirer* founded by printer Jasper Harding whose newborn son William will take over when his father retires in 1869.

Godey's Lady's Book begins publication at Philadelphia under the name *Lady's Book*. Publisher Louis Antoine Godey, 26, introduces the first U.S. periodical for women.

Fiction *The Red and the Black* (*Le Rouge et le Noir*) by French novelist Stendhal (Marie Henri Beyle), 47, who blends 18th century rationalism with romantic fervor in what he calls the emotional "crystallization" of experience.

Poetry *Poems Chiefly Lyrical* by English poet Alfred Tennyson, 21, whose book gets a poor critical reception; "Old Ironsides" by Boston medical student Oliver Wendell Holmes, 21, is published in the *Boston Daily Advertiser* and is instrumental in saving the U.S. frigate *Constitution* from being destroyed by the Navy Department which has condemned her: "Ay, tear her tattered ensign down!/ Long has it waved on high . . ."; "The Ballad of the Oysterman" by Oliver Wendell Holmes; "Mary Had a Little Lamb" by Boston editor Sara Josepha Buell Hale, 42, whose verse in the first issue of the magazine *Juvenile Miscellany* will be set to music from the song "Goodnight Ladies" in 1867.

Painting *Liberty on the Barricades* by Eugène Delacroix who sympathizes with the July Revolution.

Cyrus McCormick's reaper enabled one farmer to do the work of five and began a revolution in agricultural productivity.

Birds of America by John James Audubon, now 45, is published in the first of its several editions (*see* 1813). Audubon has been enabled by his wife's financial support to pursue his passion for painting birds from life, and his work began appearing in London 3 years ago.

Theater *Hernani* by Victor Hugo 2/25 at the Comédie Française, Paris.

Opera *I Capulleti e i Montecchi* 3/4 at Venice's Teatro de la Fenice, with music by Italian composer Vincenzo Bellini, 28, libretto from the Shakespeare play *Romeo and Juliet* of 1595.

First performances   Concerto No. 2 in F minor for Pianoforte and Orchestra by Frederic Chopin 3/17 at Warsaw; Concerto No. 1 in E minor for Pianoforte and Orchestra by Frederic Chopin 10/11 at Warsaw (the concertos will be published in the opposite order of their premieres); *Symphonie Fantastique* by French composer Hector Berlioz, 27, 12/25 at Paris; Berlioz makes extravagant use of percussion and breaks new ground in symphonic composition.

The Kentucky State House is completed at Frankfort by architect Gideon Shryock.

Louisiana's Oak Alley plantation house is completed at Vacheria by George Swaney.

"Woodman, Spare That Tree" by New York newspaper editor-poet George Pope Morris, 28, is published in the *New York Mirror* which Morris founded 7 years ago. "Woodman, spare that tree./ Touch not a single bough: In youth it sheltered me,/ And I'll protect it now" (*see* Arbor Day, 1875; Kilmer, 1913).

"In whatever proportion the cultivation of potatoes prevails . . . in that same proportion the working people are wretched," writes English political journalist William Cobbett, 67, in *Rural Rides.*

The Industrial Revolution has turned England's peasantry into half-starved paupers and has destroyed rural skills, says Cobbett (above).

French and Belgian bakers begin using minute quantities of highly toxic copper sulfate as well as the less toxic alum to whiten bread.

Domestic baking and brewing skills have been forgotten by the English peasantry, says William Cobbett (above). "Nowadays all is looked for at shops. To buy the thing ready made is the taste of the day: thousands who are housekeepers buy their dinners ready cooked" (*see* 1902).

Tinned foods from London's Donkin, Hall & Gamble Preservatory reach English food shops for the first time (*see* 1823).

Teacher's Highland Cream Scotch whisky has its beginnings in a distillery opened at Glasgow by William Teacher, 19.

The continuous still patented by Irish inventor Aeneas Coffee speeds up distilling and makes for "cleaner" whisky and gin.

U.S. duties on coffee, tea, salt, and molasses imports are reduced by Congress.

The first full cargo of bananas—1,500 stems—arrives at New York aboard Captain John Pearsall's schooner *Harriet Smith* (*see* Chester, 1804; Baker, 1870).

Abortion is made a statutory crime in the United States (*see* England, 1803; Pius XI, 1869).

The U.S. population reaches 12.9 million, including 3.5 million black slaves. The country receives 54,338 immigrants from Ireland during the year and 27,489 from England.

The population of the world reaches 1 billion, up from 750 million in 1750.

1831 The McCormick reaper that enables one man to do the work of five is demonstrated by Virginia farmer Cyrus Hall McCormick, 22, whose father tills some 1,200 acres near Lexington with nine slaves and 18 horses. Young McCormick's crude but effective horse-drawn reaper is so devised that the horse is hitched alongside it rather than behind as in the case of the 1826 Bell reaper. His reaper's knife vibrates in a line at right angles to the direction in which the machine is moving, a divider moves ahead to separate a swath from the field and turn the grain toward the blade, and a row of mechanical fingers ahead of the blade holds the straw straight to be cut. Severed stalks are deposited neatly on a platform, and the reaper permits horsepower to replace human power (*see* 1834).

The basic principle of the electric dynamo is discovered by England's Michael Faraday (*see* 1821; Sturgeon, 1823). His electromagnetic current generator consists simply of a cylindrical coil (solenoid) and a bar magnet that can be slipped into the coil, but

416

Faraday succeeds in generating electrical current October 17 and discovers electromagnetic induction. He finds by using his galvanometer that a current is registered while the magnet is being inserted, and that the current starts again in the opposite direction when the magnet is withdrawn, but that no current is registered while the magnet is stationary (see galvanometer, 1826; Gramme, 1872).

Faraday finds that if the current in a wire wrapped round an iron rod is interrupted, a current will be generated in a second wire wrapped round the rod. He is excited by the discovery that electrical energy is transferred between two circuits, but he does not see the potential for stepping down power from a high-voltage line for use with alternating current which regularly reverses its direction (see 1888).

A method for producing induced current much like that of Faraday's (above) is discovered by U.S. physicist Joseph Henry (see 1827). The unit of induction will be called a henry.

✗ Italians at Modena and Parma are inspired by last year's Paris Revolution to rise in February and demand freedom of northern Italy, and there are widespread revolts in the papal states as the reactionary Cardinal Bartolomeo Alberto Cappellari begins a 15-year term as Pope Gregory XVI. The insurrections are put down in March with help from Austrian troops, but fresh revolts break out by year's end (see Mazzini, 1832).

The first king of the Belgians Leopold I begins a 34-year reign at age 40. The prince of Saxe-Coburg is the widower of Britain's late Princess Charlotte, he is elected to the Belgian throne, a large Dutch army invades his country, but French forces sent by Louis Philippe force the Dutch to withdraw.

The Battle of Ostrolenka May 26 gives Russian forces under Count Dibich-Zabalanski a victory over Polish troops as internal disputes between moderates and radicals divide the Poles. Warsaw falls to the Russians September 8, the revolution that began last year collapses, most of the revolutionary leadership escapes to Paris, and the russification of Poland begins in provinces not occupied by Prussia or Austria (see 1772; 1918).

The Greek president Count Ioannes Antonios Kapodistrias is assassinated October 9 at age 55. The Greeks make his brother Avgoustinos, 53, provisional president.

The French Foreign Legion created by Louis Philippe to employ his Swiss and German mercenaries will serve largely in North Africa, the Middle East, and Indo-China. The Legion will attract renegades and fugitives from justice for a century and a half.

The Brazilian emperor Pedro I abdicates April 7 at age 33 and returns to Europe. He is succeeded by his 5-year-old son by his first wife who will be crowned in 1841 and who will reign until 1889 as Pedro II.

Jedediah Strong Smith is killed May 27 by Comanches on the Cimarron River in the Southwest (see 1830).

A Bengali uprising against oppressive Hindu rule is suppressed, and the Moslem leader Titu Mir is killed by government troops November 19.

India's Mysore State comes under British control as the British use the excuse of domestic misgovernment to increase their power in the subcontinent.

The Bristol Riots October 29 to 31 raise fears in London that the unrest may spread to other towns and begin a revolution. The newly appointed recorder of Bristol Sir Charles Wetherall is an outspoken critic of the Parliamentary Reform Bill that passed the Commons in September but has been thrown out by the House of Lords, supporters of the measure wreck Bristol's Mansion House and set the Bishop's Palace afire, other public buildings are attacked, the city magistrates call in troops, a bloody cavalry charge restores order, four of the rioters are executed, 22 are transported (see Reform Act, 1832).

✊ Irish Catholics resort to violence in an armed protest against enforcement of tithes to support the established Episcopal Church.

The Union of Northumberland and Durham Coalminers is founded by English miner Thomas Hepburn who demands shorter hours for coal workers.

French workers at Lyons revolt. The insurrection is put down in November but only with great difficulty as secret societies proliferate among the workers.

New York has its first labor demonstrations as stone cutters riot in protest against the use of stone cut at Sing Sing prison for buildings of the new University of the City of New York (see NYU, below; General Trades Union, 1833).

The Supreme Court rules March 18 that an Indian tribe may not sue in federal courts since the tribes are not foreign nations (Cherokee Nation v. Georgia) (see 1832).

Chief Black Hawk agrees to withdraw his tribesmen to lands west of the Mississippi (see 1830; 1832).

The Liberator begins publication at Boston where local abolitionist William Lloyd Garrison, 26, advocates emancipation of the slaves who comprise nearly one-third of the U.S. population.

Nat Turner's rebellion brings panic to the South as whites learn that the 30-year-old Virginia slave has murdered his master and all his master's family in their sleep the night of August 21. A religious zealot, Turner has convinced other slaves that he has received divine guidance, the seven companions who have helped him murder the Joseph Travis family quickly grow to a mob of more than six dozen, state militia and armed townspeople intercept the rebels 3 miles outside Jerusalem, Va., many slaves are killed including some who took no part in Turner's rebellion which has killed 60 whites in 48 hours, and while

1831 (cont.) Turner escapes for 6 weeks, he is finally apprehended, tried, convicted, and hanged November 11 at Jerusalem along with 16 accomplices.

Samuel Sharp's rebellion in Jamaica beginning 2 days after Christmas kills no whites, but the slaves force sugar estate owners at gunpoint to draw up documents freeing all their slaves, they burn canefields and other property, the British retaliate by burning the slave shacks, they hang Sharp and hundreds of others, and they flog slaves who have joined in Sharp's refusal to work without compensation, but a fall in the price of sugar has made slavery unprofitable to many planters.

The position of the magnetic North Pole is determined by Scottish polar explorer James Clark Ross, 31, with his uncle Sir John Ross (*see* 1818).

The British Association for the Advancement of Science (BAAS) is founded along lines of the earlier Gesellschaft deutscher Naturforscher (*see* 1848).

English naturalist Charles Darwin, 22, embarks on a voyage to South America and the Galapagos Islands as ship's naturalist aboard the *Beagle* (*see* 1840).

Chloroform is invented independently by Justus von Liebig and by U.S. chemist Samuel Guthrie, 49, whose chloric ether will be widely employed as an anaesthetic (*see* 1847; "laughing gas," 1799; Long's sulfuric ether, 1842).

A patent for making malleable cast iron is issued to U.S. inventor Seth Boyden, 43, who invented his process 5 years ago. Boyden had invented a process in 1819 for making patent leather and he will go on to invent a process for making sheet iron, a hat-shaping machine, and improvements in railroad locomotives and stationary steam engines.

The first Baldwin locomotives are manufactured by New Jersey industrialist Matthias William Baldwin, 35, who will soon produce a steam locomotive that goes 62 miles per hour (*see* 1830).

A cowcatcher for locomotives is invented by U.S. engineer Isaac Dripps. The cowcatcher will be used initially in 1833 on the Camden and Amboy Railroad between Bordentown and Hightstown, N.J., and when its projecting points are found to impale animals on the right of way, the prongs will be replaced by a heavy bar set at right angles to the rails.

The Mohawk and Hudson Railroad begins service August 9 as the locomotive *DeWitt Clinton* built by the West Point Foundry pulls a train of cars between Albany and Schenectady in the first link of a road that will become the New York Central in 1853.

The 102-mile Morris Canal is completed between Newark, N.J., and Easton, Pa., to carry anthracite coal to New York. By 1861 the canal will be handling 889,000 tons of coal (*see* Delaware-Raritan, 1834).

A feeder canal to the Ohio River and the Erie Canal spurs development of Columbus, Ohio, which will be chartered as a city in 1834.

The first steamboat voyage on the upper Missouri is accomplished by John Jacob Astor's American Fur Company steamboat S.S. *Yellowstone*.

A new London Bridge opens across the Thames to replace the 10th-century structure now being demolished (*see* Rennie, 1817).

New York University (NYU) has its beginnings in the University of the City of New York (*see* 1896).

Wesleyan University is founded at Middletown, Conn.

The University of Alabama is founded at Tuscaloosa.

Denison University is founded at Granville, Ohio.

Xavier College is founded at Cincinnati.

Telegraphy is pioneered by Joseph Henry (above) who sees that an electromagnet can be used to send messages over great distances by wiring the magnet to a switch, turning it on and off to attract and release a piece of iron, and thus producing a pattern of clicks. Henry exhibits his 14-inch-long device at the Albany Academy in Albany, N.Y., and he transmits signals over more than a mile of wire, but he does not patent the device nor does he put it to any practical use (*see* Morse, 1832).

G & C. Merriam is founded under the name Merriam, Little & Co. by Massachusetts printers George and Charles Merriam, 28 and 25, respectively, who move to Springfield to start the business that will become G. & C. Merriam next year. When Noah Webster dies in 1843 the Merriams will buy rights to publish his 1828 *American Dictionary*.

Nonfiction "The Autocrat of the Breakfast Table" by Oliver Wendell Holmes appears as an essay in the *New England Magazine.* Another such essay will appear next year (*see Atlantic Monthly,* 1856).

Fiction *Notre-Dame de Paris* by Victor Hugo who has become depressed over the failure of last year's Paris Revolution and by the intimacies his wife Adèle has begun with the poet-critic Charles Augustin Sainte-Beuve; *The Young Duke* by English novelist Benjamin Disraeli, 27, whose father Isaac D'Israeli abandoned Judaism in 1817 and has had his children baptized in the Anglican church.

Poetry *Autumn Leaves* (*Les feuilles d'automne*) by Victor Hugo (above); *Boris Godunov* by Russian poet Aleksandr Sergeevich Pushkin, 32, whose liberal views have cost him his government post but who will regain his position in the ministry of foreign affairs next year; *Legends of New England in Prose and Verse* by *New England Weekly Review* editor John Greenleaf Whittier, 23; "To Helen" by Edgar Allan Poe: "Thy hyacinth hair, thy classic face,/ Thy Naiad airs, have brought me home/ To the glory that was Greece/ And the grandeur that was Rome."

Painting *Salisbury Cathedral from the Meadows* by John Constable; *Le 28 Juillet 1830* by Eugène Delacroix.

The Barbizon school of French painters holds its first exhibition at Paris. The painters take their name from a village near Fontainebleau, their rural genre scenes are based on direct observation of nature, and they will soon be joined by Jean François Millet, now 17, and Théodore Rousseau, now 19.

Theater *The Gladiator* by U.S. playwright Robert Montgomery Bird, 25, 9/26 at New York's Park Theater, with Edwin Forrest as Spartacus.

Opera *La Sonnambula* 3/6 at Milan's Teatro Carano, with music by Vincenzo Bellini; *Robert le Diable* 11/21 at the Academie Royale de Musique, Paris, with music by German-born composer Giacomo Meyerbeer (Jakob Liebmann Beer), 40. Meyerbeer's work establishes French grand opera style with spectacular scenic effects, florid arias designed to show off the virtuosity of the singers, dramatic recitative, and romantic plot material; *Norma* 12/26 at Milan's Teatro alla Scala, with music by Vincenzo Bellini.

First performances Piano Concerto No. 1 in G minor by Felix Mendelssohn 10/17 at Munich.

Japan's Takashimaya retail store empire has its beginnings in a dry goods shop opened at Edo.

New York's Gramercy Park opens between 20th and 22nd Streets east of Fifth Avenue. The private park created by Samuel Ruggles will remain a green spot for more than 150 years.

Mount Auburn Cemetery opens at Cambridge, Mass. The "garden of graves" will become popular for Sunday outings.

Growing and harvesting a bushel of U.S. wheat takes 3 man-hours of work, a figure that will begin to drop through use of the McCormick reaper (above).

English novelist Benjamin Disraeli (above) writes to his sister from Cairo: "Oh the delicious fruits we have here and in Syria! Orange gardens miles in extent, citrons, limes, pomegranates; but the most delicious thing in the world is a banana, which is richer than a pineapple."

The English biscuit firm Carr's of Carlisle is started by baker Jonathan Dodgson Carr.

Gorham table silver is introduced by the Gorham and Webster Company of Providence, R.I., headed by local jeweler-silversmith Jabez Gorham, 39. Spoons, forks, thimbles, and other pieces are hand forged and hand fabricated so two men can produce only two dozen pieces per day.

Boston's S. S. Pierce Co. has its beginnings in a shop opened to sell "choice teas and foreign fruits" by local merchant Samuel Stillman Pierce who declares, "I may not make money but I will make a reputation." Pierce will ship wine from Madeira to New York to Buenos Aires and back to New York to satisfy an old Bostonian's taste for Madeira wines that have spent months at sea, his firm will send a dogsled team to fetch Russian isinglass (a gelatin made from sturgeon bladders) for S. S. Pierce jellies, the firm will can buffalo tongue, terrapin stew, and Singapore pineapple, and by going to such lengths S.S. Pierce and his descendants will make both money and a reputation.

Delmonico's Restaurant in New York is opened at 23 and 25 William Street by John and Peter Delmonico (*see* 1827; 1842).

The U.S. population reaches 13 million, Britain reaches 12.2 million, Ireland 7.7 million.

The United States will receive 599,000 immigrants in this decade, up from fewer than 400,000 in the 40 years between 1789 and 1829.

Robert Owen of 1824 New Harmony fame tries to popularize contraceptive measures more effective than the widely employed coitus interruptus method (*see* Edmonds, 1832; Knowlton, 1835).

1832 An Italian unification movement is aborted in March when Piedmontese authorities learn of plans for a June uprising planned last year by the Young Italy society started last year by the 26-year-old patriot Giuseppe Mazzini (*see* 1834).

A German unification movement is aborted in July by Austria's Prince von Metternich after a gathering of 25,000 at the Hambach Festival in May has toasted France's Marquis de Lafayette, now 74, has demanded a German republic, and has threatened armed revolt. The Six Articles adopted by the German Confederation June 28 at Metternich's insistence imposes on every German sovereign the duty of rejecting petitions of his estates that would impair his sovereignty. The right of estates to refuse supplies as a means of securing constitutional changes is repudiated by the Six Articles, and beginning in July all public meetings are forbidden, edicts against universities are renewed, and suspicious political characters are placed under surveillance.

Britain's upper middle class is enfranchised by the First Reform Act which passes the House of Lords June 4 and doubles the number of eligible British voters to 1 million. William IV has threatened to create new peers if the Lords continue to reject the reform bill as they did last year, pocket boroughs (controlled by single individuals or families) and rotten boroughs (election districts with the same voting power as other districts but with far fewer inhabitants) are abolished, seats are redistributed to create constituencies in the new towns, and millowners in the Midlands are enabled to agitate more effectively for removal of high tariffs on foodstuffs from abroad (*see* Ricardo, 1817; Wellington, 1828; Cobden, 1838; Second Reform Act, 1867).

The "spoils system" in U.S. politics gets its name January 21 in a Senate speech by U.S. senator from New York William Learned Marcy, 46, who says that he can see "nothing wrong in the rule that to the victor belong the spoils." Marcy will be governor of New York, U.S. secretary of war, and U.S. secretary of state

1832 (cont.) in the next 20 years, and politicians will continue to be able to name cronies to government jobs and to dispense favors that will enrich their friends (*see* Pendleton Civil Service Reform Act, 1883).

The U.S. Government has exclusive authority over tribal Indians and their lands within any state, rules the Supreme Court March 3 in *Worcester v. Georgia*.

The Creek sign a treaty March 24 ceding their lands east of the Mississippi to the United States.

Seminoles in Florida cede their lands to the United States May 9 in a treaty signed by 15 chiefs who agree to move west of the Mississippi (but *see* 1835).

Chief Black Hawk in the state of Illinois leads his Sauks back from west of the Mississippi, he retakes a village, and he begins a 4-month Black Hawk War that ends only when the Illinois militia massacre the warriors August 2 at Bad Axe River in Wisconsin Territory. Black Hawk surrenders after taking refuge with the Winnebagoes (*see* 1823).

Sauk and Fox tribesmen agree to remain west of the Mississippi in a treaty signed September 21.

Chicasaw lands east of the Mississippi are ceded to the United States October 14.

Vice President John C. Calhoun's Fort Hill letter of August 28 to the governor of South Carolina gives a closely reasoned classic exposition of Calhoun's theory of state sovereignty (the Doctrine of Concurrent Majority).

The Democratic-Republican party that has elected every U.S. president since Thomas Jefferson is renamed the Democratic party. Its first national convention held at Baltimore in late May has established the two-thirds majority requirement for nomination that will be followed by all future Democratic presidential conventions, and it reelects Andrew Jackson to a second term with 219 electoral votes against 49 for Henry Clay and 18 for others.

South Carolina legislators hold a state convention November 19 to protest the 1828 Tariff of Abominations and a new tariff law (below). The Ordinance of Nullification passed by the convention November 24 follows the principles of John C. Calhoun (above) in calling the tariff acts "null, void, and no law" in South Carolina.

President Jackson blasts South Carolina's "nullifiers" in a proclamation issued December 10. Jackson's Vice President John Calhoun has been replaced on the ticket by Martin Van Buren, and he resigns the vice presidency December 28 to take the Senate seat of Robert W. Hayne who has been elected governor of South Carolina.

💲 The Tariff Act passed by Congress July 14 has reduced some of the duties in the 1828 Tariff of Abominations, but it has retained the principle of protectionism.

✊ The New England Anti-Slavery Society is founded at Boston (*see* Jim Crow, below).

Parliament appoints a royal commission to investigate Britain's Poor Law which costs the nation £7 million per year, or 10 shillings per capita (*see* 1834; Malthus, 1798).

The cholera epidemic that spread through Russia in 1830 reaches Scotland, it appears in New York in June, it causes 4,000 deaths by October, and it spreads south and west. Scottish physician Thomas Latta at Leith injects saline solution to save the life of a cholera patient and pioneers a new treatment.

An anatomy act passed by Parliament ends the need of body snatching for medical research (*see* 1829).

Hodgkin's disease is described as a disorder of the "absorbent glands and spleen" by English physician Thomas Hodgkin, 34. Marked by sarcoma of the lymph nodes, the disease will be found to have a fatality rate of about 75 percent within 5 years of onset, but many victims will live 10 years and more.

Codeine is isolated from opium by French chemist Pierre Jean Robiquet, 52 (*see* morphine, 1803; heroin, 1898).

A 3-year expedition to explore the Rocky Mountains begins May 1 as French-American U.S. Army captain Benjamin Louis Eulalie de Bourneville, 36, leaves Fort Osage on the Missouri River with a wagon-train bound for the Columbia River. The expedition includes trapper-guide Joseph Reddeford Walker, now 34, of Independence, Mo.

The first steamboat on Lake Michigan reaches Fort Dearborn (*see* 1818; weekly service, 1834).

A canal is completed to connect Cleveland with the Ohio River at Portsmouth (*see* Cleaveland, 1796).

Construction begins in Indiana on the 459-mile Wabash Canal that will be completed in 1855 to connect the Ohio River with Lake Erie at Toledo.

Sweden's Gota Canal opens to connect the North Sea with the Baltic.

A screw propellor for steamships is patented by French shipbuilder Pierre Louis Frédéric Sauvage, 47, whose design will be appropriated by others (*see* Ressel, Wilson, 1827).

The first true clipper ship is built at Baltimore for merchant Isaac McKim (*see* 1790, 1816). The 143-foot 493-ton *Ann McKim* is designed for the China trade with yachtlike lines and three raking square-rigged masts (*see* 1845).

The Erie Railroad is incorporated April 24 by a special act of the New York State legislature under the name New York and Erie Railroad Co. (*see* 1851).

The New York and Harlem Railroad goes into service November 14 and is the first New York City street railway. Two horse-drawn cars travel up and down the Bowery between Prince and 14th Streets on tracks slotted deep into the pavement. Built by coachmaker John Stephenson, the horsecars that replace Abraham Bower's 5-year-old "accommodation" have a capacity of 40 passengers each, they attain speeds of 12 miles per hour, run every 15 minutes, and charge a fare of 25 cents (*see* 1834).

A modern sewing machine devised by New York inventor Walter Hunt, 36, has a needle with an eye in its point that pushes thread through cloth to interlock with a second thread carried by a shuttle. But Hunt's daughter Caroline refuses to use the machine in the corset-making establishment she proposes to open lest it put hand sewers out of work, and the Hunt machine is not patented (*see* Thimmonier, 1829; Howe, 1843; Hunt's safety pin, 1849).

Gettysburg State College is founded at Gettysburg, Pa.

New York University art professor Samuel F. B. Morse begins development of an electric telegraph that will speed communication (*see* 1827, 1837; Henry, 1831).

Nonfiction *Domestic Manners of the Americans* by English novelist Frances Milton Trollope, 52, who says of Americans, "I do not like them. I do not like their principles, I do not like their manners, I do not like their opinions." Trollope came to America in 1827 after divorcing the father of her son Anthony and the boy's two older brothers, she came to observe an experimental farm at Memphis operated by freed slaves who worked to buy the freedom of others and thus to spread freedom and dignity, but the farm was in chaos by the time she arrived and she opened The Bazaar at Cincinnati to sell novelty goods from London.

Fiction *Indiana* by French novelist George Sand (Amandine-Aurore-Lucie Dupin, Baronne Dudevant), 28, who at age 16 inherited her family's estate at Nohant, at 18 married a retired army officer to whom she has borne two children, but has lived independently at Paris for the past year, has collaborated under the pen name Jules Sand with author Jules Sandeau, 21, in writing for *Le Figaro*, and has shocked Paris by going about in trousers; *Maler Nolten* by German novelist-poet Eduard Mörike, 28.

Poetry *Faust* (second part) by Johann Wolfgang von Goethe who dies at Weimar March 22 at age 82.

Painting *Waterloo Bridge from Whitehall Stairs* by John Constable; *A Moorish Couple on Their Terrace* by Eugène Delacroix.

French caricaturist Honoré Daumier, 24, portrays Louis Philippe as Gargantua gorging himself on the earnings of the working class and spitting them back into the arms of the ruling elite, the king has him arrested and sentences him to 6 months in prison. A staffman for the periodical *La Caricature*, Daumier will later join the *Charivari* and will combine caricatures of the bourgeoisie with serious painting.

Theater *The Hunchback* by Irish playwright (James) Sheridan Knowles, 48, a cousin of the late Richard Brinsley Sheridan, 4/5 at London's Royal Theatre in Covent Garden, with Knowles as the hunchback and with Fanny (Frances Anne) Kemble, 23, as his daughter Julia. The theater managed by Fanny's father Charles Kemble, 57, is saved from bankruptcy by the successful play which opens at two New York theaters June 18.

Ballet *La Sylphide* 3/12 at the Théâtre de l'Academie Royale de Musique, Paris, with music by French composer Jean Scheitzhoeffer, choreography by Philippe Taglione (*see* 1836).

Opera *L'Elisir d'Amore* 5/12 at Milan's Teatro alla Scala, with music by Italian composer Gaetano Donizetti, 33. The libretto is based on a French comedy and introduces the comic figure Mr. Dulcamara.

First performances Overture to *The Hebrides* (Fingal's Cave) by Felix Mendelssohn 5/14 at London's Covent Garden Theater; Symphony No. 5 in D minor (*Reformation*) by Felix Mendelssohn 11/15 at Berlin's Singakademie.

Hymn "Rock of Ages" by Utica, N.Y., composer Thomas Hastings with words from the verses of 1776 by the late Augustus Montague Toplady.

Patriotic song "America" with lyrics by Boston Baptist minister Samuel Francis Smith, 23, who has written it in half an hour to the English tune "God Save the King." Schoolchildren at Boston's Park Street Church sing "America" July 4.

Musical stage The blackface song-and-dance act *Jim Crow* wins 20 encores at the City Theater on Jefferson Street in Louisville, Ky. Minstrel show pioneer Thomas Dartmouth "Daddy" Rice, 24, has seen an elderly, deformed slave named Jim Crow perform a little jump as he works in a livery stable near the theater, and he reproduces the man's hop and song: "Wheel about, turn about,/ Do jes so;/ An' everytime I wheel about/ I jump Jim Crow" (*see* Jim Crow law, 1880; Emmet's Virginia Minstrels, 1843).

Diastase is separated from barley. It is the first enzyme to be isolated (*see* Payen and Persoz, 1833).

American eating habits are deplored by Frances M. Trollope (above) who reports that American suppers are huge buffets that may include "tea, coffee, hot cake and custard, hoe cake, johnny cake, waffle cake, and dodger cake, pickled peaches, and preserved cucumbers, ham, turkey, hung beef, apple sauce and pickled oysters. . . ."

The U.S. Army's daily liquor ration is abolished.

Gooderham & Worts distillery is founded at Toronto on land granted by the Crown.

The Sachertorte is devised at Vienna by kitchen trainee Franz Sacher, 16, for a dinner prepared in honor of Prince von Metternich. The sweet cake is made of chocolate, eggs, and marmalade (*see* Sacher Hotel, 1876).

London's Reform Club is founded (*see* gas ovens, 1838).

1832 (cont.) *An Enquiry into the Principles of Population* by English scholar Thomas Rowe Edmonds says, "Amongst the great body of the people at the present moment, sexual intercourse is the only gratification, and thus, by a most unfortunate concurrence of adverse circumstances, population goes on augmenting at a period when it ought to be restrained. To better the condition of the labouring classes, that is, to place more food and comforts before them, however paradoxical it may appear, is the wisest mode to check redundancy . . . When (the Irish) are better fed they will have other enjoyments at command than sexual intercourse, and their numbers, therefore, will not increase in the same proportion as at present."

1833 Parliament orders abolition of slavery in the British colonies by August 1, 1834, in a bill passed August 23 after a long campaign by the humanitarian William Wilberforce who has died July 29 at age 73. Children under 6 are to be freed immediately, slaves over 6 are to be given a period of apprenticeship that will be eliminated in 1837, slaveowners are to be given a total of £120 million in compensation.

A factory act voted by Parliament August 29 forbids employment of children under age 9, forbids factory owners to work children between 9 and 13 for more than 48 hours per week and for more than 9 hours per day, requires that children under 13 be given at least 2 hours of schooling per day, limits working hours for children between 13 and 18 to 69 hours per week and 12 hours per day, and establishes statutory minimums of time permitted workers of whatever age to eat the food they have brought from home. Parliament passes the bill over the opposition of Tories and of many Whigs who subscribe to Adam Smith's laissez-faire principles of 1776, it sets up a system of paid inspectors, but the new law applies only to textile factories and its safeguards are inadequate.

New York trade societies join to form the General Trades' Union, trade unionism begins to supersede workingmen's political parties, but the movement will collapse in the financial panic and economic depression that will begin in 1837 (*see* 1864).

"An Appeal in Favor of That Class of Americans Called Africans" by Boston abolitionist David Lee Child and his 31-year-old bride Lydia Maria (Francis) Child proposes that blacks be educated. The idea is considered outrageous in most circles, but many supporters of slavery are converted to the abolitionist cause by the Appeal.

Canterbury, Conn., schoolmistress Prudence Crandall is imprisoned for violating a special act of the legislature directing her not to admit black girls to her school.

The American Anti-Slavery Society is founded at Philadelphia December 4 by abolitionists who include James Mott, 45.

The Female Anti-Slavery Society is founded at Philadelphia under the leadership of Lucretia Coffin Mott, 40, wife of James (above).

The threat of open conflict between the industrial North and the cotton-exporting South is ended by the Compromise Tariff Act submitted by Henry Clay of South Carolina to defuse the nullification issue. It is passed by the House of Representatives February 26 119 to 85, it is passed 29 to 16 by the Senate March 1, and it is signed into law by President Jackson.

Spain's Ferdinand VII dies at Madrid September 29 at age 48 after a repressive 19-year reign. He is succeeded by his 2-year-old daughter who ascends the throne as Isabella II to begin a 35-year reign that will be dominated first by Ferdinand's fourth wife Maria Christina of Naples (who 3 years ago persuaded Ferdinand to abolish the Salic Law in Spain by pragmatic sanction) and then by profligate courtiers.

Portugal's Maria II is restored to the throne by her father Dom Pedro who has returned from Brazil and has defeated her brother Dom Miguel with French and British aid. Miguel will be expelled from Portugal at the end of May next year by a quadruple alliance of Britain, France, Spain, and Portugal following the death of Dom Pedro, and Maria will reign until 1853 through two insurrections.

Vom Krieg by the late Prussian army officer Karl von Clausewitz is a posthumous three-volume work on the science of warfare that will be a classic in its field. Clausewitz served with the Russian Army against Napoleon in 1812, he was made a major general and director of the Allgemeine Kriegschule in 1818, but he died at age 51 in the cholera epidemic at Breslau in 1831.

The German foundling Kaspar Hauser, who was accepted by some as prince of Baden, dies December 17 at age 21 after receiving stab wounds from a person or persons unknown who called him to a rendezvous with promises of information regarding his parentage (*see* 1828).

The Oxford Movement to restore High Church traditions of the 17th century in the Church of England begins July 14 at St. Mary's, Oxford, with an assize sermon on "national apostasy" preached by clergyman-poet John Keble, 41, who criticizes the suppression of 10 Irish bishoprics. Keble is supported by his fellow at Oxford's Oriel College John Henry Newman, 32, whose "Tracts for the Times" begin appearing and who will preach at St. Mary's for the next 8 years on the need to secure for the Church of England a firm base of doctrine and discipline lest the Church be disestablished or be abandoned by High Churchmen. The movement will be called Tractarian after Newman's Tracts, it will be joined by Oriel College fellow Edward Bouverie Pusey, now 32, in 1835, and with respect to ritual observances it will be called Puseyite, but it will arouse such opposition that many Tractarians including Newman will feel compelled to leave the Church of England and become Roman Catholics.

An "analytical engine" is proposed by English mathematician Charles Babbage, 41, who in 1822 proposed a "difference engine" but who has now conceived of a large-scale digital calculator that goes far beyond his earlier device. Babbage will obtain some government financial support to develop his calculator but will finance his work largely with his own fortune (*see* 1842).

Crown Staffordshire China Company, Ltd., is founded in England.

The East India Company loses its prized monopoly in the China trade (most of it in tea) by an act of the British prime minister Charles Grey, 69, second Earl Grey.

Crown Agents for Overseas Governments and Administrations is founded by two British government clerks whose private company will buy supplies for governors of the colonies. The mail-order firm will develop into a giant operation with headquarters near London's Westminster Abbey, with offices throughout the world, and with 2,000 employees to provide banking services, supervise road building, manage civil servants' pension funds, and engage in other areas beyond purchasing (which Crown Agents will do efficiently for more than 140 years by placing bulk orders and thus obtaining far lower prices than customers could otherwise expect to pay).

The Compromise Tariff Act voted by Congress (above) provides for gradual reduction of U.S. tariffs until July 1, 1842, when no rate is to be higher than 20 percent.

Phelps, Dodge & Co. is created at New York by local metals trader Anson Greene Phelps, 51, whose warehouse at Cliff and Fulton Streets collapsed last year and who takes into partnership his 27-year-old son-in-law William Earl Dodge, a dry-goods merchant who will acquire timberlands in Georgia, Canada, and Wisconsin and who will buy copper mines on Lake Superior.

New York's Bowery Savings Bank is founded by local businessmen whose "bank of the little people" will grow to become the nation's largest savings bank.

Britain's National Provincial Bank is founded.

The Philadelphia & Reading Railroad Company is chartered April 4. Some subsidiary lines have been operating since 1831.

The Andover & Wilmington Railroad is chartered in Massachusetts. It will join with the 3-year-old Boston & Lowell and with other roads to create the Boston & Maine with 4,077 miles of track in Massachusetts, Maine, Vermont, and New York.

The first cargo of U.S. ice for India leaves Boston to begin a voyage of 4 months and 7 days. Frederic Tudor has loaded his ship *Tuscany* with 180 tons of ice—plus apples, butter, and cheese—for Lord William Bentinck and the nabobs of the East India Company at Calcutta, half the ice is lost in transit and during unloading, but the voyage nevertheless makes a profit (*see* 1805; 1846).

Atlanta, Ga., has its beginnings in a cabin built by pioneer Hardy Ivy on former Creek lands at the foot of the Blue Ridge Mountains. The town of Terminus will be founded at the site in 1837 (*see* 1843).

Experiments and Observations on the Gastric Juices and the Physiology of Digestion by William Beaumont is published. It will become a classic in clinical medicine (*see* 1822).

Oberlin College opens at Oberlin, Ohio. The first coeducational U.S. college admits blacks.

Haverford College is founded at Philadelphia by the Society of Friends.

The University of Delaware has its beginnings in the College of Delaware founded at Newark.

Wake Forest College is founded in North Carolina.

Uruguay's National University of the Republic is founded at Montevideo.

England's Durham University is reorganized under that name (*see* 1657).

France's Primary Education Law enacted June 28 gives the Church extensive control over the nation's primary schools.

The *New York Sun* launched by publisher Benjamin Day, 23, is the city's first successful 1-cent daily and challenges the competition which charges 6 cents. Day's son Benjamin will invent the Ben Day process for shading in printed illustrations.

Nonfiction "Sartor Resartus" by Scottish essayist-historian Thomas Carlyle, 38, appears in *Fraser's* magazine. The philosophy of clothing expressed in Carlyle's essay is actually a speculative discussion of creeds and systems of philosophy with strong elements of autobiography; *Last Essays of Elia* by Charles Lamb who will die late next year at age 59.

Jim Crow began as a comic minstrel show figure but grew to symbolize racial prejudice in America.

1833 (cont.) Fiction *Lelia* by George Sand whose novel *Indiana* last year asserted the right of women to love and independence. Sand begins a love affair with playwright-poet Alfred Louis Charles de Musset, 23, whose first book of poetry appeared 3 years ago and who has recently joined the staff of *La Revue des Deux Mondes.* "Ms. Found in a Bottle" by Edgar Allan Poe appears in the October 19 issue of the *Baltimore Sunday Visiter.*

Poetry *Pauline* by English poet Robert Browning, 21, whose work is poorly received.

Painting *Fifty-three Stations of Tokaido* (*Tokaido Gojusansugi*) by Japanese *ukiyoe* landscape painter Ando Hiroshige, 36 (*see* 1601).

Theater *Bertrand and Raton, or The Art of Conspiracy* (*Bertrand et Raton, ou l'art d'conspirer*) by Eugène Scribe 11/14 at the Théâtre Française, Paris.

Opera *Lucrezia Borgia* 1/26 at Milan's Teatro alla Scala, with music by Gaetano Donizetti.

First performances "Die eerst Walpurgisnacht" by Felix Mendelssohn 1/10 at Berlin's Singakademie; Symphony No. 4 in A major (*Italian*) by Felix Mendelssohn 5/13 at London's Hanover Square Rooms.

Hymn "Lead, Kindly Light" verses by Oxford University church vicar John Henry Newman (above) who has written them while traveling aboard ship from Palermo to Marseilles (*see* 1868); "God Save the Emperor" by Russian composer Alexis Feodorovich Lvov will be the Russian national hymn until 1917.

New York's Brooks Brothers takes the name H. and D. H. Brooks & Company upon the death of founder Henry Sands Brooks at age 61 (*see* 1818). Sons Henry and Daniel H. Brooks will adopt the name Brooks Brothers in 1850 (*see* 1858).

The balloon-frame house that will revolutionize U.S. residential construction is invented by Chicago carpenter Augustus Deodat Taylor who nails two-by-fours together to create a cagelike framework to which a roof and siding are nailed. Critics predict that prairie winds will blow the house up and away like a balloon, but it proves to be even sturdier than conventional houses made like barns from heavy beams that require considerable time and experience to build. Within 20 years Taylor houses will be going up all over America as teams of amateurs use handy-sized precut lumber and cheap mass-produced nails to knock houses together.

A 3-year famine begins in Japan. The suffering will be even worse than in 1783.

A reaper that will rival the McCormick reaper of 1831 is patented by Cincinnati Quaker inventor Obed Hussey, 41, whose machine will go into production next year and will be snapped up by midwestern grain farmers. McCormick's machine will not go into production until 1840 and will encounter resistance from farmers in hilly Virginia (but *see* 1847).

Farmer's Register is published for the first time in Virginia with agriculturist Edmund Ruffin, 39, as editor. Ruffin has seen farmland eroded by tobacco growers and he warns planters of the "growing loss and eventual ruin of your country, and the humiliation of its people, if the long-existing system of exhausting culture is not abandoned." "Choose, and choose quickly," says Ruffin, and he urges contour plowing, crop rotation, the use of furrows for careful drainage, and the use of lime and fertilizers to rejuvenate the soil.

Avocados are introduced from Mexico into southern Florida by horticulturist Henry Perrine.

The enzyme amylase is extracted from malt by French chemists Anselme Payen and Jean-François Persoz who observe that it converts starch into sugar (*see* Schwann, 1836; Kuhne, 1878).

An alternative to the millstones that have been used to grind grain since ancient times is devised by a Swiss millwright who replaces the stones with rollers. He uses them to reduce the grain to flour more efficiently (*see* Sulzberger, 1839).

Teetotalism is advocated by English prohibitionist R. Turner who makes a stammering speech at Preston in behalf of "teetoteetoteetotal" abstinence from alcoholic beverages and unwittingly introduces a new word to the language.

Bottled carbonated water is sold to New York merchants by English-American entrepreneur John Matthews who opens a shop at 33 Gold Street and begins to manufacture a compact apparatus for carbonation —the first soda fountain (*see* Silliman, 1807).

The diaphragm contraceptive is invented by German physician Friedrich Adolphe Wilde whose rubber cap will be popularized in years to come by physician Wilhelm Mensinga (*see* Place, 1822; Sanger, 1923).

1834 Britain's Grand National Consolidated Trades Union, organized in January by Robert Owen and John Doherty, 36, is pledged to strike for an 8-hour day. Within a few weeks the union has half a million members, but its avowed purpose of fomenting a general strike alarms the government; six workers led by George Loveless who have formed a lodge at Tolpuddle outside Dorchester are sentenced in March to be transported to New South Wales or Tasmania for 7 years. Their conviction produces demonstrations throughout the country, the prime minister Lord Melbourne refuses to receive a petition of protest bearing 250,000 signatures, a series of strikes meets with no success, Owen is intimidated, and the Grand National dissolves in October, but the Tolpuddle martyrs will be brought home in 1836 to appease the public outcry.

A new British Poor Law enacted by Parliament August 14 limits the pay of charitable doles to sick and aged paupers. The law establishes workhouses where able-bodied paupers are put to work (no able-bodied man may receive help unless he enters a workhouse), and the system that has provided a dole to supplement low wages is ended.

New York's General Trades Union organizes a National Trades Union that takes in all crafts.

Workers along the Chesapeake and Ohio Canal that was started in 1828 stage a riot January 29. President Jackson orders Secretary of War Lewis Cass to send in troops, and federal troops are used for the first time in a U. S. labor conflict.

A department of Indian affairs established by Congress June 30 sets up Indian territory west of the Mississippi. Florida Seminoles are ordered to move west October 28 in accordance with a treaty signed May 9, 1832 (see Osceola, 1835).

Unskilled U.S. workers demonstrate against abolitionists in fear that they will be displaced by black freedmen. A New York antislavery society meeting at the Chatham Street Chapel is broken up July 4 by rioters who protest the presence of some blacks in the audience, the rioting continues for more than a week, and churches and houses are destroyed.

Antiabolitionists at Philadelphia destroy the homes of 40 blacks in October.

Some 35,000 slaves are freed in South Africa as slavery is abolished throughout the British Empire amid complaints about the inadequacy of compensation to former slaveowners (see 1833; Great Trek, 1835).

The Spanish Inquisition instituted in the 13th century is finally abolished (see 1492; 1820).

A Spanish civil war that will continue for 5 years begins as the throne of Isabella II is claimed by her 46-year-old uncle Don Carlos Maria Isidro de Bourbon who is supported by the Church and by the Basques, the Catalonians, and the conservative elements of Aragon and Navarre. The pretender is opposed by Portugal, Britain, France, and supporters of Isabella who form a quadruple alliance, London suspends the Foreign Enlistment Act, and Sir George de Lacy Evans, 47, who served in the Peninsula campaign and in the American Revolution is enabled to form a foreign legion that will support Isabella.

Portugal's 6-year civil war is ended May 26 by the defeat of Miguel who leaves the country (see 1828).

The Young Europe movement is founded by Italian lawyer Giuseppe Mazzini who expands his Young Italy movement of 1832 by organizing Young Germany, Young Poland, and similar groups from headquarters at London (see 1848; 1849).

South Africa has a Kaffir War as Bantu tribesmen (called Kaffir by the Dutch who use it in the same sense that Americans use the word "nigger") invade eastern regions in irritation at the steady encroachment of Dutch cattlemen and farmers. The Bantu are driven back but only with difficulty (see Great Trek, 1835; Kaffir War, 1877).

 South Australia is founded by followers of British colonial theorist Edward Gibbon Wakefield, 38, who obtain a charter August 2 for their South Australia Association with support from the duke of Wellington and from historian George Grote, 38. The first settlers will be landed in 1836 at Kangaroo Island.

The Australian colony that will be called Victoria is settled for the first time by West Australia rancher Edward Henty and his brothers at Portland Bay. They will be joined next year by John Batman, 34, and his associates from Tasmania.

 John Jacob Astor sells his fur interests as pelts threaten to become scarce. Beaver pelts have sold for $6 apiece in peak years, enabling trappers to make $1,000 per season, but the fur companies have charged enormous prices for supplies hauled from St. Louis to summer rendezvous points, so while the beaver has been nearly exterminated, none of the trappers have made fortunes. Astor has monopolized the upper Missouri Valley fur trade, he has made himself the richest man in America, and he will now devote his efforts to administering his fortune, much of which he will invest in New York real estate (see Juneau, 1818; Astor House, 1836).

Lowell, Mass., has six corporations operating 19 mills with 4,000 looms and more than 100,000 spindles (see 1814; Thoreau, 1849).

The U.S. Senate censures President Jackson March 28 for removing deposits from the Bank of the United States. The Senate approves a resolution introduced by Henry Clay late last year, Jackson enters a formal protest April 15, and the resolution will be removed early in 1837 from the Senate Journal.

Britain's Westminster Bank, Ltd., has its beginnings in the London and Westminster Bank, a joint-stock company that will amalgamate in 1909 with the London and County Banking Company that will be founded in 1836.

The Zollverein customs union organized by some of the German states eliminates tariffs among its members (see 1853).

 The direction of an electric current induced in a circuit by moving it in a magnetic field produces an effect tending to oppose the circuit's motion, says Russian physicist Heinrich Emil Lenz, 30, who formulates a new law of electricity.

 The Delaware and Raritan Canal opens between New Brunswick, N.J., and Bordentown, Pa. The 43-mile canal will be extended 21 miles to Trenton on the Delaware River, it will be the state's chief transportation corridor, mule-drawn barges will be hauling 1.2 million tons of coal and 12 million board-feet of lumber per year from Philadelphia to New York by 1860, and the canal will remain in operation until 1933.

1834 (cont.) The Portage Railroad opens to connect Philadelphia with Pittsburgh via rail and canal.

The New York and Harlem Railroad of 1832 extends its horsecar route up Fourth Avenue to 84th Street (*see* 1837).

Hansom cabs are introduced in London. The patented safety cabs which will be called the gondolas of London have been designed by English architect Joseph Aloysius Hansom, 31, who last year designed the Birmingham town hall.

London's Baring Brothers acquires two ships and enters the China trade with the *Alexander Baring* and the *Falcon.* The merchant banking house competes with the East India Company (above).

Weekly steamboat service begins between Buffalo and Fort Dearborn (*see* 1832; Chicago, 1830; railroad, 1852).

Cornelius van Derbilt begins to multiply the $500,000 he has amassed in the steamboat trade (*see* 1829; 1850).

 Tulane University has its beginnings at New Orleans. Local merchant Paul Tulane, 33, opened a dry-goods and clothing store 12 years ago, he will make large gifts to the school beginning in 1882, and it will take the name Tulane in 1884.

Wheaton College is founded at Norton, Mass.

The University of Brussels has its beginnings.

The braille system of raised point writing devised by French educator Louis Braille, 25, will gain acceptance throughout the world (*see* Haüy, 1784). Braille has been blind since age 3, he has been teaching fellow sightless people since 1828, and his system can be used for music as well as for words.

The New Yorker Staats-Zeitung begins publication at New York. The German-language weekly will become a daily in 1849.

Fiction   *Le Père Goriot* by French novelist Honoré de Balzac, 34; *The Last Days of Pompeii* by English novelist Edward George Bulwer-Lytton, 31.

Painting   *Algerian Women at Home* by Eugène Delacroix; *The Martyrdom of Saint Symphorian* by Jean Ingres.

The Munich Glyptothek sculpture gallery is completed by Leo von Klenze, 50.

London's National Gallery is started by English architect William Wilkins, 56.

First performances   *Harold in Italy* Symphony by Hector Berlioz 11/23 at the Paris Conservatoire. Berlioz has based the work on the poem "Childe Harold" of 1818 by the late Lord Byron.

Hymn   "Jesus, Lover of my Soul" by Simeon Butler Marsh, verses by the late Methodist leader Charles Wesley.

Popular song   "Zip Coon" ("Turkey in the Straw") is published anonymously. Bob Farrel and George Washington Dixon will claim authorship.

 Chantilly racetrack opens 26 miles north of Paris.

 New York's first Fifth Avenue mansion goes up at the northeast corner of 9th Street for merchant Henry Brevoort whose lead will be followed within the year by a dozen other rich families. They will make Fifth Avenue the city's most desirable residential address.

Fire destroy's London's Houses of Parliament and part of the city October 16. A major reconstruction program begins (*see* Buckingham Palace, 1837; Trafalgar Square, 1843; Big Ben, 1858).

British wheat prices fall to £10 per ton, down from £30 in 1812.

Cyrus McCormick receives a patent for his reaper of 1831 and Obed Hussey begins manufacturing his reaper of last year (*see* 1840).

 Sardines are canned for the first time in Europe (*see* first U.S. sardine cannery, 1876).

Gas refrigeration has its beginnings in a compression machine invented in England by U.S. inventor Jacob Perkins of 1790 nail cutter fame who has lived abroad for years. Now 58, Perkins distills rubber to create a volatile liquid which is allowed to evaporate by absorbing heat from its surroundings. When the capor is compressed, it turns back to liquid, giving off heat, and by alternately compressing and expanding Perkins extracts heat from the region of expansion until he has cooled water to the point that it freezes (*see* Faraday, 1823; Gorrie, 1845; Linde, 1873).

Some 28 million acres of U.S. public lands will be offered for sale this year and next. As Americans move west of the Appalachians to take up the new lands, European immigrants will replace them.

Thomas R. Malthus dies at Haileybury, England, December 23 at age 68. Father of three (one died at age 17), Malthus has been attacked for "having the impudence to marry after preaching against the evils of a family." He has been viciously caricatured by Charles Dickens, vilified by essayist William Hazlitt, accused of defending war, plagues, slavery, and infanticide, but still holds the chair in political economy to which he was appointed in 1805.

1835 Dutch (Boer) cattlemen in South Africa begin a Great Trek to the north and east of the Orange River in irritation at Britain's abolition of slavery in 1833. Some 10,000 Boers will move to new lands beyond the Vaal River (the Transvaal) in the next 2 years, seriously depopulating the eastern part of the Cape Colony (*see* Pretorius, 1856).

Melbourne is founded in Australia and is named for the new British prime minister William Lamb, second Viscount Melbourne (*see* Victoria, 1834).

St. Petersburg, Fla., has its beginnings in a settlement at Old Tampa Bay founded by French immigrant Odet Philippe who was once a surgeon for Napoleon.

A new Seminole War against the whites in Florida Territory is precipitated by the arrest and imprisonment of the 31-year-old Seminole Osceola who has thrust his knife through the 1832 treaty that ceded Seminole lands to the United States. Osceola escapes, he and his braves kill a chief who signed the 1832 treaty, they also kill the U.S. Indian agent at Fort King, and they begin 2 years of guerilla activities against U.S. forces under General Thomas S. Jesup while Seminole women and children remain hidden deep in the Everglades (*see* 1836).

English borough government is revolutionized by the Municipal Corporation Act.

The Barakzai dynasty that will rule Afghanistan until 1929 is founded by the khan of Kabul Dost Mohammed, now 42, who gains power over the entire country, takes the title emir, and begins a 4-year reign (*see* 1826; 1838).

The last Holy Roman Emperor Francis II (Francis I as first Austrian emperor) dies March 2 at age 67 and is succeeded as emperor of Austria by his 4-year-old son who will reign until 1848 as Ferdinand I.

The first German railroad line opens between Nuremberg and Fürth.

The United States has 1,098 miles of railroad in operation.

Chemists synthesize the pain reliever salicylic acid but cannot produce a safe, effective anodyne (*see* Stone, 1793; Gerhardt, 1853).

London pathologist James Paget, 21, at St. Bartholomew's Hospital detects the parasite *Trichina spiralis* for the first time. The parasite will later be associated with trichinosis, a disease produced by eating raw or undercooked pork products or meat from bears, polar bears, rats, foxes, or marine animals (*see* von Zenker, 1860; Paget's disease, 1877).

Albion College is founded at Albion, Mich. (*see* "Sweetheart of Sigma Chi," 1912).

The *New York Herald* begins publication May 6 under the direction of Scots-American journalist James Gordon Bennett, 40, who has started the 1-cent newspaper with $500, two wooden chairs, and an old dry goods box in a cellar office. Bennett has been a staffman for the *New York Enquirer* and its successor, the *Morning Courier and New York Enquirer*.

Agence France-Presse is established under the name Agence Havas. The French national news agency will take the name France-Presse in 1945.

Nonfiction *Democracy in America (La Démocracie en Amérique)* by French aristocrat Alexis Charles Henri Maurice Clerel de Tocqueville, 35, who traveled for 9 months in 1831 through eastern Canada, New England, New York, Philadelphia, Baltimore, Washington, Cincinnati, Tennessee, and New Orleans on a commission to study the U.S penitentiary system. "Nothing struck me more forcibly than the general equality of conditions. . . . All classes meet continually and no haughtiness at all results from the differences in social position. Everyone shakes

hands"; but de Tocqueville foresees the rise of certain forces that will eventually undermine the principle of economic equality, and while the American passion for equality "tends to elevate the humble to the rank of the great . . . there exists also in the human heart a depraved taste for equality, which impels the weak to attempt to lower the powerful to their own level, and reduces men to prefer equality in slavery to inequality with freedom."

Tyranny of the majority is cited as a possible hazard of democracy by de Tocqueville (above), but he notes that law, religion, and the press provide bulwarks against democratic despotism, as he will elaborate in a second volume to be published in 1840.

Fiction *Mirgirod (Stories)* by Nikolai Gogol who will leave Russia next year to live abroad, mostly in Rome; *Arabeski (Essays and Stories)* by Nikolai Gogol includes "Nevsky Prospekt," "The Portrait," and "Notes of a Madman"; *Mademoiselle de Maupin* by Théophile Gautier espouses the doctrine of "art for art's sake" in its preface and denounces bourgeois philistinism; *Rienzi* by E. G. E. Bulwer-Lytton is based on the Roman revolt of Cola di Rienzi in 1347; *Fairy Tales (Eventyr)* by Danish novelist Hans Christian Andersen, 30, whose novel *The Improvisatore* also appears and enjoys such success that Andersen is encouraged to pursue a career as novelist and dramatist and to neglect the fairy tales that will make him famous. Included in Andersen's first volume are "The Tinderbox" ("Fyrtojet"), "The Princess on the Pea" ("Princessen paa Aerten"), "Little Claus and Big Claus" ("Lille Claus og store Claus"), and "Little Ida's Flowers" ("Den lille Idas Blomster") which will be followed in time by "The Ugly Duckling," "The Fir Tree," "The Red Shoes," "The Swineherd," "The Snow Queen" ("Snedronningen"), and "The Emperor's New Clothes" ("Kejserens nye Kloeder"); *The Yemassee* by U.S novelist William Gilmore Simms, 29, whose story about Indians will make him widely known. Simms returns from New York to his native Charleston, S.C., where his first wife died 3 years ago and where next year he will marry the daughter of a rich plantation owner.

Painting *Burning of the Houses of Lords and Commons* by J. M. W. Turner who witnessed last year's great fire after rushing from dinner with sketchbook in hand to find the spectacle being applauded by throngs of spectators on the Thames embankments; *The Valley Farm* by John Constable; *Homer in the Desert* by J. P. C. Corot who makes a second visit to Italy; *Hundred Views of Mount Fuji* by Japanese *ukiyoe* painter Katsushika Hokusai (Tetsuzo Nakashima), 75, whose *Ten Thousand Sketches* (Manga) will be published in its 15th and final volume next year (Hokusai's work includes "The Great Wave"). Baron Antoine Jean Gros drowns himself in the Seine at Meudon June 26 at age 64.

P. T. Barnum begins a career in U.S. show business. Connecticut-born promoter Phineas Taylor Barnum, 25, buys a slave woman who is alleged to have been

1835 (cont.) George Washington's nurse and to be more than 160 years old. Joice Heth will be proved to be no older than 70 when she dies next year, but Barnum will continue the well-publicized tours he has begun with a small company of carnival attractions (*see* Dutch belted cows, 1840; Tom Thumb, 1842).

Opera *I Puritani* 1/25 at the Théâtre des Italiens, Paris, with music by Vincenzo Bellini; *La Juive* 2/23 at the Paris Grand Opéra, with music by French composer Jacques Halévy, 35, libretto by playwright Eugène Scribe; *Lucia di Lammermoor* 9/26 at the Teatro San Carlo, Naples, with music by Gaetano Donizetti, libretto from the Walter Scott novel of 1818 *The Bride of the Lammermoor.*

First performances *Grand Polonaise Brillante* by Frederic Chopin 4/26 at the Paris Conservatoire.

Popular songs "Long, Long Ago" by English songwriter-novelist-playwright Thomas Haynes Bayly, 38; "Kathleen Mavourneen" with lyrics by Irish author Julia Crawford, 35.

Louisiana's Rosedown plantation house is completed in Georgian style at St. Francisville for planter Daniel Turnbull.

Mississippi's Lochinvar plantation house is completed by Scots-American Indian trader Robert Gordon who names it for the hero in the 1808 poem "Marmion" by the late Sir Walter Scott.

New York loses 674 buildings December 16 in a $15 million fire that rages in the vicinity of Hanover and Pearl Streets.

Honeybees are described by Washington Irving in *A Tour of the Prairies:* "It is surprising in what countless swarms the bees have overspread the Far West within a moderate number of years. The Indians consider them the harbinger of the white man, as the buffalo is of the red man; and say that, in proportion as the bee advances, the Indian and the buffalo retire . . . I am told that the wild bee is seldom to be met with at any great distance from the frontier. . . ."

Berlin naturalist Theodor Schwann extracts the enzyme pepsin from the stomach wall and proclaims it the most effective element in the digestive juices (*see* hydrochloric acid, 1824; Payen and Persoz, 1833; Kuhne's introduction of the word "enyzme," 1878).

Sauce Bearnaise made with tarragon vinegar originates at the Pavillon Henri IV restaurant outside Paris (*see* 1606).

Chili powder is developed in Mexico's Texas Territory by English settlers who combine various Mexican ground peppers as a convenient way to make Mexican-style dishes (*see* 1828; Gebhardt, 1894).

Russia's bonded peasant population reaches close to 11 million, up from less than 10 million in 1816. The overabundance of serfs causes problems in years when crops are short.

"Fruits of Philosophy" by Cambridge, Mass., physician Charles Knowlton, 35, is a Malthusian pamphlet advocating contraception. Knowlton is prosecuted and is imprisoned for 3 months (*see* Bradlaugh, Besant, 1877).

1836 The Alamo at San Antonio falls March 6 to a 4,000-man army commanded by the president of Mexico General Antonio Lopez de Santa Anna, 40, after an 11-day siege. The 188-man force that has garrisoned the Franciscan missionary includes William B. Travis, 26, Bowie knife inventor James Bowie, 39, and former U.S congressman from Tennessee David "Davy" Crockett, 49. The Mexicans sustain nearly 1,600 dead plus many wounded, they spare 30 U.S. noncombatants, but they kill the entire garrison, shooting five prisoners.

"Remember the Alamo" is the battle cry of U.S. Army Colonel Sidney Sherman, 31, as he helps former Tennessee Governor Samuel "Sam" Houston, 43, defeat General Santa Anna (above) and his Mexicans April 21 at the Battle of San Jacinto (*see* Austin, 1821).

The Republic of Texas is founded with Sam Houston (above) as president. J. K. and A. C. Allen found the city of Houston in southeastern Texas, and the new republic claims the territory between the Rio Grande and the Neuces Rivers (*see* 1845; King, 1853).

Seminoles in Florida and their black slaves massacre a 103-man U.S. Army force under the command of Major Francis L. Dade as the Second Seminole War continues (*see* 1835; 1837).

Arkansas is admitted to the Union as the 25th state.

Vice President Martin Van Buren, 53, is elected to the presidency with support from the outgoing President Jackson. He receives more popular votes than his four opponents combined, and he wins 170 electoral votes versus the combined total of 124 for his opponents who are led by William Henry Harrison.

Natal, Transvaal, and the Orange Free State are founded by Boer farmers who continue the Great Trek that began last year in South Africa.

Adelaide is founded in South Australia on a fertile plain that sweeps up from the coast to a line of hills. The town is named for the consort of Britain's William IV (*see* 1834).

U.S. missionary Marcus Whitman, 34, takes his wife Narcissa and Eliza Spalding to the Pacific Northwest. They are the first white women to cross the Continent (*see* 1843; 1847).

The S.S. *Beaver* tested under steam at Vancouver May 16 is the first steamboat to be seen on the Pacific Coast. Built last year in England with Boulton & Watt engines, the 101.4-foot vessel enters the Willamette River in Oregon Territory May 31 on her maiden voyage, she runs down the river under steam, and she enters the lower reaches of the Columbia River.

Of 2.35 million tons of U.S. merchant shipping some 60,000 tons are in steam.

The Erie Canal that was completed in 1825 is widened and deepened for the barge traffic which has repaid investors with toll receipts (*see* 1917).

The Long Island Railroad begins operations April 18 (*see* 1900; 1905).

The first Canadian railway opens July 21 to link Laprairie on the St. Lawrence River with St. Johns on the Richelieu.

The hot-air balloon *Nassau* carried by 85,000 cubic feet of coal gas lifts off November 7 from London's Vauxhall Gardens with three passengers in her gondola, she passes over Liège and Coblenz, and she comes to rest 18 hours and 500 miles later in the German duchy of Nassau. Balloonist Charles Green has been the first to use coal gas which he employed in the *Nassau* (then called something else) to celebrate the coronation of George IV in 1821.

The first electric cell with a long working life is developed by English chemist John Frederick Daniell, 47, who improves on the 1800 cell of Alessandro Volta by producing a cell that generates a steady current for considerable periods of time (*see* Plante, 1859).

Acetylene is discovered and identified by English chemist Edmond Davey.

Galvanized iron (coated with zinc) is invented in France.

The world's largest steel manufacturing and munitions plant has its beginnings in a French ironworks at Le Creusot purchased by French industrialist Joseph Eugène Schneider, 31, and his brother Eugène. They will develop the works into a gigantic steelmaking enterprise.

The Colt six-shooter revolver patented by Hartford, Conn., inventor Samuel Colt, 22, has an effective range of only 25 to 30 yards but will be improved and will play a major role in the opening of the West. Colt establishes the Patent Arms Manufacturing Company at Paterson, N.J., but the firm will soon fail (*see* 1846; 1871; Hayes, 1844).

Midland Bank, Ltd. is founded in England.

Barclays Bank has its beginnings in a charter granted to the new Colonial Bank founded at London. The bank will open offices next year in Jamaica, Barbados, Antigua, Dominica, Trinidad, St. Kitts, and St. Thomas in the West Indies (*see* 1925).

The University of Wisconsin is founded at Madison.

McGuffey's First and Second *Readers* are compiled for a Cincinnati publisher by Cincinnati College president William Holmes McGuffey, 36, whose *Readers* will grow to number six in the next 15 years and will be sold until 1927. They will be used to educate generations of Americans in the virtues of frugality, industry, and sobriety.

The *Toledo Blade* begins publication in Ohio.

The *Philadelphia Public Ledger* begins publication. Three journeymen printers start Philadelphia's first penny daily.

J. B. Lippincott & Co. is founded by Philadelphia book publisher Joshua Ballinger Lippincott, 23, whose son Joshua Bertram will continue the firm until 1940 when successors will take over.

Nonfiction *Evidence from the Scripture and History of the Second Coming of Christ, about the Year 1843* by U.S. religious leader William Miller, 54, whose book will lead to the founding of the Adventist Church in 1845; *The Book of Wealth: in Which It Is Proved from the Bible that It Is the Duty of Every Man to Become Rich* by U.S. clergyman Thomas P. Hunt; "Nature" by Boston essayist Ralph Waldo Emerson, 33, who says, "The inevitable mark of wisdom is to see the miraculous in the common" and who advises readers to "enjoy an original relation to the universe" (*see* Thoreau, 1837).

Fiction *Sketches by 'Boz'* by London court reporter Charles (John Huffam) Dickens, 24, whose first sketch appeared in a December, 1833, periodical and who has used the pen name 'Boz' since August; *Mr. Midshipman Easy* by retired British Navy captain Frederick Marryat, 44, whose first novel was published as *The King's Own* shortly after his retirement from the navy in 1830; *Confession d'un Enfant du Siècle* by Charles de Musset (autobiographical novel). "Maelzel's Chess-Player" by Edgar Allan Poe.

Painting *Stoke-by-Nayland* by John Constable; *Diana Surprised by Actaeon* by J. P. C. Corot.

Theater *The Government Inspector (Revizor)* by Nikolai Gogol 4/19 at St. Petersburg's Alexandrinsky Theater.

Opera *Les Huguenots* 2/29 at the Paris Opéra, with music by Giacomo Meyerbeer; *A Life for the Czar (Ivan Susanin)* 12/9 at St. Petersburg, with music by Russian composer Mikhail Ivanovich Glinka, 32, who traveled in Italy from 1830 to 1832, met Vincenzo Bellini and Gaetano Donizetti, and fell in love with Italian opera. His opera will open the season at St. Petersburg and Moscow every year hereafter until 1917.

Ballet *La Sylphide* at Copenhagen, a new version of the 1832 ballet with music by the late German composer Christoph Willibald Gluck.

Oratorio *St. Paul* by Felix Mendelssohn 5/22 (Whitsunday) at the Düsseldorf Festival, with a chorus of 364 voices and a 172-piece orchestra.

The King's Plate and the Queen's Plate horse races at Quebec begin the oldest stakes races that will be run continuously in North America.

A phosphorus match patented by Springfield, Mass., shoemaker Alonzo D. Phillips is the prototype of matches that will be used in the future to light stoves, hearthfires, and smoking tobacco (*see* Walker, 1827; Lundstrom, 1853).

Crossing the Atlantic entirely by steam was a triumph of engineering, but sailing ships often made better time.

The Arc de Triomphe ordered by Napoleon in 1806 is completed at Paris in the Place de l'Etoile. 164 feet high and 148 feet wide, it is the world's largest triumphal arch and its frieze depicts the successful campaigns of France's armies between 1790 and 1814.

New York's Astor House opens on the northwest corner of Broadway and Vesey Streets. It sets new standards of hotel luxury (*see* Tremont House, 1829; Marryat, 1838).

Iceland's Mount Hekla erupts as it did in 1597 and creates widespread destruction (*see* 1947).

U.S. frontier food is praised by Narcissa Whitman (above) who writes, "I wish some of the feeble ones in the States could have a ride over the mountains; they would say like me, victuals even the plainest kind ever relished so well before."

The first printed American menu is issued by New York's 5-year-old Delmonico's Restaurant and lists as one of its most expensive dishes "Hamburg Steak" (*see* 1899).

Some 75 percent of gainfully employed Americans are engaged in agriculture, down from 83 percent in 1820 (*see* 1853).

1837 Queen Victoria begins a 64-year reign over the British Empire June 20. The 18-year-old granddaughter of George III succeeds to the throne upon the death of her uncle William IV at age 71, but Salic law forbids female succession in Hanover and that kingdom is separated from Britain. The Hanoverian crown passes to George III's eldest surviving son the duke of Cumberland, he will reign until 1851 as Ernst August, and his son will reign as George V until Prussia annexes Hanover in 1866.

The Japanese Tokugawa shogun Ienari resigns at age 64 after a 44-year rule marked by widespread disturbances produced in part by Ienari's efforts to reform the government and improve education. Ienari has had 40 mistresses, half of his 54 children have died in infancy. He is succeeded by his 45-year-old son

Ieyoshi who will rule until 1853, and the new shogunate will be marked by increasing sentiment for restoration of imperial power and by increasing demands that Japan open her ports to foreign trade.

Michigan is admitted to the Union as the 26th state.

President Jackson recognizes the Republic of Texas on his last day in office March 3 after approval by Congress.

The Texas Rangers have their beginnings at Waco where Anson Darnell, Starrett Smith, and Jacob Gross establish Fort Fisher.

Congress increases Supreme Court membership March 3 from seven justices to nine.

A French-Canadian rebellion against British rule begins under the leadership of Louis Joseph Papineau, 51, and William Lyon Mackenzie, 42. Speaker of the legislative assembly of Lower Canada, Papineau is charged with high treason, he escapes to the United States, and he is declared a rebel after some riots and fighting in the Montreal area. Mackenzie attacks Toronto December 5, he is repulsed, he flees across the border December 13, he seizes Navy Island in the Niagara River, and he proclaims a provisional government, but he will be arrested in the United States early next year. The U.S. steamboat *Caroline* supplies the rebels but is burnt December 29 by Canadian troops who have crossed the Niagara River (*see* Durham Report, 1839).

The Seminole leader Osceola is tricked into coming out of the Florida Everglades under a flag of truce in October and is arrested with several followers when he enters the compound at St. Augustine. The action of the commanding officer General Thomas S. Jesup brings public protest, but Osceola remains a prisoner, his braves are defeated December 25 at Okeechobee Swamp by the 53-year-old Colonel Zachary Taylor who is called "Old Rough and Ready" and is promoted to brigadier general. Osceola will die early next year at Fort Moultrie near Charleston, S.C., and most of his tribespeople will be exterminated in the next few years (*see* Florida statehood, 1845).

Congress enacts a gag law to suppress debate on the slavery issue.

Alton, Ill., editor Elijah Paris Lovejoy, 34, receives a new press from the Anti-Slavery Society to replace the *Alton Observer* press that has been smashed by townspeople who favor slavery. An armed band of citizens approaches the warehouse where the new press is stored, a group of abolitionists stands guard to defend the press, one of the citizens tries to set fire to the warehouse, Lovejoy dashes into the street, and he is shot dead November 7.

Boston abolitionist Wendell Phillips, 26, hears a proslavery speaker in a meeting at Faneuil Hall December 8 compare Lovejoy's murderers (above) to the patriots of the Boston Tea Party of 1773. Phillips gave up his law career 2 years ago after seeing a Boston mob drag abolitionist William Lloyd Garrison half-naked through the streets at the end of a rope, he has never spoken in public before, but he rises in fury to denounce the previous speaker, he points to portraits of John Adams and John Hancock on the wall, he says, "I thought those pictured lips would have broken into voice, to rebuke the recreant American, the slanderer of the dead," and his eloquence sways the meeting.

 A smallpox epidemic in the Great Plains practically wipes out the Arikara, the Hidatsa, and the Mandan.

Persian cuneiform inscriptions deciphered by German archaeologist Georg Friedrich Grotefend, 62, open the way to a knowledge of life among early peoples of the Near East. The inscriptions date to 3,000 B.C. (see Rawlinson, 1846).

The essential importance of chlorophyll to photosynthesis is established by French physiologist René Joachim Henri Dutrochet, 61 (see Ingenhousz, 1779).

Recherches sur la Probabilité des Jugements by French mathematician Siméon Denis Poisson, 67, establishes rules of probability based on the incidence of death from mule kicks in the French army.

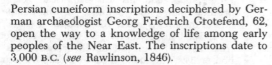 Economic depression begins in the United States following the failure in March of the New Orleans cotton brokerage Herman Briggs & Co. Inflated land values, speculation, and wildcat banking have contributed to the crisis, New York banks suspend specie payments May 10, financial panic ensues, at least 800 banks suspend specie payment, 618 banks fail before the year is out (many have deceived bank inspectors as to the amount of gold backing their banknotes), specie disappears from circulation, employers pay workers in paper "shinplasters" of dubious value and often counterfeit, 39,000 Americans go bankrupt, $741 million is lost, and the depression reduces thousands to starvation (see 1838).

The depression (above) forces every New England textile mill but one to close down. Nathaniel Stevens at North Andover expands production and works 76-hour weeks, paying above average wages of $4.50 per week plus $2 for board (see 1813; 1899).

Economic depression begins in Britain.

Congress authorizes the issue of U.S. Treasury notes not to exceed $10 million October 12 in a move to ease the nation's financial crisis.

Frankfurt banker August Belmont, 20, hears of the financial panic in New York (above) while en route to Havana to transact business for the younger Meyer Rothschild (see 1801). Belmont completes his Cuban business, he sends in his resignation to Frankfurt but offers to act as agent for the Rothschilds, he sails for New York, he rents a small office in Wall Street, and although virtually without capital he begins a business that will grow into a powerful banking house.

 Completion of the Pennsylvania Canal spurs development of Pittsburgh.

The New York and Harlem Railroad reaches Harlem with its horsecars and develops the world's first steam tram (see 1834; 1839).

London's Euston Station opens July 20 with an enormous Doric arch to serve as the city's main-line rail terminal (see Waterloo Station, 1848).

 The world's first kindergarten opens at Blankenburg, Thuringia, under the direction of German educator Friedrich Fröbel, 55 (see 1855; Peabody, 1860).

Third and Fourth McGuffey *Readers* are published (see 1836).

The University of Louisville is founded in Kentucky.

Depauw University has its beginnings in the Indiana Ashway University founded at Greencastle, Ind. The school will adopt the name Depauw in 1883.

Marshall University is founded at Huntington, Va.

Mount Holyoke Female Seminary opens November 8 at South Hadley, Mass., the first U.S. college for women. Local educator Mary Lyon, 40, proposes to give the best possible education to women of modest means and is so successful with her 80 students that she will have to turn away 400 applicants next year for lack of space.

The University of Athens is founded in Greece.

 An electric telegraph is patented by English physicist Charles Wheatstone, 35, and English electrical engineer William Fothergill Cooke (see 1845; Electric Telegraph Company, 1846).

Samuel F. B. Morse gives a public demonstration of his magnetic telegraph and files for a U.S. patent (see 1832). Morse's assistant Alfred Lewis Vail, 30, devises a Morse code using dots and dashes to represent letters in place of an earlier system that assigned numbers to letters (see 1843; 1844).

"Post Office Reform: Its Importance and Practicality" by English schoolmaster Rowland Hill, 42, urges that Britain replace the system of charging for postage on the basis of distance and number of sheets with a uniform rate based on weight in which the sender pays in advance by buying "labels" to be affixed to each letter with "cement." Hill submits his pamphlet to the prime minister William Lamb, the second Viscount Melbourne (see 1635; 1840).

The Pitman shorthand system devised by Englishman Isaac Pitman, 24, is the first scientific shorthand system. It is based on phonetics and employs lines, curves, and hooks with contractions and "grammalogues" for frequently occuring words (see Gregg, 1888).

The *New Orleans Times-Picayune* begins publication. The Spanish picayune coin still in circulation is worth 6¼ cents.

The *Baltimore Sun* begins publication May 17. Founded by local printer Arunah S. Abell, it sells at 1 cent per copy.

1837 (cont.) Little, Brown & Co. publishers is founded at Boston by Charles Coffin Little, 38, of Maine with James Brown, 37.

Nonfiction *The French Revolution* by Thomas Carlyle whose manuscript was partly burned by the manservant of John Stuart Mill, 31, chief of relations with native states for the East India Company; *History of the Reign of Ferdinand and Isabella the Catholic* by Boston historian William Hickling Prescott, 41, who is completely blind as the result of an accident in his freshman year at Harvard when he was struck in the eye by a crust of bread thrown by another student in the commons dining room. The three-volume work establishes Prescott's reputation, and he works with assistants on a history of Cortez.

"The American Scholar" is delivered as a Harvard Phi Beta Kappa address by Ralph Waldo Emerson, who calls for intellectual independence from the past, from Europe, and from all obstacles to originality.

Harvard graduate Henry David Thoreau, 19, delivers a commencement address that enlarges on Emerson's 1836 essay on "Nature" and says that man should not work for 6 days and rest on the seventh but rather should work 1 day and leave 6 free for the "sublime revelations of nature."

Fiction *The Posthumous Papers of the Pickwick Club* by Charles Dickens: "Accidents will happen—best regulated families"; "It's over, and can't be helped, and that's one consolation, as they always say in Turkey, ven they cuts the wrong man's head off"; "I think he's a wictim o'connubiality, as Blue Beard's chaplain said, with a tear of pity, ven he buried him"; *Le Curé de Village* by Honoré de Balzac; *Twice-Told Tales* by U.S. story-writer Nathaniel Hawthorne, 33.

Poetry "Hymn, Sung at the Completion of the Concord Monument" by Ralph Waldo Emerson: "By the rude bridge that arched the flood,/ Their flag to April's breeze unfurled,/ Here once the embattled farmers stood,/ And fired the shot heard round the world" (*see* 1775); Russian poet Aleksandr Pushkin is mortally wounded in a duel January 29 with an officer in the Horse Guards and dies February 10 at age 36; "A Song about Czar Ivan Vasilyevich, His Young Bodyguard, and the Valiant Merchant Kalashnikov" by Russian poet Mikhail Yuryevich Lermontov, 22, who is transferred to a regiment in the Caucasus after writing an anticourt poem following the death of Aleksandr Pushkin (above).

Baron François Gérard dies at Paris January 11 at age 66; John Constable dies at London March 31 at 60.

Theater *The Clique, or the Helping Hand (La camaraderie, ou la Courte Echelle)* by Eugène Scribe 6/19 at the Théâtre Français, Paris.

First Performance   *Requiem* by Hector Berlioz 12/5 at the Church of Les Invalides, Paris.

The Knabe Piano is introduced by German-American pianomaker William Knabe who goes into partnership with H. Gahele at Baltimore to build "pianos of quality for genteel people of means." After Gahele's death in 1855 Knabe will push sales of his pianos, he will control the southern market by 1860, and by the time he dies in 1864 the Knabe Piano Company will be the largest Baltimore manufacturing facility of any kind (*see* Chickering, 1823; Steinway, 1859).

The Bayswater Hippodrome opened June 3 in England is the world's first steeplechase racecourse.

Procter & Gamble Company is founded in Cincinnati by English-American candlemaker William Procter, 35, and his Irish-American soap-boiler brother-in-law James Gamble, 34, who peddle candles in the streets and to the Ohio River trade. They gross $50,000 their first year despite competition from 11 local soap and candle factories and from housewives who make their own soap from grease, fat, and clean wood ashes boiled in backyard kettles (*see* Ivory Soap, 1878).

Shillito's opens in Cincinnati under the name McLaughlin and Shillito, a dry goods store whose sole proprietor by 1857 will be John Shillito, now 21 (*see* Federated, 1929).

Tiffany & Co. has its beginnings in a New York "Stationery and Fancy Goods Store" that opens September 18 near City Hall. Merchant Charles Lewis Tiffany, 25, has borrowed $1,000 from his father in Connecticut, he and his partner John B. Young stock Chinese bric-a-brac, pottery, and umbrellas as well as stationery, total receipts for the first 3 days are $4.98, profits the first week total only 33 cents, but the firm will grow to be one of the world's most prestigious jewelry retailers. The store will move up to 271 Broadway in 1847, Tiffany will start manufacturing his own jewelry in 1848 and will add gold jewelry that year, he will open a Paris branch in 1850, he will adopt the firm name Tiffany & Co. in 1853, and he will open a London branch in 1868 (*see* Tiffany Diamond, 1878; Preakness Woodlawn Vase, 1873; Louis Comfort Tiffany, 1878).

Buildings and paved streets occupy only one-sixth of Manhattan Island; the rest remains planted in farms and gardens.

London completes the Thames Embankment.

London's Buckingham Palace will be the royal residence of the new queen, Victoria (above), and her successors. John Nash completed the palace last year in a Palladian-style reconstruction of a mansion built in 1704 for the duke of Buckingham, but the late William IV disliked the palace (*see* 1856).

Famine strikes Japan but the Tokugawa shogun Ieyushi refuses to open storehouses at Osaka to the starving people. A riot led by the former priest Heihachiro Oshio ends with 40 percent of Osaka in ashes, and the riots spread throughout Japan, but the shogun resists appeals to ease tax burdens on farmers who have little or no cash crop.

Charles Dickens describes widespread hunger among Britain's urban poor in early installments of his novel *Oliver Twist*. "Please, sir, I want some more," says young Oliver, as the Industrial Revolution's dislocation of society creates problems in English agriculture.

 A self-polishing steel plow that can break the heavy sod of the Illinois and Iowa prairie is fashioned by Vermont-born blacksmith John Deere, 32, at Grand Detour, Ill. Deere chisels the teeth off a discarded circular saw blade of Sheffield steel, he creates a plow with the proper moldboard curve for breaking the sod, and by saving farmers from having to pull their plows out of furrows for repeated cleaning with wooden paddles, the Deere plow will permit efficient farming in vast areas that have defied earlier efforts (*see* 1839).

The first steam-powered threshing machine is patented by Winthrop, Maine, inventors John A. Pitts and Hiram Abial Pitts whose machine separates grain from its straw and chaff (*see* Case, 1842).

The shakeout of land speculators in the economic depression (above) makes more U.S. farmland available for real farmers.

 Scottish chemist Andrew Ure, 59, dismisses the idea that Britain's factory children may have rickets for lack of sunlight. Gaslight is more progressive and quite as healthy, says Ure (*see* Gas Light and Coke Company, 1819; Steenbock, 1923).

 Tetley Tea is introduced at Huddersfield, England, where local entrepreneurs Joseph and Edward Tetley open a shop under the name Tetley Brothers—Dealers in Tea. The two have peddled their tea from a packhorse across the Yorkshire moors (*see* 1856).

Lea & Perrins Worcestershire Sauce is introduced by English chemists (pharmacists) John Wheeley Lea and William Perrins who opened a shop at 68 Broad Street in Worcester in 1823 and have sold groceries and toiletries as well as pharmaceuticals. The zesty sauce contains vinegar, oil, and spices mixed to a recipe furnished by a Lord Sandys, formerly governor of Bengal, and aged until palatable.

Some 1,200 U.S. automated flour mills produce 2 million bushels of flour in the area west of the Alleghenies, with more millions being milled by millers on the eastern seaboard who have been licensed to use the 1790 Oliver Evans patent or who infringe on it.

Treatise on Bread and Breadmaking by Sylvester Graham inveighs against refined wheat flour. Graham societies are formed and Graham hotels open in some U.S. cities as thousands of Americans follow vegetarian diets, eating day-old whole-grain bread, oatmeal gruel, beans and boiled rice prepared without salt (Graham says condiments may inflame a thirst for alcohol), and cold puddings (*see* 1829).

Society in America by English novelist-economist Harriet Martineau, 35, says of corn on the cob, "The greatest drawback is the way in which it is necessary to eat it . . . It looks awkward enough: but what is to be done? Surrendering such a vegetable from considerations of grace is not to be thought of." (Martineau visited the United States from 1834 to 1836).

"The cookery in the United States is exactly what it is and must be everywhere else—in a ratio with the degree of refinement of the population," writes Frederick Marryat of 1836 *Mr. Midshipman Easy* fame. "In the principal cities you will meet with as good cookery in private houses as you will in London, or even Paris."

1838 The first transatlantic crossings by ships powered entirely by steam are completed April 23 as two British steamers arrive at New York. The 703-ton S.S. *Sirius*, 19 days out of London, has been used until now only for cross-channel service while the 1,440-ton S.S. *Great Western*, 15 days out of Bristol, is larger and faster. Both have been designed by English engineer Isambard Kingdom Brunel, 32 (*see* surface condenser, 1830; Cunard, 1840).

The S.S. *Sirius* (above) is owned by a navigation company founded by Scottish merchant Macgregor Laird, 31, who 5 years ago organized an expedition to travel up the Niger River, an ill-fated affair in which his associate Richard Lemon Lander was mortally wounded by African natives.

The S.S. *Great Western* (above) has been named for the Great Western Railway which I. K. Brunel has been serving as chief engineer, and it is the first wooden steamship to cross the Atlantic. Brunel's father is at work on the Thames tunnel from Wapping to Rotherhithe and the younger Brunel has introduced broad gauge tracks and has constructed the Great Western's viaducts, tunnels, and bridges, including the Royal Albert Bridge across the Tmar River into Cornwall.

The first Russian railway opens to link St. Petersburg with the czar's summer palace at Tsarskoe Selo.

 British troops invade Afghanistan and advance to Kandahar. The 54-year-old governor-general of India George Eden, earl of Auckland, has sent in the troops out of exaggerated fears of Russian influence. They move on to Ghazni and Kabul, they depose the Barakzai emir Dost Mohammed who took power in 1834, and they take him to India as a prisoner (*see* 1839).

The Battle of Blood River December 16 in Natal gives Afrikaner forces a victory over Zulu natives. The Boers kill more than 3,000 Zulus and eliminate the main threat to their settlements.

 A "People's Charter" published in London May 8 calls for universal suffrage without property qualifications. William Lovett has founded the London Workingmen's Association to mobilize Britons disappointed by the Reform Bill of 1832. The charter he

1838 (cont.) has drafted contains Six Points which include payment of Members of Parliament, equal electoral areas, and other reforms, and it wins approval August 8 at a great meeting held on Newhall Hill 6 weeks after the coronation of Queen Victoria.

Britain applies the Poor Law of 1834 to Ireland and adds to the hardship of the country's famine (below). Designed to discourage paupers from seeking relief, the Poor Law makes work inside the workhouse worse than the most unpleasant sort of work to be found on the outside, and it has the effect of stimulating emigration.

The "underground railway" organized by U.S. abolitionists transports southern slaves to freedom in Canada, but slaving interests at Philadelphia work on the fears of Irish immigrants and other working people who worry that freed slaves may take their jobs. A Philadelphia mob burns down Pennsylvania Hall May 17 in an effort to thwart antislavery meetings.

The Trail of Tears takes more than 14,000 members of the Cherokee Nation from tribal lands in Georgia, Alabama, and Tennessee 800 miles westward along the Tennessee, Ohio, Mississippi, and Arkansas Rivers to Little Rock and thence to Indian territory west of the Red River. Escorted with their horses and oxen by troops under the command of General Winfield Scott, the Cherokee journey by wagon and keelboat for anywhere from 93 to 139 days, an estimated 4,000—mostly infants, children, and old people—die en route of measles, whooping cough, pneumonia, pleurisy, tuberculosis, and pellagra, and the last contingents will not reach Indian territory until March 25 of next year (some have refused to budge) (*see* 1831; 1832).

 St. Paul, Minn., has its beginnings in a settlement made by French-Canadian trapper Pierre Parrant who settles in the upper Mississippi Valley as a squatter at Fort Snelling, formerly Fort Anthony (*see* 1819). Parrant will be removed from the reservation with other squatters in 1840, and the neighboring squatter settlement will be named St. Paul the following year by missionary Lucian Galtier (*see* Minneapolis, 1847).

Kansas City is founded in November on a hill overlooking a bend in the Missouri River by Missouri frontier pioneers who include John McCoy, William Sublette, William Chick, and William Gillis. Their settlement is near Westport Landing, founded earlier as a post for the Indian fur trade and as an outfitting station for wagons to Santa Fe and Oregon Territory.

💲 An Anti-Corn Law league to oppose British protectionism is founded at Manchester by Lancashire calico printer Richard Cobden, 34 (*see* 1839).

Philadelphia's Drexel & Co. banking house has its beginnings in a brokerage firm founded by Austrian-American portrait painter Francis Martin Drexel, 46 (*see* Morgan, 1871).

 The cell theory of physiology is formulated at Jena by German botanist Matthias Jakob Schleiden, 34 (*see* 1858).

The word "protoplasm" to denote the substance of a cell body as differentiated from the cell nucleus is used for the first time by German botanist Hugo von Mohl, 33 (*see* Purkinje, 1840).

Fermentation is shown to be dependent on yeast cells by French physician Charles Cagniard de la Tour, 61 (*see* Pasteur, 1857).

Alfried Krupp, 26, visits Sheffield, England, and meets J. A. Henckel, founder of a steel mill in the Ruhr valley town of Solingen. Krupp is a son of Friedrich whose Fried. Krupp of Essen is turning out tableware on a hand mill devised by Alfried's brother Hermann (*see* 1816; 1851).

Cheney Brothers Silk Manufacturing Company has its beginnings January 2 at South Manchester, Conn., where entrepreneurs Ralph Cheney, 31, Ward, 24, Rush, 22, and Frank, 20, are joined by E. H. Arnold in putting up $50,000 to start the Mount Nebo Silk Mill. The factory opened March 31 is powered by a mill-race wheel and will be the first commercially successful U.S. silk mill. The monthly *Silk Growers' Manual* published by the firm beginning in July will grow to have a circulation of 10,000 as Americans rush to cultivate the fast-growing Chinese mulberry tree introduced at Baltimore in 1826, but a blight will strike the trees in 1844, and the native industry will be forced to depend on imported raw silk.

D. Appleton & Co. publishers is founded at New York by former dry goods merchant Daniel Appleton, 53, and his son W. H. Appleton, 24, who will open a London branch next year. By the time D. Appleton dies in 1849 his five sons will be running the firm, and by 1865 it will be second only to Harper Bros. (*see* 1817; Appleton-Century, 1933)

Nonfiction *Casanova's Memoirs Ecrits par Lui-Même*, twelfth and final volume. The first appeared in 1826, some 28 years after the roué's death at age 73 (*see* 1755).

Fiction *Oliver Twist, or the Parish Boy's Progress* by Charles Dickens who has serialized the work in his *Bentley's Miscellany* and whose sentimental story of Fagin, Bill Sykes, the Artful Dodger, and young Oliver is intended in part as an exposé of Poor Law evils. Illustrations are by caricaturist George Cruikshank, 47, who illustrated the 1836 Dickens book *Sketches by 'Boz'*; "Ligeia" by Edgar Allan Poe, whose melodramatic short story appears in the September issue of the Baltimore *American Museum* (Poe married his cousin Virginia, now 15, 2 years ago); *The Narrative of Arthur Gordon Pym* by Edgar Allan Poe; *Münchhausen* by German novelist Karl Leberecht Immerman, 42, introduces the mendacious baron who personifies the attitudes Immerman opposes with an idealized image of patriotic peasant morality; French novelist George Sand of 1832 *Indiana* fame begins a

434

9-year liaison with composer Frederic Chopin 4 years after her estrangement from poet-playwright Alfred de Musset who has taken to drink after failures to achieve reconciliation (he will never recover but despair has inspired his most creative work). Chopin at 28 is, like Musset, 6 years younger than George Sand who continues to have her novels published while scandalizing Europe with her masculine attire and cigar smoking.

 Painting *Medea* by Eugène Delacroix who is rejected for membership in the French Institute.

 Theater *Ruy Blas* by Victor Hugo 11/8 at the Théâtre de la Renaissance, Paris.

Opera *Benvenuto Cellini* 9/10 at the Paris Opéra, with music by Hector Berlioz.

Popular songs "Vive la Compagnie" is published at Leipzig as a French drinking song; "Annie Laurie" by Scottish composer Alicia Ann Spottiswoode, 28, Lady John Scott, lyrics from the 1700 poem by William Douglas; "Flow Gently, Sweet Afton" by Philadelphia composer James E. Spilman, lyrics from the 1792 poem "Afton Water" by Robert Burns.

 Goshen, N.Y., has its first trotting race, and a harness racing tradition is begun.

 Houston's Rice dry goods store opens in the Texas Republic. Massachusetts-born merchant William Marsh Rice, 22, will develop his enterprise into a large export-import and retail business (*see* Rice Institute, 1912).

 New York's Lord & Taylor moves into a four-story building at 61–63 Catherine Street, offering "Irish linens, sheeting, diapers, shawls, laces, gloves, silk and cotton hosiery, &c. &c. &c." (*see* 1826; 1853).

New York's numbered streets are divided into east numbers and west numbers according to which side of Fifth Avenue they are on.

 Regent's Park opens to the London public on 410 acres of pastureland known as Marylebone Park Fields until the park was laid out in 1812.

 Famine kills thousands in the north of Ireland as crops fail (*see* 1845).

The word "protein" is coined by Dutch chemist Gerard Johann Mulder, 36, who adapts a Greek word meaning "of the first importance" (*see* 1820; 1827; 1854).

Iron in the blood is what enables the blood to absorb so much oxygen, concludes Jöns Jakob Berzelius who pioneers an understanding of hemoglobin.

 Gas ovens are installed at London's Reform Club (*see* 1832; Sharp, 1826). Coal or wood is the common cooking fuel in most of the world, but Arab nomads use camel chips, American Indians use buffalo chips, and Eskimos use blubber oil.

A bottled chow chow mustard pickle is introduced by London's 132-year-old firm Crosse & Blackwell which has shifted in the past 20 years from supplying produce to preserving fruit, vegetables, and meat for use aboard ships bound for distant outposts of the empire. Jars and tins of truffled hare pâté from the Perigord, truffled woodcock, and other delicacies are shipped out to colonial officers.

New York's Schaefer beer has its beginnings as Prussian brewery worker Frederick Schaefer, 21, of Wetzlar emigrates to New York and obtains a position with a brewery on Broadway between 18th and 19th Streets. Schaefer and his younger brother Maximilian will purchase the brewery in 1842 and will make F. and M. Schaefer one of the first U.S. breweries to produce lager beer.

Fresh menus are printed daily at New York's 2-year-old Astor House, writes Captain Frederick Marryat (*see* 1837; Delmonico's, 1836). Marryat has arrived in the city a few months after the economic crisis of 1837 in which one-third of all New Yorkers who subsisted by manual labor were unemployed and at least 10,000 were made dependent on almshouses which were unable to prevent many from starving to death.

1839 *Report on the Affairs of British North America* by the first earl of Durham John George Lambton, 48, proposes the union of Upper and Lower Canada and the granting of governmental responsibilities to the Canadians. Lord Durham placated the rebels 2 years ago as governor-general, the report published February 11 attempts to justify the position he took before his resignation last year, and Lord John Russell introduces a resolution in Parliament June 20 to implement Durham's recommendations (*see* 1840).

Willem I of the Netherlands recognizes Belgian independence April 19. He permits the Belgians to take the western part of Luxembourg (the rest of Luxembourg remains a grand duchy with the Dutch king as grand duke).

Ottoman forces invade Syria in April to contest the claims of the 70-year-old Egyptian viceroy Mohammed Ali (*see* 1805). His general Ibrahim Pasha defeats the sultan's forces June 24 at the Battle of Nezib.

The Ottoman sultan Mahmud II dies July 1 at age 54 as his fleet surrenders voluntarily at Alexandria. Greece has won independence in Mahmud's 31-year reign, he is succeeded by his 16-year-old son, who continues the war that Mahmud has started with the Egyptian viceroy, and the new sultan will reign until 1861 as Abdul Mejid.

The Serbian prince Miloš Obrenović abdicates under pressure from opponents who have conspired with the Russians to curb the autocratic powers exercised by Miloš since 1817. He is succeeded by his 20-year-old son Milan, who rules until his untimely death late in the year, and then by his 14-year-old son who will reign until 1842 as Michael III Obrenović.

The British-Afghan War that began last year continues as the British escort the unpopular Shah Shuja, who reigned from 1803 to 1810, to Kabul and restore

1839 (cont.) him to power in place of Dost Mohammed. Agitation rises against British influence, and Afghan patriots work to restore Dost Mohammed.

An Opium War between China and Britain begins in November after Chinese official Lin Tse-hsu, 54, orders the destruction of some $6 million worth of illegal Indian opium stored by foreign merchants in Canton warehouses. Western physicians make wide use of opium but the East India Company has encouraged addiction to the poppy derivative to keep its Indian and Chinese workers subdued (*see* Hong Kong, 1842).

Denmark's Frederick VI dies December 3 at age 71 after a 31-year reign (plus 24 years as regent) in which Norway has been lost to Sweden (*see* 1814). Frederick is succeeded by his 53-year-old nephew who will reign until 1848 as Christian VIII.

💲 Britain's Anti-Corn Law League gains power by amalgamating opposition groups (*see* 1838). Cobden's league attracts workers to its cause by promising that a removal of tariffs on foreign grain will reduce food prices, give Britons more money to buy clothing, and thus create more domestic demand and more jobs in the textile industry. Promoters of the league know that lowering food prices will enable them to lower wages (*see* 1841; 1846).

Economic depression in the United States in the next few years will force Maryland and Pennsylvania to default in their interest payments to British and European bondholders.

✊ "American Slavery as It Is" by Ohio evangelist-abolitionist Theodore Dwight Weld, 35, is published as a tract favoring emancipation.

A conciliatory address against militant abolitionism is delivered by Kentucky's Henry Clay who has been trying for 15 years to gain the presidency. Consulting others before making the speech, Clay is told that it may offend ultras of both parties, but he replies, "I trust the sentiments and opinions are correct; I had rather be right than be president."

"To each according to his needs, from each according to his abilities," writes French socialist leader (Jean Joseph Charles) Louis Blanc, 28, in his essay "L'Organisation du Travail." Journalist Blanc founds *Revue du Progrès* to promote his socialist doctrines.

∞ Nauvoo, Ill. gets its name and becomes the largest city in the state as some 10,000 Mormons settle at a town on the Mississippi formerly called Commerce. The Mormons have been driven from Missouri into Illinois (*see* 1830; Brigham Young, 1846).

New England clergyman John Humphrey Noyes, 28, establishes a Bible class at Putney, Vt., where he will soon urge the establishment of a communal society (*see* Putney Community, 1846).

⚡ Steam engines are introduced on the New York and Harlem Railroad (*see* 1837; Vanderbilt, 1863).

Adams Express Company has its origins in an express service started by William Frederick Harnden, 27, who carries packages in a carpetbag on the railroads between New York and Boston.

The Chesapeake and Ohio Canal started in 1828 reaches 134 miles west of Georgetown but runs into financial difficulties (*see* 1850).

Italy gets her first railway as an 8-kilometer line opens between Naples and Portici (*see* 1859).

The first real bicycle is invented at Dumfries, Scotland, by local blacksmith Kirkpatrick MacMillan, 29, of Courthill who adds a pedal system and a brake to the frame and wheels designed by Sauerbroun and Niepce in 1816. MacMillan's 57-pound bike with its 32-inch iron-tired front wheel and 42-inch rear wheel make it possible for the first time for a person to travel under his own power faster than he can run. (*see* Michaux, 1861).

✸ Effective use of rubber is pioneered by former Philadelphia hardware merchant Charles Goodyear, 39, who has obtained rights to a sulfur process for treating rubber, has accidentally overheated a mixture of rubber, sulfur, and white lead, and stumbles on a way to "vulcanize" rubber to make a hard and durable substance that chars but does not melt. Goodyear has sold the patent on his father Amasa Goodyear's pitchfork (the first steel-tine pitchfork) to finance his experiments with raw rubber, which has been used to some extent earlier as in Macintosh raincoats (*see* 1823). Rubber's commercial value has been limited by its tendency to become sticky in hot weather and to lose its elasticity in cold weather, but Goodyear's vulcanization process will extend its uses (*see* 1844).

A power loom to weave two-ply ingrain carpets is devised by Massachusetts inventor Erastus Brigham Bigelow, 25 (*see* 1845; Horrocks, 1813).

A journal box, or housing, for the portion of a shaft or axle contained by a plain bearing is patented by Massachusetts inventor Isaac Babbitt, 40, who suggests that the box be lined with an alloy of tin, antimony, and copper that will be called Babbitt's metal.

A steam hammer that will make possible larger forgings without loss of precision is invented by Scottish engineer James Nasmyth, 31, who will patent his steam hammer in 1842.

Patek Philippe watches are introduced at Geneva, Switzerland.

⌛ *Microscopic Investigations on the Accordance in the Structure and Growth of Plants and Animals* by German naturalists Theodor Schwann and Matthias Jakob Schleiden is an exegesis of the cell theory (*see* 1835; 1838).

Ozone is discovered and named by German-Swiss chemist Christian F. Schönbein, 40.

Lanthanium is isolated as a new metallic element by Swedish chemist Carl Gustav Mosander, 42.

436

The first state-supported normal school (teacher's college) is founded at Lexington, Mass., through the efforts of Board of Education secretary Horace Mann, 33 (*see* 1852).

Boston University is founded.

The University of Missouri is founded.

Virginia Military Institute (VMI) is founded at Lexington.

Boston's Lowell Institute is founded by John Lowell, Jr., 70, to provide free lectures by eminent scholars.

Fiction *The Charterhouse of Parma (La Chartreuse de Perme)* by Stendhal who has written the novel of passion and political adventure in 7 weeks after 7 years of thought; *Nicholas Nickleby* by Charles Dickens who has serialized the novel for 20 months and has introduced readers to the bad education administered by the exploitive Mr. Squeers of Dotheboys Hall, an institution derived from the author's childhood experience; "The Fall of the House of Usher" by Edgar Allan Poe whose melodramatic tale of an intellectual confronted with the death of a beautiful woman appears in the September issue of *Burton's Gentleman's* magazine.

Poetry *Voices of the Night* by Harvard language professor Henry Wadsworth Longfellow, 32. His poem "A Psalm of Life" begins, "Tell me not, in mournful numbers,/ Life is but an empty dream!—/ For the soul is dead that slumbers,/ And things are not what they seem./ Life is real! Life is earnest!/ And the grave is not its goal . . ./ Let us, then, be up and doing,/ With a heart for any fate. . . ."

Painting *Suzanne au Bain* and *Venus Anadymone* by French painter Théodore Chassériau, 19; *Dignity and Impudence* by Edwin H. Landseer.

The Daguerrotype process of photographic reproduction discovered by Louis Daguerre in 1829 is described to a meeting of the French Academy of Arts and Sciences, August 19, but English inventor William Henry Fox Talbott, 39, claims that he produced photographs earlier than Daguerre using a camera obscura with silver chloride and common salt or potassium iodide as fixing agents. Talbot soon afterwards reveals a Calotype process that involves use of silver iodide with sodium thiosulfate used to fix the image which is a reverse image or "negative" (*see* Herschel, 1840).

The first Daguerrotype portraits to be produced in America are made by telegraph pioneer Samuel F. B. Morse who returns from a visit to Paris with the process he has learned from Daguerre. Morse teams up with English-American physician-scientist John William Draper, 28, who 3 years ago obtained his M.D. from the University of Pennsylvania and who will make important contributions to photography, photochemistry, radiant energy, and the electric telegraph (*see* 1837; telegraph line, 1843).

Opera *Oberto Conte di San Bonifacio* 11/17 at Milan's Teatro alla Scala, with music by Italian composer Giuseppe Verdi, 26.

First performances *Romeo and Juliet* Symphony by Hector Berlioz 11/24 at the Paris Conservatoire.

England's Grand National Steeplechase has its first running at Aintree near Liverpool.

Rugby rules are devised by Cambridge University student Arthur Fell (*see* Ellis, 1823).

Baseball rules are devised by West Point cadet Abner Doubleday, 19, of Cooperstown, N.Y., whose dicta call for a diamond-shaped field and two teams of nine players each (*see* 1846). England's Lady Hervey mentioned the game in a letter of November, 1784, Jane Austen mentioned it in her novel *Northanger Abbey,* Oliver Wendell Holmes played it at Harvard before his graduation in 1829, and it is only distantly related to cricket (*see* 1788).

Kingscote at Newport, R.I., is completed by English-American architect Richard Upjohn, 37, for George Noble Jones of Savannah. The house on Bellevue Avenue will be acquired by William Henry King with money acquired in the tea trade, and it will be followed by more imposing "cottages" as Newport becomes a favored summer resort for the rich.

The heath hen *Tympanuchus cupido cupido* once common throughout New England is now found only on Martha's Vineyard, Mass. A gamebird closely related to the prairie chicken, the heath hen was once an important food source, but its numbers have been reduced by market hunters (*see* 1929).

Sugar production in Jamaica, British West Indies, will fall in the next two decades to between 20,000 and 25,000 tons per year, down from 70,000 tons in 1821, as a consequence of the end of slavery.

Samuel F. B. Morse persuaded congressmen to back him in a test of the telegraph that would speed communications.

1839 (cont.) John Deere produces 10 steel plows (*see* 1838; 1842).

Congress appropriates $1,000 for the first free distribution of seeds to U.S. farmers.

Lectures on the Science of Life by Sylvester Graham urges dietary measures for good health in two volumes. Graham blames American dyspepsia and sallow complexion on fried meat, alcohol, eating too fast, and the use of "unnatural," refined wheat flour. Espousing vegetarianism, he urges readers to eat fruits, vegetables, and unbolted (unsifted) whole wheat flour in bread that is slightly stale and is to be chewed thoroughly to promote good digestion, prevent alcoholism, and diminish the sex urge.

A flour mill that employs rollers rather than millstones is built at Budapest, Hungary, by Swiss engineer Jacob Sulzberger (*see* 1833; 1870).

Some 95 chests of Assam tea arrive at London and are sold at auction. Unlike green China tea, the leaves from India are fermented and the new black tea, less astringent than green tea, begins to gain popularity (*see* 1823; duchess of Bedford, 1840).

French chef Alexis Soyer becomes chef of London's Reform Club. Soyer fled France in the 1830 revolution and has served some of England's great houses (*see* 1847).

1840 Queen Victoria marries her first cousin Albert February 10 wearing only items of British manufacture. Her husband, 3 months her junior, is a son of the duke of Saxe-Coburg-Gotha and a nephew of the king of the Belgians Leopold I.

Prussia's Friedrich Wilhelm III dies June 7 at age 69 after a reign of more than 42 years. He is succeeded by his 44-year-old son who will reign until 1861 as Friedrich Wilhelm IV.

The Treaty of London July 15 joins Britain, Austria, Prussia, and Russia against the Egyptian viceroy Mohammed Ali. The Allies offer the pasha hereditary rule of Egypt and lifetime possession of Syria on condition that he give up northern Syria, Mecca, Medina, and Crete and that he return the Ottoman fleet. He rejects the offer, the British induce the boy sultan Abdul Mejid to depose the viceroy, Paris panics at news of the treaty, the 43-year-old minister of foreign affairs Louis Adolphe Thiers urges support of Mohammed Ali, and French newspapers echo his views.

British gunboats commanded by Sir Robert Stopford bombard Beirut September 9, and the British land troops under the command of Sir Charles James Napier, 57, a veteran of the American Revolution, the war of Greek independence, and the peninsular war against Napoleon.

Beirut falls to General Napier (above) October 10, France's Louis Philippe decides not to support Mohammed Ali, Thiers resigns October 20, Acre falls to the British November 3, and Napier concludes the Convention of Alexandria November 27. Mohammed Ali agrees to return the Ottoman fleet and to give up all claims to Syria in return for hereditary rule of Egypt.

Willem I of the Netherlands abdicates October 7 at age 68 after a 26-year reign in order to marry the Roman Catholic Belgian countess d'Oultremont who is unpopular with the Dutch. His 47-year-old son succeeds him and will reign until 1849 as Willem II.

The Union Act passed by Parliament July 23 unites Upper and Lower Canada, adopts various administrative reforms, but avoids the issue of government responsibility in Canada. Parliament acts in response to last year's report by Lord Durham who dies July 28 at age 48 (*see* British North American Act, 1867).

William Henry Harrison wins election to the U.S. presidency as Whigs sing, "Oh have you heard how Old Maine went?/ She went hell-bent for Governor Kent,/ And Tippecanoe and Tyler too." The hero of the 1811 Battle of Tippecanoe wins 234 electoral votes to Martin Van Buren's 60 (but *see* 1841).

The World's Anti-Slavery Convention opens at London, but Boston abolitionist William Garrison refuses to attend, protesting the exclusion of women (*see* 1831). The U.S. antislavery movement has split into two factions in the past year largely because of Garrison's advocacy of women's rights, including their right to participate in the antislavery movement (*see* first Women's Rights Convention, 1848).

"Property is theft" ("la propriété, c'est le vol"), writes French socialist Pierre Joseph Proudhon, 31, in his treatise "What Is Property?" ("Qu'est ce-que la propriété?").

"On the Production of Heat by Voltaic Electricity" by English physicist James Prescot Joule, 22, describes efforts to measure electric current by exact quantitative data (*see* Volta, 1800). Joule's paper announces the law that the rate at which heat is produced in any part of an electric circuit is measured by the product of the square of the current and the resistance of that part of the circuit. Joule will also formulate the first law of thermodynamics—the conservation of energy law states that energy can be converted from one form to another but cannot be destroyed. A unit of energy will be named the joule in his honor (*see* Clausius, 1850; Thomson, 1851).

Zoology of the Voyage of the Beagle by Charles Darwin has no reference to the idea that struck Darwin 2 years ago when he read the T. R. Malthus *Essay on Population* of 1798. Darwin realized that living creatures in nature must compete with each other for sustenance and that nature kills off those which cannot compete, but he will not commit the notion to paper, even in pencil, for another 2 years (*see* 1831; Wallace, 1848; Spencer, 1852).

Czech physiologist Johannes Evangelista Purkinje, 53, at Breslau proposes that the word "protoplasm" be applied to the formative material of young animal embryos (*see* von Mohl, 1838).

Handbuch der Physiologie des Menschen by German physiologist Johannes Peter Müller, 39, revives ideas that go back to Aristotle and includes a reaffirmation of spontaneous generation (*see* Redi, 1668). But Müller does introduce some sound new ideas about nervous energy, reflex movements, gland structures, the embryonic development of sex organs, and other matters.

A new worldwide cholera epidemic begins. It will kill millions in the next 22 years (*see* 1830; London, 1849).

The Baltimore College of Dental Surgery established in Maryland is the first regular U.S. dental school. The American Society of Dental Surgeons is organized. The *American Journal of Dental Science* begins publication (*see* calcium, below).

The wooden steamship *Britannia* arrives at Boston on the first voyage of the government-subsidized Royal Mail Steam Packet Company established last year by Nova Scotia-born shipper Samuel Cunard, 43, in association with George and James Burns of Glasgow and David M'Iver of Liverpool. Cunard will introduce iron steamers in 1855 and in 1862 will replace paddle wheels with screw propellors to break the Black Ball line's dominance of the transatlantic packet trade and to break New York's monopoly in the trade.

More than 200 steamboats ply the Mississippi, double the number in the mid-1820s. New Orleans is the fourth largest city in America and will overtake New York in the next 10 years in volume of shipping as more than half the nation's exports move out of New Orleans.

U.S. canals cover 3,300 miles, and the nation has 2,816 miles of operating railway versus 1,331 in the United Kingdom and fewer than 300 miles in France. More than 300 U.S. railroad companies are in operation and tracks vary in gauge from 6 feet down to 4 feet 8.5 inches (*see* B&O, 1828).

From New York to Boston is an overnight steamer trip or a 6-hour train journey and costs $7.

From New York to Philadelphia by train and ferry takes 6.5 hours, down from 3 days in 1817, but it takes longer when the Delaware River freezes over, halting train-ferry service and forcing passengers to walk across the ice.

The United States has nearly 20 millionaires (*see* 1892; John Law, 1719).

The world's first adhesive postage stamps go on sale in Britain May 1 for use beginning May 6 (*see* Hill, 1837). The Penny Blacks bearing the head of Queen Victoria have been printed by U.S. inventor Jacob Perkins of 1834 compression machine fame who in 1819 developed a process and the necessary equipment for printing bank notes and has established a factory in England for printing securities. 64 million of the new stamps will be printed, and twice as many

letters are posted this year as were mailed in 1839, but British postal revenues fall drastically and will not regain their 1839 level until 1875 (*see* United States, 1847; perforating machine, 1854).

The *Cincinnati Times* is started by publisher Calvin W. Starbuck whose newspaper will have an unprecedented circulation of 125,000 and will go to nearly every post office in the United States and Canada (*see* Enquirer, 1841).

The *Memphis Commercial-Appeal* begins publication as a daily newspaper,

Fiction *Two Years Before the Mast* by Boston novelist Richard Henry Dana, 25, who sailed on a 150-day voyage aboard the brig *Pilgrim* round Cape Horn to California in 1834, returned aboard the ship *Alert* in 1836, and has had his book published anonymously; *The Pathfinder* by James Fenimore Cooper who has received wide criticism for his 1838 novels *Homeward Bound* and *Home as Found* and for his 1838 nonfiction work *The American Democrat*. Cooper has won most of the libel suits brought against him and has helped establish effective rules of libel in U.S. courts; *Tales of the Grotesque and Arabesque* by Edgar Allan Poe; *A Hero of Our Time* (*Geroi Nashevo Vremeni*) by Mikhail Lermontov.

Poetry *The Novice* (*Mtsyri*) by Mikhail Lermontov who is banished to the Caucasus once again after a duel with the son of the French ambassador; "Sordello" by Robert Browning.

Painting *Flight into Egypt* by Jean Baptiste Camille Corot; *Entry of the Crusaders into Constantinople* by Eugène Delacroix; *Christ au Jardin des Oliviers* by Théodore Chassériau.

Photography is advanced by English astronomer Frederick William Herschel, 48, whose father discovered the planet Uranus in 1781 and who first uses the word "negative" to describe the reverse image obtained last year by Fox Talbot. Talbot has pioneered the true photographic development process by waxing or oiling paper on the side opposite to the image, thus obtaining true copies (positives) of any negative by contact printing on another piece of sensitized paper, but his Calotypes take a long time and require specially constructed paper. The solvent power of sodium hyposulfite (hypo) on silver salts is discovered by Herschel, who invented contact lenses at age 35 (*see* Archer, 1851).

Theater *The Shoemaker and the King* (*El Zapatero y el Rey*), part I, by Spanish playwright Jose Zorilla y Moral, 22, 3/14 at Madrid's Teatro El Principe; *Judith* by German playwright Christian Friedrich Hebbel, 27, 7/6 at Berlin's Hoftheater; *The Glass of Water, or Causes and Effects* (*Le Verre d'Eau, ou les Effects et les Causes*) by Eugène Scribe 11/17 at the Théâtre Française, Paris.

Opera *The Daughter of the Regiment* (*La Figlia del Reggimento*) 2/11 at the Opéra-Comique in Paris, is presented under the title *La Fille du Régi-*

1840 *(cont.) ment* with music by Gaetano Donizetti; *The Favorite* (*La Favorita*) 12/2 at the Paris Grand Opéra, with music by Gaetano Donizetti.

The saxophone is invented by Belgian musical instrument maker Antoine Joseph Sax, 26, who is known as Adolphe.

Popular songs "The Two Grenadiers" ("Die beiden Grenadiere") by German composer Robert Schumann, 30, lyrics by Heinrich Heine; "Rocked in the Cradle of the Deep" by English composer Joseph Philip Knight, 28, lyrics by Emma Willard who retired 2 years ago from her Emma Willard School.

The polka is introduced to the United States by Viennese ballet dancer Fanny Elssler, 30, who introduced the dance to the Paris stage 6 years ago and who begins a U.S. tour that will add to her fortune.

Manufacture of the McCormick reaper begins with improvements added by McCormick to his original 1831 machine (*see* 1834; 1847).

A U.S. farmer requires 233 man-hours to produce 100 bushels of wheat using primitive plow and harvesting cradle, down from 300 hours in 1831 (*see* 1920).

Grapefruit trees are introduced into Florida by Don Philippe, a Spanish nobleman (*see* Lunan, 1814; sweeter grapefruit, 1900).

The first important U.S. breeding herd of quick-fattening Hereford cattle is established with stock imported from Britain by Erasmus Corning and William H. Sotham at Albany, N.Y. (*see* 1817).

The first Dutch belted cows to be seen in the United States are imported by showman P. T. Barnum who exhibits them as curiosities (*see* 1835; 1842).

Vermont and New Hampshire have some 2 million sheep, and their farmers are engaged in a profitable wool-producing industry (*see* clothing makers, 1862).

Oyster canning begins at Baltimore using bivalves from Chesapeake Bay.

France sends a naval vessel into Arcachon Bay to guard the bay's oysters from draggers and rakers (*see* 1759; Coste, 1853).

The need of calcium for proper bone development is demonstrated by Swiss chemist Charles J. Choss (*see* Humphry Davy, 1808; vitamin D, 1922).

Afternoon tea is introduced by Anna, the duchess of Bedford. The tea interval will become a lasting British tradition, but the English still drink more coffee than tea (*see* 1839; 1850; 1869).

Carling Brewing and Malting Company, Ltd., is started by London, Ontario, brewer Thomas Carling (*see* Labatt, 1847).

Scots-American Peter Ballantine starts a brewery on the Passaic River at Newark, N. J., that will brew only ale until 1880 but by 1914 will be brewing half a million barrels of beer and ale each year.

Durgin Park's opens in Boston's North Market Street where the restaurant will continue for more than 135 years. Venison, bear steak, Indian pudding, and other specialties are served at common tables.

Antoine's Restaurant has its beginnings in the Pension Alciatore founded in the French quarter of New Orleans by French-American chef Antoine Alciatore (*see* Oysters Rockefeller, 1899).

 Some 207,000 Irish and 76,000 English emigrants leave for the United States.

New York is a city of more than 312,000, up from fewer than 124,000 in 1820, but the U.S. population remains 90 percent rural.

1841 William Henry Harrison dies of pneumonia April 4 at age 68 just 1 month after taking office as U.S. president. He is succeeded by his 51-year-old vice president John Tyler.

The Egyptian viceroy Mohammed Ali agrees to give up Crete and Syria, pay tribute to the sultan, and reduce his army to 18,000 men in exchange for hereditary power in Egypt. Now 72, he will reign until he loses his mind in 1848.

The Straits Convention signed by the five great powers July 13 guarantees Ottoman sovereignty, closes the Bosporus and the Dardanelles to all foreign warships in time of peace, and marks the return of France as an international power.

Britain's Whig prime minister Viscount Melbourne resigns August 28 after a six-term ministry. The Tories come to power in a new government headed by Sir Robert Peel.

British envoys to Afghanistan Sir Alexander Burnes and Sir William Macnaghten are murdered in the continuing Afghan War (*see* 1839; 1842).

The first British consul general to Zanzibar is appointed.

New Zealand is made a British colony (*see* Maori War, 1843).

British soldier Sir James Brooke, 38, is confirmed as rajah of Sarawak by the sultan of Borneo 3 years after having helped the sultan's uncle Muda Hassim suppress a rebellion in the province by several Dyak headhunter tribes. A veteran of the East India Company's army who sustained a serious wound in the Burmese War 16 years ago, Brooke succeeded to a large property when his civil servant father died, he equipped the schooner *Royalist* and set forth to rescue the Malay Archipelago from barbarism, he will reform the Sarawak government, he will be joined by his nephew Charles Arthur Johnson in 1852, 1 year after being charged in the House of Commons with having received "head money" and otherwise abusing his power, he will return to England to defend himself, the charges will be ruled "not proven" by a royal commission sitting at Singapore, and Sir James will rule Sarawak until his death in 1868.

British forces have occupied Hong Kong since January in the continuing Opium War. The British seize Chinkiang and several coastal ports (*see* 1839; 1842).

Peru's president Agustín Gamarra invades Bolivia, but he is defeated and killed November 20 at Ingavi. Gamarra's death at age 56 plunges Peru into a civil war that will continue until 1845.

💲 Britain's new Peel ministry introduces the first peacetime British income tax and reduces import duties on raw materials and foodstuffs, thus encouraging grain imports which lower food prices and reduce the national debt by increasing customs revenues. The new tax law taxes incomes above £150 per year at 7d per pound sterling, and although the rate will fall as low as 2d in 1875, it will rise to 10s per pound sterling in the war a century hence.

✊ Providence lawyer Thomas Wilson Dorr, 36, founds a People's party to liberalize the Rhode Island charter of 1636. He submits a new, liberal constitution to extend suffrage in the state.

✴ The first emigrant train bound for the Pacific is guided through northwestern Montana Territory by Irish-American trapper and Indian trader Thomas Fitzpatrick.

U.S. lands west of Wisconsin that have not been offered for sale are estimated by Secretary of State Daniel Webster to have 30,000 to 50,000 settlers. Congress gives each head of family the right when the lands are opened for sale to buy as much as 160 acres at a minimum price of $1.25 per acre, provided that a house has been built on the land he holds and the land is under cultivation (*see* 1804; Homestead Act, 1862).

Dallas, Tex., has its beginnings in the independent Republic of Texas as Tennessee trader John Neely Bryan builds a house on the Trinity River to start a settlement that he will name after his friend George Mifflin Dallas, 49, who will become U.S. vice president in 1845 (*see* 1858).

California's Fort Ross is purchased from the Russian colonists who established it in 1811 by Swiss-American pioneer John Augustus Sutter, 38, who arrived at San Francisco 2 years ago by way of a job with the American Fur Company and a journey via Fort Vancouver, Honolulu, and Sitka. Granted lands to start a settlement by the provincial governor Juan Bautista Alvarado, Sutter has become a Mexican citizen and has thus gained title to his land grant, 50,000-acre New Helvetia, on which he has built a house and fort (*see* gold, 1848).

✴ The Prussian "needle gun" designed by gunsmith Johann Nikolas Dreyse, 54, is the world's first successful breech-loading military rifle. The bolt-action rifle uses a long, slender, needlelike firing pin to penetrate through a black-powder propelling charge and detonate a primer seated against the base of the bullet, and it will be adopted by the Prussian army in 1848 to replace the army's muzzle-loading rifles (*see* Sadowa, 1866).

A uniform system of screw threads is proposed by English mechanical engineer Joseph Whitworth, 38, who has introduced machine tools and methods that permit working tolerances to be reduced from the generally accepted 1/16 of an inch to a mere 1/1000 of an inch. Whitworth's suggestion will eventually be accepted, and the British Standard Whitworth (BSW) system will be generally adopted.

Treating indigo with potassium hydroxide is shown to produce an oil (aniline) by German chemist C. J. Fritzsche (*see* Perkin, 1856).

⚡ Cook's Tours have their beginnings in a travel service started by English printer-temperance worker Thomas Cook, 33, who has observed that the Midlands County Railway has opened an extension between Leicestershire and Loughboro where a temperance conclave is to be held. He persuades the railroad to reduce its fare to Loughboro if he will guarantee 500 passengers on a route that normally carries only 50, he organizes a group of 570 teetotalers (*see* Turner, 1833), and he charges them only 14 cents each for the 48-mile return trip (*see* London Great Exhibition, 1851).

⚡ Arc lamps for street lighting are demonstrated at Paris (*see* Brush, 1879).

⚕ Hypnosis is discovered by Scottish surgeon James Baird, 46.

Smith, Kline & French Laboratories has its beginnings in a wholesale-retail pharmaceutical firm started by Philadelphia pharmacist George K. Smith.

🎓 Brook Farm is founded at West Roxbury, Mass., by New England intellectuals who join former Unitarian minister George Ripley, 38, and his wife Sophia Dana Ripley to form a commune and school that will pursue truth, justice, and order. Shares of stock in the enterprise are sold to members who include teachers, farmers, carpenters, printers, and shoemakers, with each man and woman receiving a dollar a day for his or her labors and with housing, food, clothing, and fuel provided at cost to all members and their families. Charles A. Dana, 21, and Nathaniel Hawthorne, 37, are among the initial members, and by 1844 the commune will have grown to include four houses, work rooms, and dormitories with an infant school, a primary school, and a 6-year college preparatory course whose classes in botany, philosophy, Greek, Latin, Italian, German, music, and drawing will be attracting students from as far away as Havana and Manila (*see* 1846).

Fordham University is founded by New York Jesuits under the name St. John's College.

Manhattanville College of the Sacred Heart is founded at New York.

Otterbein College is founded at Westerville, Ohio.

📰 The *New York Tribune* is launched by publisher Horace Greeley, 30, who started the *New Yorker* with Jonas Winchester in 1834 and who merges that paper

1841 (cont.) into his new enterprise, a daily paper that will have great influence on U.S. opinion.

The *Brooklyn Eagle* begins publication at Brooklyn, N.Y.

The *Cincinnati Enquirer* begins publication.

The *Cleveland Plain Dealer* begins publication as the *Advertiser*.

The first advertising agency is started by Philadelphia entrepreneur Volney B. Palmer who sells newspaper space to out-of-town advertisers, charging the papers 25 percent of their space rates plus postage and stationery costs. By 1849 Palmer will have offices at New York, Boston, and Baltimore in addition to his Philadelphia office (*see* Carlton and Smith, 1864).

Punch begins publication at London. The new humor magazine will continue for more than 137 years.

Nonfiction "Heroes and Hero-Worship" by Thomas Carlyle whose moral essay contains the line, "No great man lives in vain. The history of the world is but the biography of great men"; "Self-Reliance" by Ralph Waldo Emerson whose moral essay contains the lines, "A foolish consistency is the hobgoblin of little minds, adored by little statesmen and philosophers and divines," and "Whoso would be a man, must be a nonconformist"; "Love" by Ralph Waldo Emerson: "All mankind(s) love a lover"; *Extraordinary Popular Delusions and the Madness of Crowds* by Scottish journalist Charles MacKay, 27.

Fiction *Barnaby Rudge, A Tale of the Riots of 'Eighty* by Charles Dickens (*see* Gordon "No-Popery" riots, 1780); *The Old Curiosity Shop* by Charles Dickens whose account of the death of Little Nell in the novel's final installment has reduced strong men to tears on both sides of the Atlantic; *The Deerslayer* by James Fenimore Cooper whose frontier figure Natty Bumpo (Leatherstocking) makes his first appearance as a young man, having been an older frontiersman in the original Leatherstocking novel *The Pioneers* of 1823, Hawkeye in the 1826 novel *The Last of the Mohicans,* and the Pathfinder in last year's novel of that title; "The Murders in the Rue Morgue" by Edgar Allan Poe in the April issue of *Graham's Magazine* at Philadelphia is the world's first detective story. Poe is editor of the magazine and his story "A Descent into the Maelstrom" appears in the May issue.

Poetry "Pippa Passes" by Robert Browning is published as part of the first in a series of pamphlets he will issue under the title *Bells and Pomegranates* between now and 1846: "The year's at the spring,/ And day's at the morn;/ Morning's at seven;/ The hillside's dew-pearled;/ The lark's on the wing;/ The snail's on the thorn;/ God's in His heaven—/ All's right with the world!" (I); *Ballads and Other Poems* by Henry Wadsworth Longfellow who includes his poems "Excelsior," "The Village Blacksmith," and "The Wreck of the Hesperus"; *The Demon* by Mikhail Lermontov who is killed July 27 at age 26 in a duel with a fellow soldier at Pyatigorsk.

 Painting *Jewish Wedding in Morocco* by Eugène Delacroix; *Père Lacordaire* by Théodore Chassériau.

 An *f*/3.6 lens for portrait cameras is produced by Viennese mathematician Joseph Petzval, 34.

Theater *London Assurance* by Irish playwright Dion Boucicault (né Dionysius Lardner Boursiquot), 20, 3/4 at London's Covent Garden Theater. Boucicault has written under the name Lee Morton.

Ballet *Giselle ou les Wilis* 6/28 at the Théâtre de l'Académie Royale de Musique, Paris, with music by French composer Adolphe Charles Adam, 38, choreography by Jean Coralli, 62, libretto by Théophile Gautier. *Giselle* will be the great classic tragedy of ballet repertory.

First performances Symphony No. 1 in B flat minor (*Spring*) by Robert Schumann 3/31 at Leipzig's Gewandhaus; Symphony No. 4 in D minor and Overture, Scherzo and Finale by Robert Schumann 12/6 at Leipzig's Gewandhaus.

Anthem "Deutschland, Deutschland über alles" is published with lyrics by German poet-philologist August Heinrich Hoffman, 43, a professor at Breslau University, whose words will be set to the music of Franz Joseph Haydn's *Emperors Quartet* and will become the German national anthem in 1922.

U.S. boxer Tim Hyer becomes the first recognized fisticuffs champion.

New York's John Street Methodist Church is completed in Italianate style just east of Nassau Street on the site of the first American Methodist church.

Shepheard's Hotel, Cairo, has its beginnings in the Hotel des Anglais opened by English entrepreneur Samuel Shepheard, 20, of Preston Capes, Northumberland. The hotel is housed in a building that occupies the site of a harem built in 1771 by the sheik Ali Bey and used as Bonaparte's headquarters in 1799, it will be called Shepheard's beginning in 1845, and it will be the last British outpost between Gibraltar and India, a mailing address and international meeting place for the pink gin set.

A New York State Fair at Syracuse begins the tradition of U.S. state fairs dedicated to the advancement of agriculture and the home arts.

Irish agriculture falls into decay with 663,153 out of 690,114 land holdings less than 15 acres. Tenant farmers raise grain and cattle to produce money for their rents while depending largely on potatoes for their own food. Whisky is at times cheaper than bread, and the price discrepancy helps produce widespread drunkenness (*see* potato failure, 1845).

Steam-powered biscuit (cookie) making machinery is employed for the first time at Reading, England.

A Treatise on Domestic Economy for the Use of Young Ladies at Home and at School elevates the subject of woman's role in the kitchen to new heights and begins a movement toward serious education in the household arts. Its author is Catharine Esther Beecher, 40, daughter of the Calvinist clergyman Lyman Beecher, president of the Lane Theological Seminary at Cincinnati.

 Ireland's population reaches 10,175,000, up from 7.7 million a decade ago. The figure will be sharply reduced by famine and emigration later in this decade.

Britain's population reaches 18.5 million with 15 million of it in England and Wales.

London is a city of 2.24 million, Paris of 935,000, Vienna of 357,000, Berlin of 300,000.

New York's population reaches 313,000 with nearly 50,000 passing through the city each year, but fewer than 140 U.S. towns have 2,500 or more.

The U.S. population reaches the 17 million mark with 12.5 percent of the people in cities of over 8,000. The country will receive 1.7 million immigrants in this decade, up from 599,000 in the 1830s.

1842 British forces in Afghanistan fall back from Kabul January 6 under pressure from Afghans under Akbar Khan who massacres all but 121 of the 3,000-man British army, Akbar's father Dost Mohammed regains the throne he held from 1835 to 1839 and will keep it until his death in 1863, a punitive force from India under General Sir George Pollock, 57, reoccupies Kabul in September, but the British and their sepoy troops withdraw from the exposed position in October on orders from London.

The Treaty of Nanking August 29 ends the Opium War that began in 1839 and opens China to wholesale exploitation by the Western powers. China cedes Hong Kong to Britain, Amoy, Canton, Foochow, Ningpo, and Shanghai are set apart as cities in which foreigners receive special privileges, including immunity from Chinese law, and in which foreigners may conduct trade under consular supervision, the treaty obliges China to pay the equivalent of $21 million in indemnities and forbids her to impose any tariff above 5 percent, the opium traffic continues (*see* T'ai P'ing Rebellion, 1850).

The young Serbian prince Michael III Obrenović leaves the country in August under pressure from opponents who resent his heavy taxation and internal reforms. They elect Aleksandr Karageorgević, 36, to succeed Michael and he begins a reign that will continue until 1858.

The Webster-Ashburton Treaty signed August 9 by U.S. Secretary of State Daniel Webster and Britain's Baron Ashburton Alexander Baring, 68, finalizes the Maine-Canadian border, but the border of the Oregon Territory remains in dispute (*see* 1845; Oregon Trail, below).

A new civil war begins in South America as Peru remains locked in the war that began last year. Uruguay's exiled former president Manuel Oribe, 46,

gains support from the Argentine dictator Juan Manuel de Rosas, 47, in an effort to subjugate Uruguay whose first president José Fructuoso Rivera, 52, has just completed a second term in office (*see* 1843).

 The Oregon Trail mapped by U.S. Army lieutenant John Charles Frémont, 29, will take thousands of emigrants westward. Frémont eloped last year with the 16-year-old daughter of U.S. Senator from Missouri Thomas Hart Benton, 60. His guide is trapper Christopher "Kit" Carson, 33, who ran away from his Kentucky home at age 17 and at 20 joined an expedition to California (*see* 1845).

A wagon train of 120 people led by physician Elijah White, 36, is the first large-scale emigration to Oregon Territory. White has been appointed Indian agent for the Northwest (*see* Whitman, 1843).

The owner of a fugitive slave may recover him under the Fugitive Slave Act of 1793, rules the Supreme Court March 1 in *Prigg v. Pennsylvania*. The 1826 Pennsylvania law that made kidnapping a slave a felony is overturned by the court which says an owner cannot be stopped from recovering a slave but says also that state authorities are under no obligation to help the slaveowner.

Congressman Joshua R. Giddings from Ohio resigns his seat March 22 after being censured by the House for introducing antislavery resolutions, but Giddings is reelected and is back in his seat May 8.

A child labor law that limits the working hours of children under 12 years to 10 per day is enacted by the Massachusetts legislature (*see* age limit, 1848; Britain, 1802).

The legality of trade unions is upheld by Massachusetts chief justice Lemuel Shaw, 61, in *Commonwealth v. Hunt*. Reshaping the common law that has held unions to be criminal conspiracies, Shaw reasons that the purpose of the Boston Journeyman Bootmakers Society is not "to accomplish some criminal or unlawful purpose" but rather to persuade "all those engaged in the same occupation to become members," and he rules that a strike for a closed shop is quite legal and that a union is not responsible for illegal acts by individuals.

Strikes and riots disrupt industrial areas in the north of England.

 Sanitary Conditions of the Labouring Population of Great Britain by English sanitary reformer Edwin Chadwick, 42, exposes the squalor of the nation's milltown slums in a report by the Poor Law commissioners. The report shows that working people have a much higher incidence of disease than do the middle and upper classes.

The Health of Towns Association is established in response to the Chadwick report (above). The citizens' group calls for the substitution of "health for disease, cleanliness for filth, enlightened self-interest

Iron horses like the Baldwin locomotive speeded inland transportation in an age of poor roads and turnpikes.

for ignorant selfishness," and demands "the simple blessings of Air, Water and Light" for everyone (*see* Engels, 1845).

The science of biochemistry is founded by German chemist Baron Justus von Liebig, 39, who suggests in *Die Thierchemie* that animal heat is produced by combustion. Liebig applies classic methodology to studying animal tissues.

The anaesthetic properties of ether in surgery are discovered by Jefferson, Ga., physician Crawford Williamson Long, 27, who performs the first recorded operation under general anaesthesia. Friends familiar with Humphry Davy's 1799 experience with nitrous oxide have asked Long to stage a "laughing gas" frolic, he has suggested that sulfuric ether will work just as well, and when he finds that some of the partygoers have bruised themselves but have experienced no pain, he uses ether on his patient James Venable while removing a cyst from Venable's neck. Long will publish his findings in 1849 (*see* 1845; Morton, 1846).

Illinois becomes the leading U.S. source of fluorspar (or fluorite, calcium fluoride, CaF_2) which will be used as a flux in metallurgy.

The calculating machine on which Charles Babbage has been working since 1833 is rejected by the British government after it has advanced £17,000 to help Babbage develop the machine (he has spent some £20,000 of his own capital). Prime Minister Robert Peel has joked, "How about setting the machine to calculate the time at which it will be of use?" but an account of Babbage's "difference engine" is published in French by an Italian engineer and is read by Augusta Ada Lovelace, 27, the only legitimate daughter of the late Lord Byron, who sees possibilities in Babbage's calculator, translates the Italian's account into English, has it published over her initials A. A. L. in Taylor's *Scientific Memoirs,* and shows the translation to Babbage. He asks why she did not write an original paper and Lady Love-

lace responds with an extension of the Italian's paper that is three times longer, corrects some serious errors in Babbage's own work, and compares his machine with the Jacquard loom of 1801 which is also programmed with punched cards. "It weaves algebraic patterns just as the jacquard loom weaves flowers and leaves," she writes, but Babbage and Lady Lovelace will lose heavily with an "infallible" betting system for horse races that employs the "difference engine" (*see* Burroughs, 1888).

The first U.S. wire suspension bridge opens January 2 to span the Schuylkill River at Fairmount, near Philadelphia. The $35,000 bridge is 25 feet wide, has a span of 358 feet, is supported by five wire cables on either side, and has been built by U.S. civil engineer Charles Ellet, Jr., 32, who has studied at the Ecole Polytechnique in Paris, is familiar with the Seguin bridge of 1825, and will be called the Brunel of America (*see* 1838; Roebling, 1845).

The Paris-Versailles train pulled by two locomotives jumps the track May 8 and catches fire. Many passengers are trapped inside the wooden carriages.

A French railway act provides for government construction of roadbeds, bridges, tunnels, and stations.

Queen Victoria makes her first railroad journey, traveling from Windsor to Paddington, London.

A new U.S. railroad opens to connect Boston with Albany, N.Y.

The University of Chile is founded at Santiago by poet-scholar Andres Bello, now 60.

Notre Dame University is founded at South Bend, Ind., by French Catholic missionary Edward Frederick Sorin, 28, who will serve as Notre Dame's first president from 1844 to 1865.

Villanova University is founded by Roman Catholics at Philadelphia.

Ohio Wesleyan University is founded at Delaware.

Iowa Wesleyan College is founded at Point Pleasant.

The Citadel is founded at Charleston, S.C.

The *Illustrated London News* begins publication in May.

The *Pittsburgh Post-Gazette* begins publication September 18 (*see* 1846).

Fiction *Dead Souls* (*Metitrye Dushi,* first part) by Nikolai Gogol whose earlier novel *Taras Bulba* appears in an enlarged, rewritten version; *Nanso Satomi Hakken* by Japanese novelist Bakin Takizawa, 75, who has taken 25 years to write the novel that is one of 300; "The Masque of the Red Death" by Edgar Allan Poe appears in the May issue of *Graham's Magazine* which sacks Poe for drunkenness; "The Mystery of Marie Roget" by Edgar Allan Poe begins appearing in the November issue of *Snowden's Ladies Companion.*

Poetry *Poems* by Alfred Tennyson whose two-volume work includes "Break, Break, Break," "Godiva," "Locksley Hall," "Morte d'Arthur," and "Sir Galahad." "In the spring a young man's fancy lightly turns to thoughts of love" ("Locksley Hall"). "The old order changeth, yielding place to new,/ And God fulfills Himself in many ways" and "More things are wrought by prayer/ Than this world dreams of" ("Morte d'Arthur"). "My strength is as the strength of ten,/ Because my heart is pure" ("Sir Galahad"); *Dramatic Lyrics* by Robert Browning includes "Incident at the French Camp" which ends, " 'You're wounded!' 'Nay,' the soldier's pride/ Touched to the quick, he said:/ 'I'm killed, sire!' And his chief beside,/ Smiling the boy fell dead"; Browning's "The Last Duchess" begins, "That's my last Duchess painted on the wall,/ Looking as if she were still alive"; *Lays of Ancient Rome* by Thomas Babington Macaulay includes "Horatius at the Bridge": "To every man upon this earth/ Death cometh soon or late./ And how can man die better/ Than facing fearful odds/ For the ashes of his fathers/ And the temple of his gods . . ."; "The Raven" by Edgar Allan Poe: "Quoth the Raven 'Nevermore' "; "The Rainy Day" by Henry Wadsworth Longfellow: "Into each life some rain must fall"; "Excelsior" by Longfellow: "The shades of night were falling fast,/ As through an Alpine village passed,/ A youth who wore 'mid snow and ice,/ A banner with the strange device/ Excelsior!"

Theater *The Shoemaker and the King* (*El Zapatero y el Rey*), part II, by José Zorrilla y Moral at Madrid's Teatro de la Cruz.

"Tom Thumb" is exhibited by P. T. Barnum who has bought Scudder's New York Museum and who has discovered the 4-year-old midget Charles Sherwood Stratton at Bridgeport, Conn., and will use him to gain world prominence. Stratton will be no taller than 25 inches until he is in his teens, at maturity he will be no more than 40 inches tall with a weight of 70 pounds, and he will be given the title General Tom Thumb by Queen Victoria (*see* 1863).

Opera *Nebuchadnazzar* (*Nabucco*) 3/9 at Milan's Teatro alla Scala, with music by Giuseppe Verdi; *Linda of Chamonix* (*Linda di Chamonix*) 5/19 at Vienna's Kärntnerthor Theater, with music by Gaetano Donizetti; *Rienzi, the Last of the Tribunes* (*Rienzi, die Letzte der Tribunen*) 10/20 at Dresden, with music by German composer Richard Wagner, 29; *Russlau and Ludmilla* 12/9 at St. Petersburg with music by Mikhail Ivanovich Glinka.

First performances Symphony No. 3 in A minor (*Scotch*) by Felix Mendelssohn 3/3 at Leipzig's Gewandhaus.

The New York Philharmonic gives its first concert December 7 with all musicians except the cellist

standing up as they play in the manner of the Leipzig Gewandhaus concerts, a practice they will continue until 1855. The cooperative will give four concerts each year until 1863 when the number will be increased to five (*see* Carnegie Hall, 1893).

Gimbels department stores have their beginnings in a Vincennes, Ind., trading post opened by Bavarian-American peddler Adam Gimbel, 26, who has acquired a 2½-story frame house from a local dentist. "Fairness and Equality of All Patrons, whether they Be Residents of the City, Plainsmen, Traders or Indians," Gimbel advertises (*see* Milwaukee, 1887).

Richmond's Thalhimer Brothers has its beginnings in a new dry goods store.

D. H. Holmes opens at New Orleans. It will be the first large dry goods store in the South to employ women and one of the first to provide free delivery.

Air-conditioning (and mechanical refrigeration) are pioneered by Florida physician John Gorrie, 39, who devises a method for lowering the temperature in his wife's sick-room at Apalachicola. Having waited in vain for ice from Maine that has been lost in the wreck of the schooner that was carrying it, Gorrie takes measures to alleviate the unbearable heat. He sets a vessel of ammonia atop a stepladder, lets it drip, and thus invents an artifical ice-making machine whose basic principle will be employed in air-conditioning (and in refrigeration) (*see* Perkins, 1834; Carré, 1858; Linde, 1873; Carrier, 1902).

Paris' church of La Madeleine is completed in Greek revival style after 36 years of construction.

New York gets its first municipal reservoir system as Croton water arrives in the city through hollowed logs that will soon be replaced with iron pipes leading to a new Murray Hill receiving reservoir on Fifth Avenue between 40th and 42nd Streets (*see* 1892).

Broadway is found swarming with untended pigs by Charles Dickens who visits New York on an American reading tour and whose observations are published in his *American Notes* which advocate abolition of slavery.

Hamburg is largely destroyed by a fire that rages in the German city from May 5 to 7 and in 100 hours ravages 4,219 buildings that include 2,000 dwellings. Property damage amounts to £7 million, 100 are killed, 20 percent of the city is left homeless, and contributions to help rebuild Hamburg pour in from other German states and principalities.

John Deere produces 100 plows and peddles them by wagon to farmers in the area of Grand Detour, Ill. (*see* 1837; 1847).

John Morrell & Co. is established by the son of George Morrell who takes over the 15-year-old firm started by his father after saving it from a financial crisis. The firm has been curing its own hams and bacons (*see* 1868).

New York gets its first shipment of milk by rail as the Erie Railroad line is completed to Goshen in Orange

1842 (cont.) County. New Yorkers are unaccustomed to milk rich in butterfat and complain of the light yellow scum atop the milk (*see* 1884).

Starch is produced from corn for the first time at Jersey City, N. J. (*see* National Starch, 1900).

France has nearly 60 sugar beet factories producing 2 pounds of sugar per capita annually (*see* 1810; 1878).

A patent for a gelatin dessert is issued to Peter Cooper of 1830 *Tom Thumb* fame, but Cooper does nothing to develop the product (*see* Jell-O, 1897).

A Budapest factory established 2 years ago by Bohemian gluemaker M. Leiner will grow to become Treforest Chemical Company, Ltd., world's largest maker of bone gelatin.

Italy's Buitoni factory produces 3,600 pounds of pasta per day (*see* 1827; 1856).

Acetic acid, found naturally in vinegar, is synthesized by German organic chemist Adolf Wilhelm Hermann Kolbe, 27.

Mott's apple cider and Mott's vinegar are introduced by Bouckville, N.Y., entrepreneur S. R. Mott.

Vienna has 15,000 coffeehouses (*see* 1683; 1925).

Delmonico's opens opposite New York's Bowling Green (*see* 1831). Lorenzo Delmonico, 19, imports European cooks and recipes for the large new hotel and restaurant, and he will popularize green vegetables, salads, and ices (*see* 1861).

Ireland is losing some 60,000 per year to emigration (*see* 1840; 1847).

1843 India's Mohammedan emirs of Sind refuse to surrender their independence to the East India Company, the British commander Sir Charles Napier provokes Anglo-Sind hostilities, he attacks a 30,000-man Baluch army February 17, and his 2,800 men defeat the Baluchs in an engagement that sees generals fighting alongside private soldiers.

The Battle of Hyderabad in March destroys the army of the Sind emirs, and Napier sends him home the one-word dispatch "Peccari" ("I have sinned," a pun that conveys his boast, "I have Sind").

Maori natives kill New Zealand settlers in the Massacre of Wairau, antiforeign outbreaks in the North follow the massacre, and a 5-year Maori War begins.

Britain makes Natal a British colony following repulsion of the Boers who have allegedly exploited the natives and who in many cases move north across the Vaal River.

Britain separates Gambia from Sierra Leone and makes it a separate crown colony (*see* 1807).

Manuel Oribe lays siege to Montevideo following withdrawal of French forces that have supported the Uruguayan president José Fructuoso Rivera. The siege will continue for 8 years.

Hawaiian independence gains recognition November 28 in a convention between Britain and France who promise not to annex the Sandwich Islands that have been ruled since 1825 by Kamehameha III (Kauikeaouli), now 30. Kamehameha obtained U.S. recognition last year and seeks closer U.S. relations.

Some 1,000 Americans who have come west on the Oregon Trail in a wagon train led by missionary Marcus Whitman settle Columbia River Valley territory that Britain claims on the basis of explorations by Francis Drake in 1579 and explorations by James Cook in 1788 (*see* 1836; 1842; Portland, 1845).

Atlanta, Ga., is named Marthasville after Martha Atlanta Thomson, daughter of Georgia Governor Wilson Lumpkin, to replace the name Terminus used since 1837 to identify the termination point at 1,050 above sea level of J. E. Thomson's Western and Atlantic Railroad (*see* 1847).

The S.S. *Great Britain* launched July 19 by I. K. Brunel is the first of the large iron-hulled screw-propellor steamships that will dominate the transatlantic trade. The six-masted, single-screw, 3,270-ton vessel is 322 feet in length overall, she carries a crew of 130 including 30 stewards, her dining room seats 360, she is the first propellor-driven ship (and the first iron ship) to cross the Atlantic, beginning in 1850 she will make 32 voyages in a 26-year career of carrying emigrants to Australia, she will serve as a cargo vessel from 1882 to 1886, and thereafter she will serve as a floating warehouse until she is scuttled in 1937.

A Chartist cooperative land association that will free working people from the tyranny of the factory and the Poor Law is urged by English social agitator Feargus O'Connor, 49, who says that settling people on the land will take surplus labor off the market and will force manufacturers to offer higher factory wages (*see* below).

Weavers at Rochdale, England, are told by social reformer George Jacob Holyoake, 26, "Anybody can see that the little money you get is half-wasted, because you cannot spend it to advantage. The worst food comes to the poor, which their poverty makes them buy—and their necessity makes them eat. Their stomachs are the waste-basket of the State. It is their lot to swallow all the adulterations on the market" (*see* cooperative society, 1844; Engels, 1845).

Inhumane treatment of mental patients is revealed to the Massachusetts legislature by former Boston schoolteacher Dorothea Lynde Dix, 41, who has seen disturbed people imprisoned with criminals and left unclothed regardless of age or sex in cold, dark, unsanitary facilities, chained to the walls in some cases and often flogged. Her detailed documented report encounters public apathy, but the legislature is moved to enlarge the Worcester insane asylum and Dix will spend the next 40 years persuading state legislators and foreign officials to build 32 new hospitals, and to restaff existing facilities with intelligent, well-trained personnel.

An indignant paper on the contagiousness of child-birth fever (puerperal fever) is published by Boston physician Oliver Wendell Holmes of 1830 *Old Ironsides* fame. Holmes has quit private practice to teach medicine at Harvard (*see* 1847; Semmelweis, 1848).

Yellow fever sweeps the Mississippi Valley and kills 13,000.

The Howe Sewing Machine is invented by Boston machine shop apprentice Elias Howe, Jr., 27, who is not familiar with Walter Hunt's machine of 1832. The Howe machine uses two threads to make a stitch that is interlocked by a shuttle (*see* 1846).

The College of the Holy Cross is founded by Jesuits at Worcester, Mass.

Congress appropriates $30,000 to enable Samuel F. B. Morse to build an experimental telegraph line between Washington, D.C., and Baltimore (*see* 1837). Morse obtains help from Ithaca, N.Y., miller Ezra Cornell, 36, and Rochester, N.Y., banker-businessman Hiram Sibley, 36, and proceeds to construct the world's first long-distance telegraph line (*see* 1844).

The typewriter is pioneered by Worcester, Mass., inventor Charles Thurber, 40, who patents a hand-printing "chirographer" with a cylinder that moves horizontally and contains a device for letter spacing (*see* Sholes, 1867).

London's *Sunday News of the World* begins publication. Circulation reaches 12,971 copies per week within a year and will grow to 6 million per week as the *News of the World* becomes the world's highest circulation newspaper.

The *Economist* begins publication in August under the aegis of London economist James Wilson, 38, who laments "that while wealth and capital have been rapidly increasing, while science and art have been working the most surprising miracles in aid of the human family . . . the great material interests of the higher and middle classes, and the physical condition of the labouring and industrial classes, are more and more marked by characters of uncertainty and insecurity."

London museum director Henry Cole sends out the world's first Christmas cards. He has designed a three-panel card that says, "A Merry Christmas and a Happy New Year" (*see* Prang, 1875).

English bookseller Daniel Macmillan, 30, opens a shop at Cambridge with his brother Alexander, 28. The firm will go into publishing next year, changing its name to Macmillan & Co.

London publisher George Routledge, 31, starts a business that will gain success in 1848 with the first of many 1-shilling classics, the "Railway Library."

Nonfiction *Either-Or* (*Euten-Eller*) by Danish philosopher Soren Aabye Kierkegaard, 30, who repudiates the objective philosophy of the Absolute propounded by the late German philosopher G. W. F. Hegel and who preaches instead a religion of acceptance and suffering based on faith, knowledge,

thought, and reality that will be called "existentialism." Holding that religion is an individual matter, Kierkegaard denounces the theology and practice of the state church; *History of the Conquest of Mexico* by Boston's W. H. Prescott.

Fiction *The Prose Romances of Edgar A. Poe;* "The Gold Bug" by Edgar Allan Poe appears in the *Philadelphia Dollar Newspaper;* "The Pit and the Pendulum" by Edgar Allan Poe appears in *The Gift;* "The Black Cat" by Edgar Allan Poe appears in the August 19 issue of the *Philadelphia United States Saturday Post;* "Carmen" by French novelist Prosper Mérimée, 40, whose short story of a Spanish cigarette factory girl will be the basis of an opera in 1875; *A Christmas Carol* by Charles Dickens whose Ebenezer Scrooge of Scrooge & Marley shares roast goose with his clerk Bob Cratchit and the whole Cratchit family: "God bless us, every one," says Tiny Tim (*see* Christmas cards, above).

Poetry "The Song of the Shirt" by Thomas Hood protests against sweated labor. The piece appears in *Punch* and makes the 2-year-old humor magazine something more than a humor magazine.

Painting *The Sun of Venice Going to Sea* by J. M. W. Turner.

John James Audubon travels up the Missouri River to Fort Union at the mouth of the Yellowstone River to sketch wild animals. Now 58, Audubon completed his bird paintings in 1839. Washington Allston dies at Cambridgeport, Mass., July 9 at age 63; John Trumbull dies at New York November 10 at age 87.

Opera *The Flying Dutchman* (*Der Fliegende Hollander*) 1/2 at Dresden's Hoftheater, with music by Richard Wagner; *Don Pasquale* 1/4 at the Theatre des Italiens, Paris, with music by Gaetano Donizetti; *A Midsummer Night's Dream* 10/14 at Potsdam's Neues Palais, with music by Felix Mendelssohn that includes a "Wedding March" that will be used in a British royal wedding in 1858 and will remain popular for generations; *The Bohemian Girl* 11/27 at London's Drury Lane Theatre, with music by Dublin-born composer Michael William Balfe, 37, lyrics by Alfred Dunn, arias that include "I Dreamt I Dwelt in Marble Halls," "The Heart Bow'd Down," and "Then You'll Remember Me."

First performances *Das Paradies und die Peri* by Robert Schumann 12/4 at Leipzig's Gewandhaus; Frederic Chopin continues his 5-year-old liaison with George Sand, but he has tuberculosis of the larynx and will die in the autumn of 1849 at age 39.

Popular songs "Columbia, the Gem of the Ocean" ("Columbia the Land of the Brave") by U.S. songwriter Thomas a Becket; "Long, Long Ago" ("The Long Ago") by English songwriter Thomas Haynes Bayly, 46; "Stop Dat Knockin' at My Door" by U.S. songwriter A. F. Winnemore; "The Old Granite State" with lyrics by Jesse Hutchinson to the revivalist hymn "The Old Church Yard" (The Hutchinson Family singers introduce the new song at a temperance meeting in New York's Broadway Temple).

447

1843 (cont.) The Virginia Minstrels give the first full-scale minstrel show 2/6 at New York's Bowery Amphitheater and are the first of the Negro Minstrel troupes that will dominate U.S. musical entertainment for most of the century. Directed by Daniel Decatur Emmet, 28, the minstrels are gaudily costumed black-faced performers who sit in a semicircle of chairs, exchange jokes based on the popular white imagination of southern black folklore, and sing songs that include Emmet's "Old Dan Tucker." The minstrel show will be the one form of American entertainment with any direct relation to American life (see Rice's "Jim Crow," 1832; "Dixie," 1859).

Skiing for sport has its beginnings at Tromso, Norway.

Cigarettes appear on a list of tobacco products controlled by a French government monopoly. It is the first known reference to the paper-wrapped miniature cigars that have been rolled in Cuba since the late 18th century (see 1856; "Carmen," above).

W. and J. Sloane has its beginnings in a New York store opened at 245 Broadway by Scots-American merchant William Sloane who at age 19 discovered a way to shoot a shuttle across the entire width of a carpet to produce the world's first piece of tapestry carpet. The store will grow tenfold in the next 39 years, a W. and J. Sloane store will open at San Francisco in 1875, a Washington, D.C., store will open in 1906, and the enterprise will grow to number more than 44 stores while other furniture and department stores will carry furniture and home furnishings made by W. and J. Sloane.

A statue of the late Lord Nelson is hoisted atop a column erected in the center of London's new Trafalgar Square completed 2 years ago in an urban redevelopment program that has cleared out some squalid courts and cheap cookshops that had given the area the name Porridge Island.

Florida's Gamble plantation house is completed in Greek revival style at Ellenton for sugar planter Robert Gamble whose sugar fields cover 3,500 acres.

Scottish settlers in New Zealand (above) strip millions of acres of forests to create sheep pastures. Deforestation for the country's burgeoning wool industry will lead to ruinous land erosion.

The Chartist Cooperative Land Association urged by Feargus O'Connor (above) will, he says, encourage intensive "spade husbandry" that will double the soil's productivity.

The J. I. Case threshing machine is introduced by former Oswego County, N.Y., farmer Jerome Increase Case, 24, who last year came West with six of the best threshing machines he could buy, sold five to prairie farmers, used the sixth to thresh wheat for farmers in Wisconsin, learned from experience the deficiencies of existing machines, and used money earned while learning to develop a superior machine. Case will build a factory at Racine, Wis., and

will develop a sales organization that will make J. I. Case the world's largest thresher producer and a major manufacturer of farm steam engines, tractors, and other farm equipment (see 1837; 1908).

300 stems of Cuban red bananas are landed at New York and are sold at 25 cents a "finger" wholesale by John Pearsall (see 1830). Now a New York commission merchant, Pearsall will go bankrupt within a few years when a banana shipment of 3,000 stems arrives in too ripe a state to be sold (see Baker, 1870).

The price of pepper imported by New Englanders from Sumatra since 1805 drops to less than 3 cents per pound (see 1873).

Japan's capital city of Edo has a population of 1.8 million and is second in size only to London (see 1657), but Japan's total population of nearly 30 million is controlled by infanticide (the Japanese call it mabiki, using an agricultural term that means "thinning out"). Hundreds of thousands of second- and third-born sons are killed each year, but daughters are generally spared since they can be married off, sold as servants or prostitutes, or sent off to become geishas (professional entertainers).

1844 A new British Bank Charter Act effectively yields control of the nation's currency to the private bankers of London's Lombard Street and permits the "Street" to share in the sovereignty of the Empire if not actually to control it. All banknotes are to be issued against securities and bullion in the bank vaults, the Bank of England may increase or decrease banknote issues at will within limits set by the act, but "the Old Lady of Threadneedle Street" may not increase the total amount of banknotes thus issued "on the Credit of such Securities, Coin and Bullion."

Shipments of gold abroad—largely to the United States—have depleted British gold reserves, joint-stock companies have issued great quantities of paper money, the Bank Charter Act (above) separates the Bank of England's banking department from its note-issuing department, and its effect will be to eliminate by gradual degrees all notes except those of the Bank of England.

The Rochdale Society of Equitable Pioneers founded by 28 poor weavers at Rochdale, Lancashire, is the first modern cooperative society (see Holyoake, 1843). The society opens a store in Toad Lane, it sells strictly for cash at local retail prices, and at year's end it divides its profits among its members. Flour, oatmeal, butter, and sugar are its only initial wares but the store soon adds tea and groceries and will later add coal, clothing, and furniture (see 1862).

Fruitlands is founded by Concord social reformer Amos Bronson Alcott, 44, whose utopian commune in northern Massachusetts does not succeed. Alcott has recently returned from a trip to England made at the expense of his friend Ralph Waldo Emerson to observe the methods of the Alcott House School, an experimental school named in his honor. He and his fellow communards at Fruitlands neglect practical necessities in their passion for talk and social reform activities, the failure of their crops reduces them to near-starvation, and they abandon the community within a few months. (Alcott will move about New England for the next 9 years, he will become superintendent of schools at Concord, Mass., in 1859, but he will gain financial security only after 1869 through the literary efforts of his daughter Louisa May.)

Wealth and Biography of Wealthy Citizens of the City of New York by *New York Sun* owner Moses Yale Beach, 44, lists some 850 New Yorkers worth $100,000 or more. Included are John Jacob Astor ($44 million), Stephen Van Rensselaer ($10 million), William B. Astor ($5 million), Peter Stuyvesant ($4 million), and Cornelius van Derbilt ($1.2 million).

"Religion is the sigh of the oppressed creature, the feelings of a heartless world, just as it is the spirit of unspiritual conditions. It is the opium of the people," writes German socialist Karl Marx, 26, in his *Introduction to a Critique of the Hegelian Philosophy of the Right.* Cologne authorities suppressed Marx's newspaper *Reiische Zeitung* last year and he has exiled himself to Paris where he meets Friedrich Engels (*see* 1845; 1847).

A prize-winning essay on Britain's "National Distress" by English author Samuel Laing, 31, reveals the effects of machinery on the country's working class: "About one-third plunged in extreme misery, and hovering on the verge of actual starvation; another third, or more, earning an income something better than that of the common agricultural labourer, but under circumstances very prejudicial to health, morality, and domestic comfort—viz. by the labour of young children, girls, and mothers of families in crowded factories; and finally, a third earning high wages, amply sufficient to support them in respectability and comfort."

The Young Men's Christian Association (YMCA) is founded at London by English dry goods clerk George Williams, 23, who has been holding meetings for prayer and bible-reading with fellow workers. The YMCA will combine interests in social welfare with those in religious wefare, it will soon have branches in France and the Netherlands, and it will spread round the world (*see* Boston, 1851).

Spain creates a Guardia Civil to police rural areas. "The Guardia Civil must not be fearsome, except to evildoers. Nor must it be feared, except by enemies of order," the organization's moral code will proclaim next year, but the Guardia Civil in its patent leather hats and green capes will become a symbol of governmental repression especially to Basques, gypsies, and anarchists.

Sweden's Charles XIV (John Bernadotte) dies at Stockholm March 8 at age 81 after a 26-year reign. He is succeeded by his 44-year-old son who will rule Sweden and Norway as Oskar I.

The Treaty of Tangier ends a French war in Morocco.

Santo Domingo gains her independence from Haiti and establishes the Dominican Republic on the island of Hispaniola (*see* 1822).

A band of 15 Texas Rangers led by Colonel John Coffee Hays, 27, attacks a party of some 300 Comanches. The Rangers kill half the Indians and intimidate the rest with Colt revolvers that can fire six shots without reloading (*see* 1837; Colt, 1836, 1846).

U.S. Democrats deadlock in convention but finally nominate the first "dark horse" presidential candidate. James Knox Polk, 48, of Tennessee campaigns with the slogan "Reoccupation of Oregon, reannexation of Texas," Congress has delayed action on annexation, the Whig candidate Henry Clay straddles the issue, an antislavery candidate splits the Whig vote in New York, and Polk wins election with 170 electoral votes to Clay's 105.

Anaesthesiology is pioneered by Boston dentist Horace Wells, 39, who has learned how to administer nitrous oxide ("laughing gas") from Gardner Q. Colton and who uses it to deaden pain while extracting his own tooth (*see* Humphry Davy, 1799). Wells will attempt a demonstration of the gas before a Harvard Medical School class next year but his patient will not be completely anaesthetized when Wells makes the extraction and the class will not be impressed (*see* Morton's ether, 1846).

Crawford Long at Jefferson, Ga., makes the first use of ether in childbirth. He administers ether to his wife during the delivery of their second child (*see* 1842; Simpson, 1847).

Vestiges of the Natural History of Creation by Scottish author-publisher Robert Chambers, 42, anticipates some conclusions that Charles Darwin will publish in 1858 and 1859. Chambers and his brother William founded the Edinburgh publishing house W. & R. Chambers 12 years ago (*see* below).

Charles Goodyear obtains the basic rubber vulcanization process patent that will dominate the rubber industry (*see* 1839). Goodyear licenses the New Haven, Conn., firm L. Candee Company to make vulcanized rubber overshoes.

Wells, Fargo & Co. has its beginnings in a new express service between Buffalo and Detroit started by entrepreneur Henry Wells, 38, who worked briefly as a messenger for the Harnden Express Company, quickly became a partner in another firm, and now starts Wells & Company with William George Fargo, 26, and another partner. Wells & Company will extend service next year to Cincinnati, Chicago, and St. Louis (*see* Harnden, 1839; American Express, 1850).

The State University of New York is founded at Albany.

Samuel F. B. Morse transmits the first telegraph message ("What hath God wrought") May 24 from the

1844 (cont.) U.S. Supreme Court room in the Capitol at Washington, D.C., to his associate Alfred L. Vail at the Mount Clare Station of the B&O Railroad at Baltimore, and Vail transmits the message back (*see* 1837; 1843). Morse will establish telegraph lines with help from Ezra Cornell and Hiram Sibley (*see* 1848).

The wood pulp paper process invented by German engineer Gottlob Keller, 38, will reduce the price of newsprint and will permit the growth of cheap mass media (*see* Burgess, 1854).

Ned Buntline's Magazine begins publication at Cincinnati but soon fails. Publisher Edward Zane Carroll Judson, 21, earned a U.S. Navy midshipman's commission at age 15, his action stories have appeared in *Knickerbocker Magazine* under the pen name Ned Buntline, he will track down and capture two fugitive murderers in Kentucky next year, and will publish the sensational *Ned Buntline's Own* at Nashville, he will be arrested the following year for shooting and killing the husband of his alleged mistress, he will somehow survive an actual lynching, and he will thereafter reestablish *Ned Buntline's Own* at New York (*see* Macready-Forrest Astor Place Theater riot, 1849; Know-Nothing party, 1854).

Nonfiction *Summer on the Lake* by U.S. transcendentalist feminist Margaret Fuller, 34, who has been giving public "conversations" at Boston since 1839 to further the education of women and has become editor of the transcendentalist magazine *The Dial*. Horace Greeley invites Fuller to become literary critic of his *New York Tribune; Chambers's Cyclopaedia of English Literature* by Robert Chambers (above) who has compiled the work with *Inverness Courier* editor Robert Carruthers, 45 (*see* 1868).

Fiction *The Life and Adventures of Martin Chuzzlewit* by Charles Dickens with illustrations by "Phiz"; *The Three Musketeers* (*Les Trois Mousquetaires*) by French novelist-playwright Alexandre Dumas, 42, whose Athos, Porthos, Aramis, and D'Artagnan cry, "All for one, one for all" (IX); *Coningsby: or, The New Generation* by English novelist-statesman Benjamin Disraeli, now 40, who has been a member of Parliament since 1837 ("Almost everything that is great has been done by youth," III); "The Purloined Letter" by Edgar Allan Poe.

Poetry *Deutschland, Ein Wintermarchen,* and *Neue Gedichte* by Heinrich Heine; "Abou ben Adhem" by Leigh Hunt whose Abou wakes "from a deep dream of peace" and finds that to "love his fellow man" is even worthier than to love the Lord; *Odes to Rosa* by the late English poet Thomas Haynes Bayly who died 5 years ago at age 42: his "Isle of Beauty" contains the line, "Absence makes the heart grow fonder"; "The Day is Done" by Henry Wadsworth Longfellow ends with the lines, "And the night shall be filled with music,/ And the cares that infest the day/ Shall fold their tents, like the Arabs,/ And silently steal away"; "The Boy's Thanksgiving Day" by Boston abolitionist Lydia Maria Francis

Child begins, "Over the River, and through the woods/ To Grandfather's house we go. . . ."

Painting *Shoeing the Mare* by Edwin Landseer; *Rain, Steam, and Speed* by J. M. W. Turner.

Theater *The Drunkard, or The Fallen Saved* by U.S. playwright William H. Smith (né Sedley), 37, and an anonymous "Gentleman" 2/12 at the Boston Museum. P. T. Barnum picks up the morality play about the evils of drink and presents it at Philadelphia, New York, and other cities (it will have frequent revivals; *see* 1854); *Don Juan Tenorio* by José Zorilla 3/28 at Madrid's Teatro de la Cruz.

Opera *Ernani* 3/9 at Venice's Teatro la Fenice, with music by Giuseppe Verdi; *Alessandro Stradella* 12/30 at Hamburg, with music by German composer Friedrich von Flotow, 33.

First performances Ouverture Le Carnaval Romain by Hector Berlioz 2/3 at the Salle Herz, Paris.

Stage musicals *Bombastes Furioso* 12/13 at Hollis 11 in the Harvard Yard is the first theatrical production of the Hasty Pudding Society of 1795. Undergraduates play female roles as well as male but works with original music and lyrics will not be presented for more than 35 years.

The polka is introduced to New York in May at the Chatham Theater by dancers Mary Ann Gannon, 15, and L. de G. Brockes after 14 years of growing popularity in Europe (*see* 1840).

Popular songs "The Blue Juanita" by U.S. songwriter Marion Dix Sullivan is about a river in Pennsylvania.

A public park for Manhattan is proposed by New York poet-journalist William Cullen Bryant of 1817 "Thanatopsis" fame who is coeditor and coowner of the *New York Post:* "Commerce is devouring inch by inch the coast of the island, and if we rescue any part of it for health and recreation, it must be done now. . . . All large cities have their extensive public grounds and gardens, Madrid and Mexico their Alamedas, London its Regent's Park, Paris its Champs Elysées, and Vienna its Prater" (*see* 1853; Olmsted, 1857).

The great auk *Pinguinus impennis* becomes extinct as the last one is killed by collectors on Eldey Island, 10 miles west of Iceland. A flightless bird resembling the penguin which once numbered in the millions, the auk for centuries swam 3,000 miles each year from its wintering grounds on North Carolina's outer banks to nesting sites on rocky islands off Iceland, Greenland, and Newfoundland, but while it was originally eaten by cod fishermen and used for bait, the bird has been wantonly shot and clubbed to death for flesh and for feathers to be sold in Europe.

A listing of foods published by French agricultural chemist Jean Baptiste Joseph Dieudonne Boussingault, 42, ranks the foods in terms of their relative value as protein sources (*see* Mulder, 1838).

Better rail transport improves British diets.

✗ Milk reaches Manchester by rail for the first time and rail shipments soon begin to London (*see* 1863). Rail transport will lower English food prices and will make fresh eggs, green vegetables, fresh fish, and country-killed meat available more quickly.

New England's Hood Dairy enterprise has its beginnings as Vermont farmer's son Harvey P. Hood, 23, moves to Boston with horse, harness, wagon, and sleigh. He starts work driving a bakery route in suburban Charlestown at $12 per month (*see* 1846).

Praktisches Kochbuch by German hausfrau Henriette Davidis-Holle is published for the first time. The cookbook will go through continuous revisions over the years and will be a classic source for upper middle-class German households.

1845 Potato crops fail throughout Europe, Britain, and Ireland as the fungus disease *Phytophthora infestans* rots potatoes in the ground and also those in storage (*see* 1739). Irish potatoes are even less resistant than potatoes elsewhere, so up to half the crop is lost.

Famine kills 2.5 million from Ireland to Moscow and is generally blamed on the wrath of God. The famine is especially severe in Ireland where so many peasants depend on potatoes for food while exporting their grain and meat, but British charity and British government relief do little to alleviate the suffering.

The English potato famine spurs free trade supporters Richard Cobden and John Bright at Manchester to lead a wide-scale agitation against the Corn Laws that prevent free imports of grain. Whig leader John Russell is converted to free trade (*see* 1846).

✗ An Anglo-Sikh War begins in India.

The Peruvian civil war that began in 1841 is ended by General Ramon Castilla, 48, who fought under the late José de Sucre for independence in the mid-1820s. Castilla begins a 15-year dictatorshop.

Florida joins the Union March 3 as the 27th state.

U.S. claims to Oregon Territory "by right of our manifest destiny to overspread and to possess the whole of the continent" are asserted in the July-August issue of the *United States Magazine and Democratic Review* by its editor John L. O'Sullivan. U.S. and British diplomats renew the 49th parallel as the boundary line between Oregon and British territory.

U.S. title to the Oregon Territory up to the Alaskan border at 54°40' is "clear and unquestionable," says President Polk in his annual message in December, but U.S. relations with Mexico are worsening and Polk does not intend war on the issue.

The first Tuesday following the first Monday in November is established by Congress as election day for electors of presidents and vice presidents.

The Republic of Texas established in 1836 is annexed to the United States over Mexican objections. Texas joins the Union as the 28th state December 29.

British archaeologist Austen Henry Layard, 28, begins 6 years of excavations at Nimrod and Kiyunik in Iraq. His work will reveal the remains of the palaces of the Assyrian kings of Nineveh (*see* 1846).

✊ *The Condition of the Working Class in England* (*Die Lage der arbeitenden Klassen in England*) by German sociologist Friedrich Engels, 25, reveals the exploitation of labor by capital. Engels has gone to live in England where his rich father has a cotton-spinning mill near Manchester and he has become friendly with Karl Marx in Paris (*see* 1844; 1847).

The Methodist Episcopal Church in America splits into northern and southern conferences after Georgia bishop James O. Andrews resists an order that he give up his slaves or quit his bishopric.

∞ The Adventist Church is founded by U.S. evangelist William Miller, now 72, whose 1836 prediction of the Second Coming in 1843 proved wrong but who has nevertheless attracted a considerable following (see Seventh Day Adventist Church, 1860).

Babism is founded by Persian religious leader Ali Mohammed of Shiraz, 26, whose followers call him the Bab (the Gate). He has influenced large numbers of Persian Moslems, but Moslem leaders call his views heretical and persecute him (*see* 1850).

✵ Portland is founded in Oregon Territory near the junction of the Columbia and Willamette Rivers. The town is named after the 213-year-old city in Maine as two New Englanders let a flip of a coin decide in favor of Portland rather than Boston.

"The Report of the Exploring Expedition to the Rocky Mountains in the Year 1842 and to Oregon and Northern California in the Years 1843–1844" by John C. Frémont is published while Frémont proceeds to California on a third congressionally funded

Famine in Ireland brought riots and death. The great hunger encouraged emigration to England and America.

1845 (cont.) expedition with Kit Carson serving once again as guide (*see* 1842; Los Angeles, 1846).

British Arctic explorer Sir John Franklin, now 59, sails in May with two Royal Navy ships on a new expedition to seek a northwest passage. Lured by unusually good weather, he ventures deep into a hitherto unknown channel where his ships will become hopelessly icebound and all hands lost.

Lawrence, Mass., is founded on the Merrimack River. The milltown for woolen production is named for the Boston firm A. (Amos) and A. (Abbott) Lawrence, the big New England textile concern founded in 1814 (*see* Lowell, 1834; Lawrence, Kans., 1854).

The *Rainbow* launched by New York naval architect John Willis Griffiths, 36, is the first of the "extreme" clipper ships that will for years be the fastest vessels afloat. Built for the China trade, the *Rainbow* is narrow in the bow, high in the stern, she has aft-displaced beams, and she begins a new era of improved clipper ships that will compete with the new screw-propelled iron steamships (*see* 1832; S.S. *Great Britain*, 1843; *Oriental*, 1850).

A compound steam engine is developed by British engineer William McNaughton.

A hydroelectric machine perfected by English inventor William Armstrong, 35, produces frictional electricity by means of escaping steam.

William Armstrong (above) patents an hydraulic crane (*see* Ellswick Engineering Works, 1847).

The Ames & Co. arms factory at Springfield, Mass., is acquired by Eliphalet Remington, 53, who has been making rifles at Ilion, N.Y., since 1828 and who will contract for government work (*see* Oliver Ames, 1803; Remington typewriter, 1874).

E. B. Bigelow of 1830 two-ply power loom fame invents the Brussels power loom for carpetmaking.

French inventor Joshua Heilman, 49, patents a machine for combing cotton and wool.

New York Life Insurance Company has its beginnings in the Nautilus Insurance Company that holds its first meeting April 12. Chartered by the state legislature May 21, 1841, the new mutual company has been founded by Pliny Freeman, who has persuaded 56 prominent New Yorkers to pledge $55,815 to start the firm. He becomes New York Life's first actuary and will direct company operations for years. The company will change its name to New York Life Insurance Company under terms of a legislative act April 5, 1849, and will soon be paying claims to relatives of cholera and yellow fever victims and to victims of Indian attacks.

Mutual Benefit Life Insurance Company is founded at Newark, N.J., by Robert L. Patterson, who will head the company until 1862.

The Lehman Brothers banking house has its beginnings in a dry goods store opened in Montgomery, Ala., by German-American merchant Henry Lehman, 23, who has come to a town founded 25 years ago that now has a population of 4,000 plus 2,000 slaves. Lehman's brother Emanuel, now 18, will join him in 2 years, the firm will be renamed H. Lehman & Bro. in 1848, it will be joined in 1850 by Mayer Lehman, now 15, and it will prosper in cotton trading and in extension of long-range credit to planters even after Henry Lehman dies of yellow fever at New Orleans late in 1855 (*see* 1858).

The United States Naval Academy is founded at Annapolis, Md.

Baylor University has its beginnings in the new state of Texas. State supreme court justice Robert Emmet Bledsoe Baylor, 52, has helped obtain the charter for the state's first Baptist college.

Belfast's Queen's College is founded by the British government for the education of Ulstermen who do not belong to the Church of England.

The telegraphic Morse code developed by Andrew Vail in 1837 will soon come into universal use as England's Charles Wheatstone and W. F. Cooke have a falling out as to who shall receive chief credit for the improved single-key telegraph to which they are granted patent rights (*see* 1837, 1844; Electric Telegraph Company, 1846; Western Union, 1850).

Scientific American begins publication August 28 at New York in a newspaper format (*see* 1946).

The *Police Gazette* begins publication. The weekly U.S. scandal sheet carries lurid illustrations.

Nonfiction *Woman in the Nineteenth Century* by feminist Margaret Fuller whose work for the *New York Tribune* has made her the leading U.S. critic.

Fiction *The Count of Monte Cristo* (*Le Comte de Monte-Cristo*) by Alexandre Dumas who gains his greatest success with his adventure story about the Marseilles sailor Edmont Dantes; *The Cricket on the Hearth* by Charles Dickens who takes his title from John Milton's poem "Il Penseroso" of 1645; *Sybil: or The Two Nations* by Benjamin Disraeli whose "two nations" are the rich and the poor "between whom there is no intercourse and no sympathy; who are as ignorant of each other's habits, thoughts and feelings as if they were dwellers in different zones, or inhabitants of different planets; who are formed by a different breeding, are fed by different food. . . ." *Tales* by Edgar Allan Poe whose story "The Purloined Letter" appears in *The Gift*.

Poetry "Home Thoughts, from Abroad" by Robert Browning: "Oh, to be in England/ Now that April's there"; *The Raven and Other Poems* by Edgar Allan Poe whose title poem has appeared in the January 29 issue of the *New York Evening Mirror* where Poe is assistant editor: ". . . And his eyes have all the seeming of a demon's that is dreaming,/ And the lamplight o'er him streaming throws his shadow on the floor;/ And my soul from out that shadow that lies floating on the floor,/ Shall be lifted—nevermore!"

Painting *Catlin's North American Indian Portfolio: Hunting, Rocky Mountains and Prairies of America* by U.S. painter-author George Catlin, 49, who 20 years ago went West with his wife and has gained the trust of the Indians, many of whom feared they would die if they were sketched or painted; *Fur Traders Descending the Missouri* by U.S. painter George Caleb Bingham, 34, who has turned to genre painting after 4 years as a Washington portraitist.

Theater *Fashion or Life in New York* by English-American playwright-actress Anna Cora Ogden Mowatt, 25, 3/24 at New York's Park Theater, 20 perfs. (a phenomenal run for the time).

Opera *Tannhauser* 10/19 at Dresden, with music and libretto by Richard Wagner who has based it on legends of a medieval German knight-minstrel who died in 1270.

Ballet *Pas de Quatre* 7/12 at His Majesty's Theatre, London, with Marie Taglioni (who made her debut in 1822 at Vienna), music by Cesare Pugni, choreography by Jules Perrot.

First performances Concerto in E minor for Violin and Orchestra by Felix Mendelssohn 3/13 at Leipzig's Gewandhaus; Concerto for Pianoforte and Orchestra in A minor by Robert Schumann 12/4 at Dresden, with Clara Weik Schumann, 26, playing the work developed by her husband from a "Fantasy" he composed shortly after their marriage in 1839.

The Mark Cross Saddlery Shop opened at Boston by local merchant Mark W. Cross will become world famous for its luggage and leather goods.

The world's first wire cable suspension aqueduct bridge opens in May to span the Allegheny River at Pittsburgh. The bridge has seven spans each 162 feet long and is the first bridge built by German-American engineer John Augustus Roebling, 38, who 4 years ago founded the first U.S. factory to make wire rope (*see* Ellet, 1842; Monongahela bridge, 1846).

New Bedford, Mass., reaches the height of its whaling trade. Manned by 10,000 seamen, the New Bedford fleet brings in 158,000 barrels of sperm oil, 272,000 barrels of whale oil, and 3 million pounds of whalebone (*see* 1775).

"Infanticide is practiced as extensively and as legally in England as it is on the banks of the Ganges," writes Benjamin Disraeli in his novel *Sybil* (above). Disraeli is criticizing the use of laudanum, the opium preparation commonly employed by British mothers and "nannies" to quiet their infants.

1846 Famine sweeps Ireland as the potato crop fails again and food reserves are exhausted. British Conservatives ascribe the famine to the divine hand of Providence and say it would paralyze trade to give away food to the Irish, Britons marshal private aid programs, Americans raise $1 million and send relief ships, but the aid programs are mismanaged, the Irish lack horses and carts for carrying imported grain to inland famine areas, they lack ovens and bakers for making bread, and at least half a million die of starvation and of hunger-related typhus.

Parliament finally repeals the Corn Law June 28. Conservatives led by Benjamin Disraeli oppose Prime Minister Robert Peel's free-trade actions, they denounce Peel for betraying his protectionist principles, but they are unable to prevent repeal of the 1828 Corn Law which is replaced by laws that reduce (and will soon virtually eliminate) duties on grain imports, reduce duties on imported cheeses, butter, and other foods, and abolish duties on live animal imports.

Repeal of the Corn Law (above) removes the favored status that Ireland has enjoyed as a supplier to the British market. Large Irish landowners (most of them absentee landlords) switch from growing wheat to raising cattle, and they throw cotters off the land so that it may be used for pasturage.

The United States moves closer to free trade July 30 with passage of the Walker Tariff Act named for President Polk's Treasury Secretary Robert S. Walker of Alabama. The act taxes luxuries at a high rate but lowers import duties and enlarges the list of items admitted duty-free.

Britain and America will both benefit in the next 15 years by the lowering and suspension of tariffs. U.S. exports will double to $306 million in the first 10 years of the Walker Tariff Act while imports will triple to $361 million, customs revenues will more than double, and U.S. customers will enjoy cheap manufactured products while Britons enjoy low food prices.

The Mexican War precipitated by President Polk begins January 13. Polk has failed in an effort to buy the New Mexico Territory from Mexico, he orders General Zachary Taylor to advance from the Neuces River to the Rio Grande, Taylor reaches the left bank of the Rio Grande March 28 and begins building a fort opposite Matamoras, the Mexicans order Taylor to retire beyond the Neuces April 12, Mexican troops cross the Rio Grande April 25 and kill a U.S. reconnoitering party in a cavalry skirmish.

The Battle of Palo Alto May 8 ends in victory for General Taylor whose 2,000 troops defeat a Mexican force of 6,000 with help from artillery pieces near the water hole of Palo Alto at the southern tip of Texas.

The Battle at Resaca de la Palma May 9 ends in a rout of the Mexicans who fall back across the Rio Grande.

President Polk sends a war message to Congress May 11 declaring that Mexico "has invaded our territory and shed American blood upon American soil," Congress declares that a state of war exists May 13 by act of Mexico, and it votes a war appropriation of $10 million and approves enlistment of 50,000 soldiers.

1846 (cont.) California's Black Bear Revolt begins June 14 as settlers in the Sacramento Valley proclaim a republic independent of Mexico and raise a flag bearing a black bear and a star at Sonoma. U.S. commander John Drake Sloat takes possession of Monterey July 7 and claims possession of California for the United States, Sloat's subordinate John Berrien Montgomery takes San Francisco July 9, Commodore Robert F. Stockton succeeds Sloat as commander of the U.S. Pacific fleet and takes Los Angeles August 13 with help from John C. Frémont (*see* 1845), and news of the naval occupation of California reaches Washington August 31.

An Oregon Treaty signed with Britain June 15 has given territory south of the 49th parallel to the United States, overriding cries of "54°40' or Fight." Britain receives land north of the parallel on the mainland and also receives Vancouver Island (*see* 1818; 1827; 1845).

Former Mexican dictator Antonio Santa Ana, now 51, takes command of the Mexican army at Mexico City September 14, but his 10,000-man force at Monterrey in northwestern Mexico sustains a defeat at the hands of 6,600 men commanded by General Taylor who occupies Monterrey September 24 after a 3-day battle.

Tampico falls November 15 to American naval forces under Commodore David Conner, and Coahuilla's capital Saltillo falls to General Taylor November 16.

Iowa is admitted to the Union December 28 as the 29th state with its capital at Des Moines.

The first Sino-American treaty is negotiated by the commander of the East India Squadron James Biddle, 63, who returns to command a Pacific Coast flotilla in the Mexican War.

The Pennsylvania Railroad is chartered April 13 for the purpose of constructing a line between Harrisburg and Pittsburgh (*see* 1851).

A suspension bridge across the Monongahela River is completed by John A. Roebling (*see* 1845; 1855).

Britain adopts a standard gauge for railroads in a move that will spur development of the nation's rail system (*see* Pennsylvania, 1852).

A pneumatic tire is patented by English inventor Robert William Thomson who equips a horse-drawn buggy with his tires (*see* Dunlop, 1888).

Of the United Kingdom's 3.2 million tons of merchant shipping some 131,000 tons are steam-driven.

Some 175 U.S. ships leave port with 65,000 tons of ice for export as Boston's Tudor Ice Company ships large tonnages to the Far East where it is sold at high prices to buy silk which is bought cheap and sold at high prices in America (*see* 1833; 1856).

Modern anaesthesiology is pioneered by Boston dentist William Thomas Green Morton, 27, who is not familiar with C. W. Long's 1842 ether discovery but who hears a lecture by chemist Charles T. Jackson, 41, and learns that inhaling sulfuric ether will cause a loss of consciousness. Morton tries ether on himself and on his dog, and he then uses it to extract a tooth from a patient who leaks news of the painless extraction to the newspapers. Boston surgeon Henry Jacob Bigelow reads the newspaper account and Morton is persuaded to demonstrate his procedure at Massachusetts General Hospital where surgeon John Collins Warren uses ether October 16 to anaesthetize a patient during an operation on a "congenital but superficial vascular tumor." Morton obtains a patent November 12, but he will be prevented from enforcing it through action taken by C. T. Jackson and C. W. Long. Ether will be called an anaesthetic at the suggestion of Oliver Wendell Holmes who writes to Morton the week he receives his patent, and the new anaesthetic finds immediate use in operations on Mexican War casualties, opening a new era in surgery (*see* 1847; cocaine, 1884).

The Smithsonian Institution is founded by Congress at Washington, D.C., with a £100,000 bequest from the late James Smithson who died in 1829 at age 64. Illegitimate son of the late duke of Northumberland Hugh Smithson Percy who died in 1786, Smithson was a chemist-mineralogist. Calamine will be renamed smithsonite because of his paper on calamines.

English Assyriologist Henry Creswicke Rawlinson, 36, deciphers an inscription of Darius I Hystapis at Behistun and opens Assyrian history to modern understanding (*see* Grotefend, 1837; Layard, 1845; Smith, 1872).

Milwaukee is incorporated. The new city on the shore of Lake Michigan is made up of several neighboring Wisconsin Territory villages (*see* 1818).

Boston aristocrat Francis Parkman, 23, journeys westward from St. Louis on the Oregon Trail but is overcome by illness (*see* 1847).

Brigham Young leads members of the Mormon Church in a trek to the Mexican Territory beyond the western limits of the United States, stopping en route to the Great Salt Lake Valley at the town of Omaha. Church founder Joseph Smith was killed 2 years ago by a mob at Carthage, Ill., and the 45-year-old Young has succeeded to the leadership of the Church of Latter-Day Saints (*see* 1839; 1847).

Bishop Hill is founded as an Illinois commune by Swedish religious dissenters.

Brook Farm at West Roxbury, Mass., celebrates the completion of a large new central building with a dance the night of March 2, but the building catches fire and burns to the ground. The commune has attracted such eminent visitors as Amos Bronson Alcott, William Ellery Channing, Ralph Waldo Emerson, and Margaret Fuller, its weekly journal the *Harbinger* has published items contributed by

Horace Greeley, James Russell Lowell, and John Greenleaf Whittier, but the new building consumed all available funds and the Brook Farm experiment will end next year.

The Putney Community organized in Vermont by John Humphrey Noyes and his followers antagonizes its neighbors (*see* 1839). Noyes preaches promiscuity and free love in what he calls the communism of the early Christian church, he opposes monogamy, his neighbors have him arrested, and they try to break up his communal society (*see* 1848).

Samuel Colt receives an order for revolvers as the Mexican War (above) produces a shortage of firearms. Texas Ranger Samuel Walker has persuaded President Polk to place the order with Colt who engages E. K. Root to help him mass-produce the revolvers with interchangeable parts at a new factory he has built at Hartford, Conn. (*see* 1851; Hays, 1844; Collins brothers, 1826).

The Howe Sewing Machine of 1843 is patented September 10, but U.S. tailors and garment makers are fearful of using Howe's machine lest they antagonize their workers. Howe's English agent pirates British royalties on the machine and there is wide infringement on the patent (*see* Singer, 1850, 1851).

German optical instrument maker Carl Zeiss, 30, opens a factory at Jena in Thuringia.

Bucknell University has its beginnings in a college founded at Bucknell, Pa.

The University of Buffalo is founded at Buffalo, N.Y.

Beloit College is founded at Beloit, Wis.

Grinnel College has its beginnings in Iowa.

The rotary "lightning press" patented by New York printing press manufacturer Richard Hoe, 34, can run 10,000 sheets per hour, a rate far faster than that of traditional flatbed presses. The type form of Hoe's press is attached to a central cylinder rather than to a flatbed and from 4 to 10 impression cylinders revolve about the central cylinder (*see* 1847).

The *Boston Herald* begins publication.

The *London Daily News* begins publication January 21. Editor of the first cheap British newspaper is Charles Dickens.

The *Pittsburgh Dispatch* begins publication February 18 (*see* 1842).

The Electric Telegraph Company is founded in England by W. F. Cooke and J. L. Ricardo, the latter a member of Parliament. The company acquires Cooke's patents of last year for £168,000 and by September of next year two British telegraph networks will be in operation, the northern system taking in most major cities from Edinburgh to Birmingham, the southern system linking London with Dover, Gosport, and Southampton. Rates will be based on distance at first, and long-distance telegraphy will be prohibitively expensive, but beginning in

March 1850 the rate will be reduced to a maximum of 10s for any distance, and competition will force the rate down to 1s or 2s for most inland telegrams by 1860.

Charles Scribner's Sons has its beginnings in the New York publishing house Baker and Scribner as Charles D. Scribner, 25, goes into partnership with Isaac D. Baker. The publisher's sons will incorporate as Charles Scribner's Sons in 1878.

Nonfiction "The Biglow Papers" by Boston poet-essayist James Russell Lowell, 27, begin appearing June 1 in the *Boston Courier*. The letters in dialect by a fictional Ezekiel Biglow discuss the Mexican War (above) and the possibility of the extension of slavery; *The People* (*Le Peuple*) by French historian Jules Michelet, 48, calls on France to unite, to find her strength in the people, to eliminate class divisions created by the industrial revolution, and to return to the ideals of the Revolution of 1789: "I have acquired the conviction that this country is one of invincible hope. With France, nothing is finished. Always everything begins anew."

Fiction *Typee* by U.S. novelist Herman Melville, 27, who at 19 sailed as cabin boy aboard a New York to Liverpool packet, at 20 sailed aboard the whaler *Acushnet* bound for the South Seas, and after 18 months jumped ship and found refuge with a companion on a jungle island of the Marquesas whose friendly but cannibal Taipi tribe he describes in a book that gains wide readership; *The Wandering Jew* (*Le Juif errant*) by French novelist Eugène Sue, 41, who has changed his name from Marie Joseph to Eugène in honor of his patron Prince Eugène de Beauharnais. Sue's 10-volume novel follows by 2 years his 10-volume *Mystères de Paris;* "The Cask of Amontillado" by Edgar Allan Poe appears in the September issue of *Godey's Lady's Book.*

Poetry *The Belfry of Bruges and Other Poems* by Henry Wadsworth Longfellow includes "The Arsenal at Springfield" and "The Arrow and the Song"; *Voices of Freedom* by John Greenleaf Whittier, now 38, includes "Massachusetts to Virginia."

Juvenile *A Book of Nonsense* by English poet-artist Edward Lear, 34, who made up nonsense rhymes to entertain the children of Edward Stanley, earl of Derby, while engaged in sketching the earl's menagerie at Knowsley Hall.

Painting *The Stag at Bay* by Edwin H. Landseer; *Pizarro Seizing the Inca of Peru* by English painter John Everett Millais, 17; *The Abduction of Rebecca* by Eugène Delacroix; *The Jolly Flatboatmen* by George Caleb Bingham; *Noah's Ark* by Edward Hicks.

Knoedler's opens at New York. French-American art dealer Michel Knoedler has bought the business started by Goupil et Cie. of Paris and opens a gallery at Broadway and 9th Street.

Theater *Maria Magdalena* by Friedrich Hebbel 3/13 at Königsberg.

1846 (cont.) First performances Symphony No. 2 in C major by Robert Schumann 11/5 at Leipzig's Gewandhaus.

Oratorios *Elijah* by Felix Mendelssohn 8/26 at England's Birmingham Musical Festival; *The Damnation of Faust (La Damnation de Faust)* by Hector Berlioz 12/8 at the Opéra-Comique, Paris.

Popular song "Jim Crack Corn, or the Blue Tail Fly" is published at Baltimore.

Baseball rules laid down by Abner Doubleday in 1839 are revised and codified by New York surveyor Alexander Cartwright of the Knickerbocker Baseball Club whose members have been playing the "New York game" since 1842 in an open area near Broadway at 22nd Street. Distances between bases are set at 90 feet, each team is to have nine players and is allowed three outs per inning and three strikes per man, but Cartwright's team is defeated 23 to 1 by the New York Nine in its first game June 19 at the Elysian Fields in Hoboken, N.J. (*see* 1884; Cincinnati Red Stockings, 1867).

Stearns & Foster Mattresses are introduced by Cincinnati entrepreneurs George S. Stearns and Seth S. Foster who open a factory at Clay and Liberty Streets using cotton obtained via the Ohio River and Canal. The firm will soon move to Lockland, Ohio, and will grow to become a major mattress producer (*see* Simmons Beautyrest, 1925).

New York's Marble Dry-Goods Palace opens on Broadway at Chambers Street where merchant A. T. Stewart will outgrow his new store and its additions in less than 15 years (*see* 1823; 1862).

New York's Trinity Church is completed in Gothic revival style on Broadway opposite Wall Street by Richard Upjohn. The spire of the new church is visible throughout the city.

New York's Grace Episcopal Church is completed on Broadway at East 10th Street by architect James Renwick, Jr., 28.

New York's Calvary Church at Fourth Avenue and 21st Street is completed by James Renwick.

Boston's William Underwood begins packing fish and shellfish in Maine (*see* 1822; deviled ham, 1867).

A portable hand-cranked ice cream freezer is invented by Nancy Johnson in New Jersey (*see* 1848).

Harvey P. Hood uses his savings to start a milk route at Charlestown, Mass., but he finds that the milk from nearby farmers is sometimes of dubious quality and that supplies are not always reliable (*see* 1844). Hood will buy a farm of his own at Derry, N.H., to produce milk whose quality he can control (*see* 1854).

Cookbooks *The Young Housekeeper's Friend* by Boston's Mrs. [Mary] Cornelius; *Miss Beecher's Domestic Receipt Book* by New York's Catharine Beecher (*see* 1841); *The Gastronomic Regenerator* by London's Alexis Soyer who gives Reform Club recipes for 2,000 elaborate dishes: written in just 10 months during which its author has supervised more than 60 servants and has managed 39 important banquets, the book will become the acknowledged classic of haute cuisine.

Dubonnet is introduced in Paris.

Irish emigration to England, Canada, Australia, and America is spurred by the famine (above) and by the repeal of the Corn Law as cotters are thrown off the land and small farmers are denied their favored status in the English market (*see* 1847).

1847 Russian anarchist Mikhail Aleksandrovich Bakunin is expelled from Paris for making a violent speech urging overthrow of absolute monarchy in Poland and Russia. The 33-year-old Bakunin will be active in European revolutionary movements in the next 2 years, he will be sentenced to death in Austria, but he will be turned over to czarist authorities in 1851 and will be sent to eastern Siberia in 1855 (*see* 1861).

The Communist Manifesto (Manifest des Kommunismus) published late in the year says, "Let the ruling classes tremble at a Communist revolution. The proletarians have nothing to lose but their chains. They have a world to win. Workers of the world, unite!" The pamphlet is the work of Karl Marx and Friedrich Engels who have been retained to write it by London's newly formed Communist League.

The Manifesto (above) calls for "1. Abolition of property in land and application of all rents of land to public purposes. 2. A heavy progressive or graduated income tax. 3. Abolition of all right of inheritance. 4. Confiscation of the property of all emigrants and rebels. 5. Centralization of credit in the hands of the state, by means of a national bank with state capital and an exclusive monopoly. 6. Centralization of the means of communication and transport in hands of the state. 7. Extension of factories and instruments of production owned by the state; the bringing into cultivation of waste lands, and the improvement of the soil generally in accordance with a common plan. 8. Equal obligation of all to work. Establishment of industrial armies, especially for agriculture. 9. Combination of agriculture with manufacturing industries; gradual abolition of the distinction between town and country, by a more equable distribution of the population over the country. 10. Free education for all children in public schools. Abolition of child factory labor in its present form. Combination of education with industrial production, etc." (*see* 1848).

Escaped slave Frederick Douglass, 30, begins publication at Rochester, N.Y., of an abolitionist newspaper, the *North Star*. Douglass' autobiography was published 2 years ago by the Massachusetts Antislavery Society and he has earned enough from lecture fees in Britain, Ireland, and the United States to buy his freedom.

Liberia is proclaimed an independent republic July 26 under the presidency of Virginia octoroon Joseph

Jenkins Roberts. The first African colony to gain independence, Liberia has been colonized since 1821 by U.S. freedmen sent across the Atlantic by the American Colonization Society which has decided that the colony should stop being dependent on American aid and which supports Roberts who has enlarged the colony and improved its economic position.

The Battle of Chapultepec September 13 ends in victory for U.S. General Winfield Scott whose men have scaled a fortified hill on the outskirts of Mexico City after a series of victories that began with the taking of Vera Cruz in March and have included triumphs at Cerro Gordo, Contreras, Churubusco, and Molino del Rey. General Santa Anna flees Mexico City which falls to General Scott.

A wagon road from Santa Fe to San Diego has been opened by some 400 men of the Mormon battalion under Lieutenant Colonel Philip St. George Cooke who arrived at the San Diego mission January 29 after having left Santa Fe 100 days earlier. Traveling through desert, mountains, and hostile Apache country, the men have dug wells along the way to establish the Santa Fe Trail that will soon be followed by thousands of California-bound émigrés.

Fur trader Charles Bent, 47, assumes his new post as governor of the New Mexico Territory, but his house at Taos is invaded January 19 by Pueblos and Mexicans, he and 12 other Anglos are killed with arrows (no women or children are touched), and a punitive expedition uses howitzers and hand grenades against Pueblos holed up in a church. 150 are killed August 19, 300 wounded (10 soldiers are killed in the action).

Nearly 15,000 Mormons led across the mountains by frontiersman Jim Bridger arrive on the shores of Great Salt Lake in Mexican territory that will soon be ceded to the United States. "This is the place," says Brigham Young, and he organizes the "State of Deseret," an independent nation with himself as president (see 1846; 1871).

Salt Lake City is founded by Brigham Young (above) who orders that avenues be made wide enough for a wagon and four oxen to make a U-turn.

Francis Parkman suffers a nervous breakdown in Oregon and is invalided home half-blind to Boston (see 1846; 1849).

The Donner Party is trapped by deep snow in the Sierra Nevada in November, months after leaving for California. 47 of the 87 emigrants will survive, some by eating the flesh of those who have died (see Borden, 1848).

Marcus Whitman is killed by Cayuse warriors in Oregon country November 27 along with his wife Narcissa and 12 other settlers who are blamed for the measles epidemic which has killed many of the Cayuse. Remnants of the Whitman group are rescued in December by Peter Skene Ogden, 53, of the Hudson's Bay Company after being held for ransom for more than 2 weeks (see 1843).

Minneapolis is founded across from St. Anthony's Falls on the west bank of the upper Mississippi (see 1838). The town takes its name from the Falls of Minnehaha combined with the Greek word for city.

Atlanta, Ga., is incorporated (see 1843).

Nitroglycerin is discovered by Italian chemist Ascanio Sobrero, 35, whose highly explosive liquid prepared from glycerol with nitric and sulfuric acid will be used chiefly in dynamite (see Nobel, 1866).

The Ellswick Engineering Works is founded by English engineer William G. Armstrong of 1845 hydraulic crane and hydroelectric machine fame. Armstrong will invent a breech-loading gun that will be the prototype of all modern artillery, and he will open a shipyard to build heavily armored Ellswick cruisers for the Royal Navy (see Maxim/Vickers, 1883; Vickers Armstrongs, Ltd., 1927).

Butterick Patterns have their beginnings in a technique invented by U.S. tailor-shirtmaker Ebenezer Butterick, 21, for printing and cutting paper dressmaking patterns that can be used with sewing machines such as the Elias Howe machine of 1843.

Steam powers a U.S. cotton mill for the first time at Salem, Mass., where the Maumkoag Steam Cotton Mill begins production.

Economic depression engulfs England, provincial banks fail, and even the 153-year-old Bank of England comes under pressure.

Canada Life Insurance Company is founded at Hamilton in Canada West. It is the first Canadian life insurance company.

Lazard Frères has its beginnings in a dry goods business opened at New Orleans by émigré French merchant Alexandre Lazard, who will take two of his brothers into partnership next year. A fire in 1849 will destroy a large section of New Orleans and will wipe out the Lazard firm, one brother will return to Sarrequemines, in Lorraine, but Alexandre and Simon Lazard will move to San Francisco, they will buy an interest in a fabric house making woolen yard goods, they will take their youngest brother Elie and their cousin Alexandre Weill into partnership, they will shift from dry goods to trading in gold, and by the 1880s they will have offices at New York, Paris, and London (see London, Paris, and American Bank, Ltd., 1884).

Nitroglycerin (above) will be used in medicine to relieve symptoms of angina pectoris (see 1768; amyl nitrate, 1867).

Ether is introduced into British surgery by London physician John Snow, 34 (see 1846; Snow, 1853).

Ether is used as an anaesthetic in obstetrics by Scottish physician James Young Simpson, 36, who discovers the anaesthetic properties of chloroform and introduces it into obstetric practice (see 1831).

457

The Penny Black bearing Queen Victoria's profile—the world's first adhesive postage stamp.

An influenza epidemic begins in London that will take some 15,000 lives in the next 2 years.

Oliver Wendell Holmes becomes dean of the Harvard Medical School and his 1843 paper on childbed fever finally gains attention (*see* Semmelweis, 1848).

The New York Academy of Medicine is founded.

The American Medical Association is founded under the leadership of upstate New York doctor Nathan Smith Davis, 30, after a Philadelphia convention attended by representatives of medical societies and medical schools.

Hostetter's Stomach Bitters are widely advertised in U.S. newspapers as a cure-all. The patent medicine is 44 percent alcohol, and it will make Colonel David Hostetter a millionaire (*see* 1867).

Smith Brothers Cough Drops have their origin in a recipe for a good-tasting cough remedy given to Poughkeepsie, N.Y., restaurateur James Smith who is soon offering afflicted patrons cough drops he has made in his kitchen. Smith's sons William and Andrew sell the cough drops to passengers on the New York-Albany stagecoaches that stop at Poughkeepsie, they will soon be installing jars of the cough drops in drugstores up and down the Hudson River and in the Catskill Mountains, and by the time they inherit the business in 1866 they will have many competitors (*see* 1870).

Liggett & Myers gets its Liggett as John Edmund Liggett, 18, joins the tobacco business started by his grandfather Christopher Fouls (*see* 1858; 1873).

City College of New York (CCNY) is founded as a tuition-free institution of higher learning that will enable thousands of poor immigrants to attain high positions in life.

Iowa State University is founded at Iowa City.

Lawrence College is founded at Appleton, Wis.

The first U.S. adhesive postage stamps go on sale July 1 in the form of Benjamin Franklin 5-cent stamps and George Washington 10-cent stamps, but use of adhesive stamps will not be made obligatory until January 1, 1856 (*see* England, 1840; Pitney-Bowes, 1920).

Richard Hoe's 1846 rotary press is installed by Arunah S. Abell's *Philadelphia Public Ledger* which prints 8,000 papers per hour and becomes the first newspaper able to publish large daily editions (*see* Bullock, 1865).

The *Philadelphia Evening Bulletin* begins publication April 12.

The *Chicago Tribune* begins publication June 10 as the *Chicago Daily Tribune* (*see* Medill, 1855).

New York's population of nearly 400,000 is served by 16 daily newspapers, including the 46-year-old *Evening Post*, the 14-year-old *Sun*, the 12-year-old *Herald*, and the 6-year-old *Tribune* (*see* 1851).

Nonfiction *History of the Conquest of Peru* by W. H. Prescott (two volumes).

Fiction *Jane Eyre* by English novelist Charlotte Brontë, 31, reflects the penury and unhappiness of Brontë's life as governess and school teacher in the story of an orphan girl who becomes a governess and falls in love with her sardonic employer, a married man named Rochester; *Wuthering Heights* by English novelist Emily Jane Brontë, 29-year-old sister of Charlotte, whose romantic novel about Catherine Earnshaw and Heathcliff has fewer sales by far than does Charlotte's book but will enjoy higher critical esteem; *Children of the New Forest* by Captain Frederick Marryat; *Omoo* by Herman Melville who arouses controversy by revealing the hypocrisy and venality of Christian missionaries in the South Pacific. Melville moves to New York where he will write some minor novels in the next few years before moving to a farm near Pittsfield, Mass.

Poetry *Evangeline* by Henry Wadsworth Longfellow whose long poem about the expulsions of the Acadians from Nova Scotia in 1755 and 1784 begins, "This is the forest primeval,/ The murmuring pines and the hemlocks. . . ."

Painting *Raftsmen Playing Cards* by George Caleb Bingham.

Theater *The String of Pearls, or The Fiend of Fleet Street* by English playwright George Dibdin Pitt, 48, 3/8 at London, a grisly melodrama about "the demon barber" Sweeney Todd; *A Caprice* (*Un Caprice*) by Alfred de Musset 11/26 at the Comédie-Française, Paris.

Opera *Macbeth* 3/14 at Florence's Teatro della Pergola, with music by Giuseppe Verdi, libretto from the Shakespeare tragedy of 1606; *I Masnadieri* 7/22 at Her Majesty's Theatre, London, with music by

458

Giuseppe Verdi; *Martha (oder Der Markt zu Richmond)* 11/25 at Vienna's Hofoper, with music by Friedrich von Flotow. The opera's tenor hero sings "The Last Rose of Summer," an old Irish air adapted to verse by Irish poet Thomas Moore, now 68, and incorporated by Flotow into the opera.

Popular song "Liebestraum" ("Dreams of Love") by Franz Liszt, lyrics by E. Freiligrath.

Paris jeweler Louis François Cartier opens a small shop that will grow to have branches in London, Geneva, Monte Carlo, Cannes, Munich, Hong Kong, Tokyo, New York, and Palm Beach, Fla. Cartier will gain favor with the French court in the next decade, he and his son Alfred will open a shop in the rue Neuve des Petits-Champs, the demands of their growing clientele will force them to open a larger salon on the Boulevard des Italiens, and they will open a clock and watchmaking department in 1880 (*see* 1898).

Hartford's G. Fox department store has its beginnings in a dry goods shop opened by merchant Gerhon Fox, who offers free delivery by wheelbarrow.

Boston's Louisburg Square is completed after 13 years of construction. S. P. Fuller designed the residential square in 1826.

Boston's Revere House opens under the management of Paran Stevens. He begins a chain that will make him the "Napoleon of hotel-keepers."

A new British Museum opens in London's Great Russell Street to replace the Montague House museum that opened in 1759. The museum's great circular reading room will be completed in 1857.

Ireland's potato crop fails again. The blight is widely ascribed to excessively damp weather rather than to any fungus disease, since the fungus is believed to feed on the rotting potatoes, not to be causing the rot.

Hawaii's Parker Ranch has its beginnings in a small parcel of land at the base of Mauna Kea volcano granted January 14 by Kamehameha III to Massachusetts-born kamaaina (long-time resident) John Palmer Parker, 57, who jumped ship to settle in the Sandwich Islands at age 19, married a granddaughter of Kamehameha 17 years later, and has served the royal family by providing hides and meat from wild cattle put ashore originally by George Vancouver from his ship *Discovery* in 1793. Parker has developed a ranching operation that will grow to embrace 227,000 acres with more than 50,000 head of Herefords—the largest privately owned ranch in the world.

Cyrus McCormick forms a partnership with Chicago's C. M. Gray and builds a three-story brick reaper factory on the north bank of the Chicago River near Lake Michigan (*see* 1834). McCormick has rejected sites at Cincinnati, Cleveland, Milwaukee, and St. Louis, deciding that Chicago may still be a swamp but it is receiving great tonnages of grain via William

Ogden's new Galena and Chicago Union Railroad and is clearly destined to become a grain transportation center (*see* 1848).

Obed Hussey introduces an improved version of his 1834 reaper, but he has moved his works to Baltimore and lacks the central geographical location (and the capital) to compete successfully with McCormick (above).

John Deere builds a factory at Moline, Ill., to produce his self-polishing steel plows (*see* 1842; 1852).

Horticulturist Henderson Lewelling arrives in Oregon Territory after having traveled by covered wagon from Iowa. He begins an industry in the Willamette Valley by planting 700 grafted fruit trees—apples, sweet cherry, pear, plum, and quince, all less than 4 feet tall (*see* 1849).

A stamping process is developed to make tin cans cheap enough for wider sale (*see* Mason, 1858; Solomon, 1861; can opener, 1865).

Canned tomatoes are put up in small tin pails with soldered lids by the assistant steward of Lafayette College, established 21 years ago near Easton, Pa.

The first ring doughnuts are introduced by Camden, Maine, baker's apprentice Hanson Crockett Gregory, 15, who knocks the soggy center out of a fried doughnut (*see* doughnut cutter, 1872).

London, Ontario, brewer John Labatt and a partner acquire a rebuilt 1832 plant and go into business in competition with Thomas Carling (*see* 1840).

England's Cadbury Brothers moves to larger premises in Birmingham as John Cadbury takes his brother Benjamin into partnership (*see* 1824). Cadbury has been roasting and grinding cocoa since 1831, he has been preparing sugar-sweetened chocolate powder and unsweetened cocoa powder, and for the past 5 years he has been offering French eating chocolate (*see* 1866; van Houten, 1828).

Charitable Cookery, or the Poor Man's Regenerator, is published at London. Its author is Reform Club chef Alexis Soyer who establishes a soup kitchen that serves 2,000 to 3,000 starving Londoners per day as the economic depression (above) creates widespread unemployment in the city.

More than 200,000 emigrants leave Ireland, up from 60,000 in 1842, and many come to America. The poor pay a fare of between £3 and £5 ($15 to $25) per head for passage aboard small sailing vessels, most of which are not inspected or regulated, and many of which are not seaworthy. Passengers provide their own food which is often inadequate when poor winds make the passage a long one.

A great migration from the Netherlands begins to the U.S Middle West.

The New York Commissioners of Emigration begin to keep accurate records for the first time. Between now and 1860 some 2.5 million immigrants will enter the United States through the port of New York alone and more than a million of these will be Irish.

1847 (cont.) New York's first Chinese immigrants arrive July 10 aboard the seagoing junk *Kee Ying* out of Canton with 35 Cantonese whose voyage has taken 212 sailing days. Several crew members jump ship, and their arrival marks the beginning of New York's Chinatown which will have some 1,000 residents by 1887.

1848 Paris students and workers seize the city in response to last year's *Communist Manifesto* and force Louis Philippe to abdicate in February. The revolutionists proclaim a new French Republic and the revolution spreads to Berlin, Budapest, Vienna, and throughout much of Europe as the *Manifesto* appears in virtually every European language.

Austria's Prince Metternich resigns March 13 at age 74 and leaves for London. Vienna puts down a revolution, but the country abolishes serfdom.

Prague has a revolution which is suppressed by Austrian troops under field marshal Prince Alfred Candidus Ferdinand zu Windisch-Graetz, 61.

Roman revolutionists assassinate the 61-year-old prime minister of the papal states Count Pellegrino Rossi and force Pope Pius IX to take refuge at Gaeta.

Milan has a revolution March 17 as the Milanese hear of the revolution at Vienna 4 days earlier and rise against their Austrian overlords.

Britain's Chartist movement of 1842 revives. Feargus O'Connor, now 54, was elected to Parliament from Nottingham last year and presents a Chartist petition that is claimed to have 6 million signatures, but a procession to support Chartism that was scheduled for April 10 is called off when the government garrisons London on suspicion that a revolt will start that day. The government announces that the Chartist petition contains fewer than 2 million signatures.

Britain suspends the Habeas Corpus Act in Ireland in July as political seething follows in the wake of last year's famine and continuing high food prices despite improvement in the potato crop. Smith O'Brien, 45, leads an insurrection in Tipperary, and he will be jailed, convicted, sentenced to death, but eventually pardoned.

Paris recalls army commander Louis Eugène Cavaignac, 46, from Algeria and appoints him minister of war, the government backs Cavaignac in putting down a June insurrection, thousands of workers die at the barricades, Cavaignac puts down the uprisings, and the French elect Prince Louis Napoleon Bonaparte, now 40, president of the republic December 10 (*see* 1851).

A child labor law to restrict the age of workers is enacted March 28 by the Pennsylvania legislature (*see* Massachusetts, 1842; Owen-Keating Act, 1916).

The first Woman's Rights Convention is held at Seneca Falls, N.Y., under the leadership of Elizabeth Cady Stanton, 33, and of Lucretia Coffin Mott of 1833 Anti-Slavery Society fame (*see* 1850).

 Wisconsin is admitted to the Union as the 30th state.

The Treaty of Guadelupe Hidalgo February 2 ends the Mexican War that began in 1846. Mexico gives up claims to lands north of the Rio Grande and cedes vast territories that include California to the United States in return for $15 million and the assumption by Washington of U.S. claims against Mexico. 35 percent of Mexican territory is lost to the United States.

Denmark's Christian VIII dies January 20 at age 51 after a reign of less than 9 years. He is succeeded by his 39-year-old son who will rule as Frederick VII until 1863 and who is plunged into a war with Prussia over Schleswig-Holstein.

The Egyptian pasha Mohammed Ali becomes imbecilic at age 79 and his adopted son Ibrahim serves as regent, but General Ibrahim dies November 10 at age 59 (*see* 1841; 1849).

Persia's Kajar shah Mohammed dies at age 38 after a 13-year reign that has brought his country to the brink of revolution and bankruptcy. He is succeeded by his 17-year-old son Nasr-ed-Din who will reign until 1896 with help (until 1852) from his able minister Taki Khan.

The Austrian emperor Ferdinand I has escaped to Innsbruck May 17 to avoid the disorder at Vienna, he has returned in mid-August, a third insurrection by students and workers has forced him to flee once again, and he abdicates December 2 after a 13-year reign in which he has been insane much of the time and confused even in his lucid moments. The 55-year-old Ferdinand is succeeded by his 18-year-old nephew who has served under Radetzky in Italy (above). He will reign until 1916 as Franz Josef I.

Switzerland becomes a federal union under a new constitution.

U.S. Whigs nominate Mexican War hero Zachary Taylor for the presidency in preference to the controversial party leaders Henry Clay and Daniel Webster, the Democrats nominate Lewis Cass of Michigan, Taylor receives 163 electoral votes to win the election with a 5 percent margin in the popular vote, Cass receives 127 electoral votes, losing New York because Free Soil party candidate Martin Van Buren has taken Democratic notes.

Gold is discovered in California January 24 by a 38-year-old New Jersey man working to free the wheel in the millrace for a sawmill he is building on the American River for Johann Sutter (*see* 1841). Sutter tries to keep James Marshall's discovery a secret in order to avoid disruption of his farm, but the news is published August 19 in James Gordon Bennett's 13-year-old *New York Herald,* and by year's end some 6,000 men are working in the goldfields (*see* 1849).

John Jacob Astor dies March 28 at age 84, leaving a fortune of $20 million acquired in the fur trade and in New York real estate. Astor has been the richest man in America (*see* 1834).

Mosler Safe Company is founded.

Principles of Political Economy by British economist-philosopher John Stuart Mill, 42, is a classic text on economics. An employee of the East India Company, Mill follows the abstract 1817 theory of David Ricardo but applies economic doctrines to social conditions and expresses them in human terms.

France's Comptoir National d'Escompte de Paris is founded to challenge the 48-year-old Banque de France which receives rights to issue banknotes throughout the country and which absorbs nine country banks and turns them into branches.

"Wage, Labour and Capital" by Karl Marx is published as a pamphlet. Marx has returned to Cologne at the outbreak of revolution, he has founded the journal *Neue Rheinische Zeitung,* but he will be expelled from Prussia next year (*see* 1867).

The Oneida Community is founded in central New York State by sawmill owner Jonathan Burt, farmer Joseph Ackley, and Vermont preacher John Humphrey Noyes who has been pressed by his neighbors to leave Vermont and has moved with 25 adherents to the communal association founded earlier by Burt and Ackley. They have asked Noyes to join them in a community made up largely of farmers and mechanics (*see* 1846; 1851).

An absolute scale of temperatures is proposed by British mathematician William Thomson, 24 (*see* thermodynamic theory, 1851).

English naturalists Henry Walter Bates, 23, and Alfred Russel Wallace, 25, travel to Brazil with only £100 between them, they journey up the Amazon to Manaus, and they go their separate ways in search of insect specimens. Wallace moves up the Rio Negro into the world's largest primeval forest and spends 40 days collecting rare butterflies and beetles, all of which will be lost when his homeward bound ship catches fire en route down the Amazon in 1852 (*see* 1858; Bates, 1863).

The American Association for the Advancement of Science (AAAS) is founded at Philadelphia on the model of the 17-year-old BAAS (*see* 1863).

U.S. anaesthesia pioneer Horace Wells is jailed in New York while under the influence of chloroform and commits suicide January 24 at age 33 in a fit of apparent despondence (*see* 1846; Simpson, 1847).

Childbed fever (puerperal fever) is shown to be contagious by Hungarian obstetrician Ignaz Philipp Semmelweis, 30, who reduces the incidence of the fever at a Vienna hospital by requiring that attending physicians wash their hands in chlorinated water (*see* 1850; Holmes, 1843).

The first British sanitary regulations are established by a public health act voted by Parliament.

An English public health service that will be a model for those of other nations is created by John Simon who is appointed London's first medical officer of health. Simon establishes the science of epidemiology by showing how environmental conditions can influence the spread and severity of disease.

London's Waterloo Station opens (*see* 1837; 1852).

The 538-ton mail clipper *Deutschland* goes into transatlantic service for the Hamburg-American Packet Company founded last year by German shipping interests.

Samuel Cunard's 9-year-old Royal Mail Steamship Line makes New York its base for transatlantic operations. The 1,422-ton wooden-hulled S.S. *Hibernia* with a service speed of 9.5 knots arrived at New York in December of last year.

The Pacific Mail Steamship Company is incorporated to employ a route across the Isthmus of Panama for California-bound gold seekers (*see* 1849).

The University of Wisconsin is founded at Madison, capital of the new state (above).

The University of Mississippi is founded at Oxford.

Muhlenberg College is founded at Allentown, Pa., by Lutherans, who name the college after the late German-American clergyman Gotthilf Muhlenberg who founded American Lutheranism in the 1740s.

Telegraph communication opens between New York and Chicago (*see* Morse, 1844; Western Union, 1856).

The Associated Press has its beginnings in the New York News Agency formed by a group of New York newspapers to avail themselves of the new telegraph connection (above). The Associated Press name will be adopted in 1856 (*see* Reuters, 1851).

New York's Astor Library is founded with a $400,000 bequest from the late John Jacob Astor (above). His son William Backhouse Astor, 56, will add another $550,000 to the library's endowment (*see* 1854).

D. Van Nostrand Co. publishers has its beginnings in a New York bookstore opened by David Van Nostrand, 37.

Fiction *Vanity Fair* by English novelist William Makepeace Thackeray, 37, introduces the unscrupulous, self-seeking adventuress Becky Sharp, but Thackeray's essential point is that society puts a premium on hypocrisy, and that a person without money or position can succeed only by violating the ethical principles to which society pays lip service; *Dombey and Son* by Charles Dickens; *Mary Barton* by English novelist Elizabeth Cleghorn Stevenson Gaskell, 38, who gains immediate success with her realistic portrayal of Manchester factory life; *Agnes Grey* and *The Tenant of Wildfell Hall* by English novelist Anne Brontë, 28, youngest of the three Brontë sisters, whose second novel is the story of a young mother seeking asylum from her husband, a drunken profligate; *La dame aux camelias* by French novelist-dramatist Alexandre Dumas, 24, bastard son of Alexandre Dumas père, whose doomed Marguerite Gautier and her lover Armand Duval will appear on the stage in 1852.

1848 (cont.) Poetry "A Fable for Critics" by James Russell Lowell whose Biglow Papers continue to appear in the *Boston Courier:* "a weed is no more than a flower in disguise"; "The Vision of Sir Launfal" by James Russell Lowell: "And what is so rare as a day in June? Then, if ever, come perfect days."

Painting *Portrait Equestre d'Ala ben Hamet, Calife de Constantine* by Théodore Chassériau.

Theater *You Can't Be Sure of Anything (Il ne Faut Jurer de Rien)* by Alfred de Musset 6/22 at the Comédie Française, Paris; *The Candle-Stick (Le Chandelier)* by Alfred de Musset 8/10 at the Théâtre Historique, Paris; *Andrea de Sarto (André de Sarto)* by Alfred de Musset 11/21 at the Comédie Française.

March "Radetzky March" by Vienna's Johann Strauss the elder who sides with the revolutionists against the emperor. The new emperor Franz Josef (above) refuses to have Strauss waltzes played at court balls.

Popular songs "Oh! Susanna!" by Pittsburgh songwriter Stephen Collins Foster, 21, is sung February 25 by G. N. Christy of the Christy Minstrels. Foster's song will be in the repertoire of every minstrel show and will be sung by gold-seekers en route to California; "Ben Bolt, or Oh! Don't You Remember" by Louisville composer Nelson Kneass, lyrics by Thomas Dunn English.

A solid gutta-percha golf ball replaces the leather-covered feather-stuffed ball used in Britain for centuries (*see* 1457). Made from a rubberlike gum produced by the sapodilla tree in Southeast Asia, the new ball travels 25 yards farther than any feather ball, professional golfer "Old Tom" Morris will begin using gutta-percha balls in 1852, but some players will claim that Morris takes unfair advantage and will not speak to him (*see* liquid-center ball, 1899).

Spain's Seville Fair has its beginnings in an April cattle market that will grow to become an annual 6-day *feria* of bullfighting, horsemanship, and flamenco dancing—the greatest fair in Europe.

The New York High Bridge goes up to carry an aqueduct that brings water from Croton Reservoir across the Harlem River to Manhattan (*see* 1842). A steel arch will replace five of the masonry arches in 1920.

Passenger pigeons are seen to mate only occasionally in the eastern United States but remain plentiful in the new state of Wisconsin (above; *see* 1813; 1871).

Famine strikes Europe. Denmark permits grain imports free of duty to relieve the hunger.

The Chicago Board of Trade has its beginnings in a commodity exchange at 101 South Water Street started by 82 local businessmen. Served by 400 vessels, 64 of them steamers, Chicago has become a major shipping point for grain and livestock from the Midwest bound for the Atlantic seaboard (*see* 1865).

Chicago's Cyrus McCormick produces 500 reapers in time for the harvest (*see* 1847; 1849).

Irrigation in U.S. agriculture is introduced by the Mormons who begin plowing the shores of Great Salt Lake (*see* 1847).

"Bartlett" pears are distributed by Dorchester, Mass., merchant Enoch Bartlett, 69. He buys them from Roxbury farmer-sea captain Thomas Brewer who some years ago introduced to America the pear known in France and England as the bon chrétien.

The American Pomological Society begins to standardize the names of apple varieties, hundreds of which are grown in U.S. orchards.

A Treatise on the Falsification of Foods and the Chemical Means Employed to Detect Them by English analytical chemist John Mitchell is published at London (*see* Accum, 1820; Hassall and Letheby, 1851).

News of last year's Donner Party experience reaches Galveston, Tex., surveyor-land agent Gail Borden, 47, who determines to find ways to make foods that will be long-lasting and portable (*see* 1849).

The Johnson Patent Ice-Cream Freezer invented by Nancy Johnson 2 years ago is patented by U.S. inventor William G. Young.

Failure of the liberal movement in the German states (above) forces hundreds of young men to flee for their lives. Many will emigrate to Wisconsin while German Jews will emigrate to New York, Boston, Cincinnati, Philadelphia, and some southern cities.

San Francisco loses three-fourths of its population in 4 months as men hurry to strike it rich in the goldfields (above).

1849 News of last year's gold discovery at Sutter's Mill brings a rush of 77,000 "Forty-Niners" to California whose population will jump in the next 7 years from 15,000 to nearly 300,000 as the goldfields yield $450 million in precious metal.

Huntington & Hopkins is founded to supply California prospectors with clothing, food, and equipment. Oneonta, N.Y., storekeeper Collis Potter Huntington, 28, has given up prospecting after 1 day, and he joins forces with Mark Hopkins, 36, who has founded the New England Trading and Mining Company and has come round Cape Horn to Sacramento with 26 men (each has put up $500 to capitalize the venture) and a year's supply of stores and equipment. Huntington & Hopkins will open an iron and hardware store at Sacramento in 1854 (*see* Central Pacific Railroad, 1861).

Canadians seek annexation to the United States as economic depression grips the country following repeal of the British Navigation Acts (below).

Britain reduces duties on food imports to nominal levels under the law passed in 1846.

U.S. commodity prices leap as a result of the California gold discoveries. Workers strike for higher wages in order to live, but wage hikes do not keep pace with rises in the cost of living.

The first gold-seekers from the East arrive at San Francisco February 29 aboard the S.S. *California,* a 1,050-ton vessel in the service of the new Pacific Mail Steamship Company. The sidewheeler is equipped to accommodate 60 saloon passengers and 150 in steerage, she left New York October 6 last year almost empty for lack of business, she stopped at Rio de Janeiro, rounded Cape Horn, stopped at Valparaiso, Callao, and Paita, picked up 70 California-bound Peruvians at Callao, found 1,500 eager would-be passengers when she arrived at Panama in mid-January, left Panama February 1 with 350 passengers, and has proceeded north via Acapulco, San Blas, Mazatlan, San Diego, and Monterey.

Railroad construction begins across the Isthmus of Panama to facilitate passage to California (*see* 1855).

The Chicago and Galena Railroad reaches Chicago and locomotive number 1, the *Pioneer,* steams into town in April to begin Chicago's career as America's transportation hub. By 1869 the city will be served by 10 railroad lines.

The B&O Railroad bridge completed across the Ohio River at Wheeling is a span of more than 1,000 feet and is the world's largest bridge. It has been built by Charles Ellet, Jr., of 1842 Schuylkill River bridge fame who 2 years ago built a suspension bridge across the Niagara River.

Some 50,000 Forty-Niners pass through St. Joseph, Mo., a town of 3,000 whose location at the northern and western terminus of Mississippi and Missouri River steamboat transport makes it a supply center for people preparing to walk the 2,000 miles to California.

The British Navigation Acts are abolished June 26 by an act of Parliament that ends restrictions on foreign shipping. U.S. clipper ships are permitted to bring cargoes of China tea to British ports (*see* 1850).

Budapest's Chain Bridge spans the Danube to link the cities of Buda and Pest that will not become one city until 1873.

Buda and Pest are occupied January 5 by Austrian troops sent by the new emperor Franz Josef to suppress the revolution that began last year. The Hungarian Diet meeting at Debreczen proclaims a republic April 13 and elects Lajos Kossuth, 46, "responsible governor-president" (dictator), Kossuth issues a declaration of independence April 19 saying that "the house of Hapsburg-Lorraine, perjured in the sight of God and man, has forfeited the Hungarian throne," Franz Josef accepts an offer of help from the Russian czar Nicholas, Russian troops invade Hungary June 17 and hand the Hungarians a decisive defeat August 9 at the Battle of Temesovar, Kossuth flees across the border into Turkey August 11, his successor surrenders to the Russians April 13, and the victors take bloody reprisals. Nine generals are hanged, four are shot.

Russia and Austria demand extradition of the Hungarian refugees including Kossuth (above). Constantinople has imprisoned Kossuth and refuses to extradite him, the sultan appeals to Britain for aid, Lord Palmerston promises support, French and British naval forces make a show of force at Besika Bay, but a British squadron that has entered the Dardanelles November 1 to escape bad weather withdraws in response to a Russian protest.

A Roman republic has been proclaimed February 9 with executive power vested in a triumvirate composed of Giuseppe Mazzini and two others with support from patriot Giuseppe Garibaldi, 42, who was forced to flee in 1834 for agitating against Austrian rule and who lived in Uruguay from 1836 until last year. France's marshal Oudinot leads an army of 86,000 French, Spanish, Austrian, Neapolitan, and Tuscan troops against Garibaldi's red-shirted army of 4,700, Garibaldi inflicts heavy losses on the advancing army April 30 but is wounded himself, he launches a costly attack on the French lines June 3, he is forced to evacuate Rome in early July, Rome is returned to Pius IX, Garibaldi narrowly escapes capture in August, he flees to the United States where he will become a naturalized citizen, but he will return to Italy in 1854 (*see* 1857).

Sardinia's Charles Albert denounces last year's armistice with Austria under pressure from radical forces, Piedmontese forces are crushed March 23 by Austria's General Radetzky, now 83, as they were at Custozza 8 months earlier, Charles Albert abdicates, and he is succeeded by his 29-year-old son who will reign until 1861 as Victor Emmanuel II of Sardinia and as king of Italy from 1861 to 1878 (*see* 1861).

Sikh forces are defeated at Chillianwalla and at Gujarat by the British who force the Sikhs to surrender at Rawalpindi. Britain annexes the Punjab by treaty with the raj.

Dresden and Baden have revolutions which are quickly suppressed.

"Resistance to Civil Government" by Henry David Thoreau describes Thoreau's 1-day imprisonment in 1845 for refusing to pay a poll tax to support the Mexican War which violated his antislavery views. The essay will be reissued under the title "On the Duty of Civil Disobedience," it says that every citizen has a duty to oppose bad government by acts of passive resistance such as not paying taxes, it calls the state essentially a malevolent institution and a threat to the individual, and it says, "that government is best which governs least" (*see* 1837; Gandhi, 1914).

Maryland slave Harriet Tubman, 29, escapes to the North and begins a career as "conductor" on the Underground Railway that started in 1838. Tubman will make 19 trips back to the South to free upward

1849 (cont.) of 300 slaves including her aged parents whom she will bring North in 1857.

The first successful power dam across the Connecticut River is completed at Holyoke, Mass.

The speed of light is established at approximately 186,300 miles (300,000 kilometers) per second by French physicist Armand H. L. Fizeau, 30.

A cholera epidemic at London wins support for the Health of Towns Association and its Great Sanitary Movement (see 1842; Snow, 1853). London clergyman Henry Moule, 48, works indefatigably to aid cholera victims, and he will invent a dry-earth system of sewage disposal.

A cholera epidemic spread by gold-rush emigrants crossing the Texas Panhandle wipes out the leadership of the Comanche tribe, but the Indians continue to resist settlement of their lands (see 1874).

The first U.S. woman M.D. graduates at the head of her class at Geneva Medical College in Syracuse, N.Y., after having been ostracized by other students. Elizabeth Blackwell, 28, will play an important role in U.S. medicine, but while women physicians will be prominent in some European countries, they will remain an insignificant minority in U.S. medicine for more than a century (see New York Infirmary, 1853).

The College of the City of New York (CCNY) has its beginnings in the Free Academy that opens on Lexington Avenue at 23rd Street. The CCNY name will be used beginning in 1866 and the college will become City University of New York (CUNY) (see 1847).

Eastern Michigan University is founded at Ypsilanti.

The *St. Paul Pioneer* begins publication in Minnesota Territory.

Nonfiction *The California and Oregon Trail* by Francis Parkman who has lost his eyesight but has embarked on the career of historian (see 1847); *Physical Geography of the Mississippi Valley* by bridge builder Charles Ellet, Jr. (above); *A Week on the Concord and Merrimack Rivers* by Henry David Thoreau.

Fiction *January* (*Janvier*) by French journalist-novelist Jean Baptiste Alphonse Karr, 41: "The more things change, the more they remain the same" (*Plus ça change, plus c'est la même chose*).

Poetry "The Bells" and "Annabel Lee" by Edgar Allan Poe who dies October 7 at age 40 after a final spree in Baltimore; "The Ballad of the Tempest, or the Captain's Daughter," by Boston publisher James Thomas Fields of Ticknor, Reed & Fields whose poem will be published in the McGuffey *Readers* (see 1836, 1837): " 'We are lost!' the captain shouted,/ As he staggered down the stairs./ But his little daughter whispered,/ As she took his icy hand,/ 'Isn't God upon the ocean,/ Just the same as on the land?' "

Painting *Rienzi* by English pre-Raphaelite painter (William) Holman Hunt, 22; *Isabella* by John Everett Millais who last year joined with Dante Gabriel Rosetti and Holman Hunt to form the Pre-Raphaelite Brotherhood; *After Dinner at Ornans* by French naturalist painter (Jean Desiré) Gustave Courbet, 30. Japanese *ukiyoe* painter Katsushika Hokusai dies at age 90 after an eccentric life in which he has moved 93 times and has changed his pen name 33 times, giving the old name each time to a student.

Theater English actor William Charles Macready, 56, plays *Macbeth* at New York's Astor Place Opera House May 10, and partisans of U.S. actor Edwin Forrest, 43, gather in the street outside, possibly at the instigation of Forrest who was mistreated at London in 1845. The mob proceeds to wreck the theater, the police are unable to disperse the rioters, the state militia is called in, and the Astor Place riot ends with 22 dead, 36 injured. Edward Z. C. "Ned Buntline" Judson is convicted of having led the riot and is sentenced to a year in prison (see 1844; 1854). *Herod and Marianne (Herodes und Marianne)* by Friedrich Hebbel 4/19 at Vienna's Burgtheater; *Genoveva* by Friedrich Hebbel 5/13 at Prague; *The Ruby (Der Rubin)* by Friedrich Hebbel 11/21 at Vienna's Burgtheater.

Opera *The Merry Wives of Windsor (Die Lustigen Weiber von Windsor)* 3/9 at Berlin's Hofoper, with music by German composer Carl Otto Ehrenfried Nikolai, 38 (who dies 2 months later), libretto from the Shakespeare comedy of 1600; *Le Prophète* 4/6 at the Paris Grand Opéra, with music by Giacomo Meyerbeer; *Luisa Miller* 12/8 at the Teatro San Carlos, Naples, with music by Giuseppe Verdi, libretto from Shiller's play *Kabale und Liebe* of 1784.

First performances *Tusso: Lament and Triumph* symphonic poem No. 2 by Franz Liszt 8/28 at Weimar's Grand Ducal Playhouse.

Viennese waltz king Johann Strauss the elder dies September 25 of scarlet fever at age 45. His 23-year-old son and namesake broke with his father nearly 5 years ago and began conducting his own orchestra at Dommayer's Casino in Heitzing, he delighted Vienna last year with his "Explosions Polka" and his "Festival Quadrille," he takes over his father's orchestra October 11, and he pursues a career that will overshadow that of his father.

Popular songs "Happy Farmer" ("Frölicher Landmann") by Robert Schumann; "Santa Lucia" by Neapolitan songwriter Teodoro Cottrau, 22; "Nelly Was a Lady" by Stephen C. Foster.

Hymn "It Came upon the Midnight Clear" by U.S. composer Richard Storrs Wills, 30, lyrics by Unitarian clergyman-poet Edward H. Sears.

The safety pin is patented by New York sewing machine inventor Walter Hunt, now 53, who sells the patent rights for $400 in order to raise money to discharge a small debt (see 1832; paper collar, 1854).

The bowler hat (derby) is introduced by London felt-hat makers Thomas Bowler, Ltd., of Southward Bridge Road who made the hat to fill an order placed by the 90-year old firm Lock Co. of St. James for their customer William Coke of Holkham, Norfolk. Coke wants protection from low overhanging branches while out shooting, and his hard derby headgear will become popular with foxhunters and businessmen.

 Harrods has its beginnings in a London grocery shop at 8 Brompton Road that has been run by Philip Henry Burden. Tea wholesaler Henry Charles Harrod, 49, of Eastcheap takes over the shop that will grow to become one of the world's largest department stores (see 1861).

Pittsburgh's Joseph Horne Co. is founded.

St. Louis's Famous Barr Co. has its beginnings in a small dry goods shop.

 The first modular prefabricated cast iron and glass "curtain wall" buildings are erected in New York at the corner of Washington and Murray Streets by former watchmaker and inventor James Bogardus, 49, who has been commissioned by local merchant Edgar H. Laing. The columns and spandrels that make up the facades are simply bolted together with the bolt heads covered by cast iron rosettes and other decorative ornaments. Bogardus will obtain a patent next year to cover his revolutionary invention, and prefabricated buildings will soon go up all over Manhattan and at Philadelphia, Baltimore, St. Louis, and other cities as well (see department store, 1862).

Reinforced concrete containing iron bars is patented by French inventor Joseph Monier, 26, whose invention will permit construction of taller buildings, bigger dams, and other structures not heretofore possible, but no reinforced concrete building of more than two stories will be erected for 54 years (see Cincinnati, 1903; Otis, 1852).

Moscow's Kremlin Palace is completed after 11 years of construction.

 A U.S. Department of the Interior that will eventually serve as custodian for the nation's natural resources is created March 5 by act of Congress and is headed by former Secretary of the Treasury Thomas Ewing who takes office as a member of President Taylor's new administration. The U.S. Patent Office established in 1790 is transferred from the State Department to the new Department of the Interior, and the Bureau of Indian Affairs established in 1834 is moved from the War Department to the new Department of the Interior which for years will serve merely as general housekeeper for the government.

 Thousands of U.S. farmers are deserted by workers who have left for California, and they are impelled to buy McCormick reapers at $100 each. McCormick has stocked warehouses throughout the upper Mississippi Valley to meet the demand, he guarantees his reapers, he lets farmers buy them on an installment plan geared to harvest conditions, he never sues a farmer for payment, but he pays his factory workers small wages for long hours of labor (see 1847; 1850).

Canada's Massey-Harris farm equipment company has its beginnings in the Newcastle Foundry and Machine Manufactory started by U.S.-born entrepreneur Daniel Massey, 51, whose son Hart Almerrin Massey will take over the plant at Bond Head on Lake Ontario in 1855 and will rename the company Massey Manufacturing Co. in 1870 (see 1890).

Basque shepherds from Argentina and Uruguay flock by the hundreds to California in quest of gold. Many will later become sheepherders on the western range (see 1907).

 Some 10,000 California gold-seekers will die of scurvy in the next few years. More thousands will avoid scurvy by eating winter purslane (*Montia perfoliata*), an herb that will be called miner's lettuce.

 Henry David Thoreau (above) laments what dambuilders are doing to the shad, a fish "formerly abundant here and taken in weirs by the Indians, who taught this method to the whites by whom they were used as food and as manure" (see Tisquantum, 1621). The shad are disappearing, says Thoreau, as "the dam, and afterward the canal at Billerica and the factories at Lowell, put an end to their migrations hitherward" (see 1834; 1858).

A "meat biscuit" is invented by Gail Borden to provide a portable food for friends leaving in July for California (see 1848). Borden makes what he calls an "important discovery . . . an improved process of preserving the nutritious properties of meat, or animal flesh, of any kind, by obtaining the concentrated extract of it, and combining it with flour or vegetable meal, and drying or baking the mixture in an oven, in the form of a biscuit or cracker." Borden will spend 6 years and will invest $60,000 in developing and promoting his "meat biscuit" (see 1851).

California gold attracted hordes of eager prospectors. A few made fortunes—at a terrible cost to the environment.

1849 (cont.) Henderson Lewelling takes his first crop of Oregon apples to San Francisco and sells all 100 of them at $5 apiece to prospectors hungry for fresh fruit (*see* 1847; scurvy, above).

Domingo Ghirardelli arrives at San Francisco and begins selling tent stores to gold-seekers. An Italian merchant who has lived in Latin America, Ghirardelli has seen cacao growing in Guatemala and he will build a San Francisco chocolate factory.

1850 An "omnibus bill" introduced January 29 by U.S. Senator Henry Clay contains compromise resolutions designed to reduce the growing polarity between North and South. California is to be admitted to the Union as a free state, territorial governments are to be set up in the rest of the territory acquired from Mexico with no congressional stipulation as to slavery in the territory, Texas is to give up her claim to part of the New Mexico Territory in return for federal assumption of the Texas state debt, slavery is to be abolished in the District of Columbia, and a stronger fugitive slave law is to be enacted.

John Calhoun attacks the Clay compromise March 4 in his "Speech on the Slavery Question," Daniel Webster supports Clay March 7 in his speech "For the Union and Constitution."

The Clayton-Bulwer Treaty negotiated April 19 between U.S. Secretary of State John Middleton Clayton, 54, and Britain's Sir Henry Lytton Bulwer regulates the interests of both countries in Central America with special reference to a proposed canal across Nicaragua (*see* Walker, 1856).

President Taylor dies of typhus July 9 at age 66 after 16 months in office. He is succeeded by his vice president Millard Fillmore, 50.

California is admitted to the Union September 9 as the 31st state.

The balance of the Mexican cession is divided at the 37th parallel into the territories of New Mexico and Utah. Texas receives $10 million for relinquishing her claims to part of the New Mexico Territory (above) (*see* below slavery actions).

China's T'ai P'ing Rebellion begins under the leadership of Kwangsi district schoolmaster and mystic Hung Hsiu-ch'uan, 38, who believes himself to be the younger brother of Jesus Christ, calls himself T'in-wang (Heavenly Prince), and calls his dynasty T'ai P'ing (Great Peace). Helped by the strategist Yang Hsiu-ch'ing, Hung leads southern peasants against the Manchu government in a civil war that will take from 20 to 30 million lives in the next 14 years (*see* 1853).

The Don Pacifico affair brings Britain and Greece close to war. David Pacifico, 66, is a British subject who served as Portuguese consul general at Athens from 1837 to 1842 and who has held substantial claims against the Greek government, an anti-Semitic mob burned his house at Athens in December of last year, the British foreign secretary Viscount Palmerston (Henry J. Temple), now 66, has ordered a squadron to the Piraeus to force a settlement of the Pacifico claims and other claims, the British embargo Greek vessels in the Piraeus and then seize some Greek ships in January, the Greeks comply with British demands April 26 under pressure, and Palmerston defends his action June 29 in a parliamentary speech that appeals to British nationalism with the phrase "civis Romanus sum."

The Persian founder of Babism Ali Mohammed of Shiraz is condemned to death for heresy and is executed in the public square of Tabriz July 9 at age 31. His follower Husayn Ali, 33, takes over the Bab's mission, he will be exiled to Baghdad, then to Constantinople, then to Adrianople, and finally to Acre, he will claim to be the leader promised by the Bab, he will take the title Bahaullah (Splendor of God), and he will preach the new faith Bahai (*see* 1845).

Britain's Amalgamated Society of Engineers organizes workers using novel principles that include large contributions from members, benefits to members, and vigorous pursuit of measures to improve wages and working conditions through direct action and collective bargaining.

A French electoral law enacted May 31 requires that a voter be resident in one place for at least 3 years as attested by a tax receipt or by an employer's affidavit. The law is directed at radical workers who tend to be migratory.

French clubs and public meetings are forbidden June 9, Republican civil servants are dismissed at the slightest provocation, homes of Republicans are searched, Republican newspapers are hit with fines and lawsuits (*see* 1851).

The first national women's rights convention is held at Worcester, Mass. It has been organized largely through efforts by reformer Lucy Stone, 33, who was graduated 3 years ago from Oberlin College and who will organize annual conventions each year for many years to come (*see* 1848; Bloomer, 1851).

A new Fugitive Slave Act passed by Congress September 18 strengthens the 1793 act by substituting federal jurisdiction for state jurisdiction (*see* Clay compromise, above). New York freedman James Hamlet is arrested by a deputy U.S. marshal at New York as a fugitive from Baltimore in the first recorded action under the new act, but the arrest arouses so much public indignation that Hamlet is redeemed and freed. The Chicago City Council moves October 21 not to sustain the new act while a mass meeting at New York October 30 resolves that the act should be sustained (*see* Boston, Syracuse, 1851; Wisconsin, 1854).

Congress abolishes flogging in the U.S. Navy.

The second law of thermodynamics, enunciated by German mathematical physicist Rudolf Julius Emanuel Clausius, 28, states that heat cannot pass from a colder body to a warmer body but only from a warmer body to a colder body. The heat-transfer

466

principle will be basic to all refrigeration and to many developments in chemistry and physics (*see* Carnot, 1824; Thomson, 1851).

The Bunsen burner invented by German chemist Robert Wilhelm Bunsen, 29, at Heidelberg University produces an intensely hot, almost nonluminous flame that leaves no sooty deposit on test tubes. It uses three volumes of air to every volume of coal gas, and it will become standard equipment in every chemical laboratory (its principle will be employed in gas stoves).

German industrialist Friedrich Bayer, 25, founds a company at Elberfield that will be called Friedrich Bayer und Co. until it is renamed Farbenfabriken vorm. Friedrich Bayer und Co. in 1881 (*see* heroin, 1898; aspirin, 1899).

A trip hammer devised by Neponsit, Mass. inventor Silas Putnam will be used by the U.S. cavalry to make horseshoe nails.

The Singer Sewing Machine invented by U.S. actor-mechanic Isaac Merrit Singer, 38, will become the world's largest-selling machine of its kind (*see* Howe, 1843). Singer's patented wood-carving machine has been destroyed in a boiler explosion, he has watched some Boston mechanics trying to repair a primitive sewing machine, and he has been inspired to devise a better one (*see* 1851).

United States use of energy is at a rate of 7,091 pounds of coal per capita, a rate many technologically advanced nations will not attain for more than 120 years, but 91 percent of U.S. energy comes from wood and the rest largely from whale oil (*see* 1859).

The first U.S. clipper ship to be seen at London arrives from Hong Kong after a 97-day voyage. The *Oriental* carries a 1,600-ton cargo of China tea and her $48,000 cargo fee nearly covers the cost of her construction. British shipbuilders are inspired to copy the *Oriental's* lines but are handicapped by English rules of taxation that consider length and beam in measuring tonnage while leaving depth untaxed. The short deep ships built at Aberdeen and on the Clyde do not approach the speed of the U.S. clipper ships which soon abandon the China trade for the more profitable business of transporting gold-seekers to California.

The S.S. *Atlantic* goes into service for Edward Knight Collins's U.S. Mail Steamship Company in competition with Samuel Cunard's 11-year-old Royal Mail Steam Packet Company. 282 feet in length overall, the 2,856-ton paddle-wheeler leaves New York April 27, she damages her side-wheels on ice off Sandy Hook, but the 200-passenger liner breaks the Royal Mail's speed record on her return voyage by crossing in 10 days, 16 hours (*see* 1852).

Luckenbach Steamship Company has its beginnings at Rondout, N.Y., where German-American entrepreneur Lewis Luckenbach acquires a tugboat and starts a towing and salvage business. Luckenbach will

be joined by others to build five tugs for use in the Philadelphia area, he will progress to oceangoing tugs, he will start the first coastwise coal barge service from Norfolk to New York and New England, and he will pioneer in the practice of towing barges in tandem against the advice of insurance underwriters who in some cases will refuse to insure barges or cargos thus towed.

Rio Grande steamboat operator Richard King, 25, and former navy commander Mifflin Kenedy are backed by Texas merchant Charles Stillman in a steamboat venture that will modernize and monopolize commercial traffic on the Rio Grande (*see* Santa Gertrudis Creek, 1853).

Cornelius van Derbilt establishes a shipping line to California via Nicaragua and cuts the prices charged by competitors (*see* 1834, 1853; Clayton-Bulwer Treaty, above).

The Illinois Central Railway receives nearly 2.6 million acres of Illinois land as a gift from Congress to become the first U.S. railroad to obtain a land grant. The Illinois Central will be chartered next year to build lines between Cairo and East Dubuque and between Centralia and Chicago, it will become the chief U.S. railroad running from North to South, and it will sell much of its land to settlers at $5 to $15 per acre.

The Louisville and Nashville Railroad Company is incorporated in Kentucky March 5. The new railroad will be profitable almost from the start, and within 80 years it will be operating more than 5,000 miles of track in 13 states of the South with 60 percent of its traffic coming from bituminous coal mines in Kentucky, Virginia, Alabama, and Illinois.

U.S. railroad trackage reaches 9,000 miles, up from little more than 3,000 in 1840. Canal mileage reaches 3,600, up from 3,300 in 1840.

The Chesapeake & Ohio Canal begun in 1828 finally reaches Cumberland, Md., which the B&O Railroad reached in 1842. The $22 million 184.5-mile canal with its 74 lift locks is obsolete, and plans to continue it 180 miles westward to Pittsburgh are abandoned, but the canal will nevertheless be used until 1924.

Land grants to U.S. railroad companies in the next 21 years will cover more territory than France, England, Wales, and Scotland combined.

American Express Company is formed by a merger of the 6-year-old Wells & Company, Livingston, Fargo & Company, and the firm of Butterfield, Wasson & Company founded last year by upstate New York entrepreneur John Butterfield, 48 (*see* Wells, Fargo, 1852; Overland Mail, 1857; traveler's cheques, 1891).

Great Britain enters a "Golden Age" of prosperity as she embraces free trade principles that remove tariffs on foodstuffs. Self-sufficient in food until now and generally even a food exporter, Britain becomes a net food importer and depends on her manufactur-

1850 (cont.) ing industry to provide the foreign exchange needed to feed her people. Food prices will rise far less swiftly than other prices and British wage increases will more than keep pace with price increases.

Irish entrepreneur William Russell Grace, 18, makes his way to Callao, Peru, after 2 years at sea and 2 more years with a Liverpool ship chandlery. Grace joins a Callao chandlery that he and his brother will take over within a few years (*see* 1865).

New York shirtmaker Oliver Fisher Winchester, 39, sets up a New Haven, Conn., factory whose success will enable him to buy control of New Haven's Volcanic Repeating Arms Company. He will reorganize it in 1857 under the name New Haven Arms Company, and he will reorganize it in 1867 under the name Winchester Repeating Arms Company (*see* Henry lever-action rifle, 1860).

Only half the children born in the United States until now have reached the age of 5. The percentage will increase dramatically.

Ignaz Semmelweis enforces antiseptic practices in the obstetric ward of Budapest's St. Rochus Hospital (*see* 1848). Semmelweis has returned to Budapest after failing to convince Viennese hospital authorities of the need for sterile conditions (*see* Pasteur, 1861; Lister, 1865).

The first textbook of histology (the study of organic tissues) is published at Würzburg. Its author is Swiss anatomist Rudolf Albert von Kölliker, 33, who was a student of Johannes Müller (*see* 1840).

The opthalmoscope invented by German physicist-anatomist-physiologist Hermann Ludwig Ferdinand Helmholtz, 29, is an instrument for examining the retina and the interior of the eye.

The University of Sydney is founded in Australia.

The University of Utah is founded at Salt Lake City.

Illinois Wesleyan University is founded at Bloomington.

The University of Dayton is founded in Ohio.

The University of Rochester is founded in New York.

The United States has 254 daily newspapers, up from 138 in 1840 (*see* 1860).

The *Portland Oregonian* begins publication.

Harper's Monthly begins publication at New York (*see* 1817; 1856).

Nonfiction *Representative Men* by Ralph Waldo Emerson.

Fiction *The Personal History of David Copperfield* by Charles Dickens whose "humble" Uriah Heep and Mr. Micawber are confined in the King's Bench debtors' prison as the author's father was confined in the Marshalsea prison: "Annual income twenty pounds, annual expenditure nineteen pounds six, result happiness. Annual income twenty pounds, annual expenditure twenty pounds ought and six, result misery" (illustrations by "Phiz"); *Pendennis* by Wil-

liam Makepeace Thackeray; *The Scarlet Letter* by Nathaniel Hawthorne whose novel is about inhumanity in Puritan New England.

Poetry *Sonnets from the Portuguese* by English poet Elizabeth Barrett Browning, 44, who expresses hesitation at burdening poet Robert Browning with an invalid wife. She married Browning 4 years ago despite her infirmity, the result of an injury sustained while saddling a horse at age 15: "How do I love thee? Let me count the ways./ I love thee to the depth and breadth and height/ My soul can reach . . ."; "In Memoriam" by Alfred Tennyson who began the elegy 17 years ago upon the death of his sister's fiancé Arthur Hallam: " 'Tis better to have loved and lost,/ Than never to have loved at all;" "Ring out, wild bells, to the wild sky,/ The flying cloud, the frosty light:/ The year is dying in the night;/ Ring out, wild bells, and let him die. . . ." "Ring out the old, ring in the new,/ Ring, happy bells, across the snow;/ The year is going, let him go;/ Ring out the false, ring in the true"; "The Building of the Ship" by Henry Wadsworth Longfellow: "Sail on, O Ship of State!/ Sail on, O Union, strong and great!/ Humanity with all its fears/ With all the hopes of future years,/ Is hanging breathless on thy fate!"

Painting *Morning, the Dance of the Nymphs* by Jean B. C. Corot; *The Stonebreakers* and *Burial at Ornans* by Gustave Courbet; *Christ in the House of His Parents* by John Everett Millais.

Gallery of Illustrious Americans by New York portrait photographer Mathew B. Brady, 27, gains national prominence for Brady (*see* 1864).

Opera *Genoveva* 6/25 at Leipzig, with music by Robert Schumann; *Lohengrin* 8/28 at the Weimar Theater, with music by Richard Wagner that includes a "Wedding March" (*see* Victoria, 1858).

P. T. Barnum engages Swedish coloratura Johanna Maria "Jenny" Lind, 30, for an American tour and pays "the Swedish nightingale" $1,000 per night plus all expenses. She opens at New York's Castle Garden 9/11 in a concert that grosses $17,864.05 and she begins a 2-year U.S. tour in which she will earn $130,000 of which $100,000 will go to charities.

Popular songs "De Camptown Races (Gwine to Run All Night)" by Stephen C. Foster; "Cheer, Boys, Cheer" by English composer-singer Henry Russell, 38, lyrics by Scottish journalist Charles Mackay.

Squash racquets is played for the first time by the boys of England's 279-year-old Harrow School (approximate year).

Anagrams is invented by a Salem, Mass., schoolteacher whose word-building game will gain wide popularity (*see* Scrabble, 1948).

Levi Strauss "bibless overalls" are introduced by Bavarian-American Levi Strauss, 20, who has arrived at San Francisco with a bundle of canvas fabric he hoped to sell to a tentmaker. Told by a miner that prospectors need sturdy pants, Strauss finds a tailor, has him make up two pairs of canvas pants, wears one pair himself and gives the other to his new friend who goes round town talking about these new pants of Levi's, and sends word to his brothers in the East to "buy up all the canvas you can lay your hands on." By 1853 Strauss will be hiring all the tailors and seamstresses he can find for his California Street pants factory, he will switch from canvas to denim, and when he finds that two pieces rarely dye to the same shades of light blue, brown, or grey, he will order a deep indigo blue that assures him of a standard color for the "blue jeans" that will be worn by generations of Americans (*see* rivets, 1874).

Sweet-Orr Company is founded at Wappingers Falls, N.Y., by local tailor James A. Orr who has split his pants panning for gold in California, has returned home, and has formed a partnership with his nephews C. E. and S. W. Sweet. They have put up a few hundred dollars to help their uncle buy six sewing machines and hire girls to operate them. Sweet-Orr will be a major producer of overalls (*see* Lee, 1911).

The Pinkerton National Detective Agency opens at Chicago under the direction of Scots-American lawman Allan Pinkerton, 31, who was elected deputy sheriff of Kane County, Ill., 4 years ago after discovering a gang of counterfeiters and leading a force to capture them. Pinkerton has recently joined the Chicago police force as its first and only detective, he has helped to apprehend the perpetrators of a series of railway and express company robberies, and he has resigned to open the Pinkerton Agency which will solve a number of railroad crimes in the next decade (*see* 1861).

San Francisco's City of Paris department store has its origin in a dry goods shop opened at the corner of Stockton and Geary Streets by French-American merchant Felix Verdier who operated a silk stocking factory at Nimes but who prefers exile to the repression that is ending the French republic (above).

St. Louis' Scruggs-Vandervoort-Barney has its origin in a dry goods store that will become a leading department store.

A 50-year period of large-scale tenement construction begins at New York (*see* 1901 tenement law).

Eight pairs of English sparrows are imported by the Brooklyn Institute to protect Brooklyn, N.Y., shade trees from caterpillars (*see* starlings, 1890).

Fire damages San Francisco May 4, June 14, and September 17.

Salmon is taken for the last time from England's Thames River which is fast becoming heavily polluted. The fish will not reappear in the Thames for more than 120 years.

Cyrus McCormick buys out William Ogden for twice the $25,000 Ogden has invested in McCormick's Chicago reaper business (*see* 1847; 1851).

The U.S. cotton crop reaches 2,136,000 bales.

California raises 15,000 bushels of wheat (*see* 1860; Glenn, 1851).

German-American entrepreneur Henry Miller begins buying up California land. The immigrant butcher has arrived at San Francisco with $6 in his pocket and instead of prospecting for gold has borrowed money to start buying property along rivers, cutting off back-country homesteaders from the water, and forcing them to sell out to him at distress prices. Learning of a new swamp lands law that permits a settler to gain title to lands that are underwater and pay nothing if he agrees to drain the land, Miller loads a rowboat atop a wagon and has himself pulled across a large stretch of dry land, whereupon he files a map of the sections with a sworn statement that he has covered the land in a rowboat. By such means, and by purchasing land from speculators who have obtained rights while working as U.S. Government inspectors, Miller will one day own more than 14.5 million acres of the richest land in California and Oregon, a territory three times the size of New Jersey (*see* 1905; Haggin and Tevis, 1877).

Jersey cows are introduced into the United States where they will be an important dairy breed noted for the high butterfat content of their milk (*see* Babcock tester, 1890).

Open-ranging longhorn cattle herds on the western plains are estimated to number 50 million head and share the prairie with 20 million head of buffalo. At age 7 or 8 the cattle's horns measure from 4 to 5 feet tip to tip, and in years past the animals have been hunted for their horns, which are used for rifle racks, buttons, spoons, and forks, and for their hides which are used for rawhide ropes, whips, buckets, clothing, and—soaked and dried—even for nails (*see* Herefords, 1840; Aberdeen Angus, 1873).

Milo maize (Kaffir corn) is introduced into the United States for use as livestock forage.

The Elberta peach is imported into the United States from China by some accounts (but *see* 1870).

The Red Delicious apple is discovered as a chance seedling in Iowa. The Red Delicious will become the leading U.S. apple variety.

A demonstration that the human liver can take the sugars broken down in digestion and build them into the complex sugar glycogen is made by French physiologist Claude Bernard, 37. It is the first evidence that the body can build up any substances of its own (*see* 1855).

Appointment of an analytical and sanitary commission to study the quality of British foods is announced by the English medical journal *Lancet* (*see* 1823; Hassall and Letheby, 1851, 1855).

The rum ration in the Royal Navy is reduced from one-quarter pint to one-eighth pint to be dispensed before the midday meal (*see* 1731; 1824).

Less than 15 percent of the world's sugar supply comes from beets (*see* 1814; 1878).

Tea catches up with coffee in popularity among the English (*see* 1840; 1869).

1850 (cont.) Folger's coffee is supplied to the growing horde of gold-seekers by San Francisco entrepreneur James Folger, who offers coffee that has been roasted, ground, and packaged at a time when most coffee drinkers are buying green coffee beans and roasting and grinding the beans themselves. Folger will obtain top quality beans from Central America that have been shipped until now only to Europe.

U.S. consumption of wheat flour reaches 205 pounds per capita, up from 170 pounds in 1830, and Americans average 184 pounds of meat, up from 178.

The first White House cooking stove is installed by Millard Fillmore (above), but the White House cooks quit in protest, preferring to use the fireplace until an expert from the Patent Office spends a day showing them how to regulate the heat with dampers.

The population of New York City reaches 700,000 with 20 percent of it foreign-born, mostly Irish.

The native population of the Hawaiian (Sandwich) Islands falls to 75,000, down from 150,000 in 1819 (*see* 1860). King Kamehameha III gives up rights to much of his lands in the Great Mahele and foreigners take over the lands.

The U.S. South has 1.8 million black slaves, 2.1 million whites. 15.7 percent of the U.S. population is black.

The world's population reaches at least 1 billion (1.24 billion by some estimates). It has twice as many people as it had in the 17th century.

1851 A complete account of thermodynamic theory that coordinates the discoveries of the past half-century is given by Glasgow mathematics professor William Thomson whose 1848 absolute scale of temperature will be called the Kelvin scale after 1892 when he is raised to the peerage by Queen Victoria and made Baron Kelvin of Largs. Thomson has developed the findings reported in 1840 by J. P. Joule, he will lay the foundations of the theory of electric oscillations, and his study of the oscillating discharge of condensers will lead to the discovery of radio waves by German physicist Heinrich Hertz in 1887.

The London Great Exhibition that opens May 1 is the world's first world's fair and in 141 days attracts more than 6 million admissions. It is intended to show British industrial achievement and prosperity, but foreign exhibits in many cases outshine British exhibits.

German steelmaker Alfried Krupp exhibits a 4,300-pound steel ingot cast miraculously in one piece; it dwarfs a 2,400-pound Sheffield "monster" casting and wins world acclaim for Fried. Krupp of Essen (*see* 1838).

The Colt revolver exhibited at the London Great Exhibition alarms British gunmakers who fear that Colt's mass-production methods will swamp their handmade guns, but gunmaker Robert Adams has patented a revolver that recocks itself each time the trigger is pulled, while the .36 caliber Colt is a single-action revolver and must be thumb-cocked for each

shot. The British master general of ordnance conducts tests September 10, Adams circulates an account that the Colt weapons misfired 10 times while no Adams weapon misfired, the *Times* says the Colt is "very good," but no official results are published. Samuel Colt presents Prince Albert and the prince of Wales with Colt revolvers, British officers use some of the other revolvers handed out by Colt to fight the "kaffirs" who are using Sioux tactics in the Cape War by attacking the British as they reload their muskets, and Colt wins over the British when he addresses the Institution of Civil Engineers November 25 and asserts that the British will never defeat the kaffirs without Colt revolvers (*see* 1846; 1871).

Scottish industrial chemist James Young, 40, patents a method for producing paraffin by dry distillation of coal. Young will manufacture naphtha, lubricating oils, paraffin oil, and solid paraffin from Bogshead coal and later from Scottish shale (*see* kerosene, 1855).

The Corliss steam engine exhibited at the London Great Exhibition (above) by Providence, R.I., engineer-inventor George Henry Corliss, 34, weighs 1,700 tons and produces 2,500-horsepower from cylinders more than 3 feet in diameter operated by 30-foot gear wheels.

The law of electromagnetic induction is enunciated by German physicist Franz Ernst Neumann, 53.

The high-tension induction coil is invented by German physicist-manufacturer Heinrich Daniel Ruhmkorff, 48.

Victoria is proclaimed a separate Australian colony (*see* 1834).

Siam's Rama III (Phra Nang Klao) dies after a 27-year reign that has seen the reopening of his country to contact with the West. He is succeeded by his 47-year-old half-brother Phra Chom Klao Mongkut who begins a 17-year reign as Rama IV. A Buddhist monk until now, the new king will build canals and roads, he will set up a printing press, he will stimulate education, he will reform the administration, he will improve the condition of slaves, he will issue Siam's first currency, he will encourage commerce with Europe and the United States, and he will import an English governess who will publish books about her experiences.

France's Third Republic ends after 3 years in a December 2 coup d'etat engineered by President Louis Napoleon Bonaparte and his half-brother Count Morny. Paris is occupied by army brigades, leading deputies are arrested in the middle of the night, and a popular uprising is quelled by the minister of war who sends his troops against the workers' street barricades. Unarmed crowds are fired upon in the Massacre of the Boulevards, and a 9-year period of repression begins (*see* Napoleon III, 1852).

Last year's Fugitive Slave Act is defied by a mob of Boston blacks who rescue the fugitive Shadrach from jail February 15. President Fillmore 3 days later calls upon Massachusetts citizens and officials to execute the law, but another fugitive slave is rescued October 1 by abolitionists at Syracuse, N.Y. (see 1854).

All Sioux lands in Iowa and some in Minnesota are ceded to the federal government by a treaty signed July 23 by Sioux chieftains.

Reform of U.S. women's clothing is urged in her magazine *The Lily* by social reformer Amelia Jenks Bloomer, 33, who will be ridiculed for wearing full-cut trousers ("bloomers") under a short skirt in public. The "bloomers" were designed by Elizabeth Smith Miller and were introduced 3 years ago at the Women's Rights Convention at Seneca Falls, N.Y.

Men and women are treated equally and all classes of work are viewed as equally honorable in the Oneida Community which has 300 converts living in communal buildings made of timber from the community's farms (see 1848). Children are reared in the "children's house" operated by men and women considered best qualified (see Newhouse trap, 1860).

The Young Men's Christian Association (YMCA) opens its first American offices at Boston and Montreal (see 1844; YWCA, 1855).

Seattle is founded in Oregon Territory. The lumber town will be given its name in 1853 to honor Chief Sealth of the Duwamish and Suquamish who befriends the first settlers (see 1884).

The Erie Railroad reaches Dunkirk on Lake Erie May 15 and becomes the first line linking New York City with the Great Lakes, providing competition for the 26-year-old Erie Canal. Begun in 1832 with state and county money, the Erie is now controlled by New York financier Daniel Drew, 53, who began his fortune as a livestock dealer who watered his stock by feeding the animals salt and letting them drink their fill to put on weight before selling them. Drew has operated steamboats on the Hudson and on Long Island Sound in competition with Commodore van Derbilt (see 1852).

The Pennsylvania Railroad reaches Pittsburgh (see 1846; 1854).

The Baltimore & Ohio reaches the Ohio River at Wheeling (see 1828; 1854).

The Hudson River Railroad opens to link New York City with East Albany (see van Derbilt, 1858).

The Missouri Pacific Railway begins laying track at St. Louis July 4 under the name Pacific Railway. The first railroad west of the Mississippi, it will grow to serve the Mississippi Valley south to Memphis and New Orleans and the Missouri Valley west to Kansas City and Pueblo, Colo., it will own majority interests in other companies to serve Texas, but it will never reach the Pacific.

Some 4,400 miles of railway track will be laid this year and next between the Atlantic seaboard and the Mississippi.

The Flying Cloud launched by Nova Scotia-born Boston shipbuilder Donald McKay, 41, is a 229-foot clipper ship and the greatest of some 40 clipper ships that will be built this year and next. 41 feet wide, 22 feet deep, and displacing 1,783 tons, she is bought by New York merchant Moses Grinnell, she sails from Pier 20 on New York's East River under the command of Marblehead master Josiah Creasy, and she sets a new record by reaching San Francisco in just under 90 days (see 1952).

Visitors to the London Great Exhibition (above) have in many cases booked their travel accommodations through Thomas Cook (see 1841; 1866).

An Australian gold rush follows the discovery by sheep ranch manager Edward Hammond Hargreaves, 35, who has found the yellow metal near Bathhurst in New South Wales. English merchant-shipper George Fife Angas, 62, who has founded South Australia, moves to Adelaide as an influx of Chinese attracted by the gold strike brings demands for legislation to keep non-white immigrants out of Australia (see 1855; Victoria, above).

The U.S. Treasury turns out nearly 4 million $1 gold pieces—tiny coins authorized by Congress 1849.

Congress votes March 3 to authorize minting of 3-cent silver coins to reduce the demand for large copper pennies.

The Williamsburgh Savings Bank is founded at Brooklyn, N.Y., in a corner of a basement of a Greek Revival church at the corner of Old Fourth and South Third Streets in the Williamsburgh section. The bank will have a building of its own by 1854 (see "Tower of Strength," 1929).

Northwestern University is founded north of Chicago in an area that will be called Evanston after physician John Evans, 36, professor of obstetrics at Chicago's Rush Medical College. Evans publishes and edits the *Northwestern Medical and Surgical Journal* and has been a leader in securing a charter for the new university.

The University of Minnesota is founded at Minneapolis.

Ripon College is founded at Ripon, Wis.

The University of Santa Clara is founded in California.

Duke University has its beginnings in North Carolina's Trinity College founded at Durham (see 1924).

The *New York Times* begins publication September 18 with Henry J. Raymond as editor of the daily newspaper (see Ochs, 1896).

The first successful cable is laid between Dover and Calais under the English Channel.

Reuter's News Service is started by German entrepreneur Paul Julius von Reuter, 35, who has pioneered in using carrier pigeons to convey messages, notably final stock prices, between Brussels and Aachen to plug the only gap in a telegraph system link-

471

Stephen Foster's most popular song had its debut June 15, 1853. It helped arouse sympathy for America's slaves.

ing the commercial centers of Berlin and Paris. Reuter moves to London to take advantage of the new cable (above) and establishes a continental cable service that will be extended from stock prices to general news and will become a worldwide news agency that will compete with the Associated Press founded 3 years ago and with other news agencies (*see* INS, 1906; UP, 1907).

The Library of Congress is damaged by fire December 24 in the Capitol at Washington and two-thirds of the collection acquired from Thomas Jefferson in 1814 is destroyed along with thousands of other volumes. Congress appropriates $100,000 to buy new books and to create a more fireproof room for the library, which by 1865 will have more than 80,000 books and will add the Smithsonian Institution's 40,000-volume library in 1866 (*see* 1897).

Nonfiction *Fifteen Decisive Battles of the World* by London University historian Edward Shepherd Creasy, 39; *The League of the . . . Iroquois* by Rochester, N.Y., lawyer-ethnologist Lewis Henry Morgan, 33, who has made the first scientific study of any Indian tribe and who will be called the "father of American anthropology."

Fiction *Uncle Tom's Cabin, or Life Among the Lowly* (first serial installments) by U.S. novelist Harriet Beecher Stowe, 40, whose sentimental tearjerker about slavery will have record sales (*see* 1852); *Moby Dick* by Herman Melville is only superficially about whaling and is possibly the greatest novel in all American literature. It will have sales of barely 50 copies in Melville's lifetime; *The House of the Seven Gables* by Nathaniel Hawthorne; *The Snow-Image and Other Twice-Told Tales* by Hawthorne.

Poetry *Romanzero* by Heinrich Heine.

Painting *Washington Crossing the Delaware* by German painter Emanuel Leutze, 35, who will emigrate to New York and Washington in 1859. John James Audubon dies at New York January 27 at age 65; J. M. W. Turner dies at Chelsea December 19 at age 76.

Sculpture *The Greek Slave* exhibited at the London Great Exhibition (above) is a marble figure completed in 1843 by U.S. sculptor Hiram Powers, now 45, who started his career in a Cincinnati waxworks, moved to Washington, D. C., in 1834 to make busts from life of U. S. statesmen, and moved in 1837 to Florence where he will live until his death in 1873. Inspired by reports that Greek prisoners were sold in slave markets by the Turks during the 1821–1829 war for Greek independence, the neoclassical nude attracts great attention, authorities set aside special hours for women who are embarrassed at viewing it in the presence of men, the work is sold in London, and Americans by the thousands pay 25 cents each to see full-sized marble copies that tour U.S. cities.

A wet collodion process for developing photographic images is published by English architect Scott Archer, 38, whose process will be used in photomechanical houses for nearly a century. A solution of nitrocellulose in alcohol-ether, collodion is iodized by Archer and is sensitized in the darkroom by immersion in a bath of silver nitrate to form silver iodide with an excess of silver nitrate. The plate is exposed in the camera, developed by pouring on a solution of pyrogallol containing acetic acid, and fixed with a strong solution of thiosulfate of soda (cyanide of potassium will later be used instead). Archer's process, which he does not patent, will quickly replace Calotype and Daguerrotype (*see* Talbot, 1841; Daguerre, 1839; Sayce and Bolton, 1864).

Theater *Dame de Pique* by Dion Boucicault at London's Drury Lane Theatre; *Love in a Maze* by Dion Boucicault 3/6 at the Princess's Theatre, London; *The Follies of Marianne* (*Les Caprices de Marianne*) by Alfred de Musset 6/14 at the Comédie Française, Paris; *An Italian Straw Hat* (*Un Chapeau de Paille d'Italie*) by French playwright Eugène Labiche, 36, 8/14 at the Théâtre de la Montansier, Paris. The five-act comedy is one of six Labiche plays performed this year (nine were produced last year, 12 will be produced next year); *Bettine* by Alfred de Musset 10/30 at the Théâtre du Gymnase, Paris.

Opera *Rigoletto* 3/11 at Venice's Teatro la Fenice, with music by Giuseppe Verdi, libretto from a Victor Hugo drama of intrigue and treachery in the French court of François I.

First performances Symphony No. 3 in E flat major (*Rhenish*) by Robert Schumann 2/6 at Düsseldorf's Geisler Hall; Hungarian Rhapsody No. 2 by Franz Liszt who has settled at Weimar with Princess Sayn-Wittgenstein.

Popular songs "Old Folks at Home" by Stephen C. Foster.

The America's Cup won by the U.S. schooner *America* August 22 will be the most coveted trophy in world ocean racing. The U.S. schooner beats seven British schooners and eight cutters in a race round the Isle of Wight to win the Royal Yacht Squadron Cup which she carries home to the United States. It will remain there despite repeated attempts by British, French, Australian, Canadian, and other world yachtsmen to outsail U.S. boats and gain—or regain—the America's Cup.

I. M. Singer patents his sewing machine and goes into partnership with his New York lawyer Edward Clark, who will defend I. M. Singer and Company from patent suits brought by Elias Howe (*see* 1846; 1850). Howe will eventually win a Massachusetts court decision and will make a fortune from royalties that Singer will pay as the sewing machine gains worldwide distribution (*see* Hunt, 1858).

Bally Shoe Factories is founded by Carl Franz Bally in the village of Schoenwend in Switzerland's Aare Valley. The Bally enterprise will develop into a worldwide shoemaking company with factories in Austria, France, Britain, South Africa, and the United States as well as in Switzerland.

The Aquascutum raincoat challenges the Macintosh raincoat of 1823. The London firm Bax and Company in Regent Street makes the new raincoat from a chemically treated wool fiber trademarked Aquascutum (*see* Burberry, 1856).

$ Boston's Jordan Marsh Company has its beginnings in a dry goods shop opened by merchants Eben D. Jordan and Benjamin L. Marsh. They will change the store's name next year to Jordan, Marsh Co., they will run their first full-page newspaper advertisement in mid-June of 1875, and the store will become Jordan Marsh Company in 1901 (*see* Boston Opera, 1909).

Lazarus Brothers opens at Columbus, Ohio, where Fred Lazarus and his brothers start a dry goods shop that will become the nucleus of Federated Department Stores (*see* 1929).

 The London Great Exhibition (above) is held in a Crystal Palace in Hyde Park constructed by the royal gardener Joseph Paxton, 50. The first great building not of solid masonry construction, the Crystal Palace is actually an immense 108-foot high greenhouse modeled after a conservatory designed by Paxton at Chatsworth in the late 1830s using newly developed techniques for making large sheets of glass, it has taken 2,000 men to build, it has consumed one-third the nation's glass output for a whole year, it is the world's largest glass-walled structure, and it is by far the largest single structure of any kind yet seen in the world, enclosing an area four times that of St. Peter's in Rome. The gas-lighted Crystal Palace will be a major influence in European railway station design for decades to come and it will be copied almost literally for a New York exposition in 1853.

 Cyrus McCormick exhibits his reaper at the London Great Exhibition, he produces 6,000 reapers, and he begins to enlarge foreign markets for his product (*see* 1849, 1879; Stanton, 1861).

Forty-Niner Hugh Glenn uses money made in the freighting business to plant wheat in California's Sacramento Valley and begins a vast agricultural empire (*see* 1865).

A 100-acre wheat field remains the largest any one man can farm.

 Ireland suffers widespread blindness as a result of the malnutrition experienced in the potato famine that began in 1846.

Articles exposing the adulteration of British foods will be published in the next 3 years by British chemist Arthur Hill Hassall and dietitian Henry Letheby who will document the whitening of bread with alum, the dilution of coffee with chicory, etc. (*see* 1850; 1855).

 Gail Borden returns from the London Great Exhibition with the Great Council Gold Medal for his meat biscuit. He has promoted it as useful for naval expeditions and other voyages (some have gone with Elisha Kent Kane, 41, who is making his first Arctic expedition), for travelers "on long journeys, through destitute regions," for explorers "in making geological and mineralogical surveys of our newly acquired territories," and for all families, "especially in warm weather" (*see* 1849).

Borden's ship encounters rough seas on the Atlantic, the two cows in the ship's hold become too seasick to be milked, an immigrant infant dies, and the hungry cries of the other infants determine Borden to find a way to produce a portable condensed milk that can keep without spoiling (*see* 1853).

Sale of wine, spirits, beer, and other intoxicating beverages has been forbidden at the London Great Exhibition (above) but tea, coffee, chocolate, cocoa, lemonade, ices, ginger-beer, and soda water have been permitted. The 61-year-old firm Messrs. Schweppe & Co. which received its first royal warrant 15 years ago has sold 177,737 dozen bottles, up from roughly 70,000 last year, and nearly 85,000 dozen of the total have been sold at the Exhibition. White Rhine wine (hock) and soda is a popular British beverage, and Schweppe's soda water is a popular mixer (*see* 1858).

The first U.S. state prohibition law is voted in Maine where the mayor of Portland Neal Dow, 47, has drafted the law, has submitted it to the state legislature, and has campaigned for its passage. An ardent temperance advocate, Dow will see his measure followed by other states (*see* 1852).

German-American brewer Valentin Blatz buys the 5-year-old City Brewery at Milwaukee and begins to increase production of Blatz Beer.

England's Huntley & Palmers biscuit works employs some 300 workers after 25 years in business.

The first U.S. cheese factory is established outside Rome, N.Y., by Jesse Williams.

1851 (cont.) Several tons of butter are shipped by rail from Ogdensburg, N.Y., to Boston in an ice-cooled wooden railcar insulated with sawdust.

The first wholesale ice cream business is founded by Baltimore milk dealer Jacob Fussell who receives milk in steady supply but who is faced with a problem of erratic demand. Fussell sells his ice cream at less than half the price charged by others and he begins to thrive.

Hawaii's Castle & Cooke food empire has its beginnings in a Honolulu mercantile house started by former missionaries Samuel Northrup Castle and Amos Starr Cooke who arrived in the Sandwich Islands aboard the *Mary Frazier* in 1837. They sever their ties with the American Board of Commissioners for Foreign Missions of Boston (*see* 1964).

China's population reaches 440 million, but Chinese census procedures have been disrupted by the Tai-p'ing rebellion that began last year. Chinese population counts will be uncertain until 1953 and even thereafter.

India has a population of 205 million, Japan 33.5, Russia 65, Turkey 27, France 36, the German states and free cities 34, the Italian states 24, Great Britain 20.9 (with 17.9 in England and Wales), Brazil an estimated 8 million including 2.5 million slaves, the United States 23.6 million with nearly half living west of the Alleghenies.

More than 250,000 Irish emigrate and the country's population falls to 6.5 million, down from 10,175,000 in 1841. Some go to South Australia (above) which has a population of 77,000, as does Victoria, while New South Wales has 190,000.

The United States will receive 2.5 million immigrants in this decade, up from 1.7 million in the 1840s.

London is the world's largest city with a population of 2.37 million. Sochow has 2 million, Peking 1.65, Canton 1.24; Changchow, Kingtehchen, Sian, and Siangtan each has 1 million, Wuhan 997,000, Constantinople 900,000, Calcutta 800,000, Hangchow 700,000, Bombay 650,000, Foochow 600,000. Paris has nearly 1.3 million and begins a rapid rise (figures include suburban environs).

1852 The safety elevator invented at Yonkers, N.Y., by master mechanic Elisha Graves Otis, 41, will lead to the development of high-rise buildings. Otis sets up ratchets along each side of an elevator shaft at the Yonkers Bedstead Manufacturing Company, he attaches teeth to the sides of the cage, the rope that holds up the cage keeps the teeth clear of the ratchets so long as the rope remains under tension, and when the tension is released the teeth grip the ratchets and hold the cage securely in place. Otis has been about to join the gold rush to California, but he changes his mind when he receives two unsolicited orders for his "safety hoister" (*see* 1854).

 The Sand River Convention signed by the British January 17 recognizes the independence of the Transvaal (*see* 1843; South African Republic, 1856).

Argentina abandons her designs on Uruguay following the defeat of the Argentine dictator Juan Manuel de Rosas February 3 in the Battle of Caseros. Insurgent Justo de Urquiza, 51, wins the battle with support from Brazilian and Uruguayan forces and Rosas flees to England.

The Burmese king Pagan Min is deposed after a 6-year reign, and Rangoon is taken by British forces as a second Burmese War begins.

New Zealand breaks apart under terms of a new constitution that provides for six provinces, each under the control of a superintendent with a provincial council elected by voters who must be property owners. A governor with a legislative council and a house of representatives exercises general administrative power, but regulation of the natives is left to the colonial office at London, and provincial governments will determine most affairs until 1875.

U.S. Democrats nominate "dark horse" Franklin Pierce of New Hampshire for president, and he wins the election by defeating Whig candidate Winfield Scott of Mexican War fame with 254 electoral votes to Scott's 42. The Whig party begins to dissolve over the slavery issue.

A Second Empire is proclaimed in France December 2 following exile of the Orléans family by Louis Napoleon who orders a plebiscite in November, finds support for revival of the empire, and begins a reign as Napoleon III that will continue until 1870.

Wells, Fargo & Co. is founded at New York by W. G. Fargo to "forward Gold Dust, Bullion, Specie, Packages, Parcels & Freight of all kinds, to and from New York and San Francisco . . . and all the principal towns of California and Oregon" (*see* 1844). Fargo will consolidate with rival stagecoach companies in 1866 and will become president of American Express in 1868 after a larger merger.

The first through train from the East reaches Chicago February 20 by way of the Michigan Southern Railway. The railroad will make Chicago more than ever the grain and meat-packing center of America.

The National Road that began as the Cumberland Road in 1811 and that reached Wheeling 6 years later finally reaches Illinois.

The Pennsylvania Railroad completes trackage between Philadelphia and Pittsburgh (*see* 1851; 1854).

Pennsylvania adopts a railroad gauge different from that of New York to prevent the Erie Railroad from passing through Pennsylvania into Ohio (*see* 1853).

A railroad that will become famous as the Rock Island Line runs its first train October 10. Pulled by a brightly painted locomotive named the *Rocket*, six yellow coaches travel 40 miles from Chicago to Joliet, Ill., in 2 hours to start service on the Chicago, Rock Island Line founded under the name Rock Island & LaSalle in 1847 by Rock Island, Ill., settler George Davenport and his associates. By February of 1854 the road will reach Rock Island in the Mississippi to give Chicago its first rail link to America's key waterway, and the road will grow to embrace 7,500 miles of track extending north to Minneapolis-St. Paul, south to Galveston, east to Memphis, and west to Denver, Colorado Springs, and Santa Rosa (see Iowa City, 1855).

Studebaker Brothers Manufacturing Co. is founded as H. And C. Studebaker at South Bend, Ind., by Pennsylvania-born wagonmaker Clement Studebaker, 21, with his older brother Henry. Brother John M. is making wheelbarrows for gold miners at Placerville, Calif., and will join the company in 1858 with $8,000 in savings from the goldfields, brothers Peter E. and Jacob F. will join thereafter, the company will be organized as Studebaker Brothers in 1868, and it will become the world's largest wagon and carriage producer (see 1902).

The first Boston area street railway begins operations with a single horsecar between Harvard Square, Cambridge, and Union Square, Somerville.

London's Paddington and King's Cross railway stations open (see 1848; 1864).

The Société Aérostatique is founded at Paris as the world's first aeronautical society (see Cayeley, 1853).

The world's first tramp steamer is launched June 30 at Jarrow, England, as the John Bowes goes into service as a collier.

The S.S. Pacific goes into transatlantic service for the Collins Line (United States Mail Steamship Company). A sister ship to the S.S. Atlantic that began service in 1850, the 2,856-ton S.S. Pacific is the first ship to cross from New York to Liverpool in less than 10 days (see 1854).

The Sovereign of the Seas launched by Donald McKay of last year's Flying Cloud fame confounds skeptics by showing that a 2,421-ton clipper ship can be practical (but see 1953).

"Coal oil" is distilled from coal tar by a Boston pharmaceutical firm. The firm will start selling its coal oil under the brand name "kerosene" when it is found that the oil is not only a lubricant but will also burn in lamps (see Young, 1851; Gessner, 1855).

An improved lamp chimney is devised by German-American inventor Christopher Dorflinger.

The first effective compulsory school attendance law in America is enacted by the Massachusetts legislature.

Boston State College is founded.

Tufts College is founded at Medford, Mass., by Hosea Ballou II, nephew of a prominent Universalist clergyman.

Antioch College is founded at Yellow Springs, Ohio, by Massachusetts educator Horace Mann (see 1839).

Mills College for Women is founded at Oakland, Calif.

The Washington Evening Star is launched as a two-page penny daily published by Joseph Borrows Tate, 34, who is bought out after 6 months by William Wallack who makes it a four-page paper and who next year will employ Crosby S. Noyes as a reporter. Noyes and four partners will buy the Star in 1867.

"Uncle Sam" is portrayed for the first time in cartoon form by the New York comic weekly Diogenes, Hys Lantern (see 1813; 1917).

The Boston Public Library opens with funds raised by public subscription in a drive led by local financier Joshua Bates, 64, a partner in London's Baring Brothers since 1828.

Nonfiction Thesaurus of English Words and Phrases by English physician-scholar Peter Mark Roget, 73, whose book will go through 28 editions before its compiler dies at age 90.

Fiction Uncle Tom's Cabin by Harriet Beecher Stowe goes through 120 U.S. editions within a year. 300,000 copies are sold in America with similar sales abroad, a popular success never before seen in publishing and rarely to be seen again; The Blithedale Romance by Nathaniel Hawthorne is a critique of the 1841–1847 Brook Farm experiment and analyzes the urge to seek Utopia and the possibly tragic effects of feminist emancipation; History of Henry Esmond by William Makepeace Thackeray; Ange Pitou by Alexandre Dumas père, now 50; A Sportsman's Sketches (Zapiski okhotnika) by Russian novelist Ivan Turgenev, 33, who is exiled to his estates for an obituary praising Nikolai Gogol, who has died February 21 at age 42.

Poetry Emaux et Camées by Théophile Gautier.

Painting Pietà by French painter Gustave Moreau, 26; Christ Washing Peter's Feet by English painter Ford Madox Brown, 31; Ophelia by John Everett Millais.

Theater Camille, the Lady of the Camellias (La Dame aux Camélias) by Alexandre Dumas fils 2/2 at the Théâtre du Vaudeville, Paris. Based on last year's novel, the play was published in 1848 but censors have delayed the production; Agnes Bernauer by Friedrich Hebbel 3/25 at Munich's Hoftheater; Uncle Tom's Cabin by George L. Aiken, 22, 9/27 at the Troy, N.Y., Museum. Adapted from the Harriet Beecher Stowe novel (above), the play will be produced throughout the country with enormous success in the North; Masks and Faces by English playwrights Charles Reade, 38, and Tom Taylor, 35, 11/20 at London's Haymarket Theatre; The Journalists (Die Journalisten) by German playwright Gustav Freytag, 36, 12/8 at Breslau.

Opera Dmitri Donskoi 4/30 at St. Petersburg, with music by Russian court pianist Anton Grigorevich

1852 (cont.) Rubinstein, 22, who is invited by the Grand Duchess Helena Pavlovich to be music director at Michael Palace and to spend the summer with her on Kammeny Island in the Neva River (*see* below).

First performances Overture to Byron's *Manfred* by Robert Schumann 6/13 at Weimar; Overture to *Julius Caesar* by Robert Schumann 8/3 at Dusseldorf's Male Choral Festival; Melody in F by Anton Rubinstein (above) at St. Petersburg. The piano piece composed on Kammeny Island is played primarily with the thumbs.

Popular song "Massa's in de Cold Cold Ground" by Stephen C. Foster.

Bright tobacco is discovered by North Carolina farmers Eli and Elisha Slade near Durham and will soon be used in Bull Durham pipe tobacco. The Slade brothers heat some of their tobacco crop over hot flues and find that the clear, golden tobacco that emerges from this curing process is sweet to smoke. They apply the process to other tobaccos but find that none reacts to flue-curing in the same way (*see* Reynolds, 1875; Camels, 1913).

Chicago merchant Potter Palmer opens a shop that will develop into the city's largest department store (*see* Marshall Field, 1865).

The Bon Marché at Paris is joined by French merchant Aristide Boucicaut who will turn the small piece-goods shop into the world's first true department store. Boucicaut institutes revolutionary retailing principles that include small markups to encourage high volume and rapid turnover to compensate for smaller gross margins, fixed and marked prices, and free entrance with no moral obligation to buy. He will soon begin extending the right to exchange merchandise or to obtain a refund, sales will increase from half a million francs this year to 5 million by 1860, and by 1870 the Bon Marché will occupy an entire city block with sales of 20 million francs in dresses, coats, underwear, shoes, millinery, and the like (*see* 1893; Louvre, 1855; Printemps, 1865; Samaritaine, 1869; Lewis's of Liverpool, 1856).

Château-sur-Mer is completed at Newport, R.I., for William S. Wetmore who has made a fortune in the China trade. The ornate Victorian mansion on Bellevue Avenue will be augmented in 1872 by Newport's first French ballroom which will be designed by Richard Morris Hunt (*see* 1839; 1895).

The Bois de Boulogne is given to Paris by Napoleon III who begins an 18-year reign with a huge program of public works under the direction of Baron Georges Eugène Haussmann, 42, who is named prefect of the Seine and who begins widening streets and opening new boulevards. Named by its inhabitants in 1308 after a pilgrimage to Notre Dame de Boulogne-sur-Mer on the Manche (English Channel), the bois has been a royal hunting ground for more than two centuries, but it will be transformed by Baron Haussmann into a 2,100-acre park modeled after London's Hyde Park.

Hydraulic mining begins in California as miners complete a 45-mile canal to bring in water at the rate of 60 million gallons per day, and gold miner Anthony Chabot devises a canvas hose with an 8-inch thick nozzle that permits gold-bearing gravel to be washed from stream banks into placer pits. This labor-saving device will devastate California hillsides as it brings tons of topsoil and gravel into bottomland for every ounce of gold extracted (*see* 1884).

The first practical movable-frame beehive is designed by Philadelphia clergyman Lorenzo Lorraine Langstroth, 42, who discovers the "bee space" of just under one-quarter inch in height and whose hive will revolutionize the beekeeping industry (*see* Huber, 1789).

The Holstein cow that will be most significant to the development of the major U.S. dairy breed arrives aboard a Dutch vessel (*see* 1625).

John Deere's plow factory at Moline, Ill., produces 4,000 plows (*see* 1847; 1855).

International Silver Company has its beginnings in the Meriden Britannia Company founded at Meriden, Conn., through a merger engineered by Horace C. Wilcox, 28, who has been acting with his younger brother Dennis as sales agent for the silverplate made at Hartford since 1847 by William, Asa, and Simeon Rogers. Rogers Brothers is included in the new company which will become the leading U.S. tableware producer.

Prohibition laws are adopted by Massachusetts, Vermont, and Louisiana (*see* 1855; Maine, 1851).

Service à la Russe is brought to England but will not be common for another 20 or 30 years (*see* 1811). Instead of dishes being placed in turn on sideboards for waiters to serve to guests, a multitude of dishes will continue to be placed before English diners simultaneously in two or three great courses and several minor courses.

Emigration from Ireland has its peak year but will continue on a large scale for years to come (*see* 1847).

The governor of California calls for land grants to encourage the continued immigration of Chinese, "one of the most worthy of our newly adopted citizens." Close to 50,000 Chinese have defied China's death-penalty law against emigration to make their way to California's goldfields, and an immigration agency (called the Chinese Six Companies after the six districts of China from which most have come) has been formed to advance money to newcomers to buy picks, shovels, and other mining supplies (*see* Central Pacific Railroad, 1861).

1853 Commodore Matthew Calbraith Perry, 59, of the U.S. Navy arrives at Edo in July with the first formal bid for U.S. relations with Japan. Perry carries a letter for the shogun from former president Millard Fillmore who dispatched Perry in November with a request for a treaty, Perry demands the treaty "as a right, and not . . . as a favor," and he leaves word that he will return in the spring for a favorable reply.

Japan's Tokugawa shogun Ieoshi dies at age 61 after a 16-year reign. He is succeeded by his 29-year-old brother Iesada who will open two Japanese ports to trade next year in order to end a civil war precipitated by the demands of Commodore Perry (above).

British forces end the Second Burmese War, Britain annexes Pegu, and Mindon Min becomes king of Burma, beginning an enlightened reign that will continue until 1878. The new king will build Mandalay and will make it the Burmese capital in 1857.

Shanghai falls to rebel forces September 7 as the T'ai P'ing Rebellion continues (see 1850). Bandits in Anhuei, North Kiangsu, and Shantung organize under the name Nien Fei and begin a 15-year campaign of plunder as imperial troops withdraw to cope with the T'ai P'ing rebels.

The French emperor Napoleon III marries the Spanish comtesse Eugènie de Montijo, 26, January 29 at the Tuileries Palace. Napoleon has failed to win the hand of a Vasa or Hohenzollern.

Portugal's Maria II (Maria da Gloria) dies November 15 at age 34 after a 27-year reign marked by insurrections in 1846 and 1851 and interrupted by a 5-year civil war during which the queen lived in England. She is succeeded by her 16-year-old son Pedro de Alcantara, the boy's father will serve as regent until 1855, and he will reign as Pedro V until his death from cholera in 1861.

Political unrest in Europe over Turkish occupation of holy places in Palestine brings Russia, France, and Britain to the brink of war (see 1854).

The Gadsden Purchase treaty signed with Mexico December 30 permits the United States to annex a tract of land south of the Gila River. Mexico receives $10 million under terms of the treaty negotiated by U.S. Minister James Gadsden, 65.

The territory acquired in the Gadsden Treaty (above) includes the best railroad route from Texas to California. The treaty also gives the United States right of transit across the Isthmus of Tehauntepec.

A survey of the most practicable transcontinental U.S. railroad routes has been financed March 3 by a congressional appropriation of $150,000, to be undertaken under the direction of the War Department (see Central Pacific, 1861; Union Pacific, 1862).

The New York Central is created as the first major U.S. rail combine by a consolidation of 10 short-line railroads between Albany and Buffalo, but gauge standards change at the New York, Pennsylvania, and Ohio state borders, and the city of Erie, Pa., tears up rails of identical gauge in order to force trains to stop at Erie (see Britain, 1846; Vanderbilt, 1867).

A railroad from Philadelphia reaches the shore of Absecon, N.J., which will become famous as Atlantic City (see 1896).

The Vienna-Trieste railway line opens through the Alps (see 1867).

India's first railway line opens to link Bombay with Thana 20 miles away. English engineer James John Berkley, 34, has built the line and will complete the Bombay-Calcutta-Madras-Nagpur line in 1856.

Parliament authorizes construction of a 3.75-mile London underground railway between Farrington Street and Bishop's Road, Paddington (see 1863).

The Boston-built clipper ship Northern Light makes a record 76-day 6-hour voyage from San Francisco to Boston.

The Great Republic launched by Donald McKay is the world's largest sailing ship, but she is too big to be a commercial success. The 4,555-ton four-masted barque has patent double topsails and a 15-horsepower steam engine on deck to handle her yards and work her pumps.

I. K. Brunel begins construction of the S.S. Great Eastern. The passenger steamer will employ paddle wheels as well as a propellor and will be slightly larger than the Great Republic (above) but no more successful commercially.

The British single-screw steamship S.S. Himalaya goes into service. The 4,690-ton ship is 340 feet in length overall and will remain in service for more than 70 years.

U.S. shipping magnate Cornelius van Derbilt acknowledges that he is worth $11 million and that his fortune brings him an annual return of 25 percent (see 1850; 1858).

The first manned heavier-than-air flying machine soars 500 yards across a valley carrying the terrified coachman of English engineer Sir George Cayley, 80, in a large glider. Cayley defined the problem of heavier-than-air flight in his 1809 paper "On Aerial Navigation" (see Wright brothers, 1903).

A London cholera epidemic is traced by physician John Snow to a busy public pump in Broad Street whose water supply is contaminated by the cesspool of a tenement in which a cholera patient resides. Asked how the epidemic can be stopped, Snow replies, "remove the pump handle" (see Snow, 1847).

A yellow fever epidemic at New Orleans kills 7,848.

Acetyl salicylic acid is synthesized by Alsatian chemist Karl Gerhardt, but the derivative of salicylic acid is not in a form pure enough to be used therapeutically (see 1793; 1835; Aspirin, 1899).

Transportation of British convicts to Tasmania is ended after a half-century in which some 67,000 convicts have been landed on the island that is now definitively renamed Tasmania to replace the name Van Diemen's Land (see 1642).

The Massachusetts Constitution Convention receives a petition to permit woman suffrage. The appeal comes from the wife of educator and social reformer

1853 (cont.) Amos B. Alcott and 73 other women (*see* Lucy Stone, 1850; Elizabeth Cady Stanton, 1860).

Brunswick, Hanover, and Oldenburg join the German Zollverein, bringing all the non-Austrian German states into the customs union founded in 1834 (*see* 1867).

A London banking firm and foreign exchange that will become the world's leading gold trader is founded by Samuel Montagu, 21, with his brother and brother-in-law. The family name Samuel has been changed to Montagu by royal license, and the new firm will help make London the clearinghouse of the international money market.

The New York Clearing House that opens October 11 at 14 Wall Street is the first U.S. bank clearinghouse. 38 banks use the facility, and total clearings for the first day amount to nearly $2 million.

The Home Insurance Company is founded by New York entrepreneurs who defy warnings that their venture is "a desperate undertaking" in light of the July 1845 Broad Street fire that wiped out practically every New York insurance company. The New York State comptroller warned in his annual report last year that mutual companies should not go outside the bounds of their own counties or, at most, beyond an adjoining county, but the Home proceeds to underwrite protection on a national scale through local agents with an initial subscription of $500,000, and within 18 months the company has 140 agents.

The *United States Review* predicts that within half a century "machinery will perform all work—automata will direct them. The only tasks of the human race will be to make love, study and be happy."

Pocket watches are produced in quantity for the first time by the American Waltham Watch Company at Waltham, Mass. More than 30 watch factories will derive from the Waltham works, but watches will not be mass-produced for nearly 40 years and wristwatches will not appear for 54 years (*see* Ingersoll, 1892).

Bausch & Lomb Optical Company is established at Rochester, N.Y., by German-American lens grinders John Jacob Bausch, 23, and Henry Lomb, 28, whose firm will become the leading U.S. producer of microscopes, field glasses, binoculars, etc.

Samuel Colt opens a Hartford, Conn., armory with 1,400 machine tools that will revolutionize the manufacture of small arms (*see* 1846; 1871).

The University of Melbourne is founded in Australia.

Washington University is founded at St. Louis (*see* Brookings, 1910).

The University of Florida is founded at Gainesville.

Brentano's has its beginnings as the leading U.S. bookselling firm. Austrian-American entrepreneur August Brentano opens a newsstand in front of New York's New York Hotel and is permitted to occupy the desirable space because he is handicapped by a withered arm. Brentano discovers that the hotel has many English guests who bet on English horse races, and he prospers by ordering newspapers from England, meeting clipper ships at dockside to obtain the papers quickly, and providing race results to eager buyers. A 35-round bareknuckle prizefight between English champion Tom Sayers and American challenger John Heenan will arouse so much interest that Brentano will sell quantities of papers at $1 each and will grow rich enough to open a basement emporium in 1860 that will grow into a large bookstore.

Nonfiction *The Stones of Venice* by English art and social critic John Ruskin, 34, whose three-volume study explains the development of Gothic architecture and its beauty in terms of the moral virtue of the medieval society that produced it, attacking "the pestilent art of the Renaissance" that arose, he says, from an immoral society.

Fiction *Bleak House* by Charles Dickens with illustrations by "Phiz"; *Peg Woffington* by Charles Reade who has adapted last year's play *Masks and Faces* at the suggestion of actress Laura Seymour who will be his housekeeper beginning next year; *Cranford* by Mrs. Gaskell; *Ruth* by Mrs. Gaskell; *Villette* by Charlotte Brontë.

Juvenile *Tanglewood Tales for Girls and Boys* by Nathaniel Hawthorne.

Poetry *Poems* by English poet-critic Matthew Arnold, 31, includes "Sohrab and Rustum," "Scholar-Gipsy," and "Requiescat."

Painting *Le Tepidarium* by Théodore Chassériau.

Theater *Gold* by Charles Reade 1/10 at London's Drury Lane Theatre.

Opera *Il Trovatore (The Troubadour)* 1/19 at Rome's Teatro Apollo, with music by Giuseppe Verdi; *La Traviata* 3/6 at Venice's Teatro la Fenice, with a libretto based on last year's Alexandre Dumas play *La Dame aux Camélias*, music by Giuseppe Verdi who has completed it in 4 weeks (the production in modern dress is a dismal failure).

First performances Fantasia on Hungarian Melodies for Pianoforte and Orchestra by Franz Liszt 6/1 at Pest's Hungarian National Theater, with Hans von Bülow as soloist; Symphony No. 1 in E flat major by French composer (Charles) Camille Saint-Saëns, 17, at Paris.

Popular songs "My Old Kentucky Home, Good Night" and "Old Dog Tray" by Stephen C. Foster.

Boston pianomaker Jonas Chickering dies at age 55 as his burnt-out factory is being replaced by a building surpassed in size only by the U.S. Capitol at Washington. The new plant has 220,000 square feet of floor space and a huge inner court for Chickering & Sons whose Thomas E., C. Frank, and George H. Chickering carry on the 30-year-old firm.

 Freehold Raceway opens at Freehold, N.J., with harness races.

The first U.S. World's Fair opens July 14 at New York in a Crystal Palace Exposition modeled on the London Great Exhibition of 1851.

The safety match is patented by Swedish inventor J. E. Lundstrom (*see* 1836; book matches, 1893).

New York's Lord & Taylor store moves into a new building at Grand and Christie Streets with a large central rotunda, cathedral windows, and carpeting. Cofounder G. W. Taylor retired last year to England (*see* 1826; 1860).

Rike's of Dayton has its beginnings in the Rike-Kumler Company that opens to give Ohio a new dry goods store.

The Mount Vernon Hotel that opens at Cape May, N.J., is the world's first hotel with private baths (*see* London's Savoy, 1889).

Charleston's 125-room Mills House opens at the corner of Meeting and Queen Streets where it has been built at a cost of $300,000 by Otis Mills, known in South Carolina as the John Jacob Astor of Charleston.

Construction of a new St. Patrick's Cathedral begins on New York's Fifth Avenue between 50th and 51st Streets. Designed in Gothic Revival style by James Renwick, it will be completed in 1879.

New York City is authorized by the state legislature to purchase land for a public park, and some 624 acres are acquired from 59th Street north to 106th Street between Fifth and Eighth Avenues (*see* Bryant, 1844; Olmsted, 1857).

The world's largest tree is discovered in California and is called the *Wellingtonia gigantea.*

Continued decline in French oyster production disturbs the government at Paris which sends the embryologist-ichthyologist Coste to study the remains of ancient Roman oyster culture at Italy's Lake Fusaro (*see* 110 B.C.; 1375).

Less than half of Americans are engaged in agriculture, down from 83 percent in 1820.

The King Ranch has its origin as Texas steamboat captain Richard King begins acquiring land on Santa Gertrudis Creek between the Rio Grande and the Neuces River (*see* 1850). King acts on the advice of his friend Robert E. Lee, 46, a colonel in the U.S. Army, and pays a Spanish family $300 for 15,500 acres—less than 2 cents per acre (*see* Kleberg, 1886).

Extreme drought parches the Southwest and lowers the prices of land and of cattle. Richard King (above) is able to buy longhorns at $5 per head.

Texas cattleman Samuel A. Maverick, 50, receives an anonymous note telling him to look after his strays on the Matagorda Peninsula or risk losing them. Maverick accepted 400 head of cattle in payment of a debt in 1845 and has never bothered to brand the animals on his 385,000-acre ranch, but he sends down a party of cowhands who round up about the same number that were turned loose on the peninsula 6 years ago, he sells the cattle to Toutant Beauregard of New Orleans, and he retires from ranching. The word "maverick" will become a generic for unbranded cattle and for political or intellectual independents who do not go along with their associates.

The first Concord grapes are exhibited to the Massachusetts Horticulture Society by Concord, Mass., horticulturist Ephraim Wales Bull, 48, who has developed the variety and who begins selling cuttings from the parent vine of the slip-skin Lambrusca-type grape at $5 per cutting. Within 10 years Concords will be growing all across America (*see* Welch, 1869).

Potato chips are invented at Saratoga Springs, N.Y., where chef George Crum of Moon's Lake House gives a mocking response to a patron who has complained that his French fries are too thick. He shaves some potatoes paper thin and sends them out to the customers—who are delighted, order more, and encourage Crum to open a restaurant of his own across the lake. Crum's new restaurant will take no reservations and millionaires including Jay Gould and Commodore van Derbilt (above) will stand in line along with everyone else.

Keebler biscuits are introduced at Philadelphia by baker Godfrey Keebler whose Steam Cracker Bakery will become a leading U.S. producer of cookies and crackers.

Gail Borden succeeds in his effort to produce condensed milk (*see* 1851). Using vacuum pans obtained from Shakers at New Lebanon, N.Y., Borden finds a formula for a product that has no burnt taste or discoloration and that lasts for nearly 3 days without souring. He travels to Washington to file a patent claim (*see* 1855).

Commodore Perry opened Japan to the West. His Caucasian nose amused the Asians, and artists exaggerated it.

1854 The Crimean War that begins March 28 will continue until 1856. British and French fleets have entered the Black Sea January 3, Russia has broken off relations with both countries February 6, the czar has ignored a February 7 Anglo-French ultimatum to evacuate the Danubian principalities by April 30, Britain and France have made an alliance with Turkey March 12, Russian troops have crossed the Danube March 20, and Britain and France declare war March 28.

Allied troops land on the Crimean Peninsula of the Ukraine in mid-September and defeat an inferior Russian force September 30 at the Battle of the Alma River.

The Battle of Balaclava October 25 ends in victory for the allies and includes a cavalry charge of Britain's Light Brigade led by the infamous Commander James Thomas Brudenell, 57, seventh earl of Cardigan, who has made a career of purchasing military commissions, fighting duels, and pursuing women (his name will survive in the cardigan sweater; that of his commanding officer Field Marshal Fitzroy James Henry Somerset, 66, baron Raglan of Raglan, will survive in the raglan sleeve coat). Cardigan is the first man to reach the lines and emerges unscathed, but Russian artillery cut down 505 of his 700 men (see Tennyson poem, below).

The Battle of Inkermann November 5 gives the allies another major victory.

The Danubian principalities have been evacuated by the Russians since August 8 and have been occupied with Turkish consent since August 22 by Austria, which gave Russia an ultimatum June 3 not to carry the war across the Balkan mountains and signed a June 14 treaty with Turkey agreeing to intervene in Bosnia, Albania, or Montenegro should any disturbance break out there.

The British withdraw from territory north of South Africa's Orange River in accordance with the convention of Bloemfontein signed February 17 with the Boers. The Orange Free State is organized by Boer settlers.

Egypt's khedive Abbas I is assassinated July 13 at age 41 by enemies in his court after a 6-year reign. He is succeeded by his 32-year-old uncle who will reign until 1863 as Said Pasha (see Suez Canal concession, below).

The Treaty of Kanagawa signed March 31 by Commodore Matthew C. Perry opens the Japanese ports of Hakodate and Shimoda to U.S. trade, makes provision for shipwrecked U.S. seamen, and establishes friendly relations with Japan. The Tokugawa shogun Iesada decides that Japan needs a defense force and asks the emperor to order Buddhist temples to contribute their great bells for gun metal.

The Elgin Treaty signed June 5 establishes reciprocity between Canada and the United States.

The Republican party has been organized February 28 at Ripon, Wis., by former Whigs and disaffected Democrats opposed to the extension of slavery. They take the name Republican from the party founded by Thomas Jefferson which became known as the Democratic-Republican party, but which dropped the last part of the name in 1828.

The Kansas-Nebraska Act passed by Congress May 20 repeals the Missouri Compromise of 1820, opens Nebraska country to settlement on the basis of popular sovereignty, provides for the organization of the Kansas Territory and the Nebraska Territory, undoes the sectional truce of 1850, and effectively destroys the Whig party whose northern members join the new Republican party (above).

 Lawrence, Kans., is founded by two parties sent out by the New England Emigrant Aid Society, a group organized by Massachusetts educator Eli Thayer, 34, to encourage emigration to Kansas. The town is named after the society's patron, Boston merchant Amos Lawrence, now 67 (see 1845; Brown, 1856).

Omaha is formally founded in the Nebraska Territory (see 1846).

The Kansas-Nebraska Act (above) is signed into law by President Pierce May 30 and opens to white settlement western lands that have been reserved by sacred treaty for the Indians.

 A Wisconsin man convicted by a federal court of rescuing a runaway slave in violation of the 1850 Fugitive Slave Act is released by the Wisconsin Supreme Court which rules that the 1850 act is unconstitutional and therefore invalid (see 1842; Dred Scott decision, 1857).

A Boston mob attacks a federal courthouse May 26 in a vain attempt to rescue the fugitive slave Anthony Burns. Federal troops are called in to escort Burns to the Boston docks for return to his southern owner, and they march the prisoner through streets lined with silent but outraged citizens.

Scots-American journalist James Redpath, 21, of Horace Greeley's *New York Tribune* travels through the slave states urging slaves to run away.

U.S. Roman Catholics are attacked on numerous occasions throughout the year by members of a new political party which holds its first national convention in November at Cincinnati. Composed of "native-born Protestants," the new American party opposes immigration and is named the Know-Nothing party by New York publisher E. Z. C. Judson (see Ned Buntline, 1844, 1849).

Fishing rights "in common with white men" are guaranteed to Quinault, Lummi, Nisqualie, Puyallup, and other Puget Sound tribes who have ceded their lands in the Northwest. The tribesmen receive treaty rights to fish for the salmon which climb the rivers of the region.

A typhus epidemic in the Russian army spreads to the British and French in the Crimea (above), it reaches Constantinople, and it is spread by merchant ships throughout Russia and Turkey.

Florence Nightingale takes 34 London nurses to Scutari. The 34-year-old superintendent of a London hospital for invalid women organizes a barracks hospital where she introduces sanitary measures that will reduce the toll of cholera, dysentery, and typhus (but disease will nevertheless take more lives in the Crimean War than will battle casualties).

"An Investigation of the Laws of Thought, on Which are Founded the Mathematical Theories of Logic and Probabilities" by self-taught English mathematician George Boole, 39, advances the first workable system substituting symbols for all the words used in formal logic. Boole's paper "The Mathematical Analysis of Logic" appeared 7 years ago and won him a professorship in mathematics at Queen's College in Cork, Ireland, despite his lack of any degree.

Smith & Wesson Revolver Company has its beginnings in a partnership formed by Massachusetts inventors Horace Smith, 46, and Daniel Baird Wesson, 29, to produce a lever-action pistol under patents they have just obtained. The rimfire pistol will be enormously popular and the company will be one of the world's largest handgun producers.

Philadelphia dentist Mahlon Loomis, 28, patents a kaolin process for making false teeth.

The first fractional distillation of crude petroleum is made by Yale chemistry professor Benjamin Silliman the younger, 38, who has been asked by New Englander George Henry Bissell, 33, to analyze a sample of Pennsylvania "rock oil" which burns better than the coal oil squeezed from asphalt, cannel coal, coal tar, and "albertite" bituminous rock (see 1852). The Pennsylvania Rock Oil Company of New York founded by Bissell and a New York partner is the first company organized to exploit the potential of Pennsylvania's petroleum deposits. Higher boiling fractions of petroleum will prove useful as lubricants, but lower boiling fractions such as gasoline will be avoided as a menace that causes lamps to explode and that is difficult to eliminate without causing complaints about pollution (see 1859; kerosene, 1855).

The Pennsylvania Railroad headed by J. Edgar Thomson, 46, opens its line between Harrisburg and Pittsburgh (see 1852; 1857).

The B&O opens its line between Baltimore and Wheeling (see 1851).

The Chicago, Burlington & Quincy Railroad is created by a merger of four small lines. Entrepreneur James Frederick Joy, 43, has engineered the merger (the new corporate name will be adopted February 14 of next year), he has been helped by Springfield, Ill., lawyer Abraham Lincoln, 45, in earlier efforts to extend the Michigan Central to Chicago, and he works to extend the Chicago, Burlington & Quincy (see Quincy Bridge, 1868).

Railroads reach the Mississippi (above), but cattlemen continue to drive Texas cattle great distances overland as drought continues in the Southwest. The first Texas longhorns to reach New York arrive after a long trek that has made their meat tough and stringy.

Passage of the Kansas-Nebraska Act (above) has been pushed by U.S. Senator from Illinois Stephen Arnold Douglas, 41, who has introduced the term "popular sovereignty" to replace the less elegant term "squatter sovereignty." Douglas has been motivated in large part by a desire to facilitate construction of a transcontinental railway.

The Vienna-Trieste rail line opens over Semmering Pass with tunnels and steep gradients that make it an engineering marvel.

The side-wheeler S.S. Arctic sinks September 27 off Cape Race, Newfoundland, after colliding with the 250-ton French iron propeller ship S.S. Vesta. A sister-ship to the S.S. Pacific that went into service in 1852, the 3,000-ton S.S. Arctic has been the largest and most splendid of the Collins Line steamships, her casualties include 92 of her 153 officers and men, and all her women and children are lost including the wife, the only daughter, and the youngest son of E. K. Collins (see 1850).

Egypt's new khedive Said Pasha (above) grants a Suez Canal concession November 30 to his long-time friend Ferdinand de Lesseps, 49, a French diplomat-promoter who has dreamed of such a canal for 25 years (see 1859; Darius, 520 B.C.).

The U.S. Mint opens a San Francisco branch and pays miners the official rate of $16 per ounce for gold (which can drop to as low as $8 per ounce in the open market but which can also go much higher than $16). The mint produces $4 million in gold coins in its first year, and will produce nearly $24 million by 1856.

Brooklyn Polytechnic Institute is founded at Brooklyn, N.Y.

University College is founded at Dublin.

Le Figaro begins publication at Paris. Local journalist Jean Hippolyte Auguste Villemessant, 42, will make the weekly paper a daily beginning in 1866 (see Coty, 1924).

The Age begins publication at Melbourne. Australian journalists John and Henry Cooke will sell out in 2 years to Ebenezer Syme for £2,000 and Syme's brother David will make The Age one of the world's leading dailies.

A papermill at Roger's Ford in Chester County, Pa., produces paper from wood pulp at low cost. Philadelphia inventor Morris Longstreth Keen, 34, boils wood in water under pressure and will found the American Wood-Paper Company in 1863.

English inventor Hugh Burgess arrives at Roger's Ford (above) where he will build a papermill to use the soda process for making paper from wood pulp

1854 (cont.) which he has developed with inventor Charles Watt (see 1798; Tilghman, 1867).

New York's Astor Library opens February 1 just below Astor Place in Lafayette Street (see 1848). None of the library's 80,000 volumes may be taken from the building, nor can a book even be removed from the shelf unless the visitor is accompanied by a library officer, but by 1873 the library will be averaging 86 visitors per day, 5 percent of them women (see Dewey, 1876; New York Public Library, 1895).

Boston's Ticknor & Fields is created by a reorganization of the 22-year-old publishing house Ticknor, Reed & Fields. The firm will begin publishing the *Atlantic Monthly* in 1857 and will gain renown by publishing the works of Emerson, Hawthorne, Holmes, Lowell, Longfellow, Thoreau (below), and Whittier along with the English authors and poets Browning, De Quincey, Leigh Hunt, and Tennyson (below) (see Dutton, 1858).

Nonfiction *Walden, or Life in the Woods,* by Henry David Thoreau: "The mass of men lead lives of quiet desperation" (I, "Economy") and "If a man does not keep pace with his companions, perhaps it is because he hears a different drummer. Let him step to the music which he hears, however measured or far away" (18, "Conclusion"); *Die Geschichte der Deutschen,* volume 1 of a massive German language dictionary by Jacob Grimm of 1815 *Grimm's Fairy Tales* fame.

Fiction *Hard Times* by Charles Dickens; *Ten Nights in a Barroom and What I Saw There* by Philadelphia novelist Timothy Shay Arthur, 45, whose work about the evils of drink will be adapted to the stage and will be the leading temperance drama for decades (see 1844; "Come Home Father," 1864).

Poetry "The Charge of the Light Brigade" by Alfred Tennyson glorifies the action by Lord Cardigan at the Battle of Balaclava (above): "Half a league, half a league, half a league onward,/ Into the Valley of Death rode the Six Hundred...."

Painting *The Reaper* by Jean François Millet; *Bonjour, Monsieur Courbet* by Gustave Courbet; *The Light of the World* by Holman Hunt.

Theater *The Courier of Lyons* by Charles Reade and Tom Taylor 6/26 at the Princess's Theatre, London.

The New York Academy of Music opens at the northeast corner of 14th Street and Irving Place (see Metropolitan Opera House, 1883; Carnegie Hall, 1891).

The Mason and Hamlin Organ Company founded at Boston by Henry Mason, 23, and Emmons Hamlin, 33, will start making pianos in 1882 and will reorganize under the name Mason and Hamlin Organ and Piano Company (see Knabe, 1837; Chickering, 1853; Steinway, 1859).

German composer Robert Schumann attempts suicide February 27 in a fit of depression (he suffered a mental breakdown in 1844 but recovered). Boatmen in the Rhine pick Schumann up after he jumps from a bridge, he is committed to an asylum 5 days later, and he will die there in 1856 at age 46.

First performances *Orpheus* (symphonic poem) by Franz Liszt 2/16 at Weimar (originally a new overture to the Gluck opera *Orfeo ed Euridice* of 1762); *Les Preludes* (Symphonic Poem No. 3) after Lamartine's *Meditationes Poetiques* by Franz Liszt 2/23 at Paris; *Mazeppa* by Franz Liszt 4/16 (Easter Sunday) at Weimar's Grand Ducal Palace; *Fest-Lange* (Symphonic Poem No. 7) by Franz Liszt 11/9 at Weimar.

Oratorio *L'Enfance du Christ* by Hector Berlioz 12/10 at the Salle Herz, Paris.

Popular song "Jeanie with the Light Brown Hair" by Stephen C. Foster.

A disposable paper collar patented by sewing machine pioneer Walter Hunt of 1849 safety pin fame will gain great popularity, but only after Hunt's death. Hunt takes pains to patent his new invention and to secure a royalty agreement for its production (see 1858).

The Otis safety elevator invented 2 years ago impresses visitors to a New York industrial fair. Elisha G. Otis has thus far sold only three of his elevators, but he has himself hoisted aloft, he orders the rope to be cut, he plunges melodramatically earthward as spectators gasp and scream, safety ratchets engage to halt his descent, and he emerges from his elevator cage saying, "All safe. All safe, ladies and gentlemen" as he sweeps the stovepipe hat from his head and takes a bow (see 1857).

New York's Marble Collegiate Church is completed on Fifth Avenue at 29th Street.

Cyrus McCormick's reaper patents are confirmed by the Supreme Court in the case of *Seymour v. McCormick.* The reaper inventor is defended by Baltimore lawyer Reverdy Johnson, 60, and by Washington lawyer Thaddeus Stevens, 62.

Ice-harvesting on Walden Pond is described by Henry David Thoreau (above) who says, "They told me that in a good day they could get out a thousand tons, which was the yield of about one acre.... They told me that they had some in the ice-houses at Fresh Pond five years old which was as good as ever.... The sweltering inhabitants of Charleston and New Orleans, or Madras and Bombay and Calcutta, drink at my well" (see 1833; 1846).

Dairyman Harvey P. Hood gives up his retail dairy route at Charlestown, Mass., to concentrate on building a supply of quality milk for other Boston area routemen (see 1846). Hood collects milk each morning from farms near his own place at Derby, N.H., loads the milk cans into a freight car attached to the one daily train into Charlestown on the Concord Railroad, and he sells the milk to peddlers who will deliver it throughout Boston (see 1890).

German-American grocer Ferdinand Schumacher, 31, starts a business that will make him the U.S. "Oatmeal King" (*see* 1856).

McSorley's Ale-House is opened in New York's East 7th Street by Irish-American publican John McSorley.

 Papal "infallibility" in all matters including those of contraception and abortion is implied by a Vatican ruling that makes the Immaculate Conception of the Virgin Mary an article of faith (*see* 1869; 1870).

1855 "The Angel of Death has been abroad throughout the land," says British orator John Bright in a February speech to the House of Commons. He urges withdrawal of British troops from Sevastopol and from the Crimea. Viscount Palmerston, now 70, becomes prime minister February 5 and will retain the position until his death in 1865.

Russia's Nicholas I dies March 2 at age 58 after having remarked that "Generals January and February" would be his best allies against British and French troops in the Crimea. The "Iron Czar" who has reigned since 1825 is succeeded by his 36-year-old son who will reign until 1881 as Aleksandr II and who will bring great reforms to Russia (*see* 1861).

Sardinia's premier Count Camillo Benso di Cavour, 45, has brought his country into the Crimean War on the side of England and France. A 10,000-man Piedmontese force helps win the Battle of Chermaia August 16.

"Here I am and here I stay" ("J'y suis, j'y reste"), says the French general Marie Edme Patrice Maurice de Mac-Mahon, 47, in the trenches before Malakoff September 8. He leads the assault on Malakoff.

Russian forces abandon Sevastopol September 11, sinking their ships and blowing up their forts to keep them from falling into enemy hands.

The Treaty of Peshawar signed March 30 creates an Anglo-Afghan alliance against Persia whose Nasir Ud-den has designs on Herat. Russian forces complete a 5-year conquest of the Syr Darya Valley that marks the beginning of a Russian advance to the Persian frontier in Central Asia (*see* 1856).

Japanese treaties are signed with Russia in February and with the Netherlands in November by the Tokugawa shogun Iesada who is called tycoon by the foreigners and is mistakenly believed to be the "secular emperor."

The first European treaty with Siam is negotiated by English diplomat Harry Smith Parke, 27, who obtains rights to establish consuls and to trade throughout the kingdom of Rama IV. Similar treaties will be signed with the United States and France next year and with other countries thereafter.

Ethiopian chief Ras Kassa, 37, deposes Ras Ali of Gondar, he conquers the rulers of neighboring Tigre, Gojjam, and Shoa, he proclaims himself king of kings, and he begins a 13-year reign as the emperor Theodore. Englishmen Walter Plowden and John Bell will help him put down rebellions by subordinates.

 Falls on the Zambezi River that will be called Victoria Falls are discovered by Scottish missionary David Livingston, 42, who has organized a great expedition northward from Cape Town through West Central Africa (*see* Stanley, 1871).

Personal Narrative by British explorer Richard Francis Burton, 34, describes a pilgrimage Burton made 2 years ago to the sacred Moslem city of Mecca disguised as a Pathan. Burton is in Africa in the company of explorer John Hanning Speke, 28 (*see* 1862).

The Amana community is founded on the Iowa frontier at a site christened Amana by Prussian-American sectarian leader Christian Metz, 61, who started his Community of True Inspiration sect in 1817 and who has led a communal society near Buffalo, N.Y., for the past 12 years. The community will be incorporated in 1859 as the Amana Society (*see* Amana Refrigeration, 1967).

The Sault St. Marie ("Soo") River Ship Canal opens to link Lake Huron and Lake Superior and to make the Great Lakes a huge inland waterway navigable by large ships. Built by engineer Charles T. Harvey with capital from Chicago, New York State, and St. Johnsbury, Vt., the "Soo" will give Chicago access to the vast iron-ore deposits of northern Michigan.

The first load of ore to go through the new "Soo" Canal (above) is shipped by the Cleveland Iron Mining Company which has been started by Samuel Livingston Mather, 38 (*see* Pickands, Mather, 1883).

A suspension bridge across Niagara Gorge is completed by John A. Roebling of 1846 Monongahela bridge fame after Charles Ellet has quit in a dispute over finance (*see* 1849). A 368-ton train crosses the 821-foot single-span Roebling bridge March 6 and is the first train to cross a bridge sustained by wire cables (*see* Cincinnati-Covington bridge, 1867).

Australian rail transport is thrown into confusion as New South Wales changes from a 5-foot 3-inch gauge to a narrower 4-foot 8.5-inch gauge while South Australia, West Australia, and Queensland adopt a 3-foot 6-inch gauge for reasons of economy.

The Lehigh Valley Railroad has its beginnings in a line built between Easton and Mauch Chunk by Pennsylvania coal mine operator Asa Packer, 50. The road will grow to have 1,364 miles of track from New York to Buffalo.

An accident on the Camden and Amboy Railroad near Burlington, N.J., August 29 kills 21, injures 75.

The Chicago & Rock Island Railroad works to extend its line to Iowa City, Iowa, in response to an offer of $50,000 if the road reaches Iowa City by December 3. With only minutes to spare, workers drag the locomotive the final 1,000 feet with ropes in −30° weather (*see* 1852; 1856).

1855 (cont.) The word "kerosene" from the Greek "keros" (wax) is coined by Long Island, N.Y., physician Abraham Gesner of Newtown Creek who makes kerosene from raw petroleum. He promotes it as a patent medicine in the absence of any lamp or stove that can burn kerosene efficiently as a fuel (*see* 1852, 1859; Young, 1851).

Continuing epidemics of cholera and typhus in the Crimea take more lives than battle wounds or food poisoning episodes, but English physician Edmund Alexander Parkes, 35, pioneers the science of modern hygiene. Parkes serves as superintendent of a civil hospital in the Dardanelles (*see* 1854).

A kind of anemia that is inevitably fatal and that will later be called pernicious anemia is described for the first time by English physician Thomas Addison, 62 (*see* Whipple, 1922; Minot and Murphy, 1924).

The Paris International Exposition that runs from May to November hails French technological and economic progress as France gains military prestige in the Crimea (above).

Commercial aluminum production is pioneered by French chemist Henri Etienne Sainte-Claire Deville, 36, who develops a method for producing the metal (*see* Wöhler, 1827; Hall, 1886).

Celluloid is patented by English chemist Alexander Parkes, 42, who has developed the plastic material from guncotton and camphor (*see* Hyatt, 1872).

The Young Women's Christian Association (YWCA) is founded at London to improve the condition of working girls by providing good food and a decent place to live for young women who live away from home (*see* 1858; YMCA, 1844, 1851).

The first U.S. kindergarten opens at Watertown, Wis., where the wife of German immigrant Carl Schurz has started the school for children of other immigrants (*see* Froebel, 1837; Peabody, 1860).

The Elmira Female College is founded at Elmira, N.Y. It will be the first U.S. institution to grant academic degrees to women (*see* Mount Holyoke, 1837; Mills, 1852; Vassar, 1861).

Berea College is founded at Berea, Ky.

Pennsylvania State University is founded.

Michigan State University is founded at East Lansing.

A telegraph line to link the Mississippi River with the Pacific Coast is authorized by Congress which commissions James Eddy and Hiram Alden to construct the line (*see* Denver, 1863).

A telegraph line is completed to link London with Balaclava in the Crimea as war continues.

The *Daily Telegraph* begins publication June 29 following repeal of England's Stamp Act. Other British papers go from weekly publication to daily, but the *Daily Telegraph* will have double the circulation of the 67-year-old *Times* by 1860, and by 1870 it will be the largest paper in the world with a circulation of more than 270,000.

The *Chicago Tribune* founded 8 years ago comes under the control of Cleveland publisher Joseph Medill, 32, who will run the paper for the next 44 years as Chicago grows from a town of 80,000 to a city of nearly 2 million (*see* McCormick, Patterson, 1910).

Leslie's Illustrated Newspaper is started at New York by English-American publisher Frank Leslie, 34, who has changed his name from Henry Carter, has gained experience as an engraver for the *Illustrated London News*, and has been a poster artist for P. T. Barnum (*see* 1842; Borden, 1857; magazine, 1906).

A teleprinter is patented by English-American inventor David Edward Hughes, 24, who will later lay out the basic principles of the "loose contact" on which hearing aids, the telephone, and other forms of the microphone will be established (*see* 1877).

Nonfiction *Familiar Quotations* by Boston publisher John Bartlett, 35, whose work will be periodically updated and reissued for well over a century; *The Age of Fable* by Boston scholar Thomas Bulfinch, 59, a son of the architect, whose work will be popular for generations as Bulfinch's *Mythology; Principles of Psychology* by English philosopher Herbert Spencer, 35, who has developed a doctrine of evolution as applied to sociology (*see* Darwin, 1858, 1859).

Fiction *Westward Ho!* by English clergyman-novelist Charles Kingsley, 36, rector of Eversley in Hampshire, who describes in vivid terms a South American landscape he has never seen; *North and South* by Mrs. Gaskell; *The Warden* by English novelist Anthony Trollope, 40, who has been a postal inspector in Ireland since 1841.

Poetry *Men and Women* by Robert Browning whose poem "Andrea del Sarto" contains the line, "A man's reach should exceed his grasp"; *Leaves of Grass* by former *Brooklyn Eagle* editor Walt (Walter) Whitman, 36, whose volume of 12 poems has been published at his own expense, receives mixed reviews, and sells few copies. Included are poems that will later be titled "Song of Myself," "I Sing the Body Electric," and "There Was a Child Went Forth." The book will be expanded in a later edition next year and a still larger third edition in 1860; "Song of Hiawatha" by Henry Wadsworth Longfellow who gave up his Harvard teaching post last year: "By the shores of Gitche Gumee,/ By the shining Big-Sea-Water...."

Painting *Interior of the Studio: A Real Allegory Summing up Seven Years of My Life as an Artist* by Gustave Courbet whose work has been rejected by the Paris Exhibition and who has mounted an exhibition of his own in a nearby shed; *The Horse Fair* by French painter Rosa (Marie Rosalie) Bonheur, 33.

Crimean War scenes are photographed using the slow wet collodion process of 1851 by English photographer Roger Fenton, but his work cannot be published for lack of technology (*see* Ives, 1886). Wood engravings of some of Fenton's scenes are printed in the *Illustrated London News* and give a new sense of reality to war, even though action scenes are impossible (*see* Brady, 1864).

Opera *The Sicilian Vespers (I Vespri Siciliana)* 6/13 at the Paris Opéra, with music by Giuseppe Verdi.

First performances   Concerto No. 1 for Pianoforte and Orchestra in E flat minor by Franz Liszt 2/17 at Weimar's Grand Ducal Palace, with Liszt at the piano under the direction of Hector Berlioz; "Te Deum" by Hector Berlioz 4/30 at Paris; *Prometheus* (Symphonic Poem No. 5) by Franz Liszt 10/18 at Braunschweig; Trio in B major by German composer Johannes Brahms, 22, 11/27 at Dodsworth's Hall, New York, with William Mason, 26, at the pianoforte.

Popular songs   "Listen to the Mockingbird" by Philadelphia barber-composer Richard Milburn, lyrics by Alice Hawthorne (Septimus Winner, who writes under his mother's maiden name); "Star of the Evening" by James M. Sayles; "Come Where My Love Lies Dreaming" by Stephen C. Foster.

The Louvre opens at Paris and the new dry goods store attracts visitors to the city's International Exposition (above). Merchants Chauchard and Heriot serve the carriage trade using principles initiated by Aristide Boucicaut at the Bon Marché in 1852.

Boston's Parker House hotel is opened in School Street by Harvey D. Parker (*see* 1925).

The malodorous Chicago River is dredged by engineers who begin to create a landfill on which an enlarged city will rise (*see* Union Stockyards, 1865).

Fairmount Water Works is built at Philadelphia where the waterworks will be the basis of 3,845-acre Fairmount Park, largest public park within any American city (*see* 1876 centennial exposition).

London's sewer system is modernized following a new cholera outbreak.

The *Milwaukee Wisconsin* reports that a New York poultry dealer has received a shipment of 18,000 passenger pigeons in a single day.

A steel plow whose working surface is remarkably smooth without being brittle is invented at South Bend, Ind., by Scots-American James Oliver, 32. The surface of Oliver's plow is made from a steel casting that is chilled more quickly than its back-supporting sections (*see* 1869; Deere, 1837).

John Deere gets his first salesman. He is joined by George W. Vinton who will travel across the United States from the East Coast to the Pacific and from the Mexican border into Canada to establish agencies for Deere "ploughs and agricultural implements" (*see* 1852; 1857).

Some 16 million bushels of U.S. wheat are exported to Europe, up from 6 million in 1853 (*see* 1860).

Food and Its Adulterations: Comprising the Reports of the Analytical Sanitary Commission of 'The Lancet' is published at London (*see* 1850; 1851). A. H. Hassall scandalizes England with reports that all but the most costly beer, bread, butter, coffee, pepper, and tea contains trace amounts of arsenic, copper, lead, or mercury, but Crosse & Blackwell announces that it has stopped coppering pickles and fruits and that it will no longer use bole armenian to color sauces.

A domestic gas oven priced at £25 is introduced by the English firm of Smith and Phillips and is one of the first such stoves to be put on the market in an age of coal and wood stoves (*see* Reform Club, 1838). Cooking fuel is so costly that hot meals in most British homes are prepared only two or three times a week, but gas ovens will not come into common use for another 40 years.

A military cookstove that can prepare food for a battalion with 47 pounds of wood instead of the usual 1,760 pounds is demonstrated August 27 by Alexis Soyer who has been chef at London's Reform Club for the past 12 years.

Gail Borden obtains a patent for his condensed milk containing sugar to inhibit bacterial growth (*see* 1853; 1856). Unsweetened condensed milk will not be canned satisfactorily until 1885.

New York's Reingold beer has its origin as German-American brewer Samuel Liebmann opens a brewery at Brooklyn.

Miller's beer has its origin as Milwaukee brewer Frederick Miller buys the Best Brothers brewery which sent the first shipment of Milwaukee beer to New York in 1852. The brewery will be rebuilt in 1888 and the company reorganized under the name Frederick Miller Brewing Company (*see* Schlitz, 1856; Pabst, 1864).

Prohibition laws are adopted by Delaware, Indiana, Iowa, Michigan, New Hampshire, New York, and by the Nebraska Territory (*see* 1852; National Prohibition Party, 1869).

A Shilling Cookery for the People by Alexis Soyer (above) contains recipes for sheep's head, boiled neck of mutton, and the like. 248,000 copies are sold.

Boston's Parker House (above) serves à la carte meals at all hours of the day instead of requiring that guests sit down at mealtimes to be served a meal dished out by the host. Its kitchen will become famous as the birthplace of the soft Parker House roll.

The New York State Immigration Commission leases Castle Garden at the foot of Manhattan to receive immigrants. 400,000 arrive in the course of the year (*see* Ellis Island, 1892).

Australia's Victoria colony acts in response to the influx of 33,000 Chinese who have helped swell the population to 333,000 from 77,000 in 1851 when gold was discovered in New South Wales. A new law restricts immigration of Chinese and provides for a poll tax of £10 on each Chinese immigrant.

Crimean War casualties brought Florence Nightingale to Russia. Most deaths came from disease.

1856 The Bessemer converter patented by English engineer Henry Bessemer, 42, decarbonizes melted pig iron with a blast of cold air to produce low-cost steel. The air's oxygen combines with carbon in the iron and dissipates it in the form of carbon dioxide, so although the Bessemer process requires ore that is relatively free of such impurities as phosphorus, the new converter will bring down the price of steel and will permit its use in many new applications (*see* Kelly, 1857).

A regenerative smelting furnace invented by German engineer Friedrich Siemens, 30, in England will lead to the development of the open-hearth process for making steel. Siemens works at his brother Wilhelm's works, and his furnace permits production of ductile steel for boiler-plate (*see* 1861).

The mauve dye produced from coal tar by English chemistry student William Henry Perkin, 18, is the world's first synthetic dye. Hoping to find a synthetic quinine that will break the Dutch monopoly in cinchona bark, Perkin winds up with a disappointing tarry black solution, but when he dips a piece of silk into the solution, he finds it is a stable dye, the first dye ever made from anything but a root, bark, or berry.

W. H. Perkin (above) has been working as assistant to German chemist August Wilhelm von Hofmann, 38, who was brought to London's Royal College of Medicine by the queen's consort Prince Albert, and von Hofmann will persuade young Perkin to develop a German aniline dye industry. Synthetic organic dyes will wreck the market for indigo and for the madder roots used to produce the dye alizarine (*see* 1857).

The Victoria Cross is established by a Royal Warrant signed in January by the queen as the Crimean War nears its end. The medal "For Valour" will be Britain's highest military decoration.

The Crimean War ends February 1 as Russia yields to an Austrian ultimatum and agrees to preliminary peace terms at Vienna.

The Congress of Paris in March neutralizes the Black Sea. Russia cedes the mouths of the Danube and part of Bessarabia, and the European powers promise to respect the independence and integrity of the Ottoman Empire.

Persian forces occupy the Afghan town of Herat and precipitate a new Anglo-Persian War.

Britain annexes the Indian province of Oudh west of Lucknow (*see* mutiny, 1857).

Boers in South Africa establish the South African Republic (Transvaal) with the year-old town of Pretoria as its capital and with Marthinus Wessels Pretorius, 37, as president (*see* 1854; 1877; 1880).

Britain makes Natal a crown colony (*see* 1843).

British and French forces seize Canton and precipitate a new Anglo-Chinese War.

U.S. adventurer William Walker, 32, sacks the Nicaraguan capital Granada, he gains U.S. recognition of his regime in May, and he becomes president in July. Walker led an armed force into the country last year at the invitation of a native revolutionary faction, he has become virtual dictator of Nicaragua, and he is planning a Central American military empire based on slave labor, agricultural development, and a cross-isthmus canal (*see* 1857).

U.S. voters elect Pennsylvania Democrat James Buchanan, 65, president after rejecting presidential aspirant Stephen A. Douglas. Buchanan receives 174 electoral votes, his Republican opponent John C. Frémont receives 114.

The Kansas-Nebraska Act of 1854 was a "swindle," says U.S. senator from Massachusetts Charles Sumner, 45, May 20 during a Senate debate on the admission of Kansas to the Union. Sumner inveighs against the act's authors Stephen A. Douglas and Andrew P. Butler of South Carolina, condemning the "harlot slavery" and the "incoherent phrases" spoken in its behalf by the 62-year-old Senator Butler. Two days later Butler's 38-year-old nephew Representative Preston Smith Brooks of South Carolina physically assaults Sumner as he sits in the Senate Chamber, beating him so badly that he will not be able to resume his duties for 3 years, but Massachusetts voters will defiantly reelect Sumner next year.

Lawrence, Kans., is sacked May 21 by pro-slavery "border ruffians" who have poured into the territory by the thousands in a move to pack the territorial legislature of "bleeding Kansas" with men who will vote to make Kansas a slave state under terms of Stephen A. Douglas's "popular sovereignty" idea.

Free Soil leaders are indicted for treason by the Kansas territorial legislature and there are pitched battles between free-soilers and slavery proponents (although some of the raids, lootings, lynchings, and murders arise out of claim-jumping rather than from the slavery issue).

Pro-slavery men along Pottawatomie Creek are attacked May 24 by Kansas abolitionist John Brown, 56, of Osawatomie and his followers. They hack five of the slavery advocates to death in revenge for the sacking of Lawrence (*see* Harper's Ferry, 1859).

Repeal of the 1807 law against trading in slaves is urged by South Carolina governor James H. Adams.

The Hatt-I-Humayun edict issued February 18 by the Ottoman sultan Abdul Mejid guarantees Christian subjects life, honor, and property, abolishes the civil power of Christian church heads, abolishes torture, reforms prisons, guarantees full liberty of conscience, opens all civil offices to every subject of the sultan, makes Christians liable for military service but permits them to buy exemption, and permits foreigners to acquire property under certain circumstances. The sweeping reforms have been forced on the Ottoman Turks by Austrian, British, and French ambassadors following the Turkish defeat in the Crimean War (above).

Neanderthal man fossils are found in the Neanderthal Valley of the German Rhineland by Johann C. Fuhrott who discovers a human skull in a stratum of rock clearly thousands of years old. French surgeon Paul Broca, 32, is the world's leading authority on skull structure and maintains that the skull is from an early form of man, quite different in some ways from modern man. He disputes Berlin physician Rudolf Virchow, 35, who says the skull is from an ordinary savage with a congenital skull malformation or bone disease (*see* Cro-Magnon, 1868; Virchow, 1858).

The worm parasite that produces kidney and liver malfunctions in the deadly snail-fever disease schistosomiasis (bilharzia) is identified by German scientist Theodore Bilharz, 31, who has come to Cairo to study the disease. He will die himself of typhus in 1862, and while typhus will be effectively controlled well within the next century, bilharzia will affect 70 percent of rural Egyptian men and will be an important factor in keeping Egypt's life expectancy to 52 long after other countries have increased their life expectancies to 70 and more.

The whaling ship *E. L. B. Jennings* returns to New Bedford, Mass., with 2,500 barrels of sperm oil after a 4½-year voyage.

Switzerland's Crédit Suisse bank is founded at Zurich.

Andrew Carnegie makes his first investment at the encouragement of his new employer and buys 10 shares of Adams Express Company stock at $50 per share. The 20-year-old Scots-American railway telegrapher has taken a position as secretary to the Pennsylvania Railroad's Pittsburgh division superintendent Thomas A. Scott, and by 1863 his

$500 investment will be returning $1,500 per year in dividends (*see* 1865; Harnden, 1839).

The Wabash and Erie Canal opens after 24 years of construction that has been marked by loss of life to cholera and loss of money to embezzlers. The 458-mile canal extending south to Evansville on the Ohio River is the largest ever dug in America, but the section below Terre Haute will close in 4 years and the rest will close down in 1874 as railroads make the canal obsolete.

The first railway bridge to span the Mississippi opens April 21 between Rock Island, Ill., and Davenport, Iowa. Built of wood resting on stone piers, the bridge is tested April 22 by a train consisting of three locomotives and eight passenger cars. The S.S. *Effie Afton* rams the 1,582-foot bridge within 2 weeks, but before the La Salle and Rock Island can sue for damages, the steamboat company files suit claiming that the bridge has blocked its right of way. The courts will call the bridge a public nuisance, but lawyer Abraham Lincoln will persuade the Supreme Court to uphold the legality of the bridge.

The Illinois Central Railroad line is completed between Chicago and Cairo, Ill.

Auburn University is founded at Auburn, Ala.

Seton Hall College is founded at South Orange, N.J.

St. Lawrence University is founded at Canton, N.Y.

Western Union Company is chartered as an amalgamation of small U.S. telegraph firms by Ezra Cornell and Hiram Sibley who financed Samuel F. B. Morse in 1844. Sibley organized the New York and Mississippi Valley Printing Telegraph Company in 1851, and he becomes president of the new Western Union whose facilities will be greatly expanded (*see* 1859).

Harper's Weekly begins publication at New York where it will continue until 1915 (*see Harper's Monthly*, 1850; Thomas Nast, 1869).

Frankfurter Zeitung begins publication at Frankfurt am Main.

Nouveau Dictionnaire de la Langue Française by French lexicographer Pierre Larousse, 39, contains Larousse's dictum, "Un dictionnaire sans examples est un squelette" (skeleton).

Nonfiction *The Rise of the Dutch Republic* by U.S. historian John Lothrop Motley, 42, who has served as secretary to the U.S. legation at St. Petersburg; *A Chronological History of the United States* by Boston historian Elizabeth Palmer Peabody, 52 (*see* kindergarten, 1860).

Fiction *It's Never Too Late to Mend* by Charles Reade details abuses, including torture, in English prisons; *Rudin* by Ivan Turgenev.

Poetry *The Panorama* by John Greenleaf Whittier contains the poems "Maud Muller" and "Barefoot Boy"; "A Farewell" by Charles Kingsley is a satiric

1856 (cont.) poem containing the line, "Be good, sweet maid, and let who can be clever."

Painting *La Source* by Jean Auguste Dominique Ingres, now 76.

Theater U.S. playwrights get their first legal copyright protection under a new law that releases a flood of dramatic productions.

Moscow's 80-year-old Bolshoi Theater gets a new 2,200-seat opera house that opens in Petrovsky Street to replace the house that opened in 1825 but was destroyed by fire 3 years ago.

The Bechstein piano is introduced by Berlin pianomaker Carl Bechstein, 30.

The Wurlitzer Company founded by German-American bank clerk Rudolph Wurlitzer, 25, will become world-famous for its organs. Grandson of the German violinmaker Hans Adam Wurlitzer, young Wurlitzer rents three small rooms and begins importing musical instruments while continuing to clerk at Cincinnati's Heidelbach and Seasongood Bank (*see* 1861).

Popular songs "Darling Nelly Gray" by Otterbein College student Benjamin Russell Hanby at Westerville, Ohio, whose song does much to arouse sympathy for America's slaves; "Gentle Annie" by Stephen C. Foster.

Cigarettes are introduced at London clubs by Crimean War veterans who have discovered them in Russia (*see* 1843). The new smokes are generally considered to be effete and effeminate, but the first British cigarette factory is opened by Crimean veteran Robert Gloag (*see* Philip Morris, 1858).

The Burberry raincoat is introduced by English tailor Thomas Burberry of Basingstoke. Made of water-repellent fabric rather than of rubberized fabric or oilskin, the Burberry coat will vie with Macintosh and Aquascutum (*see* 1823; 1851; Tielocken, 1910).

Lewis's Ltd. of Liverpool is started by London merchant David Lewis at the English port that now handles twice the shipping of London and nearly half of all British shipping. Lewis sells boys' clothing at 44 Ranelagh Street, but he will visit the Bon Marché at Paris in the 1870s, he will rename his Liverpool store the Bon Marché, and he will retain that name for years as he builds the establishment into a giant British department store.

Marshall Field moves to Chicago to begin a career that will make him a legend among merchants. The 22-year-old Pittsfield, Mass., store clerk turns down his employer's offer of a partnership, he takes a job clerking for the dry goods firm of Cooley, Wadsworth & Co., he works 18 hours a day at a yearly salary of $400, and by sleeping in the store and buying no clothes except overalls he saves half his pay (*see* 1861).

I. M. Singer and Company offers a $50 allowance on old sewing machines turned in for new Singer machines—the first trade-in allowances (*see* 1851). Sin-ger's Edward Clark has established 14 branch stores with pretty demonstrators, he follows his trade-in offer with a pioneer installment buying plan that allows $5 monthly rental fees to be applied toward ultimate purchase price, and Singer sales will increase by 200 percent within the year (*see* 1889).

New York's "Little Church Around the Corner" opens on 29th Street east of Fifth Avenue. The pastor of a more prestigious church will decline to marry a couple not of his congregation, he will suggest that they try "the little church around the corner," and the Church of the Transfiguration will become popular for weddings.

London architects enlarge the 20-year-old Buckingham Palace to give it a new south wing with a ballroom 110 feet long.

Bantu prophets in South Africa encourage tribesmen to believe that legendary heroes are about to return and drive out the whites with whom the tribesmen have warred for years. The Bantu slaughter their cattle and two-thirds of them starve to death.

The Agen plum that will be the basis of a large prune industry is introduced into California's Santa Clara Valley by French immigrant Pierre Pellier (*see* Chinese plum, 1870).

The first calf ever to be butchered in Japan is slaughtered for U.S. envoy Townsend Harris, 52, at Shimoda where he is awaiting recognition. A New York merchant who has been dispatched by President Pierce to follow up Commodore Perry's opening of Japan and to be the first U.S. consul general to that country, Harris has arrived at Shimoda in August and he has a cow milked—the first milk ever obtained for human consumption in Japan (*see* 1872).

Borden's condensed milk is rejected by New York customers accustomed to watered milk that has been doctored with chalk to make it white and with molasses to make it seem creamy (*see* 1841; 1855). Borden abandons the factory he has set up with two partners at Wolcottville, Conn., and sells a half-share in his patent to one of his partners (but *see* 1857).

Boston exports more than 130,000 tons of "fine, clear" ice from Massachusetts lakes and ponds as 363 U.S. ships sail from various ports with a total of 146,000 tons of ice, up from 65,000 on 175 ships in 1846 (*see* 1880).

Mechanical ice-making is pioneered by Australian inventor James Harrison who has emigrated from Scotland. His ether compressor makes it possible to produce beer even in hot weather (*see* Perkins, 1834; Gorrie, 1851; Carré, 1858; Linde, 1873).

Schlitz beer has its origin at Milwaukee's August Krug brewery which is taken over 7 years after its founding by German-American bookkeeper Joseph Schlitz, 25. Krug has died, Schlitz will marry his widow, he will change the name of the brewery, and he will increase its production (*see* 1874).

The German Mills American Oatmeal Factory opened at Akron, Ohio, by Ferdinand Schumacher employs water-powered millstones to grind 3,600 pounds of oatmeal per day (see 1854). U.S. farmers grow 150 million bushels of oats per year and while most goes to feed horses, Schumacher will find a large market for his oatmeal among German immigrants at Cleveland, Cincinnati, St. Louis, Philadelphia, and New York, and his mills will become Akron's leading enterprise (see 1875).

A new Buitoni pasta factory is opened at Citta di Castello in Umbria by Giovanni Buitoni, son of Giovambattista and Giulia (see 1827). The new plant goes up near the old one at Sausepolepo where Buitoni has been making semolina flour from wheat brought in by the wagonload from the distant Puglie plateau (see 1884).

Joseph Tetley & Company, Wholesale Tea Dealers opens in London's Mincing Lane (see 1837; 1888).

👫 Human understanding of the reproductive process is advanced by German botanist Nathaniel Pringsheim, 33, who observes sperm entering ova (see Hertwig, 1875).

1857 The Dred Scott decision announced by Supreme ✊ Court Chief Justice Roger B. Taney March 6 enrages abolitionists and encourages slaveowners. The fugitive slave Dred Scott, now 62, brought suit in 1848 to claim freedom on the ground that he resided in free territory, but the court rules that his residence in Minnesota Territory does not make him free, that a black may not bring suit in a federal court, and—in an obiter dicta by Taney—that Congress never had the authority to ban slavery in the territories, a ruling that in effect calls the Missouri Compromise of 1820 unconstitutional.

The Impending Crisis of the South, and How to Meet It by North Carolina farmer Hinton Rowan Helper, 28, tries to show that slavery is not only economically unprofitable, but is ruinous to small farmers such as himself who do not own slaves. Helper calls slavery "the root of all the shame, poverty, ignorance, tyranny and imbecility of the South" and he is denounced by Southerners while being hailed in the North for his courage and vision.

The world's first alimony payments are ordered by Britain's Matrimonial Causes Act which establishes that a husband's responsibility as provider continues in perpetuity after a marriage is ended.

British game laws are eased after years of harsh penalties that made anyone caught poaching liable to transportation to Australia for 7 years. Poached game has been a dietary mainstay for many families.

⚔ The Irish Republican Brotherhood is founded (see Fenians, 1858).

The Italian National Association is founded by Giuseppe Garibaldi to work for unification of the country. Garibaldi returned 3 years ago after 5 years at Staten Island, N.Y., where he worked as a candlemaker (see 1849; 1860).

Afghanistan's independence is recognized by Persia March 4 in the Treaty of Paris forced upon Persia's Nasir Ud-Din by the British.

The Sepoy Mutiny that begins May 10 at Meerut ends control of India by the East India Company. A new Enfield rifle adapted from designs by Samuel Colt has been introduced by the British Army in India, following appearances by Colt before a Parliamentary Committee on Small Arms at London, but cartridges fired by the new rifle are partially coated with grease and must be bitten open before they are loaded. Sepoys (natives) comprise four-fifths of the army in India, caste Hindus among them insist that the grease is beef fat from the sacred cow, Moslems insist it is pork fat from flesh forbidden by the Koran, and local chiefs encourage scattered revolts in hope of regaining lost privileges.

British losses in the Sepoy Mutiny (above) are small, but a massacre at Cawnpore July 15 takes the lives of 211 British women and children in one of several atrocities perpetrated by both sides.

Loyal forces from the Punjab recapture Delhi September 20 to turn the tide against the rebels (see 1858).

The Mountain Meadows Massacre in Utah Territory September 11 kills 135 California-bound emigrants. The Fancher wagon-train arrived at Salt Lake City August 3 from Arkansas with 60 men, 40 women, and 50 children, most of them Methodists. They found the Mormon capital disturbed by the fact that President Buchanan has removed Brigham Young as governor and has sent a force under General Albert Sydney Johnston, 54, to establish the primacy of federal rule in the territory. Some 300 to 400 Pah-Ute braves led by a few Mormons acting on orders from Brigham Young ambush the Fancher party some 320 miles south of Salt Lake City, the wagon-train's riflemen repulse the initial assault, the party holds out from Monday to Friday, Young's friend John D. Lee treacherously induces the emigrants to pile their arms into a wagon, and the Indians butcher to death all but a dozen or so children under age 8.

💲 Financial panic strikes New York following failure of the Ohio Life Insurance and Trust Company. A severe depression ensues in which 4,932 business firms will fail after a period of speculation and overexpansion.

Tariff duties are reduced by a new U.S. tariff act.

U.S. shipping subsidies introduced in 1845 are abandoned in response to Southern opposition.

A prime field hand in the South fetches $1,500 and up in the market, and critics such as Hinton Helper (above) point out that slavery ties up capital in human beings when it might better be employed in labor-saving improvements. 1,000 Southern families share in an income of $50 million per year, while

1857 (cont.) another $60 million is divided among 660,000 families, yet even rich slaveholders have their earnings eaten up by commissions, freight charges, tariffs, imports of manufactured goods from the North, and by the care and maintenance of slaves whose labor may actually be more costly than free labor in the North (*see 1863*).

Northwestern Mutual Life Insurance Company has its beginnings in the Mutual Life Insurance Company of Wisconsin founded at Janesville by septuagenarian John C. Johnston who has taken nearly 2 years to line up the $200,000 in life insurance policies required for the state charter. The company will move to Milwaukee in 1859, it will be renamed Northwestern Mutual in 1868, and by the end of 1868 it will have 28,000 policyholders across the country with assets of more than $4 million.

An overland California mail bill passes Congress and an Overland Mail Company is organized by John Butterfield of American Express (*see 1850*). Butterfield wins the government contract to carry mail from St. Louis to San Francisco via Little Rock, El Paso, Tucson, Yuma, and Los Angeles using the route pioneered in large part by the Mormon Batallion of Philip Cooke in 1847 (*see 1858*).

A nationwide U.S. celebration marks the linking by rail of New York and St. Louis.

The Pennsylvania Railroad extends its control through purchase and lease over the entire rail route between Philadelphia and Pittsburgh. The Pennsylvania buys up the state's chief canal system to eliminate competition (*see 1854; 1871*).

French railway construction is spurred by a new railway law that guarantees interest payments on railroad company bonds. By the end of next year France will have 16,207 kilometers of railway line, up from 3,627 in 1851.

Venice gains a rail link to other European capitals as the Milan-Venice railway is completed across a 3.5-kilometer bridge put up in 1846 to span the lagoon between San Giuliano on the mainland and the area of San Giobbea and San Lucia.

New York to San Francisco ocean freight rates drop to $10 per ton, down from as high as $60 per ton in Gold Rush days, as an excess of shipping intensifies competition and makes the industry unprofitable. Some clipper ships can cover more than 400 miles on a good day, a distance no steamship can match, but the day of the clipper ship is ending.

Nicaraguan overland transportation properties between the Atlantic and Pacific that belong to Cornelius van Derbilt's Accessory Transit Company are seized by Nicaraguan president William Walker (*see 1856*). Van Derbilt sends agents to other Central American countries and organizes an effort to oust Walker who surrenders himself May 1 to a U.S. Navy officer in order to escape capture. Walker is returned to the United States but goes back to Central America where he is arrested in November by Commodore Hiram Paulding. Returned once again to the United States, he will be captured by a British naval officer in 1860, turned over to Honduran authorities, court-martialed, and executed.

"The whale oils which hitherto have been much relied on in this country to furnish light and yearly become more scarce, may in time almost entirely fail," says the *Scientific American* June 27. The increase in U.S. literacy spurs demand for lighting (*see 1866; Drake, 1859*).

A "pneumatic" steelmaking process invented in 1847 is patented by Eddyville, Ky., steelmaker William Kelly whose patent battle with England's Henry Bessemer will combine with a shortage of sufficiently pure iron to delay adoption of oxygen steel furnaces in the United States (*see 1856; 1861; 1863*).

The cant hook (peavey) is invented on the Stillwater branch of Maine's Penobscot River where Joseph Peavey sees river drivers trying to break up a log jam and gets an idea. Peavey instructs his blacksmith son Daniel to make a clasp with lips connected by a bolt, and then to attach a hook, two rings, and a pick at the end of the handle. Peavey will also invent a hoist for pulling stumps, a clapboard-making machine, a shingle-making machine, and an undershot waterwheel, but his cant hook multiplies the efficiency of a logger and will be the basis of the Peavey Manufacturing Company (*see Frank Peavey, 1868*).

The aniline dye industry begins in England as W. H. Perkin and his father build a mauve dye works near Harrow (*see 1856; German Chemical Society, 1868*).

French chemist Louis Pasteur, 32, shows that a living organism causes the lactic fermentation that spoils milk (*see 1859*).

French physiologist Claude Bernard pioneers modern physiology by applying the biochemical methods developed by Justus von Liebig in 1842 to the living animal, combining them with physiological methods. Bernard pursues his investigations of glycogen production by the human liver (*see 1850; 1860*).

The New York Infirmary for Women and Children opens on Florence Nightingale's birthday May 12 under the direction of Elizabeth Blackwell, her younger sister Emily, and another woman doctor (*see 1849*). The loss of an eye has prevented Blackwell from achieving her ambition to practice as a surgeon, she has been unable to find a place on any other hospital staff because of her sex, and she has started the new hospital that will be run entirely by women. It will move in November 1875 to 321 East 15th Street and will remain there for more than a century.

U.S. cities have higher death rates than any other places in the world. Tuberculosis is the big killer, causing roughly 400 deaths per 100,000 population (the disease is not considered contagious), and while New York has the highest death rate, it is closely followed by Philadelphia and Boston.

The University of California is founded at Oakland, but classes will not begin until 1869. The tuition-free university will move to Berkeley when that town is settled in 1873 and the first baccalaureates will be awarded at Berkeley (*see* UCLA, 1919).

San Jose State College is founded in California.

Illinois State University is founded.

Marquette University is founded at Milwaukee.

The Universities of Bombay, Calcutta, and Madras are founded in India.

Cooper Institute is founded in New York's Astor Place by Peter Cooper of 1829 *Tom Thumb* locomotive fame. The Institute will develop into Cooper Union and will carry on extensive programs of adult education (*see* 1859).

The *Atlantic Monthly* begins publication at Boston under the editorship of James Russell Lowell whose name has been suggested by Oliver Wendell Holmes. Holmes has also suggested the magazine's name and when Lowell accepts the editorship on condition that Holmes be a contributor, Holmes revives his 1831 title "The Autocrat of the Breakfast Table" for his contributions (*see* 1858).

The *New York Tribune* sacks all but two of its foreign correspondents in an economy move (*see* financial panic, above). One of the two correspondents retained is Karl Marx.

England's *Birmingham Post* begins publication.

Fiction *Madame Bovary* by French novelist Gustave Flaubert, 36, who is prosecuted for immorality but wins acquittal; *Little Dorrit* by Charles Dickens: "Papa, potatoes, poultry, prunes, and prisms are all very good words for the lips: especially prunes and prisms"; *Barchester Towers* by Anthony Trollope who continues the Barsetshire chronicle that began with *The Warden* in 1855; "The Sad Fortunes of the Rev. Amos Barton" by English writer George Eliot (Mary Ann[e] or Marian Evans), 37, who 3 years ago began living openly with philosopher-critic George Henry Lewes, 40, a married man who cannot divorce his wife because he has failed to condemn her for having had a child by another man. Eliot, whose story is published in *Blackwood's* magazine, is a puritan at heart and calls herself Mrs. Lewes, as does Lewes, but she is shunned by proper Victorian wives.

Juvenile *Tom Brown's School Days* by English jurist Thomas Hughes, 35, whose Rugby principal Dr. Thomas Arnold says, "Life isn't all beer and skittles." Hughes worked 3 years ago with London theologian Frederick Denison Maurice, 52, to found Working Men's College.

Poetry "Santa Filomena" by Henry Wadsworth Longfellow is a tribute to Crimean War nurse Florence Nightingale: "Lo! in that house of misery/ A lady with a lamp I see. . . ." (*see* 1854).

The first Currier & Ives prints are issued as New York lithographer Nathaniel Currier, 44, takes into partnership his bookkeeper of 5 years James Merritt Ives, 33, and begins signing all his prints with the new firm name. Currier has been issuing lithographs since 1835 that illustrate U.S. manners, personages,

and notable events and has been famous since 1840 for his prints of W. K. Hewitt's lurid depiction of a fire aboard the steamship *Lexington*. Priced at from 15 cents to $3, Currier & Ives prints will be sold all over the United States and will be distributed through branch offices in European cities. Currier will retire in 1880 and his son Edward West Currier will be bought out in 1902 by Ives's son Chauncey whose firm will continue until 1907.

Theater *The Poor of New York* by Dion Boucicault 1/8 at Wallack's Theater, New York. Boucicault emigrated to New York in 1853 and has adapted *Les pauvres de Paris* by Edouard-Louis-Alexandre Brisebarre and Eugène Nus.

Opera *Simon Boccanegra* 3/12 at Venice's Teatro la Fenice, with music by Giuseppe Verdi to a libretto based on history concerning Genoa's first doge (who served from 1339 to 1344). The opera is a failure and will not be successful until 1881 when it will be given a new libretto by Arrigo Boito.

First performances Piano Concerto in A major and Symphonic Poem No. 1 (*Ce qu'on entend sur la montagne*, after Victor Hugo) by Franz Liszt 1/7 at Weimar's Grand Ducal Palace; Sonata in B minor by Franz Liszt 1/22 at Berlin, with pianist Hans von Bülow who marries Liszt's daughter Cosima, 19, August 18; the *Faust Symphony in Three Characters* (after Goethe) by Franz Liszt 9/5 at Weimar's Grand Ducal Palace; Symphony to Dante's *Divine Comedy* by Franz Liszt 11/7 at Dresden; *The Battle of the Huns (Die Hunnenschlacht)* symphonic poem by Franz Liszt 12/29 at Weimar.

The Philadelphia Academy of Music designed by Napoleon Le Brun and C. Runge opens at the corner of Broad and Locust Streets (*see* Philadelphia Orchestra, 1900).

Baltimore's Peabody Institute opens in Mount Vernon Place with a great concert hall, a lecture hall, an art collection, a reference library, and a music conservatory established with a $1.4 million gift from financier George Peabody, 62.

Hymn "We Three Kings of Orient" by English-American clergyman John Henry Hopkins, Jr., 37.

Popular song "Jingle Bells" ("One-Horse Open Sleigh") by Boston composer James Pierpont, 35.

Longchamp racetrack opens April 27 in the new Bois de Boulogne Park at Paris.

The *Harvard* constructed at Brooklyn, N.Y., is the first U.S. racing shell (*see* Henley Regatta, 1829). Built by James Mackay for the Harvard Boat Club of Cambridge, Mass., the six-oared rudderless craft is 40 feet long and 26 inches wide, it weighs 50 pounds, and it will be used in competition with similar white pine racing shells that will be built for Harvard and other American colleges (*see* 1876).

The first American Chess Congress opens at New York in the fall. Top honors go to New Orleans player Paul Charles Morphy, 20, who taught himself the

1857 (cont.) game in childhood by watching his father play, won two out of three games (the third was a draw) against a visiting Hungarian chess master before he was 13, and will tour Europe in the next 2 years, defeating all challengers and winning the unofficial world title (*see* Steinitz, 1886).

Meier & Frank opens at Portland, Oreg., where the dry goods store will become the city's leading department store.

The world's first commercial passenger elevator is installed in the five-story New York store of E. G. Haughwort at the corner of Broadway and Broome Streets. The elevator cab is completely enclosed (*see* 1854; 1861).

Louisiana's Belle Grove plantation house is completed for a sugar king whose residence is grander than any other in the South. The Palladian mansion will be destroyed by fire in 1952.

Mentmore Towers goes up in Buckinghamshire for English sportsman-art collector Mayer Amschel de Rothschild, 39, who will be elected to Parliament next year and whose son-in-law will become prime minister briefly from 1894 to 1895. The 75-room neo-Elizabethan house designed by Joseph Paxton of 1851 Crystal Palace fame is a fantasy of pierced towers in buff sandstone and pioneers the use of large plate-glass windows.

U.S. landscape architect Frederick Law Olmsted, 35, is appointed superintendent of New York's Central Park which is under construction but whose name belies the fact that it is far to the north of the city's population center (*see* 1844). Olmsted's application has been endorsed by William Cullen Bryant, by *Tribune* publisher Horace Greeley, by botanist Asa Gray, by financier August Belmont, and by author Washington Irving (now 74), but the new superintendent finds the park site filled with hog farms, bone-boiling works, and squatters' shacks which make it "a pestilential spot, where rank vegetation and miasmatic odors taint every breath of air." Work on the park becomes a relief project for city politicians struggling to cope with the economic depression (above) (*see* 1858).

Michigan State College of Agriculture opens to offer the first state institution courses in scientific and practical agriculture.

John Deere produces steel plows at the rate of 10,000 per year (*see* 1855).

The California honey industry has its beginnings at San Diego where hives of Italian honeybees are introduced. California will become the leading U.S. honey producer.

The California grape and wine industries have their beginnings at Buena Vista in the Valley of the Moon near the Sonoma Mission where Tokay, Zinfandel, and Shiras grape vines from his native Hungary are planted by Count Agoston Haraszthy de Moksa, 55. Sauk City, Wis., was founded by the count in the 1840s, he came to California in 1849, and the vines he plants are the first varietal grape vines in America (*see* 1861).

The condensed milk patented by Gail Borden in 1855 is made from skim milk devoid of all fats and of certain necessary food factors. The condensed milk will contribute to rickets in young working-class children (*see* Pekelharing, 1905).

Sales of Borden's condensed milk will be helped by *Leslie's Illustrated Newspaper* which will crusade against "swill milk" from Brooklyn cows fed on distillery mash.

Commercial production of Borden's condensed milk begins at Burrville, Conn., where Gail Borden has opened a condensing plant with financial backing from New York grocery wholesaler Jeremiah Milbank, 39, whom he has met by chance on a train. Samples are carried through the streets of New York and they now meet with more success (*see* 1856; New York Condensed Milk Company, 1858).

Durkee's Dressing is created in his kitchen by Brooklyn, N.Y., entrepreneur Eugene R. Durkee who will peddle his spiced mayonnaise-based combination salad dressing and meat sauce from door to door before selling it through retailers (*see* Glidden, 1929).

Hiram Walker's Distillery is built on the Canadian side of the Detroit River by Detroit grocer Hiram Walker, 41, who has moved west from his native Massachusetts and who also builds a small flour mill. Walkerville will be named for Walker whose family will retain control of the firm until 1926 (*see* 1933; Canadian Club, 1882).

Demand for Minneapolis flour begins in the East as a farmer in the Minnesota Territory ships a few barrels to New Hampshire in payment of a debt as economic depression makes specie payment difficult. The flour is made from winter wheat which produces a whiter flour, and since Minnesota spring wheat yields a darker flour, the demand from the East will spur efforts to refine milling methods (*see* 1874).

An English biscuit firm that will become Peak, Frean & Co., Ltd., is started at Dockhead by James Peak.

The population of Chicago reaches 93,000, up from 4,100 in 1837.

1858 An assassination attempt on France's Napoleon III and his wife kills 10 and injures 150, but the January 14 bomb explosions leave the emperor and his Eugénie untouched. The French execute Italian revolutionist Felice Orsini, 39, and his accomplice Joseph Pieri March 13 but only after Orsini has appealed to Napoleon from prison for help in freeing Italy from Austrian rule.

Napoleon meets secretly July 10 with Count Cavour at Plombières, he agrees to join Piedmont in a war against Austria provided that the war can be provoked in a way that will make it appear justified in the public opinion of Europe, he sends Prince

Jérôme on a mission to Warsaw in order to assure himself of Russian goodwill, and he signs a formal treaty with Cavour December 10 (see 1859).

Prussia's Friedrich Wilhelm IV is declared insane a year after suffering two paralytic strokes. His 61-year-old brother Wilhelm is made regent October 7.

The Serbian prince Aleksandr Karageorgević is deposed December 23 at age 52 after a weak 16-year reign. He is succeeded by the 79-year-old Miloš Obrenović who was deposed in 1839 and who will reign until his death in 1860.

The Anglo-Chinese War that began in 1856 is ended by the Treaties of Tientsin signed June 26 to 29. The Chinese agree to open 11 more ports to Britain, France, the United States, and Russia, with the Russians obtaining the north bank of the Amur by the Treaty of Aigun.

A U.S.-Japanese commercial treaty arranged by U.S. consul Townsend Harris is signed July 29 through the influence of Prime Minister Ii Naosuke, 43, who has won appointment as tairo under the shogun Iesada. Harris has pointed out the fate that China (above) has met at the hands of European imperialists and has persuaded the Japanese that a treaty with the United States will be on favorable terms and will serve to protect Japan from more rapacious Western powers. The treaty covers tariffs, provides for an exchange of diplomats, and is followed by a similar treaty August 18 with the Netherlands, August 19 with Russia, August 26 with Britain, and October 27 with France.

Japan's feeble Tokugawa shogun Iesada dies at age 34 without an heir and will be the last Tokugawa shogun of any consequence. The 12-year-old Iemochi has been appointed by Iesada as his successor, an appointment secured by Ii Naosuke (above), and he will reign until 1866.

The British Crown takes over the duties and treaty obligations of the East India Company following last year's Sepoy Rebellion and assumes responsibility for India's "protected" states (see 1686; 1947).

Minnesota is admitted to the Union as the 32nd state.

"Cotton is king," says U.S. senator from South Carolina James Henry Hammond, 41, in a speech March 4 taunting critics of the South (the phrase was used 3 years ago as the title of a book by David Christy): "You dare not make war upon cotton! No power on earth dares make war upon it. Cotton is king."

"A house divided against itself cannot stand," says former Illinois congressman Abraham Lincoln June 16 in accepting nomination as the Republican candidate for U.S. senator at Springfield. "I believe this government cannot endure permanently half slave and half free." Lincoln will be defeated by Democrat Stephen A. Douglas, but in 2 years he will win election to the presidency over Douglas and two other opponents (see 1860; railroads, 1854, 1856).

 A fugitive slave in Ohio is rescued by Oberlin College students and one of their professors. They send the man off to safety in Canada (see 1854; 1859).

Russia's Aleksandr II begins emancipating the nation's serfs (see 1861).

 London's Linnaean Society hears a paper on the survival of the fittest in the struggle for existence in nature presented by English naturalists Alfred Russel Wallace and Charles Darwin (see 1840). Wallace has developed theories of evolution while visiting the Malayan archipelago (see 1859).

The Theory of the Vertebrate Skulls is published by English biologist Thomas Henry Huxley, 33.

Die Cellularpathologie by Berlin physician Rudolf Virchow calls the cell the basic element in the life process (see Neanderthal man, 1856). Virchow has analyzed diseased tissues from the point of view of cell formation and cell structure, and he concludes that all cells arise from cells ("omnis cellula e cellula") (see von Kolliker, 1850).

Über die Konstitution und die Metamorphosen der chemischen Verbindungen und über die chemische Natur des Kohlenstoffs by German chemist Friedrich August Kekule von Stradonitz, 29, demonstrates the composition of organic molecules. He shows that they are formed by carbon atoms linked together to form long skeletal chains (see 1865).

Denver is founded in Kansas Territory that will become Colorado. The town established at the junction of the South Platte River and Cherry Creek is named in honor of Kansas Territory governor James W. Denver (see gold strike, below).

The Texas socialist community La Reunion is abandoned by its followers, who move to nearby Dallas (see 1841). The communards have been followers of

The Sepoy Rebellion ended the East India Company's century-old control of the Indian subcontinent.

1858 (cont.) the late French social philosopher and reformer Charles Fourier who died in 1837 at age 65.

The Overland Mail stage reaches St. Louis October 9 after 23 days and 4 hours on its first trip from San Francisco (*see* 1857). A westbound stage that has left at the same time reaches San Francisco October 10 after 24 days, 20 hours, 35 minutes (*see* transcontinental railroad, 1869).

The first practical sleeping car is perfected for the Chicago & Alton Railroad by Brocton, N.Y., cabinetmaker George Mortimer Pullman, 27, whose retractable upper berth doubles the sleeping car's payload (*see* 1864).

"Commodore" van Derbilt sells his New York-to-California shipping line to rivals who will operate via Panama rather than via Nicaragua (*see* 1857). Van Derbilt takes the $20 million he has gained in the shipping trade and begins buying up shares in the Harlem Railroad running out of New York City and in the Hudson River Railroad running north to East Albany (*see* 1863).

London's Chelsea Bridge is completed across the Thames. Tolls will be collected until 1879 and the bridge will be rebuilt in the 1930s.

Anatomy of the Human Body, Descriptive and Surgical by London physician Henry Gray, 33, is published for the first time. Gray is a Fellow of the Royal College of Surgeons and Gray's *Anatomy* will be a standard text for more than a century.

French schoolgirl Bernadette Soubirous, 14, at Lourdes has a vision February 11 of "a lady" dressed in a white robe with a blue sash, the first of 18 such visions that she will have through mid-July. The asthmatic daughter of a poor miller, Bernadette lives with her parents and six siblings in a one-room stone house. She is cured of her asthma, she tells local priests that "the lady" has urged her to "tell the priests to build a chapel here" at the grotto near a bend in the Gave de Pau River, she is called a sorceress, but there are reports of miraculous cures at the grotto and a chapel will be built (*see* 1866).

E. R. Squibb & Sons has its beginnings in a chemical and pharmaceutical laboratory founded by Brooklyn, N.Y., pharmacist Edward Robinson Squibb, 39, whose lower eyelids have been burned off by an ether explosion. Squibb will never be able to close his eyes completely, he will cover them with court plaster in order to sleep, but he will become a major supplier of ether to the medical profession, his firm will take the name E. R. Squibb & Sons in 1892, and German-American chemist Theodore Weicker will take over as president in 1905 to make Squibb a major pharmaceutical house.

A placer gold strike in the eastern Colorado region of Kansas Territory 90 miles from Pike's Peak begins a new gold rush to Cherry Creek (*see* Denver, above).

The American Bank Note Company is created at New York by a merger of the seven independent engraving-printing firms that have printed U.S. paper currency since the Revolution. American Bank Note will print U.S. currency until 1879 and U.S. postage stamps until 1894, and it will thereafter print currency and stamps for scores of foreign countries.

Lehman Brothers of Montgomery, Ala., opens a New York office at 119 Liberty Street after 13 years at Montgomery. Emmanuel Lehman settles in New York at age 31 (*see* Cotton Exchange, 1870).

Sewing machine inventor Walter Hunt of 1854 paper collar fame is offered $50,000 in five annual payments by Isaac M. Singer to clear up any possible patent claims, but Hunt will die in June of next year at age 62 before the first payment falls due, having derived little benefit from his Globe stove, fountain pen, breech-loading rifle, or other inventions.

Iowa State College is founded at Ames.

Oregon State University is founded at Corvallis.

Queen Victoria and President Buchanan exchange messages August 16 over the first transatlantic cable. New York paper merchant Cyrus West Field, 39, has promoted the project first proposed by Frederick Newton Gisborne, 39, he has consulted with Samuel F. B. Morse, he has founded the New York, Newfoundland, and London Telegraph Company with backing from Peter Cooper and others, Queen Victoria cables, "Glory to God in the Highest, peace on earth, good will to men," and the first commercial cable message follows (at $5 per word). London merchant John Cash whose firm J. and J. Cash makes woven name labels cables his New York representative, "go to Chicago," but the cable's electrical insulation soon fails and by October the cable is useless (*see* 1866).

The *Territorial Enterprise* begins publication at Mormon Station in the Territory of Western Utah with a press freighted in from San Francisco. Operations will soon move to Virginia City (*see* 1859).

The pen name "Artemus Ward" appears in the 17-year-old *Cleveland Plain Dealer*. Maine-born city editor Charles Farrar Browne, 24, uses the name to sign a letter to the editor allegedly written by a shrewd showman with Yankee dialect and unconventional spelling (*see* "Josh Billings," 1865).

Street & Smith Publications, Inc., has its beginnings in the *New York Weekly* published by former *New York Sunday Dispatch* bookkeeper Francis S. Street and former *Sunday Dispatch* reporter Francis Shubael Smith, 38, who buy out the *New York Weekly Dispatch* for $40,000 and rename it. Begun in 1843 as the *Weekly Universe* by Amos J. Williamson, the fiction magazine has a small circulation and Street and Smith have less than $100 between them, but Williamson agrees to wait for his money until the new owners have earned it, Street and Smith boost circulation by attracting well-known writers with enormous sums, and by 1861 their *Weekly* will have a circulation of 100,000 (*see* Nick Carter, 1886).

E. P. Dutton & Co. publishers is founded by Boston bookseller Edward Payson Dutton, 17, who buys out his partner and who will buy out Ticknor & Fields in 1864 (*see* 1854). Dutton will achieve his greatest success by joining with the London firm J. M. Dent in publishing "Everyman's Library," a series of cheap reprints of the English classics (*see* Dent, 1888).

Fiction *Dr. Thorne* by Anthony Trollope.

Poetry *The Courtship of Miles Standish* by Henry Wadsworth Longfellow; "The Deacon's Masterpiece; or, The Wonderful One Hoss Shay" by Oliver Wendell Holmes is published as a satirical poem in Holmes' *Atlantic Monthly* column "The Autocrat of the Breakfast Table": Holmes's Deacon completes his "chaise" on the day of the 1755 Lisbon earthquake and his "Logical Story" is taken by some to be a satire on the collapse of Calvinism; "The Chambered Nautilus" by Oliver Wendell Holmes is published in his *Atlantic Monthly* column with a final stanza that begins, "Build thee more stately mansions, O my soul,/ As the swift seasons roll . . ."; *Legends and Lyrics* by English poet Adelaide Ann Procter, 33, whose lyric poem "The Lost Chord" begins, "Seated one day at the organ,/ I was weary and ill at ease,/ And my fingers wandered idly/ Over the noisy keys . . ." (*see* popular song, 1877); *The Defense of Guenevere and Other Poems* by English poet-craftsman William Morris, 24.

Painting *Derby Day* by English painter William Powell Frith, 39 (*see* 1779); *Eight Bells* by U.S. painter Winslow Homer, 22; Ando Hiroshige dies at Edo October 12 at age 61.

Theater *Jessie Brown, or The Relief of Lucknow* by Dion Boucicault 2/22 at Wallack's Theater, New York; *Foul Play* by Charles Reade and Dion Boucicault 5/28 at London's Adelphi Theatre; *Our American Cousin* by Tom Taylor 10/18 at Laura Keene's Theater, New York.

England's Princess Royal is married January 25 at age 18 to Prussia's Crown Prince Frederick Wilhelm and both the 1843 Mendelssohn "Wedding March" from *A Midsummer Night's Dream* music and the 1850 Wagner "Wedding March" from the opera *Lohengrin* are played, beginning a tradition that will endure for weddings of royalty, nobility, and commoners in much of the world.

Opera *Orpheus in the Underworld* (*Orphée aux Enfers*) 10/21 at the Bouffés Parisiens in Paris, with music by German-French composer Jacques Offenbach (Jacob Eberst), 39, who was conductor at the Comédie Française from 1849 to 1855 and has been managing his own theater for 3 years.

"Le Cancan" is danced for the first time in the new Jacques Offenbach opera (above).

London's Covent Garden Opera House is completed by local architect Sir Charles Barry, 63.

Popular songs "The Yellow Rose of Texas" with music by a U.S. composer identified only as "JK";

"The Old Grey Mare (Get Out of the Wilderness)" by U.S. songwriter J. Warner whose song will be adapted as an 1860 presidential campaign song by supporters of Abraham Lincoln (above).

The McKay machine invented by South Abingdon, Mass., shoemaker Lyman Reed Blake, 23, permits production of low-cost shoes by eliminating the heavy work of hand sewing. Gordon McKay, now 37, will promote Blake's machine and it will become famous as the McKay machine.

London tobacco merchant Philip Morris opens a cigarette factory using mostly smoke-cured Latakia leaf from Turkey (*see* 1902; Gloag, 1856).

U.S. tobacco merchant John Liggett takes his brother William into partnership and the firm becomes J. E. Liggett & Brother (*see* 1847; Liggett & Myers, 1873).

New York's 40-year-old Brooks Brothers opens its first branch at Broadway and Grand Street with a custom department housed in a circular room lit from a 68-foot dome (*see* 1909).

R. H. Macy Company opens October 27 with an 11-foot storefront on New York's 14th Street. Nantucket-born merchant Rowland Hussey Macy, 36, went to sea on a whaling ship at age 15, he returned with a red star tattooed on his arm, he opened a dry goods store at Haverhill, Mass., in 1851 selling only for cash and never deviating from a fixed price, he failed after 3 years, but he will use flamboyant advertising to make his New York store more successful and while his first day's sales of ribbons, trimmings, hosiery, and gloves total only $11.06, his gross sales next year will be $90,000 (*see* 1867).

Baltimore's Hutzler Brothers Co. department store has its beginnings in the M. Hutzler & Son dry goods store opened by merchant Abram G. Hutzler and his father (*see* 1908).

Boston begins filling in its Back Bay using newly developed steamshovels and rail lines to bring gravel 9 miles from Needham. By 1882 the entire area will be filled to create land on which Commonwealth Avenue, Copley Square, and much of modern Boston will stand.

Big Ben begins chiming out the hours, half-hours, and quarter-hours in the 316-foot tall clock tower of London's Westminster Palace opened by Queen Victoria in 1852. The 13.5-ton great bell that chimes the hours solo for the 23-foot clock is tuned to the note E, it is the lowest note in the chime that strikes the quarter-hours, and it is named for Sir Benjamin Hall, Baron Llanover, who is chief commissioner of works.

Johns-Manville Corporation has its beginnings in New York's H. W. Johns Manufacturing Company started by Johns to produce paint and roofing materials (*see* 1901).

New York's Central Park opens to the public in the autumn although it remains 5 years short of completion (*see* 1857). F. L. Olmsted has been assisted by landscape architect Calvert Vaugh, and he fights pro-

1858 (cont.) posals that the park include a stadium, a race-track, a church, a permanent circus, and other installations. The park has cost $5 million, but the high cost of horsecar and elevated railway transportation will for years keep Olmsted's sylvan retreat beyond the reach of most New Yorkers (*see* 1863).

Henry David Thoreau pleads for "national preserves in which the bear and the panther, and some even of the hunter race may still exist, and not be civilized off the face of the earth—not for idle sport or food, but for inspiration and our own true recreation" (*see* Yellowstone National Park, 1872).

 The Pekin duck is introduced to Long Island by a sea captain who has brought the ducks from China to found an industry (date approximate).

Grenada in the Caribbean produces its first crop of nutmeg and mace to begin the island's career as the world's leading producer of those spices. An English sea captain bound home with spices from the East Indies presented seedlings to his hosts at the port of St. George's in 1843.

The first mechanical refrigerator is devised by French inventor Ferdinand P. A. Carré who uses liquid ammonia in the compression machine that he will demonstrate at the 1862 London Exhibition by using it to manufacture blocks of ice (*see* Harrison, 1856; Lowe, 1865; Linde, 1873).

The Mason jar, patented by New York metalworker John Landis Mason, 26, is a glass jar with a thread molded into its top and a zinc lid with a threaded ring sealer. Mason's reusable jar will be made at first by the Whitney Glass Works of Glassboro, N.J., and will free farm families from having to rely on pickle barrels, root cellars, and smoke houses to get through the winter. Urban families, too, will use Mason jars to put up excess fruits and vegetables, especially tomatoes, berries, relish, and pickles, and the jars will soon be sealed with paraffin wax, a by-product of kerosene (*see* Drake, 1859; Ball brothers, 1887).

The New York Condensed Milk Company is established by Gail Borden (*see* 1857; 1861).

London's Express Country Milk Company has its beginnings in a firm started by local milk retailer George Barham, 22, whose company will have the world's largest milk-bottling center (*see* Margarine Act, 1887).

London's meat becomes fatter and juicier as the Smithfield market receives rail shipments of ready-dressed carcasses from Aberdeen 515 miles away. Beef, mutton, pork, and veal arrive in perfect condition the night after the animals are slaughtered, and the meat is far less lean than if the animals had been driven to market as in the past.

Schweppe's Tonic Water has its beginnings in "an improved liquid known as quinine tonic water" which is patented at London. The product will be made and sold by J. Schweppe & Co. Ltd. beginning in 1880 (*see* 1851; 1953).

The mint julep is created at Old White Springs in Virginia's Allegheny Mountains. The julep is made with brandy, cut-loaf sugar, limestone water, crushed ice, and mountain mint, but the French brandy will generally be replaced by bourbon whiskey.

1859 Petroleum production begins at Pennsylvania to give the world a new source of energy and reduce demand for the whale oil, coal gas, and lard that have been used in lamps (*see* Baku, 1823). Unemployed New Haven & Hartford Railroad conductor "Colonel" Edwin Laurentine Drake, 40, has been sent to Titusville in Pennsylvania's Venange County by New York banker James Townsend, an associate of George Bissell (*see* 1854). Drake uses salt-well drilling equipment to dig into oil-bearing strata, he strikes oil August 28, his 70-foot well is soon producing 400 gallons per day (2,000 barrels per year) to begin the first commercial exploitation of petroleum in the United States and to introduce a new era of kerosene lamps and stoves (*see* Gesner, 1855; Rockefeller, 1860).

Electric home lighting is demonstrated for the first time in the United States by Salem, Mass., inventor Moses Gerrish Farmer, 39, who lights two incandescent lamps on his mantelpiece with platinum strip filaments powered by a wet-cell voltaic battery.

The first practical electric storage battery is invented by French physicist Gaston Plante, 25 (*see* Daniell, 1836; Leclanche's dry-cell battery, 1867).

 On The Origin of Species by Means of Natural Selection, or the Preservation of Favored Species in the Struggle for Life by England's Charles Darwin creates a furor by flying in the face of fundamentalist religion. Darwin's hand has been forced by Alfred Russel Wallace (*see* 1858; Scopes, 1925).

The spectrum analysis that will permit the discovery of new elements is elaborated by German physicist Gustav Robert Kirchhoff, 35, and R. W. Bunsen of 1850 Bunsen burner fame (*see* Mendeléev, 1870).

The chemical theory of fermentation advanced by the German chemist Baron von Liebig is disproved by France's Louis Pasteur whose daughter Jan dies of typhoid fever in September. Pasteur also disproves the theory of spontaneous generation and shows that while some microorganisms exist in the air like yeast, and like yeast can transform whatever they touch, other microorganisms are anaerobic and cannot survive in the presence of air (*see* 1861).

 France's Napoleon III warns the Austrian ambassador January 1 and thus leaks the secret of his alliance last year with Count Cavour. Piedmontese reserves are called up March 9, Austrian troops are mobilized April 7, an Austrian ultimatum April 23 to demobilize within 3 days is rejected by Piedmont but gives Count Cavour the provocation he has wanted, Austrian troops invade Piedmont April 29, but the Austrian general Franz Gyulai moves so slowly that the French have time to mobilize.

France declares war on Austria May 12 pursuant to the alliance Napoleon III made last year, the Piedmontese defeat Austrian forces May 30 at Palestro after peaceful revolutions have driven out the rulers of Tuscany, Modena, and Parma, French and Piedmontese forces cross the Ticino into Lombardy, and the Battle of Magenta June 4 ends with the withdrawal of Austrian troops.

The king of the Two Sicilies Ferdinand II has died May 22 at age 49 after a 19-year reign in which he has won the epithet "King Bomba" by having the chief cities of Sicily bombarded to enforce his reactionary control. He has been succeeded by his 13-year-old son Francesco who will reign for less than 2 years.

The Battle of Solverino June 24 brings cruel suffering to both sides but is indecisive (*see* Dunant, 1862).

The Austrian emperor Franz Josef finds himself short of funds and faced with revolution in Hungary, he meets with Napoleon III July 11 at Villafranca as Prince Metternich dies at age 86, and hostilities cease. Napoleon has become alarmed at all the bloodshed and at the revolutions that have been fomented by nationalists in the papal legations of Bologna, Ferrara, and Ravenna as well as in Tuscany, Modena, and Parma, and the Italian princes are returned to their thrones (*see* Garibaldi, 1860).

Sweden's Oskar I dies July 8 at age 60 after a 15-year reign. He is succeeded by his 33-year-old son who will reign as Charles XV until 1872.

Queensland in Australia is separated from New South Wales and becomes a separate colony with its capital at Brisbane (*see* 1901).

Oregon is admitted to the Union as the 33rd state.

New Mexico Territory lands occupied by the confederated bands of Pima and Maricopa tribes near the Gila River are ordered to be surveyed and set apart as a reservation by the president under terms of a February 28 act of Congress. The reservation is not to exceed 100 square miles, and $10,000 is to be given to the tribes for tools and to cover the expenses of the land survey (the 64,000-acre reservation will be enlarged to 145,000 acres in 1869).

The Fugitive Slave Act of 1850 is upheld by the Supreme Court March 7 in the case of *Ableman v. Booth* which reverses the Wisconsin court decision of 1854 that called the act unconstitutional (*see* Dred Scott, 1857).

Georgia prohibits the post-mortem manumission of slaves by last will and testament. The state legislature votes to permit free blacks to be sold into slavery if they have been indicted as vagrants.

John Brown's raid on Harper's Ferry, Va., October 16 stirs passions throughout the country. Abolitionist Brown of 1856 Pottawatomie Massacre fame leads 13 whites and five blacks into Harper's Ferry, they seize the town and its federal arsenal as a signal for a general slave insurrection that will establish a new state as a refuge for blacks, but Brown is overpowered October 18 by federal troops under Colonel Robert E. Lee who is supported by U.S. marines. John Brown is convicted of treason and he is hanged December 2 at Charlestown at age 59, but "his truth" will go marching on in the words of a popular song.

Britain's House of Commons gets its first Jewish member as Lionel Rothschild, 41, wins a parliamentary election. His son Nathan will be the first Jewish peer to sit in the House of Lords (*see* Nathan, 1815).

Suez Canal construction begins April 25 (*see* 1854). Ferdinand de Lesseps has financed the sea-level waterway between the Mediterranean and the Red Sea chiefly by selling stock to French investors, but he has sold 44 percent for nearly $20 million to Egypt's khedive Mohammed Said. 30,000 Egyptian forced laborers start work at wages above prevailing rates and they will be augmented by Arab, French, Italian, and Greek workers before hand labor is largely replaced beginning in 1863 by mechanical equipment brought from Europe to dig out nearly 2 million cubic centimeters of earth each month (*see* 1869).

The British clipper ship *Falcon* launches a new method of shipbuilding. Much smaller than the American clipper ships but longer lasting and more economical to operate, the *Falcon* is made of wooden planking on iron frames.

The Italian states still have only 1,759 kilometers of railway track (*see* 1839).

Brink's Express is started at Chicago by a Vermonter with a horse and wagon who in 1891 will begin moving bank funds and payroll money to start a business that will grow into the leading U.S. armored truck money-transport company (*see* 1950).

Last year's gold strike in the Colorado Rockies of Kansas Territory brings 100,000 prospectors determined to reach "Pike's Peak or bust."

The Comstock Lode discovered on Mt. Davidson in Washoe, Nev., is an enormous deposit of silver and gold that will yield $145 million worth of ore in the next 11 years and $397 million by 1882. Prospectors Peter O'Reilly and Patrick McLaughlin have found pay dirt on property claimed by Canadian-American prospector Henry Tompkins Paige Comstock, 39, who has been in the area for 3 years, but mining operations are impeded by a blue sand until the sand is assayed and turns out to be three-fourths silver, one-fourth gold, and worth $4,700 per ton (*see* 1873).

Comstock (above) sells his claim for almost nothing but others make fortunes, including Missouri-born prospector George Hearst, 39, whose luck has been poor in California. He pays $450 for a half-interest in a mine believed by its owner Alvah Gould to be worthless, he pays a few hundred dollars more for a one-sixth interest in the Ophir mine which will prove to be the richest in the Comstock Lode and in the Gould and Curry mine which will be the second richest.

1859 (cont.) George Hearst (above) becomes a millionaire overnight, he joins with a partner to buy the Ontario mine in Utah Territory, and he will go on to acquire other partners and other mining properties including the Homestake mine in Dakota Territory, the Anaconda copper mine in Montana Territory, and additional properties in Chile, Peru, and Mexico (*see* Anaconda, 1881; William Randolph Hearst, 1887).

Equitable Life Assurance Society is founded by New York entrepreneur Henry Baldwin Hyde, 25, who hangs a 30-foot sign across the front of a building in which he rents a one-room office with borrowed desks and chairs. Formerly a cashier for the Mutual Life Insurance Company, Hyde has been sacked for proposing the establishment of a company that will insure lives for more than $10,000 and 2 days later he rents space above the Mutual Life offices whose sign is completely dwarfed by the new Equitable sign. By January of next year Hyde will have raised the $100,000 deposit required by the New York State comptroller for life insurance companies and will have installed as president of Equitable the brother of his pastor at the Fifth Avenue Presbyterian Church. By the end of next year he will have 229 agents whom he has selected and trained (*see* 1862).

Treatise on Gout and Rheumatic Gout by London physician Alfred Baring Garrod, 40, shows that Galen in the 2nd century was wrong in blaming gout on overindulgence. A staff physician at University College Hospital, Garrod says gout comes from an excess of uric acid in the blood and can be controlled by avoiding foods high in purine and by using drugs such as colchicine (*see* Franklin, 1785).

Cocaine is isolated from coca leaves brought home from Peru by Austrian explorer Karl von Scherzer, but physicians show little interest in the potential of the drug for anaesthesia (*see* 1884).

New York's Cooper Union for the Advancement of Science and Art opens its first building at Astor Place and Fourth Avenue (*see* Cooper Institute, 1857; W. W. Norton, 1923).

Telegraph promoter Samuel F. B. Morse agrees to the formation of the North American Telegraph Association as a near-monopoly (*see* 1844; Western Union, 1856, 1866).

Rocky Mountain News is started as the first newspaper in what will soon be Montana Territory by U.S. surveyor William Newton Byers, 28, who will be publisher and editor until 1878 (*see* Montana, 1864).

Fiction *A Tale of Two Cities* by Charles Dickens whose novel of the French Revolution begins, "It was the best of times, it was the worst of times . . ."; *Adam Bede* by George Eliot wins its author her first wide success; *The Ordeal of Richard Feverel* by English novelist George Meredith, 31; *Oblomov* by Russian novelist Ivan Aleksandrovich Goncharov, 47, a rich merchant's son who last year published *Fregat Pallada* describing a voyage to Japan as secretary to a Russian mission.

Poetry *The Idylls of the King* by Alfred Tennyson whose first volume begins a series that he will complete in 1885 to bring Arthurian legend to life with verses about Arthur, Guinevere, Lancelot, the lady of Shalott, and the towers of fabled Camelot; *The Rubaiyat of Omar Khayyam of Naishapur* by English poet-translator Edward Fitzgerald, 50, who puts into graceful English quatrains the rhymed verse of a 12th-century Persian astronomer-poet: "A Book of Verses underneath the Bough,/ A Jug of Wine, a Loaf of Bread—and Thou/ Beside me, singing in the Wilderness—/ Oh, Wilderness were Paradise enow!" "And much as wine has played the Infidel,/ And robbed me of my Robe of Honor—Well,/ I often wonder what the Vintners buy/ One half so precious as the stuff they sell"; "The Moving Finger writes; and having writ,/ Moves on; nor all your Piety nor Wit/ Shall lure it back to cancel half a Line/ Nor all your Tears wash out a Word of it"; "The Children's Hour" by Henry Wadsworth Longfellow begins, "Between the dark and the daylight,/ When the night is beginning to lower,/ Comes a pause in the day's occupations/ That is known as the Children's Hour"; *Mireio* by French Provençal poet Frédéric Mistral, 29.

Painting *The Absinthe Drinker* by French painter Edouard Manet, 27; *The Angelus* by Jean François Millet; *Le Bain Turc* by Jean Auguste Dominique Ingres, now 79; *At the Piano* by U.S. émigré painter-etcher James Abbott McNeill Whistler, 25, who settles at London. Whistler lived in Russia during his teens while his father directed construction of a railroad for Czar Nicholas I, he was forced to leave West Point at age 19 for failing chemistry, and he has lived abroad since age 21.

Theater *The Octaroon, or Life in Louisiana* by Dion Boucicault 12/5 at New York's Winter Garden Theater. Boucicault has adapted the 1856 novel *The Quadroon* by Mayne Reid to create his melodrama.

Opera *The Masked Ball* (*Un Ballo Maschero*) 2/17 at Rome's Teatro Apollo, with music by Guiseppe Verdi; *Faust* 3/19 at the Théâtre Lyrique in Paris, with music by French composer Charles Gounod, 41, to a libretto based on the Goethe tragedy.

First performances Serenade for Orchestra No. 1 in D major by Johannes Brahms 3/28 at Hamburg; Concerto No. 1 for Pianoforte and Orchestra by Johannes Brahms 7/22 at Hanover.

Hymns "Ave Maria" ("Hail Mary") by Charles Gounod (above) who has based it on Johann Sebastian Bach's first prelude in *The Well-Tempered Clavier* of 1722; "Nearer My God to Thee" by Boston musician Lowell Mason, now 67, lyrics by the late Sarah Adams who wrote them in 1840 or 1841.

Popular songs "Dixie" ("I Wish I Was in Dixie's Land") by Daniel Decatur Emmet of the Virginia Minstrels is performed for the first time 4/4 at New York's Mechanics Hall, 472 Broadway; "La Paloma" by Spanish songwriter Sebastian Yradier, 50.

The Steinway Piano has its beginnings in an improved grand piano developed by German-American pianomaker Henry Engelhard Steinweg, 62—the first piano with a single cast-metal plate. The plate is strong enough to withstand the pull of strings which Steinweg has combined with an overstrung scale that both saves space and produces a much fuller tone than earlier pianos. Steinweg will call himself Steinway beginning in 1865, he established a New York piano factory with several of his sons in 1853, and his new grand piano will make Steinway & Sons world-famous.

 The first intercollegiate baseball game July 1 ends with an Amherst College team defeating a Williams team 73 to 32 in 26 innings on the grounds of the Maplewood Female Institute at Pittsfield, Mass. (see 1845; Cincinnati Red Stockings, 1869).

The Cachar Polo Club founded by British colonial officers stationed in Assam, India, is the world's first polo club.

French tightrope walker Charles Blondin (Jean François Gravelet), 35, crosses Niagara Falls on a tightrope June 30.

The world's first flying trapeze circus act is performed November 12 at the Cirque Napoleon in Paris by Jules Léotard, 21, who has practiced at his father's gymnasium in Toulouse. Safety nets will not be introduced until 1871 and Léotard meanwhile will use a pile of mattresses to cushion possible falls. The song "That Daring Young Man on the Flying Trapeze" will be written about Léotard and his name will be applied to the tights worn by acrobats and dancers.

 Gloag's Sweet Threes cigarettes made from Latakia tobacco dust wrapped in yellow tissue are introduced by London cigarette-maker Robert Gloag (see 1856); a fast worker can fill 1,250 of the thick hand-made cigarettes in a day (see Richmond, 1860).

 San Antonio's Menger Hotel opens. German-American brewer William Menger has built a three-story hotel for the Texas cowtown.

 Boston's Public Garden is established on 108 acres of filled land owned by the Commonwealth of Massachusetts (see Swan Boats, 1877).

Acquisition of land for Brooklyn's Prospect Park is authorized by the New York State legislature (see 1867; Central Park, 1858).

The world's first children's playgrounds open at Manchester, England, where horizontal bars and swings have been installed in Queen's Park and Philips Park.

 Mechanization of U.S. agriculture will be spurred by the discovery of oil at Titusville (above).

Two dozen English rabbits are introduced into Australia by landowner Thomas Austin to provide shooting sport. In 6 years Austin will have shot 200,000 rabbits on his own estate but will have killed scarcely half the rabbits on his property, and since five of the fast-multiplying animals consume more grass than one sheep, the rabbits will quickly become a major problem to sheep-raisers (see myxomatosis, 1951).

 Paraffin wax, a by-product of kerosene produced from petroleum (above), will be used to seal Mason jars used for preserving foods (see Mason, 1858).

Civilized America is published at London and ridicules Americans for calling a cock a rooster and for using similar euphemisms.

New York Tribune editor Horace Greeley visits Denver and finds that its residents subsist almost entirely on beans, bacon, and sourdough bread (see 1858). The mining town's only hotel is a tent.

The A&P retail food chain has its beginnings in the Great American Tea Company store opened at 31 Vesey Street, N.Y., by local merchant George Huntington Hartford, 26, who has persuaded his employer George P. Gilman to give up his hide and leather business and go partners in buying China and Japanese tea directly from ships in New York harbor. Both originally from Maine, the two men buy whole clipper ship cargoes at one fell swoop, they sell the tea at less than one-third the price charged by other merchants, they identify their store with flaked gold letters on a Chinese vermilion background, and they start a business that will grow into the first chain store operation (see 1863; A&P, 1869).

1860 Sicilian authorities abort an uprising against the Bourbon monarchy in April but Giuseppe Garibaldi organizes an army of 1,000 "Redshirts" at Genoa and sails May 5 for Marsala. He lands May 11, gathers recruits as he marches inland, defeats the Neapolitans May 15 at Calatafimi, takes Palermo June 6, crosses the Straits with British connivance August 22, takes Naples September 7, and supports Victor Emmanuel II of Piedmont as king of a united Italy. By November, he is back on the island of Caprera looking after his donkeys Pius IX, Napoleon III, Oudinot, and the Immaculate Conception (see 1857; 1861).

Montenegro's Danilo I is assassinated August 12 after a 9-year reign in which he has tried to reform and modernize the Balkan state. Danilo is succeeded by his 19-year-old nephew who will reign until 1918 as Nicholas I.

Serbia's Miloš Obrenović dies at Belgrade September 27 at age 80 after taking cruel vengeance on the enemies that deposed him in 1839. He is succeeded by his son Michael III Obrenović who reigned briefly from 1839 to 1842 and who will rule until his assassination in 1868. Michael will abolish the oligarchic constitution of 1839 and will work to consolidate the Balkan states under Serbian leadership.

Napoleon III increases the powers of the French Parlement in November in an effort to regain support lost by last year's war with Austria and Piedmont. A new commercial treaty with Britain has further weakened his support (below).

John Brown's raid on the federal arsenal at Harper's Ferry kindled new flames of abolitionist passion.

The world's first breech-loading rifled artillery is used August 12 in China as Armstrong 18-pounders bombard Sinho to force admission of foreign diplomats by Peking. Seventeen thousand French and British troops occupy Peking October 12 and burn the Summer Palace to punish the Chinese for seizing Harry Parkes, the 52-year-old diplomat who has been virtual governor of Canton and who was taken prisoner despite his flag of truce. Peking is forced to yield to some Western demands and to increase its indemnities (see 1842; 1853; 1864).

The U. S. Army's Fort Defiance in New Mexico Territory has been attacked April 30 by 1,000 Navajo whose sheep and goats have been shot by soldiers from the fort. Led by Manuelito, the Navajos nearly succeed in taking the fort before being driven off by musketfire (see 1861).

The United States becomes less united following the election of Abraham Lincoln as president in November with 40 percent of the popular vote (Lincoln has received 180 electoral votes, John C. Breckenridge 72 with 18 percent of the popular vote, Stephen A. Douglas 12 with 30 percent of the popular vote). South Carolina adopts an Ordinance of Secession December 20 as protest against the election (see 1861).

$ U.S. cotton exports amount to $192 million out of the nation's export total of $334 million, up from $72 million in 1850 when cotton accounted for less than half the total.

An Anglo-French treaty of reciprocity signed in January has been negotiated by English free-trade advocate Richard Cobden and opens up a wider area of trade between the two countries (see 1845). Many Frenchmen oppose the treaty and it weakens the popularity of Napoleon III (above).

John D. Rockefeller enters the oil business at age 20. A junior partner in the Cleveland produce commission firm Clark & Rockefeller, John Davison Rockefeller has been sent 100 miles to Titusville, Pa. by a group of businessmen to investigate the potential of the petroleum found last year, he reports back that petroleum has little future, but he pools his savings with those of his partner Maurice B. Clark, they invest $4,000 in the lard oil refinery of candlemaker Samuel Andrews, and Rockefeller persuades richer men to build more refineries for petroleum which he foresees as a major energy source (see 1863).

An internal combustion engine patented at Paris by Belgian inventor Jean Etienne Lenoir, 38, employs a carburetor that mixes liquid hydrocarbons to form a vapor. An electric spark explodes the vapor in a cylinder but Lenoir's engine works on illuminating gas and has no compression (see Otto, 1866).

Vladivostok is founded by Russian pioneers on the Pacific Coast.

The first expedition to cross Australia from south to north leaves Melbourne with 17 men, 26 camels, and 28 horses under the leadership of Irish-Australian Robert O'Hara Burke, 40. The group will reach the Gulf of Carpentaria next year but Burke will die of starvation on the return trip, as will his lieutenant William John Wills, 26, and another man.

East Africa is explored by German adventurer Karl Klaus von der Decken, 27. He will propose plans for a vast German colony in the area but natives will murder him in 1865.

German traders sent by Woermann and Company open a factory (trading post) on West Africa's Cameroons coast.

British colonists in Natal, South Africa, import workers from India to work their sugar plantations under 3-year indentures.

Elizabeth Cady Stanton urges woman suffrage in an address to a joint session of the New York State Legislature (see 1848; Equal Rights Association, 1866).

The Henry rifle patented by U. S. gunsmith D. Tyler Henry is the first truly practical lever-action rifle. The Winchester Repeating Arms Company will introduce an improved version, the M1866, with a .44 rimfire cartridge.

The first Winchester repeating rifle goes into production at New Haven, Conn. (see 1850; 1866).

The Oneida Community grosses $100,000 from sales of the Newhouse trap named for Community member Sewell Newhouse, who invented the device that is fast becoming the standard trap used in North America and that will eventually become the standard for most of the world. The major enterprise of the 12-year-old Community is making traps, and men of the Community have developed dishwashing machines and machines for paring apples and washing vegetables to spare themselves the tedium of kitchen chores (see tableware, 1877).

The first Japanese-built ship to reach the United States arrives at San Francisco February 16 after a 34-day voyage. The 300-ton iron steamship S.S. *Kanrinmaru* has been accompanied by the U.S. cruiser *Powhatan* and carries a delegation of 80 which proceeds to Washington, D.C., puts up at the Willard Hotel, and drinks from the hotel fingerbowls.

More than 1,000 steamboats ply the Mississippi, up from 400-odd in 1840.

French railway trackage reaches 5,918 miles, up from 336 in 1842 (*see* 1870).

Diabetes is the result of a pancreas disorder, says Paris physician Etienne Lancereaux, 31 (*see* 1869).

The clinical symptoms of acute trichinosis are noted for the first time by German pathologist Friedrich Albert von Zenker, 35, but the cause-effect relationship remains unknown (*see* 1835).

The Seventh Day Adventist Church is founded at Battle Creek, Mich., by former followers of William Miller (*see* 1835; sanitorium, 1866).

The first U.S. English-speaking kindergarten opens at Boston under the direction of Elizabeth Palmer Peabody whose school for pre-schoolers follows the lead set by Mrs. Carl Schurz in 1855. Mrs. Peabody is the sister-in-law of educator Horace Mann and of novelist Nathaniel Hawthorne.

Louisiana State University and Louisiana A&M College are founded at Baton Rouge.

Bard College is founded at Annandale-on-Hudson, N.Y.

The first Pony Express riders leave St. Joseph, Mo., April 3 and deliver mail to Sacramento, Cal., 10 days later. William Hepburn Russell, 48, has organized the Pony Express to carry mail at rates of $2 to $10 per ounce depending on distance, he keeps 80 riders in the saddle at all times of day and night, and he uses fast Indian ponies in relays to cover the 10 miles or so between each of some 190 stations (*see* 1861).

U.S. Army Signal Corps surgeon Albert J. Myer receives a $4,000 congressional appropriation to develop a wigwag system of visual signaling that he has invented.

The United States has 372 daily newspapers, up from 254 in 1850, but newspapers remain generally too expensive for the average man or woman (*see* 1909).

The Cornhill Magazine begins publication at London under the editorship of William Makepeace Thackeray whose last three novels will be published in the magazine.

Fiction   *The Mill on the Floss* by George Eliot; *The Marble Faun* by Nathaniel Hawthorne; *The Woman in White*, a pioneer detective novel by English novelist William Wilkie Collins, 36, whose historical romance *Antonina* appeared in 1850 and whose new work is serialized in the London magazine *All the Year Round; Malaeska: The Indian Wife of the White Hunter* by Anne S. W. Stephens is the first "dime novel." It is published at New York by Beadle &

Adams whose proprietors Erastus Flavel Beadle, 39, and Robert Adams moved east from Buffalo 2 years ago, have experimented with 10-cent paperbound songbooks, joke books, and etiquette books, but only now have a runaway best-seller. Beadle & Adams will publish hundreds of dime novels and thousands of Dime Library and Half Dime Library titles including the adventures of Deadwood Dick and Nick Carter (*see* 1886); *On the Eve* by Ivan Turgenev.

Poetry   "Tithonus" by Alfred Lord Tennyson who writes, "After many a summer dies the swan"; "Rock Me to Sleep, Mother" by New England poet Florence Percy (Elizabeth Chase Akers), 28, who writes, "Backward, turn backward, O time in your flight,/ Make me a child again just for tonight."

Painting   *The Guitarist* by Edouard Manet.

Theater   *The Colleen Bawn, or The Brides of Garryowen* by Dion Boucicault 3/29 at Laura Keene's Theater, New York, with John Drew in a melodrama based on the 1829 novel *The Collegians* by Gerald Griffin; *Rip Van Winkle* 12/24 at New York, with Joseph Jefferson, 31, in the title role his own dramatization of the Washington Irving story.

First performances   Serenade No. 2 in A major by Johannes Brahms 2/10 at Hamburg; Concerto for Cello and Orchestra in A minor by the late Robert Schumann 6/9 at Leipzig's Royal Conservatory.

Popular songs   "Old Black Joe" by Stephen C. Foster; "The Glendy Burk" by Stephen C. Foster; "Annie Lisle" by H. S. Thompson whose melody will be the basis of the Cornell University song "Far Above Cayuga's Waters."

The first British Open golf tournament opens at Prestwick, Scotland. U.S. sportsman begin wearing knickerbockers (plus-fours) (*see* U.S. Open, 1894).

The first world heavyweight boxing championship bout April 17 at Farnborough, Hampshire, pits U.S. champion John C. Heenan against the British champion Tom Sayers. The fight continues for 42 rounds until Sayers is unable to use his right arm, Heenan is blinded from his own blood, and the crowd breaks into the ring to stop the fight.

The longest bare-knuckle prizefight in U.S. history is held at Berwick, Me., where J. Fitzpatrick and James O'Neill battle for 4 hours, 20 minutes.

Australia's Melbourne Cup horserace has its first running in the Victoria colony.

The Checkered Game of Life board game is introduced at Springfield, Mass., lithographer Milton Bradley, 23, who has been hurt by the business recession this year. The success of the game encourages Bradley, he will found the firm Milton Bradley & Company in 1864, it will become the Milton Bradley Company in 1878, and it will be a leading producer of school materials and games.

1860 (cont.) Armstrong Cork Company has its beginnings in the John D. Glass Company founded by Pennsylvania entrepeneurs Thomas Marton Armstrong and John D. Glass: when Glass dies in 1864 his interests will be acquired by Armstrong's brother Robert and by William G. Standish, the Company will be renamed Armstrong Brothers & Company, and it will employ machinery to cut the bark off cork trees in Spain, Portugal, and North Africa (*see* Armstrong Linoleum, 1907)

The word "linoleum" is coined by English inventor Frederick Walton who has devised a process for oxidizing linseed oil to produce a cheap rubber-like material for use as a floorcovering. Other methods will be developed for solidifying linseed oil but all linoleum production will be based essentially on Walton's inventions.

Cigarette smoking increases in America. Richmond, Va., has more than 50 cigarette factories and North Carolina and Virginia together have more than 348, up from 119 in 1840 (*see* 1875; Philip Morris, 1858).

New York's Lord & Taylor dry goods store moves from its Catherine Street location of 1826 to a new five-story building at the corner of Broadway and Grand Street where its staircase is lighted by a huge $500 gas chandelier made by the 23-year-old firm Tiffany & Co. (*see* 1873).

Cleveland's Higbee Company has its beginnings in a dry goods store that will grow to become a major department store.

Alabama's Kirkwood mansion is completed in Greek revival style at Eutaw for local cotton planter Foster M. Kirksey whose family will occupy the plantation house for more than a century.

Texas cattleman Richard King takes his old steamboat partner Miflin Kenedy into partnership and the two pool their resources to import Durham cattle that will improve their breeding stock (*see* 1850; 1853; 1868).

The growth of the railroad and the steamship in the next four decades will encourage expansion of U.S. agriculture for export markets.

The U.S. wheat crop reaches 173 million bushels, more than double its 1840 level.

The U.S. corn crop reaches 839 million bushels, up from 377 million in 1840 (*see* 1870; 1885).

The U.S. cotton crop reaches 3.48 million bales of which most is shipped to Liverpool for England's booming textile industry.

Contour plowing and use of fertilizer is urged by Mississippi agronomist Eugene Hilgard who writes, "Well might the Chickasaws and Choctaws question the moral right of the act by which their beautiful, parklike hunting grounds were turned over to another race . . . Under their system these lands would have lasted forever; under ours, in less than a century the state will be reduced to the . . . desolation of the once fertile Roman Campagna" (*see* Ruffin, 1833).

Parliament passes the first British Adulteration of Food Law after physician Edward Lankester quotes recent cases in which three people have died after attending a public banquet at which green blanc-mange was served that was colored with arsenite of copper. Lankester has shown that sulfide of arsenic is used to color Bath buns yellow (*see* 1861).

Louis Pasteur sterilizes milk by heating it to 125° Centigrade at a pressure of 1.5 atmospheres (100°C is equal to 212°F). Pasteur will develop methods using lower heats to "pasteurize" milk (*see* 1857; 1861; cattle tuberculosis test, 1892; Bang's disease, 1896).

U.S. women are advised to cook tomatoes for at least 3 hours by *Godey's Lady's Book*.

The U.S. population reaches 31.4 million, double its 1840 level, with 4 million of the total foreign-born. The white birth rate is 41.4 per thousand, down from 55 in 1800, but the excess of births over deaths is still the main source of population growth.

Indian population in the United States and its territories is 300,000, down from between 600,000 and 900,000 in 1607.

U.S. population density is 10.6 people per square mile, up from four to five in 1790 although 16.1 percent of the people live in cities of 2,500 or more. Only nine cities have more than 100,000 (New York has 805,651, Philadelphia 562,529, Brooklyn 266,661, Baltimore 212,418, Boston 177,812, New Orleans 168,675, Cincinnati 161,044, St. Louis 160,773, Chicago 109,260, Buffalo 81,129, Newark 71,914, Louisville 68,033, Albany 62,367, Washington 61,122, San Francisco 56,802, and Providence 50,666).

Hawaii's native population has fallen from 150,000 in 1819 and 75,000 in 1850 to less than 37,000 as a consequence of contagious diseases introduced from Europe and America (*see* 1959).

1861 Italy unites as a single kingdom (below) while the United States disunites.

Kansas is admitted to the Union as a free state January 29 but between January and May the secession of South Carolina late last year is followed by Mississippi, Florida, Alabama, Georgia, Louisiana, Texas, Virginia, Tennessee, Arkansas, and North Carolina.

Delegates from six seceding states meet at Montgomery, Ala., February 4 and form a provisional government, the Confederate States of America. Jefferson Davis of Mississippi, now 52, is named provisional president of the CFA February 8 and is confirmed by an election in October held after seizure of federal funds and property in the South.

Civil War begins April 12 as Fort Sumter on an island in Charleston harbor is bombarded by Confederate General Pierre Gustave Toutant de Beauregard, 42, who has resigned as superintendent of the U.S. military academy at West Point to assume command of the Confederate Army.

"This country, with its institutions, belongs to the people who inhabit it," President Lincoln has said in his inaugural address March 4. "Whenever they shall grow weary of the existing government they can exercise their constitutional right of amending it, or their revolutionary right to dismember it or overthrow it."

The U.S. Army numbers 13,024 officers and men March 4 but President Lincoln calls for 42,034 volunteers to serve for 3 years and by July there are some 30,000 green recruits in and about Washington under the command of Mexican War veteran Winfield Scott, but old "Fuss and Feathers" is now 75.

The first Battle of Bull Run near the Manassas railway junction across the Potomac ends in a rout of General Irvin McDowell's Union forces by Confederate troops under the Command of General Beauregard (above) and General Joseph Eggleston Johnston, 54.

Union forces under General Nathaniel Lyon are defeated August 10 at Wilson's Creek, Mo.

Confederate forts on the North Carolina coast are captured in late August by Union forces under General Benjamin Franklin Butler, 42.

The Battle of Ball's Bluff on the Potomac October 21 ends in defeat for the Union.

President Lincoln gives General George Brinton McClellan, 34, command of all federal forces November 1. McClellan spends the winter training a 200,000-man Army of the Potomac while Union naval forces attempt to enforce an embargo on Southern ports that was ordered in April.

Detective Allan Pinkerton has gained prominence by uncovering a plot to kill president-elect Lincoln in Baltimore during Lincoln's journey to Washington for the inauguration (above). General McClellan (above) engages Pinkerton to head a department of counterespionage and Pinkerton, disguised as a Major E. J. Allen, supplies reports that exaggerate the size of Confederate troop concentrations and discourage McClellan from taking decisive action (Pinkerton will resign next year) (see 1850; Molly Maguires, 1877).

The Colorado Territory is formed February 28, the Dakota Territory March 2, the Nevada Territory March 2 (see Comstock Lode, 1859). The Arizona Territory organized August 1 consists of all of New Mexico south of the 34th parallel (northeastern New Mexico has been included in the Colorado Territory).

The Trent affair November 8 precipitates an Anglo-American crisis. Arctic explorer Captain Charles Wilkes, 63, commanding the U.S.S. San Jacinto stops the British mail packet S.S. Trent and removes former U.S. Senators John Murray Mason, 63, and John Slidell, 68, now Confederate commissioners bound for Britain and France. Secretary of State William H. Seward will avert war by releasing the two men early next year.

A united Kingdom of Italy proclaimed March 17 by the nation's parliament joins Lombardy, Piedmont, Parma, Modena, Lucca, Romagna, Tuscany, and the two Sicilies under Victor Emmanuel II of Piedmont's House of Savoy. Nice and Savoy were lost to France last year, Venetia is held by Austria and will not be united with Italy until 1866, and Rome is held by France's Louis Napoleon and will not become part of Italy, and the nation's capital, until 1870. The proclamation of unification is followed within weeks by the death at age 62 of Conte Camillo Bensodi di Cavour who has been so instrumental in creating the new kingdom (see 1842; 1866).

Prussia's Friedrich Wilhelm IV has died January 2 at age 65 after a 2.5-year period of paralysis and insanity. He has been succeeded after a 20-year reign by his 63-year-old brother who has been acting as regent and who will reign as Wilhelm I until 1888.

Portugal's Pedro V dies November 11 of cholera at age 24 after a reign of less than 9 years. He is succeeded by his 23-year-old brother who will reign as Luiz I until 1889.

France's Napoleon III extends the financial powers of Parlement and mounts a grandiose program of public works despite the quickly mounting expenses of his extravagant foreign policy. Political opposition to the emperor begins to grow at a rapid pace.

French, British, and Spanish troops land at Vera Cruz in December to force Mexico's Benito Juarez to honor his financial obligations and to resume the payments which he has suspended (see 1862).

Queen Victoria's Prince Consort Albert dies of typhoid fever December 14 at age 42.

The Ottoman sultan Abdul Mejid has died June 25 at age 38 after a reign of nearly 22 years that has been marked by reforms including the repression of slavery. He has been succeeded by his 31-year-old brother Abdul Aziz who will reign until 1876 and will obtain enormous wealth which he will squander recklessly.

 Czar Aleksandr II completes the emancipation of Russian serfs begun in 1858. He allots land to the serfs for which they are to pay over a period of 49 years, but the land is given not to individuals but rather to village communes (mirs) and is to be redistributed every 10 or 12 years to assure equality. Since a peasant may buy only half the amount of land he cultivated as a serf and will often be unable to afford his annual "redemption" payments, he will be unable to gain economic independence much less improve the land or his methods of cultivation.

Russian anarchist Mikhail Bakunin returns to Eurpoe after escaping imprisonment in Eastern Siberia and traveling home via Japan and the United States (see 1847). Bakunin will be the leading European anarchist until his death in 1876.

Chiricahua Apache chief Cochise in Arizona Territory is falsely accused of having kidnapped a white child, he appears at an army post to deny the charge, he is imprisoned, he escapes, and he takes hostages

1861 (cont.) to be exchanged for other Chiricahuas held by the U.S. Army. The exchange of hostages does not take place, the hostages are killed on both sides, the 49-year-old Cochise joins with his father-in-law Mangas Coloradas of the Mimbreno Apache in raids that threaten to drive the Anglos from Arizona (*see* 1862).

A U.S. Sanitary Commission is organized by Secretary of War Simon Cameron June 9. Educator Clara (Clarissa Harlowe) Barton, 40, quits her job at the U.S. Patent Office to organize facilities for recovering soldiers' lost baggage and to secure medicine and supplies for troops wounded in the first Battle of Bull Run (above) (*see* American Red Cross, 1881).

Dorothea Dix, now 59, wins an appointment as superintendent of women nurses for the Union.

New York's Bellevue Hospital Medical College is established with Lewis Albert Sayre, 41, as the first U.S. professor of orthopedic surgery.

The germ theory of disease has its beginnings in a paper published by Louis Pasteur that absolutely refutes the idea of spontaneous generation (*see* 1860). *"Memoire sur les corpuscles organises qui existent dans l'atmosphere"* convincingly discredits the 1748 notion and others of its kind which are still commonly believed (*see* Lister, 1865).

The Central Pacific Railroad is chartered in California to build the western section of a projected transcontinental rail link. Leland Stanford, 37, is president, Collis P. Huntington of 1849 Huntington and Hopkins fame is vice-president, Mark Hopkins is an officer, and Charles Crocker, 39, is in charge of construction. Faced with a manpower shortage due to the Civil War, Crocker approaches the Chinese Six Companies that recruits workers at $35 per head from California and from China (whose economy has been disrupted by the T'ai P'ing Rebellion). Some 9,000 of the 10,000 laborers on the Central Pacific will be Chinese (*see* 1869).

U.S. entrepreneur Henry Meiggs, 50, obtains a contract to complete a Chilean Railroad between Valparaiso and Santiago. Meiggs chartered the packet ship *Albany* in 1849 to carry New York lumber to San Francisco and made a fortune in lumber and land speculations, a credit crisis in 1854 plunged him heavily into debt but his brother was elected city comptroller and Meiggs obtained a book of city notes signed in advance by the mayor and the outgoing comptroller, he received upward of $365,000 for the notes, he absconded September 26 aboard the bark *America*, the city did not discover its loss until October 16, Don Enrique arrived with his family in Chile, his knowledge of Spanish has won him a position superintending construction of the Santiago al Sur Railroad, he will complete the new rail line in less than 2 years (several previous contractors have gone bankrupt), his success will bring him a profit of $1.5 million, and he will repay San Francisco (*see* 1871).

The velocipede developed by Parisian coachbuilder Pierre Michaux is the world's first true bicycle (*see* Macmillan, 1839). Michaux establishes La Compagnie Parisienne Ancienne Maison Michaux et Cie, he produces two prototype models that have cranks and pedals attached directly to their front wheels, and he will sell 142 cycles next year (*see* 1870).

Congress levies the first U.S. income tax August 5 to raise money needed for the Union Army and Navy. The law taxes incomes in excess of $800 at the rate of 3 percent (*see* 1872).

U.S. tariffs rise as Congress passes the first of three Morrill Acts which will boost tariffs to an average of 47 percent. Duties on tea, coffee, and sugar are increased as a war measure.

Henry du Pont, 49, obtains enough saltpeter from England to keep his Delaware powderworks producing. His firm will make 4 million pounds of gunpowder for the Union Army and will sell it for nearly $1 million in the course of the war (*see* 1814; 1872).

Jay Cooke & Company is founded at Philadelphia by banker Jay Cooke, 40 (*see* 1873).

U.S. banks suspend payments in gold December 30.

The Gatling gun invented by U.S. engineer Richard Jordan Gatling, 43, can fire hundreds of rounds per minute. It will see service in the Civil War beginning in 1864 (*see* Maxim, 1883).

The open-hearth process for making steel developed almost simultaneously by William Siemens and by French engineer Pierre Emile Martin, 37, will result in a rapid increase in steel production (*see* Siemens, 1856). Using a regenerative gas-fired furnace, the new process requires less coal than did previous methods such as the Bessemer process of 1856 (*see* Hewitt and Cooper, 1862).

Pittsburgh's Jones & Laughlin Company opens a two-stack furnace. Benjamin Franklin Jones, 37, bought an interest 10 years ago in the American Steel & Iron Works being built by Bernard Lauth outside Pittsburgh, Irish-American ironmaker James Laughlin, 55, who shipped pig iron from his Youngstown, Ohio, Falcon furnace to Pittsburgh, joined Jones and Lauth in 1854, and the new firm will become a major steel producer (*see* 1900).

Britain produces 83.6 million tons of coal, France 6.8 million, Russia 300,000.

Britain produces 3.7 million tons of iron, France 3 million, the United States 2.8 million, the German states 200,000.

MIT (The Massachusetts Institute of Technology) is founded by William Barton Rogers downriver from Harvard at Cambridge, Mass.

Vassar Female College is chartered at Poughkeepsie, N.Y., by local brewer Matthew Vassar, 69, who has made a fortune in land speculation and who endows the college that will open in 1865.

Yale awards the first American degree of doctor of philosophy (Ph.D.) (*see* Bryn Mawr, 1885).

504

The University of Colorado is founded at Boulder.

The University of Washington is founded at Seattle.

A Western Union telegraph line is completed between New York and San Francisco, one of whose hills will hereafter be called Telegraph Hill. The wire has been strung across the continent despite opposition from hostile Indians and from Confederate sympathizers who have tried to prevent it, and the telegraph brings an end to the money-losing Pony Express started last year by William Hepburn Russell (see Holladay, 1862).

L'Osservatore Romani is founded as the official newspaper of the Vatican.

Nonfiction *The History of England* by English statesman Thomas Babington Macaulay, now 61 (fifth and final volume). Macaulay was raised to the peerage in 1857 and is the 1st Baron Macaulay.

Fiction *Great Expectations* by Charles Dickens with illustrations by Marcus Stone, 21; *Silas Marner, or the Weaver of Raveloe* by George Eliot; *The Cloister and the Hearth* by Charles Reade whose romance of the Reformation is based on wide reading in literature of the period; *Framley Parsonage* by Anthony Trollope.

Poetry *The Golden Treasury of the best Songs and Lyrical Poems in the English Language* by English anthologist-poet Francis Turner Palgrave, 37, who will publish a second, enlarged series in 1897.

Painting *St. John* by New York painter John La Farge, 26; *Orphée, Le Repos* by J. B. C. Corot.

Wood-cut Engravings for Dante's *Inferno* by Gustave Doré.

Theater Lola Montez dies in obscurity at Astoria, N.Y., January 17 at age 43 and is buried in a Brooklyn cemetery under the name Mrs. Eliza Gilbert. *Siegfried's Death (Siegfrieds Tod)* by Friedrich Hebbel 1/31 at Weimar's Hoftheater; *Kriemhild's Revenge (Kriemhildes Rache)* by Friedrich Hebbel 5/18 at Weimar's Hoftheater.

First performances *Mephisto Waltz* by Franz Liszt, in January at Weimar's Grand Ducal Palace; Mass in B minor by the late Johann Sebastian Bach (see 1733) 4/24 at Berlin (first complete performance; Quartet in G minor for piano and strings by Johannes Brahms 11/16 at Hamburg's Wormer Hall.

Hymn "Abide with Me; Fast Falls the Eventide" by English composer-organist William Henry Monk, 38, lyric by the late Scottish Anglican clergyman Henry Francis Lyte who died in 1847 at age 54.

Popular songs "Aura Lea" by the U.S. composer George R. Poulton, lyrics by Cincinnati poet William Whiteman Fosdick, 36; "Maryland! My Maryland!" by Marylander James R. Randall whose lyric is set to the music of the German Christmas song "O Tannenbaum" (Randall has heard that Massachusetts troops were attacked while passing through Maryland and hopes his state will join the Confederacy); "The Va-

cant Chair, or We Shall Meet but We Shall Miss Him" by New York composer George Frederick Root, 41, who 8 years ago founded the New York Normal Institute with special attention to training music teachers. Lyrics are by H. S. Washburn.

Rudolph Wurlitzer obtains a Union Army contract to supply drums and trumpets (see 1856; 1908).

I. M. Singer sells more sewing machines abroad than in America and has profits of nearly $200,000 on assets of little more than $1 million (see 1856; 1863).

John Wanamaker, 23, opens a Philadelphia menswear shop with his brother-in-law Nathan Brown. Merchant Wanamaker will pioneer in selling all items at fixed prices with none of the haggling that has been customary between customer and clerk, and within 10 years he will be the largest U.S. menswear retailer (see 1896; Bon Marché, 1852; Strawbridge & Clothier, 1868).

Marshall Field becomes general manager of Chicago's Cooley, Wadsworth store and will become a partner next year (see 1856; 1865).

Charles Digby Harrod, 20, takes over his father's London grocery store in the Brompton Road and works to turn Harrods into a department store (see 1849). He will install a plate glass window and by 1868 he will have a weekly volume of £1,000 (see 1883).

Elisha G. Otis patents a steam-powered elevator but dies at Yonkers, N.Y., April 8 at age 50, leaving Otis Elevator Company to his sons (see 1857). The Otis elevator together with cheaper steel (above) will permit development of the high-rise building and will lead to the rise of the modern city (see 1884).

Most Russian peasants can do no more than grow enough for their own families' needs with a small surplus in good years to sell for tax money. Most cultivate with wooden plows, harvest their crops with sickles or scythes, and thresh their grain with hand flails. One-third of the peasants have no horses, another third only one horse, and even in the richer parts of Russia the soil is drained by strip farming and a shortage of fertilizer (see Stolypin, 1906).

Chicago ships 50 million bushels of U.S. wheat to drought-stricken Europe, up from 31 million in 1860 despite the outbreak of the Civil War and the shortage of farm hands.

"Without McCormick's invention, I feel the North could not win and that the Union would be dismembered," says Secretary of War Edwin M. Stanton. The McCormick reaper sells for $150, up from $100 in 1849, but McCormick offers it at $30 down with the balance to be paid in 6 months if the harvest is good and over a longer term if the harvest is disappointing (see Singer, 1856).

The California State Legislature commissions Count Agoston Haraszthy to bring select varieties of Eu-

1861 (cont.) ropean wine grapes to the state (*see* 1857). Haraszthy will obtain 100,000 cuttings that represent 300 varieties and will inaugurate the modern era of California wine production (*see* France, 1868).

A lecture to the Royal Society of Arts demonstrates that 87 percent of London's bread and 74 percent of the city's milk is still adulterated despite the Adulteration of Foods Law enacted last year (*see* 1872).

Louis Pasteur (above) confutes the Gay-Lussac theory of 1810 that the absence of oxygen is what permits food to be canned without spoilage. Pasteur also points out that since milk is alkaline rather than acid, it requires more heat for sterilization, but heating milk to 110° C. will stop the growth of "vibrios," he says, and will preserve it indefinitely (*see* 1895).

Baltimore canner Isaac Solomon reduces the average processing time for canned foods from 6 hours to 30 minutes by employing Humphry Davy's discovery that adding calcium chloride raises the temperature of boiling water to 240° F. and more (*see* 1874).

Gail Borden licenses more factories to produce his condensed milk, which the Union Army is purchasing for use in field rations. Borden's son John Gail fights for the Union, his son Lee fights with the Texas Cavalry for the Confederacy (*see* 1857; 1866).

Van Camp's Pork and Beans helps sustain Union troops in the field. Indianapolis grocer Gilbert C. Van Camp, 37, who was once a tinsmith, has created a new canned foor staple and has secured an army contract (*see* 1882).

Philadelphia butcher Peter Arrell Brown Widener, 27, obtains a government contract to supply mutton to Union troops in and about Philadelphia. Widener will pocket a $50,000 profit which he will invest in a chain of meat stores and in street railways, building a huge fortune (*see* American Tobacco, 1890).

America's first commercial pretzel bakery opens at Lititz, Pa., with local baker Julius Sturgis in charge.

Henri Nestlé begins his rise to world prominence. The 45-year-old Swiss businessman has taken a financial interest in a chemical firm at Vevey operated by Christopher Guillaume Keppel, and he assumes ownership upon Keppel's retirement (*see* 1866).

Book of Household Management by English journalist Mrs. Isabella Beeton, 25, gives precise recipes for Victorian dishes in a thick 3-pound volume whose contents appeared originally in periodicals. Mrs. Beeton gives costs and cooking times as well as ingredient quantities.

Schrafft's candy has its beginnings in a small store opened at 85 Eliot Street, Boston, by Bavarian-American confectioner William F. Schrafft. He has obtained a loan from the brother of his wife Wilhelmina at New Bedford, his gumdrops gain quick popularity (patrons send them to soldiers in the field), and he expands his operations to produce peppermint sticks, cinnamon balls, and other candy that Boston merchants buy in wholesale lots (*see* Shattuck, 1897).

Delmonico's restaurant in New York moves uptown to Fifth Avenue at 14th Street (*see* 1845; 1899).

Britain's population reaches 23.1 million while Ireland has 5.7 million, Italy 25, Russia 76.

America's 23 Northern states have a population of more than 22 million while the South has 10 million of whom more than a third are slaves.

1862 The Union gains its first major success in February as Fort Henry on the Tennessee River and Fort Donelson on the Cumberland fall to U.S. forces under Brigadier-General Ulysses S. Grant, 39, who wins a promotion to major general of volunteers.

Santa Fe falls March 4 to Confederate forces under Henry Hopkins Sibley but Southern hopes of taking over the Southwest are dashed March 27 at the Battle of Glorieta. Union forces stop Sibley in Apache Canyon at Pidgin's Ranch near Glorieta Pass.

The first naval battle between ironclad ships occurs March 8. The Confederate ironclad frigate *Merrimac* (renamed the *Virginia*) has sunk the *Cumberland* and has defeated the *Congress* in Hampton Roads but is forced to withdraw March 9 after an engagement with the Union's ironclad *Monitor*, built by John Ericsson, 59, with a revolving gun turret.

The Battle of Shiloh April 6 on the Tennessee River ends with both sides claiming victory but General Grant has been routed by the Confederacy's General Albert Sydney Johnston, 59, who is mortally wounded in the battle.

Island Number 10 below Cairo, Ill., on the Mississippi falls to Union forces April 8. Brigadier General of Volunteers John Pope, 40, begins a successful effort to split the Confederacy by gaining control of the entire length of the Mississippi.

General McClellan finally ends his long delay and sends Union forces up the peninsula between the James and York Rivers toward Richmond. The outnumbered Confederates under Joseph Eggleston Johnson and Robert E. Lee are obliged to pull back but much of the Union strength is diverted to the Shenandoah Valley by Colonel T. J. "Stonewall" Jackson. The Federal troops are withdrawn from the peninsula after sustaining heavy losses in the Battle of Fair Oaks May 31 and in the Seven Days' Battle from June 25 to July 1 at Mechanicsville, Gaines' Mill, White Oaks Swamp, and Malvern Hill.

The Second Battle of Bull Run (Manassas) August 30 ends in defeat for the Union.

The Battle of Antietam (Sharpsburg) in Maryland September 17 is indecisive but wins Massachusetts General Joseph Hooker, 47, his nickname "Fighting Joe" (camp followers of Hooker's army are called "Hooker's girls," or simply "hookers").

A Confederate force under General Braxton Bragg, 45, threatens Cincinnati but retires after an indecisive engagement at Perryville October 8 with Union troops under Don Carlos Buell, 44. Buell is relieved of his command for not having promptly pursued Bragg, who had some success at Shiloh (above), and Buell's replacement William Starke Rosecrans, 43, skirmishes with Bragg for 4 days in the Battle of Murfreesboro beginning December 31.

President Lincoln relieves General McClellan of his command in November and places the Army of the Potomac under General Ambrose Everett Burnside, 38. Robert E. Lee hands Burnside a bad defeat December 13 at the Battle of Fredericksburg, and President Lincoln will replace Burnside in January.

Britain and Spain have withdrawn their troops from Mexico April 8 when it became clear that France's Napoleon III intended to establish a Catholic Latin empire in Mexico (*see* 1861; 1863).

London has decided not to recognize the Confederacy on which Britain depends for cotton. The British are dependent on the North for grain exports (*see* *Trent* affair, 1861).

Greece's Otto I is deposed after a 29-year reign that has alienated the Greeks and has brought an assassination attempt on his wife Amalie. Otto and his queen take refuge on a British warship and return to Bavaria (*see* 1863).

Slavery is abolished in the District of Columbia April 16 by act of Congress and is abolished in U.S. territories June 19.

"My paramount object in this struggle is to save the Union," writes President Lincoln August 22 in a letter to Horace Greeley of the *New York Tribune,* "and is not either to save or to destroy slavery. If I could save the Union without freeing any slave, I would do it; and if I could do it by freeing all the slaves, I would do it; and if I could save it by freeing some and leaving others alone, I would also do that" (but *see* below).

An Emancipation Proclamation issued by President Lincoln September 22 declares that "persons held as slaves" within areas "in rebellion against the United States" will be free on and after January 1, 1863. Lincoln makes it clear that emancipation is a war aim.

Chiricahua and Mimbreno Apaches led by Cochise hold Apache Pass with 500 warriors against 3,000 California volunteers under General James Carleton until they are forced out by artillery fire. The aged Mangas Coloradas is captured, he is killed in prison, and Cochise leads his followers deep into the Dragoon Mountains from which he continues raids that will terrorize white settlers until 1871 (*see* 1861).

A Sioux uprising has begun in Minnesota August 17 under the leadership of Little Crow. The insurrection is suppressed, 306 tribesmen are sentenced to death, and 38 are hanged December 26 on a huge scaffold at Mankato.

The First Regiment of South Carolina volunteers is organized in November and is the first U.S. regiment of ex-slaves. Its commander is Boston's Colonel Thomas Wentworth Storrow Higginson, 38, formerly pastor of the Free Church at Worcester, who in 1854 purchased axes and led the unsuccessful effort to liberate the fugitive slave Anthony Burns.

The Homestead Act voted by Congress May 20 declares that any U.S. citizen, or any alien intending to become a citizen, may have 160 acres of Western lands absolutely free (except for a $10 registration fee) provided that he makes certain improvements and that he live on the tract for 5 years. Enacted to redeem an 1860 Republican campaign promise after years of excessive land speculation, the new law is to become effective January 1 (below).

English African explorer John Speke confirms that Lake Victoria is the source of the Nile—the world's longest river (*see* Burton, 1855).

The freighting firm Russell, Majors and Waddell has gone bankrupt financing the Pony Express that Western Union put out of business last year with its telegraph. Missouri entrepreneur Ben Holladay, 42, buys the bankrupt firm at public auction in March and thus acquires the Central Overland, California, and Pikes Peak Express with its government contract for hauling overland mail between Missouri and the Pacific Coast, the contract will soon be worth more than $1 million per year in federal subsidies as Holladay puts the stagecoach runs on schedule, builds new way stations, improves equipment, upgrades personnel and passenger accommodations, and extends his runs into the mining districts of Colorado, Idaho, and Montana Territory. The "Napoleon of the Plains" will make a fortune in the next 4 years before he sells out in anticipation of the effect that transcontinental railroads will have on his business (*see* 1863).

Confederate soldiers fought valiantly for their lost cause, but they could not match the North's industrial resources.

1862 (cont.) Union Pacific Railroad builders receive authority from Congress July 1 to take the timber, stone, and other material they need from public lands along the right of way they have been granted. The builders include shovel-maker Oakes Ames, 58, of Oliver Ames & Sons who wins election in November to the House of Representatives (*see* 1803; 1863; Crédit Mobilier, 1867; 1872).

Congress promises up to 100 million acres of federal lands to the Union Pacific (above), the Central Pacific, and other railroads that will connect the Mississippi with the Gulf and Pacific Coasts (*see* 1863).

The Illinois-Central facilitates Union troop movements with its north-south line (*see* 1850). The company will sell off 800,000 acres of its land to settlers.

Union Army raiders led by Captain James J. Andrews steal the Confederate locomotive *The General* April 1 and race the Western and Atlantic woodburner north in an effort to cut the rail lines and thus isolate General P. G. T. Beauregard's army at Chattanooga. Confederate soldiers give chase in the locomotive *The Texas* and catch the raiders.

England's Lancashire textile mills shut down as they run out of Southern lint from which they have been cut off by the Civil War.

The first American open-hearth steel furnace is started by New York industrialists Abram Stevens Hewitt, 40, and Edward Cooper, 38, of the iron-making firm Cooper, Hewitt (*see* Siemens, Martin, 1861).

John Hancock Life Insurance Company is founded by Boston entrepreneurs along lines laid down last year by the nonforfeiture law passed through the efforts of reformer Elizur Wright, 58.

Henry B. Hyde's 3-year-old Equitable Life Assurance Company employs hundreds of agents and writes nearly $2 million in new insurance policies as Americans are made aware of life's jeopardies by the Civil War. All New York life insurance companies enjoy nearly twice the business seen in any previous year but Equitable grows much faster than its rivals as Hyde himself will avoid the draft quite legally by hiring a substitute for $800.

The first Monte Carlo gambling casino opens in Monaco under the direction of the former manager of the casino at Bad Homburg (*see* 1878). Monaco sells Menton and Roquebrune to France.

Raynaud's disease gets its first description in a paper on "Local Asphyxia and Symmetrical Gangrene of the Extremities" by French physician P. Edouard Reynaud who attributes the symptoms to an arrest of the passage of blood to the affected parts as a result of a spasm of the arterioles. The disease will be found to be one of childhood or early adulthood and will be observed to affect females more often than males.

"Un Souvenir de Solverino" by Swiss philanthropist Henri Dunant, 34, urges the creation of volunteer societies to help the wounded on battlefields. Dunant has written his pamphlet after having witnessed terrible scenes of bloodshed and neglect at the Battle of Solverino in 1859 (*see* International Red Cross, 1863).

Ergotism breaks out in Finland where rye bread is a major component of the peasants' diet.

The Morrill Land-Grant Act provides funds to start U.S. land-grant colleges for the scientific education of farmers and mechanics (*see* below; 1890).

Fiction *Les Miserables* by Victor Hugo, now 60, whose 10-volume work depicts the injustice of French society. Hugo has been living on the island of Guernsey since his banishment by Napoleon III in 1848; *Fathers and Sons* (*Otzi i Deti*) by Ivan Turgenev introduces the term "nihilism," meaning a belief in nothing and a total rejection of established laws and institutions.

Poetry *Goblin Market and Other Poems* by English poet Christina Georgina Rossetti, 32, gives the Pre-Raphaelites their first great literary success. Rossetti's brother Dante Gabriel Rossetti, 34, is a leader of the Pre-Raphaelite Brotherhood and its rebellion against the Royal Academy of Art but his wife of 2 years succumbs to an overdose of the laudanum she has been taking to dull the pain of her tuberculosis; "Say Not the Struggle Nought Availeth" by the late English poet Arthur Hugh Clough, whose final stanza ends, "But westward, look, the land is bright."

Painting *Potato Planters* by Jean François Millet; *La Musique aux Tuileries* by Edouard Manet.

Theater *East Lynne, or The Elopement* 4/21 at Boston, is an adaptation of the novel by English novelist Ellen Price Wood, 48, whose story has been running in the *Baltimore Sun*. The melodrama will be perenially revived and will be the most popular play in U.S. stage history; *Mazeppa* 6/16 at New York's New Bowery Theater, with poet-actress Adah Isaacs Menken, 27, strapped half nude to a horse in a melodramatic adaptation of the 1819 Byron poem that creates a sensation.

Opera *Beatrice and Benedict* 8/9 at Baden-Baden, with music by Hector Berlioz, libretto from the 1599 Shakespeare play *Much Ado About Nothing*; *La Forza del Destino* 11/10 at St. Petersburg's Imperial Italian Theater, with music by Giuseppe Verdi.

First performances Scenes from Goethe's *Faust* by the late Robert Schumann, in January at Cologne; *Wallenstein's Camp* (*Valdstynov Tabor*) by Czech pianist-composer Bedrich Smetana, 37, 1/5 at Prague, a symphonic poem based on the Friedrich von Schiller play of 1798.

Kochel (K.) listings for the works of the late Wolfgang Amadeus Mozart appear in *Chronologisch-thematisches Verzeichniss* by Austrian musicographer-naturalist Ludwig Ritter von Kochel, 62, whose catalogue has an appendix listing lost, doubtful, or spurious Mozart compositions. German music scholar Alfred Eisenstein will revise the work for a 1937 reissue.

The Baldwin piano has its beginnings in a Cincinnati music shop opened by local music teacher Dwight Hamilton Baldwin, 41, who gives up teaching, loads six reed organs on a rented spring wagon, and begins selling the instruments door to door. Baldwin will soon have branch offices at Louisville and Indianapolis and will begin manufacturing pianos in 1890.

"The Battle Hymn of the Republic" appears in the February issue of *The Atlantic Monthly* with lyrics by Julia Ward Howe, 43, who helps her husband Samuel Gridley Howe, 61, in publishing the Boston abolitionist journal *The Commonwealth* which is dedicated also to prison reform, improved care for the feeble-minded, and abolition of imprisonment for debt. Howe's verse is set to the tune "Glory, Glory, Hallelujah" attributed to William Steffe.

Waltzes "Perpetuum Mobile" and "Motor Waltz" by Vienna's Johann Strauss.

Popular songs "We Are Coming, Father Abraham, 300,000 More" by Irish-American bandmaster Patrick Sarsfield Gilmore, 33, of the 24th Massachusetts Regiment, lyrics by Delaware Quaker abolitionist James Sloan Gibbons, 52; "We've a Million in the Field" by Stephen C. Foster; "The Bonnie Blue Flag" by English-American actor Harry B. McCarthy, 27, whose verses to the melody of "The Irish Jaunting Cart" were sung by McCarthy last year at Jackson, Miss., and have been revised by Mrs. Annie Chambers-Ketchum (the song will be the Confederacy's national anthem).

"Taps" is composed early in July by Army of the Potomac chief of staff General Daniel Butterfield, 31, who writes the notes for the bugle call at Harrison's Landing in Virginia. Butterfield has written the bugle call to be played at lights out and at funerals.

$ A second London Great International Exhibition includes a display of Japanese arts and crafts that stir demand for Japanese silks, prints, porcelains, bronzes, lacquer ware, and bric-a-brac (*see* 1863).

Liberty's of London has its origin as London clerk Arthur Lasenby Liberty, 18, enters the employ of a Regent Street Oriental goods merchant (*see* 1875).

An English Wholesale Society is established to supply the scores of cooperative societies that have sprung up along lines established in 1844 by the Equitable Pioneers of Rochdale, but most workers are restrained from joining such societies by the fact that they owe money to local tradespeople and must continue to live on credit.

New York department store king A. T. Stewart contributes $100,000 to the Union cause and sells uniforms at cost to the Union Army (*see* 1846). Stewart has introduced a revolutionary one-price system with each item carrying a price tag, an innovation that permits him to employ women sales clerks who can be hired more cheaply than men. Having amassed a fortune of $50 million, Stewart gives a 10 percent discount to wives and children of clergymen and schoolteachers.

The world's largest department store is erected in New York's 10th Street by A. T. Stewart (above) who has employed James Bogardus, now 62, to design the eight-story structure that is also the world's largest building with a cast-iron front (*see* 1849). It has a central court, a huge skylight, a grand stairway leading up from the spacious ground floor, and elevators to make the upper floors accessible (*see* Otis, 1861; Wanamaker, 1896).

U.S. wool production will climb from 40 million pounds to 140 million in the war years as the nation's woolen mills fill Union Army contracts and pay dividends of 10 to 40 percent.

 British crops fail and hunger is widespread, especially since thousands of millhands have been thrown out of work by a cotton famine (above).

 The Morrill Land-Grant Act voted by Congress July 2 gives the states 11 million acres of federal lands to sell, nearly twice the acreage of Senator Justin Morrill's home state of Vermont which becomes a vast sheep pasture as U.S. clothing makers shift from cotton to wool.

Nearly 470,000 settlers will apply for homesteads in the next 18 years under terms of the Homestead Act (above). Roughly one-third of these will actually receive land but while a farmer can make a living on 80 acres in the East, land in the West is generally so arid that even 160 acres will rarely permit economically viable agriculture (*see* 1909).

Starch is shown to be the product of photosynthesis by German botanist Julius von Sachs, 30 (*see* 1898; Ingenhousz, 1779).

An independent U.S. Department of Agriculture is created (*see* 1889).

The U.S. Produce Exchange is organized at New York (*see* Chicago Board of Trade, 1865).

 Union forces destroy Confederate salt works on Chesapeake Bay (*see* 1863).

Congress prohibits distillation of alcohol without a federal license but "moonshiners" continue to make whiskey.

The U.S. Navy abolishes its rum ration through the influence of Rear Admiral Andrew Hull Foote, 56, an ardent temperance advocate who has made his ship the first in the Navy to stop issuing rum rations. The ration will later be revived (*see* Daniels, 1914).

An Internal Revenue Act passed by Congress in July to finance the war effort taxes beer at $1 per barrel and imposes license fees on tavern owners.

Gulden's Mustard is introduced.

Canned soups are introduced by England's Crosse & Blackwell (*see* Campbell and Anderson, 1869).

1862 (cont.) U.S. immigration spurts as a result of the Homestead Act (above), of war-inflated farm prices, and of exemption from military service for foreigners.

1863 The Emancipation Proclamation issued last year by President Lincoln takes effect January 1 and frees nearly 4 million U.S. slaves. When the proclamation is instrumented in 1865 some 385,000 slaveowners will lose human property valued at $2 billion, but while half of all white families in South Carolina and Mississippi own slaves and 12 percent of all slaveowners have more than 20 slaves, 75 percent of all free Southerners have no direct connection with slavery.

Kit Carson and federal troops that have been joined by a band of Ute tribesmen reach Fort Defiance in Arizona Territory July 20 and begin to resettle Navajo and Apache tribespeople on a reservation at Fort Sumner in New Mexico. All captives who surrender voluntarily are to be taken to the reservation to become farmers, all males who resist are to be shot and their livestock and food supplies are to be destroyed (*see* 1862; 1864).

The Nez Perce in the Northwest are forced to sign a treaty agreeing to vacate lands coveted by the whites (but *see* 1877).

A peace treaty with the Shoshone, Washoe, and other tribes in the Nevada Territory gives more than 23 million acres of land to the tribes but most of it is desert. The Ruby Valley Treaty gives the white man rights to build railroads across the Indian lands which comprise 86 percent of the Territory (*see* 1861).

 Mosby's Rangers led by Confederate cavalry officer John Singleton Mosby, 29, operate behind Union lines in Virginia and capture Union Brigadeer General Edwin H. Stoughton with 100 of his men March 9 at Fairfax Court House. The exploit wins Mosby a promotion to captain and gains recruits for his nine-man force of irregulars (*see* "greenback raid," 1864).

Union forces suffer defeat at Chancellorsville, Va., from May 1 to May 4 but the South loses one of its best generals. Thomas Jonathan "Stonewall" Jackson, 39, who won his nickname in 1861 at the first battle of Bull Run (Manassas) is wounded by one of his own sentries May 2, his arm is amputated May 3, and he receives a letter from Robert E. Lee a few days later saying, "You are better off than I am, for while you have lost your left, I have *lost* my *right* arm." Jackson dies May 10 saying, "Let us cross the river and rest in the shade."

The Battle of Gettysburg in Pennsylvania early in July marks the turning point of the war as Southern troops are routed after the heroic Pickett's Charge of July 3. General George Edward Pickett, 38, leads his 4,500 muskets plus 10,000 men from General A. P. Hill's command from Seminary Ridge across an open plain raked by Union musket and artillery fire from three sides and ascend the slant of Cemetery Hill. Some 6,000 Southerners fall and the Confederate advance into the North is doomed.

Union troops are beaten at Chicamauga, Ga., September 19 and 20 before rallying to drive the Confederates from Lookout Mountain and Missionary Ridge and win the Battle of Chattanooga in Tennessee November 23 to 25.

West Virginia seceded from Virginia in 1861 and is admitted to the Union June 20 as the 35th state. The new state's constitution calls for gradual emancipation of slaves.

The Territory of Idaho is formed from parts of Dakota, Nebraska, Utah, and Washington.

Arizona is created as a separate territory cut from the New Mexico Territory.

French forces in Mexico occupy Mexico City June 7 and a group of exiled Mexican leaders meeting under French auspices in July adopt an imperial form of government for their country. They offer the Mexican throne to Austria's Archduke Maximilian, 31, brother of Emperor Franz Josef (*see* 1862; 1864).

Conscription for the Union Army begins July 11 under the March 3 Conscription Act which gives exemption to any man who pays $300.

Draft riots break out in Northern cities with the worst occurring at New York. Some 1,200 people are killed and thousands injured as mobs attack the Colored Orphan Asylum on Fifth Avenue between 43rd and 44th Streets, a four-story building that houses more than 200 children and a staff of matrons and attendants. The orphans are evacuated before they can be harmed but blacks throughout the city are attacked and killed. Now a city of 800,000 with some 200,000 of its people Irish, New York suffers more than $2 million in property damage as rioters tear up railroad tracks, burn hotels, and create general chaos in their battles with police and federal troops, but New York State contributes more men to the Union Army than does any other state.

Lawrence, Kan., is burned August 21 by Quantrill's Raiders led by former schoolteacher and professional gambler William C. Quantrill, 26, who helped capture Independence, Mo., last year and was mustered into the Confederate Army with his men. Captain Quantrill's 450 raiders include Jesse Woodson James, 15, his brother Frank, and Thomas Coleman "Cole" Younger, 19, who ride into Lawrence at dawn, kill 180 men, women, and children, sack the town, and burn most of its buildings, but Kansas contributes a greater percentage of its male population to the Union Army than does any other state (*see* James and Younger, 1876).

President Lincoln dedicates a national cemetery at Gettysburg (above) November 19 and makes an eloquent address ("Four score and seven years ago . . .") that will be memorized by generations of schoolchildren (". . . that government of the people, by the people, and for the people shall not perish from the earth").

Denmark's Frederick VII dies at age 55 after a 15-year reign and is succeeded by his 45-year-old cousin who will reign as Christian IX until 1906. The duchies of Schleswig and Holstein deny Danish claims of sovereignty as the 34-year-old duke of Schleswig-Holstein-Sonderburg-Augustenburg proclaims himself Frederick VIII.

The Greek Assembly chooses Britain's Prince Alfred to succeed the deposed Otto I, the British government rejects the election, the Greeks choose a 17-year-old Danish prince, and he will reign until 1913 as George I.

Egypt's khedive Mohammed Said dies at age 41 after a 9-year reign and is succeeded by his 33-year-old cousin who begins a 16-year reign as Ismail Pasha with a speech about the need for economy. But Ismail sets out to complete the modernization of Egypt and by the end of the year is hopelessly in debt and will go further into debt as he bribes newspapers to favor his vanity and buys jewels to adorn the wives in his harem (see Suez Canal, 1875).

President Lincoln signs a bill passed last year that guarantees builders of the Central Pacific and Union Pacific Railroads $16,000 for every mile of track laid on the plains, $32,000 per mile for tracks laid through intermountain stretches, and $48,000 per mile for track laid through the mountains. The bill also provides for extensive land grants along the railroads' rights of way.

Ground is broken at Sacramento, Ca., February 22 for the Central Pacific Railroad (see 1861; 1866).

Ground is broken at Omaha in Nebraska Territory December 2 for the Union Pacific Railroad (see 1862; 1865).

The Atchison, Topeka and Santa Fe Railroad is organized November 24 by Kansas abolitionist Cyrus K. Holliday, 37, of Topeka with State Senator S. C. Pomeroy of Atchison and other promoters who rename a company formed earlier as the Atchison and Topeka. They lobby in the state legislature for federal land grants and county bond issues (see 1864).

Cornelius van Derbilt gains control of the New York and Harlem Railroad (see 1839; 1858; 1864).

The Milwaukee Road (Chicago, Milwaukee, St. Paul and Pacific Railroad) has its origin in the Milwaukee and St. Paul Railroad which incorporates the Milwaukee and Mississippi begun in 1851. The road will be the first to reach Minneapolis and St. Paul (in 1867), it will enter Chicago on its own rails in 1873, it will adopt the name Chicago, Milwaukee and St. Paul in 1874, it will reach Omaha in 1882, and by 1887 it will reach Kansas City while its northwest line reaches the Missouri River near Mobridge, S. D. (see 1909).

New Zealand gets her first railroad as a state-owned line opens between Christchurch and Ferrymead.

The world's first underground railway system opens in London January 10. The London Underground carries 9.5 million passengers in its first year and will grow to cover 257 miles of track with 278 stations (see 1853; 1890; New York, 1904).

Britain and France sign commercial treaties with Belgium to begin a period of free trade. The River Scheldt reopens to free navigation for the first time since 1648.

Twin-screw steamers appear on the high seas but Bristol, Glasgow, Liverpool, Sunderland, and other British ports will produce hundreds of iron windjammers in the next two decades while U.S. ships will continue to be made of the wood that North America's vast forests make cheap and abundant.

A scarlet fever epidemic in England takes more than 30,000 lives.

A 12-year worldwide cholera epidemic begins (see 1866).

The fundamental principles of the International Red Cross movement to aid wounded soldiers and other victims of war are established at Geneva's Palais de l'Athenée where 36 experts and government delegates meet in response to Henri Dunant's 1862 appeal (see 1864).

The Naturalist on the Amazon by English naturalist H. W. Bates is published at London. Bates returned in 1859 with 8,000 new insect species (see 1848).

Congress authorizes creation of a National Academy of Sciences to advise the U.S. government in scientific matters and to promote scientific research (see AAAS, 1848; NRC, 1916).

A petroleum refinery is established at Cleveland by John D. Rockefeller (see 1860; 1865).

The Solvay process for obtaining soda (sodium carbonate) from salt (sodium chloride) is employed in a new plant built at Couillet, near Charleroi, by Belgian industrial chemist Ernest Solvay, 25, who invented the process with his brother Alfred in 1861 as a cheaper and more effective process than the 1791 Leblanc process. Salt is dissolved in water, saturated with ammonia, and allowed to trickle down a tower full of perforated partitions. Carbon dioxide produced by heating limestone to quicklime is blown into the bottom of the tower to produce sodium bicarbonate which is heated to make sodium carbonate, or soda, which will be widely used not only to make glass but also in paper, bleaches, in water treatment, and in refining petroleum (see American Solvay Process, 1881).

The first Kelly-process steel is poured at the Wyandotte Iron Works in Michigan. William Kelly's 1857 patent for the "pneumatic process" will come under the control of the only U.S. company licensed by Henry Bessemer, and the Bessemer name will come into exclusive use for the process (see 1856). Kelly will receive less than 5 percent of the royalties paid to Bessemer (see oxygen furnace, 1954).

Bethlehem Steel Company has its origin in the Saucon Iron Company founded at South Bethlehem, Pa., to make rails from local iron ores. The company soon

1863 (cont.) hires John Fritz of the Cambria Iron Company who has pioneered in making Bessemer Steel (*see* 1886).

Cotton textile production begins in Japan. The Japanese will be the world's largest cotton goods exporters by 1932.

A new U. S. gold rush begins in May as prospectors discover gold at Alder Gulch in the Idaho Territory.

Travelers Insurance Company is founded by Hartford, Conn., businessman James Goodwin Batterson, 40. It is the first U.S. accident insurance company.

The First National Bank of Chicago opens.

France's Credit Lyonnaise bank is incorporated.

The University of Massachusetts has its beginnings in the Massachusetts Agricultural College founded at Amherst. The college will be renamed in 1947.

Boston College is founded by Roman Catholics.

Le Petit Parisien begins publication under the name *Le Petite Presse*. Advertising will not develop in France as in Britain and America so French newspapers will be obliged to support themselves by offering favorable publicity to any political group that will pay but *Le Petit Parisien* will be France's largest paper by 1910 with 1.5 million circulation (*see* 1944).

Fiction *Romola* by George Eliot; *Five Weeks in a Balloon* (*Cinq Semaines en Ballon*) by French novelist Jules Verne, 35; "The Man Without a Country" by U.S. author Edward Everett Hale, 41, whose hero Philip Nolan has been exiled for his part in the treason of Aaron Burr but who has requested that he be memorialized with the epitaph, " . . . He loved his country as no other man has loved her;/but no man has deserved less at her hands"; the pen name "Mark Twain" is adopted by former Mississippi riverboat pilot Samuel Langhorne Clemens, 27, who failed as a prospector in Nevada 2 years ago and has gone to work as a Virginia City newspaper reporter using as his nom de plume the cry used by Mississippi riverboat leadsmen to indicate a 12-foot depth of water. Twain will move to San Francisco next year to work for the *San Francisco Call* and to write short stories.

Poetry *Tales of a Wayside Inn* by Henry Wadsworth Longfellow includes "Paul Revere's Ride." Friends gathered at the Red-Horse Inn at Sudbury some 20 miles from Cambridge tell tales and the landlord of the inn goes first: "Listen, my children, and you shall hear/ Of the midnight ride of Paul Revere,/ On the eighteenth of April, in Seventh-Five;/ Hardly a man is now alive/ Who remembers that famous day and year . . ."; *The Water-Babies* by Charles Kingsley: "When all the world is young, lad,/ And all the trees are green;/ And every goose a swan, lad,/ And every lass a queen;/ Then hey, for boot and horse, lad,/ And round the world away;/ Young blood must have its course, lad,/ And every dog its day."

Painting *Le dejeuner sur l'herbe* by Edouard Manet is exhibited May 15 at the Salon des Refuses in Paris and creates a furor with its depiction of a nude picknicking with two clothed men; other paintings: *Mlle. Victorine in the Costume of an Espada* and *Olympia* by Edouard Manet; *Man with Hoe* by Jean Millet (*see* Markham, 1898). Eugène Delacroix dies at Paris August 13 at age 65.

Japanese *ukiyoe* prints are discovered in London by James A. McNeill Whistler who will adopt a Japanese butterfly seal to sign his work and who will promote Japanese art in Paris (*see* 1867; 1872; Toulouse-Lautrec, 1893).

The Winged Victory of Samothrace turns up in excavations at the Greek city of Samothrace. The Louvre at Paris will exhibit the statue for well over a century.

First performances Missa Solemnis in A flat major by the late Franz Schubert 1/1 at Leipzig.

Opera *The Pearl Fishers* (*Les Pecheurs*) 9/10 at the Théâtre-Lyrique, Paris, with music by French composer Georges (Alexander César Leopold) Bizet, 25.

Popular Songs "When Johnny Comes Marching Home" by Louis Lambert (Patrick Sarsfield Gilmore). He has adapted the song "Johnny Fill Up the Bowl" which may have been adapted from the song "Johnny, I Hardly Knew Ye"; "Clementine (Down by the River Lived a Maiden)" by U.S. songwriter H. S. Thompson; "Just Before the Battle, Mother" by George Frederick Root; "The Battle Cry of Freedom" by George Frederick Root; "Weeping, Sad and Lonely, or When This Cruel War Is Over" by Henry Tucker, lyrics by Charles Carroll Sawyer; "The Rock Island Line" by Confederate soldiers: "Now the Rock Island Line/ It is a mighty good road, Oh the Rock Island Line/ It is the road to ride . . ." but while the lyrics say, "She runs down to New Orleans" the Rock Island will in fact never go beyond Eunice, La., and while the Chicago & Rock Island will be renamed the Chicago, Rock Island & Pacific in 1880 the road will not reach westward beyond Denver in the north and New Mexico in the south (*see* 1855).

Definitive rules for "soccer" are drawn up by the Football Association established this year in England (*see* rugby, 1823). Soccer will be called "association" in Britain, will be called football in most other countries, and will be popular throughout Europe and South America (*see* U.S. football, 1869; World Cup, 1930).

The first major U.S. racetrack for flat racing opens at Saratoga Springs, N.Y., which will become the center of American horseracing (*see* Travers Stakes, 1864).

The first four-wheeled roller skates are patented by New York inventor James L. Plimpton whose small boxwood wheels are arranged in pairs and cushioned by rubber pads, making it possible to maintain balance and to execute intricate maneuvers (*see* 1760). Plimpton's roller skates will lead to a widespread roller skating fad later in this decade and the fad will sweep Europe in the 1870s.

General Tom Thumb is married February 10 at New York's Grace Church on Broadway and 10th

Street to Lavinia Warren (Mercy Bunn) who stands 2 feet 8 inches in height (*see* 1842). Heavily promoted by showman P. T. Barnum, the wedding attracts huge crowds that jam the streets (the wedding party stands on a grand piano to receive guests at the Metropolitan Hotel).

 Singer Manufacturing Company is incorporated by sewing machine inventor I. M. Singer and Edward Clark who split 4,100 of the 5,000 shares between them (*see* 1861). Family incomes in America average only $500 per year and a new Singer sewing machine sells for $100 but Clark's $5 per month installment plan persuades customers to buy Singer machines which cost perhaps $40 to make including all overhead (*see* 1873).

Cincinnati's H. and S. Pogue opens at 100 West 5th Street. The dry goods shop started by Irish-American merchant Samuel Pogue, 32, and his brother Henry will grow to become a major department store.

London merchant William Whitely opens a dry goods shop in Bayswater that will incorporate a jewelry department in 1867 to make it the first British retail establishment to expand beyond drapery and haberdashery (*see* Stewart, 1846). Whitely will add a "foreign department" in 1870 to sell Oriental novelties, he will add the first store restaurant in 1872, a cleaning and dyeing department in 1874, and a hairdressing salon in 1876. Whitely's will call itself "The Universal Provider," it will employ the slogan "Anything from a Pin to an Elephant," and it will actually supply an elephant to fill an order from a Church of England clergyman.

 The Capitol dome at Washington is capped December 2 to complete the great structure on which work has been continued through the war by order of President Lincoln. Architect Thomas U. Walter has unified the work of the Capitol's three previous architects William Thornton, Benjamin Latrobe, and Charles Bulfinch. The Capitol will be landscaped with terraces designed by Frederick Law Olmsted and its rotunda will be graced with a fresco by Constantino Brumidi that will be completed in 1865.

 New York's Central Park Commission reports, "If all the applications for the erection and maintenance of towers, houses, drinking fountains, telescopes, mineral water fountains, cottages, Eolian harps, gymnasiums, observatories, and weighing scales, for the sale of eatables, velocipedes, perambulators, Indian Work, tobacco and segars, iceboats and the use of the ice for fancy dress carnivals were granted, they would occupy a large portion of the surface of the park, establish a very extensive and very various business, and give to it the appearance of the grounds of a country fair, or of a militia training ground."

Richmond has bread riots in April and Mobile has bread riots in September as the Union starves the South. Vicksburg, Miss., is starved out July 4 after a brief siege and the Union gains control of the key to the Mississippi River.

 Confederate President Jefferson Davis urges Southerners to plant corn, peas, and beans. His April message gives priority to food crops over cotton and tobacco.

Widescale rustling (theft) begins on the Texas plains as cattle there are hit by the worst winter in years.

An epidemic of cattle disease in Britain over the next 4 years will boost meat prices and will cause a boom in imports of tinned meats from Australia (*see* 1866; 1871).

The British epizootic (above) strikes hardest at Dutch cows which have proved the sturdiest milkers for keeping in urban milksheds but are the breeds most susceptible to disease. British dairymen are compelled to make wider and more efficient use of milk trains (*see* 1844), to develop water coolers on farms and at milk depots, and to use tinned-steel churns for transporting milk from the trains to urban markets.

Disruption of sugar plantations in the South sends U.S. sugar prices soaring and brings a vigorous increase in sugar planting in the Hawaiian Islands, dependent for years on the whaling industry which is now in a decline as a result of the growing use of kerosene for lamp oil (*see* 1859).

 San Francisco's Bay Sugar Refining Company is started by German-American entrepreneur Claus Spreckels, 35, who has prospered as a San Francisco grocer and brewer since 1856 (*see* 1868).

Union forces cut the South off from its salt deposits on the Louisiana Gulf Coast and destroy all its salt works in Florida, North Carolina, and Virginia.

Salt from wells in the area of Syracuse, N.Y., and Saginaw, Mich., keep the North well-supplied with salt.

Sutlers provide Union troops with canned meat, oysters, condensed milk (*see* Borden, 1861), pork and beans (*see* Van Camp, 1861), and vegetables, including green beans.

Confederate troops eat the meat-and-vegetable stew "burgoo" created by Lexington, Ky., chef Gus Jaubert but there is widespread hunger in the South.

Granula is introduced by Dansville, N.Y., sanatorium operator James Caleb Jackson, 52, who has baked graham flour dough into oven-dried bread crumbs to create the first cold breakfast food (*see* Graham, 1837; Kellogg's Granula, 1877).

Ovaltine (Ovomaltine) has its beginnings at Berne where Swiss scientist George Wander succeeds in producing a sweet-tasting malt extract which he will combine with whole milk, whole eggs, and cocoa to make a nourishing, easily digested, quickly absorbed emergency food for situations in which ordinary food may not be suitable. Wander has been assisted by a German at the University of Berne to set up a re-

New York draft riots left 1,200 dead and thousands injured as the city mob vented its fears and prejudices.

search laboratory to study the extraction of malt for use in combating infant mortality, and his son Albert will develop the product further (see 1905).

Perrier Water is introduced commercially by Source Perrier which bottles the French spring water that bubbles up from a spring near Nîmes. The water contains calcium and sparkles because of its natural carbon dioxide content.

Toronto brewer Eugene O'Keefe resigns from his O'Keefe and Company firm to start a new brewery. O'Keefe will build a lager brewery in 1879 that will make his name famous among beer drinkers.

Chase and Sanborn's Coffee has its beginnings at Boston where merchants Caleb Chase, 32, and James S. Sanborn begin selling coffee and tea (see 1878).

The Great American Tea Company founded in 1859 grows to have six stores and begins selling a line of groceries in addition to tea (see A&P, 1869).

La Villette opens at Paris. The central, hygienic slaughterhouse has been designed by Baron Georges Eugène Haussmann, prefect of the Seine since 1852.

President Lincoln proclaims the first national Thanksgiving Day October 3 and sets aside the last Thursday of November to commemorate the feast given by the Pilgrims in 1621 for their Wampanoag benefactors (see 1769). The president has acted partly in response to a plea from *Godey's Lady's Book* editor Sarah Josepha Hale, now 74, who has campaigned since 1846 for Thanksgiving Day observances and who by 1852 had persuaded people to celebrate Thanksgiving on the same day in 30 of the 32 states, in U.S. consulates abroad, and on U.S. ships in foreign waters (see Roosevelt, 1939).

Britain's 24-year-old Cunard Line enters the immigrant trade with low rates for passengers aboard its new screw propellor transatlantic ships as Ireland is hit once again by potato rot and the exodus to America is restimulated (see 1846).

President Lincoln asks Congress December 8 to establish a system for encouraging immigration.

1864 President Lincoln calls February 1 for 500,000 men to serve for 3 years or for the duration of the war.

Meridian, Miss., is occupied February 14 by General William Tecumseh Sherman, 44, who has replaced General Grant as commander of the Army of the Tennessee. He destroys railroads and supplies.

Ulysses S. Grant is commissioned Lieutenant General March 9 and is given command of all Union armies March 10.

The Army of the Potomac under General Grant and General Meade starts across the Rapidan May 3 to invade the Wilderness. Union and Confederate forces battle indecisively at the first Battle of the Wilderness near Chancellorsville, Va., May 5 to 6, and at Spotsylvania Court House May 8 to 12. "I propose to fight it out on this line if it takes all summer," says General Grant May 11 in a dispatch to Secretary of War Stanton.

Grant is defeated by General Lee June 1 to 3 at the Battle of Cold Springs Harbor and sustains 12,000 casualties. Petersburg, Va., is besieged by Union forces beginning June 19.

The Battle of Kenesaw Mountain in Georgia ends in defeat for General Sherman whose dead and wounded total 1,999 while Confederate casualties total only 270.

An attempted raid on Washington, D.C., July 9 by Confederate forces under General Jubal Anderson Early, 47, is blocked by General Lew (Lewis) Wallace, 37, who last year saved Cincinnati from being taken by the Confederacy. Wallace loses the battle but he saves the capital by gaining time for General Grant's troops to approach.

The Battle of Atlanta July 22 ends in victory for General Sherman who defeats Southern troops under General John Bell Hood, 33, after a 5-week siege. The Confederate Army has been augmented since June by boys of 17 and men from 45 to 50.

The second Battle of Atlanta (Ezra Church) July 28 ends in another defeat for General Hood who has sustained 10,000 casualties in the two battles with General Sherman losing nearly as many.

A mine is exploded beneath the Confederate fort at Petersburg, Va., July 30 but Union forces fall back with 2,864 killed and wounded, 929 missing.

"Damn the torpedoes! Four bells, Captain Drayton, go ahead!" orders Union Admiral David Glasgow Farragut, 63, at the Battle of Mobile Bay August 5. Defying Confederate torpedoes (mines) at the narrow entrance to the bay, Farragut's flagship *Hartford* proceeds into the bay and gains a victory.

General Jubal Early's Confederate cavalry is defeated September 19 at Winchester, Va., by General Philip Sheridan but 697 Union troops are killed, 3,983 wounded, 338 missing as compared with 276 Confederate dead, 1,827 wounded, 1,818 missing. Sheridan beats Early again September 22 at Fisher's Hill and October 19 at Cedar Creek as he clears the Shenandoah Valley of Southern troops (below).

General Sherman leads his army of 60,000 on a "march to the sea" beginning November 16 and proceeds to cut a mile wide swath through Georgia.

The Battle of Franklin November 30 ends in disaster for General Hood who has attempted to strike behind Sherman's lines. Hood makes a frontal assault on General John McAllister Schofield, 33, south of Nashville and sustains terrible casualties—1,750 dead including six general officers, 3,800 wounded, while Union losses total 189 dead 1,033 wounded.

The hand-cranked Gatling gun invented in 1861 is employed by Union forces which defeat General Hood at the Battle of Nashville in mid-December.

Savannah is occupied December 22 by General Sherman who sends a dispatch to President Lincoln: "I beg to present you as a Christmas gift the city of Savannah."

"It is best not to swap horses while crossing the river," President Lincoln has said June 9 in an address to a delegation from the National Union League and he has gained reelection in November with 55 percent of the popular vote, winning 212 electoral votes to 21 for the Democratic candidate General George McClellan (Lincoln has run as a Union party candidate with support from "War Democrats" and has been helped to win by General Sherman's victory at Atlanta).

Nevada has been admitted to the Union as the 36th state before the election (see Comstock Lode, 1859).

Montana Territory has been formed out of Idaho Territory May 26 as prospectors flock to the goldfields of Virginia City (see 1863).

Austria's Archduke Maximilian has accepted the throne of Mexico April 10, he has reached Mexico City June 12, and he has been helped by French troops to drive Benito Juarez across the northern border into the United States (see 1863; 1866).

Nanking is sacked by Chinese Manchu forces under Tseng Kuo-fan helped by the "Ever Victorious Army" of the British General Charles G. "Chinese" Gordon. Hung Hsiu-ch'uan takes poison, more than 100,000 are killed between July 19 and 21, and the T'ai P'ing Rebellion that began in 1850 is ended (see Korea, 1876; "Open Door Policy," 1899).

A 17-month Polish insurrection that has spread to Lithuania and White Russia has been suppressed in May. Polish autonomy is abolished (see 1815; 1918).

 The Russian language is made obligatory in Polish schools and proceedings are instituted against Polish Roman Catholic clergymen.

The Russian judiciary is reformed by the abolishment of class courts and the establishment of new courts modeled on the French system that provide jury trials for criminal offenses and provide justices of the peace to deal with minor civil suits.

Russia's Zemstvo Law establishes a system of local government boards that can levy taxes for local roads, bridges, schools, hospitals, and the like. Peasants, nobility, and townspeople are all to be represented on local zemstvos with no single class to have a majority.

Louis Napoleon acknowledges the right to strike and ends a French ban on workers' associations.

The Brotherhood of Locomotive Engineers, the Iron Moulders' International, and the Cigar Makers' National Union are organized by U.S. workingmen (see 1833; 1834; National Labor Congress, 1866).

Navajos terrorized by Kit Carson and his men are marched three hundred miles to Fort Sumner in New Mexico Territory on the "Long Walk" to the Bosque Redondo concentration camp. By December the camp contains 8,354 Navajo plus 405 Mescalero Apache but 1,200 will escape next year, and Carson will be relieved of his command in the fall of 1866 after a despotic regime in which hundreds have died of disease and starvation (see 1863; 1868).

Cheyennes go on the warpath and are supported by Arapahoe, Apache, Comanche, and Kiowa braves. Many are massacred in November at Sand Creek in Colorado Territory by U.S. troops under the command of John Chivington.

 A bronze Indian head one-cent piece whose design will remain unchanged until 1909 is issued by the U.S. Mint.

"In God We Trust" is printed on every piece of U.S. currency for the first time by order of Treasury Secretary Salmon Portland Chase, 56.

The Confederacy suffers wild inflation as $1 billion in paper currency is circulated. Gold value of the paper money falls in the first quarter of the year to $4.60 per $100 while in the North the gold value of the greenback falls to 39 cents as of July 11.

A "greenback raid" October 14 by Mosby's Rangers seizes $168,000 in Union funds which are divided among Mosby's men to buy new equipment and uniforms (see 1863).

German-American financier Joseph Seligman, 45, helps the Union cause by marketing U.S. Treasury bonds abroad. He establishes the banking house of J. & W. Seligman that will soon have offices at San Francisco, New Orleans, London, Paris, and Frankfurt am Main to augment its New York office.

New York's Guaranty Trust Company has its beginnings in the New York Guaranty and Indemnity

1864 (cont.) Company founded with a capital of $100,000. The bank will be renamed Guaranty Trust Company of New York in 1895 and by the end of 1928 it will have resources of more than $1 billion and a staff of 4,000 (*see* Morgan Guaranty, 1959).

The Bank of California is founded at San Francisco by merchants and bankers who include New Yorker Darius Ogden Mills, 39, who will serve as the bank's president until 1873 (*see* Mills Hotel, 1896).

Niihau in the Sandwich (Hawaiian) Islands is purchased from the king Kamehameha IV for $10,000 by the Robinson family that has been invited by the king to move from New Zealand and take over the 12-mile-long, 46,000-acre island that will remain in the Robinson family for well over a century. Seventh largest of the Sandwich Islands, Niihau has no streams but will raise sheep and shorthorn cattle.

Oil is discovered along Pennsylvania's Pithole Creek by a "finder" using a witch-hazel twig divining rod: a well will be pumping 250 barrels of oil per day by early January, 1865, and by the end of June four wells at the new town of Pithole will be pumping more than 2,000 barrels per day—one-third of all the oil produced in Pennsylvania. Some 3,000 teamsters will be driving wagonloads of barrels to the riverboats and to the railhead (*see* pipeline, 1866).

The Chicago North Western Railway Co. is formed by a consolidation of the 16-year-old Galena & Chicago Union Railroad with the 9-year-old Chicago, St. Paul and Fond du Lac Railroad.

The Atchison, Topeka and Santa Fe is aided by the Kansas State Legislature which accepts a federal land grant February 9 and votes to allow railroads to select additional lands within 20 miles of their lines in lieu of lands already held by settlers through preemption. The governor signs a law March 1 allowing counties to vote subsidies of up to $200,000 to railroads (*see* 1863; Atchison Associates, 1868).

Erie Railroad president Daniel Drew and New York State legislators sell New York and Hudson River Railroad stock short on the New York Stock Exchange. Cornelius Vanderbilt (who has changed his name from van Derbilt) buys up all the stock there is plus another 27,000 shares, and when Drew and the Albany legislators cannot deliver the stock they have sold there is chaos. Vanderbilt sells them stock at $285 per share so that they can deliver, many are driven to bankruptcy, and Vanderbilt gains control of the New York and Hudson (*see* 1863; 1865).

A railway sleeping car with folding upper berths is patented by George M. Pullman and Ben Field of Chicago (*see* 1858; 1865).

London's Charing Cross station opens.

The French Line paddle-wheeler *Washington* arrives at New York in June to begin 110 years of service between New York and the Channel ports by the Compagnie Genérale Transatlantique.

The drive chain is patented by English inventor James Slater whose precision-made chain was foreseen by Leonardo da Vinci. It will be used in industrial machinery and in bicycles (*see* Renold, 1880; Starley, 1870).

Britain is cut off from U.S. cotton by the Civil War (above) so a cotton thread mill at Newark, N. J., is opened by George and William Clark, grandsons of Patrick and James (*see* 1806). J&P Coats will buy an interest in a Pawtucket, R.I., thread mill in 1869 and in 1952 the two rival thread companies will merge to create Coats & Clark.

Barbituric acid is synthesized by German chemist Adolf von Baeyer, 29, and is the first barbiturate drug (von Baeyer's work will be eclipsed by that of his associate F. A. Kekule) (*see* 1858; 1865).

The Red Cross is established by the Geneva convention drawn up by an international diplomatic conference whose agreement will be signed by every major world power. The Italian Red Cross is founded at Rome while the French Red Cross has its beginnings in a new Société Française de Secours aux blesse militaires which will be merged into the French Red Cross (*see* 1863; 1865; Dunant, 1862).

Swarthmore College is founded at Swarthmore, Pa., by abolitionists who include James Mott (*see* 1833).

Bates College is founded at Lewiston, Me.

The University of Kansas is founded at Lawrence.

The University of Denver is founded in Colorado Territory.

Illustrated weeklies such as *Harper's* and *Frank Leslie's Illustrated Weekly* publish hundreds of sketches and drawings of Civil War battles, sieges, and bombardments but no magazine or newspaper has the equipment or technique needed to make halftone blocks for printing photographs (*see* 1880; Ives, 1886; Brady, below).

Houghton, Mifflin Co. publishers has its beginnings in the partnership Hurd & Houghton formed by Cambridge, Mass., publisher Henry Oscar Houghton, 41, who started at age 13 as a Burlington, Vt., printer's apprentice and who has operated the Riverside Press since 1852. George Harrison Mifflin, now 19, will join Hurd & Houghton in 1867, he will be admitted to the firm in 1872, and he will head Houghton, Mifflin Co. from 1908 until his death in 1921.

Fiction *Letters from the Underground* (*Zapiski zi podpolya*) by Russian novelist Fedor Mikhailovich Dostoievski, 44, who was convicted of conspiracy in 1849, was sentenced to be shot, was reprieved at the last moment, was sent to Siberia for 5 years, has had his review *The Times* suppressed, and has lived abroad to escape his financial troubles; *Journey to the Center of the Earth* (*Voyage au Centre de la Terre*) by Jules Verne; *Renée Mauperin* by Jules Goncourt; *The Small House at Allington* by Anthony Trollope; *Can You Forgive Her?* by Anthony Trollope is the first of six Palliser novels.

Poetry *Dramatis Personae* by Robert Browning whose poem "Rabbi Ben Ezra" contains the lines, "Grow old along with me!/ The best is yet to be,/ The last of life, for which the first was made"; *In War Time* by John Greenleaf Whittier whose poem "Barbara Frietchie" contains the lines, "'Shoot, if you must, this old gray head,/ But spare your country's flag,' she said".

 Painting *The Dead Toreador* by Edouard Manet; *Souvenir de Mortefontaine* by Jean Corot; *Homage a Delacroix* by French painter (Ignace) Henri (Joseph Theodore) Fantin-Latour, 28.

 Photography is advanced by Britons B. J. Sayce, 27, and William Blanchard Bolton, 16, who describe the preparation of an emulsion of silver bromide in collodion (*see* Archer, 1851). But the Sayce-Bolton process leaves nitrates in the emulsion (*see* 1874; Maddox, 1871).

New York photographer Mathew B. Brady, now 41, travels through the war-torn South with a wagonful of equipment to record scenes of the conflict. Brady learned to make daguerrotypes from Samuel F. B. Morse in 1840, he switched to the new wet-plate process 9 years ago, and he has poured all his money into training assistants who will help him make a photographic record of the war (*see* 1850).

 Popular songs "Beautiful Dreamer" by the late Stephen C. Foster who wrote the song a few days before his death in obscurity January 13 at age 37 in the charity ward of New York's 3-year-old Bellevue Hospital. Proceeds from Foster's songs averaged the not inconsiderable sum of $1,371.92 per year from 1849 to 1860 but Foster became ill and alcoholic and his death was hastened by poverty and drink; "All Quiet Along the Potomac Tonight" by John Hill Hewitt, now 63, lyrics by Lamar Tontaine; "Tenting on the Old Camp Ground" by Boston songwriter Walter Kittredge, 31, who wrote the song one evening last year after receiving his draft notice but who has been rejected by the army for reasons of health; "Tramp! Tramp! Tramp!" by George Frederick Root; "When the War Is Over, Mary," by John Rogers Thomas, lyrics by George Cooper; "Wake Nicodemus!" by Henry Clay Work; "Come Home, Father" by Henry Clay Work whose new temperance song will be included in performances of *Ten Nights in a Barroom* (*see* 1854); "Der Deitcher's Dog (Where, O Where Has My Little Dog Gone?)" by Septimus Winner who has adapted a German folk song.

Opera *La Belle Helène* 12/17 at Paris, with music by Jacques Offenbach.

The Travers Stakes has its first running at the year-old Saratoga racetrack at Saratoga Springs, N.Y.

English cricket player William Gilbert Grace plays his first county match at age 16 to begin a career that will make him famous as the greatest all-round cricketer in history. Grace will revolutionize the game as a batsman and his prowess will attract thousands as he becomes a celebrity throughout the Empire, not for his Bristol medical practice but for his performance in the test matches at Lord's (*see* 1787; the Ashes, 1882).

A cyclone destroys most of Calcutta October 1 and kills an estimated 70,000.

Man and Nature by pioneer ecologist George Perkins Marsh, 63, of the U.S. foreign service warns that "the ravages committed by man subvert the relations and destroy the balance which nature had established ...; and she avenges herself upon the intruder by letting loose her destructive energies.... When the forest is gone, the great reservoir of moisture stored up in its vegetable mould is evaporated.... There are parts of Asia Minor, of Northern Africa, of Greece, and even of Alpine Europe, where the operation of causes set in action by man has brought the face of the earth to a desolation almost as complete as that of the moon.... The earth is fast becoming an unfit home for its noblest inhabitants ..." Now U.S. minister to Italy, Marsh is a one-time Vermont farmer, lumber dealer, sheep raiser, lawyer, and businessman who has been in the foreign service since 1849 and who has journeyed through the Nile Valley, to Petra, to Vesuvius, through the Greek islands and the eroded hills of Tuscany, and has seen what poor land management has done to his native Vermont (*see* 1874).

California's Yosemite Valley is protected by Congress which passes a bill at the urging of Frederick Law Olmsted to preserve the valley as the first U.S. national scenic reserve "for public use, resort, and recreation (*see* 1890; Yellowstone, 1872).

Chicago's Lincoln Park is designated as such. The 120-acre cemetery will have most of its graves removed and will be expanded to embrace more than 1,000 acres of woodlands, bridle paths, playgrounds, golf courses, yacht basins, gardens, museums.

U.S. wheat prices climb to $4 per bushel and food prices rise as European crops fail and the North ships wheat to hungry Europe.

Virginia's Shenandoah Valley is the breadbasket of the South and General Philip Sheridan (above) has 50,000 troops and orders to "eat out Virginia clear and clean ... so that crows flying over it for the balance of this season will have to carry their provender with them." Loss of the Shenandoah Valley as a food source forces the South to tighten its belt.

A grasshopper plague in the Great Plains shortens the U.S. wheat crop.

France's lentil industry moves to Lorraine where colder weather kills off the insect pests that have ruined lentil crops for years.

Britain's first fish-and-chips shops will open in the next few years as steam trawlers are developed that can carry fish packed in ice. Taken from the North Sea, the fish will be kept chilled from the moment of catch until delivery to city retailers who will deep fry

1864 (cont.) fish fingers and serve them with deep-fried potatoes, all liberally doused with vinegar (*see* 1902).

The first U.S. salmon cannery opens on California's Sacramento River at Washington in Yolo County. Hapgood, Hume & Co. is founded by Andrew S. Hapgood, George W. Hume, and William Hume who pack 2,000 cases and although half the cases spoil because the cans have not all been properly sealed their cannery will soon be followed by others at San Francisco and at the mouth of every river north to Alaska (*see* 1866; 1878).

Armour Packing Company has its beginnings in a Milwaukee pork-packing firm started in partnership with John Plankinton by local commission merchant Philip Danforth Armour, 32, who has made nearly $2 million in 90 days selling short in the New York pork market. Armour went to California in his teens, dug sluiceways for goldminers at $5 to $10 per day, saved $8,000 in 5 years to give himself the wherewithal to start his business at Milwaukee, and has traveled to New York where he found pork selling at $40 per barrel. Foreseeing a Union victory as General Grant prepared to march on Richmond, Armour has sold short at more than $33 per barrel, he has covered his sales at $18 per barrel, and he has made a fortune (*see* 1868).

Pabst Beer has its beginnings as German-American brewer Frederick Pabst, 28, and an associate succeed to control of Milwaukee's Empire Brewery which produces 4,895 barrels per year (*see* 1889; Schlitz, 1856; Pabst Blue Ribbon, 1893).

Heineken Beer gets its name as Dutch brewer Gerard Adrian Heineken acquires the 272-year-old De Hooiberg brewery and develops a special yeast that will give his beer a distinctive taste.

European immigrants pour into the United States to take up free land under the Homestead Act of 1862 and to fill farm and factory jobs left vacant by Union Army draftees and by Americans gone West both to avoid the draft and to claim free land.

1865 The American Civil War ends, President Lincoln is assassinated, and a 12-year Reconstruction Era begins in the South with state legislatures run by "carpetbaggers" and "scalawags" (below).

Union forces occupy Columbia, S.C., February 17, and Charleston falls to a Union fleet February 18. Petersburg, Va., surrenders April 3 and General Grant takes Richmond the same day.

General Lee surrenders to General Grant April 9 at Appomattox Courthouse, Va., and the war is over (although the last Confederate army will not surrender until May 26 at Shreveport, La.). Lee's 28,000 hungry men are permitted to keep their private horses and sidearms.

The Union has lost 360,222 men (110,000 of them in battle) and the Confederacy has lost 258,000 (94,000 in battle) with at least 471,427 wounded on both sides.

President Lincoln is assassinated April 14 while attending a performance at Ford's Theatre in Washington, D.C., and is succeeded by his vice-president Andrew Johnson.

Actor John Wilkes Booth has climbed the stairway to Lincoln's box, he shoots the president in the head, he leaps to the stage crying "Sic semper tyrannis! The South is avenged!" and although he has broken his leg he escapes. Told of the president's death at age 66 April 15, Secretary of War Stanton says, "Now he belongs to the ages."

The 27-year-old Booth is a son of the late English-American actor Junius Brutus Booth and a brother of the eminent Shakespearean actor Edwin Thomas Booth. He is not found until April 26 when he is either killed by his captors or dies by his own hand. Several of his accomplices have tried to kill Secretary of State Seward and they are hanged July 7.

The "carpetbaggers" who move into the South are so called with contempt by Southerners who say they can put all they own in the common hand luggage called a carpetbag. Some become state legislators and U.S. congressmen, some are missionaries sent to help the freedmen who are helped in some cases also by the "scalawags"—Southerners who join with the ex-slaves to establish a new order in the South.

The British prime minister Viscount Palmerston dies October 18 at age 80. He is succeeded by Lord John Russell, now 73, who will resign next June after his reform bill fails.

The king of the Belgians Leopold I dies December 10 at age 74 after a 34-year reign that has established the Belgian monarchy. He is succeeded by his 30-year-old son Leopold Louis Philippe Marie Victor who will reign until 1909 as Leopold II and who will expand Belgian interests (and his own) in the Congo.

Boers in the Orange Free State have begun war with the Basutos that will continue until next year.

Natural laws of heredity are elucidated in a paper read to the Brünn Society for the Study of Natural Science by Austrian botanist Gregor Johann Mendel, 43, who entered an Augustinian order as a monk at age 21 and at age 35 began studying the genetics of garden peas, using peas for his experiments because the stigma of the pea flower is usually pollinated by pollen from the same flower, which means that a new plant has in effect one parent and is thus assured of pure traits, e.g., yellow, green, smooth, wrinkled, dwarf, or tall. By preventing such self-pollination, and by pollinating hundreds of pea plants with pollen from other plants, Mendel has established that "in any given pair of contrasting traits, one trait is dominant and the other recessive."

Mendel's law (above) states that the first generation of progeny of mixed parents will all be hybrids, but that in the second generation only half will be hybrids while one quarter will reflect the true trait of one parent and a second quarter the true trait of the second parent. Mendel's recognition that various dominant or recessive characteristics depend on certain basic units, later to be called genes, will be the basis of improved varieties of plant and animal life in the century to come but established scientists will not begin to appreciate Mendel's work until the turn of the century (*see* DeVries, 1900).

The structure of aromatic compounds is explained by F. A. Kekule von Stradonitz, who sets forth a doctrine of the linking of carbon atoms and originates the ring (closed-chain) theory of the benzene molecule's constitution (*see* 1858).

The Colorado River Indian Reservation is established by an act of Congress signed March 3 by President Lincoln: the reservation will ultimately contain 264,250 acres with 225,914 in Arizona's Yuma County and 38,366 in California's San Bernardino and Riverside Counties but the desolate Mojave Desert reservationland has an average high of 110 to 113°F in summer and an average low of 39° in winter.

The Ku Klux Klan organized at Pulaski, Tenn., is a secret social club of young men who hope to recapture the comradeship and excitement of the war. Their name comes from the Greek "Kuklos" meaning circle, they adopt elaborate rituals, and their curious uniform is soon discovered to terrorize superstitious blacks. They will be joined in the next few years by a majority of Southern whites as the KKK attempts to return local and state government to white, Democratic party control (*see* 1915; White Camelia, 1867).

The commandant of the Confederate prison camp at Andersonville, Ga., is convicted of "murder, in violation of the laws and customs of war" and is hanged November 10 in Washington's Old Capitol Prison at the foot of Capitol Hill. More than 12,000 Union prisoners of war died at Andersonville in 14 months, as many as 97 in a single day, but while 30,218 Union prisoners have died in various Confederate prison camps (as compared with 25,976 "rebels" who have died in Union prison camps) the execution of the 42-year-old Swiss-American Captain Henry Wirz has come after a trial in which a priest who traveled up from Savannah to give testimony was stopped by the military judges after a few minutes when it became clear that the testimony would be favorable to the defendant (Wirz has spurned an offer of a pardon if he would testify against Jefferson Davis).

The Thirteenth Amendment to the Constitution is ratified by two-thirds of the states and beginning December 18 prohibits slavery or any other denial of liberty "without due process of law."

Jamaican blacks revolt in the Morant Bay area but the insurrection is quickly suppressed by the Scottish governor of Jamaica Edward John Eyre, 40, who orders the execution of 450 natives, has many more flogged, and has 1,000 native homes burned. Eyre left home for Australia at age 17, 8 years later he

explored the region around Lake Torrens and discovered a lake that has been named after him, he crossed the Nullarbor Plain to western Australia with an aborigine companion and became the first white man to cross that desert, but his action in Jamaica creates widespread indignation in Britain. Eyre is censured and dismissed but representative government in Jamaica has been suspended and will not be restored until 1884.

The Salvation Army has its beginnings in a London mission founded in Whitechapel by itinerant English religious revivalist William Booth, 36, who says, "A man may be down but he's never out." (*see* 1878).

Rockefeller & Andrews is organized by Cleveland oil refiner John D. Rockefeller whose produce business has been made prosperous by the Civil War and who sells his share in the business to his partner Maurice B. Clark. He pays Clark $72,500 for his interest in the oil refinery of Samuel Andrews, he goes into partnership with Andrews, and by year's end they have grossed $1.2 million after having boosted capacity of the 2-year-old refinery to 505 barrels per day, twice that of any other in the area (*see* 1863; 1868).

A high vacuum mercury pump that will make the electric light bulb possible is developed by German chemist Herman Johann Philipp Sprengel, 28 (*see* Swan, 1878; Edison, 1879; but *see* also Langmuir, 1912).

Cornelius Vanderbilt orders his Hudson River Railroad employees not to connect with the New York Central (*see* 1864; 1867).

The Union Pacific Railroad that started at Omaha in 1863 reaches Kansas City (*see* 1867).

The Missouri-Kansas-Texas Railroad has its beginnings. The "Katy" will extend from St. Louis via 3,000 miles of track through Missouri to Kansas City, San Antonio, Houston, and Galveston and will adopt its formal name in 1870.

The Southern Pacific Company is organized to link San Francisco with San Diego (*see* 1876).

The Pioneer completed by George M. Pullman is the first true sleeping car with convertible berths (*see* 1864; 1867).

The first U.S. train robbery is committed May 5. An Ohio and Mississippi passenger train bound from Cincinnati to St. Louis is derailed by objects placed on the tracks near North Bend, Ohio, and armed holdup men swarm through the cars robbing passengers of money and valuables (*see* Jesse James, 1872).

The 1,700-ton St. Louis-New Orleans sidewheeler steam packet *Sultana* explodes on the Mississippi April 27 killing 1,600 out of the 2,300 aboard.

A British Locomotives on Highways Act (Red Flag Act) passed by Parliament requires that steam-powered carriages be preceded by men on foot carrying red flags (*see* 1829). Stage coach interests have ob-

1865 (cont.) tained passage of the act, it will not be repealed until 1896, and it will stifle further development of steam buses which have overcome many technical problems and are becoming highly successful (*see* 1896).

💲 Wartime inflation has reduced the value of Confederate paper money to $1.70 per $100 by January and has driven the gold value of the Union greenback to 46 cents. The Confederate money becomes worthless and the greenback will not regain its full value until the end of 1878 (*see* Greenback party, 1873).

Boston's Kidder, Peabody & Company is founded April 1 by Boston financiers Henry P. Kidder, Howard Peabody, 33, and Oliver W. Peabody who take over the banking house John E. Thayer and Brother and affiliate themselves with London's Baring Brothers & Co., Ltd.

New York's 43-year-old City Bank obtains a federal charter and becomes National City Bank (see First National, 1812; First National City, 1955).

The Hong Kong and Shanghai Bank is founded in the British crown colony and begins a banking empire.

W. R. Grace & Co. is founded at New York to engage in the South American trade under the leadership of William Russell Grace (*see* 1850; 1890).

Andrew Carnegie enters the steel business with former blacksmith Andrew Klopman (*see* 1856; 1867).

Bridgeport Brass Company is founded at Bridgeport, Conn.

✳ Pratt & Whitney Company is founded at Hartford, Conn., by Vermont-born machinist Francis Asbury Pratt, 38, and Amos Whitney. Pratt has initiated a system for making interchangeable parts used in Civil War rifles, he will invent a metal-planing machine in 1869, a gear cutter in 1884, and a milling machine in 1885, he will be instrumental in having a standard system of gauges adopted, and his Pratt & Whitney firm will become a major producer of engines as well as machine tools.

The Yale Lock is patented by Shelburne Falls, Mass., inventor Linus Yale, 44, whose improved cylinder lock for the doors of houses and business establishments will be widely used for well over a century. Yale has been marketing his Yale Monitor dial combination lock for banks but he will go into partnership with John M. Towne in 1868 under the name Yale Lock Manufacturing company, Yale and Towne will build a factory at Stamford, Conn., to produce the new cylinder lock, but Yale will die at New York Christmas Day, 1868, a few weeks after the locks have gone into production.

⚕ The value of carbolic acid as an antiseptic in treating compound fractures is discovered at Glasgow by English surgeon Joseph Lister, 38, who has read of Pasteur's 1861 findings in France (*see* microscope, 1830). Lister develops a sprayer that creates a carbolic mist and inaugurates the era of antiseptic surgery (*see* Johnson & Johnson, 1886).

The Swedish Red Cross is founded at Stockholm.

The Norwegian Red Cross is founded at Oslo.

Serious cholera, smallpox, typhus, and yellow fever epidemics will kill thousands in the next 8 years at Philadelphia, New York, Boston, Washington, Memphis, Baltimore, and New Orleans (*see* 1866).

A Sanitary and Social Chart of New York City's Fourth Ward describes overcrowding in the 30 blocks south of Chatham Square. Smallpox and typhus are found in the area and one privy is reported to be shared by 78 people.

A cholera epidemic strikes Paris in September, the daily death toll reaches 200, sulfur is burned to combat the "miasma" in the air that is held responsible despite John Snow's observations at London in 1853, and Louis Pasteur's infant daughter Camille dies in the epidemic.

🎓 Cornell University is founded at Ithaca, N.Y., by Andrew Jackson White, 32, a state senator who last year helped codify the state's school laws and create a system of training schools for teachers. White has persuaded Ezra Cornell of Western Union to provide large sums of working capital that will make use of land granted to the state under the Morrill Act of 1862, the new university will open in 1868 free of all sectarian control, and its faculty of nonresident professors will include Louis Agassiz and James Russell Lowell.

Lehigh University is founded at Bethlehem, Pa.

Fisk University is founded at Nashville, Tenn.

The University of Kentucky is founded at Lexington.

The University of Maine is founded at Orono.

Worcester Polytechnic Institute is founded at Worcester, Mass.

▌▐ Reuters News Service conveys news of President Lincoln's assassination (above) to Europe a week ahead of the competition (*see* 1851). Reuters' American agent James McClean hires a tug, overtakes the mailboat bound for Britain, and throws aboard a canister containing his dispatch (*see* Atlantic Cable, 1866).

An improved rotary press devised by Philadelphia inventor William A. Bullock draws on a continuous roll of paper and cuts the sheets before they are printed. The Hoes in New York will evolve a true web press but only after U.S. paper manufacturers develop paper strong enough to form a long web that will run over many cylinders without tearing, and only after the perfection of quick-drying inks that will permit presses to print newspapers first and cut them afterward (*see* 1846; 1870).

The Nation begins publication at New York under the direction of Irish-American journalist Edwin Lawrence Godkin, 34, who will merge his weekly journal of liberal political opinion into the *New York Post* in 1881 and will be editor-in-chief of the *Post* for 17 years beginning in 1883.

The *San Francisco Chronicle* has its beginnings in the free theater program sheet *San Francisco Dramatic Chronicle* published by local journalist Michel Harry de Young, 16, and his 18-year-old brother Charles. They will drop the word "Dramatic" in 1868 and will make the *Chronicle* a full-fledged 2 cent newspaper whose sole owner and editor-in-chief beginning in 1880 will be the younger brother.

The *San Francisco Examiner* begins publication (*see* Hearst, 1887).

Nonfiction *Sesame and Lillies* by John Ruskin who has put together a series of lectures he has given at Manchester, not about art but about reading, education, woman's work, and social morals; *Josh Billings: His Sayings* by Massachusetts-born humorist Henry Wheeler Shaw, 47, who follows the deliberately bad spelling employed by Cleveland's "Artemus Ward" and takes the part of an unlettered Yankee cracker-barrel philosopher. Shaw has turned to writing and lecturing after careers as explorer, farmer, steamboat captain, auctioneer, and real estate dealer.

Fiction *Alice's Adventures in Wonderland* by English mathematician Lewis Carroll (Charles Lutwidge Dodgson), 33, who has written his fantasy for the entertainment of Alice Liddell, second daughter of classical scholar Henry George Liddell, 54, dean of Christ Church. The book is illustrated by *Punch* cartoonist John Tenniel, 45; *Our Mutual Friend* by Charles Dickens with illustrations by Marcus Stone: "The question [with Mr. Podsnap] about everything was, would it bring a blush into the cheek of the young person [Podsnap's daughter Georgiana]" (xi); *The Belton Estate* by Anthony Trollope; "The Celebrated Jumping Frog of Calaveras County" by Mark Twain.

Poetry *Drum Taps* by Walt Whitman who has added his poem "When Lilacs Last in the Dooryard Bloom'd" as a memorial to the late president. The Department of the Interior sacks Whitman from his clerkship on charges of having included explicit sexual references in his 1855 book *Leaves of Grass* into which his new book of war poems will be incorporated, the poet finds a new job in the attorney general's office, and he will remain in Washington until he suffers a paralytic stroke in 1873; *Atalanta in Calydon* by English poet Algernon Charles Swinburne, 28, whose drama in classical form with choruses includes the lines, "When the hounds of spring are on winter's traces,/ The mother of months in meadow or plain/ Fills the shadows and windy places/ With lisp of leaves and ripple of rain"; "The Hand That Rocks the Cradle Is the Hand That Rules the World" by U.S. lawyer-poet William Ross Wallace, 46, who has gained fame with his Civil War songs "Keep Step with the Music of the Union" and "The Liberty Bell."

Juvenile *Hans Brinker, or The Silver Skates* by New York author Mary Elizabeth Mapes Dodge, 34.

Painting *Peace and Plenty* by George Innes; *Prisoners from the Front* by Winslow Homer, who produced a series of drawings for *Harper's Weekly*.

Theater *Society* by English playwright Thomas William Robertson, 36, 11/11 at the Prince of Wales's Theatre, London.

Opera *L'Africaine* (*The African*) 4/28 at the Paris Grand Opéra, with music by the late Giacomo Meyerbeer who died at Paris last year at age 72; *Tristan und Isolde* 6/10 at Munich's Royal Court Theater, with music by Richard Wagner.

Chicago's Crosby Opera House opens April 20.

Tony Pastor's Opera House opens in New York August 14 at 201 Bowery under the management of actor-clown-comedian-balladeer Antonio Pastor, 28.

Oratorio *The Legend of St. Elizabeth* by Franz Lizst 8/15 at Budapest.

First performances Symphony in B minor (*Unfinished*) by the late Franz Schubert 12/17 at Vienna.

Popular songs "Ich Liebe Dich" by Edvard Grieg, lyrics by Hans Christian Andersen, now 60; "Marching Through Georgia" by Henry Clay Work.

English racing's Triple Crown goes to the French-bred horse Gladiateur which wins the Two Thousand Guineas, the Derby, and the St. Leger.

The U.S. trotter Goldsmith Maid makes money at New Jersey harness tracks for her new owner Alden Goldsmith who will sell the 8-year-old mare in 1869 for $15,000. She will earn $100,000 in the following 2 years, Harry N. Smith will buy her in 1871 for $32,000 with a view to breeding her, he will race her instead, she will earn another $100,000 for Smith, she will go undefeated from 1871 to 1874, she will win her last race at age 20, her purses will total $364,200, and she will live to age 28.

The Stetson hat is created by Philadelphia hatmaker John Batterson Stetson, 35, who worked for years in

President Lincoln's tragic death at Ford's Theater came only 5 days after the Confederate surrender at Appomatox.

1865 (cont.) his family's hat company until he came down with tuberculosis. Stetson went West to seek a cure, he joined the gold rush to Pike's Peak in 1863, and he has returned home to open his own factory for producing the high-crowned, "10-gallon hat" destined for fame on the Western plains. Stetson's $5 "Boss of the Plains" is a modified Mexican sombrero with a 4-inch crown, a 4-inch brim that can carry 10 "galions" (ribbons) and a leather strap hatband, and it has a look of importance. A Stetson made from better materials will sell for $10, a Stetson made from pure beaver or nutria felt will sell for $30, and by 1900 Stetson will have the world's largest hat factory with a payroll of more than 3,000.

 Deering, Milliken & Co. is founded at New York by Portland, Me., textile merchants Seth M. Milliken, 29, and William Deering, 39 (*see* harvester, 1873).

B. Altman & Co. is started by New York merchant Benjamin Altman, 25, whose dry goods store will become a giant department store (*see* 1906).

Chicago's Marshall Field learns that local merchant Potter Palmer plans to retire from active work in the store he started in 1852 (*see* 1861). Field persuades Palmer to sell him an interest and when Palmer takes in Levi Leiter of Cooley, Wadsworth the three men organize a $600,000 firm under the name Field, Palmer, and Leiter with Field taking a $260,000 interest (*see* 1867).

Le Printemps in Paris is started by a former Bon Marché department head named Jauzot (*see* 1852; Louvre, 1855; Samaritaine, 1869).

 Boston City Hall is completed by architects Gridley J. Fox Bryan and Arthur Gilman.

 Trading of wheat futures begins at Chicago after years of informal speculation in "to arrive" grains during the Crimean and Civil Wars, but while the Chicago Board of Trade moves into the Chamber of Commerce Building at LaSalle and Washington Streets and deals in futures it will not be used for hedging until 1879 (*see* 1848). New York and New Orleans markets continue to be "spot" markets dealing in actual grain (*see* 1872).

California's Sacramento Valley increases its wheat production. Hugh Glenn owns 50,000 acres in the valley (*see* 1851; 1868).

 Flour milling is revolutionized by French-American milling engineer Edmund LeCroix who builds a small mill for Alexander Faribault at Northfield, Minn., and adapts a French machine to develop a middlings purifier that improves the yield of endosperm wheat particles free of bran.

"Patent" flour is introduced using a newly patented process for separating bran from granual "middlings" (farina). LeCroix (above) improves on this superior quality flour with a middlings purifier that permits continuous improvement of the flour stream as it moves through the mill. He combines the bolting cloth used for centuries to sift flour for finer granulation with fan-driven air currents used for years to clean wheat (*see* Pillsbury, 1871).

Poor yeast is responsible for poor quality U.S. bread, says Austrian stillmaster Charles Fleischmann, 31, who visits Cincinnati to attend his sister's wedding. Salt-rising bread is preferred in the North, baking soda hot bread is preferred in the South, and what little yeast bakers use is generally "slop" yeast from potato water or from the frothy "barm" at the top of ale vats, but Fleischmann will change that (*see* 1868).

Royal Baking Powder has its beginnings at Fort Wayne, Ind., where a pharmacist mixes baking soda with cream of tartar to produce a powder (*see* Standard Brands, 1929).

Goodman's matzohs (unleavened bread) have their beginnings in a Philadelphia bake shop opened at the end of the Civil War by German baker Augustus Gutkind who has sailed for America, changed his name to Goodman, and taken a job as master baker for the Union Army. Gutkind's family has made matzohs for Passover in the province of Posen since 1766 (*see* 1883).

Anheuser-Busch has its beginnings at St. Louis where German-American brewer Adolphus Busch, 26, goes into business with his father-in-law Eberhard Anheuser (*see* 1873; Budweiser, 1876).

Hamm's Beer is introduced at St. Paul, Minn., by German-American brewer Theodore Hamm, 40, who emigrated from Baden in 1854, has worked as a butcher and saloonkeeper, and opens a brewery.

Del Monte Corporation has its beginnings in a California food brokerage firm founded by James K. Armby whose company will become the Oakland Preserving Company in 1891, California Packing Corporation in 1916, and Del Monte Corporation in 1967—the leading U.S. packer of fruits and vegetables (*see* 1891).

Cans made of thinner steel come into general use and the rim round the top of each can permits the invention of the can opener that will permit cans to be opened more easily than with hammer and chisel.

A compression machine to produce artificial ice built by U.S. inventor-balloonist Thaddeus Sobieski Coulincourt Lowe, 33, pioneers artificial refrigeration. Lowe has been chief of the U.S. Army aeronautic section since 1860 (*see* water gas, 1873).

Great Western Champagne is introduced by the Pleasant Valley Wine Company of Hammondsport, N.Y. Local clergyman William Bostwick started the first New York State winery 5 years ago with Catawba grapes from his garden and he produces the state's first champagne.

Chicago's Union Stock Yards open December 25 on a 345-acre tract of reclaimed swampland southwest of the city limits. With the Mississippi virtually shut down by the Civil War, Chicago has replaced Cincinnati, Louisville, and St. Louis as the nation's meat-packing center. The city doubled its packing capacity in a single year of the war with eight new large packing plants and many small ones to serve the nine railroads that converge on Chicago and that have spent $1.5 million to build the new Stock Yards with pens that can hold 10,000 head of cattle and 100,000 hogs at any given time (see Armour, 1872; Swift, 1877).

Bookbinder's Restaurant opens at Philadelphia where it will be famous for its snapper soup.

1866 Removal of French forces from Mexico is demanded February 12 by the U.S. government which has refused to recognize the emperor Maximilian. He sends his Belgian-born wife Carlota to seek aid from Pope Pius IX and Napoleon III but the empress soon finds that Maximilian's cause is hopeless (see 1867).

Europe goes to war for 7 weeks beginning in June as French, Austrian, Hanoverian, Italian, and Prussian forces fight in three theaters with telegraphic communications playing an important part for the first time in a European war as they did in the American Civil War. The war has been precipitated by the actions of the Prussian minister-president Count Otto von Bismarck who dominates the regime of Wilhelm I and who has formed an alliance with the new kingdom of Italy.

Italian forces are defeated by the Austrians on both land and sea but Venetia, ceded earlier by Austria to France, is ceded to Italy July 3 and French troops are withdrawn from Rome in December.

The Battle of Sadowa (Koniggratz) July 3 results in a stunning victory for the Prussians under Count Helmuth von Moltke, 66, who has reorganized the army and whose forces have the advantage of breech-loading needle guns that can be fired by infantrymen from prone positions against the erect Austrians who are using muzzle-loaders (see 1841; chassepot musket, below).

The Treaty of Prague August 23 ends the European war and incorporates Hanover, Electoral Hesse, Frankfurt, and Nassau into Prussia. The Germanic Confederation of 1815 is ended and the North German Confederation excludes Austria to give Prussia domination over German territory north of the Main.

The first king of Romania is recognized October 24 by the Ottoman sultan Abdul Aziz and begins a reign that will continue until 1914 (although Romania will not obtain full independence until 1878). The 27-year-old Prince Carol of Hohenzollern-Sigmaringen has arrived at Bucharest after having traveled incognito across Austria following his proclamation as king of Wallachia and Moldavia after the kidnapping and forced abdication of Alexander Guza by Conservatives and Liberals who want a foreign prince. A new constitution has been introduced in July based on the liberal but undemocratic Belgian charter of 1831.

The Japanese shogun Iemochi dies at age 20 and is succeeded by his 29-year-old kinsman Yoshinobu who will reign briefly as the last Tokugawa shogun.

Limits to the authority of martial law and to suspension of habeas corpus in time of war are set by the Supreme Court April 3 in the case of *Ex parte Milligan* but the opinion of the Court is not handed down until December 17: "Martial law can never exist where the courts are open in the proper and unobstructed exercise of their jurisdiction."

A Civil Rights Act is passed by Congress April 9 over President Johnson's veto to secure for former slaves all the rights of citizenship intended by the 13th Amendment.

The American Equal Rights Association founded May 10 at New York is an outgrowth of the Woman's Rights Society (see Anthony, 1869).

Reconstruction begins in the South, accompanied by racial conflicts. Efforts to introduce black suffrage into the Louisiana Constitution produce a July 30 race riot at New Orleans with some 200 casualties.

The National Labor Congress convenes August 20 at Baltimore and forms the National Labor Union. President is William H. Sylvis, 38, who early in 1861 called for a national convention of workingmen to oppose the impending civil war. Sylvis has helped to reorganize the Iron-Moulders' Union and will use Washington lobbyists to promote the interests of his 600,000-member National Labor Union until his death in July, 1869 (see Knights of Labor, 1869).

The American Society for the Prevention of Cruelty to Animals (ASPCA) is founded by New York shipbuilder's son Henry Bergh, 43, who serves as first president. Chief object of the society is to stop the abuse of horses (see ASPCC, 1875).

Horses provide virtually all the power for urban transit and for agricultural production.

A crude internal combustion engine that will sell by the thousands in the German states and in England in the next 10 years is patented by Cologne engineer Nikolaus August Otto, 34, who has read of the 1860 Lenoir engine and who has obtained backing from engineer-businessman Eugen Langen, 33. Otto shares patent rights with his brother William.

The first U.S. oil pipeline is completed to connect Pithole, Pa., with a railroad 5 miles away (see 1864).

Sperm oil for lighting and lubrication sells for $2.25 per gallon, up from 43 cents in 1823 (see *Scientific American*, 1857). The high price of sperm creates a growing demand for kerosene and petroleum.

The chassepot musket adopted by the French army is an improvement on the breech-loading Prussian needle gun used by the Prussians at the Battle of Sadowa (above). Gunsmith Antoine Alphonse Chassepot, 33, has developed the new musket.

The Skoda works that will supply European armaments for future wars is founded by Czech engineer

1866 (cont.) Emil von Skoda, 27, who takes over a machine works at Pilsen. He will develop it into a factory famous for its cannon and other artillery.

The Winchester M1866 rifle is introduced by the Winchester Repeating Arms Co. (*see* 1860; 1894).

Dynamite is invented by Swedish engineer Alfred Bernhard Nobel, 33, who has studied mechanical engineering in the United States. Nobel harnesses the power of the nitrogylcerin discovered by Ascanio Sobrero in 1847. He mixes it with absorbent diatomaceous earth to create a safe blasting powder that will replace black powder (*see* 1875; 1901).

A cholera epidemic takes 120,000 lives in Prussia and 110,000 in Austria.

A cholera epidemic strikes London and an epidemic of cholera at Bristol is checked through measures instituted by physician William Budd, 55, who also stamps out an epizootic of rinderpest in British livestock (*see* 1873; Snow, 1853)

A London dispensary for women opens under the direction of English physician Elizabeth Garrett Anderson, 30, who pioneers the admission of women to the professions, including medicine.

Cholera kills some 50,000 Americans with 2,000 of the fatalities occurring at New York which creates the first U.S. municipal board of health.

New York has had recurring epidemics of cholera, scarlet fever, smallpox, typhoid fever, typhus, and yellow fever which will grow more severe in the next 7 years in Baltimore, Boston, Memphis, New Orleans, Philadelphia, and Washington as well as in New York.

Parke, Davis & Co. has its beginnings at Detroit where Hervey C. Parke invests in a laboratory founded earlier by local physician-pharmacist Samuel P. Duffield to make ether, sweet spirits of nitre, oil of wine, Hoffman's Anodyne, and similar preparations with the motto "Medicamenta Vera." Parke will be joined in 1871 by George Davis, the firm of Parke, Davis will finance expeditions to Mexico, Central America, the West Indies, and the Fiji Islands, and they will introduce pharmaceutical drugs that will include cascara sagrada, coca, Jabirandi, Jamaica dogwood, and Grindelia Robusta (*see* 1879).

The clinical thermometer is invented by English physician Thomas Clifford Allbut, 30.

Bernadette Soubirous of Lourdes enters the convent of Saint Gildard at Nevers where she will die of tuberculosis in 1879 despite administration of water from the grotto at Lourdes (*see* 1858). Reports of cures from the grotto will nevertheless continue to attract sick, blind, and infirm visitors (*see* 1926).

The Western Health Reform Institute is founded at Battle Creek, Mich., by Seventh Day Adventist prophet Ellen G. White whose sanitorium treatment combines vegetarian diet and hydrotherapy with some accepted medical methods. The "San" will in-

cubate the fledgling U.S. breakfast food industry (*see* 1860; Kellogg, 1876; Post, 1893).

The Great Tea Race from Foochow to London pits 11 clipper ships who race to minimize spoilage of the China tea in their hot holds. The skippers crowd on sail but the voyage still takes close to 3 months.

Thomas Cook initiates a system for providing hotel accomodations to implement the Cook's Tours he began in 1856 (*see* 1851; Khartoum, 1884).

London has a Black Friday May 11 as financial panic hits the city.

Postwar economic depression begins in the United States as prices begin a rapid decline following the Civil War's inflation (*see* Black Friday, 1869).

Beirut's American University is founded under the name Syrian Protestant College. The school will be renamed in 1920 and its graduates will include presidents, prime ministers, cabinet members, and ambassadors of several Middle Eastern nations.

Drew University is founded by New York financier Daniel Drew at Madison, N.J., on the centennial of American Methodism.

The University of Ottawa is founded in Ontario.

Carleton College is founded at Northfield, Minn.

A new Atlantic Cable between Britain and the United States is completed July 27 by Cyrus W. Field with backing from Peter Cooper (*see* 1858; 1879).

Western Union Telegraph absorbs two smaller telegraph companies to gain control of 75,000 miles of wire and become the first great U.S. industrial monopoly (*see* 1856; 1881).

The *Hartford Courant* begins publication on a daily basis to succeed the weekly *Connecticut Courant* that began 73 years ago.

Ginn & Co. publishers is founded by Tufts graduate Edwin Ginn, 28, who publishes *Craik's English Shakespeare* and follows it with *Allen's Latin Grammar* and *Goodwin's Greek Grammar*. Ginn will move to Rochester, N.Y., and will make his firm a major textbook house (*see* D. C. Heath, 1886).

Henry Holt Co. publishers is founded by Yale graduate Henry Holt, 26, at New York. Holt will introduce American readers to the daring novels of England's Thomas Hardy and later to the tales of Robert Louis Stevenson (*see* Harcourt, Brace, 1919; Holt, Rinehart and Winston, 1960).

G. P. Putnam and Sons is founded at New York by George P. Putnam, 52, who began campaigning at age 23 for international copyright agreements, moved to London 4 years later to open a bookstore specializing in American books, and has returned to go into business with his son.

Fiction *War and Peace* (*Voina i Mir*) by Russian novelist Count Leo (Lev Nikolaevich) Tolstoi, 38, is published in its first installment. Tolstoi, who will complete his long novel about the 1812 Napoleonic invasion in 3 years, lives on his country estate Yasnaya Polyana whose serfs he has liberated in accordance with the 1861 Emancipation Act; *Crime and Punishment* (*Prestuplenie i Nakazaniye*) by Fedor Dostoievski; *The Gambler* (*Igrok*) by Fedor Dostoievski who has dictated the novel in 1 month to fulfill an obligation to a publisher. He will marry the stenographer Anna Snitkina, 20, next year and she will bear him children as he gambles away the little money they have; *Toilers of the Sea* (*Les travailleurs de la mer*) by Victor Hugo.

Poetry *Poems and Ballads* by Algernon Charles Swinburne whose "Ballad of Burdens" carries the refrain, "Princes, and ye whom pleasure quickeneth,/ Heed well this rhyme before your pleasure tire;/ For life is sweet, but after life is death./ This is the end of every man's desire"; "Thyrsis" by Matthew Arnold; "Snow-bound" by John Greenleaf Whittier; "O Captain! My Captain!" by Walt Whitman whose elegaic ode commemorates Lincoln.

Painting *The Fifer* by Edouard Manet; *A Storm in the Rocky Mountains* by Albert Bierstadt.

Opera *The Brandenburgers in Bohemia* (*Branibori v Cechach*) 1/5 at Prague's National Theater with music by Bedrich Smetana; *The Bartered Bride* (*Prodana Nevesta*) 5/30 at Prague's National Theater, with music by Bedrich Smetana; *Mignon* 11/17 at the Opéra-Comique, Paris, with music by French composer Charles Louis Ambroise Thomas, 55.

Broadway musicals *The Black Crook* 9/12 at Niblo's Garden, with a Faustian plot by U.S. playwright Charles M. Barras, 40, a cast of 100 dancing girls in pink tights (clergymen denounce their costumes and indelicate postures as does James Gordon Bennett in his *New York Herald*), music adapted from various sources with additional music by Giuseppe Verdi, 474 perfs. (The first true Broadway musical will see many revivals and will tour for more than 40 years.)

G. Schirmer Co. is founded at New York by German-American music publisher Gustave Schirmer, 37.

New York's Steinway Hall opens in 14th Street. It will be the city's leading concert hall for more than two decades.

Estey Organ Company is founded at Brattleboro, Vt., by local plumber-investor Jacob Estey, 51, with engineer Levi K. Fuller, 25. The firm will grow to have sales of more than 1800 instruments per month.

Popular songs "Come Back to Erin" by London songwriter Claribel (Charlotte Allington Barnard); "When You and I Were Young, Maggie" by Detroit composer J. A. Butterfield, lyrics by Canadian-American journalist George Washington Johnson of the *Cleveland Plain-Dealer;* "We Parted by the River" by U.S. songwriter William Shakespeare Hays.

The New York Athletic Club is founded June 17 by John G. Babcock (who has invented the sliding seat for rowers), Henry E. Buermeyer, and William B. Curtis. They will introduce the first spiked shoes at the club's first open indoor competition November 11, 1868, at New York's Empire Skating Rink.

Cincinnati's Plum Street Temple is completed for the city's B'nai Yeshurun congregation whose Austrian-American rabbi Isaac Meyer Wise, 47, is pioneering a reform movement in U.S. Judaism by abandoning dietary laws and other orthodox practices such as segregating women, wearing beards, and keeping heads covered. The Moorish building with its twin minarets seats 1,400.

The Morris chair is introduced by English craftsman-poet-wallpaper designer William Morris, 32, whose reclining chair has a bar and notch arrangement that permits its back to be tilted to a 45-degree angle or folded flat to facilitate shipment.

The first U.S. crop report is issued by the 4-year-old Department of Agriculture. The report has been compiled by field workers who have worked to determine the nation's production of various crops.

Cattlemen discover that livestock can survive the cold of the northern Great Plains and can eat the grasses there.

Cattle from Texas are driven north for the first time on the Chisholm Trail, named after the scout Jesse Chisholm. The cattle arrive at Abilene, Kan., for shipment by rail to points east (*see* 1867; 1871; 1885).

The amino acid glutamic acid is isolated from wheat by German chemist H. Ritthausen who introduces into protein chemistry the experimental method of acid hydrolysis and the subsequent precipitation of barium or calcium salts of certain amino acids by means of alcohol (*see* monosodium glutamate, 1908).

A salmon cannery opens on the Columbia River that will be followed by canneries at the mouth of almost every river north to Alaska (*see* 1878).

The first San Francisco salmon cannery opens (*see* 1864).

A U.S. patent is issued for a tin can with a key opener.

British imports of tinned meat total 16,000 pounds.

More than 90 percent of Britain's tea still comes from China (*see* 1900; Great Tea Race, above).

Henri Nestlé formulates a combination of farinaceous pap and milk for infants who cannot take mother's milk and starts a firm under his own name to produce the new infant formula (*see* 1861; 1875; Liebig, 1867).

The Anglo-Swiss Condensed Milk Company is founded at Cham, Switzerland, by U.S. entrepreneurs Charles and George Page. Their supervisor John Baptist Meyenberg, now 18, will suggest the possibility of preserving evaporated milk in the same way as other canned foods, without sugar, but the Page brothers will enjoy such success with their sweetened condensed milk that they will reject

1866 (cont.) Meyenberg's idea and he will emigrate to America (*see* Helvetia Milk Condensing Company, 1885).

Gail Borden adopts the trademark Eagle Brand to protect his condensed milk from competitors who have appropriated the name Borden (*see* 1861). Borden has made a fortune supplying his product to the Union Army and his plant at Elgin, Ill., produces at a rate of 300,000 gallons per year (*see* 1875).

Breyer's Ice Cream is founded at Philadelphia (*see* National Dairy, 1926).

Washburn, Crosby Company is founded in Wisconsin by Maine timber baron Cadwallader Colden Washburn, 48, who served as a major general in the Union Army. Washburn has settled in Wisconsin and he erects his first flour mill on the banks of the Mississippi (*see* 1871).

Cadbury's Cocoa Essence is the first pure cocoa to be sold in Britain (*see* 1849). Richard Cadbury, 31, and his brother George, 27, have come close to failing, but they are saved by the new product which they advertise as "Absolutely Pure: Therefore Best." They have squeezed out excess cocoa butter to leave a pure, concentrated powder that need not be adulterated with the potato flour and sago flour used in all British cocoa powders up to now to counteract the natural fats (*see* van Houten, 1828). The cocoa butter made available by the process enables Cadbury Brothers to increase production of chocolate candy (*see* Bournemouth, 1879).

L. Rose Company is established at London to supply lime juice to the Royal Navy.

Major Grey's chutney made from cultivated Jamaican mangoes is introduced by Crosse & Blackwell which also introduces a marmalade.

Jack Daniel's Tennessee Sour Mash Whiskey is introduced at Lynchburg by local distiller Daniel whose nephew Lem Motlow will carry on the business, leaching the product of the stills through vats filled with 10 feet of charcoal (*see* Brown-Forman, 1956).

1867 Irish Fenians try to seize Chester in February with an attack on police barracks; they kill 12 people trying to blow up Clerkenwell jail. The revolutionary movement founded among Irish-Americans by James Stephens in 1858 spread to Ireland 2 years ago but will dissolve next year as differences arise between Stephens and more radical leaders.

The British North America Act March 29 unites Ontario, Quebec, New Brunswick, and Nova Scotia in the Dominion of Canada with its capital at Ottawa, a town of 18,000. First premier of the Dominion is John Alexander Macdonald, 52, a Scots-Canadian who has been premier of Upper Canada and who has led the federation movement.

Alaska is ceded to the United States by the Russian czar Aleksandr II in a treaty signed March 30. U.S. Secretary of State William Henry Seward has arranged the $7.2 million purchase at 1.9 cents per acre, critics ridicule "Seward's icebox," but the Senate consents April 9.

Nebraska is admitted to the Union as the 37th state.

Mexico's emperor Maximilian surrenders May 15 to Juarez forces commanded by Mariano Escobedo who have besieged Gueratero, a court martial condemns him to death, and he goes before a firing squad June 19, thus ending Napoleon III's dream of establishing an empire in Latin America.

Midway Islands in the Pacific are taken in the name of the United States August 28 by Captain William Reynolds of the U.S.S. *Lackawanna*.

The Japanese Meiji emperor Mutsuhito has ascended the throne in February at age 15 but is powerless until the Tokugawa shogun Yoshinobu abdicates in November after less than 1 year, ending the feudal military government that has controlled Japan for nearly seven centuries (*see* Meiji Restoration, 1868).

The Austro-Hungarian dual monarchy that will continue until 1918 is created in October by a compromise engineered by Hungarian statesman Ferencz Deak, 64, who has gained restoration of the Hungarian constitution from the Austrian emperor Franz Josef who will rule as king of Hungary until his death in 1916. The king-emperor has ruled with absolute power since 1848 and has no sympathy for the constitutional government under which he will now rule.

Prussia's Count von Bismarck organizes a North German Confederation under Prussian leadership. The socialist chairman of German workingmen's unions August Babel, 27, wins election to the Confederation's Reichstag.

 Das Kapital by Karl Marx is published in its first volume and urges an end to private ownership of public utilities, transportation facilities, and means of production.

The Zollverein customs union established in 1834 expands to include Baden, Bavaria, Hohenzollern, and Wurttemberg (*see* 1871).

Kuhn, Loeb & Company is founded at New York February 1 by German-American banker Abraham Kuhn and his brother-in-law Solomon Loeb who went into partnership 17 years ago at Lafayette, Ind., to sell clothing, moved to Cincinnati, retired in 1865, moved to New York to lead lives of leisure, and now open a commercial bank with $500,000 in capital. They soon make a market for U.S. government bonds and railway bonds, Kuhn will soon retire to live in Germany, Loeb will head the firm until 1885 (*see* Schiff, 1875).

Britain's Second Reform Bill passed August 15 extends suffrage, opens borough elections to all householders paying the poor rates and to all lodgers of 1 year's residence or more who pay annual rents of at least £10, opens county elections to owners of land that rents for at least £5 per year and to tenants who pay at least £12 per year, but a bill that would give women the right to vote fails (see 1905).

The Knights of the White Camelia is organized in Louisiana. Similar to the 2-year-old Ku Klux Klan, the fraternal order will spread among white supremacists throughout the former Confederate states.

A commission to conclude peace treaties with the Indians is appointed by Congress (see 1868).

The first practical dry cell battery is invented by French engineer Georges Leclanche, 28, whose electrolytic cell can provide an intermittent electric supply as required (see Plante, 1859). Leclanche's battery will be employed by the millions in the century to come for powering an endless array of industrial and consumer products (see Eveready, 1890).

Babcock & Wilcox Company is founded at Providence, R.I., by local engineers George Herman Babcock, 35, and Stephen Wilcox who patent a sectional industrial "safety" boiler designed to prevent any dangerous explosions. The firm will put up large plants at Elizabeth, N.J., and at Glasgow and will grow to become the largest U.S. producer of coal-fired boilers and a major producer of machine tools and other equipment.

Mallinckrodt Chemical Works of St. Louis has its beginnings in the G. Mallinckrodt & Co. firm founded by Missouri-born chemist Edward Mallinckrodt, 22, with his older brother Gustav and his younger brother Otto. The two younger Mallinckrodts have recently returned from 3 years of study at Weisbaden and apprenticeship at Hanover while Gustav worked for Richardson Drug Company at St. Louis. Gustav and Otto will die in the mid-1870s after helping Edward produce the first quality chemicals west of the Mississippi and Edward will go on to become the "ammonia king."

United Iron Mills is founded by Philadelphia scale manufacturer Henry Phipps, 28, in partnership with Andrew Carnegie (see 1865; Frick, 1873).

Directors of the Union Pacific Railroad sell shares at par to U.S. congressmen in the Crédit Mobilier company they have formed in an effort to stave off investigation into the high personal profits they are making on the line under construction in the West (see 1863; 1869; 1872).

Steel rail production begins in the United States which has been using rails of iron or imported steel.

Construction begins at St. Louis on the Eads Bridge that will span the Mississippi. Louisville, Ky., engineer James Buchanan Eads, 46, invented a diving bell in the 1850s, he made a fortune salvaging sunken hulls in the Mississippi, he supplied the Union with seven 175-foot ironclads in the space of 100 days in 1861, but financiers, politicians, and other engineers scoff at his proposal to sink massive stone piers through 103 feet of turbulent water to bedrock below the dense river bottom, and they ridicule his

project of cantilevering three steel spans—each more than 500 feet long. Eads proceeds to innovate fabrication techniques that are unique, imaginative, and effective, he will put nearly $7 million into the endeavor in the next 7 years, and 12 men will die in the huge pneumatic caisson of his east pier (see 1874).

A suspension bridge designed by J. A. Roebling opens to span the Ohio River between Cincinnati and Covington, Ky. (see 1855; Brooklyn Bridge, 1883).

Cornelius Vanderbilt gains control of the New York Central Railroad (see 1865). Now 72, Vanderbilt issues an order January 14 that all trains on his New York & Hudson River Railroad must terminate at East Albany, 2 miles from the Albany depot, he shows protesting legislators an old law specifically forbidding the New York & Hudson River to run trains across the Hudson River, stock in the New York Central drops sharply, and Vanderbilt buys enough to secure control by December (see 1869).

The Pullman Palace Car Company is founded by George M. Pullman with Andrew Carnegie (above) who will be its major stockholder until 1873. The new company will build cars and will operate them under contract for railway companies (see first dining car, 1868).

The Wagner Drawing Room Car designed by New York wagonmaker Webster Wagner, 50, goes into service on Commodore Vanderbilt's New York Central (above). Wagner will soon contract to use George Pullman's folding upper berth and hinged seats but when he uses the Pullman-designed equipment on Vanderbilt's Lake Shore and Michigan Southern line after 1873 Pullman will sue and the lawsuit will not yet have been settled when Wagner dies in a New York Central train collision in 1882.

The first U.S. elevated railway begins operation at New York on a single track from Battery Place to 30th Street above Greenwich Street (9th Avenue). Steam trains of the Gilbert Elevated Railway Company provide much quicker transportation than do the horse cars below and the Gilbert line will hook up within a decade to the Third Avenue Railroad that will operate between City Hall Park and 42nd Street (see 1878; subway, 1904).

An alpine rail line with 22 tunnels is completed through the 4,500-foot high Brenner Pass between Innsbruck, Austria, and Bolzano in the Trentino-Alto Adige region of Italy.

The Pacific Mail Steamship Company begins regular service between San Francisco and Hong Kong.

The first successful gallstone operation is performed June 15 by Indianapolis physician John Stough Bobbs on McCordsville, Ind., patient Mary E. Wiggins. Bobbs will be called "the father of cholecystotomy."

Amyl nitrate proves valuable in treating angina pectoris. Scottish physician Thomas Lauder Brunton, 23, who does research on circulation and on the physiological action of drugs (see nitroglycerin, 1847).

Ku Klux Klansmen and Knights of the White Camelia brought terror to Southern blacks during Reconstruction days.

Atropine is shown to block cardial effects of vagal stimulation by two German physicians (*see* 1872).

The Austrian Red Cross is founded at Vienna.

Hostetter's Stomach Bitters are advertised in the United States with claims that the product will cure dyspepsia, colic, dysentery, and bilious complaints (*see* 1847). Promoter James Cook Ayer, 49, rivals Hostetter with his patent medicine Dr. Ayer's Sarsaparilla which is 26 percent alcohol.

The New York State Legislature votes to establish a free public school system.

The University of Illinois is founded at Urbana.

Mankato State University is founded at Mankato, Minn.

West Virginia University is founded at Morgantown.

Howard University for Negroes is founded by white Congregationalists outside Washington, D.C. The founders include General O. O. Howard, director of the Freedmen's Bureau, and they arouse ridicule with their proposal to admit students of all ages, male or female, married or single, informed or ignorant.

Atlanta University is founded in Georgia. It will become a leading institution for the higher education of blacks.

The Prussian mail service owned by the Thurn und Taxis family is purchased by the government.

The first practical "writing machine" is invented by Milwaukee printer Christopher Latham Sholes, 48, who has sought a means of inscribing braille-like characters for use by the blind (*see* Braille, 1834). Court reporter Charles Weller is asked to test the machine's efficiency, he types, "Now is the time for all good men to come to the aid of the party," and Sholes will call his machine a "typewriter" (*see* 1868).

The sulfite process for producing wood pulp for papermaking is devised by U.S. inventor Benjamin Chew Tilghman, 48 (*see* 1870; Burgess, 1854).

Turin's *La Stampa* (*The Press*) has its beginnings in the *Gazetta Piedmontese*.

Paperback book publishing is pioneered by Leipzig's Reclams Universal Bibliothek which issues a paperback edition of Goethe's *Faust*.

Nonfiction *The English Constitution* by *Economist* editor Walter Bagehot, 41.

Fiction *Thérèse Raquin* by French novelist Emile Zola (Edouard Charles Antoine Zola), 27; *The Last Chronicle of Barset* by Anthony Trollope; *Under Two Flags* by French novelist Ouida (Marie Louise de la Ramée), 28, whose romance *Held in Bondage* appeared 4 years ago.

Juvenile *Ragged Dick, or Street Life in New York* is serialized in the periodical *Student and Schoolmate* published at New York under the name "Oliver Optic" by William Taylor Adams, 45. Author of the novel is Unitarian minister Horatio Alger, 35, whose more than 100 rags-to-riches novels in the next 30 years will dramatize the virtues of pluck, honesty, hard work, and marrying the boss's daughter (*see* 1871).

Poetry "Dover Beach" by Matthew Arnold: "And we are here as on a darkling plain/ Swept with confused alarms of struggle and flight./ Where ignorant armies clash by night"; *The Life and Death of Jason* by William Morris.

Painting *The Execution of Maximilian* by Edouard Manet; *Rape* by French painter Paul Cézanne, 28; the Paris World's Fair introduces Japanese *ukiyoe* prints to the West; Jean Auguste Dominique Ingres dies at Paris January 14 at age 86; Théodore Rousseau dies at Barbizon December 22 at age 55.

Theater *The Death of Ivan the Terrible* (*Smert Ioanna Groznogo*) by Count Leo Tolstoy 1/12 at St. Petersburg's Alexandrinsky Theater; *Caste* by Thomas William Robertson 4/6 at the Prince of Wales's Theatre, London; *Dora* by Charles Reade 6/1 at London's Adelphi Theatre.

Opera *Don Carlos* 3/11 at the Paris Opéra, with music by Giuseppe Verdi, libretto from the Friedrich von Schiller play of 1787; *La Grande-Duchesse de Gerolstein* 4/12 at the Variétés Théâtre, Paris, with music by Jacques Offenbach; *Romeo et Juliette* 4/27 at the Théâtre-Lyrique, Paris, with music by Charles Gounod, libretto from the Shakespeare tragedy of 1595; *Cox and Box (or The Long-Lost Brother)* 5/11 at London's Adelphi Theatre, with music by London church organist Arthur Seymour Sullivan, 25, libretto by F. C. Burnard based on the J. Maddison Mortori farce *Box and Cox*.

First performance "The Blue Danube Waltz" ("An der Schonen Blauen Daonau") by Johann Strauss 2/15 at Vienna, with lyrics from a poem by Karl Beck, 50. Sung by the Viennese Male Singing Society, the new waltz creates a sensation.

The New England Conservatory of Music is founded at Boston.

The Cincinnati Conservatory of Music is founded.

Popular songs "The Little Brown Jug" by Philadelphia songwriter R. E. Eastburn (Joseph Eastburn Winner), 32, whose older brother Septimus wrote the lyrics to "Listen to the Mocking Bird" in 1855.

Baseball's curve ball pitch is invented by Brooklyn, N.Y., pitcher William Arthur Cummings.

Washington's National baseball team tours the country and defeats the Cincinnati Red Stockings 53 to 10, the Cincinnati Buckeyes 90 to 10, the Louisville Kentuckians 82 to 21, the Indianapolis Western Club 106 to 21, and the St. Louis Union Club 113 to 26 (the teams are all amateur organizations) (see 1869).

Marquis of Queensberry rules for boxing are formulated by English athlete John Graham Chambers, 24, who has founded an amateur club to encourage boxing under the aegis of Scotland's Sir John Sholto Douglas, 23, 8th Marquis of Queensberry (see Oscar Wilde, 1895).

The Belmont Stakes has its first running and the 1.5-mile test for 3-year-old thoroughbreds is won by a horse named Ruthless. Major August Belmont II has built New York's Belmont Park racetrack and has helped to organize the Jockey Club to oversee U.S. horseracing (see Preakness, 1873).

A diamond as large as a child's marble is discovered by South African schoolboy Erasmus Jacobs on the Orange River near Hope Town but the discovery will not be made public for some years (see 1871).

Chicago's Carson, Pirie Scott & Company opens at 136 West Lake Street but will move to 118-120 State Street and will provide serious competition for Field, Leiter and Company (below). Samuel Carson and John Pirie have been operating a downstate Illinois chain of dry goods stores since 1854 and have gone into partnership with Chicago merchants George and Robert Scott and Andrew MacLeish.

Chicago's Field, Palmer & Leiter becomes Field, Leiter & Company as Potter Palmer sells his share in the store and Marshall Field joins with his brothers Henry and Joseph and with Levi Leiter and his brother Marshall to form the new firm which is capitalized at $1.2 million (see 1865; 1881).

Rich's of Atlanta has its beginnings in the M. Rich Dry Goods store, a 20- by 75-foot shop in Whitehall Street opened by Hungarian-American merchant Morris Rich, 20, with $500 borrowed from his brother William. Rich came to America with William at age 13, he changed his name from Reich, he became a foot peddler, he has learned to speak En-glish with no perceptible accent, and he will be joined by his brothers Emanuel and Danuel who will help him make M. Rich & Bros. Atlanta's paramount department store (see 1924).

New York's R. H. Macy Company stays open Christmas Eve until midnight and has record 1-day receipts of $6,000 (see 1858; 1874).

Milan's Galleria Vittoria Emanuele is completed by architect Guiseppe Mengoni, 40, to connect the busy Piazza del Duomo with the neighboring Piazza della Scala. The great glass-roofed arcade (320 yards long, 16 yards wide, 94 feet high) in the form of a Latin cross provides a meeting place for the Milanese and is so popular that when hailstones break every pane in the glass ceiling in 1869 the citizenry will reject proposals for an unbreakable roof and will insist that the glass be replaced.

Scots-American naturalist John Muir, 29, starts out late in the year on a walk that will take him 1,000 miles through Kentucky, Tennessee, Georgia, and Florida (see 1868; Sierra Club, 1892).

Alaska (above) has a Pribilof seal population of 2.5 million, down from 5 million in 1786 when the islands were discovered (see 1911).

More than half of all U.S. working people are employed on farms.

The Grange, or the Patrons of Husbandry, is founded in the upper Mississippi Valley by former U.S. Department of Agriculture field investigator Oliver H. Kelley, 41. The organization's popular name derives from its lodges, which are designated by an archaic name for barn. Avowedly nonpolitical, the Grange's stated aims are educational and social, with emphasis on reading and discussion to increase farmers' knowledge, but the discussions will inevitably turn to freight rates, high taxes, and politics (see 1876).

A patent application for barbed wire is filed by U.S. inventor Lucien Smith but no reliable machine exists to manufacture such wire in quantity (see 1873).

Chicago livestock dealer Joseph Geating McCoy, 29, buys 450 acres of land at $5 per acre in Abilene, Kan., he builds pens and loading chutes with lumber he has brought from Hannibal, Mo., he installs a pair of large Fairbanks scales, and he promises Texas ranchers $40 per head for cattle the ranchers can sell at home for only $4 per head. Abilene is "a small, dead place of about one dozen log huts . . . four-fifths of which are covered with dirt for roofing," but it is the terminus of the Kansas Pacific Railway which despite its name operates only between Chicago and Abilene. The railroad has promised McCoy one-eighth of the freight charge on each car of cattle he ships East, he sends out the first shipment (20 carloads) September 5, and by year's end some 35,000 head of longhorns have passed through Abilene, a figure that will more than double next year (see 1871; Chisholm Trail, 1866).

1867 (cont.) Prehistoric canals in Arizona Territory are cleared by the John Swilling Company to bring water from the Salt River to the fertile lands of the valley. The town of Phoenix begins growing (*see* Roosevelt Dam, 1911).

Iowa farmer William Louden modernizes dairy farming with a rope sling and wooden monorail hay carrier. Suspended beneath the peak of a barn, Louden's carrier enables a farmer to swing a load of hay without using a pitchfork, and Louden's litter carrier hauls out manure, permitting a farmer to clean a stable or dairy barn in one-tenth the time it has taken until now. Louden's contributions will make possible large, efficient dairy herds.

The Illinois and Wisconsin Dairymen's Association is founded.

Development of a synthetic butter is begun by French chemist Hippolyte Mége-Mouries, 50, at the urging of the emperor Napoleon III who may recall his uncle's encouragement of food canning and beet sugar production (*see* 1794; 1811). Mége-Mouries works with suet, chopped cow's udder, and warm milk to begin a revolution in the butter industry (*see* margarine, 1869).

The first patent baby food is introduced by Justus von Liebig whose product will be sold commercially for decades (*see* 1842; Nestlé, 1861; Clapp, 1922).

Sugar beets are introduced into Utah Territory by Brigham Young who has machinery from Liverpool carted across the continent to Salt Lake City by ox-drawn wagon, but the beet sugar factory he builds will be abandoned within 2 years (*see* 1880).

C. F. Mueller Company has its beginnings as German-American baker Christian Frederick Mueller, 27, starts selling homemade egg noodles house-to-house from a pushcart at Jersey City, N.J. His product is well received by the city's large German population, by 1870 Mueller will be buying flour by the barrel rather than by the bag, he will replace his pushcart with a horse and wagon, and his firm will become the largest U.S. producer of macaroni, spaghetti, and egg noodles.

Canned deviled ham is introduced by Boston's William Underwood & Co. (*see* 1822; red devil trademark, 1870).

Burnham & Morrill canned sweet corn is introduced by Portland, Me., entrepreneurs George Burnham and Charles S. Morrill who establish a cannery that will become famous for its clam bouillon and—most especially—for its canned baked beans (*see* 1875).

Arm & Hammer Baking Soda has its beginnings as Brooklyn, N.Y., spice dealer James A. Church closes his factory to enter the baking soda business but retains the symbolic sign of the Roman god Vulcan that identified his Vulcan Spice Mill. Church sells his product by the barrel with the help of a Colonel Powell, a 7-foot 4-inch giant of a salesman, and he will soon adopt the name Arm & Hammer Saleratus under which his baking soda will dominate the market.

Ruppert's Brewery has its start as New York brewer Jacob Ruppert, 25, buys a tract of timberland on Third Avenue between 91st and 92nd Streets to build his own brewery after 4 years of managing his father's Turtle Bay Brewery. Ruppert clears the timber from his land and erects a three-story building that will grow to become the world's largest lager brewery (*see* 1874).

Overpopulation is a red herring invented by the capitalists to justify poverty among the working class, says Karl Marx in *Das Kapital* (above). Marx rejects the idea of contraception and favors enhanced production and more equitable distribution of wealth as better ways to improve the lot of the working class.

1868 President Andrew Johnson dismisses Secretary of War Edwin M. Stanton February 18 because Stanton has supported vindictive Radical Republicans who have tried to block presidential efforts to be charitable toward the defeated Southern states. The House of Representatives votes February 21 to impeach the president "of high crimes and misdemeanors," a trial begins in the Senate March 30, and the Senate votes 35 to 19 for the president's removal May 16 but fails by one vote to achieve the two-thirds majority needed.

Military rule has continued meanwhile in the South and in June Congress authorizes readmission of the seven Confederate states on condition that black suffrage be retained (below).

A Tory government headed by Benjamin Disraeli comes to power in Britain February 29. Parliament passes an Irish Reform Bill and a Scottish Reform Bill July 13, but the Liberal party scores sweeping victories in the general elections in November. Disraeli resigns December 2, and William Ewart Gladstone, 59, begins a ministry that will continue until 1874.

Japan's Meiji Restoration ends the feudal rule that has continued since 1185 and overturns the Tokugawa shogunate that has held power since 1603 (*see* 1867). The emperor Mutsuhito signs a Charter Oath April 6 pledging himself to be guided in his rule by a deliberative assembly responsive to public opinion and thereupon gains direct control as an alliance of the Satsuma and Choshu families forces the rival Tokugawa family from power. The last Tokugawa forces are defeated July 4 in the Battle of Ueno at Edo which is renamed Tokyo (eastern capital) in November.

Japan's 16-year-old emperor (above) says in his coronation oath, "We shall summon assemblies, and in ruling the nation we shall have regard to public opinion . . . Knowledge will be sought out among the nations of the world, and thus the well-being of the empire will be ensured." The imperial family takes over Kyuju palace, a fortress-castle in the center of Tokyo that has been used by shoguns for centuries (*see* 1869).

The raja of Sarawak Sir James Brooke dies at age 65 and is succeeded by his 39-year-old nephew Sir Charles Anthony Johnson Brooke who has adopted his uncle's surname and who will reign until his death in 1917 (*see* 1841; British protectorate, 1888).

The Ethiopian emperor Theodore is defeated April 10 in the Battle of Arogee by an Anglo-Indian force under Sir Robert Napier, 58. Theodore commits suicide, the British reach Magdala April 13, and they free traders, missionaries, and envoys imprisoned since 1864 by the cruel and eccentric Theodore. Ethiopia falls into anarchy following the withdrawal of Napier who will be created first Baron Napier of Magdala by Queen Victoria (*see* 1872).

Basutoland is annexed by the British following defeat of the Basutos by the Orange Free State which protests the British action. Transvaal forces attempt to occupy Delagoa Bay but withdraw under pressure from the British.

Madagascar's Hova queen Rashoherina dies after a 5-year reign and is succeeded by Ranavalona II who will reign as queen until 1883. True power remains in the hands of her husband and first minister Rainilaiarivony, a Christian who was also married to Rashoherina and who will retain power until 1896 by marrying Ranavalona's successsor. Paris recognizes Hova supremacy in Madagascar August 8.

Siam's Rama IV dies at age 64 after a 17-year reign and is succeeded by his 15-year-old son Somdeth Phra Paraminda Maha Chulalongkorn who will rule personally beginning in 1873. The new king will abolish the feudal system and slavery, he will improve the country's laws and education, he will introduce the telegraph (1883), he will open the first Siamese railroad, and he will visit European capitals (1897) in a reign that will continue until 1910.

Spain's prime minister Ramon Maria Narvaez, duke of Valencia, dies April 23 at age 68 and absolutist rule is ended by a revolutionary proclamation issued at Cadiz September 18 by the 47-year-old admiral Juan Bautista Topete y Carballo. Isabella II has been attacked in the press for making her court favorite (an actor) Spain's minister of state and her royal forces are defeated September 28 at Alcolea by Marshal Juan Prim y Prats, 54.

Spain's Isabella II flees to France September 29, her enemies declare her deposed, and Marshal Prim forms a provisional government October 5 under the regency of the former governor of Cuba Francisco Serrano y Dominguez, 58. The new government annuls reactionary laws, abolishes the Jesuit order and other religious orders, and establishes universal suffrage and a free press.

The Serbian prince Michael III Obrenović is assassinated the night of June 10 outside Belgrade at age 43. Michael has freed Serbia from Ottoman rule, he is succeeded by his 13-year-old cousin Milan, the new prince will gain full independence for Serbia, he will take the title king in 1882, and will reign until 1889.

Russian forces occupy Samarkand.

The Republican party rejects President Johnson (above) and nominates Civil War hero Ulysses S. Grant for the presidency, selecting Schuyler Colfax of Indiana as his running mate. The Democrats nominate former New York governor Horatio Seymour but the Republicans "wave the bloody shirt" and label the Democratic party the party of treason. Grant wins 53 percent of the popular vote with 214 electoral votes to Seymour's 80.

 Readmission of the seven former Confederate states to the Union (above) is made on the "fundamental condition" that black suffrage be retained in those states forever (*see* Fifteenth Amendment, 1870).

Ratification of the 14th Amendment to the Constitution is proclaimed July 28 by Secretary of State William H. Seward: "All persons born or naturalized in the United States, and subject to the jurisdiction thereof, are citizens of the United States and of the State wherein they reside. No State shall make or enforce any law which shall abridge the privileges or immunities of citizens of the United States; nor shall any State deprive any person of life, liberty, or property, without due process of law. . . ."

Navajo chiefs are forced by U.S. military authorities to sign a treaty agreeing to live on reservations and cease opposition to whites. The August 12 treaty establishes a 3.5-million-acre reservation within the Navajo Nation's old domains (a small portion of the original Navajo holdings), and while the main reservation will grow to embrace nearly 14.5 million acres (25,000 square miles) reaching out from the Four Corners to include northeastern Arizona, northwestern New Mexico, and southwestern Utah most of it will be desert and semidesert with only 68,000 acres of farmland.

The Navajo population has declined from 10,000 to 8,000 during 5 years of military internment. When the survivors return on foot to their homeland they find that their 200,000 sheep have dwindled to just 940 and that they must learn a new way of life if they are to endure.

Congress enacts an Eight-Hour Law for U.S. government laborers but in private industry most laborers work 10 to 12 hours per day.

Cuba begins a 10-year war with Spain which has not adopted some promised reforms and which will continue to permit slavery on the island until the 1880s.

 Rockefeller, Andrews & Flagler begins a battle to drive out competition in the chaotic U.S. petroleum industry as Rockefeller develops a huge market for his kerosene by underselling coal oil and whale oil (*see* 1865). Henry Morrison Flagler, 35, moved west from his native Canandaigua, N.Y., at age 14, he has married Mary Harkness whose uncle Stephen owns a distillery at Bellemore, Ohio, that has supplied

531

1868 (cont.) whiskey sold by Clark & Rockefeller in Cleveland, he joined Rockefeller and Andrews last year, and he will persuade Harkness to loan the firm $70,000 that will permit acquisition of more refineries and pipelines as the firm grows larger and more efficient. With a capacity of 1,500 barrels per day when many competitors refine only one or two barrels, Rockefeller buys his wooden barrels at 96 cents each when other refiners pay $2.50 and he obtains a 15 cent rebate on every barrel he ships via the Lake Shore and Michigan Southern Railroad (*see* Standard, 1870).

An air brake that will permit development of modern rail travel is tested by its inventor George Westinghouse, 22, whose brake has been dismissed as a "fool idea" by Cornelius Vanderbilt. Westinghouse invented a device 3 years ago for rerailing derailed cars, he will make his air brake automatic in 1872, and the Westinghouse air brake will permit an engineer to set the brakes simultaneously throughout a whole train by means of a steam-driven air pump (*see* Union Switch and Signal, 1882).

An automatic railway "knuckle" coupler patented by former Confederate Army major Eli Hamilton Janney, 37, hooks upon impact and replaces the link and pin coupler that endangers the fingers and the lives of brakemen. Janney's coupler prevents excess sway of railcars and will become standard railway equipment in 1888.

Coil and elliptic railroad car springs invented by U.S. engineer Aaron French, 41, make rail travel more comfortable.

The Mississippi River at Quincy, Ill., is spanned by a bridge built by a company organized for the purpose by James Frederick Joy of the Chicago, Burlington & Quincy Railroad (*see* 1854). Joy has spent $1.5 million on the project in defiance of his critics and his judgment will be confirmed when the Burlington's business in the Quincy area doubles next year (*see* Hannibal Bridge, 1869; Eads, 1874).

Atchison Associates is formed in September to build the Atchison, Topeka and Santa Fe Railroad (*see* 1864). The new group will soon run out of money and control will pass to Boston financier Thomas Nickerson. He will be president of the Santa Fe from 1874 to 1880 and will obtain backing from Boston's Kidder, Peabody and from London's Baring Brothers (*see* pooling agreement, 1880).

A standard system of screw threads established by Philadelphia machine-tool maker William Sellers, 44, is adopted by the U.S. government.

The first U.S. open hearth steel furnace is built at Trenton for the New Jersey Steel and Iron Company owned by Cooper Hewitt and Company (*see* 1862).

A process for electroplating with nickel is patented by Boston inventor William H. Rimington who uses a solution prepared by dissolving refined nickel in nitric acid, then precipitating the nickel by the addition of carbonate of potash, washing the precipitate

with water, dissolving it in a solution of sal-ammoniac, and filtering it (*see* nickel steel, 1888).

Tungsten steel is invented by English metallurgist Robert Forester Mushet, 57, whose alloy is much harder than ordinary steel (*see* 1882).

The German Chemical Society is founded by chemist August W. von Hofmann, now 50, whose research in organic chemistry has advanced the aniline dye industry founded by England's W. H. Perkin in 1857. Hofmann has introduced violet dyes made from rosanaline and he will find a way to convert an amide into an amine having one less carbon atom.

Helium is discovered in the spectrum of the sun's atmosphere by amateur English astronomer Joseph Normann Lockyer, 32.

Cro-Magnon man of the Upper Paleolithic period of 38,000 B.C. is discovered in a French cave near Perigueux by archaeologist Edouard Armand Isidore Hippolyte Lartet, 67, who finds four adult skeletons and one fetal skeleton (*see* Neanderthal man, 1856).

Japan's Mitsubishi industrial empire has its beginnings as shipping magnate Yataro Iwasaki, 35, aids the Meiji Restoration (above) by transporting government troops to fight the Tokugawa forces at Edo. The son of a ronin (unemployed samurai warrior), Iwasaki has discovered and explored two remote Japanese islands, he has organized a coastal shipping service, and he is engaged in establishing the industrial complex that will prosper under the name Mitsubishi.

President Grant (above) has gained election with support from bankers and other creditors who want repayment of bonds in gold and who have called the Democrats disloyal for urging payment of the national debt in greenbacks.

U.S. business will use the "due process" clause in the 14th Amendment (above) to resist government intervention (but *see* 1877).

Metropolitan Life Insurance Company is founded at New York by a reorganization of the National Travelers Insurance Company started 5 years ago under the name National Life & Limb Insurance Co. (*see* 1879).

The University of the South begins classes at Sewanee, Tenn., 10 years after its founding by Episcopalian bishops Leonidas Polk and James H. Otey.

Wayne State University is founded at Detroit.

A patent for a typewriter is issued to Christopher Sholes, Carlos G. Glidden, and Samuel W. Soule (*see* Sholes, 1867). Sholes is encouraged by businessmen James Densmore and George Washington Yost to construct a machine whose most commonly used keys will be widely separated on the keyboard to avoid jamming and Sholes aligns the letters in an arrangement that will permit rapid fingering:

QWERTYUIOP
ASDFGHJKL
ZXCVBNM

Densmore and Yost will buy the patent from Sholes, Glidden, and Soule and will persuade the Remington Fire Arms Co. to produce the machine (*see* 1873).

The *Atlanta Constitution* is founded as a morning daily by Colonel Carey W. Styles to lead the fight for reestablishment of state government by Georgians, a fight that will be won in 1871 with the routing of "scalawags and carpetbaggers" (*see* Grady, 1879).

The *Louisville Courier-Journal* is created by a merger of two Kentucky newspapers under the editorship of Henry Watterson who will continue to direct the paper's policy until his death in 1921.

The World Almanac is published for the first time. The *New York World* has compiled a 108-page compendium of facts (mostly political including notes on Southern Reconstruction and the extension of suffrage to blacks in the North), the *Almanac* has 12 pages of advertising, annual publication will end in 1876, but *World* publisher Joseph Pulitzer will revive the *Almanac* in 1886 and it will appear every year thereafter.

The Overland Monthly begins publication at San Francisco. Editor Bret (Francis Brett) Harte, 32, has his story "The Luck of Roaring Camp" published in the second issue.

N. W. Ayer & Son is founded by Philadelphia advertising solicitor Wayland Ayer, 20, whose father has little or no part in the new advertising firm set up to represent farm journals and the religious weekly National Baptist (see "open contracts," 1875).

J. Walter Thompson has its beginnings as U.S. advertising pioneer James Walter Thompson, 20, persuades publishers of magazines such as *Godey's Ladies Book* to let him sell space in all the magazines as if they were one unit. Thompson persuades merchants to buy space in a group of magazines rather than in one at a time, the influx of new advertising enables the publishers to improve the quality of their printing, their paper, and their illustrations and to pay authors and artists better rates while selling their publications at 10 or 15 cents as advertising revenues increase their profits (*see* 1878).

Rand McNally & Company is founded by Chicago printer William Rand and his former apprentice Irish-American printer Andrew McNally, 31, who 9 years ago assumed management of the *Chicago Tribune*'s job printing shop. Specializing initially in passenger tickets, timetables, and related print jobs, Rand McNally will publish its first map in 1872 when it issues a *Railway Guide* and the firm will grow to become the world's leading mapmaker and a major publishing house.

Chambers's Encyclopaedia is published in 10 volumes (*see* 1844).

Fiction   *The Moonstone* by Wilkie Collins.

Juvenile   *Elsie Dinsmore* by U.S. author Martha Farquharson (Martha Farquharson Finley), 40, who will write the seven-volume *Mildred* series and the 12-volume *Pewit's Nest* series plus 26 *Elsie* novels.

Poetry   *Verses on Various Occasions* by John Henry Newman who includes his 1866 poem "The Dream of Gerontius."

Painting   *Zola* by Edouard Manet.

Opera   *Mefistofele* 3/5 at Milan's Teatro alla Scala, with music by Italian composer Arrigo Boito, 26; *Dalibor* 5/16 at Prague, with music by Bedrich Smetana; *Die Meistersinger von Nurnberg* 6/21 at Munich, with music by Richard Wagner; *La Perichole* 10/6 at the Théâtre des Variétées, Paris, with music by Jacques Offenbach; *Genevieve de Brabart* 10/22 at New York, with music by Jacques Offenbach in the first U.S. performance of the opera that contains an aria that will become the hymn of the U.S. Marine Corps (lyrics beginning, "From the halls of Montezuma to the shores of Tripoli . . ." will be published in 1918).

First performances   Symphony No. 1 in G minor (*Winter Dreams*) by Russian composer Petr Ilich Tchaikovsky, 27, 2/15 at Moscow; *A German Requiem* (*Ein Deutsches Requiem*) by Johannes Brahms 4/10 (Good Friday) at St. Stephans's Cathedral, Bremen; Symphony No. 1 in C minor by Austrian composer Anton Bruckner, 43, 5/9 at Linz. The work is too difficult for the orchestra but Vienna will hear a revised version in 1891; Concerto No. 2 in G minor for Piano and Orchestra by Camille Saint-Saëns 5/13 at Paris; *Tales of the Vienna Woods* (*Geschicten aus dem Wienerwald*) by Johann Strauss 6/9 at Vienna.

The Brahms Lullaby is published at Berlin with words from "Des Knaben Wunderhorn" (the second verse is by George Scherer and a Mrs. Natalia Macfarren writes English lyrics).

Hymns   "Lead, Kindly Light" ("Lux Benigna") by English clergyman-composer John Bacchus Dykes, 45, lyrics by John Henry Newman (*see* 1833); "Yield Not to Temptation" by U.S. composer Horatio Richmond Palmer, 34; "O Little Town of Bethlehem" by Philadelphia Holy Trinity Episcopal Church organist Lewis H. Redner, 37, lyrics by church rector Philips Brooks, 33.

Popular songs   "Sweet By and By" by U.S. composer Joseph P. Webster, lyrics by S. Fillmore.

The All-England Croquet Club founded at Wimbledon holds its first championship matches. Played in England for the past 12 to 15 years, the 13th century game will yield in popularity to tennis in the next 10 years (*see* 1874; 1897).

Badminton is invented at England's Badminton Hall, the Gloucestershire residence of the Duke of Beaufort Henry Charles Fitzroy Somerset, 44, whose late father promoted the Badminton Hunt. The new rac-

1868 (cont.) quet game is played with a feathered shuttle-cock which is batted back and forth across a net.

The first recorded bicycle race is held at Paris over a 2-kilometer course at the Parc de St. Cloud.

Americans observe Memorial Day (Decoration Day) for the first time May 30. The holiday commemorates the Union dead of the Civil War.

Philadelphia's Strawbridge & Clothier dry goods emporium opens at 8th Street and Market not far from John Wanamaker's 7-year-old establishment. Quaker merchants Justus Clayton Strawbridge and Isaac Hollowell Clothier are both 30, they sell only for cash, they permit no haggling over prices, and they begin a retail enterprise that will flourish.

Salt Lake City's Z.C.M.I. (Zion's Cooperative Mercantile Institution) opens under the aegis of the Church of Jesus Christ of Latter-Day Saints. Mormons are expected to trade at the new church-owned store which will drive most "Gentile" merchants out of the Utah Territory.

Amsterdam's Amstel Hotel has its beginnings in Dr. Sapphati's Palace by the Amstel. A fourth floor will be added in 1899 as the hotel grows in popularity and becomes one of Europe's grand hotels.

Ecuador and Peru are struck by earthquakes in mid-August and 25,000 die.

John Muir gets his first sight of the Golden Gate at San Francisco after having journeyed to Cuba, to Panama, across the Isthmus to the Pacific, and thence north to California. Muir moves up into the Sierra Nevadas and the Yosemite Valley (*see* 1864; 1876).

U.S. wheat prices fall to 67 cents a bushel, down from a wartime high of $4 and a postwar peak of $1.50.

Production of California wheat has been stimulated by the Crimean War and by the Civil War (*see* Glenn, 1851, 1865). The wheat has a flinty character that makes it well suited to shipment overseas and California flour is shipped not only to the Rockies but also to China, Japan, Britain, and Europe.

The 300,000-acre King-Kenedy ranch in Texas is divided between Richard King and Mifflin Kenedy (*see* 1860). King prospered through the Civil War by steamboat trade in cotton carried to British ships at Brownsville and he will use his fortune to expand the King Ranch on the Neuces River (*see* Kleberg, 1886).

The Peavey Company has its beginnings at Sioux City, Iowa, where grocery firm bookkeeper Frank Hutchison Peavey, 18, persuades his employer and another local businessman that farming will be the backbone of the West and that farmers will need implements and machinery. A nephew of the man who invented the peavey hook in 1857, young Peavey organizes the firm of Booge, Smith and Peavey to supply farmers with such items as McCormick reapers and Case threshing machines (*see* 1874).

The Planet, Jr., seed planter is patented by Moorestown, N.J., inventor Samuel Leeds Allen, 27, who has fastened two tin wash basins together with a metal band into which he has drilled holes and who has attached a handle so that his planter can be rolled over the ground. Allen will open a factory at Philadelphia in 1880 and will expand to produce a fertilizer driller, wheel hoes, potato diggers, celery hillers, and an animal trap (*see* Flexible Flyer sled, 1889).

European vineyards are ruined by Grape Phyloxera (plant lice) that have come from the United States. Roots from New York State vineyards will be used to revive the European industry.

A refrigerated railcar with metal tanks along its sides is patented by Detroit inventor William Davis who dies at age 56. The tanks are filled from the top with cracked ice to transport fish, fresh meats, and fruits (*see* 1869).

A new mechanical cooler for English trains permits quick-cooled milk to be delivered by rail in new metal containers to cities such as London, Liverpool, Manchester, and Glasgow. The milk is far safer than milk from cows kept in town sheds (*see* 1863).

Liverpool meatpacker John Morrell opens the first North American Morrell slaughterhouse at London, Ontario, after having opened Irish plants in the 1850s and a New York buying office in 1864 to obtain American bacon (*see* 1842; Ottumwa, Iowa, 1877).

Chicago meatpacker P. D. Armour adds a second plant as business booms. Armour moved from Milwaukee last year, he and his partner John Plankinton invested $160,000 to take over a slaughterhouse on Archer Avenue, and they have set up under the name Armour and Company (*see* 1864; 1869).

Libby McNeill and Libby is started by Maine-born Chicago meatpacker Arthur A. Libby, 37, who has been working with his younger brother Charles for their Chicago meatpacker uncle John C. Hancock. Arthur has decided there is no future in working for Hancock, he has established his own firm, and he is soon joined by brother Charles and by Archibald McNeill (*see* 1875).

Tabasco sauce is formulated on Avery Island off Louisiana's Gulf Coast, the island that was the Confederacy's chief source of salt during the Civil War. Edmund McIlhenny has married an Avery girl, he has settled on the 2,500-acre island, and he creates a sauce from crushed, aged red peppers, vinegar, and salt to make a piquant mixture that will be popular for generations as a condiment to be served with seafood, especially shellfish.

A sugar-refining method that takes just 8 hours instead of the usual 3 weeks is patented by San Francisco's Claus Spreckels who has gone back to Europe to study sugar manufacturing methods (*see* 1863). The California Sugar Refinery opened by Spreckels will win him the title "Sugar King" (*see* 1883).

The first U.S. production of compressed yeast begins at Cincinnati. Charles Fleischmann has emigrated from Hungary and has joined his brother Maximilian and Cincinnati yeast maker James F. Gaff to form Gaff, Fleischmann and Company (*see* 1865). He sells to local housewives from a basket at first and then by horse and wagon (*see* 1870).

White Rock Spring water has its origin at Waukesha, Wis., whose mineral springs have achieved some repute. New York railroad magnate Richard Dunbar visits Waukesha in quest of a cure for his diabetes, he drinks from one spring, he announces that he has been cured as if by magic, he builds an elaborate pavilion over the spring, and he spreads word of its miraculous powers. Another spring, much deeper than Dunbar's, will be purchased in 1871 by a certain H. M. Colver and it will be promoted as White Rock Spring (*see* Welch, 1887).

The first regularly scheduled U.S. dining car goes into service on the Chicago-Alton Railroad. George M. Pullman's *Delmonico* is named for Delmonico's restaurant at New York (*see* 1861).

Boston's Jacob Wirth Co. opens in Stuart Street where German-American restaurateur Jacob Wirth begins an enterprise that will thrive.

Former U.S. minister to China Anson Burlingame, 48, is appointed by the Peking government to head a delegation to Europe and the United States for the purpose of making treaties. The Burlingame Treaty signed at Washington July 28 defines mutual rights of immigration and emigration (*see* Hayes, 1879).

1869 The world grows smaller with the completion of the Suez Canal (below) and of a transcontinental U.S. rail link.

The Union Pacific Railroad and the Central Pacific join up May 10 at Promontory Point near Ogden in Utah Territory with a ceremony that is echoed by a nationwide celebration as travel time between New York and San Francisco is reduced to just 8 days, down from a minimum of 3 months (and often two or three times that long). The Union Pacific has been built 1,090 miles west from Omaha with $27 million in government "loans" on 13 million acres of public lands, largely with Irish labor, the Central Pacific has been built 680 miles east from Sacramento with similar government subsidies and land grants, largely with Chinese labor, and the road is completed 7 years short of the deadline set by Congress.

Central Pacific workers have laid a record 10 miles of track in 1 day. Racing to meet the Union Pacific crews, the trackmen laid 35,200 60-pound rails April 28 and spiked some 24,000 6-by-8 cross ties, each 8 feet long, to cover the 10 miles.

The Virginia & Truckee Railroad founded by Bank of California officers William Ralston, William Sharon, and Darius Ogden Mills will produce $100,000 per month in dividends for its three owners beginning in 1873 when the Big Bonanza vein opens to increase production of silver from the Comstock Lode discov-

ered in 1859. The railroad will go into receivership in 1937 and will be abandoned in 1950.

Kansas City's Hannibal Bridge opens in July and is the first permanent structure to span the Missouri River. It has been built for the Hannibal & St. Joseph Railroad by James Frederick Joy of the Chicago, Burlington & Quincy (*see* Quincy bridge, 1868).

Cornelius Vanderbilt consolidates the Hudson River and New York Central Railroads to gain a monopoly in rail transport between New York and Buffalo (*see* 1867; Lake Shore and Michigan, 1873).

A cog railway up New Hampshire's 6,293-foot Mount Washington is completed by U.S. inventor Sylvester Marsh, 66, who patented a cog rail in 1867 and who has devised special engines for ascending the highest peak in the Northeastern United States.

The Glory of the Seas is launched by Boston's Donald McKay of 1851 *Flying Cloud* fame. McKay's last sailing ship will remain in service until 1923.

The *Cutty Sark* is launched in England and sails for Shanghai to begin a 117-day voyage with 28 crewmen to handle the clipper ship's 10 miles of rigging that control her 32,000 square feet of canvas. Built for the tea trade, the ship has a figurehead wearing a short chemise, or "Cutty Sark."

The Suez Canal opens to traffic November 17, linking the Mediterranean with the Gulf of Suez at the head of the Red Sea. The canal is 103 miles long, more than 196 feet wide at its narrowest point, and 38 feet deep, and it brings Oriental ports 5,000 miles closer to Europe, 3,600 miles closer to America (*see* 1875; de Lesseps, 1859).

The rickshaw is invented at Yokohama by U.S. Baptist minister Jonathan Scobie to transport his invalid

The Iron Horse brought white ranchers and farmers to lands that had forever been the red man's hunting grounds.

1869 (cont.) wife about town. Improved models will provide employment for Scobie's converts and the gin-rickshaw will be popular in many Oriental cities.

 Chiefs of Japan's four great clans surrender their territories to the Meiji emperor Mutsuhito and the Satsuma, Choshu, Tosa, and Hizen daimyo are made governors of their former provinces (*see* 1868; Satsuma samurai rebellion, 1877).

Hyderabad's Mahbub Ali Pasha begins a 42-year reign as Nizam of a country as large as France in central India's Daccan plateau. A benevolent Moslem despot, the Nizam will order his nobles and landlords to stop collecting rents when times are bad and he will open state grain reserves when harvests are poor so that none will starve, whether Hindu or Moslem (*see* famines of 1896, 1897; Bengal, 1873, 1877).

Canada's Red River Rebellion led by Louis Riel captures Fort Garry (Winnipeg) and establishes a provisional government. A Canadian of mixed Irish and Indian blood, the 25-year-old Riel has inherited leadership from his father of Manitoba's métis (half-breeds) who believe the 2-year-old Dominion government has designs on their rights and land titles (the government has purchased 95 percent of the Northwest Territories from the 299-year-old Hudson's Bay Company for $1.5 million). Riel's government is short-lived but it will be revived (*see* 1885).

Boston expands by annexing Dorchester 2 years after having annexed Roxbury. Charlestown will be annexed in 1873 (*see* 1872 fire).

Greece agrees to evacuate Crete following a Turkish ultimatum (*see* 1908).

British debtors' prisons are abolished.

Britain's Contagious Diseases Act permits police constables to arrest female prostitutes but takes no action against their male customers.

The American Woman's Suffrage Association is started by Susan Brownell Anthony, 49, who breaks with the 3-year-old American Equal Rights Association to campaign and lecture on the need for a Constitutional amendment that will give all U.S. women the right to vote. The newspaper *Revolution* founded by Anthony last year has as its motto, "Men, their rights and nothing more; women, their rights and nothing less" (*see* 1848; 1872).

The new Wyoming Territory enacts a law giving women the right both to vote and to hold office (*see* Utah, 1870).

San Francisco has street riots July 13 against Chinese laborers (*see* Los Angeles, 1871; Chinese Exclusion Treaty, 1880, 1881).

"The only good Indians I ever saw were dead," says Civil War general Philip H. Sheridan while on a tour of the West. The Comanche chief Tochoway (Turtle Dove) has introduced himself saying he is a "good Indian."

The Noble Order of the Knights of Labor is founded by U.S. union organizers who include Uriah Smith Stephens, 48. The Garment Cutters's Association organized by Stephens in 1862 has been dissolved under pressure from Philadelphia employers, the Knights of Labor is a secret society, and its founding comes as National Labor Union president William H. Sylvis dies in July (*see* 1866; AF of L, 1886).

An African expedition to find Scottish missionary David Livingstone, 56, is organized by *New York Herald* publisher James Gordon Bennett, 28, who succeeded his father to the paper's editorship 2 years ago. Bennett commissions Welsh-American newspaper correspondent Henry Morton Stanley, 28, to find Livingstone (*see* 1871).

Wall Street has its first "Black Friday" September 24, and small speculators are ruined. Financiers Jay Gould, James Fisk, and other freebooters including President Grant's brother-in-law attempt to corner the gold market, they drive the price of gold up to $162 per ounce by noon, and they are on their way to destroying half the banks and businesses in New York when Secretary of the Treasury George Boutwell begins selling government gold and brings the price down to $133 inside 15 minutes (*see* 1873).

Goldman, Sachs & Company has its beginnings in a one-room New York basement office opened by investment banker Marcus Goldman who will be joined by his son-in-law Samuel Sachs. The firm will grow to become a major banking house.

New York's Equitable Life Assurance Society writes more than $50 million in new policies, more than all the leading British insurance companies combined (*see* 1862).

Pennsylvania oil wells produce 4.8 million barrels of crude oil (*see* 1859; Rockefeller, 1868, 1870).

Stanley Rule & Level Company at New Britain, Conn., buys the patent rights and business of Leonard Bailey who has invented the first metal plane. The Stanley-Bailey plane is cheap enough for the average craftsman to use, it has a cutter that can be adjusted easily by turning a nut, and it is much easier to sharpen than the wooden planes now widely used.

Union Bag & Paper Company has its beginnings in a patent pool formed by U.S. bagmakers to monopolize control of machines which Union Bag will lease. The company will start manufacturing its own bags in 1875 when it will make 606 million paper bags using sulfite paper from which the lignin has been removed (*see* 1899; Tilghman, 1867).

The "islets of Langerhans" in the pancreas are discovered by German medical student Paul Langerhans, 22. The tiny cells produce glucagon and insulin, ductless gland secretions that will be called hormones beginning in 1904 and that are essential to normal human metabolism (*see* 1860; 1889).

The first state board of health is established by the Massachusetts state legislature.

The Harvard Medical School rejects a demand by President Charles W. Eliot (below) that students be given written examinations. "A majority of the students cannot write well enough," says the dean, but Eliot will elevate standards at the medical school.

Harvard College names M.I.T. chemistry professor Charles William Eliot, 35, as president and Eliot begins a 40-year career in which he will contain all undergraduate studies within the college while developing graduate and professional schools. New York lawyer Christopher Columbus Langdell, 43, will be named dean of the Harvard Law School next year and will introduce the "case study" method of teaching law. Eliot will organize a graduate school of arts and sciences in 1890, and he will make the Harvard Divinity School nonsectarian.

Howard College holds its first classes at Washington, D.C., where it was organized by the Freedmen's Bureau 2 years ago.

Purdue University is founded at Lafayette, Ind.

Southern Illinois University is founded at Carbondale.

The University of Nebraska is founded at Lincoln.

Ursinus College is founded outside Philadelphia.

Pennsylvania State College is founded at Pittsburgh.

Japan's first public elementary school opens in May at Kyoto.

A cable connection with France is completed at Duxbury, Mass. Cyrus Field's 1858 cable ceased to operate after a few weeks but his new one embodies technical improvements that will make it a great success (see first transatlantic wireless message, 1901; transatlantic telephone, 1927).

La Prensa is founded at Buenos Aires by Argentine newspaper publisher Ottavio Paz whose paper will become the largest in South America (see 1870).

Harper's Weekly cartoonist Thomas Nast, 29, draws the first of many caricatures attacking New York's Tweed Ring, a group headed by State Senator William Marcy "Boss" Tweed, 46, that includes the city comptroller, the city chamberlain, and Mayor Abraham Oakey Hall, 43, and that has been bilking the city treasury out of millions of dollars. Nast is a German-American who has been with the *Weekly* since 1862 after 3 years with the *New York Illustrated News*, the *New York Times* will join in the attack on the Tweed Ring, and its ringleaders will be arrested late in 1871 (see donkey symbol for Democratic party, 1870; "Tweed" Courthouse, 1875).

George P. Rowell stabilizes the U.S. advertising business by publishing the first open, accurate list of American newspapers but agents continue to set space rates in the country's 5,411 newspapers (see Ayer, 1875; *Printer's Ink*, 1888).

Fiction *The Idiot* (*Idiot*) by Fedor Dostoievski; *L'homme qui rit* by Victor Hugo; *Phineas Finn* by Anthony Trollope; *Innocents Abroad* by Mark Twain.

Juvenile *Luck and Pluck* by Horatio Alger; *Little Women: Or Meg, Jo, Beth and Amy* by U.S. novelist Louisa May Alcott, 37, whose father Amos Bronson failed in his Fruitlands commune experiment of 1844 and who was herself forced for a time to perform menial work in order to support her family. The book will give the Alcotts financial security.

Theater *The League of Youth* (*De unges forbund*) by Norwegian playwright Henrik (Johan) Ibsen, 41, 10/18 at Christiania's (Oslo's) Christiania Theatre.

First performances Symphony No. 4 in C minor (*Tragic*) by the late Franz Schubert (1816) 2/26 at London's Crystal Palace; Symphony No. 2 (*Antar*) by Russian composer Nikolai Andreievitch Rimski-Korsakov, 25, 3/22 at St. Petersburg; Concerto in G minor for Piano and Orchestra by Edvard Grieg 4/3 at Copenhagen; Mass in E minor by Anton Bruckner 9/30 at the still incomplete Linz Cathedral; *Liebeslieder Walzer* by Johannes Brahms 10/6 at Carlsruhe.

Vienna's Staatsoper (State Opera House) opens off the Karntner Ring Strasse with 2,263 seats.

Opera *Das Rheingold* 9/22 at Munich, with music by Richard Wagner.

Popular songs "Sweet Genevieve" by U.S. composer Henry Tucker, lyrics by George Cooper, 31; "Shoo Fly, Don't Bother Me" by U.S. composer Frank Campbell, lyrics by Billy Reeves.

The Cincinnati Red Stockings complete an undefeated season, winning 56 games and tying one. First professional baseball team, the Red Stockings will remain undefeated until they fall to the Brooklyn Athletics June 14 of next year (see 1867; National League, 1876).

Rutgers defeats Princeton six goals to four November 6 in the first intercollegiate football game which is actually a form of soccer with 25 men on a team (see 1863). Boys from the College of New Jersey at Princeton have come to New Brunswick for the game (see "Boston Game," 1874).

The Cardiff Giant is "discovered" at Cardiff, N.Y., where the huge stone figure of a man has been buried secretly by a group of promoters who claim the figure is a petrified man from biblical times, citing *Genesis* 6:4 ("There were giants in the earth in those days"). Ten feet 4.5 inches long and weighing nearly 3,000 pounds, the figure is exhibited at Syracuse, Albany, New York City, and Boston, thousands pay $1 each to view the Cardiff Giant, and eminent men are taken in by the hoax before it is exposed.

Paris's Samaritaine department store is opened by a merchant named Cognacq and his wife.

Boston's Shreve, Crump & Low is opened at 226 Washington Street, corner of Winter, Summer, and Washington, by jewelers William P. Shreve, Charles H. Crump, and George D. Low whose predecessor firms date back to 1796. Shreve is a nephew of Benjamin Shreve whose Jones, Shreve, Brown & Co. has

1869 (cont.) had a handsome establishment at the corner since 1854 and has long employed Crump. The firm will move to the corner of Tremont and West Streets in 1891 and to the corner of Boylston and Arlington in July, 1930, as it becomes the Tiffany's of New England (*see* Davis Cup, 1900).

Washington's Hecht Company dry goods store is founded by Baltimore merchant Alexander Hecht.

Toronto's T. Eaton Co., Ltd., opens December 8 at 178 Yonge Street with prices clearly marked and with no bartering or credit allowed. Irish-Canadian merchant Timothy Eaton, 35, has had a general store at St. Mary's, his dry goods store will grow to become the largest Canadian retail enterprise after the Hudson Bay Company, and it will have branches at Montreal, Winnipeg, and throughout the Dominion.

 Washington's Pennsylvania Avenue is paved with wooden blocks for a mile between 1st Street and the Treasury Department building at 15th Street.

Garden City, Long Island, is started by New York department store magnate A. T. Stewart whose planned community is designed for families of moderate income.

Nashville's Maxwell House opens in Tennessee. Built at the start of the Civil War, the new hotel has served as barracks, prison, and hospital (*see* coffee, 1886).

Cairo's Mena House hotel opens to serve guests invited to the opening of the Suez Canal (above).

 "Ecology" is coined to mean environmental balance by German zoology professor Ernst Heinrich Haeckel, 35, who is the first German advocate of Charles Darwin's organic evolution theory.

Gypsy moths (*Porthetria dispar*) are brought to Medford, Mass., by French naturalist Leopold Trouvelot who hopes to start a New England silk industry. The moths escape and their larvae (which feed on leaves) will defoliate American woodlands as the moth population explodes in the next 20 years.

U.S. geologist John Wesley Powell, 35, begins explorations of the Green and Colorado Rivers in the Utah and Colorado Territories. Powell lost an arm at Shiloh in 1862 but has led summer expeditions into the Colorado Rockies for the past 2 years between teaching terms at a college in Southern Illinois (*see* 1878).

 The first U.S. plow with a moldboard entirely of chilled steel is patented by James Oliver who has established the Oliver Chilled Plow Works (*see* 1855).

The coffee rust *Hamileia vastatrix* appears in Ceylon plantations and will spread throughout the Orient and the Pacific in the next two decades (*see* 1825). The coffee growing industry will be destroyed and soaring coffee prices will lead to widescale tea cultivation (*see* 1884; tea consumption, 1898).

 A British Customs Duty Act abolishes even nominal duties on food imports (*see* 1850).

Margarine is produced commercially for the first time by France's Hippolyte Mège-Mouries. The product is patented in England under the name "butterine" (*see* 1867; 1871).

The first shipment of fresh meat from Chicago to Boston goes to market aboard the refrigerated railcar developed last year by William Davis but railroads resist losing their traffic in live animals bound for eastern markets (*see* Swift, 1877).

Armour and Company adds beef to its line of pork products (*see* 1868). Armour will start handling lamb next year (*see* chill room, 1872).

Campbell Soup Company has its beginnings in a cannery opened at Camden, N.J., by Philadelphia fruit wholesaler Joseph Campbell and icebox maker Abram Anderson. They can small peas and fancy asparagus (*see* 1894).

H. J. Heinz Co. has its beginnings at Sharpsburg, Pa., where local entrepreneur Henry John Heinz, 24, goes into business with partner L. C. Noble to pack processed horseradish in clear bottles, competing with horseradish packed in green bottles to disguise the fact that it often contains turnip fillers. Heinz has employed several local women for nearly a decade to help him supply Pittsburgh grocers with the surplus from his garden (*see* 1875).

Welch's Grape Juice has its beginnings at Vineland, N.J., where dentist Thomas Bramwell Welch develops a temperance substitute for the intoxicating wine used in his church's communion service. Welch picks 40 pounds of Concord grapes from his backyard, he pasteurizes the juice in his wife's kitchen, he bottles it, and he begins selling "unfermented wine" to nearby churches (*see* 1896; Concord grapes, 1853).

A National Prohibition party is founded in September at Chicago (*see* WCTU, 1874).

Japan's Kirin Brewery is founded at Yokohama under the name Spring Valley Brewery by U.S. entrepreneur William Copeland. Kirin Beer will become the world's second largest selling brand.

The American Woman's Home by Catherine E. Beecher and her sister Harriet Beecher Stowe deplores the popularity of storebought bread which accounts for perhaps 2 percent of all bread eaten in America.

The A&P gets its name as the 10-year-old Great American Tea Company is renamed the Great Atlantic and Pacific Tea Company to capitalize on the national excitement about the new transcontinental rail link (above). Proprietors George Huntington Hartford and George F. Gilman attract customers by offering premiums to lucky winners, they use cashier cages in the form of Chinese pagodas, they offer band music on Saturdays, and they employ other promotional efforts while broadening their line of grocery items to include coffee, spices, baking powder, condensed milk, and soap as well as tea (*see* 1876).

"Beastly contrivances" for limiting the numbers of offspring are condemned by a speaker at the annual meeting of the British Medical Association (*see* Lloyd, Wilde, 1833; U.S. "Comstock Law," 1872).

Abortion of any kind is declared an excommunicatory sin by Pope Pius IX (*see* 1870; 1930).

1870 The periodic table of elements that arranges the 63 known elements according to atomic weight (valency) is published in *The Principles of Chemistry* by Russian chemistry professor Dmitri Ivanovich Mendeléev, 36, at St. Petersburg. German chemist Julius Lothar Meyer, 60, has worked independently to make important contributions to the periodic laws of Mendeléev who begins with lithium and leaves blanks for 29 elements not yet discovered but whose discovery Mendeléev correctly predicts (*see* Dalton, 1803; germanium, 1886; Thompson, 1897).

DNA (deoxyribonucleic acid) is discovered but is not yet suspected of being the basic genetic material involved in conveying heritable characteristics (*see* Watson and Crick, 1953).

Archaeological excavations of ancient Troy are begun by German-American businessman Heinrich Schliemann, 48, who acquired U.S. citizenship in California in 1850, amassed a large fortune in the next 13 years through usurious banking and Crimean War profiteering, and has devoted himself in the past 2 years to studying sites mentioned in the writings of Homer. Schliemann has taken a 17-year-old Greek girl as his bride after studying photographs of possible candidates, he is helped in his work by Sophia Engastromenos Schliemann, the Schliemanns will antagonize professional archaeologists with their destructive amateur excavations, but they will prove Homer to be accurate by finding Priam's city where others said it could not possibly be, and they will uncover at Mycenae the world's greatest golden treasure trove.

 The Spanish queen Isabella II is persuaded to abdicate June 25 at Paris. The 39-year-old exiled queen has reigned since 1843 and is succeeded nominally by her 12-year-old son Alphonso, but the 25-year-old duke of Aosta, son of the Italian king Victor Emmanuel II, is persuaded to accept the crown and begins a brief reign as Amadeo I (*see* 1872).

The Hohenzollern prince Leopold had been offered the Spanish crown (above) and had accepted (after first refusing) but has withdrawn his acceptance at the persuasion of Prussia's Wilhelm I, head of the house of Hohenzollern, following French protests.

France's Napoleon III has wired Wilhelm (who is taking a cure at Ems) demanding a letter of apology and demanding that Wilhelm prohibit the 35-year-old Leopold from accepting any future offer to accept the Spanish crown.

The Ems Telegram (above) is made public by Prussia's Count von Bismarck with Wilhelm's permission and although Bismarck leaves out some details unsuitable for publication he makes it clear that Napo-

leon has tried to humiliate the kaiser and that Wilhelm has refused Napoleon's demands.

France declares war on Prussia July 19 and is invaded by three German armies while the French invade the Saar basin and gain a victory at Saarbrücken.

The Battle of Sedan September 1 ends in disaster for the French First Army Corps commanded by Marshal MacMahon. Napoleon himself surrenders September 2 with 80,000 men, and two German armies begin a 135-day siege of Paris September 19 as the Second Empire collapses (*see* 1871).

Italian troops enter Rome following withdrawal of French troops for the Battle of Sedan (above) and they complete the unification of the Kingdom of Italy under Victor Emmanuel II (*see* 1866).

Ireland's Home Rule Association is founded by lawyer Isaac Butt, 57, who creates a coalition of Protestants and nationalists to work for repeal of the 1801 Act of Union (*see* Parnell, 1881).

 The first through railway cars from the Pacific Coast reach New York City July 24 (*see* 1869).

Construction of the Northern Pacific Railroad begins in Minnesota (*see* 1883).

London's St. Pancras Station opens with a clock from the 1851 Great Exhibition.

French railroad trackage increases to 11,000 miles, up from 5,918 in 1860.

French lawyer Leon Gambetta, 32, pioneers air travel. Gambetta escapes from the besieged city of Paris by balloon October 8 to organize defenses against the Germans and to lead opposition against the imperial government.

The first lightweight all-metal bicycle (and the first with wire-spoked tension wheels) is patented by Coventry machinists James Kemp Starley, 40, and William Hillman who will market their Ariel cycle in September of next year at £8 (£12 with speed-gear; see velocipede, 1861; safety bicycle, 1885).

Steamships account for 16 percent of world shipping but are often slower than clipper ships.

Lloyds of London is incorporated 182 years after its founding but remains a society of private individuals who will increase in number to 6,000 "Names" that will include peers, members of Parliament, and Cabinet ministers. The "Names" will belong to more than 260 syndicates with each Name having unlimited liability for the insurance written by his syndicate (*see* 1887).

The New York Cotton Exchange is founded by 100 firms that include the 25-year-old firm Lehman Brothers of Montgomery, Ala., whose Mayer Lehman is on the Board of Governors. The U.S. cotton crop is 4.03 million bales, up from 3.48 million in 1860.

The first black U.S. legislators take their seats at Washington, D.C., as Hiram R. Revels of Mississippi takes his seat in the Senate and J. H. Rainey of South Carolina enters the House of Representatives.

1870 (cont.) Ratification of the Fifteenth Amendment to the Constitution is proclaimed March 30 by Secretary of State Hamilton Fish. The amendment forbids denial of the right to vote "on account of race, color, or previous condition of servitude" (but *see* Mississippi, 1890; Louisiana, 1898; Alabama, 1902).

A U.S.-British convention for the suppression of the African slave trade is concluded June 3 (*see* Livingstone, 1871).

Full suffrage to women is granted by the Territory of Utah (*see* Wyoming, 1869; Anthony, 1872).

The Japanese Meiji emperor Mutsuhito issues an edict in September ordering his subjects to take last names.

Standard Oil Company of Ohio is incorporated January 10 with John D. Rockefeller as president. He takes 2,667 shares in the $1 million company while 1,333 shares each are taken by his brother William, by Samuel Andrews, by H. M. Flagler, and by Flagler's 52-year-old uncle Stephen Vanderburg Harkness whose loans have helped Rockefeller and his associates (*see* 1868; 1872).

Henry Clay Frick begins construction and operation of coke ovens in the Connelsville area while working for his grandfather Abraham Overholt who dies at age 86 after 60 years of making Old Overholt Whiskey. The 21-year-old Pennsylvania farmboy works with associates and persuades Irish-American Pittsburgh judge-banker Thomas Mellon, 57, to loan the group money for their ventures (*see* 1873).

Sherwin-Williams Paint Company is founded at Cleveland by Vermont-born entrepreneur Henry Alden Sherwin, 28, who takes over a retail paint store with backing from partner Edwin Porter Williams (who puts up most of the $2,000 needed to acquire the store). Sherwin-Williams will acquire a two-story brick cooperage shop on the Cuyahoga River in 1873 to start making its own paints and it will produce 225 tons of paint mixer in the factory's first year of operation (*see* grinding machine, 1876).

"Go west, young man," says *New York Tribune* publisher Horace Greeley who picks up the phrase first published in 1851 by John L. Soule in the *Terre Haute* (Indiana) *Express.* Greeley establishes the Union Colony in Colorado Territory (it will later be. called Greeley). He has been inspired by his agricultural editor Nathan C. Meeker who digs the Territory's first irrigation canal (*see* 1888).

Smith Brothers Cough Drops are patented by William "Trade" and Andrew "Mark" whose bearded faces serve as a trademark (*see* 1847). In 1872 Smith Brothers will become the first company to offer "factory-filled" packages, and production of the cough drops will jump from 5 pounds a day to 5 tons.

The British Red Cross is founded at London.

The first Vatican Council, convened by Pope Pius IX, now 78, is the first great meeting of bishops since the Council of Trent from 1545 to 1563. Papal nuncios intimidate the bishops into favoring a decree of papal infallibility, the bishops vote 533 to 2 July 18 that the pope is infallible when he defines doctrines of faith or morals ex cathedra (from his throne) and that such dicta are "irreformable" and require no "consent of the church." The action produces a wave of anti-church legislation in the German states (*see* Lord Acton, 1887).

Women enter the University of Michigan for the first time since its founding at Ann Arbor in 1817. By the end of the 1870s there will be 154 U.S. coeducational colleges, up from 24 at the close of the Civil War (*see* Oberlin, 1833).

Hunter College for Women is founded at New York.

St. John's University is founded at Brooklyn, N.Y.

Stevens Institute of Technology is founded at Hoboken, N.J.

Syracuse University is founded at Syracuse, N.Y.

Ohio State University is founded at Columbus.

The University of Cincinnati is founded.

The University of Akron is founded.

Chicago's Loyola University has its beginnings in St. Ignatius College founded by Jesuits.

Texas Christian University is founded at Fort Worth.

Texas A&M (Agricultural and Mechanical) is founded.

Hampton Normal and Agricultural Institute is chartered in Virginia (*see* Booker T. Washington, 1881).

Only two Americans in 100 of 17 years and older are high school graduates, a figure that will rise to 76 percent by 1970. Sixty-seven percent of children between 5 and 17 are students, a figure that will rise to 78 percent by 1920 and to 87 percent by 1975.

Britain institutes compulsory education.

The British Post Office issues the world's first postcards October 1.

A rotary press built by Richard Hoe incorporates advances patented by William Bullock and prints both sides of a page in a single operation (*see* 1846; 1865). The *New York Tribune* will install the new press in its pressroom (*see* folding apparatus, 1875).

Production of paper from pulpwood begins in New England (*see* Burgess, 1854; Tilghman, 1867).

The donkey symbol that will identify the Democratic party in the United States for more than a century appears January 15 in *Harper's Weekly* where cartoonist Thomas Nast continues to caricature "Boss" Tweed and his cronies (*see* 1869). No Democrat will gain the presidency until 1884 but Nast will create the elephant symbol for the Republican party in 1874.

La Nacion begins publication at Buenos Aires to rival the paper *La Prensa* founded last year. Descendants of founder General Bartolome Mitre will control *La Nacion* for more than a century.

The *Belfast Telegraph* begins publication in Ireland.

The *Yokohama Mainichi Shinbun* begins publication in Japan but not yet on a daily basis (*see* 1871).

Dodd and Mead publishers is founded by New York publisher Frank Howard Dodd, 28, and his cousin Edward S. Mead. Dodd's father Moses W. Dodd has just retired at age 57 after achieving great success with *Elsie Dinsmore* novels, and the firm will become Dodd, Mead & Co.

Nonfiction "Civilization" by Ralph Waldo Emerson who says in his essay, "Hitch your wagon to a star."

Fiction *The Earthly Paradise* by William Morris is a collection of classical and medieval tales with illustrations by painter Edward Coley Burne-Jones, 34, who met Morris at Oxford's Exeter College; *Lothair* by Benjamin Disraeli; *The Hunting of the Snark* by Lewis Carroll; *Twenty Thousand Leagues Under the Sea* (*Vingt mille lieues sous les mers*) by Jules Verne who delights readers with Captain Nemo and his submarine; *The Mystery of Edwin Drood* by Charles Dickens who has died June 9 at age 58 leaving the work unfinished; *The Story of a Bad Boy* by Boston editor Thomas Bailey Aldrich, 33, who quit school at age 13 upon the death of his father, had a book of verse published 5 years later, and has written an autobiographical account of boyhood in Portsmouth, N. H.; *An Old Fashioned Girl* by Louisa May Alcott.

Poetry *The House of Life* by Dante Gabriel Rosetti who has been persuaded to exhume the unpublished poems he buried with his wife in 1862 and whose work establishes his reputation; "Curfew Must Not Ring Tonight" by U.S. poet Rose H. Thorpe, 20.

Painting *La perle* by J. P. C. Corot; *Un Atelier à Batignolles* by Henri Fantin-Latour.

The Boston Museum of Fine Arts is chartered in February (*see* 1909).

New York's Metropolitan Museum of Art is chartered April 13. Local real estate investor William T. Blodgett buys up three important private collections at Paris in the summer (he pays $116,180 for 174 pictures), the new museum will open in 1872 at 681 Fifth Avenue, and it will move the following year to a mansion on 14th Street (*see* 1880).

Washington's Corcoran Gallery of Art is incorporated May 14. Local banker William Corcoran, 71, made a fortune with his partner George Riggs by raising $5 million to help the government fight the Mexican War of 1846 to 1848, he retired in 1854, and he supported the Confederacy in the Civil War which he sat out in Europe (*see* 1874).

Ballet *Coppelia* 5/25 at the Théâtre Imperiale de l'Opéra, Paris, with music by French composer Clement Philibert Leo Delibes, 34. *Coppelia* will be the comic classic of the ballet repertory as the 39-year-old *Giselle* will be its tragic classic.

Opera *Die Walkure* 6/26 at Munich, with music by Richard Wagner who marries the divorcée Cosima Liszt von Bülow.

First performances *Romeo and Juliet Overture* (*Fantasia after Shakespeare*) by Petr Ilich Tchaikovsky 3/16 at Moscow; Concerto No. 3 in E flat major for Piano and Orchestra by Camille Saint-Saëns 3/17 at the Salle Playel, Paris; *Siegfried Idyll* by Richard Wagner 12/25 (his new wife's birthday) at the Wagners' Villa Tribschen on Lake Lucerne.

The first English bid to regain the America's Cup in ocean racing won by the schooner *America* in 1851 ends in failure as the *Cambria* loses 1 to 0 to the U.S. defender *Magic* in New York Bay.

New York's F. A. O. Schwarz toyshop opens on Broadway at 9th Street. German-American merchant Frederick August Otto Schwarz, 34, has worked in the Baltimore shop of his brother Henry, he will relocate to a large store in West 23rd Street, the store will net nearly $100,000 per year by 1900 selling dolls, doll houses, Kiddie Kars, rocking horses, Swiss music boxes, and the like, and it will become the world's leading toy emporium (*see* 1930).

New York City gets its first apartment house. Built by Rutherford Stuyvesant in East 18th Street from designs by Richard Morris Hunt, 43, the five-story, walk-up building is modeled on Parisian apartment buildings and is complete with concierge, but a New Yorker says, "Gentlemen will never consent to live on mere shelves under a common roof." Rents for six rooms with bath range from $1,000 to $1,500 per year, far beyond the means of New York's tenement-dwelling masses.

French citizens subscribe 40 million francs to build the Church of Sacré Coeur on Montmartre in Paris "in witness of repentance and as a symbol of hope" following the French defeat at Sedan (above).

The Louvre Palace at Paris that was started as a fortress in 1200 is finally completed as a royal residence.

Sandringham House in Norfolk is completed for Queen Victoria after 9 years of construction.

Some 4 million buffalo roam the American plains south of the Platte River by some estimates. They will be virtually wiped out in the next 4 years, leaving perhaps half a million north of the Platte (*see* 1875).

German-American lumberman Frederick Weyerhaeuser, 36, enters into a marketing agreement with other Midwestern lumbermen to form a syndicate whose headquarters Weyerhaeuser will move to St. Paul, Minn., in 1891 as he expands his timberland holdings. The Weyerhaeuser Company will grow to control more than 2 million acres of forest land from Wisconsin and Minnesota to the Pacific Northwest, the largest holding of any U.S. company (*see* 1891).

Parisians go hungry as two German armies begin a 135-day siege September 19 (above). The people eat cats, dogs, even animals from the zoo including the beloved elephants Castor and Pollux (*see* 1871).

The U.S. corn crop tops a million bushels for the first time (*see* 1885).

Mississippi steamboats proceeded majestically up and down the river. Occasional races produced great excitement.

California wheat growers produce 16 million bushels and the $20 million they receive is twice the value of all the gold mined in California for the year (*see* 1868). Great wheat farms in the Livermore and San Joaquin Valleys average nearly 40 bushels per acre with some fields producing 60 per acre (*see* 1889).

The Chinese plum that has been domesticated in Japan is introduced into California where it will be the basis of the modern plum industry (*see* Pellier's Agon plum, 1856).

Some 300 apple varieties are imported from Russia by the U.S. Department of Agriculture. Included are the Duchess, the Red Astrachan, and the Yellow Transparent.

The McIntosh apple is propagated from a seedling found on his Matilda Township homestead by Ontario nurseryman Allan McIntosh whose apple will become the dominant variety in New England and eastern New York.

The Elberta peach is introduced according to some accounts by Marshalville, Ga., orchardman Samuel Rumph who has developed the variety and has named it after his wife (but *see* 1850).

Cattle drives up the Chisholm Trail from San Antonio, Tex., to Abilene, Kan., begin on a huge scale (*see* 1867). The overland treks will bring an estimated 10 million head up the trail in the next 20 years and while Horace McCoy at Abilene does not quite fulfill his promises to Texas cattle ranchers they do receive $20 at Abilene for a steer worth $11 in Texas and that sells at Chicago for $31.50 (*see* 1871).

"Ptomaine" is coined as a word to denote certain nitrogenous compounds easily detectible by smell and in some cases poisonous. The word coined by Italian toxicologist Francesco Selmi will be applied erroneously to food contaminants which are in many cases not detectible by smell.

Porcelain rollers for flour mills are developed in Europe. Flour from rolling mills is whiter than flour from grinding mills since the dark wheat germ is flattened by the rollers into a tiny flake that is sifted off with the bran, but while the whiter flour is reduced in nutrients the loss is significant only in areas where bread remains the major part of human diets.

The porcelain rollers (above) are widely adopted in Austria and Hungary where hard wheats predominate (*see* Glasgow, 1872; Minneapolis, 1879).

Compressed yeast wrapped in tinfoil that permits shipment anywhere is marketed by Cincinnati's Gaff, Fleischmann and the yeast becomes popular even with ultraconservative bakers (*see* 1869; 1876).

Fleischmann's gin is introduced by Gaff, Fleischmann (above).

Canadian distiller Joseph Emm Seagram, 29, joins a 19-year-old firm of Waterloo, Ontario, millers and distillers that he will own by 1883. Joseph E. Seagram and Sons will become a leading Canadian whiskymaker (*see* Bronfman, 1928).

Mott's Cider and Mott's Vinegar voyage round Cape Horn to California by clipper ship in 1,000-case lots (*see* 1842; Duffy-Mott, 1900).

Banana traffic from the Caribbean to North American ports is pioneered by Wellfleet, Mass., fishing captain Lorenzo Dow Baker, 30, who is part owner of the 70-ton two-masted schooner *Telegraph of Wellfleet*. Baker buys 1,400 coconuts at 12 for a shilling and 608 bunches of bananas at a shilling each in Port Antonio, Jamaica, and puts in 11 days later at Jersey City, N.J., with the fruit beginning to turn yellow. An Italian merchant buys the fruit at Baker's offering price of $2.25 per bunch while the coconuts sell at almost no profit (*see* 1871).

The U.S. canning industry puts up 30 million cans, up from 5 million in 1860, despite the fact that it employs scarcely 600 people (*see* 1894; 1900).

The first U.S. food trademark (#82) registered by the U.S. Patent Office (above) is a red devil. It is granted to Boston's William Underwood & Co. for its "deviled entremets" (*see* 1867; 1881).

Kansas City's population reaches 32,260, up from 3,500 in 1865, as the year-old Hannibal Bridge across the Missouri helps attract residents. Chicago's population reaches 300,000, up from 93,000 in 1857.

1871 A united German Empire proclaimed January 18 in the Hall of Mirrors at Versailles inaugurates the Second Reich that will continue until November, 1918 (the First Reich was the Holy Roman Empire ended by Napoleon in 1806). Prussia's Wilhelm I is emperor and the first chancellor is Count von Bismarck who has joined the four German kingdoms of Prussia, Bavaria, Saxony, and Württemberg with the five grand duchies, 13 duchies and principalities, and three free cities (Bremen, Hamburg, and Lübeck) that have kept Germany fragmented.

Paris capitulates to German troops January 28, the French assembly accepts a peace treaty March 1, a definitive treaty is signed at Frankfurt May 10, and France agrees to cede Alsace and part of Lorraine, to pay the Germans an indemnity of 5 billion francs, and to permit an army of occupation to remain on French soil until the indemnity is paid.

Napoleon III is formally deposed March 1 by the French assembly meeting at Bordeaux because Paris has been taken over by a Communist uprising (below), the assembly declares Napoleon "responsible for the ruin, invasion, and dismemberment of France," he is released from the castle of Wilhelmshohe near Cassel where the Germans have held him prisoner, and he retires to England where he will die early in 1873 (see Prince Louis, 1879).

Basutoland is absorbed by Britain's Cape Colony and Britain annexes the diamond mines of Kimberley (below; see 1867; Rhodes, Barnato, 1880).

The Treaty of Washington signed May 8 refers settlement of the Canadian-U.S. border to the German emperor (above), refers settlement of claims against Britain for damage by the Confederate cruiser *Alabama* in the Civil War to an international commission at Geneva, and provides for partial settlement of a dispute in the North Atlantic fishery (see 1877).

British Columbia joins the Dominion of Canada July 1 with the understanding that a transcontinental railroad is to be started within 2 years and completed within 10.

The Paris Commune established in March is defeated at the end of May in a "Bloody Week" that sees 20,000 to 30,000 Parisians killed at the barricades, a death toll greater than that in the Reign of Terror of 1793 to 1794. The statesman Louis Adolphe Thiers, now 73, has been elected president of the Third Republic by the assembly February 16, the troops he has sent to seize the cannon of the Commune have refused to fire and have fraternized with the crowd, Generals Lecomte and Thomas have been seized by the crowd and executed along with hostages who have included the Archbishop Georges Darboy.

A Kulturkampf against Roman Catholics begins in Prussia (see Jesuits, 1872).

Parliament legalizes British labor unions.

Japan's restored Meiji government outlaws discrimination against the Burakumin—outcastes who live in thousands of ghettos throughout the country where for centuries they have been employed in leather tanneries. The smell of the tanneries has caused the Burakumin to be shunned by other Japanese and to be called officially "Eta" (full of filth) during Japan's long feudal period. Despite the edict from Tokyo, the Burakumin will for more than a century be denied access to other jobs and to public schools and to non-ghetto residential areas.

Scottish missionary-explorer David Livingstone sees hundreds of African women shot dead by Arab slavers or drowned in the Lualaba River at Nyangwe while trying to escape. He sends home an account of the incident to England where indignant efforts are made to force suppression of the slave trade by the sultan of Zanzibar (see 1869; 1873).

More than a dozen Chinese are killed in a race riot at Los Angeles (see 1877).

Mormon leader Brigham Young, now 70, is arrested at Salt Lake City in Utah Territory on charges of polygamy (he has 27 wives) (see 1847). The polygamy issue will delay Utah statehood until 1896.

The Indian Appropriation Act passed by Congress March 3 makes Indians wards of the federal government and discontinues the practice of according full treaty status to agreements made with tribal leaders. The act does not abrogate existing treaties but it forbids recognition of Indian tribes as nations or independent powers.

The Chiricahua Apache chief Cochise is tracked down in Arizona Territory and forced to surrender by General George Crook who has assumed command of the army in Arizona and has used other Apache as scouts (see 1862; 1872).

Dodge City, Kan., has its beginnings in a sod house built on the Santa Fe Trail 5 miles west of Fort Dodge to serve buffalo hunters. Within a year the settlement will have grown into a town with a general store, three dance halls, and six saloons and will soon be shipping hundreds of thousands of buffalo hides, buffalo tongues, and buffalo hindquarters to market via the Santa Fe Railroad that will reach Dodge City next year (see 1868; 1877).

Birmingham, Ala., is founded and incorporated at a site surrounded by iron ore, coal, and limestone deposits that were exploited in the Civil War to produce Confederate cannonballs and rifles. The town takes its name from Birmingham, England.

Kimberley is founded in South Africa and is soon the center of a great diamond industry (see 1867; 1872).

New York Herald correspondent Henry M. Stanley finds David Livingstone (above) in late October at Ujiji on Lake Tanganyika. "Dr. Livingstone, I presume," says Stanley, and he joins Livingstone in exploring the northern end of the lake, proving conclusively that the Rusizi River runs into the lake and not out of it (see 1869).

The Pennsylvania Railroad establishes a connection to New York 2 years after gaining entry to Chicago and St. Louis (see 1857; Pennsylvania Station, 1910).

The Texas Pacific Railroad that will end the Chisholm Trail cattle drives is chartered by Congress and is given a land grant but while the road's 1,800 miles of main line will extend from New Orleans to El Paso via Shreveport, Texarkana, Dallas, and Fort Worth, it will never reach the Pacific (see 1880; 1885).

1871 (cont.) Texans drive 700,000 longhorns 700 miles from San Antonio north to the Abilene stockyards, moving at 12 miles per day through open, unsettled country that provides abundant grass and water for the livestock on the "Long Drive" up the Chisholm Trail (*see* 1870).

J. G. McCoy of Abilene has been unable to collect on his contract with the Kansas, Pacific whose officers say they never anticipated such volume, but McCoy has become mayor of Abilene and has profited in real estate and other enterprises (*see* 1867).

The New York ferryboat S.S. *Westfield* explodes July 11 blowing 104 people to pieces. Her boiler was so corroded that "a knife blade could cut through the metal" but steamboat inspection remains lax and there are no rigorous design or maintenance codes.

The first full shipload of bananas lands at Boston July 28 aboard Dow Baker's 85-ton schooner *Telegraph* 14 days out of Kingston, Jamaica. Seaverns & Co. sells the fruit on commission and the firm's young buyer Andrew Preston assures Baker that a market exists for all the bananas he can obtain (*see* 1870; 1885).

South American railroad builder Henry Meiggs wins a contract from Costa Rican president Tomas Guardia to construct a national railway from Port Limon on the Caribbean 149 miles up to the country's mountain capital of San José. Meiggs is still engaged in building railroads up and down the Peruvian coast and into the Andes (*see* 1861), but he enlists the help of his nephew Minor Cooper Keith, 23, and three of Keith's brothers. The brothers will soon die of yellow fever, Meiggs himself will die at Lima in 1877, Keith will import 1,500 workmen from New Orleans, he will run out of money after building 60 miles of track, at least 4,000 men will die building the railroad, but Keith will plant bananas in the Zent Valley behind Port Limon to establish a new source of funds. He will marry the daughter of Costa Rica's ex-president José Maria Castro, and by 1883 he will be supplying bananas to shipping companies in Costa Rica, Panama, Nicaragua, and Colombia, earning enough money to complete the railroad to San José in 1890 (*see* United Fruit Company, 1899).

The first commercial Russian oil wells are sunk in the Baku suburb of Balakany on the Apsheron Peninsula that juts into the Caspian Sea (*see* 1823; 1873).

Burmah Oil Company has its beginnings in the Rangoon Oil Company started by British colonial entrepreneurs in Burma.

Machinery for separating naphtha from crude petroleum is patented by Brooklyn N.Y., oilman Henry Huttleston Rogers, 31, who went into the Pennsylvania oil fields in 1861 and who has been associated for the past 4 years with Charles Pratt & Co. in the operation of a Brooklyn refinery. Pratt, 41, and Rogers will join Rockefeller's Standard Oil Company in 1874 and Rogers will push the idea of pipeline transportation which he has originated (*see* 1866; 1864).

The 1836 Colt revolver is redesigned to extend its effective range.

The "Mauser Model 1871" breech-loading rifle is adopted by the Prussian Army (above). The rifle has been perfected by German inventor Peter Paul Mauser, 33, and his brother Wilhelm, 37, who will invent a pistol, a revolver, and a repeating rifle (the younger brother will invent the Mauser magazine rifle in 1897).

New York's Roosevelt Hospital opens in 59th Street west of Ninth Avenue. Built with a gift from James Henry Roosevelt, 71, it is one of the few U.S. hospitals to offer private rooms (at $3 to $4 per day) at a time when New York's Bellevue and most other hospitals have only crowded wards, many of them crawling with rats.

Drexel, Morgan & Co. is organized with offices in Philadelphia and on New York's Wall Street, by New York banker J. P. (John Pierpont) Morgan, 34, who joins with members of Philadelphia's Drexel family to create a powerful new banking house (*see* Drexel, 1838; Edison, 1882).

State supervision of grain warehouses begins in Illinois. When the Supreme Court sustains the action in 1877 it will lay the basis for all subsequent regulation of U.S. business by government.

Parliament abolishes purchase of British Army commissions (*see* Cardigan, 1854).

Germany goes on the gold standard December 4.

Japan's ministry of education is reorganized to promote universal education.

Smith College is established at Northampton, Mass. The late Sophia Smith inherited a fortune from her brother Austin in 1861 and left the money at her own death last year to found a college for women that will open in 1875.

The University of Arkansas is founded at Fayetteville.

Cables are laid from Vladivostok to Shanghai, Hong Kong, and Singapore via Nagasaki.

The first regular Japanese government postal service begins between Tokyo and Osaka.

Metal type and printing presses are introduced into Japan and the first Japanese daily newspaper begins publication.

Fiction *The Possessed* (*or The Demons*) (*Besy*) by Fedor Dostoievsky.

Juvenile *Tattered Tom* by Horatio Alger, who begins a new series; *Little Men* by Louisa May Alcott.

Painting *Max Schmitt in a Single Scull* by U.S. painter Thomas Eakins, 27; *Woodland Scene* by George Inness; *The Dream of Dante* by Dante Gabriel Rossetti.

Photography is advanced by British inventor Richard Leach Maddox, 55, who makes an emulsion of silver bromide using gelatin in place of collodion (*see* Sayce and Bolton, 1864). Gelatin emulsions reduce the exposure time a photographer needs from 15 seconds to as little as 1/200th of a second and Maddox's lead will be followed by J. Kennett who will market a dry, washed emulsion which a photographer can dissolve in water and use as a coating on glass to produce his own photographic plates (*see* Bolton, 1874).

 Barnum's Circus opens at Brooklyn, N.Y., and "The Greatest Show on Earth" grosses $400,000 in its first season. Showman P. T. Barnum has made a fortune promoting Jenny Lind (*see* 1850), he will enlarge his show next year, he will make it the first circus to travel the country by rail (using 65 railcars), and by 1874 he will be playing to 20,000 people per day, charging 50 cents per ticket and taking in twice his huge $5,000 per day operating cost (*see* Barnum & Bailey, 1881).

 Opera *Indigo and the Forty Thieves* 2/10 at Vienna's Theatre-an-der-Wien, with music by Johann Strauss who includes his new waltz "Ja, so singt man in der stadt wo ich geboren bin"; *Aida* 12/24 at the Cairo Opera House, with music by Giuseppe Verdi who completed the work too late for the Suez Canal opening in 1869.

Stage musical *Thespis* (or *The Gods Grown Old*) 12/26 at London's Gaiety Theatre, with music by Arthur S. Sullivan, book and lyrics by London barrister William Schwenck Gilbert, 35. The burlesque is the first Gilbert and Sullivan collaboration.

Hymn "Onward Christian Soldiers" by Arthur S. Sullivan with lyrics by London clergyman Sabine Baring-Gould, 37.

Popular songs "Chopsticks" ("The Celebrated Chop Waltz") by English composer Arthur de Lulli (Euphemia Allen), 16.

London's Albert Hall (The Royal Albert Hall of Arts and Sciences) opens with seating for 6,036.

 England's *Livonia* is defeated 4 to 1 in its bid to regain the America's Cup in ocean racing. The U.S. defenders *Columbia* and *Sappho* win two races each.

Poker is introduced to Queen Victoria at a royal party in Somersetshire by U.S. ambassador to Great Britain Robert Cumming Schenck, 62, who shows the queen how to play and at her request writes down the rules, the first written codification of the game (*see* 1821). Phrases such as "ace in the hole," "bluff," "call a bluff," "stand pat," "four-flush," "put your cards on the table," and "pass the buck" will be derived from poker.

 The Tuileries Palace at Paris is consumed by fire during the "Bloody Week" in May (above) and much of the Louvres Palace is gutted.

The Chicago Fire rages from October 8 to 9 and destroys 3.5 square miles of the city, killing perhaps 250. The fire has allegedly been started by a cow kicking over a kerosene lantern in Dekoven Street.

More than a million acres of Michigan and Wisconsin timberland are destroyed in a forest fire started by sparks from the Chicago Fire (above). The forest fire continues from October 8 to October 14 and more than 1,000 die in the logging town of Peshtigo, Wis., and in 16 surrounding communities in the worst fire tragedy in the recorded history of North America.

Passenger pigeons nesting in Wisconsin occupy 750 square miles and will continue such mass nestings until 1878 despite the October fire (above; *see* 1874).

 U.S. wheat and flour exports total 50 million bushels, while corn exports total 8 million.

Germany raises tariff barriers against food imports in a move to remain independent of France or any other country in food supply. German wheat prices will nevertheless fall 27 percent in the next 20 years and will fall 30 percent in Sweden, ruining many farmers and encouraging emigration to America.

Land planted to grain in Britain will decline by more than 25 percent in the next three decades as the railroads open up the western United States, making it unprofitable for British farmers to compete.

 The U.S. Arctic whaling fleet is trapped at the end of August by the earliest winter in memory. Thirty-two out of 39 vessels are frozen fast in the ice, New Bedford loses $1.5 million in shipping, but the seven surviving ships are able to carry all 1,200 men of the fleet safely back to New England ports.

A resolution "for the protection and preservation of the food fishes of the coasts of the United States" is signed into law by President Grant who names Spencer F. Baird to head a new U.S. Fish Commission (*see* shad, 1873).

 C. A. Pillsbury & Company is founded by Minneapolis miller Charles Alfred Pillsbury, 29, with his brother Fred, his father George, and his uncle John Sargent Pillsbury who has been governor of Minnesota. The founder became a partner 2 years ago in a small flour mill, he increased its daily capacity from 150 barrels to 200 by improving its equipment, he has turned a profit of $6,000, and he uses it to start the new firm (*see* Pillsbury's Best XXXX, 1872).

Millwright George T. Smith, 30, has made improvements in the 1865 LeCroix middlings purifier, employing a traveling brush that keeps the cloth clean and thus permits better control of air currents. Smith is persuaded to join C. A. Pillsbury & Company (above) as chief miller.

Edmund LeCroix is retained by George H. Christian to install purifiers in the Minneapolis flour mill set up by C. C. Colden in 1866 and it becomes the first large mill to be so equipped (*see* 1874).

Margarine production begins in the Netherlands as butter merchants Jan and Anton Jurgens open the world's first fully operative margarine factory at Oss after having acquired rights from Hippolyte Mège-Mouries for 60,000 francs per year (*see* 1869; United States, 1881; Jurgens, 1883).

1871 (cont.) Mountain Valley Mineral Water is offered for sale at Hot Springs, Ark., by local pharmacist John Green who has recently moved to Hot Springs from Tennessee and who has bought the Locket Spring 12 miles out of town. Green and his brother will sell their company in 1879 to St. Louis entrepreneur W. N. Benton who will promote the mineral water with testimonial health claims as a cure for dyspepsia, dropsy, torpid liver, and Bright's disease (*see* 1827).

Huntington Hartford of the A&P sends emergency rail shipments of tea and coffee to Chicago, most of whose grocery stores have burned in the great October fire (above). When the city is rebuilt, Hartford will open A&P stores (*see* 1869; 1876).

The Dominion of Canada created in 1867 takes its first census as it is joined by British Columbia (above). The country has 1,082,940 French, 846,000 Irish, 706,000 English, 549,946 Scots, and 202,000 Germans (*see* Ukrainians, 1891).

The U.S. population reaches roughly 39 million while Germany (above) has 41 million, France 36.1 million (with 1.8 million in Paris), Italy 26.8, Great Britain 26, Ireland 5.4, Japan 33, and Brazil 10 million including 1.5 million slaves.

Abortion is punishable by up to 5 years in prison under the criminal code enacted by the new German Empire (above).

1872 The Erie Ring of Wall Street speculators James Fisk and Jay Gould collapses following the January 6 shooting of Fisk by Edward S. Stokes, a business rival and a rival for the favors of Fisk's mistress, the actress Josie Mansfield. Fisk and Gould have been looting the Erie Railroad's treasury and Fisk's death draws attention to the corruption that has flourished under the Grant administration.

The *New York Sun* begins an exposure of the Crédit Mobilier formed in 1867 by Union Pacific directors.

The federal income tax imposed during the Civil War is abolished by Congress.

Britain is held responsible for Civil War depredations by the *Alabama* and other Confederate cruisers in a September 14 ruling by a Geneva court of arbitration that awards the United States government $15.5 million in damages.

A Gunpowder Trade Association organized by E. I. du Pont de Nemours controls prices of blasting and hunting powder in a market glutted with war surplus powder. Du Pont supplied the Union armies with 4 million pounds of explosives, the company is rich with profits gained in the war, it undersells competitors who do not join the association, and it forces them to yield or go out of business (*see* 1861; 1899).

John D. Rockefeller's Standard Oil Trust refines 10,000 barrels of kerosene per day and is the largest operation of its kind in the world (*see* 1870). In addition to rebates received from railroads, the Trust receives drawbacks—fixed rates that the railroads pay for every barrel of oil they carry for a Standard Oil competitor—and competitors pay five times the freight rate enjoyed by Standard Oil (*see* 1877).

The world's first industrial dynamo is perfected by Belgian electrician Zenobe Theophile Gramme, 46, who employs a ring winding of the same type invented independently by Italian physicist Antonio Pacinotti in 1860 (*see* Faraday, 1831).

Spanish Carlists (supporters of the 24-year-old Bourbon pretender to the throne) are routed at Oroquista by the forces of the new king Amadeos I, and Don Carlos has to take refuge in the Pyrenees (*see* 1873).

Sweden's Charles IV dies at Malmo September 18 at age 46 after a reign of 13 years and is succeeded by his 43-year-old brother who begins a reign as Oscar II that will continue until 1907.

Ethiopia's late emperor Theodore is succeeded by the ruler of Tigre who will reign until 1889 as the king of kings Johannes IV.

Radical Republicans renominate President Grant despite the corruption of his administration; liberal Republicans nominate New York publisher Horace Greeley of the *Tribune*. Greeley gains support from civil service reformer Carl Schurz, from malcontent Republicans who have not shared in the spoils of war and of politics, and from Democrats, but Grant wins re-election with 56 percent of the popular vote (and with 286 electoral votes to Greeley's 66). Greeley dies November 29 at age 61. Congress votes December 2 to appoint a committee to investigate the Crédit Mobilier.

Japan institutes universal military service.

Japan gets her first railway. The 18-mile line between Tokyo and Yokohama opens October 14 with ceremonies at the Shinbashi and Yokohama terminals. Financed by the Oriental Bank of England, it has been built by 16 English engineers.

A system of automatic electric signaling for railroads patented by Irish-American engineer William Robinson, 32, will be the basis for all modern automatic railroad block signaling systems.

The New York, New Haven and Hartford Railroad Company is organized with 188 miles of track that will grow to 1,800 miles. The New York and New Haven has merged with the Hartford and New Haven to create the new company and to end a competitive struggle that has ensued for nearly 20 years (*see* Shore Line route, 1893).

Boston radiates out from its City Hall to a distance of 2.5 miles, half a mile farther than in 1850, as a consequence of horsecar transportation which by 1887 will extend the congested urban area another 1.5 miles from City Hall (*see* 1852; 1857; subway, 1897).

The Jesse James gang robs its first passenger train in June after hearing that the Rock Island's eastbound train from Council Bluffs, Iowa, will be carrying $75,000 in gold. The robbers part the rails in front of the oncoming train just west of Adair on the main line between Council Bluffs and Des Moines. Engineer John Rafferty is unable to stop the train in time and is killed when his locomotive is derailed, but the gold has been delayed for another train and the James gang gets away with a mere $3,000 from the express messenger and another $3,000 from the passengers (*see* 1866; Northfield, Minn., 1876).

The Chicago & Rock Island (above) has won a government contract for all mail west of Chicago by beating the Chicago and North Western in a race between Chicago and Council Bluffs. The Rock Island 3 years ago bought an eight-wheel locomotive that had been built for the 1867 Paris International Exposition by the Grant Locomotive Works of Paterson, N.J., and the much-publicized steam engine with her boiler encased in German silver, with solid silver headlights, handles, whistles, and pumps, has beaten the Chicago and North Western by steaming the distance in 27 hours with a 19-year-old engineer in the cab and with flagmen at every crossing to keep livestock from blocking the rail bed.

The brigantine *Mary Celeste* clears New York harbor in November for Genoa with 10 men who will never be seen again. The ship will be discovered 3 weeks later sailing on a starboard tack with cargo and stores intact but without a soul aboard, a "ghost" ship whose mystery will never be solved.

Equal pay for equal work in U.S. federal employment is assured by a new law passed by Congress after lobbying by feminist Belva Ann Lockwood, 42.

Spiritualist Victoria Claflin Woodhull, 34, announces her candidacy for the U.S. presidency. A protégée of Commodore Vanderbilt (below), Mrs. Woodhull has made a fortune in Wall Street as has her sister the "magnetic healer" Tennessee Celeste Claflin, 26, and she has demanded that women be given the right to vote. But the cause of women's rights is damaged by *Woodhull and Claflin's Weekly* which defends abortion, advocates free love, and recommends licensing and medical inspection of prostitutes.

Susan B. Anthony and other women's rights advocates are arrested at Rochester, N.Y. for attempting to vote in the presidential election November 5.

Chiricahuas in Arizona Territory are promised a reservation separate from that of the Mescalero Apache and they give up their resistance to the whites. Their leader Cochise, now 60, signs a treaty with the Indian commissioner General Oliver O. Howard and retires to the new Arizona reservation where he will die in June of 1874.

Germany's Jesuits are expelled June 25 under an imperial law that is part of the new Kulturkampf.

Japanese Buddhist priests are permitted to take wives and to eat meat (*see* below).

The American Public Health Association is founded.

The Ebers papyrus discovered at Thebes by German Egyptologist Georg Moritz Ebers, 35, is the oldest known compendium of ancient Egyptian medial writings.

A cuneiform tablet deciphered by British Museum assistant George Smith, 32, bears the Gilgamesh legend of 3,000 B.C. with an Assyrian account of a great flood that conforms closely with the biblical account. Smith announces his discovery in December at a meeting of British archaeologists (*see* 1837; 1844).

German botanist Ferdinand Julius Cohn, 44, publishes the first major work on bacteriology.

Louis Pasteur publishes a classic paper on fermentation showing that it is caused by microorganisms.

"The Object and Manner of Our Lord's Return" by Pittsburgh evangelist Charles Taze Russell, 20, announces that the second coming of Christ will occur in the fall of 1874 without the awareness of mankind. Russell founds the International Bible Students' Association (*see* 1878).

The Farquharson Rifle patented by English gunsmith John Farquharson is a single-shot rifle with a falling-block action. George Gibbs of Bristol begins production of the rifle that will be produced in numerous variations by Webley, Bland, Westley Richards, and various European firms.

Calcium borate deposits from which borax can be derived are discovered near Columbus, Nev., by prospectors Francis Marion Smith, 26, and William Tell Coleman, 48, whose name will be used for the mineral: it will be called colemanite. Smith and Coleman will organize the Pacific Coast Borax Company and will gain a virtual world monopoly in the material used for making glass, porcelain, enamel, in tanning leather, and for soap. Smith will acquire additional borax deposits in California's Death Valley and will haul his ore out in huge mule-drawn wagons that will inspire the trademark "Twenty-Mule Team Borax."

Commercial production of celluloid begins under a patent obtained by Albany, N.Y., printer John Wesley Hyatt, 35, and Rockford, Ill., inventor Isaiah Smith Hyatt, in 1869 (*see* Parkes, 1855). The Hyatts have organized the Newark Celluloid Manufacturing Company, they have derived the word "celluloid" from cellulose and "oid" (meaning like), they will obtain a trademark for the word next year, and they will sell their celluloid as a substitute for ivory, horn, amber, tortoise-shell, and the like for use in billiard balls, piano keys, men's collars, buttons, dental plates, combs, and other items (*see* Eastman, 1889).

B. F. Goodrich Company is founded at Akron, Ohio, by rubbermaker Benjamin Franklin Goodrich, 30, who has been in the business since 1869. By the time he dies in Colorado in 1888 at age 46, Goodrich's company will be well established (*see* tires, 1899).

Pirelli and Co. has its beginnings at Milan where Italian entrepreneur Giovanni Battista Pirelli opens a shop that will grow to become a giant rubber company with large plantations in Java and with factories

1872 (cont.) in England, Spain, Argentina, and other countries. In less than 50 years Pirelli and Co., will have more than 30,000 employees worldwide and will have extended its activities beyond rubber to cotton mills, copper drawing mills, and other industrial enterprises.

A machine to make flat-bottomed paper bags with side pleats is patented by U.S. inventor Luther Chicks Crowell who has improved on the flat-bottomed bag machine of 1850. Crowell's machine will be improved in 1883 by a machine that will make the automatic or "flick" bag, a self-opening bag with a flat bottom and side pleats (*see* Union Bag, 1869).

Kimberly and Clark, Inc., has its beginnings in a Neenah Wis., paper mill started in the Menominee Indian Reservation by four entrepreneurs whose firm will become a major U.S. paper products manufacturer. John A. Kimberly is a part-owner of Neenah's general store while Charles B. Clark is a New York greenhorn (*see* Kotex, 1918).

Vanderbilt University is founded at Nashville, Tenn., with a grant from Commodore Vanderbilt of the New York Central.

The University of Oregon is founded at Eugene.

The University of Toledo is founded in Ohio.

Strasbourg University is founded in Alsatia.

Compulsory education in Japan is ordered in August by the new Meiji government.

The *Boston Daily Globe* begins publication March 4 with an eight-page edition that is twice the size of any of the city's other 10 dailies. Four Boston papers have morning and evening editions, most sell for 4 cents a copy, combined circulation is less than 170,000 in a metropolitan area of 500,000 with half the population in the city proper. Even the 26-year-old *Boston Herald* at 2 cents has a circulation of no more than 17,000.

Western Electric Company is founded April 2 to sell telegraph equipment and to pursue experiments on an electric telephone by company cofounder Elisha Gray, 37. The president of Western Electric is Anson Stager who is supported in his sales efforts by Enos Melancthon Barton, 29, while Gray works on his telephone (*see* Bell, 1876).

An Australian telegraph line opens to connect Adelaide with Port Darwin and is soon extended to link Australia with Java, India, and Europe.

Fiction *Under the Greenwood Tree* by English novelist-architect Thomas Hardy, 32; *Erewhon* by English satirist Samuel Butler, 37, is a utopian novel about a country devoid of machinery (the novel is issued anonymously); *Through the Looking Glass* by Lewis Carroll; *The Fiend's Delight* and *Nuggets and Dust Panned Out in California* by former San Francisco *News Letter* editor Ambrose Gwinnett Bierce, 30, who has left for a 3-year stay at London.

Painting *The Artist's Mother* (*Mrs. George Washington Whistler* or *Arrangement in Grey and Black No. 3*) by James A. McNeill Whistler; *Le Foyer de la Danse* by French painter Hilaire German Edgar Degas, 38; Gustave Doré paints London scenes. George Catlin dies at Jersey City, N.J., December 23 at age 76.

Theater *L'Arlesienne* (*The Woman of Arles*) by Alphonse Daudet 10/1 at the Vaudeville Théâtre, Paris (*see* Bizet music below).

Sarah Bernhardt (*née* Rosine Bernard), 28, begins a 10-year career with the Comédie-Française at Paris. "The Divine Sarah" will gain world renown and will continue acting even after having a leg amputated in 1914. Italian actress Eleanora Duse, 13, begins a 27-year career by appearing at Verona as Juliet in the Shakespeare tragedy of 1595.

Motion picture pioneer Eadweard Muybridge takes a sequence of photographs showing a horse running. Central Pacific Railroad president Leland Stanford has asked the 42-year-old English-American photographer to prove photographically that all four feet of a running horse are off the ground at the same time at some point in the animal's stride (*see* 1893).

Opera *Djamileh* 5/22 at the Opéra-Comique, Paris, with music by Georges Bizet, libretto from the Alfred de Musset poem *Namouna*; *La Princess Jaune* 6/12 at the Opéra-Comique, Paris, with music by Camille Saint-Saëns.

First performances *La Ronet d'Omphale* (*Omphale's Spinning Wheel*) symphonic poem by Camille Saint-Saëns 4/14 at Paris; Mass in F minor by Anton Bruckner 6/16 at Vienna; Incidental Music to *L'Arlesienne* (above) by Georges Bizet 10/1 at the Vaudeville Théâtre, Paris.

Black Jack licorice-flavored chewing gum introduced by Staten Island, N.Y., photographer Thomas Adams is the first chewing gum to be made from chicle and the first to be sold in stick form. Former Mexican president Antonio de Santa Anna, now 77, talked Adams into buying a ton of chicle in 1869, Adams has experimented fruitlessly with a project to make a rubber substitute from the latex of tropical trees such as the sapodilla, he has recalled that Indians used to chew chicle, he has added licorice flavor to the gray gum, and he goes into competition with State of Maine Pure Spruce gum magnate John B. Curtis who has been selling his gum for 20 years. Adams will sell his Tutti-Frutti gum on station platforms of the New York Elevated Railroad beginning in 1888 employing the first vending machines for chewing gum, and by 1892 the Adams Gum Company will have a six-story factory with some 250 workers (*see* Wrigley, 1892).

The first U.S. consumer protection law is enacted by Congress which makes it a federal offense to use the mails for fraudulent purposes. Post Office Chief Special Agent P. A. Woodward proceeds under the new law to prosecute "professional cheats" who are "working the most wholesale and barefaced operations, mostly through the mails, without fear of punishment."

 Montgomery Ward Company is started by Chicago mail-order pioneer Aaron Montgomery Ward, 29, whose savings were nearly consumed by last year's great Chicago fire. Ward scrapes together $1,600 and goes into business with George R. Thorne who puts up $800. Setting up shop in a 12- by 14-foot loft over a livery stable at 825 North Clark Street, Ward and Thorne call themselves "The Original Grange Supply House" and prepare a one-sheet "catalogue" to test Ward's idea that U. S. farmers, hurt by low farm prices, will respond to bargain offerings that can be shipped by rail. They list some 50 dry goods items, all priced at $1 or less, with savings of 40 percent. Ward will offer 10 days' grace on orders from Grange officials or countersigned with the Grange seal (see 1867; 1884; Sears, 1886).

Bloomingdale's has its beginnings in New York's Great East Side Store opened at 938 Third Avenue by merchant Lyman G. Bloomingdale, 31, and his brothers Joseph and Gustave (see 1886).

Simpson's opens in Toronto's Yonge Street where Scots-Canadian merchant Robert Simpson will have 13 clerks by 1880 to rival the 3-year-old T. Eaton Co. Ltd., and the much older Hudson's Bay Company.

 Romanesque architecture is introduced to America by Louisiana-born architect Henry Hobson Richardson, 34, who designed Boston's Brattle Street Church in 1870 and who this year designs Trinity Church.

Olana on the Hudson River just south of Hudson, N.Y., is completed for painter Frederic E. Church who 4 years ago traveled to Constantinople and who has commissioned architect Calvert Vaux of Central Park fame to draw up an Islamicized version of a plan drawn by Beaux Arts architect Richard Morris Hunt in 1867. A studio will be added in 1888 to the massive building of Persian-patterned bricks.

The Grand Union Hotel opens at Saratoga Springs, N.Y., where it will be a favorite hostelry for racegoers (see 1863; United States Hotel, 1875).

The Grand Bretagne Hotel opens at Athens in a large private house built in the center of town for a Triestine Greek but never occupied. The house will be enlarged and new wings added.

Boston suffers a $75 million fire that begins November 9 with an explosion in a four-story warehouse stocked with hoop skirts at the corner of Summer and Kingston Streets. The fire destroys the richest part of the city, burning 776 buildings that include granite and brick warehouses filled with merchandise and consuming 65 acres bounded by Milk and Washington Streets and Atlantic Avenue before burning itself out November 11. By 1876 the area will have been rebuilt more substantially than ever.

 Yellowstone National Park is created by a March 1 act of Congress that sets aside a 2 million acre tract of wilderness on the fast-developing frontier in Wyoming Territory. Superintendent of the first national park and the first effective wildlife sanctuary is explorer Nathaniel Pitt Langford, 39, who 2 years ago made an expedition into the area.

The New York State Forest Commission halts sales of forest lands to commercial interests (see 1892).

U.S. Grangers form cooperative ventures to purchase farm implements, machinery, feed, seed, clothing, and other necessities. Some local Granges adopt the English Rochedale plan of 1844 and in Iowa one-third of all grain elevators and warehouses are Granger-owned or controlled (see 1867; 1873).

A bumper U.S. corn crop leads to the start of a stock feeder cattle industry in the Midwest.

The Burbank potato developed by Massachusetts horticulturist Luther Burbank, 23, from a chance seedling is an improved variety that will provide Burbank with funds for developing other new varieties. He will introduce not only new potato varieties but also new tomatoes, asparagus, sweet and field corn, peas, squash, apples, cherries, nectarines, peaches, quinces, ornamental flowers, and—most especially—plums, prunes, and berries (see 1883).

The Chicago Board of Trade moves into a building of its own at LaSalle and Washington (see 1865; 1930).

Oceanography is pioneered by the British corvette H.M.S. Challenger which sets out on a 4-year voyage of 69,000 nautical miles to collect specimens and extend human knowledge of animal and plant life in the sea. The 2,306-ton wooden vessel has coal-burning steam engines to augment her sails and give her more maneuverability, her biologists collect an immense number of specimens from the sea and the sea floor. They find nothing to support the notion that some primitive forms of life survive in the deep sea that would throw light on the early history of life,

Boss Tweed provoked New York cartoonist Thomas Nast to depict political corruption with savage caricatures.

1872 (cont.) their results will be published in 50 large volumes over a period of 20 years, but like all original and productive scientific work the books will raise more questions than they answer.

Britain's pure food laws of 1860 are amended by a strict Adulteration of Food, Drink and Drugs Act. Sale of adulterated drugs is made punishable and the new act makes it an offense to sell a mixture containing ingredients added to increase weight or bulk without advising the consumer (chicory in coffee is a case in point) (*see* 1875).

The Licensing Act passed by Parliament sets strict limits on the number and kinds of places where alcoholic beverages may be sold and the hours such places may be open in an effort to curb excessive drunkenness. Riots occur in some places, the Liberal party legislation rallies publicans and brewers to the Conservative party, and the unpopularity of the new law will help topple the Gladstone government in the general elections of 1874.

British sugar consumption reaches 47 pounds per capita, up from 12 pounds per year in 1780.

Japan's Meiji emperor Mutsuhito starts a fad for beef eating among his more affluent countrymen but most Japanese cannot bear the smell of people who have eaten animal fats and few can afford beef (*see* 1868; priests, above; Townsend Harris, 1856).

Vegetarianism is satirized by Samuel Butler in his novel *Erewhon* (above). A fictional Erewhonian writes a thesis on "The Rights of Vegetables" and proves that vegetables, like animals, are alive and have feelings. The Erewhonians abandon vegetarianism after being driven by logic to eat only such things as cabbages that have died of natural causes.

The world's first large chill room is installed by Chicago's Armour and Company in a new plant at the Union Stock Yards (*see* 1865; 1869). Salt curing has been the chief way to keep perishable meats from spoiling and meat processing has been a seasonal business but Armour employs a new method that uses natural ice to maintain operations all year round (*see* refrigerated railcars, 1869). P. D. Armour's brother Simeon has opened a Kansas City slaughterhouse that can process 1,000 head of cattle in a 10-hour day.

Porcelain rollers are installed in a new flour mill built at Glasgow, Scotland (*see* 1870; Minneapolis, 1874).

Pillsbury's Best **XXXX** Flour is introduced by the 1-year-old C.A. Pillsbury Company at Minneapolis (*see* 1878).

A doughnut cutter is patented by Thomaston, Me., inventor John F. Blondell whose device has a spring-propelled rod to push out the dough of a center tube but most doughnuts continue to be made by hand (*see* 1847; Donut Corp. of America, 1920).

Grand Union Tea Company has its beginnings at Scranton, Pa., where entrepreneur Cyrus Jones, 20, opens a small store selling tea, coffee, spices, baking powder, and flavoring extracts which he also peddles door to door. Jones will be joined in the enterprise within a year by his brother Frank, a trained bookkeeper and an experienced grocery clerk, who will help young Cyrus rack up sales for the year of $12,000, a figure that will grow to well over $1 billion within a century. Grand Union will establish headquarters at Brooklyn, N.Y., in 1897.

The Café de la Paix opens at Paris in the Grand Hotel on the Boulevard des Capucines with carved pillars and landscaped ceilings.

The Paris resturant Brasserie Lipp opens on the Boulevard Saint-Germain-de-Pres under the management of an Alsatian who names it after a famous eating place in Strasbourg.

Mennonite farmers in the Crimea send four young men on a scouting expedition to America after learning that Czar Aleksandr II plans to cancel their exemption from military service, their freedom of worship, and their right to have their own schools and to speak their German language—rights granted by Catharine the Great in 1783. The young men are from well-to-do families in the Molotschna (Milk River) district and are led by Bernard Warkentin, Jr., 23, a miller's son from the village of Tjerpenije. Warkentin establishes a base in the Illinois village of Summerfield not far from East St. Louis where some Mennonite families have settled earlier and he attends McKendree College at Summerfield for a year to improve his English. After traveling with his colleagues through Pennsylvania and west to Wyoming, and from Texas through the Dakotas into Manitoba, Warkentin will write letters home that will persuade many of his countrymen to resettle, and while most will go to Manitoba because of liberal laws regarding military service many will settle in Kansas (*see* 1874).

A formula for a tampon medicated to prevent conception is contained in the Ebers papyrus found at Thebes (above).

The "Comstock Law" passed by Congress November 1 makes it a criminal offense to import, mail, or transport in interstate commerce "any article of medicine for the prevention of conception or for causing abortion." The law takes its name from New York moralist Anthony Comstock, 28, who heads the Society for the Suppression of Vice (*see* Mme. Restell, 1878).

1873 The Fourth Coinage Act passed by Congress February 12 makes gold the sole U.S. monetary standard, establishes the Bureau of the Mint, places all mint and assay office activities under control of the new Treasury Department bureau, stops coinage of 412.5-grain silver dollars, and authorizes only 420-grain trade dollars for export. The act inadvertently makes trade dollars legal tender in amounts up to $5, but a joint resolution of Congress in late July 1876 will deprive the trade dollar of its legal status (*see* Bland-Allison Act, 1878).

Demonitization of silver (above) comes in the midst of new silver discoveries in Nevada (*see* below).

President Grant's outgoing vice president Schuyler Colfax has been implicated in the Crédit Mobilier scandal that came to light last year. He was not renominated last year, but further evidence of corruption in the Grant administration continues to emerge.

"The country is fast becoming filled with gigantic corporations wielding and controlling immense aggregations of money and thereby commanding great influence and power," reports a congressional investigating committee: "It is notorious in many state legislatures that these influences are often controlling."

Germany adopts mark coinage.

Financial panic strikes Vienna in May and soon spreads to other European money centers.

Britain's "golden age" comes to an end after 23 years as Germany and the United States challenge British industrial preeminence.

European investors withdraw capital from the United States, the Wall Street banking house Jay Cooke & Company that has been financial agent for the Northern Pacific Railway fails September 18, Black Friday on the stock exchange sends prices tumbling September 19, the exchange closes for 10 days, and by year's end some 5,000 business firms have failed, millions of working Americans are obliged to depend on soup kitchens and other charities, tens of thousands come close to starvation.

The Greenback party organized by Midwesterners claims that a shortage of money is the cause of hard times. If the government will issue greenbacks until as much money is in circulation as in the boom times of 1865 the country will again enjoy prosperity, say the Greenbackers. (They also demand control of the corporations, honesty in government, conservation of natural resources, and widescale reforms.)

The U.S. financial panic enables Henry Clay Frick to acquire most of the coal and coke land in the region of Connellsville, Pa., that can be operated at a profit and when Pittsburgh steel mill operators discover that Connellsville coke is the best coke for steelmaking, the price of coke will rise from $1 per ton to $5 (see 1870). Frick will have gained control of 80 percent of the Connellsville coke output, he will be a millionaire by age 30, he will be offered a general managership by steel magnate Andrew Carnegie, and he will organize the Carnegie Company whose basic unit will be the Homestead Works (see 1892).

Silver is discovered in Nevada's Panamint Mountains and a new silver rush begins despite the February demonitization of the metal. The Great Bonanza mine is the biggest strike since the Comstock Lode of 1859.

The new Bonanza vein in the Comstock Lode is opened by mining engineers John William Mackay, 42, James Graham Fair, 41, James C. Flood, and William T. O'Brien. Fair was named superintendent of the Ophir Mine in 1865, the other partners took over the Hale & Norcross Mine a year later and then took over the Consolidated Virginia & California Mine, they were joined by Fair in 1868, and the silver vein they open February 5 will yield $150 million for Mackay and Fair who will establish the Bank of Nevada with Flood at San Francisco in 1878.

The Comstock Lode has yielded more than $120 million in silver, $80 million in gold. A millionaire miner named John Percival Jones has become a U.S. Senator from Nevada. The U.S. silver yield reaches $36 million for the year, up from $157,000 in 1860, and will continue to mount but gold production is declining from its 1854 peak.

Anglo-California Bank, Ltd., is founded at London. It will take over the San Francisco branch of New York's J. & W. Seligman (see 1864; 1909).

The First Bank of Japan is founded.

Smith Barney, Harris Upham & Co. stockbrokers has its beginnings in an office opened in December on Third Street, Philadelphia, by Charles D. Barney, 29, with help from Jay Cooke (above) who has befriended Barney since their days in Sandusky, Ohio. Edward B. Smith will start a Philadelphia investment banking firm in 1892 at age 30; John F. Harris will open a Chicago commodities trading firm in 1895 at age 32; Harris's sister Gertrude will marry John P. Upham; the Smith and Barney firms will merge in 1938; and Smith, Barney & Co., will merge with Harris, Upham & Co. in 1976.

Port Moresby is founded on the Pacific island of New Guinea by English naval commander Sir Fairfax Moresby, 87, who has been admiral of the fleet since 1870 and who half a century ago suppressed the slave trade at Mauritius. Moresby raises the British flag on the island's South Coast but London refuses to support Moresby unless Australia's colonial governments agree to assume responsibility for the territory's administration (when some colonies demur, London disavows Moresby's action).

The first Australian factory act is passed by the Victoria government at Melbourne to protect female and juvenile millhands and to maintain safe and sanitary working conditions.

Zanzibar's public slave markets close June 5 by order of the sultan Barghash Sayyid who acts under British government pressure to prohibit the export of slaves (see Livingstone, 1871).

German occupation forces begin to evacuate France following the death January 9 of the exiled Napoleon III at age 64. The Thiers government is condemned by the monarchist majority in Parlement, Thiers resigns May 24, he is succeeded promptly by Marshal MacMahon, now 64, who is elected almost unanimously, and the last German soldiers cross the border back to Germany September 16 (see 1877).

The first Spanish Republic is proclaimed February 12 by the radical majority in the cortes elected last year, the king Amadeo I abdicates the same day after a

1873 (cont.) 2-year reign in which he has been opposed as a "foreigner," the 40-year-old foreign minister Emilio Castelar y Ripoli becomes prime minister and tries to organize a centralized republic, but Carlist civil war continues (*see* 1872; 1874).

Prince Edward Island in the Gulf of St. Lawrence joins the 6-year-old Dominion of Canada July 1.

Canada's Northwest Mounted Police is established August 30 by an order-in-council. The "mounties" are to stop trading in liquor and arms with the Indians of the Northwest Territory.

Canada's first Prime Minister Sir John Macdonald resigns November 7 following charges of corruption in the last election and reports of a scandal involving the projected transcontinental railway. Macdonald will be re-elected in 1878 and will serve until his death in June, 1891.

Cornelius Vanderbilt of the New York Central gains control of the rail line between New York and Chicago by leasing the Lake Shore and Michigan Southern (*see* 1869; 1877).

Ben Holladay is dealt a heavy blow by the financial panic (above). Holladay acquired the Russell, Majors and Waddell transcontinental freight firm in 1862, he made a fortune before selling out in 1866, he has sold his steamship interests to finance a new Oregon Central Railroad, but his German bondholders will force Holladay out of the company in 1876 and he will be financially ruined.

San Francisco's first cable streetcar (and the world's first) goes into service August 1 on Clay Steet hill. English-American engineer Andrew Smith Hallidie, 37, has persuaded the city fathers to install the "end-less-wire rope way" he patented in 1871 in order to cope with the hilly streets that defy San Francisco's eight horse-drawn lines. Additional cable car lines will be installed in San Francisco and also at Los Angeles, Seattle, Denver, and Omaha (*see* 1894; Sprague, 1887, 1888).

Rochester, N.Y., lawyer George Baldwin Selden, 27, experiments with internal combustion engines in an effort to develop a lightweight engine that will propel a road vehicle that is more efficient than the "road locomotives" now used in some farm jobs (*see* 1876; Lenoir, 1860; Otto, 1866).

The White Star liner S.S. *Atlantic* runs aground April 1 off Halifax, Nova Scotia. The 420-foot steamship founders and 502 of her 931 passengers are lost.

Treatise on Electricity and Magnetism by Scottish physicist James Clerk Maxwell, 42, describes properties of the electromagnetic field and gives equations that entail the electromagnetic theory of light (*see* Hertz, 1887).

The magnetic effect of electric convection is discovered by U.S. physicist Henry Augustus Rowland, 24, who teaches at the Rensselaer Polytechnic Institute at Troy, N.Y. Rowland will investigate alternating currents.

Electricity drives machinery for the first time in history, at Vienna.

A process for manufacturing water gas discovered by Thaddeus Lowe of 1866 artificial ice fame will greatly enhance use of gaslight illumination (*see* coke oven, 1897; Welsbach mantle, 1885).

Russia's Baku oilfields increase production as Alfred Nobel of 1866 dynamite fame and his brother Ludwig invest capital to build a refinery that will make Baku the world's leading petroleum producer (*see* 1871; 1901).

"Typhoid Fever: Its Nature, Mode of Spreading, and Prevention" by English physician William Budd proves the contagious nature of typhoid fever (*see* cholera, 1866; Eberth, Koch, 1880).

Father Damien goes to the government hospital for lepers on the Hawaiian island of Molokai to care for victims of the disease that will be called Hansen's disease (*see* Hansen, 1874). Belgian missionary Joseph Damien de Veuster, 33, will contract the disease himself, he will devote the rest of his life to the work, but he will die in 1889.

New York's Bellevue Hospital establishes the Nightingale System of nurses' training (*see* Nightingale, 1854).

The University of Cape Town is founded in South Africa.

The University of South Africa is founded at Pretoria.

St. Nicholas Magazine begins publication under the editorship of Mary Elizabeth Mapes Dodge of 1865 *Hans Brinker* fame who will run the new periodical for children until her death in 1905 at age 74. Dodge will attract work by such poets as Bryant, Longfellow, and Whittier.

Nonfiction *Studies in the History of the Renaissance* by Oxford classicist Walter (Horatio) Pater, 34.

Fiction *The Gilded Age* by Mark Twain and *Hartford Courant* editor Charles Dudley Warner exposes corruption in U.S. business and politics since the Civil War; *Marjorie Daw and Other People* by Thomas Bailey Aldrich; *Around the World in Eighty Days* (*Le tour du monde en quatre-vingt jours*) by Jules Verne (*see* Nellie Bly, 1889); *The Eustace Diamonds* by Anthony Trollope.

Poetry *Les Amours jaunes* by French poet Tristan Corbière (Edouard Joachim Corbière), 28.

Painting *Le bon Bock* by Edouard Manet; *Souvenir d'Italie* by J. P. C. Corot, now 77; *Oarsmen on the Schuylkill* by Thomas Eakins. Sir Edwin H. Landseer dies at London October 1 at age 71.

Photography is advanced by German photochemist Hermann Wilhelm Vogel, 39, who discovers that adding certain dyes to photographic emulsions will increase their sensitivity.

Gelatin emulsions go on sale in London to permit any photographer "to prepare dry plates equal in sensitiveness to the best wet plates by simply pouring on the glass an emulsion and allowing it to dry," but the product introduced in July by local photographer John Burgess is not a commercial success.

♪ **Opera** *Ivan the Terrible* (*The Maid of Pskov*) 1/1 at St. Petersburg's Maryinski Theater, with music by Nikolai Rimski-Korsakov; *Le Roi l'a Dit* 5/24 at the Opéra-Comique, Paris, with music by Leo Delibes.

First performances Concerto No. 1 in A minor for Violincello and Orchestra by Camille Saint-Säens 1/19 at the Paris Conservatoire; Symphony No. 5 by the late Franz Schubert (who wrote it in 1816) 2/1 at London's Crystal Palace; Symphony No. 2 in C minor by Anton Bruckner 10/26 at Vienna; *Variations on a Theme by Haydn* by Johannes Brahms 11/2 at Vienna; *The Tempest* (Fantasy for Orchestra after Shakespeare) by Petr Ilich Tchaikovsky 12/19 at Moscow.

Popular songs "Silver Threads Among the Gold" by English composer Hart Pease Danks, 39, lyrics by Eban E. Rexford, 25; "Home on the Range" lyrics by Kansas homesteader Bruce (Brewster) Higley appear in the December issue of the *Smith County Pioneer* under the title "Oh, Give Me a Home Where the Buffalo Roam." Kansas guitarist Daniel E. Kelly writes a tune to the lyrics, it will be revised by U.S. composer William Goodwin, and it will be published in 1904 under the title "Arizona Annie."

🏃 The Preakness has its first running at Baltimore's Pimlico racetrack where the 1 3/16 mile stakes race for 3-year-olds has been named for the son of Lexington that won the Dinner Party stakes on the day the track opened in 1870. The bay colt Survivor wins the first Preakness, its owner gains possession for 1 year of the Woodlawn Vase created in 1860 by New York's Tiffany and Company. The race's namesake will be shipped to England, the Duke of Hamilton will buy the horse, and he will shoot Pimlico dead in a pique (*see* Belmont Stakes, 1867; Kentucky Derby, 1875).

⏱ Perfume manufacturing is revolutionized at Grasse in France where a new extraction process is employed to extract a solid essence from flower roots or from fragrant substances by placing them in contact with volatile fluids which dissolve essential ingredients and isolate them as they evaporate.

🌿 Liggett & Myers Tobacco Company emerges from J. E. Liggett & Brother as William Liggett sells his share in the plug (chewing) tobacco firm to George S. Myers (*see* 1858; 1911).

💲 Singer Manufacturing Company builds a huge sewing machine factory at Elizabethport, N.J.

New York's Lord & Taylor moves from its Grand Street and Broadway location to a new building at the corner of Broadway and 20th Street, the first iron frame building in New York with steam elevators. The five-story store with its mansard roof and dormer windows is lighted by gas chandeliers, it will be extended to Fifth Avenue, and it will house the growing fashion emporium until 1914 (*see* 1860).

🏛 Chicago's Grand Pacific Hotel opens at the corner of Clark Street and Jackson Boulevard where hotelman John B. Drake has built an ornate seven-story hostelry at a cost of $1.5 million.

🐟 American shad is carried across the continent and introduced into the Pacific by the U.S. Fish Commission but the fish will be popular on the West Coast only for its roe (*see* 1871; salmon, 1875).

👤 Bengal suffers a famine as rice crops fail.

🌾 DDT (dichloridiphenyl-trichlorethane) is prepared by German chemistry student Othmar Zeidler at Strasbourg who reacts chloral hydrate (the "Mickey Finn" knockout drops of the underworld) and chlorobenzene in the presence of sulfuric acid. Zeidler will describe DDT next year in the *Proceedings of the German Chemical Society* (*Berichte der Chemischen Gesellschaft*) but he has no idea of the significance of his discovery (*see* Muller, 1939).

The first Aberdeen Angus cattle to reach the United States are imported from Scotland by retired London silk merchant George Grant who brings four Angus bulls to his farm at Victoria, Kan. Foreign investment capital is pouring into the U.S. cattle ranching industry (*see* 1881).

Barbed wire exhibited at the De Kalb, Ill., county fair by Henry Rose is studied by local farmer Joseph Farwell Glidden, 60, and his friend Jacob Haish who independently develop machines for producing coil barbed wire by the mile and who obtain patents for two separate styles of barbed wire. Their "devil's rope" is destined to end the open range in the West and 80.5 million pounds of barbed wire will be manufactured in the next 74 years as the steel wire becomes important not only to farmers and ranchers but to military operations (*see* 1867; Gates, 1875).

Minnesota congressman Ignatius Donnelly complains that it costs as much to ship wheat from Minneapolis to Milwaukee as to ship the same wheat from Milwaukee to Liverpool. U.S. railroads are making deals with elevator companies, commission agents, and others to control both shipping and marketing rates and are forcing farmers to sell to the nearest elevator company, agent, or railroad at rates favorable to the buyer. Grain is often downgraded as No. 2 because it is said to be wet, frozen, or weedy, and is then sold as No. 1 grade to millers, say the farmers.

A farmers' convention at Springfield, Ill., attacks monopolies, calling them "detrimental to the public prosperity, corrupt in their management, and dangerous to republican institutions."

The Northwest Farmer's Convention at Chicago urges federal regulation of transportation rates, government-built and government-owned railroads, an end to corporation subsidies and of tariff protection for industry, a revision of the credit system, and the encouragement of decentralized manufacturing, demands called "un-American" by bankers, industrialists, and railroad operators.

1873 (cont.) The Grange reaches its membership peak of 750,000 but Ignatius Donnelly (above) compares a nonpolitical farmers' organization to a gun that won't shoot (*see* 1867; 1876).

Deering harvesters are introduced by entrepreneur William Deering, now 47, who has left Deering-Milliken in New York and has established a firm at Piano, Ill. (*see* 1865; International Harvester, 1902).

Good quality Werner harvesters made by a Grange factory in Iowa sell for half the price of a Deering or McCormick harvester. When 22 plow manufacturers agree not to sell plows to Granges except at retail prices, some Granges set up factories to make their own machines and break the "machinery rings" (*see* 1872; 1875).

Louisiana's sugar crop falls to less than one-third its 1853 level as a result of the Civil War and the emancipation of slaves. Sugar cane in many areas is replaced by rice which demands less labor.

Coor's Beer has its beginnings in the Golden Brewery started by German-American brewer Adolph Herman Joseph Coors, 26, and Jacob Schueler at Golden, Colorado Territory. Coors will buy out his partner in 1880.

St. Louis brewer Adolphus Busch becomes a full partner of his father-in-law and renames the Bavarian Brewery the E. Anheuser and Co.'s Brewing Association (*see* 1865; Budweiser, 1876).

U.S. pepper trade with Sumatra is ended by piracy and by the hostility of the natives after 937 voyages (*see* 1797; 1805).

The first successful compression system using liquid ammonia as a refrigerant is introduced by Swedish engineer Carl Linde (*see* Perkins, 1834; Gorrie, 1842; Lowe, 1865; liquefied air, 1898).

Poultry, fish, and meat that has been frozen for 6 months is eaten at a public banquet in Australia (*see* 1856; 1925).

The thermos bottle has its beginnings in the Dewar vessel invented by Scottish chemist James Dewar, 31, who will invent the thermos flask in 1892 (*see* Burger, 1904).

The Paris Council of Hygiene rules that margarine may not be sold as butter (*see* 1869; New York, 1877).

Henri Nestlé's Infant Milk Food of 1866 is introduced in the United States (*see* 1875).

Ralph's Grocery Company is founded at Los Angeles which is still a dusty town of less than 10,000.

San Francisco's population reaches 188,000 and the city has a United States Mint, cobblestone streets, and tall redwood houses.

1874 Turkey Red wheat—hard, drought-resistant, and high-yielding—is introduced into the United States by German-speaking Mennonites from Russia's Crimea (*see* 1872). The Mennonites are brought to Kansas by the Santa Fe Railroad which has been granted 3 million acres of land along its right of way and needs farmers who will occupy the land and produce crops that will generate freight revenue. Santa Fe official Carl R. Schmidt went to Russia last year and brought over a Mennonite delegation to see possible sites for settlement, he has obtained passage of a law in the Kansas legislature giving exemption from military service to those who oppose war on religious grounds, he has offered free passage to Kansas plus free transport of furniture, he has set up temporary living quarters, and the first Mennonites arrive August 16 at Hillsboro in Marion County. The 163 pioneers from 34 families pay in gold to buy 8,000 acres from the Santa Fe, they found the village of Gnadenau, a second group of 600 follows, then a third group of 1,100, and by fall the Mennonites are arriving by the thousands, each family bringing its Turkey Red seed wheat obtained originally from Turkey and planted in the Crimea for years (*see* 1895).

British troops under the command of Sir Garnet Joseph Wolseley enter the Ashanti capital Coomassie February 4 and end the second Ashanti War. Wolseley, now 40, lost an eye at Sevastopol in 1855, served in the Sepoy Mutiny of 1857, commanded an expedition to put down the Red River Rebellion in Canada 4 years ago, and he sets Coomassie afire before withdrawing.

Britain annexes the Fiji Islands.

Britain's first Gladstone ministry ends February 17 as the Tories regain power. A second Disraeli ministry begins February 21 and will continue until 1880.

Japanese troops invade Taiwan in April. Tokyo excuses the invasion by citing the death of 54 Okinawan seamen who were killed in 1871 after a shipwreck. The Japanese send delegates to China to assure the Chinese that no offense is intended, but they assert claims to Okinawa, and they agree to recall the expedition from Taiwan in October only after China agrees to pay an indemnity (*see* 1895).

Spain's 17-year-old Alphonso XII issues a manifesto from England's Sandhurst military school December 1 in response to a birthday greeting from his followers. No Alphonso has ever reigned over a united Spain but Alphonso XII proclaims himself the sole representative of the Spanish monarchy and begins a reign that will continue until his death in 1885.

A meeting of the unemployed held in New York's Tompkins Square January 13 to bring public attention to widespread poverty following last year's Wall Street collapse brings a charge by mounted police: hundreds are injured.

The first effective 10-hour day law for women is enacted May 8 by the Massachusetts legislature (*see* Supreme Court decision, 1908).

New York social worker Etta Angel Wheeler finds a little girl wandering naked through the city's slums after having been beaten, slashed, and turned out by her drunken foster mother. Appeals are made to the 8-year-old ASPCA for lack of any other agency, the American Society for the Prevention of Cruelty to

Animals decides that the child is an animal and deserving of shelter, the foster mother is prosecuted by the ASPCA for starving and abusing the 9-year-old girl, and a Society for the Prevention of Cruelty to Children (ASPCC) is organized.

Federal troops at New Orleans put down a revolt by the White League against black state government September 17.

Some 75 blacks are killed December 7 in race riots at Vicksburg, Miss.

U.S. Senator from Minnesota William Windom heads a committee that proposes a government-built, government-operated double-track freight line between the Mississippi Valley and the eastern seaboard that will prevent railroad companies from charging exorbitant freight rates (*see* 1877; farmers, 1873).

The first bridge to span the Mississippi at St. Louis is tested July 2 by seven 50-ton locomotives loaded with coal and water that chug slowly across from one bank while another seven chug across from the opposite bank, pausing at the slender junctures of the cantilevered arches on the steel arch Eads Bridge (*see* 1867). 300,000 residents and visitors crowd the levee to witness the collapse of "Eads's Folly" but the bridge holds all 700 tons. The crowd cheers, a 3-day celebration ensues with parades, band concerts, and speeches culminating in a $10,000 fireworks display, and the Eads Bridge opens to traffic July 4 with a 100-gun salvo.

The practicality of electric traction is demonstrated by Belgian-American inventor Charles Joseph Van Depoele, 28 (*see* Daft, 1885).

New York gets its first electric streetcar but the system invented by Stephen Dudley Field, 28, is hazardous and presents no immediate threat to the horsecar. One wheel of Field's streetcar—the first car to be run successfully with current generated by a stationary dynamo—picks up current carried by one of the rails. Conveyed to the car's motor, the current flows back to the other rail via a second wheel, insulated from the first, and is returned to the dynamo (*see* 1888).

Silver is found at Oro City (Leadville) in Colorado Territory where the placer gold found in 1859 has long since been exhausted. Metallurgist A. B. Wood recognizes silver-lead ores in material that goldminers have regarded merely as obstructions to their sluices. Active prospecting will begin in the spring of 1877 at Oro City which will be renamed Leadville the following year.

The leprosy bacillus is discovered by Norwegian physician Armauer Gerhard Henrik Hansen, 33, for whom the disease will hereafter properly be called Hansen's disease (*see* 1648; Father Damien, 1873).

The London School of Medicine for Women is founded by English physician Sophia Jez-Blake, 34, whose brother Thomas, 42, has just been named

headmaster of Rugby. She will gain the legal right to practice medicine in Great Britain in 1877.

The Baltimore Eye & Ear Dispensary is founded by physicians who include local opthalmologist Samuel Theobald, 28, who has introduced the use of boric acid for treating eye infections.

Improved surgical dressings are pioneered by East Orange, N.J., inventors Robert Wood Johnson, 29, and George J. Seabury who succeed in manufacturing an adhesive and medicated plaster with a rubber base (*see* 1885).

The U.S. public high school system wins support from the Supreme Court which rules against a citizen of Kalamazoo, Mich., who had brought suit to prevent collection of additional taxes. The court upholds the city's right to establish a high school and to levy new taxes to support the school.

The Chautauqua movement in U.S. education has its beginnings in a summer training program for Sunday School teachers started at Fair Point on Lake Chautauqua, N.Y., by Methodist bishop John Heyl Vincent and Akron, Ohio, farm machinery maker Lewis Miller: they begin an institution 10 miles from Lake Erie that will develop into a traveling tent show of lecturers and that will bring culture to small-town America. President Grant's appearance at Chautauqua next year will lend prestige to the movement, more than 100,000 people will be signed up for home-study correspondence courses by 1877, the Chautauqua Normal School of Languages will be started in 1879, and the Chautauqua Press will list 93 titles by 1885 by which time there will be more than 30 different Chautauquas in more than 30 states (*see* Damrosch, 1909).

St. Olaf College is founded by Norwegians at Northfield, Minn.

Colorado College is founded at Colorado Springs.

The College of Santa Fe is founded in New Mexico Territory.

The University of Adelaide is founded in Australia.

The Remington typewriter introduced by F. Remington & Sons Fire Arms Company begins a revolution in written communication. Philo Remington, 68, has headed his late father's firearms company since 1868 (*see* 1845), he has acquired sole rights to the Sholes typewriter of 1868 for $12,000, but the $125 price of the Remington typewriter is more than a month's rent for many substantial business firms and Remington produces only eight machines (*see* 1876).

The *Winnipeg Free Press* begins publication in Canada.

Yomiuri Shinbun begins publication in Japan.

Nonfiction *Encyclopaedia of Wit and Wisdom* by humorist Josh Billings who says, "It is better to know nothing than to know what ain't so."

Fiction *Far From the Madding Crowd* by Thomas Hardy; *Phineas Redux* by Anthony Trollope; "Nedda" by Sicilian short-story writer Giovanni

Early typewriters had capital letters only, and typists could not see what was being typed, but improvements came quickly.

Verga, 34, who pioneers the Italian version of naturalism that will be called *verismo; Die Messalinen Wiens* by German novelist Leopold von Sacher-Masoch, 38, from whose name the word "masochism" will be derived (*see* "sadism," 1791).

Poetry *Romances sans paroles* by French poet Paul Verlaine, 30, who in 1871 left his wife after 18 months of marriage to live with the poet Arthur Rimbaud, now 20. Verlaine was encouraged and influenced by Rimbaud, but in July of last year he shot Rimbaud in the wrist during a lovers' quarrel and he has been imprisoned to serve a 2-year sentence; *Une saison en enfer* by Arthur Rimbaud who has had his hopes dashed for a new, amoral society and for writing an unconventional new kind of poetry. Rimbaud will go into business as a North African merchant and trader and will amass a fortune before his death in 1891. *Ode* by English poet Arthur William Edgar O'Shaughnessy: "We are the musicmakers,/ And we are the dreamers of dreams. . . ."

French "Impressionists" hold their first exhibition at Paris in an "independent" show of canvases that include a harbor scene entitled *Impression: Sunrise* by Claude Monet, now 40, whose work prompts art critic Louis Leroy to call the painters "Impressionists," an epithet that will soon lose its pejorative overtone. The group includes Paul Cézanne, Edgar Degas, Edouard Manet, Manet's new sister-in-law Berthe Morisot, 33, Camille Pissarro, 44, Pierre Auguste Renoir, Alfred Sisley, 34, and beginning in 1879 will include American émigrée painter Mary Cassatt, now 30.

Washington's Corcoran Gallery of Art opens on Pennsylvania Avenue (*see* 1870).

Photography is advanced by William Blanchard Bolton, 26, who shows that nitrates (by-products of the formation of silver halide and nitrate) can be washed out of photographic emulsions through a process that will be used hereafter in developing photographs (*see* 1864; Maddox, 1871; Seed, 1879).

Theater *The Two Orphans* (*Les Deux Orphélins*) by French playwright Adolphe D'Emery, 62, 1/29 at Paris.

Opera *Boris Godunov* 1/24 at St. Petersburg's Maryinsky Theater, with music by Russian composer Modest Petrovich Mussorgsky, 34, libretto from the Aleksandr Pushkin play of 1831; *Die Fledermaus* (*The Bat*) 4/5 at Vienna's Theater-an-der-Wien, with music by Johann Strauss.

First performances *Overture to the Piccolomini* (*Max and Thekla*) by French composer (Paul Marie Theodore) Vincent d'Indy, 22, 1/25 at Paris; *Patrie Overture* in C minor by Georges Bizet 2/15 at Paris; *Requiem* by Giuseppe Verdi 5/22 at Milan's Church of San Marco. Verdi has written the work to memorialize the late poet-novelist-patriot Alessandro Manzoni, who died May 22 of last year at age 88.

Lawn tennis is patented under the name Sphairistike by British sportsman Walter Clopton Wingfield, who has adapted to outdoor play a game played for at least five centuries. Lawn tennis is introduced in Bermuda and from there into the United States.

New York's Madison Square Garden opens in April under the name Barnum's Hippodrome at the north end of the city's 38-year-old Madison Square Park on Fifth Avenue. Showman P. T. Barnum has taken over a shed used until 1871 as a freight depot for the New York and Harlem Railroad, he has spent $35,000 to remodel the roofless structure, he will sell his lease in the winter to Patrick S. Gilmore, Gilmore will rename it Gilmore's Garden and will use it for flower shows, policemen's balls, America's first beauty contest, religious and temperance meetings, and the first Westminster Kennel Club Show, while Barnum will pitch his circus tent at Gilmore's Garden each spring (*see* 1879; Gilmore, 1863; Barnum, 1871; Westminster, 1877).

The first real football game May 14 at Boston is a variation of rugby (*see* 1823; Princeton vs. Rutgers, 1869). Harvard and McGill field teams of 11 men each who run with the ball as well as kicking it in the "Boston Game," Harvard wins, a second match is held May 15, a third played at Montreal October 22 ends with Harvard winning 3 to 0, but scrimmage lines and "downs" will not be introduced until the 1880s (*see* Harvard-Yale game, 1875).

Levi Strauss blue jeans get copper rivets as the result of a joke about a prospector named Alkali who carries rock specimens in his pockets and who has had his bibless overalls riveted by a blacksmith. The riveted denims sell at $13.50 per dozen (*see* 1850; 1937).

New York's R. H. Macy Company displays its doll collection in the world's first Christmas windows, beginning a tradition that other stores will follow. Founder Macy will die at Paris in 1877 at age 55 (*see* 1867; Strauss brothers, 1888).

556

The dome of Boston's Massachusetts State House is covered in gold leaf 13 years after its first gilding.

U.S. inventor William Baldwin improves the steam radiator by screwing short lengths of one-inch pipe into a cast-iron base, but mass production of cast-iron radiators will not come for another 20 years and central heating of U.S. homes and offices will not come until the turn of the century.

British farm wages fall, farm workers strike in the east of England, and an agricultural depression begins that will lead to an exodus of farm workers into the growing milltowns. British agriculture has been undercut by foreign producers of grain and meat and begins a long decline.

A decade of drought begins on part of the western U.S. cattle range while other parts enjoy plenty of rain (see 1886).

The first shipment of Montana cattle for the East arrives at the railhead at Ogden in Utah Territory where it has been driven by cattleman James Forges from the Sun River range of Conrad Kohrs.

A paper on the feasibility of irrigating Western lands is prepared by George Perkins Marsh at the request of the U.S. Commissioner of Agriculture (see Marsh, 1864). Irrigation projects are possible, writes Marsh, if they are undertaken on a river basin scale after thorough hydrological surveys "under Government supervision, from Government sources of supply" (see Powell, 1878).

The first Peavey grain elevator goes up at Sioux City, Iowa, where farm equipment dealer Frank Peavey has heard customers complain of having no permanent market for their grain (see 1868). The 6,000-bushel "blind horse" elevator is powered literally by a blind horse walking in an endless circle while towing a post attached to an axle at the center of a circle, it saves farmers from having to haul wagonloads of grain back to the farm because they could find no buyer in town, and it will be followed by warehouses that Peavey will build with partner J. S. Meckling along the Dakota-Southern Railway between Sioux City and Yankton, S. Dak. Peavey will persuade Minneapolis flour mills that he can provide a steady supply of wheat and he will pioneer in the mass buying and selling of grain (see 1884).

A Minneapolis flour mill that employs fluted chilled steel rollers in addition to the conventional millstones is opened by C. C. Washburn who has made a fortune in Wisconsin land speculation and has served as governor of Wisconsin (see 1866; 1878; 1879; Pillsbury, 1878; Gold Medal Flour, 1880).

Food canning is improved by Allen Taylor's drop press and by use of a pressure-cooking "retort" introduced by A. K. Shriver or by Baltimore canner Isaac Solomon (see 1861). Live steam keeps the outside walls of the can under pressures comparable to those exerted by the heating contents of the can, thus speeding up the cooking of the contents without permitting the can to buckle or burst as it cools because

of any buildup in pressure during the heating process. The retort gives canners accurate control of cooling temperatures and will lead to a large-scale expansion of the industry (see Howe floater, 1876).

Margarine is introduced into the United States (see 1881; Mège-Mouriés, 1869).

The ice cream soda is invented at the semicentennial celebration of Philadelphia's Franklin Institute. Robert Green runs out of cream after making $6 per day selling a mixture of syrup, sweet cream, and carbonated water, but he substitutes vanilla ice cream and by the time the exhibition ends he is averaging more than $600 per day.

Joseph Schlitz Brewing Company is incorporated at Milwaukee with a capitalization of $200,000 (see 1856). Schlitz himself will drown next year at age 44 on a voyage to his native Germany, but his four nephews will keep management of the company in family hands for more than a century.

New York brewer Jacob Ruppert builds a new brewery with a capacity of 50,000 barrels and turns his old brewery into an ice-house (see 1867). Ruppert is making real estate investments that will make him one of the city's leading financiers (see New York Yankees, 1915).

The Women's Christian Temperance Union (WCTU) is founded at Cleveland where 135 women meet November 18 at the Second Presbyterian Church and dedicate themselves to ending the traffic in liquor. Frances Caroline Elizabeth Willard, 35, is named corresponding secretary (see National Prohibition Party, 1869; Anti-Saloon League, 1895).

The first Hutterite immigrants to America arrive at New York from Europe (see 1528). The Bonhomme colony at Yankton, S. Dak., is founded by a group speaking Tyrolean Hutterische dialect and will be followed by 200 colonies in the Dakotas, Minnesota, Montana, Washington, and the Canadian provinces of Alberta, Manitoba, and Saskatchewan; the Hutterites grow to number 20,000.

1875 The electric telephone that will revolutionize communication is pioneered by Scottish-American inventor Alexander Graham Bell, 28, who came to the United States in 1871 as a teacher of speech to the deaf and who conceived the idea of "electric speech" last year while visiting his parents at Brantford, Ontario. While trying to perfect a method for carrying more than two messages simultaneously over a single telegraph line, Bell hears the sound of a plucked spring along 60 feet of wire June 2 in the attic electrical workshop of Charles Williams at 109 Court Street, Boston. The spring has been plucked by Bell's young assistant Thomas A. Watson who is trying to reactivate a harmonic telegraph transmitter, one of several whose reeds or springs are each tuned to a different signal frequency: a contact screw has been screwed down so far that a circuit has been left unbroken that should have been broken only intermittenly and a current is being transmitted that

1875 (cont.) corresponds to a reed in Bell's room. When he hears the sound of the plucked spring he recognizes its significance and realizes that the speaking telephone can be achieved by means of a simple mechanism (*see* 1876).

The Suez Canal completed in 1869 comes under British control through the efforts of the prime minister Benjamin Disraeli who obtains a loan from the merchant banking house of Rothschild to buy up 176,752 shares in the Universal Suez Company from the profligate Egyptian khedive Ismail (*see* 1863). Ismail is deep in debt, Disraeli puts up the British Government itself as security for the £4 million loan, and he creates international consternation by purchasing control of the strategic canal (*see* 1888).

Bosnia and Herzogovina in the Balkans rise against the Turks until the Ottoman sultan Abdul Aziz meets the demands of the insurgents and promises reforms.

The Chinese emperor who will reign until 1908 assumes the throne following the death at age 19 of the T'ung Chih Manchu emperor Mu Tsung after a 12-year reign in which the dowager empress Tzu Hsi was coregent until 1873. The new 4-year-old Kuang Hsu emperor Tsai T'ien is a nephew of Tzu Hsi.

The 63-year-old Chinese general Tso Tsung-t'ang moves to suppress the Tungans of the Northern T'ien Shan who have been in revolt since 1862.

Oregon territory occupied under an 1855 treaty by the Nez Perce is opened to white settlement by President Grant (*see* Chief Joseph, 1877).

Comanche chief Quanah Parker ends his resistance to settlement of the Texas prairie by white ranchers. Parker's herd of 1,400 horses was captured and destroyed last fall by Colonel R. S. Mackenzie of the U.S. Cavalry and the chief brings his warriors into a reservation established by the government.

A Civil Rights Act that guarantees blacks equal rights in public places and bans their exclusion from jury duty is passed by Congress March 1.

The first "Jim Crow" law is enacted by the Tennessee legislature. The measure is prejudicial to blacks (*see* 1881; Rice, 1832; Florida, 1887).

New York Central tracks down New York's Fourth (Park) Avenue are lowered into a giant ditch, completed after 3 years of excavation, that places the tracks below street level. The ditch will be largely covered over by 1915 (*see* Grand Central, 1913).

London's Liverpool Street Station is completed for the Great Eastern Railway.

New York's Kuhn, Loeb & Co. investment banking house admits German banker Jacob Henry Schiff, 27, to partnership January 1, Schiff marries founder Solomon Loeb's eldest daughter Therese May 6. He will move the firm into railroad financing in 1877 by underwriting a loan to the Chicago and North Western, he will head Kuhn, Loeb after Loeb's retirement in 1885, and with help from partner Abraham Wolff

and others he will make the firm a powerful force in U.S. and international finance (*see* 1867; Kahn, 1897).

The Prudential Insurance Company of America is founded at Newark, N.J., under the name Prudential Friendly Society by Maine-born insurance agent John Fairfield Dryden, 36, with backing from local investors. Dryden will travel to London next year to study operations of that city's internationally known Prudential Assurance Company, Ltd., his company will take the name Prudential Insurance in March 1877, it will grow by selling sickness and accident insurance, Dryden will head the company from 1881 to 1911. Prudential will begin selling ordinary life insurance in 1886, and on August 20, 1896 it will advertise in *Leslie's Weekly* with a picture of the Rock of Gibraltar and the slogan, "The Prudential Has the Strength of Gibraltar" devised by J. Walter Thompson. Prudential will become a mutual company in 1915, and by 1950 it will have 80 million policyholders with $200 billion in coverage.

The Anaconda Company has its beginnings in the Montana Territory ghost town of Butte where prospector Michael Hickey finds what appears to be silver and stakes a claim. A veteran of the Union Army, Hickey discovers an old newspaper left behind by gold miners of Civil War days, he sees the headline "Grant's Armies Are Encircling Lee's Forces Like an Anaconda," and he names his mine the Anaconda (*see* Marcus Daly, 1881).

Swedish inventor Alfred Nobel of 1866 dynamite fame discovers blasting gelatin (*see* Baku oil fields, 1873; Nobel prizes, 1901).

The Fiji Islands lose 40,000 of their 150,000 inhabitants in a measles epidemic following the return of the Fiji king from a visit to New South Wales.

Science and Health by New England divorcée Mary Baker, 54, claims that the bible has helped her recover from the effects of a bad fall and explains a system of faith healing (*see* Christian Science, 1879).

The practice of osteopathy is founded by Kirksville, Mo., physician Andrew Taylor Still, 47, who lost three of his children to spinal meningitis in 1864. Still has convinced himself that all diseases are caused by abnormalities in or near bodily joints (the abnormalities will later be called osteopathic lesions or spinal joint subluxations) (*see* 1892).

The electric dental drill is patented by Kalamazoo, Mich., inventor George F. Green who will assign his patent on "electro-magnetic dental tools" for sawing, filing, dressing, and polishing teeth to Samuel S. White of Philadelphia. White's company will become the leading U.S. producer of dental equipment, but use of electric drills will await the development of lighter engines and less expensive batteries.

Vaseline petroleum jelly is introduced by the newly established Chesebrough Manufacturing Company founded by English-American entrepreneur Robert Augustus Chesebrough, 38, who has pioneered in using crude oil under burners and stills for refining oil.

Chesebrough will make kerosene and lubricating oils until 1881, but will confine himself after that to producing petroleum jelly.

Wellesley College for Women, founded in 1870, begins classes in a lavishly landscaped park round Lake Waban at Wellesley, Mass., with a main building whose central hall has a four-story glass-roofed central hall. Boston lawyer Henry Durant who profited in the Civil War by making engines and other war materiel for the Union Army has since become something of an evangelist, and has built the college. Smith College opens at Northampton, Mass. (*see* 1871).

Brigham Young University is founded at Salt Lake City in Utah Territory.

Hebrew Union College is founded at Cincinnati by Stephen M. Wise.

The first duplicating process to employ a wax stencil is perfected by New York inventor Thomas Alva Edison, 28, who has developed quadruplex telegraphy and is experimenting with parrafin paper for possible use as telegraph tape. Edison will receive a patent next year for "a method of preparing autographic stencils for printing" and will obtain a second patent for an improved method in 1880. He will license Chicago lumberman Albert Blake Dick, now 19, to use his invention. Dick will construct a flat-bed duplicator suitable for office use, employing a strong stencil fabric made from a species of hazel bush that grows only in certain Japanese islands, and the first A. B. Dick Diaphragm Mimeograph will go on sale March 17, 1887 (*see* typewriter stencil, 1888).

A high-speed newspaper folding apparatus is invented by Richard Hoe (*see* 1871).

N. W. Ayer & Son of Philadelphia offers advertisers, "open contracts" which give them access to the true rates charged by newspapers and religious journals (*see* 1868). Rates have been set up to now by advertising agents who charged whatever the traffic would bear, but Ayer will act as the advertiser's agent rather than as the newspaper's agent (*see* Rowell, 1869; Batten, 1891; ANPA resolution, 1893).

The *Chicago Daily News* begins publication December 25 and is the city's first penny newspaper (most other papers cost a nickel). Started in a small office in the same building as the *Skandinaven,* the paper is edited by local journalist Melville Elijah Stone, 27, with Percy H. Meggy and William E. Doughy.

The first American-made Christmas cards are produced at Boston by German-American lithographer Louis Prang, 51, who makes the cards for the English trade (*see* Cole, 1843). Prang's firm has been publishing $6 reproductions of famous works of art ("chromos") since 1865, but he will concentrate on introducing Christmas cards in America to develop a market that he will dominate until 1890 when cheaper imports from Germany will put him out of business (*see* Hall, 1910).

Painting *Boating at Argenteuil* by Claude Monet; *The Agnew Clinic* by Thomas Eakins. French painter J. P. C. Corot dies February 22 at age 78.

Sculpture Germany's 56-foot tall statue Hermanns-Denkmal in the Teutoberger Forest of Lower Saxony is dedicated to celebrate the triumph of the Germanic chieftain Arminus over the Roman legions of Varus in 9 A.D.

The "Hermes" produced by the Greek sculptor Praxiteles in the 4th century B.C. is unearthed at Olympia.

The "Great Chac-Mool" reclining limestone figure from the Maya-Toltec civilization of the 10th to 12th centuries A.D. in Yucatan is discovered at the entrance to a temple at Chichen-Itza.

A photoengraving process that will be the basis of an industry is patented by German-American photographer David Bachrach, Jr., 30, and Edward Levy, 29. Bachrach will establish the portrait photography firm Bachrach, Inc. Levy and his brother Max will patent an etched glass grating or screen for making halftone engravings (*see* 1893; Ives, 1886).

Opera *Carmen* 3/3 at the Opéra-Comique, Paris, with music by Georges Bizet who dies June 3 at age 36 of a throat ailment. Girls from a cigarette factory smoke on stage in Act I and the heroine sings the "Habanera." *Trial by Jury* 3/5 at London's Royalty Theatre begins a 21-year series of comic Gilbert & Sullivan operettas with librettos by W. S. Gilbert, music by Arthur S. Sullivan.

The Paris Opéra completed by French architect Jean Louis Charles Garnier, 50, has the largest stage of its kind in the world and Paris hails the structure as a worldly reply to the 530-year-old Notre Dame Cathedral. The huge stage occupies less than one-third of the 50 million franc building's total space of which more than half is taken up by foyers, galleries, and staircases that provide settings for tête-à-têtes.

A new Vienna Opera House opens with a performance of the Beethoven opera *Fidelio* of 1814.

First performances *Danse Macabre* symphonic poem by Camille Saint-Säens 1/24 at Paris; *Symphonie espagnole* for Violin and Orchestra by French composer Edouard Lalo, 52, 2/7 at Paris; *The Moldau* (*Vltava*) (symphonic poem) by Bedrich Smetana 4/4 at Prague; Concerto No. 1 for Piano and Orchestra by Petr Ilich Tchaikovsky 10/25 at Boston's Music Hall with Hans von Bülow as soloist; Concerto No. 4 in C minor by Camille Saint-Säens 10/31 at Paris; Symphony No. 3 in D major by Petr Ilich Tchaikovsky 11/19 at Moscow.

The Boston Symphony has its genesis in the Boston Philharmonic Club founded by German-American conductor Bernhard Listemann, 34 (*see* 1881).

The first organized Canadian ice hockey match is played March 3 at Montreal's Victoria Skating Rink (*see* Stanley Cup, 1893).

The Kentucky Derby has its first running at Louisville's new Churchill Downs and a small chestnut colt

1875 (cont.) named Aristides wins the 1.5 mile stakes race. Local promoter M. Lewis Clark returned from a trip to England a few years ago with plans to establish a series of races that will be comparable to the Derby Stakes at Epsom Downs, the Oaks, and other English racing classics; he predicts that within 10 years the winner of the Kentucky Derby will sell for more money than the farm on which it was raised and that one offspring of a Kentucky Derby winner will fetch more as a yearling than did his sire and dam combined. The stakes race for 3-year-olds will be shortened to 1.25 miles, it will be held early each May, and it will join with the 1 3/16 mile Preakness Stakes inaugurated in 1873 and with the 1.5 mile Belmont Stakes begun in 1867 to comprise the Triple Crown of U.S. horseracing.

The first roller skating rink opens August 2 in Belgravia, London (*see* Plimpton, 1863).

English swimmer Captain Matthew Webb, 27, crosses the English Channel from Dover to Calais August 25 in 22 hours and is the first to accomplish the feat (*see* Ederle, 1926).

The first Harvard-Yale football game is held November 12 at New Haven under "concessionary rules" that permit running with the ball and tackling (*see* 1874; Walter Camp, 1889).

R. J. Reynolds Tobacco Company has its origin in a Winston, N.C., factory set up by former tobacco peddler Richard Joshua Reynolds, 25, who has amassed $7,500 in capital working in partnership with his father. Reynolds uses $2,400 to build a 36- by 60-foot frame structure and equip it with a few crude pieces of machinery, he uses the rest to buy leaf tobacco, and he begins manufacturing pipe tobacco from burley leaf (Winston has become a center for bright tobacco production) (*see* Slade brothers, 1852; Prince Albert, 1907).

Richmond tobacco merchants Lewis Ginter and John F. Allen go into partnership to produce cigarettes from domestic bright tobacco. The cigarettes have a light smoke and a cheap price that soon wins them wide popularity (*see* 1888).

U.S. cigarette production reaches 50 million but will increase rapidly after 1882 when a cigarette manufacturing machine invented 3 years ago comes into practical commercial use. The machine that will be patented in November of next year by Albert H. Hook of New York feeds tobacco to a ribbon of paper as it is drawn from a spool, the edges pass over a gummed wheel, and a continuous cigarette is produced that the machine then cuts into separate lengths.

Liberty's of London opens at 218A Regent Street with Liberty prints and home furnishings that become so popular the shop will have to move in 1882 to larger quarters at 142–144 Regent Street (*see* 1862; 1924).

New York's "Tweed" Courthouse is completed north of City Hall at a cost of $13 million. The estimate had been $250,000 but Boss Tweed's cronies have run up huge bills including $179,729 for three tables and 40 chairs, nearly $361,000 for just a month's work by a single, solitary carpenter, but the one-time political boss is released from prison after having served a brief term for larceny and forgery (*see* 1869). Authorities rearrest Tweed in a civil action brought by the state to recover his loot, he escapes from jail in December, flees to Cuba, and proceeds to Spain disguised as a sailor, but he is recognized from a Thomas Nast cartoon, he is apprehended and returned to New York, and he will die in prison in 1878 at age 55.

A magnificent new Palmer House opens in Chicago to replace the hotel owned by merchant Potter Palmer that burned in the 1871 fire. The new hotel has a mammoth barbershop with silver dollars embedded in its floor and a lavish dining room with dishes that include broiled buffalo, antelope, bear, mountain sheep, boned quail in plumage, blackbirds, partridge, and other "ornamental dishes" (*see* 1925).

The United States Hotel opens at Saratoga Springs, N.Y., with nearly 1,000 rooms for the summer season. The new hotel calls itself the world's largest.

San Francisco's Palace Hotel opens October 2 with 755 20- by 20-foot rooms, 437 baths, five elevators, seven iron stairways, and a crystal roof over its inner court. Built with 12-foot foundations and a wrought-iron skeleton, the new hotel is supplied with water from four artesian wells and San Franciscans insist their new Palace is the world's largest city hotel, calling the United States Hotel (above) merely a resort hotel (*see* 1906).

Bangkok's Oriental Hotel opens on the Chao Phya River.

 President Grant vetoes a bill that would protect the U.S. buffalo from extinction (*see* 1870; 1879).

Arbor Day April 22 encourages Americans to plant trees on the open prairie. Nebraska agriculturist J. Sterling Morton, 43, has dreamed up the idea and within 12 years 40 states will have made April 22 an official Arbor Day (*see* Kilmer, 1913).

Earthquakes in Colombia and Venezuela May 16 take 16,000 lives.

Barbed wire is shown to be safe and effective in a demonstration put on at San Antonio, Tex., by Illinois promoter John Warne Gates, 20, who turns the main plaza of the town into a giant corral that can hold longhorned cattle (*see* Glidden, Haish, 1873). Barbed wire will begin the end of the open range in America and will launch the career of "Bet-you-a-million" Gates (*see* 1877; 1898).

U.S. Grangers fail in a scheme to produce farm equipment (*see* 1872). The Grange has bought up patents for cultivators, seeders, mowers, reapers, and many other machines and implements and it has begun to manufacture them, but the effort falls victim to patent suits, lack of capital, defective machines, and lack of cooperation in a society of rural individualists.

Combines come into use on some U.S. wheat farms.

The first American state agricultural experiment station is established at Wesleyan University in Middletown, Conn., July 20.

Luther Burbank establishes a nursery at Santa Rosa, Calif., with money obtained from the sale of his 1872 Burbank potato. Burbank will develop new forms of food and ornamental plant life by selection and cross-fertilization at Santa Rosa (*see* Shull, 1905).

The Bing cherry is developed by a Chinese orchardman in Oregon.

Apples are grown for the first time in Washington's Yakima Valley.

Navel oranges are produced at Riverside, Calif., by Jonathan and Eliza C. Tibbetts who 2 years ago obtained two trees from the USDA at Washington, which in 1871 received a dozen budded seedlings from Bahia, Brazil. The seedless winter-ripening fruit are the first ever seen in the United States and will be called Washington oranges (because the first trees came from Washington) as they proliferate to dominate California groves (*see* Valencias, 1906).

The orange crate is devised by U. S. inventor E. Bean whose 15 pound crate holds 90 pounds (about 200 pieces) and will lead to widescale marketing of the fruit (*see* Orange Growers Protective Union, 1885).

Atlantic salmon are planted in inland lakes by the U.S. Fish Commission. Land-locked salmon will be an important U.S. game fish and food fish (*see* shad, 1873; carp, 1879).

A new British Sale of Food and Drugs Law tightens restrictions against adulteration, making any adulteration injurious to health punishable with a heavy fine and making a second offense punishable with imprisonment if the seller is proved to have guilty knowledge of the adulteration (*see* 1860).

British sugar consumption rises to 60 pounds per capita, up from 47 in 1872 (*see* 1889).

Synthetic vanillin is produced by Berlin chemist Ferdinand Tiemann, 27, who patents a process for making the key flavor ingredient in natural vanilla beans.

Societé Anonymé Lactée Henri Nestlé is founded by businessmen of Vevey, Switzerland, who outbid Geneva bankers to acquire the operation of Henri Nestlé which is selling hundreds of thousands of tins of baby food each year and is the town's foremost enterprise (*see* 1866). The bankers have offered a million francs, but the Vevey businessmen offer more and provide Nestlé's wife with a coach and two horses to sweeten their proposition.

The first milk chocolate for eating is invented at Vevey (above) by the Nestlé shopman in collaboration with the foreman of Daniel Peter's chocolate factory (*see* Cadbury, 1847). They hit upon the idea of mixing sweetened condensed milk with chocolate and create a product that meets with immediate commercial success (*see* Peter and Kohler, 1904; Hershey, 1893).

The New York Condensed Milk Company begins selling fluid milk in addition to its condensed milk 1 year after the death of founder Gail Borden at age 72 (*see* 1858; 1885).

H. J. Heinz's firm Heinz & Noble is forced into bankruptcy after contracting to buy some crops that have come in more abundantly than expected, but Heinz pays off the firm's creditors with help from his wife (*see* 1869; 1876).

B&M Baked Beans are produced for use by men in the fishing fleet of Burnham & Morill Company at Portland, Me. They are the world's first canned baked beans (*see* 1867; 1927; Van Camp, 1862).

Patent rights to a tapered tin for compressed corn beef are obtained by Arthur A. Libby whose firm will export $2,500 worth of canned corned beef in 2-pound tins to London next year (*see* 1868; 1878).

A machine is invented to strip the kernels from corn cobs. It will lead to widescale canning of sweet corn (*see* Minnesota Valley Canning Company, 1903).

Steel Cut Oats are introduced by oatmeal king Ferdinand Schumacher whose new product has a flaky composition that gives it a uniformly acceptable taste and consistency (*see* 1856). Schumacher uses a new machine invented largely by his employee Asmus J. Ehrrichsen whose process is the first real innovation in milling oats, employing a series of horizontal knife blades to cut the hulled oats (groats) into a meal that has little or none of the floury residues that have made oatmeal pasty, lumpy, and glutenous. The Ehrrichsen-Schumacher process is improved upon by another Schumacher employee, William Heston, who obtains patents which he licenses Schumacher to use while reserving the right to use the new process himself (*see* Quaker Mill Company, 1877).

Hires Rootbeer has its beginnings in a recipe for an herb tea discovered by Philadelphia pharmacist Charles Elmer Hires, 24, who takes his bride on a wedding trip to a New Jersey farm. The tea is made from 16 different wild roots and berries that include juniper, pipsissewa, spikenard, sarsaparilla, wintergreen, and hops. Hires takes the recipe back to Philadelphia and begins experimenting with improved formulas (*see* 1876).

A British Trade Marks Act goes into effect and the first trademark registered is for Bass & Company Pale Ale made at Burton-on-Trent in Staffordshire since 1777.

Boston's Locke-Obers Restaurant opens under the name Frank Locke's Winter Place Wine Rooms.

Fertilization of the female egg is accomplished by a single male cell, concludes German embryologist Oscar Hertwig, 26. He has worked with sea urchins (*Arbacia punctulata*) whose female produces roughly a million eggs per season (*see* Fol, 1879).

1876 "Mr. Watson, come here. I want you," says Alexander Graham Bell March 10 in the first complete sentence to be transmitted by voice over wire. Bell has im-

1876 (cont.) proved the telephone he invented in 1875, he has been granted a patent on his 29th birthday March 3, and he uses the instrument at 5 Exeter Place, Boston, to speak with his 22-year-old assistant Thomas Augustus Watson. The patent will be challenged by Elisha Gray of the 4-year-old Western Electric Company, but Bell's claim will be upheld in the courts although Western Electric will manufacture the Bell telephone (*see* 1882).

Bell demonstrates his telephone at the U.S. Centennial Exposition that opens May 10 at Philadelphia (*see* below): the Brazilian emperor Dom Pedro II jumps out of his seat June 25 saying, "I hear, I hear!"

Bell's future father-in-law Gardiner Green Hubbard, 51, promotes the new telephone. A Boston lawyer whose daughter's deafness has led him to help found the Clarke Institution for the Deaf which he has headed since 1867, Hubbard borrows a telegraph line between Boston and the Cambridge Observatory, he attaches a telephone at each end, and in mid-October he speaks with Thomas Watson for more than 3 hours in the first sustained telephone conversation (*see* 1877).

Western Union president William Orton turns down an offer to acquire the Bell telephone (above) for $100,000, calling it a toy, a "scientific curiosity" that permits users to speak or listen but not both at once.

Thomas A. Edison is retained by Western Union (above) to improve on Bell's telephone, he builds a laboratory at Menlo Park, N.J., with $40,000 he has earned from a patented stockticker, he opens the world's first research laboratory, and he finds that carbon black makes a perfect transmitter. Edison develops a carbon transmitter that will make the telephone commercially practicable and his invention of carbonization will soon find other applications (*see* mimeograph, 1875; Swan, 1878; Cabot, 1887).

The Remington typewriter introduced at the Philadelphia Centennial Exposition (below) does not yet have a shift key (*see* 1874; 1878). Also exhibited are an envelope-making machine and the first stamped envelopes.

The U.S. Centennial Exposition opened by President Grant at Fairmount Park is called officially the "International Exhibition of Arts, Manufactures and Products of the Soil and Mine": 37 foreign nations and 26 states are represented along with innumerable private exhibitors.

All exhibits in Machinery Hall at the Centennial Exposition are powered by a great 160-horsepower engine built by the Corliss Steam Engine Company of Providence, R.I., started in 1856 by inventor George H. Corliss of 1851 London Great Exhibition fame. The Corliss engine is called the symbol of the age by Harvard historian Henry Brooks Adams, 38.

Rochester's George Selden attends the Exposition with a partner to demonstrate their patented machine for shaving and finishing barrel hoops. Selden studies the Brayton engine, developed by an Englishman living in Boston, and he notes that while the other engines exhibited operate on illuminating gas the Brayton engine employes crude petroleum fuel. It weighs 1,160 pounds and develops only 1.4 horsepower but Selden sees the possibility of a lighter, more efficiently designed engine (*see* 1873; 1879).

A four-cycle gasoline engine far more advanced than his 1866 engine is invented by German engineer Nikolaus August Otto (*see* Benz, 1885).

Korean independence from China is recognized by Japan February 26 in a treaty that opens three Korean ports to Japanese trade, permits Japan to have a resident at Seoul, and brings no protest from China.

Queen Victoria is made Empress of India under the Royal Titles Bill passed by Parliament in April and the British prime minister Benjamin Disraeli is elevated to the peerage in August and made earl of Beaconsfield.

Egyptian forces are defeated by Ethiopian troops at Gura, but then gain a crushing victory in February as the war that began last year continues.

The Ottoman sultan Abdul Aziz is deposed May 29 at age 46 after a 15-year reign, he dies 4 days later probably by his own hand but possibly as a murder victim, and he is succeeded by his 35-year-old nephew who has been imprisoned for 15 years by Abdul Aziz. Proclaimed "emperor by the grace of God and the will of the people," the nephew begins a 3-month reign as Murad V.

A Bulgarian insurrection has begun in May and Turkish irregulars are sent in to quell the uprising.

Serbia declares war on Turkey June 30 and is joined by Montenegro July 2, but the Serbs are completely defeated at Alexinatz September 1 and the Bulgarians are slaughtered by the thousands to suppress their insurrection which is ended in September.

The Ottoman sultan Murad V is declared insane and is deposed August 31. He is succeeded by his 33-year-old brother who will reign until 1909 as Abdul Hamid II.

Britons are aroused against the Turks by former prime minister William E. Gladstone whose pamphlet "The Bulgarian Horrors and the Question of the East" appears September 6 and Russia prepares for war against the Turks (*see* 1877).

A Turkish Constitution proclaimed December 23 by the 54-year-old grand vizier Midhat Pasha declares the indivisibility of the Ottoman Empire and provides for parliamentary government based on representation of all groups in society (but *see* 1877).

Mexican general Porfirio Diaz, 46, overthrows President Lerdo de Tejada and begins to restore order in a program that will stabilize the country, attract foreign capital, develop industry, build railways, promote public works, and increase commerce.

Colorado is admitted to the Union as the 38th state.

The U.S. presidential election in November ends in a dispute when neither Democrat Samuel J. Tilden of New York nor Republican Rutherford Birchard Hayes of Ohio wins the necessary 185 electoral votes (Tilden falls one vote short): two sets of returns leave 20 votes from Florida, Louisiana, Oregon, and South Carolina in dispute and there is no constitutional provision to cover the situation (see 1877).

Black militiamen have been massacred at Hamburg, S. C., in July and a race war has begun in that state.

Chiricahua Apaches in Arizona Territory are moved to a reservation occupied earlier by western Apaches and a 10-year reign of terror against white settlers in the Southwest is begun by the Chiricahua leader Geronimo who leads a band of his warriors into Mexico (see Cochise, 1872). The 47-year-old Geronimo (Jerome) has been given his name by Mexicans he raided in retaliation for the 1858 killing of his family, but his real name is Goyathalay (see 1877).

The Battle of the Little Big Horn June 25 ends in the massacre of a 264-man U.S. Seventh Cavalry force under General George Armstrong Custer, 37, at the hands of Sioux chief Sitting Bull, 42, with tribesmen under chieftains Gall and Crazy Horse. The Sioux have been angered by the slaughter of buffalo in Montana Territory by the advancing whites in the Black Hills gold rush (see Deadwood Gulch, 1875; Homestake, below; Wounded Knee, 1890).

The Turkish Constitution (above) provides for freedom of conscience, liberty of the individual, equality of taxation, and freedom of the press and education, but the new sultan will let it lapse (see 1856).

A Merchant Shipping Act designed to prevent overloading of ships and use of unseaworthy vessels is passed by Parliament after a campaign by M. P. Samuel Plimsoll, 52. A retired London coal merchant, Plimsoll is known as "the Sailors' Friend" on the strength of his 1872 book Our Seamen, and his efforts in behalf of seamen will be commemorated in the Plimsoll line on ships' hulls.

The International Association for the Exploration and Civilization of Africa is founded under the auspices of the Belgian king Leopold II.

Compagnie International des Wagons-Lits et des Grandes Express Européens is organized to bring sleeping cars to Europe. Engineer-founder Georges Nagelmakers has crossed the United States in Pullman cars (see Train Bleu, 1879).

San Francisco and Los Angeles are linked by rail September 6 as the Southern Pacific reaches Los Angeles to give that city a route to the East but high freight rates and water shortages will retard development of Los Angeles whose population will not exceed 10,000 for another few years.

The St. Louis and San Francisco (Frisco Line) is founded September 11 to take over most of the Atlantic & Pacific Railroad lines through Indian Territory.

The first carload of California fruit reaches the Mississippi Valley, but the freight rate is too steep for most growers (see Columbian Exposition, 1893).

Canada's Intercolonial Railroad opens to link Ontario with the Maritime Provinces.

A train wreck December 29 kills 83 at Ashtabula, Ohio, as a 13-year-old bridge on Cornelius Vanderbilt's Lake Shore & Michigan Southern gives way during a storm off Lake Erie and 10 cars of the Pacific Express pulled by two locomotives plunge into a creek 150 feet below, bursting into flames. A subordinate engineer was fired by the road's president in 1863 when he protested against construction of the Howe truss bridge built by the road's chief engineer.

"On the Equilibrium of Heterogeneous Substances" by Yale professor of mathematical physics Josiah Willard Gibbs, 37, extends understanding of thermodynamics. The paper will be followed by another in 1878 as Gibbs lays the theoretical groundwork for the science of physical chemistry, but the importance of his work will not be recognized for years.

The American Chemical Society is organized.

The Reichsbank that will play a major role in German economic development opens in January.

Homestake Mining Co., is founded at Lead (pronounced Leed, meaning "lode") in the Black Hills of Dakota Territory. The gold mine opened by George Hearst and Ben Ali Haggin will be the largest U.S. gold producer (see 1859; Custer, above).

Sherwin-Williams Company's H. A. Sherwin, at Cleveland, pioneers prepared, ready-to-apply paint by developing a new machine that grinds good-bodied pigments so finely and evenly that they will suspend in linseed oil (see 1870). By 1884 Sherwin-Williams will be selling $539,000 worth of paint, it

Alexander Graham Bell's telephone replaced the written word with the spoken word for instant communication.

1876 (cont.) will have profits of $36,000, and it will proceed to market varnishes and then enamels (pigments suspended in varnish) (*see* 1888).

The stillson wrench is patented by Somerville, Mass., inventor Daniel C. Stillson who has whittled a wooden model of his pipe or screw wrench.

 The Danish Red Cross is founded at Copenhagen.

Eli Lilly Company is founded May 10 at Indianapolis by former Union Army officer Eli Lilly, 38, who starts with $1,400 in capital and two employees to produce reliable medications for responsible physicians in an era dominated by patent medicines. Widower Lilly takes in his 14-year-old son Josiah Kirby in June.

A label for "Mrs. Lydia E. Pinkham's Vegetable Compound" is patented by Lynn, Mass., housewife Lydia Estes Pinkham, 57, whose husband Isaac lost all his money in the 1873 financial crash. Mrs. Pinkham has for more than a decade been concocting an herbal medicine for "woman's weakness" and related ills, a nostrum she will continue to brew in her own kitchen and for which she will write her own homely advertising until her death in 1883 (*see* 1898).

Seventh Day Adventist surgeon John Harvey Kellogg, 24, assumes management of the Western Health Reform Institute founded at Battle Creek, Mich., in 1866. A champion of vegetarianism, Kellogg will ask audiences, "How can you eat anything that looks out of eyes?" and he will develop vegetarian foods including a form of peanut butter and scores of dried cereals (*see* Granula, 1877).

 Johns Hopkins University is founded at Baltimore with a bequest from the late Baltimore financier Johns Hopkins who died 3 years ago at age 78 (*see* saccharin, 1879; hospital and medical school, 1893).

The U.S. Coast Guard Academy is founded at New London, Conn.

The University of Texas is founded at Austin.

Texas A & M (Agricultural and Mechanical College of Texas) is founded near Bryan.

 Stenotypy begins to facilitate courtroom reporting and to make records of legal proceedings more accurate. New York inventor John Colinergos Zachos patents a "typewriter and phonotypic notation" device with type fixed on 18 shuttle bars, two or more may be placed in position simultaneously, the device has a plunger common to all the bars for making impressions, and the device permits printing a legible text at a high reporting speed.

McCall's magazine begins publication in April under the name *The Queen*. Scots-American entrepreneur James McCall started the McCall Pattern Company in 1870 with a small shop at 543 Broadway, New York, and he uses the eight-page pattern and fashion periodical to promote his dress patterns, but it will grow to become a major magazine for women.

Corriere della Sera begins publication at Milan. It is the first reliable Italian newspaper, it will be Italy's one national newspaper, but even 90 years after its founding only four Italians in 10 will read any daily paper.

 "A Classification and Subject Index for Cataloguing and Arranging the Books and Pamphlets of a Library" by Amherst College librarian Melvil Dewey, 25, originates the Dewey decimal system.

Thomas Y. Crowell Company publishers is founded at New York by Boston bookbinder Thomas Young Crowell, 40, who last year invested less than $6,000 to buy the plates, bound books, and sheet stock of a bankrupt publisher of religious books. A binder for the 9-year-old textbook firm of Ginn Brothers and for other houses, Crowell is an ex-seaman who learned his craft from Boston's Benjamin Bradley.

Nonfiction *Robert's Rules of Order* by U.S. Army Engineer Corps officer Henry Martyn Robert, 39, who has been motivated by experience in civic and church groups to establish authoritative rules for smooth, democratic procedure in any self-governing organization. Robert will publish a revised and enlarged edition in 1915 at age 76.

Fiction *Roderick Hudson* by U.S. émigré author-critic Henry James, 35, who examines the moral and artistic disintegration of an American in Rome and begins a series of perceptive novels about European and American society; *The Prime Minister* by Anthony Trollope; *Marthe* by Dutch novelist Joris Karl (Charles Marie Georges) Huysmans, 28; *The Adventures of Tom Sawyer* by Mark Twain.

Poetry *The Afternoon of a Faun (L'Après midi d'un Faune)* by French poet-schoolteacher Stéphane Mallarmé, 34.

 Painting *The Spirit of '76* by Ohio painter Archibald Willard, 40, who will produce 14 versions of the canvas he has painted for the Philadelphia Centennial Exposition. The first will find a permanent home in Abbot Hall at Marblehead, Mass., but the one Willard will call his "best effort" will be a much larger canvas that will hang in the Cleveland City Hall; *Breezing Up* by Winslow Homer; *Flood at Port-Marly* by Alfred Sisley; *Le Moulin de la Galette* by Pierre Auguste Renoir.

 Theater *Peer Gynt* by Henrik Ibsen 2/24 at Oslo's Christiania Theater, with a "Peer Gynt Suite" by Edvard Grieg.

 Opera *La Gioconda* 4/8 at Milan's Teatro alla Scala, with a libretto from the Victor Hugo play *Angelo, Le Tyran de Padoue,* music by Italian composer Amilcare Ponchielli, 42, who wins acclaim for his "Dance of the Hours" ("Danze delle Ora"); *The Kiss (Hubicka)* 11/7 at Prague, with music by Bedrich Smetana; *The Golden Slippers (Vakula the Smith)* 11/24 at St. Petersburg's Maryinsky Theater, with music by Petr Ilich Tchaikovsky, libretto from a Gogol story.

The first complete performance of Richard Wagner's operatic Ring cycle opens the Festspielhaus that

Wagner has built at Bayreuth where he has lived for the past 4 years with his wife Cosima. Wagner has written the tetralogy *Der Ring des Nibelungen* over the course of 26 years and his Bayreuth Festival that begins August 13 attracts the kaiser Wilhelm I, his nephew Ludwig II of Bavaria, philosopher Friedrich Nietzsche, and many prominent composers.

The Goodspeed Opera House opens at East Haddam, Conn.

First performances Symphony No. 1 in C minor by Johannes Brahms 11/4 at Karlsruhe; *Marche Slav* by Petr Ilich Tchaikovsky 11/17 at Moscow.

Popular songs "I'll Take You Home Again, Kathleen" by U.S. songwriter Thomas P. Westendorf, 28; "Grandfather's Clock" by Henry Clay Work: "But it stopped, short—never to go again—when the old man died."

Hymns "What a Friend We Have in Jesus" by U.S. evangelist and hymn writer Ira David Sankey, 36, who has been touring since 1870 with missionary-evangelist Dwight Lyman Moody, 39, lyrics by Horatius Bonar; "The Ninety and Nine" by Ira David Sankey, lyrics by E. C. Clephane; "Trusting Jesus, that Is All" by Ira David Sankey, lyrics by E. P. Stites.

A player piano that produces music mechanically from perforated paper rolls is demonstrated at St. Louis by Scots-American inventor John McTammany, 31, who got his idea while repairing a music box during his convalescence from serious injuries sustained in the Civil War. McTammany will obtain a patent in 1881, but will lose control of his player piano manufacturing company and will die a pauper after spending income from the piano to defend his patent rights against violators.

U.S. baseball's National League is founded February 2 (*see* Cincinnati, 1869; American League, 1901).

Chicago Nationals pitcher Albert Goodwill Spalding, 26, and his brother each put up $400 to start a sporting goods business that will grow to dominate the American sports scene. Spalding will be manager, then secretary, then president of the Chicago club until 1891, he will edit *Spalding's Official Baseball Guide* beginning in 1878, the Spalding brothers will take in their banker brother-in-law William T. Brown that year, and he will provide capital with which the company will expand in 1885 to become a leading producer of baseball gloves by acquiring A. J. Reach Company, started by another ballplayer (*see* 1892).

The first Canadian bid to gain the America's Cup in ocean yacht racing ends in failure as the *Countess of Dufferin* loses 2 to 0 to the U.S. defender *Madeleine*.

The London Rowing Club four loses to the Albany Beaverwycks at Philadelphia's Centennial Regatta. *The Times* of London complains that the Albany crew's amateurs are "working mechanics" and "handicraftsmen" rather than true amateurs who row purely for recreation in leisure hours.

England's 47-year-old Henley Regatta gets its first U.S. entry as Columbia University's four-oared shell competes with British shells. The regatta will continue to be an Anglo-American event and in some years will have more entries from U.S. colleges, prep schools, and clubs than from British.

The U.S. stallion Hambletonian dies at age 27 after having sired hundreds of offspring that will make trotting horses with Hambletonian blood the dominant force in U.S. harness racing for more than a century. Hambletonian was sired by Abdallah who had been sired by Mambrino whose sire was the English horse Messenger brought to America in 1788 at age 8 (*see* Dan Patch, 1902).

B.V.D. underwear for men is introduced by New York's Bradley, Voorhees, and Day whose one-piece B.V.D.'s will be called "Babies' Ventilated Diapers" and will be given other nicknames but will become almost generic for underwear.

The Bissell Grand Rapids carpet sweeper patented by Grand Rapids, Mich., china shop proprietor M. R. Bissell is the world's first carpet sweeper (*see* vacuum cleaner, 1901). Bissell suffers from allergic headaches caused by the dusty straw in which china is packed and has devised a sweeper with a knob that adjusts its brushes to variations in floor surface and with a box to contain the dust.

Wild Bill Hickok is murdered August 2 at Deadwood in Dakota Territory at age 39. A one-time scout for the Union Army, James Butler Hickok has served as marshal at Fort Riley, Hays City, and Abilene, Kan., but he is shot from behind by Jack McCall in Deadwood's Saloon No. 10 while sitting at a poker table holding two pairs, aces and eights, that will become known as the "Dead Man's Hand."

A Northfield, Minn., attempt on a bank September 7 by Frank and Jesse James and the Younger brothers is foiled by local citizenry (*see* 1872). Two of the gang are killed in a hail of bullets, four are captured including Cole Younger and his brothers James and Robert. The James brothers escape, the Younger brothers are tried, convicted, and sent to prison. Robert Younger will die in prison in 1889, his brothers will be paroled in July, 1901, James Younger will take his own life in 1902, Cole Younger will be pardoned in 1903 and will live until 1916 (*see* James, 1882).

San Francisco's I. Magnin and Company has its beginnings in the Yankee Notions Store opened by Dutch-American seamstress Mary Ann Magnin, 27, whose husband Isaac is a woodcarver and gilder. Her needles, pins, threads, and buttons have no special distinction but Magnin will attract a wide following with the bridal trousseaux and infant layettes that she will make while raising seven children and running the shop. Her son E. John Magnin will enter the business in 1888 at age 17 and will move the store to Market Street where his brother Grover will join him while another brother will go off on his own to start the less expensive Joseph Magnin Co. (*see* 1906).

1876 (cont.) Newport's Walter Sherman House is completed by architect Henry Hobson Richardson.

Charleston's Calhoun Mansion is completed.

A bentwood cafe chair that will be standard furniture in world restaurants and saloons for nearly a century is introduced at Vienna by Gebruder Thonet (*see* Le Corbusier, 1925).

 New York's Central Park is completed after 17 years of work.

"God's First Temples—How Shall We Preserve Our Forests" by John Muir is published in a San Francisco newspaper (*see* 1868). Muir has seen sheepmen "and their hoofed locusts" overgrazing the "gardens and meadows" of the Merced River Valley above Yosemite and has heard the lumbermill saws "booming and moaning like bad ghosts" (*see* Yosemite Park, 1890).

Palm Beach, Fla., has its beginnings as cocoanuts from the wreck of the Spanish ship *Providencia* wash ashore. Palm trees seeded by the coconuts will proliferate in the area (*see* hotel, 1894).

A colony of passenger pigeons in Michigan is reported to cover an area 28 miles long and from 3 to 4 miles wide (*see* 1871; 1878).

 Famine will kill 9.6 million in Northern China and 5 million in India in the next 3 years as drought withers wheatfields in China's Shansi province and on India's Deccan Plateau.

Argentina emerges as a grain-exporting nation.

Brazil's rubber monopoly is broken by English explorer Henry A. Wickham, 30, who smuggles 70,000 seeds of the rubber tree *Hevea Brasiliensis* to the Royal Gardens at Kew whence they will be transplanted in Ceylon, India, Malaya, and the East Indies on efficient plantations that will wreck Brazil's wild rubber economy.

Hawaiian sugar is placed on the free list for importation into the United States through a treaty negotiated by Hawaiian planter Henry Alpheus Pierce Carter, 39, who has been in the mercantile business at Honolulu since age 17.

The Grange departs from its apolitical stance and begins to lobby for U.S. tax law revision including an end to tax exemption for railroad properties (*see* 1873). The Grange also demands lower interest rates, better schools, cheap textbooks, and cheaper bread, coal, and clothing.

Colorado cattleman Charles Goodnight settles one of the West's first sheepherder-cattlemen wars and heads back to Texas where he discovers an enormous valley in the Palo Duro Canyon area where 10,000 buffalo are feeding near the Canadian River (*see* 1866). After having prospered as a Colorado Territory rancher, banker, and irrigation promoter, Goodnight was wiped out in the panic of 1873, but he has recovered with money made in cattle drives. He and his cowboys drive out the buffalo and establish the Old Home Ranch, the first ranch in the Texas Panhandle. Financed by Irish-American investor John G.

Adair of Denver, Goodnight will develop the million-acre JA Ranch and the Goodnight-Adair partnership will net more than half a million dollars in 5 years.

W. Atlee Burpee & Co. is founded at Philadelphia by Canadian-American entrepreneur Washington Atlee Burpee, 18, who sells livestock by mail but who will enter the mail-order seed business in 1882.

 The first successful U.S. sardine cannery is established by New York importer Julius Wolff whose French sardine imports were interrupted by the Franco-Prussian War in 1871 (*see* 1834). Sardine canneries will soon be built at Eastport, Lubec, and other points along the Maine Coast (*see* 1881).

 Vegetarianism is embraced by Russian novelist Leo Tolstoy whose *Anna Karenina* is being serialized.

Canning becomes enormously more efficient with the introduction of the Howe "floater" which makes the tinsmith's soldering iron obsolete. A long line of cans, complete with tops and bottoms, floats slowly through the solder bath in the Howe machine picking up enough melted solder to make tight joints and permitting two men and two helpers to turn out more than 1,000 cans per day, 100 times the number one man and a helper could make in the first half of the century. In another 10 years the same number of men will be able to produce 1,500 cans per day (*see* 1895; 1897; Libby, 1891).

Delaware canner A. B. Richardson applies for a patent on a new can shape and a new method for canning boneless hams (*see* 1855). Richardson dies early in the year at age 50.

The first all-roller flour mill to be seen in America is displayed at the Philadelphia Centennial Exposition (above) but the mill is dismantled after the fair (*see* Washburn, 1874; Pillsbury, 1878).

Philadelphia fairgoers see bread and rolls raised with compressed yeast right before their eyes at a model Viennese bakery set up by Cincinnati's Gaff, Fleischmann and Company which has invested all its resources in the display to spread word about Fleischmann's Yeast (*see* 1870; 1929).

Bananas fetch 10 cents each at the Philadelphia fair. The foil-wrapped novelty gives most fairgoers their first taste of the tropical fruit (*see* Baker, 1871; Boston Fruit, 1885).

Budweiser beer wins top honors in a competition at the Philadelphia fair. The new beer has been developed by Adolphus Busch whose E. Anheuser and Co., produces 15 other brands of beer, many of them pasteurized, and introduces refrigerated railcars for all its beers (*see* 1873; Michelob, 1896).

Hires Rootbeer Household Extract is promoted at the fair with an exhibit displaying packages of dried roots, barks, and herbs (*see* 1875). Charles E. Hires has adopted the name "rootbeer" at the advice of his friend Russell Conwell, 33, who says hard-drinking Pennsylvania coal-miners will be more attracted to "rootbeer" than to "herb tea" (*see* 1886; Conwell's Temple University, 1884).

Heinz's Tomato Ketchup is introduced by Pittsburgh's H. J. Heinz who joins with his brother and a cousin to establish F. and J. Heinz (*see* 1875). Heinz packs pickles and other foods as well as the ketchup, which is 29 percent sugar (*see* 1879).

The A&P grocery chain of Huntington Hartford opens its 67th store (*see* 1871; 1880).

Glasgow grocer Thomas Johnstone Lipton opens his first shop at age 26. Lipton sailed to America at age 15 to spend 4 years learning the merchandising methods employed in the grocery section of a New York department store and he will pioneer new methods of food advertising. (He begins by having two fat pigs driven through the streets of Glasgow: painted on the pigs' scrubbed sides are the words, "I'm going to Lipton's, The Best Shop In Town for British Bacon.") (*see* 1879; tea, 1890).

The first Fred Harvey restaurant opens in the Santa Fe Railroad depot at Topeka, Kan. English-American restaurateur Frederick Henry Harvey, 41, has been in the United States since 1850, he has worked as a freight agent for J. F. Joy's Chicago, Burlington & Quincy Railroad. Joy has turned down his proposal that clean, well-run restaurants be opened for the benefit of passengers, but the Santa Fe has been receptive to the idea and Harvey's Topeka restaurant will soon be joined by others along the Santa Fe line and at other major rail depots and junctions. Harvey will also operate hotels and beginning in 1890 he will start operating a fleet of dining cars. By the time of his death in early 1901 there will be 47 Fred Harvey restaurants, all serving good food on Irish linen with Sheffield silverware, served by well-trained "Harvey Girls," plus 30 Fred Harvey dining cars and 15 Fred Harvey hotels.

Vienna's Sacher Hotel opens with a restaurant that serves the Sachertorte invented in 1832.

1877 Government regulation of U.S. business gains legal support from the Supreme Court March 1 in the case of *Munn v. Illinois*. The landmark decision sustains the state law of 1871 supervising grain elevators.

Chase National Bank is founded September 12 by New York banker John Thompson, now 75, who founded First National Bank in 1863, but sold his controlling interest in that bank 4 years ago. The new bank takes its name from the late chief justice of the Supreme Court Salmon P. Chase who originated the national banking system in 1863 when he was secretary of the treasury but who died 4 years ago at age 65. The first balance sheet published December 27 shows total resources of $1,042,009.25 (*see* 1928).

State power to fix freight rates for intrastate traffic and for interstate traffic originating within a state's borders is upheld by the Supreme Court March 1 in the case of *Peik v. Chicago and Northwestern Railroad Company*. But a later decision will limit state

regulation to intrastate shipments, it will exempt the much larger volume of freight that crosses state lines, and it will weaken the farmers' victory in the *Peik* decision (*see* 1886; Interstate Commerce Act, 1887).

Cornelius Vanderbilt has died January 4 at age 82 leaving a fortune of more than $100 million to the 38-year-old widow and the 10 children who survive him (relatively little goes to the Commodore's widow and eight daughters but his 56-year-old son William Henry receives $90 million and the four sons of W. H. receive $7.5 million among them). Vanderbilt has laid new steel rails and has built new bridges to cut running time on the New York Central between New York and Chicago from 50 hours to 24 (*see* 1873; 1902).

Callao, Lima & Oroya Railroad builder Henry Meiggs dies at Lima, Peru, September 29 at age 66 after a series of paralytic strokes leaving the world's highest railroad incomplete but his tunnel under Mount Meiggs at an altitude of 15,658 feet remains an engineering marvel (*see* 1871; Grace, 1890).

The first U.S. cantilever bridge is completed across the Kentucky River near Harrodsburg. Designed by Charles Shaler Smith for the Cincinnati Southern Railroad, the $377,500 bridge tested April 20 has three spans of 375 feet each.

Boston entrepreneur Augustus Pope converts his Hartford, Connecticut, air-pistol factory into the first U.S. bicycle factory (*see* Michaux, 1867). Pope's Columbia bicycle with its high front wheel will be popular for more than a decade until safety bicycles make it obsolete, and Pope will soon be grossing $1 million per year (*see* 1896; safety bicycle, 1885).

Standard Oil Company of Ohio president John D. Rockefeller signs a contract with the Pennsylvania Railroad that strengthens his oil-rail monopoly (*see* 1872). Rockefeller has been exploiting the Depression by buying up depressed rivals in the oil industry and gaining control of all major pipelines and of the Pennsylvania's tank cars. Secret and illegal rebates and drawbacks by the railroads give Standard Oil lower freight rates and enable the company to force competitors to merge with the Rockefeller interests (*see* 1882).

The disputed U.S. election of 1876 is decided by an electoral commission appointed January 29 and composed of five senators, five representatives, and five Supreme Court justices. All questions are decided along partisan lines (eight members of the commission are Republicans, seven are Democrats), Democrat Samuel J. Tilden is denied his marginal victory at the polls, and Rutherford B. Hayes is sworn in as president March 4, 2 days after the decision.

Walfish (Walvis) Bay on the coast of Southwest Africa is annexed by the British March 12, the South African Republic is annexed April 12 in violation of the 1852 Sand River Convention that recognized the independence of the Transvaal, and a new Kaffir War begins

1877 (cont.) that will end with the British annexing all of Kaffraria and extending their rule toward the northeast.

Queen Victoria is proclaimed Empress of India in a ceremony (durbar) held at Delhi on Disraeli's initiative. Indian princes assemble to offer their homage.

Russia declares war on Turkey April 24 as the government of Aleksandr II yields to pressure from Panslav elements. A larger war looms as the British cabinet decides July 21 to declare war on Russia if she should occupy Constantinople and if she does not make plans for immediate withdrawal. The Russians suffer reverses at Plevna, allaying fears of British intervention, but Plevna falls to the Russians December 10 and the Turks appeal for mediation (see 1878).

France has had a May 16 crisis that has threatened her survival as a republic. Premier Jules Simon has been forced to resign as Marshal MacMahon has become irritated with his weak opposition to the anticlerical position of French Leftists, but the principle of ministerial responsibility is upheld against the personal power of the Rightist president and France remains a republic (see 1873; Boulanger, 1889).

Japan's samurai warrior class rebels against the "evil counselors" of the Meiji emperor who have denied the samurai their pensions and have forbidden them to wear two swords. The Satsuma Rebellion that begins in January is crushed by September as a modern army of trained commoners is funded by a large issue of paper money.

The "Molly Maguires" make headlines after a decade of activity in Pennsylvania mining towns by the secret Irish-American terrorist society. They have been apprehended by Pinkerton detective James McParlan, 35, an Irish-American himself who 5 years ago gained admission to the fraternal Ancient Order of Hibernians, some of whose lodges have been under Molly Maguire control. Eleven members of the secret society are hanged June 21 and eight more will eventually be hanged, all through testimony given by McParlan who will later become head of Pinkerton's Denver branch and who will be involved in suppressing activities of the Western Federation of Miners in Idaho (see Haywood, 1907).

The New York Central, the Erie, the Pennsylvania, and the Baltimore & Ohio call off a long-standing rate war in April and announce a 10 percent wage cut. When the B&O announces a further 10 percent cut in mid-July, its workers begin a strike at Martinsburg, W. Va., that is soon joined by Pennsylvania Railroad workers. The Pittsburgh roundhouse is set ablaze, the strike spreads across the nation, and the railroads are shut down for a week, and the strike is not ended until federal troops are called in, firing on the workers, killing some, wounding many (both sides claim victory).

The Atchison, Topeka and Santa Fe reduces wages 5 percent August 1 and slashes conductors' salaries from a top of $120 per month to $75. The conductors strike but soon return to work at lower pay (see 1878).

A San Francisco mob burns down 25 Chinatown wash houses in July and anti-Chinese riots ensue for months. The Chinese are given little or no police protection and the situation gives rise to the phrase "not a Chinaman's chance" (see Exclusion Treaty, 1880).

Nez Perce tribespeople in the Northwest are ordered to leave or be removed forcibly after years of passive noncompliance with the treaty they signed in 1863. The 37-year-old Nez Perce leader Chief Joseph says, "I would give up everything rather than have the blood of my people on my hands. . . . I love that land more than all the world. A man who would not love his father's grave is worse than a wild animal." But in the chief's absence his braves kill several whites, U.S. troops are sent in by Howard University founder Oliver Otis Howard, now 47, the troops are nearly annihilated in the Battle of White Bird Canyon. The Nez Perce are weakened after 18 subsequent engagements, Chief Joseph leads 750 tribespeople in a retreat through nearly 1,600 miles of Rocky Mountain wilderness pursued by 600 soldiers, but he is surrounded October 5 by fresh troops under Colonel Nelson Appleton Miles, 38. Forced to surrender less than 40 miles from the safety of the Canadian border in Montana Territory, Chief Joseph says, "I am tired of fighting. Our chiefs are killed. . . . It is cold and we have no blankets. The little children are freezing to death. My people, some of them, have run away to the hills, and we have no blankets, no food. . . . I will fight no more forever."

Apaches in Arizona Territory are ordered out of the Chiricahua reservation at Warm Springs in November by General James Carleton. They are told to move to San Carlos where temperatures in summer reach as high as 140°F in a region with no game and with no food except the meagre rations issued by Indian agents. Any man, woman, or child found off the reservation is to be shot without being given a chance to surrender (see Geronimo, 1876, 1886).

Switzerland's Jews gain full citizenship and Swiss ghetto life is ended by the Emancipation Law enacted May 15.

A technique for fixing and straining bacteria is demonstrated by German country doctor Robert Koch, 33, of Wollstein who last year obtained a pure culture of the anthrax bacillus by using the eye of an ox as a sterile medium for culturing the bacillus. Koch will confirm Louis Pasteur's suggestion that every disease produced by microorganisms is produced by a specific bacillus (see tuberculosis bacillus, 1882).

The germicidal qualities of ultraviolet rays are discovered by English researchers A. Downes and T. P. Blunt whose findings will lead to new techniques for sterilization.

The cystoscope for examining the inside of the urinary bladder and introducing medication into the bladder is constructed by German surgeon-urologist Max Nitze, 28, with help from an instrument maker named Leiter.

The chronic bone disease *osteitis deformans* that will be called Paget's disease is described by London surgeon-pathologist James Paget, now 63, who first detected the *Trichina spiralis* parasite in 1835. Paget's disease will defy a century of effort to unearth its etiology and to find a specific therapy.

The Japanese Red Cross is founded at Tokyo where the Meiji emperor Mutsuhito is mobilizing forces to put down the Satsuma Rebellion (above).

Osmosis is discovered by German botanist Wilhelm Pfeffer, 32, who finds that fluids are diffused through semipermeable membrane tissues.

Oxygen, nitrogen, and other gases not heretofore considered liquefiable will be liquefied in the next year by French physicist Louis Paul Cailletet, 45 (*see* von Linde, 1898).

Barbed wire prices drop from 18 cents per pound to 8 cents as the Bessemer steelmaking process of 1856 is applied to barbed wire production. All barbed wire patents were acquired last year by the Washburn & Moen Company of Worcester, Mass., and sales of barbed wire leap from last year's 840,000 pounds to 12.86 million pounds. A ton of barbed wire represents 2 miles of three-strand "devil's rope" and sales will climb to 26.7 million pounds next year, 50.3 million in 1879, 80.5 million in 1880, 120 million in 1881 (*see* Gates, 1875, 1898).

Compulsory education for Italian children from age 6 to 9 becomes mandatory under terms of a new law but poor administration will make the law ineffectual.

Tokyo University is founded in Japan. The imperial university will be the nation's most prestigious.

The University of Manitoba is founded at Winnipeg.

The University of Detroit is founded in Michigan.

The American Museum of Natural History opens in New York just west of Central Park at 77th Street.

The first university press is founded at Baltimore's Johns Hopkins University where *The American Journal of Mathematics* begins publication. The new university is the first institution to make student needs subordinate to research demands, inaugurating the "publish or perish" system that will lead to widespread publication of pedantic papers that often have little to do with real education.

The first Bell telephone is sold in May and by August there are 778 instruments in use.

The Bell Telephone Association is organized with headquarters at New York. Founder Gardiner Hubbard gives himself and his son-in-law Bell each a 30 percent interest in the Bell patent, he gives Bell's assistant Thomas A. Watson a 10 percent interest, and he gives a 30 percent interest to investor Thomas

Sanders who put up more than $100,000 to back Bell's early experiments.

Western Union's American Speaking-Telephone Company competes with Bell, but the new Bell firm is deluged with applications for telephone agencies, and Hubbard starts leasing telephones at the rate of 1,000 per month.

The first telephone switchboard is installed May 17 in the Boston office of Edwin T. Holmes, proprietor of the Holmes Burglar Alarm Service. Bell loans Holmes 12 telephones and the switchboard at 342 Washington Street is used for telephone service by day and a burglar alarm at night.

The first telephone exchange is organized at Lowell, Mass., by local entrepreneur Charles Jasper Glidden, 20 (*see* New Haven, 1878). Glidden will quickly develop a system under the name New England Telephone and Telegraph Company and another under the name Erie Telephone and Telegraph, and he will not sell out to the Bell interests until the 1900s.

Northwestern Bell Telephone Company is founded by Lyons, Iowa, entrepreneur Joseph Cullen Root, 32.

A loose-contact telephone transmitter superior to Bell's telephone is developed by German-American inventor Emile Berliner, 26 (*see* 1878; Hughes, 1855).

A hand-cranked "phonograph or speaking machine" demonstrated by Thomas Edison November 29 records sounds on grooved metal cylinders wrapped in tinfoil. Edison has followed up on his telephone research, he shouts the verses to "Mary Had a Little Lamb" into his machine, he is astonished when the machine plays his voice back, he applies for a patent in December, and he is soon attracting paid audiences at "exhibitions" of the machine (*see* 1887).

The Farm Journal has begun publication in March. Philadelphia publisher Wilmer Atkinson, 30, sends out 25,000 copies to farmers and other rural residents within a day's ride of Philadelphia.

The *Washington Post* begins publication December 6 with a four-page edition that sells at 3 cents per copy and will have a circulation of 11,875 within a year. Publisher Stilson Hutchins, 39, calls President Hayes the "de facto president," he refers to Hayes as "His Fraudulency," he uses the term "President Tilden" in his outrage over the "crime of '76." He will buy out the competing *National Union* next year and the *Daily Republican* in 1888, but he will sell out in 1889 (*see* Meyer, 1933).

Britain's remaining restrictions on freedom of the press are ended by the court trial at London of Charles Bradlaugh, 44, and Annie Wood Besant (Ajax), 30, who have republished Charles Knowlton's Malthusian work of 1835 "Fruits of Philosophy" advocating contraception (*see* below).

 The Boston Library opens on Copley Square in a Romanesque building designed by Henry Hobson

Striking trainmen shut down U.S. railroads for a week until federal troops moved in and fired on the workers.

Richardson. Its chief benefactor has been the late Joshua Bates, a local financier who was a partner in London's Baring Brothers from 1828 until his death in 1864 at age 76 (*see* 1895).

Funk & Wagnalls Company has its beginnings in the I. K. Funk & Company publishing firm founded by U.S. clergyman-bookseller Isaac Kauffman Funk, 38, and Adam Willis Wagnalls, 34. The firm will publish *A Standard Dictionary of the English Language* in 1890 and will take the name Funk & Wagnalls the following year (*see Literary Digest,* 1890).

Fiction *Anna Karenina* by Leo Tolstoy; *The American* by Henry James; *Deephaven* (stories) by South Berwick, Me., author Sarah Orne Jewett, 27.

Juvenile *Black Beauty* by English author Anna Sewell, 57, whose "Autobiography of a Horse" will be a worldwide best seller and will remain popular for more than a century. Sewell receives a flat £20 for her manuscript and will receive no royalties.

Painting *Nana* by Edouard Manet; *Lever de Lune* by Charles François Daubigny: *The Cotton Pickers* by Winslow Homer. Gustave Courbet dies December 31 at age 58: imprisoned for 6 months in 1871 for destroying the Vendôme column at Paris, Courbet fled to Switzerland in 1873 after being sentenced to pay for the column's reconstruction.

Ballet *Swan Lake* 3/4 at Moscow's Bolshoi Theater with music by Petr Ilich Tchaikovsky. The ballet is incomplete and the production is not a success (*see* 1895).

The cakewalk is introduced into U.S. minstrel shows by the New York team Harrigan and Hart whose "Walking for Dat Cake" number imitates antebellum plantation "cakewalks."

Opera *The Sorcerer* 11/17 at London's Opera Comique, with Gilbert and Sullivan arias that in-clude "My Name Is John Wellington Wells." The operetta begins a run of nearly 6 months; *Samson et Dalila* 12/2 at Weimar's Grand Ducal Palace, with music by Camille Saint-Saëns.

First performances *Francesca da Rimini* (Fantasia for Orchestra after Dante) by Petr Ilich Tchaikovsky 3/9 at Moscow; *Les Eolides* (*The Aeolidae*) (symphonic poem) by Belgian-French composer César (August Jean Guillaume) Franck, 54, 5/13 at Paris; Symphony No. 2 in B flat major by the late Franz Schubert (who wrote it in 1815) 10/20 at London's Crystal Palace; Symphony No. 3 in D minor by Anton Bruckner 12/16 at Vienna; Symphony No. 2 in D major by Johannes Brahms 12/30 at Vienna.

Cantata *Lallah Rookh* by English composer Frederick Clay, 39, in February at the Brighton Festival with "I'll Sing Thee Songs of Araby," lyrics by Irish poet-playwright William Gorman Wills, 49.

Hymns "Where Is My [Wand'ring] Boy To-night?" by Robert Lowry; "Hiding in Thee" by Ira David Sankey, lyrics by William O. Cushing.

Popular songs "In The Gloaming" by English composer Annie Fortescue Harrison, 26, who has recently married the comptroller of Queen Victoria's household, Sir Arthur Hill, lyrics by Meta Orred; "The Lost Chord" by Gilbert & Sullivan's Arthur Sullivan who has been inspired by the fatal illness of his brother Frederick, lyrics by the late poet Adelaide A. Procter whose verse was published in 1858 and who died 6 years later at age 39; "La Paloma" ("La Colombe," "The Dove") by Spanish composer Sebastian Yradier with anonymous English lyrics.

The Westminster Kennel Club dog show is inaugurated in May at New York's 3-year-old Gilmore's Garden where 1,201 entries in the "first annual N.Y. Bench Show" compete for silver trophies produced by the 40-year-old firm of Tiffany & Co. Dog fanciers have organized the club at the Westminster Hotel on Irving Place at 16th Street, the founding members have adopted as the club's symbol the head of their pointer Sensation whose stud services they offer at $35. While no "best of show" award will be made until 1907, the first show is so popular that its scheduled 3-day run is extended for an extra day with proceeds from the fourth session going to the 11-year-old ASPCA.

The first Wimbledon lawn tennis championship matches are organized by the 9-year-old All England Croquet Club (*see* 1874; USLTA, 1881).

Singer Manufacturing Company cuts sewing machine prices in half as the U.S. economic depression continues. The move will increase sales enormously (*see* 1873; 1880).

Cincinnati's Mabley & Carew dry goods store opens in Fountain Square. Canadian-American merchant Joseph Thomas Carew, 29, is backed by his former employer Christopher Mabley of Detroit's C. R. Mabley clothing store, and he will open a Baltimore branch in 1884 (*see* Carew Tower, 1930).

Chicago's Mandel Brothers opens on State Street where Leon, Emanuel, Simon, and Solomon Mandel have been offered a lease by Marshall Field who is bent on making State Street Chicago's main shopping artery. The new department store began as Klein and Mandel in 1855.

 The first low-rent U.S. housing "project" opens at Brooklyn, N.Y., where businessman Alfred Tredway White has financed construction of cottages for workingmen at Hicks Street and Baltic, each 11.5 feet wide with six rooms. By 1880 White will have built 44 of the cottages for $1,150 each exclusive of land and he will be renting them at $14 per month. He will build 226 apartments in six-story "sun-lighted tenements" round a central court with communal bathing facilities in their basements and he will rent the four-room apartments for $1.93 per week.

New York's Jefferson Market Courthouse building is completed in Greenwich Village.

 Timber barons who are "not merely stealing trees but whole forests" are attacked by Secretary of the Interior Carl Schurz who has been named to the post by President Hayes. Schurz emigrated from his native Germany in 1848 at age 19, he practiced law at Milwaukee, served as minister to Spain, fought as a Union Army brigadeer general of volunteers, and has served as U.S. Senator from Missouri (see Muir, 1876; Forest Reserves Act, 1891).

Practical Treatise on Water Supply Engineering by U.S. hydraulic engineer John Thomas Fanning, 40, will be the standard work on the subject for years.

Swan Boats designed by Robert Paget appear on the pond of Boston's 18-year-old Public Garden with official city permission and they quickly become a major attraction for visitors.

The Fresh Air Fund started by Pennsylvania clergyman Willard Parsons brings needy city children for a visit to his rural community. Most of the children have never seen a cow and Parsons tells a friend, "We must sow this tiny seed. Its roots will strike deeper than we can possibly foresee" (see 1881).

Famine kills 4 million in Bengal.

Congress establishes a U.S. Entomological Commission to control grasshoppers which have been devastating western farms and rangelands.

California land speculators James Ben Ali Haggin, 49, and Lloyd Tevis, 53, use political influence to have Congress pass a Desert Land Act offering land at 25 cents per acre to settlers who will agree to irrigate and cultivate the land for 3 years. Haggin and Tevis have acquired hundreds of thousands of acres by buying up old Spanish land grants, often of dubious value, and they acquire 96,000 acres in the San Joaquin Valley by hiring scores of vagabonds to enter false claims which they then transfer to themselves, ousting settlers who have not yet perfected their titles under old laws and have not yet heard about the new law. The Haggin-Tevis lands will become the

basis of the Kern County Land Company (see 1890; Anaconda, 1881; Tenneco, 1961).

 Britain is awarded $4.5 million for U.S. fishing rights in the North Atlantic November 23 by the Halifax Fisheries Commission created by the Treaty of Washington in 1871.

 Argentina challenges Australia as a source of meat for Europe by sending its first refrigerator ship to France with a cargo of meat. The S.S. *Paraguay* employs an ammonia compression system devised by French engineer Charles Albert Abel Tellier, 49 (see 1876; 1880; Linde, 1873).

The first shipment of Chicago-dressed beef to reach Boston arrives in a railcar designed to prevent spoilage by Chicago meatpacker Gustavus Franklin Swift, 38, who is determined to save the cost of transporting whole live animals. Swift's partner James Hathaway has sold his interest in the firm anticipating failure, but Swift has refused to be thwarted by the railroads that demand exorbitant rates to make up for lost tonnage. He has used a railroad that has not carried livestock shipments (see 1881).

John Morrell & Co. takes over a slaughterhouse at Ottumwa, Iowa (see 1868). Morrell will build its own plant at Ottumwa next year and will begin to challenge the big Chicago meatpackers (see AMK, 1967).

A centrifugal cream separator that eliminates the need of space-consuming shallow pans and the labor of skimming the cream that rises to the top is invented by Swedish engineer Carl Gustaf Patrick de Laval, 32. By reducing the cost of producing butter, the Laval separator will lead to a vast expansion of the Danish, Dutch, and Wisconsin butter industries.

New York State outlaws the representation of margarine as "butter," but the law will be widely ignored.

Brick cheese is invented by Wisconsin cheesemaker John Jossi whose product is a more elastic, slightly milder version of Limburger (see Liederkranz, 1892).

The Quaker Mill Company begins operations at Ravenna, Ohio, making oatmeal with a process patented by William Heston (see Schumacher, 1875). Heston and his partner Henry D. Seymour register as a trademark the "figure of a man in Quaker garb," but their venture suffers for lack of business acumen and will soon be acquired by distiller Warren Corning who will use the Quaker symbol on a brand of whiskey (see Quaker Oats, 1884; 1888).

Granula is introduced at Battle Creek, Mich., by James Harvey Kellogg who has created the cold cereal breakfast food by mixing wheat, oatmeal, and cornmeal and baking half-inch thick biscuits which he grinds up and sells at 12 cents per pound in 1, 2, and 5-pound packages (see 1876; Jackson, 1863; Granola, 1881).

Tableware that will be called Community Plate silver is introduced by the Oneida Community whose Wallingford, Conn., branch has developed the silver-

1877 (cont.) ware (*see* 1860). The Community will soon convert from a communal society to a joint-stock company and will produce canned fruit, Newhouse traps, sewing silk, and Community Plate silverware under the name Oneida Community Limited.

New England Glass Works is founded by William Libbey and his son Edward who take over a 59-year-old Boston firm for which they have been Chicago representatives. Edward Drummond Libbey will have labor troubles when his father dies in 1883, he will move to Toledo, and will start the Libbey Glass Company, concentrating on cheap blown tumblers (*see* Owens, 1895).

Distillers Company, Ltd. is created by a consolidation of six Scottish distilleries which begin a great whisky cartel. The syndicate will be joined in 1919 by John Haig and Company, Ltd., in 1924 by Robert Burnett and Company, and in 1925 by Buchanan-Dewars, Ltd. (Black & White, Dewars White Label) and John Walker & Sons, Ltd. (Johnny Walker Red Label and Black Label).

The tabooed subject of contraception comes into the open at the Bradlaugh-Besant trial (above). The acquittal of Bradlaugh and Besant will lead to an end of the ban on disseminating contraceptive advice.

1878 Italy's Victor Emmanuel II dies January 9 at age 57. He has ruled the country since its unification in 1861 and he is succeeded by his 33-year-old son who will reign as Umberto I until his assassination in 1900.

Ottoman forces capitulate at Shipka Pass and ask Russia for an armistice. Russian forces take Adrianople, and a British fleet sent by Disraeli arrives at Constantinople to show support against Russia.

A London music hall ditty introduces the word "jingoism," a synonym for sabre-rattling chauvinism: "We don't want to fight, but by jingo if we do,/ We've got the men, we've got the ships, we've got the money, too."

The Treaty of San Stefano March 3 brings peace between Russia and the Ottoman Empire following a declaration of war by Athens on Constantinople. The Berlin Congress mediated by Germany's Prince Otto von Bismarck in June and July dismembers the Ottoman Empire founded in 1300. Montenegro, Romania, and Serbia become independent states, Romania receives Dobrudja, Russia receives southern Bessarabia and strategic areas in Transcaucasia. The congress divides Bulgaria into Bulgaria proper north of the Balkans, Eastern Romelia south of the Balkans, and Macedonia. Britain occupies Cyprus, France occupies Tunis, but Russian nationalists and Panslavists remain unsatisfied and the Balkans are left seething with discontent.

Italian Irredentists begin agitating to obtain Trieste and the southern Tyrol from Austria.

Chile and Bolivia verge on war over the control of nitrate deposits, essential to world production of explosives and fertilizer. Bolivia boosts the export tax on nitrates being mined by the Chilean Nitrate Company in Antofagasta, the company appeals to the Chilean government, and Bolivia temporarily rescinds the company's contract (*see* 1879).

Thomas Edison works out methods for cheap production and transmission of electrical current and succeeds in subdividing current to make it adaptable to household use. Gas company shares plummet as news of Edison's work reaches Wall Street.

Johns Hopkins professor Henry Rowland, 30, and Harvard professor John Trowbridge, 35, have helped Edison. He looks for a lamp filament that will burn for extended periods of time in a high vacuum, and he experiments with molybdenum, nickel, and platinum filaments (*see* 1879).

The Edison Electric Light Co. is founded October 15.

The first carbon filament incandescent light bulb of any value is demonstrated December 18 at a meeting of the Newcastle-on-Tyne Chemical Society. English chemist Joseph Wilson Swan, 50, has produced the bulb with help from Charles H. Stearn, but it does not achieve true incandescence and Swan will not be able to perfect it or get his lamp into volume production until 1881 (*see* Edison, 1879).

The Bland-Allison Act passed by Congress February 28 makes the silver dollar legal tender and requires that the U.S. Treasury buy $2 million to $4 million worth of silver each month. The bill introduced by Missouri congressman Richard P. Bland and Iowa congressman William B. Allison encourages prospecting for silver and will not be repealed until July 1890 (*see* Leadville, 1879).

Circulation of greenbacks is reduced by Congress May 31. $346.7 million worth of greenbacks are in circulation and by December 17 they have regained their face value for the first time since 1862.

Nearly 10,500 U.S. business firms fail as the economic depression that began in 1873 continues.

The trial of 193 young Russian revolutionaries ends in January with the acquittal of a great many of the accused but the police have special powers of "administrative exile," they pick up most of the men and women who have been acquitted, and they send them off to Siberia or elsewhere. St. Petersburg's chief of police General F. F. Trepov is shot and wounded in January by revolutionary Vera Zasulich, 26, as an act of protest against the flogging of a prisoner that had been ordered by General Trepov. Zasulich is clearly guilty, but a jury of her peers acquits her on the ground that her action was a legitimate form of political protest, a crowd cheers her as she leaves the courthouse, the authorities permit her to go abroad, and she will become an associate of Karl Marx. Another revolutionary stabs General N. V. Mezentsev with a sword August 4 in broad daylight, and systematic terrorism will begin next year (*see* 1887).

The Atchison, Topeka and Santa Fe cuts engineers' pay 10 percent April 4, most engineers and firemen strike, the railroad is closed down for 5 days, militia is called in at Emporia, Kansas, and one militiaman kills an innocent bystander, an event that leads to the arrest of several strike leaders (*see* 1877).

The Santa Fe lays tracks through Raton Pass 15 miles south of Trinidad, Colo., into New Mexico Territory. A 2,000-foot tunnel is bored through the pass 8,000 feet high in the Sangre de Cristo Mountains.

Canadian-American entrepreneur James J. Hill, 40, and his associates buy the St. Paul and Pacific Railroad which they will reorganize and extend in 1890 to create the Great Northern Railway, a road built without government subsidy (*see* Canadian Pacific, 1881; Northern Pacific, 1901).

New York's Sixth Avenue elevated opens from Rector Street to Central Park. The line will reach 155th Street in 2 years and apartment houses will rise up quickly along its route (*see* 1940).

The steamboat *J. M. White* launched on the Mississippi is the grandest ship ever seen on the river. Her smokestacks are 80 feet high, her roof bell weighs 2,880 pounds. It takes two pilots to handle her 11-foot wheel, but the $300,000 steamboat sets a new speed record by steaming from New Orleans upriver to St. Louis in 3 days, 23 hours, and 9 minutes. Riverboat traffic at St. Louis will reach more than 1.3 million tons in 1880 but will be only half that by 1885, and will be down to 347,000 tons in 1900 and 43,090 tons in 1910 as railroads displace steamboats.

The first U.S. pathology laboratory is opened at New York's Bellevue Hospital Medical College by William Henry Welch, 28 (*see* Johns Hopkins, 1893).

The first laboratory for experimental psychology is established by German psychologist Wilhelm Max Wundt, 46, who thus brings the human mind into the realm of science (*see* Pavlov, 1879; Breuer, 1882).

Mennen's Sure Corn Killer is introduced in bottles by Newark, N.J., pharmacist Gerhard Mennen, 23, who persuades other Newark druggists to stock the product and begins advertising with a singing black banjo player driven about town in a horse and wagon. Mennen will introduce Mennen's Borated Talcum Infant Powder in 1889 and will advertise it with a minstrel show to begin a business that will continue well beyond his death in 1902.

A yellow fever epidemic sweeps the U.S. Gulf Coast states and Tennessee, killing an estimated 14,000. Some 4,500 die at New Orleans alone and 5,150 die up the Mississippi at Memphis (*see* Finlay, 1881).

A smallpox epidemic strikes Deadwood in the Dakota Territory. Frontierswoman Martha Jane Canary, 26, works heroically in men's clothing to nurse the ill and renders service that will help make her legendary as "Calamity Jane."

Duquesne University is founded at Pittsburgh.

Mississippi State University is founded at Starkville.

The first commercial telephone exchange opens January 28 at New Haven, Conn. The exchange has 21 subscribers and after 6 weeks it operates at night as well as during the day (*see* 1883; Glidden, 1877).

The first telephone directory, issued February 21 by the New Haven Telephone Co., lists 50 subscribers.

The Bell company buys Emile Berliner's loose-contact telephone transmitter. Berliner patents the use of an induction coil in a transmitter (*see* 1877; gramophone, 1887).

The Remington Arms Company improves the Remington typewriter of 1876 by adding a shift key system that employs upper- and lowercase letters on the same type bar. Wyckoff, Seamens, and Benedict buy Remington's typewriter business and found the Remington Typewriter Company (*see* Underwood, 1895; Remington Rand, Inc., 1927).

Berlitz Schools of Languages have their beginnings at Providence, R.I., where German-American teacher Maximilian Delphinius Berlitz, 27, opens his own language school after 9 years of teaching French and German in a theological seminary. He goes out of town for a week, leaving his students in the care of a Frenchman who speaks no English, and when he finds that the students have made amazing progress in his absence he develops an easy-to-learn method using instructors who speak no English. By 1978 there will be close to 200 Berlitz schools worldwide.

A Cincinnati company that will become the world's largest maker of printers' inks is started by Canadian-American entrepreneur Levi Addison Ault, 26, who will be joined by Frank B. Wiborg, now 23, to form the Ault & Wiborg Co. that will become Intertype.

The *Cleveland Press* has its beginnings in the *Penny Press* started by Edward Wyllis Scripps, 24, of the Detroit *Evening News*. The Detroit paper was started 5 years ago by Scripps's English-American half-brother who helps Edward start the Cleveland paper with a substantial loan (*see* UP, 1907).

The *St. Louis Dispatch* is acquired by Hungarian-American journalist Joseph Pulitzer, 31, who will merge the *Dispatch* with the *St. Louis Post* to create the *Post-Dispatch* and begin a newspaper empire. Pulitzer arrived in America in 1864, he served in the First New York Cavalry in the Civil War, worked as a reporter for a St. Louis German-language newspaper, won election to the legislature in 1869, studied law, and was admitted to the bar 2 years ago (*see* 1883).

The *Chattanooga Times* begins publication under the direction of Cincinnati-born publisher Adoph Simon Ochs, 20 (*see* 1896).

J. Walter Thompson takes over the 14-year-old advertising firm Carlton and Smith which he joined in 1868 and begins representing general magazines (*see* 1868). Commodore Thompson's first advertisement will introduce the Prudential Insurance Company's Rock of Gibraltar trademark (*see* 1875), and in 15 years he will control the advertising in 30 publica-

1878 (cont.) tions, mostly women's magazines (*see* Curtis, 1901).

Fiction *The Return of the Native* by Thomas Hardy; *The Europeans* by Henry James.

Painting *Mme. Charpentier and Her Children* by Pierre Auguste Renoir; *Rehearsal on the Stage* by Edgar Degas; *Sierra Nevada* by Albert Bierstadt. Charles François Daubigny dies at Auvers-sur-Oise February 19 at 61.

Tiffany glass has its beginnings in a factory established by New York painter-craftsman Louis Comfort Tiffany, 30, son of the jeweler, who has studied with Venetian glassmaker Andrea Boldoni (*see* 1894).

First performances Symphony No. 4 in F minor by Petr Ilich Tchaikovsky 2/10 at Moscow; Sonata in A major for Violin and Piano by French composer Gabriel Urbain Fauré, 33, at the Trocadero Hall built for the Paris Exposition.

Opera *H.M.S. Pinafore* (or *The Lass that Loved a Sailor*) 5/25 at London's Opera Comique, with the Comedy Opera Company singing Gilbert and Sullivan arias that include "We Sail the Ocean Blue," "I Am the Captain of the Pinafore," "I Am the Monarch of the Sea," "When I Was a Lad," "Things Are Seldom What They Seem," "Carefully on Tiptoe Stealing," and "He Is an Englishman;" *The Secret* (*Tagernstvi*) 9/18 at Prague, with music by Bedrich Smetana.

The Central City Opera House opens in the Colorado mining town.

The Cincinnati Music Hall opens on Elm Street with 3,600 seats to house the May Festival that has been held since 1873.

Popular songs "Carry Me Back to Old Virginny" by pioneer black songwriter James A. Bland, 24.

Herreshoff Manufacturing Company is formed by U.S. yacht designer John Brown Herreshoff, 37, who has been blind since age 14, and his brother Nathanael Greene Herreshoff, 30. Their older brother James Brown Herreshoff, 44, has invented a sliding seat for rowboats that is used in racing shells and he will invent a fin keel for racing yachts that will be put to practical use by Herreshoff Manufacturing in 1891 when the company will begin designing yachts for the defense of the America's Cup.

President Hayes invites the children of Washington to an Easter egg roll on the White House lawn and begins an annual event.

Ivory Soap has its origin in The White Soap introduced by Cincinnati's 51-year-old Procter and Gamble Company whose chemists have perfected a hard, white, floating soap. Harley Procter, now 21, will be inspired to rename the soap Ivory while reading a psalm in church in 1882 and beginning in December of that year Ivory will be aggressively advertised with the slogan "99 and 44/100% pure" (*see* Crisco, 1911; Swan, 1940).

Cleveland paintmaker Francis H. Glidden develops a varnish that will make the Glidden Company world-famous (*see* Glidden Tour, 1905).

Mohawk Carpet Company has its beginnings at Amsterdam, N.Y., where English-American carpetmakers John, Walter, James, and Herbert Shuttleworth establish a weaving mill in the basement of a local factory with a few looms they have brought from England (*see* 1920).

Jehovah's Witnesses has its beginnings as Pittsburgh Congregationalist minister Charles T. Russell, 26, becomes pastor of an independent church at which he will preach the doctrine that Christ's second coming came invisibly in 1874 and that the world has since then been in the "Milennial Age" that will end in 1914 and will be followed by social revolution, chaos, resurrection of the dead, and—ultimately—by the establishment of Christ's kingdom on earth (*see* 1872; 1884).

The Salvation Army adopts that name (*see* 1865; Volunteers of America, 1896; Shaw drama, 1905).

Bat Masterson captures the notorious outlaw Dave Rudabaugh in Dakota Territory and is appointed U.S. marshal. William Barclay Masterson, 24, hears later in the year that his brother Edward has been gunned down while acting as marshal of Dodge City, Kan., he brings quick retribution to Edward's two killers, and he will continue as a western lawman and gambler until 1902, when he will quit to become a New York sportswriter.

Texas outlaw Sam Bass gathers a new gang at Denton 4 months after losing companions in a flight through Kansas and Missouri following a heist of $65,000 in gold and other valuables from a Union Pacific train at Big Springs, Neb. The Bass gang robs four trains near Dallas, but Bass is betrayed to the Texas Rangers. He is trapped while trying to rob a bank at Round Rock, and he is mortally wounded at age 26.

Will's Three Castles cigarettes are introduced at London (*see* 1892).

The Tiffany Diamond discovered in South Africa's Kimberly Mine (and purchased immediately by New York's Tiffany & Co.) is the largest and finest yellow diamond ever found. It weighs 287.42 carats, diamond-cutters at Paris will study it for a year before touching it, and they will turn it into a 128.51-carat stone with 90 facets (*see* Tiffany, 1837, 1909).

German-American merchant Michael Goldwater opens a general store at Prescott in Arizona Territory after years of running stores with his brother Joseph in Arizona mining towns offering gunpowder, shot, boots, clothing, whiskey, and foods that include oysters brought overland from San Francisco.

London's A. W. Gamage, Ltd., department store has its beginnings in a shop opened by merchant Albert Walter Gamage, 23.

Cleopatra's Needle is erected on London's Thames Embankment. The obelisk imported from Egypt antedates Cleopatra by many centuries.

Montreal's Windsor Hotel opens January 28.

Harvard's Memorial Hall opens at Cambridge, Mass., after 8 years of construction. The vast red brick structure memorializes the university's Civil War dead and will serve as a dining hall and theater.

A new Monte Carlo gambling casino opens to replace the original 1862 structure. Designed by Charles Garnier of 1875 Paris Opéra fame, the new casino will be completed in 1910 with a fine opera house (*see* 1913).

 Report on the Lands of the Arid Region of the United States by John Wesley Powell points out that land west of the 96th meridian is arid, that only a few areas of the Pacific Coast and the mountains receive as much as 20 inches of rain per year, that an economy based on traditional patterns of farming is not possible under these circumstances, that dry-land farming depends on irrigation, that water rights in the West are more valuable than land titles and should be tied by law to each tract of land, that only a small fraction of the land is irrigable, that the Homestead Act of 1862 must be revised if it is to apply to western lands, that western land policies and political institutions must be geared to the region's climatic conditions, that optimum irrigation will depend on large dams and canals financed and built under federal government leadership, and that the best reservoir sites should be identified and reserved at the outset (*see* 1869). Powell addresses the report to Congress and to Secretary of the Interior Carl Schurz (*see* 1877; 1888; 1909).

The last mass nesting of passenger pigeons is seen at Petoskey, Michigan (*see* 1871; 1914).

 The worst famine in history kills at least 10 million Chinese and possibly twice that number as drought continues in much of Asia as it has since 1876.

 The Matador Ranch is established in the southern Texas Panhandle by Chicago promoter Henry H. Campbell who will be backed by Scottish financiers and will spread his holdings over most of the Panhandle and up into Montana Territory (*see* Prairie Cattle Company, 1881).

The first commercial milking machines are produced at Auburn, N.Y., by Albert Durant who introduces a machine invented by L. O. Colvin.

 The first Alaskan salmon cannery is established (*see* 1866; 1890).

 The word "enzyme" is introduced by German physiologist Wilhelm Kuhne, 41, to denote the complex organic substances whose catalytic actions produce such chemical changes as digestion (*see* Payen and Persoz, 1833; Schwann, 1835; coenzymes, 1911).

Beet sugar extraction mills are demonstrated at the Paris World Exhibition. Most European countries will be encouraged by the Paris exhibit to plant sugar beets and build factories (*see* 1811; 1880).

The U.S. agency for Angostura Bitters is taken over by Venezuelan merchant George Wupperman, 26, who has married the daughter of a Hudson River steamboat fleet operator and has emigrated to New York (*see* Siegert, 1818). When Wupperman dies in 1915 leaving eight grown children, his widow Josephine will assume management of the business.

The Morgan machine that compresses beef into tins neatly and efficiently is adopted by Libby, McNeill & Libby which has been packing corned beef in tapered tins by hand (*see* 1875; 1890).

The Hutchinson Bottle Stopper invented by Charles G. Hutchinson is made of wire with a rubber washer, it seals in the carbonation of effervescent drinks when pulled up tight, and when pushed in it permits a beverage to be poured or swallowed from the bottle—but the rubber imparts a taste to the beverage (*see* Painter, 1892).

The first sugar cubes are introduced by London's Silvertown Refinery owned by sugar magnate Henry Tate, 69.

Port du Salut is registered as the name for a cheese by some French monks at the Tribunal de Commerce (*see* Port au Salut, 1816).

Charles A. Pillsbury at Minneapolis installs steel rollers to replace millstones and thus multiplies the output of his flour mills (*see* 1871; Washburn, 1874; A Mill, 1880).

The 4-year-old Washburn Mill at Minneapolis explodes, kills 18 men, wrecks 6 mills, and destroys a roundhouse, a machine shop, and a factory (*see* Washburn-Crosby, 1879).

An ice-cooled cold store is opened at Chicago by the Western Cold Storage Company (*see* 1887).

Salt wells go into production in New York's Wyoming County as a high tariff encourages production.

The first roasted coffee to be packed in sealed cans is packed by Chase and Sanborn of Boston (*see* 1863; Hills Brothers, 1900; Standard Brands, 1929).

Hills Brothers Coffee has its beginnings at San Francisco as Maine-born merchants Austin H. and Reuben W. Hills start a coffee business in the public market. The Hills brothers will open a retail shop in 1882 under the name Arabian Coffee & Spice Mills, but they will quit the retail trade 2 years later to sell through other grocers (*see* 1900).

 The Comstock Law of 1872 is applied by the antivice crusader Anthony Comstock. A Madame Restell who operates a notorious New York brothel on the northeast corner of 52nd Street and Fifth Avenue is approached by a young man who says that he is desperately poor, that his wife is pregnant, and that the birth of another child will ruin him. Mme. Restell gives him advice, provides him with medicine and instruments to produce an abortion, and is arrested by the young man who reveals himself to be Anthony

1878 (cont.)   Comstock. He refuses a $40,000 offer to drop his charges. Mme. Restell secures her release on bail, she returns to her Fifth Avenue house, and she slits her throat.

The world's first birth control clinic is opened at Amsterdam by Dutch suffragist leader Aletta Jacobs, 29, who is the first woman physician to practice in Holland (see Bradlaugh and Besant, 1877; Sanger, 1914).

1879   Thomas Edison demonstrates the first practical incandescent bulb and says it will make electric light so cheap that only the rich will be able to afford candles (see 1876; 1878). Edison has tried filaments of platinum, carbonized paper, bamboo thread, and thousands of other substances before finding the solution in a loop of cotton thread impregnated with lamp black and baked for hours in a carbonizing oven. His vacuum electric light bulb is much like the one pioneered by German chemist Herman Sprengel in 1865, and after it has burned for 45 hours he is sure it will burn for at least 100. But while electricity will provide illumination without candlewax, whale oil, coal oil, coal gas, or kerosene, its use in lighting will await development of dynamos, fuses, and sockets (see 1880; 1882).

Cleveland and San Francisco install streetlighting systems that employ arc-lamps invented by Charles Francis Brush, 30, who has devised a method for stabilizing the electric arc between carbon electrodes (see 1880).

U.S. electrical wizard Elmer Ambrose Sperry, 19, invents an improved dynamo and a new type of arc lamp (see gyroscope, 1910).

Four California oil wells and a refinery are merged by San Francisco financial interests to create the Pacific Coast Oil Company whose production will soon go entirely to John D. Rockefeller's Standard Oil Company (see 1900).

The War of the Pacific begins February 14 as Chilean troops occupy Antofagasta. Bolivia proclaims a state of war, Peru refuses to guarantee neutrality, the United States is unsuccessful in its attempts at mediation, and Chilean forces proceed to occupy the entire Bolivian coast (see 1878; 1884).

The Irish Land League is founded to campaign for independence from Britain. Irish nationalist Michael Davitt, 33, lost his right arm in a cotton mill accident at age 11, he was sent to Dartmoor Prison at 24 on treason-felony charges that he arranged to ship arms into Ireland, and he has recently returned from visiting his American-born mother and his siblings in the United States (see 1870; Parnell, 1881).

The Zulu nation founded by Shaka in 1816 is ended by British breech-loading rifles that kill some 8,000 Zulu warriors and wound more than 16,000 while 76 British officers and 1,007 men are killed in action, 17 officers and 330 men killed by disease, 99 officers and 1,286 men invalided home, 37 officers and 206 men wounded, nearly 1,000 Natal Bantu corpsmen killed. The British forces have been commanded by General Frederic Augustus Thesiger, 51, second Baron Chelmsford, the Zulu are headed by the 51-year-old Cetshwayo whose father was a half-brother of the late Shaka. The Zulu War ends only after an incredible stand by the British March 29 at Rorke's Drift where 140 soldiers—30 of them incapacitated—hold off 4,000 Zulus armed with spears and some rifles. Eleven Victoria Crosses (a record for any single action) will be awarded to the heroes of Rorke's Drift but later the same day the British lose 895 out of a force of 950 plus some 550 Bantu allies in an attack by Zulu warriors at Isandhlwana.

France's 23-year-old Prince Imperial Louis who has accompanied the British in Zululand is killed June 2 by a Zulu assegai (spear). French Anglophobes charge that the prospective Napoleon IV was killed with the connivance of Queen Victoria.

The Zulu king Cetshwayo (above) is captured by the British August 20 and sent in ill-fitting European clothes to Capetown. Zululand is divided into 13 separate kingdoms whose territory will eventually be absorbed in large part by Natal.

The Egyptian khedive Ismail is deposed by the sultan June 25 under pressure from the European powers after 16 years of profligacy. Ismail is succeeded by his 27-year-old son Tewfik who will rule until 1892.

The Afghan emir Sher Ali has died in February and has been succeeded by his 29-year-old son Mohammed Yakub who is forced 3 months later to accept the Treaty of Gandamak which allows the British to occupy the Khyber Pass on condition that they pay the emir an annual subsidy of £60,000. The Afghans rise against the British September 3, the British envoy Sir Louis Cavagnari and his escort are murdered, British troops advance on Kabul which they take October 12. Yakub is forced to abdicate October 19, and he is succeeded by his 49-year-old cousin Abd-er-Rahman who will reign until 1901, playing off the British against the Russians and thus protecting Afghanistan.

The Austro-German alliance signed October 7 has been engineered by Germany's "Iron Chancellor" Prince Otto von Bismarck after more than a year of tension between Berlin and St. Petersburg. The treaty promising mutual support in the event of an attack by Russia on either country will be renewed periodically until 1918.

A large exodus of Southern blacks to Kansas begins as restrictions against former slaves increase in states of the old Confederacy. Black migrants to Kansas early in this decade have founded the town of Nicodemus (and some have become cowboys), but their numbers have been insignificant as compared with the 6,000 freed people from Louisiana, Mississippi, and Texas who respond to the leadership of Henry Adams and Benjamin "Pap" Singleton who have selected Kansas because few blacks can afford the transportation to Liberia. While many blacks remember John Brown and regard Kansas as a modern Canaan, their departure is resisted by Southern whites who fear the loss of their labor.

U.S. women are given the right by Congress to practice law before the Supreme Court.

The Church of Christ, Scientist is chartered at Boston by Mary Baker Eddy to propagate the spiritual and metaphysical system of Christian Science (*see* 1875; newspaper, 1908).

The gonococcus bacterium *Neisseria gonorrhea* that transmits the venereal infection gonorrhea is discovered by German physician Albert Ludwig Siegmund Neisser, 24.

Russian pathologist Ivan Petrovich Pavlov, 30, shows with studies on dogs that gastric juices are produced by the stomach even without the introduction of food. Pavlov will proceed to develop the concept of acquired, or conditioned, reflex.

Standardization of pharmaceutical drugs by chemical assay is pioneered by Detroit's Parke, Davis & Company which introduces liquid Ergotae Purificatus and assures physicians that dosages will be of the exact strength specified (*see* 1866; 1897).

Lambert Pharmacal Company is founded at St. Louis by local drugstore clerk Jordan Wheat Lambert (*see* Listerine, 1922).

The *Orient* goes into service for the Orient Line's Australian passenger traffic and is the first ship to be lighted by electricity. Largest ship afloat except for the 26-year-old *Great Eastern,* the 445-foot iron vessel is a 9,500-ton single-screw steamship, but her three-cylinder 5,400-horsepower engine is supplemented by four square-rigged masts.

Electricity is used to drive a railroad locomotive for the first time at Berlin.

Le Train Bleu begins thrice-a-week service as an all-sleeper express between Calais and Rome via Nice. The train has been developed by Georges Nagelmackers (*see* 1876; Orient Express, 1883).

New York's Third Avenue "El" reaches 129th Street 1 year after reaching 67th Street.

Application for a patent on a road vehicle to be powered by an internal combustion engine is filed by George B. Selden who will not obtain the patent until 1895 (*see* 1876; Daimler, 1882).

Scotland's Firth of Tay Bridge collapses under the weight of a train in a winter storm.

Progress and Poverty by U.S. economist Henry George, 40, points out that while America has become richer and richer most Americans have become poorer and poorer. Since land values represent monopoly power, says George, a "single tax" should be imposed on landowners that would provide all the revenue needed by government and would free industry from taxes (*see* Boisguilbert, 1705). George has met the Irish nationalist Michael Davitt (above) on Davitt's visit to America.

U.S. specie payments resume January 1 for the first time since the end of 1861.

Leadville, Colo., becomes the world's largest silver camp with more than 30 producing mines, 10 large smelters, and an output of nearly $15 million (*see* 1874; Bland-Allison Act, 1878; May Company, below).

Germany's policy of free trade ends July 13 with a new protective tariff law. German industry has been depressed since the financial crisis of 1873 with its ensuing depression, imports from foreign producers have hurt German agriculture, and protectionism will spur development of German industry, transportation, and foreign trade (*see* 1914).

An era of finance capitalism that will last for more than half a century begins in the United States.

Bache & Co. has its beginnings in the New York brokerage house Leopold Cahn & Co. Jules Semon Bache, now 17, will join the firm next year (*see* 1892).

Paine, Webber, Jackson and Curtis has its beginnings in a Boston brokerage house (*see* 1942).

Metropolitan Life Insurance Company of New York begins offering small policies for wage-earners and pioneers mass insurance coverage in an age of high mortality. Agents collect small weekly premiums in cash from the working classes who most need insurance protection. The company will attract 554 English agents who will emigrate with their families, and within 3 years Metropolitan Life will have increased the number of its district offices from 3 to 50 (*see* 1868; 1915; Metropolitan Life Tower, 1909).

Aetna Life Insurance Company is founded at Hartford, Conn., with Morgan Gardner Bulkeley, 42, as its first president.

Thomas Edison's brilliance and perseverance improved the telephone and produced the phonograph and the lightbulb.

1879 (cont.) The low-priced cardboard carton is pioneered by Scots-American paper bag maker Robert Gair in New York who has set up a factory that not only produces paper bags for grocers, department stores, millers, seedmen, and other merchants but also imprints the bags with the merchants' names. When one of his workers allows a metal rule on the press to slip up so that the paper is not only printed but cut, Gair capitalizes on the blunder and designs a metal die that uses a sharp metal rule set high to cut cardboard while blunt rules are set lower to crease the cardboard for folding into cartons. Buying a secondhand press for $30, Gair fits his cutting and creasing rules to create a machine that can cut and crease 750 sheets per hour, each sheet providing 10 carton blanks to permit production of 7,500 cartons per hour (*see* 1920).

Scott Paper Company is founded at Chester, Pa., where the wholesale house will become a converter in 1885 and will specialize in making toilet tissue, paper towels, and paper napkins.

National Cash Register Company has its beginnings in a cash register patented November 4 by Dayton, Ohio, saloon-keeper James J. "Jake" Ritty whose health has been undermined by his bartenders' pilfering. Ritty took a sea voyage to Europe to recover and was inspired by a recording device on the steamship that marked the revolutions of the vessel's propellor and gave its officers a complete and accurate daily record of the ship's speed. "Ritty's Incorruptible Cashier" in its first version merely registers the amount of each cash transaction on a dial, but a second model elevates a small plate to display the amount so that both clerk and customer can see it. The inventor and his brother will develop an improved model that records each day's transactions on a paper roll so that they can be checked by a store owner against the amount of cash in the cashbox, but manufacturing the cash register will prove too big a job and Ritty will sell his business and patent rights for $1,000 (*see* Patterson, 1884).

Radcliffe College has its beginnings in classes for women started at Cambridge, Mass., by Elizabeth Cary Agassiz, 51, widow of the late naturalist Louis Agassiz who died 6 years ago at age 66 (*see* 1894).

Carlisle Training and Industrial School for Indians is founded at Carlisle, Pa., by former U.S. Army officer Richard Henry Pratt, 39, who starts the first non-reservation school for American Indians.

The multiple switchboard invented by U.S. engineer Leroy B. Firman will make the telephone a commercial success and will help increase the number of U.S. telephone subscribers from 50,000 in 1880 to 250,000 in 1890.

New York merchants urge the Bell Telephone Company to open its exchange for calls at 5 o'clock in the morning rather than at 8 and to remain open later than 6 o'clock in the evening (Fulton Fish Market dealers lead the appeal).

French interests lay the U.S. end of a new Atlantic Cable at North Eastham, Mass. (*see* Field, 1866).

The *Atlanta Constitution* founded in 1868 gets a new editor who will increase the paper's vitality. Henry Woodfin Grady, 28, has served as Atlanta correspondent for James Gordon Bennett's *New York Herald*, and has proclaimed the emergence of a "new South." He buys a quarter-interest in the *Constitution* with help from Atlantic Cable pioneer Cyrus W. Field who loans him $20,000, and his 10-year term as editor will be marked by public speeches aimed at turning Southern eyes to the future.

Asahi Shinbun begins publication at Osaka 4 years after passage of a Japanese libel law that puts editors in jail for "dangerous thoughts." Tokyo editor Riichi Ueno will replace founders Rhuhei Murayama and Noboru Kimura in 1888 and will move the paper's headquarters to Tokyo. Circulation for Osaka and Tokyo will top 150,000 by the turn of the century, and by 1975 "Rising Sun" will be publishing 100 editions per day from plants in five cities and will have a combined circulation nearly 12 million daily.

Fiction *Daisy Miller* by Henry James whose novelette will be more popular during his lifetime than anything else he will write; *The Red Room* (*Roda rummet*) by Swedish novelist August Strindberg, 30; *Creole Days* (stories) by New Orleans writer George Washington Cable, 35, who angers Southerners with his criticism of slavery, prison conditions, and the mistreatment of blacks; "The Tar Baby" by *Atlanta Constitution* staff writer Uncle Remus (Joel Chandler Harris), 30, who has perfected a written form of the black dialect heard on Georgia plantations.

Juvenile *Under the Window* by English book illustrator Kate Greenaway, 33, of the *Illustrated London News*. Her "toy-book" will popularize early 19th century costumes for childrenswear.

Painting *The Cup of Tea* by Mary Cassatt. Honoré Daumier dies at Valmondois February 11 at age 70 in a cottage given him by the late J. P. C. Corot; George Caleb Bingham dies at Kansas City July 7 at age 68.

The Chicago Art Institute is founded.

Photography is revolutionized by the Seed Dry Plate introduced by English-American photographer Miles Ainscoe Seed, 36, of St. Louis whose sensitively prepared plate can be carried anywhere, exposed, and developed later at the photographer's leisure. The dry plate will make the wet plate obsolete and will reduce the use of chemicals. Seed will incorporate the Seed Dry Plate Company in July of 1883, and he will sell out in 1902 to Eastman Kodak Company (*see* Eastman, 1880).

Opera *Eugen Onegin* 3/29 at the Moscow Conservatory, with music by Petr Ilich Tchaikovsky, libretto from the Aleksandr Pushkin poem of 1832; *The Pirates of Penzance* (or *The Slave of Duty*) 12/31 at New York's Fifth Avenue Theater, with Gilbert and

Sullivan arias that include "Model of a Modern Major-General" and "A Policeman's Lot Is Not a Happy One."

First performances Concerto in D major for Violin and Orchestra by Johannes Brahms 1/1 at Leipzig's Gewandhaus; *Slavonic Dances* by Czech composer Anton Dvorak, 37, 5/16 at Prague. Dvorak won his first public acclaim 6 years ago with the patriotic hymn "Die Erben des weissen Berges." *Variations on a Rococo Theme* for Cello and Orchestra by Petr Ilich Tchaikovsky 6/8 at Wiesbaden; Suite No. 1 in D major by Petr Ilich Tchaikovsky in December at St. Petersburg.

Vaudeville *The Mulligan Guards' Ball* 1/13 at New York's Théâtre Comique with Ed Harrigan and Tony Hart who opened in a vaudeville show at Chicago's Academy of Music in mid-July of 1873 and have toured the country mocking the pretensions of men who wear military uniforms. Harrigan and Hart will dominate U.S. vaudeville until Hart dies in 1891, Dan Collyer will replace Hart, and the new team will continue for another 5 years.

Popular songs "In The Evening by the Moonlight" by James Bland who introduces the song with Callender's Original Georgia Minstrels and who also writes "Oh Dem Golden Slippers;" "Alouette" is published for the first time in *A Pocket Song Book for the Use of Students and Graduates of McGill College* at Montreal.

New York's Madison Square Garden gets its name as railroad heir William K. Vanderbilt, 30, acquires the 5-year-old Gilmore's Garden, renames it, and announces that it will be used primarily as an athletic center. The Garden will be the scene of the National Horse Show beginning in 1883 and it will be acquired in 1887 by a syndicate of horse show sponsors including financier J. P. Morgan who will replace it in 1890 with a splendid structure of yellow brick and Pompeiian terra cotta designed by architect Stanford White (below).

F. W. Woolworth Co., has its beginnings at Watertown, N.Y., where store clerk Frank Winfield Woolworth, 27, persuades his employer to install a counter at which all goods are priced at 5 cents. He then induces one of the the firm's principals to lend him $400 with which to open a Utica store at which all items are priced at 5 cents. The store fails in 3 months, but Woolworth is staked by the same partner to try a five-and-dime store at Lancaster, Pa., which proves successful. Five-and-dimes opened by Woolworth at Philadelphia, Harrisburg, and York, Pa., and at Newark, N.J., will have indifferent success, but when he opens stores at Buffalo, Erie, Scranton, and some other cities, Woolworth will tap the low-income market and will begin to build a worldwide chain of open-shelf, self-service stores that will prosper beyond all his expectations (*see* 1900).

The May Company is started at Leadville, Colo., by German-American merchant David May, 26, who has left his Hartford City, Ind., clothing store job with $25,000 and has gone West to seek a cure for his asthma. Starting with a store of board framework covered with muslin, May sells out his stock within a few weeks as Leadville booms overnight from a town of 500 to one of 25,000 in the wake of the silver strike of 1874 (above).

The Fair opened on Chicago's State Street by German-American merchant E. J. Lehmann, 30, is a department store with "Everything for Everybody Under One Roof."

McKim, Mead & White is established by New York architects Charles Follen McKim, 32, William Rutherford Mead, 33, and Stanford White, 26. The firm will become famous for such buildings as the Century Club, the Harvard Club, the Metropolitan Club, the Players Club, and the University Club in midtown Manhattan, some Columbia University buildings, and the Boston Public Library. The firm will also make restorations in the White House at Washington, D.C.

France's Cathedral of St. Stephen at Limoges is completed after 603 years of construction.

The Boston Park system is completed by Frederick Law Olmsted—an "emerald necklace" for the city.

Belle Isle in the Detroit River is acquired for $200,000 by the city of Detroit which will reclaim land to enlarge the 768-acre island into a 985-acre park.

The last of the Southern bison herd is killed by U.S. hunters at Buffalo Springs, Tex. (*see* Grant, 1875; North Dakota, 1883).

Carp are placed in Wisconsin lakes by the U.S. Fish Commission (*see* shad, 1873; salmon, 1875). The common carp (*Cyprinus carpio*) lives up to 25 years in the wild (up to 40 in captivity) and can survive in waters above 90°F and can even withstand freezing for short periods, powers that will help it proliferate in U.S. inland waters, growing to weights of roughly 30 pounds and providing a new food source.

Britain has her worst harvest of the century, crops fail throughout Europe, demand for U.S. wheat raises prices, and the high prices bring prosperity to U.S. farmers who increase their wheat acreage as railroads build new lines to give farmers easier access to markets.

Hedging of wheat stocks by trading in futures begins on the Chicago Board of Trade that was established in 1865 (*see* Leiter, 1897; Norris, 1903).

Ireland's potato crop fails again as in 1846 and the widespread hunger produces agrarian unrest (*see* Irish Land League, above).

India has a poor crop and much of the harvest is consumed by rats which will plague many districts in the next 2 years and which will always consume a significant portion of the nation's grain stores.

McCormick's reaper sells for $1,500 in the United States, up from $150 in 1861, and there are com-

1879 (cont.) plaints that the reaper is costlier at home than in Europe (see 1875; Northwest Alliance, 1880).

The first milk bottles appear at Brooklyn, N.Y., where the Echo Farms Dairy delivers milk in glass bottles instead of measuring it into the pitchers of housewives and serving maids from barrels carried in milk wagons. Some competitors will soon follow suit (see Borden, 1885) but not all (see Hood, 1897).

Steel rollers are installed in a new Minneapolis flour mill by Hungarian engineers invited to America by C. C. Washburn of Washburn-Crosby Company (see 1866; 1878; Gold Medal Flour, 1880).

Wheatena whole wheat cooked cereal is introduced by a small bakery owner on New York's Mulberry Street who grinds the wheat, sells it in labeled packages, and advertises it in newspapers to compete with oatmeal (see Quaker, 1877). The bakery and its Wheatena will be acquired in 6 years by an Akron, Ohio, physician named Fuller who operates a firm he calls Health Foods.

Heinz's Pepper Sauce is introduced by F. and J. Heinz of Pittsburgh (see 1876; 1880).

Saccharin (benzosulfamide) is discovered accidentally at Baltimore's new Johns Hopkins University by chemist Ira Remsen, 33, and his German student Constantin Fahlberg who are investigating the reactions of a class of coal tar derivatives (toluene sulfamides). They will publish a scientific description of the new compound in February 1880 calling special attention to its sweetness. Fahlberg will file a patent claim without mention of Remsen's contribution, he will return to Germany, obtain financial backing, and organize a company to produce his sugar substitute "saccharine"—at least 300 times sweeter than sugar and a boon to diabetics (see Monsanto, 1901; Wiley, 1907; sodium cyclamate, 1937).

England's Cadbury Brothers has 250 employees and moves to the Birmingham suburb of Bournemouth (see 1866; slavery, 1901).

Thomas Lipton's British grocery store chain makes Lipton a millionaire at age 29 (see 1876; 1890).

The first Canadian Thanksgiving Day is proclaimed and is observed November 6: the day will be observed on a Monday in October beginning in 1931 (see U.S. Thanksgiving, 1863, 1939).

Gage & Tollner's opens at Brooklyn, N.Y., where restaurateurs Charles M. Gage and Eugene Tollner attract New York notables to Fulton Street with their lobster, terrapin, and other seafood dishes.

A spermatozoan is observed to penetrate an egg by Swiss scientist Herman Fol who confirms Oscar Hertwig's 1875 conclusion that a single male cell performs the act of fertilization.

A bill that would restrict Chinese immigration into the United States passes Congress but is vetoed by President Hayes who calls it a violation of the Burlingame Treaty of 1868 (see Exclusion Treaty, 1880).

1880 Lord Beaconsfield (Disraeli), now 75, loses in Britain's general elections March 8, he resigns April 18, and William Gladstone's Liberals will hold office until 1885.

"War is hell," says U.S. Civil War general William Tecumseh Sherman, now 60, in an address to a Columbus, Ohio, reunion of the G.A.R. (Grand Army of the Republic). "There is many a boy here who looks on war as all glory, but, boys, it is all hell. You can bear this warning voice to generations yet to come."

Old guard Republican "Stalwarts" try to gain a third term for President Grant, a deadlocked G.O.P. (Grand Old Party) convention selects James Abram Garfield, 48, of Ohio on the 36th ballot. He wins 214 electoral votes to 155 for the Democrats, but he beats hero Winfield S. Hancock by only 9,464 votes.

Morroco's independence is recognized July 3 in the Madrid Convention signed by the leading European powers and the United States.

French Equatorial Africa is established as a French protectorate by French explorer Pierre Paul François Camille Brazza Savorgnani, 28, who calls himself Savorgnan de Brazza and who founds Brazzaville.

Tahiti is annexed by France.

A Boer Republic independent of Britain's Cape Colony is proclaimed December 30 by Oom Paul Kruger who begins a short-lived revolt that will end with the establishment of the independent South African Republic under British suzerainty (see 1899).

The word "boycott" is introduced to the English language by an incident in Ireland's County Mayo. Tenant farmers organized by the Irish Land League refuse to harvest crops on estates managed by Charles Cunningham Boycott, 48, a retired British Army captain (see Davitt, 1879). The Land League wages a campaign of economic and social ostracism against absentee landlords and their agents, but the word "boycott" will take on a wider meaning as a weapon in economic warfare (see Parnell, 1881).

Britain's first Employers' Liability Act is passed by Parliament September 13 and grants compensations to workers for injuries.

Tennessee's 1875 "Jim Crow" law is called unconstitutional by a Federal Circuit Court (but see 1881).

Thomas Edison's 1879 incandescent bulb is patented (see Owens, 1903; Langmuir, 1912).

All of Wabash, Ind., is lighted by electricity in an April demonstration of the Brush arc-light system and a mile of New York's Broadway is illuminated by Brush arc lights December 20 (see 1879).

Wood remains a major source of energy in the United States, but use of firewood begins to decline.

Malaria is traced to a blood parasite by French army physician Charles Louis Alphonse Laveran, 35, in Algeria (see Ross, 1897).

The bacillus of typhoid fever is identified simultaneously by German bacteriologist Karl Joseph Eberth, 45, and Robert Koch who has accepted an appointment to head a Berlin University Laboratory (see 1877; Budd, 1873). The bacillus will be named *Eberthella typhi* and German bacteriologist T. A. Gaffley will confirm that it is the agent of typhoid fever in 1884 (see Wright, 1896).

Robert Koch (above) discovers a vaccine against anthrax through the accident of an assistant (see 1881).

Burroughs, Wellcome & Co., is founded at London to produce chemicals and pharmaceuticals. Cofounder Henry Wellcome, 26, is a U.S. émigré.

A pooling agreement signed February 2 resolves disputes among the Atchison, Topeka and Santa Fe, the Union Pacific, the Kansas Pacific, and the Denver, Rio Grande and Western. The Denver, Rio Grande obtains exclusive rights to build a line from Pueblo through the Royal Gorge to Leadville via a 3-foot narrow-gauge line, it pays the Santa Fe $1.4 million for work done by the Santa Fe on the Royal Gorge, and it agrees not to build a line to Santa Fe provided that the Atchison, Topeka keeps out of Denver and Leadville with its standard 56.5-inch track.

The "Chattanooga Choo-Choo" gets its name March 5 from a newspaper reporter covering the resumption of through passenger service between North and South. A Cincinnati Southern Railroad wood-burner chugs out of Cincinnati and passes through Chattanooga, Tenn., en route to New Orleans.

Elevated steam trains rumble up and down New York's Second, Third, and Sixth Avenues.

The United States has more than 100 millionaires, up from fewer than 20 in 1840 (see 1892).

Leadville, Colo., storekeeper Horace "Hod" Tabor, 53, grubstakes two starving prospectors to $64.75 worth of provisions and ends up 10 months later owning silver mines including the Matchless that will earn him as much as $4 million per year. Tabor takes as his mistress the blonde, blue-eyed divorcée Elizabeth McCourt "Baby" Doe, 23, by buying off her previous protector. He divorces his wife, and marries Baby Doe for whom he will build a Denver opera house and a mansion graced with nude statuary and 100 peacocks (see 1893).

The De Beers Mining Corporation is founded by English diamond mine operator Cecil John Rhodes, 27, and English financier Alfred Beit, also 27. The Barnato Diamond Mining Company is founded by English speculator Barnett Isaacs "Barney" Barnato, 28, whose firm will be consolidated with De Beers in 1888 to give Cecil Rhodes a virtual monopoly in the South African diamond industry (see Rhodes, 1890).

Some 539,000 Singer sewing machines are sold, up from 250,000 in 1875 (see 1873; 1889).

Japan's Fuji Bank is founded at Tokyo.

A bush roller chain patented by Swiss engineer Hans Renold improves on the James Slater drive chain of 1864. Renold has acquired Slater's small textile machine chain factory at Salford and has devised a chain with an arrangement of bushes that provide a much greater load-bearing surface than did the Slater chain (see safety bicycle, 1885).

Warner-Swasey Company is founded at Chicago by former Pratt & Whitney toolmakers Worcester Reed Warner, 34, and Ambrose Swasey, 34. The epicycloidal milling machine invented by Swasey last year is a gear-cutting device that produces true theoretical curves and thus makes possible the production of silent gears. Started with $6,000 in savings, the new firm will move to Cleveland next year and will grow to become a major producer of lathes and other machine tools and precision instruments.

The University of Southern California is founded by educators who include Marion McKinley Bovard, 33. He becomes the university's first president.

Manchester University is created by a reorganization of England's Owens College.

England's first high schools for girls open.

Parcel Post service begins in Britain (see United States, 1913).

The first British telephone directory is issued January 15 by the London Telephone Co. It lists 255 names.

The first wireless telephone message is transmitted June 3 by Alexander Graham Bell on the photophone he has invented (see Hertz, 1887; Marconi, 1895).

The *Kansas City Evening Star* is founded by publisher William Rockhill Nelson, 39 (see Nelson Gallery, 1930).

Halftone photographic illustrations appear in newspapers for the first time (see below).

The Century Company publishers is founded at New York by former Scribner & Co. editor Roswell Smith, 51, who buys out Charles Scribner with $100,000 of the $110,000 he has received from a railroad company for some land he owned out West. Smith will begin publishing *The Century Magazine* late next year (see Appleton-Century, 1933).

Longmans, Green & Co. is created by a merger engineered by London publishers Thomas Norton Longman, 31, and Hubert Henry Longman, 24, whose grandfather's uncle Thomas Longman participated in the publication of Doctor Johnson's *Dictionary* more than a century ago.

Fiction *The Brothers Karamazov* (*Brat'ya Karamazov*) by Fedor Dostoievski who caps his career with a literary masterpiece and with a patriotic speech at the unveiling of the Pushkin memorial at Moscow; Dostoevski will die early next year at age 59; *Nana* by the French novelist Emile Zola exposes the misery of life as a Parisian prostitute. "Boule de Suif" by French short-story writer Henri René Albert Guy de Maupassant, 30, is about a patriotic prostitute in the Franco-Prussian War; it will be followed by even better stories but its author is already ill with the syphilis

1880 (cont.) that will put him in a strait jacket and that will kill him at age 43 just 4 years after his younger brother dies in an insane asylum of the same disease. *Niels Lyhne* by Jens Peter Jacobsen; *The Grandissimes* by George Washington Cable; *Ben Hur, A Tale of the Christ* by former Civil War general Lew (Lewis) Wallace, now 53, who is serving as governor of the New Mexico Territory; Wallace's story of Christians in ancient Rome enjoys great popularity. *Democracy* by former Harvard history professor Henry Adams; *The Duke's Children* by Anthony Trollope.

Nonfiction *A Tramp Abroad* by Mark Twain.

Juvenile *The Peterkin Papers* by Boston author Lucretia Peabody Hale, 60, whose book *The Last of the Peterkins* will appear in 1886; *Kate Greenaway's Birthday Book* by Catherine Greenaway.

Poetry *Ultima Thule* by Henry Wadsworth Longfellow, now 73.

Painting *The Outer Boulevards* by Camille Pissarro; *Place Clichy* by Pierre Auguste Renoir; *Château de Medan* by Paul Cézanne.

New York's Metropolitan Museum of Art moves in March into a new red-brick building in Central Park at 82nd Street designed by Calvert Vaux and Jacob Wrey Mould (*see* 1870; 1888).

The first photographic reproduction in a newspaper appears March 4 in the *New York Daily Graphic.* The picture of a shanty-town is printed from a halftone produced by photographing through a fine screen with dots in the photograph representing shadows (*see* 1875; Ives, 1886; press halftones, 1897).

Photography is advanced by Rochester, N.Y., bank clerk George Eastman, 26, who works at night in his mother's kitchen to perfect a process for making dry photographic plates. Eastman goes into business producing the plates for commercial photographers (*see* Seed, 1879; roll film, 1884; Kodak, 1888).

Theater *Hazel Kirke* by Steele Mackay 2/4 at New York's Madison Square Theater, 486 perfs. (a new record). Fire destroys the drop curtain 2/26 as the audience is taking its seats, but firemen extinguish the blaze and the performance goes on as scheduled.

First performances *Tragic Overture* (*Tragische Ouvertüre*) by Johannes Brahms 12/26 at Vienna.

Popular songs "Funiculi-Funicula" by Italian composer Luigi Denza, 34, lyrics by G. Turco; "Sailing" (Sailing, over the Bounding Main) by English songwriter Godfrey Marks (James Frederick Swift), 33.

Woodward & Lothrop's Boston Dry Goods House opens at Washington, D.C.. Former Chelsea, Mass., merchants Samuel Walter Woodward, 32, and Alvin Mason Lothrop, 33, will move in January of next year from 705 Market Street to a five-story building with steam-powered elevators at 921 Pennsylvania Avenue and in 1887 they will take over a new $100,000 building at 11th and F Streets (*see* 1913).

Cologne Cathedral is completed after 634 years of construction and is the largest Gothic cathedral in northern Europe. Located near the Hohenzollern Bridge in the oldest part of the city, the dome has twin spires 515 feet high that make it the tallest structure in the world, a distinction it will hold until the Eiffel Tower is completed in 1889.

New York's Seventh Regiment Armory is completed with a 187- by 290-foot drill hall on Fourth Avenue between 66th and 67th Streets where New York and New Haven Railroad trains steam past en route to and from the Grand Central train shed built at 42nd Street in 1871.

Half of New York's population is packed into tenements on the Lower East Side, an area that accounts for a disproportionate 70 percent of the city's deaths.

Harvard's Sever Hall designed by H. H. Richardson is completed in Romanesque style—the first building in the Yard to depart from Georgian colonial style.

The Johns-Manville Company has its beginnings in Milwaukee's Manville Covering Company, started by local entrepreneur Charles B. Manville. He puts cement on neighbors' furnaces (*see* 1901).

Denver's Windsor Hotel is opened by cattle barons in Colorado and is the most elegant hostelry between San Francisco's 5-year-old Palace and Chicago's 5-year-old Palmer House (*see* Brown Palace, 1891).

California's Del Monte Hotel on the Monterey Peninsula is opened by Central Pacific Railroad boss Charles Crocker, now 58, whose $325,000 structure can accommodate 750 and will rival the finest resort hotels in the East. Guests enjoy melons, vegetables, fruits, and grapes grown in the hotel's gardens or brought down from San Francisco, and fresh flounder, pompano, rock cod, salmon, and sole from the Bay is served daily (*see* Hearst, 1887).

Tenant farmers work one-fourth of U.S. farms (which number just over 4 million).

The Northwest Alliance has its beginnings in a local founded by Chicago editor Milton George whose organization will become a leading political activist group among farmers (*see* Farmers' Alliance, 1882).

U.S. wheat production reaches 500 million bushels, up 221 percent over 1866 figures. 80 percent of the wheat is cut by machine, but wheat prices have dropped 27 percent since 1866.

U.S. export of wheat and flour combined reach 175 million bushels, up from 50 million in 1871.

Sacramento Valley, Calif., wheat grower Hugh Glenn harvests a million bushels (*see* 1865). Glenn has a thousand men working for him and they use enormous steam-powered combines to harvest 100 acres per day for as little as 25 cents per acre.

U.S. corn production reaches 1.5 billion bushels, up 98 percent over 1866 figures, and corn exports total 116 million bushels, but corn prices have dropped 15 percent since 1866. While many in Europe go hungry, Midwestern farmers burn corn for fuel; prices are too low to warrant shipping the crop to market.

Cattle drives up the Chisholm Trail reach their peak (see 1871; 1885).

Sugar beets are raised on a commercial scale for the first time in the United States (see 1878 Paris World's Fair), but only 10 percent of U.S. sugar needs are met by production of cane and beets in the continental United States and less than 0.05 percent of this will come from beets until the end of the 1880s. Another 19 percent will come from the territories of Hawaii, Puerto Rico, and the Philippines, but sugar imported from Cuba, Germany, and Java accounts for 71 percent of U.S. sugar consumption (see Spreckels, 1883; Havemeyer, 1887).

The Pillsbury A mill goes up at Minneapolis and will be the largest flour mill in the world (see 1878; 1886).

Washburn, Crosby Company of Minneapolis prepares to market Gold Medal Flour after winning a gold, a silver, and a bronze medal for flour samples it has entered in the Miller's International Exhibition (see 1879; Betty Crocker, 1921).

Thomas's English Muffins are introduced in New York by English-American baker Samuel Bath Thomas who opens a retail bakery in 20th Street between 9th and 10th Avenues and delivers to hotels and restaurants by pushcart.

"Philadelphia" brand cream cheese is introduced by a New York distributor named Reynolds who has it made for him by the Empire Cheese Company of South Edmeston, N.Y. (see Phenix Cheese, 1900).

R. T. French Company has its beginnings as New York entrepreneur Robert Timothy French goes into partnership with his eldest son George J. to operate Jackson Spice Company, grinders and packers of spices. The Frenches will merge in 1883 with a Fairport, N.Y., baking powder firm and will move their operations to Fairport. They will move to Rochester, N.Y., in 1885 (see French's Cream Salad Mustard, 1904).

Heinz's White Vinegar, Apple Cider Vinegar, and Apple Butter are introduced by Pittsburgh's F. and J. Heinz (see 1879; 1886).

More than 95 A&P grocery stores are scattered across America from Boston to Milwaukee, but the Great Atlantic & Pacific Tea Company will not have a store on the West Coast for another 50 years (see 1869; 1912).

Imported meat accounts for 17 percent of British meat consumption (see frozen beef, mutton, and lamb, below). The figure includes livestock and preserved meat, most of it salted, along with dried "Hamburg" beef and tinned, boiled mutton and beef from Australia, eaten in quantity despite its poor quality because it is half the price of fresh meat.

The first totally successful shipment of frozen beef and mutton from Australia to England arrives in early February as the S. S. *Strathleven* docks with

400 carcasses. The meat sells in London at 5½d. per pound and is soon followed by the first cargo of frozen mutton and lamb from New Zealand (see 1877).

U.S. ice shipments to tropical ports reach a high of 890,364 tons carried by 1,735 ships, up from 146,000 tons aboard 363 ships in 1856. On long voyages 40 percent of the cargo may melt but the remaining ice sells for as much as $56 per ton.

New England's ice crop fails due to an unseasonably warm winter, ice prices soar, and the high prices spur development of ice-making machines (see 1889).

Mark Twain lists American dishes he has yearned for while in Europe in his book *A Tramp Abroad* (above): buckwheat cakes with maple syrup, squash, fried chicken, Sierra Nevada brook trout, Mississippi black bass, terrapin, coon, possum, soft-shelled crabs, wild turkey, canvasback duck, succotash, Boston baked beans, chitterlings, hominy, sliced tomatoes with sugar and vinegar, sweet corn, eight kinds of hot bread, fruit pies and cobblers, and porterhouse steak for breakfast.

Los Angeles has a population of 11,183, up from 5,728 in 1870, but water shortages limit growth.

A Chinese Exclusion Treaty signed at Peking November 17 gives Washington power to "regulate, limit, or suspend" entry of Chinese laborers (see 1882).

Nearly 550,000 English and nearly 440,000 Irish immigrants enter the United States.

A pharmacy to dispense pessaries (vaginal contraceptive suppositories based on quinine in cocoa butter) is opened at Clerkenwell, England, by Walter John Rendell (see Place, 1882; Wilde, 1833).

Abortion of any kind is declared an excommunicatory sin by Pope Pius XI (see Lord Acton, 1887).

1881 Russia's Aleksandr II is assassinated March 13 at St. Petersburg at age 62 after a 26-year reign. The assassination has been organized and carried out by Sophia Perovskaya who heads a band of Nihilist terrorists of a populist fringe group and it precipitates a wave of repression and persecution as the czar is succeeded by his 36-year-old son who will reign as Aleksandr III until 1894 (see below).

Romania and Serbia win independence from Constantinople; the Serbs make an alliance with Austria.

President Garfield is mortally wounded July 2 by disappointed office seeker Charles J. Guiteau who shoots the president at a Washington, D.C., railway station. When Garfield dies September 19 at Elberon, N.J., at age 49, he is succeeded by his 50-year-old vice president Chester Alan Arthur who abandons his support of the spoils system and follows Garfield's policy of avoiding party favoritism in his appointments (see Marcy, 1832; Pendleton Act, 1883).

Irish Nationalist leader Charles Stewart Parnell, 35, agitates for home rule and is imprisoned on charges of obstructing operation of a new land policy. From

A FOUL DEED.

President Garfield's assassination, the second in 15 years, followed that of the Russian czar by less than 16 weeks.

prison Parnell directs tenant farmers to pay no rent and he thereby gains increased power (*see* 1879; 1882; Boycott, 1880).

Japanese political parties are formed.

British forces in Africa are repulsed January 28 by the Transvaal Boers at Laing's Neck and are defeated February 27 at Majuba Hill where the governor and commander-in-chief of the Natal colony Sir George Pomeroy Colley is killed at age 45. The Treaty of Pretoria concluded April 5 gives independence to the South African Republic of the Boers but under British suzerainty.

 A Century of Dishonor by U.S. author Helen Maria Fiske Hunt Jackson, 51, records government wrongs in dealing with Indian tribes. Jackson will be appointed as special commissioner next year to investigate conditions among California's Mission Indians.

A second "Jim Crow" law passed by the Tennessee legislature segregates black passengers on railroads and establishes a precedent that will be followed by similar laws throughout the South (*see* 1880; 1896).

Anti-Semitism appears in America after generations during which German Jews have mixed on equal terms with other German immigrants.

Russia's new Czar Aleksandr III (above) makes Jews the scapegoats for the assassination of his father. He also persecutes Roman Catholics but he vows to kill one-third of the country's Jews, to drive out another third, and to convert the rest, beginning a series of pogroms (massacres) that will spur emigration of millions of Jews in the next 30 years.

 The U.S. federal income tax law of 1862 is unconstitutional, the Supreme Court rules (*see* 1894).

The Anaconda Copper Company has its beginnings in the Anaconda Silver Mine opened in Montana Ter-

ritory by miner Marcus Daly, 39, who has persuaded George Hearst, Lloyd Tevis, and James B. A. Haggin to buy Michael Hickey's 1875 claim for $30,000. The silver will give out quickly but the mining operations will turn up a rich vein of copper. Daly will buy out neighboring properties, and the Anaconda will re-open as a copper mine. Daly will build a copper smelter in 1884, and he will reorganize the company with expanded holdings in 1891 under the name Anaconda Mining Company with a capitalization of $25 million (*see* Amalgamated Copper, 1899).

Meyer Guggenheim begins a mining and smelting career that will establish great fortunes. A Swiss-born Philadelphia lace and embroidery importer of 51, Guggenheim buys sight unseen a one-third interest in two lead and silver mines on the outskirts of Lead-ville, Colo., he travels out to inspect his holdings, finds that the A. Y. mine and the Minnie (both nearly 2 miles above sea-level) are flooded. He invests half his $50,000 capital to "unwater" them, and within a few months the A. Y. mine is producing 15 ounces of silver per ton of ore (*see* 1888).

The Wharton School of Finance and Commerce is established at the University of Pennsylvania with a gift from nickel miner Joseph Wharton, 55, whose Pennsylvania nickel mine has for years been the only U.S. producer of refined nickel. Wharton developed a process in 1875 for making pure malleable nickel (*see* Ritchie, 1885).

Diamond Match Company is created by a merger of the two largest U.S. match manufacturers with Ohio Columbus Barber, 40, as president. Chicago lawyer William H. Moore, 33, has effected the merger (*see* New York Biscuit, 1890).

The Atchison, Topeka and Santa Fe links up with the Southern Pacific March 8 at Deming in New Mexico Territory, the first Santa Fe through train to California leaves Kansas City March 17, but the road still has only 868 miles of its own track and despite its name it is balked by terrain from reaching Santa Fe (it will never get closer than Lamy). The 868 miles will increase to 3,600 in the next 6 years under the leadership of the Santa Fe's new president William Barstow Strong (*see* 1880; 1887).

The Southern Pacific Railway links New Orleans with San Francisco as the last spike is driven home near El Paso, Tex. Service on the Sunset route will begin in 1883 (*see* 1884).

A decade of unprecedented U.S. railroad construction begins.

Henry Villard gains control of the Northern Pacific by means of a pool he has formed to monopolize Pacific Northwest transportation. Now 46, Villard came to New York from his native Bavaria at age 18, he changed his name from Ferdinand Heinrich Gustav Hilgard to avoid being returned and drafted, and he worked for years as a journalist for the *New York Staats-Zeitung,* for James Gordon Bennett's *Herald,* and for Horace Greeley's *Tribune* (*see* 1883; 1901).

James J. Hill of the St. Paul and Pacific joins with Montreal financier George Stephen to organize a new Canadian Pacific Railway Company after the collapse of an earlier effort. Given a $25 million pledge of government aid, a 10-year deadline, and assurance that no other railroad will be permitted in the area for 20 years, Hill and Stephen hire Chicago Milwaukee & St. Paul general manager William Cornelius Van Horne, 38, to carry out the trans-Canada project (which is long overdue in light of the Dominion government's pledge to British Columbia in 1871). Van Horne moves to Winnipeg, he works his crews night and day, and by the end of summer he has built nearly 500 miles of track through forest and swamp (see 1887).

Collis P. Huntington of the Central Pacific appoints his nephew Henry Edwards Huntington, 31, as superintendent of the line he is constructing between Trimble, Tenn., and Covington, Ky., for the new Chesapeake, Ohio & South Western Railroad he is building. The younger Huntington will take over management of the Kentucky Central in 1886 and will move to San Francisco in 1892 at his uncle's request to help manage the Southern Pacific (above).

The Norfolk and Western Railroad Company is created by a reorganization of roads that began in 1837 with the City Point Railroad that ran 10 miles between Petersburg, Va., and City Point. The company will augment its 479 miles of track in this decade by acquiring other roads in Maryland and Ohio and by building new lines into the coal fields of Virginia and West Virginia and by the end of 1927 it will be operating 4,477 miles of track in six states and will have 30,000 employees.

The S. S. *Servia* goes into service for Britain's Cunard Line. It is the world's first steel ocean liner.

The motor-driven water bus (*vaporetto*) introduced at Venice will make the traditional gondola a conveyance used chiefly by tourists. By 1971 Venice will have fewer than 500 gondolas (see 1292).

An interferometer is invented by German-American physicist Albert Abraham Michelson, 29, who in 1887 will show with Edward H. Morley that the speed of light in a vaccum is the same in all inertial reference systems (coordinate systems moving at constant velocity relative to each other). The work of Michelson and Morley will lead directly to the special theory of relativity (see Einstein, 1905).

Thomas Edison's Edison Electric Light Company creates a subsidiary (The Edison Company for Isolated Lighting) to furnish factories and large department stores with individual power plants (see 1880; Edison Illuminating Company, 1882).

London's Savoy Theatre opens with the first electric illumination in any British public building. The theater has been built by Richard D'Oyly Carte, 37, who has been producing Gilbert and Sullivan operas since *Trial by Jury* in 1875 (see below).

The American Solvay Process Company is founded by U.S. entrepreneur W. B. Cogswell with backing from the Hazzard family in Rhode Island. The European Solvay family holds a half interest in the new firm (see 1863; Allied Chemical, 1920).

Scottish bacteriologist Jaime Ferran discovers a serum effective against cholera (see Koch, 1883).

A paper by Cuban physician Carlos Juan Finlay, 28, suggests that mosquitoes may spread yellow fever (see 1878; Reed, 1900).

The pneumococcus bacterium that causes pneumonia is found by U.S. Army bacteriologist-physician George Miller Sternberg, 43, who has earlier identified the malaria plasmodium and the bacilli of tuberculosis and typhoid fever.

The American Association of the Red Cross is founded by Clara Barton of Civil War fame who has done relief work in Europe during the Franco-Prussian War and has campaigned to have the United States sign a Geneva Convention (see 1861; 1882). Now 59, Barton will serve as president of the American National Red Cross until 1904 when lack of public support will require congressional action to keep the Red Cross from folding.

The Kickapoo Indian Medicine Company is founded by U.S. promoters John Healy and Texas Charley Bigelow who hire 300 Indians (none of them Kickapoos) from Indian agents, pay each one $30 per month plus expenses, and have them stage rodeos, rope tricks, and war dances to promote Kickapoo Indian Oil, Salve, Cough Cure, Pain Pills, Wart Killer, and the like. Healy and Bigelow will be joined in Pennsylvania by promoter Nevada Ned Oliver (who has never been anywhere near Nevada) who will specialize in catarrh powders made of menthol, sugar, milk, and cocaine (see cocaine, 1884).

Tuskegee Normal and Industrial Institute is founded at Tuskegee, Ala., where local blacks have invited Booker Taliaferro Washington, 25, to start the pioneer school for blacks. Washington has been instructor to 75 Indian youths at Hampton Normal and Agricultural Institute (see 1870; 1895; Carver, 1896).

Atlanta's Spelman College has its beginnings in the Atlanta Baptist Female Seminary. The school will be renamed in 1924 to honor John D. Rockefeller's mother-in-law Lucy Henry Spelman and it will be the leading U.S. college for black women.

Case School of Applied Science is founded in the home of the late Cleveland philanthropist Leonard Case on Rockwell Avenue. The school will move in 1885 to Euclid Avenue at University Circle next to the Western Reserve University started at Hudson in 1826. (Western Reserve will move to Cleveland next year to satisfy conditions of an endowment by philanthropist Amasa Stone.)

Marquette University is founded at Milwaukee.

The University of Connecticut is founded at Storrs.

The University of Pennsylvania's Wharton School is founded (see above).

1881 (cont.) Western Union Telegraph Company is created by a consolidation of the Western Union Company with two smaller telegraph companies to form a giant monopoly (*see* 1866). Financier Jay Gould and railroad magnate William H. Vanderbilt have effected the consolidation (*see* Postal Telegraph, 1886).

"The Story of a Great Monopoly" published in *The Atlantic Monthly* is an attack on John D. Rockefeller's Standard Oil Company trust by *Chicago Tribune* financial editor Henry Demarest Lloyd, 34.

Harper's Monthly commissions Henry Demarest Lloyd (above) to do a study of the Pullman Palace Car Company, but *Harper's* will reject Lloyd's work, calling it too uncritical, and will publish instead an article by economist Richard T. Ely, 27, of Johns Hopkins University. Ely will praise the physical facilities of Pullman, Ill., and its absence of saloons but he will call the town undemocratic, un-American, and feudalistic (*see* below).

Il Progresso Italo-Americano begins publication at New York. The paper will grow to become the largest-circulation foreign language daily in the city.

The *London Evening News* begins publication (*see* 1896).

Andrew Carnegie donates funds for a Pittsburgh library and begins a series of library gifts (*see* 1889).

Nonfiction *Virginibus Puerisque* (essays) by Scottish writer Robert Louis Stevenson, 30.

Fiction *The Portrait of a Lady* by Henry James; *Le Crime de Sylvestre Bonard* by French novelist Anatole France (Jacques Anatole François Thibault), 37; *The House by the Medlar Tree* (*I Malavoglia*) by Giovanni Verga; *Epitaph for a Small Winner* (*Memorias Postumas de Bas Cubas*) by Brazilian novelist Joaquim Machado De Assis, 42.

Juvenile *Heidi* (*Heidis Lehr- und Wanderjahre, Heidi Kann Brauchen, Was es Gelernst Hat*) by Swiss author Johann Heusser Spyri, 54; *Five Little Peppers and How They Grew* by U.S. author Margaret Sidney (Harriett Mulford Stone Lothrop), 37, who has married the publisher Daniel Lothrop, 50.

Painting *Sunshine and Snow* by Claude Monet; *An Asylum for Old Men* by Max Liebermann; *Luncheon of the Boating Party* by Pierre Auguste Renoir.

Sculpture *Admiral Farragut* by Irish-American sculptor Augustus Saint-Gaudens, 33, who opened studios at New York in 1873 but who will move to Cornish, N.H., in 1885. Saint-Gaudens shows a style of dramatic simplicity that has made him popular with architects such as Stanford White who has designed a pedestal for the full-length statue of the late U.S. naval hero in New York's Madison Square.

Photographic roll film is patented October 11 by Wisconsin inventor David Henderson Houston whose "photographic apparatus" is a camera whose inner end has a receptacle containing a "roll of sensitized paper or any other suitable tissue, such as gelatine or any more durable material that may be discovered, and an empty reel, upon which the sensitized band is wound as rapidly as it has been acted upon by the light" (*see* Walker, Eastman, 1884).

Barnum & Bailey's Circus is created by a merger that joins the 10-year-old P. T. Barnum circus with that of John Anthony Bailey, 34, who will gain control in 1888 (*see* Jumbo, 1882; Ringling brothers, 1907).

Opera *The Tales of Hoffmann* (*Les Contes d'Hoffman*) 2/10 at the Opéra-Comique, Paris, with music by the late Jacques Offenbach who died last October at age 61; his Barbarelle aria makes the work a *succes fou; The Maid of Orleans* (*Irleanskata dieve*) 2/13 at St. Petersburg's Maryinsky Theater, with music by Petr Ilich Tchaikovsky, libretto from the Friedrich von Schiller play of 1801; *Patience* (or *Bunthorne's Bride*) 4/23 at London's new Savoy Theatre (above) with Gilbert and Sullivan songs that include "Prithee, Pretty Maiden;" *Libusa* 5/11 at Prague, with music by Bedrich Smetana to open the new National Theater.

Lillian Russell achieves stardom at age 19 playing D'Jemma in the comic opera *The Great Mogul*, (or *The Snake Charmer*) with music by French composer Edmond Audran, 39. Born Helen Louise Leonard at Clinton, Iowa, Russell adopted her stage name last year while appearing at Tony Pastor's Opera House in New York and she has toured California in the new comic opera which she will follow with roles in *Patience* (above) and other Gilbert and Sullivan operettas. Russell will be popular for more than 20 years for her clear soprano voice and well-upholstered beauty.

First performances Concerto No. 3 in B major for Violin and Orchestra by Camille Saint-Säens 1/2 at Paris; *Academic Festival Overture* (*Academische Festouverture*) by Johannes Brahms 1/4 at the University of Breslau; Symphony No. 2 in C minor (*Little Russia*) by Petr Ilich Tchaikovsky 2/2 at St. Petersburg; Symphony No. 3 in D major by the late Franz Schubert 2/19 at London's Crystal Palace; Symphony No. 4 in E flat major (*Romantic*) by Anton Bruckner 2/20 at Vienna; Concerto No. 2 in B flat major for Pianoforte and Orchestra by Johannes Brahms 11/9 at Budapest's Redountensaal; Concerto No. 2 in G major for Pianoforte and Orchestra by Tchaikovsky 11/12 at New York's Academy of Music; Concerto in D major for Violin and Orchestra by Tchaikovsky 12/4 at Vienna.

The Boston Symphony Orchestra is founded by local banker Henry Lee Higginson, 47 (*see* 1875; 1885).

Hymn "I Am Coming" by Ira David Sankey, lyrics by Helen R. Young; "Tell It Out Among the Nations" by Ira David Sankey, lyrics by Francis R. Havergal.

March "Semper Fidelis" by U.S. Marine Corps bandmaster John Philip Sousa, 27, who took the post last year and will keep it until 1892 (*see* 1889).

The United States Lawn Tennis Association is founded May 21 by 33 U.S. clubs (*see* 1874). The USLTA will control all national tournaments in the United States and it holds its first men's championship tournaments in August at the Newport, R. I., Casino that will be host for the matches for 34 years (*see* Forest Hills, 1924).

The second Canadian bid for the America's Cup in ocean yacht racing fails. The U.S. defender *Mischief* defeats Canada's *Atalanta* 2 to 0.

Billy the Kid escapes in May while under heavy guard after 5 months in confinement on a murder conviction. He kills two deputies who try to stop him, but Sheriff Patrick F. Garrett discovers him at Fort Sumner in New Mexico Territory July 15 and shoots him dead. The New York-born western outlaw William H. Bonney, 21, has killed 21 men including a previous sheriff and within 6 weeks of his death *The True Life of Billy the Kid* is being sold in the streets of New York.

A shootout at the O.K. Corral outside Tombstone in Arizona Territory October 26 breaks up a gang headed by Ike Clanton whose brother Billy is shot along with Frank and Tom McLowry. Town marshal Virgil Earp has deputized his brothers Wyatt, 31, and Morgan, they are joined by alcoholic gambler "Doc" Holliday. Ike Clanton and Billy Claiborne escape out of town, the town suspects the Earps of murder, and Virgil Earp loses his job as marshal.

Marshall, Field & Co., is created by a reorganization of Chicago's Field, Leiter and Company (*see* 1865). In the next 25 years Field will make his firm the world's largest wholesale and retail dry goods store (*see* 1893; University of Chicago, 1891).

Detroit's J. L. Hudson Company department store has its beginnings in a menswear shop opened by English-American merchant Joseph Lothian Hudson, 34, who has worked for local retailer Christopher R. Mabley. Hudson will specialize in fire sales, he will acquire a site at Gratiot and Farmer Streets in 1891, and by 1911 he will have a store that covers an entire city block with 50 passenger elevators (*see* 1912; Hudson Motor Car Company, 1909).

Boston's William Filene, Sons & Co., opens at 10 Winter Street. Prussian-American tailor-merchant William Filene, 51, and his sons Edward P., 21, and Abraham Lincoln Filene, 16, will take over a five-story building at 445–447 Washington Street for their womenswear and accessories store (*see* 1901).

Construction of a model factory town for Pullman Palace Car employees begins on a 4,000-acre tract beside Lake Calumet outside Chicago. Pullman, Ill. (*see* above). Architect Solon Spenser Beman, 29, has designed the first all-brick U.S. city, it will have paved streets, good water supply and sewage disposal systems, it will have a shopping center arcade and a hotel named after George M. Pullman's daughter, and its rents will be fixed to give the Pull-

man Company a 6 percent return on investment (*see* 1893 strike).

New York's Dakota Apartments go up at 72nd Street and Eighth Avenue (later Central Park West), a location that seems to most New Yorkers as remote as the Dakota Territory. Financed by Singer Sewing Machine magnate Edward Clark and designed in German Renaissance style by U.S. architect Henry Janeway Hardenbergh, 34, the $2 million nine-story buildings surround a central court and will have nine hydraulic elevators to serve the Dakota's marble-floored mahogany-paneled apartments with their 15-foot ceilings.

Newport Casino at the Rhode Island resort town is completed by McKim, Mead & White.

"Cleopatra's Needle" is erected in New York's Central Park. The ancient Egyptian obelisk raised on a hill overlooking the Metropolitan Museum of Art far antedates Cleopatra as does the obelisk raised on the London Embankment in 1878.

Ring-necked pheasants from Shanghai are introduced into Oregon's Willamette Valley. The Chinese pheasant will be an important American upland game bird.

The *New York Tribune* takes over the Fresh Air Fund for city slum children that was started 4 years ago. The newspaper appeals to the public for funds to continue the program.

Drought strikes the eastern United States. New York City runs out of water and people in many cities die of heat exhaustion.

Cattle ranges in the U.S. Southwest wither in a severe drought, but cattle-raising remains profitable.

The Prairie Cattle Company of Edinburgh, Scotland, declares a 28-percent dividend. The company buys out Texas Panhandle rancher George W. Littlefield whose LIT squatter ranch claims no land rights but who receives more than $125,000 (*see* 1882).

The Beef Bonanza, or How to Get Rich on the Plains by former Union Army brevet-general James S. Brisbin, 44, encourages more British investment in U.S. cattle ventures.

A vaccine to prevent anthrax in sheep and hogs is found by Louis Pasteur (*see* 1861; Koch, 1883).

California imposes quarantine regulations to keep out insect pests and plant diseases.

The loganberry is introduced by Santa Cruz, Calif., judge James Harvey Logan who has crossed the red raspberry with a California wild blackberry. The University of California will make loganberry seeds available to the public in 1883 (*see* Boysen, 1920).

The Texas state capitol burns down; Texas legislators demand the biggest capitol building in the country with a dome at least one foot higher than the one in Washington. They arrange with a group of Chicago contractors and financiers to build the new capitol, and they trade 3 million acres of Panhandle prairie

1881 (cont.) to the Chicago syndicate. The Capitol Free-hold Land and Investment Company is formed by Chicago dry goods merchant John Villiers Farwell, 56, and his brother Charles Benjamin, 58, who is a U.S. congressman, the Farwells wind 800 miles of barbed wire round their holdings, and the XIT Ranch they establish is the largest in the Panhandle. It will soon be driving 12,000 head per year from its 200-mile Texas range 1,200 miles up the Montana Trail to the 200-mile leased XIT range in Montana Territory, the last great cattle drives from Texas.

German physician Karl von Voit at Munich suggests that a man requires 118 grams of protein per day, 500 grams of carbohydrate, and 56 grams of fat for a total of 3,055 kilocalories (see Atwater, 1902).

The first pure food laws are passed by New York, New Jersey, Michigan, and Illinois (see 1904).

A sardine cannery is put up at West Jonesport, Me., by Boston's William Underwood & Co., which has been packing lobster, clams, mackerel, and chowders since 1846 at plants in West Jonesport and Southwest Harbor (see red devil, 1870). Underwood will fry the fish in oil and will pack it under French names (see Wolff, 1876; Rogers, 1903).

The first U.S.-made margarine is produced in a West 48th Street, New York factory by Community Manufacturing Company, a subsidiary of the U.S. Dairy Company (see 1874; 1919).

Jumbo Rolled Oats are introduced by Akron, Ohio, oatmeal king Ferdinand Schumacher who imported porcelain rollers from England in 1878 and who now converts his entire oatmeal production to roller processing which eliminates the unsaleable oat flour that wasted 25 percent of the oats in his earlier process. His rolled oats save Schumacher money, they give him an advantage over competitors who have copied his steel-cut method, and they permit a housewife using a double-boiler to prepare breakfast in 1 hour, less than half the time needed for steel-cut oats and at less expense (see 1875; 1886).

Granola is adopted by J. H. Kellogg as a new name for his cold breakfast food. He has been sued for using the name Granula by the Dansville, N.Y., originators of that name (see 1877; Granose, 1895).

Chicago meatpacker Gustavus F. Swift perfects a refrigerator car to take Chicago-dressed meat to eastern butchers (see 1877). Sides of meat hang from overhead rails inside the car, and when it reaches its destination the rails are hooked up with rails inside the customer's cold storage building, making it easy to slide the meat from railcar to cold store without loss of time or change of temperature. The efficiency of Swift's system, beginning with a disassembly line from the moment of slaughter to the butchering of carcasses into primal sections, will lower the price of meat in New York, New England, and down the Atlantic seaboard.

The first British cold store opens at London which soon begins to receive shipments of chilled beef from America. When it is discovered that meat kept at 30°F maintains its quality better than meat preserved with early freezing methods, U.S. meat will begin a domination of British markets that will continue for more than 25 years (see 1877).

George Bernard Shaw embraces vegetarianism. The Irish music, art, and drama critic, now 25, receives support from his parents in Dublin to maintain his marginal London existence. ("I did not throw myself into the struggle for life," he will later say. "I threw my mother into it. I was not a staff to my father's old age: I hung on to my father's coat tails"). "A man of my spiritual intensity does not eat corpses," Shaw will say to explain his vegetarianism, and he will claim to be "seldom less than ten times as well as an ordinary carcass eater" (see 1892).

Some 669,431 immigrants enter the United States, up from 91,918 in 1861, as a decade begins that will see 5.25 million immigrants arrive.

Some 500,000 Romanian Jews will emigrate to America in the next few decades and will be joined by other Eastern European Jews and some 1.5 million Russian Jews adding new diversity to the population.

The U.S. population reaches 53 million, Great Britain has 29.7 million, Ireland 5.1, Germany 45.2, France 37.6, Italy 28.4.

1882 Electricity illuminates parts of London beginning January 12 as power from the Edison Electric Light Company at 57 Holburn Viaduct turns on street lights between Holborn Circus and the Old Bailey and incandescent bulbs go on in at least 30 buildings.

Electricity illuminates parts of New York beginning September 4 as Thomas Edison throws a switch in the offices of financier J. P. Morgan to light the offices and to inaugurate commercial transmission of electric power from the Morgan-financed Edison Illuminating Company power plant in Pearl Street. The company will soon supply current to all of Manhattan and it will develop into the Consolidated Edison Company, prototype of all central-station U.S. power companies (see 1899; Thomson, 1883).

The Electric Light Act passed by Parliament empowers local British authorities to take over privately run power stations in their areas after 21 years. By making it virtually impossible for a private electric company to recoup its investment, the new law will discourage development of power stations (no private company will generate electricity for the next 6 years and although the new law will be amended in 1888 to permit private ownership for 42 years such major cities as Manchester, Leeds, Edinburgh, and Nottingham will still have no power stations in 1890).

A draper's shop at Newcastle upon Tyne, England, is lighted by Swan lamps and becomes the world's first shop to be lighted by incandescent bulbs.

The world's first electric fan is devised by the chief engineer of New York's Crocker and Curtis Electric

Motor Company. The two-bladed desk fan is the work of 22-year-old Schuyler Skaats Wheeler.

The world's first electric flatiron is patented by H. W. Seely.

The world's first electrically lighted Christmas tree is installed in December in the New York house of Thomas Edison's associate Edward H. Johnson.

An internal combustion engine powered by gasoline is invented by German engineer Gottlieb Daimler, 48, who has worked with Eugen Langen (*see* 1886; Otto, 1866).

The Standard Oil trust incorporated by John D. Rockefeller and his associates to circumvent state corporation laws brings 95 percent of the U.S. petroleum industry under the control of a nine-man directorate. Pennsylvania lawyer Samuel C. T. Dodd has shown Rockefeller how the idea of a trust employed in personal estate law can be applied to industry and the oil trust will soon be followed by other trusts. The richest company of any kind in the world, the Standard Oil trust controls 14,000 miles of underground pipeline and all the oil cars of the Pennsylvania Railroad (*see* 1877; 1883).

Ireland's Charles Stewart Parnell and his associates are released from Kilmainham Prison May 2 after agreeing to stop boycotting landowners, to cooperate with the Liberal Party, and to stop inciting Irishmen to intimidate tenant farmers from cooperating with landlords (*see* 1880; 1881). Four days after Parnell's release the new chief secretary for Ireland and his permanent under-secretary are murdered by Fenians in broad daylight in Dublin's Phoenix Park and while the murder of Lord Frederick Cavendish and Thomas Burke is repudiated by Parnell, it leads the British to suspend trial by jury and to give the police unbridled power to search and arrest on suspicion. Public buildings in England are dynamited in a campaign of terrorism that is also disavowed by Parnell.

Canada's District of Saskatchewan is created and the town of Regina is founded on the route of the Canadian Pacific Railway being constructed by Cornelius Van Horne (*see* 1881). Regina will be headquarters for the 9-year-old Northwest Mounted Police.

A Triple Alliance is signed May 20 by Germany, Austria, and Italy. Each promises to come to the other's aid should the ally be attacked by France within the next 5 years (*see* 1887).

Alexandria is bombarded July 11 by the British fleet under Sir Beauchamp Seymour. British troops are landed to protect the Suez Canal from nationalist forces, the Egyptians are defeated September 13 by Sir Garnet Wolseley at the Battle of Tel el-Kebir. Cairo is occupied by the British September 15, and dual control of Egypt by France and Britain is abolished November 9.

Ethiopia's northern town of Assab is taken over by Italian forces who will make it the basis of Italy's Eritrean colony in 1890.

Ethiopia's Johannes IV makes a pact with his vanquished rival Menelek of Shoa and designates Menelek as his successor.

The International Association of the Congo is created out of the 1878 Belgian Comité d'Etudes du Haut-Congo and several companies are organized to exploit the region.

France claims a protectorate over the entire northwestern portion of Madagascar.

An insurrection against the French in Indo-China is launched in Tonkin.

A 3-mile limit for territorial waters is agreed upon in a Hague Convention signed by the world powers.

The tuberculosis bacillus is discovered by Robert Koch who establishes that the disease is communicable (*see* 1877). Koch's findings along with those of many other bacteriologists will lead physicians to believe that certain diseases such as beriberi are caused by bacteria rather than by dietary deficiencies (*see* Takaki, 1884; diphtheria, 1883).

Psychoanalysis is pioneered by Viennese physician Josef Breuer, 40, who discovers the value of hypnosis in treating a girl suffering from severe hysteria. Breuer induces the patient to relive certain scenes that occurred while she was nursing her sick father and he succeeds thereby in relieving her permanently of her hysteria symptoms, a success he will communicate to colleague Sigmund Freud (*see* 1895).

The St. Gothard tunnel that opens May 20 is the first great railroad tunnel through the Alps (*see* Orient Express, 1883).

Union Switch and Signal Company is organized to manufacture railroad signals invented by George Westinghouse who has made a fortune from his Westinghouse Air Brake Company (*see* 1868; gas pipelines, 1883).

"The public be damned," says U.S. railroad magnate William H. Vanderbilt to a *Chicago Daily News* reporter who asked, "Don't you run it for the public benefit?" when told that the fast *Chicago Limited* extra-fare mail train was being eliminated. "The public be damned," says Vanderbilt October 8 to reporter Clarence Dresser. "I am working for my stockholders. If the public want the train, why don't they pay for it?"

Electric cable cars are installed in Chicago where they travel 20 blocks along State Street in 31 minutes, averaging less than 2 miles per hour (*see* 1894; San Francisco, 1873).

Matson Navigation Company is started by a 33-year-old Swedish sailing captain with a loan from California sugar magnate Claus Spreckels (*see* 1868). Matson buys shares in a ship he names the *Emma Claudine* after Spreckels's sister and he begins to build a near-monopoly in San-Francisco–Honolulu shipping as trade booms in Hawaiian sugar (*see* Dollar Steamship, 1901).

1882 (cont.) Britain's Married Women's Property Act is passed by Parliament following efforts by women's rights champion Richard Marsden Pankhurst, whose widow Emmeline will campaign for woman suffrage after his death in 1898 (*see* 1903).

A wave of strikes for higher wages in the United States is touched off by higher prices that have resulted from last year's poor crops.

Manganese steel is invented by English metallurgist Robert Abbott Hadfield, 24 (*see* tungsten steel, 1868; chromium steel, 1877; nickel steel, 1888).

Oscar Wilde arrives in New York in January and says, "I have nothing to declare but my genius." Irish-born essayist Oscar Fingal O'Flahertie Wills Wilde, 27, has made himself the apostle of an art for art's sake cult. Gilbert and Sullivan burlesqued his affectations last year in their opera *Patience* with its character Bunthorne. Wilde will tour North America for a year lecturing on such subjects as "The English Renaissance of Art."

The University of South Dakota is founded.

Western Electric Manufacturing Company of Boston wins a contract February 6 to produce telephones for the Bell Company (*see* 1872; 1876). Publisher Charles Scribner has invested in the company that the Bell Company will acquire.

Harrison Gray Otis acquires an interest in the *Los Angeles Times* at age 45. A Union Army enlistee who rose to the rank of lieutenant colonel, Otis moved to California in 1876 and ran the *Santa Barbara Post* until 1879. The *Times* has absorbed the *Los Angeles Weekly Mirror;* Otis will gain full control of the Times-Mirror Company by 1886, and he will make it a powerful voice of Republican conservatism in opposition to labor unions (*see* 1910).

"When a dog bites a man that is not news, but when a man bites a dog that is news," says *New York Sun* city editor John B. Bogart.

David McKay Company is founded by Scots-American publisher David McKay, 22, who came to America at age 13. His Philadelphia publishing house gains quick success with an edition of Walt Whitman's *Leaves of Grass* and follows it with Whitman's new prose work *Specimen Days.*

Fiction *The Prince and the Pauper* by Mark Twain.

Juvenile *Pinocchio, la storia di un burratino* (little wooden boy) by Italian author Carlo Collodi (Carlo Lorenzini), 52. The marionette made by the woodcarver Gepetto comes to life and has a series of adventures and misadventures including one in which his nose grows longer every time he tells a lie.

Poetry *Canto novo* by Italian poet Gabriele D'Annunzio, 19.

Painting *Bar at the Folies Bergère* by Edouard Manet; *Self-Portrait* by Paul Cézanne; *Mr. and Mrs. John W. Field* by U.S. painter John Singer Sargent, 26, who was born abroad of U.S. parents, visited the United States in 1876 and obtained U.S. citizenship, but returned to Europe in 1877. Dante Gabriel Rosetti dies at Birchington April 10 at age 53 after making a desperate effort to give up his addiction to the soporific drug chloral hydrate.

Theater *La Belle Russe* by San Francisco playwright David Belasco, 28, 5/8 at Wallack's Theater, New York; *Ghosts* (*Gengangere*) by Henrik Ibsen 5/20 at Chicago's Arrone Turner Hall (in Norwegian); *An Unequal Match* by the late English playwright Tom Taylor 11/6 at Wallack's Theater, New York, introduces U.S. audiences to the "Jersey Lilly" Lillie Langtry (Emily Charlotte Le Breton Langtry), 30, who made her London stage debut last year. Mrs. Langtry gained her soubriquet from the painting "The Jersey Lilly" by Sir John Everett Millais for whom she posed; *Fedora* by Victorien Sardou 12/11 at the Théâtre du Vaudeville, Paris, with Sarah Bernhardt. The melodrama provides the name for a fashionable new soft felt hat with a high roll on its side brim and a lengthwise crease in its low crown.

Jumbo the elephant appears at New York's Madison Square Garden beginning April 10 in performances of Barnum & Bailey's Circus. P. T. Barnum has imported the "largest elephant in or out of captivity" (whose name has introduced the word "jumbo" to the English language), the animal stands 11 feet high at the shoulders and weighs 6.5 tons. Barnum claims it stands 12 feet high at the shoulders, measures 26 feet in length if the trunk is included, and weighs 10.5 tons. Captured 20 years ago as a baby, Jumbo has been a prime attraction at London's 56-year-old Royal Zoological Gardens since 1865 when he was acquired from the Jardin des Plantes at Paris in exchange for a rhinoceros, the London zoo has sold him to Barnum for $10,000 because he has become difficult, his sale has raised a storm of protest in England, and there will be general mourning when Jumbo is killed by a freight train on the Grand Trunk Railway at St. Thomas, Ontario, in mid-September 1885.

Opera *The Snow Maiden* (*Snyegurochka*) 2/10 at St. Petersburg, with music by Nikolai Rimski-Korsakov; *Parsifal* 7/26 at the Festspielhaus in Bayreuth, Germany, with music by Richard Wagner; *The Devil's Wall* (*Centova stena*) 10/29 at Prague, with music by Bedrich Smetana; *Iolanthe* (or *The Peer and the Peri*) 11/25 at London's new Savoy Theatre, with Gilbert and Sullivan arias that include "When Britain Really Ruled the Waves" and "Faint Heart Never Won Fair Lady."

First performances Serenade in C major for String Orchestra by Petr Ilich Tchaikovsky 1/28 at Moscow; First Modern Suite for Piano by U.S. composer Edward Alexander MacDowell, 20, 7/11 at Zurich; *1812 Overture* by Petr Ilich Tchaikovsky 8/20 at Moscow with sound effects evocative of the Battle of Borodino; *My Country* (*Ma Vlast*) by Bedrich Smetana (now totally deaf) 11/5 at Prague (the symphonic cycle includes *The Moldau*) (*see* 1875); *Song of the Fates* (*Gesang der Parzen*) by Johannes Brahms 12/10 at Basel.

London's *Sporting Times* carries an advertisement August 30 with a funereal black border: "In Affectionate Remembrance of English Cricket Which Died at the Oval on 29th of August, 1882; Deeply lamented by a large circle of sorrowing friends and acquaintances. R.I.P. N.B. The body will be cremated and the ashes taken to Australia." An English team sent to Australia next year with instructions to "bring back the ashes" will be presented with a 5-inch earthenware urn filled with ashes and cricket's most hallowed souvenir will be presented to the Marylebone Cricket Club in 1928.

The Andrew Jergens Company is founded at Cincinnati. The firm will produce soaps, cosmetics, and lotions (*see* 1901).

Jesse James dies April 3 at age 34 of a gunshot wound in the back of the head. A fugitive since the Northfield, Minn., bank robbery attempt of 1876, James has been living quietly at St. Joseph, Mo., under the name Thomas Howard. The governor has offered a large reward for the capture of James dead or alive, James has befriended fellow outlaw Robert Ford, who has shot him to get the reward, and his murder inspires a ballad that will make future generations regard James as a Robin Hood figure.

The Hatfield-McCoy feud that has simmered for years in the southern Appalachians of West Virginia and eastern Kentucky boils over in the election day shooting of Kentucky storekeeper Ellison Hatfield, brother of William Anderson "Devil Anse" Hatfield, 43, who mortally wounded Harmon McCoy of the Union Army while fighting with Confederate forces in the Civil War. Hatfield's son Johnse has precipitated the quarrel by attempting to elope with Randall McCoy's daughter Rosanna, and when Ellison Hatfield dies of his wounds three of McCoy's sons, captured earlier by an armed posse under Anse Hatfield, are murdered in retaliation, beginning a bloodbath that will continue for years as local influence is used to obtain quick release of any arrested participants. Kentucky authorities will invade West Virginia in 1888 and will seize several Hatfields, ending open warfare between the clans. "Devil Anse" Hatfield will live until late in 1921.

Only 2 percent of New York homes have water connections and while tenements have some rudimentary plumbing facilities nearly every private house has a backyard privy.

Drought continues on western U.S. ranchlands.

Edinburgh's Prairie Cattle Company pays $350,000 to acquire the Quarter Circle T Ranch of Texas Panhandle rancher Thomas Bugbee who 6 years ago drove a small herd from Kansas to the Canadian River and established the ranch (*see* 1881; 1884).

The Farmer's Alliance claims 100,000 members in 8 state alliances and 200 local alliances. The Alliance is now headed by Milton George (*see* 1880; 1889).

The bacilli that produce swine fever (hog cholera), swine erysipelas, and glanders (another livestock disease) are discovered at Berlin's Friedrich Wilhelm Institute by German bacteriologist Friedrich August Johannes Löffler, 30 (*see* diphtheria, 1884).

Germany will assume leadership of European industry in the next two decades, but the Germans will attempt to maintain self-sufficiency in food production where the British have not. The Germans will plant another 2 million acres to food crops and will use high tariffs to protect German farmers from foreign competition even though such a policy means keeping domestic food prices high.

"The evidence regarding the adulteration of food indicates that they are largely of the nature of frauds upon the consumer . . . and injure both the health and morals of the people," reports a U.S. congressional committee. The practice of fraudulent substitution "has become universal," says the committee, and it issues a list of people who have died from eating foods and using drugs adulterated with poisonous substances (*see* 1889).

Van Camp Packing Company is incorporated and packs 6 million cans of pork and beans per year for shipment to Europe as well as to many U.S. markets (*see* 1861; 1894).

Nashville, Tenn., wholesale grocer Joel Cheek quits his firm to devote full time to developing a coffee blend (*see* Maxwell House Coffee, 1886).

Canadian Club Whisky is introduced by the 25-year-old Hiram Walker distillery at Walkerville, Ontario, which has been forced by Kentucky distillers to rename its 21-year-old Walker's Club brand.

Lüchow's restaurant is opened in New York's East 14th Street by German-American restaurauteur Au-

The Brooklyn Bridge, an engineering marvel that was soon "for sale" to unwary out-of-town visitors.

1882 (cont.) gust Lüchow. The 50-seat eating place will grow until it seats more than 1,000 and employs 22 chefs.

U.S. immigration from Germany reaches its peak.

The first U.S. act restricting general immigration is passed by Congress (*see* 1875). The new law excludes convicts, paupers, and defectives and it imposes a head tax on immigrants.

The 1880 Chinese Exclusion Act takes effect and bars entry of Chinese laborers for a period of 10 years (*see* 1892). The loss of Chinese labor spurs development of machinery to clean and bone fish in California's salmon canneries (*see* 1866; 1895; Smith, 1903).

Crop failures in southern Japan bring widespread starvation. Recruiting agents sent by planters persuade peasants to emigrate to Hawaii's sugar fields; 100,000 Japanese workers and their families will move in the next 30 years (*see* 1897; 1909).

1883 The Brooklyn Bridge (Great East River Bridge) that opens May 24 links America's two largest cities and 12 people are trampled to death in the excitement. Designed by the late John Augustus Roebling, who died of a tetanus infection in 1869 at age 63 after having his leg crushed by a ferryboat while working on the great bridge, the 486-meter (1,595.5-foot) span has a steel web truss to keep it from swaying in the wind as designed by J. A. Roebling, and it has been completed by Roebling's 45-year-old son Washington Augustus, who has been crippled, half-paralyzed, and made partially blind by caisson disease (the "bends") but who observes the dedication ceremony from his house on Columbia Heights.

The Northern Pacific Railroad is completed September 8 with a "last spike" ceremony at Gold Creek in Montana Territory after 13 years of work (*see* Villard, 1881; financial struggles, 1893; 1901).

U.S. railroads adopt standard time with four separate time zones—Eastern, Central, Rocky Mountain, and Pacific. Pacific Standard Time is 3 hours behind Eastern Standard Time.

Australians complete a rail line to link Sydney in New South Wales with Melbourne in Victoria.

Norway completes the Oslo-Bergen railway across the Hardanger mountain range with nearly 60 miles of its track above the timber line. The new rail link ends the isolation of Bergen and brings it to within 8 hours of Norway's other major city (and capital).

The Calais-Nice-Rome Express from Paris goes into service. The trip to Nice takes 18 hours but will take only 14 by the end of the century.

The *Orient Express* that leaves for Constantinople October 4 from the Gare de l'Est, Paris, is Europe's first transcontinental train. The *Express d'Orient* and its route have been designed by the Compagnie Internationale des Wagon-Lits et des Grands Express Européens headed by Georges Nagelmakers and includes two sleeping cars, an elaborate dining car, a baggage wagon containing a lavish kitchen, and a mail car (*see* 1876; *Train Bleu,* 1879). The dining car and both sleeping cars are fitted with newly invented four-wheel bogies and superior springing that give passengers a steady ride even round the sharpest bends at speeds of close to 50 miles per hour, but since no direct rail link to Constantinople has been completed, the new train goes only to the Bulgarian border south of Bucharest where passengers are ferried across the Danube, taken by a less comfortable train to Varna on the Black Sea, and there put on a ship to Constantinople (*see* 1889).

Ferdinand de Lesseps of 1869 Suez fame begins work on a Panama Canal for the Compagnie Universelle du Canal Interoceanique (*see* 1889).

The Ediswan Company is started by England's Joseph Swan and Thomas Edison who has beaten Swan to obtain English patent rights to the incandescent bulb (*see* 1878; 1879). Swan has developed a new lamp filament of nitrocellulose that has advantages over the carbon filament (*see* tungsten, 1913).

The German Edison Company is established by German electrotechnician Emil Rathenau, 45, and electrical engineer Oskar Miller, 28. The new firm is the forerunner of Allgemeine Elektrizitäts-Gesellschaft (A. E. G.) which Rathenau will head.

The Thomson-Houston Electric Company is started by Philadelphia inventor Elihu Thomson, 30, and electrical engineer Edwin James Houston, 36. Thomson has invented a transformer that steps down high-voltage alternating current (*see* 1888; General Electric, 1892).

George Westinghouse pioneers control systems for long-distance natural gas pipelines and for town gas distribution networks (*see* 1882; 1885).

John D. Rockefeller's Standard Oil Trust monopoly absorbs the Tidewater Pipe Company. The trust takes the output of 20,000 wells and employs 100,000 people (*see* 1882; 1884).

The Pendleton Civil Service Reform Act passed by Congress January 16 provides for competitive examinations for positions in the federal government and establishes a Civil Service Commission to end the abuses that culminated in the assassination of President Garfield 2 years ago. The act sharply reduces the number of federal appointees who will get their jobs from elected officials under the "spoils system," it establishes a merit system for appointment and promotion based on competitive examinations, and the number of "classified" civil service workers employed on the basis of merit will be expanded by Congress, with such workers protected from loss of job through change in political administration.

French control of Tunisia is assured by the convention of Marsa signed June 8 with the bey of Tunis.

British control of Egypt is established by the new consul general Sir Evelyn Baring, 42, who receives his appointment with plenipotentiary diplomatic rank to advise the khedive but who will effectively rule the country until his retirement in 1907.

Egyptian control of the Sudan is challenged by the Mahdi Mohammed Ahmed ibn-Seyyid Abdullah of Dongola, a 40-year-old agitator and fanatic whose forces ambush the British general William Hicks, 53, and kill him November 4. The Egyptians are wiped out November 5 at the Battle of El Obeid, the self-styled prophet gains control over Kordofan, the governors of Darfur and Bahr-el-Ghazal are obliged to surrender, and the Mahdi's lieutenants attack the Red Sea ports (see 1884).

The first fully automatic machine gun is invented by American-born English engineer Hiram Stevens Maxim, 43, whose Maxim/Vickers gun will be adopted in 1889 by the British army and thereafter by every other major army. Maxim's gun is an advance over the 1861 Gatling gun in that the recoil energy of each bullet is employed to eject the spent cartridge, insert the new round, and fire it. The Maxim Gun Co. will be absorbed into Vickers' Sons and Maxim in 1896 (see 1828; Boer War, 1899; Armstrong-Vickers, 1927).

An artificial silk is developed from nitrocellulose by French chemist Hilaire Bernigaud, 44, comte de Chardonnet (see viscose rayon, 1892).

Copper ore in the Sudbury Basin of northern Ontario is discovered by builders of the Canadian Pacific Railway (see 1882; 1885).

Pickands, Mather & Co. is founded by Cleveland iron ore, coal, and pig iron dealer Samuel Mather, 32, of the Cleveland Iron Mining Company headed by his father Samuel Livingstone Mather (see 1855).

The Pittsburgh Plate Glass Company that will become the largest U.S. glassmaker and second largest paintmaker is created by a reincorporation of the New York City Plate Glass Company. Ohio River steamboat fleet operator John Baptiste Ford has persuaded former Pennsylvania Railroad president John Pitcairn that a site 20 miles north of Pittsburgh provides an ideal site for a glassworks, since soda ash is available from the Pennsylvania hills for melting purposes, the river bottom can provide grinding sand, and local mines can provide cheap coal to power grinders and polishers (see 1896; Duplate, 1927).

The League of Struggle for the Emancipation of Labor is founded in Switzerland by émigré Russian political philosopher Georgi Valentinovich Plekhanov, 26, whose organization will make the first Marxist analysis of Russian society, economics, and politics and will issue the first directives toward the creation of a Russian labor movement (see 1867; Lenin, 1895).

A German sickness insurance law enacted in May is the first of several moves by Prince Otto von Bismarck to lead the German people away from state socialism. Workers are to bear two-thirds of the cost of the insurance program, employers one third (see accident insurance law, 1884).

German pathologist Edwin Klebs, 49, describes the diphtheria bacillus (see Löffler, 1884).

Robert Koch develops a preventive inoculation against anthrax (see 1882).

Robert Koch identifies the comma bacillus that causes Asiatic cholera.

A worldwide cholera pandemic begins that will kill millions in the next 11 years.

The University of North Dakota is founded at Grand Forks.

Telegraph service begins between the United States and Brazil.

Commercial Cable Company is founded by Comstock Lode millionaire John William Mackay, now 52, and New York Herald publisher James Gordon Bennett who challenge Jay Gould's monopoly in transatlantic cable communication. Mackay and Bennett will lay two submarine cables to Europe next year and will break the Gould monopoly (see 1869; 1886).

Thomas Edison (above) pioneers the radio tube with a method for passing electricity from a filament to a plate of metal inside an incandescent light globe, and he patents the "Edison effect" (see Arnold, 1912).

Joseph Pulitzer of the St. Louis Post-Dispatch acquires the New York World from Jay Gould (above; see 1878). The paper has a circulation of 15,000 and is losing $40,000 per year, but Pulitzer will make it profitable (see 1893; Hearst, 1896; Howard, 1931).

Grit begins publication at Williamsport, Pa. The weekly for rural readers will grow in the next 94 years to have a circulation of more than 5 million.

Science magazine is founded by telephone pioneer Alexander Graham Bell and his father-in-law G. G. Hubbard. The magazine will become the organ of the 35-year-old American Association for the Advancement of Science (AAAS) (see National Geographic Society, 1888).

The Ladies' Home Journal begins publication at Philadelphia under the name Ladies' Journal. Maine-born publisher Cyrus H. K. (Herman Kotzschmar) Curtis, 32, dropped out of high school after 1 year, started a 2-cent weekly at age 13 called Young America, founded the People's Ledger at Boston in 1872, moved to Philadelphia in 1876, sold the Ledger, started the Tribune and Farmer in 1883 with a woman's page edited by his wife, who is editor of the new monthly periodical, and Curtis offers cash prizes to readers who submit the most names of possible subscribers (see patent medicine, 1892; Post, 1897).

Life magazine begins publication at New York. Edward Sandford Martin, 27, helped start the Harvard Lampoon in 1876 and his new humor magazine will continue as such for more than half a century (see Gibson Girl, 1890; Luce, 1936).

More than 2,300 Remington typewriters were sold last year. By 1885 sales will reach 5,000 per year (see 1878; 1890; Mark Twain, below).

Nonfiction Life on the Mississippi by Mark Twain is a memoir of riverboat piloting and a critique pub-

1883 (cont.) lished from the world's first typewritten book manuscript; "The Forgotten Man" by Yale political and social science professor William Graham Sumner, 43, extols the "clean, quiet, virtuous, domestic citizen, who pays his debts and his taxes and is never heard of out of his little circle.... The Forgotten Man ... delving away in patient industry, supporting his family, paying his taxes, casting his vote, supporting the church and the school. ... He is the only one for whom there is no provision in the great scramble and the big divide. Such is the Forgotten Man: He works, he votes, generally he prays—but his chief business in life is to pay."

Philosophy *Thus Spake Zarathustra* (*Also Sprach Zarathustra*) by German philosopher Friedrich Wilhelm Nietzsche, 39, is published in the first of its four parts and introduces the idea of the Superman (Ubermensch). Nietzsche's theories will be influential on German thinking 30 years hence and, especially, a half century hence.

Fiction *Treasure Island* by Robert Louis Stevenson, an adventure novel with Long John Silver's pirate song "Fifteen men on a dead man's chest—/Yo-ho-ho, and a bottle of rum! ..." Stevenson has returned to Scotland after having traveled across the Atlantic in steerage and across America in an emigrant train to pursue Fanny Van de Grift Osbourne, a married woman 11 years his senior and mother of three. He met her 7 years ago at Fontainebleau, France, married her at San Francisco in 1880, and thereafter took her to a western mining town.

Poetry *The Flemish* (*Les Flamandes*) by Flemish poet Emile Verhaeren, 28; *Poems of Passion* by Wisconsin-born poet Ella Wheeler Wilcox, 33, whose poem "Solitude" begins, "Laugh, and the world laughs with you;/ Weep, and you weep alone"; *The Old Swimmin' Hole and 'Leven More Poems* by Indiana poet James Whitcomb Riley, 34, of the *Indianapolis Journal* who includes his poem "When the Frost is on the Punkin!"

Painting *The Swimming Hole* by Thomas Eakins. Gustave Doré dies at Paris January 23 at age 51; Edouard Manet dies at Paris April 30 at age 51.

Theater *An Enemy of the People* (*En Folkefiende*) by Henrik Ibsen 1/13 at Oslo's Christiania Theater; *The Tragedy of Man* (*Az ember tragediaja*) by the late Hungarian playwright Imre Madách 9/21 at Budapest's Magyar Nemzeti Szinhaz; *Lucky Per's Journey* (*Lycko-Pers reja*) by August Strindberg 12/22.

Buffalo Bill's Wild West Show opens at Omaha, Neb., with riding, target shooting, and showmanship in an open-air spectacle that will be America's favorite entertainment of its kind for the next 20 years. Promoter William Frederick Cody, 37, is a former buffalo hunter and cavalry scout who received his nickname "Buffalo Bill" in 1869 from E. Z. C. "Ned Buntline" Judson (*see* 1844). Cody is famous for having killed and scalped the Cheyenne leader Yellow

Hand in a July 1876 duel, he will be joined in 1885 by markswoman Annie Oakley (Phoebe Mozee), "The Peerless Lady Wing-Shot," who is now 23, and for 1 year the show will include Sioux chieftain Sitting Bull (*see* Wounded Knee, 1890).

Keith & Batchelder's Dime Museum opens at 585 Washington Street, Boston, where former circus promoters Benjamin Franklin Keith, 37, and George H. Batchelder have assembled a group of sideshow freaks to support themselves during the months the circus is not on tour. Keith covers the front of the three-story building with red and blue canvas twelve-sheets advertising Siamese twins, tattooed ladies, wild men of Borneo, sword swallowers, snake charmers, Circassian beauties, and the cow that allegedly kicked over the lantern to start the Chicago fire in 1871. Keith & Batchelder employ Edward F. Albee, 26, to manage a second-floor vaudeville theater that opens at 10 in the morning with acts that include the Reed family troupe and New York song and dance comedians Joe Weber and Lew Fields (Shanfield), both 16, who go on eight times a day for $40 per week (*see* 1885).

Opera *Lakme* 4/14 at the Opéra-Comique, Paris, with music by Leo Delibes. The Bell Song "De la fille du paria" in Act II receives special applause.

New York's Metropolitan Opera House opens October 22 with a performance of the 1859 Gounod opera *Faust* sung in Italian with Christine Nilsson, 40, of Sweden as Marguerite. The 3,700-seat Met replaces the smaller Academy of Music that opened in Irving Place in 1854 and whose Old Guard have prevented the city's new millionaires from obtaining desirable boxes (*see* 1966).

First performances *The Accursed Huntsman* (*Le Chasseur Maudit*) (Symphonic Poem) by César Franck 3/31 at Paris; "Kol Nidre" by German composer Max Bruch, 45 (who has arranged a traditional Hebrew melody for cello and orchestra) 10/20; *Espana* orchestral rhapsody by French composer Emmanuel Chabrier, 42, 11/4 at Paris; *Husitska* (dramatic orchestral work) by Anton Dvorak 11/18 at Prague's Bohemian Theater; Symphony No. 3 in F major by Johannes Brahms 12/2 at Vienna.

Broadway musicals *Cordelia's Aspirations* 11/5 at the Theatre-Comique, with Ned Harrigan and Tony Hart, songs by Harrigan and Hart that include "My Dad's Dinner Pail."

Hymns "When the Mists Have Rolled Away" by Ira David Sankey, verses by Annie Herbert; "Till We Meet Again" ("God Be With You") by William Gould Tomer, verses by Jeremiah Eames Rankin.

Gold Flake cigarettes are introduced at London.

Fire guts London's Harrods store December 6, but proprietor C. D. Harrod orders new stock and enjoys record Christmas sales (*see* 1861). Harrod employs 100 clerks, bookkeepers, packers, etc. and fines latecomers a penny-halfpenny for every 15 minutes they are late (*see* 1884).

Washington's Pension building opens with a grand court enclosed by four levels of galleries and with eight massive 75-foot Corinthian columns to support its roof. Designed by General Montgomery C. Meigs to provide offices for the disbursement of pensions to war veterans and widows, the building has a court that will be the scene of at least seven presidential inaugural balls beginning in 1885.

The Stoughton house at Cambridge, Mass., is completed by Henry Hobson Richardson.

Krakatoa in the Sunda Strait between Java and Sumatra erupts August 27 in the greatest volcanic explosion since the eruption of Santorini in 1470 B.C. (*see* Tamboro, 1815). Although Santorini's explosion was roughly five times greater, Krakatoa's is heard nearly 3,000 miles away some 4 hours later, the dust that Krakatoa throws 34 miles into the air falls 10 days later at points more than 3,000 miles away, and the explosion creates a wave that wipes out 163 Indonesian villages and takes more than 36,000 lives.

White and Cree hunters in Dakota Territory discover a herd of 10,000 buffalo on the Cannon Ball River and exterminate the animals (*see* 1875; 1893).

Drought strikes the northern plains states. Railroad builder James J. Hill who is pushing his Great Northern tracks across the plains urges diversified farming. He buys 600 purebred bulls, distributes them among the farmers in the region, and offers prizes for the best cattle produced.

Purdue University chemistry professor Harvey Washington Wiley, 39, gains appointment as chief of the Division of Chemistry in the U.S. Department of Agriculture (*see* "Poison Squad," 1902).

The first absolutely pure brewers' yeast culture is introduced at Copenhagen's Carlsberg Brewery, whose owner Carl Jacobsen has backed Danish biochemist Emil Christian Hansen, 41, in his experiments to free yeast from bacteria. Yeast propagated from a single selected cell will eliminate brewing failures, and that fact is recognized by Schlitz Brewery head William J. Uihlein, who obtains a pure yeast culture from Copenhagen and brings it to Milwaukee (*see* 1874).

The first malted milk is produced at Racine, Wis., by English-American inventor William Horlick, 37, who will coin the name "malted milk" in 1886. Horlick has combined dried whole milk with extract of wheat and malted barley in powder and tablet form, and his "diastoid" is the first whole dried milk that will keep (*see* evaporated milk, 1885).

The A. Goodman bakery established at Philadelphia in 1865 moves to Manhattan where Goodman and his sons will manufacture matzohs, noodles, spaghetti, and dehydrated soups until 1946, when the firm will move to larger premises in Long Island City.

West Coast sugar refining and marketing is monopolized by San Francisco's Claus Spreckels who has obtained a large concession of land in the Sandwich (Hawaiian) Islands to keep his big refinery supplied with cane. Spreckels also uses some sugarbeets (*see* 1868; 1880; McKinley Act, 1891).

The first successful pea-podder machine is installed at Owasco, N.Y., where it replaces 600 cannery workers (*see* pea viner, 1889).

Oscar Mayer wieners have their beginnings in a Chicago retail shop opened to sell fresh and cured meats in Sedgewick Street on the North Side by German-American butcher Oscar F. Mayer, 23, who has been in America since 1873 and in Chicago since 1876. Mayer's partner in the enterprise is his brother Gottfried who has apprenticed in the art of sausage making and ham curing in Bavaria (*see* 1929).

B. H. Kroger Company has its beginnings in a Cincinnati grocery store opened by local grocery salesman Bernard H. Kroger, 23, whose 17-foot front store is called the Great Western Tea Company. Kroger has put up $372 in capital, a partner has put up $350, and Kroger buys out the partner for $1,550 by year's end. He will have four stores by mid-1885, and the firm will grow to have more than 1,250 stores in 20 states.

Some 40,000 tons of Jurgens Dutch margarine are shipped to Britain, which imports most of her margarine and butter (*see* 1876; Unilever, 1929).

Swiss hotel manager César Ritz, 33, is engaged to operate the Grand Hotel at Monte Carlo and hires as chef Auguste Escoffier, 37, who began his career at age 13 as an apprentice at his uncle's restaurant in Nice and moved at age 19 to the popular Paris restaurant Le Petit Moulin Rouge (*see* Pêche Melba, 1894).

The most lavish party yet held in America is staged March 26 at the $2 million Gothic mansion of railroad magnate William Kissam Vanderbilt, 34, on the northwest corner of New York's Fifth Avenue at 53rd Street. Vanderbilt is chairman of the Lake Shore & Michigan Southern, and it is estimated by the *New York World* (above) that his wife has spent $155,730 for costumes, $11,000 for flowers, $4,000 for hired carriages, $4,000 for hairdressers, and $65,270 for catering, champagne, music, and the like to make the $250,000 fancy-dress ball a success.

The Northern Pacific Railroad (above) sends agents to the British Isles to encourage immigration to the U.S. Northwest (*see* Santa Fe, 1874).

James J. Hill (above) sends agents to Scandinavia to encourage immigration to the territory that will be served by his Great Northern Railroad.

The Southern Immigration Association is founded to encourage European immigration to the U.S. South.

The United States has her peak year of immigration from Denmark, Norway, Sweden, Switzerland, the Netherlands, and China (*see* Exclusion Act, 1882).

U.S. contraceptive production is pioneered by German-American entrepreneur Julius Schmid, 18, a

1883 (cont.) cripple who came to New York 2 years ago from Schorndorf. He has been making "goldbeater" capping skins for bottles of perfume and other volatile liquids, using the tissue of lamb ceca which he now uses for condoms (*see* 1723; Youngs, 1920).

1884 The Linotype typesetting machine patented by German-American mechanic Ottmar Mergenthaler, 30, will revolutionize newspaper composing rooms. The Linotype has a keyboard much like that of a typewriter (*see* Sholes, 1868). Depressing a key on the keyboard releases a matrix from a magazine, and this small rod with the die of a character on its vertical edge falls into a line-composing box where little wedges automatically adjust the spaces between the words. When a line of matrices has been set, it is carried off to be cast in metal slugs made to the width of a newspaper column, the metal slugs are assembled in a form, compositors add hand-set headlines and line illustrations, and the form is ready for the press or for casting into a stereotype plate (*see* 1725; halftones, 1886; *New York Tribune,* 1886).

Le Matin begins publication at Paris.

Svenska Dagbladet begins publication at Stockholm.

The former Sudanese governor Charles "Chinese" Gordon is given executive powers by the Egyptian khedive Mohammed Tewfik and moves out to rescue Egyptian garrisons in the Sudan from the Mahdi (*see* 1883). Now 51, Gordon is refused in his requests to London for Zobeir and Turkish troops. He nevertheless manages to rescue some 2,500 women, children, and wounded men from Khartoum, but he is hemmed in at Khartoum by the Mahdi beginning March 12 (*see* 1885).

A German protectorate over the coast of Togoland is proclaimed July 5 by the German consul at Tunis, and a German protectorate over the Cameroons Coast is proclaimed by the consul a week later.

The War of the Pacific that began in 1879 between Chile and Peru ends April 4 with the Treaty of Valparaiso that deprives Bolivia of access to the sea. Victorious Chile gained the Peruvian province of Tarapaca last year in the Treaty of Ancona, and she now gains Bolivian territories that are rich in nitrates (*see* Haber process, 1908; Grace, 1890).

The political slogan "Rum, Romanism, and Rebellion" defeats the Republican "plumed knight" presidential candidate James G. Blaine, 54, and helps elect New York governor Grover Cleveland, 47, to the presidency in the first Democratic party national victory since James Buchanan won election in 1856. Allegations that Cleveland fathered an illegitimate child in his youth have produced the chant, "Ma, Ma, where's my Pa?" (Cleveland acknowledged the child and has supported it while expressing doubts in private that he was the father), and Democrats reply, "Gone to the White House, ha, ha, ha." They have won the crucial New York Catholic vote as a result of

remarks made October 9 at the Fifth Avenue Hotel by New York clergyman Samuel D. Burchard ("We are Republicans, and don't propose to have our party identify ourselves with the party whose antecedents have been Rum, Romanism, and Rebellion"), New York voters have taken exception to the remarks, and they give Cleveland a narrow 1,149-vote edge that enables the governor to win with a plurality of 20,000 votes out of a 10 million vote total and with 219 electoral votes to 189 for Blaine.

A Bureau of Labor in the Department of the Interior is established by Congress as severe coal strikes occur in Pennsylvania and Ohio (*see* 1888).

A German accident insurance law passed in June extends to practically all German wage-earner groups and is paid for entirely by employers. The measure continues efforts begun by Prince von Bismarck in last year's sickness insurance law to resist advocates of state socialism (*see* 1891).

Russia ends her poll tax, a relic of serfdom, but the beginning of industrialization in Russia is creating an industrial proletariat whose living and working conditions are no better than were those of rural serfs (*see* 1903; Plekhanov, 1883).

A Berlin conference on African affairs begins November 15 with delegates from 14 nations, including the United States, who agree to work for the suppression of slavery and the slave trade (*see* 1873; 1892).

London's Toynbee Hall—the world's first settlement house—is founded to attract well-to-do young people to "settle" in the city's slums and to serve the poor (*see* New York's University Settlement, 1886).

The diphtheria bacillus is isolated and cultured at Berlin by F. A. J. Löffler (*see* 1882; Klebs, 1883; Roux and Yersin, 1889).

The prevention of blindness from gonorrheal infection in newborn infants by using a few drops of silver nitrate solution in the eyes is discovered by Leipzig gynecologist Karl Sigismund Franz Crede, 65 (*see* Howe Act, 1890).

Open-air treatment of tuberculosis in America is pioneered by New York physician Edward Livingston Trudeau, 36, who developed consumption himself at age 25 and repaired to the Adirondack Mountains to regain his health. The Adirondack Cottage Sanatorium that Trudeau opens at Saranac, N.Y., will later be called the Trudeau Sanatorium.

The anesthetic properties of cocaine in medical practice are discovered by New York surgeon William Stewart Halsted, 31, who injects the drug to pioneer the practice of local anesthesia. A stickler for hygiene who sends his shirts to Paris to be laundered, Halsted becomes addicted to the drug derived from leaves of the South American Andes shrub *Erythroxylon coca* (or *E. truxillense*) in the course of his experiments, and although he will recover in 2 years, he will require morphine in order to function (*see* 1803; 1859; Johns Hopkins, 1893).

Lehn & Fink of Brooklyn, N.Y., has introduced cocaine (above). The firm was founded 10 years ago by entrepreneur Louis Lehn and German-American drug wholesaler Frederick William Fink, now 38, who has supplied Thomas Edison with materials for his experiments.

New York ophthalmologist Carl Killer, 27, introduces cocaine as a local anesthetic for eye surgery.

New York's Memorial Hospital has its beginnings in the New York Cancer Hospital opened at Central Park West and 106th Street by local gynecologist J. Marion Sims with support from John Jacob Astor, 62, who administers the estate of his late grandfather and namesake. The first U.S. hospital to specialize in cancer in an age when the disease is considered incurable, it will be renamed the General Memorial Hospital for the Treatment of Cancer and Allied Diseases in 1899 and will innovate use of circular wards (to avoid corners that are thought to accumulate dirt and stagnant air).

English surgeon Rickman John Godlee, 35, performs the first operation for the removal of a brain tumor November 25. Godlee is a nephew of Lord Lister.

The compound steam turbine invented by English engineer Charles Algernon Parsons, 26, exerts steam power first upon a large vane wheel and then—through slots in the casing—on another vane wheel and so on until the power of the steam is spent. The turbine develops 10 horsepower at 18,000 rpm, but Parsons will add a condenser in 1891, he will adapt the turbine to maritime use in 1897, he will be building 1,000-kilowatt turbines by 1900, and his geared turbine will appear in 1910 (see 1897).

More than 80 percent of the petroleum from U.S. oil wells is marketed by John D. Rockefeller's Standard Oil Trust (see 1882; 1892; Sherman Act, 1890).

The Central Pacific Railroad is merged into the Southern Pacific by Charles Crocker and Collis P. Huntington, who amalgamate other California railroads to create a giant competitor to the Union Pacific (see 1881; Santa Fe, 1887).

Seattle gets its first rail link to the East. Still a small lumber town, it begins to grow (see 1851).

Electric streetcars employing overhead wires appear in Germany (see Daft's trolley, 1885).

General Charles "Chinese" Cordon (above) has been conveyed to Khartoum by travel agent Thomas Cook, now 76 (see 1866). John Mason Cook, 50, has been his father's partner since 1864 and has extended Thomas Cook & Son service to America.

The London, Paris & American Bank, Ltd., of Great Britain is founded by Lazard Frères, the New York, London, Paris, and San Francisco firm of silk importers and exchange dealers (see 1847; 1909).

History of New York City by Benson J. Lossing says, "New York, unfortunately, is becoming in large degree a city of only two conspicuous classes, the rich and the poor. The great middle classes, which constitute the bone and sinew of the social structure, have been squeezed out, as it were, by the continually increasing pressure of the burden of the cost of living in the city."

National Cash Register Company is founded at Dayton, Ohio, by local coal merchant John Henry Patterson, 40, who has bought a controlling interest in the National Manufacturing Company, which has bought the Ritter cash register of 1879 and has improved it by adding a cash drawer and a bell that rings every time the drawer is opened. Patterson is ridiculed for investing $6,500 in a company that makes anything so useless, he offers the seller $2,000 to let him out of the deal, he is refused, so he changes the firm name and goes to work improving the cash register. Patterson will innovate the idea of exclusive sales territories, he will pay large commissions to salesmen, he will organize a force of well-trained service men to maintain the machines he sells, and he will make NCR prosper (see 1912; Watson, 1903).

The Watch Tower Bible and Tract Society is founded by Charles Taze Russell to publish his books, pamphlets, and periodicals (see 1878). Russell warned true Christians against political and social allegiances in his book *Food for Thinking* in 1881, and he preaches that the world is on the brink of annihilation in a monstrous battle of Armageddon after which 144,000 of all who have ever lived in the history of mankind will reappear in heaven (see Jehovah's Witnesses, 1931).

Temple University is founded at Philadelphia by Baptist clergyman Russell Herman Conwell, 41, a former lawyer who has made a fortune with his inspirational lecture "Acres of Diamonds," encouraging his listeners to take advantage of the opportunities in their "own backyards." Conwell will give the lecture more than 6,000 times before his death in 1925, and he will give all the proceeds to his university.

The Fabian Society is founded in January by young London intellectuals who aim to reconstruct society "in accordance with the highest moral responsibilities." Recognizing that deciding what courses to pursue will require "long taking of counsel," they take the name Fabian from the 3rd century B.C. Roman statesman Quintus Fabius Maximus, called "Cunctator" (delayer) because of his cautious delaying tactics against Hannibal. George Bernard Shaw joins in May, London economist Sidney James Webb, 25, and writer Beatrice Potter, 26, will soon join, Webb will marry Potter, and the Webbs will set up a socialist salon that will attract celebrated thinkers and writers.

The Waterman pen invented by New York insurance man Lewis Edson Waterman, 47, is the first practical fountain pen with a capillary feed. Waterman has 200 of the pens produced by hand, but the end of the pen must be removed and ink squirted in with an eye dropper (the lever-fill pen will not be introduced until 1904) (see Parker, 1888).

"Sportsmen" shooting from moving trains helped wipe out the bison that provided sustenance for the Plains Indians.

John C. Winston Co. publishers is founded by Philadelphia Quaker John Clark Winston, 27, who had planned to manufacture photograph albums but who publishes instead the 512-page leather-bound *Crown Book of the Beautiful, the Wonderful, and the Wise*, which he sells by subscription. The company will be capitalized at $200,000 in 1900, it will be the largest U.S. publisher of bibles within 20 years, and it will be a major textbook publisher (*see* Holt, Rinehart and Winston, 1960).

Fiction *The Adventures of Huckleberry Finn* by Mark Twain; "The Lady or the Tiger" by U.S. novelist-short story writer Frank (Francis Richard) Stockton, 50; *Against Nature* (*A Rebours*) by Joris Karl Huysmans; *The Death of Ivan Ilyich* (*Smeat' Ivana Il'icha*) by Leo Tolstoy.

Painting *Bathers at Asnieres* (*Une Baignade, Asnières*) by Georges Seurat who joins with Paul Gauguin, Paul Cézanne, and Dutch painter Vincent van Gogh, 31, in supporting the exhibiting society Les Vingt founded at Brussels by Belgian painter James Sydney Ensor, 24; *King Cophetua and the Begger Maid* by Edward Coley Burne-Jones.

A photographic film roll system invented by British photography pioneer W. H. Walker uses paper coated with emulsion.

George Eastman invents a machine to coat photographic paper continuously in long rolls and will obtain a patent for the machine in 1895 (*see* 1880). Flexible roll film will permit development of cameras more convenient to use than large plate cameras (*see* Houston, 1881; Kodak, 1888).

The Playbill has its beginnings in the *New York Dramatic Chronicle*, a one-page flyer started by local printer Frank V. Strauss. It will evolve into a slick magazine with editions in every major U.S. city.

Opera *Princess Ida* (or *Castle Adamant*) 1/5 at London's Savoy Theatre, with book, lyrics, and music by Gilbert and Sullivan; *Manon* 1/19 at the Opéra-Comique in Paris, with music by French composer Jules Massenet, 42, libretto based on the Abbé Provost story "Les Aventures du Chevalier des Grieux et de Manon Lescaut" of 1731 (*see* Puccini, 1893); *Mazeppa* in February at Moscow's Bolshoi Theater, with music by Petr Ilich Tchaikovsky, libretto from the poem by Lord Byron.

First performances Piano Suite No. 2 by Edward MacDowell 3/8 at New York; Symphony No. 7 in E major by Anton Bruckner 12/30 at Leipzig.

Broadway musical *Adonis* 9/24 at the Bijoux Theater, with Henry E. Dixey, music by Edward E. Rice, book and lyrics by William F. Gill and Henry Dixey, 603 perfs.—the first Broadway musical to have a run of more than 500 performances.

Popular songs "Love's Old Sweet Song" by Irish-born London composer James Lyman Molloy, 47, lyrics by C. Clifton Bingham, 25, beginning, "Just a song at twilight . . ."; "The Fountain in the Park" by London composer Ed Haley whose song will be given lyrics beginning, "While strolling through the park one day . . ."; "Otchi Tchorniya" with music by an unknown Russian composer.

Overhand pitching gains acceptance for the first time in major league baseball, but a batter will be allowed until 1887 to call for a high pitch or a low pitch, and the number of balls required for a walk will not be established at four until 1889.

The "Louisville Slugger" bat is introduced by the Kentucky firm Hillerich and Bradsby. German-American woodturner J. Frederick Hillerich, 50, has made bowling balls and pins and has been asked by Louisville Eclipse player Peter "the Gladiator" Browning, 26, to make an ashwood bat that will replace one Browning has broken. Browning has made his own bats of seasoned timber aged in his attic, but although he has averaged three hits per game with his homemade bats, he does even better with Hillerich's bat.

The first baseball playoff series is won by the National League's Providence, R.I., team, which defeats the New York Metropolitans of the American Association 3 games to 0 (*see* National League, 1876; American League, 1901; World Series, 1902).

The National Horse Show opens in October at New York's Madison Square Garden in East 27th Street with 352 animals in 105 classes including hunters, jumpers, harness horses, ponies, Arabians, police and fire horses, mules, and donkeys in an event that will be held annually the first week of November.

The first roller coaster opens at Coney Island, N.Y. It has been put up by former Elkhart, Ind., Sunday school teacher Lemarcus A. Thompson, who will soon be making improved models for amusement parks throughout America and Japan (*see* Steeplechase Park, 1897).

598

Gold Dust soap is introduced by Chicago's N. K. Fairbank & Co., with two black boys as the "Gold Dust Twins" trademark that will soon be used for Gold Dust washing powder and Gold Dust scouring cleanser as well.

Chicago's Montgomery Ward Company issues a 240-page catalog offering nearly 10,000 items from cutlery, harnesses, and parasols to stereoscopes, trunks, and writing paper. Still describing itself on the catalog cover as "The Original Grange Supply House," the 12-year-old mail order firm assures customers that all goods are sent "subject to examination" and that unsatisfactory items may be returned with the company paying the transportation both ways (see 1904; Sears, 1886).

A new Harrods store opens at London in September with displays of silver and brass, trunks and saddlery, cheap patent medicines, and with pay desks (see 1883). C. D. Harrod more than doubles the volume of his old store, he insists on "net cash before delivery," but he will extend limited credit to approved customers such as actresses Lily Langtree and Ellen Terry and playwright Oscar Wilde beginning next year. When Harrod sells out for £120,000 in 1889, the store will be doing an annual business of nearly £500,000 (see 1894).

New York's Dakota Apartments open at 1 West 72nd Street (see 1881).

The New York architectural firm Carrère & Hastings is founded by John Merven Carrère, 25, and Thomas Hastings.

New York's Villard Houses modeled after Rome's Canceleria are completed on Madison Avenue between 50th and 51st Streets by McKim, Mead and White for Henry Villard of the Northern Pacific who loses control of the railroad and suffers a nervous breakdown (see 1883). Villard occupies the mansion on the southerly corner but he will soon sell it to *New York Tribune* publisher Whitelaw Reid, 49, a fifth house will be built on the northeast corner of the property in 1886, and a sixth house thereafter.

New York's Chelsea Hotel has its beginnings in a 12-story brick cooperative apartment house that opens in West 23rd Street. The structure will become a hotel in 1905.

Chicago's Studebaker Building is completed by architect S. S. Berman whose structure will be renamed the Fine Arts building.

The first skyscraper goes up in Chicago (see 1885).

California outlaws the hydraulic mining that has been ruining the environment since 1852.

Ceylon's coffee output falls to 150,000 bags, down from 700,000 in 1870 when the rust disease caused by *Hamileia vastatrix* began making deep inroads (see 1869). The last shipment of coffee beans will leave the island in 1899.

Bordeaux mixture is invented by French botanist Pierre M. Alexis Millardet, 46, whose solution of copper sulfate, lime, and water effectively combats the fungus diseases attacking French vineyards and will prove effective against potato blight (see 1848).

Reaper magnate Cyrus McCormick dies March 13 at age 75, leaving a fortune of $200 million to his widow, his four sons, and his three daughters. His 25-year-old son Cyrus, Jr., assumes the presidency of the McCormick Harvesting Machine Company (see International Harvester, 1902).

Frank Peavey moves his headquarters to Minneapolis where electric lights were introduced last year and where the Minneapolis Millers Association has long been his biggest customer (see 1874). Within a year Minneapolis will be the largest U.S. wheat-receiving market and will be taking in 33 million bushels annually (see 1886).

A congressional committee reports that a number of individuals, many of them "foreigners of large means," have acquired ownership of land tracts in Texas, some of them embracing more than 250,000 acres: "Certain of these foreigners are titled noblemen. Some of them have brought over from Europe, in considerable numbers, herdsmen and other employees who sustain to them a dependent relationship characteristic of the peasantry on the large landed estates of Europe." Two British syndicates hold 7.5 million acres of land (see 1888; Prairie Cattle Company, 1882).

The Dairylea milk producers' cooperative has its beginnings in an association of Orange County, N.Y., farmers who pool their efforts to market their milk effectively in competition with Harlem River Valley farmers, who ship milk into New York City at a rate of 50,000 quarts per day. The 40-quart milk can introduced in 1876 is now standard for shipment on night trains to the city (see 1842; 1907).

Chinese farm workers comprise half of California's agricultural labor force, up from 10 percent in 1870. The Chinese have raised dikes at the mouths of the San Joaquin and Sacramento Rivers and are reclaiming millions of acres of rich farm lands (see below).

The soft-shell clam *Mya arenaria*, also called the long-neck or steamer clam, is introduced to the U.S. Pacific Coast (see shad, 1873).

Beriberi continues to plague the Japanese navy, but the director of the Naval Medical Bureau Baron Kanehiro Takaki sends two ships on a 287-day voyage during which the men on one ship are to be served a diet of meat, cooked fish, and vegetables, while the men on the other ship are to be served the usual Japanese diet of polished white rice and raw fish. Some 160 men out of 360 come down with beriberi on the second ship and 75 die, while on the first ship nobody dies, and the 16 cases of beriberi are found to occur only among men who refused to accept the prescribed diet. Takaki orders Western-style rations to be served aboard all Japanese naval vessels (see 1642; 1887; 1905).

1884 (cont.) Scurvy reappears in the British navy and a daily lemon ration is ordered aboard all British warships where the old 1795 order has lapsed.

Quaker Oats becomes one of the first food commodities to be sold in packages. Put up in cardboard cannisters, the cereal will be widely and aggressively advertised throughout the United States and Britain (*see* 1877; 1888).

Buitoni's high-gluten pasta is introduced commercially (*see* 1856; 1941).

Black and White scotch is introduced by Glasgow distiller James Buchanan.

London's first A. B. C. teashop opens near Bridge Station but is generally ridiculed. Londoners prefer the old coffee shops with high-backed benches (*see* Lyons, 1894).

A second Chinese Exclusion Act passed by Congress July 5 tightens the provisions of the 1882 act (*see* 1888; California farm workers, above).

1885 The world's first successful gasoline-driven motor vehicle reaches a speed of 9 miles per hour at Mannheim. German engineer Karl-Friedrich Benz, 41, has built the single-cylinder, chain-drive three-wheeler (*see* 1888; Mercedes, 1901; Mercedes-Benz, 1926).

The "Bicyclette Moderne" designed by French engineer G. Juzan has two wheels of equal size with a chain-driven rear wheel employing a drive chain stronger than the one on the first rear drive "Bicyclette" designed by André Guilmet in 1868 and manufactured by Meyer et Cie. The Rover Company of Coventry, England, introduces the "safety" bicycle designed by the late J. K. Starley whose vehicle has wheels of equal size, a departure from the "ordinary" whose front wheel is much larger than its rear wheel. Sewing machine inventor James Kemp Starley died in 1881 at age 51 after having designed the bicycle that has wheels 30 inches in diameter with solid rubber tires, a chain-driven rear wheel, and—like Juzan's modern "Bicyclette"—a close resemblance to a vehicle sketched in 1493 by Leonardo da Vinci or one of his associates. The new French and English models make the bicycle suitable for general use (*see* United States, 1889; pneumatic bicycle tire, 1888).

The world's first electric trolley line is installed at Baltimore by English-American electrical engineer Leo Daft, 41, who uses double overhead wires from which the passenger cars draw electricity through a small carriage called a "troller" (*see* 1888).

The Fifth Avenue Transportation Company, Ltd., is founded by New York entrepreneurs who are determined to forestall the introduction of trolley cars (above). The company's horsecars will remain in service until 1907 (*see* Fifth Avenue Coach Company, 1896).

The Congressional Limited Express goes into service on the Pennsylvania Railroad between New York and Washington, D.C.

The Missouri, Kansas, and Texas Railroad reaches the heart of the Texas cow country and ends the need to drive cattle long distances to railheads (*see* 1871).

Khartoum falls January 26 to the Mahdi Mohammed Ahmed whose forces massacre General Charles "Chinese" Gordon and his garrison just before a British relief expedition reaches the city. The Mahdi dies June 21 and is succeeded by the khalifa Abdullah el Tasshi whose dervishes gain control of all the Sudan except for the Red Sea fortresses (*see* 1896).

Italian forces establish themselves at Massawa with British encouragement and begin to expand their holdings in the East African highlands.

The king of the Belgians Leopold II assumes the title of sovereign of the Congo Free State following French recognition of the Free State and conclusion of an agreement defining the boundary between the Free State and the French Congo. Another agreement has been concluded with Lisbon giving Portugal the Kabinda Enclave; large areas of the Congo Free State are assigned to concessionaires, but the central portion is set aside as state land and as the king's private domain.

Germany annexes Tanganyika and Zanzibar.

Britain establishes protectorates in the Niger River region, in north Bechuanaland, and in southern New Guinea. British troops occupy Port Hamilton, Korea.

The Treaty of Tientsin signed June 9 recognizes the French protectorate of Tonkin in return for a promise by the French to respect China's southern frontier. The treaty has been negotiated by British diplomat Robert Hart, 50, as the Chinese general Tso Tsung-t'ang dies at age 73 urging modernization of his country.

Britain's second Gladstone ministry ends June 9. Robert Arthur Talbot Gascoyne-Cecil, 55, marquis of Salisbury, has headed the Tories since the death of Lord Beaconsfield (Disraeli) in 1881 and begins a brief ministry, but Gladstone will regain power early next year.

Spain's Alphonso XII dies of phthisis November 24 at age 27 after a 15-year reign in which he has escaped two assassination attempts. Alphonso's mother Maria Christina becomes queen regent, but his posthumous son will be born next year, will come of age in 1902, and will reign until 1931 as Alphonso XIII.

Canada's Louis Riel leads another rebellion against Dominion authorities to protest the indifference of the Ottawa government toward the grievances of western Canadians (*see* 1869). Now a U.S. citizen, Riel was requested last year to give up his Montana schoolteaching post and to lead the protest, he has broken with the Roman Catholic Church, he establishes a government of métis, and he fights Dominion troops from March to May. The troops have been sent west on the partially completed Canadian Pacific Railway (*see* 1881), Riel is defeated at Batoche, he is apprehended and charged with treason, he is

600

convicted by an English-speaking jury, and he is hanged November 16 at Regina, leaving a legacy of bitterness in Canada's western provinces.

Anti-Chinese rioting breaks out in the Washington Territory. President Cleveland issues an order November 7 calling for the troublemakers to be dispersed (*see* Seattle, 1886).

The Browning single-shot rifle is introduced by the 19-year-old Winchester Repeating Arms Company whose new weapon has been designed by Utah Territory gunsmith John M. Browning, 30, and will be enormously successful.

Westinghouse Electrical & Manufacturing Company is founded by George Westinghouse who buys up rights to the European Gaulard-Gibbs transformer and who will buy patents to the Nikola Tesla induction motor and the Tesla polyphase alternator, which will make it economically feasible to transmit power over long distances (*see* 1883; 1888).

A practical transformer for large electricity supply networks is perfected by U.S. electrical engineer William Stanley, 27, and George Westinghouse (above). The two will give the first practical demonstration of an alternating-current system in March of next year at Great Barrington, Mass., and while Thomas Edison has rejected the alternating-current system in favor of direct current, the Westinghouse Company will exploit the alternating-current system and will use it to send high-voltage current over long wires, employing transformers to step down the voltage for local distribution to houses, stores, factories, and the like (*see* 1888; Thomson, 1883).

The principle of the rotary magnetic field that will lead to the development of polyphase motors (and of Italy's hydroelectric industry) is discovered by Italian physicist-electrical engineer Galileo Ferraris, 38, who will devise transformers for alternating current.

Gas lighting gets a new lease on life from Austrian chemist Carl Auer von Welsbach, 27, who isolates the element praseodymium and patents a gas mantle of woven cotton mesh impregnated with thorium and cerium oxides, rare earths obtained from India's Travencourt sands. The Welsbach mantle is fitted over a gas jet to increase its brilliance.

Railroad Transportation, Its History and Its Laws by Yale political science instructor Arthur Twining Hadley, 29, exposes the fallacy of the 1817 Ricardian theory of free enterprise as applied to industries having large permanent investments. Hadley pinpoints the high proportion of fixed to variable costs as a source of instability and the tendency toward combination, and he is called to testify before a Senate committee that is drafting an interstate commerce bill (*see* 1887).

M. A. Hanna & Company is founded by Cleveland coal, iron, and street railway magnate Marcus Alonzo Hanna, 48, who has organized the Union National Bank and has acquired the *Cleveland Herald* and the Cleveland Opera House (*see* McKinley, 1896).

Canadian Copper Company is founded by Ohio businessman Samuel J. Ritchie to buy up claims in the Sudbury Basin of northern Ontario (*see* 1883). The copper ore turns out to be rich in nickel, which is used primarily for coins and for nickelplating, but whose value for nickel-steel alloys will soon be recognized (*see* 1888; Mond Nickel, 1900).

The Broken Hill Proprietary Company, Ltd., that will monopolize Australian iron and steel production is founded by Mount Gipps sheep station manager George McCulloch, his hired hand Charles Rasp, and 12 other partners who have staked claims to a tin mine found by Rasp in 1883. The mine has proved to be the world's largest silver-lead-zinc deposit, it will gross more than £150 million before it closes in 1939, and it will pay dividends of nearly £16 million.

The first successful U.S. appendectomy is performed (by some accounts) January 4 at Davenport, Iowa, by physician William West Grant who has diagnosed a perforated appendix in his 22-year-old patient Mary Gartside. Grant is the first U.S. physician deliberately to open the abdomen and to sever the appendix from the cecum.

The first antirabies vaccine is administered beginning July 6 to a 9-year-old Alsatian schoolboy who has been bitten on the hands and legs by a rabid dog. Louis Pasteur has developed the vaccine from weakened viruses that have aged on the dessicated spinal cords of rabbits that have died from rabies; the vaccine has worked with test animals but has never been tried with humans. Pasteur's 31-year-old assistant Pierre Paul Emile Roux, on whose work the vaccine has been based, opposes its use until the reason for its effectiveness is known, but Pasteur risks criticism by the medical fraternity and permits the vaccine to be administered to young Joseph Meister, the boy is saved from an agonizing death, and while the treatment requires a series of painful injections in the stomach, victims of bites from rabid animals flock from all over the world to be treated.

Moved by compassion to treat a young girl who was bitten 5 weeks earlier and has almost no chance of survival, Pasteur (above) is attacked when the girl dies, jealous physicians question his other successes, suggesting that perhaps Joseph Meister and the others were not really bitten by rabid animals, but Pasteur is defended by Emile Roux, and his critics are shamed (*see* Institut Pasteur, 1888).

Phagocytosis is discovered by Russian zoologist-bacteriologist Ilya Ilich Mechnikov, 40, who conducts experiments with starfish larvae in Sicily where he is recovering from a suicide attempt. Mechnikov finds that white blood corpuscles (leukocytes) engulf and destroy foreign microorganisms, and his work suggests the means by which vaccines achieve success.

Johnson & Johnson Company is founded at New Brunswick, N.J., by Robert Wood Johnson with his brothers James Wood Johnson and Edward Mead Johnson to produce a full line of pharmaceutical plasters with an India rubber base (*see* 1874; 1886).

1885 (cont.) Stanford University (Leland Stanford Junior University) is founded by railroad magnate Leland Stanford, now 61, to memorialize his son Leland, Jr., who died last year at age 15 of typhoid fever at Florence after visiting with archaeologist Heinrich Schliemann (*see* 1870). The university will open outside San Francisco in 1891.

Bryn Mawr College for Women is opened outside Philadelphia by former Quaker minister Joseph Taylor. The new college employs the only four women Ph.D.'s in the United States (*see* Yale, 1861) and along with Radcliffe will be the only college to prepare women for the Ph.D. for more than 50 years.

The Georgia Institute of Technology (Georgia Tech) is founded at Atlanta.

The University of Arizona is founded at Tucson.

McAlester College is founded at St. Paul, Minn., by members of the United Presbyterian Church.

Good Housekeeping magazine begins publication in May at Springfield, Mass. (*see* Institute, 1901).

Fiction *Germinal* by Emile Zola; *Bel Ami* and *Contes et Nouvelles* by Guy de Maupassant; *Diana of the Crossways* by George Meredith who wins his first public acclaim at age 57 for his roman à clef about the granddaughter of playwright Richard Brindsley Sheridan; *Marius the Epicurean* by Oxford essayist-critic Walter H. Pater, now 46, who expresses his ideal of the aesthetic life in his romance set in the time of ancient Rome's Marcus Aurelius; *A Mummer's Wife* by Irish novelist George Moore, 33; *King Solomon's Mines* by English novelist H. (Henry) Rider Haggard, 29, who went to Africa at age 19 as secretary to Henry Bulwer, nephew of the late novelist E. G. E. L. Bulwer-Lytton; *The Rise of Silas Lapham* by Boston novelist-editor William Dean Howells, 48, who edited the *Atlantic Monthly* from 1871 to 1881 and encouraged both Henry James and Mark Twain while writing some novels of his own.

Poetry "The Betrothed" by English journalist-poet Rudyard Kipling, 20, whose satirical poem contains the lines, "A woman is only a woman, but a good Cigar is a Smoke." Chauvinist Kipling went to India at age 15 and has worked since age 17 on the editorial staff of the *Civil & Military Gazette and Pioneer* at Lahore where his father is curator of the Lahore Museum. *A Child's Garden of Verses* by Robert Louis Stevenson, whose poem "Bed in Summer" begins, "In winter I get up at night/ And dress by yellow candle-light./ In summer, quite the other way,/ I have to go to bed by day. In "Happy Thought" Stevenson writes, "The world is so full of a number of things,/ I'm sure we should all be as happy as kings." "Little Orphant Annie" by James Whitcomb Riley, who writes, "An the Gobble-uns 'at gits you/ Ef you/ Don't/ Watch/ Out!'"

Painting *The Potato Eaters* by Vincent van Gogh.

Amsterdam's Rijkmuseum founded by Louis Bonaparte in 1808 moves into new quarters where its Rembrandts and other paintings will be displayed for more than 90 years.

Theater *The Wild Duck* (*Vildauden*) by Henrik Ibsen 1/11 at Oslo's Christiania Theater.

Keith & Batchelder's Dime Museum at Boston breaks up as Batchelder moves to Providence and as Keith acquires the Bijou Theater next door to the Dime Museum in Washington Street.

Opera *The Mikado* (or *The Town of Titipu*) 3/4 at London's Savoy Theatre, with book and lyrics by William S. Gilbert, music by Arthur S. Sullivan. Inspired by Commodore Perry's opening of Japan in 1853 and subsequent enthusiasm for things Japanese, the opera enjoys enormous success with arias that include "A Wand'ring Minstrel I," "Behold the Lord High Executioner," "I've Got a Little List," "Three Little Maids from School," "For He's Going to Marry Yum-Yum," "Here's a How-De-Do," "My Object All Sublime," "The Flowers That Bloom in the Spring," and "Tit-Willow"; *The Gypsy Baron* (*Zigeunerbaron*) 10/24 at Vienna's Theater an der Wien, with music by Johann Strauss.

First performances Suite No. 3 in G by Petr Ilich Tchaikovsky 1/24 at St. Petersburg; Prelude, Chorale, and Fugue for Piano by César Franck 1/24 at the Société Nationale, Paris; *Saugefleurie, Legend for Orchestra,* after a Tale by Robert de Bonnières by French composer (Paul Marie Théodore) Vincent d'Indy, 33, 1/25 at Paris; *Les Djinns* (Symphonic Poem) by César Franck 3/15 at the Société Nationale, Paris; Symphony No. 4 in E minor by Johannes Brahms 10/25 at Meiningen.

The Boston Pops is founded by the 4-year-old Boston Symphony. Audiences enjoy liquid refreshments during the May–June series of concerts (*see* Symphony Hall, 1900; Arthur Fiedler, 1930).

England's *Genesta* is defeated 2 to 0 by the U.S. defender *Puritan* in the first English effort to regain the America's Cup since 1871.

Parker Brothers is started at Salem, Mass., by local inventor George Swinerton Parker, 18, who has devised a game he calls Banking in which the player who amasses the most wealth is the winner. Parker will be joined by his brother and will remain head of the firm for 60 years (*see* Monopoly, 1935).

Sunlight soap is introduced by Lancashire salesman William Hasketh Lever, 34, whose free-lathering yellow soap will dominate the British market. Lever has had the soap made for him, but he will soon produce it himself (*see* Lifebuoy, 1897).

An identification system based on fingerprints is devised by English scientist Francis Galton, now 63, who has founded the science of eugenics with his 1869 book *Hereditary Genius* and subsequent books. Galton proves that fingerprints are permanent and that no two people ever have the same fingerprints.

Chicago's Home Insurance building at LaSalle and Monroe Streets is the world's first skyscraper. The

10-story marble structure completed in the fall by architect William LeBaron Jenney, 52, has a framework made partly of steel and will be enlarged by two additional stories (*see* Otis, Siemens, 1861; Tacoma building, 1888; Wainwright building, 1890).

Chicago's Board of Trade building is completed at the end of LaSalle Street. It will be the center of grain futures trading until in 1930 (*see* 1879).

Brooklyn's St. George Hotel has its beginnings in a single building that will be joined by seven more to fill the entire block bounded by Clark, Hicks, Pineapple, and Henry Streets (*see* 1929).

Bermuda's Princess Hotel opens outside Hamilton. Queen Victoria's daughter Princess Louise visited Bermuda in 1882, the visit gained an international reputation for the islands, and the new hotel is named in her honor.

Sagamore Hill is completed for Theodore Roosevelt at Cove Neck, Long Island. The 22-room, $16,975 house will be electrified in 1914.

The Carson house is completed at Eureka, Calif.

A Canadian National Parks system has its beginnings in a reserve of 10 square miles set aside by Queen Victoria in the Canadian Rockies in an area where Canadian Pacific Railway surveyors discovered hot springs in 1883. A lake in the region has been named Lake Louise in honor of the queen's daughter, whose husband the marquis of Lorne was governor-general of Canada from 1878 to 1883. The area set aside will become Banff National Park, and it begins a program that will respond to the promotion of Irish-Canadian trader-frontiersman John George "Kootenai" Brown. Waterton Lakes, Kootenay, Banff, Jasper, Yoho, Columbia Icefield, Glacier, and Mt. Revelstoke National Parks will all be set aside as such in the system (*see* Waterton-Glacier Park, 1932).

The National Audubon Society has its beginnings in a group of U.S. birdlovers organized by *Forest and Stream* editor George Bird Grinnell, 36, to protest the commercial hunting of birds and the indiscriminate slaughter of U.S. wildlife in general (*see* 1905; Boone & Crockett Club, 1887).

Memoirs of a Revolutionist (*Paroles d'un Revolté*) by Russian philosopher Prince Petr Alekseevich Kropotkin, 43, declares that the "Golden Age of the small farmer is over. . . ." He is in debt to the cattle-dealer, the land speculator, the usurer. Mortgages ruin whole communities, even more than taxes" (*see* 1861; 1905).

Barbed wire fencing of public lands in the U.S. West is prohibited by Congress February 25, and President Cleveland issues a proclamation August 7 ordering removal of all unlawful enclosures (*see* 1877).

The U.S. corn crop tops 2 billion bushels for the first time in history and is double the 1870 crop (*see* 1906). Most of the corn goes into hog and cattle feed, but U.S. cattle are still fattened largely on grass.

The Orange Growers Protective Union of Southern California is organized as the Santa Fe Railroad extends its service in the Los Angeles area (*see* 1881; 1887; California Fruit Growers Exchange, 1895).

Commercial production of calimyrna (California + Smyrna) figs begins in California, but immature figs drop off the trees until growers employ caprification, following the advice of 3rd century B.C. Greek botanist Theophrastus. The growers plant one wild (or capri) fig tree to every 100 cultivated trees, and Blastophoga wasps that live in the capri trees "set" the fruit so that it will mature on the cultivated trees.

The North American lobster catch reaches an all-time high of 130 million pounds.

The Maryland oyster catch reaches nearly 15 million bushels.

Salmonella bacteria get their name from a paper by U.S. veterinarian Daniel Elmer Salmon, 35, who describes the bacteria that produce gastroenteritis with fever when ingested with infected food. Chief of the year-old Bureau of Animal Husbandry in the Department of Agriculture, Salmon has based his paper on work done by 26-year-old researcher Theobald Smith, but the bacteria he describes will be called salmonellae.

Fresh milk in bottles is added to the line of the New York Condensed Milk Company now headed by John Gail Borden (*see* 1861; 1879; evaporated milk, 1892).

Evaporated milk is produced commercially for the first time at Highland, Ill., where the Helvetia Milk Condensing Company has been established by John B. Meyenberg, now 37, with help from local Swiss-Americans (*see* Anglo-Swiss, 1866). When Galveston, Tex., is devastated by fire in November and fresh milk is hard to obtain, Helvetia Milk donates 10 cases of its product (*see* Carnation milk, 1899).

Morton's salt is introduced by the new Joy Morton & Co. firm that will be the only nationwide U.S. marketer of salt. Thirty-year-old Joy Morton has spent 6 years with E. L. Wheeler & Company, a firm that grew out of the Alonzo Richards firm that was started as Agents for Onondaga Salt at Chicago in 1848 to market salt from Syracuse that arrived via the Erie Canal and the Great Lakes (*see* 1912).

The United Fruit Company has its beginnings in the Boston Fruit Company established by Andrew Preston and nine partners who have been persuaded to set up an independent agency to import bananas by Dow Baker (*see* 1871). Now a prosperous shipper and a partner in the Standard Steam Navigation Company, Baker has built the *Jesse H. Freeman* schooner with auxiliary steam engines that permit him to send 10,000 stem cargoes north to Boston in 10 to 12 days from his new base in Jamaica, and the new company prospers as banana harvests increase (*see* 1899).

Moxie is introduced under the name Moxie Nerve Food by Lowell, Mass., physician Augustin Thompson who was introduced by a Lieutenant Moxie to the properties of a plant that is the beverage's chief ingredient other than sparkling water.

1885 (cont.) New York's Exchange Buffet opens September 4 across from the New York Stock Exchange at 7 New Street as the world's first self-service restaurant (*see* Horn & Hardart, 1902).

Part of India's 20th century reluctance to employ family limitation methods other than sexual abstinence has its origin at Kathiawar where Mohandas K. Gandhi, 16, has sex with his pregnant 14-year-old wife while his father dies in another room of the house, an experience that will lead Gandhi in 1906 to espouse sexual abstinence (*brahmacharya*) and to support no other form of family planning for India, where his influence would be enormously supportive in helping the nation avoid a population crisis. English physicians in this century have been introducing Western medicine into India to reduce the death rate, and English moralists have eliminated the slaughter of female children and other customs that have held India's population growth in check, measures that include *suttee,* the custom of burning wives along with their dead husbands on funeral pyres. India has a population of some 265 million, up from 203.4 million in 1850.

1886 The Haymarket Massacre at Chicago gives the U.S. labor movement its first martyrs and marks the beginnings of May Day as a worldwide revolutionary memorial day. Chicago police fire into a crowd of strikers May 1, killing four and wounding many others. The 17-year-old Knights of Labor organization holds a peaceful rally May 4 in Haymarket Square to protest the shooting, someone throws a small bomb that knocks down 60 policemen, killing one and mortally wounding six others, the police fire into the crowd, and the workers sustain three times as many casualties as the police (*see* Altgeld, 1893).

Labor agitation for an 8-hour day and better working conditions makes this the peak year for strikes in 19th-century America (*see* 1825). Some 610,000 U.S. workers go out on strike, and monetary losses exceed $33.5 million.

A new American Federation of Labor (AF of L) is founded under the leadership of English-American cigarmaker Samuel Gompers, 35, who 5 years ago founded the Federation of Organized Trades and Labor Unions at Pittsburgh. Gompers will be AF of L president for 37 of the next 38 years (*see* 1902).

A streetcar strike ties up New York City public transit completely until motormen settle for $2 for a 12-hour day with a half hour off for lunch.

Seattle has anti-Chinese riots, and 400 Chinese are driven from their homes. Some are sent to San Francisco before federal troops are called in.

A municipal order discriminating against Chinese laundries is a violation of the 14th Amendment, says the Supreme Court in *Yick Mo v. Hopkins.*

The last major Indian war in the United States is ended September 4 with the capture by U.S. troops of the Chiricahua Apache chief Geronimo after 4 years of warfare on the Mexican border (*see* 1876). Captured earlier by General George Crook, Geronimo has escaped, but he has been pursued by General Henry Ware Lawton, 57, who recaptures Goyathlay and turns him over to General Nelson A. Miles, who has relieved Crook.

The U.S. settlement house movement has its beginnings in two small rooms at 146 Forsythe Street, New York, rented by ethical culture leader Stanton Coit, 29, who has returned from a visit to London's 2-year-old Toynbee Hall. An assistant to Felix Adler in the 10-year-old Society for Ethical Culture, Coit begins forming neighborhood clubs to help organize the poor to work for social improvement, and he will establish the Neighborhood Guild next year (*see* University Settlement, 1891; Hull House, 1889).

The appointment of General Georges Boulanger, 38, as minister of war January 4 stimulates French *revanchist* sentiment. A veteran of the 1870 siege of Metz in the Franco-Prussian War, Boulanger has been pushed into prominence by Georges Clemenceau, 44, a member of the Chamber of Deputies who served as a war correspondent with Ulysses S. Grant's army in the U.S. Civil War (*see* 1887).

Britain's first Salisbury ministry ends January 27 after 7 months and a third Gladstone ministry begins February 12.

An Irish home rule bill introduced in Parliament April 8 by Prime Minister William Gladstone provides for a separate Irish legislature but retains control of matters relating to the army and navy, trade and navigation, and the crown in the British Parliament where the Irish will no longer be represented. The measure is attacked by Conservatives, a secession from the Liberal Party is led by the marquis of Huntington Joseph Chamberlain, 50, who resigns from the Gladstone cabinet, the bill is defeated in July, and the third Gladstone ministry is ended July 26 by a general election which gives victory to the Conservatives. A second Salisbury ministry that will continue until 1892 takes power, and Lord Salisbury's 38-year-old nephew Arthur Balfour is made chief secretary for Ireland.

Britain annexes upper Burma following a third Anglo-Burmese war, but desultory guerrilla warfare will continue for years. The British protectorate in Burma is recognized by China July 24 in return for a continuation of a decennial tribute.

A gold rush to South Africa's Transvaal follows discovery of the yellow metal on the Witwatersrand. Diamond king Cecil Rhodes founds Consolidated Gold Fields, Ltd. (*see* De Beers, 1880; British South African Company, 1889).

Johannesburg in South Africa's Transvaal is laid out in September and soon has a population of 100,000—half of it native workers—as the world's largest gold mines begin operations (above).

The element germanium is discovered at Freiburg in Saxony by German physicist C. Winkler in a silver thiogermanate. Germanium was unknown to Dmitri Mendeléev in 1870 when he published the periodic table of elements, but he suspected its existence and assigned it an atomic weight of 72.6.

Commercial aluminum production is pioneered by Oberlin College graduate chemistry student Charles Martin Hall, 23, who uses methods developed by Humphry Davy in 1807 to liberate aluminum electrolytically from aluminum oxide (bauxite) (*see* Sainte-Claire Deville, 1855). Hall succeeds in February in separating the oxide from the bauxite, he adds cryolite (a fluoride of aluminum), and he applies electric current whose passage is resisted by the oxide, turning the electrical energy into heat and ultimately breaking down the oxide into its aluminum and oxygen components. Hall forms the Pittsburgh Reduction Co. to exploit his discovery (*see* 1888).

French metallurgist Paul Louis Toussaint Heroult, 23, discovers a process almost identical to that of Hall (above) at almost exactly the same time, but litigation over patent priority will be resolved in Hall's favor in 1893. The two will eventually become close friends and will develop the Hall-Heroult process that will be used in the aluminum industry.

The first electrolytic magnesium plant is built at Hamelingen, Germany, near Bremen. Carnalite (a double salt of magnesium chloride and potassium chloride) is used as a raw material to make magnesium, used initially in flares (*see* Dow, 1930).

Bethlehem Steel Company's John Fritz switches from commercial work to ordnance at the suggestion of Navy Secretary William C. Whitney, 45, who has made a fortune in New York City transit lines (*see* 1863; Ryan, below; U.S. Shipbuilding, 1902).

National Carbon Company is organized to produce carbons for electric arc streetlights and similar carbon products (*see* 1879; Ever Ready battery, 1890).

Newport News Shipbuilding and Dry Dock Company has its beginnings in the Chesapeake Dry Dock & Construction Company started by railroad man Collis Huntington, who has acquired the Chesapeake & Ohio Railroad. When Huntington dies in 1900 at age 80, his nephew H. E. Huntington will acquire control of the shipyard at Newport News, Va.

More than half of Britain's 7.36 million tons of merchant shipping is in steam, up from less than 9 percent in 1856.

The Supreme Court reverses its decision in the 1877 Peik case and forbids individual states to fix rates on shipments passing beyond their borders. The ruling handed down October 25 in *Wabash, St. Louis & Pacific Railway v. Illinois* says that only the federal government may regulate interstate railway rates, and the decision affects 75 percent of the volume on U. S. railroads (*see* Interstate Commerce Act, 1887).

The first trainload of California oranges leaves Los Angeles for the East (*see* Columbia Exposition, 1893).

New York's Metropolitan Traction Company organized by local financier Thomas Fortune Ryan, 35, is the nation's first holding company. Ryan started a brokerage house at age 21, he had his own seat on the New York Stock Exchange 2 years later, he has been buying up street railway franchises, and he calls his company "the great tin box." By 1900 Ryan will have beaten his rival William C. Whitney (above) for control of the Broadway surface line, and he will control nearly every other line in the city (*see* Southern Railway, 1894; Royal Typewriter, 1905).

Control of streetcar lines in Chicago's North and West Sides is gained by financier Charles Tyson Yerkes, 49, who is building up a complex corporate empire through financial maneuvers in which he aligns himself with corrupt politicians (*see* London subway, 1890).

A buggy manufacturing company that will soon be the largest in the world is started at Flint, Mich., by local entrepreneur William Crapo Durant, 24, in partnership with hardware merchant J. Dallas Dort who has acquired patent rights to a two-wheeled road cart (*see* Buick, 1905).

Gottlieb Daimler perfects his internal combustion engine of 1882 (*see* carburetor, 1892).

The first ready-to-use surgical dressings are introduced by Johnson & Johnson (*see* 1885). Robert Wood Johnson heard an address in 1876 by England's James Lister and has developed sterile dressings wrapped in individual packages and suitable for immediate use without risk of contamination. The company has begun operations with 14 employees on the fourth floor of a former wallpaper factory at New Brunswick, N.J. (*see* 1899; Mead Johnson Company, 1900).

Sophie Newcombe Memorial College is founded at New Orleans to give Tulane University a woman's adjunct.

Chicago's Haymarket Massacre grew out of a police assault on strikers. The bloodshed gave May Day new significance.

1886 (cont.) Postal Telegraph Company breaks Western Union's telegraph monopoly. Commercial Cable Company's J. W. Mackay starts the company that will be headed by his son Clarence Hungerford Mackay beginning in 1902 (see 1881; 1883; 1928).

Linotype machines are installed by the *New York Tribune,* the first newspaper to use the machines (see Merganthaler, 1884; Fotosetter, 1949).

Television is pioneered by German inventor Paul Gottlieb Nipkov, 26, who devises a rotating scanning device (see Baird, 1926).

D. C. Heath Co. publishers is founded at Boston by former Ginn Bros. representative Daniel Collamore Heath, 42, whose firm will rival Ginn Bros.

Nonfiction *Capital (Das Kapital)* by Karl Marx is published in English (see 1867).

Fiction *The Mayor of Casterbridge* by Thomas Hardy; *The Bostonians* and *The Princess Casamassima* by Henry James; *Indian Summer* by William Dean Howells whose new novel makes him the acknowledged leader of the U.S. "realist" school; *An Iceland Fisherman (Pecheur d'Islande)* by Pierre Loti; *A Drama in Muslin* by George Moore; *The Strange Case of Dr. Jekyll and Mr. Hyde* by Robert Louis Stevenson who has written the pioneer science-fiction novel in 3 days and 3 nights and rewritten it in another 3 days and nights; *Kidnapped* by Stevenson who is ill with tuberculosis and will spend the winter of 1887–1888 at the Saranac Lake, N.Y., sanatorium started 2 years ago by E. L. Trudeau; *The Romance of Two Worlds* by English novelist Marie Corelli (Mary Mackay), 31, whose works will be the favorite reading of Queen Victoria and of Italy's Queen Margherita; "The Old Detective's Pupil" by New York writer John Russell Coryell, 38, whose Nick Carter story in Street & Smith's *New York Weekly* begins the series revived in 1891 when S&S assigns Frederick Van Rensselaer Day to write a weekly Nick Carter Detective Library series (see 1858).

Juvenile *Little Lord Fauntleroy* by English-American novelist Frances Hodgson Burnett, 37, whose story of an American boy who inherits a vast estate in England is based on an actual event; *Jo's Boys* by Louisa May Alcott.

Poetry *Les Illuminations* by Arthur Rimbaud.

Painting The eighth and final show of French impressionism opens at the Maison Dorée restaurant near the Paris Opéra and includes the canvas *Sunday Afternoon on the Island of La Grande Jatte* by "neoimpressionist" Georges Seurat whose work is ridiculed by the critics. Seurat has developed a "pointillism" technique of applying paint in thousands of tiny spots rather than by brush strokes.

Other paintings *Bubbles* by Sir John Everett Millais, who was made a baronet last year; *Carnation, Lily, Lily, Rose* by John Singer Sargent. *Girl Arranging Her Hair* by Mary Cassatt; *Carnaval du Soir* by French "primitive" painter Henri Rousseau, 42.

Sculpture *The Kiss (Le Baiser)* by French sculptor Auguste Rodin, 45, whose sensuous white marble work represents the illicit Italian lovers Paolo Malatesta and Francesca da Rimini of the 13th century whose story was told by Dante Alighieri (Francesca's husband Giovanni Malatesta murdered her because she was in love with his brother Paolo).

A process for halftone engraving that uses small raised dots of varying sizes is developed by U.S. inventor Frederick Eugene Ives, 30, who 5 years ago pioneered in color photography by making the first trichromatic halftone process printing plates. Ives will also invent a process for gravure printing that will employ minute pits etched into a metal plate, and while rotogravure will replace his photogravure, the Ives halftone process will endure in photoengraving (see 1880; *New York Tribune,* 1897).

Theater The Keith-Albee Vaudeville Circuit is founded by theater managers B. F. Keith and Edward F. Albee (see 1885; Orpheum Circuit, 1897).

First performances Manfred Symphony by Petr Ilich Tchaikovsky 2/23 at Moscow; Symphonic Variations for Piano and Orchestra by César Franck 5/1 at the Salle Playel, Paris; Symphony No. 3 in C minor by Camille Saint-Säens 5/19 at London, with the composer conducting the London Philharmonic which has commissioned the work; "A Night on the Bald Mountain" by Modest Mussorgsky 10/27 at St. Petersburg; *Ophelia* by Edward MacDowell 11/4 at New York's Chickering Hall.

Popular songs "Hatikva" with lyrics by Bohemian-born English poet Naphtali Herz Imber, 30, who has come to Palestine as private secretary to a British journalist and poet. Imber's lyrics to a version of Bedrich Smetana's "The Moldau" of 1879 will be widely sung by Jews throughout the world.

The U.S. yacht *Mayflower* retains the America's Cup by defeating the English challenger *Galatea* 2 to 0.

The first world chess title goes to Bohemian chess master Wilhelm Steinitz, 50, who defeats J. H. Zukertort at London. He will hold the title until 1894.

New Yorker Steve Brodie is found in the water beneath the 3-year-old Great East River (Brooklyn) Bridge July 23 and claims to have jumped from the bridge. Nobody has witnessed the jump, and Brodie's claim is suspect since previous jumpers have fallen to their deaths, but any suicide leap—especially one from a bridge—will in many circles be called hereafter a "brodie."

The tuxedo dinner jacket is introduced by tobacco heir Griswold Lorillard to replace the tailcoat worn until now at evening social affairs. A short black coat with satin lapels modeled on the English smoking jacket, the tuxedo is worn by Lorillard in public for the first time October 10 at the Autumn Ball of the Tuxedo Park Country Club at Tuxedo, N.Y.

Johnson's Wax is introduced at Racine, Wis., by local parquet flooring peddler Samuel C. Johnson who has branched into paste wax. His S. C. Johnson & Son, Inc., will become the world's leading producer of floor wax (*see* Johnson's Glo-Coat, 1932).

Avon Products Company has its beginnings in the California Perfume Company founded by Brooklyn, N. Y., door-to-door book salesman David H. McConnell, 28, whose firm will become the world's largest cosmetic company. McConnell has been gaining admission to his customers' parlors by offering free vials of perfume, he has found more response to the perfume than to *Pilgrim's Progress* or *The American Book of Home Nursing*, so he abandons bookselling and concentrates on selling perfume.

The William J. Burns International Detective Agency has its beginnings at Columbus, Ohio, following revelations of fraud. A citizens "Committee of 100" that includes local tailor Michael Burns puts up money to hire a private investigator, the committee selects Michael's 22-year-old son William despite his father's disapproval, young Burns finds the safecracker-forger who has been spirited out of the local penitentiary to perpetrate the fraud, he obtains confessions, and he rounds up accomplices. Burns will work for the U.S. Secret Service for 14 years beginning at $3 per day in 1891, he will leave the Secret Service in 1905 to investigate fraud in San Francisco, he will start the Burns and Sheridan Detective Agency in 1909, and he will soon thereafter buy out his partner to operate under his own name (*see Los Angeles Times* bombing, 1910).

Sears, Roebuck Company has its beginnings at North Redwood, Minn., where Minneapolis & St. Louis Railroad agent Richard Warren Sears, 23, buys a consignment of $25 gold-filled "yellow watches" that a local jeweler has refused. Station agent Sears has been selling wood, coal, and lumber to local farmers and Indians, bringing in the commodities at special freight rates and shipping out the farmers' meat and berries at a profit. Sears uses the telegraph to offer the watches to other station agents at $14 each C.O.D. subject to examination, the other agents are able to undersell local jewelers, Sears makes $5,000 in 6 months, and he quits his job to go into business at Minneapolis (*see* 1887).

A model Bloomingdale's department store opens on New York's Third Avenue at 59th Street near a station of the new Third Avenue El that opened 8 years ago (*see* 1872). Bloomingdale brothers Lyman, Joseph, and Gustave have built up a thriving enterprise, specializing in whalebone for corsets, yard goods, ladies' notions, and hoop skirts with help from the El that has contributed to an uptown movement of the city's middle class. By the turn of the century, Bloomingdale's will cover 80 percent of the block from 59th to 60th Street between Third and Lexington Avenues and by 1927 the store will occupy the entire block (*see* Federated, 1929).

Chicago's Rookery building is completed in South LaSalle Street by Burnham and Root. Architects Daniel Hudson Burnham, 39, and John Wellborn Root, 36, started their firm in 1873, their 11-story Rookery has a graceful semiprivate square surrounded by shops and offices, and their pioneering design employs cast-iron columns, wrought-iron spandrel beams, and steel beams to support party walls and interior floors (*see* 1891).

A decade of intermittent drought begins on the U.S. Great Plains after 8 years of extraordinary rainfall. Close to 60 percent of U.S. range livestock die in blizzards and from lack of grass on overgrazed lands.

North Dakota rancher Theodore Roosevelt, 28, sustains heavy losses, gives up, and returns to New York to enter politics (*see* 1887; Sagamore Hill, 1885).

Buffalo hunter Charles Jesse Jones, 42, crosses the plains from Kansas to Texas and sees thousands of head of cattle lying dead from the blizzard, but coming upon some of the few remaining buffalo in the area, he finds "every animal . . . as well and wiry as a fox." Jones determines to capture bison calves and to cross them with cattle and by the turn of the century he will have established a new breed that he will name "cattalo."

The King Ranch of Texas, whose founder Richard King died last year at age 59, is inherited by his daughter Alice Gertrudis King who marries her father's 31-year-old lawyer Robert Justus Kleberg. He assumes management of the 500,000-acre ranch which now employs nearly 1,000 hands and grazes 100,000 head of cattle (he also assumes a $500,000 debt left by King at his death) (*see* 1868; 1940).

The Canadian prairie's ability to produce good wheat crops is demonstrated by Manitoba farmer Angus Mackay, 45, who plants Red Fife wheat on a field that he left fallow last year and reaps 35 bushels of hard wheat per acre (*see* Sanders, 1892).

The largest grain elevator in the U.S. Northwest if not in the world goes up in southeast Minneapolis. Frank Peavey's $3.5 million St. Anthony Elevator will burn to the ground next year destroying 1.15 million bushels of wheat but the loss will be covered by insurance, and Peavey will build a large new terminal (*see* 1884; 1899).

Fluorine is isolated by French chemist Henri Moissan, 34 (*see* Motley, 1916).

Dutch researcher Christian Eijkman, 28, is sent to Java to study beriberi, which has become a major problem in the East Indies (*see* 1896; Takaki, 1884).

Oatmeal king Ferdinand Schumacher at Akron is wiped out by a fire that destroys his new Jumbo mill, his Empire mill, and his other properties, consuming 100,000 bushels of oats plus quantities of other grains (*see* 1881). Schumacher has no insurance to cover his losses in the disastrous May fire, but he recovers in part by absorbing a small local competitor and by entering the Consolidated Oatmeal Company pool, whose members control half the nation's oatmeal trade (*see* American Cereal, 1888).

1886 (cont.) Pittsburgh's H. J. Heinz calls on London's 179-year-old Fortnum and Mason while on holiday in England and receives orders for all the products he takes out of his Gladstone bag (*see* 1880; 1888).

An Oleomargarine Act is passed by Congress to tax and regulate the manufacture and sale of margarine (*see* 1881; 1890).

Diamond Crystal Salt Company has its beginnings in the St. Clair Rock Salt Co. established by St. Clair, Mich., investors, including Charles F. Moore, who back Buffalo, N.Y., inventor J. L. Alberger and employ his new process for producing salt economically from brine deposits. The company name will be changed when chemical analysis shows the salt to be the purest yet found (*see* General Foods, 1929).

Maxwell House coffee gets its name. The 17-year-old hotel at Nashville, Tenn., serves its guests coffee made from the blend perfected by Joel Cheek who is persuaded by the praise of the guests to market his blend under the name Maxwell House (*see* 1882; Postum Cereal Company, 1928).

Salada tea has its beginnings in the Golden Tea-Pot Blend of the Salada Ceylon Tea Company introduced by Canadian wholesale grocery salesman Peter C. Larkin who is convinced that Ceylon teas will replace China teas in America as they have in England. Larkin packs Ceylon teas in a lead foil container sealed with a glue-on wraparound label, and while the name "Salada" is the name of a small Indian tea garden and has no significance, Larkin finds that people ask for "that Salada tea," so beginning in 1892 he will label his product Salada in large letters. He will run small newspaper advertisements, and he will persuade grocers to let him glue white enamel letter Salada Tea signs in their windows (*see* 1902).

White Rose is adopted as the brand name for a New York grocery wholesale house started by Joseph Seeman, 26, and his brother Sigel who pool their savings of $4,500 and borrow another $4,000 from an older brother to buy out their uncle David and his partner David Lewi (*see* White Rose Ceylon Tea, 1901).

Coca-Cola goes on sale May 8 at Jacob's Pharmacy in Atlanta, where local pharmacist John S. Pemberton has formulated a headache and hangover remedy whose syrup ingredients include dried leaves from the South American coca shrub (*see* cocaine, 1884) and an extract of Kola nuts from Africa plus fruit syrup. Pemberton has been unsuccessful with his "Globe of Flower Cough Syrup," his "Triplex Liver Pills," and other concoctions, but he has been advertising his Coca-Cola "esteemed Brain Tonic and Intellectual Beverage" since March 29. His bookkeeper Frank M. Robinson has named the product and has written the name Coca-Cola in a flowing script. Pemberton has persuaded fountain man Willis E. Venable at Jacob's to sell the beverage on a trial basis, Venable adds carbonated water, and by year's end Pemberton has sold 25 gallons of syrup at $1 per gallon, but he has spent $73.96 in advertising and

will sell two-thirds of his sole ownership in the product next year for $1,200 (*see* Candler, 1891).

Dr. Pepper is introduced as "The King of Beverages, Free from Caffeine" by Waco, Tex., chemist R. S. Lazenby who has experimented with a soft drink formula developed by a fountain man at the town's Old Corner Drug Store. The fountain man has called his drink Dr. Pepper's Phos-Ferrates.

Hires' Rootbeer is introduced in bottles, but Hires advertising emphasizes the advantages of brewing the drink at home from Hires extract (*see* 1876).

Fauchon opens on the Place de la Madeleine in Paris as an *epicerie* extraordinaire.

The Statue of Liberty is dedicated October 28 on Bedloe's Island in New York Harbor after Joseph Pulitzer's *New York World* has raised $100,000 for a pedestal that Congress had refused to fund. Designed by French sculptor Frederic Auguste Bartholdi, 52, and presented by the people of France to the people of the United States, "Liberté Eclairant le Monde" stands more than 151 feet tall and graces a pedestal that will be inscribed in 1903 with words written in 1883 by philanthropist Emma Lazarus, 37: "Give me your tired, your poor,/ Your huddled masses, yearning to breathe free,/ The wretched refuse of your teeming shore./ Send these, the homeless, tempest tossed, to me:/ I lift my lamp beside the golden door."

1887 Germany's Prince von Bismarck warns Europe against war January 11 in a speech that advocates a much larger German army while France is agitated by nationalist sentiment and demands for revenge against her victor in the Franco-Prussian War of 1870–1871. Ententes are formed among the powers, the Triple Alliance of 1882 is renewed for another 5 years and a secret Russian-German treaty is signed June 18 following Russia's refusal to renew the expiring 1881 Alliance of the Three Emperors.

An Italian-Ethiopian War begins in January, an Italian force is annihilated January 25 at Dogali, but Italy strengthens her position by backing Menelek, king of Shoa, and Ethiopia's king of kings Johannes is diverted by attacks in the north from Mahdist forces.

Britain promises to evacuate Egypt within 3 years in the May 22 Drummond-Wolff Convention with the Ottoman Turks, but the promise is made on provision that conditions are favorable, and Britain retains the right to reoccupy Egypt should the country be menaced by invasion or internal disorder. The Egyptian khedive Tewfik refuses to ratify the convention.

Britain annexes Zululand to block the Transvaal government from establishing a link to the sea.

Macao off the Chinese coast is ceded to Portugal.

France's President François Paul Jules Grévy is forced to resign December 2 at age 80 following revelations that his son-in-law Daniel Wilson has been trafficking in medals of the Legion d'honneur.

The ionic theory that electrolytes (substances that conduct electricity) split up in solution into electrically charged particles (ions) is advanced by Swedish chemist Svante August Arrhenius, 26 (*see* 1923).

The existence of electric or electromagnetic waves in the space round a discharging Leyden jar is shown by German physicist Heinrich Rudolph Hertz, 30, who has been investigating James Clerk Maxwell's 1873 electromagnetic theory of light (*see* Leyden jar, 1745). Hertz finds that the waves are propagated with the velocity of light as Maxwell had predicted.

Electricity is introduced to Japan in January by the Tokyo Electric Light Co. (Tokyo Dento Kaisha).

The Interstate Commerce Act approved by Congress February 4 orders U.S. railroads to keep their rates fair and reasonable (*see* Hadley, 1885; ICC, 1888; Elkins Act, 1903).

The Canadian Pacific Railway reaches Vancouver May 23, the first single company transcontinental railroad in America. Built by James J. Hill and W. C. Van Horne with 2,095 miles of track, the CP joins the east and west coasts of Canada and will spur migration to Canada's western provinces (*see* 1881; 1888; Canadian National, 1923).

The first Atchison, Topeka and Santa Fe train to reach Los Angeles via Santa Fe track arrives May 31, and a rate war begins between the Santa Fe and Collis P. Huntington's Southern Pacific. The Santa Fe has bought the Los Angeles and San Gabriel Valley Railroad to gain access to the city, passenger fares from Kansas City to Los Angeles drop as low as 1 dollar, and Los Angeles has a land boom.

The Sessions vertical end frame designed by Pullman Palace Car Company superintendent H. H. Sessions reduces railroad car sway and makes it safer to move from one car to another, as when going to the dining car. The company will refine the end frame to close vestibules and make a train one continuous unit.

A railroad trestle on the Toledo, Peoria & Western near Chatsworth, Ill., gives way in August and a passenger train bound for Niagara Falls with more than 600 passengers plunges into a ditch, killing more than 70, injuring nearly 300.

The first "Jim Crow" law to segregate black passengers from whites on railway cars is passed by the Florida legislature (*see* Rice, 1832; Mississippi, 1888).

Undulant fever, or brucellosis, is found to be caused by a bacterium transmitted in milk from Maltese goats and will later be found in other milk including cows' milk. The source of "Malta fever" or "Mediterranean fever," which has caused illness and even death among British military personnel, is identified by English physician David Bruce, 32 (*see* Bang, 1896; U.S. milk hygiene, 1921).

Bristol-Myers Company has its beginnings at Clinton, N.Y., where the Clinton Pharmaceutical Company is founded by local entrepreneur William McLaren Bristol, 27, in partnership with John Ripley Myers who will die in 1900.

No-Tobac is introduced by Attica, Ind., tobacco foe H. L. Kramer whose patent medicine is designed to spoil a smoker's (or chewer's) taste for tobacco. The product will fail, but the Cascarets laxative pills made of cascara sagrada introduced by Kramer to counteract No-Tobac's constipating effects will make him a fortune (*see* Sterling Drug, 1909).

Boston's Cabot Corporation has its beginnings in a lampblack firm founded by local entrepreneur Godfrey Cabot, 36, who breaks away from the family paint company to start the business that will be the basis of a vast fortune. Cabot has found that the oil and gas fields of western Pennsylvania are plagued by the sooty carbon debris of gas blowoffs and refining, he begins to build and acquire carbon black plants, he will branch off into natural gas production and distribution, and he will make his Cabot Corporation the major supplier of carbon black for electric lamp filaments, telephones, and other uses.

Cincinnati Milacron has its beginnings as Cincinnati bank clerk Frederick A. Geier joins a struggling Ohio River machine shop that he will develop into the largest U.S. producer of machine tools. Cincinnati Milling Machine will pioneer in improving milling machines by incorporating the motor drive within the machine to protect factory workers from exposed moving wheels and whirling shafts, it will introduce hydraulic controls to feed work to cutters and permit smoother performance, and it will introduce a power-controlled gear shift to eliminate the heavy manual effort needed to change the speed of tool revolutions.

The machine à calculer invented by French engineering student Leon Bolle, 18, is the first machine to automate multiplication using a direct method. Bolle's machine has a multitongued plate that constitutes a multiplication table and represents a marked advance over calculators that employ multiple additions for multiplication (*see* 1642; 1692; 1833; 1842).

The Comptometer introduced by the new Felt & Tarrant Manufacturing Company of Chicago is the first multiple-column calculating machine to be operated entirely by keys and to be absolutely accurate at all times. Local inventor Dorr Eugene Felt, 25, has gone into partnership with Robert Tarrant to produce the machine, it will be the only multiple-column key-operated calculator on the market until 1902, and by the time Felt dies in 1930 the company will have 850 employees and annual sales of $3.1 million (*see* Burroughs, 1888).

Lloyd's of London writes its first nonmarine insurance policy after 199 years of insuring only maritime carriers (*see* 1870). The great 120- by 340-foot Lloyd's underwriting room in Lime Street continues to be dominated by the Lutine Bell salvaged in 1859 from the frigate H. M. S. *Lutine* that was captured from the French in 1793 and sunk off the Dutch coast 6 years later with more than £1 million gold and

1887 (cont.) silver. The bell is still rung before important announcements—once for bad news and twice for good. The marine insurance underwritten by Lloyd's "Names" will continue to exceed nonmarine insurance until 1949.

Pratt Institute opens at Brooklyn, N.Y., to provide training for artisans and draftsmen. The school has been funded by Charles Pratt, 57, who sold his oil refinery to John D. Rockefeller in 1874 and who has been a benefactor to Amherst College and the University of Rochester.

Clark University is founded at Worcester, Mass., by educator Jonas Gilman Clark, 72.

Catholic University of America is founded at Washington, D.C.

The University of Wyoming opens at Laramie.

Occidental College is founded at Los Angeles.

Pomona College is founded at Claremont, Calif.

Chico State College is founded at Chico, Calif.

Gonzaga University is founded at Spokane, Wash.

The Perkins Institution founded in 1829 receives a request from telephone pioneer Alexander Graham Bell to examine 6-year-old Helen Adams Keller who lost her sight and hearing at 19 months of age. Teacher Anne Mansfield Sullivan, 20, of the Perkins Institution travels to the Keller home, she starts work with young Helen March 2, she quickly teaches the girl to feel objects and to associate them with words spelled out by finger signals on the palm of her hand, and Helen soon can feel raised words on cardboard and can make her own sentences by arranging words in a frame (*see* 1904).

Esperanto is invented by Polish oculist-philologist Lazarus Ludwig Zemenhof, 28, who hopes his universal language will help achieve world peace and understanding (*see* Ogden, 1929; Shaw, 1950).

Heinrich Hertz's electric waves (above) will be the basis of radio communications (*see* Marconi, 1895).

San Francisco Evening Examiner publisher William Randolph Hearst, 23, scores his first big scoop April 1 by chartering a special train to cover the fire that destroys the 7-year-old Del Monte Hotel built by Charles Crocker at Monterey. Hearst has inherited the paper from his late father George Hearst of 1859 Comstock Lode fame (*see* 1895).

The *Paris Herald* begins publication October 4 with the last of its four pages devoted to advertisements directed toward English and American visitors and émigrés. The paper is a European edition of James Gordon Bennett's *New York Herald*.

U.S. telephone listings reach 200,000 by December 31, with 5,767 in Boston and neighboring towns, 1,176 in Hartford, 1,393 in New Haven.

The Pratt Institute Free Library of Pratt Institute (above) is the first free library in New York state.

The Boston Public Library opens in a building designed by architects McKim, Mead & White.

Fiction *The Aspern Papers* by Henry James; *Plain Tales from the Hills* by Rudyard Kipling; *The People of Hemso* (*Hemsoborna*) by August Strindberg; *She* by Sir H. Rider Haggard, who has retired to a country house in Norfolk on the proceeds of his enormously popular 1885 book; *Allan Quatermain* by Sir H. Rider Haggard; *Thelma* by Marie Corelli; *A Study in Scarlet* by Scottish physician-novelist Arthur Conan Doyle, 28, who has written the book to supplement his small income and whose otherwise undistinguished work introduces the master detective Sherlock Holmes.

Painting *Moulin de la Galette* by Vincent van Gogh; *Walt Whitman* by Thomas Eakins.

Theater *Rosmersholm* by Henrik Ibsen 4/12 at Oslo's Christiania Theater; *The Father* (*Fadren*) by August Strindberg 11/14 at Copenhagen's Cosmo Theater; *Ivanov* by Russian playwright Anton Chekhov, 27, 11/19 at Moscow's Korsk Theater; *La Tosca* by Victorien Sardou 11/24 at the Théâtre de la Porte-Saint-Martin, Paris (*see* opera, 1900); *A Gown for His Mistress* (*Tailleur pour dames*) by French playwright Georges Feydeau, 24, 12/17 at the Théâtre de la Renaissance, Paris.

Opera *Ruddigore* (or *The Witch's Curse*) 1/22 at London's Savoy Theatre, with new Gilbert and Sullivan songs; *Otello* 2/5 at Milan's Teatro alla Scala, with music by Giuseppe Verdi, libretto from the Shakespeare tragedy of 1604; *The Reluctant King* (*Le Roi malgré lui*) 5/18 at the Opéra-Comique, Paris, with music by Emmanuel Chabrier.

First performances Suite in D for Trumpet, Flutes, and Strings by Vincent d'Indy 1/7 at Paris; Symphony No. 1 for Orchestra and Piano (*Symphony sur un air montagnard français*) by Vincent d'Indy 3/20 at Paris; Double Concerto in A minor for Violin, Cello, and Orchestra by Johannes Brahms 10/18 at Cologne; *Capriccio espagnol* by Nikolai Rimski-Korsakov 10/31 at St. Petersburg's Imperial Opera House; Suite No. 4 (*Mozartiana*) by Petr Ilich Tchaikovsky 11/26 at Moscow; *Pictures at an Exhibition* by Modest Mussorgsky 11/30 at St. Petersburg.

Thomas Edison invents the first motor-driven phonograph and opens a new laboratory at West Orange, N.J., that is 10 times the size of his Menlo Park laboratory of 1876. Edison's new phonograph plays cylindrical wax records (*see* 1877).

The gramophone patented by Emile Berliner of 1877 loose-contact telephone transmitter fame improves on Edison's phonograph (above) by substituting a disk and a horizontally moving needle for Edison's cylinder and vertically moving needle. The groove in Berliner's disk propels the arm of his gramophone automatically, eliminating the need for the separate drive mechanism that Edison's machine requires, but the pivoted tone arm of the gramophone has a fixed head and a tracking error that causes distortion in the music amplified through the large horn attached to its tone arm (*see* 1900; Victrola, 1906).

Tipperary beats Galway at hurling, and Limerick beats Louth at football in the first All-Ireland Championships (*see* Croke Park, 1910).

England's *Thistle* loses 2 to 0 to the U.S. defender *Volunteer* in the America's Cup ocean yacht races.

Atlanta's Piedmont Driving Club is founded by local gentlemen who restrict membership to men. The exclusive club admits members by invitation only and will exclude blacks and most Jews.

The first U.S. social register is published by New York golf promoter Louis Keller, 30, the son of a patent lawyer who owns a farm at Springfield, N.J., on which he has founded the Baltusro Golf Club. Keller has earlier helped start the scandal sheet *Town Topics*. His 100-page book sells for $1.75, it contains roughly 3,600 names based largely on telephone listings which it prints in larger type than that used in the phone company directory, it draws on the membership list of the Calumet Club at 29th Street and Fifth Avenue, and it will be followed by social registers published in most major U.S. cities, with preference given to white, non-Jewish, nondivorced residents who are considered respectable by the arbiters who compile the books.

Cannon Mills has its beginning in the Cannon Manufacturing Company founded at Concord, N.C., by James William Cannon, 35, who will introduce low-cost cotton crash towels in 1889 and terrycloth towels in 1900. Cannon sheets and towels will gain wide prominence.

 Richard Sears moves to Chicago, hires watchmaker Alvah C. Roebuck, and sells watches through clubs and by mail order, advertising in rural newspapers (*see* 1886; Sears, Roebuck, 1893).

Gimbel Brothers, Milwaukee, is opened by Jacob, Isaac, Charles, Ellis, Daniel, Lewis, and Benedict Gimbel, whose father Adam Gimbel opened the first Gimbel's at Vincennes, Ind., in 1842 (*see* 1894).

 The Grand Hotel on Mackinac Island, Mich., opens on a high bluff with 262 rooms and a wide 900-foot long veranda providing a view of ships passing through the Straits of Mackinac between Lake Michigan and Lake Huron.

Pittsburgh's Allegheny Courthouse and Jail is completed by Henry Hobson Richardson.

The W. G. Low house at Bristol, R.I., is completed by McKim, Mead & White of New York.

 The Boone & Crockett Club to protect American wildlife from ruthless slaughter by commercial market hunters is organized by a group of "American hunting riflemen" who include George B. Grinnell and Theodore Roosevelt who was defeated last year in a New York mayoralty election (*see* Grinnell, 1885). Membership in the club will be limited to 100.

Yellowstone country is made a refuge for buffalo and big game by Congress at the persuasion of Theodore Roosevelt (above; *see* Pelican Island, 1903).

 China's Hwang-ho River floods its banks. The resulting crop failures and famine kill 900,000.

 U.S. wheat prices fall to 67 cents per bushel, lowest since 1868, as the harvest reaches new heights. Britain and other importers of American wheat enjoy lower food prices.

Blizzards continue in the northern Great Plains (*see* 1886). The worst storm of the hard winter rages for 72 hours at the end of January, and millions of head of open-range cattle are killed in Montana, Kansas, Wyoming, and the Dakotas. Whole families are found frozen to death in tar-paper cabins and in dugouts, the big ranching syndicates go bankrupt, and the homesteaders that move in to start farms include former cowboys. Friction will soon begin between the farmers and the surviving ranchers.

The Hatch Act voted by Congress March 2 authorizes the establishment of agricultural experiment stations in all states having land-grant colleges.

Beriberi can be prevented by proper diet, says Japan's Baron Takaki in a report of his 1884 study published in the British medical journal *Lancet* (*see* Eijkman and Grijns, 1896).

Britain's Margarine Act establishes statutory standards for margarine, but dairy magnate George Barham does not succeed in his demand that if any coloring be allowed in margarine it should be pink, green, or—preferably—black (*see* 1858; U.S. federal coloring restriction removal, 1950).

Wesson Oil and Snowdrift Company has its beginnings in the Southern Cotton Oil Company founded at Philadelphia. The company's cottonseed-crushing mills in the Carolinas, Georgia, Arkansas, Tennessee, Louisiana, and Texas will make it the largest prime producer of cottonseed oil and the first U.S. manufacturer of vegetable shortening (*see* Wesson, 1899).

The isomeric hexose sugar mannose is isolated by German chemist Emil Fischer, 35, who works with his associate Tafel to synthesize the fruit sugar fructose. Other sugars have been isolated earlier, including glucose, galactose, and sorbose.

Sugar Refineries Company is organized by New York sugar refiner Henry Osborne Havemeyer, 40, whose 17 refineries account for 78 percent of U.S. refining capacity (*see* American Sugar Refining, 1891).

Log Cabin Syrup is introduced by St. Paul, Minn., grocer P. J. Towle, who blends maple syrup (45 percent) and cane sugar syrup to produce a product much lower in price than pure maple syrup. He markets it in a tin shaped and decorated to look like the boyhood home of his boyhood hero Abraham Lincoln (*see* Postum Company, 1927).

White Rock Mineral Springs Company is established in Wisconsin by Charles Welch with an initial capital-

Overhead pitching and new rules helped make baseball the national pastime it would remain for over a century.

ization of $100,000. Welch has bought the spring outside Waukesha and will promote "White Rock Lithia Water" throughout the country (see 1868; "Psyche," 1893).

Ball-Mason jars are introduced by Ball Brothers Glass Manufacturing Company of Muncie, Ind., which has been offered free natural gas and a generous land site to persuade it to move to Muncie where natural gas has recently been discovered. William Charles Ball, 35, and his brothers Lucius Lorenzo, Frank C., Edmund Burke, and George Alexander began making tin oil cans at Buffalo, N.Y., 10 years ago. They switched to making glass oil cans and glass fruit jars 3 years ago (see Mason, 1858).

Ice-making machines are installed to replace the blocks of ice at the Western Cold Storage Company in Chicago, but cold stores in most places continue to be cooled by harvested ice cut from lakes and hauled ashore by teams of horses (see 1878; 1889).

"Power tends to corrupt and absolute power corrupts absolutely," writes John Emerich Edward Dalberg Acton, 53, to Cambridge University professor Mandell Creighton. Lord Acton is a liberal Roman Catholic and a leader of the opposition to the papal dogma of infallibility on which is based Church resistance to most forms of birth control (see 1870).

1888 Chicago's Tacoma building, with a steel skeleton that employs load-bearing metal throughout its structure, represents the first basic advance in building construction since the medieval Gothic arch and flying buttress. The steel skeleton method of construction for tall buildings that was initiated by LeBaron Jenney's Home Insurance building of 1885 is firmly established by Chicago architect William Holabird, 33, whose firm of Holabird & Roche will be the major developer of Jenney's idea into modern office build-

ings in Chicago and will revolutionize the city's skyline with the Caxton building in 1890, the Pontiac building in 1891, the Marquette building in 1894, the Tribune building in 1901, and numerous hotels and office buildings thereafter.

The Washington Monument that will remain the world's tallest masonry structure is completed at Washington, D.C., after 40 years of on-again off-again construction. The obelisk stands 555 feet high.

"We Germans fear God, and nothing else in the world," says Prince von Bismarck February 6 in a speech in the Reichstag at Berlin. Bismarck has allowed terms of last year's Triple Alliance renewal to leak out as a discouragement to Russian and French ambitions.

Germany's Wilhelm I dies at Berlin March 9, less than 2 weeks before his 91st birthday, after a 27-year reign of Prussia and Germany that has seen the unification of Germany under Bismarck (above). Wilhelm is succeeded by his 57-year-old son Friedrich Wilhelm, but the new emperor dies June 15 of throat cancer and is succeeded in turn by his 29-year-old son who ascends the throne as Wilhelm II to begin a reign that will continue until his abdication in 1919 ends the German monarchy.

France's General Boulanger is relieved of his command after twice having come to Paris without leave. He is removed from the army list on the recommendation of a council of inquiry composed of five other generals, but although wounded in an embarrassing duel with the 60-year-old anti-Boulangist Charles Thomas Floquet, the popular "Man on Horseback" revanchist hero Boulanger is elected to the Chamber for the Nord (see 1886; 1889).

Britain establishes a protectorate over Sarawak March 17 and over North Borneo May 12, but the North Borneo Company continues to hold and administer North Borneo as it has since 1881, and Sir Charles Brooke continues to rule Sarawak as he has since 1868 (see 1946).

The Matebele king Lobengula, 55, accepts a British protectorate and signs a treaty October 30 giving the Cecil Rhodes interests exclusive mining rights in Matabeleland and Mashonaland.

U.S. voters elect Indiana Republican Benjamin Harrison, 55-year-old grandson of the ninth president William Henry Harrison, although President Cleveland actually receives a 100,000-vote plurality in the popular vote. Harrison receives 233 electoral votes to Cleveland's 168, New York makes the difference as it did in 1884, and again it is the Irish vote that swings the state, this time in reaction to a statement by the British minister to Washington that Cleveland would be friendlier to Britain than Harrison, a remark the Republicans use to support their contention that Cleveland's tariff position would favor British industrial interests.

A new law of chemistry formulated by French chemist Henri Louis Le Chatelier, 38, establishes the principle that if one of the factors in any chemical equilibrium changes, be it pressure, temperature, or something else, the system readjusts itself to minimize the change.

An alternating-current (ac) electric motor developed by Croatian-American inventor Nikola Tesla, 31, applies a variation of the rotary magnetic field principle discovered 3 years ago by the Italian Galileo Ferraris to a practical induction motor that will largely supplant direct-current (dc) motors for most uses (*see* Stanley and Westinghouse, 1885). A former Edison Company employee at West Orange, N.J., Tesla will make possible the production and distribution of alternating current with his induction, synchronous, and split-phase motors (he will also develop systems for polyphase transmission of power over long distances, and he will pioneer the invention of radio), but the Tesla Electric Company he organized last year is unsuccessful, and he will never derive much material success from his inventions (*see* 1893).

Patents for an electric railway issued 5 years ago to C. J. Van Depoele are acquired by the Thomson-Houston Electric Company of Lynn, Mass., which hires Van Depoele as an electrician. The inventor receives a patent for a carbon commutator brush (*see* 1874; General Electric, 1892).

The first successful electric trolley cars go into service February 2 at Richmond, Va., where engineer-inventor Frank Julian Sprague, 31, has laid 12 miles of track between Church Hill and New Reservoir Park (*see* Daft, 1885). A former assistant to Thomas Edison, Sprague quit 4 years ago to start the Sprague Electric Railway and Motor Company, his trolley line has 40 four-wheeled cars that can travel at 15 miles per hour and are lighted with incandescent bulbs, and within 2 years some 200 other U.S. cities will be served by electric trolley car lines (*see* 1900).

The Interstate Commerce Commission is established under terms of last year's Interstate Commerce Act. The ICC will make some efforts to protect farmers from discriminatory freight rates (but *see* California Fruit Growers Exchange, 1895; Elkins Act, 1903).

Los Angeles is linked to San Diego by a new Atchison, Topeka and Santa Fe line.

The Santa Fe builds a second line into Los Angeles from San Bernardino through Riverside and Orange counties.

The Santa Fe gains access to Chicago's Dearborn Station through acquisitions and new rail lines to give it routes from Chicago to points west.

The *Florida Special* leaves Jersey City in January on H. M. Flagler's Florida East Coast Railway. Flagler has contracted with George M. Pullman to build the fully vestibuled electrically lighted train, and its 70 passengers include Pullman (*see* hotel, below).

The Canadian Pacific Railway receives a British government mail subsidy to the Orient and begins to acquire ships for a Pacific mail route (*see* 1887; 1891).

The first Chinese railway opens between Tangshan and Tientsin. The 80-mile line will be extended to Shanghaikuan in 1894 and to Fengt'ai outside Peking in 1896.

German financiers project a Berlin-to-Baghdad railway and obtain a concession October 6 to construct a line to Angora.

A railroad line between Budapest and Constantinople has opened August 12 (*see* 1889).

A Suez Canal Convention signed at Constantinople October 29 declares the canal to be free and open to merchant ships and warships in both wartime and peacetime (*see* 1875). The canal is not to be blockaded but the sultan and the khedive are to be free to take such measures as they may "find necessary for securing by their own forces the defense of Egypt and the maintenance of public order."

The first patent for a pneumatic bicycle tire is awarded October 31 to Scottish veterinary surgeon John Boyd Dunlop, 47, at Belfast, Ireland. Advised by a physician to have his sickly son ride a tricycle, Dunlop has devised the tires to cushion the boy's ride on Belfast's cobblestone streets, using rubber sheeting and strips of linen from an old dress of his wife's. The Dunlop Rubber Company has its beginnings in a firm Dunlop establishes with entrepreneur W. H. Ducros, but he will sell the patent rights to Ducros and will derive only a small profit from his invention (*see* Michelin brothers, 1895).

Benz motor carriages are advertised for the first time at Mannheim by Karl-Friedrich Benz who organizes Firma Benz & Cie. (*see* 1885; Mercedes-Benz, 1926).

Brazil's slaves go free May 13 under terms of a law put through by a Liberal ministry under Pedro II who has ruled since 1840. The Rio Branco law of 1871 freed the children of slaves, an 1885 law freed all slaves over 60, and the new law completes emancipation without recompense to slave owners.

A U.S. Department of Labor is created by Congress, which restructures the 4-year-old Bureau of Labor, but the new department will not have cabinet status until 1903.

Anti-Chinese riots break out in Seattle (*see* Chinese Exclusion Act, below).

The Burroughs adding machine patented by St. Louis inventor William Seward Burroughs, 31, is the first successful key-set recording and adding machine (*see* Comptometer, 1887). The machine is not commercially practical, but Burroughs and three partners organize the American Arithmometer Company, they sell $100,000 worth of stock, they develop an improved model, and while the new model will not stand up to heavy use, Burroughs will obtain further capitalization, and he will produce a model in 1891 that will print out each separate entry and the final result of each computation. He will be granted patents in 1893 for the first practical adding machine, American Arithmometer will begin production of the machines, the company will move to

1888 (cont.) Detroit in 1905, and it will become the Burroughs Corporation.

Nickel steel is invented in France and gives impetus to Samuel J. Ritchie's 3-year-old Canadian Copper Company with its rich nickel ore deposits and to other nickel companies (*see* manganese steel, 1882).

The world's first commercial aluminum is produced Thanksgiving Day by C. M. Hall's Pittsburgh Reduction Company (*see* 1886; Mellon, 1891).

$ The Philadelphia Smelting and Refining Company is organized by Meyer Guggenheim, who last year took a venture in copper stock and did so well that he gives up the lace business he started in 1872 and goes into partnership with his four oldest sons (*see* 1881). Helped by all seven of his sons, Guggenheim will establish a second smelter in Mexico in 1891 and a third in 1894 (*see* ASARCO, 1899).

Andrew Carnegie gains majority ownership in the Homestead Steel Works outside Pittsburgh (*see* 1881; 1892).

Sherwin-Williams Company acquires Chicago's Calumet Paint Company, major supplier to the Pullman Company (*see* 1876; 1895).

Westvaco has its beginnings in the West Virginia Pulp and Paper Company started at Piedmont, W. Va., by Scots-American William Luke and his eldest son. Five other sons will join the enterprise to make the company a major U.S. paper producer.

The Institut Pasteur is founded at Paris with private subscriptions. The contributors have been inspired by Louis Pasteur's rabies vaccine of 1885 and include Russia's Aleksandr III, Brazil's Pedro II, and the Ottoman sultan Abdul Hamid II (*see* 1903; 1923).

Bellevue Hospital physiology professor Austin Flint, 52, at New York writes, "What has been accomplished within the past ten years as regards knowledge of the causes, prevention, and treatment of disease far transcends what would have been regarded a quarter of a century ago as the wildest and most impossible speculation."

Abbott Laboratories has its beginnings in the Ravenswood, Ill., kitchen of local physician Wallace Calvin Abbot whose firm will be incorporated under the name Abbott Alkaloidal Company. Abbott follows the radical idea of a Belgian chemist and isolates the active principles (alkaloids) of botanicals such as quinine, strychnine, and aconitine, which he promotes to other physicians.

G. D. Searle Co. has its beginnings in the Omaha pharmaceutical firm Searle & Hereth founded by Gideon Daniel Searle and a partner. The firm will move to Chicago in 1890 and will be renamed G. D. Searle Co. in 1906.

New York and New England telephone linemen work through the blizzard that strikes the Atlantic Coast between March 11 and March 14 to restore service on the new line that connects Boston with New York, but communications are disrupted by the storm and many communities are isolated for days.

A new shorthand system he calls "Light Line Phonography" is introduced by U.S. inventor John Robert Gregg. The Gregg system will largely replace the Pitman system in America (*see* 1837).

The Parker Pen Company is started at Janesville, Wis., by local telegraphy teacher George Safford Parker, 24, whose firm will become the world's largest producer of fountain pens (*see* Waterman, 1884). Parker sells John Holland pens to his students at the Valentine School in order to supplement his meager income, but the pens give trouble and Parker becomes adept at fixing faulty pens. He acquires a small scroll saw, a lathe, a cutter, and other tools to aid his repair work, and he develops a pen of his own with a superior feed (*see* 1904).

The first typewriter stencil is introduced at London by immigrant Hungarian inventor David Gestetner who 7 years ago introduced the first wax stencil duplicating machine to be marketed commercially. Chicago's A. B. Dick Company will introduce its first typewriter stencil in 1890 (*see* 1875).

The *Financial Times* begins publication at London.

The *National Geographic* begins publication in October at Washington, D.C., where the National Geographic Society is founded by Alexander Graham Bell's father-in-law Gardiner Greene Hubbard who founded the magazine *Science* with Bell 5 years ago. The new quarterly will begin monthly publication in 1896, it will publish its first photographs the same year, it will publish its first color plates in 1906, and in February 1910, it will adopt the yellow and white cover that it will retain.

McGraw-Hill Company has its beginnings as Panama, N.Y., schoolteacher James H. McGraw, 28, quits teaching and buys control of the *American Journal of Railway Appliances*. Vermont-born railroad man John A. Hill, 30, quits the Denver & Rio Grande Railroad to become editor of *Locomotive Engineer,* a publication for which he has written (*see* 1909).

Printer's Ink begins publication under the direction of advertising agent George P. Rowell whose trade magazine will campaign for honest advertising.

Di Yiddishe Folkbibliothek is founded at Kiev and is the world's first Yiddish literary annual. Founder Sholem Aleichim (Sholem Rabinovitch), 29, will raise the standards of Yiddish and will teach Russian Jews, who have been hounded since the assassination of Aleksandr II in 1881, to laugh at their troubles.

J. M. Dent Ltd. is founded at London by local bookbinder Joseph Malaby Dent, 39, who issues new editions of Charles Lamb's *Essays of Elia* of 1823 and *The Last Essays of Elia* of 1833. Dent will publish a pocket-size "Temple" edition of Shakespeare's works in 1893, and his new publishing house will achieve great success with its "Everyman's Library" series (*see* Dutton, 1858).

Nonfiction *The American Commonwealth* by Oxford professor James Bryce, 50, who sees the United States sailing in "a summer sea" and setting a course of responsible liberty that will be a model for the world. America's institutions, says Lord Bryce, are the answer to mankind's longings, "towards which, as by a law of fate, the rest of civilized mankind are forced to move," but he warns that "perhaps no form of government needs great leaders so much as a democracy," and he expresses concern that "the ordinary American voter does not object to mediocrity." *Travels in Arabia Deserta* by English explorer-poet Charles Montagu Doughty, 45, who 12 years ago learned Arabic, disguised himself as a Bedouin, and made the pilgrimage to Mecca.

Fiction *Looking Backward, 2000–1887* by U.S. socialist Edward Bellamy, 38, is a utopian novel that pictures a happy, peaceful United States of the year 2000 in which all industry has been nationalized and all wealth equitably distributed. The book sells 1 million copies and Nationalist clubs spring up to pursue the realization of Bellamy's ideas. *The Book of the Thousand Nights and a Night* by English Orientalist Richard Burton, now 67, who anticipated Doughty (above) by visiting Mecca disguised as a Pathan in 1853 and who has translated in its entirety the Arabian Nights stories known in the West until now only through expurgated stories such as "Aladdin and the Lamp." Sources of the stories are largely Persian, not Arabic, and are presented within the framework of a situation involving the Persian monarch Shahriyar and his wife Shahrazad (Scheherezade). Having had faithless wives in the past, Shahriyar has been taking a new wife each night and having her put to death in the morning, but Scheherezade ends this practice by keeping the monarch fascinated with stories, many of them bawdy. Burton's 16-volume work enjoys great success, but after his death in 1890 his wife Isabel will burn the manuscript containing his full translation of *The Perfumed Garden of Cheikh Nefzaoui: A Manual of Arabian Erotology; Robert Elsmere* by Tasmanian-born English novelist Mrs. Humphry Ward (Mary Augusta Arnold Ward), 37. U.S. publishers put out pirated editions for as little as 4 cents per copy and the Maine Balsam Fir Co. gives away a free copy with each cake of soap.

Juvenile *The Happy Prince* by Oscar Wilde, who 4 years ago married the wealthy Constance Lloyd and who has written the book of fairy tales for his 3-year-old son Cyril and his 2-year-old son Vyvyan.

Poetry "Casey at the Bat" is published June 3 in the *San Francisco Examiner* which pays Ernest Lawrence Thayer, 24, $5 for his contribution. The comic verse about baseball will be popularized by comedian-singer William DeWolf Hopper, 30, who will recite it thousands of times to enthusiastic audiences: "... And somewhere men are laughing, and somewhere children shout;/ But there is no joy in Mudville—mighty Casey has struck out."

The Kodak camera ("You Press the Button, We Do the Rest") introduced by George Eastman revolutionizes photography by making it possible for any amateur to take satisfactory snapshots (*see* 1884). The small, light, $25 camera comes loaded with a roll of stripping paper long enough for 100 exposures, the entire camera is sent to Rochester, N.Y., when the film has been entirely exposed, the exposed strip is developed and printed at Rochester, a new strip is inserted for $10, and the camera is returned to its owner with the finished prints. Eastman will explain the name Kodak by saying, "I knew a trade name must be short, vigorous, incapable of being misspelled to an extent that will destroy its identity, and, in order to satisfy the trademark laws, it must mean nothing" (*see* transparent negative film, 1889).

Painting *The Vision of the Sermon (Jacob and the Angel)* and *Still Life with Fruit, à mon ami Laval* by former Paris stockbroker (Eugène Henri) Paul Gauguin, 40, who has exhibited with the impressionists, has given up his job, has left his wife and family, but has been forced to return to Paris after running out of money on a visit last year to Martinique; *Side Show* by Georges Seurat; *Sunflowers, Arena at Arles,* and *Night Cafe* by Vincent van Gogh, who has befriended Paul Gauguin; *Place Clichy* by French painter-lithographer Henri (Marie Raymond) de Toulouse-Lautrec, 23, who has been physically deformed since his youth as the result of accidents and delicate health; *The Entrance of Christ into Brussels* by James Sydney Ensor, who uses macabre skeletons and masks with strident colors to rebel against the smugness and hypocrisy of the ruling class.

Sculpture *The Thinker (Le penseur)* by Auguste Rodin.

New York's Metropolitan Museum of Art opens its first addition and begins an expansion that will continue until the museum occupies 20 acres of Central Park (*see* 1880).

Theater *Sweet Lavender* by English playwright Arthur Wing Pinero, 33, 3/21 at Terry's Theatre, London, 684 perfs.

Opera *Le Roi d'Ys* 5/7 at the Opéra-Comique, Paris, with music by French composer Edouard Lalo who achieves his first great success at age 65; *The Yeoman of the Guard (or The Merryman and His Maid)* 10/3 at London's Savoy Theatre with Gilbert and Sullivan arias including "I Have a Song to Sing, O!"

Vienna replaces the Burgtheater of 1776 with a larger Burgtheater opera house and concert hall. The policy of permitting no curtain calls continues.

"Kaiserwalzer" by Johann Strauss restores the composer to favor with the emperor Franz Josef who stripped the waltz king of his honors 5 years ago for divorcing his second wife and marrying a young Jewish widow.

First performances *Requiem* by Gabriel Fauré in January at the Church of the Madeleine, Paris, where

1888 (cont.) Fauré has been assistant organist and choirmaster since 1877; Wallenstein Trilogy by Vincent d'Indy 2/28 at Paris; *Psyche* (Symphonic Poem for Orchestra and Chorus) by César Franck 3/10 at Paris; Concerto No. 1 for Piano and Orchestra by Edward MacDowell in April at Boston; Symphony No. 5 by Petr Ilich Tchaikovsky 11/17 at St. Petersburg.

"L'Internationale" is published with music by Belgian-born woodcarver Pierre Chrétien Degeyter, 40, lyrics by Parisian transport worker Eugène Edine Pottier, 72, who wrote the words during the Commune uprising of 1871: "Arise, ye prisoners of starvation;/ Arise, ye wretched of the earth...." It will become a worldwide Communist anthem.

"There are only about four hundred people in New York society," says social arbiter Ward McAllister, 60, in a *New York Tribune* interview (*see* social register, 1887). McAllister failed in a San Francisco law practice and traveled east to Newport, R.I., at age 22 to marry the heiress to a steamboat fortune. In 1872 he organized the Patriarchs, a group comprised of the heads of New York's oldest families on whose approval social aspirants depend.

Jack the Ripper makes headlines. London East End streetwalkers Mary Ann Nicholls, Annie Chapman, Elizabeth Stride, and their neighbors Catherine Eddowes and Mary Kelly die at the hands of one or more killers who feed the women poisoned grapes and then disembowel them. Scotland Yard can find no solution to the mystery, and it will later be alleged that agents of Queen Victoria murdered the women to hush up a scandal involving the queen's grandson Albert, duke of Clarence.

Woodbine's cigarettes are introduced in London.

Durham, N.C., tobacco merchant Washington B. Duke, 67, produces 744 million cigarettes at Durham and at his factory in New York's Rivington Street. A Confederate army veteran, Duke has leased a cigarette-making machine invented by Virginian James Bonsack, and W. Duke & Sons grosses $600,000 (*see* American Tobacco Company Trust, 1890).

Richmond, Va., cigarette makers Allen & Ginter produce more than 700 million cigarettes (*see* 1875). The Philadelphia Centennial Exposition of 1876 boosted the firm's sales.

Tobacco-chewer Thomas Edison refuses to hire cigarette smokers.

New York's R. H. Macy & Co. takes in as partners German-American merchant Isidor Straus, 43, and his brother Nathan, 40, who will become owner of the store in 1896. Isidor came to New York at age 9, started a crockery firm with his father Lazarus at age 20, and 9 years later took over the crockery and glassware department of Macy's (*see* 1874; 1901; Abraham & Straus, 1893; *Titanic*, 1912).

May Company merchant David May buys a bankrupt Denver store for $31,000, hires a brass band to attract crowds, and within a week has sold out the store's old stock at bargain prices, has remodeled the store, and has restocked it to open the May Shoe & Clothing Company store, "Goods retailed at wholesale prices" (*see* 1879; 1892).

The Ponce de Leon Hotel is opened January 10 at St. Augustine, Fla., by Standard Oil magnate H. M. Flagler, who has taken over the Florida East Coast Railway and is extending it south. Each room in the new $1.25 million hotel has electric lights and $1,000 worth of furnishings (*see* Tampa Bay Hotel, 1891; Royal Poinciana, 1894; *Florida Special*, above).

The Banff Springs Hotel opens in the Canadian Banff National Park set aside in 1885. Designed in a mixture of French château and Scottish baronial styles by New York architect Bruce Price, the five-story H-shaped wooden structure with accommodations for 280 has been built by the Canadian Pacific Railway (above) whose president William Van Horne says, "Since we cannot export the scenery we'll import the sightseers."

The Hotel del Coronado opens across the bay from San Diego, Calif., with 399 rooms around a central court in a five-story structure that has 75 baths. Put up by retired railroad executive Elisha Babcock and pianomaker H. L. Story of the Story and Clark Piano Company, the new hotel designed by James, Merrit, and Watson Reid has a main dining room whose arched ceiling is made of natural sugarpine fitted together entirely by wooden pegs. It will be the largest pillarless room in the country for years.

Washington's State, War, and Navy Department building is completed across the street from the White House by architect Alfred B. Mullett who has given the building mansard roofs and dormer windows typical of structures built since the Civil War.

The New York State Capitol building nears completion on a 3.5-acre site looming hundreds of feet above downtown Albany after more than 20 years of construction by H. H. Richardson and Leopold Elditz, but large chunks of brick begin to fall from the ceiling of the Assembly chamber.

The blizzard that strikes the U.S. Northeast in March comes on the heels of the mildest winter in 17 years and follows a warm spell in which buds have opened on trees in New York's Central Park. New York's temperature drops to 10.7°F March 12, and winds off the Atlantic build up to 48 miles per hour, bringing unpredicted snow which continues off and on into the early morning of Wednesday, March 14. The 3-day accumulation totals 20.9 inches, but snowdrifts 15 to 20 feet high have brought traffic to a standstill. Washington is isolated from the world for more than a day, 200 ships are lost or grounded from Chesapeake Bay north, at least 100 seamen die in the "Great White Hurricane," pedestrians and horses freeze to death in the streets, and at least 400 die, including former U.S. Senator from New York Roscoe Conkling, 58, who catches pneumonia and dies in mid-April.

U.S. cattlemen go bankrupt and foreign investors liquidate their American holdings after a drastic decline in cattle herds following the 1886–1887 drought on the western plains (*see* 1884).

Congress passes emergency legislation and places Major John Wesley Powell in charge of an irrigation survey to select reservoir sites, to determine irrigation product areas, and to carry out part of his 1878 plan (*see* 1889).

A new salt field is discovered in central Kansas by prospectors boring for natural gas (*see* 1892).

The American Cereal Company is created by a merger of all seven major U.S. oatmeal producers. More than 50 percent of the stock goes to Ferdinand Schumacher, whose holding is worth $2.5 million (*see* 1886), 12 percent goes to Henry Parsons Crowell for the Quaker Oats brand and the Ravenna mill he now owns (*see* 1877), and another 12 percent goes to Chicago-Cedar Rapids oatmeal producer Robert Stuart (*see* 1893).

B. Manischewitz Co. has its beginnings as the world's largest baker of matzohs and matzoh products. Russian-American baker Behr Manischewitz opens a bakery at Cincinnati, the company will establish a Jersey City plant in 1931 to make products for Passover while continuing to make other products at Cincinnati, and in later years the firm will build a plant at Vineland, N.J., to become a major producer of borscht, chicken soups, vegetable soups, gefilte fish, and other kosher foods (*see* Monarch wine, 1934).

H. J. Heinz reorganizes a food packing firm under his own name (*see* 1886; 1896).

England's Tetley tea is introduced in U.S. markets by Tetley agents Wright and Graham who merchandise Tetley's Indian and Ceylon tea through department stores such as R. H. Macy (above), a radical innovation at a time when Americans consume far more green and Formosan tea than black tea.

U.S. immigration from Britain has its peak year.

A new Chinese Exclusion Act voted by Congress October 1 forbids Chinese workers who have left the United States to return (*see* 1882; 1884; 1894).

1889 Oklahoma Territory lands formerly reserved for Indians are opened to white homesteaders by President Harrison at high noon April 22, and a race begins to stake land claims. Prior rights are claimed in many areas by "Sooners," who have entered the territory prematurely, bitter fights break out, but by sundown there are booming tent towns at Guthrie and at Oklahoma City, formerly a small water and coaling station for the Santa Fe Railroad but suddenly a city of 10,000 (*see* 1893).

A ghost dance has been ordered by the medicine man Wawoka of the Nevada Paintes following a January 1 solar eclipse which Wawoka has interpreted as a sign from the great Spirit. White men's bullets cannot penetrate the shirts worn by braves in the cere-

monial dance, Wawoka promises, and the U.S. War Department prohibits the dance lest it stir up violence (*see* Wounded Knee, 1890).

North Dakota, South Dakota, Montana, and Washington are admitted to the Union as the 39th, 40th, 41st, and 42nd states.

Austria's Archduke Rudolph is found dead January 30 with his 17-year-old mistress Baroness Marie Vetser at Rudolph's hunting lodge Mayerling outside Vienna. The beautiful Marie has been shot by the 31-year-old crown prince who has then taken his own life, leaving the Hapsburg emperor Franz Josef without an heir. His 25-year-old nephew Franz Ferdinand becomes heir-apparent (but *see* 1914).

Serbia's Milan Obrenović IV abdicates March 6 at age 34 and retires to Paris after a 21-year reign. The king has circulated scandalous reports about his estranged wife Natalie, he has extorted a divorce that is illegal in the eyes of the church, and he is succeeded by their 13-year-old son who will reign as Aleksandr I until 1903.

The French *revanchist* Boulanger threatens to overturn the Third Republic in a coup d'état, but a warrant is issued for his arrest and he flees the country April 1, taking refuge first at Brussels and then at London. Boulanger will commit suicide in 1891.

The Ivory Coast has been made a French protectorate January 10, and an Anglo-French agreement August 5 defines respective French and British spheres of influence on the Gold and Ivory Coasts and on the Senegal and Gambia Rivers.

Ethiopia's Johannes IV is killed March 12 in the Battle of Metemma fighting the Mahdists. He is succeeded after a 17-year reign by Menelek of Shoa, whose claim to the throne is supported by the Italians against those of Johannes's son Ras Mangasha. Menelek will reign as king of kings until 1911.

The British South Africa Company headed by Cecil Rhodes receives almost unlimited rights and powers of government in the area north of the Transvaal and west of Mozambique (*see* 1890).

Equatoria's Governor Emin Pasha is "rescued" by a relief expedition headed by Henry M. Stanley, who is financed largely by the king of the Belgians Leopold II, king of the Congo Free State, and by Leopold's friend Sir William MacKinnon of the Imperial British East Africa Company, both desirous of securing Equatoria and giving the Congo State an outlet to the Upper Nile. The German-born Mehmed Emin Pasha, whose Egyptian province was severed from the rest of Egypt by the Mahdi revolt in 1885, arrives at Bagamoyo in December, and he will soon be employed by the Germans, but he will be killed by Arab slave traders west of Lake Victoria in 1892.

The first Japanese constitution is promulgated.

The first Pan-American Conference opens October 2 at Washington, D.C., to cement relations among

1889 (cont.) Western Hemisphere nations. All Latin American countries except Santo Domingo send representatives, the delegates establish the Pan-American Union as an information bureau, but they reject a convention calling for the promotion of peace by arbitration, and they reject a plan of reciprocity.

Portugal's Luiz I dies October 19 at age 51 after a 28-year reign in which slavery has been abolished in every Portuguese colony. He is succeeded by his 26-year-old son, who will reign as Carlos I until 1908.

The Brazilian army deposes Pedro II November 15 after a 49-year reign and proclaims a Brazilian republic under the leadership of General Manoel Deodoro da Fonseca, 62. He will be elected president under a new constitution in 1891, but a naval revolt in late November of that year will oust him from office.

France's Compagnie Universelle du Canal Interocéanique goes bankrupt after having spent the equivalent of $287 million in an effort to build a Panama Canal that has cost the lives of some 20,000 Frenchmen and Chinese, Irish, and West Indian laborers in 5 years. The French call the Isthmus of Panama "de Lesseps' graveyard," and thousands lose their savings in the canal company's collapse.

The Maritime Canal Company of Nicaragua incorporated by Congress February 20 to build, manage, and operate a ship canal begins work October 22, but while supporters of the new company say Nicaragua has a healthier climate, opponents argue that the country has too many active volcanoes and that the Nicaragua route is too long (see 1902).

Europe's *Orient Express* completes arrangements for through travel between Paris and Constantinople without change of train (see 1883). The first through train leaves the Gare de l'Est June 1 and arrives at Constantinople in 67 hours, 35 minutes—more than 13 hours faster than in 1883 but 7½ hours slower than the time that will be standard within 10 years (see Simplon-Orient Express, 1919).

Scotland's Firth of Forth Bridge is completed by Sir John Fowler, now 72, and Sir Benjamin Baker, 49.

Europe's first electric trolley goes into service at Northfleet, Kent, England (see Richmond, Va., 1888).

Montreal's $2 million Windsor Station is opened by the Canadian Pacific Railway.

The "safety" bicycle patented in 1885 is introduced in the United States. Within 4 years, more than a million Americans will be riding the new bikes.

Rights to manufacture motor vehicles in France using the Daimler patents of 1882 and 1886 are acquired by René Panhard, 48, and E. C. Levassor who will mount the Daimler engine on a chassis in 1891 (see pneumatic tires, 1892).

Nellie Bly leaves Hoboken, N.J., November 14 in an attempt to outdo the hero of the 1873 Jules Verne novel *Le Tour du Monde en Quatre-Vingt Jours. New York World* reporter Elizabeth "Nellie Bly" Cochrane, 22, has earlier feigned madness in a successful attempt to gain admission for 10 days to New York's insane alylum on Blackwell's Island, she has persuaded her editor to give her a bold new assignment, and she leaves at just after 9:40 in the morning to break the fictional record of Phileas Fogg (see 1890).

Bird Flight as a Basis of Aviation by German engineer Otto Lilienthal, 41, shows the advantages of curved surfaces over flat ones for winged flight. Lilienthal has studied bird flight and has built gliders to prove his thesis, but he will be killed in a glider accident in 1896 (see Langley, 1896).

Cordite is patented by English chemist Frederick August Abel, 62, and Scottish chemist James Dewar of 1873 Dewar's vessel fame. The smokeless, slow-burning explosive powder is made of nitroglycerin, nitrocellulose, and mineral jelly.

A cheap new process for producing the bromine used by the pharmaceutical and photographic industries is discovered by Canadian-American chemist Herbert Henry Dow, 23, who last year received an advanced degree from Cleveland's 8-year-old Case School for Applied Science. Dow finds that by adding certain chemicals to cold brine and passing a current of air through the solution and onto scrap iron, a moisture collects on the iron that drips into a container as ferric bromine, a solution that contains a high percentage of commercial quality bromine (see 1891).

The Comptograph sold by Chicago's Felt & Tarrant Manufacturing Company in December to the Manufacturers' National Bank of Pittsburgh is the world's first recording adding machine (see 1887; 1888).

A worldwide influenza pandemic will affect 40 percent of the human race in the next 2 years (see 1918).

The bacilli of tetanus and of symptomatic anthrax are isolated by Japanese bacteriologist Shibasaburo Kitazato, 37, who works with Robert Koch at Berlin (see 1890).

The diphtheria bacillus is shown to produce a toxin in work done at the Pasteur Institute by Pierre Paul Emile Roux, now 36, and his Swiss colleague Alexandre Emile John Yersin, 26 (see Klebs, 1883; Löffler, 1884; von Behring, 1890).

Diabetes research is advanced by German physiologists J. von Mering and O. Minkowski who remove the pancreas of a dog and observe that although the animal survives, it urinates more frequently, and the urine attracts flies and wasps. When they analyze the urine, they find the dog has a canine equivalent of diabetes, which ultimately causes it to go into coma and die (see Bernard, 1855; Lancereaux, 1860; Langerhans, 1869; Sharpey-Schafer, 1916).

The Mayo Clinic has its beginnings in the St. Mary's Hospital opened at Rochester, Minn., by the Sisters of St. Francis who 6 years ago ministered to the injured left in the wake of a tornado that devastated the town. The hospital's medical staff consists of physician-surgeon William Worrall Mayo and his sons William James Mayo, 28, and Charles Horace Mayo, 24, whose clinic will grow to receive nearly 500,000 visitors per year (*see* Kendall, 1915).

The Cleveland Street scandal titillates London. Revelations appear about a West End homosexual brothel that employs post office messenger boys to gratify the appetites of clients whispered to include the Prince of Wales, his equerry Lord Arthur Somerset, 38, son of the duke of Beaufort, and the 25-year-old duke of Clarence, Prince Albert Victor Christian Edward (*see* Jack the Ripper, 1888). Some of the post office boys are bribed to go abroad so that they will not give evidence, and when one boy does give evidence against the earl of Euston, the newspaper editor who reports his testimony receives a 1-year jail sentence for libel.

The Great London dock strike from August 15 to September 16 helps extend British trade unionism from the skilled classes to the less skilled.

Chicago's Hull House opens in the South Halsted Street slums under the direction of social workers Jane Addams, 29, and Ellen Gates Starr, whose settlement house will help the poor of the city (*see* Coit, 1886; University Settlement, 1891).

"The man who dies rich dies disgraced," writes steel magnate Andrew Carnegie in an article on "the gospel of wealth." He is praised for his philanthropies by oil magnate John D. Rockefeller (*see* library benefactions, 1881; Carnegie Institute, 1900; Carnegie Institution, 1902; Carnegie Foundation, 1905; Carnegie Corporation, 1911; Rockefeller Institute, 1901).

The world's first electric elevators are installed by the Otis Company in New York's Demarest building on Fifth Avenue at 33rd Street.

Electric lights are installed at the White House in Washington, D.C., but neither President Harrison nor his wife will touch the switches. An employee turns on the lights each evening, and they remain burning until the employee returns in the morning to turn them off.

The first electric train lighting system is patented by U.S. inventor Harry Ward Leonard, 28, who worked with Thomas Edison to introduce the central station electrical system for cities (*see* 1884). Leonard will patent an electric elevator control in 1892.

I. M. Singer Company introduces the first electric sewing machines and sells a million machines, up from 539,000 in 1880 (*see* 1903).

Union Oil Company has its beginnings 75 miles northwest of Los Angeles, where prospector Lyman Stewart strikes oil in Torrey Canyon.

Barnard College opens near New York's Columbia University after 3 years of effort by Annie Nathan Meyer, 24, who has charmed and cajoled Columbia trustees and alumni. The new woman's college is named for Columbia's late president Frederick August Porter Barnard who died 6 months ago at age 80

after a long career in which he favored extending the university's educational opportunities to women.

Clemson College has its beginnings in the Clemson Agricultural College founded at Clemson, S.C.

The University of Idaho is founded at Moscow.

The New York Educational Alliance is organized by German-Jewish groups to provide education and recreation for slum dwellers on the city's Lower East Side, most of them from eastern Europe.

The *Wall Street Journal* that begins publication July 8 is the outgrowth of a daily financial news summary distributed by Dow Jones & Company, a firm organized 7 years ago by New York economists and financial reporters Charles Henry Dow, 38, and Edward D. Jones, 33. Dow has been a member of the New York Stock Exchange since 1885 and a partner in the brokerage firm Goodbody, Glyn & Dow. The Dow Jones Industrial Average will become a measure of the stock market's performance, and the *Wall Street Journal* will grow to become the second largest U.S. newspaper in terms of circulation with regional and foreign editions.

The *Memphis Commercial-Appeal* begins publication. Local cotton merchant West James Crawford, 45, has started the *Commercial* with some business associates and they soon absorb the *Appeal*.

A coin-operated telephone patented by Hartford, Conn., inventor William Gray is installed in the Hartford Bank. Gray will incorporate the Gray Telephone Pay Station Company in 1891 with backing from Amos Whitney and Francis Pratt of the 24-year-old firm Pratt & Whitney, the company will rename itself Gray Manufacturing Company, and it will install pay phones in stores, hotels, restaurants, and saloons, giving 65 percent of the take to the tele-

Elizabeth Cochrane outdid Jules Verne's fictional Phineas Fogg by girdling the earth in little more than 72 days.

1889 (cont.) phone company, giving 10 percent to the store, and keeping 25 percent for the Gray Company (local calls will cost 5 cents everywhere until 1951).

Nonfiction *Time and Free Will* (*Essai sur les données immédiates de la conscience*) by French philosopher Henri Louis Bergson, 29; *Borrowings* by a Mrs. S. B. Yule who attributes to the late Ralph Waldo Emerson the line, "If a man can write a better book, preach a better sermon, or make a better mousetrap than his neighbor, though he builds his house in the woods, the world will make a beaten path to his door." Mrs. Yule claims that Emerson made the statement in a lecture at San Francisco in 1871.

Fiction *A Connecticut Yankee in King Arthur's Court* by Mark Twain; *The Child of Pleasure* (*Il Piacere*) by Gabriele D'Annunzio.

Poetry *The Ballad of East and West* by Rudyard Kipling: "... and never the twain shall meet"; *Hot Houses* (*Serres chaudes*) by Belgian poet Maurice Polydore Marie Bernard Maeterlinck, 27.

Painting *Landscape with Cypress Tree, The Laborer, L'Hôpital de St. Paul à Saint Rémy, The Starry Night,* and *Self-Portrait with Bandaged Ear* by Vincent van Gogh who is suffering from a mental disorder and has cut off his ear and presented it to a young prostitute at Arles; *Portrait of an Old Woman* by James Ensor; *Still Life with Japanese Print* by Paul Gauguin; *The Gulf Stream* by Winslow Homer.

The Protar f.7.5 lens designed by German physicist Paul Rudolph, 31, for Carl Zeiss of Jena is the world's first anastigmatic lens to be commercially successful (*see* Tessar, 1902).

Goodwin Film & Camera Company is founded by New Jersey clergyman-inventor Hannibal Williston Goodwin, 67, who has been granted a patent on a "photographic pellicle produced from a solution of nitrocellulose dissolved in nitrobenzol or other non-hydrous and non-hydroscopic solvent and diluted in alcohol or other hydrous and hydroscopic diluent."

Hannibal Goodwin (above) has overcome curling of film by use of a celluloid varnish which remains flat when applied to a piece of glass or metal and can be sensitized with a gelatin emulsion, he has sent George Eastman at Rochester a 17-foot length of film to be coated and sensitized, Eastman has written him in mid-February that he has succeeded in coating the film with a sensitized emulsion, and 17 days later Eastman chemist Henry Reichenbock has applied for a patent on a transparent roll film produced from a solution of camphor, fusel oil, and amyl nitrate dissolved in nitrocellulose and wood alcohol. Goodwin's film will be marketed under the name An-sco by the Anthony & Scovill Company, which will be involved in litigation with Eastman until 1914, when it will receive $5 million from Eastman pursuant to a court ruling (*see* 1901; Eastman, 1888, 1895; cellulose acetate film, 1924).

Theater *The Lady from the Sea* (*Fruen fra Havet*) by Henrik Ibsen 2/12 at Oslo's Christiania Theater; *Miss Julie* (*Froken Julie*) by August Strindberg 3/14 at Copenhagen's Studentersamfundet; *The People of Hemso* (*Hemsoborna*) by August Strindberg 5/29 at Djurgardsteatern; *Before Dawn* (*Vor Sonnenaufgang*) by German playwright Gerhart (Johann Robert) Hauptmann, 26, 10/20 at Berlin's Lessingtheater. The play pioneers German naturalist drama and creates a sensation. *Honor* (*Ehre*) by German playwright Hermann Sudermann, 32, 11/27 at Berlin's Lessingtheater.

Opera *Esclarmonde* 5/18 at the Opéra-Comique, Paris, with music by Jules Massenet, who has written the title role for California soprano Sybil Sanderson; *The Gondoliers* (*or The King of Baratria*) 12/7 at London's Savoy Theatre, with Gilbert and Sullivan songs that include "I am a Courtier Grave and Serious," "Take a Pair of Sparkling Eyes," "There Lived a King," "O My Darling, O My Pet," "An Enterprise of Martial Kind," "I Stole the Prince," "Roses White and Roses Red," and "We're Called Gondoliers."

First performances Symphony in D minor by César Franck 2/12 at the Paris Conservatoire; Symphony No. 1 in D major by Bohemian composer Gustav Mahler, 29, 11/20 at Budapest.

English organist-electrician Robert Hope-Jones, 30, applies electricity to the organ for the first time. Chief electrician of the Lancashire and Cheshire Telephone Company at Birkenhead, Hope-Jones moves the console to a position that would be much too far from the pipes for a pneumatic system. He will emigrate to the United States, and before his death in 1914 he will sell his patents to the Rudolph Wurlitzer Company of North Tonawanda, N.Y. (*see* 1861; 1908; Hammond, 1934).

Japanese Musical Instrument Manufacturing Company (Nippon Gakki Siego Kabushiki Kwaisha) is founded by organ and pianomaker Torakasu Yamaha with 30,000 yen in capital. Yamaha introduced the first Japanese organ in 1885 and introduced the Yamaha piano 2 years later.

New York's Harlem Opera House opens in 125th Street. German-American cigarmaker-theatrical magnate Oscar Hammerstein, 42, has built it.

The Chicago Auditorium opens December 9 with Adelina Patti singing "Home, Sweet Home" to an audience that includes President Harrison. The new auditorium seats 3,500 and is part of a 17-story building that Louis Sullivan will complete next year.

March "Washington Post March" by John Philip Sousa.

Popular songs "Oh, Promise Me!" by U.S. composer (Henry Louis) Reginald De Koven, 40, lyrics by English drama critic Clement Scott, 48 (*see Robin Hood,* 1890); "Down Went McGinty" by Irish-American comedian Joseph Flynn.

Boston pugilist John Lawrence Sullivan, 30, defeats Jake Kilrain at Richburg, Miss., in July. The 75-round fight lasts for 2 hours, 16 minutes in 106-degree heat and is the last major bareknuckle prizefight.

The first All-America football team has a backfield and linemen selected by Yale athletic director Walter Chauncey Camp, 30, from among college varsity players across the country (see 1875; 1891).

The Flexible Flyer sled introduced by Philadelphia farm equipment maker Sam Leeds Allen of 1868 Planet, Jr. fame has runners that can be flexed over their entire length to permit turns twice as tight at twice the speed possible with other sleds. Allen's daughter Elizabeth has run her nonsteerable sled into a tree, inspiring Allen to invent the Flexible Flyer with double-thick runners whose concave channels give them steering bite and are mounted beneath boards of fine-grained oak varnished to a gleaming finish.

Richard Sears sells his 3-year-old mail-order watch business for $70,000 but soon starts another such business with a catalog of watches, watch chains, and other jewelry offered with the slogan "Satisfaction or Your Money Back" (see 1893).

The Eiffel Tower designed by French engineer Alexandre Gustave Eiffel, 57, is completed at Paris for the Universal Exhibition that opens May 6. The soaring 984.25-foot tower has a wrought-iron superstructure on a reinforced concrete base, it contains more than 7,000 tons of iron, 18,038 girders and plates, 1,050,846 rivets, and has three hydraulic elevators, one of them built by the Otis Company of Yonkers, N.Y.

London's Savoy Hotel opens August 6, the first British hotel to have private baths (see 1853). Built by Gilbert & Sullivan impressario Richard D'Oyly Carte of 1881 Savoy Theatre fame, the new hotel is built of reinforced concrete on a steel frame, it uses timber only for doors and window frames, it is Britain's first fireproof hotel, and it has 70 private bathrooms while the new Hotel Victoria on Northumberland Avenue has only four baths to serve its 500 guests. Manager of the new Savoy Hotel is César Ritz (see 1883; 1896; Escoffier, 1894).

New York's first real skyscraper opens September 27 at 50 Broadway. Architect Bradford Lee Gilbert has climbed to the top of the 13-story structure during construction and has let down a plumb line during a hurricane to show crowds gathered to watch the building collapse that it is steady as a rock.

The Johnstown Flood May 31 kills 2,000 to 5,000 Pennsylvanians in a city of 30,000. An earthen dam 90 feet high on the Conemaugh River has given way 14 miles away in the mountains, a torrent of water roars down on the city at 50 miles per hour, and its force tosses a 48-ton locomotive 1 mile.

The constitutional conventions of the new states of North Dakota and Montana (above) hear Major John Wesley Powell urge delegates to measure land values in acre-feet—the area that can be covered with 12 inches of water from irrigation or natural sources (see 1888). County lines should follow drainage divides,

says Powell, with each river valley a political unit whose inhabitants can work cooperatively, but the politicans pay little heed.

Rust finishes off Ceylon's coffee industry (see 1869). Demand increases for Latin American coffee.

The first spindle-type cotton picking machine is tested by U.S. inventor Angus Campbell whose machine will not be developed and produced commercially for more than half a century (see Rust, 1927).

Discontented southern farmers merge their farm organizations into the Southern Alliance (see 1882).

Kansas and Nebraska farmers pay 18 to 24 percent interest rates on loans, with rates sometimes going as high as 40 percent. Local brokers and then local loan companies secure funds from eastern investors and take healthy cuts for themselves.

The 27-year-old U.S. Department of Agriculture is voted cabinet rank, and J. M. Rusk becomes the first secretary of agriculture under President Cleveland.

British dairymen get their first milking machines. William Murchland at Kilmarnock, Scotland, manufactures the machines (see Colvin, 1878).

The Maine salmon catch reaches 150,000 pounds.

The Hudson River shad catch reaches an all-time high of 4.33 million pounds. The catch begins to decline, and although it will climb back up to 4.25 million pounds in 1942, it will then fall off drastically, and water pollution will spoil its taste.

A pure food law is proposed in Congress but meets with ridicule (see 1882; 1892).

A New York margarine factory employee tells a state investigator that his work has made "his hands so sore . . . his nails came off, his hair dropped out and he had to be confined to Bellevue Hospital for general debility," but the "bogus butter" made from hog fat and bleaches is widely sold as "pure creamery butter" and is no worse than "butter" made from casein and water or from calcium, gypsum, gelatin fat, and mashed potatoes (see 1890).

The first large-scale English margarine plant begins production at Godley in Cheshire. Danish entrepreneur Otto Monsted competes with U.S. and Dutch firms that are producing margarine in volume (see 1876; 1880; 1890).

English sugar consumption rises to 76 pounds per capita, up from 60 pounds in 1875, to make Britain the heaviest sugar user in the world by far.

A U.S. ice shortage caused by an extraordinarily mild winter gives impetus to the development of ice-making plants (see 1880; Western Cold Storage, 1887). By year's end the country has more than 200 ice plants, up from 35 in 1879.

C. A. Pillsbury & Company is acquired by an English syndicate and is merged with the Washburn Mill Co. of Minnesota State Senator W. D. Washburn to create Pillsbury-Washburn Flour Mills, Ltd. Pillsbury's three principal mills produce 10,000 barrels of flour

1889 (cont.) per day to make the company the world's largest flour miller, and this first major milling merger will lead to further mergers (*see* 1880; 1909; Northwestern Consolidated Milling Co., 1891).

Aunt Jemima pancake flour, invented at St. Joseph, Mo., is the first self-rising flour for pancakes and the first ready-mix food ever to be introduced commercially. Editorial writer Chris L. Rutt of the *St. Joseph Gazette* and his friend Charles G. Underwood used their life savings last year to buy an old flour mill on Blacksnake Creek, but a falloff in westward migration by wagon train has decreased demand for mill products. Faced with disaster, Rutt and Underwood have experimented for a year, and have come up with a formula combining hard wheat flour, corn flour, phosphate of lime, soda, and a pinch of salt which they package in 1-pound paper sacks and sell as Self-Rising Pancake Flour, a name Rutt changes to Aunt Jemima after attending a minstrel show at which two blackfaced comedians do a New Orleans-style cakewalk to a tune called "Aunt Jemima" (*see* 1893).

Calumet baking powder has its beginnings at Chicago where local food salesman William M. Wright turns his bedroom into a laboratory and develops a baking powder that he produces at night and sells during the day.

McCormick spices have their beginnings at Baltimore where local entrepreneur Willoughby McCormick employs two girls and a boy in a one-room factory with cellar and backyard and goes into business selling flavoring extracts, fruit syrups, juices, Iron Glue ("Sticks Everything but the Buyer") and Uncle Sam's Nerve and Bone Liniment ("For Man or Beast") (*see* 1902).

The pea viner that takes the whole pea vine and separates peas from pods in a continuous operation is introduced to expedite pea canning (*see* 1883).

Milwaukee's Pabst Brewery gets its name as the Empire Brewery produces 585,300 barrels for the year and is renamed (*see* Pabst, 1864; blue ribbon, 1893).

Lenox china is introduced by Trenton, N.J., ceramist Walter Scott Lenox, 30, who has established the Ceramic Art Company and whose porcelain will be ranked with that of England's Wedgwood and Spode.

1890 The Sherman Anti-Trust Act passed by Congress July 2 curtails the powers of U.S. business monopolies: "Every contract, combination in the form of trust or otherwise, or conspiracy in restraint of trade or commerce among the several States, or with foreign nations, is hereby declared to be illegal." But the new law will have little initial effect (*see* Clayton Act, 1914).

The Supreme Court virtually overrules its 1877 decision upholding state regulation of business March 24. The court's decision in *Chicago, Milwaukee, St. Paul Railroad v. Minnesota* denies Minnesota's right to control railroad rates and in effect reverses the court's ruling in *Munn v. Illinois*.

The Sherman Silver Purchase Act passed by Congress July 14 supersedes the Bland-Allison Act of 1878 but continues government support of silver prices (*see* 1893).

The McKinley Tariff Act passed by Congress October 1 increases the average U.S. import duty to its highest level yet, but while the average is roughly 50 percent, the act does provide for reciprocal tariff-lowering agreements with other countries.

Wall Street has a panic in November as the London banking house of Baring Brothers fails and English investors dump U.S. securities.

The Peruvian government escapes bankruptcy with help from New York financier W. R. Grace who assumes the debt of two bond issues in return for concessions that give him virtual control of nearly all the country's developed and undeveloped resources including the rich Cerro de Pasco silver mines, all the Peruvian guano deposits, 5 million acres of oil and mineral lands, and several railroad leases (*see* Grace, 1865). Peru's treasury has been drained by the War of the Pacific that ended in 1884 and by the costs of financing the railroads built by the late Henry R. Meiggs who died in 1877. Now 58, Grace has twice been elected mayor of New York (1880 and 1884), he will organize the New York & Pacific Steamship Company next year, he will later add the Grace Steamship Company, and in 1895 he will combine his New York and Peruvian holdings into William R. Grace and Company, which will expand with agricultural, banking, chemical, mercantile, and utility investments in North and South America.

Boston's Old Colony Trust is started by local banker Thomas Jefferson Coolidge, 59.

The Influence of Sea Power Upon History, 1660–1783 by U.S. naval officer-historian Alfred Thayer Mahan, 50, demonstrates the decisive role of naval strength and will have enormous influence in encouraging the world powers to develop powerful navies. Mahan's objective is to have Congress strengthen the U.S. Navy, which last year launched its first battleship but which depends chiefly on its White Squadron of three small cruisers and a dispatch boat. His book is eagerly read in Britain, which has long controlled the seas, in Russia, in Japan, and in Germany, where Kaiser Wilhelm II orders a copy placed in the library of every German warship and pushes for a strong German navy.

Germany's Prince von Bismarck is forced to resign as prime minister March 18. Kaiser Wilhelm is caricatured for having "dropped the pilot" who has united the German states and who has inaugurated signal reforms in German society.

Anglo-German disputes in East Africa are resolved July 1 in an agreement by which the Germans give up all claims to Uganda, receive the little island of Heligoland in the North Sea which Britain obtained from Denmark in 1815, and recognize the protectorate over Zanzibar established by Britain June 14.

Cecil Rhodes becomes prime minister of Africa's Cape Colony July 17 and adds the political post to his position as head of De Beers Consolidated Gold Fields and of the British South African Railway.

The German East Africa Company cedes all its territorial rights to the German government October 28.

Willem III of the Netherlands dies November 23 at age 73 after a 34-year reign. He is succeeded by his 10-year-old daughter whose mother Emma will rule as regent until 1898, but who will herself reign until 1948 as Wilhelmina I.

The Grand Duchy of Luxembourg splits from the Netherlands upon the death of Willem III (above).

The first Japanese political elections are held July 11, but suffrage is limited to males over 25 who pay taxes of at least 15 yen per year (1.1 percent of the population), so only 453,474 drop their ballots in the small black lacquer ballot boxes (*see* 1929).

The first Japanese Diet opens November 29 as members elected in July take their seats.

Idaho is admitted to the Union as the 43rd state.

Wyoming is admitted to the Union as the 44th state.

Salisbury is founded September 12 by the British South Africa Company in the Mashonaland territory that will become Rhodesia in 1893.

The United Mine Workers of America is organized as an affiliate of the 4-year-old American Federation of Labor (AF of L) (*see* 1897).

The Knights of Labor strike the New York Central Railroad August 8.

A poll tax, literacy tests, and other measures designed to restrict voting by blacks are instituted by the Mississippi state legislature. Similar restrictions will be imposed by other southern states (*see* 1898).

Sioux lands in South Dakota that were ceded to the U.S. government last year are thrown open to settlement February 10 under terms of a presidential proclamation that opens 11 million acres to homesteaders. Sioux chief Sitting Bull of 1876 Battle of the Little Big Horn fame is arrested in a skirmish with U.S. troops December 15, and he is shot dead by Indian police at Grand River as Sioux warriors of the Ghost Dance uprising try to rescue him (*see* 1889).

The "Battle" of Wounded Knee December 29 ends the last major Indian resistance to white settlement in America. Some 350 Sioux men, women, and children are massacred in South Dakota by nearly 500 troopers of the U.S. 7th Cavalry.

Java man fossils of a prehistoric human ancestor are found at Kedung Brebus, Java, by Dutch paleontologist Eugene Dubois, 32, who is serving as a military surgeon in the East Indies. The fossil evidence of *Pithecanthus erectus* is found in an earth stratum dating from the Upper Pleistocene era of 700,000 B.C.

Punch-card processing is pioneered by U.S. engineer Herman Hollerith, 30, who adapts techniques employed in the Jacquard loom of 1801 and the player piano of 1876 to devise a system for punching holes in sheets of paper to record U.S. census statistics. Patents to the Hollerith system will be acquired by the Tabulating Machine Co. (*see* Watson, 1912).

U.S. steelmaking is aided by the discovery of rich iron ore deposits in Minnesota's Mesabi region by prospector Leonidas Merritt, 46 (*see* Rockefeller, 1893).

Sun Oil Company of Ohio is founded by entrepreneur Joseph Newton Pew, 42, who in 1874 married a Titusville, Pa., girl whose family has helped develop the Pennsylvania oil fields. Pew has pioneered in pumping gas by mechanical pressure, he has patented a pump of his own invention to supply cities with heat and light, he will acquire other companies, he will merge Sun Oil of Ohio into Sun Oil Company of New Jersey in 1910, and he will market his products under the name Sunoco.

The first commercial dry cell battery is introduced under the name Ever Ready by the National Carbon Company (*see* 1886; Leclanche, 1867).

Packard Electric Company is founded at Warren, Ohio, by local engineer James Ward Packard, 27, with his brother William Doud Packard, 29 (*see* first Packard motorcar, 1900).

Nellie Bly boards the S.S. *Oceanic* at Yokohama January 7 and sails for San Francisco after having crossed the Atlantic, Europe, and Asia in her well-publicized attempt to girdle the earth in less than 80 days (*see* 1889). The *New York World* reporter is advised at San Francisco that the purser has left the ship's bill of health at Yokohama and that nobody may leave the ship for 2 weeks, she threatens to jump overboard and swim, she is put on a tug and taken ashore, her train across the continent detours to avoid blizzards and is almost derailed when it hits a handcar, but she pulls into Jersey City at 3:41 in the afternoon of January 25 after a journey of 72 days, 6 hours, 11 minutes, and 14 seconds (*see* Mears, 1913).

Ten thousand Americans die in railroad-related accidents and 80,000 are seriously injured.

The United States has 125,000 miles of railroad in operation, Britain 20,073 miles, and Russia 19,000.

London's first electric underground railway goes into service, and the coke-burning locomotives that have operated since 1863 are retired. The syndicate that has built the underground system will soon be headed by Chicago traction magnate Charles T. Yerkes who will sell his Chicago interests in 1899 and will move to London in 1900 (*see* 1886). A tube ride to any point in London on the new underground line costs twopence (*see* Budapest, 1896).

Daimler-Motoren-Gesellschaft is founded by Gottlieb Daimler at Bad Cannstatt in Germany (*see* 1886; 1901; British Daimler, 1896).

1890 (cont.) The first tetanus antitoxin is produced by Berlin bacteriologist Emil von Behring, 36, and Shibasaburo Kitazato who immunize animals by injecting minute amounts of toxin and find that the animals produce antibodies.

The first diphtheria antitoxin is produced by Emil von Behring (above), who works in Robert Koch's laboratory and whose discovery will win him the first Nobel Prize for medicine in 1901 (*see* 1891; Roux and Yersin, 1889; Biggs, 1894).

New York State requires physicians to apply prophylactic drops to the eyes of newborn infants. The state legislature enacts the Howe Law drafted by Buffalo ophthalmologist-legislator Lucien Howe, 42, and most states will enact similar laws to combat blindness caused by gonorrheal infection (*see* Crede, 1884; Barnes, 1902).

Only 3 percent of Americans age 18 to 21 attend college. The figure will rise to 8 percent by 1930.

Colgate University takes that name after 71 years as Madison University. The late soapmaker William Colgate and his sons have been large benefactors to the university at Hamilton, N.Y. (*see* 1806).

The University of Oklahoma is founded at Norman in Oklahoma Territory.

Oklahoma State University is founded at Stillwater (*see* statehood, 1907).

The *Literary Digest* begins publication with reprints of comment and opinion from other U.S. periodicals. The new weekly has been started by New York publisher I. K. Funk who publishes a *Standard Dictionary of the English Language* with his associate A. W. Wagnalls (*see* 1877; 1937; *Reader's Digest,* 1922).

"Everybody talks about the weather, but nobody does anything about it," says an editorial in the *Hartford Courant,* which attributes the line to "an author" who is either Mark Twain or associate editor Charles Dudley Warner, now 61.

Nonfiction *The Golden Bough* (first volume) by Scottish anthropologist James George Frazer, 36, who will publish 15 further volumes in the next 25 years in a monumental exploration of the cults, legends, myths, and rites of the world and their influence on the development of religion; a one-volume abridged version will be published in 1922.

Fiction *A Hazard of New Fortunes* by William Dean Howells who moved to New York from Boston 2 years ago and who shows the conflict between striking workers and capitalist interests; *Hunger (Sult)* by Norwegian novelist Knut Hamsun (Knut Pedersen), 31, who returned to Norway last year after two extended visits in America during which he worked as a farmhand, as a Chicago streetcar conductor, and as a lecturer; *The Sign of the Four,* a new Sherlock Holmes detective novel by A. Conan Doyle; *Tout Vient à Qui Sait Attendre* by English novelist-essayist Lady Mary Montgomerie Lamb Currie, 47: "Ah,

All things come to those who wait,/ They come, but often come too late."

Poetry *Poems by Emily Dickinson* is published at the urging of Lavinia Dickinson, whose late sister Emily Elizabeth died at her native Amherst, Mass., 4 years ago at age 55 without ever having had any of her work appear under her own name. The book receives a cool reception from critics but has a good enough public response to warrant publication of more Emily Dickinson poems. New volumes will appear in 1891 and 1896, and by 1945 nearly all of her many hundreds of poems will have been published and her reputation as a major U.S. poet will be secure: "Because I could not stop for Death,/ He kindly stopped for me;/ The carriage held but just ourselves/ And Immortality"; *The Sightless (Les Aveugles)* by Maurice Maeterlinck; "The Lake Isle of Innisfree" by Irish poet William Butler Yeats, 25, whose first book of poetry appeared 4 years ago. His new poem begins, "I will arise and go now, and go to Innisfree,/ And a small cabin build there...."

Painting *Poplars* by Claude Monet; *The Cardplayers* by Paul Cézanne; *On the Threshold of Eternity, Chestnut Trees in Flower, A Field Under a Starry Sky, The Auvers Stairs, Portrait of Doctor Gachet, The Town Hall of Auvers on the Fourteenth of July,* and *Crows Over the Wheat Fields* (his last work) by Vincent van Gogh, who shoots himself July 27 at Auvers and dies there 2 days later at age 37; *Breaking Home Ties* by Irish-American painter Thomas Hovenden, 49, whose work will be the most widely engraved painting in America.

The "Gibson Girl" created by New York illustrator Charles Dana Gibson, 22, makes her first appearance in the humor weekly *Life,* which has been buying Gibson drawings since 1886. Apprenticed briefly to sculptor Augustus Saint-Gaudens, Gibson studied at the Art Students League. Millions will share his conception of the ideal American girl (*see* 1902).

Theater *Beau Brummel* by U.S. playwright (William) Clyde Fitch, 25, 5/17 at New York's Madison Square Garden, with English-American actor Richard Mansfield, 36, who has commissioned the play; *The Reconciliation (Das Friedensfest)* by Gerhart Hauptmann 6/1 at Berlin's Ostendtheater, 4 perfs.

Ballet *The Sleeping Beauty* 1/15 at St. Petersburg's Maryinsky Theater, with music by Petr Ilich Tchaikovsky, choreography by Marius Petipa.

Opera *Cavalleria Rusticana* 5/17 at Rome's Teatro Costanzi, with music by Italian composer Pietro Mascagni, 27, libretto from a play by Sicilian novelist Giovanni Verga; *Robin Hood* 6/11 at the Chicago Opera House, with music by U.S. composer Reginald De Koven who includes his 1889 song "Oh, Promise Me!" in the work whose book and other lyrics are by Harry B. Smith; *Prince Igor* 11/4 at St. Petersburg, with music by the late Aleksandr P. Borodin who died early in 1887 at age 52 after years of working on the opera for his wife, an opera singer. The score has been completed by Nikolai Rimski-Korsakov and by Russian composer Aleksandr Konstantinovich Glazunov, 25 (*see* ballet, 1909); *The Trojans (Les Troyens)* 12/5 at Karlsruhe, with music by the late Hector Berlioz who died in 1869 at age 65. The opera will not be presented in its original French until a U.S. production in 1960; *Queen of Spades (Pique Dame, or Pikovaya Dama)* 12/19 at St. Petersburg, with music by Petr Ilich Tchaikovsky.

First performances *Lancelot and Elaine* by Edward MacDowell 1/10 at Boston.

Cy Young signs with the Cleveland team of the National League to begin an outstanding pitching career that will continue for nearly 23 years—with Cleveland through 1898, with the St. Louis Cardinals through 1900, with the Boston Red Sox of the American League through 1908, with the Cleveland Indians of the American League through 1911, and with the Boston Braves of the National League for part of the 1912 season. Denton True "Cy" Young, 23, wins both games of a doubleheader in October, and he will be the first pitcher to win 500 games (*see* 1904).

The first Army-Navy football game begins a long rivalry between West Point and Annapolis; Navy wins 24 to 0.

The Colonial Dames of America is founded May 23 by women who can show that their ancestors came to America before 1776 (*see* National Society, 1893).

The Daughters of the American Revolution (DAR) is organized at Washington, D.C., by four women who include two government clerks.

How the Other Half Lives by *New York Evening Sun* police reporter Jacob August Riis portrays slum life and the conditions that make for crime, vice, and disease. Writes the 51-year-old Danish-American journalist, "When the houses were filled, the crowds overflowed into the yards. In winter [there were] tenants living in sheds built of old boards and roof tin, paying a dollar a week for herding with the rats" (*see* Steffens, 1904).

A Sunlight soap factory is built by English soapmaker W. H. Lever who establishes the model industrial town of Port Sunlight (*see* 1885; Lifebuoy, 1897).

Rothman's is founded by a London tobacconist.

The American Tobacco Company is founded by James Buchanan "Buck" Duke, 33, who creates a colossal trust by merging his father Washington Duke's Durham, N.C., company with four other major plug tobacco firms. Helped by New York and Philadelphia financiers who include Peter A. B. Widener, Grant B. Schley, William C. Whitney, and Thomas Fortune Ryan, Duke is joined by tobaccoman R. J. Reynolds, and he will pyramid a group of holdings that will include the American Snuff Company, the American Cigar Company, the American Stogie Co., and United Cigar Stores (*see* 1888; 1911).

The Wainwright building completed at St. Louis by Chicago architect Louis Henry Sullivan, 33, is the first true skyscraper. Sullivan formed a partnership 9 years ago with Dankmar Adler, he finished a new addition to Chicago's Carson Pirie Scott department store at Madison and State Streets last year, his apprentices include Frank Lloyd Wright, 21, and his Wainwright building has an unbroken sweep of vertical line from base to top (tenth) story, a design that will influence architecture for years to come.

Louis Sullivan (above) completes Chicago's 17-story Auditorium building at a cost of $35 million (*see* auditorium opening, 1889).

William LeBaron Jenney completes Chicago's 16-story Manhattan building at 431 South Dearborn Street. It is the world's first tall building with metal skeleton construction throughout.

New York's 16-story Pulitzer building is completed near the Manhattan end of the Brooklyn Bridge.

Starlings are introduced into New York by local drug manufacturer Eugene Schieffelin who has failed in efforts to introduce skylarks, song thrushes, and nightingales from his native Germany. Schieffelin releases 50 pairs of starlings, he will release another 20 pairs next year, and the birds will prey upon the English sparrows that have overrun Central Park since their introduction in 1850.

Washington's Rock Creek Park is set aside after years of congressional opposition. Development is begun on an urban green belt in the nation's capital that will be 4 miles long, up to 1 mile wide, and will embrace 2,213 acres.

Yosemite National Park is created by act of Congress which also creates Sequoia National Park. Yosemite embraces 761,320 acres on California's Tuolumne River; Sequoia embraces 386,863 acres that include Mt. Whitney in the California Sierras, highest mountain in the continental United States (14,494 feet).

Alaska has 38 salmon canneries, up from one or two in 1878, and 4,000 men sail north from San Francisco each summer to catch and can the fish, returning at the end of the 6-week season. Chinese from San Francisco's Chinatown work from 6 in the morning until 8 at night to cut, clean, and can the red salmon, chinooks, silversides, and dog salmon caught largely by Italians and Scandinavians (*see* Smith, 1903).

Canada's Massey-Harris farm equipment company is created by a merger of the Massey Manufacturing Company with its chief competitor A. Harris and Son to become the largest farm equipment producer in the British Empire (*see* 1849). H. A. Massey retired to Cleveland in 1871, his son Charles moved the company to Toronto in 1878 and acquired the Toronto Light Binder before dying prematurely in 1884, and Massey is again headed by H. A. Massey, now 67, who effects the merger.

A second Morrill act passed by Congress August 30 supplements the 1862 law and establishes experiment stations, extension services, and agricultural research programs to aid U.S. farmers.

Dropping the Pilot. When Kaiser Wilhelm sacked Bismarck, the man who had united Germany, he was caricatured in *Punch*.

From 75 to 90 percent of all Kansas farms are mortgaged at interest rates that average 9 percent. Roughly one third of all farm mortgages in the state have been foreclosed in the past decade, as farmers have been prevented by drought from producing enough to keep up interest payments on loans taken out to buy farm machinery and seed.

Kansas farmers are urged to "raise less corn and more hell" by Populist party leader Mary Elizabeth Cylens Lease, 36, who began speaking in behalf of Irish home rule in 1885 and who makes 161 speeches as she stumps the state. Told by "the Kansas Pythoness" that Kansas suffers "from two great robbers, the Santa Fe Railroad and the loan companies," the farmers vote against the Republicans and send representatives of an independent party to Congress.

Third-party platforms begin to call for federal warehouses in which farmers may store their crops and receive in return certificates redeemable in currency for 80 percent of the market price, permitting them to hold crops off the market until prices improve.

Cattlemen and sheepmen engage in open conflict as the once "inexhaustible" range of 17 western states and territories becomes fully stocked with 26 million head of cattle and 20 million head of sheep competing for grass on the prairie.

The Kern County Land Company is founded by speculators Lloyd Tevis and James Ben Ali Haggin who have battled Henry Miller and Charles Lux for Kern River water rights in California, have won 75 percent of the rights, and have seen their 400,000 acres in the lower San Joaquin Valley grow (*see* 1850; 1877). The company's lands will continue to grow until they cover 2,800 square miles, an area more than twice the size of Rhode Island (*see* oil, 1936).

The Babcock Tester that accurately measures the butterfat content of milk is invented by U.S. agricultural chemist Stephen Moulton Babcock, 47, in Wisconsin. Butterfat content is used as a basis for paying farmers, and the Babcock Tester measures it by dissolving the milk's casein in sulfuric acid to liberate the butterfat which is raised by centrifugal force into a glass tube for easy measurement.

Milk is pasteurized by law in many U.S. communities despite opposition by some dairy interests and by people who call pasteurization "unnatural" (*see* 1860; Evans, 1917).

New England dairyman H. P. Hood re-enters the retail distribution business but will not pasteurize his milk until 1896 (*see* 1854). Now 69, Hood has been joined by his sons George and Gilbert who help him consolidate some of the nearly 2,000 competing milk routes in Greater Boston, establish new ones, and set up new receiving stations for milk in various parts of New England (*see* 1897).

Unsweetened condensed milk is introduced commercially by the 5-year-old Helvetia Milk Condensing Company at Highland, Ill. (*see* Borden, 1855; Meyenberg, 1885; "Our Pet," 1894).

Margarine will be improved in the next few years by the addition of vegetable oils such as palm oil and arachis oil from peanuts (*see* 1889; Lever, 1911).

Peanut butter is invented by a St. Louis physician, who has developed the butter as a health food (*see* hydrogenation, 1901; Peter Pan, 1928; Skippy, 1932).

Cudahy Packing Company is founded by Irish-American meatpacker Michael Cudahy, 38, who was brought into the business 3 years ago by P. D. Armour, has gone into partnership with Armour in South Omaha, and who now takes over Armour's interest in the Armour-Cudahy Packing Company. Cudahy will introduce methods for curing meats under refrigeration and will develop improved railroad cars, making it possible to cure meat all year round and transport it to distant cities (*see* 1910).

A key opening device for rectangular meat cans is developed by Libby, McNeill & Libby (*see* 1878; 1891).

American Biscuit & Manufacturing Company is created by a merger of western bakeries under the leadership of Chicago lawyer Adolphus Williamson Green, 47, whose new company controls some 40 bakeries in 13 states (*see* National Biscuit, 1898).

The New York Biscuit Company is created by a merger of some 23 bakeries in 10 states, including Newburyport's 98-year-old John Pearson & Son and Boston's 89-year-old Bent & Company. Boston's 85-year-old Kennedy Biscuit Works has become the largest U.S. bakery, and it joins New York Biscuit in May as Chicago lawyer W. H. Moore of 1881 Diamond Match fame contributes financing and aggressive leadership in a bid to give his New York Biscuit Company control of the entire industry.

American Biscuit (above) is headed by St. Joseph, Mo., cracker baker F. L. Sommer whose Premium Saltines are famous for their parrot trademark and their "Polly wants a cracker" slogan. Sommer is dispatched by A. W. Green to open a bakery at New York that will challenge New York Biscuit in its own territory, and a price war begins that will continue until 1898.

The first aluminum saucepan is produced at Cleveland by Henry W. Avery whose wife will use the pan until 1933 (see 1888).

Canada Dry ginger ale has its beginnings in a small Toronto plant opened by local pharmacist John J. McLaughlin to manufacture carbonated water for sale to drugstores as a mixer for fruit juices and flavored extracts. McLaughlin will soon start making his own extracts and will develop a beverage he will call McLaughlin Belfast Style Ginger Ale (see 1907).

San Miguel beer is introduced by a Manila brewer.

Thomas Lipton enters the tea business to assure supplies of tea at low cost for his 300 grocery shops (see 1879). Lipton offers "The Finest the World Can Produce" at 1 shilling 7 pence per pound when the going price is roughly a shilling higher (see 1893).

The U.S. population reaches 62.9 million with two-thirds of it rural, down from 90 percent rural in 1840.

The population of Los Angeles reaches 50,000, up from 11,183 in 1880.

1891 The papal encyclical *Rerum novarum* issued May 15 by Leo XIII (Gioacchino Pecci) points out that employers have important moral duties as members of the possessing class and that one of society's first duties is to improve the position of the workers.

German factory workers win the right June 1 to form committees that will negotiate with employers on conditions of employment, and factory inspection is made more efficient.

The world's first old age pension plan goes into effect in Germany. Introduced by Prince von Bismarck in the Old Age Insurance Act of June 1889, the plan compels all workers to contribute if they are over age 16, are fully employed, and earn more than 2,000 marks ($500) per year. Employers must contribute equal amounts, and the pension is payable at age 70 to persons who have paid premiums for a minimum of 30 years (see Britain, 1908; U.S. Social Security Act, 1935).

U.S. workers strike throughout the year for higher wages and shorter hours.

New York's University Settlement is founded by wealthy citizens to take over the work begun 5 years ago by Stanton Coit. He has gone to England as ethical culture minister to London and will head the West London Ethical Culture Society while the new society in New York urges university students to volunteer as settlers in the city slums (see 1897).

A New Orleans lynch mob breaks into a city jail March 14 and kills 11 Italian immigrants who have been acquitted of murder—the worst lynching in U.S. history. Italian workers are at the bottom of the U.S. social heap and receive lower wages than any other workers, black or white.

Jim Crow laws are enacted in Alabama, Arkansas, Georgia, and Tennessee (see Mississippi, 1888; Supreme Court decision, 1896).

Chicago's Provident Hospital is the first U.S. interracial hospital. Established by black surgeon Daniel Hale Williams, 33, the new facility incorporates the first U.S. nurses training school for black women (see open heart surgery, 1893).

A Young Turk movement of exiles from the Ottoman Empire has its beginnings in a meeting at Geneva. The Young Turks subscribe to the provisions of the 1876 constitution.

The Hawaiian king David Kalakahua dies January 20 at age 54 after a 16-year reign and is succeeded by his 52-year-old sister who will reign until 1893 as Queen Lydia Liliuokalani. The white elite which owns 80 percent of arable lands in the islands have united in the Hawaiian League to oppose Kalakahua, who has favored the interests of sugar magnate Claus Spreckels, and the sugar planters form an Annexation Club in a plot to overthrow the queen (see Spreckels, 1883; abdication, 1893).

Leander Starr Jameson, M.D., 38, is made administrator of the South Africa Company's territories. A friend of Cecil Rhodes, Jameson is a Scottish physician who came to Kimberley in 1878 and has been employed by Rhodes to negotiate with the Matabele chief Lobengula (see 1893).

African copper mining is pioneered by a 31-year-old aide to Cecil Rhodes who sends an expedition north to study outcroppings observed by the late David Livingstone. The expedition sent out by Robert Williams reports back that the copper is across the border in Katanga territory owned by the king of the Belgians Leopold II, Williams goes to Leopold and negotiates an agreement under which the Katanga Company (Union Minière du Haut Katanga) is organized April 15 (see Benguela Railroad, 1903).

A new Colorado gold rush begins as thousands rush to Cripple Creek on the slopes of Pike's Peak following a strike by prospector Robert Wommack who has found paydirt at Poverty Gulch. The Cripple Creek mines will grow in the next 20 years to become the fifth largest producer in world history, they will yield nearly $1 billion in the yellow metal, and by the end of this decade the town of Cripple Creek will have 60,000 people, 147 active mining companies, 40 grocery stores, 17 churches, 25 schools, 15 hotels, 88 doctors and dentists, nearly 100 lawyers, a stock exchange, streetcars, 8 newspapers, and 139 24-hour saloons (see 1900).

The American Express Travelers Cheque copyrighted by the 41-year-old American Express Com-

1891 (cont.) pany will become an important means of protecting travelers' funds from theft and loss. American Express guarantees checks countersigned by the purchaser, pays banks a commission for selling the checks, receives a 1 percent commission from the purchaser, and enjoys the use of what will turn out to be vast sums of money interest-free. (Thomas Cook & Sons issued the first Travelers Cheques in 1874.)

Aluminum production gets a boost from Pittsburgh banker Andrew William Mellon, 36, who invests in the Pittsburgh Reduction Company that will soon be headed by his brother Richard and finances the mortgage of a new plant at New Kensington, Pa., for the company that will become the Aluminum Company of America (Alcoa) (*see* 1888; 1945).

National Lead Corporation is created by a merger of some 25 companies that supply white lead to U. S. paint makers. The company will grow to become a leading producer of paint (Dutch Boy), solder, lead shot for the steel industry, die castings, "solid" journal bearings for freight cars, lead for storage batteries, and the oil-well drilling mud baroid.

The first commercial bromine to be produced electrolytically is introduced by Herbert H. Dow's Midland Chemical Company, which Dow has established at Midland, Mich., with backing from Cleveland sewing machine maker J. H. Osborn (*see* 1889). Dow's bromine will find a good market in the pharmaceutical and photographic industries, and Dow begins work that will develop a process for producing chlorine electrolytically (*see* 1897; ethyl, 1924).

The Carborundum Company has its beginnings in an abrasive invented at Monongahela City, Pa., by engineer Edward Goodrich Acheson who runs an electric current through a mixture of silica and carbon to produce a material hard enough for rough polishing of diamonds, rubies, sapphires, and other gemstones. The material that Acheson sells at $880 per pound will replace emery, corundum, and other sanding and polishing materials.

The Frasch process for extracting sulfur economically is patented by German-American chemist Herman Frasch, 40, who has noted that sulfur melts at a fairly low temperature and is not soluble in water. His hot-water melting process permits production of cheap sulfuric acid for making superphosphate fertilizer and for countless other purposes and will be used by Frasch in October 1895 to extract sulfur from the salt dome discovered in 1869 in Louisiana.

Oklahoma Territory lands ceded to the United States by the Sauk, Fox, and Potawatomie open to white settlement September 18 by a presidential proclamation that opens 900,000 acres (*see* 1889; 1892).

The New York Central's *Empire State Express* travels 436 miles from New York to East Buffalo in a record-breaking 7 hours, 6 minutes.

Construction begins at Vladivostok on a Trans-Siberian Railway that has been financed in part by French financiers and by London's Baring Brothers. Russian convicts will perform most of the labor on the railway which will link Moscow with the Pacific Coast (*see* 1900).

A gasoline engine that will power a road vehicle is designed by Chicopee, Mass., bicycle designer Charles Edward Duryea, 29, and his toolmaker brother Franklin (*see* 1892; Benz, 1885, 1888).

The S. S. *Empress of India,* the S. S. *Empress of Japan,* and the S. S. *Empress of China* begin service out of Vancouver as the Canadian Pacific Railway moves into shipping (*see* 1888).

The Ocean Mail Subsidy Act passed by Congress authorizes subsidization of the U.S. merchant marine (*see* 1928; 1936).

Berlin's Koch Institute for Infectious Diseases opens with great nationalistic fanfare despite revelations that Koch's tuberculosis vaccine is ineffective.

The diphtheria antitoxin produced last year by Emil von Behring has hopelessly variable results on test animals until Koch Institute bacteriologist Paul Ehrlich, 37, shows Behring how to standardize his vaccine. Ehrlich increases the amount of antitoxin produced in the blood of a horse by steadily raising the amount of toxin injected, the diphtheria vaccine is given its first human application Christmas Eve on a child dying in a Berlin hospital, the child recovers and is discharged a week later, but while Behring will be made a baron and will grow rich on royalties from commercial sale of the vaccine, he will trick Ehrlich out of his share by persuading him that he will be granted an institute of his own if he renounces commercial royalties (*see* antisyphilis drug, 1909).

The University of Chicago is founded with help from merchant Marshall Field who gives 25 acres of land on which the university buildings will be erected and who will contribute $100,000 next year, but most of the funding comes from oilman John D. Rockefeller.

Drexel Institute is founded at Philadelphia with an endowment from local banker Anthony Joseph Drexel, 65, who has been co-owner since 1864 of the *Philadelphia Public Ledger.*

California Institute of Technology is founded at Pasadena.

Oklahoma A. and M. (Agricultural and Mechanical) is founded.

Hardin-Simmons University is founded by Baptists at Abilene, Tex.

American University is founded at Washington, D.C.

The Automatic Electric Company is organized to exploit a dial telephone patented by Kansas City undertaker Almon B. Strowger, who has convinced himself that "central" is diverting his incoming calls to a rival embalmer (*see* AT&T, Gary, 1919).

The first full-service advertising agency is established March 15 at New York by George Batten, 36, who offers "service contracts" under which his agency will handle copy, art, production, and placement of advertisements. Clients are relieved of any need to maintain their own elaborate advertising departments, and Batten is compensated by the media which pay him commissions on space rates (*see* ANPA, 1893; Calkins & Holden, 1902; BBDO, 1928).

Fiction *Tess of the d'Urburvilles* by Thomas Hardy portrays human tragedies rooted in the conflict between the changing society of industrial England and the rural ways of an earlier age; *The Story of Gosta Berling* (*Gosta Berlings Saga*) by Swedish novelist Selma Lagerlöf, 32; *The Heritage of Quincas Borba* (*Quincas Borba*) by Joachim Machado De Assis; *New Grub Street* by English novelist George Gissing, 33; *The Light That Failed* by Rudyard Kipling, who has returned to England from India; *The Little Minister* by English novelist James M. (Matthew) Barrie, 31, who will turn to writing for the stage next year; *Peter Ibbetson* by English artist-novelist George Louis Palmella Busson du Maurier, 57, who has worked for years on the staff of *Punch* and whose novel is autobiographical; *The Picture of Dorian Gray* by Oscar Wilde whose novel is attacked by some critics as "decadent" and "unmanly" for portraying a beautiful hedonist who retains his youthful good looks while his portrait shows the marks of time and dissipation; *Lord Arthur Savile's Crime and Other Stories* by Oscar Wilde; *News from Nowhere* (stories) by William Morris, now 57, who describes an English socialist commonwealth; *Main-Travelled Roads: Six Mississippi Valley Stories* by U.S. short story writer (Hannibal) Hamlin Garland, 31, who grew up in Wisconsin, Iowa, and the Dakota Territory, moved to Boston in 1884 to seek a literary career, and has been encouraged by William Dean Howells; *Tales of Soldiers and Civilians* by Ambrose Bierce is based on the author's Civil War experiences and contains the story "Occurrence at Owl Creek Bridge"; "A Scandal in Bohemia" by A. Conan Doyle in the July issue of the *Strand* magazine begins regular publication of Sherlock Holmes stories.

Poetry "The English Flag" by Rudyard Kipling: "And what should they know of England who only England know?"

Painting *Toilers of the Sea* by U.S. painter Albert Pinkham Ryder, 44; *The Bath* by Mary Cassatt; *The Good Judges* by James Ensor; *The Star of Bethlehem* by Edward Coley Burne-Jones; *Hail Mary* (*la Orana Maria*) by Paul Gauguin, who settles in Tahiti where he will live until 1893, *Vase of Tulips* by Gauguin. Henri de Toulouse-Lautrec produces his first music hall posters. Georges Seurat dies at Paris March 20 at age 31.

Theater *The Duchess of Padua* by Oscar Wilde 1/26 at New York's Broadway Theater; *Hedda Gabler* by Henrik Ibsen 2/26 at Oslo's Christiania Theater; *The American* by Henry James 7/26 at London's Opera-Comique, 70 perfs. (*see* 1877 novel).

Opera *Griseldis* 5/15 at the Comédie Française, Paris, with music by Jules Massenet.

Stage musicals *Cinder-Ellen up-too-late* 12/24 at London's Gaiety Theatre with Lottie Collins in the last successful presentation of burlesque, the light musical entertainment that has been popular for half a century but that will be replaced by musical comedy. (U.S. forms of burlesque will make the term disreputable with nudity and vulgarity.) Music and lyrics by Canadian-American songwriter-minstrel show manager Henry J. Sayers, 38, songs that include "Ta-ra-ra-boom-der-ay: did you see my wife today. No I saw her yesterday: ta-ra-ra-boom-der-ay," 236 perfs.

Carnegie Hall opens May 5 in West 57th Street, New York, with a concert conducted in part by Petr Ilich Tchaikovsky, who has come from Russia at the persuasion of Oratorio Society director Walter Damrosch. Built with a $2 million gift from steel magnate Andrew Carnegie, the new hall designed by architect William Burnett Tuthill will be New York's pre-eminent concert hall until late in 1962.

The Chicago Symphony is founded under the direction of German-American conductor Theodore Thomas, who has been bringing orchestras to Chicago since 1862 (*see* Orchestra Hall, 1904).

First performances Concerto No. 1 in F sharp minor for Piano and Orchestra by Moscow Conservatory student Sergei Vassilievich Rachmaninoff, 18, who will revise the work drastically 25 years hence; "March of the Dwarfs" by Edvard Grieg; Orchestral Suite in A minor by Edward MacDowell in September at England's Worcester Festival.

Basketball is invented at Springfield, Mass., by Canadian-American physical education director James Naismith, 30, who is taking a course at the YMCA Training School in Springfield and who has been assigned with his classmates the project of inventing a game that will occupy students between the football and baseball seasons. Naismith sets up fruit baskets atop ladders and establishes rules that will be used in the first publicly held game in March of next year and will never be substantially changed.

A new Polo Grounds is erected for the New York Giants baseball club to replace a small 6,000-seat polo stadium first used by the Giants in 1883. By 1894 the Giants will set a league attendance record of 400,000 for the year (*see* 1958; Yankee Stadium, 1923).

John Joseph McGraw, 18, joins the Baltimore Orioles to begin a 41-year career in major league baseball. McGraw will be appointed manager of the New York Giants in July 1902 and will continue as player-manager until 1906, when he will retire with a lifetime batting average of .334 after having helped the Giants win two National League pennants and a World Series victory, and he will continue as manager of the Giants until June 1932,

The first football rule book is written by Walter Camp, who invents the scrimmage line, the 11-man

1891 (cont.) team, signals, and the quarterback position (*see* 1889; 1898).

💲 Atlanta's Davison-Paxon department store has its origin in a dry goods shop opened by merchants Beaumont Davison and Frederick J. Paxon whose store will become the city's second largest (*see* Rich's, 1867; R. H. Macy, 1925).

J. W. Robinson Company opens at Los Angeles across from City Hall in Spring Street. Massachusetts merchant Joseph Winchester Robinson opened his Boston Dry Goods Store early in 1883 and has moved into larger quarters.

🏛 Chicago's new Monadnock building at 53 West Jackson Street relies completely on functional form. Burnham & Root of 1886 Rookery fame have made a clean break with traditional styles of architecture and have employed advanced techniques of steel frame construction and utter simplicity of design.

Boston's Ames building goes up at the corner of Tremont and Washington Streets. The city's first skyscraper rises 13 stories above the street.

Ochre Court at Newport, R. I., is completed in late Gothic French château style for New York real estate magnate Ogden Goelet.

Denver's Brown Palace Hotel opens as prospectors crowd into Cripple Creek to make their fortunes in the goldfields (above). Carpenter Henry C. Brown arrived by oxcart at Cherry Creek in 1860 and by 1888 owned much of the miners' encampment that became Denver.

Florida's Tampa Bay Hotel goes up as railroad magnate Henry Bradley Plant of Atlanta's Southern Express Company tries to make Tampa a popular winter resort in competition with the East Coast resorts of H. M. Flagler (*see* 1888). Now 71, Plant has organized the Savannah, Florida, and Western Railroad and architect J. A. Wood has modeled Plant's ornate $3 million hotel with its 13 minarets on Granada's Alhambra Palace of 1354.

🌐 The Forest Reserves Act passed by Congress March 3 authorizes withdrawal of public lands for a national forest reserve as lumber king Frederick Weyerhaeuser expands his holdings (*see* 1870). With timber resources being consumed and wasted at an alarming rate, Secretary of the Interior John W. Noble has persuaded congressmen to insert a rider in a public lands build authorizing the president "from time to time, [to] set apart and reserve [forest lands] in any state or territory having public lands wholly or in part covered with timber and undergrowth. . . ." Some 13 million acres will be set aside in President Harrison's administration to begin a policy that will set aside more than 185 million acres of national forests in 40 states in the next 80 years (*see* 1905).

The New York Botanical Garden opens in the Bronx.

👤 Russian crops fail, millions are reduced to starvation, and the rural peasantry raids towns in search of food.

President Harrison responds to an appeal by Cassius Marcellus Clay, 81, who was Abraham Lincoln's minister to Russia. Harrison orders U.S. flour to be shipped to the Russians (*see* 1892).

🌾 Kansas farmers are bankrupted by tight money conditions. Some 18,000 prairie schooners (covered wagons) cross the Mississippi headed back east (*see* 1889; 1890; 1894).

☂ British butchers convicted of selling meat unfit for human consumption may be required on a second offense to put up signs on their shops stating their record. A Public Health Act passed by Parliament provides for the public exposure of wrongdoing.

🍴 Rath Packing Company is founded at Waterloo, Iowa, by E. F. and J. W. Rath whose firm will be a worldwide supplier of canned and smoked hams, bacon, sausage, and luncheon meats.

Beech-Nut Packing Company has its beginnings in the Imperial Packing Company founded at Canajoharie, N. Y., by Raymond Lipe, Walter Lipe, Bartlett Arkell, and John Zieley (*see* 1899).

Ceresota flour is introduced by Northwestern Consolidated Milling Company, a new firm created by a merger of six Minneapolis millers who have been disturbed by the 1889 Pillsbury-Washburn merger.

The American Sugar Refining Company is incorporated in New Jersey by H. O. Havemeyer whose 4-year-old Sugar Refineries Company is dissolved by the New York courts. "Trust certificates" in the old company are exchanged one-for-one for shares in the new company which begins taking over the entire U.S. sugar industry in one colossal trust (*see* 1892).

H. O. Havemeyer (above) will enter the coffee business in a bid to keep John Arbuckle out of the sugar business. Arbuckle, 52, is the largest individual owner of shipping under U.S. registry and is the nation's leading coffee importer (*see* Yuban, 1944).

The first machine to solder rectangular tins automatically is invented by a Libby, McNeill & Libby employee. The new machine supplements one invented earlier by Libby employee James Brown whose machine solders round tins, and it will save Libby $50,000 its first year (*see* 1890; 1906).

The "Del Monte" label that will become the leading label for U.S. canned fruits and vegetables is used for the first time. Executives of the Oakland Preserving Company at Oakland, Calif., have been inspired by Charles Crocker's 11-year-old Del Monte Hotel at Monterey and use its name to identify their premium quality fruit ("extras") (*see* 1865; 1895).

The first electric oven for commercial sale is introduced at St. Paul, Minn., by the Carpenter Electric Heating Manufacturing Company.

Coca-Cola ownership is acquired for $2,300 by Atlanta pharmacist Asa G. Candler, 40, who buys up stock in the firm but who will achieve great success only when he changes Coca-Cola advertising to end claims such as "Wonderful Nerve and Brain Tonic and Remarkable Therapeutic Agent" and "Its beneficial effects upon diseases of the vocal chords are wonderful." Candler will make Coca-Cola syrup the basis of a popular 5-cent soft drink (see 1886; 1892).

New York City has more soda fountains than saloons. *Harper's Weekly* reports that marble chips from the construction of St. Patrick's Cathedral on Fifth Avenue are being used to make sulfuric acid for the production of 25 million gallons of soda water.

New York's Gristede Brothers grocery chain begins with a carriage trade store opened by Diedrich and Charles Gristede at 42nd Street and Second Avenue.

Congress votes March 3 to establish a U.S. Office of Superintendent of Immigration (see 1894).

Canada gets her first Ukrainian immigration influx (see Mennonites, 1874). Ukrainians will comprise Canada's fourth largest population group after the French, Irish, and English.

Overpopulation begins to cause worry in Japan.

1892 The Egyptian khedive Mohammed Tewfik dies January 7 at age 39 after a 12-year reign in which he has been forced to let the British establish a virtual protectorate and has let the Mahdi take the Sudan. Tewfik is succeeded by his headstrong 17-year-old son who will reign until 1914 as Abbas II and who will retake the Sudan.

French forces depose the king of Dahomey but encounter resistance in the form of native uprisings against imperialism.

French forces under Colonel Louis Archinard defeat the Fulani on the Upper Niger and take Segu.

British explorer Sir Harry Hamilton Johnston, 34, subdues Angoni and Arab uprisings in Nyasaland.

Britain's second Salisbury ministry falls in the general election August 13 after 6 years in power; a fourth Gladstone cabinet takes office August 18.

President Harrison loses his bid for re-election as the Democrats campaign on a platform opposing the McKinley Tariff Act of 1890 and re-elect Grover Cleveland with 277 electoral votes to Harrison's 145. Cleveland wins 46 percent of the popular vote, Harrison 43 percent, the Populist candidate 22 percent.

A presidential proclamation April 19 opens some 3 million acres of Arapaho and Cheyenne lands in Oklahoma to settlement (see 1891; 1893).

Homestead, Pa., steel workers strike the Carnegie-Phipps mill in June and are refused a union contract by managing head Henry Clay Frick who calls in Pinkerton guards to suppress the strike. Men are shot on both sides, Frick himself is shot and stabbed by Polish-American anarchist Alexander Berkman, 22, but recovers, union organizers are dismissed, and the men go back to working their 12-hour shifts November 20 after nearly 5 months of work stoppage. Andrew Carnegie's income for the year is $4 million, down only $300,000 from 1891 (see 1888; Carnegie Steel Company, 1899).

"American workmen are subjected to peril of life and limb as great as a soldier in time of war," says President Harrison.

Australia has a bitter strike that closes down ports, mines, and sheep-shearing stations and is ended only by military intervention. The 7-year-old Broken Hill Proprietary Company and other mining companies will not make peace with the unions until 1923.

Arab slaveholders in the Belgian Congo rebel beginning in mid-May and are defeated November 22 by Belgian forces under Baron François Dhanis, 31. Forced labor of Congo natives is introduced December 5 in the guise of taxes to be paid in labor.

Shell Oil Company has its beginnings as English entrepreneur Marcus Samuel, 57, sends his first tanker through the Suez Canal with oil for Singapore, Bangkok, and other destinations to break the Standard Oil Company monopoly in the Far East. Samuel and his brother control the trading company of M. Samuel & Company started in 1830 by their late father and Marcus's namesake, who chose the company's shell emblem because he had earlier been in the seashell business (see Royal Dutch-Shell, 1907).

John D. Rockefeller's Standard Oil Trust is outlawed under the 1890 Sherman Act by the Ohio Supreme Court, but control of the trust properties are kept in Rockefeller hands by Standard Oil of New Jersey, a new company incorporated under a recent New Jersey holding company law that permits companies chartered at Trenton to hold stock in other corporations (see 1883; Lake Superior Consolidated Iron Mines, 1893; Supreme Court decision, 1911).

An improved carburetor that mixes vaporized fuel with air to create a combustible or explosive gas is invented by Germany's Gottlieb Daimler (see 1890; Lenoir, 1860; Maybach, 1893).

Philips and Co. begins production of incandescent electric lamps at Eindhoven, the Netherlands. Mechanical engineer Gerard Leonard Frederik Philips, 33, and his banker father founded the company last year with a staff of 10 in a vacant buckskin factory, but the firm will show no profit until 1895, when Gerard's youngest brother Anton Frederik Philips, now 18, joins the firm and proves to be a master salesman. He will obtain a contract to supply the Russian court with 50,000 lightbulbs per year, Philips will be the third largest European lamp producer by the turn of the century, it will reorganize in 1912 under the name N. V. Philips' Gloeilampenfabrieken, and by 1978 it will have more than 400,000 employees worldwide producing and selling products and services often far removed from lightbulbs.

General Electric Company is created through a merger engineered by New York financier J. P. Morgan who combines Henry Villard's Edison General Electric Company with Charles A. Coffin's Thomson-Houston Company (see 1883; MAZDA lamps, 1909).

The law of hysteresis whose application will improve the efficiency of electric motors, generators, and

1892 (cont.) transformers is discovered by German-American engineer Charles Proteus Steinmetz, 27, who fled Berlin 4 years ago to escape prosecution in connection with a socialist newspaper he was editing and who came to the United States a year later. A hunchbacked wizard, Steinmetz changed his name from Karl August Rudolf to Charles Proteus, using the nickname Proteus given him when he was a student at the University of Breslau.

The Steinmetz discovery (above) permits engineers to forecast accurately how much electric power will be lost as a result of residual magnetism in electromagnets and will result in generators and motors designed to minimize such loss (*see* 1893).

Cutler-Hammer Company is started at Milwaukee by engineer H. H. Cutler and promoter E. W. Hammer. Cutler will soon produce a "starter box" for streetcars that will permit a streetcar operator to start his motor by slowly moving a handle to the right, sending it over brass contacts, and thereby cutting out some resistance coils in succession to allow increasing amounts of current to reach the motor which accelerates as the handle is moved.

The first U.S. motorcar is produced by some accounts at Springfield, Mass., where Charles and Franklin Duryea complete a gasoline buggy with a four-cycle water-cooled engine and a rubber and leather transmission (*see* 1891; Chicago-Milwaukee race, 1895).

The first motorcar to be equipped with pneumatic tires is produced by French automakers René Panhard and E. C. Levassor (*see* 1889).

South Africa's first trains from Capetown reach Johannesburg in September and begin to generate income that will be important to the Cape Colony's finances.

Chicago's first elevated railway goes into operation to begin the "Loop" that will circle the city's downtown area. The "Alley L" line on the South Side will be expanded to serve much of the city.

The science of virology is pioneered by Russian botanist Dmitri Iosifovich Ivanovski, 28, who discovers filterable viruses (*see* Beljerinck, 1895).

Cholera is introduced into the United States August 30 by steerage passengers from the Hamburg-Amerika line ship S.S. *Moravia.*

The American School of Osteopathy is founded at Kirksville, Mo., by Andrew T. Still who will begin publishing the *Journal of Osteopathy* in 1894 (*see* 1875). The practice of osteopathy eschews use of drugs, it will spread quickly, and most states will eventually accord it legal recognition equivalent to that of orthodox medical practice.

A new method for producing viscose rayon patented by English chemists Charles Frederick Cross, 37, and Edward John Bevan is safer than the Chardonnet nitrocellulose process of 1883 and cheaper than the cuprammonium process. Cross and Bevan dissolve cellulose in a mixture of carbon disulfide and sodium xanthate, and they squirt the viscous solution through fine holes to produce spinnable fibers (*see* Little, 1902; Viscose Company, 1910).

Union Carbide Corporation has its beginnings at Spray, N.C., where local entrepreneurs Thomas Leopold Willson and James T. Morehead accidentally produce calcium carbide while trying to make aluminum in an electric furnace or to produce metallic calcium by fusing lime and coal tar. Molten slag from their operation is dumped into a nearby stream and liberates a gas, and they discover that the gas is acetylene (carbide gas) which can be used in lighting. They will establish the first commercial carbide factory at Spray in 1894, and they will found the National Carbide Sales Corporation to market acetylene (soon found to be effective for cutting metal) (*see* Claude, 1897; ferrochrome, 1897; Union Carbide, 1906).

The $1 Ingersoll pocket watch is introduced by U.S. mail-order and chain store entrepreneur Robert Hawley Ingersoll, 33. "The watch that made the dollar famous" will be a huge success, but Ingersoll's company will be insolvent by 1921, and he will sell its assets to Waterbury Clock Company of Connecticut in 1922 (*see* Timex, 1946).

Hamilton Watch Company is founded at Lancaster, Pa., by entrepreneur James Hamilton and 17 subscribers who take over the 18-year-old Adams and Perry watch factory that has been forced to suspend operations. Hamilton adds a new wing to the factory, and he introduces a "turnip" watch designed by Harry J. Cain—first Hamilton watch to meet the Time Inspection Rules established by U.S. railroads last year after a bad accident (the "watch of railroad accuracy" will be produced for 33 years).

Economic depression begins in the United States, but the country has 4,000 millionaires, up from fewer than 20 in 1840.

Bache & Co. is created by a reorganization of the 13-year-old New York brokerage house Leopold Cahn & Co. under the direction of financier Jules Semon Bache, now 30, who joined the firm as a cashier in 1880, became a partner in 1886, and will expand the firm from a one-room operation with 15 employees to a house with 37 branches and 800 employees (*see* American Glucose, 1898).

The United States Rubber Company is created by an amalgamation of four major firms under the direction of rubber importer Charles A. Flint.

The Dalton gang from Oklahoma Territory arrives at Coffeyville, Kan., the morning of October 5 with the intention of robbing two banks, but the aroused townspeople meet the gang with heavy gunfire. Former train robbers Robert Dalton, 25, and his brother Grattan fall dead along with two others.

The Illinois Institute of Technology is founded at Chicago.

The University of Rhode Island is founded at Kingston.

Ithaca College is founded at Ithaca, N.Y.

The University of New Mexico begins classes at Albuquerque in the New Mexico Territory.

A "pledge of allegiance" for U.S. schoolchildren to recite October 12 in commemoration of the discovery of America 400 years ago says simply, "I pledge allegiance to my flag, and to the Republic for which it stands, one nation, indivisible, with liberty and justice for all." Former clergyman Francis Bellamy, 36, who writes for *The Youth's Companion* has composed the pledge, generations of schoolchildren will mumble "for Richard Sands" instead of "for which it stands," "my flag" will be changed to "the flag of the United States of America" (and *see* 1954).

Telephone service between New York and Chicago begins October 18.

The *Toronto Star* begins publication.

The Ridder newspaper chain that will grow to include 19 daily newspapers, most of them in the West and Midwest, has its beginnings as German-American publisher Herman Ridder acquires the New York German-language newspaper *Staats-Zeitung und Herold* (see Knight, 1903).

Baltimore's *Afro-American* begins publication on a semiweekly basis with John Murphy as editor.

The Addressograph invented by Sioux City, Iowa, engineer Joseph Smith Duncan prints mailing addresses automatically. Duncan will obtain a patent for his "addressing machine" in 1896, his first model employs a revolving hexagonal block of wood to which he has glued rubber type torn from rubber stamps, a new name and address advances to the printing point each time the block is turned, and the process of turning the block re-inks the type. Duncan will put a more refined model into production in late July of next year from a back office in Chicago.

Fiction   *The American Claimant* by Mark Twain; *The Children of the Ghetto* by English novelist-playwright Israel Zangwill, 28, whose Russian Jewish parents came to England as refugees in 1848; *The Soul of Lillith* by Marie Corelli; *The Intruder* (*L'Innocente*) by Gabriele D'Annunzio; *The Adventures of Sherlock Holmes* by A. Conan Doyle.

Poetry   *Barrack-Room Ballads* by Rudyard Kipling includes "Gunga Din," "If," and "The Road to Mandalay"; *The Song of the Sword* by English poet William Ernest Henley, 43, includes his poem "England, My England" and his 1891 poem "Non Sum Qualis Eram Bonae Sub Regno Cynarae" with the line "I have been faithful to thee, Cynara! in my fashion." Henley lost a foot to tuberculosis at age 12, he has gathered about him a group of young writers including Kipling (above) whose imperialist sentiments jibe with his own, and he collaborates with Robert Louis Stevenson on three plays.

Painting   *The Spirit of the Dead Watching* and *Aha ce feii* (*Why, you are jealous*) by Paul Gauguin; *At the Moulin Rouge* and *Au Lit, Le Baiser* by Henri de Toulouse-Lautrec; *Woman Sweeping* by French painter Jean Edouard Vuillard, 23.

Theater   *Lady Windermere's Fan* by Oscar Wilde 2/22 at the St. James's Theatre, London. Wilde calls a cynic "a man who knows the price of everything and the value of nothing" (III). *Walker, London* by James M. Barrie 2/25 at Toole's Theatre, London; *Monsieur Goes Hunting!* (*Monsieur chasse*) by Georges Feydeau 4/23 at the Théâtre du Palais Royal, Paris; *Champignol in Spite of Himself* (*Champignol malgré lui*) by Georges Feydeau and a collaborator 11/5 at the Théâtre des Nouveautés, Paris; *Widowers' Houses* by George Bernard Shaw 12/9 at London's Royalty Theatre; *Charley's Aunt* by English actor-playwright Brandon Thomas, 36, 12/21 at London's Royalty Theatre, 1,466 perfs. (*see* 1948).

Opera   *Pagliacci* 5/21 at Milan's Teatro dal Verme, with music by Italian composer Ruggiero Leoncavallo, 34, who delights audiences with his aria "Vesti la Giubba"; *Mlada* 10/20 at St. Petersburg's Maryinsky Theater, with music by Nikolai Rimski-Korsakov that includes "Night on Mount Triglov"; *Iolanta* 12/18 at St. Petersburg's Maryinsky Theater, with music by Petr Ilich Tchaikovsky.

Ballet   *The Nutcracker Suite* (*Casse-Noisette*) 12/17 at St. Petersburg's Maryinsky Theater, with music by Petr Ilich Tchaikovsky.

First performances   *Carneval* Overture by Anton Dvorak 4/28 at Prague on the eve of the composer's departure for New York; Prelude in C sharp minor by Sergei Rachmaninoff 9/24 at Moscow; Symphony No. 8 in C minor by Anton Bruckner 12/18 at Vienna.

Popular songs   "Daisy Bell (A Bicycle Built for Two)" by English songwriter Harry Dacre (Frank Dean) who is visiting America; "The Bowery" by English-American composer Percy Gaunt, 40, lyrics by Charles H. Hoyt.

La vie Parisienne found vivid expression in the lithographs of the deformed painter Henri de Toulouse-Lautrec.

1892 (cont.) The first title match prizefight to be fought with padded gloves and according to the 25-year-old marquis of Queensberry rules is held September 7 at New Orleans. James John "Gentleman Jim" Corbett, 26, scores a knockout in the 21st round to take the heavyweight title from the "Boston Strong Boy" John Lawrence Sullivan—the "Great John L."

Chicago's 16-year-old A. G. Spalding Company acquires the Wright & Ditson Company started by cricketer-baseball player George Wright and becomes a major factor in the production of tennis balls and tennis rackets. Spalding also begins making golf clubs and balls that will so improve the game that golf will gain new popularity not only in the United States but also in Britain.

Chicago salesman William Wrigley, Jr., 30, starts selling chewing gum, which is now being made by at least 12 companies (*see* Adams, 1872). Wrigley started as a soap salesman, he offered baking powder as a premium to his wholesale soap customers, he switched to selling baking powder, he has offered two packages of chewing gum with each can of baking powder, and he has been so encouraged by the response that he turns all his efforts to selling chewing gum (*see* 1893).

Cold cream is introduced by New York apothecaries V. Chapin Daggett and Clifford Ramsdell who substitute white mineral oil for the perishable vegetable oils that have been used until now and that have made face creams turn rancid in short order.

Book matches are patented by U.S. inventor Joshua Pusey, whose matches contain poisonous white phosphorus that will be replaced by safer chemicals in 1911 (*see* Lundstrom, 1853).

Player's Navy Cut cigarettes are introduced at London.

Wills's Three Castle cigarettes are packed in the first push-up cardboard cigarette packets (*see* 1878; Imperial Tobacco Company, 1901).

Stix, Baer & Fuller is founded at St. Louis by Cincinnati merchant Charles Aaron Stix, 31, in association with J. A. Baer, L. Baer, and Aaron Fuller who remain at Fort Smith to manage the Boston Store in that town. The new dry goods store will soon be the largest department store west of the Mississippi.

St. Louis' Famous Company is acquired for $150,000 in cash by May Company founder David May and his three brothers-in-law who have prospered at Leadville and Denver (*see* 1888). Famous will acquire the 43-year-old William Barr Dry Goods Store, it will rename itself Famous-Barr, and it will become the leading St. Louis retail enterprise (*see* 1910).

New York's Judson Memorial Church is completed on Washington Square by architect Stanford White.

New York's St. John the Divine is begun on an 11.5-acre site acquired last year on Morningside Heights by the Episcopal diocese of New York for $850,000.

Planned as the world's largest cathedral, the great church, whose cornerstone is laid December 27, has been designed by George Lewis Heins and Christopher Grant La Farge who will be succeeded by Ralph Adams Cram and Frank E. Ferguson in 1911.

Brooklyn's Grand Army Plaza is graced with a Soldiers' and Sailors' Memorial Arch dedicated to the Civil War dead. The arch serves as an entrance to Prospect Park.

Marble House is completed at Newport, R.I., by architect Richard Morris Hunt for railroad heir William K. Vanderbilt, now 42. The summer "cottage" on Bellevue Avenue has lines derived from those of the Grand Trianon and Petit Trianon at Versailles and will be augmented in 1913 by a lacquered Chinese teahouse on Cliff Walk.

The Reno Inclined Elevator patented by New York inventor Jesse W. Reno March 15 is the world's first escalator. The Reno escalator will be installed in the fall of 1896 at Coney Island's Old Iron Pier, but the flat-step moving staircase patented by U.S. inventor Charles A. Wheeler August 2 is the first practical escalator. (It will never be built, but inventor Charles D. Seeberger will buy Wheeler's patent, he will incorporate its basic feature in his own improved design, he will have Otis Elevator Company produce it, and the Seeberger Escalator will be used at the Paris Exposition of 1900 and at Gimbels department store at Philadelphia in 1901.)

The Sierra Club is founded by John Muir and others to protect America's natural environment (*see* 1876; Muir Woods, 1908).

New York State's Adirondack Park is created by the state legislature which sets up the nation's largest forest reserve: "The Forest Preserve shall be forever kept as wild forest lands."

New York City gets new torrents of clean drinking water as the $24 million New Croton Aqueduct is completed after 7 years of construction (*see* 1842; Catskill system, 1917).

Famine cripples Russia, but by late January, some 3 million barrels of U.S. flour are en route to relieve the starvation that is killing millions (*see* 1891).

The Populist party polls more than a million votes in the U.S. presidential election (above) as farmers register their protest against the railroads and against farm machine makers.

The first successful U.S. gasoline tractor is produced by Waterloo, Iowa, farmer John Froelich who will organize the Waterloo Gasoline Traction Engine Company early next year. The company will be acquired by the John Deere Plow Company (*see* 1902).

Cheap grain from America and Russia depresses French farm prices. Only one French farm holding in 15 has a horse-drawn cultivator, only one in 150 has a mechanical reaper, and French farmers demand higher import duties to protect them from more efficient overseas competitors.

Canadian wheat production is advanced by druggist William Saunders, 56, who has been named to head the Dominion Experimental Farms. Saunders crosses Red Fife wheat with an early ripening variety obtained from India and produces the hardy Markham wheat strain on a farm in British Columbia (*see* Mackay, 1886).

A method for eradicating tuberculosis from dairy herds is developed by Danish veterinarian Bernhard Laurits Frederik Bang, 44 (*see* Bang's disease, 1896).

The first U.S. cattle tuberculosis test is made March 3 on a herd at Villa Nova, Pa., with tuberculin brought from Europe by the dean of the University of Pennsylvania veterinary department.

A campaign for pasteurized milk is launched by R. H. Macy partner Nathan Straus who will establish milk stations in New York and other large cities.

Congress is petitioned to hold pure food law hearings (*see* 1889; Wiley, 1902).

The *Ladies' Home Journal* announces that it will accept no more patent medicine advertisements. The *Journal* has been edited since 1889 by Dutch-American editor Edward William Bok, 29 (*see* 1883; 1904).

The Coca-Cola Company is organized by Asa Candler at Atlanta (*see* 1891; 1895).

A clamp-on tin-plated steel bottle cap with an inner seal disk of natural cork and a flanged edge is patented by Baltimore machine-shop foreman William Painter, 54, who also patents a capping machine for beer and soft drink bottles. The new bottle cap will replace the unsanitary Miller Plunger patented in 1874 and the 1878 Hutchinson Bottle Stopper which are both widely used. Painter will design an automatic filler and capper with a capacity of 60 to 100 bottles per minute, and he will establish the Crown Cork and Seal Company at Baltimore to market his bottle caps and machines (*see* Gillette, 1895; New Process Cork, 1913).

The first Hawaiian pineapple cannery opens (*see* Dole, 1902).

American Sugar Refining Company controls 98 percent of the U.S. sugar industry, and H. O. Havemeyer's Sugar Trust uses political influence to suppress foreign competition with tariff walls. The company saves itself millions of dollars per year in duties by having its raw sugar imports shortweighted (*see* 1891; 1895; Spreckels, 1897).

Evaporated milk is added to the Borden product line of the New York Condensed Milk Company (*see* 1885; Meyenberg, 1885).

Liederkranz cheese is invented by Monroe, N.Y., delicatessen man Emile Frey, 23, whose employer gives the new cheese its name after winning approval of its taste from his choral society which calls itself Liederkranz and has its own Liederkranz Hall on New York's East 58th Street. The cheese is a milder version of Limburger and will be produced by the Monroe Cheese Company (*see* 1926; Jossi, 1877; Borden, 1929).

George A. Hormel Company is founded by Austin, Minn., butcher-meatpacker George Albert Hormel, 31, (who pronounces his name with emphasis on the first syllable). Hormel converted an abandoned creamery on the Cedar River into an abbatoir last year, he slaughters 610 hogs by year's end, and he will personally split 100,000 carcasses before letting anyone else do the job as he builds a ham, bacon, sausage, and fresh pork business (*see* 1926).

Fig Newtons are introduced by the 87-year-old Kennedy Biscuit Works of the 2-year-old New York Biscuit Company. Kennedy bakery manager James Hazen has been persuaded to try out a new machine to make preserve-filled cookies invented by Philadelphian James Henry Mitchell, and he calls the cookies Newtons after having named a series of earlier cookies Beacon Hill, Brighton, and Melrose. Since the preserve most often used to fill the cookies is fig preserve, the cookies made by other New York Biscuit bakeries to fill a rising demand will be Fig Newtons (*see* National Biscuit Company, 1898).

Heublein Club Cocktails are introduced at Hartford, Conn., by the 17-year-old firm of G. F. Heublein & Bro. started by the restauranteur's sons Gilbert and Louis Heublein. The Connecticut governor's Foot Guards have ordered a gallon of Martinis and a gallon of Manhattans prepared in advance for an outing, the outing has been rained out two weekends in a row, the prepared cocktails are about to be dumped, but a dubious taste reveals that they are better than when freshly made, and the Heublein brothers are inspired to bring out the world's first bottled cocktails (*see* A-1 Sauce, 1906).

Campari aperitif is introduced by Italian entrepreneur Davide Campari whose father Gaspare opened a cafe at Milan in 1867. The younger Campari opens a factory at Sesto Giovanni to produce the aperitif after studying the art in France.

Minimum age for marriage of Italian girls is raised by law to 12.

The *padrone* system that prevails in Italian immigration to the United States is resisted by Roman Catholic missionaries who open the Church of Our Lady of Pompeii in a storefront at 113 Waverly Place, New York, to help immigrants whose passage has been paid by *padrones* to whom the immigrants are bound almost as indentured servants. The clergymen will open a church at 25 Carmine Street in 1925.

New York's immigrant receiving station moves to Ellis Island in the Upper Bay of New York Harbor after the receiving station at Castle Garden established in 1855 has received nearly 7.7 million immigrants. Castle Garden will be turned into an aquarium in 1896, and 27.5-acre Ellis Island will process immigrants until 1932.

The Geary Chinese Exclusion Act passed by Congress May 5 extends for another 10 years all existing

1892 (cont.) Chinese exclusion laws and requires all Chinese residing in the United States to register within a year or face deportation (*see* 1902).

1893 "The Significance of the Frontier in American History" by University of Wisconsin historian Frederick Jackson Turner, 31, observes that the American frontier has been the source of the individualism, the self-reliance, the inventiveness, and the restless energy that have been so characteristic of Americans but that the frontier is now ending. Turner delivers his paper at a meeting of the American Historical Association held at Chicago during the Columbian Exposition that opens to show the world what progress Chicago has made since the fire of 1871.

A vast section of northern Oklahoma Territory opens to land-hungry settlers September 16. Thousands of "Boomers" jump at a signal from federal marshals and rush in by foot, on horseback, in buggies and wagons, and on bicycles to stake and claim quarter-section farms, but as in 1889, they find that "Sooners" have sneaked across the line earlier by cover of night and have started building houses on the 165-mile by 58-mile Cherokee Strip—6 million acres purchased from the Cherokees in 1891 for $8.5 million.

West Africa is explored by English naturalist Mary Kingsley, 30, who is taken down the Ogowe River through cannibal country by Fang tribesmen. A niece of the late novelist-poet Charles Kingsley, she photographs wildlife and finds beetles never before cataloged.

Norwegian Arctic explorer Fridtjof Nansen, 32, tries to drift across the polar basin in the icebound ship *Fram.* Nansen led the first expedition to cross Greenland in 1888, he will drift for 18 months in the *Fram,* and he will then travel with a companion by sledge and skis across the ice to 86° 14' north, the northernmost point yet reached by any explorer (*see* 1909).

The Hawaiian queen Liliukoalani, who has reigned for less than 2 years, is overthrown by annexationists with support from U.S. minister John Leavitt Stevens. Armed marines from the U.S.S. *Boston* are landed January 16 to "protect" U.S. interests, the queen abdicates under duress January 17, and annexationists block U.S. efforts to restore the monarchy (*see* 1894).

Laos becomes a French protectorate as France begins to develop a new colonial empire in Indo-China. Colonel Simon Gallieni, 44, and Louis Robert Gonzalve Lyautey, 39, move to pacify a region as large as France herself with 16 million inhabitants whose country will be securely in French control by 1895.

France establishes French Guiana in South America and the Ivory Coast in Africa as formal colonies.

French colonial forces on the Niger River defeat Tuareg warriors.

Transvaal annexes Swaziland.

Natal gains self-government.

The king of the Matabele Lobengula leads a revolt against the British South Africa Company of Cecil Rhodes, but Leander Starr Jameson cuts the Matabele down with machine-gun fire October 23, suppresses the revolt, forces Lobengula to give up his capital Bulawayo, and drives the Matabele king into exile where he will die next year (*see* 1891; 1894).

Economic depression continues in America as European investors withdraw funds.

The Philadelphia and Reading Railroad goes into receivership February 20 with debts of $125 million and is soon joined by the Northern Pacific, the Union Pacific, the Erie, and the Santa Fe. Foreclosures in this decade will affect 41,000 miles of U.S. railroad track—15 percent of the total.

Wall Street stock prices take a sudden drop May 5, the market collapses June 27, 600 banks close their doors, more than 15,000 business firms fail, and 74 railroads go into receivership in a depression that will continue for 4 more years.

The Sherman Silver Purchase Act of 1890 is repealed by Congress October 31, and the United States returns to the gold standard that will be retained until April 1933. Silver prices collapse; silver barons such as Colorado's "Hod" Tabor are bankrupted (*see* 1880).

The Lake Superior Consolidated Iron Mines Company is created by oil magnate John D. Rockefeller who has loaned the Merritt brothers $420,000 to develop the Mesabi iron mines of Minnesota and to build a railroad to Duluth (*see* 1890). Rockefeller has called the loan on short notice, the Merritt brothers have not been able to pay, they have been obliged to forfeit their properties, and Rockefeller's $29.4 million company leases the properties to Henry Clay Frick of the Carnegie-Phipps mill at Homestead, Pa. (*see* 1892; Carnegie, Oliver, 1896).

Kelly's Industrial Army marches on Washington, D.C., 1,500 strong to demand relief which is not forthcoming from Congress. Led by "General" Charles T. Kelly, the army of unemployed workers from California arrives for the most part via boxcar.

Chicago's Pullman Palace Car Company reduces wages by one-fourth and obliges workers to labor for almost nothing while charging them full rents in company housing at Pullman, Ill., and charging inflated prices at company food stores (*see* 1881; 1894).

The American Railway Union is founded by socialist Eugene Victor Debs, 48, and others. Debs has been national secretary of the Brotherhood of Locomotive Firemen (*see* 1894).

Three of the men convicted of conspiracy in the 1886 Haymarket riot at Chicago are freed by the newly elected 45-year-old German-American governor of Illinois John Peter Altgeld whose action produces a storm of criticism. Altgeld has acted at the urging of Chicago lawyer Clarence Seward Darrow, 35 (*see* Haywood case, 1907).

Woman suffrage is adopted in New Zealand, which becomes the first country in the world to give women the right to vote.

New York's Henry Street Settlement is founded on the Lower East Side by social worker Lillian D. Wald, 26 (see Chicago's Hull House, 1889).

Anti-Semitism mounts in France as Jews are blamed for the collapse in 1889 of the Panama Canal Company whose bankruptcy has cost many French investors their savings. The company had been controlled by an international group of dubious character whose members were in many cases Jewish and who included Baron de Reinach and Cornelius Herz, and although Ferdinand de Lesseps and his associates are sentenced to prison in February, none of the leading figures will actually serve time (see Dreyfus, 1894).

Britain's Labour party is founded by socialists who include Scotsman James Keir Hardie, 37. A miner from age 10 to age 22, Keir Hardie organized a labor union among his fellow miners, he headed a new Scottish Labour party in 1888, and he was elected last year to Parliament.

The world's first open heart surgery operation is performed by Chicago surgeon Daniel Hale Williams who saves the life of a street fighter with a knife wound in an artery near his heart (see Williams, 1891).

The Johns Hopkins Medical School and Hospital are founded at Baltimore's 17-year-old Johns Hopkins University. Physician in chief is Canada's William Osler, 44, whose *Principles and Practices of Medicine* was published 2 years ago and who is the leading medical professor of his time. Surgery professor W. S. Halsted, pathologist W. H. Welch, and gynecological surgeon Howard Atwood Kelly, 35, will help Osler give the school a leadership unmatched in U.S. medicine (see Welch, 1878; Halsted, 1884; Flexner, 1910).

The basal metabolism test that will be used to measure human metabolic rates is devised by German physiologist Adolf Magnus-Levy, 28.

A symbolic method of calculation that will bring the complex field of alternating current within the reach of the average practicing engineer is announced by Charles P. Steinmetz whose Yonkers, N.Y., employer Osterheid and Eickemeyer has been acquired by the new General Electric Company of Schenectady, N.Y. (see 1892). The Steinmetz method will make the use of alternating current commercially feasible and will be largely responsible for the quick introduction of apparatus using alternating current on a wide scale (see Westinghouse, Stanley, 1885; Tesla, 1888).

The Klondike oil well geysers up in a marshy field on East Toledo's Millard Avenue, and a rush begins to drill wells. The Ohio city will become a major oil refinery center.

The first Ford motorcar is road tested in April by Detroit machinist Henry Ford, 30, of the Edison Illuminating Company, who has been working on his "gasoline buggy" since last year. Ford will drive his tiller-steered Quadricycle through the streets of Detroit in the early hours of June 4, 1896 (see 1899).

A float-feed carburetor for gasoline engines is developed by German engineer William Maybach, 46, who is an associate of Gottlieb Daimler (see 1892).

Greece's 3.5-mile Corinth Ship Canal opens to link the Gulf of Corinth with the Gulf of Athens.

Air brakes on U.S. railroad trains are made mandatory by federal law (see Westinghouse, 1868).

The New York, New Haven and Hartford Railroad completes its Shore Line route between New York and Boston by leasing the 500-plus miles of the Old Colony Railroad. The Old Colony controls the Boston and Providence Railroad whose 44 miles of track are needed by the New Haven (see 1872; Mellen, 1903).

A survey of Brooklyn, N.Y., schools reveals that 18 classes have 90 to 100 students each, while one classroom is jammed with 158 (see 1867).

New Mexico Highlands University is founded at Las Vegas.

Western New Mexico University is founded at Silver City.

Montana State University is founded at Missoula.

Montana State College is founded at Bozeman.

Western Montana College is founded at Dillon.

Montana School of Mines is founded at Butte.

The Field Museum is founded at Chicago with $1 million contributed by Marshall Field who will add a second $1 million and will leave the museum an additional $8 million in his will when he dies early in 1906.

Rural U.S. telephone companies begin to proliferate as the Bell patents of 1876 expire.

McClure's magazine begins publication at 15 cents a copy under the direction of Irish-American publisher S. S. (Samuel Sidney) McClure, 36, who created the first U.S. newspaper syndicate in 1884.

The American Newspaper Publishers Association (ANPA) founded in 1886 adopts a resolution agreeing to pay commission in the form of discounts to recognized independent advertising agencies and to give no discounts on space sold directly to advertisers. The resolution establishes the modern advertising agency system (see Batten, 1891; Curtis, 1901).

Joseph Pulitzer installs a four-color rotary press in hopes of reproducing great works of art in the Sunday supplement of his *New York World* (see 1883). Designed by New York's Hoe Company of 1875 folding apparatus fame, the new press will be used to produce the first colored cartoon (see 1896).

Fiction *Maggie: A Girl of the Streets* by New York newspaper reporter Stephen Crane, 21, who has the naturalistic portrayal of slum life published at his own expense.

1893 (cont.) Painting *The Cry* and *The Voice* by Norwegian postimpressionist Edvard Munch, 29; *The Boating Party* by Mary Cassatt; *Rouen Cathedral* by Claude Monet; *Hina Maruru* by Paul Gauguin.

Henri de Toulouse-Lautrec produces a color lithograph poster for the Divan Japonais, a Paris cafe at 75 Rue des Martyrs whose waitresses wear kimonos. The Duran-Ruell Galleries uses the poster to advertise an exhibition of more than 300 *ukiyoe* prints by Hiroshige and Utamara. Toulouse-Lautrec produces another Japanese style-color lithograph to promote *Aristide Bruant dans son cabaret* (see 1863).

Theater *Magda (Heimat)* by Hermann Sudermann 1/7 at Berlin's Lessingtheater; *The Girl I Left Behind Me* by David Belasco and *New York Sun* critic Franklin Fyler 1/25 at New York's Empire Theater, 208 perfs.; *The Weavers (Die Weber)* by Gerhart Hauptmann 2/26 at Berlin's Neues Theater; *A Woman of No Importance* by Oscar Wilde 4/14 at London's Haymarket Theatre; *The Second Mrs. Tanqueray* by Arthur Wing Pinero 5/28 at the St. James's Theatre, London, with Mrs. Patrick Campbell. Pinero has gained financial independence with the farces he has written since his early twenties, and he now presents the first of several "problem" plays which are considered daring and profound; *The Triumph of Death (Il trionfo della morte)* by Gabriele D'Annunzio; *The Beavercoat (Der Biberpelz)* by Gerhart Hauptmann 9/21 at Berlin's Deutsches Theater; *Hannele's Trip to Heaven (Hanneles Himmelfahrt)* by Gerhart Hauptmann 11/14 at Berlin's Königliches Schauspielhaus.

Opera *The Magic Opal* 1/19 at London's Lyric Theatre, with music by Spanish composer Isaac (Manuel Francisco) Albeniz, 32, who made his debut as a pianist at age 4, began running away from home at age 9, embarked for Puerto Rico at age 12 and wound up in Buenos Aires, was returned to Havana where his father had been stationed as a tax collector, persuaded his father to let him travel alone to New York, and played throughout the United States before returning to Spain; *Manon Lescaut* 2/1 at Turin's Teatro Reggio, with music by Italian composer Giacomo Puccini, 34, to a libretto with the same title as the Massenet opera of 1884; *Falstaff* 2/9 at Milan's Teatro alla Scala, with music by Giuseppe Verdi based on the character in the Shakespeare play *Henry IV* of 1597–1598. Verdi is 80 but his last opera shows undiminished powers of wit and composition. *Hänsel und Gretel* 12/23 at Weimar, with music by German composer Engelbert Humperdinck, 39.

First performances *Hamlet and Ophelia* by Edward MacDowell 1/28 at Boston; Sonata Tragica by Edward MacDowell 3/18 at Boston's Chickering Hall; Symphony No. 6 in B minor *(Pathetique)* by Petr Ilich Tchaikovsky 10/28 at St. Petersburg 9 days before the composer dies of cholera at age 53; Symphony No. 9 *(From the New World)* by Anton Dvorak 12/15 at New York's Carnegie Hall in a performance by the New York Philharmonic which has moved into the 2-year-old hall in West 57th Street where it will remain until 1962. Dvorak has written the symphony with snatches from black spirituals and American folk music as a greeting to his friends in Europe.

Stage musicals *A Trip to Chinatown* 8/7 at New York's Madison Square Theater, with book by Charles Hoyt, music and lyrics by Percy Gaunt, songs that include "The Bowery," "Reuben, Reuben," "Push the Clouds Away," and "After the Ball" by songwriter Chester K. Harris, 26, whose song will be the first to have sheet music sales of more than 5 million copies, 650 perfs.; *A Gaiety Girl* 10/14 at London's Prince of Wales Theatre, with music by Sidney Jones, lyrics by Harry Greenbank, 413 perfs. (the first musical comedy to be billed as such).

Popular songs "Happy Birthday to You" ("Good Morning to All") by Louisville, Ky., private kindergarten teacher Mildred Hill, lyrics by her sister Patty Smith Hill; "See, Saw, Margery Daw" by Arthur West; "Two Little Girls in Blue" by Charles Graham.

Hymn "When the Roll Is Called Up Yonder" by James M. Black.

Florenz Ziegfeld begins a 39-year show business career by engaging orchestras and musical attractions for the Columbian Exposition (above). A native of Chicago, the 25-year-old Ziegfeld profits handsomely by exhibiting the German strong man and physical culture exponent Eugene Sandow, 26.

The Stanley Cup ice hockey trophy has its beginnings in a silver cup presented to the winner of an amateur Canadian hockey match by the son of the earl of Denby, governor general of Canada. Frederick Arthur, Lord Stanley of Preston, has purchased the cup for £10 ($48.67), it will be replaced by a $14,000 silver bowl, it will become the North American professional hockey trophy beginning in 1910, and beginning in 1926 it will be awarded each year to the winner of the National Hockey League championship (see 1875; NHL, 1917).

The Chicago Golf Club opens at Wheaton, Ill., where Charles B. MacDonald has laid out the first 18-hole golf course in America.

The distance from the pitcher's mound to home plate in baseball is fixed at 60 feet, 6 inches.

The U.S. racing yacht *Vigilant* defeats England's *Valkyrie* 3 races to 0 to defend the America's Cup.

Savage Arms Company is founded at Utica, N.Y., by Jamaican-American inventor Arthur William Savage, 36, who has developed an improved magazine rifle for sportsmen.

Paris students witness the world's first striptease February 9 at the Bal des Quatre Arts. Gendarmes seize the artist's model who has disrobed for the art students, a court fines her 100 francs, the ruling provokes a riot in the Latin Quarter, students besiege

638

the Prefecture of Police, and military intervention is required to restore order.

The world's first Ferris wheel goes up at the Chicago fair (above). Designed by U.S. engineer Washington Gale Ferris, 34, the Midway amusement ride is a giant $300,000 vertical power-driven steel wheel, 250 feet in diameter, with 36 passenger cars, each seating 40 people, balanced at its rim (see 1897).

The "Clasp Locker or Unlocker for Shoes" exhibited at the Chicago fair (above) is the world's first slide fastener. U.S. inventor Whitcomb L. Judson has patented the device and has patented a machine to manufacture it (see Sundback, 1913).

Fels-Naphtha soap is introduced by Philadelphia soapmaker Joseph Fels, 39, whose 17-year-old Fels & Company has just purchased a factory in which to apply the naphtha process to making laundry soap.

Cultured pearl cultivation is pioneered by Japanese entrepreneur Kokichi Mikimoto, 35, who 5 years ago established the first pearl farm in the Shinmei inlet. Mikimoto has learned from a Tokyo University professor that if a foreign object enters a pearl oyster's shell and is not expelled the oyster will use the object as the core of a pearl. Mikimoto pulls up a bamboo basket for routine inspection July 11, and he finds a semispherical pearl, the world's first cultured pearl.

Juicy Fruit chewing gum is introduced by William Wrigley, Jr., who has been selling Lotta Gum and Vassar (see 1892). Wrigley's Spearmint chewing gum is introduced in the fall and will be the nation's leading brand by 1910 (see Wrigley Field, 1914).

The National Society of Colonial Dames is founded by U.S. women whose organization will grow to outnumber by 5 to 1 the Colonial Dames of America founded 3 years ago.

Lizzie Borden makes headlines in June when she goes on trial at Fall River, Mass. The 32-year-old spinster Lizzie Andrew Borden is charged with having killed her stepmother and then her father on the morning of August 4 last year, the sensational trial boosts newspaper circulation figures to new heights, the jury finally acquits the defendant of the double murder, but street urchins chant, "Lizzie Borden took an axe/ And gave her mother forty whacks./ And when she saw what she had done/ She gave her father forty-one."

The Bon Marché in Paris has sales of 150 million gold francs, up from 20 million in 1870, and is the world's largest department store (see 1852).

Chicago's Marshall Field and Company occupies nearly an entire city block on State Street and its wholesale store employs more than 3,000 on 13 acres of floor space (see 1881; Field Museum, above).

The name Sears, Roebuck & Company is used for the first time as the Chicago's mail-order firm racks up sales of $338,000 in baby carriages, clothing, furni-

ture, musical instruments, sewing machines, and a wide range of other merchandise. By next year its catalog will have more than 500 pages (see 1889; Rosenwald, 1895).

Brooklyn's Abraham & Straus is founded as Joseph Wechsler of Wechsler & Abraham sells his interest to Macy's Isidor and Nathan Straus and their partner Charles B. Webster (see 1888). Abraham Abraham, 59, will bring his sons-in-law Simon F. Rothschild, 32, and Edward Charles Blum, 30, into the store to counter control by the Macy interests and by the turn of the century A&S will have entrances on four sides of the block it largely occupies (see Federated, 1929).

Newark's Bamberger department store opens February 1. Merchant Louis Bamberger, 37, has worked in his native Baltimore for his uncles who run the 35-year-old store M. Hutzler & Son, he has formed a partnership with German-American merchant Felix Fuld, 24, and Louis Frank, the store has sales of $260,000 its first year, and it will be the leading store in Newark (see WOR, 1922; R. H. Macy, 1929).

Philadelphia's Lit Brothers has its beginnings in a shop at 8th and Market Streets opened by local merchants Samuel D. Lit, 23, Jacob D. Lit, 21, and their sister Rachel.

Salt Lake City's Mormon Temple is completed on the site ordained for its construction by Brigham Young in 1847. Only "worthy Mormons" who adhere strictly to church rules may enter.

New York's Herald Square takes its name as a building designed by McKim, Mead and White for James Gordon Bennett's New York Herald opens at the intersection of Broadway and Sixth Avenue.

London's Piccadilly Circus is graced with a new fountain erected as a memorial to the late Lord Shaftesbury, whose puritanical attitudes are belied by the fountain's sculptured Eros.

New York's Metropolitan Club building at Fifth Avenue and 60th Street is completed by Stanford White. Financier J. P. Morgan and his friends have commissioned the Italian Renaissance palazzo.

New York's Waldorf Hotel opens March 14 on Fifth Avenue at 33rd Street where the residence of William B. Astor has been torn down to make room for the 13-story hotel designed by architect Henry Janeway Hardenbergh with 530 rooms and 350 private baths (see Astor, 1848; Waldorf-Astoria, 1897).

Chicago's Congress Hotel opens on Michigan Avenue. It is an annex to the Auditorium Hotel built in connection with the Auditorium Theater Building completed by Louis Sullivan in 1890.

Quebec City's Chateau Frontenac Hotel opens December 18 after 19 months of construction. Modeled on a Loire Valley château by New York architect Bruce Price and built by a group of Canadians headed by Canadian Pacific Railway president William Van Horne, the 170-bedroom horseshoe-shaped

Motion pictures flickered to life with Thomas Edison's crude but prophetic kinetograph and kinetoscope.

hotel has an exterior of Glenboig bricks imported from Scotland.

 America's buffalo herd falls to 1,090 as market hunters continue to exterminate the animals (*see* 1900).

 Seabrook Farms has its beginnings in a 78-acre farm purchased by New Jersey farmer Arthur Seabrook who will raise vegetables with his wife and, later, with his son Charles (*see* 1920).

 Milwaukee's Pabst beer wins a blue ribbon at the Chicago fair (above) and will be sold hereafter as Pabst Blue Ribbon beer (*see* 1889).

White Rock soda water is promoted at the Chicago fair (above) by Charles Welch who has had the pavilion over his spring at Waukesha, Wis., dismantled and moved to Chicago, where it has been reassembled and serves as a refreshment stand (*see* 1887). White Rock executives at the fair see a painting by British artist Paul Thumann, they purchase rights to the painting *Psyche at Nature's Mirror,* and they make Thuman's scantily clad Psyche the White Rock Girl trademark (*see* 1895).

Quaker's dietetic pastry flour wins a "highest" award at the Chicago fair (above). Produced by a division of the American Cereal Company, the flour is an advance over self-rising flour.

American Cereal Company pays $7,500 to acquire the American Health Food Company, a minor competitor in the breakfast food industry.

American Cereal (above) takes advantage of the spring financial panic to acquire Pettijohn's California Breakfast Food which has promoted its wheat flakes with advertising that has attacked oatmeal (*see* Johnson, Boswell, 1755). "My *horse* eats oats," one Pettijohn advertisement has said, and it has gone on to quote a college president to the effect that few

people have the strong disposition of horses or of Scottish highlanders and that oatmeal can produce colic, flatulence, biliousness, rash, "eruptions," and other troubles. American Cereal pays $12,340 to acquire Pettijohn and its brown bear emblem on whose flank is printed, "Bear in Mind Our Trade Mark," and it spends another $50,000 to improve the Pettijohn plant and to promote the cereal in ways that do not disparage oatmeal (*see* Quaker Oats Co., 1901).

Shredded Wheat is pioneered by Nebraska lawyer Henry Drushel Perky, 50, who finds that boiled wheat helps his indigestion. Perky enlists the help of Watertown, N.Y., designer Harry Ford to design a machine that will shred wheat, he travels to Denver to interest his brother John in manufacturing the patented machine, he and his brother organize the Cereal Machine Company to make hand machines that people can use to make their own wheat biscuits, and he opens a Denver restaurant in which all foods served contain Shredded Wheat (*see* 1894).

Cream of Wheat is introduced by the Diamond Mill of Grand Forks, N.D., whose chief miller Thomson S. Amidon has suggested to mill owners George Ball, Emory Mapes, and George Clifford that they produce a cereal made of "purified" wheat middlings (*see* LeCroix, 1865). The cereal takes 15 minutes to cook (30 minutes for infants), and when New York flour brokers Lamont, Corliss & Company receive 10 cases, they wire back within 3 hours for another 50. Some 550 cases are sold the first year, and although Cream of Wheat will not show a profit until 1900, the cereal will be so popular by 1897 that its makers will move their operations to Minneapolis (*see* 1902).

Aunt Jemima pancake mix is promoted at the Chicago fair (above) by St. Joseph, Mo., miller R. T. Davis who has acquired Chris Rutt's mix of 1889 and has improved it by adding rice flour, corn sugar, and powdered milk so that it can be prepared by adding only water. Davis sets up a 24-foot high flour barrel, he arranges displays inside the barrel, and he engages the 59-year-old former Kentucky slave Nancy Green to demonstrate the Aunt Jemima mix at a griddle outside the barrel (*see* 1910; 1926).

Postum is developed to replace coffee with a nutritious beverage of wheat, molasses, and wheat bran by ulcer patient C. W. (Charles William) Post, 38, at the Western Health Reform Institute operated since 1876 by John Harvey Kellogg (*see* 1895).

Thomas Lipton registers a new trademark for the tea he has been selling since 1890 and which is sold only in packages, never in bulk. Over the facsimile signature "Thomas J. Lipton, Tea Planter, Ceylon," Lipton prints the words "Nongenuine without this signature" (*see* 1909).

Hershey's Chocolate Company has its beginnings as Lancaster, Pa., caramel maker Milton Snavely Hershey, 36, visits the Chicago fair (above) and sees chocolate-making machinery exhibited by a Dresden firm. Hershey has the machinery shipped to Lancaster and begins experiments with it in a wing of his caramel plant (*see* 1894).

Swiss chef Oscar Tschirky is engaged as maître d'hotel by New York's new Waldorf Hotel (above). Tschirky has won recognition at Delmonico's, and as Oscar of the Waldorf he will create the Waldorf salad made from bits of apple, lettuce, and mayonnaise (*see* Waldorf-Astoria, 1931).

Maxim's opens in October at 3 Rue Royale in Paris. The new restaurant will soon be famous for its elegance and its cuisine.

1894 The Wilson-Gorman Tariff Act that becomes law August 27 without President Cleveland's signature reduces U.S. tariff duties by roughly 20 percent, but lobbyists keep most of the 1890 McKinley Act's protective features intact (*see* Dingley Act, 1897).

The Wilson-Gorman Act (above) includes an income tax on incomes above $4,000 per year (*see* 1881). New York lawyer Joseph H. Choate, 62, calls the 2 percent tax "communistic, socialistic" (*see* 1895).

Economic depression continues in the United States.

Strikes cripple U.S. railroads. President Cleveland takes the position that the government has authority only to keep order, thus effectively supporting the railroad operators and their strikebreakers (*see* Roosevelt, 1902).

Some 750,000 U.S. workers strike during the year for higher wages and shorter hours.

Coxey's Army arrives at Washington, D.C., April 30 after a 36-day march of unemployed workers from Massillon, Ohio, led by sandstone quarry operator Jacob Sechler Coxey, 40. The 400 marchers demand that public works be started to provide employment and that $50 million in paper money be issued, but Coxey is arrested for walking on the grass and is forced to leave the Capitol grounds (*see* 1932).

Pullman Palace Car Company workers strike May 11 in protest against wage cuts, and a general strike of western railroads begins June 26 as Eugene V. Debs orders his railway workers to boycott Pullman (*see* 1893). Debs is indicted by a federal grand jury for interfering with the mails and with interstate commerce after U.S. troops have entered Chicago in July to enforce federal laws in the Pullman strike. Illinois governor John Peter Altgeld protests that President Cleveland has violated states' rights in sending in the troops, he claims that the press has exaggerated the size of the disorders in Chicago, the troops are withdrawn, and the strike ends 2 weeks later.

Labor Day is established as a legal holiday by a June 28 act of Congress that sets aside the first Monday in every September to honor the contribution of labor.

French Army captain Alfred Dreyfus is convicted by a court-martial of having passed military information to German agents. The 35-year-old Dreyfus will later be proved innocent, but the Dreyfus case produces a wave of anti-Semitism in France (*see* 1897).

The Dreyfus trial (above) is covered by Viennese journalist Theodore Herzl, 34, who hears the Paris mob cry, "Death to the Jews!" and who lays the foundations of political Zionism with his book *The Jewish State: An Attempt at a Modern Solution of the Jewish Question* (*see* first Zionist congress, 1897).

 Britain's fourth Gladstone ministry ends March 5 after Gladstone has shattered the Liberal party with his fight for Irish home rule. The Liberals retain power with Archibald Philip Primrose, 46, earl of Rosebery, as prime minister (*see* Mentmore, 1857).

Hungary's Lajos Kossuth dies at Turin March 20 at age 91, and his 53-year-old son Ferenc returns from exile to lead the Independence party in the Parliament at Budapest.

French president Marie François Sadi Carnot dies at age 57 after having been stabbed at Lyons June 24 by Italian anarchist assassin Santo Caserio.

Russia's Aleksandr III dies November 1 at age 49 after a 13-year reign and is succeeded by his 24-year-old son who has married Princess Alix of Hesse at Czar Aleksandr's deathbed. The new czar begins a 23-year reign as Nicholas II that will bring an end to the Russian monarchy, and 3,000 people are crushed to death at his coronation as a result of negligence by officials charged with distributing bounties.

Dahomey becomes a French colony June 22 following a March 15 Franco-German agreement on the boundary between the French Congo and the Cameroons that have been a German protectorate since 1885. French imperialists have hopes of taking over the southern part of the former Egyptian Sudan and forcing the British to evacuate Egypt by threatening to divert the course of the Nile.

The Congo Treaty signed May 12 by Britain with the king of the Belgians Leopold II gives the British a lease on a wide corridor between Lake Tanganyika and Lake Albert Edward in return for a lifetime lease to Leopold of vast territories west of the Upper Nile and north of the Congo-Nile watershed. German protests force the British to abandon their corridor and to give up the possibility of a Capetown-to-Cairo railroad, and Leopold is forced by French threats to make an agreement August 14 giving up his claim to the northern part of his lease.

The Republic of Hawaii is proclaimed July 4 with Judge Sanford Ballard Dole, 50, as president. The republic gains U.S. recognition August 7, and the royalist revolt that begins December 8 is quickly suppressed (*see* 1893; 1898).

The British ship *Kowshing* carrying Chinese troops to Korea is sunk by the Japanese July 25, the Korean regent declares war on China July 27, China and Japan declare war on each other August 1, and the Japanese win easy victories in the ensuing months. A British invitation to Germany, France, Russia, and the United States to join in a united move to intervene is rejected by Berlin and Washington (*see* 1895).

1894 (cont.) The Dutch East Indies rebel against the government of the 14-year-old Dutch queen Wilhelmina, but the revolt is suppressed. Another uprising in 1896 will be put down only with great difficulty.

A chemically inert gas he calls argon from the Greek word for inactive is discovered by Scottish chemist William Ramsay, 42, who removes from the air various known gases including nitrogen, oxygen, and carbon dioxide and finds that an inert gas remains. Ramsay and his colleague Travers will discover three other inert gases in the air and will name them krypton (hidden), neon (new), and xeon (stranger) (*see* Langmuir, 1912).

Lichens are found to consist of fungi and algae living in a symbiotic (mutually beneficial) relationship. The discovery is made by German botanist Johannes Reinke (*see* Beatrix Potter, 1902).

The *bacillus pestis*—the etiological agent of the Black Death bubonic plague—is discovered by Shibasaburo Kitazato and A. E. J. Yersin (*see* 1665; 1889; 1900).

The diphtheria antitoxin developed by Emil von Behring is introduced into U.S. medical practice by New York physician Hermann Michael Biggs, 35.

A muscle-splitting incision for appendectomies is developed by New York surgeon Charles McBurney, 49, who has discovered a tender pressure point important in the diagnosis of appendicitis (it will be called McBurney's point).

Oil is discovered at Corsicana, Tex., as a well being bored for water suddenly begins spouting oil. In 4 years nearly every Corsicanian will have an oil well in his backyard and the field will be producing 500,000 barrels per year (*see* Spindletop, 1901).

The Southern Railway System is organized by New York financier and traction magnate Thomas Fortune Ryan who puts together the Richmond and Danville and the East Tennessee, Virginia, and Georgia systems into a company that will soon embrace the South Carolina and Georgia, the Cincinnati Southern, the Alabama Great Southern, the New Orleans and Northeastern, the Georgia Southern and Florida, and the Northern Alabama to create a system that will operate 8,000 miles of railroad extending from the Potomac and Ohio Rivers to the Gulf and from the Atlantic to the Mississippi (*see* 1886).

The Sunset Limited begins service on the Southern Pacific between New Orleans and San Francisco. The once-a-week express averages 33 miles per hour to make the run in 75 hours, it will soon be running three times a week, and it will run daily beginning in 1913 (*see Sunset* magazine, 1898).

Union Station opens at St. Louis. Its design has been adapted from that of the medieval French walled city of Carcasonne.

Boston's North Station opens for the Boston & Maine Railroad (*see* South Station, 1899).

The first railroad opens across the South American Andes.

Cable cars in U.S. cities haul 400 million passengers, but trolley lines will rapidly supplant the cable cars (*see* Hallidie, 1873; Richmond, 1888). The complex cable car systems are vulnerable to breakdown, they require large inputs of energy simply to move their heavy cables, but the cars will continue to operate on the hills of San Francisco.

England's 36-mile Manchester Ship Canal opens to link Manchester with the Mersey River.

London's Tower Bridge opens to span the Thames. The £1.5 million bridge has a 200-foot center span that can be raised to permit passage of vessels; its chain suspension side spans are each 270 feet long.

Radcliffe College for Women opens at Cambridge, Mass., after 15 years of opposition by Harvard president Charles William Eliot to the classes given since 1879 by Elizabeth Cary Agassiz. The college is named for Anne Radcliffe, who in the 17th century became the first woman to make a gift to Harvard.

Multiplex telegraphy is improved by Austro-Hungarian-American physicist Michael Idversky Pupin, 36, who has studied under Hermann von Helmholtz.

A. C. W. Harmsworth acquires London's conservative *Evening News* and reorganizes the paper. Born in Dublin, Alfred Charles William Harmsworth, 29, began as a free-lance journalist at age 17, he set up a publishing house at London with his brother Harold 5 years later, and in 1888 he started the periodical *Answers to Correspondents* (later simply *Answers*) (*see Daily Mail*, 1896).

Nonfiction *Wealth Against Commonwealth*, a study of John D. Rockefeller's Standard Oil Company by Henry Demarest Lloyd who defends Eugene V. Debs (above) in legal battles arising out of the Pullman strike; *Glimpses of Unfamiliar Japan* by U.S. author (Patricio) Lafcadio (Tessima Carlos) Hearn, 44, who was born in the Ionian Islands of British-Greek parentage, has obtained a teaching position in Japan, has married a Japanese woman of a samurai family, and gives Western readers their first sympathetic view of Japanese life. Hearn will become a Japanese citizen next year, will take the name Koizumi Yakumo, and will teach at the Imperial University in Tokyo from 1896 to 1903.

Fiction *Pudd'nhead Wilson* by Mark Twain; *Trilby* by George du Maurier whose malevolent hypnotist Svengali will become a generic term for anyone who tries with evil intentions to force or persuade someone else to do his bidding (the novel creates a fashion for the trilby hat); *The Prisoner of Zenda* by English novelist Anthony Hope (Anthony Hope Hopkins), 31; *The Ebb-Tide* by Robert Louis Stevenson who based the work on a draft by his stepson Lloyd Osbourne. Stevenson suffers a stroke of apoplexy on his verandah in Samoa December 3 and dies at age 44, his body buried on the summit of Mount Vaea by the Samoans who regard him as chief; *The Memoirs of*

Sherlock Holmes by A. Conan Doyle who in December 1893 killed off his detective along with Professor Moriarty in an Austrian disaster chronicled in the *Strand* magazine (but *see* 1902).

Juvenile *The Jungle Book* by Rudyard Kipling.

Art *The Venetian Painters of the Renaissance* by Lithuanian-American art critic-historian Bernard Berenson, 29, who was graduated from Harvard 7 years ago, has studied at Oxford and at the University of Berlin, and has trained himself in the galleries of Italy to recognize the works of the Italian masters by their styles and techniques. Berenson will acquire the 18th-century Florentine mansion I Tatti and will be the ranking authority on classical art until his death in 1959.

The *Yellow Book* begins publication with London artist Aubrey Vincent Beardsley, 22, as art editor. Beardsley's black-and-white "art nouveau" drawings will achieve a fame far more enduring than their creator, who will die in 1898 at age 26.

Painting *Femme à sa toilette* by Edgar Degas. George Innes dies at Bridge of Allan, Scotland, August 3 at age 69.

Favrile glass is trademarked by Louis Comfort Tiffany, who has invented a process for staining glass by adding pigments to molten glass while it is being made instead of applying stain or burning pigments into hardened glass (*see* 1878). Tiffany achieves incomparable iridescences that he employs in free form "art nouveau" shapes to create brilliant lamps, chandeliers, vases, jewelry, and other objects.

Theater *How to Get Rid of Your Mistress* (*Un fil à la patte*) by Georges Feydeau 1/9 at the Théâtre du Palais Royal, Paris; *The Land of Heart's Desire* by William Butler Yeats 3/29 at London's Avenue Theatre; *Arms and the Man* by George Bernard Shaw 4/21 at London's Avenue Theatre. Shaw innovates the practice of having his plays published for general readership with elaborate prefaces that deal with political and social issues (his new play deflates romantic illusions of military "glory"); *Hotel Paradiso* (*L'hotel du libre echange*) by Georges Feydeau and a collaborator 12/5 at the Théâtre des Nouveautés, Paris.

Billboard has its beginnings in an eight-page monthly started by Cincinnati publishers James Hennegan and W. H. Donaldson as *Billboard Advertising*. Theater notes will be introduced beginning in mid-October 1901, a motion picture section will be added in 1907, and *Billboard* will become a U.S. show business weekly (*see Variety,* 1905).

Boston's $1 million Keith Theater opens with Weber and Fields who make $400 per week. By 1905 they will be pulling down $4,000 per week.

Opera *Thais* 3/16 at the Paris Grand Opéra, with music by Jules Massenet, libretto from a novel by Anatole France; *Werther* 4/19 at New York's Metropolitan Opera House, with music by Jules Massenet, libretto from the Goethe work of 1774; *La Navar-*

raise 6/20 at London's Covent Garden, with music by Jules Massenet.

Ballet *Afternoon of a Faun* (*L'Après-midi d'un Faune*) 12/23 at Paris, with music by French composer Claude Achille Debussy, 32, (*see* Mallarmé poem, 1876).

First performances Symphony No. 5 in B flat major by Anton Bruckner 4/9 at Graz (Bruckner will die in the fall of 1896 at age 72 leaving his Symphony No. 9 in D minor incomplete); Concerto No. 2 in D minor for Piano and Orchestra by Edward MacDowell 12/14 at New York.

The Queen's Hall opens in London's Langham Place. The auditorium will be famous for its Promenade Concerts until its destruction in 1941.

Broadway musical *The Passing Show* 5/12 at the Casino Theater, with music by Viennese-American composer Ludwig Englander, 35, book and lyrics by Sydney Rosenberg. The production introduces the revue to the musical theater.

Popular songs "Humoresque" (piano composition) by Anton Dvorak; "The Sidewalks of New York" by Irish-American composer Charles B. Lawlor, 42, lyrics by native New Yorker James W. Blake, 32 ("East side, West side, all around the town . . ."); "I've Been Working on the Railroad" is published under the title "Levee Song" in *Carmina Princetoniana*. University of Texas undergraduate John Lang Sinclair will write lyrics beginning, "The eyes of Texas are upon you . . ." for a student minstrel show that will be presented May 12, 1903.

The Penn Relays are held for the first time in April at Philadelphia.

The first U.S. Open golf tournament is held at St. Andrew Golf Club in Yonkers, N.Y., at the initiative of Scots-American golfer John Reid, who helps to organize the U.S. Golf Association (USGA) (*see* British Open, 1860; liquid center golf ball, 1899).

Yale end Frank Hinkey, 22, ends a 4-year football career in which he has been named to the All-America team four times. Weighing 157 pounds and standing 5 feet 9 inches, Hinkey will be called "the greatest football player of all time" by coach Glenn Scobey "Pop" Warner, now 23, who will coach the Carlisle Indians and will go on to coach teams at Georgia, Cornell, Pittsburgh, Stanford, and Temple.

World chess champion Wilhelm Steinitz is defeated by German chess master Emanuel Lasker, 26, who gains the world title he will hold until 1921.

The Winchester M1894 lever action rifle designed by John M. Browning is introduced by the Winchester Repeating Arms Company (*see* 1866).

England's Marks & Spencer department store chain has its beginnings in the Penny Bazaar ("Don't ask the price, it's a penny") opened at Cheetham Hill, Manchester, by Polish-born merchant Michael Marks, 31, in partnership with Thomas Spencer, 42,

1894 (cont.) whose employer loaned Marks £5 in 1884 when the Pole arrived at Leeds penniless, illiterate, and unable to speak English. Marks started as an itinerant peddler, he opened a stall in Kirkgate Market, Leeds, he has since opened stalls in six other Lancashire street markets, and he has innovated the practice of arranging wares according to price. By 1900 there will be a dozen Penny Bazaar stores (three of them in London), and by 1915 there will be 140 selling haberdashery, earthenware, hardware, household goods, stationery, and toys at the fixed price of a penny per item. Marks & Spencer will open their first store under that name at Darlington in 1922, and "Marks & Sparks" will grow to become Britain's leading retail enterprise.

Harrods at London inaugurates 7 o'clock closing hours (4 o'clock Thursdays) as its new manager Richard Burbidge, 47, ends the penny-halfpenny fines for late employees that was instituted in 1883, installs display windows, and arrives himself by 7 each morning to make "Harrods Serve the World" more than a slogan for the Knightsbridge store whose cable address is "Everything." Land is acquired beginning this year for a large new store that will not be completed until 1939.

Gimbel Brothers of Milwaukee opens a Philadelphia store that will be the city's largest retail establishment. Founding father Adam Gimbel dies at age 78, and Isaac Gimbel takes over the firm's presidency (*see* 1887; New York Gimbels, 1910).

 A London Building Act voted by Parliament limits the height of buildings to 150 feet. A development called Queen Anne's Mansions has disturbed Queen Victoria's view, and no skyscrapers will be erected in London for nearly 60 years.

Berlin's Reichstag is completed after 10 years of construction, and the German parliament moves into its new home (*see* 1933).

The Hotel Metropole in Brussels is opened by Belgian brewer Prosper Wiedemans who has acquired a bank in the Place de Bronckers and has turned it into a 100-room hotel. Wiedemans will acquire adjoining properties and will enlarge the Metropole to make it a 420-room hotel with 770 beds.

The Royal Poinciana Hotel opens at Palm Beach, Fla., with 540 rooms that will be enlarged to give it 1,300. Standard Oil millionaire H. M. Flagler has extended his Florida East Coast Railroad 200 miles south to Lake Worth and has put up the $2 million wooden hotel to accommodate winter visitors (*see* 1888; The Breakers, 1895).

Chicago's new Reliance building designed by Daniel Burnham is "a glass tower 15 stories high."

Newport's Belcourt Castle is completed on Bellevue Avenue in the Rhode Island summer resort for Oliver H. P. Belmont. The 52-room Louis XIII-style "cottage" has been designed by Richard Morris Hunt and John Russell Pope, 20.

Some 6,576 New York slum dwellers are found to be living in windowless inside rooms. Air shafts have been installed by landlords to circumvent an 1879 law passed to ban such inside rooms, but the shafts are used in many cases as garbage chutes.

 U.S. wheat sells at 49 cents per bushel, down from $1.05 in 1870. Prairie schooners headed back east have canvas covers painted with the words, "In God we trusted, in Kansas we busted."

The Carey Act passed by Congress August 18 grants 1 million acres of federally owned desert lands to certain states on condition that they irrigate the land, reclaim it, and dispose of it in small tracts to settlers. U.S. Senator Joseph M. Carey, 49, of Wyoming has sponsored the legislation.

California's Irvine Co. ranch is incorporated by James Irvine, Jr., 27, whose late father came from Ireland to seek his fortune in the goldfields, made money as a wholesale merchant in San Francisco, joined with three other men to buy up sheep rangeland from Spanish settlers who had fallen into debt to Anglo-American merchants in Los Angeles, and bought out his partners in 1876. The younger Irvine will develop a vast ranching and farming empire, including a 100,000-acre ranch in Montana.

Ralston Purina Company has its beginnings in the Robinson-Danforth Commission Company founded by St. Louis feed merchants George Robinson and William H. Danforth. They have mixed corn and oats to produce a feed that will not give horses and mules colic as corn alone may do (*see* Purina, 1897).

 A study of children in London's Bethnal Green district shows that 83 percent receive no solid food besides bread at 17 out of 21 meals per week. Scurvy, rickets, and tuberculosis are widespread in such districts as they are in many British and European industrial centers.

Our Pet evaporated cream is introduced in a 5-cent miniature can by the Helvetia Milk Condensing Company whose new product will gain wide popularity (*see* 1890; Pet Milk Company, 1923).

U.S. ice-making plants produce 1.5 million tons of machine-made ice (*see* 1889; 1926).

Minute Tapioca is introduced by Boston's Whitman Grocery Company first under the name Tapioca Superlative and then as Minute Tapioca, a name selected to honor the minutemen who fought the English at Lexington and Concord in 1775. Boston housewife Susan Stavers has obtained South American manioc (cassava) roots, imported duty-free since 1883 and used to produce starch, and she has run them through her coffee grinder to produce translucent tapioca granules that make a smooth pudding. Local publisher John Whitman has bought rights to her process, he has organized the Whitman Grocery Company, and he sells boxes of the tapioca which Stavers has sold in paper bags (*see* 1926).

Shredded Wheat maker H. D. Perky receives a visit at Denver from John Harvey Kellogg who returns to Battle Creek determined to invent a better breakfast food (*see* 1881; Granose, 1895).

H. D. Perky moves his Natural Food Company to Boston and opens a plant at Roxbury, Mass., with 11 machines to make shredded wheat (*see* 1893; 1895).

The first commercial chili (or chile) powder is developed at New Braunfels, Tex., by German-American café owner William Gebhardt, who runs pepper (capsicum) bits through a small home meat grinder three times and dries the ground pepper into a powder (*see* 1835). Gebhardt will open the first chili powder factory next year, making five cases per week and selling the product from the back of a wagon while he develops improved machines to increase production.

Van Camp pork and beans are advertised in U.S. magazines for the first time. A sample can is offered for 6 cents in the first full-page food product advertisement to appear in a national publication (*see* 1882; tuna, 1914).

Joseph Campbell Preserve Company gets a new president as Arthur Dorrance, 45, succeeds Campbell with whom he formed a new partnership in 1876 (*see* 1869; "condensed" soup, 1897).

The Hershey Bar introduced by Milton S. Hershey is 45 percent sugar, 16 to 18 percent cocoa beans, 14 percent chocolate liquor (ground up cocoal beans), 23 to 25 percent milk solids (*see* 1893; 1900).

Pêche Melba is created by Auguste Escoffier at London's 5-year-old Savoy Hotel to honor the Australian grande cantrice Madame Nellie Melba (Helen Porter Mitchell), 33, who is singing at Covent Garden. Inspired by the swan in Richard Wagner's opera *Lohengrin* of 1850, Escoffier tops a scoop of vanilla ice cream on a cooked peach half with a purée of raspberries and almond slivers.

London's first J. Lyon's teashop opens at 213 Piccadilly. Joseph Lyons operates the white-fronted shop with gold letters and begins an empire of Lyons tea shops that will sell Welsh rabbit, meat pies, canned spaghetti on toast, fried potatoes, and assorted biscuits, buns, and cakes.

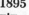 A Chinese Exclusion Treaty with the United States is signed March 17. Chinese authorities again consent to exclusion of Chinese laborers (*see* 1884; 1943).

A Bureau of Immigration is created by Congress.

An Immigration Restriction League formed by a group of Bostonians campaigns for a literacy test that will screen out uneducated undesirables. The league's efforts will be directed against Asiatics, Latins, and Slavs (*see* 1917).

1895 The x-ray or roentgen ray discovered by Bavarian physicist Wilhelm Conrad Roentgen, 50, will revolutionize diagnostic medicine by making it possible to photograph the inner organs and bone structures of animals and humans. Professor of physics since 1888 at Würzburg's Physical Institute, Roentgen notices a phenomenon November 8 while working with the cathode-ray ultravacuum tube recently invented by English physicist Sir William Crookes, 63. When a current is passed through the tube, a nearby piece of paper that has been painted with barium platinocyamide appears to fluoresce brightly. The phenomenon occurs even when the tube is covered with black cardboard, and Roentgen proves that the effect is caused by an invisible ray. He announces his discovery to the Würzburg Physical-Medical Society December 28 in his paper "Eine neue Art von Strahlen" (*see* Nobel, 1901; use in treating cancer, 1903).

Studies in Hysteria (*Studien über Hysterie*) by Viennese physician Sigmund Freud, 39, is published in collaboration with Josef Breuer (*see* 1882).

Sigmund Freud (above) has worked with Josef Breuer in treating hysteria with hypnosis, but he begins now to develop a new treatment that will be the basis of scientific psychoanalysis. "No neurosis is possible with a normal sex life," Freud will say, but he will give up sex himself at age 42, and he will suffer much of his life from stomach upsets, migraine headaches, and nasal catarrh for which he will use cocaine (*see* 1900).

Filterable viruses are discovered by Dutch botanist Marinius Willem Beljerinck, 44, who is not familiar with Dmitri Ivanovski's 1892 discovery.

 The League of Struggle for the Emancipation of the Working Class is founded at St. Petersburg by Russian revolutionary Vladimir Ilich Ulyanov, 25, who will adopt the pseudonym Nikolai Lenin. He has read the works of Karl Marx, his older brother was executed 4 years ago for plotting against the life of the czar, he travels in late April to Switzerland, he reaches an agreement with Georgi Plekhanov, he is arrested after his return, and he will be exiled to Siberia for 3 years beginning in 1897 (*see* 1900; Plekhanov, 1883).

Booker T. Washington gives a speech agreeing to withdrawal of blacks from politics if education and technical training are guaranteed to blacks. Washington makes his remarks at Atlanta's Cotton States Exposition in Piedmont Park, a fair that attracts 800,000 visitors who come to see the Liberty Bell from Philadelphia, Buffalo Bill Cody, and some 6,000 exhibits (and to hear concerts by Victor Herbert and John Philip Sousa), but the speech by Washington alienates some blacks.

Cuban insurgents stage an abortive revolution against Spanish rule, but the revolt is ruthlessly suppressed and the island left in turmoil (*see* 1898).

The Treaty of Shimonoseki April 17 ends a brief Sino-Japanese war in which the Chinese army and navy have been destroyed. China recognizes the independence of Korea, she cedes Taiwan (Formosa), the Pescadores Islands, and the Liaotung Peninsula to Japan, she agrees to pay 200 million taels in indemni-

1895 (cont.) ties, and she agrees to open four more ports to foreign commerce. Russia, Germany, and France force Japan to return the Liaotung Peninsula, but the Japanese agree only on condition that they receive another 30 million taels. France obtains territorial and commercial concessions in China's southern provinces, while Britain, France, Germany, and Russia all make huge loans to China with customs revenues as security (*see* 1897; Boxer Rebellion, 1900).

Britain's Tories regain power in the general elections and a third Salisbury ministry begins June 25. It will continue until 1902.

The name Rhodesia is given to the territory of the South Africa Company south of the Zambezi River to honor the prime minister of the Cape Colony Cecil Rhodes. Southern Rhodesia will become a British crown colony in 1923 (*see* 1965).

Tongaland is annexed by the British June 11 to block any possible access of the Transvaal to the sea via Swaziland, and Bechuanaland is attached to the Cape Colony in November.

The Jameson raid that begins December 29 is an attempt to foment rebellion against the Boer government of the Transvaal's Oom Paul Kruger, now 70. Leander Starr Jameson leads 600 men in a 140-mile dash across the Transvaal (*see* 1893; 1896).

The Delagoa Bay Railway that has opened July 8 gives Johannesburg and Pretoria an economic outlet to the sea independent of British control.

Germany's 53.2-mile Kiel (Nord-Ostsee) Ship Canal opens to connect the North Sea with the Rhine.

The Ohio Valley Improvement Association is organized October 8 at the Cincinnati Chamber of Commerce to make the Ohio a navigable channel for commerce. The U.S Army Corps of Engineers will build 49 locks and movable dams on 980 miles of river between Pittsburgh and Cairo, Ill.

A patent for a "road locomotive" powered by a "liquid hydrocarbon engine" of the compression type is granted to George B. Selden (*see* 1879; 1899).

Wilshire Boulevard opens between Los Angeles and Santa Monica on the Pacific. The thoroughfare has been built by local goldmine promoter, medical faddist, and socialist H. Gaylord Wilshire.

Pneumatic tires are put on motorcars for the first time by France's André Michelin, 42, and his brother Edouard, 36, whose Michelin & Cie. will be Europe's largest tire producer and one of the world's three leading tire companies (*see* Dunlop, 1881; Panhard and Levassor, 1892).

The first U.S. pneumatic tires are produced by the Hartford Rubber Works at Hartford, Conn., owned by the bicycle maker Pope Manufacturing Company (*see* Kelly-Springfield, 1899).

The Lanchester motorcar introduced by English engineer Frederick W. Lanchester of the Lanchester Engine Company is the first British four-wheel gasoline-powered motorcar. It has epicyclic gearing, worm drive, and pneumatic tires.

The Wolesley motorcar introduced by the Wolesley Sheep-Shearing Machine Company has a two-cylinder opposed air-cooled engine and has been designed by the Australian-born engineer Herbert Austin, 29 (*see* Austin motorcar, 1905).

A Paris-Bordeaux road race is won by an 1891 Panhard Levassor with a two-cylinder engine that has three forward speeds, no reverse, and enough speed to complete the journey in 48 hours, 47 minutes.

The first U.S. automobile race is run Thanksgiving Day on a 53.5-mile course between Chicago and Milwaukee and is won by the only American-made gasoline-powered car in the race which has been organized by Herman Kohlsaat's *Chicago Times-Herald* with a $2,000 first prize. Some 80 contestants enter the race, but only 6 are able to start; average speed over the snowy roads is 5.25 miles per hour, and the winner is James Franklin Duryea, driving a vehicle with a rigid front axle, a water-cooled engine, a steering tiller, whose up-and-down motion controls the speed, and Hartford tires (above) purchased by Charles Duryea who organizes the Duryea Motor Wagon Co. at Springfield, Mass. (*see* 1891; 1896).

The first delivery van powered by a gasoline engine is completed in December by the French firm Peugot Frères, whose vehicle runs on a 4-horsepower Daimler motor that enables it to carry a half-ton load at 9.5 miles per hour and a 650-pound load at 12 miles per hour.

The first Benz "Omnibus" goes into service in Germany with a one-cylinder rear engine that develops between 4 and 6 horsepower and has a capacity for eight passengers.

A "diesel" engine that operates on a petroleum fuel less highly refined and less costly than gasoline is invented by German engineer Rudolf Diesel, 37, whose engine has no electrical ignition system and is simpler than a gasoline engine and more trouble-free. Diesel will work with Fried. Krupp of Essen and the Augsburg-Nuremberg machine factory to build a successful engine (*see* locomotive, 1913).

The first commercial electric power from Niagara Falls is transmitted August 26 by the Niagara Falls Power Company incorporated in 1889. The company employs three 5,000-horsepower Westinghouse Electric generators that deliver two-phase currents at 2,200 volts, 25 cycles, and the power is used by the Pittsburgh Reduction Company to reduce aluminum ore (*see* Mellon, 1891).

The Sherman Anti-Trust Act of 1890 is emasculated by the Supreme Court January 21 in the case of *U.S. v. E. C. Knight Co.* H. O. Havemeyer's 3-year-old Sugar Trust is upheld by the court, which dismisses an antitrust case against the trust on the ground that control of the manufacturing process affects interstate commerce only incidentally and indirectly (*see* Clayton Act, 1914).

U.S. Treasury gold reserves fall to $41,393,000 as economic depression continues, but the New York banking houses of J. P. Morgan and August Belmont join forces to loan the Treasury $65 million in gold to be paid for at a stiff price in government bonds. Morgan has made a fortune reorganizing and consolidating railroads, but Belmont died late in 1890 at age 73.

The income tax provision in last year's Wilson-Gorman Tariff Act is ruled unconstitutional May 20 by a 5 to 4 Supreme Court decision in the case of *Pollock v. Farmers' Loan and Trust Company* (see 1913).

Sherwin-Williams Company adopts the trademark "It Covers the Earth" designed by the firm's publicity manager George Ford but foreign paint sales will never account for more than a small part of Sherwin-Williams' business (see 1888).

The London School of Economics is founded by Fabian socialists.

Northern Illinois University is founded at De Kalb.

The University of Texas at Arlington is founded.

Underwood Typewriter Company is founded by New York ribbon and carbon merchant John Thomas Underwood, 38, to develop and market a machine patented 2 years ago by Brooklyn inventors Franz X. and Herman L. Wagner, whose typewriter enables the typist to see what is being typed.

William Randolph Hearst acquires the *New York Morning Journal* from John R. McLean for $180,000 (see 1887). Hearst will call the paper's morning edition the *New York American* beginning in 1902 after acquiring the *Boston American,* the *Chicago American,* and other papers, and he will go on to publish magazines that will include *Good Housekeeping* (see 1885), *Harper's Bazaar, Town and Country,* and *Hearst's International-Cosmopolitan* (see 1905; "The Yellow Kid," 1896).

The *Denver Post* begins publication under the direction of its new proprietors Frederick Gilmer Bonfils, 35, and Harry Heye Tammen, 39, who have renamed the *Denver Evening Post.* Bonfils is an Oklahoma real estate promoter who has been running the Little Louisiana Lottery at Kansas City and who has been persuaded by Denver storekeeper H. H. Tammen to buy the *Evening Post.* The two will use sensationalist techniques to multiply circulation 20-fold in the next 12 years, but their crusades in the name of justice and public good will sometimes be more notable for flamboyance than for integrity.

Collier's Weekly magazine begins publication. New York publisher Peter F. Collier has changed the name of his *Once a Week* magazine and challenges the *Saturday Evening Post* (see Crowell, 1919).

Field and Stream magazine begins publication. The new monthly periodical for sportsmen will continue for more than 80 years.

Guglielmo Marconi pioneers wireless telegraphy. The 21-year-old Italian inventor has studied the Hertz discovery of 1887, he has set up a laboratory at his family's country house outside Bologna, and in September he transmits a message to his brother who is out of sight beyond a hill. Marconi's mother is British, and he will apply in June of next year for a British patent on his wireless (see 1896).

The New York Public Library is created by a merger of the 41-year-old Astor Library, the Lenox Library, and the Tilden Library (see Carnegie, 1901).

A new Boston Public Library opens on Copley Square in a Renaissance building by Charles McKim of McKim, Mead & White (see 1877).

Bobbs-Merrill Company publishers is founded at Indianapolis by William Conrad Bobbs, 34, who has worked since 1879 for booksellers Merrill, Meigs & Company.

Fiction   *Almayer's Folly* by British novelist Joseph Conrad, 37, who emigrated from the Ukraine, changed his name (from Joez Teodor Jozef Konrad Nalecz Korzeniowski), served for 4 years in the French merchant marine and then for 16 in the British merchant marine, and has been writing for just over a year, making himself a master prose stylist in his adopted language; *Jude the Obscure* by Thomas Hardy; *The Time Machine* by English journalist-science fiction writer H. G. (Herbert George) Wells, 28; *Esther Waters* by George Moore; *Celibates* (stories) by George Moore; *Bewilderments (Forvillelser)* by Swedish novelist Hjalmar Soderberg, 26; *The Promised Land (Det Forjaettede Land),* a trilogy by Danish novelist Henrik Pontoppidan; *The Red Badge of Courage* (novelette) by Stephen Crane, who will serve as a war correspondent in 1896 and 1897, will move to England in 1897, and will die of tuberculosis at Badenweiler, Germany, in 1900 at age 28; *The Sorrows of Satan* by Marie Corelli.

Demon Rum made temperance workers indignant. They demanded prohibition and found an ally in Thomas Nast.

1895 (cont.) Poetry *The Tentacular Cities* (*Les Villes Tentaculaires*) by Emile Verhaeren; *Majors and Minors* by U.S. poet Paul Laurence Dunbar, 23, whose first poetry collection was privately printed as *Oak and Ivory* late in 1893. Dunbar is the son of former slaves and his work is warmly praised by William Dean Howells in *Harper's* magazine. "I never saw a Purple Cow,/ I never hope to see one;/ But I can tell you, anyhow,/ I'd rather see than be one," writes *San Francisco Lark* editor Frank Gelett Burgess, 29, whose jingle gains immediate currency.

The Venice Biennale opens. The first international show of contemporary art begins a tradition that will be continued for more than 80 years.

Berthe Morisot dies at Paris March 2 at age 54.

Sculpture *The Burghers of Calais* by Auguste René Rodin breaks with tradition by showing the burghers walking in file rather than grouped in a circle or square (*see* 1347). Commissioned by the city of Calais, the work has taken Rodin 11 years.

A Pocket Kodak is introduced by Eastman Kodak, and the new camera gains immediate success (*see* transparent negative film, 1889; Brownie, 1900).

Theater *An Ideal Husband* by Oscar Wilde 1/3 at London's Haymarket Theatre; *The Importance of Being Earnest* by Oscar Wilde 2/14 at London's St. James Theatre. Wilde is called a homosexual by Sir John Sholto Douglas, marquis of Queensberry, whose son is one of Wilde's intimates, Wilde brings libel action against Queensberry, revelations are made about Wilde's personal morals, he is sentenced in May at the Old Bailey to 2 years' imprisonment for offenses he has committed, and he goes into bankruptcy soon after. *The Art of Maryland* by David Belasco 10/22 at New York's Herald Square Theater, with Mrs. Leslie Carter, 229 perfs.

The first theater showing of motion pictures takes place March 22 at 44 rue de Rennes, Paris, where members of the Société d'Encouragement à l'Industrie Nationale see a film of workers leaving the Lumière factory at Lyons for their dinner hour. The cinematographe of inventors Louis and Auguste Lumière, 31 and 33 respectively, is a vast improvement over the kinetoscope peepshow introduced last year by Thomas Edison, whose film can be viewed by only one person at a time. The 16-frame per second mechanism devised by the Lumière brothers will be the standard for films for decades (*see* 1896).

The first commercial presentation of a film on a screen takes place May 20 at New York. An audience in a converted store at 153 Broadway views a 4-minute film of a boxing match.

A ciné projector patented by U.S. inventor Charles Francis Jenkins, 28, has an intermittent motion.

A combination ciné camera and projector patented May 27 by British inventor Birt Acres has an appliance for loop-forming. Acres has filmed the Oxford-Cambridge boat race March 30, he films the Derby,

using film purchased from the American Celluloid Co. of Newark, N.J., but his associate Robert Paul will challenge his claim to sole proprietorship.

Ballet *Swan Lake* 2/8 at St. Petersburg's Maryinsky Theater, with choreography by Marius Petipa in a complete version of the 1877 ballet with music by the late Petr Ilich Tchaikovsky.

First performances Symphony No. 2 in C minor (*The Resurrection*) by Gustav Mahler 4/14 at Berlin; "Till Eulenspiegel's Merry Pranks" ("Till Eulenspiegels Lustige Streiche") by German composer Richard Strauss, 31, 11/5 at Cologne.

Popular songs "The Band Played On" by New York actor-composer John F. Palmer, lyrics by English-American actor Charles B. Ward, beginning, "Casey would waltz with a strawberry blonde...."

"America the Beautiful" by Wellesley College English professor Katharine Lee Bates, 36, will be set to the music of Samuel A. Ward's "Materna" and will become an unofficial national anthem. A climb up Pike's Peak in 1893 has inspired Bates to write her poem about America's "amber waves of grain" and "purple mountain majesty above the fruited plain ... from sea to shining sea." Revised versions will appear in 1904 and 1911.

The U.S. yacht *Defender* defeats *Valkyrie II* 3 to 0 to thwart the seventh English effort to regain the America's Cup.

The American Bowling Congress founded September 9 sets rules for a 10-pin bowling game devised to circumvent a congressional prohibition of 9-pin bowling. The new ABC will sponsor the first national tournament at Chicago in 1901 and the event will attract 41 five-man teams, 72 two-man teams, and 115 individual bowlers.

South Carolina's Pinehurst Country Club opens in December on 5,000 acres in The Barrens. Boston millionaire James W. Tufts paid $1 per acre for the property in June, he has built a hotel, stables, stores, greenhouses, a church, a post office, and the country club that will grow to have five 18-hole golf courses and will become a world-renowned golfing mecca.

The Gillette razor has its beginnings in a proposal by U.S. bottle stopper salesman King Camp Gillette, 40, for a disposable razor blade. Gillette's boss William Painter has advised him to "invent something which will be used once and thrown away" so that "the customer will come back for more" (*see* 1892) and when Gillette finds his razor dull, he says to himself, "A razor is only a sharp edge, and everything back of it is just support. Why forge a great piece of steel and spend so much time and labor in hollow grinding it when the same result can be obtained by putting an edge on a piece of steel only thick enough to hold an edge?" But he is unable to find technical expertise or financial backing to develop his idea (*see* 1901).

Sears, Roebuck & Company has sales of $750,000, up from $338,000 in 1893, and A. C. Roebuck sells his interest in the firm for $2,000 to Chicago merchant Julius Rosenwald, 33, who hires his brother-in-law Aaron Nusbaum to serve as treasurer and general manager of the mail-order house (see 1904).

Chicago's Marquette building is completed by Holabird & Roche with wide windows that flood the building's interior with light but create problems of partitioning office space.

The Prudential (Guaranty) building at Buffalo, N.Y., is completed by Louis Sullivan.

New York's Washington Arch is completed at the foot of Fifth Avenue at a cost of $128,000. The 86-foot-high arch designed by architect Stanford White commemorates the first inauguration of President George Washington.

Biltmore House at Asheville, N.C., is completed for railroad heir George Washington Vanderbilt II, 33, and is the world's largest private house. Located on an estate of 119,000 acres and built in 5 years at a cost of $4.1 million, the house has 250 rooms and is surrounded by vast forests. Forester Gifford Pinchot, 30, is employed to superintend the forests (see 1898).

The Breakers is completed by Richard Morris Hunt at Newport, R.I., for railroad heir Cornelius Vanderbilt II, 52, who is president of the New York and Harlem Railroad, chairman of the boards of the New York Central & Hudson River and of the Michigan Central, eldest brother of G. W. Vanderbilt II (above), and donor of an 1893 Yale dormitory that memorializes his son William Henry. The 70-room fireproof summer "cottage" on Ochre Point Road is modeled on palazzos at Genoa and Turin and has been completed in less than 3 years to replace the P. Lorillard house of the same name, which burned down in November 1892.

The Breakers completed at Palm Beach, Fla., is a vast rambling winter hotel financed by Florida East Coast Railroad promoter H. M. Flagler (see 1903; Royal Poinciana, 1894).

Richmond's Jefferson Hotel opens with electric lights and two toilets on every floor. The electric system will cause a fire that will destroy the hotel in 1901, but the Jefferson will reopen in 1910 with 300 rooms, each with a private bath.

Britain's National Trust is created with government funding to preserve country houses, parks, and gardens. The National Trust will protect 150 "stately homes," 100 grand gardens and landscaped parks, 17 entire villages, more than 2,000 farms, and some nature reserves (see first British national park, 1950).

The world wheat price falls to £5 per ton as North American producers make large initial offerings, but the price rises when it turns out that the Kansas wheat crop totals only 18 million bushels—less than half a million metric tons.

The U.S. Department of Agriculture sends agronomist Mark Alfred Carleton, 29, out to Kansas to investigate the wheat crop shortfall. Carleton reports that the only good drought-resistant wheat grown in Kansas is the Turkey Red wheat introduced by Russian Mennonites in 1874, and his report creates a clamor for the "miracle" wheat that will soon replace soft spring wheat completely in Kansas (see 1896).

Florida ships 30 million pieces of fruit, down from a billion last year. All the state's lemon trees were killed by a freeze last year.

The California Fruit Growers Exchange cooperative is organized to market the produce of California growers in the face of discriminatory freight rates (see 1885; Sunkist, 1919).

Boston's Sacred Cod is moved to the new Massachusetts State House after 111 years in the old State House.

A record 211.5-pound cod measuring more than 6 feet in length is caught by Massachusetts fishermen using a line trawl.

Columbia River salmon canning reaches its peak of 634,000 cases (see 1866; CRPA, 1899).

Canned foods are shown to keep from spoiling not because air has been driven out of the container but because bacteria have been killed or inhibited in their growth (see Appert, 1810; Pasteur, 1861). S. C. Prescott at the Massachusetts Institute of Technology and William Lyman Underwood conduct studies that will continue over the next 3 years and will lead to safer canning methods by producing charts giving optimum processing times and temperatures.

The botulism bacterium *Clostridium botulinum* is isolated by Belgian bacteriologist Emilie Pierre Marie Van Ermengem, 44. The anaerobic bacterium, whose toxin is twice as deadly as tetanus toxin and 12 times deadlier than rattlesnake venom, has been associated in Europe with sausages whose cases provide an airless environment, but botulism in the United States stems largely from nonacidic foods that have been improperly bottled or canned (see 1920).

Del Monte canned goods are introduced by California's Oakland Preserving Company, which also markets an ordinary line but which identifies its premium grade with the name Del Monte and a label picture of Charles Crocker's hotel on Monterey Bay, which has been rebuilt since the 1887 fire that destroyed the original structure (see 1891; 1916).

An automatic bottle-blowing machine is patented by Ohio glassmaker Michael Joseph Owens, 36, who is manager of Edward Drummond Libbey's Toledo glass factory (see 1877; 1903).

"Coca-Cola is now sold in every state of the Union," boasts Asa Candler of Atlanta, but the beverage has yet to be bottled (see 1892; 1899).

White Rock mineral water and ginger ale are promoted as mixers for alcoholic beverages by New York White Rock representative Frank T. Huntoon who decides that promoting mineral waters only with health claims shuts them out of a larger market. Gin-

1895 (cont.) ger ale, sarsaparilla, and root beer are sold under the White Rock label, but the name White Rock will soon be a generic for carbonated water (*see* 1893; Cliquot Club, 1901; Canada Dry, 1907).

The Anti-Saloon League of America is organized at Washington, D.C. (*see* W.C.T.U., 1874; Nation, 1900).

Beatrice Foods has its beginnings in the Beatrice Creamery Company at Beatrice, Neb., started by local entrepreneur George Everett Haskell, 30, whose firm will grow to become the leading U.S. marketer of processed foods and the third largest U.S. dairy company. Haskell 3 years ago acquired the bankrupt Fremont Butter and Egg Company for which he had worked at $10 per week, he will arrange with the De Laval Separator Company to finance the purchase of separators by Nebraska farmers, and by 1905, there will be 30,000 De Laval separators on Nebraska farms (*see* De Laval, 1877; Beatrice, 1905).

Postum is introduced as a coffee substitute at Battle Creek, Mich., by C. W. Post, who has quit "the San" uncured and discouraged but who has embraced Christian Science. Post sells his Postum in paper bags from hand carts (*see* 1893; Grape Nuts, 1897).

Granose, introduced in February, is the world's first flaked breakfast cereal. John Harvey Kellogg has run boiled wheat through his wife's machine for rolling out dough, he has baked the thin film in an oven, and he has been persuaded by his 35-year-old brother Will Keith Kellogg not to grind the flakes into granules but to sell them as flakes. Since a 10-ounce package sells for 15 cents, Kellogg and his brother sell 60 cent per bushel wheat at $12 per bushel retail (*see* 1894; Sanitas Corn Flakes, 1898).

Shredded Wheat biscuits develop a market. Henry D. Perky acquires a large bakery at Worcester, Mass., to satisfy the growing demand (*see* 1894; 1898).

Swans Down cake flour is introduced by Evansville, Ind., miller Addison Igleheart, whose family has been making flour at Evansville for nearly 40 years and has been selling Swans Down family flour since 1876. Igleheart develops a low-gluten cake flour from winter wheat which he has ground, sifted through silk screens, and ground again. He sells some to a cake pan salesman who needs flour to demonstrate his pans, and the salesman is so impressed that he quits selling pans to sell the new cake flour. It will be advertised in the *Ladies' Home Journal* beginning in 1898 (the first national advertising for any packaged cake flour), and in 1904, it will win grand prize for cake flour at the St. Louis exposition (*see* 1926).

Baker's Coconut Company has its beginnings as Philadelphia miller Franklin Baker accepts a cargo of fresh coconuts in lieu of cash for a consignment of flour he has shipped to a merchant at Havana who has been unable to raise cash because of Cuba's political unrest (above). When Baker finds it impossible to sell the coconuts in Philadelphia markets, he buys machinery and develops a method for producing shredded coconut meat of uniform quality, a product he promotes to local housewives. The coconut business will be so successful that Baker will sell his flour business in 2 years and will establish the Franklin Baker Co. (*see* 1927).

The first U.S. pizzeria opens in New York at 53½ Spring Street (*see* 1905).

The Cordon Bleu Cooking School opened by Marthe Distel at the Palais Royal in Paris takes a name derived from the blue ribbon worn by graduates of the school opened by Mme. de Maintenon in 1686. The Grand Diplôme of the new school on the rue Champ de Mars will become the highest credential a chef can have (*see* 1934).

The "Chantilly" silver pattern that will be the most popular U.S. flatware pattern for more than 80 years is introduced by the Gorham Company.

The word "calorie" is applied to food for the first time by Wesleyan University professor Wilbur Olin Atwater, 41, who has studied in Germany and who has established an Office of Experiment Stations in the U.S. Department of Agriculture. An agricultural chemist, Atwater takes the kilocalorie, or large calorie (the amount of heat needed to raise the temperature of a kilogram of water 1 degree Celsius—from 15°C to 16°C at a pressure of 1 atmosphere—or 4 pints of water 1 degree Fahrenheit), and he uses this calorie as a measure of the energy contained in foods for a guide to economical food buying based solely on calories per dollar (*see* 1902).

Emigration of Russians increases to 108,000 from scarcely 10,000 in 1882 as population pressures force the czar Nicholas II to ease restrictions against travel. Most of the emigration is to Siberia and is encouraged by the Trans-Siberian Railway whose construction began 4 years ago (*see* 1899).

1896 The Supreme Court upholds racial segregation by sustaining a Louisiana "Jim Crow car law" May 18 in the case of *Plessy* v. *Ferguson*. The Court lays down the doctrine that states may provide blacks with "separate but equal" facilities for education, transportation, and public accommodations." Justice John Harlan says, "The Constitution is color-blind" in a lone but vigorous dissenting opinion, but the majority ruling sets off a wave of new segregation measures that designate drinking fountains, public benches, rest rooms, railroad cars, hospitals, and theater sections "Colored" or "Whites Only" (*see* 1954).

Idaho women gain suffrage through an amendment to the state constitution.

Utah is admitted to the Union as the 45th state after Mormons agree to give up polygamous marriage.

"You shall not press down upon the brow of labor this crown of thorns, you shall not crucify mankind upon a cross of gold," says Nebraska Fundamentalist William Jennings Bryan, 36, in a speech July 8 at the Democratic National Convention. His oratory in support of free silver wins him the nomination, and the Populist party also nominates Bryan.

Ohio governor William McKinley, 53, gains the Republican presidential nomination with support from Cleveland industrialist Mark Hanna. Employers put pressure on workers to vote against "anarchy" and "revolution" lest they jeopardize their jobs, and a rise in wheat prices before election day alleviates agrarian discontent. Bryan fails to attract urban voters, and while he wins 176 electoral votes by carrying the South, the Great Plains states, and the Rocky Mountain states, he loses to McKinley who wins 271 electoral votes and gains election with a 600,000 plurality in the popular vote.

Canada gets her first French-Canadian premier as Quebec Liberal Wilfrid Laurier, 55, wins in the general elections held in June. He takes office July 11 to begin more than 15 years as premier.

Boer forces in South Africa defeat L. Starr Jameson at Krugersdorp January 1, they force him to surrender January 2 at Doorn Kop, and they turn him over to the British for trial in England, where he is convicted but receives only a light sentence (see 1895). A telegram of congratulations to Oom Paul Kruger of Transvaal from the German kaiser January 3 strains Anglo-German relations, and mutual suspicions set in among the Boers and British in South Africa.

Cecil Rhodes resigns the Cape Colony premiership January 6, a committee of the Cape Assembly finds him guilty of having engineered last year's Jameson raid. The Transvaal government signs a defensive alliance with the Orange Free State in mid-March, and it fortifies Pretoria and Johannesburg with munitions ordered from Europe (see Boer War, 1899).

British forces take Coomassie January 18 in the Fourth Ashanti War and imprison the Ashanti king.

Ethiopian warriors defeat Italian troops March 1 at Adowa and force Italy to sue for peace. The Treaty of Addis Ababa October 6 withdraws the Italian protectorate (see 1895; 1897).

Matebele tribesmen in Rhodesia begin a new uprising that continues into October.

A French expedition to claim the Sudan sets out for Fashoda under the command of Jean Baptiste Marchand, 33, who has traced the Niger River to its source and has explored the region from the Niger River to Tengrela (see 1897).

France proclaims the African island of Madagascar a French colony August 6 (see 1897).

Anglo-Egyptian troops begin a reconquest of the Sudan under the command of General Horatio Herbert Kitchener, 46, who builds a railroad as he advances. He takes Dongola September 21 (see 1885; 1898).

The shah of Persia Nasr-ed-Din is assassinated May 1 at age 65 after a 48-year reign that has seen the growth of Russian power in the country. The shah is succeeded by his incompetent 43-year-old son who will reign until 1907 as Muzaffar-ed-Din.

Armenian revolutionaries attack the Ottoman Bank at Constantinople August 26, and Ottoman forces retaliate with a 3-day massacre of Armenians.

Bulgaria's Prince Ferdinand gains recognition from Russia and then from other powers following the conversion of his 2-year-old son Boris to the Orthodox faith, but Bulgaria remains a principality of the Ottoman Empire (see 1908).

 Radioactivity is discovered in uranium by French physicist Antoine Henri Becquerel, 44 (see Klaproth, 1797; Planck, 1900; Curie, 1904).

 A system of antityphoid inoculation is originated by British pathologist Almroth Edward Wright, 35 (see Eberth, Koch, 1880).

The F. Hoffman-LaRoche & Co. AG firm that will become the world's leading ethical drug company has its beginnings as Swiss entrepreneur Fritz Hoffman-LaRoche, 27, is helped by his silk merchant father to buy out a German pharmacist with whom he formed a partnership 2 years ago. Young Hoffman-LaRoche takes over a small chemical wholesaler's plant that makes extracts, tinctures, varnish, and floor wax, and he introduces an antiseptic powder.

The Canadian Red Cross is founded.

 Gold in Canada's Klondike near the Alaskan border is discovered August 17 by U.S. prospector George Washington Carmack, 35, who has been in Alaska since 1888. A new gold rush begins (see 1897).

The Mesabi Range holdings of John D. Rockefeller's Lake Superior Consolidated Iron Mines Company are purchased by the Carnegie Corporation and by Pittsburgh's Henry W. Oliver (see 1893; 1901).

Japan's Yawata Steelworks, founded in March, is the first Japanese steelmaking firm. A 25-million yen plant will be completed in Kyushu by German engineers in 1901, and Japan will become a major world steel producer (see Fuji Steel, 1945).

A large plate glass plant is completed on the east side of the Maumee River at Toledo, Ohio, by Edward Ford, son of America's pioneer glassmaker (see 1883). Ford will establish a model town at Rossford.

 Miami, Fla., is incorporated at Fort Dallas, which last year had only 3 houses. H. M. Flagler extends his Florida East Coast Railroad to the new town and dredges its harbor (see hotel, below; Miami Beach, 1913).

 Aviation is pioneered by U.S. astronomer Samuel Pierpont Langley, 62, of the Smithsonian Institution at Washington, D.C. Langley sends a steam-powered model airplane on a 3,000-foot flight along the Potomac May 6, it is the first flight of a mechanically propelled flying machine, and he sends an improved model on a 4,200-foot flight in November (see 1903).

The Haynes-Duryea motorcar produced by the Duryea Motor Wagon Company of Springfield, Mass., is the first U.S. motorcar to be offered for public sale. Total U.S. motorcar production is 25 (see 1895; 1897).

1896 (cont.) British-Leyland has its beginnings in the Leyland Motors firm founded at the town of Leyland in Lancashire (*see* 1968).

The British Daimler Company is founded by English entrepreneur H. J. Lawson who buys a factory site at Coventry to produce a motorcar that will be favored by British royalty (*see* 1890).

Britain repeals her Red Flag Act of 1865 requiring that a man on foot carrying a red flag precede all road carriages, but the suggestion that motorcars may come to rival "light railways" brings roars of laughter from the benches in Parliament.

The first vertical four-cylinder motorcar engine is introduced by France's Panhard & Levassor, which also introduces sliding gears with a cone clutch.

The Stanley Steamer is introduced at Newton, Mass., by Francis Edgar Stanley, 47, and his twin brother Freeling O. Stanley who have prospered in making photographic dry plates but who have been inspired by a DeDion *Voiture à vapeur* they saw demonstrated in Massachusetts last year (*see* 1899).

The U.S. bicycle industry has sales of $60 million, with the average bike retailing at $100. Pope Manufacturing Company turns out one bicycle per minute (*see* 1877; 1885; Pope motorcars, 1897).

The first underground rail service on the European continent begins at Budapest where a 2.5-mile electric subway goes into operation (*see* London, 1890; Paris, 1900; Boston, 1897).

Princeton University assumes that name 250 years after being chartered as the College of New Jersey.

New York University assumes that name 65 years after being chartered as the University of the City of New York.

Adelphi College is founded at Long Island City, N.Y.

Stromberg-Carlson Telephone Manufacturing Corporation is founded by Swedish-American engineers Alfred Stromberg, 35, and Androv Carlson who have worked for the Chicago Western Telephone Construction Company. The new firm is capitalized at $50,000, the founders will sell out for $750,000 in 1902 to Rochester, N.Y., investors, and the new owners will move the company into production of radio receivers after Carlson's death in 1913 (*see* 1955).

The world's first permanent wireless installation is established in November by Marconi's Wireless Telegraph Co., Ltd. at The Needles on the Isle of Wight, Hampshire, England. The firm has been set up by Guglielmo Marconi's British relatives (*see* 1895; 1901; Braun, 1897).

The *London Daily Mail* is founded by *Evening News* publisher Alfred C. W. Harmsworth who condenses news in "the penny newspaper for one halfpenny," gains wide circulation for his new morning paper, and continues a campaign he has begun to warn Britons of the threat from Germany (*see* 1894; 1903).

The *New York Times,* published since 1851, gets a face-lift from publisher Adolph S. Ochs, now 39, who has made his *Chattanooga Times* prosper, has been married since 1883 to the daughter of Cincinnati's Rabbi Isaac Wise, and has acquired control of the *New York Times* August 18 for $75,000, most of it borrowed. The other owners assure Ochs of a stock majority if he can make the paper profitable for 3 consecutive years, he throws out the paper's romantic fiction and its tiny typefaces, he improves neglected areas such as financial news, he starts a weekly book review section and a Sunday magazine, and he adopts the slogan "All the News That's Fit to Print" (*see* 1878; 1897).

"What's the Matter with Kansas?" by *Emporia Gazette* editor William Allen White, 28, attracts national attention to White's fledgling newspaper.

"The Yellow Kid" appears in Joseph Pulitzer's *New York World* in March. The one-panel cartoon by Richard F. Outcault will appear in strip form in William Randolph Hearst's *New York Journal* beginning October 24 of next year in the *Journal's* Sunday color supplement, Pulitzer and Hearst will battle over rights to the cartoon, and the contest for readership between the two will be marked by sensationalism that will be called "yellow journalism," a phrase that will be applied to other sensationalist papers.

Scott, Foresman Co. publishers is founded at Chicago by E. H. Scott, W. C. Foresman, and Hugh Foresman to buy the George Sherwood Book Co. list. The firm will publish the "modern McGuffey" *Elson's Grammar School Readers* beginning in 1909, and by 1945 Scott, Foresman will be the largest U.S. publisher of elementary school texts as well as being a major publisher of high school and college texts.

Fiction *In His Steps* by Topeka, Kans., clergyman-author Charles Monroe Sheldon, 39, is serialized in the *Chicago Advance,* a religious weekly, while Sheldon keeps his pews filled with readings to his parishioners at the new Central Congregational Church. Sheldon's book—subtitled *What Would Jesus Do?*—will appear next year as a paperback novel, will be pirated because of a defective copyright, will be translated into 45 languages, will sell at least 8 million and possibly 30 million copies, but will net its author only a few hundred dollars. *Quo Vadis* by Polish novelist Henryk Sienkiewicz, 50, who will become world-famous for his story of Nero's Rome; *Country of the Pointed Firs* (stories) by Sarah Orne Jewett who portrays the loneliness of the isolated and declining coastal town of South Berwick, Me.

Juvenile *Frank Merriwell, or First Days at Fardale* by U.S. author Burt L. Standish (William Gilbert Patten), 30, who has written the book at the suggestion of New York publishers Street and Smith (*see* Nick Carter, 1886). Patten will write 776 Frank Merriwell novels whose weekly sales will average 125,000 copies (*see* Stratemeyer, 1899).

Poetry *A Shropshire Lad* by University College Latin professor A. E. (Alfred Edward) Housman, 37, at London: "When I was one and twenty/ I heard a wise man say,/'Give crowns and pounds and guineas/ But not your heart away . . .'" (XIII, 1); *Green Fire* by Scottish poet Fiona Macleod (William Sharp), 40, whose lyric poem "The Lonely Hunter" ends, "O never a green leaf whispers, where the green-gold branches swing:/ O never a song I hear now, where one was wont to sing./ Here in the heart of Summer, sweet is life to me still,/ But my heart is a lonely hunter that hunts on a lonely hill." Sharp has been using the pen name Fiona Macleod since 1893 to sign mystical stories and poetic prose works designed to promote a Celtic revival. *Lyrics of Lowly Life* by Paul Laurence Dunbar whose book has a sympathetic introduction by William Dean Howells that helps make the young man fashionable; *Prosas profanas* by Nicaragua's Ruben Dario whose book is a landmark in the modernista movement.

Painting *The 'Cello Player* by Thomas Eakins; *Daniel in the Lions' Den* by U.S. painter Henry Ossawa Tanner, 37, who arrived at Paris 5 years ago and will remain there; *The Vuillard Family at Lunch* by Jean Edouard Vuillard. Sir John Everett Millais dies at London August 13 at age 67.

London's National Portrait Gallery (Tate Gallery) moves from Bethnal Green into a permanent home in Westminster completed with funds contributed by sugar magnate Sir Henry Tate, now 77, who has given £80,000 and has donated 57 modern paintings. The Tate will be enlarged in 1899 and further enlarged in 1908 (*see* Duveen, 1926).

Theater *Michael and His Lost Angel* by Henry Arthur Jones 1/15 at London's Lyceum Theatre; *The Dupe (Le dindon)* by Georges Feydeau 2/8 at the Théâtre du Palais Royal, Paris; *Salomé* by Oscar Wilde 2/11 at the Théâtre de l'Oeuvre, Paris (Wilde wrote the play in French but cannot enjoy the furor it creates because he is confined in Reading Gaol); *Rosemary* by French-born English playwright Louis Napoleon Parker, 44, and Murray Carson 8/31 at New York's Empire Theater, with John Drew, 136 perfs.; *Secret Service* by U.S. playwright-actor William H. Gillette, 41, 10/5 at New York's Garrick Theatre, with Gillette as Captain Thorne, a secret agent for the Union Army, 176 perfs.; *The Sea Gull (Chayka)* by Anton Chekhov 10/17 at St. Petersburg's Alexandrinsky Theater (*see* 1898); *The Sunken Bell (Die versunkene Glocke)* by Gerhart Hauptmann 12/2 at Berlin's Deutsches Theater; *Emperor and Galilean (Kejsor og Galileer)* by Henrik Ibsen 12/5 at Leipzig's Stadttheater; *King Ubu (Ubu Roi)* by French playwright Alfred Jarry, 23 (who wrote it at age 15) 12/10 at the Théâtre de l'Oeuvre, Paris.

French comedienne Anna Held, 23, makes her U.S. debut September 21 at New York's Herald Square Theater in a lavish production of the 1884 Charles H. Hoyt play *A Parlor Match* mounted by Florenz Ziegfeld with help from Charles Dillingham, 48 perfs.

The first U.S. public showing of motion pictures April 20 at Koster and Bial's Music Hall in New York employs Thomas Edison's Vitascope, an improvement on his kinetoscope of 1893, and a projector made by Thomas Armat (*see* 1903; Lumière, 1895).

Opera *Pepita Jiminez* 1/5 at Barcelona's Liceo, with music by Isaac Albeniz; *La Bohème* 2/1 at Turin's Teatro Reggio, with music by Giacomo Puccini, libretto from "Scenes de la Vie de Bohème" by the late Henri Murger whose work appeared in the journal *Le Corsair* in the late 1840s; *The Grand Duke (or The Statutory Duel)* 3/7 at London's Savoy Theatre is the last Gilbert & Sullivan operetta (Sullivan will die in 1900, Gilbert in 1911); *Andrea Chénier* 3/23 at Milan's Teatro alla Scala, with music by Italian composer Umberto Giordano, 28; *Der Corregidor* 6/7 at Mannheim with music by German composer Hugo Wolf.

Brazil's $5 million Manaus Opera House opens some 700 miles up the Amazon where it has been built for rubber barons whose business has boomed with the growth of the bicycle industry and with increased use of motorcars and has not yet been made uneconomic by East Indian rubber plantations (*see* Wickham, 1876). The ballerina Anna Pavlova will dance at Manaus and the entire company of Milan's Teatro alla Scala will cross the ocean and ascend the Amazon for annual appearances.

First performances Suite No. 2 in E minor *(Indian)* by Edward MacDowell 1/23 at New York's Metropolitan Opera House. MacDowell accepts an invitation to head Columbia University's new department of music (but *see* 1904); Concerto in B minor for Violincello and Orchestra by Anton Dvorak 3/19 at London; Concerto No. 5 in F major for Piano and Orchestra by Camille Saint-Saëns 6/2 at Paris on the 50th anniversary of the composer's first public appearance as a pianist; "Roland (The Saracens and Lovely Alda)" by Edward MacDowell 11/5 at Boston's Tremont Theater; *Also Sprach Zarathustra* (freely after Friedrich Nietzsche) (Tone Poem) by Richard Strauss 11/27 at Frankfurt-am-Main.

Stage musicals *El Capitan* 4/20 at New York's Broadway Theater, with De Wolf Hopper in a comic opera with music by John Philip Sousa, 112 perfs.; *The Geisha* 4/25 at Daly's Theatre, London, with music by Sidney Jones, lyrics by Harry Greenback, 750 perfs.; *The Art of Maryland* 9/5 at New York's new Weber and Fields Music Hall, with Joe Weber and Lew Fields in a parody of David Belasco's legitimate stage hit *The Heart of Maryland* (*see* 1895).

Popular songs "Sweet Rosie O'Grady" by New York songwriter Maude Nugent, 19, who has been unable to find a publisher. She introduces the song herself at Tony Pastor's Opera House; "Kentucky Babe" by German-American composer Adam Geibel, 41, lyrics by Richard Henry Buck, 26; "A Hot Time in the Old Town" by U.S. violinist-composer-minstrel Theodore August Metz, 48, lyrics by end man Joe Hayden.

Quack medicine flourished in a time of great medical discoveries. Most doctors remained unaware of the progress.

The Olympic Games of ancient Greece are revived through the efforts of Greek nationalists and of French educator-sportsman Pierre de Frédy, 33, baron de Coubertin, who obtained support 2 years ago for bringing back the games banned by the Romans in 394 A.D. but held on a small scale by the Greeks in 1859, 1870, 1875, and 1889 and by the French in 1892. The late Greek-Romanian Evangelios Zappas has willed his entire fortune to reestablishing the Olympic games in Greece, the ancient Athens stadium has been renovated at a cost of $500,000, the Greek government has added $100,000 to the Zappas money, the Greek merchant George Averoff of Alexandria has given $390,000 to complete restoration of the Panathenaic Stadium, and the first modern Olympiad is held at Athens with 484 contestants from 13 nations to begin a quadrennial event that will be broadened to include athletic events undreamed of by the Greeks of ancient times (see Boston Marathon, 1897).

The world's first public golf course opens in New York's Van Cortlandt Park.

Volunteers of America is founded by a grandson of the late Salvation Army founder William Booth (see 1878). Ballington Booth has been in charge of the Salvation Army's U.S. operations, but he has had a falling out with his father, and he organizes a rival group that resembles the Salvation Army.

Atlantic City, N.J., completes a boardwalk 41 feet wide to replace a series of four narrower boardwalks built since 1870.

Wanamaker's New York opens in East 10th Street as Philadelphia merchant John Wanamaker takes over the cast-iron A. T. Stewart retail palace of 1862. Wanamaker has long since expanded his menswear store of 1861 into a department store (see 1903).

S. H. Kress & Company 5, 10, and 25-cent store opens at Memphis where merchant Samuel Henry Kress, 33, has been inspired by the success of F. W. Woolworth since 1879 and has decided to start a similar chain-store business in the South. Kress's Memphis store is an immediate success, he will soon follow it with stores in other southern cities, he will move to New York in 1900, he will have 51 stores in operation by 1907, and by the time he dies in 1955 at age 92, he will have 264 stores in his chain. Kress will be a major benefactor of Washington's National Gallery of Art, New York's Metropolitan Museum of Art, and more than 40 other U.S. art museums.

Miami's Royal Palm Hotel opens to begin the city's career as a winter resort (see above). H. M. Flagler adds the Royal Palm to the Alcazar, the Royal Poinciana, the Breakers, and the other hotels he has built at Palm Beach and Daytona (see 1903).

The Palace Hotel opens July 29 at St. Moritz, Switzerland, and gains quick popularity among Europe's wealthy resortgoers. Attracted originally by the alleged health benefits of the town's rust-red springs, English visitors to St. Moritz have invented bobsledding and have popularized tobogganing, curling, Viennese ice dancing, and Norwegian-style skiing.

London's Hotel Cecil opens on the site of Durham House and is the city's largest hotel.

César Ritz is invited by oilman Calouste Gulbenkian and others to build a hotel at Paris (see 1889; Paris Ritz, 1898; Gulbenkian, 1914).

New York's Hotel Greenwich opens under the name Mills Hotel No. 1 at 160 Bleecker Street. The hotel has been funded by philanthropist Darius Ogden Mills of 1864 Bank of California fame, it has been designed by architect Ernest Flagg, each of its 1,500 tiny bedrooms has a window overlooking either the street or one of two grassy inner courts, and it offers lodgings at 20 cents per night to poor "gentlemen" who pay 10 cents to 25 cents per meal, on which the hotel makes a small profit.

Cripple Creek, Colo., has a fire April 25 that begins when kerosene lanterns are knocked over during a dancehall fight. The fire consumes more than 30 acres of buildings including the homes of new millionaires.

A Japanese earthquake and seismic wave June 15 kill an estimated 22,000.

Turkey Red wheat is planted by farmers throughout much of Kansas, Nebraska, Oklahoma, and Texas where it will soon be the predominant winter wheat variety, and in Montana, Minnesota, and the Dakotas where farmers plant Turkey Red in the spring for fall harvesting, but the decline in the U.S. wheat crop last year has encouraged Australia, Canada, and Russia to enter the export market and to compete actively for the European market (see 1895; Kubanka, 1899).

Failure of India's wheat crop raises world prices, but increased world competition (above) keeps prices from rising too high.

U.S. botanist George Washington Carver, 32, joins Alabama's Tuskegee Institute as director of its Department of Agriculture (*see* Booker Washington, 1881; peanuts, 1921).

The bacterium of infectious abortion in cows is discovered by Danish veterinarian B. L. F. Bang who 4 years ago originated a method for eradicating bovine tuberculosis in dairy herds. Since the bacterium is one of several that cause undulant fever, or brucellosis, in humans, it will be called *Brucella abortus* (*see* Bruce, 1887), but the condition it produces in cattle will be called Bang's disease (*see* 1900; Evans, 1917).

Chickens fed polished rice are found to suffer from a disease resembling beriberi (*see* Takaki, 1887). Dutch physicians Christiaan Eijkman and Gerrit Grijns in Java make the discovery but decide that polished rice must contain a toxin that is neutralized by something in rice hulls (*see* 1906; Eijkman, 1886).

Iodine is found present in the human thyroid gland by German biochemist E. Baumann. The mineral is absent from all other human body tissues (*see* Marine, 1905).

Chemical Composition of American Food Materials is published by the U.S. Department of Agriculture. The bulletin is based on work by W. O. Atwater and others who have compiled data on the protein, fat, carbohydrate, ash, water, and refuse content of foods, and it will be revised in 1899 and 1906 (*see* 1950; Atwater, 1895).

"57 Varieties" is adopted by H. J. Heinz as an advertising slogan although the firm produces well over that number of products. Henry J. Heinz has seen a car card advertising 21 shoe styles while riding on a New York elevated train and adapts the idea (*see* 1888; 1900).

S&W canned foods have their beginning in a San Francisco wholesale grocery firm started on Market Street at the corner of Fremont Street by local entrepreneur Samuel Sussman and his cousins Gustav and Samuel I. Wormser.

Tootsie Rolls are introduced at New York by Austrian-American confectioner Leo Hirschfield, 29, whose penny candy is the first to be wrapped in paper. Hirschfield names the chewy, chocolatey confection after his 6-year-old daughter Clara whom he calls "Tootsie."

Cracker Jack is introduced at Chicago by German-American candymaker F. W. Rueckheim and his brother Louis whose candy-coated popcorn mixed with peanuts has been called "crackerjack!" by an enthusiastic salesman. The Rueckheim brothers have been in Chicago since shortly after the fire of 1871, and they have operated a popcorn stand for 20 years. They will adopt the slogan "The More You Eat, the More You Want," they will be helped by the 1908 song "Take Me Out to the Ball Game," they will sell Cracker Jack in boxes containing coupons redeemable for prizes beginning in 1910, they will pack prizes with the Cracker Jack beginning in 1912, they will use Jack and his dog Bingo in advertising beginning in 1916, and they will show them on the box beginning in 1919.

Welch's Grape Juice production moves to Watkins Glen, N.Y., close to a vast grape growing region (*see* 1869). Charles Welch has been running his father's Unfermented Wine business since 1872 (*see* 1897).

Michelob beer is introduced by Adolphus Busch of 1876 Budweiser fame whose St. Louis brewery Anheuser-Busch is the largest in the country. Michelob will be sold only on draft until 1961 (*see* 1933; 1956).

The Olympia Brewing Company is founded at Olympia, Wash., by German-American brewer Leopold F. Schmidt, whose brewery will become the largest on the West Coast.

"Little Egypt" dances nude on the table at a private dinner given at Louis Sherry's by New York playboy Barnum Seeley, grandson and heir of the late circus promoter P. T. Barnum who died 5 years ago at age 80. But while Fahrida Mahszar is widely thought to have performed the *danse du ventre*, or hootchy-kootchy, on the Midway Plaisance of Chicago's 1893 Columbian Exposition under the name "Little Egypt," she never in fact appeared there.

Fannie Farmer's Boston Cooking School Cookbook by the head of a teacher-training institution uses a precise measuring system that will make it an enduring best seller in America (but not in Europe).

National Tea Company has its beginnings in a small tea store that opens on Chicago's North Side.

S&H Green Stamps are issued for the first time by the Sperry & Hutchinson Company founded at Jackson, Mich., by local entrepreneurs Thomas A. Sperry and Shelly B. Hutchinson who issue trading stamps to store customers. Participating stores issue one S&H stamp for every 10 cents a customer spends, books filled with S&H stamps are exchangeable for merchandise at "premium parlors" set up for the purpose, the A&P will soon be a major user of S&H stamps, other companies will spring up to compete with Sperry & Hutchinson, and by 1914 trading stamps will be given out with 6 percent of all U.S. retail purchases, especially purchases at grocery stores (*see* 1951).

1897 The atom, believed by the ancient Greeks to be indivisible, turns out to have a nucleus orbited by one or more electrons (*see* Democritus, 330 B.C.). English physicist Joseph John Thomson, 41, modifies the idea formulated by John Dalton in 1803 and tabularized by Dmitri Mendeléev in 1870, he shows that the structure of each element is characterized not merely by a different atomic weight but also by an atomic number, and he shows that this number is the number of electrons orbiting the nuclei of the element's atoms (*see* Rutherford, 1911; neutron, 1932).

1897 (cont.) The parasite that causes malaria is carried by the Anopheles mosquito, says British physician Ronald Ross, 40, in famine-stricken India. Ross has been investigating the possibility that mosquitoes may spread malaria as was suggested in the case of yellow fever by Carlos Finlay in 1881, he shows that the Anopheles mosquito is the vector for malaria, and his discovery will lead to the draining of swamps where mosquitoes breed, to expanded use of window screens and mosquito netting, and—eventually—to widespread use of insecticides (*see* DDT, 1943; Laveran, 1880; Reed, 1900).

Physiological standardization of pharmaceuticals that cannot be standardized chemically is pioneered by Detroit's Parke, Davis & Company (*see* 1879).

U.S. bituminous coal miners leave the pits July 5 to begin a 12-week walkout. They win an 8-hour day, semimonthly pay, abolition of company stores that charge premium prices and keep them forever in debt, and biennial conferences with mine operators (*see* Virden, 1898; United Mine Workers, 1899).

New York's University Settlement moves into a $200,000 "castle" at the corner of Eldridge and Rivington Streets. The settlement house started by Stanton Coit in 1886 has built public baths that will serve as models for municipal public baths, and it leads the fight for a city subway system.

A new trial for France's Alfred Dreyfus is demanded by his brother Matthieu who has discovered that the handwriting on a key piece of evidence in his brother's 1894 trial was not that of Alfred but of former Austrian army officer Marie Charles Ferdinand Walsin Esterhazy, 50, a finding made early last year by French intelligence chief Colonel Georges Picquart, 43 (*see* Zola, 1898).

The first Zionist congress opens at Basel as Theodor Herzl arouses support for his dream of a Jewish homeland in Palestine that will provide a refuge for the oppressed Jews of the world (*see* 1894). Herzl will obtain an appointment with the Ottoman sultan Abdul Hamid II and although he has scant financial backing, he will offer to buy up the Turkish national debt in exchange for Jewish rights in "the Promised Land" of Palestine (*see* Balfour Declaration, 1917).

Zanzibar abolishes slavery by decree of the sultan whose country has been a British protectorate since 1890 (*see* 1873; 1884; 1892).

Belgian forces reach the Nile at Rejaf in February, they defeat the Sudan dervishes, they occupy Loda and Wadelai, they reach the Bahr-el-Ghazal region in August, but they are challenged in September by a great mutiny as the Batetelas revolt on the upper Congo in an insurrection that will last until 1900.

Madagascar's Malagasy queen Hova is deposed at the end of February.

The boundary between Dahomey and Togoland is defined July 23 by a Franco-German agreement.

French forces have taken Busa February 23, and they take Nikki November 30, bringing vigorous protests from Britain and raising the threat of war between Britain and France. (*see* 1898).

The Hawaiian Islands are annexed to the United States under terms of June 16 treaty that is ratified by the Hawaiian Senate September 9. Annexation has been pushed by the Hawaiian sugar planters, who proclaimed the Republic of Hawaii in 1894, but Japan has some 25,000 nationals in the islands and files a formal protest, warning of grave consequences (*see* 1882; 1898; 1941).

Cubans reject an offer of self-government from Spain's Liberal premier Praxades Sagasta, insisting on complete independence (*see* 1895; 1898).

Honduras in Central America has a revolution that is aided by U.S. soldier of fortune Lee Christmas who has been working as a locomotive engineer in the country. He is celebrated by his journalist friend Richard Harding Davis, 33, in the novel *Soldiers of Fortune* (*see* Zemurray, 1911).

German forces occupy Kiaochow (Chia-chou) Bay and Tsingtao in China November 14 following the murder of two German missionaries in Shantung province. The Germans have selected Tsingtao as their reward for having intervened in behalf of China against Japan in 1895, but their action precipitates a scramble for consessions in China by most of the great European powers (*see* 1895; 1899).

News of last year's Klondike gold discoveries reaches the United States in January and starts a new gold rush. The ship *Excelsior* arrives at San Francisco in July with $750,000 in Klondike gold, the *Portland* arrives at Seattle 3 days later with $800,000 in gold, and by year's end the Klondike field has yielded $22 million worth of gold.

World gold production reaches nearly 11.5 million ounces, up from 5 to 6 million per year between 1860 and 1890 but still little more than half the 22 million-ounce figure that will be reached by 1910.

The gold standard is introduced in Russia by finance minister Sergei Yulievich Witte, 48.

The gold standard is adopted by Japan March 29.

The Dingley Tariff Act passed by Congress July 24 raises U.S. living costs by increasing duties to an average of 57 percent. Rates are hiked on sugar, salt, tin cans, glassware, and tobacco, as well as on iron and steel, steel rails, petroleum, lead, copper, locomotives, matches, whisky, and leather goods, but the influx of gold from the Klondike (above) helps end the 4-year economic depression. A decade of prosperity begins in the United States.

New York's Kuhn, Loeb & Co. has admitted German banker Otto Hermann Kahn, 29, to membership January 1. A naturalized British subject, Kahn joined the New York banking firm Speyer & Co. in 1893, he stayed for 2 years, he has traveled in Europe for the past year, he has married the daughter of Kuhn, Loeb partner Abraham Wolff, and he joins with Kuhn, Loeb head Jacob Schiff and with speculator Edward Henry Harriman, 49, in reorganizing the bankrupt Union Pacific Railroad, pruning away unprofitable branch lines, and creating a simplified bond structure to replace the company's old tangle of debts (the Union Pacific will soon be able to buy control of the Southern Pacific and to buy a 40 percent interest in the Northern Pacific) (see 1901).

Continental Casualty Company is founded at Chicago and will become known as "the Lloyd's of Chicago" (see Lloyd's of London, 1870). The firm will pioneer in writing accident and health insurance at a time when state regulation of rates is lax and competition almost nonexistent (see 1911).

Dow Chemical Company is founded by Herbert H. Dow at Midland, Mich. (see 1891; 1922).

E. I. du Pont de Nemours & Co. buys the smokeless powder patents and the Squankum, N.J., powder plant of U.S. engineer and powdermaker Hudson Maxim, 44, whose brother Hiram invented the first fully automatic machine gun in 1883 (see Du Pont, 1872; 1899).

U.S. railroads are subject to the Sherman Anti-Trust Law of 1890, says the Supreme Court March 22 in a 5 to 4 decision handed down in the *Trans-Missouri Freight* case, but the "long and short haul" clause of the Interstate Commerce Act of 1887 is nullified by the court November 8 in *Interstate Commerce Commission v. Alabama Midland Railway Company.*

Boston's Boylston Street subway line between the Public Gardens and Park Street begins service September 1 and is the first U.S. subway line (see Budapest, 1896). The line will be extended within a year to the 3-year-old North Station (see New York, 1904).

Trolley service begins across New York's 14-year-old Brooklyn Bridge.

A projected Capetown-to-Cairo Railroad reaches Bulawayo in Southern Rhodesia November 4.

U.S. auto production reaches 100, up from 25 last year (see 1898).

Bicycle maker Albert A. Pope switches to motorcar production (see 1896; Pope-Tribune, 1904).

The Autocar Company has its beginnings in the Pittsburgh Motor Vehicle Company started at Ardmore, Pa., by Louis S. Clarke who introduces a three-wheeled vehicle powered by a one-cylinder air-cooled engine. Autocar will bring out a shaft-driven motorcar with a two-cylinder water-cooled engine in 1901 (see 1906).

The first large U.S. automobiles are built at Cleveland by Scots-American bicycle maker Alexander Winton, 37, who organizes the Winton Motor Carriage Company and drives one of his cars 800 miles over dirt roads to New York. By the end of next year Winton will have a patent for his vehicle and will have sold nearly 30 cars.

The Royal Automobile Club is founded at London.

The S.S. *Turbinia* attains a speed of 34.5 knots and is the first vessel to be propelled by a steam turbine (see Parsons, 1884). A jet of steam turns blades inside a rotating cylinder to propel the experimental ship.

The *Argonaut* designed by U.S. naval architect Simon Lake, 31, is the first submarine to operate successfully in open waters (see 1776; Holland, 1900).

The use of acetylene gas torches for cutting metal is given impetus by French chemist-physicist Georges Claude, 27, who shows that acetylene can be transported safely if it is dissolved in acetone (see 1903).

The first U.S. commercial high-carbon ferrochrome for plating steel is produced by acetylene promoter James T. Morehead with help from French-American metallurgist Guillaume de Chalmot (see 1892; Union Carbide, 1906).

Manufacture of high-grade coke for steelmaking is improved by the New Lowe Coke Oven invented by Thaddeus S. C. Lowe (see 1873).

A cathode-ray tube (Braun tube) that pioneers development of television and other electronic communications is invented at Strassburg by German physicist Karl Ferdinand Braun, 47, who has improved the Marconi wireless by increasing the energy of sending stations and arranging antennas to control the direction of effective radiation (see 1895). The Braun tube will be linked in 1907 to "electric vision" by Russian physicist Boris Rosing (see Baird, 1926).

"All the News That's Fit to Print" appears February 10 in a box to the left of the title of the *New York Times,* where it will remain for more than 80 years. Adolph S. Ochs has offered a $100 prize to anyone who could think up a better slogan, but the motto devised by Ochs and his editors in October of last year has not been topped.

The *Jewish Daily Forward* begins publication at 175 East Broadway, New York. Editor of the Socialist Yiddish newspaper is Polish-American novelist-journalist Abraham Cahan, 37, whose first novel was published last year under the title *Yekl: A Tale of the New York Ghetto* (see The Day, 1914).

Halftones are printed for the first time on a power press and on newsprint. The *New York Tribune* employs techniques developed by Frederick E. Ives and Stephen Horgan (see Ives, 1886).

"The report of my death was an exaggeration," Mark Twain cables the *New York Times* June 2 from London. Now 61, Twain is on a world lecture tour that will help him recoup part of the fortune he lost in the panic of 1893.

William Randolph Hearst's *New York Journal* hires *Sunday World* editor Arthur Brisbane, 32, who quits the Pulitzer paper and uses sensationalist "yellow

1897 (cont.) journalism" techniques to build the *Journal's* circulation from 40,000 to 325,000 in 6 weeks (*see* 1895; 1898).

"The Katzenjammer Kids" by German-American cartoonist Rudolph Dirks begins appearing in the *New York Journal* December 12, Arthur Brisbane's 33rd birthday (above). The antics of Hans und Fritz (who torment der Captain, der Inspector, und Momma) ape those of the German cartoon characters Max und Moritz by Wilhelm Busch (*see* 1917).

Ladies' Home Journal publisher Cyrus H. K. Curtis pays $1,000 to acquire the 76-year-old *Saturday Evening Post* (*see* 1883; Lorimer, 1899).

The *Woman's Home Companion* begins publication at Springfield, Ohio. Publisher John S. Crowell started the magazine in 1873 under the name *Home Companion*, renamed it the *Ladies' Home Companion* in 1886, and has changed its name to avoid confusion with Curtis's magazine (above; *see* 1906).

"Yes, Virginia, there is a Santa Claus," writes *New York Sun* editor Francis Church, 58, in a September 21 editorial reply to reader Virginia O'Hanlon, age 8, who has written to inquire if Santa Claus really exists: "Not believe in Santa Claus? You might as well not believe in fairies. . . . No Santa Claus! Thank God, he lives, and he lives forever" (*see* 1823).

Doubleday & Co. has its beginnings in the New York publishing house Doubleday & McClure started by Frank Nelson Doubleday, 35, with S. S. McClure of *McClure's* magazine (*see* 1893). Doubleday has spent 20 years with Charles Scribner's Sons, and he founds a firm that will become the most prolific U.S. publishing house (*see* Doran, 1907; Literary Guild, 1934).

The Monotype typesetting machine introduced by U.S. inventor Tolbert Lanston, 53, is more practical for book publishers than the Merganthaler Linotype machine of 1884. Lanston obtained his first patents for the machine in 1885, it incorporates a keyboard machine that perforates paper rolls in certain patterns, each pattern represents a character, the perforations go into a caster and release matrices from which the characters are cast in single metal types (but not in complete lines), the Monotype assembles the types automatically to form lines, and the lines are then made up into pages.

Fiction *Fruits of the Earth (Les Nourritures terrestres)* by French novelist André Gide, 28; *The Understudy (La Doublure)* by French novelist Raymond Roussel, 20; *The Nigger of the 'Narcissus'* by Joseph Conrad; *The Spoils of Poynton* and *What Maisie Knew* by Henry James; *The Invisible Man* by H. G. Wells; *Liza of Lambeth* by English novelist William Somerset Maugham, 23; *Captains Courageous* by Rudyard Kipling; *Dracula* by Dublin-born English writer Bram Stoker, 50, who is secretary and business adviser to English actor Sir Henry Irving, 59 (the first actor to be knighted). Stoker has read up on vampire folklore and on Transylvania at the British Museum

and has embellished an historic Transylvanian Vlad Dracula who did not drink blood but who did have hordes of people impaled on spears, high or low depending on their rank, and had other victims blinded, strangled, and boiled alive (*see* 1476).

Poetry *Jeanne d'Arc* by French poet Charles Peguy, 24; "Recessional" by Rudyard Kipling on the occasion of Queen Victoria's second jubilee (in the *Times* July 17): "God of our fathers, known of old/ Lord of our far-flung battle-line,/ Beneath whose awful Hand we hold/ Dominion over palm and pine—/ Lord God of Hosts, be with us yet,/ Lest we forget —lest we forget!" *Lou Pouèmo Dóu Rose* by Frédéric Mistral, now 67.

Painting *The Sleeping Gypsy* by Henri Rousseau; *Large Interior* by Jean Edouard Vuillard; *Boulevard des Italiens, Morning, Sunlight* by Camille Pissaro; *Frieze of Life* by Edvard Munch.

Theater *The Little Minister* by James M. Barrie 9/27 at New York's Empire Theater, with U.S. actress Maude Adams (Maude Kiskadden), 25, who has adopted her mother's maiden name, 300 perfs.; *The Devil's Disciple* by George Bernard Shaw 10/4 at New York's Fifth Avenue Theater, with Richard Mansfield, 64 perfs.; *The Liars* by Henry Arthur Jones 10/6 at London's Criterion Theatre; *Cyrano de Bergerac* by French playwright Edmond Rostand, 29, 12/28 at the Théâtre de la Porte-Saint-Martin, Paris, 200 perfs.

The Théâtre du Grand Guignol opens in Montmartre under the direction of Paris theatrical manager Oscar Metenier, 38, whose bloodcurdling horror plays will overshadow his farces (*see* 1815).

The Orpheum Circuit is founded by German-American theatrical promoter Gustav Walter, who arrived at San Francisco in 1874, opened the Orpheum Theater in 1887 with a 22-piece Hungarian electrical orchestra, introduced Weber and Fields of New York to California 2 years later, leased Child's Opera House at Los Angeles last year, opened a booking office at Chicago, and now opens a third theater at Kansas City. Walter will die next year on his return from a tour of Europe in search of new talent.

Opera *Fervaal* 3/12 at the Théâtre de la Monnai, Brussels, with music by Vincent D'Indy.

First performances *Istar* Symphonic Variations by Vincent D'Indy 1/10 at both Brussels and Amsterdam; Symphony No. 1 in D minor by Sergei Rachmaninoff 3/15 at St. Petersburg; *The Sorcerer's Apprentice (L'Apprenti sorcier, Scherzo d'après une ballade de Goethe)* by French composer Paul Dukas, 31, 5/18 at Paris; "Thanksgiving and Forefathers Day for Orchestra and Chorus" by Yale undergraduate Charles Edward Ives, 23, 11/25 at New Haven's Centre Church on the Green. The congregation is not receptive.

Broadway musicals *The Good Mr. Best* 8/3 at the Garrick Theatre, with book by John J. McNally and a demonstration in the third act of the new cinematograph (*see* 1895); *The Belle of New York* 9/18 at the Casino Theater, with Edna May, 17, as the Salvation Army girl Violet Gray, Harry Davenport, music by Gustave A. Kecker, book and lyrics by Hugh Martin, songs that include "The Anti-Cigarette Society," "You and I," 56 perfs.

Congress broadens U.S. copyright laws to give copyright owners exclusive rights to public performances of their works, but the new law will be widely flouted (*see* 1909; ASCAP, 1914; Victor Herbert, 1917).

March "The Stars and Stripes Forever" by John Philip Sousa, who quit the Marine Corps in 1892. Sousa has been touring the world with his own band and wrote the new march in the fall of last year while returning from England.

Popular songs "Take Back Your Gold" by U.S. composer Monroe H. Rosenfeld, lyrics by Louis W. Pritzkow; "On the Banks of the Wabash Far Away" by U.S. songwriter Paul Dresser (né Dreiser), 40; "Asleep in the Deep" by U.S. minstrel composer Henry W. Petrie, 40, lyrics by English-American writer Arthur J. Lamb, 27.

The world heavyweight boxing title changes hands March 17 in the 14th round of a match held at Carson City, Nev. New Zealand-American Robert Prometheus "Bob" Fitzsimmons, 34, knocks out the champion James J. Corbett with a "solar plexus punch" (*see* 1892; Jeffries, 1899).

The first Boston Marathon is run April 19. The Boston Athletic Association insists that the long-distance footrace be free of "professionalism, politics, and plugs"; the BAA will extend the annual 25-mile Patriot's Day race to 26 miles, 385 yards after the 1908 Olympic Games when officials will lengthen the Olympic course so that the British royal family can view the start at Windsor Castle.

John Peter "Honus" Wagner, 23, joins the National League's Louisville team to begin a notable career in baseball. The Flying Dutchman will lead the league five times in stolen bases, he will accumulate a total of 722 stolen bases, and he will have a lifetime batting average of .329.

The first Cheyenne Rodeo is held in July and begins an annual Wyoming tradition.

University of Pennsylvania freshman T. Truxton Hare, 18, begins a 4-year football career at left guard. He will play 60 minutes of every game, Walter Camp will select him four times for his All-America Team, and Truxton will help Penn win 48 of its 55 games, holding opponents scoreless in 33 games.

The United All-England Croquet Association is founded as improved mallets, wickets, and balls revive popularity for the game (*see* 1868).

Steeplechase Park opens at Coney Island, N.Y., under the management of real estate operator George Cornelius Tilyou, 35, who has invented many of the rides and fun houses himself for the large amusement area. Competing attractions will spring up in the next decade to cover 20 acres and make Coney Island the greatest amusement area in the world.

Vienna's 131-year-old Prater Park installs a 210-foot high Ferris wheel. Riders get a panoramic view of the Danube and of the city from the wheel's spacious cabins (*see* 1893; St. Louis, 1904).

Lifebuoy soap is introduced under the name Lifebudy soap by England's Sunlight soap producer W. H. Lever who has been expanding since 1888 and has acquired a controlling interest in the Curtis Davis Company of Cambridge, Mass. Lever's strong soap will be promoted as a safeguard against body odor (*see* Lux flakes, 1906).

London's Moss Bros of Convent Garden goes into the dresswear hire business to accommodate a customer who has gone broke as a stockbroker and has obtained a professional engagement as a monologuist. Started by Moses Moss in 1860 and managed by his eldest son Alfred, the secondhand clothing shop will serve generations of Englishmen, including the nobility, who will hire from Moss Bros not only morning dress and evening wear but also coronation robes, court dress, ball gowns, wedding dresses, ski clothes, and theatrical costumes.

John Ward shoes are introduced by New York jobber-retailer Frank Melville, Jr., 37, who names the men's shoes after baseball player John Ward (and after his sculptor-uncle John Quincy Adams Ward). By 1900 Melville will have John Ward shoe stores at Philadelphia, Brooklyn, and New York (*see* 1922).

Red Cross shoes are introduced by the new Cincinnati firm Krohn, Fechheimer Company founded by Irwin Krohn and Marcus Fechheimer, 33. They will sell the firm to U.S. Shoe Corporation in 1923.

Mail Pouch tobacco is introduced under the name West Virginia Mail Pouch October 15 by Wheeling, W. Va., stogie makers Aaron and Samuel Bloch who started making stogies in the back of Samuel's wholesale grocery and dry goods store in 1879. Farmers will be paid for more than half a century to let Bloch Brothers use their barns as advertising billboards for the Mail Pouch brand chewing tobacco made from flavored stogie wrapper clippings.

New York's Waldorf-Astoria Hotel is opened by John Jacob Astor IV, 30, who has had architect Henry Janeway Hardenbergh design a 17-story Astor House at 34th Street and Fifth Avenue and has combined it with the 13-story Hardenbergh-designed Waldorf Hotel opened by his estranged cousin William Waldorf Astor in 1893. The 1,000-room hotel has 765 private baths and is the largest, most luxurious hotel in the world (*see* Palm Garden Restaurant, below; new Waldorf-Astoria, 1931).

Milwaukee's Pfister Hotel opens at 424 East Wisconsin Avenue. The eight-story hotel will be enlarged.

A massive, ornate Library of Congress is completed at Washington, D.C. The Renaissance-style structure

1897 (cont.) has been built to house the books that have piled up in a room at the Capitol since 1851.

 President Cleveland sets aside 20 million acres of additional western forest reserves (*see* Harrison, 1891). Congress has passed the Forest Service Organic Act to provide enabling legislation for the establishment of a national forest system (and to make it illegal for the government to sell National Forest timber not dead or fully mature and individually marked for felling), but some senators demand that Cleveland be impeached. Cleveland vetoes bills passed to reverse his proclamation and Congress adjourns without overriding the vetoes (*see* Pinchot, 1898).

 More than 1.2 million pounds of sturgeon are landed in New York and New Jersey, but pollution is beginning to doom the Hudson River's "Albany beef" industry.

Forty-nine million pounds of shad are landed on the U.S. East Coast.

 The drought that began on the U.S. western plains in 1886 finally comes to an end.

Europe's wheat crop falls short of its needs, and wheat futures are bid up on the Chicago Board of Trade as speculator Joseph Leiter, 29, makes a spectacular effort to corner the market. Son of the one-time Marshall Field partner Levi Leiter, young Leiter has been given $1 million by his father to start a real estate business but instead has started to buy wheat futures at 65 cents per bushel and has made a neat profit which he invests in more futures, continuing to buy until he has acquired 12 million bushels for December delivery, 9 million of them from meatpacker P. D. Armour. Leiter refuses to take his profit of several million dollars in hopes of still higher profits, but Armour discovers that grain elevators at Duluth are bulging with wheat, he charters 25 lake vessels and tugs that can break through the ice to Duluth, and he sends them north to get wheat that will break Leiter's corner in the market (*see* 1898).

U.S. farmers reap profits of millions of dollars as wheat prices rise to $1.09 per bushel, highest since 1891, partly as a result of Joseph Leiter's buying of futures (above).

 Boston's H. P. Hood starts distributing milk in glass bottles instead of ladling it from large cans into customers' pitchers (*see* Brooklyn, 1879; Borden, 1885). Hood stables more than 1,200 horses (*see* 1890), his routemen must harness their horses and load their wagons before driving to the often distant points at which their rounds begin, and they must start work shortly after midnight in order to commence deliveries at four in the morning.

Double-strength "condensed" soup that will give Campbell's soup dominance in the industry will be developed in the next year by chemist John T. Dorrance, 24, a nephew of Jos. Campbell Preserve Co. president Arthur Dorrance, who has degrees from MIT and the University of Göttingen. He persuades his uncle to hire him as researcher (*see* 1894; 1898).

Grape Nuts is introduced as a health food by C. W. Post of 1893 Postum fame who includes a copy of his pamphlet *The Road to Wellsville* with each box of his ready-to-eat cold cereal of wheat and malted barley baked in the form of bread sticks. Post believes that grape-sugar (dextrose) is formed during the baking process (*see* Post Toasties, 1904).

Purina breakfast cereal is introduced by the 3-year-old St. Louis livestock food company Robinson-Danforth which names its product Purina to signify purity (*see* Ralston, 1902).

The American Sugar Refining Company makes a deal with San Francisco's Claus Spreckels to eliminate competition (*see* 1891; 1895; 1899).

Jell-O is introduced by LeRoy, N.Y., cough medicine manufacturer Pearl B. Wait whose wife Mary gives the product its name. Wait's gelatin dessert is made from a recipe adapted from Peter Cooper's recipe of 1845 The powder is 88 percent sugar (*see* 1899).

Welch's Grape Juice production moves to Westfield, N.Y. (*see* 1896). Charles Welch processes 300 tons of grapes at Westfield, a stronghold of the Women's Christian Temperance Union in the heart of the 90-mile Chautauqua and Erie grape belt along the southeastern shore of Lake Erie (*see* Bryan, 1913).

Tin cans are made more reliable by the introduction of double seams and improved crimping of body and ends (*see* 1880; 1895; aluminum, 1960).

Britons begin to eat lunch, dooming the classic British breakfast which still often includes kippers (smoked herring, split open and fried in butter), finnan haddie (smoked haddock, often from the Scottish fishing port of Findhorn), kedgeree (rice mixed with fish, usually salmon, and hard-boiled egg—a dish introduced from colonial India), roast beef, kidneys, bacon, sausages, porridge, snipe (Scotland), scones (Scotland), cold toast, butter, marmalade, treacle, eggs, and tea with milk.

Boston's William F. Schrafft Company hires confectionery salesman Frank G. Shattuck who disposes of the factory's output for the rest of the year within a few months and proceeds to open a retail candy shop in New York's Herald Square. The shop will begin serving lunch next year to become the first Schrafft's restaurant (*see* 1861; 1906).

The chef of the Palm Garden Restaurant at New York's new Waldorf-Astoria Hotel (above) earns $10,000 per year, guests must wear formal attire, and all waiters speak French, German, and English.

More than 60 cases of champagne are consumed by 900 guests in Louis XV period costumes at a $9,000 ball given February 10 by Mrs. Bradley Martin, daughter of Carnegie Steel magnate Henry Phipps, who has had a huge Waldorf-Astoria suite decorated in the manner of Versailles despite the national economic depression that has persisted since 1893.

1898 A Spanish-American War that lasts for 112 days is precipitated by a February 15 explosion that destroys the U.S. battleship *Maine* in Havana Harbor, killing 258 sailors and two officers (*see* Sagasta, 1897). The sinking of the *Maine* follows by 6 days the publication in William Randolph Hearst's *New York Journal* of a letter stolen from the mails at Havana, a private letter from the Spanish minister to the United States calling President McKinley a spineless politician (the minister has been recalled by Madrid).

Assistant Secretary of the Navy Theodore Roosevelt sends secret cable orders to the 60-year-old commander of the U.S. Asiatic squadron George Dewey who is told February 25 to proceed to Hong Kong and to prepare for an attack on the Spanish squadron in the Philippines in the event of war.

Mobilization of U.S. Army forces begins March 9, and Congress appropriates $50 million without a single dissenting vote "for national defense and each and every purpose connected therewith."

A Spanish board of inquiry attributes the destruction of the *Maine* (above) to an internal explosion, but the report of the Spanish board March 22 is disputed by a U.S. naval court of inquiry which has reported March 21 that an external cause produced the explosion. The U.S. report is made public March 28, a joint note to President McKinley from ambassadors of six great powers April 6 calls for a peaceful solution to the Cuban problem, the Spanish queen Marie-Amelie acts on advice from Pope Leo XIII and orders a suspension of hostilities against Cuban rebels to "facilitate peace negotiations," but President McKinley sends a war message to Congress April 11.

A joint resolution of Congress April 19 recognizes Cuban independence, authorizes the president to demand Spanish withdrawal from the island, and disclaims any intention to annex Cuba.

A Volunteer Army Act is passed by Congress April 22 and a Volunteer Cavalry—the "Rough Riders"—is organized by Colonel Leonard Wood of the Army Medical Corps and by Lieutenant Colonel Theodore Roosevelt (above) who resigns his navy post in May.

The first shots of the Spanish-American War are fired April 22, Spain declares that a state of war exists April 24, war is formally declared by Congress April 25, Commodore Dewey receives the news in Hong Kong April 26, and he enters Manila Bay just before midnight on the night of April 30.

The Battle of Manila Bay May 1 begins at 5:40 in the morning when Commodore Dewey says to the captain of his flagship, "You may fire when you are ready, Gridley." By the time a cease-fire is ordered at 12:30 in the afternoon, all 10 ships in the Spanish squadron have been destroyed with a loss of 381 men, while eight Americans have been slightly wounded and none killed. Dewey is elevated to rear admiral May 11.

San Juan, Puerto Rico, is bombarded May 12 by the commander-in-chief of the North Atlantic Squadron William Thomas Sampson, 58, who headed the board of inquiry into the explosion that sank the *Maine*.

Cuba's Guantánamo Bay is invaded June 10 by 623 U.S. Marines and 24 officers.

Some 16,887 U.S. troops leave Tampa, Fla., June 14 for Santiago, Cuba, singing, "There'll Be a Hot Time in the Old Town Tonight."

An Anti-Imperialist League to oppose annexation of the Philippines is founded at Boston's Faneuil Hall June 15 by leading intellectuals.

Annexation of the Hawaiian Islands has been proposed in a joint resolution of Congress introduced in the House May 4, with the imperialist sentiment fired by the Battle of Manila (above). The measure is signed by President McKinley July 7, and Hawaiian sugar planters gain free access to U.S. markets (*see* 1897; 1959).

U.S. Army forces under the command of the 63-year-old major general of volunteers William Rufus Shafter arrives off Santiago, Cuba, June 20 and disembarks 2 days later with the Rough Riders of Colonel Wood and Lieutenant Colonel Roosevelt.

The Battle of Las Guasimas June 24 is the first land battle of the war and ends in a Spanish defeat by U.S. forces under the command of the major general of volunteers Joseph Wheeler, 62, with Leonard Wood and Theodore Roosevelt pushing ahead of other troops with 1,000 regulars and Rough Riders.

The Battle of San Juan Hill July 1 to 2 ends in victory for U.S. forces under General Hamilton S. Hawkins,

Admiral Dewey's victory at Manila Bay established the United States as a Pacific power in a brief war with Spain.

1898 (cont.) whose infantry take the hill after a charge by Colonel Roosevelt and the Rough Riders who also help take Kettle Hill. Some 1,460 men and 112 officers are killed, wounded, or missing after the action.

The Battle of Santiago Bay July 3 ends with 180 Spaniards dead and 1,800 captured, while the Americans have lost only one man and have sustained one wound casualty. "Don't cheer, boys, the poor devils are dying," shouts Captain John Woodward Philip, 58, of the U.S. battleship *Texas* as the Spanish cruiser *Vizcaya* is driven ashore in flames, but only 3 percent of U.S. major caliber shells have scored hits.

Puerto Rico is invaded July 25 by U.S. troops under the command of General Nelson A. Miles who receives the surrender of Ponce July 28.

A peace protocol is signed with Spain August 12, and the war is formally ended December 10 by the Treaty of Paris. Spain withdraws from Cuba and cedes Puerto Rico, Guam, and the Philippines to the United States which pays $20 million for the Philippines (*see* 1946).

Cuba gains her independence from Spain which loses her last dominions in the Americas (*see* 1902).

The Battle of Omdurman September 2 gives Britain's General Kitchener a decisive victory over the khalifa of the Sudan Abdullah el Taashi. Kitchener takes Khartoum from the dervishes, he reaches Fashoda September 19, and he finds it occupied by French forces under the command of Major Jean-Baptiste Marchand.

France claims the left bank of the Nile, Ethiopia claims the right bank, London demands that the French evacuate the territory that Britain claims for Egypt by right of conquest, the French try to get Russian support but fail, and Paris orders the evacuation of Fashoda November 3.

Italian anarchist Luigi Luccheni has stabbed the Austrian empress Elizabeth September 10 at Geneva while she was walking from her hotel to the steamer. She has died within a few hours at age 60.

New York City becomes Greater New York under terms of an 1896 law that unites Kings County (Brooklyn), Richmond County (Staten Island), Bronx County, Long Island City, Newtown (Queens County), and Manhattan to create a metropolis of just under 3.5 million inhabitants.

French novelist Emile Zola forces a new trial of Captain Dreyfus who has been sent to the penal colony called Devil's Island off the coast of French Guiana (*see* 1897). It is revealed that the documents that convicted Dreyfus were forged by two other officers (a Colonel Henry and Major Esterhazy) and that Dreyfus was the victim of an anti-Semitic plot, but he will not be released and restored to rank until 1906.

The U.S. Supreme Court declares March 28 that a child born of Chinese parents in the United States is a citizen and cannot be denied re-entrance to the United States by the Chinese Exclusion Laws of 1880 and 1892 (*United States v. Wong Kim Ark*).

Louisiana adopts a new constitution with a "grandfather clause" that restricts permanent voting registration to whites and to blacks whose fathers and grandfathers were qualified to vote as of January 1, 1867, a clause that virtually disenfranchises blacks. Race riots and lynchings sweep the South (*see* Mississippi, 1890; Alabama, 1902).

Whites battle Indians in Minnesota.

Virden, Ill., coal mine operators attempt to break a strike by importing 200 nonunion black workers, an action that provokes violence: 14 miners are killed and 25 wounded in the October 12 Mt. Olive massacre that will lead to the formation next year of the United Mine Workers of America.

Minnesota Mining Company is acquired along with a fleet of Great Lakes ore ships and railroads in the Mesabi iron range and in the Chicago area by the Illinois Steel Company of Chicago and the Lorrain Steel Company with backing from New York's J. P. Morgan & Co. (*see* 1896; U.S. Steel, 1901).

Republic Steel Company is created by a merger of Ohio and Pennsylvania steel firms (*see* 1937).

John W. Gates becomes president of the American Steel & Wire Company, which has a virtual monopoly in barbed wire (*see* 1875). Gates has established his own barbed wire company at St. Louis and has negotiated a series of mergers and consolidations (*see* Tennessee Coal & Iron, 1906).

An 1895 Illinois inheritance tax law is sustained by the Supreme Court April 25 in *Morgan v. Illinois Trust and Savings Bank,* and Congress imposes the first U.S. federal tax on legacies June 13 in a War Revenue Act that also provides for excise duties and taxes on tea, tobacco, liquor, and amusements.

Canada's Klondike yields more than $10 million worth of gold, a quantity it will continue to average through 1904 (*see* 1897).

Radium is isolated by Polish-born French physical chemist Marie (Marja) Sklodowska Curie, 31, and her husband Pierre, 39. It is the first radioactive element (*see* 1904; uranium, 1896).

The Palmer School of Chiropractic is founded at Davenport, Iowa, by Canadian-American magnetic healer Daniel David Palmer, 53, who has developed a system of manually manipulating the joints, especially the spine, for which he makes extravagant claims. Palmer's books *A Textbook of the Science, Art and Philosophy of Chiropractic* and *The Chiropractor* will appear in 1910 and 1914, respectively.

Lydia Pinkham's Vegetable Compound is widely advertised as "The Greatest Medical Discovery Since the Dawn of History" (*see* 1876). The compound of black cohosh, liferoot plant, fenugreek seeds, and other herbs in a 21 percent alcohol solution promises to remedy female complaints. It will continue to be made and sold for another 76 years, but it is outsold by the patent medicine Pe-Ru-Na, which has a higher alcoholic content and is sold for catarrh by physician-promoter Samuel Brubaker Hartman, 68, who has made $2.5 million from Pe-Ru-Na.

Heroin is introduced under that brand name as a cough suppressant derived from opium by the 48-year-old German chemical-pharmaceutical firm Farbenfabriken vorm. Friedrich Bayer und Co. (*see* Aspirin, 1899).

Bubonic plague will kill an estimated 3 million people in China and India in the next decade (*see* 1910).

Gideons International has its beginnings at Boscobel, Wis., where traveling salesmen John H. Nicholson and Sam Hill share a room at the Central Hotel and decide to form an association of Christian businessmen (excluding those in the liquor trade) and professional men to "put the Word of God into the hands of the unconverted." The association will raise money for their work, it will place 25 bibles in a Montana hotel in 1908, and by 1976 the Gideons will be placing 16.5 million bibles per year in hotels, hospitals, prisons, schools, colleges, and other locations.

Union Carbide Company is founded by Chicago entrepreneurs to manufacture calcium carbide for the production of acetylene gas for streetlights and for home lighting which still depends largely on coal gas and kerosene (*see* 1892; 1906).

Timken Roller Bearing Axle Company is founded by German-American carriage maker Henry Timken, 67, who opened a St. Louis carriage works in 1855, patented a special type of carriage spring in 1877, and has just patented a tapered roller bearing that will make his new company the leader in its field.

The Indian motorcycle is introduced by the new Hendee Manufacturing Company of Springfield, Mass. Motorcycle pioneer George Hendee improves on earlier cycles (which have essentially been bicycles with one-cylinder gasoline engines attached), he will begin mass production in 1902, and his company will be renamed Indian Motorcycle in 1923 (*see* Daimler, 1885; Harley-Davidson, 1903).

U.S. motorcar production reaches 1,000, up from 100 last year.

The Opel motorcar is introduced by German bicycle maker Adam Opel at Rüsselsheim (*see* 1929).

The Renault motorcar is introduced at Paris (*see* Renault Frères, 1899).

Goodyear Tire and Rubber Company is founded at Akron, Ohio, by Frank Augustus Sieberling, 39, who will make it the leading U.S. tiremaker (*see* 1921).

The right of the courts to decide the reasonableness of U.S. railroad rates—and the doctrine of judicial review—is established by the Supreme Court March 7 in the case of *Smyth v. Ames*.

Lykes Brothers Shipping Line is started by U.S. entrepreneurs Frederick E. Lykes and Howell Lykes, Jr., who borrow $20,000 from their cattleman father and begin a major freighter concern by shipping cattle out of Cuba and Florida.

Standard Fruit and Steamship Company has its beginnings in the Vaccaro Brothers Company started at New Orleans by Italian-American banana importers Joseph, Felix, and Lucca Vaccaro who are helped by their brother-in-law Salvador D'Antoni to acquire the two-masted schooner *Frances* (*see* 1926).

A pilot plant to produce viscose rayon yarn that can be woven and dyed opens at Kew, Surrey, England (*see* Cross, Bevan, 1892). English inventor C. H. Stearn patents a viscose filament produced by treating wood pulp with caustic soda (sodium hydroxide) (*see* Courtalds, 1905; Little, 1902).

Northeastern University is founded at Boston.

A message to Garcia is delivered by U.S. Army Lieutenant Andrew Rowan who is sent on a secret mission in April to obtain certain information from Cuban insurgent General Calixto Garcia. Despite a breakdown in ordinary lines of communication, Rowan delivers his message, he obtains the desired information, and he returns to Washington D.C. Garcia is named to represent Cuba in negotiations with the United States for Cuban independence, but he dies at age 62 (*see* Elbert Hubbard, 1899).

William Randolph Hearst publishes special editions of the *New York Journal* from his private yacht anchored in Havana Harbor. Cowboy painter Frederic Remington had been sent to Cuba earlier by Hearst and had cabled that everything was quiet and that there would be no war, but Hearst had replied, "You furnish the pictures and I'll furnish the war." U.S. opinion is inflamed by *Journal* stories ("Remember the *Maine!*"), and the paper's circulation reaches 1.6 million May 2.

The *New York Times* drops its price from 3 cents to 1 cent and circulation triples to 75,000 within a year. By 1901 it will be over 100,000 (*see* 1897; 1913).

Sunset magazine begins publication at Los Angeles to promote business for the Southern Pacific Railroad by attracting tourists, settlers, and developers to the West. Named for the railroad's crack *Sunset Limited* between New Orleans and Los Angeles, the magazine will be sold to its staff members in 1914, they will turn it into a literary magazine, Laurence W. Lane will acquire it for $65,000 in 1928, and it will become a family magazine.

The Telegraphone patented by Danish electrical engineer Valdemar Paulsen, 29, is the world's first magnetic wire recording device (*see* 1929).

Nonfiction *Wild Animals I Have Known* by English-Canadian author Ernest Thompson Seton, 38, whose book launches him on a career; *Mr. Dooley in Peace and in War* by *New York Evening Journal* humorist Finley Peter Dunne, 31, whose book *Mr. Dooley in the Hearts of His Countrymen* also ap-

1898 (cont.) pears, beginning a series by a fictitious Chicago bartender whose witty and skeptical remarks to his silent and gloomy companion Malachi Hennessey are published in Dunne's weekly newspaper column.

Fiction "The Turn of the Screw" (story) by Henry James; *The War of the Worlds* by H. G. Wells (*see* 1938); *David Harum, A Story of American Life* by the late U.S. banker-novelist Edward Noyes Westcott who has just died at age 52: "Them that has gits"; *Evelyn Innes* by George Moore; *The Forest Lovers* by English novelist Maurice Hewlett, 37; *The Woman and the Puppet* (*La Femme et le pantin*) by French novelist-poet Pierre Louys (Pierre Louis), 28.

Poetry *From the Dawn to the Evening Angelus* (*De l'Angelus d'aube à l'angelus du soir*) by French poet Francis Jammes, 30; "The Ballad of Reading Gaol" by Oscar Wilde, who was released from prison last year after serving the 2-year sentence imposed in 1895, has emigrated to Paris, and will die there late in November 1900 at age 44: "Yet each man kills the thing he loves,/ By each let this be heard,/ Some do it with a bitter look/ Some with a flattering word,/ The coward does it with a kiss,/ The brave man with a sword!"

Glasgow's Mackintosh School of Art is founded.

Gustave Moreau dies at Paris April 18 at age 72, leaving his house and some 8,000 paintings and drawings to the French nation; Sir Edward Coley Burne-Jones dies at London June 17 at 64; Pierre C. Puvis de Chavannes dies at Paris October 10 at 73.

The Graflex camera patented by U.S. inventor William F. Folmer, 36, is the world's first high-speed multiple-split focal plane camera.

Photographs taken with artificial light are produced for the first time (*see* flash bulb, 1930).

Theater *The Dream of a Spring Morning* (*Sogno d'un mattino di primavera*) by Gabriele D'Annunzio 1/11 at Rome's Teatro Valle; *Trelawney of the "Wells"* by Arthur Wing Pinero 5/27 at the St. James's Theatre, London; *Drayman Henschel* (*Fuhrmann Henschel*) by Gerhart Hauptmann 11/5 at Berlin's Deutsches Theater; *The Seagull* (*Chayka*) by Anton Chekhov 12/17 at the Moscow Art Theater, the first effective performance of the play that failed dismally 2 years ago at St. Petersburg but that now is a brilliant success; *Ghetto* by Dutch playwright Herman Heijermans, 34, 12/24 at Amsterdam's Hollandsche Schouwburg.

Russian actor-producer Konstantin Sergeevich Stanislavski (K. S. Alekseev), 35, has founded the Moscow Art Theater (above) and will head it for 40 years. His "method" will revolutionize acting with infusions of genuine emotion.

The William Morris Agency opens on New York's 14th Street where German-American theatrical agent William Morris, 25, obtains bookings for vaudeville acts at a 5 percent commission. Morris will help build shows for vaudeville house managers and will make his firm the world's leading talent agency.

French film pioneer Léon Gaumont opens a London office in Cecil Court. English film pioneer Cecil Hepworth, 23, builds a 10-foot by 6-foot studio in his garden at Walton-on-Thames.

First performances *Pelléas and Mélisande* Orchestral Suite by Gabriel Fauré 6/21 at London's Prince of Wales Theatre for a production of the 1893 Maurice Maeterlinck play with Mrs. Patrick Campbell.

Broadway musical *The Fortune Teller* 9/26 at Wallack's Theater, with music by Irish-American conductor-composer Victor Herbert, 30, book and lyrics by Harry B. Smith, songs that include "Gypsy Love Song," 40 perfs.

Popular songs "The Rosary" by Ethelbert Nevin, 36, lyrics by Robert Cameron Rogers, 36; "When You Were Sweet Sixteen" by English-American songwriter James Thornton, 37.

Canadian-American yachtsman Joshua Slocum, 54, brings his 37-foot sloop *Spray* into Newport, R.I., June 27 after completing the first one-man circumnavigation of the world. Slocum has used only a compass, a sextant, and a "dollar clock" as navigational instruments in his 3-year voyage.

The touchdown in U.S. college football receives a value of 5 points, up from the 4 established in 1884, and athletic directors give the goal after touchdown a value of 1 point, down from 2 in 1884 (*see* 1912).

Atlantic City's Steel Pier opens with amusement park attractions (*see* boardwalk, 1896).

Louis Vuitton brands his initials on the canvas luggage he has created, hoping to discourage imitators. Once a dress packer to the empress Eugènie, the French luggage maker has gained wide acceptance for his trunks and cases, and will introduce them in the United States in 1902.

Cluett, Peabody Company is incorporated at Troy, N.Y., with a capitalization of $5 million. English-American collar- and shirtmaker George B. Cluett, 59, has lost his partner D. W. Coon, who has retired, he has started the new firm with his brother Robert and with Frederick Forrest Peabody, 39, and the firm will sell its collars, cuffs, and shirts under the brand name Arrow (*see* 1921).

International Shoe Company has its beginnings at St. Louis where local jobber John C. Roberts joins the Memphis shoe dealers Oscar and Jackson Johnson and with their cousin Edgar Rand to start a firm that will become the world's largest shoemaker. Roberts, Johnson & Rand Shoe Company leases machines from Boston's United Shoe Machinery Company and begins producing shoes. The firm will absorb Peter Shoe Company, it will purchase the Friedman-Shelby Company to add the Diamond and Red Goose brands to its line, and it will expand by adding Poll-Parrot shoes, Florsheim shoes, and other brands.

Paris jeweler Alfred Cartier takes his sons Louis, Jacques, and Pierre into the business and opens a new shop at 13 rue de la Paix (*see* 1847). Louis, 23, will become Cartier's creative genius (*see* 1902).

New York's Bonwit Teller Company is founded by merchant Edmund D. Teller, who has absorbed the fashion tailoring establishment started by Paul J. Bonwit 3 years ago at 6th Avenue and 18th Street. The partners will open a new store at Fifth Avenue and 38th Street in 1911 (*see* 1930).

New York's Condict building designed by Chicago's Louis Sullivan is completed at 65 Bleecker Street for Silas Alden Condict. The radical structure will later be called the Bayard building.

New York's Fine Arts building designed by Henry J. Hardenbergh is completed on West 57th Street where it will house the Art Students' League.

Brooklyn's Grand Army Plaza is graced with an 80-foot-high arch designed by architect John Duncan to commemorate Union Army forces in the Civil War. Stanford White creates four tall Doric columns to mark the entrance to Prospect Park, and sculptor Frederick MacMonnies works on a statue of Victory in a two-wheeled chariot drawn by four horses abreast to surmount Duncan's triumphal arch.

Chicago's Gage building on South Michigan Avenue is completed by Holabird and Roche.

Claridge's Hotel opens in London's Brook Street, where it has been rebuilt on a site occupied by an earlier hotel that operated under the name Claridge's for half a century.

The Paris Ritz opens in a 17th-century townhouse in the Place Vendôme (*see* Gulbenkian, 1896). César Ritz has found that the duc de Lauzun's property was for sale, he has suggested the name "Grand Marnier" to London liqueur maker Marnier La Postolle for La Postolle's orange-flavored cordial, La Postolle has given him the money to buy the townhouse, and Ritz opens the new hotel with 170 guest rooms (and with chef Auguste Escoffier of 1894 Pêche Melba fame) (*see* London Ritz, 1902).

A Vanderbilt mansion north of Hyde Park, N.Y., is completed for railroad heir-yachtsman Frederick William Vanderbilt, 42.

Gifford Pinchot is appointed chief forester in the U.S. Department of Agriculture. Before going to work at the Vanderbilt estate at Asheville, N.C., 3 years ago, Pinchot studied forestry in France under Sir Dietrich Brandis who founded forestry in British India, he has managed the Vanderbilt forests in the Great Smokies, and he has made long field trips (*see* 1902).

China has serious famine as the northern provinces suffer drought, while in Shantung province the Yellow River overflows its banks to create disastrous floods.

U.S. wheat futures reach $1.85 per bushel as the outbreak of the Spanish-American War (above) booms demand. Joseph Leiter has paper profits of $7 million (*see* 1897), but he holds contracts for 35 million bushels, and when wheat pours into Chicago in June, Leiter's corner on the market is broken. He not only loses his profit but winds up with a debt of $10 million which is paid by his father.

"Photosynthesis" is introduced as a new term to denote the process by which plants synthesize carbohydrates from carbon dioxide, water, and inorganic salts using sunlight for energy and chlorophyll as a catalyst (*see* Ingenhousz, 1779; von Sachs, 1862).

More U.S. troops in the Spanish-American War (above) die from eating contaminated meat than from battle wounds. The deaths raise a public outcry for reform of the meatpacking industry (*see* 1905).

Sugar prices soar following the outbreak of the Spanish-American War (above). Sugar broker George Edward Keiser started buying stock in Cuban-American Sugar Company at $5 per share and continues to buy as the price soars to $300, buying so much that he winds up controlling the company.

American Glucose Refining Company is created by New York financier Jules Bache in a $40 million consolidation of companies that include H. O. Havemeyer's 7-year-old American Sugar Refining Company (*see* Bache, 1892; U.S. Glucose, 1902).

A. E. Staley Company is started by Decatur, Ill., entrepreneur Augustus E. Staley who will make his firm the second largest U.S. corn processor after Corn Products Refining Company (*see* 1902). Staley will also be a major processor of soybeans and an important factor in the chemical industry (*see* first U.S. soybean refinery, 1922; football, 1920).

Campbell's soups appear for the first time with red and white labels whose colors have been suggested by Cornell College football uniforms (*see* 1897; 1904).

Sanitas corn flakes are introduced by the Sanitas Nut Food Company set up at Battle Creek, Mich., by J. H. Kellogg with his brother Will Keith (*see* Granose, 1895). The world's first corn flakes quickly turn rancid on grocers' shelves and have little acceptance in a market oriented toward wheat cereals (*see* 1902).

Shredded Wheat is promoted as "the perfect food" by Henry D. Perky, who embarks on a lecture tour (*see* 1895). "From the most abject physical wreck, I have succeeded, by the use of naturally organized food, in reorganizing my body into perfectly healthy condition," says Perky (who will die in 1906 at age 66). "I use no other bread or cereal food product than shredded whole wheat biscuit, and dishes made from these biscuit. I am 55 years of age and feel younger than 20 years ago." In a message to mothers, Perky's company says, "Do you know that children crave natural food until you pervert their tastes by the use of unnatural food? Unnatural food develops unnatural and therefore strong propensities and desires in children. Like begets like—pure food, pure minds" (*see* 1900).

1898 (cont.) The National Biscuit Company is formed by a consolidation of the New York Biscuit Company, American Biscuit and Manufacturing Company, United States Baking Company, and United States Biscuit Company (*see* 1890). Adolphus W. Green heads the new company, whose 114 bakeries comprise 90 percent of all major U.S. commercial bakeries.

Uneeda Biscuits are created by National Biscuit Company's A. W. Green (above) who seeks to establish a brand name that will surmount the anonymity of the cracker barrel seen in every grocery shop. Green decides to concentrate the company's efforts behind a flaky soda cracker, he retains N. W. Ayer & Son of Philadelphia as his advertising agency, and he is advised by Ayer's Henry N. McKinney that a manufacturer must "insure his future sales by adopting a trade name and trade dress which will belong exclusively to him by trademark and trade right." McKinney suggests the name Uneeda Cracker, Green changes it to Uneeda Biscuit, the name is registered December 27 with the U.S. Patent Office (*see* 1900).

Pepsi-Cola is introduced by New Bern, N.C., pharmacist Caleb Bradham who has been mixing fountain drinks since 1893 and has developed a cola drink formula (*see* 1902).

Mechanical refrigeration is advanced by Swedish inventor Carl von Linde who perfects a machine that liquefies air (*see* 1873; Freon 12, 1931).

Annual British tea consumption averages 10 pounds per capita, up from 2 pounds in 1797 (*see* 1869).

Louis Sherry's opens on New York's Fifth Avenue at 44th Street. French-American caterer-confectioner Louis Sherry has operated a four-story establishment since 1881 to serve New York's carriage trade, and his new restaurant will be among the city's finest for 21 years (*see* Delmonico's, 1899).

1899 The boll weevil *Anthonus grandis* crosses the Rio Grande from Mexico and begins to spread north and east through the U.S. cotton-growing states. The weevil will destroy vast acreages of cotton and will have a devastating effect on agriculture in the South and on the U.S. economy in general (*see* 1916; 1921).

An "Open Door" policy in China proposed by U.S. Secretary of State John Milton Hay, 61, receives support from the great powers who agree that all the imperialist countries shall have equal commercial opportunity in spheres of special interest (*see* 1900).

The Boer War begins in South Africa October 12 as President Kruger of the Boer republic acts to block suspected British moves toward acquiring the rich Transvaal with its gold mines (*see* 1886). Equipped with Krupp artillery, the Boers lay siege to Mafeking October 13, to Kimberley October 15, and to Ladysmith November 2. British forces are equipped with Vickers-Maxim weapons supplied by Basil Zaharoff, 49, a Turk who has become chairman of Vickers and who also supplies the Boers, building a personal fortune (*see* 1900; Maxim, 1883).

West Africa's Ashanti stage their last uprising against the British. Colonial officer Sir Fredric Hodgson has provoked the Ashanti by demanding that they surrender the Golden Stool of Friday that has been their sacred symbol of power for the past century. Hodgson wants the throne so that he may sit upon it as governor of the Gold Coast, but the tribesmen lay siege to his fortress, and it is 2 months before he and his wife can escape to the coast.

"The White Man's Burden" by Rudyard Kipling appears in *McClure's* magazine. The *Times* of London calls it "an address to the United States."

The Action Française right-wing political movement founded by Charles Maurras, 31, attracts support from the Paris newspaper *Action Française*, edited by pamphleteer Léon Daudet, 32, who rallies the defeated opponents of Alfred Dreyfus with royalist and nationalist invective.

The United Mine Workers of America, organized under the leadership of Illinois coal miner John Mitchell, 29, joins anthracite coal workers with bituminous coal workers who formed a union 9 years ago and who struck the mines in 1897 (*see* Virden, Ill., massacre, 1898). U.S. Mines continue to employ thousands of boys barely into their teens (*see* 1902).

New York's Consolidated Edison Company is created by a merger of the Edison Illuminating Company with the Consolidated Gas Company controlled by the Rockefeller family and William Whitney (*see* 1882; power failure, 1965.)

Nippon Electric Company is founded with 92 employees and 200,000 yen in capital. Owned 54 percent by Western Electric Co., the firm will grow to be Japan's largest producer of electric equipment with more than 30,000 employees by 1966.

Worthington Pump and Machinery Company has its beginnings in the International Steam Company started with a stock offering by New York's Lehman Brothers in that firm's first venture into underwriting (*see* Cotton Exchange, 1870).

The Taylor-White process for heat-treating high-speed tool steels increases cutting capacities of blade edges by 200 to 300 percent. Philadelphia engineers Frederick Winslow Taylor, 43, and Maunsel White, 43, have developed the process.

Carnegie Steel Company is created by a consolidation of various steel properties controlled by Andrew Carnegie (*see* Homestead strike, 1892; U.S. Steel, 1901).

Armco Steel Company has its beginnings in the American Rolling Mill Company founded at Middleton, Ohio, by Cincinnati entrepreneur George M. Verity, 34, who joined Sagendorph Iron Roofing and Corrugated Company at age 22, became manager the following year, and reorganized the firm in 1891 under the name American Steel Roofing Company. Verity has developed a continuous wide-sheet roller mill at great cost and after many failures, his process revolutionizes the manufacture of sheet steel, his mill on the Miami River will turn out its first steel sheets in February of 1901, and he will license other firms to use his process (*see* 1906).

National Steel Company is created through a merger engineered by Chicago lawyer W. H. Moore who organized New York Biscuit in 1890 and American Tin Plate last year (*see* 1929).

American Steel Company is founded by W. H. Moore (above) with help from his brother James (*see* American Can, 1901).

Amalgamated Copper Company is founded in April by German-American entrepreneur Leonard Lewisohn, 51, and his younger brother Adolph who last year erected the Raritan Copper Works at Perth Amboy, N.J., and who have received backing for the $65 million firm from Standard Oil Company executives William Rockefeller and Henry Huddleston Rogers and from New York banker James Stillman. Amalgamated buys the Anaconda mine at Butte, Mont., from Marcus Daly (*see* 1881), the Anaconda Company will be incorporated in 1911, and it will acquire Amalgamated in 1915.

American Smelting and Refining Company (ASARCO) is created by the Lewisohns, William Rockefeller, and H. H. Rogers (above) who merge leading U.S. copper producers into a $75 million combination as the growing use of electricity increases demand for copper wire. ASARCO capitalization will soon be increased to $155 million.

The Guggenheim family refuses to join the ASARCO copper trust (above) and chooses instead to compete with the trust (*see* 1888). Meyer Guggenheim forms alliances with mine owners, he gives them financial backing in many cases, and he starts the Guggenheim Exploration Co. to seek new ore deposits (*see* 1901).

E. I. du Pont de Nemours is incorporated in Delaware (*see* 1872). Du Pont has been making dynamite since 1880 and now controls 90 percent of U.S. blasting powder production and 95 percent of U.S. gunpowder production (*see* 1902; Nobel, 1866).

International Paper Company is created by a merger of nearly 30 U.S. and Canadian paper companies. International will purchase large timber tracts in Maine and California and will build up a national marketing organization based at New York.

Union Bag & Paper Corporation is reorganized to create a $27 million trust that tries to squeeze out competitors such as International Paper (*see* 1869).

J. P. Stevens & Company is founded at New York with $25,000 and 21 employees by John P. Stevens, a grandson of the late Nathaniel Stevens who has worked at $150 per year for the commission house that handles goods from the Stevens family mills at North Andover (*see* 1813; 1837). Stevens will make deals with southern cotton mills, he will invest in the ones that show promise, and he will make J. P. Stevens a leader in the U.S. textile industry.

Renault Frères is founded in March by French motorcar producers Louis and Marcel Renault (*see* 1898; glass-enclosed motorcar, 1900).

FIAT (Fabrica Italiana Automobili Torino) is founded July 1 at Turin by cavalry lieutenant Giovanni Agnelli, 33, and eight partners with a capitalization of 800,000 lire ($152,400). FIAT completes 10 three-horsepower motorcars by November and will grow to become Europe's largest automaker and Italy's largest industrial firm (*see* tractors, 1919; "Topolino," 1936).

French racing driver Camille Jenatzy drives a La Jamais Contente at a speed of 67.79 miles per hour.

U.S. auto production reaches 2,500, up from 1,000 last year.

Henry Ford joins the new Detroit Automobile Company as chief engineer (*see* 1893; 1901).

A group of financiers acquires the Selden road locomotive patent rights. They will bring a lawsuit for infringement of the patent next year and will win (*see* 1895; 1903).

A Stanley Steamer driven by F. E. Stanley climbs to the top of Mount Washington (*see* 1896).

Locomobile Company of America is founded by *Cosmopolitan* magazine publisher J. B. Walker who has bought out F. E. Stanley (above) and his brother for $250,000 with backing from several associates. Locomobile takes over the Stanley plant at Newton, Mass., but the directors of the new company will soon have a falling out, and the Stanley twins will take over the company (*see* 1902).

The first U.S. clincher tires are introduced at Akron, Ohio, by B. F. Goodrich Company which produces 19-ply rubber tires in sizes ranging from 28 X 2½ inches to 36 X 3 inches (*see* 1872; Brunswick, 1923).

Kelly-Springfield pneumatic tires are introduced at Springfield, Ohio, by the Rubber Tire Wheel Company (*see* Hartford Rubber Works, 1895).

American Car and Foundry Company (ACF) is founded at Berwick, Pa., to compete with the Pullman Palace Car Company. The founders include Charles Lang Freer, 43, who has been building railroad cars since age 17, and ACF will become the world's largest maker of freight cars.

Boston's South Station opens to complement the North Station built in 1894.

Boston's last horsecar runs December 24. A trolley line replaces the horsecar as Boston extends its 2-year-old subway, the first in America.

United Fruit Company is incorporated by banana exporter Minor C. Keith and the Boston Fruit Company which has been distributing Keith's fruit since the failure of his New Orleans distributor (which cost Keith $1.5 million) (*see* 1871; 1885). Andrew Preston is president of the firm created by the merger, Keith is first vice president, and United Fruit controls 112 miles of railroad with 212,494 acres of land, more

Wall Street panicked when Jay Cooke & Son failed. The stock exchange closed for 10 days, 5,000 business firms failed.

than 61,000 acres of it in production (*see* 1929; Tropical Radio Telegraph, 1910).

United Fruit's Minor C. Keith sees an opportunity for passenger traffic on the company's banana boats and charters four new ships built originally for the U.S. Navy. The Great White Fleet established by Keith includes the S.S. *Farragut*, the S.S. *Admiral Dewey*, the S.S. *Admiral Schley*, and the S.S. *Admiral Sampson*, each of which carries 53 passengers and 35,000 bunches of bananas (*see* 1904).

A violent hurricane sweeps Puerto Rico August 8, killing 2,000 and leaving thousands more homeless. U.S. Army Medical Corps assistant surgeon Bailey Kelly Ashford, 25, is assigned to a hospital treating native victims of the storm and finds that 75 percent are anemic. When he examines their feces, Bailey finds hookworm eggs, and when he treats patients who have not responded to arsenic, iron, or improved diet with thymol and epsom salts, Ashford eliminates hookworm and sharply reduces the death toll from anemia (*see* Froelich, 1789; Stiles, 1902).

A cholera pandemic begins that will continue until 1923, affecting much of the world.

Zinc oxide adhesive plasters are introduced by Johnson & Johnson, which has developed them in cooperation with some leading U.S. surgeons (*see* 1886). The new plasters avoid irritation to delicate skin, thus giving relief to patients, yet they have greater strength and better sticking qualities that will make them valuable to surgeons (*see* 1916; Band-Aid, 1921).

Aspirin (acetylsalicylic acid) is perfected by German researchers Felix Hoffman and Hermann Dreser who have developed the powdered analgesic (pain-killer) and fever reducer from coal tar. Less irritating

to gastrointestinal tracts than salicylic acid, the drug will be made less irritating still by the addition of the neutral salt calcium glutamate, it will be marketed by prescription under the tradename Bayer Aspirin beginning in 1905, and it will become the world's largest selling over-the-counter drug (*see* Gerhardt, 1853; Heroin, 1898; Sterling Drug, 1919).

The School and Society by University of Chicago philosopher-psychologist John Dewey, 39, pioneers progressive education by challenging traditional teaching methods based on lectures, memorization, and mechanical drill. Dewey suggests that education is a process of acculturation, an accumulation and assimilation of experience whereby a child develops into a balanced personality with wide awareness.

San Francisco State College is founded in California.

The University of Northern Arizona is founded at Flagstaff.

Western Illinois University is founded at Macomb.

Simmons College is founded at Boston.

Saturday Evening Post publisher G. H. K. Curtis appoints his literary editor George Horace Lorimer, 32, editor-in-chief (*see* 1897). The *Post's* circulation remains below 2,000, but Lorimer will build it to more than 3 million in the next 38 years by attracting such writers as Stephen Crane, Joseph Conrad, Theodore Dreiser, Jack London, Frank Norris, Booth Tarkington, O. Henry, John Galsworthy, Willa Cather, Mary Roberts Rinehart, Stephen Vincent Benet, Sinclair Lewis, John P. Marquand, Ring Lardner, and F. Scott Fitzgerald (*see* J. W. Thompson, 1901).

Nonfiction *The Theory of the Leisure Class* by University of Chicago social scientist Thorstein Bunde Veblen, 42, declares that decorum (or etiquette) and refined tastes are adopted by society as evidence of gentility because they can be acquired only with leisure. Certain foods and beverages are esteemed for the same reason, and so is drunkenness. Veblen introduces such concepts as "conspicuous consumption," "conspicuous waste," and "vicarious" consumption and waste to explain social behavior that has either defied explanation or has gone unexamined.

Fiction *The Gentleman from Indiana* by "Hoosier" novelist (Newton) Booth Tarkington, 30; *Stalky and Co.* (autobiographical stories) by Rudyard Kipling who derides the cult of compulsory games; *The Promised Land* (*Ziemia obiecana*) by Polish novelist Wladyslaw Reymont, 32; *Dom Casmurro* by Joaquim Machado De Assis; "A Message to Garcia" (short story) by Buffalo, N.Y., publisher Elbert Green Hubbard, 43, who 4 years ago established the Roycroft Press to publish the literary magazine *The Philistine* whose contents he writes entirely himself. Hubbard moralizes about self-reliance and perseverance in a story based on an incident from last year's Spanish-American War; *The Amateur Cracksman* by English novelist Ernest William Hornung introduces the gentleman burglar Raffles.

668

Juvenile The first of some 30 *Rover Boys* adventure novels by U.S. author Edward Stratemeyer, 36, will lead to the establishment in 1906 of the Stratemeyer Literary Syndicate with hack writers fleshing out plots and characters devised by Stratemeyer who has been turning out books since 1894 in the Horatio Alger style. Published under various pen names, the books will include *The Motor Boys* (by "Clarence Young"), *Tom Swift* (by "Victor Appleton"), *The Bobbsey Twins* (by "Laura Lee Hope"), *The Boy Scouts* (by "Lieutenant Howard Payson"), *The Hardy Boys* (by "Franklin W. Dixon"), and *Nancy Drew* mysteries (by "Carolyn Keene"). The books will sell by the millions, and when Stratemeyer dies in 1930, his daughter Harriet, now 6, and her sister Edith will take over the syndicate and will continue the various series. Harriet Stratemeyer Adams will still be writing books in the late 1970s, and the books will still be fattening the profits of publishers Grosset & Dunlap, started now by Scots-American bookkeeper Alexander Grosset, 29, and salesman George Dunlap, 31.

Painting *Two Tahitian Women* by Paul Gauguin; *Paysages et interieurs* (lithographs) by Jean Edouard Vuillard. Alfred Sisley dies at Muret-sur-Loing January 29 at age 59.

Sculpture *The Puritan* by Augustus Saint-Gaudens.

Theater *Barbara Frietchie* by Clyde Fitch 10/23 at New York's Criterion Theater, with Julia Marlowe, 83 perfs.; *Uncle Vanya* (*Dyadya Vanya*) by Anton Chekhov 10/26 at the Moscow Art Theater; *Ashes* (*Cenizes*) by Spanish playwright Ramon Maria del Valle Inclan, 33, 12/7 at Madrid's Teatro de Larra; *The Tenor* (*Der Kammersang*) by German playwright Benjamin Franklin Wedekind, 35, 12/10 at Berlin's Neues Theater.

Opera *Cinderella* (*Cendrillon*) 5/24 at the Paris Opéra-Comique, with music by Jules Massenet.

First performances Concerto No. 2 in D minor for Piano and Orchestra by Edward MacDowell 3/5 at New York's Chickering Hall; Symphony No. 1 in E minor by Finnish composer Jean (Johann Julius Christian) Sibelius, 33, 4/26 at Helsinki; Catalonia Suite No. 1 for Orchestra by Isaac Albeniz 5/27 at the Théâtre Noveau, Paris; "Enigma" Variations on an Orchestral Theme by English composer Edward (William) Elgar, 42, 6/19 at London (conductor Hans Richter revises the score and adds a coda to create a version that Elgar conducts at the Worcester Festival); "Sea Pictures Songs for Chorus and Orchestra" by Edward Elgar 10/5 at the Norwich Festival.

Stage musicals *Floradora* 11/11 at London's Lyric Theatre, with music by Leslie Stuart, lyrics by Ernest Boyd-Jones and Paul Rubens, songs that include the second-act number beginning, "Tell me, pretty maiden, are there any more at home like you? . . ." 455 perfs.

Popular songs "My Wild Irish Rose" by New York songwriter Chauncey Olcott, 41; "O Sole Mio!" ("Oh, My Sun!") by Neapolitan composer Edoardo di Capna, 35, lyrics by Giovanni Capurro, 30; "Hello, Ma Baby" by New York composer Joseph E. Howard, lyrics by Ida Emerson that begin, "Hello, ma baby,/Hello, ma honey,/Hello, ma ragtime gal. . . ."

Scott Joplin's "Original Rag" and "Maple Leaf Rag" are the first ragtime piano pieces to appear in sheet music form. Joplin, 30, was a bandleader at the 1893 Columbian Exposition at Chicago, has been taking courses in harmony and composition at the George Smith College for Negroes in Sedalia, Mo., has been playing piano at Sedalia sporting houses that include the Maple Leaf Club, and has developed a ragged-type style, heavily syncopated, that publisher John Stark discovers at Sedalia and that will be exploited by other pianists.

"Lift Every Voice and Sing" by Florida songwriters John Rosamond Johnson, 26, and his brother James Weldon Johnson, 28, will be called the black national anthem. James Weldon became the first black to be elected to the Florida bar 2 years ago, the Johnson brothers will move to New York in 1901 to begin a brief career as a songwriting team, but James Weldon will soon go back to school to prepare for a larger career (*see* 1912).

English tea magnate Thomas Lipton has *Shamrock I* built as a racing yacht in the first of five efforts he will make to regain the America's Cup, but his boat is defeated 3 to 0 by the U.S. defender *Columbia*.

U.S. prizefighter James J. Jeffries, 24, wins the world heavyweight title from Bob Fitzsimmons June 9, with an 11th round knockout in a match held at Coney Island, N.Y. Jeffries will retire undefeated in March 1905 and will be succeeded by Marvin Hart, who will be defeated at Los Angeles in 1906.

A liquid-center gutta percha golf ball invented by Cleveland golfer Coburn Haskell with help from a B. F. Goodrich scientist replaces the solid gutta percha ball used since 1848. The "bouncing billy" is soon replaced by a ball with tightly wound rubber threads wrapped round a solid rubber core, and A. G. Spalding will acquire rights to the new ball (*see* 1892).

"I wish to preach, not the doctrine of ignoble ease, but the doctrine of the strenuous life," says the governor of New York Theodore Roosevelt April 10 in a speech at Chicago.

Missouri becomes the "show me" state. Congressman Willard D. Vandiver, 45, addresses a naval dinner at Philadelphia and says, "I come from a state that raises corn and cotton and cockleburs and Democrats, and frothy eloquence neither convinces nor satisfies me. I am from Missouri. You have got to show me."

The S. S. Kresge chain-store empire has its beginnings in a 5-and-10-cent store opened by Detroit merchant Sebastian Spering Kresge, 31, whose firm will have 677 stores in 27 states by 1940 (*see* 1962).

1899 (cont.) Chicago's Carson Pirie Scott & Co. opens a large new department store designed by Adler and Sullivan in State Street at Madison.

New York's University Club is completed by McKim, Mead and White in West 54th Street at Fifth Avenue.

The New York Yacht Club building on West 44th Street is completed with galleonlike windows by architect Whitney Warren, 20.

Washington's Post Office building is completed at Pennsylvania Avenue and 12th Street with a great glass-roofed court. The Romanesque revival granite building is topped by a clock tower.

London's Carlton House Hotel opens in Waterloo Place near the Carlton Club and Carlton House Terrace. César Ritz of the 10-year-old Savoy Hotel is employed as manager, and Louis Escoffier of the year-old Paris Ritz is placed in charge of the restaurant kitchen (*see* London Ritz, 1902).

Wisconsin's last wild passenger pigeon is shot (*see* 1878; 1914).

Mount Rainier National Park is created by act of Congress. The parkland embraces 242,000 acres of dense forests and meadows radiating from the slopes of an ancient 14,408-foot volcano in Washington State and contains the greatest single-peak glacial system in the United States.

A Refuse Act passed by Congress empowers the U.S. Army Corps of Engineers to prosecute polluters. The law provides for fines of up to $2,500 for oil spills and similar acts of pollution, but it will not be enforced.

The Columbia River Packers Association is created by seven chinook salmon canneries at the mouth of the river, one of which packs its fish under the name Bumble Bee. CRPA will acquire several sailing vessels in 1901, will load them with lumber, coal, building and canning materials, and will build a cannery on the Nushagak River at Bristol Bay in northwestern Alaska that will be followed by many more CRPA Alaskan canneries (*see* 1938).

The Russian grain harvest is 65 million tons, double the harvest of 30 years ago, as 200 million acres are planted to grain.

Kubanka durum wheat from southeastern Russia is introduced by U.S. cerealist Mark Carleton into North Dakota, which will be the leading U.S. producer of the wheat most suitable for macaroni and spaghetti (*see* 1901; Carleton, 1895; Kharkov, 1900).

The first U.S. concrete grain elevator is erected at the western edge of Minneapolis by Frank C. Peavey who has expanded with new grain elevators throughout the Northwest and is paying huge insurance premiums on the wooden elevators and their contents (*see* 1886). Peavey has sent his son-in-law Frank T. Heffelfinger and Minneapolis builder C. F. Haglin to Europe in search of the best method for storing grain, they have returned with praise for a Romanian concrete elevator, and Peavey has defied the conventional wisdom that only wood has the necessary "give" for storing grain. Skeptics call his 80-foot-tall concrete tank "Peavey's Folly" and predict that it will explode when grain is drawn out of its bottom, but the concrete elevator proves its critics wrong and will lead to the replacement of wooden elevators throughout the country (*see* 1900).

The first Colorado beet sugar refinery is built at Grand Junction and the American Beet Sugar Company is organized.

The American Sugar Refining Company trust has almost a 100 percent monopoly in the U.S. sugar industry (*see* 1897; 1907).

Coca-Cola is bottled for the first time by Chattanooga, Tenn., lawyers Benjamin F. Thomas and Joseph B. Whitehead who have traveled to Atlanta and have persuaded Asa Candler to let them try bottling the beverage under contract (*see* 1895). Seven parent bottlers will be given contracts to establish local bottling companies and supply them with syrup, the parent bottlers will be acquired over the years by the Coca-Cola Company (the last one in 1974), but most Coca-Cola continues to be dispensed at soda fountains from syrup mixed with carbonated water (*see* Britain, 1910; distinctive bottle, 1916).

Jell-O is acquired for $450 from Pearl Wait by his LeRoy, N.Y., neighbor Orator Francis Woodward who has just started a company to produce a cereal he calls Grain-O (*see* 1897; 1906).

United Fruit Company is incorporated (*see* above).

The California Fruit Canners Association is created by a consolidation of 11 old-line companies which represent nearly half the California packers and which include Dawson & Cutting, the first commercial fruit packers in the West, and the firm of Italian-American John Mark Fontana (*see* 1916).

C. A. Swanson & Sons has its beginnings in the Jerpe Commission Company started at Omaha by Swedish-American grocer Carl A. Swanson with local entrepreneurs Frank D. Ellison and John P. Jerpe. Started with $456 in capital, the firm will be incorporated in 1905 with a capitalization of $10,000 and will prosper in poultry, eggs, and butter (*see* 1945).

The New York Condensed Milk Company becomes Borden's Condensed Milk Company, which will be renamed the Borden Company in 1919 and Borden, Inc. in 1968 (*see* 1892; Liederkranz cheese, 1929).

Carnation evaporated milk is supplied in 16-ounce cans to Klondike-bound gold seekers by Elbridge Amos Stuart who has set up a small plant at Kent, Wash., near Seattle with help from John Meyenberg of the Highland, Ill., Helvetia Condensed Milk Company (*see* Our Pet, 1894). An Indiana Quaker who became a grocer at El Paso, Tex., Stuart has come to suspect that bad milk is the cause of so many children dying of "summer complaint" and has invested his savings in a new process to manufacture canned, sterilized, evaporated milk (*see* 1906).

Wesson Oil is developed by Southern Oil Company chemist David Wesson, 38, who introduces a new method for deodorizing cottonseed oil (*see* 1887). Wesson's vacuum and high-temperature process will revolutionize the cooking oil industry and will largely overcome the prejudice against cottonseed oil, which until now has been deodorized only by heating it with a steam coil and blowing live steam through it at atmospheric pressure (*see* 1900; Wesson Oil and Snowdrift Co., Inc., 1925).

Beech-Nut Packing Company is adopted as the new name for the 8-year-old Imperial Packing Company of Canojoharie, N.Y., to suggest the beechwood fires whose smoke is used in the smokehouse that cures the company's ham and bacon. Beech-Nut has specialized also in fancy pail lard, it has acquired U.S. patent rights to a German vacuum jar, and it perfects a superior flint glass jar for its bacon (*see* coffee, 1924).

Armenian-American confectioner-peddler Peter Paul Halajian at Naugatuck, Conn., advertises "Good candies at low prices. See our mixed candy at 10¢ a pound, three pounds for 25¢. . . . Fruits and nuts of all kinds. Peter Paul" (*see* 1919).

Jewel Tea Company has its beginnings in a door-to-door peddling operation that will grow to become Jewel Companies, a major U.S. food market chain.

Oysters Rockefeller is invented at the 59-year-old New Orleans restaurant Antoine's which names the dish of oysters baked with spinach and bacon after the head of the Standard Oil Company trust.

New York's Delmonico's Restaurant moves uptown from 26th Street to Fifth Avenue at 44th Street, across the avenue from Louis Sherry's (*see* 1896; 1861; 1922).

Chopped beefsteak is called Hamburg steak in America, says a new French-German-English dictionary of foods published under the title *Blueher's Rechtschreibung* (*see* 1836; Louis Lassen, 1900).

Emigration of Russians increases to more than 223,000, up from 108,000 4 years ago, as the 8-year-old Trans-Siberian Railway encourages settlement along its right-of-way.

"Conspicuous consumption" and "conspicuous waste" require such large expenditures that they are "probably the most effectual of the Malthusian prudential checks" on population growth and make for low birthrates in some classes of society, writes Thorstein Veblen in *Theory of the Leisure Class* (above).

1900 The Boer War continues in South Africa where Frederick Sleigh Roberts (Bobs Bahadur), 67, arrives January 10 to replace Sir Redvers Henry Buller, 60, as commander-in-chief with Lord Kitchener as his chief of staff. Buller retains command of an army, but it is cavalry commander John Denton Pinkstone French, 47, who relieves Kimberley February 15 after a 4-month Boer siege. General Roberts surrounds the Boer leader Piet Arnoldus Conje near Paardeberg and forces him to surrender February 27 after he has run out of food and ammunition, General Buller relieves Ladysmith February 28 after nearly 4 months of siege, Bloemfontein falls to Roberts March 13, and Mafeking is finally relieved May 17 after a 215-day siege in which Colonel Robert Stephenson Smyth, 43, baron Baden-Powell of Gilwell, has resisted the Boers (*see* Boy Scouts, 1908).

Johannesburg falls to the British May 31, General Buller takes Pretoria June 5, Roberts and Buller join forces at Vlakfontein July 4, Britain annexes the Orange Free State and the Transvaal (they become the Orange River Colony and the Transvaal Colony), President Kruger flees to Delagoa Bay and voyages to Europe in hopes of obtaining German support, but the kaiser Wilhelm II denies the aged Kruger an audience October 6.

General Roberts hands over his command to Lord Kitchener and is created first earl Roberts of Kandahar, Pretoria, and Waterford as the Boers resort to guerrilla warfare in their efforts to drive out the British. Lord Kitchener places some 120,000 Boer women and children in British concentration camps, where 20,000 will die of disease and neglect.

A "Boxer Rebellion" rocks China beginning June 20 as foreign legations at Peking are besieged by members of a militia force who have murdered the German minister to Peking and who are being encouraged by an antiforeigner clique at the Manchu court led by the dowager empress Tz'u Hsi, 66, who has ruled China for 39 years. The siege of the legations is lifted August 14 by an international expeditionary force, but at least 231 foreign civilians, most of them missionaries, are killed in various parts of China, and Russian troops retaliate for mid-July Chinese bombardments across the Amur River by driving thousands of Chinese civilians to their death in the river. The Russians seize southern Manchuria in the fall (*see* 1901; Japanese, 1904).

Italy's Umberto I is assassinated July 29 at age 56 by an anarchist at Monza. Umberto is succeeded after a 22-year reign by his 30-year-old son who will reign until 1946 as Victor Emmanuel III.

Britain's "Khaki" election October 16 results in a victory for the Conservatives who retain power under the 70-year-old marquis of Salisbury.

President McKinley campaigns for re-election with "the full dinner pail" slogan symbolizing Republican prosperity and receives a plurality of nearly a million popular votes. The Democratic ticket headed by William Jennings Bryan and former vice president Adlai E. Stevenson wins only 155 electoral votes as compared with 292 for the Republicans, but thousands of workers cast their votes for the Socialist party candidate Eugene Victor Debs.

Russia's Nikolai Lenin returns from exile January 29 after 3 years in Siberia with his wife and mother-in-

1900 (cont.) law. He sets up residence at Pskov while awaiting the release of his wife from Ufa, and on July 16, he emigrates to Switzerland to begin a 5-year exile. In December, Lenin begins publication at Munich of the newspaper *Iskra* (the *Spark*) which takes its name from an 1825 poem by an exile in Siberia who said, "The spark will kindle a flame!" (*see* 1895; 1903).

The International Ladies Garment Workers Union is founded June 3 by cloakmakers who meet in a small hall on New York's Lower East Side. The union's seven locals represent 2,310 workers in New York, Newark, Philadelphia, and Baltimore. By 1904 the ILGWU will have 5,400 members in 66 locals in 27 cities (*see* 1909 strike).

Only 3.5 percent of the U.S. work force is organized. Employers are free to hire and fire at will and at whim (*see* United Mine Workers, 1899; 1902).

The National Consumers League has its beginnings in the Consumers League for Fair Labor Standards founded by New York social worker Florence Kelley, 41, who last year joined the Henry Street Settlement after 8 years at Chicago's Hull House (*see* 1893; Addams, 1889). Conscientous consumers, says Kelley, will not want to buy goods made in substandard factories or finished in tenements, and she is joined by Josephine Goldmark and others in a campaign against child labor and tenement sweatshops. The League works for minimum wage laws, shorter hours, improved working conditions, occupational safety, better conditions for migrant farm labor, and consumer protection in the form of pure food and drug laws (*see* "Poison Squad," 1902; Triangle Shirtwaist fire, 1911).

A new quantum theory that will have enormous impact on scientific thinking is enunciated by German physicist Max Karl Ernst Ludwig Planck, 42, who says that bodies that radiate energy do not emit the energy constantly but rather in discrete parcels which he calls quantums (*see* Einstein, 1905).

Genetic laws revealed by Gregor Mendel in 1865 become generally known for the first time as Mendel's published work is discovered and Mendelian laws are made public by Dutch botanist Hugo De Vries, 52, at the University of Amsterdam, by German botanist Karl Erich Correns, 35, and by Austrian botanist Erich Tschermak von Seysenegg, 29, who work independently of each other (*see* Bateson, 1902).

The palace of Knossus on the Greek island of Crete is unearthed by English archaeologist Arthur John Evans, 49, who has been conducting excavations on the island for the past 7 years and who has discovered pre-Phoenician script. Evans will work for 8 years to reveal the seat of an ancient "Minoan" culture.

The yellow fever virus is shown to be transmitted by the *Aëdes aegypti* mosquito. A U.S. Public Health Commission headed by Major Walter Reed, 49, of the Army Medical Corps demonstrates the role of the mosquito after having been alerted to the possibility by C. J. Finlay (*see* 1881; Havana, 1901).

The U.S. death rate from diphtheria is 43.3 per 100,000, from influenza and pneumonia 181.5 per 100,000, from infant diarrhea and enteritis 108.8, from tuberculosis 201.9, from typhoid fever and paratyphoid 35.9, from cancer 63, from diabetes mellitus 917, and from heart disease 123.1 (*see* 1922).

Infant mortality in the United States is 122 per 1,000 live births, in England and Wales 154, and in India 232 (*see* 1951).

Average age at death in the United States is 47.

Bubonic plague strikes Honolulu in epidemic form. A large section of the city's Chinatown is condemned and burned under fire department supervision to kill the plague-bearing rats, but the fire gets out of control and much of the city is destroyed.

The first U.S. bubonic plague epidemic begins at San Francisco. The body of a dead Chinese is discovered March 6 in the basement of Chinatown's Globe Hotel, local authorities try to hush up the cause of death, but 120 others will be stricken before the plague ends in February of 1904, and all but three will die (San Francisco will have another plague epidemic in 1907, as will Seattle; New Orleans will have one in 1914 and 1919, and Los Angeles will have one in 1924).

The Interpretation of Dreams (*Traumdeutung*) by Sigmund Freud is based on psychoanalytic techniques that lean heavily on dream analysis (*see* 1895; first international meeting, 1908).

A new process for cracking petroleum to obtain gasoline is invented by U.S. chemist Charles Skeele Palmer, 42, who will sell rights to the process to Standard Oil Company in 1916 (*see* Houdry process, 1936).

John D. Rockefeller's Standard Oil Company buys the Pacific Coast Oil Company (*see* 1879; 1911).

The first British gasoline-powered motorbuses go into service in January as single-deck buses begin operating in Norfolk.

The first international championship motorcar race is held June 14 from Paris to Lyons. Five entries from Belgium, France, Germany, and the United States compete for the Gordon Bennett Cup put up by New York publisher James Gordon Bennett who has lived abroad since 1877. The cars all finish, all run over dogs en route, and the winner is a French Panhard that has averaged 38.5 miles per hour.

Only 144 miles of U.S. roads are hard-surfaced, but by year's end there are 13,824 motorcars on the road.

Franklin, Peerless, and Stearns motorcars are introduced. The air-cooled engine Franklin is made by Herbert H. Franklin, 34, whose sales will peak at 14,000 in 1929.

The Packard motorcar introduced at Warren, Ohio, has a chain-driven, one-cylinder, 12-horsepower engine and three forward speeds (see 1890).

The Auburn motorcar introduced by the Auburn Automobile Company of Auburn, Ind., is a single-cylinder runabout with solid tires and a steering tiller. Frank and Morris Eckhardt of the Eckhardt Carriage Company have started the firm with $2,500 in capital; they will produce a two-cylinder model in 1905, a four in 1909, and a six in 1912 (see 1924).

White steam cars and trucks are introduced by the White Company of Cleveland, a sewing machine firm headed by Walter White whose New England-born father Thomas invented a sewing machine in 1859, moved to Cleveland in 1866, and has developed the company now run by his sons Windsor, Rollin, and Walter. The first gasoline-powered White motorcars will appear in 1910.

France's Renault Frères introduces the first glass-enclosed two-passenger motorcar.

Firestone Tire & Rubber Company is founded August 3 at Akron, Ohio, by U.S. entrepreneur Harvey Samuel Firestone, 32, who has patented a method for attaching tires to rims. Firestone invests $10,000 to start the new firm (see 1908).

The first U.S. National Automobile Show opens November 10 at New York's Madison Square Garden with 31 exhibitors. Contestants compete in starting and braking, and exhibitors demonstrate hill-climbing ability on a specially built ramp.

Trolley cars provide transportation in every major U.S. city 12 years after the opening of the first trolley line in Richmond. Some 30,000 trolley cars operate on 15,000 miles of track (see 1917).

Excavation begins in March on a New York subway system that will be the largest in the world (see 1904).

The Paris Metro underground rail service begins operations (see London, 1891; Budapest, 1896; Boston, 1897). The Metro will grow to become the world's third largest subway (second largest in terms of passenger traffic; it will carry more than a billion passengers per year).

The Trans-Siberian Railway opens between Moscow and Irkutsk (see 1891; 1904).

U.S. railroads charge a freight rate that averages 75 cents per ton-mile, down from $1.22 in 1883. The Great Northern charges only $35 for a railcar traveling 500 miles between St. Paul, Minn., and Minot, N.D., while the Chicago and North Western charges only $40 for a railcar traveling the 750 miles between Chicago and Pierre, S.D.

Atlantic Coast Line Railroad is created with 1,760 miles of track. The 64-year-old Richmond and Petersburg has grown by absorption and consolidation. It has just absorbed the 66-year-old Wilmington and Weldon, it will gain 2,378 miles of track in 1902 by acquiring the Plant system, whose lines extend from Charleston to Tampa, and by 1928 it will have a total of 5,105 miles.

The Pennsylvania Railroad acquires control of the Long Island Railroad that will soon be the nation's largest passenger carrier (see 1836; 1905).

Illinois Central engineer Jonathan Luther "Casey" Jones, 36, of Jackson, Tenn., pulls his six-coach *Cannonball Express* into Memphis on the night of April 29, he learns that the engineer for the return run is ill, and he volunteers to replace him. Highballing at 75 miles per hour through Mississippi to make up for lost time, Jones rounds a gentle curve at 4 in the morning and sees a freight train stalled on the track dead ahead. Hand upon the throttle, Jones yells at his fireman to jump, he plows into the freight, he is killed by a wood splinter driven through his head, and while the collision is only one of 27 rear-end collisions on U.S. railroads in the month of April, a ballad will make it famous.

The Hay-Pauncefote Treaty February 5 includes a British renunciation of rights to build a Panama canal. Parliament rejects the treaty (see 1901).

The Chicago Sanitary and Ship Canal opens to link Lake Michigan with the Des Plaines River. The 33.8-mile canal connects the Great Lakes with the Mississippi and the Gulf of Mexico (see Joliet, 1673).

Only 25 percent of the U.S. commercial shipping fleet remains in sail, down from 56 percent in 1870. More than 60 percent of world shipping is in steamships, up from 16 percent in 1870.

The first modern submarine is purchased by the U.S. Navy. Invented by Irish-American engineer John Phillip Holland, 60, the submarine *Holland* uses electric motors under water and internal combustion engines on the surface, employing water ballast to submerge (see Bushnell, 1776; Lake, 1897).

The first rigid airship is launched by retired German general Ferdinand von Zeppelin, 62, who will go on to build many such lighter-than-air craft (see 1928).

Cody, Wyo., is founded by William "Buffalo Bill" Cody in order to have the Chicago, Burlington & Quincy Railroad run a spar to the large tracts of land that Cody has acquired in the area of the Shoshone River's south fork.

Molybdenite is discovered by a forest ranger on 13,500-foot Bartlett Mountain near Climax, Colo. The ranger sends samples of the blue-gray ore containing the rare metal molybdenum to Greenwood, Neb., banker Hugh Neal who advises him to stake claims which will be patented in 1905. The Climax mine will prove the world's largest deposit of molybdenum ore (see American Metal Company, 1916).

The Cripple Creek gold field discovered in Colorado 9 years ago yields $20 million worth of gold per year and is second only to South Africa's Transvaal goldfield discovered in 1886. It is far larger than the Klondike field discovered 4 years ago.

1900 (cont.) Mond Nickel Company buys up claims in the Sudbury district of northern Ontario. The English firm has developed a successful method for refining nickel (*see* Canadian Copper, 1885; Wharton, 1881; International Nickel, 1902).

Crucible Steel Company is created by a merger of several small U.S. firms that make high-grade industrial steel.

Jones & Laughlin Steel Co. is created August 1 by a reorganization of the Jones & Laughlin Co., Ltd. with Benjamin Franklin Jones, Jr., as president (*see* 1861).

Moody's Manual of Railroads and Corporation Securities begins publication under the direction of New York financial analyst John Moody, 32, who has worked for 10 years in the banking house Spencer Trask & Co. Moody will establish the investor's monthly *Moody's* magazine in 1905, and his annual *Moody's Analyses of Investments* will appear beginning in 1909.

Quebec's Caisse Populaire credit union is founded at Levis across the St. Laurence River from Quebec City by journalist-parliamentary clerk Alphonse Desjardins, whose cooperative banking system is based on European systems set up since the middle of the century to protect working people from the usurious interest rates usually charged by moneylenders. Desjardins has learned of the hardships caused by usurers, his Caisse Populaire is the first American credit union, he will help start the first U.S. credit union in 1909 at the textile mill town of Manchester, N.H., his Quebec operation will grow to have assets of more than $7 billion with 1,251 branches to serve 3.33 million Quebecois, and while U.S. credit unions will have combined assets of barely $1 billion by 1950, the figure will expand to $38 billion by 1977.

England's Birmingham University is founded largely through efforts by colonial secretary Joseph Chamberlain, now 64, who has effected passage of the Commonwealth of Australia Bill which is given royal assent July 9 and who will be first chancellor of the new university beginning next year.

A U.S. College Entrance Examination Board is founded to screen applicants to colleges. The College Board Scholastic Aptitude Tests will be graded on a scale of 200 to 800, and colleges will use SAT scores as a supplement to secondary-school records and other relevant information in judging qualifications of applicants, but SAT scores will never be more than approximate and will have a standard error of measurement in the area of 32 points.

Carnegie Institute of Technology is founded at Pittsburgh with a gift from steel magnate Andrew Carnegie.

The *Daily Express* is founded by London newspaperman Cyril Arthur Pearson, 34, who will lose his eyesight beginning in 1912 but who will amass a fortune that he will devote to helping blind soldiers and sailors (*see* Beaverbrook, 1916).

One U.S. home in 13 has a telephone.

Nonfiction *The Century of the Child* by Swedish feminist Ellen Karoline Sofia Key, 51, a teacher at Stockholm for 19 years until last year and now a lecturer at the People's Institute for workingmen.

Fiction *Sister Carrie* by U.S. novelist Theodore Dreiser, 29. Publisher Frank N. Doubleday hastily withdraws the book when his wife says it is too sordid, the small edition goes almost unnoticed, and Dreiser suffers a nervous breakdown; *Monsieur Beaucaire* by Booth Tarkington; *Lord Jim* by Joseph Conrad; *Love and Mrs. Lewisham* by H. G. Wells; *The Life and Death of Richard Yea-and-Nay* by Maurice Hewlett; *The Master Christian* by Marie Corelli; *The Flame of Life* (*Il fuoco*) by Gabriele D'Annunzio has been inspired by the actress Eleanora Duse, now 41, with whom D'Annunzio has had a long love affair.

Juvenile *Claudine at School* (*Claudine à l'École*) by French author Colette (Sidonie Gabriele Claudine Colette), 27, is a semiautobiographical series of stories that will have many sequels; *The Wizard of Oz* by Chicago newspaperman Lyman Frank Baum, 44, who last year won immediate success with his first book *Father Goose: His Story* (*see* stage musical, 1901); *Little Black Sambo* by English author Helen Bannerman, whose East Indian hero thwarts his tiger pursuers by turning them to butter.

Poetry *Almas de violeta* by Spanish poet Juan Roman Jiminez, 19, whose impressionism is based on scenes of his native Andalusia.

Painting *Le Moulin de la Galette* by Spanish painter Pablo Ruiz y Picasso, 19, who will move from Barcelona to Paris in 1903; *La Modiste* by Henri de Toulouse-Lautrec; *Still Life with Onions* by Paul Cézanne; *Nude in the Sun* by Pierre Auguste Renoir; *The Wyndham Sisters* by John Singer Sargent.

Noa Noa by Paul Gauguin is an account of the painter's first years in Tahiti from 1891 to 1893. Gauguin returned to Tahiti in 1895.

The Brownie box camera introduced by Eastman Kodak Company sells at $1, it puts photography within reach of everyone, and it makes Kodak a household name (*see* Pocket Kodak, 1895). The new camera's six-exposure film sells for 15 cents (*see* acetate film, 1924; Kodachrome, 1935).

Theater *Schluck und Jau* by Gerhart Hauptmann 1/3 at Berlin's Deutsches Theater; *You Never Can Tell* by George Bernard Shaw 5/2 at London's Strand Theatre; *St. John's Fire* (*Johannisfeuer*) by Hermann Sudermann 10/5 at Berlin's Lessing theater; *Mrs. Dane's Defence* by Henry Arthur Jones 10/9 at Wyndham's Theatre, London; *Michael Kramer* by Gerhart Hauptmann 12/21 at Berlin's Deutsches Theater.

"The Great Houdini" gains wide publicity by executing an escape from London's Scotland Yard, h becomes a main attraction at London's Alhambra Theatre, and he begins a 4-year tour of the Continent. U.S. escape artist Ehrich Weiss, 26, has adopted the name Houdini from the French magician Jean Eugene Robert-Houdin. He has studied Robert-Houdin's work, his book *The Unmasking of Robert-Houdin* in 1908 will show that the Frenchman's dexterity was much exaggerated, and he will far surpass Robert-Houdin's reputation with feats such as having himself shackled in irons, locked into a roped and weighted box, dropped overboard from a boat, and emerging with a smile before baffled audiences (*see* 1926).

New York's Theatrical Syndicate headed by booking agent Charles Frohman, 40, is challenged by the Shubert brothers of Syracuse, N.Y., who lease the Herald Square Theater. Lithuanian-American theatrical manager Sam S. Shubert, 24, and his Syracuse-born brothers Lee, 25, and J. J. (Jacob J.), 20, begin a 10-year battle with Frohman, A. L. Erlanger, and Marc Klaw by renting theaters to producers against whom the syndicate discriminates. The Shuberts will soon become producers themselves, Sam will be killed in a 1905 train wreck, the other two brothers will triumph over the syndicate (which is, in effect, a theatrical trust), and they will develop the most far-flung privately controlled theatrical organization in the world (*see* Shubert Theater, 1913).

Opera *Louise* 1/2 at the Opéra-Comique in Paris, with music by French composer Gustave Charpentier, 39; *Tosca* 1/14 at Rome's Teatro Costanzi, with music by Giacomo Puccini. The libretto is based on an 1887 tragedy by Victorien Sardou, now 69, about the 1796 political strife in Rome between Bonapartists and monarchists. *The Tale of Tsar Saltan* (*Skazka o Tsarye Saltanye*) 11/3 at Moscow, with music by Nikolai Rimski-Korsakov that includes his violin piece "The Flight of the Bumble-Bee."

Boston's 2,500-seat Symphony Hall designed by McKim, Mead and White of New York opens October 15 at the corner of Massachusetts and Huntington Avenues (*see* 1881).

The Philadelphia Orchestra is organized by wealthy residents who engage German conductor Fritz Scheel to direct the new orchestra's members in its first concert November 16 at the city's 43-year-old Academy of Music.

First performances "Alborado de Gracioso" by French composer Maurice (Joseph) Ravel, 24, 1/6 at the Société Nationale, Paris; *The Dream of Gerontius* by Edward Elgar (text by Cardinal Newman) 10/3 at England's Birmingham Festival.

Broadway Musicals *Fiddle-dee-dee* 9/16 at Weber & Fields Music Hall, with Joe Weber, Lew Fields, Lillian Russell, De Wolf Hopper, David Warfield, songs that include "Rosie, You are My Posie (Ma Blushin' Rosie)" by John Stromberg, lyrics by Edgar Smith, 262 perfs.

Popular songs "A Bird in a Gilded Cage" by New York composer Harry Von Tilzer (Harry Gumm), 28, lyrics by Arthur J. Lamb.

The trademark "His Master's Voice" with a painting by Francis Barraud of a fox terrier named Nipper listening attentively to a horn gramophone appears on gramophone records (the first records with circular paper title-labels) issued by Eldridge Johnson's Consolidated Talking Machine Company of Camden, N.J., a firm that will become the Victor Company (*see* Berliner, 1877).

The Olympic Games held at Paris attract 1,505 athletes from 16 nations. France is the unofficial winner, but government bureaucrats take over the games and nearly ruin the Olympics before the event is returned to the Olympic Committee headed by the baron de Coubertin.

Christy Matthewson leaves Bucknell University to join the New York Giants, but pitches so poorly that New York sells him to the Cincinnati Red Stockings. Right-hander Christopher Matthewson, 20, will be bought back, he will pitch his first full season for the Giants in 1903, he will win 30 games, his 267-strike-out record will stand for 50 years, he will be nicknamed "Big Six" after a famous fire engine, and he will have a lifetime record of 372 wins, 187 losses, and 2,499 strikeouts.

The first Davis Cup tennis matches open August 8 at Brookline, Mass., and continue to August 10. A U.S. team defeats a British team to gain possession of an $800 silver cup donated by Harvard senior Dwight Filley Davis, 21, who has commissioned the Boston Jeweler Shreve, Crump & Low to design and produce the challenge cup.

The Junior League of the New York College Settlement is founded by postdebutante Mary Harriman,

Ragtime began a new musical genre that would lead to jazz, the distinctively American music that later swept the world.

675

1900 (cont.) daughter of financier Edward Harriman, who organizes a group to aid a local settlement house. Debutantes flock to join the league, which will be followed by Junior Leagues of Baltimore, Brooklyn, Philadelphia, and (by 1906) of Boston. By 1920, there will be 39 Junior Leagues engaged in civic-improvement projects, and Dorothy Whitney (Mrs. Willard) Straight will organize them into the Association of Junior Leagues of America.

Chicago's Everleigh Club is opened at 2131–33 Dearborn Street by local entrepreneurs Minna and Ada Everleigh, 23 and 21, respectively, who have each received a $40,000 inheritance from their late Kentucky lawyer father and who have used the money to buy and refurbish a bordello to begin an 11-year career running the country's most elegant sporting house. Visitors require letters of introduction, they are entertained by string quartets and other pleasures, and the Everleigh Club will remain in business until rival madams subsidize a crusade that will force Chicago's mayor to close down the wealthy Everleigh sisters.

Kansas City has 147 houses of pleasure, with the most elegant being that of Annie Chambers whose $100,000 mansion is graced with a larger-than-life portrait of Annie dressed in a swirl of roses and gauze but little else.

One U.S. home in seven has a bathtub; showers are even rarer.

F. W. Woolworth controls 59 stores, up from 28 in 1895, and has sales in excess of $5 million. Inspired perhaps by A&P storefronts, Woolworth adopts a bright carmine-red storefront with gold-leaf lettering and molding for all his stores (*see* 1912).

Earthquakes rock Ecuador and Peru in mid-August, killing thousands.

A hurricane strikes Galveston, Tex., September 8 and kills between 6,000 and 8,000 people in the worst recorded natural disaster in North American history. Thousands more are injured, and property damage amounts to $17 million.

Some 2 million mustangs (wild horses) roam the U.S. prairie, but the nation has fewer than 30 head of bison, down from 1,090 in 1893. Longhorn cattle are also close to extinction (*see* 1850).

Brazil's Northeastern Hump remains 40 to 50 percent forested, but the figure will drop to 5 percent in the next 70 years. Deforestation will lead to erosion and water problems.

U.S. wheat fetches 70 cents a bushel as 34 percent of the crop is exported, and corn brings 33 cents a bushel as 10 percent of the crop is exported. Texas steers bring $4.25 per hundredweight, but the price index for U.S. farm products will rise by a spectacular 52 percent in the next decade as more efficient transport (above) enables Britain and Europe to import North American grain at low rates.

Mark Carleton makes another trip to Russia and returns with hard red Kharkov wheat, a winter variety that withstands winter-kill and gives high yields (*see* 1899; 1914).

The first full-size concrete grain elevator in North America goes up at Duluth, Minn., where "elevator king" Frank C. Peavey's 3.3 million bushel elevator reduces insurance rates on stored grain by 83 percent and more (*see* 1899). The Peavey elevator makes wood obsolete for building large elevators.

Steam tractors appear on wheatfields of the U.S. Pacific Northwest, but their main use is to draw portable threshing machines, many of which are still pulled by 40 horses driven abreast.

The world has 100 million acres of irrigated cropland, up from 20 million in 1880.

The first sluice gate on the Colorado River brings irrigation water from Arizona to California's Imperial Valley (*see* Salton Sea, 1905).

The average U.S. farm worker produces enough food and fiber for seven people, up from 4.5 in 1860.

Some 2.5 horsepower is available to each man working on a U.S. farm, up from 1.5 in 1850 (*see* 1930).

Honeydew melons are introduced into the United States (year approximate).

Grapefruit become an important food in the United States as botanical development makes the fruit sweeter. U.S. citrus growers will account for 90 percent of world grapefruit production.

Capper's Farmer begins publication in December at Topeka, Kans., under the name *Missouri Valley Farmer.* Journalist Arthur Capper, 35, has worked for the *New York Tribune* and other papers.

The amino acid tryptophan is isolated by English biochemists Frederick Gowland Hopkins, 39, and S. W. Cole (*see* niacin, 1945; Hopkins, 1906).

Thirteen amino acids have now been isolated, of which eight will be found essential to adult human nutrition (*see* Rose, 1949).

Milk bottles are introduced in England but only for pasteurized milk (*see* Borden, 1885; Hood, 1897). Most British milk remains unpasteurized, and milk bottles will not be widely used for another two decades (*see* 1901; 1942).

Regulations limiting bacteria in U.S. milk to 1 million per cubic centimeter prove difficult to enforce despite growing use of pasteurization (*see* 1890). Contaminated milk remains a major source of food-borne disease (*see* Evans, 1917).

Mead Johnson Company is founded at Evansville, Ind., to produce the infant cereal Pablum that will be sold through physicians' recommendations. Founder Johnson is a brother of Johnson & Johnson's Robert Wood Johnson (*see* 1886; Metrecal, 1958).

Battle Creek, Mich., has 42 breakfast cereal plants (*see* Kellogg; 1898; Post, 1897).

A model Shredded Wheat factory at Niagara Falls, N.Y., is put up by Henry D. Perkey with backing from financiers who include Darius Ogden Mills, now 75, whose 1896 Mills Hotel has been augmented by a chain of flophouses along New York's Bowery. A picture of the "Palace of Light" factory will appear on every package of Shredded Wheat, and the new factory will also produce Shredded Wheat crackers called Triscuits (*see* 1898; National Biscuit Company, 1928).

Uneeda Biscuits have sales of more than 10 million packages per month, while all other packaged crackers sell scarcely 40,000 per month (*see* 1898). N. W. Ayer advertising copywriter Joseph Geisinger poses his 5-year-old nephew Gordon Stile in boots, oil hat, and slicker holding a box of Uneeda Biscuits, and a photographer takes a picture that will become a famous trademark (*see* Animal Crackers, 1902).

Per capita U.S. wheat flour consumption averages 224 pounds, up from 205 pounds in 1850 (*see* 1920).

Per capita U.S. sugar consumption averages 65.2 pounds per year.

National Sugar Manufacturing Company is incorporated in New Jersey (*see* Jack Frost trademark, 1913).

National Starch Manufacturing Company is founded (*see* 1842; 1906).

World beet sugar production reaches 5.6 million tons, a figure that will more than quadruple in the next 64 years.

Milton S. Hershey sells his Lancaster Caramel Company for $1 million in cash to the American Caramel Company but retains his chocolate manufacturing equipment (*see* 1894). Hershey rents a wing of his old plant from its new owners so that he may continue making chocolate bars which will have sales next year of $622,000 (*see* 1903).

Typical U.S. food prices: sugar 4 cents per pound, eggs 14 cents per dozen, butter 24 to 25 cents per pound. Boarding houses offer turkey dinner at 20 cents and supper or breakfast at 15 cents, but a male stenographer earns $10 per week and an unskilled girl $2.50.

H. J. Heinz erects an electric sign six stories high with 1,200 lights to tell New Yorkers about the "57 Good Things for the Table" that include Heinz tomato soup, Heinz tomato ketchup, Heinz sweet pickles, India relish, and peach butter (*see* 1896; 1905).

Wesson Oil is put on the market by the Southern Oil Company (*see* 1899). The pure cottonseed oil has been made palatable by David Wesson who will work from 1901 to 1911 on a process for hydrogenating cottonseed oil (*see* 1925; Normann, 1901).

Duffy-Mott Company is created by a merger of W. B. Duffy Cider Company at Rochester, N.Y., with the S. R. Mott Company (*see* 1842; apple sauce, 1930).

The Empire Cheese plant that has made Philadelphia brand cream cheese since 1880 burns down at South Edmeston, N.Y., and a new company unintentionally misspelled Phenix Cheese by its farmer-founders resumes production (*see* Kraft, 1904).

The hamburger is pioneered at New Haven, Conn., where Louis Lassen grinds 7 cents per pound lean beef, broils it, and serves it between two slices of toast (no catsup or relish) to customers at his 5-year-old three-seat Louis Lunch (but *see* 1899; 1904).

The *Guide Michelin* published at Paris is the first systematic evaluation of European restaurants. Financed by tire producers André and Edouard Michelin, the *Guide* rates restaurants using a system of three stars (worth a special journey), two stars (worth a detour), or one star, and will be updated periodically (*see* 1934).

U.S. physical culturist Bernarr Macfadden, 32, opens a New York restaurant at 487 Pearl Street at which most items sell for 1 cent. Other restaurants generally charge 15 cents for a full dinner, most bars offer free lunches, but Macfadden sets new lows. His penny prices help promote the *Physical Culture* magazine he has been publishing since 1898 (*see* 1919).

Kansas prohibitionist Carry Moore Nation, 54, declares that since the saloon is illegal in Kansas, any citizen has the right to destroy liquor, furniture, and fixtures in any public place selling intoxicants. She begins a campaign of hatchet-wielding through Kansas cities and towns, and although she will be arrested, fined, imprisoned, clubbed, and shot at, she will persevere (*see* Anti-Saloon League, 1895; 18th Amendment and Volstead Act, 1919).

San Francisco's Hills Bros. begins packing roast ground coffee in vacuum tins to begin a new era in coffee marketing. It is the beginning of the end for the coffee roasting shops common now in every town and the coffee mill seen in almost every U.S. kitchen (*see* 1878; Chase and Sanborn, 1878).

The North American population reaches 81 million, up from 5.7 million in 1800, and begins a growth that will reach 355 million by 1978.

The U.S. population reaches 76 million with 10.3 million of the total foreign born, roughly 9 million black or of mixed blood, 237,000 native American Indian or partly Indian, 90,000 Chinese, 24,000 Japanese.

Half of all U.S. working women are farmhands or domestic servants (*see* 1960).

Some 45.8 million Americans are rural inhabitants, 30.2 million urban residents.

The country has 12 million Roman Catholics, 6 million Methodists, 5 million Baptists, 1.5 million Lutherans, 1.5 million Presbyterians, 1 million Jews, 700,000 Episcopalians, 350,000 Mormons, 80,000 Christian Scientists, and 75,000 Unitarians.

The population of the world reaches 1.65 billion, and 16 cities of the world have population of 1 million or more (*see* 1901; 1960).

20th CENTURY

1901 Queen Victoria dies January 22 at age 81 after a reign of nearly 64 years in which the United Kingdom has grown from a country of 25 million to one of 37 million. The queen's 59-year-old son succeeds to the throne as Edward VII to begin a 9-year reign.

The Commonwealth of Australia created January 1 has joined New South Wales, Queensland, South Australia, Victoria, Tasmania, the Northern Territory, and West Australia.

The Boer War continues in South Africa. Lord Kitchener builds a chain of blockhouses to combat guerrilla activities, and he starts destroying Boer farms. Boer forces invade the Cape Colony under James Hertzog and Christian de Wet, but British troops repel the Boers, and when Louis Botha raids Natal, he has no success (*see* 1800; 1902).

"Speak softly and carry a big stick," says Vice President Roosevelt September 2 in a speech at the Minnesota State Fair in which he lays down a rule for U.S. foreign policy: "There is a homely adage which runs, 'Speak softly and carry a big stick; you will go far.' If the American nation will speak softly and yet build and keep at a pitch of the highest training a thoroughly efficient navy, the Monroe Doctrine will go far."

The Peace of Peking September 7 ends the Boxer Rebellion that began last year. China is obliged to pay indemnities to the world powers.

President McKinley is shot at point-blank range September 6 with a .32 caliber Ivor-Johnson revolver fired by Polish-American anarchist Leon Czolgosz, 28, during the president's visit to the Pan-American Exposition at Buffalo, N.Y. The wounds are not properly dressed, McKinley dies of gangrene September 14 at age 58, and Theodore Roosevelt at age 42 becomes the youngest chief executive in the nation's history (Cleveland's Mark Hanna calls him "that damned cowboy").

The Spindletop gusher that has come in January 10 at Beaumont, Tex., gives John D. Rockefeller's Standard Oil Trust its first major competition. The Gulf Coast oil field was located in 1892 by one-armed lumberman Patillo Higgins, now 36, and he has leased some 600 acres to Slavic-American Anthony F. Luchich (Lucas), who has been drilling since July 1899 into a salt dome on the field abandoned as unproductive by Standard Oil prospectors. Lucas has been backed by Pittsburgh financiers John H. Galey and Colonel J. M. Guffey, he has drilled some 700 feet into the Big Hill, and he has struck oil that spouts 110,000 barrels per day, flowing wild for 9 days before it can be brought under control.

The Beaumont Field (above) contains more oil than the rest of the United States combined, Spindletop establishes Texas as the major petroleum-producing state, Higgins has a 10 percent interest in the Lucas lease and becomes a millionaire overnight, and the Gulf Oil Company has its beginnings as Galey and Guffey (above) get backing from Pittsburgh banker Andrew W. Mellon and his brother Richard, who take 40 percent of the new J. M. Guffey Petroleum Company (*see* aluminum, 1891; Texas Co., 1902).

A 60-year concession to explore for oil in four-fifths of Persia is acquired for $20,000 by New Zealander William Knox D'Arcy who has made a fortune in Australian gold mining. D'Arcy will sell his concession in 1908 to Burmah Oil Company, which will be backed by the British government in forming the Anglo-Persian Company, which will begin Middle Eastern petroleum production (*see* 1908).

More than half the world's oil output is from Russia's Baku oil fields which have been developed by Ludwig Nobel, brother of dynamite inventor Alfred Nobel, and by Rothschild interests (*see* 1871). Nobel has devised the world's first oil tankers and tank cars and has installed Europe's first pipeline, but the world's major supplier of petroleum is the United States, which will produce as much as two-thirds of the world's export oil for 20 years (*see* Baku, 1946).

Allis-Chalmers Manufacturing Company is organized at Milwaukee in a merger of Chicago's Fraser & Chalmers Company, producers of mining machinery, with the interests of the late Milwaukee lawyer Edward Phelps Allis who died in 1889 at age 64. Allis took over a local flour milling machinery maker when it went bankrupt in 1861 after 14 years in business, he built up the company, the new company will erect a huge factory on the outskirts of Milwaukee in 1903, Allis-Chalmers will start making electrical equipment in 1904, and it will grow to become a major U.S. producer of steam turbines, hydroelectric units, high-voltage transformers, farm machinery (*see* 1935), and other capital-goods equipment.

A mercury-vapor electric lamp is invented by U.S. electrical engineer Peter Cooper Hewitt, 40, whose father Abram Stevens Hewitt produced the first American-made steel in 1870.

Sylvania Electric Company is organized to manufacture light bulbs (*see* General Telephone & Electronics, 1958).

Wall Street panics May 9 as brokerage houses sell off stock so they can raise funds to cover their short positions in Northern Pacific Railroad stock. Financiers Edward H. Harriman, Jacob Schiff of Kuhn, Loeb & Co., and James Stillman of New York's National City Bank vie for control of the railroad controlled by J. P. Morgan and by James J. Hill of Canadian Pacific. Stillman's City Bank is the repository of John D. Rockefeller's Standard Oil Company money (*see* Charles Stillman, 1850), Harriman and Schiff have acquired control of the Union Pacific, the Southern Pacific, and the SP's subsidiary the Central Pacific, they seek control of the Chicago, Burlington & Quincy to gain access to Chicago, the rivals for the Northern Pacific bid up the price of stock in the road to $1,000 per share, but they grow frightened when other stock prices collapse in the panic, they let short-sellers cover their positions at $150 per share, and they join forces to form the Northern Securities Company, a holding company that controls not only the Northern Pacific but also the Great Northern and the Chicago, Burlington & Quincy (*see* Kahn, 1897; Supreme Court ruling, 1904).

United States Steel Company is created by J. P. Morgan (above), who underwrites a successful public offering of stock in the world's first $1 billion corporation, nets millions for himself in a few weeks of hard work, and pays $492 million to Andrew Carnegie for about $80 million in actual assets in order to eliminate the steel industry's major price cutter. Carnegie personally receives $225 million in 5 percent gold bonds and is congratulated on being "the richest man in the world" by Morgan who merges Carnegie's properties with other steel properties to create a company that controls 65 percent of U.S. steelmaking capacity (*see* Bethlehem, 1905).

John D. Rockefeller's Lake Superior Consolidated Iron Mines Company, whose Mesabi range properties have been leased by Andrew Carnegie, is absorbed into United States Steel (above) to prevent Rockefeller from starting a rival company (*see* 1893).

Inland Steel Company opens its first steel mill in the sand dunes of Indiana Harbor east of Chicago on Lake Michigan. The company has been started by former Cincinnati junk dealer-iron founder Joseph Block and his sons.

Meyer Guggenheim and his sons gain control of the American Smelting and Refining Company by buying out Leonard Lewisohn, and they merge their properties into the ASARCO copper trust (*see* 1899). Daniel Guggenheim, 45, becomes chairman of ASARCO's executive committee, four Guggenheim sons are on the board of directors, and the Guggenheims begin to extend the copper trust's operations into areas that include Chilean copper and nitrate mines, Bolivian tin mines, Alaskan gold mines, and Belgian Congo copper mines, diamond mines, and rubber plantations. A nitrate extraction process developed by E. A. Cappelen Smith will be called the Guggenheim process (see *Titanic*, 1912; Chuquicamata mine, 1923).

The American Can Company is created by a merger of 175 U.S. can makers engineered by W. H. Moore of 1899 National Steel fame and Indiana banker Daniel Reid. The Can Trust turns out 90 percent of U.S. tin-plated steel cans (*see* Continental Can, 1904).

Monsanto Chemical Company is founded at St. Louis with a capitalization of $5,000 by entrepreneur John Francis Queeny, 42, who gives the new company his wife's maiden name and starts making saccharin (*see* Remsen, Fahlberg, 1879). Queeny's initial arrangements with patentees soon expire, the company is obliged to buy its intermediates in Switzerland and to go into competition with a firm that both dominates the market and controls the source of basic supplies, Monsanto will show no profit until 1905, but it will expand to become a major producer of alum, caffeine, caustic soda, chlorine, phenolphthalein, salicyclic acid, and hundreds of other chemicals for industry, agriculture, and medicine (*see* phenol, 1914).

A hydrogenation process invented by English chemist William Normann saturates unsaturated and polyunsaturated fatty acids to keep them from turning rancid. The process will find wide application in soapmaking and in the production of edible fats and foods containing oils (*see* below).

Nobel Prizes are awarded for the first time from a fund (initially $9.2 million) established by Alfred B. Nobel of 1866 dynamite fame, who has added to his fortune by investments in Russia's Baku oil fields (above). "Inherited wealth is a misfortune which merely serves to dull a man's faculties," said Nobel in 1895, and he has willed that his fortune be invested "in safe securities ... the interest accruing from which shall be annually awarded in prizes."

The first Nobel Prize in physics is awarded to Germany's W. C. Roentgen for his x-ray discovery.

M'KINLEY SHOT

Stranger Fires Two Bullets Into His Stomach.

His Condition Is Serious But He Is Still Living.

Taken to the Hospital on the Pan American Exposition Grounds.

America's third presidential assassination in 36 years put "Rough Rider" Theodore Roosevelt in the White House.

1901 (cont.)   The first Nobel Prize for medicine is awarded to Germany's Emil von Behring for his diphtheria antitoxin.

The Rockefeller Institute for Medical Research is founded by Standard Oil Company's John D. Rockefeller. Unlike European laboratories which are built around individuals such as the Pasteur Institute founded in 1888, the Rockefeller Institute offers facilities to groups of collaborating investigators and establishes a new pattern that others will follow (*see* John McCormick Institute, 1902; Phipps Institute, 1903; Rockefeller Sanitary Commission, 1909).

Life expectancy at birth for U.S. white males is 48.23 years and for white females, 51.08 years.

Adrenaline (epinephrine) is isolated by Japanese-American chemist Jokichi Takamine, 47, a consultant to Parke, Davis & Company, and by Armour & Company scientists working with Johns Hopkins Medical School chemist-pharmacologist John Jacob Abel, 44. Secreted by the medullary portion of the adrenal glands, levo-methylaminoethanolcatchetol ($C_9H_{13}ON_3$) is the first ductless gland secretion to be isolated by man. It will be used in medicine as a heart stimulant, to constrict the blood vessels, and to relax the bronchi in asthma; it will be synthesized, but it will be obtained more economically from the glands of cattle, even though it takes 12,000 head of cattle to produce 1 pound of the hormone that raises blood pressure (*see* Bayliss, Starling, Dakin, 1904).

Mosquito controls virtually rid Havana of yellow fever. General Leonard Wood, now 41, and Major William C. Gorgas, 47, of the U.S. Public Health Service have put in the controls (*see* 1900; Panama, 1903).

Sterling Products Company is founded to produce and market over-the-counter drugs. Sterling will introduce Danderine in 1906 (*see* Cascarets, 1909).

The Russian minister of propaganda is assassinated February 27 in reprisal for his repression of student agitators.

British chocolate heir William Cadbury visits Trinidad and is told that cocoa workers in Portugal's African islands of Sao Thomé and Principe are, for all practical purposes, treated as slaves (*see* 1879; 1902).

Alabama adopts a new constitution with literacy tests and a grandfather's clause designed to disenfranchise blacks (*see* Louisiana, 1898).

Booker T. Washington of Tuskegee Institute is entertained at a White House dinner October 16 by President Roosevelt. Reprisals are taken against southern blacks by outraged whites (*see* 1895).

The Fore River Ship & Engine Company is incorporated. Former Bell Telephone research director Thomas A. Watson quit Bell's employ in 1881 to open a machine shop at East Braintree, Mass., with F. O. Wellington. He and Wellington have been receiving U.S. Navy contracts since 1896 (*see* Bethlehem, 1913).

Dollar Steamship Company is founded by San Francisco lumberman Robert Dollar, 57, with the 129-foot ship S.S. *Newsboy*. The American President Lines, Ltd., will have its beginnings in 1924 when Dollar will launch the S.S. *President* at age 80 to give himself a round-the-world passenger line.

The Second Hay-Pauncefote Treaty November 18 gives the United States sole rights to construct, maintain, and control a trans-isthmian canal (*see* 1900). Washington assumes the obligation to assure passage through such a canal to ships of all nations (*see* 1902).

The Mercedes motorcar is introduced by German automaker Gottlieb Daimler to satisfy the Austrian consul at Nice. Emil Jellinek has offered to buy and distribute 36 Daimlers on condition that the cars be named after his 11-year-old daughter Mercedes, thus undertaking to sell nearly an entire year's production of the motorcars (*see* 1890; Mercedes-Benz, 1926).

Detroit automaker R. E. Olds moves his assembly plant to his hometown of Lansing, Mich. (*see* 1897). Copper and lumber baron Samuel L. Smith has financed the Olds Motor Works, and Olds markets 600 curved-dash "Oldsmobile" runabouts, a number he will increase to 5,000 by 1904 (*see* Reo, 1904).

The Detroit Automobile Company goes bankrupt after having sold only four or five of its cars in 2 years. Chief engineer Henry Ford is hired as experimental engineer by the men who buy Detroit Automobile's assets, and when a Ford-designed car wins a major race, some former Detroit Automobile Company stockholders form the Henry Ford Company, giving Ford one-sixth of the stock in the new company, which he will soon quit (*see* 1903).

The Apperson motorcar is introduced.

The Pierce "motorette" is introduced by Buffalo, N.Y., automaker George N. Pierce, 55 (*see* 1904).

John North Willys enters the motorcar business by selling two of the new Pierce "motorettes" (above). Willys is a 27-year-old Elmira, N.Y., sporting goods retailer who saw his first automobile (a Winton) on a trip to Cleveland last year and who has become a Pierce dealer (*see* 1902).

New York City streetcars and elevators are converted to electric power, but horsecars continue to move up and down Fifth Avenue (*see* 1885; 1907).

The American Locomotive Company is organized by a group of family-owned locomotive builders to challenge the Baldwin Locomotive Company founded in 1831. By 1906 the new company will be turning out nearly 3,000 locomotives per year, it will continue to produce more than 1,000 per year until 1914, and it will produce the Berliet motorcar from 1905 to 1914 but will abandon auto production after losing $9 million in the venture.

The Uganda Railway is completed December 26 to link Mombasa with Lake Victoria.

The U.S. College Entrance Examination Board conducts its first examinations.

The U.S. Army War College is founded at Washington, D.C., by Secretary of War Elihu Root. The college will move in 1951 to Carlisle, Pa.

Idaho State University is founded at Pocatello.

Whittier College is founded at Whittier, Calif.

Texas Women's University is founded at Denton.

Guglielmo Marconi receives the first transatlantic wireless message December 12 in Newfoundland (*see* 1896). An English telegrapher at Poldhu, Cornwall, has tapped out the letter "S," and Marconi picks it up with a kite antenna. He will build a station at Glace Bay, Nova Scotia, next year, and he will send the first readable message across the Atlantic to begin regular transatlantic wireless service (*see* 1903).

The American Multigraph Company is founded at Cleveland to produce the newly patented Multigraph, the first machine designed to print from a typed or handwritten image.

The *Winnipeg Free Press* names John Wesley Dafoe, 34, editor. Canadian minister of the interior and superintendent of Indian affairs Sir Cliffort Sifton, 40, has acquired the paper, he hires Dafoe, and the new editor will run the *Free Press* for more than 40 years, making it Canada's most powerful newspaper.

J. Walter Thompson Company receives a letter from the Curtis Publishing Company in Philadelphia which applies the ANPA rules of 1893 to its *Ladies' Home Journal, Saturday Evening Post,* and *Country Gentleman* magazines. The 10 percent agency commission for placing advertisements in Curtis magazines will be followed by other magazines and will rise to 15 percent (*see* 1878; Resor, 1916).

Andrew Carnegie gives the New York Public Library $5.2 million to open its first branches (*see* 1895). Within 55 years, the library will have 75 branches staffed by 2,000 plus three mobile units, and its operating costs will be $8 million per year (*see* 1911).

Nonfiction *Up from Slavery* by Booker T. Washington (above).

Fiction *Buddenbrooks* by German novelist Thomas Mann, 26, who has rejected his publisher's order to cut the manuscript in half. The first edition is only 1,000 copies, but a second, cheaper edition will have sales of more than a million copies in Germany and tens of thousands in other countries. *Martin Birck's Youth* (*Martin Bircks Ungdom*) by Hjalmar Soderberg; *Kim* by Rudyard Kipling; *Erewhon Revisited* by Samuel Butler; *Sister Teresa* by George Moore; *Graustark* by Lafayette, Ind., *Daily Courier* city editor George Barr McCutcheon, 35, whose novel about a fictional kingdom achieves great popular success; *The Octopus* by Frank Norris dramatizes the struggle of California wheat growers against the Southern Pacific Railroad.

Juvenile *Mrs. Wiggs of the Cabbage Patch* by Alice Hegan Race.

Poetry *The Garden of Kama and Other Love Lyrics from India,* arranged in verse by English poet Laurence Hope (Adela Florence Cory Nicolson), 36, who lived much of her life in India. Her "Kashmiri Song" begins, "Pale hands I loved beside the Shalimar. . . ."

Painting *The Gold in Their Bodies* by Paul Gauguin; *Girls on the Bridge* by Edvard Munch; *Cat Boats, Newport* by Childe Hassam, 41; *Femme Retroussant Sa Chemise* by U.S. painter Henri de Toulouse-Lautrec, who dies in his mother's arms September 9 at the Château de Malrome at age 36.

Sculpture *Mediterranean* by French sculptor Aristide (Joseph Bonaventure) Maillol, 39.

The Goodwin nitrocellulose film patent of 1889 is acquired upon the death of its inventor Hannibal Goodwin by Anthony & Scovill, a company that will become Ansco (*see* Anthony, 1852; Agfa, 1927).

Theater *The Climbers* by Clyde Fitch 1/21 at New York's Bijou Theater, with Amelia Bingham, 163 perfs.; *The Three Sisters* (*Tri Sestry*) by Anton Chekhov 1/31 at the Moscow Art Theater; *Lover's Lane* by Clyde Fitch 2/6 at New York's Manhattan Theater; *The Wedding* (*Wesele*) by Polish playwright-painter Stanislaw Wyspianski, 32, 3/16 at Cracow's Teatr Slawackiego; *The Marquis of Keith* (*Der Marquis von Keith*) by Frank Wedekind 10/11 at Berlin's Residenztheater; *If I Were King* by Irish playwright-novelist Justin Huntly McCarthy, 40, 10/14 at New York's Garden Theater, with Edward H. Sothern, 56 perfs.; *The Last of the Dandies* by Clyde Fitch 10/24 at His Majesty's Theatre, London; *The Way of the World* by Clyde Fitch 11/4 at Hammerstein's Victoria Theater, New York, with Elsie de Wolfe, 35 perfs.; *The Conflagration* (*Der rote Hahn*) by Gerhart Hauptmann 11/27 at Berlin's Deutsches Theater; *The Girl and the Judge* by Clyde Fitch 12/4 at New York's Lyceum Theater, with Anne Russell, 125 perfs.

Opera *Fire Famine* (*Feuersnot*) 11/21 at Dresden, with music by Richard Strauss.

First performances Symphony No. 6 in A major by the late Anton Bruckner 3/14 at Stuttgart (first complete performance); *Menuet Antique* by Maurice Ravel 4/13 at Paris; *Cockaigne* Overture (In London Town) by Edward Elgar 6/20 at the Queen's Hall, London; Concerto No. 2 in C minor for Piano and Orchestra by Sergei Rachmaninoff 10/14 at Moscow; Pomp and Circumstance March in D major by Edward Elgar 10/19 at Liverpool; Symphony No. 4 in G major by Gustav Mahler 11/28 at Munich.

Broadway musicals *Captain Jinks of the Horse Marines* 2/4 at the Garrick Theatre, with H. Reeves Smith, Ethel Barrymore, book by Clyde Fitch, music by T. Maclaglen, lyrics by female impersonator William H. Lingard, and a song that begins "I'm Captain Jinks of the Horse Marines, / I feed my horse on pork and beans, / And often live beyond my means, / I'm

1901 (cont.) a captain in the army," 168 perfs.; *The Governor's Son* 2/25 at the Savoy Theatre, with music, book, and lyrics by George Michael Cohan, 23, who began touring in vaudeville with his parents, began writing songs for the act in his teens, gained his first popular success at age 17 with "Hot Tamale Alley," and followed it 3 years later with "I Guess I'll Have to Telegraph My Baby," 32 perfs.

Popular songs "I Love You Truly" by U.S. songwriter Carrie Jacobs-Bond, 39; "Mighty Lak' a Rose" by the late Ethelbert Nevin, who has just died at age 39, lyrics by *Atlanta Constitution* poet-journalist Frank L. Stanton, 44; "Boola Boola" by Yale undergraduate Allan M. Hirsch.

Baseball's American League is organized by teams whose annual pennant winner will compete beginning in 1903 with the top team of the 25-year-old National League in World Series playoffs.

The U.S. America's Cup defender *Columbia* with rigging by Nat Herreshoff defeats Sir Thomas Lipton's *Shamrock II* 3 to 0.

The Arlberg Ski Club is founded at St. Christoph.

Jergen's Lotion for chapped hands is introduced by Cincinnati's 19-year-old Andrew Jergens Company, whose product will dominate the market for more than 70 years.

The first practical electric vacuum cleaner is invented by British bridge builder and wheel designer Hubert Booth. His Vacuum Cleaner Co. Ltd. sends vans round to houses and uses the Booth machine to suck dust out of houses via tubes (*see* Spangler, Hoover, 1907; Electrolux, 1921).

King C. Gillette raises $5,000 to start a safety razor company and sets up a factory above a Boston fish store (*see* 1895). MIT graduate William E. Nickerson refines Gillette's idea for a safety razor and develops processes for hardening and sharpening sheet steel (*see* 1903).

The Imperial Tobacco Company of Great Britain and Ireland is created by Sir William Henry Wills, 71, the first Baron Winterstroke, whose grandfather and father-in-law started a tobacco and snuff business at Bristol in the 18th century (*see* Wills's Three Castles, 1878; 1892). Baron Winterstroke's cousin Sir George Alfred Wills, 47, helps him effect a merger of British manufacturers and establish a company that will produce pipe tobacco and cigarettes.

New York's R. H. Macy Company moves into a new building on Herald Square between 34th and 35th Streets that replaces the old 14th Street Macy's and that will grow to become the world's largest department store building (*see* 1888; 1912).

Boston's William Filene, Sons & Co. becomes William Filene's Sons Company following the death of founder William Filene at age 71. Filene is succeeded by his son Edward who moves the store to 453–463 Washington Street, trebles its floor space,

and soon re-leases the former store at 445–447 Washington Street as an annex for babies' and children's wear (*see* 1881; Automatic Bargain Basement, 1909).

The Elms at Newport, R.I., is completed for Philadelphia coal magnate Edward Julius Berwind, 53—the world's largest individual owner of coal mines. Architect Horace Trumbauer has modeled the huge Bellevue Avenue "cottage" on the 18th-century Château d'Agnes at Asnières near Paris and has surrounded it with a high wall that encloses extensive gardens.

New York's Carnegie mansion for steel magnate Andrew Carnegie (above) is completed on Fifth Avenue at 92nd Street by Babb, Cook and Willard. The six-story 64-room neo-Georgian house has wood panels carved by Scottish and Indian craftsmen, a utilities basement fitted like a steamship engine room, a conservatory, and a large garden opposite Central Park.

New York's Benjamin N. Duke mansion on Fifth Avenue at 78th Street is completed for a founder of the American Tobacco Company Trust.

A new tenement house law is passed in New York, whose 83,000 "old law" masonry and wood tenements house 70 percent of the city's population. Strung end to end like railroad cars, the old six-story tenements have only tiny airshafts to provide light and air between their 90-foot ends, they crowd 10 families into 25- by 100-foot lots, and their minimal communal plumbing is indoors only because outhouses would consume land used for building.

New York's Harlem begins its rise following the start of construction of a Lenox Avenue subway line that triggers a real estate boom. The uptown Manhattan area will be overbuilt with apartment houses, many buildings will be unoccupied, and the razing of structures for Macy's department store (above), for Pennsylvania Station, and for large hotels, office buildings, and lofts in the Tenderloin area west of Herald Square is forcing blacks to seek new homes. Black real estate operator Philip A. Payton will seize the opportunity, he will guarantee premium rates to landlords, he will make good housing available for the first time to black New Yorkers, and Harlem will become America's largest black community. It will be a model community until overcrowding in the 1920s turns it into a ghetto.

Johns Manville Company is created by Milwaukee's 21-year-old Manville Covering Company which buys out New York's 43-year-old Johns Manufacturing Company. Johns Manville will import asbestos (45 percent silica, 45 percent magnesia, 10 percent water) from Canadian mines, and it will become the world's largest insulation company (*see* 1927).

The first Statler Hotel is completed for Buffalo's Pan-American Exposition by local restaurateur Ellsworth Milton Statler, 37, whose temporary 2,100-room structure will be replaced by a more solid Statler Hotel in 1904 (*see* St. Louis, 1904).

One fourth of U.S. agricultural produce is exported, according to testimony given at hearings of the U.S. Industrial Commission.

The Industrial Commission (above) hears a government witness testify that a steam sheller can shell a bushel of corn in 1.5 minutes versus 100 minutes for the same job done by hand and that a wheat combine can do in 4 minutes what it would take a man 160 minutes to reap, bind, and thresh by hand.

 Obesity and heart disease are observed for the first time to have a strong correlation (*see* 1913).

The hydrogenation process invented by William Normann (above) turns polyunsaturated fats into saturated fats that will be linked to heart disease when it is found that the human liver can synthesize serum cholesterol from saturated fats.

The amino acids valine and proline are isolated.

Beriberi kills thousands in the Philippines following introduction of polished white rice by U.S. occupation authorities (*see* 1898; Grijns, 1906).

 Statutory standards for milk are established to protect British consumers, but pasteurization is not required. British milk remains a source of diseases that include undulant fever and tuberculosis of the bone (*see* Evans, 1917).

The Good Housekeeping Institute is founded by *Good Housekeeping* magazine, published since 1885. The institute is to investigate all products before they can be shown editorially or advertised in the magazine, and seals of approval are awarded to acceptable products.

 The hydrogenation process invented by William Normann (above) extends the shelf life of foods containing fats.

The first soluble "instant" coffee is invented by Japanese-American chemist Satori Kato of Chicago who sells the product at the Pan American Exposition at Buffalo (*see* G. Washington, 1909).

White Rose Ceylon tea is introduced by New York's Seeman Brothers (*see* 1886; Redi-Tea, 1953).

Clicquot Club ginger ale is introduced by Boston entrepreneur H. Earle Kimball, whose beverage will be the first nationally advertised ginger ale. Kimball has started a company with an investment of less than $25,000, he has named his ginger ale after the French champagne Veuve Clicquot introduced in 1796; he will soon spend $1 million a year in advertising (*see* White Rock, 1895; Canada Dry, 1907).

The Quaker Oats Company is founded by H. P. Crowell and Robert Stuart who will sell all their brands under the Quaker name (*see* 1888; 1893). Crowell and Stuart have failed in effort to consolidate 21 other millers with the American Cereal Company and thus control more than 95 percent of U.S. oat-milling capacity, but they will drop nonstandard packages, and their holding company will be roughly twice the size of their major competitor, Great Western Cereal, maker of Mother's Oats (*see* 1911).

The *Settlement Cookbook* by Milwaukee settlement house worker Lizzie Black (Mrs. Simon Kander) is published with funds raised by volunteer women through advertisements after the settlement house directors have refused a request for $18 to print a book that would save students in a class for immigrants from having to copy recipes off the blackboard. The book will earn enough money in 8 years to pay for a new settlement house building, it will be a perennial best seller, and it will have sales of half a million copies in the next 75 years, with the slogan "The way to a man's heart" taken from the phrase "The way to a man's heart is through his stomach" from the novel *Willis Parton* by the late Sara Payson Willis Parton, who wrote under the name Fanny Fern before her death in 1872 at age 61.

Oddenino's is opened in London's Regent Street by Italian restaurateur Cavaliere Auguste Oddenino.

 London's population reaches 6.6 million, while New York has 3.44, Paris 2.7, Berlin 1.9, Chicago 1.7, Vienna 1.7, Wuhan 1.5, Tokyo 1.45, St. Petersburg 1.3, Philadelphia 1.3, Constantinople 1.2, Moscow 1.1, Sian 1, Calcutta 950,000, Canton 900,000, Los Angeles 103,000, Houston 45,000, Dallas 43,000.

Europe's population reaches above 400 million, up from 188 million in 1800, with 56.4 million in Germany, 39.1 million in France, 34 in Austria, 33.2 in Italy. China has an estimated 373 million, India 284, Japan 44, Russia 117, Great Britain and Ireland 41.4, the United States more than 76.

Some 9 million immigrants will enter the United States in this decade.

Girls in Western cultures menstruate for the first time at about age 14, down from age 17 in the late 18th century. The age of menarche will decline to 13 by the end of this century.

1902 The Anglo-Japanese Alliance signed January 20 ends the "splendid isolation" of Britain and recognizes Japan's interests in Korea. If either party should become involved in war with a third party, its ally is to remain neutral, but if the war should expand to involve any other power or powers, then the ally is obligated to enter the conflict (*see* 1904).

Spain declares the posthumous son of the late Alphonso XII of age on his 16th birthday May 16. Alphonso XIII begins a reign that will continue until 1931 despite several attempts on his life.

The Treaty of Vereeniging signed May 31 ends the Boer War. The Boers accept British sovereignty in South Africa, the British promise £3 million for rebuilding Boer farms.

The British prime minister Lord Salisbury retires July 11 at age 72 (he will die next summer) and is succeeded by his nephew Arthur James Balfour, 53, who will head the government until 1905.

1902 (cont.) Cuba is established as an independent republic. Washington withdraws the U.S. troops that helped the Cubans gain independence from Spain in 1898.

Venezuela refuses to meet her debt obligations and British, German, and Italian warships blockade Venezuelan ports December 19. The blockade will continue until February of next year, when Venezuelan dictator Cipriano Castro will agree to arbitration by a Hague Tribunal commission.

 Portugal declares national bankruptcy.

Imperialism: A Study by English economist John Atkinson Hobson, 44, is a comprehensive critique of economic imperialism that will influence German theorists Rosa Luxembourg and Rudolf Hilferding. Through their writings it will shape the thinking of the Russian Nikolai Lenin.

International Nickel Company is created by a merger of Canadian Copper Company and Orford Copper Company effected by J. P. Morgan at the behest of Charles M. Schwab and other steel magnates. Orford has a plant at Bayonne, N.J., it has found a way to refine nickel from ore it buys from Canadian Copper (*see* 1885), and it sells its nickel in Europe in competition with the Rothschild-controlled firm Le Nickel, which obtains its ore from New Caledonia in the Pacific. England's Mond Nickel Company (*see* 1900) will be merged into International Nickel Company of Canada in 1928, and despite some competition from the Falconbridge Nickel Mines that will be organized in 1930 and from other minor firms, INCO will meet 90 percent of the world's nickel needs.

United States Steel Company has two-thirds of U.S. steelmaking capacity. Only public opinion and a sense of noblesse oblige restrain its near-monopoly (*see* 1901; Bethlehem Steel, 1905).

E. I. du Pont Company's Eugene du Pont dies January 28 at age 68. His sons Thomas Coleman, 39, Pierre Samuel, 32, Irenee, 26, and Lammot, 22, pay $22 million to acquire the firm founded by their great-grandfather in 1802 (*see* 1899; 1906).

President Roosevelt works through his attorney general Philander C. Knox, 49, to institute antitrust proceedings against various U.S. corporations. Roosevelt departs from the policies of the late President McKinley which he had pledged himself to continue.

 History of the Standard Oil Company by Ida Minerva Tarbell, 44, appears in *McClure's* magazine installments. It reveals that John D. Rockefeller controls 90 percent of U.S. oil-refining capacity and has an annual income of $45 million.

The Texas Company is founded to battle Rockefeller interests. Former Standard Oil Company executive Joseph Cullinan receives backing from financier Arnold Schlaet and enlists the support of Texas governor James Hogg and of John W. Gates (*see* 1898). Now 47, Gates has lost a fortune in Wall Street, he has

agreed to stop his "bear" raids on the stock market, and he helps Cullinan buy up oil fields near Gulf Oil's Spindletop Hill in East Texas (*see* 1901) and to build up a marketing organization that will cover the United States and much of the world (*see* 1903; Cal-Tex, 1933; Texaco, Inc., 1959).

Italian railway workers strike through January and February in a demand for recognition of their union. A general strike threatens as Turin gas company employees walk out, but all railway workers who belong to the army reserve are called up by the government, and a settlement is mediated in June.

United Mine Workers leader John Mitchell leads his 147,000 anthracite coal workers out of the pits May 12 to begin a 5-month strike that cripples the United States. Mine operators and railroad presidents have rejected an invitation from Mitchell to attend a conference, they continue to oppose unionization, and George F. Baker of the Philadelphia and Reading Coal & Iron Company says July 17, "The rights and interests of the laboring man will be protected and cared for—not by the labor agitators, but by the Christian men to who God in His infinite wisdom has given the control of the property interests of this country. . . ."

By September, the price of anthracite in New York has climbed from $5 per ton to $14, and the poor who buy by the bucket or bushel pay a penny per pound, $20 per ton. Schools close to conserve fuel, people buy oil, coke, and gas stoves, mobs in western towns seize coal cars, and by October the price of coal in New York is $30 per ton.

Montana copper magnate William Andrews Clark, 63, heats his 121-room Fifth Avenue New York mansion with a furnace that consumes 17 tons of coal per day. Clark has sold most of his interests at Butte to Marcus Daly (*see* 1899), he resigned his Senate seat in 1900 after charges of election fraud were supported by a Senate committee that reported him "not duly and legally elected," but he will soon move to an even larger house (*see* 1904).

President Roosevelt brings about a settlement of the coal strike that one writer hails as "the greatest single event affecting the relations of capital and labor in the history of America." But while the strikers gain pay raises, they do not win recognition of their union as bargaining agent for their rights.

Smuggler-Union mine manager Arthur Collins is assassinated November 19 in his home at Telluride, Colo., following settlement of a violent strike against the mine by the Western Federation of Miners. Four hundred national guardsmen will go into Telluride next year to suppress the WFM.

Membership in the AF of L reaches the million mark (*see* Gompers, 1886; Department of Labor, 1913).

London's William Cadbury sees an advertisement for the sale of a Sao Thomé cocoa plantation. Workers are listed as assets at so much per head, and there is a strong suggestion of slavery in the advertisement (see 1901; 1903).

France's Panama Canal Company offers to sell its interests to the United States and reduces its asking price January 4 from $109 million to $40 million (see de Lesseps, 1883). Adoption of the Panama route in preference to a Nicaraguan route is recommended January 18 by the Isthmian Canal Commission in a supplementary report to President Roosevelt. The Isthmian Canal Act passed by Congress June 28 authorizes the president to acquire the Panama Canal Company's concession, to arrange terms with the Colombian government, and to proceed with construction of a canal. If it is not possible to obtain title and necessary control, the canal is to be built through Nicaragua (see 1903).

United States Shipbuilding Company is organized by U.S. Steel executive Charles Michael Schwab, 40, who merges Bethlehem Steel into the new company as a source of plates for ships (see 1886; 1905).

Seaboard Air Line Railway is created through merger or consolidation of nine roads with 1,162 miles of track running southward from Richmond, Va., through the Carolinas and Georgia. By 1928 the road will have 4,500 miles of track extending into Alabama and Florida.

The *Twentieth Century Limited* goes into service June 15 to begin a 65-year career on the route between New York and Chicago. The New York Central's new luxury express has two buffet, smoking, and library cars, two observation cars, and 12 section drawing-room and stateroom cars, it reduces running time on the 980-mile "water-level route" to 20 hours—down from 24 in 1877—but the *Limited's* 49 miles per hour average is well below the 61.3 miles per hour averaged on the 184-mile route of the *Paris-Calais Express.*

The *Broadway Limited* goes into service June 16 for the Pennsylvania Railroad to begin a career of more than 75 years on the route between New York and Chicago. Staffed with barbers, maids, valets, and secretaries to rival the Central's *Twentieth Century Limited* (above), the new luxury express makes the 904-mile run in 20 hours.

Egypt's *Cairo-Luxor Express* goes into service with sleeping cars.

The Isotta-Fraschini motorcar introduced by Milan's Fabbrica Automobili Isotta-Fraschini is a powerful, costly machine with a four-cylinder engine that develops 29 horsepower. Cesare Isotta and Vincenzo Fraschini started out as agents for Renault Frères, they have assembled the Renault Voiturette, they will open a large factory in 1905, they will sell a controlling interest to France's Lorraine-Dietrich in 1907, and production will continue until 1949.

Henry Ford's 70-horsepower "999" racing car driven by Bernard Eli "Barney" Oldfield, 24, sets an unofficial speed record on Detroit's Grosse Point track by

covering 5 miles in 5 minutes, 20 seconds (see 1901; Ford Motor Company, 1903).

The American Automobile Association (AAA) is founded March 4 by nine automobile clubs meeting at Chicago. The organization for the "development and introduction of the automobile" will provide members with emergency road service, it will help them plan tours, and it will work in behalf of new highway construction.

The Studebaker motorcar is introduced at South Bend, Ind., by the 50-year-old firm Studebaker Brothers which has produced more than 750,000 wagons, buggies, and carriages. Its first automobile is an electric car.

The Marmon motorcar is introduced by Indianapolis automaker Howard C. Marmon, 26, whose father Daniel is head of Nordyke and Marmon, a leading producer of milling machinery. The Marmon has an air-cooled overhead valve V-twin engine and a revolutionary lubrication system that uses a drilled crankshaft to keep its engine bearings lubricated with oil fed under pressure by a gear pump.

The Overland motorcar is introduced at Indianapolis (see Willys, 1907).

John North Willys sells four Pierce motorcars and obtains the Elmira, N.Y., agency for the Rambler car made at Kenosha, Wis. (see 1901; 1903).

A new Locomobile is introduced with a front-mounted, vertical, four-cylinder, water-cooled engine and is the first U.S. motorcar to use heat-treated steel alloys.

A. O. Smith Company is founded by Milwaukee bicycle maker A. O. Smith, who begins making motorcar frames. Smith has taken over his father's baby carriage factory and has converted it to bicycle production, but he turns to making frames and will become a leading supplier to major automakers.

Mendel's Principles of Heredity—a Defence by English biologist William Bateson, 41, supports the work by Hugo De Vries and others published 2 years ago. Bateson has explored the fauna of salt lakes in western Central Asia and in northern Europe and will introduce the term "genetics" (see 1926).

Elementary Principles in Statistical Mechanics by Yale physicist Josiah Willard Gibbs, 63, helps establish the basic theory for physical chemistry. Gibbs's work *On the Equilibrium of Heterogeneous Substances* appeared in the late 1870s.

The Carnegie Institution of Washington, established with a $10 million gift from Andrew Carnegie, will devote its efforts to scientific research (see Shull, 1905; Flexner, 1910).

Rayon is patented by U.S. chemist A. D. (Arthur Dehon) Little, 39, who has produced the new cellulose fiber with a new process (see Cross, Bevan, 1892; Courtauld, 1905; Viscose Company, 1910; Celanese, 1918; nylon, 1935).

J. P. Morgan dominated U.S. finance for years, creating trusts, averting panics, making himself immensely rich.

 The hormone secretin manufactured by glands on the wall of the small intestine is discovered by English physiologists William Maddock Bayliss, 42, and Ernest Henry Starling, 36, who will introduce the word "hormone" in 1904. Working at London's University College, Bayliss and Starling find that secretin acts on the liver to increase the flow of pancreatic juice when the acid contents of the stomach enter the duodenum.

Hookworm disease is reported to be endemic in the U.S. South by Charles Wardell Stiles, 35, chief of the Division of Zoology of the U.S. Public Health Service, in an address to the Sanitary Conference of American Republics meeting at Washington, D.C.

The General Education Board that will help reform U.S. medical education and will work to conquer hookworm disease in the South is established by John D. Rockefeller (see 1901; 1909).

The John McCormick Institute for Infectious Disease is established by reaper heir Harold Fowler McCormick and his wife Edith in memory of a son who has died in infancy of scarlet fever. An antitoxin for scarlet fever will be developed at the institute.

A noncaustic antiseptic that can be used to prevent eye infections such as gonorrheal infection in newborn infants is announced by Philadelphia chemist Albert C. Barnes, 31, and his German-American colleague Herman Hille, 31, who quit their jobs 3 days later and form a partnership (see Crede, 1884). The "silver vitellin" they say they have developed is really a silver-gelatin colloid that they will market as Argyrol and that will be used almost universally to protect newborn infants from infection that causes blindness (see 1904).

The Canadian Medical Act establishes a central national registration for physicians and uniform standards for all licensed practitioners. Passage of the act has been pushed by physician Thomas George Roddich, 56, who is a Conservative member of the Dominion House of Commons.

United Drug Company is organized by Boston druggist Louis K. Liggett and 39 other U.S. pharmacists who put up $4,000 each to buy a central manufacturing business in Boston's Leon Street.

The Boer War (above) has lost the British five times as many men to disease as to enemy action.

Cecil Rhodes dies in Africa March 26 at age 49 and leaves £6 million for public service plus $10 million to endow 170 scholarships for British, German, and American youths to study at Oxford University. The scholarships will be available to men only until 1976.

 Calkins & Holden advertising is founded at New York by U.S. advertising pioneers Earnest Elmo Calkins, 34 (who has been deaf since age 6) and Ralph Holden. The first modern advertising agency, Calkins & Holden will create advertising campaigns and displays rather than simply placing advertisements prepared by its clients. It will set up a typographical department at a time when other agencies simply send material to newspapers to have the papers set it in type as they see fit (see Batten, 1891).

Nonfiction Varieties of Religious Experience by Harvard philosopher-psychologist William James, now 60, whose Gifford Lectures at the University of Edinburgh comprise a classic reconciliation of science and religion; Rebellion in the Backlands (Os Sertos) by Brazilian engineer-journalist Eyclydes da Cunha, 36, who covered an 1896 uprising led by a religious fanatic in Brazil's sertao (backlands) and whose sympathetic treatise on history, sociology, geology, and geography amounts to a national epic.

Fiction The Wings of the Dove by Henry James, younger brother of the Harvard professor (above); Anna of the Five Towns and The Grand Babylon Hotel by English novelist (Enoch) Arnold Bennett, 35; Mrs. Craddock by W. Somerset Maugham; "Youth and Two Other Stories" by Joseph Conrad; The Supermale (Le Surmale) by Alfred Jarry; The Virginian by U.S. novelist Owen Wister, 42, whose account of a greenhorn's misadventures in Wyoming will be famous for its line, "When you call me that, smile!" The Pothunters by English humorist P. G. (Pelham Grenville) Wodehouse, 21, who will quit his bank job next year to conduct a column in the London Globe and will become famous for his characters Bertie Wooster, Jeeves, Mr. Mulliner, and Psmith; The Hound of the Baskervilles by A. Conan Doyle who has been forced by public demand to announce that his Baker Street detective Sherlock Holmes escaped death when he fell into the mountain crevasse with the arch-criminal Professor Moriarty in December of 1893 (the new book has been serialized in The Strand magazine).

The Times Literary Supplement (TLS) begins publication January 17 as part of the Times of London.

The journal of reviews, poems, and commentary will continue for more than 75 years.

Juvenile *Just So Stories for Little Children* by Rudyard Kipling, who has been given the idea by his U.S. publisher's son. Young Nelson Doubleday will receive 1 cent per copy in royalties until he dies of cancer in 1949; *The Tale of Peter Rabbit* by English artist-writer-naturalist Beatrix Potter, 36, who has been the first person in England to establish the fact that lichens represent a merging of algae and fungi but whose efforts in botany have been frustrated by the male scientific establishment (*see* Reinke, 1894). Written originally as an illustrated letter to the son of her former governess, *Peter Rabbit* was printed privately in 1900 but is published now by F. Warne and Co., whose editor Norman Warne will be engaged to marry Potter but who will die in 1905 before their marriage. Peter, Mopsy, Flopsy, and Cottontail will be followed by 22 more books that Potter will write and illustrate in the next 11 years.

Poetry *Salt Water Ballads* by English poet John Masefield, 24, who ran away to sea at age 13. His "Sea Fever" contains the lines, "I must down to the sea again, to the lonely sea and the sky,/ And all I ask is a tall ship and a star to steer her by ..."; *Songs of Childhood* by English poet Walter (John) de la Mare, 29; *Captain Craig* by U.S. poet Edwin Arlington Robinson, 32.

Painting *Waterloo Bridge* by Claude Monet; *Horseman on the Beach* by Paul Gauguin, who is dying of syphilis in the Marquesa Islands to which he moved last year; *Ladies Acheson, Misses Hunter, The Duchess of Portland*, and *Lord Ribblesdale* by John Singer Sargent. Albert Bierstadt dies at New York February 18 at age 72.

Illustrator Charles Dana Gibson signs an agreement October 23 accepting an offer from *Collier's Weekly* to draw only for *Life* and *Collier's* for the next 4 years and to do 100 double-page drawings for *Collier's* for $100,000 (*see* 1890).

Crayola brand crayons are introduced by the Easton, Pa., firm Binney & Smith. Founder's son Edwin Binney has developed the crayons by adding oil and pigments to the black paraffin and stearic acid marking devices sold by the firm, and his mother has suggested the name Crayola.

Sculpture *Comin' Through the Rye* (*Off the Range*) by Frederick Remington (bronze).

The Tessar f.4.5 antistigmatic lens designed by Paul Rudolf is introduced by Carl Zeiss of Jena (*see* 1889).

Theater *The Joy of Living* (*Es lebe das Leben!*) by Hermann Sudermann 2/1 at Berlin's Deutsches Theater; *Cathleen ni Houlihan* by William Butler Yeats and Lady Gregory (Isabella Augusta Persse Gregory, 50) 4/2 at St. Teresa's Hall, Dublin; *The Lower Depths* (*Na dne*) by Maksim Gorki 10/25 at the Moscow Art Theater (Gorki was arrested last year after publication of his seditious prose-poem "Burevest-

nik"); *The Admirable Crichton* by James M. Barrie 11/4 at the Duke of York's Theatre, London; *Old Heidelberg* by German playwright Wilhelm Meyer-Forster, 40, 11/22 at Berlin; *Henry of Arnë* (*Der arnë Heinrich*) by Gerhart Hauptmann 11/29 at Vienna's Hofburgtheater; *The Darling of the Gods* by David Belasco and John Luther Long 12/3 at New York's Belasco Theater, 182 perfs.; *Earth Spirit* (*Der Erdgeist*) by Frank Wedekind, 12/17 at Berlin's Keines Theater; *The Girl with the Green Eyes* by Clyde Fitch 12/25 at New York's Savoy Theatre, with Lucile Watson, 108 perfs.

Opera *Le Jongleur de Notre Dame* 2/18 at Monte Carlo with music by Jules Massenet; *Pélleas et Mélissande* 4/30 at the Opéra-Comique, Paris, with music by Claude Debussy, libretto by Maurice Maeterlinck. Scots-American soprano Mary Garden, 28, sings the female lead; *Adriana Lecouvrer* 11/6 at Milan's Teatro Lirico, with music by Italian composer Francesco Cilea, 36; *The Girls of Vienna* (*Wiener Frauen*) 11/25 at Vienna's Theater-an-der-Wien, with music by Franz Lehar.

Enrico Caruso makes his first phonograph recordings March 18 at Milan's Hotel di Milano where U. S. recording engineer Fred Gaisberg, 30, of the Emile Berliner London branch and his brother Will have converted a room into a recording studio using six large crates of equipment. The 39-year-old tenor is appearing at the Teatro alla Scala, he has agreed to perform 10 songs and arias for £100, the Gaisbergs have wired London asking authority to spend that much, the London office has wired a flat refusal, the Gaisbergs go ahead nevertheless, the disks go on sale in London record shops in May, and they will be reissued periodically for more than 75 years.

First performances Symphony No. 2 in C minor by Russian composer Aleksandr Nikolaievitch Skriabin, 30, 1/25 at St. Petersburg; *L'après-midi d'un faune* (Symphonic Poem) by Claude Debussy (*see* 1894); Symphony No. 2 by Jean Sibelius 3/8 at Helsinki; *Pavane pour une Infante defoute* by Maurice Ravel 4/5 at the Societé Nationale, Paris; Symphony No. 3 in D minor by Gustav Mahler 6/9 at Krefeld.

Broadway musicals *A Chinese Honeymoon* 6/22 at the Casino Theater, with music by Hungarian-American composer Jean Schwartz, 23, lyrics by William Jerome, songs that include "Mr. Dooley," 376 perfs.; *Twirly Whirly* 9/11 at the Weber and Fields Music Hall, with Lillian Russell, music by John Stromberg, lyrics by Robert B. Smith, songs that include "Come Down Ma Evenin' Star," 244 perfs.

Popular songs "In the Good Old Summertime" by Welsh-American composer-minstrel George Evans, 42, lyrics by Ren Shields, 34; "Bill Bailey, Won't You Please Come Home" by Hughie Cannon; "In the Sweet Bye and Bye" by Harry Von Tilzer, lyrics by Vincent P. Bryan; "Pardon Me, My Dear Alphonse, After You, My Dear Gaston" by Harry Von Tilzer, lyrics by Vincent P. Bryan; "Oh, Didn't He Ramble" by Will Handy (Bob Cole and J. Rosamond Johnson);

1902 (cont.) "Under the Bamboo Tree" by Bob Cole; "The Land of Hope and Glory" by Edward Elgar, lyrics by Eton master Arthur Christopher Benson, 40.

The Rose Bowl football game has its beginnings in a game played January 1 at Pasadena, Calif., as part of the Tournament of Roses held since 1890. Michigan defeats Stanford 49 to 0 as halfback William M. "Willie" Heston leads a backfield coached by Fielding "Hurry Up" Yost, whose team scores 644 points in the fall against 12 for its opponents (see 1916).

Dan Patch breaks the harness racing mark set by his sire Joe Patchen. The 6-year-old mahogany stallion runs a mile in 2:00¾, a full second below his sire's fastest speed, he goes on to equal Star Pointer's record of 1:59¼, and Minneapolis feed merchant Marion Willis Savage of the International Stock Food Company acquires the trotter for $60,000.

The Teddy Bear introduced by Russian-American candy story operator Morris Michtom and his wife of Brooklyn, N.Y., has movable arms, legs, and head. The Michtoms have seen a cartoon by Clifford Berryman in the November 18 *Washington Evening Star* showing President "Teddy" Roosevelt refusing to shoot a mother bear while on a hunting trip. They obtain the president's permission to use his nickname, and their brown plush toy Teddy Bear creates a sensation (see 1903).

The brassiere is invented by French fashion designer Charles R. Debevoise, but it will have little popularity until the introduction of elastic (see 1914).

New York Philip Morris Corporation is founded with the help of New York tobacco importer Gustav Eckmeyer, who has been exclusive agent for English Ovals and other cigarettes produced by Philip Morris of London. The new firm will soon introduce Marlboro cigarettes (see 1858; 1910).

Paris jeweler Louis Cartier creates 27 diamond tiaras for the coronation of Britain's Edward VII. Cartier opens a London branch in New Bond Street with his brother Jacques in charge (see 1898; 1917).

Tiffany & Co. founder Charles Lewis Tiffany dies at Yonkers, N.Y., February 18 at age 90, leaving an estate of $35 million.

New York's Saks 34th Street specialty store opens under the management of former Siegel, Cooper department store executive Andrew Saks and two other Siegel, Cooper executives (see Saks Fifth Avenue, 1924).

New York's Franklin Simon Company opens at Fifth Avenue and 38th Street. Merchant Simon, 37, started as a $2.50 per week clerk with Stern Brothers at age 13 and his fashion store is the first important store north of 34th Street (see 1962).

The Dayton Company is founded by Minneapolis merchant and banker George D. Dayton. His department store will become the city's largest.

J. C. Penney Company has its beginnings in the Golden Rule store opened at Kemmerer, Wyo., April 14 by merchant James Cash Penney, 26, and his wife. Penney went to work at age 19 for J. M. Hale & Brother at Hamilton, Mo., for $2.27 per month, he moved to Colorado 5 years ago at the advice of his physician and got a job at Longmont near Denver working for merchant T. M. Callahan, and the firm sent him to work in its store at Evanston, Wyo. Callahan has given him an opportunity to open a store on his own and has sold him a one-third interest for $2,000. The first day's receipts amount to $466.59 after remaining open from dawn to midnight, by the end of the first year it has done $29,000 worth of business, and Penney will move to a better location in 1904 (see 1908).

New York's "Flatiron" building is completed southwest of Madison Square by Chicago architect Daniel Burnham, whose steel-frame Fuller building soars 20 stories high and brings people from far and near to ascend to its top for the panoramic view. The building's shape inspires viewers to call it something other than the Fuller building.

Hungary's Houses of Parliament are completed after 9 years of construction on the Rudolph Quay of the Danube at Budapest. Designed in an imposing Gothic style by Aimery Steindl, the building has a dome 325 feet high.

The London Ritz Hotel built by owners of the 3-year-old Carlton House opens in Piccadilly on the site of Walsingham House (see Paris Ritz, 1898). Hotel accountant William Harris organizes the Ritz Hotel Development Corporation to build other Ritz caravansaries that will soon rise at Evian, Mentone, Lucerne, Salsomaggiore, Rome, Naples, Madrid, Barcelona, Buenos Aires, Montreal, Boston, and Atlantic City, N.J. (see New York's Ritz-Carlton, 1910).

New York's Algonquin Hotel opens at 59 West 44th Street with 143 suites and 192 rooms to begin a career as gathering place for actors, painters, musicians, and literati. Desk clerk Frank Case, 32, has persuaded owner Albert Foster to name it the Algonquin rather than the Puritan, he will himself acquire ownership for $717,000 in 1927, and he will operate the hotel until his death in 1946.

New Hampshire's Mount Washington Hotel opens at Bretton Woods with a long veranda from which guests may gaze at the mountains of the Presidential Range (see world monetary conference, 1944).

Old Faithful Inn at Wyoming's Yellowstone National Park is completed by architect Robert C. Reanor. Wings will be added in 1913 and 1927.

Rosecliff is completed at Newport, R.I., by New York architect Stanford White for Mrs. Hermann Oelrichs, daughter of the late San Francisco mining and banking magnate James Fair. Last of the great Newport "cottages," Rosecliff is a 40-room French château with a Court of Love designed by sculptor Augustus Saint-Gaudens after one at Versailles.

Whitehall is completed at Palm Beach by Carrère and Hastings for Florida East Coast Railway magnate Henry M. Flagler and his third bride. Flagler has told the architects to "build me the finest home you can think of," they have put up a 73-room, $2.5 million Spanish-inspired temple with massive Doric columns and gigantic urns, the 6-acre waterfront home has been finished in 8 months, and the *New York Herald* calls it "more wonderful than any palace in Europe, grander and more magnificent than any other private dwelling in the world."

New York's George W. Vanderbilt house at 647 Fifth Avenue is completed by Richard H. Hunt and complements the Morton Plant house next door.

Modern air conditioning is pioneered in a Brooklyn, N.Y., printing plant. U.S. engineer Willis Haviland Carrier, 26, designs a humidity control process to accompany a new air-cooling system for the plant (*see* 1911; Gorrie, 1842).

The National Reclamation Act (Newlands Act) passed by Congress June 17 authorizes the federal government to build great irrigation dams throughout the West. The act is based on ideas championed by Major John Wesley Powell (who dies at Haven, Me., September 23 at age 78), but small farmers in years to come will charge that the legislation's chief beneficiaries are large farmers (below).

"Forest and water problems are perhaps the most vital internal questions of the United States," says President Roosevelt in his first State of the Union message. The president asks for a federal reclamation program and for a sound plan to use forest reserves (he has been influenced by Gifford Pinchot and by F. H. Newell, an aide to the late Major Powell).

Crater Lake National Park is created by act of Congress on 160,290 acres of Oregon wilderness.

The Boundary Waters Canoe Area created in northern Minnesota embraces roughly a million acres of virgin pine forest.

Mont Pelée on the French Caribbean island of Martinique erupts May 8, inundating the capital and commercial center St. Pierre with molten lava and ashes that destroy the city's harbor and kill between 30,000 and 50,000. The 4,430-foot volcano has given premonitory signals, but the people of St. Pierre have been preoccupied with an imminent local political contest, they have ignored the warnings, 10 percent of the island is devastated as further eruptions occur May 20 and August 30, the *Roddam* is the only ship in the harbor that escapes destruction, and Martinique's capital shifts to Fort de France.

European countries sign a convention to eliminate the capture of migrating birds with lime-smeared sticks and iron traps, but the pact does not prohibit use of nets (*see* 1960).

The National Reclamation Act (above) encourages family farms by limiting to 160 acres the size of indi-

vidual holdings entitled to federal water and by specifying that such water is to go only to owners who are bona fide residents. A 1926 amendment will let larger landowners have water provided that they sign contracts agreeing to sell acreage exceeding the 160-acre limit within 10 years at a government-approved price that does not include the value added by the federal water.

International Harvester Company is founded at New York by Cyrus McCormick, Jr., who persuades J. P. Morgan to underwrite a trust that merges the four leading U.S. harvesting machine makers. Charles Deering of William Deering & Co. is chairman of the board, McCormick is president, and International Harvester controls 85 percent of all U.S. harvesting machine production (*see* 1873; 1884; 1912).

The Hart-Parr Company of Charles City, Iowa, builds the first gasoline tractors, some of them 11-ton monsters so difficult to start that farmers leave them running all night.

Hookworm disease is a major cause of malnutrition in the U.S. South, says Charles W. Stiles (above). Southerners are not inherently lazy, says Stiles, but the disease is sapping their energy (*see* Rockefeller Sanitary Commission, 1909).

W. O. Atwater recommends a diet containing 150 grams of protein per day for working men (*see* 1896). Karl von Voit at Munich raises his 118-gram estimate of 1881 to 145 grams (but *see* Chittenden, 1904).

A survey in the English city of Leeds shows that in the poorest sections, half the children are marked by rickets and 60 percent have bad teeth.

A survey of English milk consumption shows that in middle-class families the average person drinks 6 pints per week, while in the lower middle class the average is 3.8 pints, among artisans 1.8 pints, and among laborers 0.8 pints. Britain is Europe's biggest meat eater and smallest milk drinker.

Fish-and-chips shops (below) will make a significant contribution to raising protein levels of urban English diets.

A "Poison Squad" of young volunteers tests the safety of U.S. foods for Harvey W. Wiley of the Department of Agriculture (*see* 1883; 1907).

Congress limits substitution of margarine for butter.

Britain establishes statutory limits for butter.

Britain imports £50 million worth of meat and £4.1 million worth of fish. The average Englishman consumes more than 56 pounds of cheap imported meat per year as U.S. pork, Argentine beef, and New Zealand lamb flood the market.

An English writer is told by an old Hampshire woman, "Nothing's good enough now unless you buys it in a public house or a shop. It wasn't so when I was a girl. We did everything for ourselves, and it were better, I tell 'e. We kep' a pig then—so did

1902 (cont.) everyone; and the pork and brawn it were good, not like what we buy now. We put it mostly in brine, and let it be for months; and when we took it out and boiled it, it were red as a cherry and white as milk, and it melted just like butter in your mouth.... And we didn't drink no tea then.... We had beer for breakfast then, and it did us good. Better than all these nasty cocoa stuffs we drink now.... And we had a brick oven then and could put a pie in and a loaf and whatever we wanted and it were proper victuals."

Corn Products Company is created by a merger of United States Glucose Company with National Starch Company (*see* 1900). The new starch trust controls 84 percent of U.S. starch output (*see* Corn Products Refining Company, 1906).

Barnum's Animal Crackers are introduced by the National Biscuit Company which controls 70 percent of U.S. cracker and cookie output (*see* 1898). The new animal-shaped crackers appear just before Christmas in a box topped with a white string so that it may be hung from Christmas trees, and it joins the line of Nabisco products that includes Uneeda Biscuits, Premium Saltines, Social Tea Biscuits, Ginger Snaps, Nabisco Sugar Wafers, Jinjer Wafers, Zuzus, Lemon Snaps, Vanilla Wafers, Saltinas, Crown Pilot Crackers, and other brands including Fig Newtons, many in In-er-Seal cartons (*see* Fig Newton, 1892; Lorna Doone, Oreo, 1912; Loose-Wiles, 1903).

Ralston Purina Company gets its name as officials of the 8-year-old Robinson-Danforth Commission Company at St. Louis make an arrangement with officials of the Ralston Health Club, a worldwide organization established by Washington, D.C., university professor Albert Webster Edgerly, 50, who is sometimes called "Dr. Ralston" and whose book *Complete Life Building* propounds simple rules and facts about common foods and promotes good nutrition, urging readers to avoid heavy use of preservatives and artificial sweeteners. Ralston Purina promotes its 3-year-old Purina breakfast food and introduces Ralston cereals that will compete with Quaker Oats, Post, and Kellogg (*see* 1932; Purina, 1899).

Kellogg's Sanitas corn flakes are made lighter and crisper and are given a malt flavoring to improve their sales appeal and enable them to compete with its many imitators (*see* 1898; 1906).

Cream of Wheat maker Emory Mapes hires a Chicago restaurant waiter to pose for photographs at $5 per hour and creates a trademark that will make the cereal famous (*see* 1893). The first national advertising for Cream of Wheat is placed in the *Ladies' Home Journal* by the J. Walter Thompson agency, but the copy is by Emory Mapes (*see* 1939).

Force Wheat Flakes are introduced in Britain in June to give Britons their first taste of a dried breakfast food. The cereal is made by the Force Food Company of Canada, a subsidiary of the Buffalo, N.Y., firm run by Edward Ellsworth, who has hired Char-

les Rhoades away from Kellogg's Sanitas Nut Food Company and who advertises Force in the United States with widely read verses about "Sunny Jim" (*see* H-O Oats, 1924).

"Prices That Stagger Humanity," headlines Joseph Pulitzer's *New York World* in a campaign against the "beef trust" (24 cents a pound for sirloin steak, 18 cents for lamb chops, pork chops, or ham).

Drake Bakeries is founded by New York baker Newman E. Drake. The Borden Company will acquire the company in 1946 and will promote its Devil Dogs, Yankee Doodles, Ring Dings, Yodels, and other products.

Hawaiian Pineapple Company, Ltd., is founded by James Drummond Dole, 25, whose father is a first cousin of Hawaii's governor Sanford Dole. Young Dole visited the islands during his years at Harvard, he gave up his original plan of starting a coffee plantation, and last year he staked out a 12,000-acre homestead 23 miles outside Honolulu at Wahiawa. He has set out 75,000 pineapple plants, he has financed the new company by selling $20,000 worth of stock to friends in Boston and San Francisco, and he will pack 1,893 cases of fruit next year (*see* 1909).

Salada tea is introduced in New York (*see* 1886). In the next 20 years, Salada will build a modern packing plant at Boston, it will move its headquarters to that city, and its tea will become the largest-selling in Canada, second largest in North America.

The Pepsi-Cola Company is founded in North Carolina (*see* 1898). Caleb Bradham gives up his pharmacy to devote full time to Pepsi-Cola (*see* 1903).

Sheffield Farms is created by a merger of New York milk dealers whose businesses go back in some cases to 1841. Sheffield's president is Loton Horton whose uncle is a prominent ice-cream maker (*see* 1925).

Willoughy McCormick adopts the trade name Banquet Brand for his spices (*see* 1890).

Horn & Hardart Baking Company's Automat opens in Philadelphia's Chestnut Street. The first automatic restaurant is so popular that Philadelphia will soon have scores of Automats, and the first New York Automat will open in 1912 at 1551 Broadway (*see* Exchange Buffet, 1885). Horn & Hardart has paid a German importer $30,000 for the mechanism that permits patrons to drop nickels into slots to open glass doors and obtain food from compartments that are refilled by employees behind the scenes.

Fish-and-chips shops open to serve London's working class. Fast deep-sea trawlers extend British fishing operations to Iceland and the White Sea, they pack the fish in ice, they ship it by rail the day it is landed, and the London shops serve it with fried potatoes and vinegar (*see* 1864).

Fouquet's opens to give Paris a new restaurant of *haute cuisine*.

Le Guide Culinaire by Auguste Escoffier is a manual for professional chefs that refines and simplifies earlier standards and will become a classic.

Immigration to the United States sets new records. Most of the arrivals are from Italy, Austro-Hungary, and Russia.

Congress establishes a Bureau of the Census.

The Chinese Exclusion Act of 1882 is revised to prohibit immigration of Orientals from U.S. island territories such as Hawaii and the Philippines and to make the exclusion permanent (*see* 1943).

1903 The Wright brothers pioneer flying (below), the Trans-Siberian Railway is completed (below), and U.S. gunboat diplomacy expedites construction of a Panama Canal.

The Hay-Herran Treaty signed January 22 by U.S. Secretary of State John Hay and the foreign minister of Colombia provides for a 6-mile strip across the Isthmus of Panama to be leased to the United States for $10 million plus annual payments of $250,000. The United States had favored a route across Nicaragua, but French engineer-promoter Philippe Jean Bunau-Varilla, 42, has made a deal with New York lawyer William Cromwell of Sullivan and Cromwell, he has approached Cleveland industrialist Mark Hanna and has persuaded him to favor the route across Panama, and Cromwell has made a $60,000 contribution to the Republican party. The Senate consents to the treaty March 17, and the treaty gives $40 million to stockholders in the French canal company, many of whom are now U.S. speculators, while stipulating that Colombia is to give up all rights to sue for any portion of the $40 million and is to give up all police powers in the contemplated canal zone.

The Colombian Senate votes unanimously August 12 to reject the Hay-Herran Treaty (above), President Roosevelt calls the Colombians "Dagos," "cat-rabbits," "homicidal corruptionists," and "contemptible little creatures," Bunau-Varilla (above) meets in room 1162 of New York's Waldorf-Astoria Hotel with a physician who works for the cross-isthmus railroad represented by William Cromwell (above), he provides the man with a secret code, he gives him a declaration of independence and a flag for a new Panamanian republic that Mme. Bunau-Varilla has designed and stitched up, he supplies the draft of a new constitution for the contemplated republic, and he provides the physician with transportation back to Panama.

The U.S. cruiser *Nashville* arrives in Panamanian waters November 3, Panama declares her independence from Colombia, the railroad refuses to transport Colombian troops sent to put down the provincial revolt, Secretary Hay recognizes Panama's independence November 6, Bunau-Varilla (above) is named Panamanian ambassador to the United States November 6, and on November 18 Bunau-Varilla signs a treaty with the United States

on the same general terms as those rejected by Colombia in the Hay-Herran Treaty—granting "rights in perpetuity . . . as if [the United States] were the sovereign" but not granting sovereignty.

New York financier J. P. Morgan receives $40 million for transfer to French canal company stockholders whose names lawyer William Cromwell refuses to divulge to a Senate committee. Cromwell receives $800,000 for his legal services.

Serbian conspirators assassinate Aleksandr I Obrenović June 10. They also murder his wife Draga and some 20 members of the court of the 27-year-old king who has reigned since 1889 and has ruled personally since 1893. The Serbian assembly votes June 15 to elect the 59-year-old prince Peter Karageorgević to succeed Aleksandr, he will reign until 1921 as Peter I, but the new king is a puppet of the conspirators who assassinated Aleksandr and who restore the constitution of 1889.

A Macedonian insurrection against Constantinople ends after roving bands of Serbs, Greeks, and Bulgarians have ravaged the country. A Russo-Austrian reform program organizes a gendarmerie with Moslem and Christian constables assigned according to the makeup of local populations, the reformers appoint foreign officers, and they reorganize the Macedonian financial system.

Resentment against the Russian czar Nicholas II mounts as famine takes a heavy toll (below) and as industrial wages fall beginning in October while food prices rise (*see* 1905).

Bolsheviks (extremists) led by Nikolai Lenin split off from Mensheviks (moderates) at the London Congress of the Social Democratic party (*see* 1900; 1905).

Failure of the Russians to evacuate Manchuria under last year's Russo-Chinese agreement brings Japanese notes which the Russians contemptuously ignore (*see* 1904).

British forces complete the conquest of northern Nigeria.

Authorities at Boston indict local politician James Michael Curley, 29, and his brother Thomas on charges of having taken civil service examinations for job applicants (*see* 1904).

"Everybody is talking about Tammany men growing rich on 'graft,' " says New York political boss George Washington Plunkitt, 61, "but nobody thinks of drawing the distinction between honest graft and dishonest graft. There's an honest graft, and I'm an example of how it works. I would sum up the whole thing by saying, 'I seen my opportunities and I took 'em.' " A long-time opponent of civil service reforms, Plunkitt will leave an estate valued at between $500,000 and $1.5 million when he dies late in 1924.

The Elkins Act passed by Congress February 19 strengthens the Interstate Commerce Act of 1887. The new law forbids U.S. railroads to deviate from published rate schedules, and it holds railroad offi-

1903 (cont.) cials personally liable in cases of rebating (*see* Hepburn Act, 1906).

The Western Pacific Railroad Company is incorporated. The new transcontinental road will operate 1,189 miles of track between San Francisco and Salt Lake City, and it will connect with the Great Northern, the Union Pacific, and the Denver & Rio Grande Western.

The New York, New Haven, and Hartford begins a campaign to take over trolley and steamship lines and monopolize New England transportation in violation of the Interstate Commerce Act of 1887, the Sherman Act of 1890, and the laws of Massachusetts (*see* 1893). New York financier J. P. Morgan is a director of the road, he installs Charles Sanger Mellen as president, and he helps Mellen expand the New Haven's interests (*see* Boston & Maine, 1909).

Construction begins in March on a 1,200-mile railroad from Africa's west coast through the center of Angola into the copper-rich Katanga district. The Benguela Railroad begun by Robert Williams of 1891 copper mine pioneering fame on a concession from the Portuguese queen Marie-Amélie will reach 300 miles inland by 1913 but will not reach the copper mines until 1931.

The Trans-Siberian Railway is completed with the exception of a 100-mile stretch along the mountainous shores of Lake Baikal. Built in 12 years, the new rail line will bring hundreds of thousands of settlers into the black-soil wheat-growing areas of central Asia (*see* 1904).

The Wright brothers make the first sustained manned flights in a controlled gasoline-powered aircraft. Dayton, Ohio, bicycle mechanics Wilbur Wright, 36, and Orville Wright, 32, have built their *Flyer I* with a chain-drive 12-horsepower motorcycle engine whose cast aluminum engine block gives it a high strength-to-weight ratio. Near Kill Devil Hill at Kitty Hawk, N.C., December 17, they achieve flights first of 120 feet, then of 852 feet, but while a number of newsmen witness the event only three U.S. newspapers report it (*see* 1905).

German aviation pioneer Karl Jatho, 30, claims that he made a successful flight August 5, more than 4 months before the Wright brothers (above). Jatho built a gasoline-powered biplane in 1899 and will establish an aircraft works at Hanover in 1913.

The Chadwick motorcar introduced by U.S. engineer Lee Sherman Chadwick is a four-cylinder, 24-horsepower vehicle that goes 60 miles per hour and sells for $4,000 (*see* Chadwick Six, 1906).

Ransome E. Olds drives a racing car over a measured mile at Daytona Beach, Fla., in 1 minute, 6 seconds.

Alexander Winton drives a car at 68 miles per hour at Daytona Beach (*see* 1897). Winton has enlarged his factory to cover 13 acres. He employs 1,200 men.

The Ford Motor Company is incorporated June 16 with $28,000 raised by 12 stockholders who include

John and Horace Dodge. Henry Ford receives 225 shares in exchange for his design and 17 patents on its mechanism, production begins in a converted wagon factory on Detroit's Mack Avenue, and the $750 Model A Ford introduced by the company has a two-cylinder, 8-horsepower chain-drive engine mounted under its seat. The half-ton vehicle has a 72-inch wheelbase, it is 99 inches in length overall, its steering wheel is on the right, and 658 will be sold by next March (*see* Oldfield, 1902; Model T, 1908).

The Association of Licensed Automobile Manufacturers is formed to purchase rights to use the 1895 Selden patent at a royalty of 1.25 percent of the retail price of each automobile sold. Selden will soon be receiving a royalty on nearly every U.S.-made motorcar, but Ford Motor Company (above) refuses to join the Association (*see* 1899; 1911).

John North Willys sells 20 cars and takes on the Detroit car made by the Detroit Auto Vehicle Company (*see* 1902; 1907).

The first true automobile license plates are issued September 1 by the State of Massachusetts whose example is soon followed by all states.

Two-thirds of all U.S. motorcars sell at prices below $1,375, but most are too small, too light, and too unreliable to present serious competition to the horse and buggy, much less to the railroad.

A Packard leaves San Francisco for New York May 23 and arrives after 52 days in the first successful transcontinental trip by a motorcar under its own power, but sales of motorcars in the United States are discouraged by the poor quality of roads (*see* New York to Seattle race, 1909).

The Harley-Davidson motorcycle is introduced by Milwaukee draftsman William Harley, patternmaker Arthur Davidson, mechanic Walter Davidson, toolmaker William Davidson, and a German draftsman who is familiar with European motorcycles and with the DeDion gasoline engine. Some 50 Harley-Davidson bikes will be produced by 1906, the company will be incorporated in 1907, and by 1917 production will reach 18,000 per year as Harley-Davidson becomes the leading U.S. motorbike producer.

New York's Williamsburg Bridge opens to traffic December 19 and provides a second link between Brooklyn and New York to supplement the 20-year-old Brooklyn Bridge. The new $24.1 million 4.88-meter bridge is the first major suspension bridge with steel towers instead of masonry towers (*see* Queensboro and Manhattan bridges, 1909).

A new bottle-blowing machine permits volume production of electric light bulbs, whose high cost has discouraged widespread use of electric lighting. Michael J. Owens has improved his 1895 machine to create a completely automatic mechanism containing more than 9,000 parts. With the new machine, two men can produce 2,500 bottles per hour and as many light bulbs (*see* Langmuir, 1912).

Texaco, Inc. (The Texas Company) has its beginnings at Sour Lake, Tex., where prospectors bring in an oil well in January to give the new company its first major discovery. The Sour Lake Field will still be producing 1,400 barrels of oil per day in 1977 (*see* 1902; SoCal's Bahrein strike, 1932).

Oil gushes out of a new well on Osage Nation land in Oklahoma Indian Territory. The town of Bartlesville springs up near Jake Bartle's trading post (*see* 1905; Phillips Petroleum, 1917).

 U.S. anthracite coal miners win shorter hours and a 10 percent wage hike from President Roosevelt's Anthracite Coal Commission, but the commission refuses to recognize the United Mine Workers as bargaining agent for the miners (*see* 1902; Colorado, 1913, 1914).

Congress votes February 14 to create a Department of Commerce and Labor with its secretary to be a member of the president's cabinet (*see* Department of Labor, 1913).

The Supreme Court upholds a clause in the Alabama State Constitution denying blacks the right to vote. The court hands down the ruling April 27 in the case of *Giles v. Harris.*

Britain's WSPU (Women's Social and Political Union) is founded October 3 by Emmeline Goulden Pankhurst, 45, and like-minded women who meet at Pankhurst's house and begin to work through the Independent Labour party to achieve their goal of voting rights for women (*see* 1882; 1905).

Agents of the king of the Belgians Leopold II commit atrocities against natives in the Congo, reports British consul Roger David Casement, 39. He has conducted a government investigation of the rubber trade in lands of the Upper Congo owned personally by the king (*see* 1905).

William Cadbury visits Lisbon to investigate the question of alleged slavery in the Portuguese African cocoa islands Sao Thomé and Principe (*see* 1902). Portuguese authorities tell Cadbury that his suspicions are unfounded and invite him to see for himself (*see* 1905).

The Springfield Rifle that will become general issue in the U.S. Army and in some foreign armies is developed at the 108-year-old U.S. arsenal at Springfield, Mass. The M1903 gets its name from the Springfield Armory marking on its receiver ring (*see* 1926).

The Fouce torch invented by French inventor Edmond Fouce is the first safe, practical oxyacetylene torch for welding metals (*see* Claude, 1897). It will increase demand for acetylene and for oxygen (*see* 1907; Union Carbide, 1892, 1911).

 Typhus is shown to be transmitted only through the bite of the body louse. French physician Charles Jean Henri Nicolle, 37, reports on studies of the ancient plague that he has made as director of an outpost in Tunis, North Africa, of the Institut Pasteur.

The electrocardiograph is pioneered by Dutch physiologist Willem Einthoven, 43, at Leyden who invents a string galvanometer that will be developed into an instrument which will expand knowledge of the heart's functioning and will be used routinely to examine patients with potential or actual heart disease.

The inhibitory effects of x-rays on carcinomas and other cancerous growths is noted for the first time by German surgeon Georg Clems Perthes, 34 (*see* Roentgen, 1895).

The Phipps Institute for the Study, Treatment, and Prevention of Tuberculosis is established by steel magnate Henry Phipps at Philadelphia (*see* 1905).

John D. Rockefeller of Standard Oil contributes $7 million to fight tuberculosis.

"Typhoid Mary" gets her name as New York has an outbreak of typhoid fever with 1,300 cases reported. The epidemic is traced to one Mary Mallon who is a carrier of the disease (but not a victim) and who takes jobs that involve handling food, often using assumed names. Typhoid Mary refuses to stop, she will be placed under detention in 1915, and she will remain confined until her death in 1938.

New York's Bankers Trust Company is incorporated March 24 with $1.5 million in capital and surplus. The company will acquire Mercantile Trust (founded 1868) in 1911 and Manhattan Trust (founded 1871) in 1912, Astor Trust (formerly Sixth National Bank) in 1917, and by 1928 it will have assets of more than $734 million.

National Cash Register executive Thomas John Watson, 29, is given a budget of $1 million by John Henry Patterson to start a company that will pose as a rival to NCR but that will actually take control of the U.S.

Wilbur and Orville Wright made the first sustained manned flights in a controlled gasoline-powered aircraft.

693

1903 (cont.) secondhand cash register business (*see* 1884). Watson's Cash Register and Second Hand Exchange opens in New York's 14th Street, it undersells competitors and drives them out of business or forces them to sell out, and it will be followed up by Watson with similar operations in Philadelphia and then in Chicago (*see* THINK, 1908).

India's Tata iron and steel empire has its beginnings in Orissa where a hill of almost solid iron ore is discovered by Dorabji Jamsetji Tata, 44, and his kinsman Shapurji Saklatvala, 29. Son of an Indian cotton mill magnate, Tata starts an iron and steel company that together with his father's cotton mills will be the basis of India's modern industrial development.

Utah Copper Company is organized to mine ore at Bingham, Utah. The growing use of electricity and of the telephone has created a shortage of copper wire, and the Bingham mine provides cheap production of copper from low-grade ore.

The American Brass Company is created by a merger of U.S. copper companies that include the Guggenheim family's American Smelting and Refining Company, the United Copper firm controlled by Montana mine operator Frederick Augustus Heinze, 34, and the Amalgamated Copper Company controlled by Standard Oil Company's H. H. Rogers and Anaconda Company's Marcus Daly.

Western Michigan University is founded at Kalamazoo.

The University of Puerto Rico begins classes at Rio Piedras.

Guglielmo Marconi sends a wireless greeting January 19 from President Roosevelt to Britain's Edward VII (*see* 1901). Marconi has built four 250-foot wooden towers anchored in cement at South Wellfleet, Mass., he uses electrical waves generated by a 3-foot spark gap rotor, an operator working a huge key transmits the message at the rate of 17 words per minute, and while Marconi has arranged for a station at Glace Bay, Nova Scotia, to relay the message, the signal is so powerful that the wireless station 3,000 miles away at Poldhu in Cornwall picks it up direct (*see* 1907).

The Pacific Cable links San Francisco with Honolulu January 1 and with Manila July 4. President Roosevelt sends a message from San Francisco to Manila, it is relayed round the world, and it is returned to the president in 12 minutes.

The Knight newspaper chain that will merge with the Ridder chain in 1974 has its beginnings at Akron, Ohio, where local lawyer Charles L. Knight buys a part interest in the *Akron Beacon Journal*. By 1974 there will be 16 Knight newspapers up and down the U.S. East Coast (*see* Ridder, 1892).

The *London Daily Mirror* begins publication. The new tabloid started by *Daily Mail* publisher Alfred C. W. Harmsworth will have a circulation of more than a million by 1909 and will spawn two competitors.

Madrid's *ABC* begins publication. Journalist Torcuato de Tena y Alvarez-Ossorio will make his weekly paper a daily beginning in 1905 and will see the three-column tabloid achieve large circulation.

Redbook magazine begins publication in May under the name *Red Book*. The "Great Ten Penny Short Story Magazine" published by Chicago's Red Book Corporation (which also puts out a *Blue Book* and a *Green Book*) will carry short stories by H. G. Wells, Jack London, and other leading writers (*see* 1921).

Pulitzer prizes have their beginning in an agreement signed by *New York World* publisher Joseph Pulitzer April 10 to endow a school of journalism at Columbia University. Pulitzer has made a fortune since acquiring the *World* in 1883, and he specifies that $500,000 of his $2 million gift shall be allotted for "prizes or scholarships for the encouragement of public service, public morale, American literature, and the advancement of education."

The prix Goncourt is awarded for the first time from a fund established in 1895 by the late French writer Edmond de Goncourt who died the following year. His Académie Goncourt will honor the best French novel published each year, and the prix Goncourt will be France's most prestigious literary prize.

Fiction *The Way of All Flesh* by the late Samuel Butler who died last year at age 66; *The Ambassadors* by Henry James; *The Riddle of the Sands* by Anglo-Irish Boer War veteran Robert Erskine Childers, 33, whose story of an imaginary German raid on England will be a classic for small boat enthusiasts (beginning in 1908 Childers will devote himself to agitating for full dominion status for Ireland); *The Pit* by the late Frank Norris who died in late October of last year at age 32 but whose new work exposes price rigging by wheat speculators on the Chicago Board of Trade. Norris had planned to write a trilogy whose third volume (*The Wolf*) would have been an account of U.S. wheat relieving a European famine, but the author was sent by the *San Francisco Chronicle* to report a trip from Cape Town to Cairo in 1899, he enlisted in the British Army at the outbreak of the Boer War, he was captured by the Boers, he contracted fever, and he died at San Francisco leaving his "epic of wheat" incomplete; *The Call of the Wild* by California author John Griffith "Jack" London, 27, who at 17 shipped out as a common seaman aboard a sailing vessel that reached Japan, and who joined the Klondike gold rush at age 21; *The People of the Abyss* by Jack London (above) who lived for a period in the slums of London.

Juvenile *Rebecca of Sunnybrook Farm* by New York author Kate Douglas Wiggin, 47.

Painting *The Old Guitarist, La Celestina, La Vie, Sick Child* by Pablo Picasso; *Child with Puppet* by Henri Rousseau. Paul Gauguin dies of syphilis in the

Marquesas Islands May 18 at age 54; James A. McNeill Whistler dies at London July 17 at age 69; Camille Pissarro dies at Paris November 13 at age 73.

Britain creates the National Art Collections Fund to prevent works of art from leaving the country.

Steuben Glass Works is founded by British-American designer Frederick Carder, 35, who will head the firm until 1932 and who will not retire until he is 96. Carder's lustrous Aurene technique will produce glass rivaling in its iridescent color the Favrile designs of Louis Comfort Tiffany, now 55 (see 1878).

Theater *The Hour-Glass* by William Butler Yeats 3/14 at Dublin's Moleworth Hall; *The King's Threshold* by W. B. Yeats and Lady Gregory 3/14 at Dublin's Moleworth Hall; *Rose Bernd* by Gerhart Hauptmann 10/31 at Berlin's Deutsches Theater; *The County Chairman* by George Ade 11/24 at Wallack's Theater, New York, 222 perfs.; *Glad of It* by Clyde Fitch 12/28 at New York's Savoy Theater, with John Barrymore, 21, 32 perfs. A nephew of actor John Drew, Barrymore is the younger brother of Lionel, 25, and Ethel, 24, who have been on the stage since ages 6 and 14 respectively. "The Great Profile" will become a matinee idol and will be famous for his Hamlet beginning in 1924.

Fire engulfs Chicago's Iroquois Theater December 30. Matinee patrons rush for the exits and 602 die in the panic despite heroic efforts by comedian Eddie Foy, 47, to calm the crowd.

Film Edwin S. Porter's *The Great Train Robbery* is the first motion picture to tell a complete story (see 1896). Produced by Edison Studios and photographed at the Paterson, N.J., freight yards of the Delaware & Lackawanna Railroad, the 12-minute epic establishes a pattern of suspense drama that future moviemakers will follow.

Opera *L'Étranger* (*The Stranger*) 1/7 at the Théâtre de la Monnaie, Brussels, with music by Vincent d'Indy; *Tiefland* (*The Lowlands*) 11/15 at Prague's Neues Deutsches Theater, with music by Eugen d'Albert.

Enrico Caruso makes his New York debut November 21 singing *Rigoletto* at the 20-year-old Metropolitan Opera House. The Italian tenor has made a worldwide reputation since his debut at Milan's Teatro alla Scala in 1899, he will be the Met's leading tenor for years, and he will have a repertoire of more than 40 operatic roles (see 1902; Victrola, 1906).

Cantata "Hiawatha" by English composer Samuel Coleridge-Taylor, 28, 11/16 at Washington, D.C.

First performances *Transfigured Night* (*Verklärte Nacht*) sextet by Austrian composer Arnold Schoenberg, 28, at Vienna. The work is based on the Richard Dehmel poem *Weib und die Welt*.

Broadway musicals *The Wizard of Oz* 1/21 at the Majestic Theater, with Fred Stone and Dave Montgomery in a musical extravaganza based on the L.

Frank Baum novel of 1900, 293 perfs.; *Whoop-Dee-Doo* 9/24 at the Weber & Fields Music Hall, with Weber and Fields, music by W. T. Francis, book and lyrics by Edgar Smith, 151 perfs.; *Babette* 11/16 at the Broadway Theater, with Vienna-born Metropolitan Opera soprano Fritzi Scheff, 21, music by Victor Herbert, book and lyrics by Harry B. Smith, 59 perfs.; *Babes in Toyland* 10/13 at the Majestic Theater, with music by Victor Herbert, songs that include the "March of the Toys" and the title song (lyrics by Glen MacDonough), 192 perfs.

Popular songs "Dear Old Girl" by Theodore F. Morse, lyrics by Richard and Henry Buck; "Bedelia" by Jean Schwartz, lyrics by William Jerome; "Ida, Sweet as Apple Cider" by U.S. minstrel Eddie Leonard; "Sweet Adeline" by U.S. composer Henry W. Armstrong, 24, lyrics by Richard H. Gerard, 27, whose words will be sung by generations of barbershop quartets (the song will be used as a campaign theme for Boston mayoralty candidate John W. "Honey Fitz" Fitzgerald); "Waltzing Matilda" by Australian Marie Cowan who has adopted the 1818 Scottish song "Thou Bonny Wood of Craigie Lee" by James Barr, lyrics by Andrew Barton "Banjo" Peterson, 39, who has adapted an Australian bush ballad. ("Matilda" is Aussie slang for a knapsack; a "swagman" is a worker.)

New York's "Tin Pan Alley" gets its name from songwriter-publisher Harry von Tilzer. He receives a visit from songwriter-journalist Monroe H. Rosenfeld, who has earned little from his 1897 song "Take Back Your Gold" and other hits. Rosenfeld notices that von Tilzer's piano has a peculiarly muffled tone, von Tilzer explains that other tenants of the building at Broadway and 28th Street have demanded that piano players make less noise, he has used newspapers to reduce volume, Rosenfeld says, "It sounds like a tin pan," von Tilzer says, "Yes, I guess this is tin pan alley," and Rosenfeld repeats the phrase in his *New York Herald* music columns.

Waltz "Gold and Silver Waltz" by Franz Lehar who wrote it for an elaborate ball given last year by the Princess Metternich.

New York's Barnard College holds its first Greek Games to begin an annual competition between freshmen and sophomores. The young women vie for laurel wreaths in discus throwing, hurdling, chariot racing, hoop relay races, torch relay races, choreography, lyrics, costume design, and other events.

The U.S. yacht *Reliance* rigged by Nat Herreshoff and built by a syndicate headed by J. P. Morgan defends the America's Cup by defeating Sir Thomas Lipton's *Shamrock III* 3 to 0.

The first World Series baseball playoffs pit the American League's Boston team against the National League's Pittsburgh team. Boston wins 5 games to 3.

The Little Brown Jug becomes the trophy for the annual Michigan-Minnesota football game.

1903 (cont.) The Teddy Bear introduced last year by Morris Michtom encounters a challenge from the German firm Steiff Co. founded in 1880 at Giengen in Swabia by crippled seamstress Margarete Steiff. Her nephew Richard claims to have designed a plush bear last year with jointed limbs and a movable head, he shows it at the Leipzig Fair with little success, but a U.S. buyer sees the bear on the last day of the fair and orders 3,000. The wholesale firm Butler Brothers takes Michtom's entire output of Teddy Bears (the firm will call itself Ideal Novelty and Toy Company beginning in 1938, it will later shorten its name to Ideal Toy Company, and it will become the world's largest manufacturer of dolls).

King C. Gillette escapes bankruptcy after having gone $12,000 into debt (*see* 1901). Boston investor John Joyce advances funds to permit marketing of the Gillette safety razor and Gillette sells 51 razors, 168 blades (*see* 1904).

Singer Manufacturing Company sells 1.35 million sewing machines, up from 1 million in 1889 (*see* 1913).

A new Wanamaker Department Store at New York replaces the A. T. Stewart store of 1862 which Wanamaker has operated since 1896. Designed by Chicago's Daniel H. Burnham and Company, the enormous 15-story department store fills the block between Broadway and Fourth Avenue from 9th to 10th Streets and has no inner courtyards.

New York's Bergdorf Goodman has its beginnings in a tailoring firm for affluent women founded by Rochester-born tailor Edwin Goodman, 26. He buys out his elderly Alsatian-American partner for $15,000, he moves from a private house in 19th Street to a building in West 32nd Street, and he will move in 1914 to 616 Fifth Avenue (*see* 1928).

England's Westminster Cathedral is completed in Byzantine style with striped brick and stone. Architect John Francis Bentley died last year at age 63.

Cincinnati's Ingalls building is the world's first skyscraper with a reinforced concrete framework (*see* Monier, 1849). First reinforced concrete building of more than two stories, the 16-story $400,000 structure at Fourth and Vine Streets revolutionizes the construction industry. It is named for Big Four Railroad president Melville E. Ingalls, but the Cincinnati Transit Company will acquire it in 1959 and will rename it the Transit building.

The New York Stock Exchange building is completed at 8 Broad Street between Wall Street and Exchange Plaza.

New York's Whitehall building at Battery Park is completed with 20 stories. Another 14 stories will be added in 1911 to give the building 550,000 square feet of rentable floor space.

Kykuit is completed for Standard Oil magnate John D. Rockefeller on the 4,180-acre estate he acquired 10 years ago in the Pocantico Hills north of New York. The 14-room Victorian stone mansion commands a view of the Hudson and Saw Mill Rivers; its Dutch name means "lookout" (*see* 1908).

Boston's Fenway Court is completed by department store heiress Isabella Stewart Gardner to house her art collection.

Grand Canyon's Angel Lodge and El Tovar are opened by the Santa Fe Railroad which has built a branch from its main line at Williams to bring tourists to the canyon's rim. The new hotels are operated by the sons and son-in-law of the late Fred Harvey who died early in 1901 (*see* 1876). Some 17 hotels, 47 restaurants, and 30 dining cars are under Fred Harvey management as are food services on San Francisco Bay ferries (*see* national park, 1919).

Fire destroys Florida's 8-year-old Breakers at Palm Beach. H. M. Flagler orders construction of a new hotel that will replace the vast wooden structure and will become a winter resort hotel favored by millionaires (*see* 1925).

Florida acquires title to the Everglades swamp, the largest area ever conveyed in a single patent issued by the U.S. Land Department. Drainage operations will begin in 1906 (*see* national park, 1947).

President Roosevelt designates Florida's Pelican Island a National Wildlife Refuge, a seabird sanctuary where the fowl will be safe from the plume hunters who shoot birds to obtain feathers for milliners. Roosevelt thus begins a fish and wildlife reserve system that will set aside 30 million acres of U.S. lands in the next 70 years.

Wind Cave National Park is established in South Dakota's Black Hills by act of Congress. The 28,000-acre park has herds of bison, elk, deer, and pronghorn antelope with limestone caverns and prairie dog towns.

Russia's harvest fails again as it did in 1891. Since millions of Russians live at the edge of starvation even in the best of years, the crop failure produces famine that kills millions.

The Philippine Islands are self-sufficient in rice but will not be self-sufficient again until 1968.

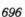 A machine that cuts off a salmon's head and tail, splits the fish open, cleans it, and drops it into hot water all in one continuous operation is devised by U.S. inventor A. K. Smith. The Smith machine adjusts itself automatically to the size of the fish, and it will be called the "Iron Chink" because it replaces Chinese hand labor in West Coast canneries (*see* Chinese Exclusion Act, 1882; 1902).

A patent application for a sardine cannery machine similar to Smith's (above) was filed last year by Arthur R. Rogers of the Underwood sardine cannery at Jonesport, Me. (*see* 1881). A patent will be granted in 1905 for the Rogers machine which according to the patent application will "separate the fish according to sizes and feed them to my improved apparatus for severing their heads and tails and cleaning them."

A San Pedro, Calif., packer puts white albacore tunafish into cans and launches a major industry (*see* Van Camp, 1914).

 The ABC of Nutrition by San Francisco food faddist Horace Fletcher launches a fad by urging readers to chew their food carefully if excessively (32 times). Fletcher is a 5-foot 6-inch importer of Oriental goods who has used strict diet to reduce his weight from 217 pounds to 152 and has thus regained good health.

Sanka Coffee is introduced by German coffee importer Ludwig Roselius who has received a shipload of beans that were soaked with seawater by a storm and who has turned the beans over to researchers. They have suggested the possibility of removing caffeine from coffee beans without affecting the delicate flavor of the beans, they have perfected a process to do just that, and Roselius has named the product Sanka, using a contraction of the French *sans caféine* (*see* 1923).

Best Foods, Inc., has its beginnings in the Simon Levi Company founded by New York food wholesaler Simon Levi with 10,000 square feet of warehouse space and a horsedrawn delivery wagon (*see* Hellmann's, 1932; Corn Products Refining Co., 1958).

The Owens Bottle Machine Company is founded by M. J. Owens (above) (*see* Owens-Illinois Glass, 1929).

Minnesota Valley Canning Company is founded to pack sweet corn at La Seur, Minn., where promoter Silver Smith has persuaded 67 local merchants to put up $100 each for construction of a cannery (*see* peas, 1907; Green Giant, 1925, 1935).

Sunshine Biscuit Company has its beginnings in the Loose-Wiles Biscuit Company started by Kansas City bakers Jacob Leander Loose, 53, James S. Loose, and John H. Wiles who break away from the 5-year-old National Biscuit Company trust. Loose–Wiles will build a bakery at Boston in 1908, and in 1912 it will build a "thousand window bakery" at Long Island City, N.Y., to make Sunshine Biscuits that will be promoted on the premise that they are more wholesome than biscuits made in traditional basement bakeries (*see* 1946; Hydrox, 1910).

England's William Normann receives a patent for his 1901 process of hydrogenating fats and oils.

Milton S. Hershey breaks ground at Derry Church, 13 miles east of Harrisburg, Pa., for a chocolate factory whose products will dominate the chocolate candy and beverage industry by taking milk chocolate out of the luxury class. Hershey lays out Chocolate Avenue and Cocoa Avenue, he builds new houses for his workers to rent or buy, and he constructs the Hammelstown and Campbelltown Electric Street Railway to connect his cornfield at Derry Church (soon to be called Hershey) with five neighboring towns in the area which he has selected because it is a major milk-producing region with a good water supply and with good rail links to U.S. ports and consumer markets (*see* 1900; 1908).

The name Pepsi-Cola is trademarked by Caleb Bradham who sells 7,968 gallons of his syrup as compared with 881,423 for Coca-Cola syrup (*see* 1902; 1907).

Members of the New York Riding Club assemble at Louis Sherry's 5-year-old Fifth Avenue restaurant for a dinner given by millionaire horseman C. K. G. Billings. The floor of the banquet room is sodded, and the guests sit on their horses, eating off small tables attached to their saddles while sipping champagne from tubes connected to their saddlebags.

Caloric Stove Corporation has its beginnings in the Caloric Gas Stove Works founded at Philadelphia by German-American stovemaker Samuel Klein, 47.

1904 Japanese naval forces attack Port Arthur in southern Manchuria February 8, bottling up a Russian squadron and launching the largest war thus far in history —the first war in which armored battleships, self-propelled torpedoes, land mines, quick-firing artillery, and modern machine guns will be used. Concerned at Russia's failure to withdraw from Manchuria and by her continuing penetration of Korea, the Japanese follow their sneak attack with a declaration of war February 10, they defeat the Russians at the Yalu River May 1, they occupy Dairen May 30, they besiege Port Arthur and occupy Seoul, they defeat a Russian force at Liaoyang in China in October, and they force the Russians to pull back to Mukden (*see* 1905).

Russia's able but ruthless minister of the interior Viacheslav Plehve is assassinated July 28. A Zemstvo congress meets at St. Petersburg in November and demands that civil liberties be granted and that a representative assembly be convened (*see* 1905).

Herero and Hottentot tribesmen in German Southwest Africa rise against German colonial forces in an insurrection that will continue until early 1908. The revolt will be suppressed only after methodical campaigns by a force of 20,000 German troops.

The new republic of Panama adopts a constitution February 13 and elects Manuel Amador Guerrero as her first president (*see* 1903). Colombia's president José Marroquin is succeeded by Rafael Reyes, 54, who represented his country at Washington last year in the negotiations relating to Panama and who assumes dictatorial rule.

"The nineteenth century was the century of the United States. The twentieth century belongs to Canada," says Canadian prime minister Sir Wilfred Laurier, now 63.

President Roosevelt wins re-election with 336 electoral votes against 140 for the Democratic candidate Judge Alton B. Parker of New York, who has been nominated in preference to William Jennings Bryan.

Boston's James Michael Curley and his brother are convicted in November of taking civil service examinations for job applicants, but on the day they begin serving time they are elected to the offices of alderman and state representative (*see* 1903). The Curley

1904 (cont.) brothers are supported by New York's Tammany Hall and the public excuses their offense on the ground that "they did it for their friends."

Marie Curie discovers two new radioactive elements —radium and polonium—in uranium ore (pitchblende) and receives her doctorate at the Sorbonne (*see* 1898; Becquerel, 1896; McMillan, 1940).

The first practical photoelectric cell is devised by German physicists Julius Elster, 50, and Hans Friedrich Geitel, 49 (*see* first electron radio tube, below).

The Supreme Court rules in a 5 to 4 decision that the Northern Securities Company of 1901 violates the Sherman Act of 1890. The court decision orders dissolution of the railroad trust.

The first tunnel under the Hudson River is completed March 8 but will not open officially until February 25, 1908. The Hudson & Manhattan Railroad Company headed by William Gibbs McAdoo, 41, has built two single-track tubes, each more than a mile long, to connect Jersey City with Manhattan.

The first New York City subway line of any importance opens to the public October 27. The Interborough Rapid Transit (IRT) line runs from Brooklyn Bridge north under Lafayette Street, 4th Avenue, and Park Avenue to 42nd Street, west to Broadway, and north to 145th Street, completing the run in 26 minutes with a train of five copper-sheathed wooden cars, each seating 56, with red-painted roofs. Tickets cost 5 cents each, 111,000 people ride the first day, 319,000 the second, and 350,000 the third as New York inaugurates a system that will grow to cover more than 842 miles—the largest rapid transit system in the world. Tiles bearing visual symbols will identify stations with names such as Astor Place rather than street numbers to aid the city's polyglot population.

The Trans-Siberian Railroad opens to link Moscow with Vladivostok some 3,200 miles away (*see* 1903). It is the longest line of track in the world.

A new rail line reaches the lower Rio Grande Valley of Texas and opens up the region for citrus fruits and vegetables on lands irrigated with river water.

The New York excursion boat S.S. *General Slocum* catches fire in the Hudson June 15 while carrying 1,400 German-Americans from the Lower East Side to Locust Grove on Long Island Sound for a Wednesday picnic sponsored by the German Lutheran Church of Sixth Street. More than 1,030 die, the tragedy shatters the German community in the Lower East Side, a court finds the paddle-wheeler's captain guilty of criminal negligence and sentences him to 10 years at hard labor in Sing Sing, and more Germans move uptown to settle in Yorkville.

The British passenger liner S.S. *Baltic* goes into service to begin a 29-year career. The largest passenger ship yet built, the 23,884-ton vessel is 726 feet in length overall—26 feet longer than the S.S. *Celtic* launched in 1901 or the S.S. *Cedric* launched last year and more than 2,500 tons larger than either.

The S.S. *Kaiser Wilhelm II* built 2 years ago for the North German Lloyd line sets a new transatlantic record in June by steaming from Sandy Hook to Eddystone, off Plymouth, in 5 days, 12 hours.

The Tropical Fruit Steamship Company, Ltd., is founded by the United Fruit Company which has contracted with shipyards to build three new refrigerator ships (*see* 1899). The company will operate its new S.S. *San José*, S.S. *Limon*, and S.S. *Esparta* under British colors (*see* 1910; radio equipment, below).

Cadillac Motor Car Company is created by a reorganization of the Detroit Automobile Company under the aegis of Henry Martyn Leland, 61 (*see* 1901; General Motors, 1909; self-starter, 1911).

The Pierce Arrow and Great Arrow begin the George N. Pierce Company on a career as the leading U.S. producer of luxury motorcars (*see* 1901). The company produces 50 Great Arrows and sells them at $3,000 to $5,000 each (*see* Glidden Tour, 1905).

A. A. Pope opens a plant at Toledo, Ohio, and introduces the Pope-Tribune at $650 (*see* 1897; Willys, 1907).

The Maxwell motorcar introduced by J. D. Maxwell gains quick popularity. The 1914 model will have the first adjustable front seat (*see* Chrysler, 1923).

The Reo introduced by R. E. Olds has a steering wheel instead of a tiller (*see* 1901). Olds has left the Oldsmobile Company in a dispute with Frederick Smith on the size and price of motorcars to be produced by the company.

La Fabrica de Automoviles La Hispano-Suiza is founded at Barcelona by Swiss-born engineer Mark Birkigt, 26, and others who reorganize a bankrupt Spanish firm started in 1899. Birkigt will make the Hispano-Suiza a luxury motorcar, but the company's real success will come from its buses, trucks, industrial engines, and aircraft engines.

U.S. reformers organize the National Child Labor Committee to promote protective legislation (*see* Owen-Keating Act, 1916).

E. F. Hutton and Company is founded by New York stockbroker Edward Francis Hutton, 28, whose brokerage house will be the first to serve California by wire service (*see* Birdseye, 1926).

William C. Gorgas is sent to Panama to eliminate the yellow fever that is discouraging construction of a cross-isthmus canal (*see* 1901; 1906).

Adrenaline (epinephrine) is isolated by English chemist Henry Drysdale Dakin, 24, and German chemist F. Stolz (*see* Takamine, 1901).

The National Tuberculosis Association is established in the United States to raise money for research that will fight consumption.

New York's Mt. Sinai Hospital is founded on upper Fifth Avenue.

The Chinese Red Cross is established at Peking and Shanghai.

Sales of Argyrol and Ovoferrin total more than $93,000 and net Albert Barnes and his colleague Herman Hille more than $44,000 in profits. They open offices at London and at Sydney, Australia (see 1902; 1907).

Dr. Scholl's arch-support is patented by Illinois medical school graduate and former shoemaker-salesman William Scholl, 24, who will advertise himself as "foot doctor to the world" and who will promote corn, callus, and bunion pads to ease aching feet.

Helen Keller is graduated magna cum laude from Radcliffe College and begins to write about blindness, a subject taboo in women's magazines because so many cases are related to venereal disease (see Argyroll, 1902; Keller, 1887). Keller has learned to speak at Boston's Horace Mann School for the Deaf by feeling the position of the tongue and lips of others, making sounds, and imitating the lip and tongue motions. She has learned to lip-read by placing her fingers on the lips and throat of the speaker while the words spoken were spelled out on the palm of her hand, her book *The Story of My Life* appeared in 1902 and was followed last year by her book *Optimism*, she will begin lecturing in 1913 to raise money for the American Foundation for the Blind, her teacher Anne Sullivan will remain with her until her death in 1936, and Keller will continue to work for the blind and deaf until her own death in 1968.

Bethune-Cookman College has its beginnings in a cabin rented at Daytona, Fla., by Mary McLeod Bethune, 29, who opens her Daytona Normal and Industrial Institute for Negro Girls with five students. Bethune makes potato pies for workmen building the nearby Clarendon Hotel, she earns $5 for a down payment on some land, and she solicits funds to build Faith Hall (see 1923).

The wireless radio distress signal letters CQD adopted January 1 mean "stop sending and listen" (see SOS, 1906).

United Fruit Company (above) installs commercial radio equipment on its ships and is the first to do so. The firm depends on radio communications to determine when and where bananas are available for loading (see 1910).

The diode thermionic valve invented by English electrical engineer John Ambrose Fleming, 55, is the first electron radio tube (see De Forest, 1906).

Parker Pen Company's George S. Parker obtains a patent May 3 for a lever mechanism that makes it easier to fill his pen's rubber sac (see 1888). Parker has gained success with his "Lucky Curve" hard rubber feed bar which minimizes leakage since it provides a continuous capillary passage between nib and barrel wall (the feed bar is curved at the end, it extends up into the ink chamber to touch the wall of the barrel, and when the pen is placed in the pocket, nib up, the ink all drains into the pen's reservoir). All fountain pens including Parker's have barrels of black hard rubber (the only available ink-resistant material that can be easily heated and formed), the upper end of the pen barrel is sealed to maintain a vacuum equal to the weight of the column of ink, careful adjustment of the feed-bar groove's cross-sectional area allows a slow flow of air bubbles that reduce the vacuum and release more ink, and tiny slits cut in the bottom of the ink channel aid capillarity (see "Big Red," 1921).

Nonfiction *The Shame of the Cities* by *McClure's* magazine managing editor (Joseph) Lincoln Steffens, 38, whose exposé of squalor in America's urban centers creates a sensation; *Mont Saint Michel and Chartres* by Henry Adams is privately printed; his study of medieval life, art, and philosophy will be published in 1913.

Fiction *The Late Mattia Pascal* (*Il fu Mattia Pascal*) by Italian novelist Luigi Pirandello, 37, whose beautiful wife became an incurable schizophrenic last year after hearing that her father-in-law's sulfur mine was flooded to the financial ruination of her husband's family and her own; *Peter Camenzind* by German novelist-poet Hermann Hesse, 27, who has quit a theological seminary in rebellion against his Protestant missionary father and has worked as a mechanic and bookseller; *Nostromo* by Joseph Conrad; *The Golden Bowl* by Henry James; *Green Mansions* by English naturalist-writer W. H. Hudson, 63, whose Rima the bird-girl gains him his first large success; *Reginald* by English short story writer Saki [H. H. (Hector Hugh) Munro], 35, who takes his pen name from the female cup-bearer in the last stanza of Edward Fitzgerald's translation of *The Rubáiyát of Omar Khayyám* published in 1859. Born in Burma, Munro was raised by two maiden aunts in Devonshire, he joined the Burma police in which his father had served, but he resigned after a year for reasons of health; *Lucky Peter* (*Lykke Per*) by Henrik Pontoppidan; *Esau and Jacob* (*Esau e Jaco*) by Joachim Machado De Assis; *Cabbages and Kings* by New York short story writer O. Henry (William Sydney Porter), 42, who was charged 8 years ago with embezzling funds from an Austin, Tex., bank in which he worked from 1891 to 1894. Porter fled to Honduras to escape prosecution, returned when he heard his wife was mortally ill, was convicted after her death, and served 3 years of a 5-year prison term; *The Sea Wolf* by Jack London who spends 6 months covering the Russo-Japanese war (above); *Freckles* by Indiana novelist Gene Stratton Porter, 41.

Poetry "Alcione" by Gabriele D'Annunzio.

The Salon d'Automne at Paris exhibits paintings by Paul Cézanne, Odilon Redon, and others but is dominated by the canvases *Charity* and *Hope* by the late Pierre Cecile Puvis de Chavannes who died in 1898.

Japan proved herself a great naval power, overcoming beriberi in the ranks and sinking a Russian fleet.

Other paintings *Mont Sainte Victoire* by Paul Cézanne; *Thames* by Claude Monet who begins to concentrate on the *Nymphaes* (water lilies) which will occupy him until his death in 1926; *Harvest Day* by German impressionist Emil Nolde (Emil Hansen), 37, who will soon turn to religious paintings; *The Wedding* by Henri Rousseau. Henri Fantin-Latour dies at Bure, Orne, August 25 at age 68.

Sculpture *The Hand of God* (bronze) by Auguste Rodin.

The Christ of the Andes is dedicated at Uspallato Pass on the Chilean-Argentine border to honor the peaceful settlement of disputes between the two countries since declaring their independence from Spain in 1817 and 1816. The 14-ton, 26-foot high monument is the work of Argentine sculptor Mateo Alonzo who has molded the figure from the bronze of old Argentine cannon.

 Theater *The Cherry Orchard* (*Vishnyovyy Sad*) by Anton Chekhov 1/17 at the Moscow Art Theater (Chekhov dies July 2 at Badenweiler in the Black Forest at age 44); *Riders to the Sea* by John Millington Synge 1/25 at Dublin's Moleworth Hall; *The Daughter of Jorio* (*La figlia di Iorio*) by Gabriele D'Annunzio 3/2 at Milan's Teatro Lirico, with Eleanora Duse; *Pandora's Box* (*Die Büchse der Pandora*) by Frank Wedekind at Nuremberg's Intimes Theater; *Candida* by George Bernard Shaw 4/20 at London's Royal Court Theatre, with Kate Rorke in the title role, 6 matinee perfs.; *The College Widow* by George Ade 9/20 at New York's Garden Theater, 278 perfs.; *The Music Master* by Charles Klein 9/26 at New York's Belasco Theater, with David Warfield, 288 perfs., *How He Lied to Her Husband* by George Bernard Shaw 9/26 at New York's Berkeley Lyceum, with Arnold Daley, 18 perfs.; *John Bull's Other Island* by George Bernard Shaw 11/1 at London's Royal Court Theatre, with Granville Barker in a satire about Shaw's native Ireland, 6 matinee perfs.; *Leah Kleschna* by C. M. S. McClellan 12/12 at New York's Manhattan Theater, with Mrs. Fiske, Charles Cartwright, George Arliss, 631 perfs.; *On Baile's Strand* by William Butler Yeats and Lady Gregory 12/27 at Dublin's new Abbey Theatre off O'Connell Street; *Peter Pan, or The Boy Who Would Not Grow Up* by James M. Barrie 12/27 at the Duke of York's Theatre, London, with Maude Adams.

Opera *Jenufa* (*Jeji Pastorkyna Jenufa, Her Fosterdaughter*) 1/21 at Brno in Austrian Moravia, with music by Czech composer Leos Janacek, 49; *Madama Butterfly* 2/17 at Milan's Teatra alla Scala, with music by Giacomo Puccini who has seen the play *Madame Butterfly* at London. Staged originally by David Belasco in New York, the play about the opening of Japan is based on the short story "Madame Butterfly" which appeared in the January 1900 issue of *Century* magazine (the new opera is a fiasco in its initial production).

The London Symphony Orchestra gives its first concert in June under the direction of Hans Richter. Principal conductors in the future will include Sir Edward Elgar, Pierre Monteux, and André Previn.

First performances *Kossuth* Symphony by Hungarian composer Béla Bartók (Nagyszentmiklos), 23, 1/13 at Budapest; Symphony No. 2 in B flat major by Vincent d'Indy 2/28 at Paris; Quartet in F by Maurice Ravel 3/5 at the Societé Nationale, Paris; *In the South* (*Alassio*) Overture by Sir Edward Elgar (knighted this year) 3/18 at London's Covent Garden Theatre; Symphony No. 5 in C sharp minor by Gustav Mahler 10/18 at Cologne.

Chicago's $1 million Orchestra Hall is completed by Daniel Burnham in French Renaissance style at 216 South Michigan Avenue.

Edward MacDowell leaves Columbia University where he has encountered opposition from conservative academicians (*see* 1896). He retires to his farm at Peterborough, N.H., he will die there in 1908 at age 46, and his widow Marian will found the MacDowell Colony to provide a summer residence for U.S. composers, authors, and artists.

Russian ballet dancer-choreographer Michel Mikhaylovich Fokine, 24, proposes sweeping changes to the management of the Imperial Ballet at St. Petersburg. Fokine made his debut on his 18th birthday, the management rejects all his suggestions, but he will see them accepted. "Dancing should be interpretive," says Fokine. "It should not degenerate into mere gymnastics. The dance should explain the spirit of the actors in the spectacle. . . . For such interpretive dancing, the music must be equally inspired. In place of the old-time waltzes, polkas, pizzicati and calops, it is necessary to create a form of music which expresses the same emotion as that which inspires the movements of the dancer. The ballet must no longer be made up of 'numbers,' 'entries,' and so on. It must show artistic unity of conception. The action of the ballet must never be interrupted to allow the danseuse to respond to the applause of the public" (*see* 1907).

Broadway musicals *Piff! Paff!! Pouf!!!* 4/2 at the Casino Theater, with Eddie Foy, music by Jean Schwartz, lyrics by William Jerome, songs that include "The Ghost That Never Walked," 264 perfs. (plus a week at the Majestic Theater beginning 12/26); *Higgledy-Piggledy* 10/12 at the Weber Music Hall, with Anna Held, Marie Dressler, Fred M. Weber, music by Maurice Levy, lyrics by Edgar Smith, 185 perfs.; *Little Johnny Jones* 11/17 at the Liberty Theater, with book, music, and lyrics by George M. Cohan, songs that include "Give My Regards to Broadway" and "Yankee Doodle Boy," 52 perfs.

Popular song "Frankie and Johnny" by songwriter Hughie Cannon whose song is published under the title "He Done Me Wrong, or Death of Bill Bailey."

The Olympic Games held at St. Louis attract 1,505 contestants from seven countries. The games are held as part of the Louisiana Purchase Exposition that belatedly celebrates the centennial of the 1803 purchase of the Louisiana Territory from France, and French athletes take most of the medals.

The first major league "perfect" game is pitched May 5 by Boston Red Sox pitcher Cy Young who faces 27 batters in nine innings and does not let one of them reach first base (*see* 1890). After Young's death in 1955 the Cy Young Award will be established for the best pitcher in the major leagues each year, and the award will later be given to the best in each league.

No World Series is held because John McGraw of the New York Giants refuses to have his team play the Boston Red Sox.

The first cement stadium is built at Harvard with a capacity of 40,000. A colonnade that adds additional seats will be added in 1910 as college football grows to become a major spectator sport, and steel stands will be added in 1919 to turn the horseshoe-shaped stadium into an enclosed oval (*see* Yale Bowl, 1914).

Auction bridge is invented as a variation on the card game Whist played since the early 16th century if not longer. The highest bidder names the trump suit (*see* contract bridge, 1925).

An International Exposition opens a year late at St. Louis to commemorate the centennial of the 1803 Louisiana Purchase. The Ferris wheel from the 1893 Chicago Midway is moved to St. Louis.

Colgate Ribbon Dental Cream is introduced by the 98-year-old William Colgate Company. The firm will be incorporated in 1908 under the name Colgate & Co., and its dental cream will become the leading U.S. dentifrice (*see* Colgate-Palmolive-Peet, 1928; Crest, 1955).

The Gillette razor is patented November 15, sales soar to 90,844 (up from just 51 last year), blade sales reach 123,648 (up from 168), and the figures will soon

be multiplied a thousandfold. King C. Gillette pays $62,500 to buy out an investor who paid $250 for 500 shares in 1901.

 Montgomery Ward distributes its first free catalogs after having sold catalogs for years at 15 cents each. The company mails out more than 3 million of the 4-pound books.

Sears, Roebuck distributes more than a million copies of its spring catalog (*see* 1895). Sears has set up its own printing plant but still uses woodcuts for more than half its illustrations and may be keeping the art of wood engraving alive (*see* 1907).

New York's Astor Hotel opens on Seventh Avenue between 44th and 45th Streets. John Jacob Astor IV of 1897 Waldorf-Astoria fame has had the new 660-room hotel constructed in classic French style.

New York's St. Regis Hotel opens at Fifth Avenue and 55th Street. John Jacob Astor IV (above) has financed construction of the luxurious new hotel.

New York's Ansonia Hotel opens at Broadway and 73rd Street. Phelps, Dodge copper heir William Earl Dodge Stokes, 52, has had the structure designed by architect Paul E. M. DuBoy and has named it in honor of his maternal grandfather Anson Greene Phelps, founder of the Ansonia Brass & Copper Company at Ansonia, Conn.

San Francisco's St. Francis Hotel opens on Union Square.

The Hotel Jefferson opens in St. Louis in time to receive visitors to the city's International Exposition.

Ellsworth M. Statler of 1901 Buffalo Exposition fame opens a 2,257-room Inside Inn for St. Louis fairgoers and has a profit of $300,000 by fall (*see* 1905).

Philadelphia's Bellevue Stratford Hotel opens in September at South Broad Street and Walnut to replace an earlier structure. The 400-room hotel will be nearly doubled in size and will be given a roof garden in 1913 as it becomes the city's social center.

Montana copper magnate W. A. Clark moves into a 130-room New York mansion on Fifth Avenue at 77th Street. The new house is considered vulgar and Norman Hapgood writes in *Collier's* magazine, "If architecture is frozen music, this edifice is frozen ragtime discord" (*see* 1902; Goethe, 1829).

Buffalo's Martin House is completed by Frank Lloyd Wright.

Harlem's Kortwright Apartments on Sugar Hill open with 29 luxury units at 1990 Seventh Avenue. The first blacks will move into the building in 1926.

The *New York Times* moves into a new 25-story Times Tower at Broadway and 42nd Street December 31 and Longacre Square becomes Times Square. The move is marked with a midnight fireworks display that will become, in modified form, a New Year's Eve tradition and will continue even after the *Times* moves to larger quarters in West 43rd Street and the Times Tower changes hands.

1904 (cont.) Fire destroys 75 city blocks in the heart of downtown Baltimore February 7 and 8. More than 1,300 buildings are gutted.

Much of Toronto is destroyed by fire April 19.

A Japanese exhibit at the New York Botanical Garden introduces a blight that begins to wipe out the American chestnut tree *Castanea dentata* whose timber has been a valuable building material and whose nuts have been an important food source.

An entente cordiale settles Anglo-French disputes in the Newfoundland fishery.

Caterpillar Tractor Company has its beginnings in the Holt Manufacturing Company of Stockton, Calif., whose Benjamin Holt tests a steam tractor November 24. Golden Meadow Developing Co. will buy the first production model in 1906 for use in Louisiana delta land (*see* 1925).

Most English farmers have turned from raising grain and meat animals which cannot compete with imports to dairy farming, market gardening, poultry raising, and fruit growing. They are unable to meet the demand for butter, cheese, and lard, much of which is imported—along with Dutch margarine— from Denmark and North America. Most English fruit goes into jams whose manufacture is being improved and which becomes highly popular as an auxiliary to margarine.

Britain's Interdepartmental Committee on Physical Deterioration publishes a report demonstrating the alarming extent of poverty and ill health in British slums. One out of four infants dies in its first 12 months in some areas, the committee reports, and it deplores the rapid decline in breast-feeding, due in part to the employment of married women in industry, but due mostly to the chronic ill-health that makes women incapable of producing milk. 33 percent of the children surveyed are actually hungry (*see* School Meals Act, 1906).

Xerophthalmia is reported among Japanese infants whose diets are devoid of fats (*see* Denmark, 1917).

A man can work hard and remain healthy on less than 50 grams of protein per day, says Yale physiological chemist Russell Henry Chittenden, 48. In his book *Physiological Economy in Nutrition* he disputes Atwater and Voit (*see* 1902), he gives evidence to support his contention, he claims that he personally feels better on a low-protein diet, and he urges such diets for all older people.

An exposé of the U.S. patent medicine business is launched by the *Ladies' Home Journal* (*see* 1892; 1898; Adams, 1906).

Pure Food Law advocates take space at the St. Louis Exposition to dramatize the fact that U.S. foods are being colored with potentially harmful dyes.

The hamburger gains popularity at the St. Louis Exposition (above) where the chopped beef specialty is fried and sold by German immigrants who live in South St. Louis (*see* Lassen, 1900).

The ice cream cone is introduced at the St. Louis fair by Syrian immigrant pastrymaker Ernest A. Hamwi who sells waferlike Zalabia pastry at a fairground concession, serving them with sugar and other sweets. When a neighboring ice cream stand runs out of dishes, Hamwi rolls some of his wafers into cornucopias, he lets them cool, and he sells them to the ice cream concessionaire. But an ice cream cone mold patent has been issued earlier in the year to Italian immigrant Italo Marchiony who claims he has been making ice cream cones since 1896 and who is joined by other claimants who challenge Hamwi's right to call himself the ice cream cone originator.

Iced tea is created at the St. Louis fair by English tea concessionaire Richard Blechynden when sweltering fairgoers pass him by, but as in the case of the ice cream cone (above), evidence will be produced of prior invention.

Green tea and Formosan tea continue to outsell black tea 5 to 1 in the United States.

Tea bags are pioneered by New York tea and coffee shop merchant Thomas Sullivan who sends samples of his various tea blends to customers in small handsewn muslin bags. Finding that they can brew tea simply by pouring boiling water over tea bag in a cup, the customers place hundreds of orders for Sullivan's tea bags which will soon be packed by a specially developed machine.

The Thermos bottle is introduced by German entrepreneur Reinhold Burger who has seen a commercial potential for the Dewar vacuum flask of 1892 and who has offered a prize for the best name to be used for the vacuum flask. The Thermos bottle will have wide use in lunch boxes, picnic hampers, and such, U.S. rights to the word "Thermos" bottle will be obtained by the King-Seeley Thermos Co., but the firm will lose exclusive rights in 1962 after surveys show that 68 percent of Americans think the word is a generic for any vacuum-insulated bottle.

Continental Can Company is organized by U.S. entrepreneur Edwin Norton of Norton Brothers who helped to create American Can in 1901 but who leaves the Can Trust and is joined by some other canmakers. Continental will supply such companies as Campbell (below) and William Underwood until Campbell starts making its own cans in 1936, and it will continue thereafter to rival American Can.

Campbell's Pork and Beans is introduced by the Joseph Campbell Preserve Company (*see* 1900).

The Campbell Kid cartoon characters that will be used to advertise Campbell's products are created by Philadelphia artist Grace Gebbie Drayton (*see* Joseph Campbell Company, 1905).

Derby Foods, Inc., is acquired by the Swift Beef Trust. Incorporated in Illinois under the name E. K. Pond Packing Company in 1888, Derby is a producer of pickled meat products (*see* peanut butter, 1928).

French's Cream Salad Mustard is developed by George F. French and is introduced by Rochester's R. T. French Company (see 1880). Milder than other mustards, it will become the world's largest selling prepared mustard and will outsell all others combined in the U.S. market (see Worcestershire sauce, 1930).

Post Toasties is introduced by the Postum Company under the name Elijah's Manna, but the name arouses the wrath of clergymen, Post is denied a trademark for his new corn flakes by the British government, and he quickly renames the product (see 1897). Postum is the world's largest single user of molasses, C. W. Post's personal fortune last year was estimated at $10 million, and his company netted $1.3 million last year (see 1906).

Anderson, Clayton & Company is started at Oklahoma City by local stenographer William Lockhart Clayton, 24, with his brothers-in-law Monroe D. and Frank E. Anderson. The cotton merchant partnership will become the world's largest, most powerful cotton firm and a leading food company. It will move to Houston, Tex., in 1916 (see Chiffon margarine, Seven Seas salad dressings, 1965).

The Baltimore Fruit Exchange is founded by Italian-American merchant Giuseppi Di Giorgio, 30, who entered the fruit business at age 14 as helper to a New York fruit jobber. Di Giorgio will buy California's Earl Fruit Company in 1911 and will enter the transcontinental fruit shipping and commission business (see 1919).

Swiss General Chocolate Company, Peter and Kohler, Amalgamated is created by a merger of Kohler Chocolate and Peter Chocolate (see 1818; 1866). The firm signs a 99-year agreement giving Nestlé the rights to market Peter, Kohler, and Nestlé chocolate brands (see 1905; 1911).

1905 Russian forces at Port Arthur surrender to Japanese besiegers January 2 and the Russians are defeated by five Japanese armies at Mukden in early March.

A fleet of 32 Russian vessels sent round the Cape of Good Hope to relieve Port Arthur is sunk by Japan's Admiral Togo in the Battle of Tsushima Strait that rages between Japan's island of Kyushu and the Korean mainland from May 27 to 29.

Norway obtains her independence from Sweden after 91 years of union. A popular plebiscite August 13 ratifies a decision of the Storting, the Swedish Riksdag acquiesces September 24, a treaty of separation is signed October 26, Denmark's Prince Charles is elected king of Norway, and he assumes the throne at age 33 to begin a 52-year reign as Haakon VII.

President Roosevelt mediates the dispute between Russia and Japan and a treaty of peace is signed September 5 at Portsmouth, N.H., after a month of deliberations. Both nations agree to evacuate Manchuria, Russia cedes the southern half of Sakhalin Island,

Japan's paramount interest in Korea is recognized, Russia transfers to Japan the lease of the Liaotung Peninsula and the railroad to Ch'angchun, but riots break out in Tokyo to protest the failure of Japanese diplomats to obtain an indemnity.

Britain's Balfour ministry ends December 4 and the Liberals take over with a cabinet headed by Sir Henry Campbell-Bannerman, 69.

A Russian revolution has begun after a peaceful workers' demonstration led by a priest was machine-gunned January 9 in front of the Winter Palace at St. Petersburg on orders from the czar. News of "Bloody Sunday" incites the nation, the grand duke Serge is murdered February 4 by revolutionary terrorists at Moscow, and peasants seize land, crops, and livestock from landlords.

Russian sailors aboard the cruiser *Potemkin* mutiny in July at Odessa, a general strike is called in October, and on October 17 Nicholas II is obliged to grant a constitution, establish a parliament (Duma), and grant civil liberties to placate the people.

Nikolai Lenin returns from exile and hails the workers' first Soviet (council) at St. Petersburg, but the czar's concessions (above) are withdrawn one by one, the revolt begun December 9 under the leadership of the Moscow Soviet is bloodily repressed by Christmas, and the Duma will be suspended by June 1906 (see 1917; Lenin, 1903; *Pravda*, 1912. Dates in this account are Julian calendar dates and are 13 days behind dates in the Gregorian calendar of 1582 which Russia will not use until January 31, 1918).

Pogroms begin in Russia. Terrorists of the anti-Semitic "Black Hundreds" will kill an estimated 50,000 Jews by 1909.

A 5½ month strike by Fall River, Mass., textile workers ends successfully January 8.

The Industrial Workers of the World (IWW) is formed as a new organization of U.S. working men who call themselves one big union for all the workers and attack the AF of L for accepting the capitalist system. Most of the "Wobblies," as they are popularly called, are members of the radical Western Federation of Miners (see Haywood, 1907; Lawrence, 1912).

A New York law limiting hours of work in the baking industry to 60 per week is ruled unconstitutional by the Supreme Court April 17 in the case of *Lochner v. New York*. The owner of a Utica bakery had been convicted of violating the law, but the court rules that Lochner's right of contract is guaranteed under the 14th Amendment and that "the limitation of the hours of labor does not come within the police power...." A dissenting opinion by Justice Oliver Wendell Holmes says that the word " 'liberty' is perverted" when it is used to prevent the state from limiting hours of work as "a proper measure on the score of health," and that "a constitution is not intended to embody a particular economic theory, whether of paternalism ... or of laissez-faire."

1905 (cont.) The Niagara Movement to abolish all racial distinctions in the United States joins 29 black intellectuals from 14 states who meet at Fort Erie, N.Y., under the leadership of Atlanta University professor William Edward Burghardt DuBois, 37 (*see* NAACP, 1909).

The Asiatic Exclusion League founded by U.S. racists seeks to ban Japanese immigration (*see* 1908).

China boycotts U.S. goods to protest U.S. laws barring entry of educated Chinese along with Chinese workers (*see* 1902).

English Quaker Joseph Burtt spends 6 months at cocoa plantations on the African islands of Sao Thome and Principe at the suggestion of cocoa magnate William Cadbury and observes that nearly half of the newly arrived laborers at one plantation died with a year. Working conditions are tantamount to slavery, Burtt reports (*see* 1903; 1909).

English suffragist Emmeline Pankhurst begins propagandizing her cause with sensationalist methods that will include arson, bombing, hunger strikes, and window smashing (*see* 1903; 1906).

"Sensible and responsible women do not want to vote," writes former president Grover Cleveland in the April *Ladies' Home Journal:* "The relative positions to be assumed by men and women in the working out of our civilization were assigned long ago by a higher intelligence than ours."

A paper on the special theory of relativity by Swiss theoretical physicist Albert Einstein, 26, is published at Bern and revises traditionally held Newtonian views of space and time. Einstein introduces the equation $E = mc^2$ in "The Electrodynamics of Moving Bodies" ("Zur Elektrodynamik bewegter Körper") and predicts that light (or radio) waves moving from one planet to another will be bent off their path by a massive body like the sun, slowing them down for a fraction of a second.

The first major epidemic of poliomyelitis since the disease was first identified in 1840 breaks out in Sweden (*see* 1916).

Procaine (novocaine) is introduced into clinical use by German surgeon Heinrich Friedrich Wilhelm Braun, 43. The local anaesthetic will find wide use in dentistry.

A U.S. Public Health Service antimosquito campaign ends a yellow fever epidemic that has killed at least 1,000 at New Orleans, the last epidemic of the disease in the United States (*see* Havana, 1901).

The Phipps Tuberculosis Dispensary is established by steel magnate Henry Phipps at Baltimore's Johns Hopkins Hospital (*see* 1893; 1903).

Compulsory vaccination laws are upheld by the Supreme Court which rules in the case of *Jacobson v. Massachusetts* that enacting and enforcing such laws is within the police power of any state.

Vicks VapoRub is introduced under the name Vick's Magic Croup Salve by the new Vick Chemical Company founded at Greensboro, N.C., by former drug wholesaler Lunsford Richardson, 52. The mentholated salve is compounded of camphor, menthol, spirits of turpentine, oil of eucalyptus, cedar leaf oil, myristica oil, nutmeg, and thymol mixed in a petroleum base, and by the time Richardson dies in 1919 it will have annual sales of $11 million.

Wildcat oil prospectors in Oklahoma Territory make a big strike in the Glenn Pool near a village on the Arkansas River called by its residents Tulsey Town. It will quickly be built up into Tulsa, "Oil Capital of the World."

U.S. auto production reaches 25,000, up from 2,500 in 1899 (*see* 1907).

The Society of Automotive Engineers (SAE) is founded to standardize U.S. automotive parts. Andrew L. Riker of Locomobile is president, Henry Ford is first vice president, John Wilkinson of Franklin is third vice president (*see* 1911).

A Napier driven by Arthur MacDonald sets a speed record of 104.651 miles per hour at Daytona Beach.

A Stanley Steamer sets a speed record of 127 miles per hour, but its quiet, nonpolluting external combustion engine requires a 30-minute warm-up and must take on fresh water every 20 miles (*see* 1899).

The floundering Buick Motorcar Company started by Flint, Mich., plumbing supply merchant David Dunbar Buick, 50, is taken over by Flint millionaire William C. Durant whose 19-year-old Durant-Dorn Carriage Company has made him the richest man in town (*see* 1906).

The first Glidden Tour is held in July, and the contest that emphasizes reliability is won by George N. Pierce's son Percy driving a Pierce Great Arrow (*see* 1904; Glidden varnish, 1878). The 34 entries include cars built by Cadillac, Packard, Peerless, Locomobile, and six European makers including Napier, Panhard, and Darracq, but the Pierce Great Arrow is judged superior to the rest. The first six-cylinder Pierce will be introduced in 1907, the George N. Pierce Company will be renamed the Pierce-Arrow Company in 1909, and the Pierce will be the ultimate U.S. luxury car until 1918 (*see* 1914).

The first Vanderbilt Cup race is held October 8 at Hicksville, Long Island, on a 10-lap course over a 30-mile circuit. A French Panhard averaging 52.2 miles per hour beats five Mercedes machines, two other Panhards, two Fiats, two Pope-Toledos, a Renault, a Packard, a Clement-Bayard, a Simplex, a De Dietrich, and a Royal Tourist.

Britain holds her first Tourist Trophy motorcar race.

England's Austin motorcar is introduced by a new company started by former Wolesley designer Herbert Austin (*see* 1895; British Motors, 1952).

The first automobile taxicabs are introduced in Paris by the 6-year-old firm of Renault Frères.

London's Inner Circle rail lines are electrified.

The Long Island Railroad that has been controlled since 1900 by the Pennsylvania installs a low-voltage third rail system and becomes the first U.S. railroad completely to abandon steam locomotion.

"The Railroads on Trial" by Ray Stannard Baker, 35, is published in *McClure's* magazine. The series of articles will be instrumental in the fight for railroad regulation (*see* Hepburn Act, 1906).

The Wright brothers improve their flying machine of 1903 to the point where they can fly a full circle of 24.5 miles in 38 minutes, a feat they demonstrate at Dayton, Ohio. Their machine will be patented in May of next year, and they will give a series of exhibitions in the United States and Europe to popularize flying (*see* Wilbur, 1908; Orville, 1909).

Bethlehem Steel Company is founded by Charles M. Schwab who determines to build a great competitor to United States Steel Corporation (*see* 1902). Bethlehem begins as the parent company of Schwab's United States Shipbuilding Company, seven of whose nine companies are small shipbuilding firms (*see* 1907).

Bolivian store clerk Simon Ituri Patino, 43, at Cochabamba is sacked by his German employer for extending $250 in credit to a poor Portuguese miner and is forced by the store owner to pay the miner's bill. The miner leaves town and leaves Patino his mine. The store clerk recruits cocoa-drugged local Indians to work the mine's outcroppings, and the property turns out to be a fabulous deposit of tin ore that will be the basis of a $200 million fortune for Simon Patino and that will make Bolivia a rival of Malaya, Burma, and the Dutch East Indies as a world tin source. Patino's Consolidated Tin Smelters, Ltd., will be the world's largest tin smelting company.

Ingersoll-Rand Corporation is created by a merger of the Ingersoll-Sargent Company with the Rand Drill Company headed by Jasper Raymond Rand, 30, whose father started making drills and compressors in 1871.

The Carnegie Foundation for the Advancement of Teaching is founded with a $10 million gift from Andrew Carnegie (*see* Carnegie Institution, 1902; Carnegie Corporation, 1911).

The Village Press is founded at Park Ridge, Ill., by typographer-printer Frederic Goudy, 40, who designs all his own typefaces. Some will be widely used by other printers.

L. C. Smith & Brothers sells its first typewriter to the *New York Tribune* for the paper's newsroom. The Syracuse, N.Y., firm will for years be the largest producer of typewriters.

Royal Typewriter Company is founded by New York financier Thomas Fortune Ryan who puts up $220,000 to back inventors Edward B. Hess and Lewis C. Meyers (*see* Southern Railway, 1894). The Royal typewriter has innovations that include a

friction-free ball-bearing one-track rail to support the weight of the carriage as it moves back and forth, a new paper feed, a shied to keep erasure crumbs from falling into the nest of type bars, a lighter and faster type bar action, and complete visibility of words as they are typed.

The *Chicago Defender* begins publication May 5. Publisher Robert S. Abbott, 35, has the first issues printed on credit, he sells 300 copies of the 2-cent paper, but the *Defender* is the first important black newspaper and within 12 years it will be so widely read in the South that critics will credit (and blame) it for inspiring a migration of blacks to the North (the *Defender* will become a daily beginning in 1956).

The Copley newspaper chain has its beginnings as Chicago utilities magnate Ira C. Copley, 41, buys the *Aurora* (Ill.) *Beacon.* Copley has pioneered in developing coin-slot gas meters, he will soon acquire papers in Elgin, Joliet, and Springfield to further his political ambitions, he will gain election to Congress in 1910, he will buy the *San Diego Union* and *Evening Tribune* in 1928, and he will develop a powerful right-wing voice that will be carried on by an orphan Copley will adopt in 1920.

William Randolph Hearst acquires *Cosmopolitan* magazine for $400,000.

Nonfiction *The Life of Reason* (volume 1 of five volumes) by Spanish-American philosopher George Santayana (Jorge Ruis Santayana y Burrais), 42, who writes, "Those who cannot remember the past are condemned to repeat it."

Fiction *The House of Mirth* by New York novelist Edith Wharton, 43, who gains her first popularity with a fictional analysis of the stratified society she knows so well as the wife of a rich banker and of that society's reaction to change; *The Tower of London* (*Rondon-to*) and *I Am a Cat* (*Waga hai wa neko de aru*) by Japanese novelist Soseki Natsume, 38, who was graduated in English at Tokyo University in 1893, studied at London from 1900 to 1902, and in his second novel presents a witty, satirical view of the world as seen through the eyes of his cat; *Where Angels Fear to Tread* by English novelist E. M. (Edward Morgan) Forster, 26, of the Bloomsbury Group; *Kipps* by H. G. Wells; *The Lake* by George Moore; *The Four Just Men* by English novelist Edgar Wallace, 30, who gains fame with a thriller based on an antiestablishment concept; *Small Town Tyrant* (*Professor Unrat*) by German novelist Heinrich Mann, 34, who will be overshadowed by his older brother Thomas, but whose novel will be made into the 1929 film *The Blue Angel; The Jungle* by U.S. novelist Upton Beall Sinclair, 27, who has been given a $500 advance by the Socialist periodical *The Appeal to Reason.* Sinclair has lived for 7 weeks among the stockyard workers of Chicago, his Lithuanian hero Jurgis is lured by steamship company posters to emigrate and takes a job in the stockyards of "Packington," Jurgis encounters a variety of capitalistic evils, and Sinclair is hailed by novelist Jack London

1905 (cont.) who says, "What *Uncle Tom's Cabin* did for the black slaves *The Jungle* has a large chance to do for the white slaves of today" (*see* below, meatpacking).

Poetry *The Book of Hours* (*Stundenbuch*) by Austrian poet Rainer Maria Rilke, 30; *Präludien* by German poet Ernst Stadler, 22; *Cantos of Life and Hope* (*Canto de vida y esperanza*) by Nicaraguan poet Ruber Dario (Felix Rubeli Garcia Sarmiento), 38.

Painting *Boy with Pipe, Seated Harlequin with Red Background, Young Acrobat on a Ball, At the Lapin Agile, The Absinthe Drinker,* and *Family of Saltimbouques* by Pablo Picasso who arrives at Paris and begins his "pink period"; *Les Grandes Baigneuses* by Paul Cézanne; *The Hungry Lion* by Henri Rousseau; *La Noce à Nino-Patte-en-l'Air, The Couple,* and *The Dance* by French painter-engraver Georges Rouault, 34; *The Marlborough Family* by John Singer Sargent.

Les Fauves create a sensation at the Salon d'Automne in Paris with paintings that free color to speak with new and unprecedented intensity. The magnification of Impressionism is pioneered by artists who include Henri Matisse, 36, Maurice de Vlaminck, 29, and André Derain, 25, they are called "wild beasts" ("les fauves") by French critic Louis Vauxcelles, and their works include Matisse's *The Open Window, Collioure, Girl Reading,* and *La Joie de Vivre,* Vlaminck's *The Pond at Saint-Cucufa,* and Derain's *The Mountains, Collioure.*

New York's 291 Gallery at 291 Fifth Avenue is opened by local photographer Alfred Stieglitz, 41, with a group of other photographers Stieglitz calls the "photo-secessionists" (they include Luxembourg-born photographer Edward Jean Steichen, 26, who opened a studio at 291 Fifth Avenue in 1902 after 2 years of study in Europe with sculptor Auguste Rodin and others). The new gallery will show only photographs until 1908, but will then begin to give Americans their first look at work by Henri Matisse (above), Pablo Picasso, the late Henri de Toulouse-Lautrec, and others.

Sculpture *The Bather* by German sculptor Wilhelm Lehmbruck, 24.

Theater *The Well of the Saints* by John Millington Synge 2/4 at Dublin's Abbey Theatre; *Hidada* (*Hidada, oder Sein und Haben*) by Frank Wedekind 2/18 at Munich's Schauspielhaus, under the title *Karl Hetmann, the Dwarf-Giant* (*Karl Hetmann, der Zwergriese*); *Elga* by Gerhart Hauptmann 3/4 at Berlin's Lessingtheater; *Alice-Sit-by-the-Fire* by James M. Barrie 4/5 at the Duke of York's Theatre, London; *Man and Superman* (minus Act III) by George Bernard Shaw 5/23 at London's Royal Court Theatre, with Granville Barker, Edmund Gwenn; *The Dance of Death* (*Dodsdansen forsta delen and anla delen*) by August Strindberg in September at Cologne's Residenztheater; *No Mother to Guide Her* by U.S. actress-melodramatist Lillian Mortimer 9/5

at Detroit's Whitney Theater; *The Squaw Man* by Edward Milton Royle 10/23 at Wallack's Theater, New York, with William S. Hart, 722 perfs.; *Mrs. Warren's Profession* by George Bernard Shaw 10/30 at New York's Garrick Theater, with Mary Shaw, Arnold Daly (who are prosecuted for performing in an "immoral" play), 14 perfs. (London's Lord Chamberlain has refused to license the play about a woman whose income is derived from houses of prostitution. London will not see a production until 1926.) *The Girl of the Golden West* by David Belasco 11/14 at New York's Belasco Theater, with Blanche Bates, 224 perfs.; *Major Barbara* by George Bernard Shaw 11/28 at London's Royal Court Theater, with Annie Russell, Granville Barker, Louis Calvert, in a "discussion in three acts" about a Salvation Army officer. Shaw wrote a letter to a Dublin newspaper at age 18 after hearing U.S. evangelists Dwight Moody and Ira Sankey, he signed the letter "S," and he said that if this sort of thing was religion then he, on the whole, was an atheist.

Harvard's 47 Workshop opens under the direction of English professor George Pierce Baker, 39, who gives a course in practical playwrighting at Radcliffe that he will begin teaching next year at Harvard under the title English 47. Dramatic works by Baker's students will be produced at the workshop, Baker will teach at Harvard until 1924, thereafter he will teach at Yale, and his students will include Eugene O'Neill, Sidney Howard, and George Abbott.

Variety begins publication at New York under the direction of former *Morning Telegraph* editor Sime Silverman, 32. He will turn his weekly show business newspaper into a daily published at Hollywood, Calif., in September of 1933, but will die 3 weeks later (*see* 1935).

Film Cecil Hepworth's *Rescued by Rover.*

Opera *Salome* 12/9 at Dresden's Hofoper, with music by Richard Strauss, libretto based on the 1896 play by the late Oscar Wilde. Soprano Marie Wittich had originally refused to sing the title role's sensuous song to the imprisoned John the Baptist praising his body, his hair, his mouth, saying, "I won't do it, I'm a decent woman." After the opera's first performance at New York's Metropolitan Opera House January 22, 1907, J. P. Morgan will forbid further performances and *Salome* will not be revived at the Met until 1934; *The Merry Widow* (*Die lustige Witwe*) 12/28 at Vienna's Theater-an-der-Wien, with music by Franz Lehar, libretto by Victor Leon and Leo Stein. By 1910 the opera will have had 18,000 performances in 10 different languages.

First performances *Pélleas and Mélissande* (Symphonic Poem) by Arnold Schoenberg 1/26 at Vienna; Introduction and Allegro in G minor for Strings by Edward Elgar 3/8 at the Queen's Hall, London; *The Divine Poem* Symphony No. 3 in C minor by Aleksandr Skriabin 5/29 at the Théâtre du Châtelet, Paris. (Skriabin has deserted his wife and four chi dren in Russia to live openly with his pretty mistress Tatyana Schloezer in Switzerland. She believes in his messianic visions of transforming the world through music and will bear him three children.) *La Mer* (tone poem) by Claude Debussy 10/15 at Paris; Symphony No. 5 in C sharp minor by Gustav Mahler 10/18 at Paris.

Isadora Duncan opens a dancing school for children at Berlin. The 27-year-old U.S. dancer, who gives birth to a child out of wedlock, has developed a spontaneous style that tries to symbolize music, poetry, and elements of nature.

March "Die Parade der Zinnsoldaten" by German composer Leon Jessel, 34, whose work will be called "Parade of the Wooden Soldiers" in English.

"Claire de Lune" by Claude Debussy is published as part of a suite for piano.

New York's Juilliard School of Music has its beginnings in the Institute of Musical Art founded by Frank Damrosch and James Loeb (*see* 1920).

Broadway musicals *Fontana* 1/14 at the Lyric Theater, with Douglas Fairbanks, 21, in a minor role, music by Raymond Hubbell, book by S. S. Shubert and Robert B. Smith, lyrics by Smith, 298 perfs., *Mlle. Modiste* 12/25 at the Knickerbocker Theater, with Fritzi Scheff, music by Victor Herbert, book and lyrics by Henry Blossom, songs that include "Kiss Me Again" and "I Want What I Want When I Want It," 262 perfs.

Popular Songs "Wait Till the Sun Shines, Nellie," by New York Tin Pan Alley composer Albert von Tilzer, 27, lyrics by Andrew B. Sterling; "What You Goin' to Do When the Rent Comes Round?—Rufus Rastus Johnson Brown" by Harry von Tilzer, lyrics by Andrew B. Sterling; "My Gal Sal" (or "They Called Her Frivolous Sal") by Paul Dresser; "In My Merry Oldsmobile" by Gus Edwards, 26, lyrics by Vincent Bryan, 22; "I Don't Care" by Harry O. Sutton, lyrics by Jean Lewis, that will be popularized by vaudeville star Eva Tanguy; "In the Shade of the Old Apple Tree" by Egbert Van Alstyne, lyrics by Henry Williams (both are song pluggers for the publishing house Remick); "Will You Love Me in December as You Do in May?" by Ernest R. Ball, lyrics by New York law student James J. Walker, 24.

Ty Cobb signs with the Detroit Tigers to begin an outstanding baseball career. Outfielder Tyrus Raymond Cobb, 18, has been nicknamed "the Georgia Peach" by sportswriter Grantland Rice for his prowess with the Augusta team of the South Atlantic League, he will play 22 seasons for Detroit and two more for the Philadelphia Athletics before retiring in 1928, he will have a lifetime batting average of .367 with a record 4,191 hits, he will score a record 2,244 runs, he will play a record number of 3,033 games, he will bat above .300 for a record 23 games, and he will steal a record 829 bases.

The New York Giants win the World Series by defeating the Philadelphia Athletics 4 games to 1.

The University of Michigan Wolverines coached by Fielding Harris "Hurry Up" Yost end a 5-year streak of 27 games in which the team has lost only once, has been tied once, and has run up 2,821 points against 42 for the opposition.

U.S. "boy wonder" billiard player Willie Hoppe, 18, wins his first world championship after 10 years of barnstorming the country with pool and billiard exhibitions. William Frederick Hoppe won the Young Masters 18.2 balkline championship at 16 and will win the world's 18.1 title next year at Paris and the world's 18.2 title the following year. By the time he retires in October 1952, Hoppe will have won 51 world billiard titles.

Palmolive Soap is introduced by Milwaukee's 42-year-old B. W. Johnson Soap Company whose Caleb Johnson has bought a new soap milling machine he saw at the St. Louis Exposition last year. The toilet soap is made from a formula that includes some hydrogenated palm and olive oils, using the hydrogenation process invented by England's William Normann in 1901, it will be advertised with the slogan "Keep that Schoolgirl Complexion," and the Johnson Company will be reincorporated in 1917 under the name The Palmolive Company (*see* Palmolive building, Colgate-Palmolive, 1928).

Commercial rayon production begins in July at an English factory built on the outskirts of Coventry by Samuel Courtauld, 29, who has bought English rights to the Stearn patent of 1898 for £25,000. French and German companies have bought foreign rights and begin production in competition with Courtauld (*see* Little, 1902; Viscose Company, 1910).

Washington's Garfinckel specialty store chain has its beginnings in a shop opened by merchant Julius Garfinckel.

Sigmund Freud in Vienna fathered psychosomatic medicine, but his emphasis on sex antagonized opponents.

1905 (cont.) The first Spiegel mail-order catalog offers furniture at terms as low as 75 cents down and 50 cents per month. Started just before the Civil War, the Chicago furniture store will give up its retail store and will broaden its catalog offerings to include apparel and general merchandise as it builds a business whose sales will peak at $24 million in 1929.

The Cullinan Diamond found in South Africa weighs 3,106 carats—the largest gem-quality diamond ever discovered. It will be cut into stones for the British Crown jewels and for the collection of the British royal family.

New York's Tiffany & Co. sells a pearl necklace for $1 million. It is the largest single sale in the store's 68-year history, and it will not be surpassed for at least 72 years (see 1906).

 New York's DeLamar Mansion on Madison Avenue at 37th Street is completed in Beaux Arts Parisian townhouse style by architect C. P. H. Gilbert.

New York's Fraunces Tavern of 1763 is rebuilt almost from scratch by architect William Mersereau with a museum upstairs.

New York's Gotham Hotel opens October 2 in West 55th Street. Designed by H. Hobard Weekes, the 20-story 400-room Gotham is a near-mate to the ornate St. Regis Hotel that opened last year across Fifth Avenue.

A new Statler Hotel opens at Buffalo, N.Y., to replace the temporary Outside Inn put up by E. M. Statler for the Pan American Exposition of 1901. Statler advertises "a room and a bath for a dollar and a half," and he will develop a chain of Statler Hotels—Boston and Cleveland in 1912, Detroit in 1915, St. Louis in 1918, and other cities (see New York's Hotel Pennsylvania, 1922; Hilton, 1954).

Cleveland's Shaker Heights suburb has its beginnings in a 1,400-acre tract of land owned by the Shaker church east of the city. Real estate developers Oris Paxton Van Sweringen, 26, and his brother Mantis, 24, have secured parcels of land in the tract, they borrow heavily to acquire a total of 4,000 acres, they will develop it into a model suburban community with winding roadways, round artificial lakes, and with restrictive covenants to control architecture, but their investment will not pay off until they persuade the Cleveland Street Railways Company to extend a line to Shaker Heights by offering to pay 5 years' interest on the cost of laying tracks (see Nickel Plate Railroad, 1916).

President Roosevelt creates a Bureau of Forestry in the U.S. Department of Agriculture February 1 with Gifford Pinchot as chief forester (see 1902). Congress passes a bill transferring U.S. forest reserves from the Department of the Interior to the USDA, and the reserves are soon designated National Forests as Pinchot works to make the Forest Service a defender of the public lands against private interests (see "conservation," 1907).

The Wichita Mountains Refuge for big game is established by President Roosevelt in Oklahoma Territory.

The National Audubon Society is founded (see Grinnell, 1885).

Water from the Colorado River has been diverted to California by sluice gates built since 1900 and is creating the Salton Sea (see Laguna Dam, 1909).

 Plant hybridization methods pioneered by Luther Burbank in 1875 are studied by U.S. botanist George Harrison Shull, 31, who journeys to Santa Rosa, Calif., on a grant from the Carnegie Institution established 3 years ago (see 1921).

More than 17 million acres of California's vast Sacramento valley are owned by 100 men while in the San Joaquin valley many individuals own tracts of 100,000 acres and more.

Roughly 12 acres of farmland are cultivated for every American. The number will fall rapidly as the population increases and as land is made more productive.

 Vitamin research is pioneered at the University of Utrecht where Dutch nutritionist C. A. Pekelharing finds that mice die on a seemingly ample diet but survive when their diet includes a few drops of milk. Pekelharing concludes that "unrecognized substances" must exist in food (see 1906).

Iodine compounds are found useful in treating goiter by Cleveland physician David Marine, 25, who has moved West from Baltimore and who has been struck by the fact that every dog in town—and many of the people—have goiters. Marine begins a campaign for the iodization of table salt (see Baumann, 1896; Kendall, 1915).

 A bill that would require patent medicine bottles to carry labels showing their ingredients is rejected by the Massachusetts House of Representatives. The $100 million-a-year patent medicine industry spends some $40 million a year in advertising, and newspapers lobby against legislation that would hinder sales of "cancer cures" and other nostrums, many of which contain cocaine, morphine, and up to 40 percent alcohol. The Proprietary Association of America has devised advertising contracts that will be canceled if legislation hostile to patent medicines is enacted, and the newspapers' conflict of interest is exposed by journalist Mark Sullivan, 31, in the November 4 issue of *Collier's* (see Pure Food and Drug Act, 1906).

U.S. meatpacking conditions are exposed by Upton Sinclair in *The Jungle* (above). The 308-page best seller has eight pages devoted to such matters as casual meat inspection, lamb and mutton that is really goatmeat, deviled ham that is really red-dyed minced tripe, sausage that contains rats killed by poisoned bread, and lard that sometimes contains the remains of employees who have fallen into the boiling vats. Sinclair's book makes many Americans turn vegetarian, sales of meat products fall off, and Congress is aroused (see Meat Inspection Act, 1906).

Articles on the Beef Trust by Charles E. Russell are published in *Everybody's* magazine.

Dissolution of the Beef Trust is ordered January 20 by the Supreme Court in *Swift v. United States,* but the court order will merely change the form of the Trust.

Holly Sugar Corporation has its beginnings in a beet sugar refinery at Holly, Colo. The company will become the largest U.S. independent processor of sugarbeets with nine factories scattered through Colorado, Wyoming, Montana, Texas, and California.

Some 41 million cases of canned foods are packed in the United States. The figure will rise in the next 25 years to 200 million (*see* 1935).

The Joseph Campbell Preserve Company is renamed the Joseph Campbell Company and advertises in *Good Housekeeping* magazine: "21 Kinds of Campbell's Soups—16 million cans sold in 1904" (*see* 1904; Franco-American, 1915).

Heinz Baked Beans are test marketed in the north of England by Pittsburgh's H. J. Heinz Co. which is incorporated this year. British working class wives are advised by advertising that baked beans make a nourishing meal for men returning from work (Heinz beans will be canned at Harlesden beginning in 1928, and baked beans will be consumed in Britain at twice the U.S. rate per capita).

Anchor Hocking Glass has its beginnings in the Hocking Glass Company founded by former Ohio Flint Glass Company decorator Isaac Jacob Collins, 30, who will merge his firm with the Anchor Cap Co. in 1937 to create Anchor Hocking Corporation.

Royal Crown Cola has its beginnings at Columbus, Ga., where local grocery wholesaler Claude A. Hatcher starts bottling soft drinks under the name Royal Crown. The Union Bottling Works will soon be organized by Hatcher Grocery (*see* 1912).

Nebraska's 10-year-old Beatrice Creamery Company acquires large creamery companies at Topeka, St. Louis, and Denver. Continental Creamery at Topeka has rights to the name Meadow Gold Butter and exclusive creamery rights to National Biscuit Company's In-er-seal package developed by the Peters Machinery Company (*see* 1928).

Nestlé merges with its major competitor Anglo-Swiss Condensed Milk Company (*see* 1866; 1918; Swiss General Chocolate, 1904).

Ovomaltine is introduced by Swiss entrepreneur Albert Wander and will be called Ovaltine in the English-speaking countries (*see* 1863). Made of malt extract, evaporated milk, powdered eggs, and cocoa powder, the beverage powder will be prescribed by physicians whose patients are convalescing or suffering from wasting disease. (The Wander Company of North America will erect an Ovaltine Food Products Plant at Villa Park, Ill., in 1917).

The New York pizzeria opened on Spring Street in 1895 is acquired by an Italian-American restaurateur for $200 (*see* 1953).

Louis Sherry's 7-year-old Fifth Avenue, New York, restaurant is the scene of a ball given by Equitable Life Assurance Society heir James Hazen Hyde who denies reports that the ball cost $100,000 (he says it cost only $20,000).

1906 The San Francisco earthquake April 18 is the worst ever to hit an American city. The tremor of the San Andreas fault at 5:13 A.M. and its ensuing 3-day fire destroy two-thirds of the city, kill at least 452, leave 250,000 homeless, and destroy property estimated at more than $400 million in value.

Congress appropriates $2.5 million for relief aid and New York bankers loan hundreds of millions to rebuild the city (*see* 1907).

San Francisco banker A. P. (Amadeo Peter) Giannini, 35, manages to rescue the gold and securities in his vault. Giannini built his stepfather's wholesale produce business into the largest in the city, he sold out his share in 1901, he founded his Bank of Italy in 1904, he has been making loans to small farmers and businessmen, he has defied banking orthodoxy by actively soliciting customers, and he is the only banker in town with enough capital to make loans for rebuilding. Giannini's reliance on gold reserves will enable him to survive the financial panic next year (*see* Bank of America, 1928).

J. P. Morgan and steel magnate John W. Gates purchase Tennessee Coal & Iron Co. (*see* 1898; 1907).

E. I. du Pont de Nemours has bought up or has otherwise absorbed the other members of the 34-year-old Gunpowder Trade Association (the Powder Trust) and has a near-monopoly in the U.S. powder industry. Du Pont produces 100 percent of the privately made smokeless powder and from 60 to 70 percent of five other kinds of explosives (*see* 1902; 1912).

 Denmark's Christian IX dies January 29 at age 87 after a 42-year reign and is succeeded by his 62-year-old son who will reign until 1912 as Frederick VIII.

The British battleship H.M.S. *Dreadnought* launched February 10 has ten 12-inch guns and is the first battleship whose guns are all so large. Berlin decides in May to increase tonnages of German battleships, to add six cruisers to the fleet, and to widen the Kiel Canal to permit passage of larger ships.

The British foreign secretary Sir Edward Grey, 44, assumes a "moral obligation" to support France in the event of a German attack, but the Cabinet will not learn of his pledge to the French until 1911.

London forces the Ottoman Turks to cede the Sinai Peninsula to Egypt.

The sultan of Morocco accepts French and Spanish control of reforms in his country following the Al-

1906 (cont.) geciras Conference at which France and Spain have agreed to reaffirm Morocco's independence and integrity. The country will nevertheless be the scene of international crises for years to come.

A Tripartite Pact July 4 declares the independence of Ethiopia but divides the country into British, French, and Italian spheres of influence.

The All-India Moslem League is founded by the 29-year-old Aga Khan III (Aga sultan Sir Mahomed Shah).

Japanese authorities expose and abort an anarchist plot to assassinate the emperor.

A world diplomatic conference revises the Geneva Convention of 1864.

 The third law of thermodynamics formulated by German chemist Walter Herman Nernst, 42, states that specific heats at the absolute zero of temperature (minus 273.12°C) become zero themselves. Nernst's discovery will make it possible to calculate the actual values of constants that characterize chemical reactions (*see* Haber, 1908).

Psychology of Dementia Praecox by Swiss psychologist Carl Gustav Jung, 31, breaks new ground. Jung meets Sigmund Freud for the first time and has doubts as to the sexual aspects of Freud's theory of psychoanalysis (*see* 1895; 1898; 1908).

The Wasserman test developed by German physician August Wasserman, 40, and (independently) by Hungarian physician Lazlo Detre is a specific blood test for syphilis (*see* Ehrlich, 1909).

The word "allergy" coined by Austrian pediatrician Clemens von Pirquet, 32, begins to replace the word "anaphylaxis" introduced a few years ago.

Rocky Mountain spotted fever is shown to be transmitted by the bite of a cattle tick. U.S. pathologist Howard Taylor Ricketts, 35, makes the discovery; the toxin spread by ticks will be called *Rickettsia*.

 Brownsville, Tex., has a race riot following an August 13 incident in which the town of 7,000 has allegedly been shot up by a few blacks from a crack all-black infantry batallion stationed on the outskirts of Brownsville 19 days earlier. One resident has reportedly been killed and a woman raped, the townspeople make reprisals, the truth of the situation will never be established, but President Roosevelt orders November 6 that three companies of black troops be given dishonorable discharges.

A Living Wage by U.S. Roman Catholic clergyman John A. Ryan condemns any wage system that is unable to provide workers with basic comforts, security, and recreation.

Mother Earth is founded by Lithuanian-American anarchist Emma Goldman, 37, and Alexander Berkman who has just been released from prison after having served time for an attempt on the life of Henry Clay Frick in the Homestead Strike of 1892. The anarchist journal will be suppressed in 1917 and its editors imprisoned (*see* 1919).

The term "suffragettes" is coined by a *London Daily Mail* writer for women such as Emmeline Pankhurst and her daughters Christabel, 26, and Sylvia, 24, who campaign for woman suffrage (*see* 1905). London barrister Frederick Pethick-Lawrence, 35, and his wife Emmeline, 39, support the Pankhursts (*see* 1913).

France's Captain Dreyfus is restored to rank following vindication of his case and is given the decoration of the Légion d'Honeur (*see* 1898). Now 47, Dreyfus will live until 1935.

The American Jewish Committee is founded by U.S. Jews, mostly of German descent, to protect the civil and religious rights of Jews and to fight prejudice.

San Francisco's board of education orders segregation of Oriental children in city schools 6 months after the earthquake (above). The Japanese ambassador registers an emphatic protest October 25, and the order is rescinded (*see* Hayashi, 1907).

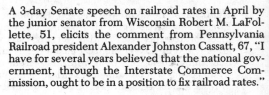 A 3-day Senate speech on railroad rates in April by the junior senator from Wisconsin Robert M. LaFollette, 51, elicits the comment from Pennsylvania Railroad president Alexander Johnston Cassatt, 67, "I have for several years believed that the national government, through the Interstate Commerce Commission, ought to be in a position to fix railroad rates."

The Hepburn Act passed by Congress June 29 extends the jurisdiction of the Interstate Commerce Commission established in 1887 and gives the ICC powers to fix railroad rates (*see* Elkins Act, 1903).

Excavation of the Panama Canal is begun by the U.S. War Department (*see* 1903; 1914; Gorgas, 1904).

The first Grand Prix motorcar race is organized by the Automobile Club de France which announced after last year's Gordon Bennett Cup race that it would take no further part in races which required that every part of a competing vehicle be made in the country represented by that vehicle. The 2-day 1,248-kilometer race pits 23 French cars against six Italian and three German cars, and it is won by a Renault with Michelin detachable rims that can be removed by unscrewing eight nuts.

Rolls-Royce, Ltd., is incorporated March 16 by English balloonist and motoring enthusiast Charles Stewart Rolls, 29, son of Lord Llangattock, and automaker Frederick Henry Royce, 43, who has produced an almost silent-running motorcar with a six-cylinder engine that produces from 40 to 50 horsepower. C. S. Rolls and Co. has sold F. H. Royce and Company motorcars on an exclusive basis for nearly 2 years, the new firm will move from Manchester to Derby in 1908, and it will discontinue all previous models to concentrate on the Silver Ghost, a machine that has been driven "14,371 miles nonstop," has proved that a gasoline-powered car can run as smoothly as a steam-driven car, and will remain in production for 19 years during which Rolls-

Royce, Ltd., develops a reputation for making the world's most luxurious motorcars.

Lagonda Motor Co., Ltd., is founded at Staines, Middlesex, by Ohio-born English entrepreneur Wilbur Gunn, who has won the London-Edinburgh motorcycle trial and who will make a fortune supplying motorcars to the Russian nobility. Lagonda is the French form of the Indian name for Buck Creek, the stream near Gunn's hometown Springfield, Ohio.

The Autocar Company of Ardmore, Pa., improves its 1897 model by adding acetylene headlights and kerosene side lamps, but like most cars the new model still has a steering rudder not a steering wheel.

The Chadwick Six built by L. S. Chadwick runs more smoothly than any four-cylinder motorcar and will have a major influence on U.S. automakers (*see* 1903). Chadwick will quit making four-cylinder cars, he will incorporate the Chadwick Engineering Works at Pottstown, Pa., in March of next year, he will road-test the first production model Chadwick Six in late April, and he will sell it at $5,500. Chadwick will quit the company in 1911 to join the Perfection Stove Company, and he will later head that firm, but Chadwick motorcars will remain in production until 1915.

W. C. Durant's Buick Company produces 2,295 motorcars, up from no more than 28 in 1904 (*see* 1905; General Motors, 1908).

The *North American Review* reports that more Americans have been killed by motorcars in 5 months than died in the Spanish-American War.

Princeton University president (Thomas) Woodrow Wilson, 49, says of the motorcar, "Nothing has spread socialistic feeling in this country more than the use of the automobile. To the countryman, they are a picture of the arrogance of wealth, with all its independence and carelessness" (but *see* 1909).

The Mack truck is introduced by former Brooklyn, N.Y., wagonbuilders John, William, and Augustus Mack who have moved to Allentown, Pa., and have produced a 10-ton vehicle of considerable power that begins a reputation for "built like a Mack truck" bulldog stamina.

Kennecott Copper Company has its beginnings in an Alaskan mine. The spread of electricity and of telephone communications continues to boost demand for copper wire.

Chicago's Union Carbide Company has been discouraged in its promotion of acetylene lighting by the spread of electric lighting, but the firm buys a metals research laboratory and acquires the ferrochrome alloy business developed by James Morehead and Guillaume de Chalmot in 1897 (*see* 1898; 1911).

The first silicon steel for electrical use to be made in America is produced by American Rolling Mills whose boss George Verity has adopted a process invented by Britain's Robert Hadfield of 1882 manganese steel fame and promoted by George Westinghouse (*see* Verity, 1899).

Weirton Steel Company has its beginnings in a West Virginia tinplate mill acquired by former U.S. Steel plant manager Ernest Tener Weir, 30, who will make Weirton a major independent plate producer (*see* National Steel, 1929).

The University of California opens a Davis campus.

Western Kentucky University is founded at Bowling Green.

Eastern Kentucky University is founded at Richmond.

"The men with the muckrakes are often indispensable to the well-being of society," says President Roosevelt April 14 in an address to the Gridiron Club at Washington, D.C., "but only if they know when to stop raking the muck and to look upward . . . to the crown of worthy endeavor." Roosevelt has in mind John Bunyan's reference in *Pilgrim's Progress* (1684) to "a man who could look no way but downwards, with a muckrake in his hand," and he has in mind also such magazines as *McClure's* (1902, 1905) and books such as *The Pit* (1903) and *The Jungle* (1905).

The *American Magazine* begins publication at New York where "muckrakers" Lincoln Steffens, Ida Tarbell, Ray Stannard Baker, and others acquire the 30-year-old *Frank Leslie's Popular Monthly*, change its name, and start a periodical that will continue for 50 years (*see* Crowell, 1911).

Crowell Publishing Company of Springfield, Ohio, is acquired by New York's American Lithographic Company whose boss Joseph Fairchild Knapp, 42, pays $750,000 to buy the *Women's Home Companion* and *Farm & Fireside* which Knapp will retitle *Country Home* (*see* 1897; 1911).

International News Service (INS) is founded by William Randolph Hearst whose wire service will compete with the AP founded in 1848 (*see* Brisbane, 1897; United Press, 1907).

A three-electrode vacuum tube amplifier that will be the basis of an electronics revolution is developed by U.S. inventor Lee De Forest, 33, whose Audion will permit the development of radio. De Forest will broadcast the voice of operatic tenor Enrico Caruso in 1910 (*see* 1916; Tesla, 1888; Fleming, 1904).

The International Radio Telegraph convention at Berlin adopts the distress call SOS to replace the CQD (Stop Sending and Listen) call adopted 2 years ago by Marconi International Communications and agrees to drop the CQD call completely after 1912.

The first radio broadcast of voice and music booms out of Brant Rock, Mass., Christmas Eve and is picked up by ships within a radius of several hundred miles. Canadian-American engineer Reginald Aubrey Fessenden, 40, patented a high-frequency alternator in 1901 that generates a continuous wave

1906 (cont.) instead of the intermittent damped-spark impulses now being used for transmission of wireless signals, he organized the National Electric Signalling Corporation in 1902 to sponsor his experiments, he has engaged Swedish-American electrical engineer Ernst Frederik Werner Alexanderson, 28, to build a large 80-kilohertz alternator for the station he has set up at Brant Rock, his equipment features a receiver circuit of his own invention that blends an incoming radiofrequency signal with another, slightly different, signal produced locally to yield a beat frequency in the audible range, and this heterodyne circuit will be generally adopted in radio broadcasting (*see* Armstrong's superheterodyne, 1917; RCA, 1919).

Nonfiction *The Education of Henry Adams* by Henry Brooks Adams, now 68, whose classic autobiographical work, privately printed, will be published in 1918 to acquaint the world with his dynamic theory of history; *The Devil's Dictionary* by Ambrose Bierce, now 64, who is the Hearst correspondent at Washington, D.C.: "Admiration: our polite recognition of another's resemblance of ourselves"; "Bore: a person who talks when you wish him to listen"; "Cynic: a blackguard whose faulty vision sees things as they are, not as they ought to be"; "Destiny: a tyrant's authority for crime and a fool's excuse for failure"; "Epitaph: an inscription on a tomb, showing that virtues acquired by death have a strong retroactive effect"; "Edible: good to eat, and wholesome to digest, as a worm to a toad, a toad to a snake, a snake to a pig, a pig to a man, and a man to a worm"; "Once: enough"; "Politics: the conduct of public affairs for private advantage."

Fiction *The City of the Yellow Devil* (*Gorod Zholtogo D'yavola*) by Maksim Gorki who was imprisoned last year for his revolutionary activity but who has had his sentence commuted to exile at the intervention of Western writers. Gorki has come to America to collect funds for the Bolshevik cause, he has been ostracized since the revelation that his traveling companion is not his wife, and his novel is an attack on the American way of life; *The Man of Property* by English novelist John Galsworthy, 39, who introduces readers to Soames Forsyte and begins *The Forsyte Saga* that he will continue until 1922; *Young Torless* (*Die Verwirrungen des Zöglings Torless*) by Austrian novelist Robert Musil, 25; *Puck of Pook's Hill* by Rudyard Kipling who will win next year's Nobel prize for literature; *Broken Commandment* (*Hakai*) by Japanese novelist Shimazaki Toson (Shimazaki Haruki), 34, whose autobiographical work breaks his father's commandment not to reveal that he and his family are members of Japan's outcast *eta* group (*see* 1871); *With Grass for Pillow* (*Kusamakura*) by Soseki Natsume; *Little Boy* (*Bocchan*) by Soseki Natsume who makes use of his experience as a schoolteacher in the 1890s; *The Four Million* (stories) by O. Henry who gains renown for "The Furnished Room" and "The Gift of the Magi"; *White Fang* by Jack London.

Poetry *Poems* by English poet Siegfried Sassoon, 20; "The Highwayman" by English poet Alfred Noyes, 26: "The wind was a torrent of darkness among the gusty trees,/ The moon was a ghostly galleon tossed upon cloudy seas,/ The road was a ribbon of moonlight over the purple moor,/ And the highwayman came riding, up to the old inn-door"; *Partage de midi* by French poet Paul Claudel, 38.

Painting *Portrait of Gertrude Stein, Two Nudes, Self-Portrait with a Palette, The Organ Grinder, The Flower Vendors, Boy Leading a Horse* by Pablo Picasso; *The Red Trees* by Maurice Vlaminck; *Westminster Bridge, The Houses of Parliament, Port of London* by André Derain; *Street Decked Out with Flags at Le Havre* by Raoul Dufy; *At the Theater* and *Tragedian* by Georges Rouault; *The Way Down to the Sea* by English painter Augustus (Edwin) John, 27; *Coltaltepetl* by Mexican painter Diego Rivera, 20. Paul Cézanne dies of diabetes at Aix-en-Provence October 22 at age 67.

Sculpture *Chained Action* by Aristide Maillol.

Theater *And Pippa Passes* (*Und Pippa tanzt!*) by Gerhart Hauptmann 1/19 at Berlin's Lessingtheater; *The Marquis of Bradomin* (*El marques de Bradomin*) by Ramon Maria del Valle Inclan 1/25 at Madrid's Teatro de la Primera; *Captain Brassbound's Conversion* by George Bernard Shaw 3/20 at London's Royal Court Theatre, with Frederick Kerr, Edmund Gwenn; *Caesar and Cleopatra* by George Bernard Shaw 3/31 at Berlin (in German), 10/31 at New York's New Amsterdam Theater, with Forbes Robertson, Gertrude Elliott, 49 perfs.; *The Silver Box* by John Galsworthy 9/25 at London's Royal Court Theatre; *The Great Divide* by U.S. playwright William Vaughan Moody, 37, 10/3 at New York's Princess Theater with Henry Miller, 238 perfs.; *The New York Idea* by U.S. playwright Langdon Elwyn Mitchell (John Philip Varley), 44, 11/18 at New York's Lyric Theater, with Mrs. Fiske, George Arliss; *The Doctor's Dilemma* by George Bernard Shaw 11/20 at London's Royal Court Theatre, with William Farren, Jr., Granville Barker; *Brewster's Millions* by U.S. playwrights Winchell Smith, 35, and Byron Ongley (who have adapted the George Barr McCutcheon novel of 1902) 12/31 at New York's New Amsterdam Theater, with a cast that includes "George Spelvin," a name Smith has invented to designate a player who doubles in another role.

First performances *Jour d'été à la montagna* by Vincent d'Indy 2/18 at Paris; Symphony No. 6 by Gustav Mahler 5/27 at Essen.

Opera *Quattro Rusteghi* (*The School for Fathers*) 3/19 at Munich, with music by Ermanno Wolf-Ferrari; *The Wreckers* (*Standrecht*) 11/11 at Leipzig, with music by English composer Dame Ethel Smyth.

The Victrola is introduced by the Victor Talking Machine Company whose Eldridge Johnson has enclosed the gramophone horn in a cabinet (*see* "His

Master's Voice," 1900). Johnson signed up operatic tenor Enrico Caruso in 1901, and he makes recordings by having Caruso sing directly into a horn while solo instrumentalists play into other horns (*see* 1922).

Broadway musicals *Forty-Five Minutes from Broadway* 1/1 at the New Amsterdam Theater, with songs by George M. Cohan that include "Mary's a Grand Old Name" and the title song, 90 perfs.; *George Washington, Jr.* 2/12 at the Knickerbocker Theater, with George M. Cohan, songs by Cohan that include *"You're a Grand Old Flag,"* 81 perfs.; *His Honor the Mayor* 5/28 at the New York Theater, with songs that include "Waltz Me Around Again, Willie (Around, Around, Around)," by Ren Shields, lyrics by Will D. Cobb, 30, 104 perfs.; *The Red Mill* 9/24 at the Knickerbocker Theater, with music by Victor Herbert, book and lyrics by Henry Blossom, songs that include "Every Day Is Ladies Day with Me," 274 perfs.

Popular songs "China Town, My China Town" by Jean Schwartz, lyrics by William Jerome; "School-Days" by Will D. Cobb, lyrics by Gus Edwards; "Anchors Aweigh" (march and two-step) by U.S. Naval Academy musical director Charles A. Zimmerman, 45, and midshipman Alfred H. Miles, 23.

French singer Maurice Chevalier, 18, tours the provinces, develops a unique insinuating style, returns in triumph to Paris with an incandescent smile, appears at the Folies Bergère, begins a 10-year romance with the popular dancer-actress "Mistinguett" (Jeannes Marie Bourgeois, 34), and is launched on a 60-year show business career.

The National Collegiate Athletic Association (NCAA) is founded January 12 after a 1905 season that saw 18 American boys killed playing football and 154 seriously injured. President Roosevelt has called representatives of Harvard, Yale, and Princeton to the White House and has held a meeting to find ways to stop the growing roughness of football, a game still played with little protective gear, but in 1909 33 boys will die playing football and 246 will sustain major injuries as the sport grows in popularity (*see* 1939).

The forward pass is legalized in football (*see* 1913).

University of Chicago quarterback Walter H. Eckersall winds up his college football career after 3 years of brilliant play for coach Alonzo Stagg.

Canadian prizefighter Tommy Burns wins the world heavyweight championship February 23 by defeating Marvin Hart in a 20-round match at Los Angeles.

The first Newport-Bermuda yacht race is held over a 635-mile course to begin an ocean sailing competition that will continue for more than 70 years.

"Tinker-to-Evers-to-Chance" becomes a sportswriter catchphrase to denote efficient teamwork. Chicago Cubs shortstop Joe Tinker, 26, second baseman Johnny Evers, 27, and first baseman Frank Chance, 29, give the club an airtight infield that en-ables the Cubs to win 116 games, lose only 36, and take the National League pennant.

The Chicago White Sox win the World Series by defeating the Cubs (above) 4 games to 2.

The world's first ski course is laid out at Zürs by Vorarlberg skier Viktor Sohm whose pupils include Hannes Schneider, 16.

The permanent wave introduced by London hairdresser Charles Nestle takes 8 to 12 hours and costs $1,000. Only 18 women avail themselves of Nestle's service, but by the time the permanent wave is introduced in the United States in 1915, it will be much cheaper and will take far less time (*see* Buzzacchini, 1926; Nestle Colorinse, 1929).

Lux Flakes are introduced by England's Lever Brothers for chiffons and other fine fabrics (*see* Lifebuoy, 1897; Rinso, 1918; Lux Toilet Form, 1925).

General Cigar Company is created through a joint venture funded by Chicago's Sears, Roebuck and New York financier Henry Goldman of the 37-year-old firm Goldman, Sachs. General Cigar will gain wide distribution for its Robert Burns, William Penn, Shakespeare, Van Dyck, and White Owl brands.

New York architect Stanford White, now 52, is shot dead June 25 at the roof garden restaurant atop Madison Square Garden, which he designed in 1889. His murderer is Pittsburgh millionaire Harry K. Thaw whose wife Evelyn Nesbit Thaw was a chorus girl and was White's mistress before her marriage. Thaw will win acquittal on an insanity plea.

The murder of Cortland, N.Y., factory girl Grace Brown, 19, makes world headlines in July. A capsized rowboat found in Big Moose Lake in the Adirondacks the morning of July 13 leads to a search, a 13-year-old boy spots a young woman's body in 8 feet of water early in the afternoon, police arrest 22-year-old Chester Gillett at a nearby resort July 14, and they charge him with murder. Raised by missionary parents at Kansas City, young Gillett took a job last year as foreman at his uncle's shirtwaist factory in Cortland, where the employees included Grace Brown, daughter of a local farmer. Pregnant by Gillett, Brown wrote him pitiful letters begging him to marry her and finally threatening to go to his family with her story. Gillett has ambitions to marry a society girl he has met, he wrote to Brown asking her to travel with him to the Adirondacks, where he said he would marry her. He signed the register at the Glenmore Hotel "Carl Graham and wife of Albany" upon his arrival by train the morning of July 12, and he took Brown out on the lake that afternoon in a hired rowboat. Gillett will be executed next year at Auburn prison (*see* novel *An American Tragedy,* 1925).

San Francisco's Emporium saves its facade in Market Street from the fire (above) and is soon able to restock and resume trade (*see* 1896; H. C. Capwell, 1927).

The Call–Chronicle–Examiner

SAN FRANCISCO, THURSDAY, APRIL 19, 1906.

EARTHQUAKE AND FIRE: SAN FRANCISCO IN RUINS

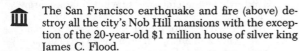

San Francisco shook and burned, more than 450 died, property losses exceeded $400 million.

The fire destroys San Francisco's leading fashion store I. Magnin, but the store reopens in 3 months on Van Ness Avenue (*see* 1876; 1909).

New York's B. Altman & Co. moves from its Sixth Avenue and 18th Street premises of 1865 to Fifth Avenue at 34th Street where the department store will cover a full city block by 1914. Altman will die in 1913 and will bequeath his $20 million collection of paintings by Botticelli, Filippo Lippi, Holbein, and Rembrandt to the Metropolitan Museum of Art along with his Chinese enamels and porcelains.

New York's Tiffany & Co. moves into a new building at Fifth Avenue and 37th Street where it will remain until it moves to 57th Street in 1940 (*see* 1905).

The Fuller Brush Company has its beginnings in the Capitol Brush Company founded at Hartford, Conn., by Nova Scotia-born merchant Alfred Carl Fuller, 21. He quits his job as salesman for another brush company, develops a machine for making twisted-wire brushes, produces brushes at night, sells them door-to-door by day, and builds a line of brushes with specific uses (*see* 1910).

The San Francisco earthquake and fire (above) destroy all the city's Nob Hill mansions with the exception of the 20-year-old $1 million house of silver king James C. Flood.

San Francisco's 31-year-old Palace Hotel uses up the water it has stored in vain attempts to save neighboring structures. Fire consumes the hotel but construction begins on a new Palace Hotel and on other new hotels, houses, and office buildings.

New York's Colony Club clubhouse designed by Stanford White (above) is completed at 120 Madison Avenue for the club founded 5 years ago by J. P. Morgan's sister Anne, Mrs. Borden Harriman, and Mrs. Helen Barney.

New York's Pierpont Morgan Library is completed by McKim, Mead & White adjacent to J. P. Morgan's brownstone in East 36th Street to house the banker's prodigious collection of rare books, manuscripts, documents, and incunabula (books printed before 1501). A north wing will enlarge the Renaissance palazzo in 1962 and it will be further enlarged in 1976.

Gary, Ind., has its beginnings as the U.S. Steel Corporation breaks ground for a new milltown on Lake Michigan. The town will be named to honor U.S. Steel's chairman Elbert Henry Gary, 60.

Forest Hills, N.Y., is founded by Brooklyn lawyer Cord Meyer, who has bought six large farms totaling about 600 acres in Queens. He has named the area Forest Hills because of its proximity to Forest Park and its high rolling ground (*see* tennis stadium, 1924).

Mesa Verde National Park is created by act of Congress. The 52,074-acre park in southern Colorado contains prehistoric cliff dwellings.

Platt National Park is created by act of Congress. The 912-acre park in Oklahoma Territory contains mineral springs.

A typhoon hits Hong Kong September 19 killing some 50,000.

Agrarian reforms to end the communal (mir) system of landholding established in Russia in 1861 are introduced by the country's new prime minister Pyotr Arkadevich Stolypin. Peasants are permitted to withdraw from a commune, to receive their shares of the land, and to own and operate the land privately (*see* kulaks, 1926; 1928).

The U.S. corn crop exceeds 3 billion bushels, up from 2 billion in 1885 (*see* 1963).

The King Ranch of Texas grows by acquisition to cover nearly a million acres with 75,000 head of cattle and nearly 10,000 horses (*see* 1886; 1940).

Florida's citrus groves are frozen by an ice storm.

California orange growers begin to set out Valencia orange seedlings to raise fruit that will mature in the summer and will make the state a year-round source of oranges, but most California oranges continue to be the Washington navels introduced in 1875.

A Pure Food and Drug bill introduced by U.S. senator from Idaho Weldon B. Heyburn encounters Republican opposition. U.S. senator from Rhode Island Nelson W. Aldrich asks, "Is there anything in the existing condition that makes it the duty of Congress to put the liberty of the United States in jeopardy?.... Are we going to take up the question as to what a man shall eat and what a man shall drink, and put him under severe penalties if he is eating or drinking something different from what the chemists of the Agricultural Department think desirable?"

But the Heyburn Bill (above) regulates producers and sellers, not consumers, and its prohibitions are only against selling diseased meat, decomposed foods, or dangerously adulterated food, and its requirements are only that labels give truthful descriptions of contents (*see* 1903; Wiley, 1902; Sinclair, 1905).

The Heyburn Bill (above) is passed by the Senate February 21 by a 63 to 4 vote following pressure by the 59-year-old American Medical Association on Senator Aldrich, the measure is passed by the House June 23 by a 240 to 17 vote, and it is signed into law by President Roosevelt.

A meat inspection amendment to the Agricultural Appropriation Bill is introduced by U.S. senator from Indiana Albert J. Beveridge and is passed without dissent, but the measure does not provide for federal funding of meat inspection.

The Neill-Reynolds report prepared by settlement house workers Charles P. Neill and James Bronson Reynolds is made public by President Roosevelt June 24 and inspires Congressman James W. Wadsworth to introduce a meat inspection amendment in the House that provides for federal funding of meat inspection. The Wadsworth measure passes both houses of Congress and is signed into law by President Roosevelt.

The Great American Fraud by New York journalist Samuel Hopkins Adams, 35, exposes the fraudulent claims and hazardous ingredients of U.S. patent medicines. The book has been serialized in *Collier's*.

Protein nutrition research is pioneered by Cambridge University biochemists Frederick Gowland Hopkins, 45, and H. G. Willcock who find that mice fed "zein" from corn plus the amino acid tryptophan (which Hopkins has isolated with S. W. Cole) will live twice as long as mice fed "zein" alone.

A British School Meals Act to provide free meals for children is passed by Britain's Liberal government under pressure from the emerging Labour party. Many schoolchildren have been unable to profit from their education because they have come to school without breakfast, and the new measure permits local authorities to add up to a halfpenny per pound to taxes in order to fund a school meals program.

A new explanation for beriberi is suggested by Dutch physician Gerrit Grijns (*see* 1896). The disease may be caused not by a toxin in rice hulls, says Grijns, but rather by the absence of some essential nutrient in polished rice (*see* Suzuki et al., 1912).

The Battle Creek Toasted Corn Flake Company is incorporated February 19 by W. K. (Will Keith) Kellogg, 46, and St. Louis insurance man Charles D. Bolin who puts up $35,000 to start the company whose stock is owned largely by Kellogg's brother J. H. even though the younger Kellogg has his signature printed on each package. W. K. Kellogg runs the company and devotes two-thirds of his budget to advertising (*see* 1902; Sweetheart of the Corn, 1907).

Post Toasties corn flakes are perfected by C. W. Post (*see* 1904; 1914).

Corn Products Refining Company is created out of the 4-year-old Corn Products Company by Standard Oil Company director E. T. Bedford whose "gluten trust" controls 90 percent of U.S. corn refining capacity. The company's Karo syrup will soon be a household name (*see* 1913; 1916).

Planters Nut and Chocolate Company is founded at Wilkes-Barre, Pa., by Italian-American entrepeneur Amedeo Obici, 29, who came to America at age 11 and who has expanded a peanut stand into a store and restaurant. In partnership with his future brother-in-law Mario Peruzzi, Obici starts a firm that will be incorporated in 1908 with $50,000 in capital, will show its first profits in 1910, and by 1912 will be using so many raw peanuts that Obici will open his own shelling plant and will buy direct from farmers to avoid being squeezed by middlemen (*see* Mr. Peanut, 1916).

"The milk from contented cows" is adopted by E. A. Stuart's Carnation Milk. The slogan has been created by a Chicago advertising man (*see* 1899).

Libby, McNeill & Libby adds catsup, bulk pickles, and bottled pickles to its line of canned meats (*see* 1891). Libby buys a milk condensery at Morrison, Ill., and begins packing canned milk (*see* 1908).

A.1 Sauce is introduced to the United States from England by Hartford's G. F. Heublein & Bro. The sauce was created in the 1820s by a chef to George IV (*see* cocktails, 1892; Smirnoff, 1939).

The "hot dog" gets its name from a cartoon by Chicago cartoonist Thomas Aloysius "Tad" Dorgan, 29, who shows a dachshund inside a frankfurter bun.

Sales of Jell-O reach nearly $1 million. Francis Woodward once offered to sell the brand for $35 but he stops making Grain-O to devote all his efforts to Jell-O (*see* 1899; Postum Cereal Company, 1925).

Frank G. Shattuck Co. is founded by Schrafft Candy Company salesman Frank Shattuck to operate retail stores (*see* 1897). Backed by George Frederick Schrafft and his brother William Frederick, Shattuck has opened a shop with a restaurant in New York's Herald Square, he will open more, and by 1928 there will be 29 Schrafft restaurants in New York, four in Boston, one in Syracuse.

The U.S. population reaches 85 million, Britain 38.9, Ireland 4.3, France 39.2, Germany 62, Russia over 120. China's population approaches 400 million.

India's population nears 300 million, up from little more than 200 million in 1850. Indian attorney Mohandas Gandhi, now 37 and practicing in South Africa, takes a vow of chastity (*brahmacharya*) and will oppose other means of limiting population in India (*see* 1885; political activity, 1914).

1907 A U.S. economic crisis looms as a result of drains on the money supply by the Russo-Japanese War of 1905, the demands imposed by the rebuilding of San Francisco following last year's earthquake and fire,

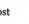

715

1907 (cont.) several large railroad expansion programs, and the fact that a late season has tied up farmers' cash. New York Stock Exchange prices suddenly collapse March 13, a July 4th address by Princeton University president Woodrow Wilson urges an attack on the illegal manipulations of financiers rather than on corporations, and "malefactors of great wealth" are attacked by President Roosevelt in a speech August 20.

Standard Oil Company of Indiana is indicted for having received secret rebates on shipments of crude oil over the Chicago and Alton Railroad. Federal district court judge Kenesaw Mountain Landis, 41, imposes a fine of more than $29 million on 1,462 separate counts, but the decision against the subsidiary of John D. Rockefeller's Standard Oil Company of New Jersey will be reversed on appeal.

Financier J. P. Morgan acts singlehandedly to avert financial panic following a rush by depositors October 23 to withdraw their money from New York's Knickerbocker Trust Company, a bank run that is followed by others at Providence, Pittsburgh, Butte, and at New York's Trust Company of America.

J. P. Morgan (above) obtains a pledge of $10 million in John D. Rockefeller money from National City Bank president James Stillman, he obtains $10 million in specie from the Bank of England which arrives via the new ship *Lusitania* (below), he gets support from First National Bank president George Baker and from financiers Edward H. Harriman and Thomas Fortune Ryan, he promises New York mayor George McClellan $30 million at 6 percent interest to keep the city from having a default on some short-term bonds, and he locks up some leading New York trust company presidents overnight in his new library in East 36th Street until 5 o'clock in the morning of November 4.

President Roosevelt permits United States Steel to acquire the Tennessee Coal, Iron and Railroad Company for $35.3 million in U.S. Steel bonds despite questions as to the legality of the acquisition in light of the 1890 Sherman Anti-Trust Act. The president's action saves the Wall Street brokerage firm of Moore & Schley from collapse, faith is restored, and the stock market recovers.

Oklahoma is admitted to the Union as the 46th state.

A Franco-Japanese treaty signed June 10 guarantees "open door" access of both France and Japan to China and recognizes the special interests of Japan in Fukien and in parts of Manchuria and Mongolia.

The Korean emperor Kojong (I T'ae-wang) who has reigned since 1864 abdicates July 19 at age 55 under pressure from the Japanese who occupy his country. He is succeeded by a figurehead controlled by the Japanese, and Korea becomes a Japanese protectorate under terms of a treaty signed July 25 (*see* 1904; 1910).

The Persian shah Muzaffar ud-Din dies at age 54 after a weak reign of 11 years. He is succeeded by his 35-year-old son who will reign until 1909 as Mohammed Ali. The reactionary Persian prime minister is assassinated in August. The ministry of Atabegi-Azam is replaced by a liberal ministry headed by Nasir ul-Mulk.

An Anglo-Russian entente concluded August 31 resolves differences between Britain and Russia in Persia and elsewhere in Asia. The entente follows by 2 days a Russian note recognizing British preeminence in the Persian Gulf.

The new Persian shah attempts a coup d'etat December 15 and imprisons the new liberal prime minister, but popular uprisings throughout the country force him to yield (*see* 1908).

Sweden's Oskar II has died December 8 at age 78 after a 35-year reign in which he also ruled Norway until 1905. He is succeeded by his popular 49-year-old son who will reign until 1950 as Gustavus V.

Britain grants dominion status to New Zealand.

Austria institutes universal direct suffrage.

Norway grants woman suffrage June 14.

Western Federation of Miners leader "Big Bill" Haywood goes on trial at Boise, Idaho, on charges of having helped murder the former governor of Idaho Frank R. Steunenberg in 1905. A miner since age 15, the 38-year-old William Dudley Haywood helped found the IWW in 1905, local lawyer William E. Borah, 42, heads the prosecution (and later wins election to the U.S. Senate), Haywood's lawyer Clarence S. Darrow of Chicago shows that Haywood's accuser has perjured himself, Haywood wins acquittal, and the WFM quits the IWW in protest against the violent direct-action tactics favored by the "Wobblies" (*see* Darrow, 1893, 1910).

Gulf Oil Company is founded by a reorganization of the Guffey Oil Company (*see* Spindletop, 1901).

Royal Dutch-Shell is created by a merger of Henri Deterding's Royal Dutch Oil Company with the 10-year-old Shell Transport and Trading Company of English oilman Marcus Samuel, now 72 (*see* 1892; Anglo-Persian, 1914).

Canadian-American entrepreneur Cyrus Eaton, 23, travels to Manitoba to secure a franchise for an electric power plant. A protege of John D. Rockefeller, Eaton obtains the franchise with backing from former associates of Rockefeller, and when the backers back out because of the financial panic (above), Eaton borrows money and builds the plant himself. He will sell it in 2 years at a good profit and he will proceed to develop gas and electric companies in hundreds of cities throughout the Midwest and Southwest (*see* Continental Gas and Electric, 1912).

U.S. motorcar production reaches 43,000, up from 25,000 in 1905 (*see* 1908).

Willys-Overland Motors is established by autodealer John North Willys who buys the Overland Automobile Company of Indianapolis and moves it to the old

Pope-Toledo plant at Toledo, Ohio. Willys has opened an auto agency in New York City, and he cannot obtain enough cars to fill all his orders (*see* 1903; 1910).

A "valveless" engine is perfected by Wisconsin agriculturist Charles Knight who introduces a windowed sleeve between piston and cylinder and engineers it to cover and uncover inlet and outlet ports, eliminating the valve gear that makes engines noisy with "play" between cams, tappets, and the valves needed to cope with expansion caused by heating (*see* Willys-Knight, 1915).

The Brush motorcar is introduced at $500. A Cadillac is advertised at $800 in the April issue of *Collier's* magazine, a Ford Model K sells for $2,800, but horses sell for $150 to $300.

New York City horsecars give way to motorbuses, but most urban transit is by electric trolley car and subway (*see* 1904; 1932; Fifth Avenue Transportation Company, 1885).

Taximeter cabs imported from Paris appear in New York in May to give the United States its first successors to hansom cabs.

The Bendix Company is founded by U.S. inventor Vincent Bendix, 25, who left his Moline, Ill., home at age 16 to study mechanics at New York. The Bendix starter drive that Bendix will perfect in the next 5 years will lead to the development of a self-starter for motorcars (*see* Bendix brake, 1912; Kettering's self-starter, 1911).

Trials by Britain's Royal Automobile Club begin a shift from steam wagons to trucks and tractors powered by internal combustion engines.

The Lancia motorcar has its beginnings at Turin where Italian engineer Vincenzo Lancia and his partner Claudio Fogolin produce a 24-horsepower Alfa which is soon followed by a six-cylinder Dailfa, a Beta, and a Gamma. They will move into a larger factory and will produce the first commercially successful Lancia (the Theta) which will develop 70 horsepower at 2,200 rpm.

The first long-distance motorcar rally begins June 10 as five cars leave Peking for Paris. The newspaper *Le Matin* has promoted the event, and the winner is a 40-horsepower Italia driven by Prince Scipione Borghese who arrives at Paris August 10 (*see* 1908).

The S.S. *Lusitania* launched by Britain's Cunard Line makes her maiden voyage in September and follows it soon after with a voyage in which she carries specie from the Bank of England to relieve the U.S. financial crisis (above). The 31,550-ton *Lusitania* is 790 feet in length overall with four screws, she can carry 2,000 passengers and a crew of 600, and she is by far the largest liner yet built (but *see* 1915).

The S.S. *Mauretania* launched by the Cunard Line will remain in service until 1935. Slightly smaller than her sister ship the S.S. *Lusitania* (above), the four-screw *Mauretania* burns 1,000 tons of coal per day and requires a "black squad" of 324 firemen and trimmers to feed her furnaces (*see* 1910).

Great Britain and Ireland have 23,100 miles of operating railway, Canada 22,400 miles, Austria-Hungary 25,800, France 29,700, Germany 36,000, Russia 44,600, India 29,800, the United States 237,000.

Union Station at Washington, D.C., is completed by Chicago architect Daniel Burnham of Burnham & Root. The new terminal is modeled on the Baths of Diocletian and the Arch of Constantine at Rome.

 Embryology is advanced by Yale zoologist Ross Granville Harrison, 37, who perfects a method of culturing animal tissues in a liquid medium and makes it possible to study tissues without the variables and mechanical difficulties of *in vivo* examinations. The method will permit Harrison to make discoveries about embryonic development and will facilitate research by others.

Electrical high-frequency "radio" surgery is invented by radio pioneer Lee De Forest (*see* 1906).

Bubonic plague kills 1.3 million in India (*see* 1910).

Sales of Argyrol and Ovoferrin top $250,000 with net profits of more than $186,000, and Albert Barnes buys out his partner Herman Hille for $350,000 (*see* 1904). Barnes will be a millionaire within 7 years as Argyrol comes into universal use to protect newborn infants against blindness from gonorrheal infection.

SKF (Svenska Kullager Fabriken, or Swedish Ball Bearing Factory) is founded at Göteborg by Swedish engineer Sven Gustav Wingquist, 30, who has perfected a superior ball bearing using a steel alloy that contains chrome and manganese. Wingquist's ball bearings are almost frictionless, his $28,000 company will be worth $28 million by 1919, it will grow to have 14 factories in seven countries including one at Stuttgart and four in the Philadelphia area, and SKF will be Sweden's largest industrial enterprise.

Bethlehem Steel Company's Saucon Mills open at Bethlehem, Pa., to roll wide-flanged girders and beams that are lighter (and therefore cheaper) than conventional riveted girders but just as strong. Bethlehem has acquired patents from inventor Henry Grey and will license other steelmakers to manufacture Grey beams on a royalty basis (*see* 1905; 1912).

The first U.S. company to produce oxygen for oxyacetylene torches is founded by a group of manufacturers who make carbon electrodes used to power electric furnaces that produce alloying metals (*see* Fouce, 1903; Union Carbide, 1911).

The American Cyanamid Company founded July 22 by U.S. entrepreneur Frank Sherman Washburn, 46, builds a plant on the Canadian side of Niagara Falls to produce calcium cyanamid for nitrogen fertilizer using the European Frank-Caro process for fixation

1907 (cont.) of atmospheric nitrogen. German chemists Adolf Frank, now 73, and Nidodem Caro, now 36, developed the process in the late 1890s, it requires vast amounts of power, Washburn has obtained backing from tobacco magnate James B. Duke, he uses local limestone, and by the end of 1909 American Cyanamid will have an annual production capacity of 5,000 tons (*see* Haber process, 1908; Lederle, 1930).

The University of Saskatchewan is founded at Saskatoon.

The University of Hawaii is founded at Honolulu.

The University of Redlands is founded at Redlands, Calif.

Wireless telegraphy service begins October 18 between the United States and Ireland (*see* Marconi, 1901; United Fruit, 1910; Sarnoff, 1912).

The United Press is founded to compete with the Associated Press founded in 1848 and the Hearst International News Service (INS) started last year. The new wire service is created by a merger of Publishers' Press, owned since 1904 by newspaper publisher Edward Wyllis Scripps, now 53, and the Scripps-McRae Press Association in which Scripps has been a partner since 1897. Roy Wilson Howard, 24, heads UP's New York office and will be UP president in 5 years (*see* 1925; *Cleveland Press,* 1878; UPI, 1958).

Rube Goldberg starts work with the *New York Evening Journal* to begin a career as cartoonist. San Francisco graduate engineer Reuben Lucius Goldberg, 24, will have his cartoons syndicated beginning in 1915, he will often show elaborate machines he has devised to perform simple tasks, and his ludicrous inventions will appear for nearly 60 years.

George H. Doran Company is founded at Toronto by local publisher George H. Doran, 38, who will move to New York next year and who will merge with F. N. Doubleday in 1927 to form Doubleday, Doran & Co. (*see* Doubleday, 1897; Literary Guild, 1934).

Nonfiction *The Autobiography of a Super-Tramp* by English poet William Henry Davies, 37, with a preface by George Bernard Shaw; *Pragmatism* by William James who retires from Harvard at age 65.

Fiction *The Secret Agent* by Joseph Conrad whose "agent" is no individual but is rather the anarchy that works unseen within any society; *The Longest Journey* by E. M. Forster; *The Iron Heel* by Jack London.

Juvenile *The Wonderful Adventures of Nils* (*Nils Holgerssons underbara resa*) by Selma Lagerlof.

Poetry "Barrel-Organ" by Alfred Noyes: "Go down to Kew in lilac-time, in lilac-time, in lilac-time;/ Go down to Kew in lilac-time (it isn't far from London)"; *Songs of a Sourdough* by English banker-poetaster Robert William Service, 33, whose bank transferred him to the Yukon late in 1904 and who will leave the North for good in 1912. Service's poems include "The Cremation of Sam McGee" and

"The Shooting of Dan McGrew": "A bunch of the boys were whooping it up in the Malamute saloon;/ The kid that handles the music-box was hitting a jag-time tune;/ Back of the bar, in a solo game, sat Dangerous Dan McGrew,/ And watching his luck was his light-o'-love, the lady that's known as Lou."

An exhibition of Cubist paintings at Paris begins a radical departure from expressionist and impressionist painting. Georges Braque, 25, Fernand Léger, 26, and others lead the movement to reduce nature to its geometric elements.

Other paintings *Les Demoiselles d'Avignon* by Pablo Picasso; *Young Sailor II* and *Luxe, Calme et Volupté* by Henri Matisse; *Blackfriars Bridge* and *The Bathers* by André Derain; *Amor and Psyche* by Claude Monet; *Rooftops of Montmagny* by French painter Maurice Utrillo, 23, illegitimate son of the painter Suzanne Valadon who has been legally adopted by Spanish writer Miguel Utrillo; *The Snake Charmer* by Henri Rousseau; *Cavalry Charge on the Southern Plains* by Frederic Remington; *Forty-Two Kids* by New York painter George Wesley Bellows, 25, who gains his first success with a picture of urchins tumbling, swimming, diving, and playing round a New York dock and follows it with *Stag at Sharkey's* inspired by Tom Sharkey's boxing arena.

Sculpture *Mother and Child* by Wilhelm Lehmbruck. Augustus Saint-Gaudens dies at Cornish, N.H., August 3 at age 59.

The North American Indian by U.S. photographer Edward S. Curtis, 39, is published in its first volume. Financed by J. P. Morgan who has pledged up to $75,000 to support the project, Curtis continues to photograph Indians who include Chief Joseph of the Nez Perce, his work will appear in 300 20-volume sets printed at a cost of nearly $1.5 million, and the sets will sell at from $3,000 to $3,500 each, depending on the binding.

Bell & Howell Company is founded by Chicago movie projectionist Donald H. Bell, 39, and camera repairman Albert S. Howell, 28, with $5,000 in capital. The firm will pioneer in improving equipment for motion picture photography and projection (Bell will sell out to Howell in 1921) (*see* 1909; 1911; Kodak, 1929; Percy, 1949).

Theater *Don Juan in Hell* (Act III of *Man and Superman*) by George Bernard Shaw 1/4 at London's Royal Court Theatre, with Ben Webster, Mary Barton; *The Truth* by Clyde Fitch 1/7 at New York's Criterion Theater, 34 perfs.; *The Playboy of the Western World* by John M. Synge 1/26 at Dublin's Abbey Theatre (the play produces riots at the theater and in the streets of Dublin); *The Maidens of the Mount* (*Die Jungfrau vorn Bischofsberg*) by Gerhart Hauptmann 2/2 at Berlin's Lessingtheater; *The Philanderer* by George Bernard Shaw 2/25 at London's Royal Court Theatre; *The Life of Man* (*Zhizn cheloveka*) by Russian playwright Leonid Nikolayevich Andreyev, 35, 2/22 at St. Petersburg's V.F. Kommissarzhevsky Theater; *A Flea in Her Ear* (*La puce à l'oreille*) by Georges Feydeau 3/2 at the Théâtre des Nouveautés, Paris; *The Rising of the Moon* by Lady Gregory 3/9 at Dublin's Abbey Theatre; *The Witching Hour* by U.S. playwright Augustus Thomas, 50, 4/18 at Hackett's Theater, New York, 212 perfs.; *The Man of Destiny* by George Bernard Shaw 6/4 at London's Royal Court Theatre, with Dion Boucicault as young Napoleon Bonaparte, 8 matinee perfs.; *A Grand Army Man* by David Belasco and others 10/16 at New York's new Stuyvesant Theater on 44th Street, with David Warfield, William Elliott, Antoinette Perry (the theater will be renamed the Belasco in September 1910).

The Barnum & Bailey Circus created in 1881 becomes the Ringling Bros. Barnum & Bailey Circus. Albert C. Ringling, 55, and his brothers Otto, 49, Alfred T., 45, Charles, 44, and John, 41, have purchased The Greatest Show on Earth and will continue touring it round the country (*see* "Weary Willie," 1921).

Samuel Lionel "Roxy" Rothafel, 25, turns a dance hall in back of his father-in-law's Forest City, Pa., saloon into a motion picture theater with a second-hand screen and projector. The Minnesota-born showman charges 5 cents admission and will soon attract the attention of vaudeville magnate B. F. Keith.

Broadway musicals *The Honeymooners* 6/13 at the Aerial Garden, with George M. Cohan and his songs, 167 perfs.; *The Follies of 1907* 7/18 at the Jardin de Paris on the roof of the New York Theater, with 50 "Anna Held Girls" in an extravaganza staged by Florenz Ziegfeld, now 38, who married comedienne Anna Held 10 years ago. She writes lyrics to Vincent Scotto's song "It's Delightful to Be Married (The Parisian Model)," show girls appear in a swimming pool in a simulated motion picture production, *The Follies* enjoys a run of 70 perfs., and opulent new editions will appear each year until 1931 (with the exceptions of 1926, 1928, and 1929) featuring chorus lines composed of beautiful girls chosen with an eye to slenderness of figure as Ziegfeld creates a new ideal to replace the ample figure now in vogue; *The Talk of the Town* 12/3 at the Knickerbocker Theater, with Victor Moore, music and lyrics by George M. Cohan, songs that include "When a Fellow's on the Level with a Girl That's on the Square," 157 perfs.

Opera *The Legend of the Invisible City of Kitesch and of the Maiden Fevrona* 2/7 at St. Petersburg's Maryinsky Theater, with music by Nikolai Rimski-Korsakov; *Ariane et Barbe Bleu* 5/10 at the Opéra-Comique, Paris, with music by Paul Dukas; *The Merry Widow* 6/8 at Daly's Theatre, London, with music by Franz Lehar, 778 perfs. (*see* 1905).

First performances Introduction and Allegro for Harp and String Orchestra, Flute, and Clarinet by Maurice Ravel 2/22 at Paris; Symphony No. 3 in C major by Jean Sibelius 9/25 at Helsinki.

Ballet *The Dying Swan* (*Le Cygne*) 12/22 at St. Petersburg's Maryinsky Theater, with Anna Pavlova dancing to music by Camille Saint-Saëns for *Le Carnival des Animaux* but adapted by Michel Fokine.

Popular songs "Marie of Sunny Italy" by Russian-American singing waiter-songwriter Irving Berlin, 19, who has changed his name from Israel Baline; "Dark Eyes" ("Sérénade Espagnole") by Neil Moret; "On the Road to Mandalay" by composer Oley Speaks, 33, with lyrics based on the 1890 poem by Rudyard Kipling; "The Caissons Go Rolling Along" by Edmund L. Gruber, who has written it for a reunion in the Philippine Islands of the U.S. Fifth Artillery that helped defeat the Spanish in 1898 (Gruber's song will not be published until February 1918).

The world's first permanent ski school opens at St. Anton in the Austrian Arlberg region of the Alps under the direction of Hannes Schneider, who will develop one system for teaching the sport to tourists and another for teaching selected local skiers who will spread the Schneider techniques throughout Europe (*see* 1906).

U.S. West Coast pitcher Walter Perry Johnson, 19, signs with the Washington Senators of the American League to begin a 21-year career with the Senators. Johnson will win the nickname "Big Train" for his fast ball, he will pitch 802 games, he will win 414, and he will record 3,497 strikeouts in 5,923 innings (his 1913 record of pitching 56 consecutive scoreless innings will stand for 55 years).

The Chicago Cubs win the World Series with Tinker, Evers, and Chance in the infield helping to defeat the Detroit Tigers 4 games to 0 after one game has ended in a tie.

Australian long-distance swimmer Annette Kellerman, 22, is arrested for indecent exposure at Boston's Revere Beach where she has appeared in a skirtless one-piece bathing suit. Even infants will be required to wear complete bathing costumes on U.S. beaches for more than 25 years.

Uncle Sam's 3 Coin Register Bank is introduced by the Durable Toy and Novelty Company. 6 inches high, 4 inches wide, 5 inches deep, and made of heavy-gauge steel, the bank takes nickels, dimes, and quarters, it registers the input with figures displayed in a little window.

France's l'Oréal perfume and beauty product empire is started by chemist Eugène Schueller whose firm will become the world's largest supplier of hair products, employing 1,000 biologists and 22,000 production and research workers.

Persil is introduced by Henkel & Cie. of Düsseldorf. It is the world's first household detergent but is not suitable for heavy-duty laundry use (*see* Tide, 1946).

The first complete, self-contained electric washing machine is introduced by the Hurley Machine Company of Chicago which puts its Thor machine on the market.

1907 (cont.) The Maytag Pastime washer introduced by the Parsons Band Cutter and Self-Feeder Company of Newton, Iowa, is a sideline to the farm equipment produced by the company which Frederick Louis Maytag, 50, has headed since 1893. The washer has a corrugated wooden tub with a hand-operated dolly inside, Maytag will add a pulley mechanism in 1909 to permit operation of the machine from an outside power source, he will introduce an electric washing machine in 1911, but Maytag's entry into the washer field is primarily to solve the problem of seasonal slumps in the farm implement business (*see* 1922).

Armstrong Linoleum is introduced by the Armstrong Cork Company founded in 1860.

The Hoover Vacuum Cleaner has its beginnings in an electric vacuum cleaner invented by J. Murray Spangler who has improved on the cleaner patented by H. C. Booth in 1901. Spangler's machine will be manufactured by U.S. industrialist W. H. Hoover, now 58, whose Hoover Suction Sweeper Company will become the Hoover Company in 1922.

 Alfred Dunhill, Ltd., opens in London's Duke Street near Piccadilly Circus. Former harness maker Dunhill has founded a tobacco shop that will become world famous, he will patent a "motorist's pipe" with a wind screen that will enjoy wide popularity until the motorcar industry installs windshields, the first Dunhill lighter will appear in 1924, and Dunhills will be acquired by Rothman International.

Prince Albert Tobacco is introduced by the 32-year-old R. J. Reynolds Company. It will soon be the leading U.S. pipe tobacco (*see* Camels, 1913).

 Bullock's is opened March 4 at Los Angeles by John Gillespie Bullock, 36, who will erect a 10-story building on Broadway in 1912. The Canadian-American merchant is backed by his former employer Arthur Letts, 45, an English-American whose dry goods store at Broadway and 4th Street will become The Broadway Store (*see* Bullock's Wilshire, 1929).

Neiman-Marcus opens September 10 at Dallas, and its initial stock is practically sold out at the end of 4 weeks. The two-story fashion emporium at the corner of Elm and Murphy Streets has been started by former Atlanta advertising agency president A. L. Neiman, his wife Carrie, and his brother-in-law Herbert Marcus who have been offered the choice of selling out for $25,000 in cash or receiving stock in the Coca-Cola Company plus the Missouri franchise for Coca-Cola syrup. They have opted for the cash, they start the store with $30,000 in capital ($22,000 of it from Neiman), they invest $12,000 in carpeting and fixtures for the store which they lease at $750 per month, and Carrie Neiman stocks it with $17,000 worth of tailored suits for women, evening gowns, furs, coats, dresses, and millinery for the women of Dallas, a city of 86,000 with 222 saloons (*see* 1913).

Sears, Roebuck distributes more than 3 million copies of its fall catalog (*see* 1904; 1927).

 The Washington Cathedral that will be completed in 1976 goes up in the nation's capital. The great Gothic structure has been designed by London architect George F. Bodley and his Bostonian pupil Henry Vaughan, architect Philip Hubert Frohman will take over in 10 years, and Frohman will lengthen the nave from 246 feet to 534 feet (*see* 1964).

The New York Customs House on the south side of Bowling Green is completed by Cass Gilbert.

Atlantic City's Marlborough Blenheim Hotel opens on the Boardwalk at the New Jersey resort city.

The Monmouth Hotel opens at Spring Lake, N.J. to replace a hotel of the same name that opened in 1892 but has burned down.

New York's Plaza Hotel opens October 1 on the Grand Army Plaza just south of Central Park on a site formerly occupied by the Alfred Gwynne Vanderbilt mansion. The $12 million 1,000-room hotel has been designed by Henry Janeway Hardenbergh in the French Renaissance Beaux-Arts style he has used for the Waldorf of 1893, the Astor House of 1897, the Willard of 1901, and the Astor of 1904.

San Francisco's Fairmont Hotel has opened April 17 on the Nob Hill site formerly occupied by the mansion of the late James G. "Bonanza Jim" Fair. Nearly completed before last year's earthquake and fire, the Fairmont will be augmented in 1961 by a 29-story tower containing 252 additional rooms.

A new St. Francis Hotel goes up on San Francisco's Union Square to replace the hotel that opened in 1904 but was destroyed by last year's fire.

Berlin's Hotel Adlon opens on Pariser Platz.

Rome's Excelsior Hotel is opened by Swiss hotelman Baron Pfyffer d'Altishofen.

 U.S. chief forester Gifford Pinchot seizes upon the word "conservation" to describe his philosophy (*see* 1905). He has learned that government forests in India are called "conservancies." The word "conservation" will soon come into general use, but it will be variously interpreted (*see* 1908).

U.S. senators from Idaho, Montana, Oregon, Washington, and Wyoming force President Roosevelt to sign an appropriations bill containing a rider that repeals the Forest Preservation Act of 1891. The president signs a proclamation 10 days later creating 16 million acres of new forests in the five states, forests that cannot be cut for timber, and before the Roosevelt administration expires early in 1909 it will have set aside 132 million acres in forest reserves.

Potlatch Forests, Inc., has its beginnings in the Potlatch Lumber Company founded by lumbermen who include Charles Augustus Weyerhaeuser, 41, with mills at Elk River and Potlatch, Idaho (*see* 1891).

America's Basque sheep herders form a mutual aid society at Boise, Idaho (*see* 1849).

The Dairymen's League, Inc., is founded by New York, New Jersey, Pennsylvania, Connecticut, Massachusetts dairy farmers whose herds total 50,000 cows. The farmers begin efforts to break industry domination by city dealers and to obtain higher prices for their milk (*see* 1919).

Pellagra is observed for the first time in Mississippi where cornmeal is a dietary staple (*see* 1771; 1913).

Researches on the Chemistry of Proteins by German chemist Emil Fischer, 55, is based on the Nobel laureate's work in synthesizing simple sugars, purine derivatives, and peptides.

The Prolongation of Life by Russian bacteriologist Ilya Mechnikov, now 62, suggests that "friendly bacteria" in yogurt will crowd out "poisonous bacteria" that shorten human life. Mechnikov has convinced himself that Bulgarian peasants live to advanced ages because they eat so much yogurt, but his theory will be substantially disproved (*see* 1885; Gayelord Hauser, 1950).

Saccharin and other benzoic acid derivatives should be banned from use in food, says Department of Agriculture chemist Harvey W. Wiley. New York congressman James S. Sherman says saccharin has saved his canning firm thousands of dollars per year, Wiley interrupts him at a White House conference to say, "Yes, Mr. President, and everyone who eats these products is deceived, believing he is eating sugar, and moreover his health is threatened by this drug!" President Roosevelt replies angrily, "Anybody who says saccharin is injurious is an idiot! Dr. Rixey gives it to me every day." Wiley has developed important refining techniques for the sugar industry, Ira Remsen heads the scientific board named by the president to review the data on saccharin, and the board's final report in 1910 will conclude that a continuing daily consumption of 300 milligrams of saccharin presents no hazard (*see* 1879; sodium cyclamate, 1937).

The American Sugar Refining trust is discovered to have defrauded the government out of import duties (*see* 1899). Several company officials are convicted, and more than $4 million is recovered by the government (*see* Domino Sugar, 1911).

The Coca-Cola Company buys out its Atlanta advertising agency (*see* 1899; Neiman-Marcus, above; Britain, 1909; distinctive bottle, 1916).

Pepsi-Cola sales increase to 104,000 gallons, up from 7,968 gallons in 1903, as Caleb Bradham establishes a network of 40 bottling plants (*see* 1920).

Canada Dry Pale Dry Ginger Ale is registered as a trademark by John J. McLaughlin who has eliminated the dark brown color of his Belfast Style Ginger Ale and has also eliminated the sharpness found in other ginger ales (*see* 1890). McLaughlin calls his product "the Champagne of Ginger Ales" and demand for the beverage will soon oblige him to bottle it at Montreal and Edmonton (*see* 1922).

"The Sweetheart of the Corn" is adopted by the Kellogg brothers as an advertising symbol for Kellogg's Corn Flakes (*see* 1906). Kellogg stenographer Fanny Bryant is photographed with her arms full of corn stalks, and the Kellogg brothers are excommunicated by the Seventh Day Adventist Church which moved its headquarters 4 years ago from Battle Creek to Tacoma, Md., outside Washington, D.C. (*see* 1911; 40% Bran Flakes, 1915).

The Minnesota Valley Canning Company at Le Seur starts packing peas in addition to sweet corn (*see* 1903; giant symbol, 1925).

The first canned tunafish is packed at San Pedro, Calif., by A. P. Halfhill (*see* Van Camp, 1914).

The Japanese diplomat Tadasu Hayashi, 57, sends Washington a note in mid-February that will be the basis of a gentlemen's agreement next year. An executive order by President Roosevelt one month later excludes all Japanese laborers coming from Canada, Hawaii, or Mexico from entry to the continental United States.

An immigration act passed by Congress February 20 excludes undesirables, raises the head tax on arrivals to $4, and creates a commission to investigate.

Nearly 1.29 million immigrants enter the United States, a new record that will not be surpassed.

1908 The Haber process for synthesizing ammonia that will free the world from its dependence on Chilean nitrates for making explosives and nitrogen fertilizers is invented by German chemist Fritz Haber, 40, and his colleague W. H. Nernst of 1906 third law of thermodynamics fame. Using far less energy and at much lower cost than the Frank-Caro process used earlier (*see* American Cyanamid, 1907), the Haber process combines nitrogen and hydrogen directly,

Henry Ford's Model T flivver came in any color you wanted, so long as it was black. Almost anybody could afford one.

1908 (cont.) using as a catalyst iron (plus some aluminum, potassium, and calcium) and employing high temperatures. Since ammonia is one part nitrogen to three parts hydrogen, it can easily be reduced to nitric acid for munitions or to sulfate of ammonia or sodium nitrate for fertilizers.

The Haber process (above) will be adapted by German industrial chemist Karl Bosch, now 34, and will be employed by Badische-Anilin-und-Soda Fabrik to produce sulfate of ammonia and sodium nitrate but mostly to make nitric acid (*see* 1914).

The Geiger counter to detect radioactive radiations is developed by German physicist Hans Geiger, 26, and New Zealand-born British physicist Ernest Rutherford, 37, at Manchester University. A high-voltage wire runs down the center of a cylinder in a near vacuum, alpha particles passing through the gas in the cylinder cause it to ionize into charged particles, and a pulse of electrical current for each alpha particle can be observed on a dial. Geiger will improve the counter in the 1920s with help from W. Muller to distinguish between alpha particles and beta and gamma rays by reduced voltage and to produce clicks through a loudspeaker (*see* Rutherford, 1911).

Portugal's licentious Carlos I is assassinated February 1 along with the crown prince in the streets of Lisbon after a reign of nearly 19 years. The 44-year-old king is succeeded by his 18-year-old younger son who will reign until 1910 as Manoel II and who ends the dictatorship of his father's prime minister Joao Franco that began in 1906.

Egypt's Mustapha Kamel dies February 10 at age 34 and his death deals the reviving nationalist movement a heavy blow. The khedive moves to counteract nationalism November 10 by appointing as premier the Christian Copt Butros Ghali and Egypt's Moslems stage violent demonstrations.

The British prime minister Sir Henry Campbell-Bannerman, recuperating from a heart attack suffered last November, makes a speech in the House of Commons February 13 but resigns April 5 and dies April 22. He is succeeded by Herbert Henry Asquith, 55, earl of Oxford and Asquith, whose Liberal ministry will continue until 1916.

The Persian shah Mohammed Ali succeeds in a coup d'etat June 23 with help from the Cossack Brigade and secret support from the Russian legation (*see* 1907). He shuts down the Persian assembly, he imposes martial law at Teheran, and many liberal leaders are killed (*see* petroleum production, below).

The Battle of Marakesh August 23 ends in defeat for the Moroccan sultan Abd-al-Aziz IV who has met the ransom demands of the brigand Raisuli to avert foreign wars, but whose actions have provoked his older brother Mulay Hafid to revolt. Insurgents proclaimed Mulay Hafid sultan at Marakesh in May of last year, Fez has proclaimed him sultan in January, Berlin announces September 3 that Germany will recognize the new sultan, the French seize German

deserters from the French Foreign Legion, Franco-German relations grow tense, but Mulay Hafid agrees to respect French and Spanish interests as accepted by his brother after the Algeciras Conference in 1906, and he begins a 4-year reign as Abd-al-Hafiz.

Austria annexes Bosnia and Herzogovina October 6, and the action produces consternation in Russia, Serbia, Montenegro, and Turkey. Berlin supports Vienna, London and Paris support the objections of Russia, Turkey, and the Balkan nations, Crete aggravates the crisis October 7 by proclaiming union with Greece, Turkey boycotts Austrian goods, and a London naval conference opens December 2.

The Congo State of the aged Leopold II is annexed to Belgium October 18 by an act of the Belgian parliament which begins to remove the abuses that have existed in the Congo since 1885.

President Roosevelt adheres to the tradition against a third term, and the Republicans nominate Roosevelt's secretary of war William Howard Taft, 50, of Cincinnati to succeed Roosevelt. Taft has served as governor of the Philippines, he has quelled a potential rebellion in Cuba, he has organized construction of the Panama Canal, and he easily defeats the Democrats who have nominated William Jennings Bryan for the third and last time, winning 321 electoral votes to 162 for the "Great Commoner."

The Supreme Court upholds railroad official William Adair who has fired an employee for belonging to a union. A law that prohibits discrimination against union labor in interstate commerce violates the 5th Amendment, the court rules January 27 in *Adair v. United States*.

The Danbury Hatters' case (*Loewe v. Lawlor*) brings a Supreme Court ruling February 3 that the Sherman Act of 1890 applies to combinations of labor as well as to management combinations. The court rules that a nationwide secondary boycott against D. E. Loewe & Co. by the United Hatters of North America in support of a striking Danbury, Conn., local is a conspiracy in restraint of trade.

The Supreme Court sustains Oregon's 10-hour day law for women in industry February 4 in *Muller v. State of Oregon*.

The Federal Bureau of Investigation (FBI) established as a division of the Department of Justice will be used in many cases against labor organizers (*see* J. Edgar Hoover, 1919).

The Supreme Court hands down prison sentences December 3 to AF of L officers Samuel Gompers, John Mitchell, and Frank Morrison for violating an injunction against a boycott of the Buck's Stove and Range Company.

Britain enacts legislation granting noncontributory old-age pensions of 5 shillings per week to poor people over age 70 (*see* Germany, 1891; British taxes, 1909; U.S. Social Security Act, 1935).

A race riot at Springfield, Mass., is reported by New York journalist Willing English Walling, who describes the plight of U.S. blacks in an article for the liberal weekly *The Independent.* "What large and powerful body of citizens is ready to come to their aid?" Walling asks and he gets a response from New York social worker Mary White Ovington (*see* NAACP, 1909).

Petroleum production begins in the Middle East May 26 as drillers employed by William Knox D'Arcy strike oil at Masjid-i-Salaman (Mosque of Solomon) and begin tapping what will prove in the 1930s to be the world's largest reservoir of oil. British cabinet member Winston Churchill, now 33, persuades London to buy up D'Arcy's 1901 concession from the shah of Persia (above) and to establish the Anglo-Persian Company which begins commercial exploitation of the new oilfield (*see* Gulbenkian, 1914; Anglo-Iranian, 1935; British Petroleum, 1954).

Hughes Tool Company is founded by Houston entrepreneur Howard Robard Hughes whose steel-toothed rock drilling bits will enjoy a monopoly in the petroleum industry. Hughes runs the first successful rock bit in an oil well at Goose Creek, Tex., and revolutionizes oil-drilling technology that has been based until now on a pulverizing technique. The device Hughes patents is the first to utilize rolling cone cutters, and by the time Hughes's son and namesake inherits the business in 1924 Hughes Tool will be making profits of $1 million per year.

Continental Oil Company has its beginnings in Oklahoma where Pittsburgh lawyer-oilman Ernest Whitworth Marland, 34, strikes oil on Ponca Indian lands. Marland used geological surveys to open West Virginia's Congo oil field in 1904, he sank 54 wells without a dry hole and made a fortune, he lost his money last year in the depression, he has come to Oklahoma and has noticed a geologic outcropping in a Ponca cemetery, he has been helped by rancher George Miller to obtain drilling rights in the cemetery and on surrounding leased lands, he will build a refinery at Ponca City, he will found the Marland Oil Company in 1920, and he will increase his holdings to control an estimated 10 percent of the world's oil supply (*see* 1929).

The Model T Ford that will soon outsell all other motorcars is introduced by Henry Ford whose $850.50 "flivver" has a wooden body on a steel frame that makes it "stronger than a horse and easier to maintain." The Model T comes only in black (*see* 1903; 1911).

U.S. auto production reaches 63,500 with at least 24 companies producing motorcars.

Harvey S. Firestone sells Henry Ford 2,000 sets of tires for the Model T (above) and begins a lasting relationship with Ford Motor Company (*see* 1900). Firestone will acquire a 2,000-acre Liberian rubber plantation in 1924 and 2 years later will lease a million acres for 99 years.

AC Spark Plug Company is founded by Buick Motor Car president W. C. Durant with French-American motorcycle specialist Albert Champion.

Champion Spark Plug Company has its beginnings in a Boston garage where Frank D. Stranahan, 26, and his 22-year-old brother Robert Allen Stranahan, just out of Harvard, begin manufacturing spark plugs, magnetos, coils, and other electrical equipment for motorcars. They will move to Toledo in 1910 and will go into business with Albert Champion (above) under the name Champion Spark Plug Co. Robert Stranahan will secure an order from Henry Ford, Champion will merge in 1921 with the Jeffery-Dewitt Co. founded by Joseph Arthur Jeffery, 35, Jeffery-Dewitt will become the Champion Porcelain Co., and Champion will be the sole supplier of spark plugs to Ford Motor Company until 1961.

W. C. Durant's Buick Motor Car Co. introduces a White Streak model and builds 8,820 motorcars.

General Motors Company is founded by W. C. Durant (above), who brings other carmakers together into a holding company (*see* 1906). Durant's bankers tell him that Henry Ford's company (above) is not worth the $8 million in cash that Ford demands, so Ford does not join (*see* Cadillac, Oakland, 1909; Storrow, 1910).

AC Spark Plug Company (above) will become a General Motors subsidiary. Together with Champion (above) it will dominate the business.

Automotive pioneer Charles Stewart Mott, 33, sells a 49 percent interest in his Flint, Mich., auto factory to General Motors (above) and will sell the remainder in 1913. A scion of the Mott cider and vinegar family, Mott went to work at age 24 for an uncle at Utica, N.Y., who made bicycle wheels and wheels and axles for motorcars, he has taken over the enterprise and moved it to Flint, and he will be a director of General Motors from 1913 until his death in 1975.

A high-wheeled International Harvester auto buggy is introduced at $750 while other simply constructed cars sell at prices between $750 and $900—more than most Americans earn in a year.

The Hupmobile is introduced by Detroit's Hupp Motor Car Company at the Detroit Automobile Show.

Less than 2 percent of all U.S. farm families own motorcars, but there are 200,000 cars on the road, up from 8,000 in 1900 (*see* 1923).

The C.I.T. (Commercial Investment Trust) finance company that will be a major factor in automobile installment buying has its beginnings at St. Louis where German-American merchant Henry Ittleson, 37, quits his job as merchandise manager of the May Company to launch the enterprise that he will move to New York in 1915. C.I.T. will concentrate at New York on automobile financing, but accounts receivable financing will account for the bulk of its business for some years (*see* GMAC, 1919).

A New York to Paris motorcar race sponsored by the *New York Times* and *Le Matin* begins February 12

1908 (cont.) at Times Square, 250,000 spectators line 8 miles of snowy New York roads to watch the contestants set out for Paris via Detroit, Cleveland, Chicago, Salt Lake City, San Francisco, Tokyo, Vladivostok, Irkutsk, Novosorirs, Moscow, Berlin, Bonn, and Brussels, a distance of 13,341 miles. U.S. contestant George Schuster, 35, driving a Thomas Flyer made by the 9-year-old E. R. Thomas Motor Company of Buffalo, N.Y., thwarts a scheme by a French contestant to buy up all available gasoline at Vladivostok; he wins the race, arriving at Paris in 169 days.

The gyrocompass invented by German engineer Hermann Anschutz-Kampfe, 36, indicates true north by sensing the rotation of the earth and then pointing the rotor axis toward the North Pole even when a ship is rolling in high seas.

French aviation pioneer Henri Farman, 34, flies a Voison biplane from Bouy to Reims in the first city-to-city flight. Farman will develop the Farman biplane with his 31-year-old brother Maurice, and he will build an aircraft factory at Boulogne Billancourt (*see* 1916).

Wilbur Wright completes a flying machine for the U.S. War Department, the aircraft crashes September 17 killing Lieutenant Thomas A. Selfridge who has flown as a passenger on the test flight, but Wright will repair the plane, it will pass U.S. Army tests in June of next year, and the Wright brothers will obtain the first government contract by producing a plane that can carry two men, can fly for 60 minutes, and can reach a speed of 40 miles per hour.

Wilbur Wright (above) wins the Michelin Cup in France by completing a 77-mile flight December 21 in 2 hours, 20 minutes (*see* 1905; 1909).

The Hejaz Railway to the Holy Places of Mecca and Medina is completed by Arab engineers after 8 years of construction (*see* T. E. Lawrence, 1917).

New York's 4-year-old IRT Broadway subway line is completed to Kingsbridge in the Bronx.

Two subway tunnels open to traffic at New York. The McAdoo Tunnel goes under the Hudson River to Hoboken (*see* 1904), another tunnel connects Bowling Green in Lower Manhattan with Brooklyn's Joralemon Street across the East River.

The King Edward VII Bridge opens to span the River Tyne at Newcastle.

The first international meeting of psychiatrists opens at Salzburg, Austria, with participants who include Sigmund Freud and Carl Gustav Jung (*see* 1906). Also present are Eugen Bleuler, 51, Alfred Adler, 38, Abraham Arden Brill, 34, Ernest Jones, 30, and while psychoanalysis will begin to gain repute and support in reputable international medical circles next year when Freud and Jung are invited to speak at Clark University in Worcester, Mass., the resistance to Freudian and Jungian techniques and philosophies will remain strong.

Buerger's disease gets its name as Viennese-American physician-surgeon Leo Buerger, 29, describes a vascular disease (thromboangiitis obliterans) that affects chiefly the peripheral arteries and sometimes the veins, especially in young men, and will be confused with atherosclerosis.

Ex-Lax Company is founded by Hungarian-American pharmacist Max Kiss, 25, who came to New York penniless 10 years ago, learned English, and learned from a physician aboard ship while traveling home for a visit to his family about the newly developed Bayer laxative phenopthalein. Kiss has developed a chocolate-flavored phenopthalein formula that he will promote in movie theaters with a film he will make using neighborhood children as actors.

U.S. banks close as the economic depression continues. Westinghouse Electric Co. goes bankrupt.

New York City's Progress Towards Bankruptcy by a former official in the city comptroller's office notes that New York's population has increased by 35 percent since 1898 from 3.27 million to 4.42 million but that the cost of servicing the city's debt has risen 189 percent, the cost of running the Board of City Records has increased by 207 percent, the College of the City of New York requires an appropriation 182 percent higher than in 1898, and library appropriations have climbed by 425 percent.

Thomas J. Watson makes an easel presentation to National Cash Register Company salesmen and writes the word "THINK" at the head of every sheet of paper (*see* 1903). NCR president J. H. Patterson sees the presentation and orders that "THINK" signs be made up for every NCR office (*see* 1910).

The University of Alberta is founded at Edmonton.

The University of British Columbia is founded at Vancouver.

The University of the Philippines is founded at Manila.

Youngstown State University is founded at Youngstown, Ohio.

Reed College is founded at Portland, Ore.

The first professional school of journalism opens at the University of Missouri.

The *Christian Science Monitor* begins publication November 25 at Boston (*see* Eddy, 1879).

The *Times* of London is acquired by *London Daily Mail* and *Daily Mirror* publisher A. C. W. Harmsworth, viscount Northcliffe, who was made a baronet 3 years ago (*see* 1788; 1903; Astor, 1922).

"Mutt and Jeff" in William Randolph Hearst's *San Francisco Examiner* March 29 is the first comic strip to appear daily with the same cartoon figures. Cartoonist Harry Conway "Bud" Fisher, 23, will continue the strip until his death in 1954.

La Nouvelle Revue Francaise begins publication at Paris under the direction of André Gide and Jean

Schlumberger; the literary review will gain wide influence.

Fiction *Penguin Island* (*L'île des Pingouins*) by Anatole France, who satirizes short story writer Guy de Maupassant; *La Retraite Sentimentale* by Colette who last year divorced Henry Gauthier-Villars; *The Outcast* (*L'esclusa*) by Luigi Pirandello; *Old Wives' Tale* by Arnold Bennett who has quit as assistant editor of *Woman* to devote himself to writing; *A Room with a View* by E. M. Forster; *The Man Who Was Thursday* by H. G. Wells; *An Ocean Tramp* by English marine engineer-novelist William McFee, 27, who will continue writing at sea until 1922 and at Westport, Conn., thereafter; *Spring* (*Haru*) by Shimazaki Toson; *Ayres Memorial* (*Memorial de Aires*) by Joaquim Mechado De Assis; *Holy Orders* by Marie Corelli.

Juvenile *The Wind in the Willows* by Scottish writer Kenneth Grahame, 49, whose stories will be dramatized by A. A. Milne; *Anne of Green Gables* by Canadian novelist Lucy Maud Montgomery, 35, who begins a series of Anne books about the Canadian wilderness.

Poetry *New Poems* (*Neue Gedichte*) by Rainer Maria Rilke.

Painting Cubism appears at the Paris Salon in an exhibition of paintings in "little cubes" by Pablo Picasso and Georges Braque.

Other paintings *Murneau* by Wassily Kandinsky; *The Doge's Palace, The Contarini Palace, The Palazzo Dario, San Giorgio Maggiore,* and *The Grand Canal, Venice,* by Claude Monet; *Nude Against the Light* and *After Dinner* by Pierre Bonnard; *Nu Rouge* by Russian painter Marc Chagall, 21; *Père Juniet's Cart* and *Zeppelins* by Henri Rousseau; *Harmony in Red* by Henri Matisse who gains international fame by exhibiting his work at New York's Steiglitz-Photo-Secession 291 Gallery; *The Lord Mayor of Liverpool* by Augustus John; *North River* by George Bellows.

The Ash Can school of U.S. realist art has its beginnings in an exhibition of work by The Eight—a group that includes cartoonist George Luks who has worked on "The Yellow Kid," William James Glackens, John French Sloan, 37, and Everett Shinn, 32. Influenced by Thomas Eakins, they have revolted against academicism with encouragement from painter Robert Henri, 43.

Sculpture *The Kiss* by Romanian-French sculptor Constantin Brancusi, 32, who has evolved a "primeval" style of stone and wood carving.

Theater *The Ghost Sonata* (*Spöksonaten*) by August Strindberg 1/21 at Stockholm's Intimate Theater; *Getting Married* by George Bernard Shaw 5/12 at London's Haymarket Theatre; *The Tragedy of Nan* by John Masefield 5/24 at London's New Royalty Theatre; *The Man from Home* by Booth Tarkington and Harry Leon Wilson 8/17 at New York's Astor Theater, with William Hodge, 496 perfs.; *What Every Woman Knows* by James M. Barrie 9/3 at the Duke of York's Theatre, London; *The Blue Bird* (*L'Oiseau bleu*) by Maurice Maeterlinck 9/30 at the Moscow Art Theater; *Days of Our Life* (*Dui nashey zhizni*) by Leonid Andreyev 11/6 at St. Petersburg's Novy Theater; *Salvation Nell* by Edward Sheldon 11/17 at Hackett's Theater, New York, with Mrs. Minnie Madden Fiske.

Stage musicals *The Three Twins* 6/15 at New York's Herald Square Theater, with music by Karl Hoschna, book and lyrics by U.S. playwright Otto Abels Harbach, 35, songs that include "Cuddle Up a Little Closer," "Yama Yama Man" (lyrics by Collin Davis), 288 perfs.; *The* (Ziegfeld) *Follies* 6/15 at New York's Jardin de Paris, with Hollywood comedienne Nora Bayes (Dora Goldberg Norworth), 28, book and lyrics mostly by Harry B. Smith, music by Maurice Levi and others, songs that include "Shine On, Harvest Moon" by Nora Bayes, lyrics by her husband Jack, 120 perfs.; *The Chocolate Soldier* (*Der tapfere soldat*) 11/14 at Vienna's Theater-an-der-Wien, with music by Oscar Strauss, libretto from the George Bernard Shaw play *Arms and the Man* of 1894.

First performances *Brigg Fair* by Frederick Delius 1/18 at London; Symphony No. 2 in E minor by Sergei Rachmaninoff 1/26 at Moscow; *Romanian Rhapsody No. 1* by Romanian composer Georges Enesco, 27, 2/7 at Paris; *Rapsodie Espagnole* by Maurice Ravel 3/15 at Paris; Symphony No. 7 in D major by Gustav Mahler 9/19 at Prague; *Poem of Ecstasy* by Aleksandr Skriabin late in the year at St. Petersburg; Symphony No. 1 in A flat major by Sir Edward Elgar 12/3 at Manchester; *In a Summer Garden* by Frederick Delius 12/11 at London.

The Brooklyn Academy of Music opens November 4 on Lafayette Avenue between Ashland Place and St. Felix Street, replacing a structure that opened in 1861.

New York's Metropolitan Opera House hires Giulio Gatti-Casazza, 40, from Milan's Teatro alla Scala. Gatti-Casazza will mastermind the Met until 1935 and will raise it to new heights of artistic and financial success.

A 65-note coin-operated player piano is introduced by the Rudolph Wurlitzer Company to augment its 44-note electric Pianino introduced 6 years ago. The old player piano sells for $500, the new one for $700 (*see* Wurlitzer, 1861; McTammany, 1876).

Popular songs "Take Me Out to the Ball Game" by Albert von Tilzer, lyrics by Jack Norworth (above) that popularize the confection Cracker Jack introduced in 1896; "Sunbonnet Sue" by Gus Edwards, lyrics by Will D. Cobb; "It's a Long Way to Tipperary" by English songwriters Harry Williams and Jack Judge.

The Chicago Cubs win the World Series by defeating the Detroit Tigers 4 games to 1 with help from Tinker and Evers and Chance.

1908 (cont.)   University of Michigan center Adolph "Germany" Schulz ends a brilliant football career for the Wolverines. Standing 6 feet 4 inches and weighing 245 pounds, Schulz has been fast as well as large and is remembered especially for a game against a powerful Pennsylvania eleven in which he held off Penn for 45 minutes until carried off the field (whereupon Penn scored more than 30 points in 15 minutes).

The Boy Scouts of Britain is founded under the leadership of Boer War hero Robert Stephenson Smyth, baron Baden-Powell of Gilwell, who held Mafeking through a 215-day siege in 1900 (*see* Boy Scouts of America, 1910; Girl Guides, 1910).

Mother's Day is observed for the first time at Philadelphia. Suffragist-temperance worker Anna May Jarvis, 44, attended a memorial service last year at the Methodist Church in Grafton, W.Va., for her mother Anna Reeves Jarvis who died at Philadelphia May 9, 1905, she conceived the idea of an annual worldwide tribute to mothers, and she will agitate for a national U.S. Mother's Day (*see* 1913).

Palm Beach cloth has its origin in a lightweight fabric of long-staple cotton and mohair from Angora goats created by U.S. chemist William S. Nutter who sells the patent to Goodall Worsted Company of Sanford, Me. Palm Beach brand fabric will revolutionize summer menswear beginning in the 1930s.

J. C. Penney buys out T. M. Callahan's interest in two western stores and begins a chain that will have 22 stores by 1911 with headquarters at Salt Lake City (*see* 1902). By the time Penney moves his headquarters to New York in 1913 he will have 48 stores and by 1916 he will have 127 (*see* 1927).

Baltimore's Hutzler Brothers Company department store incorporates after 50 years of doing business under the name M. Hutzler & Son. The store is headed by David Hutzler whose father and brother Abram started the enterprise.

New York's Singer building opens at Broadway and Liberty Street. The 41-story structure towers over the financial district.

New York's Apthorp apartment house on Broadway at 79th Street is completed by Clinton & Russell on a site formerly occupied by the Charles Apthorp mansion on land once occupied by the country house of Baron John Cornelius Van den Heuven.

New York's Graham Court apartment house is completed by Clinton & Russell at Seventh Avenue and 116th Street. Erected by William Waldorf Astor, the "Apthorp of Harlem" is an Italian Renaissance structure with huge rooms, 14-foot ceilings, fireplaces, and a large inner courtyard.

A New York mansion for German-American banker Felix Moritz Warburg, 37, of Kuhn, Loeb & Co. is completed in Renaissance château style at 1109 Fifth Avenue.

A Pocantico Hills, N.Y., mansion of fieldstone is completed in Georgian style for Standard Oil magnate John D. Rockefeller, Jr., on the vast 4,180-acre estate acquired by his father in 1893 (*see* Kykuit, 1903).

Minnesota's National Farmers Bank building is completed by Louis Sullivan at Owatonna.

Chicago's La Salle Hotel opens. The $6.5 million 22-story luxury hotel has 800 guest rooms and will be a Loop landmark for 68 years.

Boston's neighboring city of Chelsea has a fire April 12 (Palm Sunday) that destroys one-third of the town before burning itself out in late afternoon.

Los Angeles city engineer William Mulholland devises a plan to bring water from the Owens River in the Sierras to Los Angeles via a $25 million cement and steel aqueduct. The Mulholland plan will permit irrigation of the San Fernando Valley (*see* farmers, 1924; Parker Dam, 1939).

Muir Woods National Monument is created by presidential proclamation. The 500-acre forest of California redwoods and sequoias is on land donated to the federal government by William Kent, U.S. congressman from Marin County (*see* Hetch Hetchy, 1913).

Grand Canyon National Monument is created by President Roosevelt who acts under provisions of the 1906 Antiquities Act to protect Arizona's spectacular canyon from private land speculators (*see* 1919).

President Roosevelt appoints Gifford Pinchot to head a new National Conservation Commission (*see* 1907).

President Roosevelt calls a White House Conference on Conservation to publicize the cause.

President Roosevelt appoints Liberty Hyde Bailey, 50, to head a new Country Life Commission. Horticulturist-botanist Bailey is director of Cornell University's agricultural experiment station.

Less than 60 heath hens remain on Martha's Vineyard. They constitute the world's last colony of the birds once plentiful in New England (*see* 1839; 1916).

A mysterious fireball explodes the morning of June 30 over Tunguska in Siberia, it creates shock waves felt miles away, its thermal currents set great tracts of tundra woodlands afire, and the mushroom cloud and "black rain" that follow it inflict a scabby disease on reindeer herds. Irkutsk, Batavia, Moscow, St. Petersburg, Jena, and Washington, D.C., record seismic shocks. Russian scientists will not visit the sparsely populated area until 1927, they will find no meteorite fragments, and some will later speculate that the fireball was a crippled alien space vehicle powered by atomic energy.

An earthquake rocks Sicily December 28, killing some 75,000 in and about Messina.

Nearly 90 percent of the horsepower used on English and Welsh farms comes from horses (*see* 1939).

J. I. Case Company turns to selling gasoline tractors after 66 years of producing farm equipment that has made it the leading U.S. maker of farm steam engines (*see* Froelich, 1892; Edison, 1895).

Half of all Americans live on farms or in towns of less than 2,500, and the country has 6 million farms.

The flavor enhancer monosodium glutamate (MSG) that gives a meaty flavor to vegetable diets is isolated from seaweed by Tokyo University chemist Kikunae Ikeda, who calls the white salt "aginimoto," meaning "the essence of taste." The Japanese firm Ajinimoto will become the world's leading MSG producer, and the name Ajinimoto will become a generic for MSG in Japan (*see* 1934; 5'-inosinic acid, 1913).

Folger Coffee Company moves from San Francisco to Kansas City, Mo. (*see* 1850; Procter & Gamble, 1963).

A fruit canning plant that will be the world's largest canning and freezing plant is built at Sunnyvale, Calif., by Libby, McNeill & Libby (*see* 1906; 1909).

New England entrepreneur Hugh Moore develops a vending machine that sells drinking water at a penny per cup in individual paper cups that will be improved and sold as Dixie Cups (*see* 1909).

M. S. Hershey incorporates his 4-year-old business and builds a 20-room mansion 100 yards from his thriving chocolate bar factory (*see* 1903; 1911).

A gentlemen's agreement binding Japan to issue no further passports to coolies for immigration directly to the United States is concluded February 18 as the Japanese acquiesce to last year's order by President Roosevelt barring Japanese immigration (*see* 1924).

1909 The arsenic compound formulated by Paul Ehrlich to fight syphilis is the first antibacterial therapeutic drug and pioneers chemotherapy in medicine (*see* diphtheria, 1891). The German bacteriologist is now 56, his compound Number 592 is effective in destroying the trypanosomes that cause syphilis in mice and produces no side effects or aftereffects, his purer, more soluble variant Number 606 will prove effective next year in treating human victims of syphilis, and the drug will be marketed under the name Salvarsan. Ehrlich's arsphenamine will reduce the incidence of syphilis in England and France by 50 percent in the next 5 years, but while his work will lead to the discovery of new antibacterial agents, many will attack his syphilis cure on the ground that it encourages sin (*see* Fleming, 1928; Domagk, 1935).

Austrian pathologist Karl Landsteiner, 41, looks into the reasons why donors' blood sometimes causes clotting in recipients' blood and establishes the existence of different blood types (*see* 1818). Further research will reveal that there are four essential blood types: O, A, B, and AB; knowledge of compatability will make blood transfusions safe (*see* Rh factor, 1940).

Congress bans the import of opium for anything but medical purposes. Opium derivatives are widely used in the anodynes codeine and morphine as they were in the earlier anodyne laudanum, and a tincture of opium is effective in treating some intestinal disorders (*see* Heroin, 1898).

John D. Rockefeller gives $530 million for worldwide medical research. The Standard Oil Company head is the world's first billionaire (*see* Rockefeller Institute, 1901).

The Rockefeller Sanitary Commission that will become the Rockefeller Foundation in 1913 begins a campaign to eradicate hookworm disease in the South (*see* 1619; Stiles, 1902).

A theory of the gene formulated by Columbia University zoologist Thomas Hunt Morgan, 43, breaks new ground in the study of heredity.

The nucleic acids RNA and DNA are discovered by Russian-American chemist Phoebus Theodore Levene, 40 (*see* 1870; Watson and Crick, 1953).

The first man to reach the North Pole arrives April 6 at latitude 90° north. U.S. explorer Robert Edwin Peary, 52, accompanied by his black aide Matthew A. Henson and four Eskimos, plants the 46-star American flag at the Pole, and he returns to find that a companion from an earlier expedition claims to have beaten him to the Pole (the claim by surgeon Frederick A. Cook will prove false but only after a long controversy).

Constantinople recognizes Austrian annexation of Bosnia and Herzegovina January 12, Vienna pays the Turks £2.2 million in indemnity, the Russians cancel a £20 million Turkish indemnity in return for Constantinople's recognition of Bulgarian independence, and internal strife disrupts the Ottoman Empire.

The 76-year-old Ottoman grand vizir Kiamil Pasha is deposed February 13 and is succeeded by the 50-year-old Hussein Hilmi Pasha, the First Army Corps composed chiefly of Albanians revolts at Constantinople April 13 and forces Hilmi Pasha to resign, a 25,000-man army of liberation arrives from Macedonia April 24, a 5-hour battle ensues, and leaders of the April 13 revolt are executed.

The 66-year-old Ottoman sultan Abdul Hamid II, who has reigned since 1876, is deposed April 26 by unanimous vote of the Turkish parliament, he is exiled to Salonica, and he is succeeded by his helpless 64-year-old brother who will reign as Mohammed V until 1918.

The Persian shah Mohammed Ali Shah who has reigned since 1907 is deposed July 16 by the Bakhtaiari tribal chief Ali Kuli Khan, who has taken Teheran 4 days earlier. A Russian force has invaded northern Persia, has raised the siege of Tabriz March 26, and has occupied the city for the shah with savage brutality which has aroused the Bakhtaiari who replace the shah with his 12-year-old son. Ahmad Shah will reign until 1925, but he will be entirely under the control of radical elements.

Britain, France, Russia, and Italy withdraw their forces from Crete in July and the island becomes part of Greece.

The king of the Belgians Leopold II dies December 17 at age 74 after a reign of nearly 41 years in which

Mexican revolutionists divvied up the country's large landholdings among the long-disenfranchised *campesinos*.

he has exploited the Congo and has amassed great wealth at the expense of the Africans. He is succeeded by his 34-year-old nephew who will reign until 1934 as Albert I.

Japanese forces begin a 36-year occupation of Korea which is in a state of insurrection following the abdication of her emperor in 1907. Japan will formally annex Korea next year and will rename the country Chōsen.

The Valor of Ignorance by U.S. military expert Homer Lea, 32, makes predictions about future world history. Japan will be an aggressive power, says Lea, and will make war on the United States beginning with an attack on Hawaii (*see* 1941).

Nearly two decades of Hawaiian plantation disturbances erupt in a strike by exploited Japanese workers. It is the first major Hawaiian strike (*see* 1882).

Labour in Portuguese West Africa by William Cadbury draws attention to conditions of slavery in São Thomé and Principe (*see* 1905). Cadbury has visited both places and has persuaded two other Quaker cocoa and chocolate firms (Fry and Rowntree) to join the Cadbury firm in a boycott of cocoa from the Portuguese African islands, but while working conditions in Sao Thomé improve, the system of cocoa slavery remains.

The NAACP (National Association for the Advancement of Colored People) is organized at New York following a January meeting in the apartment of W. E. Walling with social worker Mary W. Ovington and immigrant leader Henry Moscowitz who begin "a revival of the Abolitionist spirit." The new organization is headed by W. E. B. DuBois and is supported by social worker Jane Addams of Chicago, educator John Dewey, journalist Lincoln Steffens, Rabbi Ste-

phen Wise, 35, and 49 others, including six blacks (*see* 1908; 1910).

A 3-month strike of some 20,000 U.S. garment workers begins November 22. The workers belong to the Ladies' Waist Makers' Union Local 25 of the 9-year-old International Ladies' Garment Workers Union (ILGWU), and they will win most of their demands (but *see* Triangle Shirtwaist Factory fire, 1911).

Bakelite is discovered by Belgian-American chemist Leo Hendrik Baekeland, 46, whose plastic material is the world's first polymer. Baekeland's synthetic shellac is made from formaldehyde and phenol, Bakelite products will be used initially for electrical insulation, and the chemist starts a company to market a molding powder used for shaping Bakelite products (*see* Union Carbide and Carbon, 1939).

Synthetic rubber is produced by German chemist Karl Hoffman of Farbenfabriken Bayer who makes it from butadiene, a gas derived from butane.

The first crossing of the English Channel by a man in a heavier-than-air machine is made July 25 by French engineer Louis Blériot, 36, who produces a monoplane and flies it from Calais to a field near Dover in 37 minutes (*see* Alcock and Brown, 1919).

Orville Wright demonstrates the success of the Wright brothers' airplane and wins assurance of its acceptance by the U.S. Army in July (*see* 1908). The brothers will establish the American Wright Co. to manufacture aircraft (*see* Curtiss-Wright, 1929).

The first international air races are held at Reims in France to compete for a cup offered by *New York Herald* publisher James Gordon Bennett. U.S. inventor-aviator Glenn Hammond Curtiss, 31, wins with an airplane and motor of his own design (*see* 1910).

A U.S. aircraft factory is founded by Glenn L. Martin, 23, who will receive his first government contract in 1913. Martin will form the Glenn L. Martin Co. at Cleveland in 1917 and he will move the company to Baltimore in 1929 (*see* Douglas, 1920).

The New York, New Haven, and Hartford Railroad buys a majority interest in the Boston and Maine, but Boston lawyer Louis Dembitz Brandeis, 50, fights the aggrandizement of New Haven president C. S. Mellen whose poor administration is wrecking the finances of his company (*see* 1903). Both the New Haven and the B&M will be forced to omit dividends to their stockholders in 1913, Mellen will be obliged to resign, and in 1914 the New Haven will be forced to divest itself of its trolley line and steamship interests (*see* 1935).

The Chicago, Milwaukee, and St. Paul Railroad reaches Seattle and becomes the seventh line to link the Mississippi to the Pacific Coast (*see* 1863).

The first transcontinental U.S. motorcar race pits two Model T Fords against an Acme, an Itala, a Shawmut, and a Stearns (which fails to start). Five cars leave New York June 1, and a Ford wins the race, arriving

728

June 22 at Seattle where the Alaska-Yukon Pacific Exposition is being held.

U.S. automobile production reaches 127,731, up from 63,500 last year.

The Hudson Motor Car Company is founded by R. D. Chapin and Howard Earle Coffin, 35, with backing from Detroit department store magnate J. L. Hudson (see 1881). Coffin is a veteran of the Olds Motor Works and has designed the Chalmers motorcar for the Chalmers-Detroit Motor Company (see 1916).

Marmon motorcars switch to water-cooled engines, and the first Marmon to compete at the new Indianapolis Speedway performs well enough to bring the car some publicity (see 1902; 1916; Indianapolis 500, 1911).

General Motors Corporation acquires the Cadillac Motor Company from Henry M. Leland for $4.5 million (see 1904). Cadillacs are made with interchangeable parts and in that respect are unusual in the fledgling automotive industry (see 1916; self-starter, 1911; Lincoln, 1922).

General Motors Corporation acquires the Oakland Motor Car Company. The firm has a factory at Pontiac, Mich., producing motorcars designed by A. P. Brush (see 1924; Pontiac, 1926).

One Iowa farmer in 34 has a motorcar, while in New York City only one family in 190 has one, reports *Collier's* magazine. The magazine calls the motorcar the greatest social force in America—greater even than rural free mail delivery, the telephone, or university extension services (see Wilson, 1906).

Western Auto Supply Company is founded by Kansas City bookkeeper George Pepperdine, 23, who opens a mail-order house to supply parts for Model T Fords which are sold minus tires, fenders, tops, windshields, and lights—items that can cost a buyer as much as the car itself. By 1915 Pepperdine's company will be grossing $229,000 per year and will have a second plant at Denver to produce parts for the Model T (see 1927).

New York's Queensboro Bridge opens March 30 to carry traffic across the East River between Manhattan and Queens. Built primarily to carry trolley cars, the $17 million span is the first important double-deck bridge.

New York's Manhattan Bridge opens December 31 to carry traffic between Manhattan and Brooklyn and is the third such link. The $31 million span is the first important double-deck suspension bridge.

Italy's Alfa-Romeo motorcar company has its origin in the Anonima Lombarda Fabbrica Automobila (ALFA) at Milan. Entrepreneurs have split with France's Alexandre Darracq, they take over Darracq's Milan branch, but they will move to Rome in 1920 and will operate under the name Alfa-Romeo.

 Britain institutes new tax measures in order to finance her social security programs (see 1908). Chancellor of the Exchequer David Lloyd George's budget imposes a supertax at the rate of 6d per pound on incomes exceeding £5,000 per year, and steep taxes are imposed on estates (see 1915).

A gold strike that will make Canada the world's third largest producer after South Africa and Russia is made by prospector Benny Hollinger who has pursued reports of "white rocks" in the Porcupine Lake area of eastern Ontario. When Canadian gold production peaks in 1941, the country will have 146 gold mines including the Hollinger and Dome mines and will be producing 5.3 million ounces per year.

The first Lincoln head penny, issued by the Philadelphia Mint, replaces the Indian head penny that has been in circulation since 1864. The new 1-cent piece will not be redesigned until 1959.

The Payne-Aldrich Tariff Act signed into law by President Taft August 5 abolishes the import duty on hides to help the U.S. shoe industry but maintains high duties on iron and steel and raises duties on silk, cotton goods, and many minor items (see 1897; Underwood-Simmons Act, 1913).

The Sixteenth Amendment to the U.S. Constitution providing for an unapportioned income tax is submitted to the 46 states for ratification (see 1913).

The Anglo-Californian Bank is founded at San Francisco (see Lazard Frères, 1884).

Edison MAZDA lamps introduced by the General Electric Company and the National Electric Company use a trade name based on that of the Persian god of light Ahura Mazda (see Langmuir, 1912).

Walter Reed Army Medical Center opens at Washington, D.C., on a site bounded by Georgia Avenue, M Street, Fern Street, and Appen Street N.W.

Kansas bans public drinking vessels, the first state to take such action.

The Public Cup Vendor Company is incorporated by Hugh Moore with backing from a New York investment banker who puts up $200,000 to start the company. It distributes free dispensers to offices, schools, and other customers who contract to buy the paper Dixie Cups (see 1908).

Cascarets are acquired by Sterling Products Company (see 1901; Kramer, 1887; Syrup of Figs, 1912).

The Walgreen's drugstore chain has its beginning in a pharmacy opened by Chicago pharmacist Charles Rudolph Walgreen, 35, who will popularize the soda-fountain-lunchcounter. His chain will grow to become the nation's largest (see 1934).

The United States has 2,600 daily newspapers to serve her 90 million people (see 1958).

New York's weekly *Amsterdam News* begins publication. The paper's circulation will peak at 100,000, the nation's largest nonreligious black weekly.

Condé Nast takes over *Vogue* magazine, started late in 1892 as a fashion and society weekly. The 35-year-

1909 (cont.) old former *Collier's* advertising manager has organized the Home Pattern Company as a side venture to make and sell dress patterns under an arrangement with Cyrus H. K. Curtis's *Ladies' Home Journal, Vogue* has a circulation of only 22,500, Nast will make it a monthly, he will hire Edna Woolman Chase as editor in 1914, and she will make *Vogue* the world's leading fashion magazine in a 38-year career that will see the launching of British and French editions (*see* 1915).

The United States Copyright Law passed by Congress March 4 takes effect July 1 and will protect U.S. authors, publishers (and composers) under terms that will remain unchanged for 68 years. The law gives copyright owners exclusive rights "to print, reprint, publish, copy, and vend the copyrighted work." The courts will develop an ill-defined doctrine of "fair use" by which to decide cases involving charges of copyright infringement, taking into account the nature of the copyrighted work, the amount of material copied, and the effect of the use on the copyright owner's potential market (*see* below, music).

The McGraw-Hill Book Company is created by a merger of the book publishing interests of rival magazine publishers James McGraw and John Hill (*see* 1888), each of whom has developed a group of magazines, McGraw's in the electrical and transportation industries, Hill's in the mechanical and engineering fields. Hill will die in 1916 and his five magazines will be merged with those of McGraw in 1917 to create the McGraw-Hill Publishing Company (*see Business Week*, 1929).

A futurist manifesto published by Italian poet-publicist Emilio Filippo Tommaso Marinetti, 33, advocates rejection of the past, abandonment of syntax and grammatical rules.

Fiction *The Peasants (Chlopi)* by Wladyslaw Reymont; *The River Sumida (Sumida-gawa)* by Japanese novelist Kafu Nagai, 30, who has returned to Tokyo after 5 years in America and France to find the city horribly modernized; "The Tatooer" (story) by Japanese writer Jamichiro Tanizaki, 23, who brings out the hidden motivations of sexual fascination; *Actions and Reactions* (stories) by Rudyard Kipling; *Tono-Bungay* by H. G. Wells who shows the excesses of patent medicine exploitation in the first of a series of novels about contemporary life; *Martin Eden* by Jack London; *A Girl of the Limberlost* by Gene Stratton Porter; *The Circular Staircase* by U.S. mystery novelist Mary Roberts Rinehart, 32.

Poetry *Handful of Songs (Gitangali)* by Bengali poet Rabindranath Tagore, 48, whose work will be promoted in the West by William Butler Yeats.

Painting *Eiffel Tower* by French painter Robert Delaunay, 24, who introduces brilliant color to cubism after having experimented with post-impressionism and fauvism (he will paint the Eiffel Tower at least 30 times); *The Dance* (panel) and *Woman in Green with a Carnation* by Henri Matisse; *Standing Nude* by Pierre Bonnard; *The Equatorial Jungle* by

Henri Rousseau; *Violincellist* by Amedeo Modigliani; *Robin* by Augustus John; *El Picador* by Diego Rivera; *Both Members of This Club* (prizefighters) by George Bellows; Alfred Steiglitz introduces U.S. watercolorist John Cheri Marin, 38, to New York with a show at his Photo-Secession 291 Gallery. Frederick Remington dies near Ridgefield, Conn., December 26 at age 48.

The Boston Museum of Fine Arts is completed (*see* 1870).

Munich's Modern Gallerie opens under the direction of local art dealer Justin Thannhauser, 17, whose father opened a Munich gallery 5 years ago. He turns that gallery into a focal point for work by "Die Brücke" ("The Bridge") expressionists Edvard Munch (who is working on a mural for Oslo University), Paul Klee, 29, Wassily Kandinsky, and others. Thannhauser will open his biggest gallery in 1927 at Berlin.

Theater *The Easiest Way* by U.S. playwright Eugene Walter, 35, 1/19 at New York's Stuyvesant (Belasco) Theater, with Joseph Kilgour, 157 perfs.; *Strife* by John Galsworthy 2/21 at the Duke of York's Theatre, London; *Griselda* by Gerhart Hauptmann 3/6 at Vienna's Hofburgtheater; *Earl Birger of Bjalbo (Bjalb-Jarlen)* by August Strindberg 3/26 at Stockholm's Swedish Theater; *The Fortune Hunter* by Winchell Smith 9/4 at New York's Gaiety Theater, with John Barrymore, 345 perfs.; *The Melting Pot* by Israel Zangwill 9/17 at New York's Artef Theater after a year on the road, with Walker Whiteside, 136 perfs. The play introduces the "melting pot" phrase to describe America's amalgam of nationalities and races (*see* de Crèvecoeur, 1782); *Anathema (Anatema)* by Leonid Andreyev 10/2 at the Moscow Art Theater; *The Tinker's Wedding* by John Millington Synge 11/11 at His Majesty's Theatre, London; *Liliom* by Hungarian playwright Ferenc Molnar, 31, 12/7 at Budapest's Vigszinhaz; *The City* by Clyde Fitch 12/21 at New York's Lyric Theater, with Walter Hampden, 190 perfs.

Film William Ranon's *Hiawatha*.

Bell & Howell Company's Albert S. Howell eliminates the "flicker" from motion pictures with a standard camera that permits precise control of film movement (*see* 1907; 1911).

Opera *Elektra* 1/25 at Dresden's Konigliches Operhaus, with music by Richard Strauss, libretto by Hugo von Hofmannsthal; *Le Coc d'Or (The Golden Cock)* 9/24 at Moscow's Zimin Theater, with music by the late Nikolai Rimsky-Korsakov.

The Boston Opera House opens November 8 with ovations to merchant Eban Jordan of Jordan-Marsh whose benefactions have made the house possible.

Ballet *Prince Igor* 5/18 at the Théâtre du Châtelet, Paris, with music by the late Nikolai Rimsky-Korsakov from the opera of 1890, choreography by Russian impressario Sergei Pavlovich Diaghilev, 37, who founds the Ballet Russe and employs dancer Waslaw Nijinsky, 19, an incredible performer who made his debut 2 years ago with Diaghilev's Imperial Ballet at St. Petersburg. Michel Fokine takes over the Imperial Ballet.

The London Symphony gives its first concert June 9.

First performances *Die Todtinsel (The Island of the Dead)* (Symphonic Poem, after a picture by A. Bocklin) by Sergei Rachmaninoff 5/1 at Moscow; Concerto No. 3 in D minor for Piano and Orchestra by Sergei Rachmaninoff 11/28 at New York.

The new United States Copyright Law (above) secures exclusive rights to composers and/or publishers to print, publish, copy, vend, arrange, record by means of gramophone or any other mechanical device, and perform publicly for profit original musical compositions, and affords protection against infringement for a period of 28 years and a renewal period of the same length (*see* 1897; ASCAP, 1914).

The Chautauqua movement founded in 1874 gains a musical aspect as Walter Damrosch, 47, brings his New York Symphony Orchestra to Chautauqua, N.Y. The Chautauqua will become an important training center for U.S. musical talent.

Broadway musicals *The* (Ziegfeld) *Follies* 6/14 at the Jardin de Paris, with Nora Bayes, Jack Norworth, Eva Tanguay, Russian-American actress-singer Sophie Tucker (Sonia Kalish), 25, music by Maurice Levi and others, book and lyrics chiefly by Harry B. Smith, 64 perfs.; *Old Dutch* 11/22 at the Herald Square Theater, with Lew Fields, English-American dancer Vernon Blythe Castle, 22, and with 9-year-old Helen Hayes (Bown) making her first New York appearance (she has been a professional actress since age 5), book by Edgar Smith, music by Victor Herbert, lyrics by George V. Hobart, 88 perfs.

Popular songs "By the Light of the Silvery Moon" by Gus Edwards, lyrics by Edward Madden; "Meet Me Tonight in Dreamland" by Leo Friedman, 40, lyrics by Beth Slater Whitson, 30; "I Wonder Who's Kissing Her Now" by Joseph E. Howard and Harold Orlob, 24, lyrics by William M. Hough, 27, and Frank R. Adams, 26; "Put on Your Old Grey Bonnet" by Percy Wenrich, 24, lyrics by Stanley Murphy; "Casey Jones" by Eddie Newton, lyrics by T. Lawrence Seibert (*see* 1900); "On Wisconsin!" (march) by W. T. Purdy.

Philadelphia's Shibe Park is completed for Connie Mack's Athletics at a cost of $1 million. The Athletics defeat the Boston Red Sox 8 to 1 on opening day; the 23,000-seat ball park will be Connie Mack Stadium beginning in 1953, and it will remain in use until 1970.

"Tris" Speaker signs with the Boston Red Sox to begin a 19-year American League career. Texas-born centerfielder Tristram E. Speaker, 21, will have a lifetime batting average of .344.

The Pittsburgh Pirates win the World Series by defeating the Detroit Tigers 4 games to 3.

A field goal in football receives a value of 3 points, down from 4 in 1904, 5 in 1883.

The celluloid Kewpie Doll with a head that comes to a point is patented by New York author-illustrator Rose Cecil O'Neill, 35, whose creation will be the basis of a mold that will be made in 1913 by Pratt Institute art student Joseph L. Kallus. The doll will make $1.5 million for O'Neill who wears a toga at her Greenwich Village salons.

Selfridge's opens in London's Oxford Street and is Britain's first large department store. U.S. merchant Gordon Selfridge, 52, has had a successful career at Chicago's Marshall Field & Company, his new store will rival Harrods and Marks & Spencer, and it will become as famous as Marshall Field's.

The first British F. W. Woolworth store opens in Liverpool's Church Street (*see* 1900). By 1958 there will be 1,000 British Woolworth stores (*see* 1912).

Filene's Automatic Bargain Basement opens at Boston and is the first of its kind (*see* 1881). Merchant Edward A. Filene marks down merchandise automatically 25 percent after 12 days, 50 percent after 18, and 75 percent after 24 with anything still remaining after 30 days donated to charity (*see* 1912).

New York's 91-year-old Brooks Brothers closes its two downtown stores and reopens at Broadway and 22nd Street near the city's most fashionable residential district. A Brooks Brothers branch opens at Newport, R.I. (*see* 1858; 1915).

San Francisco's I. Magnin moves into a new four-story building at Grant and Geary Streets that it will outgrow by 1919 (*see* 1906).

The first International Conference on City Planning meets in late May at Washington, D.C. It has been organized largely at the initiative of the secretary of New York's Committee on Congestion of Population Benjamin C. Marsh who has helped prepare a new privately printed book on city planning which begins, "A city without a plan is like a ship without a rudder."

"Make no little plans," says Chicago architect Daniel Burnham in his "Plan for Chicago of 1909." Little plans "have no magic to stir men's blood," argues Burnham, but while his Chicago plan will spur that city and many others to adopt sweeping master plans to guide their growth, some utopian master plans will be too inflexible to allow for the unpredictable social, economic, and political forces that interact to shape cities.

Chicago's Frederick G. Robie house completed by Frank Lloyd Wright at 5757 South Woodlawn Boulevard is the world's first house to be built on a slab foundation, to incorporate garages in its structure, to have roof overhangs calculated on an astronomical basis for maximum lighting in winter and maximum shade in summer, and to employ indirect lighting and rheostats (dimmers) for lighting control.

1909 (cont.) New York's 36-story Metropolitan Life Insurance Tower is completed by Napoleon Le Brun & Sons with a 46th-story observation floor on Madison Square at 23rd Street. The tower will be the world's tallest building until 1913.

New York's Alwyn Court apartments are completed in French Renaissance style on Seventh Avenue at 58th Street.

Congress enacts legislation to prevent any private builder in Washington, D.C., from putting up a structure more than 130 feet high, but the 11-story Cairo Hotel erected in 1894 is permitted to stand.

 A U.S. National Bison Refuge is created near Moise, Mont. (*see* 1900; 1910).

U.S. lumber production reaches its peak.

U.S. forester Aldo Leopold, 22, arrives in the Southwest just out of Yale and sees six immense areas, each larger than 500,000 acres, stretching roadless across Arizona and New Mexico. "Like winds and sunsets," Leopold will write in *Sand County Almanac*, "wild things were taken for granted until progress began to do away with them.... Now we face the question whether a still higher 'standard of living' is worth its cost in things natural, wild and free."

Soil is indestructible, says a report issued by the U.S. Bureau of Soils which has made the first National Soil Survey (*see* 1933; 1934).

A river and harbors bill enacted by Congress empowers the U.S. Army Corps of Engineers to construct locks and dams on U.S. waterways.

 Laguna Dam is completed on the Colorado River north of Yuma, Ariz., to irrigate more desert land.

Colorado is the most irrigated state in the nation with more than 3 million acres under irrigation (*see* Union Colony, 1888).

Acreage allotted under the Homestead Act of 1862 is doubled by Congress following the failure of tens of thousands of homesteaders in arid regions of the West for lack of enough land. But it takes at least four sections of land (2,560 acres) to support a family raising livestock in the West, so the new act is inadequate (*see* 1916; Powell, 1878).

The first Kibbutz is started at the Jordan Valley village of Degania Aleph in Palestine which is part of the Ottoman Empire.

 Smelt are planted in the Great Lakes where they will become an important food fish species.

 Libby, McNeill & Libby buys its first pineapple lands on the Hawaiian island of Oahu. Libby will pack 29,000 cases of pineapple next year (*see* 1908; Alaskan salmon, 1912).

Hawaiian Pineapple Company's James Dole summons his competitors to a meeting as a glut of pineapple production depresses prices (*see* 1902). Dole packs 242,822 cases and the growers agree to undertake a program of advertising to win acceptance for canned pineapple in the big eastern U.S. markets,

the first advertising campaign for a commodity by any growers' association (*see* 1911; Sunkist, 1919).

Strawberries are frozen for market in the Pacific Northwest (*see* Birdseye, 1914).

U.S. ice cream sales reach 30 million gallons, up from 5 million in 1899. Philadelphia has 49 ice cream manufacturing plants and 52 ice cream "saloons."

J. L. Kraft Bros & Co. is founded at Chicago by James Lewis Kraft, his accountant Oliver Blackburn, and his brothers Charles, Herbert, Fred, Norman, and John with an investment that totals $15,000. Kraft goes into competition with Phenix Cheese Corp. (*see* 1900; 1915; Kraft-Phenix, 1928).

C. A. Pillsbury & Company is leased from its British owners and is then brought back under U.S. ownership and control (*see* 1889; Bake-Offs, 1949).

Coca-Cola is exported to Britain for the first time (*see* 1899; 1907; distinctive bottle, 1916).

Thomas Lipton begins blending and packaging his tea at New York. Lipton's U.S. business will be incorporated in 1915, and 3 years after his death in 1931 his picture will begin appearing on the red and yellow packages that identify Lipton products (*see* 1893; 1914).

G. Washington soluble coffee powder is introduced by Brooklyn, N.Y., kerosene lamp maker George Constant Louis Washington, 38. Born in Belgium, Washington settled in Guatemala 2 years ago after making a small fortune in kerosene lamps, and when he noticed a fine powder on the spout of a silver coffee carafe he began experiments that led to the development of the powder for making instant coffee (*see* Kato, 1901; Nescafé, 1938).

1910 A coalition of rebellious congressmen led by Republican George W. Norris, 48, of Nebraska curtails the powers of Speaker Joseph Gurney Cannon, 73, and excludes him from the House Rules Committee March 19. The congressmen establish a system of seniority that will control committee chairmanships for more than 65 years.

Britain's Edward VII dies May 6 at age 68 after a 9-year reign of peace and prosperity. He is succeeded by his 44-year-old second son who will reign as George V until his death in 1936.

The Republic of South Africa, independent of Great Britain, is established May 31 under terms of the South Africa Act approved by Parliament in September of last year. The new Union of South Africa has dominion status, it unites the Cape Colony, the Orange River Colony, Natal, and Transvaal, its legislative seat is at Capetown, its seat of government is at Pretoria, and its prime minister is Boer statesman Louis Botha, 47, who will continue in the post until his death in 1919.

The French Congo is renamed French Equatorial Africa and is redivided into the colonies of Gabon, Middle Congo, and Ubanghi-Shari.

Egypt's Coptic premier Butros Ghali is assassinated by a nationalist fanatic.

Montenegro proclaims herself an independent Balkan kingdom August 28, and the 69-year-old prince who obtained recognition of his country's independence in the Treaty of Berlin in 1878 receives the title king by a vote of the national legislature. He begins a 9-year reign as Nicholas I.

The Portuguese monarchy founded in 1143 by Afonso Henriquez ends October 4 in a revolution at Lisbon. Manoel II flees to England (where he will live as a country gentleman until his death in 1932) after a 2-year reign, and a republic is proclaimed with a provisional government headed by scholar-writer Teofilo Braga, 67.

A Mexican social revolution begins as Francisco Indalecio Madero, 37, leads opposition to President Porfirio Diaz who has controlled the country since 1876 and who has allowed the lands of its 6 million Indians and 8 million *mestizos* to fall into the possession of large white landowners. The exploited peons start breaking up the large land-holdings and distributing farmland among the *campesinos* (see 1911).

China abolishes slavery.

German peasants still work 18-hour days and are treated little better than serfs.

A French general strike is averted by Prime Minister Aristide Briand, 48, who forces an end to a railroad strike begun by the Confédération Générale du Travail (CGT). Briand calls all railroad workers "to the colors" and the CGT orders the men back to work.

The average U.S. workingman earns less than $15 per week, his working hours range from 54 to 60 hours, and there is wide irregularity of employment.

Chicago clothing workers who include 23-year-old Sidney Hillman revolt against low wages and piecework as they begin agitating for a stronger union in the men's clothing industry. U.S. clothing workers participated in more strikes during the last quarter of the 19th century than did workers in any other industry, and their activity accelerates (see Amalgamated Clothing Workers, 1914).

The International Ladies' Garment Workers Union (ILGWU) wins a 9-week strike for New York cloakmakers (see 1909; Dubinsky, 1932).

A bomb exploded October 1 at the *Los Angeles Times* kills 20 men. Authorities arrest James McNamara, 28, and his brother John, 27, on charges of having placed the bomb to silence opposition to organized labor by Harrison Gray Otis, now 73 (see 1882), Chicago lawyer Clarence Darrow defends the McNamara brothers, but they will confess their guilt next year following exposure of the facts by detective William J. Burns who in the past 5 years has uncovered political corruption in San Francisco, kickback schemes in the railroad industry, land frauds in the Northwest, and other crimes including bank embez-

zlements. Burns will become head of the FBI for 4 years beginning in 1921 (see 1886; 1908).

The Mann White Slave Traffic Act passed by Congress June 25 discourages interstate transportation of women for immoral purposes. Newspaper stories about prizefighter Jack Johnson have inspired passage of the law (see 1915).

The "great white hope" James J. Jeffries comes out of retirement to challenge heavyweight champion Jack Johnson but loses July 4 (below). Race riots ensue at Boston, Cincinnati, Houston, New York, and Norfolk, three blacks are killed at Uvalda, Ga., as white bigots vent their rage at the continuing supremacy of the first black prizefight champion.

The National Association for the Advancement of Colored People (NAACP) is founded at New York (see Dubois, 1909). Eight out of 10 U.S. blacks still live in the 11 states of the Old Confederacy, but a "great migration" begins that will bring more than 2 million blacks to the North (see 1940).

Women in Washington State gain the right to vote in a constitutional amendment adopted November 8 (see California, 1911).

New York's Pennsylvania Station opens to train traffic September 8. The Pennsylvania Railroad's late president Alexander Johnston Cassatt had proposed erecting a hotel on the terminal's air rights, but he was dissuaded on the ground that the railroad had an obligation to give New York a monumental gateway, and he died in 1906 at age 67. Covering two square blocks between Seventh and Eighth avenues from 31st Street north to 33rd, the $112 million granite and travertine terminal has been modeled by McKim, Mead, and White on the warm room of Rome's ancient Baths of Caracalla with 84 doric columns each 35 feet high and with 150-foot ceilings in its vast waiting room (see 1966).

A trans-Andean railroad linking Argentina with Chile is completed following plans made by U.S. entrepreneur William Wheelwright who began the road before his death at age 75 in 1873.

U.S. financiers are permitted through the intercession of President Taft to join a consortium of French, British, and German financiers in underwriting China's Hukuang Railroad.

Sperry Gyroscope Company is established at Brooklyn, N.Y., by Elmer A. Sperry of 1879 dynamo and arc lamp fame to manufacture a gyroscopic compass and other instruments invented by Sperry to stabilize ships in rough waters (see patent, 1913).

The Cunard liner S. S. *Mauretania* sails from Cobh to New York in 4 days, 20 hours, and 41 minutes to set a new transatlantic speed record (see 1907).

England's Bristol Aeroplane Company has its beginnings in the British and Colonial Aeroplane Company started in the village of Filton on the outskirts of Bristol by English stockbroker George White with

1910 (cont.) £25,000 in capital. The company will establish flying schools at Brooklands and Larkhill, and it will produce aircraft for Australia, Bulgaria, France, India, Italy, Romania, Russia, Spain, and Turkey (*see* 1920).

The *London Daily Mail* offers a £10,000 prize for the winner of an air race from London to Manchester. The prize goes to French aviator Louis Paulhan, 27, who this year reaches a height of 4,149 feet in a plane he flies at Los Angeles.

Rolls-Royce's C. S. Rolls flies from Dover to Calais and back without stopping, but he is killed later in the year to become the first English aviation victim (*see* 1906; Blériot, 1909).

Glenn Curtiss flies from Albany to New York in 150 minutes to break the long-distance speed record and win a $10,000 prize put up by Joseph Pulitzer's *New York World* (*see* 1909; 1919).

"Barney" Oldfield drives a mile in 27⅓ seconds at Daytona Beach, Fla., to set a 131.724-mile per hour speed record that will stand for years.

The United States has 1,000 miles of concrete road, up from 144 in 1900 (*see* surfaced roads, 1921).

Steel begins to replace wood in U.S. automobile bodies (*see* Ford Model T, 1908, 1911; Budd, 1912).

Safety glass is patented by French poet-chemist Edouard Benedictus, who has accidentally knocked over a test tube lined with a film left by evaporation of a nitrocellulose mixture. Benedictus has observed that the cracked glass has not shattered (*see* Triplex Safety Glass Company, 1926).

W. C. Durant is forced out of General Motors and is replaced by Boston financier James J. Storrow of Lee, Higginson (*see* 1912; Chevrolet, 1911).

John North Willys produces 18,200 motorcars, up from 4,000 last year and 465 the year before (*see* 1917; 1915).

A Sears, Roebuck Model L sells for $370, a Reo runabout for $500, a Maxwell for $600, a Hupmobile for $750.

Cities Service Company is organized by New York banker Henry Latham Doherty, 40, as a holding company for public utility and petroleum properties.

Briggs & Stratton Company is started at Milwaukee to produce air-cooled gasoline engines.

Medical Education in the United States and Canada shows that three-fourths of North American medical schools are inadequate and that only the Johns Hopkins school founded at Baltimore in 1893 is a match for the great medical schools of Europe. U.S. physician Abraham Flexner, 44, has used a $14,000 grant from the 8-year-old Carnegie Institution to inspect 155 medical schools, and the Flexner Report spurs a $600 million reform program in medical education.

Washington University president Robert Somers Brookings, 60, at St. Louis is inspired by the Flexner Report (above) and embarks on a program that will make his university's medical school second to none within 3 years. Other U.S. universities are similarly motivated to elevate medical school standards.

"Every day, in every way, I'm growing better and better" is suggested as a slogan for autosuggestive healing by French pharmacist Émile Coué, 28, who has studied hypnotism and who will develop a system of psychotherapy called Couéism.

Sickle cell anemia is identified for the first time by Chicago physician James Bryan Herrick, 49, but is not yet given that name. The disease of the blood protein hemoglobin will be found to affect up to 50 percent of people in some African tribes and from 0.25 to 3 percent of U.S. blacks, although as many as 10 percent of U.S. blacks may carry the sickle cell trait which in itself has no ill-effects and will be found common among nonblacks in India, Turkey, Greece, and southern Italy wherever there is a prevalence of malaria (children with the trait will be found to have a high degree of resistance to some kinds of malaria). The actual anemia in which the blood cells take on a crescent-shaped appearance occurs only in the offspring of parents who both have the trait, it is often extremely painful, it kills most of its victims before age 21, and few live beyond age 40 (*see* 1922).

Tularemia is recognized in ground squirrels of Tulare County, Calif., by physician George Walter McCoy, 34, who with his colleague Charles Willard Chapin will name the responsible organism *Bacterium tularense*. An epizootic of wild rabbits and other animals that is communicable to humans, tularemia is the first distinctly American disease and will remain a threat to people preparing wild rabbits for cooking without taking proper precautions.

A Paris fashion for imitation sable and sealskin encourages amateur Chinese hunters to trap Manchurian marmots, many of which are infected with bubonic plague. An epidemic of the plague transmitted by unhealthy marmots will kill 60,000 in Manchuria and China in the next 2 years, and in the next 9 years it will kill 1.5 million in China and India.

The American Viscose Company that will be the first successful U.S. producer of rayon is founded under the name Viscose Company at Marcus Hook, Pa., by Britain's Courtaulds, Ltd. (*see* 1905). The company will start producing rayon from spruce pulp steeped in caustic soda beginning in 1911, it will have a monopoly protected by patents and by U.S. tariff laws, and it will control U.S. rayon production for years (*see* Little, 1902; DuPont, 1920; Celanese, 1925).

Minnesota Mining and Manufacturing Company is founded at St. Paul, Minn., in a reorganization of a firm set up 3 years ago to work a "corundum" deposit near Crystal Bay on the north shore of Lake Superior (*see* Carborundum, 1891). The "corundum" has turned out to be a low-grade anorthosite unsuitable for heavy-duty abrasives, and the company has quit mining to turn its efforts to producing a poor-quality sandpaper (*see* Scotch brand tape, 1925).

British-made steel is one-third more costly than German or U.S.-made steel because Britain's steel mills have failed to install coke ovens and to employ other technological advances.

Chile's enormously productive Chuquicamata copper mine is acquired by the U.S. copper trust ASARCO that has been controlled since 1901 by the Guggenheim family (*see* 1923).

National Cash Register has sales of $100,000 (*see* THINK, 1908). The cash registers have been improved by the addition of a small electric motor that eliminates manual operation, a motor invented by Dayton, Ohio, electrical engineer Charles Franklin Kettering, 34 (*see* automobile self-starter, 1911; antitrust conviction, 1912).

The first "Morris Plan" bank opens at Norfolk, Va., and pioneers in granting personal bank loans at a time when people who want to borrow money are generally obliged to ask family or friends or to go to loan sharks, pawn shops, or eleemosynary institutions that make compassionate loans to relieve distress. The Fidelity Loan and Trust Company founded by Norfolk lawyer Arthur J. Morris, 29, makes 1-year loans to locally employed citizens of good character, Morris requires two cosigners, he obliges borrowers to repay in monthly installments, he deducts 6 percent in advance to give his bank an actual interest return of 11.6 percent, and by 1920 there will be Morris Plan banks in 37 states (*see* National City Bank, 1928).

The Wall Street brokerage house Salomon Brothers is founded by Arthur, Herbert, and Percy Salomon to trade in short-term securities and conduct a money-brokerage business. The firm will become the largest partnership in the financial district.

White, Weld & Co. is created by a reorganization of the 14-year-old Wall Street banking house Moffat & White. Alexander Moss White takes Francis Minot Weld, 35, into partnership.

Southern Methodist University is founded at Dallas.

Kent State University is founded at Kent, Ohio.

Bowling Green State University is founded at Bowling Green, Ohio.

The Mann-Elkins Act passed by Congress June 18 amends the Interstate Commerce Act of 1887 to regulate telephone, telegraph, and cable companies. The new law declares such companies to be common carriers subject to ICC regulations (*see* Federal Communications Act, 1934).

American Telephone and Telegraph chief Theodore N. Vail has himself elected president of Western Union and abolishes the 40- to 50-cent charge for placing telegraph messages by telephone. Vail has acquired a controlling interest in Western Union from the Jay Gould estate for $30 million in AT&T stock, and while the courts will force AT&T to sell its Western Union stock in 1914, free placement of telegraph messages by telephone will continue even after Vail resigns his presidency (*see* 1913).

Tropical Radio Telegraph Company is founded by United Fruit Company to provide uninterrupted radio contact between the United States and Central America (*see* 1904). United Fruit has been handling 77 percent of world banana exports, it is shipping fruit to Europe, and it will make Tropical Radio Telegraph a subsidiary in 1913 (*see* 1929; ITT, 1920).

The *Pathé Gazette* shown in Britain and the United States is a pioneer film newsreel. French cinematographer Charles Pathé, 47, and his brother Emil have become Paris agents for the Edison phonograph, they have acquired filmmaking equipment invented by British instrument maker Robert Paul while on a visit to London, they have obtained financial support, and they will set up production units in Britain, the United States, Italy, Germany, Russia, and Japan.

The *Pittsburgh Courier* begins publication March 10 under the management of local attorney Robert L. Vann, 22.

Chicago Tribune editor Robert W. Patterson dies and is succeeded by Robert Rutherford McCormick, 30, and his cousin Joseph Medill Patterson, 31. They will be coeditors until 1925, although Patterson will devote most of his time to his New York enterprises beginning in 1919. A nephew of the late reaper inventor, McCormick will build the Chicago paper's circulation from 200,000 to 892,000 (1.4 million on Sunday) in the next 45 years, he will make the *Tribune* the world's greatest newspaper in terms of advertising revenue, and he will establish a radio station with the call letters WGN (for "world's greatest newspaper") (*see* "The Gumps," 1917; *New York Daily News,* 1919; Tribune Tower, 1925).

Carry Nation fought saloons in Kansas and carried her violent temperance crusade across the country.

1910 (cont.) *Women's Wear Daily* begins publication at New York under the direction of journalist Edmund Fairchild whose tradepaper for the garment industry will be the basis of a publishing empire.

Hallmark, Inc., has its beginnings in a wholesale card jobbing company started at Kansas City by Nebraskan Joyce Clyde Hall, 18, and his brother who will soon start dealing in greeting cards (*see* Pring, 1875). The Hall brothers will buy an engraving plant in 1916 to produce their own Hallmark cards, and their company will become the world's largest manufacturer of greeting cards.

Fiction *Clayhanger* by Arnold Bennett begins a trilogy about the ugly life in the "five towns" that are the center of England's pottery industry; *Howards End* by E. M. Forster; *Prester John* by Scottish novelist John Buchan, 35; *The History of Mr. Polly* by H. G. Wells; *La Vagabonde* by Colette, who marries Henry de Jouvenal; *The Notebook of Malte Laurids Brigge* (*Die Aufzeichnungen des Malte Laurids Brigge*) by Rainer Maria Rilke.

Juvenile *The Secret Garden* by Frances Hodgson Burnett; *Rewards and Fairies* by Rudyard Kipling.

Poetry *A Handful of Sand* (*Ichiaku no suna*) by Japanese poet Takuboku Ishikawa, 25, whose tanka in the traditional 31-syllable form have a content that is not traditional (Ishikawa will die of tuberculosis in 1912); *Five Great Odes* (*Cinq Grandes Odes*) by Paul Claudel; *The Town Down the River* by Edwin Arlington Robinson includes his poem "Miniver Cheevy" (who "loved the days of old" but was "born too late . . . called it fate,/ And kept on drinking").

Painting *Nude with Apple* by William Glackens; *Nudes in the Forest* (*Nue dans la forêt*) by Fernand Léger; *Blue Nude, The Dance,* and *Music* by Henri Matisse, who shows the influence of a Munich exhibition of Near Eastern art; *Yadwiga's Dream, Exotic Landscape,* and *Horse Attacked by Jaguar* by Henri Rousseau, who dies at Paris September 2 at age 66; Holman Hunt dies at London September 7 at age 83; Winslow Homer dies at Prout's Neck, Me., September 29 at age 74.

Russian painter Wassily Kandinsky, 43, produces the world's first nonrepresentational paintings.

Sculpture *Standing Woman* by Wilhelm Lehmbruck.

Theater *Deirdre of the Sorrows* by John M. Synge 1/13 at Dublin's Abbey Theatre; *Chantecler* by Edmond Rostand 2/7 at the Théâtre de la Porte-Saint-Martin, Paris, with Lucien Guitry in the title role; *Justice* by John Galsworthy 2/21 at the Duke of York's Theatre, London; *Misalliance* by George Bernard Shaw 2/23 at the Duke of York's Theatre, London, 11 perfs. (in repertory); *Old Friends* and *The Twelve-Pound Look* by James M. Barrie 3/1 at the Duke of York's Theatre, London; *The Dragon's Head* (*La farsa infantil de la cabeza del dragón*) by Ramon Valle Inclan 3/5 at Madrid's Teatro de la Conventa;

Get-Rich-Quick Wallingford by George M. Cohan 9/19 at New York's Gaiety Theater, with Hale Hamilton as J. Rufus Wallingford in a comedy based on a novel by George Randolph Chet, 424 perfs.; *The Guardsman* (*A testor*) by Ferenc Molnár 11/19 at Budapest's Vigszinhaz.

Films Joseph A. Golden's *The New Magdalene* with Pearl White; D. W. Griffith's *Ramona* with Mary Pickford.

Animated motion picture cartoons are pioneered by *Brooklyn Eagle* cartoonist John Randolph Bray, 31, using a "cel" system he has invented and that will be used by all future animators. Each cartoon frame is a photograph of several layers of celluloid transparencies, the only layers that change from frame to frame are those that involve movements of figures, backgrounds (and some figures) remain constant, and the technique avoids the distracting moves that existed when each frame was drawn entirely by hand and it reduces production costs enormously. Bray's cartoon "The Dachshund and the Sausage" is acquired by Pathé (above), Bray develops a "Colonel Heeza Liar" cartoon based roughly on Theodore Roosevelt, he will employ animators Max and David Fleischer who will create "Popeye" cartoons (*see* 1929), Paul Terry who will produce "Terry Toons," and Walter Lantz who will create "Bugs Bunny" (*see* 1937; Disney, 1928).

Ballet *Scheherezade* 6/4 at the Théâtre National de l'Opéra, Paris, with music by the late Nikolai Rimski-Korsakov, choreography by Michel Fokine. Waslaw Nijinsky of Serge Diaghilev's Ballet Russe dances the role of the Favorite Slave. *The Firebird* 6/25 at the Paris Opéra, with music by Russian composer Igor Federovich Stravinsky, 28; Tamara Karsavina, 25, dances the title role, Michel Fokine dances the role of Ivan Czarevich in the ballet commissioned by Serge Diaghilev.

Opera *Macbeth* 11/30 at the Opéra-Comique, Paris, with music by Swiss composer Ernest Bloch, 30. One critic says, "This music is barbarian—simply cruel torture to the ear."

First performances Three Piano Pieces by Arnold Schoenberg 1/14 at Vienna; *Mother Goose* (*Ma Mère l'Oye*) by Maurice Ravel 4/20 at Paris. The four-handed piano piece will have its first orchestrated performance early in 1912; Fantasia on a Theme by Thomas Tallis for Double String Orchestra by English composer Ralph Vaughan Williams, 37, 9/6 at Gloucester Cathedral; Symphony No. 8 in E flat major by Gustav Mahler 9/12 at Munich's Exposition Concert Hall, with 146 orchestral players, two mixed choruses of 250 voices each, a children's choir of 350, and 7 vocal soloists.

The London Palladium opens December 26 with 2,500 seats. The Palladium will be London's most popular theater for vaudeville and revues beginning with one-night musical comedy turns.

Broadway musicals *Tillie's Nightmare* 5/5 at the

Herald Square Theater, with Marie Dressler, music by A. Baldwin Sloane, lyrics by Edgar Smith, songs that include "Heaven Will Protect the Working Girl" based on the 1898 song "She Was Bred in Old Kentucky," 77 perfs.; *The (Ziegfeld) Follies* 6/20 at the Jardin de Paris, with singer Fannie Brice (Fannie Borach), 18, who won a Brooklyn talent contest 5 years ago singing "When You Know You're Not Forgotten by the Girl You Can't Forget," who left school to start a theatrical career, and who has been hired at $75 per week by Florenz Ziegfeld. Music by Gus Edwards and others, book and lyrics by Harry B. Smith, 88 perfs.; *Madame Sherry* 8/30 at the New Amsterdam Theater, with songs that include "Every Little Movement Has a Meaning All Its Own" by Karl Hoschna and Otto Harbach, "Put Your Arms Around Me, Honey" by Albert von Tilzer, lyrics by Junie McCree, 45, 231 perfs.; *Naughty Marietta* 11/7 at the New York Theater, with music by Victor Herbert, book and lyrics by Rida Johnson Young, songs that include "Tramp! Tramp! Tramp!," "I'm Falling in Love with Someone," "Ah, Sweet Mystery of Life," 136 perfs.

Popular songs "Come, Josephine, in My Flying Machine" by German-American composer Fred Fisher, 35, lyrics by Canadian-American Alfred Bryan, 39; "Mother Machree" by Chauncey Olcott and Ernest R. Ball, lyrics by Rida Johnson Young; "Down by the Old Mill Stream" by Tell Taylor, 34; "A Perfect Day" by Carrie Jacobs-Bond; "Let Me Call You Sweetheart" by Leo Friedman, lyrics by Beth Slater Whitson; "Some of These Days" by Shelton Brooks; " 'Opie'—The University of Maine Stein Song" by Norwegian-American composer E. A. Fenstad, 40, lyrics by 1906 University of Maine graduate Lincoln Colcord, 27 (*see* Rudy Vallee, 1928).

World heavyweight champion Jack Johnson handily defeats former titleholder James J. Jeffries July 4 at Reno, Nev. (above).

Spanish matador Juan Belmonte kills his first bull July 24 at age 18 in the new ring at El Arahal.

The All-Ireland Championship finals played since 1887 move into Dublin's Croke Park where they will be played each year (except in 1947 when New York's Polo Grounds will host the games in an effort to revive interest in Gaelic football among Irish-Americans).

Chicago's Comiskey Park opens.

Connie Mack's Philadelphia Athletics win the World Series by defeating the Chicago Cubs 4 games to 1.

The Boy Scouts of America is founded by U.S. painter-illustrator Daniel Carter "Uncle Dan" Beard, 60, whose book *Boy Pioneers and Sons of Daniel Boone* was published last year. Beard has been inspired by the 2-year-old British organization founded by Lord Baden-Powell.

The Camp Fire Girls of America is founded by Luther Halsey Gulick, 45, who helped James Naismith invent the game of basketball in 1891 at the YMCA College at Springfield, Mass. Now director of physical education for New York City public schools and a social engineer for the Russell Sage Foundation, Gulick is assisted by his wife.

The Girl Guides is founded by Lord Baden-Powell (above) with his sister Agnes, 52 (*see* Girl Scouts of America, 1912).

Father's Day is observed for the first time June 19 at Spokane, Wash., where the local YMCA and the Spokane Ministerial Association have persuaded the city fathers to set aside a Sunday to "honor thy father." The idea has come from local housewife Mrs. John Bruce Dodd, 28, who has been inspired by the selflessness and responsibility of her father William Smart, a Civil War veteran who raised his daughter and her five brothers after the early death of his wife.

"And this is good old Boston,/ The home of the bean and the cod,/ Where the Lowells talk only to Cabots/ And the Cabots talk only to God," says John Bossidy in a toast at the midwinter dinner for alumni of the College of the Holy Cross at Worcester. Bossidy paraphrases a toast made in 1905 by a member of the Harvard Class of 1880 who said, "Here's to old Massachusetts,/ The home of the sacred cod,/ Where the Adamses vote for Douglas,/ And the Cabots walk with God."

The Elizabeth Arden beauty salon chain has its beginnings in a New York beauty treatment parlor started by Canadian-American beauty shop secretary Florence Nightingale Graham, 25, who first goes into business with Elizabeth Hubbard, has a falling out with her partner, borrows $6,000 from a cousin, and opens a Fifth Avenue shop under the name Elizabeth Arden inspired by the 1864 Tennyson poem *Enoch Arden.* Graham repays the loan within 4 months, she will move farther uptown and will open a Washington, D.C., branch in 1915, and by 1938 there will be 29 Elizabeth Arden salons.

The Tielocken coat that will be called the trenchcoat beginning in 1914 is introduced by Burberry's (*see* 1856). Tied and locked closed with a strap and buckle, the coat will be augmented by buttons, epaulettes, and rings for hanging grenades.

U.S. cigarette sales reach 8.6 billion with 62 percent of sales controlled by the American Tobacco Trust created in 1890. The tobacco companies spend $18.1 million to advertise their brands (*see* 1911; 1913).

May Department Stores Company is incorporated to replace the partnership of founder David May and his three brothers-in-law. The corporation adds the M. O'Neill store at Akron, Ohio, to its Denver and St. Louis stores (*see* 1892; Cleveland, 1914).

New York's Gimbel Brothers Department Store opens on Greeley Square between 32nd and 33rd Streets (*see* 1894; Saks Fifth Avenue, 1924).

The Fuller Brush Company is incorporated in a reorganization of the 4-year-old Capitol Brush Company.

1910 (cont.) By 1920 the firm will have sales of nearly $12 million per year as A. C. Fuller builds a corps of independent door-to-door salesmen.

Barcelona's Casa Mila is completed by Spanish architect Antonio Gaudi, 58, after 5 years of construction.

Chicago's Blackstone Hotel opens on Michigan Avenue at Balbo Avenue. Architect Benjamin Marshall has been retained by hotelman Tracy Corey Drake, 46, whose father John B. Drake built the Grand Pacific Hotel in 1873 (*see* Drake Hotel, 1919).

Madrid's Ritz Hotel opens October 23 with 200 bedrooms and salons, 100 baths.

New York's Ritz-Carlton Hotel opens just before Christmas on Madison Avenue between 46th and 47th Streets. Real estate heir Robert Walton Goelet, 27, has been persuaded by architect Charles Wetmore and Ritz Hotels syndicator William Harris to build the 12-story luxury hotel which has an inner garden with a duck pond (*see* Harris, 1902). To quiet street noises, the new hotel will have Madison Avenue's cobblestones replaced with wood blocks from 42nd to 48th Streets, paying for the work that the city has refused to finance, but switch engines in the nearby Grand Central yards will continue to disturb guests for some years to come. Goelet will have bought up most of the shares in Ritz Hotels Development by 1927, Joseph Widener will finance a Philadelphia Ritz, but César Ritz will die in an insane asylum in 1912 (*see* Boston Ritz, 1927).

Boston's Charles River Dam is completed to maintain the water level of the Charles River and to remove the flats exposed at low tide.

Wyoming's Shoshone Dam is completed by the Bureau of Reclamation. The arch of rubble on the North Platte River rises 328 feet high.

Glacier National Park in Montana is created by act of Congress which sets aside more than a million acres of lakes, peaks, glaciers, and Rocky Mountain flora and fauna (*see* 1932).

Conservationist Gifford Pinchot is elected president of the National Conservation Association following his removal from the Forestry Service by President Taft after a policy dispute with Secretary of the Interior Richard Achilles Ballinger (*see* 1908). Pinchot has accused Ballinger of reversing President Roosevelt's conservation policies.

Florida orange shipments finally regain their 1894 levels, but Florida's northern groves have been abandoned and population in the Orlando area has suffered a huge decline.

Blueberry cultivation is revolutionized by New Jersey botanist Frederick Coville who develops a plump, almost seedless blueberry that will be the basis of a multimillion-dollar industry.

Cudahy Packing Company moves to Chicago after 20 years at Omaha and will remain at Chicago for 40 years (*see* 1890; 1950).

The world's first glass-lined milk car goes into service on the Boston & Maine Railroad for Boston's Whiting Milk Company.

70 percent of U.S. bread is baked at home, down from 80 percent in 1890 (*see* 1924).

Aunt Jemima pancakes are sold throughout the United States as pancakes become a year-round staple served at many meals rather than just at winter breakfasts (*see* 1893; Quaker Oats, 1926).

Hydrox "biscuit bon-bons" are introduced by the Loose-Wiles Biscuit Company (*see* 1903; Oreo, 1912).

Vichyssoise is invented in the kitchen of New York's new Ritz-Carlton Hotel (above) by chef Louis Diat, 32, whose cold soup is an adaptation of France's hot *soupe bonne femme*.

The U.S. population reaches 92 million with 13.5 million of it foreign-born. Just over half live in cities and towns of 2,500 or more, up from 21 percent in 1860 (in Germany, 34.5 percent of the people live in cities of 20,000 or more, up from 18.4 percent in 1885).

The U.S. Immigration Commission winds up nearly 4 years of study with a 41-volume report that recommends restricting immigration, especially of unskilled labor (*see* 1917).

1911 A nuclear model of the atom proposed by Ernest Rutherford at the University of Manchester is comprised largely of a positively charged nucleus surrounded by electrons (*see* Thomson, 1897; Geiger counter, 1908; Bohr, 1913).

U.S. explorer Hiram Bingham, 35, discovers the Inca city of Macchu-Pichu that escaped the notice of the Spanish conquistadors. Bingham's missionary grandfather developed a written language out of Hawaiian, his missionary father did the same for the language of the Gilbert Islands, Bingham makes his discovery at an altitude of 8,200 feet in the Peruvian Andes where jungle growth covers the long-deserted Inca city.

Norwegian explorer Roald Amundsen, 39, arrives at the South Pole December 14 with four fellow Norwegians and 17 ravenous huskies. The men survive on seal blubber, they appease the dogs by killing one sledge dog and feeding it to the others, they are the first to reach the Pole , but five British explorers led by Robert Falcon Scott, now 43, will be less lucky. They will reach the Pole January 18 of next year, but with each man pushing a sledge whose load averages 190 pounds the daily ration of 4,800 calories will be inadequate and the men will starve to death.

Mexico's president Porfirio Diaz is overthrown May 25 (*see* 1910). Revolutionist Francisco Madero opposed the re-election of Diaz last year but was forced to flee to the United States, he has led a military campaign against Diaz and established a new capital May 11 at Ciudad Juarez, he makes himself president November 6, and he begins an administration that will continue for 15 months (*see* 1913).

A military coup that establishes a new Honduras "banana republic" favorable to his interests is engineered by Bessarabian-American banana grower Samuel Zemurray, 34, who for the past 6 years has been shipping fruit from lands he has bought along the country's Cuyamel River. Zemurray loans former Honduras president General Manuel Bonilla enough money to buy the yacht *Hornet*, he sends Bonilla out to the yacht in his own private launch at Biloxi, Miss., with a case of rifles, a machine gun, and ammunition, and he provides him with the services of soldiers of fortune Guy "Machine Gun" Molony and Lee Christmas (*see* 1897). When Bonilla and his cohorts oust the old Honduras government Zemurray gains valuable concessions (*see* United Fruit Company, 1929).

Britain's House of Lords loses its veto power under the Parliament Act passed by the Lords August 10 after a threat from Prime Minister Herbert Asquith that he will have enough peers created to carry the measure.

Britain's House of Commons for the first time votes salaries for its members. Each M.P. is to receive £400 per year under terms of the measure adopted August 10, 6 weeks after the coronation of George V.

Russian Premier Pyotr Arkadevich Stolypin is assassinated September 1 in the presence of Nicholas II at the Kiev Opera House. An informer for the czar's secret police fires a revolver at point-blank range.

The Black Hand Serbian secret society founded at Belgrade in May works to reunite Serbs living within the Austrian and Ottoman Empires with their kinspeople in Serbia. "Unity or Death" ("Unedinjenje ili Smrt") is the society's slogan, but while the Black Hand will influence Serbian policies in the Balkan wars, its leader Colonel Apis Dimitrievič will clash with the Serbian government and will be executed with two colleagues in June of 1917.

Italy declares war on Turkey September 29, and the Tripoli coast is bombarded by the Italian fleet which makes the first offensive use of aircraft in an attack that begins a war which will continue for more than a year.

A revolution begins in China that will end the 267-year Ch'ing dynasty of the Manchus, will propel China into the 20th century, and will begin the decline of such customs as having men wear humiliating pigtails and having women's feet painfully deformed by binding them.

Chinese revolutionary leader Sun Yat-sen, 45, returns from 16 years of exile in Hawaii, England, and the United States. The first graduate of Hong Kong's new College of Medicine, Sun is elected president of the United Provinces of China in December by a revolutionary provisional assembly at Nanking.

A Japanese woman's liberation movement is launched by Racho Hiratsuka, but Japan will not give women the vote until 1946.

California women are granted suffrage by constitutional amendment (*see* New York, 1917).

New York's Triangle Shirtwaist Factory at Washington Place and Greene Street has a fire March 25 and 146 people are killed, most of them sweatshop seamstresses who are unable to escape. The tragedy brings new demands for better working conditions (*see* IWW Lawrence strike, 1912).

A British Trade Disputes act guarantees the right to strike and to picket peacefully.

A limited British National Insurance program legislated by Parliament in December provides unemployment insurance for 2.25 million workers in trades such as building and engineering that are especially subject to layoffs. Funded by contributions from workers, employers, and the state, the program provides benefits for a maximum of 15 weeks.

John D. Rockefeller's Standard Oil Company trust is broken up by the Supreme Court May 15 in a ruling in the case of *Standard Oil Co. of N.J. v. United States,* but the court rules only against "unreasonable" restraints of trade where a company has "purpose or intent" to exercise monopoly power in violation of the Sherman Act of 1890 (*see* below, tobacco trust decision). The trust is reorganized into five separate corporations plus some smaller ones—Standard Oil of New Jersey will later be called Esso and then Exxon, Standard Oil of California (SoCal), Standard Oil of Indiana, Standard Oil of Ohio (Sohio), and Standard Oil of New York (which will later be called Socony-Vacuum, then Mobil). Also Atlantic Refining (which will become Atlantic Richfield in 1967), Vacuum Oil Company, Prairie Oil & Gas, Buckeye Pipe Line Co., and Anglo-American Oil, Ltd. (*see* 1902).

An electric self-starter for motorcar and truck engines is invented by C. F. Kettering who last year provided National Cash Register with an electric motor for its register drawers. Kettering's Dayton Engineering Laboratories (Delco) is given a contract to supply 4,000 self-starters by Cadillac boss Henry M. Leland after he has lost a good friend who was killed while trying to crank a woman's balky engine (*see* Leland, 1909; Ford, 1919; General Motors, 1918).

Electric Auto-Lite Company is started at Toledo, Ohio, by Clement O. Miniger to make ignition sets (starting motors, distributors, coils, generators) and sparkplugs. By 1929 Electric Auto-Lite will be a major supplier of ignition sets to Ford, Essex, Hudson, Hupmobile, Jordan, Nash, Packard, Peerless, and Pierce, and it will rival Delco (above) (*see* 1930).

The first SAE handbook on standardization is published by the 6-year-old Society of Automotive Engineers. Beginning with spark plugs and carburetor flanges, the SAE will standardize screw threads, bolts, nuts, and all other automotive components (*see* lubricating oil, 1926).

Ford Motor Company wins a court decision that the Ford engine is fundamentally different from the G.

1911 (cont.) B. Selden engine on which patents are about to expire anyway. Ford has refused to pay royalties to G. B. Selden's 8-year-old association which has received $5.8 million in royalties from other automakers (Selden himself has received only $200,000, the rest having gone to lawyers, management executives, sales promotion, and production commissions).

Chevrolet Motor Company is founded by former General Motors head W. C. Durant (*see* 1910). He teams up with Swiss-American racing car driver Louis Chevrolet, 32, who has been in the United States since 1901, and they produce the first Chevrolet motorcars in a New York plant at 57th Street and 11th Avenue (*see* 1915).

The first Indianapolis 500 (mile) motorcar race is held May 30. A Marmon Wasp averages 75 miles per hour to win (*see* 1909).

Finishing 11th in the Indianapolis 500 (above) is the first Stutz motorcar which averages 68 miles per hour despite tire troubles that have forced it to make persistent pit stops. Built by Indianapolis engineer Harry C. Stutz, 35, the car earns the slogan "the car that made good in a day" (*see* 1913).

A transcontinental U.S. motorcar race organized by Philadelphia auto distributor John Guy Monihan begins June 26 at Atlantic City, N.J. Finalists arrive at Los Angeles August 10 after covering 4,731 miles.

The first Monte Carlo Rally is won by a 25-horse-power Turcat-Mery.

An eight-valve four-cylinder Bugatti wins its class in the Grand Prix du Mans. The first all-Bugatti car, it has been designed by Italian automaker Ettore Bugatti, 30, who has lived in France since his teens, built his first motorcar at age 17, and will dominate auto racing for more than 20 years.

Tolls on New York's Williamsburg Bridge of 1903 are removed at midnight July 19.

The last horse-drawn bus of the London General Omnibus Company goes out of service. The city had 1,142 licensed horse-drawn buses and the same number of motor buses at the end of October of last year, but while at least one horse-drawn bus will continue running (over Waterloo Bridge) until 1916, the horse is now rapidly being replaced by motorbuses and motorcars and trucks in major world cities.

A record transcontinental airplane flight is completed by Calbraith P. Rogers who flies a Wright biplane from Sheepshead Bay, N.Y., to Long Beach, Calif., in 3½ days of flying time. The trip actually takes 84 days as the engine of the *Vin Fizz Flyer* quits in the air six times and Rogers crashes 12 times, but he collects $11,285 of the $50,000 in prize money put up by publisher William Randolph Hearst.

The first airplane with an enclosed passenger cabin is the six-passenger Blériot *Berline* built for Parisian Henri Deutsch de la Neurthe.

Nellie Bly's 1889–1890 round-the-world record of 72 days is beaten by André Jaeger-Schmidt, who circles the earth from Paris to Paris in 39 days, 19 hours, traveling by ship and rail (*see* Mears, 1913).

The British White Star passenger liner S.S. *Olympic* arrives at New York June 21 to begin service that will continue until 1935. With an overall length of 892 feet, the 45,300-ton triple screw ship is by far the largest liner yet built, she carries 2,500 passengers, and she is the first to have a swimming pool.

The Santa Fe *Deluxe* goes into service December 2 between Chicago and Los Angeles. Passengers pay $25 extra fare each on the weekly 63-hour passenger express to enjoy services that include a barbershop, a library, a stenographer, ladies' maids, daily market reports, bathing facilities, a club car, a Fred Harvey dining car, four Pullman sleeping cars whose compartments and drawing rooms have brass beds, and telephones at terminals en route (*see* 1926).

 U.S. Postal Savings service opens January 3 at 48 second-class post offices under terms of legislation signed last June by President Taft. Deposits reach $11 million in 11 months, and the money is distributed among 2,710 national and state banks.

The Purchasing Power of Money by Yale political economy professor Irving Fisher, 44, advances the thesis that prices rise in proportion to the supply of money and the velocity with which money circulates. Fisher pioneers in "indexing" the economy with price indexes, cost-of-living indexes, etc. (*see* Bureau of Labor Consumer Price Index, 1913).

Theory of Economic Development by Moravian economist Joseph Alois Schumpeter, 28, will influence other economists' thinking especially after it is translated into English in 1934. A professor at the University of Graz, Schumpeter will be appointed to a Harvard chair in 1932.

Continental Assurance Company is founded to sell life insurance. The firm is an offshoot of the 14-year-old Continental Casualty Company which has prospered by selling disability insurance to railroad employees and which has absorbed many of its competitors, the two companies have the same directors and chief executives but separate shareholders, and they will merge at the end of 1967 to form the holding company CNA Financial Corp.

Chicago's Union Carbide Company acquires the oxygen company founded 4 years ago to supply users of oxyacetyline torches (*see* 1907; 1917).

 Southern pine trees used now only for turpentine and naval stores prove useful as pulp sources for kraft paper, a strong brown packaging paper made by a sulfate process that uses an alkaline instead of an acid (as in the sulfite process) to remove the noncellulose lignin from pulp ("Kraft" is German for strength). The discovery will revolutionize the paper industry and will bring new prosperity to parts of the South.

The Carnegie Corporation of New York is created with a $125 million gift from Andrew Carnegie to encourage education (*see* 1905; Flexner, 1910).

Connecticut College for Women is founded at New London.

Skidmore College for Women is founded at Saratoga Springs, N.Y.

The first direct telephone link between New York and Denver is established May 8.

The *American* magazine founded 5 years ago is acquired by J. F. Knapp's Crowell Publishing Company for $40,000 in cash and $396,000 in Crowell preferred stock (*see Collier's,* 1919).

The *London Observer* that began publication in 1791 is acquired by John Jacob Astor, grandson of Viscount Astor of Hever Castle (*see* 1899; 1922).

The Official Secrets Act passed by Parliament August 22 makes it a criminal offense to publish any official government information not intended for publication. No British journalist will defy the law until 1977.

Olivetti Company is founded at Ivrea west of Milan in the Piedmont by electrical engineer Camillo Olivetti, 43, who has designed and built the first Italian typewriter. Few Italian firms have accepted steel-nibbed pens, much less typewriters, but by year's end Olivetti has received an order for 100 machines from the Italian Navy and by 1933 his plant will be producing 24,000 machines per year. The company will sell its typewriters in 22 foreign countries, but most will be sold through Olivetti retail shops in Italy (*see* Underwood, 1959).

France's Gallimard publishing house has its beginnings in the firm La Nouvelle Revue Francaise-Librairie Gallimard founded by dilettante Gaston Gallimard, 30, with André Gide and Jean Schlumberger to publish works by contributors to the 3-year-old review. Gallimard will become the nation's leading publisher and will join the Hachette group founded in 1826.

Nonfiction *The Concise Oxford Dictionary* (COD).

Fiction *Death in Venice* (*Der Tod in Venedig*) by Thomas Mann; *Ethan Frome* by Edith Wharton; *Under Western Eyes* by Joseph Conrad; *Zuleika Dobson* by English critic-essayist-caricaturist Max Beerbohm, 39, whose satire about an adventuress at Oxford will be his only novel; *Life Everlasting* by Marie Corelli; *The Innocence of Father Brown* by English essayist-poet-novelist G. K. (Gilbert Keith) Chesterton, 37, whose detective hero is modeled on his friend Father O'Connor, who will receive Chesterton into the Roman Catholic Church in 1922; *The Phantom of the Opera* by French mystery writer Gaston Leroux, 43; *Death of a Nobody* (*Mort de quelqu'un*) by French novelist Jules Romains (Louis Farigoule), 26; *Sanders of the River* by Edgar Wallace; *Mr. Perrin and Mr. Traill* by New Zealand-born English novelist Hugh

Walpole, 27; *The Wild Geese* (*Gan*) by Japanese surgeon-novelist Ogai Mori, 49, whose 1909 autobiographical work *Vita Sexualis* (*Ita Sekusuarisu*) attacked the naturalist contention that man has no control over his sexual instinct; *Jennie Gerhardt* by Theodore Dreiser; *Mother* by U.S. novelist Kathleen Thompson Norris, 31, whose novels will be serialized in women's magazines for more than 30 years.

Juvenile *Mother Carey's Chickens* by Kate Douglas Wiggin; *Jim Davis* by John Masefield.

Poetry *The Everlasting Mercy* by John Masefield; "World's End" ("Weltende") by German poet Jacob van Hoodis (Has Davidsohn), 24, is the world's first expressionist poem; "The Female of the Species" by Rudyard Kipling: "But the she-bear thus accosted rends the peasant tooth and nail./ For the female of the species is more deadly than the male."

Painting *The Red Studio* and *The Blue Window* by Henri Matisse; *Gabrielle with a Rose* by Pierre Auguste Renoir; *Man with a Guitar* by Georges Braque; *Accordionist* by Pablo Picasso; *Church at Chatillon* by Maurice Utrillo; *I and the Village* by Marc Chagall, who arrived at Paris last year.

Sculpture *Kneeling Woman* by Wilhelm Lehmbruck.

Theater *The Rats* (*Die Ratten*) by Gerhart Hauptmann 1/13 at Berlin's Lessingtheater; *The Scarecrow* by U.S. playwright Percy Mackaye, 35, 1/17 at New York's Garrick Theater, 23 perfs.; *Mrs. Bumpsted-Leigh* by U.S. playwright Harry James Smith, 31, 4/3 at New York's Lyceum Theater, with Mrs. Minnie Maddern Fiske, 64 perfs.; *Fanny's First Play* by George Bernard Shaw 4/19 at London's Little Theatre, with Christine Silve, Harcourt Williams, Reginald Owen, 622 perfs.; *The Martyrdom of Saint Sebastian* by Gabriele D'Annunzio 5/22 at the Théâtre du Châtelet, Paris, with music by Claude Debussy. Ballet dancer Ida Rubinstein plays the lead role but D'Annunzio's works have been placed on the index of forbidden books by the Vatican 2 weeks earlier and the archbishop of Paris warns Roman Catholics not to attend performances on threat of excommunication; *Disraeli* by Louis Napoleon Parker 9/18 at Wallack's Theater, New York, with George Arliss, 280 perfs.; *The Return of Peter Grimm* by David Belasco 10/17 at New York's Belasco Theater, with David Warfield, 231 perfs.; *The Garden of Allah* by English novelist Robert Smythe Hichens, 47, and Mary Hudson 10/21 at New York's Century Theater, in a drama based on the 1905 novel by Hichens, 241 perfs.; *Everyman* (*Jedermann*) by Hugo von Hofmannsthal 12/1 at Berlin's Zirkus Schumann; *Oaha, the Satire of Satire* (*Oaha, die Satire der Satire*) by Frank Wedekind 12/23 at Munich's Lustspielhaus; *Kismet* by English-American playwright Edward Knoblock, 37, 12/25 at New York's Knickerbocker Theater with Otis Skinner, 184 perfs.

Films D. W. Griffith's *The Indian Brothers*; D. W. Griffith's *Fighting Blood* with Blanche Sweet; D. W.

ALEXANDER'S RAGTIME BAND

BY IRVING BERLIN

Ragtime music gave the world a new beat that anticipated the American jazz idiom. Scott Joplin lived to see it.

Griffith's *The Lonedale Operator* with Blanche Sweet; William Humphreys' *A Tale of Two Cities* with Maurice Costelli, Norma Talmadge.

Bell & Howell Company's Albert S. Howell develops a continuous printer that makes copies of motion picture films automatically and economically to permit mass distribution of films (*see* 1909).

The Keystone Company is founded by Canadian-American motion picture pioneer Mack Sennett, 27, who changed his name from Michael Sinnott when he came to New York in 1904 to begin a stage career in burlesque and the circus. Sennett has been working with D. W. Griffith at the Biograph Studios in New York (*see* Chaplin, 1913).

Opera *Der Rosenkavalier* (*The Knight of the Rose*) 1/26 at Dresden's Hofoper, with music by Richard Strauss, libretto by Hugo von Hofmannsthal; *Natoma* 2/8 at New York's Metropolitan Opera House, with Mary Garden, John McCormack, music by Victor Herbert; *L'Heure Espagnole* 5/19 at the Opéra-Comique, Paris, with music by Maurice Ravel; *The Jewels of the Madonna* (*I Gioielli della Madonna*, or *Der Schmuck der Madonna*) 12/23 at Berlin's Kurfuersten Oper, with music by Ermanno Wolf-Ferrari.

Ballet *Le Spectre de la Rose* at Monte Carlo's Théâtre de Monte Carlo, with music by the early 19th century composer Carl Maria von Weber, choreography by Michel Fokine; *Petrouchka* 6/13 at the Théâtre du Châtelet, Paris, with Waslaw Nijinsky dancing the title role opposite Tamara Karsavina, music by Igor Stravinsky, who departs from his earlier romanticism to introduce bitonality and to employ syncopation with unconventional meters.

First performances *Prometheus, the Poem of Fire* by Aleksandr Skriabin 3/15 at Moscow's Bolshoi Theater, in a pioneer multimedia effort to blend color and music; Symphony No. 4 by Jean Sibelius 4/3 at Helsinki; "Valses Nobles et Sentimentales for Piano" by Maurice Ravel 5/9 at the Salle Gaveau, Paris; Symphony No. 2 in E flat major by Sir Edward Elgar 5/24 at a London music festival.

Broadway musicals *The Pink Lady* 3/13 at the New Amsterdam Theater with Hazel Dawn, music by Belgian-American composer Ivan Caryll, 312 perfs. (the hit makes pink the year's fashion color); *La Belle Parée* 3/20 at Lee Shubert's Winter Garden Theater, with Russian-American blackface minstrel singer Al Jolson, 24, who has changed his name from Asa Yoelson, vaudeville entertainer George White, 21, who has changed his name from Weitz, music by New York composer Jerome David Kern, 26, and others, lyrics by Edward Madden and others, 104 perfs.; *The Ziegfeld Follies* 6/26 at the Jardin de Paris with the Dolly Sisters [Viennese dancers Jennie (Jan Szieka Deutsch) and Rosie (Roszka Deutsch), both 18], Leon Errol, 80 perfs.; *Betsy* 12/7 at the Casino Theater, with music by Leslie J. Stuart.

Popular songs "Alexander's Ragtime Band" by Irving Berlin popularizes the ragtime music that Scott Joplin pioneered in 1899: "Everybody's Doin' It" by Irving Berlin popularizes the Turkey Trot dance invented by dancer Vernon Castle and his 18-year-old bride Irene Foote Castle; "I Want a Girl (Just Like the Girl that Married Dear Old Dad)" by Harry von Tilzer, oedipal lyrics by Will Dillon, 34; "Memphis Blues" by W. C. (William Christopher) Handy, 38, who adapts a campaign song he wrote in 1909 for a Memphis mayoralty candidate. Handy has assimilated black spirituals, work songs, and folk ballads with a musical form called "jass" and has employed a distinctive blues style with a melancholy tone achieved by use of flatted thirds and sevenths; "All Alone" by Albert von Tilzer, lyrics by Will Dillon; "When I Was Twenty-One and You Were Sweet Sixteen" by Egbert Van Alstyne, lyrics by Henry H. Williams; "Goodnight Ladies" by Egbert Van Alstyne, lyrics by Henry Williams; "Oh, You Beautiful Doll" by Nathaniel Davis Ayer, 24, lyrics by Seymour Brown, 26; "My Melancholy Baby" by Erne Burnett, 27, lyrics by Maybelle E. Watson that will be replaced next year with new lyrics by George A. Norton, 33; "Down the Field" (Yale football march) by Stanleigh P. Freedman, lyrics by C. W. O'Connor; "Little Grey Home in the West" by English composer Hermann Lohr, 40, lyrics by Miss D. Eardley-Wilmot, 28; "Roamin' in the Gloamin' " by Scottish songwriter and music hall entertainer Harry Lauder (MacLennan), 41; "A Wee Doch-an-Doris" by Harry Lauder, lyrics by Gerald Grafton.

Connie Mack's Philadelphia Athletics win the World Series by defeating John McGraw's New York Giants 4 games to 2.

Harvard freshman Charles Brickley, 18, begins a notable football career by kicking four field goals to defeat a Princeton freshman eleven 12 to 0.

Lee Riders have their beginnings in the H. D. Lee garment factory built at Salina, Kan., by the H. D. Lee hardware store whose notions department carries overalls made by an eastern supplier who is usually late in his deliveries. Henry David Lee, 62, made a fortune in the late 1880s by selling his Ohio kerosene plant to John D. Rockefeller's Standard Oil Company, he moved West to regain his health and started a bank, a flour mill, an ice plant, and a wholesale hardware company, he went into the wholesale grocery business in 1889, and by the turn of the century H. D. Lee Mercantile Company was the biggest wholesale grocer and jobber in the Midwest supplying customers with everything from canned beans and canned salmon to horse collars. The new garment factory at Salinas produces overalls, jackets, and dungarees of blue denim that will be called Lee Riders beginning in the 1920s (*see* 1926).

The Supreme Court breaks up James B. Duke's American Tobacco Company Trust of 1890 in its May 29 ruling in the case of *United States v. American Tobacco Company.* The firms that emerge from the trust include American Tobacco, P. Lorillard (*see* 1789), Liggett & Myers (*see* 1873), R. J. Reynolds (*see* 1875), and the British-American Tobacco Company (*see* Brown & Williamson, 1927).

The American Snuff Company that has been part of the Tobacco Trust (above) breaks into three equal parts—American Snuff, G. W. Helme Company, and United States Tobacco Company whose major brands include Copenhagen Snuff and Bruton.

German architect Walter Adolf Gropius, 28, designs a steel skeleton building whose only walls are glass "curtain walls" for the Fagus factory at Alfeld. Gropius will create a stir with his model factory at the 1914 Werkbund Exhibition at Cologne (*see* Bauhaus, 1918).

Rome's Victor Emmanuel II monument designed by Giuseppi Sucani is completed after 28 years of construction. The ornate structure symbolizes the achievement of Italian unity in 1861.

Paris' Plaza-Athenée Hotel is created by a combination of two luxury hotels.

Taliesin East is completed at Spring Green, Wis., by architect Frank Lloyd Wright (*see* 1909; Taliesin West, 1938).

New York's $9 million Public Library main branch on Fifth Avenue between 40th and 42nd Streets is completed by architect Thomas Hastings of Carrère and Hastings. The terraced Fifth Avenue entrance is guarded by lions sculpted by E. C. Potter.

A paper that will be the basis of modern air conditioning is presented to the American Society of Mechanical Engineers by Willis H. Carrier (*see* 1902). "Rational Psychometric Formulae" is based on 10 years of work that have initiated a scientific approach to air conditioning (*see* Carrier Corporation, 1915).

China's Yangtze River floods its banks. An estimated 100,000 are killed by the flood waters.

Roosevelt Dam on the Salt River in Arizona Territory is completed by the Bureau of Reclamation as part of the first large-scale irrigation project. The 284-foot high rubble masonry arch has a crest length of 1,125 feet, it creates a reservoir with a capacity of 1.64 million acre-feet. and it will make the region round Phoenix a rich source of fruits and vegetables.

Forest Physiography by U.S. geographer Isaiah Bowman, 33, is the first detailed study of the physical geography of the United States.

The Appalachian Forest Reserve Act is passed by Congress to appropriate funds for purchasing forest lands to control the sources of important streams in the White Mountains and the southern Appalachians (*see* Appalachian Trail, 1921).

Famine reduces 30 million Russians to starvation. Nearly one quarter of the peasantry is affected, but 13.7 million tons of Russian grain, mostly wheat, are shipped abroad (*see* 1947).

A Belgian Congo concession to develop a plantation of 1.88 million acres is granted by the king of the Belgians Albert I to Lever Brothers head W. H. Lever, Lord Leverhulme, on condition that Lever pay minimum wages and establish schools and hospitals. Lever has bought 200,000 acres in the Solomon Islands of the Pacific and has planted 17,000 acres to coconut palms, he founds Huiléries du Congo Belge, and he plants oil palm trees to create oils for his soaps and margarines (*see* Lux flakes, 1906; Rinso, 1918).

U.S. entrepreneur Haroldson Lafayette Hunt, 22, invests a small inheritance in Arkansas Delta cotton land after having worked his way through the West and Southwest since leaving home at age 16. Hunt will increase his holdings in Arkansas and Louisiana to some 15,000 acres in the next few years (*see* 1920).

An improved combine that harvests, threshes, and cleans wheat is devised by U.S. inventor Benjamin Holt (*see* Industrial Commission, 1901).

The Pribilof Island seal population that had fallen to 2.5 million when Alaska was acquired by the United States in 1867 falls to 150,000 following years of operations by the Alaska Commercial Company. The United States, Canada, Japan, and Russia sign a Fur Seal Treaty agreeing to preserve the seals from extinction.

The Columbia River salmon catch reaches a record 49 million pounds that will never be reached again (*see* 1866; 1938).

The 1906 Pure Food and Drug Law provision against advertising that is "false or misleading in any particular" does not apply to far-fetched declarations of therapeutic or curative effects, rules the Supreme Court (*see* Sherly Amendment, 1912).

The word "vitamines" is introduced by Polish biochemist Casimir Funk, 27, who works at London's Lister Institute. If the enzymes discovered by the

1911 (cont.) late Wilhelm Kuhne in 1878 are to work properly they require coenzymes in some cases, Funk discovers, and he calls these coenzymes "vitamines" in the mistaken belief that they all contain nitrogen and are all essential to life (*see* 1912; Drummond, 1920).

Crisco is introduced by Cincinnati's Procter & Gamble of 1878 Ivory Soap fame. It is the first solid hydrogenated vegetable shortening (*see* Normann, 1901; Spry, 1936).

Domino brand sugar is introduced by the American Sugar Refining Co., (*see* 1907; Jack Frost, 1913).

Riviana Foods, Inc., has its beginnings in the Southern Rice Sales Company founded at New Orleans by local rice dealer Gordon S. Orme and New York salesman Julius R. Ross who has been sent to New Orleans to sell a shipment of imported black-eyed peas. Southern's medium grain rice will be promoted within a few years under the name River Brand Fluffy White Rice, and when production of long-grain rice increases the company will introduce it under the brand name Carolina Gold Rice. Southern will change its name to River Brand Rice Mills, Inc., and in 1965 will become Riviana Foods, Inc.

Quaker Oats Company is enabled by a sharp business recession to acquire the Mother's Oats brand which has annual sales of $5 million (*see* 1901). The Great Western Cereal Company which is Quaker's major competitor is forced to abandon its Fort Dodge, Iowa, and Joliet, Ill., oat-milling facilities in order to save its profitable wheat flour business, it sells its oat mills and brand name to Quaker for $1 million in cash plus the market value of the mills' grain inventory, and Quaker will sell the same cereal under both the Quaker and Mother's labels (*see* Puffed Wheat, Puffed Rice, 1913).

Corn flakes are produced under 108 brand names at Battle Creek, Mich., but Kellogg's and Post Toasties lead the pack (*see* 1906; 1907). W. K. Kellogg buys out the last of his brother's holdings in the Battle Creek Toasted Corn Flake Company, going $330,000 into debt in order to gain virtually complete ownership of the company that will become the Kellogg Corporation (see W. K. Kellogg Foundation, 1930; 40% Bran Flakes, 1915).

The Fasting Cure by Upton Sinclair is a food fad book. Sinclair has moved to California (*see* 1905; EPIC, 1934).

Mass production of canned pineapple is made possible by Henry Ginaca's invention of a machine that can remove the shells from 75 to 96 pineapples per minute, coring each one and removing its ends.

James Dole's Hawaiian Pineapple Company packs more than 309,000 cases, up from less than 234,000 last year (*see* 1909; 1922).

The first canned chile con carne and tamales are produced at San Antonio, Tex., by William Gebhardt who will receive 37 patents for his machinery innovations (*see* 1896).

M. S. Hershey, Inc., has sales of $5 million (*see* 1908; 1918).

The Swiss chocolate firm Peter, Cailler & Kohler Chocolates Suisses S.A. is created as the Cailler Chocolate firm founded in 1819 is acquired by the Swiss General Chocolate Company, Peter and Kohler in which Nestlé has a 29 percent interest (*see* 1904; 1920).

New York's Ellis Island has a record 1-day influx of 11,745 immigrants April 17 (*see* 1892). Two steamship companies have more than 5,000 ticket agents in Galicia alone, some Germans buy tickets straight through from Bremen to Bismarck, N.D., and the U.S. population is at least 25 percent foreign-born in nearly every part of the country outside the South.

The U.S. population reaches 94 million while Great Britain has 40.8 million, England and Wales 36 million, Ireland 4.3, France 39.6, Italy 34.6, Japan 52, Russia 167, India 315, China 425.

1912 The S.S. *Titanic* of the Royal Mail Line scrapes an iceberg in the North Atlantic on her maiden voyage, she sustains a 300-foot slash, and she sinks in 2½ hours on the night of April 15. The three-screw passenger liner of 46,328 tons is 882 feet in length overall, she is the world's largest passenger liner, and she has been called "unsinkable," but only 711 of the 2,224 aboard are saved, and the 1,513 lost include such prominent millionaires as R. H. Macy's Isidor Straus, 67, copper heir Benjamin Guggenheim, 47, and traction heir Harry Elkins Widener, 27, who goes down clutching a 1598 edition of Bacon's essays (*see* Widener Library, 1915; Sarnoff, below).

New Mexico and Arizona are admitted to the Union as the 47th and 48th states.

The Seventeenth Amendment providing for election of U.S. Senators by direct popular vote is adopted by 37 states and begins the end of the "millionaire's club" that has dominated the U.S. Senate.

U.S. Marines are landed in Honduras in February, in Cuba 4 months later, and in Nicaragua in August to protect American interests. The marines will not be withdrawn from Nicaragua until 1933.

The Japanese emperor Mutsuhito dies July 30 at age 60 after a 45-year reign that has restored imperial power (*see* 1867; 1868). He is succeeded by his son Yoshihito, 33, who will reign as the emperor Taisho until 1926 and whose reign will see Japan become a world power of the first rank, but the death of Mutsuhito is shared by the general Maresuke Nogi who is the principal of a school for the imperial family and who commits *seppuku* with his wife by immolation.

The Kuomintang (Chinese Nationalist party) is founded by Sun Yat-sen (*see* 1911; 1924).

Denmark's Frederick VIII dies after a 6-year reign and is succeeded by his 41-year-old son who will reign until 1947 as Christian X.

A Balkan War begins October 18 as the Ottoman Turks conclude the Treaty of Lausanne with Italy and promise to withdraw troops from Tripoli while Italy promises to withdraw troops from the Dodecanese Islands and to restore them to the Turks.

Montenegro has declared war on Turkey October 8, the Turks have declined October 12 to undertake reforms in Macedonia demanded by the great powers, Constantinople has declared war on Bulgaria and Serbia October 17, the Greeks join the conflict, and the Turks suffer major reverses.

Bulgarian forces triumph October 22 at Kirk Kilisse in Thrace, the Serbs gain a victory October 24 to 26 at Kumanovo, and Bulgarian troops under the 55-year-old commander in chief Mikhail Savov win the Battle of Lule Burgas October 28 to November 3 that brings them to the last lines of defense before Constantinople, but the Russians warn that they will use their fleet to resist a Bulgarian occupation of Constantinople, and the Bulgarians fail in an attack on the Turkish lines.

The Serbs overrun northern Albania and reach the Adriatic November 10, they gain victory at Monastir November 15 to 18, but Austria declares her opposition to Serbia having access to the Adriatic and announces her support for an independent Albania. Austria and Russia begin to mobilize but an armistice December 3 ends most of the conflict.

Former U.S. president Theodore Roosevelt bolts the Republican party to run for re-election on a Progressive party that is called the "Bull Moose" party because Roosevelt has said he felt "fit as a bull moose," he is wounded October 14 by an assassin in Wisconsin, but he wins 88 electoral votes and 28 percent of the popular vote. President Taft wins only 8 electoral votes and 23 percent of the popular vote, Socialist Eugene Debs polls more than 900,000 votes, but New Jersey governor Woodrow Wilson receives 435 electoral votes and 42 percent of the popular vote to give the Democrats control of the White House for the first time since Grover Cleveland left office in 1897.

Lawrence, Mass., textile workers walk out January 12 in a strike led by IWW agitators (see 1905). The strike is successful and wins prominence for the International Workers of the World among textile workers throughout the East (see 1913).

Congress extends the 8-hour day to all federal employees, but in private industry most workers labor 10 to 12 hours per day 6 days per week.

A minimum wage law for women and children legislated in Massachusetts is the first state law of its kind.

The *New York Times* Neediest Cases Fund Christmas charity is started by publisher Adolph S. Ochs.

Electric light bulbs are made longer lasting by General Electric Company research chemist Irving Langmuir, 31, who discovers that filling incandescent bulbs with inert gases will greatly increase the illuminating life of tungsten filaments developed by his colleague W. D. Coolidge (see 1913). Confuting conventional wisdom that the vacuum in the light bulb is what permits its filament to burn so long, Langmuir shows that bulbs with poor vacuums are no worse than those with the best vacuums, but that adding nitrogen gas (which does not react with the tungsten filament) will avoid evaporation of the filament and will prolong the life of the bulb. Langmuir, who has been experimenting with chemicals since age 7, will substitute argon for nitrogen (see 1894).

Oklahoma's Wheeler Well No. 1 comes in and begins making a fortune for wildcatter Thomas Baker Slick, 28, who has leased more than 100,000 acres of Oklahoma oil lands. The discovery well that starts gushing in March is in the Cushing field.

Petroleum reserves for the U.S. Navy are established at Elk Hills and Buena Vista Hills, Calif., as the navy converts it ships from coal to diesel (see Teapot Dome, 1915).

Turkish Petroleum Company is founded to exploit reserves that have been discovered in Mesopotamia.

Continental Gas and Electric Company is organized by Cleveland's Cyrus Eaton. It is the first great utility holding company (see 1907; Insull, 1932).

E. I. du Pont de Nemours divests itself of some explosives factories by court order. Stockholders receive securities in two new companies, Atlas Powder and Hercules Powder, but the courts permit Du Pont to retain its 100 percent monopoly in military powder (see 1906).

Some 30 National Cash Register Company officers including J. H. Patterson and Thomas J. Watson are indicted for criminal conspiracy in restraint of trade (see 1903). Patterson dismisses Watson, who will become general manager of the Computer-Tabulating-Recording Company (C-T-R), a holding company with a subsidiary that employs Herman Hollerith and has acquired the Hollerith punched card patents of 1890 (see IBM, 1924).

Bethlehem Steel's Charles M. Schwab journeys to France and buys Chile's Tofo Iron Mines from the Schneider interests. The Chilean mines contain 50 million tons of ore with iron content 10 percent better than Lake Superior ores (see 1907; 1913).

Libbey-Owens Corporation is created by a merger of the Owens Bottle Machine Company and the operations of Toledo glassmaker E. D. Libbey (see Owens, 1895, 1903).

E. D. Libbey (above) buys the patents of Toledo plate-glass maker Irving Wightman Colburn and supports Colburn while he develops the process that by 1916 will be turning out hundreds of yards of plate glass in a continuous flow at an enormous plant that Libbey-Owens will build at Charlestown, W. Va.

Cellophane is perfected at Zurich by Swiss chemist Jacques Edwin Brandenberger, who patented a less

1912 (cont.) satisfactory transparent film in 1908 (*see* Du Pont, 1926).

Monroe Calculating Machine Co. is founded at Newark, N.J., by U.S. entrepreneur Jay Randolph Monroe, 29, to produce a machine invented by Frank Stephen Baldwin, 74. The Arithmometer patented by Baldwin in 1874 was the first adding machine sold in the United States. Baldwin patented a calculating machine in 1902, he met Monroe last year, and he has refined his machine with an independent shaft for carrying balances and a reverse order for dividing and calculating (*see* Litton, 1957).

Freeport Sulphur Company is founded in July and begins mining sulfur November 12 in the coastal plain of the Texas Gulf Coast, using the Frasch process of 1891.

The world's first amphibious aircraft is designed and built by German-American engineer Grover Loening, 24, who was graduated 2 years ago from Columbia University with the first U.S. master's degree in aeronautics. Loening's "aeroboat" brings him to the attention of Orville Wright who will hire him next year as his assistant and as manager of Wright Aircraft's Dayton, Ohio, factory.

The Fokker aeroplane is introduced by Dutch aircraft designer Anthony Herman Gerard Fokker, 22, who opens a factory at Johannesthal, Germany, and who will build another such factory next year at Schwerin (*see* 1916; 1922).

Sopwith Aviation Co., Ltd., is established at Kingston-on-Thames by English aeronaut Thomas Octave Murdoch Sopwith, 24 (*see* Hawker, 1921).

The world's first aeronautical library is established at Auteuil by French engineer A. G. Eiffel of 1889 Eiffel Tower fame. Now 80, Eiffel investigates air currents in the world's first laboratory of aerodynamics.

Bendix Brake Company is founded by Vincent Bendix who has begun production of his Bendix starter drive and whose new firm will be the first mass producer of four-wheel brakes for motorcars (*see* 1907; Bendix Aviation, 1929).

Buick Division chief Charles William Nash, 48, becomes president of General Motors and brings in American Locomotive Works manager Walter P. Chrysler, 37, to head Buick (*see* Durant, 1910; Nash Motors, 1916; Chrysler, 1923).

Seven companies produce half of all U.S. motorcars (*see* 1923).

More than 22 percent of all U.S. motorcars are Fords which come out of Ford factories at the rate of 26,000 per month (*see* 1911; assembly line, 1913).

Edward G. Budd Manufacturing Co. is founded by Philadelphia entrepreneur Edward Gowan Budd, 41, who has developed a sheet metal stamping process and who will soon undertake production of steel truck and passenger car bodies for General Motors.

Edward G. Budd (above) will obtain his first volume orders in 1915 from John and Horace Dodge, he will have 4,700 employees by the end of 1918, he will start the Budd Wheel Co. at Detroit in 1921 (the two companies will merge 6 months before Budd's death late in 1946). Budd will produce the first stainless-steel airplane body in 1931, will become a major builder of railroad cars, will become a major supplier to Ford Motor Company, and will become the fourth largest U.S. user of steel.

The Supreme Court orders the Union Pacific Railroad and the Southern Pacific to dissolve their merger. The ruling is handed down December 2 in the case of *United States v. Union Pacific Railroad Co.* (*see* 1897 ruling).

Brazil's Madeira-Mamoro Railway opens after 6 years of construction that has cost 6,000 lives and the equivalent of 3 tons of gold. Rubber barons have financed the 255-mile road to circumvent 19 major waterfalls, the road permits resumption of Bolivian rubber shipments, but malaria, yellow fever, beriberi, snakebites, wild animals, and curare-tipped arrows from hostile natives have taken a heavy toll, and the Amazon Basin rubber boom will soon collapse as East Indian and African plantations undercut the price of wild rubber.

The first diagnosis of a heart attack in a living patient is reported in the December 7 issue of the *Journal of the American Medical Association* by Chicago physician James B. Herrick (*see* sickle cell anemia, 1910). Herrick points out that what may seem to be acute indigestion, food poisoning, angina pectoris, or something else may in fact be due to a blood clot (thrombosis) in the coronary artery which is what generally destroys a segment of the heart muscle to produce a myocardial infarction which has been considered until now merely a medical curiosity seen only at autopsy as an inevitable consequence of ageing. Herrick's 55-year-old patient (a banker) has survived only 52 hours, but Herrick shows that heart attacks need not be fatal, further work will show that clots generally occur in coronary arteries that have been damaged by arteriosclerosis (or atherosclerosis), that they set off a series of physiologic responses that cause chest pain and abdominal discomfort, and that they can be prevented to some extent, but heart disease remains a relatively minor cause of death among Americans as compared with tuberculosis and pneumonia (*see* 1921).

The Pituitary Body and Its Disorders by Boston surgeon Harvey Cushing, 43, advances knowledge of the pituitary gland and its relation to diabetes.

Harvard physiologist Walter Bradford Cannon, 41, shows that hunger sensations are experienced whenever the empty stomach of a medical student contracts vigorously, and that the contractions progressively increase in frequency and intensity as a fast is prolonged. Cannon hypothesizes that the vagus nerves may carry gastric impulses to the medulla, the posterior portion of the brain.

California Syrup of Figs is acquired by Sterling Products which adds the laxative product to its Cascarets (*see* 1909; Bayer Aspirin, 1919).

Rice University is founded under the name Rice Institute with a bequest from the late Texas merchant William Marsh Rice, who was chloroformed to death by his valet in New York 12 years ago at age 84 (*see* 1838). Boston architect Ralph Adams Cram has designed the new university at Houston.

Memphis State University is founded in Tennessee.

The Montessori Method by Italian educator Maria Montessori, 42, describes her success at teaching slum children between the ages of 3 and 6 how to read. First woman graduate of Rome University medical school, Montessori begins a movement of Montessori schools for teachers.

The Kallikak Family by U.S. psychologist Henry Herbert Goddard, 46, relates feeblemindedness to crime and causes a sensation. Goddard invented the word "moron" in 1910. Last year he tested the school population of a New Jersey town and revised the Binet-Simon I.Q. test for U.S. use (*see* 1916).

The wireless message "S.S. *Titanic* ran into iceberg. Sinking fast" is picked up accidentally by Russian-American wireless operator David Sarnoff, 20, who is manning a station set up by John Wanamaker in his New York store window ostensibly to keep in touch with the Philadelphia Wanamaker's but actually is a publicity stunt (*see* 1903). Sarnoff relays the message from the *Titanic* (above) to another steamer which reports that the liner has sunk but that some survivors have been picked up. President Taft orders other stations to remain silent and Sarnoff remains at his post for 72 hours, taking the names of survivors and making his own name familiar to millions of newspaper readers (*see* 1917).

An SOS in Morse code—three dots, three dashes, three dots—is adopted as a universal distress signal by an International Radio-Telegraph Conference.

Irving Langmuir's work on vacuums (above) will be applied to the development of an improved radio tube whose patents will be major assets of Radio Corporation of America (*see* 1919).

The first effective high-vaccum tube for amplifying electric currents is produced by Bell Laboratories physicist H. D. Arnold (*see* Edison, 1883; Langmuir, above; transistor, 1948).

Britain nationalizes her telephone system. The action by Parliament follows that of most European countries and brings demands for the nationalization of American Telephone and Telegraph Company (*see* 1910; Burleson, 1913).

AT&T's Western Union buys U.S. rights to a multiplex device that permits up to four messages to be sent at once over the same circuit. The multiplex takes advantage of the difference between the speed of mechanical impulses and the speed of electrical impulses.

Pravda begins publication to voice the ideas of Russia's underground Communist party (*see* 1905) with Vyacheslav Molotov (Vyacheslav Mikhailovich Skryabin), 22, as editor. Nikolai Lenin uses the Russian word for truth and while *Pravda* will publish only one view of the truth, the newspaper's circulation will grow to 10.3 million, making it the world's largest.

The S. I. Newhouse newspaper chain has it beginnings at Bayonne, N.J., where a local lawyer has acquired controlling interest in the foundering *Bayonne Times* as payment for a legal fee and sends his 17-year-old office boy Samuel I. Newhouse to take charge, offering him half the paper's profits in lieu of salary. By the time he is 21 Newhouse will have earned a law degree at night school and will be earning $30,000 per year from the newspaper. He will persuade his employer to join him in buying the *Staten Island Advance* in 1922, and by 1955 the Newhouse chain will include the *Long Island Press,* the *Newark Star-Ledger,* the *Syracuse Post-Standard, Herald-Journal,* and *Herald-American,* the *St. Louis Globe-Democrat,* the *Portland Oregonian,* and the *Portland Oregon-Journal* (*see* 1967).

Fiction *The Autobiography of an Ex-Colored Man* by U.S. poet-essayist James Weldon Johnson of 1899 "Lift Every Voice and Sing" fame. He will not acknowledge authorship until 1927; *Jean-Christophe* by French novelist-playwright Romain Rolland, 46; *The Sea and the Jungle* by *London Morning Leader* staffman H. M. (Henry Major) Tomlinson, 39; *'Twixt Land and Sea* (stories) by Joseph Conrad includes "The Secret Sharer" and "The Inn of the Two Witches"; *The Unbearable Bassington* by Saki (H. H. Munro); *The Financier* by Theodore Dreiser; *Riders of the Purple Sage* by former New York dentist Zane Grey, 37, who will have a top best-seller every year from 1917 through 1926.

Poetry *Duino Elegies* by Rainer Maria Rilke who enters a period of existential self-revelation and will not complete the *Elegies* until 1922; *Ripostes* by U.S. émigré poet Ezra Loomis Pound, 27, who went abroad to live 4 years ago and published his first book at Venice a year later under the title *A lume spento.* Pound pioneers an antipoetical imagism which he will abandon in 2 years for a vorticism which will relate to painting and sculpture (*see* 1925); *A Dome of Many-Coloured Glass* by Boston poet Amy Lowell, 36, sister of Harvard president Abbott Lawrence Lowell, 56. Barely 5 feet tall and weighing 250 pounds, the poet defies convention by smoking cigars, cursing in public, and taking another woman into her life and home, but she will publish 10 more volumes of poetry in the next 13 years and each will be more popular than the last.

Painting *September Morn* (*Matinée de Septembre*) by French painter Paul Emile Chabas, 43 (*see* 1913); *The Violin* by Pablo Picasso; *Homage à Picasso* by Spanish cubist Juan Gris (José Victoriano González), 25; *Woman in Blue* by Fernand Léger who has a

1912 (cont.) one-man show at the Galerie Kahnweiler; *The Cattle Dealer* by Marc Chagall; *The Life of Christ* and *St. Mary of Egypt Among Sinners* by Emil Nolde; *The Artillery* by French painter Roger de la Fresnaye, 27; *McSorley's Bar* and *Sunday, Women Drying Their Hair* by John French Sloan; *Woolworth Building* by watercolorist John C. Marin.

Georges Braque invents collage.

Theater *The Marchioness Rosalind (La Marquesa Rosalinda)* by Ramon del Valle Inclan in January at Madrid's Teatro de la Princesa; *Death and Damnation (Tod und Teufel)* by Frank Wedekind 4/29 at Berlin's Künstlerhaus Werkstatt der Werdenden; *Epic Voices (Voces de gesta)* by Ramon del Valle Inclan 5/26 at Madrid's Teatro de la Princesa; *Gabriel Schilling's Flight (Gabriel Schillings Flucht)* by Gerhart Hauptmann 6/14 at Bad Lauchstadt's Goethe Theater; *The Yellow Jacket* by George C. Hazelton and J. Harry Beurimo 11/4 at New York's Fulton Theater, 80 perfs.; *The Wolf (A farkas)* by Ferenc Molnár 11/9 at Budapest's Magyar Szinhaz; *The Tidings Brought to Mary (L'Annonce faite à Marie)* by Paul Claudel 12/20 at the Théâtre de l'oeuvre, Paris; *Peg O' My Heart* by J. Hartley Manners 12/20 at New York's new Cort Theater, with the playwright's bride Laurette Taylor, 605 perfs.

The Minsky brothers take over New York's Winter Garden Theater for bawdy burlesque productions.

Films *Queen Elizabeth* with Sarah Bernhardt is shown July 12 at New York's Lyceum Theater and is the first feature-length motion picture to be shown in America. U.S. rights to the 40-minute French film have been acquired by Hungarian-American nickelodeon chain operator Adolph Zukor, 39, a former furrier who has resigned as treasurer of Loew's Enterprises and who has persuaded theatrical producer Charles Frohman to join him in investing $35,000 in the venture. Zukor and Frohman earn $200,000 showing the film on a reserved seat basis in theaters across the country, and they form Famous Players Co. to produce films of their own (*see* Lasky, 1913).

Other films D. W. Griffith's *Her First Biscuit* with Mary Pickford (Gladys Smith); D. W. Griffith's *The Musketeers of Pig Alley* with Lillian Gish.

Universal Pictures Corporation is created by a merger of U.S. film producers who include German-American cinema pioneer Carl Laemmle, 45. He will have sole control of Universal from 1920 to 1936, and he will be the first to promote the personalities of his film performers as "movie stars," hiring Mary Pickford, now 19, from the rival Biograph Studios of D. W. Griffith (above) (*see* United Artists, 1919).

Ballet *Daphnis et Chloe* by Sergei Diaghilev's Ballet Russe 6/8 at the Théâtre du Châtelet, Paris, with music by Maurice Ravel, choreography by Michel Fokine. Waslaw Nijinsky dances the role of Daphnis, Tamara Karsavina is Chloe.

First performances Symphony No. 9 in D flat major by the late Gustav Mahler 6/26 at Vienna; *Shep-herd's Key* by Australian-English composer Percy Aldridge Grainger, 30, 8/19 at Queen's Hall, London; *Five Pieces for Orchestra (Fünf Orchesterstrücke)* by Arnold Schoenberg 9/3 at a London Promenade Concert; *Two Pictures (Ket Kap) for Orchestra* by Béla Bartók 10/5 at Budapest; *Pierrot Lunaire: Three Times Seven Melodies for Reciter, Piano, Piccolo, Bass Clarinet, Viola, and Cello* by Arnold Schoenberg 10/16 at Berlin's Choralionsaal.

Broadway musicals *The Isle o' Dreams* 1/27 at the Grand Opera House, with Chauncey Olcott, music by Ernest R. Ball, lyrics by Olcott and George Graf, Jr., 26 (who has never been to Ireland), songs that include "When Irish Eyes Are Smiling," 32 perfs.; *The Passing Show* 7/22 at the Winter Garden Theater, with Willie and Eugene Howard, music by Louis A. Hirsch, lyrics by Harold Atteridge, 136 perfs.; *The Ziegfeld Follies* 10/21 at the Moulin Rouge, with Leon Errol, Vera Maxwell, 77 perfs.; *The Firefly* 12/12 at the Lyric Theater, with music by Rudolf Friml, lyrics by Otto Harbach, songs that include "Giannina Mia," 120 perfs.

Popular songs "Waiting for the Robert E. Lee" by Lewis F. Muir, lyrics by L. Wolfe Gilbert; "When the Midnight Choo Choo Leaves for Alabam" by Irving Berlin; "Moonlight Bay" by Percy Wenrich, lyrics by Edward Madden; "That Old Gal of Mine" by Egbert Van Alstyne, lyrics by Earle C. Jones; "The Sweetheart of Sigma Chi" by Albion College sophomores F. Dudleigh Vernor, 20, and Byron D. Stokes, 26, who wrote the song in their freshman year; "Bulldog" and "Bingo Eli Yale" by Yale sophomore Cole Porter, 19.

The Maxixe is introduced to U.S. dancefloors.

English golfer Harry Vardon, 42, wins the British PGA 12 years after winning the U.S. Open. Born on the Isle of Jersey, Vardon has invented the overlapping "Vardon grip" and will be among the top five players in the British Open 16 times in 21 years.

The Boston Braves receive that name from New York political contractor James E. Gaffney. He has bought Boston's National League franchise with two other New York investors and takes over a club that has been called at various times the Beaneaters, the Triumvirs, the Doves, and the Rustlers. The new name is suggested by Gaffney's Tammany Hall affiliations and the Braves begin the season with veteran pitcher Cy Young (*see* 1890; Milwaukee, 1953).

Boston's 33,437-seat Fenway Park is completed for the Red Sox who changed their name from the Red Stockings in 1907.

The Boston Red Sox win the World Series by defeating the New York Giants 4 games to 3.

The Olympic Games at Stockholm attract 4,742 contestants from 27 countries.

Oklahoma Indian James Francis "Jim" Thorpe, 24, wins both the pentathlon and the decathlon at the fifth Olympiad (above), scoring 8,412 points out of a possible 10,000 in the decathlon and winning four firsts in the pentathlon. Thorpe returns to score 25 touchdowns and 198 points for the Carlisle Indian School at Carlisle, Pa., and he is named halfback for the second year on Walter Camp's All-America team. A man of Sac and Fox ancestry, Thorpe will lose his Olympic gold medals when he admits to having played semi-professional baseball during his summer vacation last year, thus losing his amateur status, and his name will be stricken from the Olympic record books at the insistence of the Amateur Athletic Union (AAU), but he will be rated the greatest athlete and football player of the first half of the twentieth century.

The fourth down is added to U.S. football and a touchdown is given a value of six points, up from the five point value established in 1898. The football field is standardized at 360 feet by 160 feet including end zones 10 feet deep, a pass completed to the end zone is scored as a touchdown, and the football is reduced in girth from 27 inches at the middle to between 22½ and 23 inches (*see* 1929).

Harvard sophomore halfback Huntington R. "Tack" Hardwick begins a 3-year era in which coach Percy Haughton's eleven will rack up 29 wins, no losses.

Princeton athletic star Hobart Amery Hare "Hobey" Baker, 20, is named head of the hockey team and achieves legendary feats in football, golf, track, swimming, and gymnastics as well. As football captain, Baker will drop-kick a 43-yard field goal to tie Yale.

The Girl Scouts of America has its beginnings March 12 at Savannah, Ga., where Juliette Gordon Low, 52, starts the first troop of Girl Guides in America (*see* England, 1910). The Girl Guides will be renamed the Girl Scouts next year and headquarters will be established at New York City.

Hadassah is founded by Baltimore-born Jewess Henrietta Szold, 52, who will make the sisterhood of U.S. Jewish women a Zionist organization beginning in 1916 and who will head the group until 1926. Szold has been disappointed in love by Talmudic scholar Louis Ginzberg, 39, whose first books she has translated, but who 4 years ago met Adele Katzenstein in Berlin and married her.

R. H. Macy's Nathan Straus is shaken by the loss of his brother Isidor on the *Titanic* (above) and sells his interest in the store to Isidor's sons Jesse Isidor Straus, 40, Percy Seldon Straus, 36, and Herbert N. Straus, 30 (*see* 1901; Thanksgiving Day parade, 1924).

New York merchant Henri Bendel moves his 20-year-old clothing store from 520 Fifth Avenue to 10 West 57th Street where it will prosper.

Detroit's J. L. Hudson dies a bachelor at age 65 and his nephews Richard, Oscar, Joseph, and James Webber take over Hudson's vast department store and his automotive interests (*see* 1881; 1909; 1928).

L. L. Bean, Inc., of Freeport, Me., is started by local merchant Leon Leonwood Bean, 40, who has invented the Maine Hunting Shoe and who goes into partnership with his brother Gus to open a small clothing store. Ninety of the first 100 hunting shoe orders are returned because the shoes' leather tops have separated from their rubber bottoms, but Bean solves the problem with a combination of stitching and glue, he makes good on all the returns, and he begins a mail-order sporting goods empire whose sales will top $1 million per year by 1937, $3.5 million by the time Bean dies in 1967, and $41 million by 1977 with sales of North Maine Woods shirts, chamois shirts, and down vests supplementing sales of the Maine Hunting Shoe.

A new Filene's store with a 7-foot doorman opens in Boston September 3 at the corner of Washington and Summer Streets in a building designed by Chicago's Daniel Burnham (*see* Automatic Bargain Basement, 1909). Edward Filene will hold free tea dances beginning in 1919, and although his Automatic Bargain Basement is losing money and will continue to lose money for 7 more years, it will then become profitable and will endure as a Boston institution (*see* Federated, 1929).

F. W. Woolworth Co. is incorporated by Frank Woolworth who absorbs the five-and-dime chains established by four of his erstwhile partners (*see* 1909; 1919; Woolworth Building, below).

New York's 60-story Woolworth building goes up near City Hall. The 792-foot tall "Cathedral of Commerce" designed by architect Cass Gilbert will be the world's largest habitable structure until 1931.

New York's 998 Fifth Avenue luxury apartment house is completed in Italian Renaissance style by W. S. Richardson of McKim, Mead and White opposite the Metropolitan Museum of Art on 81st Street.

New York's 635 Park Avenue luxury apartment house is completed by J. E. R. Carpenter at 66th Street with one apartment to a floor.

New York's McAlpin Hotel opens at Broadway and 34th Street on a site acquired from Jay Gould in 1877

Grazing an iceberg proved fatal to the "unsinkable" *Titanic*— and to 1,513 of her 2,224 passengers.

1912 (cont.) by David H. McAlpin. The 24-story $7.1 million hotel has 1,515 rooms, it is the world's largest, and McAlpin will add a 185-room annex in 1919.

New York's Vanderbilt Hotel opens on lower Park Avenue at 34th Street.

The Beverly Hills Hotel opens on a hilltop outside Los Angeles where it will be a favorite haunt of motion picture people.

The Manila Hotel opens formally July 4. A dance for 500 waltzers inaugurates the five-story 265-room hotel on Manila Bay.

France's Normandy and Golf Hotels open with a gambling casino at Deauville.

Boston's Copley-Plaza Hotel opens in Copley Square on a site formerly occupied by the Museum of Fine Arts (*see* Sheraton, 1941).

Montreal's Ritz Hotel opens New Year's Eve with 267 rooms. The Ritz will remain Montreal's preeminent hotel for more than 65 years.

 Alaska's 6,715-foot Katmai volcano erupts and buries Kodiak Island 100 miles away under 3 feet of ashes while darkening skies over most of Alaska.

Japanese cherry trees given to the United States as a goodwill gesture from the royal family are destroyed when found to be infected with insects and disease (*see* 1904 chestnut blight). A second shipment of cherry trees is planted at Washington, D.C., where the trees will blossom each spring to make the Tidal Basin a perennial tourist attraction.

Wild boars are introduced into the United States from Germany by an American who represents a group of English investors. George Gordon Moore encloses a game refuge in the North Carolina Appalachians, he builds a large log lodge with indoor plumbing, and he stocks the refuge with 12 bison, 14 elk, 6 Colorado mule deer, 34 black bears, and 14 young wild boars, most of which will escape to mate with free-roaming "mountain-rooter" sows to begin a feral swine population that will grow to number more than 1,200.

 A new Homestead Act reduces from 5 years to 3 years the residence requirement of U.S. homesteaders (*see* 1909; 1916).

Dissolution of the International Harvester Trust of 1902 is ordered by the U.S. Department of Justice (but *see* 1918).

Ocean Spray Cranberry Sauce is introduced by the Cape Cod Cannery Company which buys berries from farmers who cultivate 26,000 acres. President of the company is Boston lawyer Marcus L. Urann who has been developing cranberry bogs in Plymouth County and who has opened a new cranberry sauce cannery at Hanson (*see* 1930; Hall, 1816).

Charles Seabrook goes into partnership with his father Arthur on the family's New Jersey truck farm (*see* 1893). An agricultural innovator, young Charles

has installed overhead irrigation on the farm whose size he will increase in the next few years to 273 acres. By 1914 Seabrook Farms will be selling 200 carloads of produce, mostly in the New York and Philadelphia markets, and by 1917 Seabrook will be cultivating more than 3,000 acres of owned and leased land (*see* cannery, 1920).

 An anti-beriberi compound is extracted from rice hulls by Japanese biochemists J. Suzuki, T. Shimamura, and S. Ohdake (*see* 1906; 1933).

The fat-soluble nutrient that will later be called vitamin A is discovered in butter and egg yolks by U.S. biochemists Elmer Verner McCollum, 33, and Marguerite Davis who establish that it was a lack of this nutrient that caused C. A. Pekelharing's Dutch mice to die prematurely in 1905 when given no milk. A similar discovery is made by Yale biochemists Thomas B. Osborne, 53, and Lafayette B. Mendel, 40.

Die Vitamine by Casimir Funk suggests that beriberi, rickets, pellagra, and sprue may all be caused by "vitamine" deficiencies (*see* 1911).

 The Sherley Amendment to the U.S. Pure Food and Drug Law of 1906 prohibits farfetched declarations of therapeutic or curative effects (*see* 1911; "Marmola," 1931; Wheeler-Lea Act, 1938).

A Truth in Advertising code is adopted by the Associated Advertising Clubs of America.

A U.S. postal regulation requires all advertising in the media to be labeled "advt."

 Libby, McNeill & Libby buys an Alaskan salmon cannery. Libby will operate an extensive fishing fleet with as many as 14 salmon canneries and will continue to market salmon under the Libby label even after it sells the fleet and canneries in 1959 (*see* 1909; tomato juice, 1923).

 Morton's Table Salt is introduced in a blue and white asphalt-laminated paper cannister with an aluminum pouring spout (*see* 1885). Beginning in 1914 the cannister will bear the slogan "When It Rains It Pours" and a trademark depicting a little girl holding an umbrella in the rain while holding a Morton's Salt cannister upside down in her other hand with salt pouring from its open spout.

Hellmann's Blue Ribbon Mayonnaise is introduced by German-American delicatessen owner Richard Hellmann, 35, who has operated Hellmann's Delicatessen at 490 Columbus Avenue in New York since 1905. Hellmann will build a three-story mayonnaise factory in Astoria, Long Island, next year, he will incorporate under the name Richard Hellmann's, Inc., in 1916, he will build a larger Astoria plant in 1922, and by 1927 he will have plants at Chicago, San Francisco, Atlanta, Dallas, and Tampa (*see* 1927).

The Prince Macaroni Company is started on Prince Street in Boston's North End by three Italian-Americans. The firm will expand in the next 20 years to outgrow its Prince Street quarters, it will move to Lowell, but it will remain Prince Macaroni.

Oreo Biscuits are introduced by the National Biscuit Company whose two chocolate-flavored wafers with a cream filling compete with the Hydrox "biscuit bon bons" introduced in 1910. The name will be changed in 1958 to Oreo Cream Sandwich.

Lorna Doone cookies are introduced by the National Biscuit Company (above). The shortcake cookies are named for the 1869 novel by Richard Doddridge Blackmore, still required reading in many schools.

Royal Crown Ginger Ale and Chero-Cola are bottled by the Union Bottling Works at Columbus, Ga., which reorganizes under the name Chero-Cola Company and issues franchises to bottle Chero-Cola to other Georgia bottlers (see 1914; Hatcher, 1905).

The A&P begins an expansion program under John Hartford, a son of the founder (see 1876). From its present base of nearly 500 stores, the chain will open a new A&P store every 3 days for the next 3 years as it stops providing charge accounts and free delivery and bases its growth on one-man "economy" stores that operate on a cash and carry (see 1929).

The first self-service grocery stores open independently in California. The Alpha Beta Food Market opens at Pomona, Ward's Groceteria opens at Ocean Park, and they are soon followed by the Bay Cities Mercantile Company's Humpty Dumpty Stores (see Saunders, 1916).

Mory's opens at New Haven to serve Yale University students and professors.

1913 The assembly line introduced at the Ford Motor Company reduces the time required to assemble a motorcar from 12.5 hours to 1.5 hours. Devised with the help of engineer Clarence W. Avery, Ford's line reverses the disassembling line used by Chicago and Cincinnati meatpackers, factories producing a wide variety of products will convert to assembly line production, the line will revolutionize much of industry, but it will increase worker boredom and will permit industry to hire unskilled and semiskilled workers at wages lower than those of skilled workers.

A commercial ammonia plant employing the Haber process of 1908 begins production at Ludwigshafen, Germany. The ammonia is used primarily for making explosives.

The Sixteenth Amendment to the Constitution proclaimed in force February 25 by Secretary of State Philander C. Knox empowers Congress to levy graduated income taxes on incomes above $3,000 per year. The income tax will bring drastic changes to the lifestyles of a few thousand rich Americans, but the very rich will find loopholes for avoiding taxes.

A sensational report published February 28 by the House Committee on Banking and Currency exposes the "money trust" that controls U.S. financial power. U.S. congressman from Louisiana Arsene P. Pujo heads the committee that has called witnesses including financier J. P. Morgan (who dies at Rome March 31 at age 75 leaving a vast estate).

Economic Interpretation of the Constitution by Columbia University history professor Charles A. Beard, 39, points out that America's founding fathers were all men of property when they drafted the Constitution in 1787. Beard suggests certain consequent inequities.

The Rockefeller Foundation is created by John D. Rockefeller of Standard Oil (below).

U.S. import duties are reduced May 8 by the Underwood-Simmons Tariff Act which lowers tariffs by an average of 30 percent and represents the first real break in tariff protection since the Civil War. Agricultural implements, raw wool, iron ore, pig iron, and steel rails are admitted duty-free under the new law, and tariffs on raw materials and foodstuffs are substantially reduced.

Many U.S. manufacturers are hurt by the reduction and elimination of tariffs (above), and pressure mounts for restoration of tariff protection (see 1922).

The United States has 40 percent of world industrial production, up from 20 percent in 1860.

The average English worker still earns less than £1 per week ($5 in U.S. currency) while American workers average more than $2 per day (see Ford, 1914).

A Federal Reserve System designed to reform U.S. banking and currency is created by the Glass-Owen Currency Act signed into law by President Wilson December 23. The legislation drafted to prevent panics such as the one in 1907 establishes 12 Federal Reserve banks in America's 12 major cities and requires member banks to maintain cash reserves proportionate to their deposits with the Fed—which loans money to the banks at low rates of interest relative to the rates the banks charge customers.

The amount of money in circulation at any given time is determined by the Board of Governors of the Federal Reserve System (above) which provides elasticity to the supply of currency and can act to control inflation (see Banking Act, 1935).

Bethlehem Steel's Charles M. Schwab acquires the Fore River Shipbuilding Corporation of Massachusetts and makes Eugene Grace, 37, president of Bethlehem. Grace will develop Bethlehem into the world's second largest steelmaker (see 1912; Watson, 1901; Sparrows Point, 1916).

The first Indian head/buffalo 5-cent piece is issued by the U.S. Mint to replace the Liberty Head nickel that has been in circulation since 1883. The new coin will not be superseded until 1938.

A monthly Consumer Price Index is computed to help the U.S. Bureau of Labor Statistics determine the fairness of wage levels (see Fisher, 1911).

A U.S. Department of Labor is created by the new Wilson administration in response to demands by the AF of L which now has 2 million members.

The IWW takes Paterson, N.J., silk workers out on 5-month strike to protest against installation of improved machinery (see 1912; Luddites, 1811).

1913 (cont.) The Colorado Fuel and Iron Company is struck by the United Mine Workers, two mines are set afire by strikers protesting policies of the firm controlled by Standard Oil Company's John D. Rockefeller, 27 strikers are killed (*see* Ivy Lee, below; Ludlow massacre, 1914).

U.S. suffragettes march 5,000-strong down Washington's Pennsylvania Avenue March 3 following Alice Paul, 27, who founds the National Woman's Party to spearhead the movement for woman suffrage. Crowds of angry, jeering men slap the demonstrators, spit at them, and poke them with lighted cigars, a brawl stops the march before it can reach the White House, 40 people are hospitalized, and it takes a cavalry troop from Ft. Myer to restore order.

English suffragette Emmeline Pankhurst draws a 3-year sentence for inciting her supporters to place explosives in the house of the Chancellor of the Exchequer David Lloyd George as part of her campaign to gain the vote for British women (*see* 1906). Pankhurst will serve only 1 year and will devote part of it to a hunger strike (*see* 1918; Gandhi, 1914).

The Prisoners' Temporary Discharge for Ill Health Act passed by Parliament in April aims to thwart militant suffragettes who stage hunger strikes. Suffragettes call it the Cat and Mouse Act.

The Universal Negro Improvement Association is founded in Jamaica, British West Indies, by social reformer Marcus Moziah Garvey, 26 (*see* 1916).

The Anti-Defamation League to fight anti-Semitism in America is founded by the 70-year-old B'Nai B'rith (Sons of the Covenant). Started as a New York fraternal organization, B'Nai B'rith has become an international group, and its ADL will work to counteract prejudice through community projects and legal action.

 Mexico's President Madero is deposed by the 58-year-old military leader Victoriano Huerta and is shot dead February 22 at age 39 while allegedly trying to escape his captors after less than 2 years in office. The United States refuses to recognize Huerta as president (*see* 1914).

Greece's George I is assassinated at Salonica March 18 at age 67 after a reign of nearly 50 years. The former Danish prince is succeeded as king of the Hellenes by his 44-year-old son who will reign as Constantine I until 1917 (*see* 1920).

The Treaty of London May 30 resolves last year's 6-week Balkan War between the Ottoman Turks and the Greek-Bulgarian-Serbian coalition, but a 32-day Second Balkan War begins June 29 when a Bulgarian commander orders an attack on Serbo-Greek positions. Bucharest and Constantinople declare war and Bulgaria is quickly defeated, but political crises continue in the Balkans (*see* 1914).

A new model of the atom devised by Danish physicist Niels Bohr, 28, violates classical electromagnetic theory but successfully accounts for the spectrum of hydrogen. Bohr applies Max Planck's quantum theory of 1900 to Ernest Rutherford's nuclear atom of 1911 (*see* 1939; Rutherford, 1919).

Some 34 percent of the world's electrical equipment is made in Germany, 19 percent in the United States.

A patent on "tungsten and method for making the same for use as filaments of incandescent electric lamps" is granted to General Electric Company researcher William David Coolidge, 39, who 5 years ago produced the first ductile tungsten by using high temperatures to draw the metal into fine filaments. Long-burning tungsten filament bulbs will replace the Swan-Edison carbon filament bulbs in use until now (*see* 1879; Owens, 1903; Langmuir, 1912).

The Keokum Dam on the Mississippi River is completed to produce hydroelectric power.

The Hetch Hetchy Dam on California's Tuolumne River is funded by Congress to provide water and hydroelectric power for San Francisco. Congressman William Kent of 1908 Muir Woods fame votes to build the dam that will destroy what John Muir, now 75, has called "the Tuolumne Yosemite."

World coal reserves are estimated by an International Geological Congress at Toronto which takes 1 foot as the minimum workable thickness of seams down to depths of 4,000 feet and 2 feet as the minimum for seams at lower depths. North America is judged to have more than 5 trillion metric tons of coal, Asia 1.3 trillion, Europe 784 billion, South America 33 billion, Africa 58 million, Oceania 170 million (*see* Paley Commission Report, 1952).

World petroleum production reaches 407.5 million barrels, up from 5.7 million in 1870. Most of the output comes from wells in the United States and in Russia's Caspian Sea and Caucasus Mountain oilfields (*see* Persia, 1908, 1914; Venezuela, 1922).

Sales of U.S. luxury motorcars priced from $2,500 to $7,500 reach 18,500 with Packard leading the field (2,300 cars), paced by Pierce Arrow (2,000). White, Franklin, Locomobile, and Peerless provide healthy competition.

Cadillac is the leading make in the $1,500 to $2,500 range and will enter the luxury market next year with a V8 model.

The Deusenberg Motor Company is founded at St. Paul, Minn., by Fred S. and August S. Deusenberg. The German-American bicycle makers (and bike racers) opened a garage at Des Moines, Iowa, in 1903, they produced their first motorcar in 1904 under the name Mason, and they have sold their Iowa company to the Maytag Washing Machine Company which is selling their original car as a Maytag (*see* 1907; 1919).

The Stutz Motor Car Company is organized by Harry C. Stutz, who merges his Stutz Auto Parts Company with the Ideal Motor Car Company (*see* 1911; Stutz Bearcat, 1914).

Some new Ford models sell for as little as $550 F.O.B. Detroit, and the price will soon drop to $490 (*see* 1925; assembly line, above).

The Dodge brothers John and Horace break with Ford and become independent while continuing to own stock in Ford which builds a big new plant at Highland Park, Mich. (*see* 1914; 1919).

The first South American subway line opens at Buenos Aires.

New York's Grand Central Station opens at 42nd Street and replaces the shed that has existed on the site since 1871 as a terminal for New York Central and New York, New Haven and Hartford passenger trains. The open cut that has carried trains down Fourth Avenue to 42nd Street is being paved over to create Park Avenue on which no public transportation or commercial vehicles will be permitted.

Henry M. Flagler's Florida East Coast Railway reaches Key West, but Flagler dies at West Palm Beach May 20 at age 83. 3,000 men have worked for 7 years to complete the rail link to the Keys, yellow fever has killed hundreds, and hurricanes will destroy the line in 1926 and 1935.

The first diesel-electric locomotives go into service in Sweden. Diesel-electrics will generally replace steam locomotives, but inventor Rudolf Diesel jumps or falls overboard from the Antwerp-Harwich mail steamer the night of September 30 and is lost at age 55 (*see* 1895; first U.S. diesels, 1924).

New York Evening Sun reporter John Henry Mears, 35, circles the world in a record 35 days, 21 hours, 36 seconds (*see* Jaeger-Schmidt, 1911). A nephew of National Biscuit Company president A. W. Green, Mears leaves New York on the Cunard Line's S. S. *Mauretania* carrying a package of Uneeda Biscuits, he arrives at Fishguard, Wales, he proceeds by train to London, he crosses the Channel by ship, he proceeds by train to Paris and on to Berlin, to St. Petersburg, and on to Manchuria via the Trans-Siberian Railway, he crosses by ship to Japan, he proceeds by ship to Vancouver, he flies to Seattle, and he completes the 21,066-mile journey by train via Chicago (*see* Wiley Post, 1931).

The German passenger liner S. S. *Imperator* that will become the S. S. *Berengaria* in 1919 goes into service on the North Atlantic. The 52,022-ton ship has four screws, she is 919 feet in length overall, and she will continue in service for 25 years (*see* 1914).

Elmer A. Sperry receives a patent for his stabilizer gyroscope (*see* 1910; rail defect detection, 1923).

The Moore-McCormack line that will become a major U.S. shipping line to South America is started at 5 Broadway in New York by cargo solicitor Bert Moore and tugboat captain Emmett McCormack, both 31. They put up $5,000 each to go into business leasing ships on charter (*see* 1915).

The first multimotored aircraft is built and flown by Russian aeronautical engineer Igor Ivan Sikorsky, 24, who 4 years ago built a prototype helicopter (*see* 1939; autogyro, 1923).

Lord Northcliffe of the *London Daily Mail* offers a £10,000 prize for the first nonstop transatlantic crossing by aeroplane. No pilot has topped the distance record of 628.15 miles set last year, and many regard the offer as an empty publicity stunt (*see* 1919).

Camel cigarettes are introduced by R. J. Reynolds Company which made no cigarettes before joining the Tobacco Trust in 1890 (*see* 1911). Camels are made largely from a flue-cured bright tobacco much like the tobacco discovered in 1852 by Eli and Elisha Slade, but they also contain a sweetened burley from Kentucky combined with some Turkish tobaccos that make them the first of the modern blended cigarettes. Their package design has been inspired by "Old Joe," a dromedary in the Barnum & Bailey circus menagerie, and they are backed in their first year by a $1.5 million advertising campaign (*see* 1917).

Chesterfield cigarettes are introduced by Liggett & Myers which is well known for its Fatima, Picayune, and Piedmont brands (*see* 1873; 1926).

Tobacco companies spend $32.4 million to advertise their various brands in the United States, up from $18.1 million in 1910 (*see* Lucky Strike, 1916).

The American Cancer Society is founded at a time when 9 out of 10 cancer patients die of the disease. The percentage of mortality will fall sharply but the incidence of cancer will increase.

The Schick test for determining susceptibility to diphtheria is developed by Hungarian-American physician Bela Schick, 36, at New York's Mount Sinai Hospital.

Lambarene Hospital in French Equatorial Africa is founded by French Protestant missionary-physician Albert Schweitzer, 38, who will be famous for his "reverence for life."

Parcel Post service is inaugurated by the U.S. Post Office Department January 1 after more than two decades of agitation by Populist politicians and farmers who hope to ship produce to market via Parcel Post. The service has been opposed by American Express, Adams Express, United States Express, and Wells Fargo, but by year's end packages are being mailed at the rate of 300 million per year, mail-order firms such as Montgomery Ward and Sears, Roebuck receive up to five times as many orders as last year, while sales of rural merchants are depressed.

Nationalization of U.S. telephone and telegraph communications is proposed by Postmaster General Albert Burleson who notes that the Constitution provided for federal control of the postal system and would have provided for federal control of other means of communication had they existed (*see* Britain, 1912). AT&T president Theodore N. Vail tells

1913 (cont.) stockholders, "We are opposed to government ownership because we know that no government-owned system in the world is giving as cheap and efficient service as the American public is getting from all its telephone companies," but while U.S. long-distance rates are indeed lower than in Europe, local calls generally cost more.

AT&T president Vail (above) has his vice president N. C. Kingsbury meet with Attorney General George Wickersham, the company divests itself of its Western Union holdings to avoid antitrust action, it loses $7.5 million by the divestiture, it halts plans to take over some midwestern telephone companies, but it retains its valuable Western Electric acquisition (*see* 1910; dial telephone, 1919).

New York public relations pioneer Ivy Ledbetter Lee, 36, persuades John D. Rockefeller, Jr., to travel to Colorado and to speak personally to the miners, an act that improves relations between the Rockefeller family and the outraged strikers (above). An advocate of frank and open dealing with the public, Lee will help make the Rockefellers famous for their philanthropies—partly by having John D. Sr. hand out dimes to schoolchildren.

The Rockefeller Foundation is chartered in New York by John D. Rockefeller, Sr., at the advice of Frederick T. Gates, formerly head of the American Baptist Education Society, who has become a confidant to the senior Rockefeller. The new foundation will be a major force in improving world health, world agriculture, and education and it will work toward world peace (*see* 1914).

The *New York Times* adopts an eight-column configuration that it will continue until September 7, 1976. The new format adopted April 1 expands the seven-column measure used since December 4, 1865.

"Toonerville Folks" introduces newspaper comic strip readers to the Powerful Katrinka, the Terrible-Tempered Mr. Bang, Mickey "Himself" McGuire, Aunt Eppie Hogg, and the Toonerville Trolley that Meets All the Trains. The new strip by cartoonist Fontaine Fox, 29, will be retitled the "Toonerville Trolley" and it will continue until 1955.

W. A. Schaeffer Pen Company is founded at Fort Madison, Iowa, by jeweler Walter A. Schaeffer, 46, whose fountain pens will compete with those made by Waterman and Parker.

Harper's Bazar is purchased by William Randolph Hearst who will change the magazine's name to *Harper's Bazaar* in 1929. The publication for women has been published since 1867 by Harper Brothers.

The first U.S. crossword puzzle is published December 21 in the weekend supplement of the *New York World*. English-American journalist Arthur Wynne has seen similar puzzles in 19th century English periodicals for children and in the *London Graphic,* and he has arranged squares in a diamond pattern with 31 clues which are for the most part simple word

definitions: 2-3 "What bargain hunters enjoy," five letters; 13-21 "A boy," three letters; 22-23 "An animal of prey," four letters (sales, lad, lion) (*see* Simon & Schuster, 1924).

Prentice-Hall, Inc., publishers is founded by New York University economics teacher Charles W. Gerstenberg, 31, and his colleague Richard Prentice Ettinger, 20, who use their mothers' maiden names and publish Gerstenberg's book *Methods of Corporation Finance.* The new house will establish a mail-order department in 1923 and a trade department in 1937.

Nonfiction *The Tragic Sense of Life (Del sentimento tragico de la vida)* by Basque philosopher-novelist-poet-dramatist Miguel De Unamuno, 49, whose early realistic novel *Paz en la guerra* appeared in 1897. Man can exist, says Unamuno, only by resisting the absurdity and injustice of the fact that death brings oblivion, and he urges readers to base their "faith" in "doubt," which alone gives life meaning.

Fiction *Swann's Way (Du Côté de chez Swann)* by French novelist Marcel Proust, 42, whose memories of childhood have been revived by tasting shell-shaped madeleine cakes dipped in tea and who will follow his psychological novel with six more, all under the title *Remembrance of Things Past (A la Recherche du temps perdu); The Boys in the Back Room (Les Copains)* by Jules Romains; *The Happy-Go-Lucky Morgans* by Welsh poet-novelist Edward Thomas, 35; *Sons and Lovers* by English novelist D. H. (David Herbert) Lawrence, 38; *O Pioneers* by former *McClure's* magazine managing editor Willa Sibert Cather, 39, who grew up on the Nebraska frontier; *Virginia* by Virginia novelist Ellen Anderson Gholson Glasgow, 39, whose first novel appeared in 1900; *Polyanna* by U.S. novelist Eleanor Porter, 45; *Dr. Fu Manchu* by English mystery novelist Sax Rohmer (Arthur Sarsfield Wade), 30.

Poetry *General William Booth Enters Heaven* by U. S. poet (Nicholas) Vachel Lindsay, 33; *The Tempers* by Rutherford, N.J., poet-physician William Carlos Williams, 40; *Dauber* by John Masefield; *Stone (Kamen)* by Russian poet Osip Mandelstam, 21; *Eve* by Charles Peguy.

The Armory Show that opens February 17 at New York's huge 69th Regiment Armory on Lexington Avenue at 25th Street gives Americans their first look at Cubism. Represented are the late Paul Cézanne, Henri Paul Gauguin, Vincent Van Gogh, and other impressionists, but what shocks most of the 100,000 visitors are works by French-American sculptor Gaston Lachaise, 31, U.S. cubist Charles Sheeler, 30, U.S. realist Edward Hopper, 31, U.S. watercolorist John Cheri Marin, and the canvas *Nude Descending Staircase* by French-American Dadaist Marcel Duchamp, 26. The show moves to the Chicago Art Institute, where students burn French postimpressionist Henri Matisse in effigy, and then to Boston. Roughly 250,000 see the show, and while most are upset the show ushers in a new era of acceptance for unromantic art expression.

Other paintings *Henry James* by John Singer Sargent; *L'Ennui* by Walter Sickert; *The Violin* by Pablo Picasso; *Battle of Lights, Coney Island* by Joseph Stella.

Anthony Comstock of the New York Society for the Suppression of Vice sees a copy of last year's Paul Chabas painting *September Morn* May 13 in the window of New York art dealer Braum & Co. on West 46th Street (*see* Comstock Law, 1872). Now 69, Comstock demands that the picture be removed from the window because it shows "too little morning and too much maid," Chicago alderman "Bathhouse John" Coughlin vows that the picture will not be displayed publicly in Chicago, but oilman Calouste Gulbenkian will acquire the oil and it will wind up at New York's Metropolitan Museum of Art.

Sculpture *Standing Youth* by Wilhelm Lehmbruck; *Sea God* by Swedish sculptor Carl Milles (Carl Emil Wilhelm Anderson), 38 (granite); *The Little Mermaid* (bronze) by Danish sculptor Edvard Eriksen, 37.

Theater *Vladimir Mayakovsky—A Tragedy* by Russian playwright-poet Vladimir Vladimirovich Mayakovsky, 20, who performs in his own play at Moscow; *Romance* by Edward Sheldon 2/10 at Maxine Elliott's Theater, New York, with Doris Keane, 160 perfs; *Jane Clegg* by Irish playwright St. John Ervine, 29, 6/19 at London, with Sybil Thorndike; *Androcles and the Lion* by George Bernard Shaw 9/1 at the St. James's Theatre, London, with O. P. Heggie, Ben Webster, Leon Quartermaine, 52 perfs.; *The Seven Keys to Baldpate* by George M. Cohan, who has adapted a novel by Earl Der Biggers, 9/22 at New York's Astor Theater, with Wallace Eddinger, 320 perfs.

New York's Shubert Theater opens on West 44th Street.

New York's Palace Theater opens March 24 at Broadway and 47th Street. Other vaudeville houses have a top price of 50 cents, the new Palace charges $2, and B. F. Keith of Boston and his partner Edward F. Albee in the Keith Circuit's United Booking Office present a bill that includes a wire act, a Spanish violinist, a one-act play by George Ade, a condensed Viennese operetta, the Eight London Palace girls, comedians McIntyre and Hardy, and comedian Ed Wynn, 26. The Palace has no success, however, until May 5 when Sarah Bernhardt opens for a 2-week engagement that is extended for another week and a half. Pantomime juggler W. C. Fields (William Claude Dukenfield), 33, who joins the act the week of May 10 began his career at age 14 and played a command performance before England's Edward VII in 1901.

Actors' Equity Association is founded May 26 at New York's Pabst Grand Circle Hotel with Francis Wilson

as president, Henry Miller as vice president. Actors' Equity will set up contracts under which actors are employed and will maintain a benefit system for its membership, but it will not obtain recognition as the trade union of the acting profession until its members strike in August 1919.

Films D. W. Griffith's *Judith of Bethulia* with Blanche Sweet, Henry B. Walthall, Mae Marsh in the first American-made four-reel film; Cecil B. DeMille's *The Squaw Man* with Dustin Farnum in the first full-length feature to be filmed at Hollywood, Calif.; *The Count of Monte Cristo* with James O'Neill whose son Eugene has been released from a tuberculosis sanatorium and will enroll next year in George Pierce Baker's 47 Workshop at Harvard; *The Perils of Pauline* produced by a Hearst-controlled company whose cliff-hanger films are designed to bring audiences back each week; Colin Campbell's *The Spoilers* with William Farnum; Mack Sennett's *Barney Oldfield's Race for Life* with Sennett, Mabel Normand.

Charlie Chaplin signs a $150 per week contrast with moviemaker Mack Sennett who has discovered English actor-dancer Charles Spencer Chaplin, 24, in New York.

The Jesse L. Lasky Feature Play Company is founded by vaudeville producer Jesse Louis Lasky, 32, his Polish-American brother-in-law Samuel Goldwyn, 30, and playwright Cecil Blount DeMille, 31, who has selected Hollywood for making *The Squaw Man* (above) because California has an abundance of sunshine. Goldwyn is a glovemaker whose business has been made unprofitable by the new Underwood–Simmons Tariff Act (above) which has lowered duties on imported gloves, the Lasky firm will merge with Adolph Zukor's Famous Players to create Famous Players-Lasky, the studio will become Paramount Famous Players—Lasky Corporation in 1916, and it will continue under that name until 1932 when it will become Paramount Pictures (see M-G-M, 1924).

Ballet *The Rites of Spring* (*Le Sacre du Printemps*) 6/13 at the Théâtre du Châtelet, Paris, with Serge Diaghilev's Ballet Russe, choreography by Waslaw Nijinsky, music by Igor Stravinsky. Outraged audiences stage violent demonstrations at Stravinsky's wild dissonances and tumultuous rhythms which begin a new epoch in music.

Sol Hurok begins a 60-year career as musical impressario by persuading Russian-American violinist Efrem Zimbalist, 24, to play a recital for a Socialist party gathering in New York's Brownsville section. The 25-year-old Russian-American Hurok has started a New York musical society called Music for the Masses to give popular-priced Sunday afternoon concerts which he will move from Madison Square Garden to the 4,000-seat Hippodrome, and he will introduce Americans to the Russian ballerina Anna Pavlova before presenting the Ballet Russe (above) in its first American tour.

"The Temptation of Saint Pankhurst." *Life* magazine spoofed the woman suffrage movement's leader Emmeline Pankhurst.

Opera *Penelope* 3/4 at Monte Carlo, with music by Gabriel Fauré; *La Vida Breve* (*The Short Life*) 4/1 at Nice, with music by Spanish composer Mañuel de Falla, 36; *L'Amore dei tre re* (*The Love of Three Kings*) 4/10 at Milan's Teatro alla Scala, with music by Italian composer Italo Montemezzi, 37.

First performances *Garrelieder* for Vocal Soloists, Mixed Chorus, and Orchestra by Arnold Schoenberg 2/23 at Vienna with a text based on an 1868 poem by the late Danish poet Jens Peter Jakobsen; *Deux Images* (symphonic diptych) by Béla Bartók 2/26 at Budapest; *Kammersimphonie* by Arnold Schoenberg 3/31 at Vienna's Musikvereinsaal; *Six Pieces for Orchestra* by Schoenberg's student Anton von Webern, 29, 3/31 at Vienna's Musikvereinsaal; *Falstaff* Symphonic Study in C minor (with two interludes in A minor) by Sir Edward Elgar in October at England's Leeds Festival.

Broadway musicals *The Sunshine Girl* 2/3 at the Knickerbocker Theater, with Vernon and Irene Castle doing the Turkey Trot, music by John L. Golden, lyrics by Joseph Cawthorne, 160 perfs.; *The Passing Show* 6/10 at the Winter Garden Theater, with Charlotte Greenwood, a runway to bring the show's scantily clad chorus girls close to the audience, music chiefly by Sigmund Romberg, lyrics chiefly by Harold Atteridge, 116 perfs.; *The Ziegfeld Follies* 6/16 at the New Amsterdam Theater, with Ann Pennington, Elizabeth (Fanny) Brice, Leon Errol, 96 perfs.; *Sweethearts* 9/8 at the New Amsterdam Theater, with music by Victor Herbert, lyrics by Robert B. Smith, 136 perfs.; *High Jinks* 12/10 at the Lyric Theater, with music by Rudolf Friml, book and lyrics by Otto Hauerbach (later Harbach) and Leo Ditrichstein, songs that include "Jim," "Come Hither Eyes," "Something Seems Tingle-lingeling," 213 perfs.

Popular songs "Peg O' My Heart" by Fred Fisher, lyrics by Alfred Bryan; "You Made Me Love You (I Didn't Want to Do It)" by Italian-American composer James V. Monaco, 28, lyrics by Joe McCarthy, 28; "Ballin' the Jack" by Chris Smith, lyrics by James Henry Burris; "If I Had My Way" by James Kendis, lyrics by Lou Klein; "He'll Have to Get Under—Get Out and Get Under" by Grant Clarke and Byron Gay, lyrics by Byron Gay that make fun of the growingly popular motorcar; "Now Is the Hour (Maori Farewell Song)" by New Zealand songwriters Maewa Kaihan, Clement Scott, Dorothy Stewart.

Ebbets Field opens for the National League's Brooklyn Dodgers whose outfield includes Charles "Casey" Stengel, 23. (The Dodgers will not adopt that name until 1932.)

The New York Yankees adopt that name as the Highlanders of the American League move into the 22-year-old Polo Grounds at 155th Street and Eighth Avenue as tenants of the New York Giants (see Ruppert, 1915; Yankee Stadium, 1923).

Connie Mack's Philadelphia Athletics win the World Series, defeating the New York Giants 4 games to 1.

Knute Rockne revolutionizes football by making brilliant use of the forward pass to defeat an Army eleven and change the course of the game. Norwegian-American Knute Kenneth Rockne, 25, is captain of the Notre Dame varsity, he receives 17 out of 21 passes thrown by Charles "Gus" Dorais, he gains 243 yards, and Notre Dame beats Army 35 to 13.

The first U.S. deck shuffleboard game is played on a hotel court at Daytona, Fla. The game will be popular with elderly retirees (see Miami Beach, below).

The Casino of Monte Carlo has an historic run of one color. Black comes up 26 times in succession at a roulette wheel August 18, theoretically returning 1.35 billion francs on a 20 franc stake, but gamblers bet so heavily on red that the house wins several million francs for La Société Anonyme des Bains de Mer et Cercle des Etrangers à Monte Carlo which always averages about 125 percent return on invested capital each year.

Coco Chanel pioneers sportswear for women at a new boutique in Deauville that features berets and open-necked shirts in an age when women of fashion adorn themselves with feathers and huge hats. Gabrielle Chanel, 30, gained her nickname at age 20 while entertaining the 10th Light Horse Regiment in the small garrison town of Moulins, she became a Paris milliner while mistress to Etienne Balsan, she is now mistress to English businessman Arthur Capel, her lovers will include England's second duke of Westminster who owns 17 Rolls-Royces and has mammoth greenhouses in which pears and peaches ripen all year round, and she will make sweaters the fashion of the rich as Chanel knitwear gains world fame (see Chanel No. 5, 1920).

Pennsylvania makes Mother's Day a state holiday (*see* Jarvis, 1908; Wilson, 1914).

Brillo Manufacturing Corporation is founded by New York lawyer Milton B. Loeb, 26, whose client (a manufacturing jeweler) has developed a method for cleaning aluminum cooking utensils using steel wool with a special reddish soap that gives the vessels a brilliant shine.

The first dependable slide-fastener and efficient machines to manufacture it commercially are developed by Swedish-American inventor Gideon Sundback, 33, who attaches matching metal locks to a flexible backing, each tooth being a tiny hook that engages with an eye under an adjoining hook on an opposite tape (*see* Judson, 1893; "zipper," 1926). Sundback will patent improvements on his slide fastener in 1917 and will assign the patents to the Hookless Fastener Co. of Meadville, Pa., which will manufacture the Talon slide fastener (*see* YKK, 1934).

 Singer Manufacturing Company sells 2.5 million sewing machines, 675,000 of them in Russia.

Neiman-Marcus in Dallas burns in the spring. Filene's Basement in Boston (*see* 1909) sells the stock while Neiman-Marcus builds a new store (*see* 1907).

A new Woodward & Lothrop store opens October 30 in Washington, D.C., where Woodies will expand (*see* Palais Royal, 1946).

 New York's Woolworth building opens in April (*see* 1912).

New York's Equitable building goes up on lower Broadway. The world's largest office building has been financed by a syndicate that includes Thomas Coleman of E. I. du Pont de Nemours who has put up $30 million (*see* 1915).

New York's General Post Office building opens on Eighth Avenue between 31st and 33rd Streets across from the 3-year-old Pennsylvania Station. Designed by McKim, Mead, and White with two blocks of Corinthian columns, the building's front is inscribed with lines written by the Greek historian Herodotus about the couriers of Xerxes in the 5th century B.C. : "Neither snow, nor rain, nor heat, nor gloom of night stays these couriers from the swift completion of their appointed rounds."

New York's Grand Central Station (above) has a mammoth concourse designed by Reed and Stern with a Beaux Arts facade designed by Warren and Wetmore.

Carrère and Hastings completes a marble Fifth Avenue mansion for steel magnate Henry Clay Frick between 70th and 71st Streets.

Cincinnati's Union Central Insurance building is completed on the site formerly occupied by the Chamber of Commerce building at Fourth and Vine Streets. The $2.5 million 34-story skyscraper is the second highest building in the world after New York's 60-story Woolworth building (above).

Houston's Rice Hotel opens May 17. Built by local banker-lumberman Jesse Jones, 39, the city's first deluxe hotel will receive guests for more than 60 years (*see* Shamrock, 1949).

The Greenbrier opens at White Sulphur Springs, W. Va. The Chesapeake & Ohio Railroad's 650-room resort hotel has 6,500 acres of surrounding woodlands, bridle paths, golf courses, mineral baths, swimming pools, and tennis courts.

Miami Beach, Fla., begins its career as a winter resort. Avocado grower John S. Collins, 76, has begun a bridge across Biscayne Bay to link the sandbar to the mainland. Carl Graham Fisher, 41, who has just made $5 million by selling the Prest-O-Lite acetylene automobile lamp company he acquired for almost nothing, loans Collins $50,000 to complete the bridge, and in February he goes into business with Collins, selling lots at auction while building concrete bulkheads along the shore. Fisher and Collins will build 27 miles of bulkheads, they will add 2,800 acres to Miami Beach's present 1,600 acres in the next 10 years by dredging, pumping, and filling in land over mangrove roots. By 1923 they will have built the Lincoln, Flamingo, Nautilus, King Cole, and Boulevard Hotels to augment the Royal Palm built by the late H. M. Flagler in 1896 (*see* 1924).

 Ohio's Great Miami River floods its banks at Columbus March 25 after a 5-day rainfall that has dropped 10 inches of water. The flood kills 351, injures hundreds more, and creates property damage amounting to $100 million.

Congress passes a bill to protect migratory game and insectivorous birds.

"Trees" by *New York Times* Book Review editor and poet Alfred Joyce Kilmer, 27, appears in the August issue of *Poetry* magazine and wins worldwide acclaim: "I think that I shall never see, a poem lovely as a tree ..." (*see* song, 1922).

Forest Lawn Cemetery at Tropico (Glendale), Calif., is taken over by Missouri-born metallurgist-promoter Hubert Eaton, 30, who will use showmanship and salesmanship to expand the tiny cemetery into a vast enterprise with branches in Hollywood Hills, Cypress, and Covina Hills. Encouraged by an old college friend, Eaton embraces the new concept of selling burial plots "before need," he will write "The Builder's Creed" on New Year's Day of 1917, and he will make Forest Lawn a showplace of more than 1,200 acres of towering trees, sweeping lawns marked with bronze memorial tablets rather than with tombstones, splashing fountains, flowers, birds, bronze and marble statues, a Memorial court of Honor with stained glass windows and with a great mausoleum in which one may be buried only if voted that honor by the Forest Lawn Council of Regents, and with small churches modeled on famous ones in Europe. Eaton will add a mortuary and a crematory,

757

1913 (cont.) he will charge admission to visitors, he will forbid artificial flowers, and he will make Forest Lawn the final resting place for 8,000 Californians per year.

Avocados on southern California ranches are practically wiped out by a great freeze that spares only one variety out of more than 100. The Fuerte (Spanish for strength) variety will provide the basis for a revived commercial avocado industry.

Rabbits fed large amounts of cholesterol and animal fats are shown to develop hardening of the arteries (arteriosclerosis) by Russian pathologist Nikolai Anichkov (see Keys, 1953).

Pellagra kills 1,192 in Mississippi. The U.S. Public Health Service sends Hungarian-American physician Joseph Goldberger, 39, to study the disease which is known to affect at least 100,000 in the Deep South (see 1907; 1915).

The U.S. Pure Food and Drug Law of 1906 is amended to make it more effective as was done last year (see Tugwell, 1933).

The flavor-enhancer 5'-inosinic acid discovered by Tokyo University chemist Shintaro Kodama is 10 to 20 times more effective than the monosodium glutamate (MSG) discovered in 1908 and marketed under the name Ajinimoto.

A Jack Frost figure of a boy is introduced as a trademark for the Jack Frost brand of sugar sold by National Sugar Manufacturing Company (see 1900).

Corn Products Refining Company is obliged by antitrust action to sell its half interest in Penick & Ford, a New Orleans firm that produces Brer Rabbit Molasses and Vermont Maid Maple Syrup. One-third of the company is acquired by E. T. Bedford's son Frederick Thomas Bedford (see 1906; 1916; 1921).

Welch's Grape Juice is served instead of wine at a dinner given for the British ambassador by U.S. Secretary of State William Jennings Bryan. Prohibitionist Bryan becomes a target for cartoonists who make Welch's a household name (see 1897; Daniels, 1914).

Peppermint Life Savers are introduced by Cleveland, Ohio, chocolate manufacturer Clarence Crane as a summer item to sell when chocolate sales decline. Crane uses a pharmaceutical company's pill-making machine to create the uniquely-shaped peppermint with the hole in the middle which he advertises "for that stormy breath," and when streetcar advertising salesman Edward J. Noble, 31, happens to buy some he tries to persuade Crane to use car cards for his advertising. Crane offers to sell the product for $5,000, Noble finds a partner, they buy Crane's trademark and small stock of peppermints for $2,900, and they start producing hand-wrapped rolls of Life Savers in a New York loft under the name Mint Products, Inc. (see 1920).

Quaker's Puffed Rice and Quaker's Puffed Wheat are introduced by the Quaker Oats Company whose Chicago advertising agency Lord & Thomas is headed by Albert D. Lasker, 33. He has discovered that the factory making Quaker "Wheat Berries" and "Rice Berries" employs a mechanism resembling a blunt cannon to puff the grains up to eight times their normal size (see Anderson, 1902), he renames the cereals, his chief copywriter Claude Hopkins comes up with the slogan "The Grains That Are Shot from Guns," and the advertising will puff sales 20- to 30-fold (see 1911; Aunt Jemima acquisition, 1926).

New Process Cork Company is started by New York inventor Charles E. McManus to compete with the Crown Cork & Seal Company founded by William Painter in 1892. McManus patents a process for granulating natural cork and mixing it with a binder to form an economical substitute for pure, unadulterated cork, he will gain control of Crown Cork & Seal, he will create Crown Cork International, and the firm will produce half the world's bottle caps.

New York's first Nedick's orange drink and frankfurter stand opens. Entrepreneurs Robert T. Neely and Orville Dickinson start an enterprise that will blossom into a $12 million chain.

1914 A World War begins in Europe July 28 one month after the assassination of the heir to the Austrian throne in Bosnia. Riding in a 1912 Graf und Stift motorcar at Sarajevo, the 51-year-old archduke Franz Ferdinand and his wife are killed by tubercular high school student Gavrilo Prinzip who has been hired by Serbian terrorists to kill the nephew of the emperor Franz Josef.

Austrian militarists have been spoiling to enter the wars that have embroiled the Balkans since 1912, and Vienna uses the incident at Sarajevo in June as an excuse to declare war on Serbia.

The war quickly widens as Germany declares war on Russia August 1 and on France August 3. Neutral Belgium is invaded by German troops August 4 and Britain declares war on Germany.

"The lamps are going out all over Europe; we shall not see them lit again in our lifetime," says British secretary of state for foreign affairs Sir Edward Grey.

German forces slip past Belgian fortifications at Liège in a night attack and the Belgians fall back to Brussels.

Montenegro declares war on Austria August 5, Serbia declares war on Germany August 6, Austria declares war on Russia August 6, Montenegro declares war on Germany August 8, Britain and France declare war on Austria August 12.

French defensive strategy has ignored the possibility of a German invasion through Belgium and has counted on a Russian advance in the East. A French invasion of Lorraine designed to regain territory lost in the Franco-Prussian War of 1870 to 1871 is stymied by the Germans who drive the French out of Lorraine with heavy French casualties.

Belgian forces fall back on Antwerp and destroy the bridges over the Meuse as the Germans enter Brussels August 20.

Some 250,000 French *poilus* fall in the Battle of the Frontiers between August 14 and August 25, but news of the staggering loss is censored and will not appear until after the war.

Japan declares war on Germany August 23 and on Austria August 25. The Japanese produce munitions for Russia and the other Allied powers, they begin to land forces in Shantung for an attack on the German position at Tsingtao, and a British detachment joins them (*see* 211 demands, 1915).

German colonial forces in Togoland surrender August 26 to an Anglo-French force. Britain and France divide the German African colony between them.

The Battle of Tannenberg August 26 to 30 ends in crushing defeat for a large Russian army that has invaded east Prussia under the leadership of General Aleksandr Vasilievich Samsonov, 55, to take pressure off the French on the Western Front. Another Russian army under General Paul Rennenkampf, 60, fails to support Samsonov, German forces under General Paul von Hindenburg, 66, and General Erich Ludendorff, 49, surround the Russians and take 100,000 prisoners with help from General Hermann von Francois, 48, executing a plan developed by Colonel Max Hoffman, 45. General Samsonov shoots himself, General Rennenkampf will be executed in 1918.

The Russians rename their 211-year-old capital Petrograd because St. Petersburg sounds German (*see* Leningrad, 1924).

The first German air raid strikes Paris August 30 as German aircraft drop small explosives on the city.

The Battle of the Marne September 5 to 12 ends the German advance. French and British troops force the Germans to withdraw west of Verdun but are unable to dislodge them from north of the Aisne.

The Battle of the Masurian Lakes September 6 to 15 brings further defeat to the Russians, this time at the hands of the 65-year-old German general August von Mackensen. 125,000 Russians are taken prisoner and the Germans advance to the lower Niemen River.

Three British cruisers are sunk in September by the German submarine U-9 which retaliates for the sinking of three German cruisers at Helgoland bight August 28.

Ghent falls to the Germans October 11 as they try to reach the Channel ports in a rush to the sea, but while Bruges is taken October 14 and Ostend October 15, the Belgians flood the district of the Yser and the German push fails.

The Battle of Ypres October 30 to November 24 pits German troops against French and British troops in trench warfare that will consume huge numbers of soldiers on both sides in the next 4 years as the conflict becomes a war of position in which the front line will not shift more than 10 miles.

Odessa, Sevastopol, and Theodosia on the Black Sea are suddenly bombarded October 29 by a Turkish fleet that includes two German cruisers. Russia declares war on Turkey November 2, Britain and France declare war on Turkey November 5, and Britain proclaims the annexation of Cyprus which the British have occupied since 1878.

A British squadron under Rear Admiral Sir Christopher George Francis Maurice Craddock, 62, is surprised off the Chilean coast November 1 by the German vice admiral Graf Maximilian von Spee, 63. The British are defeated off Coronel, Craddock loses the *Monmouth* and goes down with his flagship the *Good Hope;* the *Gloucester* escapes.

The Battle of the Falkland Islands December 8 ends in victory for a British squadron under Rear Admiral Sir Frederick Charles Doveton Sturdee, 65, who surprises Graf Spee as he prepares to attack the Falklands while en route home from his triumph over Admiral Craddock (above). Spee goes down with his flagship the *Scharnhorst,* his two sons and 1,800 other men are also lost, the *Gneisenau, Leipzig,* and *Nürnberg* are sunk, only the *Dresden* escapes.

Russian forces meanwhile have forced von Mackensen to fall back from Warsaw and have forced the Austrians to retreat to Cracow. The Battle of Cracow from November 16 to December 2 brings heavy casualties to both sides. New divisions diverted from the western front bolster German resistance in early December after Russian troops threaten to surround the Germans following the November battles of Lodz and Lowicz. Lodz falls to the Germans December 6, but Austrian forces fail to break through the Russian lines before Cracow and the Russians will remain within 30 miles of the city through the winter.

Serbian troops drive out the Austrians in early December after winning the Battle of Kolubara, and the city of Belgrade taken by the Austrians December 2 is retaken by the Serbs December 15.

The French government has moved to Bordeaux out of fear that Paris will fall to the Germans. French passions against "the Bosch" have eclipsed the scandal of March 16 when the 55-year-old editor of *Le Figaro* Gaston Calmette was killed in his office by the wife of French minister of finance Joseph Caillaux, 51, who had been accused of financial irregularities in office by Calmette.

U.S. forces occupy Vera Cruz April 21 following a series of hostile acts by Mexicans including an incident in which a party of U.S. Marines which landed at Tampico for supplies was briefly detained. President Huerta has refused a demand by Admiral Mayo to give the U.S. flag a 21-gun salute, President Wilson sends a fleet to Tampico, President Huerta is forced to resign July 15 under pressure from the 55-year-old Vesustiano Carranza who is hostile to U.S. interests, and Mexico is plunged into civil war between Carranza and his lieutenant Francisco "Pancho" Villa, 37 (*see* 1916).

1914 (cont.) Northern and southern Nigeria are united.

South Africa's prime minister Louis Botha puts down a pro-German Boer revolt. He takes command of troops that enter German South-West Africa.

Britain proclaims a protectorate over Egypt December 18. The khedive Abbas Hilmi who has reigned since 1892 is deposed December 19 and is succeeded by the 60-year-old Hussein Kamil who will be khedive until 1917.

Swedish-American IWW leader Joe Hill, 34, is arrested January 13 on charges of having been one of two masked men who gunned down Salt Lake City grocer John Morrison and his son the night of January 10. Hill had sought medical attention 90 minutes after the murder, telling a physician on the other side of town that he had been shot in an argument over another man's wife, but while Morrison was wounded in a similar attack long before Hill came to work in the Utah copper mines, and his killing has apparently been connected with the earlier attack ("We've got you now," one of the masked men had said), and while no motive can be shown for Hill to have committed the crime when he is brought to trial in June, he is nevertheless convicted. Born Joel Hagglund, Joe Hill called himself Joseph Hilstrom when he came to the United States in 1903, he has written essays, letters, and songs for the Wobbly newspapers *Industrial Worker* and *Solidarity*, his songs have included "The Preacher and the Slave" which contained the phrase "pie in the sky," and he has had a major influence in furthering the IWW cause (*see* 1915).

The Ludlow massacre April 20 climaxes a struggle by Colorado coal miners struggling for recognition of their United Mine Workers union (*see* 1913). A battle with state militia near Trinidad ends with 21 dead including two women and 11 children caught in tents that have been set ablaze, angry strikers take possession of the Colorado coalfields, and they do not yield until federal troops move in June 1.

The Amalgamated Clothing Workers of America is formed by a dissident majority within the manufacturer-oriented United Garment Workers Union (*see* 1910; 1918).

Suffragettes march on the Capitol at Washington June 28 to demand voting rights for U.S. women. The march is staged within hours of the assassination of Sarajevo (above) (*see* Jeanette Rankin, 1916).

Mohandas Gandhi returns to India at age 45 after 21 years of practicing law in South Africa where he organized a campaign of "passive resistance" to protest his mistreatment by whites for his defense of Asian immigrants. Gandhi has read Henry David Thoreau's 1849 essay "On the Duty of Civil Disobedience" and he attracts wide attention in India by conducting a fast—the first of 14 such fasts that he will stage as political demonstrations and that will inaugurate the idea of the political fast (*see* 1930; Sarah Wright, 1647; Irish demonstrators, 1920).

Threats of labor troubles in early January have led Henry Ford to offer workers a minimum wage of $5 per day—more than twice the average U.S. wage and more than the average English worker earns in a week. The $5-a-day wage idea is largely the brainchild of James Couzens, 42, who met Ford in 1903, borrowed heavily in order to invest $2,500 in the new Ford Motor Company, and has become Ford's second in command.

A Federal Trade Commission established by Congress September 26 to police U.S. industry is designed only to prevent unfair competition (*see* Raladam case, 1931; Wheeler-Lea Act, 1938).

The Clayton Anti-Trust Act voted by Congress October 15 toughens the federal government's power against combinations in restraint of trade as outlawed by the Sherman Act of 1890. The new law contains provisions to protect labor (*see* Celler-Kefauver, 1950).

"The maxim of the British people is 'business as usual,' " says First Lord of the Admiralty Winston Churchill November 9 in a speech at London.

Membership in British cooperative societies reaches 3.8 million (*see* Rochdale, 1844).

Japanese prime minister Count Gombei Yamamoto, 62, and Japanese navy minister Viscount Makoto Saito, 56, are held "morally responsible" for having permitted high-ranking navy personnel to accept bribes for placing large orders with Germany's Siemens-Schuckertwerke AG and then with England's Vickers' Sons and Maxim for communications equipment. Several scapegoats go to jail but Yamamoto and Saito are merely retired to the naval reserve. Yamamoto will become prime minister again in 1923, Saito will become prime minister in 1932.

The Panama Canal opens to traffic August 3 just as Germany declares war on France (above). Built essentially on French plans at a total cost of 30,000 lives and some $367 million in U.S. money (on top of the $287 million lost by the French in the 1880s), the canal uses a system of locks to carry ships 50.7 miles between deep water in the Atlantic and deep water in the Pacific (*see* 1903).

The Houston Ship Canal opens to give Houston an outlet to Galveston Bay on the Gulf. The 50-mile canal will make the Texas city a deep-water port and a major shipping point for U.S. grain.

The Cape Cod Ship Canal opens to link Buzzards Bay with Cape Cod Bay, Mass. The 17.4-mile canal enables coastal shipping to avoid the voyage round the Cape.

The White Star Line passenger vessel S.S. *Britannic* launched February 26 is a sister ship of the S.S. *Titanic* that went down in 1912 (*see* 1916).

The Hamburg-American Line's S.S. *Vaterland* that will become the S.S. *Leviathan* in 1919 arrives at New York from Cherbourg May 21 on her maiden voyage to begin a 24-year career on the North Atlantic. The 56,282-ton ship is 950 feet in length overall, has four screws, and can accommodate 4,000 passengers, 1,134 in crew.

The S.S. *Bismarck* that will become the S.S. *Majestic* in 1919 begins a 26-year career on the North Atlantic. The 56,621-ton German passenger liner is 954 feet in length overall and has four screws.

The Canadian Pacific's S.S. *Empress of Ireland* collides with another ship May 29 in the Gulf of St. Lawrence and sinks with a loss of 1,023 lives.

The Cunard Line's S.S. *Aquitania* arrives at New York June 15 on her maiden voyage. The 47,000-ton British passenger liner is 901 feet in length overall, she can accommodate 3,250 passengers, 1,000 in crew, and she is double-skinned with an average of 15 feet between her inner and outer shells.

U.S. auto production reaches 543,679 with Model T Fords accounting for more than 300,000 of the total. The country has fewer than 100,000 trucks, most of them delivery vans (*see* 1921).

A large Dodge Brothers factory goes up at Hamtramck, Mich., where Horace and John Dodge pioneer in making all-steel bodied motorcars and achieve immediate success (*see* 1913). Both brothers will die in 1920 (*see* Dillon, Chrysler, 1928).

The Stutz Bearcat is introduced with a design patterned on the White Squadron racing cars that won victories last year. Stutz also produces family cars while the Bearcat provides lively competition for the Mercer made at Trenton, N.J.

Pierce-Arrow's Herbert B. Dawley patents the fender-inset headlamps used in the 1913–1914 Pierce-Arrow Model 48 B-2. They will hereafter be a distinctive mark of the luxury car that rivals Packard in the high-priced motorcar market.

Greyhound Lines, Inc., has its beginnings in the Mesabi Transportation Co. founded at Hibbing, Minn., by Swedish-American diamond-drill operator Carl Eric Wickman, 30, who had opened a Hupmobile and Goodyear Tire agency but was unable to sell the Hupmobile. He runs the car on a regular schedule across the range to nearby Alice charging iron miners 15 cents one way, 25 cents roundtrip (local taxis charge upwards of $1.50 each way). Wickman takes in a partner, he is soon building his own bodies and mounting them on truck chassis, and by 1918 he will have 18 buses operating in northern Minnesota with annual earnings of $40,000 (*see* 1922).

Cleveland sets up the world's first red-green traffic lights August 5 at Euclid Avenue and East 105th Street.

Gulf Oil Company distributes the first U.S. automobile maps (*see* Gulf, 1901). The 10,000 maps show roads and highways in Allegheny County, Pa., and other oil companies soon follow Gulf's lead. Road maps distributed free by service stations will encourage automobile travel (and gasoline consumption).

The British government increases its equity in the 6-year-old Anglo-Persian Company to protect Royal Navy fuel supplies, and Armenian oilman Calouste Gulbenkian negotiates one of history's largest petroleum deals between Anglo-Persian and the 7-year-old Royal Dutch-Shell Company (*see* Ritz, 1896). Gulbenkian turns down the consortium's offer of a shilling per ton royalty on all the oil drilled, he points out that the shilling may decline in value, he obtains as payment for his services a royalty to be paid in actual oil—2.5 percent to come from Anglo-Persian, 2.5 percent from Royal Dutch-Shell—and he will receive 5 percent of all the oil produced in the Middle East for the rest of his 86 years (*see* Iraq, 1927; Anglo-Iranian, 1935).

The U.S. Navy establishes a new oil reserve at Teapot Dome, Wyo. (*see* 1912; 1921).

Monsanto Chemical Company of St. Louis starts making phenol (carbolic acid) for U.S. physicians cut off from German imports. Monsanto is the first firm outside Germany to make the disinfectant (*see* 1901).

The hookworm control program started in the South by the Rockefeller Foundation 5 years ago reaches its peak of activity, but in many areas barefoot hookworm victims are reinfected soon after treatment.

New York City has only 38 more public schools than in 1899 despite an increase of more than 300,000 in enrollment. The overcrowded schools turn away 60,000 to 75,000 children each year for lack of space.

The teletype machine introduced by German-American inventor Edward E. Kleinschmidt, 38, speeds communications. Kleinschmidt will merge with his only competitor in 1928 to create the Morkun-Kleinschmidt company that will become the Teletype Corporation that American Telephone & Telegraph will buy for $30 million in 1930.

The *Sunday Post* begins publication at Glasgow and gains a readership that will grow until it reaches close to 80 percent of everyone in Scotland over age 15.

The *New Republic* begins publication at New York. The political weekly will compete with the *Nation* founded in 1865.

The *Day* begins publication at New York to compete with the *Forward* founded in 1897. The new Yiddish newspaper incorporates a section in English and by 1917 it will have a circulation of 65,369 as compared with 148,500 for the *Forward*.

Nonfiction *A Preface to Politics* by New York writer Walter Lippmann, 25.

Fiction *Dubliners* (stories) by émigré Irish author James Joyce, 32, who has had trouble getting published in Ireland and who ekes out a living as an English teacher at Trieste; *A Portrait of the Artist as a Young Man* by James Joyce; French novelist Henri-Alban Fournier, 28, is killed early in the war (his body will never be found). Fournier is well known for his novel *Le Grand Meaulnes* published last year under

1914 (cont.) the nom de plume Alain-Fournier; *The Vatican Swindle (Les Caves du Vatican)* by André Gide; *Recaptured (L'Entrave)* by Colette; *Mist (Niebla)* by Miguel de Unamuno; *The Titan* by Theodore Dreiser; *Penrod* by Booth Tarkington; *A Springtime Case (Otsuyagorishi)* by Junichiro Tanizaki; *Kokoro* by Natsume Soseki; *Tarzan of the Apes* by U.S. novelist Edgar Rice Burroughs, 39, whose story about the son of an English peer raised by apes will have 26 sequels; he will also write many science fiction novels.

Poetry *The Congo and Other Poems* by Vachel Lindsay; *North of Boston* by San Francisco-born poet Robert Lee Frost, 40, who moved to England in 1912 but who will return next year to New England where he taught school from 1906 to 1912. "The Death of the Hired Man" contains the line, "Home is the place where, when you have to go there, they have to take you in," and "Mending Wall" contains the line, "Good fences make good neighbors"; *Canti Orfico* by Italian poet Dino Campana, 29; *Starting Point (Der Aufbrach)* by German poet Ernst Stadler, who wins the Iron Cross but is killed at Ypres at age 31; French poet Charles Peguy dies September 5 leading his troops at the Battle of the Marne.

Painting *The Violin* and *Ma Jolie* by Pablo Picasso; *The Guitarist* by Georges Braque; *The Red Studio* by Henri Matisse; *George Bernard Shaw* by Augustus John; *The Creator* by Paul Klee, who visits Tunisia and "discovers" color but who will work only in watercolors until after 1918; *The Bride of the Wind* by Oscar Kokoschka; *Backyards, Greenwich Village* by John Sloan.

London's Old Vic Shakespeare Company opens at a theater that was given its name in 1833 for the princess who became Queen Victoria 4 years later.

Theater *The Bow of Odysseus (Der Bogen das Odysseus)* by Gerhart Hauptmann 1/17 at Berlin's Deutsches Künstlertheater; *The Exchange (L'echange)* by Paul Claudel 1/22 at the Théâtre du Vieux Colombes, Paris; *Too Many Cooks* by U.S. playwright Frank Craven, 33, 2/24 at New York's 39th Street Theater, with Craven, 223 perfs.; *Pygmalion* by George Bernard Shaw 4/11 at His Majesty's Theatre, London, with Sir Herbert Beerbohm Tree, 61, as Professor Higgins, Mrs. Patrick Campbell, now 47, as the Covent Garden flower girl Eliza Doolittle whose shocker "Not bloody likely" in Act III helps give Shaw another commercial success, 118 perfs.; *The Hostage (L'otage)* by Paul Claudel 6/5 at the Théâtre de l'oeuvre, Paris; *On Trial* by U.S. playwright Elmer Rice (Elmer L. Reizenstein), 21, 8/19 at New York's Candler Theater, 365 perfs.

Films Mack Sennett's *Tillie's Punctured Romance* with Charlie Chaplin, Marie Dressler, Mabel Normand, Chester Conklin, Mack Swain, Charles Bennett, and the Keystone Kops in the first U.S. feature-length comedy; Mack Sennett's *Curses! They Remarked;* Charlie Chaplin's *Between Showers;* D. W. Griffith's *The Mother and the Law* attacks factory owners who pose as public benefactors; D. W. Griffith's *The Battle of Elderberry Gulch.*

Opera *Francesco da Rimini* 2/19 at Turin's Teatro Regio, with music by Italian composer Riccardo Zandonai, 30; *Marouf, Savetier de Caire* 5/15 at the Opéra-Comique, Paris, with music by Henri Rabaud.

First performances "On Hearing the First Cuckoo in Spring" by Frederick Delius 1/20 at London. Delius is losing his eyesight to syphilis; *London Symphony* by Ralph Vaughan Williams 3/27 at London.

Broadway musicals *Sari* 1/3 at the Liberty Theater, with music by Emmanuel Kelman, lyrics by C. C. S. Cushing and Eric Heath, songs that include "Love's Own Sweet Song," 151 perfs.; *Shameen Dhu* 2/2 at the Grand Opera House, with Chauncey Olcott, Rida Johnson Young, songs that include "Too-Ra-Loo-Ral, That's an Irish Lullaby" by Michigan-born songwriter James Royce Shannon, 32 perfs.; *The Ziegfeld Follies* 6/1 at the New Amsterdam Theater, with Ed Wynn, Ann Pennington, Leon Errol, music by Dave Stamper, Raymond Hubbell, and others, lyrics by Gene Buck and others, 112 perfs; *The Passing Show* 6/10 at the Winter Garden Theater, with Marilyn Miller making her debut at age 14, barelegged chorus girls, music chiefly by Sigmund Romberg, lyrics chiefly by Harold Atteridge, 133 perfs.; *The Girl From Utah* 8/24 at the Knickerbocker Theater with songs that include "They Didn't Believe Me" by Jerome Kern, lyrics by Herbert Reynolds (M. E. Roache), 120 perfs.; *Chin-Chin* 10/20 at the Globe Theater, with music by Henry Williams, lyrics by Joe Judge, songs that include "It's a Long Way to Tipperary," 295 perfs.; *The Only Girl* 11/2 at the 39th Street Theater, with music by Victor Herbert, lyrics by Henry Blossom, songs that include "You're the Only Girl for Me," 240 perfs.; *Watch Your Step* 12/8 at the New Amsterdam Theater, with Vernon and Irene Castle doing the Castle Walk, Fanny Brice, music and lyrics by Irving Berlin, songs that include "Play a Simple Melody," 175 perfs.

Popular songs "Keep the Home Fires Burning" by Welsh-born London composer David Ivor Davies, 21, lyrics by American-born poetess Lena Guklbert Ford, who will die in a zeppelin raid on London in 1918; "There's a Long, Long Trail" by Zo (Alonzo) Elliott, 23, who wrote the music while attending college in the United States, lyrics by W. Stoddard King, 25; "Colonel Bogey March" by London composer Kenneth J. Alford (F. J. Ricketts); "St. Louis Blues" by W. C. Handy; "12th Street Rag" by Euday L. Bowman, 27; "The Missouri Waltz" by John Valentine Eppel, 43; "When You Wore a Tulip and I Wore a Big Red Rose" by Percy Wenrich, lyrics by Jack Mahoney, 32; "A Little Bit of Heaven (And They Called It Ireland)" by Ernest R. Ball, lyrics by J. Keirn Brennan; "By the Beautiful Sea" by U.S. composer Harry Carroll, 22, lyrics by Harold R. Atteridge.

The American Society of Composers, Authors, and Publishers (ASCAP) is founded in New York to protect the interests of music writers, lyricists, and publishers (see 1909 copyright law). ASCAP will defend its members against illegal public performances for profit of copyrighted musical compositions, will protect them against other forms of infringement, and will collect license fees for authorized performances (see Victor Herbert, 1917; BMI, 1939).

The Millrose Games are held for the first time January 28 at New York's Madison Square Garden. The indoor track meet is named for the country estate of department store executive Lewis Rodman Wanamaker, 50, who began the Millrose Athletic Association in 1908 and whose Millrose Games include as a major event the Wanamaker Mile footrace.

Walter Hagen wins the U.S. Open at age 21 to begin a remarkable golfing career. Upstate New York golfer Walter Charles Hagen will win the Open again in 1919, he will win the Professional Golfers' Association (PGA) title in 1921 and again from 1924 to 1927, he will win the British Open in 1922 and again in 1924, 1928, and 1929, and he will also win the Canadian Open and the French Open.

Chicago's Wrigley Field is completed at a cost of $250,000 for the Chicago Cubs by local restaurateur Harry Weeghman who will sell the ballpark to chewing gum magnate William Wrigley, Jr., in 1919. Wrigley will expand the park's seating capacity several times to seat 46,000, he will run it until his death in 1932, but by the mid-1970s the centerfield bleacher area will have been roped off, wider seats and wider aisles will have been installed, and the seating capacity will have been reduced to 37,741.

The Boston Braves win the World Series by defeating Connie Mack's Philadelphia Athletics 4 games to 0.

Barcelona's El Sport bullring opens with 19,582 seats and is the second largest in Spain. The 19-year-old matador Joselito (José Miguel Isidro del Sagrado Corazon de Jesus Gómez y Gallito) kills six giant bulls in the arena at Madrid July 3, making 25 quites, placing 18 banderillos, and making 242 passes with cape and muleta.

The Yale Bowl is completed at New Haven, Conn., at a cost of $650,000. The 61,000-seat football stadium will be enlarged to seat 74,786 as college football becomes a major sporting attraction.

The first national Mother's Day is proclaimed by President Wilson whose wife Ellen will die August 6. The second Sunday in May will become the biggest business day of the year for U.S. restaurants and flower shops (see 1913; "M-O-T-H-E-R," 1915).

Helena Rubinstein challenges Elizabeth Arden for leadership in the fledgling U.S. cosmetics industry (see 1910). The 44-year-old Rubinstein left her native Poland to seek a husband in Australia at age 19, she made $100,000 in 3 years selling a skin cream she formulated from ingredients that included almonds and tree bark, she has opened a salon in London, and she is the reigning beauty adviser to French and British society. The 4 foot 11 inch cosmetician will introduce medicated face creams and waterproof mascara, she will pioneer in sending saleswomen out on road tours to demonstrate proper makeup application, and she will develop a $60 million business by the time of her death at age 94 in 1965.

The elastic brassiere that will supplant the corset now in common use is patented in November by Mary Phelps Jacob who as a New York debutante devised the prototype bra with her French maid before a dance, using two pocket handkerchiefs, some pink ribbon, and thread. A descendant of steamboat pioneer Robert Fulton, Jacob was asked by friends to make bras for them, a stranger asked for a sample and enclosed a dollar, she has been encouraged to engage a designer to make drawings, she will make a few hundred samples of her Backless Brassiere with the help of her maid, but will find them hard to sell, and she will sell her patent to the Bridgeport, Conn., corset firm Warner Brothers Company which will acquire for $15,000 a patent that will later be estimated to have a value of $15 million.

Doublemint chewing gum is introduced by William Wrigley, Jr. (see 1893; 1921; Wrigley Field, above).

Germany's 107th Regiment of Leipzig leaves its trenches December 14 and follows a band playing Christmas carols. Singing lustily and distributing gifts to the enemy, the Germans play football (soccer) with the enemy in the afternoon, hostilities resume December 15.

New York's Lord & Taylor department store moves into a new Fifth Avenue store at 38th Street after 41 years at Broadway and 20th Street (see 1873).

New York's B. Altman store on Fifth Avenue at 34th Street is enlarged after 8 years to fill the entire block east to Madison Avenue.

"Your Government Needs YOU!" Alfred Leete's poster helped Britain recruit men for the muddy trenches of France.

1914 (cont.) A new eight-story May Company department store goes up on Cleveland's Public Square as the chain adds the Forest City to its Denver, St. Louis, and Akron locations. The May Company's Famous-Barr store in St. Louis is the city's leading department store, up from seventh position when it was acquired in 1892 (*see* 1910; Los Angeles, 1923).

New York's St. Thomas Episcopal Church at Fifth Avenue and 53rd Street is completed by architect Bertram Goodhue of Cram, Goodhue & Ferguson.

New York's Municipal building is completed by McKim, Mead and White near the Manhattan end of the Brooklyn Bridge in Chambers Street at Centre Street. The 25-story office complex houses city administrative offices.

New York's Biltmore Hotel opens across from the new Grand Central Terminal. The 21-story Biltmore has been erected by John McEntee Bowman who will build Biltmores at Atlanta, Providence, Havana, Palm Beach, Los Angeles, and other cities (*see* Commodore, 1919; Miami Biltmore, 1925).

The Essex and Sussex Hotel opens at Spring Lake, N.J., with 250 rooms and huge wooden verandas.

Grossinger's opens at Ferndale, N.Y., to provide New York sweatshop workers with a vacation boarding house that will grow to become a 1,500-acre Catskill Mountain resort. Austro-Hungarian immigrants Malke and Selik Grossinger begin an enterprise that will one day serve nearly 1,500 guests per week (*see* Concord, 1935).

The passenger pigeon that once dominated U.S. skies becomes extinct September 1 as the last known bird of the species dies in the Cincinnati Zoo (*see* 1878).

Paul Bunyan and his blue ox Babe appear in promotional pamphlets for the Red River Lumber Co. of Minneapolis and Westwood, Calif. Advertising writer W. B. Laughhead has created the "folk hero" unknown to lumberjacks.

The relief ship S.S. *Massapequa* reaches Belgium in November with a cargo of food sent by the Rockefeller Foundation to aid the starving Belgians.

Berlin places German food supplies and allocations under government control December 26, and London thereupon declares all foodstuffs on the high seas to be contraband.

Some 200,000 British schoolchildren receive free meals under the School Meals Act of 1906 (*see* Milk in Schools Scheme, 1931, 1934).

British farmers produce less than one-fourth the nation's grain needs. Nearly 4 million acres of arable British lands have passed out of cultivation as Canada and India have emerged as major suppliers.

German scientists develop mercury fungicide seed dressings that will prevent losses to plant diseases. In years to come, the mercury will take severe tolls of wildlife and even of some human life (*see* 1969).

U.S. ranchers herd cattle with Model T Fords.

U.S. farmhands begin annual migrations north from Texas, traveling in Model T Fords and harvesting crops as they ripen up to the Canadian border.

The Smith-Lever Act passed by Congress May 8 provides for agricultural extension services by USDA county agents working through the land-grant colleges established under the 1890 Morrill Act. An outgrowth of work done by Seaman Knapp and Theodore Roosevelt, the act authorizes federal appropriations to support state and local funding of farm and home demonstration agents.

A national 4-H Club is founded 14 years after the first such club was organized in Macoupin County, Ill. Sponsored by the U.S. Department of Agriculture, the 4-H Club is directed toward youths in rural areas, it aims to improve "head, heart, hands, and health," and it will help end prejudice against "book farming" along scientific lines.

George Washington Carver reveals the results of experiments that show the value of peanuts and sweet potatoes in replenishing soil fertility (*see* Carver, 1896). Southern planters have in many instances been ruined by the boll weevil and begin turning to peanut and sweet potato culture, especially when Carver shows the many peanut by-products he has produced in his laboratory—not only flour, molasses, and vinegar but also cheese, milk, and coffee substitutes, synthetic rubber, plastics, insulating board, linoleum, soap, ink, dyes, wood stains, metal polish, and shaving cream (*see* cotton production, 1921).

Fish freezing is pioneered by Clarence "Bob" Birdseye, a 28-year-old New Yorker trading furs in Labrador. He notices that fish caught through the ice freeze stiff the instant they are exposed to the air and taste almost fresh when defrosted and cooked weeks later (*see* 1917).

Van Camp Seafood Company is founded by Indianapolis packer Frank Van Camp whose father Gilbert began packing pork and beans in 1861 and who is persuaded by his son Gilbert to sell the family's Midwestern operation and to enter the fast-growing California tunafish packing business (*see* 1903). The father and son buy the California Tunny Packing Company of San Pedro, they contract with operators of 35 to 40 small Japanese-owned albacore boats to buy all the albacore the boats can catch and to accept deliveries 7 days a week, and by October they have developed a new method—purse-seining—to increase tuna catches. Within a year the Van Camps will be building a new fleet of 15 modern 40-foot albacore boats, they will turn the new boats over to the fishermen at no cost, and by finding new tuna banks off the Mexican Coast, rushing the catch back to the San Pedro cannery by tender, and lowering the price of canned tuna they will pioneer in making tunafish an American staple rather than a costly delicacy (*see* 1922).

U.S Navy secretary Josephus Daniels orders that Welch's Grape Juice be served in place of the navy's traditional rum grog (see 1923; Bryan, 1913).

Beer sales are barred in the state of Washington. Seattle Brewing and Malting Company president Louis Henrich moves operations to San Francisco and renames his company Rainier.

Chero-Cola has sales of more than $611,000, and the Chero-Cola Company files an application to register the name Chero-Cola. A lawsuit to bar use of the name is instituted by the Coca-Cola Company and litigation will continue for years (see 1912; 1918).

Some margarine is now made entirely of vegetable oil combinations, but Americans consume 5 pounds of butter for every pound of margarine (see 1890; Lever, 1911).

National Dairy Corporation has its beginnings as Chicago businessman Thomas H. McInnerney, 47, acquires ownership of the Hydrox Company, a wholesaler of artificial ice, ginger ale, and ice cream. Formerly general manager of New York's Siegel Cooper department store, McInnerney will increase Hydrox sales in the next 9 years from $1 million to $4 million (see 1923).

The Kelvinator Company is organized to produce refrigerators (see 1918; Nash-Kelvinator, 1935).

Postum Cereal Company founder C. W. Post commits suicide May 9 at his Santa Barbara, Calif., home in a fit of depression at age 59. His only child is Marjorie Merriweather Post, 27, and she becomes owner and operator of the company (see Post Toasties, 1906; incorporation, 1922; Jell-O, 1925).

Large-scale pasta production begins in the United States which has imported almost all of its macaroni and spaghetti from Naples but which has been cut off from Italian sources by the outbreak of the European war (above) (see Carleton, 1899).

Italian-American pasta maker Vincent La Rosa and his five sons start a company at Brooklyn, N.Y., that will later move to Warminster, Pa. V. La Rosa & Sons, Inc., will make macaroni, spaghetti, egg noodles, and prepared Italian-style foods in plants at Warminster and Milwaukee.

Thomas Lipton expands his retail grocery empire to include some 500 shops (see 1909). Lipton has acquired tea, cocoa, and coffee plantations, meatpacking plants, and factories, and he has at least 20 British retail grocery rivals.

The term "birth control" is introduced by U.S. feminist Margaret Higgins Sanger, 31, in her publication *The Woman Rebel.* Sanger exiles herself to England in order to escape federal prosecution for publishing and mailing *Family Limitation,* a brochure that deals with contraception (see Brooklyn clinic, 1916).

915 The Great War in Europe grows more intense. Casualty lists mount for both sides on the eastern and western fronts and a German U-boat (submarine) blockade of Great Britain begins February 18.

British naval forces attack the Dardanelles beginning February 19 to prevent the Germans who have seized control of Turkey from blocking supplies to Russia via the Bosporus and the Black Sea. British action has been requested by the Russians to relieve pressure on their defenses in the oil-rich Caucasus, but four British warships are sunk by mines March 18 in an effort to force the Narrows, and British admiral John de Robeck withdraws, thus losing an opportunity to seize the Dardanelles at a time when the Turks have no supplies and are practically defenseless (see Gallipoli, below).

Turkey charges the Armenians with taking Russia's side and begins deporting the entire population of Armenia, massacring all who resist. Some 1.75 million Armenians will be deported and at least 600,000 will be starved to death in the Mesopotamian Desert.

British troops land on Turkey's Gallipoli Peninsula beginning April 25, but Turkish artillery pins down British, French, and Austrian units and the Turkish commander Mustapha Kemal, 34, says to his troops, "I do not order you to attack. I order you to die."

The first sea lord of the admiralty Sir John Arbuthnot Fisher, 74, had proposed the Gallipoli campaign (above) but he has turned against the idea and has resigned. ("Damn the Dardanelles. They will be our grave.") When the British abandon the campaign in December, the blame for its costly failure falls on the first lord of the admiralty Winston Churchill, now 41.

The Germans use chlorine gas April 22 at the Second Battle of Ypres, the first use of poison gas by any warring power. Greenish-yellow clouds of gas choke French colonial troops who flee in panic, but Canadians plug the 4½ mile gap left by the routed Africans.

Torpedoes from the German submarine U-20 hit the Cunard Line passenger ship S.S. *Lusitania* at 2:10 o'clock in the afternoon of May 7 off the coast of Ireland, and the huge vessel sinks in 18 minutes killing 1,198 who include 128 U.S. citizens, among them railroad magnate Alfred Gwynne Vanderbilt, 38, and New York theatrical magnate Charles Frohman, 75, who goes down with the ship saying, "Why fear death? It is the most beautiful adventure in life" (the line is reminiscent of one in the 1904 James M. Barrie play *Peter Pan*). It will turn out that the 8-year-old *Lusitania* carried 173 tons of rifle ammunition, shrapnel casings, fuses, and contraband food from the United States but had no escort and remained on course despite recent U-boat sightings in the area.

"There is such a thing as being too proud to fight," says President Wilson May 10 in a speech at Philadelphia, and the sinking of the *Lusitania* (above) with large numbers of women and children fires world opinion against the Germans. "We have come to the parting of the ways," says presidential aide Colonel Edward M. House, 57, and although the formal protest sent to Berlin May 13 is milder than Wilson's original denunciation, pacifist Secretary of State William Jennings Bryan resigns June 8.

1915 (cont.) Italy declares war on Austria May 23, turning against her former ally in hopes of obtaining territory along the Adriatic and in the Alps. The Italians will launch four offensives during the war but will accomplish nothing but the loss of 250,000 troops on a 60-mile front along the Isonzo River (*see* Caporetto, 1917).

France gives General Henri Philippe Benoni Omer Joseph Pétain, 59, command of an army June 15.

German authorities in occupied Brussels arrest British Red Cross nurse Edith Louisa Cavell, 50, August 4 on charges of having assisted Allied military prisoners to escape. Tried and convicted, she is executed by a firing squad October 12 along with a Belgian who has provided guides, British propagandists use her death to inflame public sentiment against the savage Boche and ignore the fact that the French have shot a woman for a similar offense.

Warsaw falls to the Germans August 7, and by September the Russians have lost all of Poland, Lithuania, and Courland, along with nearly 1 million men.

General Pétain (above) launches a great attack in Champagne September 25 and follows it with a report containing principles of a new tactical doctrine.

Italy has declared war on Turkey August 21, Bulgaria declares war on Serbia October 14, Britain declares war on Bulgaria October 15 and is joined by Montenegro, France declares war on Bulgaria October 16, Russia and Italy follow suit October 19.

The 21 demands presented by Tokyo to Peking January 18 have included the demands that Japan take over German rights in Shantung, that Japanese leases in southern Manchuria be extended to 99 years with commercial freedom for the Japanese in Manchuria, that China give Japan a half-interest in the Han-yeh-p'ing Company which operates iron and steel mills at Han-yang, iron mines at Ta-yeh, and a colliery at P'ingshan, and that China declare her determination not to lease or cede any part of her coast to any power. The Chinese have given modified acceptance to these four demands but have set aside others calling for railway concessions in the Yangtze River Valley which is within Britain's sphere of influence and for Japanese advisers in Chinese political, financial, and military affairs.

Henry Ford charters the ship S.S. *Oscar II,* he calls it the *Peace Ship,* and he sails for Europe December 4 with a party of advisers in a vain but much-publicized attempt to "get the boys out of the trenches by Christmas."

The La Follette Seaman's Act passed by Congress March 4 abolishes prison sentences for U.S. merchant marine sailors who desert ship and contains other provisions that improve the lot of merchant seamen. The act crowns a long campaign by International Seamen's Union chief Andrew Furuseth, 61, who works ceaselessly in behalf of his membership, living a monastic life and accepting a salary equal only to the union scale wage of an able-bodied seaman.

U.S. Pullman car porters (called "George" because they are George Pullman's "boys") earn a minimum wage of $27.50 per month. Asked by the U.S. Commission on Industrial Relations if the wage is high enough, Pullman's general manager replies, "All I can say is that you can get all the men you require to do the work." Porters' wages will rise to $48.50 per month by 1919 and will increase in that year to $60 per month for nearly 400 hours of work or 11,000 miles, whichever is logged first, the Pullman Palace Car Company will pay overtime at the rate of 60 cents per 100 miles or 25 cents per hour, but porters will continue to pay for their own meals and will be obliged to buy their own uniforms and equipment out of salaries and tips (*see* Randolph, 1925).

IWW organizer Joe Hill is executed by a firing squad November 19 (*see* 1914). Hill has been in prison for 22 months while appeals for a new trial have been entered by the Swedish government, by AF of L president Samuel Gompers, and by President Wilson, they have all been rejected by Utah officials, and on the eve of his execution Hill has wired "Big Bill" Haywood, "Don't waste any time in mourning. Organize." The message will help make Joe Hill a legend among working men (*see* Haywood, 1907).

U.S. racial tensions are heightened by D. W. Griffith's full-length motion picture *The Birth of a Nation* which has racist aspects (below).

Black prizefighter Jack Johnson loses his world heavyweight title at Havana where the fight has been held because Johnson has been a fugitive from U.S. justice (below). He has inflamed white prejudice by his marriage to a white woman and by his lavish life-style, he was convicted in 1912 of violating the Mann Act of 1910, he skipped bond, and he has been living abroad with his wife.

A new Ku Klux Klan is started Thanksgiving night on Stone Mountain near Atlanta by William Joseph Simmons who revives the name from the KKK of the 1860s and who makes it an instrument of bigotry. A preacher, traveling salesman, and promoter of fraternal organizations, Simmons obtains a legal charter from the state of Georgia and calls his KKK a "high class, mystic, social, patriotic, benevolent association" dedicated to "white supremacy," the protection of Southern womanhood, and "Americanism." His "invisible empire" of Kleagles and Grand Dragons will be promoted through advertising developed by Edward Young Clark, it will attract membership of nearly 100,000 throughout the country within 6 years, it will concentrate political power to elect U.S. senators, congressmen, and state officials, and it will employ terrorist tactics against blacks, Jews, and Roman Catholics most especially in the South and Midwest (*see* 1925).

The Thompson submachine gun (Tommy gun) is introduced by U.S. brigadier-general John Taliaferro Thompson, who organizes the Auto-Ordnance Company to build the lightweight, semiautomatic infantry shoulder rifle.

The worst train wreck in British history kills 227 and injures 246 as a Scottish express plows into an earlier minor wreck May 22 at Gretna Junction north of Carlisle at Quintinshill. A Scottish regiment of 500 men is reduced to 72.

The Pennsylvania Railroad electrifies 20 miles of main line track between Philadelphia and Paoli (which becomes a switching point for steam engines to and from the west).

The Tunkhamnock Viaduct is completed across a valley in Pennsylvania. The $12 million 2,375-foot concrete bridge cuts 39 miles off the route of the Delaware, Lackawanna & Western Railroad.

The Fruehauf tractor trailer has its beginnings at Detroit where local blacksmith-wagonmaker August Fruehauf, 47, and his associate Otto Neumann create the first trailer for the Model T Ford of local lumber dealer Frederick M. Sibley, Jr., who wants to transport a boat to his new summer place on an upstate Michigan lake. The Fruehauf Trailer Company founded in February of 1918 will become the world's largest maker of tractor trailers pulled by sawed-off trucks (tractors) to compete with railroads.

New York's Fifth Avenue Coach Company starts designing and assembling its own buses to replace the French de Dions and English Daimlers it has imported since 1907. The new 34-seat double-decker coaches are powered by 40-horsepower four-cylinder Knight sleeve-valve engines (below) (see 1936).

The 1,000,000th Ford motorcar rolls off the assembly line and Ford produces more than 500,000 Model T cars, up from 300,000 last year (see 1913; 1927).

Willys-Overland produces 91,780 motorcars, up from 18,200 in 1910, and is the world's second largest automaker. Willys has absorbed several other firms and its sales are helped by the patented Willys-Knight sleeve-valve engine that employs two simple sleeves in each cylinder, moving silently up and down on a film of oil without springs, valves, or camshafts (see 1907; New York buses, above).

The Chevrolet Motor Company is incorporated in Delaware by W. C. Durant after having sold 16,000 motorcars since 1911. Durant offers General Motors stockholders five shares of Chevrolet stock for every share of GM whose stock is being acquired in the open market by Pierre S. du Pont, and GM stock climbs from 82 January 2 to a high for the year of 558 (see 1916).

General Tire and Rubber Company is founded by U.S. entrepreneur William O'Neill, 30, and his father who each put up $50,000 of the initial capital of $200,000. The younger O'Neill will make General a major tire producer (fifth largest after Goodyear, Goodrich, Firestone, and U.S. Rubber) and a leading factor in the entertainment, communications, and aerospace industries (see 1945).

The excursion boat *Eastland* suddenly turns over July 24 in the Chicago River while carrying 2,000 picnickers bound for a Western Electric Company outing—812 drown.

Moore-McCormack Lines buys its first ship (see 1913). Moore and McCormack pay $15,000 down to buy a $90,000 freighter, they load her with a cargo of dynamite that no other shipper will touch, they send her to Brazil, and she is the first U.S. flagship to enter Rio harbor in 26 years.

 British income taxes rise to an unprecedented 15 percent as the Great War drains the nation's financial resources (see 1909; 1918).

The state of Delaware begins revising its corporation laws to adopt "suggestions" forwarded by New York lawyers. New Jersey has had the lion's share of corporate charters and has been called "the Mother of Trusts," but President Wilson has persuaded New Jersey legislators to outlaw a series of abusive practices, the New York lawyers recognize that corporate franchise taxes will be valuable to a state as tiny as Delaware, and that state's legislators liberalize their laws to attract corporations which will soon make Delaware the leading charterer of the largest industrial corporations.

New York's Metropolitan Life Insurance Company becomes a mutual company with profits going to the policyholders instead of to stockholders (see 1879; weight tables, 1942).

A typhus epidemic in Serbia kills 150,000.

The Mayo Foundation for Medical Education and Research is founded by the University of Minnesota with a $2.5 million gift from C. H. and W. J. Mayo of the Mayo Clinic at Rochester, Minn. (see 1880).

Thyroxine is isolated by Mayo Foundation researcher Edward Calvin Kendall, 29. Deficiencies of the thyroid hormone produce goiters which C. H. Mayo (above) has made a career of removing surgically (see Marine, 1905; Akron, 1916).

The disposable scalpel is patented by U.S. inventor Morgan Parker, 23, who will establish the Bard-Parker Company next year and who will merge it in 1956 with Becton, Dickinson Co. of Rutherford, N.J., which he will head until his retirement in 1965.

The "Sippy" diet for gastric ulcers is promoted by U.S. physician Bertram W. Sippy who observes that the elimination of "rough foods," the administration of alkaline drugs, and frequent feedings of milk and cream produce "an accurate neutralization of all free hydrochloric acid during the time that food and its accompanying secretion are present in the stomach" (see Prout, 1824).

 Emory University is founded at Atlanta under the name Methodist College with support from Coca-Cola's Candler family. The university is an outgrowth of the manual labor school Emory College founded at Oxford in 1836.

Harvard's Harry Elkins Widener Library opens in the Yard. A memorial to the *Titanic* victim of 1912, the world's largest college library has been erected with funds contributed by Widener's mother.

1915 (cont.) Long-distance telephone service between New York and San Francisco begins January 25. Alexander Graham Bell, now 68, repeats the words of 1876 ("Mr. Watson, come here . . .") to Thomas Watson in San Francisco, the call takes 23 minutes to go through and costs $20.70, but Americans sing "Hello, Frisco" written for *The Ziegfeld Follies* by Louis Hirsch and Gene Buck.

Adventures of Teddy Tail—Diary of the Mouse in Your House by English cartoonist Charles Folkard appears in the *London Daily Mail* April 5, the mouse ties a knot in its tail April 9 to rescue a beetle that has fallen down a hole, and the first British newspaper comic strip begins a career that will continue for more than 40 years.

Direct wireless communication between the United States and Japan begins July 27.

Japanese engineer Tokuji Hayakawa invents the first mechanical pencil and markets it under the brand name Sharp. Proceeds will enable the inventor to start the Hayakawa Electric Company that will market a wide range of products under the Sharp name.

Condé Nast takes over *House and Garden* magazine which has only 10,000 readers and little advertising (*see Vogue*, 1909).

Alfred A. Knopf and Co. publishers is founded at New York with $5,000 in capital by former Doubleday, Page editor Alfred Abraham Knopf, 23. He will marry his assistant Blanche Wolf, now 21, next year, they will choose a Russian wolfhound (borzoi) as their colophon, and they will achieve their first success with an American edition of the 1904 romance *Green Mansions* by W. H. Hudson (*see* 1960).

Fiction *The Good Soldier* by former *English Review* editor Ford Madox Ford, 41, who has changed his name from J. L. Ford Hermann Hueffer; *Of Human Bondage* by W. Somerset Maugham; *The "Genius"* by Theodore Dreiser; *Wood and Stone* by English novelist John Cowper Powys, 43; *Pauline* by English novelist Compton Mackenzie, 32; *The Rainbow* by D. H. Lawrence whose book is suppressed in November 2 months after publication; *Rashomon* by Japanese novelist Ryunosuke Akutagawa, 23, who gives a cynical, psychological twist to an old folktale; "The Gentleman from San Francisco" ("Gospodin iz San-Francisco") by Russian poet-writer Ivan Alekseyevich Bunin, 45, whose short story satirizes Western bourgois civilization and expresses a pessimistic philosophy that will dominate his later works; *The Thirty-Nine Steps* by John Buchan; *The Sea Hawk* by English novelist Rafael Sabatini, 39; *The Star Rover* by Jack London; *Gino Bianchi*, a work of prose satire by Italian poet Piero Jahier, 31.

Poetry *Chicago Poems* by *Chicago Daily News* writer Carl Sandburg, 37, who calls his city "Hog Butcher for the World/ Tool Maker, Stacker of Wheat,/ Player with Railroads and the Nation's Freight Handler;/ Stormy, husky, brawling,/ City of the Big Shoulders"; *A Spoon River Anthology* by Chicago lawyer-poet Edgar Lee Masters, 46, whose sombre free-verse monologues are written as if spoken from the graveyard by former residents of a fictitious Illinois town. The book creates a sensation, it will go through 70 editions in the next 25 years, and it will be translated into several foreign languages; English poet Charles Sorley dies in battle at age 19; English poet Rupert Brooke of the Royal Navy dies April 23 of blood poisoning at age 27 after having been weakened by sunstroke. Buried on the Aegean island of Skyros, Brooke has written, "If I should die, think only this of me:/ That there's some corner of a foreign field/ That is for ever England."

Painting *Harlequin* by Pablo Picasso; *The Bride Stripped Bare by Bachelors* by Marcel Duchamp is the world's first Dada-style painting; *Birthday* by Marc Chagall; *Flower Pot in a Window* by U.S. watercolorist Charles Ephraim Burchfield, 22, who will be graduated next year from the Cleveland School of Art (he has worked in a factory to earn his tuition).

Sculpture *Woman Combing Hair* by Russian sculptor Aleksandr Archipenko, 28.

Theater *The Unchastened Woman* by Louis Kaufman Anspacher 10/9 at New York's 39th Street Theater, 193 perfs.; *He Who Gets Slapped* (*Tot, kfopoluchayet poshicheedony*) by Leonid Andreyev 10/27 at Moscow's Dramatic Theater; *John Ferguson* by St. John Ervine 11/30 at Dublin's Abbey Theatre.

Films D. W. Griffith's *The Birth of a Nation* with Lillian Gish, Mae Marsh, Henry B. Walthall contains such cinematic innovations as the close-up, the pan (panoramic shot), the flashback, and the use of a moving camera in addition to its element of racism (above); Cecil B. DeMille's *Carmen* with Geraldine Farrar; William S. Hart's *Pinto Ben* with William S. Hart; Frank Powell's *A Fool There Was* with Theda Bara (Theodosia Goodman) who is billed as "the vamp" ("Kiss me, my fool").

Opera *Madame Sans Gêne* 1/25 at New York' Metropolitan Opera House, with Geraldine Farrar a Catherine Huebscher, music by Italian compose Umberto Giordano, libretto from a play by Victoria Sardou and E. Moreau.

First performance Symphony No. 5 in E flat majo by Jean Sibelius 12/8 at Helsinki.

Broadway musicals *The Passing Show* 5/29 at th Winter Garden Theater, with Marilyn Miller, bar tone John Charles Thomas in his Broadway debu music chiefly by Leo Edwards and W. F. Peter, lyri by Harold Atteridge, 145 perfs.; *The Ziegfeld Folli* 6/21 at the New Amsterdam Theater, with W. Fields, Ed Wynn, George White, Ann Penningto music by Louis A. Hirsch, Dave Stamper, and othe 104 perfs.; *The Blue Paradise* 8/5 at the Casino Th ater, with Vivienne Segal, music by Edmund Eysle book by Edgar Smith based on a Viennese oper lyrics by Herbert Reynolds (M. E. Roche), songs th include "Auf Wiedersehn," 356 perfs.; *The Princess Pat* 9/29 at the Cort Theater, with Al Shean, music by Victor Herbert, book and lyrics by Henry Blossom, 158 perfs.; *Very Good Eddie* 12/23 at the Princess Theater, with music by Jerome Kern, lyrics by Schuyler Greene, 341 perfs.; *Stop! Look! Listen!* 12/25 at the Globe Theater, with music and lyrics by Irving Berlin, book by Harry B. Smith, 105 perfs.

Popular songs "Pack up Your Troubles in Your Old Kit Bag" by Welsh-born London composer Felix Powell and his brother George Asaf (George Henry Powell), 35; "I Didn't Raise My Boy to Be a Soldier" by Al Piantadosi, who has plagiarized a melody by Harry Haas), lyrics by Alfred Bryan; "Paper Doll" by Johnny Black; "There's a Broken Heart for Every Light on Broadway" by Fred Fisher, lyrics by Howard Johnson; "M-O-T-H-E-R, a Word that Means the World to Me" by Theodore More, lyrics by Howard Johnson; "Nola" by New York Tin Pan Alley pianist-composer Felix Arndt, 26.

The New York Yankees and the American League franchise purchased for $18,000 in 1903 by Frank Farrell and William Deveny is purchased January 11 for $460,000 by brewer Jacob Ruppert and engineer Tillinghast l'Hommidieu Houston (*see* Ruppert, 1874; Babe Ruth, 1920).

Rogers Hornsby signs with the St. Louis Cardinals and makes his major league debut late in the season at age 19. The Texas-born athlete will lead the National League in batting, home runs, and runs batted in (the triple crown) in 1922 and 1925, he will set a league record batting average of .424 in 1924, and by 1957 he will have a lifetime batting average of .358, surpassed only by Ty Cobb's .367.

The Boston Red Sox win the World Series by defeating the Philadelphia Phillies 4 games to 1.

The "great white hope" Jess Willard, 32, wins the world heavyweight title April 15 at Havana with a 26th round knockout victory over Jack Johnson (above). Willard will hold the title until 1919.

Harvard beats Yale 41 to 0 in the final gridiron appearance of Harvard star athlete Edward W. "Eddie" Mahan, 23, who has been an all-American halfback in 1913 and 1914 and who is selected by Walter Camp once again for the all-America team. Except for a loss to Cornell this year Harvard has won all its games for the past 3 years and Mahan crowns his career by scoring four touchdowns against Yale and kicking five extra points. Only 165 pounds, Mahan is also a star baseball player and he will pitch the first five innings of an exhibition game next spring to win a 1-0 victory for Harvard over the world champion Boston Red Sox.

New York's Brooks Brothers moves from Broadway and 22nd Street into a large new Madison Avenue store at 44th Street where it will remain for more than 60 years (*see* 1909; Garfinckel's 1946).

J. W. Robinson opens a new Los Angeles store on 7th Street between Grand and Hope. The store will be doubled in size in 1923 and will be modernized in 1934 (*see* 1891; Palm Springs, 1947).

Kansas City's Muehlbach Hotel opens May 17 on 12th Street between Baltimore and Wyandotte. Built by local brewer George Muehlbach, the 12-story hotel has 450 rooms and will be augmented in 1953 by an 18-story tower and convention center that will give it an additional 300 rooms.

New York's Equitable building is completed at 120 Broadway between Pine and Cedar Streets (*see* 1913). The new office building contains 1.2 million square feet of floor space on a plot of just under one acre, it has nearly 30 times as much floor space as was contained in its site, it exploits its site as no building has ever done before, and it raises protests and demands for a zoning law that will prohibit such buildings (*see* 1916).

New York's Willard Straight mansion on Fifth Avenue at 94th Street is completed for diplomat Willard Dickerman Straight, 35, who will die of pneumonia in Paris early in December 1918.

Carrier Corporation is founded under the name Carrier Engineering Corporation by air-conditioning pioneer Willis H. Carrier and six other young engineers who pool $32,600 to start the company (*see* 1911; Empire Theater, 1917).

Rocky Mountain National Park is created by act of Congress on 262,000 acres of Colorado wilderness land that includes 107 named peaks above 10,000 feet in elevation.

Germany's War Grain Association confiscates all stocks of wheat, corn, and flour at fixed prices, suspends private transactions in grain, fixes a bread ration, and orders municipalities to lay up stores of preserved meat as Britain blockades German ports.

A U.S. vessel with a cargo of wheat for Britain is sunk by a German cruiser.

The U.S. wheat crop totals 1 billion bushels for the first time as American farmers respond to high wartime wheat prices by plowing and planting millions of acres never before planted (*see* 1921; 1934).

The Hessian fly introduced in 1776 causes $100 million worth of damage to the U.S. wheat crop which nevertheless breaks all records.

Cuban sugar production is owned largely by U.S. and other foreign interests. Americans own 40 percent, other foreigners 20 percent.

The German warship *Kronprinz Wilhelm* puts into Newport News, Va., with 50 sailors suffering from beriberi (*see* Suzuki, 1912; Williams, 1933).

Pellagra is shown to be the product of Southern diets based largely on corn and not a disease spread by any bacteria (*see* 1913). Joseph Goldberger of the U.S. Public Health Service has conducted tests using inmates of Mississippi's Rankin prison who have volunteered to go on corn product diets in return for sentence reductions (*see* 1771; Elvehjem, 1936).

Poison gas that seared the lungs and blistered the skin brought new horrors to trench warfare in Europe.

The National Dairy Council is established by U.S. dairy interests which set up the agency for nutrition research partly at the suggestion of E. V. McCollum (*see* 1912).

The cancer-causing properties of coal tar are demonstrated by Japanese chemists Katsusaburo Yamagiwa and Koichi Ichikawa who paint rabbits' ears with coal tar in the first experiments that produce cancer in animals (*see* Kennaway, 1933).

Absinthe is outlawed for sale in France. The aromatic liqueur made from wormwood (*Artemisia absinthium*) and other herbs produces blindness and death among habitual users.

Kraft processed cheese is introduced by Chicago's J. L. Kraft and Bros. which has developed a process that arrests the bacterial curing of cheese without subjecting it to such high temperatures as to cause oil separation (*see* 1909). Processed cheese packed initially in tins will hereafter comprise a growing part of Kraft's cheese business (*see* Kraft-Phenix, 1928; National Dairy Corporation, 1928).

Kellogg's 40% Bran Flakes are introduced by the Battle Creek Toasted Corn Flake Company (*see* 1911; 1919).

Franco-American Food Company is acquired by the Joseph Campbell Company which will market the canned soups, canned spaghetti, and other products of the New Jersey firm (*see* 1905; 1922).

Pyrex glass is developed by Corning Glass researchers Eugene C. Sullivan and William C. Taylor whose heat-resistant and shock-resistant borosilicate glass will be used in Pyrex oven dishes and coffeemakers that will be popular in U.S. kitchens.

Safeway Stores begins its rise to leadership in U.S. food retailing. American Falls, Idaho, merchant Mar-

ion B. Skaggs, 27, buys his father's grocery store for $1,088 and is helped by five brothers to start a network of stores that within 11 years will cover 10 states with 428 retail outlets (*see* 1926).

1916 The general theory of relativity announced by Albert Einstein revolutionizes the science of physics (*see* 1905). Now at the University of Berlin and a director of the Kaiser Wilhelm Institute, Einstein has evolved the theory from his work in the geometrization of physics and the integration of gravitational, accelerational, and magnetic phenomena which he will unite into a unified field theory represented by a single set of equations (*see* 1929).

The U.S. National Academy of Sciences founded in 1863 starts a National Research Council (NRC).

The World War in Europe takes a heavy toll (below), the United States remains neutral while chasing Mexican bandit Pancho Villa (below), the Irish rise against the British in a great Easter rebellion (below), and an Arab revolt against the Turks begins in the Hejaz (below).

Britain withdraws her forces from the Gallipoli by early January without further losses but the Battle of Verdun on the Western Front from February 21 to July 11 takes 350,000 French lives and nearly as many German lives. Krupp of Essen supplies the Germans with 3,000 new cannons per month while Allied artillery fire Vickers shells produced under a fuse patent licensed by Krupp in 1904.

Berlin has notified Washington that German U-boats will treat armed merchantmen as cruisers, the "extended" U-boat campaign has begun March 1, three Americans have perished in the sinking of the unarmed French steamer S.S. *Sussex* March 24 in the English Channel, and Washington has warned Berlin that the United States will sever diplomatic relations unless the Germans abandon "submarine warfare against passenger and freight-carrying vessels." Berlin replies in early May that merchant vessels "shall not be sunk without warning and without saving human lives unless they attempt to escape or offer resistance."

The British hospital ship S.S. *Britannic* sinks in 5 minutes November 21 after hitting a mine en route to pick up 3,500 wounded from the Aegean island of Lemnos for transfer to Naples. The ship has 1,134 aboard and 30 are killed, most of them by the *Britannic's* own propellers.

Pancho Villa has raided Columbus, N. Mex., March 9 killing 17 Americans, and a U.S. punitive expedition has moved into Mexico March 15 under the command of General John J. Pershing, 55 (*see* 1914). Pershing has orders to "capture Villa dead or alive" but he is unable to catch the Mexican and will withdraw in early February of next year.

U.S. Marines land in Santo Domingo in May to restore order. U.S. occupation will continue until 1924

770

Ireland's Easter rebellion beginning April 24 lasts a week but has little popular support. Former British consular official Roger Casement has had no success in raising a brigade of Irish war prisoners in Germany, a German U-boat has landed him April 20 to support the Irish Republican Brotherhood led by Patrick Henry Pearse, 37, but German aid fails to materialize (see Casement, 1903). While 150,000 Irish volunteers fight for the king in Flanders, some 2,000 rebels at Dublin rise against the British, whose police arrest the leaders of the uprising. The people hiss the rebel leaders but they become martyrs when they are convicted of treason and hanged August 3 (see 1919).

The Battle of Jutland (Skagerrak) May 31 to June 1 ends with heavy losses to British and German naval forces, but the German fleet escapes the larger British fleet.

A U.S. National Defense Act passed by Congress June 3 provides for an increase in the standing army by five annual stages to 175,000 men with a National Guard of 450,000 and an officers' reserve corps. The Wilson administration emphasizes "preparedness" as sentiment against neutrality increases.

Britain's refusal to permit U.S. imports of German knitting needles needed in U.S. mills has drawn a sharp protest from Washington in May, and Washington protests again when the London Official Gazette blacklists some 30 U.S. firms under the British Trading with the Enemy Act of July 18.

French pilots in Spads and Nieuports gain control of the air from the Germans who have held mastery for a year flying Fokkers equipped with A. H. G. Fokker's device that permits pilots to fire through their revolving propellers (see 1912). The British introduce new De Havillands and Farman Experimentals in July, and the German ace Max Immelman, 26, is shot down July 18. (He has invented the air combat maneuver that will be known as the Immelman turn.)

French aircraft designer Marcel-Ferdinand Bloch, 24, has introduced the first variable-pitch propellor to give French pilots an edge over the Germans. First graduate of France's first aeronautical school in 1911, Bloch married the daughter of a rich furniture maker and set up an aircraft factory in 1912 with backing from his father-in-law (see 1947).

The Escadrille Americaine has gone into combat May 15 with seven U.S. volunteer pilots flying Nieuports in support of the French. Kiffin Rockewell downs a German plane May 18 for the Escadrille's first victory. The German ambassador at Washington complains in November that the U.S. flyers violate American neutrality, Paris orders that the group be called simply Escadrille 124, its members protest and call themselves the Lafayette Escadrille. The group will never number more than 30 men at a time, but 45 men will serve in the Lafayette Escadrille.

The Battle of the Somme from July to mid-November is the bloodiest battle in history and follows the largest artillery barrage in history (1,437 British guns rain 1.5 million shells on the enemy along an 18-mile front in the course of 7 days). July 1 is the bloodiest day in British history with 57,470 British casualties, including 19,240 dead, 35,493 wounded, 2,152 missing, 585 taken prisoner. The Germans sustain 8,000 casualties July 1 and the artillery is heard as far away as Hampstead Heath, England. The 140-day offensive involves 3 million men along a front of some 20 miles, the Allied armies lose 794,000 men, the Central Powers lose 538,888, the Allies drive the Germans back no more than 7 miles at any point, and the Germans will regain most of the lost ground in 1918.

The British attack July 1 (above) begins 2 minutes after five gigantic mines dug under the German lines are blown up at 7:28 in the morning, Boer War veteran General Henry Seymour Rawlinson has ordered the daylight attack to accommodate French artillery observers despite the known advantages of attacking at first dawn, 66,000 British troops come out of the trenches and advance on the enemy in a ceremonial step of 1 yard per second, Tyneside Scotsmen march to bagpipes while the 8th East Surreys come out kicking footballs, 14,000 fall in the first 10 minutes by one account, General Rawlinson has not coordinated his artillery barrage with the needs of his infantry, and one-third of all the British shells fired are duds.

Commander-in-chief of British forces General Douglas Haig is found to have said at a War Council April 14 of last year, "The machine gun is a much overrated weapon and two per battalion is more than sufficient." Like other top officers, Haig does not visit the front lines and says he considers it his duty not to, lest the sight of wounded men affect his judgment.

The Black Tom explosion July 30 blows up munition loading docks at Jersey City, N.J., killing 7 men, injuring 35, and destroying $40 million worth of property. It is widely believed that German saboteurs have set off the explosion.

More of Europe is drawn into the Great War. Germany and Austria have declared war on Portugal in March, Romania declares war on Austria August 27, Italy declares war on Germany August 28, Germany, Turkey, and Bulgaria declare war on Romania.

The first tanks to be used in warfare go into action September 15 in the Battle of the Somme (above). British writer and Boer War veteran Ernest Dunlap Swinton, 48, has invented the machines.

"I believe that the business of neutrality is over," says President Wilson in late October to the Cincinnati Chamber of Commerce. "The nature of modern war leaves no state untouched."

President Wilson wins re-election on a platform that includes the slogan "He kept us out of war," but he believes he has lost until the late returns from California give him 23 more electoral votes than his Re-

1916 (cont.) publican opponent Justice Charles Evans Hughes of the Supreme Court. Wilson's 4,000-vote edge in California gives him 277 electoral votes to 254 for Hughes, who receives 46 percent of the popular vote to Wilson's 49 percent.

German Zeppelins follow up last year's raids on England with 41 more such raids. The worst comes October 13, and on November 28 the Germans make their first airplane raid on London. The Germans have introduced the Albatross and Halberstadt planes and have begun flying in formation.

An Arab revolt against the Ottoman Turks has begun June 5 with an attack on the garrison at Medina, which has surrendered June 10. The 60-year-old grand sherif of Mecca Husein Ibn-Ali had supported the Turks but has switched sides at the persuasion of his 31-year-old third son Faisal and of English archaeologist-soldier T. E. (Thomas Edward) Lawrence, 27. Husein is proclaimed king of the Arabs October 29 and founds the Hashemite dynasty that will rule the newly independent Hejaz until 1924.

Polish general Jozef Pilsudski, 49, obtains recognition of an independent Poland from the Central Powers November 16. Pilsudski 2 years ago organized an independent Polish army of 10,000, acting in secret. He has fought with Austria against Russia, but he has resigned his command because of German and Austrian interference in Polish affairs (see 1918).

The Austro-Hungarian emperor Franz Josef dies November 21 at age 86 after a 68-year reign. He is succeeded by his 29-year-old grandson who became heir to the throne in 1914 when the archduke Franz Ferdinand was assassinated at Sarajevo, and he will reign until 1918 as Karl I.

Britain's Asquith government resigns December 4 and a war cabinet takes over. The new prime minister is Welshman David Lloyd George, 63, who succeeded Lord Kitchener as secretary of state for war in July when Kitchener went down with H.M.S. *Hampshire* off the Orkneys, torpedoed while en route to Russia for secret talks.

The odious Russian faith-healer Grigori Efimovich Rasputin, 45, who has ingratiated himself with the court by promising a cure for the hemophilia that afflicts the czarevich, dies December 31 at Petrograd at the hands of a group of noblemen bent on ridding Russia of the monk's corrupting influence on Nicholas II and the czarina Aleksandra (see 1918; Bolshevik revolution, 1917).

The Russian port of Murmansk is founded on the Barents Sea 175 miles north of the Arctic Circle to receive Allied war materiel. Warm currents from the Gulf Stream keep the port open year round even when some ports to the south are frozen.

Russia's Nikolai Lenin puts out a pamphlet under the title "Imperialism, the Highest Stage of Capitalism." He makes the ideas expressed by John Hobson in his book *Imperialism* of 1902 the official view of the Communist party (see 1917; *Pravda*, 1907).

Constitutionality of the U.S. federal income tax under the amendment adopted in 1913 is upheld by the Supreme Court January 24 in the case of *Brushaber v. Union Pacific Railroad Company*.

The Wealth and Income of the People of the United States by economist Willford Isbell King last year pointed out the increasing concentration of income in the hands of the few, an indication of the need for a graduated income tax. In 1910, King observed, the richest 1.6 percent of U.S. families received 19 percent of the national income, up from 10.8 percent in 1890. While the richest 2 percent of the population received 20.4 percent of the national income and averaged $3,386 per capita in income, the poorest 65 percent received 38.6 percent and averaged $197.

Hetty Green dies July 3 at age 80 leaving an estate of more than $100 million that has made her the richest woman in America. Henrietta Howland Robinson Green inherited $10 million from her father and from a maternal aunt at age 29, she kept her finances separate from those of her late husband Edward H. Green whom she married in 1867, she multiplied her fortune with investments in stocks, government bonds, mortgages, and Chicago real estate while living penuriously, her son lost a leg because she would not hire a physician to treat him, and the eccentric "witch of Wall Street" has been living in a small Hoboken, N.J., apartment.

Bethlehem Steel's Charles M. Schwab pays $49 million to acquire the Pennsylvania Steel Company formerly controlled by the Pennsylvania Railroad. The company has a plant at Steelton, ore mines in Cuba, more in Pennsylvania, and—most important—a tidewater steel mill on Chesapeake Bay at Sparrows Point, Md., where Bethlehem will create a vast shipyard as it continues to prosper on government shipbuilding contracts (below).

A new 10-cent piece is introduced by the U.S. Mint along with a new 25-cent piece and a new 50-cent piece. The Mercury dime will be minted for the next 30 years, the quarter with its standing figure of Liberty will be changed slightly next year but will not be replaced until 1932, and the new half-dollar with a walking figure of Liberty will not be superseded until 1948.

Reynolds Metals Company is founded by Richard S. Reynolds, a nephew of the late R. J., to make foil wrappings for Camels and other R. J. Reynolds cigarettes (see 1918; aluminum, 1945).

Lucky Strike cigarettes are introduced by American Tobacco Company (see 1911). The new brand will soon outsell the company's Sweet Caporal and Pall Mall brands and will challenge the Camels brand launched 3 years ago by R. J. Reynolds (see 1918; 1925).

U.S. cigarette production reaches 53.1 billion, up from 35.3 billion in 1912.

"Peace, it's wonderful," says New York's "Father Divine" and he organizes the Peace Mission movement. Local evangelist George Baker, 42, and his followers will establish a communal settlement at Sayville, Long Island, that they will soon have to abandon, but Father Divine will garner a substantial following in the next 45 years preaching a renunciation of personal property, complete racial equality, and a strict moral code in the more than 170 Peace Mission settlements, or "heavens," that he will open. Tobacco, cosmetics, liquor, motion pictures, and sex will be totally banned.

U.S. iron and steel workers return to work January 13 at East Youngstown, Ohio, after receiving a 10 percent wage hike, but there are 2,000 strikes by U.S. workers in the first 7 months of the year alone.

A San Francisco Preparedness Parade July 22 is disrupted by a bomb explosion that kills 9 and wounds 40. Labor leader Thomas J. Mooney, 34, is accused along with Warren K. Billings, 22, of having planted the bomb, both protest their innocence, Mooney is convicted and condemned to death, Billings is given life imprisonment. Mooney's sentence will be commuted late in 1918, he will be released early in 1939, Billings will be released late in 1939 and will be pardoned in 1961, but acrimony over the affair will continue for the next 25 years.

The Owen-Keating Act passed by Congress September 1 forbids shipment in interstate commerce of goods on which children under 14 have worked or on which children from 14 to 16 have worked more than 8 hours per day (but *see* Supreme Court, 1918).

The Adamson Bill signed by President Wilson September 3 averts a strike by railroad brotherhoods by providing for an 8-hour day on interstate railroads with time and a half for overtime.

A Workmen's Compensation Act passed by Congress September 7 brings 500,000 federal employees under a program to protect them from disability losses.

The first U.S. congresswoman is elected by Montana voters. She is Jeanette Rankin, 36.

Marcus Garvey moves to New York and establishes U.S. headquarters for the Universal Negro Improvement Association (*see* 1913; 1920).

The term "I.Q." (intelligence quotient) is introduced in *The Measurement of Intelligence* by Stanford University psychologist Lewis Madison Terman, 39, who presents the first test for measuring intelligence that will be widely used. The Stanford-Binet test is a revision of the Binet-Simon scale (*see* 1912).

The word "insuline" for the hormone produced by the islets of Langerhans in the human pancreas is introduced by English physiologist Edward A. Sharpey-Schafer, 60 (*see* 1869; Banting, 1922).

A medical student accidentally discovers the anticoagulant powers of the drug heparin, obtained from animal lungs. Swedish biochemist J. Erik Jorpes, now 21, will identify the structure of heparin in the early 1930s and will help make the potent blood thin-

ner a standard therapy for blood clots in the leg caused by thrombophlebitis, for some heart attacks, and for certain lung conditions, as well as for preventing formation of blood clots after major surgery.

X-ray technology is revolutionized by General Electric's William D. Coolidge of 1913 tungsten filament fame. He patents a hot-cathode x-ray that will replace the cold aluminum-cathode tube and will be the prototype of all future x-ray tubes (*see* 1895).

A U.S. poliomyelitis epidemic strikes 28,767 in midsummer and fall. Some 6,000 die, 2,000 of them in New York, and thousands more are crippled (*see* 1905; Franklin Roosevelt, 1921).

Johnson & Johnson acquires the 94-year-old Chicopee Manufacturing Corporation as the war in Europe booms demand for the firm's surgical dressings (*see* 1899). The New Jersey firm makes the move to assure itself of adequate textile materials (*see* Band-Aid, 1921).

A Federal Highway act voted by Congress July 11 authorizes a 5-year program of federal aid to the states for construction of post roads on a 50–50 basis.

Henry Ford buys a site on Detroit's River Rouge for a gigantic new motorcar plant. Ford's Model T gets 20 miles per gallon of gasoline.

W. C. Durant regains control of General Motors whose president Charles W. Nash resigns (below). GM is reorganized as a Delaware corporation.

Cadillac Motor Car Company is set up as a division of General Motors (above) (*see* 1909).

General Motors will absorb the manufacturing facilities of W. C. Durant's Chevrolet Company (*see* 1915), it will absorb the Hyatt Roller Bearing Company whose 43-year-old chief Alfred P. Sloan is a protégé of Cadillac's Henry M. Leland, it will absorb the Dayton Engineering Laboratories (Delco) whose C. F. Kettering is a friend of Leland (*see* 1911), and it will absorb the New Departure Manufacturing Company, a producer of roller bearings (*see* Fisher Body, 1918).

Nash Motors is founded by former GM chief Charles W. Nash (above), who purchases the Thomas B. Jeffery Company of Kenosha, Wis., which started making bicycles in 1879 and introduced the Rambler motorcar in 1902 (*see* Nash-Kelvinator, 1935).

The Marmon 34 priced at $2,700 and up is introduced with a "scientific lightweight" engine of aluminum. Designed by Howard Marmon with his Hungarian-American engineer Fred Moskovics and Alanson P. Brush, the car's only cast-iron engine components are its cylinder sleeves and its one-piece "firing head." Body, fenders, hood, transmission case, differential housing, clutch cone wheel, and radiator shell are all of aluminum, but the car has problems and is unable to compete with the new Cadillac V8.

The Hudson Super-Six is introduced by the 7-year-old Hudson Motor Car Company which sells 26,000

1916 (cont.) vehicles and becomes the leading U.S. maker of high-priced motorcars (*see* closed sedan, 1922).

The first mechanically operated windshield wipers are introduced in the United States. Electric windshield wipers will not be produced until 1923.

U.S. railroad trackage reaches its peak of 254,000 miles, up from 164,000 in 1890. The total will decline, but only marginally.

Cleveland's Van Sweringen brothers acquire the Nickel Plate system (the New York, Chicago & St. Louis Railroad). Seeking the right of way for a streetcar extension to connect their 11-year-old Shaker Heights suburb with Cleveland, the Van Sweringens learned that the Nickel Plate system was for sale, they have found backers, and they start a railroad empire that will grow to include the Erie, the Père Marquette, the Chesapeake & Ohio, the Missouri Pacific, and the Toledo, St. Louis and Western—a network of 21,000 miles of track—before it falls apart in the early 1930s (*see* Cleveland Terminal Tower Building, 1930).

A U.S. Shipping Board is created September 7 by act of Congress.

The German freight submarine *Deutschland* that arrived at Baltimore July 9 with a cargo of dyestuffs arrives in November at New London, Conn., with a cargo of chemicals, gems, and securities.

Bethlehem Steel (above) builds submarines for the British and obtains a U.S. government contract for 88 vessels to be built on a cost-plus basis with half the savings under estimated costs to go to Bethlehem. The ships will be built for $93 million, $48 million below the estimate, and Bethlehem will have a profit of $24 million.

Todd Shipyards is founded by New York shipbuilder William H. Todd, 42, after a Naval Appropriations Act passed by Congress August 29 authorizes appropriation of $313 million for a 3-year naval construction program. The Battle of Jutland (above) has demonstrated the value of dreadnoughts and light cruisers.

The Bryan-Chamorro Treaty with Nicaragua gives the United States exclusive rights to build a canal through that country and thus prevents anyone else from building a rival to the Panama Canal that opened in 1914. Nicaragua receives $3 million and is thus enabled to pay off its debts to U.S. bankers, but the new pact is criticized by the *New York Times* which says that the "dollar diplomacy" of former president Taft and his secretary of state Philander C. Knox has been made to "more nearly resemble ten-cent diplomacy" by President Wilson.

U.S. petroleum companies raise gasoline prices 7 cents per gallon above 1914 levels as the European war and mounting domestic demand create shortages. Engineers predict that world petroleum reserves will be exhausted within 30 years (but *see*

Lake Maracaibo, 1922; east Texas, 1930; Saudi Arabia, 1933; Alaska, 1968; North Sea, 1969).

Sinclair Oil and Refining Company is organized by U.S. entrepreneur Harry Ford Sinclair, 40, who has put together some small Midwestern refineries and a pipeline company and who floats a $16 million bond issue in Wall Street. By 1923 Sinclair will have added the Freeport and Tampico Oil Corporation and Pennsylvania's Union Petroleum Company, and Sinclair Oil will have corporate assets of $412 million (*see* Teapot Dome, 1921).

New York's American Metal Company pursues explorations of the Climax, Col., molybdenite mine found in 1900 under the direction of its Denver office head Max Schott. The steel alloy potentials of molybdenum remain largely unknown but American Metal will eventually acquire the Climax property and will become American Metal-Climax (later Amax).

Russell Sage College for Women is founded at Troy, N.Y., by philanthropist Margaret Olivia Slocum Sage, 88, whose late husband died 10 years ago at age 90 leaving her $70 million amassed as an associate of Jay Gould in his railroad security manipulations. Sage's second wife, she established the Russell Sage Foundation for improving social and living conditions in the United States with a $10 million gift in 1907, and she has given liberally to Cornell, Princeton, Rensselaer Polytechnic Institute, and the Emma Willard School.

W. M. A. Beaverbrook begins a vast publishing empire by gaining control of London's 16-year-old *Daily Express.* Canadian cement magnate William Maxwell Aitken Beaverbrook, 37, has been representing the Ottawa government at the Western Front, by 1918 he will be British minister of information and will control the *Sunday Express,* and by 1923 he will control the *Evening Standard.*

El Universal begins publication at Mexico City. Local journalist Felix F. Palavaicini, 35, sets new standards by publishing news rather than editorial opinion on his daily front page (*see* 1917).

The first radio news is broadcast by Lee De Forest who has established a radio station (*see* 1906; 1922; Conrad, 1920).

Cincinnati advertising man Stanley Burnet Resor, 37, buys out New York's J. Walter Thompson Company advertising agency (*see* Curtis, 1901). Thompson hired Resor 8 years ago to open a Cincinnati office, he will use testimonial advertisements beginning next year for Pond's Face Cream, he will attract such clients as Ford Motor Company, Lever Brothers, and Fleischmann's Yeast, and he will increase JWT's 1916 billing of $3 million a hundredfold.

Nonfiction *A Heap o' Livin'* by English-American journalist Edgar Albert Guest, 35, of the *Detroit Free Press* who says, "It takes a heap o' livin' to make a house a home." His book will have sales of more than a million copies.

774

Fiction *The Golden Arrow* by English novelist Mary (Gladys Meredith) Webb, 35; *Grass on the Wayside* (*Michigusa*) by Satsume Soseki; *Gharer baire* by Hindu poet-novelist Rabindranath Tagore (Ravindranatha Thakura), now 55, whose novel in the Bengali vulgate creates a controversy by moving away from the traditional Bengali literary language in which Tagore has written numerous poems, plays, songs, and short stories that helped him win a 1913 Nobel prize (Tagore has used the £8,000 he won to maintain the school he started in 1901 at Santiniketan, Balpur, Bengal); *Casuals of the Sea* by William McFee; *Greenmantle* by John Buchan who is serving on the British headquarters staff in France; *Kingdom of the Dead* (*De Dodes Rige*) by Henrik Pontoppidan; *You Know Me, Al* (stories) by *Chicago Tribune* sportswriter Ring (Ringgold Wilmer) Lardner, 31.

Poetry *The Man Against the Sky* by Edwin Arlington Robinson; *The Jig of Forslinby* by U.S. poet Conrad Potter Aiken, 27, who calls his work a "poetic symphony"; *Six Poems* by Edward Thomas; *Sea Garden* by U.S. poet H. D. (Hilda Doolittle) Aldington, 30, who married the English imagist poet Richard Aldington in 1912 but will divorce him after the war and return to America; *Twentieth Century Harlequinade and Other Poems* by English poet Edith Sitwell, 29, and her brother Osbert, 23; *The Buried Harbor* (*Il Porto Sepolto*) by Italian poet Giuseppe Ungaretti, 28; U.S. poet Alan Seeger, 28, is killed in action July 4 at Belloy-en-Santerre. Seeger enlisted in the French Foreign Legion at the outbreak of the war and leaves behind lines that include, "I have a rendezvous with Death/ At some disputed barricade,/ When Spring comes back with rustling shade/ And apple-blossoms fill the air."

Painting *The Three Sisters* by Henri Matisse; *The Disquieting Muse* by Italian painter Giorgio de Chirico, 28; *Naturaleza muerta, El rastro* by Diego Rivera. Thomas Eakins dies at Philadelphia June 25 at age 71; Odilon Redon dies at Paris July 6 at age 76.

The Dada artistic and literary movement launched at Zurich will lead to surrealism next year. German pacifist writer Hugo Ball, 30, Alsatian painter-sculptor-writer-poet Hans (or Jean) Arp, 29, Romanian-born French poet Tristan Tzara (Sami Rosenstock), 20, and their adherents believe that Western culture has betrayed itself by its easy acceptance of the World War. They protest against all bourgeois notions of meaning and order with chaotic experiments in form and language (*see* Duchamp, 1915).

The *Saturday Evening Post* buys its first Norman Rockwell illustration from *Boys' Life* illustrator Norman Rockwell, 22, who dropped out of Mamaroneck, N.Y., High School 6 years ago to work for the monthly magazine of the Boy Scouts of America. Rockwell has been art director of *Boys' Life* since 1913, but he will now draw mostly for the *Saturday Evening Post* which will buy an average of 10 Norman Rockwell covers per year until it ceases weekly publication in 1969.

Sculpture *The Fallen* by Wilhelm Lehmbruck; *Naid* fountain (bronze) by Carl Milles.

Theater *Moses* by English poet-artist Isaac Rosenberg, 26; *A Kiss for Cinderella* by James M. Barrie 3/16 at Wyndham's Theatre, London; *A Night at an Inn* by Lord Dunsany 4/23 at New York's Neighborhood Playhouse; *The Mask and the Face* (*La maschera e il volto*) by Italian playwright Luigi Chiarelli, 35, 5/31 at Rome's Teatro Argentina; *Good Gracious Annabelle* by U.S. playwright Clare Kummer 10/31 at New York's Republic Theater, with Lola Fisher, Roland Young, Walter Hampden, 111 perfs.; *Bound East for Cardiff,* a one-act play by U.S. playwright Eugene Gladstone O'Neill, 27, 11/16 at New York's Provincetown Playhouse; *The White-Haired Boy* by Irish playwright Esme Stuart Lennox Robinson, 30, 12/13 at Dublin's Abbey Theatre.

Films Herbert Brenon's *War Brides* with Alla Nazimova; Otto Ripart's *Homunculus* and *The Revenge of Homunculus;* John Emerson's *The Mystery of the Leaping Fish* with Douglas Fairbanks; William S. Hart's *Hell's Hinges* with Hart.

Opera *Ariadne auf Naxos* 10/4 at Vienna, with music by Richard Strauss, libretto by Hugo von Hofmannsthal.

Stage musicals *Robinson Crusoe, Jr.* 2/17 at New York's Winter Garden Theater, with Al Jolson, music by Sigmund Romberg and James Hanley, book and lyrics by Harold Atteridge and Edgar Smith, 139 perfs.; *The Ziegfeld Follies* 6/12 at New York's New Amsterdam Theater, with W. C. Fields, Fanny Brice, Ina Claire, Ann Pennington, music by Louis Hirsch, Jerome Kern, and Dave Stamper, 112 perfs.; *The Passing Show* 6/22 at New York's Winter Garden Theater, with Ed Wynn, music chiefly by Sigmund Romberg, lyrics chiefly by Harold Atteridge, songs that include "Pretty Baby" by Tony Jackson and Egbert van Alstyne, lyrics by German-American songwriter Gus Kahn, 30, 140 perf.; *Chu Chin Chow, A Musical Tale of the East* 8/31 at His Majesty's Theatre, London, with a book by Oscar Asche, 45, who has created an extravaganza out of the pantomine *The Forty Thieves,* music by Frederick Norton, 2,238 perfs. (the musical will continue through the war and beyond); *The Century Girl* 11/16 at New York's Century Theater, with Hazel Dawn, Marie Dressler, Elsie Janis, Leon Errol, music by Irving Berlin and Victor Herbert, lyrics by Berlin and Henry Blossom, songs that include Berlin's "You Belong to Me," 200 perfs.

First performances *Scythian Suite* by Russian composer Serge Sergeevich Prokofiev, 24, 1/29 at Petrograd's Imperial Maryinsky Theater.

Popular songs "Roses of Picardy" by London composer Haydn Wood, 34, lyrics by lawyer-publisher Fred E. Weatherly, 68; "I Ain't Got Nobody" by Spencer Williams, 27, lyrics by Roger Graham, 31; "La Cucaracha" ("The Cockroach") is published at Mexico City and at San Francisco; "Ireland Must Be

1916 (cont.) Heaven for My Mother Came from There" by Fred Fisher, lyrics by Joe McCarthy and Howard E. Johnson.

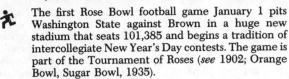

The first Rose Bowl football game January 1 pits Washington State against Brown in a huge new stadium that seats 101,385 and begins a tradition of intercollegiate New Year's Day contests. The game is part of the Tournament of Roses (see 1902; Orange Bowl, Sugar Bowl, 1935).

The first PGA (Professional Golfers Association) tournament opens at the Siwanoy Country Club, Bronxville, N.Y.

The Boston Red Sox win the World Series by defeating the Brooklyn Dodgers 4 games to 1.

Tokyo's Imperial Hotel is completed by Frank Lloyd Wright near the Imperial Palace with Mayan architectural features. It is ornate and sprawling, but it is soundly engineered (see 1923 earthquake).

San Francisco's Clift Hotel is completed at 495 Geary Street by local attorney Frederick Clift. The 14-story hotel will be given a new wing and three additional floors in 1926 to make it a luxurious 400-room hotel with high ceilings and thick sound-proofed walls.

Miami's $16 million James Deering mansion Vizcaya is completed for the farm equipment heir. Roofing tile for the coraline stone Florida house once covered an entire Cuban village (the Cubans have been given new roofs), a 300-year-old travertine marble fountain from the town square of the Italian village Bassano di Surti near Rome has been placed in Vizcaya's Fountain Garden (the Italians have been given a modern water system), the estate has 10 acres of formal gardens including the Fountain Garden modeled after Rome's Villa Albani, and the house has 45 telephones, oversize brine-cooled refrigerators, marble floors, and two elevators.

The first U.S. zoning law is enacted in New York City partly as a response to the Equitable building completed last year, partly as a result of a full-page newspaper advertisement headlined "Shall We Save New York?" and sponsored by merchants who include B. Altman & Co., Arnold Constable & Co., Gimbel Brothers, Lord & Taylor, R. H. Macy & Co., and Saks & Co. (see set-back law, 1923).

Winfield Hall at Glen Cove, Long Island, is completed for dime store magnate F. W. (Frank Winfield) Woolworth by architect Charles P. H. Gilbert whose 62-room "summer villa" has a Gothic library, a Baroque music room, a Georgian dining room, and French Empire bedrooms copied from a Napoleon palace in Compiègne.

Double-shell enameled bathtubs go into mass production in the United States to replace the cast-iron tubs with roll rims and claw feet that have been standard for decades.

The U.S. National Park Service in the Department of the Interior is created by act of Congress August 20.

California's Lassen Volcanic National Park is created by act of Congress. The 107,000-acre park embraces a still-active volcano.

Hawaii Volcanoes National Park is created under the name Hawaii National Park. The 220,345-acre park on the island of Hawaii will be renamed in 1961.

Acadia National Park has its beginnings. John D. Rockefeller, Jr., donates 5,000 acres of his family's Mount Desert Island in Maine to the nation; President Wilson proclaims it a national monument (see 1919).

The Ecological Society of America is founded.

Florida's Gulf Coast has a "red tide" caused by a proliferation of the dinoflagellate plankton *Gymnodinium breve*. The red tide kills millions of fish whose nervous systems are immobilized by the expelled waste of *G. breve* (see 1932).

A German War Food Office is established as Britain's naval blockade forces strict rationing of food.

A German potato blight contributes to starvation that kills 700,000 and weakens morale in the army.

France sets a maximum wheat price of 33 francs per quintal (220 pounds) to the farmer and sets controls on butter, cheese, and oil cakes. Parisians line up in milk queues.

A British Departmental Committee on Food Prices is established after a sharp rise in food prices by June has brought complaints of profiteering. Two-thirds of Britain's sugar came from Austria-Hungary before the war and sugar prices have risen steeply.

British bread prices begin to move up from 9½d per 4-pound loaf, an Order in Council empowers the Board of Trade to regulate food supplies and fix prices, but the president of the Board of Trade tells the House of Commons in October that there is no need to establish a Ministry of Food or to appoint a Food Controller: "We want to avoid any rationing of our people in food."

Port of London Authority chairman Hudson Ewbanke Kearley, 60, viscount Devenport, is appointed Food Controller in December but the government is not prepared to ration food. Lord Devenport appeals to the public to make voluntary sacrifices (see 1917).

British fuel shortages motivate Parliament to pass a "summer time" act and most European governments do the same, advancing clocks one hour to make the most of available light. British farmers protest that they must milk their cows in the dark and must then wait idly until the sun has evaporated the dew before they can harvest hay (see Congress, 1918).

A Federal Farm Loan Act passed by Congress July 17 provides for Farm Loan Banks throughout the United States and creates a Federal Farm Loan Board. The legislation makes it easier for U.S. farmers to obtain credit with which to buy land, acquire farm machinery, and generally improve their productivity (see Agricultural Credits Act, 1923).

A Stockraising Homestead Act doubles the amount of land allowed under the Homestead Act of 1909, but even 640 acres—a full square mile—is too small in many arid areas (*see* 1862). Failed homesteaders will soon sell their land to stockmen bent on acquiring large ranches (*see* Taylor Grazing Act, 1934).

U.S. wheat farmers have another bumper crop but the average corn farmer produces little more than 25 bushels per acre.

The first hybrid seed corn is shipped by Funk Brothers of Bloomington, Ill., to a Jacobsburg, Ohio, farmer who pays $15 per bushel for the seed (*see* East and Shull, 1921; Golden Bantam, 1933).

The boll weevil reaches the Atlantic coast (*see* 1899; 1921).

The Japanese beetle *Popilla japonica* whose grubs have arrived in the roots of imported nursery stock appears for the first time in America at Riverton, N.J. The beetle will proliferate and damage millions of dollars worth of fruits and vegetables.

Vitamin B is isolated by E. V. McCollum who believes it to be just one coenzyme (*see* 1912; Drummond, 1920; Smith, Hendrick, 1928).

The first large-scale study of iodine's effect on human goiter is conducted by U.S. physicians David Marine and E. C. Kendall (*see* 1905; Mayo Clinic, 1915). Girls in some Akron, Ohio, schools are given tablets containing 0.2 gram of sodium iodide, and the incidence of goiter in susceptible teenage girls given the tablets is found to drop markedly (*see* table salt, 1921).

The relationship between fluorides and tooth decay is studied by Colorado Springs, Col., dentist Frederick S. Motley who finds that his patients' teeth are mottled but contain few cavities. Motley begins to trace this to the fact that the city's drinking water contains fluoride salts in a concentration of two parts per million (*see* Dean, 1933).

A mechanical home refrigerator is marketed for the first time in the United States, but its price of $900 discourages buyers who can buy a good motorcar for the same money (*see* 1925; Kelvinator, 1918; Frigidaire, 1919; GE, 1927).

Filled milk made with vegetable oil to replace butterfat is made in quantity in the United States to the consternation of dairymen (*see* 1923).

The Corn Products Refining Company "gluten trust" organized by E. T. Bedford in 1906 is broken up by the courts, but Bedford retains control of a major share of U.S. corn refining capacity (*see* 1913; 1923).

California Packing Corporation is incorporated at San Francisco with a $16 million Wall Street underwriting promoted by George N. Armsby, son of Jacob (*see* 1865; Del Monte, 1891). Now the largest U.S. fruit and vegetable canner, Calpak operates 61 canneries including some in Washington, Oregon, and Idaho, and it owns a 70 percent interest in the Alaska

Packers Association whose Star Fleet continues as the last commercial sailing fleet to fly the American flag (*see* 1893; 1930; Del Monte Corporation, 1967).

Wilson & Co. is founded at Chicago in a reorganization of the meatpacking firm Sulzberger & Sons which started as Swarzchild and Sulzberger in 1853, built a slaughterhouse at Cedar Rapids in 1871, bought a Kansas City plant in 1893, moved to Chicago in 1908, bought an Oklahoma City plant in 1911, and in 1913 became the first U.S. meatpacker in Brazil. The company is taken over by Thomas E. Wilson, head of the 2-year-old Wilson Sporting Goods Company (*see* Ling-Temco-Vought, 1967).

"Mr. Peanut" is introduced by the Planters Nut and Chocolate Company which moved 3 years ago from Wilkes Barre, Pa., to Suffolk, Va., in the heart of the peanut growing country and has opened a shelling factory (*see* 1906). Planters has conducted a contest among Suffolk high school students to find an appropriate trademark, the winning sketch has been an anthropomorphized peanut, a commercial artist has added a monocle and a crooked leg to the initial sketch (which won its designer a $5 prize), and the company will be helped by Mr. Peanut to grow in the next 20 years into a huge enterprise (*see* 1961).

Coca-Cola adopts the distinctive bottle shape that will identify it for the next 58 years—a slimmer model of the waist-bulging bottle of 1913 made at Terre Haute, Ind., by Chapman S. Root of the Root Glass Company. The Supreme Court rules that if Coca-Cola is to claim a distinctive name it must contain some derivatives of cola beans and coca leaves but does not rule against the use of these substances in denatured form (*see* 1910; Woodruff, 1919).

The Orange Crush Company is incorporated at Chicago by entrepreneurs who employ a process de-

"I Want You." James Montgomery Flagg's poster, based on the 1914 British poster, attracted U.S. recruits in 1917.

1916 (cont.) veloped by N. C. Ward employing an orange concentrate obtained from the California Fruit Growers Exchange (*see* 1895). Orange Crush consists primarily of carbonated water and sugar, it will be introduced into Canada and Latin America in the 1920s, and within 65 years it will be sold in more than 65 countries (*see* Hires, 1962).

The Piggly-Wiggly opened at Memphis, Tenn., by food merchant Clarence Saunders begins the first supermarket chain and will make its founder a fortune in the stock market (*see* California, 1912; San Francisco, 1923; King Kullen, 1930).

Nathan's Famous frankfurters have their beginning in a Coney Island, N.Y., hot dog stand at the corner of Stillwell and Surf Avenues opened by Polish-American merchant Nathan Handwerker, 25, who sells his franks at 5 cents each—half the price charged by Feltman's German Gardens on Surf Avenue where Handwerker has worked weekends as a counterman while making $4.50 per week as a delivery boy in the Lower East Side. Handwerker has invested his life savings of $300 in the hot dog stand, he works 18 to 20 hours per day with his 19-year-old bride Ida who laces the franks with her secret spice recipe, and he prospers (*see* 1917).

The first birth control clinic outside Holland is opened at 46 Amboy Street, Brooklyn, by Margaret Sanger who distributes circulars printed in English, Italian, and Yiddish to announce the opening (*see* 1914). The clinic is raided by the police, Sanger is jailed for 30 days, she founds the New York Birth Control League after her release, and she begins publication of the *Birth Control Review* (*see* 1921).

1917 The German high command resumes unrestricted U-boat attacks despite the probability that such attacks will bring the United States into the European war. Bolstering German confidence is the strength of the Hindenburg line on the western front and the collapse of Russian opposition on the eastern front as revolution begins in Russia (below).

British intelligence intercepts a wireless message January 17 from the German foreign secretary Arthur von Zimmermann to the German ambassador Count Johann von Bernstorff at Washington. Decoded, the Zimmermann note says, "We intend to begin unrestricted submarine warfare. We shall endeavor to keep the United States neutral. In the event of this not succeeding we make Mexico a proposal of alliance on the following basis: Make war together, make peace together, generous financial support, and an understanding on our part that Mexico is to recover the lost territory in Texas, New Mexico, and Arizona."

Berlin notifies Washington January 31 that unrestricted submarine warfare will begin the next day, the United States severs relations with Germany February 3, Latin American nations including Brazil and Peru follow suit, China severs relations with Germany March 14.

Eleven U.S. senators conduct a filibuster to block arming of U.S. merchant ships running the gauntlet of German U-boats. President Wilson denounces the senators March 4 saying, "A little group of willful men, reflecting no opinion but their own, have rendered the great government of the United States helpless and contemptible."

Russian troops mutiny March 10 following 2 days of strikes and riots at Petrograd, the czar Nicholas II en route home by private train March 15 has the train pulled into a siding and abdicates in favor of his brother Michael, Michael abdicates March 16 in favor of a provisional government headed by Prince Georgi Evgenievich Lvov, 55, the Romanov dynasty founded in 1613 comes to an abrupt end.

Nikolai Lenin and other Bolshevik leaders arrive at Petrograd in April. The German high command has sent them by sealed railroad carriage from Switzerland across Germany in a calculated move to undermine the pro-Ally provisional government (above) (*see* revolution, below; Lenin, 1905).

The United States declares war on Germany April 6, 4 days after President Wilson has sent a war message to the Senate. General Pershing has been recalled from his pursuit of the Mexican bandit Pancho Villa and he is named to head an American Expeditionary Force as the French and British sustain enormous losses on the western front.

Canadian troops take Vimy Ridge in the Battle of Arras that lasts from April 9 to May 4, but while the British army commanded by General Edmund Allenby advances 4 miles, it is unable to effect a breakthrough.

French troops mutiny after sustaining cruel losses in April and after hearing of mutiny among Russian troops on the eastern front. French authorities relieve General Robert Georges Nivelle, 61, of his command but exonerate him from blame for the failure of his plans, they replace him with General Pétain who tries to restore order as the mutiny sweeps through 16 corps, the government executes 23 socialist and pacifist agitators, but the brunt of the Allied war effort falls on the British Tommy as the French *poilu* loses heart for continuing the war.

More than half the 875,000 tons of Allied shipping lost in April is British, but Prime Minister Lloyd George prevails on the Admiralty to try convoying merchant vessels. Convoys begin May 10, German U-boats continue their depredations and sink 8 million tons by October 10, but the German submarine campaign has lost so much force that the United States is able to increase troop shipments.

An embargo proclamation issued by President Wilson July 9 places exports of U.S. foodstuffs, fuel, iron, steel, and war materiel under government control.

U.S. destroyers sent by President Wilson help blockade German ports and convoy merchant ships bound for Britain.

The Jones Act passed by Congress March 2 makes Puerto Rico a U.S. territory and makes Puerto Ricans U.S. citizens. Voting is made compulsory, the selective service act is extended to Puerto Rico at the request of the San Juan government, and Puerto Rico drafts 18,000 men into the U.S. Army.

The Danish West Indies which include the Virgin Islands of St. Thomas, St. Croix, and St. John with 26,000 inhabitants become U.S. territory March 31 upon Senate ratification of a treaty giving Denmark $25 million for the 132 square miles of land involved.

"Lafayette, we are here," says U.S. Colonel Charles E. Stanton July 4 at the tomb of Lafayette in Paris but U.S. troops do not go into action until October 27.

The Battle of Passchendaele from July 31 to November 10 costs the British 400,000 men.

Russia's Lvov government (above) is replaced July 7 by a new provisional government headed by minister of war Aleksandr Feodorovich Kerenski, 36, who takes office as prime minister while Russian troops pull back on all fronts (see revolution, below).

Aqaba in Arabia falls to Arab forces led by Colonel T. E. Lawrence who attacks Turkish garrisons and breaks the Turkish communications link by disrupting the Hejaz Railway. Baghdad has been in British hands since March 11.

German colonial troops gain a victory in mid-October at Mahiwa and invade Portuguese East Africa.

French dancer Mata Hari (Gertrud Margarete Zelle), 41, is convicted of having spied for the Germans and is executed October 15 at St. Lazare.

Caporetto in the Julian Alps near Italy's Austrian border is bombarded in late October by German and Austrian artillery. Troops move in beginning October 24 in heavy fog in an effort to reach the Tagliamento River, but while nearly 300,000 Italians are taken prisoner in the 2-month Caporetto campaign and more than 300,000 desert, the Germans and Austrians make little real progress.

The Balfour Declaration is issued November 2 by British foreign secretary Arthur J. Balfour, now 69, as British troops invade Palestine and take it from the Ottoman Turks who have held it since 1516 (Jerusalem falls to the British December 9). Says Balfour, the British government favors "the establishment in Palestine of a national home for the Jewish people and will use their best endeavours to facilitate the achievement of that object, it being clearly understood that nothing shall be done which may prejudice the civil and religious rights of existing non-Jewish communities in Palestine" (see Herzl, 1897; Passfield Paper, 1930).

The Battle of Passchendaele ends November 10 with the British completely demoralized, but the Battle of Cambrai that begins November 20 gives the British some success initially. 300 British tanks launch a surprise raid in the first great tank attack of the war, but the Germans counterattack November 30 and recover most of the territory they have lost.

A Bolshevik revolution begins at Petrograd the night of November 6 (October 24 according to the Julian calendar still used in Russia). Commissar Aleksandr B. Belyshev, 24, aboard the cruiser *Aurora* anchored in the Neva River fires, on party orders, a blank shot from the ship's foredeck gun, housewives waiting in endless breadshop queues have been demonstrating in protest, they are joined by soldiers from the Petrograd garrison, by sailors from Kronstadt, and by the factory workers' Red Guards who seize government offices and storm the Winter Palace of the Romanovs.

Aleksandr Kerenski (above) has been forced to accept Bolshevik support to resist the efforts of the 64-year-old general Lavr Georgievich Kornilov to make himself dictator, the Bolsheviks have secured a majority in the Petrograd Soviet under the leadership of revolutionist Leon Trotsky (Lev Davydovich Bronstein), 40, who was expelled from France last year and has returned from exile in the United States and England to support Lenin (above) who is behind the coup of November 6.

The Kerenski government falls, Kerenski himself escapes with his life and goes into hiding (he will later take sanctuary abroad), and a new government headed by Lenin takes office November 7 under the name Council of People's Commissars. Trotsky is commissar for foreign affairs and a 39-year-old Georgian who calls himself Josef Stalin (Iosif Vissarionovich Dzhugashvili) is commissar for national minorities.

Russian serfs seize the landlords' fields as the Bolsheviks initiate plans to make Moscow the nation's capital.

The Extraordinary Commission to Combat Counter-Revolution founded by revolutionist Felix Dzerzhinsky, 42, December 20 is a secret police organization designed to protect the Council of People's Commissars (above) and to crush opposition. The Cheka will later be called the GPU and will subsequently become the KGB.

Race riots at East St. Louis, Ill., July 2 leave 39 dead, hundreds injured.

New York blacks led by W. E. B. Du Bois and James Weldon Johnson of the NAACP walk in silence 15,000 strong down Fifth Avenue to protest the violence at East St. Louis (above).

The Congressional Union for Woman Suffrage pickets the White House to urge presidential support of the woman suffrage amendment. President Wilson endorses equal suffrage in the states October 25 when he speaks at the White House before a group from the New York State Woman Suffrage party, and 20,000 women march in a New York suffrage parade October 27.

New York adopts a constitutional amendment November 6 and becomes the first state to grant equal voting rights to women (see 1918).

1917 (cont.) The first U.S. woman governor takes office in Texas. Mrs. James "Ma" Ferguson, 42, fills the vacancy left by her husband who has been impeached and removed from office, but no woman will be elected governor in her own right until Connecticut elects Mrs. Ella Grasso in 1974.

Typhus sweeps Russia to compound the problems of defeat and revolution (above). The epidemic will kill up to 3 million in the next 4 years (*see* 1918; Armand Hammer, 1921).

Phillips Petroleum Company is founded at Bartlesville, Okla., by local banker Frank Phillips, 43, and his brother Lee Eldas Phillips, 40, who have made money in local wells (*see* 1903). The Phillips brothers sold most of their properties to Tidal Oil Company last year, they have retained some Oklahoma acreage that Tidal would not accept, the Great War has doubled oil prices and has motivated Frank Phillips to drill on his remaining property, his first well is a gusher, the company has a gross income of $218,000 in its first 6 months, by 1922 it will have net assets of more than $50 million and will earn $3 million on a gross of $12.5 million, Phillips will adopt the brand name "Phillips 66" in 1927 (using the number of the U.S. highway under construction near the company's first refinery), by the end of the 1920s Phillips will be an integrated company with refineries, pipelines, filling stations, and subordinate ventures in petrochemicals, carbon black, and liquified natural gas, and in 1930 Phillips will buy Independent Oil & Gas Company headed by younger brother Waite Phillips, now 34 (*see* North Sea, 1969).

The Gerber-Covington oil pool is discovered east of Enid in Oklahoma's Cherokee Strip.

Humble Oil Corporation is organized by nine Texas and Oklahoma investors who in some cases will retain a strong minority interest for 40 years—long after the company has been largely absorbed by Standard Oil Company of New Jersey. When Jersey Standard merges all its domestic properties in 1960, Humble will be the nation's second largest domestic oil firm with the largest U.S.-flag tanker fleet, six major refineries, thousands of miles of pipeline, thousands of wells, and marketing outlets in 40 states.

Use of electric signs in the United States is restricted November 16 to conserve energy.

U.S. trolley car ridership reaches 11 billion with 80,000 electric streetcars plying 45,000 miles of track, up from 30,000 trolley cars on 15,000 miles of track in 1900. Connecting lines make it possible to travel from New York to Boston by trolley and even for more than 1,000 miles from eastern Wisconsin to central New York State, paying a nickel to ride to the end of each line (*see* 1939).

New York's Erie Canal is replaced after 92 years by a modern barge canal 12 feet deep, 75 to 200 feet wide, 524 miles long. The old canal has been made obsolete by steam power and the new barge canal makes use of an additional 382 miles of canalized lakes and rivers between Albany and lakes Ontario and Erie (*see* 1825; 1836).

New York City's Hell Gate Bridge (the New York connecting railroad bridge) is completed across the East River to permit trains from Boston to enter Manhattan via the Bronx.

Kansas City's Union Station is completed. It is the nation's second largest railway terminal.

A "Stop-Look-Listen" warning sign for railroad crossings is designed by a Seattle, Wash., safety lecturer for the Puget Sound Power Company to replace the "Watch for Engines" sign in common use.

The worst train wreck in world history occurs December 12 at Modane, France, where a passenger train jumps the tracks killing 543, injuring hundreds more. Three U.S. train wrecks in Pennsylvania, Oklahoma, and Kentucky kill 20, 23, and 46, respectively.

U.S. auto production reaches 1,745,792, up from 543,679 in 1914. Model T Fords account for 42.4 percent of the total.

Japan's Datsun motorcar has its beginnings in the DAT introduced by the 5-year-old Kwaishinska Motor Car Works of Tokyo founded by K. Den, R. Aoyama, and A. Takenchi. The firm will merge in 1926 with Jidosha Seizo Jitsuyo of Osaka, it will devote all its production to trucks until 1930, and it will adopt the rising sun emblem in 1932.

Germany's BMW (Bayerische Motoren Werke) is created at Munich by a reorganization of Bayerische Flugzeugwerke. The company will introduce the world's first six-cylinder high-altitude aircraft engine and a 550-horsepower nine-cylinder aircraft engine, but it will be noted for its high-speed motorcycles before turning to sportscar production under the name Bavarian Motor Works.

Chance Vought Company is founded by U.S. aeronautical engineer and designer Chance Milton Vought, 27 (*see* United Aircraft, 1929).

The Anglo-American Corporation of South Africa is founded by German-born South African mining magnate Ernest Oppenheimer, 37, whose firm will grow to control 95 percent of the world's diamond supply (*see* Rhodes, Barnato, 1880).

Union Carbide and Carbon Corporation is created in November by a merger of Union Carbide Company, the Linde Company, the Prest-O-Lite Corporation, and the National Carbon Company famous for its Eveready flashlights and batteries. The new company finds itself swamped immediately with government orders for activated carbon for gas masks, helium for dirigibles, ferrozirconium for armorplating, and other war-related products (*see* Union Carbide, 1911; petrochemicals, 1920; Prestone, 1926).

U.S. tax revenues from income taxes for the first time pass revenues from customs duties (*see* 1913). By 1920 income tax revenues will be 10 times those from customs duties.

The United States has more than 40,000 millionaires, up from 4,000 in 1892. Millionaire railroad equipment salesman and trencherman James Buchanan "Diamond Jim" Brady dies April 13 at Atlantic City, N.J., at age 60, 3 months after the death at Denver of "Buffalo Bill" Cody (who died bankrupt at age 70).

A superheterodyne circuit that greatly increases the selectivity and sensitivity of radio receivers over a wide band of frequencies is developed by U.S. Army Signal Corps major Edwin Howard Armstrong, 26, whose circuit will become the basic design for all amplitude modulation (AM) radios (see 1906; FM, 1933).

Marketing of a simple "radio music box" is urged on the American Marconi Company. Marconi employee David Sarnoff of 1912 *Titanic* fame says his plan will make the radio "a 'household utility' in the same sense as the piano or phonograph" (see 1920).

U.S. journalist Dorothy Day, 19, quits her job on the IWW newspaper *The Call* and joins *The Masses,* a U.S. Communist party newspaper that is soon suppressed (see 1933).

Excelsior begins publication at Mexico City. The daily will become Mexico's leading newspaper.

"The Gumps" appears February 12 in the *Chicago Tribune* whose publisher Joseph Medill Patterson has dreamed up the comic strip and has given it its name (see 1910). Cartoonist Sidney Smith, 30, has created the characters based on real people, and in mid-March of 1922 he will be signed to the first $1 million cartoon contract with a guarantee of $100,000 per year and a new Rolls-Royce (see 1955).

The "Katzenjammer Kids" that began appearing in 1897 is renamed "The Captain and the Kids" as German names become unpopular in America. The comic strip moved 5 years ago from Hearst's *New York Journal* to Pulitzer's *New York World.*

Grey Advertising, Inc., has its beginnings in an art studio started by New York entrepreneur Lawrence Valenstein, 18, who has borrowed $100 from his mother to open an office whose walls are grey. Valenstein will employ Arthur Cornell Fat, now 13, as an office boy, the two will become equal partners, Grey will represent garment trade accounts at first, and it will grow to become the fifth largest U.S. agency.

The *World Book* encyclopaedia is published in its first edition. It will grow to 22 volumes in the next 60 years, and its sales will grow to exceed those of any other encyclopaedia.

Nonfiction *A Son of the Middle Border* (reminiscences) by Hamlin Garland; *Parnassus on Wheels* by U.S. essayist Christopher Darlington Morley, 27, is the odyssey of a horse-drawn library.

Fiction *The Book of the Martyrs* (*Vie des Martyrs*) with war stories by French novelist Denis Thévenin (Georges Duhamel), 35; *South Wind* by Scottish novelist-scientist Norman Douglas, 48, who has settled on the Italian island of Capri which he idealizes as

"Nepenthe"; *Nocturne* by English novelist Frank Swinnerton, 33; *The Rise of David Levinsky* by Jewish *Daily Forward* editor Abraham Cahan.

Juvenile *Understood Betsy* by Vermont novelist Dorothy Canfield Fisher, 38.

Poetry *Renascence and Other Poems* by Maine-born poet Edna St. Vincent Millay, 25, whose title poem appeared 5 years ago and won her a sponsor who has put her through Vassar; *Prufrock and Other Observations* by émigré U.S. poet T. S. (Thomas Stearns) Eliot, 28, who expresses his disenchantment in modern life with "The Love Song of J. Alfred Prufrock"; *The Chinese Nightingale and Other Poems* by Vachel Lindsay; *Merlin* by Edwin Arlington Robinson; "La Jeune Parque" by French poet Paul Valéry, 45, who dedicates his first great poem to André Gide and follows it with "Aurore"; *Diary of a Newlywed Poet* (*Diario de un Poeta Recien Casado*) by Spanish poet Juan Ramon Jiminez, 36; English poet T. E. Hulme is killed in action after 3 years with the artillery in France.

"I Want You," says Uncle Sam in a recruitment poster painted by New York illustrator James Montgomery Flagg, 40, who has used his own face as a model for the stern-visaged Uncle Sam (see 1813; 1852). U.S. Army recruitment officers distribute some 4 million copies.

The term "surrealism" coined by French man of letters Guillaume Apollinaire (Wilhelm de Kostrowitzky), 37, denotes antiestablishment art (see Dada, 1916; Breton, 1924).

Dutch painter Piet Mondrian (Pieter Cornelis Mondriaan), 45, founds the art review *De Stihl* with Theo van Doesburg. Mondrian has evolved a purely abstract style using only horizontal and vertical lines, the three primary colors, and shades of black, white, and grey.

Painting *John D. Rockefeller* by John Singer Sargent; *Piano Lesson* by Henri Matisse; *Nude at the Fireplace* by Pierre Bonnard; *Crouching Female Nude* by Amedeo Modigliani; *Forward* by Marc Chagall; *Ladies in Crinoline* by Wassily Kandinsky. Albert Pinkham Ryder dies at Elmhurst, N.Y., March 28 at age 70; Edgar Degas dies at Paris September 27 at age 83; he has been blind since 1909.

Sculpture *Man with Mandolin* by Jacques Lipschitz; *Dancing Girls* (bronze) and *Cerberus* (granite) by Carl Milles. Auguste Rodin dies at Mendon November 17 at age 77.

Theater *The Old Lady Shows Her Medals* and *Seven Women* by James M. Barrie 4/7 at London's New Theatre; *Right You Are—If You Think You Are* [*Cosi e (se vi pare)*] by Luigi Pirandello 6/18 at Milan's Teatro Olimpio; *The Silken Ladder* (*La scala di seta*) by Luigi Chiarelli 6/28 at Rome's Teatro Argentina; *Dear Brutus* by James M. Barrie 10/17 at Wyndham's Theatre, London; *In the Zone* by Eugene O'Neill 10/31 at New York's Provincetown Play-

1917 (cont.) house (one-act play); *The Long Voyage Home* by Eugene O'Neill 11/2 at the Provincetown Playhouse (one-act play); *Why Marry?* by U.S. playwright Jesse Lynch Williams, 46, 12/25 at New York's Astor Theater, with Estelle Winwood (Pulitzer prize, 1918).

The Empire Theater at Montgomery, Ala., installs the first theater air-conditioning (*see* Carrier, 1911). Within 40 years every major U.S. theater will be air-conditioned.

Films D. W. Griffith's *Hearts of the World* with Lillian and Dorothy Gish has been financed by London to arouse U.S. sympathies against the Germans but the United States enters the war before the film is released; Clarence Badger's *Teddy at the Throttle* with Gloria Swanson, Wallace Beery; Charlie Chaplin's *The Cure;* Emilio Ghione's *The Gray Rats.*

Ballet *Les Femmes de Bonne Humeur* 4/12 at Rome's Teatro Constanza, with Leonide Massine, music by the 18th century composer Domenico Scarlatti, book by French playwright Jean Cocteau, 27, choreography by Massine; *Parade* 5/18 at the Théâtre du Châtelet, Paris, with music by Erik Satie, choreography by Leonide Massine, scenery by Pablo Picasso (the first cubist ballet).

First performances *Trois Poèmes Juifs* by Ernest Bloch 3/23 at Boston's Symphony Hall; *Israel* Symphony by Ernest Bloch 5/3 at New York's Carnegie Hall; *Schelomo (Solomon)* Hebrew Rhapsody for Violoncello and Orchestra by Ernest Bloch 5/13 at New York's Carnegie Hall.

Austrian pianist Paul Wittgenstein, 30, loses his right arm at the Russian front, thus apparently ending a promising career that was interrupted by the war. But in the postwar years Wittgenstein will commission and perform works for the left hand by composers such as Richard Strauss, Maurice Ravel, Sergei Prokofiev, Paul Hindemith, and Benjamin Britten.

Stage musicals *Have a Heart* 1/11 at New York's Liberty Theater, with Louise Dresser, Thurston Hall, book and lyrics by Guy Bolton and P. G. Wodehouse, music by Jerome Kern, 76 perfs.; *Love o'Mike* 1/15 at New York's Shubert Theater, with Peggy Wood, Clifton Webb, book by Thomas Sydney, music by Jerome Kern, lyrics by Harold B. Smith, 192 perfs.; *The Maid of the Mountain* 2/10 at Daly's Theatre, London, with music by Harold Fraser-Simson and James W. Tate, book by Frederick Lonsdale, lyrics by Harry Graham, F. Clifford Harris, (Arthur) Valentine, songs that include "Love Will Find a Way," 1,352 perfs.; *Oh, Boy!* 2/20 at New York's Princess Theater, with Marion Davies, Edna May Oliver, music by Jerome Kern, book and lyrics by Guy Bolton and P. G. Wodehouse, songs that include "Till the Clouds Roll By," 463 perfs.; *The Passing Show* 4/26 at New York's Winter Garden Theater, with De Wolf Hopper, music chiefly by Sigmund Romberg, lyrics chiefly by Harold Atteridge, songs that include "Goodbye Broadway, Hello France" by Billy Baskette, lyrics by C. Francis Reisner and Benny Davis,

196 perfs.; *The Ziegfeld Follies* 6/12 at New York's New Amsterdam Theater, with blackface comedian Eddie Cantor (né Isidore Itzkowitz), 25, W. C. Fields, Will Rogers, Fanny Brice, music by Raymond Hubbell and Dave Stamper with a patriotic finale by Victor Herbert, 111 perfs.; *Maytime* 8/17 at New York's Shubert Theater, with Peggy Wood, Charles Purcell, music by Sigmund Romberg, book and lyrics by Rida Johnson Young, songs that include "Will You Remember (Sweetheart)," 492 perfs.; *Leave It to Jane* 9/28 at New York's Longacre Theater, with music by Jerome Kern, book and lyrics by Guy Bolton based on George Ade's play *The College Widow* of 1904, 167 perfs.; *Over the Top* (revue) 11/28 at New York's 44th Street Roof Theater, with comedian Joe Laurie, dancer Fred Astaire (né Austerlitz), 18, and his sister Adele, music by Sigmund Romberg and others, 78 perfs.; *Going Up* 12/25 at New York's Liberty Theater, with Frank Craven, Donald Meek, music by Louis A. Hirsch, book and lyrics by Otto Harbach based on the 1910 play *The Aviator,* 351 perfs.

Popular songs "Over There" by George M. Cohan, who writes the song for the American Expeditionary Force embarking for the war in Europe; "You're in the Army Now" by Isham Jones, lyrics by Tell Taylor and Ole Olssen; "Hail, Hail the Gang's All Here" by U.S. composer Theodore Morse who has adapted a melody by the late Arthur S. Sullivan from Act II of the 1879 Gilbert & Sullivan opera *The Pirates of Penzance,* lyrics by D. A. Esrom (Morse); "Smiles" by Lee S. Roberts, lyrics by O. Will Callahan; "For Me and My Gal" by George W. Meyer, 33, lyrics by Edgar Leslie, 32, and E. Ray Goetz, 31; "They Go Wild, Simply Wild, Over Me" by Fred Fisher, lyrics by Joe McCarthy; "Oh Johnny, Oh Johnny, Oh" by Abe Olman, 29, lyrics by Edward Rose, 42; "The Bells of St. Mary's" by Australian-born London composer A. Emmet Adams, 27, lyrics by actor-playwright Douglas Furber, 31.

"The Darktown Strutters' Ball" by Shelton Brooks is recorded as the first jazz record; "Tiger Rag" is published as a one-step with music by D. J. LaRocca of the Original Dixieland Jazz Band.

Jazz pioneer Joseph "King" Oliver, 32, moves to Chicago following the shutdown of New Orleans red-light district sporting houses by military authorities. A cornetist in Kid Ory's band, Oliver is replaced by his student Louis Daniel Armstrong, 17, who in 1922 will join Oliver's Creole Jazz Band in Chicago and in 1924 will join Fletcher Henderson's orchestra in New York.

Composer Victor Herbert is upheld by the Supreme Court in a suit against Shanley's Cafe in New York for using his songs without permission. The decision by Justice Holmes supports ASCAP, which Herbert helped start 3 years ago and which issues licenses to hotels, restaurants, dance halls, cabarets, motion picture theaters, and other establishments to play music controlled by ASCAP members.

The Chicago White Sox win the World Series by defeating the New York Giants 4 games to 2.

The National Hockey League (NHL) is organized November 22 at Montreal with teams from Montreal (the Canadians and the Wanderers), Quebec, Ottawa, and Toronto. The first U.S. team to join will be the Boston Bruins in 1924, followed by the Pittsburgh Pirates in 1925 and the New York Rangers, Chicago Black Hawks, and Detroit Cougars (later Redwings) in 1926, but the U.S. teams will be comprised almost entirely of Canadian-born players.

The first NHL hockey team to use artificial ice is the Toronto Arenas, whose name will be changed to the St Patricks in 1919 and to the Maple Leafs in 1926. Hockey has been played until now only on natural ice, and games have been canceled when warm spells prevented play.

 U.S. cigarette production reaches 35.3 billion, up from below 18 million in 1915. Camel cigarettes have 30 to 40 percent of the U.S. market 4 years after their introduction.

General Pershing cables Washington, "Tobacco is as indispensable as the daily ration; we must have thousands of tons of it without delay," but Nikolai Lenin (above) finds smoking intolerable and forbids smoking on the train that takes him to Petrograd.

 Paris jeweler Pierre Cartier, who opened the first New York Cartier salon in 1908 on a Fifth Avenue mezzanine, gives financier Morton F. Plant a two-strand Oriental pearl necklace in exchange for Plant's Renaissance-style mansion at Fifth Avenue and 52nd Street. The building will remain New York Cartier headquarters for more than 60 years (*see* 1902). Pierre's brother Louis, now 42, designed the first wristwatch 10 years ago for French aviator Santos Dumont, and he will introduce the Tank watch next year as a tribute to the men of the American Tank Corps.

 New York's American Telephone and Telegraph building is completed by architect Welles Bosworth at 195 Broadway with eight Ionic colonnades on a Doric order—more columns than any other building in the world.

Invaders of the czar's Winter Palace at Petrograd (above) find themselves in a building of 1,050 rooms with 117 staircases, 1,786 windows, and a 290-square foot map of Russia in emeralds, rubies, and semiprecious stones. The soldiers and sailors are awed by the opulence and leave the palace unmolested.

 A new Catskill water system aqueduct opens to provide New York City with 250 million gallons daily of the purest, best-tasting water of any major American metropolis (*see* 1892).

Alaska's Mount McKinley National Park is established by act of Congress. The park embraces nearly 2 million acres which include large glaciers, spectacular wildlife (caribou, Dall sheep, grizzly bears,

moose, wolves), and the highest mountain (20,300 feet) in North America. Called Denali (the Great One) by local Indians, the mountain was given its name in 1896 by William A. Dickey, then just out of Princeton and prospecting for gold on the Sustina River after hearing of William McKinley's nomination for the presidency.

Halifax, Nova Scotia, is destroyed December 6 by an explosion that levels two square miles, kills 1,654, and blinds, maims, or disfigures 1,028. The Norwegian relief ship *Imo* loaded with supplies for war-torn Europe has plowed into the French munitions ship *Mont Blanc* loaded with 4,000 tons of TNT, 2,300 tons of picric acid, 61 tons of other explosives, and a deck cargo of highly flammable benzene which has been ignited and has touched off the explosives. A tidal wave created by the explosion washes the city's remains out to sea.

 Britain's House of Commons is stunned by news that 2 million tons of shipping have been lost to German U-boats and that the country has only 3 to 4 weeks' supply of food in stock (above).

Britain's war bread beginning in February is made from flour milled at an extraction rate of up to 81 percent with a compulsory admixture of 5 percent barley, oat, or rye flour to stretch available supplies.

Food Controller Lord Devenport asks heads of families to limit their family bread consumption to 4 pounds per person each week, meat consumption to 2.5 pounds, sugar to three-quarters of a pound.

British retail food prices rise to 94 percent above July 1914 levels by the end of March. A 4-pound loaf of bread fetches a shilling and a Royal Commission reports that rising prices and faulty food distribution are creating industrial unrest.

200,000 Berlin factory workers strike for a week in April to protest a reduction in bread rations.

Well-to-do Britons miss sugar, butter, and white bread, but price increases after July are at only one-fourth the rate earlier and the subsidization of bread by the government keeps food relatively cheap as compared with other commodities. Mostly because the war has ended unemployment, British working class diets actually improve.

 U.S. mining engineer Herbert C. Hoover, 43, is named Food Administrator having served as chairman of the Commission for Relief in Belgium. Hoover encourages U.S. farmers with the slogan "Food Can Win the War."

The U.S. Food Administration's Grain Corporation buys, stores, transports, and sells wheat and fixes its price at $2.20 per bushel under terms of the Lever Act passed August 10 to establish government control over food and fuel.

Drought begins on the Western plains.

The American Dietetic Association is founded at Cleveland.

Russia's Bolshevik revolution replaced czarist tyranny with a tyrannical "dictatorship of the proletariat."

British military conscription finds that only three out of nine Britons of military age are fit and healthy. Poor nutrition is blamed.

Britain's Medical Council reports that at least half the children in industrial towns have rickets (*see* 1902).

Xerophthalmia is observed in Danish children whose diets are lacking in butterfats. Denmark has been exporting her butter to the warring powers even at the expense of her domestic needs, and dietary deficiency is endangering the children's eyesight (*see* Japan, 1904; McCollum, 1912).

U.S. bacteriologist Alice Evans, 36, begins work that will show the ability of the bacterium which causes contagious abortion (Bang's disease) in cattle to be passed to human beings, notably via raw milk, and to produce undulant fever or brucellosis (*see* Bruce, 1887; Bang, 1896). The dairy industry and the medical profession will oppose Evans, but the compulsory pasteurization of U.S. milk in the late 1920s will be achieved largely through her efforts in the next 9 years (*see* dairy practices, 1921).

Clarence Birdseye returns to his native New York to pursue the commercial exploitation of his food-freezing discoveries (*see* 1914). Birdseye has spent 3 years in Labrador and he has learned to freeze cabbages in barrels of seawater (*see* 1923).

The first national advertising for Del Monte brand canned fruits and vegetables appears April 21 in the *Saturday Evening Post* (*see* California Packing Corporation, 1916). Calpak acquires the Hawaiian Preserving Company which owns pineapple fields and a cannery on Oahu, it will acquire canneries in the next decade in Wisconsin, Minnesota, Illinois, and Florida, it will start growing and packing pineapples in the Philippines, and it will enter the canned sar-

dine and tuna industries (*see* Del Monte properties, 1919; Del Monte Corporation, 1967).

Acme Markets is incorporated. The company will be a major U.S. retail food chain.

Nathan Handwerker counters rumors spread by his Coney Island rivals who say that 5-cent hot dogs cannot be of the best quality (*see* 1916). Handwerker hires college students to stand round his counters wearing white jackets with stethoscopes hanging out of their pockets and word spreads that doctors from Coney Island Hospital are eating Nathan's hot dogs.

A law requiring that U.S. immigrants pass a literacy test in any language is enacted January 29 over a second veto by President Wilson. Inspired by the Immigration Restriction League founded in 1894, the law has been passed by previous Congresses but has been vetoed, it becomes law February 5, and it excludes immigrants from most of Asia and the Pacific Islands, but refugees from religious persecution are exempted from having to take the tests to relieve the distress of Russian Jews (*see* 1921).

The U.S. population passes the 100 million mark after three centuries of growth.

1918 The worst pandemic to afflict mankind since the Black Death of the mid-14th century sweeps through Europe, America, and the Orient killing 21.64 million—more than 1 percent of the world's population—while the European War ends after having killed some 10 million (*see* below). The "Spanish" influenza (which actually began in China) affects 80 percent of the people in Spain, the first U.S. cases appear August 27 at Boston where two sailors report to sick bay at Commonwealth Pier, by August 31 the Navy Receiving Ship has 106 flu cases, by mid-September the flu has spread all over the East Coast, nearly 25 percent of Americans fall ill, some 500,000 die including 19,000 at New York, schools are closed, parades and Liberty Loan rallies are banned, hospitals are jammed, coffin supplies are exhausted at Baltimore and Washington.

The Fourteen Points for a just and generous peace outlined by President Wilson January 8 in a message to Congress are intended to counter the Russian Bolsheviks, who have released secret agreements revealing Allied plans to carve up the German Empire. Wilson calls for "open covenants openly arrived at" and for self-determination of government by Europe's peoples, he asks for the creation of a League of Nations to preserve the peace, but he has failed to obtain advance Allied agreement to his proposals.

Russia's new Bolshevik government withdraws from the "capitalist-imperialist" war March 3 by signing the Treaty of Brest-Litovsk with Germany. Russia abandons all claims to Poland, Lithuania, the Ukraine, the Baltic provinces, and Finland.

Finnish soldier-statesman Baron Carl Gustaf Emil von Mannerheim, 51, recaptures Helsinki from the

Bolsheviks who had seized it. Mannerheim will obtain Russian recognition of Finland's sovereignty in 1919 and will head an independent republic (*see* 1939).

German and Austrian expeditionary forces are sent to clear the Bolsheviks out of the Ukraine, and 7,000 U.S. troops are sent to occupy the Russian Pacific port of Vladivostok.

German forces have launched a major offensive on the Western Front from March 21 to April 5 and have gained ground against French and British armies depleted of able fighting men and almost devoid of reserves, but the tide of war has turned with the entry of U.S. troops.

The Lafayette Escadrille of 1916 becomes the U.S. Pursuit Squadron February 18. The 94th Pursuit Squadron founded in March under the command of French-American pilot Raoul Lufbury, 32, includes U.S. pilot Eddie (Edward Vernon) Rickenbacker, 27.

German air ace Baron Manfred von Richthofen, 26, leads the "Flying Circus" that downs dozens of Allied aircraft but is shot down himself April 21. The Red Baron is credited with 80 kills and the Allies bury him with full military honors.

Raoul Lufbury (above) is killed in action May 7 and French pilot René Fonck, 24, of "Les Cigones" Groupe de Combat No. 12 shoots down 6 German fighter planes in 45 seconds May 9. Fonck repeats the feat September 26 and by war's end has shot down 127 enemy planes.

The U.S. Second and Third Divisions stop a German offensive in early June with support from some disorganized French units. U.S. Marines capture Belleau Wood north of Château-Thierry June 6 and hold Belleau Wood through 19 days of repeated German attempts to dislodge them.

Eddie Rickenbacker engages 7 German planes in a dogfight September 25, he will win the Congressional Medal of Honor for his performance in the encounter, and by war's end his combined balloon and aircraft kills will total 26.

U.S. ace Frank Luke, 22, takes off in his Spad September 29 in defiance of his commanding officer who has grounded him. Luke has shot down 16 enemy planes, 10 German Fokkers have gone up expressly to seek him out, he downs two of the Fokkers before an antiaircraft shell fragment hits him in the shoulder, he goes down behind enemy lines, he empties his pistol at approaching soldiers, and they shoot back, mortally wounding Luke 16 days after he first went into combat.

Russia's royal Romanov family is shot to death July 16 at Yekaterinburg by order of the Bolsheviks 4 days after others of the Russian nobility have been assassinated elsewhere. Nicholas II, the czarina Aleksandra, their daughters Olga, Tatiana, Marie, and Anastasia, their son Alexis, Prince Dolgorolkoff, their physician, a nurse, and a lady in waiting are all put to death July 16 or within a few weeks of that date, but rumors will persist that one or more of the daughters has somehow been spared.

Bulgaria's Ferdinand I abdicates October 4 at age 57 after a 32-year reign following defeat of Bulgarian forces in September at Dobropole in Macedonia. Ferdinand leaves Sofia and is succeeded by his 22-year-old son who will reign until 1943 as Boris I.

The British attack with 450 tanks at the Battle of Amiens in August and the Germans are forced to fall back to the Hindenburg line after British and French offensives in September.

General Pershing makes his first major offensive in mid-September at Saint-Mihiel and forces the Germans to give up salients they have held since 1914. The Americans take 15,000 prisoners and the Allies push north and east in the battles of the Argonnes and Ypres from late September to mid-October.

Mutiny breaks out in the German fleet at Kiel October 28 and spreads quickly to Hamburg, Bremen, Lübeck, and all of northwestern Germany. Revolution breaks out November 7 at Munich.

Germany's Wilhelm II abdicates November 8 and hostilities on the western front end November 11 in an armistice signed by Germany and Allies.

The Great War has killed 1.8 million Germans, 1.7 million Russians, 1.4 million French, 1.2 million Austrians and Hungarians, between 750,000 and 950,000 British, 460,000 Italians, 325,000 Turks, and 115,000 Americans. Some 20 million have been blinded, maimed, mutilated, crippled, permanently shell-shocked, or otherwise disabled.

A Congress of Oppressed Nationalities, most of them ruled by the Hapsburgs, has been held at Rome in April, and Italy has recognized the unity and independence of the new Yugoslav nation organized in 1917. The Kingdom of the Serbs, Croats, and Slovenes is proclaimed December 4 under the regency of Serbia's 30-year-old Prince Aleksandr Karageorgević who will become Yugoslavia's Aleksandr I in 1921.

The Czechoslovak National Council at Paris has organized a provisional government October 14 with Thomas Garrigue Masaryk, 68, as president and with Eduard Beneš, 34, as foreign minister. The council has issued a declaration of independence October 28.

Hungary has had a revolution that ended the Hapsburg monarchy October 31, and a republic is proclaimed November 16.

The Austrian emperor Karl I who ascended the throne in 1916 at the death of Franz Josef is forced to renounce participation in the government of Austria November 11 and of Hungary November 13.

A Polish republic has been proclaimed November 3 at Warsaw. Poland quickly comes under the control of General Josef Pilsudski who was imprisoned by the Germans in 1916 when his troops refused to join the

1918 (cont.) Central Powers against the Allies but who has been released after the collapse of the Central Powers.

Hailed as a U.S. war hero is Tennessee doughboy Alvin Cullum York, 30, whose petition for exemption as a conscientious objector was denied by his draft board. In the battle of the Argonne Forest October 8, Private York of the 82nd Infantry Division led an attack on a German machine gun nest that killed 25 of the enemy and he then almost singlehandedly captured 132 prisoners and 35 machine guns. Promoted to sergeant November 1, York will be awarded the Congressional Medal of Honor and the French Croix de Guerre.

The Owen-Keating Child Labor Law of 1916 is called an unconstitutional encroachment on states' rights by the Supreme Court June 3 in the case of *Hammer v. Dagenhart*. Justice Holmes dissents (*see* Fair Labor Standards Act, 1938).

The Amalgamated Clothing Workers Union begins striking against open shops, sweat shops, and piece work pay (*see* 1914). The union will stage at least 534 strikes in the next 6 years and will claim victory in 333 (*see* 1937).

IWW leaders are found guilty of conspiring against the prosecution of the war. Heavy fines and prison sentences handed down to some 100 leaders by Judge Kenesaw Mountain Landis at Chicago will be sustained by the U.S. Circuit Court of Appeals.

British women over age 30 gain the right to vote under terms of the Fourth Franchise Bill which also grants suffrage to all men over age 21. Emmeline Pankhurst has favorably influenced masculine opinion by persuading women to do war work and has helped obtain passage of the bill (*see* 1913; 1928).

A resolution providing for a U.S. Woman Suffrage Amendment passes the House of Representatives in January, but the Senate rejects the resolution for the third time October 1 (*see* 1919).

U.S. Fuel Administrator Harry A. Garfield orders all plants east of the Mississippi to shut down January 16 if they are not producing essential war materials. Purpose of the order is to conserve coal needed for troop transports, warships, and merchant vessels, the order remains in effect for 5 days, and it is followed by nine Monday closings.

Broadway theaters close February 12 to conserve energy.

The Fuel Administration orders four lightless nights per week beginning July 24 to conserve fuel for the coming winter. The order remains in effect until November 22.

A head-on collision between two trains on the Nashville, Chattanooga, and St. Louis Railway in Tennessee June 22 kills 99 and injures 171 in an all-time high for U.S. railroad mismanagement.

New York's worst subway accident kills 97 and injures 100 November 2 as a train jumps the track at 30 miles per hour approaching the new Prospect Park station of the Brooklyn Rapid Transit Service. The train is manned by supervisors in the absence of striking motormen who belong to the Brotherhood of Locomotive Engineers, it is traveling at five times the speed limit, many of its cars are wooden, and it is wrecked at the Malbone Street Tunnel of the Brighton Beach line that runs along Fulton Street and Franklin Avenue to Coney Island.

The General Motors Corporation acquires a controlling interest in Detroit's Fisher Body Company which will become a GM division (*see* 1916).

Some 46 percent of fracture cases in the U.S. Army result in permanent disability, chiefly by amputation, and 12 percent of fracture cases are fatal (*see* 1937).

Typhus takes a heavy toll in Galicia, the Ukraine, and the Black Sea region (*see* 1917). The International Red Cross helps fight the disease.

The alkaloid drug ergotamine is extracted from the ergot fungus *Claviceps purpura* (*see* 857). Useful in small doses as a muscle and blood vessel contractant, the drug will be used to treat migraine attacks and to induce abortion (*see* ergonovine, 1935).

Emergency tent hospitals go up throughout America as the Spanish influenza epidemic (above) taxes regular hospital facilities. Trolley conductors, store clerks, and others wear masks to avoid contracting the flu.

Inflation begins in Germany. The mark will decline in value by 99 percent in terms of gold over the course of the next few years (*see* 1922).

British income taxes rise to 30 percent, up from 15 percent in 1915, as the national debt climbs to an unprecedented £8 billion (which the British express as £8 thousand million).

Celanese Corporation of America is founded at Cumberland, Md., by Swiss-American chemist Camille Edward Dreyfus, 40, who worked with his brother Henri beginning in 1910 to produce cellulose acetate lacquers and plastic film to replace flammable cellulose nitrate photographic film and came up with good-quality acetate film yarns in 1913 after 20,000 experiments. Reacting purified wood pulp or cotton linters with acetic anhydrase, the Dreyfus brothers form a primary solution that is hydrolized into a white flocculent mass, washed clean of acid, and formed into a flake that can be dissolved in acetone to produce a spinning solution. Volume production at Cumberland will be delayed by a flood until 1924, but Dreyfus will commission silk mills to weave fabrics of "artificial silk" to Celanese specifications, the $2.90 per pound that Celanese will charge for its 150-denier yarn will be reduced to $1.42 by 1930, to 60 cents by 1935, and to 54 cents by 1939 as the company finds ways to cut costs, and Celanese Corporation will become the largest producer of acetate rayon and a major producer of viscose rayon and other synthetic fibers.

The first U.S. airmail stamps are issued as regular service begins between Washington, D.C., and New York (the 24-cent stamps show a biplane in flight, but some of the stamps are accidentally printed with the plane inverted and the faulty stamps become rare collectors' items).

The first official U.S. mail flight never makes it to New York. The pilot discovers on his first takeoff attempt that someone has forgotten to fill the fuel tank, and after he does take off he becomes lost over Maryland and has to land in a cow pasture (*see* 1921).

Henry Ford's Stout Air Line has been the first airline to carry mail but has been hampered by Ford's refusal to open his Detroit airport on Sundays.

David Low joins the *London Star* at age 27 to pursue a career as political cartoonist. The New Zealand-born Australian will transfer to the *Evening Standard* in 1927 and will become famous for his Colonel Blimp satirization of the British ruling class.

The *Boston Post* reaches a circulation of 540,000 and claims the widest readership in America. The *Post* sells for 1 cent while the *Globe* and the *Herald* have joined most other U.S. dailies in going to 2 cents.

"Believe It or Not!" is published for the first time by *New York Globe* sports cartoonist Robert LeRoy Ripley, 24, who sketches figures of men who have set records for such unlikely events as running backward and broad jumping on ice. Encouraged by reader response to pursue his quest for oddities, Ripley will move to the *New York Post* in 1923, syndication of his cartoons will begin soon after, and "Believe It or Not!" will eventually be carried by 326 newspapers in 38 countries.

Nonfiction *Eminent Victorians* by English writer (Giles) Lytton Strachey, 58, introduces a new genre of biography by injecting imagined conversations and taking other liberties while debunking the Victorian eminences of Florence Nightingale and such.

Fiction *The Four Horsemen of the Apocalypse* by Spanish novelist Vicente Blanco-Ibanez, 51, breaks all world records for book sales; *Man of Straw (Der Untertan)* by Heinrich Mann; *Tarr* by English novelist (Percy) Wyndham Lewis, 33, who is also an avante-gard poet and painter; *My Antonia* by Willa Cather; *The Magnificent Ambersons* by Booth Tarkington.

Poetry *Poems* by the late English poet Gerard Manley Hopkins who died in 1889 at age 45. His rich rhythmic system will inspire a new generation of poets; *The Dark Messengers (Los Heraldos Negros)* by Peruvian poet César Vallejo, 26; *Cornhuskers* by Carl Sandburg whose poem "Prairie" says, "I speak of new cities and new people./ I tell you the past is a bucket of ashes . . ." Sandburg's poem "Grass" says, "Pile the bodies high at Austerlitz and Waterloo./ Shovel them under and let me work—/ I am the grass; I cover all;" English poet-playwright-painter Isaac Rosenberg is killed in action April 7 at age 27;

poet Wilfred Owen is awarded the Military Cross for gallantry and is killed in action November 4 at age 25; France's Guillaume Apollinaire dies November 9 of influenza and of a head wound received in March of 1916. Dead at age 38, Apollinaire leaves behind erotic poems relating battle action and sexual desire: "Two shell-bursts/ A pink explosion/ Like two bared breasts/ Snooking their tips/ HE KNEW LOVE/ What an epitaph."

Painting *Gartenplan* by Paul Klee; *Engine Rooms* by Fernand Léger; *Act* and *Portrait of Mme. Zboroski* by Amedeo Modigliani; *Scottish Girl* by Juan Gris; *Friends* and *Saxonian Landscape* by Oskar Kokoschka; *Bathing Man* by Edvard Munch; *Odalisques* by Henri Matisse; *Portrait of Igor Stravinsky* by Robert Delaunay; *Still Life: Dead Game* by André Derain; *Still Life with Coffee* by Spanish painter Joan Miró, 25; *Landscape of Piquey* by Diego Rivera; *The Night Wind* by Charles Burchfield.

Sculpture *Seated Youth* by Wilhelm Lehmbruck who will die by his own hand at age 38 in late March of next year at Berlin; *Sunglitter* by Carl Milles.

Theater *Deburau* by French playwright-actor Sacha Guitry, 32, 2/9 at Paris, with Guitry himself (matinees only since Paris is under bombardment by German cannon); *Sea Battle (Seeschlacht)* by German physician-playwright Richard Goering, 30, 3/3 at Berlin's Deutsches Theater; *Lightnin'* by Winchell Smith and Frank Bacon 8/26 at New York's Gaiety Theater, with Bacon as Lightnin' Bill Jones, 1,291 perfs.; *Mystery Bouffe (Misteriya Buff)* by Vladimir Mayakofsky 11/7 at Petrograd's Malevich Communal Theater; *The Moon of the Caribees* by Eugene O'Neill 12/20 at New York's Playwrights Theater.

The first Pulitzer prize for drama is awarded to Jesse Lynch Williams for his 1917 comedy *Why Marry?* which continues at New York's Astor Theater.

Warner Brothers Pictures is incorporated in California by Polish-American cinematists Harry Warner, 36, and Albert, 34, with their Canadian-born brother Jack, 26, and a fourth brother Sam. The older brothers grossed a handsome return last year by filming Ambassador James W. Gerard's book *My Four Years in Germany* which they produced at New York's Vitagraph studios, but they will have little success in Hollywood until 1926.

Louis B. Mayer Pictures Corporation is organized at Los Angeles by Russian-American movie theater operator Louis Burt Mayer, 33, who in 1915 bought New England rights to D. W. Griffith's *Birth of a Nation* for an unprecedented $25,000 and who has decided to make films himself (*see* M-G-M, 1924).

Films Alan Dwan's *A Modern Musketeer* with Douglas Fairbanks; Marshall Neilan's *Amarilly of Clothesline Alley* with Mary Pickford, Norman Kerry; Marshall Neilan's *Stella Maris* with Mary Pickford; Charlie Chaplin's *Shoulder Arms* and *A Dog's Life*; J. Gordon Edwards's *Salome* with Theda Bara; J. G. Edwards's *When a Woman Sins* with

1918 (cont.) Theda Bara; F. Richard Jones's *Mickey* with Mabel Normand, George Nichols; Walter Edwards's *A Pair of Silk Stockings* with Constance Talmadge; Abel Gance's *The Tenth Symphony*.

Opera *Where the Lark Sings* (*Wo die Lerche singt*) 2/1 at Budapest's Königstheater, with music by Franz Lehar; *Duke Bluebeard's Castle* (*A Kekszakallu Herceg Vara*) 5/24 at Budapest, with music by Béla Bartók; *Il Trittico* 12/14 at New York's Metropolitan Opera House, with music by Giacomo Puccini who has written a trio of short operas—*Il Tabarro*, *Suor Angelica*, and *Gianni Schicchi*.

First performances Classical Symphony by Serge Prokofiev 4/21 at Petrograd; *The Legend of the World at Play* (*Le Dit des Jeux du Monde*) by Swiss composer Arthur Honegger, 26, 12/2 at Paris.

The Cleveland Orchestra that will grow to rival the New York Philharmonic, the Boston Symphony, and the Philadelphia Orchestra is founded by a group headed by Adella Prentiss Hughes, a sister-in-law of the English author Rupert Hughes. The founders engage Russian-American conductor Nikolai Sokoloff, 32, to lead the new orchestra (*see* 1931).

Broadway musicals *Oh, Lady! Lady!* 2/1 at the Princess Theater, with music by Jerome Kern, book and lyrics by Guy Bolton and P. G. Wodehouse, 219 perfs.; *Sinbad* 2/14 at the Winter Garden Theater, with Al Jolson, book by Harold Atteridge, music by Sigmund Romberg and others, songs that include "My Mammy" by U.S. composer Walter Donaldson, 25, lyrics by Joe Young, 20, and Sam M. Lewis, 33, "Rock-a-by Your Baby with a Dixie Melody" by Jean Schwartz, lyrics by Joe Young and Sam M. Lewis, 164 perfs.; *Oh, Look!* 3/7 at the Vanderbilt Theater, with songs that include "I'm Always Chasing Rainbows" by Harry Caroll, who has adapted Chopin's Fantaisie Impromptu in C sharp minor, lyrics by Joseph McCarthy, 68 perfs.; *The Passing Show* 7/25 at the Winter Garden Theater, with Marilyn Miller, Fred and Adele Astaire, Eugene and Willie Howard, Charles Ruggles, Frank Fay, music chiefly by Sigmund Romberg and Jean Schwartz, lyrics chiefly by Harold Atteridge, songs that include "Smiles" by J. Will Callahan and Lee G. Robert, and with June Caprice singing "I'm Forever Blowing Bubbles" by John William Kellette, lyrics by Jean Kenbrovin (James Kendis, James Brockman, Nat Vincent), 124 perfs.; *The Ziegfeld Follies* 6/18 at the New Amsterdam Theater with Eddie Cantor, Will Rogers, Marilyn Miller, W. C. Fields, music by Louis A. Hirsch, 151 perfs.; *Yip Yip Yaphank* 8/19 at the Century Theater with a cast of 350 recruits from Camp Upton at Yaphank, Long Island, music and lyrics by Irving Berlin, songs that include "Oh, How I Hate to Get Up in the Morning," "Mandy," "Soldier Boy," 32 perfs.; *Sometime* 10/4 at the Shubert Theater, with vaudeville trooper Mae West, 26, singing songs that include "Any Kind of Man" by Bohemian-American composer-songwriter Rudolf Friml, 38, 283 perfs.

Popular songs "Till We Meet Again" by Richard A. Whiting, 27, and Canadian-American Richard B. Egan; "K-K-K-Katy" by Canadian-American songwriter Geoffrey O'Hara, 36; "After You're Gone" by Henry Creamer, 39, lyrics by Turner Layton, 24; "Somebody Stole My Gal" by Leo Wood; "Beautiful Ohio" by Robert A. King, lyrics by Ballard MacDonald.

The Original Dixieland Jazz Band tours Europe at year's end and spreads appreciation for the American musical idiom.

Exterminator wins the Kentucky Derby after starting as a late entry 30 to 1 longshot. The chestnut gelding goes on to win a record 34 stakes races.

The Boston Red Sox win the World Series by defeating the Chicago Cubs 4 games to 2.

The Raggedy Ann Doll introduced by a New York firm is based on a doll produced last year to promote sales of the first book of Raggedy Ann stories. *Indianapolis Star* political cartoonist John Gruelle, 37, found the handmade rag doll in his attic last year and gave it to his tubercular daughter Marcella, they named it Raggedy Ann through a combination of neighbor James Whitcomb Riley's "Little Orphant Annie" of 1885 and Riley's poem "The Raggedy Man," the doll inspired Gruelle to make up stories which he told to entertain Marcella, she died holding the doll in March of 1916 after being vaccinated by a contaminated needle, Gruelle's book will have 25 sequels, and the Raggedy Ann doll will grow to become a $20 million per year business.

Rinso is introduced by Lever Brothers. It is the world's first granulated laundry soap (*see* Lux Flakes, 1906; Lux Toilet Form, 1925).

Kotex is introduced under the name "Celucotton" by Kimberly & Clark Company of Neenah, Wis., whose German-American chemist Ernst Mahler, 31, has developed a wood-cellulose substitute for cotton to fill the desperate need for dressings and bandages in European field hospitals (*see* 1872). When word reaches Wisconsin that Red Cross nurses are using Celucotton for sanitary napkins, the company begins development of the first commercial sanitary napkin which will be introduced under the name Kotex in 1921 (*see* Kleenex, 1924; Tampax, 1936).

Camel cigarettes are the favorite smoke among U.S. forces in France and enjoy a 40 percent share of the U.S. market as R. J. Reynolds dies at age 68. Camel sales are trailed by American Tobacco's Lucky Strike and by Liggett & Myers's Chesterfield.

The International Church of the Four-Square Gospel is founded at Los Angeles by Canadian-American evangelist Aimee Semple McPherson, 28, a divorcée who has arrived penniless but who offers hope and salvation to Southern and Midwestern migrants who have moved to Southern California. McPherson will build a large following that will provide funds to build the huge Angelus Temple from which her ser mons will be broadcast over a radio station she will purchase with funds contributed by the faithful. The sermons will be preceded by patriotic-religious music played by a 50-piece band, and the McPherson movement, based largely on faith healing, adult baptism, and Fundamentalist spectacle, will attract a wide following (see 1923).

 The Staatliches Bauhaus founded at Weimar by German Architect Walter Gropius of 1911 "curtain wall" fame combines two art schools in a revolutionary center that interrelates art, science, technology, and humanism. The Bauhaus will move to a new Gropius-designed building at Dessau in 1925 but will be closed in 1933 (see 1937).

New York's St. Vincent Ferrer Church at Lexington Avenue and 68th Street is completed by Bertram Goodhue of Cram, Goodhue & Ferguson.

New York's Racket and Tennis Club on Park Avenue between 52nd and 53rd Streets is completed by McKim, Mead and White in Florentine palazzo style.

Washington's Wardman Park Hotel opens on Woodley Road NW for hotelman Harry Wardman.

The Broadmoor Hotel opens at Colorado Springs.

 The Dutch States-General appropriates money to drain the Zuider Zee for the creation of fertile dry land. The Dutch will build dams, dykes, sluiceways, watergates, canals, and locks to "impolder" more than 800,000 acres that will increase the territory of the Netherlands by 7 percent.

British food rationing begins with sugar January 1 and is extended in February to include meat, butter, and margarine. By summer it includes all important foodstuffs except bread and potatoes. Fresh meat is rationed by price and consumers are required to buy from a particular butcher to avoid deception. Ration books are issued in July and the bacon ration is raised from 8 ounces per week to 16 ounces. Other rationed commodities include 8 ounces of sugar, 5 ounces of butter and/or margarine, 4 ounces of jam, 2 ounces of tea (weekly).

Potatoes are rarely available in British markets and the milling extraction rate is raised to 92 percent, up from 81 percent last year, with soy and potato flour mixed in to stretch Britain's short wheat supplies. The bread is dark and unattractive.

France rations bread and restricts consumption of butter, cream, and soft cheese. Manufacture and sale of all confectionery is banned.

U.S. sugar rationing begins July 1 with each citizen allowed 8 ounces per week. U.S. Food Administrator Herbert Hoover asks for voluntary observance of wheatless Mondays and Wednesdays, meatless Tuesdays, porkless Thursdays and Saturdays, and the use of dark "Victory bread."

All food regulations are suspended in the United States in late December but remain in effect in Britain and Europe.

 Prime Minister David Lloyd George asks British women to help bring in the harvest.

A "summer time" daylight saving law is enacted by Congress, which follows the example of Britain and Europe. The new law angers U.S. farmers as it has angered the British (see 1916) and Congress will repeal the law next year, overriding President Wilson's veto.

More horses and mules are on U.S. farms than ever before, and enormous acreages are planted to oats for the animals, whose numbers will now decline.

International Harvester's share of the U.S. harvesting machine industry falls to 65 percent, down from 85 percent in 1902. A dissolution decree obtained by the Department of Justice from a District Court is dismissed by the Supreme Court (see 1912; 1927).

U.S. Corn Belt acreage sells for two and three times 1915 prices.

 Cod-liver oil is shown to contain an agent that cures rickets. English researcher Edward Mellanby gives recognition to a treatment used by North Sea mothers for generations (see McCollum, 1921).

Yale biochemists Lafayette Benedict Mendel and B. Cohen show that guinea pigs cannot develop vitamin C (ascorbic acid) and fall prey to scurvy even more easily than do humans (see Drummond, 1920; Szent-Györgyi, 1928).

 The North American lobster catch falls to a low point of 33 million pounds, down from its all-time high of 130 million pounds in 1885.

 The U.S. Food Administration orders severe limitations on use of sugar in less essential food products, including soft drinks. As shortages of sugar continue, the Administration prepares to declare the entire soft drink industry nonessential and to order the industry closed down for the duration, but the threat fails to materialize and sugar prices begin to soar (see 1920; American Sugar Refining, 1919).

Chero-Cola has sales of close to $1.5 million and establishes its own sugar refinery to maintain its supply (see 1914; 1920).

Hershey Chocolate Company is donated to the Milton Hershey School for orphan boys established by Hershey in 1909. The school will retain 100 percent ownership until 1927, when some stock will be sold to the public in order to raise funds.

Nestlé sales have been multiplied like Hershey's by wartime demand (see 1905). Nestlé has 100 milk condenseries in the United States plus scores in other countries.

The Kelvinator refrigerator is introduced (see Nash-Kelvinator, 1935).

Americans call sauerkraut "liberty cabbage" and German toast becomes "French toast."

1918 (cont.) The first automatic pop-up toaster is patented by U.S. inventor Charles Strite.

Italian-American pasta maker Emanuele Ronzoni, 48, acquires American-made macaroni machinery and incorporates under his own name. Production manager for the past 12 years of a Brooklyn, N.Y., macaroni factory, Ronzoni has seen the growing demand for American-made pasta products, he will be helped first by his two daughters and then by his three sons, he will have so much success supplying the Italian-American market with macaroni, spaghetti, and egg noodles that he will build a large Long Island City factory in 1925, and he will start selling under the Ronzoni name in 1932.

Contadina canned tomato sauce is introduced by the Hershel Fruit Products Company of Hershel, Calif.

1919 The Versailles Peace Conference opens January 18 outside Paris with delegates from 27 victorious nations and one week later adopts a unanimous resolution to create a League of Nations whose members will protect each other against aggression and will devote itself to such matters as disarmament, labor legislation, and world health (*see* Wilson's Fourteen Points, 1918).

A new German republic is established with its constituent assembly at Weimar, a Thuringian city far to the southwest of Berlin where the traditions are humanistic rather than militaristic. The national assembly meets February 6 to draw up a constitution which is adopted July 31 but the country is embroiled in communist uprisings mixed with conspiracies to reestablish the monarchy.

The Third International founded at Moscow March 2 is an organization dedicated to propagating communist doctrine with the avowed purpose of producing worldwide revolution. This Comintern will unite Communist groups throughout the world.

"I have been over into the future and it works," says author-journalist Lincoln Steffens to U.S. financier Bernard Baruch after a visit to Russia, but that country is embroiled in civil war between the Bolshevik Red Army and a White Russian Army led by General Anton Denikin with Allied support.

General Denikin (above) routs Red Army forces in the Caucasus February 3 to 9 but the Red Army captures Kiev February 3, invades Estonia, enters the Crimea April 8 one day after the Allies have evacuated Odessa, and takes Ufa June 9. Anglo-White Russian forces defeat the Red Army August 10 in North Dvina but the Red Army takes Omsk November 15 and Kharkov December 13.

British troops occupy Archangel September 27 but withdraw from Murmansk October 12.

Sinn Fein party members of Parliament have proclaimed an independent Irish Republic January 21 and have organized a Parliament of their own. Their Dail Eireann includes Sinn Fein president Eamon de Valera, 37, but the British suppress the Dail Eireann

September 12 and war begins November 26 between the Sinn Fein and British regulars (*see* 1916; 1920).

Romania has annexed Transylvania January 11, a Bolshevist coup overthrows the Hungarian government March 21, monarchists regain control August 1, Romanian forces invade Hungary, they take Budapest August 4, they force Hungary's Communist premier Béla Kun, 34, to take refuge at Vienna, they plunder Hungary, but they are induced to withdraw November 14 (*see* 1920).

Montenegro deposes her king Nicholas I April 20 and votes for union with Yugoslavia.

Greek troops land at Smyrna May 15 with Allied support and Italian troops land in Anatolia. Turkish war hero Mustapha Kemal organizes resistance to further dismemberment of the Ottoman Empire beginning May 19 but the new sultan Mohammed VI dismisses him July 8 and outlaws him July 11. Kemal declares himself independent of the sultan August 5 at the Turkish Nationalist Congress (*see* 1915; 1923).

The Treaty of Versailles signed June 28 obliges Germany to accept sole responsibility for having caused the Great War. Germany returns to France the Alsace-Lorraine conquests of 1871, she cedes other territories to Belgium and Poland, she cedes her colonies to the Allies to be administered as mandates under the League of Nations, and she agrees to pay large reparations (below).

The Treaty of Saint-Germain signed September 10 obliges Austria to recognize the independence of Czechoslovakia, Hungary, Poland, and Yugoslavia. Austria agrees to pay heavy reparations and to cede the territories of Galicia, Istria, the Trentino, South Tyrol, and Trieste.

The Treaty of Neuilly signed November 27 obliges Bulgaria to recognize Yugoslavian independence, to give up her Aegean seaboard, and to pay $445 million in reparations.

France acquires mandate control of Syria from Turkey and of Togo and Cameroons in Africa from the Germans.

The U.S. Senate rejects the Versailles Treaty (above) and rejects U.S. membership in the League of Nations. President Wilson has suffered a stroke October 2, his left side is paralyzed, and he is powerless to fight isolationists led by Republican Senator John Cabot Lodge of Massachusetts who have particularly attacked Article X of the treaty which insures the permanence of the territorial boundaries agreed upon at Versailles. The president has called this "the heart of the covenant" but critics assail it and the Senate vote November 19 fails to come up with the two-thirds majority needed for ratification.

Berlin authorities arrest socialist agitators Karl Liebknecht, 48, and Rosa Luxemburg, 49, after an insurrection inspired by their Spartacus party. They are murdered January 15 while being transferred from military headquarters to prison.

U.S. authorities release anarchists Emma Goldman and Alexander Berkman from prison but deport them with more than 200 others to Soviet Russia which Goldman will describe in her 1923 book *My Disillusionment with Russia* (*see* 1906).

Supreme Court Justice Oliver Wendell Holmes formulates a "clear and present danger" test for defining conditions under which the constitutional right of freedom of the speech may be abridged. "When a nation is at war," says Holmes March 3 in the espionage case of *Schenck v. United States,* "many things that might be said in times of peace are such a hindrance to its effort that their utterance will not be endured so long as men fight. . . ."

The Supreme Court upholds conviction of Russian propagandists opposing U.S. intervention in Russia. Justices Holmes and Brandeis dissent from the ruling handed down November 10 in *Abrams v. United States.* Holmes says, "Only the emergency that makes it immediately dangerous to leave the correction of evil counsels to time warrants making any exception to the sweeping command, 'Congress shall make no law . . . abridging the freedom of speech,'" but federal authorities deport 249 Russians December 21 aboard the transport ship S.S. *Buford.*

The House of Representatives unseats Wisconsin socialist congressman Victor Berger November 10, Berger's district reelects him in December, but the House will declare his seat vacant next January.

The International Labor Office (ILO) is created by the League of Nations.

Labor unrest rocks the United States. Four million workers go out on strike or are locked out.

Boston police strike September 9 in protest against pay scales that range from 25 cents per hour for 83-hour weeks down to 21 cents per hour for 98-hour weeks despite wartime inflation. Only 427 of the city's 1,544-man force remain on duty to protect against the orgy of lawlessness that ensues, gangs of men, often drunk, roam the streets robbing, looting, raping, and beating up other citizens, Governor Calvin Coolidge goes to bed at 10 and does not learn about the rioting until next morning, he sends state militia into Boston September 12, the 1,117 strikers are dismissed, AF of L leader Samuel Gompers asks that they be reinstated, Coolidge wires Gompers September 14, "There is no right to strike against the public safety by anybody, anywhere, at any time."

Steelworkers at Gary, Ind., start a strike September 22 to force United States Steel Corporation to recognize their union, but the strike will end in 110 days without success. One-third of the workers labor 7 days a week.

AF of L leader in the steel strike (above) is former IWW organizer William Zebulon Foster, 38, who will soon emerge as the leading figure in the American Communist movement.

United Mine Workers Union leader John Llewellyn Lewis, 39, begins a strike of bituminous coal miners November 1 but Attorney General Alexander Palmer obtains an injunction under the 1917 Lever Act whose wartime powers remain in effect. The strike ends November 9.

Serving as special assistant to A. M. Palmer (above) is lawyer John Edgar Hoover, 24, who in 2 years will become assistant director of the Federal Bureau of Investigation (FBI) (*see* 1908). Hoover handles deportation cases involving alleged Communist revolutionaries (above).

The Amritsar Riots for Indian self-government produce a massacre April 10. The local British commander calls out his troops and without giving the demonstrators adequate warning has the men fire on an unarmed mob, killing 379, wounding 1,200. General Dyer is forced to resign after a commission of inquiry has censured his action.

The *Dearborn Independent* is published for the first time by automaker Henry Ford and reveals a tone of anti-Semitism.

A 19th Amendment to the Constitution granting women suffrage is adopted by a joint resolution of Congress June 20 and sent to the states for ratification (*see* 1920).

Race riots occur in 26 U.S. cities throughout the year. Washington, D.C., has riots July 19 as white soldiers and sailors attack black ghetto sections. Chicago has riots beginning July 27 as a disturbance at a Lake Michigan beach spreads to the city's Black Belt leaving 15 whites and 23 blacks dead, hundreds seriously injured.

Airmail service got off the ground with difficulties that included a printing error in the first airmail stamps.

1919 (cont.) English economist John Maynard Keynes, 36, foresees that high reparations imposed on Germany would upset the world economy. Leader of the British Treasury team at Versailles, Keynes resigns to write in opposition to the reparations plan (*see* 1936).

The Treaty of Versailles (above) obliges Germany to pay large reparations that include not only billions of dollars, francs, pounds, lire, etc., but also merchant ships and fishing ships plus large quantities of coal to be delivered in the next 10 years to France, Belgium, and Italy.

Germany loses 72 percent of her iron ore reserves as Lorraine is given back to France under terms of the Versailles Treaty. The second largest iron producer in 1913, Germany will be seventh largest as the Germans concentrate mining and steelmaking in the Ruhr Basin.

The U.S. Bayer Company whose German parent has been making aspirin since 1899 is seized as spoils of war by U.S. alien property custodian Francis P. Garvan. The I. G. Farbenindustrie affiliate is purchased by Sterling Drug Company (*see* 1912) which will market Bayer Aspirin and will become a major U.S. over-the-counter drug house.

Inflation begins in France which has suffered enormous property damage as well as human destruction in the Great War. The buying power of the franc in terms of gold will decline by 78 percent in the next 8 years (*see* 1926; 1928).

The war has cost the United States nearly $22 billion from April 1, 1917, through April of this year and nearly $9 billion has been loaned to the Allied powers. Americans have paid high taxes to fund the war effort and have contributed $400 million in cash and materials to the Red Cross War Council.

The cost of living in New York City is 79 percent higher than it was in 1914, says the Bureau of Labor Statistics (*see* 1913).

A Wall Street boom in "war baby" stocks sends prices to new highs. Baldwin Locomotive is up 360 percent over 1917 levels, Bethlehem Steel up 1,400 percent, General Motors up 940 percent.

U.S. chemical engineer John Merrill Olin, 26, joins his father Franklin W. Olin as first vice president of the 27-year-old Olin Corporation (*see* 1944).

E. I. du Pont de Nemours has $49 million in wartime profits even after paying out dividends of $141 million to stockholders. The company's explosives have fired 40 percent of the Allied shells in the war, it has met at least half the domestic U.S. requirements for dynamite and black blasting powder, and it begins to acquire other chemical companies and to enlarge its holdings in General Motors Corporation which it will soon control (*see* 1912; GM, 1908, 1957; Sloan, 1929).

Andrew Carnegie dies August 11 at age 83 in his Berkshire Hills mansion at Lenox, Mass., after having given away some $350 million in philanthropic contributions that inspired other U.S. millionaires to be philanthropic (*see* 1889).

The Twentieth Century Fund to advance research and education on economic questions is established by Boston merchant Edward Filene.

"A Method of Reaching Extreme Altitudes" by U.S. physicist Robert Hutchings Goddard, 36, predicts the development of rockets that will break free of Earth's gravitational pull and reach the moon. Goddard has devised the first two-stage rocket and received a grant from the Smithsonian Institution 2 years ago (*see* 1926; *New York Times,* 1921).

The NC-4 flying boat designed by U.S. aeronautical engineer Jerome Clarke Hunsaker, 33, for Curtiss Aeroplane & Motor Company makes the first transatlantic crossing by a heavier-than-air machine, leaving Newfoundland May 16 and arriving at Lisbon May 27 with a five-man crew under U.S. Navy Lieutenant Commander Albert C. Read (Curtiss has produced more than 4,000 JN-4 "Jenny" biplanes for training army and navy pilots in the war) (*see* 1911).

The Sopwith biplane *Atlantic* takes off from Newfoundland May 18 powered by a 350-horsepower Rolls-Royce engine and with 400 gallons of fuel. Pilot Harry G. Hawker, 27, and navigator K. Mackenzie Grieve fly 1,000 miles towards Ireland in quest of the £10,000 prize offered by Lord Northcliffe in 1913 for the first nonstop transatlantic flight, but engine trouble forces them to ditch, a Danish tramp steamer picks them up, London gives them a hero's welcome, and the *Daily Mail* gives them a £5,000 consolation prize (*see* 1921).

A Vickers Vimy bomber powered by two Rolls-Royce Eagle engines achieves the first nonstop transatlantic flight June 14 and wins the *Daily Mail*'s £10,000 prize. Royal Flying Corps pilot John William Alcock, 27, was captured by the Turks after bombing Constantinople during the war, he makes the 1,960-mile flight from Newfoundland to Ireland in 16 hours, 12 minutes accompanied by navigator Arthur Whitten-Brown, but they land ingloriously in a bog and Alcock dies later in the year in a plane crash (*see* Lindbergh, 1927).

French-American restaurateur-hotel proprietor Raymond Orteig, 49, offers a $25,000 prize for the first solo nonstop New York to Paris flight. Orteig operates New York's Brevoort and Lafayette hotels.

German aircraft engineer Hugo Junkers, 60, opens an aircraft factory at Dessau. Junkers will design the first all-metal airplane to fly successfully and he will establish one of the first regular mail and passenger airlines in Europe.

KLM (Koninklije Luchtvaart Maatschappig voor Nederland an Kolonien) is founded by Dutch banking and business interests. The Dutch national airline will begin scheduled flights between Amsterdam and London May 17 of next year.

Europe's *Orient Express* becomes the Simplon-Orient Express. Suspended in 1914, the fabled 36-year-old luxury train avoids passing over any German or Austrian soil by using the 12-mile Simplon Tunnel that opened through the Alps in 1906 between Brig, Switzerland, and Domodossola, Italy (*see* 1929).

The 5-year-old German passenger liners S.S. *Vaterland* and S.S. *Bismarck* are handed over to the British as war reparations and are renamed the S.S. *Leviathan* and the S.S. *Majestic*.

Merritt-Chapman & Scott is created by a merger of the Merritt Wrecking Organization, Chapman Derrick & Wrecking Company, and T. A. Scott Company. The new firm is the largest ship salvage company in the Western Hemisphere, it will acquire additional companies beginning in 1929, and it will take over inland salvage operations.

Henry Ford assumes full control of the now enormous Ford Motor Company. Ford has lost a lawsuit brought by stockholders who include the Dodge brothers but he takes all his capital plus some borrowed funds and buys up all the outstanding shares in the company, paying more than $105 million, and returning roughly $12.5 million for every $5,000 invested in 1908 (*see* 1920).

Electric starters become optional on the Model T Ford but most Model T's are still started by hand-cranking the engine (*see* Kettering, 1911).

Henry Ford builds a motorcar factory in his family's ancestral home town of Cork in Ireland.

The Bentley motorcar is introduced by former London taxi fleet manager W. O. (Walter Owen) Bentley, 31, who created the B.R. 2 "Merlin" rotary engine that powered the Sopwith Camel during the war. Bentley's 3-litre racing car is the forerunner of machines that will win at Le Mans and that will lead to luxury sedans (*see* Rolls-Royce, 1931).

The Citroën motorcar is introduced by French munitions-maker André Gustave Citroën, 41, who turns his factory over to producing motorcars that can be sold at low prices. Citroën will go bankrupt in 1934 and will lose control of his company but the Citroën will remain a major French automobile (*see* 1955).

The Deusenberg brothers set up shop at Indianapolis to make motorcars after selling John North Willys the war plant at Elizabeth, N.J., they set up to build aviation engines and a 160-horsepower tractor engine (*see* 1913; 1922; Willys, 1915; Durant, 1921).

General Motors Acceptance Corporation (GMAC) is founded by General Motors Corporation, now 28.7 percent owned by du Pont interests (above). The GM subsidiary will become the world's largest automobile financing company (*see* 1939).

Oregon imposes the first state gasoline tax February 25.

Amerada Petroleum Company is founded by Dallas petroleum geologist Everett Lee De Golyer, 32.

U.S. Plywood Company is founded by New York entrepreneur Lawrence Ottinger, 35, who borrows $500 from his mother to obtain exclusive rights to casein glue discovered during the war by the federal government's Forest Products Laboratory at Madison, Wis. Ottinger has supervised inspection and production of aircraft plywood for the U.S. Army during the war, he buys and resells surplus Italian government plywood, he is the first to market plywood in standard sizes, but while Leo Baekeland of 1909 Bakelite fame patented a resinous bond for wood plies in 1912, plywood production will remain primitive until the "Tego process" of 1926.

The Eastman School of Medicine and Dentistry is founded at the University of Rochester by photography pioneer George Eastman whose company supplies the new motion picture industry with its raw film stock (*see* School of Music, below).

UCLA (University of California at Los Angeles) opens to give the 51-year-old university a new campus.

Dial telephones are introduced November 8 at Norfolk, Va., by American Telephone & Telegraph Company which has earlier rejected dial phones but which has been threatened by a telephone operators' strike (*see* AT&T, 1912).

The Automatic Electric Company founded in 1891 is acquired by entrepreneur Theodore Gary who will make a fortune selling dial equipment to the Bell System before eventually licensing Western Electric Company to make dial telephones using the Strowger patents (*see* General Telephone, 1955).

U.S. Navy officials advise General Electric Company president Owen D. Young, 45, that GE's high-frequency Alexanderson alternator is vital to long-distance wireless communications and must remain in U.S. hands. British Marconi has offered $5 million for rights to the alternator but the Navy urges GE to start its own radio company.

Radio Corporation of America (RCA) is founded by Owen D. Young (above) who loans Ernst Alexanderson to RCA which will employ him as chief engineer for 5 years (*see* 1906). RCA will acquire the Victor Company and will become a radio-phonograph colossus but anti-trust court actions will separate RCA from GE (*see* Victrola, 1906; NBC, 1926).

Ha'aretz (*The Land*) begins publication at Tel Aviv under the direction of Palestinian journalists who include Gershon Agronsky.

The *New York Daily News* begins publication June 26 under the direction of *Chicago Tribune* veteran Joseph Medill Patterson who tells his editors, "Tell it to Sweeney—the Stuyvesants will take care of themselves." Patterson will make the *Daily News* the first successful U.S. tabloid and the most widely read U.S. newspaper of any kind (*see* 1910; 1921).

"Gasoline Alley" by *Chicago Tribune* staff cartoonist Frank King, 36, capitalizes on America's growing fas-

1919 (cont.) cination with the motorcar. Popularity of the new comic strip will zoom when its main character Walt adopts foundling Skeezix in 1921, and it will be the first strip in which characters grow and age.

True Story magazine is started by New York physical culture enthusiast Bernarr Macfadden, now 51, who has been publishing *Physical Culture* magazine since 1898. *True Story* will reach a peak circulation of more than a million as it titillates readers with suggestive morality stories and as Macfadden goes on to publish a host of movie, romance, and detective story magazines while publishing daily newspapers in 10 cities including the *New York Evening Graphic* (*see Liberty,* 1931; Fawcett, 1922).

Captain Billy's Whiz Bang is launched at Minneapolis by former World War army captain Wilford H. Fawcett, who quickly turns his mimeographed off-color joke sheet into a 25-cent pocket size monthly which his sons haul to local dealers on coaster wagons (*see True Confessions,* 1922).

Collier's Weekly is acquired by J. F. Knapp's Crowell Publishing Company which pays $1.75 million for a majority stock interest. Crowell will pour $15 million into the magazine over the next 15 years before *Collier's* becomes profitable (*see* 1896; 1911; 1925).

E. Haldeman–Julius Little Blue Books are published at Girard, Kan., beginning with Oscar Wilde's *Ballad of Reading Gaol* of 1898 and Edward Fitzgerald's *The Rubaiyat of Omar Khayyam* of 1859. Local publisher Emanuel Julius-Haldeman, 30, married Marcet Haldeman in 1916 and prefixed his surname to hers, he has been publishing the socialist weekly the *Appeal to Reason* founded by Julius A. Wayland in 1895, and his 10-cent Little Blue Books will grow to have annual sales of 500,000 copies.

Harcourt, Brace, Inc., publishers is founded at New York by former Henry Holt editor Alfred Harcourt, 38, after a dispute with Holt, now in his late seventies, over a new book Harcourt has bought from the English philosopher-mathematician Bertrand Russell (*see* Holt, 1866). Harcourt takes with him Holt's production chief Donald Brace and takes also Holt's most promising novelist Sinclair Lewis (*see* 1960).

Nonfiction *Introduction to Mathematical Philosophy* by Bertrand Russell; *Epistle to the Romans* (*Der Römerbrief*) by Swiss Protestant Reformed theologian Karl Barth, 33, who champions dialectic theology; *The Waning of the Middle Ages* by Dutch historian Johan Huizinga, 47, whose work will appear in English translation in 1924; *The American Language* by *Baltimore Evening Sun* staffman H. L. (Henry Louis) Mencken, 39, who coedits *The Smart Set* with drama critic George Jean Nathan. Mencken's scholarly analysis of the differences between English English and American English will be supplemented in 1945 and 1948; *Prejudices* (essays) by H. L. Mencken who will publish five additional books under the same title in the next 8 years; *Ten Days That Shook the World* by U.S. war correspondent

John Reed, 32, who witnessed the 1917 October revolution in Russia. Reed will organize and lead a U.S. Communist Labor party, will edit its journal, *The Voice of Labor,* will be indicted for sedition, will escape to Russia, and will die of typhus in October of next year before reaching his 33rd birthday.

Fiction *La Symphonie pastorale* by André Gide; *A New Life* (*Shinsei*) by Shimazaki Toson; *Within a Budding Grove* (*A l'ombre des jeunes filles en fleurs*) by Marcel Proust (Goncourt prize); *The Moon and Sixpence* by W. Somerset Maugham; *Jurgen* by Virginia author James Branch Cabell, 40, whose medieval romance is suppressed on charges of obscenity but will win wide acclaim through the 1920s; *Winesburg, Ohio* by Chicago writer Sherwood Anderson, 43, whose vignettes refute sentimental notions of untroubled rural life; *Java Head* by U.S. novelist Joseph Hergesheimer, 39, who makes vivid the glory days of Salem, Mass., in the flush of its China trade prosperity; *My Man Jeeves* by P. G. Wodehouse; *Lad, a Dog* by New Jersey author Albert Payson Terhune, 47.

Poetry *War Poems* by Siegfried Sassoon who won the Military Cross in 1917, threw it into the sea, made a public announcement of his refusal to serve further, but returned to France last year and was wounded a second time; *Marlborough* by the late Charles Sorley; *Boy* (*Ragazzo*) by Piero Jahier; *Altazor* by Chilean poet Vicente Huidobro, 26; *Poems* by U.S. poet Michael Strange (Blanche Oelrichs), who has divorced Philadelphia millionaire Leonard Thomas and will marry John Barrymore next year.

Painting *The Murder* by Edvard Munch; *La Marchesa Casati* and *Gypsy Woman with Baby* by Amedeo Modigliani whose health is failing as a result of tuberculosis, alcoholism, and drug addiction; *Pierrot and Harlequin* by Pablo Picasso; *Follow the Arrow* by Fernand Léger; *Dream Birds* by Paul Klee; *Dreamy Improvisation* and *Arabian Cemetery* by Wassily Kandinsky; *Samson and Delilah* by Max Liebermann; *Nympheas* by Claude Monet; *Anywhere Out of the World* by Marc Chagall; Pierre Renoir dies at Caques-sur-Mer December 17 at age 78.

Sculpture *Archer* (bronze and granite) by Carl Milles; *Bird in Space* (bronze) by Constantin Brancusi (*see* 1926).

Theater *The Last Days of Mankind* (*Die letzten Tage der Menschheit*) by Austrian playwright-poet Karl Kraus; *King Nicholas, or Such Is Life* (*König Nicolo, oder so ist das Leben*) by Frank Wedekind 1/15 at Leipzig's Schauspielhaus; *Up in Mabel's Room* by U.S. playwrights Willson Collison, 26, and Otto Harbach 1/15 at New York's Eltinge Theater 229 perfs.; *Augustus Does His Bit* by George Bernard Shaw 3/12 at New York's Guild Theater, with Norma Trevor, 111 perfs.; *Elius Erweckung* by Frank Wedekind 3/16 at Hamburg's Kammerspiele; *Tête d'Or* by Paul Claudel 3/30 at the Théâtre du Gymnase, Paris; *The Fall and Rise of Susan Lenox* by George V. Hobart 6/9 at New York's 44th Street Theater, with Alma Tell; *Transfiguration* (*Di*

Wandlung) by German playwright Ernst Toller, 26, 8/30 at Berlin's Tribüne Theater. Toller is sentenced to 5 years in prison for his political activities; *Hercules* (*Herakles*) by Frank Wedekind 9/1 at Munich's Prinzregenztheater; *Adam and Eva* by Guy Bolton and George Middleton 9/13 at New York's Longacre Theater, 312 perfs.; *The Gold Diggers* by Avery Hopwood 9/30 at New York's Lyceum Theater, with Ina Claire, Ruth Terry, 282 perfs.; *Clarence* by Booth Tarkington 9/20 at New York's Hudson Theater, with Alfred Lunt, 306 perfs.; *Mr. Pim Passes By* by A. A. (Alan Alexander) Milne, 37, 12/1 at Manchester's Gaiety Theatre. *Punch* contributor Milne wrote two comedies while fighting in France; *Aria Da Capo* by Edna St. Vincent Millay 12/15 at New York's Provincetown Playhouse.

Films Robert Wiene's *The Cabinet of Dr. Caligari* with Werner Krauss, Conrad Veidt; Fritz Lang's *Half-Caste*; Abel Gance's *J'Accuse* and *Madame Dubarry*; Erich von Stroheim's *The Devil's Passkey*; D. W. Griffith's *Broken Blossoms* with Lillian Gish, Richard Barthelmess; Victor Fleming's *Till the Clouds Roll By* with Douglas Fairbanks, Kathleen Clifford; D. W. Griffith's *Fall of Babylon* with Constance Talmadge, Elmer Layton; D. W. Griffith's *Scarlet Days* with Richard Barthelmess, Carol Dempster; Cecil B. DeMille's *Male and Female* with Gloria Swanson, Bebe Daniels, Thomas Meighan (based on the James M. Barrie play *The Admirable Crichton*); Lambert Hillyer's *Branding Broadway* with William S. Hart; Charlie Chaplin's *Sunnyside*.

United Artists, Inc., is founded at Hollywood by D. W. Griffith, Charlie Chaplin, romantic star Mary Pickford, and matinee idol Douglas Fairbanks who have set up the firm to increase their share of the profits from the films they make. Now 36, Fairbanks will marry Pickford next year and both will continue making films selected, financed, and distributed (but not produced) by United Artists (*see* 1951).

Paramount-Famous Players-Lasky Corporation opens a 6-acre Astoria, N.Y., film studio with a stage 225 feet by 126 by 60. Paramount will sell the studio to the U.S. Army in 1942.

Ballet *The Three-Cornered Hat* 7/22 at London's Alhambra Theatre, with Leonide Massine of the Ballet Russe as the Miller, Tamara Karsavina as the Miller's wife, music by Manuel de Falla, choreography by Massine.

Opera *Die Frau ohne Schatten* 10/10 at Vienna's Opernhaus, with music by Richard Strauss, libretto by Hugo von Hoffmansthal; The St. Louis Municipal Opera opens its first season with a performance of the light opera *Robin Hood*.

The Eastman School of Music is founded at the University of Rochester with a gift from photography pioneer George Eastman (*see* medicine above).

Scottish music hall favorite Harry Lauder is knighted at age 48 by George V for his recruitment efforts in the Great War. Sir Harry lost his only son in the war.

Broadway musicals *The Velvet Lady* 2/3 at the New Amsterdam Theater, with Jed Prouty, Eddie Dowling, music by Victor Herbert, lyrics by Henry Blossom, 136 perfs.; *The Whirl of Society* 3/5 at the Winter Garden Theater, with Al Jolson, George White, Blossom Seeley (who runs up and down the aisles via a runway across the pit which also gives audiences a closer look at the chorus girls), music by Louis A. Hirsch, lyrics by Harold Atteridge, 136 perfs.; (George White's) *Scandals* 6/2 at the Liberty Theater, with White, "dimple-kneed" Ann Pennington, music by Richard Whiting, book and lyrics by White, Arthur Jackson, 128 perfs.; *The Ziegfeld Follies* 6/16 at the New Amsterdam Theater, with Marilyn Miller, Eddie Cantor, Eddie Dowling, Van and Schenck, music and lyrics by Irving Berlin, Dave Stamper, Gene Buck, songs that include "Sweet Sixteen" by Stamper and Buck, "A Pretty Girl Is Like a Melody" by Berlin whose song will be the *Follies* theme, 171 perfs.; *The Ziegfeld Midnight Frolic* 10/2 at the New Amsterdam Roof, with Fanny Brice, Ted Lewis, Will Rogers, W. C. Fields, Chic Sale, music and lyrics chiefly by Dave Stamper and Gene Buck, songs that include "Rose of Washington Square" by James F. Hanley, lyrics by Ballard MacDonald; *Apple Blossoms* 10/7 at the Globe Theater, with Fred and Adele Astaire, music by Austrian-American violinist Fritz Kreisler, 44, and U.S. composer Frederick Jacobi, 28, book and lyrics by William Le Baron, songs that include "I'm in Love," "Who Can Tell," "You are Free," "Little Girls, Good-bye," 256 perfs.; *The Passing Show* 10/23 at the Winter Garden Theater, with Charles Winninger, James Barton, Reginald Denny, music chiefly by Sigmund Romberg, lyrics chiefly by Harold Atteridge, 280 perfs.; *Buddies* 10/26 at the Selwyn Theater, with Peggy Wood, Roland Young, music and lyrics by B. C. Hilliam, songs that include "My Buddies," 259 perfs.; *Irene* 11/18 at the Vanderbilt Theater, with Edith Day, music by Harry Tierney, lyrics by Joseph McCarthy, songs that include "Castle of My Dreams," "In My Sweet Little Alice Blue Gown," 670 perfs.

Popular songs "Swanee" by New York Tin Pan Alley composer George Gershwin, 21, lyrics by Irving Caesar, 24, who has been inspired by the 1851 Stephen Foster song "Old Folks at Home." Al Jolson will record the song early next year; "Dardanella" by Felix Bernard, 22, and Johnny Black, lyrics by Fred Fisher; "How 'Ya Gonna Keep 'Em Down on the Farm? (After They've Seen Pa-ree)" by Walter Donaldson, lyrics by Sam M. Lewis and Joe Young; "Oh, What a Pal Was Mary" by Pete Wendling, lyrics by Edgar Leslie and Bert Kalmar; "Missouri Waltz" by Frederick Knight Logan (who got the melody from a young black guitarist), lyrics by J. R. Shannon (James Royce); "Smilin' Through" by Arthur A. Penn; "Cielito Lindo" ("Beautiful Heaven") by Mexican composer Quirino Mendoza y Cortez; "The World Is Waiting for the Sunrise" by English composer Ernest Seitz, lyrics by Eugene Lockhart; "Let the Rest of the

1919 (cont.) World Go By" by Ernest R. Ball, lyrics by J. Keirn Brennan.

New York's Roseland Ballroom opens December 31 at 1658 Broadway (51st Street) where it will remain (one flight up) until 1956 when it will move to 239 West 52nd Street. Proprietor Louis J. Brecker, 21, opened a Philadelphia Roseland at Chester and 12th Street 3 years ago while attending the Wharton School but has moved to New York to escape Philadelphia's blue laws.

Wimbledon tennis champion Mrs. Lambert Chambers is defeated after six triumphs in singles competition by France's Suzanne Lenglen, 20, who began tournament play at age 12, won the world hard court championship at 15, and will not be beaten until 1926 except for one loss by default.

Jack Dempsey wins the world heavyweight boxing championship July 4 by a third round knockout over champion Jess Willard at Toledo, Ohio. William Harrison "Jack" Dempsey, 24, is called the "Manassa Mauler" because he comes from Manassa, Colo., and he will hold the crown until 1926 (see 1921).

U.S. racing gets its first Triple Crown winner as the chestnut colt Sir Barton wins the Kentucky Derby, the Preakness, and the Belmont Stakes in a feat that will not be repeated until 1930.

The Cincinnati Reds win the World Series by defeating the Chicago White Sox 5 games to 3 (but see 1920).

The Green Bay Packers is founded as a professional football team by halfback-coach Curly Lambeau who will remain head coach of the Wisconsin team until 1949 (see NFL, 1920).

The pogo stick is patented by U.S. inventor George B. Hansburg, 32, whose bouncing metal stick will be ridden by thousands in the 1920s and will be the basis of a dance number in *The Ziegfeld Follies*.

F. W. Woolworth dies April 8 at age 67 leaving a fortune of $67 million. There are 1,000 Woolworth stores in the United States plus many in Britain, and the chain has annual sales of $107 million (see 1912).

New York's Commodore Hotel opens January 28 with 2,000 rooms—the largest hotel in the world. Built by John McEntee Bowman of 1914 Biltmore fame on a site adjoining Grand Central Station, the 33-story Commodore is named to honor the late New York Central Railroad magnate Commodore Cornelius Vanderbilt (see Hotel Pennsylvania, 1922).

Hilton Hotel Corporation has its beginnings at Crisco, Tex., where entrepreneur Conrad Nicholson Hilton, 31, uses his life savings of $5,000 to finance the purchase of the small Mobley Hotel. Hilton was a partner in his father's mercantile interests at San Antonio, N. Mex., before the war, he will soon acquire several other small Texas hotels, and he will build a new hotel at Dallas in 1925 (see 1945).

Chicago's Drake Hotel opens on Lake Shore Drive with 800 rooms. Hotelman Tracy Corey Drake put up the luxurious Blackstone Hotel 9 years ago.

 Grand Canyon National Park is established by act of Congress. The 673,575-acre park in Arizona includes the most spectacular part of the Colorado River's great 217-mile canyon (see hotels, 1903).

Zion National Park is established by act of Congress. The 147,035-acre park in Utah is rich in colorful canyon and mesa scenery.

Lafayette National Park is established by act of Congress on Maine's 41,634-acre Mount Desert Island (see Rockefeller, 1916). First national park east of the Mississippi, it will be renamed Acadia National Park in 1929.

Del Monte Properties Co. is incorporated in California to manage 25 square miles of land on the Monterey Peninsula south of San Francisco which includes California's first golf course. Major stockholder and president is Samuel F. B. Morse, 34, a grandnephew of the telegraph pioneer who will scrape guano from offshore rocks to use as fertilizer for his Cypress Point, Pebble Beach, and Del Monte golf courses. Seals will take over the rocks and will prevent their original pelican and cormorant populations from returning.

MacMillan Export Company is founded by Vancouver lumberman H. R. (Harvey Reginald) MacMillan, 34, who will make his firm the largest in British Columbia. MacMillan became chief forester of the province in his late twenties and has urged expansion of lumbering and reforestation.

 Belgian food prices drop by 50 percent and British food prices by 25 percent but prices remain high elsewhere in Europe. German ports are blockaded until July 12.

French beef, mutton, pork, and veal prices have increased nearly sixfold since 1914, reports *Le Petit Journal*, and egg, cheese, and butter prices have increased fourfold. France removes restrictions on the sale of beans, peas, rice, eggs, and condensed milk, and then on bread, but while the wartime ban on sugar imports is lifted the import duty on sugar is raised to almost prohibitive levels.

Eastern Europe has famine as a result of poor crops and the shortage of manpower. Vienna cuts bread rations to 4 ounces per week in late December.

U.S. food prices remain far above 1914 levels. Milk is 15 cents per quart, up from 9 cents. Sirloin steak is 61 cents per pound, up from 32 cents. Fresh eggs are 62 cents per dozen, up from 34 cents.

Famine in eastern Europe (above) boosts demand for U.S. wheat. Prices soar to $3.50 per bushel and farmers are encouraged to plant wheat on land never before tilled (see 1921; 1934).

Di Giorgio Farms is organized by Giuseppi Di Giorgio who started the Baltimore Fruit Exchange in

1904 and who has begun buying acreage in California's San Joaquin Valley.

Italy's FIAT begins making tractors as Europe's agriculture struggles to revive.

Malnutrition in famine-stricken Vienna (above) is studied by a team of scientists from Britain's year-old Accessory Food Factors Committee. Harriette Chick and her colleagues find scurvy common among infants and note a serious increase in rickets, and they prove the success of good nutrition in curing rickets.

England's Edward Mellanby finds that rickets is not an infection as has been widely believed but is produced by a dietary vitamin deficiency (see 1918; Drummond, McCollum, 1920; McCollum, 1922).

The U.S. Pure Food and Drug Law of 1906 is amended once again to eliminate loopholes (see 1912; 1913; but see Kallet, Schlink, 1932).

U.S. margarine production reaches a level of 1 pound to every 2.4 pounds of butter, up from 1 to every 5 in 1914 (see 1881; 1921).

The Dairymen's League founded in 1907 is reincorporated at New York under the name Dairymen's League Cooperative Association. Its members will pool their milk and will sell it at different prices depending on how it will be used (see 1921).

An 18th amendment to the Constitution prohibiting sale of alcoholic beverages anywhere in the United States is proclaimed in January to go into effect January 16, 1920; a War Prohibition Act passed last year goes into effect at the end of June to continue until demobilization. The Prohibition Enforcement Act (Volstead Act) passed over President Wilson's veto October 28 defines as "intoxicating" any beverage containing 0.5 percent alcohol or more (see 1920).

Thirsty Americans flock to Havana whose Sloppy Joe's is called the national American saloon.

Compania Ron Bacardi, S.A., is incorporated in Cuba by Facundo and Jose Bacardi and Henri Schueg, sons and son-in-law of Catalan Facundo Bacardi who started the distillery. They have run the rum company as a partnership for some years following the death of the senior Bacardi.

American Sugar Refining Company enters production by acquiring Central Cunagua, a Cuban sugar plantation of 100,000 acres with a huge mill (central), a railroad, and a town of 1,000 (see 1911; 1920).

Coca-Cola Company's Asa G. Candler turns 68 and sells out for $25 million to a group headed by Ernest Woodruff (see 1916; 1923).

Peter Paul Manufacturing Company is incorporated at New Haven, Conn., by candymaker Peter Paul Halajian and five other Armenian-Americans (see 1899). Their first candy bar is a blend of coconut, fruits, nuts, and chocolate sold under the name Konabar (see Mounds, 1921).

"Sunkist" is burned into the skin of a California orange with a heated fly swatter by California Fruit Growers Exchange executive Don Francisco, 27, who urges that citrus fruit marketed by the Exchange be stamped with the name. It will be the first trademark to identify a fresh fruit commodity (see 1895; Chiquita Banana, 1944).

The Fleischmann Company launches a national advertising campaign to urge housewives to buy bakery bread instead of baking at home. The company now sells most of its yeast to commercial bakers (see 1876; Standard Brands, 1929).

Kellogg's All-Bran is introduced by the Battle Creek Toasted Corn Flakes Company (see 1915; 1922).

Frigidaire is selected as the name of a new refrigerator produced by W. C. Durant's General Motors Company (above) which has paid $56,000 to acquire Guardian Refrigerator Company, a one-man firm that was close to bankruptcy. The name has come out of a contest sponsored by GM which will make Frigidaire the world's leading name in refrigerators.

U.S. ice cream sales reach 150 million gallons, up from 30 million in 1909.

The Eskimo Pie has its beginnings in the "I-Scream-Bar" chocolate-covered ice cream stick patented by Danish-born candy store proprietor Christian Nelson of Onawa, Iowa (see 1921; Good Humor, 1920).

Louis Sherry's New York restaurant closes after 21 years on Fifth Avenue. The Louis Sherry name will survive as a brand name for ice cream and chocolates.

Massive relocations of ethnic minorities begin in Europe. The Treaty of Neuilly (above) sanctions the exchange of 46,000 Bulgarian Greeks for 120,000 Greek Bulgarians (see Lausanne, 1923).

1920 Russia's civil war continues as the Bolsheviks struggle to consolidate control of the country in the face of opposition from the Poles and Letts who capture Dvinsk January 5. The White Russian admiral Aleksandr Kolchak is defeated at Krasnoyarsk and is executed by the Red Army February 7 at age 45, 1 day before the Bolsheviks take Odessa.

Novorossiisk on the Black Sea falls to the Red Army March 28 and the White Russian Army of Anton Denikin collapses. The Ukraine is overrun in late April by Polish troops under Marshal Jozef Pilsudski who take Kiev May 7 but are driven out June 11 despite support from the Ukrainians.

The Red Army takes Pinsk July 27 and crosses into Poland but is defeated August 14 to 16 by Polish forces supported by French general Maxime Weygand who forces the Bolsheviks to give up their Polish conquests.

Russia's Polish War ends October 12 in a peace treaty signed at Tartu and the Red Army is freed to push back the White Russian forces of Baron Petr Nikolaevich Wrangel, 42, who has taken over much of southern Russia. Wrangel is forced back to the Crimea November 1, he loses Sevastopol November

Nikolai Lenin rallied Russians against evil Western "imperialists," but he welcomed Western capital investment.

14, he is obliged to evacuate his troops to Constantinople, and the Russian counterrevolution is ended.

The Baltic states Estonia, Latvia, and Lithuania are recognized as independent nations by the Bolshevik government after unsuccessful efforts to make them part of the new U.S.S.R. (Union of Soviet Socialist Republics). The republics were created during the Bolshevik Revolution of 1917 (see 1940).

Berlin is seized March 13 in a right-wing German Putsch headed by the American-born journalist Wolfgang Kapp, 51, who is supported by irregular troops under General von Luttwitz, 60, in a move to restore the monarchy. The disbanded troops led by the Erhardt Brigade wear swastikas on their helmets, they have come from fighting in the Baltic provinces to destroy "Bolshevik republicanism," the legitimate government escapes to the provinces, Kapp is made chancellor and orders a general strike, he is supported by General Ludendorff, but he fails to gain foreign recognition, the army remains generally uncommitted, Kapp is hampered by the general strike, he is opposed by the Security Police, he soon finds that he has no authority, and he flees the city March 17 (see Hitler, 1923).

Hungary loses nearly three-quarters of her territory and two-thirds of her population in the Treaty of Trianon signed June 4 by the regent Admiral Nikolaus Horthy (Miklos de Nagybanya Horthy), 52, who will serve as regent until 1944. Western Hungary is given to Austria, Slovakia to Czechoslovakia, Croatia-Slavonia to Yugoslavia, the Banat of Temesvar in part to Yugoslavia and in part to Romania which also receives Transylvania and part of the Hungarian plain.

Greece's King Alexander dies of blood poisoning October 25 at age 27 after a 3-year reign (he has been bitten by a pet monkey). His father Constantine, who abdicated in 1917, resumes the reign he began in 1913 and continues the disastrous war against Turkey.

British reinforcements have arrived in Ireland May 15 to support His Majesty's forces against attacks by Sinn Fein political militants who continue resistance to British regulars and to the new "Black and Tans" made up of Royal Irish Constabulary recruits who are issued khaki tunics and trousers and dark green caps that are almost black. Nicknamed after a familiar breed of Irish hounds, the Black and Tans have been helping the British suppress Irish nationalists since March, and they take reprisals for nationalist acts of terrorism.

The Government of Ireland Act passed by Parliament December 23 gives Northern Ireland and Southern Ireland the right to elect separate parliaments of their own with each to retain representatives in the British Parliament at London (see 1919; 1921).

Two agitators for Irish independence (above) die in an English prison after fasting for 75 days in a protest demonstration (see Gandhi, 1914). Cork Lord Mayor Terence James MacSwiney, 41, collapses on the fifteenth day and physicians are unable to save him.

Mexico's president Venustiano Carranza is killed May 21 by an assassin in the employ of the insurgent generals Adolfo de la Huerta, Alvaro Obregon, and Plutarco Elias Calles. The 39-year-old Obregon has taken Mexico City and is elected president August 31 following the surrender of Pancho Villa who is given a handsome estate on which he will live until his assassination in 1923.

"America's present need is not heroics but healing; not nostrums but normalcy," says presidential hopeful Warren Gamaliel Harding, 54, of Ohio in a speech at Boston May 10. The handsome, genial, but colorless senator is nominated by the Republicans and is opposed by Ohio's Democratic governor James M. Cox, 50, who wins only 34 percent of the popular vote and receives only 127 electoral votes against 404 for Harding.

The League of Nations meets for the first time November 15 in its new headquarters at Geneva but its membership includes neither the U.S.S.R. nor the United States. U.S. membership has been rejected finally March 19 by the Senate whose opposition has been led by the Senator from Massachusetts Henry Cabot Lodge (see 1919).

Five men kill a factory guard and paymaster April 15 at South Braintree, Mass., and escape in a stolen motorcar with a steel box containing a payroll of $15,776.51. Factory worker Nicola Sacco, 20, and fish peddler Bartolomeo Vanzetti, 32, are picked up May 5 in a car that contains propaganda leaflets attacking the U.S. government and all other governments, they are arrested for the April 15 murder and robbery, and they are prosecuted as "Reds" by U.S. Attorney General Mitchell Palmer (see 1927).

President Wilson rules May 5 that the Communist Labor Party of America is outside the scope of U.S. deportation laws.

The American Civil Liberties Union is founded by social reformers who include Methodist minister Harry F. Ward, 47, Clarence Darrow, Upton Sinclair, Jane Addams, Helen Keller, Roger Williams, 36, former War Labor Policies Board chairman Felix Frankfurter, 37, and socialist Norman Mattoon Thomas, 35. FBI agents soon infiltrate the ACLU (see 1908).

Norman Thomas (above), a former clergyman, will staunchly oppose both Communism and Fascism, but he will advocate such radical ideas as low-cost public housing, the 5-day work week, minimum wage laws, and the abolition of child labor (Congress will ultimately pass laws supporting them all), and he will be a quadrennial Socialist party candidate for president from 1928 through 1948.

Britain orders unemployment insurance for all workers except domestic servants and farm workers (see allowances for dependent relatives, 1921).

The first Universal Negro Improvement Association international convention opens at Liberty Hall in New York's Harlem under the leadership of Marcus Garvey who has founded UNIA branches in nearly every U.S. city with a sizeable black population (see 1916). Some 25,000 delegates from 25 nations attend and Garvey begins to exalt African beauty and to promote a "back to Africa" movement with a plan for resettlement in Liberia (see 1847; 1924).

Woman suffrage is proclaimed in effect August 26 following Tennessee's ratification of the 19th amendment and women voters help elect Harding (above).

The League of Women Voters is founded to give impartial, in-depth information on candidates, platforms, and ballot issues.

A bomb explosion September 16 scars the J. P. Morgan bank building, it kills 30, it injures 100, and it causes $2 million in property damage.

The Amalgamated Clothing Workers of America begins a 6-month strike in December against sweat shops and nonunion shops. Now 100,000 strong, the union workers find themselves locked out by New York, Boston, and Baltimore clothing manufacturers who charge the union leadership with "Sovietism" and demand a return to piecework pay. The manufacturers will lose an estimated $10 million before the strike ends in June of next year, the workers will accept a 15 percent wage cut while promising to increase productivity by 15 percent, but clothing makers will agree to a union shop and to a continuation of the 44-hour week (see 1918; 1937).

London's Croydon Airport is designated in March as the city's terminal for air traffic from the Continent. Regular KLM Royal Dutch Airline flights between Rotterdam and London begin May 17 (see 1919).

QANTAS (Queensland and Northern Territories Air Service) begins service in Australia in November.

Regular air service begins between Cuba and Key West, Fla. (see Trippe, 1923).

Douglas Aircraft Company is founded by former Glenn L. Martin Company aircraft designer Donald Douglas, 28, who has quit to start his own firm in order to produce the large, safe, relatively slow commercial plane which he has designed but which Martin has refused to produce (see 1924).

England's Bristol Aeroplane Company acquires rights to manufacture the Cosmos radial engine and starts a department that will produce the nine-cylinder, air-cooled Jupiter radial engine (see British and Colonial, 1910). Bristol has built 4,500 fighter planes during the war and has developed the Bristol Pullman, first cabin airliners, from the trimotor Bristol Braemar bomber (see 1935).

U.S. motorcar production increases with Ford Model T cars accounting for 54.57 percent of all cars sold.

Nearly two-thirds of the world's petroleum is supplied by U.S. wells (see Venezuela, 1922).

Hunt Oil Company has its beginnings as Arkansas-Louisiana planter H. L. Hunt is hit by the collapse of farm prices and is impelled to start dealing in oil leases in the new Arkansas oilfields (see 1911). Hunt will build up capital, he will begin drilling his own wells, and within 4 years he will have made his first million dollars (see Hunt Oil, 1936).

The "Ponzi scheme" bilks thousands of Bostonians out of their savings. Italian-American "financial wizard" Charles Ponzi, 38, offers a 50 percent return on investment in 45 days, 100 percent in 90 days, and by late July his Securities and Exchange Company at 27 School Street is taking in hundreds of thousands of dollars per day. Ponzi says he has found that a 1-cent reply coupon issued in Spain as a convenience by international postal agreement is exchangeable at any U.S. post office for a 6-cent stamp and that he has agents buying up millions of coupons throughout Europe and is making a 5 cent profit on each. The idea is called ridiculous by Boston financier Clarence Walker Barron, 65, who publishes a financial daily that will later become *Barron's Weekly*. It is theoretically possible to make a few thousand dollars by manipulating postal reply coupons but certainly no more, says Barron.

Charles Ponzi (above) replies to critics that he has invented his postal coupon story to keep Wall Street speculators from divining his real secret, but by late afternoon of July 26 the Suffolk County district attorney announces that Ponzi has agreed to accept no more funds until his books can be audited.

Charles Ponzi (above) continues to reimburse investors at 50 to 100 percent interest, his supporters claim that he is being attacked by "unscrupulous bankers," but it soon develops that Ponzi has been convicted of a swindle in Montreal and that the "wizard" with the mansion in Belmont and the chauffeur-driven Locomobile has merely been paying out part of what he has been taking in. At least $8 million of the $15 million he has accepted will never be ac-

1920 (cont.) counted for, his noteholders will receive 12 cents on the dollar, six banks will fail as a result of the Ponzi scheme, and Ponzi will serve 3.5 years in Plymouth County Jail (he will escape a further 7- to 9-year term by jumping bail of $14,000 in 1925).

Allied Chemical and Dye Corporation is created largely at the initiative of William H. Nichols whose General Chemical Company is a major producer of sulfuric acid. Allied's largest single component is the Barret Company, leading U.S. producer of roofing products, and the new corporation includes also National Aniline and Chemical Company, American Solvay Process Company (*see* Cogswell, 1881), and Semet-Solvay Company.

Union Carbide and Carbon Corporation establishes a chemical company that will pioneer development of petrochemicals. Union Carbide also acquires the Haynes Stellite Company to expand its metallurgical capabilities in the field of corrosion- and heat-resistant metal alloys.

E. I. du Pont de Nemours acquires U.S. rights to the Chardonnet viscose rayon process of 1883 from France's Comptoir des Textiles Artificiels and sets up the DuPont Fibersilk Company at Buffalo, N.Y. (*see* 1919; cellophane, 1924).

The Robert Gair Company buys up three firms from which it has been buying jute and paperboard, it adds a strawboard mill, and it becomes an integrated packaging company (*see* 1879).

The world's first radio broadcasting station begins broadcasting November 2 to give results of the Harding-Cox election (above) and nearly 300,000 listeners hear the returns. KDKA has been set up at East Pittsburgh by Westinghouse engineer Frank Conrad, 46 (*see* radio advertising, 1922).

David Sarnoff proposes a plan for manufacturing $75 radio music boxes and predicts that at least a million could be sold in 3 years (*see* 1917; National Broadcasting Company, 1926).

International Telephone and Telegraph (ITT) is founded by Puerto Rican sugar broker Sosthenes Behn, 38, and his brother Hernand to run telephone and telegraph operations in Cuba and Puerto Rico (*see* Tropical Radio Telegraph, 1910). The Behn brothers were born in the Virgin Islands of Danish-French parents and have acquired a small San Juan telephone business to satisfy a bad debt (*see* 1925).

"Winnie Winkle the Breadwinner" by cartoonist Martin Michael Branner, 31, begins in September in the 15-month-old *New York Daily News.*

Pitney-Bowes Postage Meter Company is founded to produce a postage meter acceptable to the U.S. Post Office as Congress enacts legislation enabling the Post Office to accept first class mail not stamped with adhesive stamps (*see* 1847). Arthur H. Pitney, 49, is a former Chicago wallpaper company employee who saw the firm's postage stamps being stolen by office workers and who developed an early postage meter in 1901; Walter Bowes, 38, is a former Adressograph

Company salesman who bought the Universal Stamping Machine Company in 1908 and who has been selling a high-speed postmarking and stamp-canceling machine to the Post Office (which has rejected a postage meter Bowes has proposed because it did not completely protect the government's stamp revenues). Advised by the Post Office to team up with Pitney whose self-locking meter does protect stamp revenues, Bowes has merged his firm with Pitney's, the new company takes over the Universal Stamping Machine plant at Stamford, Conn., it produces meters that rent for $10 per month, and the first metered letter is posted December 10.

Nonfiction *Outline of History* by H. G. Wells who intends it to replace "narrow nationalist history by a general review of the human record." "Human history becomes more and more a race between education and catastrophe," says Wells; *The Storm of Steel* (*In Stahlgewittern*) by German author Ernst Jünger, 25.

Fiction *This Side of Paradise* by former New York advertising agency copywriter F. (Francis) Scott (Key) Fitzgerald, 23, who takes his title from a line in a 1915 poem by the late Rupert Brooke; *The Age of Innocence* by Edith Wharton, Pulitzer prize; *Main Street* by U.S. novelist Sinclair Lewis, 35, who satirizes smalltown America; *Cheri* by Colette; *Women in Love* and *The Lost Girl* by D. H. Lawrence.

Poetry *A Few Figs from Thistles* by Edna St. Vincent Millay: "My candle burns at both ends;/ It will not last the night;/ But, ah, my foes, and, oh, my friends—/ It gives a lovely light."

New York's Société Anonyme, Inc., is founded by Marcel Duchamp, Philadelphia-born Dadaist photographer-painter-sculptor Man Ray, 30, and Katherine S. Dreier who will open the city's first modern art museum (*see* Phillips Collection, 1921; Museum of Modern Art, 1929).

Painting *Portrait of Josie West* by Missouri painter Thomas Hart Benton, 31; *February Thaw* by Charles Burchfield; *Church* by U.S. cubist Lyonel (Charles Adrian) Feininger, 49; *Guitar, Book, and Newspaper* by cubist Juan Gris; *The Tug Boat* by Fernand Léger; *L'Odalisque* by Henri Matisse; *Reclining Nude* by Amedeo Modigliani who dies at Paris January 25 at age 35.

Theater *Beyond the Horizon* by Eugene O'Neill 2/2 at New York's Morosco Theater, with Richard Bennett in O'Neill's first full-length play, 111 perfs.; Pulitzer prize; *The Outlaw* (*Loupeznik*) by Czech journalist-playwright Karel Capek, 29, 3/2 at Prague's National Theater; *The White Savior* (*Der Weisse Heiland*) by Gerhart Hauptmann 3/28 at Berlin's Grosses Schauspielhaus; *The Skin Game* by John Galsworthy 4/21 at the St. Martin's Theatre, London; *Mary Rose* by James M. Barrie 4/22 at London's Haymarket Theatre; *I'll Leave It to You* by English actor-playwright Noel (Pierce) Coward, 20, 7/21 at London's New Theatre, with Coward, Moya Nugent, 37 perfs.; *The Bat* by Mary Roberts Rinehart and Avery Hopwood 8/23 at New York's Morosco Theater, with Effie Ellsler in a dramatization of Rinehart's 1908 novel *The Circular Staircase,* 867 perfs.; *East of Suez* by W. Somerset Maugham 9/2 at His Majesty's Theatre, London; *The First Year* by U.S. actor-playwright Frank Craven 10/20 at New York's Little Theater, with Craven, 760 perfs.; *The Emperor Jones* by Eugene O'Neill 11/1 at New York's Provincetown Playhouse, with Charles S. Gilpin as the Pullman porter who becomes dictator of a tropical island and disintegrates morally. The play moves uptown to the Selwyn Theater 12/27, it will move to the Princess Theater a month later, 204 perfs.; *Heartbreak House* by George Bernard Shaw 11/10 at New York's Garrick Theater, with Helen Westley, Dudley Digges, 125 perfs.; *Masses and Men* (*Massen Menschen*) by Ernst Toller 11/15 at Nuremberg's Stadttheater; *The Makropolous Secret* (*Vec Makropulos*) by Karel Capek 11/21 at Prague's National Theater.

Films   D. W. Griffith's *The Love Flower* with Richard Barthelmess, Carol Dempster; D. W. Griffith's *The Idol Dancer* with Richard Barthelmess, Clarine Seymour; Lambert Hillyer's *The Tollgate* with William S. Hart; Buster Keaton's *The Saphead;* George Melford's *The Round Up* with Roscoe (Fatty) Arbuckle.

Ballet   *Le Boeuf sur le toit* (*The Nothing-Doing Bar*) 2/21 at the Théâtre des Champs-Elysées, Paris, with famous circus clowns and acrobats, music by Darius Milhaud, scenario by Jean Cocteau; *Pulcinella* 5/15 at the Théâtre National de l'Opéra, Paris, with Leonide Massine, Tamara Karsavina, music by Igor Stravinsky based on scores by Giambattista Pergolesi, choreography by Massine, scenery and costumes by Pablo Picasso.

Broadway musicals   (George White's) *Scandals* 6/7 at the Globe Theater with Ann Pennington, comic Lou Holtz, music by George Gershwin, lyrics by Arthur Jackson, 134 perfs.; *The Ziegfeld Follies* 6/22 at the New Amsterdam Theater with Fanny Brice, W. C. Fields, Moran and Mack, Van and Schenck, music and lyrics by Irving Berlin, Victor Herbert, Joseph McCarthy, Harry Tierney, Gene Buck, and others, songs that include "Love Boat" with music by Victor Herbert, 123 perfs.; *Sally* 12/21 at the New Amsterdam Theater with Marilyn Miller, Leon Errol, music by Jerome Kern, lyrics by B. G. (George Gard) DeSylva, 25, songs that include "Look for the Silver Lining," 570 perfs.; *The Passing Show* 12/29 at the Winter Garden Theater, with Eugene and Willie Howard, Marie Dressler, Janet Adair, music by Jean Schwartz, lyrics by Harold Atteridge, songs that include "In Little Old New York," 200 perfs.

New York's Juilliard Foundation is established with a legacy left by the late French-American textile merchant Augustus D. Juilliard who in 1874 started a New York firm that earned him a fortune. Juilliard died last year at age 83 and stipulated in his will that income from the legacy be used to further music in America. The Juilliard Graduate School will be founded in 1924, the foundation trustees 2 years later will take over the Institute of Musical Art founded in 1905, and in 1946 the two schools will be combined under the name Juilliard School of Music.

First performances *Chant de Nigamon* (Symphonic Poem) by Arthur Honegger 1/3 at Paris; *Le Tombeau de Couperin* Suite for Orchestra by Maurice Ravel 2/28 at Paris; *La Valse,* a choreographic poem by Maurice Ravel 12/12 at Paris.

Popular songs   "Avalon" by Al Jolson and Vincent Rose who have lifted the melody from the aria "E Lucevan Le Stelle" in Giacomo Puccini's opera *Tosca* of 1900. Puccini and his publishers will be awarded damages of $25,000 plus all future royalties from the song; "I'll Be with You in Apple Blossom Time" by Albert von Tilzer, lyrics by Neville Fleeson; "The Japanese Sandman" by Richard Whiting, lyrics by Raymond Egan; "Margie" by U.S. songwriter Con Conrad (Conrad K. Dober), 28, lyrics by J. Russel Robinson, 28, and Benny Davis, 27; "Whispering" by U.S. composer John Schonberger, 28, lyrics by Richard Coburn (Frank D. de Long), 34; "When My Baby Smiles at Me" by U.S. composers Bill Munro and Harry von Tilzer, lyrics by Andrew B. Sterling and comedian Ted Lewis (Theodore Leopold Friedman), 28, who introduced the song 2 years ago at Rector's Cafe in New York: "Mon Homme" by French composer Maurice Yvain, 29, lyrics by Jacques-Charles.

Babe Ruth signs with the New York Yankees January 3 to begin a 14-year career as "Sultan of Swat" for New York. Yankee owner Jacob Ruppert has acquired the 24-year-old Boston Red Sox pitcher George Herman Ruth for $125,000 plus promises of a large loan, his new left-hander sets a slugging average record of .847 in his first season with New York, Ruth hits 54 home runs, bats .376, scores 158 runs, and makes the Yankees the first team in any sport to draw more than a million spectators, nearly double the team's 1919 gate (*see* 1923).

The "Black Sox" scandal threatens to undermine the prestige and popularity of America's national pastime as eight members of last year's Chicago White Sox baseball team are indicted in September for fraud in connection with last year's 5 to 3 World Series loss to Cincinnati. Chicago judge Kenesaw Mountain Landis, now 53, presides over the grand jury that hears the case, he will be named first commissioner of professional baseball in January of next year, and in one of his first rulings he will ban the eight indicted Chicago players from organized baseball for life.

The Cleveland Indians win the World Series by defeating the Brooklyn Dodgers 5 games to 2 in the last Series that will require 5 victories.

U.S. tennis player William Tatem "Bill" Tilden, Jr., wins his first national singles title at age 27 and becomes the first American to win the men's singles at Wimbledon, England. Tilden will dominate world tennis in the next 5 years and will remain undefeated in Davis Cup singles play until 1925 (*see* 1927).

1920 (cont.) British golf champion Joyce Wethered, 19, wins the English Ladies championship to begin a decade of triumph in which she will be virtually unbeatable.

The Olympic Games at Antwerp attract 2,741 athletes from 26 nations. U.S. athletes excel.

Spanish bullfighter José Gomez y Ortega, 25, is fatally gored May 16 at Talavera de la Reina to end the career of "Joselita" (or "Gallita"), who has killed more than 1,565 bulls in the arena.

Sir Thomas Lipton's *Shamrock IV* is defeated 3 to 2 by the U.S. defender *Resolute* in its challenge for the America's Cup.

Man o' War loses the Kentucky Derby but wins both the Preakness and the Belmont Stakes to close out a spectacular racing career in which he has been the odds-on favorite in every race he entered. The big chestnut colt is retired to stud.

The National Football League (NFL) is organized as the American Professional Football Association by men who include Joe Carr who founded the Columbus Panhandles in 1904, and 1918 University of Illinois star end George Stanley Halas, 25 (*see* Green Bay Packers, 1919). Halas obtains one of the original $100 franchises in behalf of the Staley Starch Company of Decatur, Ill. (*see* 1898), he will move the team to Chicago in 1922, he will rename it the Bears, he will make it commercially viable in 1925 by hiring "Red" Grange, and he will revolutionize football in the 1930s by perfecting the T formation that will make the game a contest of speed and deception with increased use of the forward pass.

Chanel No. 5 is introduced by "Coco" Chanel whose perfume will become the world's most popular fragrance (*see* 1913).

Antoine de Paris creates the mannish shingle bob haircut that will replace the conventional bob introduced by dancer Irene Castle in 1914. Polish-born hairdresser Antek Cierplikowski, 35, calls himself Monsieur Antoine (*see* Seligman and Latz, 1927).

The first Miss America beauty queen is crowned at Atlantic City, N.J., to begin a lasting tradition.

Loehmann's opens at Brooklyn, N.Y., where former A. T. Stewart & Company coat buyer Frieda Mueller Loehmann, 47, and her son Charles have invested $800 to start a woman's specialty shop that will have little success until it becomes a discount store. Loehmann pays cash to buy surplus dresses at reduced prices from garment makers in cash-short Seventh Avenue, she passes the savings on to her customers, she will shift entirely to discounting in 1922, and she will shop for bargains until 2 weeks before her death in 1962 by which time Loehmann's will have annual sales of $3 million (son Charles will open a Bronx Loehmann's in 1930 that will develop into a 34-store chain in 13 states by offering bargains from stores with plain pipe racks, communal dressing rooms, and a cash only, no returns policy).

A New York real estate tax abatement law that will stimulate construction of more than $1 billion worth of housing in New York City alone is passed by the legislature after a warning by Governor Alfred E. Smith that the state has a serious housing shortage (as does Britain, most of Europe, and much of America).

An English Renaissance limestone palace for Standard Oil heir Harold I. Pratt is completed on New York's Park Avenue at 68th Street. The building will later house the Council of Foreign Relations.

Barely 20 percent of America's virgin forest lands remain uncut.

Russia suffers a disastrous drought. Nikolai Lenin appeals to the U.S. Communist party for a report on American agricultural methods (*see* famine, 1921).

The American Farm Bureau Federation is founded. The Farm Bureau Federation will become the driving force behind mobilizing the political efforts of U.S. farmers.

The Federal Trade Commission orders the separation of the Deering and McCormick harvesting machines manufactured by International Harvester Corporation. The FTC acts under terms of the Clayton Act of 1914 (*see* 1918; 1927).

The U.S. soybean harvest reaches 1 million bushels, a figure that will increase more than 600 times in the next half-century (*see* 1924).

The boysenberry is developed by U.S. breeder Rudolph Boysen who crosses blackberries, raspberries, and loganberries to create a new variety but does not capitalize on his berry (*see* Knott, 1933).

Prohibition (below) will force California vineyard owners to diversify their production, to market as table grapes much of the fruit that has gone into wines and brandies, and to improve their methods of producing raisins which will soon be marketed under the Sunmaid label.

"Vitamines" become vitamins through the efforts of British biochemist J. C. Drummond who observes that not all coenzymes are amines (*see* Funk, 1911). Drummond labels the fat-soluble vitamin "A," the water-soluble vitamin "B," and the antiscorbutic vitamin "C," and with help from O. Rosenheim he finds that the human liver can produce vitamin A from the provitamin carotene widely available in fruits and vegetables.

A substance in cod-liver oil that can cure rickets and xerophthalmia is discovered by E. V. McCollum who has been at Johns Hopkins since 1917 (*see* 1917; Mellanby, 1918). Xerophthalmia is an abnormal dryness of the eye membranes and cornea that can lead to blindness (*see* vitamin D, 1922).

Botulism from commercially canned food strikes 36 Americans, 23 die, and the U.S. canning industry is motivated by falling sales to impose new production safety standards (*see* 1925).

Overfishing of the Sacramento River forces the closing of San Francisco's last salmon cannery (*see* 1866).

MacFisheries, Ltd., is started by William Hasketh Lever of England's Lever Brothers. It will become the world's largest chain of fish stores.

National Prohibition of sales of alcoholic beverages in the United States goes into effect January 16. A mock funeral for "John Barleycorn" is held January 15 at Norfolk, Va., by evangelist William Ashley "Billy" Sunday, 57, who has agitated for Prohibition but whose popularity now begins to fade. A farewell party to alcohol is given at New York's Park Avenue Hotel the evening of January 15 with tables draped in black.

Prohibition booms sales of coffee, soft drinks, and ice cream sodas, but consumption of alcoholic beverages will continue through illegal sales and homemade "bathtub gin."

The world sugar price drops from 30 cents per pound in August to 8 cents in December.

M. S. Hershey loses $2.5 million in the collapse of world sugar prices and other large sugar consumers also take heavy losses.

Pepsi-Cola's Caleb Bradham has bought sugar at 22 cents per pound, he loses $150,000, and Pepsi-Cola heads toward bankruptcy (see 1907; Guth, 1933).

Chero-Cola sales top $4 million, up more than 100 percent over 1918 sales, but the company ends the year with debts of over $1 million that will not be entirely paid off until 1926 (see 1918; 1928).

Howdy is introduced by St. Louis soft drink maker Charles L. Rigg who gets backing from local coal merchant Edmund Ridgway. The new drink will have some success until citrus growers push through laws in some legislatures requiring that orange-flavored drinks contain real orange pulp and orange juice (see Orange Crush, 1916; 7-Up, 1929).

American Sugar Refining Company sells the sugar from its newly acquired Central Cunagua at an average price of 23.5 cents for the year. The company nets $5.4 million, reinvests it in 200,000 additonal acres of sugar fields, buys two small islands with a combined area of 350 square miles, and builds a new *central* (sugar mill).

A new Life Savers plant opens at Port Chester, N.Y., and Edward J. Noble's Mint Products, Inc., is renamed Life Savers, Inc. (see 1913). Noble has increased sales by packaging his candy in resealable foil to preserve their flavor, by placing his nickel Life Savers next to the cash register at every United Cigar store and at many other stores, and by having the cashiers include nickels in every customer's change (see American Broadcasting, 1943; Beechnut-Life Savers, 1956).

The Good Humor created by Youngstown, Ohio, confectioner Harry Burt is a chocolate-covered ice cream bar on a stick. Burt has read about the "I-Scream-Bar" patented last year by Christian Nelson and will obtain his own patent in 1924 (see 1926).

Baby Ruth is introduced by Chicago's Curtiss Candy Company founded 4 years ago in a back room over a North Halstead Street plumbing shop by candymaker Otto Young Schnering, now 28. Schnering has used his mother's maiden name for the company and he names his 5-cent chocolate-covered candy roll of fudge, caramel, and peanuts after the daughter of the late President Cleveland (see 1923).

U.S. flour consumption drops to 179 pounds per capita, down from 224 pounds in 1900, as Americans eat more meat, poultry, fish, and vegetables while reducing consumption of baked goods and pasta.

Donut Corporation of America is founded by New York baker Adolph Levitt, 37, who has seen Red Cross workers dispensing doughnuts during the war and who sees an opportunity for a company to develop an automatic doughnut-making machine whose buyers will provide a market for a standardized mix.

La Choy Food Products, Inc., has its origin in a fresh-grown bean sprout business developed by Detroit grocer Wallace Smith who teams up with Ilhan New, a Korean he has known since both were students at the University of Michigan. Smith and New sell their bean sprouts in cans and glass jars (see 1922).

Seabrook Farms builds a modern cannery adjacent to the railroad tracks in the center of the New Jersey farmlands being cultivated by Charles Seabrook (see 1912; Birdseye, 1925).

U.S. food prices will fall 72 percent in the next 2 years as farm prices plummet.

The U.S. population reaches 105.7 million. Urban residents (54 million) for the first time exceed rural residents (51.5 million) but one in every three Americans still lives on a farm, a proportion that will drop in the next 50 years to one in 22.

The world population reaches 1.86 billion.

Abortion is legalized in Soviet Russia by a decree of the Lenin government at Moscow, but while Russian physicians are not permitted to refuse an abortion where a woman is no more than 2.5 months pregnant they are ordered to discourage patients from having abortions, especially in first pregnancies (see 1936).

Abortion is made illegal in France to compensate for the population loss experienced in the Great War. Severe fines and prison sentences are ordered for anyone who administers or receives an abortion, but the law will be widely flouted. Within 50 years the number of illegal abortions will climb to an estimated 500,000 per year with bungled abortions causing an estimated 500 deaths per year.

Youngs Rubber Company is founded by U.S. entrepreneur Merle Leland Youngs, 33, to make Trojan brand condoms that will compete with Julius Schmid's Shiek and Ramses brands (see 1883). Trojans will become the largest-selling condoms sold through U.S. drugstores, Youngs will head the Hol-

1920 (cont.) land-Ramos Corporation beginning in 1947, and he will die without issue in 1958 at age 71 (*see* 1923).

1921 Russian sailors mutiny at Kronstadt beginning February 23 as the nation's economy collapses (below). Bolshevik authorities put down the mutiny by March 17 but only with considerable bloodshed.

The Holmogor concentration camp that Bolshevik authorities open at Archangel is the world's first such camp. The Soviet government will establish many such camps and at least 10 million prisoners will die in the camps in the next 32 years.

British coal miners walk out of the pits March 31.

U.S. workers strike as employers cut wages by 10 to 25 percent. United States Steel Corporation cuts wages three times during the year and the Railroad Labor Board cuts wages 12 percent July 1.

The AF of L elects Samuel Gompers president for the 40th time at age 71.

The Supreme Court calls an Arizona picketing law invalid. The decision comes December 19 in the case of *Truax v. Corrigan*.

Persia has a bloodless coup February 20 as former Cossack trooper Riza Khan Pahlevi, 44, expels all Russian officers from the country and starts a new regime. Russia's Nikolai Lenin gives up special rights in Persia, he frees her of obligations to Russia, and he gives Persia joint command of the Caspian Sea.

A Russo-Turkish treaty signed March 16 recognizes Turkish possession of Kars and Ardaha in return for Turkey's retrocession of Batum. The treaty follows by 3 days an Italian agreement to evacuate Anatolia in return for economic concessions, but hostilities continue between Greece and Turkey. The Turks prevent the Greeks from reaching Angora only by desperate efforts.

Syria's Faisal I arrives at Basra June 23 and is placed on the throne of Iraq 2 months later by the British high commissioner Sir Percy Cox who has conducted a plebiscite that showed 96 percent of the Iraqi people in favor of having Faisal as king. He will reign until his death in 1933 and he establishes the Hashimite dynasty that will continue thereafter.

The Battle of Anual in Morocco July 21 brings defeat to a Spanish army at the hands of Rifs under the command of Abd'-el-Krim, 36. An anarchist has assassinated the Spanish prime minister Eduardo Dato Iradier March 8, General Fernandez Silvestre commits suicide when the Rifs kill 12,000 of his 20,000 men, and news of the disaster at Anual produces a political crisis at Madrid (*see* 1923).

Portugal has a revolution following the assassination in October of a founder of the 11-year-old republic.

Yugoslavia's Peter I has died August 16 at age 77 after less than 3 years as monarch of the new nation. He is succeeded by his 33-year-old son who will reign until 1934 as Aleksandr I (*see* 1929).

The Japanese prime minister Takashi Hara is assassinated by a fanatic November 4 at age 67.

Billy Mitchell sinks the former German battleship *Ostfriesland* July 21 to prove his contention that a strategic air force makes large navies obsolete. Brigadier General William Mitchell, 41, led a mass bombing attack of nearly 1,500 planes in 1918, his Martin M-2 bombers are twin-engined biplanes whose 418-horsepower Liberty engines give them a top speed of 98 miles per hour, and the 22,800-ton *Ostfriesland* is the first capital warship to be sunk by bombs from U.S. planes.

The U.S.S. *Jupiter* converted from an 11,050-ton collier is the first U.S. aircraft carrier. She has a stem-to-stern flight deck 534 feet (163 meters) in length and will be commissioned for fleet service in September of next year as the U.S.S. *Langley*.

The Washington Conference on Limitation of Naval Armaments that opens November 12 hears U.S. Secretary of State Charles Evans Hughes say, "Competition in armament must stop." Hughes announces that the United States is prepared to scrap immediately 15 old battleships and to cancel construction of nine new battleships and six new cruisers, some of them 85 to 90 percent complete. Naval power is generally believed to have given the Allies the margin of victory in the Great War and the announcement that Washington is prepared to scrap two-thirds of the U.S. battleship fleet stuns the conferees, many of whom believe that America would be committing naval suicide (*see* 1922).

Southern Ireland gains Dominion status December 6 in a treaty signed with Britain. The Catholic Irish Free State (Eire) embraces 26 of Ireland's 32 counties but the six counties in Protestant Northern Ireland remain part of the United Kingdom and conflict between the two will continue for well over half a century (*see* 1920; IRA, 1922).

 A New Economic Policy (NEP) sponsored by Nikolai Lenin is announced by Russia's Communist Party as industrial and agricultural production fall off and shortages become acute in food, fuel, and transportation.

The NEP (above) abolishes food levies to placate Russia's peasants and a limited grain tax is substituted. Some freedom of trade is restored to enable the peasants to dispose of their surpluses and some private commercial enterprises are permitted in the cities (*see* Armand Hammer, below).

A Russian plea for resumption of trade relations is rejected March 25 by U.S. Secretary of State Charles Evans Hughes who refuses such trade so long as Communism prevails.

The United States has nearly 20,000 business failures and by September nearly 3.5 million Americans are out of work. President Harding calls an Unemployment Conference under the chairmanship of Commerce Secretary Herbert Hoover.

British unemployment reaches 2.5 million in July but then begins a gradual drop to 1.2 million where it will remain until 1930. Seven million Britons take wage cuts and the unemployed are given allowances for dependent relatives.

The British Medical Association estimates that a family of five needs 22s 6½d per week for food to maintain proper health, but as unemployment reaches its peak in July the dole is 29s 3d per week and rents in even the worst slum tenements average 6s per week.

The U.S. General Accounting Office is created by act of Congress and is the first federally funded arm of Congress since the Library of Congress was established in 1800. The G.A.O. will be a congressional watchdog on federal spending.

A new silver dollar is minted to replace the coin that has been in circulation. The new coin has the word "Peace" under the eagle on one side, it has the Liberty head on the opposite side, and it will not be superseded for 50 years.

The New York Curb Exchange moves into a new building of its own in Trinity Place following decades in which members have transacted business by signaling from curbstone street positions to clerks located in windows of surrounding buildings (see American Stock Exchange, 1953).

Heart disease becomes the leading cause of death in America after 10 years of jockeying for the lead with tuberculosis. Coronary disease accounts for 14 percent of U.S. deaths and the figure will increase to 39 percent in the next 50 years.

The Council of the American Medical Association refuses to endorse an A.M.A. resolution proposed in 1917 that would oppose use of alcohol as a beverage and would discourage its use as a therapeutic agent. More than 15,000 physicians and 57,000 druggists and drug manufacturers applied for licenses to prescribe and sell liquor in the first 6 months after passage of the Volstead Act in 1919 and by 1928 physicians will be making an estimated $40 million per year by writing prescriptions for whiskey.

Former U.S. secretary of the Navy Franklin Delano Roosevelt, 39, is stricken with poliomyelitis while vacationing at Campobello Island off Nova Scotia. Popularly called infantile paralysis, the disease is widespread in North America and it will leave Roosevelt crippled for life (see 1916; Georgia Warm Springs Foundation, 1927).

Columbia University Medical School graduate Armand Hammer, 22, goes to Russia to help the Lenin government cope with its postwar disease plagues and to collect $150,000 owed to his father's company for drugs shipped during the Allied blockade of Russian ports. Hammer's Russian-American father is in Sing Sing prison for having performed an alleged abortion, he travels to the Urals, he barters a million tons of U.S. wheat for a fortune in furs, caviar, and precious stones, and he meets late in August with Nikolai Lenin who persuades him to take a concession to operate an asbestos mine in the Urals. The mine will not be successful but Hammer and his brother Victor, 21, will open an export-import business at Moscow that will serve as agents for Ford Motor Company, Parker Pen, U.S. Rubber, Underwood Typewriter, and nearly three dozen other foreign companies.

Psychodiagnostics by Swiss psychiatrist Hermann Rorschach, 36, introduces the Rorschach Test, based on subjects' reactions to inkblots, to probe the unconscious.

Band-Aid brand adhesive bandages are introduced by Johnson & Johnson of New Brunswick, N.J., which will diversify its product line in this decade to offer items such as Johnson's Baby Cream (see 1916).

Electric light bulb production efficiency is improved by the Corning Glass Works which installs a new ribbon machine that turns out between 21,000 and 31,000 bulbs per hour (see 1903; Langmuir, 1912).

A depletion allowance for petroleum-producing companies is granted by an act of Congress to encourage exploration of potential new petroleum reserves as America increases her consumption of gasoline. The 27.5 percent depletion allowance tax incentive will be cut to 22 percent in 1969.

The Teapot Dome scandal that will help tarnish the Harding administration has its beginnings as Navy Secretary Edwin Denby transfers control of naval oil reserves to the Department of the Interior whose secretary Albert Fall secretly leases Teapot Dome to private oil operators Harry Sinclair and Edward Doheny (see 1915). Sinclair and Doheny will lose their leases after a congressional investigation in 1923 but they will be acquitted in 1928 of charges that they bribed Secretary Fall.

IF YOU DON'T COME IN SUNDAY DON'T COME IN MONDAY.

THE MANAGEMENT

U.S. sweatshop operators resisted efforts by union men to organize garment workers in the big-city loft factories.

1921 (cont.) The antiknock properties of tetraethyl lead as a gasoline additive are discovered by U.S. chemist Thomas Midgley, 32, who is helped by General Motors to establish the Ethyl Corporation (*see* 1923).

The Port of New York Authority created April 30 by New York State and New Jersey will administer marine terminals, tunnels, bridges, and other facilities that will include airports, helicopter pads, rail terminals, bus terminals, and office buildings serving 164 million commuters per year and 42 million air passengers (*see* bus terminal, 1950; PATH, World Trade Center, 1962).

Berlin's Avus Autobahn opens to traffic September 10. Originally planned in 1909 and nearly complete when the Great War stopped construction, the Autobahn is the world's first highway designed exclusively for motor traffic and with controlled access, it runs 6.25 miles from the Grunewald to the suburb of Wannsee, a 26-foot grass mall separates its two 26-foot wide carriageways, and it is spanned by 10 ferroconcrete bridges.

A Federal Highway Act passed by Congress November 9 begins to coordinate state highways and to standardize U.S. roadbuilding practice (*see* 1944; Route 66, 1932).

The United States has 387,000 miles of surfaced road by year's end, up from 190,476 in 1909 (*see* 1930).

More than a million trucks travel on U.S. roads and highways, up from 100,000 in 1909.

Generators become standard equipment on Model T Fords which account for 61.34 percent of all U.S. motorcars sold.

Durant Motors, Inc., is founded by W. C. Durant who has again been forced out of General Motors Corporation but who has raised $7 million to start a new venture (*see* 1916). Durant acquires the Bridgeport, Conn., plant of the bankrupt Locomobile Company to build a Durant luxury car that will supplement the $850 Durant Four and the medium-priced Durant Six made at Muncie, Ind., and he pays $5.25 million to acquire the Willys plant at Elizabethport, N.J., which is the world's most modern auto factory (*see* Deusenberg, 1919). The Willys-Overland Company has gone bankrupt and its receivers sell Durant the Willys design for a new medium-priced Flint motorcar that Durant intends to market (*see* Star, 1922; Willys-Overland, 1936).

GM's share of the U.S. motorcar market reaches 12 percent and GM begins a rapid expansion under the leadership of Alfred Sloan.

The Wall Street banking house Dillon, Read acquires control of the Goodyear Tire & Rubber Company (*see* 1898). F. A. Sieberling loses $15 million in 1 day but he starts Sieberling Rubber Company, a firm that will become a significant factor in the tire industry.

The *New York Times* runs an editorial explaining that Robert H. Goddard's rockets cannot possibly work because there is nothing in outer space for the rockets' exhausts to push against (*see* 1919; 1926).

English pilot Harry G. Hawker dies July 12 at age 29 in a crash of the Nieuport Goshawk he is testing for T. O. M. Sopwith's Hawker Engineering Co., Ltd., which Sopwith renamed in Hawker's honor last year (*see* 1912; 1919).

The first transcontinental U.S. day-night flight encourages Congress to support airmail service. Mail pilot Jack Knight lands at Omaha February 22 after a 248-mile flight from North Platte, Neb., he learns that no pilot is available for the next leg, he flies on through heavy snow to Iowa City and refuels, he flies on to Chicago, he completes 672 miles in 10 hours, and two other pilots take the plane through to New York, setting a transcontinental flight record of 33 hours, 20 minutes (*see* 1918; Doolittle, 1922).

Two-way weekly airmail service between Cairo and Baghdad begins in June. The Royal Air Force reduces the time it takes a letter from London to reach Baghdad to between 5 and 10 days, down from 28 days before the airplane.

The British Broadcasting Company (BBC) has its beginnings (*see* 1922).

Pittsburgh's radio station KDKA is founded (*see* 1920; 1922).

Cincinnati's WLW radio station is started by local auto parts producer Powel Crosley, 35, who moves his ham station 8CR transmitter from his house to his factory and has it licensed under the call letters WLW. Crosley will organize the Crosley Radio Corporation in 1923 and will be active not only in broadcasting but also in baseball and in the production of radios, refrigerators, washing machines, other appliances, and (briefly) a subcompact automobile (*see* 1946; first night baseball game, 1935).

The *Sunday News* is launched by New York's 2-year-old *Daily News*. By 1925 it will be outselling all other Sunday papers with help from its comic strips.

"Tillie the Toiler" by cartoonist Russ Westover challenges the 2-year-old comic strip "Winnie Winkle."

"Smitty" by cartoonist Walter Bendt appears for the first time November 29 in the *Chicago Tribune*.

Dell Publishing Company is founded by New York publisher George T. Delacorte, Jr., 27, and former *New York World* Sunday editor William A. Johnston whose magazine *Sweetheart Stories* begins an empire. In 10 years Dell will be publishing 14 magazines, most of them pulp, confession, and movie fan magazines that will include *Modern Screen* and *Modern Romances*.

The Parker Duofold fountain pen ("Big Red") is introduced by the Parker Pen Company of Janesville, Wis., at $7 but is considered by many to be too large for comfortable writing.

Nonfiction *The Story of Mankind* by Dutch-American historian Henrik Willem Van Loon, 39.

Fiction *Three Soldiers* by U.S. novelist John Roderigo Dos Passos, 25, who last year published *One Man's Initiation—1917* to describe his experiences in the U.S. Army medical corps; *Memoirs of a Midget* by Walter De La Mare; *Alice Adams* by Booth Tarkington; *Scaramouche* by Rafael Sabatini; *Mavis of Green Hill* by U.S. novelist Faith Baldwin, 28, whose books will be serialized in magazines for women and will be second in popularity only to those of Kathleen Norris (*see* 1911); *The Mysterious Affair at Styles* by English mystery writer Agatha (Mary Clarissa Miller) Christie, 30, who introduces the detective Hercule Poirot, late of the Belgian Surete.

Poetry *Il Canzoniere* by Italian poet Umberto Saba (Umberto Poli), 38; *Second April* by Edna St. Vincent Millay; *English Poems* by Portuguese poet Fernando Pessoa, 33, who was brought up in South Africa; *The Pillar of Flame (Ognenny stolp)* by Russian poet Nikolai Gumilyov; *Anno Domini* by Russian poet Anna Akhmatova (Anna Gorenko), 32, who has defied her father's objections to her career.

The Phillips Collection opens at Washington, D.C., the first U.S. modern art museum. Collector Duncan Phillips, 35, will be director until his death in 1966.

Painting *Gray Day* by German painter George Grosz, 28, is a savage portrayal of German society; *Odalisque in Red Trousers* by Henri Matisse; *Still Life With Guitar* by Georges Braque; *Three Women* by Fernand Léger; *Three Musicians* by Pablo Picasso; *Composition with Red, Yellow and Blue* by Piet Mondrian; *The Fish* by Paul Klee; *The Kiss* by Edvard Munch; *Bull Durham* by U.S. cubist Stuart Davis, 26.

Theater *Diff'rent* by Eugene O'Neill 1/4 at New York's Provincetown Playhouse, 100 perfs.; *The Green Goddess* by Scottish playwright William Archer, 65, 1/18 at New York's Booth Theater with George Arliss, 440 perfs.; *R.U.R. (Rossum's Universal Robots)* by Karel Capek 1/25 at Prague's National Theater; *A Punch for Judy* by Philip (James Quinn) Barry, 24, 4/18 at New York's Morosco Theater; *Six Characters in Search of an Author (Sei Pei Personaggi in Cerca d'Autore)* by Luigi Pirandello 5/10 at Rome's Teatro Valle (Pirandello committed his wife Antonietta to an insane asylum in 1918 and has been obsessed by characters in his dreams); *If* by Lord Dunsany 5/30 at London's Ambassadors Theatre; *Dulcy* by U.S. playwrights George Simon Kaufman, 31, and Marc (Marcus Cook) Connelly, 30, 8/13 at New York's Frayzee Theater, 246 perfs.; *Getting Gertie's Garter* by Wilson Collison and Avery Hopwood 8/21 at New York's Republic Theater, with Hazel Dawn, 120 perfs.; *A Bill of Divorcement* by English playwright Clemence Dane (Winifred Ashton), 33, 10/10 at New York's George M. Cohan Theater, with Katherine Cornell, Charles Waldron, 173 perfs.; *Anna Christie* by Eugene O'Neill 11/2 at New York's Vanderbilt Theater, with Pauline Lord as Anna Christopherson in the story of a prostitute's fight for redemption, 177 perfs., Pulitzer prize.

"Weary Willy" makes his bow at Ringling Bros. Barnum & Bailey's circus. Clown Emmet Kelly, 22, will make the sad-faced character his role for 50 years.

Films Fred Niblo's *The Three Musketeers* with Douglas Fairbanks; D. W. Griffith's *Way Down East* with Lillian Gish, Lowell Sherman, Richard Barthelmess; D. W. Griffith's *Dream Street* with Carol Dempster, Ralph Graves; Fritz Lang's *Destiny;* Fritz Lang's *Spies;* Fred Niblo's *The Four Horsemen of the Apocalypse* with Italian-American vaudeville dancer Rudolph Valentino (originally Rodolpho d'Antonguolla), 26; George Melford's *The Shiek* with Rudolph Valentino; Henry King's *Tol'able David* with Richard Barthelmess; Alfred E. Green and Jack Pickford's *Little Lord Fauntleroy* with Mary Pickford; Charlie Chaplin's *The Kid* with Chaplin; Sam Wood's *Peck's Bad Boy* with Jackie Coogan; James Cruze's *Leap Year* with Roscoe (Fatty) Arbuckle, whose arrest in connection with the death of a young woman creates a scandal that suggests widespread use of drugs in the film capital and ends Arbuckle's career.

New York musicians organize Local 802 of the American Federation of Musicians. The powerful local will negotiate contracts with the Metropolitan Opera, the League of New York Theaters, and recording companies.

Isadora Duncan opens a Moscow school for the dance at the invitation of the Soviet government (*see* 1905). Now 43, Duncan meets and marries Russian poet Sergei Aleksandrovich Esenin, 26, who 2 years ago founded the imagist group and is known as the "poet laureate of the Revolution." He and Duncan, neither speaking the other's language, will tour the United States; many will call them Bolshevist spies (*see* 1927).

Ballet *The Buffoon (Le chout)* 5/17 at the Théâtre Gaité-Lyrique, Paris, with music by Sergei Prokofiev. He came to America last year and has married Lina Ivanovna Llubera whose mother is Russian; *The Sleeping Princess* 11/2 at London's Alhambra Theatre, with Bronislava Nijinska, music by Igor Stravinsky, choreography by Marius Petipa.

Opera *Mörder, Hoffnung der Frauen,* and *Das Nusch-Nuschi* 6/4 at Stuttgart, with music by German composer Paul Hindemith, 25; *Katya Kananova* 10/23 at Brno, with music by Leo Janicek; *The Love for Three Oranges* 12/30 at Chicago, with music by Sergei Prokofiev.

Stage musicals *Shuffle Along* 5/23 at New York's 63rd Street Music Hall, with teenager Josephine Baker in an all-black revue, songs that include "Love Will Find a Way" and "I'm Just Wild About Harry" by Eubie (James Hubert) Blake, 38, and Noble Sissle, 32, 504 perfs.; *Two Little Girls in Blue* 5/31 at New York's George M. Cohan Theater, with music by Vincent Youmans, 23, and P. Lannin, lyrics by Arthur Francis (Ira Gershwin), songs that include "Oh Me! Oh My!" 134 perfs.; *The Ziegfeld Follies* 6/21 at New York's Globe Theater, with Fanny Brice singing the torch song "My Man" published at Paris last year under the title "Mon Homme" and made poignant by the fact that Brice is married to gambler Nick Arnstein (English lyrics by Alfred Willametz). "Sec-

1921 (cont.) ond Hand Rose" by James F. Hanley, lyrics by Grant Clark, is another *Follies* hit, 119 perfs.; *The Co-Optimists* 6/27 at London's Royalty Theatre, with music and lyrics by Melville Gideon, songs that include "When the Sun Goes Down," "Tampa Bay," 500 perfs.; (George White's) *Scandals* 7/11 at New York's Liberty Theater, with White, Ann Pennington, Lou Holtz, music by George Gershwin, lyrics by Arthur Jackson, songs that include "Drifting Along with the Tide," 97 perfs.; *Tangerine* 8/9 at New York's Casino Theater, with book by Philip Bartholomae and Guy Bolton, music by Carlo Sanders, lyrics by Howard Johnson, 337 perfs.; *The Greenwich Village Follies* 8/31 at New York's Shubert Theater, with Ted Lewis, songs that include "Three O'Clock in the Morning" by Spanish composer Julian Robledo, 34, lyrics by New York lyricist Dolly Morse (Dorothy Terrio), 31, 167 perfs.; *Blossom Time* 9/21 at New York's Ambassador Theater, with book and lyrics by Dorothy Donelly who has adapted the German operetta *Das Dreimädelhaus* based on the life of composer Franz Schubert, music by Sigmund Romberg whose proceeds from the show will be roughly 2,000 times what Schubert earned from all his music, 592 perfs.; *The Music Box Revue* 9/22 at New York's Music Box Theater, with Irving Berlin, songs by Berlin that include "Say It with Music," 440 perfs.; *Bombo* 10/6 at New York's Jolson Theater, with Al Jolson singing numbers by Sigmund Romberg, with book and lyrics by B. G. DeSylva. Jolson soon interpolates "My Mammy" by Walter Donaldson, lyrics by Joe Young and Sam M. Lewis, "Toot, Toot, Tootsie" by Dan Russo, lyrics by Gus Kahn and Ernie Erdman, "April Showers" by Louis Silvers, 32, lyrics by Jack Yellen, "California, Here I Come" by Joseph Meyer, lyrics by Jolson and B. G. DeSylva, 219 perfs.; *The Perfect Fool* 11/7 at New York's George M. Cohan Theater, with Ed Wynn, book, music, and lyrics by Wynn, songs that include "Daisy" by Wynn and "My Little House" by George Gershwin, lyrics by Irving Caesar and B. G. DeSylva; *Kiki* 11/29 at New York's Belasco Theater, with Lenore Ulric, songs that include "Some Day I'll Find You" by Zoel Parenteau, lyrics by Schuyler Green, 600 perfs.

First performances *Pastorale d'Été* by Arthur Honegger 2/17 at Paris; *Le Roi David* Symphonic Psalm for Chorus and Orchestra by Arthur Honegger 6/11 at the Jorot Theater in Mezieres outside Lausanne; *The Lark Ascending* Romance for Violin and Orchestra by Ralph Vaughan Williams 6/14 at London; Concerto No. 3 for Piano and Orchestra by Sergei Rachmaninoff 12/16 at Chicago.

Popular songs "Ain't We Got Fun" by Richard A. Whiting, lyrics by Gus Kahn and Raymond Egan; "There'll Be Some Changes Made" by U.S. composer Benton Overstreet, lyrics by Billy Higgins; "I'm Nobody's Baby" by Milton Ager and Lester Santly, lyrics by Benny Davis; "All by Myself" by Irving Berlin; "My Mammy" by Walter Donaldson, lyrics by Joe Young and Sam M. Lewis; "The Sheik of Araby" by Ted Snyder, Harry B. Smith, Francis Wheeler; "Fire Dance" ("Danse Rituelle du Feu") by Manuel de Falla, lyrics by Martinez Serra, 41.

Basketball star Nat Holman, 24, joins the Boston Celtics and with Dutch Leonard begins a 9-year career in which the Celtics will win 720 games out of 795. Professional basketball gains respectability for the first time as Holman continues to coach the C.C.N.Y. team he began coaching last year.

Boxing has its first $1 million gate July 2 at Boyle's Thirty Acres in Jersey City where heavyweight champion Jack Dempsey defeats French challenger Georges Carpentier by a fourth round knockout. The handsome Carpentier won the world light-heavyweight title by defeating Battling Levinsky in a Jersey City bout held October 20 of last year and the bout with Dempsey has been promoted by Tex Rickard of Madison Square Garden. It begins at just after 3 o'clock in the afternoon, it draws more than 90,000 spectators who pay $1.7 million for tickets, and it earns $300,000 for Dempsey, $215,000 for Carpentier.

The New York Giants win the World Series by defeating the New York Yankees 5 games to 3.

Spanish bullfighter Juan Belmonte retires at age 29 after matador Manuel Granero is killed in the ring at Madrid in May, but the millionaire founder of modern bullfighting will return several times before finally devoting himself exclusively to the breeding of bulls for the *corrida*.

World chess champion Emanuel Lasker is defeated after having held the title for 27 years. Cuban chess master Jose Raul Capablanca y Granperra, 33, wins the title that he will hold until 1927.

Centre College of Danville, Ky., upsets the Harvard football team 6 to 0 with a 32-yard reverse run in the third period by Centre quarterback Alvin "Bo" McMillin.

Drano is introduced by Cincinnati's P. W. Drackett & Sons, Inc., whose drain cleaner consists of crystals containing sodium hydroxide (caustic lye). The company was founded in 1910 by entrepreneur Philip Wilbur Drackett to distribute chemicals (*see* 1933).

Electrolux vacuum cleaners are introduced by Swedish electric lamp salesman Axel Wenner-Gren, 40, who has founded the Electrolux Company to produce the machines that will be the world's top-performing vacuum cleaners. Wenner-Gren's company will also be a major factor in the refrigerator industry.

Ingersoll Watch Company is acquired by the Waterbury Clock Company after having sold 100 million watches worldwide (*see* 1892; Timex, 1946).

The Van Heusen collar is introduced by Phillips Jones Corporation which has acquired rights to the starchless but stiff collar invented by John M. van

Heusen, 52. The collar is made from multiple ply, interwoven fabrics and van Heusen has patented collars, cuffs, neckbands, and other articles made in whole or in part from such fabrics.

The Arrow shirt is introduced by Cluett, Peabody Co. as demand increases for collar-attached shirts. Research director Sanford Lockwood Cluett, 47, develops a "Sanforizing" process to limit shrinkage (*see* 1898).

P. K. chewing gum is introduced by William Wrigley, Jr., now 60, whose son Philip Knight Wrigley, 26, will head the firm following Wrigley's death in 1932 (*see* 1914; Wrigley building, 1924).

U.S. cigarette consumption reaches 43 billion, up from 10 billion in 1910 despite the fact that cigarettes are illegal in 14 states. Anticigarette bills are pending in 28 other states, college girls are expelled for smoking, but the tobacco companies promote the addiction to nicotine.

The Oxford Group is founded at Oxford University by German-American evangelist Frank Nathan Daniel Buchman, 43, who claims to have had a vision of the Cross in the English lake district in 1908. Buchman has served as a missionary for the YMCA in Japan, Korea, and India, he works to "change" lives through his First Century Christian Fellowship, and he will organize groups in the Scandinavian countries, Canada, the United States, South America, and Latin America (*see* Moral Rearmament, 1939).

New York's Cunard building is completed on Bowling Green across from Cass Gilbert's Customs House of 1907. The 21-story structure has been designed by Benjamin Wistar Morris with an assist from Thomas Hastings, it stands on the site once occupied by Delmonico's Hotel (which became Stevens House but was demolished in 1919), and it has a Great Hall with elaborately decorated domed vaults designed by Ezra Winter.

San Francisco's 22-story Standard Oil building is completed at the corner of Sansome and Bush.

Watts Tower is begun at Los Angeles by Italian-American tile-setter Simon Rodia, 41, who uses only hand tools, shells, glass, and other found objects to build a structure that will awe visitors for decades.

The Los Angeles Ambassador Hotel opens with 532 rooms on a 24-acre expanse of sports facilities.

Chicago's Field Museum of Natural History founded in 1893 opens in a new building overlooking Grant Park.

Coe Hall on Long Island's north shore, near Oyster Bay, N.Y., is completed for industrialist William Robertson Coe by the architectural firm Walker & Gillette. The 65-room Elizabethan style country house is surrounded with 400 acres of rare plants and trees from Europe and Asia.

Hot Springs National Park is created by act of Congress. Set aside as a government reservation in 1832,

the 3,535-acre park in Arkansas contains 47 mineral hot springs.

An Appalachian Trail for hikers is proposed by U.S. forester Benton MacKaye, 42, who is first president of the Wilderness Society. Extending nearly 2,000 miles from Georgia's Springer Mountain to Maine's Mt. Katahdin, the wilderness footpath will in large part follow the Great Indian Warpath that existed in the 18th century from Creek Territory in Alabama into Pennsylvania, but its diverse parts will be unified by MacKaye.

Famine kills 3 million Russians. Frozen corpses are piled 20 feet high in the streets waiting for the ground to thaw so that burial pits can be dug. Millions of people are saved by relief aid organized by U.S. Secretary of Commerce Herbert C. Hoover whose American Relief Administration raises more than $60 million in response to an appeal by Russian writer Maksim Gorky.

A Russian Famine Relief Act passed by Congress December 22 authorizes the expenditure of $20 million for the purchase of seed, grain, and preserved milk to be sent to Russia.

Lincoln Steffens is persuaded by American Communist Harold M. Ware to donate more than $70,000 in lecture fees to buy tractors and other farm equipment for Russia. Ware has made a study of U.S. farming methods in response to last year's request by Nikolai Lenin and he notes that Russia has fewer than 1,500 tractors, many of them unrepairable wrecks (*see* 1922).

U.S. farmers overproduce on acreage planted during the war and farm prices in July fall to levels 85 percent below 1919 highs. Cotton is 11 cents per pound, down from 42 cents; corn is 42 cents per bushel, down from $2; wheat is $1, down from $3.50.

The Harding administration tries to relieve the agricultural depression with an emergency tariff act imposing high duties on imports of wheat, corn, meat, sugar, wool, and other farm products.

Cotton production in Georgia and South Carolina is cut in half by the ravages of the boll weevil (*see* 1916; 1924).

Botanist George Washington Carver of the Tuskegee Institute testifies before the House Ways and Means Committee on the value of peanuts which are planted increasingly by Georgia and South Carolina farmers (*see* Carver, 1914).

A hybrid corn variety that will yield far more per acre than conventional corn is perfected by Harvard biologist Edward Murray East, 42, of the Connecticut Agricultural Experiment Station, and Princeton botanist George Harrison Shull (*see* 1905; 1930).

Cod-liver oil is found to be a preventive against rickets by vitamin pioneer E. V. McCollum who observes that rats fed large amounts of calcium develop bone deformities much like those seen in rickets but that

1921 (cont.) the deformities are prevented if a little cod-liver oil is added to the rats' rations (*see* 1918; 1922).

U.S. embryologist Herbert McLean Evans, 39, at the University of California, Berkeley, shows with rat studies that mammals other than humans require an "anti-sterility" factor in their diets if they are to reproduce (*see* vitamin E, 1935).

Salt iodized with potassium iodide is introduced by U.S. table salt makers but iodization is not made mandatory (*see* 1924; Akron study, 1916).

The Fundaments of Our Nutrition by Swiss physician M. O. Bircher-Benner, 54, recommends ingestion of more uncooked foods.

Good dairy practices are legislated in several states to improve the safety of U.S. milk which often reaches consumers with a bacteria count of 500,000 or more per cubic centimeter (*see* 1900). Undulant fever, brucellosis, bacillary dysentery, infectious hepatitis, typhoid fever, tuberculosis, and other diseases are transmitted by contaminated milk.

Wholesale butter prices in the New York market fall to 29 cents per pound, down from 76 cents during the war. Imports of Danish butter have increased and Americans are using more margarine.

U.S. butter is "scored" on a point system that gives 45 points for top flavor, 25 points on the basis of composition, 15 on color, 10 on salt content, 5 on the wooden butter tub used for packaging. Butter that scores 92 out of a possible 100 is called extra grade or "New York extras," but out of 622 Minnesota creameries only 200 make butter good enough to command the premium price paid for 92-score "New York extras."

Land O' Lakes Butter, Inc., has its beginnings in the Minnesota Cooperative Creameries Association formed by Meeker County, Minn., creameries. The federation will burgeon into a Minneapolis-based empire of midwestern dairy farmers.

Bel Paese semisoft cheese is introduced by Italian cheesemaker Egidio Galbani.

Food canning is advanced by Cambridge, Mass., chemist Bradley Dewey, 34, who discovers the first water-based latex sealing compound. The sealant will be used inside the crimped rims by which tops and bottoms are attached to cans and Dewey's firm Dewey & Almy will be a major producer of the sealant and of the machines used to apply it (*see* synthetic rubber, 1939).

The name "Betty Crocker" is developed by Washburn, Crosby Company of Minneapolis. The firm runs a contest to promote its Gold Medal Flour and letters from contestants are answered by the fictitious food authority Betty Crocker (*see* 1880; 1924).

The first automatic doughnut-making machine is introduced (*see* Donut Corporation of America, 1920).

Molasses prices drop to 2 cents per gallon, down from 20 cents last year. Penick & Ford, Ltd., which makes Brer Rabbit Molasses and Vermont Maid maple syrup loses $9.5 million (*see* Corn Products Refining, 1913; sugar price drop, 1920; R. J. Reynolds, 1965).

World cocoa prices collapse in the absence of any futures market mechanism. Speculative "hoarders" have used bank credits to buy up cocoa beans produced from October through January in anticipation of the usual price advances but when the banks suddenly begin calling the loans the cocoa is thrown on the market, prices break nearly 20 cents per pound, and losses are sustained by cocoa merchants and importers as well as by outside speculators who are in many cases ruined (*see* Cocoa Exchange, 1925).

Mounds candy bars are introduced by the Peter Paul Manufacturing Company incorporated 2 years ago. The coconut and bittersweet chocolate bar is made from a formula devised by former chemist George Shamlian and its immediate success encourages Peter Paul to build a plant at Naugatuck, Conn. (*see* automatic production, 1932).

The Eskimo Pie replaces the "I-Scream-Bar" of 1919 as Omaha, Neb., candymaker Russell William Stover, 33, teams up with Christian Nelson to sell franchises for the manufacture and sale of the chocolate-covered ice cream bars (*see* 1922; Good Humor, 1920).

Wise Potato Chips are introduced by Berwick, Pa., grocer Earl V. Wise who finds himself overstocked with old potatoes. He peels them, slices them with an old-fashioned cabbage cutter, follows his mother's recipe for making potato chips, packages the chips in brown paper bags, and sells them in his grocery store (*see* George Crum, 1853; peeling machines, 1925).

Lindy's Restaurant opens at 1626 Broadway in New York under the management of German-American restaurateur Leo "Lindy" Lindeman, 33, whose cheesecake will be favored by newspapermen, politicians, and theater people for half a century.

Sardi's Restaurant opens in West 44th Street, New York, under the direction of Italian-American restaurateur Vincent Sardi, 35, whose place will be an unofficial theatrical club for more than half a century. Sardi will move to 234 West 44th Street in 1927 when his first building is razed to make way for construction of the St. James Theater.

The U.S. population reaches 107 million. Biologist Raymond Pearl notes that the rate of population increase has been declining since 1914 and predicts that it will reach a peak of 197,274,000 in the year 2100 (*see* 1939; biometrics, 1923).

Some 900,000 immigrants enter the United States in the fiscal year ending June 30.

The Dillingham Bill (Emergency Quota Act) enacted by Congress May 19 establishes a quota system to restrict immigration. Entry is permitted only to 3 percent of the people of any nationality who lived in the United States in 1910 (*see* 1924).

The American Birth Control League is started by Margaret Sanger (*see* 1916; 1923).

The Mothers' Clinic for Constructive Birth Control is started in England by paleobotanist Marie Carmichael Stopes, 41, whose book *Radiant Motherhood* was published last year.

The population of Great Britain reaches 42.7 million. Germany has 30 million, France 39.2, Italy 38.7, Brazil 30, Japan 78, Russia 136.

1922 Postwar political and economic convulsions are marked by new treaties, new violence, and the emergence of new nations and regimes—an independent Egyptian monarchy, an Italian fascist dictatorship, and an independent Irish Free State.

Japan agrees February 4 to return Shantung to China where rival war lords engage in civil war.

The Washington Conference ends February 6 after nearly 3 months with a naval armaments treaty that provides for a 10-year period during which no new ships of more than 10,000 tons with guns larger than 8 inches in width are to be built by Britain, France, Italy, Japan, or the United States. Britain and the United States are then to be permitted totals of 525,000 tons each, Japan 315,000 tons, France and Italy 175,000 tons each.

Submarine warfare and use of poison gas are restricted by the Washington Conference (above).

The Permanent Court of International Justice opens February 15 at The Hague.

The Kingdom of Egypt is proclaimed March 15 as the sultan Ahmed Fuad who succeeded his brother Hussein Kamil in 1917 assumes the title of king 2 weeks after the termination by Britain of her protectorate over Egypt. The Sudan remains under joint Anglo-Egyptian sovereignty and Fuad I begins a reign that will continue until 1936.

The Irish Republican Army (IRA) is formally constituted in March "to safeguard the honor and independence of the Irish Republic." A militant arm of the Sinn Fein political party that has stood for a free, undivided Ireland since the Easter Rising of 1916, the IRA will be disavowed by responsible Irish political leaders but it will continue for more than half a century to employ terrorist tactics in a civil war within the Irish Free State (Eire) and in Ulster.

The dominion status granted to Ireland last year by Britain is rejected by President de Valera who has resigned January 9 and who organizes a new Republican Society. De Valera begins an insurrection against his erstwhile colleagues Arthur Griffith and Michael Collins who have formed a new government, and the terrorism used earlier against the British is now used also against Irishmen as well.

British field marshal Sir Henry Hughes Wilson, 58, who has urged severe coercion of the Sinn Fein, is murdered by Sinn Fein terrorists, the president of the Dail Eireann Arthur Griffith dies suddenly August 12, the prime minister Michael Collins is mortally wounded August 22 at age 30 while repelling an IRA assault, William T. Cosgrove is elected September 9 to succeed Griffith, a Constitution for the Irish Free State is adopted by the Dail October 24, the IRA leader Erskine Childers of 1903 *Riddle of the Sands* fame is court-martialed and executed by a firing squad November 24, the Irish Free State is officially proclaimed December 6, the parliament of Northern Ireland votes December 7 to remain outside the Free State, and the last British troops leave the Free State December 17.

The German foreign minister Walter Rathenau has been murdered June 24 at age 55 by nationalist reactionaries. Son of the industrialist who helped found the German Edison Company in 1883, Rathenau had signed the treaty of Rapallo April 16 recognizing Soviet Russia as a great power and resuming relations with the Lenin government, and he signed a pact May 15 ceding Upper Silesia to Poland (*see* Kapp, 1920; Hitler, 1923).

Greece's Constantine I abdicates under pressure for a second time in late September. (He will die of a brain hemorrhage at age 54 early next year at Palermo.) He is succeeded by his 32-year-old son who will reign briefly as George II, will regain the throne in 1935, and will reign until 1947.

Britain's Lloyd George cabinet resigns October 19 after Conservatives, meeting at the Carlton Club, vote to quit the coalition government. Canadian-born Scotsman Andrew Bonar Law, 64, heads a new Conservative government.

The Turkish sultanate at Constantinople is ended November 1 by Mustapha Kemal whose forces have taken Smyrna from the Greeks in September (but have seen the city largely destroyed by fire) and who has accepted neutralization of the Dardanelles in exchange for the return of Adrianople and Eastern Thrace. The sultan Mohammed VI flees and his cousin Abdul Mejid is proclaimed caliph.

A fascist dictatorship in Italy begins in late November as Benito Mussolini is summoned by Victor Emmanuel III to form a ministry and is granted dictatorial powers so that he may restore order and bring about reforms. The 39-year-old journalist-politician has campaigned in his *Popolo d'Italia* against Communism, he has organized his Fascio di Combattimento in Milan into a political party, he has won support from Italian business interests fearful of Communism, and he has led his black-shirted Fascisti in a "March on Rome" October 28, but Mussolini's dictatorial powers are to expire at the end of next year (*see* 1923).

 Moscow signs commercial treaties and trade agreements with Italy and Sweden.

A modified Franco-German reparations agreement permits Germany to pay with raw materials such as coal but Britain places the burden of war debts on

Germany's postwar inflation reduced the value of the mark until it took more than 4 trillion marks to buy $1.

the United States. The Balfour note states that Britain would expect to recover from her European debtors only the amount which the United States expects from Britain.

The Reparations Commission adopts a Belgian proposal August 31 permitting Germany to pay reparations in installments on Treasury bills.

Germany's stock market collapses in August and the mark falls in value from 162 to the dollar, down to more than 7,000 to the dollar (*see* 1923).

A U.S. business revival led by the automobile industry begins 7 years of prosperity.

The Fordney-McCumber Tariff Act passed by Congress September 19 cancels the low tariffs of the 1913 Underwood Act and puts tariffs back to the levels of the 1909 Payne-Aldrich Act. The new law gives the president power to raise or lower duties by 50 percent in order to equalize production costs but presidents will use that authority in 32 out of 37 cases to further increase duties in response to appeals for protection by U.S. business and labor.

The Federal Reserve Board created in 1913 sets up a bankwire system to eliminate physical transfer of securities from one city to another and thus avoid theft, loss, or destruction of negotiable Treasury certificates. A Federal Reserve Bank taking in a certificate for delivery to another Federal Reserve Bank retires the certificate and instructs its sister bank by teletype to issue a new one (*see* 1968).

Henry Ford makes more than $264,000 per day and is declared a billionaire by the Associated Press.

The Lincoln Motor Company started last year by Cadillac founder Henry M. Leland is acquired for $12 million by Ford Motor Company president Edsel Ford (*see* Lincoln-Mercury, 1939).

The Star, introduced by Durant Motors, Inc., is a $348 motorcar built to compete with Ford's Model T, but Ford reduces the price of the Model T to stifle Durant's threat of competition (*see* 1921).

The Chevrolet division of General Motors is placed under the control of Danish-American engineer William Knudsen, 43, who has left Ford. Using mass assembly methods and Du Pont paints in a variety of colors, Knudsen will soon overtake Ford's black Model T (*see* Model A, 1927).

The first closed sedan is introduced by Hudson at a price only slightly above that of a touring car (*see* 1918; 1932).

The Model A Deusenberg introduced by Deusenberg Automobile and Motor Company of Indianapolis is the first U.S. production motorcar with hydraulic brakes, the first with an overhead camshaft, and the first U.S. straight eight. Ninety-two of the luxury cars are sold, a number that will rise to 140 in 1923 (*see* 1919).

Checker Motors Corporation has its beginnings in the Checker Cab Manufacturing Corporation founded at Kalamazoo, Mich., by Russian-American entrepreneur Morris Markin, 29, whose taxicab manufacturing plant will be renamed in 1958.

State Farm Mutual Automobile Insurance Company is founded by Bloomington, Ill., entrepreneur George J. Mecherle whose firm will be the leading U.S. automobile insurer by 1942. State Farm offers reduced rates to rural drivers (whose accident rate is lower than that of urban drivers) and accepts only drivers whose cars are fully paid for.

Minnesota bus pioneer Carl Wickman sells his interests in Mesabi Transportation Co. for something over $60,000 and begins to buy out small bus lines between Duluth and Minneapolis (*see* 1914; 1926).

The first all-metal U.S. airplane is built by engineer William Bushnell Stout, 42, who will sell his commercial aircraft company to Ford Motor Company in 1925, will start a passenger airline in 1926, and will sell it to United Aircraft and Transport in 1929.

Dutch aircraft designer A. H. G. Fokker emigrates to America where he will establish the Fokker Aircraft Corporation of America at Hasbrouck Heights, N.J. (*see* 1912; 1916; Juan Trippe, 1927).

The first coast-to-coast flight in a single day is made in September by U.S. Army Air Corps Lieutenant James Harold Doolittle, 25, who flies a DH4b from Pablo Beach, Fla., to San Diego and covers the 2,163-mile distance in 21 hours, 28 minutes flying time.

Oil is discovered near the shores of Lake Maracaibo, Venezuela, by a company controlled by Royal Dutch-Shell (*see* 1914). Gushing for 9 days, the new well spills nearly a million barrels into the lake before it is capped. Gulf Oil and Standard Oil of Indiana hold adjacent leases and the major oil companies will make Venezuela one of the world's leading petroleum producers.

U.S. coal miners strike for nearly 6 months to protest wage cuts. The massive strike by the United Mine Workers AF of L cripples U.S. industry and begins a period of chronic depression in the coal mining industry, whose operators will employ cutthroat competition to remain viable.

A 13 percent wage cut announced by the Railroad Labor Board May 28 affects 400,000 U.S. railway workers who strike from July 1 through the summer.

Coal miners at Herrin, Ill., riot in protest against the use of strike breakers June 22 to 23, 26 men are killed, but both coal and railroad workers return to their jobs, defeated, in September.

An enzyme discovered by Scottish bacteriologist Alexander Fleming, 41, breaks down bacterial cell walls. Fleming calls his lysozyme "the dissolving enzyme" (see penicillin, 1928).

Ur on the Euphrates River in Iraq is discovered by English archaeologist Charles Leonard Woolley, 42, who finds Sumerian temple ruins dating to 2600 B.C. and gives historical reality to the ancient Mesopotamian civilization of Sumer of which there has been only legendary knowledge.

The tomb of Egypt's King Tut (the 18th Dynasty pharaoh Tutankhamen who reigned from 1358 B.C. to 1350 B.C.) is discovered November 26 at Luxor in the Valley of the Kings by English Egyptologist George Edward Stanhope Molyneux, 56, earl of Carnarvon, and Howard Carter, 49. Of the 27 pharaohs buried near Thebes only the minor pharaoh Tutankhamen has been spared having his tomb looted.

Montecatini Chemical Company is founded by Italian industrialist Guido Donegani, 45, who gains support from Benito Mussolini (above) and who will make Montecatini Italy's second largest industrial power after FIAT (see 1899). The company will grow into a multinational empire (see 1945).

Dow Chemical Company chemists develop a process to make phenol production more efficient. The Hale-Britton process developed by William J. Hale (son-in-law of founder Herbert H. Dow) and Edgar C. Britton, 31, will permit cheap production of orthophenylphenol and paraphenylphenol that Dow will market as insecticides, germicides, and fungicides under the brand name Dowicides.

The U.S. death rate from diphtheria falls to 14.6 per 100,000, down from 43.3 in 1900; from influenza and pneumonia to 88.3, down from 181.5; from infant diarrhea and enteritis to 32.5, down from 108.8; from tuberculosis to 97, down from 201.9; from typhoid and paratyphoid fever to 7.5, down from 35.9; but from cancer the death rate is 86.8 per 100,000, up from 63 in 1900; from heart diseases it is 154.7, up from 123.1; and from diabetes mellitus it is 91.7, up from 18.4.

The hormone insulin isolated from canine pancreatic juices gives diabetics a new lease on life, the first treatment for the disease other than diet restrictions. Canadian medical researchers Frederick Grant Banting, 31, and Charles Herbert Best, 23, have isolated insulin (Banting calls it "isletin"), they use it to save the life of 14-year-old Leonard Thompson who is dying in Toronto General Hospital, and they will license Eli Lilly Company of Indianapolis to make the first commercial insulin (see Sharpey-Schafer, 1916; zinc protamine insulin, 1937).

Sickle cell anemia gets its name 12 years after its discovery by Chicago physician James B. Herrick in a 20-year-old West Indian student (see 1910). The hereditary disease strikes thousands worldwide.

U.S. electrical engineer Vannevar Bush, 32, helps start a company to produce the S-tube, a gaseous rectifier developed by inventor C. G. Smith that greatly improves the system of supplying electricity to radios (see analog computer, 1930).

Radio is used for the first time as an advertising medium. New York station WEAF (later WNBC) begins running paid commercials to establish a pattern of private control of U.S. public airwaves: "What have you done with my child," radio pioneer Lee De Forest will ask. "You have sent him out on the street in rags of ragtime to collect money from all and sundry. You have made of him a laughingstock of intelligence, surely a stench in the nostrils of the gods of the ionosphere" (see 1906; WJZ, below; NBC, 1926).

A half interest in the Westinghouse radio station WJZ at Newark, N.J., is acquired by David Sarnoff, who will acquire the other half with some associates in 1923. The station has studios in the Waldorf-Astoria Hotel on Fifth Avenue at 34th Street (see 1920).

Newark's WOR radio station begins broadcasting February 22. The Bamberger station founded by department store magnate Louis Bamberger will be sold to Mutual Broadcasting Company in 1933.

The BBC (British Broadcasting Corporation) is organized under the leadership of English engineer John Charles Reith, 33, a 6-foot, 6-inch tall misanthrope who will run the BBC for the next 16 years and will make it one of Britain's most revered institutions, supported by the public in the form of license fees.

The U.S. Independent Telephone Association is advised by AT&T that the big Bell system will take over no more independents without giving advance notice to the I.T.A. and will buy no company unless it fits logically into nearby Bell facilities and is clearly in the public interest.

The Times of London is purchased for $7 million by John Jacob Astor, grandson of Viscount Astor of Hever Castle (see 1899; Harmsworth, 1908). Astor was a British army officer in the war and will be the first baron Astor of Hever (see Thomson, 1953).

The *New York Daily Mirror* is started as a tabloid competitor of the 3-year-old *Daily News* by publisher William Randolph Hearst who this year buys the *Washington Herald,* the *Oakland Post-Enquirer,*

1922 (cont.)   the *Los Angeles Herald,* the *Syracuse Telegram,* and the *Rochester Journal* (*see* 1963).

The *Reader's Digest* appears in February with articles "of lasting interest" condensed from books and from other magazines into a pocket-size monthly. Former St. Paul, Minn., book salesman De Witt Wallace, 32, and his bride Lila Acheson Wallace, 32, have 1,500 subscribers whose numbers will grow to more than 200,000 by 1929 as the *Digest* plants some of its articles in other magazines and then condenses them. The magazine will accept no advertising until 1955 and by the 1970s it will be publishing 29 million copies per month in 13 languages (*see* 1933).

True Confessions magazine is started by Wilford H. Fawcett to compete with Bernarr MacFadden's 3-year-old *True Story* magazine. Fawcett's 3-year-old *Captain Billy's Whiz Bang* will reach a circulation of 425,000 per month next year (*see* 1928).

Better Homes and Gardens magazine begins publication at Des Moines, Iowa, under the direction of Edwin Thomas Meredith, now 46, who started *Successful Farming* in 1902 and who has served as Secretary of Agriculture under President Wilson.

Krocodil begins publication at Moscow. The illustrated supplement to the newspaper *Worker (Rabochy)* will develop into a political humor magazine.

The Racing Form is acquired for $500,000 by Hearst circulation director Moses Louis Annenberg, 44, and two other Hearst executives who take over the daily tip-sheet established a few years ago by Chicago newspaperman Frank Buenell. Annenberg will buy the *Morning Telegraph,* his chief competitor, he will quit the Hearst organization in 1926, he will go into partnership with Chicago gambler Monte Tennes to control bookie joints with leased wires to racetracks, and he will force his *Racing Form* partners to sell their interests to him for more than $2 million (*see* 1936).

Charles Atlas wins the "World's Most Perfectly Developed Man" contest sponsored by *Physical Culture* magazine publisher Bernarr MacFadden. Italian-American Angelo Siciliano, 28, is a former 97-pound weakling who has built himself up with "dynamic tension" exercises which he claims to have developed after watching a lion at the zoo, he will win MacFadden's contest again next year, he will open a Manhattan gymnasium in 1926, and by 1927 his Charles Atlas, Ltd., will be taking in $1,000 per day from students who subscribe to his mail-order physical culture course.

Nonfiction   *Decline of the West (Der Untergang des Abendlandes. Umrisse einer Morphologie der Weltgeschichte)* by German writer Oswald Spengler, 42, who predicts the eclipse of Western civilization; *Etiquette—The Blue Book of Social Usage* by New York divorcee Emily (Price) Post, 48, who has found the manners of Americans far inferior to those of their social counterparts in Europe; *Public Opinion* by Walter Lippmann.

Fiction   *Ulysses* by James Joyce. All reputable publishers have refused the stream of consciousness account of a day in the lives of Dubliner Leopold Bloom and his wife Molly, but Paris bookseller Sylvia Beach has published it under the imprint of her bookshop's name Shakespeare & Co. Irish critic Æ (George William Russell) of the *Irish Homestead* calls it "the greatest fiction of the twentieth century;" *Siddharta* by Hermann Hesse, who visited India in 1911, has undergone psychoanalysis, and has developed a Jungian mixture of depth psychology and Indian mysticism to probe the fantasies of adolescents; *The Bridal Canopy (Haknasath Kallah)* by Hebrew novelist Samuel Joseph Agnon, 44, who changed his name from Czaczkes when he moved from his native Galicia in 1909; *The Dream (Le Songe)* by French novelist Henry de Montherlant, 26; *A Kiss for the Leper (Le Baiser au lépreux)* by French novelist François Mauriac, 37; *The Enormous Room* by U.S. poet E. E. (Edward Estlin) Cummings, 27, who drove an ambulance in France and served afterward in the U.S. Army (he will sign his poetry "e. e. cummings"); *The Beautiful and the Damned* by F. Scott Fitzgerald; *Tales of the Jazz Age* (stories) by F. Scott Fitzgerald with illustrations by John Held, Jr., 32; *Babbitt* by Sinclair Lewis, who examines the conformist, complacent, conservative American businessman and introduces a new pejorative; *Captain Blood* by Rafael Sabatini; *Jigsaw* by London debutante Barbara Carter, 21, whose first novel enjoys huge success, earns its author £150, and launches her on a career.

Juvenile   *The Voyages of Dr. Doolittle* by English civil engineer Hugh Lofting, 36, who was wounded in 1917 and has turned to writing and illustrating. His book about a physician who can talk to the animals begins a series.

Poetry   *The Wasteland* by T. S. Eliot indicts the 20th century with innovative metrics and diction in a style perfected with the help of Ezra Pound. The eloquent work links numerous allusions explained in lengthy notes; *Anabasis (Anabase)* by French poet-diplomat Saint-John Perse (Marie René Auguste Alexis Saint-Léger Léger), 34, whose epic poem about the Greek Xenophon of 401 B.C. has landscapes reflective of the Gobi desert through which the poet traveled while stationed in China; *Tristia* by Osip Emilyevich Mandelstam who has developed an elliptical and metaphorical language; *Clouds (Moln)* by Swedish poet Karin Boye, 22; *Trilce* by César Vallejo.

The Fugitive magazine appears in April. The poetry monthly will continue until December 1925 with contributions by Vanderbilt University poets and writers who include John Crowe Ransom, 33, (John Orley) Allen Tate, 22, and Robert Penn Warren, now 16.

The *New York Times Book Review* appears for the first time as a separate section of the newspaper.

Painting   *Twittering Machine* by Paul Klee; *Before the Bell* by Max Beckmann; *The Farm* by Joan

Miró; *Still Life with Guitar, Harlequin,* and *Mother and Child* by Pablo Picasso; *Sunset* and *Maine Islands* by John Marin.

Theater *The Cat and the Canary* by U.S. playwright John Willard 2/7 at New York's National Theater with Florence Eldredge, Henry Hull; *To the Ladies* by Marc Connelly and George S. Kaufman 2/20 at New York's Liberty Theater, 128 perfs.; *Back to Methusaleh* by George Bernard Shaw 2/27 at New York's Garrick Theater (Parts I and II) with Dennis King, Margaret Wycherley, (Parts III and IV) 3/6, (Part V) 3/13, 72 perfs. total; *Loyalties* by John Galsworthy 3/8 at St. Martin's Theatre, London; *The Hairy Ape* by Eugene O'Neill 3/9 at New York's Provincetown Playhouse (and then uptown at the Plymouth Theater) with Louis Wolheim, 127 perfs.; *Abie's Irish Rose* by U.S. playwright Anne Nichols, 30, 5/23 at New York's Fulton Theater, a play about a mixed marriage, 2,532 perfs. (a new record); *The Machine Wreckers* (*Die Maschinensturmer*) by Ernst Toller 6/30 at Berlin's Grosses Schauspielhaus; *The Fool* by Channing Pollock 10/23 at New York's Times Square Theater with James Kirkwood, Lowell Sherman, 773 perfs.; *The World We Live In* (*The Insect Comedy*) by Karel and Josef Capek 10/31 at New York's Al Jolson Theater, with Mary Blair as a butterfly, Vinton Freedley as a male cricket, 112 perfs.; *Rain* by U.S. playwrights John Colton and Clemence Randolph 11/7 at New York's Maxine Elliott Theater, with Jeanne Eagels as Sadie Thompson in a dramatization of the W. Somerset Maugham short story "Miss Thompson," 321 perfs.; *The '49'ers* by Marc Connelly and George S. Kaufman 11/13 at New York's Cort Theater, with Howard Lindsay, Ronald Young, Ruth Gilmore, 16 perfs.; *The Texas Nightingale* by Zoe Akins 11/20 at New York's Empire Theater, 31 perfs.

The Treasurer's Report is presented at an amateur revue and the comedy monologue by *Life* magazine drama critic Robert Charles Benchley, 33, launches Benchley on a new career as humorist.

"Texas" Guinan begins her career as Prohibition era New York nightclub hostess. Mary Louise Cecilia Guinan, 38, goes to work as mistress of ceremonies at the Cafe des Beaux Arts and is soon hired away by Larry Fay of El Fey from whose club she will move to the Rendezvous, the 300 Club, the Argonaut, the Century, the Salon Royal, the Club Intime, and to several Texas Guinan Clubs that will serve bootleg Scotch at $25 a fifth, bootleg champagne at $25 a bottle, plain water at $2 a pitcher. The clubs will charge from $5 to $25 cover to the "butter-and-egg men"; Texas Guinan ("give the little girl a great big hand") will welcome customers from her seat atop a piano with the cry, "Hello, sucker!"

Films Frederick W. Murnau's *Nosferatu* with Max Schreck as Count Orlock (Dracula); Rex Ingram's *The Prisoner of Zenda* with Lewis Stone, Alice Terry; Allan Dwan's *Robin Hood* with Douglas Fairbanks,

Wallace Beery; Fred Niblo's *Blood and Sand* with Rudolph Valentino; D. W. Griffith's *Orphans of the Storm* with Dorothy and Lillian Gish who leave Griffith's Biograph Studios; the documentary *Nanook of the North* by British explorer-writer-director Robert Joseph Flaherty, 28.

The San Francisco Opera has its first season, beginning a rise that will make it second in the United States only to New York's Metropolitan Opera.

Hollywood Bowl opens. The 17,000-seat outdoor California amphitheater will present concerts, opera, and ballet.

Austria's Salzburg Mozart Festival has its first season to begin a lasting August tradition in the city's Festspielhaus (Festival Hall), Mozarteum, Landestheater, Mirabell Castle, and Marionette Theater.

First performances Pastoral Symphony by Ralph Vaughan Williams 1/26 at London.

Broadway musicals *The Ziegfeld Follies* 6/5 at the New Amsterdam Theater, with Will Rogers, Ed Gallagher, Al Shean, Olsen and Johnson, music by Dave Stamper, Louis A. Hirsch, Victor Herbert, and others, book and lyrics by Ring Lardner, Gene Buck, and others, songs that include "Mister Gallagher and Mister Shean," 541 perfs.; *George White's Scandals* 8/22 at the Globe Theater, with W. C. Fields, music by George Gershwin, lyrics by E. Ray Goetz, B. G. De Sylva, and W. C. Fields, Paul Whiteman and His Orchestra, songs that include "I'll Build a Stairway to Paradise" with lyrics by B. G. De Sylva and Arthur Francis (Ira Gershwin), 88 perfs.; *The Gingham Girl* 8/28 at the Earl Carroll Theater, with music by Albert von Tilzer, lyrics by Neville Fleeson, songs that include "As Long as I Have You," 322 perfs.; *The Passing Show* 9/20 at the Winter Garden Theater, with Eugene and Willie Howard, Janet Adair, Fred Allen, music largely by Alfred Goodman, lyrics mainly by Harold Atteridge, songs that include "Carolina in the Morning" by Walter Donaldson, lyrics by Gus Kahn, 95 perfs.; *Little Nellie Kelly* by George M. Cohan 11/13 at the Liberty Theater, with Elizabeth Hines, 276 perfs.

Popular songs "Way Down Yonder in New Orleans" by Henry Creamer and Turner Layton; "Chicago" by Fred Fisher; "Georgia" by Walter Donaldson, lyrics by Howard Johnson; "My Buddy" by Walter Donaldson, lyrics by Gus Kahn; "Blue" by Lou Handman, lyrics by Grant Clarke and Edgar Leslie; "Water Boy" by Avery Robinson, lyrics by Howard Johnson; "I'll See You in My Dreams" by Isham Jones, lyrics by Gus Kahn; "On the Alamo" by Isham Jones, lyrics by Gus Kahn; "Trees" by Oscar Rasbach, lyrics by Joyce Kilmer (*see* 1913 poem); "Goin' Home" by Anton Dvorak, lyrics by William Arms Fisher (*see* 1893 symphony).

Recording in acoustically correct studios rather than by singing or playing directly into horns is made possible by a Western Electric Company research team led by J. P. (Joseph Pease) Maxfield, 34, whose phono-

1922 (cont.) graph record graver chisels vibrations into wax at the rate of 30 to 5,500 wiggles per second (*see* Victrola, 1906). Electric impulses derived from sound waves as in the telephone vibrate the graver with augmented power to improve the fidelity of phonograph records (*see* vinylite records, 1946, 1948).

Gene Sarazen wins the U.S. Open at age 21 to begin a notable golf career. Sarazen dropped out of school in his early teens to help support his family, changed his name from Saraceni, went to work as a caddy in his native Harrison, N.Y., and goes on from his triumph at the Open to win the Professional Golfers Association (PGA) tournament, a feat he will repeat next year by beating Walter Hagen.

The New York Giants win the World Series by defeating the New York Yankees 4 games to 0 after one game has ended in a tie.

Princeton's football "team of destiny" beats Chicago 21 to 18 after trailing 18 to 7 with 12 minutes left to play. Faking a punt from behind his goal line at Chicago's Alonzo Stagg Field, Princeton quarterback Jack Cleaves throws a pass that advances the ball to midfield, end Howard Gray picks off a Chicago fumble and runs it into the end zone with 6 minutes to go, Burly Crum scores a second touchdown on a fourth down line plunge in the closing minutes, and Chicago fails by inches to score again as the clock runs out.

Mah-Jongg is introduced in America and a nationwide craze begins for the ancient Chinese game. The 144-tile sets will outsell radios within a year.

Listerine fights bad breath, says the 43-year-old Lambert Pharmacal Company of St. Louis which has been making the antiseptic solution for at least 42 years (*see* Lister, 1865). Advertising man Milton Fuessle has suggested the new appeal, a clipping from the British medical journal *Lancet* reveals that the medical term for bad breath is "halitosis," and Gerard Barnes Lambert, 34, seizes upon the word as the basis for advertising. Lambert will take Fuessle to New York, he will found the advertising agency Lambert and Feasley (he says Fuessle's name is too hard to pronounce), he will huckster Listerine with human-interest story advertisements and with the claim that the product kills millions of germs on contact (although the bacteria in any human mouth number in the *billions*), he will be spending $5 million per year on advertising by late 1928 when he will sell his stock in Lambert Pharmacal for $28 million (at $115 per share; the stock will subsequently climb to $151 but will drop to $8 within a year).

The Maytag Gyrofoam washing machine introduced by the Newton, Iowa, firm outperforms all other washing machines yet takes up only 25 square inches of floorspace (*see* 1907). Now 65, F. L. Maytag has built his own aluminum foundry to cast the tubs for his new machine, he will discontinue all other prod-

ucts next year, and by 1926 his sales volume will be $53 million, up from $2 million last year.

The Hall-Mills murder case makes world headlines. Children looking for mushrooms in a field across the Raritan River from New Brunswick, N.J., early in the morning of September 16 find the bodies of overweight clergyman Edward H. Hall, 44, and a member of his church choir Eleanor Mills, 34, wife of a local gardener and mother of two. Both have been shot in the head, they have been dead for 36 hours, and police find notes suggesting that they have been lovers (Hall's widow Frances is a Johnson & Johnson heiress and about 10 years his senior) (*see* 1926).

The first Thom McAn shoe store opens October 14 on New York's Third Avenue near 14th Street with men's shoes at $3.99 per pair. Melville Shoe Company vice president and founder's son (John) Ward Melville, 35, served during the Great War under J. Franklin McElwain, head of the Quartermaster Corps shoe and leather division. He and McElwain have developed the idea of a mass-produced shoe to be sold through a chain of low-priced stores with Melville Shoe and the J. J. McElwain Company of Nashua, N.H., sharing in the profits. Melville has found the name Thomas McCann in a roster of Scottish golf professionals and has abbreviated the name to make it distinctive; by 1927 there will be 370 Thom McAn stores with prices kept low by limiting the number of styles and colors produced, and Melville Shoe will acquire J. J. McElwain in 1939.

The Lincoln Memorial dedicated May 30 at Washington, D.C., contains a 19-foot seated figure of the 16th president carved out of Georgia marble by sculptor Daniel Chester French, now 72. The $2,940,000 monument beside the Potomac has taken 7 years to build.

Kansas City's Country Club Plaza Shopping Center designed by developer Jesse Clyde Nichols, 42, is the world's first large decentralized shopping center. Nichols wrote a Harvard graduate thesis on the economics of land development, he has visited English "garden city" developments, he has collected architectural ideas in Spain, and he pursues construction of the 6,000-acre Country Club district that will occupy 10 percent of downtown Kansas City, Mo.

"Ribbon windows"—rows of glass evenly divided by vertical concrete slabs—are innovated in a plan for an office building by German architect Ludwig Mies Van Der Rohe, 35, who will employ the design in many European and American buildings.

New York's 2,200-room Hotel Pennsylvania is completed as the world's largest on Seventh Avenue across from the Pennsylvania Station by hotelman E. M. Statler with funds supplied by the Pennsylvania Railroad (*see* Commodore, 1919; Chicago's Stevens Hotel, 1927).

New York's last horsedrawn fire apparatus makes its final appearance December 22. Equipment from

Brooklyn's Engine Company 205 at 160 Pierrepont Street races to put out a fire.

 Australia moves to protect her koala bears after fur trappers have killed 8 million in less than 4 years and have nearly wiped the marsupial out of existence.

 Small private farms are permitted in Soviet Russia by Nikolai Lenin to help the nation produce more food (see Stalin, 1928).

Harold M. Ware arrives in Russia with 21 tractors, other farm machinery, seeds, supplies, and food (see 1921). Ware is assigned to lands in the Urals where he and his volunteer associates seed most of 4,000 acres in winter wheat and encourage peasants to give up their holdings and join a collective (see 1925).

U.S. farmers remain in deep depression with a few exceptions such as California citrus growers (below).

Agricultural marketing cooperatives exempt from antitrust law restrictions are authorized by the Capper Volstead Act passed by Congress February 18. The co-ops are subject to supervision by the Secretary of Agriculture who is to prevent them from raising prices "unduly."

A Grain Futures Act passed by Congress September 21 curbs speculation that is thought to have contributed to the collapse of grain prices in 1920. The new act, which supersedes an August 1921 act that has been declared unconstitutional by the Supreme Court, limits price fluctuations within any given period on U.S. grain exchanges.

The first U.S. soybean refinery is built at Decatur, Ill., by A. E. Staley (see 1898). Staley removes at least 96 percent of the oil from soybeans and sells the residue, or cake, to the feed industry for use in commercial feeds, or to farmers to mix with other ingredients as a protein supplement for livestock (see 1923).

California becomes a year-round source of oranges as Valencia orange production catches up with navel orange production (see 1875; 1906; Sunkist, 1919).

James Dole's Hawaiian Pineapple Co., Ltd., buys the 90,000-acre Hawaiian island of Lanai, 60 miles from the company's Honolulu cannery, to give Dole 20,000 acres of land that can be planted in pineapples (see 1911). Fourteen other Hawaiian packers are now canning pineapple but Dole's company is by far the largest, producing 1.5 million cases out of the 4.8 million industry total, and Hawaiian Pineapple Company shareholders receive a 23 percent dividend (see Castle & Cooke, 1964).

 Vitamin D is isolated by E. V. McCollum who uses it in successful treatment of rickets. The newly found vitamin is found to play some role in raising the amount of calcium and phosphate deposited in bones but the mechanism remains a mystery (see 1923).

Experimental dogs are found to produce hemoglobin quickly and avoid anemia when fed liver in tests made by University of Rochester pathologist George Hoyt Whipple, 44 (see Minot and Murphy, 1924).

 The last European case of botulism that will be traced to a commercial canner is reported (see United States, 1925).

Van Camp Sea Food Company merges with White Star Canning and two other nearly bankrupt San Pedro, Calif., tuna packers after being hurt by the 1921 economic deflation and the collapse of wartime markets (see 1914). The new Van Camp Sea Food Co., Inc., increases production and sales but lacks the equipment needed to make extended cruises and overcome the circumstances that make tuna fishing a seasonal business limited to albacore (see 1924).

Quality Bakers of America, Inc., is formed as a cooperative purchasing service by independent wholesale bakers whose survival is threatened by the giant competition emerging with the growth of chain stores and chain bakeries. The co-op will become the industry's largest such group with nearly 100 U.S. members and with more than 30 bakers in Australia, Bermuda, Canada, and Mexico who in some cases will opt to buy advertising services from QBA (see Sunbeam Bread, 1942).

Pep breakfast food is introduced by the Battle Creek Toasted Corn Flake Company which changes its name to the Kellogg Company (see 1919; 1928).

The Postum Cereal Company is incorporated (see Post, 1914; Jell-O, 1925).

The Campbell Soup Company is established by a renaming of the Joseph Campbell Company (see 1932; Franco-American, 1915).

La Choy Food Products is incorporated by Detroit's Wallace Smith and Ilhan New who begin canning bean sprouts in metal cans (see 1920; 1937).

Clapp's Vegetable Soup is introduced as the first U.S. commercially prepared baby food by Rochester, N.Y., restaurant manager Harold H. Clapp and his 30-year-old wife Anna Louise Alberger Clapp who has begun canning the soup for neighbors' children after using it to help nurse her infant son Jack through an illness at the suggestion of her physician. The Clapps will promote the idea into a national baby food marketing business which they will sell to Johnson and Johnson Company (see Gerber, 1927).

Canada Dry Ginger Ale opens its first U.S. bottling plant on New York's 38th Street to avoid the long costly haul from Canada and the high tariff on imports (see 1907; Fordney-McCumber Act, above). Shipments from the new plant begin April 28 and a full-page newspaper advertisement prepared by N. W. Ayer & Son of Philadelphia carries the headline, "Down from Canada Came Tales of a Wonderful Beverage." The ginger ale sells at 35 cents per 12-ounce bottle but meets with immediate success despite its high price.

Eskimo Pies produce $30,000 per week in royalties but legal defense against patent infringers is so costly that Russell Stover sells his share in the company to Christian Nelson for $30,000 and uses the money to

1922 (cont.) open the first Russell Stover candy shop (*see* 1921; Reynolds, 1924).

New York's Delmonico's Restaurant closes after 91 years as the city's top eating place.

1923 French troops occupy Germany's rich Ruhr Basin beginning January 11. The Germans have defaulted on coal deliveries promised at Versailles in 1919 and German inflation soars out of control (below).

Adolf Hitler, 34, stages a "Beer Hall Putsch" at Munich November 8 as the mark falls to below 1 trillion to the dollar. Hitler's National Socialist German Workers' (Nazi) political party founded early in 1919 by Munich locksmith Anton Drexler is not socialist and does not represent the workers but it capitalizes on Germany's social unrest.

Hitler takes over Munich's vast Bürgerbräukeller with help from General Erich Ludendorff and seizes the city government, the authorities promptly oust the Nazis, a court next year will sentence Hitler to 5 years in prison, he will serve 9 months before being paroled (*see* 1925; 1933).

Benito Mussolini secures his fascist dictatorship by dissolving Italy's nonfascist parties July 10 and by forcing a law through the parliament November 14. Any party that wins the largest number of votes in an election shall have two-thirds of the seats in the parliament even though it may gain no more than 25 percent of the popular vote (*see* 1922; 1924).

A Bulgarian coup d'état June 9 overthrows Prime Minister Aleksandr Stamboliski whose dictatorial policies in behalf of the peasants have antagonized the army, the Macedonians, and others. Stamboliski is shot dead June 14 while allegedly trying to escape.

The Union of Soviet Socialist Republics (Russia, the Ukraine, White Russia, and Transcaucasia) established on paper January 1 becomes a reality July 6.

Jordan (Transjordania) becomes an autonomous state May 26. Occupying 80 percent of Palestinian territory, the British protectorate is headed by Emir Abdullah ibn Husein, 40-year-old son of the king of Hejaz. Britain will recognize Jordanian independence early in 1928 but will retain military control and some financial control.

A Turkish republic is founded by General Mustafa Kemal who has destroyed the political power wielded for centuries by Moslem leaders of the old Ottoman Empire (*see* 1915; 1919). He has defeated the Greek army bent on occupying Turkey, the assembly at Angora elects him president August 13, and makes Angora the national capital October 13. He will make Turkey a modern nation—abolishing the veil for women, ordering the Turks to dress in Western clothes, substituting the Roman alphabet for the Arabic, and introducing the Gregorian calendar of 1582 (*see* 1924; Treaty of Lausanne, below).

The Spanish garrison at Barcelona mutinies September 12 and the Marquis de Estella General Miguel

Primo de Rivera, 53, issues a manifesto that day suspending the constitution and proclaiming a directorate comprised of army and navy officers. General Primo has the approval of Alfonso XIII for his bloodless coup, he takes Barcelona, proclaims martial law throughout Spain, dissolves the cortes, suspends trial by jury, imposes rigid press censorship, and jails or exiles his liberal opponents.

The British prime minister Andrew Bonar Law has resigned May 20 after 209 days in office (he dies October 30 at age 65). His chancellor of the exchequer Stanley Baldwin, 55, has headed a new Conservative cabinet since May 22, but the general elections in November give the Labour party its first great victory (*see* 1924).

Nikolai Lenin establishes the first Soviet forced-labor camp in the Solovetsky Islands northwest of Archangel (*see* Holmogor concentration camp, 1921). Slave labor in the next 30 years will build 9 new Russian cities, 12 railway lines, 6 heavy industry centers, 3 large hydroelectric stations, 2 highways, and 3 ship canals (*see* Stalin ship canal, 1933).

A minimum wage law for women in the District of Columbia passed by Congress in 1918 is unconstitutional, the Supreme Court rules April 9 in the case of *Adkins v. Children's Hospital* (*see* 1937).

The National Woman's party founded by Alice Paul in 1913 meets at Seneca Falls, N.Y., and endorses an Equal Rights Amendment drafted by Paul who calls it the Lucretia Mott amendment.

United States Steel Corporation reduces its 12-hour day to an 8-hour day August 2 following the lead set by American Rolling Mill Company in 1916 (*see* 1899). Big Steel will hire an additional 17,000 workers in the next year and will raise wages but the company will still increase its profits.

The German mark falls to 7,260 to the U.S. dollar January 2 and Berlin has food riots when 14 municipal markets close because of a strike against higher prices charged at the stalls and booths in the markets.

The German mark falls to 160,000 to the dollar by July and unemployment combines with inflation to create social unrest (*see* Hitler, above); 1.5 million are unemployed, 4.5 million are employed only part time, yet prices continue to rise and by July 30 the mark has depreciated to 1 million to the dollar.

The German mark falls to 13 million to the dollar in September, to 130 billion to the dollar by November 1, and to 4.2 trillion to the dollar by the end of November. Prices rise so fast that workers are paid daily —and then several times a day. Middle class savers and pensioners are wiped out, formerly affluent Germans dispose of their possessions in order to eat, German peasants refuse to part with their eggs, milk, butter, or potatoes except in exchange for articles of tangible value and they fill their houses with pianos, sewing machines, Persian rugs, even Rembrandts (*see* 1924).

Income taxes paid by thousands of leading Americans appear in newspapers pursuant to terms of a tax disclosure law passed by Congress through efforts by U.S. Senator George W. Norris of Nebraska, an insurgent Republican. John D. Rockefeller, now 83, is reported to have paid only $124,266, but his son John D., Jr., has paid $7.4 million under the relatively low prevailing rates. Henry Ford is reported to have paid nearly $2.47 million in federal income taxes.

U.S. corporate profits will increase by 62 percent in the next 6 years and dividends to stockholders will increase by 65 percent. Income of U.S. workers will increase by 11 percent.

Shields and Company is founded by former Merrill, Lynch & Co. partner Paul Vincent Shields, 33, who has quit to open his own brokerage house.

Atlas Corporation is founded by U.S. entrepreneur Floyd Odlum, 31, who soon gains control of the Goldman Sachs Trading Corp.

Anaconda Company acquires Chile's Chuquicamata copper mine for $70 million from the Guggenheim family which retires from the copper business (see 1910; first Guggenheim foundation, 1924).

A Siberian gold rush begins as Soviet prospector Voldimar P. Bertin encounters independent Yakut prospector Mikhail P. Tarbukin working a rich stake he has found near Aldan and persuades him June 19 to join forces with the state prospecting party. Tarbukin will receive an Order of Lenin and an Order of the Red Banner, Soviet troops will move into Aldan early in 1925 to restore order after a series of robberies and murders, and the Aldan fields will produce hundreds of tons of gold per year for more than half a century.

Russia recovers rapidly from her 1921–1922 famine and approaches prewar levels of agricultural and industrial production.

Burlington Mills is founded as U.S. cotton prices fall to 11 cents per pound, down from 44 cents last year. Textile executive J. Spencer Love, 27, of Gastonia, N.C., sells his mill at auction for $200,000, he retains his outworn machines, he moves them to Burlington whose Chamber of Commerce has agreed to underwrite a $250,000 stock offering and sell the stock to local investors, he produces a coarse cotton dress fabric that promptly goes out of fashion, but Love will make Burlington the largest U.S. rayon producer and the firm will become the world's largest diversified textile producer.

Dutch-American physicist Peter Joseph Wilhelm Debye, 39, works out a mathematical explanation for electrolysis. Metallic salts disassociate in solution into ions (charged atoms), Debye explains, and he shows why the disassociation does not always appear to be complete (see Arrhenius, 1887).

Tetanus toxoid developed by French bacteriologist Gaston Ramon, 37, of the Pasteur Institute will lead to widescale immunization against the infection.

Introduction to Medical Biometry and Statistics by Johns Hopkins biologist Raymond Pearl, 44, establishes the foundation of what will be called biometrics (see population figures, 1921).

Scots-Canadian physiologist John James Rickard McLeod, 47, who interpreted last year's Banting-Best insulin discovery shares the Nobel award with Frederick G. Banting.

U.S. oil magnate Harry F. Sinclair wins the Kentucky Derby with his horse Zev and sails for Russia with an offer to buy the Baku oil fields (see 1901). Laughing off a congressional investigation of his role in the Teapot Dome scandal that broke 2 years ago, Sinclair and his retinue occupy two decks of the ship *Homeric* and by some accounts his attempt to buy the Baku fields comes close to succeeding.

Tetraethyl lead is introduced as a fuel additive by the new Ethyl Corporation (see Midgley, 1921). The lead is mixed three parts to two with ethylene dibromine, a derivative of bromine, to eliminate engine "knock" and yet leave no lead deposit in an engine (see Dow, 1924).

Aeroflot begins operations July 15 with a six-passenger ANT-2 flight from Moscow to Nizhny Novgorod. The plane takes 3.5 hours to cover the 200-mile distance, but the new airline will grow to become the world's largest and will make parts of Russia accessible within hours where they once took days and even weeks to be reached overland.

Sabena (Société Anonyme Belge d'Exploitation de la Navigation Aérienne) is founded. It will be the Belgian national airline.

Pan American World Airways has its beginnings in a New York City plane taxi service started by local bond salesman Juan Terry Trippe, 24, who quits his job and joins his friend John Hambleton in buying

The Jazz Age as portrayed by cartoonist John Held, Jr., who sometimes teamed up with novelist F. Scott Fitzgerald.

1923 (cont.) nine U.S. Navy flying boats that are about to be scrapped (*see* 1925).

Boston's Logan International Airport has its beginnings in the Municipal Airport that opens in September. Local judge Edward Lawrence Logan, 48, commanded the 101st U.S. Infantry in the Great War, and the city will rename its airport in Logan's honor after his death in 1939.

Templehof Airport opens in Berlin on the site of the Kaiser's parade ground before the Great War. The new airport records 100 civilian flights by year's end (*see* Lufthansa, 1929).

German aircraft designer Wilhelm Messerschmitt, 25, establishes an aircraft manufacturing firm under his own name while continuing to work as an engineer for Bayerische Flugzeugwerke. Messerschmitt designed his first plane during the war at age 18.

The autogyro is invented by Spanish aeronaut Juan de la Cierva, 27. The aircraft has a large horizontal free-running rotor plus a conventional propellor for forward power but it has no conventional wings (*see* Sikorsky helicopter, 1913; 1939).

Consolidated Aircraft Corporation is founded at Buffalo, N.Y., by U.S. aviation pioneer Reuben H. Fleet, 36, who helped to inaugurate the first regular airmail service between New York, Philadelphia, and Washington in 1918. Fleet will transfer operations to San Diego in 1935 and will merge with Vultee.

Canadian National Railways is created by a takeover of bankrupt roads and a merger of the roads with the government-owned Grand Trunk and Intercolonial roads to form a government-owned rail network larger than any other system in the Western Hemisphere. Canadian National has 20,573 miles of track —7,000 miles more than the Canadian Pacific.

A device for detecting and measuring defects in railroad rails is invented by Elmer Sperry of 1913 gyroscope fame. Sperry will perfect the device in 1928 and the first Sperry detector cars will go into service in November of that year produced by Sperry Products, Inc., of Hoboken, N.J. (*see* Sperry Rand, 1955).

U.S. auto production reaches 3,780,358, up from 543,679 in 1914; 51.85 percent are Fords.

More than 13 million cars are on U.S. roads and 108 U.S. companies are engaged in adding to the total, but 10 automakers account for 90 percent of sales.

Annual model style changes that make older models stylistically obsolete are inaugurated by major U.S. automakers in a move that will force smaller companies out of the market and will prevent new companies from entering. Forty-three U.S. companies will be making motorcars by 1926, there will be only 10 by 1935, and no new domestic manufacturer will succeed in cracking the market after this year (*see* Kaiser, 1946). The planned obsolescence of motorcars will be a major part of automotive marketing.

Walter P. Chrysler becomes president of a reorganized Maxwell Motor Company and begins to develop a line of innovative new motorcars (*see* Buick, 1912). Now 48, Chrysler quit his position as president of the General Motors Buick division 3 years ago in a dispute with GM president W. C. Durant and has helped reorganize Willys-Overland (*see* 1924).

The Hertz Drive-Ur-Self System is founded by Chicago's Yellow Cab Company president John D. Hertz, who buys a company that started in 1918 with 12 used cars operating out of a lot in South Michigan Avenue. Hertz will be the world's largest auto rental concern (*see* General Motors, 1925).

B. F. Goodrich Company acquires the Brunswick Tire Company from Brunswick-Balke-Collender which is compelled by a break in the rubber market to dispose of its lucrative automobile tire business (*see* 1872; clincher tires, 1899). Brunswick will continue to be a leading producer of bowling balls, and Goodrich becomes a major tire producer.

Bethune-Cookman College is founded at Daytona, Fla., by a merger of Mary McLeod Bethune's 19-year-old Daytona Normal and Industrial Institute for Negro Girls with the Cookman Institute for Men at Jacksonville. Bethune will head the college until 1942 and will make its slogan "Enter to Learn, Depart to Serve."

Glassboro State College is founded at Glassboro, N.J.

Texas Tech University is founded at Lubbock.

Zenith Radio Corporation is founded by Chicago auto-finance entrepreneur Eugene F. McDonald, Jr., 33, who obtains exclusive rights to market the products of the Chicago Radio Laboratory founded by former U.S. Navy radio electricians Karl E. Hassel, 27, and R. H. G. Matthews who have developed the trademark Z-Nith from the call letters of their amateur radio station 9ZN. Hassel and Matthews constructed a longwave radio receiver for the *Chicago Tribune* in 1919, the newspaper was able to pick up news dispatches from the Versailles peace conference and thus gain a 12- to 24-hour lead over papers using the jammed Atlantic Cable, Major Edwin H. Armstrong has licensed Chicago Radio to produce sets using his patents, McDonald has raised $330,000 to start Zenith, and he also starts the National Association of Broadcasters with himself as president (*see* Armstrong, 1917; FM, 1940).

London Radio Times begins publication. Circulation will reach 9 million by 1950.

Published March 3 at New York is Volume 1, No. 1 of newsweekly *Time,* a venture that will mushroom into a vast publishing empire. Based on rewrites of wire service stories with little additional reporting, the new magazine is put out by Henry Robinson Luce, 24, and his Yale classmate Briton Hadden who resigned last year from their jobs as reporters for the *Baltimore News.* Hadden will die in 1929 after having established a distinctive *Time*style by inverting sentences and by inventing such words as "socialite," "GOPolitician," "cinemaddict," and "tycoon" (meaning a business magnate) (*see Fortune*, 1930; *Newsweek*, 1933).

The Gannett Company is founded by upstate New York publisher Frank Ernest Gannett, 47, who assembles four regional newspapers including the *Rochester Times-Union* and the *Rochester Democrat and Chronicle* into an enterprise that will grow to encompass 55 papers in 17 states and Guam.

"Skippy" is introduced by cartoonist Percy Crosby, 32, whose new comic strip features the adventures of a winsome young boy.

"Moon Mullins" is introduced by cartoonist Frank Willard, 32, whose new comic strip features adventures of a roughneck ne'er-do-well, his kid brother Kayo, his Uncle Willie and Aunt Mamie, and Lord and Lady Plushbottom.

Young and Rubicam, Inc., is founded at New York by former Lord and Thomas advertising copywriter John Orr Young, 36, with Raymond Rubicam, 32, who has recently coined the slogan "The Priceless Ingredient" for E. R. Squibb (*see* 1858). Starting with the Pennsylvania Crude Oil account, Y&R wins the Postum account December 15.

A. C. Nielsen Company is founded by Chicago electrical engineer-market researcher Arthur Charles Nielsen, 26, who will develop indexes to provide information on distribution in various industries including food, drugs, and pharmaceuticals. Nielsen ratings for the broadcast media will be used by advertisers and their agencies in selecting shows for sponsorship and placement of commercials.

W. W. Norton Company publishers has its beginnings in the People's Institute Publishing Company founded by New York editor William Warder Norton who hires a stenographer to transcribe lectures given at the People's Institute of Cooper Union (*see* 1859). Norton sells "Lectures in Print" to subscribers, friends will persuade him to bind the lectures into books, and he will enjoy such success with the first five that he will break with Cooper Union and go into business as W. W. Norton Company.

Nonfiction *I and Thou* (*Ich und Du*) by Austrian philosopher Martin Buber, 45; *The Theme of Our Time* (*El Tema de Nuestro Tiempo*) by Spanish essayist José Ortega y Gasset, 40; *The Prophet* by Syrian-American mystic Kahlil Gibran, 40, whose work about man's relation to his fellowman will sell 5 million copies in the next 50 years and will provide a solid financial base for the 8-year-old New York publishing house Alfred A. Knopf; *The Dance of Life* by English scientist (Henry) Havelock Ellis, 64, who says, "Freud regards dreaming as fiction that helps us to sleep; thinking we may regard as fiction that helps us to live; Man lives by imagination"; *My Life and Loves* (first volume) by Frank Harris.

Fiction *Confessions of Zeno* (*La conscienza di Zeno*) by Italian novelist Italo Svevo (Ettore

Schmitz), 62, who studied English at Trieste under James Joyce; *Genitrix* by François Mauriac; *The Good Soldier Svejk* (*Osudy dobreho vojaka Svejka za svet ove valky*) by the late Czech novelist Jaroslav Hasek who has died at age 40. Hasek deserted the Austrian army in 1916 to join the free Czechoslovak forces fighting for independence from Russia, he joined the Russian Communist party in 1918 and served as a political commissar with the Red Army, he returned to Prague 2 years ago and has died with his bawdy attack on bourgeois values incomplete; *The Marsden Case* by Ford Madox Ford; *Riceyman Steps* by Arnold Bennett; *Antic Hay* by English novelist-critic Aldous Huxley, 29, whose grandfather was the biologist Thomas Henry Huxley and whose brother Julian, 36, is an Oxford biologist.

Poetry "Stopping by Woods on a Snowy Evening" by Robert Frost: "The woods are lovely, dark and deep./ But I have promises to keep,/ And miles to go before I sleep,/ And miles to go before I sleep"; *Harmonium* by Connecticut poet-life insurance company lawyer Wallace Stevens, 44; *The Harp-Weaver and Other Poems* by Edna St. Vincent Millay who wins the Pulitzer prize, marries, and moves to Austerlitz, N.Y., in the Berkshires: "Euclid alone has looked on Beauty bare" (Sonnet 22, II, 11–12); *Sonnets to Orpheus* by Rainer Maria Rilke; *Red Candle* by Chinese poet Wen I-tuo, 24, who came to America last year but who will return to China in 1925; *Collected Poems* by Vachel Lindsay who includes "In Praise of Johnny Appleseed"; *Spring and All* by William Carlos Williams; *Come Hither*, a "collection of rhymes and poems for the young of all ages" by Walter de la Mare.

Painting *The Lovers* (neoclassical), *Lady with the Veil* (neoclassical), *Melancholy* (expressionist), and *Women* (surrealist) by Pablo Picasso; *Thomas Hardy* by Augustus John; *Circles in the Circle* by Vassily Kandinsky; *Ivry Town Hall* by Maurice Utrillo; *Village in Northern France* by Maurice de Vlaminck; *On the Banks of the River Marne* by Raoul Dufy; *Love Idyll* by Marc Chagall; *The Trapeze* by Max Beckmann.

Murals *Entering the Mine, Miners Being Searched, Freeing of the Peon, The First of May, The Revolution Will Bear Fruit!* and others by Diego Rivera at Mexico City; *Revolutionary Trinity* by José Clemente Orozco; *The Workman Sacrificed* by David Afaro Siqueiros; Diego Rivera begins work on 239 frescos for the Secretariat of Public Education.

Theater *The Young Idea* by Noel Coward 2/1 at London's Savoy Theatre, with Coward, Herbert Marshall, Ann Trevor, 60 perfs.; *Icebound* by U.S. playwright Owen Davis, 49, 2/10 at New York's Sam Harris Theater, with Boots Wooster, 171 perfs., Pulitzer prize; *You and I* by Philip Barry 2/19 at New York's Belmont Theater with Lucille Watson, 140 perfs.; *The Adding Machine* by Elmer Rice 3/9 at New York's Garrick Theater, with Dudley Digges as

1923 (cont.) Mr. Zero, Edward G. Robinson as Shrdlu, Helen Westley, 72 perfs.; *The Incorruptible Man* (*Der Unbestechliche*) by Hugo von Hofmannsthal 3/16 at Vienna's Raimund Theater; *The Shadow of a Gunman* by Irish playwright Sean O'Casey, 43, 4/9 at Dublin's Abbey Theatre, a play about the Easter Rising of 1916 in which O'Casey was nearly shot; *Poppy* by U.S. playwright-lyricist Dorothy Donelly 9/3 at New York's Apollo Theater, with former *Ziegfeld Follies* juggler W. C. Fields who has been helped by showman Philip Goodman to develop the fraudulent character Eustace McGargle that Fields will portray for 20 years, 346 perfs.; *Outward Bound* by English playwright Sutton Vane, 34, 9/17 at London's Everyman Theatre; *Hinkemann* (*Der deutsche Hinkemann*) by Ernst Toller 9/19 at Leipzig's Altes Theater; *White Cargo* by U.S. playwright Leon Gordon 11/5 at New York's Greenwich Village Theater, with Richard Stevenson, Annette Margules as Tondeleyo, 678 perfs.; *Saint Joan* by George Bernard Shaw 12/28 at New York's Garrick Theater, with Winifred Lenihan, Morris Carnovsky, 214 perfs.

Films Wallace Worsley's *The Hunchback of Notre Dame* with Lon Chaney; Erich von Stroheim's *Greed* with Gibson Gowland as McTeague, Zasu Pitts as his wife Trina, Jean Hersholt in the first film version of the 1899 Frank Norris novel *McTeague;* James Cruze's *The Covered Wagon* with J. Warren Kerrigan, Lois Wilson, Alan Hale; Rex Ingram's *Where the Pavement Ends* with Ramon Novarro, Alice Terry; Cecil B. DeMille's *The Ten Commandments* with Theodore Roberts as Moses, Estelle Taylor, Richard Dix, Nita Naldi; Sam Taylor and Tim Whelan's *Safety Last* with Harold Lloyd; John Griffith Wray's *Anna Christie* with Blanche Sweet; Charlie Chaplin's *A Woman of Paris* with Edna Purviance, Adolphe Menjou.

First performances Symphony No. 6 by Jean Sibelius 2/19 at Helsinki; Symphony No. 1 in E minor (*Nordic*) by U.S. composer Howard Hanson, 26, 5/30 at Rome; *The Black Maskers* suite by U.S. composer Roger Huntington Sessions, 26, 6/23 at Smith College, Northampton, Mass. Sessions has written the incidental music for a performance of the play by Leonid Andreyev; *Dance Suite* (*Tancsuit*) for Orchestra by Béla Bartók 11/19 at Budapest.

Ballet *Facade* 6/12 at London's Aeolian Hall, with Edith Sitwell reading her poetry, music by English composer Howard Walton, 21 (*see* 1931); *Les Noces* (*The Wedding*) 6/14 at the Théâtre Gaiété-Lyrique, Paris, with Felicia Dubrovska, music and lyrics by Igor Stravinsky, choreography by Bronislava Nijinska; *La Creation du Monde* 10/25 at the Théâtre des Champs Elysées, Paris, with Jean Borlin, 30, music by Darius Milhaud, choreography by Borlin, scenery, costumes, and curtain by Fernand Léger.

Stage musicals André Charlot's revue *Rats* 2/21 at London's Vaudeville Theatre, with Gertrude Lawrence (Gertrud Alexandra Dagmar Lawrence Klasen), 24, music by Philip Braham, book and lyrics by Ronald Jeans; *The Passing Show* 6/14 at New York's Winter Garden Theater, with George Jessel, music by Sigmund Romberg and Jean Schwartz, book and lyrics by Harold Atteridge, 118 perfs.; *George White's Scandals* 6/18 at New York's Globe Theater, with music by George Gershwin, lyrics by E. Ray Goetz, B. G. DeSylva, Ballard MacDonald, 168 perfs.; *Helen of Troy, N.Y.* 6/19 at New York's Selwyn Theater, with Helen Ford, music and lyrics by Bert Kalmar and Harry Ruby, book by George S. Kaufman and Marc Connelly, 191 perfs.; *Artists and Models* 8/20 at New York's Shubert Theater, with Frank Fay, seminude showgirls, music by Jean Schwartz, book and lyrics by Harold Atteridge, 312 perfs.; André Charlot's revue *London Calling* 9/4 at the Duke of York's Theatre, London, with Noel Coward, Gertrude Lawrence, music and lyrics mostly by Coward, songs that include "You Were Meant for Me" by Eubie Blake, lyrics by Noble Sissle; *The Greenwich Village Follies* 9/20 at New York's Winter Garden Theater, with music by Louis Hirsch and Con Conrad, lyrics by Irving Caesar and John Murray Anderson, 140 perfs.; *The Music Box Revue* 9/22 at New York's Music Box Theater, with Grace Moore, music and lyrics by Irving Berlin, 273 perfs.; *The Ziegfeld Follies* 10/20 at New York's New Amsterdam Theater, with Fanny Brice, Paul Whiteman and his Orchestra, music by Dave Stamper, Rudolf Friml, Victor Herbert, and others, 233 perfs.; *Runnin' Wild* (black revue) 10/29 at New York's Colonial Theater, with a title song by A. Harrington Gibbs, lyrics by Joe Grey and Leo Wood, "Charleston" by Cecil Mack (Richard C. McPherson), 40, and Jimmy Johnson, 29, whose song launches a national dance craze; *Kid Boots* 12/31 at New York's Earl Carroll Theater, with Eddie Cantor, music by Harry Tierney, lyrics by Joseph McCarthy, songs that include "Polly Put the Kettle On," 479 perfs.; *The Song and Dance Man* 12/31 at New York's George M. Cohan Theater, with Cohan, Robert Cummings, music and lyrics by Cohan, 96 perfs.

Popular songs "Yes, We Have No Bananas" by Frank Silver and Irving Cohn; "Nobody's Sweetheart" by Gus Kahn, Ernie Erdman, Billie Meyers, Elmer Schwebel; "Who's Sorry Now?" by Ted Snyder, lyrics by Bert Kalmar, Harry Ruby; "I Cried for You" by Gus Arnheim and Abe Lyman, lyrics by Arthur Freed; "Nobody Knows You When You're Down and Out" by Jimmy Cox; "Mexicali Rose" by Jack B. Tenny, lyrics by Helen Stone; "It Ain't Gonna Rain No Mo' " by Wendell Woods Hall, 27, who has adapted an old folk song.

"Down Hearted Blues" is recorded by Philadelphia blues singer Bessie Smith, 25, whose first record has sales of 2 million copies and launches a career that will not falter until the late 1920s.

The Wightman Cup donated by Philadelphia sportswoman Hazel Hotchkiss Wightman, 34, for the winner of a U.S.-British women's tennis tournament will do for women's tennis what the Davis Cup of 1900 is doing for men's tennis.

The Winged Foot Country Club is founded at Mamaroneck, N.Y., by the New York Athletic Club.

Washington's Congressional Country Club opens on River Road May 23 with 632 active members.

New York's Yankee Stadium opens April 19, draws a sell-out crowd of more than 60,000, and turns away thousands for lack of seats. Colonel Jacob Ruppert has built the $2.5 million stadium with help from Tillinghast l'Hommedieu Houston (who will soon sell his share in the club to brewer Ruppert), Babe Ruth hits a three-run home run in the third inning of the inaugural game, and the Yankees beat the Boston Red Sox 4 to 1.

The New York Yankees win their first World Series by defeating the New York Giants 4 games to 2.

The Dempsey-Firpo fight at the New York Polo Grounds September 14 sees Argentine fighter Luis Angel Firpo, 29, knock Jack Dempsey out of the ring and into the laps of ringside sportswriters, but Dempsey knocks down the "Wild Bull of the Pampas" nine times, wins in two rounds, and retains his title.

U.S. cigarette production reaches 66.7 billion, up from 52 billion in 1921, as overseas sales increase.

The Schick magazine razor is patented April 24 by U.S. World War veteran Colonel Jacob Schick, 45, who during the war invented a machine that enabled a worker to fill 25 gas masks per minute where it had earlier taken 35 minutes to fill one mask.

The Schick dry shaver patented November 6 by Colonel Schick (above) is the world's first practical electric shaver (see 1930).

Maidenform brassieres are introduced by Russian-American entrepreneur Ida Rosenthal, 36, and her English-American partner Enid Bissett who last year opened a dress shop on New York's West 57th Street and gave away sample brassieres with a little uplift because they did not like the fit of their dresses on flat-chested "flappers." Capitalized at $4,500, the new Maidenform Company will move its operations next year to Bayonne, N.J., and by 1928 it will have a volume of nearly $500,000 per year despite the flapper look that deemphasizes breasts (see 1914).

President Coolidge lights the first White House Christmas tree to begin a lasting tradition.

The May Company acquires the 44-year-old Hamburger & Sons store in downtown Los Angeles for $4.2 million and adds a Los Angeles May Company to its Denver, St. Louis, Akron, and Cleveland stores (see 1914; Baltimore, 1927).

Ohrbach's opens October 4 in New York's 14th Street on a site occupied until last year by a penny arcade that Adolph Zukor opened in 1903. The arcade burned down, Austrian-American merchant Nathan M. Ohrbach, 38, has acquired the property and has put up a dress shop in partnership with Max Wiesen, his advertised bargains attract such crowds that windows are broken, 20 people suffer minor in-

juries, the store will have sales of more than $15 million next year, and when partner Wiesen sells out in 1928 for $625,000 he will have increased his initial investment tenfold (see Los Angeles, 1948).

Aimee Semple McPherson dedicates Angelus Temple at Los Angeles January 1 with a large rotating illuminated cross visible for 50 miles (see 1918). McPherson uses special effects to produce thunder, lightning, and wind that illustrate her "foursquare gospel" and help fill her 5,000-seat temple.

St. Bartholomew's Church at New York is completed by Bertram Goodhue on Park Avenue between 50th and 51st Streets in Moorish style.

New York City adopts a new setback law that limits the height and configuration of buildings as luxury apartment houses and hotels go up on Park Avenue (see Grand Central, 1913; zoning laws, 1916; 1961).

New York's Bowery Savings Bank building is completed across from Grand Central Station at 110 East 42nd Street by York & Sawyer. The Bowery's banking room has massive counters that are almost dwarfed by the immense ceiling height with great marble columns, mosaics, and chandeliers which make it a palatial paean to capitalism.

The Los Angeles Biltmore Hotel is completed by New York architects Schultze and Weaver.

Rio de Janeiro's Copacabana Palace Hotel is opened by Rio entrepreneur Otavio Guinle whose eight-story hotel in Louis XIV style will make Copacabana Beach a fashionable resort.

Tokyo and Yokohama are destroyed by earthquake and fire September 1. Six prefectures are affected, 91,000 are killed, 13,000 are missing, 752,000 are injured, 83,000 houses are completely destroyed and 380,000 partially destroyed, property damage totals nearly $3 billion, but the Imperial Hotel at Tokyo completed by Frank Lloyd Wright in 1916 is left intact. Tokyo will be rebuilt on the traditional pattern of Edo with houses numbered according to the years in which they were built.

"Falaise" is completed at Port Washington, N.Y., for copper magnate Harry F. Guggenheim who names the Long Island Norman mansion after the birthplace of William the Conqueror.

An Agricultural Credits Act provides for 12 Federal Intermediate Banks to help U.S. agricultural and livestock interests which remain in deep depression (see 1921; 1922).

U.S. wheat farmers try to persuade each other to plant less but overproduction continues in the absence of any effective farm organization.

Grasshoppers plague Montana. Forming a cloud 300 miles long, 100 miles wide, and half a mile high, the locusts devour every green blade, leaf, and stalk, leaving holes in the ground where green plants grew.

1923 (cont.) Soybean cultivation increases in eastern states with encouragement from higher freight rates that make it costly to feed cows with cottonseed from the Cotton Belt or with bran from Minneapolis flour mills (*see* Staley, 1922; McMillen, 1934).

Birdseye Seafoods, Inc., is opened on New York's White Street by Clarence Birdseye who has received patents on his quick-freezing process but who lacks the means to gain public acceptance. Birdseye is forced into bankruptcy (*see* 1917; 1925).

Irradiating foods with ultraviolet light can make them rich sources of vitamin D, says University of Wisconsin biochemist Harry Steenbock, 37, and he files for a patent on his discovery. Researchers including Alfred Hess at Columbia University have found that ultraviolet light from the sun and from mercury-vapor lamps can cure rickets (*see* McCollum, 1922), Steenbock has followed up on their studies, and he has found that stimulating the provitamins in foods can enable the human liver to convert them into vitamin D (*see* 1927; Rosenheim and Webster, 1926).

Congress calls filled milk a menace to health. The Filled Milk Act passed after pressure from dairy interests forbids use of nondairy ingredients (including low-fat vegetable oil to replace butterfat) in anything that is called (or looks like) a milk product but the courts will overturn the law in 1973 (*see* 1916).

Pet Milk Company is created by a reorganization of the Helvetia Milk Condensing Company which moved to St. Louis in 1921 (*see* "Our Pet," 1894).

National Dairy Corporation is organized at New York by Thomas McInnerny who says the dairy industry is bigger than the automobile or steel industry but needs some organization to control the quality and service of its many small, local companies (*see* 1914). McInnerny obtains help from Wall Street to sell $50 million in stock that provides capitalization for the giant holding company which consolidates 168 companies and will acquire many others (*see* 1928).

Welch's Grape Jelly is introduced (*see* 1897; Welch-ade, tomato juice, 1927).

The first commercially canned tomato juice is introduced by Libby, McNeill & Libby which has expanded with plants in Ontario and in Washington State, has put up additional plants in California, and has acquired a Hawaiian pineapple plantation on Molokai. Libby's tomato juice is described as "hay-like" and its color is "brownish" (*see* 1929).

Synthetic citric acid is produced by fermentation and becomes an important food and beverage additive (*see* Scheele, 1784).

A "Method of Making Grape Sugar (Dextrose)" that will be the basis of a multibillion dollar industry is patented by Corn Products Refining Company research chemist William B. Newkirk, 35, who has obtained the first pure dextrose from corn by finding a way to expel the corn molasses that impairs quality and flavor. The Newkirk method involves making coarse dextrose crystals from which the molasses can be removed, it will consume millions of bushels of corn each year, and it will produce a pure crystalline dextrose with important uses in bakery products, beverages, candy, preservatives, and processed foods —and in pharmaceuticals and intravenous feeding solutions for hospital patients (*see* 1916; Bosco, 1955).

Japan's Suntory brand "Scotch" Whisky is introduced by Suntory, Ltd., which will start a chain of bars and restaurants in the mid-1950s. The chain will grow to have 25,000 establishments and Suntory, Ltd., will claim in the mid-1970s to have the largest-selling brand of Scotch in the world.

U.S. sugar consumption reaches 106.39 pounds per capita, up from 65.2 pounds in 1900. Some of the sugar goes into illegal "moonshine" whiskey.

Coca-Cola Company's Ernest Woodruff is succeeded by his son Robert W. Woodruff, 33, who will give the soft drink worldwide distribution (*see* 1919; 1929).

Sanka Coffee is introduced in the United States (*see* Roselius, 1903; Postum Company, 1928).

Candymaker Russell Stover opens a factory at Denver to produce Mrs. Stover's Bungalow Candies (*see* 1922). Stover will open a second factory in 1925 at Kansas City, he will open a third in 1942 at Lincoln, Neb., and by the time he dies in 1954 at age 66 there will be 40 Russell Stover stores and some 2,000 department stores and drugstores will be selling Russell Stover candies.

The Milky Way candy bar is developed in the Midway district between Minneapolis and St. Paul by confectioner Frank C. Mars, 39, who has heretofore found little success. Possibly inspired by his own astronomical name, Mars names his creation after the distant star galaxy and he will see his Milky Way sales leap in 1 year from $72,800 to $792,000 as popularity grows for his mixture of milk chocolate, corn syrup, sugar, milk, hydrogenated vegetable oil, cocoa, butter, salt, malt, egg whites, etc. (*see* 1930).

The Butterfinger candy bar is introduced by Chicago's Curtiss Candy Company whose boss Otto Schnering has promoted Baby Ruth by chartering an airplane and parachuting candy bars down over Pittsburgh, causing a massive traffic jam as people rushed into the streets to scramble for the free candy. The chocolate-covered honeycomb peanut butter Butterfinger bar will be dropped along with Baby Ruth on cities in 40 states and the stunt will help make Curtiss brands national favorites (*see* 1920; Standard Brands, 1964).

The Popsicle has its beginnings in New Jersey where Oakland, Calif., lemonade mix salesman Frank Epperson is demonstrating his product. Epperson accidentally leaves a glass of lemonade on a windowsill overnight, he wakes in the morning to find the lemonade frozen round a spoon left in the glass, and he applies for a patent on his "Epsicle" (*see* 1924).

A supermarket of sorts opens in San Francisco where a large steel-frame building opens on the site of a former baseball field and circus ground with 68,000 square feet of selling space and room to park 4,350 automobiles (shoppers are offered free parking for one hour). The Crystal Palace sells food, drugs, cigarettes, cigars, and jewelry and has a barber shop, a beauty parlor, and a cleaning establishment, it will sell liquor as well as food after 1934, and by 1937 the Crystal Palace will be setting sales records—200 tons of lemons, 250 tons of oranges, 300 tons of apples in one year, five carloads of eggs in a month, 51,000 pounds of sugar in 1 hour (see Saunders, 1916; King Kullen, 1930).

The restaurant La Pyramide opened at Vienne by French restaurateur Fernand Point, 26, near a Roman pyramid that was the turn of a chariot racetrack, will become a gastronomic mecca (see 1955).

The Treaty of Lausanne signed in July between Turkey and Greece begins a massive transfer of 190,000 Greeks from Turkey to Greece and of 388,000 Moslems from Greece to Turkey (see Neuilly, 1919).

The Sanger Research Bureau is opened with a birth control clinic at New York by the American Birth Control League whose president James F. Cooper and his associate Herbert Simonds are persuaded by Margaret Sanger to start the Holland-Rantos Company, first U.S. company to manufacture rubber diaphragm contraceptives for women (see Wilde, 1833; Sanger, 1921). The diaphragm provides women with their first means of avoiding pregnancy independent of a man's use of a condom (but see 1929).

1924 Nikolai Lenin dies of sclerosis January 21 at age 53, the city of Petrograd is renamed Leningrad, and a triumvirate takes power as Josef Stalin begins a power struggle with Leon Trotsky (see 1918). Ruling with Stalin are Lev Borisovich Kamenev (né Rosenfeld), 40, and Grigori Evseevich Zinoviev (né Hirsch Apfelbaum), 40 (see 1926; Zinoviev letter, below).

Russia gives up the czar's "ill-gotten gains" at the expense of China, returns her Boxer Rebellion indemnity of 1900 for use in Chinese education, and sends advisers to China's Kuomintang national congress at Canton. Sun Yat-sen admits Communists to the Kuomintang (see 1911; Chiang Kai-shek, 1925).

Britain's first Labour government takes office January 22 under James Ramsay MacDonald, 57, who opposed British participation in the war and who recognizes the U.S.S.R. February 1. Britain signs a commercial treaty in which the Soviet Union gives British goods most-favored nation treatment but the United States refuses to recognize the U.S.S.R. unless she acknowledges her foreign debts and restores alien property, a position stated last year by Secretary of State Charles Evans Hughes.

The Ottoman dynasty founded in 1290 by Osman the Conquerer ends March 3 as Turkey's president Mustapha Kemal abolishes the caliphate and banishes all members of the house of Osman (see 1923; 1930).

Benito Mussolini's Italian fascists use pressure tactics to gain control of the electoral machinery and poll 65 percent of the vote in elections held early in April.

Italian Socialist deputy Giacomo Matteotti, 39, is murdered June 10 by Mussolini's Fascisti whose illegal acts of violence have been detailed in Matteotti's book The Fascisti Exposed (see 1923). Most of the nonfascist third of the Italian chamber secedes June 15 vowing not to return until the government has been cleared of complicity in the Matteotti murder, demands are made that the fascist militia be disbanded, Mussolini disavows any connection with the murder, he dismisses all those implicated, but he imposes strict press censorship July 1 and he forbids opposition meetings August 3. Prominent Fascist party members will be tried for the murder in 1926 but none will receive more than a light sentence.

Persia's premier Riza Khan Pahlevi establishes government control throughout the country after having subdued the Bakhtiari chiefs of the southwest and the Sheik Khazal of Mohammerah who has been supported by the British and by the Anglo-Persian Oil Company (see 1923; 1925).

The Hejaz is invaded by the 44-year-old Wahabi sultan of Nejd Abdul'-Aziz ibn-Saud who conquers the country and forces the 68-year-old Hashimite king Husein' ibn-Ali to abdicate in favor of his eldest son Ali' ibn-Husein, 46 (see Saudi-Arabia, 1932).

Marcus Garvey's plan for resettlement of U.S. blacks is rejected by the Liberian government which fears that Garvey's motive is to foment revolution (see 1920). Garvey will be convicted next year of fraudulent dealings in the Black Star Steamship Company that he has founded but that has gone bankrupt, his 5-year sentence will be commuted by President Coolidge, but he will be deported back to Jamaica in 1927 (see Rastafarians, 1930).

President Coolidge wins reelection on a platform of "Coolidge Prosperity." Unable to decide between President Wilson's son-in-law William Gibbs McAdoo of California and New York's Catholic governor Alfred E. Smith, the Democrats have nominated New York corporation lawyer John W. Davis on the 103rd ballot at the convention in New York's Madison Square Garden, but Davis wins only 136 electoral votes and 29 percent of the popular vote against 382 electoral votes and 54 percent of the popular vote for Coolidge. (Progressive candidate Robert M. La Follette is supported by the Socialists and wins 13 electoral votes, 17 percent of the popular vote.)

Britain's Labour government falls November 4 after the general election October 29 has given the Conservatives a great victory, partly through the release October 25 of the so-called Zinoviev letter, possibly a forgery, allegedly written by Comintern chief Grigori E. Zinoviev (above) and calling on British Communists to "have cells in all units of the troops," especially those based in big cities or near munitions plants. Stanley Baldwin heads a new government

Benito Mussolini glorified himself with propaganda techniques that masked the brutality of his fascist rule in Italy.

that denounces British treaties with Russia November 21. He will remain prime minister until 1929.

Albania proclaims herself a republic December 24.

 Germany's ruinous inflation ends as Berlin issues a new Reichsmark, imposes strict new taxes, and makes a sharp cut in the availability of credit for business expansion. The new Reichsmark is backed 30 percent by gold and its value is set at 1 billion old marks (which cease to be legal tender and are withdrawn from circulation under terms of a plan devised by a commission headed by Chicago banker Charles Gates Dawes, 59).

The Dawes Plan (above) which goes into effect September 1 reorganizes the Reichsbank under Allied supervision, it sets World War reparations to be paid by Germany; and it provides for an Allied loan to Germany of 800 million gold marks, $110 million of it to come from the United States.

International Business Machines Corporation (IBM) is organized at New York by former National Cash Register executive Thomas J. Watson who has changed the name of C-T-R to IBM (see 1912; Mark I computer, 1944).

Dean Witter and Co. is founded by San Francisco stockbroker Dean Witter, 37, with his brothers Jean C., 32, and Guy, 30; brother John, 22, will join the firm next year.

Massachusetts Investors Trust, founded by Boston financiers, is the first U.S. mutual fund.

 Imperial Airways is formed in April by a merger of Britain's Handley-Page Transport, Instone Air Lines, Daimler Airways, and the British Marine Air Navigation Co. (see BOAC, 1939).

The first round-the-world flights are completed in August by two U.S. *World Cruisers* designed and produced by California manufacturer Donald Douglas (*see* 1920). Powered by Liberty engines and able to fly for 18 hours without refueling, the planes have taken nearly 5 months but only 15 flying days and their much-publicized circumnavigation wins Douglas a $750,000 U.S. Army order for 50 XO observation planes (*see* DC-1, 1933).

The Daniel and Florence Guggenheim Foundation whose funds will go mostly to support aerospace research is set up at New York by former copper king Daniel Guggenheim, now 68 (*see* Chuquicamata mine, 1923; Goddard, 1926).

The first U.S. diesel electric locomotive is placed in service by the Central Railroad of New Jersey (*see* Sweden, 1913). The 300-horsepower Ingersoll-Rand engine uses General Electric electrical components and is installed in a locomotive built by the American Locomotive Company of Schenectady, N.Y. It will remain in service until 1957 (*see* 1948).

The first Chrysler motorcar is introduced by the Maxwell Motor Company (*see* 1923). The car has four-wheel hydraulic brakes, a high compression engine, and other engineering advances (*see* 1925).

The 24-year-old Auburn Automobile Company is joined by Chicago executive E. L. (Erret Lobban) Cord, 30, who gives Auburn's unsold inventory of 700 cars some cosmetic touch-ups, nets the firm $500,000, and breathes new life into the company which is now owned by Chicago financiers who include William Wrigley, Jr., but which is producing only six cars per day. Cord will double sales next year, he will introduce a new model, he will outperform and undersell the competition, and he will become president of Auburn in 1926 (*see* Dusenberg, 1926; 8-115, 1928).

Oakland automobiles made by General Motors Corporation become the first cars to be finished with DuPont Duco paints which cut days off the time required to paint an automobile (*see* 1909; Du Pont, 1915; Pontiac, 1926).

Ford produces nearly 2 million Model T motorcars for the second year in a row and drops the price of a new touring car to a low of $290, making a durable automobile available to Americans even of modest means. More than half the cars in the world are Model T Fords (*see* 1926; Model A, 1927).

The 497-meter Bear Mountain Bridge opens at Peekskill, N.Y., to carry motorcar traffic across the Hudson River (*see* George Washington Bridge, 1931).

The Bronx-Whitestone, Cross-Bay, Henry Hudson, Throgs Neck, Triborough, and Verrazano Bridges will be built in the next 44 years by New York's Robert Moses, 35, who is named president of the Long Island State Park Commission by Governor Alfred E. Smith. Moses will also build the Bruckner, Clearview, Brooklyn-Queens, Cross-Bronx, Gowanus, Long Island, Major Deegan, Prospect, Nassau, Sheridan, Staten Island, Throgs Neck, Van Wyck, and Whitestone Expressways, the Harlem River Drive and the West Side Highway, and the Belt, Cross Island, Cross-County, Grand Central, Interborough, Northern State, Meadowbrook, Laurelton, Sunken Meadow, Mosholu, and Hutchinson River Parkways, but he will build with no master plan and his projects will favor private automobile travel at the expense of mass transit.

Ethyl Corporation's Thomas Midgley, Jr., and C. F. Kettering of General Motors make a deal with Dow Chemical to obtain 100,000 pounds of ethylene dibromide per month at 58 cents per pound. Ethyl combines the chemical with tetraethyl lead to make a gasoline additive that eliminates engine knock (*see* 1923).

A synthetic gasoline development program is started by Germany's I. G. Farben chemical cartel whose top executive Karl Bosch, 50, is advised by his experts that rising gasoline prices will make gasoline derived from coal competitive with gasoline derived from petroleum. Germany has no domestic sources of petroleum and lacks foreign exchange but she has abundant coal reserves, she faces an energy crisis, and Farben is impressed by some expert forecasts that world petroleum reserves will be exhausted within a few decades (*see* 1916). An industrial chemist who has adapted the Haber process of 1908 to commercial ammonia production, Bosch predicts that synthetic gasoline will soon undersell gasoline produced from petroleum.

The streptococcus that incites scarlet fever is isolated by U.S. physician George Frederick Dick, 43, and his wife Gladys, 24. They will devise the Dick skin test for susceptibility to the disease.

Diabetes is shown to be more than simply a disorder of the pancreatic gland (*see* Banting, Best, 1922). Argentine physiologist Bernardo Alberto Houssay, 37, demonstrates that the pituitary gland is involved in human sugar breakdown (*see* 1937).

Kleenex is introduced under the name Celluwipes by Kimberly Clark and is the first disposable handkerchief. Ernst Mahler of 1918 Kotex fame has developed the product from celucotton, the name will be changed to Kleenex 'Kerchiefs, and it will be shortened subsequently to the one word Kleenex.

Duke University gets its name and begins the rise that will make it a great seat of learning. American Tobacco Company president James Buchanan "Buck" Duke who has made earlier gifts to the 86-year-old Trinity College at Durham, N.C., announces that he will donate $40 million if the school will change its name. The offer is widely criticized but Duke adds another $7 million October 1, he dies 9 days later at age 67, and Trinity College becomes Duke University.

The Brookings Institution is founded under the name Robert Brookings Graduate School of Economics and Government with a gift from St. Louis philanthropist-educator Robert Somers Brookings, 74, who has made a fortune in woodenware.

England's Summerhill School is founded at Leiston in Suffolk by Scottish schoolmaster A. S. (Alexander Sutherland) Neill, 38, and his wife Ada Lindesay-Neustatter Neill who renounce all discipline, all direction, all moral training, and all religious training. Neill is determined to make the school fit the child instead of making the child fit the school, he makes the coeducational boarding school self-governing, attendance at classes and sports is made optional, and the Summerhill School which permits children to develop in their own way will be widely influential.

U.S. radio set ownership reaches 3 million but most listeners use crystal sets with earphones to pick up signals from the growing number of radio stations.

The *New York Herald-Tribune* is created by a merger of the Gordon Bennett-Horace Greeley newspapers. *Tribune* editor Ogden Mills Reid, 42, heads the new daily that will give the *New York Times* healthy competition until 1966.

Le Figaro in Paris is acquired after 70 years of publication by Corsican-born French perfume maker François Coty, 50, who has long since changed his name from Francesco Giuseppe Spoturno and who will make the paper a vehicle for his profascist views.

"Little Orphan Annie" appears October 5 in the *New York Daily News. Chicago Tribune* staff cartoonist Harold Lincoln Gray, 30, has helped Sidney Smith draw "The Gumps," he has developed a blank-eyed, 12-year-old girl character together with her dog Sandy, her guardian Oliver "Daddy" Warbucks, and his manservant Punjab, the comic strip will campaign against communism, blind liberalism, and other threats to free enterprise and rugged individualism, and it will continue beyond Gray's death in 1968.

The Saturday Review of Literature begins publication August 2 under the editorship of Yale English professor Henry Seidel Canby, 45, who has edited the weekly *Literary Review* of the *New York Post* since 1920. J. P. Morgan president Thomas W. Lamont has sold the *Post* to Cyrus H. K. Curtis of Philadelphia, Curtis has discontinued the *Literary Review,* Lamont has given *Time* magazine publisher Henry R. Luce backing to continue the literary weekly with Canby as editor, and Canby is supported by William Rose Benét, 38, Amy Loveman, and Christopher Morley (*see* 1936).

The American Mercury begins publication. The new monthly is edited by H. L. Mencken and by drama critic George Jean Nathan, 42, of *Smart Set.*

The Dial Press is founded by former Henry Holt editor Lincoln MacVeagh, 33, with backing from his Harvard classmate Scofield Thayer who publishes *The Dial.*

Simon and Schuster is founded by Richard Leo Simon, 25, and New York journalist Max Lincoln Schuster, 27. The first book published by the new house is a collection of crossword puzzles (*see* 1913).

1924 (cont.) Nonfiction *Manifesto of Surrealism (Manifeste de surréalisme)* by French poet-essayist André Breton, 28, who has been a member of the Dadaist movement and whose October Manifesto inaugurates a new movement (*see* Apollinaire, 1917). Breton becomes editor of *La Revolution Surréaliste; With Lawrence in Arabia* by U.S. journalist Lowell Jackson Thomas, 32, brings prominence to English archaeologist-soldier T. E. Lawrence who has refused a knighthood and the Victoria Cross for his World War exploits in the Arabian desert (*see* 1916; 1926).

Fiction *The Magic Mountain (Der Zauberberg)* by Thomas Mann who uses the setting of a sanatorium to explore the sickness of contemporary European civilization; *A Passage to India* by E. M. Forster who has produced no new novel since 1910; *Precious Bane* by Mary Webb; *The Green Hat* by Armenian-English novelist Michael Arlen, 30, who has changed his name from Dikran Kuyumijian and who becomes an instant celebrity on the strength of his best-seller which will earn him $500,000 in royalties; *Some Do Not* by Ford Madox Ford; *The Fleshly and the Meditative Man (L'homme de chair et l'homme reflet)* by French (Breton) novelist-poet Max Jacob, 48; *The Green Bay Tree* by U.S. novelist Louis Bromfield, 27; "Salt," "The Letter," and other short stories by Russian author Isaak Emmanuilovich Babel, 30, in the magazine *Left; So Big* by U.S. novelist Edna Ferber, 37, whose best seller wins a Pulitzer prize.

Juvenile *Bambi* by Austrian critic-magazine writer Felix Salter, 57, whose anthropomorphic tale of a fawn will be translated into English by U.S. magazine editor Whittaker Chambers; *When We Were Very Young* by A. A. Milne who has written the verses to amuse his 4-year-old son Christopher Robin and whose first edition sells out on publication day. Illustrations are by *Punch* contributor Ernest Howard Shepard, 44, who illustrated Kenneth Grahame's 1908 book *The Wind in the Willows.*

Poetry *Veinte poemas de amor y una cancion desesperada* by Chilean poet Pablo Neruda (Neftali Ricardo Reyes), 20, who won recognition last year with his *Crepusculario* and who will go abroad in 1927 as Chilean consul first at Rangoon, then in Java, then at Barcelona; *Tamar and Other Poems* by California poet Robinson Jeffers, 37, who has built a high rock tower at Carmel Bay and has lived in seclusion with his wife since the outbreak of war in 1914; *The Man Who Died Twice* (novel in verse) by Edward Arlington Robinson; *Chills and Fever* by Vanderbilt University teacher-poet John Crowe Ransom, now 40; *The Ship Sails On* by Nordahl Grieg.

Painting *Sugar Bowl* by Georges Braque; *Daughter Ida at the Window* by Marc Chagall; *The Birthday* by Marc Chagall; *Catalan Landscape* by Joan Miró; *Venice* by Oskar Kokoschka; *The Dempsey-Firpo Fight* by George Bellows (*see* 1923).

Eastman Kodak Company replaces its highly flammable celluloid film with a photographic film made of cellulose acetate (*see* Reichenbach, Goodwin, 1889; Ansco, 1901; 1927; Kodachrome, 1935).

Theater *Hell Bent fer Heaven* by U.S. playwright Hatcher Hughes, 43, 1/4 at New York's Klaw Theater, 122 perfs., Pulitzer prize; *The Show-Off* by U.S. playwright George Kelly, 37, 2/4 at New York's Playhouse Theater, with Louis John Bartels, Lee Tracy, 575 perfs.; *Beggar on Horseback* by George S. Kaufman and Marc Connelly 2/12 at New York's Broadhurst Theater, with Osgood Perkins, Spring Byington, 164 perfs.; *Juno and the Paycock* by Sean O'Casey 3/3 at Dublin's Abbey Theatre. O'Casey has been supporting himself with pick and shovel on a road gang but his play's 2-week run earns him royalties of £25 and the success encourages him to quit the job and devote his energies to writing; *Welded* by Eugene O'Neill 3/17 at New York's 39th Street Theater, 24 perfs.; *All God's Chillun Got Wings* by Eugene O'Neill 5/15 at New York's Provincetown Playhouse, with former Rutgers football star Paul Bustill Robeson, 26, playing a black man married to a white woman (Mary Blair). The Ku Klux Klan threatens reprisals, the Salvation Army and the Society for the Suppression of Vice warn that "such a play might easily lead to racial riots or disorder and if there is any such possibility police powers can be exercised," police officers are stationed throughout the theater opening night, the director reads the first scene, but no violence occurs throughout the play's run; *Each in His Own Way (Ciascuno a suo modo)* by Luigi Pirandello at Milan's Teatro dei Filodramatici; *What Price Glory?* by New York playwrights Laurence Stallings, 28, and Maxwell Anderson, 35, 9/3 at New York's Plymouth Theater, with Louis Wolheim as Captain Flagg, Brian Donlevy as Corporal Gowdy, 299 perfs.; *Desire Under the Elms* by Eugene O'Neill 11/11 at New York's Greenwich Village Theater, with Walter Huston, 208 perfs. (the play moves uptown after 2 months, first to the Earl Carroll Theater, then to the George M. Cohan Theater); *They Knew What They Wanted* by U.S. playwright Sidney Coe Howard, 33, 11/24 at New York's Garrick Theater, with Pauline Lord, Glenn Anders, Richard Bennett, 414 perfs., Pulitzer prize, 1925; *The Man With a Load of Mischief* by English playwright Ashley Dukes, 39, 12/7 at London; *The Vortex* by Noel Coward 12/16 at London's Royalty Theatre, with Coward, Mary Robson, 224 perfs.; *The Youngest* by Philip Barry 12/22 at New York's Gaiety Theater, with Henry Hull, 104 perfs.

Films Jean Renoir's *Greed* with Erich von Stroheim (*see* 1923); Mauritz Stiller's *Gosta Berling's Saga* with 19-year-old Swedish actress Greta Garbo whose name Stiller has changed from Gustaffson; Paul Leni's *Waxworks* with Conrad Veidt as Ivan the Terrible, Emil Jannings as Haroun-al-Raschid, Werner Kraus as Jack the Ripper; Serge Mikhailovich Eisenstein's *Strike;* Fernand Léger's *Ballet Mécanique;* D. W. Griffith's *America;* D. W. Griffith's *Isn't Life Wonderful?* with Carol Dempster, Neil Hamilton; F. W. Murneau's *The Last Laugh* with Emil

Jannings; Henry King's *Romola* with Lillian and Dorothy Gish, William Powell, Ronald Colman; Victor Seastrom's *He Who Gets Slapped* with Lon Chaney, Norma Shearer, John Gilbert; John Ford's *The Iron Horse* with George O'Brien, Madge Bellamy; Henry Beaumont's *Beau Brummel* with John Barrymore, Mary Astor; Raoul Walsh's *The Thief of Baghdad* with Douglas Fairbanks; Herbert Brenon's *Peter Pan* with Betty Bronson; James Cruze's *Merton of the Movies* with Glenn Hunter; Ernst Lubitsch's *The Marriage Circle* with Adolphe Menjou, Marie Prevost; Fritz Lang's *Kriemhild's Revenge;* Frank Lloyd's *The Sea Hawk* with Milton Sills; Buster Keaton and Donald Crisp's *The Navigator* and *Sherlock, Jr.* with Keaton; Hal Roach's *Jubilo, Jr.* with Our Gang (Mary Korman, Mickey Davids, Joe Cobb, Farina, Jackie Condon); Sidney Olcott's *Monsieur Beaucaire* with Rudolf Valentino; Jean Renoir's *La Fille de l'Eau.*

Metro-Goldwyn-Mayer (M-G-M) is founded by vaudeville theater magnate Marcus Loew, 54, who has absorbed the 6-year-old Louis B. Mayer Pictures Corporation and who buys Goldwyn Pictures Corporation from which Samuel Goldwyn has resigned (*see* 1917). Goldwyn will control Samuel Goldwyn, Inc., Ltd., from 1926 to 1941 and will continue to produce films through the 1950s, winning fame as a producer and notoriety for such expressions as "Include me out" and "In two words, impossible."

Columbia Pictures is founded by Harry Cohn, 33, who 6 years ago joined Universal Pictures as secretary to Carl Laemmle, learned the rudiments of picturemaking, and 2 years later formed the CBS Sales Company which he has reorganized.

Music Corporation of America (MCA) is founded by Chicago physician Jules C. Stein, 28, who has done postgraduate work at Vienna and has just published a definitive work on telescopic spectacles. To help pay his way through medical school Stein has played violin and saxophone in his own dance band, he has booked dance bands into hotels, nightclubs, and summer resorts on a commission basis, and he starts a company that will innovate the one-night stand at a time when most bookings have been for the season. Beginning with Guy Lombardo and His Royal Canadians, Stein will sign up most of the big bands before moving on to sign variety acts, radio talent, and movie stars to exclusive MCA contracts.

Opera *Erwartung* (*Expectation*) 6/6 at Prague's Neues Deutsches Theater, an expressionistic one-character mimodrama with music by Arnold Schoenberg; *Hugh the Drover, or Love in the Stocks* 7/4 at His Majesty's Theatre, London, with music by Ralph Vaughan Williams; *Die glückliche Hand* 10/14 at Vienna's Volksoper, with music by Schoenberg.

Ballet *Les Biches* 1/6 at the Théâtre de Monte Carlo, with Polish dancer Leon Woizikovsky (*né* Wojcikowski), 24, and other members of Sergei Diaghilev's Ballet Russe, music by French composer

Francis Poulenc, 24, choreography by Bronislava Nijinska; *Les Fâcheux* 1/19 at the Théâtre de Monte Carlo, with Sergei Diaghilev's Ballet Russe, music by French composer Georges Auric, 24; *Schlagobers* 5/9 at the Vienna State Opera with Tilly Losch, 19, music by Richard Strauss; *Mercure* ("poses plastiques") 6/14 at the Théâtre de la Cigale, Paris, with music by Eric Satie, sets and curtains by Pablo Picasso that overshadow Leonide Massine's choreography; *Le Train Bleu* 6/20 at the Théâtre des Champs-Elysées, Paris, with Bronislava Nijinska and other members of the Ballet Russe, music by Darius Milhaud, choreography by Nijinska, libretto by Jean Cocteau, curtain by Pablo Picasso, costumes by Coco Chanel.

George Balanchine quits the Soviet State Dancers while on tour in Paris, he joins Sergei Diaghilev's Ballet Russe, he changes his name from Georgi Meilitonovitch, and at age 20 begins a career that will make him the world's leading choreographer (*see* 1932).

Serge Koussevitsky begins a 25-year career as director of the Boston Symphony. The 50-year-old émigré Russian conductor and bass fiddle virtuoso has adopted the French version of his name Sergei Alexandrovitch Kussevitzky (*see* Tanglewood, 1934).

Philadelphia's Curtis Institute of Music is founded by publishing heiress Mary Louise Curtis Bok.

First performances *Rhapsody in Blue* by George Gershwin 2/12 at New York's Aeolian Hall with Paul Whiteman's Palais Royal Orchestra accompanying the pianist-composer who completed the piano score January 7 after 3 weeks of work. Composer Ferde Grofe, 31, has orchestrated the *Rhapsody* for piano and jazz ensemble; Symphony No. 7 in C major by Jean Sibelius 3/24 at Stockholm; *Tzigane,* Concert Rhapsody for Violin and Orchestra by Maurice Ravel 4/26 at London, with Hungarian virtuoso Yelly d'Aranyl as soloist; "Pacifica 231" by Arthur Honegger 5/8 at Paris; Concerto for Piano, Wind Instruments, and Double-Basses by Igor Stravinsky 5/22 at Paris; *The Pines of Rome* (*Pini di Roma*) (Symphonic Poem) by Ottorini Respighi 12/14 at Rome.

Broadway musicals *André Charlot's Revue of 1924* 1/9 at the Times Square Theater, with Jack Buchanan, Beatrice Lillie, Douglas Furber, music by Philip Braham, lyrics by Furber, songs that include "Limehouse Blues," 138 perfs.; *The Ziegfeld Follies* 6/24 at the New Amsterdam Theater, with Will Rogers, Vivienne Segal (who will be joined in the spring of next year by W. C. Fields and Ray Dooley), music by Raymond Hubbell, Dave Stamper, Harry Tierney, Victor Herbert, and others, 520 perfs.; *George White's Scandals* 6/30 at the Apollo Theater, with music by George Gershwin, lyrics by B. G. DeSylva, songs that include "Somebody Loves Me" with additional lyrics by Ballard MacDonald, 192 perfs.; *Rose-Marie* 9/2 at the Imperial Theater, with Mary Ellis, Dennis King, music by Rudolf Friml, lyrics by Otto

1924 (cont.) Harbach and Oscar Hammerstein II, 29, songs that include "Indian Love Call" and the title song, 557 perfs.; *The Passing Show* 9/3 at the Winter Garden Theater, with James Barton, Harry McNaughton, music by Sigmund Romberg and Jean Schwartz, lyrics by Harold Atteridge, 104 perfs.; *Greenwich Village Follies* 9/16 at the Shubert Theater, with the Dolly Sisters, Moran and Mack, music and lyrics by Cole Porter, songs that include "I'm in Love Again," "Babes in the Woods," 127 perfs.; *Dixie to Broadway* 11/22 at the Broadhurst Theater, with Florence Mills in an all-black revue, music by George Meyer and Arthur Johnston, lyrics by Grant Clarke and Roy Turk, 77 perfs.; *Lady Be Good* 12/1 at the Liberty Theater, with Fred Astaire and his sister Adele dancing to music by George Gershwin, lyrics by Ira Gershwin, songs that include "Oh, Lady Be Good," "Somebody Loves Me," 184 perfs.; *The Student Prince of Heidelberg* 12/2 at the Jolson Theater, with music by Sigmund Romberg, lyrics by Dorothy Donnelly, songs that include "Deep in My Heart, Dear," "Welcome to Heidelberg," "Student Life," "Drinking Song," 608 perfs.

Bix Beiderbecke begins a 6½ year career that will make the name Bix immortal in the annals of jazz. Iowa-born cornetist Leon Bix Beiderbecke, 20, records "Fidgety Feet" February 18 at the Gennett Studios in Richmond, Ind.

Popular songs "I'll See You in My Dreams" and "It Had to Be You" by Isham Jones, lyrics by Gus Kahn; "Tea for Two" by Vincent Youmans, lyrics by Irving Caesar and Clifford Grey; "California, Here I Come" by Joseph Meyer, 32, lyrics by Al Jolson, B. G. DeSylva; "Lazy" by Irving Berlin; "What'll I Do" by Irving Berlin; "When My Sugar Walks Down the Street" by Gene Austin, Jimmy McHugh, Irving Mills; "Everybody Loves My Baby (But My Baby Don't Love Nobody But Me)" by Jack Palmer and Spencer Williams; "There's Yes Yes in Your Eyes" by Joseph H. Saintly, lyrics by Cliff Friend; "Amapola (My Pretty Little Poppy)" by James M. LaCalle, lyrics by Albert Gamse; "When Day Is Done" is published at Vienna under the title "Madonna" with music by Viennese composer Robert Katscher; B. G. DeSylva (above) will write English lyrics.

 Wembley Stadium opens for the British Empire Exhibition at Middlesex, England, with seating capacity for nearly 100,000.

Forest Hills, Long Island, completes a tennis stadium for the West Side Tennis Club which held USLTA championship matches from 1915 to 1920 at Forest Hills. The matches that began in 1881 have been held for the past 3 years at Philadelphia's Germantown Cricket Club but will be held hereafter at Forest Hills. Bill Tilden wins the men's singles, Helen Wills wins the women's singles, and a U.S. team headed by Tilden defeats Australia to win the Davis Cup.

The first winter Olympics open at Chamonix and the games at Paris attract 3,385 contestants from 45 nations. Finnish track star Paavo Nurmi, 27, wins the 1,500-meter and 5,000-meter runs, but U.S. athletes win the largest number of medals overall.

The Washington Senators win the World Series by defeating the New York Giants 4 games to 3.

University of Illinois halfback Harold "Red" Grange, 21, receives the opening kickoff from undefeated Michigan State, runs it back 95 yards for a touchdown, scores three more touchdowns in the next 12 minutes, and scores a fifth later in the game. Grange will be nicknamed the "Galloping Ghost" by sportswriter Grantland Rice and will be selected for the All-America Team 3 years in a row.

Notre Dame University has an undefeated season thanks to a backfield that Grantland Rice (above) calls the "Four Horsemen": Don Miller (162 pounds), Elmer Layden (162), Jim Crowley (164), and Harry Stuhldreher.

 The Leopold-Loeb case makes headlines and builds the reputation of lawyer Clarence Darrow, now 67. Chicago students Nathan Leopold and Richard Loeb, both 19 and both sons of wealthy families (Loeb's father is a Sears, Roebuck vice president), murder 14-year-old Robert Franks in cold blood. Darrow introduces novel forms of evidence based on psychiatric examinations and saves Leopold and Loeb from the gallows (they are sentenced to life imprisonment but Loeb will be killed in prison) (*see* Darrow, 1911).

Florida's notorious Ashley gang is broken up by federal agents after 14 years of bank robberies, hijackings, and (more recently) rum running on the Atlantic Coast.

Chicago florist-bootlegger Dion O'Banion is shot dead November 10 by a gunman who walks into his flower shop with a companion and guns him down as the companion shakes O'Banion's hand. The ensuing funeral sets new records for gaudy display as Hymie Weiss (Earl Wajchiechowski) takes over the O'Banion mob to challenge Johnny Torrio and Al Capone for control of the liquor traffic.

Jarman Shoe Company is founded at Nashville, Tenn., by local entrepreneur James Franklin Jarman, 57, who has raised $130,000 in capital and who asks his son Walter Maxey Jarman, 19, to quit MIT and join him in the business of producing $5 Jarman's Friendly Fives. The company will have annual sales of more than $1 million by 1926 and young Maxey Jarman will be secretary-treasurer (*see* 1932).

Barney's opens on New York's Seventh Avenue at 17th Street. Merchant Barney Pressman will make his discount store the nation's largest menswear retailer.

Saks Fifth Avenue opens just south of St. Patrick's Cathedral with window displays that feature $1,000 raccoon coats, chauffeurs' livery, and a $3,000 pigskin trunk. New York merchant Bernard F. Gimbel

39, and Horace Saks, 42, merged their stores at Greeley Square last year (see Gimbels, 1910), they bought a parcel of land uptown, their store is the first large specialty shop north of 42nd Street, and it sells out its stock of silver pocket flasks the first day.

New York's R. H. Macy Company opens a 20-story building west of Macy's existing store on Herald Square. Two further additions in 1928 and 1931 will make Macy's the world's largest department store under one roof, a store with more than 2 million square feet of floor space (see 1901; Davison-Paxon, 1925).

The first Macy's Thanksgiving Day parade moves 2 miles from Central Park West down Broadway to Herald Square to begin an annual promotion event designed to boost Christmas sales.

Rich's of Atlanta moves into a large new building at Broad and Alabama Streets. Founder Morris Rich died 2 years ago at age 75 but the new store that bears his name has 800 employees.

Liberty's of London opens a new shop in Great Marlborough Street with a gabled facade, stained glass windows, and an antiqued interior made from teak and oak timbers from the ships H.M.S. *Hindustan* and H.M.S. *Impregnable* (see 1882).

Zale Corp. has its beginnings at Wichita Falls, Tex., where Russian-American merchant Morris Bernard Zale, 22, opens a jewelry store that will grow to become the world's largest retail jewelry chain. Zale has fled anti-Semitism in Europe, he will pioneer in selling jewelry on credit, and by 1977 Zale Corp. will have annual sales of nearly $700 million.

The Federal Reserve Bank of New York building at 35 Liberty Street is completed in the style of a massive Florentine palazzo of Indiana limestone, Ohio sandstone, and ironwork (see Fort Knox, 1935).

Chicago's Wrigley building is completed in May with a 32-story tower on Michigan Avenue for the William Wrigley Jr. Company. Designed by Graham, Anderson, Probst, and White, the building has 442,000 square feet of office space and is the first large building north of the Chicago River.

Quebec City's 31-year-old Chateau Frontenac Hotel is completed with a tower that dominates the city.

Detroit's Book-Cadillac Hotel opens with a main lobby of Venetian grandeur. Its walls are of Breche Violette marble trimmed with Alabama marble, its bronze railings rest on black walnut beams, and its ceiling has gold leaf panels emblazoned with the arms of the sieur de Cadillac.

New York's 18-story, 1,200-room Roosevelt Hotel opens in the block bounded by 45th and 46th Streets and Vanderbilt and Madison Avenues. The $10 million hotel is convenient to Grand Central.

Lima's Gran Hotel Bolivar opens with 350 rooms to begin half a century as Peru's central meeting place for businessmen, social leaders, and politicians.

Palm Beach, Fla., mansions designed by architect Addison Mizener, 52, go up for U.S. millionaires. Mizener builds Villa de Sarmiento for A. J. Drexel Biddle, Casa Bendita for John S. Philips, Concha Marina for George and Isabel Dodge, La Guerida for Rodman Wanamaker II, and El Sclano for Harold S. Vanderbilt, but his greatest project is El Mirasol, an enormous Moorish palace with 25 acres of lawn and a 20-car garage for J. P. Morgan partner E. T. (Edward Townsend) Stotesbury of Philadelphia (see Boca Raton, 1925).

An Oil Pollution Act is passed by Congress to update the Refuse Act of 1899 but prosecution of violators will be lax.

Jones Beach and other New York area parks and beaches including Belmont Lake, Captree, Hecksher, Hither Hills, Hempstead Lake, Valley Stream, and Wildwood will be built under the aegis of Robert Moses (above).

Miami Beach promoter Carl Fisher hires publicity man Steve Hanagan who will flood newspapers with pictures of Florida "bathing beauties" to convey the idea that the Atlantic at Miami Beach in January is warmer than the Pacific at Los Angeles in August.

The first effective chemical pesticides are introduced (see DDT, 1939).

Nearly two-thirds of the commercial fertilizer sold in the United States goes to Southern farmers who use it to push cotton to earlier maturity in order to frustrate the timetable of the boll weevil (see 1921).

Owens Valley, Calif., farmers armed with shotguns sit atop the Los Angeles water gates and blow up the city's aqueduct 17 times to prevent drainage of water from their lands. State militia drive off the farmers but the conflict will continue for more than 50 years as the Owens Valley dries up.

Van Camp Sea Food Company of San Pedro, Calif., has its credit with American Can Company canceled for not paying long overdue bills after it has diversified to pack summer citrus fruits and produce, the cannery is shut down, the company goes into receivership, but a heavy run of sardines encourages Frank Van Camp to borrow money, he goes back into business, he makes enough profit to pay off much of the firm's debts, and he will regain control of the company in 1925 (see 1922; 1926).

California-canned olives cause 16 deaths from botulism in the Midwest. All inventories of canned olives are ordered to be destroyed and food brokers refuse to handle lesser known brands of canned fruits and vegetables such as those of Van Camp (above).

Eating liver is shown to prevent and cure pernicious anemia in humans (see Addison, 1855). Boston physicians George Richards Minot, 39, and William Parry Murphy, 32, have studied G. H. Whipple's 1922 discoveries and they show that liver feedings have at least limited value in treating the disease (see Cohn, 1926; Lilly, 1928; Castle, 1929).

1924 (cont.) Continental Baking Company is incorporated with headquarters at Chicago to manage a sprawl of nearly 100 plants that produce bread and cake under dozens of different labels. Continental will become the leading U.S. bakery firm (*see* Wonder Bread, Hostess Cakes, 1927).

Thirty percent of U.S. bread is baked at home, down from 70 percent in 1910.

The H-O Company is acquired by Standard Milling Company of Kansas City. H-O produces H-O Oats and Presto Flour along with the breakfast food Force which is made by H-O Company of Canada and still enjoys wide sale in the United Kingdom (*see* 1902).

Wheaties is introduced by Washburn, Crosby Company of Minneapolis which will soon advertise the wheat-flake cereal (4.7 percent sugar) as "the breakfast of champions" (*see* 1921; General Mills, 1929).

Distillers Corporation, Ltd., is founded by Canadian distiller-bootlegger Samuel Bronfman, 33, and his brother Allan, 28, who borrow the name of Britain's 47-year-old Distillers Company, Ltd., and build their first distillery at Ville La Salle outside Montreal (*see* Distillers Corporation-Seagram, 1928).

Beech-Nut Coffee is introduced by Beech-Nut Packing Company (*see* 1899; baby foods, 1931).

The average American consumes 17.8 pounds of butter per year, 6.8 pounds of ice cream, 4.5 pounds of cheese, more than 350 pounds of fluid milk (nearly one pint per day).

The Good Humor is patented by Harry Burt (*see* 1920; Brimer, 1926).

Eskimo Pie Company is acquired by U.S. Foil Company head Richard S. Reynolds who has been supplying Eskimo Pie with metal foil (*see* 1922).

The Epsicle is patented by Frank Epperson who will sell the patent to the Joe Lowe Corporation founded in 1902 by food processor Joe Lowe, now 41. Lowe will market the Epsicle under the name Popsicle and will rename his company the Popsicle Corporation (*see* 1923).

The Stouffer Restaurant chain has its beginnings in the Stouffer Lunch opened on a busy Cleveland street corner by Wharton School of Business graduate Vernon Bigelow Stouffer, 22, with an initial investment of $12,000. The lunch counter will grow into a nationwide operation of restaurants, inns, food services, and food products.

The Johnson-Reed Immigration Act passed by Congress May 26 limits the annual quota from any country to 2 percent of U.S. residents of that nationality in 1890 (*see* Dillingham Bill, 1921).

Japanese are totally excluded from immigration by the new act (above) despite a warning by the Japanese ambassador of grave consequences if the United States should abandon the Gentlemen's Agreement.

Close relatives of U.S. citizens are permitted to enter as nonquota immigrants under the Johnson-Reed Act (above) and no restrictions are placed on immigration from Canada or Latin America. Immigration from Canada, Newfoundland, Mexico, and South America has its peak year.

1925 *Mein Kampf* (*My Battle*) by Adolf Hitler is published in its first part (*see* beer hall putsch, 1923). Hitler has dictated the book to his aide (Walter Richard) Rudolf Hess, 31, while in prison, he will complete it in 1927, and he says "The great masses of the people . . . will more easily fall victims to a great lie than to a small one" (*see* 1933).

The first president of the German Reich Friedrich Ebert dies February 28 at age 53 after 6 years of fighting left-wing and right-wing extremists.

Soviet authorities catch and shoot British spy Sidney Reilly (*né* Sigmund Georgevich Rosenblum), who once persuaded the British mission to Moscow to finance a scheme to destroy the Bolsheviks by parading Lenin and Trotsky without their trousers through the streets of Moscow.

Britain's Conservative government rejects a Geneva protocol for the peaceful settlements of international disputes. Czechoslovakia's Eduard Benes and Greece's Nicolaos Sokrates Politis have drafted the protocol, but it has met with opposition from the Dominion governments such as that of Canada's Raoul Dandurand, who has said, "We live in a fireproof house, far from inflammable materials."

A protocol signed by the world powers June 17 bars use of poison gas in war. An arms traffic convention signed the same day governs international trade in arms and munitions.

The Locarno Conference of October 5 to 16 results in the Locarno Treaty signed December 1 to guarantee Franco-German and Belgo-German frontiers by mutual agreement, by arbitration treaties between World War antagonists, and by mutual assistance treaties that give Europe some sense of security.

France recognizes that Germany has not bound herself against aggression to the south and east. She begins construction along the Franco-German border of the heavily fortified Maginot Line named for French politician André Maginot, 48.

Norway annexes Spitzbergen.

Britain declares Cyprus a crown colony.

Persia's majlis gives Reza Khan Pahlevi dictatorial powers in February, the majlis declares the absent shah deposed October 31, the assembly proclaims Reza Khan shah December 13, and Reza Shah Pahlevi begins a reign that will continue until his abdication in 1941 (*see* 1924).

Cancer kills Chinese republican leader Sun Yat-Sen at Peking March 12 at age 57. Sun's Kuomintang army controls Canton and surrounding areas, students at Shanghai demonstrate against "unequal treaties" May 30 until British forces open fire to disperse the demonstrators, Canton has similar demonstrations June 23, China boycotts British goods and shipping, the Kuomintang appoints General Chiang Kai-shek, 39, commander in chief in September, Chiang makes a Soviet general his unofficial chief of staff, and by year's end he has defeated Sun's opponent Chen Chiung-ming, 50, to bring Kwangtung and Kwangsi Provinces under Kuomintang control (see 1926).

$ "The business of America is business" says President Coolidge January 17 in an address to the Society of American Newspaper Editors.

The Corrupt Practices Act passed by Congress makes it "unlawful for any national bank, or any corporation . . . to make a contribution or expenditure in connection with any election to any political office" but the new law permits an individual donor to give up to $5,000 to a political campaign committee and places no limit on the number of committees that may receive such contributions (see 1972).

President Coolidge tells Congress he opposes cancellation of French and British war debts. The foreign press has called Uncle Sam "Uncle Shylock" for refusing even to scale down the debts but Coolidge says privately, "They hired the money, didn't they?"

Britain's chancellor of the exchequer Winston Churchill returns to the gold standard at the prewar gold and dollar value of the pound—123.27 fine grains of gold or 4.86 dollars to the pound. Parliament and the people respond with enthusiasm but the move makes British coal, steel, machinery, textiles, ships, cargo rates, and other goods and services 10 percent above world prices, and the result is unemployment and wage cuts (see strike, 1926).

Barclay's Bank (Dominion, Colonial, and Overseas) is created through an amalgamation engineered by London banker Frederick Craufurd Goodenough who puts together three banks to realize a 9-year dream of organizing a worldwide bank (see 1836).

The Ku Klux Klan founded in 1915 stages a parade August 8 at Washington, D.C., with 40,000 marchers in white hoods.

The Brotherhood of Sleeping Car Porters is organized by A. Philip Randolph, 36, who is publisher of The Messenger, a monthly New York magazine devoted to black politics and culture. Monthly wages for Pullman porters have been raised in the past year to $67.50 per month, up from a minimum of $27.50 in 1915; Randolph will work to raise them further.

The Autobiography of Mother Jones by Irish-American union organizer Mary Harris Jones, 95, says, "I am always in favor of obeying the law, but if the high-class burglar breaks the law and defies it, then I say we must have a law that will defend the nation and our people." Jones has grown up in the U.S. labor movement and has been imprisoned on occasion for violent activities in behalf of West Virginia and Colorado coal miners, her slogan has been "Pray for the

dead and fight like hell for the living," and to illustrate the abuses of child labor she tells of meeting a boy of 10 and asking him why he was not in school. "I ain't lost no leg," says the boy, and Jones tells her readers that "lads went to school when they were incapacitated by accidents" in the mines and mills.

The Kelly Air Mail Act passed by Congress authorizes the U.S. Post Office Department to sign contracts with private companies for carrying the mail at rates ranging up to $3 per pound, rates that amount to government subsidies for airlines.

Commercial air service between Detroit and Chicago is inaugurated by Henry Ford April 13.

Colonial Air Transport starts carrying mail between New York and Boston. The company has been created by a merger of Boston's Colonial Airways with Eastern Air Transport, a line organized by Juan Trippe and John Hambleton with backing from Cornelius Vanderbilt Whitney and William H. Vanderbilt (see 1923; Cuba, 1927).

Chrysler Corporation is created by a reorganization of Maxwell Motor Co. (see 1924; Dodge, 1928).

Chrysler, Ford, and General Motors produce at least 80 percent of U.S. motorcars and will increase their share of the market.

The Yellow Truck and Coach Manufacturing Company is acquired by General Motors from Chicago taxi fleet operator John Hertz who also sells GM his Hertz Drive-Ur-Self System (see 1923; 1953).

Henry Ford has 10,000 U.S. dealers, up from 3,500 in 1912. Each agency is required to stock at least one of each of the 5,000 parts in a Model T (43 percent of the parts retail for 15 cents each or less).

Most Ford dealers receive their cars knocked down since seven knocked-down cars can be shipped in the

Tennessee's "Monkey Trial" pitted Scripture against Darwin. Teacher John Scopes (center) had dared to defy the law.

1925 (cont.) railroad boxcar space required for only two assembled cars and a good mechanic can assemble the Model T in half a day. A new Ford roadster sells for $260 F.O.B. Detroit.

Britain's Vauxhall Motors is acquired by General Motors Corporation.

The Crescent Limited goes into service between New Orleans and New York via the Southern Railway, the West Point Route, the Louisville & Nashville, and the Pennsylvania. The luxury train charges a $5 premium over the regular fare.

The Vickers balanced vane hydraulic pump is developed by U.S. engineer Harry F. Vickers, 26, who 3 years ago founded the Vickers Manufacturing Company. His pump will be a basic product used especially in the oil industry (*see* Sperry Corp., 1937).

Synthetic rubber is pioneered by Belgian-American clergyman-chemist Julius Arthur Nieuwland, 47, at Notre Dame University. Nieuwland passes acetylene gas through a solution of ammonium chloride and gas and his casual reference to the resulting product will inspire Du Pont chemists to develop a product that Du Pont will introduce in 1931 under the name Du-Prene (*see* Semon, 1926).

Malignant diphtheria strikes Nome, Alaska. Local physician Curtis Welch of the U.S. Public Health Service fears an epidemic that will jeopardize 11,000 lives in the area. He wires for antitoxin, a dog team sets out from Shaktolik January 27, fresh teams relay the antitoxin as temperatures drop below –50°F, "musher" Leonard Seppala crosses Norton Sound on pack ice heaving in the ground swell of the Bering Sea as a blizzard sweeps in with winds of 80 miles per hour, and veteran musher Gunnar Kasson arrives at Nome February 2 at 5:36 in the morning. The teams have covered 655 miles in 5.5 days (the previous record was 9 days), and the antitoxin arrives in time to prevent an epidemic (*see* Behring, Ehrlich, 1891).

Soviet Russia has her last major outbreak of cholera (*see* 1855).

Cooley's anemia is described by Detroit physician Thomas Benton Cooley, 54. The hereditary blood disorder impairs the synthesis of hemoglobin, it is incurable, it kills its victims at an average of 20, and it has been common for thousands of years in the Mediterranean, the Middle East, the Philippines, and parts of India and China.

The Menninger Clinic opens in a farmhouse at Topeka, Kan., where local country doctor Charles F. Menninger, 63, starts a group practice for the mentally ill with his sons Karl, 32, and William, 26. Their "total environment" approach has been inspired by a 1908 visit by C. F. Menninger to the Mayo Clinic at Rochester, Minn., they will operate on C. F.'s premise that no patient is untreatable, they employ a family atmosphere with physical exercise and a team of multidiscipline doctors for each patient, and they begin a revolution in treating mental illness.

New York's Columbia-Presbyterian Hospital opens on upper Broadway at 168th Street. It is a joint effort by Columbia University and Presbyterian Hospital.

The Scopes "Monkey Trial" makes headlines in July as Dayton, Tenn., schoolteacher John T. Scopes, 25, goes on trial for violating a March 13 law against teaching evolution in the state's public schools. Scopes has tested the law by acquainting his classes with the 1859 teachings of Charles Darwin, he is defended by Chicago attorneys Clarence Darrow and Dudley Field Malone, he is prosecuted by former secretary of state William Jennings Bryan, he is fined $100, and Bryan dies of apoplexy July 26.

The John Simon Guggenheim Foundation is established by mining magnate Simon Guggenheim, 57, and his wife in memory of their son John who died 3 years ago at age 17. Guggenheim Fellowships endowed by the foundation will enable thousands of Americans to pursue studies that will result in works which will win seven Nobel prizes and 31 Pulitzer prizes in the next half century.

Bennington College for Women is founded at Bennington, Vt.

The University of Miami is founded at Coral Gables, Fla., with support from local real estate promoter George Edgar Merrick (below).

Hebrew University is founded at Jerusalem by émigré U.S. Zionist Judah Leon Magnes, 48.

Freedom of speech and of the press "are protected by the First Amendment from abridgment by Congress [and] are among the fundamental personal rights and 'liberties' protected by the due process clause of the Fourteenth Amendment from impairment by the states," rules the Supreme Court June 8, but the court upholds the conviction of a man under the New York Criminal Anarchy Act of 1902. Benjamin Gitlow's pamphlet "The Left Wing Manifesto" called for "mass strikes," "expropriation of the bourgeoisie," and the establishment of a "dictatorship of the proletariat," the court rules in *Gitlow v. New York* that this "is the language of direct incitement," but Justice Holmes observes that "every idea is an incitement" and Justice Brandeis joins in the dissent.

The Scripps-Howard newspaper chain is created as New York newspaperman Roy Howard of 1907 UP fame moves up to co-directorship of the Scripps-McRae chain. Howard broke the news of the 1918 World War armistice 4 days early by acting on a tip and he will bring new dynamism to the newspapers in the chain (*see* 1927).

The *New Yorker* begins publication in February with backing from Fleischmann's Yeast heir Raoul Fleischmann, 39. Edited by journalist Harold Wallace Ross, 33, the 32-page, 15 cent weekly magazine of satire, fiction, social commentary, and criticism has a cover drawing by Rea Irvin of a Regency dandy (who will be named Eustace Tilley) contemplating a butterfly through a magnifying glass. The magazine quickly attracts the talents of cartoonists Peter Arno (Curtis Arnoux Peters), 21, and Helen Hokinson, 26, and of advertising writer E. B. (Elwyn Brooks) White, 26, who will write most of the "Talk of the Town" items that begin each issue. Humorist James Grover Thurber, 30, will become a *New Yorker* regular after receiving rejection slips for his first 20 submissions.

Cosmopolitan magazine is created by a merger of *Hearst's International Magazine* with an earlier *Cosmopolitan* under the editorship of Raymond Land, 47, who will publish works by Louis Bromfield, Edna Ferber, Fannie Hurst, Rupert Hughes, Sinclair Lewis, Somerset Maugham, Dorothy Parker, O. O. McIntyre, Booth Tarkington, and P. G. Wodehouse (*see* 1905).

Collier's editor William Ludlow Chenery sends three staff writers on a nationwide tour to report on Prohibition. They find a breakdown in law enforcement of all kinds and *Collier's* becomes the first major magazine to call for a repeal of the 18th Amendment that has been in effect since January 1920. The magazine loses 3,000 readers but gains 400,000 new readers (*see* 1919).

Parent's Magazine is started by New York bachelor George Joseph Hecht, 30, who quits his family's prosperous hide and skin business, raises $50,000 from family and friends, and launches a monthly magazine devoted to raising children.

Japanese radio broadcasting begins March 22.

American Telephone and Telegraph Company's Western Electric Company splits off its international holdings in anticipation of antitrust action. ITT's Sosthenes Behn and his brother Hernand get backing from the J. P. Morgan banking house to obtain International Western Electric for $30 million and become owners of a network of overseas manufacturing companies that will compete with Siemens, with the Ericson firm of Sweden, but not with AT&T which will use ITT as its export agents under a mutual agreement not to compete with ITT abroad while ITT refrains from competing with AT&T in the United States (*see* 1920; Geneen, 1959).

Bell Laboratories is established by AT&T (above) to consolidate research and development for the Bell System's telephone companies (*see* transistor, 1948).

The Viking Press publishers is founded by New York law graduate Harold K. Guinsburg, 26, and former Alfred E. Knopf promotion man George S. Oppenheimer, 27, who start out with $50,000 in capital (Guinsburg's family has prospered in the Kleinert dress shield business). They obtain a backlist to carry their overhead by acquiring the 20-year-old firm of B. W. Huebsch whose authors include James Joyce, D. H. Lawrence, Sherwood Anderson, and Thorstein Veblen. Huebsch is persuaded to join Viking as editor-in-chief and the new house opens with a 1925 list that includes *The Book of American Spirituals* edited by James Weldon Johnson and arranged by his brother Rosamond (*see* 1899; Literary Guild, 1927).

The Modern Library is purchased for $225,000 from Boni and Liveright by the firm's vice president Bennett Alfred Cerf, 27, with Donald S. Klopfer, 23. They begin building the clothbound line of reprints into a low-priced, 400-title line that will sell more than 50 million copies in the next 50 years (*see* Random House, 1927).

Nonfiction *Mein Kampf* (above); *The Tragedy of Waste* by New York economist Stuart Chase, 37, who deplores not only the waste of U.S. natural resources but of manpower and of the human spirit that is being sacrificed to total mechanization in industry and agriculture; *In the American Grain* by U.S. poet William Carlos Williams.

Fiction *The Trial* (*Der Prozess*) by the late Austrian novelist Franz Kafka who died last year of tuberculosis at age 41 and had intended that his incomplete manuscripts be burned. His friend Max Brod, 41, has edited the work that captures the frantic nightmare of injustice that pervades German society under the Weimar Republic; *Childhood* (*Detstvo Luvers*) by Soviet novelist Boris Pasternak, 35, who has revised the first chapter of a novel whose remaining manuscript pages he has lost; *The Desert of Love* (*Le Desert de l'Amour*) by François Mauriac; *No More Parades* by Ford Madox Ford; *Pastors and Masters* by English novelist Ivy Compton-Burnett, 33; *Mrs. Dalloway* by English novelist Virginia Woolf, 43, who experiments with stream-of-consciousness technique; *Serena Blandish, or The Difficulty of Getting Married* (anonymous) by English novelist Enid Bagnold, 36; *Pauline* by French novelist-poet Pierre Jean Jouve, 38; *Jew Süss* by German novelist-playwright Lion Feuchtwanger, 41; *An American Tragedy* by Theodore Dreiser is based on the Gillett-Brown murder case of 1906; *Barren Ground* by Ellen Glasgow who gains her first critical success at age 51; *The Great Gatsby* by F. Scott Fitzgerald; *Arrowsmith* by Sinclair Lewis; *The Professor's House* by Willa Cather; *Manhattan Transfer* by John Dos Passos; *Gentlemen Prefer Blondes* by California novelist-scriptwriter Anita Loos, 32, who started writing scenarios for D. W. Griffith at age 15 and whose gold-digging Lorelei Lee will be famous for generations; *The House Without a Key* by U.S. playwright-novelist Earl Der Biggers, 41, whose Charlie Chan detective mystery is the first of many; *The Fellowship of the Frog* by Edgar Wallace.

Juvenile *The Childhood and the Enchanters* (*L'Enfant et les Sortilèges*) by Colette.

Poetry *The Cantos* (volume 1) by Ezra Pound; "The Hollow Men" by T. S. Eliot whose poem has reference to the straw figures hung in London streets each day to celebrate Guy Fawkes Day which commemorates discovery of the 1605 Gunpowder Plot: "This is the way the world ends, not with a bang but a whimper"; *Cuttlefish Bones* (*Ossi di seppia*) by antifascist Italian poet Eugenio Montale, 29; *Color* by Harlem, N.Y., poet Countee Cullen, 22.

1925 (cont.) Painting *Three Dancers* by Pablo Picasso; *The Apprentice* by Georges Rouault; *The Drinking Green Pig* by Marc Chagall; *Tower* by Lyonel Feininger. George Bellows dies at New York January 8 at age 42; John Singer Sargent dies in England April 15 at age 69; Roger de la Fresnaye dies of tuberculosis at Grasse November 27 at age 40.

Sculpture *Rima* by Jacob Epstein who has been inspired by the W. H. Hudson novel *Green Mansions* of 1904 to create the statue for London's Hyde Park; *The Duke of Marlborough* by Jacob Epstein.

The Leica camera introduced by E. Leitz G.m.b.H. of Wetzlar, Germany, is a revolutionary miniature 35 millimeter camera invented by Oskar Bernack. It takes a 36-frame film roll, has a lens that can be closed down to take pictures with great depth of field or opened for dim lighting conditions, has fast and slow shutter speeds that permit action pictures, and has interchangeable lenses that permit telephotography (*see* "candid camera," 1930; Nikon, 1948).

Germany's leading photographic film producer A. G. für Analin (Agfa) is acquired by I. G. Farbenindustrie (*see* Bayer, 1919; Ansco, 1927).

Theater *Is Zat So?* by James Gleason and Richard Taber 1/5 at New York's 39th Street Theater, with Gleason, Eleanor Parker, Robert Armstrong in a prizefight comedy, 618 perfs.; *Processional* by U.S. playwright John Howard Lawson, 29, 1/12 at New York's Garrick Theater, with George Abbott, June Walker, Ben Grauer, 96 perfs.; *Fallen Angels* by Noel Coward 4/21 at London's Globe Theatre, with Tallulah Bankhead, Edna Best, 158 perfs.; *Hay Fever* by Noel Coward 6/8 at London's Ambassadors Theatre, with Marie Tempest, Ann Trevor, 337 perfs.; *Veland* by Gerhart Hauptmann 9/19 at Hamburg's Deutsches Schauspielhaus; *The Butter and Egg Man* by George S. Kaufman 9/23 at New York's Longacre Theater, 243 perfs.; *Craig's Wife* by George Kelly 10/12 at New York's Morosco Theater, with Chrystal Herne, 289 perfs., Pulitzer prize 1926; *Lucky Sam McGarver* by Sidney Howard 10/21 at New York's Playhouse Theater, with John Cromwell, Clare Eames, 29 perfs.; *In a Garden* by Philip Barry 11/16 at New York's Plymouth Theater, with Laurette Taylor, Louis Calhern, 73 perfs.; *Easy Virtue* by Noel Coward 12/7 at New York's Empire Theater, with Jane Cowl, Joyce Carey, 147 perfs.

Films E. A. Dupont's *Variety* with Emil Jannings; Sergei Eisenstein's *The Armored Cruiser Potemkin;* Rupert Julian's *The Phantom of the Opera* with Lon Chaney; King Vidor's *The Big Parade* with John Gilbert, Renee Adoree; Fred Niblo's *Ben Hur* with Ramon Novarro, Francis X. Bushman, May McAvoy, Clare McDowell; Abel Gance's *Napoleon;* Erich von Stroheim's *The Merry Widow* with Mae Murray, John Gilbert; Tod Browning's *The Unholy Three* with Lon Chaney, Mae Bush, Matt Moore, Victor McLaglan; Josef von Sternberg's *Salvation Hunters* with derelicts from the Long Beach, Calif., waterfront; Charlie Chaplin's *The Gold Rush* with Chaplin, Mack Swain; Fred Niblo's *Don Q* and *Son of Zorro,* both with Douglas Fairbanks; George Fitzmaurice's *The Dark Angel* with Vilma Banky, Ronald Colman; Clarence Brown's *The Eagle* with Rudolph Valentino, Vilma Banky, Louise Dresser in a filmplay based on a Pushkin story; Harry Hoyt's *The Lost World* with Wallace Beery as Professor Challenger, Lewis Stone, Lloyd Hughes; Malcolm St Clair's *Woman of the World* with Pola Negri, Charles Emmet Mack; Henry King's *Stella Dallas* with Belle Bennett, Alice Joyce, Lois Moran, Douglas Fairbanks, Jr.; Alfred Hitchcock's *The Pleasure Garden;* Herbert Brenon's *A Kiss for Cinderella* with Betty Bronson, Esther Ralston; Rupert Julian's *Three Faces East* with Jetta Gondal, Rupert Julian; D. W. Griffith's *Poppy* with W. C. Fields; Harold Lloyd's *The Freshman* with Harold Lloyd; Sam Taylor and Fred Newmeyer's *Go West* with Buster Keaton.

Opera *Wozzeck* 1/14 at Berlin's State Opera is the first full-length atonal opera. Austrian composer Alban Berg, 40, has based his music on the George Buchner tragedy of 1836. *L'Enfant et les Sortilège* 3/21 at Monte Carlo, with music by Maurice Ravel.

Ballet *Les Matellots (The Sailors)* 6/17 at the Théâtre Gaiété-Lyrique, Paris, with music by Georges Auric, choreography by Leonide Massine.

First performances Symphony for Organ and Orchestra by U.S. composer Aaron Copland, 24, 1/11 at New York, with Nadia Boulanger; Concerto for Violin and Orchestra in D minor (*Concerto Accademico*) by Ralph Vaughan Williams 11/6 at London's Aeolian Hall.

Stage musicals *Big Boy* 1/7 at New York's Winter Garden Theater, with Al Jolson, songs that include "It All Depends on You" by Ray Henderson, lyrics by B. G. DeSylva and Lew Brown (Russian-American writer Lewis Bronstein, 31), "If You Knew Susie Like I Know Susie" by Joseph Meyer, lyrics by B. G. DeSylva, 188 perfs.; *No, No Nanette* 3/11 at London's Phoenix Theatre, with Binnie Hale (Beatrice Mary Hale-Munro), 25, music by Vincent Youmans, lyrics by Irving Caesar and Otto Harbach, songs that include "Tea for Two," "I Want to Be Happy"; *On with the Dance* (revue) 4/30 at London's Pavilion Theatre, with Nigel Bruce, Hermione Baddeley, music by Noel Coward and Philip Braham, book and lyrics by Coward, 229 perfs.; *The Garrick Gaieties* 6/8 at New York's Garrick Theater, with Sterling Holloway, Romney Brent, music by local composer Richard Rodgers, 23, lyrics by Lorenz Hart, 27, songs that include "Manhattan," "Sentimental Me," 1- perfs. (plus 43 beginning 5/10/26); *Artists and Models* 6/24 at New York's Winter Garden Theater, with music by J. Fred Coots, Alfred Goodman, Maurice Rubens, lyrics by Clifford Grey, songs that include "Follow Your Stars," "Take a Little Baby Home with You," 411 perfs.; *Dearest Enemy* 9/18 at New York's Knickerbocker Theater, with Helen Ford, music by Richard Rodgers, lyrics by Lorenz Hart, book by Herbert Fields based on the Revolutionary War leg end about Mrs. Robert Murray delaying General Howe, songs that include "Here in My Arms," 286 perfs.; *The Vagabond King* 9/21 at New York's Casino Theater, with Dennis King, music by Rudolf Friml, lyrics by Bryan Hooker, songs that include "Only a Rose," "Some Day," "Song of the Vagabonds," 511 perfs.; *Sunny* 9/22 at New York's New Amsterdam Theater, with Marilyn Miller, Jack Donahue, Clifton Webb, music by Jerome Kern, lyrics by Otto Harbach and Oscar Hammerstein II, songs that include "Who," 517 perfs.; *The Charlot Revue* 11/10 at New York's Selwyn Theater, with Beatrice Lillie, Gertrude Lawrence, Jack Buchanan, songs that include "Poor Little Rich Girl" by Noel Coward, "A Cup of Coffee, a Sandwich, and You" by Joseph Meyer, lyrics by Billy Rose and Al Dubin, 138 perfs.; *The Cocoanuts* 12/8 at New York's Lyric Theater, with the Four Marx Brothers, Margaret Dumont, book by George S. Kaufman, music and lyrics by Irving Berlin, 218 perfs.; vaudeville monologist Art Fisher has given the Marx Brothers their nicknames and has helped develop their characters: Groucho (Julius Henry), 30, is a moustached wit, Harpo (Arthur), 32, is an idiotic kleptomaniacal mute harpist, Chico (Leanard), 34, is a pianist and confidence man who serves as Harpo's interpreter, Zeppo (Herbert) is straight man; *Tip-Toes* 12/28 at New York's Liberty Theater, with Queenie Smith, Jeanette MacDonald, Robert Halliday, music by George Gershwin, lyrics by Ira Gershwin, book by Guy Bolton and Fred Thompson, songs that include "Sweet and Low-Down," "Looking for a Boy," 194 perfs.

They Laughed When I Sat Down at the Piano but When I Started to Play!—" is the headline for a U.S. School of Music advertisement written by New York copywriter John Caples, 25, who has quit the engineering department of New York Telephone Company to join Ruthrauff and Ryan.

"The Charleston" is introduced to Paris by "Bricktop," a 30-year-old redheaded American who arrived penniless from her native Harlem last year and who has become hostess at a Place Pigalle nightclub. Ada Beatrice Queen Victoria Louisa Virginia Smith du Conge begins a half-century as nightclub hostess.

Popular songs   "Yes, Sir! That's My Baby!" by Walter Donaldson and Gus Kahn; "I Love My Baby (My Baby Loves Me)" by Harry Warren, 32, lyrics by Austrian-American writer Bud Green, 28; "Sleepy Time Gal" by Ange Lorenzo and Richard A. Whiting, lyrics by Joseph R. Alden and Raymond B. Egan; "Sweet Georgia Brown" by Ben Bernie, Maceo Pinkard, and Kenneth Casey; "Alabamy Bound" by Ray Henderson, lyrics by B. G. DeSylva, Bud Green; "Dinah" by Harry Akst, 31, lyrics by Sam M. Lewis and Joe Young; "Sometimes I'm Happy" by Vincent Youmans and Irving Caesar; "Always" by Irving Berlin; "Remember" by Irving Berlin; "Five Feet Two, Eyes of Blue" by Ray Henderson, lyrics by Sam M. Lewis and Joe Young; "I'm Sitting on Top of the World"; by Ray Henderson, lyrics by Sam M. Lewis and Joe

Young; "Don't Bring Lulu" by Ray Henderson, lyrics by Billy Rose and Lew Brown; "I Dreamed I Saw Joe Hill Last Night" by Earl Robinson, lyrics by Alfred Hayes (*see* 1915); "Moonlight and Roses" by Ben Black and Neil Moret with a melody based on H. Lemare's "Andantino"; "Valentine" by French composer Henri Christine, 58, lyrics by Albert Willemetz; "Jealousy" ("Jalousie, a 'Tango Tzigane' [Gypsy Tango]") by Danish violinist-composer Jacob Gade, 46; "Show Me the Way to Go Home" by London songwriters Reg Connelly, 27, and Irving King (Jimmy Campbell), 22.

Grand Ole Opry goes on the air November 28 as *WSM Barn Dance* over Nashville, Tenn., radio station WSM owned by National Life and Accident Insurance Company ("We Shield Millions"). When the Saturday night show's name is changed late in 1927 to *Grand Ole Opry* it will be featuring Uncle Dave Macon, now 55, as "the Dixie Dewdrop" and he will be supported by or followed by such country music stars as the Fruit Jar Drinkers, the Gully Jumpers, Dr. Humphrey Bates and the Possum Hunters, Uncle Jimmy Thompson, Fiddling Arthur Smith, and Roy Acuff, now 22, who will run for governor of Tennessee in 1948.

The Rose Bowl Game at Pasadena January 1 is won by Knute Rockne's Notre Dame "Four Horsemen" but Stanford junior fullback Ernest A. Nevers stars by gaining 114 yards through the line and punting for an average of 42 yards. Nevers missed much of the 1924 season because both his ankles were broken but he plays in the Rose Bowl with his legs so tightly taped that circulation is nearly cut off, and he goes on to lead Stanford to a 27 to 14 fall upset over the University of California, handling the ball on all but three plays to defeat Cal for the first time in 8 years.

Philadelphia's Soldiers Field opens with 165,000 seats. The new stadium will be the scene of Army-Navy football games and other events.

The New York Giants professional football team is founded by Timothy J. Mara.

New York's Madison Square Garden is demolished after a 35-year career in which it has been the scene of prizefights, 6-day bicycle races, rodeos (beginning in 1923), horse shows, and last year's Democratic National Convention. The old Garden is replaced by a new $5.6 million Garden designed by Tex Rickard's architect Thomas W. Lamb; the new Garden on Eighth Avenue between 49th and 50th Streets opens November 28, it will be used for circuses, hockey games, horse shows, basketball games, ice shows, political rallies, and track meets until February 1968, but it is designed principally for boxing and wrestling matches and has poor sightlines for other events.

The Wood Memorial introduced at New York in April is a test for 3-year-old thoroughbreds prior to the Kentucky Derby in May.

Former Columbia baseball star Henry Louis "Lou" Gehrig, 22, joins the New York Yankees as a first

1925 (cont.) baseman and begins a 14-year career of 2,130 consecutive games in which he will have a batting average of .341 (*see* 1939).

"Lefty" Grove is acquired for a record $100,600 by Connie Mack for the Philadelphia Athletics. The 25-year-old pitcher Robert Moses Grove begins a 17-year major league career in which he will strike out 2,266 batters and will record a lifetime earned run average of 3.06.

The Pittsburgh Pirates win the World Series by defeating the Washington Senators 4 games to 3.

Contract bridge is invented by railroad heir and yachtsman Harold S. Vanderbilt, 41, while on a Caribbean cruise. A variation on the 21-year-old game of auction bridge, the new game will eclipse auction bridge and whist beginning in 1930 when Romanian-American expert Eli Culbertson will defeat Britain's Lieutenant-Colonel W. T. M. Butler in a challenge match at London's Almack's Club that will bring the game wide publicity (*see* Goren, 1936).

Floyd Collins makes headlines in late January after being trapped inside a Kentucky cave he had been exploring with companions. Search parties try to reach him before it is too late but Collins is found dead February 16 under a boulder that has pinned him fast for 18 days.

Scotch Tape gets its name from a Detroit automobile plant car painter. The Minnesota Mining and Manufacturing Company founded in 1910 has developed a masking tape to facilitate two-tone paint jobs, but a 3M employee has eliminated the adhesive from the center of the tape to save money. The new tape does not stick, an angry painter tells a 3M salesman to "take this tape back to those Scotch bosses of yours and have them put adhesive all over the tape," 3M replaces the missing adhesive, and will make Scotch a brand name for a full line of adhesive tapes.

The Simmons Beautyrest mattress is introduced by Zalmon Simmons, Jr., whose father started the Simmons Company at Kenosha, Wis., in 1870. The company acquired two mattress-making firms 6 years ago and Simmons has perfected another inventor's innerspring mattress whose coils are contained in individual cloth pockets, permitting stress on one group of coils to be distributed throughout the mattress.

Chester H. Roth Co. is founded by New York entrepreneur Chester H. Roth, 23, whose hosiery commission firm will grow to have sales of $56 million per year by 1958 when he will merge with Julius Kayser Company to create a colossus whose hosiery, lingerie, gloves, and swimsuits will have annual sales of nearly $550 million by 1975.

Lux toilet soap is introduced by Lever Brothers under the name Lux Toilet Form. The white milled soap will challenge Palmolive and Procter & Gamble's Cashmere Bouquet (*see* 1905; Lux Flakes, 1906; Rinso, 1918; Unilever, 1929).

U.S. cigarette production reaches 82.2 billion, up from 66.7 billion in 1923.

Old Gold cigarettes are introduced by P. Lorillard. The firm is well known for its Murad cigarettes and their slogan "Be nonchalant—light a Murad," and Old Golds will gain popularity with the slogan "Not a cough in a carload" (*see* 1911; Kent, 1952).

"Blow some my way," says a woman to a man lighting a cigarette in advertisements by Liggett & Meyers for its 12-year-old Chesterfield brand. The advertisement breaks a taboo by suggesting that women smoke.

Lucky Strike cigarettes are promoted by George Washington Hill, 41, who succeeds his father Percival Hill as head of American Tobacco (*see* 1918). Young Hill will introduce the slogan "Reach for a Lucky instead of a sweet" (*see* 1931).

"Pretty Boy" Floyd begins a 12-year career in which he will rob more than 30 Midwestern banks and will kill 10 people. Charles Arthur Floyd, 18, robs a local post office of $350 in pennies at St. Louis.

Al Capone takes over as boss of Chicago bootlegging from racketeer Johnny Torrio who retires after sustaining gunshot wounds. Alphonse Capone of Cicero, Ill., is a 26-year-old Italian-American who has been a lieutenant of Torrio and who last year had Torrio's chief rival Dion O'Bannion gunned down in his flower shop. Capone soon controls not only bootlegging but also gambling, prostitution, and the Chicago dance hall business while his agents on the Canadian border and in the Caribbean help him grow rich by smuggling huge quantities of whiskey and rum into the United States (*see* 1927).

Izzy and Moe are dismissed as Prohibition agents after having made 4,392 arrests in just over 5 years with a 95 percent record of convictions. Isadore Einstein and Moe Smith are both in their mid-forties, each weighs more than 225 pounds although neither is taller than 5 feet 7 inches, and they are discharged because they have antagonized their superiors by getting too much personal publicity for their ingenious and successful, if undignified, stratagems for apprehending Prohibition law violators.

New York's R. H. Macy Company gains control of Atlanta's Davison-Paxon Company department store (*see* 1891; 1924; Bamberger's, 1929).

Gimbel Brothers acquires Philadelphia's Kaufmann & Bauer store which will be renamed Gimbel Brothers in 1928 (*see* Saks Fifth Avenue, 1924; Pittsburgh Gimbels, 1940).

Filene's in Boston opens a branch at Wellesley and begins a suburban expansion that will see Filene's stores at Hyannis, Northampton, Winchester, Worcester, Belmont, Chestnut Hill, and other locations (*see* 1912; Federated, 1929).

Gamble-Skogmo, Inc., has its beginnings at Fergus Falls, Minn., where Hudson-Essex motorcar dealers Bertin Clyde Gamble, 27, and Phil Skogmo begin selling auto parts to inaugurate a retail empire that will grow in 50 years to have more than 3,400 department stores, specialty shops, grocery stores (Red Owl), drugstores (Snyder's), and mass merchandising stores (Tempo and Buckeye Mart) throughout America and Canada, mostly in small towns, with annual sales of $1.5 billion.

 A Paris Exposition Internationale des Arts Décoratifs displays a two-story apartment designed by Swiss-born architect Charles Edouard Jeanneret, 38, who calls himself Le Corbusier and who calls his apartment Le Pavillon de l'Esprit. Its spacious rooms are furnished with a minimum of furniture which includes bentwood chairs introduced by Gebrüder Thonet of Vienna in 1876 but never used as modern furniture until now. Le Corbusier also employs as decorative objects bistro wineglasses, laboratory flasks, seashells, industrial equipment, and ethnic rugs and hangings.

The term "Art Deco" will be derived half a century hence from the Paris Exposition (above) but not from the pioneering ideas of Le Corbusier.

Potsdam's Einstein Tower is completed by German architect Eric Mendelsohn, 38.

Chicago's Tribune Tower is completed in May on Michigan Avenue at Tribune Place for "The World's Greatest Newspaper." New York architects John Mead Howells and Raymond M. Hood have designed a 36-story Gothic skyscraper 58 feet taller than the 32-story Wrigley building completed last year.

New York's Ritz Tower is completed on Park Avenue at 57th Street by Carrère & Hastings. The 42-story tower is an elegant apartment building.

The Brooklyn Museum is completed by McKim, Mead and White.

Washington's Mayflower Hotel opens February 18 with 1,000 rooms. The inaugural ball for President Coolidge is held at the Mayflower in March.

Paris's Bristol Hotel opens.

Boston's Parker House opens on Tremont Street to replace the hotel opened in 1855.

Chicago's Palmer House opens at State and Monroe Streets to replace the hotel built in 1875.

Chicago's Hotel Sherman is completed at the corner of Clark and Randolph Streets.

Memphis's Peabody Hotel opens with 617 rooms to replace the Peabody that had been the city's social center for 56 years.

The Breakers at Palm Beach, Fla., is replaced after 22 years by a $6 million hotel with 600 guest rooms and suites, two conference wings, two 18-hole golf courses, 12 tennis courts, indoor and outdoor swimming pools and a private beach, a fountain modeled after one in the Boboli Gardens of Florence, a lobby inspired by Genoa's Palazzo Larega, and a general design inspired by Rome's Villa Medici.

Florida's Boca Raton Hotel is completed 25 miles south of Palm Beach by Addison Mizener who provides the $10 million 450-room hotel with an artificial lake, islands, and gondolas. Financed by utility magnate Clarence H. Geist, the Boca Raton has indoor and outdoor swimming pools.

The Miami Biltmore at Coral Gables, Fla., is completed by John McEntee Bowman of 1914 New York Biltmore fame and Coral Gables promoter George Edgar Merrick whose late father Solomon Greasley Merrick was a Congregationalist minister who moved to Florida from Cape Cod in 1898, acquired 160 acres of land near the Everglades, and built a homestead he called Coral Gables. The younger Merrick acquired an adjacent tract in 1922, he called it Coral Gables, and he set out to build the first Miami subdivision as a resort for respectable older people who could not afford Carl Fisher's Miami Beach (see 1913). The new $7 million Miami Biltmore has a 250-foot outdoor swimming pool and a 300-foot replica of Spain's Tower of Giralda at Seville.

The bubble of inflated Florida land values breaks as investors discover the lots they have bought are in many cases underwater. The hordes of Florida real estate promoters turn out to include a man named Charpon who is actually Charles Ponzi of 1920 "Ponzi scheme" notoriety.

The first motel opens December 12 at San Luis Obispo, Calif. James Vail's Motel Inn with accommodations for 160 guests is located on one of the busiest U.S. motor routes.

William Randolph Hearst moves into his San Simeon castle La Cuesta Encantada overlooking the Pacific on 240,000 acres of ranchland. He has spent an estimated $50 million to build the Hispano-Moorish Casa Grande and its adjoining buildings (the place requires a staff of 50).

Washington's Firenze estate with a 59-room pseudo-Tudor mansion on a 22-acre site bordering Rock Creek Park is completed by architect Russell Kluge for heiress Blanche Estabrook Roebling O'Brien.

 The worst tornado in U.S. history cuts through Missouri, Illinois, and Indiana March 18 killing 689, injuring thousands, and causing millions of dollars worth of property damage.

Harold Ware returns to Russia with 26 volunteers and $150,000 worth of U.S. farm equipment, seeds, and supplies (see 1921; 1922). Ware demonstrates mechanized farming on 15,000 acres of land in the northern Caucasus and he is selected by Moscow to oversee a program of organizing huge mechanized state farms for the improvement of agricultural efficiency throughout Russia, a post he will hold until 1932 (see Stalin, 1928).

Caterpillar Tractor Company is created by a merger of Holt Manufacturing Co. (see 1904) and C. L. Best Tractor Co., founded by California manufacturer Clarence Leo Best, 47. The firm will build a large factory at Peoria, Ill.

Chiang Kai-shek fought rival warlords to unify China but betrayed the revolutionary ideals of Sun Yat-sen.

 Night blindness (nyctalopia) is shown to be related to vitamin A deficiency by U.S. physiologists L. S. Fredericia and E. Holm who find that rats do not see well in dim light if their diets are lacking in vitamin A (*see* McCollum, 1920; Wald, 1938).

 U.S. refrigerator sales reach 75,000, up from 10,000 in 1920 (*see* 1929; GE refrigerator, 1927).

A deep-freezing process for cooked foods is developed by Clarence Birdseye with Charles Seabrook (*see* 1923; 1912). Tightly packed in a small carton, the food is encased in a metal mold and several such molds are placed in a long metal tube that is immersed in a low-temperature brine solution to produce a quick-contact process that Birdseye patents (*see* 1926).

Jell-O is merged into the Postum Company (*see* 1906; 1926).

Wesson Oil and Snowdrift Company, Inc., is created by a reorganization of the Southern Cotton Oil Company (*see* Wesson Oil, 1900; Hunt Foods, 1960).

The New York Cocoa Exchange is established by merchants, importers, and brokers who hope to avoid repetition of the disastrous price break of 1921 and who adopt rules modeled on those of the Cotton Exchange and the Chicago Board of Trade.

Automatic potato-peeling machines are introduced that will permit widescale production of potato chips.

Wise Potato Chips become so popular that Earl Wise builds a 32- by 75-foot concrete block plant at Berwick, Pa., to replace the remodeled garage in which he has been producing chips since 1921. By 1942 the plant will have expanded to embrace more than 40,000 square feet of floor space.

A giant wearing a bearskin and carrying a club is adopted for the promotion of Minnesota Valley Canning Company products but the advertising symbol does not inspire customers to buy (*see* 1907; Burnett's jolly Green Giant, 1935).

Vienna has 1,250 coffeehouses, down from 15,000 in 1842.

 Birth control wins the endorsements of the New York Obstetrical Society, the New York Academy of Medicine, and the American Medical Association after persuasion by New York obstetrician Robert L. Dickinson who obtains a $10,000 Rockefeller Foundation grant for research in contraception.

1926 Josef Stalin establishes himself as virtual dictator of the Soviet Union, beginning a 27-year rule that will de-emphasize world revolution but will bring new repression to Soviet citizens and terror to Russia's neighbors. The Politburo expels Leon Trotsky and Grigori Zinoviev in October.

U.S. troops have landed in Nicaragua beginning May 2 to preserve order and protect U.S. interests in the face of a revolt against the new president Emiliano Chamorro, who resigns under pressure in the fall.

The French fleet bombards Damascus May 8 in an effort to suppress the great insurrection of the Druses that began last year. Paris proclaims Lebanon a republic May 23.

Chiang Kai-shek succeeds the late Sun Yat-sen as leader of the Chinese revolutionary party and begins the unification of China under the Kuomintang, which holds power only in the south. Chiang takes Wuchang in October and establishes that city as his seat of power (*see* 1925; 1927).

The Japanese emperor Yoshihito dies December 25 at age 47 after a 14-year reign. He is succeeded by his 25-year-old son, who has been acting as regent during the 5-year illness of Yoshihito. The new emperor Hirohito will reign for more than half a century, and the influence of Japan's army and navy will increase enormously in the next 15 years (*see* Mukden, 1931).

 France stabilizes the franc at 20 percent of its prewar value and thus virtually wipes out the savings of millions of Frenchmen. The devaluation will have the effect of making the French Europe's greatest gold hoarders (*see* 1928).

A gigantic German steel cartel is created by a merger of major mining enterprises with the Rhine-Elbe Union steel company that has been built up by Albert Vogler, 49, with help from the late Hugo Stinnes, Nazi industrialist Emil Kirdorf, 79, and Nazi steelmaker Fritz Thyssen, 53. The new United Steel Works (Vereinigte Stahlwerke) is rivaled only by the great Krupp works at Essen.

 The doctoral thesis of English physicist Paul Adrien Maurice Dirac, 24, advances a formal theory that will hereafter govern the study of submicroscopic phenomena. A cofounder of the modern theory of quantum mechanics, Dirac will extend his theory in the next 4 years to embrace ideas of relativity (*see* Einstein, 1916; 1929; Heisenberg, 1927).

A wave model of the atom constructed by Austrian physicist Erwin Schrödinger, 39, makes a major contribution to modern quantum theory (*see* Planck, 1900). Schrödinger has seized upon a radical theory advanced by the French physicist Louis-Victor de Broglie that the electron, like light, should exhibit a dual nature, behaving both as particle and as wave, and in the Schrödinger model electrons wash round the nucleus.

The Theory of the Gene by Columbia University zoologist Thomas Hunt Morgan, 60, proves a theory of hereditary transmission that will be the basis for all future genetic research. Morgan's book *The Physical Bases of Heredity* appeared in 1919 and he has conducted experiments with fruit flies to pinpoint the location of genes in the chromosomes of the cell nucleus (*see* Bateson, 1902; Watson, Crick, 1953).

A British General Strike cripples the nation from May 3 to May 12 as members of the Trade Union Congress rally to the slogan, "Not a penny off the pay; not a minute on the day." The strike begins with a lockout May 1 by private coal mine operators whose workers refuse to accept a pay cut averaging 13 percent and refuse to work an extra hour each day. The mine operators have been forced to cut wages and increase hours by the action of Chancellor of the Exchequer Winston Churchill who has returned to the gold standard, thus squeezing export industries such as coal which must compete with German and Polish producers and with oil producers. Railwaymen, printing trade workers, building trade workers, truckdrivers, dockworkers, iron- and steelworkers, chemical industry workers, and some power company workers walk out in sympathy with the coal workers in accordance with strategy devised by Transport Workers chief Ernest Bevin, 42.

The Royal Navy trains its guns on British strikers who try to prevent ships from off-loading food and other relief materials in support of the great strike (above), economist John Maynard Keynes has termed the action by Winston Churchill "featherbrained" and "silly," but while 3 million workers respond to Ernest Bevin's strike call volunteers who include most of the students of Oxford and Cambridge maintain essential services. The sympathy strike is called off May 12, but the coal miners who average $14.60 per week in wages continue to resist any wage cut or lengthening of hours until November 19 when they capitulate unconditionally. The mine workers accept the terms of the mine operators plus drastic layoffs; they will not strike again until 1972.

The Railway Labor Act (Watson-Parker Act) passed by Congress sets up a five-man board of mediation appointed by the president to settle railway labor disputes (*see* 1934).

Ford Motor Company plants introduce an 8-hour day and a 5-day work week beginning September 5.

The rocket launched March 16 by physicist Robert H. Goddard is the first liquid fuel rocket, it demonstrates the practicality of rockets, and it convinces Goddard that rockets will one day land men on the moon (*see* 1921). Goddard sends his rocket on a 2.5-second flight from a field on his Aunt Effie's farm near Auburn, Mass., it travels 184 feet at a speed of only 60 miles per hour and it reaches a height of only 41 feet, but Goddard writes in his diary, "It looked almost magical as it rose, without any appreciably greater noise or flame." He continues his research, and beginning in 1930 he will get financial support from copper heir Harry Guggenheim at the advice of Charles A. Lindbergh and from the Daniel and Florence Guggenheim Foundation established in 1924.

U.S. Navy explorer Richard Evelyn Byrd, 36, and pilot Floyd Bennett, 35, take off May 9 from Spitzbergen in a trimotor Fokker monoplane, they fly 700 miles to the North Pole, they circle the pole 13 times, and they return in 15.5 hours.

The first contract airmail flight has taken off February 15 from Dearborn, Mich. The Ford Pullman all-metal monoplane lands at Cleveland.

Scheduled U.S. airline service begins April 6. A Varney Air Lines two-seat Laird Swallow biplane piloted by Leon D. Cuddeback, 28, flies 244 miles on a contract mail route from Pasco, Wash., to Boise, Idaho, and proceeds to Elko, Nev., with 200 pounds of mail.

Charles Augustus Lindbergh, 24, takes off from St. Louis April 15 on the first regularly scheduled mail flight between St. Louis and Chicago. Lindbergh is chief pilot for Robertson Aircraft Corporation whose owners Frank and William Robertson have three DH-4 biplanes (*see* 1927; American Airways, 1930).

Trans World Airlines has its beginnings in the Western Air Express Company (*see* 1930).

Northwest Airlines has its beginnings in the Northwest Airways Company that begins service between Chicago and St. Paul.

The Air Commerce Act passed by Congress encourages the growth of commercial aviation by awarding mail contracts.

The Army Air Corps is created by act of Congress.

Philadelphia's 533-meter Benjamin Franklin Bridge opens to traffic.

The Florida Keys link of the Florida East Coast Railway completed in 1912 is destroyed September 19 by a hurricane which further deflates the boom in Florida real estate (*see* 1925; 1935; Overseas Highway, 1938).

Chicago's Union Station opens to serve four large railroads.

The Chief departs from Chicago's Dearborn Station November 14 to begin daily Santa Fe service between Chicago and Los Angeles with seven cars including four sleeping cars, a diner, a club car, and an observation lounge car. The 63-hour run will be reduced to 58 hours in 1929 and to 56 hours in 1930 (*see* 1911; *Super Chief*, 1936).

1926 (cont.) Greyhound Corporation is incorporated to compete with intercity passenger rail service (*see* 1922). General Motors Corporation will be the largest Greyhound stockholder until 1948 (*see* 1929).

The *Delta Queen* is launched at Cincinnati and the paddlewheel passenger steamer goes into service between the Queen City and New Orleans. Fare for the 7-day trip on the Ohio and Mississippi Rivers is $35.

Standard Fruit and Steamship Company is created at New Orleans by a reorganization of the banana importing firm Vaccaro Brothers (*see* 1898). Standard Fruit has a fleet of refrigerated steamships and extensive banana lands in Honduras that challenge the United Fruit Company monopoly (*see* 1964).

The Pontiac motorcar is introduced by General Motors which renames its Oakland (*see* 1924).

The Chrysler Imperial is introduced by Chrysler Corporation. The luxury model will continue in production with styling and engineering changes for more than 50 years.

The Model T Ford sells for $350 new with a self-starter but is losing ground to GM's Chevrolet (*see* 1922; Model A, 1927).

The Deusenberg Automobile and Motor Company is acquired by E. L. Cord's Auburn Automobile Company (*see* 1924; Model J, 1929).

S.A.E. viscosity numbers to standardize engine lubricating oils are established by the Society of Automotive Engineers which assigns heavy oil the number 50 and light oil the number 10 (*see* 1911).

Prestone is introduced by Union Carbide and Carbon Company (*see* 1920). The first ethylene glycol antifreeze for motor vehicle radiators, it retails at $5 per gallon.

The Triplex Safety Glass Company of North America is founded by U.S. entrepreneur Amory L. Haskell who has obtained U.S. rights to the 1910 patent of Edouard Benedictus. Haskell begins production on one floor of the Lipton Tea factory at Hoboken, N.J., and receives assistance from Henry Ford to build his own factory, but the initial price of safety glass is $8.80 per square foot and it costs a Cadillac owner $200 to replace all the glass in his car with safety glass (*see* 1927; Sloan, 1929).

Safety glass windshields are installed as standard equipment on high-priced Stutz motorcar models.

A power steering unit patented by Waltham, Mass., inventor Francis Wright Davis, 38, is installed in a 1921 Pierce-Arrow Runabout. Formerly chief engineer of Pierce-Arrow's trucking division, Davis and his master craftsman George Jessup will demonstrate the power steering unit to Detroit automakers beginning next year, but commercial production of cars with power steering will not come until 1951.

U.S. auto production reaches 4 million, up nearly eightfold from 1914 (*see* 1927).

The Mercedes-Benz supercharged SS sportscar is introduced by the new German motorcar giant Daimler-Benz created by a merger of Daimler Motoren-Gesellschaft with Firma Benz & Cie. (*see* 1886; Jellinek, 1901; diesel, 1936).

The Maserati Neptune and Trident racing cars are introduced by Italian automakers Alfieri, Ettore, and Ernesto Maserati who have built cars for other racing companies since 1914.

Synthetic rubber is pioneered by B. F. Goodrich Rubber Company chemist Waldo Lonsbury Semon, 28, who uses catalysts in an effort to extract the chlorine from the polymer polyvinyl chloride. Semon polymerizes PVC into a white powder, he plasticizes the PVC powder with agents such as tricreylphosphate, and he produces a workable synthetic that can be rolled and treated like rubber. Semon's product is odorless, weatherproof, age-resistant, and acid-resistant, and will be introduced commercially in 1933 under the name Koroseal (*see* Nieuwland, 1925; butadiene, 1939).

Sintered carbide is introduced by Fried. Krupp of Essen whose nonferrous metal alloy on a tungsten carbide base enables machine tools to cut steel at 150 meters per minute instead of 8 meters.

The semi-automatic .30 M1 rifle that will be adopted by the U.S. Army in 1936 is patented by Canadian-American inventor John C. Garand, 38.

An improved waterproof cellophane that will revolutionize packaging is developed by E. I. du Pont chemists William Hale Church and Karl Edwin Prindle (*see* Brandenberger, 1912). Du Pont has been making cellophane at Buffalo, N.Y., since early 1924, selling it initially for $2.65 per pound.

Father Coughlin makes his first radio broadcast October 17 over Detroit's station WJR to begin a career of nearly 20 years. Detroit priest Charles Edward Coughlin, 34, will broadcast sermons marked by racial bigotry and right-wing sentiments (*see* 1934).

The grotto of Lourdes that has been famous since 1858 attracts new attention after French housewife Augustine Augault is relieved overnight of a fibroid tumor of the uterus that has swelled her weight from 77 pounds to 102. The tumor has been diagnosed as such by physicians but after Mme. Augault is carried on a stretcher in the procession of the Blessed Sacrament at Lourdes it is found to have disappeared by 30 Catholic and non-Catholic physicians, a "miracle" that will help lead to the canonization of Sister Bernadette in 1933 (*see* 1866).

Ergotism from infected rye breaks out in the Soviet Union and in some places affects half the population (*see* LSD, 1943; Pont Saint Esprit, 1951).

Reading University is founded in England.

Long Island University (LIU) is founded at Brooklyn, N.Y.

Sarah Lawrence College for Women is founded at Bronxville, N.Y., by local real estate developer William V. Lawrence who names the college for his wife.

Scripps College is founded at Claremont, Calif.

The first successful demonstration of television is given by Scottish inventor John L. Baird, 28, but his mechanical system based on the van Nipkov rotating disk of 1886 has serious limitations (*see* 1927).

The first motion picture with sound is demonstrated (*see* below; 1927; de Forest, 1923).

The National Broadcasting Company (NBC) is founded November 11 by David Sarnoff whose nine-station network soon has 31 affiliates (*see* 1920; 1927).

General Telephone Corporation has its beginnings in the Associated Telephone Utilities Corporation founded by Southern Wisconsin investor Sigurd L. Odegard who gets backing from Chicago utilities magnate Marshall E. Sampsell and acquires a Long Beach, Calif., telephone company (*see* 1935).

Amazing Stories magazine is founded by Luxembourg-born U.S. inventor and science-fiction enthusiast Hugo Gernsback, 42, who came to America at age 20 to promote an improved dry cell battery he had invented and whose Electro Importing Company, founded a year later, was the world's first radio supply house. Gernsback started publishing *Modern Electrics* in 1908 and began publishing *Radio News* in 1919.

Publicis is founded by French advertising man Marcel Bleustein-Blanchet, 19, who will develop an international network of independently controlled local advertising agencies, the largest such network in Europe. By 1929 Publicis will be the exclusive advertising representative for 18 French government radio stations.

The Book-of-the-Month Club is founded by New York advertising men Maxwell Byron Sackheim, 35, and Harry Scherman, 39, who quit the Ruthrauff and Ryan agency in 1919 to start Sackheim & Scherman. They are joined by Charles and Albert Boni and Robert Haas to start a cut-rate mail-order enterprise that will market some 300 million hardcover books in the next 50 years. Titles are chosen by an editorial board consisting of *New York World* columnist Heywood Broun, 37, Henry Seidel Canby of Yale, author Dorothy Canfield Fisher, author Christopher Morley, and Kansas publisher William Allen White, and the first selection goes out April 16 to 4,750 members (*see* below; Literary Guild, 1927).

William Morrow & Co. publishers is founded by Irish-American editor William Morrow, 52, of Frederick A. Stokes publishers.

Nonfiction   *History of England* by Cambridge University historian G. M. (George Macaulay) Trevelyan, 50; *Dictionary of Modern English Usage* by English lexicographer H. W. (Henry Watson) Fowler, 68; *The Story of Philosophy* by New York educator-author Will (William James) Durant, 40, whose best-seller will have sales of well over 2 million copies and will be translated into several foreign languages. Durant became director of the radical Labor Temple School

at age 29, he presented the material in his new book in a series of adult education lectures, and he then had E. Haldeman-Julius publish them in a series of 5-cent Little Blue Books; *Seven Pillars of Wisdom* by T. E. Lawrence (*see* Lowell Thomas, 1924) whose 280,000-word account of World War desert fighting appears in a 30 guinea limited edition. A 130,000-word abridged version will be published next year under the more appropriate title *Revolt in the Desert,* and the full book will be issued for general circulation after Lawrence's death in a motorcycle accident in 1935; *Microbe Hunters* by U.S. bacteriologist Paul de Kruif, 36, who helped Sinclair Lewis with his 1925 novel *Arrowsmith* and now gives a popular account of the discoveries by Louis Pasteur, Robert Koch, Paul Ehrlich, and others.

Fiction   *Lolly Willowes* by English novelist Sylvia Townsend Warner, 33, is the first selection of the new Book-of-the-Month Club (above); *The Counterfeiters (Les Faux Monnayeurs)* by André Gide; *Debits and Credits* (stories) by Rudyard Kipling whose son was killed in 1915, and whose preoccupation with imperialism and anti-German sentiment has put him out of touch with his contemporaries, but who is still capable of such gems as "The Garden" and "The Wish House"; *The Plumed Serpent* by D. H. Lawrence; *A Man Could Stand Up* by Ford Madox Ford; *The Castle (Das Schloss)* by the late Franz Kafka; *The Bullfighters (Les Bestiairs)* by Henry de Montherlant; *Blindness* by English novelist Henry Green (Henry Vincent Yorke), 21; *The Sun Also Rises* by U.S. novelist Ernest Miller Hemingway, 27, who quotes émigrée author Gertrude Stein, now 52, in an epigraph that says, "You are all a lost generation," a line Stein heard her garageman use in scolding a young mechanic who did not make proper repairs on her Model T Ford; *The Labala* by U.S. novelist Thornton Niven Wilder, 29; *Soldier's Pay* by Mississippi novelist William Cuthbert Faulkner, 28, who added the "u" to his name when he published a volume of poetry 2 years ago; *Under the Sun of Satan (Sous le soleil de Satan)* by French novelist Georges Bernanos, 38; *Before the Bombardment* by English novelist Osbert Sitwell, 34; *Stamboul Train* by English novelist Graham Greene, 26; *The Murder of Roger Ackroyd* by Agatha Christie; *Clouds of Witness* by Dorothy Sayers; *Show Boat* by Edna Ferber; *Smoky* by U. S. cowboy novelist Will James, 34.

Poetry   *The Close Couplet* by U.S. poet Laura Riding, 25; *White Buildings* by U.S. poet Hart Crane, 27; *A Drunk Man Looks at the Thistle* by Scottish poet Hugh MacDiarmid (C. M. Grieve), 34; *The Weary Blues* by U. S. poet Langston Hughes, 24, who has been helped by Vachel Lindsay and who receives the Witter Bynner Undergraduate Poetry Award; *Enough Rope* by U.S. poet-author Dorothy Rothschild Parker, 33, who is well-known for her 1920 advertising line "Brevity is the soul of lingerie" and will be better known for "Men seldom make passes/ At girls who wear glasses," for putting down an ac-

1926 (cont.) tress with the line, "She ran the whole gamut of emotions from A to B," and for the verse, "Guns aren't lawful; Nooses give;/ Gas smells awful;/ You might as well live."

Juvenile *Winnie-the-Pooh* by A. A. Milne who delights readers with Pooh-bear, Tigger, Piglet, Ee-ore, Kanga and baby Roo, Owl, and other companions of Christopher Robin; *Fairy Gold* by Compton Mackenzie; *The Little Engine that Could* by U.S. author Watty Piper (Mabel C. Bragg), illustrations by George and Doris Haumon.

Painting *Lover's Bouquet* by Marc Chagall; *Several Circles* by Wassily Kandinsky; *The Red House* by Edvard Munch; *Lady Ottoline Morrell* by Augustus John; *Terrace in Richmond* by Oskar Kokoschka; *The Last Jockey* by Belgian surrealist René Magritte, 27. Mary Cassatt dies at her country house outside Paris June 14 at age 81 (she has been blind for years); Claude Monet dies at Giverny December 5 at age 86.

Sculpture *Draped Reclining Figure* by Henry Moore; *The Visitation* by Jacob Epstein; *Europa* fountain by Carl Milles; New York's Collector of Customs classifies Constantin Brancusi's *Bird in Space* of 1919 "a manufacture of metal" subject to 40 percent duty, photographer Edward Steichen who has imported the *Bird* claims it is a work of art and thus exempt from duty under existing laws, a judge rules that while the *Bird* may not imitate nature it is a work of art according to the "so-called new school of art" which espouses abstraction.

Theater *The Great God Brown* by Eugene O'Neill 1/23 at New York's Greenwich Village Theater, with William Harrigan, 171 perfs.; *The Plough and the Stars* by Sean O'Casey 2/8 at Dublin's Abbey Theatre, 133 perfs.; *The Queen Was in the Parlour* by Noel Coward 8/24 at Martin's Theatre, London; *Broadway* by U.S. playwrights Philip Dunning and George Abbott 9/16 at New York's Broadhurst Theater, with Lee Tracy, 332 perfs.; *And So to Bed* by English playwright J. B. Fagan 9/26 at the Queen's Theatre, London, in a play about the 17th century diarist Samuel Pepys; *White Wings* by Philip Barry 10/15 at New York's Booth Theater, 31 perfs.; *Caponsacchi* by U.S. playwright Arthur Frederick Goodrich, 48, 10/26 at Hampden's Theater, New York, with Goodrich's brother-in-law Walter Hampden as the canon Giuseppe Gaposacchi, from Robert Browning's dramatic monologues *The Ring and the Book* of 1868 and 1869, 269 perfs.; *Dorothea Augermann* by Gerhart Hauptmann 11/20 at Vienna's Theater in der Josefstadt, Munich's Kammerspiele, and 15 other German theaters; *"This Was a Man"* by Noel Coward 11/23 at New York's Klaw Theater, 31 perfs.; *The Constant Wife* by W. Somerset Maugham 11/29 at New York's Maxine Elliott Theater, 295 perfs.; *The Silver Cord* by Sidney Howard 12/20 at New York's John Golden Theater, with comedienne Sarah Hope Crews, Margalo Gilmore, Earle Larimore in a play about mother-son love, 112 perfs.; *In Abraham's Bosom* by U.S. playwright Paul Eliot

Green, 32, 12/30 at New York's Provincetown Playhouse, with Jules Bledsoe, 123 perfs. (many after the play moves uptown to the Garrick Theater), Pulitzer prize 1927.

Films Alan Crosland's *Don Juan* with John Barrymore opens August 6 at New York's 20-year-old Manhattan Opera House and is accompanied by sound electrically recorded on disks in the Warner Brothers Vitaphone process developed by Western Electric Company engineers. Film czar Will H. Hays, 47, who has headed the Motion Picture Producers and Distributors of America (MPPDA) since 1922 appears on screen and is heard predicting that Vitaphone will revolutionize the industry, the film gets an enthusiastic response in October when it is shown at Grauman's Egyptian Theater in Hollywood, but few exhibitors are willing to install the costly equipment necessary for Vitaphone, and better established film studios will have no part of it (*see* 1927).

Other films Fritz Lang's *Metropolis;* Sergei Eisenstein's *October;* Vsevolod Pudovkin's *Mother* with Vera Baranovskaia; Jean Renoir's *Nana* with Catherine Hessling, Werner Krauss; Raoul Walsh's *What Price Glory?* with Victor McLaglen, Dolores Del Rio; Victor Seastrom's *The Scarlet Letter* with Lillian Gish, Lars Hanson; King Vidor's *A Boheme* with Lillian Gish, John Gilbert, René Adorée; James Cruze's *Old Ironsides* with Charles Farrell, Esther Ralston, Wallace Beery; Malcolm St. Clair's *The Grand Duchess and the Waiter* with Adolphe Menjou, Florence Vidor; Herbert Brenon's *Beau Geste* with Ronald Colman, Noah Beery, Neil Hamilton; Albert Parker's *The Black Pirate* with Douglas Fairbanks; Frank Tuttle's *Kid Boots* with Eddie Cantor, Clara Bow; Clarence Brown's *Kiki* with Norma Talmadge, Ronald Colman; Richard Rosson's *Fine Manners* with Gloria Swanson, Eugene O'Brien; Buster Keaton's *The General* and *The Battling Butler* with Buster Keaton; Hal Roach's *Putting Pants on Philip* with English comic Stan (Arthur Stanley Jefferson) Laurel, 36, and Georgia-born comic Oliver (Oliver Nowell) Hardy, 34; George Fitzmaurice's *Son of the Sheik* with Rudolph Valentino who dies of peritonitis at New York's Polyclinic Hospital August 23 at age 31 after surgery for an inflamed appendix and two perforated gastric ulcers. The screen idol has come to New York to promote his new film, press agents hired by Joseph Schenck of United Artists capitalize on his death, his body lies in state at Frank E. Campbell's funeral parlor on Broadway, fans line up for 11 blocks to view the remains, and 100,000 mourners file past the ornate coffin.

Harry Houdini makes headlines August 6 by remaining underwater for 91 minutes in an airtight case containing only enough air to sustain a man for 5 or 6 minutes. The 52-year-old escape artist has practiced breath control and has remained absolutely still in order to minimize his oxygen consumption, but the Great Houdini suffers a subsequent stomach injury and dies of peritonitis October 31.

Opera *Judith* (drama with music) 2/13 at Monte Carlo, with music by Arthur Honegger; *Turandot* 4/25 at Milan's Teatro alla Scala, with music by the late Giacomo Puccini who died 2 years ago at age 66.

Ballet   Martha Graham makes her first solo appearance April 18 at New York's 48th Street Theater. Now 31, Graham studied at Los Angeles with Ruth St. Denis, 49, and Ted Shawn, 35, she performed as lead dancer in the ballet *Xochitl* in 1920, she joined the *Greenwich Village Follies* in 1923, she will form her own dance troupe, and she will improvise a highly individual choreography. Graham will continue dancing until 1970. *The Miraculous Mandarin* 11/27 at Cologne, with music by Béla Bartók.

First performances   Symphony No. 7 in C major by Jean Sibelius 4/3 at Philadelphia's Orchestra Hall; Symphony No. 1 by Soviet composer Dmitri Shostakovich, 19, 5/12 at Moscow (it is the student's diploma piece); *Ballet Mecanique* by U.S. composer George Antheil, 26, 6/19 at Paris. The work was written originally for an abstract film and is scored for instruments that include a player piano and an airplane engine. *Portsmouth Point* Overture by William Walton 6/22 at Zurich's Tonhalle.

Broadway musicals   *The Girl Friend* 3/17 at the Vanderbilt Theater, with music by Richard Rodgers, lyrics by Lorenz Hart, songs that include "The Blue Room," "The Simple Life," "Why Do I," 301 perfs.; *The Garrick Gaieties* 5/10 at the Garrick Theater, with Sterling Holloway, Romney Brent, music by Richard Rodgers, lyrics by Lorenz Hart, songs that include "Mountain Greenery," 174 perfs.; *George White's Scandals* 6/14 at the Apollo Theater, with Ann Pennington introducing the dance step the Black Bottom that will rival the Charleston, songs that include "The Birth of the Blues" by Ray Henderson, lyrics by B. G. DeSylva and Lew Brown, 424 perfs.; *Countess Maritza* 9/18 at the Shubert Theater, with Yvonne D'Arle, music by Viennese composer Emmerich Kalman, book and lyrics by Harry B. Smith who has adapted a Viennese operetta, 318 perfs.; *Honeymoon Lane* 9/20 at the Knickerbocker Theater, with Eddie Dowling, Pauline Mason, Kate Smith, music by James F. Hanley, lyrics by Dowling, songs that include "The Little White House (At the End of Honeymoon Lane)," 317 perfs.; *Oh, Kay* 11/8 at the Imperial Theater, with Gertrude Lawrence, music by George Gershwin, songs that include "Do, Do, Do" and "Someone to Watch over Me" with lyrics by Ira Gershwin, "Heaven on Earth" and the title song with lyrics by Ira Gershwin and Howard Dietz, 256 perfs.; *The Desert Song* 11/30 at the Casino Theater, with Vivienne Segal, Robert Halliday, music by Sigmund Romberg, lyrics by Oscar Hammerstein II and Otto Harbach, songs that include "Blue Heaven" and "One Alone," 471 perfs.; *Peggy-Ann* 12/27 at the Vanderbilt Theater, with Helen Ford, music by Richard Rodgers, lyrics by Lorenz Hart, songs that include "Where's that Rain-

bow?" 333 perfs.; *Betsy* 12/28 at the New Amsterdam Theater, with Al Shean, Belle Baker, music by Richard Rodgers, lyrics by Lorenz Hart, songs that include also Irving Berlin's "Blue Skies," 39 perfs.

Josephine Baker opens her own Paris nightclub at age 20 after having risen to fame in *La Revue Nègre* and starring at the *Folies Bergère* in a G-string ornamented with bananas. The U.S. émigrée darling of European cafe society will begin a professional singing career in 1930, she will be naturalized as a French citizen in 1937, and she will continue performing until shortly before her death in 1974.

Popular songs "Muskrat Ramble" by New Orleans jazz cornetist Edward "Kid" Ory (lyrics will be added in 1937); "Baby Face" by Benny Davis and Harry Akst; "What Can I Say After I've Said I'm Sorry?" by Walter Donaldson and bandleader Abe Lyman; "Charmaine" by Hungarian-American composer Erno Rapee, 35, lyrics by Lew Pollak, 31; " 'Gimme' a Little Kiss, Will 'Ya' Huh?" by Roy Turk, Jack Smith, and Maceo Pinkard; "Bye Bye Blackbird" by Ray Henderson, lyrics by Mort Dixon; "If I Could Be with You One Hour Tonight" by Henry Creamer and Jimmy Johnson; "In a Little Spanish Town" by Mabel Wayne, lyrics by Sam M. Lewis and Joe Young; "When the Red, Red Robin Comes Bob, Bob, Bobbin' Along" by Harry Woods.

U.S. tennis star Helen Wills loses to France's Suzanne Lenglen in "the match of the century." Bill Tilden loses the Davis Cup singles tournament to France's René Lacoste, but the United States retains the Davis Cup for the seventh year.

U.S. golfer Bobby Jones loses the U.S. Golf Association Amateur championship to George Von Elm but wins the U.S. Open.

Gertrude Ederle becomes the first woman to swim the English Channel and beats the world record by nearly 2 hours. The 19-year-old New York Olympic champion failed in a Channel attempt last year, she arrives at Dover August 6 after 14 hours, 31 minutes in the water, she has been forced by heavy seas to swim 35 miles in order to cover the 21-mile distance from Cape Gris-Nez near Calais, and she suffers permanent loss of hearing (*see* Chadwick, 1951).

Gene Tunney wins the world heavyweight boxing championship held by Jack Dempsey since 1919. New York prizefighter James Joseph Tunney, 28, gains a 10-round decision September 23 at Philadelphia, he will beat Dempsey again next year, and he will retire undefeated in 1928 (*see* 1927).

English cricket ace Sir John Berry Hobbs, 44, scores 16 centuries in first-class cricket.

Cushioned cork-center baseballs are introduced.

The St. Louis Cardinals win the World Series by defeating the New York Yankees 4 games to 3.

German swimmer H. Vierkotter breaks Gertrude Ederle's Channel record (above) by swimming the Channel in 12 hours, 40 minutes.

1926 (cont.) The permanent wave invented by Charles Nestle in 1906 is improved by Italian hairdresser Antonio Buzzacchino who invents a new method that will make the "permanent" widely fashionable.

Slide fasteners are called "zippers" for the first time after a promotional luncheon at which English novelist Gilbert Frankau, 42, has said, "Zip! It's open! Zip! It's closed!" (*see* Sundback, 1913). Elsa Schiaperelli will use zippers in her 1930 line and when the general patents expire the following year the zipper will come into wide use in men's trousers, windbreakers, and sweaters and in women's dresses and other apparel (*see* YKK, 1934).

The first blue jeans with slide fasteners are introduced by H. D. Lee Company which has opened plants at Kansas City, South Bend, Trenton, and Minneapolis to produce its one-piece Union-Alls and Lee Riders. Lee also introduces U-shaped saddle crotches and rise and seat proportions graduated with individual waists and inseams (*see* 1911; 1936).

John Powers, Inc., inaugurates a fashion model agency industry that will grow to gross upwards of $1 billion per year. New York actor John Robert Powers, 30, has overheard a businessman saying he wanted a group of attractive people to pose for a magazine advertisement, Powers has rounded up some friends and has delivered the photograph, he has bound up a catalogue of pictures and distributed them to advertising agencies, and he has gained backing from Sir Herbert Beerbohm Tree to open the world's first model agency.

Palmolive-Peet Company is created by a merger of the Palmolive Company with the Peet Brothers firm founded in 1872 by William, Robert, and Jesse Peet (*see* 1928; Palmolive soap, 1905).

 Chicago bootlegger Al Capone's Hawthorne Hotel headquarters are sprayed with machine gun fire in broad daylight September 20 by gunmen firing from eight touring cars that parade single file through the streets of the suburban area but no one is killed and the cars disappear into the traffic.

Illegal liquor traffic is estimated to be a $3.6 billion per year business and has spawned a gigantic underworld of criminal activity since 1919. Widespread defiance of the Prohibition laws is encouraging citizens to flout other laws and the "Noble Experiment" is clearly a failure (*see* Capone, 1927; Wickersham Commission, 1931).

The Hall-Mills murder of 1922 makes new headlines. New Jersey police arrest Frances Stevens Hall September 29 and charge her with having murdered her husband and his mistress, the case goes to trial in October, a jury turns in a not guilty verdict December 3, and the case remains a mystery.

Municipal zoning ordinances authorized by state governments are upheld by the Supreme Court in the case of *Euclid v. Ambler Realty Company* on the ground that "states are the legal repository of police power." The Department of Commerce publishes a "Standard State Zoning Enabling Act" to serve as a model for state legislatures (*see* 1916; 1961).

A Limited Dividend Housing Companies Law passed by the New York State legislature permits condemnation of land for housing sites, abatement of local taxes, and other measures to encourage housing construction. Limits on rents and profits are required, and income limitations are set for tenants.

A Montauk Beach, Long Island, summer resort is projected by Miami Beach promoter Carl Fisher who buys 10,000 acres to build a resort that he hopes will attract as many buyers as his Florida properties (*see* 1913). Fisher has $6 million in cash, $6 million in quick assets, and Florida property valued at $25 million which he mortgages to build a $12 million hotel with golf course, swimming pool, and polo grounds, but by the end of 1929 he will have lost most of his money and the Montauk Beach Hotel will be a vacant monument to miscalculation.

New York's 39-story Paramount building opens in Times Square with a Paramount Theater for Adolph Zukor's Paramount-Publix Corporation.

New York's Taft Hotel opens November 15 under the name Manger Hotel. Designed by architect H. Craig Severance, the $10 million hotel has 20 floors with 1,250 rooms, it has been built by Julius and William Manger, 33 and 27, who operate 17 smaller New York hotels (including the Great Northern, the Navarre, the Endicott, the Wolcott, the Woodstock, and the Martha Washington), and it will be enlarged in 1931 to 2,000 rooms and renamed the Taft.

Philadelphia's Benjamin Franklin Hotel opens with 1,200 rooms at Chestnut Street and 9th.

Philadelphia's Warwick Hotel opens at 17th Street and Locust one block east of Rittenhouse Square. The 20-story Warwick will be enlarged by an addition in 1928 to give it a total of 550 rooms.

San Francisco's Hotel Mark Hopkins opens in December on the hilltop site at the corner of California and Mason Streets atop Nob Hill. The new 19-story, 418-room hotel replaces a Gothic house commissioned by the late Mark Hopkins and completed after his death at age 65 in 1878 (the building housed the Hopkins Art Institute until it was destroyed in the 1906 fire) (*see* Top o' the Mark, 1939).

The Los Angeles Central Library is completed by Bertram Goodhue in a mixture of Spanish colonial and Beaux Arts styles.

Otis Elevator Company is challenged by the Westinghouse Company which acquires the patents and engineering skills of several sizeable companies that include Otis's chief competitors. Westinghouse elevators will vie with Otis elevators in America's proliferating skyscrapers.

 The U.S. Forest Service identifies 55 million acres of U.S. wilderness area. The largest area found in the survey covers 7 million acres (*see* 1961).

Trofim Denisovich Lysenko gains notice for the first time in the Soviet Union. The 28-year-old agronomist puts ideology ahead of science and he will have enormous influence on Soviet farm policies (*see* 1935).

Liberian lands are opened to rubber cultivation by Harvey Firestone who has promoted rubber tree plantations in the Philippines and in South America since 1900 and has become Ford Motor Company's major tire supplier. Firestone will plant 6,000 acres to rubber trees in the next decade.

An oral liver extract to treat pernicious anemia is developed by Harvard physician Edwin Joseph Cohn, 33 (*see* 1930; Minot and Murphy, 1924; Castle, 1929; blood plasma, 1941).

The B vitamin is shown to be more than one vitamin (*see* McCollum, 1916). Joseph Goldberger shows that rats can be cured of pellagra on a diet from which the heat-labile part of vitamin B has been removed (*see* 1915; Smith and Hendrick, 1928).

Sunlight is shown to convert the sterol ergesterol into vitamin D in animals (*see* Steenbock, 1923). The findings of British biochemists O. Rosenheim and T. A. Webster explain why children who do not get enough sunlight are vulnerable to rickets (*see* 1930).

California's tuna packing industry collapses as albacore disappear from offshore waters. San Pedro packs only 51,223 cases, down from 358,940 last year, and the San Diego pack drops to less than 14,600, down from 95,000.

Van Camp Sea Food Company is saved by its sales manager Roy P. Harper, 33, who has introduced the brand names Chicken of the Sea and White Star (*see* 1924). Harper decides to promote yellow-fin tuna which can be packed all year round, and by eliminating all flakes, packing the yellow-fin in solid pieces, and calling it "Fancy" tuna Harper creates a demand for fish heretofore scorned because its flesh is not the white meat associated with albacore (*see* 1962).

A frozen goose is cooked and served to Postum Cereal Company boss Marjorie Merriweather Post whose yacht is being provisioned at Gloucester, Mass. (*see* 1914). Post's chef has obtained the bird from General Seafoods Company, a small freezing plant on Gloucester's Fort Wharf that is operated by Clarence Birdseye who has developed a belt freezer and is selling quantities of frozen fish but is on the verge of bankruptcy (*see* 1925). Post seeks out Birdseye, she is impressed by his freezing process, but while his business is for sale at $2 million the purchase is opposed by Post's board of directors and her husband stockbroker Edward F. Hutton (*see* General Foods, 1929).

Minute Tapioca is acquired by Postum Cereal Company (*see* Stavers, 1894).

Igleheart Brothers and its Swans Down cake flour is acquired by Postum Cereal Company (*see* 1895).

Aunt Jemima Mills is acquired by Quaker Oats Company for $4 million (*see* 1910; 1913).

Hormel Flavor-Sealed Ham is introduced by George A. Hormel & Company and is the first ham in a can to be produced by a U.S. meatpacker. Hormel has been slaughtering upwards of a million hogs per year since 1924, its canned ham is produced by means of a process patented by Hamburg, Germany, inventor Paul Jorn, and it meets with immediate success (*see* 1892; Spam, 1937).

Machine-made ice production in the United States reaches 56 million tons, up from 1.5 million in 1894 (*see* 1889). Much of it is used to chill illegal beer, highballs, and cocktails (above).

The Good Humor Corporation is formed by some Cleveland businessmen following the death of Harry Burt (*see* 1924). Some of the franchises offered for sale are bought by Tennessee entrepreneur Tom Brimer (*see* 1929).

Flavored yogurt is introduced in Paris by Spanish yogurt-maker Isaac Carasso who moves from Barcelona and opens a factory to serve the larger French market but finds that the French prefer plain yogurt (*see* 1941; Dannon, 1942).

Liederkranz cheesemaker Monroe Cheese Company moves to Van Wert, Ohio, to obtain a dependable supply of fresh milk (*see* 1892; Borden, 1929).

Safeway Stores, Inc., is created by a merger. Marion Skaggs joins his chain of 428 grocery stores with the Sam Seelig Company of southern California to create a chain of 466 stores that will grow to surpass the A&P in sales by 1973 (*see* 1915; 1931).

First National Stores is created by a merger of Boston's 31-year-old Ginter Company with the O'Keefe Company and the John T. Connor Company.

IGA (Independent Grocers' Alliance Distributing Company) is launched at Poughkeepsie, N.Y., where

Flying the Atlantic solo on one engine made "the Lone Eagle" a world hero and gave aviation a dramatic boost.

1926 (cont.) 69 retail grocers from the East and Midwest meet in the fall to organize a defense against inroads on their sales by such corporate chain store giants as A&P and First National (above). IGA will develop its own brands of coffee and other products and will grow to include more than 3,600 stores in 46 states.

New York's Palm Restaurant opens on Second Avenue between 44th and 45th Streets. Italian-American restaurateurs Pio Bozzi and John Ganzi intended to name their place Parma after the capital of their native Italian province Emilia. They have been frustrated by a city clerk who has licensed the place under the name Palm.

Ideal Marriage, Its Physiology and Technique by Dutch gynecologist Th. H. Van de Velde, 53, says that "a fundamental principle of the Roman Catholic sexual code, which corresponds with precepts in Protestant and Jewish doctrine, is the rejection of all actions to prevent conception," but he notes that the methods of contraception "known and practiced today often contravene the demands of Ideal Marriage by diminishing stimulation, disturbing and dislocating normal relations, offending taste. . . ."

1927 Chinese Generalissimo Chiang Kai-shek takes Hangchow in February with combined units of the Kuomintang and the Kungch'antang (Communists), Shanghai and Canton fall a few weeks later, Nanking is looted and burned March 24, and the warlord era of Chinese history is ended. Chiang negotiates with bankers and industrialists at Shanghai where he once operated a brokerage business, he is promised from $3 million to $10 million if he will break with Moscow, and he reverses his earlier political philosophy by overthrowing the Leftist government at Hangchow and establishing a Rightist National Revolutionary Government at Nanking with Communists and left-wing elements excluded. Despite questions as to the legality of his divorce from the mother of his son, Chiang marries Wellesley-educated Christianized Soong Mei-ling, 26, December 1 and allies himself with one of China's richest, most powerful families. Mei-ling's father Charles Soong returned from America to become a publisher and distributor of bibles, amassing a fortune by investing his profits at high returns; her sister Ching-ling is the widow of Sun Yat-sen, and her brother T. V. (Tse-ven) is a Harvard-educated economist who will help unify China's currency and set up a central banking system (*see* 1926; Peking, 1928).

"I do not choose to run," says President Coolidge in an August 2 statement to the press that takes him out of contention for the 1928 presidential nomination.

Josef Stalin expels Leon Trotsky from the Central Committee of the Communist party in November.

Charles A. Lindbergh lands the single-engine monoplane *Spirit of St. Louis* at Le Bourget Airfield, Paris, May 21 at 10:24 in the evening after completion of the first non-stop solo flight across the Atlantic (*see*

1926; Alcock, Whitten-Brown, 1919). Backed by St. Louis businessmen, Lindbergh paid $10,580 for the plane built by San Diego aircraft designer T. Claude Ryan, 29, with a 220-horsepower, nine-cylinder Wright Aeronautical Whirlwind engine, he has spent 8 weeks at the Ryan factory supervising every detail of construction, he made his first test flight April 28, a crude periscope enables him to see what lies ahead since his forward vision is blocked by the gasoline tank and engine, he has declined a radio in order to save weight for 90 more gallons of gasoline, he took off in the rain from Roosevelt Field, Long Island, at 7:55 in the morning of May 20 so heavily laden with 451 gallons of gasoline that he barely cleared some telephone wires, he has navigated by dead reckoning to cover 3,600 miles (1,000 miles of it through snow and sleet) in 33 hours, 29 minutes, he wins the $25,000 prize offered by Raymond Orteig in 1919, and he becomes a world hero. Hailed as "The Lone Eagle," Lindbergh rejects motion picture, vaudeville, and commercial offers totalling $5 million.

An uncertainty principle that melds physics and philosophy is announced by German physicist Werner Heisenberg, 26, who has been working with Max Born, 45, at Germany's Göttingen University. Heisenberg points out that certain pairs of variables describing motion—velocity and position, or energy and time—cannot be measured simultaneously with absolute accuracy because the measuring process itself interferes with the quantity to be measured, so while quantum mechanics provides valuable information it is useful only within limits of tolerance since no events can be described with zero tolerance (*see* Planck, 1900; Dirac and Shrödinger, 1926).

Fossil remains of Pithecanthropus pekinsis (Peking man) dating to between 400,000 and 300,000 B.C. are found at Choukoutien, near Peking, by Canadian anatomist Davidson Black, 42.

A stone spearhead found embedded between the ribs of an Ice Age bison skeleton near Folsom, N.Mex., is the first of many such finds that will indicate the presence of glacial man in 8,000 B.C.

Peruvian aerial survey pilot Toribio Mexta Xesspe flying over the barren plains of southern Peru sees long lines in the shape of birds, animals, and reptiles. Visible only from the air, the mysterious drawings, enormous in size, were made by the pre-Inca Nazca civilization that flourished for a milennium before being absorbed by the Inca about 700 A.D.

Sacco and Vanzetti die in the electric chair at Dedham Prison August 23 despite worldwide efforts to have Massachusetts authorities drop charges against the two for lack of evidence (*see* 1920). A note passed to Nicola Sacco in 1925 from convicted bank cashier murderer Celestino F. Madeiros said, "I hereby confess to being in the South Braintree shoe company crime and Sacco and Vanzetti was not in said crime" but the district attorney refused to investigate. The defense has filed eight motions for a new trial since

848

1921 but the state's Supreme Judicial Court has upheld Justice Webster Thayer in early April, ruling on law, not on evidence. "I know the sentence will be between two classes, the oppressed class and the rich class," Sacco has said. Bartolomeo Vanzetti has appealed to Governor Alvan T. Fuller for a pardon and a Dartmouth professor has filed an affidavit alleging that Judge Thayer said to him, "Did you see what I did with those anarchistic bastards the other day?" Governor Fuller (a millionaire Cadillac dealer) has appointed a review committee at the request of 61 law professors, the committee comprised of Harvard president A. Lawrence Lowell, MIT president Samuel W. Stratton, and former probate judge Robert A. Grant has upheld the jury verdict July 27, public demonstrations in behalf of Sacco and Vanzetti have no effect, but efforts to gain retroactive pardons will contine until 1977, when a new Massachusetts governor will grant the posthumous pardon.

Petroleum prospectors in northern Iraq strike oil October 14 near Kirkuk. Baba Gurgur No. 1 gushes oil 140 feet in the air at a rate of 80,000 barrels per day, it takes the drillers 10 days to bring the well under control and to prevent the oil from reaching the Eternal Fire (Baba Gurgur) a mile and a half away that has been burning for thousands of years where natural gas seeps out of the earth. The well has been financed by Iraq Petroleum Company, Ltd., a new cartel created by French, British, U.S., and Iraqui interests with help from Calouste Gulbenkian who receives a 5 percent interest in the oilfield (see 1914).

French World War flying ace Charles Nugesser, 35, vanishes in May while trying to fly the Atlantic (see Lindbergh, above). Nugesser shot down 45 enemy planes during the war.

U.S. pilot Clarence Duncan Chamberlin, 34, takes off from Roosevelt Field, New York, June 4 and flies 3,911 miles nonstop in 42.5 hours to Saxony, Germany, carrying junk dealer Charles A. Levine who has financed the flight.

U.S. Navy Commander Richard E. Byrd makes the first radio-equipped transatlantic flight June 29 in a trimotored Fokker monoplane piloted by Lieutenant Bernt Balchen, and Bert Acosta with Radioman George O. Noville completing the crew.

U.S. Army Air Corps lieutenants Lester J. Maitland and Albert F. Hegenberger make the first successful flight from San Francisco to Honolulu June 28.

The Norden bombsight is invented by Dutch-American inventor Carl Lucas Norden, 47, and his engineer associate Theodore H. Barth who work to improve the device. The 90-pound Mark XV bombsight that Norden will perfect in 1931 with help from Frederick I. Entwhistle of the U.S. Navy will have 2,000 parts and will remain a closely guarded military secret until it is patented in 1947 (when jet planes will have made it obsolete).

Pan American Airways is founded by Juan Trippe who obtains exclusive rights from Cuban president Gerardo Machado y Morales to land at Havana and begins mail service between Key West, Fla., and Havana with Fokker F-7 single-engine monoplanes (see 1925; 1929).

U.S. mail planes fly nearly 6 million miles and carry 37,000 passengers (see 1929).

Tokyo's Chikatetsu subway opens. The system will grow to have eight lines with 102.9 miles of track.

U.S. railroads begin to introduce centralized traffic control (CTC) that permits automatic control of two-way traffic on single tracks and makes single-track operations nearly as efficient as double-track.

The 46-mile Chesapeake and Delaware Ship Canal opens to connect the bay with the Delaware River.

The Ford Model A is introduced to succeed the Model T that has been the U.S. standard for nearly 20 years. U.S. auto production falls to 3,093,428, down nearly 900,000 from 1926 as a result of Ford's stoppage for retooling to produce a car that will compete with Chevrolet. The 15 millionth Ford to come out of the Ford plant is driven by Henry Ford and his son Edsel, now 34.

More than 20 million cars are on the U.S. road, up from 13,824 in 1900.

Sweden's Volvo motorcar is introduced as a four-cylinder engine touring car with a top speed of 37 miles per hour. Göteborg industrialist Assar Gabrielsson and engineer Gustaf Larsson have built a factory and turned out a car to challenge the dominance of imported cars in the Swedish market.

A 1,000 horsepower "Mystery Sunbeam" driven by Major Henry O'Neil de Hane Segrave averages 203.79 miles per hour at Daytona Beach, Fla., May 29.

The Buffalo Peace Bridge opens August 4 to link Canada and the United States.

The Holland Tunnel opens November 12 to connect Canal Street, Manhattan, with Jersey City and give motor vehicles a road link under the Hudson River, the first alternative to New York-New Jersey ferry boats. Clifton Milburn Holland, the tunnel's chief engineer, died in 1924 just 2 days before diggers from east and west met below the Hudson.

The first compulsory state automobile insurance law is passed by the Massachusetts legislature.

Duplate Corporation is created by Du Pont and Pittsburgh Plate Glass to make safety glass using Du Pont pyrolin and Pittsburgh plate (see 1883). PPG will buy out Du Pont's interest in Duplate in 1930 (see 1929).

Safety glass windshields for Model A Fords and Lincolns are ordered by Henry Ford. Triplex Safety Glass contracts to supply half of Ford's needs and licenses Ford to produce the rest himself (see 1926).

The end of the Model T (above) deals a heavy blow to the 18-year-old Western Auto Supply Company whose $11.5 million in annual sales derive largely from Model T parts. The company has 31 retail stores

1927 (cont.) and will become a vast retail chain enterprise dealing not only in automobile parts but also in hardware, cheap watches, flashlights, electrical appliances, and drugstore items (*see* Pepperdine College, 1937).

The S.S. *Ile de France* arrives at New York on her maiden voyage. The 43,000 ton French Line "Boulevard of the Atlantic" has a plane-launching catapult on her afterdeck to speed mail delivery.

The Iron Lung invented by Harvard professor Philip Drinker, 40, has an airtight chamber that employs alternating pulsations of high and low pressure to force air in and out of a patient's lungs. Drinker uses two discarded household vacuum cleaners and other cast-off machinery to create the Drinker Respirator that will be manufactured by Warren E. Collins, Inc., of Boston and will be used for the first time in mid-October of next year to treat a small girl at Boston Children's Hospital who is suffering from respiratory failure due to poliomyelitis.

The Georgia Warm Springs Foundation treatment center for fellow victims of poliomyelitis is founded by Franklin D. Roosevelt (*see* 1921). The center will be operated in years to come by the National Foundation March of Dimes (*see* 1938).

Britain's Vickers-Armstrongs, Ltd., is created by a merger of Vickers' Sons and Maxim with W. G. Armstrong, Whitworth and Co., Ltd. (*see* 1847; 1883).

Underwood Elliott Fisher Company is created by a merger of the Underwood Typewriter Company with the bookkeeping machine maker Elliott-Fisher (*see* Underwood, 1895). The firm will acquire the Sundstrand adding machine and in 1945 will become the Underwood Company (*see* Olivetti, 1959).

J. P. Morgan and Company acquires control of Johns-Manville Company (*see* 1901). Morgan's senior partner Thomas W. Lamont buys up more than half the outstanding shares and drives the price of the stock from 55 up to 126.

Transatlantic telephone service begins January 7 between London and New York: 3 minutes of conversation cost $75, or £15.

A television image dissector tube is invented by Utah engineer Philo Taylor Farnsworth, 21, who has been inspired by accounts of work done in the Soviet Union by Boris Rosing to transmit moving pictures by electricity.

The first U.S. demonstration of television is given April 7 in the auditorium of New York's Bell Telephone Laboratories by AT&T president Walter S. Gifford who lets a large group of viewers see Commerce Secretary Herbert C. Hoover in his office at Washington while hearing his voice over telephone wires (*see* BBC, 1936).

Development of television is thwarted by the fact that it takes a frequency band of 4 million cycles, versus only 400 for an ordinary radio band, to transmit the 250,000 elements needed for a clear picture.

David Sarnoff's year-old National Broadcasting Company has so many radio stations that it splits up into a Blue Network and a Red Network (*see* American Broadcasting, 1943; CBS, 1928).

The Futura typeface designed by Germany's Paul Ronner for the Bauerische Giesserei, Frankfurt, will gain wide popularity in the next five decades.

Roy Howard acquires the *New York Telegram* for the Scripps-Howard newspaper chain (*see* 1925; 1931).

Remington Rand, Inc., is created by U.S. manufacturer James Henry Rand, 40, whose late father and namesake started a business at New York in 1898 manufacturing bank ledgers and bookkeeping equipment. The younger Rand has built up a business of his own with the American Kardex Co., he merged it with the Rand Company in 1922, he absorbed Irving Fisher's Index Visible, Inc., and Melvil Dewey's Library Bureau in 1925, and last year he acquired several other companies including the Remington Typewriter Company (*see* 1878; Sperry Rand, 1955).

Doubleday, Doran & Company publishers is created by Frank Nelson Doubleday, now 65, who absorbs the George H. Doran Company (*see* 1897; 1907). The firm will shorten its name to Doubleday & Company in 1946 (*see* Literary Guild, 1934).

Coward-McCann Co. publishers is founded by former Bobbs-Merrill editor Thomas Ridgway Coward, 31, and sales manager James A. McCann, 42.

The Literary Guild of America sends out its first selection in March to 5,732 subscribers. The new book club was incorporated last year by Samuel W. Craig with support from Harold Guinzburg of Viking Press, it has been inspired by the success of the Book-of-the-Month Club established last year, its first book is a biography of the anti-vice crusader Anthony Comstock by Heywood Broun and Margaret Leech, and the Guild offers 12 such books per year, each averaging $3 in price, for $18 paid in advance or $19 in installments. By January 1929 the Guild will have 70,000 subscribers as its editor-in-chief Carl Van Doren selects titles that attract demand (*see* 1934).

Nonfiction *Main Currents in American Thought: An Interpretation of Literature from the Beginning to 1920* by University of Washington professor Vernon Louis Parrington, 56, who will win a 1928 Pulitzer prize for his interpretation of the development of American thought which he sees to be based on a concept of democratic idealism; *The Story of a Wonder Man* (autobiography) by Ring Lardner.

Fiction *Der Steppenwolf* by Hermann Hesse; *Flight Without End* (*Die Flucht ohne Ende*) by Austrian novelist Joseph Roth, 33, who shows the collapsed Austro-Hungarian Empire as seen through the eyes of a returned officer; *Amerika* by the late Franz Kafka; *Jalna* by Canadian novelist Mazo de la Roche, 42, who wins the *Atlantic Monthly's* $10,000 prize and gains overnight fame and fortune after years of hard work and poverty; *Mr. Weston's Good*

Wine by English novelist T. F. Powys, 52, brother of J. C. Powys; *Celibate Loves* (stories) by George Moore; *The Left Bank* (stories) by Welsh-Creole author Jean Rhys, 33; *Death Comes for the Archbishop* by Willa Cather, whose new novel is based on the 19th century French-American clergyman Jean Baptiste Lamy who built the first cathedral in the Southwest at Santa Fe; *Elmer Gantry* by Sinclair Lewis, whose novel of religious charlatanism is the year's U.S. best seller; *The Treasure of the Sierra Madre* (*Der Schatz der Sierra Madre*) by German novelist Ben Traven (Ret Marut); *archy and mehitabel* by *New York Tribune* humorist Donald Robert Perry "Don" Marquis, 44, whose cockroach archy is the reincarnation of a poet and whose alley cat mehitabel has rowdy misadventures; *The "Canary" Murder Case* by U.S. critic-novelist S. S. Van Dine (Willard Huntington Wright), 39, whose detective Philo Vance will win a wide following; *The Unpleasantness at the Bellona Club* by Dorothy Sayers.

Poetry "American Names" by U.S. poet Stephen Vincent Benét, 29; *The Women at Point Sur* by Robinson Jeffers; *Tristram* by Edwin Arlington Robinson whose verse novel is a best seller; "Launcelot" by Edwin Arlington Robinson; *Leitenant Schmidt* by Boris Pasternak is a verse epic.

Painting *Seated Woman* by Pablo Picasso; *Glass and Fruit* by Georges Braque; *Figure with Ornamental Background* by Henri Matisse; *Man with Newspaper* by René Magritte; *Manhattan Bridge* by Edward Hopper; *Radiator Building, New York* by U.S. painter Georgia O'Keeffe, 39, who married photographer Alfred Steiglitz of the 291 Gallery 3 years ago; *Egyptian Impression* by U.S. cubist Charles Demuth, 43; *Lonesome Road* by Thomas Hart Benton. Juan Gris dies at Boulogne-sur-Seine outside Paris May 11 at age 40.

Sculpture *Floating Woman* by Gaston Lachaise; *Madonna and Child* by Jacob Epstein; *Folkinga* fountain by Carl Milles.

A new Ansco camera film factory goes up at Binghamton, N.Y., with financing and technical assistance from Germany's I. G. Farbenindustrie's Agfa division to help Agfa compete with Eastman Kodak which has obtained tariff increases and has cut prices to squeeze out Ansco and Agfa (*see* Ansco, 1901; Agfa, 1925; U.S. seizure, 1942).

Theater *Saturday's Children* by Maxwell Anderson 1/26 at New York's Booth Theater, with Ruth Gordon, Roger Pryor, 310 perfs.; *The Marquise* by Noel Coward 2/16 at London's Criterion Theatre, 129 perfs.; *The Second Man* by U.S. playwright S. N. (Samuel Nathan) Behrman, 34, 4/11 at New York's Guild Theater, with Alfred Lunt, Lynn Fontanne, Margalo Gilmore, Earle Larimore, 178 perfs.; *Burlesque* by George Manker Wattes and Arthur Hopkins 9/1 at New York's Plymouth Theater, with Barbara Stanwyck, Hal Skelly, Oscar Levant, 372 perfs.; *The Trial of Mary Dugan* by Bayard Veilleur 9/19 at New York's National Theater, with Ann

Harding, Rex Cherryman, Robert Cummings, 437 perfs.; *Porgy* by U.S. novelist-playwright DuBose Heyward, 42, and his wife Dorothy 10/27 at New York's Guild Theater, 367 perfs. (*see* Gershwin opera, 1935); *The Oil Islands* (*Die Petroleuminseln*) by Lion Feuchtwanger 10/31 at Hamburg's Deutsches Schauspielhaus; *The Road to Rome* by U.S. playwright Robert Emmet Sherwood, 31, 11/31 at The Playhouse, New York, with Jane Cowl, 440 perfs.; *Paris Bound* by Philip Barry 12/27 at New York's Music Box Theater, with Hope Williams, 234 perfs.; *The Royal Family* by George S. Kaufman and Moss Hart 12/28 at New York's Selwyn Theater, with a book based on the history of the Barrymore family, 345 perfs.

Hollywood's Grauman's Chinese Theater opens.

Films Alan Crosland's *The Jazz Singer* is the first full-length talking picture to achieve success. Warner Brothers executive producer Darryl Francis Zanuck, 25, has given Al Jolsen his film debut, the film opens at New York October 6, it contains only brief sequences of dialogue and singing, but the sound-on-disk Warner Brothers Vitaphone system introduces a new era of "the talkies" that will end the careers of some movie stars (*see* 1926; 1929).

Other films (all silent) Sergei Eisenstein's *The Ten Days That Shook the World;* Carl Dreyer's *The Passion of Joan of Arc* with Maria Falconetti; Abel Gance's *Bonaparte;* Walter Ruttman and Karl Freund's *Berlin: The Symphony of a Great City;* Josef von Sternberg's *The Last Command* with Emil Jannings; Josef von Sternberg's *Underworld* with George Bancroft, Evelyn Brent; René Clair's *Le Chapeau de Paille d'Italie* with Albert Prejean, Olga Tschechova; Fred Niblo's *Camille* with Gilbert Roland, Norma Talmadge; Paul Leni's *The Cat and the Canary* with Creighton Hale, Laura LaPlante, Tully Marshall; Clarence Brown's *Flesh and the Devil* with Greta Garbo, John Gilbert, Lars Hansen; Victor Fleming's *The Way of All Flesh* with Emil Jannings; F. W. Murneau's *Sunrise* with Janet Gaynor, George O'Brien; Frank Borzage's *Seventh Heaven* with Janet Gaynor as Diane, Charles Farrell as Chico; William A. Wellman's *Wings* with Clara Bow, Charles "Buddy" Rogers, Richard Arlen, Gary Cooper; William K. Howard's *White Gold* with Jetta Goudel, George Bancroft; Herbert Brenon's *Beau Geste* with Ronald Colman, Neil Hamilton, Noah Beery; Cecil B. DeMille's *The King of Kings* with H. B. Warner; Sidney Franklin's *Quality Street* with Marion Davies, Conrad Nagel; Erich von Stroheim's *Wedding March* with Stroheim, Fay Wray; Ernst Schoedsack and Merian C. Cooper's *Chang,* shot on location in Siam; Tod Browning's *The Unknown* with Lon Chaney, Joan Crawford; Sam Wood's *The Fair Co-ed* with Marion Davies, John Mack Brown; Sam Taylor's *My Best Girl* with Mary Pickford, Buddy Rogers; Sam Wood's *Rockies* with Marion Davies, John Mack Brown; James W. Horne's *College* with Buster Keaton; Buster Keaton's *The General* with Keaton.

1927 (cont.) The Academy of Motion Picture Arts and Sciences is founded May 11 by Louis B. Mayer of M-G-M (*see* 1924). Annual awards of the Academy will be called "Oscars" by movie columnist Sidney Skolsky (now a 22-year-old press agent), first president of the Academy is Douglas Fairbanks, first winners of the gold statuette (which is 92.5 percent tin) are William Wellman for *Wings,* Emil Jannings for best actor, 21-year-old Janet Gaynor for best actress.

Opera *The King's Henchman* 2/17 at New York's Metropolitan Opera House, with music by U.S. composer Deems Taylor, 41, libretto by Edna St. Vincent Millay who sees four printings of the libretto in book form sell out in 20 days. Millay contributes proceeds of her pamphlet "Justice Denied in Massachusetts" to the defense of Sacco and Vanzetti (above), she will make a personal appeal to the governor that he spare the men, and she will be arrested in the deathwatch outside the Boston Court House the night of their execution; *Mahagonny* 7/17 at Germany's Baden Baden festival, with music by German composer Kurt Weill, 27, libretto by German playwright Bertolt Brecht, 29: the one-act singspiel (song-play) will be expanded into *The Rise and Fall of the Town of Mahagonny* which will open 3/9/30 at Leipzig; *Le Pauvre Matelot* 12/16 at the Opéra-Comique, Paris, with music by Darius Milhaud.

First performances Concerto No. 4 in G minor for Piano and Orchestra by Sergei Rachmaninoff 3/18 at Philadelphia's Academy of Music, with Leopold Stokowski conducting the Philadelphia Orchestra; *Arcana* by French-American composer Edgar Varese, 34, 4/8 at Philadelphia's Academy of Music; Symphony in E minor by Roger Sessions 4/22 at Boston's Symphony Hall.

The Pittsburgh Symphony Society is founded.

Broadway musicals *Rio Rita* 2/2 at the new Ziegfeld Theater on Sixth Avenue at 54th Street, with music and lyrics by Harry Tierney and Joseph McCarthy, songs that include the title song, 494 perfs. Now 58, Florenz Ziegfeld has hired *Follies* set designer Joseph Urban, a Viennese sculptor-painter-architect, to design the modern theater that will stand for 40 years; *Hit the Deck* 4/25 at the Belasco Theater, with music by Vincent Youmans, lyrics by Leo Robbins and Clifford Grey, songs that include "Join the Navy," "Hallelujah," 352 perfs.; *The Ziegfeld Follies* 8/16 at the Ziegfeld Theater, with Eddie Cantor, Ruth Etting, music and lyrics entirely by Irving Berlin, 167 perfs.; *Good News* 9/6 at the 46th Street Theater, with music by Ray Henderson, lyrics by B. G. DeSylva and Lew Brown, songs that include "The Best Things in Life Are Free," "Lucky in Love," "Flaming Youth," "Just Imagine," 551 perfs.; *My Maryland* 9/12 at the Jolson Theater, with a book based on the 1899 Clyde Fitch play *Barbara Frietchie,* music by Sigmund Romberg, 312 perfs.; *A Connecticut Yankee* 11/3 at the Vanderbilt Theater, with William Gaxton, Constance Carpenter, music by Richard Rodgers, lyrics by Lorenz Hart, songs

that include "My Heart Stood Still," "Thou Swell," 418 perfs.; *Funny Face* 11/22 at the Alvin Theater, with Victor Moore, William Kent, music by George Gershwin, lyrics by Ira Gershwin, songs that include "The Babbitt and the Bromide," 244 perfs.; *Delmar's Revels* 11/28 at the Shubert Theater, with Frank Fay, Bert Lahr, Patsy Kelly, music by Jimmy McHugh, lyrics by Dorothy Fields, 112 perfs.; *Show Boat* 12/27 at the Ziegfeld Theater, with Helen Morgan as Julie LaVerne, book by Edna Ferber, music by Jerome Kern, lyrics by Oscar Hammerstein II, songs that include "Bill," "Can't Help Lovin' that Man," "Ol Man River," "Only Make Believe," "Life on the Wicked Stage," "Why Do I Love You," 527 perfs.

The Varsity Drag is introduced to U.S. dance floors.

"Duke" Ellington begins a 5-year engagement at New York's Cotton Club during which radio broadcasts will bring national recognition to the 28-year-old Edward Kennedy Ellington.

Radio music *The A&P Gypsies* debut in January over NBC's Blue Network. The violinists will give way to Harry Horlick's Orchestra which will continue for 10 years; *Cities Service Concerts* debut 2/18 and will continue each Friday evening into the mid-1950s (60 minutes until 1940, 30 minutes thereafter).

Popular songs "Black and Tan Fantasy" by Duke Ellington (above), lyrics by "Bubber" Miller; "Me and My Shadow" by Al Jolson and pianist Dave Dreyer, 33, lyrics by Billy Rose; "Chloe" by Neil Moret, lyrics by Gus Kahn; "Diane" by Irving Rapee, lyrics by Lew Pollak to exploit the film *Seventh Heaven;* "Girl of My Dreams" by Sunny Clapp; "Ain't She Sweet" by Milton Ager, lyrics by Jack Yellen; "I'm Looking Over a Four Leaf Clover" by Harry Woods, lyrics by Mort Dixon; "Let a Smile Be Your Umbrella" by composer Sammy Fain, 25, lyrics by Irving Kahal, Francis Wheeler; "My Blue Heaven" by Walter Donaldson, lyrics by George Whiting, 43; " 'S Wonderful" and "Strike Up the Band" by George Gershwin, lyrics by Ira Gershwin; "Mississippi Mud" by Harry Burris of the Rhythm Boys (Burris, Al Rinker, and "crooner" Harry Lillis "Bing" Crosby, 26) who sing with Paul Whiteman and his Orchestra, lyrics by James Cavanaugh.

"He's Got the Whole World in His Hand" is published for the first time in the *Journal of American Folklore.*

The first all-electric jukeboxes are introduced by the Automatic Musical Instrument Company of Grand Rapids, Mich., and the Seeburg Company of Chicago. Large-scale mass production will begin in 1934 and by 1939 there will be 350,000 jukeboxes in U.S. bars, restaurants, and other establishments.

Capehart Automatic Phonograph Company of America is founded by Indianapolis entrepreneur Homer Earl Capehart, 30, who has acquired the patent rights of a Cleveland inventor named Small to manufacture a coin-operated phonograph with an automatic device that not only selects a record and places it on the turntable but then also turns the record over and plays its flip side. Capehart will acquire rights to a device invented by Columbia Phonograph Company engineer Ralph Erbe and in 1929 will introduce an improved record changer, shifting from jukeboxes to home consoles for the luxury market.

U.S. dancer Isadora Duncan is strangled to death at Nice September 14 at age 49 when her long scarf is entangled in a rear wheel of the sports car being demonstrated to her by an automobile salesman with whom she has become enamored (*see* 1921).

The first Golden Gloves boxing tournament opens March 11 at New York's Knights of Columbus center and at Brooklyn's Knights of St. Anthony's center, the finals are held March 28 at Tex Rickard's new Madison Square Garden, witnessed by a record crowd of 21,954, with an estimated 10,000 turned away for lack of space. The Golden Gloves had been proposed by *New York Daily News* sportswriter Paul Gallico in a February 14 back page headline and feature story, the event will continue for more than 50 years, attracting thousands of contenders who will include Emile Griffith, Gus Lesnevich, Floyd Patterson, Ray Robinson, and José Torres.

U.S. tennis star Bill Tilden loses at Philadelphia's Germantown Cricket Club to French star René Lacoste who avoids Tilden's backhand, beats him 6-3, 4-6, 6-3, 6-2, and wins the Davis Cup, ending domination of the cup by English speaking countries and beginning a 6-year period in which France will hold the cup and will sweep the Wimbledon matches.

California tennis star Helen Wills wins her first Wimbledon singles title at age 21. "Little Miss Poker Face" won her first U.S. national championship at age 17 and will remain undefeated until she loses at Wimbledon in 1933.

Golfer Tommy Armour wins the U.S. Open at age 30. The Scotsman goes on to win the Canadian Open.

The first Ryder Cup golf match ends in victory for a team of U.S. professionals led by Walter Hagen who defeat a British team at Worcester, Mass., to gain possession of the £750 silver cup put up by English seed magnate Samuel Ryder, 54. A British team won an unofficial match held last year at Wentworth, Surrey, the U.S. team includes Tommy Armour (above), British teams will win in 1929 and 1933, but U.S. teams will dominate the biennial matches.

Gene Tunney retains his world heavyweight boxing crown by surviving Jack Dempsey's seventh round knockout punch at Chicago's Soldier Field September 22. A new rule requires that a fighter go to a neutral corner after he has knocked down his opponent, but Dempsey ignores the referee's order and stands over the fallen Tunney. Paul Gallico of the *New York Daily News* (above) will write that Tunney "was out. No question about it. His mind was gone," but 15 seconds elapse before the referee reaches the count of nine, Tunney rises from the "long count," and he goes on to win the decision.

Babe Ruth hits his 60th home run of the season September 30 off a pitch by Washington's Tom Zachary to set a record that will stand for 30 years.

The New York Yankees win the World Series by defeating the Pittsburgh Pirates 4 games to 0.

University of Michigan end Benjamin G. "Bennie" Oosterban ends 3 years as college football's most brilliant pass receiver. Grantland Rice names him to the All-America team for the third time and Oosterban goes on to graduation with nine varsity letters after a career that included one season in which he led the Big Ten Conference not only in football scoring but also in basketball, was the leading hitter in baseball, and was a champion discus thrower.

University of Minnesota sophomore Bronislaw "Bronko" Nagurski begins a 3-year career in which he will make otherwise mediocre Minnesota teams difficult to beat. Grantland Rice will name Nagurski to the All-America eleven only in his senior year.

World chess champion José Raoul Capablanca loses to Russian-born French master Aleksandr Aleksandrovich Alekhine, 35, who will hold the title until 1935, will regain it in 1937, and will hold it until his death in 1946 (*see* 1921).

Frances Heenan "Peaches" Browning, 16, sues millionaire New York real estate operator Edward W. "Daddy" Browning, 52, for divorce in a White Plains, N.Y., courthouse after less than a year of marriage. The January trial produces testimony that titillates newspaper readers.

The first U.S. Antoine's beauty salon opens in New York's 3-year-old Saks Fifth Avenue store where Seligman & Latz, Inc., changes the name of its Georgian Beauty Salon (*see* Antoine de Paris, 1920). Hairgoods wholesale salesman Sidney Seligman 44, and ladies' neckwear salesman Edward K. Latz formed a partnership in 1911, Latz's brother Israel joined the firm in 1913, they opened their first beauty salon in a Cincinnati department store in 1914, they have obtained exclusive U.S. rights to the name Antoine's, and they will soon have more than 100 salons.

Super Suds introduced by Colgate and Company is a laundry and dishwashing soap product composed of quick-melting hollow beads rather than flakes or powder (*see* Rinso, 1918; Tide, 1946).

The Cyclone roller coaster opens June 26 at Coney Island, N.Y., with a 100-second ride that takes screaming passengers up and down nine hills and over connecting tilted curves for 25 cents each.

Brown & Williamson Tobacco Company is acquired by British-American Tobacco which will increase production and distribution of Sir Walter Raleigh and Kool cigarettes.

The Snyder-Gray murder trial makes world headlines. Queens Village, Long Island, housewife Ruth

The "talkies" gave Hollywood its voice and made motion pictures a powerful influence throughout the world.

Snyder and her corset salesman lover Henry Judd Gray kill New York magazine art editor Albert Snyder, with a sashweight March 20 in a suburban sex triangle. A jury convicts the pair, and they will die in the electric chair at Sing Sing early next year.

Al Capone has an income for the year of $105 million, an all-time record for the highest gross income ever received by a private U.S. citizen (see 1925; 1926). Most of the Chicago gangster's money derives from bootleg liquor operations and he takes in $35 million more than Henry Ford will make in his best year (see 1929; tax evasion, 1931).

The Supreme Court rules that illegal income is taxable, thus giving the federal government a powerful new weapon against the underworld.

 J. C. Penney opens his 500th store and goes public (see 1908). By the time the stock is listed on the New York Stock Exchange in 1929 the company will have 1,495 stores (see 1971).

Sears, Roebuck and Company distributes 15 million of its general catalogs, 23 million of its semiannual sales catalogs and other catalogs. Virtually every rural American home has a Sears or Montgomery Ward mail-order catalog (see 1907).

The May Company acquires a major Baltimore store for $2.3 million, renames it the May Company, and adds a Baltimore outlet to other stores (see 1923).

San Francisco's Emporium acquires Oakland's H. C. Capwell Company and creates the Emporium-Capwell Corporation (see 1906). The store will open several branches in the 1950s.

 Ottawa's Canadian Parliament building is completed to replace the building finished in 1867 but destroyed in 1916 except for its Gothic library.

The Free Library of Philadelphia building is completed in French Renaissance style on Vine Street between 19th and 20th Streets.

Radburn, N.J., is designed by U.S. architects Clarence S. Stein, 46, and Henry Wright whose aim is not to make the most economical use of land but the most economical use of people with details planned to protect residents from air pollution, the abrasive effects of noise, needless tensions, fears, and alienation. Completion of the first modern "new town" will be delayed for economic reasons but Stein will go on to design Chatham Village outside Pittsburgh, Sunnyside Gardens in Long Island, and Kitimat in British Columbia.

The American Insurance Union Citadel at Columbus, Ohio, opens with 47 floors at Broad and Front Streets.

New York's Graybar building is completed on Lexington Avenue adjoining Grand Central Station. The 30-story building named for the Graybar Electric Company has more than 1 million square feet of rentable floor space—more than any other office building in the world.

New York's Delmonico Hotel opens on Park Avenue at 59th Street with 32 floors, 500 rooms.

New York's Sherry-Netherland Hotel opens on Fifth Avenue and 59th Street. Built by Schultze & Weaver, the hotel has 37 floors.

Boston's Ritz Hotel opens May 18 at the corner of Arlington and Newberry Streets overlooking the Public Garden.

Boston's Statler Hotel opens with 1,150 rooms on 14 floors. Hotel pioneer Ellsworth M. Statler will die in April of next year at age 65.

Washington's Hay-Adams Hotel opens on Lafayette Square. Armenian-American architect Mihran Mesrobian, 38, has designed the hotel to replace the Romanesque Hay-Adams houses built in the 1880s by the late Henry Hobson Richardson for author Henry Adams and former secretary of state John Hay.

Chicago's Stevens Hotel opens on Michigan Avenue between Balbo Avenue and 8th Street. The 3,000-room Stevens is the largest hotel in the world (see Conrad Hilton, 1945).

London's May Fair Hotel opens on a site formerly occupied by Devonshire House. The red brick block has 400 rooms on eight floors.

Honolulu's Royal Hawaiian Hotel opens at Waikiki Beach. Alexander & Baldwin has financed the new hotel.

Mar-a-Lago is completed at Palm Beach, Fla., for Postum Cereal head Marjorie Merriweather Post and her husband E. F. Hutton. Shaped like a crescent with a 75-foot tower and surrounded by 17 acres with guest houses, staff quarters, cutting gardens, and nine-hole golf course, the 115-room mansion ha taken 4 years to complete, three ships from Genoa have brought the Dorian stone for its outer walls, the ancient red roofing tiles have come from Cuba along with black and white marble inlay for the floors, Post has picked up 38,000 antique Spanish tiles for indoor wall decoration, and she has helped Palm Beach survive an economic depression by hiring all available local craftsmen to work on the $7 million project.

Minneapolis-Honeywell Corporation is created by a merger of Minneapolis Heat Regulator Company and Honeywell Heating Specialties Company of Wabash, Ind. William Sweatt, 59, and his family own Minneapolis Heat, Mark Honeywell, 53, owns Honeywell Heating, the new corporation has a 75 percent share of the market for oil-burner thermostat controls, and it will expand by acquiring Time-O-Stat Controls Co. of Elkhart, Ind., in 1931, Philadelphia's Brown Instrument Company in 1934, and others (see 1949).

April flood waters in the lower Mississippi Valley cover 4 million acres and cause $300 million in property loss (see Flood Control Act, 1928).

More than 100 people are swept to their deaths by a Vermont flood in early November after 11 inches of rainfall in 2 days. The Winooski, Lamoille, and White Rivers rise to destroy most of Vermont's covered bridges, the flood waters wash away houses and mills, and they cover 7,000 acres with rock gravel.

Georgia-Pacific Corp. has its beginnings in the Georgia Hardwood Lumber Company of Augusta, purchased by entrepreneur Owen Robertson Cheatham, 24, for $12,000. His grandfather has warned him, "Stay out of the timber business. In 20 years, all of the timber will be cut down." But Cheatham will expand his operations throughout the Southeast, he will acquire a plywood operation at Portland, Ore., in 1947, he will rename the company Georgia-Pacific Corp. in 1948, and he will make it a multinational colossus with papermills, chemical plants, and extensive oil, gas, coal, and mineral reserves.

The mechanical cotton picker perfected by Texas inventor John Daniel Rust, 35, and his 27-year-old brother Mack will have a profound social impact on the South when marketing of the machine begins in 1949 (see Campbell, 1889). The Rust cotton picker inserts a long spinning spindle with teeth into the cotton boll, winds up the cotton, picks it out, and is kept wet to facilitate removal of the cotton from the teeth, it picks a bale of cotton in one day, and it will spur migration of blacks to northern cities as it reduces the need for field hands.

The Supreme Court refuses a Federal Trade Commission request for further dissolution of the International Harvester Trust whose McCormick and Deering harvesting machines have been separated by the court order of 1920.

Harry Steenbock patents his 1923 discovery of vitamin D irradiation and assigns the patent to the Wisconsin Alumni Research Foundation, rejecting all commercial offers (see Borden's vitamin D fortified milk, 1933; but see also 1946).

Your Money's Worth by U.S. economist Stuart Chase and engineer F. J. (Frederick John) Schlink, 35, says, "We are all Alices in a Wonderland of conflicting claims, bright promises, fancy packages, soaring words, and almost impenetrable ignorance." Schlink has spent several years with the National Bureau of Standards which tests products before the federal government will buy them and he wonders why private citizens do not have the advantage of such testing (see Chase, 1925; Consumers' Research, 1929).

Wonder Bread is introduced in a balloon-decorated wrapper by Continental Baking Company which moves its headquarters to New York as Kansas City baking executive M. Lee Marshall becomes board chairman (see 1924; sliced bread, 1930).

Campbell Taggart, Inc. is chartered July 14 at Kansas City with $3 million in capital by Win M. Campbell and A. L. Taggart who take over the Manor Baking Co. which began selling its products December 8, 1925, with home delivery by horse and wagon. Campbell-Taggart will move its headquarters to Dallas in 1939 and will grow in 50 years to have 80 plants in North and South America and Europe.

United Biscuit Company is incorporated to challenge National Biscuit and Loose-Wiles for a share of the U.S. biscuit, cracker, and cookie market. The new holding company operates 12 regional baking companies (see Keebler, 1966).

Hostess Cakes are introduced by Continental Baking (above; see Twinkies, 1930).

Lender's Bagel Bakery is founded at West Haven, Conn. It will become the largest U.S. bagel baker.

American Sugar Refining Company's share of the U.S. sugar market falls to 25 percent, down from nearly 100 percent in 1899, but its 16-year-old Domino brand remains the top-selling table sugar. National Sugar Refining with its 14-year-old Jack Frost brand controls 22 percent of the market and while 13 other U.S. companies refine imported raw sugar none has more than a 7 percent share of market.

Homogenized milk is introduced by the Borden Company, but other milk is still sold with cream at the top that must be mixed before the milk is poured.

Gerber Baby Foods Company has its beginnings at Fremont, Mich., where local food processor Daniel F. Gerber, 28, is told by doctors to feed his sick daughter Sally strained peas (see Clapp, 1922). Gerber finds that strained baby foods are commercially available but are expensive, are sold only in a few parts of the country, and are available only at pharmacies and only by doctors' prescription (see 1928).

A General Electric refrigerator with a "monitor top" that contains an hermetically sealed compressor is introduced. It will make GE the industry leader by 1930 (see 1929).

1927 (cont.) Hellmann's Mayonnaise is acquired by the Postum Cereal Company which extends distribution throughout the United States (*see* 1912; 1932).

Log Cabin Products is acquired by the Postum Cereal Company which will reduce the maple syrup content of Log Cabin Syrup from its 1887 level of 45 percent down to 3 percent as maple prices rise.

Walter Baker Chocolate Company is acquired by the Postum Cereal Company (*see* 1824).

Franklin Baker Company is acquired by the Postum Cereal Company (*see* coconut, 1895).

B&M Brick Oven Baked Beans are introduced by Burnham & Morrill of Portland, Me. (*see* 1875).

Welch's Tomato Juice and the carbonated grape drink Welch-ade are introduced (*see* 1923; 1945).

Marriott's Hot Shoppe opens at Washington, D.C., at the corner of 14th Street and Park Road Northwest. Utah-born Mormon John Willard Marriott, 27, has invested his savings of $1,000 plus $1,500 in borrowed capital to obtain an exclusive franchise to sell A&W Root Beer in Washington, Baltimore, and Richmond using syrup obtained from two Westerners named Allen and Wright, his business has fallen off in the fall, he has hired a barbecue cook and has borrowed some recipes from the chef of the nearby Mexican Embassy, and he puts his bride Alice behind the stove to make hot tamales and chile con carne. The nine-seat root beer stand will grow in the next 45 years into the Marriott Corporation with 36 Hot Shoppes, eight Big Boy Coffee Shops, 29 Roy Rogers Family Restaurants, five Farrell's Ice Cream Parlour Restaurants, and numerous business, hospital, and other institutional food service operations plus hotels to serve between 600,000 and 700,000 people per day in 34 states and 15 foreign countries.

German physiologists Bernard Zondek and S. Ascheim discover a sex hormone that will lead to the first early test for pregnancy.

Birth control pioneer Margaret Sanger organizes the first World Population Conference (*see* 1921; International Planned Parenthood Federation, 1948).

1928 Penicillin is discovered to have antibacterial properties that will launch an "antibiotic" revolution in medicine. Scottish bacteriologist Alexander Fleming at St. Mary's Hospital, London, who discovered "the dissolving enzyme" in 1922, notices that no bacteria have grown in the vicinity of some *Penicillium notatum* fungus that has accidentally fallen into a preparation of bacteria he was about to throw away (*see* 1929; Florey, 1940).

The Basis of Sensation by English physiologists Edgar Douglas Adrian, 39, and Charles Scott Sherrington, 67, presents work that will enable physicians to understand disorders of the nervous system. Adrian has worked out the mechanism by which nerves carry messages to and from the brain.

Eli Lilly introduces Liver Extract No. 43 to treat pernicious anemia (*see* Cohn, 1926; Castle, 1929).

Peking surrenders to Chiang Kai-shek who last year renamed the city Peiping (northern peace). Chiang is elected president of China (*see* 1931).

The Kellogg-Briand Pact (Pact of Paris) is signed August 27 by 63 world powers whose representatives renounce war. Devised by U.S. Secretary of State Frank B. Kellogg, 72, and French foreign minister Aristide Briand, 66, the pact is implemented in September by the League of Nations.

The Albanian Republic proclaimed in 1925 becomes a kingdom under former prime minister Ahmed Bey Zogu, 33, who has changed his name to Scanderbeg II and who is crowned as Zog I to begin an 18-year reign of which the last 7 will be spent in exile.

Mexico's president Alvaro Obregon is assassinated July 17 at age 48 after having been elected to a second term July 1 in a country dominated by former president Plutarco Elias Calles, 51, who will continue his control until 1935 (*see* Cardenas, 1934).

U.S. voters elect Herbert Hoover president with 444 electoral votes against 87 for his Democratic opponent Alfred E. Smith, the Catholic governor of New York. Smith loses five states of the "Solid South" and obtains only 41 percent of the popular vote as compared with 58 percent for Hoover (below).

Bolivia and Paraguay go to war December 6 over the Chaco Territory. Paraguay appeals to the League of Nations; the Pan-American Conference that held its sixth meeting early in the year at Havana offers to mediate, but skirmishes will continue until April 4, 1930, when the two countries will reach a temporary truce agreement (*see* 1932).

Italy abolishes woman suffrage May 12 under a new law that restricts the franchise to men 21 and over who pay syndicate rates or taxes of 100 lire. The law reduces the electorate from nearly 10 million to only 3 million and requires that voters approve or reject in toto the 400 candidates submitted by the Fascist grand council.

British women gain the vote on the same terms as men under provisions of a July 2 act of Parliament.

The first Soviet Five-Year Plan launched by Josef Stalin in October will bring liquidation or exile to Siberia for millions of *kulaks* (rich peasants) who resist collectivization of agriculture (below).

The National Conference of Christians and Jews is founded to fight U.S. bigotry following the defeat of Catholic presidential candidate Alfred E. Smith (above).

The French franc has been devalued June 24 from 19.3 cents U.S. to 3.92 cents. The disguised repudiation of the national debt wreaks havoc on France's *rentier* class (*see* 1926).

"We in America today are nearer the final triumph over poverty than ever before in the history of any land," says Republican presidential candidate Herbert Hoover (above). "The slogan of progress is changing from the full dinner pail to the full garage," says Hoover, and his opponent misquotes him as saying, "A chicken in every pot and two cars in every garage" (see Henri IV, 1606).

"The American system of rugged individualism" is hailed by candidate Hoover October 22 in a speech at New York.

The Bank of America comes under the control of San Francisco banker A. P. Giannini who pays $510 per share for 35,000 of the outstanding 65,000 shares in the 116-year-old bank (see Giannini, 1906). Giannini will absorb the Bowery East River National Bank and the Commercial Exchange National Bank, he will form Bancamerica Corporation as a securities underwriting affiliate, and he will make Bank of America the nation's largest bank (see BankAmericard, 1958).

Personal bank loans are pioneered by New York's National City Bank which goes into competition with the Morris Plan started in 1910 and offers loans to employed borrowers on terms similar to those offered by Morris Plan banks.

Continental-Illinois Bank & Trust Company is created by a merger of Chicago's Continental National Bank with the Illinois Merchants Trust Company. The $1 billion financial institution will dominate Midwest banking.

New York's Chase National Bank has grown since 1877 to become the largest commercial bank in America, exceeded in size internationally only by London's Midland, Barclays, and Lloyds banks (see 1930).

The Jones-White Merchant Marine Act passed by Congress May 22 gives private U.S. shipping interests federal subsidies to help them compete with foreign lines (see 1936).

Amelia Earhart, 30, flies from Newfoundland to Burry Port, Wales, June 17. The U.S. aviatrix is the first woman to fly the Atlantic (see 1937).

Newark Airport opens in September. The 68-acre, $1.75 million field will grow to cover 2,300 acres (see La Guardia, 1939).

The German dirigible Graf Zeppelin arrives October 15 at Lakehurst, N.J., after covering 6,630 miles in 121 hours on her first commercial flight. The voyage from Friedrichshafen inaugurates transatlantic service by lighter-than-air craft (see 1900; 1937).

Lockheed Aircraft designer John Northrop quits the small Burbank, Calif., company to start his own firm. Gerard Vultee, 27, succeeds Northrop as chief engineer, he will redesign the Lockheed Vega for speed, and he will design the Sirius for Charles Lindbergh and his wife Anne (see 1927; Lockheed, 1932; American Airlines, 1930).

New York's Goethals Bridge and Outerbridge Crossing open to connect Staten Island with New Jersey.

Plymouth motorcars are introduced by Chrysler Motors to compete with Ford and Chevrolet. "Look at all three," says Walter Chrysler in advertisements featuring Plymouths with high compression engines and hydraulic brakes.

DeSoto motorcars are introduced by Chrysler Motors. The medium-priced cars will remain in production until 1961.

A new 112-horsepower Chrysler Imperial "80" is advertised as "America's most powerful automobile."

Stutz advertises a 113-horsepower model.

E. L. Cord's Auburn Automobile Company comes out with an eight-cylinder, 115-horsepower model which is advertised with a picture of 115 stampeding horses. Auburn's boat-tailed speedster travels at 108.6 miles per hour at Daytona, Fla., in March and later in the year averages 84.7 miles per hour for 25 hours at Atlantic City, N.J. (see 1924; 1930).

Florida's Tamiami Trail opens in April to link Miami with Fort Myers on the Gulf Coast. The 143-mile highway through the Everglades has taken 11 years to build and has cost more than $48,000 per mile.

The Pioneer Yelloway bus that reaches New York from California is the first transcontinental bus. Wesley E. Travis founded the Pioneer Yelloway System in 1919 over his father's old stagecoach routes. His larger competitor Pickwick Stages operates as far east as Kansas City (see Greyhound, 1929).

U.S. crude oil consumption reaches a rate of 7.62 barrels per capita while the rest of the world averages 0.19 barrel.

The Boulder Dam Project Act passed by Congress December 21 commits the federal government to participate in the production of hydroelectric power (see Kaiser, 1931).

American Negro: A Study in Racial Crossings by Northwestern University anthropology professor Melville Jean Herskovits, 33, advances the thesis that U.S. blacks constitute a homogeneous and culturally definable population group.

Coming of Age in Samoa by American Museum of Natural History anthropologist Margaret Mead, 26, is based on studies made while living with the natives on the Pacific island. Mead's book on the development of social behavior among adolescents on the island stresses the impermanence of human values.

The world's first combined radio, cable, and telegraph service company is created by a merger of Clarence Mackay's Commercial Cable-Postal Telegraph Company with International Telephone and Telegraph (ITT) (see International Western Electric, 1925). Mackay's father broke Western Union's telegraph monopoly in 1886, he inherited J. W. Mackay's communications empire in 1902, he completed a transpacific cable in 1903, he established wire communications with southern Europe via the Azores in 1907, he put a cable into service between New York and Cuba in 1907 and from Miami to Cuba in 1920,

1928 (cont.) and in 1923 he completed a wire link to northern Europe via Ireland.

Columbia Broadcasting System (CBS) is founded by Congress Cigar Company advertising manager William S. Paley, 27, who has been receiving $50,000 per year from his father's firm and who last year committed the company to an advertising contract of $50 per week with Philadelphia's 225-watt radio station WCAU while his father was away on vacation. Young Paley was criticized for making the contract, but he has seen sales of La Palina cigars soar in response to radio advertising, he sells some of his stock in Congress Cigar to raise upwards of $275,000, he buys into the financially ailing United Independent Broadcasters (which controls the Columbia Phonograph Company), he is elected president of the 22-station network September 26, he keeps CBS solvent by selling a 49 percent interest to Adolph Zukor's Paramount-Publix motion picture firm (broadcasting 16 hours per day over long-line telephone wires costs $1 million per year), he will move CBS to New York next year, and he will make the network a rival to David Sarnoff's NBC (*see* ABC, 1943).

Philco radios are introduced by Philadelphia Storage Battery Company and will soon be the world's largest-selling radios. The firm was started in 1906 with $10,000 in capital, sold $15 million worth of radio batteries last year, has started making radio sets after hearing Radio Corporation of America announce that a new AC tube will soon make radio batteries unnecessary, and will soon change its name to Philco Corporation. Philco will start assembly line production next year and by 1934 will be selling more than twice as many radios as Radio Corporation.

The Majestic Radio is introduced with a dynamic loudspeaker by the Grigsby-Grunow Company but the leading producer of radios is Atwater Kent, which popularizes the new AC tube made by RCA.

The first regularly scheduled television programs are broadcast beginning May 11 by Schenectady, N.Y., General Electric station WGY (*see* 1927; BBC, 1936).

Batten, Barton, Durstine & Osborn, Inc. (BBDO) is created by a merger September 15 of New York's 37-year-old George Batten Company with the 9-year-old firm Barton, Durstine & Osborn headed by Bruce Barton, 42, Roy S. Durstine, 42, and Alex Osborn, 40. Both companies have been at 383 Madison Avenue since 1923, BDO has been using radio for its client Atwater Kent since 1925, and the new agency has 113 clients, 600 employees, and branch offices at Boston, Buffalo, and Chicago.

Modern Mechanics is introduced as a new monthly magazine by Fawcett Publications (*see* 1922).

The *Atlanta World* begins publication as a 5-cent black daily.

The Oxford English Dictionary (*O.E.D.*) is published in 12-volume form after 44 years of work, most of it by Scottish editor-in-chief James A. H. Murray who died in 1915 at age 78. The 15,487-page work will be published in a two-volume Compact Edition with magnifying glass in 1971, and will be further supplemented in 1972 and thereafter to provide authoritative information on English word origins, usages, and pronunciations.

Fiction *Lady Chatterley's Lover* by D. H. Lawrence, who is dying of tuberculosis at Florence, is an explicit account of the sex relations between the wife of a crippled English peer and their lusty gamekeeper Mellors, privately printed because it is denied publication in England (*see* 1959); *The Well of Loneliness* by English novelist (Marguerite) Radclyffe Hall, 44, whose novel about a lesbian attachment between a young girl and an older woman encounters censorship problems; *Orlando* by Virginia Woolf; *The Last Post* by Ford Madox Ford; *The Children* by Edith Wharton; *All the Conspirators* by English novelist Christopher Isherwood, 24; *Nadja* by surrealist André Breton; *Southern Mail* (*Courrier-Sud*) by French aviator-novelist Antoine de Saint-Exupéry, 28; *The Cockpit* by U.S. novelist James Gould Cozzens, 25; *Mr. Buttsworthy on Rampole Island* by H. G. Wells; *Envy* (*Zavist*) by Soviet novelist Yuri Oleska, 29; *Point Counter Point* by Aldous Huxley; *The Bridge of San Luis Rey* by Thornton Wilder; *The Childermass* by Wyndham Lewis; *Some Prefer Nettles* (*Tade kuu muhi*) by Junichiro Tanizaki; *The Eclipse* by Chinese novelist Shen Yen-ping (Mao Tun), 32; *Time Regained* (*Le Temps Retrouvé*) by Marcel Proust is the last of his *Remembrance of Things Past* novels; *Decline and Fall* by English novelist Evelyn Waugh, 25; *The Mystery of the Blue Train* by Agatha Christie.

Juvenile *The House at Pooh Corner* by A. A. Milne; *Millions of Cats* by Wanda Gag.

Poetry *Gypsy Ballads* (*Romancero gitano*) by Spanish poet-dramatist Federico Garcia Lorca, 30, whose imaginary gypsies are based only in part on the real gypsies of Andalusia. They live in a world of childlike innocence that is brutalized by modern civilization in the form of the Civil Guard founded in 1844; *Nine Experiments* by English poet Stephen Spender, 19; *John Brown's Body* by U.S. poet Stephen Vincent Benét who is in France on a Guggenheim Fellowship and who wins a Pulitzer prize; *Mr. Pope and Other Poems* by U.S. poet (John Orley) Allen Tate, 28; *The Dead Water* (*Ssu-shui*) by Chinese poet Wen-I-To, 29; *The Cantos* (II) by Ezra Pound.

Painting *Seated Odalisque* by Henri Matisse; *Still Life with Jug* by Georges Braque; *Wedding* by Marc Chagall; *Black Lilies* by Max Beckmann; *The Titanic Days,* by René Magritte; *Girl on Sofa* by Edvard Munch; *Nightwave* by Georgia O'Keeffe; *Conversation, Country Dance, Louisiana Rice Fields,* and *Crapshooters* by Thomas Hart Benton; *Sixth Avenue and Third Street* by John Sloan.

Sculpture *Diana* fountain by Carl Milles.

The Philadelphia Museum of Art opens.

Theater *Marco Millions* by Eugene O'Neill 1/9 at New York's Garrick Theater, 92 perfs.; *Cock Robin* by Philip Barry and Elmer Rice 1/12 at New York's 48th Street Theater, 100 perfs.; *Strange Interlude* by Eugene O'Neill 1/30 at New York's John Golden Theater, with Lynn Fontanne, Glenn Anders, Earl Larimore, and Tom Powers in a long Freudian study of women with Elizabethan monologistic asides (the curtain rises at 5:30, descends at 7 for an 80-minute dinner interval, rises again at 8:20, and does not fall until after 11), 426 perfs., Pulitzer prize; *The Captain from Kopenick* (*Der Hauptmann von Kopenick*) by Karl Zuckmayer 3/5 at Berlin's Deutsches Theater; *Lazarus Laughed* by Eugene O'Neill 4/9 at the Pasadena Playhouse in California; *Skidding* by U.S. playwright Aurania Rouverol 5/21 at New York's Bijou Theater, with Marguerite Churchill, 448 perfs.; *The Front Page* by former *Chicago Daily News* staffman Ben Hecht, 34, and former *Hearst's International Magazine* staffman Charles MacArthur, 33, 8/14 at New York's Times Square Theater, with Lee Tracy, Osgood Perkins, Dorothy Stickney, 276 perfs.; (MacArthur marries actress Helen Hayes 8/17); *Machinal* by Sophie Teadwell 9/7 at New York's Plymouth Theater, with Jean Adair, Clark Gable, Zita Johnson in an expressionist drama based on the Ruth Snyder–Judd Gray murder case of last year, 91 perfs.; *Elmer the Great* by George M. Cohan and Ring Lardner 9/24 at New York's Lyceum Theater, with Walter Huston, 40 perfs.; *Squaring the Circle* (*Kvadratura Kruga*) by Soviet playwright Valentin Katayev, 31, 9/28 at the Moscow Art Theater, more than 800 perfs.; *Topaze* by French playwright Marcel Pagnol, 33, 10/9 at the Théâtre des Variétés, Paris; *The Far-Off Hills* by Esme Stuart Lennox Robinson 10/22 at Dublin's Abbey Theatre; *The Humiliation of the Father* (*Le père humilié*) by Paul Claudel 11/26 at Dresden's Schauspielhaus; *Holiday* by Philip Barry 11/26 at New York's Plymouth Theater, with Hope Williams, 229 perfs.; *Wings Over Europe* by English playwrights Robert M. B. Nichols, 31, and Maurice Browne 12/12 at New York's Martin Beck Theater, with Alexander Kirkwood as physicist Francis Lightfoot, who has discovered the secret of an atomic bomb, 90 perfs.; *Giants in the Earth* by U.S. playwright Thomas Job, 28 (who has adapted the epic novel by Ole Rolvaag) 12/17 at Carleton College, Northfield, Minn.

Films Walt Disney's *Steamboat Willie* introduces Mickey Mouse in the first animated cartoon with a sound track. U.S. animator Walter Elias Disney, 26, has produced the film under license from J. R. Bray who patented the "cel" system in 1910, his Mickey Mouse will be the basis of a vast entertainment and promotion empire, he will start a *Silly Symphony* series of black and white cartoon short subjects featuring Donald Duck, Pluto, and other cartoon characters, and they will rival Mickey Mouse in worldwide popularity (*see* 1931; 1938).

Other films King Vidor's *The Crowd* with Emil Jannings, Marlene Dietrich, James Murray, Eleanor Boardman (silent); René Clair's *Italian Straw Hat;* Josef von Sternberg's *The Last Command* with Emil Jannings; Ernst Lubitsch's *The Patriot* with Emil Jannings; F. W. Murneau's *Four Devils* with Janet Gaynor; Frank Borzage's *Street Angel* with Janet Gaynor; Luis Buñuel's *Un Chien Andalou* with Pierre Batcheff, painter Salvador Dali, and Buñuel; Charlie Chaplin's *The Circus* with Chaplin; Juri Taritch's *Czar Ivan the Terrible;* Vsevlod Pudovkin's *The End of St. Petersburg;* Joe May's *Homecoming* with Lars Hansen; F. Richard Jones's *The Gaucho* with Douglas Fairbanks; George Fitzmaurice's *Lilac Time* with Gary Cooper, Colleen Moore; Fred Niblo's *The Mysterious Lady* with Greta Garbo; Henry Beaumont's *Our Dancing Daughters* with Joan Crawford, John Mack Brown; W. S. Van Dyke's *White Shadows in the South Seas* with Raquel Torres, Monte Blue; Ted Wilde's *Speedy* with Harold Lloyd; King Vidor's *Show People* with Marion Davies, William Haines; Charles F. Reisner's *Steamboat Bill, Jr.* with Buster Keaton.

Radio comedy, variety *Amos 'n Andy* 3/19 over Chicago's WMAQ, with white actors Freeman Fisher Gosden, 28, and Charles J. Correll, 38, impersonating the black co-owners of the "Fresh-Air Taxicab Company of America" along with nearly all the other roles including Kingfish, Lightnin', and Madame Queen. The daily 15-minute comedy show will be broadcast nationally by David Sarnoff's NBC beginning next year and will soon reach 40 million listeners, two-thirds of the available audience, as movie theaters interrupt their programs to let audiences hear the show that will become a weekly half-hour program beginning in 1943 (*see* 1949); *The National Farm and Home Hour* debuts to attract U.S. farm family audiences.

Opera *The Three-Penny Opera* (*Die Dreigroschenoper*) 8/31 at Berlin's Theater am Schiffbauerdamm, with Lotte Lenya as Jenny, music by her husband Kurt Weill, book and lyrics by Bertolt Brecht who has transposed the *Beggar's Opera* of 1728 into the idiom of Germany's Weimar Republic.

Stage musicals *Rosalie* 1/10 at New York's New Amsterdam Theater, with Marilyn Miller, Frank Morgan, Jack Donahue, music by George Gershwin and Sigmund Romberg, lyrics by Ira Gershwin and P. G. Wodehouse, book by Guy Bolton and William Anthony McGuire, 335 perfs.; *The Three Musketeers* 3/13 at New York's Lyric Theater, with Dennis King as D'Artagnan, Vivienne Segal, Reginald Owen as Cardinal Richelieu, Clarence Derwent as Louis XIII, music by Rudolph Friml, songs that include "March of the Musketeers," 318 perfs.; *This Year of Grace* 3/22 at the London Pavilion, with Jessie Matthews, Tilly Losch, Melville Cooper, book, music, and lyrics by Noel Coward, songs that include "A Room with a View," "World Weary," "Dance, Little Lady," 316 perfs.; *Present Arms* 4/26 at New York's Mansfield Theater, with Charles King, Busby Berkeley, music

1928 (cont.) by Richard Rodgers, lyrics by Lorenz Hart, songs that include "You Took Advantage of Me," 155 perfs.; *Blackbirds of 1928* 5/9 at New York's Liberty Theater, with Bill "Bojangles" Robinson, songs that include "Digga Digga Do" and "I Can't Give You Anything but Love" by Jimmy McHugh, lyrics by Dorothy Fields, 518 perfs.; *George White's Scandals* 7/2 at New York's Apollo Theater, with Harry Richman, Ann Pennington, Willie and Eugene Howard, music by Ray Henderson, lyrics by B. G. DeSylva and Lew Brown, 240 perfs.; *Good Boy* 9/15 at New York's Hammerstein Theater, with Eddie Buzzell, songs that include "I Wanna Be Loved by You" by Herbert Stothard, Bert Kalmar, and Harry Ruby, 253 perfs.; *The New Moon* 9/10 at New York's Imperial Theater, with Robert Halliday, Evelyn Herbert, music by Sigmund Romberg, lyrics by Oscar Hammerstein II and others, songs that include "One Kiss," "Lover, Come Back to Me," "Softly, as in a Morning Sunrise," "Wanting You," "Stout-Hearted Men," 509 perfs.; *Paris* 10/8 at New York's Music Box Theater, with Irene Bordoni, music and lyrics by Cole Porter and E. Ray Goetz, songs that include "Let's Fall in Love" with lyrics that begin, "Let's do it . . . ," 195 perfs.; *Hold Everything* 10/10 at New York's Broadhurst Theater, with Bert Lahr, Jack Whiting, Victor Moore, Ona Munson, music by Ray Henderson, lyrics by B. G. DeSylva and Lew Brown, songs that include "You're the Cream in My Coffee," 413 perfs.; *Animal Crackers* 10/23 at New York's 44th Street Theater, with the Four Marx Brothers, Margaret Dumont, book by George S. Kaufman and Morrie Ryskind, music and lyrics by Bert Kalmar and Harry Ruby, 191 perfs.; *Treasure Girl* 11/8 at New York's Alvin Theater, with Gertrude Lawrence, Clifton Webb, music by George Gershwin, lyrics by Ira Gershwin, songs that include "I've Got a Crush on You," "I've Got a Feeling I'm Falling," "Oh, So Nice," 68 perfs.; *Whoopee* 12/4 at New York's New Amsterdam Theater, with Eddie Cantor, music and lyrics by Walter Donaldson and Gus Kahn, songs that include "Love Me or Leave Me," "Makin' Whoopee," 379 perfs.

Hollywood musicals Victor Fleming's *The Awakening* with Vilma Banky as Marie, Walter Byron, Louis Wolheim, and the song "Marie" by Irving Berlin.

First performances Symphonic Piece by Harvard music professor Walter Hamor Piston, 34, 3/6 at Boston's Symphony Hall. Piston was graduated summa cum laude from Harvard in 1924 and has studied at Paris with Paul Dukas and Nadia Boulanger. Variations for Orchestra by Arnold Schoenberg 12/2 at Berlin; *America: An Epic Rhapsody in Three Parts for Orchestra* by Ernest Bloch with a text from poems by Walt Whitman 12/20 and 12/21 at New York, Boston, Philadelphia, Cincinnati, Chicago, and San Francisco; *An American in Paris* by George Gershwin 12/13 at New York's Carnegie Hall with Gershwin at the piano.

Rudy Vallee forms his own band and opens at New York's Heigh-Ho Club with a megaphone to amplify his voice. The first "crooner," 27-year-old Hubert Prior Vallee is a self-taught saxophonist who worked his way through a year at the University of Maine and 3 years at Yale with interruptions for musical engagements, he received his bachelor's degree from Yale last year, he sings the Maine "Stein Song," and he makes his theme song "My Time Is Your Time."

Lawrence Welk starts a small band and launches a half-century career with broadcasts to rural South Dakota audiences from a Yankton radio station. The 24-year-old accordionist will call his music "Champagne Music" beginning in 1938 and will write his own theme song "Bubbles in the Wine."

The Mills Brothers cut their first record to begin a career that will continue for more than half a century. The Piqua, Ohio, singers include Herbert, 18, Harry, 16, Donald, 15, and John, Jr. (who will die in 1936 during a performance at Philadelphia).

Popular songs "The Breeze and I" by Ernesto Lecuona, lyrics by Al Stillman; "Sweet Sue—Just You" by Victor Young, 28, lyrics by Will J. Harris, 28; "Sweet Lorraine" by Rudy Vallee's piano player Cliff Burwell, 28, lyrics by Mitchell Parish, "I'll Get By" by Fred Ahlert, 36, lyrics by Roy Turk, 36; "Carolina Moon" by Joe Burke and Benny Davis; "She's Funny That Way" by Neil Moret, lyrics by Billy Rose and E. Y. Harburg.

The Olympic Games at Amsterdam attract 3,905 contestants from 46 countries. U.S. athletes win the most medals.

U.S. Olympic swimming champion Johnny Weissmuller, 25, retires after having set 67 world records and having won three Olympic gold medals for the U.S. swimming team. Weissmuller will have a Hollywood screen test in 1930 and will make 19 films in 18 years portraying Tarzan, the jungle man created by novelist Edgar Rice Burroughs in 1914.

Spanish picadors and their horses are given some protection by a law requiring that horses wear a mattresslike armor strapped over one side and under the belly and that picadors wear steel armor over their right legs.

Portugal outlaws the killing of bulls in the ring but permits bullfighting to continue without killing.

Jimmy Foxx joins Connie Mack's Philadelphia Athletics at age 20 to begin a career in which he will break Babe Ruth's home run average (see 1920). The Athletics will trade James Emory Foxx to the Boston Red Sox in 1935, he will move to the Chicago Cubs in 1942, and he will play his final season for the Philadelphia Phillies in 1945.

The New York Yankees win the World Series by defeating the St. Louis Cardinals 4 games to 0.

The Boston Garden opens. The new arena will host basketball and hockey games, track meets, and other events.

Colgate-Palmolive-Peet Company is created by a merger of the 122-year-old Colgate Company with the 2-year-old Palmolive-Peet Company. The new firm has assets of more than $63 million with combined sales of $100 million and is in a position to challenge the leadership of Cincinnati's 91-year-old Procter & Gamble Company whose sales have grown to $156 million.

Welcome Wagon International, Inc., has its beginnings at Memphis, Tenn., where advertising agency head Thomas W. Briggs introduces new residents to his clients by hiring agents to make personal calls. Briggs cites the frontier custom of sending a covered wagon loaded with supplies out to meet westward-bound migrants and thus encourage them to settle, 2,200 U.S. cities will have Welcome Wagon offices by 1967, 80,000 merchants will support the organization, and it will employ 6,000 hostesses.

New York's Bergdorf Goodman moves north from 616 Fifth Avenue to occupy a new marble building on the site of the former Cornelius Vanderbilt mansion at Fifth Avenue at 58th Street opposite the Plaza.

Detroit's J. L. Hudson acquires its leading competitor Newcomb & Endicott and erects a new building on Woodward Avenue (*see* 1912; 1946).

Boston's Wm. Filene's Sons acquires R. H. White Company and will operate the store as a Filene subsidiary until 1944 (*see* 1912; Federated, 1929).

New York's General Motors building is completed by Shreve & Lamb in West 57th Street.

The New York Athletic Club building is completed on Central Park South and Seventh Avenue.

New York's Tudor City is completed by Fred F. French Company between Second and Third Avenues from 40th Street north to 43rd. The 12-building complex includes 3,000 apartments, 600 hotel rooms, restaurants, private parks, and shops.

New York's Beresford Apartments designed by Emery Roth with three castle-like towers go up on Central Park West at 81st Street just north of the Museum of Natural History.

New York's 42-story Pierre Hotel is completed by Schultze & Weaver on Fifth Avenue at 61st Street.

The Beverly Wilshire Hotel is completed on Rodeo Drive at Beverly Hills, Calif.

London's Grosvenor House hotel opens in Park Lane with 467 rooms on eight floors.

Detroit's 47-story Greater Penobscot building is completed at Griswold and First Streets.

The Breuer chair designed by Hungarian-born architect Marcel Lajos Breuer, 26, is introduced by Vienna's Gebrüder Thonet (*see* bentwood chair, 1876).

California's 3-year-old St. Francis Dam near Saugus gives way March 12, killing 450.

A Flood Control Act passed by Congress May 15 provides an estimated $325 million to be spent over the course of 10 years for levee work on the lower Mississippi (*see* 1927).

A Florida hurricane in September causes Lake Okeechobee to overflow, killing 1,836.

Bryce Canyon National Park is created by act of Congress. The park in southern Utah embraces 36,010 acres of amphitheaters, pinnacles, spires, and walls carved by natural erosion.

Collectivization of Soviet agriculture is ordered by Josef Stalin in the first Five-Year Plan (above). Peasants burn their crops, slaughter their livestock, and hide their grain from state collectors (but *see* 1931).

World leadership in scientific plant breeding and genetic livestock development is held by the Soviet Union largely as a result of biological research programs developed by Nikolay Ivanovich Vavilov to benefit socialist agriculture (but *see* 1940).

Vitamin C (ascorbic acid) is isolated from capsicums (peppers) at the Cambridge, England, laboratory of Frederick Gowland Hopkins by Hungarian-born biochemist Albert Szent-Györgyi von Nagyrapolt, 35, who finds the capsicums nearly four times as rich in the antiscurvy vitamin as lemons (*see* Lind, 1747; Hopkins, 1906; King, 1932).

Vitamin B is shown to be at least two vitamins by U.S. biochemists M. I. Smith and E. G. Hendrick who name the heat resistant vitamin G, or B_2 (*see* 1926; McCollum, 1916; Warburg, 1932).

At least 1,565 Americans die from drinking bad liquor, hundreds are blinded, and many are killed in bootlegger wars. Federal agents and Coast Guardsmen are making 75,000 arrests per year and enforcement of Prohibition laws is costing U.S. taxpayers millions of dollars, but the laws are openly flouted.

Distillers Corporation-Seagram is organized in March by Samuel and Alan Bronfman who last year acquired the Joseph E. Seagram & Sons company founded in 1870 (*see* 1924). The Bronfmans are ship-

The crash of New York Stock Exchange values wiped out many investors and began a decade of economic depression.

1928 (cont.) ping hundreds of thousands of gallons of liquor that winds up in the United States despite Prohibition laws and they will make Seagram the world's largest producer of alcoholic beverages (*see* 1933).

Glyceride emulsifiers are employed for the first time in U.S. foods such as baked goods, shortenings, margarines, and ice creams.

Peter Pan Peanut Butter is introduced by Swift Packing Company's E. K. Pond division and is the first hydrogenated, homogenized peanut butter and the first to have national advertising and promotion (*see* 1890; Normann, 1901). E. K. Pond has been licensed to use a process invented in 1923 by Alameda, Calif., food processor J. L. Rosefield to stabilize peanut butter by replacing a significant part of its natural peanut oil with hydrogenated peanut oil and the new brand (which will soon be marketed by Swift's Derby Foods division) takes its name from the 24-year-old James M. Barrie drama (*see* Skippy, 1932).

Peanut butter cracker sandwich packets are introduced under the name NAB by National Biscuit Company which sells the 5-cent packets through newsstands, drugstores, candy counters, and other such retail outlets (*see* Ritz, 1931).

The Shredded Wheat Company, whose basic patent expired before 1912, is acquired for $35 million in stock by National Biscuit Company (above). The name "shredded wheat" will be declared common property by the Supreme Court in 1938 (*see* 1900).

The Calumet Baking Powder Company is acquired by the Postum Cereal Company (*see* Wright, 1895).

The Cheek-Neal Coffee Company that markets Maxwell House Coffee is acquired by Postum Cereal.

Sanka Coffee distribution rights are acquired by Postum Cereal (*see* 1903; 1933; General Foods, 1929).

Baby foods are advanced by Daniel Gerber who develops improved methods for straining peas and finds by a market survey that a large market exists for such foods if they can be sold cheaply through grocery stores (*see* 1927). Gerber advertises in *Child's Life* magazine and offers six cans for a dollar (less than half the price of baby foods sold at pharmacies) to customers who will send in coupons filled out with the names and addresses of their grocers (*see* 1929).

Glidden Food Products Company acquires the Portland Vegetable Oil Company and the Wisconsin Food Producers Company to which it will add Chicago's Troco Margarine Company and additional margarine makers to gain a captive market for its refinery operations (*see* 1929).

Beatrice Creamery Company acquires the Pioneer Creamery of Galesburg, Ill., for $1.5 million with help from Clinton Howard Haskell, a nephew of Beatrice's late founder (*see* 1905). Pioneer's salty Holland brand butter is popular in New England markets and by the fall of next year Beatrice will be operating 50 subsidiary companies, 30 creameries,

33 milk plants, 54 ice-cream plants, and dozens of cold storage warehouses, ice plants, and the like from Ohio to Montana.

J. L. Kraft & Co. buys out its leading competitor, Phenix Cheese, which has been making processed cheese under license from Kraft, and creates the largest U.S. cheese company under the name Kraft-Phenix (*see* 1900; 1915; National Dairy Corp., 1929).

Breakstone Foods is acquired by National Dairy Corp. which also acquires General Ice Cream (*see* 1923).

Klim powdered milk is introduced by the Borden Company which has acquired the Merrell-Soule Company which has originated Klim. Borden is acquiring hundreds of other companies to maintain its lead over National Dairy (above).

The Eskimo Pie patent of 1919 is invalidated by the courts but the old "I-Scream-Bar" has such a large share of the market that the action has little effect on sales (*see* 1924).

Rice Krispies are introduced by the W. K. Kellogg Company. The new breakfast food is 10 percent sugar (*see* Pep, 1922; Raisin Bran, 1942).

Nehi Corporation is created by a reorganization of the Chero-Cola Company whose nearly 500 bottling plants are mostly in the South (*see* 1920; Royal Crown Cola, 1934).

"I say it's spinach and I say the hell with it," reads E. B. White's caption to Carl Rose's *New Yorker* magazine cartoon showing a child refusing to eat broccoli. The vegetable has only recently been introduced into the United States from Italy by D'Arrigo Brothers, an enterprising grower in northern California's Santa Clara Valley.

Schrafft's Candy Company moves into a large new Boston plant at 529 Main Street (*see* 1897; 1929).

New York's Barricini Candy Company is founded.

1929 $ Wall Street stock prices crash beginning Tuesday, October 24, following a drop in U.S. iron and steel production and a rise in British interest rates to 6.5 percent that has pulled European capital out of the U.S. money market. An unprecedented 16.4 million shares trade October 24, the Dow Jones Industrial Average plummets 30.57 points, liquidation of securities continues as speculators are forced go sell stock they have bought on margin, and $30 billion in capital disappears—a sum almost equal to the dollar cost of the 1914–1918 war to the United States (*see* 1930).

Some 513 Americans have incomes above $1 million for the year and a dozen have incomes above $5 million. The rate of normal income tax on the first $7,500 of net income is 1.5 percent with exemptions of $1,500 for a single person and $3,500 for a married person or head of household. At $12,000 per year the tax rate climbs to 5 percent plus a surtax that is graduated up to 20 percent on $100,000, but while a married man with an income of $100,000 may pay as much as $16,000 in tax he will probably find legal ways to avoid paying that much.

Seventy-one percent of U.S. families have incomes below $2,500 which is generally considered the minimum necessary for a decent standard of living. The average weekly wage is $28 (*see* 1932).

Britain's unemployment rate tops 12.2 percent with more miners and workmen idle than in the General Strike of 1926. Most working class families in the Welsh coal fields exist on a dole of about $7 per week and corner pubs close down for lack of trade.

Unilever is created by a merger of Britain's Lever Brothers with the Dutch margarine-making firm Anton Jurgens founded in 1883. Unilever is the first multinational firm in the soap and food industries.

Owens-Illinois Glass Company is created by the Owens Bottle Machine Company which buys Illinois Glass Company for $19.6 million in cash and securities. The income of Owens Bottle Machine has been mostly from patent royalties (*see* 1903; 1918; 1940).

National Steel Company is founded by tinplate magnate Ernest T. Weir who merges his Weirton Steel Company with Detroit's Great Lakes Steel Corporation and Cleveland's M. A. Hanna Company to create a $120 million steelmaking colossus (*see* 1906; Hanna, 1885).

Bigelow-Sanford Company is created by a merger of the Bigelow-Hartford firm of Connecticut and of Lowell, Mass., with the Sanford carpetmaking firm of Amsterdam, N.Y.

Edsel Ford announces an increase in the minimum daily wage at Ford Motor Company plants December 2. The wage goes from $6 up to $7 but wages in virtually all industries will soon decline (*see* 1933).

Albert Einstein announces that he has found a key to the formulation of a unified field theory—a group of equations applicable not only to gravitation but also to electromagnetics and subatomic phenomena (*see* 1916; 1939).

Leon Trotsky is expelled from the Soviet Union in January some 14 months after having been thrown out of the Communist Party on charges of having engaged in antiparty activities. Josef Stalin removes Trotsky's threat to his dictatorship (*see* 1924; 1940).

Nikolai Bukharin is expelled from the Communist Party November 17 after having headed the Third International since 1926. Other members of the Rightist opposition are expelled and Stalin is left to rule as undisputed dictator.

Yugoslavia's Aleksandr I proclaims a dictatorship January 5 and dissolves the Croat and all other parties January 21. The Kingdom of the Serbs, Croats, and Slovenes becomes Yugoslavia officially October 3 in a move to end historic divisions of the realm.

Britain's Labour Party wins the general election on May 30 and Ramsay MacDonald forms a second cabinet June 5 that will hold power for more than 2 years. Diplomatic relations with Moscow resume October 1.

The Lateran Treaties ratified by the Italian parliament June 7 restore temporal power to the pope over the 108.7-acre Vatican City in Rome, the Italian government agrees to pay an indemnity of 750 million lire in cash and 1 billion lire in government bonds, and the pope leaves the Vatican July 25 after years of virtual imprisonment.

Japan's last parliamentary election for more than 16 years is held with big red lacquer ballot boxes. Twenty percent of the population is eligible to vote as compared with 1.1 percent in 1891, but suffrage remains limited to men of 25 and older (Japanese militarists will soon take over the government and will put an end to free elections).

A dispute over Jewish use of Jerusalem's Wailing Wall leads (in August) to the first large-scale Arab attacks on Jews, many of whom are killed (*see* 1930).

A Mississippi lynch mob of 2,000 burns an accused black rapist alive, a coroner's jury returns a verdict of death "due to unknown causes," and Mississippi governor Theodore G. Bilbo says the state has "neither the time nor the money" to go into the matter. But total U.S. lynchings for the year number 10, down from 23 in 1926, 97 in 1909.

U.S. auto production tops 5 million with minor makes accounting for 25 percent of sales. The 5 million figure will not be reached again for 20 years (*see* 1932).

General Motors Corporation buys the German Opel Motorcar Company founded in 1898.

GM's Chevrolet Division introduces a model with a six-cylinder engine and advertises that the new Chevy costs no more than a four-cylinder car.

General Motors president Alfred P. Sloan opposes a suggestion by Lammot du Pont, 49, that Chevrolets be equipped with safety glass (*see* Duplate, 1927). GM's Cadillacs and La Salles have recently been equipped with Duplate glass but Sloan points out that Packards have not been equipped with safety glass and their sales have not suffered. "I do not think that from the stockholder's viewpoint the move on Cadillac's part has been justified," writes Sloan, and while he acknowledges that nonshatterable glass "is bound to come" he resists changes that will reduce GM profits: "Accidents or no accidents, my concern in this problem is a matter of profit and loss."

The first motorcar with front-wheel drive is introduced by E. L. Cord's Auburn Automobile Company (*see* 1928).

The Model J Deusenberg introduced by E. L. Cord's Deusenberg, Inc., is a "real Duzy" (*see* 1926). The costly 265-horsepower luxury car will go 112 to 116 miles per hour and will be built until 1936 for affluent Americans and Europeans.

The first station wagon in introduced by Ford Motor Company which equips a Model A with a boxy wooden body that provides extra space for cargo and passengers.

1929 (cont.)   The first mobile home trailer is displayed in New York showrooms by the Hudson Motor Car Company (*see* 1922). Aviation pioneer Glenn H. Curtiss has invented the trailer.

Greyhound Corp. buys out Pioneer Yelloway System for $6.4 million (*see* 1926; 1928). Greyhound has sold $2 million in stock to Floyd Odlum's Goldman Sachs Trading Corp., $480,000 in stock to the Southern Pacific Railway, $330,000 in stock to the Pennsylvania Railroad (*see* 1934).

Scuderia Ferrari is founded at Modena December 1 by former Alfa Romeo racing driver Enzo Ferrari, 31, with a few partners to sell Alfas in three provinces (Scuderia means stable, or racing team) (*see* 1940).

Curtiss-Wright Corporation is created by a merger of American Wright Company with Curtiss Aircraft (*see* 1909; 1910; General Motors, 1933).

Grumman Aircraft Engineering Corporation has its beginnings in a Baldwin, Long Island, aircraft repair shop opened by Leroy Grumman and Leon "Jake" Swirblul. William T. Schwendler, 24, is chief engineer.

United Aircraft & Transport Corporation is created by U.S. aeronautical engineer and designer Chance Vought, now 39, who merges his 12-year-old Chance Vought aircraft manufacturing firm with the Pratt & Whitney Aircraft Co. and the Boeing Airplane Co.

Bendix Aviation Corporation is started by Vincent Bendix who will merge his various radio and motorcar and aviation equipment-making firms into the new corporation (*see* 1912; Bendix Trophy, 1930).

U.S. commercial airlines fly 30 million miles, up from 6 million in 1927, and carry 180,000 passengers, up from 37,000.

Delta Air Lines begins passenger service June 17 under the name Delta Air Service with three six-passenger Travelaire monoplanes powered by 300-horsepower Wright "Whirlwind" engines flying at 90 miles per hour between Dallas and Jackson, Miss., via Shreveport and Monroe, La. Delta was organized late last year under the leadership of former agricultural extension service county agent C. E. Woolman, 39, who pioneered in using airplanes to dust cotton crops with arsenate of lead and calcium arsenate in order to protect them from boll weevil damage.

Pan American Airways starts daily flights between Miami and Havana and flies three times weekly between Miami and San Juan, Miami and Nassau, and San Juan and Havana (*see* 1927; 1935).

Pan American consultant Charles A. Lindbergh opens a route through Central America to the Panama Canal Zone, Pan Am acquires Cia Mexicana de Aviacion and wins a mail contract to Mexico City, and by year's end Pan Am has routes totaling 12,000 miles, up from 251 at the end of last year (*see* 1930).

Panagra (Pan American Grace Airways) is created by Pan American (above) and W. R. Grace and Company to provide air service to South American cities. Each company puts up $500,000 to start Panagra.

London's Heathrow Airport has its beginnings in Richard Fairey's Great West Aerodrome used mainly for experimental flights (*see* 1946; Gatwick, 1936).

Lufthansa is organized as the German national airline and Berlin's 6-year-old Tempelhof Airport gains new importance. By 1936 it will be Europe's busiest air travel center.

The *Graf Zeppelin* that was launched last year completes the first round-the-world flight of any kind. The dirigible carries nine commercial passengers 19,000 miles in 21 days, 7 hours.

The S.S. *Bremen* goes into service July 10 and sets a new transatlantic speed record for passenger liners. The North German-Lloyd line vessel crosses from Cherbourg to New York in 4 days, 17 hours, 42 minutes, cutting 3 hours off the record set by the S.S. *Mauretania* in 1910.

The *Simplon-Orient Express* is struck by a blizzard in early February beyond the Bulgarian-Turkish border and is frozen fast for 5 days at Tcherkesskeuy. Temperatures fall well below the freezing point inside the wagon-lits, food, water, and fuel give out, and the situation is saved only by the cooperation of crew and passengers, some of whom work with pick and shovel to tunnel out and buy food and fuel from Turkish peasants at staggering prices (*see* 1919; 1932).

Continental Oil Corporation (CONOCO) is created by J. P. Morgan & Co. The New York banking house took over the Marland Oil Company 2 years ago from polo player E. W. Marland and merges it with the Continental Oil Company of Maine which it has also taken over (*see* 1908; Consolidation Coal, 1967).

The first clinical application of crude penicillin is made January 9 at St. Mary's Hospital, London, by Alexander Fleming who treats an assistant suffering from an infected antrum by washing out the man's sinus with diluted penicillin broth, successfully destroying most of the staphylococci (*see* 1928; 1931).

The first Blue Cross nonprofit tax-exempt health insurance association is organized at Dallas, Tex. where local schoolteachers whose unpaid bills have been a burden to Baylor University Hospital make an arrangement with the hospital. Each teacher is guaranteed up to 21 days' free use of a semiprivate room and other hospital services on condition that small monthly fees be paid in advance on a regular basis. The program will quickly spread to all hospitals in the area with a central agency to collect the fees and the Blue Cross trademark of the American Hospital Association (the national association of voluntary hospitals) will be used by agencies throughout the country that meet AHA standards. By 1935 Blue Cross will have half a million subscribers and a Blue Shield program set up by medical societies and local doctors' guilds will provide surgical insurance (*see* 1940

Hypertension (high blood pressure) and fatal heart disease are linked for the first time by Harvard physician Samuel Albert Levine, 38, who notes that 60 out of 145 heart attack patients have been hypertensive. In more than 90 percent of hypertension cases, the cause cannot be found and the patient is said to have "essential" hypertension, a misnomer dating to a time when so many people had high blood pressure that it was considered essential, but while hypertension produces no symptoms unless it is very severe it will prove a major factor in heart fatalities (*see* 1949).

Insulin shock treatment for schizophrenia is introduced by Austrian-American psychiatrist Manfred J. Sakel, 29, who uses overdoses of insulin to produce shock and finds it effective in many cases (*see* Banting, Best, 1922; Thorazine, 1954).

The Murry and Leoni Guggenheim Foundation to promote dental science is founded by copper magnate Murry Guggenheim, 71, and his wife.

Gang warfare in Chicago reaches a peak of brutality the morning of February 14 in the "St. Valentine's Day massacre." Seven members of the George "Bugs" Moran gang are rubbed out at 10:30 in a North Clark Street garage and bootleg liquor depot as mobsters vie for control of the lucrative illicit liquor trade (police suspect that members of the Al Capone gang have done the killing) (*see* 1927; 1931).

Chicago has 498 reported murders, New York 401, Detroit 228, Philadelphia 182, Cleveland 134, Birmingham 122, Atlanta and Memphis 115 each, New Orleans 111.

"The so-called method of coeducation is false in theory and harmful to Christian training," proclaims Pope Pius XI December 31 in his encyclical *Divini illius magistri.*

Basic English by Cambridge University philologist C. K. (Charles Kay) Ogden, 40, proposes universal adoption of a basic international vocabulary of 850 English words he has developed after working with I. (Ivor) A. Richards, now 36, on their 1923 book *The Meaning of Meaning.* Ogden points out that 30 percent of the world's population has English as its mother tongue or as the government language (he has India in mind) and he says his easily learned basic English could help promote world peace.

An airmail letter crosses the United States in 31 hours at a cost of 25 cents postage for 3 ounces.

The United States has 20 million telephones, up from 10 million in 1918 and twice as many as all the rest of the world combined. Most are wooden boxes hung on walls with cranks to ring Central, but many tall tubelike phones are in use with hooks to hold their receivers, and French phones are beginning to appear with mouthpiece and receiver in one piece.

The Blattnerphone designed by German film producer Louis Blattner is the world's first tape recorder. Based on patents obtained by German sound engineer Kurt Stille, the device employs steel tape rather than the wire used in the Poulsen recorder of 1898, it is the first successful magnetic recorder with electronic amplification, and Blattner uses it for adding synchronized sound to the films that he makes at the Blattner Color and Sound Studios at Ellstree, England. The BBC will acquire the first commercially produced Blattnerphone in 1931 (*see* plastic tape, 1935).

U.S. radio sales total nearly $950 million as Americans pay $118 and up for elaborate console model Atwater Kent and Stromberg-Carlson sets with seven tubes and built-in superpower magnetic speakers to hear Amos 'n' Andy, Rudy Vallee, and Graham MacNamee's NBC sports broadcasts (*see* Stromberg-Carlson, 1896; *The Goldbergs,* below).

The Motorola auto radio invented by University of Illinois engineering school graduate Paul Vincent Galvin, 34, is the first commercially successful radio for automobiles. Galvin started a business in a Chicago garage last year with $565 in capital, he will develop it into the Motorola Company, but while his first radio plays in a moving automobile it is twice the size of a tackle box, its bulky speaker is stuffed under the floorboards, and its audio qualities leave much to be desired.

Benton & Bowles advertising is founded by New York agency executives William Benton, 29, and Chester Bowles, 38, who will pioneer in radio advertising and will make their firm a major agency for General Foods (below). They will be millionaires within 6 years (*see* Muzak, 1940).

Business Week magazine begins publication September 7 at New York. The new McGraw-Hill publication will have lost $1.5 million by the end of 1935 but will turn the corner to become the leading magazine of its kind. In many years it will be the leading magazine of any kind in terms of advertising pages.

Redbook magazine is acquired by the McCall Corporation (*see* 1875; 1903; Norton Simon, 1969).

"Herblock" begins a career as political cartoonist that will continue for half a century. Herbert Lawrence Block, 19, draws editorial page cartoons for the *Chicago Daily News,* he will move to Cleveland in 1933 to work for the Newspaper Enterprise Association (NEA), and in 1946 he will join the *Washington Post* which will syndicate Herblock cartoons to some 200 U.S. newspapers.

"Popeye" appears for the first time in the 10-year-old "Thimble Theatre" drawn by New York cartoonist Elzie Crisler Segar, 34, whose one-eyed, spinach-loving sailor with corncob pipe and outsize sense of chivalry will soon be joined by girl friend Olive Oyl and hamburger-loving pal Wimpy (*see* spinach growers, 1937).

Farrar and Rinehart publishers is founded by Doubleday, Doran editors John Chipman Farrar, 33, and Stanley M. Rinehart, Jr., 32, with Stanley's brother Frederick R., 27. The Rineharts are sons of the mys-

1929 (cont.) tery novelist Mary Roberts Rinehart (*see* 1909; Farrar Straus, 1946; Holt, Rinehart and Winston, 1960).

Nonfiction *Middletowne: A Study in Contemporary American Culture* by U.S. sociologists Robert Staughton Lynd, 37, and his wife Helen Merrell Lynd, 32, who break new ground in American sociology by applying methods and approaches used in studying primitive peoples to the Midwestern city of Muncie, Ind., and allying sociology with anthropology; *Goodbye to All That* (autobiography) by Robert Graves; *Is Sex Necessary?* by *New Yorker* magazine humorists E. B. White and James Thurber; *The Adventurous Heart* (*Das abenteuerliche Herz*), essays by Ernst Jünger whose ideas have been taken over in part by the Nazis.

Fiction *The Time of Indifference* (*Gli indifferenti*) by Italian novelist Alberto Moravia (Alberto Pincherle), 22, whose portrayal of petty middle-class corruption in Rome is interpreted by many as a criticism of Italian society under Benito Mussolini. The government has persuaded the literary establishment to avoid references to real problems and issues and the Moravia novel creates a sensation. *Les Enfants Terribles* by French novelist Jean Cocteau, 40; *All Quiet on the Western Front* (*Im Westen nichts Neues*) by German novelist Erich Maria Remarque, 30, whose novel sells 2.5 million copies in 25 languages in 18 months; *Look Homeward, Angel* by NYU English instructor Thomas Clayton Wolfe, 29, whose inchoate autobiographical typescript about the Gant (Wolfe) family of Asheville, N.C., has been organized and edited with the help of Scribner's editor Maxwell Evarts Perkins, 45, who has also been F. Scott Fitzgerald's mentor; *Sartoris* by William Faulkner who depicts the fictional town of Jefferson in the fictional Yoknapatawa County of Mississippi and begins an account of antebellum society's fall and the rise of the unscrupulous Snopes clan; *The Sound and the Fury* by William Faulkner; *A Farewell to Arms* by Ernest Hemingway; *The Last September* by Irish-born English novelist Elizabeth Bowen, 30; *Living* by Henry Green; *Sido* by Colette; *Berlin-Alexanderplatz* by German novelist-psychiatrist Alfred Doblin, 51; *Wolf Solent* by John Cowper Powys; *The Innocent Voyage* by English novelist Richard Hughes, 29, whose novel will be retitled *A High Wind in Jamaica* next year and will sell upwards of 3 million copies. Hughes is credited with having written the first radio play, transmitted by the BBC in 1924 with the title "Danger," and he charms (and shocks) readers with his story of children seized by pirates en route home to England from Jamaica (Hughes has never been to the West Indies); *The Near and the Far* by English novelist L. H. (Leo Hamilton) Myers, 48; *The Fortunes of Richard Mahoney* by Australian novelist Henry Handel Richardson (Ethel Florence Roberta Richardson), 59; *I Thought of Daisy* by U.S. novelist-critic Edmund Wilson, 34; *The Magnificent Obsession* by U.S. novelist Lloyd Douglas, 52; *Dodsworth* by Sinclair Lewis; *Dawn Ginsbergh's Revenge* (magazine pieces) by New York humorist S. J. (Sidney Joseph) Perelman, 25; *Claudia* by U.S. novelist Rose Franken, 31; *Red Harvest* and *The Dain Curse* by former Pinkerton detective (Samuel) Dashiell Hammett, 35; *The Roman Hat Mystery* by New York advertising and publicity writers Frederick Dannay and Manfred Bennington Lee, both 29, who write under the name Ellery Queen.

Poetry *Blind Fireworks* by Irish poet Louis Mac-Neice, 22, expresses social protect; *Poets, Farewell* by Edmund Wilson.

Painting *Woman in Armchair* by Pablo Picasso; *Fool in a Trance* by Paul Klee; *Love Idyll* by Marc Chagall; *Composition with Yellow and Blue* by Piet Mondrian; *Sailing Boats* by Lyonel Feininger; *Black Flower and Blue Larkspur* by Georgia O'Keeffe; *Cotton Pickers* (*Georgia*) by Thomas Hart Benton; *John B. Turner—Pioneer* and *Woman with Plants* (a portrait of his mother) by Iowa genre painter Grant Develson Wood, 37; Robert Henri dies at New York July 12 at age 64.

New York's Museum of Modern Art opens November 8 on the 12th floor of the Hecksher building at 730 Fifth Avenue with an exhibition of works by the late French impressionists Paul Cezanne, Paul Gauguin, Georges Seurat, and Vincent Van Gogh. Director of the museum is Alfred H. Barr, Jr., 27, who will be its guiding spirit for some 38 years (*see* 1939).

Eastman Kodak Company introduces 16 millimeter film with motion picture cameras and projectors for home use (*see* Kodachrome, 1935).

Theater *Street Scene* by Elmer Rice 1/10 at The Playhouse in New York, with Mary Servoss, Leo Bulgakov, Erin O'Brien Moore, Beulah Bondi, 601 perfs., Pulitzer prize; *Journey's End* by London insurance man-playwright Robert C. Sherriff, 33, 1/21 at London's Savoy Theatre, 594 perfs. (Sherriff served as a lieutenant at Vimy Ridge in the East Surrey Regiment's Ninth Batallion, his play fills audiences with the horror of wartime trench life, and it is staged in Paris, Berlin, and New York); *Dynamo* by Eugene O'Neill 2/11 at New York's Martin Beck Theater, with Dudley Digges, Glenn Anders, Helen Wylie, Claudette Colbert, 50 perfs.; *The Bedbug* (*Klop*) by Vladimir Mayakofsky 2/13 at Moscow's Meyerbold Theater; *Marius* by Marcel Pagnol 3/9 in Paris, with Raimu as Cesar, Pierre Fresnay as Marius; *Strictly Dishonorable* by U.S. playwright Preston Sturges 9/18 at New York's Alvin Theater with Muriel Kirkland who falls ill in December and is replaced by Antoinette Perry's 17-year-old daughter Marguerite Perry, 557 perfs.; *The Silver Tassle* by Sean O'Casey 10/11 at London's Apollo Theatre; *Berkeley Square* by John L. Baldridge 11/4 at New York's Lyceum Theater, with Leslie Howard, Margalo Gillmore, 229 perfs.; *Amphitryon '38* by French playwright Jean Giraudoux, 47, 11/8 at the Comédie des Champs-Elysées, Paris.

Radio drama *The Goldbergs* 11/20 with Gertrude Berg, 30, in the role of Molly Goldberg in a series initially titled *The Rise of the Goldbergs* (see 1949).

Warner Brothers Company acquires the Stanley Company of America to gain control of some 250 U.S. theater outlets and free itself of distribution worries (see 1918; *The Jazz Singer*, 1927).

Films Josef von Sternberg's *The Blue Angel* with Marlene Dietrich, Emil Jannings (Dietrich's song "Falling in Love Again" was composed by Friedrich Hollander, 33, who will emigrate to Hollywood); G. W. Pabst's *Pandora's Box* with Louise Brooks; Vsevelod I. Pudovkin's *Storm over Asia* with Valeri Inkizhinov, A. Dedintsev in a story about the British Army's attempt to take over Mongolia (silent); Alfred E. Green's *Disraeli* with George Arliss, Joan Bennett; William Wellman's *Wings* with Gary Cooper; Victor Fleming's *The Virginian* with Gary Cooper, Walter Huston; Merian C. Cooper and Ernst B. Schoedsack's *The Four Feathers* with Richard Arlen, Fay Wray, Clive Brook, William Powell; Alan Dwan's *The Iron Mask* with Douglas Fairbanks; Sidney Franklin's *Wild Orchids* with Greta Garbo; Lionel Barrymore's *His Glorious Night* with John Gilbert whose silent screen lover image is destroyed when audiences hear his tenor actor voice; Alfred Suntell's *The Cocoanuts* with the Marx Brothers.

Hollywood musicals Roy Del Ruth's *The Desert Song* is the first "all-talking and singing operetta"; Henry Beaumont's *The Broadway Melody* ("100% All Talking + All Singing + All Dancing!") with George M. Cohan's 1904 song "Give My Regards to Broadway," songs by Irving Thalberg protegés Nacio Herb Brown, 33, and Arthur Freed (originally Grossman), 35, that include "You Were Meant for Me" and "The Wedding of the Painted Doll" (a color sequence helps the film gross $4 million for M-G-M at a time when motion picture theater admission prices average 35 cents); Charles Riesner's *Hollywood Revue of 1929* with Conrad Nagel, Jack Benny, Rudy Vallee, Joan Crawford, Norma Shearer, John Gilbert, John Barrymore, Marie Dressler, Marion Davies, Buster Keaton, Nacio Herb Brown-Arthur Freed songs that include "Singin' in the Rain," some sequences in Technicolor (the musical numbers are recorded first and then synchronized to the action on the screen rather than recorded directly on the sound track as in *The Broadway Melody*, above); King Vidor's *Hallelujah* with an all-black cast (theaters in the South refuse to show the film) and with Irving Berlin songs that include "The End of the Road," "Swanee Shuffle"; *Innocents of Paris* with Maurice Chevalier singing "Louise" by Jack Whiting, lyrics by Leo Robin; Ernst Lubitsch's *The Love Parade* with Maurice Chevalier and Jeanette MacDonald singing "Dream Lover" and "The March of the Grenadiers" by Victor Schertzinger; Rouben Mamoulian's *Applause* with Helen Morgan; Roy Del Ruth's *The Gold Diggers of Broadway* with songs that include "Tip Toe Through the Tulips" and

"Painting the Clouds with Sunshine" by Joe Burke, 45, lyrics by Al Dubin, 38; Charles King's *Chasing Rainbows* with songs by Jack Yellen that include "Happy Days Are Here Again!" (the song will be used as the theme for Franklin D. Roosevelt's 1936 presidential campaign); W. S. Van Dyke's *The Pagan* with Ramon Novarro, music by Nacio Herb Brown, lyrics by Arthur Freed, songs that include "Pagan Love Song"; David Butler's *Sunny Side Up* with Janet Gaynor, Charles Farrell, music by Ray Henderson, lyrics by B. G. DeSylva and Lew Brown, songs that include "I'm a Dreamer," "If I Had a Talking Picture of You," and the title song.

Stage musicals *Follow Thru* 1/9 at New York's 46th Street Theater, with Jack Haley, Irene Delroy, music by Ray Henderson, lyrics by B. G. DeSylva and Lew Brown, songs that include "Button up Your Overcoat," 403 perfs.; *Spring Is Here* 3/11 at New York's Alvin Theater, with Glenn Hunter, music by Richard Rodgers, lyrics by Lorenz Hart, songs that include "With a Song in My Heart," 104 perfs.; *Sing for Your Supper* 4/24 at New York's Adelphi Theater, with Earl Robinson, music by Lee Warner and Ned Lieber, lyrics by Robert Sous, songs that include "Ballad for Americans," 60 perfs.; *The Little Show* 4/30 at New York's Music Box Theater, with Fred Allen, Portland Hoffa, Libby Holman, Bettina Hall, Peggy Conklin, Clifton Webb, Romney Brent, music by Arthur Schwartz and others, lyrics by Howard Dietz, songs that include "I Guess I'll Have to Change My Plan," "Moanin' Low" (music by Ralph Rainger), "Caught in the Rain" (music by Henry Sullivan), "Can't We Be Friends" (music by Kay Swift), 321 perfs.; *Hot Chocolates* 6/20 at New York's Hudson Theater, with Louis Armstrong in an all-black revue, songs that include "Ain't Misbehavin'" by Thomas "Fats" Waller and Henry Brooks, lyrics by Andy Razaf, 219 perfs.; *Show Girl* 7/2 at New York's Ziegfeld Theater, with Ruby Keeler, Jimmy Durante, Duke Ellington and his Orchestra, music by George Gershwin that includes the ballet "An American in Paris," lyrics by Ira Gershwin and Gus Kahn, songs that include "Liza" sung by Al Jolsen in the audience to his wife Ruby Keeler onstage, 111 perfs.; *Bitter Sweet* 7/18 at His Majesty's Theatre, London, with Peggy Wood, book, music, and lyrics by Noel Coward, songs that include "I'll See You Again," "Zigeuner," 697 perfs.; *Sweet Adeline* 9/3 at New York's Hammerstein Theater, with Helen Morgan as Addie Schmidt, music by Jerome Kern, book and lyrics by Oscar Hammerstein II, songs that include "Why Was I Born," "Don't Ever Leave Me," "Here Am I," 234 perfs.; *George White's Scandals* 9/23 at New York's Apollo Theater, with Willie Howard, songs by Irving Caesar, George White, and Cliff Friend, 161 perfs.; *June Moon* 10/9 at New York's Broadhurst Theater, with book by George S. Kaufman and Ring Lardner, music and lyrics by Lardner, 273 perfs.; *Fifty Million Frenchmen* 11/27 at New York's Lyric Theater, with William Gaxton, music and lyrics by Cole Porter, songs that include "You Do

"His Master's Voice" stopped winding down as electricity made the wind-up gramophone obsolete.

Something to Me," 254 perfs.; *Wake Up and Dream* 12/30 at New York's Selwyn Theater, with Jack Buchanan, music and lyrics by Cole Porter, songs that include "I'm a Gigolo," "What Is this Thing Called Love?" 136 perfs.

The Chicago Civic Opera building completed at 20 West Wacker Drive has a 3,800-seat auditorium to challenge the Chicago Auditorium that opened late in 1889. The building also has a penthouse suite for utility magnate Samuel Insull (*see* 1932).

Opera *Sir John in Love* 3/21 at London's Royal College of Music, with music by Ralph Vaughan Williams that includes "Fantasia on Greensleeves"; *The Gambler* 4/29 at the Théâtre Royal de la Monnaie, Brussels, with music by Serge Prokofiev, libretto from the Dostoievski novel of 1866; *Happy End* 8/31 at Berlin's Theater am Schiffbauerdamm, with music by Kurt Weill, book and lyrics by Bertolt Brecht.

Ballet *The Prodigal Son* 5/21 at the Sarah Bernhardt Theater, Paris, with the Ballet Russe, music by Serge Prokofiev.

First performances Symphony No. 3 by Serge Prokofiev 5/17 at Paris; *Amazonas* (Symphonic Poem) by Heitor Villa-Lobos 5/30 at Paris; Concerto for Viola and Orchestra by William Walton 10/3 at London, with Paul Hindemith as soloist; Concerto for Viola and Orchestra by Darius Milhaud 12/18 at Amsterdam; Symphony for Chamber Orchestra by Anton von Webern 12/18 at New York's Town Hall.

Guy Lombardo and his Royal Canadians open at New York's Roosevelt Hotel where the group directed by Canadian-American bandleader Guy Albert Lombardo, 27, will play dance music each winter for decades. A December 31 radio broadcast begins a national New Year's Eve tradition.

Popular songs "Stardust" by Hoagy (Hoagland) Carmichael, 29, lyrics by Mitchell Parish; "St. James Infirmary" by Joe Primrose; "Honeysuckle Rose" by Thomas "Fats" Waller, 25, lyrics by Andy Razaf; "Siboney," "Say Si Si," "Blue Night," and "Two Hearts that Pass in the Night" by Cuban composer Ernesto Lecuona who has written them all January 6; "Just a Gigolo" by Italian composer Leonello Casucci, English lyrics by Irving Caesar.

The Orthophonic phonograph developed by Western Electric Company engineer H. C. Harrison is an improved electric gramophone that will replace wind-up mechanical record players.

English racetrack bookmakers at Newmarket rage at the installation of a totalizator that gives odds 40 percent longer than those offered by the bookies. Invented by Australian engineer J. Cruickshank, the tote introduces pari-mutuel betting and will be installed at U.S. tracks beginning in 1931 by British Automatic Totalisator, Ltd.

Australian cricketer Donald G. Bradman achieves a world record by scoring 452 not out.

Connie Mack's Philadelphia Athletics win the World Series by defeating the Chicago Cubs 4 games to 1.

The football used in U.S. intercollegiate championship play is reduced in girth to 22 to 22½ inches.

Yale sophomore Albert James "Albie" Booth comes off the bench October 26 with Army leading 13 to 0 and carries the ball 33 times to score 21 points and upset the Black Knights. "Little Boy Blue" stands only 5-feet 6-inches and weighs 144 pounds but 80,-000 spectators hail his prowess and Booth begins a career that will make him a football legend.

The Japanese Mah-jongg Association is founded as the Chinese game gains popularity.

Williams Electronics Co. has its beginnings in a pinball machine company founded by U.S. entrepreneur Harry Williams, 24, who will invent the "tilt" mechanism that makes the machine go dead temporarily when a player nudges it too hard. Williams will also invent the kickout hole and will make his machines "talk" with bells and gongs.

The first crease-resistant cotton fabric is introduced by Tootal's of St. Helens, England.

Nestle Colorinse is introduced in 10 shades. It is the first home-applied hair coloring and one shade is a blue-grey that will be popular among elderly women (*see* permanent wave, 1906; Clairol, 1931).

Federated Department Stores is created by a loose confederation of three stores put together by Columbus, Ohio, retailer Fred Lazarus, Jr., 44, of the 78-year-old firm Lazarus Brothers. Brooklyn's 36-year-old Abraham & Straus and the 48-year-old Boston store Filene's join with Lazarus Brothers in the chain that will be joined next year by the 57-year-old New York store Bloomingdale's and thereafter by Shillito's of Cincinnati, Rikes of Dayton, the Boston Store of Milwaukee, Goldsmith's of Memphis, Feley's of Houston (1951), Burdine's of Miami (1956), Sanger-Harris of Dallas, Levy's of Tucson, Bullock's and I. Magnin in California, and other stores that will make Federated the largest U.S. store chain.

Filene's (above) acquires an adjoining building to give it an entire Boston city block bounded by Washington, Summer, Hawley, and Franklin Streets.

Newark's 36-year-old Bamberger's department store has sales of $35 million and is taken over by New York's R. H. Macy Company following the death of Bamberger partner Felix Fuld (*see* Institute of Advanced Study, 1930; Davison-Paxon, 1925; O'Connor Moffat, 1945).

Gimbel Brothers has combined sales of $124 million, up from $17 million in 1907 (*see* Saks, 1924).

New York's Chanin building is completed at 122 East 42nd Street by builder Irwin S. Chanin. The building towers 56 stories above Grand Central Station.

New York's 34-story New York Central building is completed north of Grand Central at 46th Street on Park Avenue (*see* Pan Am Building, 1963).

New York's 39-story Fuller building is completed at East 57th Street and Madison Avenue.

New York's Riverside Church is completed on Riverside Drive at 122nd Street.

New York's Temple Emmanuel is completed on Fifth Avenue at 65th Street.

Chicago's 40-story Union Carbide and Carbon building is completed at 200 North Michigan Avenue.

The *Chicago Daily News* building completed over a railroad right of way by Holabird and Root at 400 West Madison Street is a $10 million Indiana limestone structure.

The 32-story Foshay Tower at Minneapolis is completed by utility magnate Wilbur F. Foshay, 48, whose $25 million 12-state utility empire goes into receivership in November. A sign over Foshay's desk reads, "Why worry? It won't last. Nothing ever does." (Foshay will be sentenced to 15 years at Leavenworth Penitentiary for misrepresenting his earnings, but by 1931 he will be vice president of a Colorado granite company owned by Chicago drugstore magnate Charles Walgreen.)

Brooklyn's Williamsburgh Savings Bank "Tower of Strength" is completed for the 78-year-old savings institution. It will remain Brooklyn's tallest building for more than half a century.

American Radiator & Standard Sanitary Corporation is created by a merger of New York's American Radiator Company and Pittsburgh's Standard Sanitary Manufacturing Company to join the world's two leading companies in their respective fields. The merger has been engineered by American Radiator's Clarence Mott Woolley, 64, who has spent 43 years promoting cast-iron radiators both in Europe and in the United States and who acquires C. F. Church Manufacturing Company, a maker of toilet seats.

Harvard College receives a $13 million gift for construction of undergraduate residential houses from Standard Oil magnate Edward S. Harkness whose father Stephen Harkness financed John D. Rockefeller in 1870 and who has earlier gifted Yale with funds for undergraduate housing. Eliot, Lowell, Kirkland, Leverett, Winthrop, and Dunster Houses will be built in the next few years with Harkness money.

New York's 740 Park Avenue luxury apartment house is completed at 71st Street by Rosario Candela with a 34-room four-floor apartment for John D. Rockefeller complete with gymnasium, billiard room, and accommodations for five live-in servants.

New York's 1185 Park Avenue apartment house is completed between 92nd and 93rd Streets. The opulent residential block has a large inner courtyard.

New York's Carlyle Hotel opens on Madison Avenue at 76th Street.

Brooklyn's St. George Hotel gets a 31-story tower that gives it a total of 2,600 rooms and the world's largest swimming pool (120 by 40 feet with slightly salty water).

Philadelphia's Barclay Hotel opens in Rittenhouse Square. The 200-room Barclay will be the city's most elegant hotel.

Toronto's Royal York Hotel opens.

Paris gets a new luxury hotel as the George V opens on the Champs Elysées.

Prague's Cathedral of St. Vitus is completed after 585 years of construction.

The Tugendhat house at Brno in Czechoslovakia is completed by Mies van der Rohe, now 43, and his mistress Lilly Reich, 44.

Xanadu is completed 80 miles east of Havana, Cuba, for Irenée du Pont, 52, with high wood-beamed ceilings, seven bedrooms, and a nine-hole golf course on a 450-acre estate near Varadero Beach.

Atlantic City, N.J., opens an $8 million Convention Hall on the Boardwalk; its arena can seat 41,000.

The Barcelona chair designed by Mies van der Rohe and Lilly Reich (above) makes its debut at the German pavilion of the Barcelona Fair. The chair has a chrome steel X frame with leather-covered foam rubber cushions.

Africa's Serengeti National Park has its beginnings in a 900 square mile lion sanctuary set aside by the colonial government after complaints by professional hunters that people are going into the bush with Model T Fords to slaughter lions (*see* 1940).

One heath hen is left in America, down from 2,000 in 1916, and the male of the species seen on Martha's Vineyard has no mate. It will be extinct after 1931.

The Agricultural Marketing Act passed by Congress June 15 encourages farmers' cooperatives and provides for an advisory Federal Farm Board with $500 million in revolving funds to buy up surpluses in or-

1929 (cont.) der to maintain prices. The funds are inadequate and since farmers cannot be persuaded to produce less, farm prices continue to drop.

Half of all U.S. farm families produce less than $1,000 worth of food, fiber, or tobacco per year and 750,000 farm families produce less than $400 worth.

Signs of drought begin to appear in the U.S. Southwest and upper Great Plains (*see* 1930).

Soviet biologist Nikolai Vavilov endorses the government's push toward collectivized farms as a shortcut to scientific agriculture (*see* 1928; 1930).

Danish biochemist Carl Peter Henrik Dam, 34, finds that he can produce severe internal bleeding in chickens if he puts them on a fat-free diet (*see* vitamin K, 1935).

Harvard physician William B. Castle finds that pernicious anemia can be prevented only if the gastric juices contain an "intrinsic" factor necessary for the absorption of an "extrinsic" factor in foods (*see* Minot and Murphy, 1924; Cohn, 1926; vitamin B_{12}, 1948).

A survey in Baltimore shows that 30 percent of children have rickets. A similar study in London's East End shows that 90 percent of children have rickets (*see* Steenbock, 1923; 1927).

Consumers' Research is started at Washington, N.J., by F. J. Schlink who sets up a testing organization that will do for consumers what the Bureau of Standards does for government purchasing agents (*see* 1927). Schlink begins publication of the magazine *Consumer Bulletin* (*see* 1932).

General Mills, Inc., is created by a merger of the 63-year-old Minneapolis milling firm Washburn, Crosby Company with 26 other U.S. milling companies. General Mills is the world's largest miller.

General Foods Corporation is created out of the 34-year-old Postum Company which gets backing from Wall Street's Goldman, Sachs Trading Company to acquire Clarence Birdseye's firm and its patents for $20 million plus the Diamond Crystal Salt Company (*see* 1886; 1928; 1930).

Standard Brands, Inc., is created in a merger engineered by J. P. Morgan Company that combines Chase and Sanborn, the Fleischmann Company, and the Royal Baking Powder Company which has recently introduced Royal Gelatin Desserts to compete with Jell-O (*see* Planter's 1961).

Diamond Crystal Salt (above) is acquired by General Foods for cash plus 100,000 shares of General Foods common stock but by the time the stock transfers have been completed the value of the stock has fallen from between 70 and 75 down to 42 in the general market collapse. Under General Foods management Diamond Crystal will overproduce its slow-selling grades, it will be forced to dump thousands of tons of unsold salt into the St. Clair River, and by 1935 it will be losing nearly $500,000 per year (*see* 1953).

Kraft-Phenix Cheese Company is acquired by National Dairy Corporation for $33 million in stock and $33 million in bonds plus more than $6 million in cash (*see* 1923; 1928). Kraft-Phenix sells well over 200 million pounds of cheese—close to 40 percent of all the cheese consumed in the United States—and has sales of more than $86 million with net profits of more than $4.6 million.

Monroe Cheese Company is acquired by the Borden Company which begins to market Liederkranz on a nationwide basis (*see* 1892; 1926).

General Foods (above) contracts with Seabrook Farms to develop machines for packaging frozen produce and to produce frozen lima beans under the Birds Eye label (*see* 1925; 1931).

U.S. electric refrigerator sales top 800,000, up from 75,000 in 1925, as the average price of a refrigerator falls to $292, down from $600 in 1920. The average price will fall to $169 by 1939 and the new refrigerators will use less electricity (*see* GE, 1927).

United Fruit Company acquires Samuel Zemurray's Cuaymel Fruit Company after having acquired 22 other competitors since 1899 (*see* Honduras military coup, 1911). Now 52, Zemurray receives 300,000 shares of United Fruit Company stock with a value in November of $31.5 million and he is the largest stockholder (*see* 1932).

E. R. Durkee & Company is acquired by the Glidden Company which will begin selling all its food products under the name Durkee Famous Foods (*see* 1857; 1928; 1962).

Libby, McNeill & Libby adopts a new method of pressing tomatoes for a juice that will make Libby's Tomato Juice the world's largest-selling brand (*see* 1923). Libby packs 100,000 cases of tomato juice but the figure will jump next year to 739,000 cases and to 4.5 million in 1931 (*see* pineapple juice, 1933).

Coca-Cola Company has gross sales of $39 million and begins using the advertising theme "The Pause That Refreshes."

Seven-Up is introduced under the name Lithiated Lemon by St. Louis bottler Charles Grigg of 1920 Howdy fame who markets the highly carbonated lemon-lime soft drink in 7-ounce bottles and sells 10,500 cases (*see* 1933).

Good Humor franchiser Tom Brimer has eight of his trucks blown up after refusing to pay protection money to Chicago racketeers but the trucks are insured (*see* 1926). The resulting publicity is so good for sales that Brimer is able to pay stockholders a 25 percent dividend and one stockholder acquires a 75 percent interest in the company for $500,000.

Oscar Mayer wieners are trademarked with a yellow paper ring on every fourth wiener to break the tradition of anonymity in meat sales (*see* 1883). The company will develop a machine in 1944 that will encircle each wiener with the yellow band bearing the Oscar Mayer name.

Daniel Gerber begins selling strained baby foods through grocery stores (*see* 1928). Using leads supplied by mail-order customers, Gerber salesmen drive cars whose horns play "Rock-a-Bye Baby," they sell 590,000 cans in 1 year, and other food processors are inspired to enter the baby food market (*see* Beechnut, 1931; Libby, 1934).

A&P stores grow in number to 15,709 and the chain has sales of more than $1 billion (*see* 1912; 1937).

Grand Union operates 685 stores, has some 120 home delivery routes traveled by 1,100 salesmen, and has sales of $37 million (*see* 1872).

Boston's W. F. Schrafft & Sons merges with the Frank G. Shattuck Company which operates Schrafft's restaurants (*see* 1906; 1928; 1967).

The sex hormone "estrone" is isolated by German chemist Adolph Butenandt, 26, and U.S. biochemist Edward Adelbert Doisy, 36 (*see* androgen, 1931).

"Sanger's Clinic" is raided by New York police officers but Sanger continues to campaign for birth control (*see* 1923; International Planned Parenthood Federation, 1948).

1930 Wall Street prices break again in May and June after an early spring rally that has seen leading stocks regain between one-third and one-half their losses of last year. As more investors realize the economic realities of the business depression, stock prices begin a long decline that will carry them to new depths (*see* 1932).

U.S. unemployment passes 4 million and national income falls from $81 billion to less than $68 billion.

Economic studies that will culminate in the formulation of a Gross National Product (GNP) index of national wealth are initiated by Russian-American economist Simon Kuznets, 29, who begins teaching economic statistics at the University of Pennsylvania. The Kuznets studies will embrace national earnings, income levels, and productivity.

The Smoot-Hawley Tariff Bill is approved by Congress in a special session called by President Hoover despite a petition against the measure signed by 1,028 economists. Signed into law by President Hoover June 17, the act raises tariffs to their highest levels in history—higher even than under the Payne-Aldrich Act of 1909—and it embraces a Most Favored Nations policy first introduced in 1923. Certain nations are granted large tariff concessions under an arrangement that will continue for more than 45 years.

Other countries raise tariffs in response to the Smooth-Hawley Tariff Act (above).

A general world economic depression sets in as world trade declines, production drops, and unemployment increases.

A $230 million Public Buildings Act has been voted by Congress March 31 and a $300 million appropriation for state road-building projects has been voted April 4 to create jobs.

A Committee for Unemployment Relief is appointed by President Hoover in October. Four and one-half million Americans are unemployed, says Hoover.

$100 million to $150 million in appropriations for new public works construction is requested by President Hoover December 2 in his message to Congress and a $116 million public works bill is passed by Congress December 20.

More than 1,300 banks close during the year. New York's Bank of the United States with 60 branches and 400,000 depositors closes December 11.

New York's Chase National Bank becomes the world's largest by merging with the Equitable Trust Company and with Interstate Trust to create a bank with deposits of more than $2 billion and resources of nearly $3 billion, but Chase will be surpassed by A. P. Giannini's Bank of America (*see* 1928; 1955).

The W. K. Kellogg Foundation is established at Battle Creek, Mich., by breakfast food pioneer William Keith Kellogg who retired last year from the presidency of the W. K. Kellogg Company (*see* 1906; 1951).

A London Naval Conference convenes January 21 and ends 3 months later with a treaty signed by Britain, the United States, France, Italy, and Japan who agree to limit submarine tonnage and gun-caliber and to scrap certain warships. Japanese militarist factions attack government policy in signing the treaty (*see* below; 1931).

Spanish dictator Miguel Primo de Rivera resigns January 28 for reasons of health and dies March 16 at age 59 after having ruled the country since September of 1923. Spanish students agitate for a republic and the monarchy of Alfonso XIII is denounced (*see* 1931).

The Ethiopian empress Zanditu dies April 2 after a troubled reign of 14 years and is succeeded by the 39-year-old Ras Tafari who took the name Haile Selassie when he was proclaimed king (negus) in June of 1928. He is proclaimed king of kings November 2 with the title Haile Selassie I (*see* 1935).

Italy's Benito Mussolini comes out May 24 in favor of revising the Versailles Treaty.

Romania's king Michael is removed from the throne June 8 after a 3-year reign and is succeeded by his father who has returned from exile June 6 and who begins a 10-year reign as Carol II at age 37. The new king has electrified the country by arriving from Paris by airplane and he is soon joined by his 26-year-old mistress Magda Lupescu who will have great influence on Carol.

The last Allied troops leave the Rhineland June 30.

Constantinople is renamed Istanbul and Angora is renamed Ankara by the Turkish president Mustafa Kemal (*see* 1923; 1935).

Peru's president Augusto Leguia resigns August 25 and flees the country after 11 years in office. Colonel Luis Sanchez Cerro has led a military revolt and will be elected president next year but will be assassinated at the end of April, 1933.

1930 (cont.) Argentina has a revolution September 5. President Hipolito Irigoyen who served in that office from 1916 to 1922 was elected again in 1928 but he is driven from the presidency by the 62-year-old José Francisco Uriburu who brings the country's big landowners and business interests back to power after 14 years of social reform.

Brazil has a revolution in October led by the governor of Rio Grande do Sul Getulio Dornelles Vargas, 47, who accepts the presidency October 26 and forces Washington Luis Pereira de Souza to resign 4 days later. Vargas will be dictator of Brazil until 1945.

The Japanese prime minister Yuko Hamaguchi who has supported acceptance of the London Naval Conference program (above) is shot by assassins November 14 and will die in May of next year (see 1931).

The last Allied troops leave the Saar December 12 (see 1935).

Slavery in Liberia is reported March 8 by a U.S.-League of Nations commission.

A civil disobedience campaign against the British in India begins March 12 under the leadership of Mahatma Gandhi who has been empowered by the All-India Trade Union Congress to begin the demonstrations (see 1914). Called Mahatma (meaning greatsouled, or sage) for the past decade, Gandhi leads a 165-mile march to the Gujurat Coast on India's Arabian Sea and produces salt by evaporation of seawater in violation of the law as a gesture of defiance against the British monopoly on salt production.

France enacts a workmen's insurance law April 30.

South Africa's white women are given the vote May 19 but blacks of both sexes remain disenfranchised.

A halt in Jewish immigration to Palestine so long as unemployment persists among the Arabs is suggested October 20 in the Passfield Paper on Palestine presented by the British secretary for colonies Sidney James Webb, 71, first baron Passfield (see Balfour Declaration, 1917; White Paper, 1939).

The Institute for Advanced Study at Princeton University is established with an initial endowment of $5 million from department store magnate Louis Bamberger, now 75, and his sister Mrs. Felix Fuld. They have been urged by Abraham Flexner of 1910 Flexner Report fame to charter a new type of institution dedicated to "the usefulness of useless knowledge" and it will attract such minds as Albert Einstein, Thorstein Veblen, J. Robert Oppenheimer, Wolfgang Pauli, and John Von Neumann.

The planet Pluto is discovered March 18 by astronomers at the Lowell Observatory in Flagstaff, Ariz., who give the ninth planet its name.

Chicago's Adler Planetarium opens with a projector manufactured by Germany's Carl Zeiss Corporation. First planetarium in the Western Hemisphere, it has been built with a gift from local merchant Max Adler.

The first analog computer is placed in operation by Vannevar Bush and some associates who have de-vised a "differential analyzer" (see Babbage, 1833 1842; Bush, 1922; Mark I, 1944).

Plexiglass is invented by McGill University research student William Chalmers whose thermoplastic polymer of methyl methacrylate is light in weight and can be bent when heated into any shape desired It will be marketed in Britain as Perspex.

Dow Chemical Company produces more than a million pounds of magnesium (see Ethyl, 1924). The price of magnesium has dropped to 48 cents per pound, down from $5 in 1917 when it was widely used in flares to illuminate battlefields.

Rastafarians in Jamaica, British West Indies, hail the new Ethiopian emperor Haile Selassie (above) as the living God, the fulfillment of a prophesy by Marcus M. Garvey who is said to have declared, "Look to Africa, where a black king shall be crowned, for the day of deliverance is near" (see Garvey, 1924). Members of the new sect will withdraw from Jamaican society, they will call white religion a rejection of black culture, they will insist that blacks must leave "Babylon" (the Western world) and return to Africa they will contribute to Jamaican culture (notably to the island's reggae music), but Rasta extremists will traffic in ganja (marijuana) and will engage in acts of violence.

United Airlines is created by a merger of Boeing Transport with National Air Transport. United uses Ford Tri-Motor planes to cut flying time from New York to San Francisco to 28 hours.

Transcontinental and Western Air (TWA) is created by a merger and receives a government mail contract (see 1926; Hughes, 1939).

American Airlines has its beginnings in American Airways founded by Auburn motorcar maker Erret Cord who merges Robertson Aircraft with other small firms (see Lindbergh, 1926). Needing 20 single-engine, 12-place planes for a Midwest shuttle service Cord starts Airplane Development Corporation to produce the planes, he places his brother-in-law Donald Smith in charge, and Smith hires Gerard Vultee from Lockheed and sets him up in a small hangar at Grand Central Airport, Los Angeles (see Vultee 1928; Cord Corp., American Airlines, 1934).

The first airline stewardess begins work in mid-May for United Airlines (above). Boeing Air Transport agent Steve Stimpson at San Francisco has suggested that commercial aircraft carry "young women as couriers," United has hired Ellen Church and told the registered nurse and student pilot to hire seven other nurses—all aged 25, all single, no more than 5-feet 4-inches tall and 115 pounds with pleasant personalities—and they serve cold meals and beverages pass out candy and chewing gum, and comfort airsick passengers. Women cabin attendants will serve to help allay public fears of flying.

Braniff Airways is founded with a route from Tulsa Oklahoma City to Wichita Falls, Tex. Oklahoma in surance man Tom E. Braniff, 46, backed his younger brother Paul 2 years ago in starting an air service to carry passengers at low rates over the 116-mile route between Tulsa and Oklahoma City, he sold the failing airline last year after extending service to Kansas and Missouri, he has founded the new airline that he will expand to reach Kansas City early next year, and Braniff Airways will grow to cover the Southwest with routes to South America.

Pan American Airways begins flights to South America (*see* 1929; 1935).

National Airlines has its beginnings in the National Airlines Taxi Service started by Chicago aircraft distributor George T. Baker, 29, who will obtain a 142-mile Florida airmail route between St. Petersburg and Daytona Beach in 1934. Baker will shorten his company name to National Airlines in 1937 and he will get a Miami to Jacksonville route in 1938.

By year's end three transcontinental air routes are in service but passenger flights are irregular (*see* American's Mercury flight, 1936).

Wiley Post, 31, wins the first Bendix Trophy Air Race flying the *Winnie Mae* owned by his Oklahoma oilman employer Floyd C. Hall. Bendix has offered a prize for the winner of the Los Angeles to Chicago race that will become a transcontinental race beginning next year (*see* Bendix, 1929; Post, 1931).

British aviatrix Amy Johnson, 27, arrives in Australia May 24 after making the first solo flight by a woman from London. She follows the 19½ day flight with a record 6-day solo flight from England to India.

The British dirigible R101 burns October 5 northwest of Paris at Beauvais on her maiden voyage to Australia. The disaster takes 54 lives.

Aristotle Socrates Onassis buys six freighters for $20,000 each as the worldwide economic depression reduces demand for cargo vessels. Built for the Canadian National Railways at $2 million each, the freighters will serve as the nucleus of a large fleet for the shrewd 29-year-old Greek tobacco and shipping millionaire. He will buy his first tanker in 1935, he will increase his tanker fleet until he has 50 that include 15 supertankers capable of carrying more than 200,000 tons each, and he will build a shipping, whaling, airline, and real estate empire of more than $600 million (*see* Olympic Airways, 1957).

Pittston Corp. is founded in January by Erie Railroad stockholders who have paid $20 million to acquire the anthracite carrier from Cleveland's Van Sweringen brothers (who had acquired the Erie with backing from J. P. Morgan & Co.).

General Motors Corporation acquires two locomotive manufacturing companies that will give GM a virtual monopoly in the market (*see* 1961).

An electric passenger train travels on Delaware and Lackawanna tracks between Hoboken and Montclair, N.J., in a test run by Thomas Edison, now 84, who will die next year.

Atlanta's Union Station opens April 18 at Pryor and Wall streets.

The first South American subway line opens October 18 at Buenos Aires. The Lacroze line of the Ferrocarril Terminal Central de Buenos Aires has been built by 3,000 men in 21 months (*see* Mexico City, 1970).

The Oakland-Alameida Tunnel opens to traffic under San Francisco Bay.

The Detroit-Windsor Tunnel opens to traffic under the Detroit River November 3 to supplement the Ambassador Bridge that opened in November of last year. Like the Oakland-Alameida Tunnel (above), it has been built of prefabricated tubes floated over a trench and sunk like sections of pipeline.

The Longview Bridge opens to span the Columbia River in Washington State with 366 meters of cantilevered steel.

The Mid-Hudson Bridge opens at Poughkeepsie, N.Y., to span the Hudson. Builder of the suspension bridge is Polish-American engineer Ralph Modjeski, 69, who has gained a reputation with the McKinley Bridge at St. Louis, the Broadway Bridge at Portland, Ore., and other bridges including some at Chicago. He will complete the Huey P. Long Bridge in 1935.

U.S. motorcar sales drop off sharply but the country has an average of one passenger car for every 5.5 persons, up from one for every 13 in 1920. Ford sells 1 million Model A's, down from 2 million last year. Chevrolet sales drop only 5 percent.

Japan has 50,000 motorcars as compared with 23 million in the United States, 18,000 in China, 125,000 in India, 4,822 in Syria.

The United States has 694,000 miles of paved road, up from 387,000 in 1921, plus 2.31 million miles of dirt road (*see* 1940).

A 16-cylinder Cadillac is introduced by General Motors Corporation whose founder is sold out by his bankers as Wall Street prices collapse once again. W. C. Durant of 1922 Star fame liquidated his fortune in common stocks early last year but he plunged back into the market when prices plummeted, his Durant Motors, Inc., will be liquidated in 1933, and Durant will be personally bankrupt by 1936.

Free-wheeling is introduced by Studebaker Corp.

Electric Auto-Lite Company merges with Motor Meter Gauge & Equipment Company and becomes a major supplier of ignition systems to Chrysler Corporation (*see* 1911; Plymouth, De Soto, 1928). Chrysler has been embarrassed at having to buy its electrical equipment from GM's Delco-Remy division.

 U.S. gasoline consumption rises to nearly 16 billion gallons, up from 2.5 billion in 1919.

World oil prices collapse after wildcatter Columbus M. Joiner, 71, brings in a gusher October 3 in Rusk County, eastern Texas, to open a huge new oilfield. Joiner will sell out to H. L. Hunt for $40,000 in

1930 (cont.) cash, $45,000 in short-term notes, and a guarantee of $1.2 million from future profits, his field will produce at least 3.6 billion barrels of oil, and it will make H. L. Hunt the richest man in America (see 1920; 1936).

The protein-splitting enzymes pepsin, trypsin, and chymotrypsin are crystallized by Rockefeller Institute biochemists John Ward Northrup, 39, and Moses Kunitz (see Schwann, 1835; chymotrypsin, 1935).

The Human Mind by Menninger Clinic psychiatrist Karl Menninger explains that psychiatry is a legitimate and relatively uncomplicated source of help for mentally disturbed persons, it popularizes a previously arcane subject, and although written for medical students it finds a wide market (see 1925).

Tincture of merthiolate is introduced by Eli Lilly Company and quickly gains widespread popularity for painting cuts and scratches although it had no success until given a little alcohol to make it sting and some vegetable dye to make it show on the skin.

Lederle Laboratories is acquired by American Cyanamid Company (see 1907). The firm will be a major producer of biological vaccines and serums, vitamin products, and veterinary products such as hog cholera serum and a vaccine effective against equine encephalitis ("blind staggers") (see 1938).

Old Dominion University is founded at Norfolk, Va.

Brooklyn College is founded at Brooklyn, N.Y.

Some 4.3 percent of Americans are illiterate, down from 20 percent in 1870. The figure will fall to 2.4 percent in the next 30 years but nearly 5 million Americans will remain illiterate.

U.S. radio set sales increase to 13.5 million, up from 75,000 in 1921. U.S. advertisers spend $60 million on radio commercials (see 1922; FCC, 1934).

Lowell Thomas begins a nightly radio network news program September 29. The program will run on both NBC and CBS for a year, NBC will carry it from 1931 to 1946; CBS will carry it from 1946 until May 14, 1976 (see 1924).

McCann-Erickson, Inc., is created by a merger of the H. K. McCann Company with the Erickson Company. Harrison King McCann, 50, is president, A. W. Erickson is board chairman, the new advertising agency has its headquarters at New York.

The *Daily Worker* begins publication at London. The Communist Party organ will continue until 1941.

Fortune magazine is launched by Henry R. Luce of *Time* whose new monthly business magazine has 182 pages in its first issue and sells at newsstands for $1 ($10 per year by subscription) (see 1923; 1936).

William Randolph Hearst owns 33 U.S. newspapers whose circulation totals 11 million.

"Blondie" is introduced by King Features comic strip cartoonist Murat Bernard "Chic" Young, 29, who earlier drew a strip called "Dumb Dora." His jazz-age flapper heroine is married to playboy Dagwood Bumstead, their antics will make "Blondie" the most widely syndicated of all cartoon strips, more than 1,600 U.S. newspapers plus some foreign papers will carry the strip, and the huge sandwiches created by Bumstead on evening forays to the refrigerator will become widely known as "dagwoods."

Nonfiction *The Revolt of the Masses* (*La rebelion de las masas*) by Ortega y Gasset, who has sought the historical basis for modern social ills but who tends toward rhetoric and oversimplification; *Bring 'Em Back Alive* by U.S. zoo and circus supplier Frank Buck, 46, who has been making expeditions since 1911 to capture wild birds and animals.

Fiction "Machine" ("Kikai") by Japanese short story writer Riichi Yokomitsu, 32, for whom the 1923 Tokyo earthquake is a symbol of the machine culture and of modern utilitarianism; *East Wind, West Wind* by U.S. novelist Pearl Comfort Sydenstricker Buck, 38, who was raised in China by her Presbyterian missionary parents and who wrote the book while aboard ship headed for America; *Mitsou* by Colette; *Flowering Judas* (short stories) by U.S. author Katherine Anne Porter, 40; *A Room of One's Own* by Virginia Woolf who champions the cause of independence for women; *Brief Candles* by Aldous Huxley; *As I Lay Dying* by William Faulkner; *The Apes of God* by Wyndham Lewis; *Thy Servant a Dog* (stories) by Rudyard Kipling; *Job* (*Hiob*) by Joseph Roth; *Laughing Boy* by U.S. novelist Oliver Hazard Perry La Farge, 28, who writes about the Navajo; *Cimarron* by Edna Ferber; *Destry Rides Again* by U.S. pulp writer Max Brand (Frederick Schiller Faust), 38, who averages roughly two books per month; *Vile Bodies* by Evelyn Waugh; *Murder at the Vicarage* by Agatha Christie whose detective Jane Marple will appear in 14 other mystery novels; *It Walks by Night* by U.S.-English detective novelist John Dickson Carr, 25, who will sometimes write as Carter Dickson or Carr Dickson; *The Maltese Falcon* by Dashiell Hammett.

Poetry *The Bridge* by Hart Crane who has taken the 47-year-old Brooklyn Bridge as a symbol of man's creative power. The book's many poems explore the essence of the American destiny, but its mixed reception contributes to the poet's growing insecurity and he will jump or fall from a ship bound for the United States from Mexico and will drown April 27, 1932; *20 Poems* by Stephen Spender; *The Cantos* by Ezra Pound (third volume); "Ash Wednesday" by T. S. Eliot is a religious poem of self-abnegation; "Spring Comes to Murray Hill" by New York poet Ogden Nash, 28, appears in the *New Yorker* magazine; Nash will soon join the magazine's staff and will be celebrated for such verses as "Candy is dandy/ But liquor is quicker," lines that will often be misattributed to Dorothy Parker.

Painting *American Gothic* by Grant Wood who portrays his sister and his dentist as rural farmfolk and helps launch the American native regionalist style; *Fall of Cuernevaca* and *Cortez and his Merce-*

naries by Diego Rivera for Mexico City's Palacio de Cortez; *Cold Buffet* by George Grosz; *Self-Portrait with Saxophone* by Max Beckmann.

Sculpture *Tiare* by Henri Matisse; *Poseidon* fountain by Carl Milles (Gothenburg); *Diana* fountain by Carl Milles (Chicago).

Kansas City's Nelson Gallery is founded with a $13 million trust fund set up by the late *Kansas City Star* editor-publisher William Rockhill Nelson who died in 1915 at age 74 (*see* 1880). The art gallery will be housed in the Nelson mansion surrounded by 20 acres of lawn, it will be noted for its Oriental collection, but the will of the late colonel stipulates that no artist's work may be purchased until the artist has been dead for at least 30 years.

A *London Graphic* writer coins the phrase "candid camera" to describe the intimate and often irreverent Leica portraits of statesmen by German photographer Erich Solomon who in 1932 will take a rare (and illegal) picture of the U.S. Supreme Court in session (*see* Leica, 1925).

Flashbulbs patented September 23 by German inventor Johannes Ostermeir are introduced 7 weeks earlier by General Electric Company. A small filament in the "flash lamp" heats up when connected to a source of electricity, the heat ignites foil inside the bulb, and the foil flashes to produce a fireless, smokeless, odorless, noiseless (but blinding) light.

Theater *Children of Darkness* by U.S. playwright Edwin Justus Mayer, 33, 1/7 at New York's Biltmore Theater; *Tonight We Improvise* (*Questa sera si recita a soggetto*) by Luigi Pirandello 1/25 at Königsberg's Neues Schauspielhaus, 4/14 at Turin's Teatro di Turino; *The Bathhouse* (*Banya*) by Vladimir Mayakovski 1/30 at Leningrad's Peoples' House, 3/16 at Moscow's Meyerhold Theater; *As You Desire Me* (*Come tu mi vuoi*) by Luigi Pirandello 2/18 at Milan's Teatro de Filodrammatici; *The Green Pastures* by Marc Connelly 2/21 at New York's Mansfield Theater, is an adaptation of a 1928 collection of tales by Roark Bradford, 34, depicting heaven, the angels, and the Lord as envisioned by a black country preacher for a Louisiana congregation, 640 perfs.; *Hotel Universe* by Philip Barry 4/14 at New York's Martin Beck Theater, with Ruth Ford, Glenn Anders, Earl Larimore, Morris Carnovsky, 81 perfs.; *Moscow Is Burning* (*Moskva gorid*) by Vladimir Mayakovski 4/21 at Moscow's Circus I (Gostsirk I); *The Barrets of Wimpole Street* by Dutch-English playwright Rudolph Besier, 52, at England's Malvern Festival (the play will open next year at New York's Empire Theater with Katherine Cornell and will run for 370 performances); *Private Lives* by Noel Coward 9/24 at London's Phoenix Theatre, with Coward, Gertrude Lawrence, Laurence Olivier, Coward's song "Someday I'll Find You," 101 perfs.; *Once in a Lifetime* by George S. Kaufman and Moss Hart 9/24 at New York's Music Box Theater, with Kaufman and Spring Byington, 401 perfs.; *The Greeks Had a Word*

for It by Zoe Akins 9/25 at New York's Sam H. Harris Theater, with Dorothy Hull, Varree Teasdale, Muriel Kirkland, 253 perfs.; *The Sailors of Cattaro* (*Die Matrosen von Cattaro*) by German playwright Friedrich Wolff, 42, 11/8 at Berlin's Lobe Theater; *Grand Hotel* by W. A. Drake who has adapted the Vicki Baum novel 11/13 at New York's National Theater, with Henry Hull, Sam Jaffee, 459 perfs.; *Alison's House* by U.S. novelist-playwright Susan Glaspell, 48, 12/1 at New York's Civic Repertory Theater, 41 perfs., Pulitzer prize.

Radio drama *The Lone Ranger* 1/20 over Detroit's WXYZ begins with the overture from the Rossini opera *Guillaume Tell* of 1829 and an announcer saying, "A fiery horse with the speed of light, a cloud of dust and a hearty 'Hi-yo Silver'—the Lone Ranger rides again." The serial has been developed from *Curly Edwards and the Cowboys* by James E. Jewell, 23, who will soon give his masked hero an Indian friend—Tonto—who will call the Lone Ranger "Kemo Sabe" (trusting brave), the name of a Michigan summer camp operated by the father of the girl Jewell will marry; *Death Valley Days* 7/30 on NBC Blue Network stations. New York advertising writer Ruth Cornwall Woodman has researched background for the show by visiting Panamint City, she introduces "The Old Ranger" to give the story authenticity, the series will move to CBS in 1941, and it will continue until 1945.

U.S. moviegoing increases as all film studios rush to make "talkies" and as a new Vitascope widens theater screens.

Films Clarence Brown's *Anna Christie* with Greta Garbo, Charles Bickford ("Garbo Talks!" say the advertisements); Richard Wallace's *The Right to Love* with Ruth Chatterton is the first picture to be shown with a new process that eliminates popping, crackling, grating, and other surface noises; D. W.

Artist Grant Wood portrayed vanishing rural archetypes in his genre painting *American Gothic*.

1930 (cont.) Griffith's *Abraham Lincoln* with Walter Huston, Una Merkel; Luis Buñuel's *L'Age d'Or;* René Clair's *Under the Roofs of Paris (Sous les Toits de Paris)* with Albert Prejean; Colin Clive's *Journey's End* with Ian Maclaren, Anthony Bushnell; Josef von Sternberg's *Morocco* with Marlene Dietrich, Gary Cooper, Adolphe Menjou; Howard Hawks's *The Dawn Patrol* with Richard Barthelmess, Douglas Fairbanks, Jr.; Howard Hughes's *Hell's Angels* with Ben Lyon, Jean Harlow; Lewis Milestone's *All Quiet on the Western Front* with Lew Ayres; Robert Milton's *Outward Bound* with Leslie Howard, Beryl Mercer, Douglas Fairbanks, Jr.; Frank Borzage's *Liliom* with Charles Farrell; Alfred Hitchcock's *Murder* with Herbert Marshall, Norah Baring; Raoul Walsh's *The Big Trail* with John Wayne; Mervyn Le-Roy's *Little Caesar* with Edward G. Robinson; George Hill's *The Big House* with Wallace Beery, Chester Morris; Henry King's *Lightnin'* with Will Rogers, Louise Dresser, Joel McCrea; John Cromwell's *Tom Sawyer* with Jackie Coogan; George Hill's *Min and Bill* with Wallace Beery, Marie Dressler; Alfred E. Green's *Old English* with George Arliss; Lloyd Bacon's *Moby Dick* with John Barrymore, Joan Bennett; Roy Del Ruth's *Three Faces East* with Erich von Stroheim, Constance Bennett; Norman McLeod's *Monkey Business* with the Marx Brothers; Victor Heerman's *Animal Crackers* with the Marx Brothers; William McGann's *On the Border* with Rin-Tin-Tin; Ross Lederman's *The Man Hunt* with John Loder, Rin-Tin-Tin.

U.S. cigarette companies produce 123 billion smokes, up from less than 9 billion in 1910. Hollywood helps make cigarette smoking seem sophisticated as film directors have actors light up to fill awkward interludes with "business."

Hollywood musicals William A. Seiter's *Sunny* with Marilyn Miller in a film version of the 1925 Broadway success; Edward H. Sloman's *Puttin' on the Ritz* with Harry Richman, Joan Bennett, songs by Irving Berlin; Ernst Lubitsch's *Monte Carlo* with Jeanette MacDonald, Jack Buchanan, music by Richard A. Whiting and W. Frank Harling, lyrics by Leo Robin, songs that include "Beyond the Blue Horizon"; Hobart Henley's *The Big Pond* with Maurice Chevalier, Claudette Colbert, music by Sammy Fain, lyrics by Irving Kahal and Pierre Norman, songs that include "You Brought a New Kind of Love to Me."

Stage musicals *Strike Up the Band* 1/14 at New York's Times Square Theater, with Bobby Clark, Red Nichols Band (which includes Benny Goodman, Gene Krupa, Glenn Miller, Jimmy Dorsey, and Jack Teagarden), music by George Gershwin, lyrics by Ira Gershwin, book by George S. Kaufman, songs that include "Soon," "I've Got a Crush on You," and the title song, 191 perfs.; *Nine-Fifteen Revue* 2/11 at New York's George M. Cohan Theater, with Ruth Etting, music by local composer Harold Arlen (*né* Hyman Azbuck), 24, lyrics by Ted Koehler, songs that include "Get Happy," 7 perfs.; *Lew Leslie's In-* *ternational Revue* 2/15 at New York's Majestic Theater, with Gertrude Lawrence, Harry Richman, music by Jimmy McHugh, lyrics by Dorothy Fields, songs that include "Exactly Like You," "On the Sunny Side of the Street," 96 perfs.; *Simple Simon* 2/18 at New York's Ziegfeld Theater, with Ed Wynn, Ruth Etting, music by Richard Rodgers, lyrics by Lorenz Hart, songs that include "Ten Cents a Dance," "I Still Believe in You," 135 perfs.; *Fine and Dandy* 9/23 at New York's Erlanger Theater, with Joe Cook, Eleanor Powell, Dave Chasen, music by Kay Swift, lyrics by Paul James (Swift's husband James Warburg), book by Donald Ogden Stewart, songs that include "Can This Be Love?" 255 perfs.; *Girl Crazy* 10/14 at New York's Alvin Theater, with Ethel Merman, music by George Gershwin, lyrics by Walter Donaldson and Ira Gershwin, songs that include "I Got Rhythm," "Embraceable You," "Little White Lies," "But Not for Me," "Bidin' My Time," 272 perfs.; *Three's a Crowd* 10/15 at New York's Selwyn Theater, with Libby Holman, Fred Allen, Clifton Webb, songs that include "Body and Soul" by Johnny Green, lyrics by Robert Sourt, 25, and Edward Heyman, 23, "Something to Remember You By" and "The Moment I Saw You" by Arthur Schwartz, lyrics by Howard Dietz, 272 perfs.; *The Garrick Gaieties* 10/16 at New York's Guild Theater with Sterling Holloway, Rosalind Russell, Imogene Coca, songs that include "I'm Only Human After All" by Russian-American composer Vernon Duke (Vladimir Dukelsky), 27, lyrics by E. Y. Harburg and Ira Gershwin, "Out of Breath and Scared to Death of You" by Johnny Mercer and Everett Miller, 158 perfs.; *Lew Leslie's Blackbirds of 1930* 10/22 at New York's Royale Theater, with Ethel Waters, Ceci Mack's Choir, songs that include "Memories of You" by Eubie Blake, lyrics by Andy Razaf, 57 perfs.; *Sweet and Low* 11/17 at New York's 46th Street Theater, with George Jessel, Fanny Brice, songs that include "Outside Looking In" by Harry Archer and Edward Ellison, "Cheerful Little Earful" by Harry Warren, Ira Gershwin, and Billy Rose, 184 perfs.; *Smiles* 11/18 at New York's Ziegfeld Theater, with Marilyn Miller, Bob Hope, Eddie Foy, Jr., Fred and Adele Astaire, songs that include "Time on My Hands" by Vincent Youmans, lyrics by Harold Adamson and Polish-American writer Mack Gordon, 26, "You're Driving Me Crazy" by Walter Donaldson, 63 perfs.; *Ever Green* 12/3 at London's Adelphi Theatre, with Jessie Matthews, music by Richard Rodgers, lyrics by Lorenz Hart, songs that include "Dancing on the Ceiling," 254 perfs.; *The New Yorkers* 12/8 at New York's Broadway Theater, with Hope Williams, Ann Pennington, Jimmy Durante, Lew Clayton, Eddie Jackson, music and lyrics by Cole Porter, songs that include "Love for Sale," "Go into Your Dance," 168 perfs.

Nazi thug Horst Wessel dies in a Berlin hospital February 23 at age 22 of blood poisoning. Painter S. Epstein, tailor Peter Stoll, and barber Hans Ziegle will be convicted of having shot Wessel the night

January 14 in a street brawl over a "Lucie of Ander-platz," the Nazis will make a martyr of Wessel, and his "Horst-Wessel-Lied," set to music plagiarized from a Hamburg waterfront ballad and containing such lines as "When Jewish blood drips off your trusted pen-knife/ We march ahead with twice as steady step," will be the Nazi anthem.

Opera *The Nose* 1/13 at Leningrad, with music by Dmitri Shostakovich (who includes an orchestral sneeze and other novel effects), libretto from a story by Nikolai Gogol; *Von heute auf morgen* (*From Today until Tomorrow*) 2/1 at Frankfurt's Municipal Theater with music by Arnold Schoenberg; *Neues vom Tage* (*The News of the Day*) 6/8 at Kroll's Theater, Berlin, with music by Paul Hindemith.

Ballet *The Golden Age* (*Zolotoy Vyek*) 10/26 at Leningrad, with music by Dmitri Shostakovich.

First performances Suite for Orchestra by Walter Piston 3/28 at Boston's Symphony Hall; Symphony No. 2 (*Romantic*) by Howard Hanson 11/28 at Boston's Symphony Hall.

Popular songs "Georgia on My Mind" by Hoagy Carmichael, lyrics by Stuart Gorrell; "When It's Sleepy Time Down South" by Leon Rene, Otis Rene, and Clarence Muse; "Sleepy Lagoon" by Eric Coates, lyrics by Jack Lawrence; "Dream a Little Dream of Me" by F. Andrée and W. Schwandt, lyrics by Gus Kahn; "Three Little Words" by Harry Ruby, lyrics by Bert Kalmar (for the film *Amos 'n' Andy*); "Walkin' My Baby Back Home" by Roy Turk, Fred E. Ahlert, Harry Richman; "Little White Lies" by Walter Donaldson; "It Happened in Monterey" by Mabel Wayne, lyrics by William Rose (for John Murray Anderson's film *King of Jazz* with Paul Whiteman); "Sing You Sinners" by Franke Harling, lyrics by Sam Coslow; "Them There Eyes" by Maceo Pinkard, William Tracey, and Doris Tauber; "I'm Confessing—That I Love You" by Doc Dougherty and Ellis Reynolds.

New York's Brill building opens at 1619 Broadway. Its 11 stories are soon occupied by Tin Pan Alley publishers and bandleaders.

The first Hambletonian Stakes trotting race is held at Good Time Park in Goshen, N.Y., to begin a harness racing tradition that will continue until 1956 when the race will be moved to Du Quoin, Ill.

Gallant Fox wins racing's Triple Crown by taking the Kentucky Derby, the Preakness, and the Belmont Stakes.

U.S. golfer Robert Tyre "Bobby" Jones, 28, wins the "Grand Slam" of golf by taking the Open and Amateur tournaments in both the United States and Great Britain.

German prizefighter Max Schmeling, 24, is fouled by U.S. heavyweight champion Jack Sharkey, 27, in the fourth round of a title bout at New York June 12. Schmeling wins the title but will lose it back to Sharkey in 1932.

The Philadelphia Athletics win the World Series by defeating the St. Louis Cardinals 4 games to 2.

The first World Cup football (soccer) competition is organized by the Fédération Internationale des Associations Football headed by France's Jules Rimet, 57. Uruguay and Argentina win the semifinals by defeating Yugoslavia and the United States; Uruguay wins the World Cup by defeating Argentina 4 to 2 in the incomplete stadium at Montevideo.

Sir Thomas Lipton's *Shamrock V* is defeated 4 to 0 by the U.S. defender *Enterprise* in Lipton's final bid to gain the America's Cup. Lipton will die next year at age 81.

Schick Dry Shaver, Inc., is founded by Colonel Jacob Schick who will begin production next year at Stamford, Conn., and will sell 3,000 of his electric shavers at $25 each (*see* 1923). Sales will reach 10,381 in 1932 and while Schick will die in July of 1937 at age 59 nearly 1.85 million of his shavers will have been sold by the end of that year.

Breck Shampoo is introduced by John H. Breck, Inc., of Springfield, Mass., whose president John H. Breck, 53, started losing his hair at an early age, developed hair preparations that he began selling in 1908, and incorporated his firm last year. Breck shampoos in three formulations for oily, dry, and normal hair will be introduced in 1933, Beautiful Hair Breck signs with pastel paintings of women will appear in 1936, and by 1939 Breck hair preparations will be sold through 15,000 beauty salons (*see* 1946).

Judge Crater disappears in early August. New York Tammany lawyer Joseph Force Crater, 41, has been appointed in April by Governor Franklin D. Roosevelt to fill an unexpired term on the New York Supreme Court, he interrupts his summer vacation to return to New York, he withdraws all the cash in his bank account (just over $5,000), he sells $16,000 worth of stocks, dines with friends, steps into a taxi in front of the restaurant, and is never heard of again.

Bonwit Teller moves into a new Fifth Avenue store at 56th Street acquired from Stewart & Company (*see* 1898). Paul Bonwit will retire in 1934 and will sell the company to Floyd Odlum of Atlas Corporation which will add two floors to the building in 1938 and will start a new 12-story addition in 1939. Hoving Corporation will buy out the Atlas interest in 1946.

F. A. O. Schwartz moves uptown from 31st Street to a large new toy store in New York's new Squibb Building (below; *see* 1870).

The Chicago Board of Trade building completed by Holabird and Roche at 141 West Jackson Boulevard towers 45 stories above the city and will be Chicago's tallest building for 40 years.

Chicago's Merchandise Mart is completed by Marshall Field and Company which will sell it to New York financier Joseph P. Kennedy in 1945. The world's largest commercial building, the $35 million Mart covers two square blocks and rises 18 stories with a 25-story tower.

1930 (cont.) Chicago's Palmolive building is completed by Holabird and Roche. The $6 million, 37-story structure is topped with a Lindbergh Beacon that flashes 500 miles out over Lake Michigan.

Cleveland's 52-story Terminal Tower building has opened January 26. The north wing of the $110 million building put up by the Van Sweringen brothers is a hotel built several years ago (*see* Nickel Plate system, 1916).

Atlanta's $1 million City Hall is completed in March by Ten Eyck Brown.

Cincinnati's Carew Tower is completed for the Mabley & Carew department store founded in 1877.

San Francisco's Royal Dutch-Shell tower is completed with 29 floors at a cost of $4 million.

Albany's Alfred E. Smith office building is completed for New York State legislators.

New York's 35-story Squibb building is completed by Ely Jacques Kahn on Fifth Avenue at 58th Street.

The *New York Daily News* building opens June 25 with 718,000 square feet of floor space. Rising 467 feet high above East 42nd Street, the skyscraper has been designed by John M. Howells, Raymond M. Hood, and J. André Fornithran.

An insulated window glass that will be marketed as Thermopane is developed by U.S. inventor C. D. Haven.

New York's San Remo Apartments designed by Emory Roth go up on Central Park West between 74th and 75th Streets.

Lefrak City raises the first of 20 18-story apartment house towers that the Lefrak Corporation will erect on 32 acres of the old Astor estate in New York's Corona, Queens, section. The all-white apartment complex with 20,000 middle-class residents will be 25 percent black by 1972 and 70 percent by 1976.

New York's 38-story Barbizon-Plaza Hotel opens May 12 at 58th Street and Sixth Avenue. The $10 million hotel has 1,400 rooms, two concert auditoriums, a glass-enclosed roof for athletics, art galleries, numerous studios for artists and sculptors, and immediate financial troubles. The value of the hotel will fall to $4.5 million by 1933 and the Barbizon will be sold that year for $2,500 in cash to a buyer who will assume the building's debts of nearly $6 million.

New York's St. Moritz Hotel opens October 1 at Central Park South and Sixth Avenue on a site formerly occupied by the New York Athletic Club. The new 35-story, 1,000-room hotel designed by Emery Roth has been erected by Harris H. and Percy Uris with a sky room restaurant. The mortgage on the hotel will be foreclosed by the Bowery Savings Bank in mid-March of 1932, but it will be acquired soon afterward by private owners for $4 million.

New York's Essex House Hotel is completed in December on Central Park South just east of the year-old New York Athletic Club at Seventh Avenue. The 45-story, 1,286-room Seville Towers (as it is called) will not open until late next year and it will be in the hands of the Reconstruction Finance Corporation until 1946 when it will be acquired by private owners for $6 million.

Cincinnati's 29-story Netherlands Plaza Hotel has opened January 27 with 800 rooms.

Washington's Shoreham Hotel opens with 900 rooms on Calvert Street just off Connecticut Avenue.

New York's River House opens at 435 East 52nd Street on the East River. Designed by Bottomley, Wagner & White, the lower floors of the palatial 26-story cooperative apartment house contain the River Club with its swimming pool, tennis courts, squash courts, and ballroom. A dock on the river provides mooring for yachts.

New York's 322 East 57th Street luxury apartment house is completed by Harry M. Clawson of Caughey & Evans with duplex living rooms 18 feet high.

New York's London Terrace apartment complex opens between 9th and 10th Avenues from 23rd Street north to 24th. The 1,670-unit complex has a block-long private garden, a solarium, a swimming pool, and doormen dressed as London "Bobbies."

New York's Majestic Apartments designed by Irwin S. Chanin Company go up on Central Park West between 71st and 72nd Streets. The twin-towered Majestic has wide banks of windows streamlined round its corners.

A 43-room mansion is completed at 60 East 93rd Street for the divorced wife of railroad heir William K. Vanderbilt, Jr.

 Carlsbad Caverns National Park is established by Congress on 46,753 acres of underground chambers in southern New Mexico.

Dutch elm disease kills some trees in Cleveland and Cincinnati in its first attacks on the American elm *ulmus americanus.* A fungus first observed in Holland in 1919, the blight has been introduced in elm burl logs shipped from Europe to be made into veneer for furniture. Within 40 years it will have killed some 13 million trees and will be destroying 400,000 elms each year in 30 states and Canada, wilting or shriveling leaves in June or July, yellowing them prematurely, killing young trees sometimes in 1 year and older ones in 3 or 4 as fungus spores are spread by underground root grafts and by two kinds of bark beetles. The loss of America's foremost shade tree will have a marked effect on the environment of many American cities and towns.

Some 25 percent of Americans live on or from the farm, many of them on subsistence farms that operate outside the money economy. The total number of U.S. farms is roughly 6.3 million (*see* 1931).

Major U.S. crops produce barely $8 per acre and the average annual farm income is $400 per family.

Four out of 10 U.S. farms are worked by tenant farmers as compared with nine out of 10 British farm one-third of farms in western Europe, 78 percent of Australian farms, and 40 percent of Argentine farms.

Fifty-five percent of agricultural workers on Soviet farms are employed on collective farms (*see* Stalin's Five-Year Plan, 1928).

The mortgage debt of U.S. farms is $9.2 billion, up from $3.2 billion in 1910. Farmers have borrowed heavily to buy the machines they need to remain competitive.

Twenty percent of the North American work force is employed in agriculture as compared with 7 percent in Britain, 25 percent in France, 40 percent in Japan.

Farmers in the Corn Belt begin to drop their resistance to hybrid corn as they see test plantings which demonstrate dramatically how the new corn can increase yields (*see* 1921; Bantam, 1933).

A Grain Stabilization Corporation is established in the Department of Agriculture to buy up surpluses that are depressing farm prices but the $500 million appropriated to fund the corporation's activities is not nearly sufficient (*see* Commodity Credit Corporation, 1933).

Northwest Colorado cowranges are opened to sheep grazing by Colorado-Utah rancher James Monaghan, 38, who started working as a cowhand in summer roundups at age 16 and who is now president of the Rio Branco Wool Growers' Association. Monaghan will become an historian beginning in 1945.

Monfort of Colorado, Inc., has its beginnings in a feedlot started by rancher Warren H. Monfort on a farm he has inherited a mile outside Greeley. Monfort will have cattle on feed all year round by 1934 and by 1968 he will have 100,000 head of cattle fattening on alfalfa, grain, and sugar beets.

The broiler chicken is developed by poultry farmers on the Delmarva (Delaware-Maryland-Virginia) Peninsula. The broiler will replace the spring chicken that has kept chicken a seasonal food and has limited consumption of chicken which remains costlier than red meat.

"With the introduction of agriculture mankind entered upon a long period of meanness, misery, and madness, from which they are only being freed by the beneficent operation of the machine," writes English philosopher Bertrand Russell in *The Conquest of Happiness*.

Unprecedented drought parches the U.S. South and Midwest. A $45 million Drought Relief Act is voted by Congress December 20.

The *Star of Alaska* makes her final trip north from San Francisco to the Alaskan salmon canneries and the era of the great Star square-riggers is ended (*see* 1893; California Packing, 1916).

Vitamin D is isolated in its crystalline form calciferol and is soon being used to fortify butter, margarine, and other foods (*see* Borden's milk, 1933).

A concentrate 100 times as potent as liver for treating pernicious anemia is developed by Edwin J. Cohn at Harvard Medical School (*see* 1926; 1929; 1948).

Labeling of substandard canned goods is ordered by the McNary-Mapes Amendment to the 1906 Food and Drug Act. The move has been urged by the National Canners Association as a safety measure and to eliminate competition from shoddy goods.

Birds Eye Frosted Foods go on sale for the first time March 6 at Springfield, Mass. Frozen peas, spinach, raspberries, cherries, loganberries, fish, and various meats are introduced by General Foods but the packets are kept in ice-cream cabinets, they are not readily visible, and they sell at relatively high prices (35 cents for a package of peas) (*see* 1929; 1931).

Dry ice (solid carbon dioxide) is introduced commercially in the United States for such purposes as keeping ice cream cold.

Sliced bread is introduced in the United States under the Wonder Bread label by Continental Baking (*see* 1927). Consumers are suspicious at first but soon accept it enthusiastically.

The Toastmaster automatic toaster is introduced by the McGraw-Electric Company of Elgin, Ill.

Hostess Twinkies are introduced by Continental Baking (above). A Continental bakery at Chicago has been turning out little sponge cakes for shoppers to use as the basis of strawberry shortcakes and when the strawberry season ends bakery manager James A. Dewar, 33, hits on the idea of filling the cakes with sugary cream to keep the cake line in production year round. A St. Louis sign advertising "Twinkle Toes Shoes" inspires him to call the cakes Twinkies.

Jiffy brand biscuit mix is introduced by Chelsea Milling Company of Chelsea, Mich. (*see* Bisquick, 1931).

The International Apple Shippers Association offers its fruit on credit to jobless men who will peddle apples on streetcorners and will help the association dispose of its vast surplus. By November some 6,000 men are selling apples on New York sidewalks and more thousands are selling apples in other cities, but by the spring of next year the apple sellers will be called a nuisance and City Hall will order them off the streets of New York.

Mott's Apple Sauce is introduced by the Duffy-Mott Company (*see* 1900; Mott's Apple Juice, 1938).

Ocean Spray Preserving Company merges with Cranberry Products Company of New Egypt, N.J., and with A. D. Makepeace Company of Wareham, Mass., to create the cranberry growers' cooperative Cranberry Canners, Inc. (*see* 1912). The co-op will be joined in 1940 by the Wisconsin Sales Company and in 1941 by Washington and Oregon growers and its name will be changed in 1946 to National Cranberry Association (*see* 1959).

Sterling Salt Company is acquired by International Salt Company which will adopt Sterling as the trademark for all its salt products. Sterling table salt will be introduced in 1934.

1930 (cont.) French's Worcestershire Sauce is introduced in 5-ounce, paper-wrapped bottles with glass and cork stoppers by Rochester's R. T. French Company of 1904 cream salad mustard fame. The company has imported an English chemist who has perfected a piquant Worcestershire sauce made of soy sauce, garlic, anchovies, tamarinds, distilled vinegar, corn syrup, sugar, salt, spices, and flavoring, and while the package will be changed the wood-aged product will not be (*see* Lea and Perrins, 1823; potatoes, 1946).

Snickers candy bars are introduced by Mars, Inc., which obtains national distribution and racks up sales of $24.6 million with net profits of nearly $2.3 million (*see* 1923; 1932).

The Better Homes and Gardens Cookbook is a U.S. best seller. It will have sales of some 18 million copies in the next 45 years and will be the all-time best selling U.S. cookbook.

The first true supermarket opens in August at Jamaica, Long Island, where former Kroger Grocery and Baking Co. store manager Michael S. Cullen, 46, opens the King Kullen Market in an abandoned garage and meets with instant success. Cullen has written Kroger president William H. Albers suggesting a plan for "monstrous stores . . . away from the high-rent districts" that will attract customers with aggressive price-cutting. "I could afford to sell a can of milk at cost if I could sell a can of peas and make two cents," Cullen has written, but his letter has been intercepted by another Kroger executive. "King Kullen, the world's greatest price wrecker—how does he do it?" (*see* 1923; Big Bear, 1932).

Jack & Charlie's 21 Club opens in January at 21 West 52nd Street, New York. Restaurateur John Karl "Jack" Kriendler, 31, and his accountant cousin Charles "Charlie" Berns, 28, have been operating speakeasy saloons since 1923 and they have been subsidized in effect by the Rockefellers, who have purchased their lease at 42 West 49th Street to clear the block for construction of Rockefeller Center (*see* 1931). Kriendler and Berns store their illicit liquor behind secret walls and devise an arrangement that permits the bartender to push a button at the first sign of a raid by federal Prohibition enforcement agents, tilting the shelves of the bar to send all bottles down a chute to smash in the cellar and thus destroy the evidence that the agents need for a conviction. They will prosper at the new location and will acquire the building at 19 West 52nd Street in 1935.

Benito Mussolini's Italy makes abortion a crime "against the integrity and health of the race" but illegal abortions continue at a rate of more than half a million per year.

A human egg cell is seen for the first time through a microscope (*see* spermatozoa, 1677). B. Kraus and D. Ogino in Japan discover that human ovaries generally release maternal eggs 12 to 16 days before menstruation but about one woman in four will be found to be wildly erratic in her menstrual cycle and all women will be found to be erratic for a few months after the birth of a child.

Production of better quality contraceptives is encouraged by a U.S. court decision that extends trademark protection to contraceptive devices. Economic depression makes large families increasingly burdensome to breadwinners.

The encyclical *Casti connubii* issued December 31 by Pope Pius XI says, "Any use whatsoever of matrimony exercised in such a way that the [sex] act is deliberately frustrated in its natural power to generate life is an offense against the law of God and of nature, and those who indulge in such are branded with the guilt of a grave sin." But the "rhythm" system of birth control favored by the Catholic Church is an inadequate form of contraception for reasons suggested above and increasing numbers of Roman Catholics are employing artificial methods of birth control including abortion.

The world's population reaches close to 2 billion with much of it in the grip of economic depression.

The U.S. population reaches 122.8 million and emigration from the United States for the first time in history exceeds immigration.

1931 Financial panic and economic depression engulf most of the world. Vienna's Kreditanstalt goes bankrupt May 11, possibly as a result of French opposition to an Austro-Hungarian credit union, and the panic spreads to Germany where the Darmstadter und National Bank closes.

The Bank of England advances money to Austria but Britain's own financial position is shaky (below).

President Hoover proposes a 1-year moratorium on payments of war debts and reparations June 20 and when Germany's Danatbank goes into bankruptcy July 13 it precipitates a general closing of German banks that continues until August 5.

Britain receives a French-American loan August 1 but London and Glasgow have riots September 10 to protest government economy measures, naval units mutiny September 15 to protest pay cuts, Britain is forced to abandon the gold standard once again September 21, and the pound sterling falls in value from $4.86 to $3.49.

Canadian tariffs have been raised June 18. It is estimated that the new customs duties will cut off two thirds of the goods imported from the United States.

U.S. motorcar sales collapse and Detroit lays off another 100,000 workers, reducing employment in automobile plants to 250,000, down from 475,000 in 1929. Two out of three Detroit workers (and 8 out of 10 Detroit blacks) are totally or partially unemployed and while the situation will improve unemployment will remain high in Detroit until 1942 (*see* 1933).

Stabilization of Industry by General Electric Company president Gerard Swope, 58, outlines the "Swope Plan" for economic recovery. Leave the problem in the hands of business, says Swope, and let trade associations develop national economic plans to revive the economy.

2,294 U.S. banks fail, up from 1,352 last year.

Brown Brothers Harriman & Co. is created by a merger of the New York banking house Brown Brothers that dates back to 1818 and the Harriman Brothers & Co. firm started by the late railroad securities speculator Edward H. Harriman who died in 1909 at age 61. Harriman's 40-year-old son William Averell will head the Union Pacific Railroad beginning next year (*see* Sun Valley, 1936).

Reynolds & Co. is founded by tobacco heir Richard S. Reynolds, 22, with John D. Baker and Thomas F. Staley, 27.

Loeb, Rhoades & Co. (Carl M. Loeb Roades & Co.) is founded by New York investment banker John Langloth Loeb, 28, who married a Lehman at age 24.

The Nevada State Legislature enacts a 6-week residency law for divorce-seekers in a move to generate revenue for the Depression-struck state which has almost no tax base since most of its lands are federally owned. Nevada grants 5,260 divorces, up from 2,500 in 1928, and 4,745 of the divorce decrees are handed down at Reno which becomes the boom town divorce capital of the world (*see* gambling, below).

U.S. unemployment reaches above the 8 million mark. Hunger marchers petition the White House December 7 for a guarantee of employment at a minimum wage but they are turned away.

President Hoover recommends an emergency Reconstruction Finance Corporation and a public works administration in his annual message to Congress December 8 (*see* 1932).

Japan abandons the gold standard December 11.

Spain's Alfonso XIII leaves the country April 14 after forces favoring a republican form of government have won a big victory in municipal elections. The king who has reigned since 1886 is declared guilty of high treason November 12, he is forbidden to return, the royal property is confiscated, a new constitution is adopted December 9, and a Spanish Republic is created that will continue until 1939 (*see* 1936).

Britain's Labour government resigns August 24 in a disagreement over remedies for the nation's financial crisis, but Prime Minister Ramsay MacDonald heads a new coalition cabinet that will retain power until mid-1935.

The Mukden Incident September 19 is used by the Japanese as an excuse for occupying Manchuria. An alleged railway explosion is cited as provocation, Kirin is seized September 21, and within 5 months the Japanese will have taken Harbin and the three eastern provinces (the action is in large measure a reprisal for China's boycott of Japan's cotton textiles).

China's Nationalist president Chiang Kai-shek comes under pressure from Communist forces led by Mao Tse-tung, 37. He is prevented by the Communists and by the Yangtze floods (below) from mounting any military effort against the Japanese (*see* 1934).

Production of atomic energy is pioneered by Columbia University physicist Harold Clayton Urey, 38, and two colleagues who discover heavy water (deuterium oxide) whose molecules consist of an atom of oxygen and two atoms of deuterium (heavy hydrogen, a rare isotope of hydrogen). The discovery will lead to the separation of other isotopes including the separation of the fissionable uranium 235 from the more common U238 (*see* Cockroft, Chadwick, 1932).

The Six Companies to construct Boulder Dam on the Colorado River is organized by U.S. engineer Henry John Kaiser, 49, who coordinates the capabilities of six contractors (*see* 1930). Kaiser has built miles of highway from California up the West Coast into British Columbia and in Cuba and he has built a number of cement plants (*see* 1936).

Scottsboro, Ala., makes headlines as a shouting mob surrounds the county courthouse where nine black youths are being tried on charges of having raped two white women aboard a freight car March 25 after the blacks allegedly threw some white hoboes off the train. A white mob pulled the blacks from the train when it arrived at Paint Rock, Ala., the defendants Harwood Patterson, Olen Montgomery, Clarence Norris, Ozie Powell, Willie Robertson, Charlie Weems, Eugene Williams, Andy Wright, and Roy Wright have been transferred to Scottsboro to prevent their being represented by counsel, they are defended only by a reluctant lawyer who has been assigned to the case by the presiding judge and given no preparation, the jury discounts testimony by a physician, and the 3-day trial ends April 9 with eight of the defendants sentenced to death and the ninth to life imprisonment. The physician has testified that he examined Victoria Price, 21, and Ruby Bates, 17, of Huntsville shortly after the alleged rape and that while he found dried semen he found no live spermatozoa and no blood.

The Supreme Court will reverse the Scottsboro convictions (above) in October of next year in a landmark ruling that defendants in capital cases in state courts must have adequate legal representation.

The "Scottsboro Boys" (above) will have a new trial in Alabama in 1933, the trial will end in conviction, and the Supreme Court will again reverse the convictions with a landmark ruling that blacks may not be systematically excluded from grand and trial juries. New York civil rights lawyers Shad Polier, 25, and Samuel S. Leibowitz, 38, will take up the cause, a third trial with one black on the jury will end in conviction, but some of the indictments will be dropped, the sentences will be commuted to life imprisonment, the defendants will serve a total of 130 years behind bars (one will not be paroled until 1951).

Out of work and out of funds: the grim realities of the Great Depression made radical proposals look good.

Harlan County, Ky., coal miners and deputized guards have a gunfight May 4 at Evarts following 4 years of strikes and labor-management battles. The Harlan County Coal Operators Association began spending heavily in 1927 to terrorize miners and their families with strong-arm tactics in a move to combat efforts by the United Mine Workers to organize the men, the conflict has come to a head, the fight ends with three guards and one miner left dead, untold numbers of others are carried dead or dying into the hills.

 Swissair has its beginnings in an airline started with private capital that will continue to control at least 75 percent of the national airline.

Seversky Aircraft Corporation is founded by Russian-American aeronautical engineer Alexander Procofieff de Seversky, 37, who lost a leg in the World War. His company will manufacture pursuit planes (see Republic Aviation, 1939).

New York's Floyd Bennet Field opens at the south end of Brooklyn's Jamaica Bay. The first city-owned airport takes its name from the late aviation pioneer who died in 1928 at age 37 (see 1926; La Guardia, 1939).

Wiley Post circles the earth in the Winnie Mae (see 1930). Flying with Harold Gatty as navigator, Post flies across the Atlantic to the British Isles, across Europe and Soviet Russia, and back to the United States in 8 days, 15 hours, and 51 minutes, a feat he will repeat in 1933 in 7 days, 18 hours, and 49 minutes flying solo to become the first pilot to circle the earth alone (see 1935; Hughes, 1938).

Omaha's Union Station opens. The magnificent new terminal serves the seven railroads that converge on the Nebraska city.

New York's George Washington Bridge opens October 24 to span the Hudson River between Manhattan and New Jersey. The 1,067-meter bridge is the world's largest suspension bridge and its 90,000 tons of deadweight are suspended from four 3-foot cables made by John A. Roebling's Sons Company of Trenton, N.J. (see Brooklyn Bridge, 1883; Golden Gate, 1937).

The Bayonne (Kill Van Kull) Bridge opens to traffic. The 504-meter span is the world's longest steel arch bridge.

Auburn motorcar sales soar to 28,130 and profits equal those of 1929 after a depressing 1930 sales year. E. L. Cord signs up 1,000 new Auburn dealers as his car climbs from 23rd place in retail sales to 13th on the strength of the new Auburn 8-98 whose 286.6-cubic inch Lycoming engine is far more powerful than any other in the price class (the costliest sells for $1,395). The new Auburn is the first rear-drive motorcar with a frame braced by an X cross member and it is the first moderately priced car with L.G.S. Free Wheeling (but see 1937).

The four-cylinder Ford Model A has a 103.5-inch wheelbase, it develops 40 horsepower at 2,200 rpm, and it sells at between $430 and $595.

The four-cylinder Plymouth has a 110-inch wheelbase, it develops 56 horsepower at 2,800 rpm, and it sells at between $535 and $645.

The six-cylinder Chevrolet has a 109-inch wheelbase, it develops 50 horsepower at 2,600 rpm, and it sells at $475 to $635 and up.

Bentley Motors, Ltd., is acquired from W. O. Bentley by Rolls-Royce, Ltd., which will market a Rolls-Royce motorcar under the Bentley name using a different front grill (see 1919).

 Penicillin is used successfully at England's Royal Infirmary in Sheffield to relieve two cases of gonococcal ophthalmitis in children who have contracted gonorrhea from their mothers at birth (see Argyrol, 1902; Fleming, 1928; 1929). Penicillin is also used at the Royal Infirmary to relieve a colliery manager suffering from severe pneumococcal infection of the eye but no further efforts will be made until the end of the decade to pursue the chemotherapeutic potentials of penicillin (see Florey, 1940).

Alka-Seltzer is introduced by Miles Laboratories of Elkhart, Ind., which has been producing Dr. Miles Nervine tonic for nearly 50 years. An analgesic and antacid for headaches, hangovers, and upset stomachs, Alka-Seltzer is a tablet made from sodium bi-carbonate, mono-calcium phosphate, acetyl-salicylic acid (aspirin), and citric acid, it fizzes when dropped in water, and it will gain quick acceptance among dyspeptics even though its aspirin content may upset stomachs. Within 40 years Miles will be selling 2.5 billion Alka-Seltzer tablets per year and will have 1 percent of the U.S. aspirin market, 21 percent of the antacid market.

Chicago mobster Al Capone of 1929 St. Valentine's Day massacre notoriety is found guilty of evading $231,000 in income taxes and is sentenced by a Chicago federal court to 11 years' imprisonment and a $50,000 fine (*see* 1939).

U.S. underworld boss Salvatore Maranzano is assassinated in a murder engineered by Italian-American Charles "Lucky" Luciano, 34, who restructures the U.S. Mafia into a federation of "families" (*see* 1936).

Prohibition is not working, reports President Hoover's Wickersham Committee headed by former Attorney General George Woodward Wickersham, 73.

Starr Faithfull makes lurid headlines June 8 when her body—clad only in a silk dress—washes up on the beach at Long Beach, N.Y. The beautiful 25-year-old woman has been dead since June 5, suicide notes are produced some weeks later, but the cause of her death will remain a mystery.

A 1925 Minnesota "gag law" that banned publication of a "malicious, scandalous and defamatory newspaper, magazine, or other periodical" is ruled unconstitutional by the Supreme Court in *Near v. Minnesota,* the first case in which provisions of a state law are held to restrict personal freedom of speech and press without due process, and a decision that incorporates provisions of the First Amendment into the 14th.

The *New York World Telegram* begins publication in February as Roy Howard of the Scripps-Howard newspaper chain pays $5 million—$8.69 per reader —to obtain the Associated Press franchise and the goodwill of Pulitzer's *New York World* and *Evening World,* which he merges with the *Telegram* to create the new evening paper. Joseph Pulitzer's son Ralph, 52, has sustained losses averaging $430,000 per year for the past 5 years and is happy to sell.

Liberty magazine is acquired from the *Chicago Tribune* by Bernarr Macfadden in exchange for his *Detroit Mirror* tabloid which the *Tribune* will abandon after 16 months while Macfadden builds *Liberty* into a major periodical.

"Dick Tracy" has its beginnings in the *Chicago Tribune's* new comic strip "Plainclothes Tracy" introduced by former Hearst syndicate cartoonist Chester Gould, 30, whose jutting-jawed detective is never without his snap-brim hat. The strip will be popular for more than 45 years and will reach nearly 100 million readers each day in 600 U.S. newspapers and hundreds of foreign newspapers.

"Mickey Mouse" by Walt Disney makes his first appearance as a comic strip figure (*see* 1928).

"Felix the Cat" by Otto Mesmer makes his first appearance as a comic strip drawn by Pat Sullivan (*see* 1919).

"Starch ratings" for the measurement of magazine readership (editorial matter and advertising) are established by former Harvard business psychology professor Daniel Starch, 48, who has been research director of the American Association of Advertising Agencies since 1924 and has pioneered in the past decade in measuring advertising readership and radio audiences (*see* Hooper, 1934).

Nonfiction *Axel's Castle* (critical pieces) by Edmund Wilson.

Fiction *Night Flight (Vol de nuit)* by Antoine de Saint-Exupéry; *L'Homme approximate* by Romanian surrealist novelist Tristan Tzara (Sami Rosenstock), 35; *African Confidence (Confidence Africaine)* by French novelist Roger Martin du Gard, 30; *Afternoon Men* by English novelist Anthony Powell, 26; *Prince Jali* by L. H. Myers; *The Waves* by Virginia Woolf; *Sanctuary* by William Faulkner; *Tropic of Cancer* by U.S. émigré novelist Henry Miller, 39, whose earthy novel will not be permitted in the United States for decades; *Boy* by Irish novelist James Hanley, 30, whose book is suppressed; *The Dream Life of Balso Snell* by U.S. novelist Nathanael West (Nathan Wallenstein Weinstein), 27, who has developed a style derived from Dadaism and surrealism in the arts; *After Leaving Mr. Mackenzie* (stories) by Jean Rhys; *The Good Earth* by Pearl Buck; *Grand Hotel* by Austrian-American novelist Vicki Baum, 43 (*see* play, 1930). *Hatter's Castle* by Scottish physician-novelist A. J. (Archibald Joseph) Cronin, 35, who has given up his lucrative London West End practice for reasons of health; *S.S. San Pedro* by James Gould Cozzens; *The Glass Key* by Dashiell Hammett.

Poetry *Strophe* by Greek poet George Seferis, 31; *The Loosening* by English poet Ronald Bottrall, 25.

Painting *The Persistence of Memory* by Spanish surrealist Salvador Dali, 27, whose work was first exhibited 5 years ago at Barcelona and whose limp watches and clocks draped over barren landscapes gain wide attention and ridicule; *The Breakfast Room* by Paul Bonnard; *The Trick-Riders* by Marc Chagall; *Still Life with Studio Window* by Max Beckmann; *Market Church* by Lyonel Feininger; *The Ghost Vanishes* by Paul Klee who begins teaching at Düsseldorf; *The Dance* by Henri Matisse who has been commissioned to paint the murals by Argyrol king Albert Barnes; *Route 6, Eastham* by Edward Hopper; *Man, Woman, and Child* by Joan Miró; *Zapatistas* by José Clemente Orozco.

The Whitney Museum of American Art is founded by railroad heiress Gertrude Vanderbilt Whitney, 54, whose husband Harry Payne Whitney died last year at age 58.

Sculpture Rio de Janeiro's *Christ the Redeemer* is dedicated atop Corcovado (Hunchback Mountain). The 125-foot tall concrete work by French sculptor Paul Maximilian Landowski, 56, has outstretched arms that span 92 feet, it weighs 1,145 tons, and it has been completed by Brazilian engineer Heitor da Silva Costa; *Genesis* by Jacob Epstein; *Mlle. Pognany* by Constantin Brancusi.

The first exposure meter for photographers is invented by William Nelson Goodwin, Jr., of the Weston Electrical Instrument Corporation at Newark,

1931 (cont.) N.J., whose Photronic Photoelectric Cell will be introduced commercially in February of next year. Goodwin's meter contains a dial calculating device for translating brightness values into camera aperture settings, and since it changes light energy directly into electrical energy it requires no batteries.

 Theater *Tomorrow and Tomorrow* by Philip Barry 1/13 at New York's Henry Miller Theater, with Zita Johnson, Osgood Perkins, Herbert Marshall, 206 perfs.; *Green Grow the Lilacs* by U.S. playwright Lynn Riggs, 30, 1/26 at New York's Guild Theater, with Helen Westley, Lee Strasberg, June Walker, Franchot Tone, 64 perfs.; *Fanny* by Marcel Pagnol; *Farce of the Chaste Queen (Farsa y licencia de la rena castiza)* by Ramon de Valle Inclan 6/3 at Madrid's Teatro Munoz Seca; *The House of Connelly* by Paul Green 10/5 at New York's Martin Beck Theater, with Stella Adler, Franchot Tone, Clifford Odets, Rose McClendon, 81 perfs.; *Cavalcade* by Noel Coward 10/13 at London's Drury Lane Theatre, 405 perfs.; *The Left Bank* by Elmer Rice 10/5 at New York's Little Theater, 242 perfs.; *Mourning Becomes Electra* by Eugene O'Neill 10/26 at New York's Guild Theater, with Alla Nazimova and Alice Brady in a play based on the 5th Century B.C. Greek tragedies, 150 perfs.; *Judith* by Jean Genet 11/4 at the Comédie des Champs-Elysées, Paris; *Counsellor-at-Law* by Elmer Rice 11/6 at New York's Plymouth Theater, with Paul Muni, 292 perfs.; *Springtime for Henry* by English playwright Benn W. Levy, 31, 12/9 at New York's Bijou Theater, with Leslie Banks, Nigel Bruce, 199 perfs.

The Westport Country Playhouse has its first season at Westport, Conn. Lawrence Langner and his wife Armina Marshall of the Theatre Guild in New York have founded the summer theater in an old tannery (*see* American Shakespeare Theatre, 1955).

Films Charlie Chaplin's *City Lights;* William Wellman's *Public Enemy* with James Cagney, Jean Harlow, Mae Clark (who gets half a grapefruit in her face); Josef von Sternberg's *Dishonored* with Marlene Dietrich; Josef von Sternberg's *An American Tragedy* with Sylvia Sidney, Phillips Holmes, Frances Dee; Karl Froelich's *Mädchen in Uniform* with Hertha Thiele, Dorothea Wieck; G. W. Pabst's *Comradeship (Kameradschaft)*; G. W. Pabst's *The Three Penny Opera (Die Dreigroschenoper)*; Sergei Eisenstein's *Thunder over Mexico;* Jean Renoir's *The Bitch (La Chienne)*; Jean Renoir's *Bondel Saved from Drowning;* René Clair's *A Nous la Liberté;* Frank Capra's *Platinum Blonde* with Jean Harlow; Wesley Ruggles's *Cimarron* with Richard Dix, Irene Dunne in the first Western to win an Academy Award; Archie Mayo's *Svengali* with John Barrymore; Tod Browning's *Dracula* with Bela Lugosi; James Walsh's *Frankenstein* with Boris Karloff; Norman Taurog's *Skippy* with Jackie Cooper; Norman Z. McLeod's *Monkey Business* with the Marx Brothers; Robert Flaherty and F. W. Murneau's documentary *Tabu* with Reri.

U.S. movie theaters show double features to boost business. Many unemployed executives spend their afternoons at the movies.

Radio drama and comedy *Little Orphan Annie* 4/6 over NBC Blue Network stations. Sponsored by the makers of Ovaltine and based on the comic strip that began in 1924, the show will continue until 1943 ("Who's that little chatterbox?/ The one with pretty auburn locks?/ Who can it be?/ It's Little Orphan Annie ..."); *Lum and Abner* over KTHS at Hot Springs, Ark., moves to Chicago's NBC station in July, and begins 22 years of daily episodes at the Set 'Em Down Store operated by Lum Edwards (Chester Lauck, 29) and Abner Peabody (Norman Goff, 24); *The Easy Aces,* with comedian Goodman Ace, 32, and his wife Jane Epstein Ace whose *Easy Aces* will continue until 1945 and whose *Mr. Ace and Jane* will continue until 1955.

Cleveland's Severance Hall opens February 5 with a concert by the Cleveland Orchestra under the direction of Nikolai Sokoloff who has been conducting the group since 1918. The new concert hall has been built with a bequest from the late Standard Oil Company treasurer John Long Severance who died in 1913 at age 74. It provides a permanent home for the orchestra which has grown from 55 performers to 85.

Congress votes March 3 to designate "The Star Spangled Banner" the U.S. national anthem (*see* 1814).

Kate Smith makes her radio debut May 1 singing "When the Moon Comes over the Mountain" on CBS stations. Kathryn Elizabeth Smith, 22, has played comic fat girl roles in Broadway shows, she has finally won a singing role at New York's Palace Theater, she begins a radio career that will continue for nearly half a century, she will sing Irving Berlin's "God Bless America" in a 1938 Armistice Day broadcast, and she will acquire exclusive air rights to the song Berlin wrote originally for his 1918 show *Yip-Yip Yaphank* but laid aside.

Cantata *Belshazzar's Feast* for Baritone, Chorus, and Orchestra by William Walton 10/10 at Leeds.

First performances Concert Music for String Orchestra and Brass Instruments by Paul Hindemith 4/3 at Boston's Symphony Hall in a concert celebrating the Boston Symphony's 50th anniversary; "Amphion Suite" by Arthur Honegger 6/23 at the Paris Opéra; "Grand Canyon Suite" by Ferde Grofe 11/22 at Chicago's Studebaker Hall in a concert by Paul Whiteman and his Orchestra.

Ballet *Façade* 4/26 at London's Cambridge Theatre, with Antony Tudor, Alicia Makarova, Frederick Ashton, music by William Walton, choreography by Ashton (*see* 1923); *The Lady of Shalott* 11/12 at London's Mercury Theatre, with Frederick Ashton, music by Jean Sibelius, choreography by Ashton.

London's Royal Ballet has its beginnings in the Sadler's Wells Ballet founded by Ninette de Valois whose small opera ballet company will grow to become Britain's national ballet company.

Broadway musicals *America's Sweetheart* 2/10 at the Broadhurst Theater, with music by Richard Rodgers, lyrics by Lorenz Hart, songs that include "I've Got Five Dollars," 135 perfs.; *Billy Rose's Crazy Quilt* 5/19 at the 44th Street Theater, with Rose's wife Fanny Brice, music by Harry Warren, lyrics by Rose and Mort Dixon, songs that include "I Found a Million Dollar Baby—in a Five and Ten Cent Store," 79 perfs.; *The Little Show* 6/1 at the Music Box Theater, with Beatrice Lillie, Ernest Truex, music and lyrics by Noel Coward, songs that include "Mad Dogs and Englishmen," written by Coward last year while motoring between Hanoi and Saigon, "Cat's Cradle," 136 perfs.; *The Band Wagon* 6/3 at the New Amsterdam Theater, with Fred and Adele Astaire in their last appearance together on the first revolving stage to be used in a musical, music by Arthur Schwartz, lyrics by Howard Dietz, songs that include "Dancing in the Dark," "High and Low," "New Sun in the Sky," "I Love Louisa," 260 perfs.; *The Ziegfeld Follies* 7/1 at the Ziegfeld Theater, with Helen Morgan, Ruth Etting, Harry Richman, music by Walter Donaldson, Dave Stamper, and others, lyrics by E. Y. Harburg and others, 165 perfs.; *Earl Carroll's Vanities* 7/27 at the new 3,000-seat Earl Carroll Theater on 7th Avenue at 50th Street, with William Demarest, Lillian Roth, naked chorus girls, music mostly by Burton Lane plus Ravel's "Bolero," lyrics by Harold Adams, songs that include "Goodnight, Sweetheart" by English songwriters Ray Noble, James Campbell, and Reg Connelly, 278 perfs.; *George White's Scandals* 9/14 at the Apollo Theater, with Willie Howard, Rudy Vallee, Ray Bolger, Ethel Merman, music and lyrics by Ray Henderson and Lew Brown, songs that include "This Is the Missus," "The Thrill Is Gone," "That's Why Darkies Were Born," "Life Is Just a Bowl of Cherries," 202 perfs.; *Everybody's Welcome* 10/13 at the Shubert Theater, with Tommy and Jimmy Dorsey, Ann Pennington, Harriet Lake (Georgia Sothern), songs that include "As Time Goes By" by Herman Hupfield (see film *Casablanca*, 1942), 139 perfs.; *The Cat and the Fiddle* 10/15 at the Globe Theater, with Bettina Hall, Georges Metaxa, Eddie Foy, Jr., music by Jerome Kern, lyrics by Otto Harbach, songs that include "She Didn't Say 'Yes,'" "The Night Was Made for Love," 395 perfs.; *The Laugh Parade* 11/2 at the Imperial Theater, with Ed Wynn, music by Harry Warren, lyrics by Mort Dixon and Joe Young, songs that include "You're My Everything," 231 perfs.; *Of Thee I Sing* 12/26 at the Music Box Theater, with Victor Moore as Alexander Throttlebottom, William Gaxton as John P. Wintergreen, music by George Gershwin, lyrics by Ira Gershwin, songs that include "Love Is Sweeping the Country," "Wintergreen for President," "Who Cares?" and the title song, 441 perfs., Pulitzer prize 1932 (the first for any musical).

Popular songs "Mood Indigo" by Duke Ellington, lyrics by Albany Bigard, Irving Mills; "Heartaches" by Al Hoffman, lyrics by John Klenner; "Marta (Rambling Rose of the Wildwood)" by Moises Simons, lyr-

ics by L. Wolfe Gilbert; "I Don't Know Why I Love You Like I Do" by Fred E. Ahlert, lyrics by Roy Turk; "Where the Blue of the Night Meets the Gold of the Day" by Fred E. Ahlert, lyrics by Roy Turk (crooner Bing Crosby records the song and will make it his theme song); "I Love a Parade" by Harold Arlen, lyrics by Ted Koehler; "Take Me in Your Arms" by Fred Markush, lyrics by Mitchell Parish; "Just One More Chance" by Arthur Johnston, lyrics by Sam Coslow; "I Surrender, Dear" by Harry Burris of the Rhythm Boys, lyrics by Gordon Clifford; "That's My Desire" by Helmy Kresa, lyrics by John Klenner; "Love Letters in the Sand" by J. Fred Coots, lyrics by Nick and Charles Kenny; "Out of Nowhere" by Edward Heyman and John Green; "(I'll Be Glad When You're Dead) You Rascal You" by Sam Theard; "That Silver Haired Daddy of Mine" by Texas-born Oklahoma radio "singing cowboy" Orvon "Gene" Autry, 24, who will sell more than 5 million copies of the song; "Got a Date with an Angel" by English composers Jack Waller and Joseph Tunbridge, lyrics by Clifford Grey and Jimmie Miller; "Sally" by English songwriters Harry Leon (Sugarman), Will E. Haines, and Leo Towers (for the film *Sally in Our Alley* with Gracie Fields); "Lady of Spain" by English composer Tolchard Evans, 30, lyrics by Stanley Demerell, 51, and Bob Hargreaves.

H. Ellsworth Viner, Jr., wins the U.S. Lawn Tennis Association's Men's Singles title, Mrs. Helen Wills Moody wins the Women's Singles.

Francis Ouimet wins the U.S. Golf Association Amateur.

The St. Louis Cardinals win the World Series by defeating the Philadelphia Athletics 4 games to 3.

Knute Rockne has died in an airplane crash in Kansas March 31 at age 43 (*see* 1913). Rockne took over as head coach at Notre Dame in 1918 and his teams have won 105 games and tied 5 out of 122 for a percentage record of .897.

Clairol hair dye is introduced by U.S. chemists' broker Lawrence Gelb, 33, who has acquired the formula in Europe (*see* Nestle Colorinse, 1929). Gelb builds a research laboratory and plant at Stamford, Conn., and tries to create a U.S. market for hair dyes (*see* Miss Clairol, 1950).

Stanley Home Products Company is started by former Fuller Brush salesman Fink Stanley Beveridge, 51, who sets up shop in the bottom of a Westfield, Mass., tobacco shed with six dealers and seven clerks and secretaries. Beveridge will have little success until 1937 when he will follow the lead of such companies as Aluminum Cooking Utensil Company (Wear-Ever) and will use home parties to sell his brushes and mops, beginning a great upsurge that will make Stanley Home Products a major retailer of household chemicals, personal aids, and vitamins as well as brushes (*see* Fuller, 1906; Tupperware, 1945).

Lucky Strike cigarettes outsell Camels for the first time as American Tobacco Company challenges the

1931 (cont.) lead of R. J. Reynolds (*see* Hill, 1925). The lead will alternate between the two brands for the next 20 years as cigarette advertising helps to build radio broadcasting in America and as the radio helps build cigarette consumption.

∞ Jehovah's Witnesses adopt that name under the leadership of Joseph Franklin "Judge" Rutherford, 62, who has headed the International Bible Students' Association since the death of Charles Taze Russell in 1916. Rutherford proselytizes with the slogan "Millions now living will never die" (*see* 1884).

The Black Muslims have their beginnings at Detroit where local Baptist teacher Elijah Poole, 34, becomes an assistant to Wali Farad who has founded the Nation of Islam. Poole changes his name to Elijah Muhammad, he will establish Muhammad's Temple of Islam No. 2 at Chicago in 1934, Farad will thereupon mysteriously disappear, Muhammad will assume command of the growing sect as the Messenger of Allah, and by 1962 there will be at least 49 Temples of Islam with an estimated 250,000 followers (*see* Malcolm X, 1952).

💲 The Nevada State Legislature legalizes gambling. California entrepreneur Raymond Smith opens Harolds Club in Reno's Virginia Street naming the gambling casino after one of his sons, he advertises Harolds Club with billboards along western highways, and he begins a thriving enterprise.

🏛 New Delhi opens in India. The planned capital has been designed by English architects Sir Edwin Landseer Luytens, 62, and Sir Herbert Baker, 69, who have taken some inspiration from Christopher Wren and from Pierre L'Enfant (*see* 1667; 1790).

New York's Chrysler building opens at the corner of Lexington Avenue and 42nd Street and is for a few months the tallest building in the world. The 77-story, 1,048-foot structure of steel and concrete is capped with a stainless steel crown made by Fried. Krupp of Essen.

New York's Empire State building opens on the site formerly occupied by the Waldorf-Astoria Hotel of 1897 at Fifth Avenue and 34th Street where it will stand as the world's tallest building for more than 40 years. Erection of the 102-story skyscraper has been guided by Paul Starrett, 65, who supervised construction of the Flatiron building in 1902 and who in 1922 founded the firm of Starrett Brothers with Ralph and William Aiken Starrett.

New York's Waldorf-Astoria Hotel opens October 1 on a full-block site from 49th to 50th Street between Park and Lexington Avenues leased from the New York Central Railroad. The 2,200-room hotel built by Thompson-Starrett Company has a 44-story tower and employs the old Waldorf's maître d'hôtel Oscar Tschirsky who is paid $30,000 per year and who has been so heavily promoted as Oscar of the Waldorf that his calling cards are so inscribed.

London's Dorchester Hotel opens in Park Lane.

New York's Parc Vendome Apartments open with 600 units in four buildings just east of 9th Avenue on 57th Street.

New York's Century Apartments designed by Irwin S. Chanin's architect Jacques Delamarre open on Central Park West between 62nd and 63rd Streets where the Century Theater of 1909 designed by Carrère and Hastings has been torn down.

New York's 500 Fifth Avenue office tower is completed just north of the New York Public Library of 1911 at 42nd Street. The 59-story building has been designed by Shreve, Lamb & Harmon who also designed the Empire State Building (above).

New York's General Electric building opens under the name RCA-Victor Building on Lexington Avenue at 51st Street. The 50-story, 570-foot tower designed by Schultze & Weaver will soon be taken over by General Electric.

New York's McGraw-Hill building at 330 West 42nd Street is completed by Raymond M. Hood with horizontal bands of blue-green terra-cotta.

Rockefeller Center construction begins on a three-block midtown Manhattan site leased by John D. Rockefeller in 1928 with the intention of building a new Metropolitan Opera House. The 23-year lease given by Columbia University will be renewed periodically and the university will receive $3.5 million per year in rent on the $125 million office building development.

Philadelphia's Convention Hall is completed at 34th Street and Vintage Avenue with seats for 13,000 and room on stage for another 1,000. The Renaissance-style hall has been designed by U.S. architect Philip Cortelyou Johnson, 25.

🌐 U.S. air pollution is deplored by the U.S. Public Health Service which issues a study early in the year reporting that "the contamination of the atmosphere by smoke from the chimneys of private houses, office buildings, industrial plants, steam engines, tugs and steamships has become a serious matter in several of the larger cities . . ." but while one-fifth of the natural light of New York City is estimated to be cut off by smoke the chief concern in most of the country is that factories are idle and are not belching forth the smoke that came with prosperity.

China's Yangtze River overflows its banks and floods 40,000 square miles causing widespread famine (*see* Chiang Kai-shek, above).

Some 75 percent of Soviet farms remain in private hands despite the Five-Year Plan begun by Josef Stalin in 1928 to encourage collective farms and state farms. Liquidation of kulaks is intensified.

A National Coffee Department is established in Brazil where collapse of the world coffee market has brought economic disaster and has helped precipitate a revolt in the southern provinces by Getulio D. Vargas, 48. The Coffee Department will supervise the destruction of large quantities of Brazil's chief export item in order to maintain good prices in the world market (*see* Nescafé, 1938).

The U.S. wheat crop breaks all records and drives down prices. Many Kansas counties declare a moratorium on taxes to help farmers survive, but elsewhere farmers are forced off the land as banks foreclose on mortgages (*see* Farm Mortgage Financing Act, 1934).

The United States has 7.2 million operating farms, up from some 6.3 million last year, with more than a billion acres of farmland in production and with the world's highest rate of cultivated food crop acreage per capita. By 1935 the number of farms will be down to 6.84 million and by 1969 3.45 million.

British diets are found to be so poor that an Advisory Committee on Nutrition is organized. New marketing schemes for farmers are launched to put food within reach of more Britons and a Milk in Schools Scheme subsidizes milk so that children may have it at cheap prices (*see* 1934).

Pregnant women with nutritional megaloblastic anemia respond to diets containing autolysed yeast, British medical researcher Lucy Wills discovers at Bombay (*see* Mitchell and Snell, 1944).

Vitamin A is isolated by Swiss chemist Paul Karrer, 42 (*see* 1920; 1925; 1937).

A U.S. company sued by the FTC for false advertising is upheld by the Supreme Court in the case of *FTC v. Raladam.* A product called Marmola contining some thyroid extract is advertised as "a scientific remedy for obesity," but while the Court agrees with the American Medical Association that the advertising is dangerously misleading it rules that such advertising is not unfair to competition (*see* Clayton Act, 1914; Wheeler-Lea Act, 1938; Regimen, 1965).

Taste perception is found by researchers to be largely an inherited trait. Many more non-Europeans than Europeans (or white Americans) are capable of tasting the chemical phenylthiocarbamide (PTC) according to the research.

Salt is used for the first time in baby foods by Daniel Gerber's Fremont Packing Company which adds salt to make its products more acceptable to mothers (*see* 1929). Infants' taste buds are not sufficiently developed to discern any difference but sales resistance has come from mothers who taste their babies' food (*see* 1941; MSG, 1951).

Beech-Nut Baby Foods are introduced by Beech-Nut Packing Company which brings out a line of 13 strained baby and junior foods in glass jars (*see* 1924). The foods will be sold on a national basis within the next year and will lead other baby food makers to market their products in jars.

U.S. mechanical refrigerator production tops 1 million units, up from 5,000 in 1921. By 1937 the industry will be producing refrigerators at the rate of nearly 3 million per year (*see* 1929).

Freon 12 (dichlorodifluoromethane) refrigerant gas is adopted by the Frigidaire division of General Motors and by most other makers of mechanical refrigerators to replace ammonia and other more dangerous gases. Invented by Thomas Midgley of Ethyl Corporation and C. F. Kettering of General Motors, Freon 12 is produced by a Du Pont-General Motors subsidiary.

Birds Eye Frosted Foods go on sale across the United States as General Foods expands distribution (*see* 1930). Birds Eye frozen lima beans are produced by Seabrook Farms, but only a few retail grocers have freezer cases for displaying frozen foods (*see* 1940).

Bisquick is introduced by General Mills. The prepared mix for biscuits contains sesame seed oil to keep its flour and shortening from turning rancid and it has been named by General Mills president D. D. Davis whose new product competes with Jiffy brand biscuit mix introduced last year by Chelsea Milling.

Ballard Biscuits made from refrigerated dough and packaged in cylindrical containers under pressure are introduced by Ballard & Ballard, Inc., of Louisville, Ky.

Wyler's Bouillon Cubes are introduced by Chicago entrepreneur Silvain S. Wyler who imports the cubes made to his own formula in Holland and Switzerland. Wyler's product line will grow to include four kinds of bouillon cubes, beef and chicken gravy mixes, dehydrated oregano and mint leaves, a meat tenderizer, dehydrated mixed vegetable flakes, and dried soup greens.

New York's Hotel Bar Butter is introduced with a package showing a silhouette of the New York skyline with hotels that include the new Waldorf-Astoria.

Safeway Stores reach their peak of 3,527 outlets (*see* 1926). The company will close many of its smaller grocery stores and will open huge supermarkets.

The male sex hormone androgen is isolated by Germany's Adolph Butenandt (*see* 1929).

Birth control receives guarded endorsement from the Council of Churches of Christ in America.

U.S. birth rates and immigration to the United States will decline in this decade for economic reasons.

The U.S. population reaches 124 million. Great Britain has 46 million, Germany 65, France 42, Italy 41, the Indonesian islands 61, Japan 65, Soviet Russia 148, India 338, China perhaps 440.

1932 Splitting the atom for the first time in history presents the possibility of a vast new energy source. English physicist John Douglas Cockroft, 35, and his associate Ernest Walton use a voltage multiplier they developed in the 1920s to accelerate charged subatomic particles to extremely high velocities. They use this "atomic gun" to bombard lithium with protons, and the alpha particles (helium nuclei) they produce show that the protons have reacted with the lithium

1932 (cont.) nuclei to produce helium (*see* Thomson, 1897; Joliot-Curie, 1934).

The neutron discovered by English physicist James Chadwick, 41, is a particle similar in mass to the proton but without an electric charge (*see* electron, 1897). Since it is neutral, the neutron easily penetrates atoms and permits efficient splitting of atomic nuclei for developing atomic reactors.

The world's first practical cyclotron built by University of California physicist Ernest Orlando Lawrence, 31, is an accelerator that propels atomic particles in spiral paths by the use of a constant magnetic field.

Oil wells within the city limits of Oklahoma City are drilled by local attorney Robert Samuel Kerr, 35, and his brother-in-law James L. Anderson who have acquired control of a contract drilling firm and have borrowed money to post $200,000 liability bonds in a gamble that large oil companies have refused to take. Kerr and Anderson will make a profit of some $2 million on the venture (*see* Kerr-McGee, 1937).

Standard Oil Company of California (SoCal) prospectors in Bahrein strike oil in early June with their first well in the British protectorate in the Persian Gulf. Production will reach 20,000 barrels per day by 1936, and SoCal will take in the Texas Company as an equal partner to avail itself of Texaco's marketing facilities in the Far East (*see* 1903; 1933).

 The kingdom of Saudi Arabia is established by the Bedouin king of Hejaz Abdul-Aziz ibn-Saud, now 52. He renames Hejaz and Nejd, whose independence was recognized by Britain in 1927 (*see* oil, 1933).

The British Union of Fascists is founded by former Labour party M.P. Sir Oswald Mosley, 36, who last year quit the party in protest against its defeatist attitude toward unemployment and started a new party based on principles more socialistic than fascistic. Mosley will become a supporter of Italy's Benito Mussolini and Germany's Adolf Hitler, and he will demand expulsion of Britain's Jews (*see* 1936; 1940).

Eamon de Valera is elected president of Ireland in March, he suspends Irish land annuity payments, and a tariff war between Britain and Ireland begins in July (*see* 1922). The de Valera government will encourage diversification of Irish agriculture and will make efforts to achieve industrial self-sufficiency, but the loss of the country's chief export market brings a collapse of its cattle industry and worsens the economic depression in Ireland (*see* 1935).

Siam's absolute government is ended June 24 by European-educated radicals who capture the king Rama VII (Prajadhipok) and hold him captive briefly until he agrees to a constitution and to the establishment of a senate (*see* 1935).

A Swedish socialist government comes to power September 24 with Per Albin Hansson, 47, as prime minister. He will continue as prime minister until his death in 1946, and Sweden's Social Democratic party will retain power until 1976.

"I pledge you, I pledge myself, to a new deal for the American people," says New York governor Franklin D. Roosevelt as he accepts the Democratic party nomination for president at Chicago.

New York City's playboy mayor James John "Jimmy" Walker, 51, resigns September 1 during an investigation of corruption by a state legislative commission headed by Judge Samuel Seabury, 59 (*see* song 1905).

Franklin D. Roosevelt wins election to the presidency by gaining 472 electoral votes and 57 percent of the popular vote as compared with 59 electoral votes and 40 percent of the popular vote for President Hoover, who carries only six states as economic depression worsens.

The average U.S. weekly wage falls to $17, down from $28 in 1929. "Breadlines" form in many cities.

Some 1,616 U.S. banks fail, nearly 20,000 business firms go bankrupt, there are 21,000 suicides, and expenditures for food and tobacco fall $10 billion below 1929 levels.

U.S. industrial production falls to one-third its 1929 total, and the U.S. Gross National Product (GNP) falls to $41 billion, just over half its 1929 level.

Wall Street's Dow Jones Industrial Average drops to 41.22 July 28, down from its high of 381.17 September 3, 1929. It is the lowest point it will reach.

A Reconstruction Finance Corporation has been authorized by Congress January 22 to help finance industry and agriculture in accordance with President Hoover's request of last year.

Communism is endorsed by prominent U.S. intellectuals who say that only the Communist party has proposed a real solution to the nation's problems. Among the endorsers are poet-novelist Sherwood Anderson, novelist Erskine Caldwell, novelist John Dos Passos, novelist Theodore Dreiser, writer Waldo Frank, writer Granville Hicks, teacher Sidney Hook, writer Matthew Josephson, and journalist Lincoln Steffens.

Chicago utilities magnate Samuel Insull, now 73, runs into financial difficulties, and three of his largest companies go into receivership. Once Thomas Edison's private secretary, Insull has overextended himself to pay $65 million for Cyrus Eaton's shares in Commonwealth Edison and Peoples Gas Light and Coke, but while Eaton made $15 million in profit and has seen his own net worth rise to $100 million, the Cleveland utility and steel magnate has been reduced in net worth to less than $5 million by the Wall Street collapse (*see* 1912). Insull is indicted on charges arising out of his activities as president of Chicago Edison, Commonwealth Edison, Peoples Gas Light and Coke, and other companies, but he will avoid arrest for 2 years and will be acquitted after trials in 1934 and 1935.

The AF of L reverses its long-standing position against unemployment insurance and urges that work be spread through a 30-hour week with some "economic planning" by the federal government.

Unemployment reaches between 15 and 17 million by year's end, 34 million Americans have no income of any kind, and Americans who do work average little more than $16 per week.

An Emergency Relief and Reconstruction Act passed by Congress July 21 gives the RFC (above) power to lend $1.8 billion to the states for relief and self-liquidating public works projects.

A Home Loan Act passed by Congress July 22 establishes 12 federal home loan banks that will lend money to mortgage loan institutions. The measure is designed to rescue the banks that are being forced to close and is augmented by a moratorium on first-mortgage foreclosures ordered by the controller of the currency August 26.

Germany has 5.6 million unemployed; Britain, 2.8 million.

Britain abandons free trade for the first time since 1849 and imposes tariffs and quantitative restrictions on many farm imports while subsidizing British farmers to help them survive the Depression. Imperial preferences are introduced to favor imports from colonial and Commonwealth countries, with special preferences given to dairy products, meat, and wheat from Australia, Canada, and New Zealand.

Mahatma Gandhi begins a "fast unto death" to protest the British government's treatment of India's lowest caste "untouchables" whom Gandhi calls *harijans*—"God's children." Gandhi's campaign of civil disobedience has brought rioting and has landed him in prison, but he persists in his demands for social reform, he urges a new boycott against British goods, and after 6 days of fasting he obtains a pact that improves the status of the "untouchables" (*see* 1930; 1947).

Dearborn, Mich., police fire into a crowd of 3,000 men, women, and children demonstrating outside the Ford Motor Company plant March 7. Four are killed, 100 are wounded, and the wounded are hand-cuffed to their hospital beds on charges of rioting.

The Norris-La Guardia Act passed by Congress March 23 prohibits the use of injunctions in labor disputes except under defined conditions and outlaws "yellow-dog contracts" that make workers promise not to join any labor union. Sponsored by Nebraska congressman George William Norris, now 70, and New York City congressman Fiorello Henry La Guardia, 49, the bill helps establish labor's right to strike, picket, and conduct boycotts.

David Dubinsky (*né* Dobnievski) becomes president of the International Ladies Garment Workers Union (ILGWU) at age 40. The Polish-American organizer launches a membership drive that will triple the union's membership in 3 years.

"Bonus Marchers" descend on Washington beginning in May as some 25,000 poverty-stricken World War veterans demonstrate to obtain "bonuses" authorized by the Adjustment Compensation Act of 1924 but not due until 1945. Hoping to get roughly $500 each, the veterans camp out with wives and children in the city's parks, dumps, empty stores, and warehouses. Sun reporter Drew Pearson, 34, sees "no hope on their faces."

Tanks, gas grenades, and cavalry and infantry armed with machine guns and bayonetted rifles are used to disperse the demonstrators (above) from their main camp on Anacostia Flats and elsewhere in an operation commanded by U.S. Army Chief of Staff Douglas MacArthur, 52, Major Dwight David Eisenhower, 41, Major George Smith Patton, Jr., 45, and other officers. More than 100 casualties are sustained in the violence of July 28, but President Hoover maintains that the Bonus Marchers are "communists and persons with criminal records" rather than veterans.

U.S. motorcar sales fall to just over 1 million, down from more than 5 million in 1929.

Sales of Ford passenger cars to farmers fall to 55,000, down from 650,000 in 1929.

Ford halts production of its Model A introduced in 1927 as it tools up to introduce the first low-priced V-8. Ford loses millions of dollars and lays off workers to reduce payroll costs from $145 million (1929) to $32 million (1933).

The Hudson Terraplane is introduced with stream-lined styling (*see* 1922; AMC, 1954).

Some 25 percent of U.S. auto glass is safety glass. Many states enact legislation requiring safety glass in windshields (*see* Sloan, 1929).

General Motors Corporation forms a subsidiary to acquire electric streetcar companies, convert them

Mahatma Gandhi in India defied the British raj with "passive resistance" that culminated in independence.

1932 (cont.) to GM motorbus operation, and resell them to local entrepreneurs who will agree to buy only GM buses as replacement vehicles (*see* New York, 1936; criminal conspiracy conviction, 1949).

U.S. Route 66 opens to link Chicago and Los Angeles with a 2,200-mile continuous highway that will be called the "Main Street of America." Soon lined with motor courts, Burma-Shave signs, two-pump service stations, and curio shops, Route 66 carries truckers and motorists west via St. Louis, Joplin, Oklahoma City, Amarillo, Gallup, Flagstaff, Winona, Kingman, Barstow, and San Bernardino.

The first patent application for a parking meter is made in December by *Oklahoma City News* editor Carl C. Magee, who will be granted rights in 1936. Magee will apply in 1935 for a patent on a refined version of his 1932 parking meter. 174 Dual Park-O-Meters made by the Dual Parking Meter Company will be installed in Oklahoma City in July 1935, 300 more will be ordered when their success is demonstrated (police officers will be obliged to explain that no jackpots can be expected by those who deposit coins), and meters of the improved design will appear in the streets of major world cities in the next few decades.

Washington's Arlington Bridge across the Potomac is completed by McKim, Mead and White of New York.

London's Lambeth Bridge of 1862 is replaced by a new bridge across the Thames.

Sydney, Australia, completes its Harbour Bridge to connect the city with its suburban areas. It is the world's largest arch bridge.

Japan's Bridgestone Tire Company is founded by entrepreneur Shojiro Ishibashi, whose name means "stone bridge." His company will become the world's eighth largest rubber manufacturer.

Europe's Simplon-Orient Express becomes the Arlberg-Orient Express as it inaugurates a new route closer to the original route of 1883. The 6-mile Arlberg Tunnel avoids the long detour into Italy and takes the luxury train from Switzerland eastward to Austria and thence to Istanbul (*see* 1929; 1952).

New York's Independent subway system opens September 10 to extend service into areas not served by the BMT or by the 28-year-old IRT (*see* 1933).

The Welland Sea Canal of 1829 opens to connect Lake Erie and Lake Huron after having been rebuilt to accommodate vessels up to 600 feet in length with a 22-foot draft.

California's Lockheed Aircraft Company is acquired from its receivers in bankruptcy for $40,000 by a group formed by Boston's Lee, Higginson banking house and aircraft designer Lloyd Carl Stearman, 33, who becomes the first president of the revived Lockheed Company (*see* Northrop, Vultee, 1928). Stearman worked in partnership with Clyde Cessna and Walter Beech in 1924 to produce the Travel Air, a pioneer civilian production plane, and after being nearly wiped out in 1929, he merged his Stearman Aircraft Company at Wichita with United Aircraft which produces his Stearman training planes. Stearman will head Lockheed for several years, he will design airplanes and spacecraft that will include the Lockheed Electra, and he will design swing-wings for the F-111 fighter-bomber.

Beech Aircraft Corporation is founded at Wichita, Kan., by Walter H. Beech (above) and his wife Olive Ann, 28, who will head the company after Beech's death in 1950 (*see* Beech Bonanza, 1945).

The Benzedrine Inhaler is introduced by Smith Kline & French Laboratories whose nasal decongestant uses amphetamine as its active ingredient. The drug will be employed in treating hyperkinetic children, it will be prescribed for obesity, and it will be the basis of a "speed" culture based on drug abuse.

New York Hospital moves into a huge new facility on York Avenue with 1,165 beds. It will remain the city's largest private voluntary hospital (*see* 1791).

The Experiment in International Living is founded by Syracuse University official Donald Beates Watt, 39, who will direct the program until 1950. An estimated 250,000 young people—including 50,000 Americans—will live with families in countries other than their own in the next 45 years under the aegis of the organization whose purpose is to foster international understanding and goodwill.

Boise State College is founded in Idaho.

Laurence Institute of Technology is founded at Southfield, Mich.

British Broadcasting Corporation (BBC) takes over the responsibility of developing television from the Baird Company (*see* 1926; 1927; 1936).

The Walter Winchell Show begins on U.S. radio December 4 featuring *New York Daily Mirror* columnist Walter Winchell, 35: "Good evening, Mr. and Mrs. America and all the ships at sea. . . ."

William Esty Co. is founded by New York advertising executive William Cole Esty, 38, who has quit the J. Walter Thompson Co. because that agency will accept no cigarette or liquor accounts. Esty's first client is the R. J. Reynolds Company, and he develops a campaign for Camel cigarettes.

The *Family Circle* begins publication at Newark, N.J., early in September with 24 pages. The first magazine to be distributed exclusively through grocery stores, the weekly is given away free to shoppers at two eastern grocery chains and will have a circulation of 1.44 million by 1939 (*see* 1946; *Woman's Day*, 1937).

Nonfiction *Death in the Afternoon* by Ernest Hemingway indulges the novelist's obsession with bullfighting.

Fiction *Laughter in the Dark* by Russian novelist Vladimir Nabokov, 33; *Brave New World* by Aldous

Huxley, who projects a world in the "Year of Our Ford" when people will go not to the movies but to the "feelies," where men will be attended by "pneumatic" girls (a word borrowed from T. S. Eliot's poem "Whispers of Immortality"), and where human reproduction will be controlled by the state; *A Lesson in Love* (*La Naissance du jour*) by Colette; *Salavin* by Georges Duhamel; *Radetzkymarsch* by Joseph Roth; *The Knot of Vipers* (*Le Noeud de Viperes*) by François Mauriac; *Journey to the End of the Night* (*Voyage au bout de la nuit*) by French physician-novelist Louis-Ferdinand Céline (Henri-Louis Destouches), 38; *Little Man, What Now?* (*Kleiner Mann —was nun?*) by German novelist Hans Fallada (Rudolf Ditzen), 30; *The Memorial* by Christopher Isherwood; *Snooty Baronet* by Wyndham Lewis; *Black Mischief* by Evelyn Waugh; *Poor Toni* by Scottish novelist-poet-critic Edwin Muir, 45; *Limits and Renewals* (stories) by Rudyard Kipling; *Light in August* by William Faulkner; *Tobacco Road* by U.S. novelist Erskine Caldwell, 29, who depicts the depravity of poor whites in Georgia's sharecropper society; *The Case of the Velvet Claws* by California lawyer Erle Stanley Gardner, 43, who started writing occasional detective stories in 1921, has been averaging more than a million words of pulp magazine writing each year since 1928, and will follow his Perry Mason detective novel with dozens in the same vein; *Death Under Sail* by English physicist-novelist C. P. (Charles Percy) Snow, 27; *The Crime of Inspector Maigret* by Franco-Belgian novelist Georges Simenon, 29.

Juvenile *Little House in the Big Woods* by Missouri novelist Laura Ingalls Wilder, 65, who begins a series of eight volumes that will appear in the next 11 years to recount her girlhood in the Midwest of the late 19th century; *L'Histoire de Babar* (*The Story of Babar, the Little Elephant*) by French artist-writer Jean De Brunhoff, 33, whose book will sell 50,000 copies in French before being translated into English. De Brunhoff will die of tuberculosis in 1937 but his book and its sequel, *Travels of Babar*, will be followed by further Babar adventures produced by his son.

Poetry "Anna Livia Plurabelle" by James Joyce, whose daughter Lucia is troubled by mental disease that will be diagnosed as schizophrenia; *Poems* by Stephen Spender; *Late Arrival* (*Sent pa jorden*) by Swedish poet Gunnar Ekelöf, 25.

Painting *Girl Before a Mirror* by Pablo Picasso; *Christ Mocked by Soldiers* by Georges Rouault; *Sacre Coeur* by Maurice Utrillo; *Professor Sauerbruch* by Max Liebermann, now 85; *Sacco and Vanzetti* by Lithuanian-American painter Ben (Benjamin) Shahn, 33, who produces 23 gouaches inspired by the execution in 1927; *Daughters of the American Revolution* by Grant Wood; *Butterfly Chaser* by Thomas Hart Benton.

Sculpture *Standing Woman* by Gaston Lachaise; *Head of a Woman* by Pablo Picasso; *Jonah* fountain by Carl Milles; *Prospero and Ariel* by English sculptor Eric Gill, 50, for London's Broadcasting House.

Motorized and hand-cranked "stabiles" by U.S. sculptor-painter Alexander Calder, 34, create a stir in Paris. "Le Cirque Calder" exhibited in 1926 consisted of small wire sculptures of animals and acrobats; Dadaist-surrealist Jean Arp has suggested the word "stabile." Calder follows his stabiles with hanging "mobiles" that move with air currents (Marcel Duchamp has suggested the name).

Polaroid film invented by Harvard College dropout Edwin Herbert Land, 23, is the world's first synthetic light-polarizing film. Land opens the Land-Wheelwright Laboratories at Boston with former Harvard physics instructor George Wheelwright and the firm will produce polarizing filters for cameras beginning in 1935 (*see* sunglasses, 1936; camera, 1947).

Theater *The Animal Kingdom* by Philip Barry 1/12 at New York's Broadhurst Theater with William Gargan, Leslie Howard, Ilka Chase, 183 perfs.; *There's Always Juliet* by U.S. playwright John Van Druten 2/15 at New York's Empire Theater, with Edna Best, Herbert Marshall, 108 perfs.; *Night Over Taos* by Maxwell Anderson 3/9 at New York's 48th Street Theater, with J. Edward Bromberg, Morris Carnovsky, Clifford Odets, 13 perfs.; *Too True to Be Good* by George Bernard Shaw 4/4 at New York's Guild Theater, with Beatrice Lillie, Hope Williams, Leo G. Carroll, Claude Rains, 57 perfs.; *Another Language* by Rose Franken 4/25 at New York's Booth Theater, with Margaret Hamilton, Margaret Wycherly, Dorothy Stickney, 344 perfs.; *The Ermine* (*L'ermine*) by French playwright Jean Anouilh, 21, 4/26 at the Théâtre de l'oeuvre, Paris; *Dinner at Eight* by George S. Kaufman and Edna Ferber 10/22 at New York's Music Box Theater, with Constance Collier, 232 perfs.; *Autumn Crocus* by U.S. playwright C. L. Anthony 11/19 at New York's Morosco Theater, with Patricia Collinge, Francis Lederer, 210 perfs.; *Biography* by S. N. Behrman 12/12 at New York's Guild Theater, with Earle Larimore, Ina Claire, 283 perfs.

Washington's Folger Library opens. The great Shakespearean collection has been funded by the late Standard Oil Company chairman Henry Clay Folger who died 2 years ago at age 73.

Radio comedy shows *The Jack Benny Show* 5/2 on NBC stations with violinist-comedian Benny, 38, who has changed his name from Benjamin Kubelsky, has toured in vaudeville (originally as Ben K. Benny), appeared last year in *Earl Carroll's Vanities*, and begins a radio show that will continue for 23 years with the help of Benny's wife Mary Livingston, Don Wilson, Dennis Day, Eddie "Rochester" Anderson, and scriptwriters who will work endless variations on the themes of Benny's stinginess, his Maxwell car, his violin playing, and his age. Perpetually 39, Benny will later move to CBS, will move to television in 1955, and will continue for another 10 years. *The Fred Allen Show* 10/23 on CBS stations with former

1932 (cont.) vaudeville juggler Allen, 38, who has changed his name from John Florence Sullivan. His 1-hour *Linit Show* will become the *Salad Bowl Revue* for Hellmann's mayonnaise, the *Sal Hepatica Revue* for Bristol-Myers, the *Texaco Star Theater* for the Texas Company, and finally *The Fred Allen Show*, its cast will include Allen's wife Portland Hoffa, it will become a half-hour show beginning June 28, 1942, it will introduce "Allen's Alley" December 13 of that year, it will reach an audience of 20 million, and it will continue until June 29, 1949, when Allen's guest will be Jack Benny (above).

Radio serial debuts *One Man's Family* 4/28 over NBC stations in San Francisco, Los Angeles, and Seattle from 9:30 to 10 in the evening created and written by Carleton Errol Morse, 30. The weekly program will be expanded to the entire NBC network in mid-May of next year and will continue as a daily 15-minute show from June 5, 1950, through May 1959, with 3,256 episodes recounting events in the lives of Henry and Fanny Barbour and their children Paul, Hazel, Claudia, Cliff, and Jack. *Just Plain Bill* 9/19 over CBS stations. The series has been devised by Frank Hummert and Anne Ashenhurst, who will marry Hummert in 1935 (both work for Chicago's Blackett & Sample advertising agency). *Betty and Bob* 10/10 over NBC Blue Network stations is another new soap opera developed by Frank Hummert and Anne Ashenhurst, whose productions will dominate daytime radio. The show will continue until mid-March of 1940. *Buck Rogers in the Twenty-Fifth Century* 11/7 over CBS stations. The children's adventure show will continue until late March 1947.

Films   Edmund Goulding's *Grand Hotel* with Greta Garbo, Joan Crawford, John and Lionel Barrymore, Lewis Stone, Wallace Beery, Jean Hersholt; Merian C. Cooper and Ernest Schoedsack's *King Kong* with Fay Wray, Bruce Cabot; Lewis Milestone's *Rain* with Joan Crawford, Walter Huston; G. W. Pabst's *Don Quixote* with Fyodor Chaliapin, George Robey; Howard Hawks's *Scarface* with George Raft; Fritz Lang's *M* with Peter Lorre; Mervyn LeRoy's *I Am a Fugitive from a Chain Gang* with Paul Muni; Jack Conway's *Arsene Lupin* with John and Lionel Barrymore; James Whale's *The Old Dark House* with Charles Laughton, Melvyn Douglas, Raymond Massey, Gloria Stuart, Lilian Bond, Boris Karloff; Carl Dreyer's *Vampyr*; Cecil B. DeMille's *The Sign of the Cross* with Fredric March, Elissa Landi, Claudette Colbert, Charles Laughton; Josef von Sternberg's *Shanghai Express* with Marlene Dietrich, Clive Brook; George Cukor's *A Bill of Divorcement* with John Barrymore, Katharine Hepburn (Bryn Mawr '28); Ernst Lubitsch's *Trouble in Paradise* with Herbert Marshall, Miriam Hopkins, Kay Francis; Josef von Sternberg's *Blonde Venus* with Marlene Dietrich, Herbert Marshall, English-American actor Cary Grant (Archibald Alexander Leach), 28; Archie Mayo's *Night After Night* with Mae West, George Raft; Jack Conway's *Red-Headed Woman* with Jean Harlow; Edward Cline's *Million-Dollar Legs* with W. C. Fields, Jack Oakie; James Cruze, H. Bruce Humberstone, Stephen Roberts, William A. Seiter, Ernst Lubitsch, and Norman Taurog's *If I Had a Million* with Gary Cooper, George Raft, W. C. Fields.

Stage musicals   *Face the Music* 2/17 at New York's New Amsterdam Theater, with Mary Boland, music and lyrics by Irving Berlin, songs that include "Manhattan Madness," "Let's Have Another Cup of Coffee," 165 perfs.; *Words and Music* 9/16 at London's Adelphi Theatre, with Joyce Barbour, Ivy St. Helier, John Mills, music and lyrics by Noel Coward, songs that include "Mad Dogs and Englishmen," "Mad About the Boy," "Journey's End," "Let's Say Goodbye," 164 perfs.; *Earl Carroll's Vanities* 9/27 at New York's Broadway Theater, with Milton Berle, Helen Broderick, music by Harold Arlen and Richard Myers, lyrics by Ted Koehler and Edward Heyman, songs that include "I Gotta Right to Sing the Blues," 87 perfs.; *Americana* 10/5 at New York's Shubert Theater, with music by Jay Gorney, Harold Arlen, Richard Myers, Herman Hupfield, lyrics by E. Y. Harburg, songs that include "Brother, Can You Spare a Dime" (music by Gorney), 77 perfs.; *Music in the Air* 11/8 at New York's Alvin Theater, with Al Shean, Walter Slezak, music by Jerome Kern, lyrics by Oscar Hammerstein II, songs that include "I've Told Every Little Star," 334 perfs.; *Take a Chance* 11/26 at New York's Apollo Theater, with Jack Haley, Ethel Merman, Sid Silvers, music by Nacio Herb Brown, Vincent Youmans, and Richard Whiting, lyrics by B. G. DeSylva, songs that include "You're an Old Smoothie," 243 perfs.; *Gay Divorce* 11/29 at New York's Ethel Barrymore Theater, with Fred Astaire, Claire Luce, music and lyrics by Cole Porter, songs that include "Night and Day," 248 perfs.; *Walk a Little Faster* 12/7 at New York's St. James Theater, with Beatrice Lillie, Bobby Clark, music by Vernon Duke, lyrics by E. Y. Harburg, songs that include "April in Paris," "That's Life," 119 perfs.

Ballet   *Cotillon* 4/12 at Monte Carlo's Théâtre de Monte Carlo, with the new Ballets Russe de Monte Carlo organized by George Balanchine, music by the late Emmanuel Chabrier; *Jeux d' Enfants (Children's Games)* 4/14 at Monte Carlo, with Irina Baronova, Tamara Tommanova, David Lichine, music by the late Georges Bizet, choreography by Leonide Massine, scenery and costumes by Joan Miró.

Hollywood musicals   Frank Tuttle's *The Big Broadcast* with Kate Smith, George Burns and Gracie Allen, the Mills Brothers, the Boswell Sisters, Cab Calloway, and Bing Crosby, who begins regular radio broadcasts; Rouben Mamoulian's *Love Me Tonight* with Maurice Chevalier, Jeanette MacDonald, music by Richard Rodgers, lyrics by Lorenz Hart, songs that include "Lover," "Mimi," "Isn't It Romantic."

New York's Radio City Music Hall opens December 27 in Rockefeller Center with 6,200 seats. A mighty Wurlitzer organ and a 100-piece orchestra accompany vaudeville acts presented by showman Samuel

"Roxy" Rothafel, but the world's largest indoor theater fails to attract crowds and will not gain success until it renames its high-kicking "Roxyette" chorus girls "Rockettes" and shows motion pictures.

First performances Four Orchestral Songs by Arnold Schoenberg 2/21 at Frankfurt-am-Main; Suite for Flute and Piano by Walter Piston 4/30 at Trask's Yaddo outside Saratoga Springs, N.Y.; *From the Gayety and Sadness of the American Scene* by U.S. composer Roy Harris, 34, 12/29 at Los Angeles.

Popular songs "Say It Isn't So" and "How Deep Is the Ocean" by Irving Berlin; "I Don't Stand a Ghost of a Chance with You" by Victor Young, lyrics by Bing Crosby and Ned Washington; "I'm Getting Sentimental Over You" by George Bassman, lyrics by Ned Washington; "(I'd Love to Spend) One Hour With You" by Richard Whiting, lyrics by Leo Robin; "Don't Blame Me" by Jimmy McHugh, lyrics by Dorothy Fields; "Yours" by Gonzalo Roig, lyrics by Albert Gamse; "It Don't Mean a Thing if It Ain't Got that Swing" by Duke Ellington, lyrics by Irving Mills; "Willow Weep for Me" by Ann Ronell.

 The Olympic Games at Los Angeles attract 2,403 contestants from 39 countries. California athlete Mildred "Babe" Didrikson, 18, wins the javelin throw and sets a new record of 11.7 seconds for the 80-meter hurdles.

Jack Sharkey regains the world heavyweight boxing title June 21 by a 15-round decision over Germany's Max Schmeling at the new Garden Bowl in Long Island City, New York. "We wuz robbed!" cries Schmeling's manager Joe Jacobs.

Pitcher J. H. "Dizzy" Dean plays his first full season with the St. Louis Cardinals to begin a brief but dazzling career with the Gas House Gang. The 22-year-old Dean will lead the National League in strikeouts for the next 3 years.

Ducky Medwick joins the Cardinals (above) to begin an 8-year career with the team. Joseph Michael Medwick, 20, will be traded to the Brooklyn Dodgers in 1940, then to the New York Giants, then to the Boston Braves, then back to the Dodgers before retiring in 1948 with a lifetime batting average of .348

The New York Yankees win the World Series by defeating the Chicago Cubs 4 to 0. With the third game tied 4 to 4 October 1 and with two strikes against him, Babe Ruth leers at his hecklers, points to the flagpole at the right of the scoreboard in center field, and hits the next pitch out of Wrigley Field.

The Washington Redskins professional football team has its beginnings in the Boston Braves team organized by George P. Marshall.

The Army-Navy football game played since 1890 moves from New York to the University of Pennsylvania's Franklin Field at Philadelphia. The game will move in 1936 to the huge Philadelphia Municipal Stadium built in an unsuccessful attempt to outbid Los Angeles for this year's Olympic Games.

 Revlon Company is started by New York cosmetics salesman Charles Revson, 26, with his brother Joseph, 28, and chemist Charles Lachman, 35. When employer Elka Cosmetics rejects his ultimatum that he be made national distributor, young Revson rents a loft in the New York garment district, borrows money at 2 percent per month, and with Lachman's help develops a superior opaque nail enamel which he promotes with exotic names such as Tropic Sky rather than with the descriptive identifications dark red, medium red, pink, etc., that have been traditional. Concentrating on beauty salons, Revlon obtains distribution by use of intimidation. Volume for the first 10 months is only $4,055.09, and the Revsons' 22-year-old brother Martin rejects suggestions that he join the firm, saying that someone in the family had better make some money (he will cling to his $35 per week Wall Street brokerage clerk position until 1935). Revlon will start distributing through drugstores in 1937, using salesmen who "accidentally" destroy displays set up by the competition, and by 1941 the firm will have a virtual monopoly on beauty salon sales (*see* 1940).

General Shoe Corporation is founded by Maxey Jarman, who takes over the Jarman Shoe Company started by his father in 1924. Jarman renames the firm that he will control completely after his father's death in 1938 (*see* 1950).

Johnson Glo-Coat floor wax is introduced by the S. C. Johnson Company of Racine, Wis. (*see* 1886; Frank Lloyd Wright building, 1939; Kleer, 1964).

 Parliament cigarettes are introduced by Benson & Hedges. The premium-priced brand has a filter-tip "mouthpiece" and comes in a box (*see* Viceroy, 1936).

The Zippo lighter designed by Blaisdell Oil Company owner George Grant Blaisdell, 37, is introduced by the Zippo Manufacturing Co. of Bradford, Pa.

 The kidnapping of Charles A. Lindbergh, Jr., March 1 makes world headlines. The aviation pioneer pays a $50,000 ransom for his child's safe return, but the body of the 20-month old infant is found 2 months later on Lindbergh's New Jersey estate while 5,000 federal agents comb the country (*see* 1934).

A Phoenix court convicts Winnie Ruth Judd, 27, of having killed two women, dismembering one body, and shipping both to Los Angeles in a truck (blood seeping from the trunk has led to the discovery of the bodies). Sentenced to be hanged, Judd will later be declared insane, she will be sentenced to a mental institution for life, but she will escape seven times and will be at large for 7 years from 1962 to 1969.

Philadelphia's Savings Fund Society building at 12 South 12th Street is completed by George Howe and William Lescaze and is the first major international-style skyscraper to be built in the United States. The 36-story structure has 32 office floors which are visually separate from a vertical circulation spine with floor and spine all floating on a curved-corner base.

1932 (cont.) New York's 80 Pine Street skyscraper is completed with 66 floors in the Wall Street area.

New York's Port Authority building between Eighth and Ninth Avenues from 15th to 16th Streets is completed by Cass Gilbert, now 73, with 2.3 million square feet of rentable space.

Pittsburgh's 42-story Gulf Refining Company building is completed at Grant Street and 7th Avenue.

The Nebraska State Capitol building is completed at Lincoln. It was designed by the late Bertram Grosvenor Goodhue, who died in 1924 at age 55.

London's Cumberland Hotel opens across from the Marble Arch with 900 rooms.

 Drainage of the Zuider Zee is completed in the Netherlands to open up new farmland (*see* 1918).

"Every European nation has a definite land policy and has had one for generations," Franklin Roosevelt tells the Democratic convention (above). "We have none. Having none, we face a future of soil erosion and timber famine ..." (*see* Civilian Conservation Corps, 1933; Soil Erosion Service, 1933).

Waterton-Glacier International Peace Park is created by the United States and Canada. The new park embraces 22-year-old Glacier National Park.

 Famine in the Ukraine and in the Caucasus kills thousands.

More Americans are hungry or ill-fed than ever before in the nation's history. Nearly a million go back to the land.

Distribution to needy Americans of 40 million bushels of wheat held by the Federal Farm Bureau is authorized by Congress March 7 with the distribution to be handled by the Red Cross. Another 45 million bushels of wheat are added July 5, plus 250 million pounds of cotton.

 U.S. farm prices fall to 40 percent of 1929 levels.

Wheat falls to below 25 cents a bushel, oats to 10 cents, sugar to 3 cents per pound, cotton and wool to 5 cents per pound.

Iowa Farmers' Union militants start a 30-day strike August 9 to protest low farm prices. "Stay at home! Sell nothing!" say union members, who smash the windshields and headlights of farm trucks they catch going to market and block highways with chains and logs to enforce their strike.

 A breakthrough in vitamin B research is made at Germany's Kaiser Wilhelm Institute for Biology. Nobel laureate Otto H. Warburg, 49, and his associates find a yellow coenzyme that catalyzes the transfer of hydrogen atoms (*see* vitamin B$_2$—riboflavin, 1935).

Vitamin C (ascorbic acid) is isolated by University of Pittsburgh biochemist Charles Glen King, 36 (*see* 1933; Szent-Györgyi, 1928).

 100,000,000 Guinea Pigs by Consumer's Research engineer Arthur Kallet, 29, and F. J. Schlink relates horror stories that dramatize the dangers in some foods, drugs, and cosmetics sold despite the Pure Food and Drug Act of 1906 and its amendments (*see* Schlink, 1929). The book becomes a best seller, and Kallet splits with Schlink to start a rival organization at Mount Vernon, N.Y.—Consumers Union.

 Florida's Gulf Coast has its worst red tide since 1916. Millions of fish are killed (*see* 1946).

 United Fruit Company profits drop, and the company's stock falls in value to $10.25 per share, down from $105 in November of 1929. Samuel Zemurray sees his holdings decline in value to $4.5 million, down from $31.5 million, he persuades United Fruit's other directors to appoint him to the newly created post of general manager, he regains control of the company's Latin American properties, and the stock climbs back to $26 within a few weeks on the strength of Zemurray's prestige alone (*see* 1929; Chiquita banana, 1944).

Ralston Purina Company begins a sharp upward course under the direction of Donald Danforth, 33, who takes over from his father (*see* 1902). Danforth will move Ralston Purina into new consumer food areas in the next 24 years and will increase sales from $19 million to more than $400 million.

Campbell's tomato juice is introduced by Campbell Soup Company (*see* 1923; Libby's, 1929, 1933).

Sacramento tomato juice has its beginnings in the Bercut-Richards Packing Company founded by Wheatland, Calif., machinist Thomas Richards who was called in last year by a small fruit canning cooperative to solve some production problems. Richards has been helped by Peter and Henri Bercut to buy the Sacramento facility which he will turn from packing fruit to canning tomato juice under the Sacramento label.

Norton Simon, Inc. has its beginnings in the Val Vita Foods Company started by California entrepreneur Norton Simon, 25, who has bought a bankrupt Fullerton orange juice bottling company for $7,000. Simon creates a line of canned fruits and vegetables, his sales the first year are $43,000, they will grow in 2 years to more than $500,000, and in 10 years to nearly $9 million (*see* 1942).

Frito corn chips are introduced by San Antonio, Tex., candymaker C. Elmer Doolin who goes into a local cafe for a sandwich, is served a side dish of corn chips created by Mexican cartoonist-cafe owner Gustavo Olguin, acquires the recipe for $100, and goes into business with his mother and his brother Earl using a converted potato ricer to cut *tortilla* dough into strips. Brother Earl develops a machine to force the dough out under pressure, and the Doolins license local companies to make Fritos using machinery purchased at cost with Doolin-trained personnel, taking a royalty on each package sold (*see* Frito-Lay, 1961).

Hellmann's mayonnaise is acquired from General Foods by Best Foods, Inc., which will merchandise it as Hellmann's Real Mayonnaise in eastern markets and as Best Foods mayonnaise in western markets (*see* 1903; 1927; Corn Products Refining Co., 1958).

Skippy peanut butter is introduced by Rosefield Packing Company of California, whose J. L. Rosefield cancels his exclusive licensing agreement with Swift's Derby Foods to use the Rosefield process in making its Peter Pan peanut butter (*see* 1928). Rosefield markets his own brand named after the comic strip started the same year he invented his process (1923) and he also introduces the first smooth-base peanut butter that contains chunks of roasted peanuts. Rosefield will patent a new type of cold-processed hydrogenated peanut oil in 1950, and by 1954 Rosefield Packing will have nearly 25 percent of the U.S. peanut butter market. Best Foods (above) will acquire Rosefield Packing in 1955.

Mounds candy bars are sold in packages of twin bars at the same nickel price formerly charged for one bar as Peter Paul converts a soap-wrapping machine to handle candy bars and uses machinery to replace hand wrapping while switching from a foil wrap to cellophane (*see* 1921; Almond Joy, 1947).

Three Musketeers candy bars are introduced at a nickel by Mars, Inc. (*see* 1930; M&Ms, 1940).

Big Bear Super Market opens at Elizabeth, N. J., and is the first large cut-rate self-service grocery store (*see* King Kullen, 1930). Local entrepreneurs Robert M. Otis and Roy O. Dawson have put up a total of $1,000 to take over an empty car factory on the outskirts of town, their Big Bear the Price Crusher store has 50,000 square feet of pine tables displaying meats, fruit, vegetables, packaged foods, radios, automobile accessories, and paints, and after 1 year they have made a profit of $166,000 by selling Quaker Oats oatmeal at 3 cents a box, pork chops at 10 cents a pound. Traditional grocers persuade local newspapers to refuse Big Bear advertising and push through a state law against selling at or below cost, but Big Bear is quickly imitated by Great Tiger, Bull Market, Great Leopard, and others as the supermarket revolution gathers force (*see* Food Fair, 1933).

Harry's Bar opens at the end of Venice's Grand Canal at the intersection of the Calle Valleresso. Italian restaurateur Giuseppe Cipriani, 32, names it after Harry Pickering, an American who used to drink at the Hotel Europe owned by Cipriani's father and who has loaned Giuseppe half of the $10,000 he needed to open the hotel-style bar that will expand into a restaurant.

1933 Adolf Hitler begins 12 years as dictator of the German Reich, Franklin D. Roosevelt begins 12 years as president of the United States, Antonio de Oliveira Salazar begins 37 years as dictator of Portugal.

Adolf Hitler comes to power as chancellor January 30 on a rising tide of German nationalism and economic unrest. Fire destroys the Reichstag at Berlin February 27, Hitler's Nazis immediately accuse the Communists of having started the fire, they fabricate a case against Dutch Communist Marinus Van der Lubbe, 23, who is tried and promptly executed, but Nazi leader Hermann Goering, 40, is accused at the trial of having set the fire himself (the accusation comes from Georgi Dimitrov, who will later be premier of Bulgaria) (*see* 1947).

The National Socialist German Workers (Nazi) party wins 44 percent of the votes in the Reichstag elections March 5, the Nationalist party supported by industrialists who include Fritz Thyssen and Alfried Krupp wins 8 percent of the votes, the Nationalists throw their support to Hitler by helping to pass an Enabling Act March 23, and the Nazi regime is given dictatorial powers.

Portuguese prime minister and finance minister Antonio de Oliveira Salazar, 44, drafts a new constitution that will make the most backward country in Europe a "unitary and corporative republic"—a fascistic dictatorship based on political repression that dictator Salazar will head for more than 37 years and that will keep the country backward.

Austrian chancellor Engelbert Dollfuss, 40, proclaims a dictatorship March 7 and soon after dissolves the Bundesversammlung as antigovernment agitation increases following the success of the Nazis in Germany. Dolfuss prohibits parades and assemblies as of March 8, but Austrian Nazis stage a giant demonstration and riot March 29, and when the government forbids the wearing of uniforms by members of any political party, Hitler retaliates by imposing a tax of 1,000 marks on any German who visits Austria, thus ruining Austria's tourist business (*see* 1934).

Japan announces that she will withdraw from the League of Nations in 1935. The League suffers its first serious setback.

U.S.-Soviet relations are established November 16 for the first time since the 1917 revolution.

Chicago mayor Anton Joseph Cermak, 59, is mortally wounded February 15 at Miami by an assassin who is thought to have been aiming at President-elect Roosevelt but who may simply be a hired gangland hit man.

New York's Tammany Hall is unseated by Fiorello Henry La Guardia of 1932 Norris-La Guardia Act fame who wins election as mayor on a reform-fusion ticket and begins 12 years at City Hall.

$ Detroit defaults on its $400 million debt February 14 when bank closings prevent completion of a $20 million emergency loan. The city has been caught between reduced tax revenues and the need for greater welfare support arising from the collapse of the automobile industry, and the debt will not be fully repaid until 1963.

President Roosevelt enters the White House March 4 with more than 15 million Americans out of work and says, "The only thing we have to fear is fear itself." Blacks, unskilled workers, and workers in

Franklin D. Roosevelt's New Deal measures helped Americans survive the Depression without a revolution.

heavy industry are especially affected by the widespread unemployment, but even Americans with jobs have had their wages and hours reduced. Wage-earner incomes are 40 percent below 1929 levels.

A nationwide bank holiday is proclaimed March 5 by presidential order, and an embargo is placed on gold exports.

The Emergency Banking Act passed by Congress March 6 gives the president control over banking transactions and foreign exchange, forbids hoarding or export of gold, and authorizes banks to open as soon as they are determined by bank examiners to be solvent. Banks begin to reopen March 13, and by March 16 about 75 percent of all Federal Reserve banks are back in business.

All private gold holdings must be surrendered to Federal Reserve banks in exchange for other coin or currency, says a presidential order issued April 5.

The United States abandons the gold standard April 19 by presidential proclamation. A currency stabilization plan proposed by the gold standard countries meeting in July at a World Monetary and Economic Conference at London is rejected by President Roosevelt. In October the president authorizes the Reconstruction Finance Corporation to buy newly mined gold at $31.36 per ounce, 27 cents above the world market price.

The U.S. national income falls to $40.2 billion, down from $87.8 billion in 1929, and the national wealth falls to $330 billion, down from $439 billion.

A Federal Emergency Relief Act passed by Congress May 12 establishes a $500 million fund that can be distributed in grants to the states. Former social worker Harry Lloyd Hopkins, 43, is appointed federal administrator of emergency relief, and he per-

suades the president to establish a Civil Works Administration (CWA) November 9 to provide emergency jobs for 4 million unemployed Americans through the winter (see 1934; WPA, 1935).

The Home Owners Loan Corporation is established by Congress June 13 as mortgage foreclosures average 1,000 per day. In the next 4 years the HOLC will grant emergency loans of more than $4 billion to prevent foreclosures (see 1931).

A National Industrial Recovery Act (NIRA) passed by Congress June 16 provides for "codes of fair competition" in industries and for collective bargaining with labor, whose unions have dropped in membership from 3.5 million to less than 3 million. Industry agrees to shorten working hours and in some cases to limit production and fix prices (see Supreme Court decision, 1935).

The first NRA Blue Eagle signs of cooperation with the National Recovery Administration appear in store and factory windows August 1: "We Do Our Part."

Typical annual U.S. earnings are $3,382 for a physician, $4,218 for a lawyer, $2,250 for an engineer, $8,663 for a congressman, $907 for a construction worker, $216 for a hired farm hand, $260 for a sleep-in domestic servant ($21.66 per month), $3,111 for a college teacher, $1,227 for a public school teacher (5,000 Chicago schoolteachers storm the banks for back pay April 24 after having been paid for 10 months in scrip).

A Stetson hat sells for $5, a gas stove for $23.95 (see truck, motorcar, and food prices below).

Dun & Bradstreet, Inc. is created by a merger of New York's R. G. Dun & Company with Cincinnati's Bradstreet Company. Dun was founded in 1859 by mercantile authority Robert Graham Dun and has published Dun's Review since 1893; Bradstreet was founded by John M. Bradstreet in 1849 under the name Bradstreet's Improved Mercantile Agency; Dun & Bradstreet will provide financial data and credit ratings of U.S. business firms and business executives, many of whom are now in serious straits.

A National Labor Board established by President Roosevelt August 5 under the NRA (above) works to enforce the right of collective bargaining under the chairmanship of U.S. Senator Robert F. Wagner, 56, of New York (see NLRB, 1934; Wagner Act, 1935).

Lynchings spread across the South. Forty-two blacks are killed by lynch mobs.

Saudi Arabia's Abdul-Aziz ibn-Saud gives Standard Oil Company of California a 60-year exclusive concession to explore for oil on a 320,000 square mile tract of desert (see 1932). Ibn-Saud receives a loan of $170,327 from SoCal, which has recently begun pumping oil on the Persian Gulf island of Bahrein and which will soon find that its concession overlies the world's richest petroleum reserve. To help exploit the Saudi Arabian reserve, SoCal makes a 50—

50 arrangement with the 31-year-old Texas Company, forming Arabian American Oil Company (Aramco) to produce the petroleum and CalTex to market it through the Texas Company's outlets in Europe, Africa, and Asia (Aramco will later take in other partners, including the Saudi Arabian government, which will acquire full ownership in 1976).

Gasoline sells for 18 cents a gallon in America.

The Tennessee Valley Authority Act passed by Congress May 18 creates a Tennessee Valley Authority (TVA) to maintain and operate a power plant at Muscle Shoals, Ala.

The Dnieper River Dam is completed in the Soviet Ukraine. Construction of the 810,000-horsepower hydroelectric installation has been directed by Hugh Lincoln Cooper, 68, who built the Muscle Shoals Dam in Alabama, and it will save 3 million tons of coal per year.

The Baltic-White Sea Stalin Ship Canal opens in the Soviet Union to link Povenets on Lake Onega with Belmorsk on the White Sea. The 140-mile canal has been built in 2 years with slave labor at a cost of some 250,000 lives, but its shallow draft and primitive wooden locks will soon make it obsolete (*see* 1923; Moscow-Volga Canal, 1937).

The Illinois Waterway linking the Great Lakes with the Gulf of Mexico via the Mississippi River opens officially at Chicago June 22.

The S. S. *Europa* of the North German-Lloyd line crosses from Cherbourg to New York in 4 days, 16 hours, 48 minutes and breaks the transatlantic speed record set by her sister ship the S. S. *Bremen* in 1929.

The Italian line's S. S. *Rex* sets a new transatlantic speed record by crossing from Cherbourg to New York in 4 days, 13 hours, 58 minutes.

United Fruit Company's Great White Fleet grows to number 95 vessels (*see* 1899; Zemurray, 1932).

Air France is founded August 30 by a merger of France's Aeropostale with another line.

The DC-1 is introduced by Douglas Aircraft, and 25 of the planes are ordered by TWA, whose management has suggested construction of the Douglas Commercial aircraft. It can carry 12 passengers at 150 miles per hour (*see* 1924; 1930; DC-3, 1936).

General Motors gains control of North American Aviation, a holding company that controls Curtiss-Wright, Sperry Gyroscope, Ford Instrument, Berliner-Joyce Aircraft, and Eastern Air Transport and is a major stockholder in most other important U.S. aviation companies (*see* 1934).

General Motors assumes leadership in U.S. motorcar sales, with Chrysler second, Ford third.

The Marmon Automobile Company goes into receivership in May (*see* 1916).

A new Pontiac coupe sells for $585, a new Chevrolet half-ton pickup truck for $650, a 1929 Ford for $580.

New York's new Independent subway line begins the F train from 179th Street in Jamaica to Manhattan and thence to Coney Island's Stillwell Avenue station. The trip takes 85 minutes.

The D train goes into service on the BMT from 205th Street in the Bronx to Coney Island's Stillwell Avenue station—an 85-minute journey for 5 cents.

The A train goes into service on the BMT. The new express will be extended from 207th Street in Manhattan to Far Rockaway or Lefferts Boulevard—a journey of 100 minutes for 5 cents (*see* song, 1941).

Gangsters thought to include Pretty Boy Floyd open fire with machine guns June 17 in front of Kansas City's 16-year-old Union Station and kill hoodlum Frank Nash together with four law enforcement officers who were escorting Nash.

The first pure chemical carcinogen (cancer-causing chemical) is isolated by British biochemist Ernest Kennaway who shows that a polycyclic aromatic hydrocarbon from subtotal combustion will cause cancer in test animals (*see* 1915). Such hydrocarbons are found in air pollution, auto exhausts, and cigarette smoke.

The influenza virus is isolated for the first time following a London epidemic (*see* 1918 pandemic).

A neurotropic vaccine against yellow fever is developed by French researchers who use a strain of attenuated yellow fever virus (*see* Walter Reed, 1900).

Dow Chemical Company opens a plant at Kure Beach, N.C., to produce bromine from seawater (*see* magnesium, 1930).

Dow Chemical starts building a plant at Long Beach, Calif., to produce iodine from oil field brine. Dow will break the British-Chilean nitrate monopoly in iodine and will bring the price of iodine down from $4.50 per pound to 81 cents.

Southern Colorado State College is founded at Pueblo.

West Georgia College is founded at Carrollton.

Black Mountain College is founded at Black Mountain, N.C.

Monmouth College is founded at Long Branch, N.J.

"Fireside chats" begin on radio March 12 as President Roosevelt starts, "My friends . . ." and tries to calm Depression fears and win support for New Deal measures being undertaken to restore the nation's economic health. The president urges listeners to have faith in the banks.

Frequency modulation (FM) to provide static-free radio reception is perfected by radio pioneer Edwin H. Armstrong of 1917 superheterodyne circuit fame, who proved in 1915 that radio waves and static have the same electrical characteristics. Armstrong has insisted that any attempt to eliminate static without

1933 (cont.) some radically new principle would be fruitless and that hundreds of patents for static eliminating devices are worthless (*see* Zenith, 1940).

The first "walkie-talkie" portable two-radio sets are developed by U.S. Army Corps engineers with help from Paul V. Galvin of 1929 Motorola fame, who has built up a multimillion dollar business.

IBM enters the typewriter business by acquiring a firm that has been trying for 10 years to perfect an electric office typewriter. Once part of Northeast Electric Company, Electromatic Typewriters, Inc., is now independent (*see* International Business Machines, 1924; IBM Selectric, 1961).

Newsweek magazine has its beginnings February 17 in a weekly news magazine published under the name *News-Week* by English-American journalist Thomas John Cardel Martyn who has created the magazine to rival Henry R. Luce's 10-year-old *Time* (*see* 1937; 1961).

The *Washington Post* changes hands June 1 as California-born Wall Street copper and chemical millionaire Eugene Meyer, 57, outbids Evalyn McLean, wife of owner Edward B. (Ned) McLean, who is wearing the Hope diamond but cannot match Meyer's bid of $825,000 for the bankrupt paper (*see* 1877). Chief force behind President Hoover's creation of the Reconstruction Finance Corporation last year, Meyer serves as an RFC director, he will battle Franklin D. Roosevelt's New Deal, but his daughter Katharine will marry New Dealer Philip L. Graham, now 17, in 1940 and the *Post* will become a progressive force in U.S. journalism (*see* 1954).

The *Catholic Worker* begins publication with the aim of uniting workers and intellectuals in joint efforts to improve farming, education, and social conditions. Founder Dorothy Day gets support from French-American editor Peter Maurin, who has developed a program of social reconstruction he calls "the green revolution." The new monthly will become an organ for pacifism and social justice, and it will have a circulation of 150,000 within 3 years.

The *Reader's Digest* publishes its first original signed articles. The *Digest* departs from its 11-year-old policy of digesting from other publications and begins to plant feature stories in other magazines for subsequent publication in *Digest* versions (*see* 1922; 1955).

Esquire magazine is launched in October by former advertising copywriter Arnold Gingrich, 29, who has been editing *Apparel Arts* at Chicago since 1931 and who is backed by advertising man William Weintraub, 34, and David Smart. Intended initially to be a men's fashion quarterly distributed through clothing stores and department stores, *Esquire* publishes a story by Ernest Hemingway in its first issue, it features risqué cartoons and drawings of scantily clad women, and despite its high cover price of 50 cents, it quickly sells out on newsstands, begins monthly publication, and in its first 3 years will sell 10 million copies with the help of good writing by Scott Fitzgerald, John Dos Passos, Albert Camus, Aldous Huxley, William Faulkner, Clarence Darrow, H. L. Mencken, Dorothy Parker, Damon Runyon, William Saroyan, Georges Simenon, John Steinbeck, and other leading writers.

"Smilin' Jack" is introduced by cartoonist Zack Terrell Mosley, 26, who began flying lessons last year and who sells his new comic strip to the *Chicago Tribune* and *New York News* syndicate.

"Alley Oop" is introduced August 7 by cartoonist V. T. Hamlin, 33, whose caveman hero will begin moving to other eras of history by means of a remarkable time machine. The new comic strip will be syndicated by NEA Service beginning in April 1939.

The American Newspaper Guild is founded at Washington, D.C., in December to protect city room employees. *New York World-Telegram* reporter Heywood C. Broun, 45, is elected president.

Reynal & Hitchcock publishers is founded by Eugene Reynal of Blue Ribbon Books and Curtice Hitchcock of Macmillan and Stokes, whose new house has its first success publishing Adolph Hitler's *Mein Kampf* in English. The firm will prosper by publishing the *Mary Poppins* books by P. L. Travers.

Nonfiction *The Autobiography of Alice B. Toklas* by émigrée U.S. author-critic Gertrude Stein whose book is actually her own autobiography rather than that of the woman who has been her companion and secretary since 1907. "A rose is a rose is a rose," writes Stein who is famous for being more concerned with the sound and rhythm of words than with intelligibility. *Down and Out in Paris and London* by English writer George Orwell (Eric Blair), 30, whose health was broken by the climate while serving in the Burma Imperial Police and who has experienced poverty as a struggling writer.

Ulysses by James Joyce is ruled acceptable for publication in the United States by Justice John M. Woolsey of the U.S. District Court at New York who rules that the "dirty" words in the 1922 book are appropriate in context and not gratuitous. The case against U.S. government censorship has been brought by Bennett Cerf of Random House who has retained lawyers Morris Ernst, 45, and Alexander Lindsay.

Fiction *Man's Fate* (*La Condition Humaine*) by French novelist André Malraux, 32, wins the Concourt Prize. The novel deals with the undercover struggle against imperialism in Indochina; *The Tales of Jacob* (*Die Geschichten Jaacobs*) by Thomas Mann; *The Bark Tree* (*Le Chiendant*) by French novelist Raymond Queneau, 30; *La Chatte* by Colette; *Fontamara* by Italian novelist Ignazio Silone (Secondo Tranquili), 33, whose anti-Fascist work exposes the plight of Italy's southern peasants; *The Forty Days of Musa Dagh* (*Die vierzig Tage des Musa Dagh*) by Franz Werfel; *All Night at Mr. Stanyhurst's* by English novelist Hugh Edwards, 35; *Opening Day* by

English novelist David Gascoyne, 17; *A Glastonbury Romance* by John Cowper Powys, now 61; *From a View to Death* by Anthony Powell; *Lost Horizon* by English novelist James Hilton, 33, who fascinates readers with a fictional Shangri-la in the Himalayas of Tibet; *Miss Lonelyhearts* by Nathanael West whose advice-to-the-lovelorn newspaper columnist becomes involved with some of his correspondents; *God's Little Acre* by Erskine Caldwell; *The Last Adam* by James Gould Cozzens; *Murder Must Advertise* and *Hangman's Holiday* by Dorothy Sayers.

Poetry *Residence on Earth* (*Residencia en la tierra*) by Pablo Neruda, who has published the work in individual pieces between 1925 and 1931 during a period of spiritual nihilism.

Painting *The Dance* by Henri Matisse.

Germany suppresses all modernistic painting in favor of superficial realism.

Murals *Man at the Crossroads* by Diego Rivera for New York's Radio City Music Hall. The mural is destroyed because it contains a portrait of Nikolai Lenin, but Rivera uses the proceeds of the work to pay for the expenses of frescoes that he executes gratis for New York's New Workers School. *Quetzelcoatl and the Old Order, The Legend of the Races, Stillborn Education,* and *Latin America* by José Clemente Orozco for Dartmouth College.

Sculpture *The Palace at Four A.M.* by Swiss sculptor-painter Alberto Giacometti, 31.

Theater *Design for Living* by Noel Coward 1/24 at New York's Ethel Barrymore Theater, with Coward, Alfred Lunt, Lynne Fontanne, 135 perfs.; *Alien Corn* by Sidney Howard 2/20 at New York's Belasco Theater, with Katherine Cornell, 98 perfs.; *The Enchanted* (*Intermezzo*) by Jean Genet 2/27 at the Comédie des Champs-Elysées, Paris; *Both Your Houses* by Maxwell Anderson 3/6 at New York's Royale Theater, with Morris Carnovsky, Walter C. Kelly, Mary Phillips, Jerome Cowan, Sheppard Strudwick in a polemic against political corruption, 120 perfs., Pulitzer Prize; *Men in White* by U.S. playwright Sidney Kingsley, 27, 9/26 at New York's Broadhurst Theater, with Morris Carnovsky, Luther Adler, Elia Kazan, Clifford Odets, 367 perfs., Pulitzer Prize 1934; *Ah, Wilderness* by Eugene O'Neill (his only comedy) 10/2 at New York's Guild Theater, with George M. Cohan as Nat Miller, William Post, Jr., Elisha Cook, Jr., Gene Lockhart, Philip Moeller, Ruth Gilbert, 289 perfs.; *Tovarich* by French playwright Jacques Duval (Jacques Boularan), 42, 10/13 at the Théâtre de Paris, 800 perfs.; *Mulatto* by Langston Hughes 10/24 at New York's Vanderbilt Theater, with Rose McClendon, 270 perfs.; *Tobacco Road* by U.S. playwright Jack Kirkland, 31, who has adapted last year's Erskine Caldwell novel 12/4 at New York's Masque Theater, with Henry Hull as Jeeter Lester, 3,182 perfs. (the play will run into the 1940s and will break the record of *Abie's Irish Rose* which opened in 1927; *see* 1939); *Twentieth Century* by Ben Hecht and Charles MacArthur 12/29 at New York's Broadhurst Theater, with Eugenia Leontovich as Lilly Garland, Moffat Johnston as Oscar Jaffe, 152 perfs.

Radio drama and variety shows *Oxydol's Own Ma Perkins* continues the soap opera serial genre with daily 15-minute shows sponsored by Procter & Gamble. Actress Virginia Payne, 23, plays the title role she will continue for 27 years. *Don McNeill's Breakfast Club* 6/23 on Chicago radio. Host McNeill, 26, has changed the name of the Pepper Pot and begins a long career of getting studio laughs. *The Romance of Helen Trent* 7/24 is a soap opera developed by Frank Hummert and Anne Ashenhurst, whose show is carried on CBS network stations beginning 10/3. *Jack Armstrong the All-American Boy* 7/31 on Chicago's KBBM with St. John Terrell, who is soon replaced by Jim Ameche. Creator of the show is Robert Hardy Andrews, the sponsor is the 9-year-old "Breakfast of Champions" Wheaties produced by General Mills, the theme song begins, "Wave the flag for Hudson High, boys/ Show them how we stand,/ Ever shall our team be champions,/ Known throughout the land," and the show will continue until 1951.

Sally Rand attracts thousands to the Chicago World's Fair that opens May 27 to celebrate a Century of Progress. The 29-year-old fan dancer gets star billing at the "Streets of Paris" concession on the Midway, she does a slow dance to Debussy's "Clair de Lune" wearing only ostrich plumes, and she is credited with making the fair a success as jobless Americans flock to Chicago in search of fun.

Films Alexander Korda's *The Private Life of Henry VIII* with Charles Laughton; George Cukor's *Dinner at Eight* with John Barrymore, Jean Harlow; Frank Lloyd's *Cavalcade* with Diana Wynyard, Clive Brook, Ursula Jeans; Lowell Sherman's *Morning Glory* with Katharine Hepburn, Adolphe Menjou, Douglas Fairbanks, Jr.; Lowell Sherman's *She Done Him Wrong* with Mae West as Diamond Lil ("Come up and see me sometime"), Cary Grant, Gilbert Roland; Wesley Ruggles's *I'm No Angel* with Mae West, Cary Grant in a film version of the 41-year-old "sex queen's" stage hit; Gustav Machaty's *Ecstasy* with Hedy Lamarr; Raoul Walsh's *Sailor's Luck* with James Dunn, Sally Eilers; James Cruze's *I Cover the Waterfront* with Ben Lyon, Claudette Colbert; Stewart Warner's *The Eagle and the Hawk* with Fredric March, Cary Grant, Jack Oakie, Carole Lombard; Ernst Lubitsch's *Design for Living* with Gary Cooper, Fredric March, Miriam Hopkins; George Cukor's *Little Women* with Katharine Hepburn, Joan Bennett, Francis Dee, Jean Parker, Paul Lukas; Frank Lloyd's *Berkeley Square* with Leslie Howard; Jean Vigo's *Zero for Conduct* (*Zero de conduit*); Edward Sutherland's *International House* with W. C. Fields, George Burns, Gracie Allen, Bela Lugosi, Cab Calloway, Rudy Vallee, Sterling Holloway; Leo McCarey's *Duck Soup* with the Marx Brothers; James Whale's *The Invisible Man* with Claude Rains; Frank Capra's *The Bitter Tea of General Yen* with Barbara Stanwyck in the first film to be shown at New York's new Radio City Music Hall (*see* 1932).

1933 (cont.) Twentieth Century Pictures is organized by Hollywood film producers who include Darryl Zanuck of Warner Brothers, who will merge the new studio with Fox Studios in 1935 to create Twentieth Century Fox.

Hollywood musicals Lloyd Bacon's *42nd Street* with Warner Baxter, Bebe Daniels, Dick Powell, Ruby Keeler, George Brent, music and lyrics by Al Dubin and Harry Warren, songs that include "Shuffle Off to Buffalo" and "You're Getting to Be a Habit with Me"; Mervyn LeRoy's *Gold Diggers of 1933* with Ginger Rogers, Dick Powell, Joan Blondell, choreography by Busby Berkeley, music and lyrics by Al Dubin and Harry Warren, songs that include "We're in the Money," "Shadow Waltz"; Raoul Walsh's *Going Hollywood* with Bing Crosby, Marion Davies, music by Nacio Herb Brown, lyrics by Arthur Freed, songs that include "Temptation"; Lloyd Bacon's *Footlight Parade* with James Cagney, Joan Blondell, Ruby Keeler, Dick Powell, choreography by Busby Berkeley, music by Sammy Fain, lyrics by Irving Kahal, songs that include "By a Waterfall," "Honeymoon Hotel"; Harry Joe Brown's *Sitting Pretty* with Ginger Rogers, Jack Oakie, Jack Haley, music and lyrics by Harry Revel and Mack Gordon, songs that include "Did You Ever See a Dream Walking?"; Thornton Freeland's *Flying Down to Rio* with Dolores Del Rio, Gene Raymond, Fred Astaire and Ginger Rogers (a new dance team), music by Vincent Youmans, lyrics by Gus Kahn and Edward Ellison, 31, songs that include "Carioca," "Orchids in the Moonlight," and the title song; Robert Z. Leonard's *Dancing Lady* with Joan Crawford, Fred Astaire, Clark Gable, Franchot Tone, music by Burton Lane, lyrics by Harold Adamson, songs that include "Everything I Have Is Yours"; Constantin Bakaleinikoff's *Let's Fall in Love* with Gregory Ratoff, Ann Sothern, Betty Furness, music by Harold Arlen, lyrics by Ted Koehler, songs that include the title song; Walt Disney's *The Three Little Pigs* (animated) with music and lyrics by Frank E. Churchill, songs that include "Who's Afraid of the Big Bad Wolf."

Broadway musicals *Strike Me Pink* 3/4 at the Majestic Theater, with Lupe Velez, Jimmy Durante, Hope Williams, music by Ray Henderson, lyrics by B. G. DeSylva and Lew Brown, songs that include "It's Great to Be Alive," "Love and Rhythm," "Let's Call It a Day," "Home to Harlem," 105 perfs.; *As Thousands Cheer* 9/30 at the Music Box Theater, with Marilyn Miller, Clifton Webb, Ethel Waters, book by Irving Berlin and Moss Hart, music and lyrics by Berlin, Edward Heyman, and Richard Myers, songs that include "Harlem on My Mind," "Heat Wave," "Easter Parade," 400 perfs.; *Let 'Em Eat Cake* by George S. Kaufman and Morrie Ryskind 10/21 at the Imperial Theater, with William Gaxton as John P. Wintergreen, Victor Moore as Alexander Throttlebottom, music by George Gershwin, lyrics by Ira Gershwin, 90 perfs.; *Roberta* (initially *Gowns by Roberta*) 11/18 at the New Ambassadors Theater, with Ray Middleton, George Murphy, Bob Hope, Fay Templeton, Tamara Geva, Sydney Greenstreet, music by Jerome Kern, lyrics by Otto Harbach, songs that include "Smoke Gets in Your Eyes," "The Touch of Your Hand," "Yesterdays" ("Lovely to Look At" will be added for a 1935 film version), 295 perfs.

Opera *Arabella* 7/1 at Dresden's Staatsoper, with music by Richard Strauss, libretto by Hugo von Hofmannsthal.

Ballet *Les Presages* (*Destiny*) 4/13 at Monte Carlo's Théâtre de Monte Carlo, with music by Petr Ilich Tchaikovsky, choreography by Leonide Massine.

George Ballanchine forms his own company and calls it Les Ballets (*see* 1932; 1934).

Choreographer Ted Shawn opens a school for male dancers at Lee, Mass. (*see* Martha Graham, 1926). Shawn has left his wife Ruth St. Denis. His school will be disbanded, but it will be the basis of the Jacob's Pillow Dance Festival that Shawn will inaugurate in October 1941.

First performances Concerto for Piano and Orchestra No. 2 by Béla Bartók 1/23 in a Frankfort radio broadcast; Concerto in C major for Two Pianos and Orchestra by Ralph Vaughan Williams 2/1 in a BBC broadcast; *School for Scandal* Overture by Samuel Barber 8/30 at Philadelphia's Robin Hood Dell; Concerto for Piano, Trumpet, and String Orchestra by Dmitri Shostakovich 10/15 at Leningrad; *Charterhouse Suite* by Ralph Vaughan Williams 10/21 at the Queen's Hall, London.

Popular songs "Basin Street Blues" by Spencer Williams whose work was published in small orchestra parts 4 years ago; "Only a Paper Moon" by Harold Arlen, lyrics by E. Y. Harburg, Billy Rose; "Lazybones" by Hoagy Carmichael, lyrics by vocalist Johnny Mercer, 23; "Love Is the Sweetest Thing" by Ray Noble; "Stormy Weather—Keeps Rainin' All the Time" by Harold Arlen, lyrics by Ted Koehler; "Dolores" by Frank Loesser, lyrics by Louis Alter (for the film *Las Vegas Nights*); "Sophisticated Lady" by Duke Ellington, lyrics by Irving Mills, Mitchell Parish; "I Wanna Be Loved by You" by Johnny Green, lyrics by Billy Rose, Edward Heyman; "In a Shanty in Old Shanty Town" by Joe Young, John Siros, Little Jack Little; "I Cover the Waterfront" by Johnny Green, lyrics by Richard Heyman; "It Isn't Fair" by bandleader Richard Himber, Frank Warshauer, Sylvester Sprigato, lyrics by Himber; "Minnie the Moocher" by bandleader Cabell "Cab" Calloway, 26, who plays at Owney Madden's Cotton Club in Harlem, lyrics by Irving Mills (when Calloway forgets the lyrics he "scat" sings "Hi-de-hi-hi" and gets an enthusiastic audience response); "The Old Spinning Wheel" by Billy Hill; "I Like Mountain Music" by Frank Weldon, lyrics by James Cavanaugh; "Maria Elena" by Spanish songwriter Lorenzo Barcelata.

Italian prizefighter Primo Carnera, 26, of Argentina wins the world heavyweight title June 29. The 260-pound "bull from the pampas" knocks out Jack Sharkey in the sixth round of a championship bout at Long Island City.

England's Frederick J. Perry wins the U.S. Lawn Tennis Association's men's singles; Helen Hull Jacobs wins the women's singles.

Baseball's first All-Star Game is played July 6 at Chicago's Comiskey Field. The American League defeats the National League 4 to 2.

The New York Giants win the World Series by defeating the Washington Senators 4 games to 1.

The Philadelphia Eagles football team is founded by Bert Bell; the Pittsburgh Steelers team is founded by Art Rooney.

The Dy-Dee-Doll that sucks water from a bottle and wets its diaper is introduced by New York's Effanbee Doll Company, which has acquired patent rights from the doll's Brooklyn inventor Marie Wittman. More than 25,000 of the new dolls are sold in its first year.

Dreft is introduced by Cincinnati's Procter & Gamble Company for dishwashing in hard-water areas west of the Appalachians. The hymolal-salt detergent is costlier than soap but will prove a popular addition to the Ivory soap, Oxydol, Camay, Crisco line of P&G products (see Persil, 1907; Tide, 1946; Surf, 1949).

Windex for cleaning windows is introduced by Cincinnati's Drackett Company of 1921 Drano fame.

Philip Morris cigarettes are introduced in the United States (see 1858; 1902). Page boy Johnny Roventini from the 3-year-old Hotel New Yorker delivers the Call for Philip Morris slogan over a portion of Ferde Grofe's 2-year-old Grand Canyon Suite on radio stations April 17 and will continue to promote the brand for 20 years.

Sheraton Corporation of America has its beginnings at Cambridge, Mass., where Boston entrepreneur Ernest Henderson, 36, and his Harvard classmate Robert Lowell Moore take over the Continental Hotel that opened the day the stock market crashed in 1929. By 1937 Henderson and Lowell will have bought up stock for as little as 50 cents a share in Standard Investing Corporation, they will use the firm's capital to finance acquisitions that will include a small Boston residential hotel called the Sheraton despite its Hepplewhite decor, and they will use the name Sheraton to identify all their properties (see Copley-Plaza, 1941).

New York's 70-story RCA building opens at 30 Rockefeller Plaza in May as construction of Rockefeller Center proceeds under the direction of Reinhard and Hoffmeister, Corbet Harrison and MacMurray, and Hood and Fouilhoux who will design all the buildings put up in this decade. The small British building opens in May and La Maison Française opens in September, both on Fifth Avenue.

The Tennessee Valley Authority (above) will control floods in the Tennessee Valley region.

The Civilian Conservation Corps (CCC) created by Congress March 31 under the Unemployment Relief Act (Reforestation) will enlist more than 3 million young men in the next 8 years. The CCC will plant more than 2 billion trees, will build small dams, will aid in wildlife restoration, and will tackle erosion problems (see 1935).

Oregon's Tillamook Burn in August wipes out 12 billion board feet of virgin timber. Friction from a falling tree has touched off the fire that advances along an 18-mile front, littering beaches for 30 miles with charred fragments and raining still smoldering debris on ships 100 miles at sea.

A Soil Erosion Service started by the U.S. Department of Agriculture will help farmers learn tilling methods that will minimize erosion. The seriousness of the problem gains recognition when a great dust storm November 11 to 13 sweeps South Dakota topsoil as far east as Albany, N.Y. (see 1909; 1935).

The Tennessee Valley Authority (above) will improve agriculture in the Tennessee Valley region.

U.S. farm prices drop 63 percent below 1929 levels as compared with 15 percent for industrial prices since industrialists can control production more effectively than can farmers. Cotton sells in February at 5.5 cents per pound, down from a 1909–1914 average of 12.5 cents, and wheat sells for 32.3 cents per bushel, down from an average of 88.4 cents.

An Agricultural Adjustment Act (AAA) voted by Congress May 12 authorizes establishment of an Agricultural Adjustment Administration (AAA) within the Department of Agriculture.

An Emergency Farm Bill becomes law in June, and the AAA (above) sets out to restore farm income by reviving 1909–1914 average prices for wheat, dairy products, cotton, tobacco, corn, rice, sugar, hogs, and peanuts.

Secretary of Agriculture Henry Agard Wallace, 44, orders limitation procedures to compensate for the fact that the AAA (above) was established after most crops were planted and pigs were farrowed. Some 400,000 farrowed pigs are ordered to be destroyed and 330,000 acres of cotton to be plowed under.

The Commodity Credit Corporation in the U.S. Department of Agriculture is created to buy surpluses and to handle any subsidies payable to farmers for reducing their crop acreage (see 1930; 1935).

A Farm Credit Act passed by Congress June 16 consolidates rural credit agencies under a Farm Credit Administration.

Midwestern farmers strike in October to force up prices by withholding products from market. They complain that the AAA has no real power (see 1932).

The world wheat price falls to an historic low of £4 per ton, where it will remain through 1934.

1933 (cont.) At least a million destitute U.S. farm families are given direct government relief. While farm prices begin to inch up, a farmer must pay the equivalent of 9 bushels of wheat for a pair of work shoes, up from 2 bushels in 1909.

Roughly 25 percent of U.S. workers are engaged in agriculture, down from nearly 50 percent in 1853 (*see* 1950).

Golden Cross Bantam corn is introduced (*see* East, Shull, 1921). The first commercial hybrid grain to be planted on a large scale, it permits farmers to increase their yields, which now average 22.8 bushels of corn per acre of land (*see* 1950).

The boysenberry developed by Rudolph Boysen in 1920 is rediscovered by Anaheim, Calif., grower Walter Knott, 43, who makes it the basis of Knott's Berry Farms. Knott harvests 5 tons of the long, dark, reddish-black berries per acre.

An anti-beriberi vitamin substance is isolated from rice husks by U.S. biochemist Robert R. Williams, 47, who was born in India and who began his professional career in Manila where beriberi is a major health problem. It takes a ton of rice husks to produce less than 0.2 ounce of the substance (*see* Suzuki, 1912; vitamin B_1—thiamine, 1936).

A heat-stabile B vitamin is isolated by Austrian chemist Richard Kuhn, 33, at Berlin's Kaiser Wilhelm Institute (*see* 1932; vitamin B_2—riboflavin, 1935).

Vitamin C (ascorbic acid) is synthesized by Swiss chemist Tadens Reichenstein and his associates (*see* King, 1932).

Milk fortified with vitamin D is offered to the public for the first time by the Borden Company (*see* 1930). Children are the chief victims of vitamin D deficiency, and children are the chief consumers of milk.

Epidemiological studies relating fluoride intake and tooth decay are undertaken by H. Trendley Dean of the U.S. Public Health Service (*see* 1916; 1939).

A Consumer Advisory Board is included in the National Recovery Administration (NRA, above).

Rexford Guy Tugwell is named assistant secretary of agriculture and is given command of the Food and Drug Administration. A 42-year-old professor of economics at Columbia University and a self-proclaimed Socialist, Tugwell vows to give "human rights" priority over "property and financial rights," and he begins campaigning for a new pure food and drug law (*see* 1938).

"Reg. Penna. Dept. Agr." appears on packages of crackers, pasta, snack foods, and similar foods following passage of a Pennsylvania state law ordering that bakeries and other premises producing such foods be licensed and be inspected periodically for minimum cleanliness and worker health. Any company producing such foods must have its production facilities inspected, wherever they may be, if the foods are to be sold in Pennsylvania.

Ritz crackers are introduced by National Biscuit Company and will be the world's largest selling crackers within 3 years. Crisper and less fluffy than soda crackers, Ritz crackers are butter crackers made with more shortening than soda crackers and without yeast, they are spread with a thin coating of coconut oil and are sprinkled with salt after baking, 5 million of the crackers are baked, and by 1936, production will be at the rate of 29 million per day (*see* Shredded Wheat acquisition, 1928).

Sanka brand decaffeinated coffee is acquired by General Foods (*see* 1903; 1928).

Campbell's chicken noodle soup and Campbell's cream of mushroom soup are introduced (*see* tomato juice, 1932; can production, 1936).

Stokely-Van Camp is created by a merger of Stokely Brothers and Van Camp (*see* 1898; Frank Van Camp, 1914). Stokely has grown by acquiring other canning companies, Van Camp has added to its pork and beans and catsup line by canning New Orleans-style kidney beans, hominy, Vienna sausage, and other items (*see* Hawaiian pineapple, 1944).

Pineapple juice is introduced to Americans at the Chicago World's Fair (above) by Libby, McNeill & Libby, which has 17 booths at the fair to sell Libby's juices, including the tomato juice introduced in 1929.

Tree-Sweet canned orange juice is introduced by Tree-Sweet Products, Inc., of California. Los Angeles investment banker W. K. McCracken has put up less than $12,000 to back an inventor who has developed a new method for canning orange juice that retains more flavor and nutrients than other methods. McCracken calls the process Instovac (*see* 1948).

Sunsweet prune juice is introduced by the Duffy-Mott Company under an agreement with Sunsweet Growers, Inc., a California cooperative that grows and processes prune plums. Sunsweet is the first commercial prune juice (*see* 1930; 1938).

Margarine made from soybeans is produced in public demonstrations at the Ford Motor Company's Industrialized American Barn at the Chicago Fair (above). Ford chemical engineer Robert Boyer, 34, has developed soy plastics for horn buttons, gearshift handles, and control knobs and is working on ways to substitute soybean forms for conventional foods (*see* 1937).

More than 11 percent of U.S. grocery store sales are made through 18,000 A&P stores (*see* 1929; 1930).

Food Fair, Inc., has its beginnings at Harrisburg, Pa., where Samuel Friedland, 36, and George Friedland, 31, rent a garage with 10,000 square feet of floor space for $150 per month and open the Giant Quality Food Price-Cutter supermarket. Starting with a kosher butcher shop at Middletown, N.Y., in 1919, the Friedlands moved to Harrisburg in 1920. They sell butter at 19½ cents per pound, eggs at 12 cents per dozen, oranges at 7 cents per pound, their first week's sales amount to $15,000, they open a second store at Reading, they will open a third and a fourth next year at York and Baltimore, and by 1950 Food Fair will be the nation's seventh largest food chain with 112 supermarkets (*see* Big Bear, 1932).

More typical U.S. food prices: butter 28 cents per pound, margarine 13 cents, eggs 29 cents a dozen, oranges 27 cents a dozen, milk 10 cents a quart, bread 5 cents per 20-ounce loaf, sirloin steak 29 cents per pound, round steak 26 cents, rib roast 22 cents, ham 31 cents, bacon 22 cents, leg of lamb 22 cents, chicken 22 cents, pork chops 20 cents, cheese 24 cents, coffee 26 cents, rice 6 cents, potatoes 2 cents, sugar 6 cents (but *see* typical earnings, above).

Sugar falls to 1.3 cents per pound in New York, and Puerto Rico has widespread hunger as wages are reduced (*see* 1920).

The prohibition against sale of alcoholic beverages in the United States that began early in 1920 ends December 5 as Utah becomes the 36th state to ratify the 21st Amendment repealing the 18th Amendment after an estimated 1.4 billion gallons of hard liquor have been sold illegally. Twenty-two states and hundreds of counties remain dry by statute or local option, and some states permit sale only in stores controlled by a state monopoly.

Repeal (above) finds roughly half the whiskey aging in U.S. rack warehouses owned by National Distillers Corporation (Old Grand Dad, Old Taylor, Old Crow, Old Overholt, Mount Vernon).

Schenley Distillers Corporation is organized at New York by entrepreneur Lewis S. Rosenstiel, 42, who takes the name from the Schenley, Pa., location of Joseph S. Finch Company, a rye distillery that forms part of the new corporation, which will be the leading U.S. distiller until 1937 and which will lead again from 1944 to 1947. Also included are the Old Quaker distillery at Lawrenceburg, Ind., and the Kentucky distilleries of George T. Stagg at Frankfort, James E. Pepper at Lexington, and New England Distillers at Covington.

Schenley Distillers (above) owns 25 percent of the whiskey in U.S. rack warehouses, and 25 percent of the corporation's stock is owned by Lewis Rosenstiel.

Most of the remaining whiskey in U.S. rack warehouses is owned by Frankfort Distilleries (Four Roses) and Glenmore (Kentucky Tavern), which will be acquired by Distillers Corporation-Seagram (*see* 1928). Seagram will build a large distillery at Lawrenceburg, Ind., to produce 5 Crown, 7 Crown, Kessler, and other whiskey brands that will dominate the market (*see* 1934).

Hiram Walker, Inc., will build a large distillery at Peoria, Ill., to produce the Imperial, Ten High, Walker's Deluxe, and other brands that will supplement its Canadian Club brand introduced in 1882. Walker is now controlled by Harry C. Hatch who bought the firm in 1926 for $114 million which included $9 million for the goodwill attached to Canadian Club.

Prohibition's "Texas" Guinan has died November 5 at age 49, leaving an estate of only $28,173, although she is known to have banked well over $1 million in the mid-1920s (*see* 1922).

Brewing Corporation of America is founded by Cleveland entrepreneurs who take over an abandoned auto plant with money received in the liquidation of Peerless Motor Company. They will introduce Carling's and Black Label beer next year (*see* 1943).

Sale of 3.2 beer has been legalized by Congress April 7, and the first team of Clydesdale horses to promote Budweiser beer has appeared a day later. Anheuser-Busch has survived Prohibition by producing commercial yeast and sarsaparilla.

7-Up is promoted as a mixer for alcoholic beverages by Charles Grigg of St. Louis who renames his Lithiated Lemon and sells 681,000 cases of the soft drink (*see* 1929).

Repeal (above) dampens the boom in most soft drinks and in ice cream sodas.

Coca-Cola sales tumble to 20 million gallons of syrup (2.5 billion drinks), down from a 1930 peak of 27.7 million gallons (3.5 billion drinks).

A new automatic fountain mixer that mixes the exact amounts of syrup and carbonated water is introduced by Coca-Cola Company at the Chicago Fair (above). The mixer eliminates the chance of error by a counterman.

Pepsi-Cola is acquired by Loft candy store chief Edward Guth who begins to bottle the drink in 12-ounce bottles (*see* 1920; Mack, 1934).

E. and J. Gallo Winery Company has its beginnings in a California winery purchased by entrepreneurs Ernest Gallo, 24, and Julio, 23, who sink their savings of $5,900 into an operation that will become the largest U.S. wine producer.

Josef Stalin imposed ruthless totalitarian rule that stifled opposition to his control of Soviet Russia.

903

1933 (cont.) Grape production in the Chautauqua-Erie grape belt of New York State declines precipitously as the repeal of Prohibition (above) reduces consumer demand for grapes to be used for home wine-making. The New York growers use little or no fertilizer or insect spray, they average little more than 1 ton per acre, they receive only $20 per ton, and they have lost the table grape market to California growers.

New York entrepreneur Jacob M. Kaplan, 40, acquires a small winery at Brocton, N.Y., and establishes a floor price of $50 per ton for grapes, guaranteeing the price before the grapes are picked. Kaplan has prospered in West Indian sugar and rum ventures during Prohibition, he hires chemists and mechanical engineers to produce a uniform beverage efficiently and economically, and he encourages growers to improve their farms and vineyards and to concentrate on growing Concord grapes (see 1945).

Gallagher's Steak House opens at 228 West 52nd Street, New York, with steak, a baked potato, and salad for $1.75 but with nothing stronger than 3.2 beer until December. Former *Ziegfeld Follies* girl Helen Gallagher is the widow of vaudevillian Ed Gallagher of Gallagher and Shean fame.

Adolf Hitler (above) encourages production of more "Aryans" by offering cash incentives to Germans who will marry and cash awards for each new infant born. The policy will increase German birth rates in the next few years (see Lebensborn, 1935).

1934 France verges on civil war following the suicide January 3 of Russian-born promoter Serge Stavisky who has been accused of issuing fraudulent bonds against the security of the municipal pawnshop at Bayonne, has evidently engaged in other dubious speculations, and has been protected from legal action by corrupt government ministers and deputies. A high official in the public prosecutor's office at Paris is found murdered, allegations are made that he was killed to protect some well-known leaders in the government, both Communists and right-wing Fascist and Royalist groups say the scandal demonstrates the corruption and inefficiency of the democratic government, Paris has serious riots February 6, 7, and 9, a general strike ensues, and the republic is saved only by the establishment of a coalition government of officials untouched by the Stavisky affair.

The king of the Belgians Albert I dies February 17 at age 58 after a 25-year reign and is succeeded by his 32-year-old son who will reign until 1950 as Leopold III.

The Austrian chancellor Engelbert Dollfuss issues a decree in February dissolving all political parties except for his own Fatherland Front. He antagonizes Vienna's working class by ordering police raids on Socialist headquarters and a bombardment of the Socialist housing unit, the Karl Marx Hof (see below).

A Nazi blood purge June 30 kills at least 77 party members alleged to have plotted against Adolf Hitler in Germany. Raids by Nazi storm troopers eliminate the party's radical wing, and the victims include the Sturm Abteilungen group of Ernst Röhm and supporters of Gregor Strasser, both of whom are killed.

Austrian Nazis seize the Vienna radio station July 25, force the staff to broadcast a report that Chancellor Dollfuss (above) has resigned, enter the chancellory, and shoot Dollfuss dead. Italy and Yugoslavia concentrate troops on the frontier and Berlin disavows any connection with the attempted coup.

Power and Earth (*Macht und Erde*) by German geographer Karl Haushoker, 67, implies that a dynamic Germany has the natural right to grasp all of Eurasia and to dominate the oceanic countries. Based in part on British political geographer Halfor John Mackinder's 1904 paper "The Geographical Pivot of History," Haushoker's theories of geopolitics will help shape Adolf Hitler's demands for *lebensraum* (living space; see Saar Basin, 1935).

Germany's President von Hindenburg dies August 2 at age 87, and a plebiscite August 19 gives Adolf Hitler 88 percent of the votes needed to assume the presidency. Hitler retains the title *der führer*.

Yugoslavia's Aleksandr I is assassinated October 9 at age 45 along with French Foreign Minister Louis Barthou at Marseilles as the king arrives for a state visit. The assassin is a Macedonian terrorist working with Croat revolutionists headquartered in Hungary, war between Yugoslavia and Hungary is averted by the League of Nations, which has admitted Soviet Russia September 18, and Aleksandr is succeeded by his 11-year-old son who will reign until 1945 as Peter II, with Aleksandr's cousin Prince Paul as regent.

Chinese Communist forces under Mao Tse-tung leave Kiangsi in October with Nationalist Kuomintang armies in pursuit. In the Long March that will last until October of next year, Mao's forces will be on the move for 268 days out of 368, they will travel 6,000 miles to Yunnan, they will cross 18 mountain ranges and six major rivers, but 68,000 of Mao's 90,000 men will be lost in continual rear-guard actions against Kuomintang troops (see 1931; 1937).

The Mexican Constitution is amended to extend the term of the presidency to 6 years, the 39-year-old minister of war and marine General Lazaro Cardenas is elected president July 2, he promises to "revive the revolutionary activity of the masses," and although he has been chosen by strongman Plutarco Calles, he regards Calles as too conservative and will force him into exile next year.

Josef Stalin's close collaborator Sergeo Mironovich Kirov, 46, is assassinated December 1 at Leningrad. The assassination reveals the strength and desperation of the opposition to Stalin within the Communist party, and many of the party's most prominent older leaders will be convicted in spectacular trials that follow the incident at Leningrad (see 1937).

Italian and Ethiopian troops clash at Ualual December 5 on the frontier between Italian Somaliland and Ethiopia. Benito Mussolini will use the incident as an excuse to invade Ethiopia next year.

India's All-India Congress Socialist party is founded.

Italian physicist Enrico Fermi, 33, bombards uranium with neutrons and produces transuranium elements (*see* 1938; Becquerel, 1896; Chadwick, 1932; Segre, 1937).

French physicist Irene Joliot-Curie, 38, and her husband Frederic Joliot-Curie, 34, bombard aluminum with alpha particles (helium nuclei) from a naturally radioactive source and turn the aluminum into a radioactive form of phosphorus, but Mme. Joliot-Curie's mother Marie Curie dies July 4 of pernicious anemia at age 66 (*see* 1904; Cockcroft, Walton, 1932).

Patterns of Culture by Columbia University social anthropologist Ruth Benedict, 47, breaks new ground. Benedict studied anthropology for the first time at age 32, she enrolled at Columbia 2 years later to study under Franz Boas, and she will replace Boas as dean of the anthropology department upon his retirement in 1936 (*see* 1928; 1946).

President Roosevelt tells Congress January 4 that costs of the U.S. national economic recovery program will reach $10.5 billion by June 20, 1935.

The price of gold that has been progressively raised since late October 1933 from its long-maintained level of $20.67 per ounce is stabilized by the U.S. Treasury in January at $35 per ounce, a price that will be maintained for 40 years.

The Export-Import Bank of Washington is created February 12 with $11 million in capital to help finance and facilitate exports and imports of commodities; $10 million of the $11 million has come from the Reconstruction Finance Corporation (RFC) organized in 1932.

Secretary of State Cordell Hull persuades Congress that the high tariffs of the 1930 Smoot-Hawley-Grundy Act have contributed to world depression and that high tariffs should be replaced by mutual tariff relaxation agreements with other countries. The Reciprocal Trade Agreement Act passed by Congress June 12 gives the president power to negotiate trade pacts without advice or consent of the Senate, and the first such pact is signed August 24 with Cuba. Reciprocal tariff-cutting agreements will be made with 18 foreign nations in the next 4 years, and they will bring an increase in world trade.

A Sugar Act establishes annual U.S. sugar import quotas based on anticipated consumption. The act allows prices much higher than world prices in order to help friendly nations that sell to the United States.

The Johnson Debt Default Act passed by Congress April 13 forbids additional loans to any country in default of debt payments to the United States.

The Swiss Bank Secrecy Act is voted by the parliament to protect the accounts of Jews in Nazi Germany. Numbered accounts have four- or five-digit numbers that depositors write out in script, the number in script becomes the depositor's signature, only two or three senior bank officials know the name of the depositor, and while Swiss law says that banks may not furnish information about such accounts even to Swiss tax authorities (tax evasion is not a criminal offense in Switzerland) and while numbered accounts will be used to safeguard the fortunes of U.S. racketeers, Communist espionage agents, and Latin American and Oriental dictators the Swiss banks do insist on background knowledge of depositors and do cooperate with police or authorized investigators in cases of criminal fraud and forgery.

A Securities and Exchange Commission (SEC) is created by Congress June 6 to limit bank credit for speculators and to police the securities industry. Wall Street speculator Joseph Patrick Kennedy, 45, is named in July to head the new commission despite opposition from New Dealers and from leading newspapers. (Kennedy is the father of 9 and will hold the post for 431 days before being named to head the U.S. Maritime Commission.)

Security Analysis by English-American financier Benjamin Graham, 40, pioneers modern security analysis, it will remain the standard text for more than 40 years, and it will have sales of more than 100,000 copies. Starting out at $12 per week with a job writing stock and bond prices on a Wall Street brokerage house blackboard, Graham went into business with Jerome Newman in 1926 to start the Graham-Newman Corporation investment fund, he was a millionaire before age 35, and his book emphasizes the importance of a stock's book value—the physical assets of the company issuing the stock.

The Liberty League to oppose New Deal economic measures is formed in August as a bipartisan group that includes the du Ponts, Alfred Sloan and William Knudsen of General Motors, J. Howard Pew of Sun Oil Company, Sewell Avery of Montgomery Ward, and politicians who include Democrats Alfred E. Smith and John Jacob Raskob.

A Civil Works Emergency Relief Act is passed by Congress February 15 to appropriate another $950 million for the continuation of civil works programs and direct relief aid.

Relief Administrator Harry L. Hopkins reports April 13 that 4.7 million U.S. families are on relief.

Demagogic welfare schemes proliferate in America. U.S. senator from Louisiana Huey Pierce Long, 40, presents in the Senate his Share Our Wealth Program, an "every man a king" wealth redistribution scheme.

Massachusetts Democratic party boss James Michael Curley is elected governor at age 59 and will undertake large, costly public works programs in the next 2 years that will be compared to those of Huey Long.

1934 (cont.) Long Beach, Calif., physician Francis E. Townsend urges an Old Age Revolving Pension Plan to be financed by a 2 percent transaction tax. The Townsend Plan is to assure $200 per month for every unemployed American over age 60.

Upton Sinclair campaigns as Democratic candidate for governor of California and announces an End Poverty in California (EPIC) Plan.

Royal Oak, Mich., radio priest Father Charles Coughlin organizes a National Union for Social Justice based on radical inflation (*see* 1926).

A National Railroad Adjustment Board is created by Congress to guarantee railway workers the right to organize and to bargain collectively through representatives of their own choosing (*see* 1926).

A National Labor Relations Board (NLRB) is created June 19 by a joint resolution of Congress to replace the National Labor Board established under the NRA last year.

A summertime wave of strikes takes U.S. workers off the job and includes the nation's first general strike. It is called at San Francisco July 16 to show sympathy for a strike of 12,000 International Longshoremen's Association stevedores led by Australian-American organizer Harry Bridges, 32.

The United States joins the International Labor Organization (ILO) that was started in 1919.

The Warsaw Convention signed by representatives of the United States and of many European countries provides for a uniform liability code and uniform documentation on tickets and cargo for international carriers. Liability for loss of life or injury is limited to $8,300 except where willful misconduct can be proved (the convention is designed to keep fledgling airlines from being put out of business by large damage suits).

American Airlines, Inc., is created by a reorganization of the 4-year-old American Airways Company, whose E. L. Cord loses control of the airline (*see* below).

Continental Air Lines has its beginnings in the Southwest division of Varney Air Transport founded by former Varney president and former United Airlines director Louis H. Mueller, 38, who flies mail between El Paso and Pueblo, Calif. Continental will become a major domestic passenger carrier.

The Cord Corporation is organized to absorb Auburn Automobile Company, Checker Cab Manufacturing, Columbia Axle, New York Shipbuilding, and Aviation Manufacturing Corporation which includes the Vultee Aircraft division (*see* 1930).

Gerard Vultee designs a V-11 attack bomber that will be purchased by Brazil, China, Turkey, and the U.S.S.R., but he and his young wife will be killed in 1938 when their Stinson crashes into an Arizona peak in a snow squall while en route to Los Angeles from Washington, D.C. (*see* 1930).

North American Aviation begins production of a military training plane designed by J. H. "Dutch" Kindelberger, 39, who was formerly chief draftsman for Glenn L. Martin and chief engineer for Douglas Aircraft (*see* General Motors, 1933; Mustang, 1940).

The Chrysler Airflow is introduced by Chrysler Motors which also introduces overdrive. One model of the streamlined Airflow has the world's first curved one-piece windshield, and the car contains many innovative advances, but only 11,292 will be sold. By 1937 Chrysler will abandon the radical design as a costly miscalculation of public acceptance.

Greyhound Corp. cuts fares between New York and Chicago to as little as $8 in a rate war with competing bus lines (regular fare is $16). Greyhound operates 1,800 33-passenger nickel-plated buses in 43 states, it buys the buses from General Motors Truck Co. for $10,000 on a cost-plus contract, it pays its drivers $175 per month plus a mileage rate, and it grosses $30 million (*see* 1929).

The *City of Salina* goes into service between Kansas City and Salina, Kan., to begin a new era of streamlined passenger trains on U.S. railroads. The new Union Pacific train has air-conditioned cars of aluminum alloy made by Pullman.

A new Burlington Zephyr train goes into service between Chicago and Denver using diesel engines that begin the end of steam power on U.S. railroads (*see* 1924). The streamlined passenger train hits a top speed of 112.5 miles per hour and averages 77.6 miles per hour on a 1,017-mile nonstop run between the two cities May 26.

The Chessie trademark of a sleeping cat is adopted by the Chesapeake & Ohio Railroad to symbolize its smooth roadbed. The C&O has grown to serve Washington, Richmond, White Sulphur Springs in West Virginia, Cincinnati, Columbus, Cleveland, Toledo, Detroit, and other points in the Midwest.

Britain's Cunard Line that began in 1839 as the Royal Mail Steam Packet Company becomes the Cunard-White Star Line by merging with the White Star Line that was acquired by the Royal Mail Steam Packet Company in 1927 (*see Queen Mary*, 1936).

The Chinese ship *Weitung* burns January 21 on the Yangtze River; 216 lives are lost.

The S.S. *Morro Castle* catches fire off Asbury Park, N.J., September 8; 125 lives are lost.

The first practical radar tests are conducted March 20 at Kiel Harbor by German navy Signals Research Chief Rudolf Kuhnold who has developed a 700-watt transmitter working on a frequency of 600 megacycles plus a receiver and disk reflectors. Kuhnold succeeds in receiving echoes from signals bounced off the battleship *Hesse* anchored 600 yards away, and in October he picks up echoes from a ship 7 miles away in a demonstration before high-ranking naval officers at Pelzerhaken near Lübeck. Signals are also received accidentally from a seaplane flying through the beam (the first detection of aircraft by radar) and

70,000 Reichsmarks ($57,500) are appropriated for developing Kuhnold's idea (*see* Watson-Watt, 1935).

A Federal Communications Commission (FCC) is created June 10 by Congress to supervise the U.S. telephone, telegraph, and radio industries. Radio stations are to be given 3-year licenses, licensees and license-applicants are to show that they serve, or intend to serve, the "public interest, convenience, and necessity," but licenses will, in fact, be granted and renewed almost automatically over the next 25 years.

The Mutual Network headed by New York radio station WOR is established to compete with NBC and CBS (*see* WOR, 1922; American Broadcasting, 1943).

Mary Margaret McBride begins broadcasting over New York's WOR to begin a career of more than 20 years as First Lady of Radio. Using the name "Martha Deane," the 34-year-old newspaper and magazine writer is supposed to be a grandmother with a large family who gives out household hints, but on her third day she interrupts her own program to announce that she does not cook very well and dislikes housekeeping intensely. McBride will move to CBS in 1937 with a program under her own name, she will move to NBC in 1941, she will pack Yankee Stadium in 1949 with 40,000 fans paying homage to her 15 years on the air, and she will move to the American Broadcasting Company in 1950.

"Hooper ratings" for the measurement of radio audiences are established by former Daniel Starch Associates researcher C. E. (Claude Ernest) Hooper, 36, who uses telephone interviews to find out what programs respondents are listening to at any given time rather than depending on recall surveys. The Hooper service will be acquired by A. C. Nielsen Co. in 1950 (*see* 1923; Starch, 1931; Gallup, 1935).

France bans advertising on government radio stations.

Hill & Knowlton is founded at New York by Cleveland public relations counsel John Wiley Hill, 43, in partnership with Don Knowlton. The new firm will make a reputation in the next few years by counseling large steelmakers faced with labor problems and it will grow to become the world's largest PR firm.

"Terry and the Pirates" by comic-strip cartoonist Milton Arthur Caniff, 27, establishes an adult adventure story line with an Oriental setting and reflects such current events as the Japanese invasion of China. The *Chicago Tribune—New York Daily News* syndicate strip will employ explicit sexiness to attract a wide following for Caniff's movie tradition heroes Pat Ryan and Terry and for villains such as The Dragon Lady (*see* 1947; Flip Corkin, 1942).

"Li'l Abner" by comic-strip cartoonist Al Capp (Alfred Gerald Caplin), 35, is set in the fictitious hamlet of Dogpatch, Ky. Capp has been ghost-drawing "Joe Palooka" for Ham Fisher, his new strip begins appearing in a few newspapers, and it will soon be syndicated to hundreds of papers.

"Flash Gordon" by comic-strip cartoonist Alex Raymond is a world-of-tomorrow adventure strip that sets new standards of cartoon artistry and competes with the popular 25th-century strip "Buck Rogers." Syndicated by King Features, the new strip is by a former assistant to Chic Young on "Blondie."

"Jungle Jim" by Alex Raymond (above) is another new adventure strip.

The *Chicago Tribune* adopts simplified spelling of 80 words to correct an "unspeakable offense to common sense," but although the *Tribune* will make "catalog" and "epilog" widely used alternatives to "catalogue" and "epilogue," the paper will revert in 1975 from "thru" and "thoro" to the conventional "through" and "thorough."

The Merriam-Webster *Dictionary of the English Language,* first published by Noah Webster in 1828, is updated with a second edition: " 'Like' introducing a complete clause, or an incomplete clause in which the predicate, and sometimes the subject, is to be supplied from the context, is freely used only in illiterate speech and is now regarded as incorrect" (*see* 1961).

The Literary Guild, founded in 1927, is acquired by Doubleday, Doran, Inc., which has had a minority interest since 1929. The Guild has changed its membership terms and is selling new books at a flat rate of $2 each plus a few cents carrying charge. Frank Nelson Doubleday has died January 30 at age 72, but his firm will make the Literary Guild and its 5-year-old Junior Guild the basis of a book club empire that will include two dozen mail-order book clubs.

The *Partisan Review* begins publication to give U.S. intellectuals a new literary magazine.

Nonfiction *Leaves and Stones (Blatter und Steiner,* essays) by Ernst Jünger.

Fiction *Seven Gothic Tales* by Danish novelist Isak Dinesen (Karen Dinesen, 49, the baroness Blixen) who married her cousin in 1914, lived with him until 1921 on the British East African coffee plantation her parents purchased for them, and has written her book in English; *I, Claudius* and *Claudius the God and His Wife Messaline* by Robert Graves; *And Quiet Flows the Don (Tikhiy Don)* by Soviet novelist Mikhail Aleksandrovich Sholokhov, 29; *Rickshaw Boy (Lo-l'o hsiang-tzu)* by Chinese novelist Lao She (Shu Ch'ing-ch'un), 36, who has returned to China after studying in England from 1924 to 1930 (an English translation will appear in 1945 with a happy ending added by the translator); *Burmese Days* by George Orwell; *Weymouth Sands* by John Cowper Powys; *The Bachelors (Les Celibataires)* by Henry de Montherlant; *Tender Is the Night* by F. Scott Fitzgerald, whose central character Dick Diver is modeled on former émigré Gerald Murphy, 46, a dilettante painter of some talent who last year returned to New York to take over management of his late father's Mark Cross luggage and haberdashery shop; *Appointment in Samarra* by *New Yorker* mag-

1934 (cont.) azine writer John Henry O'Hara, 29; *A Cool Million* by Nathanael West; *The Young Manhood of Studs Lonigan* by Chicago novelist James Thomas Farrell, 30, whose *Young Lonigan* appeared in 1932 and whose *Judgment Day* will appear next year to complete the depiction of a deteriorating Chicago and of a brash, aimless blue-collar Chicagoan; *Summer in Williamsburg* by Brooklyn, N.Y., novelist Daniel Fuchs, 25; *Call It Sleep* by New York novelist Henry Roth, 28, whose book will not gain popularity until the 1960s; *I Can Get It for You Wholesale* by New York novelist Jerome Weidman, 22, whose comic novel is about the garment district; *Such Is My Beloved* by Canadian novelist Morley Callaghan, 31; *Seven Poor Men of Sydney* and *The Salzburg Tales* by Australian novelist Christina Stead, 32; *The Materassi Sisters (Sorelle Materassi)* by Italian novelist Aldo Palezzeschi (Aldo Giurlani), 49; *A Handful of Dust* by Evelyn Waugh; *Goodbye, Mr. Chips* by James Hilton; *Long Remember* by U.S. novelist MacKinlay Kantor, 30; *Daring Young Man* (stories) by California-born short story writer William Saroyan, 26, whose lead story is "The Daring Young Man on the Flying Trapeze"; *The Postman Always Rings Twice* by U.S. detective novelist James M. (Mallahan) Cain, 42; *Fer-de-lance* by U.S. detective novelist Rex (Todhunter) Stout, 48, who retired to France 7 years ago with $400,000 gained by selling an Educational Thrift System, a deposit program for children, to U.S. bankers. Stout's fortunes have been reduced by the Depression, but his overweight detective Nero Wolfe will make him prosperous once again. *Murder on the Orient Express* by Agatha Christie, whose new Hercule Poirot novel is published in the United States as *Murder on the Calais Coach; The Nine Tailors* by Dorothy Sayers; *The Thin Man* by Dashiell Hammett.

Juvenile *Mary Poppins* by Australian-born English author P. (Pamela) Travers, 28, whose wonder-working English governess will appear in a series of books.

Poetry *The Cantos* (fourth volume) by Ezra Pound; *Variations on a Time Theme* by Edwin Muir; *The Masterless Hammer (Le Marteau sans maître)* by French poet René Char, 21.

Painting *The Bullfight* by Pablo Picasso; *Homage to Mack Sennett* by René Magritte; *William Tell* by Salvador Dali; *The Ballad of the Jealous Lover of Lone Green Valley, Lord, Heal the Child, Homestead, Ploughing It Under,* and *Going Home* by Thomas Hart Benton.

Mexican muralists Diego Rivera, José Clemente Orozco, and David Afaro Siqueiros return to Mexico following the election of General Cardenas to the presidency (above).

Theater *Thunderstorm* by Chinese playwright Tsao Yu (Wan Chia-pao), 24, who adopts a style similar to that of Greek tragedy. He awes Peking audiences with the disruptive powers abroad in the world, but his play is perceived as an attack on the tyranny of the traditional family system. *Days Without End* by S. N. Behrman 1/18 at Henry Miller's Theater, New York, with Earle Larimore, Stanley Ridges, Ilka Chase, 57 perfs.; *The Joyous Season* by Philip Barry 1/20 at New York's Belasco Theater, with Lillian Gish, Jane Wyatt, 16 perfs.; *Conversation Piece* by Noel Coward 2/16 at His Majesty's Theatre, London, with Coward, Moya Nugent, Yvonne Printemps, Louis Hayward, George Sanders, 177 perfs.; *They Shall Not Die* by U.S. playwright John Wexley 2/21 at New York's Royale Theater, with Claude Rains, Ruth Gordon, Tom Ewell, Helen Wesley, and Dean Jagger in a play suggestive of the Scottsboro case, 62 perfs.; *Yellow Jacket* by Sidney Howard and Paul de Kruif 3/6 at New York's Martin Beck Theater, with James Stewart, Myron McCormick in a play about the conquest of yellow fever, 79 perfs.; *Merrily We Roll Along* by George S. Kaufman and Moss Hart 9/9 at New York's Music Box Theater, with Kenneth McKenna, Jessie Royce Landis, Mary Philips, 155 perfs.; *The Distaff Side* by John Van Druten 9/25 at New York's Booth Theater, with Mildred Natwick, Sybil Thorndike, Estelle Winwood, 177 perfs.; *The Children's Hour* by U.S. playwright Lillian Hellman, 29, 11/20 at Maxine Elliott's Theater, New York, with Eugenia Rawls in a play that hints at sexual abnormalities, 691 perfs.; *Rain from Heaven* by S. N. Behrman 11/24 at New York's Golden Theater, with Jane Cowl in a play that protests Nazi treatment of German Jews, 99 perfs.; *Professor Mamlock* by Friedrich Wolf 12/8 at Zurich's Schauspielhaus; *Valley Forge* by Maxwell Anderson at New York's Guild Theater, with Philip Merivale, George Coulouris, Margalo Gilmore, 58 perfs.; *Accent on Youth* by Samson Raphaelson 12/25 at New York's Plymouth Theater, with Constance Cummings, 229 perfs.

British National Films is founded at Ellstree, England, by English miller J. Arthur Rank, 46, who will soon gain control of the Odeon Circuit with its 142 sumptuous theaters plus the Gaumont theatre chain founded in the 1890s. Rank will have studios at Denham, Pinewood Studios, and Shepherd's.

The Hays Office is created by the U.S. film industry's MPPDA (Motion Picture Producers and Distributors of America, Inc.), which hires former Postmaster General Will H. Hays, now 55, to administer a production code established by the industry. No exposure of female breasts, no suggestion of cohabitation or seduction, and no unconventional kissing are among the prohibitions that will be enforced.

Shirley Temple makes her first full-length film at age 6 and follows Hamilton McFadden's *Stand Up and Cheer* (in which she steals the show by singing "Baby Take a Bow") with Alexander Hall's *Little Miss Marker* and David Butler's *Bright Eyes* (in which she sings "The Good Ship Lollypop"). All dimples and curly hair, Temple will go on to star in half a dozen other Hollywood films in the next 4 years.

Other films   Howard Hawk's *Twentieth Century* with John Barrymore, Carole Lombard; John Ford's *The Lost Patrol* with Victor McLaglen, Boris Karloff; Frank Capra's *It Happened One Night* with Clark Gable, Claudette Colbert (*see* below); Victor Fleming's *Treasure Island* with Jackie Cooper, Wallace Beery; Jack Conway's *Viva Villa* with Wallace Beery, Leo Carillo, Fay Wray; Rowland V. Lee's *The Count of Monte Cristo* with Robert Donat, Elissa Landi, Louis Calhern, Sidney Blackmer; Rouben Mamoulian's *Queen Christina* with Greta Garbo, John Gilbert; Paul Czinner's *Catharine the Great* with Elizabeth Bergner; Paul Czinner's *Ariane* with Elizabeth Bergner; John Stahl's *Imitation of Life* with Claudette Colbert, Louise Bevers; Jean Benoit-Levy and Marie Epstein's *La Maternelle;* Jacques Feydeu's *Carnival in Flanders* (*La Kernesse Heroique*); Jean Vigo's *L'Atalante;* Yasujiro Ozu's *Ukigusa Monogatari;* Edward Cline's *Peck's Bad Boy* with Jackie Cooper; Mitchell Leisen's *Death Takes a Holiday* with Fredric March, Evelyn Venable, Gail Patrick; Frank Borzage's *Little Man, What Now?* with Douglass Montgomery, Christian Rut in an exposé of the roots of Nazism; King Vidor's *Our Daily Bread;* Robert Flaherty's documentary *Man of Aran;* William Beaudine's *The Old-Fashioned Way* with W. C. Fields; Norman Z. McLeod's *It's a Gift* with W. C. Fields in a remake of Field's silent film *The Old Army Game;* W. S. Van Dyke II's *The Thin Man* with William Powell and Myrna Loy as Nick and Nora Charles; John Cromwell's *Of Human Bondage* with Bette Davis, Leslie Howard, Frances Dee; John Cromwell's *Spitfire* with Katharine Hepburn, Robert Young, Ralph Bellamy.

Radio drama   *The Lux Radio Theater* 10/14 on NBC stations. The show will move to CBS in late July of next year, it will continue until mid-1954, and it will then return briefly to NBC; *The Aldrich Family* 10/17 on NBC stations with Ezra Stone as Henry Aldrich. The show will continue until 1953.

Opera   *Lady Macbeth of the Mzensk District* 1/22 at Leningrad's Maly Opera House, with music by Dmitri Shostakovich. *Pravda* denounces the music, calling it "a deliberate and ugly flood of confusing sound . . . , a pandemonium of creaking, shrieking, and clashes," another critic calls it "unSoviet, unwholesome, cheap eccentric, tuneless and leftist"; *Merry Mount* 2/10 at New York's Metropolitan Opera House, with music by Howard Hanson; *Four Saints in Three Acts* 2/20 at New York's 44th Street Theater, with music by U.S. composer Virgil Garnett Thompson, 37, libretto by Gertrude Stein whose opera is not about saints, is not presented in three acts, but adds to the fame of Gertrude Stein with such bewildering lines as "Pigeons in the gass, alas."

The Glyndebourne Festival Opera has its first season 54 miles south of London on the 640-acre estate of Audrey and John Christie. The London Philharmonic provides music for the June to August performances in the Christies' 800-seat opera house.

The Berkshire Music Festival has its first season on the 210-acre Tappan family estate outside Lenox, Mass., whose grounds can accommodate up to 14,000 concertgoers. The Boston Symphony will take over the Festival in 1936 under the direction of Serge Koussevitzky, a disastrous rainstorm will halt a concert August 12, 1937, and the Boston Symphony will erect a 6,000-seat "Shed" with fine acoustics in 1938.

First performances   *Sacred Music* (*Avodath Hakodesh*), *a Sabbath Morning Service for Baritone Cantor, Chorus, and Orchestra* by Ernest Bloch 1/12 at Turin (radio broadcast); *Symphony: 1933* by Roy Harris 1/26 at Boston's Symphony Hall; *The Enchanted Deer* (*Cantata Profana*) by Béla Bartók 5/25 at London in a performance by the BBC Wireless Chorus and the BBC Symphony; Concerto for String Quartet and Orchestra after the Concerto Grosso Op. 6 No. 7 by G. F. Handel by Arnold Schoenberg 9/26 at Prague (Schoenberg has been in the United States since October of last year); *Rhapsody on a Theme of Paganini* for Piano and Orchestra by Sergei Rachmaninoff 11/7 at Baltimore in a concert by the Philadelphia Orchestra.

Stage musicals   *The New Ziegfeld Follies* 1/4 at New York's Winter Garden Theater, with Fanny Brice, Jane Froman, Vilma and Buddy Ebsen, Eugene and Willie Howard in a production staged by Ziegfeld's widow Billie Burke, music by Vernon Duke and others, lyrics by E. Y. Harburg and others, songs that include "I Like the Looks of You," "The Last Roundup" by Billy Hill, "Wagon Wheels" by Peter DeRose, lyrics by Billy Hill, 182 perfs.; *Conversation Piece* 2/16 at His Majesty's Theatre, London, with Noel Coward, Louis Hayward, George Sanders, book, music, and lyrics by Coward, songs that include "I'll Follow My Secret Heart," 177 perfs.; *Life Begins at 8:40* 8/27 at New York's Winter Garden Theater, with Bert Lahr, Ray Bolger, Brian Donlevy, music by Harold Arlen, lyrics by Ira Gershwin and E. Y. Harburg, songs that include "Fun to Be Fooled," "You're a Builder Upper," "Let's Take a Walk Around the Block," 237 perfs.; *Anything Goes* 11/21 at New York's Alvin Theater, with William Gaxton, Ethel Merman, Victor Moore, book by Guy Bolton, P. G. Wodehouse, Howard Lindsay, and Russel Crouse, music and lyrics by Cole Porter, songs that include "The Gypsy in Me," "I Get a Kick Out of You," "You're the Top," "Blow, Gabriel, Blow," "All Through the Night," and the title song, 420 perfs.; *Thumbs Up* 12/27 at New York's St. James Theater, with Bobby Clark, Ray Dooley, Sheila Barrett, songs that include "Autumn in New York" by Vernon Duke, "Zing! Went the Strings of My Heart" by James Hanley, 156 perfs.

Hollywood musicals   Elliott Nugent's *She Loves Me Not* with Bing Crosby, Miriam Hopkins, Kitty Carlisle, music by Ralph Rainger, lyrics by Leo Robin, songs that include "Love in Bloom."

Popular songs   "The Beer Barrel Polka" (*"Skoda Lasky"*) by Czech songwriters Jaromir Vejvoda,

Duststorms ruined 100 million acres of U.S. croplands, forcing "Okies" and "Arkies" to move west to California.

Wladimir A. Timm, and Vasek Zeman (English lyrics by Lew Brown will be published in 1939); "What a Difference a Day Makes" (*"Cuando vuelva a tu lado"*) by Spanish composer Marcia Greves, English lyrics by Stanley Adams; "Miss Otis Regrets" by Noel Coward, who has written it for *Bricktop* (*see* 1925); "June in January" by Ralph Rainger, lyrics by Leo Robin; "Blue Moon" by Richard Rodgers, lyrics by Lorenz Hart; "Stars Fell on Alabama" by Frank Perkins, lyrics by Mitchell Parish; "Solitude" by Duke Ellington, lyrics by Eddie De Lange and Irving Mills; "I Only Have Eyes for You" by Harry Warren, lyrics by Al Dubin; "The Very Thought of You" by Ray Noble; "Love Thy Neighbor" by Harry Revel, lyrics by Mack Gordon; "Deep Purple" by Peter DeRose, lyrics by Mitchell Parish; "Little Man You've Had a Busy Day" by Mabel Wayne, lyrics by Maurice Sigler and Al Hoffman; "The Object of My Affection" by U.S. songwriters Pinky Tomlin, 25, Coy Poe, and Jimmie (James W.) Grier, 36; "Hands Across the Table" by French composer Jean Delettre, English lyrics by Mitchell Parish; "Alla en el Rancho Grande" by Mexican composer Sylvano R. Ramos, lyrics by Bartley Costello; "Tumbling Tumbleweed" by Bob Nolan; "Carry Me Back to the Lone Prairie" by Carson Robinson; "You and the Night and the Music" by Arthur Schwartz, lyrics by Howard Dietz (for the film *Revenge with Music*); "With My Eyes Wide Open I'm Dreaming" by Mack Gordon and Harry Revel (for the film *Shoot the Works*); "You Oughta Be in Pictures" by U.S. composer Dana Suesse, 22, lyrics by Edward Heyman; "On the Good Ship Lollipop" by Richard A. Whiting, lyrics by Sidney Clare (for the film *Bright Eyes,* above); "Isle of Capri" by Will Grosz, lyrics by Jimmy Kennedy; "Winter Wonderland" by Felix Bernard, lyrics by Dick Smith.

Le Jazz Hot by French critic Hugues Panassié, 22, is the first book of jazz criticism.

The Hammond organ patented by Chicago clockmaker Laurens Hammond, 39, is the world's first pipeless organ. The 275-pound instrument has a two-manual console with pedal clavier and a power cabinet but no reeds, pipes, or vibrating parts, it costs less than a penny per hour to operate, and it will lead to a whole generation of electrified instruments.

The School of the American Ballet is founded by George Balanchine with help from Boston philanthropist Lincoln Kirstein (*see* 1933).

Harlem's Apollo Theater is opened by entrepreneurs Leo Brecher and Frank Schiffman who have bought the failing burlesque theater Hurtig and Seaman's, changed its name, and changed its policy of barring black patrons. Schiffman books blues singer Bessie Smith into the Apollo and makes it the leading U.S. showcase for black performers.

Prizefighter Max Baer, 25, knocks out Primo Carnera June 13 in the 11th round of a title bout at Long Island City and wins the world heavyweight championship he will hold for exactly 1 year.

The World Cup football (soccer) competition is won by Italy, which defeats Czechoslovakia 2 to 1 in overtime at Rome's Stadio Torino.

Pitcher Leroy Robert "Satchel" Paige, 28, breaks Dizzy Dean's 30-game winning streak as he strikes out 17 men and allows no runs in a Hollywood All-Stars game while Dean strikes out 15 and lets one run score. Paige starts 29 games in 29 days, and his team wins 104 out of 105 games as he continues to pitch for the Bismarck, S. Dak., team for which he pitched 31 games last year and won 27. Paige will pitch in the Negro National League for the Crawford Giants of Pittsburgh, the Homestead Grays of Baltimore, and the Kansas City Monarchs, clinching the Negro World Series title for the Monarchs in 1942 and pitching 64 scoreless innings for the team in 1946 (*see* 1948).

The St. Louis Cardinals win the World Series by defeating the Detroit Tigers 4 games to 3 after winning the pennant on the last day of the season.

The U.S. ocean yacht *Rainbow* defeats England's *Endeavour* 4 to 2 to retain the America's Cup.

The Masters golf tournament for professionals at Georgia's Augusta National Golf Club begins a tournament that will continue for more than 40 years. The Masters will be one of golf's annual classics [along with the U.S. Open, the British Open, and the Professional Golfers Association (PGA) contests].

U.S. men's underwear sales slump after moviegoers see Clark Gable remove his shirt in the film *It Happened One Night* (above) to reveal that he wears no undershirt. Sales of men's caps have declined as a result of the association of men's caps with hoodlums in gangster movies.

The Washeteria that opens April 18 at Fort Worth, Tex., is the first launderette. Proprietor J. F. Cantrell has installed four washing machines and charges by the hour.

YKK (Yoshida Kabushiki-kaisha) is founded by Japanese entrepreneur Tado Yoshida, 26, whose firm will become the world's largest producer of zippers (*see* Sundback, Talon, 1913). Yoshida has found himself out of a job when his employer was charged with tax evasion and went bankrupt, he has invested $170 and has employed two former associates to start a new business, within a few months he has hired 10 girls to run his machines, and he imitates U.S.-made zippers for the growing Japanese clothing industry.

Clyde Barrow, 24, and Bonnie Parker die in a hail of bullets May 23 on a road 50 miles east of Shreveport, La., after a 2-year career in which they have casually killed 12 people in Texas, Oklahoma, Missouri, and Iowa. Their most successful robbery netted them no more than $3,500 and the father of one of their gang members has told the police where to watch for them. Texas Ranger Frank Hamer, sheriff's deputy Ted C. Hinton, and four other sheriff's deputies have set up an ambush, Bonnie and Clyde drive into the trap at 85 miles per hour, the lawmen riddle them with 50 bullets, and they die holding a machine gun and a sawed-off shotgun, respectively.

John Dillinger, 32, leaves the Biograph Theater in Chicago July 22 not knowing that a woman friend has betrayed him. FBI agents shoot him dead after an 11-year career in which he has robbed banks in Indiana, Ohio, Illinois, and Wisconsin.

New York police arrest German-American furrier Bruno Richard Hauptmann September 20 for possession of ransom money paid to recover Charles A. Lindbergh, Jr., in 1932. Hauptmann says he received the gold certificates from a former partner in the fur business and denies any connection with the Lindbergh kidnapping (*see* 1936).

The U.S. Army turns over Alcatraz Island in San Francisco Bay to the Bureau of Prisons which will convert the "Rock" into a federal prison. The army has used the island since 1854, it is 1,650 feet long and 450 feet wide, the army built a three-story cell block for military prisoners in 1909, and before the Bureau of Prisons abandons it in 1963, Alcatraz (Spanish for pelican) will house the most notorious U.S. criminals including Al Capone, George (Machine-gun) Kelly, and Robert Stroud.

The Worldwide Church founded by U.S. evangelist Herbert W. Armstrong, 37, adjures its members to observe the sabbath on Saturday, to celebrate Passover but not Christmas, and to follow kosher dietary laws. Armstrong and his son Garner Ted will use radio to attract a wide following.

Charles R. Walgreen opens the world's first superdrugstore at Tampa, Fla., and begins a revolution in drug chain merchandising by using open display cases for nonprescription drugs and by carrying merchandise not sold at drugstores until now. Walgreen operates drugstores in 37 states and retires at age 61 (*see* 1909).

 San Francisco's Coit Tower is completed by Arthur Brown, Jr.

 A *Field Guide to the Birds* by Boston painter-ornithologist Roger Tory Peterson, 26, takes up where John James Audubon left off (*see* 1843). Peterson's book will go into nearly 50 printings in the next 40 years and will sell more than 1.7 million copies.

Great Smoky Mountains National Park is created by act of Congress for full development. Established for protection and administration in 1930, the park along the North Carolina-Tennessee border embraces 515,226 acres in the highest mountain range east of the Mississippi.

Dust storms in May blow some 300 million tons of Kansas, Texas, Colorado, and Oklahoma topsoil into the Atlantic. At least 50 million acres lose all their topsoil, another 50 million are almost ruined, and 200 million are seriously damaged (*see* Soil Conservation Act, 1935).

The Taylor Grazing Act passed by Congress June 28 sets up a program to control grazing and prevent erosion of western grasslands. The new law effectively closes the public domain to homesteading (*see* Stockraising Homestead Act, 1916).

Western ranchers begin two decades of wholesale slaughter of wild horses to clear the disintegrating ranges. The horsemeat fetches 5 or 6 cents a pound (it is sold for human food, dog food, and chicken feed), the government pays a bounty to encourage the horse hunters, and by 1952 the wild horse population will be 33,000 down from 2 million in 1900.

 The Taylor Grazing Act (above) establishes grazing districts under the control of the Department of the Interior.

The western dust storms (above) are an aftermath of imprudent plowing during the Great War, when farmers planted virgin lands to wheat in order to cash in on the high grain prices then prevailing.

"Okies" and "Arkies" from the Dustbowl begin a trek to California that will take 350,000 farmers west within the next 5 years.

Mexico's agrarian revolution that began in 1910 will be pushed forward by President Cardenas (above), who will resume distribution of the land to the Pueblos and who will also work to build the power of organized labor.

The *Erzengungsschlacht* program to expand domestic food production is started in Nazi Germany. By 1937 the country will be producing 90 percent of the food it consumes.

Drought reduces the U.S. corn crop by nearly a billion bushels, and the average yield per acre falls to 15.7 bushels, down from 22.8 last year (wheat yields average 11.8 bushels per acre).

U.S. soybean acreage increases to 1 million (*see* 1924; 1944).

1934 (cont.) The potential of soybeans as a livestock feed is seen by Fort Wayne, Ind., sugar beet processor Dale W. McMillen. He buys German processing machinery and establishes Central Soya, a company that will be a major factor in the fast-growing U.S. soybean industry (*see* Staley, 1922).

A Farm Mortgage Financing Act passed by Congress January 31 creates a Federal Farm Mortgage Corporation to help farmers whose mortgages are being foreclosed (*see* 1931).

A Crop Loan Act passed by Congress February 23 authorizes loans to farmers to tide them over until harvest time.

The Frazier-Lemke Farm Bankruptcy Act passed June 28 allows mortgage foreclosures to be postponed for 5 years (but *see* 1935).

A "Milk in Schools" scheme improves nutrition among British schoolchildren by supplying one-third pint of milk each day to nearly half of all elementary school pupils. The children either pay nothing or get the milk at extremely low cost (*see* 1906; 1931).

Phenylketonuria (PKU) is described for the first time. The condition affects infants who lack enzymes needed to metabolize the amino acid phenylalanine and may cause mental retardation if not quickly diagnosed and remedied by putting the infant on a diet low in phenylalanine.

Pyridoxine (vitamin B_6) is discovered at Cambridge University by Hungarian-born biochemist Paul Gyorgy, 40, who finds a coenzyme that cures dermatitis in rats. It will be synthesized in 1939.

U.S. food-buying patterns begin shifting to larger consumption of red meats (especially beef and pork), fruits, green vegetables, and dairy products as industrial earnings start to improve.

MSG (monosodium glutamate) is produced commercially for the first time in the United States, which has depended until now on the flavor enhancer Ajinimoto imported from Japan (*see* 1908; 1947).

Tillie Lewis Foods Company has its beginnings in Flotill Products, Inc., in California's San Joaquin Valley. Brooklyn, N.Y., divorcée Myrtle (Tillie) Ehrlich, 28, has been advised by the U.S. Department of Agriculture that pomodoro Italian canning tomatoes cannot be grown in the United States, she has taken her savings and sailed for Italy, she has met an Italian pomodoro canner on the ship, she has convinced him that the tomatoes can be grown in California, she has persuaded him to loan her $10,000 and some pomodoro seed, she has moved to California, she has persuaded the Pacific Can Company of Stockton to build a plant that she can rent, and she has used the loan from Florindo del Gaizo to start Flotill Products. When del Gaizo dies in 1937, Ehrlich will borrow $100,000 to buy his interest in Flotill. She will marry AF of L western director Meyer Lewis in 1947, and she will sell her Tillie Lewis Food Company to Ogden Corporation for $6 million.

A new chilling process for meat cargoes improves on the process used in 1880 on the S.S. *Strathleven*.

Pepsi-Cola Corporation is acquired by Walter Mack, who will promote Pepsi's 12-ounce bottle to challenge Coca-Cola (*see* 1933; 1939).

Royal Crown Cola is introduced by Nehi Corporation (*see* 1928; 1959; Hatcher, 1905; Diet-Rite, 1962).

Carvel's frozen custard stand opens at Hartsdale, N.Y. Greek-American entrepreneur Thomas A. Carvel, 27, has changed his name from Carvelas, he will have 21 soft ice cream stores by 1950, and by 1976 he will have 680 franchised stores in 14 states.

Seagram's 7 Crown blended whiskey is introduced by Distillers Corporation-Seagram, which will make 7 Crown by far the largest-selling U.S. whiskey (*see* 1933; 1947).

Monarch Wine Company is founded at Brooklyn, N.Y., to produce kosher sacramental wines for use on religious occasions in place of homemade wines. Monarch will lease the name Manischewitz to gain acceptance for its strong, aromatic wine made from native American vitis labrusca grapes, it will bottle wines under 17 other labels, it will grow to become the largest U.S. producer of fruit wines (such as blackberry, cherry, elderberry, and loganberry), it will produce more champagne than America imports from France, its winery will grow to cover four city blocks, and Manischewitz wines will become popular with gentiles as well as with Jews (*see* 1888).

The Los Angeles Farmers Market opens at 6333 West Third Street with stalls that rent for 50 cents a day on 30-day leases. Started by 17 farmers who have had trouble selling their produce, the market will grow to cover three acres of buildings with 18 acres of parking space and with 160 individually owned stalls selling such items as Monzano bananas, Texas mustard greens, snow peas, black radishes, fresh figs, Louisiana sugar cane, Minnesota white veal, racks of lamb, country-style apple and potato sausages, German pumpernickel bread, fresh angelica, loganberries, and loquats.

Le Cordon Bleu outgrows its 39-year-old Paris quarters in the Palais Royale and is moved by Mme. Distel to 120 Rue du Faubourg St. Honoré (*see* 1945).

The *Guide Michelin* published since 1900 by the French tire firm to evaluate European restaurants is given an elongated format. A green jacket will be adopted in 1939.

The Dionne quintuplets born May 28 at Callander, Ontario, are the world's first five infants on record to be born at one delivery and to survive. Elzire Dionne is a 24-year-old mother of six, she is delivered of five girls by her physician Allen R. Dafoe, 51, and the infants Emilie, Yvonne, Cecile, Marie, and Annette average 2 pounds 11 ounces each.

1935 A plebiscite conducted by the League of Nations January 13 shows that voters in the Saar Basin prefer reunion with the German Reich 9 to 1 over union with France or continuation of rule by the League, which has administered the region since 1919. The League returns the Saar to Germany March 1.

Adolf Hitler denounces Versailles Treaty clauses that provide for German disarmament, but Berlin signs an agreement with London promising not to expand the German navy to a size larger than 35 percent of the Royal Navy.

Adolf Hitler organizes the Luftwaffe to give Germany a military air capability. Reich minister for air forces is Nazi Reichstag president Hermann Goering, who served in the air force in the Great War.

The U.S. Army Air Corps has its beginnings in the General Headquarters Air Force established under the command of Brigadier General Frank Maxwell Andrews, 51. It is the first independent U.S. strategic air force.

Turkey's president Mustafa Kemal adopts the name Kemal Ataturk (see 1930; 1938).

Persia becomes Iran by order of Reza Shah Pahlevi who has controlled the country since 1925.

The Soviet Comintern founded in 1919 responds in June to the growth of Fascism abroad. It approves Communist participation in "Popular" front governments with other leftists or moderates (see 1943).

Siam's Rama VII (Prajadhipok) abdicates March 2 after a 10-year reign in which the Siamese have abolished absolute royal power. He is succeeded by his 10-year-old nephew who will reign until his assassination in 1946 as Rama VIII (Ananda Mahidol).

Britain's third Baldwin ministry begins June 7 as Stanley Baldwin, now 67, replaces Ramsay MacDonald as head of the coalition cabinet. An Anglo-German naval pact is signed June 18 (see above).

Italian troops invade Ethiopia October 3. France has ceded part of French Somaliland to Italy and has sold Italy shares in the Ethiopian Railway but Benito Mussolini has rejected further concessions offered by France and Britain in mid-August (see 1896; 1936).

Josef Stalin decrees that Soviet children above the age of 12 are subject to the same punitive laws that apply to adults—8 years in a labor camp for stealing corn or potatoes, for example, or 5 years for stealing cucumbers.

Nazi SS (Schutzstaffel) leader Heinrich Himmler, 35, starts a Lebensborn (life source) state breeding program to produce an Aryan "super race." He encourages young women of "pure blood" to volunteer their services as mates of SS officers to contribute blond, blue-eyed babies who will grow into thin-lipped narrow-nosed "Nordic beings" to carry on the "thousand-year Reich."

The Nuremberg Laws enacted by the Nazi Party congress meeting at Nuremberg September 15 deprive Jews of German citizenship, they forbid intermarriage with Jews, and they make intercourse between "Aryans" and Jews punishable by death to prevent "racial pollution."

The basic definition of a Jew published November 14 defines the categories of mixed offspring, or mischlinge. The first degree includes anyone with two Jewish grandparents, the second degree anyone with one Jewish grandparent.

Belfast has anti-Catholic riots in July. Northern Ireland expels Catholic families, and Catholics in the Irish Free State make reprisals.

The National Labor Relations Act (Wagner-Connery Act) passed by Congress July 5 creates a National Labor Relations Board and reasserts the right of collective bargaining. The right was contained in section of the NRA code of 1933 that the Supreme Court has struck down (see below).

The Committee for Industrial Organization (CIO) is founded by dissidents within the AF of L who advocate industrial unionism but who have been outvoted by craft union advocates at the AF of L's November convention at Washington, D.C. The dissidents elect United Mine Workers president John L. Lewis chairman of the CIO and they elect a 39-year-old Scots-American UMW vice president named Philip Murray chairman of the CIO's Steel Workers Organizing Committee (see 1936).

The United Automobile Workers (UAW) holds it first convention at Detroit and receives a charter from the AF of L (see 1936).

"We must quit this business of relief" and create 3.5 million jobs for "employables," says President Roosevelt January 7 in an address to a joint session of Congress.

An Emergency Relief Appropriation Act passed by Congress April 8 authorizes nearly $5 billion to provide "work relief and to increase employment by providing useful projects."

A Works Progress Administration (WPA) is created by executive order May 6, with Harry L. Hopkins as WPA administrator.

A National Youth Administration (NYA) is created June 26 as a division of the WPA (above) to provide jobs for 4.2 million young people seeking work.

The National Industrial Recovery Act (NRA) of 1933 is ruled unconstitutional by the Supreme Court May 27 in the case of Schechter Poultry Corporation v. United States.

The Railway Pension Act of 1934 is ruled unconstitutional by the Supreme Court June 27 in the case of Railroad Retirement Board v. Alton Railway Company, but a Railway Retirement Act is passed by Congress to replace the 1934 law. Railroads and their employees are each to contribute 3.5 percent of the first $300 earned each month to build a retirement fund.

The Social Security Act passed by Congress August 14 provides a system of old-age annuities and unemployment insurance benefits. Drafted by Eastman

1935 (cont.) Kodak Company treasurer Marion Bayard Folsom, 41, the act provides for state aid to be matched by federal aid of up to $15 per month for needy retirees over age 65, with employers and employees taxed equally to support the program. The tax is to begin in 1937 at 1 percent and is to rise by steps to 3 percent in 1949, qualified employees are to be able to retire at age 65 beginning January 1, 1942, and are to receive payments of from $10 to $15 per month for the rest of their lives, and widows and orphans are to receive payments beginning in 1940.

The Social Security Act (above) provides for a fund to help states pay allowances to workers who have lost their jobs. Beginning with 1936 payrolls, employers are to set aside for this purpose a 1 percent tax in the first year, 2 percent the second, and 3 percent the year after, with employees contributing half the amount set aside.

Internal Revenue Service figures for the year are reported by President Roosevelt in a monopoly message. One-tenth of 1 percent of U.S. corporations own 52 percent of all corporate assets reported and earn 50 percent of all corporate income. Less than 5 percent own 87 percent of all corporate assets, and less than 4 percent earn 87 percent of all net profits reported by all U.S. corporations.

A Revenue Act passed by Congress August 30 seeks to achieve some diffusion of wealth. The law provides for inheritance and gift taxes but critics protest that the law means double taxation for recipients of stock dividends and clippers of bond coupons.

The Banking Act signed into law by President Roosevelt August 23 reorganizes the Federal Reserve System created in 1913 and increases its authority. It establishes an open market committee to buy and sell government securities held by the Federal Reserve Banks and thus control the nation's money supply. The banking reform also regulates checking accounts and requires that banks contribute to the support of the Federal Deposit Insurance Corporation that protects depositors from default or theft.

Fort Knox is established in Kentucky to serve as a repository for U.S. gold bullion. The army guards the gold and the government assures foreign bankers that they can redeem every $35 in U.S. paper currency for an ounce of gold from Treasury Department stores at Fort Knox (which do not begin to approach the amounts of gold stored for the accounts of various nations in the vaults of the Federal Reserve Bank building put up at New York in 1924).

Britain and Ireland conclude a cattle and coal agreement that enables the Irish to ship some of their meat surplus, but the disastrous Anglo-Irish tariff war will not end until February of next year when Dublin will agree to pay land annuities (*see* 1932; 1938).

Josef Stalin urges productivity increases in November and encourages individual initiative with extra pay for notable efficiency, giving official recognition to the Stakhanovite movement based on the achievement of coal miner Aleksei Grigorievich Stakhanov, 29. Working at a coal face in the Donets Basin the night of August 30, Stakhanov and his crew reportedly mined 102 tons of coal in a single shift of 5 hours 45 minutes—14 times the normal rate. Virtually illiterate, the stocky miner has used other members of the crew to shore up the shaft with timbers while he hewed the coal, departing from the previous time-consuming process of alternating between cutting coal and erecting timbers. Soviet propagandists publicize a locomotive engineer who is said to have increased the average speed of freight trains to that of passenger trains; but most workers live by the saying, "As long as the bosses pretend they are paying us a decent wage we will pretend that we are working," and productivity will remain low.

Morgan Stanley & Co., Inc., is founded by J. P. Morgan's grandson Henry Sturgis Morgan, 34, his fellow Morgan J. P. partner Harold Stanley, 49, and four other J. P. Morgan bankers.

U.S. entrepreneur John D. MacArthur, 38, buys Bankers Life & Casualty Company of Chicago for $2,500 and begins the career that will make him a billionaire. Brother of playwright Charles MacArthur of 1928 *The Front Page* fame and brother-in-law of actress Helen Hayes, John began at age 17 as a salesman for his brother Alfred's Central Standard Life of Chicago, he will use a dubious mail-order insurance scheme to make Bankers Life highly profitable, and by 1976 he will be rivalled in wealth only by shipping magnate Daniel K. Ludwig.

Toledo's Libbey Glass Company is acquired for $5 million by Owens-Illinois, which will market Libbey-Owens glass (*see* 1883).

Sulfa drug chemotherapy is introduced by German biochemist Gerhard Domagk, 40, to launch a new era in medicine that will revolutionize treatment of infectious diseases including certain forms of pneumonia and will reduce the hazards of peritonitis in abdominal surgery. Director since 1927 of I. G. Farbenindustrie at Elberfield, Domagk and his colleagues have injected 1,000 white mice with fatal doses of streptococci and have then treated them with prontosil, an azo dye patented in 1931 by Farbenfabriken Bayer of 1899 aspirin fame, which has turned out to have antibacterial properties (all the white mice recovered, and the same results have been obtained with rabbits). Prontosil will be developed into sulfanilamide, which will be followed by other sulfonamides (*see* Ehrlich, 1909; Dubos, 1939; penicillin, 1928, 1940; streptomycin, 1943).

The proteinaceous nature of viruses is demonstrated by Rockefeller Institute biochemist Wendell Meredith Stanley, 31, who shows that viruses are not submicroscopic organisms as is commonly believed.

The protein-splitting enzyme chymotrypsin is isolated from pancreatic juice by U.S. biochemist John H. Northrup of 1930 pepsin fame.

Ergonovine is extracted from the ergot fungus *Claviceps purpurea,* and the alkaloid proves an effective tool in obstetrics (*see* Stearns, 1808; ergotamine, 1918). The alkaloid content of the fungus will be raised by selective breeding from 0.02 percent to 0.5 percent, and the product will be marketed under the name Ergothetrine in Britain (*see* ergotism, 857).

The first wearable electronic hearing aid is produced by British inventor A. Edwin Stevens, who founds a company he calls Amplivox to produce the 2½ pound device (*see* Zenith, 1943).

The French Line passenger ship S.S. *Normandie* goes into service on the North Atlantic for the Compagnie Generale Transatlantique and arrives at New York June 3 after having crossed from Southampton in a record 4 days, 11 hours, 42 minutes. The 79,280-ton luxury liner with four screws is 1,029 feet in length overall and has an 80-foot swimming pool (*see* 1942).

Greek entrepreneur Stavros S. Niarchos, 26, begins a shipping fleet that will rival the maritime empire of Aristotle Onassis (*see* 1930). Niarchos persuades his flour miller uncles to buy six British freighters at Depression prices of $20,000 each so that they can import their own wheat and avoid middlemen, he will quit the employ of his uncles to start his own firm in 1939, and by mid-1940 he will be operating seven tramp freighters (*see* 1945).

The Lower Zambezi railroad bridge opens January 14 in Africa and will be the world's longest railroad bridge until December (*see* below).

A railroad bridge designed by McKim, Mead and White opens to span the Cape Cod Canal of 1914 at Buzzards Bay, Mass.

Newark's Pennsylvania Station opens March 23. Lawrence Grant White of McKim, Mead and White has designed the new terminal.

A hurricane September 2 completely wipes out the Florida East Coast Railroad line between Florida City and Key West that was repaired after the hurricane of 1926. The new storm sweeps across the keys and kills 400 (*see* overseas highway, 1938).

The Huey P. Long Bridge completed December 10 at Metairie, La., is 4.35 miles long—the world's longest railroad bridge.

General Motors Corporation begins a program of dieselizing U.S. railroad locomotives (*see* 1930; 1941).

Twin stainless steel Zephyrs go into service on the Burlington Route. The Budd-built trains have a cruising speed of 90 miles per hour, and they cut 3.5 hours off the 882-mile round trip between Chicago and the twin cities of Minneapolis and St. Paul (*see* 1934).

The Bristol Blenheim light bomber has its beginnings in a twin-engine transport monoplane introduced by the English aircraft firm (*see* 1920; Bristol-Siddeley, 1959).

The B-17 bomber demonstrated for the U.S. Army by Boeing Aircraft is the first four-engine, all-metal, low-wing monoplane.

Bell Aircraft Company is founded at Buffalo, N.Y., by former Consolidated Aircraft general manager Lawrence Bell, 40, and his assistant Ray P. Whitman, 52, following the removal of Consolidated operations to California.

Pilot Wiley Post sets out on a pleasure trip to the Orient with his humorist friend Will Rogers, now 55. Their plane crashes near Point Barrow, Alaska, August 15 and both men are killed (*see* 1931).

The first official trans-Pacific air mail flight leaves San Francisco November 22, and the China Clipper flying boat of Juan Trippe's Pan American Airways arrives November 29 at Manila after having flown 8,210 miles with stops at Honolulu, Midway, Wake, and Guam (*see* 1930). The new San Francisco-Manila route gives Pan Am a total of 40,000 miles versus 24,000 for Air France, 23,600 for Lufthansa, 21,000 for British Imperial, 11,700 for KLM, 10,500 for Soviet Russia's Aeroflot.

Moscow's Metropol subway opens in May with 5.5 miles of track that will grow to become a 105-mile system with more than 90 stations. The new subway has stations modeled after the great U.S. railroad terminals with magnificent murals, and chandeliers.

The Toyota motorcar is introduced in prototype by Japan's Toyoda Automatic Loom Works whose Sakichi Toyoda received £100,000 from a Lancashire firm in 1929 for rights to produce his advanced loom in England. Toyoda has used the money to develop a motorcar design and has put his son Kiichiro in charge of the venture. Kiichiro has sent an engineer to the Packard works at Detroit as a tourist, and the engineer has acquired enough information to set up an assembly line (*see* 1937).

English racing driver Sir Malcolm Campbell, 50, drives his *Bluebird* at 276 miles per hour over sand at Daytona Beach, Fla.

Nash-Kelvinator Corporation is created by a merger of Nash Motors with the Kelvinator Corporation (*see* 1914; Charles Nash, 1916; American Motors, 1954).

The Motor Carrier Act passed by Congress August 9 places U.S. interstate bus and truck lines under control of the Interstate Commerce Commission.

The Rural Electrification Administration established by President Roosevelt's executive order May 11 will underwrite rural electric cooperatives and provide loans for transmission lines. Only 10 percent of 30 million U.S. rural residents have electrical service, but with help from the REA, 90 percent of U.S. farms will have electricity by 1950.

An estimated 6.5 million windmills have been produced in the United States in the past half-century. Most have been used to pump water or to run sawmills, but some "wind generators" have produced small amounts of electricity.

1935 (cont.) Britain's Anglo-Persian Company of 1914 becomes the Anglo-Iranian Company as Persia becomes Iran (above) (*see* British Petroleum, 1954).

Polyethylene, developed by the Alkali Division of Britain's Imperial Chemical Industries, is the first true "plastic" ever made from the polymerization of ethylene. Two years ago, company chemists found small specks of a white solid material when they opened their retort after an attempt to force a copolymerization between liquid ethylene and an aldehyde, using extremely high temperatures to link small molecules into long chains, and their polyethylene will find wide use in packaging (*see* 1953).

Nylon, developed by E. I. du Pont chemist Wallace Hume Carothers, 39, is a synthetic polymide that will replace silk, rayon, and jute in many applications. Carothers has combined adipic acid and hexamethylenediamine to form long filaments of what he calls "polymer 66." Drawing the filaments out to a certain length aligns the polymer chains and pulls them to their full extent, making the filaments strong and durable but giving them many of the characteristics found in silk and wool (*see* 1937).

George Washington Carver joins the U.S. Department of Agriculture's Bureau of Plant Industry and pursues experiments in the industrial use of the peanut (*see* 1921).

Radar (radio detecting and ranging) is pioneered by Scottish physicist Robert Alexander Watson-Watt, 43, of Britain's Government Radio Research Station, who begins setting up radar warning systems on the British Coast, but his installations require enormous antenna towers (the longer the wavelength transmitted, the larger the antenna needed), and Watson-Watt uses wavelengths of roughly 50 centimeters (*see* Hertz, 1887; Kuhnold, 1934; MIT, 1940).

The first tape recorder to use plastic tape is produced in Berlin, where AEG introduces the Magnetophon with a tape of speed of 30 inches per second. Its performance is inferior to that of the 1920 Blattnerphone, but its operating cost is (*see* 1940).

General Telephone Corporation of New York is created by New York bankers who reorganize the bankrupt Associated Telephone Utilities (*see* 1926). The new holding company will be run by the bankers until 1955 (*see* GTE, 1958).

The American Institute of Public Opinion (Gallup poll) is founded by Iowa statistician George H. Gallup, 34, who has been launched on his career as pollster by *Des Moines Register* and *Tribune* publisher Gardner Cowles, 32, who has hired Gallup to gauge reader reaction to newspaper features (*see* 1936).

The *Minneapolis Star* is acquired by Gardner Cowles (above), who is building an empire of publishing and broadcasting properties (*see Look,* 1937).

This Week is launched by Crowell-Collier's Joseph P. Knapp, whose Sunday newspaper magazine supplement will be carried by scores of metropolitan papers (*see Collier's,* 1919).

Ted Bates, Inc. advertising is founded by former Benton & Bowles executive Theodore Lewis Bates, 33, whose agency will specialize in hard-sell advertisements for package goods and cigarettes.

Nonfiction *My Country and My People* by Chinese scholar Lin Yutang, 40, who has studied comparative literature at Harvard and at Leipzig and has arrived in America after 12 years in China during which he has observed the rise of Sun Yat-Sen and Chiang Kai-shek. Lin has invented an index system for Chinese characters and has helped formulate a Romanization system for written Chinese.

Fiction *Gyakko* (*Doke no hana*) by Japanese novelist Osamu Dazai (Shuji Tsushima), 26; *Before the Dawn* (*Yoakemae*) by Shimasaki Toson; *Wheel of Fortune* (*Le ambizoni sbagliate*) by Alberto Moravia whose second novel is ignored by reviewers under pressure from Fascist authorities; *It Can't Happen Here* by Sinclair Lewis who projects a fascist takeover of America and warns Americans against complacency about the totalitarian governments that are tightening their grip on Japan and much of Europe; *Holy Ireland* by Irish novelist Norah Hoult, 37; *A Clergyman's Daughter* by George Orwell; *Mr. Norris Changes Trains* by Christopher Isherwood; *Rajah Amahr* by L. H. Myers; *The Stars Look Down* by A. J. Cronin; *A Crime* (*Un Crime*) by Georges Bernanos; *The Last Puritan* by philosopher George Santayana; *Tortilla Flat* by California novelist John Ernst Steinbeck, 33, whose work about the Spanish-speaking "paisanos" of Monterey is a best seller; *Of Time and the River* and *From Death to Morning* (stories) by Thomas Wolfe.

Juvenile *National Velvet* by Enid Bagnold.

Poetry *Monologue* (*Alleenspraak*) by Afrikaans poet N. P. van Wyk Louw, 29; *Poems* by English poet William Empson, 29.

Painting *Minotauromachy* by Pablo Picasso; *The Soda Fountain* by William Glackens; *Senators* by U.S. social realist painter-cartoonist William Gropper, 37, who has done the work on assignment from *Vogue* magazine. Max Liebermann dies at Berlin February 8 at age 87; Gaston Lachaise dies at New York October 18 at age 53.

Kodachrome is introduced for 16-millimeter movie cameras by Eastman Kodak Company which has acquired production rights from U.S. concert violinist Leopold Godowsky, Jr., 35, and his pianist co-inventor Leopold Damrosch Mannes, 35, who have devised a three-color dye-coupling process with help from a team of Eastman scientists. Godowsky and Mannes met as students at New York's Riverdale Country School in 1916, they have studied physics and chemistry at the University of California and at Harvard while continuing their music careers, Godowsky married George Gershwin's sister Frances in 1931, and the two have been working with Eastman at Rochester since July 1931 (*see* 1936).

Theater *Waiting for Lefty* by U.S. playwright Clifford Odets, 28, 1/5 at New York's Civic Repertory Theater on 14th Street, 168 perfs.; *The Old Maid* by Zoe Akins 1/7 at New York's Empire Theater, with Judith Anderson, Helen Mencken, 305 perfs., Pulitzer Prize; *Point Valaine* by Noel Coward 1/16 at New York's Ethel Barrymore Theater, with Alfred Lunt, Lynn Fontanne, Broderick Crawford, 55 perfs.; *Awake and Sing* by Clifford Odets 2/19 at New York's Belasco Theater, with Morris Carnovsky, Stella Adler, John Garfield, 209 perfs.; *Till the Day I Die* and *Waiting for Lefty* by Clifford Odets 3/26 at New York's Longacre Theater with a top price of $1.50 per seat in a production by the Group Theater founded 4 years ago by Odets and director Lee Strasberg, 33, 136 perfs.; *There Was a Prisoner* (*Y avait un prisonnier*) by Jean Anouilh 3/21 at the Théâtre des Ambassadeurs, Paris; *Night Must Fall* by Welsh-born English playwright Emlyn Williams, 29, 5/31 at London's Duchess Theatre; *Winterset* by Maxwell Anderson 9/25 at New York's Martin Beck Theater, with Burgess Meredith, Richard Bennett, Margo in a play based on the Sacco-Vanzetti case, 195 perfs.; *Bright Star* by Philip Barry 10/15 at New York's Empire Theater, with Lee Tracy, Julie Hayden, 7 perfs.; *Dead End* by Sidney Kingsley 10/28 at New York's Belasco Theater, with Joseph Dowling as the gangster "Baby Face" Martin, Sheila Trent, 268 perfs.; *Murder in the Cathedral* by T. S. Eliot 11/1 at London's Mercury Theatre—a play based on the death of the archbishop of Canterbury at the hands of Henry II's knights in 1170: "The last temptation is the greatest treason:/ To do the right deed for the wrong reason" (I), 180 perfs.; *Tiger at the Gates* (*La Guerre de Troie n'aura pas lieu*) by Jean Giraudoux 11/21 at the Théâtre de l'Athenée, Paris; *Boy Meets Girl* by U.S. playwrights Bella (Cohen) and Samuel Spewack, both 36, 11/27 at New York's Cort Theater, with Jerome Cowan, Garson Kanin, Everett Sloane, 669 perfs.

Maxwell Anderson's *Winterset* (above) wins the first annual New York Drama Critics' Circle Award.

The American National Theater and Academy (ANTA) created July 5 by act of Congress has been funded through the efforts of New York socialite Mary Stewart French, 45, who has been troubled by U.S. government neglect of the performing arts as compared with European government support of music, dance, and the theater. French has pawned her family diamonds, she has presented benefits, and has received support from Eleanor Roosevelt

Radio drama and comedy *Backstage Wife* debuts 4/5 on NBC radio to begin a new soap opera scripted by Frank and Anne Hummert; *Fibber McGee and Molly* 4/16 on NBC Blue Network stations with Jim (James Edward) and Marian Driscoll Jordan in a comedy series that began under another name in 1931. The series is sponsored by Johnson's wax and will continue until 1952; *Gang Busters* (*G-Men*) 7/20 on NBC stations dramatizes the death of John Dillin-

ger last year. Developed by Phillips H. Lord, the show will move to CBS early next year and will continue for more than 20 years.

Films Frank Lloyd's *Mutiny on the Bounty* with Charles Laughton, Clark Gable, Franchot Tone; Alfred Hitchcock's *The 39 Steps* with Robert Donat, Madeleine Carroll; George Cukor's *David Copperfield* with Freddie Bartholomew, W. C. Fields, Lionel Barrymore, Basil Rathbone, Madge Evans, Maureen O'Hara; John Ford's *The Informer* with Victor McLaglen; Clarence Brown's *Anna Karenina* with Greta Garbo, Fredric March, Freddie Bartholomew, Maureen O'Sullivan; Richard Boleslawski's *Les Miserables* with Fredric March, Charles Laughton, Cedric Hardwicke; Rowland V. Lee's *Cardinal Richelieu* with George Arliss; William Dieterle's *The Story of Louis Pasteur* with Paul Muni; Josef von Sternberg's *Crime and Punishment* with Peter Lorre; Irving Pichel and Lansing C. Holden's *She* with Helen Gahagan; Max Reinhard and William Dieterle's *A Midsummer Night's Dream* with James Cagney, William Powell, Olivia de Havilland, Joe E. Brown, Mickey Rooney; Henry Hathaway's *Lives of a Bengal Lancer* with Gary Cooper, Franchot Tone, C. Aubrey Smith; George Stevens's *Alice Adams* with Katharine Hepburn, Fred MacMurray; George Cukor's *Sylvia Scarlett* with Katharine Hepburn, Cary Grant, Edmund Gwenn; Rouben Mamoulian's *Becky Sharp* with Miriam Hopkins, Billie Burke in the first full-length Technicolor feature; Paul Czinner's *Escape Me Never* with Anna Neagle; Herbert Wilcox's *The Little Damozel* with Anna Neagle; Howard Hawks's *Ceiling Zero* with James Cagney, Pat O'Brien; Fred Zinneman's *The Wave;* Michael Curtiz's *Captain Blood* with Errol Flynn; David Butler's *The Littlest Rebel* with Shirley Temple, Bill Robinson; William Keighley's *G-Men* with James

Adolf Hitler promised Germans a new order based on "racial purity," repression, and preparation for military aggression.

917

1935 (cont.) Cagney; Leo McCarey's *Ruggles of Red Gap* with Charles Laughton, Mary Boland, Zasu Pitts; James Whale's *The Bride of Frankenstein* with Elsa Lanchester, Boris Karloff; Jean Renoir's *Toni;* Sam Wood's *A Night at the Opera* with the Marx Brothers.

"HICKS NIX STICKS PIX" headlines *Variety* July 17. The 30-year-old show business newspaper reports that rural audiences reject motion pictures with bucolic stories and characters.

Hollywood musicals   Mark Sandrich's *Top Hat* with Fred Astaire and Ginger Rogers, Irving Berlin songs that include "Cheek to Cheek," "Isn't It a Lovely Day to Be Caught in the Rain," "Top Hat, White Tie, and Tails"; Archie Mayo's *Go into Your Dance* with Al Jolson, Ruby Keeler, Helen Morgan, Glenda Farrell, Patsy Kelly, Al Dubin-Harry Warren songs that include "About a Quarter to Nine" and "She's a Latin from Manhattan"; Busby Berkeley's *Gold Diggers of 1935* with Dick Powell, music by Harry Warren, lyrics by Al Dubin, songs that include "Lullaby of Broadway"; A. Edward Sutherland's *Mississippi* with Bing Crosby, W. C. Fields, Joan Bennett, music by Richard Rodgers, lyrics by Lorenz Hart, songs that include "It's Easy to Remember but So Hard to Forget"; Roy Del Ruth's *Folies Bergère* with Maurice Chevalier, Ann Sothern, Merle Oberon.

Stage musicals   *Spread It Abroad* at London with Cyril Ritchard, Madge Evans, songs that include "These Foolish Things Remind Me of You" by Jack Strachey and Harry Link, lyrics by Holt Marvell; *At Home Abroad* 9/19 at New York's Winter Garden Theater, with Beatrice Lillie, Eleanor Powell, Ethel Waters, Eddie Foy, Jr., music by Arthur Schwartz, lyrics by Howard Dietz, songs that include "Hottentot Potentate," 198 perfs.; *Jubilee* 10/12 at New York's Imperial Theater, with Melville Cooper, Mary Boland, Montgomery Clift, music and lyrics by Cole Porter, songs that include "Begin the Beguine," "Just One of Those Things," 169 perfs.; *Jumbo* 11/16 at the New York Hippodrome, with Jimmy Durante, a live elephant, music by Richard Rodgers, lyrics by Lorenz Hart, songs that include "Little Girl Blue," "The Most Beautiful Girl in the World," 233 perfs.; *George White's Scandals* 12/24 at New York's New Amsterdam Theater, with Bert Lahr, Willie and Edgar Howard, Rudy Vallee, music by Ray Henderson, lyrics by Jack Yellen, 110 perfs.

Opera   *Porgy and Bess* 10/10 at New York's Alvin Theater, with Todd Duncan, J. Rosamond Johnson, music by George Gershwin, lyrics by Ira Gershwin and DuBose Heyward whose 1927 stage play *Porgy* has provided the libretto and arias that include "I Got Plenty o' Nuttin'," "Summertime," "I Loves You, Porgy," "It Ain't Necessarily So," 124 perfs.

Your Hit Parade debuts on radio in April. The program of song hits is sponsored by the American Tobacco Company and promotes Lucky Strikes.

Benny Goodman opens at the Palomar Ballroom in Los Angeles August 21 and is hailed as the King of Swing. Clarinetist-bandleader Benjamin David Goodman, 26, uses arrangements by Fletcher Henderson to introduce a new "big band" jazz style, he starts a *Let's Dance* radio program of "swing" music, and he begins a long career that will be helped by such sidemen as Lionel Hampton, Gene Krupa, and Teddy Wilson (*see* 1938).

Jazz music of black or Jewish origin is banned from German radio beginning in October.

Popular songs: "The Music Goes Round and Round" by Edward Farley and Michael Riley, lyrics by "Red" Hodgson; "I Can't Get Started" by Vernon Duke, lyrics by Ira Gershwin; "I Won't Dance" by Jerome Kern, lyrics by Otto Harbach and Oscar Hammerstein II; "Stairway to the Stars" by violinist Matt Malneck and Frank Signorelli, lyrics by Mitchell Parish; "Goody Goody" by Matt Malneck and Johnny Mercer; "I'm in the Mood for Love" by Jimmy McHugh and Dorothy Fields; "A Little Bit Independent" by Joseph A. Boyle, lyrics by Edgar Leslie; "Moon Over Miami" by Joe Burke, lyrics by Edgar Leslie; "In a Sentimental Mood" by Duke Ellington; "I'm Gonna Sit Right Down and Write Myself a Letter" by Fred E. Ahlert, lyrics by Joe Young; "Red Sails in the Sunset" by Hugh Williams (Will Grosz), lyrics by Jimmy Kennedy.

The Orange Bowl game is held for the first time January 1 at Miami. Bucknell defeats Miami 26 to 0.

The Sugar Bowl game is held for the first time January 1 at New Orleans. Tulane beats Temple 20 to 14.

College football's Heisman Memorial Trophy is awarded for the first time by New York's Downtown Athletic Club, whose first athletic director is former University of Pennsylvania football coach John Heisman, 58. Heisman has started the Touchdown Club of New York to honor all college players who have scored on the gridiron, the first award winner chosen by sportswriters and sportscasters is University of Chicago halfback John J. "Jay" Berwanger, 21, and the trophy will be awarded annually after Heisman's death next year to honor not only the recipient but also the man who introduced the center snap, the vocal "hike" as a signal for starting play, the hidden-ball play, the scoreboard listing downs and yardage, etc., and who was a leader in the fight to legalize the forward pass and to reduce games into quarters rather than halves.

The first major league night baseball game is played May 14 at Cincinnati's Crosley Field. A button pressed by President Roosevelt at Washington turns on 363 lights of 1,000 kilowatts each mounted on eight giant towers to illuminate the field and to begin a new era in "America's favorite pastime."

The Detroit Tigers win the World Series by defeating the Chicago Cubs 4 games to 2.

Hot Springs, Va., golf caddy Samuel Jackson "Sammy" Snead, 22, becomes a professional golfer to begin an outstanding career.

Eddie Arcaro wins a race on a gelding named No More at Chicago's Washington Park to begin a 26-year career that will win stakes races of well over $23 million. George Edward Arcaro, 19, will be the top money winner 6 years, he will twice bring home Triple Crown winners (Kentucky Derby, Preakness, Belmont Stakes), and he will generally pocket a flat 10 percent of the winnings.

James J. Braddock, 29, wins the world heavyweight title from Max Baer June 13 at Long Island City, N.Y. Braddock gains a 15-round decision over Baer.

Monopoly is introduced by Parker Brothers of Salem, Mass., which rejected the board game in 1933 because it took too long to play, involved concepts such as mortgages and interest that players would find confusing, and had rules that were too complex. Unemployed engineer Charles B. Darrow, 36, of Germantown, Pa., has adapted the Landlord's Game devised at the turn of the century by one Lizzie J. Magie to popularize the ideas of Henry George (see 1879), who believed that capitalism could work only if no one were permitted to profit from the ownership of land. Quakers at a school in Atlantic City, N.J., have given local place names to the board properties, but Darrow's patent will make him a millionaire.

Max Factor of Hollywood opens a super-colossal salon in the film capital. Now 58, the Russian-born cosmetics magnate came to America at age 27, became a Hollywood makeup man in his late thirties, and has a factory that employs 250 people producing cosmetics and wigs.

Fred and "Ma" Barker of the notorious Karpis-Barker gang are slain January 16 by federal agents outside Ocklawaha, Fla.

Louisiana governor Huey Long is shot to death September 8 by physician Carl Austin Weiss who has determined to end the dictatorial ambitions of the 42-year-old Kingfish who dies in the arms of Nazi-sympathizer Gerald L. K. Smith. Slot machines by the hundreds have been installed in New Orleans with Long's approval by New York underworld boss Frank Costello.

Newark, N.J., mobster Dutch Schulz (Arthur Flegenheimer), 33, is mortally wounded October 23 by gunmen from a newly organized New York crime syndicate who walk into his saloon headquarters and shoot him down along with his three companions. A major figure in liquor bootlegging during Prohibition, Flegenheimer has twice in the last 2 years been tried and acquitted for evading income taxes on the proceeds of his various rackets.

Allied Stores Corporation is created by a reorganization of Hahn Department Stores whose stock plummeted from $57 per share in 1929 to less than $1 in 1932. Headed since 1933 by former Frederick Loeser & Company of Brooklyn president B. Earl Puckett, 37, Allied Stores' profits have increased since their 1933 low of $25,000 and will be up to $20 million by 1948 as Puckett decentralizes management responsibility.

The League of Nations moves into a gleaming white $6 million palace completed for the League at Geneva.

New York's 41-story International Building at 630 Fifth Avenue opens in Rockefeller Center in May.

The U.S. Supreme Court moves from its chamber in the Capitol building to a dazzling white Vermont marble building of its own designed by the late New York architect Cass Gilbert who died last year at 75.

Williamsburg, Va., regains its colonial splendor after 8 years of recreation funded by a $94.9 million gift from John D. Rockefeller, Jr. Boston architect William G. Perry, 52, has supervised the work of restoring 40 buildings on a 178-acre site (see 1699).

The first U.S. public housing project opens December 3 on New York's Lower East Side, where a row of tenements owned by Vincent Astor at 3rd Street and Avenue A has been demolished. Governor Herbert Lehman, Eleanor Roosevelt, and Mayor Fiorello La Guardia attend the opening of the eight-building complex built by the City Housing Authority that was founded in February of last year with a promised grant of $25 million. In the next 40 years the CHA will build 228 projects with 167,000 apartments to house 560,000 persons, and other cities will build similar projects.

The Concord opens at Kiamesha Lake, N.Y., to rival the Catskill resort hotel Grossinger's started in 1914. Jeris hair tonic millionaire Arthur Winarick has acquired a small family hotel that he will expand into a 10-story structure with indoor and outdoor swimming pools, eight indoor tennis courts, ski slopes with snow-making machines, indoor and outdoor skating rinks, the world's largest nightclub, and endless helpings of blintzes, potato pancakes, bagels, and lox (smoked salmon).

The first Alvar Aalto molded plywood furniture comes off the production line set up west of Helsinki at Artek Oy in Turku by Finnish architect Alvar Aalto, 37, who has designed chairs of molded birch plywood in bent plywood frames for the Paimio Tuberculosis Sanatorium located north of Helsinki.

The Richter scale for measuring the intensity of earthquakes is devised by U.S. seismologist Charles Richter, 35, who records ground motion in seismographs. Each increase of one number means a 10-fold increase in magnitude (the San Francisco earthquake of 1906 is judged to have been a quake of 8.3 on the Richter scale—10 times greater than a quake of 7.3).

Shenandoah National Park in Virginia's Blue Ridge Mountains is created by act of Congress. John D. Rockefeller, Jr., has used matching funds to encourage North Carolina, Tennessee, and Virginia to preserve the Blue Ridge, and the new 193,593-acre park provides vistas of the Piedmont and the Shenandoah Valley.

The Wilderness Society is founded by U.S. conservationists to work for the preservation of wilderness

1935 (cont.) areas and of wildlife through educational and scientific programs and through cooperation with state and local citizen groups.

The Civilian Conservation Corps (CCC) created in 1933 reaches its peak enrollment of 500,000.

Dust storms in western states stop highway traffic, close schools, and turn day into night.

A Soil Conservation Act is signed by President Roosevelt who names Hugh Hammond Bennett, 54, to head the new Soil Conservation Service (see Soil Erosion Service, 1933). Bennett estimates that soil erosion is costing the United States $400 million in diminished productivity alone each year, and he works to make Americans soil-conscious.

U.S. farm prices begin to rise as the Commodity Credit Corporation purchases surplus farm commodities for distribution among needy Americans (see 1933; AAA, 1938).

The United States has 6.81 million operating farms, down from 7.2 million in 1931.

A Resettlement Administration created by executive order April 30 works to move people from poor lands to better lands under the direction of administrator Rexford Guy Tugwell (see 1933).

The Frazier-Lemke Farm Bankruptcy Act of 1934 is unconstitutional, the Supreme Court rules May 27 in *Louisville Joint Stock Land Bank v. Radford.*

One-third of U.S. farmers receive U.S. Treasury allotment checks for not growing food and other crops or are committed to receive such checks under terms of the AAA law of 1933, but drought holds down production more than New Deal planting restrictions do (see Supreme Court decision, 1936).

A new harvester introduced by Allis-Chalmers Company is smaller and lighter than a conventional combine but is capable of harvesting almost any kind of crop. Allis-Chalmers has a 14.1 percent share of the U.S. harvester market as compared with 32 percent for International Harvester, but its new harvester will raise Allis-Chalmers's share to 45.6 percent by next year, while International Harvester's will fall to less than 12 percent (see 1901; 1937).

Canada's Parliament establishes a Wheat Board with headquarters at Winnipeg, Manitoba, to handle barley, oat, and wheat exports and to tell farmers how much they can plant each year with a guarantee that will sell their crops.

Five Acres and Independence by Maurice Grenville Kains, 67, is a practical guide to conducting a small farm. The book becomes a best seller as thousands of urban Americans go back to the land.

Fertilized eggs removed from the uterus of a rabbit are stored alive for several hours in a special blood serum and are transplanted surgically into the uterus of a virgin rabbit, where they will mature to permit virgin birth (see calf, 1950).

Soviet agronomist T. D. Lysenko calls his more scientific critics "Trotskyite bandits" and enemies of the state. Josef Stalin hears him, he says, "Bravo, comrade Lysenko, bravo," and Lysenkoism becomes Soviet agricultural gospel (see 1926; Vavilov, 1940).

 Kwashiorkor is found to be associated with a maize diet. British Colonial Medical Service physician Cicely D. Williams, 42, described a deficiency disease 2 years ago with symptoms that include edema, bloated stomach, cracked skin, red or dirty gray hair, and even dwarfism, the disease is common among infants at Accra in the Gold Coast, Williams gives the disease's African name in a report to the British medical journal *Lancet,* and she says it is the disease "the deposed baby gets when the next one is born," indicating that it may be caused by a lack of mother's milk (see 1951).

Vitamin E (alpha-tocopherol) is isolated from wheat germ oil at the University of California, Berkeley, by biochemists Herbert McLean Evans, now 53, and Oliver and Gladys Emerson (see 1921; 1938).

Vitamin K—essential for blood "Koagulation"—is isolated by Danish biochemist C. P. H. Dam and by U.S. biochemist Edward A. Doisy and his associates at St. Louis University (see 1937; Dam, Doisy, 1929).

 Eat, Drink and Be Wary by consumer advocate F. J. Schlink relates horror stories related to food contamination (see 1932; 1933; Sinclair, 1905; Tugwell, 1933).

U.S. fish cutters discover that the small white fillet of ocean perch from the Atlantic tastes much like freshwater perch. This launches a boom in the industry.

A record 42-pound lobster is caught off the coast of Virginia.

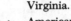 Americans consume 50 million chickens but pay more for poultry than for red meat (see 1965).

U.S. food packers ship 240 million cases of canned goods, up from 160 million in 1931 (see 1940).

The 1925 "giant" symbol of Minnesota Valley Canning is turned into the Jolly "Ho Ho Ho" Green Giant by Chicago advertising copywriter Leo Burnett, 43, who colors the giant green, dresses him in leaves, and starts a new advertising agency under his own name (see 1936; 1950).

ReaLemon lemon juice is introduced by Chicago entrepreneur Irvin Swartzberg, whose physicians have told him to start the day with lemon juice and water but who has become tired of squeezing lemons. Swartzberg starts the Puritan Company to supply lemon juice to bars, hotels, restaurants, and industrial users, he will sell ReaLemon to consumers by 1941.

Beer in cans is introduced for the first time by Krueger Beer of Newton, N.J.

Canadian distillers are sued by the U.S. government for $60 million in taxes and duties evaded during Prohibition. The amount will be lowered to $3 million, and half of it will be paid by Distillers Corporation-Seagram (see 1933; 1943).

Alcoholics Anonymous is started at New York June 10 by ex-alcoholic Bill Wilson, 40, and his former drinking companion Dr. Robert H. Smith, who takes his last drink and works with Wilson to share with other alcoholics the experience of shaking the disease. The AA organization is denied funding by John D. Rockefeller, Jr., who says that money will spoil its spirit (the organization will spread through church groups). The anonymity of "Bill W." will not be broken until his death in 1971, and he will be called by English novelist Aldous Huxley "the greatest social architect of our time" (*see* Synanon, 1958).

The first hot meals to be served in the air are served on Pan American Airways Clipper flights (above).

Chicago printing salesman Duncan Hines, 55, sends out a pamphlet in lieu of a Christmas card, he lists his favorite eating places, and he receives so many requests for copies that he goes into business leasing "Recommended by Duncan Hines" signs for as much as $20 per year. Guidebooks by Hines will be published under titles that will include *Adventures in Good Eating* and *Lodging for a Night* (*see* 1954).

Ireland amends her criminal code to make it a felony to sell, import, or advertise any form of birth control device or method.

Japan's population reaches 69.2 million, up from 34.8 million in 1872. Emigration to Manchuria eases population pressures to some extent, and the birth rate falls to 14.4 per thousand, down from its peak of 15.3 in 1930, but overpopulation causes mounting anxiety.

1936 Britain's George V dies January 20 at age 70 after a reign of nearly 26 years and is succeeded by his 41-year-old son Edward, who assumes the throne as Edward VIII. The new king is in love with the 39-year-old American divorcée Wallis Warfield Simpson, he abdicates December 10 to marry her, and he is succeeded by his 41-year-old brother, who will reign until 1952 as George VI.

Adolf Hitler takes advantage of the Ethiopian crisis to denounce the 1925 Locarno Pacts and to reoccupy the Rhineland March 7. A Rome-Berlin Axis is formed October 25, and Japan signs an Anti-Comintern Pact with Germany November 25.

Egypt's Ahmed Fuad dies April 28 at age 68 after a reign of more than 18 years, first as sultan, then as king. He is succeeded by his 16-year-old son Farouk who will reign until 1952, and Britain agrees August 27 to withdraw from all of Egypt except for the Suez Canal zone.

Italian forces take Addis Ababa May 5, and on May 9 Italy proclaims the annexation of Ethiopia. The African nation is joined with Eritrea and Italian Somaliland to create Italian East Africa, but Ethiopia will regain her independence with British help late in 1941 and will take over Eritrea in 1952.

Barefoot Ethiopian warriors by the hundreds of thousands have been killed by Italian bombs and mustard gas while Benito Mussolini's son-in-law Conte Galeazzo Ciano has expressed rapture at the beauty of bombs "opening like red blossoms" on Ethiopia's highlands. "I am here today to claim the justice that is due to my people," says the Ethiopian emperor Haile Selassie June 30 in an address at Geneva to the League of Nations. "God and history will remember your judgment," says the emperor, and as he steps down he murmurs, "It is us today. It will be you tomorrow."

A Spanish civil war begins July 18 as army chiefs at Mililla in Spanish Morocco start a revolt against the weak government at Madrid. Insurgent generals Francisco Franco, 44, and Emilio Mola, 49, are supported by most of the army and the air force, and the revolt spreads rapidly to the garrison towns of Cadiz, Seville, Saragossa, and Burgos in Spain. Commanding large Moorish contingents, Franco and Mola form a Junta of National Defense July 30 at Burgos. They are soon joined by German and Italian "volunteers," and while Russia supplies the government loyalists with advisers and equipment, the nonintervention policies of Britain, France, and the United States serve the interests of Franco and Mola.

The Spanish insurgents (above) obtain arms from Germany and Italy, they lay siege to Madrid November 6, and the republican government immediately begins executing rightist political prisoners and military officers lest they be freed by the Fascists.

"The fifth column" will take Madrid, says General Mola (above) when asked which of his four columns will capture the city. He refers to sympathizers within Madrid, but resistance is stiffened by the Communist orator La Pasionaria (Dolores Ibarruri, 41), who has said July 18, "They shall not pass" (No pasaran) and who exhorts housewives to take lunch to their husbands in the trenches and to pour boiling oil on any Fascists who enter the city.

An International Brigade of anti-Fascists rallies to the Spanish Loyalist cause, 82 Americans embark for France as "tourists" on the S.S. *Normandie* Christmas Day to join the fight, by February of next year several thousand Americans will be in the Lincoln Brigade, and by April 1939 some 3,100 Americans will have fought in Spain and half will have died.

Nicaragua has a coup d'etat June 2. The National Guard led by General Anastasio Somoza, 40, deposes President Juan Sacasa, Somoza will be president for 10 years beginning next year, and his family will continue his dictatorship for more than 30 years thereafter.

President Roosevelt wins re-election to a second term with 61 percent of the popular vote, which reaches an unprecedented 45 million. Governor Alfred M. Landon, 59, of Kansas denounces New Deal encroachments on American business and American institutions, but the Democrats denounce "economic royalists" who are indifferent to the needs of the people, they point to the economic progress made since 1933, and they win 523 electoral votes, capturing every state but Maine and Vermont, as compared with eight for Landon who receives 37 percent of the popular vote (*see* Gallup poll, below).

1936 (cont.) Nazi Germany's Gestapo is taken over by Heinrich Himmler and is combined with the regular police force. Started by Hitler in 1933, the secret police (*Geheime Staatspolizei,* or Gestapo) will compile dossiers on virtually every German to suppress political opposition.

A Great Purge begins in the Soviet Union. The *Yezhovschina* will take an estimated 8 to 10 million lives in the next 2 years as Josef Stalin liquidates his political enemies (*see* 1937).

The sit-down strike is pioneered February 14 by United Rubber Workers of America employees who receive pink layoff slips at 3 in the morning and who refuse to leave Plant No. 2 of the Goodyear Tire and Rubber Company.

Sit-down strikers occupy the General Motors Chevrolet body plant at Flint, Mich., with CIO backing after five members of the United Automobile Workers Union have been laid off at GM's Fisher Body plant in Atlanta for wearing union buttons (*see* 1937).

Philip Murray of the CIO organizes the United Steel Workers of America (*see* 1935; Homestead Strike, 1892; Republic Steel, 1937).

The AF of L suspends CIO unions (*see* 1935).

The Supreme Court rules June 1 that a New York minimum wage law for women passed in 1933 is unconstitutional. The Court hands down the decision in the case of *Morehead v. New York ex. rel. Tipaldo* (*see* Fair Labor Standards Act, 1938).

Sir Oswald Mosley leads an anti-Jewish march down London's Mile End Road October 12 (*see* 1932, 1940).

The General Theory of Employment, Interest and Money by John Maynard Keynes advances the idea that massive economic depressions such as the one now engulfing the world are not necessary. Depressions can be avoided, says Keynes, by fairly simple governmental action such as investment in public works, encouragement of capital goods production, and stimulation of consumption to help restore the economic equilibrium. Once this is achieved, the capitalist system will resume its normal long-term growth rate with the Gross National Product increasing by 2.5 percent each year to double national income every 30 years or so, a growth that is much faster than can be achieved under any other economic system (*see* British general strike, 1926).

Some 38 percent of U.S. families (11.7 million families) have incomes of less than $1,000 per year. The Bureau of Labor Statistics places the "poverty line" at $1,330.

The Robinson-Patman Act passed by Congress June 20 to supplement the Clayton Anti-Trust Act of 1914 forbids U.S. manufacturers to practice price discrimination including use of advertising allowances to favored customers such as chain stores.

France, Switzerland, and the Netherlands abandon the gold standard September 27.

The French franc is devalued October 2.

The Italian lira is devalued October 4.

Germany embarks on a Four-Year Plan October 19, with Hermann Goering as economic minister.

The Ford Foundation for Human Advancement is established by Ford Motor Company president Edsel Ford (*see* 1927; 1943).

Sulfa drugs discovered in Nazi Germany come into use in the United States after further development by U.S. pharmaceutical firms (*see* 1935; 1937).

The Robert Wood Johnson Foundation is founded by the Johnson & Johnson family to advance U.S. health care delivery. The funds assets will exceed $1 billion by 1975, making it second only to the Ford Foundation (above).

The Merchant Marine Act passed by Congress June 29 provides for federal subsidies to U.S. shipowners to make up the difference between what foreign shipping lines pay to man and maintain their ships and the higher operating costs U.S. shipping lines must pay (*see* Jones-White Act, 1928).

Some 39,000 U.S. maritime workers tie up all West Coast ports beginning October 30 in a strike that spreads to eastern and Gulf Coast ports. The strike will last for nearly 3 months before seamen vote to accept tentative agreements.

National Bulk Carriers is founded at New York by U.S. shipbuilder Daniel K. Ludwig, 39, who started his career at age 9 by raising a sunken vessel and who has pioneered in developing a technique for side-launching newly built ships. Ludwig has also developed a welding process to replace riveting in shipyards (*see* 1941).

The S.S. *Queen Mary* goes into service on the North Atlantic for the Cunard-White Star Line. The 80,774-ton passenger liner has four screws, measures 1,019.5 feet overall, and has been built at Clydebank by John Brown & Co., Ltd. which built the *Lusitania,* the *Aquitainia,* the *Empress of Britain,* and H.M.S. *Hood.*

London-Paris night ferry service begins in October to provide the cheapest luxury route between the two capitals. Passengers leaving Victoria Station at 9 o'clock in the evening (10 o'clock in summer) have their sleeping cars loaded aboard Channel steamers at Dover and offloaded at Dunkirk, permitting morning arrival at the Gare du Nord in Paris.

The *Super Chief* leaves Chicago's Dearborn Station May 12 with nine Pullman cars pulled by diesel locomotives. The new weekly luxury train put into service by the Santa Fe reduces traveling time between Chicago and Los Angeles to just over 39 hours, much faster than *The Chief* that has been in service since 1926, and Santa Fe officials contract with Philadelphia's Edward G. Budd Company to buy nine new stainless steel air-conditioned cars that will accommodate 104 passengers and a crew of 12.

The DC-3 introduced by Douglas Aircraft is a powerful two-engine, 21-passenger aircraft built at the urging of C. R. Smith of American Airlines. The Model T of commercial aviation will prove that commercial aircraft can be profitable if flown fully loaded, Douglas will sell more than 800 within 2 years, the DC-3 will make Douglas the leader in commercial aircraft, and Douglas will produce more than 10,000 military versions (the British will call them Dakotas, the U.S. Navy R-4D's, the Air Transport Command C-47's) (see 1933; 1938).

The American Airlines Mercury flight to Los Angeles leaves Newark Airport in late October carrying 12 passengers who will occupy sleeper berths plus two motion picture celebrities who pay a premium over the standard $150 fare to occupy the private Sky Room compartment of the Douglas Sleeper Transport version of the new DC-3 (above). The flight departs at 5:10 in the afternoon, it flies to Memphis, Dallas, Phoenix, and on to Glendale, Calif., where it arrives at 9:10 the following morning, just 20 minutes after estimated time of arrival.

London's Gatwick Airport opens with direct rail connections to the city and with covered access to aircraft from a circular terminal building. The 189-acre airport will remain in use for 20 years and will be replaced in 1958.

Soviet aviator Valeri Pavlovich Chkalov, 32, flies nonstop from Moscow to Nikolaevsk on the Amur River within a year after having received the Order of Lenin for his exploits as a test pilot (see 1937).

New York City's electric streetcar system is converted in part to a system employing GM buses made by General Motors Corporation, which has obtained control of the city's surface transit lines through stock purchases (see 1932; 1949; Pacific Coast Lines, 1938).

New York's Fifth Avenue Coach Company replaces its open-air, double-decker omnibuses with closed double-deckers that are called "Queen Marys" and will remain in operation until 1953 (some open-air double-deckers will remain in service until late in 1948). The fare on Fifth Avenue is 10 cents, but subways and other bus lines continue to charge 5 cents (see 1896; 1907; higher fares, 1947).

New York's Triborough Bridge opens July 11 to link Manhattan, Queens, and the Bronx. The 1,380-foot suspension bridge spans the East River and charges a 25-cent toll for passenger cars.

New York's Henry Hudson Bridge opens December 12 to link Manhattan's Upper West Side with the Riverdale section of the Bronx and with the Westchester parkways beyond. The 800-foot steel arch bridge across the Harlem River has a 10-cent toll.

The Cord 810 introduced by Auburn-Deusenberg-Cord of Auburn, Ind., is a sleek modern motorcar with advanced features that include disappearing headlights (see 1934; 1937).

The Willys-Overland Company is reorganized and renews production of low-priced motorcars (see 1915; Jeep, 1940).

The Ford V8 is unveiled in November (see 1932).

The Topolino (Little Mouse) is introduced by Italy's 37-year-old Fiat whose CR-32 biplane is Francisco Franco's chief fighter plane in the Spanish Civil War (above). Fiat's popular-priced "people's car" will not be replaced on the assembly lines until 1948.

The world's first production passenger car to operate on diesel fuel is introduced by Germany's Mercedes-Benz (see 1926; Diesel, 1895).

Hunt Oil Company is founded by H. L. Hunt, whose firm will soon be the largest independent U.S. producer of oil and natural gas (see Joiner, 1930). Hunt has expanded his operations into Oklahoma and Louisiana and then into the great East Texas field, he will move his headquarters to Dallas next year, and he will develop properties that will yield him an income of roughly $1 million per week.

A California discovery well that will lead to major oil production in Kern County is brought in at 8,000 feet by Shell Oil drillers who have used new seismograph techniques on land owned by Kern County Land Company (see 1890). Seventy-five percent of Kern County Land revenues will soon be coming from oil well royalties, but the company will continue to be a major producer of cattle, potatoes, and other farm products (see Tenneco, 1968).

The Houdry process for cracking oil to produce gasoline is introduced commercially by Sun Oil Company and Socony-Vacuum, joint owners of the catalytic process invented by French-American engineer Eugene F. Houdry, 44, who is the fils in Houdry & Fils, a French steelmaking firm. Houdry has used bauxite as a catalyst to develop a way to produce upwards of 80 percent gasoline from the lowest grade crude oil and refinery residuum without producing a gallon of fuel oil on which profit is nil or minimal. Thermal cracking of crude oil by the Palmer method of 1900 or the Bosch method of 1924 has required pressures of up to 3,000 pounds per square inch and temperatures of up to 1,200°F, but the Houdry process requires pressures of only 20 to 40 psi and temperatures of only 900°F.

Boulder Dam (Hoover Dam) is completed on the Colorado River after 21 months of construction on the border between Arizona and Nevada. Concrete for the $175 million project has been set with cooling tubes to hasten a process that would otherwise have taken a century, and its giant hydroelectric generators produce cheap power for southern California, Arizona, and Nevada. The dam is 726 feet high and 1,244 feet wide, and will be renamed in 1947 to honor the president who authorized its construction (see below; Kaiser, 1931; Bonneville, 1937).

The right of the TVA to dispose of surplus hydroelectric power is upheld February 17 by the Supreme

"Put your trust in Japanese military," said this poster addressed to Chinese peasants. "Return to your homes."

Court in the case of *Ashwander v. Tennessee Valley Authority.* The ruling is a victory for the New Deal.

Last year's Bituminous Coal Conservation Act (Guffey Act) designed to replace the NRA code in the bituminous coal industry is ruled unconstitutional by the Supreme Court in *Carter v. Carter Coal Company et al.*

The world's first electronic television system is set up by the 14-year-old British Broadcasting Corporation (BBC) (*see* 1939; Baird, 1926).

The Canadian Broadcasting Corporation is founded.

The *Philadelphia Inquirer* is acquired for a reported $15 million, including $4 million in cash, by publisher Moses L. Annenberg, who is netting $1 million per year from his *Racing Form* and *Morning Telegraph* and from his racing wire activities (*see* 1922; 1939).

The *Saturday Review of Literature* founded in 1924 loses some of the subsidy it has been receiving from banker Thomas W. Lamont, Henry Seidel Canby resigns his editorship to devote more time to the Book-of-the-Month Club, and Harvard lecturer Bernard De Voto, 39, is hired to replace him. Lamont will end his subsidy completely in 1938, the struggling magazine will be helped by Harry Scherman of the Book-of-the-Month Club, who will furnish the magazine with his membership list at no cost, and De Voto will be replaced by assistant editor George Stevens, now 32 (*see* 1939).

The Gallup poll started last year gains prominence by forecasting accurately the outcome of the November presidential elections (above) and discredits the *Literary Digest,* which had predicted a victory for Governor Landon on the basis of mailings to telephone company subscribers and automobile owners,

most of whom are Republicans. Now published by its founder's son Wilfred John Funk, the 46-year-old *Digest* will fold next year; Gallup poll predictions will become a permanent part of U.S. political life.

LIFE magazine begins publication November 23 and will continue weekly publication through 1972. The new picture magazine gains enormous success from the start for *Time-Fortune* publisher Henry R. Luce, who has acquired the name from the publishers of the defunct humor magazine that began in 1883.

England's Penguin Books, Ltd., begins a paperback revolution in book publishing. Bodley Head managing director Allen Lane, 34, quits to launch the new firm with £100 in capital, and he issues paperback editions of good literary works at 6 pence per copy (they will find their chief retail outlet initially in F. W. Woolworth Co. stores) (*see* Pocket Books, 1939).

Nonfiction *Mathematics for the Millions* by English zoology professor Lancelot Hogben, 40, whose popularization will be translated into 30 languages and will go through 45 U.S. printings; *Inside Europe* by *Chicago Daily News* correspondent John Gunther, 35, will have sales of more than 500,000 copies; *How to Win Friends and Influence People* by U.S. public-speaking teacher Dale Carnegie, 48, will be a best-seller for 10 years. Carnegie will offer his "Dale Carnegie Course in Effective Speaking and Human Relations" in cities throughout America and in 45 foreign countries. *The Flowering of New England* by U.S. scholar Van Wyck Brooks, 50, is a study of U.S. literary history and wins a Pulitzer Prize.

Fiction *U.S.A.* by John Dos Passos whose novel *The Forty-Second Parallel* completes a trilogy about postwar America that began with *The Big Money* in 1930 and *1919* in 1932; *Absalom! Absalom!* by William Faulkner; *In Dubious Battle* by John Steinbeck; *Eyeless in Gaza* by Aldous Huxley who calls chastity "the most unnatural of the sexual perversions" (XXVII); *Black Spring* by Henry Miller; *Keep the Aspadistra Flying* by George Orwell; *The Weather in the Streets* by English novelist Rosamond Lehman, 33; *Strange Glory* by L. H. Myers; *Check to Your King* and *Passport to Hell* by New Zealand novelist-poet Robin Hyde (Iris Wilkinson), 30; *Mr. Visser's Descent into Hell (Meer Visser's hellevaart)* by Dutch novelist Simon Vestdijk; *The Gift* by Vladimir Nabokov; *The Brothers Ashkenazi (Di brider Ashkenazi)* by Polish-American novelist Isaac Bashevis Singer, 32, who is on the staff of New York's *Jewish Daily Forward; Gone With the Wind* by Atlanta novelist Margaret Mitchell, 36. Macmillan editor Harold Latham, 49, has changed the title from *Tomorrow is Another Day,* he has changed the heroine's name from Pansy to Scarlett O'Hara, the 1,037-page Civil War romance gains instant success, it will receive a 1937 Pulitzer Prize, and by 1939 it will have sold 2 million copies. *Drums Along the Mohawk* by U.S. novelist Walter D. Edmonds, 33; *Double Indemnity* by James M. Cain.

Juvenile *The Story of Ferdinand* by New York writer Munro Leaf, 31, with illustrations by Robert Lawson is the story of a Spanish bull who rejects the macho tradition and refuses to fight in the ring. Written in 40 minutes, Leaf's story will be translated into 61 languages, but it is attacked initially as a "pro-Fascist tract" by some and by others as "red propaganda" or a bitter satire on pacifism. The story will be sold for $800 (divided between Leaf, Lawson, and the publisher) to be made into a Walt Disney animated film.

Poetry "The People, Yes" by Carl Sandburg; *Twenty-Five Poems* by Welsh poet Dylan Thomas, 22; *Reality and Desire* (*La realidad y el deseo*) by Spanish poet Luis Cernuda, 32. Spanish Falangists seize poet-playwright Federico Garcia Lorca August 19 and kill him near his Andalusian birthplace of Fuente Vaqueros as the civil war devastates Spain.

Painting *The Black Flag* by René Magritte; *Composition in Red and Blue* and *Composition in Yellow and Black* by Piet Mondrian; *The Old King* by Georges Rouault; *George C. Tilyou's Steeplechase Park* and *End of the 14th Street Crosstown Line* by Reginald Marsh; *Mujer tehuana* and *El vendedor de coles* by Diego Rivera.

Kodachrome is introduced in August by Eastman Kodak Company in 35-millimeter cartridges and in a paper-backed rollfilm (*see* 1935). The 18-exposure 35-millimeter cartridge sells for $3.50 with processing included and makes color photography as easy for an amateur as black-and-white photography (*see* Kodacolor, 1944).

Theater *Sunrise* by Wan Chia-pao at Peking; *The Astonished Heart* (six scenes) and *Red Peppers* (one scene, with music) by Noel Coward 1/9 at London's Phoenix Theatre; *Hands Across the Sea, Family Album* (one scene, with music), *Fumed Oak* (two scenes), and *Shadow Play* (one scene, with music) by Noel Coward 1/13 at London's Phoenix Theatre; *Ethan Frome* by Owen Davis 1/21 at New York's National Theater, with Ruth Gordon, Raymond Massey, Pauline Lord, Tom Ewell in a dramatization of the 1911 Edith Wharton novel, 120 perfs.; *The Horns of Don Friolera* (*Las Cuernos de don Friolera*) by Ramon Maria de Valle Inclan 2/14 at Madrid's Teatro de la Zarzuela; *End of Summer* by S. N. Behrman 2/17 at New York's Guild Theater, with Ina Claire, Osgood Perkins, Mildred Natwick, Van Heflin, Shepperd Strudwick, 121 perfs.; *Idiot's Delight* by Robert Sherwood 3/29 at New York's Shubert Theater, with Alfred Lunt and Lynn Fontanne in an antiwar drama, 300 perfs., Pulitzer Prize; *The Women* by U.S. playwright Clare Booth, 44, 7/9 at New York's Ethel Barrymore Theater, with Ilka Chase, Jane Seymour, Margalo Gilmore, Arlene Francis, Audrey Christie, Doris Day, Marjorie Main, Ruth Hammond, 657 perfs.; *Reflected Glory* by George Kelly 9/21 at New York's Morosco Theater, with Tallulah Bankhead, 127 perfs.; *Stage Door* by George S. Kaufman and Edna Ferber 10/22 at New York's Music Box Theater, with Margaret Sullavan, Tom Ewell, 169 perfs.; *French Without Tears* by English playwright Terence Rattigan, 25, 11/6 at London's Criterion Theatre, 1,039 perfs.; *Tonight at 8:30* by Noel Coward 11/24 at New York's National Theater, 118 perfs.; *You Can't Take It With You* by George S. Kaufman and Moss Hart 12/14 at New York's Booth Theater with Frank Wilcox, Josephine Hull, Ruth Attaway, George Tobias, 837 perfs., Pulitzer Prize 1937; *Days to Come* by Lillian Hellman 12/15 at New York's Vanderbilt Theater, with Florence Eldridge, 7 perfs.; *Brother Rat* by V.M.I. graduates John Monks, Jr., and Fred F. Finklehoff 12/16 at New York's Biltmore Theater, with Eddie Albert, Frank Albertson, Ezra Stone, José Ferrer, 577 perfs.

Films Charlie Chaplin's *Modern Times* expresses the common man's horror at the dehumanizing technology of the assembly line; Archie Mayo's *The Petrified Forest* with Humphrey Bogart, Leslie Howard, Bette Davis; Robert Z. Leonard's *The Great Ziegfeld* with William Powell, Myrna Loy, Frank Morgan; Mervyn LeRoy's *Anthony Adverse* with Fredric March, Olivia de Havilland; George Cukor's *Camille* with Greta Garbo, Robert Taylor, Lionel Barrymore; Ernst Lubitsch's *Desire* with Marlene Dietrich, Gary Cooper; Lewis Milestone's *The General Died at Dawn* with Gary Cooper, Madeleine Carroll, Akim Tamiroff; Michael Curtiz's *The Charge of the Light Brigade* with Errol Flynn; Fritz Lang's *Fury* with Sylvia Sidney, Spencer Tracy; William Wyler's *Dodsworth* with Walter Huston, Paul Lucas, Maria Ouspenskaya; Julien Duvivier's *Pepe le Moko* with Peter Lorre; Jean Renoir's *The Lower Depths* with Jean Gabin, Louis Jouvet; Alexander Korda's *Rembrandt* with Charles Laughton, Gertrude Lawrence, Elsa Lanchester; William Cameron Menzies's *The Shape of Things to Come* with Raymond Massey, Ralph Richardson; William Wyler's *These Three* with Miriam Hopkins, Merle Oberon, Joel McCrae in a film version of the Lillian Hellman play *The Children's Hour;* Mark Sandrich's *A Woman Rebels* with Katharine Hepburn, Herbert Marshall; Gregory La Cava's *My Man Godfrey* with Carole Lombard, William Powell; Frank Capra's *Mr. Deeds Goes to Town* with Gary Cooper, Jean Arthur; John Ford's *Prisoner of Shark Island* with Warner Baxter; David Butler's *Captain January* with Shirley Temple, Guy Kibbee; Irving Cummings's *Poor Little Rich Girl* with Shirley Temple, Alice Faye, Jack Haley; Pare Lorentz's documentary *The Plow that Broke the Plains;* Henry Hathaway's *Trail of the Lonesome Pine* with Sylvia Sidney, Henry Fonda, Fred MacMurray is the first outdoor film in full Technicolor.

Hollywood musicals Roy Del Ruth's *Born to Dance* with James Stewart, tap dancer Eleanor Parker, songs by Cole Porter that include "Easy to Love" and "I've Got You Under My Skin"; Roy Del Ruth's *Broadway Melody of 1936* with Eleanor Parker, Jack Benny, Robert Taylor, songs by Nacio Herb Brown and Arthur Freed that include "I Gotta Feelin' You're Foolin'," "You Are My Lucky Star"; George

1936 (cont.)   Stevens's *Swing Time* with Ginger Rogers, Fred Astaire, music by Jerome Kern, lyrics by Dorothy Fields, songs that include "A Fine Romance" and "The Way You Look Tonight"; Mark Sandrich's *Follow the Fleet* with Fred Astaire, Ginger Rogers, Randolph Scott, Harriet Hilliard, Betty Grable, songs by Irving Berlin that include "Let's Face the Music," "Let Yourself Go," "We Saw the Sea"; Norman Taurog's *Rhythm on the Range* with Bing Crosby, Martha Raye, songs that include "I'm an Old Cowhand from the Rio Grande" by Johnny Mercer; James Whale's *Show Boat* with Paul Robeson, Irene Dunne, Helen Morgan, songs by Jerome Kern and Oscar Hammerstein II from the 1927 Broadway musical; William Thiele's *The Jungle Princess* with Dorothy Lamour, Ray Milland, music by Frederick Hollander, lyrics by Leo Robin, songs that include "Moonlight and Shadows"; W. S. Van Dyke II's *San Francisco* with Clark Cable, Jeanette MacDonald, Spencer Tracy, music by Bronislaw Kaper and Walter Jurmann, lyrics by Gus Kahn, songs that include the title song.

Broadway musicals   *The Ziegfeld Follies* 1/30 at the Winter Garden Theater, with Bob Hope, Eve Arden, Josephine Baker, Judy Canova, Fanny Brice, music by Vernon Duke, George Gershwin and others, lyrics by David Freedman, Ira Gershwin, and others, songs that include "I Can't Get Started" by Vernon Duke, lyrics by Ira Gershwin, 227 perfs. (after an interruption caused by Fanny Brice's illness); *On Your Toes* 4/11 at the Imperial Theater with Ray Bolger, Tamara Geva, and George Church dancing in the ballet *Slaughter on Tenth Avenue,* music by Richard Rodgers, lyrics by Oscar Hammerstein II, 315 perfs.; *Red, Hot and Blue* 10/29 at the Alvin Theater with Ethel Merman, Jimmy Durante, Grace and Paul Hartman, Bob Hope, book by Howard Lindsay and Russel Crouse, music and lyrics by Cole Porter, songs that include "De-Lovely," "Down in the Depths on the 90th Floor," 183 perfs.; *The Show Is On* 12/25 at the Ethel Barrymore Theater with the same cast as *The Women* (above), songs that include "By Strauss" by George Gershwin, lyrics by Ira Gershwin, "Little Old Lady" by Hoagy Carmichael, lyrics by Stanley Adams, 202 perfs.

Opera   *The Poisoned Kiss* (or *The Empress and the Necromancer*) 5/12 at Cambridge (and later at the Sadler's Wells Theatre, London), with music by Ralph Vaughan Williams.

Ballet   *L'Epreuve d'Amour* (*The Proof of Love*) 4/4 at the Théâtre de Monte Carlo, with Vera Nemchinova as Chung-Yang, André Egelevsky as the lover, music by Wolfgang Amadeus Mozart, choreography by Michel Fokine; *Don Juan* 6/25 at London's Alhambra Theatre, with Anatole Vilzak, André Egelevsky as the lover, music by Christoph Willibald Gluck, choreography by Michel Fokine.

First performances   *Peter and the Wolf March* by Sergei Prokofiev 5/2 at a Moscow children's concert, Prokofiev returned from exile last year and will remain in the U.S.S.R. until his death in 1953; Symphony No. 3 in A minor by Serge Rachmaninoff 11/6 at Philadelphia's Academy of Music; *Prelude Arioso and Fughetta in the Name of Bach* by Arthur Honegger 12/5 at Paris.

Negro Folk Songs as Sung by Lead Belly is published with songs that include "Good Night, Irene" by U.S. chain-gang veteran Huddie "Lead Belly" Ledbetter, now 48. Song collector Alan Lomax, 20, and his father John Avery Lomax met Lead Belly 2 years ago while recording American ballads, they begin touring the country with Lead Belly, and they introduce him to audiences on radio, on college campuses, in concert halls, and at night clubs where he plays a 12-string guitar.

Nick's opens in New York's Greenwich Village. Nick Rongetti's place at 7th Avenue and 10th Street will attract jazz lovers for 27 years to hear Sidney Bechet, George Bruno, Eddie Condon, Wild Bill Davison, Bud Freeman, Bobby Hackett, Max Kaminsky, Ray McKinley, Miff Mole, Pee Wee Russell, Zutty Singleton, Willie (The Lion) Smith, Johnny Windhurst, and others.

"Roll On, Columbia" by U.S. folksinger Woody Guthrie is based on the music of "Goodnight, Irene" (above) by Huddie Ledbetter and John Avery Lomax. Now 24, Woodrow Wilson Guthrie quit school in his native Oklahoma at age 15 to play the harmonica in Houston barbershops and pool halls, he returned home to study guitar, and he has appeared on radio singing his song "Those Oklahoma Hills" and other original works. Alan Lomax has suggested to the Department of the Interior that they hire Guthrie to propagandize in the Northwest against the private power companies that use Hollywood stars to attract crowds to public meetings where speakers urge the people to vote against public power projects, Guthrie has hitchhiked to Portland, the government has provided him with a car and chauffeur to follow the course of the river, and he writes 26 songs in 26 days (*see* 1938).

Popular songs   "Until The Real Thing Comes Along" by Mann Holiner, Alberta Nichols, Sammy Cahn, Saul Chaplin, and L. E. Freeman; "Sing, Sing, Sing" by Louis Prima; "Boo-Hoo" by Carmen Lombardo (brother of bandleader Guy Lombardo) and John Jacob Loeb, lyrics by Eddic Hcyman; "A Melody from the Sky" by Louis Alter, lyrics by Sidney D. Mitchell (for the film *Trail of the Lonesome Pine*); "The Night Is Young and You're So Beautiful" by Dana Suesse, lyrics by Billy Rose and Irving Kahal; "Poinciana" by Nat Simon, lyrics (Spanish) by Manuel Llisco, (English) Buddy Denis.

The Olympic Games held at Berlin attract 4,069 contestants from 51 countries. U.S. track star Jesse Owens, 22, wins four gold medals, setting new Olympic and world records for the 200-meter sprint and the running broad jump (26 feet, 5 5/16 inches). Owens runs anchor on the 400-meter relay team that breaks the world record, and he ties the Olympic record for the 100-meter sprint. Too embarrassed at the defeat by a black of Germany's "master race" Aryan athletes, Chancellor Hitler leaves the stadium and lets someone else present Owens with his medals.

High school athlete Bob Feller signs with the Cleveland Indians, he strikes out seven St. Louis Cardinal batters including Leo Durocher, 29, in an exhibition game, he makes his first major league start in August, and within a few weeks he has tied the major league record of 17 strikeouts in one game. Robert W. A. Feller, 17, will pitch for the Indians for 20 years.

Joe DiMaggio signs with the New York Yankees and begins a 13-year career in which his batting average will never fall below .300, will average .325, and will peak at .381 in 1938. San Francisco-born Joseph Paul DiMaggio, Jr., 21, will play until 1952, with a 3-year hiatus between 1943 and 1945.

The New York Yankees win the World Series by defeating the New York Giants 4 games to 2.

"Slingin' Sammy" Baugh ends an outstanding college football career in which he has passed for 38 touchdowns in three seasons with Texas Christian University and has completed 274 passes out of 599 in a time when few teams throw more than 10 passes per game. The 22-year-old quarterback will sign an extravagant $8,000 per year contract with the Washington Redskins next year, beginning a professional career that will continue until 1952.

Winning Bridge Made Easy by Philadelphia lawyer Charles Henry Goren, 35, makes a radical departure from the dominant "honor-trick" method devised by Ely Culbertson for evaluating a hand (*see* Vanderbilt, 1925). Goren gives up his law practice to devote himself to refining his bidding system.

Britain's Butlinlands holiday resort empire has its beginnings at Skegness on England's east coast where entrepreneur William "Billy" Butlin, 35, opens a holiday camp with accommodations for 1,000 and enjoys such success that he will have to double the camp's size within a year and open another 2 hours from London at Clacton. Butlin will invite every member of Parliament who voted for the new Holiday with Pay Bill to opening ceremonies at Clacton and within 40 years Butlin will be providing low-cost family vacations for more than a million Britons each year at camps of 5,000 to 12,000 each.

Polaroid lens sunglasses are introduced by the Land-Wheelwright Laboratories that will rename itself the Polaroid Corp. next year (*see* 1932; camera, 1947).

Kansas City's H. D. Lee Company adopts a hair-on-hide leather label and opens a Lee Rider plant in Levi Straus's San Francisco backyard (*see* 1926).

Bass Weejuns introduced at $12 a pair by G. H. Bass & Co. of Wilton, Me., begin a fashion for slip-on moccasin "loafers" that will gain wide popularity among both men and women.

Tampax, Inc., is founded at New Brunswick, N.J., to produce the cotton tampon with string attached patented by Denver physician Earl Haas. Women since ancient times have used absorbent rags during their menstrual periods but no commercial tampon has been available until now (*see* Kotex, 1918).

Charles "Lucky" Luciano draws a 30- to 50-year prison sentence after a New York jury convicts him of compulsory prostitution (*see* 1931). Authorities will release Luciano in 1946 and will deport him to his native Italy.

Japanese authorities arrest Tokyo geisha Sada Abe on charges of having stabbed her unfaithful lover to death in his sleep, castrating him, and carrying his reproductive organ about in her obi (sash) for days while eluding the police.

Bruno Richard Hauptmann dies in the electric chair at the New Jersey State Prison in Trenton April 3. Hauptmann protests his innocence of having kidnapped and killed Charles A. Lindbergh, Jr., in 1932, the evidence against him is far from conclusive, but anti-German sentiment has helped to seal his fate.

 New York's American Museum of Natural History opens a Memorial Hall dedicated to the late Theodore Roosevelt.

Skidmore, Owings & Merrill has its beginnings in the firm Skidmore & Owings founded by U.S. architects Louis Skidmore, 39, and Nathaniel Alexander Owings, 33, who will take John Ogden Merrill, 39, into partnership in 1939. Gordon Bunshaft, 27, will be chief designer beginning next year and will become a partner in 1946.

Sun Valley Lodge ski resort opens near Ketchum, Idaho, where Union Pacific Railroad board chairman W. Averell Harriman has built the lodge to compete with the Canadian Pacific and its Banff–Lake Louise resorts (*see* 1885). Harriman takes up skiing to promote the sport and to promote Sun Valley.

 Ice chokes the Ohio River for months.

President Roosevelt signs an Omnibus Flood Control Act into law.

 The Agricultural Adjustment Act of 1933 is ruled unconstitutional by the Supreme Court January 6 in *United States v. Butler,* but the New Deal uses soil conservation as the basis for a new effort to limit planting. The Soil Conservation and Domestic Allotment Act passed by Congress February 29 pays farmers to plant alfalfa, clover, and lespedeza rather than soil-depleting crops such as corn, cotton, tobacco, and wheat.

Drought reduces U.S. crop harvests and brings new hardship to farmers and consumers.

Boulder Dam on the Colorado River (above) creates a lake 115 miles long (Lake Mead) whose waters are used to irrigate 250,000 acres.

T. D. Lysenko's sensationalist agricultural nostrums gain full sway over Soviet agriculture (*see* 1935).

1936 (cont.) Soviet geneticist Nikolai Vavilov shows that the white potato *Solanum tuberosum* could not possibly have originated in Virginia as is commonly believed (*see* 1530; 1597; Vavilov, 1929, 1940).

A 4-year program begins in Nazi Germany to produce synthetic (*ersatz*) replacements for raw materials such as fats and livestock fodder.

The butter yellow dye p-dimethyaminoaobenzene is dropped from use in foods following revelations by Japanese biochemist M. Yoshida that the dye produces liver tumors in test rats.

Vitamin B$_1$ is synthesized by Robert R. Williams who gives it the name thiamine (*see* 1933; 1937).

Vitamins *Plus* is introduced by a new company formed by entrepreneurs who include former Hearst magazine editor Henry Sell, 46. The diet supplement includes liver and iron, it is introduced at booths set up in cosmetic departments at Marshall Field, Saks Fifth Avenue, Gimbels, and Lord and Taylor, and Vitamins *Plus* is soon being sold nationwide through mail-order advertising (*see* Sell's Liver Paté, 1941).

Campbell Soup begins manufacturing its own cans and will become the world's third largest producer of food cans simply by supplying its own needs (*see* 1933; Continental Can, 1904).

Minnesota Valley Canning adds asparagus to its line of Green Giant canned vegetables (*see* 1935; 1950).

Spry is introduced by Lever Brothers to compete with the hydrogenated vegetable shortening Crisco introduced by Procter & Gamble in 1911. Within a year Spry will have sales of $12 million versus $25 million for Crisco.

The name "Betty Crocker" is used by General Mills as a signature for responses to consumer inquiries. The fictitious authority is portrayed as a gray-haired homemaker, an image that will see four revisions in the next 36 years as Betty Crocker emerges as a major brand name for various General Mills products (*see* 1924; Kix, 1937).

The Waring Blender, designed by U.S. bandleader Fred M. Waring, 36, begins mechanizing kitchen chores.

The first Giant Food Store supermarket is started at Washington, D.C., by entrepreneurs Jacob J. Lehrman, 25, and N. M. Cohen, who pioneer self-service food retailing in the nation's capital.

The Chunky chocolate bar containing Brazil nuts and raisins is introduced by New York Delancey Street candymaker Philip Silverstein.

Dave Chasen's opens at Beverly Hills, Calif. Russian-American vaudeville straight man Dave Chasen, 37, uses a $3,000 loan from *New Yorker* magazine editor Harold Ross to start the chili and sparerib restaurant that will soon attract celebrities with specialities such as hobo steak—New York cut steak broiled on a layer

of rough salt and dipped in hot butter just before it is served.

Howard Johnson restaurants have their beginnings at Orleans on Cape Cod where Wollaston, Mass., restaurateur Howard Johnson has persuaded young Reginald Sprague to open an eating place that Johnson will supply with ice cream, fried clams, and frankfurters (*see* 1928; 1937).

The Joy of Cooking by St. Louis housewife Irma S. Rombauer gives recipes in the most minute detail, telling the cook exactly what to look for. Rombauer had a private edition printed 5 years ago for her grown children and her daughter Marion Rombauer Becker, 33, will coauthor future editions.

The 1920 Soviet decree legalizing abortion is revoked, and a new law restricts abortions to cases in which pregnancy endangers the life of the woman or in which the child is likely to inherit a specified disease (*see* 1955).

A U.S. Circuit Court of Appeals judge rules that the purpose of the 1872 Comstock law, liberalized in 1929, "was not to prevent the importation, sale, or carriage by mail of things which might intelligently be employed by conscientious and competent physicians for the purpose of saving life or promoting the well-being of their patients." The ruling is made in a case brought by birth-control advocate Hannah Stone.

The U.S. population reaches 127 million, while Great Britain has 47 million, France 44, Germany 70, the Soviet Union 173, Japan 89, China 422, India 360, Brazil 35.

1937 Moscow "show trials" begin January 23 as Josef Stalin purges the Communist party and the Soviet army of alleged Trotskyites. Grigori L. Pyatakov, 47, is executed January 31, Karl Bernardovich Radek, 52, is condemned to serve 10 years in prison, Marshal Mikhail Nikolaevich Tukhachevski, 44, is convicted of treason by a military tribunal and is executed June 12 along with seven other generals, and hundreds of others are liquidated or sent to Siberia.

Spain's General Mola dies in an airplane crash as civil war continues, with more than 10,000 Germans and from 50,000 to 75,000 Italians supporting General Franco. He commands several hundred thousand insurgents against the Republican Army, which is supported by an International Brigade of Russians, Britons, other Europeans, and Americans (*see* 1936).

Malaga falls to General Franco February 8 as the insurgents advance with Italian aid, but the road from Madrid to Valencia remains intact, and Italian troops are defeated March 18 at Brihuega by Loyalists who capture large stores of equipment.

The defenseless Basque town of Guernica is annihilated on the afternoon of April 26 by German Junker and Heinkel bombers that drop explosive and thousands of aluminum incendiary projectiles for more than 3 hours while Heinkel fighters strafcivilians who have fled into the fields (*see* Picasso mural, below).

Almeria is bombarded May 31 by four German warships in reprisal for a Loyalist air attack on the *Deutschland,* Bilbao falls to the insurgents June 18 after weeks of heavy fighting and aerial bombing, Basque resistance collapses, Gijon falls October 21 as Franco breaks resistance in the Asturias, the Spanish government moves from Valencia to Barcelona October 28, a naval blockade of the entire Spanish coast is announced by General Franco November 28, but a Loyalist counter-offensive begins December 5, and Teruel falls to the Loyalists December 19.

The British prime minister Stanley Baldwin retires May 28 at age 69 and is succeeded by his chancellor of the exchequer (Arthur) Neville Chamberlain, 58, who attempts to appease Adolf Hitler.

Iraq's dictator General Bakr Sidqi is assassinated by a Kurd August 11 following conclusion of a nonaggression pact signed in July by Turkish, Iraqi, Iranian, and Afghan diplomats.

Japanese forces invade China July 7 as the new prime minister Prince Fumimaro Konoye, 46, embarks on an undeclared war that will continue until 1945. Peking falls to the Japanese July 28, Tientsin July 29, Shanghai November 8, Nanking December 13, and Hanchow December 24. Some 200,000 civilians are executed at Nanking, and this massacre, combined with merciless bombing of the Chinese cities, rouses world opinion against Japan.

The *Panay* incident of December 12 produces tension between Japan and Britain and the United States. British and U.S. ships near Nanking are attacked by Japanese bombers, but Japan's explanations are accepted in Washington, and the world powers are distracted from the aggression in China by events in Europe.

Last year's German-Japanese anti-Comintern pact is joined by Italy November 6, and Rome withdraws from the League of Nations December 11. Mussolini began the year by concluding a "gentlemen's agreement" with Britain in which each has agreed to maintain the independence and integrity of Spain and to respect each other's interests and rights in the Mediterranean, and an Italian-Yugoslav treaty signed March 25 has guaranteed existing frontiers and maintenance of the status quo in the Adriatic.

Brazil's President Getulio Vargas proclaims a new constitution November 10 after 7 years in office, he closes the Congress, and he begins nearly 15 years of dictatorship which he says is not Fascist but which will have all the earmarks of fascism.

A magnetic resonance method for observing the spectra of atoms and molecules in the radio-frequency range is invented by Austrian-American physicist Isidor Isaac Rabi, 39, at Columbia University. Rabi's invention will make it possible to deduce the mechanical and magnetic properties of atomic nuclei.

The first laboratory-made element is produced by Italian physicist Emilio Gino Segre, 32, working with Enrico Fermi (*see* 1934). They bombard molybdenum with deuterons and neutrons to produce an element with the atomic number 43 that probably does not exist in nature but that will be called technetium (*see* nuclear fission, 1938; McMillan, 1940).

Albanian Moslems rebel in mid-May against a government decree that forbids the veiling of women and against the dictatorial rule of Zog I.

Germany's Buchenwald concentration camp opens July 16 on a plateau overlooking Weimar. The first inmates are mostly political prisoners of every religious belief, but most of the 238,980 inmates that will ultimately be sent to Buchenwald will be Jews, and 56,545 will die in the camp's gas chambers.

German Jews are evicted from trade and industry, they are ordered to wear yellow badges displaying the six-pointed "star of David," and they are barred from all parks, places of entertainment, health resorts, and public institutions (*see* Nuremberg laws, 1935; Kristalnacht, 1938).

Romanian Jews are forbidden to own land and are barred from the professions at year's end by legislation put through by the newly installed prime minister Octavian Goga, 56, who takes office despite the fact that his National Christian party gained only 10 percent of the votes in the election.

The United Automobile Workers (UAW) is recognized by General Motors Corporation February 11 as sole bargaining agent for workers in all GM plants. The action is taken to end the union's sit-down strike, but 4,470 other strikes idle plants throughout the country, and most of them are sit-down strikes.

Henry Ford says, "We'll never recognize the United Auto Workers Union or any other union" and he employs a "service department" of 600 goons armed with guns and blackjacks to prevent unionizing of Ford workers (*see* 1932).

United States Steel Corporation permits unionization of its workers March 2 to avoid a strike by the United Steel Workers, CIO (*see* 1936).

The United Steel Workers Union meets with resistance from "little steel" firms, which include Bethlehem with 82,000 workers, Republic with 53,000, Youngstown Sheet and Tube with 27,000, and National, American Rolling Mills, and Inland with a combined total of some 38,000.

The principle of a minimum wage for women is upheld by the Supreme Court March 29. The Court's ruling in the case of *West Coast Hotel v. Parrish* reverses some earlier decisions.

The National Labor Relations Act of 1934 is upheld by a series of 5 to 4 Supreme Court decisions beginning April 12.

The Social Security Act of 1935 is upheld by the Supreme Court May 24.

1937 (cont.) Republic Steel is struck and picketed by workers singing "Solidarity Forever" and "I Dreamt I Saw Joe Hill Last Night" (*see* 1915). Republic's $130,000 a year boss Tom Girdler says he would rather go back to hoeing potatoes than give in to union organizers, and on Memorial Day May 30, he has Chicago police attack the demonstrators. Four are killed, three others mortally wounded, and 84 injured as the police fire on unarmed strikers and brutally assault wives and children.

The CIO claims a membership of 3.5 million by September with more than 500,000 in the United Steel Workers Union as the violence at Republic Steel (above) is followed by other incidents of police repression accompanied by further deaths and injuries.

Jersey City, N.J., mayor Frank Hague, 61, is questioned in a legislative investigation as to his right to forbid picketing and distribution of labor circulars on the city's streets. "I am the law," replies Hague, who has been mayor for 20 years and will remain mayor for another 10.

Amalgamated Clothing Workers president Sidney Hillman obtains a settlement with the Clothing Manufacturers Association of the United States and establishes a bargaining pattern that will be used throughout the industry (*see* 1918). Hillman has organized all but a handful of men's clothing workers (*see* Office of Production Management, 1941).

$ The U.S. economic recovery that has progressed for 4 years falters beginning in midyear. Business activity suffers a sharp drop, and Wall Street's Dow Jones Industrial Average falls from its post-1929 high of 194.40.

"I see one-third of a nation ill-housed, ill-clad, ill-nourished," President Roosevelt has said in his second inaugural address January 20. The inauguration date has been moved from March 4 under terms of the 20th Amendment.

John D. Rockefeller dies May 23 at age 97. Andrew W. Mellon dies August 26 at age 82 (*see* art, 1941).

The Miller-Tydings Act is passed by Congress to allow manufacturers to fix resale prices of brand-name merchandise in states where legislatures have authorized price-fixing contracts. Designed to prevent predatory pricing and ruinous price wars, the new fair trade law has been devised as an exception to the Sherman Anti-Trust Law of 1890 and permits a manufacturer to determine the minimum price at which his products may be sold at retail outlets.

The Folklore of Capitalism by Washington attorney Thurman Arnold, 46, shows how antitrust laws have actually promoted the growth of industrial monopolies in the United States "by deflecting the attack on them into purely moral and ceremonial channels." Arnold will be named U.S. assistant attorney general next year and in the next 5 years will file more than 200 suits alleging conspiracies in restraint of trade.

Crown Zellerbach Corporation is created by a merger of Crown Willamette Paper Company, the largest U.S. West Coast papermaker, with the Zellerbach Paper Company founded in 1870.

⚕ A closed-plaster method of treating compound fractures, introduced by Barcelona physician Jose Trutta Raspall, uses principles developed by Lincoln, Nebraska, physician H. Winnett Orr to save fracture victims in the Spanish Civil War (above) and reduce the need for amputation.

Diabetics are treated successfully for the first time with zinc protamine insulin, which reduces the need for diet therapy (*see* 1924; 1942).

The Neurotic Personality of Our Time by German-American psychoanalyst Karen Danielsen Horney, 52, is published.

U.S. children die after being treated with an elixir of the antibacterial drug sulfanilamide containing the solvent diethylene glycol (*see* 1936; Food, Drug and Cosmetics Act, 1938).

⚡ Germany retires her 9-year-old *Graf Zeppelin* after 144 ocean crossings that have carried more than 13,000 passengers. The big dirigible is replaced by the *Hindenburg,* which carries 50 passengers in private cabins at 78 miles per hour, but the new dirigible is filled with hydrogen gas, she explodes and burns at Lakehurst, N.J., May 6, and the brief era of transatlantic travel by dirigible is ended (*see* Pan Am, 1939).

U.S. aviatrix Amelia Earhart disappears July 2 on a Pacific flight from New Guinea to Howland Island (*see* 1928). Earhart was married in 1931 to New York publisher George Putnam.

Soviet aviator V. P. Chkalov flies nonstop over the North Pole from Moscow to Vancouver, covering 5,400 miles that include 3,100 over ice fields (*see* 1936).

Soviet Russia opens the 80-mile Moscow-Volga Ship Canal to give Moscow access to the Volga (*see* Stalin Ship Canal, 1933).

Hong Kong's C. Y. Tung shipping line is founded by Chinese shipowner Chao-Yung Tung, 25, whose father-in-law has a monopoly on much of the Chinese coastal shipping trade and who was himself made vice president last year of the Tientsin Shipowners Association. Tung has moved to Hong Kong at the outbreak of hostilities with Japan (above), and he will build a fleet that will rival those of the Greek shipowners Aristotle Onassis and Stavros Niarchos.

San Francisco's Golden Gate Bridge opens May 27 across San Francisco Bay to link the city with Marin County. Like the Longview cantilever bridge of 1930 and the George Washington Bridge of 1931, the new 1,280-meter (4,200-feet) Golden Gate Bridge has been designed by U.S. bridge engineer Joseph Baermann Strauss, now 67, and is the world's longest suspension bridge (*see* Verrazano Bridge, 1964).

New York's West Side Highway opens as an elevated six-lane motorcar and truck route along the Hudson

River from the Battery to 72nd Street (where it becomes the Henry Hudson Parkway).

An automatic transmission for automobiles is introduced by General Motors under the name Hydramatic Drive as optional equipment for 1938 Oldsmobiles. Similar transmissions have been used on London buses for 12 years and will be employed increasingly on U.S. passenger cars, first as optional equipment, then as standard.

Vickers, Inc., is acquired by Sperry Corporation (*see* 1925). The Midwest company has pioneered in developing hydraulic systems that will be used in automatic transmissions, power brakes, and similar applications (*see* Sperry-Rand, 1955).

Packard Motor Car Company sells a record 109,518 cars, most of them medium-priced "120" models.

Stutz Motor Company files for bankruptcy. The firm has produced fewer than 700 cars since 1930 and none since 1935.

Pierce-Arrow Company ceases production. The company will be sold at auction in May of next year.

Auburn, Cord, and Deusenberg motorcars pass into history as Auburn's E. L. Cord returns from his Surrey estate and sells his motorcar holdings. Cord moved to England to escape kidnap threats on his children.

Kerr-McGee Oil Company is founded by Oklahoma City's Robert S. Kerr and former Phillips Petroleum geologist Dean Anderson McGee, 34, in a reorganization of the Kerlyn Oil Company (*see* 1932).

The first offshore Louisiana oil wells are drilled by Standard Oil Company of New Jersey.

Bonneville Dam is dedicated on the Columbia River in Oregon. Like last year's Boulder Dam and like the Golden Gate Bridge (above), the new hydroelectric installation has been masterminded by Henry J. Kaiser (*see* 1931; 1941).

Queens College is founded at Flushing, N.Y.

St. John's College is founded at Annapolis, Md., where former University of Virginia professor Stringfellow Barr, 40, and University of Chicago administrator Scott Buchanan, 42, take over the King William's School founded in 1696 and begin a Great Books program that revives the principles of a classical education.

Pepperdine College is founded at Los Angeles with a gift from Western Auto Supply magnate George Pepperdine, now 51, who has amassed a fortune of $10 million (*see* 1909; 1927). Pepperdine will lose his money and will testify in 1950 that his personal assets are no more than $1.

The emergency three-digit telephone number 999 comes into use in Britain to summon police, firefighting, or ambulance aid. Britain's example will be followed by countries in Europe, the Far East, and South America (*see* New York, 1968).

Xerography is pioneered by New York prelaw student Chester Floyd Carlson, 31, whose dry-copying process will revolutionize duplication of papers in offices, schools, and libraries. Photostats are costly, carbon copies are often blurred, and few can be made at one time, but Carlson has seen the demand for multiple copies of patent specifications and other documents while working in the patent department of a New York electronics firm, and he sees possibilities in a process based on principles of photoconductivity and electrostatics. Taking a sulfur-coated zinc plate, Carlson gives it an electrostatic charge by rubbing it with a handkerchief in the dark, he places over it a transparent celluloid ruler, and he then exposes the zinc plate to light for a few seconds, neutralizing the charge except where the markings of the ruler have blocked the light. Dusting lycopodium powder over the plate and blowing away the excess, Carlson is left with a perfect image of the ruler (*see* 1938).

Newsweek magazine begins publication at New York to compete with Henry R. Luce's 14-year-old *Time*. Real estate heir Vincent Astor, 42, and railroad heir W. Averell Harriman, 45, have been publishing *Today,* they merge that news weekly with T. J. C. Martyn's 4-year-old *News-Week,* and they bring in as editor former assistant secretary of state Raymond Moley, 51, *Today* and install McGraw-Hill president Malcolm Muir as publisher (*see* 1961).

Look magazine begins publication at New York to compete with Henry R. Luce's *LIFE. Des Moines Register* publisher Gardner Cowles launches the biweekly picture magazine that will continue until 1971.

Women's Day appears in October as the A&P launches a 3-cent monthly women's service magazine for distribution in A&P stores. The food chain

Pablo Picasso's *Mother with Dead Child* expressed rage at the 1937 Fascist attack on Spanish civilians at Guernica.

1937 (cont.) will sell the magazine to Fawcett Publications in 1958.

"Prince Valiant" by Canadian-American cartoonist Harold Rudolph "Hal" Foster, 44, is a new comic strip based on legends of knights in armor and Arthurian chivalry.

Nonfiction *Spanish Testament* by Hungarian-born French journalist Arthur Koestler, 32, who fell into Fascist hands at the fall of Malaga while covering the Spanish Civil War for the *London News Chronicle*, was condemned to death as a spy, was released after months of imprisonment and torture only after British authorities brought pressure, and will have an abridged form of the book published in 1942 under the title *Dialogue with Death; Four Hundred Million Customers* by U.S. businessman Carl Crow, 54, is a book about the potential in trade with China.

Fiction *The Road to Wigan Pier* by George Orwell who examines the conditions of the unemployed in the north of England; *Coming from the Fair* by Norah Hoult; *Mouchette* (*Nouvelle Histoire de Mouchette*) by Georges Bernanos; *Mad Love* (*L'amour fou*) by André Breton; *The Gift* by Vladimir Nabokov; *The Revenge for Love* by Wyndham Lewis; *The Citadel* by A. J. Cronin; *The Young Desire It* by Australian novelist Seaforth Mackenzie (Kenneth Mackenzie), 24; *Turning Wheels* by English novelist Stuart Cloete, 38, who sold his South African dairy farm 4 years ago and has returned to England; *To Have and Have Not* by Ernest Hemingway; *Of Mice and Men* by John Steinbeck; *Low Company* by Daniel Fuchs; *The Late George Apley* by U.S. novelist John Phillips Marquand, 43, who is best known for his Mr. Moto detective stories in the *Saturday Evening Post* but whose novel will win a 1938 Pulitzer Prize; *Serenade* by James M. Cain; *The Education of H*y*m*a*n K*a*p*l*a*n* by U.S. humorist sociologist Leonard Q. Ross (Leo Calvin Rosten), 29, who came to America from Poland as an infant and who finds poignant humor in the efforts of New York immigrants to gain education in the city's free adult education classes; *Remembering Laughter* by U.S. novelist Wallace Stegner, 28; *Beat to Quarters* by English novelist C. S. (Cecil Scott) Forester, 38, who begins a Captain Horatio Hornblower trilogy that will be completed with *Ship of the Line* next year and *Captain Horatio Hornblower* in 1939; *The Hobbit* by Oxford philologist J. R. R. (John Ronald Reuel) Tolkien, 45; *Dark Frontier* and *Uncommon Danger* by London advertising agency director-detective novelist Eric Ambler, 28, whose second book is published in the United States as *Background to Danger; Busman's Holiday* by Dorothy Sayers.

Juvenile *And to Think That I Saw It on Mulberry Street* by U.S. writer-illustrator Dr. Seuss (Theodor Seuss Geisel), 33.

Poetry *Collected Poems* by T. S. Eliot includes "Chamber Music," "Pomes Penyeach," and "Ecce Puer"; *The Cantos* (fifth volume) by Ezra Pound; *The Man with the Blue Guitar* by Wallace Stevens;

The Semi-Circle (*Die Halve Kring*) by N. P. van Wyk Louw.

Painting *Guernica* by Pablo Picasso who has been commissioned to produce a mural for the Spanish Republic's pavilion at the Paris World's Fair. After 6 months of doing nothing, Picasso has worked in a 6-week burst of outraged energy to complete a cubist canvas nearly 26 feet long filled with bedlam and terror that expresses the painter's horror at the brutality of modern warfare; *Revolution of the Viaducts* by Paul Klee; *Still Life with Old Shoe* by Joan Miró; *Woman with a Mandolin* by Georges Braque; *The Pleasure Principle* and *Not to Be Reproduced* by René Magritte; *Echo of a Scream* by David Alfara Siqueiros; *Hollywood* by Thomas Hart Benton. H. O. Tanner dies at Paris May 25 at age 77.

Sculpture *Consummatum Est* by Jacob Epstein.

London's Tate Gallery opens a Duveen Gallery endowed by local art dealer Joseph Duveen, Baron Duveen of Milbank, now 68.

New York's Parke Bernet art auction firm is founded by Major Hiram Parke and Otto Bernet.

Agfacolor film in 35-millimeter cartridges is introduced by Germany's A. G. Fur Analin (Agfa) and by Ansco (*see* 1927; Kodachrome, 1935; 1936).

The fastest film made is Eastman Kodak's black-and-white Super-X with a Weston rating of 32 (*see* Weston exposure meter, 1931; ASA ratings, 1947).

Popular Photography magazine begins publication at Chicago in May.

Theater *High Tor* by Maxwell Anderson 1/9 at New York's Martin Beck Theater, with Burgess Meredith, Peggy Ashcroft, 171 perfs.; *The Masque of Kings* by Maxwell Anderson 2/8 at New York's Shubert Theater with Dudley Digges, Henry Hull, Margo, 89 perfs.; *Yes, My Darling Daughter* by U.S. playwright Mark Reed 2/9 at The Playhouse, New York, with Peggy Conklin, Lucille Watson, 405 perfs.; *Traveler Without Luggage* (*Le voyageur sans baggage*) by Jean Anouilh 2/16 at the Théâtre de Mathurius, Paris; "*Having Wonderful Time*" by Austrian-American playwright Arthur Kober, 36, 2/20 at New York's Lyceum Theater, with Katherine Locke, Jules Garfield, Cornel Wilde, 132 perfs.; *The Ascent of F.6* by Christopher Isherwood and W. H. Auden 2/26 at London's Mercury Theatre; *Electra* (*Electre*) by Jean Genet 5/13 at the Théâtre de l'Athenée, Paris; *Room Service* by John Murray and Allen Boretz 5/19 at New York's Cort Theater, with Sam Levine, Eddie Albert, Betty Field, 500 perfs.; *Golden Boy* by Clifford Odets 11/23 at New York's Belasco Theater, with Jules Garfield, Lee J. Cobb, Karl Malden, Elia Kazan in a play about prizefighting, 250 perfs.; *Of Mice and Men* by John Steinbeck 11/23 at New York's Music Box Theater, with Art Lund as Lennie, 207 perfs. (director George S. Kaufman has polished Steinbeck's efforts to present his story on the stage while Steinbeck gathers material for his novel *The Grapes of Wrath*).

Radio drama and comedy *The Guiding Light* by Irma Phillips, 27, 1/25 over NBC features the Rev. John Rutledge (the show will move to CBS radio in 1947 and will continue on radio to 1956 while beginning on television in 1952); *Our Gal Sunday* by Frank and Anne Hummert 3/29: "the story of an orphan girl named Sunday from the little town of Silver Creek, Colorado, who in young womanhood married England's richest, most handsome lord, Lord Henry Brinthorpe—the story that asks the question, Can this girl from a mining town in the West find happiness as the wife of a wealthy and titled Englishman? (the show will continue until early in 1959); *The Charlie McCarthy Show* 5/9 over NBC, with ventriloquist Edgar Bergen, 34, and W. C. Fields, who appears until December (the show will continue until 1948 and will be on CBS from 1949 to 1954); *Grand Central Station* over NBC Blue Network stations: "As a bullet seeks its target, shining rails in every part of our great country are aimed at Grand Central Station, heart of the nation's greatest city. Drawn by the magnetic force of the fantastic metropolis, day and night great trains rush toward the Hudson River, sweep down its eastern bank for 140 miles, flash briefly by the long red row of tenement houses South of 125th Street, dive with a roar into the two-and-a-half mile tunnel which burrows beneath the glitter and swank of Park Avenue, and then—EEEESSSHHHHhhh—Grand Central Station, crossroads of a million private lives! gigantic stage on which are played a thousand dramas daily" (the show will move to CBS and later to ABC).

Films Jean Renoir's *Grand Illusion (La Grande Illusion)* with Erich von Stroheim, Jean Gabin; Jean Renoir's *A Day in the Country;* Marcel Pagnol's *Harvest* with Fernandel, Marguerit Moreno, music by Arthur Honegger; William K. Howard's *Fire Over England* with Laurence Olivier, Vivien Leigh; Harold Shuster's *Wings of the Morning* with Henry Fonda, Annabella (first British film in Technicolor); William Wellman's *A Star Is Born* with Janet Gaynor, Fredric March; Sidney Franklin's *The Good Earth* with Luise Rainier, Paul Muni; John Ford's *The Life of Emile Zola* with Paul Muni; Victor Fleming's *Captains Courageous* with Spencer Tracy, Freddie Bartholomew; John Cromwell and W. S. Van Dyke's *The Prisoner of Zenda* with Douglas Fairbanks, Jr., Ronald Colman, Madeleine Carroll; Frank Capra's *Lost Horizon* with Ronald Colman, Sam Jaffe, Thomas Mitchell, Edward Everett Horton; Lloyd Bacon's *Marked Woman* with Bette Davis, Humphrey Bogart; John Ford's *The Hurricane* with Dorothy Lamour, Jon Hall; Leo McCarey's *The Awful Truth* with Cary Grant, Irene Dunne; Gregory La Cava's *Stage Door* with Katharine Hepburn, Adolphe Menjou, Lucille Ball, Ginger Rogers; George Stevens's *Quality Street* with Katharine Hepburn, Franchot Tone; Norman Z. McLeod's *Topper* with Cary Grant, Constance Bennett, Roland Young, Billie Burke; Anatole Litvak's *Mayerling* with Charles Boyer, Danielle Darrieux; Michael Curtiz's *Kid Galahad* with

Edward G. Robinson, Bette Davis, Humphrey Bogart, Wayne Morris; Julien Duvivier's *Pepe Le Moko* with Jean Gabin; Robert Flaherty and Zoltan Korda's *Elephant Boy* with Sabu; Pare Lorentz's documentary *The River;* John Ford's *Wee Willie Winkie* with Shirley Temple, Victor McLaglen; Alan Dwan's *Heidi* with Shirley Temple, Jean Hersholt; George B. Seitz's *A Family Affair* with Mickey Rooney as Andy Hardy, Lionel Barrymore as Judge James Hardy in the first of a series that will continue off and on for 21 years, with Lewis Stone as Judge Hardy, Fay Holden as Mrs. Hardy, and girlfriends who will include Ann Rutherford, Judy Garland, Lana Turner, Esther Williams, Kathryn Grayson, and Donna Reed.

The first Bugs Bunny cartoon is released by Warner Brothers. *Porky's Hare Hunt* features the voice of Mel Blanc, 29, who creates the voices of Bugs Bunny, Porky Pig, and others who will include Daffy Duck, Woody Woodpecker, and Speedy Gonzales. It takes 125 people to make one 6½ minute cartoon, but audiences are delighted with Bugs Bunny's "What's up, Doc?" and "That's all, folks" (*see* 1910).

The Thalberg Memorial Award inaugurated by the 10-year-old Academy of Motion Picture Arts and Sciences honors the late M-G-M producer Irving Grant Thalberg, who died of pneumonia in September of last year at age 37 after a brilliant career that began as secretary to Universal Pictures president Carl Laemmle.

Hollywood musicals Mark Sandrich's *Shall We Dance* with Ginger Rogers, Fred Astaire, music by George Gershwin (who dies July 11 of a brain tumor at age 38), lyrics by Ira Gershwin, songs that include "They Can't Take That Away from Me," "Things Are Looking Up," "They All Laughed," "Slap That Bass," "Let's Call the Whole Thing Off," and the title song; George Stevens's *Damsel in Distress* with Fred Astaire, George Burns, Gracie Allen, music by George Gershwin, lyrics by Ira Gershwin, songs that include "Nice Work If You Can Get It," "A Foggy Day in London Town"; W. S. Van Dyke's *Rosalie* with Eleanor Powell, Nelson Eddy, Frank Morgan, music and lyrics by Cole Porter, songs that include "In the Still of the Night" and the title song; Roy Del Ruth's *On the Avenue* with Dick Powell, Madeleine Carroll, Alice Faye, music and lyrics by Irving Berlin, songs that include "I've Got My Love to Keep Me Warm"; Frank Tuttle's *Waikiki Wedding* with Bing Crosby, Martha Raye, songs that include "Sweet Leilani" by Harry Owen, "Blue Hawaii" by Leo Robin, lyrics by Ralph Rainger; Ray Enright's *Ready, Willing and Able* with Ruby Keeler, Jane Wyman, songs that include "Too Marvelous for Words" by Richard Whiting, lyrics by Johnny Mercer; Robert Florey's *Mountain Music* with Martha Raye, Bob Burns, songs that include "Good Morning" by Sam Coslow.

Stage musicals *Babes in Arms* 4/14 at New York's Shubert Theater, with Ray Heatherton, Alfred Drake, music by Richard Rodgers, lyrics by Lorenz Hart, songs that include "My Funny Valentine,"

1937 (cont.) "The Lady Is a Tramp," "Johnny One Note," "I Wish I Were in Love Again," "Where or When," 289 perfs.; *I'd Rather Be Right* 11/2 at New York's Alvin Theater, with George M. Cohan as President Roosevelt, book by George S. Kaufman, music by Richard Rodgers, lyrics by Lorenz Hart, songs that include "Have You Met Miss Jones?" 290 perfs.; *Pins and Needles* 11/27 at New York's Labor Stage Theater, with music and lyrics by Harold Rome, songs that include "Nobody Makes a Pass at Me," 1,108 perfs. (the musical is sponsored by the International Ladies Garment Workers Union [ILGWU], no cast member receives more than $55 per week, 12 new songs will be added, and the show will set a new record for musicals with its long run); *Me and My Gal* 12/16 at London's Victoria Palace Theatre, with Lupino Lane as the Cockney from Lambeth who turns out to be 17th baron and 8th viscount of Hareford, book and lyrics by English playwright L. Arthur Rose, 50, and Douglas Furber, music by Noel Gay, songs that include "The Lambeth Walk," 1,646 perfs.; *Between the Devil* 12/22 at New York's Imperial Theater, with Jack Buchanan, Evelyn Laye, music by Arthur Schwartz, lyrics by Howard Dietz, songs that include "By Myself," 93 perfs.

Ballet *Les Patineurs* (*The Skaters*) 2/16 at the Sadler's Wells Theatre, London, with Margot Fonteyn, music by Giacomo Meyerbeer, choreography by Frederick Ashton; *Francesca da Rimini* 7/15 at London's Royal Opera House in Covent Garden, with Lubov Tchernicheva, music by Petr Ilich Tchaikovsky, choreography by David Lichine, 36.

Opera *Lulu* 6/2 at Zurich's Municipal Theater, with music by the late Alban Berg, who died late in 1935 at age 50.

The National Broadcasting Company starts the NBC Symphony with Arturo Toscanini as conductor. Now 70, Toscanini has been replaced as conductor of the New York Philharmonic after 8 years but will continue as conductor of the NBC Symphony until his retirement in 1954.

Avery Fisher invests $354 to start a hi-fi business that will make him a millionaire. The 31-year-old entrepreneur rents a small loft on New York's West 21st Street, he buys RCA Photophone amplifiers that are being used in movie theaters, he adds Western Electric speakers, an FM tuner, and a turntable, he creates some of the world's first component systems, and by the early 1960s he will account for 50 percent of U.S. hi-fi component sales. Along with Herman Hosner Scott, Paul Klipsch, Frank McIntosh, and others, Fisher breaks new ground in raising the quality of musical sound reproduction (*see* 1969).

First performances *Voice in the Wilderness* (*Le Voix dans le desert*) Symphonic Poem for Orchestra and 'Cello Obbligato by Ernest Bloch 1/21 at Los Angeles; Concertino by Walter Piston 6/20 in a CBS radio broadcast from New York; *Variations for String Orchestra on a Theme by Frank Bridge* by English composer Benjamin Britten, 23, in August at

Salzburg. Britten has been a student of Bridge since age 12 and has had his own work performed since 1934; Concerto for Violin and Orchestra in D minor by the 19th century German composer Robert Schumann (who wrote it in 1853) 11/26 at Berlin's Deutsches Opernhaus; Symphony No. 5 by Dmitri Shostakovich 11/21 at Leningrad (critics hail it as a model of Soviet music and Shostakovich regains his ideological good standing); *A Boy Was Born* by Benjamin Britten 12/21 in a BBC broadcast.

Popular songs "That Old Feeling" by Sammy Fain, lyrics by Lew Brown; "Once in a While" by Michael Edwards, lyrics by Bud Green; "The Nearness of You" by Hoagy Carmichael, lyrics by Ned Washington; "Somebody Else Is Taking My Place" by Russ Morgan, lyrics by Dick Howard and Bob Ellsworth; "The Dipsy Doodle" by bandleader Larry Clinton; "Moon of Manakoora" by Alfred Newman, lyrics by Paramount songwriter Frank Loesser, 27 (for the film *The Hurricane*); "Harbour Lights" by Jimmy Kennedy and Hugh Williams (Will Grosz).

War Admiral wins the Kentucky Derby and goes on to win the Triple Crown despite the challenge of Seabiscuit. The Bay Dancer son of Man o' War breaks the record for a mile and a half as he wins the Belmont Stakes (*see* 1938).

Joe Louis gains the world heavyweight title June 22 by knocking out James J. Braddock in the eighth round of a title bout at Chicago. Joseph Louis Barrow, 23, is the youngest fighter ever to win the championship and will hold it for exactly 12 years—longer than any other man, but while he will have grossed an estimated $4.23 million by the time he retires undefeated in 1949, the Brown Bomber will never be a millionaire.

Don Budge wins all his Davis Cup singles and doubles tennis matches and regains the cup for the United States for the first time in 10 years. John Donald Budge, 22, won the national doubles with his partner Gene Mako last year at Forest Hills, he takes the U.S. singles title, he defeats Germany's Baron Gottfried von Cramm in a five-set singles triumph at Wimbledon to take the British title, and he wins the Australian championship as well.

The U.S. ocean yacht *Ranger* built and skippered by Harold S. Vanderbilt successfully defends the America's Cup against England's *Endeavour II* skippered by Sir Thomas Sopworth in the last America's Cup competition between J class boats (*see* 1958).

The New York Yankees win the World Series by defeating the New York Giants 4 games to 1.

Nylon is patented by E. I. du Pont's W. H. Carothers, who assigns the patent to Du Pont (*see* 1935). The first completely man-made fiber will have wide uses not only in clothing but also as a substitute for canvas in sailboat sails, for sisal in ships' hawsers, for hog bristles in brushes, etc. (*see* toothbrush, 1938; nylon stockings, 1940; Terylene-Dacron, 1941).

Levi Strauss Company modifies its blue jeans, covering hip-pocket rivets with thread following complaints by schoolteachers that the rivets scratch desk seats (see 1874; 1964).

The Babee-Tenda infant chair invented by George B. Hansburg of 1919 pogo stick fame will not tip over. Now 50, Hansburg has devised the chair for his first granddaughter Norma.

 "Falling Water" is completed by Frank Lloyd Wright at Bear Run, Pa. Wright has built the dramatic country house for department store magnate Edgar Kaufmann.

New York's Time-Life building opens in September at 1 Rockefeller Plaza with 36 floors (see 1959).

The U.S. Housing Authority (USHA) created by Congress September 1 in the Wagner-Steagall Act provides financial assistance to the states in an effort to remedy the nation's housing shortage (and to provide work in the construction trades).

New York's Harlem River Houses are completed at 151st Street and the Harlem River Drive, where seven red-brick buildings of between four and five stories have been built as the first federally financed and federally constructed public housing in the city. Graced with trees and spacious plazas, the buildings have been erected following 1935 Harlem riots demanding decent low-cost housing; the rents are low, and the carefully screened tenants are provided with a nursery, a health clinic, and social rooms.

New York's Hampshire House is completed in October on 59th Street between Sixth and Seventh Avenues after 7 years of interrupted construction. The 550-room, 37-story structure opens as an apartment-hotel.

German architect Walter Gropius is called to Harvard, where he will continue Bauhaus methods as professor of architecture (see 1911). In self-imposed exile from Nazi Germany since 1934, Gropius has been working with London architect Maxwell Fry to design the Village College residence in Cambridgeshire. He joins Hungarian-American designer-photographer Laszlo Moholy-Nagy, 42, in organizing the New Bauhaus at Chicago that will be reorganized in 1939 as the Institute of Design and that will have a major impact on architectural design.

The Palais de Chaillot is completed at Paris on a site formerly occupied by Trocadero Castle.

Cape Hatteras National Seashore is set aside by act of Congress as the first national seashore. Congress stipulates that the "area shall be permanently reserved as a primitive wilderness and no development of the project or plan for the convenience of visitors shall be undertaken which would be incompatible with the preservation of the unique flora and fauna or the physiographic conditions now prevailing."

Drought ends in the United States, but stem rust attacks the wheat crop as it did in 1935 (see 1941).

U.S. spinach growers erect a statue to the comic-strip sailor Popeye, who is credited with having boosted consumption of the vegetable (see 1929; New Yorker cartoon, 1928).

Allis-Chalmers Company improves its rubber-tired tractor and sells a lightweight tractor and combine as a package for $1,000, while competition charges $1,000 each for a tractor and combine. The new equipment propels Allis-Chalmers from nowhere to third place in the U.S. farm equipment industry (see 1935).

Vitamin A is isolated as crystals from fish liver oils by U.S. biochemists A. N. Holmes and R. E. Corbet (see Karrer, 1931).

Vitamin K is produced in crystalline form (see 1935).

Synthetic thiamine (vitamin B$_1$) is manufactured in the United States and Switzerland at $450 per pound, but further research will soon reduce the price to a few cents per pound (see 1936; 1938).

Pepperidge Farm bread is introduced by Connecticut entrepreneur Margaret Fogarty Rudkin, 40, who sets up an oven in her husband's former polo pony stable on the family's 120-acre Pepperidge Farm and makes whole-wheat bread which she sells first to neighbors and then through a New York City fancy food retailer (see 1940).

Spam is introduced by George A. Hormel & Co., whose 12-ounce canned luncheon meat product will become the world's largest selling canned meat.

Soy protein "analogs" that will be used as substitutes for bacon and other animal protein foods are pioneered by Ford Motor Company scientists trying to develop a synthetic wool fiber. They spin a textile filament from soybean protein and create a vegetable protein that can be flavored to taste much like any animal protein food (see 1949; Boyer, 1933).

The artificial sweetener sodium cyclamate that is 30 times sweeter than sugar but has none of the bitter aftertaste of the saccharin discovered in 1879 is discovered by University of Illinois chemist Michael Sveda (see 1964).

Kix corn puff cereal is introduced by General Mills.

La Choy Food Products founder Wallace Smith is killed by a bolt of lightning, founder Ilhan New left the firm in 1930, but La Choy builds its first plant at Detroit (see 1922; 1942).

Britain gets her first frozen foods as Wisbech Produce Canners Ltd. of Wisbech in Cambridgeshire introduces frozen asparagus in May at 2 shillings, 3 pence a pack, strawberries in June at 1 shilling, 2 pence per 8-ounce pack, garden peas in July at 9 pence per 6-ounce pack, and sliced green beans in August at 1 shilling, 2 pence per 6-ounce pack. Wisbech's S. W. Smedley has developed his own freezing process after studying American techniques on a visit to the United States, but Britain has only 3,000 home refrigerators as compared with more than 2 million in the United States.

1937 (cont.) Home freezers become commercially important for the first time in the United States as frozen food sales increase, but relatively few Americans have anything more advanced than an icebox. Icemen continue to make regular deliveries to most U.S. middle-class households.

The A&P begins opening supermarkets, as do other major U.S. food chains. Three or four smaller stores are closed down for every A&P supermarket opened (*see* 1929; 1958; King Kullen, 1930; Big Bear, 1932).

The supermarket shopping cart introduced at Oklahoma City June 4 begins a revolution in food buying. Sylvan N. Goldman, 38, owns Standard Food Markets and Humpty Dumpty Stores, he has created the cart to enable his customers to buy more than can fit in the wicker baskets they carry, he has taken some folding chairs, put them on wheels, raised the seats to accommodate a lower shopping basket, placed a second basket on the seat, and used the chair back as a handle. Four U.S. companies will develop the shopping cart into a computer-designed chromed-steel cart that can be nested in a small area.

Howard Johnson restaurants become a franchised operation as restaurateur Johnson hits upon the idea of franchising after having found it impossible to obtain bank financing for restaurants (*see* 1936). Johnson locates property which he leases to a Cambridge, Mass., widow who invests first $5,000 and then another $25,000, he constructs a building, he hires employees, he charges a small fee for the franchise but takes no part of the profits, he retains exclusive rights to supply food including 28 flavors of ice cream, menus, table mats, and other items, and he starts a chain of franchised orange-roofed restaurants whose design, and operation he will rigidly control (*see* 1952).

Cookbook *Serve It Forth* by Scots-Irish California gastronome and prose stylist M. F. K. (Mary Frances Kennedy) Fisher, 29.

Contraception receives a virtually unqualified endorsement from an American Medical Association committee on birth control (*see* 1940).

The first state contraceptive clinic opens March 15 at Raleigh, N.C. The State Board of Health introduces a program for indigent married women in its regular maternity and child health service.

Islam's Grand Mufti issues a fatwa permitting Moslems to take any measure to avoid conception to which both man and woman agree.

1938 Adolf Hitler vows to "protect" the 10 million Germans living outside the Reich, he annexes Austria in March, and he engineers an April 10 plebiscite which shows that 99.75 percent of Austrians desire union with the Third Reich.

The Austrian *Anschluss* (above) draws protests from Britain and France, but they appease the führer at Munich in September by permitting him to take the Sudetenland, a 16,000-square-mile territory that comprises nearly a third of Czechoslovakia and contains a third of her inhabitants.

"I believe it is peace for our time . . . peace with honor," says the British prime minister Neville Chamberlain in a speech given upon his return from Munich (above; *see* 1939).

"I am convinced that it is wiser to permit Germany eastward expansion than to throw England and France, unprepared, into a war at this time," writes Charles A. Lindbergh September 23 to U.S. Ambassador to Britain Joseph P. Kennedy. Lindbergh has made surveys of British, German, and Soviet airpower, and he argues that Britain could not possibly win a war in Europe even with U.S. aid.

London has announced postponement of any Palestine partition January 4, Jewish terrorist Solomon ben Yosef has been executed June 29, Arab markets are bombed in Jerusalem, Haifa, and Jaffa either by Jewish or Arab terrorists, 20 Jews are massacred October 2 at Tiberias, Arab extremists seize Bethlehem and the old section of Jerusalem, which are retaken by British troops October 10 and October 18, respectively, a new British commission reports November 9 that all partition proposals are impractical, and by year's end there are 25,000 to 30,000 British troops in Palestine (*see* 1930; 1939).

Japanese forces in China follow their successes of last year by taking Tsingtao January 10 after destruction by the Chinese of some Japanese factories in the area. The Japanese advance along the Hankow Railway and through Shansi Province, they reach the Yellow River March 6, but they suffer several reverses as Chinese guerrillas retain control of the countryside.

Amoy falls to the Japanese May 10, Japanese and Russian forces clash on the Chinese-Siberian border from July 11 to August 10, Japanese forces land at Bias Bay near Hong Kong October 12, Canton falls October 21, Hankow is taken October 25. Capturing Canton permits the Japanese to cut the Canton-Hankow Railway that supplies Chinese forces in the interior with war matériel from abroad.

Spanish insurgents sever Loyalist territory in Castile from Barcelona and Catalonia, the opposing forces remain deadlocked along the Ebro River through most of the summer, a great insurgent drive begins in Catalonia December 23, and the Loyalists are forced back toward Barcelona. Some Italian troops have been withdrawn from Spain following an Anglo-Italian pact signed April 16, but a force of 40,000 remains to support Generalissimo Francisco Franco.

Turkey's Kemal Ataturk dies November 10 at age 57 after an administration of 15 years in which he has established a modern republic. Unanimously elected to succeed him as president in a vote by the national assembly is the 54-year-old Ismet Inonu, who has been responsible for many of the reforms accomplished since 1923 and who begins an administration that will continue until 1950.

France's colonies of Corsica and Tunisia are demanded in December by Italy's Benito Mussolini.

Polish forces have occupied the Teschen area of Czechoslovakia October 2 after having sent a note September 29 demanding cession of the territory seized by the Czechs in the Polish-Russian war of 1920. Hungarian claims in Slovakia and Ruthenia are championed by Poland.

Britain and Ireland resume friendly relations after concluding a 3-year agreement to remove tariff barriers (see 1935). Britain turns over coast defense installations to Eire, and Dublin agrees to pay £10 million to satisfy land-annuity claims.

The Declaration of Lima is adopted December 24 by representatives of 21 American nations meeting at a Pan-American conference in Peru. The Latin-American countries and their North American neighbors agree to consult in the event that the "peace, security, or territorial integrity" of any state is threatened, and they reaffirm absolute sovereignty in the face of fears that Europe's Fascist powers may attempt takeovers in the Americas.

Mexico has nationalized her petroleum industry March 18 and has revoked licenses granted to British and U.S. oil companies to operate in Mexico. Oil is a natural resource that belongs to all the Mexican people, the Cardenas government has said; it has expropriated properties valued at $450 million, and it has proposed oil barter agreements with Germany, Italy, and other nations to exchange oil for manufactured goods imported up to now largely from Britain and the United States.

The first nuclear fission of uranium is produced December 18 by German physicist Otto Hahn, 59, who has found that the nucleus of certain uranium atoms can be split into two approximately equal halves, releasing not only energy but also neutrons that can, in turn, split further uranium atoms (see Fermi, 1934). Hahn is assisted by his colleague Fritz Strassman and by Austro-Swedish physicist Lise Meitner, 60, who will be helped by her nephew Otto Frisch, 34, to work out the implications of Hahn's observations (see Bohr, Einstein, 1939).

Austrian Jews are deprived of their civil rights and of their means of livelihood by the Nazis (above), and Jewish shops and homes are plundered.

Anti-Jewish legislation is enacted in Italy.

The greatest pogrom in German history begins November 9 following the assassination of Paris embassy official Ernst Edouard vom Rath November 7 by German-born Polish Jew Herschel Grynzpan, 17, who has heard of the mistreatment of thousands of Polish Jews (including members of his own family) after their deportation from Germany. Jewish shop windows ("crystal") are smashed in the Kristalnacht riots, shops, homes, and synagogues are looted, demolished, and burned, and between 20,000 and 30,000 Jews are carried off to concentration camps (see 1939; Buchenwald, 1933).

A Committee to Investigate Un-American Activities is created by the House of Representatives under the chairmanship of Texas congressman Martin Dies, 36, who has turned against the New Deal which he originally supported. The Dies Committee begins investigating Nazi activities in the United States but soon turns to investigating Communist activities, and while most of the committee's charges will be based on hearsay, circumstantial evidence, or slander, Dies will claim that his committee is more effective in exposing Communist subversion than is the FBI.

The Fair Labor Standards Act (wage and hour law) passed by Congress June 15 limits working hours of some 12.5 million U.S. workers in the first national effort to place a floor under wages and a ceiling on hours. Working hours for the first year after the new law takes effect are limited to 44 per week with the limit to be reduced to 42 for the second year and to 40 for every year thereafter. Longer work weeks are permitted only if overtime work is paid for at 1½ times the regular rate. A minimum of 25 cents per hour is prescribed for the first year and 30 cents for the next 6 years (see Minimum Wage Act, 1949).

The new minimum wage law (above) wipes out overnight the 40,000-worker needlework industry of Puerto Rico where the hourly rate for *skilled* workers has been 25 cents.

The Congress of Industrial Organizations (CIO) is formally organized in November to succeed the Committee for Industrial Organization formed in 1935. John L. Lewis is elected CIO president November 18 (see 1946).

Equal accommodations for Missouri law students regardless of race are ordered by the Supreme Court December 12 in *Missouri ex. rel. Gaines v. Canada.*

Germany's trade balance shows a deficit of 432 million marks. The country has been bankrupt since 1931 by ordinary capitalist standards, and Reichsbank president Horace Greeley Hjalmar Schacht, 61, warns that the country's enormous armament program must be curtailed lest the catastrophic inflation of 15 years ago recur.

President Roosevelt asks Congress for help in stimulating the U.S. economy as business remains in recession with 5.8 million Americans still unemployed. Congress reduces corporation profits taxes May 27 and passes an Emergency Relief Appropriations Act June 21.

A Temporary National Economic Committee (TNEC) to study the concentration of economic power in America is established by President Roosevelt and is approved by Congress. The TNEC will operate under the direction of U.S. senator from Wyoming Joseph Z. O'Mahoney, and it will examine the effect of the concentration of economic power on the decline in competition.

A new Jefferson head nickel is issued by the U.S. Mint to supersede the Indian head nickel that has been in

Herald Examiner

NEW AUSTRO-GERMAN EMPIRE

Hitler Crosses Border on Way to Capital;
3,000 German Troops Fly Into Vienna

'No Power Can Drive Us Out,'
Fuehrer Tells Cheering 250,000

Adolf Hitler's annexation of Austria brought Europe closer to war. Appeasement at Munich delayed the inevitable.

circulation since 1913. The Jefferson Memorial now being constructed at Washington, D.C., is depicted on one side of the new coin (*see* 1943).

Wall Street's Dow Jones Industrial Average falls to 98.95, down from a 1937 high of 194.40, but it rebounds to 158.41 by year's end.

A Civil Aeronautics Authority (CAA) created by act of Congress June 23 moves to regulate the growing U.S. aviation industry. Named to head the new authority is former Life Savers magnate Edward J. Noble, now 56 (*see* 1920; American Broadcasting, 1943).

Howard Hughes sets a new round-the-world speed record in July, flying a twin-engine Lockheed plane from California to California in 3 days, 19 hours, 14 minutes, 28 seconds. Now 32, Hughes has $3 million per year in Hughes Tool Company profits to finance his flying exploits and his Hollywood filmmaking (*see* 1908; Post, 1931; Odum, 1947; TWA, 1939).

Eastern Airlines is created out of North American Aviation's Eastern Air Transport by World War flying ace E. V. "Eddie" Rickenbacker who buys into North American with backing from Standard Oil heir Laurence Rockefeller, 28 (*see* North American, 1933). Now 48, Rickenbacker has worked in the auto industry and for several aircraft and airline companies, he will make Eastern a major carrier, and he will obtain routes up and down the East Coast and to Mexico and the Caribbean.

Northrop Aircraft Company is started by John Knudsen Northrop, now 42, whose company was acquired last year by Douglas Aircraft (*see* 1928).

Douglas Aircraft has sales of $28.4 million as its DC-3 of 1936 gains popularity. Douglas solicits orders for a new four-engine DC-4, but Boeing goes into production with a four-engine 307 that challenges Douglas for leadership in the commercial aircraft industry (*see* B-17, 1935; TWA, 1940).

McDonnell Aircraft Corporation is founded by former Glenn L. Martin Company project engineer James Smith McDonnell, Jr., 39, who will make McDonnell Aircraft a leading producer of military aircraft (*see* McDonnell-Douglas, 1967).

El Capitan goes into service February 22 between Chicago and Los Angeles for the Santa Fe. The new once-a-week all-coach express has two chair cars, a baggage-dormitory coach, a lunch-counter/tavern car, and a chair observation car; it carries 192 passengers, and it operates on the same schedule as the *Super Chief* that went into service 2 years ago.

The San Diegan goes into service March 27 for the Santa Fe. The new express between Los Angeles and San Diego makes two round-trip runs each day, and the trip takes 2½ hours.

General Motors Corporation joins with Standard Oil of California to organize Pacific Coast Lines, a firm that will convert West Coast electric street railways into motorbus lines (*see* 1932; 1939).

The Florida Overseas Highway brings Key West to within 5 hours' driving distance of Miami. The new road employs spans built by Henry Flagler for his Florida East Coast Railway of 1912, which was repaired after the hurricane of 1926 but was completely wiped out by the hurricane of 1935.

The Volkswagen ("people's car"), with an air-cooled rear engine, is assembled by hand in Nazi Germany, and the cornerstone for a Volkswagen factory is dedicated May 26 at Wolfsburg on the Mittelland Canal 40 miles east of Hanover in Lower Saxony. The car has been designed on commission from Adolf Hitler by Austrian automotive engineer Ferdinand Porsche, 42, whose low-cost "beetle" will not go into mass production for more than 10 years. More than 18 million of the "beetles" will eventually be sold to exceed the Model T Ford's record (*see* 1949).

Fiberglas is perfected by Owens-Illinois Glass Company and the Corning Glass Works. The material, made of fine glass filaments, can be spun into yarn and woven into fabrics or used as insulating material.

Teflon (Fluon) is discovered accidently by Du Pont chemist Roy Joseph Plunkett, 28, whose polytetrafluoroethylene plastic is an excellent electrical insulation material that is stable over a wide range of temperatures and is resistant to most corrosive agents. Discovered while working on refrigerants, Teflon will have many industrial uses, it will be marketed under the name Fluon by Britain's Imperial Chemical Industries, and it will be used as a coating for cooking utensils (*see* below).

The first U.S. state law requiring medical tests for marriage license applicants is enacted April 12 by the New York State Legislature.

The March of Dimes to finance research that will combat poliomyelitis is founded under the leadership of President Roosevelt's former law partner Basil O'Connor, 46.

The first life tables showing reduced life expectancy for smokers are published in a report to the New York Academy of Medicine by Johns Hopkins Medical School professor Raymond Pearl who says, "Smoking is associated with a definite impairment of longevity. This impairment is proportional to the habitual amount of tobacco usage by smoking, being great for heavy smokers and less for moderate smokers" (*see* Muller, 1939).

The first high-definition color television demonstration is made February 4 at London's Dominion Theatre, Tottenham Court Road, by John L. Baird, who transmits color films and shows them on a 9- by 12-foot screen via a 120-line-per-inch system (*see* 1926). Baird transmits live action in color from the Baird Studios at Crystal Palace less than 2 weeks later, but commercial development is blocked by Baird's refusal to consider electronic transmission in place of mechanical transmission (*see* Goldmark, 1940).

The first true Xerox image is produced October 22 at Astoria, Queens, by Chester Carlson with the help of a German refugee physicist (*see* 1937). The electrophotographic image is imprinted on wax paper which has been pressed against an electrostatically charged 2- by 3-inch sulfur-coated zinc plate that has been dusted with lycopodium powder: Carlson is attending New York Law School night classes, he will be admitted to the bar in 1940, and he will receive his first patent that year for the process he will call "xerography," using the Greek word *xeros* for dry, but he will fail in his initial attempts to gain financial backing to pursue his project (*see* 1944).

The ballpoint pen is patented by Hungarian chemist George Biro and his brother Ladislao J. Biro, a Budapest printer's proofreader. The Biro brothers will emigrate in 1943 to Argentina, where they will obtain financial backing from British financier Henry Martin, who will set up a factory in England with Frederick Miles to produce pens that will not leak at high altitudes for use by the Royal Air Force. The French company Bic will acquire the Martin-Miles firm and will develop a cheaper throwaway pen.

The Biro brothers (above) have invented a veinlike tube that fits inside a pen barrel and moistens the ball at the pen's tip by capillary attraction, but their ballpoint pen will achieve its potential only after Austrian-American chemist Franz Seech in California develops a viscous fluid with a dye that forms a film on any surface when exposed to air (*see* 1945).

Picture Post is launched by British publisher Edward Hulton, who models the photo weekly on Henry R. Luce's *LIFE* (*see* 1936). Hulton's late father inherited proprietorship of the *London Evening Chronicle, Sunday Chronicle, Daily Dispatch, Daily Sketch,* and *Sporting Chronicle* from his father in 1904 and

went on to acquire the *Evening Standard* and *Illustrated Sunday Herald* before his death in 1925.

"Superman" is introduced in comic books by Cleveland cartoonists Jerry Siegel, 24, and Joseph Shuster, 24, who developed their superhuman Clark Kent newspaperman hero while in high school and who have finally sold it to Detective Comics, Inc., which publishes the first "Superman" episode in the June issue of *Action Comics,* paying the two young men $10 per page to give them an income of $15 each per week. "Superman" will begin appearing in newspapers in the early 1940s and will be the basis of radio and television serials and endless merchandise spin-offs but Detective Comics, Inc., has acquired all rights, and "Superman's" originators will derive little financial reward until the syndicators agree late in 1975 to provide them with pensions.

Information, Please! debuts May 17 over NBC radio to begin a 14-year run. Former Simon & Schuster editor Clifton Paul Fadiman, 34, is moderator, the quiz show panel selected by NBC producer Dan Goldenpaul includes *New York Times* sportswriter John Kieran, 46, pianist Oscar Levant, 32, *New York Post* columnist Franklin Pierce Adams, 47, and guests, and any listener who sends in a question that stumps the experts receives a 24-volume set of the *Encyclopaedia Britannica.*

The War of the Worlds broadcast October 30 over CBS stations gives a dramatic demonstration of the power of radio. Orson Welles's Mercury Theater of the Air presents a radio version of the 1898 H. G. Wells novel, and its "news" reports of Martian landings in New Jersey are so realistic that near-panics occur in many areas despite periodic announcements that the program is merely a dramatization.

Nonfiction *It Is Later Than You Think* by Russian-American critic Max Lerner, 36; *Homage to Catalonia* by George Orwell antagonizes British leftists by showing how Stalinists have suppressed Trotskyist and anarchist elements in Spain's independent left. Orwell joined the Republican side after going to Spain as a journalist late in 1936, his book was turned down by a left-wing publisher, it will sell only 600 copies in his lifetime, and it will not be published in the United States until after his death in 1950; *With Malice Toward Some* by U.S. writer Margaret Halsey, 28, who spent a year in Devon, England, where her husband was an exchange professor.

Fiction *Nausea (La Nausée)* by French novelist Jean-Paul Sartre, 33; *But the World Must Be Young (Men ung ma verden ennu vaere)* by Nordahl Grieg is a novelistic critique of Stalinism; *The Death of the Heart* by Elizabeth Bowen; *Brighton Rock* by Graham Greene is his first explicitly "Catholic" novel; *Ferdyduke* by Polish novelist Witold Gombrowicz, 34; *Scoop* by Evelyn Waugh is a spoof on British foreign correspondents that thinly veils actual fact; *Out of Africa* by Isak Dinesen; *The Forest of a Thousand Demons (ogboju ode rinn igbo irummale)* by

1938 (cont.) Nigerian novelist (and Yoruba chief) Daniel O. Fagunwa, 28; *Tropisms (Tropismes)* by Russian-born French novelist Nathalie Sarrante, 36; *Chosen People* by Seaforth Mackenzie; *The Code of the Woosters* by P. G. Wodehouse; *The Fathers* by Allen Tate; *Young Man with a Horn* by U.S. novelist Dorothy Dodds Baker, 31, has been inspired by the music, if not the life, of the late Bix Beiderbecke who died of lobar pneumonia at age 28 in August 1931 (*see* 1924); *Epitaph for a Spy* and *Cause for Alarm* by Eric Ambler; *Dynasty of Death* by U.S. novelist Taylor Caldwell, 38, who 7 years ago obtained her bachelor's degree at the University of Buffalo, studying nights while working as a court stenographer by day.

Juvenile *The Man of Bronze* by former New York telegrapher Kenneth Robeson (Lester Dent), 32, whose "Doc Savage" adventure novel will be followed in the next 7 years by another 164 such novels as Dent turns out a new 60,000-word "Doc Savage" adventure almost every month; *The 500 Hats of Bartholomew Cubbins* by Dr. Seuss.

Poetry *The Odyssey* (*I Odysseia*) by Greek (Cretan) poet Nikos Kazantzakis, 55, whose 33,333-line "modern sequel" has been influenced by the French philosopher Henri Bergson, now 79; *Dreams Begin Realities* by U.S. poet Delmore Schwartz, 25.

Painting *Italian Women* by Georges Rouault; *Cradling Wheat* by Thomas Hart Benton. William Glackens dies at Westport, Conn., May 22 at age 68; German expressionist Ernst Ludwig Kirchner dies at Davos, Switzerland, June 15 at age 58 a year after the Nazis confiscated more than 600 of his works.

The Minox camera introduced by a Latvian factory is shaped like a Mounds candy bar 3 inches long and uses 35-millimeter film. Production will move to Germany in 1946, and the Germans will develop a Minox with a built-in light-sensitive exposure meter and with a shutter speed of up to 1/500th of a second.

Theater *The Restless Heart* (*La Sauvage*) by Jean Anouilh 1/10 at the Théâtre de Mathurius, Paris; ". . . one-third of a nation . . .": *A Living Newspaper* by U.S. playwright Arthur Arent, 32, 1/17 at New York's Adelphi Theater (Federal Theater Project), 237 perfs.; *Bachelor Born* by U.S. playwright Ian Hay 1/25 at New York's Morosco Theater, with Peggy Simpson, Helen Trenholme, 400 perfs.; *Shadow and Substance* by Paul Vincent Carroll 1/26 at New York's Golden Theater, with Cedric Hardwick, Sara Allgood, Julie Hayden, 274 perfs.; *On Borrowed Time* by Paul Osborn 2/3 at New York's Longacre Theater, with Dudley Digges, Dorothy Stickney, Dickie Van Patten in a dramatization of the Lawrence E. Watkin novel, 321 perfs.; *Our Town* by Thornton Wilder 2/4 at New York's Henry Miller Theater, with Martha Scott, Frank Craven, Philip Coolidge, 336 perfs., Pulitzer Prize 1939; *What a Life* by Clifford Goldsmith 4/13 at New York's Biltmore Theater, with Ezra Stone as Henry Aldrich, Eddie Bracken, Betty Field, 538 perfs.; *Purgatory* by William Butler Yeats, now 73, 8/10 at Dublin's Abbey Theatre; *Thieves' Carni-*

val (*Le bal des voleurs*) by Jean Anouilh 9/17 at the Théâtre des Arts, Paris; *The Corn Is Green* by Emlyn Williams 9/20 at London's Duchess Theatre; *Kiss the Boys Goodbye* by Clare Booth 9/28 at Henry Miller's Theater, New York, with Millard Mitchell, Helen Claire, Benay Venuta, 286 perfs.; *The Fabulous Invalid* by George S. Kaufman and Moss Hart 10/8 at New York's Broadhurst Theater (the "invalid" being the legitimate theater), 165 perfs.; *Abe Lincoln in Illinois* by Robert Sherwood 10/15 at New York's Plymouth Theater, with Raymond Massey in the title role, 472 perfs., Pulitzer Prize 1939 (declined); *Rocket to the Moon* by Clifford Odets 11/24 at New York's Belasco Theater, with Morris Carnovsky, 131 perfs.; *Here Come the Clowns* by Philip Barry 12/7 at New York's Booth Theater, with Eddie Dowling, Madge Evans, Russell Collins, 88 perfs.

Radio drama *Young Widder Brown* 7/26 over NBC stations. Created by Frank and Anne Hummert, the new soap opera will continue daily until late June 1956.

Films Serge Eisenstein's *Aleksandr Nevsky;* Mark Donskoi's *The Childhood of Maksim Gorky;* Michael Naszynsky's *The Dybbuk;* Marcel Pagnol's *The Baker's Wife* with Raimu; Alfred Hitchcock's *The Lady Vanishes* with Michael Redgrave, Margaret Lockwood, Paul Lukas, Dame May Witty; Anthony Asquith and Leslie Howard's *Pygmalion* with Howard, Wendy Hiller; Michael Curtiz's *The Adventures of Robin Hood* with Errol Flynn; Edmund Goulding's *The Dawn Patrol* with Errol Flynn; Victor Fleming's *Test Pilot* with Clark Gable, Spencer Tracy, Myrna Loy; George Cukor's *Holiday* with Katharine Hepburn, Cary Grant; Howard Hawks's *Bringing Up Baby* with Katharine Hepburn, Cary Grant; William Wyler's *Jezebel* with Bette Davis, Henry Fonda, George Brent; Jeff Musso's *The Puritan* with Jean-Louis Barrault; Richard Wallace's *The Young in Heart* with Janet Gaynor, Douglas Fairbanks, Jr., Paulette Goddard; George Stevens's *Vivacious Lady* with Ginger Rogers, James Stewart; Norman Taurog's *The Adventures of Tom Sawyer* with Tommy Kelly, May Robson; William A. Seiter's *Room Service* with the Marx Brothers; Irving Cummings's *Little Miss Broadway* with Shirley Temple; Allen Dwan's *Rebecca of Sunnybrook Farm* with Shirley Temple.

Hollywood musicals Walt Disney's *Snow White and the Seven Dwarfs* is the first full-length animated cartoon feature, Snow White sings "Some Day My Prince Will Come" and "One Song," dwarfs Doc, Grumpy, Happy, Sleepy, Dopey, Sneezy, and Bashful sing "Heigh-Ho" and "Whistle While You Work," music by Frank Churchill, lyrics by Larry Mose; Ray Enright's *Hard to Get* with Dick Powell, Olivia de Havilland, music by Harry Warren, lyrics by Johnny Mercer, songs that include "You Must Have Been a Beautiful Baby"; George Marshall's *The Goldwyn Follies* with Bobby Clark, music by the late George Gershwin, lyrics by Ira Gershwin, songs that include "Love Walked In," "Love Is Here to Stay," "I Was Doing All Right," "I Love to Rhyme"; Wesley Ruggles's *Sing You Sinners* with Bing Crosby, Fred MacMurray, Donald O'Connor, songs that include the Franke Harling-Sam Coslow title song, "Small Fry" by Hoagy Carmichael, lyrics by Frank Loesser; George Archimbaud's *Thanks for the Memory* with Bob Hope, songs that include the title song by Ralph Rainger, lyrics by Leo Robin (it will become Hope's theme song) and "Two Sleepy People" by Frank Loesser.

Stage musicals   *Right This Way* 1/4 at New York's 46th Street Theater, with Tamara, Guy Robertson, Joe E. Lewis, music by Sammy Fain, lyrics by Irving Kahal, songs that include "I Can Dream, Can't I?" 15 perfs.; *Operette* 3/16 at His Majesty's Theatre, London, with Peggy Wood, music and lyrics by Noel Coward, songs that include "The Stately Homes of England," 133 perfs.; *I Married an Angel* 5/11 at New York's Shubert Theater, with Dennis King, Vera Zorina, Vivienne Segal, music by Richard Rodgers, lyrics by Lorenz Hart, songs that include "Spring Is Here" and the title song, 338 perfs.; *Helzapoppin* 9/22 at New York's 46th Street Theater, with Ole Olsen and Chic Johnson who delight audiences with their slapstick and sight gags, music by Sammy Fain, lyrics by Irving Kahal and Charles Tobias, songs that include "I'll Be Seeing You," 1,404 perfs.; *Knickerbocker Holiday* 10/19 at New York's Ethel Barrymore Theater, with Walter Huston, music by Kurt Weill, book and lyrics by Maxwell Anderson, songs that include "September Song," 168 perfs., *Leave It to Me* 11/9 at New York's Imperial Theater, with ingénue Mary Martin, 24, doing a simulated striptease to Cole Porter's song "My Heart Belongs to Daddy" (other songs include "You Never Know," "At Long Last Love," and "Some Gentlemen Don't Like Love,") 307 perfs. (Porter was injured last year in a fall from a horse and will be confined to a wheelchair for the rest of his life); *The Boys from Syracuse* 11/23 at New York's Alvin Theater, with Jimmy Savo, Eddie Albert in a story about the Shubert brothers, music by Richard Rodgers, lyrics by Lorenz Hart, songs that include "Falling in Love with Love," "Sing for Your Supper," "This Can't Be Love," 235 perfs.

Opera   *Mathis der Maler* (*Matthias the Painter*) 5/28 at Zurich's Stadtheater, with music and libretto by Paul Hindemith who has based it on the life of the German painter Matthias Grünewald (Mathis Gothart Nithart) who died in 1528. The opera had been scheduled to open at Berlin in 1934 but was banned by the Nazis.

Ballet   *St. Francis* 7/21 at London's Drury Lane Theatre, with music by Paul Hindemith, choreography by Leonide Massine; *Billy the Kid* 10/9 at the Chicago Civic Opera House, with music by Aaron Copland, choreography by Eugene Loring.

First performances   Symphony No. 3 by Howard Hanson 3/26 in an NBC Orchestra radio concert; *The Incredible Flutist* (ballet music) by Walter Piston 3/30 at Boston's Symphony Hall; Symphony No. 1 by

Walter Piston 4/8 at Boston's Symphony Hall; Quartet in G minor for Piano and Strings by Ernest Bloch 5/5 at Los Angeles; Concerto No. 1 in D major for Piano and Orchestra by Benjamin Britten in August at Queen's Hall, London.

Benny Goodman and His Orchestra give the first Carnegie Hall jazz concert at New York January 17 with guest performers who include Count Basie and members of the Basie and Duke Ellington orchestras (*see* 1935). Pianist Jess Stacy plays "Sing Sing Sing."

Glenn Miller begins touring with a big band of his own after years of playing trombone and arranging music for Tommy and Jimmy Dorsey and for Ray Noble. Now 39, Miller will achieve enormous success next year with his recordings of "In the Mood," "Sunrise Serenade," and "Moonlight Serenade" (which will become his theme song) (*see* 1942).

Woody Guthrie identifies himself with the labor movement and travels the country singing his songs "Hard Traveling," "Blowing Down This Dusty Road," "Union Maid," and "So Long (It's Been Good to Know You)." Guthrie will support the cause of organized labor with his "Talking Union" album and with personal appearances (*see* 1936).

Popular songs   "Two Sleepy People" by Hoagy Carmichael, lyrics by Frank Loesser; " I Get Along Without You Very Well (Except Sometimes)" by Hoagy Carmichael, lyrics by Jane Brown Thompson; "You Go to My Head" by J. Fred Coots, lyrics by Haven Gillespie; "I Let a Song Go Out of My Heart" by Duke Ellington, lyrics by Irving Miller, Henry Nemo, John Redmond; "One O'Clock Jump" by Count Basie; "Camel Hop" by Mary Lou Williams; "Sent for You Yesterday (and Here You Come Today)" by Eddie Durham, Count Basie, and vocalist Jimmy Rushing; "F. D. R. Jones" by Harold Rome; "The Flat Foot Floogie" by Slim Gaillard, Slam Stewart, Bud Green (who have been forced to change the word "floozie" to "floogie"); "A-Tisket, A-Tasket" by Ella Fitzgerald and Van Alexander (a hunchback arranger for the Chick Webb band who will die next year); "Cherokee" by Ray Noble (whose song will be the theme for bandleader-tenor saxophonist Charlie Barnet); "I Hadn't Anyone Till You" by Ray Noble.

The samba and the conga are introduced to U.S. dancefloors.

 The third World Cup football (soccer) finals are held at Colombes, France, an Italian team wins by defeating Hungary 4 goals to 2, but no further World Cup games will be held until 1950.

Don Budge wins the Australian, French, British, and U.S. singles tennis championships, a "grand slam" never before accomplished and one that will not be duplicated for 24 years.

The New York Yankees win the World Series by defeating the Chicago Cubs 4 games to 0.

War Admiral starts as a 1-4 favorite over Seabiscuit in a November match race at Pimlico before a crowd of 40,000, but Seabiscuit wins (*see* 1937).

1938 (cont.) Fiberglas (above) will largely replace wood in pleasure boat hulls, surfboards, skis, etc.

Gropius House is completed by architect Walter Gropius, whose new residence at Lincoln, Mass., gives new direction to residential architecture.

Taliesin West is completed at Paradise Valley outside Phoenix, Ariz., by Frank Lloyd Wright, whose new home will also serve as a teaching center (see 1911).

The Cloisters opens in New York's Tryon Park. A gift from the Rockefeller family to the Metropolitan Museum of Art, the medieval European nunnery is filled with art treasures that include a unicorn tapestry.

The Hardoy sling chair is introduced by New York's Knoll Associates, which also distributes the Barcelona chair of 1929 designed by Mies van der Rohe.

Olympic National Park is created by act of Congress to protect 896,660 acres of Pacific Northwest rain forest, glaciers, and meadows that support a herd of rare Roosevelt elk.

A Flood Control Act is passed by Congress to authorize public works on U.S. rivers and harbors.

A tropical hurricane strikes Long Island and much of New England without warning September 21, and in a few hours wreaks more havoc than the Chicago fire of 1871 or the San Francisco earthquake and fire of 1906. The storm takes 680 lives, destroys 2 billion trees, causes $400 million in property damage, and inflicts great and lasting environmental damage, but 60 colonies of beavers in New Jersey's Palisades Park busily man their dams through the blow and minimize flooding of 42,000 acres of land and highways.

An International Convention for the Regulation of Whaling institutes voluntary conservation quotas, but the killing of whales by Japanese, Norwegian, and Russian ships goes on virtually unabated.

Efforts are initiated to help salmon and steelhead trout ascend the Columbia River via fish "ladders" as the river's fishing industry is threatened by power dams, such as the year-old Bonneville dam, that have cut the fish off from spawning grounds.

Albacore tuna are found in large schools off the Oregon Coast, and salmon fishermen who have been supplying the Columbia River Packers Association since 1899 turn to tuna fishing (see Van Camp, 1926). The Packers Association adopts the brand name Bumble Bee for its canned tuna after having used it for years to identify its canned salmon and builds the first tuna cannery in the Northwest, setting it up alongside its salmon cannery at Astoria, Ore. (see 1945).

Restrictions on planting most U.S. crops are relaxed by a revised Agricultural Adjustment Act that even supplies farmers with lime and mineral fertilizers to increase yields. The new AAA begins direct crop-subsidy "parity" payments to farmers based on 1910–1914 farm prices.

The Commodity Credit Corporation established by the new AAA (above) supports U.S. farm prices by buying up surpluses for an "Ever-Normal Granary" designed to protect the nation against drought and plant diseases, to distribute surpluses among the needy, and to pay export subsidies that will encourage foreign sales by "equalizing" U.S. farm prices with lower world prices (see 1940 wheat exports; food stamps, 1939).

Arizona's 286-foot high Bartlett Dam is completed.

Florida's Fairchild Tropical Garden is founded at Coconut Grove to honor former U.S. Department of Agriculture botanist and worldwide agricultural explorer David Grandison Fairchild, 69, who retired 10 years ago after a 39-year career in which he brought back more than 200,000 plant specimens which included species important to U.S. agriculture. A son-in-law of the late Alexander Graham Bell, Fairchild continues his expeditions as an adviser to the U.S. Department of Agriculture.

Nicotinic acid (niacin) is found to prevent pellagra (see 1915; Elvehjem, 1936).

Enrichment of bread with the B_1 vitamin thiamine synthesized by Robert R. Williams 2 years ago is proposed at a scientific meeting in Toronto (see 1940).

Pantothenic acid is isolated by U.S. biochemist Roger John Williams, 45, brother of the thiamine pioneer. The minor B vitamin is present in many foods.

Vitamin E (alpha-tocopherol) is synthesized by Paul Karrer and is found to be an effective antioxidant (see Karrer, 1931; Evans, Emerson, 1935).

Studies of the chemistry of vision in poor light are begun by Harvard biologist George Wald, 31, who will show the importance of vitamin A in avoiding nyctalopia, or night blindness (see 1925; 1931).

The last reported U.S. case of "the milksick" occurs as dairies virtually wipe out the often fatal disease by pooling their milk from a variety of herds. Also called the slows or the trembles, the disease is transmitted in the milk of cows that have eaten white snakeroot (*Eupatorium rugosum*).

A new U.S. Food, Drug and Cosmetic Act updates the Pure Food and Drug Act of 1906 (see 1912; 1913; Tugwell, Schlink, 1933). The new law establishes standards of identity for most food products but while the possible basic ingredients of about 400 such products are required to be listed in the Code of Federal Regulations, only "optional" ingredients such as salt, sugar, and spices are required to be listed on labels. The new law is stricter than the old one, but it will be challenged on the grounds that it is still not sufficiently protective of consumers' health (see Delaney, 1950).

The Wheeler-Lea Act gives the Federal Trade Commission jurisdiction over advertising that may be false or misleading even if it does not represent unfair competition (see 1931). The FTC is given special powers to regulate advertising of foods, drugs, cosmetics, and therapeutic devices.

The American Chamber of Horrors by Ruth De Forest Lamb details abuses in the U.S. food industry.

U.S. consumption of beef and dairy products continues to increase by 2 to 3 percent as it has been doing each year through most of the decade.

A can of meat put up in 1824 is discovered. Its contents are fed to test rats with no observable ill effects.

The Cryovac deep-freezing method of food preservation is developed by the Boston firm of Dewey and Almy (*see* Birdseye, Seabrook, 1925).

Mott's apple juice is introduced by the Duffy-Mott Company (*see* 1930; Sunsweet prune juice, 1933).

Nescafé is introduced in Switzerland by the Nestlé Company, which has been asked by the Brazilian government to help find a solution to Brazil's coffee surpluses. Nestlé has spent 8 years in research to develop the instant coffee product (*see* G. Washington, 1906; 1909; Instant Maxwell House, 1942).

Teflon (above) has a low coefficient of friction that will make it popular as a coating for nonstick frying pans and other cooking utensils.

Detroit's London Chop House opens across from the Penobscot Building with steak dinners at 75 cents and scotch and soda at 25 cents. University of Michigan dropout Lester Gruber, 33, will be joined by his brother Samuel next year, and they will make the Chop House Detroit's leading bar and restaurant.

1939 World War II begins 1 week after the August 23 signing of a mutual nonaggression pact between Nazi Germany and Soviet Russia. Adolf Hitler has occupied Bohemia and Moravia, he has annexed Memel, his foreign minister Joachim von Ribbentrop, 46, signs the pact with Josef Stalin's new commissar of foreign affairs V. M. Molotov, and German troops and aircraft attack Poland September 1.

Britain and France declare war on Germany September 3 as a German U-boat sinks the British ship *Athenia* off the Irish Coast. H.M.S. *Courageous* is sunk September 19.

Soviet troops invade Poland from the east September 17, Warsaw surrenders to the Germans September 27, and Poland is partitioned September 28 between Germany and the U.S.S.R.

The Spanish Civil War has ended March 28 with the fall of Madrid to Francisco Franco. German and Italian forces have been withdrawn from Spain by late June, and Spain will be neutral in the new European war after having lost upwards of 410,000 in battle or by execution (more than 200,000 have died of starvation, disease, or malnutrition, and the death total is estimated by some at well over 1 million).

The Romanian premier Armand Calinescu is assassinated September 21 by members of the pro-Fascist Iron Guard (*see* 1940).

A British expeditionary force of 158,000 is in France by late September, but a U.S. nonintervention move-

ment is spearheaded by former president Herbert Hoover, who is supported by Theodore Roosevelt, Jr., by U.S. senator from Virginia Harry F. Byrd, by U.S. senator from Idaho William Borah, by U.S. senator from Montana Burton K. Wheeler, by Henry Ford, and by Charles A. Lindbergh.

Charles A. Lindbergh makes his first anti-intervention speech on U.S. radio September 17. He had been living abroad to escape publicity since the kidnapping and murder of his infant son in 1932 and the execution of the child's alleged killer in 1936, and he argues that Stalin is as much to be feared as Hitler (*see* 1938; 1941).

"I cannot forecast to you the action of Russia. It is a riddle wrapped in a mystery inside an enigma," says Winston Churchill October 1 in a radio broadcast. Churchill has been made first lord of the admiralty as of September 3 (*see* 1915; 1926; 1940).

Finland is invaded by Soviet troops November 30 (*see* 1940). Former president Herbert Hoover organizes a drive for Finnish relief December 5, and Congress grants Finland $10 million in credit for agricultural supplies.

The Hatch Act passed by Congress August 2 bars U.S. federal employees from taking an active role in political campaigns. The purpose of the measure is to keep party politics out of government agencies and prevent a return of the spoils system (*see* 1883).

The Battle of the River Plate December 13 off the South American coast ends with the British cruiser H.M.S. *Exeter* sustaining heavy damage from the guns of the German pocket battleship *Graf Spee* which is driven into Montevideo Harbor by the Exeter's sister cruisers H.M.S. *Ajax* and H.M.N.Z.S. *Achilles*. The *Graf Spee* is scuttled in the harbor December 17 by orders from Adolf Hitler to keep her from falling into British hands.

 German foreign minister von Ribbentrop sends a circular to diplomatic and consular offices January 25 under the title "The Jewish Question, a Factor in Our Foreign Policy for 1938": "It is not by chance that 1938, the year of our destiny, saw the realization of our plan for Greater Germany as well as a major step towards the solution of the Jewish problem.... The spread of Jewish influence and its corruption of our political, economic, and cultural life has perhaps done more to undermine the German people's will to prevail than all the hostility shown us by the Allied powers since the Great War. This disease in the body of our people had first to be eradicated before the Great German Reich could assemble its forces in 1938 to overcome the will of the world."

The S.S. *St. Louis* of the Hamburg-Amerika Line leaves Hamburg May 13 with 937 Jewish refugees from Nazi oppression and is the last major shipload to leave before the war begins. The passenger list has been approved by Joseph Goebbels, all passengers hold seemingly valid Cuban visas, but they are refused admission at Havana. The United States ac-

1939 (cont.) cepts 25,957 German immigrants per year under the Immigration Act of 1924 and refuses admittance to the passengers of the *St. Louis,* which heads back for Germany, but Britain, France, Belgium, and Holland agree at the last moment to admit the refugees.

An international conference to organize facilities for Jewish emigration is convened at Evian by President Roosevelt, delegates from 30 nations hold discussions, but nothing is accomplished.

The United Jewish Appeal (UJA) is founded at New York to raise funds for Jewish relief.

A British White Paper that in effect repudiates the Balfour Declaration of 1917 is issued by London, which rules Palestine under a League of Nations mandate (*see* 1938). Admissions to Palestine are limited to 50,000 for the next 5 years, and while the White Paper does authorize the admission of 25,000 Jewish refugees, it envisions the establishment of an independent nation that will be predominantly Arab with Jewish immigration restricted (*see* 1941).

The Jewish population of Europe is 9.5 million but will decline sharply in the next 6 years. Few will escape the holocaust that begins now for Czechoslovakian and Polish Jews who suffer at the hands of the Nazis as the German and Austrian Jews have suffered for the past year and more.

Marian Anderson tries to rent Constitution Hall at Washington, D.C., for a concert and is refused because of her race by the Daughters of the American Revolution, who own the hall. The 37-year-old black contralto has been acclaimed by many European critics as the world's greatest, she is supported by Eleanor Roosevelt and other DAR members who resign from the organization, and she draws an audience of 75,000 at the Lincoln Memorial Easter Sunday.

The possibility of self-sustaining nuclear fission is proved March 3 at Columbia University in New York by Enrico Fermi, Hungarian-American physicist Leo Szilard, 41, and their colleagues John Ray Dunning, 31, C. B. Pegram, and Walter N. Zinn, 32 (*see* 1938).

The nuclear research at Columbia (above) confirms European findings that the absorption of a neutron by a uranium nucleus sometimes causes the nucleus to split into approximately equal parts with the release of enormous amounts of energy. These findings by O. R. Frisch and L. Meitner last year are discussed by their Danish colleague Niels Bohr with Albert Einstein at Princeton, N.J., where the work at Columbia is also discussed (*see* Bohr, 1913; Einstein, 1929; U-235, 1940).

Albert Einstein writes to President Roosevelt, "Some recent work by E. Fermi and L. Szilard which has been communicated to me in manuscript leads me to expect that the element uranium may be turned into a new and important source of energy in the near future. Certain aspects of the situation which has arisen seem to call for watchfulness and, if necessary,

quick action on the part of the Administration. . . . In the course of the last four months it has been made almost certain . . . that it may become possible to set up a nuclear chain reaction in a large mass of uranium, by which vast amounts of power and large quantities of radium-like elements would be generated. . . . This new phenomenon would lead also to the construction of bombs."

An Advisory Committee on Uranium is appointed in the autumn by President Roosevelt after he is advised that German physicists have split the uranium nucleus by assaulting it with neutrons (*see* first controlled chain reaction, 1942).

Fluorescent lighting that is far less consuming of energy than incandescent lighting is introduced by General Electric Company, which has developed it with the advice of U.S. physicist Arthur Holly Compton, 47, of the University of Chicago.

U.S. chemist Linus Carl Pauling, 38, develops a resonance theory of chemical valence by which he has been able to construct models for a number of anomalous molecules, notably the benzene molecule, which have not been explainable by conventional chemical terms. Pauling has applied quantum mechanics to the problem of how atoms and molecules enter into chemical combination with each other, he produces a full account of chemical bonding, and his paper "The Nature of the Chemical Bond and the Structure of Molecules and Crystals" will win him a 1954 Nobel Prize (*see* Heisenberg, 1925; Dirac and Schrodinger, 1926).

The first commercial transatlantic passenger air service begins June 28 as 22 passengers and 12 crew members take off from Port Washington, N.Y., for Marseilles via the Azores and Lisbon aboard the Pan American Airways *Yankee Clipper,* a Boeing aircraft powered by four 1,550-horsepower Wright Cyclone engines (*see* 1935). Pan Am has been providing air service to the Caribbean, South America, and the Pacific but has been thwarted from starting the transatlantic service earlier by British-American diplomatic disputes over airport landing rights. The *Yankee Clipper* has separate passenger cabins, a dining salon, a ladies' dressing room, a recreation lounge, sleeping berths, and a bridal suite, the flight takes 26.5 hours, and the one-way fare is $375.

British Overseas Airways (BOAC) is created by a reorganization of Imperial Airways under the leadership of former BBC director J. C. W. Reith, who has been chairman of Imperial Airways since last year and who will be BOAC chairman until next year (*see* 1922; Imperial, 1924). Reith will be appointed minister of information, minister of transport, minister of works and buildings, and first commissioner of works.

The first turbojet aircraft is tested August 24 at Rostock-Marienehe and is demonstrated in October for high officials of the German Luftwaffe. The Heinkel He-178 with a centrifugal flow engine has been designed by Hans von Ohain.

British aircraft designers work on a jet plane that uses a turbojet engine designed in 1930 by Frank Whittle, whose Gloster-Whittle E.28/39 will be test flown for the first time in mid-May 1941.

Howard Hughes buys control of Transcontinental and Western Airlines (TWA) from the Wall Street banking house Lehman Brothers (*see* 1931; 1938). Hughes will develop TWA into Trans World Airways and will control it until 1966, by which time he will have expanded his patrimony into a fortune of $1.5 billion and will have made TWA a transatlantic competitor of Pan American (above).

Allegheny Airlines is founded. It will grow to become the sixth largest U.S. domestic passenger line.

New York's La Guardia Airport opens in the fall under the name North Beach Airport (*see* Newark, 1928; Idlewild, 1948).

Republic Aviation Corporation is created by a reorganization of Seversky Aircraft (*see* 1931; 1942).

The first American-made helicopter is flown by Igor Sikorsky, now 50, who has been in the United States since 1919 and who has made the helicopter for United Aircraft Corporation at Bridgeport, Conn. (*see* Chance Vought, 1929).

Lear, Inc., is founded by William P. Lear (*see* 1924). The company will fill more than $100 million worth of contracts in the next 6 years, supplying aircraft navigation devices developed by Lear (*see* 1962).

The first PT boats are completed for the Finnish navy by Higgins Industries, Inc., of New Orleans, a firm started under the name Higgins Lumber & Export in 1922 by Andrew Jackson Higgins, now 53, whose 1931 *Dixie Greyhound* riverboat traveled 1,150 miles upriver to St. Louis in 72 hours despite delays caused by propellers bent on submerged logs. Higgins will build PT (propeller torpedo) boats for the British and U.S. navies beginning next year, and in 1942 the company will be given a $385 million order for upwards of 200 Liberty ships.

The Trans-Iranian Railway is completed in January after nearly 12 years of construction to link the Caspian Sea with the Persian Gulf. The new railway has been built entirely with Iranian capital.

The Pacemaker goes into service on the New York Central for the Chicago run with a fare of just over $30 round trip in fancy coaches.

The Trail Blazer goes into service on the Pennsylvania Railroad to compete with the New York Central on the Chicago run.

U.S. interurban streetcar trackage falls to 2,700 miles as buses replace trolleys (*see* 1917; General Motors, 1932; criminal conspiracy conviction, 1949).

New York's Bronx-Whitestone Bridge opens to connect the Bronx with Queens and to facilitate access to the new La Guardia Airport (above) and to the World's Fair that opens in April. The new bridge is 701 meters in length.

Connecticut's Merritt Parkway opens in June with 38 miles of landscaped road winding through Fairfield County to link New York's Hutchinson River Parkway with Milford.

The Lincoln Mercury is introduced by Ford Motor Company's Edsel Ford (*see* Continental, 1941).

Fewer than 60 percent of U.S. families own automobiles. The figure will rise to 80 percent by 1964.

General Motors, Ford, and Chrysler are each indicted for attempting to monopolize the U.S. automobile financing market by allegedly coercing dealers to use GMAC, Ford, or Chrysler financing facilities (*see* GMAC, 1919). The indictments against Ford and Chrysler are dropped in exchange for promises that they will stop coercing their dealers if GM is convicted, but while that conviction will be handed down in 1941, GM will not be required to give up its GMAC subsidiary, nor will Ford or Chrysler be obliged to divest itself of its financing subsidiary. By the mid-1950s, GMAC will be the world's largest auto-financing company and will be averaging 18.7 percent per year in net profits.

 A pilot plant for making synthetic rubber is opened by U.S. chemist Bradley Dewey of 1921 canning technology fame, who has conducted research on rubberlike elastomers and who will complete one of the first U.S. synthetic rubber plants in 1942 (*see* Semon, 1926; Goodrich tire, 1940).

Synthetic rubber research is resumed by Union Carbide and Carbon Corporation which acquires the Bakelite Corporation and pursues studies of butadiene as a source of synthetic rubber (*see* Bakelite, 1909; Dow, Goodyear, 1940).

Permanente Cement Company is founded by industrialist Henry J. Kaiser of 1937 Bonneville Dam fame to supply materials for the Shasta Dam that he will complete in 1945 (*see* shipyards, 1941).

Stuka dive bombers of the German Luftwaffe rained death and destruction on European cities in World War II.

1939 (cont.) Nylon is introduced commercially by E. I. du Pont (*see* Carothers, 1937; first nylon stockings, 1940).

Hewlett-Packard, Inc., is founded by California engineers William Redington Hewlett, 26, and David Packard, 27, whose firm will become the leading U.S. producer of electronic instruments.

 Britain's richest 10 percent holds 88 percent of the nation's wealth, down from 92 percent in 1912. The top 10 percent commands 34.6 percent of the nation's after-tax personal income (*see* 1946).

France is hardly any richer than she was in 1914 and is ill-prepared to fight a war (*see* 1940).

Seventeen percent of the U.S. work force remains largely unemployed, but while the actual number of unemployed men and women has fallen from 15 million in 1933 down to 9.5 million, even Americans with jobs have relatively low average incomes.

Somewhat more than 4 million Americans declare incomes above $2,000 for the year, 200,000 declare incomes of more than $10,000, 42,500 declare incomes of more than $25,000. Only 3 percent of the population has enough income to pay income tax at all, and 670,000 taxpayers account for 90 percent of all income taxes collected.

Your Income Tax by New York accountant J. K. (Jacob Kay) Lasser, 42, helps Americans understand and prepare their tax returns.

U.S. Steel Corporation reports a net income of $41 million on sales of $857 million after a 1938 deficit (*see* 1964). The average U.S. Steel employee has worked an average of just over 25 hours per week at an average wage of just under 90 cents per hour, and his average wage of about $1,600 per year is $100 more than the average earned by General Motors Corporation employees. Both companies employ roughly 220,000 people.

The Oxford Group's Moral Rearmament movement gains a wide following in Britain (*see* 1921).

A rabies epidemic begins in Poland and spreads among foxes, bats, and other mammals, including dogs and cows. By 1950 the disease will be in Germany, it will advance at the rate of about 25 miles per year, and the first case of a rabid dog in more than 50 years in Britain will be reported in 1969.

French-American bacteriologist René Jules Dubos, 38, at the Rockefeller Institute for Medical Research, isolates two agents from swamp soil that are effective against a broad spectrum of gram-positive bacteria but are too toxic for internal use by humans. Dubos isolates tyrocidine and gramicidine, establishing procedures that his former teacher Selman A. Waksman will adopt (*see* streptomycin, 1943; penicillin, 1940).

Opening ceremonies of the New York World's Fair at Flushing Meadows in April are telecast by the National Broadcasting Company. The telecast is picked up by from 100 to 200 experimental receivers set up in the New York metropolitan area and is seen by 1,000 viewers (*see* 1945; BBC, 1936).

"Sooner than you realize it, television will play a vital part in the life of the average American," say advertisements for the World's Fair telecast (above) placed by Du Mont Television Receivers, Inc., a division of Allen B. Du Mont Laboratories, Inc., at Clifton, N.J., started in 1931 by former De Forest Radio chief engineer Allen Balcom Du Mont, now 38 (*see* 1948).

FM radio receivers are put on the market for the first time (*see* Armstrong, 1933; Zenith, 1940).

Some 27.5 million U.S. families have radios, up from 10 million in 1929, and 45 million sets are in use in the United States.

"This is London," says CBS correspondent Edward R. Murrow, 31, who ends his broadcasts with the tagline "Goodnight and good luck." Murrow's will become the best known voice on U.S. radio in the next 7 years.

Peabody Awards are inaugurated by the Georgia University School of Journalism for "recognition of outstanding public service by stations, networks and individuals in broadcasting." The awards are named in memory of the late Georgia-born banker-philanthropist George Foster Peabody, who died last year at age 86 after a postretirement career of promoting educational work in the South.

The Parker 51 fountain pen is introduced by the Parker Pen Company of Janesville, Wis., which has been headed since 1933 by Kenneth Parker, 44. He has helped design the sleek new pen (*see* 1921).

"Batman" is launched by U.S. cartoonist Bob Kane, whose comic-book hero is accompanied by a youthful Robin and will soon be syndicated to newspapers.

Glamour magazine is launched in April by Street & Smith Publications, Inc. to reach working women beyond the age of its 4-year-old *Mademoiselle*.

Saturday Review of Literature editor George Stevens hires Norman Cousins, 27, as executive editor in December. Cousins has been managing editor of *Current History,* he will be named editor of the *Saturday Review* in 1942, he will get new financial backing from Dallas petroleum geologist Everett Lee De Golyer, and he will make the biweekly more than a literary review.

 Pocket Books, Inc., Americanizes the paperback revolution in publishing begun by Britain's Penguin Books in 1936. The new paperback house started by Robert de Graff and Simon & Schuster puts out 25-cent reprints of major and minor literary classics using enormous and fast new rubber-plate rotary presses that permit printing of paperbacks in large economical quantities at a unit cost of pennies. Most authors, agents, and hardcover publishers agree to permit paperback reprints, but Willa Cather will stipulate in her will when she dies in 1947 that none of her books may be issued in paperback (*see* Avon, 1941; Popular Library, 1942; Bantam, 1945).

Nonfiction *Language in Action* by Canadian-American semanticist S. I. (Samuel Ichiye) Hayakawa, 33, whose lucid popularization will be retitled *Language in Thought and Action*.

Fiction *Finnegans Wake* by James Joyce, who will die of a perforated ulcer in 1941 and whose allegory has epic dimension but is too difficult for wide readership; *On the Marble Cliffs* (*Auf den Marmorklippen*) by Ernst Jünger, whose allegorical novel is a protest against Germany's Nazis; *Mister Johnson* by Anglo-Irish novelist Joyce Cary, 51; *Alberte* (trilogy) by Norwegian novelist Cora Sandel (Jara Fabricius), 59; *The Grapes of Wrath* by John Steinbeck, whose novel is based on observations made while traveling with migrant farm families from the Oklahoma Dust Bowl, produces a reaction almost comparable to that of *Uncle Tom's Cabin* in 1852 and will win a 1940 Pulitzer Prize; *The Day of the Locust* by Nathanael West, who portrays the moral degeneration of Hollywood where he has been employed as a screenwriter since 1936 (West will be killed in an automobile accident near El Centro, Calif., in late December of next year at age 37); *The Web and the Rock* by the late Thomas Wolfe, who died in mid-September of last year at age 37 but whose manuscripts are in the hands of Harper & Brothers editor Edward Aswell, who will work them into two further novels; *Night Rider* by U.S. novelist-poet Robert Penn Warren, now 34; *Wind, Sand and Stars* by Antoine de Saint-Exupéry; *Goodbye to Berlin* by Christopher Isherwood; *How Green Was My Valley* by British novelist Richard Llewellyn (Richard David Vivian Llewellyn Lloyd); *Mrs. Miniver* by English novelist-poet Jan Struther (Joyce Mastone Anstruther Graham), 38; *Black Narcissus* by English novelist Rumer Godden (Mrs. Laurence Foster), 30; *Hangover Square* by English novelist Patrick Hamilton, 34; *Party Going* by Henry Green; *Love and Death* by English novelist Llewelyn Powys, who dies of tuberculosis at age 55; *The Girls* (*Les Jeunes Filles*) by Henry de Montherlant; *Tropic of Capricorn* by Henry Miller; *Pale Horse, Pale Rider* (stories) by Katherine Anne Porter; *Wickford Point* by John P. Marquand; *Mask of Dimitrios* by Eric Ambler (*A Coffin for Dimitrios* in the United States); *The Big Sleep* by U.S. detective novelist Raymond Thornton Chandler, 51, who introduces the private eye Philip Marlowe.

Poetry *Autumn Journal* by Louis MacNeice; *Occasions* (*le occasioni*) by Eugenio Montale; *Human Poems* (*Poemas humanas*) by César Vallejo; *Return to My Native Land* (*Cahier d'un retour au pays natal*) by Martinique poet Aimé Césaire, 26; *A Heart for the Gods of Mexico* by Conrad Aiken.

Juvenile *Madeline* by Austrian-American novelist Ludwig Bemelmans, 41, who illustrates his own work (which will outlive his new novel *Hotel Splendide*); *Mike Mulligan and His Steam Shovel* by U.S. author Virginia Lee Burton.

 New York's Museum of Modern Art (MOMA) moves into a handsome new building at 11 West 53rd Street (*see* 1929).

Grandma Moses gains overnight fame after engineer-art collector Louis Caldor sees work by the primitivist Anna Mary Robertson, 79, displayed in a drugstore window at Hoosick Falls, N.Y. Caldor drives to Robertson's farm, buys all 15 of her paintings, and exhibits three of them at the new Museum of Modern Art (above) in a show entitled "Contemporary Unknown Painters." Grandma Moses will continue painting until shortly before her death at age 101 in December 1961.

Other paintings *Ubermut* by Paul Klee; *Poison* and *Objective Stimulation* by René Magritte; *Seated Man* by Willem de Kooning; *Persephone, Susannah and the Elders, Threshing Wheat, Roasting Ears,* and *Weighing Cotton* by Thomas Hart Benton; *John Brown* by John Steuart Curry; *Handball* by Ben Shahn; *Retrato de Pita Amor* by Diego Rivera.

 Theater *The White Steed* by Paul Vincent Carroll 1/10 at New York's Cort Theater, with Barry Fitzgerald, Jessica Tandy, George Coulouris, 136 perfs.; *The American Way* by George S. Kaufman and Moss Hart 1/21 at New York's Center Theater in Rockefeller Center, with Fredric March, Florence Eldridge, 164 perfs.; *The Little Foxes* by Lillian Hellman 2/15 at New York's National Theater, with Tallulah Bankhead, Carl Benton Reid, Dan Duryea, Patricia Collinge, 191 perfs.; *Family Portrait* by Lenore Coffee and William Joyce Cowan 3/8 at New York's Morosco Theater, with Judith Anderson, Philip Truex, 111 perfs.; *The Philadelphia Story* by Philip Barry 3/28 at New York's Shubert Theater, with Katharine Hepburn, Lenore Lonergan, Shirley Booth, Van Heflin, Joseph Cotten, 96 perfs.; *My Heart's in the Highlands* by William Saroyan 4/13 at New York's Guild Theater, 43 perfs.; *No Time for Comedy* by S. N. Behrman 4/17 at New York's Ethel Barrymore Theater, with Katherine Cornell, Laurence Olivier, Margalo Gilmore, 185 perfs.; *After the Dance* by Terence Ratigan 6/21 at the St. James's Theatre, London; *Ondine* by Jean Genet 8/3 at the Théâtre de l'Athenée, Paris; *Skylark* by Samson Raphaelson 10/11 at New York's Belasco Theater, with Gertrude Lawrence, 250 perfs.; *The Man Who Came to Dinner* by George S. Kaufman and Moss Hart 10/25 at New York's Music Box Theater, with Monty Wooley as Sheridan Whiteside and with Cole Porter's song "What Am I to Do," 739 perfs.; *The Time of Your Life* by William Saroyan 10/25 at New York's Booth Theater, with Eddie Dowling, Julie Haydon, Gene Kelly, Celeste Holm, William Bendix, Reginald Beane, 185 perfs., Pulitzer Prize; *Margin for Error* by Clare Booth 11/3 at New York's Plymouth Theater, with Otto Ludwig Preminger, 264 perfs.; *Life with Father* by Howard Lindsay and Russel Crouse 11/8 at New York's Empire Theater, with Lindsay and Dorothy Stickney in a comedy based on the book by Clarence Day, 3,244 perfs. (a new record); *Key Largo* by Maxwell Anderson 11/27 at New York's Ethel Barrymore Theater,

1939 (cont.) with Jose Ferrer, Paul Muni, Uta Hagen, 105 perfs.; *Mornings at Seven* by U.S. playwright Paul Osborn 11/30 at New York's Longacre Theater, with Dorothy Gish, Russell Collins, Enid Marley, 44 perfs.

W. C. Fields is honored February 16 by a banquet at the Masquer's Club in Hollywood with guests who include Groucho Marx, Bob Hope, Jack Benny, Edgar Bergen, Milton Berle, Red Skelton, George Burns, and writer-sociologist Leo Rosten. Asked to say something following the eulogy by William Collier, Sr., Rosten says, "The only thing I can say about W. C. Fields, whom I have admired since the day he advanced upon Baby LeRoy with an ice pick, is this: any man who hates dogs and babies can't be all bad."

Films Victor Fleming's *Gone with the Wind* with Vivien Leigh as Scarlett O'Hara, Clark Gable as Rhett Butler, Leslie Howard as Ashley Wilkes, Olivia de Havilland as Melanie Hamilton. Produced by David O. Selznick with a screenplay by Sidney Howard based on the 1936 novel by Margaret Mitchell, GWTW has its world premiere December 15 at Atlanta, it runs 222 minutes and must be interrupted with an intermission.

Other films Jean Renoir's *The Rules of the Game* (*La Regle du Jeu*); Marcel Carne's *Daybreak* (*Le Jour Se Leve*) with Jean Gabin, Jules Berry, Arlette; Ernst Lubitsch's *Ninotchka* with Greta Garbo; George Cukor's *The Women* with Joan Crawford, Norma Shearer, Paulette Goddard, Rosalind Russell, Joan Fontaine, Hedda Hopper; Edmund Goulding's *The Old Maid* with Bette Davis, Miriam Hopkins; Edmund Goulding's *Dark Victory* with Bette Davis, George Brent, Humphrey Bogart, Ronald Reagan; John Ford's *Stagecoach* with John Wayne, Claire Trevor; William Wellman's *Beau Geste* with Gary Cooper, Brian Donlevy, Ray Milland, Robert Preston, Susan Hayward; George Stevens's *Gunga Din* with Cary Grant, Douglas Fairbanks, Jr., Victor McLaglen, Sam Jaffe; Zoltan Korda's *Four Feathers* with Ralph Richardson, C. Aubrey Smith, June Duprez, Clive Baxter; Carol Reed's *The Stars Look Down* with Michael Redgrave, Margaret Lockwood, Emlyn Williams; Sidney Lanfield's *The Hound of the Baskervilles* with Basil Rathbone, Nigel Bruce; Anatole Litvak's *Confessions of a Nazi Spy* with George Sanders, Francis Lederer; William Dieterle's *Juarez* with Paul Muni; Gregory Ratoff's *Intermezzo* with Ingrid Bergman in a remake of a successful 1936 film with Bergman; William Wyler's *Wuthering Heights* with Laurence Olivier, Merle Oberon; Sam Wood's *Goodbye, Mr. Chips* with Robert Donat, Greer Garson; William Dieterle's *The Hunchback of Notre Dame* with Charles Laughton; Lewis Milestone's *Of Mice and Men* with Burgess Meredith, Lon Chaney, Jr.; Henry King's *Stanley and Livingstone* with Spencer Tracy; George Marshall's *Destry Rides Again* with James Stewart, Marlene Dietrich; Frank Capra's *Mr. Smith Goes to Washington* with Gary Cooper, Jean Arthur; John Ford's *Young Mr. Lincoln* with Henry Fonda; Herbert Wilcox's *Nurse Edith Cavell* with Anna Neagle in a remake of his 1928 silent film *Dawn* that was banned by the British government.

Hollywood musicals Victor Fleming's *The Wizard of Oz* with Judy Garland (Frances Gumm, 17), Ray Bolger, Bert Lahr, Jack Haley, Frank Morgan, Margaret Hamilton, music by Harold Arlen, lyrics by E. Y. Harburg, songs that include "Somewhere Over the Rainbow," "Follow the Yellow Brick Road," "We're Off to See the Wizard"; Ray Enright's *Going Places* with Dick Powell, Ronald Reagan, Anita Louise, music by Harry Warren, lyrics by Johnny Mercer, songs that include "Jeepers Creepers."

Radio music *The Dinah Shore Show* 8/6 on NBC Blue Network stations with singer Dinah Shore.

Broadcast Music, Inc. (BMI) is founded October 14 by U.S. radio networks to build "an alternate source of music suitable for broadcasting" in competition with the ASCAP monopoly founded in 1914 (*see* 1917). ASCAP has boosted its license fees and the networks balk at paying the higher fees (*see* 1940).

Broadway musicals *The Streets of Paris* 6/19 at the Broadhurst Theater, with Brazilian Carmen Miranda singing "South American Way," music by Jimmy McHugh and others, lyrics by Al Dubin and others, 274 perfs.; *George White's Scandals* 8/28 at the Alvin Theater, with Willie and Eugene Howard, Ben Blue, Ann Miller, Ella Logan, the Three Stooges in the 13th and final edition of the *Scandals*, music by Sammy Fain, lyrics by Jack Yellen, songs that include "Are You Having Any Fun," 120 perfs.; *Too Many Girls* 10/18 at the Imperial Theater, with Desi Arnaz, Eddie Bracken, Van Johnson, Richard Kollmar, Marcy Wescott, music by Richard Rodgers, lyrics by Lorenz Hart, songs that include "I Didn't Know What Time It Was," 249 perfs.; *Very Warm for May* 11/17 at the Alvin Theater, with Grace McDonald, Jack Whiting, Eve Arden, June Allyson, Vera Ellen, music by Jerome Kern, lyrics by Oscar Hammerstein II, songs that include "All the Things You Are," 59 perfs.; *Du Barry Was a Lady* 12/6 at the 46th Street Theater, with Bert Lahr, Ethel Merman, Betty Grable, music and lyrics by Cole Porter, songs that include "Friendship," "Do I Love You?," 408 perfs.

First performances Sonata No. 1 for Piano and Orchestra (*Concord*) by Charles Ives (who wrote it between 1911 and 1915) 1/20 at New York's Town Hall; Symphony No. 3 by Roy Harris 2/24 at Boston's Symphony Hall; Concerto No. 2 for Violin and Orchestra by Béla Bartók 4/23 at Amsterdam (Bartók flees the Germans in the fall); Symphony No. 6 by Dmitri Shostakovich 12/3 at Moscow.

Oratorio *Joan of Arc at the Stake* (*Jeanne d'Arc au bucher*) 5/6 at the Théâtre Municipal, Orleans, with music by Arthur Honegger, libretto by Paul Claudel.

Frank Sinatra joins bandleader Harry James to sing with a new band that James is assembling. The 23-year-old New Jersey roadhouse singer will leave within a year to join the Tommy Dorsey band, he will break his contract with Dorsey in 1942, and he will take an 8-week engagement at New York's Paramount Theater to begin a career as idol of teenage "bobby-soxers."

Popular songs "There'll Always Be an England" by English songwriters Ross Parker and Hughie Clark; "I'll Never Smile Again" by U.S. songwriter Ruth Lowe, a former pianist in an all-girl band who has written the song in memory of her late husband; "Heaven Can Wait" by Jimmy Van Heusen, lyrics by Eddie De Lange; "And the Angels Sing" by trumpet player Ziggy Elman (Harry Finkelman), who has adapted a Jewish folk tune, lyrics by Johnny Mercer; "Ciribiribin" by composer A. Pestalozza, who has adapted an Italian folk tune, lyrics by Jack Lawrence (bandleader-trumpet player Harry James promotes the song); "Undecided" by U.S. bandleader Charlie Shavers, lyrics by Sid Robin; "Moonlight Serenade" by Glenn Miller, lyrics by Mitchell Parish (see 1938); "In the Mood" by Joe Garland, lyrics by Andy Razaf; "All or Nothing at All" by Arthur Altman, lyrics by Jack Lawrence; "The Lady's in Love with You" by Burton Lane, lyrics by Frank Loesser; "Scatterbrain" by Kahn Keene, Carl Bean, Frankie Masters, lyrics by Johnny Burke; "South of the Border" by Jimmy Kennedy and Michael Carr; "Three Little Fishes" by Saxie Dowell.

Rudolph the Red-Nosed Reindeer by a Montgomery Ward advertising copywriter is printed up with illustrations, and some 2.3 million copies of the story in verse are given away (see 1949).

Ted Williams is brought up to the Boston Red Sox to begin a brilliant career as outfielder and hitter. The 20-year-old Theodore Samuel Williams started with the San Diego Padres at age 16, he was acquired by the Red Sox for their farm club 2 years later, and he will play 19 seasons for Boston. His 1941 batting average of .406 will be the highest since the 1924 Rogers Hornsby record of .424 and his lifetime batting average for 2,292 games will be .344.

Mel Allen begins broadcasting Yankee baseball games for New York's CBS radio station at age 26. Allen will be the "voice of the Yankees" for 25 years and will be famous for his "going, going, gone" and his "how about that!" but New York has been the last city to permit broadcasting big league games on a daily basis, and it has taken *Journal-American* sportswriter Bill Slocum, Jr., to persuade club owners that broadcasting the games will not hurt attendance (the broadcasts will actually boost attendance).

Yankee "Iron Horse" Lou Gehrig is stricken with a rare and fatal form of paralysis (amyotropic lateral sclerosis), takes himself out of the lineup April 30, travels to the Mayo Clinic for examination, and bids a tearful farewell to Yankee fans July 4 with a lifetime batting average of .340. Gehrig is appointed a New York City parole commissioner by Mayor La Guardia and will serve until his death in early June 1941.

The New York Yankees win the World Series by defeating the Cincinnati Reds 4 games to 0.

A Baseball Hall of Fame is established at Cooperstown, N.Y., to celebrate the "centennial" of the national pastime. Players honored by installation in the Hall of Fame are all deceased with the exception of Connie Mack, now 76, whose Philadelphia Athletics have won five World Series since he assumed management of the team in 1901.

Football helmets are made mandatory in U.S. college football competition (see NCAA, 1906).

University of Chicago president Robert M. Hutchins stuns the athletic world by announcing that the university is quitting the Big 10 Conference and abandoning intercollegiate football.

Cup-sizing for brassieres is introduced by the Warner Brothers Company of Bridgeport, Conn., whose designer Leona Gross Lax, 48, has developed the concept (see 1914).

Philadelphia Inquirer publisher Moses L. Annenberg is indicted by a federal grand jury at Chicago for having evaded $1.26 million in income taxes between 1932 and 1936 (see 1936). Including interest and penalties, Annenberg owes the government more than $5.5 million in the largest case of tax evasion in history, he will pay $9.5 million in taxes, penalties, and future interest, and he will serve time in federal prison at Lewisburg, Pa., until shortly before his death in July 1942 (see Seventeen, 1944).

Al Capone is released from prison, but his mind has been destroyed by syphilis while in Alcatraz (see 1931). The gangster retires to his estate at Miami Beach and will vegetate there until his death in 1947.

Pall Mall cigarettes in a new 85-millimeter length are the first U.S. "king-sized" cigarettes. American Tobacco Company's George Washington Hill lengthens the 2-year-old brand to make it 15-millimeters longer than other cigarettes and claims that the longer length "travels the smoke, and makes it mild."

Tabakmissbrauch und Lungencarcinom by German physician F. H. Muller relates smoking to lung cancer (see Pearl, 1938; Ochsner, 1945).

The Johnson Wax Research Tower designed by Frank Lloyd Wright is completed at Racine, Wis.

U.S. motels and tourist courts number 13,500, while the country has 14,000 year-round hotels each with 25 guest rooms or more. The number of motels will increase to more than 41,000 in the next 20 years as America embraces the automobile culture and the number of year-round hotels will fall to just over 10,000 (see Holiday Inns, 1952).

Earthquakes kill thousands in Chile.

Parker Dam is completed across the Colorado River near Parker, Ariz., as part of the $220 million Colorado River Aqueduct System which taps 1 billion gallons of water per day from the river, lifts it nearly one-quarter of a mile high, and transports it across 330 miles of desert and mountain to the 3,900-square mile Metropolitan Water District of Los Angeles (see

1939 (cont.) Mulholland, 1908). Located 155 miles below the 3-year-old Boulder Dam, the new $13 million project has been built up from 234 feet below the river bed.

 DDT is introduced as a persistent low-cost hydrocarbon pesticide developed by Swiss chemist Paul Muller, 40, of the Geigy Company and is applied almost immediately and with great success against the Colorado potato beetle which is threatening Switzerland's potato crop (*see* 1943; Zeidler, 1873; typhus, 1944; Osborne, 1948; Carson, 1962).

Japanese beetles menace crops in much of the United States (*see* 1916).

Nearly 25 percent of Americans are still on the land, but the average farm family has a cash income of only $1,000 per year.

Germany has stockpiles of 8.5 million tons of grain as World War II begins (above).

Russia is obligated under the August 23 nonaggression treaty pact (above) to supply Germany with 1 million tons of wheat per year and to expedite delivery of Manchurian soybeans.

 The first U.S. food stamp program is instituted in May by the U.S. Department of Agriculture to feed the needy of Rochester, N.Y. The program will continue until 1943 (*see* 1964).

Britain imposes rationing of meat, bacon, cheese, fats, sugar, and preserves in fixed quantities per capita, allocating supplies equally and keeping prices at levels people can afford. Britain is the largest buyer of food in the world market, absorbing 40 percent of all food sold in international trade.

 British bread and margarine are enriched and fortified with vitamins and minerals. Britons increase consumption of milk, potatoes, cheese, and green vegetables.

The American Institute of Nutrition revives the idea of fortifying staple foods with vitamins and minerals (*see* 1936; 1941).

Fluoridation of U.S. drinking water is urged by C. J. Cox of Pittsburgh's Mellon Institute (*see* Dean, 1933; Grand Rapids, Newburgh, 1945).

Zinc is shown to be an essential trace element. British biochemists David Keilin and T. Mann demonstrate that the mineral is essential to the human enzyme carbonic anhydrase, which is needed by the body to eliminate carbon dioxide waste.

 Consolidated Foods, Inc., has its beginnings as Montreal shoe-wholesaler Nathan Cummings, 42, takes an option to buy a Baltimore sugar and coffee wholesaler for $1.2 million. Cummings will exercise the option in 1941 and will begin an amalgam of food retailers and processors under the name Consolidated Groceries (*see* 1951; 1954).

The first precooked frozen foods are introduced under the Birds Eye label by General Foods Corporation, which markets a chicken fricasee and criss-cross steak (*see* 1931). Competitors come out within the year with frozen creamed chicken, beef stew, and roast turkey (*see* Morton Packing, 1940).

A 5-minute Cream of Wheat is introduced to compete with quick-cooking Quaker Oats, which reduced its cooking time in 1922 from 15 minutes to 5 (*see* 1902).

Lay's potato chips are introduced by Atlanta's H. W. Lay Company founded by Herman Warden Lay, 30, who has taken over the Barrett Food Products Company for which he was a route salesman in 1932 (*see* Frito-Lay, 1961).

Rights to Smirnoff Vodka are acquired for $14,000 by G. F. Heublein & Bro. of Hartford, Conn. (*see* 1892). John G. Martin, 33, who heads the company, is the English-American grandson of Heublein founder Gilbert F. Heublein, he has helped bring the company back into the liquor business in the past 6 years, and he employs Russian émigré Rudolph Kunett, whose Smirnoff Company has been grossing $36,000 per year but is close to bankruptcy (*see* 1946).

Pepsi-Cola challenges Coca-Cola with a radio jingle written for $2,500 by Bradley Kent and Austen Herbert Croom to the old English hunting song "D'ye Ken John Peel": "Pepsi-Cola hits the spot/ Twelve full ounces, that's a lot/ Twice as much for a nickel, too/ Pepsi-Cola is the drink for you" (*see* 1934; 1949).

San Francisco's Top o' the Mark opens in May atop the 13-year-old Mark Hopkins Hotel, which was built without a bar because of Prohibition. Copper magnate Daniel C. Jackling has given up his 19th floor penthouse suite, builder George D. Smith has persuaded the board of directors to invest $100,000 in remodeling the space, and the fancy bar earns back the $100,000 in 3 months and 20 days as visitors flock to the Top o' the Mark.

French restaurateur Henri Soulé, 36, arrives at New York to operate the French Pavilion restaurant at the World's Fair (above; *see* Pavillon restaurant, 1941).

Thanksgiving Day is celebrated November 23—the fourth Thursday in the month rather than the last Thursday. Federated Department Stores chief Fred Lazarus, Jr., has persuaded President Roosevelt that a longer Christmas shopping season will help the economy, the president has changed the date by proclamation, and within a few years most states will enact legislation making November's fourth Thursday Thanksgiving Day (*see* 1863; Federated, 1929).

 The population of Palestine (above) reaches 1.4 million, including 900,000 Moslems, 400,000 Jews, 100,000 Christians (*see* 1948).

A U.S. Census Bureau official predicts that the U.S. population will increase from its present level of 131 million to a peak of 136 million and will then begin a long, gradual decline that will bring it down to 126 million by 1980 (*see* Pearl, 1921).

1940   The fall of France, Belgium, the Netherlands, Luxembourg, Denmark, Norway, and Romania to the Germans leaves Britain and Russia dependent on

950

U.S. aid to resist the Nazi attempt at world domination (*see* below).

Soviet Russia takes 16,173 square miles of Finland and annexes the Baltic nations Estonia, Latvia, and Lithuania with German concurrence (*see* below).

German troops seize Denmark and Norway in April a few weeks after peace is concluded between Finland and the U.S.S.R. A Nazi government is set up at Oslo under Norwegian Nazi Vidkun Quisling, 52, but native resistance elements work to frustrate the Quisling regime.

The *Blitzkrieg* (lightning war) that begins May 10 rains destruction on Rotterdam and other Dutch cities from the air while German armies sweep without warning into the Lowlands. They cross the Meuse at Sedan May 12, Rotterdam surrenders May 13, Wilhelmina and her court escape to London, the Dutch armies surrender May 14, and the German mechanized divisions race into Belgium and northern France toward the Channel ports, cutting off British and Belgian forces in Flanders from the collapsing French forces under General Maxime Weygand, 72, who has taken command as commander in chief.

Winston Churchill succeeds Neville Chamberlain as Britain's prime minister after Chamberlain's resignation May 7 following bitter attacks in the House of Commons. "I have nothing to offer but blood, toil, tears, and sweat," Churchill tells the Commons May 13, but he makes clear the British objective: "Victory: victory at all costs, victory in spite of all terror, victory however long and hard the road may be: for without victory there is no survival."

Amiens and Arras fall to the Germans May 21, Belgium capitulates May 28, and evacuation of British and French troops from Dunkirk begins May 29.

"We shall not flag or fail," says Prime Minister Churchill to the Commons June 4: "We shall fight in France, we shall fight on the seas and oceans, we shall fight with growing confidence and growing strength in the air, we shall defend our island, whatever the cost may be, we shall fight on the beaches, we shall fight on the landing grounds, we shall fight in the fields and in the streets, we shall fight in the hills; we shall never surrender."

Dunkirk is evacuated by June 4 after 5 days of frenzied efforts to take some 200,000 British troops and 140,000 French from the beaches before they can be captured by the advancing Germans. Ships and small boats of all sorts are employed to ferry the men across the Channel to England, but 30,000 are killed or taken prisoner.

Italy declares war on France and Britain June 10. "The hand that held the dagger has plunged it into the back of her neighbor," says President Roosevelt.

German troops enter Paris June 14, a French appeal for U.S. aid is declined June 15 as the French fortress at Verdun falls to the Germans, France's head of state Paul Reynaud is replaced June 16 by Marshal Henri-Philippe Petain, and the 83-year-old Petain asks for an armistice a day later.

France signs an armistice with Hitler June 22 at Compiègne and signs an armistice with Mussolini June 24 as the French capital moves to Vichy.

Soviet troops have moved into Estonia, Latvia, and Lithuania beginning June 17 following an ultimatum that charged the Baltic countries with hostile activities. They are incorporated into the U.S.S.R. July 21.

Soviet troops invade Romania June 27 after Carol II has refused demands to cede Bessarabia and Bukovina to the U.S.S.R. Berlin rejects Carol's appeals for aid (*see* below).

French fleets at Oran in North Africa are sunk July 3 by the Royal Navy and France's Vichy government breaks off relations with Britain 2 days later.

Night bombing of German targets by the Royal Air Force begins July 9 as Hitler's Luftwaffe intensifies air attacks on Britain. Ninety German bombers are shot down over Britain between July 15 and July 21, and 180 German planes are shot down August 15 as the Battle of Britain reaches its peak, with Spitfires attacking Stukas (*Sturzkampflugzeng*) equipped with wind-whistles to terrify the populace.

"Never in the field of human conflict was so much owed by so many to so few," says Prime Minister Churchill August 20 in a speech to the Commons praising the Royal Air Force (RAF) whose Spitfire pilots have frustrated the Luftwaffe, but an all-night German air raid on London 3 days later begins the Blitz.

British Fascist Sir Oswald Mosley has been taken into custody in May and locked up in Brixton Prison after saying, "I know I can save this country and that no one else can" (*see* 1936). The former Lady Cynthia Curzon has long since divorced Mosley, and when he married Diana Mitford at Berlin 4 years ago his only guests were Adolf Hitler and Joseph Goebbels.

Russian revolutionary Leon Trotsky has escaped a raid on his Mexican villa in May when Soviet agents armed with machine guns invaded the premises, but NKVD agent Ramon Mercader, 26 (alias Frank Jacson, alias Jacques Mornard), posing as a friend, has stabbed Trotsky with an ice pick August 21, killing him at age 61. Mercader will serve 20 years in prison.

Berlin has proclaimed a blockade of British waters August 17 and by September the daily bombing of London is killing hundreds each day and injuring thousands as Hitler prepares to invade Britain.

Washington hands over 50 U.S. destroyers to London September 3 in exchange for rights to build U.S. air and naval bases on British territory in Newfoundland and in the Caribbean, but German U-boats sink 160,000 tons of British shipping in September and sink the S.S. *Empress of Britain*, carrying children to Canada, October 2.

Resistance to German occupation authorities remained strong in Europe through the bleakest years of the war.

Romanian authorities have arrested the 58-year-old dictator Ion Antonescu in July for opposing territorial concessions to the U.S.S.R. (above) but have released him. He is appointed premier September 5, he forces the abdication of Carol II who flees the country September 6 after a 10-year reign, and Carol is succeeded by his 19-year-old son Michael who will reign until the end of 1947 (*see* below).

The Axis created September 27 at Berlin joins Germany, Italy, and Japan in a 10-year military and economic alliance. Adolf Hitler and Benito Mussolini meet a week later in the Brenner Pass, German forces seize Romania's Ploesti oil fields October 7, and Italy demands strategic points in Greece October 28.

Britain responds to a Greek appeal for aid by postponing a Middle East offensive and sending troops in early November to occupy Suda Bay, Crete.

The British have stopped passage of war matériel through Burma to China in mid-July at the request of Japan; they reopen the Burma Road October 18.

Japan's Prince Fumumaro Konoye has become premier in mid-July with a mandate to reorganize the government along totalitarian lines, British garrisons are withdrawn August 9 from Shanghai and northern China, and Japanese forces begin occupying French Indo-China September 26 after receiving permission from the Vichy government to use several ports and three airfields in Indo-China.

The $8.4 billion budget submitted by President Roosevelt January 3 has had $1.8 billion earmarked for defense. "I should like to see this nation geared . . . to production of 50,000 planes a year," the president has said later, and he has asked in May for an additional $1.275 billion for defense. Congress has appropriated $1.49 billion June 11 in a Naval Supply Act, it has appropriated another $1.8 billion June 26, it has appropriated $4 billion for the army and navy September 9, and it has appropriated another $1.49 billion for defense October 8.

The first peacetime military draft in U.S. history begins October 29.

The Popular Democratic Party that will control Puerto Rico until 1977 comes to power with the election of party founder Luis Munoz Marin, 42, who started the PDP in 1938. President Roosevelt next year will appoint Rexford Guy Tugwell governor of Puerto Rico and he will work with Munoz Marin to improve the island's economy.

President Roosevelt wins re-election to a precedent-shattering third term with 54 percent of the popular vote. His Republican opponent Wendell L. Willkie, 48, of New York is a former utilities company president who has attacked the Tennessee Valley Authority but who has generally liberal, internationalist views that have won him the nomination against isolationists Robert A. Taft of Ohio, Arthur Vandenberg of Michigan, and Thomas E. Dewey of New York and that win him 44 percent of the popular vote but only 82 electoral votes to President Roosevelt's 449.

The British battleship H.M.S. *Jervis Bay* is sunk in the Atlantic November 4, but a British attack on Taranto a week later cripples the Italian fleet.

Coventry in England's industrial Midlands is pulverized by the Luftwaffe November 10. British intelligence has alerted Prime Minister Churchill to the fact that the raid on Coventry was imminent, but Churchill has made the decision not to evacuate the city lest the Germans discover that their secret code has been broken with help from a device acquired last year in the fall of Poland.

Hungary joins the Axis November 20, and Romania joins November 23. Rioting spreads across Romania beginning November 27 after 64 officials of the Carol government are executed by the Iron Guard of the dictator Ion Antonescu.

More than 4,550 Britons are killed in November air raids, but the anticipated German invasion of Britain does not materialize.

The British Eighth Army commanded by General Archibald Percival Wavell, 57, opens a North African offensive December 9 with an attack on Sidi Barrani which has been in Italian hands since mid-September. The Italians are driven across the Libyan border December 15, and Mussolini's forces in Italian Somaliland are driven out of El Wak a day later.

Persecution of Jews by the Nazis is extended to Poland, Romania, the Netherlands, and other occupied territories. A densely populated Jewish area in Czestochowa is surrounded by SS troops in January, thousands of half-naked men and women are herded into a large square, they are beaten until they bleed, and they are kept standing for hours in the frosty night air while young girls are taken into the synagogue, forced to undress, raped, and tortured.

The Katyn Forest Massacre in March kills 10,000 Polish officers captured by the Red Army when it entered Poland 6 months ago. Imprisoned 15 miles west of Smolensk, the Poles are gunned down and buried in mass graves after having their hands bound behind their backs with a rope looped round their necks.

The Alien Registration Act (Smith Act) passed by Congress June 28 requires that aliens be fingerprinted and makes it unlawful to advocate overthrow of the U.S. government or to belong to any group advocating such overthrow.

⚡ The rare isotope uranium 235 is isolated from its more abundant chemical twin uranium 238 by means of a gaseous diffusion process developed by a Columbia University research team headed by J. R. Dunning (see 1939). He shows that the isotope is the form of uranium that readily undergoes fission into two atoms of nearly equal size, thus releasing prodigious amounts of energy (the gaseous diffusion process will be the major source of uranium 235 used for fueling atomic reactors).

The first transuranium element is discovered by U.S. physicist Edwin Mattison McMillan, 32, at the University of California, Berkeley. The radioactive element is heavier than uranium and is called neptunium by McMillan, who will soon discover another, still heavier, transuranium element which he will call plutonium (see Seaborg, 1941).

A continuous coal-digging machine that will revolutionize coal mining is developed by Consolidation Coal Company president Carson Smith and engineer Harold Farnes Silver, 39. The machine will be purchased in 1947 by Joseph Joy, now 56, whose Joy Manufacturing Company will dominate coal-mining equipment production. Six banks of cutter chains moving at 500 feet per minute will enable the Joy machine to dig out a series of vertical slices 18 inches deep and to bore a tunnel up to 18 feet wide.

U.S. unemployment remains above 8 million, with 14.6 percent of the work force out of work.

U.S. income taxes are increased June 25 by a Revenue Act designed to yield $994.3 million. A second Revenue Act passed October 8 provides for excess profits taxes on corporation earnings.

An Export Control Act passed by Congress July 2 gives the president power to halt or curtail export of materials vital to U.S. defense. Export of aviation gasoline outside the Western Hemisphere is embargoed July 31, and export of scrap iron and steel to Japan is embargoed in October after large quantities of the metals have been shipped to the Axis partner, whose ambassador in Washington calls the action "an unfriendly act."

The first Social Security checks go out January 30 and total $75,844, a figure that will rise to $4.9 billion in 35 years as some 31 million U.S. pensioners become eligible for Social Security benefits. The first check goes to Vermont widow Ida May Fuller, 35, who receives $22.54 and will receive more than $20,000 before she dies in 1975 at age 100 (see 1935).

The U.S. Gross National Product (GNP) is $99 billion, down from $103 billion in 1929. Government spending accounts for 18 percent of the total, up from 10 percent in 1929 (see 1950).

⚡ The world's largest passenger liner is completed in Britain and goes into service as a troop transport. Powered by steam turbines that develop 168,000 horsepower and give her a normal sea speed of 28.5 knots (32.8 miles per hour), the 83,673-ton ship is 1,031 feet in length overall and will go into commercial service for the Cunard Line after the war as the S.S. *Queen Elizabeth*.

The MIG-1 fighter plane named for Soviet mathematician and aircraft designer Mikhail I. Gurevich, 48, is introduced by Moscow's Aircraft Factory No. 1. The refined MIG-3 will be flown by Soviet pilots beginning next year (see MIG-15, 1947).

The Mustang fighter plane is designed and produced in 127 days by North American Aviation's "Dutch" Kindelberger and John Leland Atwood, 35 (see 1934). The P-51 Mustang is powered by the same 1,000-horsepower Rolls-Royce engine that powers the Spitfire, which is winning the Battle of Britain.

The first commercial flight using pressurized cabins takes off July 8 as a Transcontinental & Western Air Boeing 307-B Stratoliner goes into service between New York's 1-year-old La Guardia Airport and Burbank, Calif., with a stop at Kansas City. The plane carries 33 passengers by day and 25 at night (24 of the seats are in compartments convertible into 16 sleeping berths), and flying time is 14 hours going west, 11 hours, 55 minutes going east.

Rohr Industries, Inc., has its beginnings in San Diego's Rohr Aircraft Company founded by former Ryan Aeronautical Corporation engineer Frederick Hilmer Rohr, 44, who specializes in making the complex metal plumbing for aircraft engines and then delivering the complete power package for installation on commercial and military planes.

The first Ferrari racing car competes without success in the last prewar Mille Miglia race in April (see 1929). Ferrari calls his cars simply 815 because his contract with Alfa Romeo bars him from using the name Ferrari on any car. Scuderia Ferrari will produce oleodynamic grinding machines until 1945.

The Jeep designed by Karl K. Pabst, consulting engineer to the Bantam Car Company of Butler, Pa., is a lightweight four-wheel-drive, general-purpose (GP) field vehicle powered by a four-cylinder Continental engine. The U.S. Army places orders for 70 preproduction models, and in November, both Ford Motor Company and Willys-Overland submit prototype models for testing by the army. The Willys MB design will be accepted as standard in the summer of next year, both companies will be given production

1940 (cont.) contracts, and nearly 649,000 Jeeps will be produced in the next 5 years, with Willys completing a new Jeep every 80 seconds at the peak of its production (*see* 1945).

The United States has 1.34 million miles of surfaced road, up from 694,000 in 1930, plus 1.65 million miles of dirt road (*see* 1950).

The Pennsylvania Turnpike is completed from Carlisle to Irvin, 11 miles east of Pittsburgh, and is the first tunneled U.S. superhighway. The $70 million, 160-mile turnpike uses seven tunnels to speed motor traffic through the Alleghenies and bypass towns along the way, but while the 160-mile trip takes only 2½ hours, the remaining 40 miles to Pittsburgh takes another hour or more.

The Arroyo Seco Parkway dedicated in December is the first Los Angeles freeway. In 30 years, some 60 percent of downtown Los Angeles will be taken up with highways and parking lots as the freeways transform the city to make Los Angeles a sprawling collection of suburbs dependent on the automobile and doomed to a smoggy environment.

New York's Queens Midtown Tunnel opens to link Manhattan and Queens.

Construction begins on a Brooklyn-Battery Tunnel (*see* 1950).

New York's Sixth Avenue "El" of 1878 is torn down, and the scrap metal is sold to Japan before enactment of the Export Control Act (above). The avenue will be renamed the Avenue of the Americas, but natives will continue to call it Sixth, and it will remain a wide, dingy thoroughfare of pawn shops and such for another 20 years.

Some 26,630 trolley cars serve U.S. transportation needs, down from 80,000 in 1917. The number will drop to 1,068 by 1975.

A new Chevrolet coupe sells for $659 F.O.B. Flint, a Pontiac station wagon sells for $1,015 F.O.B. Pontiac, a Studebaker Champion sells for $660 F.O.B. South Bend, a Nash sedan sells for $795 F.O.B. Kenosha, and a Packard sells for between $867 and $6,300 F.O.B. Detroit (lowest prices advertised).

The first commercial synthetic rubber tires are exhibited June 5 by B. F. Goodrich Company of Akron, whose Ameripol tires have been made of butadiene synthesized from soap, gas, petroleum and air.

 Goodyear Dow Corporation is formed by Goodyear Tire and Rubber and Dow Chemical to produce synthetic rubber from styrene and butadiene. The only U.S. producer of synthetic rubber has been Du Pont, which makes 2,468 long tons of neoprene this year employing research done by the late J. A. Nieuwland (*see* 1925; 1942).

President Roosevelt acts to build U.S. natural crude rubber reserves in the event of a cutoff of supplies from the Far East. The Rubber Reserve Company created by the president in June is under the Reconstruction Finance Corporation (*see* 1942).

 The world's first electron microscope is demonstrated April 1 at the RCA Laboratories at Camden, N.J. Ten feet high and 700 pounds in weight, the microscope has been developed by RCA engineers supervised by Russian-American research executive Vladimir Kosma Zworykin, 50, and it can magnify up to 100,000 diameters. The electron microscope will permit scientific studies impossible with conventional microscopes.

The Lascaux caves with wall drawings that show how man lived at least 16,000 years ago are discovered by schoolboys near Périgueux in France.

Race, Language, and Culture by Franz Boas, now 82, crowns a long career in anthropology (*see* 1934).

 "Penicillin as a Chemotherapeutic Agent" in the August 24 issue of the *Lancet* reports studies by Australian-born British pathologist Howard W. Florey, 42, at the Sir William Dunn School of Pathology. Florey and his German refugee colleague Ernest Chain have developed Alexander Fleming's penicillin of 1928 into an agent that will become the world's major weapon against infections and chronic diseases (*see* Dubos, 1939; world supply, 1942).

The sulfa drug sulfadiazine is announced by Lederle Laboratories chemist Richard Owen Roblin, 33 (*see* sulfanilamide, 1935).

U.S. Blue Cross health insurance programs have 6 million subscribers, up from 500,000 in 1935, but Blue Shield surgical insurance covers only 260,000 (*see* 1950).

The Rh factor in blood (named for the rhesus monkeys used in research) is discovered by blood type pioneer Karl Landsteiner, who is now with the Rockefeller Institute for Medical Research at New York (*see* 1909). Landsteiner's colleague Alexander S. Wiener has participated in the discovery.

The albumin, globulin, and fibrin fractions of blood plasma are separated by Harvard's Edwin J. Cohn (*see* pernicious anemia, 1930). The American Red Cross and the U.S. Navy will use albumin in the next 6 years to treat shock, globulin to treat various forms of infection, and fibrin to stop hemorrhages while serum gamma globulin will be used in years to come for mass immunization against measles, poliomyelitis, and other epidemic diseases.

Celiac patients in Dutch hospitals improve after Nazi occupation authorities requisition all wheat and rye flour. Hospital authorities discover that celiac disease (nontropical sprue) comes from an intolerance for gluten, the major protein in wheat and rye.

 Iona College is founded at New Rochelle, N.Y.

The letter V begins appearing on walls in German-occupied Belgium. Two Belgians working for the BBC in London have instigated the campaign, knowing that for Flemish-speaking Belgians the V stands for "vrijheid" (freedom), and for French-speaking

Belgians the V stands for "victoire" (victory). The letter is soon scrawled on walls all over Europe, even in countries where the words for freedom and victory do not begin with V.

MIT establishes a radiation laboratory in November to pursue experiments in radar (see Watson-Watt, 1935). The British invention is helping to win the Battle of Britain against the Luftwaffe (above).

The magnetic plastic tape recorder is improved by German technicians H. J. von Braunmuhl and W. Weber who apply a high-frequency bias to the oxide-coated tape of the AEG Magnetophone of 1935 (see Sony, 1950).

An FM radio station started at Chicago by Zenith Radio's Eugene McDonald will survive to become the world's oldest. Zenith will produce the lion's share of U.S. FM radio sets (see 1923; Armstrong, 1933; hearing aid, 1943).

Color television is pioneered by Hungarian-American engineer Peter Carl Goldmark, 34, of CBS whose system requires special receivers. It will give way in the 1950s to an RCA system whose signals will be compatible with conventional black and white TV signals (see 1939; long-playing records, 1948).

Newsday begins publication at Long Island City, N.Y., where copper heir Harry F. Guggenheim and his third wife Alicia Patterson start a daily paper.

PM begins publication at New York. The evening tabloid started by Chicago department store heir Marshall Field III contains no advertising.

"Brenda Starr" by Chicago cartoonist Mrs. Dale Messick, 34, depicts the comic strip adventures of a 23-year-old reporter for the *Flash*. Her heroine will meet Basil St. John in 1945 and will marry him in 1975 without either having aged a day.

Nonfiction *To the Finland Station* by Edmund Wilson.

Fiction *The Man Who Loved Children* by Christina Stead; *The Thibaults* (in eight volumes) by Roger Martin du Gard; *The Heart Is a Lonely Hunter* by U.S. novelist Carson Smith McCullers, 23; *The Tartar Steppe* (*Il deserto de Tartari*) by Italian novelist Dino Buzzati, 34; *Kallocain* by Karin Boye; *The Seed* (*Kimen*) by Norwegian novelist Tarjei Vesaas, 43; *The Ox-Bow Incident* by U.S. novelist Walter van Tilburg Clark, 31; *For Whom the Bell Tolls* by Ernest Hemingway; *You Can't Go Home Again* by the late Thomas Wolfe; *My Name is Aram* (stories) by William Saroyan; *The Power and the Glory* by Graham Greene; *The Pool of Vishnu* by L. H. Myers; *On a Darkling Plain* by Harvard English instructor Wallace Earle Stegner; *Native Son* by U.S. novelist Richard Wright, 31, who joined the Communist party in 1932, moved to New York in 1937 to edit the *Daily Worker,* and last year received a Guggenheim fellowship; *Journey into Fear* by Eric Ambler; *Ten Little Niggers* by Agatha Christie, whose new detec-

tive novel will be published in America first as *And Then There Were None* and later as *Ten Little Indians.*

Poetry *The Man Coming Toward You* by U.S. poet Oscar Williams, 40; *Spain, Take Thou This Cup from Me* (*Espana, aparta de me este caliz*) by César Vallejo; *Cantos* by Ezra Pound.

Painting *The Romanian Blouse* by Henri Matisse; *Sky Blue* by Wassily Kandinsky; *Circus Caravan* by Max Beckmann; *The Red Mask* by Rafillo Tamayo; *Stump in Red Hills* by Georgia O'Keeffe; *The Hailstorm* and *After Many Springs* by Thomas Hart Benton; *Death and Fire* by Paul Klee who dies at Muralto-Locarno, Switzerland, June 29 at age 60. Jean Edouard Vuillard has died at La Baule, France, June 21 at age 71.

Theater *The Male Animal* by James Thurber and playwright-actor Elliott Nugent, 40, 1/9 at New York's Cort Theater, with Nugent, Gene Tierney, 243 perfs.: *My Dear Children* by playwrights Catherine Turney and Jerry Horwin 1/31 at New York's Belasco Theater, with John Barrymore, 117 perfs.; *The Fifth Column* by Ernest Hemingway and Benjamin Glazer 3/26 at New York's Alvin Theater, with Lenore Ulric, Lee J. Cobb, Franchot Tone, 87 perfs.; *There Shall Be No Night* by Robert Sherwood 4/29 at New York's Alvin Theater, with Alfred Lunt, Lynn Fontanne, Sydney Greenstreet, Richard Whorf, Montgomery Clift, 115 perfs., Pulitzer Prize; *Johnny Belinda* by U.S. playwright Elmer Harris, 62, 9/18 at New York's Belasco Theater, with Helen Craig, Horace McNally, 321 perfs.; *George Washington Slept Here* by George S. Kaufman and Moss Hart 10/18 at New York's Lyceum Theater, with Ernest Truex, Jean Dixon, 173 perfs.; *Old Acquaintance* by John Van Druten 12/23 at New York's Morosco Theater, with Jane Cowl, Kent Smith, 170 perfs.; *My Sister Eileen* by Joseph A. Fields and Jerome Chodorov 12/26 at New York's Biltmore Theater, with Shirley Booth, Jo Ann Sayers, Morris Carnovsky in a play based on Ruth McKinney's book, 865 perfs.

Films John Ford's *The Grapes of Wrath* with Henry Fonda, Jane Darwell; John Ford's *The Long Voyage Home* with John Wayne, Thomas Mitchell, Barry Fitzgerald; George Cukor's *The Philadelphia Story* with Katharine Hepburn, Cary Grant, James Stewart; Michael Curtiz's *The Sea Hawk* with Errol Flynn; Raoul Walsh's *They Drive by Night* with George Raft, Humphrey Bogart, Ann Sheridan, Ida Lupino; Alfred Hitchcock's *Foreign Correspondent* with Joel McRae, Laraine Day; Mervyn LeRoy's *Waterloo Bridge* with Vivien Leigh, Robert Taylor; William Keighley's *Torrid Zone* with James Cagney, Ann Sheridan; Sam Wood's *Kitty Foyle* with Ginger Rogers, Dennis Morgan; Robert Z. Leonard's *Pride and Prejudice* with Laurence Olivier, Greer Garson, Edna May Oliver; William Dieterle's *Dr. Ehrlich's Magic Bullet* with Edward G. Robinson, Ruth Gordon, Otto Kruger; Ludwig Berger, Tim Whelan, and Michael Powell's *The Thief of Baghdad* with Sabu,

1940 (cont.) Rex Ingram, June Duprez, Conrad Veidt; Jean Renoir's *La Femme de Boulanger;* Frank Borzage's *The Mortal Storm* with Margaret Sullavan, James Stewart; Edward Cline's *The Bank Dick* with W. C. Fields; Edward Cline's *My Little Chickadee* with W. C. Fields, Mae West; Preston Sturges's *The Great McGinty* with Brian Donlevy.

Radio *Truth or Consequences* debuts 3/23 over four CBS stations. Originated, produced, and emceed by New York announcer-actor-writer Ralph Livingstone Edwards, 26, the spoof on giveaway quiz shows will move to NBC and will continue until 1951, when it will become a television show.

🎵 **Hollywood musicals** Walt Disney's *Fantasia* with animated visualizations of musical classics that include "The Sorcerer's Apprentice" featuring Mickey Mouse and "A Night on Bald Mountain"; Walt Disney's *Pinocchio* with music by Leigh Harline, lyrics by Ned Washington, songs that include "When You Wish Upon a Star."

Broadway musicals *Two for the Show* 2/8 at the Booth Theater, with Eve Arden, Betty Hutton, Keenan Wynn, Alfred Drake, songs that include "How High the Moon" by Morgan Lewis, lyrics by Nancy Hamilton, 124 perfs.; *Higher and Higher* 4/4 at the Shubert Theater, with Jack Haley, Marta Eggert, music by Richard Rodgers, lyrics by Lorenz Hart, songs that include "It Never Entered My Mind," 84 perfs.; *Louisiana Purchase* 5/28 at the Imperial Theater, with William Gaxton, Victor Moore, Vera Zorina, Irene Bordoni, music and lyrics by Irving Berlin, songs that include "It's a Lovely Day Tomorrow," 444 perfs.; *Cabin in the Sky* 10/25 at the Martin Beck Theater, with Ethel Waters, Todd Duncan, Dooley Wilson, Rex Ingram, J. Rosamond Johnson, music by Vernon Duke, book and lyrics by John Latouche and Ted Felter, songs that include "Taking a Chance on Love," 156 perfs.; *Panama Hattie* 10/30 at the 46th Street Theater, with Ethel Merman, Arthur Treacher, Betty Hutton, music and lyrics by Cole Porter, songs that include "Let's Be Buddies," 501 perfs.; *Pal Joey* 12/25 at the Ethel Barrymore Theater, with Gene Kelly, Vivienne Segal, June Havoc, music by Richard Rodgers, lyrics by Lorenz Hart, book based on the new collection of stories by John O'Hara, songs that include "Bewitched," "I Could Write a Book," "Zip," 344 perfs.; *All in Fun* (revue) 12/27 at the Majestic Theater, with Bill Robinson, Imogene Coca, songs that include "It's a Big, Wide, Wonderful World" by John Rox, 3 perfs.

First performances *Les Illuminations* song cycle by Benjamin Britten 1/30 at London, based on the 1886 poems by Arthur Rimbaud; Concerto for Violin and Orchestra by Paul Hindemith early in the year at Amsterdam (Hindemith moves to the United States); Concerto in D minor for Violin and Orchestra by Benjamin Britten 3/30 at New York's Carnegie Hall; Divertimento for String Orchestra by Béla Bartók 6/11 at Basel; *Fantasia de Movementos Mixtos* for Violin and Orchestra by Heitor Villa-Lobos

11/1 at the Colon Theater, Buenos Aires; Concerto for Violin and Orchestra by Arnold Schoenberg 12/6 at Philadelphia; Kammersimphonie No. 2 by Arnold Schoenberg 12/15 at New York.

Opera *Izaht* 4/16 at Rio de Janeiro's Municipal Theater with music by Heitor Villa-Lobos.

The Metropolitan Opera of the Air sponsored by the Texas Company (later Texaco Inc.) begins Saturday afternoon broadcasts that will be heard throughout the United States and Canada for more than 38 years; *The Bell Telephone Hour* 4/29 over NBC stations will continue Monday evenings for 18 years.

U.S. radio networks continue to resist ASCAP demands for higher fees (*see* BMI, 1939). ASCAP has withdrawn music controlled by its members and does not permit the networks even to use birds trained to sing the music. The boycott will not end until the parties reach a compromise late next year.

Popular songs "The Last Time I Saw Paris" by Jerome Kern, lyrics by Oscar Hammerstein II; "Bless 'em All" by English songwriters Jimmie Hughes and Frank Lake; "Tuxedo Junction" by U.S. bandleader Erskine Hawkins, William Johnson, and Julian Dash, lyrics by Buddy Feyne; "Beat Me, Daddy, Eight to the Bar" by Don Raye, Hughie Prince, and Eleanore Sheehy; "I Hear a Rhapsody" by George Frogos and Jack Baker; "Blueberry Hill" by Al Leurs, Larry Stock, and Vincent Rose; "Back in the Saddle Again" by Ray Whitley and cowboy singer Gene Autry; "You Are My Sunshine" by Louisiana singer James Houston (Jimmie) Davis, 37, and Charles Mitchell. Davis will use the song to win the Louisiana governorship in 1944 and 1960.

Muzak is acquired by former New York advertising man William Benton who pays $135,000 to take over a small company that pipes "background music" into restaurants and bars on leased telephone wires under a system originated by World War I brigadier general George O. Squire and put into operation in 1925 by a public utility holding company. Benton will expand Muzak by piping it into factories, retail stores, offices, and even elevators and will sell the company at a $4.2 million profit (Bowles left Benton & Bowles in 1935 after having made more than $1 million in 6 years and since 1937 has been vice-president of the University of Chicago, where he has organized the popular radio forum *Chicago Round Table*).

🏃 The Olympic Games Committee cancels the games scheduled for Tokyo and Helsinki on account of the war.

Roosevelt Raceway opens at Westbury, Long Island, for harness racing with parimutuel machines legalized last year by the New York State Legislature (*see* 1929). Lawyer George Morton Levy, 52, who defended mobster Lucky Luciano against Thomas E. Dewey in 1936, has invested most of his personal fortune in the new track and has cajoled former business associates into putting up money to bring night harness racing to New York, and he pays mobster Frank Costello more than $200 per week to keep Roosevelt Raceway free of bookmakers. The track built on the site of Roosevelt Airfield will lose money for its first 4 years, but Levy will introduce the mobile starting gate that avoids false starts, he will abolish the prevailing heat system, he will make a fortune from his racing interests, and he will build a new $20 million high-rise Roosevelt Raceway in 1957.

The Cincinnati Reds win their first World Series since the infamous 1919 "Black Sox" Series by defeating the Detroit Tigers 4 games to 3.

The first nylon stockings go on sale in the United States May 15. Competing producers have bought their nylon yarn from E. I. du Pont de Nemours (see 1937; Britain, 1946).

Cotton fabrics hold 80 percent of the U.S. textile market at the mills, down from 85 percent in 1930. Man-made fabrics, most of them cellulose fabrics such as rayon and acetate, have increased their market share to 10 percent (see 1950).

Swan soap introduced by Lever Brothers lathers better than the Ivory soap introduced by Procter and Gamble in 1878. P&G has stolen Lever's secret and has improved its Ivory, an out-of-court settlement in 1944 will oblige P&G to pay Lever some $10 million for its industrial espionage, but Lever's new floating soap will never provide serious competition to Ivory.

Matching Lips and Fingertips introduces the first Revlon lipsticks. The promotion is launched by the first full-color Revlon advertising and the first two-page Revlon magazine spread (see 1932).

Tiffany & Co. moves uptown into a large new store at Fifth Avenue and 57th Street, New York, after 34 years at 37th Street. The new store is the first fully air-conditioned store of any kind.

New York's Parkchester housing project opens with 12,000 apartments of which only 400 have more than two bedrooms. The first project "village" to be financed by Metropolitan Life Insurance Company, Parkchester has a population density of 62 families per acre (see Stuyvesant Town, 1947).

Kings Canyon National Park is established by act of Congress in California's High Sierras. Incorporated as a detached section of the new 460,331-acre reserve is the former General Grant National Park with its giant sequoia trees.

Isle Royale National Park is established by act of Congress on the largest island in Lake Michigan. The 539,341-acre park has an outstanding moose herd.

Serengeti National Park is created by the British in Tanganyika, who have added land to the 900-square-mile lion sanctuary set aside in 1929, have included the Ngorongoro Crater, and have extended the list of protected species to include giraffes, buffalo, rhinoceroses, and most carnivores. Serengeti is the first national park in East Africa.

Black markets flourish in occupied and unoccupied France. Bread and other food staples are rationed, and consumers pay premium prices to obtain more than their allotted rations.

Some 3 million tons of U.S. wheat are exported under the export subsidy program started in 1938. The subsidy averages 27.4 cents per bushel to equalize the higher U.S. price with the world price of wheat.

Argentina ships wheat and other foodstuffs to Europe. She will become the richest nation in South America in the next 5 years.

Berlin orders wholesale slaughter of Danish livestock to boost German morale with extra "victory rations" and to save on fodder, gambling that the war will be short. Cattle numbers are reduced by 10 percent, hogs by 30 percent, poultry by 60 percent, and by next year Danish output of animal products will fall to 40 percent below 1939 levels.

Soviet geneticist Nikolai Vavilov is arrested and imprisoned in an underground cell for his opposition to T. D. Lysenko, who will dominate Soviet agriculture until 1964 with his unscientific ideas (see 1936; 1942).

An estimated 90 percent of Western Europe's livestock will be destroyed in the next 5 years, and major pure-bred stock-raising centers will be reduced or eliminated.

Santa Gertrudis cattle developed over the last 18 years by King Ranch boss Robert J. Kleberg, Jr., 44, are recognized as a new breed by the U.S. Department of Agriculture. The cattle have the cherry red coloring and the beef quality of the English shorthorn that was first imported into the United States in 1834 and that represents five-eighths of Santa Gertrudis genetic stock, but the animals have the small hump, the heavy forequarters, and the hardiness of the Indian Brahma breed introduced into the United States in 1854. Santa Gertrudis steers reach a weight of 2,300 pounds and give up to 71.9 percent meat.

King Ranch drought problems have been countered by Kleberg's late father, who dug deep artesian wells, developed trench silos, brought in the first British breeds to run open on the western range, persuaded the Missouri Pacific to run a rail line through the ranch, established the town of Kingsville, and cultivated citrus, palm, and olive trees (see 1886). The younger Kleberg has made an arrangement with Humble Oil & Refining Company to receive royalties on oil and gas pumped from King Ranch lands, which now cover nearly a million acres, an area roughly the size of Rhode Island. The ranch is the largest single beef cattle producer in America.

Nearly one-third of the U.S. farmland tilled in 1930 —some 160 million acres—has been withdrawn from cultivation under programs instituted by the Soil Conservation Administration (see 1935).

The U.S. soybean crop reaches 78 million bushels, up from 5 million in 1924 (see 1945).

1940 (cont.) The United States has more than 6 million farms, but while 100,000 farms have 1,000 acres or more, some 2.2 million have fewer than 50 acres (*see* 1959).

The B vitamin biotin is isolated by U.S. biochemist Vincent Du Vigneaud, 39, who finds that a substance known as vitamin H is identical with the coenzyme R found in leguminous plants and is, in fact, a B vitamin. Du Vigneaud will elucidate the structure of biotin in the next 2 years, but while two kinds of dermatitis in infants will be found to respond to biotin therapy, no natural biotin deficiency will be observed in humans.

Vitasoy is introduced in Hong Kong by local entrepreneurs whose protein soft drink meets with little success until it is promoted with advertising that says, "Vitasoy will make you grow taller, stronger, prettier."

The U.S. Food and Drug Administration (FDA) that was established in 1906 is transferred from the Department of Agriculture to the Federal Security Agency, which will become the Department of Health, Education, and Welfare in 1953.

U.S. red meat consumption reaches 142 pounds per capita on an average annual basis. The figure will increase to 184 pounds in the next 30 years.

The United States imports 70 percent of the world coffee crop, up from 50 percent in 1934.

A freeze-drying process for food preservation is discovered (*see* Maxim, 1964).

Controlled atmosphere (CA) storage is used for the first time on McIntosh apples whose ripening is slowed by storage in gas-tight rooms from which the oxygen has been removed and replaced with natural gas. The process has been developed by Cornell University professor Robert M. Smock.

Nearly 15,000 U.S. retail stores are equipped to sell frozen foods, up from 516 in 1933.

Morton Packing Company is founded at Louisville, Ky. The firm will enter the frozen food business in the late 1940s with a line of chicken, turkey, and beef pot pies to which it will later add fruit pies (*see* 1955).

Arnold bread has its beginnings at Stamford, Conn., where Paul Dean Arnold, 32, and his wife Betty find an old brick oven lined with English tile. They bake a bread loaf with a distinctive taste and launch a major baking enterprise.

Demand for Pepperidge Farm bread obliges Margaret Rudkin to rent some buildings at Norwalk, Conn., and to expand her baking facilities (*see* 1937; 1961).

Duraglas is introduced for deposit bottles and brings a boom to Owens-Illinois Glass (*see* 1929). The new bottle glass can stand up to repeated use by soft drink bottlers.

Cellophane-wrapped meat is sold for the first time by the A&P (*see* 1926).

Hors d'Oeuvres and Canapes by U.S. cooking authority James Beard, 37, launches Beard on a career that will make his name a household word (*see* 1949).

Gourmet magazine is founded at New York by former *National Parent-Teachers* magazine publisher Earle Rutherford MacAusland, 46.

New York's Toots Shor restaurant opens at 51 West 51st Street. Philadelphia-born saloonkeeper Bernard "Toots" Shor, 35, is a one-time B.V.D. salesman who stands 6 feet 2, weighs 250 pounds, and was a speakeasy bouncer for mobster Owney Madden during Prohibition. He will make his place popular among hard-drinking sports fans, he will sell his lease in 1958 for $1.5 million, he will open a new place at 33 West 52nd Street, and he will relocate to other locations.

McDonald hamburger stands have their beginning in a drive-in opened near Pasadena, Calif., by movie theater co-owners Richard and Maurice McDonald of Glendora (*see* 1948).

M&M candies have their beginning in a candy-coated chocolate produced for the U.S. military by Forrest E. Mars and Bruce E. Murrie (*see* Mars, Inc., 1923; 1930; 1932).

Seven out of 10 U.S. blacks still live in the 11 states of the old Confederacy, but the figure is down from 8 out of 10 in 1910 (*see* 1960).

Birth control receives public endorsement from Eleanor Roosevelt.

The population of the world reaches 2.3 billion, with roughly 500 million in China. Eighty percent of the world still lives in agricultural villages, says French geographer Max Sorre.

1941 World War II explodes into a worldwide conflict as German troops invade Soviet Russia and Japanese forces attack at Pearl Harbor (below).

A Lend-Lease program to aid the Allies is recommended by President Roosevelt January 6 in a congressional message that defies widespread isolationist sentiment.

The $17.5 billion budget submitted to Congress by President Roosevelt January 8 includes nearly $11 billion for national defense.

Congress authorizes $7 billion in Lend-Lease aid March 27 and authorizes another $6 billion October 28 and an additional $10 billion December 15 for Lend-Lease and for the U.S. armed forces.

Yugoslavia has a revolution March 27 and is invaded April 6 by German troops.

Greece is invaded by the Germans April 6.

The America First Committee is founded in April by a group of isolationists headed by *Chicago Tribune* publisher Robert R. McCormick and Sears, Roebuck chairman Robert E. Wood, who are joined by Charles A. Lindbergh, U.S. Senators Borah, Byrd, Wheeler, and others.

Hitler aide Rudolf Hess flies to Scotland May 10 on an undisclosed mission. The British interne him.

German paratroops invade Crete May 20. The British withdraw from the Greek island 12 days later.

The German battleship *Bismarck* escapes into the Atlantic May 24 and sinks the British dreadnought *Hood,* but British air and naval forces sink the *Bismarck* May 27.

British forces arrive in Iraq May 31 and prevent Axis sympathizers from taking over the government.

British and Free French troops invade Syria and Lebanon in early June to prevent a German takeover of those countries.

Jewish terrorists in Palestine use violence to fight for independence from Britain. The Stern Gang founded by Polish-born underground leader Abraham Stern assassinates officials, it bombs military installations and oil refineries, and although the British will kill Stern next year, his followers will continue the struggle (*see* 1939; 1945).

German troops invade Soviet Russia June 22, they advance rapidly against the Soviet army whose leaders have been to a large extent liquidated in Josef Stalin's political purges of the late 1930s, and they lay siege to Leningrad. British intelligence predicts a Soviet collapse in 10 days, U.S. intelligence says 3 months, German soldiers carry no winter clothing, but by December the *Wehrmacht* is fighting 360 Soviet divisions when it had anticipated fighting fewer than 200.

The Atlantic Charter comes out of secret meetings held off the coast of Newfoundland from August 9 to August 12 by President Roosevelt and Prime Minister Churchill. The charter contains eight articles of agreement on war aims.

Iran is invaded in late August by British and Soviet troops, Reza Shah Pahlevi abdicates September 16 after a reign of 16 years, and he is succeeded by his 21-year-old son Mohammed Reza Pahlevi who is more inclined to cooperate with the Allies.

President Roosevelt issues an order September 11 that German or Italian vessels sighted in U.S. waters are to be attacked immediately.

The U.S. destroyer *Kearny* is torpedoed by a German U-boat off Iceland October 17.

The U.S. destroyer *Reuben James* is sunk by a German U-boat October 31; 100 lives are lost.

Pearl Harbor on the Hawaiian island of Oahu comes under attack Sunday morning, December 7 (December 8, Tokyo time) from 360 carrier-based Japanese planes led by Mitsuo Fuchida, 38, the Japanese lose only 29 planes, but the attack corps cripples the U.S. Pacific fleet, sinking the battleships U.S.S. *Arizona, Oklahoma, California, Nevada,* and *West Virginia,* damaging three other battleships, inflicting major damage on three cruisers and three destroyers, destroying 200 U.S. planes, and killing 2,344 men. The

American public is told only that the U.S.S. *Arizona* has been sunk and the U.S.S. *Oklahoma* capsized.

The attack on Pearl Harbor at 7:50 A.M. Honolulu time (1:20 P.M. in Washington) has come without declaration of war. It is only at 9 P.M. Washington time that the Japanese foreign minister advises the U.S. Embassy at Tokyo that a state of war exists between the United States and Japan.

December 7 is "a date that will live in infamy," says President Roosevelt in an address to Congress December 8. The Senate votes 82 to 0 for a declaration of war on Japan, the House votes 388 to 1 for war (Congresswoman Jeanette Rankin votes against it as she did in 1917), and President Roosevelt signs the declaration at 4:10 P.M.

Japan declares war on Britain as well as on the United States. Japanese forces land in Malaya and Siam December 8.

H.M.S. *Prince of Wales* and H.M.S. *Repulse* are sunk by the Japanese off the Malayan coast December 9.

Japanese forces land on Luzon in the Philippines December 10; they take Guam in the Marianas December 11.

Germany declares war on the United States December 11 and thus makes it possible for President Roosevelt to end U.S. neutrality in the European war. Italy echoes the German declaration, and the United States declares war on Germany and Italy.

Romania declares war on the United States December 12 and Bulgaria follows suit December 13.

U.S. admiral Chester W. Nimitz, 56, is given command of the Pacific Fleet December 17 and replaces Admiral H. E. Kimmel, who has been relieved of his command as has Lieutenant General Walter C. Short. Both are held responsible for not having been

Pearl Harbor brought the United States into the war, exploding isolationist sentiment in no uncertain way.

1941 (cont.) prepared for the Japanese surprise attack on the U.S. naval base at Pearl Harbor (above).

Some 80,000 to 100,000 Japanese troops are landed at the Gulf of Lingayen December 22 for a major invasion of the Philippines.

Wake Island falls to the Japanese December 23.

Hong Kong is taken by the Japanese December 25.

President Roosevelt has called in his January 6 message to Congress for a world with the Four Freedoms protected—freedom of speech and expression, freedom of religion, freedom from want, freedom from fear.

Adolf Hitler has given the signal for the "Final Solution" to Europe's "Jewish problem." Adolf Eichmann proposes "killing with showers of carbon monoxide while bathing" but the cyanide gas Zyklon B is found more effective.

Some 3,000 Jewish men, women, and children are machine-gunned to death by German SS units in the suburbs of Minsk and Mogilev while German military authorities stand by.

Babi Yar 30 miles outside Kiev is the scene of a September 29 massacre as Nazi invasion forces machine-gun to death between 50,000 and 96,000 Ukrainians of whom at least 60 percent are Jews.

Estonian, Galician, Latvian, Lithuanian, Polish, and Russian Jews flee at the approach of advancing German troops. Jews caught by the Germans are drafted into labor gangs, driven into ghettos, forced into military brothels, massacred with machine guns, or shipped in freight cars to detention camps where many are found dead on arrival. Jewish shops, factories, department stores, libraries, synagogues, and cemeteries are plundered and destroyed.

A U.S. Fair Employment Practice Committee (FEPC) is created by President Roosevelt June 25 after a march by 50,000 blacks on Washington has been threatened by A. Philip Randolph of the Brotherhood of Sleeping Car Porters to protest unfair employment practices in war industry and in the government (*see* Randolph, 1925).

The transuranium element plutonium with the atomic number 94 is isolated at Berkeley by University of California physicists Glenn Theodore Seaborg, 29, and Edwin M. McMillan, who last year discovered neptunium. The Pu 239 isotope of plutonium shows promise of having a higher energy yield from nuclear fission than uranium (*see* 1942).

Grand Coulee Dam begins generating power on the Columbia River in eastern Washington. The world's largest hydroelectric installation has been built by contractors organized by Henry J. Kaiser of 1937 Bonneville Dam fame (*see* shipyards, below).

An Office of Scientific Research and Development (OSRD) is created by President Roosevelt June 28, with Vannevar Bush as director (*see* analog computer, 1930).

An Office of Production Management (OPM) has been created by the president January 7, with William S. Knudsen of General Motors Corporation as director general and with Sidney Hillman of the Amalgamated Clothing Workers Union as associate director general.

An Office of Price Administration and Civilian Supply (OPA) created by the president April 11 has New Deal economist Leon Henderson, 45, as its head, but wartime inflation increases the general price level by 10 percent for the year.

The U.S. Treasury issues war bonds to help reduce the amount of money in circulation. Priced to yield 2.9 percent return on investment, the Series E savings bonds come in denominations of from $25 to $10,000.

U.S. tax rates are increased sharply in nearly all categories September 20 in an effort to raise more than $3.5 billion for war-related expenditures.

Merrill Lynch Pierce Fenner & Beane is created by a merger that puts together the world's largest securities and commodities brokerage house. New York stockbroker Charles E. Merrill, 58, formed a partnership in 1915 with Edmund C. Lynch, he transferred the firm's brokerage business and much of its staff to E. A. Pierce & Company to enter the investment banking business in 1930, he merged with Pierce and E. A. Cassatt last year, and he now merges with the firm Fenner & Beane. Winthrop Hiram Smith, now 48, will join the firm in 1958, the name will become Merrill Lynch Pierce Fenner & Smith, and it will be shortened to Merrill Lynch & Co. in the 1970s.

Henry Kaiser (above) establishes a chain of seven Pacific Coast shipyards north of Richmond, Calif., at the outbreak of the Pacific war in December. Kaiser shipyards will use prefabrication and assembly line methods to set new speed records in shipbuilding (*see* 1942).

Welding Shipyards, Inc., is founded at Norfolk, Va., by Daniel K. Ludwig (*see* 1936).

An Office of Defense Transportation is established December 18 by President Roosevelt.

U.S. motortruck production reaches 4.85 million, up from 3.5 million in 1931 (*see* 1951).

U.S. auto production reaches 3.3 million.

The Lincoln Continental is introduced by Ford Motor Company's Edsel Ford (*see* 1939).

There are 32.6 million cars on the U.S. road, up from 20 million in 1927 (*see* 1950).

The first U.S. diesel freight locomotives go into service for the Atchison, Topeka and Santa Fe (*see* General Motors, 1935). Built by the Electromotive Division of General Motors Corporation, the new 5,400-horsepower diesels eliminate water problems in desert country and reduce hotbox problems on downgrades with a dynamic braking system. Running time between Chicago and California is cut from 6 days to 4 days, with only five brief stops en route, and the sound of the steam engine whistle begins to fade from the American scene (*see* 1957).

"The Sad Sack" is originated by former Walt Disney cartoonist George Baker, 25, whose cartoon strip will appear in *Yank* beginning next year (*see* 1942).

London's *Daily Worker* is suppressed January 21.

Parade magazine, founded by Marshall Field III, begins publication in May for newsstand distribution. The *Washington Post* takes over the picture magazine in August for distribution with its Sunday edition, other papers acquire distribution rights, and by 1978 *Parade* will go out with 124 Sunday papers, reaching well over 20 million readers.

Germany abandons Gothic type May 31 in favor of Roman type.

Nonfiction *Escape From Freedom* by German-American psychoanalyst-philosopher Erich Fromm, 41, who studies the meaning of freedom and authority; *The Mind of the South* by U.S. journalist W. (Wilbur) F. Cash who dies July 2 at age 40; *Let Us Now Praise Famous Men* by *Time* magazine film critic James Agee, 31, and *Fortune* magazine photographer Walker Evans, 37, who have studied the plight of Alabama sharecroppers and who confront Americans with rural poverty in the South; *Black Lamb and Gray Falcon* by English woman of letters Rebecca West (Cecily Adams), 49, whose book is a two-volume diary of her trip to Yugoslavia in 1937.

Fiction *The Fancy Dress Party* (*La mascherata*) by Alberto Moravia enrages Benito Mussolini who personally censors the novel when he realizes that the South American dictator portrayed by Moravia represents Il Duce; *Darkness at Noon* by Arthur Koestler, who completed the novel in a Vichy concentration camp; *Scum of the Earth* by Arthur Koestler, who shows the misery inside Vichy concentration camps; *A Woman of the Pharisees* (*La Pharisienne*) by François Mauriac; *The Pasquier Chronicles* (*Chronique des Pasquier*) by Georges Duhamel; *Conversation in Sicily* (*Conversazione in Sicilia*) by Italian novelist Elio Vittorini, 37; *The Blind Owl* (*Buf-i-Kur*) by Iranian novelist Sadig Hidayat, 37; *Herself Surprised* by Joyce Cary; *A Curtain of Green* (stories) by Mississippi writer Eudora Welty, 32; *The Seventh Cross* (*Das siebte Kreuz*) by émigrée German novelist Anna Seghers (Netty Radvanyi), 41; *Reflections in a Golden Eye* by Carson McCullers; *The Last Tycoon* by the late F. Scott Fitzgerald, who died of a heart attack at age 44 in December of last year, leaving incomplete his novel based roughly on the late M-G-M producer Irving Thalberg; *What Makes Sammy Run?* by U.S. novelist Budd Schulberg, 27, whose father is a leading Hollywood screenwriter-producer. Many take Schulberg's Sammy Glick as the typical American success story. *Mildred Pierce* by James M. Cain; *The Keys of the Kingdom* by A. J. Cronin is the U.S. fiction best seller; *H. M. Pulham, Esq.* by John P. Marquand who calls

it "a very sad book about a completely frustrated individual"; *Saratoga Trunk* by Edna Ferber; *The Song of Bernadette* by Franz Werfel; *Storm* by University of California English instructor George Rippey Stewart, 46.

Poetry *55 Poems* by U.S. poet Louis Zukofsky, 37; *Poems de la France malheureuse* by Jules Supervielle; *Raka* by N. P. van Wyk Louw; *La Crève-Coeur* by French novelist-poet Louis Aragon, now 44, who has served with distinction against the Germans.

Juvenile *Curious George* by German-American writer-illustrator H. A. (Hans Augusto) Rey, 43, and his wife Margaret, whose monkey George will appear in six sequels (the Reys were living in Paris in June of last year but were able to bicycle south before the arrival of the German *Wehrmacht*, reached Lisbon, sailed to Rio where they had worked together in 1935 and had married, and arrived at New York in October of last year).

Avon Books is founded by William Randolph Hearst. The new paperback house will compete with Pocket Books, Inc. (*see* 1939; Popular Library, 1942; Bantam, 1945).

Mount Rushmore National Monument attracts visitors to South Dakota following the death of native American sculptor John Gutzon de la Mothe Borglum who suffered a fatal heart attack March 6 at age 73. Borglum has developed new methods of stoneworking to carve 60-foot high heads of George Washington, Thomas Jefferson, Abraham Lincoln, and Theodore Roosevelt out of the living rock. His son Lincoln works to improve the collar and lapels on Washington's coat, Jefferson's collar, Lincoln's head, and Roosevelt's face, but he will leave the massive work incomplete.

The National Gallery of Art opens at Washington, D.C., where a $15 million bequest from the late Pittsburg financier Andrew W. Mellon has financed construction of the rose-white Tennessee marble building. Mellon died in the summer of 1937 at age 82, leaving an art collection acquired at the persuasion of the London art dealer Baron Duveen of Milbank, now 72. Gallery director David Edward Finley, 50, has supervised construction of the building that also will house the Dale, Kress, Rosenwald, and Widener collections.

Painting *Nighthawks* by Edward Hopper; *New York Under Gaslight* by Stuart Davis; *Little-Known Bird of the Inner Eye* by Seattle painter Morris Graves, 31; *Divers Against Yellow Background* by Fernand Léger. Robert Delaunay dies at Montpelier, France, October 25 at age 56.

Theater *Arsenic and Old Lace* by U.S. playwright Joseph Kesselring, 39, 1/10 at New York's Fulton Theater with Josephine Hall, Jean Adair, Boris Karloff, 1,437 perfs.; *Native Son* by Richard Wright and Paul Green 3/24 at New York's St. James Theater, with Canada Lee, 114 perfs. (see 1940 novel); *Watch on the Rhine* by Lillian Hellman 4/1 at New York's

1941 (cont.) Music Box Theater, with Paul Lukas, Mady Christians, Anne Blythe, George Coulouris, 378 perfs.; *Mother Courage, A Chronicle of the Thirty Years' War* (*Mutter Courage und ihre Kinder*) by Bertolt Brecht 4/19 at Zurich's Schauspielhaus; *Blithe Spirit* by Noel Coward 7/2 at London's Piccadilly Theatre, 1,997 perfs. (a new record for a London stage play); *Candle in the Wind* by Maxwell Anderson 10/22 at New York's Shubert Theater, with Helen Hayes, Lotte Lenya, 95 perfs.; *Junior Miss* by Jerome Chodorov and Joseph Fields 11/18 at New York's Lyceum Theater, with Patricia Peardon, 16, as Judy Graves, Lenore Lonergan as Fuffy Adams, 710 perfs.; *Angel Street* by playwright Patrick Hamilton 12/5 at New York's Golden Theater, with Judith Evelyn, Vincent Price, 1,295 perfs.; *In Time to Come* by U.S. playwrights Howard Koch, 39, and John Huston, 35, 12/8 at New York's Mansfield Theater with Richard Gaines as Woodrow Wilson, Nedda Harrigan as Mrs. Wilson, House Jameson as Senator Lodge, Russell Collins as Col. House, 40 perfs.

Films Orson Welles's *Citizen Kane* with Welles, Joseph Cotten, Everett Sloane, Agnes Moorehead, George Coulouris. Publisher William Randolph Hearst is portrayed with only minor fictionalization in an allegory on the theme of idealism corrupted by power (the film is not reviewed or advertised in any Hearst newspaper).

Other films John Huston's *The Maltese Falcon* with Humphrey Bogart, Sydney Greenstreet, Peter Lorre, Mary Astor, Elisha Cook, Jr.; Howard Hawks's *Sergeant York* with Gary Cooper; John Ford's *How Green Was My Valley* with Roddy McDowell, Donald Crisp, Sara Allgood, Walter Pidgeon, Maureen O'Hara; Gabriel Pascal's *Major Barbara* with Wendy Hiller, Rex Harrison; Charlie Chaplin's *The Great Dictator;* Alfred Hitchcock's *Rebecca* with Joan Fontaine, Laurence Olivier, George Sanders; John Cromwell's *So Ends Our Night* with Fredric March, Margaret Sullavan; Irving Rapper's *One Foot in Heaven* with Fredric March, Martha Scott; Sam Wood's *King's Row* with Ann Sheridan, Robert Cummings, Ronald Reagan; Charles Vidor's *Ladies in Retirement* with Ida Lupino, Louis Hayward, Evelyn Keyes; Michael Curtiz's *The Sea Wolf* with Edward G. Robinson, Ida Lupino, John Garfield; George Cukor's *A Woman's Face* with Joan Crawford, Melvyn Douglas; William Wyler's *The Little Foxes* with Bette Davis; Mitchell Leisen's *Hold Back the Dawn* with Charles Boyer, Olivia de Havilland; George Cukor's *Two-Faced Woman* with Greta Garbo (her last film), Melvyn Douglas, Constance Bennett; Alexander Hall's *Here Comes Mr. Jordan* with Robert Montgomery, Evelyn Keyes; George Stevens's *Penny Serenade* with Cary Grant, Irene Dunne; Edward Cline's *Never Give a Sucker an Even Break* with W. C. Fields, Margaret Dumont; Preston Sturges's *The Lady Eve* with Barbara Stanwyck, Henry Fonda; Preston Sturges's *Sullivan's Travels* with Joel McCrae, Veronica Lake; Walt Disney's *Dumbo.*

Radio comedy *Duffy's Tavern* premieres in April on CBS Network stations with Ed Gardner, who opens each show with the line, "Duffy's Tavern, where the elite meet to eat. Archie the manager speaking, Duffy ain't here. Oh, hello, Duffy" (Duffy will never appear).

West Coast musical *Jump for Joy* is an all-black revue with songs that include "I Got It Bad and That Ain't Good" by Duke Ellington, lyrics by Paul Francis Webster, Henry Newman, Irving Mills.

Broadway musicals *Lady in the Dark* 1/23 at the Alvin Theater with Gertrude Lawrence, Danny Kaye, music by Kurt Weill, lyrics by Ira Gershwin, songs that include "Jenny (the Saga of)," "My Ship," "Tchaikovsky," 162 perfs. (Kaye, 28, has changed his name from David Daniel Kominsky, he has married Sylvia Fine while working in the Catskill Mountain "borscht circuit," and he has been helped by her witty songs); *Best Foot Forward* 10/1 at the Ethel Barrymore Theater, with Rosemary Lane, Nancy Walker, June Allyson, songs by Hugh Martin and Ralph Blane that include "Buckle Down, Winsocki," 326 perfs.; *Let's Face It* 10/29 at the Imperial Theater with Danny Kaye, Eve Arden, Nanette Fabray, music and lyrics by Cole Porter, songs that include "Ace in the Hole," "You Irritate Me So," and Danny Kaye patter songs with lyrics by Sylvia Fine (above), 547 perfs.; *Sons O'Fun* 12/1 at the Winter Garden Theater with Olsen and Johnson, Carmen Miranda, Ella Logan, music by Sammy Fain and Will Irwin, lyrics by Jack Yellen and Irving Kahal, songs that include "Happy in Love," 742 perfs.

First performances *Symphonic Dances* for Orchestra by Sergei Rachmaninoff 1/4 at Philadelphia's Academy of Music; Concerto for Violincello and Orchestra by Paul Hindemith 2/7 at Boston's Symphony Hall, with Gregor Piatigorsky as soloist; Concerto for Violin and Orchestra by Samuel Barber 2/7 at Philadelphia's Academy of Music, with Albert Spalding as soloist; Symphony No. 1 by U.S. composer Paul Creston (né Joseph Guttoveggio), 34, 2/22 at the Brooklyn Academy of Music; *Latin-American Symphonette* by Morton Gould 2/22 at Brooklyn; *Ballad of a Railroad Man* for Chorus and Orchestra by Roy Harris 2/22 at Brooklyn; *Sinfonia da Requiem* by Benjamin Britten 3/29 at New York's Carnegie Hall. Tokyo commissioned the work in 1939 for the 2,600th anniversary of the Japanese imperial dynasty in 1940 but rejected it, calling it too Christian; *A Symphony in D for the Dodgers* by U.S. composer Robert Russell Bennett, 46, 5/16 in a radio concert broadcast from New York; Piano Sonata by Aaron Copland 10/21 at Buenos Aires; Symphony No. 2 by Virgil Thomson 11/17 at Seattle; Symphony in E flat major by Paul Hindemith 11/21 at Minneapolis; *Scottish Ballad* for Two Pianos and Orchestra by Benjamin Britten 11/28 at Cincinnati; Symphony No. 1 by U.S. composer David Diamond, 26, 12/21 at New York's Carnegie Hall.

Luftwaffe night raiders have destroyed the Queen's Hall, London, with incendiary bombs May 10.

A BBC broadcast from London June 27 has urged the subjugated peoples of Europe to adopt the Morse code signal for the letter V (for Victory)—three dots and a dash—and to whistle the opening motive of Symphony No. 5 by Ludwig van Beethoven whenever Nazi soldiers are around. London's Westminster chimes have added the four notes on the hour.

Popular songs "Lili Marlene" by German composer Norbert Schultze (who also wrote "Bombs on England"), lyrics by World War I German soldier Hans Leip, who wrote them before going to the Russian front in 1916, combining the name of his girlfriend with that of a friend's girl), English lyrics by London publisher Jimmy Phillips and lyricist Tommy Connor, who adapt the song Allied troops have learned from German prisoners of war and from German radio (German publishers will receive royalties beginning in 1958); "Blues in the Night" by Harold Arlen, lyrics by Johnny Mercer; "(There'll Be Blue Birds Over) the White Cliffs of Dover" by English songwriters Nat Burton and Walter Kent; "We Did It Before (and We Can Do It Again)" by Cliff Friend, lyrics by Charlie Tobias; "I Don't Want to Walk Without You" by Jule Styne and Frank Loesser; "I Don't Want to Set the World on Fire" by Eddie Seiler, Sol Marcus, Bennie Benjamin, Eddie Durham; "Take the A Train" by Duke Ellington and Billy Strayhorn (see New York subway, 1933); "How About You?" by Burton Lane, lyrics by Ralph Freed; "I'll Remember April" by Don Raye, Gene DePaul, Pat Johnston; "Elmer's Tune" by Chicago undertaker's assistant Elmer Albrecht, lyrics by Sammy Gallop and bandleader Dick Jurgens; "Racing with the Moon" by Johnny Watson, lyrics by Watson's wife Pauline Pope and bandleader Vaughn Monroe; "This Love of Mine" by Sol Parker and Henry Sanicola, lyrics by Frank Sinatra; "Why Don't You Do Right" by blues songwriter Joe McCoy; "Yes Indeed!" by Sy Oliver; "Daddy" by University of Pennsylvania Wharton School student Bob Troup, who wrote the song last year for the Penn freshman Mask and Wig show; "Deep in the Heart of Texas" by Don Swander, 36, and his wife June Hershey Swander, 32 (who has never been in Texas); "Jersey Bounce" by Billy Plate, Tony Bradshaw, Edward Johnson, Robert B. Wright; "The Hut-Sut Song" by Leo V. Killion; "Cow-Cow Boogie" by Don Raye, Gene DePaul, and Benny Carter; "Chattanooga Choo-Choo" by Harry Warren, lyrics by Mack Gordon (see Glenn Miller, 1942); "Why Don't We Do This More Often" by Allie Wrubell, lyrics by Charlie Newman; "Let's Get Away from It All" by Matt Dennis (a Tommy Dorsey protegé), lyrics by Tom Adair; "Boogie Woogie Bugle Boy" by Don Raye and Hughie Prince; "Anniversary Waltz" by Al Dubin and Dave Franklin.

Stan Musial plays for the St. Louis Cardinals beginning late in the season and has a batting average of .426 for 12 games. Stanley Frank Musial, 22, will have a lifetime batting average of .331 in 22 seasons and a career total of 3,630 hits, a record second only to that of Ty Cobb (see 1905).

The New York Yankees win the World Series by defeating the Brooklyn Dodgers 4 games to 1.

Dacron (Terylene) is pioneered by English chemist John Rex Whinfield, 40, who produces a new polyester fabric made from terephthalic acid and ethylene glycol. The fiber used to make the fabric will be marketed after the war under the name Terylene by Britain's Imperial Chemical Industries and under the name Dacron by E. I. Du Pont de Nemours (see nylon, 1939; Orlon, 1948).

New York gangster Abe "Kid Twist" Reles "falls" to his death November 12 from a sixth-story Coney Island hotel window in the presence of a six-man police bodyguard. Reles last year informed to the Brooklyn district attorney, his testimony attributed 130 hired killings between 1930 and 1940 to a national crime syndicate called Murder Incorporated, and his testimony will lead to the execution of mob figures who include Louis "Lepke" Buchalter (see Kefauver Committee hearings, 1950).

Boston's 29-year-old Copley Plaza Hotel is acquired by the Sheraton Corporation, which will shock Bostonians in 1951 by renaming the landmark hotel the Sheraton-Copley (see 1933; Sheraton-Cadillac, 1951).

Quality Inns is founded to franchise motel operations. By 1977 the company will have 300 franchised motels, hotels, and recreational lodging facilities with more than 31,000 rooms in the United States, Canada, and Europe.

Russia has her most severe winter in 30 years, and Leningrad (above) has no heat, no electricity, and little food. The Luftwaffe destroys food stocks stored in wooden buildings, and besieged Leningraders eat cats, dogs, birds, jelly made of cosmetics, and soup made from boiled leather wallets. Those able to work are given a bread ration of half a pound per day, others receive only two slices, and the bread is often made of low-grade rye flour mixed with sawdust, cellulose residues, and cottonseed cake. Thousands die of starvation, and before the siege is lifted in 1944, from 20 to 40 percent of Leningrad's 3 million people will have died in 900 days of hunger and hunger-related disease (see Stalingrad, 1942).

Britain has received her first U.S. Lend-Lease shipments of U.S. food April 16 just in time to avert a drastic food shortage. By December, 1 million tons of U.S. foodstuffs have arrived.

Germany is the best-fed of the European combatant nations. A rationing plan provides Germans with at least 95 percent of the calories received in peacetime—2,000 calories per day.

Soviet citizens outside Leningrad receive an estimated 1,800 calories per day, but people in occupied Finland, Norway, Belgium, and the Netherlands receive less than 1,800, and those in the Baltic states, Poland, France, Italy, Greece (and the other Balkan countries) are lucky to get 1,500.

1941 (cont.) Mexico's wheat harvest is reduced by half as stem rust devastates the crops in Queretaro, Guanajuato, Michoacan, and Jalisco—states that comprise the nation's breadbasket. Mexico is obliged to spend $30 million (100 million pesos) year after year to import corn and wheat, leaving less money for imported machinery, power generators, chemicals, and dozens of other desperately needed imports.

A program to improve Mexican agriculture is begun at the urging of U.S. Secretary of Agriculture Henry A. Wallace by the Rockefeller Foundation. University of Minnesota rust specialist Elvin C. Stakman, 56, Cornell University soil expert Richard Bradford, 46, and Harvard University plant geneticist Paul C. Mangelsdorf, 42, are sent to Mexico, and they submit a blueprint for redeveloping the country's rural economy (*see* Harrar, 1942).

A National Nutritional Conference for Defense is convened by President Roosevelt to study causes for the physical defects found in so many young men called up by the draft. Mayo Clinic nutrition specialist Russell M. Wilder heads a group of experts from the National Research Council, the American Medical Association, and the American Public Health Association in a study of the eating habits of 2,000 representative U.S. families (*see* 1943).

Only 30 percent of U.S. white bread is enriched with vitamins and iron. South Carolina becomes the first state to pass a law requiring enrichment.

The average fat content of U.S. frankfurters is 19 percent, up from 18 percent in 1935 (*see* 1969).

Sell's liver paté has its beginnings in a paté made from pork livers, pork fat, onions, defatted wheat germ, milk powder, and yeast developed by publisher-promoter Henry Sell, who last year sold his Vitamins *Plus* to Vick Chemical Company (*see* 1905; 1936). Sell is helped by a Waldorf-Astoria chef who adds seasonings to the product which will be sent in Red Cross parcels to U.S. prisoners of war held in Axis prison camps (*see* 1945).

Spice Island Company has its beginnings in an herb farm started by San Francisco stockbroker Frederick Johnson, whose company will be an important producer of vinegar, spices, and other food products.

A big "Mc" is adopted as a trademark by the House of McCormick (*see* 1921). The company will build a potato dehydration plant in Maine next year at the request of the U.S. Army, and it will work on developing DDT (*see* Muller, 1939).

Daniel Gerber's Fremont Canning Company sells a million cans of baby food per week (*see* 1929, 1948).

Paris yogurt maker Isaac Carasso returns to Barcelona, winds up his European affairs, and emigrates to New York. Carasso is protected from Nazi seizure by an order from Francisco Franco that shields Sephardic Jews (*see* 1926; Dannon, 1942).

Buitoni Foods Corporation is organized at New York by Italian pasta maker Giovanni Buitoni, who has sung at Carnegie Hall to publicize his products but who has been isolated in the United States since late 1939 by the outbreak of war in Europe. Buitoni's new U.S. company will produce pasta and related canned and frozen foods (*see* 1883).

Cheerios breakfast food is introduced by General Mills. It is 2.2 percent sugar.

The Chemex coffee maker designed by Peter Schlumbohn is introduced by New York's Chemex Corporation.

Casserole Cookery by Baltimore author Marian Tracy is published. It will be the vademecum of war brides and of young housewives for years to come.

Basic U.S. food prices by December are 61 percent above prewar prices.

New York's Le Pavillon opens October 15 at 51 East 55th Street under the direction of Henri Soule, who ran the restaurant at the 1939 and 1940 World's Fair French Pavilion. The new eating place has a staff of 40 and charges $1.75 for a table d'hote luncheon of hors d'oeuvre, plat du jour, dessert, and coffee.

The U.S. population reaches 132 million, Great Britain has 47 million, France 40, Germany with its annexed territories 110, the U.S.S.R. with its annexed territories 181, Japan 105 (up from 89 million in 1936), Brazil 41, India 389, and China about 500.

1942 The world's first controlled, self-sustaining nuclear chain reaction is achieved December 2 at the University of Chicago's Stagg Field by a small team organized in June under the name Manhattan Engineering District. The team includes physicists Enrico Fermi, Leo Szilard, and the Hungarian-American Edward Teller, 34, it will now move to the Los Alamos National Laboratory in New Mexico, and its membership will be enlarged (*see* 1939; plutonium, 1941; atomic bomb, 1945).

The Japanese take Manila January 2, they invade the Dutch East Indies January 10, but they suffer their first major sea loss in late January at the Battle of Macassar Strait when U.S. and Dutch naval and air forces attack a Japanese convoy.

President Roosevelt calls in January for production in 1942 of 60,000 planes, 45,000 tanks, 20,000 antiaircraft guns, and 6 million deadweight tons of merchant shipping. His $59 billion budget submitted January 7 has more than $52 billion earmarked for the war effort.

An Inter-American Conference assembles 21 representatives at Rio de Janeiro January 15 to coordinate Western Hemisphere defenses against aggression, the conference adopts a unanimous resolution January 21 calling for severance of relations with the Axis powers, and the group sets up an Inter-American Defense Board in March.

The bazooka antitank weapon developed at the Frankfort Arsenal by Edward J. Uhl, 24, and Leslie A. Skinner, 40, is tested for the first time in May.

Napalm (napthenic acid and palmetate) developed by Harvard chemist Louis F. Fieser, 43, in response to a U.S. Army request is a jellied gasoline incendiary that will increase the effective range of flamethrowers and slow down the rate of burning. Prominent up to now for developing the blood-clotting agent vitamin K, Fieser produces an inexpensive derivative of petroleum and palm oils that will find wide use as a canister filler for air-to-ground bombs.

Singapore falls to the Japanese February 15. The big guns of the British naval base have fixed emplacements and point out to sea, making them useless against the Japanese who approach from the Malayan interior.

An Allied squadron is wiped out in the Battle of the Java Sea late in February, and the Japanese land in the Solomon Islands March 13, threatening the vital route to Australia.

U.S. troops on the Bataan peninsula in the Philippines surrender to the Japanese April 9.

Tokyo is raided April 18 by 16 B-25 bombers from the U.S. carrier *Hornet* under the command of Major James Harold "Jimmy" Doolittle, 45, who also bombs Yokohama and other cities before landing in China. Three U.S. flyers die in crash landings; the Japanese capture 11 others and execute three as "war criminals."

The Burma Road is cut by the Japanese, who capture Lashio April 29. China's Chiang Kai-shek is given U.S. support in his resistance to Japanese aggression. U.S. cargo planes deliver supplies from India over "the hump" (the Himalayas), and Chiang's chief of staff General Joseph Warren "Vinegar Joe" Stilwell, 59, begins the 478-mile Ledo Road from India to Burma to link up with the old Burma Road.

The Japanese sustain heavy losses in early May at the Battle of the Coral Sea, but they sink the U.S. carrier *Lexington*.

Mandalay falls to the Japanese May 2 as they complete their conquest of Burma.

The U.S. garrison at Corregidor in the Philippines surrenders May 6. General Jonathan Mayhew Wainwright III, 59, and his men are taken prisoner.

Cologne is raided by the RAF on the night of May 30 in the first 1,000-bomber attack on German industrial targets.

U.S. carrier-based planes stop the Japanese at the Battle of Midway in early June.

Attu and Kiska in the Aleutians are occupied by the Japanese June 7.

Eight German agents are captured by the FBI June 28 after being landed by a U-boat on Long Island.

Tobruk in Libya is taken by German field marshal Erwin Rommel June 21. The Axis forces reach El Alamein 70 miles from Alexandria before being checked by British forces under the command of General Bernard L. Montgomery.

Dieppe on the French coast is raided August 19 by Canadian commando troops, but the attack is aborted by German defenders; 3,500 Canadians are lost.

The Battle of Stalingrad begins August 22. The Germans have captured Sevastopol in the Crimea July 2 after an 8-month siege, and they launch an offensive against the Volga River center for shipment of oil from the Caucasus, a city of 500,000 whose population will dwindle to 1,515 in the barbaric 5-month battle. The Russians will lose 750,000 troops, the Germans will lose 400,000, the Romanians nearly 200,000, the Italians 130,000, the Hungarians 120,000, and Axis survivors will be sustained in many cases only by cannibalism before 22 German divisions, reduced to 80,000 men, surrender early next February.

The German battleships *Scharnhorst, Gneissenhau,* and *Prinz Eugen* have escaped from the occupied French harbor of Brest to the Baltic in February, but they avoid Allied naval vessels and aircraft.

U-boat activity off the U.S. Atlantic Coast takes a heavy toll of merchant ships bound for British and Russian ports with war matériel, foodstuffs, and men. A dimout extending 15 miles from the coast is ordered April 28 to make it harder for the U-boats to sight their quarry at night.

The Women's Auxiliary Army Corps (WAAC) is established by act of Congress May 14. *Houston Post* editor Oveta Culp Hobby, 37, is sworn in as director.

The Office of Strategic Services (OSS) is created by executive order June 13. World War I hero William Joseph "Wild Bill" Donovan, 59, is named director of the military intelligence organization.

The WAVES (Women Accepted for Voluntary Emergency Service) is authorized by act of Congress July 30. Named to head the women's branch of the Naval Reserve is Wellesley College president Mildred H. McAfee, 42.

A British-U.S. force of 400,000 under the command of General Dwight D. Eisenhower lands at Casablanca, Oran, and Algiers November 7 and 8 in an armada of 500 transports convoyed by 350 naval vessels. Vichy French garrisons at Casablanca, Oran, and Algiers are overpowered after brief fighting, and an armistice is arranged by the Vichy government's 61-year-old Admiral Jean-François Darlan who is assassinated December 24.

The French fleet at Toulon is in large part scuttled by its crews November 27 to keep the ships from falling into German hands.

"I have not become the King's First Minister in order to preside over the liquidation of the British Empire," says Prime Minister Churchill November 10 in a speech at the Mansion House. Immediate independence of India has been demanded by Mahatma Gandhi and other Indian leaders who have been arrested but later released (*see* 1947).

U.S. factories poured out a torrent of war material to help Allied troops defeat the Axis powers.

Unoccupied France is occupied by German troops November 11.

The first surface-to-surface guided missile is launched December 24 at Peenemunde by German rocket engineer Wernher von Braun, 30, who tests his buzz bomb (*see* 1944).

Deputy Gestapo chief and Reich "protector" of Czechoslovakia Reinhard Heydrich is assassinated May 31 by Czech patriots. The 38-year-old Heydrich has been known as der Henker (the Hangman), and his death brings swift and terrible retribution.

The Czech village of Lidice in Bohemia is burned by the Germans June 6 after every male has been executed in reprisal for the assassination of Reinhard Heydrich (above). Only one man is reported to have escaped, and the female population is abused by the Germans.

Some 30,000 Parisian Jews are rounded up by 2,000 police officers July 16. They are bused out of the city to Nazi concentration camps; only 30 will survive.

Some 7,000 French Jews including infants and children are locked into a stadium for 8 days without water or toilet facilities.

A methodical annihilation of all European Jews within their reach is begun by Adolf Hitler and his Gestapo chief Heinrich Himmler. Some 8,000 Greek Jews from Salonika are transferred to concentration camps in the mountains of Macedonia, and another 45,000 will be deported in the next 3 years, leaving scarcely 500 in the city (*see* Poland, 1943).

Some 110,000 Japanese-Americans living in coastal Pacific areas are placed in concentration camps under terms of Executive Order 9066 issued by President Roosevelt February 19. No similar moves are taken against Japanese-Americans in the Hawaiian Islands or in the U.S. East and Midwest, nor are measures taken against alien Germans or Italians, but native-born U.S. citizens of Japanese ancestry are rounded up along with Japanese aliens and interned in remote areas of Arizona, Arkansas, inland California, Colorado, Idaho, Utah, and Wyoming, where they live in tar-papered barracks heated with coal stoves and guarded by military police armed with rifles. The interned Japanese-Americans (two-thirds are U.S. citizens) lose an estimated $400 million in property of which $38.5 million will be repaid by the U.S. government in the mid-1950s.

The Congress of Racial Equality (CORE) is founded by University of Chicago students under the leadership of James Leonard Farmer, 22, who becomes its national chairman. The organization will use passive resistance tactics pioneered by Mahatma Gandhi in India and will employ sit-in techniques to end racial segregation and discrimination (*see* 1961).

 The entire world supply of penicillin is barely enough to cure one serious case of meningitis (*see* 1943; Florey, 1940).

Oral drugs for diabetics are pioneered by French medical researcher André Loubatiére, who discovers that sulfa drugs are closely related chemically to para-amino benzoic acid (PABA) and produce a lowering of blood sugar levels (*see* Domagk, 1935).

New York's Metropolitan Life Insurance Company tries to correct inadequacies in its desirable height-weight ratio tables. The age scale is eliminated, and three classes of "frame size" are introduced with ranges of desirable weight rather than single figures (overweight policy holders are considered poor mortality risks).

The first Kaiser Foundation Hospital is dedicated by U.S. industrialist Henry J. Kaiser (below). The 54-bed facility at Oakland, Calif., will develop into the Kaiser Foundation Health Plan and will often be called Kaiser-Permanente after the creek in the Santa Cruz Mountains where Kaiser built his first cement plant (the plan will be a pioneer program in continuing health maintenance).

The Beveridge Plan of English economist William Henry Beveridge, 63, is a comprehensive report embodying proposals for postwar "cradle-to-grave" social security in Britain. Master of Oxford's University College, Beveridge is chairman of Britain's Inter-Departmental Committee on Social Insurance and Allied Services (*see* National Health Service, 1946).

An Emergency Price Control Act voted by Congress January 30 gives the Office of Price Administration (OPA) power to control prices (*see* 1941).

A General Maximum Price Regulation Act voted by Congress April 28 freezes 60 percent of U.S. food items at store-by-store March price levels.

Congress appropriates $26.5 billion for the navy February 2 and brings total war costs since June 1940 to $116 billion. Another $42.8 billion is appropriated for the army June 30, and by July 1 the nation is spending $150 million per day.

The Revenue Act of 1942 is the largest in U.S. history. Designed to produce $9 billion, it contains provision for a 5 percent victory tax on all incomes above $624 for the duration of the war.

An Office of Economic Stabilization is created by President Roosevelt who asks Supreme Court Justice James F. Byrnes, 63, to resign and become economic stabilization director. An order issued by Byrnes October 27 limits salaries to $25,000 per year.

More than 3.6 million American men remain unemployed, but the number has fallen from 9.5 million men and women in 1939. The ranks of the unemployed dwindle rapidly as war plants, shipyards, oil fields, and recruiting offices clamor for manpower.

Zinc-coated steel pennies are issued by the U.S. Mint under an Emergency Coinage Act designed to release copper for war production (silver nickels are issued to free nickel for the war effort). By the time the last wartime coins are issued in 1945, they will be made from salvaged shell casings.

Paine, Webber, Jackson and Curtis is created by a merger of two Boston brokerage houses, one of which was founded in 1879. Paine, Webber will grow to become one of the six largest houses in Wall Street.

Germany's General Aniline and Film Corporation is seized by the U.S. government under terms of trading-with-the-enemy laws. The company had been transferred to Swiss ownership in 1939, but the Justice Department claims that Interhandel is a front for the I. G. Farben chemical cartel (GAF will be sold to U.S. private interests in 1965, Swiss owners will receive roughly one-fourth of the proceeds, and the U.S. government will put its share into a Special War Claims Fund to reimburse plaintiffs for losses suffered in World War II).

The last new U.S. automobile that will be produced until 1945 rolls off the Ford assembly line February 10 as auto plants turn to producing tanks, Jeeps, aircraft, and other war matériel on cost-plus contracts under the direction of the War Production Board set up by executive order January 16 with former Sears, Roebuck executive Donald M. Nelson, 49, as WPB director.

A tire-rationing plan has been issued in January by the OPA (above), but experts warn that stronger measures are needed. "Unless corrective measures are taken immediately [to conserve rubber], this country will face both a military and a civilian collapse," say Wall Street sage Bernard Baruch, now 72, Harvard University president James Bryant Conant, 49, and Chicago University physicist Arthur H. Compton.

All but 3 percent of U.S. crude rubber needs have been supplied by Far Eastern sources now cut off by the Japanese, and the nation's stockpile of rubber is only 660,000 tons. Civilian consumption has been running at the rate of between 600,000 and 700,000 tons per year, and U.S. synthetic rubber plants produced only 12,000 tons last year (see 1940).

Mexico agrees in September to sell its entire production of guayule for U.S. rubber production until the end of 1946.

Nationwide gasoline rationing is ordered in September, chiefly to reduce rubber consumption. Rationing had begun in May on the East Coast, where tanker shipments have been reduced by German U-boat sinkings, but more than 200 congressmen have requested and received X stickers entitling them to unlimited supplies of gasoline. All U.S. motorists are assigned A, B, or C stickers as of December 1. Those with A stickers are allowed 4 gallons per week, which will later be reduced to 3 gallons, but nearly half of all motorists obtain B or C stickers, which entitle them to supplementary rations because their driving is essential to the war effort, or to public health, or for similar reasons. Truckers are given T stickers permitting them unlimited amounts of gasoline or diesel fuel, but pleasure driving is banned, and a 35-mile-per-hour speed limit is established on highways.

New York's East River Drive opens May 26 with ceremonies led by Mayor La Guardia. The roadbed between 23rd and 34th Streets is filled with bricks and rubble left from air raids on London and donated by the British government, but the new drive that cuts Manhattan off from the East River is poorly drained and will flood in heavy rains.

The Alcan International Highway opens officially November 30. The road has been built by the United States to link Alaska with the Canadian province of Alberta.

The French Line passenger ship S.S. *Normandie* that went into service in 1935 has been gutted by fire and has capsized in February at her New York pier while being converted for troop transport service. She will be repaired, righted, and will serve as the S.S. *Lafayette* until 1946.

The Liberty ship *Robert E. Peary* is launched November 9 by the Kaiser Shipyards on the Pacific Coast. Her keel was laid 4 ½ days earlier, she is delivered November 12, and she is the first of some 1,460 Liberty-class cargo vessels and other ships that Kaiser will build during the war (see 1941).

Henry Kaiser has built the first steel mill on the Pacific Coast to produce steel for his shipyards, and he has built a magnesium plant as well. He manufactures aircraft, Jeeps, and other war matériel in plants he has acquired for the purpose (see aluminum, 1945; Kaiser Foundation Hospital, above).

Aerojet Corporation is founded by Theodore von Karman to manufacture small jet assistance takeoff motors for U.S. military and (especially) naval aircraft (see Goddard, 1926; Aerojet-General, 1945).

The IL-2 Stormovik dive bomber designed by Soviet aircraft designer Sergei Vlandimirovich Ilyushin, 48, goes into volume production for use against the

1942 (cont.) U.S.S.R.'s German invaders. Some 36,000 of the heavily armored planes will be produced, the plane will serve as the Soviet equivalent of the U.S. DC-3 introduced in 1936, and Eddie Rickenbacker will call it "the best plane for its purpose in the world."

The Office of War Information (OWI) is created by President Roosevelt June 13, with CBS commentator and novelist Elmer Holmes Davis, 52, as its director.

Yank begins publication June 17 under the direction of Colonel Egbert White, 48, who puts out the weekly armed forces magazine with help from *Chattanooga Times* general manager Adolph Shelby Ochs, *Saturday Evening Post* editor Robert Martin Fuoss, and *Liberty* magazine art editor Alfred Strasser. White worked as a sergeant on *Stars and Stripes* in 1918 and has risen through the ranks.

Flip Corkin makes his first appearance in Milton Caniff's comic strip "Terry and the Pirates," which has been appearing since 1934. The new cartoon character is modeled on Caniff's friend Captain Philip G. Cochran, 32, whose exploits in the war will nearly match those of Flip Corkin.

Negro Digest is started by Chicago publisher-insurance executive John Harold Johnson, 24, who has worked his way up from office boy at the Supreme Liberty Life Insurance Company while studying at the University of Chicago and at Northwestern. The first issue has sales of 3,000, but the monthly's circulation will soar to 100,000 when Eleanor Roosevelt writes a piece for its feature series "If I Were a Negro" (*see Ebony,* 1945).

Nonfiction *Victory Through Airpower* by Alexander de Seversky (*see* Republic Aviation, 1939); *Admiral of the Ocean Sea: A Life of Christopher Columbus* by Harvard history professor Samuel Eliot Morison, 55, who has made several voyages following the route of the Great Navigator. Morison is appointed U.S. historian of naval operations with the rank of lieutenant commander and will write a 15-volume *History of U.S. Naval Operations in World War II; The Spanish Labyrinth* by émigré English writer Gerald Brenan, 48, who was caught at Malaga when the Spanish Civil War erupted; "The Myth of Sisyphus," a philosophical essay by French man of letters Albert Camus, 29, who has joined the Resistance against France's Nazi occupation forces; *Generation of Vipers* by U.S. author Philip Gordon Wylie, 40, introduces the term "Momism" to describe the emasculating American matriarchy.

Fiction *Flight to Arras* (*Pilote de la guerre*) by Antoine de Saint-Exupéry; *The Stranger* (*L'etranger*) by Albert Camus; *The Family of Pascal Duarte* (*La familia di Pascal Duarte*) by Spanish novelist Camilio José Cela, 26; *Pied Piper* by English novelist Nevil Shute (Nevil Shute Norway), 43; *To Be a Pilgrim* by Joyce Cary; *The Moon Is Down* by John Steinbeck; *The Just and the Unjust* by James Gould Cozzens; *Put Out More Flags* and *Work Suspended* by Evelyn Waugh.

Poetry *And Suddenly It's Night* (*Ed e subito sera*) by Italian poet Salvatore Quasimodo, 41; *The Man Without a Way* (*Mennen a tan vag*) by Swedish poet Eric Lindegren, 32; *Blood for a Stranger* by U.S. poet Randall Jarrell, 28.

Painting *Patience* by Georges Braque; *L'Oiseau bleu* by Pierre Bonnard; *Red Landscape* by Graham Sutherland; *John Brown Going to His Hanging* by U.S. painter Horace Pippin, 54; *July Hay* and *Negro Soldier* by Thomas Hart Benton. Walter Sickert dies at Bath January 23 at age 81; Grant Wood dies at Iowa City February 12 at age 49.

Theater *The Apollo of Bellac* (*L'Appolon de Bellac*) by Jean Genet 6/16 at Rio de Janeiro's Muncipal Theater; *The Eve of St. Mark* by Maxwell Anderson 10/7 at New York's Cort Theater, with Aline MacMahon, William Prince, Matt Crowley, Martin Ritt, 291 perfs.; *Without Love* by Philip Barry 11/10 at New York's St. James Theater, with Katharine Hepburn, Elliot Nugent, Audrey Christie, 113 perfs.; *The Skin of Our Teeth* by Thornton Wilder 11/18 at New York's Plymouth Theater, with E. G. Marshall and Florence Eldridge as Mr. and Mrs. Antrobus, Fredric March, Tallulah Bankhead, Montgomery Clift, 359 perfs., Pulitzer Prize.

Films Noel Coward and David Lean's *In Which We Serve* with Coward, John Mills, Celia Johnson, Michael Wilding (with a score by Coward); Michael Curtiz's *Casablanca* with Humphrey Bogart, Ingrid Bergman (Dooley Wilson sings "As Time Goes By" from the 1931 Broadway musical flop *Everybody's Welcome* with music by Herman Hupfeld); John Huston's *In This Our Life* with Bette Davis, Olivia de Havilland, George Brent, Dennis Morgan; Orson Welles's *The Magnificent Ambersons* with Joseph Cotten, Tim Holt, Agnes Moorehead, Dolores Costello; Luchino Visconti's neorealistic *Ossessione* (*Obsession*) with a screenplay based without permission on the 1934 James M. Cain detective novel *The Postman Always Rings Twice;* George Stevens's *Woman of the Year* with Katharine Hepburn, Spencer Tracy; George Cukor's *Keeper of the Flame* with Katharine Hepburn, Spencer Tracy; Irving Rapper's *Now, Voyager* with Bette Davis, Paul Henreid, Claude Rains; Frank Tuttle's *This Gun for Hire* with Alan Ladd, Veronica Lake; Preston Sturges's *The Palm Beach Story* with Claudette Colbert, Joel McCrae; William Wyler's *Mrs. Miniver* with Greer Garson, Walter Pidgeon; Walt Disney's *Bambi*; John Farrow's *Wake Island* with Brian Donlevy, William Bendix, Robert Preston; W. S. Van Dyke II's *Journey for Margaret* with Margaret O'Brien, Robert Young, Loraine Day; Lucas Demare's *The Gaucho War* (*La Guerra Gaucha*); Ernst Lubitsch's *To Be or Not to Be* with Jack Benny, Carole Lombard (her last film).

Hollywood musicals David Butler's *The Road to Morocco* with Bing Crosby, Bob Hope, Dorothy Lamour, music by Jimmy Van Heusen, lyrics by Johnny Burke, songs that include "Constantly," "Moonlight Becomes You," and the title song; George Marshall's

Star-Spangled Rhythm with Bing Crosby, Bob Hope, Dorothy Lamour, Ray Milland, Veronica Lake, Susan Hayward, Alan Ladd, Paulette Goddard, Cecil B. DeMille, songs that include "That Old Black Magic" and "Old Glory" by Harold Arlen, music by Johnny Mercer; Busby Berkeley's *For Me and My Gal* with Judy Garland, Gene Kelly; William A. Seiter's *You Were Never Lovelier* with Fred Astaire, Rita Hayworth, music by Jerome Kern, lyrics by Johnny Mercer, songs that include "Dearly Beloved," "I'm Old Fashioned," and the title song; Victor Schertzinger's *The Fleet's In* with William Holden, Dorothy Lamour, Betty Hutton, Eddie Bracken, music by Schertzinger, lyrics by Johnny Mercer, songs that include "Arthur Murray Taught Me Dancing in a Hurry" and "Tangerine"; Irving Cummings's *Springtime in the Rockies* with Betty Grable, Carmen Miranda, Cesar Romero, Jackie Gleason, Charlotte Greenwood, songs that include "I Had the Craziest Dream" by Harry James, lyrics by Mack Gordon; Mark Sandrich's *Holiday Inn* with Bing Crosby, Fred Astaire, music and lyrics by Irving Berlin, songs that include "White Christmas," a holiday number that will break all marks for record sales.

First performances Diversions on a Theme for Piano for Left Hand and Orchestra by Benjamin Britten 1/16 at Philadelphia's Academy of Music (*see* Wittgenstein, 1917); Imaginary Landscape No. 3 by U.S. composer John Milton Cage, Jr., 29, 3/1 at Chicago. The work is scored for an electric oscillator, buzzers of variable frequency, Balinese gongs, generator whine, a coil, tin cans, and a marimbula; Symphony No. 7 (*Leningrad*) by Dmitri Shostakovich (who was airlifted out of the beleaguered city last year) 3/1 at Moscow; Second Essay for Orchestra by Samuel Barber 4/16 at New York's Carnegie Hall; *Lincoln Portrait* (Symphonic Poem) by Aaron Copland, *Mark Twain* by Jerome Kern, and *The Mayor La Guardia Waltzes* by Virgil Thomson 5/14 at Cincinnati; *Bachianos Brasileiras* No. 9 for Orchestra by Heitor Villa-Lobos 6/6 at New York; *Choros* No. 6, No. 9, and No. 11 by Heitor Villa-Lobos 7/5 at Rio de Janeiro.

Ballet *Romeo and Juliet* 4/6 at New York's Metropolitan Opera House, with Jerome Robbins, Hugh Laing, Antony Tudor, Alicia Markova, Sono Osato, music by the late Frederick Delius, choreography by Tudor; *Pillar of Fire* 4/8 at New York's Metropolitan Opera House, with Hugh Laing, Antony Tudor, Nora Kaye (as Hagar), music by Arnold Schoenberg, choreography by Tudor; *Rodeo* 10/16 at New York's Metropolitan Opera House, with Agnes George de Mille, 37, music by Aaron Copland, choreography by de Mille; *Metamorphoses* 11/25 at New York's City Center, with Tanaquil LeClerq, Todd Bolender, music by Paul Hindemith, choreography by George Balanchine; *Gayeneh* 12/9 at Molotov, with music (including a "Saber Dance") by Armenian Soviet composer Aram Khatchaturian, 39.

Broadway musicals *Star and Garter* 1/24 at the Music Box Theater, with Bobby Clark, Gypsy Rose Lee, Georgia Sothern in an extravaganza mounted by showman Mike Todd, songs that include Harold Arlen's "Blues in the Night" and Irving Berlin's "The Girl on the Police Gazette," 609 perfs.; *By Jupiter* 6/2 at the Shubert Theater, with Ray Bolger, music by Richard Rodgers, lyrics by Lorenz Hart, 427 perfs.; *This Is the Army* 7/24 at the Broadway Theater, with an all-soldier cast for the benefit of the Army Emergency Relief Fund, music, book, and lyrics by Irving Berlin, songs that include "I Left My Heart at the Stage-Door Canteen," the title song, and songs from Berlin's 1918 musical *Yip-Yip-Yaphank*, 113 perfs.

Popular songs "Warsaw Concerto" by English composer Richard Addinsell, 38; "When the Lights Go on Again" by Eddie Seiler, Sol Marcus, Bennie Benjemen; "Praise the Lord and Pass the Ammunition" by Frank Loesser, who quotes a remark alleged to have been made by a U.S. Navy chaplain at Pearl Harbor last year; "Don't Get Around Much Anymore" by Duke Ellington, lyrics by Bob Russell; "Paper Doll" by Johnny S. Black; "In the Blue of Evening" by Alfred A. D'Artega, lyrics by Tom Adair; "My Devotion" by Ric Holman and Johnny Napton; "There Will Never Be Another You" by Harry Warren, lyrics by Mack Gordon (for the film *Iceland*); "I've Heard That Song Before" by Jule Styne, lyrics by Sammy Cahn (for the film *Youth on Parade*); "I'm Glad There Is You" by pianist Paul Madeira Mertz who has played with the Dorsey brothers and with the late Bix Beiderbecke; "Serenade in Blue" by Harry Warren, lyrics by Mack Gordon; "Who Wouldn't Love You" by Carl Fischer, lyrics by Bill Carey (whose song will be popularized by bandleader Kay Kyser); "Jingle Jangle Jingle" by Joseph J. Lelley, lyrics by Frank Loesser; "One Dozen Roses" by bandleader Dick Jergens and Walter Donovan, lyrics by Roger Lewis and Country Washburn; "Perdido" by Juan Tizol, lyrics by H. J. Lengsfelder, Erin Drake.

The first "golden record" is presented February 10 to Glenn Miller, whose 1941 hit "Chattanooga Choo Choo" has been sprayed with gold by RCA-Victor in recognition of the record's having sold more than 1 million copies. Miller disbands his orchestra late in the year, he will join the U.S. Army Air Force as a major, he will organize a large orchestra that will broadcast to troops in every theater of the war, but he will disappear in mid-September of 1944 on a flight from England to Paris.

Garden State Racetrack opens under the management of New Jersey entrepreneur Eugene V. Mori, 44, who has sold stock in the venture door-to-door to obtain the $1 million needed to acquire the franchise.

New York City's pinball machines are outlawed by the City Council under a law pushed through by Mayor La Guardia, who says schoolboys are stealing nickels and dimes from their mothers' pocketbooks to feed the machines that are feeding the underworld. The law takes effect in January, and machines made by Harry Williams and others are smashed

1942 (cont.) with a sledgehammer by La Guardia for news photographers (most of the confiscated machines are dumped into the ocean).

The St. Louis Cardinals win the World Series by defeating the New York Yankees 4 games to 1.

 Nevada divorces are ruled valid throughout the United States by the Supreme Court.

Boston's Cocoanut Grove nightclub becomes a roaring holocaust Saturday night, November 28. The club is packed with nearly 1,000 patrons of whom 492 die and 270 are injured.

 Famine kills some 1.6 million Bengalese as the rice crop near Bombay is ruined by fungus disease.

Oxfam is founded to fight world famine by Oxford University classical scholar Gilbert Murray, 76.

Millions of Europeans live in semistarvation as German troops cut off areas in the Ukraine and North Caucasus that have produced half of Soviet wheat and pork production. Food supplies fall to starvation levels in German-occupied Greece, Poland, and parts of Yugoslavia.

U.S. sugar rationing begins in May after consumers have created scarcities by hoarding 100-pound bags and commercial users have filled their warehouses. One-sixth of U.S. sugar supplies have come from the Philippines, which are in Japanese hands, U.S. householders are asked by ration boards to state how much sugar they have stockpiled, ration stamps are deducted to compensate, the weekly ration averages 8 ounces per person, but it will rise to 12 ounces.

Hoarding of coffee leads to coffee rationing, which begins in November.

 "Victory Gardens" are cultivated by Americans in backyards and in communal plots as vegetables become scarce, especially in California, where two-thirds of the vegetable crop has been grown by Japanese-Americans (*see* above). Forty percent of all U.S. vegetables are produced in nearly 20 million Victory Gardens but the number will fall as interest flags.

Britons "Dig for Victory" and raise vegetables in backyard gardens.

Soviet geneticist Nikolai Vavilov dies of malnutrition in the prison where he has been confined since 1940. Vavilov's anti-intellectual rival T. D. Lysenko advises Josef Stalin to switch from traditional grain crops to millet, which requires less moisture.

Washington State plant pathologist J. George Harrar, 36, is persuaded by Elvin C. Stakman of the Rockefeller Foundation to leave his new post as head of the state university's plant pathology department at the end of the school year and to lead the program to redevelop Mexico's rural economy (*see* 1941; 1943).

Florida becomes the leading U.S. producer of oranges, passing California.

 Forty-two percent of U.S. white bread is enriched with B vitamins and iron, up from 30 percent last

year. Louisiana and South Carolina enact laws requiring that corn staples be enriched.

British flour extraction rates are raised to 85 percent to stretch wheat supplies. The higher extraction rate raises levels of vitamins and minerals in British bread (which remains unrationed; *see* 1916).

 U.S. troops stationed in Britain are forbidden to drink local milk, which is not pasteurized. Little of Britain's milk is pasteurized, and many diseases that affect Britons are ascribed to unpasteurized milk (*see* 1900).

 K rations are packed for U.S. troops by Chicago's Wrigley Company (*see* 1893). Each combat ration contains "defense" biscuits and compressed Graham biscuits, canned meat or substitute, three tablets of sugar, four cigarettes, and a stick of Wrigley's chewing gum. The breakfast ration includes also a fruit bar and soluble coffee (*see* below), the dinner ration includes flavored and plain dextrose tablets and a packet of lemon-juice powder, and the supper ration includes bouillon powder and a bar of concentrated chocolate called "Ration D."

Instant Maxwell House coffee has its beginnings in the soluble coffee for K rations (above) that has been developed for the armed forces by General Foods at its Hoboken, N.J., Maxwell House coffee factory. The coffee will be introduced to the public after the war as Instant Maxwell House (*see* Nescafé, 1938).

U.S. soft drink companies are permitted enough sugar to meet quotas of from 50 to 80 percent of the production attained in the base year 1941 but with no limit on sales to the armed forces. Pepsi-Cola has a much smaller 1941 base than Coca-Cola and is unable to import Mexican sugar as such without having it subject to ration rules, so Pepsi builds a plant just across the border and imports syrup until the government says syrup is sugar and halts its import.

Milk deliveries in most U.S. cities are reduced to alternate days, and in some cities horse-drawn milk wagons reappear.

Dannon yogurt is introduced in New York by Swiss-born Spanish émigré Joe Metzger, who goes into business with Isaac Carasso (*see* 1941). Metzger employs his 23-year-old son Juan at the company's Bronx factory, the factory turns out 200 8-ounce jars per day initially and sells them at 11 cents each to the mostly ethnic New York yogurt market, but Dannon will relocate next year at Long Island City and will increase its production (*see* 1950).

Kellogg's Raisin Bran is introduced by the Kellogg Company (*see* 1928). The new breakfast food is 10.6 percent sugar (*see* 1950).

Hunt Foods, Inc., is organized by Norton Simon who liquidates his Val Vita Foods Corporation of 1932, takes a personal profit of $2 million, and changes the name of the 52-year-old Hunt Brothers Packing Company of Hayward, Calif., which he has acquired. Simon introduces the private label canned foods of the Hunt Brothers under the Hunt name, he will buy other private label canneries, and he will take advantage of wartime food and tin shortages to give the Hunt label national recognition (*see* 1945).

La Choy Food Products sells its Detroit plant to the government and moves to a 25-acre site at Archbold, Ohio (*see* 1937). La Choy will be the largest single customer for Michigan celery which it will use along with mushrooms from Pennsylvania, bamboo shoots and water chestnuts from postwar Taiwan, mung beans from Oklahoma, Texas, Thailand, and South America, and domestic flour and soybeans to become the world's largest producer of canned Chinese food.

Sunbeam bread is introduced by some members of the 20-year-old Quality Bakers of America, who adopt the "Miss Sunbeam" trademark.

How to Cook a Wolf by M. F. K. Fisher helps Americans cope with wartime food shortages.

1943 The tide of war turns against the Axis in the Pacific, in North Africa, in Italy, and on the Russian front.

Anzac (Australian-New Zealand-Canadian) and U.S. forces take the southeastern tip of New Guinea from the Japanese January 22 and assure the safety of Australia from Japanese invasion.

Allied forces take Guadalcanal in the Solomon Islands February 8 after heavy fighting.

The Battle of the Bismarck Sea in early March ends with U.S. Liberator and Flying Fortress bombers sinking an estimated 21 Japanese transports bound for New Guinea with 15,000 troops.

Allied forces take the Japanese air base at Munda in the Solomons August 5 and destroy more than 300 Japanese planes 2 weeks later in attacks on the Wewak airfield in New Guinea.

U.S. troops that landed at Sitka in the Aleutians in May retake Kiska August 15.

Tripoli falls to the British Eighth Army January 23. Axis forces in Tunisia retreat with the British in hot pursuit.

The Casablanca Conference attended by President Roosevelt, Prime Minister Churchill, General Giraud, and General de Gaulle ends January 27 with the appointment of General Dwight D. Eisenhower as commander of unified forces in North Africa.

Berlin rushes reinforcements to Tunisia, the Germans take Kasserine Pass February 22, but U.S. troops retake the pass 4 days later. Tunis falls to the British May 7, Bizerte falls to the Americans the same day, and Axis resistance ends in North Africa.

British paratroopers and U.S. airborne troops invade Sicily July 9 and 10. More than 500 U.S. bombers raid Rome July 19.

Benito Mussolini and his cabinet resign under pressure July 25. Marshal Pietro Badoglio, 72, takes over.

Allied armies take Messina August 17, they cross the Straits of Messina, and they invade Southern Italy as representatives of the new Badoglio regime (above) sign an armistice with Allied officers at Algiers.

Italy has surrendered unconditionally, the Allied high command announces September 8, but German forces in Italy resist the Allied advance.

The U.S. Fifth Army lands at Salerno September 9 and sustains heavy losses. The Americans take Naples October 1 as German forces seize Rome and other major Italian cities.

Heavy bombing of industrial centers in Germany and occupied France has begun on a continuous basis in January.

Soviet troops relieve Leningrad's 17-month siege in February, but the Germans will blockade the narrow corridor to the city more than 1,200 times in the next year and starvation will continue. By January of next year the city's population will have shrunk from 3 million to 560,000.

The Germans lose 500,000 men in 3 months of heavy winter fighting as the Russians retake Kharkov and other key cities, but the Germans mount a spring offensive and recapture Kharkov March 15.

The Kremlin quietly dissolves the Comintern in May in consideration of the wartime alliance between the Communists and the Western Allies (*see* 1935).

The Battle of Kursk that begins July 5 involves 6,000 German and Russian tanks and 4,000 planes. It ends after a week of heavy fighting in a victory for the Soviet Fifth Army but while the Germans have lost 70,000 men, 2,000 tanks, 1,392 planes, and 5,000 vehicles the Russian losses are at least comparable.

Soviet forces retake Kharkov August 23 with help from increased Soviet industrial output and with U.S. war matériel including steel, industrial machinery, planes, and motor vehicles supplied via Archangel, Vladivostok, and the Persian Gulf.

Soviet forces retake Smolensk September 25 and retake Kiev on the Dnieper River November 6.

The Moscow Conference in late October establishes a European advisory commission on terms of German surrender, separation of Austria from Germany, and destruction of Italy's Fascist regime.

The United Nations has its beginnings in a brief congressional resolution drafted by freshman congressman J. William Fulbright, 38, of Arkansas (*see* Conference on Food and Agriculture, below; Fulbright awards, 1946).

The United Nations Relief and Rehabilitation Administration (UNRRA) is established November 9 by an agreement signed at Washington.

The Teheran Conference in late November is attended by President Roosevelt, Prime Minister Churchill, and Premier Stalin. They discuss an Allied military landing in France and agree to set up an advisory commission to study European problems.

Allied forces have landed on Bougainville in the Solomons November 1 following the bombing of Rabaul in New Britain by Allied planes since October 12.

1943 (cont.) Tarawa and Makin in the Gilbert Islands are taken by U.S. troops in late November. Allied forces land on Cape Gloucester, New Britain, December 26.

France's Pas de Calais area is attacked December 24 by 3,000 Allied planes that include 1,300 from the U.S. Eighth Air Force.

 The Battle of the Warsaw Ghetto that begins Passover Eve, April 18, ends 6 weeks later with 5,000 German troops killed and wounded, but 5,000 Jews have been killed defending themselves against German tanks and artillery. Some 500,000 Jews had been locked into an area that formerly accommodated half that number, and while thousands have escaped to join the Polish resistance, some 20,000 are deported to such death camps as Auschwitz (Oswiecim), Birkenau, Belzec, Chmelno, Maidenek, and Sobibor. Jews at Bialystock, Tarnow, and other Polish cities offer resistance, but few will survive the genocidal Nazi holocaust.

The plan for the "extermination of the Jews" is well advanced, says SS führer Heinrich Himmler October 4 in a speech to his Gruppenführer (lieutenant generals), despite pleas to spare this or that "exceptional" Jew. The Nazi elite force will not be deflected from their objective, says Himmler, and while he says "we will never speak of it" in public, the destruction of the Jews will remain forever "an unwritten and never-to-be-written page of glory."

The SS in Denmark begins rounding up Danish Jews in October after having left them untouched since 1940, but the Danes help most of their Jewish compatriots escape to safety in Sweden.

U.S. Secretary of the Interior Harold L. Ickes is ordered by President Roosevelt to take over soft coal mines threatened with strikes, but United Mine Workers boss John L. Lewis defies threats to send in troops. "They can't dig coal with bayonets," says Lewis.

A West Virginia state law requiring schoolchildren to salute the flag or face expulsion is ruled invalid by the Supreme Court June 14 in the case of *West Virginia Board of Education v. Bernette.*

A Detroit race riot is quelled by federal troops June 22 after 34 have died in 2 days of disturbances that have involved thousands.

Harlem has a race riot August 1.

 The $109 billion budget submitted to Congress by President Roosevelt January 11 has had $100 billion earmarked for the war effort.

A "hold-the-line" anti-inflation order is issued by President Roosevelt in April at a time when the wholesale price index published monthly by the Labor Department's Bureau of Statistics since 1913 stands at 103.1. By August 1945, the price index will have risen only to 105.8, thanks to price controls.

A "Pay-As-You-Go" Current Tax Payment Act is voted June 9 by Congress which adopts a plan

proposed by R. H. Macy chairman Beardsley Ruml, 49. The act provides for income taxes on wages and salaries to be withheld by employers from paychecks.

Ford Motor Company president Edsel Ford dies at age 49 and bequeaths 90 percent of his stock in the company to the Ford Foundation he set up in 1936. More than 40 percent of the company's stock has been owned by Edsel Ford, and his will employs a tax avoidance scheme engineered by Wall Street investment banker Sidney Weinberg, 52, chairman of Goldman, Sachs (*see* 1947).

The Nuffield Foundation for medical, scientific, and social research is created by British automaker William Richard Morris, 66, Viscount Nuffield, who has made a fortune with his Morris Motors, Ltd.

Rent control in the United States is imposed by federal law and takes effect in November. The controls will expire in 1950 but will be continued by New York State and some other states and will be continued thereafter by New York City.

 The "Big Inch" pipeline to carry Texas oil to the eastern seaboard is completed, and the ban on nonessential driving is revoked in September following a dramatic decline in highway traffic deaths.

Penicillin is applied for the first time to the treatment of chronic diseases (*see* 1942; 1945).

The word "antibiotic" is coined by Rutgers University microbiology professor Selman Abraham Waksman, 43, who finds the actinomycete *Streptomyces grisens* in the soil of a field and in the throat of a child (*see* streptomycin, 1944).

The "Pap" test for detecting cervical cancer is recognized by the medical establishment after 15 years of work by Greek-American physician George Nicholas Papanicolaou, 60, who developed the vaginal smear test at Cornell University in 1928 to diagnose the cancer that has been the leading cause of death among U.S. women. The test is based on exfoliative cytology (microscopic study of cells shed by bodily organs), and within 20 years it will have reduced cancer of the cervix to number three as a cause of death among U.S. women.

The Infant and Child in the Culture of Today by Yale University psychoclinician Arnold L. Gesell, 63, and his assistant Frances Ilg says that the infant should not be subjected to totalitarian rule but should be given autonomy. Subtitled *The Guidance of Development in Home and Nursery School,* the book is based on pioneering studies based in part on the use of motion pictures to determine normal behavior in children and to establish norms, it gives parents rules to enable them to anticipate the developmental stages of their growing children, and it goes through 12 printings in 1 year (*see* Spock, 1946).

The hallucinogenic properties of LSD (lysergic acid diethylamide) are discovered accidentally by Swiss chemist Albert Hofmann of Sandoz A.G., who is "seized by a peculiar sensation of vertigo and restlessness. . . . With my eyes closed, fantastic pictures of extraordinary plasticity and intensive color seemed to surge toward me. After two hours this state gradually wore off." Hofmann has swallowed a derivative of ergot, he has spectacular hallucinations when he ingests a quarter of a milligram of the compound, and his findings will spur research in psychopharmacology (*see* ergot, 857 A.D.; Gaddum, 1953).

Production of synthetic hormones is pioneered by U.S. chemist Russell Marker, 41, who discovers a cheap source of the hormone progesterone in the barbasco plant that grows wild in Mexico. Using an extract from the root of this member of the Dioscorea family, Marker works in a Mexico City pottery shop, he produces 2,000 grams of progesterone worth $80 per gram in just 2 months, he will join a small Mexican drug firm to form Syntex, S.A., and another group of chemists will buy him out (*see* below; cortisone, 1947).

The American Broadcasting Company (ABC) is created by Life Savers millionaire Edward Noble (*see* 1920). NBC has been ordered by the Federal Communications Commission to divest itself of one of its two radio networks, Noble writes a check for $8 million to acquire the 16-year-old Blue Network, he turns it into ABC, and he sets out to rival NBC and CBS.

A $40 electric hearing aid is introduced by Zenith Radio Corporation whose boss Eugene McDonald has lost the hearing in one ear following an automobile accident and who has found that the only available hearing aids sell for between $150 and $200 (*see* 1935; 1952).

Cartoonist Bill Mauldin, 21, is shipped overseas and joins the Mediterranean staff of the U.S. Army newspaper *Stars and Stripes*. William Henry Mauldin will cover campaigns in Italy, France, and Germany, and the miseries of his grimy G.I. characters Willie and Joe will reflect those of countless enlisted men enduring the hardships of war.

Foote, Cone and Belding, Inc., is founded by former Lord & Thomas advertising agency executives Emerson Foote, 36, Fairfax Mastick Cone, 40, and Don Belding, 45, following the retirement of Lord & Thomas president Albert Lasker, now 63, who has made a vast fortune promoting the wares of such clients as American Tobacco Company and who begins to give financial support to cancer research.

Popular Library is started as a new U.S. paperback publishing house to compete for the growing market begun in 1939 by Pocket Books (*see* Avon, 1941; Bantam, 1945).

Nonfiction *Christianity and Democracy* by French philosopher Jacques Maritain, 61, who became a Roman Catholic in 1906 and who champions the cause of liberal Catholicism; *Being and Nothingness* (*L'Etre et le Néant*) by Jean Paul Sartre, who was captured at the fall of France in June 1940, was held prisoner of war until April 1941, and has been engaged in the resistance against occupation forces.

Fiction *Arrival and Departure* by Arthur Koestler; *The Man Without Qualities* (*Der Mann ohne Eigenschaften*) by the late Robert Musil, who fled Germany after the 1938 Anschluss, was refused refuge by the United States, and died last year in Switzerland at age 62, leaving his novel unfinished; *Dead Fires* (*Fogo Morto*) by Brazilian novelist José Lins do Rego; *The Fountainhead* by Russian-American novelist Ayn Rand, 38; *The Big Rock Candy Mountain* by Wallace Stegner.

Juvenile *The Little Prince* (*Le Petit Prince*) by Antoine de Saint-Exupéry who has joined the Free French forces in North Africa; *Johnny Tremain: A Novel for Young and Old* by U.S. author Esther Forbes, 52, who has won a Pulitzer prize for a biography of Paul Revere.

Poetry *Four Quartets* by T. S. Eliot; *Western Star* by Stephen Vincent Benét who dies at New York March 13 at age 44.

Painting *Prodigal Son, Wreck of the Ole '97, Night Firing of Tobacco, Sugar Cane*, and *Picnic* by Thomas Hart Benton; *Broadway Boogie-Woogie* by Piet Mondrian; *The Juggler* and *Crucifixion* by Marc Chagall; *Odysseus and Calypso* by Max Beckmann; *The Thanksgiving Turkey* by Grandma Moses. Chaim Soutine dies August 9 at age 49 while undergoing surgery in a Paris hospital; Marsden Hartley dies at Ellsworth, Me., September 2 at age 66.

Theater *The Patriots* by Sidney Kingsley 1/29 at New York's National Theater, with Madge Evans, Francis Reid, 157 perfs.; *The Good Woman of Setzuan* (*Der gute Mensch von Sezuan*) by Bertolt Brecht 2/4 at Zurich's Schauspielhaus; *Harriet* by F. Ryerson and Cohn Claues 3/3 at New York's Henry Miller Theater, with Helen Hayes, 377 perfs.; *Kiss and Tell* by F. Hugh Herbert 3/17 at New York's Biltmore

Bill Mauldin's sardonic cartoons deglamorized war and found humor at the expense of army brass.

1943 (cont.) Theater, with Joan Caulfield as Corliss Archer, Robert White as Dexter Perkins, 103 perfs.; *Tomorrow the World* by U.S. playwrights James Gow and Arnaud d'Usseau 4/14 at New York's Ethel Barrymore Theater, with Ralph Bellamy, Shirley Booth, Skippy Homeier, 500 perfs.; *Present Laughter* by Noel Coward 4/29 at London's Haymarket Theatre, with Coward, Joyce Carey, 38 perfs. (plus 528 beginning 4/16/47); *This Happy Breed* by Noel Coward 4/30 at London's Haymarket Theatre, with Coward, Joyce Carey, 38 perfs. (alternating with *Present Laughter,* above); *The Voice of the Turtle* by John Van Druten 12/8 at New York's Morosco Theater, with Margaret Sullavan, Audrey Christie, Elliott Nugent, 1,557 perfs.; *While the Sun Shines* by Terence Rattigan 12/24 at London's Globe Theatre, 1,154 perfs.

New York Times theatrical caricaturist Al Hirschfeld, 40, introduces the name of his newborn daughter Nina into his drawings and begins a puzzle game that will continue for more than 35 years. Hirschfeld's drawings have appeared on the drama pages of the *Times* for 20 years, and his circus sketch includes a poster with the legend "Nina the Wonder Child."

The New York City Center of Music and Drama opens on West 55th Street, where the city has acquired the 55th Street Shriners Auditorium for nonpayment of taxes. Mayor La Guardia has proposed that the city have a popular-priced performing arts center, and City Council president Newbold Morris has suggested that the Shriners Auditorium be turned into a "theater for the people."

Films The Soviet documentary *Stalingrad;* Roy Boulting's *Desert Victory;* Zoltan Korda's *Sahara* with Humphrey Bogart; Hal Wallis's *Air Force* with John Ridgely, John Garfield, George Tobias; Richard Rossen's *Corvette-225* with Randolph Scott; Michael Curtiz's *Mission to Moscow* with Walter Huston; Akira Kurosawa's *Sanshiro Sugata;* Henri-Georges Clouzot's *Le Corbeau* with Pierre Fresnay, Ginette Leclerc (Clouzot and Fresnay are accused of unpatriotic activity for having made the picture); Alfred Hitchcock's *Shadow of a Doubt* with Teresa Wright, Joseph Cotten, Hume Cronyn; Robert Stevenson's *Jane Eyre* with Orson Welles, Joan Fontaine, Peggy Ann Garner; William Wellman's *The Ox-Bow Incident* with Henry Fonda; George Stevens's *The More the Merrier* with Jean Arthur, Joel McCrae, Charles Coburn; William Wellman's *Lady of Burlesque* with Barbara Stanwyck as ecdysiast Gypsy Rose Lee; Henry King's *The Song of Bernadette* with Jennifer Jones; Mervyn LeRoy's *Madame Curie* with Greer Garson; Sam Wood's *For Whom the Bell Tolls* with Gary Cooper, Ingrid Bergman, Katina Paxinou, Akim Tamiroff; Herman Shumlin's *Watch on the Rhine* with Paul Lukas, Bette Davis; René Clair's *Forever and a Day* with Edmund Goulding, Cedric Hardwicke, Charles Laughton, Claude Rains, and dozens of other British actors and actresses; Billy Wilder's *Five Graves to Cairo* with Franchot Tone, Ann Baxter, Erich von Stroheim, Akim Tamiroff.

Hollywood musicals Gregory Ratoff's *Something to Shout About* with Don Ameche, Janet Blair, songs by Cole Porter that include "You'd Be So Nice to Come Home to"; Edward H. Griffith's *The Sky's the Limit* with Fred Astaire, Joan Leslie, Robert Benchley, songs that include "My Shining Hour" and "One for My Baby" by Harold Arlen, lyrics by Johnny Mercer; Tim Whelan's *Higher and Higher* with Frank Sinatra, Michele Morgan, Jack Haley, songs that include "I Couldn't Sleep a Wink Last Night" by Jimmy McHugh, lyrics by Harold Adamson; Curtis Bernhardt's *Happy Go Lucky* with Mary Martin, Dick Powell, songs that include "Let's Get Lost" and " 'Murder,' He Says" by Jimmy McHugh, lyrics by Frank Loesser; Edward Sutherland's *Dixie* with Bing Crosby, Dorothy Lamour, songs that include "Sunday, Monday or Always" and "If You Please" by Jimmy Van Heusen, lyrics by Johnny Mercer.

First performances *Freedom Morning* Symphonic Poem for Orchestra, Tenor, and Chorus by Marc Blitzstein 4/28 at London, with Richard Hayes as soloist and a chorus of 200 black U.S. aviation engineers; Symphony No. 8 by Dmitri Shostakovich 11/4 at the Moscow Conservatory; Symphony No. 4 by Howard Hanson 12/3 at Boston's Symphony Hall.

Ballet *Mother Goose Suite* in October at New York's Central High School of the Needle Trades Auditorium, with music by the late Maurice Ravel.

Broadway musicals *Something for the Boys* 1/7 at the Alvin Theater, with Ethel Merman, book by Harold and Dorothy Fields, music and lyrics by Cole Porter, songs that include "Hey, Good Lookin' " 422 perfs.; *Oklahoma!* 3/31 at the St. James Theater, with Alfred Drake, Celeste Holme, Howard da Silva, a book based on the 1931 Broadway play *Green Grow the Lilacs,* music by Richard Rodgers, lyrics by Oscar Hammerstein II, songs that include "Oh, What a Beautiful Morning," "People Will Say We're in Love," "All or Nothing," "Kansas City," "I Cain't Say No," "Pore Jud," "The Surrey with the Fringe on Top," "I Want to Be Happy" (lyrics by Irving Caesar), and the title song (lyrics by Otto Harbach), 2,212 perfs.; *The Ziegfeld Follies* 4/1 at the Winter Garden Theater, with Milton Berle, music by Ray Henderson with music by Harold Rome interpolated, lyrics by Jack Yellen and others, 553 perfs.; *One Touch of Venus* 10/7 at the Imperial Theater, with Mary Martin, Kenny Baker, music by Kurt Weill, libretto by S. J. Perelman and Ogden Nash, lyrics by Nash, songs that include "Speak Low," "West Wind," 567 perfs.; *Carmen Jones* 12/2 at the Broadway Theater, with Muriel Smith, drummer Cosy Cole, music by the late Georges Bizet, book and lyrics by Oscar Hammerstein II, 503 perfs.

Popular songs "Do Nothin' Till You Hear from Me" by Duke Ellington, lyrics by Bob Russell; "Comin' in on a Wing and a Prayer" by Jimmy McHugh, lyrics by Harold Adamson; "Holiday for Strings" by David Rose; "Mairzy Dotes" by Milton Drake, Al Hoffman, Jerry Livingston; "I've Heard That Song Before" by

Jule Styne and Sammy Cahn; "How Many Hearts Have You Broken?" by Al Kaufman, lyrics by Marty Symes; "San Fernando Valley" by Gordon Jenkins (title song for film); "They're Either Too Young or Too Old" by Arthur Schwartz, lyrics by Frank Loesser (for David Butler's film *Thank Your Lucky Stars*); "Tico-Tico" by Brazilian composer Zequinha Abreu, lyrics by Aloysio Oliveira; "Besame Mucho" by Mexican songwriter Consuelo Velazquez.

Count Fleet wins the Kentucky Derby and goes on to win U.S. racing's Triple Crown but injures his leg coming down the stretch at Belmont Park. He is retired to stud.

Mexico City's Hipodromo de las Americas opens. Wall Street "bear" Ben Smith has bankrolled the $2 million racetrack.

The New York Yankees win the World Series by defeating the St. Louis Cardinals 4 games to 1.

Americans are told to "use it up, wear it out, make it do or do without." Shoes are rationed beginning February 7, but while Britons are allowed only one pair per year, the U.S. ration is three pairs, only slightly below the 3.43 bought on average in 1941.

Sneakers are impossible to find, and schoolboys are obliged to buy shoes with reclaimed rubber soles that leave black marks on gymnasium floors.

Rubber, metal, paper, silk, and nylon are all collected for recycling, and housewives who wash and flatten tins for recycling save kitchen fats to be exchanged for red ration points at the butcher's (*see* below).

The Pentagon, completed January 15 at Arlington, Va., is the world's largest office building and provides space for the vast and growing number of U.S. war administrators. The $83 million, five-story, five-sided building has 6.5 million square feet of floor space, 17 miles of corridors, and 7,748 windows.

The Jefferson Memorial is dedicated at Washington, D.C., on land reclaimed from the Potomac. The monument contains a 19-foot bronze statue of the nation's third president.

Rent control (above) will prevent landlords from raising rents by more than a small percentage each year and will be a factor in discouraging new housing construction in New York City.

The Mexican volcano Paricutin emerges in a Michoacan cornfield in February and begins eruptions that will continue for 7 years. The new volcano buries some nearby populated areas under lava and ashes, it threatens a wide area, and it will grow to a height of 820 feet from its base.

A United Nations Conference on Food and Agriculture at Hot Springs, Ark., from May 19 to June 3 provides for a UN Food and Agricultural Organization (FAO; *see* 1945).

DDT is introduced to fight insect pests that destroy U.S. crops (*see* Muller, 1939).

Mexican wheat production is spurred by research undertaken with support from the Rockefeller Foundation (*see* Stakman, Harrar, 1942). Mexican agricultural output will increase by 300 percent in the next 25 years, while the country's population increases by 70 percent (*see* Borlaug, 1944).

Plowman's Folly by Kentucky soil and crop expert Edward H. Faulkner says that plowing interferes with the natural capillary action of the soil. Faulkner recommends disk harrowing which works green vegetation into the soil and, he says, will mean less erosion, will require less fertilizer, and will produce better crops.

Rinderpest kills most of Burma's livestock. Since animals provide most of the country's power for irrigation and cultivation, the Burmese rice crop declines, and little is left for export to Bengal (*see* 1944).

Japan has her worst rice crop in 50 years. The daily 1,500-calorie subsistence level cannot always be met.

U.S. meat rationing begins March 29, but the ration is 28 ounces per week, and meat production rises by 50 percent. Meat consumption actually rises to 128.9 pounds per capita on an annual basis as the wartime economic boom puts more money into working people's pockets and as meat prices are rolled back to September 1942 levels. G.I.'s are served 4.5 pounds of meat per week (navy men get 7 pounds), and creamed chipped beef is a staple of service chow lines as Washington takes 60 percent of prime and choice beef and 80 percent of utility grade beef.

An estimated 20 percent of U.S. beef goes into black market channels, bacon virtually disappears from stores, western cattle rustlers kill and dress beef in mobile slaughterhouses and sell the meat to packing houses, and wholesalers force butchers to buy hearts, kidneys, lungs, and tripe in order to get good cuts of meat.

Butchers upgrade meat, selling low grades at ceiling prices and at the ration point levels of top grade.

Less than one-fourth of Americans have "good" diets according to a nutrition study undertaken in 1941.

"Recommended Dietary Allowances" for various nutrients are published for the first time by the Food and Nutrition Board, National Academy of Sciences-National Research Council.

Bread-enrichment laws pass the Texas and Alabama legislatures. Seventy-five percent of U.S. white bread is enriched with iron and some B vitamins, up from 30 percent in 1941.

Japan acts to prevent beriberi, which is disabling many civilians. The Tokyo government distributes no white rice and orders citizens to eat *haigamai* (brown rice) or *hichibuzuki mai* (70 percent polished rice), but many, if not most, Japanese laboriously hull their *hichibuzuki mai* to obtain the white, glutinous, nutritionally deficient rice they prefer.

"Converted" rice is developed by Texas produce broker Gordon Harwell with English food chemist

1943 (cont.) Eric Huzenlaub by pressure-cooking rough, unhulled rice in a way that diffuses the outer bran layers into the kernels' starchy protein and then steaming the rice in a way that partially gelatinizes the starch to seal in the vitamins. Vacuum-dried and then air-dried to restore its original moisture content, the rice is then hulled and its bran removed, leaving a product that retains 80 percent of the natural B vitamins in rough rice, or paddy.

Uncle Ben's converted rice will be marketed after the war by Harwell (above), and it will later be enriched with added B vitamins.

U.S. butter consumption falls to 11 pounds per capita, down from 17 pounds in the 1930s, as Americans forgo some of their 4 ounces per week ration in order to save red stamps for meat. Butter is often unavailable, since most butterfat is employed to make cheese for Lend-Lease aid.

U.S. margarine is subject to a 10 percent federal tax if artificially colored (¼ cent per pound if colored by the consumer or used uncolored). Millions of householders use vegetable dye to color their white margarine yellow, but as more consumers turn to margarine, Eleanor Roosevelt campaigns for a repeal of the margarine tax (*see* 1950).

Cheese is rationed at the rate of 4 pounds per week per capita but requires red stamps that may also be used for meat. Americans ate cheese at a rate of 2.5 pounds per week before the war, but home economists estimate that the country's most affluent one-third ate cheese at the rate of 5 pounds per week, while the poor ate scarcely 1 pound.

Sale of sliced bread is banned by Agriculture Secretary Claude Wickard in a move to hold down prices.

Flour, fish, and canned goods join the list of rationed foods, but coffee is derationed in July. Americans eat far better than do citizens of the other belligerent nations (Britons enjoy only about two-thirds of what Americans are allowed under rationing programs).

Cleveland's Tip Top and Forest City Breweries are acquired by Brewing Corporation of America, which thus reaches a brewing capacity of 1 million barrels per year (*see* 1933).

Frankfort Distillers and its well-known Four Roses and Paul Jones brands are acquired by Distillers Corporation–Seagram as U.S. distillers produce alcohol for synthetic rubber production (*see* 1933).

The Chinese Exclusion Acts of 1882 and 1902 are repealed by a Chinese Act signed into law by President Roosevelt December 17. The new act makes Chinese residents of the United States eligible for naturalization and permits immigration of an annual quota of 105 Chinese (*see* 1965).

Development of oral contraceptives is pioneered by chemist Russell Marker (above), whose Syntex, S.A. will become a major supplier of raw materials for oral contraceptives (*see* Pincus, 1955; Enovid 10, 1960).

1944 Allied troops land 25 miles south of Rome at Anzio and Nettuno January 22, but while the Germans have just withdrawn their patrols in the area to reinforce the Gustav line at Cassino to the south, General J. P. Lucas commanding the U.S. VI Corps misses the opportunity to advance on Rome. He has his men dig foxholes for 2 days to consolidate their beachhead, the delay gives the Germans time to rush in reinforcements, German fire from the Alban Hills pins down the 50,000 U.S. and British soldiers, the Allies build up their forces to 125,000, but the road to Rome has been closed, the Allies are unable to launch an offensive until May 23 when they receive enough air support to advance on Rome, and they finally take the city from the Germans June 4 after sustaining 25,000 casualties.

D day, June 6, sees 176,000 Allied troops landing at Omaha Beach, Utah Beach, and other Normandy beaches under the supreme command of General Eisenhower whose forces take Cherbourg June 6.

Allied plans for Operation Overlord have been stolen by an intrepid German spy at Istanbul and are in Nazi hands, but the German high command has been led to believe that the Normandy landings are a diversion to draw Hitler's panzer divisions south to Normandy while 30 divisions strike at Calais. General Rommel tries to persuade General von Runstedt and the Führer that the Normandy landing is the real thing, Allied intelligence uses its knowledge of the secret German code to keep abreast of the split in German top-level thinking, the flow of false information is redoubled, and Rommel does not receive the support that would have driven the invaders back into the sea.

Soviet troops have recaptured Novgorod January 20, have relieved Leningrad completely a week later, have reached the border of prewar Poland in February, have taken Krivoi Rog in the Ukraine February 22 after trapping 10 German divisions near Cherkassy, have crossed the Dniester March 19, have retaken Odessa April 10, have retaken Sevastopol May 9, and are clearing the Crimea and the Ukraine of German invaders.

From 60,000 to 100,000 Germans are trapped at Sevastopol and surrender, but they are killed by the Russians who round up 300,000 to 500,000 Crimean Tartars who had welcomed the Germans and send them into exile in Central Asia.

Minsk falls to the Russians July 3, and 100,000 Germans are captured.

Berlin has been bombed January 20 by the RAF whose planes dropped 2,300 tons of bombs in an action that provoked protests February 9 in the House of Lords where bombing of German cities was criticized. Daylight attacks have begun March 6 by U.S. high-level bombers using the Norden bombsight first developed in 1927 and still a U.S. secret.

Buzz bombs with warheads of nearly 1 ton each begin falling on Britain September 8 as the Germans retaliate (*see* below).

Allied forces in the Pacific take Kwajalein Island February 6, they attack the main Japanese Central Pacific base at Truk in mid-February, they land on Eniwetok in the Marshalls February 17, they land at Hollandia in New Guinea April 22, and B-29 bombers attack Japan's home island of Kyushu June 15.

The Battle of the Philippine Sea June 19 ends with a loss of 402 Japanese planes, while only 27 U.S. planes are downed.

The U.S. Army Air Corps has nearly 80,000 aircraft by July and employs more than 2.4 million men.

Saipan in the Marianas falls to U.S. forces July 8.

Iceland attains the status of an independent republic July 17. A sovereign state since 1918 but a dependency of Denmark, the country discovered by the Vikings in 874 has been occupied since May 1940 by British and then by U.S. forces to prevent its seizure by Germany, but withdrawal of U.S. troops will not begin until the end of 1959.

Adolf Hitler survives an assassination attempt July 20 and continues to direct the *Wehrmacht* as it falls back before advancing Allied armies. Some of Hitler's generals have plotted against him, a bomb explodes, but the Führer is unhurt.

Soviet troops cross the Curzon line in Poland July 23, the Kremlin recognizes the Lublin Committee of Polish Liberation in Moscow July 26 as the governing authority of a liberated Poland, Warsaw rises against the Germans August 1 on orders from General Bor-Komorowski (Tadeusz Komorowski), 49, of the Polish underground, who responds to an appeal by Moscow Radio, but Soviet troops are unable to come to the support of Bor-Komorowski, the Germans crush the uprising and inflict heavy losses, and Bor-Komorowski and a few survivors are forced to surrender after 2 months of ferocious fighting.

Allied forces cross the Loire August 11, the U.S. Seventh Army lands in southern France August 15 and begins moving up the Rhine Valley, the U.S. Third Army of General George S. Patton, Jr., reaches the Seine August 19, the Allies exterminate the German Seventh Army in the Falaise Gap from August 13 to August 20, French troops retake Marseilles August 23, and French and U.S. troops liberate Paris August 25 after more than 4 years of German occupation.

General de Gaulle enters Paris August 25, and the French provisional government moves 5 days later from Algiers to Paris.

Romania surrenders to Soviet forces August 24, the Red Army enters Bucharest August 30, Moscow declares war on Bulgaria September 5, Soviet columns enter Sofia September 16, and Belgrade falls October 20 to Soviet and Yugoslav partisan forces.

Antwerp falls to the Allies September 4, Brussels is liberated September 5, but British airborne troops landed September 17 at Eindhoven and Arnhem are unable to outflank the German Westwall defenses and sustain heavy losses before the survivors are withdrawn.

Buzz bombs take an increasing toll in Britain despite efforts by Allied bombers to knock out the German factories producing the bombs and to destroy launching sites. Designed by German rocket expert Werner von Braun, the liquid-fueled missiles are called V-2 bombs (*Vergelt::ngswaffe Zwei*, revenge weapon two), more than 1,000 will land in Britain, they will kill more than 2,700, and they will maim and injure an additional 6,500.

Athens is retaken by the Allies October 13, and Aachen in the Netherlands is taken October 21.

Guam in the Pacific has been retaken in August by Allied forces, which take Peleliu in the Palaus in October and begin carrier-based raids on Formosa (Taiwan), where 300 Japanese planes are destroyed October 12.

The Philippines are invaded by Allied forces October 20, and superfortress raids on Tokyo from Saipan begin November 24.

President Roosevelt wins re-election to a fourth term with 53 percent of the popular vote and 432 electoral votes. His Republican opponent is New York governor Thomas E. Dewey who receives 46 percent of the popular vote but fails to carry his home state and winds up with only 99 electoral votes. Roosevelt has dumped his vice president Henry A. Wallace because he is thought to be too liberal for southern voters, the president has been discouraged from naming WPB boss Donald Nelson as his running mate because of Nelson's womanizing, and so the vice president-elect is U.S. senator from Missouri Harry S. Truman, 60, who has gained national recognition by chairing a special Senate "watchdog" committee to investigate possible profiteering on national defense projects.

The German battleship *Tirpitz* is sunk November 12.

The German submarine *U-505* has been seized June 4 off French West Africa in the first capture at sea of any foreign warship since 1815. A U.S. task force commanded by Admiral Daniel V. Gallery, 43, of the carrier *Guadalcanal* has taken the *U-505* and obtained valuable military secrets, including a German radio code and a new type of torpedo, but the coup is kept secret so that the Germans will believe the submarine has sunk.

Strasbourg falls to the Allies November 24, but the Battle of the Bulge that begins December 16 takes a heavy toll of U.S. troops as the Germans launch an offensive in the Ardennes Forest of Belgium that will continue into January of next year.

"Nuts," says General Anthony McAuliffe December 22 to German demands that he surrender his 101st Airborne Division at Bastogne, which is held against overwhelming odds and is relieved December 26 by

1944 (cont.) units of General Patton's Third Army headed by Colonel Wendell Blanchard, 41, whose tanks have come 150 miles in 19 hours.

Budapest is surrounded by Soviet forces December 27.

Nazi troops gun down 335 Italians in the Fosse Ardeatine caves beside the Appian Way outside Rome March 24 in reprisal for the killing of 35 German soldiers by partisans. Of the dead, 255 are civilians, 68 are soldiers, and the status of 12 will remain a mystery, but all are victims of Herbert Kappler, the 37-year-old SS colonel who has ordered the massacre.

Nazi authorities jail Hungarian bishop Josef Mindszenty, 52, for prohibiting Roman Catholics to say a Mass and to sing a government-ordered Te Deum "in thanksgiving for the successful liberation of the town [Budapest] from the Jews" (*see* 1948).

Amsterdam Jew Otto Frank and his family are betrayed to the Gestapo August 4 after more than 2 years in hiding and are deported with eight others in the last convoy of cattle trucks to the extermination camp at Auschwitz. Frank's 15-year-old daughter Anne has her head shaved at Auschwitz (the Reich uses women's hair for packing round U-boat pipe joints and for other purposes), but she is not gassed with the others. She will be shipped to the Bergen-Belsen concentration camp and will die there in March of next year, probably of typhus, but three notebooks left behind at 263 Prinsengracht in Amsterdam will be found to contain her diary chronicling the period in which she and her family hid from the Gestapo (*see* Broadway play, 1955).

An American cannot be denied the right to vote because of color, rules the Supreme Court. The April 3 decision in *Smith v. Allwright* is handed down in a case involving a Texas primary election.

An American Dilemma by Swedish sociologist Gunnar Myrdal explores the history of U.S. black-white relationships and examines the moral and psychological dilemmas posed by years of professing equality while practicing inequality.

The first automatic, general-purpose digital computer is completed at Harvard University, where it has been built under the aegis of Engineering School mathematics professor Howard Hathaway Aiken, 44, with a $5 million grant from IBM (*see* Watson, 1924; Bush, 1930). The Harvard-IBM Mark I Automatic Sequence Controlled Calculator has 760,000 parts and 500 miles of wire, it requires 4 seconds to perform a simple multiplication and 11 seconds to perform a simple division, and it is subject to frequent breakdown (*see* ENIAC, 1946).

More than 100 Italians and possibly twice that many are killed March 2 in a railway tunnel 2 miles from Balvano by carbon monoxide fumes. Most of the victims are black-market operators who have been obtaining chocolate, cigarettes, and other scarcities (often from Allied troops) and trading them for eggs, meat, and olive oil from country people for sale at high prices in Naples.

A Federal Highway Act passed by Congress November 29 establishes a new U.S. National System of Interstate Highways. The arterial network of 40,000 miles is planned to reach 42 state capitals and to serve 182 of the 199 U.S. cities with populations above 50,000 (*see* 1955; 1956).

Liquid natural gas (LNG) bursts out of two East Ohio Gas Company storage tanks at Cleveland October 20 and creates a firestorm that kills 131 people. Two million gallons of LNG flow down the streets and into the sewers, exploding at the slightest spark, gutting 29 acres of houses and stores, burning birds to death in midair as they fly over the city, and creating anxiety about the safety of LNG.

The first kidney machine to filter noxious wastes out of the blood of patients with kidney disease is produced by Dutch physician Willem J. Kolff, 33, who uses the clinical apparatus in secret to save the lives of Dutch partisans in German-occupied Holland. A surgical operation is required to insert the machine's large tubes into an artery and vein, the machine is used only for brief emergency treatment of waste-product buildup, but improvements will be made (*see* Scribner, 1960).

Chromatography is refined by British biochemists Archer John Porter Martin, 34, and Richard Laurence Millington Synge, who follow up on work done in 1906 by Mikhail S. Tsvett. Their paper chromatography permits separation of complex mixtures such as protein molecules into their constituents (such as amino acids), a separation not practical with ordinary chemical methods, and it will make possible new biological discoveries (*see* Smith, Folkers, 1948).

A typhus epidemic threatens Naples but is stopped by widespread spraying of DDT to kill lice (*see* Muller, 1939).

The first operation to save a "blue baby" is performed November 9 at Baltimore's Johns Hopkins Children's Hospital by surgeon Alfred Blalock, 45, who proceeds on the premise advanced by his colleague Helen Taussig, 46, that anoxemia can be cured by bypassing the pulmonary artery. Prevented by a congenital pulmonary artery defect from getting enough blood into their lungs, many infants have been born blue, have grown progressively weaker, and have either died or have been doomed to chronic invalidism, but the surgical technique developed by Blalock and Taussig will permit blue babies to live normal lives (and to have normal color).

The antibiotic streptomycin is introduced by Selman A. Waksman (*see* 1943).

Wallace Laboratories is sued by the Federal Trade Commission, which begins 16 years of litigation to force removal of the word "liver" from the name of Carter's Little Liver Pills. The name will be changed to Carter's Little Pills in 1960 after 11,000 pages of testimony and a Supreme Court decision.

💲 A British Pay-As-You-Earn (PAYE) income tax program is instituted beginning April 6 (*see* U.S. Ruml plan, 1943).

A United Nations Monetary and Financial Conference at Bretton Woods, N.H., in July establishes the International Bank for Reconstruction (World Bank) and the International Monetary Fund as the Western powers look to the economic problems that will face the world after the war. The monetary system formulated at Bretton Woods pledges every participating country to keep its currency within a percentage point or two of an agreed dollar value, and the IMF is designed to provide moral suasion and credit to keep the system alive. The system will remain in effect until March 1973, when stability rules will be generally disregarded following a 1971 U.S. move unlinking the dollar from any gold value.

The $70 billion budget submitted to Congress January 10 is sharply reduced from last year's budget, but President Roosevelt observes in November that the war is costing the United States $250 million per day, and he opens a sixth War Loan Drive for $14 billion.

Theory of Games and Economic Behavior by Hungarian-American mathematician John von Neumann, 40, and German-American economist Oskar Morgenstern, 42, presents a theory that can be applied to any situation in business, diplomacy, or military strategy in which a decision maker confronts a problem in which he is not in complete control of all the variables affecting the outcome. Von Neumann's 25-page paper "Toward a Theory of Games" appeared in 1928, Morgenstern approached the concept the same year in his first book on business forecasting, and the two met in 1939.

Road to Serfdom by Viennese-American economist Friedrich August von Hayek, 45, attacks Keynesian economic theories.

Textron, Inc., is founded by U.S. parachutemaker Royal Little, 48, who adopts a name coined by the J. Walter Thompson advertising agency and who will turn Textron into the first business "conglomerate" in 1955. A nephew of rayon pioneer Arthur D. Little, Royal Little dropped out of Harvard after 1 year to serve as an officer in World War I, he apprenticed himself without pay to learn silk manufacturing with Cheney Brothers (*see* 1838), he built up his Atlantic Rayon Corporation through mergers, he took over his New Hampshire competitor Suncook Mills last year, and he makes plans to create a giant that will dominate the textile industry (*see* 1948).

Ralph M. Parsons, Inc., is organized by U.S. engineer Ralph Parsons, 48, who at age 13 opened an Amagansett, Long Island, garage and machine shop with his brother, studied steam and machine design at Brooklyn's Pratt Institute, and became a specialist in oil refinery engineering. Parsons breaks with his partner Stephen D. Bechtel, 44, who will rival Parsons in obtaining worldwide engineering contracts.

Olin Industries, Inc., is created by a consolidation of John M. Olin's Olin Corporation with Winchester Repeating Arms Co., Western Cartridge Co., and other firms (*see* 1919; Olin Mathieson, 1954).

🎓 The G.I. Bill of Rights (Servicemen's Readjustment Act) enacted by Congress June 22 will finance college educations for millions of U.S. war veterans.

📰 *Al Akhbar* begins publication at Cairo. Twin publishers Aly and Mustapha Amin, 30, begin the weekly *Akhbar el Yom* in addition to their daily newspaper.

Parisien Liberé begins publication at Paris under the direction of advertising man Emilien Amaury, 33, who has started clandestine Resistance papers during the war while serving as Vichy government director of propaganda favoring large families. The de Gaulle government has expropriated the daily *Le Petit Parisien* on charges of having collaborated with the enemy, it has placed Amaury in charge of the 81-year-old paper, he has renamed it, and he will make *Parisien Liberé* a commercial success with a daily circulation of more than 800,000 and with 22 regional editions.

Le Monde begins publication at Paris December 19 to succeed the prewar paper *Le Temps* which had become a mouthpiece for the French steel trust, the big private banks, and the foreign office. Directeur Hubert Beuve-Mery has General de Gaulle's blessings to make *Le Monde* an independent paper, he will run it for 25 years, and he will make it the most prestigious paper in France.

Seventeen magazine begins publication in September. Publishing heir Walter H. Annenberg, 36, has started the periodical for young girls (*see* 1939; TV Guide, 1953).

✒ Fiction *Winter Tales* by Isak Dinesen; *The Ballad and the Source* by Rosamond Lehmann; *The Golden Fleece* by Robert Graves; *There Were No Windows* by Norah Hoult; *The Dwarf* (*Dvargen*) by Par Lagerkvist; *Dangling Man* by Canadian-American novelist Saul Bellow, 29; *A Bell for Adano* by *Time* magazine journalist-novelist John Richard Hersey, 30; *A Walk in the Sun* by U.S. war novelist Harry Peter M'Nab Brown, 27; *Strange Fruit* by U.S. novelist Lillian Smith, 47, whose novel is the year's U.S. fiction best seller although it is banned by Boston's Watch and Ward Society; *The Lost Weekend* by U.S. novelist Charles Reginald Jackson, 41, whose story of alcoholism is a best seller; *The Razor's Edge* by W. Somerset Maugham.

🖌 Painting *Three Studies for Figures at the Base of a Crucifix* by English painter Francis Bacon, 34, whose asthma has kept him out of military service; *Effervescence* by Hans Hoffmann; *Plantation Road* by Thomas Hart Benton; *Pelvis III* by Georgia O'Keeffe. Edvard Munch dies at his estate outside Oslo January 23 at age 80; Piet Mondrian dies at New York February 1 at age 71; sculptor Aristide Maillol dies in an

979

D-Day on the Normandy beachhead cost many Allied lives, but the successful landing opened the road to Paris.

automobile accident near Banyuls-sur-Mer October 5 at age 82.

Kodacolor is introduced by Eastman Kodak Company whose new color negative film makes it possible to take color snapshots with low-priced cameras. Eastman will bring out an improved indoor-outdoor Kodacolor film in 1956 (*see* Kodachrome, 1936; Ektachrome, 1946).

Theater *Decision* by U.S. playwright Edward Chodorov 2/2 at New York's Belasco Theater, with Georgia Burke in a political melodrama about fascism in America and U.S. race relations, 160 perfs.; *Antigone* by Jean Anouilh 2/4 at the Théâtre de l'Atelier in occupied Paris; *The Searching Wind* by Lillian Hellman 4/12 at New York's Fulton Theater, with Cornelia Otis Skinner, Dudley Digges, Montgomery Clift, 318 perfs.; *No Exit* (*Huis Clos*) by Jean-Paul Sartre 5/27 at the Théâtre du Vieux-Colombier in occupied Paris; *Anna Lucasta* by U.S. playwright Philip Yordan, 30, 8/30 at New York's Mansfield Theater, with Hilda Simons, Canada Lee, John Tate, 957 perfs.; *I Remember Mama* by John Van Druten (who has adapted Kathryn Farber's book *Mama's Bank Account*) 10/19 at New York's Music Box Theater, with Mady Christians, Frances Heflin, Joan Tetzel, Marlon Brando, Oscar Homolka, 714 perfs.; *Harvey* by U.S. playwright Mary Coyle Chase, 37, 11/1 at New York's 48th Street Theater, with Frank Fay as an alcoholic with an imaginary rabbit friend, 1,775 perfs., Pulitzer Prize; *Dear Ruth* by U.S. playwright Norman Krasna, 35, 12/13 at New York's Henry Miller Theater, 683 perfs.; *O Mistress Mine* (*Love in Idleness*) by Terence Rattigan 12/20 at London's Lyric Theatre, with Alfred Lunt and Lynn Fontanne.

Films John and Ray Boulting's *Henry V* with Laurence Olivier in a British propaganda version of Shakespeare's 1599 tragedy; Mervyn LeRoy's *Thirty Seconds Over Tokyo* with Clark Gable, Walter Pidgeon; Sergei Eisenstein's *Ivan the Terrible* (Part 1); Fritz Lang's *Ministry of Fear* with Ray Milland; George Cukor's *Winged Victory* with Lon McCallister, Jeanne Crain; Alfred Hitchcock's *Lifeboat* with Tallulah Bankhead, William Bendix, John Hodiak, Canada Lee; Preston Sturges's *Hail the Conquering Hero* with Eddie Bracken, Ella Raines, William Demarest; Otto Preminger's *Laura* with Clifton Webb, Gene Tierney; Billy Wilder's *Double Indemnity* with Barbara Stanwyck, Fred MacMurray, Edward G. Robinson; Preston Sturges's *The Miracle of Morgan's Creek* with Eddie Bracken, Betty Hutton, William Demarest; George Cukor's *Gaslight* with Ingrid Bergman, Charles Boyer; Howard Hawks's *To Have and Have Not* with Humphrey Bogart, Lauren Bacall; Clarence Brown's *National Velvet* with Mickey Rooney and 12-year-old Elizabeth Taylor.

Hollywood musicals Vincente Minelli's *Meet Me in St. Louis* with Judy Garland, songs by Hugh Martin and Ralph Blane that include "The Trolley Song," "The Boy Next Door," the title song, and "Have Yourself a Merry Little Christmas"; Leo McCarey's *Going My Way* with Bing Crosby, Barry Fitzgerald, songs that include "Would You Like to Swing on a Star?" and "Too-ra-Loo-ra-Loo-ra"; Mark Sandrich's *Here Come the Waves* with Bing Crosby, music and lyrics by Harold Arlen and Johnny Mercer, songs that include "Ac-cent-tchu-ate the Positive"; Charles Vidor's *Cover Girl* with Rita Hayworth, Gene Kelly, music by Jerome Kern, lyrics by Ira Gershwin, songs that include "Long Ago (and Far Away)"; Robert Siodmak's *Christmas Holiday* with Gene Kelly, Deanna Durbin, songs by Frank Loesser that include "Spring Will Be a Little Late This Year."

First performances *Symphonic Metamorphosis of Themes by Carl Maria von Weber* by Paul Hindemith 1/20 at New York's Carnegie Hall; *Ode to Napoleon* by Arnold Schoenberg 1/23 at Carnegie Hall (the ode is based on a poem by Lord Byron); *Jeremiah* by New York Philharmonic assistant conductor Leonard Bernstein, 25, 1/28 in a concert by the new Pittsburgh Symphony; Concerto for Piano and Orchestra by Arnold Schoenberg 2/6 in an NBC Symphony concert broadcast from New York; Symphony No. 2 (dedicated to the Army Air Forces) by Corporal Samuel Barber 3/3 at Boston's Symphony Hall; Symphony No. 2 by Walter Piston 3/5 at Washington, D.C.; *Theme with Variations According to the Four Temperaments* by Paul Hindemith 9/3 at Boston's New England Mutual Hall; *Capricorn Concerto* by Samuel Barber (who has named it after the Mount Kisco, N.Y., estate he shares with Gian-Carlo Menotti) 10/8 at New York's Town Hall; Theme and Variations in G minor for Orchestra by Arnold Schoenberg 10/20 at Boston's Symphony Hall; *Fugue on a Victory Tune* by Walter Piston 10/21 at New York's Carnegie Hall; Concerto for Orchestra by Béla Bartók 12/1 at Boston's Symphony Hall.

Ballet *Fancy Free* 4/18 at New York's Metropolitan Opera House with Jerome Robbins, John Kriza, and Harold Laing as the Three Sailors, music by Leonard Bernstein (above), choreography by Robbins; *Appalachian Spring* 10/30 at the Library of Congress, Washington, D.C., with Martha Graham, music by Aaron Copland; *Herodiade* 10/30 at the Library of Congress, with Martha Graham, music by Paul Hindemith, text from a poem by Stéphane Mallarmé.

Broadway musicals *Mexican Hayride* 1/28 at the Winter Garden Theater, with Bobby Clark, June Havoc, book by Herbert and Dorothy Fields, music and lyrics by Cole Porter, songs that include "Count Your Blessings," 481 perfs.; *Hats Off to Ice* 6/22 at the Center Theater, with ice skaters performing to music and lyrics by John Fortis and James Littlefield, 889 perfs.; *The Song of Norway* 8/21 at the Imperial Theater, with music based on works by Edvard Grieg, book and lyrics by Robert Work and George "Chet" Forest, songs that include "Strange Music," 860 perfs.; *Bloomer Girl* 10/5 at the Shubert Theater, with Celeste Holm as Evalina, music by Harold Arlen, lyrics by E. Y. Harburg, songs that include "Evalina," "It Was Good Enough for Grandma," 653 perfs.; *On the Town* 12/28 at the Adelphi Theater, with Sono Osato, Betty Comden, Adolph Green, Nancy Walker, music by Leonard Bernstein, dances derived from the ballet *Fancy Free*, 563 perfs.

Radio *The Perry Como Show* debuts with former Canonsburg, Pa., barber Perry Como, 32, whose soft, easygoing style will make him popular with millions.

Popular songs "I'll Walk Alone" by Jule Styne, lyrics by Sammy Cahn (for the film *Three Cheers for the Boys*); "I'm Making Believe" by James V. Monaco, lyrics by Mack Gordon (for the film *Sweet and Low Down*); "Don't Fence Me In" by Cole Porter (for the film *Hollywood Canteen*); "Jealous Heart" by Nashville country music singer Jenny Lou Carson; "That's What I Like about the South" by Andy Razaf; "Moonlight in Vermont" by Karl Senssdorf, lyrics by John Blackburn; "Linda" by Ann Ronell; "Sentimental Journey" by Ben Homer, Bud Green, and Les Brown; "Candy" by Mack Davis, Joan Whitney, and Alex Kramer; "Twilight Time" by Buck Ram, Morty Nevins, and Artie Dunn; "It Could Happen to You" by Jimmy Van Heusen, lyrics by Johnny Mercer (for the film *And the Angels Sing*); "Nancy (with the Laughing Face)" by Jimmy Van Heusen and comedian Phil Silvers; "Rum and Coca-Cola" by Jeri Sullivan and Paul Baron, lyrics by comedian Morey Amsterdam; "You're Nobody Till Somebody Loves You" by Russ Morgan, Larry Stock, and James Cavanaugh; "You Always Hurt the One You Love" by Robert Allan and Doris Fisher; "I Should Care" by Paul Westerly, Sammy Cahn, and Alex Stordahl (for the film *Thrill of a Romance*); "I've Got a Lovely Bunch of Cocoanuts" by English songwriter Fred Heatherton.

 The St. Louis Cardinals win the World Series by defeating the St. Louis Braves 4 games to 2.

 San Francisco's I. Magnin is purchased by Bullock's (*see* Magnin's Seattle, 1925; Bullock's Wilshire, 1929).

 The Fort Greene Houses completed at Brooklyn, N.Y., will be New York's largest public housing project for years to come. The apartment buildings occupy 38 acres and provide 3,500 apartments to house 14,000 people (*see* Co-Op City, 1968).

 Big Bend National Park in Texas is established by act of Congress. Located in a bend of the Rio Grande River, the new park occupies 708,221 acres of mountainland and desert.

 Bengal's rice crop fails again as it did in 1942. Millions starve, some because they refuse to accept wheat flour (*see* Burma's rinderpest, 1943).

 Britain cuts her food imports to half their prewar levels. Domestic wheat production has increased by 90 percent, potato production by 87 percent, vegetable production by 45 percent, sugar beet production by 19 percent despite the manpower shortage.

A "Green Revolution" moves forward outside Mexico City as former E. I. Du Pont plant pathologist Norman Borlaug, 30, joins the Rockefeller Foundation effort to improve Mexican agricultural production (*see* 1943; Salmon, 1945; black stem rust, 1951).

The average yield per acre in U.S. cornfields reaches 33.2 bushels, up from 22.8 in 1933 (*see* 1968).

U.S. soybean acreage reaches 12 million as new uses for the beans are found in livestock feed, sausage filler, breakfast foods, enamel, solvent, printing ink, plastics, insecticides, steel-hardening, and beer (*see* McMillen, 1934). Henry Ford predicts that in 5 years soybean milk will be produced at 3 cents per quart, and the cow will be obsolete.

U.S. farm acreage will decline by 7.3 percent in the next 20 years, dropping by 1.3 million acres per year. Some 27 million acres of noncroplands will be converted to farm use (mostly in Florida, California, Washington, Montana, and Texas), but 53 million acres of croplands will be taken out of production and shifted to use for homesites, factory sites, highways, and the like.

 Folic acid (folacin) is isolated by U.S. biochemists H. Mitchell and E. Snell. The B vitamin is thought at first to be effective against pernicious anemia, but while that will be disproven, the vitamin does cure macrocytic anemia by stimulating the regeneration of both red blood cells and hemoglobin.

Bread enrichment laws are enacted by the Kentucky and Mississippi legislatures.

 Bread, flour, oatmeal, potatoes, fish, fresh vegetables, and fruit other than oranges remain unrationed in Britain. Prices are controlled so that the average householder has about half the food budget available for unrationed foods after buying rationed foods plus foods whose distribution is controlled or allocated on a "points" basis.

1944 (cont.) U.S. meat consumption rises to 140 pounds per capita, up from 128.9 last year, as national income rises to $181 billion, up from $72.5 billion in 1939. A large proportion of the meat is sold through black-market channels organized by criminal elements.

Prepackaging of foods is tested by Ohio State University in cooperation with Ohio Boxboard, E. I. du Pont, Oliver Machine, Hussman Refrigeration, the Atlantic Commission Company, and the A&P, whose executives look beyond the war and explore ways to reduce losses in food distribution. By 1961, 88 percent of U.S. supermarkets will be prepackaging all or some of their produce, and 90 percent will be prepackaging all fish, smoked meats, and table-ready meats in transparent film (*see* polyethylene, 1935).

Only 10 U.S. grocers have completely self-service meat markets. The figure will increase to 5,600 by 1951, to 11,500 by 1956, and to 24,100 by 1960, when 55 percent of all meat sold at retail will be from self-service cases.

Seabrook Farms establishes its own brand after 13 years of packaging frozen food for General Foods to sell under the Birds Eye label and for other companies to sell under their own labels. Seabrook sales will grow in the next 12 years to more than $27 million (*see* Snow Crop, 1957).

Stokely-Van Camp moves into Hawaiian pineapple canning (*see* 1933; 1956).

Chiquita Banana is introduced by the United Fruit Company in a move to make bananas a brand-name item rather than a generic commodity (*see* Sunkist, 1919). The bananas are advertised on radio with a tune composed by Len MacKenzie and performed by Ray Bloch's orchestra with vocalist Patti Clayton singing Garth Montgomery's lyrics, "I'm Chiquita Banana/ And I've come to say,/ Bananas have to ripen in a certain way:/ When they are fleck'd with brown and have a golden hue/ Bananas taste the best and are the best for you./ You can put them in a salad/ You can put them in a pie-aye/ Any way you want to eat them/ It's impossible to beat them/ But bananas love the climate of the very, very tropical equator/ So you should never put bananas in the refrigerator" (copyright 1945 Maxwell-Wirges Publications, Inc.).

Yuban coffee is acquired by General Foods. The coffee was developed before 1920 by the late sugar-coffee merchant John Arbuckle as a "*yu*letide *ban*-quet" for his friends and customers.

The G.I. Bill of Rights (above) will provide 4 percent home loans to veterans with no down payment required. The law will subsidize a postwar building boom and will encourage a mass exodus from U.S. cities that will deplete major metropolitan areas of middle-income taxpayers (*see* Levittown, 1947).

A large-scale migration of Americans from rural to urban areas begins. The shift will create major problems in cities.

1945 World War II ends in Europe May 8 and in the Pacific August 14, but only after major new military and naval activity (*see* below) and after the deaths of three of the world's five leading heads of state.

Massive operations in the Pacific and in Europe mark the closing months of the war. U.S. forces invade the Philippines in force January 9 under the command of General Douglas MacArthur who enters Manila February 4 and completes recovery of the city within 3 weeks.

1,000 U.S. bombers raid Berlin February 3 and drop tons of explosives, British Lancasters raid Dresden February 13 with phosphorus and high explosive bombs that create a firestorm which kills an estimated 135,000, the U.S. 1st Army crosses the Ludendorff Bridge left standing at Remagen by the retreating Wehrmacht and occupies Cologne March 7, by March 10 the Allies control the west bank of the Rhine from Nijmegen in the Netherlands to Koblenz.

The U.S. 9th Army reaches the Rhine opposite Düsseldorf by March 16 and joins with the 1st Army to take more than 325,000 German prisoners in the Battle of the Ruhr.

More than 100 U.S. B-24 bombers raid Tokyo the night of March 9, they rain incendiaries on the city, and they start fires that kill more than 124,000.

U.S. troops invade Mindinao in the Philippines beginning March 10.

U.S. forces take Iwo Jima March 16 after nearly a month of heavy fighting that has taken thousands of American lives on the Pacific island.

The League of Arab States organized March 22 unites Egypt, Iraq, Jordan, Lebanon, Saudi Arabia, Syria, and Yemen in coordinating efforts toward achievement of complete independence and mutual cooperation. By 1974 the League will include 20 Arab states including Algeria, Tunisia, Morocco, Lebanon, Kuwait, Quatar, Bahrain, Oman, Somalia, Sudan, and Mauretania.

Palestinian terrorists cripple railroads with dynamitings and scuttle British police launches used to apprehend illegal immigrants. Polish-born militant Menahem Begin, 32, leads the Irgun Zvai Lenmi that spearheads opposition to British control of Palestine (*see* 1948).

President Roosevelt dies April 12 of a cerebral hemorrhage at Warm Springs, Ga., 2 months after a Yalta Conference with Prime Minister Churchill and Premier Stalin in which the three powers have pledged "unity of purpose and of action." Dead at age 63, FDR had been preparing for a conference at San Francisco where the charter of a United Nations organization is to be drafted.

FDR (above) is succeeded by his vice president Harry S. Truman.

Nuremberg falls to the U.S. 7th Army April 21 as Russian forces reach the suburbs of Berlin.

Russian and U.S. patrols meet April 25 on the Elbe just to the south of Berlin, they celebrate far into the night with whiskey, vodka, and accordion music, Adolf Hitler's hope that the alliance between Capitalists and Communists will collapse is shattered, and Heinrich Himmler begins surrender negotiations.

Benito Mussolini and 12 of his former Cabinet officers are executed April 28 at Lake Como. German armies in Italy surrender unconditionally April 29.

Adolf Hitler commits suicide April 30 at age 56 in the Reich Chancellery at Berlin as Soviet troops converge on the city.

Hitler aide Martin Bormann, 45, is seen May 2 in a tank crossing Berlin's Weidenammer Bridge. Bormann will not be positively identified hereafter but rumors will persist that he is alive and living in Argentina or Chile.

Germany surrenders unconditionally May 7. President Truman proclaims May 8 V-E (Victory in Europe) Day.

U.S. forces regain Okinawa in the Ryukyus from the Japanese June 21 after nearly 3 months of fighting in which it has taken half a million Americans to subdue 110,000 Japanese. The U.S. death toll is 49,151.

Washington announces reconquest of the Philippines July 5.

Full air war against Japan's home islands of Honshu and Kyushu begins July 10 from bases in the Marianas and Okinawa.

Carrier-based air attacks on Tokyo begin July 17 after U.S. planes have dropped leaflets threatening Japan with aerial destruction unless she surrenders unconditionally.

An atomic bomb is tested successfully in the desert near Alamogordo, N.M., July 18 (below).

The U.S.S. *Indianapolis* is torpedoed July 30 at 2 minutes after midnight and sinks 12 minutes later in the Indian Ocean 3 days after having delivered essential components of the atomic bomb to Tinian in the Marianas. The heavy cruiser has sent no S.O.S. because her main communications center has been destroyed, her survivors are not spotted by a Navy pilot until August 2, and by that time most of her 1,996 officers and men have drowned, or have been killed by sharks, or in some cases have been murdered by crazed brothers in arms. Only 316 survive, and while the ship's commander is court-martialed in December on charges of having failed to run a zigzag course in a war zone, the charges will be dropped in February of next year, and the captain will be promoted to rear admiral after he retires next year.

Japanese air ace Saburo Sakai downs a U.S. B-29 over Japan in early August to end a career in which he has blasted 64 Allied aircraft out of the skies from the cockpit of his Mitsubishi Zero fighter. Sakai lost one eye in combat, he has flown half-blind, and he has only recently accepted a commission as commander after years of refusal.

The Potsdam Conference ends August 2 after 16 days of deliberations by President Truman, Generalissimo Josef Stalin, and Prime Minister Churchill who is replaced July 28 by the new British prime minister Clement R. Attlee whose Labour party has defeated Churchill's Conservatives in the general elections. The world leaders agree that Germany is to be disarmed and demilitarized, that her National Socialist institutions are to be dissolved, that her leaders are to be tried as war criminals, and that democratic ideals are to be encouraged in postwar Germany with restoration of local self-government and freedom of speech, press, and religion subject to military security requirements. Manufacture of war matériel is to be prohibited and production of metals, chemicals, and machinery essential to war is to be controlled.

Tokyo rejects the Potsdam Declaration calling upon Japan to surrender. U.S. planes drop leaflets over Hiroshima August 4 warning, "Your city will be obliterated unless your Government surrenders."

The atomic bomb (code name "Little Boy") dropped on Hiroshima August 6 is a 10-foot long, 9,000 pound device with the explosive power of 20,000 tons of TNT. The U.S. Army Air Force Boeing B-29 bomber *Enola Gay* piloted by Paul Tibbets, Jr., has flown from the Pacific atoll of Tinian, the bombardier drops "Little Boy" from an altitude of 32,000 feet. The bomb explodes 660 yards above the city and flattens 4 square miles of Hiroshima, 100,000 Japanese die outright, close to another 100,000 will die from burns and radiation sickness, hundreds will be disfigured.

The atomic bomb (code name "Big Boy") dropped on Nagasaki in Kyushu August 9 by the B-29 bomber *Bock's Car* is a plutonium-core bomb with the same explosive power as "Little Boy." It kills 75,000 Japanese outright and many of the 75,000 survivors will die from burns and radiation sickness. Leaflets dropped earlier had threatened "a rain of ruin the like of which has never been seen on earth."

Japan sues for peace August 10. President Truman proclaims V-J (Victory over Japan) Day August 14.

World War II ends after nearly 6 traumatic years in which an estimated 54.8 million have died, most of them civilians. Many millions more are left crippled, blind, mutilated, homeless, orphaned, and impoverished. Europe has 10 million displaced persons. The war has directly involved 57 nations, but the Soviet Union, Germany, China, and Japan have borne the lion's share of casualties. Counting only military personnel, the U.S.S.R. has lost 7.5 million, Germany nearly 2.9 million, China 2.2 million, Japan 1.5 million, Britain nearly 398,000, Italy 300,000, the United States more than 290,000, France nearly 211,000 including colonial troops (but not including 36,877 prisoners of war who died in captivity), Canada 39,139, Australia 29,395, New Zealand 12,262, South Africa 8,681, India 36,092, the rest of the British Empire 21,085.

1945 (cont.) U.S. forces land in Japan August 28. General George C. Marshall is named supreme commander of Allied occupation forces.

Formal Japanese surrender terms signed September 2 aboard the U.S.S. *Missouri* in Tokyo Bay provide for Soviet control of Outer Mongolia, Chinese sovereignty over Inner Mongolia, Manchuria, Taiwan, and Hainan, U.S. and Soviet occupation of Korea until a democratic government can be established. Japan cedes the Kuril Islands and the southern part of Sakhalin to the U.S.S.R. Emperor Hirohito is to remain Japanese head of state, but the Japanese high command and military establishment is to be disbanded, and a U.S. army of occupation is to rule Japan.

Japanese forces in China, estimated to number 1 million, capitulate formally September 9 at Nanking. Their leaders sign surrender papers with representatives of Chiang Kai-shek.

The British at Singapore accept formal surrender of Japanese forces in Southeast Asia (estimated to number 585,000) September 12. The British reoccupy Hong Kong.

Soviet troops liberate Auschwitz January 26 but find fewer than 3,000 prisoners at the Polish death camp where more than 1 million have died in SS gas chambers. The SS has removed the rest to camps inside Germany. General Patton liberates Buchenwald April 11 after 60,000 have died there, Dachau is liberated April 24, but the Allies are able to rescue only 500,000 of whom many will die of the effects of hunger and disease.

The Nazi genocide has killed an estimated 14 million "racial inferiors" including Poles, Slavs, gypsies, and close to 6 million Jews.

The World Zionist Congress demands admission of 1 million Jews to Palestine in a statement issued August 13 (*see* terrorists above).

French women gain the right to vote for the first time under terms of a new enfranchisement bill.

U.S. private Eddie Slovik has died January 31 before a firing squad, the first American to be executed for desertion since the Civil War. A Detroit plumber before the war, Slovik was drafted last year after having been rejected earlier, his commanding officer in basic training recognized his "total inability" and tried to obtain his discharge or at least a transfer to a noncombat unit, it took Slovik 6 weeks to locate his unit after being shipped overseas, he claimed to have deserted and said he would desert again, he signed a "confession" calculated to keep him out of combat, General Eisenhower approved his execution.

The possibility of a new energy source (as well as of a nuclear holocaust that would end civilization) is raised by the atomic bomb that is tested successfully July 18 at Alamogordo, N. Mex., and is then dropped on Hiroshima and Nagasaki (above).

The first Soviet atomic chain reaction is achieved by physicist Igor Kurchatov (see 1949).

U.S. gasoline and fuel oil rationing ends August 19.

Consolidation Coal Company absorbs Pittsburgh Coal Company in a merger that creates a vast new mining behemoth under the leadership of George Hutchinson Love, 44. Consolidation was once controlled by the Rockefellers, Pittsburgh Coal is controlled by the Mellon family, and while the two big companies between them lost $100 million in the 15 years between 1925 and 1940, the new Consolidation Coal Company will be profitable (*see* 1956; 1967).

 Penicillin is introduced on a commercial basis following work by a large Anglo-American research team.

Streptomycin is introduced commercially.

"A distinct parallelism between the incidence of cancer of the lung and the sale of cigarettes" is observed by New Orleans surgeon Alton Ochsner, 49, in an address at Duke University (which has been endowed with a fortune derived from tobacco sales; *see* 1924). "The increase is due to the increased incidence of smoking and . . . smoking is a factor because of the chronic irritation it produces," says Ochsner.

Flying Tiger Line, Inc., is founded by former U.S. fighter pilot Robert W. Prescott, 32, who takes the nickname of General Claire Chennault's American Volunteer Group with which he flew from late 1941 until July 1942 when the group was disbanded after many sorties against the Japanese. Starting with four planes and 16 employees, Prescott will make Flying Tiger Line the world's largest air cargo firm.

A B-25 light bomber flies into New York's Empire State Building July 28, tearing a hole between the 78th and 79th floors, killing all three men aboard, and killing 10 early Sunday morning churchgoers.

The Beechcraft Bonanza two-engine private plane is introduced by Beech Aircraft of Wichita, Kan.

General Tire and Rubber Company buys a half-interest in Aerojet Corporation for $75,000 (*see* 1942); General Tire will acquire a controlling interest and will rename the firm Aerojet-General (*see* 1915).

Greek shipping magnate Stavros Niarchos buys oil tankers with $6 million in insurance money received for six sunken ships. Driving hard bargains, making a profit of $3.2 million on a $101,000 investment in one deal, Niarchos expands his fleet which will number 80 vessels by the late 1960s and will have made him a fortune of $400 million (*see* 1935).

U.S. automobile companies convert to passenger car production. A redesigned CJ-2A Universal Jeep goes into production in September at the Willys-Overland plant in Toledo, Ohio (*see* 1940; Brazil, 1965).

Henry Ford steps down from the presidency of Ford Motor Company at age 82 and yields control of the shattered organization to his 28-year-old grandson Henry Ford II as production of civilian passenger cars resumes. Edsel Ford's widow Eleanor Clay Ford and her mother had threatened to sell their stock in the company if the founder would not relinquish control. Eleanor's son Henry Ford II immediately dismisses Harry Bennett, who has ruled the Ford empire through sycophants by fear and terror, and he raids other companies to create a new management team headed by Bendix Aviation president Ernest R. Breech, 48, who will join Ford next year as executive vice president (*see* 1947).

The Bank of France is nationalized.

Family allowances are introduced in Britain.

A U.S. tariff act empowers the President to encourage reciprocal trade by reducing tariffs to 25 percent of original schedule rates (*see* 1934; GATT, 1947).

A revenue act passed by Congress November 8 provides for nearly $6 billion in tax reductions.

The U.S. Gross National Product (GNP) for the year is $211 billion, double the booming 1929 figure, even though strikes have closed down Ford, General Motors, and other plants. Bituminous coal mines are shut down by strikes through much of the fall.

The International Bank for Reconstruction and Development comes into being December 27; 21 countries have subscribed nearly $7.2 billion to the World Bank with nearly $3.2 billion of the total coming from the United States. The bank's first loans will be made to France in May of 1947 at interest rates of 3 and 3¼ percent (*see* Bretton Woods, 1944).

Rockwell Manufacturing Company is created by a renaming of the Pittsburgh Equitable Meter Company started with Mellon family support in 1927 by Pittsburgh engineer Willard F. Rockwell, now 56, who began the firm by acquiring the water and gas-meter division of the Westinghouse Company. Rockwell has expanded Pittsburgh Equitable by acquiring some 18 other companies in such areas as valves, recording indexes, and registers, and he is also chairman of the board of Timken-Detroit Axle Company which has supplied 80 percent of U.S. Army axle requirements during the war, partly because Rockwell was a U.S. Army colonel during World War I (*see* Rockwell Spring & Axle, 1953).

Aluminum Company of America (Alcoa) is judged by a U.S. Court of Appeals to have held a 90 percent monopoly in U.S. aluminum ingot production before the war, but the monopoly enjoyed by the Mellons for more than half a century will soon be ended (*see* 1891). Reynolds Metals Company has been producing ingots with government encouragement during the war (*see* 1916), Kaiser Aluminum is created for the purpose by Henry J. Kaiser and takes over some government-built aluminum plants, and several U.S. copper companies will soon enter the industry.

World copper reserves are estimated at 100 million tons. The world will use roughly that much copper in the next 30 years, but the reserve will then be 300 million tons as a result of new discoveries.

Fuji Steel is founded by Japanese industrialist Shigeo Nagano who will merge his company with Yawata Steel in the late 1960s to make Fuji a major world steel producer (*see* Yawata, 1896). Japan's steel industry has suffered relatively little damage in the war.

Italy's Montecatini chemical colossus has had 70 percent of its productive capacity destroyed in the war but it begins to rebuild under the leadership of general manager Carlo Faines (*see* 1922). The company directs its first efforts toward rebuilding nitrogen plants for fertilizers.

The top 8.5 percent of Americans hold 20.9 percent of U.S. personal wealth, down from 32.4 percent of personal wealth in 1929.

General Education in a Free Society is the report of a Harvard faculty committee on the objectives of a liberal education. The 264-page book recommends sweeping changes that many U.S. colleges will adopt.

Ballpoint pens go on sale October 29 at New York's Gimbel Brothers 3 weeks after production has been started by Chicago promotor Milton Reynolds, 53, who has seen the Ladislao Biro pen while visiting Buenos Aires on business in June (*see* 1938). Reynolds has developed a ballpoint pen different enough to get around existing patents, he went into production October 6, he is producing 70 pens per day, and Gimbels quickly sells out at $12.50 each with the initial promise that the pens will write underwater. Some banks suggest that ballpoint pen signatures may not be legal, but the new pens do not leak at high altitudes and they will make it practical to handwrite multicopy business and government forms using carbon paper. Reynolds has capitalized his venture at $26,000, but after 1 month he has made a net profit of more than $500,000, by early 1946 he will be producing 32,000 pens per day, and he will be employing 800 workers as ballpoint pens begin to supplant fountain pens.

Arthur Godfrey Time debuts 4/30 on CBS network radio stations and will continue for 27 years. Host Arthur Michael Godfrey, 41, began as a Washington, D.C., radio announcer in 1930 after 10 years in the U.S. Navy and Coast Guard, he began a regular morning show in 1941, he makes sport of his sponsors as he has done since the 1930s, and he begins to gain a nationwide following that will grow by some estimates to number 70 million.

Meet the Press debuts 10/5 on a New York radio station with *American Mercury* magazine publisher Lawrence E. Spivak, 44, moderating a "spontaneous, unrehearsed weekly news conference of the air." Journalists interview prominent news figures on the show which will go on NBC television beginning in November 1947, and will be moderated by Spivak until November 1975.

Some 5,000 U.S. homes have television sets—bulky receivers with tiny screens that pick up what little

1945 (cont.) programming is available from the handful of stations in operation. But the world is on the edge of a communications revolution that will see television sets in nearly every home of every developed country (*see* 1939; 1948).

Ebony magazine begins publication in November and the black-oriented U.S. picture monthly sells out its initial press run of 25,000 copies. Publisher is John H. Johnson of 1942 *Negro Digest* fame whose Johnson Publishing Company will introduce *Tan* in 1950 and *Jet* in 1951 as Johnson increases his holdings in Supreme Liberty Life Insurance Company (he will be the major stockholder by 1964 and will later be chairman of the board).

Bantam Books is founded by New York publisher Ian Ballantine, 29, who starts a new paperback house to compete with Pocket Books, Avon Books, and Popular Library (*see* 1939; 1941; 1942).

Nonfiction *The Yogi and the Commissar* by Arthur Koestler; *Black Boy* (autobiography) by Richard Wright.

Fiction *The Animal Farm: A Fairy Story* by George Orwell whose allegorical fable contains the line, "All animals are created equal, but some animals are more equal than others"; *The Age of Reason* (*L'age de raison*) and *The Reprieve* (*Le Sursis*) by Jean-Paul Sartre, first two novels in a trilogy; *Christ Stopped at Eboli* (*Cristo si e fermato ad Eboli*) by Italian novelist Carlo Levi, 43, who reveals the social and human problems of Lucania where he was confined in the mid-1930s for antifascist activities; *The Serpent* (*Ormen*) by Swedish novelist Stig Dagerman, 22; *Krane's Cafe* (*Kranes Konditori*) by Cora Sandel; *Grape-harvest* (*Vindima*) by Portuguese novelist-poet-physician Miguel Torga (Adolfo Coelho Da Rocha), 38; *The Crack-Up,* an incomplete novel by the late F. Scott Fitzgerald whose widow Zelda will die in 1948 when the Asheville, N.C., mental hospital where she is a patient is destroyed by fire; *Prater Violet* by Christopher Isherwood; *Brideshead Revisited* by Evelyn Waugh who was received into the Catholic Church in 1930 and who now becomes more positive in advancing the message of the Church; *Loving* by Henry Green; *A Fearful Joy* by Joyce Cary; *Cannery Row* by John Steinbeck; *Forever Amber* by U.S. novelist Kathleen Winsor, 29.

Juvenile *Stuart Little* by E. B. White of the *New Yorker* magazine whose protagonist is a mouse; *The Famous Invasion of Sicily by the Bears* (*La Famosa Invasione degli Ursi in Sicilia*) by Dino Buzzati.

Painting *Red Man–White Man–Black Man* by U.S. painter Mark Tobey, now 55, who was converted to the Baha'i World Faith in 1918; *Rice Threshing* by Thomas Hart Benton; *Brass Band* by Russian-American expressionist Max Weber, now 64; *For Internal Use Only* by U.S. abstractionist Stuart Davis, now 50; *Great Tenochtitlan* and *The Market in Tiangucio* by Diego Rivera for Mexico City's Palacio Nacional;

German graphic artist Käthe Kollwitz dies outside Dresden at Moritzburg Castle April 22 at age 77.

Sculpture *Red Pyramid* (mobile) by Alexander Calder; *Family Group* by Henry Moore.

Theater *The Hasty Heart* by U.S. playwright John Patrick, 39, 1/3 at New York's Hudson Theater, with John Lund, Richard Basehart, 207 perfs.; *Dark of the Moon* by U.S. playwrights Howard Richardson, 26, and William Berney, 24, 3/14 at New York's 46th Street Theater, with music by Walter Hendl, 28, based on "The Ballad of Barbara Allen" and other folk songs, 322 perfs.; *The Glass Menagerie* by Mississippi-born playwright Tennessee (Thomas Lanier) Williams, 34, 3/31 at New York's Plymouth Theater, with Laurette Taylor, Eddie Dowling, Julie Haydon, Anthony Rose, 561 perfs.; *State of the Union* by Howard Lindsay and Russel Crouse 11/14 at New York's Hudson Theater, with Myron McCormack, Ralph Bellamy, 765 perfs., Pulitzer prize; *Dream Girl* by Elmer Rice 12/14 at New York's Coronet Theater, with Wendell Corey, Betty Field (Mrs. Rice), 348 perfs.; *The Madwoman of Chaillot* (*La Folle de Chaillot*) by Jean Giraudoux 12/19 at Paris; *Home of the Brave* by Arthur Laurents 12/27 at New York's Belasco Theater, a play about anti-Semitism in the U.S. Army, 69 perfs.

Films Marcel Carné's *Children of Paradise* (*Les Enfants du Paradis*) with Jean-Louis Barrault; Sergei Eisenstein's *Ivan the Terrible* (Part 2); William Wellman's *The Story of G.I. Joe* with Burgess Meredith as Ernie Pyle, Robert Mitchum; Billy Wilder's *The Lost Weekend* with Ray Milland, Jane Wyman; Alfred Hitchcock's *Spellbound* with Gregory Peck, Ingrid Bergman; Vincente Minnelli's *The Clock* with Judy Garland, Robert Walker; John Ford's *They Were Expendable* with Robert Montgomery, Donna Reed; Lewis Milestone's *A Walk in the Sun* with Dana Andrews, Richard Conte; Herman Shumlin's *Confidential Agent* with Charles Boyer, Lauren Bacall, Peter Lorre; René Clair's *And Then There Were None* with Barry Fitzgerald, Walter Huston, Judith Anderson, Louis Hayward; Max Ophuls's *The Earrings of Madame De . . .* with Charles Boyer, Danielle Darrieux; Elia Kazan's *A Tree Grows in Brooklyn* with Dorothy McGuire, Peggy Ann Garner, James Dunn, Joan Blondell; Akira Kurosawa's *The Man Who Tread the Tiger's Tail*.

Hollywood musicals Walter Lang's *State Fair* with Jeanne Crain, Dana Andrews, music by Richard Rodgers, lyrics by Oscar Hammerstein II, songs that include "It Might as Well as Be Spring," "It's a Grand Night for Singing."

Stage musicals *Up in Central Park* 1/27 at New York's Century Theater, with music by Sigmund Romberg, book by Herbert and Dorothy Fields, lyrics by Dorothy Fields, 504 perfs.; *Carousel* 4/19 at New York's Majestic Theater, with John Raitt as Billy Bigelow (Liliom), Jan Clayton as Julie Jordan, music by Richard Rodgers, lyrics by Oscar Hammerstein II, book based on the Ferenc Molnar play *Liliom* of 1909, songs that include "If I Loved You," "June Is Bustin' Out All Over," "You'll Never Walk Alone," 890 perfs.; *Perchance to Dream* 4/21 at the London Hippodrome, with Ivor Novello, Muriel Barron, Margaret Rutherford, book, music, and lyrics by Novello, 1,022 perfs.; *Sigh No More* (revue) 8/22 at London's Piccadilly Theatre, with Joyce Grenfell, Madge Elliott, Cyril Ritchard, music and lyrics by Noel Coward, songs that include "I Wonder What Happened to Him," "The End of the News," "Wait a Bit, Joe," "Matelot," "Never Again," and the title song, 213 perfs.; *Billion Dollar Baby* 12/21 at New York's Alvin Theater, with Joan McCracken, Mitzi Green, Bill Talbert, music by Morton Gould, lyrics by Betty Comden and Adolph Green, 219 perfs.

Opera   *Peter Grimes* 6/7 at the Sadler's Wells Theatre, London, with music by Benjamin Britten, libretto from the 1810 poem "The Borough" by George Crabbe.

First performances   Symphony No. 5 in B flat major by Serge Prokofiev 1/13 at Moscow while an artillery salute outside the concert hall celebrates news of a great Soviet victory on the Vistula; Symphony No. 9 by Dmitri Shostakovich 11/3 at Leningrad; Prelude for Orchestra and Mixed Choir by Arnold Schoenberg 11/18 at Los Angeles; String Quartet No. 2 in C by Benjamin Britten 11/21 at London on the 250th anniversary of the death of Henry Purcell.

Austrian composer Anton von Webern dies at Mittersill, near Salzburg, September 15 at age 61 after being shot by a trigger-happy U.S. military policeman outside his son-in-law's villa.

Ballet   *Undertow* 4/10 at New York's Metropolitan Opera House, with Hugh Laing, Alicia Alonso, music by William Schuman, choreography by Antony Tudor.

Popular songs   "It's Been a Long, Long Time" by Jule Styne, lyrics by Sammy Cahn; "Till the End of Time" by Buddy Kay and Ted Mossman who have adapted Chopin's Polonaise in A flat; "For Sentimental Reasons" by William Best, lyrics by Deke Watson; "I'm Beginning to See the Light" by Don George, Johnny Hodges, Duke Ellington, and Harry James; "Les Trois Cloches" ("While the Angelus Was Ringing") by French songwriter Jean Villard; "La Mer" by French singer-songwriter Charles Trenet, 32; "Laura" by David Raksin, lyrics by Johnny Mercer (title song for last year's film); "There Must Be a Way" by Sammy Gallop, David Saxon, Robert Cook; "Let It Snow! Let It Snow! Let It Snow!" by Jule Styne, lyrics by Sammy Cahn.

"Move on Up a Little Higher" is recorded by U.S. gospel singer Mahalia Jackson, 34, and scores a huge success. Seven other hymns recorded by Jackson will have sales of more than a million copies each and will include "I Believe," "I Can Put My Trust in Jesus," and "He's Got the Whole World in His Hands."

Pitcher Warren Spahn, 24, returns from the European war to resume a career with the Boston Braves that was interrupted after four games in 1942.

The Detroit Tigers win the World Series by defeating the Chicago Cubs 4 games to 3.

Aerosol spray insecticides begin a revolution in packaging. The commercial "bug bombs" employ a Freon-12 propellant gas developed by two U.S. Department of Agriculture researchers in 1942, they have been used during the war to protect troops from malaria-carrying mosquitoes, the new spray cans are heavy and costly to produce, but they will soon be replaced by lightweight tin and aluminum cans that will employ lower pressure propellants and that will lead to widespread use of aerosol spray products (*see* Freon-12 refrigerant gas, 1931; Redi-Wip, 1947; Ablanalp, 1953).

Conrad Hilton opens the Conrad Hilton Hotel at Chicago and takes over Chicago's 20-year-old Palmer House with backing from local building supply magnate Henry Crown, 49 (*see* 1943). The U.S. Army has occupied the 3,000-room Stevens Hotel that opened in 1927, Hilton purchases control of the hotel, and he renames it (*see* 1947).

The Food and Agriculture Organization (FAO) of the United Nations establishes headquarters at Rome with English agriculturist John Boyd Orr as director.

The semidwarf wheat variety Norin 10 whose 2-foot stems respond quickly to water and fertilizer and do not fall over (lodge) from the weight of their grain heads is discovered in Japan by U.S. Department of Agriculture agronomist Samuel C. Salmon, 60, who is traveling with General MacArthur's occupation force as a cereal improvement expert to help the

Nuclear fission raised fearsome questions. Would it end dependence on fossil fuels or would it destroy the world?

1945 (cont.) Japanese in their reconstruction. Salmon finds Norin 10 on a visit to the Morioka experimental station in northern Honshu, he returns to the United States with some seeds which he grows in quarantine, Norin 10 proves to be extremely susceptible to leaf stripe and powdery mildew, but Salmon's fellow agronomist Orville Vogel crosses the Japanese wheat with resistant strains of American wheat. Grains developed from Norin 10 will increase wheat harvests in India and Pakistan by more than 60 percent.

The U.S. soybean crop reaches 193 million bushels, up from 78 million in 1940.

The chemical 2,4-D (2,4-dichlorophenoxyacetic acid) that was patented as a plant growth regular by E. I. du Pont in 1943 is patented as a general weed killer by American Chemical Paint Company which will sell 2,4-D for killing dandelions and plantain weed without harming lawns. The first selective plant killer, 2,4-D will be found to destroy broad-leafed plants such as bull thistle, cocklebur, ragweed, and wild mustard while leaving food crops such as corn and wheat unharmed, thus increasing crop yields by destroying moisture- and nutrient-consuming weeds without laborious cultivation.

The University strawberry developed by the University of California agriculture station will make strawberries a long-season widely grown commodity.

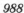 Wakefield Seafoods, Inc., has its beginnings in Wakefield Deep Sea Trawlers, Inc., and is the first company to develop modern techniques for processing and freezing Alaska king crab. Entrepreneur Lowell Wakefield was piloting a herring seiner off Alaska's Kodiak Island in 1939 when he came upon a mountain of live king crabs left by an exceptionally low tide after a severe storm, and when the U.S. Fish and Wildlife Service made a survey of Alaskan waters in 1940, Wakefield followed the government boat whose gear he borrowed in 1941 when the $100,000 appropriated for the survey ran out. Wakefield and his wife Jessie have evolved a method of cooking crabmeat and then freezing it, he has mortgaged his house and sold stock to buy a 143-foot trawler, and by the time she makes her second voyage she will be hauling in 800 crabs per hour and processing and freezing the big crabs as they are caught (*see* 1968).

Columbia River Packers Association executive Thomas F. Sandoz travels to Japan and contracts with Japanese fishermen to supply CRPA's Astoria albacore cannery with foreign tuna (*see* 1938; 1950).

Japan mobilizes schoolchildren to gather more than a million metric tons of acorns for use in flourmaking to supplement scarce wheat and rice stocks.

CARE (Cooperative for American Remittances to Europe) is founded as a private relief organization to help deal with the misery widespread on the Continent. Ready-assembled U.S. food packages of good quality are shipped to the European families and friends of people in America for $10 each, including transportation, with delivery guaranteed at a time when packages sent through normal channels are highly susceptible to loss, theft, or damage.

Peasoup powder sent to relieve hunger in Italy is only reluctantly accepted because it is so unfamiliar, but powdered eggs become familiar everywhere.

U.S. food rationing on all items except sugar ends November 23, but food remains scarce in most of the world. Black markets exist throughout Europe.

The amino acid tryptophan that is abundant in milk is found by nutrition researchers to be a provitamin that triggers production of niacin (vitamin B 3) by the human liver. The discovery solves the mystery of resistance to pellagra among infants who receive enough milk (*see* 1900; 1906; Elvehejm, 1936).

Bread-enrichment laws are enacted in Alabama, Georgia, Hawaii, Indiana, Maine, New Hampshire, New York, North Carolina, North Dakota, South Dakota, Washington, West Virginia, and Wyoming.

The first attempts to fluoridate community water supplies to reduce the incidence of dental caries in children are made in the United States. The fluoridation program at Grand Rapids, Mich. is followed by a program at Newburgh, N.Y., but the moves arouse widespread political opposition (*see* Dean, 1933; Cox, 1939; Britain, 1955).

Self-styled nutritionist Carlton Fredericks is convicted of practicing medicine without a license and is fined $500. The 37-year-old New York broadcaster has a doctorate in communications, he will serve as a paid consultant to companies making diet supplements, he will continue broadcasting, and he will author books full of dubious health claims.

Some 85 percent of U.S. bread is commercially baked, up from 66 percent in 1939.

Frozen orange juice is pioneered by U.S. food processors who use knowledge gained in wartime production of powdered orange juice. They develop an easily frozen sludge of concentrated juice that can be reconstituted to taste far more like fresh-squeezed juice than does ordinary canned juice (*see* 1946).

Welch Grape Juice Company is acquired by winemaker J. M. Kaplan who has built his upstate New York winery into National Grape Corporation (*see* 1933; Welch, 1927). Kaplan has encouraged the six small farmers' cooperatives that supply him with grapes to form a new, stronger cooperative, and he has made an arrangement with the new National Grape Co-operative Association, Inc., to set aside part of the sale price of each case of goods and accumulate funds for eventual purchase of National Grape Corporation by the cooperative. Welch Grape Juice is a household name but the company's $9 million per year business is declining and Kaplan has been persuaded to buy it by the farmers. He scraps the hundreds of thousands of 5-gallon glass carboys used to store grape juice at the Welch plants, he replaces them with refrigerated stainless steel tanks, and he installs modern equipment (*see* 1956).

The name "Coke" is registered for the first time as a trademark for Coca-Cola (*see* 1942; 1955).

Omaha's C. A. Swanson & Sons begins to develop a line of canned and frozen chicken and turkey products under the Swanson label using experience gained in World War II when nearly all the firm's poultry was shipped to the armed forces. Called the Jerpe Commission Company until now, the 45-year-old company has been owned since 1928 by Carl A. Swanson (*see* "TV" Dinners, 1954).

Sell's Liver Paté is introduced commercially (*see* 1941). The product will be joined in the next few years by such Sell's Specialities as canned Braised Beef, Beefsteak and Kidney, and Corned Beef Hash.

Hunt Foods, Inc., has sales of $19 million with after-tax profits of $530,000 (*see* 1942). Norton Simon buys United Can & Glass Company to give Hunt its own container production facility and he buys Ohio Match Company to give the firm millions of match-covers on which to print the slogan "Hunt for the Best," plugging Hunt Tomato Sauce and other Hunt products (*see* 1946).

Tupperware Corporation is founded by former E. I. du Pont chemist Earl W. Tupper, who has designed plastic bowls and cannisters with a patented seal that permits them to be stored on their sides or upside down without leaking, a feature that will be demonstrated at Tupperware Home Parties.

Le Cordon Bleu reopens at 24 rue du Champs de Mars near Les Invalides in Paris under the direction of Belgian entrepreneur Mme. Elizabeth Brassard after having been closed by the war (*see* 1934). Brassard will run the school for more than 30 years, and her students will include Americans Audrey Hepburn and Julia Child (*see* 1961).

Paris's Lasserre Restaurant opens on the newly renamed Boulevard Franklin D. Roosevelt. The restaurant will be world-famous for its cuisine and wine list.

One third of the world's Jews have died in Nazi death camps in the last 6 years, including an estimated 4 million killed with cyanide gas at the Auschwitz-Birkenau extermination camp in southern Poland.

An estimated 54.8 million people have died in World War II, including 25 million in the Soviet Union, 7.8 million in China, and more than 6 million in Poland which has lost more than 22 percent of her people.

1946 "From Stettin in the Baltic to Trieste in the Adriatic, an iron curtain has descended across the Continent," says former prime minister Winston Churchill March 5 in an address at Westminster College in Fulton, Mo. President Truman is in the audience that hears the British statesman say that Moscow's totalitarian dominance has produced a decline of confidence in "the haggard world."

An Austrian Republic with frontiers as of 1937 has gained recognition from the Western powers January 7, Albania has proclaimed herself a People's Republic January 11, Yugoslavia has adopted a new Soviet model constitution January 31, Hungary has proclaimed herself a republic February 1, Italy's Victor Emmanuel III abdicates May 9 at age 76 after a 46-year reign, his 41-year-old son Umberto proclaims himself king, a referendum June 2 rejects the monarchy 12.7 million to 10.7 million, Umberto II joins his family at Lisbon June 3, and the nation becomes a republic. Italy loses the Dodecanese Islands to Greece and parts of her northern territory to France June 27, Bulgaria becomes a People's Republic September 15 following a referendum against the monarchy, Greece's George II returns to Athens September 28 following a plebiscite favoring retention of the monarchy, Bulgarian Communist Georgi Dimitrov returns from Moscow November 21 to become premier (*see* 1933).

The United Nations General Assembly opens its first session January 10 at London with Paul Spaak of Belgium as president, the UN Security Council meets for the first time January 17 at London, Norwegian Socialist Trygve Lie is elected UN Secretary-General February 1, the Security Council meets March 25 at New York's Hunter College, the League of Nations assembly dissolves itself April 18, the UN General Assembly meets at New York October 23, New York is selected as permanent UN headquarters December 5, and 9 days later the UN accepts a gift of $8.5 million from John D. Rockefeller, Jr., toward purchase of property in Turtle Bay on New York's East River for permanent UN headquarters.

British and French forces begin evacuating Lebanon March 10, Moscow agrees to withdraw troops from Iran April 5 on the promise that reforms will be made in Azerbaijan. Transjordan proclaims herself independent May 25, after gaining British recognition.

Britain's "Lord Haw Haw" (William Joyce) has been hanged January 3 at London's Wandsworth Prison after having been convicted of treason. Born in Brooklyn, N.Y., of Irish and English parents, Joyce emigrated to England in 1905, he applied for a British passport in 1933, he was a prominent supporter of the British Fascist Oswald Mosley, he fled to Germany in late August of 1939 and made propaganda broadcasts to Britain, he was arrested in Denmark last year, and he was prosecuted for treason on the ground that he carried a British passport at the start of the war and thus owed allegiance to the Crown.

Romania's wartime premier Ion Antonescu is sentenced to death May 17.

The Nuremberg Tribunal returns verdicts September 30. Twelve leading Nazis are sentenced to death including Joachim von Ribbentrop and Hermann Goering (who commits suicide by taking poison), Rudolf Hess and Walter Funk are sentenced to life imprisonment, Franz von Papen and Hjalmar Schacht are acquitted.

1946 (cont.) Paris recognizes Vietnamese independence within the French Union March 4, but hostilities with native Communists continue as Ho Chi Minh tries to drive out the French and unite Indo-China. The French retaliate by proclaiming an autonomous Republic of Cochin China at Saigon June 1, they bombard Haiphong November 23, they kill 6,000, and a long struggle begins.

China's civil war resumes April 14 after a truce of more than 3 months negotiated by U.S. General George C. Marshall, the Nationalist government returns from Chungking to Nanking May 1, another truce stops hostilities for 6 weeks beginning May 12, the Kuomintang reelects President Chiang Kai-shek October 10, a Sino-American treaty of friendship, commerce, and navigation is signed November 4, a national assembly meets November 15 without Communist representation, and the Chinese adopt a new constitution December 25.

The king of Siam Rama VIII is found dead of a bullet wound June 9 at age 21 after an 11-year reign. His brother Phumiphon Aduldet will reign as Rama IX beginning May 5, 1950, after he returns from school in Switzerland, and the Siamese accept a UN verdict October 13 that they return to Indo-China the provinces they acquired in 1941 as allies of Japan.

The Philippines gain independence from the United States July 4 under provisions of the McDuffie-Tydings Act of 1934. The Philippine Republic headed by President Manuel A. Roxas tries to subdue the Communist-led Huks (Hukbalahaps) peasant party that has appropriated lands in central Luzon.

The Cheribon Agreement initialed by Dutch and Indonesian diplomats November 15 follows conclusion of a truce in the fighting between Indonesians and Dutch and British forces, the Dutch agree to recognize the Indonesian Republic (Java, Sumatra, Madura) and to the establishment of the United States of Indonesia which will include also Borneo, the Celebes, the Sunda Islands, and the Moluccas to be joined in equal partnership with the Netherlands under the Dutch Crown. The last British troops leave Indonesia November 29 (*see* 1949).

Sarawak is ceded to the British Crown by the rajah Sir Charles Brooke (*see* 1888).

Juan Peron wins election as president of Argentina February 24 at age 50 and begins a rule that will continue until 1955.

Mexico elects Miguel Alemán Valdés president July 7, and the election of the civilian leads to closer U.S. ties. The 44-year-old Alemán is the first civilian president, he appoints a cabinet of economic experts, and he begins a program of industrialization, electrification, irrigation, and improvement of transportation.

ENIAC (electronic numerical integrator and computer) is the world's first automatic electronic digital computer and makes the Mark I electromechanical computer of 1944 obsolete. Constructed at Harvard, ENIAC is a massive device that employs 18,000 radio tubes and large amounts of electric power, it operates on the principle that vacuum tubes can be turned on and off thousands of times faster than mechanical relays, it can make some 4,500 additions per second, and although its tubes are not reliable and it functions only for brief periods, ENIAC begins a revolution in industrial technology. University of Pennsylvania electrical engineers John Presper Eckert, 27, and John William Mauchly, 39, have developed ENIAC following Mauchly's visit with University of Iowa scientist John Vincent Atanasoff, now 41, who has invented basic concepts of computer technology (*see* transistor, 1948; Remington-Rand, 1950).

The word "automation" is coined by Ford Motor Company engineer Delmar S. Harder, 54, for the system he has devised to manufacture automobile engines. Harder's completely automatic process produces a new engine every 14 minutes, it reduces production time from 21 hours, and it is the first complete self-regulating system applied to manufacturing (*see* assembly line, 1913).

Polish Jews who have survived the holocaust are killed at Kielce in a pogrom July 14.

Italian women are given the vote for the first time.

Japanese women gain the right to vote as U.S. occupation authorities make sweeping changes in Japanese society; 89 women stand for election to the Diet and 34 win seats in the April 10 elections.

Paris brothels are closed by La Loi Marthe Richard named for the 58-year-old member of the French Assembly who has campaigned against the enslavement of women in houses of prostitution. Mme. Richard became the sixth woman in the world to fly an airplane 34 years ago, she served as a spy in World War I, she stole the German plan for U-boat attacks on U.S. troopship convoys from the bedroom of naval attaché Hans von Krohn in Spain. Her legislation does not outlaw prostitution, but bordellos are no longer licensed, medical examinations are dropped, and demimondaines are obliged to solicit in the streets.

An Indian Claims Commission is established by Congress to settle once and for all the disputes that have been smoldering for nearly a century over lands taken by the white man.

Bombay removes social disabilities of the city's untouchables, but prejudice against the *harijans* continues.

A National Health Service Bill enacted by Parliament makes medical services free to all Britons. The effect of the new measure will be to lower dramatically Britain's infant mortality rate and maternal death rate to levels below those in the United States, and to reduce death rates from bronchitis, influenza, pneumonia, tuberculosis, and some other diseases to levels below U.S. rates (*see* 1947).

The Common Sense Book of Baby and Child Care by New York psychiatrist Benjamin Spock, 43, will be used to raise a generation of children along permissive lines of behavioral standards. Spock wrote the book while serving in the war as a Navy Medical Corps lieutenant colonel in charge of severe disciplinary cases, it will be retitled as *Baby and Child Care,* and it will become an all-time best seller.

$ Housing shortages and pent-up demand for consumer goods lead to runaway prices and rising wage demands in much of the world. Strikes idle some 4.6 million U.S. workers during the year with a loss of 116 million man-days, the worst stoppage since 1919.

Some 260,000 electrical workers strike General Electric, Westinghouse, and General Motors January 15.

Some 263,000 meat packers strike January 16.

Some 750,000 steel workers strike January 20.

Parliament repeals the British Trades Disputes Act of 1927 February 13, it legalizes certain kinds of strikes, and it frees labor unions of most restrictions on political activities.

The British Government takes over the Bank of England February 14.

A wage-pattern formula announced by President Truman February 14 entitles U.S. labor to 33 percent wage increases that equal the rise in the cost of living since January 1941.

An employment act passed by Congress February 20 declares that maximum employment must be the government's policy goal.

President Truman reestablishes the Office of Economic Stabilization February 21 to control inflation. He names Chester Bowles to direct the office.

U.S. troops seize the country's railroads May 17 in the face of imminent strikes. A brief strike ends when President Truman recommends wage boosts.

Parliament nationalizes the British coal industry in May with a law that is to take effect January 1, 1947.

U.S. troops seize American soft coal mines May 22 to end a strike begun April 1. John L. Lewis has brought his United Mine Workers back into the AF of L late in January (*see* 1936), he leads his soft coal workers out on strike November 21 in defiance of a federal injunction, he is fined $3.5 million December 4, and the workers return to the pits December 7.

The Office of Price Administration (OPA) expires June 29 when the President vetoes a Compromise Price Control act, but Congress revives the OPA July 25 with a new Price Control act.

Canada institutes Family Allowances. Sales of children's shoes jump from 762,000 pairs per month to 1,180,000 as Canadian parents receive financial aid.

Hungary suffers the worst inflation in world history as the gold pengo of 1931 falls in value to 130 trillion paper pengos in June. The government prints 100-trillion pengo notes.

The U.S. Mint issues a new 10-cent piece bearing the profile of Franklin D. Roosevelt to replace the Mercury dime in circulation since 1916. The new Roosevelt dime will not be superseded in design for 30 years but will decline in value in those 30 years.

Wall Street's Dow Jones Industrial Average reaches a post-1929 high of 212.50, but falls to 163.12.

High meat prices bring demands that President Truman resign, but food prices soften when the government withdraws from the market during the summer and prices break when the OPA (above) removes price ceilings in the fall.

Meat price controls end October 15, and President Truman issues an executive order November 9 lifting all wage and price controls except controls on rents and on prices for sugar and rice.

The U.S. inflation that will continue for at least 32 years begins December 14 as President Truman removes curbs on housing priorities and on housing prices by executive order. President Roosevelt's inflation control order of April 1943 kept prices from climbing more than 29 percent from 1939 to 1945 as compared with a 63 percent jump in the 1914 to 1918 period, but Truman is more worried about a possible postwar depression than about inflation.

 U.S. military authorities conduct the first Bikini Atoll atomic bomb tests in the Pacific in July.

The McMahon Act passed by Congress August 1 establishes a civilian U.S. Atomic Energy Commission. Former TVA director David E. Lilienthal is sworn in November 1 as the AEC's first chairman.

Application for a U.S. patent on a nuclear fusion (hydrogen) bomb is filed by mathematician John (Janos) von Neumann (*see* 1944) and German-born physicist Klaus Emil Julius Fuchs, 35 (*see* Eniwetok, 1952; Fuchs, 1950).

Jet Propulsion Laboratories researchers at the California Institute of Technology find that a liquid polysulfide polymer is the ideal propellant for rockets since it not only works as a fuel but also bonds directly to the walls of rocket shells, eliminating the need for heavy mechanical supports. Thiokol Corporation makes the polymer and will become a major supplier to the aerospace industry (*see* 1938).

Soviet petroleum production begins a major expansion that will make the U.S.S.R. the world's largest oil producer within 30 years. Soviet engineers exploit deposits between the Volga River and the Ural Mountains where prospectors first found oil in the 1930s.

Kuwait Oil Company is founded on a 50–50 basis by Gulf Oil and Anglo-Iranian Oil which will make Kuwait the Middle East's largest oil-producing nation. The company will produce 1 billion barrels of Kuwait oil in the next 8 years and another billion barrels in the following 3 years (*see* Getty, 1949).

Dutch windmills dwindle to 1,400, down from 9,000 in the 1870s. The number will fall to 991 by 1960 and to 950 by 1973 despite government efforts to pre-

1946 (cont.) serve the polder mills that have kept the Netherlands from being flooded during the war.

Wagon Lits/Cook, Ltd., is created by an amalgamation of La Compagnie Internationale des Wagon Lits and Thomas Cook & Sons.

London's Heathrow Airport opens on a formal basis May 21 (*see* 1929). The airport has been used since January for flights to Buenos Aires.

British transatlantic passenger air service to North America starts July 1 as BOAC begins flying Lockheed Constellations between London and New York. Scheduled flying time is 19 hours, 45 minutes.

Pan American Airways inaugurates the great circle route to Tokyo.

SAS (Scandinavian Airlines System) is created by a consolidation of Sweden's AB Aerotransport, Denmark's DDL, and Norway's DNL to operate on transatlantic routes.

Cathay Pacific Airways is founded at Hong Kong.

Air India is created July 29 by a reorganization of Tata Air Lines which flies passengers at low rates to all the largest cities of India. Weekly Constellation service from Bombay to London via Cairo and Geneva will begin June 8, 1948, Air India will become a state corporation in 1953, it will be serving Nairobi, Hong Kong, and Tokyo by 1955, and by 1960 it will be serving Djakarta, Darwin, Sydney, Tashkent, Moscow, Prague, Frankfurt, and New York.

Alitalia (Aerolinee Italiane Internazionali) is created September 15 with British European Airways holding 30 percent of the shares in the new company.

IATA (International Air Transport Association) is founded. The trade association has 63 member airlines within a year and begins to set policies related to traffic, rates, and fares.

The DC-6 introduced by Douglas Aircraft can carry 70 passengers at 300 miles per hour with cargo, mail, and luggage (*see* 1938). Douglas has been the leading U.S. aircraft producer during the war but is only slightly ahead of Lockheed in sales, and its backlog of military and civilian orders has dropped behind those of Lockheed and Consolidated-Vultee (*see* DC-7, 1953).

Kaiser-Frazer automobiles are introduced in a venture that will mark the last major bid to challenge the established powers of the U.S. automobile industry. Henry J. Kaiser of Kaiser Aluminum has started the new company with former Willys-Overland president Joseph Washington Frazer, 54 (*see* 1950).

The Crosley compact car is introduced by Cincinnati appliance and electronics maker Powel L. Crosley (*see* 1921). Crosley's $250 four-passenger convertible sedan and his $325 convertible coupe (which doubles as a quarter-ton truck) are less than 12 feet long, they are powered by a two-cylinder air-cooled engine, they have top speeds of 45 miles per hour and 35

miles per gallon of gasoline, but they have little appeal to U.S. buyers. A four-cylinder engine with overhead camshaft will replace the original engine, but production will peak at only 30,000 cars per year in 1948 (*see* Henry J, 1950).

Bermuda permits motorcars to operate on the island after a half-century ban on vehicles other than bicycles, horsedrawn carriages and wagons, and motortrucks for special purposes.

Vespa motor scooters are introduced in Italy to provide cheap if noisy transportation. Aircraft maker Enrico Piaggio has had his works at Pontadera destroyed by Allied bombers, he has had his chief engineer Corradino d'Ascanio design the scooter to give him a product with which he can resume production, and he calls it by the Italian name for wasp.

Colleges and universities throughout the world struggle to cope with swollen enrollments after years in which many have gone bankrupt or come close. U.S. college enrollments reach an all-time high of more than 2 million as returning veterans crowd classrooms with help from the G.I. Bill of Rights legislation passed in 1944.

The University of Binghamton is founded in New York.

Portland State University is founded in Oregon.

Lake Superior State College is founded at Sault Ste. Marie, Mich.

Mississippi Valley State College is founded at Itta Bena.

Westchester Community College is founded at White Plains, N.Y.

Marlboro College is founded at Marlboro, Vt.

Fulbright awards for an international exchange of students and professors are initiated August 1 as President Truman signs into law a bill introduced by U.S. Senator J. William Fulbright of Arkansas who was a Rhodes scholar in 1925 (*see* 1902). 120,000 Fulbright fellowships will be awarded in the next 30 years, a master of Oxford's Pembroke College will tell Fulbright, "You are responsible for the largest and most significant movement of scholars across the face of the earth since the fall of Constantinople in 1453," and Fulbright alumni by 1976 will include 41 past or present heads of states.

The BBC Third Programme begins in September to give British radio listeners more variety.

Xerography wins support from the Rochester, N.Y., firm Haloid Company whose research director John H. Dessauer has seen an article on "electrophotography" by Chester F. Carlson in a July 1944 issue of *Radio News* (*see* 1944). Dessauer and Haloid Company president Joseph C. Wilson, 36, travel to Columbus, Ohio, they see experiments conducted by the Batelle Memorial Institute, Haloid invests $10,000 to acquire production rights, and within

6 years the firm will raise more than $3.5 million to develop what will be called the Xerox copier (*see* 1950).

Die Welt (*The World*) begins publication at Hamburg under supervision of British occupation authorities. The new German daily soon has an Essen edition to give it a combined circulation of 500,000, a Berlin edition will appear beginning next year, the three editions will have a combined circulation of more than 1 million by 1949, and German publisher Axel C. Springer will acquire *Die Welt* for $1 million in 1953.

Der Spiegel (*The Mirror*) begins publication under the name *Diese Woche* (*This Week*). West German publisher Rudolf Augstein has modeled the weekly newsmagazine on *Time* and *Newsweek,* he soon renames it, and he will make *Der Spiegel* a powerful voice in European publishing (*see* 1962).

Scientific American magazine is acquired after 101 years of publication by former *LIFE* magazine science editor Gerard Piel, 31, who will be joined by *LIFE* staffmen Dennis Flanagan, 27, and Donald H. Miller, Jr., in broadening the appeal of the monthly as science grows in its impact on the lives and careers of more Americans.

Holiday magazine begins publication. Philadelphia's Curtis Publishing Company will continue the monthly travel magazine until 1970.

Family Circle magazine begins monthly publication in September after 14 years as a weekly supermarket giveaway. The cover price is 5 cents, the September issue has 96 pages, some chains drop the magazine, others accept it as a profit-making item.

The Revised Version of the New Testament published after 17 years of work revises the *American Standard Version* of 1901. Forty-four Protestant denominations have appointed a committee of 22 biblical scholars headed by Yale University Divinity School dean Luther A. Weigle, 65. The committee's *Revised Standard Version of the Old Testament* will appear in 1952 (both Bibles are based on the King James version of 1611).

Farrar, Straus & Company publishers is founded by former Farrar & Rinehart partner John C. Farrar (*see* 1929) and Roger W. Straus, 29, who will achieve their first success next year with Carlo Levi's novel *Christ Stopped at Eboli.* The new house will become in turn Farrar, Straus & Young, Farrar, Straus and Cudahy, and Farrar, Straus & Giroux.

Nonfiction *The Chrysanthemum and the Sword: Patterns of Japanese Culture* by Ruth Benedict who has never been to Japan but whose book will nevertheless be a classic in its field; *Hiroshima* by John Hersey whose documentary account of last year's nuclear attack on the Japanese city occupies the entire August 31 issue of the *New Yorker* magazine and then appears in book form; *Journal, 1939–42* by André Gide; *The Art of Plain Talk* by Viennese-American author Rudolph Flesch, 35.

Fiction *Zorba the Greek* (*Vois Kai Politeia Tou Alexi Zorba*) by Nikos Kazantzakis; *The President* (*El Señor Presidente*) by Guatemalan novelist Miguel Asturias, 47; *The Berlin Stories* by Christopher Isherwood; *The Member of the Wedding* by Carson McCullers; *Memoirs of Hecate County* (stories) by Edmund Wilson; *Ladders to Fire* by U.S. novelist Anaïs Nin, 32; *Willowaw* by U.S. novelist Gore Vidal, 21; *All the King's Men* by Robert Penn Warren; *The Big Clock* by New York poet-novelist Kenneth Fearing, 44; *Back* by Henry Green; *Miracle de la rose* by French playwright Jean Genet; "The Idiot" ("Hakuchi") by Japanese short-story writer Ango Sakaguchi, 40, who during the war came out against nationalism in "My Personal View of Japanese Culture" ("Nippon Bunka Shikan"); "The Courtesy Call" by Japanese short-story writer Osamu Dazai (Shuji Shimazu), 37, who has been the victim of a wartime air raid, has said that he was deceived by the emperor, and expresses a nihilistic feeling of despair (he will commit suicide in 1948 by throwing himself into a Tokyo reservoir); *The Foxes of Harrow* by U.S. novelist Frank Garvin Yerby, 30; *This Side of Innocence* by Taylor Caldwell; *B. F.'s Daughter* by John P. Marquand; *Mr. Blandings Builds His Dream House* by *Fortune* magazine editor Eric Hodgins, 46, who describes his own tribulations after buying an old farmhouse on Long Mountain Road in New Milford, Conn., but while Hodgins was forced to sell the house last year for $38,000 after having spent $56,000 to restore it, his book will make him a fortune; *I, the Jury* by U.S. comic-strip writer Frank Morrison "Mickey" Spillane, 28, whose raunchy Mike Hammer detective novel emphasizes sex, sadism, and violence, is scorned by critics, wins immediate popular success, and begins Spillane on a new career.

Poetry *Deaths and Entrances* by Dylan Thomas; *Paterson* by William Carlos Williams; *Lord Weary's Castle* by U.S. poet Robert Lowell, 29, who has served a term in prison for his pacifism in World War II; *The Double Image* by English poet Denise Levertov, 23.

Painting *Faun Playing the Pipe* and *Françoise with a Yellow Necklace* by Pablo Picasso whose mistress Françoise Gilot will give birth next year to his son Claude; *Cow with Umbrella* by Marc Chagall; *Composition with Branch* by Fernand Léger; *Head of Thorns* by Graham Sutherland.

Pablo Picasso founds a pottery at Vallauris in the south of France.

Ektachrome color film is introduced by Eastman Kodak Company and is the first color film a photographer can process himself. Much faster than the Kodachrome film introduced in 1935 and 1936, the new film is available initially only in transparency sheet form, but Eastman will introduce Ektachrome in roll film sizes next year and will increase its speed in 1955 and again in 1959 (*see* Kodacolor, 1942; Tri-X, 1954).

The United Nations struggled to find peaceful solutions to the problems that divided a war-weary world.

Photographer Alfred Stieglitz dies at New York July 13 at age 82 leaving his 58-year-old widow Georgia O'Keeffe.

 Theater *Those Ghosts!* (*Questi fantasmi!*) by Italian playwright Edouardo De Filippo 1/12 at Rome's Teatro Eliseo; *Born Yesterday* by U.S. playwright-screenwriter Garson Kanin, 34, 2/4 at New York's Lyceum Theater, with Judy Holliday (as the not-so-dumb blonde played in Boston by Jean Arthur), Paul Douglas, Gary Merrill, 1,642 perfs.; *Santa Cruz* by Swiss playwright Max Frisch, 34, 3/7 at Zurich's Schauspielhaus; *Beaumarchais, or the Birth of Figaro* by Friedrich Wolf 3/8 at Berlin's Deutsches Theater; *A Phoenix Too Frequent* by English playwright Christopher Fry, 38, 4/25 at London's Mercury Theatre; *The Winslow Boy* by Terence Rattigan 9/6 at London's Lyric Theatre, 215 perfs.; *The Iceman Cometh* by Eugene O'Neill 10/9 at New York's Martin Beck Theater, with James Barton, Carl Benton Reid, Dudley Digges, 136 perfs.; *The Chinese Wall* (*Die chinesische Mauer*) by Max Frisch 10/10 at Zurich's Schauspielhaus; *Filomenca Marchurano* by Edouardo De Filippo 11/7 at Naples; *The Respectful Prostitute* (*La putain respecteuse*) by Jean-Paul Sartre 11/8 at the Théâtre Antoine, Paris; *Another Part of the Forest* by Lillian Hellman 11/20 at New York's Fulton Theater, with Patricia Neal, Mildred Dunnock, 182 perfs.

Films Jean Cocteau's *Beauty and the Beast* with Jean Marais; Vittorio De Sica's *Shoe Shine*; Roberto Rosselini's *Open City* with Anna Magnani, Aldo Fabrizi; Luigi Zampa's *To Live in Peace* with Aldo Fabrizi; David Lean's *Brief Encounter* with Trevor Howard, Celia Johnson in an adaptation of Noel Coward's one-act play *Still Life*; Compton Bennett's *The Seventh Veil* with James Mason, Ann Todd; William Wyler's *The Best Years of Our Lives* with Fredric March, Myrna Loy, Teresa Wright, Dana Andrews, Harold Russell, Virginia Mayo; Frank Capra's *It's a Wonderful Life* with James Stewart, Lionel Barrymore, Thomas Mitchell, Donna Reed, Henry Travers; Robert Siodmak's *The Killers* with Burt Lancaster, Ava Gardner; Robert Siodmak's *The Spiral Staircase* with Dorothy McGuire, George Brent, Ethel Barrymore; Mitchell Leisen's *To Each His Own* with Olivia de Havilland, John Lund; King Vidor's *Duel in the Sun* with Jennifer Jones, Joseph Cotten, Gregory Peck, Lionel Barrymore; Alfred Hitchcock's *Notorious* with Cary Grant, Ingrid Bergman; John Ford's *My Darling Clementine* with Henry Fonda, Victor Mature, Linda Darnell; Jean Negulesco's *Three Strangers* with Sydney Greenstreet, Peter Lorre, Geraldine Fitzgerald; Howard Hawks's *The Big Sleep* with Humphrey Bogart, Lauren Bacall, Martha Vickers; Edmund Goulding's *The Razor's Edge* with Tyrone Power, Gene Tierney; Charles Vidor's *Gilda* with Rita Hayworth singing "Put the Blame on Mame"; Wolfgang Staudte's *The Murderers Among Us*; Kenji Mizoguchi's *Utamaro and His Five Women*; Tay Garnett's *The Postman Always Rings Twice* with Lana Turner, John Garfield; Clarence Brown's *The Yearling* with Gregory Peck, Jane Wyman, Claude Jarman, Jr.

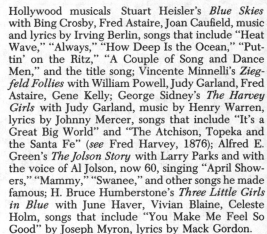 Hollywood musicals Stuart Heisler's *Blue Skies* with Bing Crosby, Fred Astaire, Joan Caufield, music and lyrics by Irving Berlin, songs that include "Heat Wave," "Always," "How Deep Is the Ocean," "Puttin' on the Ritz," "A Couple of Song and Dance Men," and the title song; Vincente Minnelli's *Ziegfeld Follies* with William Powell, Judy Garland, Fred Astaire, Gene Kelly; George Sidney's *The Harvey Girls* with Judy Garland, music by Henry Warren, lyrics by Johnny Mercer, songs that include "It's a Great Big World" and "The Atchison, Topeka and the Santa Fe" (*see* Fred Harvey, 1876); Alfred E. Green's *The Jolson Story* with Larry Parks and with the voice of Al Jolson, now 60, singing "April Showers," "Mammy," "Swanee," and other songs he made famous; H. Bruce Humberstone's *Three Little Girls in Blue* with June Haver, Vivian Blaine, Celeste Holm, songs that include "You Make Me Feel So Good" by Joseph Myron, lyrics by Mack Gordon.

Stage musicals *Lute Song* 2/6 at New York's Plymouth Theater, with Mary Martin, Yul Brynner, music by Raymond Scott, lyrics by Bernard Harrigan, songs that include "Mountain High, Valley Low," 142 perfs.; *St. Louis Woman* 3/30 at New York's Martin Beck Theater, with Pearl Bailey heading an all-black cast, music by Harold Arlen, lyrics by Johnny Mercer, songs that include "Come Rain or Come Shine," 113 perfs.; *Call Me Mister* 4/18 at New York's National Theater, with Betty Garrett, music and lyrics by Harold Rome, book by Arnold Auerbach and Arnold Horwitt, songs that include "South America, Take It Away," 734 perfs.; *Annie Get Your Gun* 5/16 at New York's Imperial Theater, with Ethel Merman, Ray Middleton, book based on the life of markswoman Phoebe "Annie Oakley" Mozee of Buffalo Bill's Wild West Show (*see* 1883), music and lyrics by Irving Berlin, songs that include "Anything You Can Do," "Doin' What Comes Naturally," "The Girl That I Marry," "You Can't Get a Man with a Gun," "I Got the Sun in the Morning," "There's No Business Like Show Business," 1,147 perfs.; *Pacific 1860* 12/19 at London's Theatre Royal in Drury Lane, with Mary Martin, music and lyrics by Noel Coward, 129 perfs.

Opera *The Medium* 5/8 at Columbia University's Brander Matthew Theater, New York, with music by Italian-American composer Gian-Carlo Menotti, 34; *The Rape of Lucretia* 7/12 at Glyndebourne, with music by Benjamin Britten.

The New York City Ballet Company has its beginnings in the Ballet Society founded by George Balanchine and Lincoln Kirstein of 1934 School of American Ballet fame; they will rename the Society in 1948.

Ballet *The Serpent Heart* 5/10 at Columbia University's McMillin Theater, New York, with Martha Graham, music by Samuel Barber, choreography by Graham; *The Four Temperaments* 11/20 at New York's Central High School of the Needle Trades, with Gisella Caccialanza, Tanaquil LeClercq, Todd Bolender, music by Paul Hindemith, choreography by George Balanchine.

The Juilliard Quartet founded by the Juilliard School's new president William Howard Schuman, 35, is a resident string quartet.

First performances Symphony in Three Movements by Igor Stravinsky 1/24 at New York's Carnegie Hall; *Metamorphosen* by Richard Strauss 1/25 at Zurich; Concerto for Clarinet and Orchestra by Darius Milhaud 1/30 at the Marine Barracks, Washington, D.C.; Concerto No. 3 for Piano and Orchestra by the late Béla Bartók 2/8 at Philadelphia's Academy of Music. Bartók died in poverty at New York last September at age 64; Concerto for Oboe and Chamber Orchestra by Richard Strauss 2/26 at Zurich; Scherzo a la Russe by Igor Stravinsky 3/22 at San Francisco; Sonatina No. 2 for 16 Wind Instruments by Richard Strauss 3/25 at Winterthur, Switzerland; *Ebony Concerto* by Igor Stravinsky 3/25 at New York's Carnegie Hall, with Woody Herman as clarinet soloist; Concerto for Violoncello and Orchestra by Samuel Barber 4/5 at Boston's Symphony Hall; Symphony No. 3 by Charles Ives 4/5 at New York; *The Bells* symphonic suite by Darius Milhaud 4/26 at Chicago; *The Unanswered Question* (*A Comic Landscape*) by Charles Ives (who wrote it in 1908) 5/11 at Columbia University, New York; *For Those We Love* requiem by Paul Hindemith 5/14 at New York's City Center, with Robert Shaw's Collegiate Chorale, text from the Walt Whitman poem "When Lilacs Last in the Dooryard Bloom'd"; Concerto No. 3 for Piano and Orchestra by Darius Milhaud 5/26 at Prague; Symphony for Strings by William Schuman (above) 7/12 at London; Symphonie No. 3 (*Liturgique*) by Arthur Honegger 8/17 at Zurich's Tonhalle; String Quartet No. 2 by Charles Ives (who wrote it between

1907 and 1913) 10/7 at New York's Town Hall; Quartet No. 2 for Strings by Ernest Bloch 10/9 at London's Wigmore Hall; Symphony No. 3 by Aaron Copland 10/18 at Boston's Symphony Hall; Concerto for Cello in E major by Aram Khatchaturian 10/30 at Moscow; Concerto No. 2 for Violoncello and Orchestra by Darius Milhaud 11/28 at New York's Carnegie Hall; Ricercari for Piano and Orchestra by U.S. composer Norman Dello Joio, 33, 12/19 at New York's Carnegie Hall; Symphony No. 2 by Darius Milhaud 12/20 at Boston's Symphony Hall; *Minstrel Show* by Morton Gould 12/21 at Indianapolis.

The first vinylite phonograph record appears in October. RCA-Victor issues a new recording of the 1895 Richard Strauss work *Till Eulenspiegels Lustige Streiche,* but vinylite will not displace shellac until the perfection of long-playing records (*see* 1948).

Popular songs "La Vie en Rose" by Italian-born Paris composer Louiguy (Louis Guglielmi), 30, lyrics by French chanteuse Edith Piaf (Edith Givanna Gassion), 31; "(Get Your Kicks on) Route 66" by Bob Troup; "To Each His Own" by Raymond B. Evans, 31, lyrics by Jay Livingston, 31 (title song for film); "Tenderly" by Walter Gross, lyrics by Jack Lawrence; "Linda" by Jack Lawrence; "You Call Everybody Darling" by Sam Martin, Ben Trace, Clem Walls; "Ole Buttermilk Sky" by Hoagy Carmichael and Jack Brooks (for the film *Canyon Passage*); "Seems Like Old Times" by Carmen Lombardo and John Jacob Loeb; "The Christmas Song (Chestnuts Roasting on an Open Fire)" by U.S. songwriter-vocalist Mel Torme and Robert Wells.

World chess champion Aleksandr Alekhine dies March 24 at age 54 on the eve of a title match against Soviet chess master Mikhail Botvinnik, 35, who has beaten five other seeded World Chess Federation players including Polish-American chess master Samuel Reshevsky, 35, who held the U.S. title from 1936 to 1944. The world title will remain vacant until 1948.

King Ranch 3-year-old Assault wins U.S. racing's Triple Crown.

The St. Louis Cardinals win the World Series by defeating the Boston Red Sox 4 games to 3.

The Army-Navy football game nearly ends in an upset for Army whose team has won 27 games straight. Army All-America stars Felix "Doc" Blanchard ("Mr. Inside") and Glenn Woodward Davis ("Mr. Outside") put Army ahead 21 to 6 by halftime, but a Navy team that has won only one game in eight all season narrows the lead to 21 to 18, gains a first down on the Army three with 90 seconds remaining, and just misses pulling an upset (*see* 1947; 1950).

An automatic Pinspotter displayed in prototype at a national bowling tournament in Buffalo, N.Y., by American Machine and Foundry Company (AMF) begins a revolution in bowling. Devised by Pearl River, N.Y., inventor Fred Schmidt, the patented vacuum Pinspotter has been rejected by Brunswick

1946 (cont.) Balke-Collender Company which will scramble to catch up with AMF as bowling becomes the leading U.S. participation sport.

Tide is introduced by Procter & Gamble and is the first detergent strong enough for washing clothes as well as dishes (*see* Persil, 1907). By the end of 1949 one out of every four U.S. washing machines will be using Tide.

The Westinghouse Laundromat introduced by the Westinghouse Company is a front-loading machine that requires a low-sudsing soap or detergent.

British-made nylon hosiery go on sale in December. The stockings are the first nylon consumer goods made in Britain (*see* 1940).

The Lewyt Vacuum Cleaner is introduced by U.S. entrepreneur Alex Lewyt, 37, who has designed a quiet, mobile cleaner to compete with Hoover, Electrolux, and others and has organized a network of salesmen and mail-order agents. By the end of his first year Lewyt has sold 100,000 vacuum cleaners and has $3 million in orders.

Timex watches are introduced by Norwegian-American entrepreneur Joakim Lehmkuhl, 51, who in 1940 was sent to New York by the Norwegian government in exile to take charge of the Norwegian Shipping Center and in 1943 was elected president of the Waterbury Watch Company, famous for its Ingersoll watch (*see* 1892). Lehmkuhl has made Waterbury Watch a wartime producer of timing mechanisms for bomb and artillery shell fuses and now moves the company back into watch production, dropping the Ingersoll name because it is associated with the $1 price. While $1 will no longer buy a watch, Lehmkuhl's mass-produced Timex at $6.95 and up will soon account for 40 percent of U.S. wristwatch sales as Waterbury Watch becomes U.S. Time Corporation (*see* Polaroid, 1950).

The bikini swimsuit designed by French couturier Louis Reard is modeled at a Paris fashion show July 5, 4 days after the first U.S. atomic bomb test (above) and creates a sensation. The scanty bikini will become popular in Europe but will not be widely seen on U.S. beaches until the 1960s.

Estée Lauder has its beginnings as New York investor Joseph Lauder, 38, goes into partnership with his wife Estée to market a few products developed by her Viennese-American uncle, a cosmetic chemist. The new firm will compete with Elizabeth Arden, Helena Rubinstein, Revlon, and the rest, it will have annual sales of $1 million by 1960, and by 1975 its annual sales will be above $100 million.

Beautiful Hair Breck full-page color magazine advertising appears for the first time (*see* 1930). Breck will open a New York salon in 1951.

London police answer a summons June 21 and rush to a Notting Hill hotel where the mutilated nude corpse of a 32-year-old woman has been found in bed with its ankles tied to the bedposts. Mrs. Margery

Aimee Gardner has separated from her husband and was dancing the evening of June 20 at a London nightclub with Neville George Clevely Heath, 29, who has a history of passing himself off as a military officer and who has signed the hotel register for the room in which Margery Gardner's body has been found. A woman walking her dog at Bournemouth soon after discovers the mutilated body of another young woman, Doreen Marshall. The police arrest Heath, a jury finds him guilty of both murders, and he is hanged October 26.

Detroit's J. L. Hudson opens a new 12-story building that gives Hudson's the world's second largest department store building. Its 2,124,316 square feet of floor space make it only slightly smaller than New York's R. H. Macy building in Herald Square (*see* 1928; Northland, 1954).

Washington's Woodward & Lothrop buys its chief competitor for $5.7 million. Founded in 1877 by Abraham Lisner, the Palais Royal took that name in 1893 when it moved to 11th and G Streets, and Woody's buys it from S. S. Kresge.

New York's Brooks Brothers is acquired by Garfinckel's, a Washington, D.C., retailer which will increase Brooks Brothers volume from its present $5.6 million to more than $50 million in the next 30 years. The 31-year-old main store at 346 Madison Avenue has branches at Boston, Newport, and Palm Beach, but new Brooks Brothers branches will open at San Francisco in 1959, at Pittsburgh in 1960, at Los Angeles in 1965, at Atlanta in 1967, at Washington, D.C., in 1968, at Scarsdale, N.Y., in 1969, at Cincinnati and St. Louis in 1971, at Houston in 1972, and elsewhere as the Brooks sack suit and button-down (polo) collar become *de rigeur* in the U.S. establishment.

War-torn Europe and Japan rebuild their cities out of the rubble left by the worst destruction in the history of warfare. Some European cities such as Warsaw are rebuilt in part from photographs to resemble their prewar appearance, Tokyo is rebuilt as it was after the 1923 earthquake with houses numbered according to the order in which they were built.

The Flamingo Hotel goes up at Las Vegas to begin the transformation of the Nevada city into a resort of grandiose hotel-casinos (*see* legalized gambling, 1931). "Murder Incorporated" veteran Benjamin "Bugsy" Siegel has put up the Flamingo with backing from syndicate boss Meyer Lansky, 42 (Siegel will be killed in June of next year by Chicago and New York mobsters).

Intercontinental Hotel Corp. is founded by Pan American Airways which enters the hotel business at the request of the State Department.

An earthquake in the Aleutian Trench April 1 shifts the sea floor and creates a seismic wave (*tsunami*). It plucks the Scotch Cap lighthouse from a rock 45 feet above the sea on Unimak, reaches Hawaii 5 hours later, kills 173, and injures 163.

The worst red tide in U.S. history begins in November on Florida's west coast, killing fish and shellfish by the millions and spurring efforts by the U.S. Fish and Wildlife Service to seek solutions to the control of *G. breve* (*see* 1916; 1932).

Meals for Millions is organized to relieve world hunger. The non-profit nonsectarian foundation with headquarters at Santa Monica, Calif., will develop high-protein foods for distribution to hungry people.

A world wheat shortage forces Britain to ration bread which was never rationed during the war. Restrictions on most other staple foods ensue.

Blizzards destroy wheat crops throughout Europe. Freak storms sweep over much of Britain at harvest time, wrecking crops in Suffolk after a wet summer has ruined hay crops in the north, in the mountains of Wales, and on the southern moors.

TEPP (tetraethyl pyrophosphate) is introduced by American Cyanamid Company whose new insecticide leaves no residue and will be widely used by fruit growers to kill orchard mites and aphids. Developed by German chemist Gerhard Schrader as part of a Nazi chemical warfare research program, TEPP has been found by British and U.S. intelligence agents in occupied Germany.

Chlordane introduced by U.S. chemist Julian Hyman is the first U.S.-developed chlorinated hydrocarbon pesticide (*see* DDT, 1939). Royal Dutch-Shell's Chemical Company will acquire Hyman's small firm.

A National School Lunch Act is passed by Congress as food prices soar (*see* Britain, 1906).

Vitamin D irradiation patents granted to Harry Steenbock in 1927 are invalidated by court rulings that say Steenbock's finding was a "discovery" rather than a patentable invention. Even a farmer who lets his alfalfa lie exposed to the ultraviolet rays of the sun would technically be infringing on the patents which have produced $9 million in royalties to the Wisconsin Alumni Foundation and have funded research programs and professors' salaries.

Not by Bread Alone by Canadian-born Arctic explorer Vilhjalmur Stefansson, 67, claims that a high-fat diet is far superior in every respect to a so-called "balanced" diet. Stefansson and his erstwhile companion of Arctic days Karsten Anderson participated in the late 1920s in a year-long supervised experiment at New York's Bellevue Hospital in which each man averaged between 2,620 and 2,650 calories per day of which at least 2,100 was derived from animal fat and the balance from animal protein (no eggs or dairy products were included), they thrived on the diet, and their "Eskimo diet" will be the basis of many best sellers (*see* Keys, Pennington, 1953).

U.S. bread consumption drops as wheat and flour are exported to starving Europe. Domestic shortages lead to a compulsory long-extraction program, and demand for flour whiteners jumps as Americans are put off by bread that is not as white as usual.

Sunshine Biscuits, Inc., is created as Loose-Wiles Biscuit Co. of 1910 Hydrox fame changes its name. The company is a major producer of pretzels, potato chips, popcorn, peanuts, and other snack foods in addition to its saltines, Hi-Ho crackers, Cheez-It crackers, and other brands and is second only to National Biscuit as a biscuit, cookie, and cracker maker.

Self-rising corn meal is marketed for the first time.

French's Instant Potato is introduced by Rochester's R. T. French Company of 1930 Worcestershire Sauce fame. The operation will be moved to Shelley, Ida., in 1951 and will use only Russet potatoes for the precooked mashed potato product.

Hunt Foods has made "price at time of shipment" contracts with its customers and holds most of them to those contracts when prices break in the fall. Hunt has 9-month sales of $48 million with after-tax profits of $5 million (*see* 1945; Snider Catsup, 1952).

An electric rice saucepan that will revolutionize Japanese cooking and will begin a vast Panasonic electronics empire is introduced by entrepreneur Konoskuke Matsushita, 55, whose saucepan is the first low-priced Japanese electrical cooking appliance. Matsushita started in 1918 with an investment of $50 to manufacture electrical adapter plugs.

U.S. frozen orange juice sales reach 4.8 million 6-ounce cans, but the product is not acceptable to most consumers. A "cutback" technique for overconcentrating orange juice and then adding fresh juice to the concentrate is developed by Louis Gardner MacDowell who is helped by C. D. Atkins and E. L. Moore to refine the process and produce a concentrate whose sweetness, flavor, and acidity are more uniform after dilution than fresh-squeezed orange juice. The new frozen concentrate will find wide acceptance and will boom demand for oranges, which are now in such oversupply that Florida growers have been cutting down trees and replacing them with avocado trees (*see* 1945; 1947).

Libby, McNeill & Libby enters the frozen food business and markets its first frozen products at Milwaukee in November (*see* baby foods, 1934).

Mrs. Paul's Kitchens is started to market frozen deviled crabs in 6-ounce packages at 59 cents retail. Philadelphia entrepreneur Edward J. Piszek, 29, goes into partnership with short-order cook John Paul, they each invest $450, and they find ready acceptance for their product (*see* Wakefield, 1945). Piszek has spent 5 years learning the food business with Campbell Soup, he has won a degree in business administration at the University of Pennsylvania night school, his job at General Electric has been jeopardized by the company's strike (above), and he begins a company that will have distribution west to the Pacific by 1960 with a Mrs. Paul's line that will include frozen fried scallops, precooked fish cakes, fish sticks, and frozen onion rings.

1946 (cont.) The Moscow Mule made of Smirnoff Vodka and ginger beer served in a copper mug is invented at the Cock 'n Bull Restaurant in Los Angeles by restaurateur Jack Morgan and Heublein boss John G. Martin (*see* 1939). The new cocktail will help boom vodka sales in America (*see* 1948).

U.S. birthrates soar as returning servicemen begin families and add to existing ones. The nation has 3,411,000 births, up from 2,858,000 last year.

The United States has 140 million people, Britain 46 million, France 40, West Germany 48, East Germany 18, Spain 21, Brazil 45, Mexico 22, the U.S.S.R. 194, Japan 73, Korea 24, China 455, India 311.

Some 2.5 million Sudeten Germans are transferred to Germany and some 415,000 Karelian Finns are moved to Finland.

Palestine has some 650,000 Jews, many of whom have immigrated illegally to find sanctuary from European persecution. The country has 1.05 million Arabs (*see* 1948).

1947 The Truman Doctrine outlined in a presidential message to Congress March 12 announces plans to aid Greece and Turkey and proposes economic (and military) aid to countries threatened by Communist takeover.

The Marshall Plan proposed at Harvard Commencement exercises in June by Secretary of State George C. Marshall would give financial aid to European countries "willing to assist in the task of recovery."

The General Agreement on Tariffs and Trade (GATT) signed by the major world powers will lead to a significant lowering of tariff barriers, will end some tariff discrimination, and will help revitalize world trade.

President Truman asks Congress November 17 to appropriate $597 million for immediate aid to France, Italy, and Austria. Congress authorizes $540 million December 23 for interim aid to France, Italy, Austria, and China and in the next 40 months will authorize $12.5 billion in Marshall Plan aid to restore the economic health of free Europe (and halt the spread of Communism) (below).

U.S. occupation authorities in Japan break up the *zaibatsu* that has controlled the nation's industry, but the old family companies that formed the consortium will remain strong factors in the Japanese economy (they include the Mitsubishi, the Mitsui, the Sumitomo, and others).

Henry Ford dies April 7 at age 83, and his will leaves 90 percent of his Ford Motor Company stock to the Ford Foundation (*see* Edsel Ford, 1943). The federal tax paid by Ford's heirs amounts to only $21 million on a taxable estate of $70 million since the bulk of the $625 million fortune has been placed tax free in the Ford Foundation which becomes the richest philanthropic organization in the history of the world. Ford's heirs are left in control of the Ford Motor

Company, and the Ford Foundation is provided with more funds for useful projects in education and other fields (*see* 1950).

 An article signed "X" in the July issue of *Foreign Affairs* magazine proposes a policy of "containment" toward the Soviet Union. The author is the new head of the State Department's policy planning staff George Frost Kennan, 43, who helped set up the U.S. embassy at Moscow in 1943, his article analyzes in detail the structure and psychology of Soviet diplomacy, Secretary of State Marshall and his successors will adopt the essentials of Kennan's policy, and Kennan will serve briefly as U.S. ambassador to Moscow from 1952 to 1953.

A Central Intelligence Agency (CIA) authorized by Congress in response to an order by President Truman works to counter activities by Moscow which is pouring money into Western Europe and is attempting through local Communist parties to establish Communist governments in various countries. The president has acted on the advice of Secretary of State Marshall and Defense Secretary James V. Forrestal (*see* below).

Greece's George II dies April 1 at age 56 after a second reign of 12 years. He is succeeded by his brother Paul, 45, who will reign until 1964.

Denmark's Christian X dies April 20 at age 76 after a 35-year reign and is succeeded by his 48-year-old son who will reign as Frederick IX until 1972.

India gains her independence from Great Britain August 15 and becomes a dominion following endorsement of a plan to partition the subcontinent by the Moslem League and the All-India Congress. Jawaharlal Nehru, 58, becomes the first prime minister of Hindu India.

Pakistan is set up as an independent Moslem state bordering India to the west and east with her capital at Karachi and with Mohammed Ali Jinnah, 71, of the Moslem League as governor general. A dispute over control of Kashmir is referred to the United Nations December 30 after millions have been killed in bloody riots that have ensued partition (*see* 1948).

Romania's Michael abdicates under Communist pressure December 30 after a 7-year reign. The Romanian monarchy begun by Carol I in 1866 is ended and Romania becomes a Communist nation.

 India outlaws "untouchability" in the age-old caste system, but discrimination against the people Mahatma Gandhi calls *harijans*—who represent 15 percent of the population—will continue for decades (*see* 1932; 1946).

The first U.S. major league black baseball player signs with the Brooklyn Dodgers (*see* below).

Congress forbids the CIA (above) to have "police, subpoena, law enforcement powers or internal security functions" inside the United States lest the agency conflict with the FBI and jeopardize the privacy of American citizens, but beginning in the 1950s and especially after 1967 the agency's operatives will undertake domestic surveillance activities, including break-ins, surreptitious mail inspections, and telephone wiretaps, and they will compile intelligence files on at least 10,000 Americans in violation of the National Security Act.

A "Hollywood Black List" of alleged Communist sympathizers compiled at a conference of studio executives meeting at New York's Waldorf-Astoria Hotel contains the names of an estimated 300 writers, directors, actors, and others who are either known or suspected to have Communist party affiliations or who have invoked the Fifth Amendment against self-incrimination when questioned by the 9-year-old House Committee to Investigate Un-American Activities. The "Hollywood Ten" who refuse to tell the committee whether or not they have been Communists are Alvah Bessie, Herbert Biberman, Lester Cole, Edward Dmytryk, Ring Lardner, Jr., John Howard Lawson, Albert Maltz, Samuel Ornitz, Adrian Scott, and screenwriter Dalton Trumbo, 39, who has in fact been a party member since 1943.

The "Hollywood Ten" (above) all draw short prison sentences for refusing to testify. Dalton Trumbo's screen credits include the 1943 film *Tender Comrade* with Ginger Rogers whose mother has tearfully testified before the Dies Committee that her daughter had to utter the "Communist line" in the film—"Share and share alike—that's democracy" (*see* 1950).

The Taft-Hartley Act passed over President Truman's veto June 23 restricts organized labor's power to strike, outlaws the closed shop (which requires that employers hire only union members), prohibits use of union funds for political purposes, introduces an 80-day "cooling off" period before a strike or lockout can begin, and empowers the government to obtain injunctions where strikes "will imperil the national health or safety" if allowed to occur or to continue.

U.S. coal mines return to private ownership June 30 after having been operated by the federal government since May 22 of last year. The United Mine Workers threaten a new strike but receive a wage boost of 44.375 cents per hour July 7.

The United Mine Workers withdraw from the AF of L in December as they did in 1936.

 British electricity production is nationalized under a new British Electricity Authority that takes over 550 private electric companies.

Britain's first atomic pile comes into operation in August at Harwell.

The Texas Company sells a half-interest in its European market to Standard Oil Company of California for $147 million (*see* 1933). SoCal will sell a 30 percent interest to Standard of New Jersey and a 10 percent interest to Socony-Vacuum for $450 million.

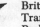 British transportation is nationalized under a new Transport Company that is given responsibility by Parliament for organizing and rehabilitating the nation's bankrupt and antiquated railroads. 3,000 British trucking firms are reorganized under the new Transport Company (*see* 1948; 1953).

New York City transit fares advance to 10 cents March 30 after having remained at 5 cents since the subway opened its first line in 1904 (Fifth Avenue buses have charged 10 cents for years, and fares in most other U.S. cities have been 10 cents for some time). Irish-American Transport Workers Union president Michael J. Quill, 41, has made a deal with Mayor O'Dwyer's labor relations assistant Theodore W. Kheel, 32, to support the 10-cent fare in return for a generous labor contract (*see* 1953).

The first tubeless automobile tires are introduced by B. F. Goodrich Company which produces tires that seal themselves when punctured.

The round-the-world speed record set by Howard Hughes in 1938 falls August 10 when U.S. pilot William P. Odum arrives at Chicago's Douglas Airport after a flight of 73 hours, 5 minutes, 11 seconds—more than 18 hours faster than the 1938 record.

A U.S. Bell X-1 reaches Mach 1.06 (750 miles per hour) October 10 and breaks the sound barrier that has been broken until now only by planes diving earthward with help from gravitational pull.

The "Spruce Goose" built and flown by Howard Hughes taxis across Long Beach Harbor in California November 2 and takes off for a 1-mile flight at a maximum altitude of 70 feet. Made largely of birch and the largest aircraft ever built, the 140-ton eight-engine seaplane has a wingspan of 320 feet, Hughes has built it as a prototype troop transport, but the Pentagon rejects the Hughes design and the huge plane goes into storage, never to fly again.

Avions Marcel Dassault Breguet Aviation is founded by French aviation pioneer Marcel-Ferdinand (Bloch) Dassault of 1916 variable pitch propellor fame who survived 3 years' imprisonment at Buchenwald, has converted to Roman Catholicism, and has adopted the pseudonym used by one of his brothers in the French resistance ("dassault" means literally "on the attack"). Now 55, Dassault will produce Mirage fighter planes and will make his company France's leading aeronautical firm.

The theory that "all massive rotating bodies are magnetic" is advanced by British physicist Patrick Maynard Stuart Blackett, 50, at the University of Manchester. Blackett has worked on cosmic rays and especially on the electrical particles known as "mesons."

The Hammurabi law code of the 18th century B.C. is reconstructed from excavations made at Nippur before 1900 by British archaeologist Francis Steele.

Development of an "atomic clock" that will determine geological age and will clear up many mysteries

1947 (cont.) of archaeology and anthropology is begun by U.S. chemist Willard Frank Libby, 38, who discovers that all organic materials contain carbon-14 atoms which decay at a measurable rate. Libby's discovery will make it possible for the first time to date organic archaeological remains within narrow limits of time.

Dead Sea scrolls of parchment that contain all but two small parts of the Old Testament Book of Isaiah are discovered by a Bedouin boy in a cave northwest of Palestine's Dead Sea. Written in the 1st century B.C. by Jews of the obscure, ascetic Essene sect which was later wiped out by the Romans, the parchments have been wrapped in yards of cloth, covered with pitch, and hidden in an earthenware jar, they will be sold piecemeal by the Bedouin who found them at Qumran, they will greatly expand knowledge of ancient Judaism, and they will be followed by several more finds of biblical manuscripts in the area.

Sexual reproduction is found to occur in bacteria, a finding that will open up a whole new world of study and that will lay the groundwork for future work in bacterial genetics. The discovery is made by Columbia University graduate student Joshua Lederberg, 22, and Yale geneticist Edward Lawrie Tatum, 37.

U.S. national health insurance comparable to that in Britain is resisted by the American Medical Association (see Britain, 1946). The Wagner-Murray-Dingell Bill is called "socialized medicine" by the AMA, and the bill never reaches the floor either of the Senate or of the House of Representatives.

Oklahoma faith healer Oral Roberts, 29, claims to pray for God's help in healing the ill and deformed who are then healed by God himself. Evangelist Roberts will start the healing ministry Healing Waters, Inc., next year, he will appear frequently on radio and television, and his Pentecostal Holiness Church will grow to have 2 million members by 1960.

California State College is founded at Los Angeles.

Sacramento State College is founded in California.

Sony Corporation has its beginnings in the Tokyo Telecommunications Company (Tokyo Tsushin Kogyo) started by Japanese electrical engineer Masaru Ibuka, with backing from sake brewing heir Akio Morita, 26. Ibuka has worked on infrared detection devices and a telephone scrambler for the military, he has taken over a gutted and boarded-up Tokyo department store, and he has started a factory to produce shortwave converters for radio sets that will enable listeners to receive news from abroad. Morita has read about Ibuka's device and joins him in founding the company that will be renamed Sony Corporation in 1958 (see tape recorder, 1950).

Channel Master, Inc., is founded by former U.S. merchant marine radio operator Joseph Resnick, 23, who borrows $7,000 to start a company that will make television antennas. Resnick will sell the company to the Avnet, Inc., conglomerate for $50 million in 1967 but will die 2 years later at age 45.

The *Chicago Sun-Times* is created by Marshall Field III whose New York newspaper *PM* had no advertising (see 1940). Field has acquired the more conventional *Chicago Sun* and merges it with the *Chicago Times* (see 1959).

"Steve Canyon" makes its debut on newspaper cartoon pages. After 13 years of drawing "Terry and the Pirates," Milton Caniff leaves the "Terry" strip to be carried on by others.

Nonfiction *Gamesmanship* by British Broadcasting Company writer Stephen Potter, 47; *The Proper Bostonians* by former Harvard *Crimson* editor Cleveland Amory, 29.

Fiction *The Plague* (*La Peste*) by Albert Camus; *The Twins of Nuremberg* (*Die Zwillingen von Nurnberg*) by German novelist Hermann Kesten, 47; *Nekya* (*Nekyia*) by German novelist Hans Erich Nossack, 46; *The Woman of Rome* (*La Romana*) by Alberto Moravia; *The Path of the Nest of Spiders* (*Il sentiero de nidi di ragno*) by Italian novelist Italo Calvino, 24; *Under the Volcano* by English novelist Malcolm Lowry, 38; *Tea with Mrs. Goodman* by English novelist Philip Toynbee, 31; *Querelle of Brest* (*Querelle de Brest*) by Jean Genet; *Hetty Dorval* by Canadian novelist Ethel Wilson, 57; *The Middle of the Journey* by U.S. novelist-critic Lionel Trilling, 42; *Euridice* by Jose Lins do Rego; *Thousand Cranes* by Yasunari Kawabata hints that all behavior is rooted in sexual neuroticism (which can be relieved by contemplating landscape); *The Setting Sun* (*Shayo*) by Osamu Dazai examines an aristocratic family which has been forced at the end of the war to cope with a new life devoid of its former wealth and prestige. Japan's new poor will be called Setting Sun people (*shayo-zoku*); *Tales of the South Pacific* by U.S. writer James (Albert) Michener, 40, who served in the Pacific during the war; *The Victim* by Saul Bellow who begins to probe the self-sacrifice demanded by society versus the human need to be an individual; *Gentleman's Agreement* by U.S. novelist Laura Zametkin Hobson, 47, who examines the covert anti-Semitic practices that have become institutionalized in U.S. society; *The Wayward Bus* by John Steinbeck.

Poetry "Day After Day" ("Giorno dopo Giorno") by Salvatore Quasimodo.

Painting *Ulysses with His Sirens* by Pablo Picasso; *A Bunch of Flowers* by Maurice de Vlaminck; *Young English Girl* by Henri Matisse; *M. Plume, Portrait of Henri Michaux* by Jean Dubuffet; *Das Matterhorn* by Oskar Kokoschka; *Betrothal II, Dark Green Painting, The Plan and the Song,* and *Agony* by Arshile Gorky. Pierre Bonnard dies at Le Cannet north of Cannes January 23 at age 79.

Sculpture *Three Standing Figures* by Henry Moore; *The Pointing Man* by Alberto Giacometti; *Riders* by Marino Marini.

The Polaroid Land Camera patented by Edwin H. Land of 1932 polaroid lens fame develops its own films within its body and produces a sepia photographic print in 60 seconds (*see* 1948).

ASA ratings developed by the American Standards Association standardize U.S. film speeds.

Theater *All My Sons* by U.S. playwright Arthur Miller, 32, 1/29 at New York's Coronet Theater, with Ed Begley, 328 perfs.; *The Prophet's Diamond* (*Il diamante del profeta*) by Italian playwright Carlo Terron, 33, 4/2 at Rome's Teatro Valle; *Command Decision* by U.S. playwright William Wister Haines, 39, 10/1 at New York's Fulton Theater, with James Whitmore, Paul Kelly, 408 perfs.; *Medea* by Robinson Jeffers 10/20 at New York's National Theater, with Judith Anderson, John Gielgud, Florence Reed, 214 perfs.; *Ring Around the Moon* (*L'invitation au château*) by Jean Anouilh 11/4 at the Théâtre de l'Atelier, Paris; *A Streetcar Named Desire* by Tennessee Williams 12/3 at New York's Ethel Barrymore Theater, with Marlon Brando, 23, as Stanley Kowalski, Jessica Tandy as Blanche DuBois, Kim Hunter, Karl Malden, 855 perfs., Pulitzer prize.

Tony Awards are established by the American Theatre Wing to honor outstanding Broadway plays, directors, performers, scenic designers, costumers, etc. The name Tony honors Antoinette Perry who headed the Theatre Wing during World War II and they rival the Oscars awarded since 1928 by the Motion Picture Academy of Arts and Sciences.

The first Cannes Film Festival opens in May on the French Riviera to begin an annual event at the Festival Palace one block from the Carlton Hotel and at 11 commercial movie theaters.

Films   Charlie Chaplin's *Monsieur Verdoux*; Maurice Cloche's *Monsieur Vincent*; Michael Powell and Emeric Pressburger's *Black Narcissus* with Deborah Kerr, Flora Robson, Sabu, Jean Simmons; Michael Powell and Emeric Pressburger's *I Know Where I'm Going* with Wendy Hiller, Roger Livesey, Finlay Currie; Carol Reed's *Odd Man Out* with James Mason; David Lean's *Great Expectations* with John Mills, Valerie Hobson, Jean Simmons, Martita Hunt; Zoltan Korda's *A Woman's Vengeance* with Charles Boyer, Ann Blyth; Robert Rossen's *Body and Soul* with John Garfield, Lilli Palmer; Irving Rapper's *The Voice of the Turtle* with Eleanor Parker, Ronald Reagan; Edmund Goulding's *Nightmare Alley* with Tyrone Power, Joan Blondell, Colleen Gray; Elia Kazan's *Gentleman's Agreement* with Gregory Peck, Dorothy McGuire, John Garfield, Celeste Holm; Roberto Rosselini's *Paisan;* Elia Kazan's *Boomerang* with Dana Andrews, Jane Wyatt, Lee J. Cobb.

The Edinburgh Festival of the Arts has its first season. The annual summer event will attract performing artists to Scotland from all over the world.

Opera   *The Telephone* 2/18 at New York, with music by Gian Carlo Menotti together with a revised version of his last year's opera *The Medium; The Trial of Lucullus* 4/18 at the University of California, Berkeley, with music by Roger Sessions, libretto from the Bertolt Brecht radio play of 1939; *The Mother of Us All* 5/7 at Columbia University's Brander Matthews Hall, New York, with Dorothy Dow as Susan B. Anthony, music by Virgil Thomson, libretto by the late Gertrude Stein who died at Paris last July at age 72; *Les Mamelles de Tiresias* 6/3 at the Opéra-Comique, Paris, with music by Francis Poulenc, libretto from a surrealist play by Guillaume Apollinaire; *Albert Heering* 6/20 at Glyndebourne, with music by Benjamin Britten.

Ballet   *Night Journey* 5/3 at Cambridge, Mass., with Martha Graham, music by William Schuman; *The Seasons* 5/17 at New York, with music by John Cage.

First performances   Symphony No. 2 by Roger Sessions 1/9 at San Francisco; Symphony No. 4 by Arthur Honegger 1/21 at Basel; *Symphonia Serena* by Paul Hindemith 2/1 at Dallas; Concerto for Violin and Orchestra in D minor by George Antheil 2/9 at Dallas; Symphony No. 3 by Morton Gould 2/16 at New York's Carnegie Hall; *Bachianas Brasilieras No. 3* for Piano and Orchestra by Heitor Villa-Lobos 2/19 in a CBS Orchestra broadcast; Concerto for Piano and Orchestra by Paul Hindemith 2/27 at Cleveland's Severance Hall, with Jesus Maria Sanroma as soloist; Suite for Hamonica and Orchestra by Darius Milhaud 5/28 at Paris with Larry Adler as soloist; *Bachianas Brasilieras No. 8* by Heitor Villa-Lobos 8/6 at Rome; Symphony No. 6 in E flat minor by Serge Prokofiev 10/10 at Leningrad; Symphony No. 3 (*Hymnus Ambrosianus*) by Darius Milhaud 10/30 at Paris.

Broadway musicals   *Finian's Rainbow* 1/10 at the 46th Street Theater, with Ella Logan, David Wayne, music by Burton Lane, lyrics by E. Y. Harburg, songs that include "If This Isn't Love," "How Are Things

The CIA was created to counter Soviet espionage activities but it would sometimes exceed its authority.

1947 (cont.) in Glocca Mora," "Old Devil Moon," "Look to the Rainbow," "When I'm Not Near the Girl I Love," "That Great Come-and-Get-It-Day," 725 perfs. The musical breaks new ground with social commentary on subjects ranging from the population explosion to the maldistribution of wealth; *Brigadoon* 3/13 at the Ziegfeld Theater, with James Mitchell, David Brooks, music by Frederick Loewe, book and lyrics by Alan Jay Lerner, 28, songs that include "The Heather on the Hill," "Come to Me, Bend to Me," "Almost Like Being in Love," "There But for You Go I," 581 perfs.; *High Button Shoes* 10/9 at the Century Theater, with Phil Silvers, Nanette Fabray, Helen Gallagher, music by Jule Styne, lyrics by Sammy Cahn, songs that include "Papa, Won't You Dance with Me," 727 perfs.; *Allegro* 10/10 at the Majestic Theater, with John Battles, John Conte, music by Richard Rodgers, lyrics by Oscar Hammerstein II, songs that include "A Fellow Needs a Girl," "The Gentleman Is a Dope," 315 perfs.; *Angel in the Wings* 12/11 at the Coronet Theater, with Paul and Grace Hartman, Elaine Stritch, music by Bob Hilliard, lyrics by Carl Sigman, songs that include "Civilization (Bongo, Bongo, Bongo)," "Big Brass Band from Brazil," 197 perfs.

Hollywood musical   George Seaton's *The Shocking Miss Pilgrim* with Betty Grable, music by the late George Gershwin, lyrics by Ira Gershwin, songs that include "The Back Pay Polka," "For You, for Me, for Everyone."

Popular songs   "Ballerina" by Carl Sigman, lyrics by Bob Russell; "Golden Earrings" by Ray Evans and Victor Young, lyrics by Jay Livingston (title song for Mitchell Leisen's film); "Feudin' and Fightin' " by Burton Lane and Al Dubin; "I'll Dance at Your Wedding" by Ben Oakland, lyrics by Herb Magidson; "Ivy" by Hoagy Carmichael; "Open the Door, Richard" by Jack McKea and Dan Howell, lyrics by Dusty Fletcher and John Mason; "Too Fat Polka" by Ross MacLean and Arthur Richardson; "Woody Woodpecker" by George Tibbles and Ramey Idriss.

Jackie Robinson signs with the Brooklyn Dodgers and starts the season at first base, the first black baseball player in the major leagues. John Roosevelt Robinson, 28, will continue through the 1956 season and will have a lifetime batting average of .311.

The New York Yankees win the World Series by defeating the Brooklyn Dodgers 4 games to 3.

English cricket attracts 2 million paying customers. The figure will drop to 500,000 by 1970 as the game loses its attraction for many Britons.

The death of Manolete August 28 plunges Spain into mourning. The multimillionaire matador Manuel Rodriguez has been fatally gored by a Miura bull in the small 8,268-seat ring at Linares and dies at age 30 after a career that has made him a legend.

The Columbia football team upsets unbeaten Army October 26, beating the cadets 21 to 20 after Army has won 32 games without a loss. Columbia is behind 20 to 7 at the half, the third period is scoreless, but Columbia quarterback Gene Rossides completes 20 of his 30 passes, 8 of them to Bill Soviacki, Columbia goes ahead 21 to 20, and it holds its 1 point lead for the last 7½ minutes of play.

The "New Look" designed by Paris couturier Christian Dior late last year lowers skirt lengths to 12 inches from the floor, pads brassieres, unpads shoulders, adds hats, makes present wardrobes obsolete, and wins quick support from fashion magazines and from the $3 billion U.S. garment industry. U.S. women resist the new fashion briefly, but then succumb and slavishly adopt not only long, full peg-top skirts, V-necks, curving waists, sloping shoulders, and frothy blouses, but also clogs, espadrilles, spike-heeled "naked sandals," and fezzes trimmed with veils and feathers.

UFOs (Unidentified Flying Objects) make headlines. Boise, Idaho, businessman Kenneth Arnold, 32, claims to have seen nine shiny, pulsating objects flying over the Cascade Mountains at speeds of up to 1,700 miles per hour while flying his two-seat plane from Chehalis to Yakima June 24. "They seemed to be alive in the center, to have the ability to change their density," he says, the Civil Aeronautics Administration expresses doubts that "anything would be flying that fast," other UFO sightings are reported, some 15 million Americans will claim to have seen UFOs in the next 25 years, more than half of all Americans will say they believe in the existence of such objects which many will say are manned by creatures from other planets, but professional airline pilots will have more mundane explanations.

Ajax cleanser is introduced by Colgate-Palmolive-Peet Co. Its silica sand is more likely to scratch than the feldspar used in other cleansers, but Ajax requires less elbow grease and soon outsells Bon Ami, Dutch Cleanser, and other feldspar cleansers (*see* Comet, 1956).

Macy's Missouri-Kansas is created by New York's R. H. Macy Company which gains control of Kansas City's John Taylor Dry Goods Store (*see* 1945).

New York's Bloomingdale's opens its first branch store.

J. W. Robinson of Los Angeles opens a Palm Springs branch (*see* 1891). It will open a Beverly Hills store in 1952 and a Pasadena store in 1958.

New York's postwar building boom begins with a 21-story story office building at 445 Park Avenue erected by Tishman Brothers.

New York's 33-story Esso building, designed by Carson and Lundin, opens in Rockefeller Center.

New York's Stuyvesant Town, financed by Metropolitan Life Insurance Company, opens from 14th Street north to 20th between First Avenue and East River Drive. The huge middle-income apartment complex houses 8,755 families (*see* Parkchester, 1940).

New York's Peter Cooper Village is completed from 20th to 23rd Streets just north of the Metropolitan Life project (above). Roomier and higher-priced, it has been designed by the same architects.

Levittown goes up on Long Island to help satisfy the booming demand for housing. Builder Abraham Levitt and his sons employ experience gained by building houses for the navy during the war. Their nearly identical houses are built on concrete slabs with no basements, crews assemble the houses using precut materials. They erect the mass-produced houses round village greens with shops, a playground, and a community swimming pool. The modest prices include major appliances, and by 1951 there will be more than 17,000 Levittown houses (see 1951).

The San Juan Hilton put up by Conrad Hilton begins a Puerto Rico building boom (see 1945; 1949).

The Eames side chair designed by Charles Eames, 40, is introduced by the Herman Miller Furniture Company of Zeeland, Mich. The revolutionary chair made of contour-moulded plywood on a frame of aluminum tubing won top prize in a 1940 Museum of Modern Art Organic Design Competition, but the aluminum has been replaced by chrome-plated steel.

Lippincott and Margulies is founded by U.S. engineer J. Gordon Lippincott, 38, and French-American designer Walter Margulies, 33, who came to America in 1939 to design the French Pavilion for the New York World's Fair. The new design firm will have a major impact on U.S. industrial design, packaging, and corporate symbols (Lippincott and Margulies will be responsible for changing U.S. Rubber to Uniroyal, Cities Service Company to Citgo, American Metals Climax to AMAX, and American Brake Shoe to Abax).

Everglades National Park in Florida is established by act of Congress. The 1.4 million acre reserve of subtropical wilderness embraces open prairies, mangrove forests, freshwater and saltwater areas, and abundant wildlife.

No trace of man in the "crystal clear" Pacific is observed by Norwegian anthropologist-explorer Thor Heyerdahl, 32, who crosses 4,300 miles of open Pacific in 101 days on a balsa raft he calls *Kon-Tiki*.

Pittsburgh begins a program of huge proportions to clean its smoky air and to modernize (see 1816). The city's air is so thick with smoke that streetlights must often be turned on all day even in fair weather (see Donora smog, 1948).

Iceland's Mount Hekla volcano erupts as it has 13 times since 1104 and causes widespread destruction.

New York City and its environs are crippled December 26 by a 25.8-inch snowfall, the worst since 1888 when 20.9 inches fell. The blizzard lasts 16 hours, but while suburban trains are stopped the storm is not accompanied by the savage winds of 1888 and the drifts are not so high.

 British agriculture sustains a £20 million loss March 16 as a gale blows across England's Fens knocking down trees and creating floods that destroy potatoes, root crops, and poultry flocks. Homes and farm buildings are ruined and floods make planting impossible.

More than a quarter of Britain's sheep and lamb flock is killed by snowstorms that isolate hundreds of farms. Two-thirds of the valuable hill wool is lost and 30,000 head of cattle die or have to be shot.

The rat poison Warfarin discovered by University of Wisconsin biochemist Karl Paul Link, 46, is introduced to fight the rodent which consumes a large portion of the world's grain production each year. The anticoagulant is based on the chemical coumarin which occurs in spoiled sweet clover and causes animals to bleed to death by interfering with vitamin K which enables the liver to produce the blood-clotting chemical prothrombin. The D-Con subsidiary of Sterling Drug, Inc., will be the best-known maker of Warfarin, royalty payments will enrich the Wisconsin Alumni Research Foundation (WARF) by several millions of dollars before patents expire in 1964, but the first Warfarin-resistant rats will be discovered near Glasgow, Scotland, in 1958.

Parathion is introduced by American Cyanamid Company (see TEPP, 1946). The new organic phosphorus insecticide is highly toxic to humans but will be widely employed to fight Florida red scale, the red spider, aphids, and leaf hoppers, initially in Florida citrus groves.

Toxaphene is introduced by Hercules Chemical Company. The new insecticide made from chlorinated naval stores (turpentine and pine rosin) will be used to protect cotton, soybeans, wheat, corn, alfalfa, sorghum, tomatoes, spinach, beans, potatoes, sunflowers, peaches, and other crops, it will prove effective against grasshoppers and against the boll weevil, and it will be the most widely used insecticide in the United States.

The drug chloramphenicol is introduced to fight livestock diseases.

Reports begin to come in of fly and mosquito strains that have developed resistance to DDT and to the British-developed benzene hexachloride.

U.S. agricultural chemical production reaches nearly 2 billion pounds, up from 100 million in 1934.

New Holland Company is acquired by Sperry Corporation (see Vickers, 1937). The Pennsylvania firm has pioneered in developing a twine-tie baler (see Sperry-Rand, 1955).

A rice-farming boom begins in the lower Mississippi valley.

 Widespread food shortages continue in the wake of World War II and the situation is exacerbated by crop failures. President Truman urges meatless and eggless days October 5 to conserve grain for hungry Europe, and a Friendship Train leaves Los

1947 (cont.) Angeles November 8 for a cross-country tour to collect food for European relief.

The Soviet Union continues food rationing until December but exports grain despite widespread hunger at home just as the czarist government did in 1911.

 Philippine health authorities begin the "Bataan experiment" in an effort to solve the problem of beriberi (*see* thiamine, 1936, 1937). The study will show that beriberi incidence is reduced by nearly 90 percent in an area where people are given rice fortified with thiamine, niacin, and iron, while there is no reduction in beriberi in a control population.

 U.S. sugar rationing ends June 11.

Almond Joy candy bars are introduced to augment the popular Mounds bars by Peter Paul which has survived the war by importing coconuts via small schooners from Honduras, El Salvador, Nicaragua, and other Caribbean countries (*see* 1932).

The 5-cent Hershey bar contains 1⅛ ounces of chocolate (but *see* 1968).

Nestlé S.A. becomes Nestlé Alimentana S.A. following acquisition of Fabrique de Produits Maggi with its 11 plants and the Maggi holding company Alimentana S.A. of Kempttal, Switzerland (*see* 1884; Nescafé, 1938; Quik, 1948).

Reddi-Wip is introduced by Reddi-Wip, Inc., whose founder Marcus Lipsky advertises aerated "real" whipped cream in pressurized cans. Reddi-Wip is the first major U.S. aerosol food product (*see* 1945; Ablanalp, 1953; Hunt-Wesson, 1969).

U.S. frozen orange juice concentrate sales reach 7 million cans, up from 4.8 million last year, but the fledgling concentrate industry has been brought to the brink of ruin by a glut of fresh oranges that has dropped prices from $4 per box to 50 cents and by an oversupply of canned single-strength juice. Snow Crop is the major distributor of concentrate and sells out to Clinton Foods after its distributors have gone broke by the dozens.

Minute Maid Corporation has its beginnings in the Vacuum Foods Company headed by John M. Fox, 34, whose pioneer orange concentrate producing firm has lost $371,000 in the past year and who finds himself with more than $500,000 tied up in retail packages bearing the Snow Crop label (above). Fox goes from door to door at Hingham, Mass., he gives each householder a free can of concentrate and the names of local grocery stores where the product can be purchased, and when stocks are cleaned out he is convinced that he has a desirable product. Fox obtains a $50,000 loan from William A. Coolidge whose Cambridge, Mass., firm initiated the development of citrus concentrates for the U.S. Army in 1942, and Coolidge gets venture capitalist John Hay (Jock) Whitney interested in Vacuum Foods (*see* 1949).

Chun King Corporation is founded by Hibbing, Minn., food salesman Jeno Paulucci, 29, who borrows $2,500, rents a quonset hut at nearby Grand Rapids that has been used as a rutabaga cannery, sets up a hydroponic garden to grow bean sprouts, and starts packing chicken chow mein in cans. Within a few weeks Paulucci is selling 300 cases per day by giving demonstrations of his product at supermarkets, and he looks for larger facilities at Duluth (*see* 1951).

Monosodium glutamate (MSG) is marketed for the first time under the Ac'cent label (*see* 1908; 1934; "Chinese Restaurant Syndrome," 1968).

McCormick & Co. merges with San Francisco's A. Schilling & Co., a coffee, spice, and extract house established in 1881 (*see* 1941). McCormick achieves national distribution and begins expanding into Latin America.

The antioxidant BHA (butylated hydroxyanisole) is introduced commercially in the United States to retard spoilage in foods.

The first commercial microwave oven is introduced by the Raytheon Company of Waltham, Mass., whose Percy LeBaron Spencer, 53, has accidentally discovered that microwaves used for signal transmission will cook food (a chocolate bar in Spencer's pocket has been melted by the agitation of molecules produced by the microwaves). Raytheon's oven employs an electronic tube (magnetron) developed in 1940 by John Randall and H. A. H. Boot of England's Birmingham University for British radar, it cooks quickly by agitating molecules with 2,400 megahertz microwaves to create internal frictional heat, but while it can bake a potato in 5 minutes, it requires 10 minutes for two potatoes (*see* Amana, 1967).

Seagram's 7 Crown becomes the world's largest selling brand of whiskey and will hold that position for more than 30 years (*see* 1934). By 1971 Seagram will be selling 7.5 million cases of 7 Crown per year, half a fifth for every American man, woman, and child.

1948 Hindu extremists assassinate Mahatma Gandhi, now 78, January 30. Many Hindus resent Gandhi's agreement to last year's partition of India and Pakistan.

Communists take over Czechoslovakia in a coup d'etat February 25 and former Czech president Edouard Beneš dies September 3 at age 65.

The State of Israel is proclaimed May 14 as the British mandate over Palestine expires. The British have withdrawn their forces under pressure from the terrorist Irgun, the "Stern Gang," and the Haganah, thousands of Arabs have fled the country, Polish-born British biochemist and Zionist leader Chaim Weizmann takes office as provisional president at age 73, Polish-Palestinian David Ben-Gurion, 61, who has been chairman of the Jewish Agency for Palestine since 1935 heads the government as prime minister and minister of defense, and Israel opens her doors to the world's Jews.

President Truman recognizes the new Jewish homeland against the advice of Secretary of State Marshall (who says the President is acting for reasons of domestic politics).

The Arab Legion of Transjordan enters Jerusalem, Egypt joins the attack on Israel May 15 and bombs the temporary capital at Tel Aviv, but Israeli defenders throw back the Arab and Egyptian invaders.

Yugoslavia is expelled June 28 from the Communist Information Bureau (Cominform) for alleged doctrinal errors and for hostility to the Soviet Union. Marshal Tito denies the charges a month later, the Yugoslav Communist party supports Tito and then purges itself of all Cominform supporters.

Soviet occupation forces in Germany set up a blockade July 24 to cut off rail and highway traffic between West Germany and Berlin. An airlift begins July 25 with U.S. and British aircraft flying in food and supplies for the more than 2 million people of West Berlin, the airlift is carrying 4,500 tons per day by September, and it will continue until September of next year.

The phrase "cold war" is coined by U.S. presidential adviser Bernard Baruch.

A new Selective Service act passed by Congress June 24 provides for the registration of all U.S. men between 18 and 25 with men between 19 and 25 to be inducted for 21 months' service. Registration begins August 30 to initiate a program that will continue for 25 years.

British Commonwealth country citizens gain the status of British subjects in the British Citizenship Act passed by Parliament July 30.

Alger Hiss, 43, supplied Soviet agents with classified U.S. documents while working in the State Department in the 1930s, says *Time* magazine senior editor Whittaker Chambers, 47, in testimony before the House Un-American Activities Committee August 3. Hiss is president of the Carnegie Endowment for International Peace; he sues Chambers for slander. Chambers will produce a microfilm he has kept hidden in a pumpkin at his Westminster, Md., farm. A federal jury at New York indicts Hiss for perjury December 15, and his first trial will end in a hung jury (but *see* 1950).

Richard Milhous Nixon, 35, pushes a congressional investigation of the Hiss affair (above). Nixon won election in 1946 by suggesting that his opponent H. Jerry Voorhis had Communist support.

The Republic of Korea is proclaimed at Seoul August 15 with Synghman Rhee, 73, as president, but the Korean People's Democratic Republic proclaimed September 9 in North Korea challenges the Rhee regime and claims dominion over the entire country (*see* 1949).

India's Jawaharlal Nehru sends troops into Hyderabad September 13, they enter the city of Hyderabad 4 days later, the 62-year-old Nizam of Hyderabad Sir Osman Ali Khan Bahadur has ruled the 82,000-square mile state since 1907 and has refused to join India or grant parliamentary government and has appealed to the United Nations, he surrenders and is permitted to retain his title, palaces, and private property (which includes a harem of 42 concubines), but his annual income of $50 million is reduced to an allowance of $900,000.

Wilhelmina of the Netherlands abdicates September 4 at age 68 after a 58-year reign and is succeeded by her 39-year-old daughter Juliana.

Sweden's Count Folke Bernadotte is assassinated by Jewish terrorists September 17 while serving as UN mediator in Palestine (above).

President Truman wins re-election with 303 electoral votes to 189 for his Republican opponent Thomas E. Dewey of New York who receives 45 percent of the popular vote while Truman receives 49.5 percent. The Democratic vote has been splintered by the States' Rights Democratic party (Dixiecrats) whose presidential candidate J. Strom Thurmond of South Carolina has received 39 electoral votes (but less than 3 percent of the popular vote) and by other minority party candidates including Henry Wallace (Progressive) and Norman Thomas (Socialist), but Truman has campaigned vigorously to confound poll-takers and embarrass the *Chicago Tribune* which has hit the streets with a front-page headline proclaiming Dewey the winner.

A quantum theory of electrodynamics far more powerful than the 1926 Dirac theory or the 1927 Heisenberg theory is developed by U.S. physicist Richard Phillips Feynman, 30, with Julian Schweinger.

Cybernetics by MIT mathematician Norbert Wiener, 53, summarizes results of studies Wiener has made in communication and information control. Derived from the Greek word for steersman, Wiener's title will come into common use to cover the whole field of information control by automated machines such as computers while Wiener works over the next 16 years to elaborate on the possibilities of cybernetics and to warn of its dangers (*see* 1950).

The transistor is developed at Bell Telephone Laboratories as a substitute for the glass vacuum tube pioneered by Bell Labs physicist H. D. Arnold in 1912. The tiny but rugged three-electrode solid-state transistor developed by physicists William Shockley, 38, John Bardeen, 40, and Walter H. Brattain, 46, will permit miniaturization of electronic devices such as computers, radios, and television sets and will lead to the development of guided missiles (*see* Texas Instruments, 1954; mesa, 1954).

The Kurdistan village of Jarmo dating to 6800 B.C. is excavated by a University of Chicago archaeological team headed by Robert J. Braidwood, 41.

Soviet scientific committees are purged following a denunciation of hostile geneticists by T. D. Lysenko.

 An apartheid platform favoring separation of the races in South Africa wins election May 26 for a Nationalist Afrikander bloc which defeats a United and Labour party coalition headed by Jan Christiaan Smuts, now 78 (*see* 1949).

1948 (cont.) The NAACP convention at Kansas City decides to give up the fight for equalization of separate black facilities and to push instead for integration, especially of educational institutions (*see* 1896; 1909; 1954).

The right of homeowners to discriminate in selling their property is denied by the Supreme Court in the case of *Shelley v. Kramer*. A restrictive covenant in a deed had prohibited sale of a house to blacks, but the court rules that the government may not enforce private acts of discrimination.

Hungarian police arrest Jozef Cardinal Mindszenty December 26 for his anti-Communist statements (*see* 1944). Cardinal Mindszenty will have a show trial next year, he will be sentenced to death, but the sentence will be commuted to life imprisonment (*see* 1956).

A U.S. energy crisis in mid-January brings urgent requests for voluntary reductions in the use of gasoline, fuel oil, and natural gas. Long a net exporter of oil, the United States has become a net importer through the development of low-cost petroleum sources in Venezuela and the Middle East.

Foreign crude oil, mostly from Venezuela, will capture 18 percent of the U.S. market in the next 10 years (*see* 1958).

Arabian-American Oil (Aramco) sells a 30 percent interest to Standard Oil of New Jersey and a 10 percent interest to Standard Oil of New York in order to broaden marketing of its Saudi-Arabian oil (*see* 1933). SoCal and Texas Company each retain a 30 percent interest (*see* 1973).

U.S. railroads shift from coal-fired steam locomotives to diesel-electric locomotives in a move that will eliminate a major market for coal and that will lead to a 36 percent decline in coal mine output in the next 25 years and an increase in demand for oil (*see* 1924; Paley report, 1952).

British railroads are nationalized January 1.

U.S. railroads are operated by the U.S. Army beginning May 10 on presidential orders (below).

The Canadian Pacific adds an airline to its railway and shipping line. The CP acquires routes that will link Canada's major cities to much of the world.

The first jet aircraft to fly the Atlantic arrive in Labrador July 12. Six RAF de Havilland Vampires complete the crossing from Britain.

The Vickers Viscount flown July 16 is the first British turboprop airliner.

The Soviet Air Force adopts the IL-28 jet bomber designed by S. V. Ilyushin (*see* 1942). The new aircraft will be the backbone of Soviet airpower for 15 years.

New York's Idlewild International Airport is dedicated by President Truman July 31. The world's largest commercial airport relieves some of the pressure from the city's 9-year-old La Guardia Airport but is much farther from midtown Manhattan (*see* 1963).

The Land-Rover introduced at the Amsterdam Motor Show April 30 by England's Rover Company of Solihull, Warwickshire, is a Jeep-like vehicle designed for civilians (*see* Universal Jeep, 1945).

The Porsche sportscar is introduced. It has been designed by Volkswagen designer Ferdinand Porsche.

The first automobile air conditioner is put on the market. The crude affair is designed to be installed under the dashboard but will be followed by factory-installed air conditioning that will be found in an estimated 46 million U.S. motorcars within 25 years.

A new 1949 Ford four-door sedan sells in the fall for $1,236 F.O.B. Detroit.

The Honda motorcycle is introduced by Japanese entrepreneur Soichiro Honda, 38, whose company will be the world's leading motorbike producer by 1958. The first Honda motorcar will appear in 1963.

Michelin Cie. introduces the world's first radial tires.

The Liberian Maritime Law adopted by the Liberian Legislature in December will make ships flying the Liberian "flag of convenience" the largest merchant fleet in the world. The "flag of convenience" system began in 1940 to permit the United States to send aid to Britain while preserving technical neutrality, and it has been exploited by former Secretary of State Edward R. Stettinius, Jr., who has founded the Liberia Company to develop Liberian iron ore reserves and other natural resources. Drawing on the experience of the world's leading admiralty lawyers, the Liberian Legislature has drafted bills creating an International Trust Company of Liberia to administer the maritime program that will produce 8 percent of the nation's Gross National Product while permitting major shipping companies (and oil companies) to operate more cheaply and profitably by avoiding use of U.S. crews and shipyards that would be required by U.S. registry, by freeing themselves from certain inspection requirements, and by taking advantage of Liberian tax laws to conceal income. The tanker *World Peace* built by Greek shipowner Stavros Niarchos will fly the Liberian flag next year and will be the first ship registered under the new law.

A Foreign Assistance Act passed by Congress April 3 implements the 1947 Marshall Plan. The act authorizes spending of $5.3 billion in the first year for economic aid to 16 European countries, it creates the European Recovery Program (ERP) and the Economic Cooperation Administration (ECA), and Studebaker boss Paul G. Hoffman is appointed Economic Cooperation Administrator of the ERP.

U.S. production, employment, and national income reach new highs but renewed strikes bring a third round of inflationary wage boosts.

An Income Tax Reduction Act has become law April 2 over President Truman's veto and has given further impetus to inflation. Speaking at Spokane, Wash., June 9, Truman calls the 80th Congress "the worst we've ever had."

Some 360,000 soft coal workers strike from mid-March to mid-April demanding $100 per month in retirement benefits at age 62.

President Truman orders the Army to operate the railroads beginning May 10 to prevent a nationwide rail strike. The railroads will be operated under U.S. Army control until 1952.

General Motors grants an 11-cent per hour wage increase to the United Automobile Workers May 25. The contract signed by GM's Charles E. Wilson and the UAW's Walter P. Reuther includes a cost-of-living clause based on the Consumer Price Index of the Bureau of Labor Statistics (see 1913; 1949).

The U.S. cost-of-living index reaches an all-time high in August, and Congress passes an Anti-Inflationary Act to "protect the Nation's economy against inflationary pressures."

Curbs on installment buying are ordered by the Federal Reserve System's Board of Governors.

A new Franklin head 50-cent piece is issued by the U.S. Mint to replace the Liberty walking coin that has been in circulation since 1916. The new half-dollar with the Liberty Bell on one side will not be superseded until 1964.

France is exhausted by the war and her gold reserves have fallen to 487 tons, down from 5,000 tons in 1932 (see Monnet, 1953).

Textron, Inc., becomes the world's first business conglomerate as Royal Little diversifies by acquiring Cleveland Pneumatic Tool Company, a leading producer of aircraft landing struts (see 1944). Little has found the textile industry too cyclical, he proposes the idea of a conglomerate that will employ management skills to improve the performance of firms in completely unrelated fields, he will acquire Pathé Industries in 1950 to put Textron into the newsreel and real estate business (Pathé owns some of the Van Sweringen properties in Cleveland put together some 30 years ago), and he will spin off some of Textron's unprofitable textile subsidiaries late in 1952 (see Textron American, 1955).

The United Nations establishes a World Health Organization (WHO) with headquarters at Geneva. The United States accepts membership June 14.

Britain's National Health Insurance Program goes into operation July 5. The program operates under legislation enacted by Parliament in 1946 and provides Britons with free medical treatment.

The adrenal hormone cortisone synthesized by Mayo Foundation biochemist Philip Showalter Hench, 52, and his colleague Edward C. Kendall of 1915 thyroxine fame brings new relief to arthritis victims. Hench administers a dose of his compound E September 21 to a 20-year-old woman incapacitated by arthritis, she is active again 4 days later, and Hench then treats 13 other arthritics with similar dramatic results. By early next year Hench and Kendall will show motion pictures of patients treated with synthetic corti-

sone who are able to run after being bedridden for years with arthritis (see ACTH, 1949; prednisone, 1955).

U.S. chemist Percy L. Julian, 49, finds a low-cost method for synthesizing cortisone (above). The method will make cortisone widely available and will make Percy a millionaire (he will use his fortune to support the civil rights movement).

The antibiotics aureoymycin and chloromycin are developed.

Dramamine is developed by Johns Hopkins physicians who discover accidentally that an antiallergy drug relieves motion sickness. A clinic patient being treated for hives (urticaria) with beta-diaminoethyl-bendohydryl-ether-8-chlorothyeophyllinate reports that taking 50 milligrams by mouth before boarding a streetcar prevents the motion sickness she has usually experienced. Control groups on the U.S. troop transport *General Ballou* test the drug while en route from New York to Bremerhaven for occupation duty.

Hadacol is introduced by Louisiana state senator Dudley J. LeBlanc whose tonic contains 12 percent alcohol. LeBlanc has started a company with $2,500 in borrowed capital, he promotes Hadacol with health claims and show business techniques, and he makes the product such a success that he will be able to sell the company for more than $8 million in 3 years.

Sexual Behavior in the Human Male by Indiana University zoologist Alfred Charles Kinsey, 54, indicates that many sex acts thought heretofore to be perversions are so common as to be considered almost normal. Kinsey has conducted interviews with some 18,500 men and women throughout America with funds provided by the National Research Council and the Rockefeller Foundation. The "Kinsey Report" arouses great controversy.

Brandeis University is founded at Waltham, Mass.

Voice of America radio broadcasts to foreign countries are funded by Congress January 27 as part of an overseas information program established by the Mundt Act (see Radio Free Europe, 1949).

One million U.S. homes have television sets, up from 5,000 in 1945, and while the sets are still large cabinets with small screens, the programming begins to improve and more TV stations go into operation (see Ed Sullivan, Bill Boyd, below).

Earl "Madman" Muntz enters the embryonic television set business at Los Angeles after a meteoric career as used car dealer and promoter of Kaiser-Frazer automobiles (see Kaiser, 1946). The 33-year-old Muntz will sell as many as 4,500 sets in a single weekend, he will have annual gross sales of as much as $55 million, he will hire 400 disc jockeys to plug Muntz TV on radio, he will print slogans such as "Stop Staring at Your Radio" on the backs of Chicago street car transfers, but he will be forced into bankruptcy in 1955.

Israel gained independence, offered refuge to the world's oppressed Jews, and fought off Arab invaders.

U.S. News and World Report begins publication to compete with *Time* and *Newsweek*. Editor-columnist David Lawrence, 59, has edited *U.S. News* since 1933 and merges it with the *World Report* he founded 2 years ago.

"Pogo" makes its debut in the *New York Star,* successor to the Marshall Field tabloid *PM.* Cartoonist Walt (Walter Crawford) Kelly, 35, is a former Walt Disney animator whose Okefenokee Swamp opossum will move to the *New York Post* upon the demise of the *Star* next year, will be in 225 newspapers worldwide by 1952, and will be in 450 by the late 1960s. Commenting on the ecological crisis, Pogo will say, "We have met the enemy and he is us."

"Rex Morgan, M.D." by Toledo, Ohio, psychiatrist-cartoonist Dal Curtis (Nicholas Dallis), 36, is a comic strip about a general practitioner. It will be syndicated to hundreds of newspapers, Dallis will start the comic strip "Judge Parker" in 1952, and he will add the comic strip "Apartment 3-G" in 1961.

Ogilvy & Mather, Inc., advertising has its beginnings in the New York agency Hewitt, Ogilvy, Benson & Mather founded by English copywriter–opinion researcher David Mackenzie Ogilvy, 37, with former J. Walter Thompson executive Anderson Fowler Hewitt, 40.

Nonfiction *The Seven Storey Mountain* by French-American Trappist monk Thomas Merton, 33, creates a sensation with its autobiographical revelations. Once a jazz musician, Merton entered Our Lady of Gethsemani Monastery at Bardstown, Ky., in 1941 under the name Frater M. Lewis.

Fiction *Intruder in the Dust* by William Faulkner; *The Young Lions* by U.S. novelist Irwin Shaw, 35; *The Naked and the Dead* by U.S. infantry veteran Norman Mailer, 25, whose novel excoriates the hy-

pocrisy of war; *Guard of Honor* by James Gould Cozzens whose war novel about a Florida military air base brings attention to his neglected earlier novels; *Remembrance Rock* by Carl Sandburg; *Confessions of a Mask* (*Kamen no kokuhaku*) by Japanese novelist Yukio Mishima (Kimitake Hiraoka), 23, who gains quick celebrity and some notoriety for his semiautobiographical novel of a homosexual with strong sadistic impulses; *Other Voices, Other Rooms* by U.S. novelist Truman Capote, 23; *The World Is a Wedding* (stories) by Delmore Schwartz; *Circus in the Attic* (stories) by Robert Penn Warren; *The Atom Station* (*Atom stooin*) by Icelandic novelist Halldor Laxness, 46; *The Aunt's Story* by Australian novelist Patrick White, 36; *The Corner That Held Them* by Sylvia Townsend Warner; *Concluding* by Henry Green; *Portrait of a Man Unknown* (*Portrait d'un inconnu)* by Nathalie Sarrante; *The City and the Pillar* by Gore Vidal; *The Heart of the Matter* by Graham Greene; *Cry the Beloved Country* by South African novelist Alan Stewart Paton, 45, principal of the Diepkloof Reformatory since 1935, who indicts the apartheid society of his native land; *The Stain in the Snow (La Neige etait sale)* by Georges Simenon.

Poetry *The Pisan Cantos* (72 to 84) by Ezra Pound who wrote them during his imprisonment at the end of World War II. Now 63, Pound was arrested by U.S. military authorities in Italy and indicted for treason in connection with profascist anti-Semitic propaganda broadcasts he made for the Italians. Judged mentally unfit to face trial, Pound has been confined to St. Elizabeth's Hospital at Washington, D.C., where he will remain until 1958.

Abstract expressionism in painting is pioneered by Wyoming-born painter Jackson Pollock, 36, whose *Composition No. 1* (*tachisma*) combines splashes and splotches of multihued paints on canvas to help launch a new school of "action painting" that will radically alter the direction of American art. Pollock's spashes, he says, are controlled by personal moods and unconscious forces.

Christina's World by Pennsylvania-born painter Andrew Nelson Wyeth, 31, captures the youthful vigor and anguish of Cushing, Me., cripple Christina Olsen, 55, in a work that will be widely reproduced. Wyeth, whose late father N. C. Wyeth was killed 3 years ago with a grandson when his automobile was struck by a train, was trained by N. C., illustrated the Brandywine edition of *The Merry Adventures of Robin Hood* at age 12, and has been working largely in tempura since 1946.

Other paintings *Sunday Dream in the Alameida Park* by Diego Rivera for Mexico City's Hotel Prado; *The Red Violin* by Raoul Dufy; *Poker Night* by Thomas Hart Benton; *The Betrothed* by Arshile Gorky who takes his own life at New York July 3 at age 43.

The Nikon camera introduced by Japan's Nippon Kogaku K.K. is a 35-mm rangefinder camera designed to compete with the German Leica that has been famous since 1925. Organized by the Mitsubishi group in 1917, Nippon Kogaku has been making lenses under the Nikkor trade name since 1932 but has never before made cameras (*see* 1959).

The Polaroid Land Camera goes on sale for the first time November 26 at Boston's Jordan Marsh department store (*see* 1947; 1950).

Theater *The Antigone of Sophocles* (*Die Antigone des Sophokles*) by Bertolt Brecht 2/15 at the Stadttheater in Chur, Switzerland; *Mr. Roberts* by U.S. playwrights Thomas Heggen, 26, and Joshua Logan, 39, 2/18 at New York's Alvin Theater, with Henry Fonda, David Wayne, Robert Keith, 1,157 perfs.; *The Lady's Not for Burning* by Christopher Fry 3/11 at the London Art Theatre; *The Caucasian Chalk Circle* (*Der kaukasische Kreidekreis*) by Bertolt Brecht (based on the Chinese drama *The Circle of Chalk*) 5/4 at Carleton College, Northfield, Minn. (in English); *Mr. Puntila and His Hired Man* (*Herr Puntila und sein Knecht Matti*) by Bertolt Brecht 6/5 at Zurich's Schauspielhaus; *Summer and Smoke* by Tennessee Williams 10/6 at New York's Music Box Theater, with Anne Jackson, Margaret Phillips, 100 perfs.; *State of Siege* (*L'etat de siège*) by Albert Camus 10/27 at the Théâtre Marigny, Paris; *The Cry of the Peacock* (*Ardele, ou La marguerite*) by Jean Anouilh 11/4 at the Théâtre de l'Atelier, Paris; *Playbill* (*The Browning Version* and *Harlequinade*) by Terence Rattigan 11/8 at London's Phoenix Theatre; *Anne of the Thousand Days* by Maxwell Anderson 12/8 at New York's Shubert Theater, with Joyce Redman as Anne Boleyn, Rex Harrison as Henry VIII, 286 perfs.

Television variety shows and drama *The Original Amateur Hour* 1/18 with host Ted Mack who will continue until 1970; *The Ed Sullivan Show* (initially *The Toast of the Town*) in June with *New York Daily News* columnist Edward Vincent Sullivan, 45, as master of ceremonies. Sullivan has been hired by CBS program development manager Worthington Miner, 47, to emcee the new TV variety show that introduces comedians Dean Martin and Jerry Lewis in its first program and will continue on Sunday nights until 1971; *Hopalong Cassidy* 11/28 on NBC TV with actor Bill Boyd in the title role of television's first Western series.

Films Vittorio de Sica's *The Bicycle Thief;* Roberto Rosselini's *The Miracle* with Anna Magnani and Federico Fellini (who wrote the story); Laurence Olivier's *Hamlet* with Olivier, Jean Simmons, Felix Aylmer; Michael Powell and Emeric Pressburger's *The Red Shoes* with Moira Shearer, Marius Goring; John Huston's *The Treasure of the Sierra Madre* with Humphrey Bogart, Walter Huston, Tim Holt; John Huston's *Key Largo* with Humphrey Bogart, Lauren Bacall, Edward G. Robinson; David Lean's *Oliver Twist* with Alec Guinness, Robert Newton, Anthony Newley, John Howard Davies; Alexander Mackendrick's *Tight Little Island* with Joan Greenwood; Or-

son Welles's *The Lady from Shanghai* with Rita Hayworth, Everett Sloane; Anatole Litvak's *The Snake Pit* with Olivia de Havilland; H. C. Potter's *The Time of Your Life* with James Cagney, William Bendix, Broderick Crawford; Howard Hawks's *Red River* with John Wayne, Montgomery Clift; John Ford's *Fort Apache* with John Wayne, Henry Fonda, Shirley Temple; Billy Wilder's *A Foreign Affair* with Jean Arthur, Marlene Dietrich, John Lund; George Cukor's *A Double Life* with Ronald Colman, Signe Hasso, Shelley Winters; Henry Cornelius's *Passport to Pimlico* with Stanley Holloway, Margaret Rutherford; William Dieterle's *Portrait of Jennie* with Jennifer Jones, Joseph Cotten, Ethel Barrymore, Lillian Gish; George Stevens's *I Remember Mama* with Irene Dunne, Barbara Bel Geddes; Joseph L. Mankiewicz's *A Letter to Three Wives* with Jeanne Crane, Linda Darnell, Ann Sothern, Kirk Douglas; Akira Kurosawa's *The Drunken Angel.*

Hollywood musicals Vincente Minnelli's *The Pirate* with Judy Garland, Gene Kelly, music and lyrics by Cole Porter, songs that include "Be a Clown"; John Berry's *Casbah* with Yvonne de Carlo, Tony Martin, Peter Lorre, music by Harold Arlen, lyrics by Leo Robin, songs that include "For Every Man There's a Woman," "Hooray for Love."

Broadway musicals *Look, Ma, I'm Dancing* 1/29 at the Adelphi Theater, with Nancy Walker, Harold Lang, music and lyrics by Hugh Martin, songs that include "Shauny O'Shay," 188 perfs.; *Where's Charley* 10/11 at the St. James Theater, with Ray Bolger in an adaptation of the 1892 English comedy *Charley's Aunt,* music and lyrics by Frank Loesser, songs that include "Once in Love with Amy," "My Darling, My Darling," "The New Ashmolean Marching Society and Students' Conservatory Band," 792 perfs.; *As the Girls Go* 11/13 at the Winter Garden Theater, with Bobby Clark, Irene Rich, music by Jimmy McHugh, lyrics by Harold Adamson, songs that include "It Takes a Woman to Make a Man," 420 perfs.; *Lend an Ear* 12/16 at the National Theater, with music and lyrics by Charles Gaynor, songs that include "I'm Not in Love," "When Someone You Love Loves You," 460 perfs.; *Kiss Me Kate* 12/30 at the New Century Theater, with Alfred Drake, Patricia Morrison, Lisa Kirk, Harold Lang in an adaptation of the 1596 Shakespeare comedy *The Taming of the Shrew,* music and lyrics by Cole Porter, songs that include "We Open in Venice," "I've Come to Wive It Wealthily," "I Hate Men," "Another Opening, Another Show," "Why Can't You Behave," "Were Thine that Special Face," "Too Darn Hot," "Where Is the Life that Late I Led," "Always True to You in My Fashion," "So in Love," "Tom, Dick or Harry," "Wunderbar," "Brush Up Your Shakespeare," 1,077 perfs.

Soviet composers Aram Khatchaturian, Serge Prokoviev, and Dmitri Shostakovich are rebuked February 11 by the Central Committee of the Communist Party which calls their work an expression of "bour-

1948 (cont.) geois decadence." The scolding comes on the heels of a denunciation by Soviet cultural czar Andrei Zhdanof who has accused the composers of "failing in their duties to the Soviet people."

The Aldeburgh Festival founded by composer Benjamin Britten has its first season 100 miles northeast of London.

Opera *The Beggar's Opera* 5/24 at England's Cambridge Arts Theatre, with music by Benjamin Britten; *Magdalena* 7/28 at Los Angeles, with music by Heitor Villa-Lobos.

Cantatas *Knoxville: Summer of 1915* by Samuel Barber 4/19 at Boston's Symphony Hall, with text by James Agee; *Saint Nicolas* by Benjamin Britten 6/5 at the Aldeburgh Festival (above) and in July at the 100th anniversary of St. Nicolas College, Lancing, Sussex; *A Survivor of Warsaw* by Arnold Schoenberg 11/4 at Albuquerque, N. M.

Ballet *Fall River Legend* 4/22 at New York's Metropolitan Opera House, with Alicia Alonso, John Kriza, music by Morton Gould, choreography by Agnes de Mille; *Orpheus* 4/28 at the New York City Center, with Maria Tallchief as Eurydice, Tanaquil LeClercq as the leader of the Bacchantes, music by Igor Stravinsky, choreography by George Ballanchine; *Cinderella* 12/27 at London's Royal Opera House in Covent Garden, with Moira Shearer, music by Serge Prokofiev, choreography by Frederick Ashton.

First performances Symphony No. 3 in E major by Walter Piston 1/9 at Boston's Symphony Hall; Symphony No. 4 by U.S. composer David Diamond, 32, 1/23 at Boston's Symphony Hall; *Mandu-Carará* (Symphonic Poem) by Heitor Villa-Lobos 1/23 at New York; *Fantasy for Trombone and Orchestra* by Paul Creston 2/12 at Los Angeles; *The Seine at Night* (Symphonic Poem) by Virgil Thomson 2/24 at Kansas City; Concerto No. 1 for Violin and Orchestra by David Diamond 2/29 at Vancouver; Symphony No. 6 by Ralph Vaughan Williams, now 75, 4/21 at London; Symphony No. 4 (*1848*) by Darius Milhaud 5/20 at Paris; Symphony No. 2 by Roger Sessions 6/9 at Amsterdam; *Toccata* by Walter Piston 10/14 at Bridgeport, Conn.; *Sinfonietta* by Francis Poulenc 10/24 in a BBC Orchestra concert from London; *Mass* by Igor Stravinsky 10/27 at Milan; Concerto No. 2 for Violin and Orchestra by Darius Milhaud 11/7 at Paris; *Wheat Field at Noon* by Virgil Thomson 12/7 at Louisville; Concerto for Piano by Howard Hanson 12/31 at Boston's Symphony Hall; Symphony No. 5 by George Antheil 12/31 at Philadelphia's Academy of Music.

The long-playing 12-inch vinyl plastic phonograph record demonstrated at New York June 18 by CBS engineer Peter Goldmark turns at a rate of 33⅓ revolutions per minute instead of the usual 78 rpm, has 250 "Microgrooves" to the inch, plays 45 minutes of music, and begins a revolution in the record industry (*see* 1946; Goldmark's color television, 1940).

Goldmark also unveils a lightweight pickup arm and a silent turntable for his LP records (*see* 1949).

Popular songs "Tennessee Waltz" by Redd Stewart and Pee Wee King; "On a Slow Boat to China" by Frank Loesser; "Manana—Is Soon Enough for Me" by Peggy Lee and Dave Barbour; "Nature Boy" by Eden Ahbez; "It's a Most Unusual Day" by Jimmy McHugh, lyrics by Harold Adamson (for Richard Thorpe's film *A Date with Judy*); "Candy Kisses" by George Morgan; " 'A' — You're Adorable" by Buddy Kaye, Fred Wise, and Sidney Lippman; "Red Roses for a Blue Lady" by Sid Tepper and Roy Beaumont; "Baby, It's Cold Outside" by Frank Loesser; "You're Breaking My Heart" by Pat Genaro and Sunny Skylar; "Buttons and Bows" by Jay Livingston and Ray Evans (for Norman Z. McLeod's film *Paleface* with Bob Hope and Jane Russell); "Enjoy Yourself—It's Later than You Think" by Carl Sigman, lyrics by Herb Magidson; "Pigalle" by French songwriter Georges Ulmer; "Sleigh Ride" by Leroy Anderson, 39, lyrics by Mitchell Parish; "I'll Be Home for Christmas" by Kim Gannon, Walter Kent, Buck Ram.

The Olympic games are held for the first time since 1936. A record 6,005 contestants from 59 nations compete at London with U.S. athletes taking the lion's share of medals.

Soviet chess master Mikhail Botvinnik wins the world title he will hold until 1957, will regain it the following year, and will hold it until 1960.

Citation with Eddie Arcaro up wins U.S. racing's Triple Crown. No horse will win it again until in 1973.

The Cleveland Indians win the World Series by defeating the Boston Braves 4 games to 2 with help from pitchers Bob Feller and Satchel Paige, now 42 (*see* 1934).

Scrabble is copyrighted by Newtown, Conn., entrepreneur James Brunot who has taken over the "crossword game" played with wooden tiles on a board from his friend Alfred M. Butts who invented the game in 1931 and called it Criss-Cross. Brunot renames the game and begins manufacturing it. Scrabble will be produced beginning in 1952 by the Bay Shore, Long Island, firm Selchow & Righter, Brunot will receive a royalty of 5 percent on the retail price until 1971 when Selchow & Righter will acquire the game outright, Scrabble will be produced in six languages, and it will be so popular that sales will rival those of the Parker Brothers game Monopoly introduced in 1935.

Dial soap is introduced by Chicago's Armour and Company which employs the bacteria-killing chemical hexachlorophene discovered in World War II to produce the world's first deodorant soap. Armour will build a factory next year at McCook, Ill., with capacity for processing 100 million pounds of fats and oils per year for the new soap that will become the largest-selling U.S. toilet soap.

New York's E. J. Korvette pioneers discount retailing. Local merchant Eugene Ferkauf, 28, has been unable to persuade his father to discount sales at the family's two Rex Luggage Company shops near Grand Central Station, he opens a second-floor discount luggage and appliance store in West 46th Street under the name E. J. Korvette, by 1953 he will have a five-store chain in Manhattan and suburban New York with sales of $9.7 million, by 1956 he will have a chain of cut-rate department stores with sales of $55 million (see 1962).

Lord & Taylor opens a Scarsdale, N.Y., store. Headed since 1946 by Dorothy Shavers, the New York specialty store continues the move to suburbia begun in 1941; it will open stores at Bala Cynwyd (1955), Garden City (1956), Washington, D.C. (1959), and elsewhere.

Ohrbach's opens a Los Angeles store on Wilshire Boulevard (see 1923; 1954).

A killer smog on the Monongahela River south of Pittsburgh affects 43 percent of the 12,000 residents of Donora, Pa. Sulfur from burning coal at the local steel mill combines with dampness in the air to produce sulfuric acid that causes headache, nausea, vomiting, and irritation of the eyes, nose, and throat; 22 die within a few days, and U.S. Steel closes down its Donora mill.

Our Plundered Planet by U.S. zoologist Fairfield Osborne, 51, expresses concern about the growing use of DDT (see 1943; Carson, 1962).

The U.S.S.R.'s last remaining centers of pure biological research are taken over by Lysenkoites and fall into the hands of people who oppose hybridization (see Lysenko, 1940). The centers were organized at the Lenin Academy of Agricultural Science and at the Institute of Genetics by the late Nikolai Vavilov who died in 1942 (see 1954).

U.S. corn is now 75 percent hybrid (see Golden Cross Bantam, 1933; record yield, 1955).

Maine's Atlantic Sea-Run Salmon Commission begins a program of removing old dams that bar fish from migrating upstream to spawning grounds (see Columbia River, 1938). The Commission starts to restock rivers such as the Aroostook, the Dennys, the Machias, the East Machias, the Narraguagus, the Penobscot, the Pleasant, the Sheepscot, and the Union (see Anadromous Fish Act, 1965).

Vitamin B$_{12}$ (cyanocobalamin) is isolated as a red crystalline substance from animal livers, and pernicious anemia is made containable by relatively inexpensive monthly B$_{12}$ injections (see Castle, 1929). English biochemist E. L. Smith and U.S. Merck Laboratories biochemist Karl A. Folkers, 41, have used bacterial response and chromatography to isolate the vitamin (see 1944; Hodgkin, 1955).

All 13 vitamins considered essential to human health have now been isolated and some synthesized.

The Organic Front by New York electrical manufacturer and food faddist J. I. (Jerome Irving) Rodale, 50, makes extravagant claims for alleged health benefits from eating vegetables and fruits grown without chemical fertilizers or pesticides. Rodale has been inspired by the work of English agriculturist Albert Howard who used locally available organic wastes as fertilizer in the Indian state of Indore for lack of more efficient fertilizers (see *Prevention*, 1950).

The first full-sized British supermarket is opened January 12 at Manor Park, London, by the London Co-Operative Society (see 1951).

U.S. sales of frozen orange juice concentrate leap to more than 12 million 6-ounce cans (see 1947; Minute Maid, 1949).

TreeSweet Products Co. leases a processing plant at Ft. Pierce, Fla., in the heart of the citrus-growing Indian River country and adds canned Florida citrus juices to its California line (see 1933; 1956).

"V-8" Cocktail Vegetable Juice introduced by Campbell Soup Company is a mixture of tomato, carrot, celery, beet, parsley, lettuce, watercress, and spinach juices (see Swanson, 1955).

Nestlé's Quik chocolate milk additive is introduced in the United States to compete with Ovaltine which dominates the market (see 1905). By 1976 Quik will have 64 percent of the $110 million market.

Gerber Products Company sells 2 million cans and jars of baby food per week (see 1941; MSG, 1951).

U.S. sales of oregano will increase by 5,200 percent in the next 8 years as demand is boosted by the growing popularity of pizza pies and other Italian specialties discovered by servicemen in Europe (see 1953).

The Salton Hotray to keep food warm is introduced by Polish-American engineer Lewis Salton, 37, who has been employed by RCA since his arrival as a refugee by way of Lithuania, Siberia, Japan, and Panama. Salton quits his $8,000 per year RCA job and goes into business with three employees in a 1,000 square foot New York loft in Reade Street, but he has little initial success as consumers rush to buy toasters and coffeemakers while showing little interest in new products.

The McDonald hamburger stand that opened in 1940 at Pasadena, Calif., is turned into a self-service restaurant by the McDonald brothers who begin to franchise the name McDonald to other fast food entrepreneurs. The McDonalds install infrared heat lamps to keep French fried potatoes warm (see 1952).

The Baskin-Robbins ice cream chain begins its growth as California entrepreneur Burton "Butch" Baskin merges his small chain with the small chain begun by the Snowbird Ice Cream stand at Adams and Palmer streets in Glendale that was opened December 7, 1945, by Irvine Robbins, now 30. Baskin-Robbins will soon be selling ice cream in more than 100 flavors including Blueberries 'N Cream, Pralines 'N Cream, Huckleberry Finn, Baseball Nut, New England Maple, Chocolate Divinity, and Nuts to You,

1948 (cont.) and by 1976 they will have 1,600 franchised outlets in the United States, Canada, Japan, and Europe.

Smirnoff Vodka sales are promoted by use of the new Polaroid camera (above). Heublein executives tour the country showing bartenders how to make the Moscow Mule cocktail invented 2 years ago in Los Angeles, they take Polaroid pictures of the bartenders drinking the cocktail, and a fad develops that helps to popularize the liquor that will soon be sold with the double-entendre advertising slogan "It Leaves You Breathless." Heublein will develop a series of vodka drinks including the vodka Martini, the Screwdriver (vodka and orange juice), and the Bloody Mary (vodka, tomato juice, lemon juice, Worcestershire sauce), and by the mid-1970s vodka will be outselling whiskey in the United States.

A Displaced Persons act voted by Congress June 25 authorizes 400,000 homeless people to settle in the United States, but the D.P.s are charged to the quotas of their countries under the Johnson-Reed Law of 1924 (*see* McCarran-Walter Act, 1952).

The International Planned Parenthood Federation is founded by birth control pioneer Margaret Sanger (*see* 1927; Pincus, 1951).

A "Eugenic Protection" law that authorizes abortion is enacted in occupied Japan whose population is nearly 80 million, up from 64.5 million in 1930.

The new state of Israel (above) occupies four-fifths of Palestine and has an Arab population of 200,000 remaining after another 500,000 have fled.

The Food and Agriculture Organization (FAO) of the United Nations predicts that the world will have 2.25 billion mouths to feed by 1960 (*see* 1945; 1960).

1949 The Western powers pledge cooperation as the Soviet Union breaks the U.S. nuclear monopoly and as Communists take over China.

Dean Gooderham Acheson, 55, replaces George Marshall as U.S. secretary of state January 7, Andrei Vyshinsky replaces V. M. Molotov as Soviet foreign minister March 4.

President Truman proposes four major courses of U.S. action in his inaugural address January 20. Point Four calls for "a bold new program for making the benefits of our scientific advances and industrial progress available for the improvement and growth of underprivileged areas."

China's Chiang Kai-shek resigns his presidency January 21 as Nationalist armies suffer reverses at the hands of the Communists who have taken Tientsin January 15 (*see* below).

Paris recognizes Vietnamese independence within the French Union March 8. The former emperor of Annam Bao Dai heads the state which includes Cochin China, but France retains the right to maintain military bases (*see* 1946; 1950).

Newfoundland joins the Dominion of Canada March 31 and becomes the tenth province.

The North Atlantic Treaty Organization (NATO) created by a treaty signed at Washington April 4 joins the United States, Canada, Iceland, Britain, France, Denmark, Norway, Belgium, the Netherlands, Luxembourg, Italy, and Portugal in a pledge of mutual assistance against aggression within the North Atlantic area and of cooperation in military training, strategic planning, and arms production.

The North Atlantic Treaty Organization (above) gives approval to President Truman's Point Four program of technical assistance to aid world peace (above).

The International Court of Justice of the United Nations hands down its first decision April 9. The court holds Albania responsible for incidents that occurred in the Corfu Channel in 1946 and awards damages to Britain.

The Republic of Eire is formally proclaimed April 18 at Dublin. London recognizes Irish independence May 17 but reaffirms the position of Northern Ireland within the United Kingdom.

The Council of Europe statute signed May 5 at London establishes a Committee of Ministers and a Consultative Assembly with Council headquarters at Strasburg. The statute is signed by Belgium, Denmark, France, Britain, Ireland (Eire), Italy, Luxembourg, the Netherlands, Norway, and Sweden who will be joined by Greece, Iceland, and Turkey.

Siam is renamed Thailand May 11.

The Berlin blockade is officially lifted by Soviet authorities May 12, but the Berlin airlift continues until September 30 when it ends after having completed 277,264 flights (*see* 1948).

The German Federal Republic (West Germany) is established May 23 with headquarters at Bonn.

The German Democratic Republic (East Germany) is established October 7 under Soviet control.

The Hashemite Kingdom of Jordan is created June 2 by a renaming of the 3-year-old Kingdom of Transjordan ruled by Abdullah (*see* 1951).

China's Chiang Kai-shek is made head of a Supreme Council July 16 and begins removing his Nationalist forces to Formosa (Taiwan). U.S. aid to Nationalist China ends August 5.

The U.S. Defense Department is created August 10 by a retitling of the War Department under terms of the National Security Act of 1947. The first secretary of defense James V. Forrestal has died May 22 at age 57 after jumping from a window at the Bethesda naval hospital which he entered in March after resigning from the cabinet with symptoms of nervous exhaustion and depression.

Civil war looms in Korea, reports a UN Commission September 2 (*see* 1950).

A Soviet atomic bomb is developed by physicists who include chiefly Andrei Dmitriyevich Sakharov, 28, who won a doctorate at age 26, and 1925 German Nobel laureate Gustav Hertz, 62, whose uncle Heinrich Hertz pioneered the wireless in 1887. President Truman announces September 23, "We have evidence that in recent weeks an atomic explosion occurred in the U.S.S.R."

The People's Republic of China is proclaimed October 1 at Peking with Mao Tse-tung as chairman of the central people's administrative council and Chou En-lai as premier and foreign minister. Removal of Nationalist forces from the mainland to Taiwan is completed by December 8.

Continued U.S. support of the United Nations is pledged by President Truman October 24 in ceremonies dedicating the new UN site at New York.

Washington imposes stringent controls November 8 on export of all strategic commodities to prevent their reshipment to Soviet bloc countries.

The Geneva Conventions adopted by most of the world powers provide for "free passage of all consignments of essential foodstuffs, clothing, and tonics intended for children under fifteen, expectant mothers, and maternity cases" in event of war, but the conventions do not specifically outlaw sieges, blockades, or "resource denial" operations (see 1962).

Indonesia elects Achmed Sukarno president December 16, the Dutch grant independence December 27 after 4 years of hostilities, the United States of Indonesia is established with its capital at Jakarta (Batavia), and President Sukarno begins an administration that will continue until 1968 (see 1945; 1959).

A South African apartheid program goes into effect in June under terms of the South African Citizenship Act which suspends automatic granting of citizenship to Commonwealth immigrants after 5 years and which bans marriages between Europeans (meaning whites) and non-Europeans (meaning blacks or "coloreds") (see 1948; 1950).

"Tokyo Rose" goes on trial for treason in July at San Francisco. Los Angeles-born UCLA graduate Iva Toguri D'Aquino, 34, is one of at least a dozen Tokyo radio announcers who were called "Tokyo Rose" by English-speaking listeners in the Pacific during the war, she did the work under pressure from Japanese secret police after being caught in Tokyo at the outbreak of the war, she refused to renounce her U.S. citizenship as did two other women announcers (who thus could not be charged with treason), she married a Portuguese national in 1945, government officials threaten and intimidate defense witnesses, the prosecution bribes a witness to give false testimony and tries to bribe an AP reporter to lie on the witness stand, the trial lasts 13 weeks and costs some $750,000, the judge's instructions make it impossible for the jury to acquit, the jury finds D'Aquino innocent of eight alleged overt acts of treason but guilty on one count of having tried to undermine U.S. morale. Sentenced to 6 years in prison, she will serve 6½.

New York dancer Paul Draper, 29, and harmonica player Larry Adler sue a Greenwich, Conn., woman for libel after Red-baiting columnist Westbrook Pegler has picked up her accusations that Draper and Adler have Communist sympathies (see Trumbo, 1947). Draper has melded tap dancing with the poses and movements of classical ballet, he has choreographed his tap dances to jazz and to music by Handel, Bach, and Beethoven, he has teamed up with Adler to earn $100,000 per year with nightclub performances, the Greenwich woman wants to cancel a concert she has booked, the libel case ends in a hung jury, but Draper and Adler are unable to obtain further bookings (see Red Channels, 1950).

Hungarian officials arrest foreign minister Laszlo Rajk June 16 on charges of conspiracy and begin a wholesale purge of Hungarian Communists accused of deviating from pro-Soviet policy.

Poland has a purge in November of prominent members of the United Workers' party central committee who are accused of having "Titoist" sympathies (see Tito, 1948).

British dock workers strike in June and close ports.

Australian coal workers strike the mines June 27 and do not return until mid-August when emergency legislation authorizes the government to send in troops to work the mines.

U.S. coal workers strike September 19, President Truman invokes the Taft-Hartley Act September 30, the miners refuse to obey the injunction, and 20 UMW leaders are cited for contempt. They win acquittal and the strike is settled.

A new Minimum Wage act passed by Congress October 26 amends the Fair Labor Standards Act of 1938 and raises the minimum hourly wage from 40 cents to 75 cents (see 1955).

U.S. steelworkers strike October 1 and do not return until November 11. The 500,000 workers win company-paid pensions but no wage boosts.

A new U.S. transcontinental speed record is set February 8 by an Air Force XB-47 jet bomber which crosses the country in 3 hours, 46 minutes at an average speed of 607 miles per hour (see Glenn, 1957).

The first nonstop round-the-world flight is completed March 2 by Air Force pilots flying the B-50 Superfortress Lucky Lady II which has been refueled in midair and which arrives at Fort Worth, Tex., after a 23,452-mile flight of 94 hours, 1 minute (see 1947).

Chicago's O'Hare Airport is named in honor of the late Lieutenant Commander Edward H. "Butch" O'Hare who earned a Congressional Medal of Honor in 1942 for having shot down five Japanese bombers and crippling a sixth, but who died in 1943 at age 29. Originally called Orchard Place, O'Hare Airport will surpass Chicago's Midway Airport by 1961 to become the world's busiest air travel facility; by 1972 it will be handling 2,000 flights per day.

1949 (cont.) The *Chicago Zephyr* begins service between Chicago and San Francisco via the Burlington, the Rio Grande, and the Western Pacific Railroads with Vista Dome coaches for sightseeing (*see* 1934).

General Motors Corporation, Standard Oil Company of California, Firestone Tire, and other companies are convicted of having criminally conspired to replace electric transit lines with gasoline or diesel buses (*see* 1932; 1936; 1938). GM has replaced more than 100 electric transit systems in 45 cities with GM buses and will continue this program despite the court action (the company is fined $5,000, its treasurer is fined $1) (*see* 1955).

U.S. auto production reaches 5.1 million and catches up after 20 years with the 1929 record.

Germany's Volkswagen begins commercial production and is introduced into the United States, but only two of the odd-looking "beetles" are sold in America (*see* 1938; 1955).

Saab-Scania AB is founded in Sweden to compete with the 22-year-old Volvo group.

World petroleum reserves outside the United States and the Soviet bloc territories are 90 percent controlled by seven major oil companies. Standard Oil Company of New Jersey, Standard Oil Company of California, Gulf Oil, the Texas Company, Socony-Vacuum, Royal Dutch-Shell, and Anglo-Iranian control 88 percent of crude oil production, 77 percent of refining capacity, 85 percent of cracking capacity, two-thirds of all privately owned tankers, and every important pipeline.

John Paul Getty obtains a concession for his Pacific Western Company to drill for petroleum in the Neutral Zone established in 1924 between Saudi Arabia and Kuwait. The 56-year-old oil magnate made his first million by age 23, he has been battling for years to gain control of the Tide Water Associated Oil Company owned largely by Standard Oil of New Jersey (above), the desert in his new concession will turn out to cover one of the world's largest petroleum reserves, and the oil will make Getty the world's richest man (*see* 1951).

More than 75 percent of all bits used in oil drilling anywhere in the free world are supplied by Hughes Tool Company which leases the drills in the United States to keep dulled bits from being retipped and sold at lower prices (*see* 1908). Mounted on three cones, the Hughes rock bit can drill into rock formations at speeds of up to 180 feet per hour, its only significant competitor is Reed Roller Bit Company, and Reed must pay Hughes a 15 percent royalty on every rock bit it supplies to drillers.

Bauxite deposits in Jamaica, British West Indies, are acquired by Reynolds Metals Company as a source of raw material for aluminum production (*see* 1945). The Reynolds move will be followed by Alcoa, Kaiser Aluminum, Canada's Aluminium Company, and others who will buy 225,000 acres of Jamaica land rich in aluminum ore.

Minneapolis-Honeywell Corporation establishes an independent Aeronautical Division that will take the company into advanced military technology (*see* 1927). Minneapolis-Honeywell produced an autopilot for bombers during World War II and it begins acquisitions that will move it into electronics.

A Communist bloc Council for Mutual Economic Assistance is created January 18 at Moscow to further economic cooperation between the Soviet Union and her satellites. Poland joins the Council a week later.

The salary of the U.S. president is raised to $100,000 per year by Congress January 19 with a tax-free allowance of $50,000 for expenses.

The General Services Administration is created by Congress to serve as an independent federal agency with responsibilities for managing government property and records economically and efficiently. The GSA will construct and operate buildings, distribute supplies, stockpile critical materials, and dispose of government surpluses.

United Automobile Workers at General Motors plants accept a slight wage cut as a business recession produces a decline in the cost of living (*see* 1948).

U.S. unemployment reaches 5.9 percent, up from 3.8 percent last year, and the Dow Jones Industrial Average on Wall Street falls to 161 at midyear, down from 193 a year earlier, but while most consumer prices drop, housing and medical care costs increase.

The average American steelworker has $3,000 per year to spend after taxes, the average social worker $3,500, a high school teacher $4,700, a car salesman $8,000, a dentist $10,000. Typical prices include a new Cadillac for $5,000, a gallon of gasoline 25 cents, a man's gabardine suit $50, a 10-inch table TV set $250, a pack of cigarettes 21 cents, a pound of pork 57 cents, a pound of lamb chops $1.15, a bottle of Coca-Cola 5 cents, a quart of milk 21 cents, a loaf of bread 15 cents, a dozen eggs 80 cents.

Japanese reparation payments are terminated May 12 by the Far Eastern Commission to spur Japan's economic recovery.

U.S. aid amounting to $5.43 billion for the European Recovery Program has been authorized by Congress in a Foreign Assistance bill enacted April 19 (*see* 1947).

A $20 million loan to Yugoslavia is extended by the U.S. Export-Import Bank September 8 to help the Tito government resist Soviet domination (*see* 1948).

The British pound is devalued from $4.03 to $2.80 September 18. Most European nations follow the British move and devalue their currencies.

Nationalization of Britain's iron and steel industries takes effect November 24.

The adrenocorticotropic hormone ACTH produced by the human pituitary gland to stimulate the adrenal glands is synthesized from liver bile acid by

Merck Laboratory researchers (*see* cortisone, 1948). Upjohn researchers will use microbes to produce ACTH more cheaply.

Effective lowering of blood pressure through use of powdered root from the tropical plant *Rauwolfia serpentina* is reported in the prestigious *British Heart Journal* by Indian physician Rustom Jal Vakil (*see* 1952).

A landmark 16-year epidemiological study of heart disease begins at Framingham, Mass., under the direction of Harvard physician William B. Kannel and his associates. 2,282 men and 2,846 women will be selected at random from the town's population of 25,000 and their records over the next 16 years will suggest associations between diet and the risk of premature death from heart disease (*see* Keys, 1953). Factors of heredity, cigarette smoking, and lack of exercise will also prove to increase heart disease risk.

The antibiotic oxytetracycline is developed by biochemists of Charles Pfizer & Company which will be awarded a patent on the drug in 1955, but tetracycline will be introduced under the trade name Achromycin by American Cyanamid's Lederle Laboratories in 1953, and Lederle will maintain a large share of the market for the drug.

The antibiotic chloramphenicol is introduced by Parke, Davis under the trade name Chloromycetin and is hailed as the first major breakthrough against typhoid fever.

The antibiotic neomycin is isolated by Selman Waksman (*see* streptomycin, 1943).

Billy Graham gains prominence with a tent crusade at Los Angeles that leads to the conversion of an Olympic track star, a noted gambler, and a notorious underworld syndicate figure. Born in North Carolina, the 31-year-old evangelist has just become first vice president of Youth for Christ International.

Radio Free Europe begins beaming world news to listeners behind the Iron Curtain from an operations base at Munich (*see* Voice of America, 1948). General Lucius D. Clay has helped to start the organization and is chairman of the board, he asks for private contributions to help fund Radio Free Europe, but nearly all its support comes from the CIA.

American Telephone & Telegraph Company is charged with having monopolized the telephone instrument market in violation of the Sherman Act of 1890. AT&T may be a "natural monopoly," says the Department of Justice, but the manufacture of telephones is by no means a natural monopoly, and the Justice Department asks the company to break its Western Electric division into three separate companies so as to permit competition in telephone instrument production and installation.

The first typesetting machine that dispenses with metal type is introduced by the Intertype Corporation of Brooklyn, N.Y., which installs its Intertype Fotosetter Photographic Line Composing Machine at the Rochester, N.Y., plant of the Stecher-Traung

Lithograph Corporation. (*see* Mergenthaler, 1884; Photon process, 1953).

New York's Doyle Dane Bernbach advertising agency is created by former Grey Advertising creative director William Bernbach, 38, who joins with Ned Doyle and Maxwell Dane, 43, to start the shop that will popularize the Volkswagen (above), the Polaroid Land camera, and other products. DDB will set new standards of creative, tasteful advertising.

Nonfiction *The Second Sex* (*Le Deuxième Sexe*) by French philosopher-novelist Simone de Beauvoir, 41, will be the bible of feminists (*see* 1953); *The Need for Roots* (*L'Enracinement*) by the late French writer Simone Weil who died in 1943 at age 34 of voluntary starvation in England after refusing to eat more than her compatriots were receiving from Nazi occupation authorities.

Fiction *Conjugal Love* (*L'Amore Coniugale e Altri Racconti*) by Alberto Moravia whose prostitutes are his most sympathetic characters; *The House on the Hill* (*La Casa in Collina*) by Italian novelist Cesare Pavese, 41; *Iron in the Soul* (*The Troubled Sleep* or *La Mort dans l'Ame*) by Jean-Paul Sartre; *The Oasis* by U.S. novelist Mary McCarthy, 37; *The House of Incest* by Anaïs Nin; *The Sheltering Sky* by émigré U.S. novelist Paul Bowles, 39; *The Man with the Golden Arm* by Chicago novelist Nelson Algren, 40, whose story of drug addiction is the top U.S. best seller (Algren has started a love affair with Simone de Beauvoir, above); *Point of No Return* by John P. Marquand; "No Consultation Today" ("Honjitsu Kyushin") by Japanese short story writer Masuji Ibuse, 51; "The Lottery," an allegory by U.S. novelist Shirley Jackson, 30; *The Third Man* by Graham Greene; *Nineteen Eighty-Four* by George Orwell who will die of tuberculosis at age 46 in January 1950.

China became a Communist people's republic. Mao Tse-tung's entry into Shanghai ended the power of Chiang Kai-shek.

1949 (cont.) *Nineteen Eighty-Four* by George Orwell (above) is a chilling projection of a totalitarian state whose authorities exercise mind control ("Big Brother Is Watching You"). Orwell introduces the inverted graffiti "Ignorance Is Strength" and "Freedom Is Slavery" along with such portmanteau words as "Newspeak," "bellyfeel," and "doublethink." "Who controls the past controls the future; who controls the present controls the past," says one of Orwell's characters (compare Santayana, 1905).

Harvard's Lamont Library, named to honor J. P. Morgan chairman Thomas W. Lamont, opens in the Yard. Thousands of alumni have contributed to its endowment fund, but it will admit no women, except in summer, until 1967.

Poetry *The Arrivistes* by U.S. poet Louis Simpson, 26.

Painting *Red Sun* by Marc Chagall; *The Studio* by Raoul Dufy; *Number 2* by Jackson Pollock; *Somerset Maugham* by Graham Sutherland. José Clemente Orozco dies at Mexico City September 7 at age 65; James Ensor dies at Ostend November 19 at age 89.

Sculpture *Lazarus* by Jacob Epstein.

Theater *Death of a Salesman* by Arthur Miller 2/10 at New York's Morosco Theater, with Lee J. Cobb as salesman Willie Loman, Mildred Dunnock, Arthur Kennedy, Cameron Mitchell, 742 perfs., Pulitzer prize; *Detective Story* by Sidney Kingsley 3/23 at New York's Hudson Theater, with Ralph Bellamy, Les Tremayne, Alexander Scourby, Maureen Stapleton, Joseph Wiseman, 581 perfs.; *Romulus the Great* (*Romulus der Grosse*) by Swiss playwright Friedrich Dürrenmatt, 28, 4/25 at Basel's Stadttheater; *The Just Assassins* (*Les Justes*) by Albert Camus 12/15 at the Théâtre Hebertot, Paris.

Television drama *The Goldbergs* 1/17 on CBS, is the first TV situation comedy. Derived from the radio show first aired in 1929, the show stars Molly Berg, it will continue until late June of 1951, and it will be followed by dozens of "sitcoms"; *Amos 'n Andy* becomes a weekly TV program with black actors (*see* 1928; 1965).

The National Academy of Television Arts and Sciences makes its first Emmy Awards.

Films Carol Reed's *The Third Man* with Orson Welles, Joseph Cotten, Trevor Howard, Valli; Carol Reed's *The Fallen Idol* with Ralph Richardson, Michel Morgan, Bobby Henrey; Robert Rossen's *All the King's Men* with Broderick Crawford, Mercedes McCambridge; John Ford's *She Wore a Yellow Ribbon* with John Wayne; Clarence Brown's *Intruder in the Dust* with David Brian, Claude Jarman, Jr.; Ken Annakin, Arthur Crabtree, Harold French, and Ralph Smart's *Quartet* with Ian Fleming, Dirk Bogarde, Mai Zetterling, and others in four Somerset Maugham stories; George Cukor's *Adam's Rib* with Spencer Tracy, Katharine Hepburn; Nicholas Ray's *They Live by Night* with Farley Granger, Cathy

O'Donnell; Raoul Walsh's *White Heat* with James Cagney; Henry King's *Twelve O'clock High* with Gregory Peck; Allan Dwan's *Sands of Iwo Jima* with John Wayne; Sam Wood's *The Stratton Story* with James Stewart, June Allyson; Jacques Tati's *Jour de Fête;* Yasujiro Ozu's *Late Spring*.

Broadway musicals *South Pacific* 4/7 at the Majestic Theater, with Ezio Pinza, Mary Martin, Myron McCormick, Juanita Hall, Betta St. John, William Tabbert, music by Richard Rodgers, lyrics by Oscar Hammerstein II, book based on James Michener's tales of U.S. military personnel in World War II posts, songs that include "Some Enchanted Evening," "Younger Than Springtime," "I'm in Love with a Wonderful Guy," "This Nearly Was Mine," "I'm Gonna Wash that Man Right Out of My Hair," "A Cockeyed Optimist," "Honey Bun," "You've Got to Be Carefully Taught," "Dites-moi Pourquoi," "There Is Nothing Like a Dame," "Happy Talk," "Bali Ha'i," 1,925 perfs.; *Miss Liberty* 6/15 at the Imperial Theater, with Philip Borneuf, music and lyrics by Irving Berlin, songs that include "Let's Take an Old Fashioned Walk," 308 perfs.; *Bloomer Girl* 10/15 at the City Center Theater, with Celeste Holm as Evelina, Joan McCracken, music by Harold Arlen, lyrics by E. Y. Harburg, 653 perfs.; *Lost in the Stars* 10/30 at the Music Box Theater, with Todd Duncan, music by Kurt Weill, lyrics by Maxwell Anderson, book based on Alan Paton's 1948 novel *Cry the Beloved Country,* 273 perfs.; *Gentlemen Prefer Blondes* 12/8 at the Ziegfeld Theater, with Carol Channing, music by Jule Styne, lyrics by Leo Robin, book based on the 1925 novel, songs that include "A Little Girl from Little Rock," "Diamonds Are a Girl's Best Friend," "Bye Bye Baby," 740 perfs.

Opera *Let's Make an Opera* 6/14 at Aldeburgh's Jubilee Hall, with music by Benjamin Britten, libretto by Eric Crozier.

Ballet *Beauty and the Beast* 12/20 at the Sadler's Wells Theatre, London, with music by the late Maurice Ravel, choreography by South African-born dancer-choreographer John Cranko, 22.

First performances Spring Symphony for Soprano, Alto, and Tenor Soli, Mixed Chorus, Boys' Choir, and Orchestra by Benjamin Britten 7/9 at Amsterdam; *Concerto Symphonique* for Piano and Orchestra by Ernest Bloch 9/3 at the Edinburgh Festival; Phantasy for Violin and Piano Accompaniment by Arnold Schoenberg 9/13 at Los Angeles; Concerto for Organ, Brasses, and Woodwinds by Paul Hindemith 11/14 at Boston's Symphony Hall.

CBS introduces improved long-playing vinyl plastic phonograph records (*see* RCA, 1946; Goldmark, 1948). RCA Records introduces small 45 rpm LPs that require large spindles.

Stereo components such as amplifiers, turntables, and speakers enjoy a sales boom.

The first LP record catalog is published in October by Cambridge, Mass., record shop proprietor William Schwann whose 26-page listing of 674 entries from 11 companies will grow in 25 years to list some 50,000 LPs in a book of more than 250 pages.

Popular songs "Melodie d'Amour" by French songwriter Henri Salvador; "Bonaparte's Retreat" by Peewee King; "Dear Hearts and Gentle People" by Sammy Fain, lyrics by Bob Hilliard; "I Don't Care If the Sun Don't Shine" by Mark David; "Scarlet Ribbons (for Her Hair)" by Evelyn Danzig, lyrics by Jack Segal; "Mona Lisa" by Jay Livingston and Ray Evans; "Huckle-Buck" by Andy Gibson, lyrics by Roy Alfred; "Room Full of Roses" by Tim Spencer; "Daddy's Little Girl" by Bobby Burke and Horace Gerlah; "The Harry Lime Theme" by Anton Karas (for the film *The Third Man*); "Rudolph the Red-Nosed Reindeer" by U.S. songwriter Johnny Marks, 40, who has adapted the verse published in 1939.

U.S. prizefighter Ezzard Charles, 27, gains the world heavyweight championship June 22 by winning a 15-round decision over Joe Walcott at Chicago following the retirement of Joe Louis March 1. Louis will come out of retirement and will lose a 15-round decision to Charles at New York September 27 of next year to make Charles undisputed champion.

The New York Yankees win the World Series by defeating the Brooklyn Dodgers 4 games to 1.

Silly Putty is introduced by New Haven, Conn., advertising man Peter C. L. Hodgson, 37, who has discovered a substance developed by General Electric Company researchers looking for a viable synthetic rubber. The useless silicone substance can be molded like soft clay, stretched like taffy, bounced like a rubber ball, and can pick up printed matter when pressed down on newsprint, but it has no market until Hodgson borrows $147 to buy a batch from GE, hires a Yale student to separate the stuff into one-ounce globs, packages it in clear compact plastic cases at $1 each, advertises it in a catalogue of toys he is preparing for a local store, and finds that Silly Putty is an immediate success.

Surf laundry detergent is introduced by Lever Brothers whose advertising claims that no rinsing is needed after washing. Procter & Gamble responds by advertising that its 3-year-old detergent Tide washes clothes "so miracle clean no rinsing needed," and the claim is echoed by Colgate's Fab (*see* 1956; Dash, 1954).

Clothes rationing ends in Britain.

"Fire and Ice" is introduced by Revlon whose new lipstick and nail enamel shade is promoted with a frankly sexual approach in advertisements featuring model Suzy Parker (*see* 1940).

A federal Housing Act sponsored by U.S. Senator Robert Taft of Ohio is passed by Congress July 15 to provide federal aid for slum-clearance projects and for building low-rent public housing.

Title 1 of the new Housing Act (above) encourages municipalities to acquire and resell substandard areas at prices below cost for private redevelopment.

Fresh Meadows Housing Development goes up in Queens, N.Y., with funds advanced by New York Life Insurance Company. The 166-acre development contains a mixture of row houses, low- and high-rise apartment buildings, schools, a theater, and a regional shopping center.

A two-bedroom U.S. house sells typically for $10,000 while a five-bedroom New York apartment rents for $110 per month. A four-bedroom duplex cooperative apartment in the East 60's near Park Avenue with a two-story living room and a wood-burning fireplace in its 16 × 21-foot library sells for $8,250 with annual maintenance of $2,970, an eight-room co-op on Fifth Avenue in the 70's with three bedrooms, a 30 × 17-foot living room, and a view of Central Park sells for $7,434 with annual maintenance of $3,591.

New York architect Philip Johnson puts up a glass house at New Canaan, Conn., to serve as his residence.

Houston's Shamrock Hotel opens March 17 (St. Patrick's Day) and eclipses the city's 26-year-old Rice Hotel. The new hotel has been built by wildcat oil millionaire Glenn McCarthy.

New York's prestigious 18-year-old Waldorf-Astoria Hotel is taken over by Conrad Hilton (*see* 1947).

Jamaica's Tower Isle Hotel opens at Ochos Rios as Caribbean resort hotel construction increases.

Boston's John Hancock building is opened September 29 with official ceremonies conducted by Mayor Curley. The 26-story building is the city's tallest and has been built to provide headquarters for the city's leading insurance company (*see* 1862; 1968; Prudential Tower, 1964).

The Nobel Peace Prize is awarded to the UN's FAO chairman Lord John Boyd Orr of Brechin (*see* 1945). Lord Boyd Orr observes that "hunger, which is the worst manifestation of poverty, is also the fundamental cause of the rebellion of the Asians against the economic domination of the European powers, a rebellion that cannot be put down with bombs and guns as long as these peoples remain convinced that their hunger and their poverty are sufferings to which they are not condemned by necessity."

Famine ravages the new People's Republic of China (above). The nation's cereal grain production falls to 110 million tons, down from 150 million before the war when the population was smaller (*see* 1952).

The Rust cotton picker of 1927 goes into mass production at Allis-Chalmers Corp. in Milwaukee and at Ben Pearson, Inc., in Pine Bluff, Ark.

The Brannan Plan advanced by U.S. Secretary of Agriculture Charles F. Brannan, 45, proposes to increase U.S. food production without taking the profit out of farming. The plan employs a formula used by sugar beet and wool producers and would pay farmers directly the difference between the market price of a commodity and the price needed to give the farmer a fair profit, it gives the consumer the benefit

1949 (cont.) of lower prices produced by greater supply, but it provides no payment for the 2 percent of farm operators who earn more than $20,000 per year and sell 25 percent of U.S. farm products. Brannan Plan supporters compare the plan to the minimum wage law of 1938 and the Social Security Law of 1935, but opponents call it socialism and Congress votes it down. The Price Parity Act passed October 31 supports wheat, corn, cotton, rice, and peanut prices at 90 percent of 1910–1914 levels through 1950, 80 to 90 percent through 1951, 75 to 90 percent on a sliding scale thereafter.

Latin America becomes a net grain importer after having been a net exporter for years, but some parts of Latin America are beginning to feel the effects of a "green revolution" (see Borlaug, 1944).

Eight "essential" amino acids are shown to be necessary for human needs, a smaller number than is needed by rats. University of Illinois nutritionist William Cumming Rose, 62, feeds students and rats on diets completely lacking in protein but containing pure amino acids, and he shows that the human body can create additional amino acids if supplied with isoleucine, leucine, lysine, methionine, phenylalinine, threonine, tryptophan, and valine.

Threonine has not been considered an essential amino acid but Rose (above) demonstrates its importance. Since rice is deficient in tryptophan, rice eaters will suffer protein deficiencies unless their diets include a source of threonine (which is abundant in beans).

Meat, dairy products, and sugar remain in short supply in Britain and sales are restricted.

The first edible vegetable-protein fiber made from spun soy isolate is introduced (see 1937). Chemical engineer Robert Boyer files for patents on a process for dehulling soybeans by putting them through a series of rollers that turn them into flakes, bathing the flakes in the hydrocarbon solvent hexane to extract their oil, heating the oil-hexane mixture to drive off the hexane, milling the oil flakes into a flour that is more than 50 percent protein, and further processing the flour to make it 90 percent protein (see 1957).

Prepared cake mixes are introduced by General Mills and Pillsbury.

Pillsbury Bake-Offs are inaugurated to develop recipes using Pillsbury flour. Both men and women are eligible to compete in the contest which will be held annually, and beginning in 1968 contestants will be permitted to use Pillsbury mixes or refrigerated products as well as Pillsbury flour.

Sara Lee Cheese Cake is introduced by Chicago baker Charles Lubin, 44, who believes that a market exists for a refrigerated cream cheese cake. Lubin has founded Kitchens of Sara Lee which he has named after his daughter and which will become one of the world's largest bakeries (see 1953).

Frozen orange juice concentrate sales continue to soar (see 1948). The boom is accelerated by a story in the June issue of *Reader's Digest*.

Minute Maid Orange Juice is promoted by crooner Bing Crosby who acquires 20,000 shares of stock in Vacuum Foods Company on the advice of John Hay Whitney in exchange for a daily 15-minute radio show that pushes concentrate sales. Vacuum Foods renames itself Minute Maid Corp. (see 1947; 1953).

Pepsi-Cola's sugar content is reduced and its recipe is standardized by former Coca-Cola Company executive Alfred N. Steele, 48, who replaces Walter Mack as head of Pepsi (see 1934; 1939). Pepsi-Cola bottlers add their own sugar while Coca-Cola bottlers buy syrup from the Atlanta company that contains sugar. Former advertising agency executive Steele sells Pepsi as "the light refreshment" to make the point that it contains less sugar than Coke (see 1950).

Cookbook   *The Fireside Cookbook* by James Beard.

1950 Communist North Korean forces invade the Republic of South Korea June 25, 4 months after the signing of a Sino-Soviet treaty at Moscow, and a Korean War begins that will continue until late July of 1953. UN Secretary-General Trygve Lie urges UN members to support South Korea June 27 and President Truman that day orders U.S. air and sea forces to "give the Korean government troops cover and support" (below).

Alger Hiss has been found guilty January 25 of having committed perjury in concealing his membership in the Communist party (see 1948). He will go to prison in March of next year after exhausting all appeals.

German-born physicist Klaus Fuchs is found guilty March 1 of having given British atomic secrets to Soviet agents. Fuchs was hired by the British to do nuclear research in 1941 although he was a known Communist, he was a member of the British-American team that developed the atomic bomb beginning in 1943, his work at Los Alamos, N.Mex., made him privy to the design, construction, components, and detonating devices of the bomb, he will serve 10 years in prison, and his U.S. confederate Harry Gold is sentenced to 30 years' imprisonment.

Soviet possession of an atomic bomb is announced March 8 by Marshal K. E. Voroshilov (see 1949).

President Truman has advised the Atomic Energy Commission January 31 to proceed with development of the hydrogen bomb (see 1946, 1952).

King of the Belgians Leopold III returns after 6 years in exile (he was a German prisoner of war from 1940 until 1945), his return July 22 is followed a day later by Socialist demonstrations against him at Brussels he abdicates August 1 after a 16-year reign, and he is succeeded by his 19-year-old son Baudouin.

UN forces land at Inchon in South Korea September 14 and 12 days later recapture Seoul from the Communists who had taken the capital June 28. General

Douglas MacArthur has been commander of UN forces in Korea since July 8 and has directed the counteroffensive.

Chiang Kai-shek has resumed the presidency of Nationalist China following British recognition of the People's Republic of China (*see* 1949).

The United States recognizes Vietnam, supplies arms to Saigon, sends a military mission to advise the Vietnamese on how to use the arms, and signs a military assistance pact with France, Cambodia, Laos, and Vietnam (*see* 1949; 1951).

Chinese Communist forces invade Tibet following rejection of Peking's offer to permit Tibet regional autonomy if she will join the Communist system.

Brazil re-elects former dictator Getulio Vargas president October 3 following economic difficulties including rising inflation that have persisted since Vargas was forced to resign in 1945. Vargas will continue in office until forced to resign again in 1954.

Sweden's Gustavus V dies October 29 at age 92 after a 43-year reign. His 66-year-old son succeeds to the throne and will rule as Gustav VI Adolf until 1973.

President Truman escapes an assassination attempt November 1. White House guards outside the Blair-Lee House, occupied by the Trumans during a White House remodeling, shoot two Puerto Ricans, one fatally, after the Puerto Ricans have killed one guard and wounded another (*see* 1954).

French forces withdraw from the northern frontier of Indo-China November 3, and General MacArthur reports a massing of Chinese Communists in North Korea 2 days later.

Libya prepares for the independence that will take effect beginning in 1952 in accordance with last year's vote by the UN General Assembly. Mohammed Idris el-Senussi is proclaimed king December 3 and will rule as Idris I until 1969.

South Africa refuses to place South West Africa under UN trusteeship.

U.S.-Spanish diplomatic relations are resumed at year's end.

A U.S. state of emergency is proclaimed December 16 following reversals by UN forces in Korea at the hands of the Communist North Koreans.

Chinese forces cross the 38th parallel in Korea December 28, raising the possibility of a war between China and the West (*see* 1951).

Johannesburg has riots January 29 as blacks begin to protest the apartheid program that went into effect last year (*see* 1951).

London dockworkers strike from April 19 to May 1.

A U.S. Communist "witch-hunt" that will continue for the next 4 years is started by U.S. Senator Joseph McCarthy, 41, of Wisconsin who addresses a Republican women's club at Wheeling, W.Va., and claims to have a list of a great many "known Communists"

employed by the State Department. McCarthy is called to testify by the Senate Foreign Relations Committee, his charges are denied by the Senate committee July 20, and McCarthy claims congressional privilege to protect himself from retaliation for his campaign of character assassination (*see* 1951).

The McCarran Act (Control of Communists Act) is passed by Congress September 20 over President Truman's veto. The act calls for severe restrictions against suspected Communists, especially in sensitive positions and during emergencies.

Red Channels by former U.S. Naval Intelligence officer Vincent Hartnett is published anonymously and makes sweeping accusations of Communist subversion in the American entertainment industry (*see* Hollywood Black List, 1947; Adler and Draper, 1949). The paperback book will lead to hearings before the House Committee to Investigate Un-American Activities, scores of actors, choreographers, playwrights, musicians, producers, directors, and screenwriters will be defamed and given no opportunity to defend themselves, dozens will be barred from employment on suspicion of using the films, the stage, radio, and television as vehicles for Communist propaganda. Abe Burrows, Edward Dmytryk, Elia Kazan, Clifford Odets, Jerome Robbins, and others will survive by collaborating with the blacklisters, but others will serve prison terms or at best will have their careers crippled for years by the *Red Channels* accusations. They will include Bertolt Brecht, Alvah Bessie, Charlie Chaplin, Norman Corwin, José Ferrer, John Garfield, Jack Gilford, Lee Grant, Dashiell Hammett, Canada Lee, Ring Lardner, Jr., Arthur Miller, Zero Mostel, Larry Parks, Dore Schary, and Dalton Trumbo (who has moved to Mexico after a year in prison and is grinding out screenplays under a pseudonym) (*see* Lillian Hellman, 1952).

President Truman requests a $10 billion war fund plus internal economic controls July 10. The Defense Production Act passed by Congress September 8 establishes a system of priorities for materials, it provides for wage and price stabilization, and it curbs installment buying.

The Revenue Act passed by Congress September 23 increases income taxes and corporation taxes.

The Celler-Kefauver Amendment to the Clayton Anti-Trust Act of 1914 "puts teeth" into the Clayton Act by curbing mergers of U.S. business firms. Written by congressman Emmanuel Celler of New York and U.S. senator Estes Kefauver of Tennessee, the new law stops companies from buying up stock in other companies, but large corporations will find other ways to achieve mergers and the number of corporate mergers in years to come will dwarf this year's number of 219 (*see* 1960).

General Motors Corporation announces 1949 profits of nearly $656.5 million, a new high for any U.S.

1019

1950 (cont.) corporation. GM signs a 5-year contract May 23 granting United Auto Workers employees pensions and wage boosts.

AF of L membership reaches roughly 8 million, CIO membership 6 million.

The U.S. Gross National Product (GNP) reaches $284 billion, up from $99 billion in 1940 and $103 billion in 1929. Government spending accounts for 21 percent of the total, up from 18 percent in 1940, 10 percent in 1929 (*see* 1960).

The U.S. Consumer Price Index for all goods and services will rise by 10 percent in the next decade.

The Federal Reserve Board estimates December 25 that four out of 10 U.S. families are worth at least $5,000 and 1 in 10 has assets of at least $25,000.

The Ford Foundation distributes $24 million in grants a year after coming into the bulk of its 1943 and 1947 bequests (*see* 1954).

French foreign minister Robert Schuman proposes a plan for pooling West European coal and steel resources. The Schuman Plan will eventually develop into the European Economic Community (*see* 1957).

 The Brink's robbery at Boston January 17 breaks all previous records for losses to armed robbers. Seven men wearing Navy pea jackets, chauffeurs' caps, and crepe-soled shoes enter Boston headquarters of the 91-year-old Brink's Express Company shortly after 7 o'clock in the evening, they don Hallowe'en masks, and they force five Brink's employees to turn over $1,218,211 in cash plus $1,557,000 in money orders. J. Edgar Hoover calls the job a Communist conspiracy, the FBI will spend $129 million in efforts to apprehend the perpetrators, it will arrest 10 men only days before the statute of limitations expires, two will die before coming to trial, eight will be sentenced, but only $50,000 of the take will ever be recovered.

An investigation of U.S. criminal activities undertaken by U.S. Senator from Tennessee Estes Kefauver begins hearings May 26 at Miami. The committee studies testimony by the late Abe "Kid Twist" Reles (*see* 1941) and when it moves its hearings to Washington, N.J., it hears gambler-racketeer William "Willie" Moretti testify that he never heard the word "Mafia" in his life.

The "Ten Most Wanted Criminals" list is issued for the first time in a publicity move by the U.S. Federal Bureau of Investigation (FBI). Several criminals are arrested after being identified by citizens who saw their pictures in newspapers, magazines, or post offices, and in the next 24 years some 300 criminals on the "most wanted" list will be located.

The Federal Bureau of Investigation by U.S. critic Max Lowenthal condemns FBI activities. Lowenthal is subpoenaed by the House Committee to Investigate Un-American Activities and copies of the book are soon hard to find at bookstores.

 U.S. railroads are seized by federal troops August 25 on orders from President Truman to avert a scheduled strike (*see* 1948).

Le Mistral between Paris and Nice goes into service for the French National Railways which has welded and polished seams between track lengths to eliminate the clickety-clack of the wheels. The new electric luxury passenger train has a barbershop and other amenities not found on U.S. trains and covers the 676-mile route in 9 hours, 8 minutes.

Stockholm's T-line subway opens with modern stations, inaugurating a system that will grow to have 60 miles of track with 94 stations.

U.S. railroad trackage for passenger traffic will decline in the next 22 years from 150,000 to 68,000, and electric railway trackage will decline from 9,600 miles to 790 as bus lines replace rail transit and as more and more Americans drive automobiles (*see* General Motors, 1949).

U.S. auto production reaches 6.7 million, up from 5.1 million last year. Used car sales are above 13 million.

Auto registrations show one passenger car for every 3.75 Americans, up from one for every 5.5 in 1930 (*see* 1960). Americans own some 40 million cars, up from 32.6 in 1941, and the figure will more than double in the next 25 years until every U.S. family has an average of 1.4 automobiles.

The Henry J is introduced by Henry J. Kaiser and his son Edgar whose compact car has a four-cylinder engine and goes 25 miles per gallon of gasoline (*see* 1946). A six-cylinder engine will be added, but the Henry J costs nearly $2,000 and is outsold by Volkswagen among the relatively few Americans who will accept compact cars in lieu of secondhand larger cars. Some 127,000 Henry J's will be sold plus another 2,300 that will be sold by Sears, Roebuck under the name Allstate in 1952 and 1953, but the make will be discontinued in 1954 and the larger Kaiser make will expire in 1955.

The United States has 1.68 million miles of surfaced road, up from 1.34 million in 1940, and only 1.31 million miles of dirt road, down from 1.65 (*see* 1960).

A second Tacoma-Narrows bridge opens to traffic across Washington's Puget Sound. The new suspension bridge is an 853-meter span.

New York's Brooklyn-Battery Tunnel whose construction was interrupted by the war opens May 25 and carries nearly twice the traffic that had been anticipated.

New York's Port Authority Bus Terminal opens on Eighth Avenue between 40th and 41st Streets. The new bus terminal will handle upwards of 7,000 buses and 200,000 passengers per week and will be the world's busiest.

Tranquilizer drugs (ataraxics) that eliminate anxiety and excitement without making users too drowsy are developed by Wallace Laboratories of Carter Products, Inc., and by Wyeth Laboratories. Chemists B. J. Ludwig and E. C. Piech at Wallace in New Brunswick, N.J., have synthesized meprobamate (methyl+propyl+carbamate) to produce the new tranquilizers (see Miltown, Equanil, 1954).

A poll of U.S. physicians reveals that penicillin is prescribed for roughly 60 percent of all patients.

Blue Cross programs cover 37 million Americans, up from 6 million in 1940, but most Americans have no health insurance (see 1969; Britain, 1948).

The U.S. ranks tenth among all countries in terms of life expectancy for men, but its ranking will drop sharply in the next decade and a half (see 1967).

Prevention magazine begins publication with articles promising good health to readers who will supplement their diets with rose-hip tablets, dolomite pills, and other vitamin and mineral products. J. I. Rodale of 1948 *Organic Front* fame has been publishing *Organic Farming* since 1942, he prints his anti-establishment digest-sized monthlies on cheap paper, he makes sensational promises based on anecdotal evidence, he receives hearty support from advertisers of diet supplements, and despite the dubious claims made in *Prevention* it will reach a circulation of close to 2 million in the next 25 years by exploiting antipathy to the medical profession.

Pope Pius XII proclaims the dogma of the bodily assumption of the Virgin Mary.

The National Council of the Churches of Christ in the United States is created by 25 Protestant and four Eastern Orthodox church groups with 32 million members.

The first Xerox copying machine is produced by the Haloid Company of Rochester, N.Y. (see Carlson, 1937; Haloid, 1946; model 914, 1960).

The first Japanese tape recorder is produced by Tokyo Tsushin Kogyo (Sony) whose expansion has been financed by Akio Morita (see 1947). Electrical engineer Masaru Ibuka has seen an American tape recorder, he makes one that weighs nearly 40 pounds, uses tape made from rice paper, and sells for nearly $500, and although he has few buyers at first, some 50,000 orders come in when Morita tours Japanese schools and gives demonstrations that persuade teachers to buy the tape recorder as a teaching device (see 1940; 1952).

U.S. television set sales begin a rapid rise (see 1948). By June more than 100 TV stations operate in 38 states, and while the U.S. census for the year shows that 5 million homes have sets, the figure is belied by sales figures that show 8 million sets in use (45 million U.S. homes have radios).

George Bernard Shaw dies at Ayot St. Lawrence, England, November 2 at age 94, leaving part of his vast fortune to develop an improved alphabet with 40 to 44 letters that will represent every sound in the English language.

"Peanuts" by *St. Paul Pioneer Press* cartoonist Charles Monroe Schulz, 27, is accepted by the United Press Syndicate and begins appearing in eight newspapers. Schulz's comic strip characters Charlie Brown ("good grief"), Lucy, Snoopy (a dog), Linus, Schroeder, and Pig Pen will make "Peanuts" popular with readers of more than 900 newspapers by 1970 and will be the basis of books, television shows, and countless manufactured items.

Nonfiction *The Lonely Crowd* by University of Chicago social sciences professor David Riesman, Jr., 41, and sociologists Reuel Denney and Nathan Glazer attracts wide attention with its analysis of inner-directed, outer-directed, and other-directed character types. Nineteenth century Americans were typically inner-directed, say the authors, and were driven by personal ambition to be highly competitive, even ruthless, in their attempts to master their worlds. Twentieth century Americans are more likely to be "other-directed," working to get ahead within a group while adjusting to the needs of others, so where earlier Americans pioneered new production efficiency, the emphasis is now on efficient administration of established businesses and on salesmanship (see Whyte, 1956); *The Human Use of Human Beings* by Norbert Wiener warns against the abuse of the new technology; *Worlds in Collision* by Russian-American physician Immanuel Velikovsky, 55, draws on mythology, archaeology, astronomy, and other disciplines to evolve a theory that the Earth barely avoided colliding with several other celestial bodies sometime about 3,200 B.C.. The curator of New York's Hayden Planetarium announces that he will stage a star show to illustrate the book's thesis and is summarily dismissed.

Fiction *The Short Life* (*La vida breve*) by Uruguayan novelist Juan Carlos Onetti, 41; *The Moon and the Bonfire* (*La luna e il falo*) by Cesare Pavese; *Anton Wachter* (eight novels) by Simon Vestdijk; *Barrabas* by Par Lagerkvist whose sinister robber represents mankind, lacking the capacities of Christ but aware of its lack; *The Wall* by John Hersey deals with the 1943 Warsaw ghetto uprising against the Nazis; *A Town Like Alice* by Nevil Shute; *The Grass Is Singing* by Rhodesian novelist Doris Lessing, 31; *The Preacher and the Slave* by Wallace Stegner deals with the late labor organizer Joe Hill; *Across the River and into the Trees* by Ernest Hemingway; *Nothing* by Henry Green.

Poetry *Canto General* by Pablo Neruda who lived through the Civil War in Spain from 1935 to 1939, returned to Chile in 1945 after working for Spanish Republican refugees at Paris, and has been publishing his epic hymn to virgin America since 1947.

Juvenile *The Thirteen Clocks* by James Thurber.

Painting *King David* by Marc Chagall; *Corps de Dame* by Jean Dubuffet; *The Constructors* by Fernand Léger; *Zulma* by Henri Matisse; *Chief* by Franz Kline; *Tundra* by Barnett Newman. Max Beckmann dies at New York December 27 at age 66.

Korean hostilities lowered the temperature of the cold war to chilly new levels, raising fears of an atomic war.

Sculpture *Seven Figures and a Head* by Alberto Giacometti; *The Goat* by Pablo Picasso.

Polaroid Corporation replaces its sepia print of 1947 with a black-and-white print, but the new print fades and a crisis develops until company chemists come up with a new film. Polaroid introduces a new "electric eye" shutter that will automatically select shutter speeds between 1/10 and 1/1,000 of a second for the camera's fixed F/5.4 lens. Polaroid contracts with U.S. Time Corporation to produce Polaroid Land Cameras (*see* Timex, 1946; high-speed film, 1960).

The Eastman Kodak Colorama at New York's Grand Central Station presents spectacular scenic views 18 feet high and 60 feet in length back-lighted by 600 metal arc lamps that burn 24 hours a day.

Theater *The Member of the Wedding* by Carson McCullers 1/5 at New York's Empire Theater, with Ethel Waters, Julie Harris, and Brandon de Wilde in a drama based on the 1946 McCullers novel, 501 perfs.; *Venus Observed* by Christopher Fry 1/18 at the St. James's Theatre, London; *The Cocktail Party* by T. S. Eliot 1/21 at New York's Henry Miller Theater, with Alec Guinness, Kathleen Nesbitt, Irene Worth, 409 perfs.; *Come Back, Little Sheba* by U.S. playwright William Motte Inge, 37, 2/15 at New York's Booth Theater, with Shirley Booth, Sidney Blackmer, Joan Loring in a play that was given its first production last year by the Theatre Guild at its Westport, Conn., summer playhouse, 191 perfs.; *Judith* (*Giuditta*) by Carlo Terron 5/2 at Milan's Teatro Nuovo; *The Bald Prima Donna* (*La Cantatrice chauve*) by French playwright Eugène Ionesco, 38, 5/11 at the Théâtre des Noctambules, Paris (Ionesco uses meaningless platitudes to convey the sterility of modern life); *Affairs of State* by French playwright Louis Verneuil 9/25 at New York's Royale Theater, with Reginald Owen, Celeste Holm, Sheppard Strudwick, 610 perfs.; *The Rehearsal (La*

répétition, ou L'amour Pani) by Jean Anouilh 10/25 at the Théâtre Marigny, Paris; *Trial of the Innocent* (*Processo agli innocenti*) by Carlo Terron 11/7 at Milan's Teatro Oden; *The Country Girl* by Clifford Odets 11/10 at New York's Lyceum Theater, with Paul Kelly, Uta Hagen, 235 perfs.; *Bell, Book, and Candle* by John Van Druten 11/14 at New York's Ethel Barrymore Theater, with Lili Palmer, Rex Harrison, 233 perfs.

Films Billy Wilder's *Sunset Boulevard* with Gloria Swanson, William Holden, Erich von Stroheim; David Lean's *Breaking Through the Sound Barrier* with Ralph Richardson, Ann Todd, Nigel Patrick; Robert Hamer's *Kind Hearts and Coronets* with Alec Guinness; Charles Crichton's *The Lavender Hill Mob* with Alec Guinness; John and Ray Boulting's *Seven Days to Noon* with Barry Jones, Olive Sloane; Antony Pelassier's *The Rocking Horse Winner* with Valerie Hobson, John Mills, John Howard Davies; Max Ophuls's *La Ronde;* Jean Cocteau's *Orpheus* with Jean Marais; Giuseppe De Santis's *Bitter Rice* with Silvana Mangano, Vittorio Gassman, Raf Vallone; Michelangelo Antonioni's *Story of a Love Affair* with Ferdinando Sarmi, Lucia Bose; Alf Sjoberg's *Miss Julie* with Anita Bjork, Ulf Palme; Fred Zinneman's *The Men* with Marlon Brando; Joseph Mankiewicz's *All About Eve* with Bette Davis, Anne Baxter, Celeste Holm; John Ford's *Wagonmaster;* Anthony Asquith's *The Winslow Boy* with Robert Donat, Margaret Leighton; Michael Gordon's *Cyrano de Bergerac* with Jose Ferrer; John Huston's *The Asphalt Jungle* with Sterling Hayden, Louis Calhern, Jean Hagen, Marilyn Monroe (née Norma Jean Mortensen), 24; Vincente Minnelli's *The Father of the Bride* with Spencer Tracy, Elizabeth Taylor, Joan Bennett.

Television shows *What's My Line* 2/2 on CBS stations, with emcee John Charles Daley and panelists Arlene Francis, Dorothy Kilgallen, anthologist Louis Untermeyer who try to guess the occupations of guests. Publisher Bennet Cerf will replace Untermeyer in 1952 and the show will continue until 9/3/67; *Your Show of Shows* debuts on NBC stations with comedians Sid Caesar, Imogene Coca, Carl Reiner, and Howard Morris. Developed by NBC executive Sylvester "Pat" Weaver, Jr., 41, the show will continue with 160 weekly programs until 1954.

Opera *The Consul* 3/15 at New York, with music by Gian Carlo Menotti; *The Triumph of St. Joan* 5/9 at Sarah Lawrence College, Bronxville, N.Y., with music by Norman Dello Joio; *Bolivar* 5/12 at the Paris Opéra, with music by Darius Milhaud.

Ballet *Judith* 1/4 at Louisville, with Martha Graham, music by William Schuman; *The Age of Anxiety* 2/26 at the New York City Center, with Jerome Robbins, music by Leonard Bernstein.

First performances   Concerto for Piano and Orchestra by Francis Poulenc 1/6 at Boston's Symphony Hall, with Poulenc as soloist; Concerto for Piano and Orchestra by Paul Creston 1/11 at Washington, D.C.; *Timon of Athens* symphonic portrait by David Diamond 2/1 at Louisville; Concerto for Violin and Orchestra by William Schuman 2/10 at Boston's Symphony Hall, with Isaac Stern as soloist; Sinfonietta in E major by Paul Hindemith 3/1 at Louisville; Concerto No. 4 for Piano and Orchestra by Darius Milhaud 3/3 at Boston's Symphony Hall; Concerto for Cello by Virgil Thomson 3/21 at Philadelphia's Academy of Music; *Variations and Fugue on a Theme by Purcell* by Benjamin Britten 5/2 at Boston's Symphony Hall; Concerto for French Horn and Orchestra by Paul Hindemith 6/8 at Baden-Baden; *Fantasia (Quasi Variazione)* on the "Old 104th" Psalm Tune for Piano, Orchestra, Organ, and Chorus by Ralph Vaughan Williams 9/16 at Gloucester's Three Choirs Festival; Symphony No. 3 by Paul Creston 10/27 at Worcester, Mass.; Symphony No. 3 by David Diamond 10/30 at Boston's Symphony Hall; Concerto for Clarinet, String Orchestra, Harp, and Piano by Aaron Copland 11/6 in an NBC Symphony Orchestra broadcast, with Benny Goodman as soloist; *Concerto Grosso* by Ralph Vaughan Williams 11/18 at London; Short Symphony by U.S. composer Howard Swanson, 41, 11/23 at New York's Carnegie Hall; Concerto for Clarinet and Orchestra by Paul Hindemith 12/11 at Philadelphia's Academy of Music, with Benny Goodman as soloist.

Cantata   *On Guard for Peace* by Serge Prokofiev 12/19 at Moscow.

Washington Post critic Paul Hume writes a disparaging review of a song recital by Margaret Truman and receives a letter in longhand from the President on White House stationery dated December 6: "Mr. Hume: I have just read your lousy review of Margaret's concert. I've come to the conclusion that you are an eight-ulcer man on four-ulcer pay.... Some day I hope to meet you. When that happens, you'll need a new nose, a lot of beefsteak for black eyes, and perhaps a supporter below."

Broadway musicals   *Call Me Madam* 10/12 at the Imperial Theater, with Ethel Merman as U.S. Ambassador to Luxembourg Perle Mesta, music and lyrics by Irving Berlin, songs that include "Hostess with the Mostes' on the Ball," "It's a Lovely Day Today," "The Ocarina," "The Best Thing for You," 644 perfs.; *Guys and Dolls* 11/24 at the 46th Street Theater, with Robert Alda, Vivian Blaine, Sam Levene, Isabel Bigley, music and lyrics by Frank Loesser, songs that include "Luck Be a Lady," "Fugue for Tinhorns," "I've Never Been in Love Before," "A Bushel and a Peck," "Adelaide's Lament," "Sue Me," "If I Were a Bell," 1,200 perfs.; *Out of this World* 12/21 at the New Century Theater, with William Eythe, Charlotte Greenwood, Peggy Rea, music and lyrics by Cole Porter, songs that include "Use Your Imagination," 157 perfs.

The Mambo is introduced from Cuba to U.S. dance-floors where it will be a standard Latin dance step.

Popular songs   "Dearie" by Bob Hilliard and Dave Mann; "Hoop-Dee-Doo" by Frank Loesser; "If I Knew You Were Comin' I'd 'Ave Baked a Cake" by Al Hoffman, Bob Merrill, Clem Watts; "It's So Nice to Have a Man Around the House" by Harold Spina, lyrics by Jack Elliott; "Music! Music! Music!" by Stephen Weiss and Bernie Baum; "My Heart Cries for You" by Percy Faith and Carl Sigman; "Rag Mop" by Johnnie Lee Wills and Deacon Anderson; "Sam's Song" by Lew Quadling, lyrics by Jack Elliott; "Sentimental Me" by Jim Morehead and Jimmy Cassin; "Sunshine Cake" by James Van Heusen, lyrics by Jimmy Burke (for the film *Riding High*); "Cherry Pink and Apple Blossom White" by Louiguy, lyrics by Jacques Larme (English lyrics by Mack David); "Silver Bells" by Jay Livingston and Ray Evans (for the film *The Lemon Drop Kid*).

New York's Birdland opens on Broadway with alto saxophonist Charles Christopher "Charlie" Parker, 30, who moved to Harlem from his native Kansas City in 1939 and has become known as "Yardbird" or simply "Bird" through his "bepop" progressive jazz style. Parker will be a leading exponent of bepop until his death March 12, 1955, after making his last appearance at Birdland.

Uruguay edges Brazil 5 to 4 and wins the fourth World Cup football (soccer) competition, the first held since 1938, as it won the first one in 1930. The cup is officially called the Jules Rimet Trophy, some 200,000 spectators fill the three tiers of Rio's unfinished Maracana Stadium for the opening games and the finals, but Germany is excluded.

Yonkers Raceway opens at Yonkers, N.Y., with grandstand seats for 15,885 harness racing fans. Wolverine Harness Raceway opens at Livonia, Mich., with grandstand seats for 12,000.

Florence Chadwick swims the English Channel August 20 and beats the record set by Gertrude Ederle in 1926. The 31-year-old San Diego stenographer crosses from France to England in 13 hours, 20 minutes (*see* 1951).

The New York Yankees win the World Series by defeating the Philadelphia Phillies 4 games to 0 after the Phillies have won the National League pennant on the last day of the regular season by defeating the Brooklyn Dodgers with a 10th inning three-run homer by Dick Sisler.

Navy defeats Army in a 14 to 2 upset for the first Navy football victory since 1947 and the first loss by the West Point cadets in 29 games.

Orlon is introduced by E. I. du Pont de Nemours which began developing the wool-like polymerized acrylonitrile fiber in 1941 under the direction of William Hale Church of 1926 waterproof cellophane fame (*see* Dacron, Terylene, 1941).

1950 (cont.)   Cotton's share of the U.S. textile market falls to 65 percent, down from 80 percent in 1940, and man-made fibers—mostly rayons and acetates—increase their share to more than 20 percent (*see* 1960).

Miss Clairol is introduced by Lawrence Gelb's Clairol Company whose new hair-coloring takes only half the application time needed by other hair colorings (*see* 1931; "Does She or Doesn't She," 1956).

Maxey Jarman's General Shoe Corporation acquires W. L. Douglas of Brockton, Mass., and begins a series of other acquisitions that will include Johnston & Murphy (*see* 1932; 1953; Celler-Kefauver amendment, above).

Otis Elevator Company installs the first passenger elevators with self-opening doors in the Atlantic Refining building at Dallas. Self-service elevators will force thousands of elevator operators to seek other means of employment.

New York's United Nations Secretariat building is completed by Wallace R. Harrison and consultants to provide offices for the UN's 3,400 employees on land overlooking the East River.

Twelve new office buildings are completed in New York with more than 4 million square feet of floor space.

Manhattan House opens in New York between Second and Third Avenues from 65th Street north to 66th. The handsome new apartment block has been designed by Skidmore, Owings & Merrill with an assist from Mayer & Whittlesey.

U.S. suburban land values will rise in the next decade by 100 percent to 3,760 percent as middle-class whites desert the cities (*see* Levittown, 1947).

Bermuda's Castle Harbour Hotel opens in March with 300 rooms.

Smokey the Bear becomes a symbol for forest fire prevention. Found clinging to a charred tree in New Mexico's Lincoln National Forest, the badly burned black bear cub orphan is flown by rangers to Santa Fe, his burned paws are treated, and he is nursed back to health at the home of a game warden, he is shipped to the National Zoo at Washington, D.C., and posters appear showing Smokey and carrying the message, "Only You Can Prevent Forest Fires." Smokey will be officially retired as the Forest Service symbol in May of 1975 and will die in late 1976.

Park District National Park is designated December 28 as the first British national park.

A Chinese agrarian reform law is promulgated by party leader Liu Shao-Chi who says, "The industrialization of China should be based on the vast market of rural China." It will be impossible to industrialize the new China without radical agrarian reform, he maintains, but while Mao Tse-tung says that China's future lies in mobilizing the peasantry, Liu follows Marxist orthodoxy and insists that large farms depend on chemical fertilizers, electrification, tractors

and other farm machinery, agronomists, and engineers. Most of the nation's budget goes to industrialization, but China's agricultural output nevertheless begins a rapid rise (*see* 1949; 1952).

U.S. farm prices will rise 28 percent in the next year as the Korean War (above) fuels inflation and boosts food prices.

The average U.S. farm worker produces enough food and fiber for 15.5 people, up from 7 in 1900 (*see* 1963).

The percentage of the U.S. available work force employed on the land falls to 11.6 percent, down from 25 percent in 1933, and 20 percent of U.S. farmers will quit the land in the next 12 years (*see* 1960).

Insects damage $4 billion worth of U.S. crops, consuming more food than is grown in New England, New York, New Jersey, and Pennsylvania combined.

The boll weevil which has destroyed at least $200 million worth of U.S. cotton each year since 1909 destroys $750 million worth.

More than 75 percent of U.S. farms are electrified, up from 33 percent in 1940.

The first calf born of a virgin mother is born at the University of Wisconsin (*see* rabbit, 1935). Transplantation of fertilized ova will permit new developments in animal breeding.

World fisheries' production reaches its prewar level of 20 million tons per year (*see* 1960).

Oyster production from the coast of Connecticut south to New Jersey reaches 3.3 million bushels (*see* 1966).

Only 82 Atlantic salmon are landed on the Maine coast, less than a thousand pounds as compared with 150,000 in 1889. Dams and pollution have reduced spawning (*see* Danish fishermen, 1964).

The Columbia River Packers Association joins with Pacific American Fisheries to form the Excursion Inlet Packing Company and build a plant 60 miles west of Juneau, Alaska (*see* 1945). CRPA built a cannery at Bellingham, Wash., in 1946 to process fish from Puget Sound and the Fraser River, and it will acquire the Hawaiian Tuna Packers Association tuna cannery at Honolulu in 1956 to can the skipjack tuna known in the islands as aku (*see* 1959).

Composition of Foods—Raw, Processed, Prepared (Handbook No. 8) is issued by the U.S. Department of Agriculture and lists 751 items that include some frozen foods (*see* 1895; 1963).

Look Younger, Live Longer by German-American food faddist Gaylord Hauser, 51, promises health miracles to those who will eat the "wonder foods" yogurt, wheat germ, brewers' yeast, blackstrap molasses, and powdered skim milk. A condensation of the book appears in *The Reader's Digest* and boosts demand for the "wonder foods" as the book becomes a best seller (*see* below).

A House Select Committee on Chemicals in Food and Cosmetics begins 3 years of hearings at Washington under the chairmanship of Brooklyn, N.Y., Democrat James J. Delaney (*see* Swanson, 1956).

✗ "Not in a quarter century have the food markets of Paris been fuller or more tempting," writes Genêt (Janet Flanner, 53) in *The New Yorker* magazine. "In the Rue du Faubourg–Saint-Denis, there is a two-hundred-yard stretch of food shops and street barrows. The hucksters shout their prices and the shop apprentices have become barkers, standing at the shop doors and bawling about the luscious wares inside.... The street barrows are filled with hairy leeks and potential salads. The Rue du Faubourg–Saint-Denis is not a rich district of the city, but these days it offers a Lucullan supply. Food is still what Parisians buy if they can. It is a nervous means of getting satisfaction, a holdover from the lean days of the Occupation."

Dannon Yogurt sales are stimulated by the Gayelord Hauser claims (above) (*see* Metzger, 1942). The company added a strawberry-flavored yogurt in 1947 and a vanilla-flavored yogurt in 1948 to augment its plain yogurt, but while Dannon will move to a larger plant in Long Island City next year, its sales will slump in 1952 as the Hauser-inspired yogurt fad wanes (sales will nevertheless remain at higher levels).

Kretschmer Wheat Germ sales double to $1.5 million as Saginaw, Mich., wheat germ producer Charles H. Kretschmer, Jr., cashes in on the boom started by Gayelord Hauser (above).

Cyclamates are introduced commercially for use as artificial sweeteners (*see* Sveda, 1937).

Sucaryl is introduced by Abbott Laboratories. Sales of the cyclamate-based artificial sweetener will reach $16 million by 1970 and will account for 20 percent of the direct market for cyclamates.

Sugar Pops breakfast food is introduced by the Kellogg Company (*see* 1942; 1952).

Coca-Cola's share of the U.S. cola beverage market is 69 percent, Pepsi-Cola's is 15 percent, but Coke's share will drop in the next 10 years to 52 percent while Pepsi's share will rise to 31 percent (*see* 1949).

Nineteen synthetic colors are used in U.S. foods. The number will decline to 11 by 1967.

Green Giant Company is adopted as the name of the Minnesota Valley Canning Company whose Green Giant symbol has helped make it the largest U.S. canner of peas and corn (*see* 1936; beans, 1958).

Cudahy Packing Company moves from Chicago back to Omaha (*see* 1910). Headquarters will be moved to Phoenix, Ariz., in 1965.

A federal tax of 10 cents per pound on U.S. margarine is removed as are all federal restrictions on coloring margarine yellow. Butter is in such short supply that retail prices often top $1 per pound and U.S. consumers turn increasingly to margarine whose average retail price is 33 cents per pound versus an average of 73 cents for butter.

Betty Crocker's Picture Cookbook is a U.S. best seller (*see* General Mills, 1936).

Minute Rice is introduced by General Foods.

New York's Coach House Restaurant is purchased by Greek-American engineer Leon Lianides who will study in France and will make the Waverley Place restaurant (located in a former carriage house of John Wanamaker) a top New York dining spot.

The Diners Club is founded to give credit card privileges at a group of 27 New York area restaurants. Entrepreneur Ralph Schneider, 40, starts with 200 cardholders who pay an annual membership fee for the card that will be accepted within a few years at hotels, motels, car rental agencies, airline ticket counters, and retail shops as well as at restaurants in most of the United States and in many foreign countries (*see* 1965).

👫 The population of the world reaches 2.52 billion.

The U.S. population has doubled since 1900 and while the urban population will increase by only 1.5 percent in the decade ahead, the suburban population will increase by 44 percent as Americans flee to the suburbs, partly to escape the decaying social milieu of the inner cities.

1951 The South Korean capital of Seoul falls January 4 to ✗ North Korean and Communist Chinese forces who penetrated UN defenses on the 38th parallel at the end of last year but who lose the capital to UN forces March 14.

General MacArthur offers to discuss an end to the Korean conflict with Peking, but his offer is rejected March 29 and MacArthur makes public his call for air attacks on the People's Republic of China.

General MacArthur is relieved of his command April 11 by President Truman. The 71-year-old general returns to Washington, he is hailed as a hero and is urged to run for election as President, but he retires to private life after a farewell address to a joint session of Congress in which he quotes a World War I British Army song: "Old soldiers never die; they simply fade away."

A Korean cease-fire and armistice talks are proposed June 23 by Soviet UN representative Jacob A. Malik, an offer to negotiate an armistice is broadcast by U.S. General Matthew B. Ridgway, truce talks open July 8 at Kaesong, but UN aircraft allegedly bomb Kaesong, and negotiations break off August 23.

A U.S.-Philippine mutual defense pact is signed August 30 and is the first of several security pacts among anti-Communist powers in the Far East.

A U.S.-Japanese mutual security pact is signed September 8. U.S. troops are permitted to remain in Japan indefinitely to assist UN operations in the Far East and no other nation is to have Japanese bases without U.S. consent.

1951 (cont.) Communist attacks on Hanoi in French Indo-China are repulsed by General De Lattre de Tassigny and the Communists revert to guerilla tactics (*see* 1953).

Iran's senate and majlis have named Mohammed Mossadegh premier April 29. The leader of the extremist National Front will hold power for nearly 15 months (*see* below).

Jordan's Abdullah has been assassinated July 20 at Jerusalem, his heir Emir Talal is proclaimed king by the national assembly September 5, but the new king will be declared unfit to rule within the next year (*see* 1949; 1953).

Egyptian restrictions that prevent Israel-bound ships from using the Suez Canal are protested by a resolution of the United Nations Security Council, but the U.S.S.R., the People's Republic of China, and India abstain. Egypt abrogates her 1936 alliance with Britain October 27 and abrogates also the condominium agreement of 1899 covering the Sudan.

"Heartbreak Ridge" in Korea has fallen to UN forces September 23 after 37 days of bitter fighting to gain the strategic heights north of Yanggu.

New peace negotiations are begun October 25 at Panmunjom, but a 30-day "trial" armistice ends December 27.

Britain's Labour government falls in the general elections after 6 years in power. Winston Churchill becomes prime minister once again at age 77, but most of the social programs innovated by the Labour government remain in place under the new Conservative government that takes office October 27.

British diplomats Guy Burgess and Donald Maclean have fled in late June to the Soviet Union and are suspected of having transmitted classified information to the Communists. British double agent H. A. R. "Kim" Philby has told Burgess and Maclean that their cover has been blown and that British intelligence agents are moving in on them (*see* 1963).

Found guilty of having sold U.S. atomic secrets to Soviet agents are Ethel Rosenberg, 35, her 34-year-old husband Julius, and their friend Morton Sobell. Mrs. Rosenberg's brother David Greenglass worked at the Los Alamos nuclear research station in New Mexico (*see* 1953; Fuchs, Gold, 1950).

U.S. federal agencies are directed by President Truman August 10 to support a program that would disperse industrial plants in order to prevent total destruction in the event of a nuclear war.

More stringent classification of security information by government agencies is ordered by President Truman September 25.

An atomic bomb is exploded November 1 over the Nevada desert in the first U.S. war maneuver involving troops and nuclear weapons.

Former secretary of state George C. Marshall, now 70, is called a Communist agent by U.S. Senator Joseph McCarthy who has been unable to prove or even to show any real evidence that anyone in the State Department is guilty of any subversive activity (*see* 1950). McCarthy has been attacked by U.S. Senator Millard Tydings of Maryland for perpetrating "a fraud and a hoax," but he continues his campaign of accusations (*see* 1954).

The world's first thermonuclear reaction is set off May 8 by U.S. nuclear scientists headed by Edward Teller.

The first power-producing nuclear fission (atomic) reactor is built by the U.S. Atomic Energy Commission established in 1946 (*see* 1958; Calder Hall, 1956; Jersey Central Power and Light, 1963).

Iran's oil industry is nationalized by the new extremist National Front government headed by Mohammed Mossadegh (above) who abrogates a 1933 concession treaty signed with London. The decree of nationalization takes effect May 2 retroactive to March 20, Britain appeals to the International Court of Justice May 26, the court rules against Iran July 5, President Truman appeals for a compromise and sends W. Averell Harriman to urge a settlement, Iranian forces occupy the Abadan oil fields September 27, evacuation of Anglo-Iranian Oil Company personnel from Abadan is completed October 4, Iran agrees December 10 to resubmit the issue to the International Court of Justice, and the dispute will continue until August of 1954.

John Paul Getty gains control of Skelly Oil Company and of Tidewater Oil which has been renamed Mission Corporation (*see* 1949). Getty thus gains control also of a complex of real estate, insurance, marketing, and manufacturing firms that include Spartan Aircraft Company (*see* Getty Oil, 1956).

A Pennsylvania Railroad derailment at Woodbridge, N.J., kills 85 and injures hundreds as a temporary track proves inadequate for the train's speed.

The United States has 8.62 million trucks, up from 4.85 million in 1941 (*see* 1961).

Power steering is installed in 10,000 Chrysler Crown Imperial sedans and convertibles. The mechanism patented by Francis Wright Davis in 1926 has been used in U.S. Army armored vehicles during World War II, the patents have expired, and General Motors will begin mass production of power steering next year using improved Davis designs.

New York's First Avenue becomes one-way northbound and Second Avenue becomes one-way southbound beginning June 4 as U.S. cities try to speed up traffic flow in streets choked with trucks and passenger cars (*see* parking, 1955; Seventh and Eighth Avenues, 1954).

The New Jersey Turnpike opens November 5 to speed traffic between New York and Philadelphia. The 118-mile toll road will receive 2 billion tolls in its first 25 years.

President Truman appoints a commission to study U.S. health needs and to recommend ways for meeting those needs.

Ergotism breaks out August 17 in the south of France where people in the town of Pont-Saint-Esprit have eaten rye bread made by baker Pierre Briand and other bakers. 300 people are affected, 50 go insane, and three die in the largest epidemic since the Russian outbreak of 1926 (see LSD, 1943). French wage levels only now regain their Depression levels of 1938, and the ergotism episode is in part a consequence of heavy dietary reliance on cheap rye bread (see Monet, 1953).

South Africans are color-classified and issued cards by the Department of the Interior to prove that they are white, black, or colored as the government moves to enforce its apartheid policies (see 1949).

Florida NAACP state secretary Harry T. Moore and his wife Harriet are killed Christmas night in a bombing of their house at Mims. Moore has protested the failure of Florida's governor Millard F. Caldwell to "take effective action" following the lynching of Jesse James Payne in 1946, his killing is thought to be associated with that protest 3 years ago, but no arrests will ever be made in the Moore killings.

The largest U.S. peacetime budget in history is submitted by President Truman January 15 with much of the $71.6 billion earmarked to meet the Korean emergency (above).

Stock purchase margin requirements are raised by the Federal Reserve Board January 16 from 50 to 75 percent in a move to discourage credit expansion.

U.S. wages and salaries are frozen January 26 by the Wage Stabilization Board which orders the second wage-salary freeze in less than 9 years.

"Margin" profit ceilings on more than 200,000 consumer items are ordered February 27 by the Office of Price Stabilization.

State "fair trade" price-fixing laws are ruled not binding on retailers in a Supreme Court decision May 21. Price wars begin immediately and department stores are mobbed.

The Defense Production Act is extended July 31, but with reduced anti-inflation powers.

U.S. income tax receipts reach a record high of $56.1 billion.

The W. K. Kellogg Foundation established in 1930 becomes a major philanthropic organization as breakfast food pioneer Will Keith Kellogg dies October 6 at age 90 and leaves the bulk of his fortune to the foundation. Its assets for more than 20 years will be surpassed only by those of the Rockefeller and Ford Foundations and the Carnegie Corporation.

The Univac computer is introduced by Remington Rand Corporation which has acquired the ENIAC electronic computer of 1946, has renamed it, and introduces it on a commercial basis for use by business firms and scientific laboratories (see IBM, 1953; Sperry-Rand, 1955).

Numbers in Color (*Nombres en Couleur*) by Belgian educator Emile-Georges Cuisenaire, 60, explains the author's method of teaching children to count by having them associate numbers and colors and thus learn the basics of addition and subtraction. Colored wooden Cuisenaire rods range in length from 1 to 10 centimeters and will be used throughout the world.

CBS broadcasts color television programs on a commercial basis beginning June 25, but conventional sets cannot pick up the signals in black and white (see Goldmark, RCA, 1954).

A new coaxial cable carries the first transcontinental U.S. television broadcast September 4.

See It Now with Edward R. Murrow debuts live coast to coast November 18 on CBS stations via coaxial cable (above).

Bell Telephone gives transistors their first commercial application October 10, using them in a trunk dialing apparatus and initiating long-distance "direct dial" telephone service (see transistor, 1948).

The volume of U.S. telephone calls is so great that without dial systems it would require nearly half the nation's adult population to operate switchboards (see 1919).

Local U.S. telephone call rates begin jumping from 5 cents to 10 cents. By 1953 the rate will be 10 cents in every state except Rhode Island, and while that state will go the dime rate in 1957 Louisiana will return to the nickel rate in 1956.

La Prensa is suppressed April 13 by Argentine dictator Juan Peron who reacts to criticism by the 82-year-old newspaper and who easily puts down a minor military uprising in late September.

"Dennis the Menace" is launched by U.S. cartoonist Henry King "Hank" Ketcham, 30, who has been inspired by a neighbor's comment on his 5-year-old son. The new cartoon strip meets with almost instant success and will be syndicated to some 750 papers.

Nonfiction *God and Man at Yale: The Superstition of Academic Freedom* by 1950 graduate William Frank Buckley, 25.

Fiction *The Rebel* (*L'Homme Revolte*) by Albert Camus who refutes communism because it leads to totalitarianism; *Adam, Where Art Thou?* (*Wo warst du Adam?*) by German novelist Heinrich Böll, 34, who was wounded in World War II and gives a vivid account of the Nazi collapse; *The Conformist* (*Il Conformista*) by Alberto Moravia; *The Catcher in the Rye* by U.S. novelist J. D. (Jerome David) Salinger, 32, whose hero Holden Caulfield seeks the pure and the good and eschews the "phonies"; *From Here to Eternity* by U.S. novelist James Jones, 30, who has served in the regular army and was encouraged by the late Maxwell Perkins at Scribner's; *The Caine Mutiny* by U.S. novelist Herman Wouk, 36, who will

1951 (cont.) win a 1952 Pulitzer prize; *Lie Down in Darkness* by U.S. novelist William Styron, 26; *Mr. Beluncle* by English novelist V. S. (Victor Sawden) Pritchett, 51; *The Loved and the Lost* by Morley Callaghan; *The Troubled Air* by Irwin Shaw who deals with the Communist witchhunt in America; *A Question of Upbringing* by Anthony Powell begins a 12-volume *roman à fleuve; The Ballad of the Sad Cafe* (stories) by Carson McCullers; *The Grass Harp* (stories) by Truman Capote.

Poetry *The Mills of the Kavanaughs* by Robert Lowell.

Painting *Christ of St. John of the Cross* by Salvador Dali; *Massacre in Korea* by Pablo Picasso; *T-1951-I* by Hans Hartung; *The Frozen Sands No. 1* by Adolph Gottlieb; *#3-1951* by Clifford Still; Diego Rivera completes murals for Mexico City's waterworks. John F. Sloan dies at Hanover, N.H., September 7 at age 80.

Sculpture *Baboon and Young* by Pablo Picasso.

Theater *Second Threshold* by Philip Barry 1/2 at New York's Morosco Theater, with Clive Brook, Betsy von Furstenberg, 126 perfs.; *The Rose Tattoo* by Tennessee Williams 2/3 at New York's Martin Beck Theater, with Maureen Stapleton, Don Murray, 306 perfs.; *Count Oderland (Graf Oderland)* by Max Frisch 2/10 at Zurich's Schauspielhaus; *The Lesson (La leçon)* by Eugène Ionesco 2/20 at the Théâtre de Poche, Paris; *The Autumn Garden* by Lillian Hellman 3/7 at New York's Coronet Theater, with Florence Eldredge, Kent Smith, Jane Wyatt, 101 perfs.; *A Sleep of Prisoners* by Christopher Fry 4/3 at Oxford's University Church; *Don Juan's Wife (La moglie di don Giovanni)* by Edouardo De Filippo 5/5 at Turin; *The Love of Four Colonels* by English playwright Peter Ustinov, 29, 5/23 at Wyndham's Theatre, London; *The Fourposter* by Jan de Hartog 10/24 at New York's Ethel Barrymore Theater, with Jessica Tandy, Hume Cronyn, 632 perfs.; *I Am a Camera* by John Van Druten 11/28 at New York's Empire Theater, with Julie Harris as Sally Bowles, William Prince as Christopher Isherwood, 262 perfs.

U.S. television drama *Search for Tomorrow* 9/9 on CBS (daytime); *Love of Life* 9/9 on CBS (daytime); *I Love Lucy* 10/15 on CBS, with Lucille Ball whose show will continue to 5/6/1957; *Kukla, Fran & Ollie* becomes an NBC Network show after having appeared on local Chicago television. Live actress Fran Allison plays opposite puppets worked by Burr Tillstrom in programs that will run for 3 years on NBC and then for 3 years on ABC-TV.

United Artists, Inc., loses $100,000 per week and is taken over from its surviving partners Charlie Chaplin and Mary Pickford by New York lawyers Arthur B. Krim, 41, and Robert S. Benjamin, 42. They acquire a 50 percent interest on condition that they make the 32-year-old firm profitable by 1954.

Films John Huston's *The African Queen* with Katharine Hepburn, Humphrey Bogart, Robert Morley; Alfred Hitchcock's *Strangers on a Train* with Robert Walker, Farley Granger; John Boulting's *The Magic Box* with Robert Donat and Maria Schell in a biography of motion picture pioneer William Friese-Greene (who actually contributed little to the development of motion pictures but whose role was exaggerated in a recent biography); Anthony Asquith's *The Browning Version* with Michael Redgrave, Jean Kent, Nigel Patrick; Charles Crichton's *The Lavender Hill Mob* with Alec Guinness; Alexander Mackendrick's *The Man in the White Suit* with Alec Guinness; Mario Zampini's *Laughter in Paradise* with Alistair Sim, Joyce Grenfell; Elia Kazan's *A Streetcar Named Desire* with Marlon Brando, Vivien Leigh; Ingmar Bergman's *Summer Interlude;* Akira Kurosawa's *Rashomon* with Toshiro Mifume; Anatole Litvak's *Decision Before Dawn* with Oskar Werner, Richard Basehart, Gary Merrill, Hildegarde Neff; George Stevens's *A Place in the Sun* with Montgomery Clift, Elizabeth Taylor in a new film version of the 1925 Dreiser novel *An American Tragedy;* Mervyn LeRoy's *Quo Vadis* with Robert Taylor, Deborah Kerr; Vincente Minnelli's *Father's Little Dividend* with Spencer Tracy, Joan Bennett, Elizabeth Taylor; Robert Rossen's *The Brave Bulls* with Mel Ferrer, Anthony Quinn.

Hollywood musicals Vincente Minnelli's *An American in Paris* with Gene Kelly, Leslie Caron, Oscar Levant, music by the late George Gershwin; Walt Disney's *Cinderella* with music by Al Hoffman and Jerry Livingston, lyrics by Mack David, songs that include "A Dream Is a Wish Your Heart Makes," "Bibbidi Bobbidi Boo," "So This Is Love."

Broadway musicals *The King and I* 3/29 at the St. James Theater, with Gertrude Lawrence, Yul Brynner, music by Richard Rodgers, lyrics by Oscar Hammerstein II, book based on Margaret Landon's novel *Anna and the King of Siam* based in turn on diaries kept by the late Anna Lewin-Owen (see Phra Chom Klao Mongkut, 1851), songs that include "Getting to Know You," "Hello, Young Lovers," "We Kiss in a Shadow," "Shall We Dance," "Whistle a Happy Tune," 1,246 perfs.; *A Tree Grows in Brooklyn* 4/19 at the Alvin Theater, with Shirley Booth, Johnny Johnston, music by Arthur Schwartz, lyrics by Dorothy Fields, songs that include "Make the Man Love Me," "Look Who's Dancing," "I'll Buy You a Star," 267 perfs.; *Flahooley* 5/14 at the Broadway Theater, with Bil Baird, Cora Baird, Yma Sumac, music by Sammy Fain, lyrics by E. Y. Harburg, songs that include "Here's to Your Illusions," 40 perfs.; *Top Banana* 11/1 at the Winter Garden Theater, with Phil Silvers, music and lyrics by Johnny Mercer, 350 perfs.; *Paint Your Wagon* 11/12 at the Shubert Theater, with Eddie Dowling, Ann Crowley, music by Frederick Loewe, lyrics by Alan Jay Lerner, songs that include "They Call the Wind Maria," "I Talk to the Trees," "I Still See Elisa," 289 perfs.

Opera *The Pilgrim's Progress* 5/26 at London's Covent Garden, with music by Ralph Vaughn Williams,

The Rake's Progress 9/11 at the Venice Festival, with music by Igor Stravinsky; *Ivan IV* (*Ivan the Terrible*) 10/12 at the Grand Théâtre de Bordeaux, with music by the late Georges Bizet; *Billy Budd* 12/1 at London's Covent Garden, with music by Benjamin Britten, libretto from Herman Melville's last complete work (Melville finished *Billy Budd, Foretopman* in 1891 but it was not published until 1924); *Amahl and the Night Visitors* 12/24 on the NBC Television Opera Theater, with music by Gian Carlo Menotti who has written the first opera for television.

Ballet *The Miraculous Mandarin* 9/6 at the New York City Center, with Melissa Hayden, Hugh Laing, music by the late Béla Bartók, choreography by Todd Bolender; *The Pied Piper* 12/4 at the New York City Center, with Tanaquil LeClerq, Jerome Robbins, music by Aaron Copland, choreography by Robbins.

Cantata *The Sons of Light* by Ralph Vaughan Williams 5/6 at London, with a chorus of 1,000 schoolchildren.

First performances Symphony No. 2 by Charles Ives (who wrote it between 1897 and 1901) 2/23 at New York's Carnegie Hall (Ives declines Leonard Bernstein's invitation to attend, but he does hear part of the performance on his housemaid's radio—he does not own one himself—and he comes out of her room dancing a jig); *Suite Archaïque* by Arthur Honegger 2/28 at Louisville; Symphony No. 5 (*Di tre re*) by Arthur Honegger 3/9 at Boston's Symphony Hall; Symphony No. 4 by Walter Piston 3/30 at Minneapolis; *Monopartita* by Arthur Honegger 6/12 at Zurich; *Stabat Mater* by Francis Poulenc 6/13 at Strasbourg.

Count Basie organizes a new band that will tour the United States and Europe. It will be even more successful than Basie's prewar band (*see* 1935).

Le Crazy Horse Saloon opens in a former coal cellar off the Champs-Elysées in Paris. Ex-painter, ex-decorator, ex-antique dealer, ex-restaurateur Alain Bernardin, 32, hires the Slim Briggs orchestra from Houston, offers Europe's first strip-tease show, and creates a sensation.

Popular songs "In the Cool, Cool, Cool of the Evening" by Hoagy Carmichael, lyrics by Johnny Mercer (for Frank Capra's film *Here Comes the Groom*). "Kisses Sweeter Than Wine" by Joel Newman, lyrics by Paul Campbell; "Unforgettable" by Irving Gordon; "I'm in Love Again" by Cole Porter; "My Truly, Truly Fair" by Bob Merrill; "Mockin' Bird Hill" by Vaughn Horton; "Too Young" by Sid Lippman, lyrics by Sylvia Dee; "If" by Tolchard Evans, lyrics by Robert Hargreaves and Stanley J. Domerell; "Mixed Emotions" by Stuart F. Loucheim; "Domino" by Louis Ferrani, lyrics by Jacques Plante (English lyrics by Don Raye); "Be My Love" by Nicholas Brodszky, lyrics by Sammy Cahn (for Norman Taurog's film *The Toast of New Orleans*); "Be My Life's Companion" by Milton De Lugg and Bob Hilliard; "Come on-a My House" by Ross Bagdasarian and

William Saroyan; "Cold, Cold Heart" by Hank Williams.

"Sugar Ray" Robinson (Walker Smith) wins the world middleweight boxing title February 4 at Chicago by beating Jake LaMotta who gave the 30-year-old Robinson his only defeat in 123 professional fights just 8 years earlier minus 1 day. Robinson loses the title July 10 to Randy Turpin, he regains it September 12, and he relinquishes it to try for the lightheavyweight crown.

"Jersey Joe" Walcott wins the world heavyweight title July 18. The 37-year-old Walcott knocks out Ezzard Charles in the seventh round of a championship bout at Pittsburgh.

Frank Sedgman wins the U.S. Lawn Tennis Association men's singles, Maureen Connolly wins the women's singles.

A college basketball scandal at New York rocks the sports world. The courts will find several college players guilty of taking payoffs from gamblers to throw games, some will serve jail terms, all will lose their chances to play professional basketball.

Willie Mays joins the New York Giants lineup in center field. Willie Howard Mays, Jr., 20, will play his first full season in 1954, he will win the National League's batting championship that year with a .345 average, he will continue with the Giants when they move from the Polo Grounds to San Francisco's Candlewick Park in 1957, and he will remain a stalwart of the team until 1972.

Mickey Mantle joins the New York Yankees at center field and plays alongside Joe DiMaggio who handles left field (*see* 1936). Mickey Charles Mantle, 19, plays only 96 games and he sets a league record of 111 strikeouts, but he shows that he can hit the ball out of the park, he will be a Yankee star for 17 years

Television changed people's lives more than radio ever had done. Not all of TV's contributions were beneficial.

1951 (cont.) beginning next season, and his batting average in his 10 peak years will be above .300.

Baseball's most exciting moment in history comes October 3 when New York Giants third baseman Robert Brown "Bobby" Thompson, 27, hits a three-run homer in the last half of the ninth inning of the third playoff game of the National League pennant race to beat the Brooklyn Dodgers 5 to 4 at the Polo Grounds. The Giants win the pennant after having come from 13½ games behind to tie the Dodgers and force the playoff.

The New York Yankees win their third consecutive World Series by defeating the New York Giants (above) 4 games to 2.

Florence Chadwick becomes the first woman to cross the English Channel from England to France (see 1950). She makes the crossing from Dover September 11 in 16 hours and 22 minutes, and she will break that record October 12, 1955, when she makes the same swim in 13 hours and 33 minutes.

The first Pan-American Games are held at Buenos Aires. Only Western Hemisphere athletes may compete.

The world's first sky-diving championship is held in Yugoslavia. Parachute jumpers compete for prizes.

 The Chemise Lacoste is exported to the United States for the first time by the French firm Izod Company which has contracted with lawn tennis star René Lacoste to use the "alligator" symbol associated with him since he helped France win the Davis Cup in 1927. The long-tailed all-cotton "alligator" tennis shirt will become a U.S. status symbol.

Marimekko is founded by Finnish textile designer Armi Ratia who has lost two brothers and a brother-in-law in the war. U.S. architect Benjamin Thompson will bring the prints to his Cambridge, Mass., Design Research shop in 1959 and Marimekko prints will gain wide popularity through D/R promotion.

Victor Gruen Associates, Inc., is founded by Austrian-American architect Victor Gruen, 48, who has designed shopping centers, store fronts, and some of the structures at the 1939 New York World's Fair. Gruen's architecture-engineering-urban planning firm will have a major impact on U.S. building design and city planning (see Fort Worth Plan, 1952).

Pittsburgh's Alcoa building is completed by Harrison & Abramovitz with 30 stories clad in aluminum.

Pittsburgh's U.S. Steel and Mellon building is completed by Harrison & Abramovitz and rises 41 stories.

A second Levittown is started by Levitt and Sons for 17,000 families in Bucks County, Pa., with schools and churches to be built on land donated by the developers (see 1947). A third Levittown will have 12,000 homes in New Jersey by 1965 with houses of three basic designs in a variety of color schemes commingled on each street. The three- to four-bedroom houses sell for between $11,500 and $14,500 each

including major appliances, and the low prices encourage thousands of Americans to leave the city and move into suburban developments that sprawl across the landscape as scores of builders adopt the methods pioneered by Levitt.

Detroit's 27-year-old Book-Cadillac Hotel becomes the Sheraton-Cadillac.

 The worst floods in U.S. history inundate Kansas and Missouri; 41 die between July 2 and 19, 200,000 are left homeless, property damage reaches $1 billion.

U.S. food prices climb steeply in the Korean War inflation. The nation suffers a beef shortage as affluent consumers increase their demand.

A British beef shortage leads to the consumption of 53,000 horses for food.

Indian government food policies are protested with a huge demonstration organized by the Socialist party at New Delhi.

Congress votes June 15 to loan India $190 million to buy U.S. grain (see P.L. 480, 1954).

The United States agrees to supply Yugoslavia with $38 million in food aid.

Britain produces enough food to supply half her domestic needs, up from 42 percent in 1914 when the population was 35 million versus 50 million today.

British farms have 300,000 tractors, up from 55,000 in 1949.

A 2-year drought begins in Australia that will kill off millions of head of livestock and will force rationing of butter.

Australian sheep-raisers introduce the virus disease myxomatosis that is endemic in South America in an effort to kill off the rabbits which are consuming enough grass to feed 40 million sheep (see Austin, 1859). The introduction of hawks, weasels, snakes, and other predators has not appreciably reduced the rabbits' numbers, hundreds of thousands of miles of costly rabbit-proof fencing has not stopped them, but rabbits infected with the virus are released, the disease is communicated by mosquitoes and other insects, and in some areas 99 percent of the rabbits are eliminated before natural resistance to myxomatosis becomes dominant (see France, 1952).

An irradiation method for sterilizing male insects and releasing them to mate with females who will die without reproducing is developed by U.S. entomologist Edward F. Knipling, 42, who has been with the U.S. Department of Agriculture since 1931. Knipling finds a new way to control insect populations biologically rather than chemically (see 1954).

 Kwashiorkor is found to be a worldwide disease among children and is shown to be caused by dietary protein deficiency in infancy (see 1935). The disease goes by different names in different countries.

 The Supreme Court rules in the case of *62 Cases of Jam v. The United States* that "within the understanding of ordinary English speech, a product should be deemed misbranded if it imitates another food, unless its label bears the word 'imitation.'"

Gerber Products Company starts using MSG (monosodium glutamate) in its baby foods to make them taste better to mothers (*see* MSG, 1934, 1969).

Tropicana Products, Inc., is founded at Bradentown, Fla., to produce chilled, pasteurized grapefruit and orange juice. Italian-American entrepreneur Anthony T. Rossi, 51, established a business in the late 1940s to pack chilled fruit sections in glass jars. He will develop ways to extract juice by varying degrees depending on the quality of the fruit (*see* 1955).

Ore-Ida Foods, Inc., has its beginnings as produce farmers outside Ontario, Ore., pool their resources to buy a frozen food factory in the town. The group will buy a second factory at Burley, Idaho, in 1960 and will merge with some other small companies in 1961 to form Ore-Ida Foods.

Jeno Paulucci's Chun King Corporation moves into a new plant with 2 million cubic feet of production and storage space (*see* 1947). Paulucci has outgrown his earlier Duluth plant and is spending 10 percent of his sales receipts on advertising as he expands operations to grow his own celery and mushrooms (*see* 1967).

Parks Sausages are introduced by Baltimore's H. G. Parks, Inc., founded by local sausagemaker Henry G. Parks, 34, whose firm will grow to become the seventh largest black-owned enterprise in America.

Nathan Cummings acquires two California companies to expand the food company he began with the acquisition of a Baltimore sugar and coffee wholesaler in 1941 and of the Chicago food wholesaler Sprague-Warner in 1942 (*see* 1939). Gentry Foods is a major processor of dehydrated onions, garlic, and pepper products, Union Sugar is a major beet sugar refiner (*see* Consolidated Foods, 1954).

Ballard and Ballard of Louisville and its 20-year-old frozen, oven-ready biscuit package are acquired by the Pillsbury Company which will make refrigerated products an important part of its line (*see* 1949).

Trading stamps are revived by the small King Soopers grocery chain at Denver which begins offering S&H green stamps in June (*see* Sperry and Hutchinson, 1896). The stamps have largely fallen out of use except as a means of getting round price-cutting laws in the 1930s, but by 1953 five of Denver's six grocery chains and many of the city's independent grocery stores will be offering trading stamps (*see* 1959).

Britain's first supermarket chain begins operations in September. Premier Supermarkets opens its first store in London's Earls Court (*see* 1948).

L'Ecole des Trois Gourmandes opens at Paris. The French cooking school for Americans is conducted by Julia Child, 39, with Simone Beck and Louisette Bertholle (*see* 1961).

The U.S. population reaches 153 million, the U.S.S.R. has 172 million, China 583 million, India 357, Pakistan 76, Japan 85, Indonesia 78, Britain 50, West Germany 50, Italy 47, France 42, Brazil 52.

Infant mortality in India is 116 per thousand, down from 232 in 1900. In the United States it is 29, down from 122 in 1900, and in Britain it is 30.

New York and its suburban areas have a population of 12.3 million, London has 8.4 million, Paris 6.4, Tokyo 6.3, Shanghai 6.2, Chicago 5, Buenos Aires 4.8, Calcutta 4.6, Moscow 4.2, Los Angeles 4, Berlin 4.4, Leningrad 3.2, Mexico City 3.1, Bombay 2.9, Peking 2.8.

Development of an oral contraceptive for humans is urged by Margaret Sanger who visits Gregory Pincus at the Worcester Foundation and asks him to follow up on his experiments on fertility in animals (*see* 1948). Now at Boston University, Pincus and his colleagues decide to study the possible contraceptive action of the hormone norethisterone (*see* 1954).

1952 Britain's George VI dies of lung cancer February 6 at age 56 after a reign of more than 15 years (the king was a heavy smoker). His 25-year-old daughter flies home from a visit to East Africa and ascends the throne as Elizabeth II to begin a long reign in which the British Empire will decline from 40 nations to no more than 12 with the British monarch having an effective voice in only one.

Canada's first Canadian governor-general has taken office January 24 in the person of Vincent Massey, 64-year-old scion of the Massey-Harris farm equipment family whose brother Raymond is a prominent actor. Massey will serve until 1959.

A Cuban military coup March 10 overthrows President Prio Socarras and replaces him with General Fulgencio Batista y Zaldivar who ruled as dictator from 1933 to 1940 and who will rule as dictator again until the beginning of 1959.

Puerto Rico adopts a new Constitution and becomes a self-governing commonwealth associated with the United States (*see* 1898; 1954).

Peking accuses U.S. forces in Korea of using germ warfare. U.S. Air Force planes bomb North Korean hydroelectric plants June 23.

Egypt's dissolute king Farouk I abdicates July 26, 3 days after a coup by General Mohammed Neguib. Farouk has reigned for 16 years, he is succeeded by his infant son Fuad who will not reign. General Neguib forms a government September 7, Egypt and Sudan sign an agreement October 13 over use of water from the Nile, and the Egyptian Constitution of 1923 is abolished December 10 (*see* 1954).

Jordan's schizophrenic king Talal is deposed August 11 after a brief reign. He is succeeded by his 16-year-old son Hussein who will reign for more than 26 years despite at least 10 attempts on his life and countless conspiracies to depose him.

1952 (cont.)   Moscow ousts U.S. Ambassador George F. Kennan October 3. Kennan has commented on the isolation of Western diplomats in Moscow and the Kremlin demands his recall.

President Truman has relieved General Eisenhower of his post as Supreme Allied Commander at his own request in April, General Matthew Ridgway has succeeded to the post, General Mark Clark has replaced Ridgway in the Far East, and the Republican party nominates Eisenhower to run for the presidency against the Democratic nominee Governor Adlai Stevenson, 52, of Illinois.

U.S. Senator Richard M. Nixon of California is nominated to run with General Eisenhower (above) but is accused of having received a "slush fund" of $18,000 from some California businessmen. Nixon appears on television September 23 and gives a speech that begins, "I come before you tonight as a candidate for the vice presidency and as a man whose honesty and integrity have been questioned ..."; he denies that any of the money in question went for his personal use but adds, "I did get something, a gift after the nomination. It was a little cocker spaniel dog, black and white, spotted. Our little girl Tricia, 6, named it 'Checkers.' The kids, like all kids, love the dog. Regardless of what they say about it, we are going to keep it." The speech produces more than 1 million favorable letters and telegrams, the Republicans win 55 percent of the popular vote and 442 electoral votes on the strength of "Ike" Eisenhower's enormous popularity, the Democrats receive only 89 electoral votes with 44 percent of the popular vote.

Former Czech Communist party secretary Rudolf Slansky and former Czech foreign minister Vladimir Clementis go on trial for treason November 27.

President-elect Eisenhower visits Korea December 2 in fulfillment of a campaign promise. An Indian proposal for a Korean armistice is adopted by the UN General Assembly December 3 but is rejected by Peking December 15.

Israel's president Chaim Weizmann has died November 7 and is succeeded December 8 by Itzhak Ben-Zvi, the choice of the Israeli knesset.

Communist "witch-hunts" continue in the United States, but the House Committee to Investigate Un-American Activities is defied May 22 by playwright Lillian Hellman who testifies that she is not a "Red" but who will not say whether or not she was 3 or 4 years ago because such testimony "would hurt innocent people in order to save myself." "I cannot and will not cut my conscience to fit this year's fashions," says Hellman but others are less resistant and many careers are ruined (see 1950; 1951).

South Africa's apartheid racial legislation has been invalidated March 20 by the Nation's Supreme Court, Prime Minister Daniel F. Malan introduces legislation April 22 to make the parliament the highest court, the bill is passed, demonstrations against "unjust" racial laws begin June 26, demonstrators are arrested through July, and leaders of the movement say that deliberate violations of the law will continue until all the jails in the country are filled.

A Mau Mau insurrection against Kenya's white settlers begins October 20. London declares a state of emergency and dispatches a cruiser and a battalion of troops (see 1953).

Malcolm X joins U.S. Black Muslim leader Elijah Mohammed following his release from prison after having served 6 years on a conviction of armed robbery. The 27-year-old disciple has educated himself while in prison, he has read the teachings of Elijah Mohammed, he has adopted the new faith, he has changed his name from Malcolm Little, and he will become the sect's first "national minister" in 1963 (see 1931; 1965).

Mycenaean texts of 1450 B.C. are deciphered by archaeologist Michael Ventris who does for the inscriptions of the Minoan civilization what Champollion's work in 1822 and earlier did for the inscriptions of ancient Egypt.

King Solomon's Ring by Austrian animal behaviorist Konrad Lorenz, 45, shows that Darwinian natural selection processes operate not only in shaping physical form but also in determining behavioral characteristics.

The United States Lines passenger ship S.S. *United States* leaves New York July 3 on her first transatlantic voyage and sets a new record. Built with immense 240,000-horsepower steam turbines that can push her at 50 miles per hour and convertible to a troopship that can transport 14,000 men, the $79 million 53,000-ton vessel is 990 feet in length overall, she can carry 1,750 passengers, and she makes the crossing of 2,949 nautical miles in 3 days, 10 hours, 40 minutes, averaging 35.59 knots per hour (more than 40 mph).

The Volga-Don Ship Canal opens between the Volga and Don Rivers in the Soviet Union. The 62-mile waterway provides a link for the Baltic–Black Sea route.

Europe's Arlberg-Orient Express is rerouted via Salonica following last year's closing of the Turkish-Bulgarian border (see 1932; 1962).

London's last tram runs July 6 as motorbuses replace streetcars.

British Motors Corporation is created by a merger of Austin Motor Company and Morris Motors, Ltd. (see Austin, 1905; Morris, 1913; Motor Holdings, 1955).

Jet aircraft passenger service is inaugurated by a British DeHavilland Comet which jets from London to Johannesburg and covers the 6,724-mile distance in less than 24 hours (see 1948; 1958).

General Dynamics Corporation is founded by U.S. entrepreneur John Jay Hopkins whose Electric Boat Company division at Groton, Conn., will build the world's first nuclear submarines beginning with the *Nautilus* in 1954. General Dynamics will move into aircraft in 1954 by acquiring Consolidated Vultee, it will enter the electronics industry in 1955 by acquiring Stromberg-Carlson, it will proceed to move into shipbuilding, coal mining, building materials, and other fields, and by 1968 General Dynamics will be an aerospace and defense industry conglomerate making missile submarines and F-111 fighter jets with annual sales of $2.6 billion.

An atomic (nuclear fission) bomb developed by British physicists is tested October 2 over the Monte Bello Islands near Australia. Britain joins the United States and the U.S.S.R. as a nuclear power.

The world's first nuclear-fusion (hydrogen) device is exploded November 1 by the U.S. Atomic Energy Commission (see von Neumann, Fuchs, 1946; Truman, 1950). The test at the Eniwetok proving grounds in the Pacific is the first full-scale thermonuclear explosion in history (see 1951; Bikini, 1954).

"Sooner or later, the nation will have to return to heavier reliance on abundant coal," says the President's Materials Policy Commission headed by CBS chairman William S. Paley (see 1928). "The nation could reduce consumption and physical waste of liquid fuels with little or no inconvenience," says the Paley Commission report, but while it predicts that U.S. demand for electricity will double in the next 2 decades, the demand will in fact quadruple and the Commission's recommendation of "an appropriate federal agency designated to undertake . . . a continuing broad appraisal of the nation's long-term energy outlook" is not instrumented.

President Truman orders federal seizure of U.S. steel mills April 8 to avert a nationwide strike, the steel companies take legal action to block government operation of the mills, the Supreme Court rules June 2 that the executive order was illegal, and 600,000 CIO steelworkers walk out June 23 to begin a 53-day strike.

The U.S. government returns the nation's railroads to private control May 23 after 21 months of operation by federal troops (see 1950).

U.S. income tax receipts reach a record $69.6 billion but the nation has a record peacetime deficit of $9.3 billion as the Korean conflict continues to drain U.S. resources.

War-inflated food prices are so high that General Eisenhower uses them as a campaign issue in his presidential campaign (above), but farm prices will fall 22 percent in the next 2 years and food prices will fall as a consequence.

Congress amends the Social Security Act of 1935 to increase benefits to the elderly by 12.5 percent and to permit pension recipients to earn as much as $75 per month without loss of benefits.

Australian cattleman-prospector Langley George Hancock, 43, discovers a mountain of solid iron ore in the Hammersley Range when his light plane is forced off course and he sees rust-colored outcroppings. Hancock will keep the location of his find secret for 10 years until a change in state mining laws permits him to stake his claim, but he gets in touch with the worldwide mining concern Rio Tinto which will make an agreement with Kaiser Aluminum and will exploit the ore deposit that will bring Hancock an estimated $250 million, making him the richest man in Australia (see 1964).

A poliomyelitis epidemic strikes more than 50,000 Americans, 3,300 die, thousands are left crippled.

The Salk vaccine against polio is tested by U.S. microbiologist Jonas Edward Salk, 38, whose hypodemic vaccine is based on killed viruses and employs a method of virus culture developed in the laboratory of Children's Hospital at Boston by bacteriologists John Franklin Enders, 55, with Frederick Chapman Robbins, 36, and Thomas Huckle Weller, 37 (they will all share in a 1954 Nobel prize). Enders helped Harvard bacteriology professor Hans Zinsser develop the first antityphus vaccine in 1930 and he will apply the Enders-Robbins-Weller culture method to developing a measles vaccine (see 1962).

The thyroid hormone tri-iodothyronine is isolated by British biochemist Rosalind Pitt-Rivers and others.

Reserpine is isolated by Swiss chemists employed by CIBA under the direction of Emil Schlitter who produce pure crystals of the active ingredient in *Rauwolfia serpentina* (see Vakil, 1949). Boston heart specialist Robert Wallace Wilkins, 45, observes that reserpine not only reduces high blood pressure but also reduces anxiety (see LSD and serotinin, 1953).

Isoniazid is introduced to fight tuberculosis by Hoffman-La Roche, Inc., of Nutley, N.J., which has employed work in organic chemistry by research chemist H. Herbert Fox, 37. A brand name of isonicotinic acid hydrozide, Isoniazid will be found to produce tumors in test mice but it will not be shown to produce tumors in humans and it will be such an effective prophylactic against TB that it will remain in use despite some alarmists.

Chlorpromazine is developed to intensify the action of standard sedatives. The antihistamine was synthesized in the late 1940s and its new potential has been found by chemists at the French pharmaceutical firm Rhone-Poulenc (see Thorazine, 1954).

The first pocket-size transistor radios introduced under the Sony name by Japanese tape recorder maker Masaru Ibuka who returns from a visit to the United States with a license from the Western Electric Company division of American Telephone & Telegraph (see 1950; Shockley, 1948). Western Electric engineers have told Ibuka that 95 out of 100 transistors coming off production lines are defective and must be discarded, and that to make a profit it would be necessary to charge $6 for a transistor alone when vacuum tube radios sell for as little as $6.95 complete, but Ibuka has improved the technology of transistor production, he has cut the reject rate from 95 percent to 2 percent, and he has reduced the cost from $6 to a fraction of one dollar (see 1959).

1952 (cont.) *The Today Show* debuts January 16 on NBC television stations with Chicago radio personality Dave Garroway, 38, serving as master of ceremonies for the 2-hour news and interview show developed by Sylvester "Pat" Weaver, Jr. Working out of a street-level studio with a window facing on New York's Rockefeller Center street traffic, Garroway is soon joined by chimpanzee J. Fred Muggs whose presence encourages children to turn on the TV set.

Most major countries of the world have TV stations and receiving sets, but while the U.S. TV system employs 525 lines to the inch and produces a sharper image than the one produced by the 450-line British Broadcasting Company system, European countries have adopted a 625-line system that produces far better resolution. France and Monaco will institute 819-line systems, but Britain, the United States, Japan, and Latin America will be locked into their coarser image systems and will thus pay the penalty of leadership (*see* Japan, 1953; BBC-2, 1964).

The first videotape is demonstrated November 11 at Bing Crosby Enterprise Laboratories in Beverly Hills, Calif., by inventors John Mullin and Wayne Johnson.

Some 17 million U.S. homes have TV sets by year's end, up from 5 to 8 million in 1950.

The first transistorized hearing aids are introduced December 29 by Sonotone Corporation of Elmsford, N.Y. (*see* 1935; transistor, 1948).

The Duane Jones case discourages U.S. advertising agency account executives from taking accounts to start their own agencies. A New York jury October 28 awards $300,000 plus any accumulated profits in the Scheideler, Beck and Werner agency to box-top king Duane Jones, 52, whose Duane Jones Company executives are ruled to have conspired with executives of the Manhattan Soap Company to move the account (industry rumor has it that Jones is rarely sober after 11 o'clock in the morning).

The *National Enquirer* founded in 1926 by a former Hearst advertising executive is taken over by Generoso Pope, Jr., 25, whose father made a fortune in sand and gravel and has published the New York Italian-language newspaper *Il Progresso*. The *Enquirer* has become little more than a tout sheet, but Pope will emphasize crime, gore, miracle cures, gossip, and sex to build circulation that will pass 4 million per week by 1975 and will multiply his $75,000 investment hundreds of times over.

Mad magazine has its beginnings in the *Mad* comic book that begins publication in August with 32 pages in full color satirizing other comic books and even making fun of itself. Founder-editor Harvey Kurtzman will develop a freckled, big-eared, cow-licked idiot boy character, comedian Ernie Kovaks will name the boy Melvin Cowznofski, he will become infamous as Alfred E. Neuman ("What—Me Worry?"), and publisher William Gaines will sell his E. C. (Entertaining Comics) Publications to Warner Communications, Inc.

 Nonfiction *Witness* by Whittaker Chambers; *The Irony of American History* by U.S. theologian Reinhold Niebuhr; *The Power of Positive Thinking* by New York clergyman Norman Vincent Peale, 54, of the Marble Collegiate Church; *Amy Vanderbilt's Complete Book of Etiquette* by former International News Service columnist Amy Vanderbilt, 43, whose 700-page book is a source book of customs, mores, and manners by a first cousin to the late railroad magnate Commodore Vanderbilt (*see* Post, 1922).

Fiction *Men of Good Will* (*Les Hommes de bonne volonté*) by Jules Romains; *The Works of Love* by U.S. novelist Wright Morris, 32; *Wise Blood* by U.S. novelist Flannery O'Connor, 27; *The Groves of Academe* by Mary McCarthy; *Player Piano* by U.S. novelist Kurt Vonnegut, Jr., 29, who 5 years ago joined the public relations staff of General Electric at Schenectady, N.Y., and who has been inspired to write a science-fiction work on the technocratic tendencies of modern industrial society; *The Natural* by New York novelist Bernard Malamud, 38; *The Long March* by William Styron; *The Old Man and the Sea* by Ernest Hemingway whose short novel, expanded from a piece first published in *Esquire* in 1934, appears first in *LIFE* magazine, then in book form, and helps Hemingway win a Nobel prize; *East of Eden* by John Steinbeck; *Doting* by Henry Green.

Juvenile *Charlotte's Web* by E. B. White.

Poetry *A Mask for Janus* by U.S. poet W. S. Merwin, 25; *Rod of Incantation* by English poet Francis King, 29; "Do not go gentle into that good night" by Dylan Thomas whose father last year seemed close to death and who was inspired to write "Rage, rage against the dying of the light."

 Painting *The Green Night* by Marc Chagall; *The Pink Violin* by Raoul Dufy; *End of Autumn* by Georges Rouault; *Woman I* by Willem de Kooning; *Mountains and Sea* by U.S. painter Helen Frankenthaler, 25; *Red Painting* by Ad Reinhardt.

Sculpture *Madonna and Child* by Jacob Epstein; *Dancer* by Marino Marini.

 Theater *The Waltz of the Toreadors* (*La valse des toréadors*) by Jean Anouilh 1/10 at the Comédies de Champs-Elysées, Paris; *The Shrike* by U.S. playwright Joseph Kramm 1/15 at New York's Cort Theater, with Jose Ferrer, Judith Eveylyn, 161 perfs., Pulitzer prize; *Jane* by S. N. Behrman 2/1 at New York's Coronet Theater with Edna Best, Basil Rathbone, 100 perfs.; *The Deep Blue Sea* by Terence Rattigan 3/5 at London's Duchess Theatre; *The Marriage of Mr. Mississippi* (*Die Ehe des Herrn Mississippi*) by Friedrich Dürrenmatt 3/26 at Munich's Kammerspiele; *The Chairs* (*Les chaises*) by Eugène Ionesco 4/22 at the Théâtre Lanery, Paris; *Quadrille* by Noel Coward 9/12 at London's Phoenix Theatre, with Alfred Lunt, Joyce Carey; *The Time of the Cuckoo* by Arthur Laurents 10/15 at New York's Empire Theater, with Shirley Booth, Dino DiLuca, 263 perfs.; *Dial 'M' for Murder* by English playwright Frederick Knott 10/29 at New York's Plymouth Theater, with John Williamson, 552 perfs.; *No Peace for the Ancient Faun* (*Non c'e pace per L'antico fauno*) by Carlo Terron 11/7 at Milan's Teatro di Via Mazzoni; *The Mousetrap* by Agatha Christie 11/25 at London's 453-seat Ambassadors Theatre, with Richard Attenborough and his wife Sheila Sims in a melodrama that will move March 25, 1974, to the larger St. Martin's Theatre and that will still be playing when Christie dies in 1976; *The Seven-Year Itch* by U.S. playwright George Axelrod, 30, 11/20 at New York's Fulton Theater, with Tom Ewell, Neva Patterson, 1,141 perfs.

Films Fred Zinneman's *High Noon* with Gary Cooper, Grace Kelly; John Huston's *The Red Badge of Courage* with Audie Murphy, Bill Mauldin; René Clement's *Forbidden Games* (*Jeux Interdits*); Vittorio de Sica's *Umberto D;* Henri-Georges Clouzot's *The Wages of Fear* with Yves Montand; Claude Autant-Lara and Yves Allegret's *The Seven Deadly Sins* with Michel Morgan, Gerard Philippe; Alessandro Baselti's *Times Gone By* with Gina Lollabrigida, Vittorio de Sica; Cuzio Malaparte's *Strange Deception* (*Il Cristo Proibito*) with Raf Vallone; Jacques Becker's *Casque d'Or* with Simone Signoret; Luis Buñuel's *The Young and the Damned* (*Los Olvidados*); Ingmar Bergman's *Monika;* Yasujiro Ozu's *The Flavor of Green Tea Over Rice;* Akira Kurosawa's *Ikuru;* Kenji Mizoguchi's *The Life of O-Haru;* Charlie Chaplin's *Limelight* with Chaplin, Claire Bloom; John Ford's *The Quiet Man* with John Wayne, Maureen O'Hara, Barry Fitzgerald; Elia Kazan's *Viva Zapata!* with Marlon Brando; George Cukor's *Pat and Mike* with Katharine Hepburn, Spencer Tracy; Lucas Demare's *After the Silence*.

Hollywood musicals Gene Kelly and Stanley Donen's *Singin' in the Rain* with Kelly, Debbie Reynolds, Donald O'Connor, Jean Hagen, Cyd Charisse in a spoof on early talking pictures with songs that include "My Lucky Star," "Broadway Melody," "Good Morning," and the title song; Charles Vidor's *Hans Christian Andersen* with Danny Kaye, music and lyrics by Frank Loesser, songs that include "Anywhere I Wander," "Ugly Duckling," "Inchworm," "Thumbelina."

Broadway musicals *New Faces* 5/16 at the Royale Theater, with Eartha Kitt, Alice Ghostley, songs that include "Love Is a Simple Thing" by Jane Carroll, lyrics by Arthur Siegal, "Monotonous" by Arthur Siegal, lyrics by Jane Carroll, Nancy Graham, 365 perfs.; *Wish You Were Here* 6/25 at the Imperial Theater, with Sheila Bond, Jack Cassidy, music and lyrics by Harold Rome, songs that include "Where Did the Night Go?" and the title song, 598 perfs.

Opera *Trouble in Tahiti* 6/12 at Brandeis University, Waltham, Mass., with music and libretto by Leonard Bernstein.

First performances Symphony, *Die Harmonie der Welt* by Paul Hindemith 1/24 at Basel; Symphony

No. 4 by Paul Creston 1/30 at Washington, D.C.; *Symphonie Concertante* in E minor by Serge Prokofiev 2/18 at Moscow, with Mstislav Rostropovich as soloist; *The Meeting of the Volga and the Don Rivers* by Serge Prokofiev 2/22 on Moscow Radio; Three Spiritual Folk Songs by the late Anton von Webern 3/16 at Columbia University's McMillin Theater, New York; *Walt Whitman* symphonic essay by Paul Creston 3/28 at Cincinnati; Symphony No. 4 by Morton Gould 4/13 at West Point, N.Y.; *Water Music* by John Cage 5/2 at New York; Romance in D flat for Harmonica, String Orchestra, and Piano by Ralph Vaughan Williams 5/3 at New York, with Larry Adler as soloist; *West Point Suite* by Darius Milhaud 5/30 at West Point, N.Y.; Symphony No. 7 in C sharp minor by Serge Prokofiev 10/11 at Moscow; Concerto for Tap Dancer and Orchestra by Morton Gould 11/16 at Rochester, N.Y.; Symphony No. 7 by Roy Harris 11/20 at Chicago; Concerto for Violin by Gian Carlo Menotti 12/5 at Philadelphia's Academy of Music; *Sea Piece with Birds* by Virgil Thomson 12/10 at Dallas.

Television *The American Bandstand* debuts in January on ABC network stations. Host Dick Clark, 22, will continue to MC the show for more than 25 years.

Dave Brubeck and his San Francisco quartet pioneer "modern" or "progressive" jazz. David Warren Brubeck, 31, makes his New York debut and begins a 15-year career of innovation that will give jazz music a new complexity of rhythm and counterpoint.

Popular songs "Lullaby of Birdland" by George Shearing, lyrics by B. Y. Forster; "Takes Two to Tango" by Al Hoffman and Dick Manning; "Do Not Forsake Me" by Dmitri Tiomkin, lyrics by Ned Washington (for the film *High Noon*); "Till I Waltz Again with You" by Sidney Prosen; "Don't Let the Stars Get in Your Eyes" by Slim Willet; "Your Cheatin' Heart" by Hank Williams; "Wheel of Fortune" by Bennie Benjamin and George Weiss; "Blue Tango" by Leroy Anderson; "Pittsburgh, Pennsylvania" by U.S. songwriter Bob Merrill (née Henry Lavin), 30; "Jambalaya—in the Bayou" by Hank Williams; "Delicado" by Waldyr Azevedo, lyrics by Jack Laurence; "Here in My Heart" by Pat Genaro, Lou Levinson, and Don Borelli; "Count Your Blessings (Instead of Sheep)" by Irving Berlin (for Michael Curtiz's 1954 film *White Christmas*); "I Saw Momma Kissing Santa Claus" by Tommy Conner.

The Olympic Games at Helsinki attract 5,867 contestants from 69 nations. U.S. athletes win the largest number of medals as Bob Mathias triumphs in the decathlon event.

Australia retains the Davis Cup by defeating a U.S. team. Australia's Frank Sedgman wins the USLTA's men's singles title, Maureen Connolly wins the women's singles.

Eddie Arcaro wins his fifth Kentucky Derby riding Hill Gail.

Senator McCarthy exploited fears of communism in America and found wide support despite his recklessness.

Rocky Marciano wins the world heavyweight title that he will defend six times before retiring undefeated in 1956. Brockton, Mass., fighter Rocco Francis Marchegianao, 28, knocks out Jersey Joe Walcott September 23 in the 13th round of a title bout at Philadelphia.

The New York Yankees win the World Series by defeating the Brooklyn Dodgers 4 games to 2.

"Never wear a white shirt before sundown," says an advertisement for Hathaway shirts in the October 18 *New Yorker.* Four out of five shirts sold in America are white shirts but the ratio will fall to two out of five in the next 15 years, and all-cotton shirts will give way to blends of cotton and synthetic fibers.

Gleem toothpaste is introduced by Cincinnati's Procter & Gamble which begins a major effort to penetrate the dentifrice business (*see* Crest, 1955).

Kent filter-tipped cigarettes are introduced by P. Lorillard of 1925 Old Gold fame whose new premium-priced brand is named after the company's top executive (*see* 1957; Viceroy, 1936).

New York's Lever House opens April 29 on Park Avenue between 53rd and 54th Streets. Designed by Gordon Bunshaft of Skidmore, Owings & Merrill, the 24-story glass-walled building takes up far less of its site than the law permits, it is hailed for its aesthetics, a traveling gondola suspended from its roof enables window cleaners to wash the structure's 1,404 panes of heat-resistant blue-green glass, but the windows are sealed, the centrally air-conditioned building makes profligate use of energy, and it will be a model for energy-wasting architectural extravangazas that will be constructed throughout much of the world.

The Fort Worth Plan presented by Victor Gruen Associates is the first U.S. proposal for reclaiming a downtown city area by banning automobiles from the central business district and turning it into a pedestrian shopping mall. The plan will not be instrumented (*see* Gruen, 1951; Northland, 1954).

The first Holiday Inn opens on U.S. Highway 70 at Memphis where local builder Kemmons Wilson puts up a motel with a swimming pool, with air-conditioning and a television set in every room, with free ice, free baby cribs, free kennels and dog food for family pets, and no charge for children under 12 who share their parents' accommodations. Wilson took his wife and five young children on a trip to Washington, D.C., last year and decided that the motel business was "the greatest untouched industry in America."

A 4-day London smog in December raises the city's death toll to three times its normal level. Ninety percent of the 4,703 dead are over age 45 and the Ministry of Health blames the contaminated air on irritant oxides of sulfur and other substances from coal smoke. One pollution expert estimates that in a bad fog year such as this a heaped teaspoonful of black powder enters the lungs of each Londoner (*see* 1955).

Rabbits infected with myxomatosis are released in France and the disease brings a sharp decrease in the French wild rabbit population (*see* 1951; 1953).

A giant Soviet tree-planting program undertaken by T. D. Lysenko is a fiasco but Lysenkoism continues to dominate Soviet agriculture (*see* 1948; 1954).

China's cereal grain production rises to 163 million tons, up from 110 million in 1949, but Asia's rice crop falls below the level of prewar harvests while populations have increased by roughly 10 percent from prewar levels (*see* 1956).

Drought reduces U.S. grain harvests. Farmers in Alabama, Georgia, Kentucky, Maine, Massachusetts, South Carolina, and Tennessee are declared eligible for disaster loans August 1, but while the drought will last for 5 years and will be even more intense than the drought of the 1930s, its effects will be tempered by tree stands planted in the Depression years and by contour plowing and new tilling methods which combine to conserve available moisture and prevent the creation of a new Dust Bowl (*see* 1953).

Nearly half of U.S. farms have tractors, up from one-quarter in 1940.

The Declaration of Santiago extends the maritime and fisheries jurisdictions of Chile, Ecuador, and Peru to 200 miles from their coastlines, but the United States maintains her 3-mile limit and most other nations limit their jurisdictions to 12 miles (*see* 1966; Jefferson, 1793).

Kellogg's Sugar Frosted Flakes are introduced. The new cereal is 29 percent sugar (*see* 1950; 1953).

No-Cal Ginger Ale is introduced by Kirsch Beverages, Inc., of Brooklyn, N.Y., whose Russian-American founder Hyman Kirsch, now 75, started a soft-drink business in 1904 with a 14- by 30-foot store in Brooklyn's Williamsburg section. Physicians at the

Kingsbrook Medical Center founded by Kirsch asked the company in 1949 to develop a sugar-free, salt-free soft drink for use by obese, diabetic, and hypertensive patients, the new ginger ale uses cyclamates in place of sugar, it is the first palatable sugar-free soft drink, and it begins a revolution in the soft drink industry (see cyclamates, 1950; Diet-Rite Cola, 1962).

Pream powdered instant cream for coffee is introduced by M. and R. Dietetic Laboratories, Inc., of Columbus, Ohio (see Coffee-Mate, 1961).

New York State repeals its law against selling yellow-colored margarine, but other dairy states continue to prohibit sale of such margarine (see 1943; 1967).

Hunt Foods, Inc., buys the Snider catsup brand name and Snider catsup plants from General Foods. Norton Simon broadens distribution of the brand (see 1946; Wesson Oil and Snowdrift, 1960).

Howard Johnson opens his 351st restaurant, making his Maine to Miami chain the world's largest (see 1937). Johnson has added a chain of higher priced Red Coach Grills, he has had 12 years' experience operating 24 eating places on the Pennsylvania Turnpike, he wins a franchise to operate 10 restaurants on the new 118-mile New Jersey Turnpike, he hires Pavillon restaurant chef Pierre Franey to upgrade the quality of Howard Johnson dishes, and he sells frozen Howard Johnson specialties through supermarkets (see 1960).

The first Holiday Inn (above) has a restaurant on the premises serving food at reasonable prices.

McDonald's begins to challenge the Howard Johnson empire (above) as Ray Kroc persuades the McDonald brothers to let him franchise their outlets to operators who will open McDonald stands throughout the country (see 1940; 1948). Kroc has received such a large order for milkshake mixers from the McDonald brothers that he has flown out to California to investigate, and he soon has hamburger stands with golden arches opening everywhere (see 1961).

The Population Council is founded by John D. Rockefeller, Jr., "to stimulate, encourage, promote, conduct, and support significant activities in the broad field of population."

A contraceptive tablet made of phosphated hesperiden is developed by Chicago's G. D. Searle laboratories (see Pincus, Hoagland, 1954).

The McCarran-Walter Immigration and Nationality Act, passed over President Truman's veto, becomes law June 27. The new law removes the ban on Asian and African immigrants to the United States, and it permits spouses and minor children to enter as non-quota immigrants, but it extends the national origins quota system set up by the Johnson-Reed Act of 1924 and critics point out that while Britain uses only half her quota of 65,000, Italy has a 20-year waiting list for her quota of 5,500 (emerging nations of Africa and Asia have token quotas of 100 each) (see 1965).

1953 "We wish to suggest a structure for the salt of deoxyribose nucleic acid (DNA)," begins a one-page article in the April 25 issue of the British monthly Nature. U.S. genetic researcher James Dewey Watson, 25, and English geneticist Francis H. C. Crick, 37, of Cambridge University write, "This structure has novel features that are of considerable biological interest" and in the following (May 30) issue they develop some of the implications of their model which has the basic structure of a double helix and shows how the genetic material in animal and human cells can duplicate itself. The experiments of Watson and Crick are soon confirmed by research studies conducted throughout the world (see 1926; 1961; Ochoa, 1955).

Josef Stalin dies March 5 at age 73 after having ruled the Soviet Union since 1928. Stalin is succeeded as Chairman of the Council of Ministers by World War II aircraft and tank production chief Georgi Maximilianovich Malenkov, 51, who will head the U.S.S.R. until 1958. The Soviet minister of internal affairs L. P. Beria is dismissed July 10 and is shot as a traitor December 23, Nikita Sergeevich Khrushchev, 58, is named first secretary of the Communist party.

Yugoslavia has adopted a new constitution January 12 and Marshal Tito has been elected 2 days later as first president of a Yugoslav Republic (see 1948).

Swedish diplomat Dag Hammarskjöld, 48, is elected Secretary-General of the United Nations March 31 and will hold the post until his death in 1961.

Cambodia's Norodom Sihanouk seizes all government buildings in a bid for complete independence after French colonial officers sign protocols May 9 giving Cambodia "full sovereignty" in military, judicial, and economic matters. The French start building a huge entrenched camp at Dien-bienphu in an effort to retain Vietnam and Cochin-China and their 250,000-man army is opposed by a Communist army only half as large (see 1951; 1954).

A 10-year campaign for independence of Kenya in East Africa from Britain is initiated by the 63-year-old Kikuyu tribal leader Kamau wa Ngengi who calls himself Jomo Kenyatta and who has organized the Mau Mau ("Hidden Ones"). Kenyatta and five other Kikuyu are convicted April 8 of masterminding a terrorist campaign to drive the whites from Kenya, the conviction is quashed July 15 by the Kenya Supreme Court, and the ruling is upheld September 22 by the East African Court of Appeals.

Korean War hostilities end July 27 with an armistice signed at Panmunjom near the 38th parallel.

Ethel Rosenberg and her husband Julius have been executed June 19 for transmitting U.S. atomic secrets to Soviet agents, and a new series of U.S. atomic tests begins in the Nevada desert.

A Soviet hydrogen device is exploded August 12 and physicist Andrei Sakharov is elevated to full mem-

1953 (cont.) bership in the Soviet Academy of Sciences. Sakharov will break with the Soviet establishment in 1968 and will win a Nobel prize in 1975.

U.S. atomic scientist J. Robert Oppenheimer is charged in December with having Communist sympathies and with possible treason. Now 49, Oppenheimer has helped to build the atomic bomb but has opposed building a hydrogen bomb (*see* 1954).

Iran's Shah Mohammed Reza Pahlevi regains power August 19 through a coup engineered and financed by the CIA to prevent a Soviet takeover.

Saudi Arabia's ibn Saud who founded the kingdom in 1926 and saw it renamed Saudi Arabia in his honor 6 years later dies November 9 at age 73. He is succeeded by his son who will reign ineptly until 1964 as Saud ibn Abdel Aziz.

The South African Parliament votes February 24 to give Prime Minister Daniel F. Malan dictatorial powers to oppose black and Indian movements against the nation's "unjust" apartheid laws (*see* 1952). The South African Supreme Court may no longer invalidate the prime minister's laws.

A new Danish constitution lowers the nation's voting age to 23.

The U.S. Department of Justice tells Charlie Chaplin that he will not be permitted to re-enter the United States until he can satisfy the Immigration Office that he is not a dangerous and unwholesome character. Now 64 and still a British subject, the actor-producer joins the long list of motion picture people who have been blacklisted because of their alleged Communist sympathies and "subversive, un-American" opinions.

A criminal investigation into the "international oil cartel" is called off by outgoing President Truman who has attacked Standard Oil Company of New Jersey, Gulf Oil, the Texas Company, Socony-Mobil, Standard Oil of California, and their big foreign colleagues Anglo-Iranian and Royal Dutch-Shell. Truman has been advised by General Omar N. Bradley that the criminal charges are against the interests of national security and a grand jury investigation is dropped by the Justice Department 3 months after President Eisenhower takes office January 20. The Justice Department files a civil complaint accusing the oil companies of having conspired to restrain interstate and foreign commerce and to monopolize commerce between the United States and foreign nations (*see* 1960).

President Truman's executive order of January 16 creating a U.S. Navy petroleum reserve out of offshore oil lands is canceled by Congress which passes the Tidelands Oil Act May 22 giving coastal states title to the submerged lands. The Supreme Court will uphold the act within a year.

A giant uranium deposit in Ontario's Algoma Basin is found by some 80 field men using Geiger counters in a search organized by Brooklyn-born Toronto mining stock speculator Joseph Herman Hirshhorn, 54, who stakes 1,400 claims covering 56,000 acres. Hirshhorn obtained rights 3 years ago to mine uranium on 470 square miles of territory round Lake Athabasca and established Rix Athabasca, the first Canadian uranium mine to operate on private risk capital. He will share his Algoma Basin find with the Rothschild-backed Rio Tinto Company, Ltd., of London, a 90-year-old firm that is now selling its Spanish copper, sulfur, and iron pyrite properties and is looking for new ventures. Hirshhorn will acquire a 55 percent interest in Rio Tinto Mining Company of Canada, Ltd., and will make it a leading world supplier of the ore used to produce fuel for nuclear energy (*see* iron ore, 1964).

An Atoms for Peace program is proposed by President Eisenhower December 8 in a speech to the United Nations General Assembly. The United States, says Eisenhower, can help other nations harness the power of nuclear energy for peaceful purposes that will divert emphasis from exploitation of nuclear fission for military applications and the new Soviet regime (above) agrees to exploratory talks.

The Vickers Viscount powered by Rolls-Royce turboprop Dart engines goes into service for British Overseas Airways (BOAC). A total of 438 of the new passenger aircraft will be sold, including 82 to U.S. airlines, and Rolls-Royce will make more than 6,000 Dart engines.

The DC-7 propellor plane is introduced by Douglas Aircraft and sells for well over $1.5 million as compared with the DC-3 of 1936 which cost less than $100,000. Douglas has been slow to move into production of commercial jet aircraft and will not build its DC-8 jet until forced by pressure from Boeing whose 707 will give Boeing leadership in the commercial aircraft industry (*see* 1956; Comet, 1952).

Japan Airlines (JAL) is organized to give the Japanese a national overseas airline.

Britain's road transport is denationalized in May just before the coronation of Elizabeth II (*see* 1947).

German Volkswagens are sold in Britain for the first time (*see* 1949).

The Hertz Drive-Ur-Self System launched in 1923 and acquired by General Motors Corporation in 1925 is acquired by the Omnibus Corporation which sells its interests in the Fifth Avenue Coach Company and the New York City Omnibus Corporation. Omnibus Corporation will change its name to Hertz Corporation in November of next year (*see* RCA, 1967).

New York City subway fares rise to 15 cents July 25, up from 10 cents in 1947. Ridership on New York subways will decline by 33 percent in the next 23 years, and ridership on Eighth Avenue line trains such as the A Train will decline by 42 percent as fares continue to rise and as the Transit Authority reduces frequency of trains (*see* 1966).

The last of New York's double-decker Fifth Avenue buses go out of service (*see* 1936). The buses have required fare collectors in addition to drivers, and rising labor costs have made them uneconomic.

TRW (Thompson-Ramo-Wooldridge) has its beginnings in a California "think tank" started under the name Ramo-Wooldridge by former Hughes Aircraft physicist-engineers Simon Ramo and Dean Wooldridge, both 40, who have been discouraged by the eccentricities of Howard Hughes and by the highhanded interference of Hughes Tool Company executives. Hughes has been the major supplier of advanced electronics to the U.S. Air Force in the Korean conflict (above), but Ramo-Wooldridge is quickly given an Air Force contract to handle systems engineering and technical direction for the entire ICBM (Intercontinental Ballistic Missiles) program beginning with Atlas, Titan, and Thor missiles. Cleveland valve-maker Thompson Products, Inc., loans Ramo-Wooldridge $500,000 and will soon invest $20 million in the firm (see 1958).

Litton Industries is founded by former Hughes Aircraft executive Charles B. "Tex" Thornton, 40, with Hughes assistant controller Roy Ash and Hughes engineer Hugh W. Jamieson. A $1.5 million stock offering in the new California electronics firm is underwritten by New York's Lehman Brothers, the company acquires a small microwave-tube company operated by Charles Litton at San Carlos, Calif., and while the company will have made a profit of only $154,000 after 9 months on sales of $3 million, it will grow quickly. By the end of its fourth fiscal year (July 31, 1958) it will have profits of $4 million on sales of $100 million (see 1957).

The IBM 701 is the first IBM computer (see ENIAC, 1946; Univac, 1950). The scientific electronic computer competes in the market with Remington Rand's scientific and business computer (see 1955).

A new catalytic process for producing polyethylene plastic invented by German chemist Karl Ziegler uses atmospheric pressure instead of the 30,000 pounds per square inch pressure required by the I.C.I. process of 1935. Ziegler is director of the Max Planck Institute for Coal Research at Mülheim in West Germany, his process ushers in a new era of low-cost plastics, and foreign companies besiege the Institute with applications for rights to use the Ziegler process.

A plastic valve mechanism for aerosol cans developed by U.S. inventor Robert H. Abplanalp, 30, sharply lowers production costs. The Abplanalp valve will lead to the marketing of countless consumer products propelled by freon gas from low-cost containers (see 1945; ozone-question, 1958).

Wall Street's Dow Jones Industrial Average begins the year at 293.79—87.38 short of the 1929 high— but falls back to 255.49 by year's end (see 1954).

The American Stock Exchange is created by a renaming of the New York Curb Exchange whose members have not traded from curbs since 1921.

All U.S. federal agencies are ordered to curtail new requests for personnel and construction by the new Eisenhower administration in early February. Agencies are asked to recommend ways that the Truman budget may be cut.

Federal tax reductions should be postponed until the budget is balanced, says President Eisenhower.

Per capita state taxes have increased from $29.50 to $68.04 since 1943, the Census Bureau reveals.

Some 63.4 million Americans are gainfully employed by September and unemployment falls to its lowest point since the close of World War II.

France must industrialize if she is to surmount poverty, says General Planning Commission chief Jean Monnet whose Monnet Plan will lead to increased industrialization (see 1951; 1959).

L&M cigarettes with "Alpha-Cellulose" filter tips are introduced by Liggett & Myers and are advertised as "just what the doctor ordered."

Tareyton filter-tipped cigarettes are introduced by American Tobacco Company, but U.S. per capita cigarette consumption will decline 8.8 percent in the next 2 years.

"Cancer by the Carton" is published in the *Reader's Digest* and warns against smoking.

The strong possibility that excessive cigarette smoking contributes to lung cancer and heart disease is expressed in several U.S. medical journal reports.

Tobacco-tar condensates can induce cancer on the skin of mice, say Ernest L. Wynder, 31, and Evarts Graham of the Sloan-Kettering Institute of Cancer Research at New York. They report their findings in *Cancer Research*.

A new U.S. Department of Health, Education and Welfare established by Congress April 11 incorporates most of the functions of the Federal Security Agency. Former WAC commander Oveta Culp Hobby is named first secretary of HEW.

Cryosurgery pioneered by U.S. physician Henry Swan II, 40, lowers body temperature to slow circulation and permit dry-heart surgery.

LSD is a potent "antagonist" of the chemical substance serotinin that has just been found to exist in the human brain (see Hofmann, 1943). English biochemist John Gaddum shows that while serotinin makes muscles contract, LSD blocks the ability of serotinin to stimulate the contraction of certain muscles (see 1955).

Japanese television broadcasting begins February 1 as NHK airs its first TV programs. A pioneer radio firm that was reorganized on a nonprofit basis in 1950, NHK will grow to have two radio networks and two TV networks whose stations will outnumber those of commercial Japanese TV companies.

The U.S. television industry has revenues of $538 million thanks in part to heavy support by cigarette advertisers. Radio advertising revenues amount to

1953 (cont.) $451 million and take their first downturn since the Depression of the 1930s (*see* 1968).

TV Guide begins publication April 3 with pocket-size weekly program listings. Publisher Walter H. Annenberg has merged his 9-year-old *Seventeen* magazine with his late father's *Philadelphia Inquirer* and racing publications to create Triangle Publications (*see* 1922; 1936), he has bought out small publishers who have started TV listing publications at New York, Philadelphia, Washington, Baltimore, and Chicago, and he has created a book with 10 regional editions. *TV Guide* has a circulation of 1.5 million by the end of its first year and will grow to have a circulation of more than 15 million as its regional editions proliferate to more than 80.

L'Express begins publication at Paris under the direction of *Elle* editor Françoise Giroud, 37, and her lover-economist Jean-Jacques Servan-Schreiber, 30. In 10 years they will turn the journal of leftist opinion into a highly successful newsmagazine modeled on *Time* and *Newsweek*.

Playboy magazine begins publication in December with a nude calendar photograph of screen comedienne Marilyn Monroe. Chicago publisher Hugh Hefner, 27, has been a department store advertising copywriter and a subscription writer for *Esquire,* he has started his frankly sexist magazine with an initial investment of $10,000, he features nude photography and ribald cartoons, and he begins an empire that will embrace Playboy Clubs, Playboy Books, and Playboy Products (*see Penthouse,* 1969).

Canadian newspaper proprietor Roy Thompson, 59, moves to Britain and begins an empire that will include hundreds of newspapers and magazines worldwide, five book publishing firms, a travel agency, and other enterprises. Thompson will first acquire control of the *Scotsman,* then of Scottish television, in 1959 he will gain control of the Kemsley Newspapers, Ltd., including the *Sunday Times,* and in 1966 he will gain control of the *Times* of London.

A photographic type-composing machine far more advanced than the 1949 Fotosetter is introduced by Photon, Inc., whose Higonnet-Moyroud machine is produced under license from the Graphic Arts Research Foundation, Inc. Operated from a standard typewriter keyboard at full electric typewriter speed, the machine delivers film negatives instead of metal type.

Nonfiction *The Second Sex* in an English translation of the 1949 book by Simone de Beauvoir which is called "a pretentious and inflated tract on feminism" by Topeka, Kan., psychiatrist Karl Augustus Menninger, 60, but is called "one of the few great books of our time" by U.S. author Philip Wylie whose 1942 book *Generation of Vipers* introduced the term "Momism"; *A Stillness at Appomattox* by U.S. historian (Charles) Bruce Catton, 54, is the third in a trilogy of Civil War histories.

Fiction *Acquainted with the Night (Und sagte kein einziges Wort)* by Heinrich Böll who points for the first time to the moral vacuum that underlies the "economic miracle" of postwar Western Germany; *Chapel Road (De Kapellekensbaan)* by Flemish novelist Louis Paul Boon, 41; *The Erasers (Les Gommes)* by French novelist Alain Robbe-Grillet, 31, who rejects conventional character and plot and develops an idiom of his own; *The Adventures of Augie March* by Saul Bellow; *Go Tell It on the Mountain* by U.S. émigré novelist James Baldwin, 29, who has gone to Paris to escape U.S. prejudice against blacks and homosexuals; *The Invisible Man* by U.S. novelist Ralph Waldo Ellison, 39, who wins a National Book award for his novel about black identity which a 1965 *Book Week* poll will call "the most distinguished single work" published in the previous 20 years; *The Garden to the Sea* by Philip Toynbee; *Too Late the Phalarope* by Alan Paton; *Martereau* by Nathalie Sarraute; *For Esme, with Love and Squalor* (nine stories) by J. D. Salinger; *Casino Royale* by London novelist Ian (Lancaster) Fleming, 45, who was personal assistant to Britain's Director of Naval Intelligence during World War II, is now foreign manager of Kemsley Newspapers, and begins a series of thrillers based on an imaginary British Secret Service agent named James Bond whose 007 prefix means that he is allowed to kill in line of duty; *Battle Cry* by U.S. Marine Corps veteran Leon Uris, 29. A dozen publishers had rejected the manuscript but reviewers hail it as the first "positive" major novel of World War II and it becomes a best seller; *Junkie* by U.S. novelist William Lee (William Seward Burroughs), 39, a grandson of the adding machine inventor. He has been a heroin addict since 1944 and will remain one until 1957.

Poetry *The Waking* by U.S. poet Theodore Roethke, 45; *Poems, 1940–1953* by U.S. poet Karl Shapiro, 40; *Poems* by English poet Elizabeth Jennings, 27.

Doubleday Anchor Books introduced by the 56-year-old publishing giant introduces a new line of quality paperbacks.

The *Paris Review* begins publication. Former Harvard *Lampoon* editor George Ames Plimpton, 26, has started the literary review with Harold L. Humes, Peter Matthiessen, John Train, and other friends.

Painting *Study after Velázquez: Pope Innocent X* by Francis Bacon; *Eiffel Tower* by Marc Chagall; *Apples* by Georges Braque; *The Snail* by Henri Matisse; *Cry of the Seagull* by Max Ernst; *Edge of August* by Mark Tobey; *Woman and Bicycle* by Willem de Kooning. Raoul Dufy dies at Forcalquier, France, March 23 at age 75; John Marin dies at Addison, Me., October 1 at age 82; Francis Picabia dies at Paris November 30 at age 74.

Sculpture *King and Queen* by Henry Moore.

Theater *The Crucible* by Arthur Miller 1/22 at New York's Martin Beck Theater, with Arthur Kennedy, Jennie Egan, Walter Hampden in an account of the 1692 Salem witch trials intended as a parallel to the persecution of alleged Communist sympathizers in the United States, 197 perfs.; *Picnic* by William Inge 2/19 at New York's Music Box Theater, with Ralph Meeker, Janice Rule, Paul Newman, Kim Stanley, Eileen Heckhart, 477 perfs., Pulitzer prize; *Camino Real* by Tennessee Williams 3/19 at New York's Martin Beck Theater, with Eli Wallach, Frank Silvera, Jo Van Fleet, Martin Balsam, Barbara Baxley, Hurd Hatfield, Michael Griggs, 60 perfs.; *Medea* (*Medée*) by Jean Anouilh 3/26 at the Théâtre de l'Atelier, Paris; *Under Milk Wood* by Dylan Thomas 5/3 at Harvard's Fogg Museum; *Don Juan, or the Love of Geometry* (*Don Juan oder Die Liebe zur Geometrie*) by Max Frisch 5/5 at Berlin's Schillertheater; *Tea and Sympathy* by Robert Anderson 9/30 at New York's Ethel Barrymore Theater, with Deborah Kerr, John Kerr, 712 perfs.; *The Teahouse of the August Moon* by John Patrick 10/15 at New York's Martin Beck Theater, with John Forsythe, David Wayne, 1,027 perfs., Pulitzer prize 1954; *The Sleeping Prince* by Terence Rattigan 11/5 at London's Phoenix Theatre, with Laurence Olivier, Vivien Leigh; *The Angel Comes to Babylon* by Friedrich Dürrenmatt 12/22 at Munich's Kammerspiele.

Ontario's Stratford Festival opens in a tent with Alec Guinness playing Shakespearean roles under the direction of Tyrone Guthrie, with sets designed by Tanya Moiseiwitsch. The 6-week inaugural season plays to an audience of 68,000 and has a box office gross of $200,000. A 2,258-seat auditorium will replace the tent, the season will lengthen to 22 weeks, the audience will grow to more than 500,000, and the box office will take in more than $4 million by 1976 (*see* American Shakespeare Theatre, 1955).

Films Henry Koster's *The Robe* with Richard Burton, Jean Simmons, and Victor Mature is the first film to be produced in CinemaScope. Designed to counter the inroads that television is making on movie theater receipts, CinemaScope employs screens much wider than those used for conventional films and has a stereophonic soundtrack; Arch Oboler's *Bwana Devil* with Robert Stack is the first three-dimensional film and represents another effort to compete with television (audiences need Polaroid viewers to see the 3-D film).

More notable films Fred Zinneman's *From Here to Eternity* with Burt Lancaster, Montgomery Clift, Deborah Kerr, Frank Sinatra; George Stevens's *Shane* with Alan Ladd, Jean Arthur, Brandon De Wilde; William Wyler's *Roman Holiday* with Audrey Hepburn, Gregory Peck; Joseph L. Mankiewicz's *Julius Caesar* with Marlon Brando, James Mason, John Gielgud; Charles Walters's *Lili* with Leslie Caron, Mel Ferrer; Stuart Heisler's *The Star* with Bette Davis, Sterling Hayden, Natalie Wood; Jacques Tati's *Mr. Hulot's Holiday* (*Les Vacances de M. Hulot*); Billy Wilder's *Stalag 17* with William Holden, Don Taylor, Otto Preminger; Yasujiro Ozu's *Tokyo Story;* Akira Kurosawa's *The Seven Samurai;* Kenji Mizoguchi's *Ugetsu;* Ingmar Bergman's *Sawdust and Tinsel;* Federico Fellini's *I Vitelloni;* Charles Frend's *The Cruel Sea* with Jack Hawkins.

 Hollywood musical Vincente Minnelli's *The Band Wagon* with Fred Astaire, Cyd Charisse, Jack Buchanan, Nanette Fabray, Oscar Levant, music by Arthur Schwartz, lyrics by Howard Dietz, songs that include "That's Entertainment," "Triplets," "By Myself," "Shine on Your Shoes."

Broadway musicals *Hazel Flagg* 2/11 at the Mark Hellinger Theater, with Helen Gallagher, music by Jule Styne, lyrics by Bob Hilliard, songs that include "Every Street's a Boulevard in Old New York," 190 perfs.; *Wonderful Town* 2/25 at the Winter Garden Theater, with Rosalind Russell, music by Leonard Bernstein, book based on the 1940 stage play *My Sister Eileen,* lyrics by Betty Comden and Adolph Green, songs that include "Ohio," "A Quiet Girl," "Conga!" 559 perfs.; *Can Can* 5/7 at the Shubert Theater, with Gwen Verdon, book by Abe Burrows, music and lyrics by Cole Porter, songs that include "I Love Paris," "C'est Magnifique," "It's All Right with Me," 892 perfs.; *Me and Juliet* 5/28 at the Majestic Theater, with Isabel Bigley, Joan McCracken, music by Richard Rodgers, lyrics by Oscar Hammerstein II, songs that include "No Other Love," 358 perfs.; *Comedy in Music* 10/2 at the John Golden Theater, with Danish pianist Victor Borge in a one-man show, 849 perfs.; *Kismet* 12/3 at the Ziegfeld Theater, with Alfred Drake, Richard Kiley, music based on the works of Aleksandr Borodin, lyrics by Robert Wright and George "Chet" Forest (Forrest Chichester, Jr., 38), songs that include "Baubles, Bangles and Beads," "Stranger in Paradise," "This Is My Beloved," 538 perfs.

First performances *Suite Hebraique* by Ernest Bloch 1/1 at Chicago; Symphony No. 7 (*Sinfonia Antartica*) by Ralph Vaughan Williams 1/14 at Manchester; *Sinfonia breve* and Concerto No. 2 in G minor for Strings by Ernest Bloch 4/11 in a BBC Symphony concert broadcast; *Te Deum* and *Orb and Sceptre* march by Sir William Walton 6/2 at London for the coronation of Elizabeth II; Symphony No. 5 by Darius Milhaud 10/16 in a radio concert broadcast from Turin; *Atomic Bomb* symphonic fantasy by Japanese composer Masao Oki, 52, 11/6 at Tokyo; Symphony No. 10 by Dmitri Shostakovich 12/17 at Leningrad.

Cantata *Une Cantate de Noël* by Arthur Honegger 12/12 at Basel.

Opera *The Harpies* 5/25 at New York, with music and lyrics by Marc Blitzstein (who wrote it in 1931); *Gloriana* 6/8 at London's Covent Garden, with music by Benjamin Britten, libretto by William Plomer.

1953 (cont.) Ballet *Fanfare* 6/2 at London's Covent Garden, with music by Benjamin Britten, choreography by Jerome Robbins.

U.S. ballet dancer Merce Cunningham, 33, of the Martha Graham Company creates his first solo and starts his own dance company. Cunningham rejects traditional tenets of ballet and modern dance, revolts against literary, musical, and body-language associations in dance, and espouses a formal definition of ballet to which he will adhere for more than 25 years.

Popular songs "April in Portugal" by Portuguese composer Raul Ferrão, lyrics by José Galherdo (English lyrics by Jimmy Kennedy); "I'm Walking Behind You" by English songwriter Billy Reid; "Crying in the Chapel" by Artie Glenn; "I Believe" by Erwin Drake, Irvin Graham, Jimmy Shirl, and Al Stillman; "Rags to Riches" by Richard Adler and Jerry Ross; "Ruby" by Heinz Roemheld, lyrics by Mitchell Parish (for King Vidor's film *Ruby Gentry*); "Oh! My Pa-pa" by Paul Burkhard (for the Swiss film *Fireworks*), English lyrics by John Turner and Geoffrey Parsons; "Eternally" ("The Terry Theme") by Charlie Chaplin (for the film *Limelight*), lyrics by Geoffrey Parsons; "You. You. You." by Lotar Olias, lyrics by Robert Mellin; "Hi-Lili, Hi-Lo" by Bronislau Kapes, lyrics by Helen Deutsch (for the film *Lili*); "That's Amore" by Harry Warren, lyrics by Jack Brooks (for Norman Taurog's film *The Caddy*); "Ebb Tide" by Carl Sigman; "That Doggie in the Window" by Bob Merrill.

🏃 Dark Star wins the Kentucky Derby to give Native Dancer his only defeat in 22 races.

Australian tennis prodigy Ken Rosewall wins the Australian and French singles title at age 18. Only 5 feet 7, Rosewall is the youngest player to win the championships, he will be the oldest player to win the French title when he takes it again in 1968 and the oldest to win the Australian title when he takes it again in 1972 at age 37.

Australia retains the Davis Cup by defeating the U.S. tennis team.

Maureen Connolly wins the "Grand Slam" of tennis by taking the Australian, French, English, and U.S. women's singles championships.

Ben Hogan wins the U.S. Open and Masters golf tournaments, breaks the Masters record by five strokes, and wins his first British Open.

The Boston Braves become the Milwaukee Braves as U.S. major league baseball teams begin a geographical realignment spurred in part by the fact that the airplane has reduced travel time (*see* Aaron, 1954; Atlanta, 1966).

The New York Yankees win the World Series by defeating the Brooklyn Dodgers 4 games to 3 and gain the championship for an unprecedented fifth consecutive time.

∞ The Church of Scientology is founded at Washington, D.C., by former U.S. science fiction writer L. (La-

fayette) Ronald Hubbard, 42, who bases the new church on his best-selling 1950 book *Dianetics: The Modern Science of Mental Health*. Man is essentially a free and immortal spirit who can achieve his true nature only by freeing himself of emotional encumbrances of the past through counseling ("auditing"), says Hubbard, his "applied religious philosophy" will make him a fortune, but British authorities in 1968 will refuse entry to Scientology students and teachers on the ground that Scientology is "socially harmful" and that its "authoritarian principles and practices are a potential menace to the well-being of those so deluded as to become followers."

💲 New York's I. Miller women's shoe firm is acquired by Maxey Jarman's General Shoe Corporation which adds Miller's high-priced women's shoes to the medium and low-priced women's shoes it has been selling since 1936 when it acquired the J. K. Orr Shoe Company (*see* 1950). Jarman acquires the New York menswear and shoe retailer Whitehouse & Hardy to give him an outlet for Johnston & Murphy shoes (*see* Hoving Corporation, 1956).

🌐 Floods devastate Europe's North Sea coastal areas. More than 2,000 are killed.

French rabbits infected with myxomatosis are released in Britain. The disease will wipe out most of the country's wild rabbits (*see* 1952).

🌾 Nikita Khrushchev (above) defies warnings by agronomists that rainfall in the Kazakhstan Soviet Republic is undependable. He orders virgin lands in Kazakhstan to be plowed and planted with grain that will increase Soviet food production (*see* 1963).

Drought in the U.S. Midwest worsens and sections of 13 states are declared disaster areas (*see* 1952). Southern Missouri has an even dryer season than in 1936, pastures are dead to the grass roots, and farmers dump cattle on the market at sacrifice prices.

🍎 A correlation between coronary heart disease and diets high in animal fats is pointed out by University of Minnesota physiologist Ancel Keys, 49, who observes that the incidence of heart disease tends to be higher in communities where animal fats comprise a large part of people's diets (*see* Anichkov, 1913; Kannel, 1949; Keys, Yudkin, 1957).

The Du Pont (Pennington) weight loss diet issued by U.S. physician Alfred W. Pennington is one of many variations on the low-carbohydrate high-fat "Eskimo" diet. Pennington has helped portly E. I. du Pont de Nemours executives lose weight (*see* Stefansson, 1946; Taller, 1961; Stillman, 1967).

Carotene, the provitamin of vitamin A, is synthesized from acetone and acetylene by researchers at Basel, Switzerland (see 1920; Khorana, 1959).

☂ The U.S. Food and Drug Administration (FDA) is placed in the new Department of Health, Education and Welfare (above).

Some 93 Japanese will be fatally poisoned in the next 7 years as a result of eating fish and shellfish contaminated with mercury wastes discharged into rivers at Minamata Bay in Kyushu and at Niigata in Honshu. Many more will go blind, lose the use of limbs, or suffer brain damage from mercury poisoning (see Huckleby family, 1969).

A process that converts nonfat dry milk into crystals that retain all the protein, mineral, and vitamin content of fresh skim milk is discovered by U.S. dairy scientist David D. Peebles.

U.S. meatpackers begin moving out of Chicago to plants closer to western feedlots (see 1865; 1960).

The first underground freezer storage room is opened at Kansas City by local mine operator Leonard Strauss who sees potential for food storage in the city's mined-out limestone quarries. Strauss employs the constant 45 to 54 degree temperature of the caves to reduce cooling costs, and his room will grow in the next 14 years into the world's largest refrigerated warehouse, handling 8 million pounds per day.

U.S. pizzerias grow to number at least 15,000, and there are at least 100,000 stores where ready-made refrigerated or frozen pizzas may be purchased (see oregano, 1948). The americanized pizza pies are thin, round layers of bread dough laden with tomato paste, mozarella cheese, olive oil, pepper, and oregano with optional extras that may include anchovies, eggs, mushrooms, onions, or sausages, the pizzas are baked on bricks or in metal ovens, and a few pizzerias offer the Sicilian pizza which is baked in a pan and is slightly thicker and more breadlike (see Shakey's, 1954).

Sara Lee Kitchens proves that properly frozen baked goods can be mass marketed successfully. Sara Lee Cheese Cake has been selling at 79 cents since 1949 and sales have mushroomed (see 1956).

Sugar Smacks breakfast food is introduced by the Kellogg Company. The new cereal is 56 percent sugar (see 1952; 1955).

Diamond Crystal Salt Company is acquired from General Foods by Charles F. Moore, grandson of the company's founder and head of the General Foods division since last year (see 1886; 1929). Moore is helped by members of his family to buy the assets of the division and return it to family ownership, and Diamond Crystal will earn more money in its first 3 years under Moore's management than it did in 24 years as a General Foods division.

Minute Maid Corporation pays its first common stock dividend as orange concentrate sales top $36 million. Minute Maid's net profits exceed $1 million (see 1949; 1954).

Candy rationing ends in Britain.

Schweppes Tonic Water is bottled for the first time in the United States and is sold under the name Schweppes Quinine Water to comply with an FDA order based on the allegation that "Tonic Water" implies therapeutic virtues. A franchise with the

Pepsi-Cola Company is negotiated by Sir Frederick Hooper and Commander Edward Whitehead, 45, the latter becomes president of Schweppes (USA), but he is warned that bottling the drink in America and reducing its price will lose the luxury market. A 75 percent price drop and advertisements featuring Commander Whitehead will gain a large share of the market for Schweppes (see 1858).

"Irish Coffee" is introduced at San Francisco's Buena Vista Cafe at the foot of Hyde Street hill on the Beach Street cable car line. The mixture of coffee, cream, sugar, and Irish whisky was discovered in Ireland by San Francisco Chronicle columnist Stanton Delaplane, 45, he has given the recipe to proprietors Jack Koeppler and George Freedberg, and the drink soon accounts for 40 percent of the Buena Vista's business.

White Rose Redi-Tea is introduced by New York's Seeman Brothers. It is the world's first instant iced tea (see 1901).

Population control is urged by New York zoologist-conservationist Fairfield Osborne. His 1948 book Our Plundered Planet warned of possible hazards in DDT, his new book The Limits of Our Earth argues that the collapse of ancient civilizations was due in part to misuse of available natural resources.

1954 The 9 to 0 decision handed down by the Supreme Court May 17 in the case of Brown v. Board of Education declares racial segregation in public schools unconstitutional, the ruling overturns the "separate but equal" doctrine laid down in the 1897 case of Plessy v. Ferguson, Chief Justice Earl Warren orders the states to proceed "with all deliberate speed" to integrate educational facilities, but Topeka, Kan., requests time to formulate a plan for racial balance. It was at Topeka that the father of Linda Brown, now 11, brought the 1951 action that has led to the court's

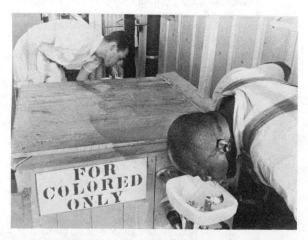

"Separate but equal" was accepted in the South until the U.S. Supreme Court ruled that segregation was unconstitutional.

1954 (cont.) landmark decision, and Topeka will repeat its request for more time for the next 20 years (*see* Little Rock, 1957, 1958).

 France appeals for U.S. aid to relieve her troops surrounded at Dien-bienphu in Indo-China (*see* 1953). President Eisenhower declares that defeat of Communist aggression in Southeast Asia is vitally important to the United States, but he declines to deploy U.S. airpower to relieve the siege of Dien-bienphu.

"The French are going to win," says the chairman of the U.S. Joint Chiefs of Staff Admiral Arthur W. Radford, "it is a fight that is going to be finished with our help."

President Eisenhower outlines the "domino theory" first voiced by newspaper columnist Joseph W. Alsop, Jr., 43: "You have a row of dominoes set up. You knock over the first one, and what will happen to the last is that it will go over very quickly." But Eisenhower resists "hawkish" suggestions by Vice President Nixon, Secretary of State John Foster Dulles, and Admiral Radford (above), and he refuses to send U.S. forces to Vietnam.

A Geneva Conference of world powers meeting from April 26 to July 21 divides Vietnam at the 17th parallel into North Vietnam and South Vietnam. Ho Chi Minh, 64, takes power as president of the Communist "Democratic Republic" of North Vietnam after 9 years of leading guerilla forces.

South Vietnam gains "complete independence" in "free association" with France under terms of a treaty signed June 4 by the French premier with South Vietnam's Prince Bau Loa who is replaced June 14 by Ngo Dinh Diem (*see* 1953; 1955).

"Free Puerto Rico!" cries Lolita Lebron March 1 from the gallery of the House of Representatives and she fires the first of eight shots that injure five congressmen. The 28-year-old divorcée and her three confederates have pulled out concealed weapons to stage their demonstration, each will serve at least 23 years in prison (they will reject parole offers lest they appear repentant or acceptive of U.S. law).

A resolution to bar communism from the Western Hemisphere is approved in March by the Tenth Inter-American Conference meeting at Caracas. Guatemala dissents.

Guatemala has charged January 29 that Nicaragua is planning to invade Guatemala with support from several other Latin American states and with tacit U.S. consent. A major shipment of Communist-made arms to Guatemala is reported March 17 by the U.S. State Department, Guatemala's foreign minister declares May 21 that his country has been forced to buy arms from Communist sources because it has been boycotted by the United States and left defenseless.

A reshuffling of the Egyptian military government that has held power since 1952 replaces General Mohammed Naguib Bey as premier. He is succeeded by the 36-year-old Colonel Gamal Abdel Nasser April 17, and a treaty signed with Britain October 19 provides for British withdrawal from the Suez Canal Zone within 20 months. Britain is to give up its rights to the base at Suez, but the Egyptians agree to keep it in combat readiness and to permit British entry in the event of an attack on Turkey or any Arab state by an outside power (*see* 1956).

An Algerian revolt against France breaks out October 31 under the leadership of the Front de Liberation (FLN) (*see* 1957).

German reunification is rejected by Soviet Russia in a meeting at Berlin of British, French, U.S., and Soviet foreign ministers.

Canada and the United States agree to build a "DEW" Line (Distant Early Warning Line) of radar stations across northern Canada to alert Canadian and U.S. authorities of the approach of aircraft or missiles over the Arctic.

Senator Joseph McCarthy conducts hearings from April 22 to June 17 as chairman of the Senate Permanent Investigations Subcommittee, and he charges that a Communist spy ring is operating at the U.S. Army Signal Corps installation at Fort Monmouth, N.J. (*see* 1951). The hearings are televised across the country, McCarthy accuses the secretary of the Army of concealing evidence, the secretary retains Boston lawyer Joseph Nye Welch, 63, to represent him, McCarthy makes a vicious charge against one of Welch's assistants, Welch says, "Until this moment, Senator, I think I never really gauged your cruelty or recklessness. . . . Have you no sense of decency, sir, at long last? Have you left no sense of decency?"

The Senate votes 67 to 22 December 2 to support a resolution of condemnation against Senator McCarthy for misconduct.

The Atomic Energy Commission revokes J. Robert Oppenheimer's security clearance, President Eisenhower follows suit, the AEC appoints a board to investigate Oppenheimer, the board clears Oppenheimer of disloyalty charges, but it votes two to one that Oppenheimer's imprudent associations have made him a security risk and upholds revocation of the physicist's security clearance (*see* 1953) (Oppenheimer will receive the AEC's Fermi Award in 1963 after the anti-Communist frenzy stirred up by Senator McCarthy has abated).

 The U.S. Atomic Energy Commission explodes a nuclear-fusion (hydrogen) "device" at Bikini Atoll in the South Pacific (below) (see 1956; Eniwetok, 1952).

The first nuclear-powered submarine is launched in January. Built at the insistence of Rear Admiral Hyman George Rickover, the U.S. Navy's *Nautilus* has been preceded by a nuclear-powered surface vessel —the Soviet ice-breaker *Lenin* (*see* 1958).

The world's first nuclear power station begins producing electricity for Soviet industry and agriculture June 27. The station 55 miles from Moscow at Obninsk has an effective capacity of 5,000 kilowatts.

Participation of U.S. private industry in the production of nuclear power gains congressional approval August 30 in amendments to the McMahon Atomic Energy Act of 1946.

Federal Power Commission price regulation of U.S. natural gas piped interstate is upheld by the Supreme Court June 7 in an historic 5-3 decision handed down in the case of *Phillips Petroleum v. U.S.* The Court rules that Phillips is a natural gas company within the meaning of the Natural Gas Act of 1938, the FPC freezes the well-head price of natural gas, 106 companies say the commission has gone beyond the court decision and that the price freeze is illegal and unworkable, U.S. Senator Lyndon B. Johnson of Texas says he will urge congressional action to solve problems raised by the court decision, the Supreme Court refuses to reverse its ruling in the Phillips case, the FPC chairman denies that his commission seeks to socialize the industry and says it will set rates high enough to provide profits necessary for risking capital to explore and develop new natural gas reserves. The industry will work for decades to have the well-head price of natural gas deregulated but will meanwhile promote wasteful uses of natural gas including its use as a boiler fuel to generate electricity.

The Dixon-Yates contract permitting private companies to supply energy to the Tennessee Valley Authority gets President Eisenhower's signature November 11, but the propriety of the contract comes under attack and the president will cancel it in 8 months.

President Eisenhower's Atoms for Peace plan of last year is implemented November 15 by the donation of more than 200 pounds of fissionable material. The plan is approved unanimously by the General Assembly of the United Nations December 4.

A solar battery developed by Bell Laboratories of American Telephone & Telegraph makes it possible to convert sunlight directly to electric power.

U.S. gasoline prices average 29 cents per gallon in October, up from 21 cents in 1944.

British Petroleum Company, Ltd., (BP) is created by a renaming of the Anglo-Iranian Petroleum Company founded in 1908 as Anglo-Persian Petroleum.

The first practical silicon transistor is introduced by Texas Instruments, Inc., whose president John Erik Jonsson, 53, has brought the price of germanium transistors down from $16 to $2.50 (*see* Shockley, 1948; Sony, 1952). Silicon transistors are much cheaper than germanium transistors and will increase sharply the use of solid-state electronic components, booming sales for Jonsson's Texas Instruments (formerly Geophysical Service, Inc.).

Electronic computers are applied for the first time to business uses. Twenty computers are shipped to commercial customers (*see* Univac, 1950; IBM, 1955).

The oxygen furnace for steelmaking is installed for the first time in the United States by McLouth Steel, a small Detroit firm with less than 1 percent of U.S. steel ingot capacity. Perfected in 1950 by a tiny Austrian company, the oxygen furnace is the first major technological breakthrough at the ingot level for steelmaking since the 19th century, it is being installed by West German and Japanese steelmakers as they modernize their production facilities, but it will not be adopted by Jones & Laughlin until 1957 or by Bethlehem and United States Steel until 1964.

The New York State Thruway opens to traffic June 24. Toll revenue from the 559-mile road between New York and Buffalo is projected to reach $68 million by 1975 and its vehicular traffic is projected to reach 108 million trips by that time, but the revenue figure will be attained by 1963 and the traffic figure by 1965.

New York's Seventh Avenue is made one-way southbound and Eighth Avenue is made one-way northbound (*see* 1951). Traffic flow is speeded by from 25 to 40 percent, but the Fifth Avenue Coach Company complains that it has lost customers on its Seventh and Eighth Avenue routes and the Transport Workers Union opposes further one-way avenues (*see* Broadway, 1956).

American Motors Corporation (AMC) is created by a merger of Hudson Motor Car Company and Nash-Kelvinator (*see* 1922; 1935; Rambler, 1959).

Studebaker-Packard Corporation is created by a merger of Studebaker Corporation and Packard Motors (*see* 1930; 1964).

The Mercedes 300 SL introduced by Germany's Daimler-Benz employs the first fuel-injection system for automobiles. Daimler-Benz engineer Rudolf Uhlenhaut has adapted a system developed by the firm for aircraft in 1935.

The IL-14 introduced in Soviet Russia replaces the IL-12 that has been the Soviet DC-3 (*see* 1948; 1962).

Convair (formerly Consolidated Vultee Aircraft) is merged into General Dynamics Corporation (*see* 1934; 1952).

Wall Street's Dow Jones Industrial Average finally passes the 381.17 high of 1929 and closes the year above the 404 mark.

Only 154 Americans have incomes of $1 million or more, down from 513 in 1929.

A U.S. taxpayer with an income of $100,000 may now pay more than $67,000 in taxes, up from $16,000 or less in 1929, and the individual tax exemption is $600, down from $1,500 in 1929. Income taxes will be reduced slightly next year, but the average tax rate, including surtax, is just above 20 percent and taxpayers in top brackets pay 87 percent.

Olin-Mathieson Chemical Corporation is created by a merger of Olin Industries, Inc., with Mathieson Chemical Corp. (*see* 1944; Squibb, 1952).

New York's Chemical Bank (initially Chemical Corn Exchange Bank) is created by a merger of the Chemi-

1954 (cont.) cal Bank and Trust Company with the Corn Exchange Bank (*see* Chase Manhattan, Citibank, 1955).

The Ford Foundation gives away $67.8 million (*see* 1950). Some $34 million goes to education, $18 million to international programs, the rest to programs in economics, public affairs, and the behavioral sciences (*see* 1956).

 The first mass poliomyelitis immunization shots are administered February 23 to schoolchildren at Pittsburgh (*see* Salk, 1952).

Open-heart surgery is introduced by Minneapolis physician C. (Clarence) Walton Lillehei, 35 (*see* Williams, 1893).

Success in treating psychotic patients with the drug chlorpromazine is reported by Montreal physicians Heinz Lehmann and G. E. Hanrahan who have obtained the drug from France's Poulenc, Ltd. (*see* 1952). Researchers at Philadelphia's Smith Kline & French have found chlorpromazine useful in preventing vomiting and the firm will introduce the drug under the brand name Thorazine.

Thorazine (above) will effect a large-scale reduction in the hospitalization of mental patients by dramatically increasing recovery from schizophrenia.

Miltown is introduced by Wallace Laboratories, Equanil is introduced by Wyeth Laboratories (*see* 1950; Librium, 1960).

President Eisenhower proposes a "reinsurance" plan that will encourage private initiative to strengthen U.S. health services. A survey of medical costs reveals that 16 percent of U.S. families go into debt each year in order to pay for treatment.

Dramatic evidence of the dangers in smoking are presented by U.S. epidemiologists E. (Edward) Cuyler Hammond, 42, and Daniel Horn, 38, who report on a 2-year study of 187,783 U.S. men aged 50 to 69 of whom 11,870 have died. Of the deceased, 7,316 were smokers and the 11,870 figure is larger by 2,265 than it would have been statistically if none of the men had smoked. More than half the deaths have been from coronary heart disease, 14 percent from lung cancer, another 14 percent from all other forms of cancer (including carcinomas of the esophagus and the larynx), with gastric ulcers, pneumonia, and influenza ranking high among causes of death. Daniel Horn gives up smoking (*see* Surgeon General's Report, 1964).

 Sales of Viceroy cigarettes take a sensational leap as U.S. smokers demand filter-tipped cigarettes (*see* 1936). The Viceroy filter is changed from cotton to cellulose acetate which will quickly become the standard filter material (*see* 1955).

 The U.S. Air Force Academy is created by act of Congress. The first class of 306 cadets will be sworn in July 11 of next year at Lowry Air Force Base, Denver; the Cadet Wing will move into permanent quarters north of Colorado Springs in 1958.

C. W. Post College is founded at Greenvale, N. Y., with a gift from cereal heiress Marjorie Merriweather Post. The new college is part of Long Island University.

 RCA introduces the first U.S. color television sets but color reception is unreliable at best. No other company will enter the color TV market on a sustained basis until 1959, when the courts will settle patent suits brought against RCA by Zenith Corporation and others (*see* Zenith, 1963).

A black and white TV set with a 19-inch screen retails at $187 in the United States.

The world has 94 million telephones of which 52 million are in the United States.

The Washington Post Company buys out the *Washington Times-Herald,* its only morning competition, March 17 for $8.5 million. Within 5 years, the *Post* will overtake the *Washington Star* in advertising lineage. The company also buys out the CBS interest in WTOP-Radio and TV started by CBS in 1949 (*see* 1933; *Newsweek,* 1961).

Sports Illustrated begins publication August 16. The new weekly magazine will lose $26 million for Time-Life, Inc., before it becomes profitable in 1964.

American Heritage Publishing Company is started with two partners by former Time-Life editor James Parton, 41, to publish magazines that will include *American Heritage, Horizon,* and *Americana* plus illustrated history books.

Nonfiction *McCarthy and His Enemies* by William F. Buckley, Jr., recognizes the excess of the Wisconsin senator but supports his campaign against U.S. Communists.

Fiction *The Thaw (Ottepel')* by Soviet novelist Ilya Grigoryevich Erenburg, 63, supplies the name for a new trend in Soviet literature and refers for the first time to the iniquities experienced under the regime of the late Josef Stalin; *Felix Krull (Die Bekenntnisse des Hochstaplers Felix Krull)* by Thomas Mann; *The Unguarded House (Haus ohne Hüter)* by Heinrich Böll; *People of the City* by Nigerian (Ibo) novelist Cyprian Ekwensi, 33; *The Radiance of the King (Le Regard du Roi)* by West African novelist Camara Laye, 26; *Lord of the Flies* by English novelist William Golding, 43; *Bonjour Tristesse* by French novelist Françoise Sagan, 19; *Under the Net* by English novelist Iris Murdoch, 35; *Live and Let Die* by Ian Fleming; *The Blackboard Jungle* by New York novelist Evan Hunter, 28; *Tunnel of Love* by U.S. comic novelist Peter De Vries, 44; *The Ponder Heart* by Eudora Welty; *The Bride of Innisfallen* (stories) by Eudora Welty; *Pictures from an Institution* by poet Randall Jarrell.

Poetry *Collected Poems* by Wallace Stevens; *The Desert Music* by William Carlos Williams.

Painting *Crucifixion* by Salvador Dali; *Les Vaga-bonds* by Jean Dubuffet; *Sylvette* by Pablo Picasso; *The Red Roofs* by Marc Chagall; *Acrobat and Horse* by Fernand Léger; *Colonial Cubism* by Stuart Davis; *Collection* by U.S. painter Robert Rauschenberg, 28; *Painting T* by Hans Hartung. Reginald Marsh dies at Bennington, Vt., July 3 at age 56; André Derain dies at Chambourcy, France, September 10 at age 74; Henri Matisse dies at Nice November 3 at age 84.

Sculpture The Iwo Jima Memorial Monument dedicated at Washington, D.C., honors the U.S. Marine dead of all wars. Based on a World War II photograph taken in March 1945 by Joe Rosenthal, the monument has six bronze figures that each stand approximately 32 feet high; *Two Dancing Figures* by English sculptor Lynn Chadwick.

Tri-X film is introduced by Eastman Kodak Company, which also introduces Tri-X motion picture film and Royal Pan sheet film. The new high-speed (200 ASA) Tri-X black and white roll film permits photography under difficult lighting conditions (it can be rated at more than 1,000 ASA and pushed in the darkroom).

Theater *The Caine Mutiny Court-Martial* by Herman Wouk 1/2 at New York's Plymouth Theater, with Lloyd Nolan as Lieutenant Commander Philip Francis Queeg, Henry Fonda, John Hodiak, 415 perfs.; *The Reluctant Debutante* by English playwright William Heatherton, 30, 8/24 at London's Cambridge Theatre, 752 perfs.; *Separate Tables (Table by the Window* and *Table Number Seven)* by Terence Rattigan 9/22 at the St. James's Theatre, London, with Eric Portman, 726 perfs.; *The Tender Trap* by U.S. playwrights Robert Paul Smith and Max Shulman 10/13 at New York's Longacre Theater, with Robert Preston, 101 perfs.; *Ladies of the Corridor* by Dorothy Parker and Arnaud d'Usseau 10/21 at New York's Longacre Theater, with Betty Field, June Walker, Edna Best, Vera Allen, Walter Matthau, Sheppard Strudwick, 45 perfs.; *The Rainmaker* by N. Richard Nash 10/28 at New York's Cort Theater, with Geraldine Page, Richard Coogan, 125 perfs.; *The Bad Seed* by Maxwell Anderson (from the novel by William March) 12/8 at New York's 46th Street Theater, with Patty McCormack, Nancy Kelly, Eileen Heckart, 332 perfs.

Howard Hughes writes a personal check for $23,489,478 March 31 to buy up the outstanding stock of Radio-Keith-Orpheum Corporation. Hughes has held a controlling interest in RKO since 1948, when he paid nearly $9 million for stock in the fifth largest Hollywood studio, stockholder suits have accused him of running the studio with "caprice, pique, and whim," and RKO has lost more than $20 million while other studios have made money (*see* 1955).

Films Elia Kazan's *On the Waterfront* with Marlon Brando, Eva Marie Saint, Rod Steiger, Karl Malden; Laslo Benedik's *The Wild One* with Marlon Brando; John Huston's *Beat the Devil* with Humphrey Bogart, Gina Lollabrigida, Robert Morley in a screen-play by Huston and Truman Capote; Alfred Hitchcock's *Rear Window* with James Stewart, Grace Kelly, Wendell Corey; Henry Cornelius's *Genevieve* with Kay Kendall, Kenneth More; John Sturges's *Bad Day at Black Rock* with Spencer Tracy, Robert Ryan, Ernest Borgnine; Richard Fleischer's *20,000 Leagues Under the Sea* with Kirk Douglas, James Mason; Satyajit Ray's *Pather Panchali;* Teinosuke Kinugasa's *Gate of Hell;* Kenji Mizoguchi's *Ugetsu;* Kenji Mizoguchi's *Sansho the Bailiff;* Akira Kurosawa's *The Seven Samurai;* Henri-Georges Clouzot's *Diabolique* with Clouzot's wife Vera and Simone Signoret.

Television play *The Bachelor Party* by Paddy Chayefsky.

Opera *The Threepenny Opera* 3/10 at New York's off-Broadway Theatre de Lys, with Kurt Weill's widow Lotte Lenya who played Jenny in the original 1928 Berlin production. Marc Blitzstein has written the new English language version; *The Turn of the Screw* 9/14 at Venice's Teatro la Fenice, with music by Benjamin Britten, libretto from the Henry James story; *Troilus and Cressida* 12/3 at London's Covent Garden, with music by William Walton, libretto from the Chaucer poetry of the late 14th century; *The Saint of Bleeker Street* 12/27 at New York's Broadway Theater, with music by Gian Carlo Menotti.

Oratorios *Moses and Aaron* by the late Arnold Schoenberg 3/12 at Hamburg's Musikhalle; *Prayers of Kierkegaard* by Samuel Barber 12/3 at Boston's Symphony Hall.

Ballet *The Legend of the Stone Flower* 2/12 at Moscow's Bolshoi Theater, with music by the late Serge Prokofiev.

Cantata *Hodie* by Ralph Vaughan Williams 9/8 at Worcester Cathedral.

First performances *De Profundis* for Mixed Chorus a capella by the late Arnold Schoenberg 1/29 at Cologne; *Washington's Birthday* by Charles Ives 2/21 in a CBS radio broadcast of chamber music (Ives dies at New York May 19 at age 79); Concerto No. 4 for Piano and Orchestra by Darius Milhaud 4/30 at Haifa, Israel; *The Odyssey of a Race (Odisseia de uma raca)* by Heitor Villa-Lobos 5/30 at Haifa; String Quartet No. 2 by Roger Sessions 5/31 at Haifa; Concerto in F minor for Bass Tuba and Orchestra by Ralph Vaughan Williams, now 82, 6/13 at London; Quartet No. 4 for Strings by Ernest Bloch 7/28 at Lenox, Mass.; *In Memoriam Dylan Thomas*, Dirge, Canons, and Song by Igor Stravinsky 9/20 at Los Angeles.

Stage musicals *The Boy Friend* 1/14 at Wyndham's Theatre, London, with music and lyrics by English songwriter Sandy (Alexander Galbraith) Wilson, 29, songs that include "I Could Be Happy with You," 2,084 perfs.; *The Pajama Game* 5/13 at New York's St. James Theater, with John Raitt, Janis Paige, music and lyrics by Richard Adler and Jerry Ross, book by Richard Bissell, songs that include "Hey, There,"

1954 (cont.) "There Once Was a Man," "7½ Cents," "Hernando's Hideaway," 1,063 perfs.; *Peter Pan* 10/20 at New York's Winter Garden Theater, with Mary Martin, Cyril Ritchard, Margalo Gilmore, music by Mark Charlap with additional music by Jule Styne, lyrics by Carolyn Leigh, 27, with additional lyrics by Betty Comden and Adolph Green, songs that include "I'm Flying," "Never Never Land," "Tender Shepherd," "I Won't Grow Up," "I've Gotta Crow," 152 perf.; *Fanny* 11/4 at New York's Majestic Theater, with Ezio Pinza, William Talbert, book by S. N. Behrman and Joshua Logan based on sketches by Marcel Pagnol, music and lyrics by Harold Rome, 888 perfs.; *House of Flowers* 12/30 at the Alvin Theater, with Pearl Bailey, Diahann Carroll, Juanita Hall, music by Harold Arlen, lyrics by Arlen and Truman Capote, 165 perfs.

Hollywood musical George Cukor's *A Star Is Born* with Judy Garland, James Mason, music by Harold Arlen, lyrics by Ira Gershwin, songs that include "The Man That Got Away."

Popular songs "Three Coins in the Fountain" by Jule Styne, lyrics by Sammy Cahn (title song for Jean Negulesco's film); "Mister Sandman" by Pat Ballard; "If I Give My Heart to You" by Jimmie Greene, Al Jacobs, and Jimmy Brewster; "The Naughty Lady of Shady Lane" by Sid Tepper and Roy C. Bennett; "Little Things Mean a Lot" by Edith Lindeman and Carl Stutz; "Cross Over the Bridge" by Bennie Benjamin and George Weiss; "Sh-Boom" by James Keyes, Claude Feaster, Carl Feaster, Floyd F. McRae, and James Edwards; "Shake, Rattle and Roll" by Charles Calhoun; "Papa Loves Mambo" by Al Hoffman, Dick Manning, and Bix Reichner; "The Happy Wanderer" by German composer Friedrich W. Mölter, lyrics by English writer Antonia Ridge.

Elvis Presley makes his first commercial recording at age 19 and achieves some success with "That's All Right, Mama" and "Blue Moon of Kentucky." Guitarist-vocalist Elvis Aaron Presley will sign an agreement next year with RCA-Victor which will promote "Elvis the Pelvis" with TV appearances, Presley will begin a motion picture career in 1956, and he will be a major factor in the rock and roll music style that will dominate the popular music scene in the late 1950s and 1960s.

The ChaChaCha based on the classic Cuban Danzon is introduced to U.S. dancefloors where it will be a standard Latin dance step.

Quebec City's first Winter Carnival opens in February. Local businessmen have organized the 10-day event to attract visitors with street dances, costume balls, ice-sculpture championships, a conoe race across the ice-clogged St. Lawrence River, speed skating, barrel-jumping, skiing, and snow-shoeing contests, and other attractions.

English track star Roger Bannister, 25, runs the mile in 3 minutes, 59.4 seconds May 6 at Oxford to break the 4-minute barrier and thus make history.

The St. Louis Browns become the Baltimore Orioles.

Hank Aaron joins the Milwaukee Braves to begin a baseball career that will span 2 decades. Henry Louis Aaron, 20, will surpass the lifetime home-run record of Babe Ruth in 1974.

Sportswriter Grantland Rice dies of a stroke at New York July 13 at age 73. Obituaries quote his immortal verse, "When the Great Scorer comes/ To mark against your name,/ He'll write not 'won' or 'lost,'/ But how you played the game."

The New York Giants win the World Series by defeating the Cleveland Indians 4 games to 0.

West Germany wins the World Cup in football (soccer) by upsetting a heavily favored Hungarian team 3 to 2 at Bern's Wanddorf Stadium.

President Eisenhower modifies the U.S. pledge of allegiance June 14. He orders that the phrase "one nation, under God" replace "one nation, indivisible" (see 1892).

Veterans Day becomes a national holiday to replace Armistice Day, a legal holiday celebrated each November 11 since 1928 under terms of a 1926 resolution of Congress to commemorate the end of World War I (see Uniform Monday Holiday Act, 1968).

The World Council of Churches organized at Amsterdam in 1948 convenes at Evanston, Ill.

The Unification Church is founded by Korean evangelist Sun Myung Moon, 34, who claims to have received a vision on a hillside in Korea at age 16 that gave him the "key to righteousness and restoration of the Kingdom of Heaven on Earth." Moon will develop a theology based on platitudes, rabid anti-Communism, and pop history supported by bits of numerology, astrology, and scientology (see Hubbard, 1950). Moon's supporters will claim that the Bible is written in code and that only Moon has broken the code.

Cleveland suburban housewife Marilyn Sheppard dies at home July 4 at age 31. Police accuse her osteopath-surgeon husband Samuel Sheppard, 30, of having murdered his wife and a jury will convict Sheppard after a much-publicized trial.

Ohrbach's takes over New York's James McCreery store in West 34th Street and moves uptown from its 14th Street location of 1923 (see Los Angeles, 1953).

Detroit's Northland opens in March with 100 stores in the world's largest shopping center. The $30 million project designed by Victor Gruen Associates includes a J. L. Hudson branch that is the largest department store erected since the 1920s, and the new suburban shopping center is a monument to the American exodus from the inner city (see Gruen, 1951; Southdale, 1957).

Geodesics, Inc., and Synergetics, Inc., are established in a reorganization of the Dymaxion Dwelling Machines Company organized in 1944 to produce seven-room circular aluminum Dymaxion houses and geodesic domes designed by Buckminister Fuller.

Holiday Inns of America, Inc., is organized by Kemmons Wilson of Memphis who last year built three more motels and who has been joined by Memphis builder Wallace E. Johnson (*see* 1952). In 8 years there will be more than 280 Holiday Inns with 30,000 rooms in 35 states, Canada, and Puerto Rico and 63 will be wholly owned by HIA, Inc. (*see* 1963).

Statler-Hilton Hotels, Inc., is created by Conrad Hilton who acquires a controlling interest in the rival Statler Hotel chain of nine hotels that began with the Buffalo Statler of 1905. The Hilton group was the world's largest hotel chain before buying into Statler and by 1966 it will include more than 60 U.S. hotels plus dozens of hotels abroad (*see* 1949; 1955).

The Fontainebleau Hotel opens at Miami Beach, Fla., with 900 rooms. Russian-American architect Morris Lapidus, 51, has designed the $13 million 14-story resort hotel.

Clouds of radioactive coral dust rain down on the Japanese fishing boat *Lucky Tiger* following the U.S. explosion of a hydrogen device at Bikini Atoll (above) and the dust falls subsequently on small Micronesian Islands downwind. People exposed to the fallout will be observed in the next 2 decades to suffer from thyroid gland nodules and cancerous tumors, loss of thyroid function in some cases, and leukemia as a result of exposure to radioactive iodine 131 isotopes.

An International Convention for the Prevention of Pollution of the Sea with Oil is assembled.

Lake Erie produces 75 million pounds of commercial fish and remains relatively unpolluted.

Congress acts to relieve world hunger and to put a prop under U.S. farm prices. Public Law 480 empowers the Department of Agriculture to buy surplus wheat, butter, cheese, dry skim milk, vegetable oils, and other surplus foods for donation abroad or to sell for native currency.

An Agricultural Trade and Development Act to protect U.S. farmers from world market collapse is passed by Congress.

Congress passes a Watershed and Flood Prevention Act to protect farmers from water erosion.

The U.S. Department of Agriculture fires its attaché at Tokyo because he does not meet "security requirements." Russian-American agricultural economist Wolf Isaac Ladejinsky, 55, had charge of Japanese land reform under General MacArthur, his only interest in revolution is in a green revolution, the government will admit its error, and Ladejinsky will work on land reform in South Vietnam at the urging of President Eisenhower.

A breakthrough in wheat genetics achieved by University of Missouri plant geneticist Ernest Robert Sears, 44, does for wheat genetics what Russia's Dmitri Mendeléev did for chemistry in 1870. Sears shows that specific chromosomes in wheat can be substituted to achieve desired changes, and he raises hopes for new hybrid wheat strains that will raise yields and will increase resistance to disease and drought.

Tiny cobs of corn found in the valley of Tehuacan southeast of Mexico City is the first wild corn ever found that can seed itself. The cobs date to 5,000 B.C.

Large-scale planting of new hybrid grain varieties in the Soviet Union is ordered by party leader Nikita Khrushchev who overrides Lysenkoite objections (*see* 1952).

Screwworm flies on the Caribbean island of Curaçao are wiped out in 4 months in a test program using sterilized males (*see* Knipling, 1951).

Congress passes a pesticides amendment to the Food, Drug and Cosmetic Act of 1938 requiring that pesticide makers show their data to the Food and Drug Administration as well as to the U.S. Department of Agriculture (*see* 1947).

No direct evidence of human illness arising from pesticide residues in food is reported by a British group established by the Minister of Agriculture and the Ministries of Fisheries, Health, and Food, but the group recommends appointment of an advisory committee to keep the problem under scrutiny in light of new and possibly dangerous compounds being introduced at a growing rate.

Antibiotic feed supplements are permitted in Britain after tests confirm their value and show no undesirable effects. U.S. livestock producers use $50 million worth of the supplements.

Molybdenum is identified as an important trace element. The mineral is contained in the human enzyme xanthine oxidase needed to convert purines into uric acid (*see* Garrod, 1859).

Let's Eat Right to Keep Fit by Los Angeles nutritionist Adelle Davis, 51, claims that large daily vitamin and mineral doses can prevent and cure a variety of ills. Davis recommends 2 grams of ascorbic acid (vitamin C) per day to prevent the common cold, she opposes milk pasteurization, she favors water fluoridation (but will later reverse her position), and she advocates eating fertile eggs and eating vegetables and fruits grown without chemical fertilizers or pesticides (*see* Rodale, 1948; 1950).

Frozen "TV" Brand Dinners are introduced by Omaha's C. A. Swanson & Sons which has been marketing frozen chicken, beef, and turkey pies (*see* 1945; Campbell, 1955).

Consolidated Foods Corporation is founded by Nathan Cummings whose Consolidated Grocers Company has acquired a number of minor food producers (*see* 1951). Consolidated Foods will grow into a mammoth business (*see* Ocoma, 1955).

Minute Maid Corporation reaches a sales volume of $100 million by paying $40 million to acquire the Snow Crop division of Clinton Foods (*see* 1947; 1953). Minute Maid gains a complete line of frozen fruits, vegetables, fish, poultry, and various prepared foods in addition to Snow Crop's citrus concentrates,

Computer technology used electronic data processing to solve problems previously insoluble and to end work tedium.

but Minute Maid will start losing money on Snow Crop after 1 year as private label competition becomes stronger in the frozen food industry (*see* Seabrook, 1957).

Use of the antioxidant BHA (butylated hydroxyanisole) in U.S. foods is approved by the FDA (*see* 1947). The additive will be widely employed to avoid rancidity and the breakdown of fatty acids and ascorbic acid (vitamin C) in breakfast foods, chicken pot pies, cooking oils, dehydrated soups, potato chips, salted nuts, shortenings, and other products.

Trix breakfast food is introduced by General Mills. The new cereal is 46.6 percent sugar (*see* 1941; 1958).

U.S. October food prices: round steak 92 cents per pound, up from 45 cents in 1944; sugar 52 cents (5-pound bag), up from 34 cents; bread 17 cents per 1-pound loaf, up from 9 cents; coffee $1.10 per pound, up from 30 cents; eggs 60 cents per dozen, down from 64 cents; milk 45 cents per half gallon, up from 29 cents; butter 72 cents per pound, up from 50 cents; lettuce 19 cents per head, up from 12 cents (*see* 1964).

Duncan Hines makes his first trip to Europe and returns asserting that American food is better than European (*see* 1935).

The Shakey's pizza parlor chain has its beginnings in a Sacramento, Calif., pizzeria opened by local entrepreneur Sherwood "Shakey" Johnson and his wartime buddy Edward Plummer who invest $850 each to start the place. Franchised pizza parlors will make Johnson and Plummer millionaires (*see* 1953; 1958).

U.S. births will remain above 4 million per year for the next decade.

An oral contraceptive pill is developed by Gregory G. Pincus and Hudson Hoagland at the Worcester Foundation (*see* Sanger, 1951). The pill employs norethisterone and is the result of work done by Pincus, Hoagland, and Min-Cheh Chang (*see* 1955).

1955 The Soviet Union recognizes the independence of West Germany January 15, Soviet premier Georgi M. Malenkov resigns February 8, Malenkov is succeeded by Marshal Nikolai A. Bulganin who reaffirms Sino-Soviet ties and appoints Marshal Georgi K. Zhukov minister of defense.

British prime minister Winston S. Churchill resigns April 5 at age 81 and is succeeded by former secretary of state for foreign affairs Sir Anthony Eden.

The presidium of the U.S.S.R.'s Supreme Soviet cancels treaties of friendship with Britain and France May 7, West Germany is admitted to NATO May 9, and eight European Communist powers sign the Warsaw Pact May 14.

Austria formally regains her sovereignty July 27 by the Treaty of Vienna, and occupation troops withdraw from the country.

South Vietnam has civil war beginning at Saigon April 28. Supporters of Premier Ngo Dinh Diem, 54, defeat supporters of the chief of state Bao Dai and force Binh Xuyen rebels out of the capital May 2 after 5 days of heavy fighting. Diem asks France to move her troops to the northern frontier for action against the Communist Vietminh or to withdraw completely; Paris agrees May 20 to deploy troops against the Vietminh. Peking promises North Vietnam $338 million in economic aid July 7 in an agreement with President Ho Chi Minh. South Vietnam's chief of state Bao Dai dismisses Premier Diem October 18, Diem refuses to resign, a referendum October 23 gives him an overwhelming vote over Bao Dai, and he proclaims a South Vietnamese Republic October 26 with himself as president (*see* 1954; 1960).

Peronist power in Argentina ends September 19 as a military junta stages a coup that overthrows dictator Juan Peron after 9 years in which Peron has created Latin America's first and only labor movement, a force of considerable economic and political power. Peron has nationalized Argentina's British-owned railroads, he has established a "Third World" bloc in international affairs, and while he has lost popularity since his suppression of the newspaper *La Prensa* in 1951 and the death of his wife Eva to cancer the following year, he still has a large following (*see* 1973).

Cook County Democratic party chairman Richard J. Daley, 53, wins the Chicago mayoralty race and begins a 21-year career as mayor of the second largest U.S. city. A machine politician in the old tradition, Daley will use patronage to control the Illinois state vote and to obtain tax breaks and zoning law favors for real estate and other interests that support him.

Black political leader Lamar D. Smith, 63, is shot to death in front of the Lincoln County Courthouse at Brookhaven, Miss., after seeking to qualify blacks to vote. The shooting is witnessed by more than 20 people, including several blacks, but nobody admits to having seen anything and no witnesses testify against the three white men charged with the murder.

Black minister George W. Lee is killed gangland style at Belzoni, Miss., after a week of terror during which blacks' property has been vandalized by whites. The blacks have refused to send their children to racially segregated schools, the whites have retaliated by refusing credit to blacks at local schools, and Lee had campaigned for black voting rights.

Segregation of public golf courses, parks, swimming pools, and playgrounds is ruled unconstitutional by the Supreme Court November 7 in a decision based on the 1954 ruling in *Brown v. Board of Education*.

An end to racial segregation on interstate buses and trains is ordered November 25 by the Interstate Commerce Commission which also prohibits segregation in terminal waiting rooms. Montgomery, Ala., seamstress Rosa Parks refuses to give up her seat on a downtown bus to a white man (*see* King, 1956).

Synthesis of ribonucleic acid (RNA) is announced by Spanish-born New York University biochemist Severo Ochoa, 49. RNA is a basic constituent of all living tissues and Ochoa has taken a giant step toward the creation of life in the laboratory out of inert materials (*see* Watson, Crick, 1953; Kornberg, 1957).

The mesa introduced by the Bell Telephone Laboratories of American Telephone & Telegraph Company is a new kind of transistor (*see* 1948).

The IBM 752 computer shipped in February is the first IBM business computer, and by August IBM has reduced Univac's lead to 30 installations versus 24 (*see* 1951). By August of next year IBM will have 76 installations to Univac's 46 with orders for 193 machines versus 65 for Univac, and while there are few intrinsic differences between the computers, IBM employs superior salesmanship and will be far ahead of its competitor by late next year.

U.S. motorcar sales reach an unprecedented 7,169,908 of which fewer than 52,000 are imported, but sales of small foreign cars led by Volkswagen will now begin a rapid rise (*see* 1949; 1959; 1968).

The first Chevrolet V8 engine motorcar is introduced, but half of all new cars have six-cylinder engines which are superior for city driving, only marginally less powerful in accelerating from 0 to 30 miles per hour, and far more efficient in their use of fuel (*see* Ford V8, 1932). By 1976 nearly 70 percent of all U.S. motorcars will have V8 engines, only 21.8 percent sixes, 8.5 percent four-cylinder engines.

The Ford Thunderbird is introduced in the form of a two-seat sportscar.

The Volkswagen Kharmann-Ghia two-seat sportscar is introduced with a body by Kharmann of Osnabrück designed by Ghia of Turin, Italy.

The Citroën DS-19 introduced at the October Automobile Show in Paris is the first new Citroën model in 2 decades. The $2,000 car has been designed by G. Berton for S.A. André Citroën, and some 1.4 million of the cars will be sold at steadily rising prices before Citroën is absorbed in 1974 by Peugot which will halt production in 1975 (*see* Fiat, 1968).

New York's Long Island Expressway opens to traffic and is inadequate for the volume of traffic.

The Tappan Zee Bridge opens to traffic at Tarrytown, N.Y. The cantilever span across the Hudson is 1,212 meters in length.

President Eisenhower submits a 10-year $101 billion highway construction program to Congress (*see* 1956).

The President's Advisory Committee on Transportation recommends reduction of federal controls to stimulate a return to competitive conditions in transportation but an intracity transit-free enterprise has worked to restrict competition.

Gasoline and diesel buses have replaced some 88 percent of U.S. electric streetcar systems (*see* 1949; General Motors, 1956).

New York City's Third Avenue "El" makes its last run in May and is torn down after 77 years of operation (*see* Sixth Avenue "El," 1940).

New York City institutes alternate side of the street parking regulations to facilitate street-cleaning as U.S. cities continue to seek solutions to the problem of traffic choked by private automobiles.

Rome's first subway opens to link the city's central railroad station to a convention center and government building complex south of the city. The subway was planned by the late Benito Mussolini.

Prednisone is introduced for treating arthritis and other conditions. The new steroid drug has far fewer side effects than cortisone (*see* Hench, 1949; Kefauver, 1957).

More than 100 cases of paralytic poliomyelitis develop among Americans injected with certain lots of the Salk vaccine that have been produced by Cutter Laboratories which has failed to inactivate the polio virus through a manufacturing error. The Salk vaccine is nevertheless judged highly effective in combatting paralytic polio (*see* 1954).

Blindness in children afflicted with retrolental fibroplasia is proved to be the result of treating premature infants with high doses of oxygen. Increased incidence of such blindness has been noted since 1940.

Reserpine is found by U.S. National Heart Institute researchers to deplete the brain's supply of the chemical substance serotinin (*see* 1952; LSD, 1953).

The U.S. federal minimum wage rises from 75 cents per hour to $1 August 12 by act of Congress.

1955 (cont.) A contract signed with American Can Company and Continental Can August 13 wins the United Steel Workers of America the first 52-week guaranteed annual wage in any major U.S. industry.

The AF of L and the CIO merge December 2 in a pact engineered by Walter Reuther and George Meany who at age 62 assumes the presidency of the combined AFL-CIO that he will hold for more than 23 years. Some 12 million U.S. workers are unionized, a number that will increase to 20 million in the next 20 years.

A staff report issued by the U.S. Senate Committee on Banking and Currency observes that "less than one percent of all American families owned over four-fifths of all publicly held stocks owned by individuals."

First National City Bank is created March 30 by a merger of New York's 133-year-old National City Bank with the 92-year-old First National Bank of New York. Citibank assets rival those of Chase Manhattan.

Chase Manhattan Bank is created March 31 by a merger of New York's 78-year-old Chase National Bank with the 156-year-old Bank of the Manhattan Company. Chase Manhattan is second in assets only to the Bank of America.

New York's Bankers Trust Company retains its name after a merger with Public National Bank that makes 52-year-old Bankers Trust a rival to Chase Manhattan and First National City (*see* Chemical Corn Exchange, 1954; Morgan Guaranty Trust, 1959).

H.&R. Block is started by Kansas City tax accountants Henry Wohlman Bloch, 32, and Richard A. Bloch, 29, who use the firm name Block to avoid mispronunciation. Specializing in low-cost mass-produced income tax returns, the Bloch brothers will open franchised offices in every major U.S. city. By 1977 they will be preparing 10 percent of all U.S. tax returns (25 percent in some cities) and will have annual incomes of some $3 million each as their company becomes the largest in the business.

Textron American is incorporated as the first business conglomerate. Royal Little has acquired the giant 56-year-old American Woolen Company and has taken control of Robbins Mills from J. P. Stevens, but he will now move Textron out of textiles which account for more than 80 percent of Textron sales (*see* 1948). By the end of next year Little will have given cash and Textron American stock to acquire firms making test equipment, heavy machinery, chain saws, plastics, electromechanical equipment, cement, aluminum, plywood, and veneers, and by the time he retires in 1962 Textron will be one of America's 100 largest companies with active interests in aerospace, agrochemicals, electronics, lenses, and metals. By 1963 the company will be completely out of textiles and will have set a course that other conglomerates will follow (*see* ITT, 1959).

Sperry-Rand Corporation is created by a merger of Sperry Corporation and Remington-Rand Corporation whose boss James H. Rand, now 68, has made it the nation's leading computer maker (*see* Univac, above). Sperry is a major producer of electronic weaponry, hydraulic equipment, and farm machinery (*see* Vickers, 1937; New Holland, 1947).

Whirlpool Corporation is created by a merger of a St. Joseph, Mich., company that has been supplying Sears, Roebuck with Kenmore laundry equipment, an RCA division that makes gas and electric ranges and air-conditioning equipment, and Seeger Refrigeration Company which supplies Sears, Roebuck with Coldspot refrigerators and freezers. The Michigan firm has been the largest U.S. maker of laundry equipment, its president Elisha Gray II, 48, is a grandson of the telephone pioneer (*see* 1872). He engineers the merger, and he heads the new firm.

The Dreyfus Fund is created by New York stockbroker Jack J. Dreyfus, Jr., 40, who has acquired the open-end Nesbett Fund, has renamed it, and increases its holdings from $2.3 million to $5.6 million by year's end. Dreyfus will buy 400 shares of the still unlisted Polaroid Corporation at 31⅞ and will see it rise to 6,372 (not counting stock splits).

General Telephone Corporation expands by acquiring Theodore Gary & Company which owns Automatic Electric Company and whose shareholders receive 1.5 shares of General Telephone for each share of Gary (*see* 1935; dial telephone, 1919; General Telephone and Electronics, 1958).

General Dynamics absorbs Stromberg-Carlson Company (*see* 1896; 1952). A pioneer in making radios, Stromberg-Carlson has become a major producer of electronics and communications equipment.

The *National Review* begins publication. The biweekly journal of conservative political opinion is published and edited by William F. Buckley, Jr.

The *Village Voice* begins publication at New York in October. Daniel Wolf and Edward Fancher have started the 12-page 5-cent weekly with $15,000, its initial circulation is 2,500, but Wolf and Fancher will increase the circulation and will sell the *Voice* in 15 years for $3 million.

The *Reader's Digest* abandons its 33-year-old position against taking advertisements but refuses to accept cigarette advertising.

"Ann Landers Says" is introduced in the *Chicago Sun-Times* by journalist Esther Pauline Friedman Lederer, 37, whose confidential column will be syndicated to hundreds of newspapers as will that of her twin sister Pauline who will write the "Dear Abby" column under the name Abigail Van Buren. Lederer married her husband Jules in 1939, she has seen him found Budget Rent-a-Car and prosper, but she will divorce him in 1975.

"Dondi" is introduced by comic strip cartoonists Gus Edson and Irwin Hasen. Edson has been drawing "The Gumps" since taking it over from Sidney Smith in 1935, he will continue drawing that strip until 1957, and he will turn out "Dondi" strips with Hasen until 1966 when Hasen will continue on his own.

Nonfiction *The Guinness Book of World Records* by London sportswriter Ross McWhirter, 30, and his twin brother Norris whose book will have sales of more than 24 million copies in 14 languages in the next 20 years; *Auntie Mame* by *Foreign Affairs* promotion manager Patrick Dennis (Edward E. Tanner III), 34, whose story of a rich young orphan and his eccentric aunt has been rejected by 10 publishers but becomes a best seller that will be made into a play, a film, and a Broadway musical.

Fiction *Lolita* by Vladimir Nabokov whose tale of a middle-aged European's love for a passionate 12-year-old American "nymphet" is a satire that reverses the usual contrast between American innocence and European worldliness; *The Ginger Man* by Brooklyn-born Irish novelist J. P. (James Patrick) Donleavy, 29, whose comic protagonist Sebastian Dangerfield rebels against the middle-class conventions of Dublin and London; *The Quiet American* by Graham Greene; *Andersonville* by MacKinlay Kantor; *A Good Man Is Hard to Find* (stories) by Flannery O'Connor; *Lord of the Rings* by J. R. R. Tolkien; *Witness for the Prosecution* by Agatha Christie.

Juvenile *Eloise* by U.S. entertainer Kay Thompson, 43, whose heroine lives at the Plaza Hotel.

Poetry "Howl" by U.S. beatnik poet Allen Ginsberg, 29, who reads it at Berkeley, Calif., and wins acclaim in the youth underground; *Journey to Love* by William Carlos Williams; *The Less Deceived* by English poet Philip Larkin, 33; *Good News of Death* by Louis Simpson.

Painting *The Women of Algiers* by Pablo Picasso; *The Lord's Supper* by Salvador Dali; *Italian Square* by Giorgio De Chirico; *Circus* by French painter Bernard Buffet, 27; *Double Portrait of Birdie* by U.S. painter Larry Rivers, 31, who has painted two views of his mother-in-law in the nude; *Bed* and *Rebus* by Robert Rauschenberg; *Flag and Target with Plaster Casts* by U.S. painter Jasper Johns, 25. Nicolas de Staël dies at Antibes March 16 at age 41; Fernand Léger dies at Gif-sur-Yvette, Seine-et-Oise August 17 at age 74; Maurice Utrillo dies at Dax in Landes November 5 at age 71.

Theater *Bus Stop* by William Inge 3/2 at New York's Music Box Theater, with Kim Stanley, Albert Salmi, 478 perfs.; *Cat on a Hot Tin Roof* by Tennessee Williams 3/24 at New York's Morosco Theater, with Barbara Bel Geddes, Ben Gazzara, Mildred Dunnock, folk singer Burl Ives as "Big Daddy," 694 perfs., Pulitzer prize; *Inherit the Wind* by Jerome Lawrence and Robert E. Lee 4/21 at New York's National Theater, with Paul Muni as Clarence Darrow, Ed Begley as William Jennings Bryan in a drama based on the Scopes "monkey trial" of 1925, 806 perfs.; *Waiting for Godot* 8/3 at London's Theatre Arts Club. Anglo-Irish playwright Samuel Becket, 49,

was secretary to the late James Joyce, he wrote the play in French, it was presented to Paris audiences 2 years ago, and it is an expression of man's anxiety and suffering as to his origin and destination; *A View from the Bridge* by Arthur Miller 9/29 at New York's Coronet Theater, with J. Carroll Naish, Van Heflin, Eileen Heckart, Jack Warden, 149 perfs.; *The Diary of Anne Frank* by Frances Goodrich and Albert Hackett 10/5 at New York's Cort Theater, with Joseph Schildkraut, Susan Strasberg, 717 perfs., Pulitzer prize 1956; *A Hatful of Rain* by U.S. playwright Michael Gazzo, 32, 11/9 at New York's Lyceum Theater, with Ben Gazzara, Shelley Winters, Frank Silvera, Anthony Franciosa in a play about drug addiction, 398 perfs.

The American Shakespeare Theatre has its first season at Stratford, Conn., a town founded in 1623 by settlers from Stratford-upon-Avon. The Theatre Guild's Lawrence Langner and Armina Marshall who opened the Westport Country Playhouse in 1931 have founded the new Shakespeare repertory theater (*see* Ontario, 1953).

Films Ingmar Bergman's *Smiles of a Summer Night;* Delbert Mann's *Marty* with Ernest Borgnine in an adaptation of the 1953 Paddy Chayefsky television script; Daniel Mann's *The Rose Tattoo* with Anna Magnani, Burt Lancaster; Elia Kazan's *East of Eden* with Julie Harris, James Dean, Raymond Massey, Burl Ives; Nicholas Ray's *Rebel Without a Cause* with Natalie Wood, Sal Mineo, James Dean (who is killed September 30 in an automobile accident at age 24); Billy Wilder's *The Seven Year Itch* with Marilyn Monroe, Tom Ewell; Alfred Hitchcock's *To Catch a Thief* with Cary Grant, Grace Kelly; Richard Brooks's *Blackboard Jungle* with Glenn Ford, Ann Francis; David Lean's *Summertime* with Katharine Hepburn, Rossano Brazzi in a film version of the Arthur Laurents play *Time of the Cuckoo;* Kenji Mizoguchi's *Princess Yang Kwei Fei;* Jean Renoir's *French Can-Can.*

Radio-Keith-Orpheum Corporation becomes R.K.O.-General in July as Howard Hughes sells the motion picture subsidiary of his R.K.O. Pictures holding company to General Tire and Rubber Company for $25 million (*see* 1954; Aerojet, 1945). Hughes merges the rest of R.K.O. into Atlas Corporation in return for an 11 percent stock interest in Atlas.

Disneyland opens July 17 at Anaheim 25 miles south of Los Angeles. Mickey Mouse originator Walt Disney of WED Enterprises has mortgaged his life insurance, his stockholdings, his house, and his furniture to acquire an orange grove, cut it down, and finance construction of the Jungle River Ride, the Mark Twain paddle-wheeler ride, and other attractions of Adventureland, Frontierland, Fantasyland, and Tomorrowland for the $17 million 244-acre amusement park. Disney will assemble a 27,500-acre tract near Orlando, Fla., to build a Disneyland East that will be part of a vacation resort, but chain-smoker Disney will die of lung cancer at age 65 in mid-December 1965 and will never see Walt Disney World.

1955 (cont.) Television shows *Captain Kangaroo* 10/3 on CBS network stations, with actor Robert James Keeshan, 28, hosting the morning show for preschoolers. Keeshan has appeared on the NBC afternoon show *Howdy Doody*, his new show will continue for more than 2 decades, and it will win a 1958 award as "the only one which puts the welfare of the children ahead of that of the sponsor . . . which instructs them in safety, ethics, and health without interrupting the serious business of entertaining them at the same time"; *The Mickey Mouse Club* in October on ABC network stations, with "Mouseketeers" Annette Funicello, Cubby O'Brien, Karen Pendleton, Cheryl Holdridge. Host of the afternoon show is Jimmie Dodd who has composed the march "M-I-C-K-E-Y M-O-U-S-E" and who will keep the *Mickey Mouse Club* going until 1958.

Hollywood musicals Richard Quine's *My Sister Eileen* with Betty Garrett, Janet Leigh, Jack Lemmon, Bob Fosse; Jean Negulesco's *Daddy Long Legs* with Fred Astaire, Leslie Caron, songs that include "Something's Gotta Give" by Johnny Mercer.

Broadway musicals *Silk Stockings* 2/24 at the Imperial Theater, with Hildegarde Neff as Ninotchka, George Tobias, Julie Newmar, Don Ameche, David Opatashu, music and lyrics by Cole Porter, songs that include "All of You," 478 perfs.; *Damn Yankees* 5/5 at the 46th Street Theater, with Gwen Verdon, music and lyrics by Richard Adler and Jerry Ross, songs that include "Whatever Lola Wants," "You've Got to Have Heart," "Two Lost Souls," 1,019 perfs.; *Pipe Dream* 11/3 at the Sam S. Shubert Theater, with Helen Traubel, music by Richard Rodgers, lyrics by Oscar Hammerstein II, based on the John Steinbeck novel *Sweet Thursday*, songs that include "All at Once You Love Her."

The Vienna State Opera House reopens after having been nearly completely destroyed by wartime bombing and gunfire.

First performances Symphony No. 8 by Heitor Villa-Lobos 1/14 at Philadelphia's Academy of Music; Symphony No. 5 (*Sinfonia Sacra*) by Howard Hanson 2/18 at Philadelphia's Academy of Music; Symphony No. 6 by Walter Piston 11/25 at Boston's Symphony Hall.

The Merengue introduced to U.S. dance floors by New York dancing teacher Albert Butler, 61, and his wife Josephine is an adaptation of a Dominican one-step that combines the rumba and the *paso doble*.

Popular songs "Rock Around the Clock" by William "Bill" Haley; "Maybellene" by U.S. guitarist-blues singer Charles Edward Anderson "Chuck" Berry, 29, Russ Frato, and Alan Freed. Berry scores an immediate hit that he will follow with "Roll Over, Beethoven," "Rock 'n Roll Music," "Memphis," and other triumphs; "Memories Are Made of This" by Terry Gilkyson, Richard Debny, and Frank Miller; "Love Is a Many-Splendored Thing" by Sammy Fain, lyrics by Paul Francis Webster (title song for Henry King's film); "Cry Me a River" by Arthur Hamilton;

"Love and Marriage" by James Van Heusen, lyrics by Sammy Cahn (for a TV production of Thornton Wilder's *Our Town*); "Dance with Me, Henry" by Etta James; "Domani" by Italian composer Ulpio Minucci, lyrics by Tony Velona.

Swaps beats the favorite Nashua to win the Kentucky Derby but Nashua comes back to defeat Swaps in a match race and will be retired to stud next year, the first race horse to be syndicated for more than $1 million.

The Philadelphia Athletics become the Kansas City Athletics as baseball broadens its geographical base.

The Brooklyn Dodgers win their first World Series by defeating the New York Yankees 4 games to 3.

U.S. cigarette consumption resumes its rise after a 2-year drop as the industry increases its advertising, especially on network television. R. J. Reynolds promotes its filter-tipped Winstons, American Tobacco its cork-tipped king-size Herbert Tareytons with their activated charcoal filter, P. Lorillard its Old Gold filters, Philip Morris its Benson & Hedges and Marlboro filters, Brown & Williamson its new filter-tipped Kools and Raleighs.

U.S. shopping centers increase in number to 1,800, and the total rises rapidly as Americans move out of the central cities to live in the sprawling suburbs (*see* Country Club Plaza, 1922; Northland, 1954).

Nieman-Marcus opens at Houston after merging with that city's Ben Hoffman, Inc. (*see* 1907). The Dallas store will open branches at Fort Worth, Atlanta, St. Louis, Washington, D.C., and elsewhere.

France's Notre Dame du Haut at Ronchamp is completed by Le Corbusier.

New York's Mobil Oil building (Socony Mobil building) is completed by Harrison & Abramovitz in East 42nd Street between Third and Lexington Avenues as a building boom begins on Third Avenue following removal of the elevated railway (above). The 43-story structure contains 1.6 million square feet of floor space and is almost entirely covered with embossed panels of stainless steel.

The United States has 30,000 motels or motor courts, up from 10,000 in 1935.

The Istanbul Hilton opens in Turkey.

The Eden Roc Hotel designed by Morris Lapidus opens on Collins Avenue at Miami Beach.

The London Clean Air Act passed in October bans the burning of untreated coal to prevent a recurrence of the killer smog of 1952 and to save an estimated $4.5 million that has been spent each year to repair the corrosion damage and clean up the 75,000 tons of soot that rained down on the city. The new law will permit 80 percent more sunshine to reach London, birds will return to the city, grass will grow, churches and other historic buildings will be cleaned and will be returned to their original white stone appearance for the first time in centuries as restoring companies remove soot packed up to 9 inches deep.

Rapid collectivization of Chinese agriculture is proposed by Chairman Mao Tse-tung of the Central People's Government (see 1950). Other Chinese leaders fear a repetition of the Soviet Union's experience in the years from 1928 to 1931, but Mao prevails and peasants who resist are liquidated.

Dwarf indica rice is introduced into Taiwan (Formosa). Higher yielding than most varieties, the new rice requires lots of fertilizer and insecticides.

Hurricane Janet hits Granada in the British West Indies and destroys 75 percent of the island's nutmeg trees (see 1843; 1858). Granada's trees have supplied 40 percent of world nutmeg and mace production, the only other major prime source is the tiny island of Siaoe north of the Celebes whose shipments are delayed by troubles in Indonesia, and since it takes 2 months for the nutmeg to reach Singapore and another 2 months to reach New York, the price of nutmeg rises from 35 cents per pound to over $2.

The National Farmers Organization (NFO) is founded in the United States.

One-tenth of U.S. families are found by a USDA survey to be living on nutritionally "poor" diets, a healthy improvement over 1943 findings.

Composition of vitamin B_{12} (cyanocobalamin) is discovered by British biochemist Dorothy Hodgkin who raises hopes that the vitamin can be synthesized for low-cost treatment of pernicious anemia and other deficiency diseases (see 1948).

The first British fluoridation of community drinking water is begun November 17 in Anglesey (see 1945).

Crest is introduced by Procter & Gamble as a new toothpaste containing stannous fluoride (see Gleem, 1952). Crest will become the top-selling dentifrice in the United States and will lead other makers to introduce fluoride toothpastes.

Gorton's of Gloucester moves into a new $1.5 million freezing plant it has leased at Gloucester, Mass. The 200-year-old firm begins producing frozen fish sticks and frozen fish dinners to supplement its traditional codfish cake business (see General Mills, 1968).

Consolidated Foods acquires Ocoma Foods of Omaha, Neb., to enter the frozen poultry parts, frozen prepared foods, and butter business (see 1954). By year's end Consolidated's 15 wholesalers and processors have combined assets of $78 million and annual sales of $225 million, figures that will soon be dwarfed as Nathan Cummings continues to expand (see Sara Lee, 1956).

Campbell's Soup Company enters the frozen foods business by acquiring control of C. A. Swanson & Sons, originator of the "TV Dinner" (see 1954). Campbell's will expand the Swanson line of 11 prepared frozen items to 65 items in the next 17 years.

Continental Baking acquires Morton Packing Company and will make it the largest U.S. producer of pot pies, fruit pies, cream pies, and frozen bread dough (see Morton, 1940; Continental, 1930). Morton will also produce TV dinners casseroles, cakes, sweet goods, English muffins, and other products (see 1968).

Special K breakfast food—4.4 percent sugar—is introduced by the Kellogg Company (see 1953; 1958).

Corn Products Refining Company acquires the chocolate-flavored milk supplement Bosco, Kasco dog food, and NuSoft fabric softener to supplement its Argo starch, Mazola corn oil, and Karo syrup (see 1923; Knorr, 1957).

Coca-Cola Company uses the name "Coke" officially for the first time (see 1945; Minute Maid, 1960; Tab, 1963).

Tropicana's Anthony Rossi builds a port at Cape Canaveral, Fla. (see 1951). Unable to expand his fleet of trucks for shipping chilled orange juice to northern markets, Rossi buys an 8,000-ton ship with stainless steel tanks, builds a bottling plant at Whitestone, Queens, and begins sending juice north by ship, a practice he will later abandon in favor of rail and truck shipment (see 1962).

Fernand Point of the Restaurant de la Pyramide at Vienne dies at the gastronomic mecca March 4 at age 58 (see 1923). His widow will continue to operate the ultimate expression of France's *haute cuisine*.

Lum's, Inc., has its origin in a Miami Beach frankfurter stand that will grow into a chain of more than 390 restaurants in the United States, the Caribbean, Spain and West Germany. Local attorney Clifford Perlman, 29, will buy the 41st Street stand which specializes in steamed frankfurters in beer, and by 1961 he will have four Lum's stands in Miami Beach.

Colonel Sanders' Kentucky Fried Chicken has its origin as Corbin, Ky., restaurateur Harland Sanders, 65, travels the country in an old car loaded with pots and pans and a "secret blend of herbs and spices" looking for prospective licensees. The roadside restaurant Sanders operated for 25 years has been ruined by a new highway that diverted traffic from his location, his only income is a $105 monthly Social Security check, but Sanders will franchise hundreds of "finger-lickin' good" fast food operators in the next 9 years and will receive 3 percent of their gross sales in return for use of his name, spices, milk and egg dip, gravy mix, and paper supplies (see 1964).

The U.S. Census Bureau reveals that the American population increased by 2.8 million last year, the largest 1-year advance on record.

Legalized abortion on demand subject to certain safeguards is resumed in the Soviet Union, but abortion and birth control are discouraged (see 1936).

The Planned Parenthood Federation of America holds conferences on abortion.

The Fifth International Conference on Planned Parenthood convenes at Tokyo and hears Gregory Pincus speak about inhibition of ovulation in women who have taken progesterone or norethynodrel, active ingredients in newly developed contraceptive

1955 (cont.) pills that will soon be spoken of collectively as The Pill (*see* 1954). The new oral contraceptive has a failure rate of only one pregnancy per thousand women per year (*see* Puerto Rico study, 1957).

1956 Europe's Communist bloc countries have insurrections following the denunciation of the late Josef Stalin and his policies by Nikita Khrushchev who speaks out against Stalin February 14 at the 20th Soviet Communist Party Conference.

Polish workers riot at Poznan June 28 to protest social and economic conditions under the Communist regime. More than 100 demonstrators are killed as the militia moves in to suppress the riots, trials of the rioters end abruptly October 10, removal of Soviet officers from the Polish Army is demanded by several Polish Communists October 16, but Polish and Soviet frontier troops exchange fire as the former Soviet officer Marshal Konstantin K. Rokossovsky orders his Polish troops to take positions near Warsaw.

Former Polish Workers' party secretary general Wladyslaw Gomulka has been freed and rehabilitated after 5 years in prison, and he becomes first secretary of the Polish Communist party October 21.

Hungarian university students meet the evening of October 22 and put together a list of 16 demands while expressing solidarity with the Polish rebels (above). The petition is put up throughout Budapest during the night on trees, on walls, and at tram stops, and the students make plans to present their demands to the minister of internal affairs who is also the head of the secret police.

Budapest's Bem Square is mobbed with students beginning at 4:30 in the afternoon of October 23 as the ministry of internal affairs retracts its denial of permission to hold a rally, the students are joined by truckloads of workers, and the crowd moves toward Parliament Square 2 miles away as its numbers swell to more than 100,000 men and women demanding democratic government, the return of former premier Imre Nagy to power, withdrawal of Soviet troops, and the release of Jozsef Cardinal Mindszenty who has been held in solitary confinement since the end of 1948.

Imre Nagy is restored as premier October 24 to appease the Hungarian demonstrators, the Stalinist head of the Communist party Erno Gero is replaced October 25 by Janos Kadar, but the revolt begins to spread across Hungary.

Soviet troop withdrawal from Poland begins October 25, but several Soviet divisions from East Germany have entered Poland a few days earlier and they remain. Marshal Rokossovsky plots to overthrow Party Secretary Gomulka, Polish attacks on Soviet Army installations at Liegnitz are suppressed by Polish militia using tear gas, the Soviet military coup against Gomulka is aborted by betrayal of his plans, Rokossovsky returns to Moscow October 28, and the Polish prelate Stefan Cardinal Wyszinski is released from custody October 29.

Soviet forces withdraw from Budapest October 30, Cardinal Mindszenty is released from prison the same day, Premier Nagy goes on the radio to promise Hungarians free elections and a prompt end to one-party dictatorship, Nagy denounces the Warsaw Pact of 1954 November 2, and 2 days later the Hungarian defiance is crushed by 16 Soviet divisions supported by 2,000 tanks. Premier Nagy is ousted, he is replaced by Janos Kadar (above) who will continue as premier until 1965, and Cardinal Mindszenty takes refuge in the U.S. embassy at Budapest where he will occupy the top floor for 15 years and will be supported by funds from U.S. Roman Catholic bishops.

The United Nations General Assembly condemns Soviet interference in Hungary in a resolution November 4, the UN calls for an investigation, the last rebel stronghold on Csepel Island in the Danube falls to Soviet forces November 14, and the Russians seize Imre Nagy November 22 as he leaves the Yugoslav embassy at Budapest.

The United States offers asylum to Hungarian "freedom fighters" November 29, but the Eisenhower administration makes no other effort to intervene and takes no action until after the president's reelection (below).

The University of Alabama has expelled its first black student Autherine Lucy March 1 in defiance of a federal court order reversing her suspension by the university's president and trustees.

Southern congressmen issue a manifesto March 11 pledging to use "all lawful means" to overturn the Supreme Court's desegregation ruling of 1954.

A Supreme Court ruling April 23 outlaws racial segregation in intrastate public transportation.

Martin Luther King, Jr., 27, organizes a boycott of Montgomery, Ala., public transportation. The black clergyman-civil rights leader leads a protest against racial discrimination.

South Africa's Nationalist government has revealed plans January 13 to remove 60,000 mixed-blood "coloreds" from the Cape Province voting roll, and on August 25 the government orders more than 100,000 nonwhites in Johannesburg to leave their homes within a year to make room for whites (*see* 1953; 1961).

A U.S. Supreme Court ruling March 26 upholds a federal law passed in 1954 to compel witnesses to testify in cases involving national security. The court rules in *Ullmann v. United States* that the witnesses will have immunity from prosecution equivalent to the protection guaranteed by the Fifth Amendment.

A Supreme Court ruling handed down April 3 in the case of *Pennsylvania v. Nelson* excludes the states from punishing persons for sedition. The national government has "occupied the field" under the Smith Act of 1940, says the high court.

Chinese who resist communization continue to be liquidated as they have been since 1949 (and especially since 1952) and as they will be for another 4 years. By 1960 some 26.3 million Chinese will have been killed according to some estimates, the largest massacre in world history.

Hungarians stage a general strike in December to protest the Janos Kadar regime (above). Some 150,000 people leave the country and they include some of the nation's best minds.

Soviet occupation of Hungary (above) has been dictated by Marshal Georgi K. Zhukov after a long debate in the Politburo where a majority has initially opposed military action. Soviet ordnance contains only intermediate ballistic missiles that can reach certain strategic areas of southern Europe only if launched from bases in Hungary, Zhukov has insisted on having those bases, and Moscow has responded also to pressure from its allies at Peking who have urged suppression of the Hungarian revolution lest world Communism disintegrate.

The Polaris missile developed at the Woods Hole, Mass., Oceanographic Institute can be launched underwater from submarines and can carry a nuclear warhead (see hydrogen bomb, below).

Sudan is proclaimed an independent democratic republic January 1 and joins the Arab League January 19, increasing membership in the league to nine.

Jordan and Israel accept UN truce proposals January 24, the Declaration of Washington issued February 1 by President Truman and Prime Minister Eden reaffirms joint Anglo-American policy in the Mideast, Moscow states February 12 that sending U.S. or British troops to the Mideast would violate the UN Charter, a military alliance of Egypt, Saudi Arabia, and Yemen is signed April 21 at Jedda, a cease-fire between Israel and Jordan is arranged by Dag Hammarskjöld of the UN and takes effect April 29, cease-fires between Israel and Lebanon and between Israel and Syria take effect May 1.

Egypt announces June 4 that she will not renew the Suez Canal Company's concession after it expires in 1968, the last British troops leave the Suez Canal base June 13, President Nasser seizes the canal July 26 under a decree outlawing the Suez Canal Company, British and French nationals leave Egypt August 2, British families are airlifted out of the Canal Zone August 9, President Nasser boycotts a London conference on the Suez August 16 and rejects 18-nation proposals on the Suez September 10.

The Suez dispute (above) is submitted to the UN Security Council September 23 by Britain and France, Israeli troops invade the Sinai Peninsula October 29, Israel accepts an October 30 Anglo-French ultimatum calling for a cease-fire and for withdrawal of troops 10 miles from the Suez Canal, but Egypt does not accept, Egyptian airfields are bombed by the French and British October 31, the United States sends aid to Israel, Jordan refuses to permit RAF planes to use bases in Jordan for operations against Egypt, Gaza falls to British forces November 2, the

UN General Assembly adopts a Canadian resolution November 4 to send an international force to the Mideast, but Britain and France abstain, British paratroops land at Port Said November 5 to recover control of the canal that Prime Minister Eden says is vital if his country is not to starve, Moscow threatens to use rockets if Britain and France do not accept a cease-fire in Egypt, the cease-fire begins November 7 but Britain says she will evacuate her troops only upon the arrival of a UN force, the UN force arrives November 15, the last Anglo-French forces leave Port Said December 22, and the UN fleet begins clearing the canal of scuttled ships December 27.

Pakistan becomes an Islamic republic February 29 but remains within the British Commonwealth.

France recognizes Tunisian independence March 20 and Habib Bourguiba accepts the premiership April 10 at the invitation of the bey of Tunis (see 1957).

Spain recognizes Moroccan independence April 7, 5 weeks after French recognition (see 1957).

Britain grants Gold Coast independence September 18 (see Ghana, 1957).

President Eisenhower wins re-election against a second challenge from Democratic hopeful Adlai Stevenson despite the president's illness and despite warnings that in the event of his death he would be succeeded by his controversial vice president Richard M. Nixon. The popular "Ike" polls 57 percent of the popular vote and wins 457 electoral votes while Stevenson polls only 42 percent of the popular vote and wins 73 electoral votes, but the Democrats retain control of Congress.

"History is on our side. We will bury you!" says Nikita Khrushchev to Western ambassadors November 17 at a reception in the Kremlin.

Soviet troops crushed uprisings in Poland and Hungary, a reminder that satellite nations were puppets of Moscow.

1956 (cont.) The world's first airborne hydrogen bomb is exploded May 21 as the U.S. Atomic Energy Commission conducts a new series of nuclear tests in the Pacific (see 1954; Britain, 1957).

The first full-scale use of nuclear fuel to produce electricity is achieved at England's Calder Hall where the first turbine goes into operation August 20 and where power is fed into the grid of the Central Electricity Authority beginning October 17. Designed to generate some 90,000 kilowatts of power, the Calder Hall installation also manufactures the artificial nuclear fuel plutonium for military purposes (see 1954; United States, 1958).

Direct responsibility for long-term financing of Britain's electric utilities industry is assumed by the government in the Finance Act passed by Parliament. The utilities have been nationalized since 1948.

Uranium ore bodies are found north of Saskatchewan's Lake Athabasca. They will make Saskatchewan the world's leading uranium producer (see 1953).

Canada pledges to help India develop nuclear energy for peaceful purposes in an agreement signed by Prime Minister Louis St. Laurent with Prime Minister Jawahrlal Nehru. India will complete nuclear power reactors north of Bombay at Trapur in 1969 and will explode a nuclear device in May 1974, but peaceful application of nuclear energy for India will not come until later.

Libya's first oil well comes into production on a concession granted by Idris I to the Libyan American Oil Company. Rights to the oil go to U.S. explorer-archaeologist Wendell Phillips, 35, who has persuaded the king that an independent company will work harder to develop Libya's petroleum resources than will any of the seven world oil giants.

Getty Oil Company is created by a reorganization of John Paul Getty's Pacific Company and is the world's largest personally owned oil producer and distributor (see 1951). Getty's Saudi-Arabian wells have been producing since 1953 and Getty Oil will coordinate his interests in various other areas.

Pocahantas Fuel Company of Virginia is acquired by Consolidation Coal Company which has been taking over other coal companies and which will continue to expand by acquisition (see 1945). Pocahantas Fuel is a major producer of high-grade metallurgical coal.

Britain imposes petrol (gasoline) rationing December 17 as a result of the Suez crisis (above).

The Federal Aid Highway Act passed by Congress June 29 authorizes construction of a 42,500-mile network of roads to link major U.S. urban centers, with 90 percent of the $33.5 billion cost to be borne by the federal government (see 1944). The new legislation indirectly subsidizes trucking firms, intercity bus lines, motor vehicle producers, and oil companies, while railroads are left unsubsidized and will depreciate and abandon their unprofitable passenger services. The system is to be completed by 1972, and while that target date will prove beyond reach, some 38,000 miles of the Interstate Highway System will be open by 1976.

The first Midas Muffler shop has opened April 20 at Macon, Ga. The franchised chain specializing in exhaust system replacement will grow to have 1,000 shops in seven countries on three continents.

U.S. traffic accidents kill 6.28 people for every 100 million miles traveled. The rate will drop to 3.57 by 1974 and the rate on the interstate highways (above) will be 1.55.

The world's first containership port opens at Elizabeth, N.J., where the Port of New York Authority has paid $3.5 million to buy 40 acres for the new facility. The first container ship is a converted tanker with simple trailer vans on her decks, but containerships will revolutionize cargo handling by reducing the need for longshoremen, and Elizabeth will remain the world's leading containerport.

The Italian passenger liner S.S. *Andrea Doria* collides in a heavy fog 60 miles off Nantucket Island, Mass., July 24 with the Swedish liner S.S. *Stockholm*. The 29,500-gross-ton Italian ship has used improper radar procedure, she has turned to her left at the last moment rather than to her right, her engine room is missing a watertight door, she has diminished her stability by failing to ballast her empty fuel tanks, and she goes down in 225 feet of water the next morning with a loss of 52 lives. Also lost is a $200,000 automobile handmade in Italy for the Chrysler Corporation. This sophisticated prototype vehicle had employed advanced construction and engineering features.

General Motors Corporation announces 1955 earnings of more than $1 billion after taxes and is indicted for using anticompetitive actions to obtain an 85 percent monopoly on the U.S. market for new buses (see 1949; 1955). GM is charged by the Justice Department with having induced municipal transit systems to adopt bus specifications which only GM buses could meet, with having entered into long-range requirement contracts with bus company operators, and with having installed a GM officer and director as board chairman and leading stockholder of GM's chief competitor in bus-making (see 1965).

New York makes Broadway one-way southbound below 47th Street (see 1954; 1957).

Boeing Aircraft and Douglas Aircraft battle for leadership in the commercial jet aircraft industry (see 1953). Boeing 707s are ordered by American Airlines, Air France, Air India, and eight other airlines, while United Airlines, Trans Canada, SAS, and nine other airlines order Douglas DC-8s, but Boeing orders will exceed Douglas orders by three to one within a year (see 1958).

An Aeroflot Tupolev-104 airliner takes off from Moscow September 15 and makes the first scheduled passenger flight from Moscow to Irkutsk, Siberia. The Tupolev-104 is the world's first passenger jet.

The Ford Foundation sells 20 percent of its Ford Motor Company stock to Wall Street investors, permitting the public to buy into Ford for the first time and bringing in some $643 million to the Foundation which announces that it will give away more than $500 million in the next 18 months, $150 million more than it has given away in the 20 years it has been in operation (*see* 1950; 1954).

Wall Street's Dow Jones Industrial Average peaks at 521.05.

IBM signs a consent decree under which it agrees to sell its tabulating and computer machines as well as leasing them, thus ending a legal skirmish with the Department of Justice. IBM agrees also to offer purchasers the same services other than maintenance that it provides to leasers and to do so without separate charge, and it agrees to establish a separate subsidiary to conduct its service bureau operations (*see* 1955; 1969).

Investors Overseas Services (IOS) is founded at Paris by U.S. promoter Bernard Cornfeld, 29, who sells mutual fund shares to U.S. servicemen stationed overseas and to French investors whose bank savings earn interest well below the annual rate of inflation. Born in Istanbul, raised in Brooklyn, Cornfeld recruits salesmen, he starts building a worldwide syndicate that will soon account for nearly 16 percent of all Dreyfus Fund sales (*see* 1955), he will move his headquarters to Geneva in the fall of 1958, and he will be a multimillionaire within a few years.

The University of South Florida is founded at Tampa.

Nonfiction *The Organization Man* by *Fortune* editor William Hollingsworth Whyte, Jr., 39, argues that a new collective ethic has arisen from the bureaucratization of society and is replacing the old Protestant individualist code. The new ethic, says Whyte, assumes that the source of creative effort is no longer the individual but is rather the group, and that "belongingness" rather than personal fulfillment has become the ultimate need of the individual (compare Riesman, 1950); *The Art of Loving* by Erich Fromm; *Profiles in Courage* by U.S. Senator from Massachusetts John Fitzgerald Kennedy, 39, examines John Quincy Adams, John Peter Altgeld, Thomas Hart Benton, Sam Houston, Daniel Webster, and other prominent men of American history.

Fiction *The Last Hurrah* by Boston novelist Edwin O'Connor, 38, whose fictional Frank Skeffington is based on the politician James Michael Curley, now 81, whose autobiography *I'd Do It Again* will appear next year; *The Floating Opera* by U.S. novelist John Barth, 26, whose nihilist hero decides after a comic analysis not to commit suicide; *The Fall* (*La Chute*) by Albert Camus; *A Certain Smile* (*Un Certain Sourire*) by Françoise Sagan; *The Towers of Trebizond* by Rose Macaulay who produces her most successful novel at age 75; *Thin Ice* by Compton Mackenzie, now 73; *Anglo-Saxon Attitudes* by English novelist-

playwright Angus Wilson, 43; *A Tangled Web* by Irish poet-novelist-critic Cecil Day Lewis, now 52, who gains great success with his detective novel; *The Butterfly of Dinard* (*La farfalla di Dinard*), prose sketches by poet Eugenio Montale; *Diamonds Are Forever* by Ian Fleming who takes the title for his new James Bond thriller from the advertising slogan used by South Africa's De Beers Consolidated Mines; *Peyton Place* by U.S. novelist Grace Metalious.

Poetry "Zima Junction" ("Stantsiya Zima") by Russian poet Yevgeny Yevtushenko, 23, who presents problems that tormented him after Stalin's death in 1953 when the poem was written and reopens long forbidden themes; *The False and the True Green* by Salvatore Quasimodo; "Chaka" by Senegalese poet Leopold Sedar Senghor, 50; *Platero and I* (*Platero y yo*) by Spanish poet Juan Ramon Jimenez, 75; *Collected Poems* by English poet Kathleen Raine, 48.

Painting *Self-portrait* by Bernard Buffet.

Lyonel Feininger dies at New York January 13 at age 84; Emil Nolde dies at Seebüll near the Danish border April 15 at age 88; Jackson Pollock is killed in an automobile accident on Long Island, N.Y., August 17 at age 44.

Theater *The Visit* (*Der Besuch der alten Dame*) by Friedrich Dürrenmatt 1/29 at Zurich's Schauspielhaus; *Romanoff and Juliet* by Peter Ustinov 4/2 at the Manchester Opera House, England; *The Chalk Garden* by Enid Bagnold 4/4 at London's Theatre Royal, 658 perfs.; *The Quare Fellow* by Brendan Behan 5/24 at the London Theatre Royale in Stratford after a 1954 opening at Dublin's Pike Theatre; *Look Back in Anger* by English playwright John Osborne, 27, 5/8 at London's Royal Court Theatre, with Kenneth Haigh, Mary Ure, Alan Bates in a play that expresses the frustration of radical youth by means of a strident attack on the middle class; *A Long Day's Journey into Night* by the late Eugene O'Neill 11/7 at New York's Helen Hayes Theater, with Fredric March, Florence Eldredge, Jason Robards, Jr., Bradford Dilman, Katherine Ross in an autobiographical play about alcoholism and drug addiction by the playwright who died late in 1953 at age 65, 390 perfs., Pulitzer prize; *The Matchmaker* by Thornton Wilder 12/5 at New York's Royale Theatre, with Ruth Gordon, Arthur Hill in a play that will be the basis of the 1964 musical *Hello, Dolly!*, 486 perfs.

Television drama *As the World Turns* 4/2 on CBS (daytime) *Edge of Night* 4/2 on ABC (daytime).

Films Ingmar Bergman's *The Seventh Seal*; Federico Fellini's *La Strada* with Anthony Quinn, Giuletta Massina, Richard Basehart; Laurence Olivier's *Richard III* with Olivier, John Gielgud, Ralph Richardson, Claire Bloom; Jules Dassin's *Rififi*; Cecil B. DeMille's *The Ten Commandments* with Charlton Heston, Yul Brynner, Anne Baxter, Edward G. Robinson; Mike Todd's *Around the World in 80 Days* with David Niven, Cantinflas, Shirley MacLaine; Joshua Logan's *Bus Stop* with Marilyn Monroe, Ei-

1956 (cont.) leen Heckart, Don Murray; George Stevens's *Giant* with James Dean, Elizabeth Taylor, Rock Hudson; Anatole Litvak's *Anastasia* with Ingrid Bergman, Yul Brynner, Helen Hayes, Akim Tamiroff; John Ford's *The Searchers* with John Wayne, Jeffrey Hunter; Alexander Mackendrick's *The Lady-killers* with Alec Guinness, Peter Sellers; Alexander Mackendrick's *Sweet Smell of Success* with Burt Lancaster, Tony Curtis; Stanley Kubrick's *The Killing* with Sterling Hayden; Albert Lamorisse's *The Red Balloon* with Lamorisse's son Pascal; Satyajit Ray's *The Apu Trilogy* (which will be completed in 1959); Kenji Mizoguchi's *Street of Shame* with Machiko Kyo; Terry Morse and Inoshiro Honda's *Godzilla, King of the Monsters* with Raymond Burr.

Stage musicals *My Fair Lady* 3/15 at New York's Mark Hellinger Theater, with Julie Andrews, 20, as Eliza Doolittle, Rex Harrison as Professor Higgins, book based on the Bernard Shaw play *Pygmalion* of 1914, music by Frederick Loewe, lyrics by Alan Jay Lerner, songs that include "Why Can't the English Teach Their Children How to Speak," "The Rain in Spain," "The Street Where You Live," "I'm Getting Married in the Morning," "I've Grown Accustomed to Her Face," "I Could Have Danced All Night," 2,717 perfs.; *Mr. Wonderful* 3/22 at New York's Broadway Theater, with Sammy Davis, Jr. and Sr., Chita Rivera, music by Jerry Bock, 27, lyrics by Larry Holofcener and George Weiss, songs that include "Too Close for Comfort," 388 perfs.; *South Sea Bubble* 4/25 at London's Lyric Theatre, with Vivien Leigh, Alan Webb, Joyce Carey, music and lyrics by Noel Coward, 276 perfs. (originally produced at the Westport Country Playhouse in 1951 under another title with Claudette Colbert); *The Most Happy Fella* 5/3 at New York's Imperial Theater, with Robert Weede, Art Lund, Jo Sullivan, book based on the Sidney Howard play *They Knew What They Wanted* of 1924, music and lyrics by Frank Loesser, songs that include "Big 'D' " and "Standing on the Corner," 676 perfs.; *Li'l Abner* 11/10 at the St. James Theater, with Peter Palmer as Abner Yokum, Edith Adams as Daisy Mae, Charlotte Rae as Mammy Yokum, Stubby Kaye, Julie Newmar, Tina Louise, music by Gene de Paul, lyrics by John Meyer, songs that include "Jubilation T. Cornpone," 693 perfs.; *Bells Are Ringing* 11/29 at the Sam S. Shubert Theater, with Judy Holliday, Jean Stapleton, music by Jule Styne, lyrics by Betty Comden and Adolph Green, songs that include "Just in Time," "The Party's Over," 924 perfs.

Opera *The Ballad of Baby Doe* 7/7 at Colorado's Central City Opera House with music by U.S. composer Douglas Stuart Moore, 61, to a libretto by John Latouche based on the career of silver magnate Horace Tabor and his widow (see 1880; 1893).

The Joffrey Ballet company is founded by U.S. dancer-choreographer Robert Joffrey.

First performances *Proclamation* for Trumpet and Orchestra by Ernest Bloch 2/3 at Houston; *Modern Psalm* for Speaker, Mixed Chorus, and Orchestra by the late Arnold Schoenberg 5/29 at Cologne; *Johannesburg Festival* Overture by William Walton 9/25 at Johannesburg; *Robert Browning* Overture by the late Charles Ives 10/14 at New York's Carnegie Hall.

Popular songs "Love Me Tender" by Elvis Presley and Vera Walson; "Hound Dog" by Jerry Leiter and Mike Stoller; "Heartbreak Hotel" by Elvis Presley, Mae Boren Axton, Tommy Durden; "I Walk the Line" by U.S. singer-composer John R. "Johnny" Cash, 24, who last year made his first record "Hey, Porter," and followed it with "Folsom Prison Blues." Cash begins appearances on the 31-year-old *Grand Ole Opry* radio and television show out of Nashville and while he will become addicted in the mid-1960s to amphetamines and barbiturates, he will rehabilitate himself with medical assistance and by the mid-1970s will be drawing bigger crowds than ever and earning well over $1 million per year; "Since I Met You, Baby" and "I Almost Lost My Mind" by U.S. composer Ivory Joe Hunter, 45, whose two records will sell more than a million copies each and will help make Hunter a living legend as he writes country music and rhythm and blues numbers that will include "My Wish Came True" and "I Need You So" for Elvis Presley, Pat Boone, and Sonny James; "Around the World in 80 Days" by Victor Jones, lyrics by Harold Adamson for the film (above); "Que Será, Será (What Will Be, Will Be)" by Jay Livingston and Ray Evans; "Canadian Sunset" by Eddie Haywood, lyrics by Norman Gimbel; "See You Later, Alligator" by Robert Guidry.

The Olympic games are held at Melbourne with 3,539 contestants from 67 nations. Soviet Russia is the winner for the first time in history.

Brazilian soccer player Edson Arantes "Pele" do Nascimento, 15, signs with the Santos team to begin an 18-year career of 1,253 games in which he will score 1,216 goals to become the world-famous athletic figure known in Brazil as Perola Negra (Black Pearl), in Chile as El Peligro (The Dangerous One), in France as La Tulipe Noir (Black Tulip), and in Italy as Il Re (The King). Pele will be signed by the New York Cosmos in 1975 to a $7 million 3-year contract that will make him the world's highest-paid team athlete.

The New York Yankees win the World Series by defeating the Brooklyn Dodgers 4 games to 3 after losing last year's Series to the Dodgers by the same one-game margin. Don Larsen of the Yankees pitches the first "perfect" game in Series history, allowing no hits in the fifth game (see Cy Young, 1904).

U.S. prizefighter Floyd Patterson, 21, wins the world heavyweight title November 30 by knocking out Archie Moore, 42, in the fifth round of a championship match at Chicago.

"Does she or doesn't she?" ask advertisements for Miss Clairol hair coloring that show children with mothers to convey the idea that hair-coloring is not just for women of dubious virtue (see 1950). The ads bid for beauty salon acceptance by answering the question, "Only her hair-dresser knows for sure" (Bristol-Myers will acquire Clairol in 1959).

Raid insect spray is introduced by the S. C. Johnson Company (see 1932; 1964).

Comet cleanser is introduced by Procter & Gamble to compete with Colgate's Ajax (see 1947). The silica sand product will soon be the largest-selling household cleanser.

Salem Cigarettes are introduced by R. J. Reynolds Company whose new brand will overtake Brown & Williamson's Kools and will be the leading brand of mentholated cigarettes within 18 months.

New York's Hoving Corporation is acquired by Maxey Jarman of General Shoe who thus gains control of Bonwit Teller and of Tiffany & Co. (see 1953; 1957).

New York's Coliseum opens April 28 in Columbus Circle. The $35 million convention center replaces Grand Central Palace on Lexington Avenue that has been used for the boat show, the flower show, and other traditional events.

Hilton Hotel Corporation divests itself of New York's Roosevelt Hotel, Washington's Mayflower, and the Hotel Jefferson at St. Louis in compliance with a Justice Department consent decree.

General Development Corporation is founded to create residential housing communities throughout Florida. Toronto financier-promoter Louis Chesler starts the company with the Mackle brothers Frank, Elliott, and Robert whose father Francis Elliott Mackle, Sr., started a Florida construction firm in 1910 and who have been associated with Chesler for several years. Port Charlotte, Port Malabar, and Port St. Lucie will be among the major General Development Corporation projects (see Arvida, 1958).

Britain's Clean Air Act begins a systematic ban on burning of soft coal and other smoky fuels (see 1955).

Georgia's Buford Dam is completed on the Chattahoochee River in February to create a reservoir and to make Lake Lanier a recreation area with 540 miles of shoreline.

Virgin Islands National Park is established by act of Congress. The park embraces most of the island of St. John—15,150 acres of green hills and sandy beaches that have been donated by Laurence Rockefeller.

Rock paintings which establish that the immense Sahara Desert was once fertile land are found 900 miles southeast of Algiers. The paintings and engravings found in the Tibesti Mountains by French archaeologist Henri Lhote, 53, date to 3,500 B.C.

Efforts to collectivize Polish agriculture are ended after a decade marked by little success. Poland's Wladyslaw Gomulka (above) reverses collectivization policies.

Some 100 million Chinese peasant families are forced into large collective farms called Agricultural Producers' Cooperatives. The farms produce a record 180 million tons of grain, up from 163 million in 1952, but partly for reasons of weather the harvest fails to match the rate of China's population growth.

A soil bank plan to ease the problem of declining U.S. farm income is proposed by President Eisenhower in a special January 9 message to Congress. A program to pay farmers for withdrawing land from production is authorized by Congress May 28 (see AAA, 1938).

India is granted a $300 million food loan August 29 to buy surplus U.S. farm products that are depressing domestic American prices (see P.L. 480, 1954).

Standard Fruit Company begins banana operations in Costa Rica (see 1926; 1959).

The disease-prone Gros Michel banana grown in Central America and the Caribbean islands since 1820 is replaced in many areas by the Cavendish (Valery) banana which is less vulnerable to disease and less likely to be blown down in hurricanes since it grows on a shorter plant. The industry shifts to Ecuador which was not a major exporter before the war but which rarely has high winds, provides good growing conditions, and will become the world's leading banana exporter within a decade, accounting for half the bananas shipped to the United States.

U.S. congressmen's wives are lectured by actress and health food enthusiast Gloria Swanson, now 57, on the hazards in American foods. The women will persuade their husbands to support a Food Additives Amendment to the Food, Drug and Cosmetic Act of 1938 which New York congressman James J. Delaney has been pushing without success (see 1950; 1958).

La Leche League International, Inc., is founded with headquarters at Franklin Park, Ill., to "help mothers who wish to breast-feed their infants" and to encourage breast-feeding.

TreeSweet Products Company switches from canning juices to producing frozen concentrates at a new $5 million plant at Ft. Pierce, Fla. (see 1947).

Stokely-Van Camp builds a Minnesota plant to produce frozen pies (see 1944).

Welch's Grape Juice has sales of $40 million for the year and is acquired from Jacob Kaplan by the National Grape Co-operative Association whose 4,500 member grape-growers become the first farmers in history to own an international business (see 1945).

U.S. canners ship 700 million cases of canned goods, up from 400 million in 1940 (see 1963).

Sara Lee Kitchens is acquired after 7 years of independent operation by Consolidated Foods which will expand Sara Lee's frozen foods line to include fruit pies, Bavarian cream pies, dinner rolls in transparent oven baking bags, ravioli, lasagna, beef stroganoff,

1956 (cont.) chicken and noodles au gratin, beef and pepper stew, etc. (*see* Lubin, 1949; Consolidated, 1955).

Beech-Nut Life Savers, Inc., is created by a merger of Beech-Nut Packing Company and Life Savers, Inc. Beech-Nut has been selling chewing gum since 1910 and candy-coated Beechies chewing gum since 1933 (*see* 1920; 1928; 1931).

Imperial Margarine is introduced by Lever Brothers. "The first margarine unconditionally guaranteed to bring you the tantalizing flavor formerly found only in the expensive table spread" is soon among the top four margarine brands, competing with Kraft's Parkay, Best Foods' Blue Bonnet, and Lever's own Good Luck brands.

Busch Bavarian beer is introduced by Anheuser-Busch, Inc., to augment its 80-year-old Budweiser brand and its 60-year-old Michelob brand.

Jack Daniel's whiskey is acquired by Brown-Forman, Inc., which pays $18.5 million in cash to owners who include the heirs of Lem Motlow whose Uncle Jack first made the Tennessee whiskey in 1866. Lynchburg, Tenn., has been dry since 1909, but the whiskey enjoys wide popularity elsewhere.

Washington's Rive Gauche restaurant opens at Wisconsin Avenue and M Street N.W. under the direction of French-American restaurateur Blaise Gherardi, 46.

French chef Paul Bocuse, 30, quits La Pyramide at Vienne to join his father Georges in the restaurant at Collonges-au-Mont-d'Or just north of Lyons. The restaurant was founded in 1765 by his great-great-great-great-great-grandfather Michel Bocuse, a miller who opened a tavern serving fried fish from the Saone, goat cheese from neighboring farms, and Mont d'Or wine. Georges Bocuse will die next year, Paul will win his first Michelin star a year later, and in 1965 he will win his third Michelin star.

1957 The Treaty of Rome signed March 25 establishes a European Economic Community (the Common Market). Belgium, France, West Germany, Italy, Luxembourg, and the Netherlands remove mutual tariff barriers to promote the economy of Europe and make it a viable competitor with Britain and the United States.

A French-Soviet trade pact has been signed February 11, Britain relaxes restrictions on trade with the People's Republic of China May 30, British tourists traveling to dollar areas receive an allowance increase June 4, and Britain decontrols most rents June 6 despite opposition from the Labour party.

The European Atomic Energy Community (Euratom) is created by a treaty signed at Rome March 25 (*see* 1958).

West German nuclear physicists announce April 12 that they will not cooperate in the production or testing of nuclear weapons, Japan sends Moscow a note April 20 protesting Soviet nuclear tests, and the British explode their first thermonuclear bomb in the megaton range May 15 at Christmas Island in the Pacific.

"Misuse of nuclear energy could lead to the annihilation of mankind," warn scientists gathered for the first Pugwash Conference of Nuclear Scientists at the Nova Scotia birthplace of Cleveland industrialist Cyrus Eaton (*see* Insull, 1932). Now 73, Eaton has traveled in Eastern Europe, he has held two previous conferences to advance peaceful exchange of information, he has turned his attention to the problem of preventing a nuclear holocaust, the Pugwash Conference includes three Soviet nuclear scientists and one from the People's Republic of China, and it concludes that "unrestricted warfare would be a disaster of unprecedented magnitude."

The National Committee for a Sane Nuclear Policy (SANE) is started by U.S. founders who include psychoanalyst Erich Fromm, whose book *The Sane Society* appeared 2 years ago and whose *The Art of Loving* was published last year.

Britain's discredited prime minister Sir Anthony Eden resigns January 9 and is replaced by the 62-year-old (Maurice) Harold Macmillan of the publishing family who will continue as PM until 1963.

President Eisenhower begins a second term by extending the Truman Doctrine of 1947 to the Mideast. The president enunciates the Eisenhower Doctrine for protecting the Mideast from Communist aggression, he sends aid to Jordan, and he asks Congress to authorize him to send U.S. armed forces to the Mideast if necessary.

Premier Bulganin of the U.S.S.R. and Premier Chou En-lai of the People's Republic of China announce January 18 that they will support the Mideast against Western aggression.

Israel rejects a February 2 UN resolution calling upon her to withdraw her troops from Egypt's Gaza Strip and other occupied Egyptian territory unless she receives more UN assurance that her own territory will be protected, the United States indicates that she will apply economic sanctions against Israel if the UN requires such action, but Washington assures Tel Aviv that the United States will support "free passage" through the Gulf of Aqaba.

Israel announces withdrawal of her troops from the Gaza Strip and the Gulf of Aqaba area March 1 on the "assumption" that the UN Emergency Force will administer the Gaza Strip and that navigation in the Gulf of Aqaba will continue.

Ghana becomes the first African state south of the Sahara to attain independence. The newly independent Gold Coast unites with the UN trust territory of British Togoland March 6, Ghana takes that name from a Sudanic empire that flourished between the 4th and 10th centuries, and Kwama N. Nkrumah begins a 15-year rule of the country.

Prime Minister Macmillan and President Eisenhower meet in the Bermuda Conference from March

21 to 24 and reestablish the relationship strained by last year's Suez crisis. The United States agrees to make certain guided missiles available to Britain.

The Aga Khan dies July 11 at age 79 after 73 years as spiritual and temporal leader of the Ismailis whose numbers have grown to some 20 million. The immensely rich Aga Sultan Sir Mohammed Shah has owned the world greatest racing stables and he is succeeded by his 21-year-old grandson Shah Karim, a Harvard student who becomes Aga Khan IV.

Algerian FLN terrorists disrupt France but President René Coty restates the government's refusal to grant independence (see 1954). The French Parlement votes Premier Bourges-Mannoury special powers July 18 to suppress the FLN (see de Gaulle, 1958).

Tunisia deposes the bey of Tunis July 25, proclaims herself a republic, and elects Habib Bourguiba president (see 1956). President Bourguiba asks for U.S. aid September 12 following border clashes with French and Algerian troops, Washington and London agree November 14 to supply small arms, and Tunisia announces November 18 that she has rejected a Soviet arms offer.

Morocco's Sherifian Empire becomes the Kingdom of Morocco August 11, 5 months after signing a treaty of friendship and alliance with Tunisia (above). The sultan Sidi Mohammed II becomes King Mohammed V and will reign until his death in 1961.

Syria ousts three U.S. embassy officials August 13 on charges of having plotted to overthrow President Shukri al-Kuwatly, Washington asks Syrian embassy officials to leave, President Eisenhower charges Moscow with trying to take over Syria, and he reaffirms the Eisenhower Doctrine September 21 (above). The Syrian president meets at Cairo with President Nasser, he meets in Syria September 25 with the premier of Iraq and the king of Saudi Arabia, and the meetings bolster Arab solidarity.

Norway's Haakon VII dies September 21 at age 85 after a 52-year reign and is succeeded by his 54-year-old son who ascends the throne as Olaf V. Norway's Labor party is returned to power October 7.

Moscow has complained to Istanbul September 11 of Turkish troop concentrations on the Syrian border, Nikita Khrushchev writes October 12 to British and European labor and socialist parties urging them to try to stop U.S. and Turkish aggression in the Mideast, Syria declares a state of emergency October 16, and U.S. secretary of state John F. Dulles warns Moscow against an attack on Turkey.

The Soviet minister of defense Marshal Zhukov is relieved of his duties October 26. Vyacheslav Molotov is exiled to Siberia for conspiring against Nikita Krushchev.

 Sputnik I launched by the Soviet Union October 4 is the world's first man-made Earth satellite. The 184-pound sphere orbits the Earth once every 90 minutes in an eliptical orbit, it is followed in November by Sputnik II which weighs more than 1,000 pounds and carries a live dog, but New York Times correspondent Harrison Salisbury in Moscow hears a Russian say, "Better to learn to feed your people at home before starting to explore the moon."

Alabama grocery chain truckdriver Willie Edwards, 25, is accused by Ku Klux Klansmen of having made remarks to a white woman, he is forced at pistol point January 23 to jump to his death from the Tyler Goodwin Bridge into the Alabama River, his body is found downriver in Lowndes County in late April. Since January 23 was his first day on the truck route, it will be demonstrated that Edwards was not the man sought by the Klan.

Little Rock, Ark., has a school integration struggle as officials try to instrument the Brown v. Board of Education decision by the Supreme Court in 1954. Jeering crowds led by Arkansas governor Orval Faubus prevent nine black children from entering Central High School in September, and President Eisenhower sends in federal troops to quell the disorder (see 1958).

The first U.S. civil rights law since Civil War reconstruction days is passed by Congress September 9. The law establishes a Civil Rights Commission, it provides federal safeguards for voting rights, and it is enacted despite opposition from such Southerners as Senator Strom Thurmond of South Carolina who spoke continuously for 24 hours and 18 minutes against the bill August 29 a new filibuster record.

Britain's Report of the Committee on Homosexual Offences and Prostitution is issued in September by the committee headed by Reading University chancellor Sir John Wolfenden, 51, and recommends an end to punitive laws against homosexuality "between consenting adults in private." The Wolfenden Report also calls for an end to the requirement that "annoyance" be established before a constable may book a prostitute for soliciting a customer above the age of 21, but the recommendation on homosexuality is what creates a controversy. London's Evening Standard calls the recommendation "bad, retrogade, and utterly to be condemned," Lord Rothermere's Daily Mail observes that "great nations have fallen and empires decayed because corruption became socially acceptable," but the Times comments that "adult sexual behavior not involving minors, force, fraud or public indecency belongs to the realm of private conduct, not of criminal law" and the Wolfenden Report is supported by the Church of England (see Street Offences Act, 1959).

A Great Leap Forward launched by Mao Tse-tung in the People's Republic of China puts more than half a billion peasants into 24,000 "people's communes." The people are guaranteed food, clothing, shelter, and child care, but deprived of all private property.

Synthetic DNA is produced by Stanford University biochemist Arthur Kornberg, 39, and his associates (see Watson, Crick, 1953; RNA, 1955). The chemical and physical structure of Kornberg's DNA is identi-

Europe's Common Market eliminated trade barriers that had put European companies at a commercial disadvantage.

cal with that of the actual genetic material, but it is biologically inert (*see* 1961; 1967).

 A National Cancer Institute is funded by Congress to seek cures for the disease that is second only to heart disease as a cause of death in the United States.

The antibiotic rifampia that will be used successfully to cure "incurable" tuberculosis is developed in Italy.

Darvon (propoxyphene) is introduced by Eli Lilly. Chemically related to the methadone discovered in 1953, the new pain-killing drug will be prescribed by physicians as a nonaddictive alternative to the opiate codeine, it will become one of the most common U.S. prescription drugs, it costs 10 times as much as aspirin, it will be found no more effective than aspirin for most uses, and it will be charged by the federal Bureau of Narcotics and Dangerous Drugs in 1973 with being an addictive drug.

The pharmaceutical industry is found to be peculiarly vulnerable to monopolistic control in a Senate investigation led by Estes Kefauver of Tennessee. World War II injuries have spurred the development of miracle drugs which were mostly unknown 20 years ago, and Kefauver says the industry "is charging all the traffic will bear in selling its new drugs," making profits of roughly 20 percent of total investment, double the average for other manufacturers.

Prednisone has a captive market of arthritis sufferers, says Senator Kefauver (above), and the 2-year-old drug is being sold at 30 cents per tablet while small, independent laboratories sell it in wholesale lots for as little as 2 cents per tablet. Large pharmaceutical firms point out that their development costs are enormous (*see* Kennedy, 1962).

 British bank interest rates rise to 7 percent.

A University of Wisconsin study shows that 20 percent of Americans still live below the "poverty line" (*see* 1959).

The effect on consumers of increasing mergers by U.S. automakers, steel companies, bread bakers, and pharmaceutical firms is investigated by Senator Kefauver (above).

Monroe Calculating Machine Company is acquired for $18 million in stock and cash by Litton Industries whose sales of $40 million per year are roughly equal to those of Monroe (*see* 1912; 1953). Litton will soon acquire the Swedish firm Svenska Dataregister that is giving National Cash Register its first serious competition.

E. I. du Pont's 23 percent ownership of General Motors Corporation stock creates conditions that violate the antitrust laws, says the Supreme Court June 3. Du Pont is ordered to divest itself of its GM stock (*see* 1915; 1929).

Union Carbide Corporation is created by a shortening of the name of the Union Carbide and Carbon (*see* 1920). The company has some 400 U.S. and Canadian plants plus affiliated companies.

Germany's Fried. Krupp agrees to supply the Soviet Union with a chemical plant and a synthetic fiber complex. Krupp has diversified from steelmaking.

Gulf+Western Industries has its beginnings December 30 in a group of small auto part companies put together by Austrian-American entrepreneur Charles G. Bluhdorn, 27, who will be a millionaire by age 30 as he creates a new business conglomerate (*see* Litton, above; Textron, 1955). Bluhdorn will acquire New Jersey Zinc, E. W. Bliss (a manufacturer of heavy machinery), Desilu Productions (whose *I Love Lucy* series has been on television since 1951), Paramount Pictures, South Puerto Rico Sugar, Consolidated Cigar, Parker Pen, and other firms.

The Wankel rotary engine produced at Lindau on Lake Constance by German engineer Fritz Wankel, 55, is the first new internal combustion engine since the Benz and Daimler engines of the 1880s and the 1895 diesel engine. Wankel replaces the up-down movement of oblong pistons in cylinders with a triangular disk that rotates inside a round cylinder. The slightly curved sides of the disk leave some space for the moving and expanding gases on at least two of its three sides, and the rotating disk opens and closes intake and exhaust valves automatically.

The Wankel engine (above) has only two moving parts and while it consumes slightly more fuel than conventional engines, it is smaller, it weighs 25 percent less, it works more smoothly, and it costs less to build in mass production. The first automobile to employ the new engine will be the German NSU, but Japan's Toyo Kgoyo will use a Wankel engine to power its Mazda beginning in 1968 as foreign automakers rush to obtain licenses for using the rotary engine that will also be used in pumps and other nonautomotive applications.

Armand Hammer comes out of retirement at age 60 to head the failing Occidental Petroleum Company in which he has invested $60,000 "for fun" after being told by his tax counsel to find a money-losing tax shelter. Occidental sold last year at 18 cents a share on the Los Angeles Stock Exchange, its net worth was $34,000, but Hammer will build its revenues from $1 million per year to more than $1 billion, and he will make it the 11th largest U.S. oil producer and the 20th largest U.S. firm of any kind (see 1921).

An International Atomic Energy Agency is established.

A nonstop round the world flight by three U.S. Air Force jets is completed January 18. The jets have averaged more than 500 miles per hour.

A new transcontinental speed record of 3 hours, 20 minutes, 8.4 seconds across the United States is set by U.S. Marine Corps major John Herschel Glenn, 36 (see 1962).

Greece's Olympic Airways is purchased in bankruptcy from the Greek government by shipowner Aristotle Onassis who will have Olympic operating at a profit by 1963 (see 1930).

Diesel power on U.S. railroads eclipses steam power. The last Atchison, Topeka and Santa Fe steam locomotive is retired from service August 27 after 88 years of Santa Fe steam operation (see 1941).

New York's last trolley car is retired from service across the Queensboro Bridge as motorbuses replace streetcars in most major U.S. cities (see General Motors, 1956; Washington, 1962).

New York's Avenue of the Americas (Sixth Avenue) is made one-way northbound despite objections from the Fifth Avenue Coach Company and the Transport Workers Union (see 1956; 1960).

Michigan's Macinac Straits Bridge opens at Mackinaw City. The $100 million 1,158-meter span is the world's longest suspension bridge.

The Edsel is introduced by Ford Motor Company which has invested some $250 million to develop a line of cars to compete with General Motors Corporation's Oldsmobile. The Edsel will be a colossal failure, and the failure will raise doubts about the effectiveness of market research.

Detroit labor leader Jimmy (James Riddle) Hoffa, 44, gains control of the International Brotherhood of Teamsters which is ousted from the AFL-CIO on charges of corruption. Hoffa organized his fellow Kroger grocery chain warehousemen into a union when he was 17, he won a brief strike, he obtained an AF of L charter for his local the following year, and he will make the Teamsters one of the country's most powerful labor unions (see 1964).

Control Data Corporation is organized to produce computers designed by Minneapolis engineer-mathematician Seymour R. Cray, 32, whose Model 1604 will be one of the first transistorized computers and

whose Model 6600 will be the first commercially successful "super" computer (see transistor, 1948). The 6600 will be a mainstay of atomic energy laboratories and other scientific research labs.

Some 1,000 electronic computers are shipped to U.S. and foreign customers, up from 20 in 1954 (see 1960).

The Hidden Persuaders by former *Collier's* magazine staffwriter Vance (Oakley) Packard, 43, suggests that advertisers are experimenting with audiovisual "subthreshold effects" to insinuate their messages past people's conscious guard. Packard cites a *Times* of London speculation that such techniques might be used for political indoctrination.

Condé Nast Publications, Inc., is acquired by the S. I. Newhouse newspaper chain (see *Vogue*, 1909; Newhouse, 1912, 1967).

Nonfiction *Memoirs of a Catholic Girlhood* by Mary McCarthy; *Where Did You Go? Out. What Did You Do? Nothing* by Robert Paul Smith.

Fiction *Doktor Zhivago* by Boris Pasternak; *Arturo's Island* (*L'Isola di Arturo*) by Italian novelist Elsa Morante, 39, wife of Alberto Moravia; *Pnin* by Vladimir Nabokov; *Jealousy* (*La Jalousie*) by Alain Robbe-Grillet; *The Wind* (*Le Vent*) by French novelist Claude Simon, 44; *On the Beach* by Nevil Shute who foresees the last days of a world destroyed by nuclear holocaust; *A Choice of Enemies* and *The Apprenticeship of Duddy Kravitz* by Canadian novelist Mordecai Richler, 26; *The Assistant* by Bernard Malamud; *That Awful Mess on Via Merulana* (*Que Pasticciaccio Brutto de Via Merulana*) by Italian novelist Carlo Emilio Gadda, 64; *The Fountain Overflows* by Rebecca West; *Gimpel the Fool* (stories) by Isaac Bashevis Singer; *O Pays, Mon Beau Peuple* by French West African novelist Sembene Ousmane, 34, who has returned to his native Senegal after working as a Marseilles dockhand and whose novel will be translated into Slovak, Hungarian, Romanian, German, and Bulgarian; *From Russia with Love* by Ian Fleming; *On the Road* by U.S. novelist Jack (Jean-Louis) Kerouac, 35, who wrote the novel in 3 weeks in 1951 typing on 20-foot strips of art paper whose ends he pasted together. Kerouac's novel about the "beat generation" describes people "who never yawn or say a commonplace thing, but burn, burn, burn like fabulous yellow roman candles exploding like spiders across the stars and in the middle you see the blue centerlight pip and everybody goes 'Awww!' "

Poetry *Opus Posthumous* by Wallace Stevens who died in early August 1955 at age 75; "Piedra del Sol" by Mexican poet Octavio Paz; *Collected Poems* by the late Scottish poet Norman Cameron who died in 1953 at age 48.

Juvenile *The Cat in the Hat* by Dr. Seuss begins a series of "Beginner Books," "Bright and Early Books," and "Big Beginner Books." His new book will be translated into many foreign languages and will have sales of between 8 and 9 million in the next

1957 (cont.) 20 years; *Little Bear* by Danish-American author Else Holmelund Minarik will be translated into 17 foreign languages including Urdu and Bengali, it will have U.S. sales of 1 million in the next 20 years, and it begins a series of "I Can Read Books."

Painting *Brown Swiss* by Andrew Wyeth; *Painting with Red Letter 'S'* by Robert Rauschenberg; *New York, N.Y.* by Ellsworth Kelly; *Summer* by Sam Francis; *Portrait of Hugo Kastor* by Raphael Soyer; *1975-D No. 1* by Clyfford Still; *Annette* by Alberto Giacometti; *Mujeres peinandose* and *Sandias* by Diego Rivera who dies at Mexico City November 25 at age 70.

Theater *The Potting Shed* by novelist Graham Greene 1/29 at New York's Bijou Theater, with Sybil Thorndike, Leueen MacGrath, Carol Lynley, Frank Conroy, 157 perfs.; *Orpheus Descending* by Tennessee Williams 3/21 at New York's Martin Beck Theater, with Maureen Stapleton, Cliff Robertson, 68 perfs.; *The Entertainer* by John Osborne 4/10 at London's Royal Court Theatre, with music by John Addison; *A Moon for the Misbegotten* by the late Eugene O'Neill 5/2 at New York's Bijou Theater, with Wendy Hiller, Franchot Tone, Cyril Cusack, 68 perfs.; *The Rope Dancers* by Morton Wishengrad 11/20 at New York's Cort Theater, with Siobhan McKenna, Art Carney, Theodore Bikel, 189 perfs.; *Look Homeward, Angel* 11/28 at New York's Ethel Barrymore Theater, with Jo Van Fleet, Anthony Perkins, Arthur Hill in a play based on the Thomas Wolfe novel of 1929, 564 perfs., Pulitzer prize; *The Dark at the Top of the Stairs* by William Inge 12/5 at New York's Music Box Theater, with Pat Hingle, Teresa Wright, Eileen Heckart, 468 perfs.

Films Ingmar Bergman's *Wild Strawberries;* Federico Fellini's *Nights of Cabiria;* Satyajit Ray's *Aprajito;* David Lean's *Bridge on the River Kwai* with William Holden, Alec Guinness, Jack Hawkins, Sessue Hayakawa; Akira Kurosawa's *Throne of Blood* with Toshiro Mifune; Stanley Kubrick's *Paths of Glory* with Kirk Douglas, Ralph Meeker; Elia Kazan's *A Face in the Crowd* with Andy Griffith, Patricia Neal, Lee Remick, Walter Matthau; Sidney Lumet's *12 Angry Men* with Henry Fonda; Martin Ritt's *Edge of the City* with John Cassavetes, Sidney Poitier, Jack Warden, Ruby Dee; Nunnally Johnson's *Three Faces of Eve* with Joanne Woodward, David Wayne, Lee J. Cobb; Billy Wilder's *Witness for the Prosecution* with Marlene Dietrich, Tyrone Power, Charles Laughton, Elsa Lanchester; Mikhail Kalatozov's *The Cranes Are Flying;* Billy Wilder's *Love in the Afternoon* with Gary Cooper, Audrey Hepburn, Maurice Chevalier, and songs that include "Fascination" by F. D. Marchetti and Maurice de Feraudy and "C'est Si Bon" by Henri Betti and André Hornez.

Hollywood musicals George Cukor's *Les Girls* with Gene Kelly, Mitzi Gaynor, Taina Elg; Stanley Donen's *Funny Face* with Fred Astaire, Audrey Hepburn, Kay Thompson, model Suzy Parker.

Broadway musicals *The Ziegfeld Follies* 3/1 at the Winter Garden Theater, with Beatrice Lillie, Billie de Wolfe, Jane Morgan in the 24th and final edition of the *Follies* 50 years after its first opening. Music by Sammy Fain, Jack Lawrence, Michael Myers, and others, lyrics by Howard Dietz, Carolyn Leigh, and others, 123 perfs.; *New Girl in Town* 5/14 at the 46th Street Theater, with Gwen Verdon, Thelma Ritter in a musical version of the 1921 Eugene O'Neill play *Anna Christie*, music and lyrics by Bob Merrill, songs that include "Sunshine Girl," 431 perfs.; *West Side Story* 9/26 at the Winter Garden Theater, with a book based on the Shakespeare tragedy *Romeo and Juliet* of 1595, music by Leonard Bernstein, lyrics by Stephen Sondheim, songs that include "Tonight," "Maria," 732 perfs.; *Jamaica* 10/31 at the Imperial Theater with Lena Horne, Ricardo Montalban, Ossie Davis, music by Harold Arlen, lyrics by E. Y. Harburg, 558 perfs.; *The Music Man* 12/19 at the Majestic Theater, with Robert Preston, music and lyrics by Meredith Willson, songs that include "Seventy-Six Trombones," "Gary, Indiana," "Till There Was You," 1,375 perfs.

Opera *Dialogues des Carmelites* 1/26 at Milan's Teatro alla Scala, with music by Francis Poulenc, libretto from the novel and play by the late Georges Bernanos; *Die Harmonie der Welt* 8/11 at Munich, with music by Paul Hindemith (*see* Kepler, 1619).

Ballet *The Prince and the Pagodas* 1/1 at London, with music by Benjamin Britten; *Agon* 6/17 at Los Angeles, with music by Igor Stravinsky, now 75.

First performances *Declaration* symphonic variations by Morton Gould 1/20 at Washington's Constitution Hall; Concerto for Cello by William Walton 1/25 at Boston's Symphony Hall; Jekyll and Hyde Variations by Morton Gould 2/2 at New York's Carnegie Hall; Symphony No. 2 by the late Charles Ives (who wrote it between 1897 and 1901) 2/22 at New York's Carnegie Hall; *Lydian Ode* by Paul Creston 2/24 at Wichita, Kan.; Symphony No. 6 by David Diamond 3/8 at Boston's Symphony Hall; Symphony No. 5 by Arthur Honegger 3/9 at Boston's Symphony Hall; Symphony No. 4 by Walter Piston 3/30 at Minneapolis; Symphony No. 10 by Heitor Villa-Lobos 4/4 at Paris; *Song of Democracy* by Howard Hanson 4/9 at Washington, D.C.; Concerto No. 2 for Piano and Orchestra by Dmitri Shostakovich 5/10 at Moscow, with Maxim Shostakovich as soloist; *Monopartita* by Arthur Honegger 6/12 at Zurich; *Stabat Mater* by Francis Poulenc 6/13 at Strasbourg; Polyphonie X for 17 Solo Instruments by French composer Pierre Boulez, 26, 10/6 at the Donaueschippu Festival of Contemporary Music; Toccata for Orchestra by Paul Creston 10/18 at Cleveland's Severance Hall; *Apocalypse* (Symphonic Poem) by Gian Carlo Menotti 10/19 at Pittsburgh; Symphony No. 11 (*1905*) by Dmitri Shostakovich 10/30 at Moscow; *Erosion, or The Origin of the Amazon River* (Symphonic Poem) by Heitor Villa-Lobos 11/7 at Louisville; Symphony No. 3 by Roger Sessions 12/26 at Boston's Symphony Hall.

Popular songs "All the Way" by James Van Heusen, lyrics by Sammy Cahn (for Charles Vidor's film *The Joker Is Wild* with Frank Sinatra); "April Love" by Sammy Fain, lyrics by Paul Francis Webster (title song for Henry Levin's film); "Bye Bye, Love" by Felice and Boudleaux Bryant; "Young Love" by Carole Joyner and Ric Cartey; "Tammy" by Jay Livingston and Ray Evans (for Joseph Pevney's film *Tammy and the Bachelor*); "School Day" by Chuck Berry; "A White Sport Coat—and a Pink Carnation" by Marty Robbins; "Jailhouse Rock" by Jerry Leiber and Mike Stoller; "Old Cape Cod" by Claire Rothrock, Milt Yakers, and Allan Jeffrey.

Motown Corporation is founded by entrepreneur Berry Gordy, Jr., 30, who invests $700 to start a recording company whose "Motown Sound" will figure large in popular music for more than 2 decades.

Middleweight boxing champion Sugar Ray Robinson, now 36, loses the title January 2 to Gene Fullmer, regains it from Fullmer May 2, and loses it again September 23 to Carmen Basilio.

U.S. tennis pro Althea Gibson, 29, wins the women's singles and doubles titles at Wimbledon, returns to a ticker-tape parade in New York, and wins the U.S. women's singles championship at Forest Hills. Gibson was the first black to enter the national grass-court championship tournament at Forest Hills in 1950 and the following year became the first black American to be invited to play at Wimbledon.

The Milwaukee Braves win the World Series by defeating the New York Yankees 4 games to 3.

The Frisbee is introduced by the Wham-O Manufacturing Co. of San Gabriel, Calif., whose public relations man has found Yale students tossing metal pie tins produced since Civil War days by the Frisbie Pie Company of Bridgeport, Conn. The plastic Frisbee launches a new sport whose first world champion will be crowned in 1968.

New York mobster Frank Costello is grazed in the head by a .32 caliber bullet May 2 in the lobby of the Majestic apartment house where he lives. His would-be assassin Vincent (the Chin) Gigante escapes, Costello rushes to the emergency room of Roosevelt Hospital, he is not badly hurt, but police search his pockets and find a slip showing more than $1 million in winnings from his gambling casinos.

Mafia lieutenant Frank (Don Cheech) Scalice is shot four times in the head June 17 while shopping for peaches at a Bronx fruit stand. Scalice is a henchman of Murder, Inc., boss Albert Anastasia.

Albert Anastasia is killed October 25 in the barbershop of New York's Park-Sheraton Hotel by two gunmen reputedly in the pay of Vito Genovese.

Apalachin, N.Y., makes headlines when police find 58 Mafia members from all over the United States gathered November 14 at the home of Joseph Barbara. Included are Vito Genovese, Joseph Bonanno, Carlo Gambino, Joseph Profaci, Jerry Catena, and Mike Miranda.

George "Bugs" Moran dies of lung cancer while serving a 10-year prison term for bank robbery.

P. Lorillard changes the filter design on its 5-year-old Kent cigarette to improve flagging sales. The new Kent micronite filter draws more easily, but the tar content of the smoke is nearly doubled and the nicotine content more than doubled.

Newport mentholated filter cigarettes are introduced by P. Lorillard.

New York's Henri Bendel is acquired by Maxey Jarman's General Shoe Corporation (*see* 1912; 1956) (General Shoe will become Genesco in 1959).

Southdale at Minneapolis is completed by Victor Gruen of 1954 Northland fame whose firm will develop auto-free environmental plans for Rochester and other U.S. cities. Southdale is a covered, heated, air-conditioned shopping center with 75 shops.

New York's Tishman building goes up at 666 Fifth Avenue between 52nd and 53rd Streets. The new 38-story office tower has a million square feet of floor space, it is one of 16 new office buildings with 5.5 million square feet of floor space that are completed in the city this year, but it will be ridiculed as the crate that the Seagram building came in (*see* 1958).

Philadelphia's Sheraton Hotel opens with 865 rooms.

Florida's Americana Hotel is completed at Bal Harbour just north of Miami Beach by Morris Lapidus who has been engaged by hotelmen Laurence Tisch, 33, and his brother Preston Robert Tisch, 30. Starting in 1946 with $124,000 in capital, the Tisch brothers have operated the 575-room Traymore and the 700-room Ambassador at Atlantic City and New York's 800-room Belmont Plaza, they have spent $17 million to build the Americana, and they will create an empire of hotels and movie theaters (*see* Loew's 1959).

Los Angeles adopts a revised building code that permits construction of high-rise buildings. The code reflects earthquake-stress engineering technology.

China's Great Leap Forward (above) virtually eliminates houseflies, mosquitoes, rats, and bedbugs over wide areas in a prodigious outburst of human energy.

The world's longest river dam is completed on India's Mahanadi River. The 83,523-foot Hirakud Dam stretches for nearly 16 miles.

Chinese cereal grain production rises to 200 million tons after having increased in the past 7 years at an annual rate of 8 percent while the rest of the world has never exceeded a rate of 3 percent.

Huge irrigation projects add 100 million acres of irrigated cropland to China's agricultural resource and give the nation 60 times as much irrigated cropland as Europe. The Chinese work to bring under control the Yellow River that has for centuries overrun its banks 2 years out of 3 to create floods that have produced havoc, famine, and desolation.

1957 (cont.) Diets high in saturated fats are related to atherosclerotic heart disease, says University of Minnesota nutritionist Ancel Keys in a paper published in the *Journal of the American Medical Association* (see 1953; Anichkov, 1913; Kannel, 1949). Keys shows that male Japanese have low rates of heart disease but that rates rise when they adopt Western diets.

Ancel Keys (above) is challenged by British nutrition researcher John Yudkin at London's Queen Elizabeth Hospital who suggests that the rising rate of heart disease may be explained quite as reasonably (if not more so) by the fact that Western people ingest far more sugar than in earlier times (see 1964).

Nitrite poisoning creates a scandal in Germany where butchers are found to be using sodium nitrite to make meat look fresh and red, exposing consumers to the hazards of methemoglobinemia. An excess of nitrite can turn blood hemoglobin into methemoglobin which cannot provide oxygen to the cells, and gross excesses can be hazardous, especially to children whose total blood volume is relatively low and whose stomachs are much less acid than those of adults. Lack of acidity makes it easier for intestinal bacteria to turn nitrates into nitrites. Methemoglobinemia can produce dizziness, fatigue, nausea, even death.

U.S. per capita consumption of margarine overtakes butter consumption for the first time. The average American uses 8.6 pounds of margarine per year versus 8.3 pounds of butter (see 1960).

Miracle Pack Prepared Foods are introduced by Seabrook Farms, Inc. (see 1944). Entrees such as beef goulash and chicken cacciatore are quick frozen in individual portions and sealed in transparent polyester-polyethylene bags that are ready to be dropped into boiling water. In 14 minutes the food is cooked, the bag is snipped open at one end, and the contents are emptied onto a plate. Frozen vegetables for "waterless cooking" will be added to the line next year.

Minute Maid Corporation's Snow Crop frozen vegetable and fruit business (but not its citrus concentrates) is acquired by Seabrook Farms (above) (see 1954).

Corn Products Refining Company diversifies by acquiring C. H. Knorr, Europe's largest producer of dehydrated soups (see 1955; Best Foods, 1958).

Soy protein technology is advanced by a new process that mixes high-protein soy flour with an alkaline liquid to create a spinning solution which is fed under pressure into spinning machines (see 1949). Engineers at Worthington Foods, General Mills, and Ralston Purina will develop improvements on this spinning technique, and engineers at Swift and Archer-Daniels-Midland will adapt extrusion methods from the plastics industry to develop new meat analogs from soy protein isolate (see Bac*Os, 1966).

New York's Forum of the Twelve Caesars Restaurant opens on West 48th Street with toga-clad waiters serving pheasant baked in clay and chilling wine in buckets made of upended centurion helmets. Restaurant Associates, Inc., president Joseph Baum, 38, has acquired 12 huge 18th century portraits of Roman emperors from designer William Pahlman to grace the walls of the new restaurant.

The Gino's hamburger-chicken fast food stand empire that will expand in the next 17 years to have 340 franchises in the mid-Atlantic states is started by Baltimore Colts defensive end Gino Marchetti.

The United States has a record number of births: 4.3 million babies are born.

An intensive trial of birth-control pills to prevent unwanted births is undertaken in Puerto Rico by Gregory Pincus and Boston gynecologist John Rock, 67 (see 1955; Enovid 10, 1960).

71 world cities have populations of more than 1 million, up from 10 in 1914.

1958 Nikita Krushchev replaces Nikolai Bulganin as chairman of the Soviet Council of Ministers March 27, he visits Peking in August, and Bulganin is dismissed from the Communist Party Presidium September 6.

A United Arab Republic has been proclaimed February 1 in a union of Egypt and the Sudan with Syria under the leadership of Egypt's President Nasser.

The Arab Federation created February 14 joins Iraq and Jordan under Iraq's Faisal II, but a coup engineered by General Abdul Karim al-Kassem assassinates Faisal July 14 along with his infant son and his premier, General Abdul Karim proclaims a republic, Jordan's Hussein succeeds Faisal as head of state, but he dissolves the Arab Federation August 1.

Lebanon is torn by riots allegedly provoked by the United Arab Republic (above), UN observers move in to guard against illegal movement of troops or arms into the country, U.S. troops from the 6th Fleet land near Beirut beginning July 15 as President Eisenhower vows to protect U.S. lives and property and to defend Lebanese sovereignty and independence, a new government comes to power in Lebanon, and U.S. troops are withdrawn October 25.

France names General de Gaulle premier May 31 after an Algerian crisis has threatened civil war. Agents of the Algerian rebels commit acts of violence within France as the open revolt that began in 1954 continues under the direction of French military leaders who have seized control of Algeria.

Paris withdraws French troops from all of Tunisia except for Bizerte June 17 after months of conflict in which French planes have bombed the Tunisian village of Sakiet-Sidi-Youssef killing 79. Tunisia joins the Arab League October 1.

France approves a Fifth Republic by a vote of more than four to one in a popular referendum September 28, the Gaullist Union gains control of the French assembly in the November elections, General de Gaulle is named president of the republic for a 7-year term to begin January 8 of next year, and France gives her overseas possessions 6 months to decide whether to become departments of the republic or to become autonomous members of a French Community (see 1959).

Guinea is proclaimed an independent republic October 2 with Sekou Toure as president following a popular referendum in which the people have rejected membership in the French Community (above), the only French colony in Africa to take such action.

The Malagasy Republic (Madagascar) becomes an autonomous state within the French Community (above) October 14, and her action is followed November 25 by Senegal, November 28 by Gabon, the new Republic of the Congo (Middle Congo), Mauritania, and Mali (French Sudan), December 1 by the New Central African Republic (Ubangi Shari), and December 4 by Dahomey and Ivory Coast.

The Federation of the West Indies has come into being January 3 with 3 million people scattered over 77,000 square miles that embrace the British colonies Antigua, Barbados, Dominica, Grenada, Jamaica, Montserrat, St. Kitts-Nevis-Anguilla, St. Lucia, St. Vincent, Tobago, and Trinidad.

A symbol for total nuclear disarmament that will become a universal peace symbol is introduced in an Easter march at Aldermaston, England, by English philosopher Bertrand Russell, now 86, but a plan for a denuclearized zone in Central Europe is rejected by the United States in April and by Britain in May.

Mutual inspection to enforce an atomic test ban is proposed by President Eisenhower April 8.

The North American Air Defense Command is established by Canada and the United States May 12.

Hungary's ex-premier Imre Nagy is executed by the Communist regime after a secret trial in mid-June (see 1956).

An Anglo-U.S. agreement to cooperate in the development of nuclear weapons is signed July 3.

The Soviet Union resumes nuclear testing September 30 after having suspended such tests in June, but a voluntary moratorium on nuclear weapons testing goes into effect November 4 with Britain, the U.S.S.R., and the United States agreeing to the moratorium (see France, 1960).

The John Birch Society is founded by U.S. right-wing candy manufacturer Robert Welch, 58, at Belmont, Mass. The name of the new political group is inspired by that of a U.S. Army officer who was killed in China by Communists 10 days after the end of World War II while working as an intelligence operative for the Office of Strategic Services (OSS).

President Eisenhower is called a conscious agent of the international Communist conspiracy by Robert Welch (above) whose John Birch Society will grow to have more than 60,000 members, will publish the

monthly magazine *American Opinion,* and will support more than 400 American Opinion bookstores.

Moroccan women gain the right to choose their own husbands. Rabat restricts polygamy.

Britain's First Offenders Act prohibits magistrates from imprisoning any adult first offender if there is a more appropriate way of dealing with the offense.

The U.S. Civil Rights Commission swears in six members January 3 and begins operations.

An employee of the Bethel Baptist Church at Birmingham, Ala., finds a dynamite bomb beside the church June 29 and moves it to an open area where it explodes without injuring anyone. The church's pastor Fred L. Shuttlesworth is a civil rights leader and authorities will arrest a Ku Klux Klan leader, now 34, in 1977 on charges of trying to blow up the black church.

The Supreme Court meets in a special term and rules unanimously September 29 that schools at Little Rock, Ark., must integrate according to schedule (see 1957). The Court's decision in *Cooper v. Aaron* implements its ruling in the 1954 case of *Brown v. Board of Education.*

"The torrent of foreign oil robs Texas of her oil market" and costs the state $1 million per day, says the chairman of the Texas Railroad Commission which controls production in the state. The Commission reduces Texas oil wells to 8 producing days per month (see 1959).

Indonesia's President Sukarno bans operations of the Royal Dutch-Shell Group in his country.

The first U.S. atomic power station for peaceful purposes is dedicated May 26.

The European Atomic Energy Community (Euratom) consisting of Belgium, France, Italy, Luxembourg, the Netherlands, and West Germany receives a U.S. pledge November 8 to supply uranium for 20 years and to loan Euratom $135 million.

The M-14 .30-caliber rifle is adopted by the U.S. military. It is a fully automatic version of the M-1 Garand rifle used in World War II and in Korea.

The cost of 100,000 computerized multiplication computations falls to 26 cents, down from $1.26 in 1952, says IBM (see 1964).

Transatlantic jet service is inaugurated by Pan American World Airways and British Overseas Airways (BOAC) (see London-Johannesburg, 1952).

The Boeing 707 goes into service to challenge the British-built Comet for leadership in the aircraft industry. The first U.S.-built commercial jet, the 707 beats out Douglas Aircraft which will not have its DC-8 in service until next year and beats out Consolidated-Vultee whose Convair 880 will not start flying until 1960. Lockheed has stuck with its Electra turboprop propeller jet and loses out in the race as pure jets begin to make other planes obsolete (see McDonnell-Douglas, 1967).

1958 (cont.) A new transatlantic speed record is set by U.S. Air Force jets flying from New York to London in 5 hours, 28 minutes. Prevailing easterly winds will make the eastward flight time shorter than the westward for commercial jetliners whose regular flights will average less than 1 hour longer than the Air Force record.

A U.S. Navy X15 rocket plane flies at speeds reaching 3,900 miles per hour—nearly six times the speed of sound—and at peak altitudes of 300,000 feet. Navy test pilot John B. McKay, 35, is at the controls.

The first U.S. Earth satellite is launched.

The first domestic U.S. 707 flight takes off December 10. National Airlines has rented two of the big Boeing jets from Pan Am for the winter season in a bid to take business away from Eastern Airlines.

The first voyage under the North Pole is completed by the 4-year-old U.S. atomic submarine *Nautilus*.

London busdrivers strike from May 5 to June 21.

London gets its first parking meters.

The Chevrolet Impala is introduced.

Syanon is founded in a rented storefront at Ocean Park, Calif., by former alcoholic Charles "Chuck" Dederich, 44, who starts weekly discussion groups with friends from Alcoholics Anonymous in an effort to rehabilitate alcoholics and drug addicts (*see* AA, 1935). Dederich and his colleagues evolve a new form of therapy that will revolutionize rehabilitation programs and will lead to the establishment of Syanon communities in several parts of the United States, in Puerto Rico, and in England as drug abuse increases (*see* Phoenix House, 1967).

Acupuncture is used for the first time as an anaesthetic after nearly 5,000 years of use in medical therapy in China (*see* Shen Nung, 2700 B.C.).

U.S. unemployment reaches a postwar high of more than 5.1 million, and the Department of Labor reports that a record 3.1 million Americans are receiving unemployment insurance benefits. Economic recession grips the nation with nearly one-third of major industrial centers classified as having "substantial" unemployment.

The upper 1 percent of Americans enjoys nearly 9 percent of the nation's total disposable income, down from 19 percent of disposable income in 1929. 64 percent of households have incomes above $4,000 per year, up from 40 percent in 1929, but white families average twice as much as nonwhite families.

The median U.S. family income is $5,087, up from $3,187 in 1948 (half of all families have incomes below the median, half above), but prices have climbed along with incomes.

A house that cost $47,409 in 1948 sells for $59,558, a family size Chevrolet that sold for $1,255 sells for $2,081, a gallon of gasoline has climbed from 25.9 cents to 30.4 cents, a pair of blue jeans that sold for $3.45 sells for $3.75, a pair of men's shoes that sold for $9.95 sells for $11.95, a daily newspaper that cost 3 cents now costs 5 cents, a year's tuition at Harvard that cost $455 costs $1,250, a hospital room that cost $13.09 per day costs $28.17, a pound of round steak that costs 90.5 cents costs $1.04, a Nathan's hot dog that cost 20 cents costs 25 cents, a ticket to a Broadway musical that cost $6.00 costs $8.05.

Some prices have come down: a ranch mink coat that cost $4,200 in 1948 costs $4,000, a roundtrip flight to London from New York that cost $630 costs $453.60, a phone call from New York to Topeka, Kan., that cost $1.90 costs $1.80 (day rate), a pound of chicken that cost 61.2 cents has come down to 46.5 cents.

The Affluent Society by Harvard economics professor John Kenneth Galbraith, 49, decries the overemphasis on consumer goods in the U.S. economy and the use of advertising to create artificial demand for such goods. More of the nation's wealth should be allocated to public purposes, says Galbraith.

BankAmericard is introduced by California's Bank of America whose new credit card costs the consumer nothing and relieves subscribing merchants of credit worries in return for a small percentage of each retail sale charged to the card. Card users are charged 18 percent interest on unpaid balances and 12 percent interest on cash advances obtained by presenting the card at teller windows (*see* 1966).

The American Express Credit Card is introduced by the American Express Company which charges an annual fee to subscribers who use the card to charge air fares, auto rentals, hotel and motel rooms, restaurant meals, and other expenses. American Express sets out to overtake Diners Club which started the travel and entertainment card business in 1950 (*see* travelers cheques, 1891).

General Telephone and Electronics Corporation is created by a merger of General Telephone Corporation and the 57-year-old Sylvania Electric Company which has grown to become a major electronics producer (*see* General Telephone, 1955).

TRW (Thompson-Ramo-Wooldridge) is created by a merger of Cleveland's Thompson Products Company whose annual sales are $275 million with Ramo-Wooldridge whose sales are $65 million (*see* 1953).

SCM, Inc., (Smith-Corona Marchant) is created by a reorganization of Cleveland's typewriter firm Smith-Corona, Inc., which acquires Marchant Calculators, Inc., and changes its corporate name (*see* 1905).

A U.S. National Defense Education Act authorizes federal spending of $480 million over 4 years for "strengthening science, mathematics, and foreign language instruction." Title III of the act gives a boost to sales of textbooks and tape recorders.

U.S. first class postal rates climb to 4 cents per ounce, up from the 3-cent level that has prevailed since July 1932 (*see* 1963).

U.S. television sets number an estimated 41 million, up from 5 to 8 million in 1950.

U.S. daily newspapers number 357, down from 2,600 in 1909, as more Americans rely on radio and television for the news.

UPI (United Press International) is created by a merger of the 51-year-old United Press with the 52-year-old Hearst International News Service.

Nonfiction *Parkinson's Law* by Englishman Cyril Northcote Parkinson, 49, satirizes the growth of bureaucracy: "Work expands so as to fill the time available for its completion"; "Expenditure rises to meet income"; "Expansion means complexity, and complexity, decay. Or: the more complex, the sooner dead"; *Only in America* by North Carolina newspaper editor Harry Golden, 56.

Fiction *The Ugly American* by U.S. novelists Eugene Burdick and William J. Lederer who are attacked by the State Department for their revelations of arrogance, insensitivity, and stupidity on the part of U.S. diplomats in the developing countries; *Things Fall Apart* by Nigerian novelist Chinna Achebe, 28; *The City and the Dogs* (*La ciudad y los perros*) by Peruvian novelist Mario Vargas Llosa, 22; *Memed, My Hawk* (*Ince Memed*) by Turkish novelist Yasar Kemal, 36; *The Leopard* (*Il gatto pardo*) by the late Sicilian novelist Prince Giuseppe Tomasi di Lampedusa who died last year at age 61; *Leech* (*Kjop ikke Dondi*) by Cora Sandel; *The Grass* (*L'Herbe*) by Claude Simon; *The Middle Age of Mrs. Eliot* by Angus Wilson; *Spinster* by New Zealand novelist Sylvia Ashton-Warner, 53, whose first novel is a story of a hard-drinking but inspired teacher and is based on personal experience; *Saturday Night and Sunday Morning* by English novelist Alan Sillitoe, 30, who draws on his experiences as a Nottingham factory worker; *The Ordeal of Gilbert Pinfold* by Evelyn Waugh; *The Dharma Bums* by Jack Kerouac; *Some Came Running* by James Jones; *Breakfast at Tiffany's* (stories) by Truman Capote; *Exodus* by Leon Uris; *Dr. No.* by Ian Fleming.

Poetry *Selected Poems 1928–1958* by U.S. poet Stanley Kunitz, 53; *Words for the Wind* by Theodore Roethke.

"Pop Art" is pioneered by Robert Rauschenberg who creates a semiabstraction with a hole into which he inserts four Coca-Cola bottles.

Other painting *Three Flags* by Jasper Johns; *Four Darks on Red* by Mark Rothko; *Blue on a Point* by Sam Francis; *Peace* by Pablo Picasso whose hand extending a bouquet will be widely reproduced; Georges Rouault dies at Paris February 13 at age 86; Maurice de Vlaminck dies at Rueil-la-Gadeliére outside Paris October 11 at age 82.

Theater *The Garden District* (*Suddenly Last Summer* and *Something Unspoken*) by Tennessee Williams 1/7 at New York's York Theater, with Anne Meacham; *Two for the Seesaw* by U.S. playwright

William Gibson, 42, 1/16 at New York's Booth Theater, with Henry Fonda, Anne Bancroft as Gittel Mosca, 750 perfs.; *Sunrise at Campobello* by U.S. playwright (and former M-G-M production chief) Dore Schary, 52, 1/30 at New York's Cort Theater, with Ralph Bellamy as Franklin D. Roosevelt, Mary Fickett as Eleanor, 556 perfs.; *Epitaph for George Dillon* by John Osborne and Anthony Creighton 2/11 at London's Royal Court Theatre; *Biedermann and the Firebugs* (*Biedermann und die Brandstifter*) by Max Frisch 3/29 at Zurich's Schauspielhaus; *The Killer* (*Tueur sans gages*) by Eugène Ionesco 4/4 at Darmstadt's Landestheater; *The Birthday Party* by English playwright Harold Pinter, 27, 4/28 at the Arts Theatre, Cambridge, England; *Variations on a Theme* by Terence Rattigan 5/8 at London's Globe Theatre; *Five Finger Exercise* by English playwright Peter Shaffer, 32, 7/17 at London's Comedy Theatre; *A Touch of the Poet* by the late Eugene O'Neill 10/2 at New York's Helen Hayes Theater with Tom Clancy, Eric Portman, Kim Stanley, Betty Field, 284 perfs.; *The Hostage* by Brendan Behan 10/14 at London's Theatre Royal, Stratford; *The World of Suzie Wong* by Paul Osborne 10/14 at New York's Broadhurst Theater, with France Nuyen, William Shattner, 508 perfs.; *The Pleasure of His Company* by Cornelia Otis Skinner and Samuel Taylor 10/22 at New York's Longacre Theater, with Skinner, Cyril Ritchard, 474 perfs.; *The Resistible Rise of Arturo Ui* (*Der aufhaltsame Aufstieg des Arturo Ui*) by Bertolt Brecht 11/10 at Stuttgart; *The Disenchanted* by Budd Schulberg and Harvey Breit (based on Schulberg's novel) 12/3 at New York's Coronet Theater, with Jason Robards, Jr. (and Sr.), Rosemary Harris, Salome Jens, George Grizzard, 189 perfs.; *The Cold Wind and the Warm* by S. N. Behrman 12/8 at New York's Morosco Theater, with Eli Wal-

Peace symbols mushroomed amidst rattling of atomic swords and anxieties about a war that could destroy mankind.

1958 (cont.) lach, Maureen Stapleton, Vincent Gardenia, Morris Carnovsky, Suzanne Pleshette, 120 perfs.; *JB* by Archibald MacLeish 12/11 at New York's ANTA Theater, with Raymond Massey, Christopher Plummer, Pat Hingle, 364 perfs., Pulitzer prize.

Films   Jack Clayton's *A Room at the Top* with Laurence Harvey, Simone Signoret; Roy Baker's *A Night to Remember* with Kenneth More; John Ford's *The Horse Soldiers* with John Wayne, William Holden; Ingmar Bergman's *The Magician* with Max von Sydow; Delbert Mann's *Separate Tables* with Rita Hayworth, Deborah Kerr, David Niven, Wendy Hiller, Burt Lancaster; Edward Dmytryk's *The Young Lions* with Marlon Brando, Montgomery Clift, Dean Martin, Hope Lange; Alfred Hitchcock's *Vertigo* with James Stewart, Kim Novak, Barbara Bel Geddes; Stanley Kramer's *The Defiant Ones* with Tony Curtis, Sidney Poitier; Richard Brooks's *Cat on a Hot Tin Roof* with Elizabeth Taylor, Paul Newman, Burl Ives; Jacques Tati's *Mon Oncle;* Satyajit Ray's *The Music Room;* Akira Kurosawa's *The Hidden Fortress* with Toshiro Mifune; Ándrzej Wajda's *Ashes and Diamonds* with Zbigniew Cybulski.

Hollywood musical   Vincente Minnelli's *Gigi* with Leslie Caron, Maurice Chevalier, Louis Jourdan, music by Frederick Loewe, lyrics by Alan Jay Lerner, songs that include "Thank Heaven for Little Girls," "The Night They Invented Champagne," and the title song.

Stage musicals   *Irma la Douce* 7/17 at London's Lyric Theatre with Elizabeth Seal, Keith Mitchell, Clive Revill, music by French composer Marguerite Monmot, book and lyrics by Alexandre Breffet, Julian More, Monty Norman, David Heath, 1,512 perfs.; *Flower Drum Song* 12/1 at New York's St. James Theater, with Pat Suzuki, Juanita Hall, Myosuki Umeki, Larry Blyden, music and lyrics by Richard Rodgers and Oscar Hammerstein II, 601 perfs.

The Spoleto Festival founded by Italian composer Gian Carlo Menotti has its first season 90 miles northeast of Rome.

Opera   *Vanessa* 1/15 at New York's Metropolitan Opera with music by Samuel Barber, libretto by Gian Carlo Menotti; *Noye's Fludde (Noah's Flood)* 6/18 at Orford Church, Suffolk, with music by Benjamin Britten, libretto from the 14th century *Chester Miracle Play.*

First performances   Concerto No. 2 for Piano and Orchestra by Dmitri Shostakovich 5/10 at Moscow; *Nocturne* song cycle for tenor and small orchestra by Benjamin Britten 10/16 at Leeds.

Popular songs   "Diana" by Canadian rock singer-composer Paul Anka, 15, who begins a meteoric rise to stardom. Anka will have three hit records within a year and will have made his first $1 million by age 17; "Satin Doll" by Duke Ellington, Billy Strayhorn, and Johnny Mercer; "Volare" ("Nel Blue, Dipinto di Blu") by Italian composer Dominico Modugno, English lyrics by Mitchell Parish; "Everybody Loves a Lover" by U.S. composer Robert Allen, lyrics by Richard Adler; "Sugartime" by Charlie Phillips and Odis Echols; "Twilight Time" by Morty Lewis, lyrics by Buck Ram; "Catch a Falling Star" by Paul Vance and Lee Pockriss; "The Chipmunk Song (Christmas Don't Be Late)" by Ross Bagdasarian.

The first Grammy Award given by the National Academy of Recording Arts and Sciences goes to the Italian song "Volare" (above), but the Burbank, Calif., organization comes under fire from much of the recording industry for favoring older, more conservative, white, middle-of-the-road artists over youth-oriented performers.

Sugar Ray Robinson wins the middleweight boxing title for a record fifth time March 25 at Chicago Stadium in a 15-round decision over Carmen Basilio.

Ashley Cooper wins the U.S. Lawn Tennis Association's men's singles championship, Althea Gibson wins the women's singles.

Arnold Palmer wins the Masters title at Augusta, Ga., plus two other golf championships and earns an impressive $42,000. Now 28, Palmer won the U.S. amateur title 4 years ago, he turned professional soon after, and he will be the most popular golfer since Bobby Jones.

The U.S. ocean yacht *Columbia* designed by Olin J. Stephens, 50, defends the America's Cup successfully against the English challenger *Sceptre* in the first America's Cup competition since 1937. The 12-metre yachts are much smaller than the pre-war "J"-class boats that nobody can now afford to build.

The New York Giants become the San Francisco Giants and play their first season at Candlewick Park.

The Brooklyn Dodgers become the Los Angeles Dodgers and play their first season at Chavez Ravine.

The New York Yankees win the World Series by defeating the Milwaukee Braves 4 games to 3.

Brazil wins her first World Cup in football (soccer), defeating Sweden 5 to 2. Pele scores two of the Brazilian goals (*see* 1956).

U.S. intercollegiate football rules change to give teams the option of trying for a two-point conversion after touchdown by running the ball or passing it from the 3-yard line. A kick between the goal posts from the 2 yard line is still worth only one point.

Baltimore Colts quarterback John Unitas, 25, leads his team to the National Football League championship, defeating the New York Giants to begin an outstanding career with the Colts that will continue through the 1960s. Professional football starts to become a national obsession as 189 CBS affiliate TV stations carry the NFL championship game (*see* Super Bowl, 1967).

Nebraska police and National Guardsmen mount roadblocks in late January and organize posses to hunt down a "mad dog" killer who has shot Marion Bartlett of Lincoln and his wife Velda through the head, clubbed their younger daughter to death and run off with Caril Fugate, Mrs. Bartlett's 14-year-old daughter by a previous marriage. Charles Starkweather, 19, has just lost his job as helper on a garbage truck, he proceeds to kill seven more people in the next 3 days before Wyoming police catch him January 30, and he will die in the electric chair June 25 of next year.

 Arvida Corporation is created to take over 100,650 acres of Florida land owned by former Aluminum Corporation of America chairman Arthur Vining Davis, 91. Arvida will be second in Florida real estate only to General Development Corporation.

The Havana Hilton opens March 27. The $21 million hotel will be the Havana Libre beginning next year.

Brasilia's Presidential Palace is completed by Oskar Niemeyer.

Milan's Pirelli building is completed by Pier Luigi Nervi and G. Ponti.

Rome's Palazzetto dello Sport is completed by Pier Luigi Nervi.

New York's Seagram building goes up on Park Avenue between 52nd and 53rd Streets where the Montana Apartments have been razed to make way for the new bronze-sheathed curtain-wall office tower designed by Ludwig Mies van der Rohe and Philip Johnson with an assist by Kahn & Jacobs (see 1959).

New York's Polo Grounds and Brooklyn's Ebbets Field become available for new housing sites as the baseball teams move to California (above).

 U.S. scientists begin testing Earth's radiation shield of ozone to discover what effects if any have been caused by atmospheric testing of nuclear weapons and by the growing number of high-altitude flights by military and commercial jet aircraft. Ozone is an unstable form of oxygen containing three atoms instead of the usual two and serves as a barrier at altitudes of from 50,000 to 135,000 feet against undue exposure to the sun's ultraviolet rays which can cause human skin cancer. The ozone layers will be found to increase in the next 13 years, but will then begin to shrink, possibly as a result of being broken up by chlorine gas which is released from freon gas by ultraviolet rays in the atmosphere at altitudes of 12 to 15 miles (see freon 12 refrigerant, 1931; Abplanalp's plastic aerosol valve, 1953). Nearly a million tons of freon will be released into the atmosphere each year by the 1970s, mostly from aerosol cans, and environmentalists will suggest the possibility that the Earth's ozone layer is being depleted.

U.S. Atomic Energy Commission physicist Willard Libby says the United States is the "hottest place in the world" in terms of radioactivity largely as a result of fallout from recent Soviet and British nuclear tests in the atmosphere (see Libby, 1947).

 Iceland extends her fishery limits to 12 miles offshore. The move will produce conflicts with British fishing vessels (see 1966).

Whalers kill 6,908 blue whales, the largest creatures ever to inhabit the Earth. When hunting of blue whales ceases in 1965, only one blue whale will be found and it will be estimated that fewer than 1,000 remain in the seas.

 China's wheat crop reaches 40 million tons, 2 million more than the U.S. crop, and cereal grain production jumps 35 percent above last year's levels despite a poor rice crop, but total food production falls far short of estimates. The dearth of food encourages peasants to neglect the grain crops of the collectives and to raise vegetables and livestock which they can sell privately, if illegally (in some communes half the land is privately cultivated) (see 1957; 1959).

The United Fruit Company agrees to establish a competitor in the banana industry. The February 4 agreement settles a 4-year antitrust suit brought by the U.S. government (see 1944; AMK, 1968).

 Enrichment of U.S. rice is made mandatory by law, but the new law does not apply to short-grain rice in the northern states where that rice is a dietary staple among some ethnic groups.

Folk Medicine by Vermont physician D. C. (DeForest Clinton) Jarvis, 77, extolls the alleged virtues of cider vinegar and honey. The food fad book is published by Henry Holt and Company at the insistence of Texas oilman Clinton Williams Murchison, 63, who is a major Holt stockholder and who has become a disciple of the Jarvis notions, the first printing is 5,000 copies, and by the end of next year more than 200,000 copies will have been sold.

 A food additives amendment to the Food, Drug and Cosmetic Act of 1938 passed by Congress permits no food additives other than those used widely for many years and "generally recognized as safe" (GRAS list) unless the FDA agrees after a thorough review of test data that the new additive is safe at the intended level of use.

A "cancer clause" is inserted in the new amendment (above) by Brooklyn, N.Y., congressman James J. Delaney (see Gloria Swanson, 1956). The Delaney clause states that if *any* amount of any additive can be shown to produce cancer when ingested by humans or test animals, *no* amount of that additive may be used in foods for human consumption (see cyclamates, 1969).

Sweet 'n Low sugarless sweetener is introduced by the Cumberland Packing Company of Brooklyn, N.Y., which uses saccharin in place of sugar.

Cocoa Puffs breakfast food, introduced by General Mills, is 43 percent sugar (see 1954; 1959).

1958 (cont.) Cocoa Krispies breakfast food is introduced by the Kellogg Company. The new cereal is 45.9 percent sugar (*see* 1955; 1959).

Best Foods, Inc., is acquired by Corn Products Refining Company along with its Skippy Peanut Butter, Hellmann's Mayonnaise, and other brands as Corn Products continues to expand and diversify (*see* Skippy, 1932; Hellmann's, 1912, 1932; Knorr, 1957; CPC International, 1959).

Green Giant canned beans are introduced (*see* 1950; 1961).

Pizza Hut opens at Kansas City to begin a franchise chain that will grow into the largest group of U.S. pizzerias. Within 16 years Pizza Hut will have gross sales of $114 million, followed closely by Shakey's with annual sales of $100 million (see 1953).

Le Drugstore, created by Publicis director Marcel Blaustein-Blanchet, opens near the Arc de Triomphe at Paris serving American-style hamburgers, sandwiches, and elaborate desserts topped with whipped cream from aerosol cans (*see* Redi-Wip, 1947). Dripping with chrome and plastic, Le Drugstore will inspire dozens of imitations in Paris and scores of imitations in France's provincial cities.

A&P stockholders agree December 12 to make voting shares in the food store chain available to the public after 99 years of private ownership.

The James Beard Cookbook is published (*see* 1949).

China's birth control program of 1954 ends as China begins a Great Leap Forward (above) (*see* 1960).

Birth control is deplored by English Roman Catholic economist Colin Clark who writes in the magazine *Nature*, "When we look at the British in the seventeenth and eighteenth centuries, at the Greeks in the sixth century B.C., the Dutch in the seventeenth century, and the Japanese in the nineteenth century, we must conclude that the pressure of population upon limited agricultural resources provides a painful but ultimately beneficial stimulus, provoking unenterprising agrarian communities into greater efforts in the fields of industry, commerce, political leadership, colonization, science, and [sometimes . . .] the arts."

Abortion in the United States by Great Neck, Long Island, physician's wife Mary Steichen Calderone reports on conferences of the Planned Parenthood Federation but is almost totally ignored (*see* 1955; Colorado, 1967).

1959 Cuban dictator Fulgencio Battista resigns January 1 after nearly 7 years in power and flees to Dominica and thence to Miami as rebel leader Fidel Castro, 32, captures Santiago 1 day after taking the provincial capital of Santa Clara. Castro's forces take Havana January 3 and Castro assumes office as premier February 16 after a 2-year rebellion, he arrives at Washington on an unofficial visit April 15, and 2 days later he calls his revolution "humanistic," not Communist.

Alaska and Hawaii are admitted to the Union as the 49th and 50th states.

Moscow urges Japan to end her agreement permitting U.S. bases on Japanese soil. The May 4 note from the Kremlin invites Tokyo to accept a Soviet guarantee of permanent neutrality.

Tibet's Dalai Lama escapes to India March 31 and receives asylum after a rising against the Chinese garrison at Lhasa, the new Chinese puppet government seals the border to India which refuses to recognize the Dalai Lama as head of a "separate" Tibetan government functioning in India. Chinese and Indian forces have border clashes.

Mao Tse-tung steps down as China's chief of state April 27 in favor of Liu Shao-chi but Mao remains chairman of the Communist Party.

Singapore becomes self-governing June 3.

Indonesia's constituent assembly is dissolved July 5 by President Sukarno who moves his nation toward a new "Guided Democracy" regime that will grow progressively more authoritarian as Sukarno's Communist Party (PKI) grows more powerful.

The Federal State of Mali is created January 17 by a merger of the African republics Senegal and French Sudan a week after Michel Debre is installed as premier of France's Fifth Republic.

Premiers of the 12 autonomous republics in Africa's French Community confer at Paris in early February with President de Gaulle.

Rwanda is torn in November by a great uprising of Hutu (Bahutu) tribesmen against the minority Tutsi (Batutsi) aristocracy in the UN mandated territory that is governed by Belgian administrators. Rwanda's monarchy is abolished and thousands of Tutsi refugees flee across the borders into the Belgian Congo (where anti-European riots at Leopoldville killed 71 in early January), Uganda, and Tanganyika.

Ceylon's prime minister Sirimavo Bandaranaike dies September 26 of wounds inflicted by an assassin 3 months after conclusion of a trade pact with Peking.

Switzerland's electorate votes February 1 to reject a proposed amendment to the constitution that would permit women to vote in national elections and to run for national office.

Japanese-Americans who renounced their citizenship in 1942 when they were placed in concentration camps under Executive Order 9066 regain full citizenship May 20 but receive no compensation for the losses they incurred as a result of their relocation.

The Street Offences Act passed by the British Parliament July 16 makes it an offense "for a common prostitute to loiter or solicit in a secret or public place for the purpose of prostitution," and says "A constable may arrest without warrant anyone he finds in a street or public place and suspects, with reasonable cause, to be committing an offence under this section." English and Welsh prostitutes will circumvent the new law by posting their telephone numbers at newsstands or by buying dogs and "walking" them as an excuse for being in the streets (*see* 1957).

U.S. Army MP corporal Roman Duckworth refuses to move to the back of a Trailways bus and a Mississippi peace officer shoots him dead. The black serviceman had been en route to his wife's sickbed on emergency furlough.

The UN General Assembly votes November 10 to condemn racial discrimination anywhere in the world including South Africa.

Cologne has anti-Semitic riots December 24.

President Eisenhower speaks out February 18 against continued emergency aid to the unemployed. He says the nation's economy is on a "curve of rising prosperity."

A University of Michigan study shows that 10 percent of U.S. families live on the "poverty line" and 20 percent live below the line (see 1957).

One American with an income of $20 million pays no federal taxes, five with incomes of more than $5 million each pay no federal taxes, one with an annual income of nearly $2 million has paid no federal taxes since 1949 (see 1960).

Vice President Nixon opens an American exhibit at Moscow and engages in a public debate with Soviet Premier Khrushchev. The dialogue takes place in a model kitchen and Nixon boasts of America's material progress and abundance of consumer goods (see Galbraith, 1958).

France demonstrates the industrial strides she has taken under the Monnet Plan of 1953 by producing twice as much steel as in 1929. The nation uses four times as much electricity as in 1929 and manufactures nearly five times as many cars and trucks.

A nationwide U.S. steel strike begins July 15.

The Landrum-Griffin Act passed by Congress September 14 marks the first major change in U.S. labor law since the Taft-Hartley Act of 1947. The new law requires labor unions to file annual financial reports with the secretary of labor but it includes a "bill of rights" for labor.

Washington seeks a Taft-Hartley Act injunction to halt the steel strike (above) October 19. The United Steelworkers challenge the validity of the Taft-Hartley injunction provision but the Supreme Court upholds the entire act November 7.

The Lincoln head penny that has been in circulation for 50 years is redesigned to show the 37-year-old Lincoln Memorial.

Morgan-Guaranty Trust Company is created by a merger of New York's J. P. Morgan and Company with the city's 95-year-old Guaranty Trust Company. The new bank has $4 billion in assets and becomes the fourth largest U.S. bank (Bank of America has $11.3 billion in assets, Chase Manhattan $8.3 billion, First National City $8 billion).

International Telephone and Telegraph Company (ITT) names former Raytheon Corporation executive vice president Harold Sydney Geneen, 49, to the ITT presidency (see 1925). Geneen will turn ITT into a giant conglomerate (see Textron, 1955).

Reynolds Metals Company acquires Britain's largest aluminum producer British Aluminium (see 1945).

Underwood (Typewriter) Company is acquired by Italy's giant Olivetti Company which has grown to become a major producer of computers as well as of typewriters (see 1911; 1927).

The RCA 501 computer introduced by Radio Corporation of America is the world's first fully transistorized computer (see 1948). New York Life Insurance Company takes delivery of the first 501 in June and RCA, while losing a fortune in its efforts to develop color television, works on the smaller 301 computer that will challenge IBM and Sperry-Rand in the booming data processing business.

The St. Lawrence & Great Lakes Waterway dedicated by Queen Elizabeth June 26 opens to give ocean-going vessels access to Great Lakes ports as far west as Duluth, some 2,342 miles from the Atlantic. The Seaway can accommodate vessels of up to 25-foot 9-inch draught—80 percent of the world's saltwater fleet—but it will prove costly to maintain.

The S.S. *Rotterdam,* launched by the Holland-American Line, is a 38,645-ton luxury liner.

The first U.S. nuclear-powered merchant ship is launched July 21 at Camden, N.J.

Hovercraft are pioneered by English engineer Christopher Sydney Cockerell, 46, who has been experimenting since 1953 with ways to reduce the friction round the hulls of boats and who demonstrates his SRN-1 hovercraft with a crossing of the English Channel on a cushion of air. The hovercraft industry will be well established within 6 years as ferries and patrol boats come into use.

The Bristol Britannia powered by Rolls-Royce engines is approved for commercial aviation. The 133-passenger Britannia is the first large turboprop aircraft.

Japanese automakers produce 79,000 cars, up from just 110 in 1947. Most of the cars are Datsuns and Toyotas and the number will increase to 3.2 million by 1970.

U.S. Volkswagen sales reach 120,000, up from 29,000 in 1955, while total sales of foreign-made U.S. cars such as British Fords, the General Motors Opel, and Chrysler's Simca top 120,000.

The Ford Falcon is Detroit's first major response to the competition from Volkswagen and other foreign compact cars. Chevrolet tools up to market a rear-engined Corvair compact (see Mustang, 1964).

The American Motors Rambler is introduced to give AMC a 14-foot 10-inch compact entry designed to compete with Volkswagen and the new Ford Falcon (above; see 1954).

1959 (cont.) The average U.S. automobile wholesales at $1,880, up from $1,300 in 1949.

President Eisenhower imposes mandatory quotas on U.S. oil imports in response to pleas from domestic producers, saying the move is based on reasons of national security. The import quotas effectively subsidize domestic producers of crude oil and force U.S. consumers to pay higher prices for gasoline and home heating oil.

Skull fragments found with crude stone tools in Tanganyika's Olduvai Gorge by British anthropologist-paleontologist Louis S. B. Leakey, 56, suggest that Australopithecene man-ape lived at least 1.78 million years ago. Potassium-argon dating shows that volcanic ash surrounding the fossils is that old.

Russian archaeologist Tatiana Proskouriakov finds a pattern of dates indicating a list of important events in the lives of certain Mayan individuals in the Yucatán. The find enables scholars to decipher the periods in which certain rulers reigned and thus to establish dynasties, but scholars will argue about whether the Mayan styphs represent ideas, words, or both.

The first complete amino acid sequence of the enzyme ribonuclease sheds some light on the chemical composition of the enzyme that helps break down ribonucleic acid (RNA), one of the two fundamental chemicals that determine normal and abnormal growth in living things. Rockefeller University scientists William H. Stein, 47, Stanford Moore, 45, and others work up the sequence (see Crick and Watson's DNA research, 1953, 1961).

The birth defect phocomelia in which flipperlike stubs are produced in place of one or more normal arms or legs appears in 12 cases seen in West German clinics that have not observed a single case in the last 5 years (see 1960).

The first transistorized TV set is introduced by Japan's Sony Corporation which last year changed its name from Tokyo Tsushin Kogyo (see Ibuka, 1952). The portable black-and-white Sony TV receiver will be followed next year by the first transistorized color TV set which will employ a picture tube developed years earlier by Ernest O. Lawrence of 1932 cyclotron fame who played a leading role in developing the atomic bombs that destroyed Hiroshima and Nagasaki in 1945.

India gets her first television and villagers travel for hundreds of miles to visit six community TV centers at New Delhi where mounted police are required to keep the crowds away from the receivers. TV stations will be built at Bombay, Amritsar in Punjab, Srinigar in Kashmir, Madras in South India, and Calcutta in East India by 1966, but locally made receiving sets will cost $425 and the average per capita income is below $80 per year.

Color TV is introduced in Cuba.

South Africa decides not to introduce any television. The decision will stand for 16 years.

Chicago becomes a two-publisher city as Marshall Field's *Sun-Times* buys the *Daily News* from publisher John S. Knight and the *Tribune* buys the *Herald-American* from the Hearst Corporation.

France legalizes press censorship by adopting a new article in the Constitution. Newspapers which disagree with the Gaullist government will be seized and closed down and papers will be impounded on frequent occasion until March 1965.

A U.S. Post Office ban on distributing the 1928 D. H. Lawrence novel *Lady Chatterley's Lover* is lifted by a federal district court at New York July 21 despite protests that the book uses such words as "fuck" and "cunt" and is explicit in its descriptions of the sex act. New York's Grove Press has distributed an unexpurgated version of the book, has been challenged by Postmaster Arthur E. Summerfield, and is upheld in *Roth v. the United States* by Judge Frederick van Pelt Bryan, 55, who is deluged with letters calling him a dirty old man. His 30-page decision rules not only that the book is not obscene but also that the Postmaster General is neither qualified nor authorized to judge the obscenity of material to be sent through the mails, that he is empowered only to halt delivery of matter already judged obscene.

Atheneum publishers is founded by Simon Michael Bessie, Alfred A. Knopf, Jr., and Hiram Haydn.

Nonfiction *The Elements of Style* by E. B. White who has adapted a manual by the late William Strunk, Jr., who was White's teacher at Cornell in 1919 and who died in 1946. White will revise the work for a second edition in 1972.

Fiction *The Poorhouse Fair* by U.S. novelist John Hoyer Updike, 27; *Goodbye, Columbus* (stories) by U.S. author Philip Milton Roth, 26; *Advertisements for Myself* by Norman Mailer; *Henderson the Rain King* by Saul Bellow; *The Naked Lunch* by William Burroughs; *Malcolm* by U.S. novelist James Purdy, 36; *The Mansion* by William Faulkner; *Dear and Glorious Physician* by Taylor Caldwell; *Advise and Consent* by U.S. novelist Alan Drury, 41; *Memento Mori* by Scottish novelist Muriel Spark, 41; *The Planetarium* (*Le Planetarium*) by Nathalie Sarraute; *Aimez-Vous Brahms?* by Françoise Sagan; *The Impossible Proof* (*Unmögliche Beweisaufnahme*) by Hans Erich Nossack; "The Loneliness of the Long Distance Runner" (story) by Alan Sillitoe; *Goldfinger* by Ian Fleming.

Poetry *A Dream of Governors* by Louis Simpson; *Heart's Needle* by U.S. poet W. D. Snodgrass, 33.

Painting *Numbers in Color* by Jasper Johns; *Jill* by U.S. painter Frank Stella, 23; *Bronze Tet* by Morris Louis; *Virginia Site* by Kenneth Noland; *Le Champ de Mars* by Marc Chagall.

Sculpture *Figure Lying on its Side* by Kenneth Armitage. Sir Jacob Epstein dies at London August 19 at age 78.

New York's Guggenheim Museum opens on Fifth Avenue between 88th and 89th Streets to house the collection of the late copper magnate Solomon R. Guggenheim whose mentor Hilla Rebay induced him to buy dozens of canvases by the late abstractionist Wassily Kandinsky (*see* Wright, below).

The Nikon F 35-mm. single-lens reflex camera is introduced by Nippon Kogaku K.K. whose rangefinder cameras enabled *LIFE* magazine photographers to provide sharp coverage of the Korean conflict (*see* 1948; Nikkormat, 1965).

Theater *A Taste of Honey* by English playwright Shelagh Delaney, 20, 2/10 at London's Wyndham Theatre, a play directed by Joan Littlewood about a pregnant adolescent who is expecting a black baby and who is befriended by a homosexual youth, 617 perfs.; *A Majority of One* by Hollywood screenwriter Leonard Spigelgass, 50, 2/16 at New York's Shubert Theater, with Gertrude Berg, Cedric Hardwicke, 558 perfs.; *Sweet Bird of Youth* by Tennessee Williams 3/10 at New York's Martin Beck Theater, with Paul Newman, Geraldine Page, 378 perfs.; *Raisin in the Sun* by U.S. playwright Lorraine Hansberry, 29, 3/11 at New York's Ethel Barrymore Theater, with Sidney Poitier, Ruby Dee, Diana Sands, Claudia McNeil, 530 perfs. (Hansberry has taken her title from a Langston Hughes poem containing the line, "What happens to a dream deferred?/ Does it dry up/ Like a raisin in the sun?"); *The Connection* by U.S. playwright Jack Gelber, 27, 7/5 at New York's off-Broadway Living Theater, with Leonard Hicks, Ira Lewis in a play about drug addiction, 722 perfs.; *The Zoo Story* by U.S. playwright Edward Franklin Albee, 21, 9/28 at Berlin's Schillertheater Wehrstatt (Albee was adopted as an infant by Reed A. Albee, son of the late Keith-Albee vaudeville circuit manager E. F. Albee whose namesake will see his play open in mid-January of next year at New York's Provincetown Playhouse); *The Miracle Worker* by William Gibson 10/19 at New York's Playhouse Theater, with Patty Duke as Helen Keller, Anne Bancroft as Annie Sullivan in a stage version of the 1957 *Playhouse 90* television drama, 702 perfs.; *Sergeant Musgrave's Dance* by English playwright John Arden, 29, 10/22 at London's Royal Court Theatre; *The Blacks* (*Les nègres*) by Jean Genet 10/28 at the Théâtre de Lutèce, Paris; *The Tenth Man* by Paddy Chayefsky 11/5 at New York's Booth Theater, 623 perfs.; *The Andersonville Trial* by U.S. playwright Saul Levitt, 46, 12/29 at Henry Miller's Theater, New York, with George C. Scott, Jr., Albert Dekker.

The Loew's Theater chain is acquired from Metro-Goldwyn-Mayer by hotelmen Laurence and Preston Tisch who will rename their parent company Loew's, Inc.

Films Alain Resnais's *Hiroshima, Mon Amour* with Emmanuelle Rosa; Marcel Camus's *Black Orpheus* set in Rio; François Truffaut's *The 400 Blows;* Jean-Luc Goddard's *Breathless* with Jean-Paul Belmondo, Jean Seberg; Michelangelo Antonioni's *L'Avventura* with Monica Vitti; Claude Chabrol's *Leda* with Jean-Paul Belmondo; Billy Wilder's *Some Like it Hot* with Jack Lemmon, Tony Curtis, Marilyn Monroe; Otto Preminger's *Anatomy of a Murder* with James Stewart, Lee Remick; Alfred Hitchcock's *North by Northwest* with Cary Grant, Eva Marie Saint, James Mason; William Wyler's *Ben Hur* with Charlton Heston, Jack Hawkins, Stephen Boyd; Walt Disney's *The Sleeping Beauty;* Alexei Batalov's *The Overcoat;* Kon Ichakawa's *Fires on the Plain;* John and Ray Boulting's *I'm All Right, Jack* with Peter Sellers in a comedy that satirizes Britain's worsening labor-management relations; George Stevens's *The Diary of Anne Frank* with Millie Perkins, Joseph Schildkraut, Shelley Winters.

Stage musicals *Once Upon a Mattress* 5/11 at New York's Phoenix Theater, with Carol Burnett, Jack Gilford, music by Mary Rodgers, lyrics by Marshall Barer, 458 perfs.; *Gypsy* 5/21 at New York's Broadway Theater, with Ethel Merman, Jack Klugman, book by Arthur Laurents based on the life of stripteaser Gypsy Rose Lee, music by Jule Styne, lyrics by Stephen Sondheim, songs that include "Small World," "Together Wherever We Go," "Everything's Coming Up Roses," 702 perfs.; *Lock Up Your Daughters* 5/28 at London's new Mermaid Theatre, with music by Laurie Johnson, lyrics by Lionel Bart (né Lionel Begleiter), 28, 328 perfs.; *At the Drop of a Hat* 10/8 at New York's John Golden Theater, with Englishmen Michael Flanders and Donald Swan, music and lyrics by Flanders and Swan, 217 perfs.; *Take Me Along* 10/22 at New York's Shubert Theater, with Jackie Gleason, Walter Pidgeon, Robert Morse, music and lyrics by Bob Merrill, 448 perfs.; *The Sound of Music* 11/16 at New York's Lunt-Fontanne Theater, with Mary Martin, Theodore Bikel, Kurt Kazner, music by Richard Rodgers, lyrics by Oscar Hammerstein II, songs that include "Climb Every Mountain," "Do-Re-Mi," "Edelweiss," "My Favorite Things," and the title song, 1,443 perfs.; *Fiorello!* 11/23 at New York's Broadhurst Theater, with Tom Bosley as the late Mayor La Guardia, Howard da Sylva, Ellen Hanley, music by Jerry Bock, lyrics by Sheldon Harnick, songs that include "Politics and Poker," 796 perfs.

First performances *Pittsburgh* Symphony by Paul Hindemith 1/30 at Pittsburgh; Missa Brevis in D for treble voices and organ by Benjamin Britten 7/22 at Aldeburgh; Concerto in E flat for Violincello and Orchestra No. 1 by Dmitri Shostakovich 10/4 at Leningrad, with Mstislav Rostropovich as soloist.

Popular songs "The Children's Marching Song" by M. Arnold (for the film *The Inn of the Sixth Happiness*); "High Hopes" by James Van Heusen, lyrics by Sammy Cahn (for the film *A Hole in the Head*); "I'm Just a Lonely Boy" by Paul Anka; "Put Your Head on My Shoulder" by Paul Anka; "Waterloo" by John Loudermilk and Marijohn Wilkin.

Swedish prizefighter Ingemar Johansson, 26, wins the world heavyweight crown June 26 by knocking out Floyd Patterson in the third round of a title match at New York.

Cuba si! Yanqui no! Fidel Castro replaced dictatorship with a Marxist regime, the first in the Western Hemisphere.

The Los Angeles Dodgers win the World Series by defeating the Chicago White Sox 4 games to 2 after the White Sox have taken their first pennant since the "Black Sox" scandal of 1919.

 Spring filter-tipped cigarettes are introduced by P. Lorillard.

A housing bill passed by Congress September 23 authorizes expenditure of $1 billion over a 2-year period with $650 million earmarked for slum clearance.

New York's Guggenheim Museum (above) has been designed by Frank Lloyd Wright who dies April 9 at age 89. The building has a dramatic circular inner ramp employed by Wright earlier on a smaller scale.

New York's Seagram building is completed opposite the 41-year-old Racquet and Tennis Club on Park Avenue (see 1958). The bronze-clad, 40-story building rises from a plaza landscaped with fountains and gingko trees (see Four Seasons, below).

New York's Time-Life building at 1271 Avenue of the Americas opens in December. Harrison, Abramovitz, and Harris has designed the 48-story building to replace the 1 Rockefeller Plaza building of 1937 (now the General Dynamics building).

China suffers catastrophic crop failures (see 1958, 1960).

A corn farmer must have at least 1,000 acres to be a viable producer, says the U.S. Department of Agriculture, but 1 million U.S. farms contain fewer than 50 acres. The country has 3.7 million farms, down from more than 6 million in 1940 when 2.2 million farms had fewer than 50 acres, and 136,000 farms have 1,000 acres or more, up from 100,000 in 1940.

U.S. cranberry growers react to a contamination scare (below) by marketing fresh berries following a drop in cranberry sauce sales, but the growers will receive a government subsidy early next year to compensate them for berries free of residue that they could not sell because of the depressed market.

The Food and Drug Administration seizes 0.25 percent of the U.S. cranberry crop and orders cranberries from Washington and Oregon off the market. Residues of the weed-killer aminotriazole have contaminated a tiny fraction of the nation's crop, but all cranberry sauce sales fall off as the headlines alarm consumers (below).

The FDA bans use of diethylstilbestrol (DES) for emasculating cocks and promoting the growth of capons (see Dodds, 1938). University of Iowa researchers have developed DES in the past few years for poultry raisers, but feminizing effects have been observed in a restaurant worker who has eaten chicken necks containing residues from DES pellet implants (cattle raisers will continue to use DES in feed).

A U.S. study shows that overweight has a strong correlation to atherosclerotic heart disease (see 1949).

Metrecal is introduced by the 59-year-old Mead Johnson Company of Evansville, Ind. The weight-reducing aid is a powdered mix of soybean flour, minerals, vitamins, and other ingredients and will be widely imitated.

Libby McNeill & Libby sells its salmon canneries at Bristol Bay, Kodiak Island, Cook Inlet, and other Alaskan locations to CWC Fisheries, a company established by Columbia River Packers Association and Ward's Cove Packing Company (see 1912; 1950). CRPA will change its name to Bumble Bee, it will build a tuna cannery at Cambridge, Md., in 1961, and it will process Atlantic skipjack, yellowfin, and albacore tuna for sale under the Bumble Bee brand.

Congress approves a 2-year extension of a program for foreign disposal of surplus U.S. farm commodities. Some $250 million worth of surplus food is to go to needy Americans through food stamps (see 1939; 1964).

U.S. supermarkets number 32,000 and account for 69 percent of all food store sales although they comprise only 11 percent of food stores.

Trading stamps given out by food stores increase prices by only 0.6 percent, says a U.S. Department of Agriculture study and the report is advertised by Sperry & Hutchinson, Inc. (see 1951). Some 200,000 U.S. retailers offer trading stamps with S&H green stamps accounting for 35 to 40 percent of the market. By year's end Sperry & Hutchinson has over $80 million in cash and securities plus large interests in real estate, department stores, and other retail outlets, some of which it has financed.

Minute Maid Corporation proves to the Florida Citrus Commission that frost-damaged oranges can be used successfully in concentrates (see 1954). After several years of wild fluctuations in profit and loss,

Minute Maid uses earth-moving machines to build 10-foot walls round 7,000 acres of marsh to reclaim land in the Florida savannahs that has been under water 9 months of the year. The company plants citrus trees from whose fruit it will make frozen juice concentrates and it develops programs that permit growers to participate in the retail prices of concentrates and thus assure Minute Maid of a constant supply of fruit. Coca Cola Company will acquire Minute Maid next year.

Royal Crown Cola Co. is created by a reorganization of Nehi Corp. (see 1928; 1934; Diet-Rite, 1962).

Frosty O's sugar-coated breakfast food is introduced by General Mills (see 1958; 1961).

Concentrate breakfast food—9.9 percent sugar—is introduced by Kellogg (see 1958; 1961).

CPC International is incorporated to combine Corn Products Refining Company with Best Foods, Inc. (see 1958).

New York's Four Seasons restaurant and The Brasserie open in the new Seagram Building (above). The posh Four Seasons and the 24-hour Brasserie are operated by Restaurant Associates, Inc.

The flavor-enhancer 5'-nucleotides, marketed in Japan, is 10 to 20 times stronger than monosodium glutamate (MSG) (see 1947). U.S. marketing will begin in 1902.

The National Cranberry Association changes its name to Ocean Spray Cranberries, Inc., expands production and distribution of Cranberry Juice Cocktail, and introduces Dietetic Cranberries in response to consumer resistance to cranberry sauce (above; see 1930). The association harvested its first million-barrel crop in 1953 and adopts new promotion ideas that will boost cranberry consumption in years to come (see Cranapple, 1965).

Hawaii (above) has a native population of 12,000, down from 37,000 in 1860.

Congress authorizes admission of some 57,000 additional immigrants without regard to quotas established by the 1952 McCarran-Walter Act. Preference is given to resident aliens and to relatives of U.S. citizens (see 1965).

1960 Soviet ground-to-air missiles at Sverdlovsk down a U.S. supersonic U-2 spy plane flying at 60,000 feet May 1. The Russians capture CIA agent pilot Francis Gary Powers, 30, with his electronic sensing equipment, the United States admits to having sent aerial reconnaisance flights over Soviet territory, and Premier Khrushchev cancels a Paris summit meeting with President Eisenhower.

Premier Khrushchev threatens July 9 at Moscow to use Soviet rockets to protect Cuba from U.S. military intervention as President Eisenhower declares that the United States will never permit a regime "dominated by international communism" to exist in the Western Hemisphere. Fidel Castro has signed an agreement at Havana February 13 with Soviet first deputy premier Anastas I. Mikoyan providing for $100 million in Soviet credit to Cuba and the Soviet purchase of 5 million tons of Cuban sugar, Castro has threatened June 23 to seize all American-owned property and business interests to counter U.S. "economic aggression," President Eisenhower has cut Cuba's sugar quota by 95 percent July 6.

The Monroe Doctrine of 1823 has died a "natural death," says Premier Khrushchev at a news conference July 12. The U.S. State Department reaffirms the Monroe Doctrine July 14 and accuses Khrushchev of trying to set up a "Bolshevik doctrine" for worldwide Communist expansion.

Cuba nationalizes all banks and all large commercial and industrial enterprises October 14, the United States imposes an embargo October 19 on all exports to Cuba except for medical supplies and most foodstuffs, Washington sends a note to the Organization of American States October 28 charging that Cuba has received substantial arms shipments from the Soviet bloc (see 1961).

France has exploded her first atomic bomb February 13 over the Sahara Desert in southwestern Algeria, joining the "atomic club" of the United States, the U.S.S.R., and Britain. She begins a series of atmospheric nuclear tests that will continue for some years in Africa and in the Pacific.

French and Belgian colonies in Africa gain independence beginning with French Cameroun January 1 and followed by Togo April 27, the Malagasy Republic (Madagascar) June 26, the Independent Congo Republic June 30, Somalia (French and Italian Somaliland) July 1, Ghana July 1, Dahomey August 1, Upper Volta in August, Ivory Coast August 7, Chad August 11, the Central African Republic August 13, Gabon August 17, Mali August 20, Niger September 3, Senegal September 5, Nigeria October 11, the Islamic Republic of Mauretania November 28.

The new Independent Congo Republic (above) headed by President Joseph Kasavubu and Premier Patrice Lumumba quickly dissolves into chaos. Separatist Moise Tshombe proclaims an independent Katanga, separatist Albert Kalonji proclaims an independent Kasai, Congolese troops mutiny, Premier Lumumba appeals to the UN for aid, the UN demands withdrawal of Belgian forces, the Security Council votes to send in UN troops, Secretary-General Dag Hammarskjöld leads UN forces into Katanga, President Kasavubu and Premier Lumumba dismiss each other, and the Congo army commander Colonel Joseph D. Mobutu takes over the government (see 1961).

The presidents of Guinea, Ghana, and Mali agree December 24 to unite their republics.

Cyprus gains independence August 16 from the British who have held the Mediterranean island since 1878. The new Cypriot republic elects Archbishop

1960 (cont.) Macharios president but Greek and Turkish interests will vie for control of Cyprus (*see* 1964).

The United Nations establishes the International Development Association (IDA) with headquarters at Washington, D.C.

The Japanese premier asks President Eisenhower June 16 to cancel a scheduled visit to Japan following 3 weeks of anti-American protest demonstrations by leftist groups. U.S. and Japanese diplomats have signed a treaty of mutual security and cooperation January 19 at Washington, the Japanese Diet approves the treaty June 19, and it takes effect June 23.

U.S. senator from Massachusetts John F. Kennedy, 43, wins election to the presidency by defeating Vice President Richard M. Nixon, who wins 219 electoral votes to Kennedy's 303, but the first Roman Catholic to be elected president wins by a scant popular vote margin of 113,057 out of more than 69 million. (502,773 go to minority party candidates including U.S. Senator from Virginia Harry F. Byrd, Jr., 45, who wins 15 electoral votes).

South Vietnam's President Ngo Dinh Diem regains power November 12 following a coup by the paratroop brigade at Saigon. Dissident groups, collectively called the Vietcong (Vietnamese Communists), meet secretly December 20 and organize the National Front for the Liberation of South Vietnam.

South Africa's Sharpeville massacre March 21 draws a sharp U.S. State Department protest. Some 20,000 blacks have besieged a police station in a Johannesburg suburb to demonstrate against a law requiring all blacks to carry papers. The police open fire, killing 56, wounding 162 (of whom 16 die). The pass law is suspended March 26 but violence continues. Whites arm themselves and 30,000 blacks march on Capetown March 30 to demand the release of their leaders.

U.S. blacks begin "sit-in" demonstrations February 1 at Greensboro, N.C., lunch counters. The town's eating places are desegregated July 25.

Southern senators begin a filibuster February 29 to block civil rights legislation. Sessions continue round the clock until March 5 to set a filibuster record of 82 hours, 3 minutes, but Congress passes a Civil Rights Act May 6 authorizing federal referees where patterns of discrimination against black voters exist. The Department of Justice brings its first sweeping civil rights suit September 13, charging a plot to obstruct black voting in Tennessee.

A state may not change the boundaries of a city to exclude black voters, the Supreme Court rules November 14 in the Tuskegee, Ala., gerrymander case *Gomillion v. Lightfoot* (*see* 1812).

The first privately financed nuclear power plant opens at Dresden, Ill., just south of Chicago. Within 14 years Commonwealth Edison will be producing more than 30 percent of its power from nuclear reactors but most utility companies will continue to use fossil fuels (*see* Consolidated Edison, 1962).

Coal supplies 45 percent of U.S. energy needs, a figure that will decline in the next 15 years to less than 18 percent as power plants and homeowners switch to oil and natural gas (*see* Paley Commission, 1952).

Twenty-nine U.S. oil companies go on trial in a U.S. district court at Tulsa, Okla., on charges of conspiring to raise and fix crude oil and gasoline prices. The defendants are sustained by federal judge Royce H. Savage who says, "The evidence does not rise above the level of suspicion."

Grand juries indict General Electric, Westinghouse, Allis-Chalmers, and 26 other U.S. producers of heavy electrical equipment for involvement in the largest conspiracy in restraint of trade in the 70-year history of the Sherman Act. Fines totaling more than $1.92 million will be levied and seven jail sentences will be handed down plus 24 suspended sentences.

The Organization of Petroleum Exporting Companies (OPEC) meets for the first time September 14 at Baghdad and forces a retraction of the decrease in oil prices by Standard Oil of New Jersey which has unilaterally rolled back prices by 4 to 14 cents per barrel. The five charter members of OPEC include Saudi Arabia, Iran, Iraq, Kuwait, and Qatar but the organization will grow to include Abu Dhabi, Algeria, Gabon, Libya, Nigeria, Indonesia, Ecuador, and Venezuela.

Some 2,000 electronic computers are delivered to U.S. business offices, universities, laboratories, and other buyers. The figure will more than double in the next 4 years and debate will rage as to whether computers wipe out jobs or create new ones (*see* Luddites, 1811–1813).

The laser (light amplification by stimulated emission of radiation) perfected by research physicist Theodore Maiman at the Hughes Laboratory in Malibu, Calif., can cut metal quickly and will find wide use in delicate welding (including retinal eye operations). U.S. inventor R. Gordon Gould, 40, coined the term laser 3 years ago at Columbia University, he had his notebook showing the basic laser concept notarized, but physicists Charles H. Townes and Arthur Schawlow applied for a patent first and were the first to publish their findings in scientific journals. Gould has tried to interest defense officials in his potential "death ray," but Gould was involved in some left-wing political activities in the early 1940s, the Defense Department has classified his patent application secret, they have denied him security clearance, and they have confiscated his notebooks. By 1977, laser sales will reach an estimated $1 billion per year as scientists use lasers for determining distances, relaying communications, projecting three-dimensional holograph pictures, and exploring nuclear applications.

The Bulova Accutron tuning fork watch introduced October 25 is the world's first electronic wristwatch. Its tuning fork vibrates 360 times per second—144 times as fast as the balance oscillators in conventional hand-wound, automatic, and electric watches—and it is accurate to within 1 minute per month.

FDA researcher Frances Kelsey keeps thalidomide off the U.S. market by delaying approval of a Cincinnati firm's application to market the tranquilizer under the brand name Kevadon. Produced by a West German pharmaceutical house and widely used in Britain and West Germany for sleeplessness, nervous tension, asthma, in cough medicines, and for relief of nausea in early pregnancy, thalidomide is said to have no side effects, but Kelsey notes that the drug is not effective in making animals sleepy. She observes that some British patients have complained of numbness in feet and fingers after using the drug, and she points out that phocomelia is becoming endemic in West Germany where 83 such birth defects appear at the clinics that saw 12 last year (see 1961).

Librium is approved for marketing by the FDA February 24 and Roche Laboratories releases the antianxiety drug. Polish-American research chemist Leo H. Sternbach, 52, and his associates have developed Librium by treating a quinazoline with methylamine. Librium sales will far surpass those of the meprobamates (see Miltown, 1954; Valium, 1963).

Aldactone is introduced by G. D. Searle & Company whose sprinolactone drug counteracts high blood pressure and edema (see Aldactazide, 1961). Searle has failed to report the existence of "malignant mammary tumors" in test animals as recorded on individual work sheets in laboratories where Aldactone was administered to the animals.

The Journal of the American Medical Association carries an article by a group of scientists who report that they have synthesized ara-A (9-beta-D-arabinofuranosyladenine) while looking for anticancer agents but have found it useless and have discarded it. An employee of an Italian branch of Detroit's Parke, Davis and Co. scoops up a thimble-size quantity of Neapolitan earth in November and sends it to Detroit in a plastic-lined manila envelope as Parke, Davis employees have been doing thousands of times since 1940. The package sent in by Cicillo Aldo will prove to contain a microorganism that contains ara-A and Parke, Davis researchers will report in July 1974 that the microorganism is effective against herpes virus, a usually fatal disease.

A 10-year campaign against malaria begins in Indonesia where the disease kills an estimated 120,000 per year and accounts for between 10 and 15 percent of all infant mortalities. The Indonesians will use equipment supplied by the World Health Organization, largely with U.S. funds, to drain mosquito-infested swamps, they will conduct house-by-house spraying with DDT, they will adopt a program to detect and treat malaria victims, and by 1964 Java

will be free of malaria except for a few isolated areas on the southern coast (see 1969).

Seattle physician Belding Scribner improves the kidney machine devised by Dutch physician Willem J. Kolff in 1944. Scribner develops a way to put tubes into a large artery and a fat vein so that they can be left in place for months or even years to facilitate treatment with artificial kidneys of patients with permanently impaired organs.

The U.S. Gross National Product (GNP) is $503 billion, up from $284 billion in 1950; government spending accounts for 27 percent of the total, up from 21 percent in 1950.

President Eisenhower acts to curb a rising deficit in the nation's balance of payments and a drain on U.S. gold reserves. He orders a reduction of government spending abroad November 16 and the Defense Department 9 days later takes steps to limit sharply the number of dependents accompanying servicemen stationed abroad.

President Eisenhower warns against the "military-industrial complex" that works to maintain high levels of spending for the defense establishment.

More than 25 million Americans declare incomes of $5,000 or more, 5.3 million declare incomes of more than $10,000, more than 500,000 declare more than $25,000 (up from 42,500 in 1939). Thirty-two million taxpayers pay 90 percent of all income taxes collected with more than 25 percent of the population paying some income tax.

Britain's richest 10 percent holds 83 percent of the nation's wealth, down from 88 percent in 1939.

West Germany's industrial production reaches 176 percent of Germany's 1936 level as an "economic miracle" progresses in Bremen, Cologne, Düsseldorf, Frankfurt, Hamburg, Leipzig, Stuttgart, and other German cities.

U.S. corporate mergers total 844, up from 219 in 1950 when Congress passed the Celler-Kefauver amendment to strengthen the Clayton Anti-Trust Act of 1914 (see 1966).

Teledyne, Inc., is founded by former Litton Industries engineer Henry Singleton, 44, and his colleague George Kozmetsky; each invests $225,000. The company seeks out government electronics contracts; it will acquire scores of small- to medium-sized companies, most of them privately owned, Teledyne sales will reach $86.5 million by 1965, more than $1 billion by 1969, and $2 billion by 1977 from microcomputers, drone aircraft, specialty metals, insurance, and consumer products.

The Erie Lackawanna Railroad is created by a merger of the 99-year-old Erie and the slightly younger Delaware, Lackawanna and Western.

U.S. auto registration figures show one passenger car for every three Americans, a number that will increase in the next decade. Fifteen percent of U.S.

1960 (cont.) families have more than one car, up from 7 percent in 1950.

There are 74 million motorcars on the U.S. road, up from 32.6 million in 1941.

The United States has 2.17 million miles of surfaced road by year's end, up from 1.68 million in 1950, and 951,100 miles of dirt road, down from 1.31 million.

New York City makes Third Avenue one-way northbound July 17 and Lexington Avenue one-way southbound, but conversion of Fifth and Madison Avenues to one-way traffic is fought by merchants, the Fifth Avenue Coach Company, and the Transport Workers Union (see 1957; 1966).

Harbor Freeway opens at Los Angeles and gives access to the west side of town.

Britain's Daimler Motor Company merges into Jaguar Cars, Ltd.

Echo I launched by the United States August 12 is the world's first communications satellite (see 1962).

Television debates between Senator Kennedy and Vice President Nixon (above) give Kennedy the edge that enables him to win the election more by his appearance and manner than by anything he says. The debates reveal the power of television in politics, but TV debates will not be used in a presidential election again until 1976.

The Xerox 914 copier begins a revolution in paperwork reproduction (see 1950). The first production line Xerox copier is called the 914 because it makes copies of up to 9 by 14 inches on ordinary paper.

Typesetting by computer is introduced at the Imperimerie National in Paris.

The Pentel introduced by Tokyo's Stationery Company in August is the world's first felt-tip pen.

Holt, Rinehart and Winston is created by a merger of the 87-year-old publishing house Henry Holt with the big textbook publishers Rinehart and Winston founded respectively in 1929 and 1884 (see 1967).

Harcourt, Brace & World is created by a merger of the 41-year-old publishing house Harcourt, Brace with the World Book Company founded in 1905 by the late Casper W. Hodgson. The merger has been engineered by Harcourt, Brace president William Jovanovich, 40.

Time-Life Books is created by Time, Inc., to repackage editorial material developed by *Time* and *LIFE*.

The New American Library is acquired by the Los Angeles Times Mirror Company, which in 2 years will stop publishing the *Evening Mirror* after losing $25 million on the paper in 14 years. Signet and Mentor books will make NAL the largest U.S. paperback house.

U.S. paperback book sales reach an annual rate of more than 300 million.

Nonfiction *Growing Up Absurd* by U.S. novelist-poet-psychologist-philosopher Paul Goodman, 49, is a study of youth and delinquency that uses materials from literature, psychology, and political theory.

Fiction *The Trial Begins* (*Sud Idyot*) by Russian novelist Andrei Sinyavsky, 25; *Set This House on Fire* by William Styron; *Rabbit, Run* by John Updike who captures the tedium of smalltown life; *The Sotweed Factor* by John Barth whose fanciful historical novel has roots in the 1708 work by Ebenezer Cook; *The Nephew* by James Purdy; *The Magician of Lublin* by Isaac Bashevis Singer; *The Human Season* by U.S. novelist Edward Lewis Wallant, 34; *The Violent Bear It Away* by Flannery O'Connor; *All or Nothing* by John Cowper Powys, now 88; *The Flanders Road* (*La Route des Flandres*) by Claude Simon; *The Key* (*Kagi*) by Junichiro Tanizaki.

Poetry *What a Kingdom It Was* by U. S. poet Galway Kinnell, 33; *To Bedlam and Half Way Back* by U.S. poet Anne Sexton, 32.

Painting *The Final Veteran* by Larry Rivers; *The Postcard* by René Magritte; *Alpha* by Morris Louis, *Whirl* by Kenneth Noland.

Polaroid Corporation introduces a new high-speed film with an ASA rating of 3,000—10 times faster than the average speed of previous Polaroid films (see 1950; color film, 1962).

Theater *Toys in the Attic* by Lillian Hellman 2/25 at New York's Hudson Theater, with Maureen Stapleton, Jason Robards, Jr., 556 perfs.; *The Room* and *Dumb Waiter* by Harold Pinter 3/8 at London's Royal Court Theatre. Written in 4 days, *The Room* bewildered audiences at England's Bristol University in 1957 but Pinter's "theatre of the absurd" has a successful run; *The Best Man* by Gore Vidal 3/31 at New York's Morosco Theater, with Melvyn Douglas, Lee Tracy, Frank Lovejoy, 520 perfs.; *The Balcony* (*Le balcon*) by Jean Genet 5/18 at the Théâtre du Gymnase, Paris; *A Man for All Seasons* by English playwright Robert Bolt, 36, 9/1 at London's Globe Theatre; *Period of Adjustment* by Tennessee Williams 11/10 at New York's Helen Hayes Theater, with James Daley, Barbara Baxley, 132 perfs.; *All the Way Home* by Tad Mosel 11/30 at New York's Belasco Theater, with Coleen Dewhurst, Arthur Hill, Lillian Gish in a play based on the only novel by the late James Agee, 334 perfs., Pulitzer prize.

Films Federico Fellini's *La Dolce Vita* with Marcello Mastroianni, Anita Ekburg, Anouk Aimee; Roberto Rosselini's *General Della Rovere* with Vittorio De Sica; Ingmar Bergman's *The Virgin Spring* with Max von Sydow; Alfred Hitchcock's *Psycho* with Janet Leigh, Anthony Perkins; Tony Richardson's *The Entertainer* with Laurence Olivier; Stanley Kubrick's *Spartacus* with Kirk Douglas, Laurence Olivier; Jack Cardiff's *Sons and Lovers* with Dean Stockwell, Trevor Howard, Wendy Hiller; Robert Montgomery's *The Gallant Hours* with James Cagney; Richard Brooks's *Elmer Gantry* with Burt Lancaster, Jean Simmons; J. Lee Thompson's *Flame over India* with Kenneth More, Lauren Bacall; Jules Dassin's *Never on Sunday* with Melina Mercouri; Basil Dearden's *The League of Gentlemen* with Jack Hawkins, Nigel Patrick, Bryan Forbes, Richard Attenborough; John and Faith Hubley's *Moonbird* (animated short).

Opera *A Midsummer Night's Dream* 6/11 at Aldeburgh's Jubilee Hall, with music by Benjamin Britten, libretto from the Shakespeare comedy of 1595.

Cantata *Carmen Baseliense, Cantata Academica* by Benjamin Britten 7/1 at Basel University, for the university's 500th anniversary.

Oratorio *The Manger* (*El Pesebrio*) by Pablo Casals, now nearly 84, 12/17 at Acapulco.

First performances Symphony No. 4 by Roger Sessions 1/2 at Minneapolis; *Lincoln, The Great Commoner* by the late Charles Ives (who wrote it in 1912) 2/10 at New York's Carnegie Hall; *Music for Amplified Toy Pianos* by John Cage 2/25 at Wesleyan University, Middletown, Conn.; Sinfonietta in E major by Paul Hindemith 3/1 at Louisville; Symphony No. 9 by Darius Milhaud 3/29 at Fort Lauderdale, Fla.; *San Francisco Suite* by Ferde Grofe 4/23 at San Francisco; *Missa pro Defunctis* by Virgil Thomson 5/14 at Pottstown, N.Y.: Symphony No. 2 by Sir William Walton 9/2 at Edinburgh; *Tocata Festiva* by Samuel Barber 9/30 at Philadelphia's Academy of Music; Concerto No. 2 for Violin and Orchestra by Walter Piston 10/14 at Pittsburgh; Symphony No. 7 by William Schuman 10/21 at Boston's Symphony Hall; Concerto No. 2 for Violin and Orchestra by Paul Creston 11/12 at Los Angeles.

Stage musicals *Fings Ain't Wot They Used t'Be* 2/4 at London's Garrick Theatre, with music and lyrics by Lionel Bart, 886 perfs.; *Bye Bye Birdie* 4/14 at New York's Martin Beck Theater, with Dick Van Dyke, Chita Rivera, Kay Medford, music and lyrics by Charles Strouse and Lee Adams, songs that include "Put on a Happy Face," 607 perfs.; *The Fantasticks* 5/3 at New York's 153-seat off-Broadway Sullivan Street Playhouse, with music by Harvey Schmidt, lyrics by Tom Jones, songs that include "Try to Remember," 7,400+ perfs.; *Oliver* 6/30 at London's New Theatre, with Keith Hamshere as Oliver, music and lyrics by Lionel Bart, book based on the Charles Dickens novel of 1837, songs that include "Food, Glorious Food," "Consider Yourself," "You've Got to Pick a Pocket or Two," "As Long as He Needs Me," "I'd Do Anything," "Who Will Buy," "Reviewing the Situation," 2,618 perfs.; *The Unsinkable Molly Brown* 11/3 at New York's Winter Garden Theater, with Tammy Grimes, music and lyrics by Meredith Willson, 532 perfs.; *Camelot* 12/3 at New York's Majestic Theater, with Richard Burton, Julie Andrews, Robert Goulet, music by Frederick Loewe, lyrics by Alan Jay Lerner, songs that include "If Ever I Would Leave You," the title song, 873 perfs. (the new musical is based on Arthurian legend, President-elect John F. Kennedy attends a performance, and his administration will be identified with the romance of Camelot); *Wildcat* 12/11 at New

York's Alvin Theater, with Lucille Ball, Keith Andes, music by Cy Coleman, lyrics by Carolyn Leigh, songs that include "Hey, Look Me Over," 171 perfs.; *Do Re Mi* 12/26 at New York's St. James Theater, with Phil Silvers, Nancy Walker, music by Jule Styne, lyrics by Betty Comden and Adolph Green, book by Garson Kanin, 400 perfs.

Popular songs "Never on Sunday (The Children of Piraeus)" by Greek songwriter Manos Hadjidakis, 35, for the Jules Dassin film (above); "The Second Time Around" by Sammy Cahn, lyrics by James Van Heusen; "The Twist" by Hank Ballard is recorded by Ernest "Chubby Checker" Evans, 19, and launches an international dance craze. Checker performs at the small Peppermint Lounge bar off New York's Times Square, he moves on to the Copacabana night club, he earns close to $1 million in a single year, and discotheques at which patrons dance to phonograph records blossom to cash in on the new teenage dance sensation; "Itsy Bitsy Teenie Weenie Yellow Polka Dot Bikini" by Lee Pockriss and Paul J. Vance; "Cathy's Clown" by Don Everly and his brother Phil; "Chain Gang" by Sam Cooke; "Green Fields" by Terry Gilkyson, Richard Dehr, and Frank Miller.

The summer Olympic Games at Rome attract 5,396 contestants from 84 countries. The unofficial winner is the U.S.S.R. which repeats its triumph of 1956.

World chess champion Mikhail Botvinnik loses the title for the second time May 10 after having held it from 1948 to 1957 and again from 1958 until now. The new champion is Soviet chess master Mikhail Tal, 23, who will hold the title for just over a year.

Floyd Patterson regains the world heavyweight boxing championship June 20 by knocking out Sweden's Ingemar Johansson in the fifth round of a title bout at New York.

The Pittsburgh Pirates win the World Series by defeating the New York Yankees 4 games to 3.

Cotton's share of the U.S. textile market falls to 65 percent, down from 68 percent in 1950, while man-made fabrics increase their share to 28 percent with polyesters commanding 11 percent of the market (*see* 1970).

Brooklyn, N.Y., Mafia leaders Albert and Lawrence Gallo revolt from the Joseph Profaci organization and force Profaci to share more income with them.

Chicago Police Superintendent Orlando W. Wilson estimates that Chicago has had 976 gangland killings since 1919.

Convicted kidnapper-rapist Caryl Chessman dies in the gas chamber at San Quentin May 2 at age 38 after nine stays of execution since he was sent to Death Row July 3, 1948.

Brasilia becomes Brazil's federal capital by order of President Kubitshek. The new city in the uplands occupies a site that 3 years ago had only three non-Indian inhabitants, planner Lucio Costa has laid it out, Oscar Niemyer has designed its buildings, and in

1960 (cont.) 6 years it will have a population of 200,000 including 90,000 civil servants.

Boston's Mayor John F. Collins invites U.S. urban planning expert Edward J. Logue, 38, to create and administer an ambitious program for the one-time "hub of the universe." Logue has masterminded a pioneering urban renewal program in New Haven, Conn., and in the next few years will transform shabby Scollay Square into Government Center, will revitalize Roxbury, and will modernize other parts of Boston, using somewhat ruthless measures that employ the powers of eminent domain to override local zoning and building codes and to relocate residents without giving them any voice in the planning.

New York's Park Avenue continues its building boom with the 53-story Union Carbide building by Skidmore, Owings & Merrill between 47th and 48th Streets.

Eleven new Manhattan office towers give the city more than 6.8 million square feet of new rentable floor space.

Pittsburgh's Gateway Center is completed by Harrison & Abramovitz and rises 22 stories high.

Chicago's McCormick Place is completed. The 10-acre lakefront convention center has a 5,000 seat auditorium.

Detroit's Cobo Hall is completed. The $54-million lakefront exhibition center will be a popular convention site.

An earthquake near Concepción, Chile, May 22 creates seismic waves (*tsunamis*) that shatter every coastal town between the 36th and 44th parallels. Traveling 442 miles per hour, the waves reach Hilo, Hawaii, after midnight and move on to Japan. The death toll is roughly 1,000.

China's grain production falls below 1952 levels as the Great Leap Forward program of 1957 reduces harvests and produces starvation in the country that now has 100 million more mouths to feed than in 1952, but strict rationing avoids the famine tolls of pre-Mao times (*see* 1961; 1963).

Grain worth $6 billion piles up in U.S. government-owned storage facilities, congressmen file vigorous complaints about storage costs, but the reserves will drop to less than $1 billion worth in the decade ahead as U.S. grain relieves world hunger (*see* India, 1966).

Ten percent of the U.S. work force is on the farm, down from 18 percent in 1940, 11.6 percent in 1950.

U.S. corn yields per acre are up 75 percent over 1940, wheat yields are up 63 percent, livestock productivity is up 45 percent, milk production per cow, 30 percent, egg production per hen, 65 percent.

It takes 8 to 10 weeks and just 7 pounds of feed to produce a meaty broiler chicken in the United States, down from 12 to 15 weeks and 12 pounds of feed for a scrawnier (but tastier) broiler in 1940.

The world fisheries catch reaches 40 million tons, up from half that amount in 1950.

Large Soviet fishing fleets move south from Newfoundland's Grand Banks using equipment far superior to that employed by U.S. fishermen to pursue the herring which is plentiful off the U.S. Atlantic Coast. Followed by well-equipped Canadian and eastern European fleets, the Soviet trawlers and purse seiners will reduce herring populations by 90 percent and will virtually wipe out the haddock which has been the lifeblood of Boston fishermen.

Fish in the Mississippi begin to die by the millions as pollution lowers oxygen levels in the water.

Red No. 2 food dye receives provisional acceptance from the Food and Drug Administration which will renew such acceptance periodically for years despite mounting evidence that the amaranth sodium salt containing sulfur and naphtha produces defects in some animals and thus may be hazardous for humans.

Aluminum cans for food and beverages are used for the first time commercially but 95 percent of U.S. soft drinks and 50 percent of beer is sold in returnable bottles that are used 40 to 50 times each. Where seamless, extruded cans are used they have an edge over cans with seams in terms of safety but while steel cans are biodegradable the new aluminum cans present environmental problems of litter (*see* 1962).

U.S. margarine consumption reaches 9.4 pounds per capita, up from 8.6 pounds in 1957; butter consumption falls to 7.5 pounds, down from 8.3 (*see* 1963).

U.S. beef consumption reaches 99 pounds per capita.

Iowa Beef Processors, Inc., is founded at Denison, Iowa, by former Sioux City cattle buyers who include Currier J. Holman, 49. Iowa Beef will grow from a single slaughterhouse at Denison to become the world's largest meatpacker (larger than Swift, Armour, Wilson, Morrell, and Cudahy combined) but Holman will be convicted of having ties with a distributor who bribed supermarket executives and butchers' union officials.

Chicago's last packing house closes as packers shift activities to the west.

Sell's Specialties is acquired by Boston's William Underwood Co. (*see* liver pate, 1945).

Seabrook Farms is acquired by New York's Seeman Brothers (*see* 1957).

Minute Maid Corp. is acquired by the Coca-Cola Company (*see* 1957).

Hunt Foods and Industries, Inc. merges with Wesson Oil and Snowdrift Co. (*see* 1925, 1952; Wakefield, 1968; Norton Simon, Inc., 1969).

Dole Corporation is created by a renaming of the 58-year-old Hawaiian Pineapple Company started by James Dole (*see* 1922; Castle & Cooke, 1964).

Howard Johnson has 607 independently-owned restaurants in his franchise and is the third largest U.S. food distributor, surpassed only by the U.S. Army and

Navy (*see* 1952). Now 63, Johnson has a family-owned enterprise that operates 296 restaurants.

Boston's Pier Four restaurant, opened by Anthony Athanas, 49, is a harborside dining place built on abandoned landfill and is soon the world's largest restaurant. Albanian-American restaurateur Athanas started with the Hawthorne Restaurant at Lynn in 1938 and he has built up a chain of five Boston area operations.

Enovid 10 is introduced in August by G. D. Searle Company of Skokie, Ill., where the first commercially available oral contraceptive has been developed by a team headed by biochemist Byron Riegel, 53 (*see* Puerto Rican test, 1957). Fifty women at Birmingham, England, cooperate with Searle to make the first British test of an oral contraceptive (the 5 mg. Conovid pills that will be introduced next year will be the first oral contraceptives sold in Britain).

The Pill (above) sells at 55 cents each and costs a woman $11 per month. Condoms continue to account for $150 million of the $200 million U.S. contraceptive business with diaphragms and spermicidal creams and gels accounting for most of the rest.

More than 34 percent of U.S. women over age 14 and 31 percent of all married women are in the labor force, up from 25 percent of women over age 14 in 1940. Only 10 percent of working women are farmhands or servants, down from 50 percent in 1900.

Forty-eight percent of U.S. blacks live outside the 11 states of the old Confederacy, up from 30 percent in 1940.

U.S. population density approaches 50 per square mile, up from 10.6 in 1860, and nearly 70 percent of the population is urban.

Populations of 1 million or more are recorded by 141 world cities, up from 16 in 1900. Tokyo has 9.6 million, New York and London 7.7 million each, Shanghai 6.2 million, Moscow 5, Mexico City 4.8, Buenos Aires 4.5, Bombay 4.1, Sao Paulo more than 4 million, up from 250,000 in 1900, 1 million in 1929.

The world population tops 3 billion, up from 2 billion in 1930 (*see* 1948 FAO prediction).

1961 Breaking the genetic code that determines the inheritance of all physical characteristics opens new possibilities for preventing inherited disorders. James D. Watson and Francis H. C. Crick show that chromosomes consist of long helical strands of the substance DNA (*see* 1953) and many scientists say their discovery is comparable to the discovery of fire, the invention of the wheel, and the development of the written alphabet (*see* Khorana, 1966).

Cuba's Fidel Castro demands that the U.S. embassy staff at Havana be reduced to 11, Washington severs relations January 3, two major Cuban opposition groups set up a revolutionary council at New York in late March with former Cuban premier José Miro Cardona as president, Cardona urges all Cubans to revolt against Castro, and Cuban Foreign Minister Raul Roa charges at the UN April 15 that U.S. and Latin American forces are preparing to invade Cuba.

The Bay of Pigs invasion April 17 to 20 ends in disaster and embarrassment for the United States. Some 1,600 Cuban exiles trained by the CIA in Florida, Louisiana, and Guatemala land near the Bahia de los Cochinos in an inept and ill-supported effort to overthrow the Castro government, Castro's forces repel the invaders with heavy loss of life.

Premier Khrushchev demands April 18 that the invasion of Cuba be halted, he promises to aid Cuba, President Kennedy replies that the United States will not permit outside military intervention, and Kennedy asserts April 20 that the United States will take steps to halt Communist expansion if U.S. security is threatened.

Premier Castro announces May 17 that Cuba will exchange prisoners taken at the Bay of Pigs (above) for 500 U.S. bulldozers, negotiations break down June 30, and Castro declares himself a Marxist-Leninist December 2. He announces formation of a united party to bring Communism to Cuba.

Dominican dictator Rafael Leonidas Trujillo is killed May 30 at Ciudad Trujillo by an eight-man assassination team that has caught the 70-year-old generalissimo unguarded. Trujillo has controlled the country directly or indirectly since 1930 and Ciudad Trujillo is renamed Santo Domingo following his death.

President Kennedy and Premier Khrushchev confer at Vienna June 3 to 4 and issue a joint communique reaffirming support for the neutrality of Laos and stating that they have discussed disarmament, a nuclear test ban, and the German question.

Rocket ships soared from science fiction into reality. A U.S.-Soviet space race propelled space age development.

1961 (cont.) A Soviet memorandum issued June 4 urges demilitarization of Berlin. Premier Khrushchev declares June 15 that Moscow will conclude a treaty by year's end and will "rebuff" any Western move to enforce rights of access to West Berlin. London, Paris, and Washington reject Soviet proposals to make Berlin a free city. President Kennedy makes a national address on the Berlin crisis July 25 and proposes a 217,000-man increase in the armed forces and a $3.4 million boost in defense spending to meet the "world-wide Soviet threat."

East German authorities close the border between East and West Berlin August 13, and the Berlin Wall erected from August 15 to August 17 stops movement from East Berlin to West Berlin. The East German parliament has built the Berlin Wall in response to a communique from Warsaw Pact nations appealing for a halt in the mass exodus of East Berliners to the West.

Some 1,500 troops enter Berlin in mid-August to reinforce the Western garrison, East Berlin authorities block entry of U.S. civilians October 26 demanding that the civilians show identity papers, U.S. and Soviet tanks move briefly to the Friedrichstrasse crossing point but they are withdrawn October 28.

China's Premier Chou En-lai walks out of a Soviet party congress at Moscow October 23 heralding a break in Sino-Soviet relations.

Premier Khrushchev declares November 7 that he is willing to postpone settlement of the Berlin issue.

The African charter of Casablanca proclaimed January 7 by the heads of state of Ghana, Guinea, Mali, Morocco, and the United Arab Republic meeting at Casablanca announces that a NATO-like organization of African states will be established.

Congolese ex-premier Patrice Lumumba is killed January 17, the Katanga government announces his death February 13 saying that hostile tribesmen murdered Lumumba, but Moscow charges UN Secretary-General Dag Hammarskjöld with having been an "accomplice" in the murder and withdraws recognition of Hammarskjöld. The UN Security Council demands an inquiry into Lumumba's death and urges use of force to prevent civil war in the Congo.

The Peace Corps of Young Americans for overseas service is created March 1 by President Kennedy who has said in his inaugural address, "Ask not what your country can do for you—ask what you can do for your country." Peace Corps volunteers will work to improve education, agriculture, and living standards in Latin America, Asia, and Africa.

Algiers is seized April 21 by insurgent French troops led by General Maurice Challe, the insurrection is put down, loyal French troops reoccupy Algiers April 26, the rebel leaders are tried and convicted July 11, General Salan and others are sentenced in absentia to death as talks proceed to give Algeria independence (see 1958; 1962).

Sierra Leone in west Africa becomes an independent monarchy within the British Commonwealth.

Tanganyika in east Africa gains full internal self-government May 1 with Julius Nyerere as premier.

The United States of the Congo is founded May 12 with her capital at Leopoldville as hostilities continue in the Congo.

Angola begins an insurrection against the Portuguese and will continue hostilities until Lisbon offers independence in 1974.

Rwanda has been proclaimed a republic January 28 and Gregoire Kayibanda is proclaimed president October 26 following new elections in which the Hutu party has gained victory.

South Africa severs her ties with the British Commonwealth May 31 and becomes a republic with Charles R. Swart as president. Ghana refuses to recognize the new republic.

UN Secretary-General Dag Hammarskjöld is killed September 18 at age 56 when his plane crashes in the Congo en route to a meeting with the governor of Katanga Moise Tshombe whose army is fighting UN forces attempting to disarm Katanga troops. U Thant of Burma is unanimously elected to succeed Hammarskjöld November 3, he has served as acting secretary general and has ordered UN commanders in the Congo to take all necessary action to restore the UN position at the Katanga capital of Elizabethville, and a cease-fire goes into effect December 21.

Syrian troops revolt September 28, the Syrian revolutionary command sets up a civilian government, it proclaims independence from the United Arab Republic September 29.

The first manned space ship circles the earth April 12 in 89.1 minutes at an altitude of 187.7 miles. Soviet astronaut Yuri Aleskeyevich Gagarin, 27, makes the orbit in the space vehicle Vostok I, and astronaut (or cosmonaut) Gherman Titov, orbits the earth 17 times less than 4 months later (see Glenn, 1962).

U.S. Navy Commander Alan B. Shepard, Jr., makes the first U.S. manned space expedition May 5.

A thermonuclear device tested in the Novaya Zemlya area of the U.S.S.R. October 30 creates a shock wave that circles the earth in 36 hours, 27 minutes. Experts estimate the power of the device at upwards of 57 megatons (57 million tons of trinitrotoluene—TNT) and two more shock waves follow the first.

The UN General Assembly condemns South Africa's apartheid policies April 13.

"Freedom riders" begin a civil rights demonstration at Birmingham, Ala., May 4 in a move organized by the 19-year-old bi-racial Congress of Racial Equality (CORE) to overturn segregation practices in the Deep South. A white mob attacks the freedom riders May 20 at Montgomery, Ala., U.S. marshals sent in by Attorney General Robert F. Kennedy restore order and maintain safe passage for travelers in interstate commerce, but similar demonstrations occur in Louisiana and other states (*see* Supreme Court, 1962).

Britain's minister of health Enoch Powell increases British Health Service charges February 1.

Phocomelia deforms 302 newborn infants in West Germany, a Hamburg physician notes that mothers of several of the infants have been taking the tranquilizer drug thalidomide, and the German Ministry of Health issues a warning to physicians (*see* 1960; 1962).

Aldactazide (spironolactone hydrochlorathiazide) is introduced by G. D. Searle to counteract high blood pressure and edema (*see* Aldactone, 1960).

An Alliance for Progress that will spur economic and social development of Latin-American countries which cooperate with the United States is formed at Punta del Este, Uruguay, and is announced by President Kennedy in March. Agrarian reform and tax reform are major objectives of the new *Alianza* created in August by an agreement signed by the United States and 19 Latin-American countries which are promised $10 billion in U.S. aid over a 10-year period.

A Latin-American free trade association comes into force June 2.

U.S. ambassador to the United Nations Adlai Stevenson urges that the developed countries of the world each contribute 1 percent of their Gross National Product to the development of the emerging nations.

The British farthing ceases to be legal tender as of January 1.

The South African Rand becomes legal tender February 14 as South Africa adopts the decimal system.

Britain's Chancellor of the Exchequer Selwyn Lloyd announces an austerity program July 17 to improve the nation's trade deficit. His emergency budget imposes a hold on wages and raises the bank rate from 5 percent to 7 percent.

New York's First National City Bank offers fixed-term certificates of deposit that pay a higher rate of interest than is permitted on savings accounts. Citibank offers the CDs in denominations as low as $500 and other banks soon follow suit as depositors seek ways to keep inflation from eroding their savings.

The U.S. Gross National Product reaches $521 billion, up 60 percent since World War II as measured in constant dollars.

Ling-Temco-Vought (LTV) is created by Texas entrepreneur James J. Ling, 38, who started Ling Electric Company in the late 1940s with $6,000 earned in some quick real estate deals. He merges his company with Temco Electronics and merges Ling-Temco with Chance Vought Corporation despite objections from the Justice Department as he begins a new conglomerate (*see* United Aircraft, 1920; Wilson, 1967).

The S.S. *France* launched by the Compagnie Generale Transatlantique is the longest and probably the last of the great transatlantic passenger liners. Measuring 1,035.2 feet in overall length, the $81.3 million 66,348-ton French Line ship will make her maiden voyage from Le Havre to New York beginning February 3 of next year.

The S.S. *Canberra* is launched for the Cunard Line. The 44,807-ton passenger liner is 818.5 feet in length.

The first London minicabs are introduced March 6 by Carline of Wimbledon which begins to replace the large, comfortable Austin taxicabs in London.

Britain's Standard-Triumph International is merged into Leyland Motors, Ltd.

The Department of Justice indicts General Motors Corporation for having forced most U.S. railroads to buy locomotives made by GM's ElectroMotive Division or risk having GM cars shipped by other carriers. The criminal proceedings will be dropped in December of 1964.

The United States has 11.7 million trucks, up from 8.62 million in 1951.

U.S. television programming is a "vast wasteland," says F.C.C. chairman Newton N. Minow, 35, in a May address to the National Association of Broadcasters convention at Washington, D.C. "I invite you to sit down in front of your television set when your station goes on the air, and stay there. You will see a vast wasteland—a procession of game shows, violence, audience participation shows, formula comedies about totally unbelievable families ... blood and thunder ... mayhem, violence, sadism, murder ... private eyes, more violence, and cartoons ... and, endlessly, commercials—many screaming, cajoling, and offending. ..."

The IBM Selectric typewriter designed by Eliot Fette Noyes, 51, is introduced by International Business Machines (*see* computer, 1955). The Selectric has a moving "golf ball" cluster of interchangeable type, it will be linked in 1964 to a magnetic tape recorder that will permit automated, individually addressed original copies of any letter, and by 1975 it will account for an estimated 70 to 80 percent of the electric typewriter market.

Newsweek magazine is purchased from the Vincent Astor estate by the *Washington Post* Company whose president Philip L. Graham, 46, is the son-in-law of the late Eugene Meyer (*see* 1937).

Harper & Row is created by a merger of New York's 144-year-old Harper Bros. with the Evanston, Ill., textbook publishing house Row, Peterson & Co.

The Merriam-Webster Dictionary, whose Second Edition appeared in 1934, appears in an updated Third Edition that brings protests from self-appointed guardians of the language. The editors have dropped the label "colloquial," saying they will not attempt to dictate usage, and they list "like" as a conjunction with no suggestion of impurity.

1961 (cont.) Nonfiction *The Wretched of the Earth* by Frantz Fanon who has supported Algerian nationalism, has gone to Moscow in search of treatment for leukemia, has come to the United States for medical help, but dies at Washington, D.C., of double pneumonia December 6 at age 36; *Nobody Knows My Name* (essays) by James Baldwin who returned to the United States from France in 1957 but will live much of his life abroad.

Fiction *Cat and Mouse* (*Katz und Maus*) by Günter Grass; *A House for Mr. Biswas* by Trinidadian novelist V. S. (Vidiadhur Surajprasad) Naipaul, 29; *Catch-22* by U.S. novelist Joseph Heller, 38, who has taken 7 years to write his work about a World War II bomber group that is a metaphor for U.S. society: "There was only one catch and that was Catch-22, which specified that a concern for one's own safety in the face of dangers that were real and immediate was the process of a rational mind. Orr was crazy and he could be grounded. All he had to do was ask: and as soon as he did he would no longer be crazy and would have to fly more missions. Or be crazy to fly more missions and sane if he didn't, but if he was sane he had to fly them. If he flew them he was crazy, didn't have to; but if he didn't want to he was sane and had to . . ."; *The Fox in the Attic* by Richard Hughes; *A New Life* by Bernard Malamud; *A Shooting Star* by Wallace Stegner; *Report to Greco* by the late Nikos Kazantzakis who died in 1957; *The Pawnbroker* by Edward Lewis Wallant; *The Prime of Miss Jean Brodie* by Muriel Spark; *Debbie Go Home* (stories) by Alan Paton; *The Spinoza of Market Street* (stories) by Isaac Bashevis Singer; *Mrs. Golightly* (stories) by Ethel Wilson; *Seduction of the Minotaur* by Anaïs Nin; *The Shipyard* (*El astillero*) by Juan Carlos Onetti; *A Passion in Rome* by Morley Callahan; *Franny and Zoey* by J. D. Salinger; *Riders in the Chariot* by Patrick White; *Thunderball* by Ian Fleming; *A Burnt Out Case* by Graham Greene.

Poetry Soviet authorities denounce Yevtgeny Yetvushenko for a poem about the Nazi massacre of Ukrainians at Babi Yar in 1941. "No monument stands over Babi Yar./ A drop sheer as a crude gravestone./ I am afraid," the poem begins, and critics interpret the verse as a protest against Soviet anti-Semitism.

Painting *Still Life with Lamp Light* by Pablo Picasso; *Blue II* by Joan Miró; *Omicron* by Morris Louis; *New Madrid* by Frank Stella; *Still-Life No. 14* by Tom Wesselmann; *Parts of the Face* by Larry Rivers; *Year of Meteors* and the diptych *EAT/DIE* by U.S. abstract impressionist Robert Indiana (Robert Clark), 34, who recalls Depression days when roadside diners made from converted railway cars flashed the word EAT at a time when many Americans could not afford a decent meal. Augustus John dies at Fordingbridge, Hampshire, October 31 at age 83; Grandma Moses (Anna Mary Robertson Moses) dies at Hoosick Falls, N.Y., December 13 at age 101.

The Barnes Foundation established by the late Argyrol magnate Albert C. Barnes opens to the public at Merion, Pa., 10 years after the death of the chemist at age 79 in an automobile accident. Housed in a 39-year-old French-style mansion, the Barnes collection includes more than 100 Renoirs, vast numbers of Cézannes, Matisses, Rousseaus, Soutines, and Picassos, and case after case of African, Egyptian, Greek, and medieval sculpture. It has an estimated value of $100 million, but the Foundation has agreed to open the collection on a limited basis only after taxpayer suits threatened its tax-exempt status.

Kodachrome II color film introduced by Eastman Kodak Company is 2½ times faster than the Kodachrome introduced in 1936 (*see* Ektachrome, 1946; Instamatic, 1963).

Theater *The American Dream* by Edward Albee 1/24 at New York's off-Broadway York Theater, 370 perfs.; *Mary, Mary* by U.S. playwright Jean Kerr, 37, 3/8 at New York's Helen Hayes Theater, with Barbara Bel Geddes, Barry Nelson, 1,572 perfs.; *Luther* by John Osborne 6/26 at Nottingham's Theatre Royale; *Purlie Victorious* by U.S. playwright Ossie Davis, 44, 9/28 at New York's Cort Theater, with Davis as Purlie Victorious Judson, Ruby Dee, Godfrey Cambridge, Alan Alda, 261 perfs.; *Gideon* by Paddy Chayefsky 11/9 at New York's Plymouth Theater, with Fredric March, George Segal, 236 perfs.; *Andorra* by Max Frisch 11/2 at Zurich's Schauspielhaus; *The Detour* (*Der Abstecher*) by German playwright Martin Walser, 34, 11/28 at Munich's Werkramm Theater der Kammerspiele; *The Night of the Iguana* by Tennessee Williams 12/28 at New York's Royale Theater, with Patrick O'Neal, Bette Davis, Margaret Leighton, Alan Webb, 316 perfs.

Films Roman Polanski's *Knife in the Water;* François Truffaut's *Jules and Jim;* Stanley Kramer's *Judgment at Nuremberg* with Spencer Tracy, Burt Lancaster, Richard Widmark, Maximilian Schell, Montgomery Clift; John Huston's *The Misfits* with Marilyn Monroe, Montgomery Clift, Clark Gable (who dies 11/16 at age 59); Robert Rossen's *The Hustler* with Jackie Gleason (as "Minnesota Fats"), Paul Newman, Piper Laurie, George C. Scott; Daniel Petrie's *Raisin in the Sun* with Sidney Poitier, Claudia McNeil, Ruby Dee, Diana Sands, Ivan Dixon; Blake Edwards's *Breakfast at Tiffany's* with Audrey Hepburn, George Peppard, Martin Balsam, Patricia Neal, Mickey Rooney; Elia Kazan's *Splendor in the Grass* with Natalie Wood, Warren Beatty, Zohra Lampert, Pat Hingle, Audrey Christie, Sandy Dennis, Barbara Loden; Walt Disney's *101 Dalmatians;* Samuel Bronston's *El Cid* with Charlton Heston, Sophia Loren; Alan Resnais's *Last Year at Marienbad;* Vittorio De Sica's *Two Women* with Sophia Loren, Eleanora Brown, Jean-Paul Belmondo; Pier Paolo Pasolini's *Accatone;* Satyajit Ray's *Two Daughters;* Yasujiro Ozu's *The End of Summer;* Jack Clayton's *The Innocents* with Deborah Kerr, Michael Redgrave, Martin Stephens, Pamela Franklin in a film version of the 1898 Henry James short story "The Turn of the Screw"; George Pollock's *Murder She Said* with Margaret Rutherford (as Miss Marple), James Robertson Justice, Arthur Kennedy.

Hollywood musicals   Robert Wise's *West Side Story* with Natalie Wood, Rita Moreno, Richard Beymer, choreography by Jerome Robbins.

Stage musicals   *Carnival* 4/13 at New York's Imperial Theater, with Anna Maria Alberghetti, Kaye Ballard, Jerry Orbach, music and lyrics by Bob Merrill, 719 perfs.; *Stop the World I Want to Get Off* 7/23 at the Queen's Theatre, London, with Anthony Newley, 29, music and lyrics by Leslie Bricusse, 30, and Newley, songs that include "Gonna Build Me a Mountain," "What Kind of Fool Am I?" 485 perfs.; *Milk and Honey* 10/10 at New York's Martin Beck Theater, with Robert Weede, Mimi Benzell, Molly Picon, music and lyrics by Jerry Herman, songs that include "Shalom," "That Was Yesterday," 543 perfs.; *How to Succeed in Business Without Really Trying* 10/14 at New York's 46th Street Theater, with Robert Morse, Rudy Vallee, book by Shepherd Mead, music and lyrics by Frank Loesser, songs that include "I Believe in You," "Brotherhood of Man," 1,417 perfs.; *Subways Are for Sleeping* 12/27 at New York's St. James Theater, with Sydney Chaplin, Carol Lawrence, Orson Bean, music by Jule Styne, lyrics by Betty Comden and Adolph Green, songs that include "Comes Once in a Lifetime," 205 perfs.

Oratorio   *Jacob's Ladder* (*Die Jakobsleiter*) by the late Arnold Schoenberg 6/17 at Vienna.

First performances   *Gloria* by Francis Poulenc 1/20 at Boston's Symphony Hall; Symphony No. 7 by Walter Piston 2/10 at Philadelphia's Academy of Music; Symphony No. 12 (*The Year 1917*) by Dmitri Shostakovich 10/9 at Leningrad.

Popular songs   "Moon River" by Henry Mancini, lyrics by Johnny Mercer (for the film *Breakfast at Tiffany's*); "It Was a Very Good Year" by Ervin Drake.

Bob Dylan begins singing at Greenwich Village, New York, coffeehouses, is discovered by Columbia Records vice-president John Hammond, and releases his first album. The 20-year-old Minnesotan has changed his name from Robert Zimmerman in honor of the late Welsh poet Dylan Thomas and he will provide civil rights demonstrators and student protest movements of the 1960s with their anthems "Blowin' in the Wind" and "The Times, They Are A-Changin'."

The Supremes sign a contract with Berry Gordy's 4-year-old Motown Corporation and cut their first records. Detroit singers Diana Ross, Mary Wilson, and Florence Ballard are still in their teens but as The Supremes they will make eight gold records in less than 2 years and will have seven top records.

U.S. saxophonist John William Coltrane gains his first wide acclaim at age 35 with a December 1 recording of his John Coltrane Quartet.

Mikhail Botvinnik regains the world chess title May 12 by defeating Mikhail Tal and winning the cham-

pionship for an unprecedented third time at age 49 (*see* 1960; 1963).

The Minnesota Twins play their first season.

Roger Maris of the New York Yankees breaks Babe Ruth's home run record of 60 October 1 at Yankee Stadium, but purists will maintain that the ball Ruth hit was heavier and that Ruth set his record in a 154-game season while the October 1 game is the 163rd (and last) Yankee game for 1961.

The New York Yankees win the World Series by defeating the Cincinnati Reds 4 games to 1.

U.S. cigarette makers spend $115 million on television advertising, up from $40 million in 1957 (*see* Surgeon General's Report, 1964; Banzhaf, 1966).

The Death and Life of Great American Cities by U.S. social critic Jane Jacobs observes that cities were safer and more pleasant when they consisted of neighborhood communities where people lived in relatively low-priced buildings, knew their neighbors, and lived in the streets and on their doorsteps rather than in the depersonalized environment characteristic of modern cities (*see* Genovese murder, 1964).

The City in History by Lewis Mumford is published.

New York adopts a new zoning resolution that permits buildings to contain a maximum of 12 times as much floor space as the area of the original site with special bonuses for enlightened land use (*see* 1916: the Equitable Building of 1915 contained nearly 30 times as much floor space as was contained in its land site). Chief effect of the new resolution will be to encourage architects to set off their buildings with open plazas.

A new Equitable Building designed by Skidmore, Owings & Merrill goes up on New York's Avenue of the Americas between 51st and 52nd Streets.

New York's Chase Manhattan Bank building is completed by Skidmore, Owings & Merrill in lower Manhattan on a site bounded by William, Nassau, Liberty, and Pine Streets. The 60-story glass and aluminum tower gives the financial district its first open plaza.

New York's First National City Bank building completed on Park Avenue takes up the entire block between 53rd and 54th Streets, extending east to Lexington Avenue. Citibank acquired the site for the 39-story tower from the estate of the late Vincent Astor who had intended to erect a building with an open plaza such as that of the Seagram Building immediately to the south.

Century City goes up on a 180-acre site in west Los Angeles formerly owned by Twentieth Century Fox studios. Aluminum Corporation of America (Alcoa) pursues a grandiose scheme for a city within a city that will provide homes for 12,000 with office and retail space for 20,000, a scheme projected by New York real estate operator William Zeckendorf.

1961 (cont.) Haleakala National Park is established by act of Congress in the new state of Hawaii. It's 26,403 acres include the dormant 10,023-foot Haleakala Volcano.

The Hawaii legislature enacts the first statewide land-use zoning plan, setting aside some land for agriculture, some for conservation, and some for urban development.

A study by the California Wildland Research Center reveals that only 17 million acres of U.S. wilderness remain, down from 55 million in 1926. Virgin land has been disappearing for 35 years at the rate of a million acres per year; the largest single unit of wilderness remaining embraces 2 million acres (*see* 1964).

A conference aimed at preserving Africa's wildlife convenes in Tanganyika in September.

China suffers further crop failures (*see* 1960; 1963).

Widespread mechanical harvesting of processing tomatoes for use in canning, ketchup, paste, sauces, tomato juice, and tomato soup begins in California as farmers plant the tough-skinned VF 145-B7879 variety developed by researchers at the Davis campus of the University of California. Rising labor costs have threatened the industry in California which produces much of the world's processing tomatoes, the new tomato will prove extremely sensitive to temperature variations and its yield per acre will be relatively low, but improved varieties will be introduced and by 1975 California will be producing more than 7 million tons of processing tomatoes per year, up from 1.3 million in 1954 (table tomatoes will continue to be picked by hand partly because machine-harvested tomatoes must be in rows separated by wide spaces to permit passage of machines).

Britain and Iceland settle a fisheries dispute but controversy over fishing rights in the North Atlantic will continue with "cod wars" between the two.

Calories Don't Count by Brooklyn, N.Y., physician Herman Taller, 52, is a U.S. best seller. The book urges overweight people to cut out carbohydrates and increase consumption of fats (*see* Stefansson, 1946; DuPont diet, 1953; Stillman, 1967).

Pepperidge Farm, Inc., is acquired by Campbell Soup Company (*see* 1940).

Planters Nut and Chocolate Company is acquired by Standard Brands (*see* 1916; 1929; Curtiss, 1964).

Frito-Lay, Inc., is created by a merger of Atlanta's H. W. Lay Company and the Frito Company of Dallas (*see* 1932; 1939; Pepsico, 1965).

R. J. Reynolds Company acquires Pacific Hawaiian Products Company and its Hawaiian Punch as the big tobacco company begins to diversify (*see* Winston, 1955). Developed in the late 1930s and distributed nationally since 1950, Hawaiian Punch contains some pineapple, papaya, guava, passionfruit, and other juices but is nearly 90 percent water and sugar (*see* Penick and Ford, 1965).

Sprite is introduced by Coca-Cola Company. The new lemon-lime drink competes with 7-Up (*see* 1933; Tab, 1963).

Coffee-Mate nondairy creamer is introduced by Carnation Company (*see* Pream, 1952). The powder is made of corn syrup solids, vegetable fat, sodium caseinate, and various additives (*see* "contented cows," 1906).

Country Corn Flakes breakfast food is introduced by General Mills (*see* 1959).

Total breakfast food is introduced by General Mills which will promote the cereal for its nutritional qualities (*see* Lucky Charms, 1964).

Green Giant enters the frozen foods business with frozen June peas, niblet corn, green beans, and baby lima beans frozen in a pouch with butter sauce (*see* 1958).

Canned pet foods are among the three top-selling categories in U.S. grocery stores. Americans feed an estimated 25 million pet dogs, 20 million pet cats.

McDonald's hamburger stands begin a vast proliferation as Ray Kroc buys out the McDonald brothers and acquires all rights to the McDonald name (*see* 1952). Kroc has organized a chain of more than 200 stands, he has borrowed $2.7 million to buy out the McDonalds, and he will build McDonald's into a chain of more than 3,500 outlets in the United States plus more in Europe, Japan, and Australia.

Mastering the Art of French Cooking by Julia Child, Simone Beck, and Louisette Bertholle demystifies good French cooking (*see* 1951; Child, 1963).

A birth control clinic opens at New Haven, Conn., but is forced to close after 9 days. The order will not be rescinded for nearly 4 years (*see* New York, 1929; Supreme Court, 1965).

The Lippes Loop intrauterine device for contraception developed by Buffalo, N.Y., physician Jack Lippes will be implanted within 8 years in an estimated 8 million women worldwide.

China's population reaches an estimated 650 million, India has 445 million, the U.S.S.R. 215, the United States 185 (up from 141 at the close of World War II), Indonesia 100, Pakistan 97, Japan 95, Brazil 73, West Germany 58, the United Kingdom 54.

New York and its suburban environs have a population of 14.2 million, Tokyo 10 million, London 8.3, Paris 7.7, Shanghai more than 7, Buenos Aires 6.9, Los Angeles 6.6, Chicago more than 6, Moscow 5.2, Mexico City 5, Calcutta 4.5, Bombay 4.2, Peking 4.2, Philadelphia 3.7.

1962 The Cuban missile crisis in October produces a tense nuclear confrontation between the United States and the Soviet Union. U.S. aerial surveillance has discovered Soviet offensive missile and bomber bases in Cuba, President Kennedy orders an air and sea "quarantine" of Cuba to prevent shipment of arms to Fidel Castro, Attorney General Robert Kennedy meets with the Soviet ambassador Anatoly Dobrynin at the Soviet embassy, he learns that Moscow will withdraw the missiles with their atomic warheads from Cuba if U.S. nuclear missiles are withdrawn from Turkey, President Kennedy rejects the deal when it is publicly offered by Premier Khrushchev, but U.S. General Lauris J. Norstad who opposes quick removal of the 15 obsolescent Jupiter rockets from Turkey is unexpectedly retired from his post as NATO commander, Khrushchev agrees to dismantle the Cuban missile sites and remove them, the Cuban blockade is ended, and the U.S. missiles in Turkey are quietly removed.

Soviet authorities have released U.S. espionage pilot Gary Powers February 10 in exchange for Soviet espionage agent Colonel Rudolf Abel who has been in U.S. hands since 1957 (see Powers, 1960).

South Vietnamese forces launch "Operation Sunrise" March 22 to eliminate Vietcong guerillas. U.S. money, arms, and field observers help the South Vietnamese. The international control commission on Indo-China, composed of Canadian, Indian, and Polish representatives, reports June 2 that North Vietnam is supplying the Vietcong rebels in violation of the 1954 Geneva agreement on Vietnam, but Polish representatives do not sign the report.

Civil war threatens in the Independent Congo Republic following President Joseph Kasavubu's repudiation of the Fundamental Law of May 1960. Fighting breaks out at Stanleyville January 13, UN Secretary-General U Thant orders UN troops in the Congo to stop the fighting, the Katanga assembly agrees February 15 to reunite Katanga with the Congo, but new fighting breaks out in October between Katanga troops and the forces of the central government.

An organization of African states is established in early February by leaders of 20 nations meeting at Lagos, Nigeria, but the rebel Algerian provisional government is not invited and violence continues in Algeria where the head of the illegal Secret Army Organization (OAS) has issued a manifesto calling for the mobilization of Algerians against a cease-fire with France.

The Lagos meeting (above) is boycotted by Ghana, Guinea, Mali, Morocco, and the United Arab Republic whose ministers meet at Casablanca in April and agree to set up an African common market.

Ghana's Kwama N. Nkrumah declares a general amnesty for refugee Ghanians May 5 and orders the release of many political prisoners.

Burundi in Central Africa gains full independence from Belgium July 1 with a monarchical government dominated by the Tutsi (Batusi and Watusi) minority. Attempts to overthrow the government by Hutu tribesmen will be defeated and Tutsi from Burundi will attack Rwanda until 1967.

Paris proclaims Algerian independence July 3, 3 days after a national referendum in which the Algerians have voted for independence by nearly 6 million to 16,534. Leaders of the Algerian provisional government have a falling out that leads to a civil war which continues until mid-September, but in late September the Algerian national assembly asks Mohammed Ben Bella to form a cabinet and he will be president until he is deposed in 1965.

Eritrea becomes an integral part of Ethiopia after 10 years of union on a federal basis but conflict will persist between the Moslem Eritreans and the Christian Ethiopians.

Jamaica, B. W. I., becomes an independent dominion within the British Commonwealth August 6. Trinidad and Tobago obtain independence from Britain August 31.

Uganda becomes an independent state within the British Commonwealth October 9. The country adopts a federal form of government to overcome the reluctance of Buganda's king Sir Edward Mutesa II to abandon the privileged position of his tribe and his country, but conflict will continue between President Mutesa and Milton Obote (see 1966).

Tanganyika becomes a republic December 9 with Julius K. Nyerere as president.

Western Samoa gains independence from New Zealand.

U.S. manufacturing firms with federal contracts of $50,000 or more are ordered January 29 to report the number of blacks on their payrolls.

Minimum wages for migratory Mexican workers in the United States are established March 9 by regulations issued by the Labor Department.

The National Farm Workers Association (NFWA) to represent stoop-labor in California's Coachella, Imperial, and San Joaquin Valleys is founded by community leader Cesar Estrado Chavez, 32 (see 1965).

U.S. court action to halt racial segregation in hospitals built with federal funds is ordered by the Justice Department May 8.

Southern School News reports that at least some token school integration has taken place in response to the Supreme Court decision of 1954 in all Southern states except Alabama, Mississippi, and South Carolina but that practically no action has been taken in Northern school districts.

Israeli authorities hang Adolf Eichmann May 21 in punishment for his concentration camp activities during World War II.

Racial tension grips the U.S. South as black student James Howard Meredith, 29, attempts to enter the University of Mississippi which has been ordered to admit the Air Force veteran by a federal appelate court whose order has been upheld by the Supreme Court. Rioting breaks out on the "Old Miss" campus September 30 despite a televised appeal by President Kennedy for peaceful desegregation, Meredith is accompanied by U.S. marshalls, federal troops are

The Berlin Wall exemplified cold war hostilities between East and West. Stalin's ghost still hung over Europe.

sent to stand guard on the campus and to maintain order beginning October 1, and Meredith begins 10 months at the campus living under constant federal guard (*see* 1966).

A New Orleans federal appeals court orders the Justice Department to bring criminal proceedings against Mississippi's governor Ross Barnett who has interfered with the court's order to admit black students to "Old Miss" (above).

The Supreme Court reverses the convictions of six Freedom Riders who were convicted in Louisiana after trying to desegregate a bus terminal.

Harlem Youth Opportunities Unlimited (HARYOU) is founded by City College of New York psychology professor Kenneth Bancroft Clark, 48, to combat unemployment among youth in the New York ghetto and to supplement local teaching facilities.

President Kennedy embargoes nearly all trade with Cuba February 3 (*see* cigars, below).

President Kennedy reduces tariff duties on some 1,000 items March 7 to increase foreign trade.

African ministers meeting at Casablanca in April (above) agree not only to establish a common market but also to set up an African payments union and an African development bank.

Wall Street's Dow Jones Industrial Average falls to 535.76, down from 734.91 late last year.

Electronic Data Systems, Inc., is founded by Dallas IBM salesman H. Ross Perot, 32, whose new data processing firm will earn him a fortune of some $600 million when EDS goes public in 1968.

The first U.S. Earth orbits are made February 7 by astronaut John Glenn who is launched into space and who makes three orbits in the Mercury capsule

Friendship 7, covering 81,000 miles at an altitude of 160 miles (*see* 1961; 1969; Glenn, 1957).

John Foster Dulles International Airport opens 24 miles from downtown Washington to supplement Baltimore's Friendship Airport and Washington's National Airport. Named after former President Eisenhower's secretary of state, Dulles is the first civil airport specifically designed to handle jet aircraft, its terminal has been designed by Eero Saarinen, and its ingenious mobile lounges are adjustable to the height of any aircraft door and save passengers from having to make the long finger corridor walk to the loading gate that is necessary at other airports.

Lear Jet Corporation is founded by William P. Lear who sells his interest in Lear, Inc., to start the new company that will be the leading producer of private jet aircraft within 5 years (*see* 1939).

The IL-62 jet designed by S. V. Ilyushin goes into service for Aeroflot (*see* 1954; 1968).

Paris and London sign an agreement November 29 for joint design and development of a supersonic passenger plane (*see* 1969).

The 17.7-mile Chesapeake Bay bridge-tunnel-highway opens to link Cape Charles, Va., with Norfolk, replacing the ferry that has operated for years at the entrance to Chesapeake Bay.

Europe's Arlberg-Orient Express goes out of service May 27 after nearly 79 years of operation between Paris and Istanbul and the Simplon-Orient Express ends service as well. Both have been victims of the airplane that has cut travel time between Paris and Istanbul to 2 hours.

Consolidated Edison Company announces plans to build a million kilowatt nuclear generating station at Ravenswood, Queens, in the heart of New York City. The Atomic Energy Commission rejects the proposal but approves construction of a plant 28 miles north of the city at Indian Point on the Hudson River (*see* 1963; Chicago, 1960).

Britain and France remove thalidomide from the market (*see* 1960; 1961). The *Washington Post* credits Food and Drug Administration researcher Frances Kelsey with having prevented thalidomide-produced birth defects in thousands of U.S. infants (July 15 editorial), she receives praise in the Senate for her "courage and devotion to the public interest," President Kennedy gives her a medal for distinguished service in a White House ceremony, but U.S. physicians have received thousands of sample packages of Kevadon and they have given a few to expectant mothers.

The thalidomide affair (above) spurs Congress to pass the Kefauver legislation giving the FDA extensive new authority to regulate the introduction of new drugs. The new law also contains provisions to prevent drug firms from overcharging and from confusing buyers of prescription drugs.

President Kennedy has requested a law that will police the pharmaceutical industry in a message that asked also for a broad program of consumer protection, a "Consumer Bill of Rights" that would include a "Truth in Lending" law and a "Truth in Packaging" law (see 1968; 1966).

The first successful measles vaccine is produced by John F. Enders, now 65, but it will not be introduced until 1966 (see Salk, 1952).

The Essalen Institute encounter group mental therapy center is founded at Big Sur, Calif., by entrepreneurs Michael Murphy, 32, and Richard Price who will attract such psychologists and psychotherapists as Fritz Perls.

Cigar smokers are the chief U.S. victims of President Kennedy's embargo on trade with Cuba (above). U.S. cigar sales exceed 6 billion per year with 95 percent of Cuban cigars rolled and wrapped in U.S. plants, but without Cuban tobacco cigar sales will fall to 5.3 billion per year by 1976 despite population growth.

COMSAT (Communications Satellite Corporation) is created by Congress to handle space communications on a profitmaking basis under government supervision (see Echo I, 1960; Early Bird, 1965).

Telstar I is launched the night of July 10. The new satellite is used to transmit the first live transatlantic telecasts between the United States and Britain.

Some 90 percent of U.S. households have at least one TV set. Thirteen percent have more than one.

American Broadcasting Company (ABC) begins color telecasts for 3.5 hours per week beginning in September, 68 percent of NBC prime evening time programming is in color, but CBS confines itself to black and white after having transmitted in color earlier. All three networks will be transmitting entirely in color by 1967.

NBC's Tonight Show introduces Johnny Carson as host beginning October 1 after 8 years in which Steve Allen has been host. "Hee-e-e-e-re's Johnny" will introduce the show for more than 16 years.

West Germany's Der Spiegel publishes an exposé of Defense Minister Franz Josef Strauss revealing the weakness of German armed forces despite the expenditure of large sums of money. Staff members of Der Spiegel are arrested in late October on orders from Strauss, Chancellor Adenauer accepts Strauss's resignation under pressure from public opinion, but Der Spiegel publisher Rudolf Augstein will not be released from prison for 4 months (see 1946).

Former Vice President Richard M. Nixon holds a press conference in November after losing a bid to defeat California governor Edmund G. "Pat" Brown by nearly 300,000 votes: "As I leave you I want you to know—just think how much you're going to be losing. You won't have Nixon to kick around any more, because, gentlemen, this is my last press conference." Nixon complains that the press has been

against him ever since his attacks on Alger Hiss in the late 1940s.

Nonfiction *The Gutenberg Galaxy* by Canadian critic-teacher Marshall McLuhan, 51, says, "The medium *is* the message" and television can save mankind. The spoken word is richer in meaning and more capable of carrying a complex message ("hotter") than the written or printed word, says McLuhan, so whereas the invention of printing strained man's limited visual sense the electronic media have no such limitation; *Travels with Charley in Search of America* by John Steinbeck.

Fiction *One Day in the Life of Ivan Denisovich* (*Odin den v zhizni Ivana Denisovicha*) by Soviet novelist Aleksandr Isayevich Solzhenitsyn, 44, is based on years spent in Siberian forced labor camps and has been completed with help from *Novy Mir* editor-poet Aleksandr Tvardovsky; *One Flew Over the Cuckoo's Nest* by U.S. novelist Ken Kesey, 27, is a satire on the dehumanization of Western society based in part on the author's experiences as a mental hospital employee; *The Reivers* by William Faulkner, who dies at his home in Oxford, Miss., July 6 at age 64; *Letting Go* by Philip Roth; *Ship of Fools* by Katherine Anne Porter; *Aura* by Mexican novelist Carlos Fuentes, 33; *Clockwork Orange* by English novelist Anthony Burgess (Jon Anthony Burgess Wilson), 45; *Morte d'Urban* by J. F. Powers; *Another Country* by James Baldwin; *The Golden Notebook* by Doris Lessing; *Wolf Willow* by Wallace Stegner; *The Garden of the Finzi Continis* (*Il giardino dei Finzi Contini*) by Italian novelist Giorgio Bassani, 46; *Pale Fire* by Vladimir Nabokov; *Reinhart in Love* by U.S. novelist Thomas (Louis) Berger, 38.

Poetry *The Jacob's Ladder* by Denise Levertov; *Pictures from Bruegel* by William Carlos Williams; *All My Pretty Ones* by Anne Sexton; *A Sad Heart at the Supermarket* by Randall Jarrell; *Silence in the Snowy Fields* by U.S. poet Robert Bly, 36.

Painting *Fool's House* by Jasper Johns; *Ace* by Robert Rauschenberg; *Silver Skies* by James Rosenquist; *Star* by Robert Indiana; *Blam!* and *Head, Red and Yellow* by U.S. "pop" artist Roy Lichtenstein, 39, who has employed comic strip techniques; *100 Cans* (of Campbell's Beef Noodle Soup) and *Green Coca-Cola Bottles* by U.S. "pop" artist Andy Warhol, 32; *White-Dash Blue* by Ellsworth Kelly; *Cantabile* by Kenneth Noland; *Stripes* by Morris Louis who dies of lung cancer at Washington, D.C., September 7 at age 50 leaving behind nearly 600 unsold works. Franz Kline has died in New York May 13 at age 52.

Polaroid Corporation introduces color film invented by Edwin H. Land (see 1947). The high-speed film produces color prints in 60 seconds while Polaroid's black-and-white film produces prints in 10 seconds.

Theater *The Physicist* (*Die Physiker*) by Friedrich Dürrenmatt 2/21 at Zurich's Schauspielhaus; *Oh, Dad, Poor Dad, Mama's Hung You in the Closet and We're Feeling So Sad* by U.S. playwright Arthur Ko-

1962 (cont.) pit, 24, 2/26 at New York's off-Broadway Phoenix Theater, 454 perfs.; *The Knack* by English playwright Ann Jellicoe, 34, 3/27 at London's Royal Court Theatre; *A Thousand Clowns* by U.S. playwright-cartoonist Herb Gardner, 27, 4/5 at New York's Eugene O'Neill Theater, with Jason Robards, Jr., Sandy Dennis, 428 perfs.; *Chips with Everything* by English playwright Arnold Wesker, 29, 4/27 at London's Royal Court Theatre, with Frank Finlay, John Kelland; *The Rabbit Race* (*Esche und Angora*) by Martin Walser 9/23 at Berlin's Schillertheater; *Who's Afraid of Virginia Woolf?* by Edward Albee 10/13 at New York's Billy Rose Theater, with Arthur Hill as George, Uta Hagen as Martha, 664 perfs.; *Lord Pengo* by S. N. Behrman 11/19 at New York's Royale Theater, with Charles Boyer, Agnes Morehead, Henry Daniell, 175 perfs.; *Never Too Late* by U.S. playwright Sumner Arthur Long, 41, 11/27 at New York's Playhouse, with Paul Ford, Maureen O'Sullivan, Orson Bean, 1,007 perfs.; *Exit the King* (*Le roi se meurt*) by Eugène Ionesco 12/5 at the Théâtre de L'Alliance, Paris.

Films Michelangelo Antonioni's *La Notte* with Jeanne Moreau, Monica Vitti; Pietro Germi's *Divorce, Italian Style* with Marcello Mastroianni; Francois Truffaut's *Shoot the Piano Player;* Ingmar Bergman's *Winter Light;* David Lean's *Lawrence of Arabia* with Peter O'Toole, Omar Sharif, Alec Guinness; John Frankenheimer's *The Manchurian Candidate* with Laurence Harvey, Frank Sinatra, Janet Leigh, Angela Lansbury; Robert Mulligan's *To Kill a Mockingbird* with Gregory Peck; John Huston's *Freud* with Montgomery Clift; Stanley Kubrick's *Lolita* with James Mason, Sue Lyon, Shelley Winters, Peter Sellers; Robert Aldrich's *What Ever Happened to Baby Jane?* with Bette Davis, Joan Crawford; Peter Ustinov's *Billy Budd;* Akira Kurosawa's *Yojimbo* with Toshiro Mifune; Satyajit Ray's *Devi.*

Broadway musicals *No Strings* 3/15 at the 54th Street Theater, with Diahann Carrol, Richard Kiley, music and lyrics by Richard Rodgers, songs that include "The Sweetest Sounds," 580 perfs.; *A Funny Thing Happened on the Way to the Forum* 5/8 at the Alvin Theater, with Zero Mostel, Jack Guilford, book by Burt Shevelove and Larry Gelbert, music and lyrics by Stephen Sondheim, songs that include "Comedy Tonight," 964 perfs.; *Little Me* 11/17 at the Lunt-Fontanne Theater, with Sid Caesar, Joey Faye, Virginia Martin, book by Neil Simon, music by Cy Coleman, lyrics by Carolyn Leigh, songs that include "Real Live Girl," 257 perfs.

First performances Symphony No. 8 by Roy Harris 1/17 at San Francisco; Symphony No. 7 by David Diamond 1/26 at Philadelphia's Academy of Music; Symphony No. 12 by Darius Milhaud 2/16 at the University of California, Davis; War Requiem by Benjamin Britten 5/30 at the new Coventry Cathedral; Symphony No. 8 by Lincoln Center president William Schuman 10/4 at New York's new Philharmonic Hall (below); Symphony No. 13 by Dmitri Shostakovich 12/18 at Moscow, with voices singing words by poet Yegveny Yetvushenko that deal harshly with anti-Semitism. Premier Khrushchev suppresses the work.

New York's Philharmonic Hall opens September 23 as part of the new Lincoln Center for the Performing Arts that is nearing completion on Columbus Avenue between 62nd and 66th Streets on a site acquired with federal aid and built with contributions of more than $165 million. The 2,863-seat concert hall designed by Max Abramovitz becomes the new home of the New York Philharmonic after 69 years at Carnegie Hall, it will be renamed Avery Fisher Hall in 1974 (*see* Fisher, 1937, 1969), but its acoustics are so poor that it will undergo repeated guttings and redesigns until 1976 (*see* Opera House, 1966).

Opera *Katerina Ismailova* 12/20 at Moscow, with music by Dmitri Shostakovich who has revised his politically unacceptable 1934 opera Lady Macbeth of the Mzensk district.

"We Shall Overcome" is copyrighted by Nashville, Tenn., schoolteacher Guy Carawan who has added rhythmic punch to a song that will be the hymn of the U.S. civil rights movement and will be sung in protest demonstrations throughout the world. Royalties from the song will go to the Highlander Folk Center at Monteagle, Tenn., whose late co-director Zilphia Horton learned the song from striking black tobacco workers at Charleston, S.C., in the mid-1940s and taught it to folk singer Peter Seeger in 1947 and to Frank Hamilton (who added a verse).

Popular songs "Those Lazy, Hazy, Crazy Days of Summer" by Hoagy Carmichael, lyrics by Charles Tobias; "Days of Wine and Roses" by Henry Mancini, lyrics by Johnny Mercer (title song for Blake Edwards's film about alcoholism); "Ramblin Rose" by Noel and Joe Sherman; "The Wanderer" by Ernest Maresca; "Addio, Addio" by Migliacci and Domenico Mudugno; "I Left My Heart in San Francisco" by George Cory, lyrics by Douglas Cross; "Marty" by Johnny Burke; "The Lonely Bull" by California trumpet player-vocalist-composer Herb Alpert, 27; "Surfin' Safari" by the Beach Boys Brian Nelson, 20, Dennis Wilson, 17, Mike Love, 21, Al Jardine, 19, and Carl Wilson, 25.

Brazil retains the World Cup in football (soccer) by defeating Czechoslovakia 3 to 1 at Santiago, Chile, and wins without Pele who has torn a thigh muscle in an earlier game with the Czechs.

Australian tennis star Rod Laver, 23, wins the Grand Slam by taking the national championships of Australia, France, Britain, and the United States. He will repeat the feat in 1969.

Ohio golfer Jack William Nicklaus, 22, wins the U.S. Open by defeating Arnold Palmer in a playoff.

The New York Mets play their first season. The new team replaces the New York Giants and the Brooklyn Dodgers. The Los Angeles Dodgers and the San Francisco Giants play their first seasons, as do the Houston Astros.

The New York Yankees win the World Series by defeating the San Francisco Giants 4 games to 3.

The first Australian bid for the America's Cup in ocean yacht racing fails as the U.S. defender *Weatherly* defeats *Gretel* 4 races to 1.

Sonny Liston wins the world heavyweight boxing title September 25. The 28-year-old fighter knocks out Floyd Patterson in the first round of a championship bout at Chicago.

 New York's E. J. Korvette takes over the W. and J. Sloane store on Fifth Avenue at 47th Street and turns it into a discount department store while Sloane moves into the store on Fifth at 38th Street occupied since 1902 by Franklin Simon. Korvette's Eugene Ferkauf has parlayed his $4,000 investment of 1948 into a fortune of $50 million.

K Mart discount stores are opened by the 63-year-old S. S. Kresge Company whose five-and-ten-cent stores are losing money. By 1977 Kresge will have sales second only to those of Sears, Roebuck & Co.

Montreal's Place Ville Marie gets its first high-rise buildings with underground galleries built according to a plan put forward by New York developer William Zeckendorf.

New York's Americana Hotel opens September 24 on Seventh Avenue at 52nd Street. The 50-story, 2,000-room hotel was designed by Morris Lapidus.

Puerto Rico's Americana Hotel opens November 29 with 440 rooms in a 16-story structure on a 5-acre beachfront site in San Juan's Isla Verde section.

Silent Spring by U.S. biologist Rachel Louise Carson, 55, warns of dangers to wildlife in the indiscriminate use of persistent pesticides such as DDT (*see* 1943; Osborne, 1948).

Alaskan Eskimos are found to have high concentrations of Cesium-137 in their bodies as a result of having eaten caribou meat which is their staple food. The caribou have grazed on lichens and have absorbed fallout dust from atmospheric nuclear tests.

Petrified Forest National Park in Arizona is established by act of Congress. The 94,189-acre park embraces Indian ruins, petrified wood, and colorful desertland.

Maine's Baxter State Park is designated as such to honor former governor Percival P. Baxter who has spent 31 years acquiring piecemeal a 202,000-acre tract which he presents to the state of Maine. The park encompasses scenic forestland surrounding 5,273-foot Mt. Katahdin, Maine's highest peak.

Britain has a cold spell that freezes outdoor house pipes, interferes with plumbing, and creates general misery (*see* 1963).

Florida loses nearly 8 million citrus trees as temperatures fall to 24°F. and remain below freezing.

An International Rice Research Institute (IRRI) is established in the Philippines at Los Banos following a tour of Asian hunger areas by Rockefeller Foundation experts who include Paul Mangelsdorf, J.

George Harrar, Warren Weaver, Edwin J. Wellhausen, and Robert F. Chandler. The IRRI is supported by both the Ford and Rockefeller Foundations and by the Philippine government (*see* IR5, IR8, 1964).

The average Asian eats more than 300 pounds of rice per year as compared with 6 pounds in the West and many rice-consuming nations including the Philippines do not produce enough for domestic needs. IRRI (above) will advance the "Green Revolution" but while per capita food production in the developing countries has increased in the past decade at an annual rate of 0.7 percent it will increase at an annual rate of only 0.2 percent in the decade ahead.

Van Camp Sea Food Company is acquired by Ralston Purina Company (*see* 1926; 1961). Van Camp's Chicken of the Sea and White Star brands have made it the world's largest tuna packer.

Diet-Rite Cola is introduced nationally by Royal Crown Cola Company and is the first sugar-free soft drink to be sold to the general public nationwide in addition to diabetics. The cyclamate-sweetened cola will soon have powerful competitors (*see* 1952; 1963).

Hires Root Beer is acquired by Crush International, Inc., of Evanston, Ill. (*see* Orange Crush, 1916; Hires, 1886). The root beer is now sold mostly in bottles but Hires extract is still sold for homemade root beer.

Tab-opening aluminum end cans for soft drinks and beer developed with backing from Aluminum Corporation of America make their first appearance. Pittsburgh's Iron City Beer in tab-opening cans is test-marketed in Virginia, many brewers question whether the cans are worth their extra cost, many consumers cut their fingers opening the cans, but can designers improve the tabs, Schlitz will introduce beer in the self-opening cans on a national scale in February of next year, more than 40 brands will be sold in the cans by July, more than 65 by August, 70 percent of beer cans will be self-opening by 1965, and more than 90 percent by 1970. Discarded tabs will be a hazard for bare feet on U.S. beaches and will contribute to environmental deterioration.

Twenty-five percent of U.S. potato consumption is accounted for by canned, frozen, and dehydrated potatoes.

New York's La Grenouille opens at 3 East 52nd Street. French-American restaurateur Charles Masson, 48, has perfected his skills under Henri Soulé at Le Pavillon and his new French restaurant will become a favorite haunt of the fashion world.

China resumes the birth control campaign suspended in her Great Leap Forward Program of 1958.

A proposal by the World Health Organization that it offer family-planning advice brings rebukes by 30 countries (but *see* 1965).

Pope John XXIII convenes Vatican II October 11, less than a century after Vatican I was convened in 1869. The world's population has tripled since 1869 to 3.1 billion.

1963 The assassination of President John F. Kennedy November 22 ends an administration of 34 months that have seen the initiation of domestic social programs that Kennedy's successor will carry out. The president slumps in the seat of his open Lincoln Continental as his motorcade approaches the Dallas World Trade Center for a scheduled speech, the rifle bullets that killed him are thought to have come from the sixth floor of the Texas School Book Depository in Elm Street, Lyndon Baines Johnson is sworn in as president en route by plane to Washington.

President Kennedy's alleged assassin Lee Harvey Oswald, 24, is a Marine Corps veteran who has spent some time in the U.S.S.R., has married the daughter of a colonel in the KGB, and has handed out literature for the Fair Play for Cuba Committee at New Orleans. Dallas police arrest Oswald 80 minutes after the assassination on charges of having killed patrolman J. D. Tipit. Dallas nightclub operator Jack Ruby, 52, shoots Oswald to death November 24 in the basement of the Dallas city jail as police are moving the suspect to safer quarters, and millions watch the shooting on television (*see* Warren Commission, 1964).

"Ich bin ein Berliner," President Kennedy has said June 26 in a speech at West Berlin during a 4-day visit to West Germany. Kennedy has pledged support for efforts to defend West Berlin from Communist encroachment, to reunify Germany, and to work toward European unity. West German chancellor Konrad Adenauer resigns October 16 at age 87 and is succeeded by Ludwig Erhard, 84.

Britain's Profumo-Christine Keeler scandal makes world headlines. War Minister Lord John Dennis Profumo is charged with having been intimate with call girl Christine Keeler, 21, to whom he was introduced naked in a swimming pool by Viscount Astor's osteopath friend Stephen Ward who has his own cottage at Astor's Cliveden estate. Profumo is married to actress Valerie Hobson, but the real scandal arises from the fact that Keeler is sleeping with Soviet naval attaché Evgeny "Honeybear" Ivanov, a known spy attached to the Russian embassy who has asked Keeler to find out from Profumo when nuclear warheads will be delivered to West Germany. Profumo confesses to the affair and resigns in early June, Keeler draws a 9-month sentence in December for perjury and conspiracy to obstruct justice.

British journalist H. A. R. Philby disappears from Beirut and the Soviet Union gives him asylum July 30.

Israeli premier David Ben Gurion has resigned June 16 at age 76 and has been succeeded by former finance minister Levi Eshkol. Israeli and Syrian forces battle August 20 along the demilitarized zone north of the Sea of Galilee but UN truce observers persuade both sides to accept a cease-fire August 25.

The Federation of Malaysia formally established September 16 joins Malaya, Singapore, Sarawak, and North Borneo.

The British prime minister Harold Macmillan resigns for reasons of health October 18 at age 69. Queen Elizabeth asks the earl of Home Sir Alexander Douglas Home, 60, to form a new cabinet, he resigns his peerages and calls himself Sir Alec Douglas-Home, and he is the first prime minister to have no seat either in the House of Lords or in the Commons.

The South Vietnam government of Ngo Dinh Diem falls the night of November 1 in a coup engineered by General Duong Van Minh and other anti-Communist officers. Diem has been president since the republic was proclaimed in 1955 but his opponents kill him along with his security chief as civil war continues in Vietnam.

 "I have a dream," says Martin Luther King, Jr., in a ceremony January 1 at the Lincoln Memorial in Washington to commemorate the centennial of the Emancipation Proclamation: "I have a dream that one day, on the red hills of Georgia, sons of former slaves and the sons of former slaveowners will be able to sit down together at the table of brotherhood. . . ."

Indigent defendants in all U.S. criminal cases are ordered to be provided by the states with the services of defense attorneys. The Supreme Court makes the ruling March 18 in the case of *Gideon v. Wainright*.

Convictions by lower courts in cases of sit-ins to protest discriminatory practices by retail establishments are reversed by the Supreme Court May 20.

Women are guaranteed equal pay for equal work in legislation enacted by Congress June 10, but the law will prove difficult to enforce.

Alabama's National Guard is federalized June 11 by President Kennedy who orders Governor George C. Wallace to permit two black students to be enrolled at the University of Alabama.

NAACP leader Medger Evers, 37, is murdered June 12 in the doorway of his home at Jackson, Miss., right after a presidential broadcast on civil rights.

President Kennedy asks Congress June 19 to enact far-reaching civil rights legislation that will include provisions to bar discrimination in the use of privately owned public facilities.

More than 200,000 black and white Americans conduct a "march on Washington" August 28 to demonstrate support for civil rights.

Public schools in three Alabama cities are desegregated after President Kennedy has again federalized Alabama's National Guard in the face of Governor Wallace's continued opposition.

Four black Alabama schoolchildren are killed and 19 people are injured Sunday, September 15, when a bomb explodes at Birmingham's 16th Street Baptist Church while 200 are attending services. The deaths of Denise McNair, 11, Carole Robertson, 14, Addie Mae Collins, 14, and Cynthia Wesley, 14, provoke racial riots, police dogs are used to attack civil rights demonstrators, and two black schoolboys—Virgil

Wade, 13, and Johnnie Robinson, 16—are killed later the same day.

The first commercial nuclear reactor is installed by Jersey Central Power and Light whose 640 million kilowatt Oyster Creek plant is the first nuclear power plant large enough to compete with coal and oil fuel. The Jersey Central plant will be followed by much larger installations, 41 nuclear plants will be ordered in the next decade, 56 nuclear plants will account for 8 percent of total U.S. energy production by 1975, but growth of nuclear power will be delayed by the rising price of uranium, by worries about nuclear disasters, and by rising construction costs, and demand for electric power will fall far short of forecasts.

A nuclear-powered electric power station on the Hudson River is opened at Indian Point, N.Y., by Consolidated Edison Company (*see* fish kill, below).

Italy's Enel is founded in February to consolidate 1,200 electric plants into a single national electric energy agency under terms of a nationalization law.

The nuclear-powered submarine U.S.S. *Thresher* sinks April 10 in 8,400 feet of water 220 miles off Cape Cod killing all 129 men aboard in the worst submarine disaster of all time. The ship has put to sea with no sure way of blowing water out of her ballast tanks in an emergency at low depths and the Portsmouth Naval Shipyard has failed to test silver-brazed joints with soundwaves.

Two-thirds of the world's automobiles are in the United States (which has one-sixth of the world's population).

Trolley car service ends at Baltimore where electric trolleys were first introduced just 88 years and 84 days earlier. Buses replace the trolleys November 4.

New York renames Idlewild Airport John F. Kennedy (JFK) Airport.

An artificial heart to take over the functions of blood circulation during heart surgery is used for the first time by Houston surgeon Michael Ellis De Bakey, 54.

Valium is introduced in December by Roche laboratories whose chemist Leo Sternbach synthesized the benzodiazepine anti-anxiety drug in 1959 and which has been awaiting Food and Drug Administration approval. Five to 10 times more potent than Librium as a muscle-relaxant and anti-convulsant, Valium has no more unwanted side effects than Librium, it costs more than Librium, and it will soon be even more widely prescribed than Librium (*see* 1960).

A federal grand jury at Washington, D.C., indicts Richardson-Merrell, Inc., and three of its scientists on charges of having supplied the Food and Drug Administration with falsified data in order to receive approval for marketing the cholesterol-lowering drug MER/29. The drug produces cateracts (usually operable), hair loss, and severe skin reactions in thousands of users, the company pleads no contest to 8 of 12 counts, MER/29 will be removed from the market, Richardson-Merrell will be fined the maximum

permissible $80,000, but the firm has profits of nearly $17.8 million, up $276,000 over 1962 profits.

Krebiozen cannot prevent cancer, says the Food and Drug Administration, which prosecutes promoters of the substance. Yugoslavian-American physician Steven Durovic, 65, and his lawyer brother Marko, 62, arrived in the United States in 1949 with half a teaspoonful of the substance which Stevan claimed to have developed in Argentina from the blood serum of horses stimulated by injections of a fungus extract, the Durovics have won support from famed physiologist Andrew C. Ivy, now 70, dozens of people insist that Krebiozen is effective, it will enrich the Durovics by some $4 million before it is outlawed, but the FDA shows that it is simply mineral oil with or without traces of the amino acid creatinine.

Laetrile cannot cure cancer, says the FDA, which finds no evidence to support claims that amygdalin injections are effective. Produced from apricot pits, which contain cyanide, laetrile was patented in 1950 by U.S. promoter Ernst T. Krebs, who was fined last year and will be fined again in 1966 but who will get rich from his alleged cancer "cure." Krebs will die in 1970, his son and namesake will call laetrile "vitamin B17." Former Canadian test pilot Andrew R. L. McNaughton, 46, will gain right-wing support for laetrile, Mexican physician Ernesto Rodriguez Contreras, 47, will give laetrile injections to desperate cancer victims who will flock to his Clinica Del Mar on the Tijuana oceanfront, some states will legalize laetrile in the late 1970s, but the FDA calls it a "cruel fraud."

Pope John XXIII dies June 3 at age 81 after a 5-year papacy and is succeeded by Cardinal Giovanni Battista Montini, 66, who becomes Pope Paul VI.

Reading the Lord's Prayer or verses from the Bible in U.S. public schools is held unconstitutional June 17. The Supreme Court ruling in the case of *School*

An assassin's bullet ended the brief presidency of John F. Kennedy. Charges of conspiracy found wide credence.

1963 (cont.) *District of Abington Township v. Schempp* caps a campaign by atheist Madalyn Murray O'Hair, 44.

 British entry into the European Economic Community established in 1957 is vetoed after objections are raised by France's President De Gaulle.

U.S. unemployment reaches 6.1 percent by February but U.S. factory workers average more than $100 per week for the first time in history.

More than 50 million U.S. taxpayers support the Treasury, up from 4 million in 1939. Most income taxes are paid by payroll withholdings (*see* 1943).

New Hampshire conducts the first state lottery—a sweepstakes ostensibly to raise money for state education. The state ranks last in terms of state aid to education, the lottery will neither raise this ranking nor will it contribute more than 3 percent of state education aid in any year, but other states will follow New Hampshire's example as politicians seek substitutes for income taxes and postpone fundamental tax reforms and adequate funding for social services.

The U.S. federal budget is nearly $100 billion, up from $9 billion in 1939. Almost half the total goes for military appropriations as U.S. involvement in Southeast Asia begins to escalate.

An inflation begins in Indonesia that will depreciate the currency 688-fold in the next 7 years (*see* 1965).

U.S. federal employees number 2.5 million, up from 1.13 million in 1940.

U.S. entrepreneur Anthony De Angelis whose Allied Crude Vegetable Oil & Refining Company grosses more than $300 million per year is found to have obtained credit using empty storage tanks as collateral (nobody has bothered to check the tanks). Biggest factor in the vegetable oil industry, De Angelis goes bankrupt, his bankruptcy wipes out the New York Stock Exchange firm Ira Haupt & Company along with a subsidiary of American Express Company, and some small investors are ruined.

Wall Street's Dow Jones Industrial Average plummets 21 points in 30 minutes at news of the Kennedy assassination (above), but the market recovers.

A "hot line" emergency communications link between Washington and Moscow to reduce the risk of accidental war goes into service August 30 under an agreement signed June 20. The line will operate via satellite beginning early in 1978.

U.S. first class postal rates go to 5 cents per ounce, up from 4 cents in 1958 (*see* 1968).

New York City newspapers resume publication April 1 after a 114-day strike but the Hearst Corporation's financially weakened *New York Mirror* ceases publication October 15 after 41 years in which it has built up a circulation surpassed in the United States only by that of the *New York Daily News* (*see* 1966).

Zenith Radio Corporation and the Sylvania division of General Telephone and Electronics begin producing their own color picture tubes for television sets after having bought the tubes for years from Radio Corporation of America. Both companies pay royalties to RCA which controls basic patents but Zenith will grow to surpass RCA as the leading U.S. producer of color TV sets.

CBS acquires Los Angeles TV station KTTV for less than $10.4 million after 12 years of joint ownership with the Times Mirror Company headed by Norman Chandler, 60, and his son Otis, 32. The Chandler family has a dominant position in Los Angeles real estate, its New American Library is the leading U. S. paperback book publisher, it will be the leading U.S. publisher of bibles and a major printer of telephone directories, and it will make the *Los Angeles Times* the nation's largest standard size general newspaper in terms of circulation and the world's largest in terms of advertising volume.

 Nonfiction *The Feminine Mystique* by U.S. feminist Betty Goldstein Friedan, 42, who argues that women as a class suffer various forms of discrimination but are victimized especially by a system of delusions and false values that encourages them to find personal fulfillment through their husbands and children (*see* NOW, 1966); *Parlez-Vous Franglais?* by Sorbonne University professor René Etiemble who describes the extent to which English has invaded the French language despite efforts by the Academie Française founded in 1635. Etiemble calculates that some 5,000 common Anglo-American words such as *le pullover* and countless technical terms have infiltrated the language not to mention 1,300 bits of advertising jargon (but English, of course, is full of French words such as "mystique"); *The Fire Next Time* (essays) by James Baldwin.

Fiction *Dog Years* (*Hundejahre*) by Günter Grass; *Acquainted With Grief* (*La cognizione del dolore*) by Carlo Emilio Gadda; *Honey for the Bears* by Anthony Burgess; *Cat's Cradle* by Kurt Vonnegut, Jr.; *Big Sur* by Jack Kerouac; *The Second Stone* by U.S. novelist-critic Leslie Fiedler, 46; *Raise High the Roofbeam, Carpenters* and *Seymour: An Introduction* by J. D. Salinger; *The Tenants of Moonbloom* by the late Edward Lewis Wallant who died last year at age 36; *The Bell Jar* by the late U.S. poet Sylvia Plath who has taken her own life at age 31 and whose novel is an autobiographical account of manic depression; *The Icicle* (*Fantasticheskiye Povesti*, stories) by Andrei Sinyavsky; *The Spy Who Came in from the Cold* by English novelist John Le Carre (David Cornwell), 31; *V* by U.S. novelist Thomas Pynchon, 26; *The Centaur* by John Updike

Juvenile *Where the Wild Things Are* by Maurice Sendak; *The Wolves of Willoughby Chase* by U.S. author Joan Aiken, daughter of poet-novelist Conrad Aiken.

Poetry *At the End of the Open Road* by Louis Simpson.

The *New York Review of Books* begins publication on a bi-weekly basis September 26.

Painting *Homage to the Square "Curious"* by German-American painter Joseph Albers, now 75, who was a master at Weimar's Bauhaus for 10 years until 1933 and has been a major force on U.S. painters and architects ever since; *Nomad* by James Rosenquist; *Yellow Half* by Kenneth Noland; *Map* by Jasper Johns; *Red, Blue, Green* by Ellsworth Kelly; *Whaam!* and *Hopeless* by Roy Lichtenstein; *Great American Nude No. 44* and *Still-life No. 34* by Tom Wesselmann; *Man and Child* by Francis Bacon. Georges Braque dies at Paris August 31 at age 81.

Eastman Kodak Company introduces Kodak Instamatic cameras that can be loaded with film cartridges. Eastman also introduces Kodachrome-X, Ektachrome-X, and Kodacolor-X films with twice the speed of their predecessors (*see* 1936; 1944; 1946; Kodachrome II, 1961).

Theater *The Milk Train Doesn't Stop Here Anymore* by Tennessee Williams 1/16 at New York's Morosco Theater, with Hermione Baddeley, Mildred Dunnock, 69 perfs.; *The Deputy* (*Der Stellvertrecar*) by German playwright Rolf Hochhuth, 31, 2/23 at Berlin's Theater am Kurfurstendamm; *Barefoot in the Park* by Neil Simon 10/23 at New York's Biltmore Theater, with Elizabeth Ashley, Robert Redford, Mildred Natwick, Kurt Kaszner, 1,502 perfs.; *Mr. Krott, Larger Than Life* (*Über lebengross Herr Krott*) by Martin Walser 11/30 at Stuttgart's Staatstheater.

Films Tony Richardson's *Tom Jones* with Albert Finney; Federico Fellini's *8½* with Marcello Mastroianni; Martin Ritt's *Hud* with Patricia Neal, Paul Newman, Melvyn Douglas, Brandon de Wilde; John Sturges's *The Great Escape* with Steve McQueen, Richard Attenborough, James Garner, James Coburn, Donald Pleasance; Ralph Nelson's *Lilies of the Field* with Sidney Poitier; John Huston's *The List of Adrian Messenger* with Kirk Douglas, George C. Scott; Robert Wise's *The Haunting* with Julie Harris, Claire Bloom; Louis Malle's *The Fire Within;* Lindsay Anderson's *The Sporting Life* with Richard Harris; George Pollock's *Murder at the Gallop* with Margaret Rutherford (as Miss Marple), Robert Morley, Flora Robson; Stanley Kramer's *It's a Mad, Mad, Mad, Mad World* with Spencer Tracy, Edie Adams, Milton Berle, Sid Caesar, Ethel Merman; Ingmar Bergman's *The Silence;* Luchino Visconti's *The Leopard* with Burt Lancaster, Claudia Cardinale, Alain Delon; Alfred Hitchcock's *The Birds* with Rod Taylor, Jessica Tandy, Tippi Hedren, Suzanne Pleshette; John and Faith Hubley's *The Hole* (animated short).

Opera *The Long Christmas Dinner* 3/13 at New York's Juilliard School of Music with music by Paul Hindemith, libretto from a play by Thornton Wilder.

Cantatas *Cantata Misericordia* by Benjamin Britten in September at Geneva for the 100th anniversary of the Red Cross; *Song of Human Rights* by Howard Hanson 12/10 at Washington D.C., with a text that includes excerpts from President Kennedy's inaugural address.

Stage musicals *Half a Sixpence* 3/21 at London's Cambridge Theatre, with Tommy Steele, music and lyrics by David Hendon, book by Douglas Cross based on the H. G. Wells novel *Kipps* of 1905, 677 perfs.; *She Loves Me* 4/23 at New York's Eugene O'Neill Theater, with Barbara Cook, Jack Cassidy, music by Jerry Bock, lyrics by Sheldon Harnick, 39, songs that include "Days Gone By," 301 perfs.

The Beatles score their first big success with a recording of "I Want to Hold Your Hand." The Liverpool rock group includes songwriters John Lennon, 23, and Paul McCartney, 22, who are supported by George Harrison, 20, and drummer Ringo Starr, 24, who has replaced the original Beatles drummer Peter Best. Their long hair will be widely imitated and their music will raise rock to new heights of artistry and popular appeal.

World chess champion Mikhail Botvinnik is defeated at Moscow May 20 by Soviet chess master Tigran Petrosian, 33, who will hold the title until 1969.

The Los Angeles Dodgers win the World Series by defeating the New York Yankees 4 games to 0.

A British train robbery August 8 nets $7 million, mostly in banknotes. A team of robbers stop a train near Cheddington, 36 miles northwest of London.

Newsweek magazine copygirl Janice Wylie, 21, and her roommate Emily Hoffert, 23, are brutally stabbed to death August 28 in their apartment at 57 East 88th Street, New York. Police arrest delivery boy George Whitmore, 19, he confesses to the murders but later recants amid allegations of police beatings to force the confession, a court will convict Richard Robles, and he will go to prison for life.

Pecos, Tex., financier Billie Sol Estes, 43, is convicted of selling finance companies $24 million worth of mortgages on nonexistent fertilizer tanks. He will serve 6 years of a 15-year sentence for mail fraud and conspiracy to defraud.

New York's Pan Am building is completed above the 50-year-old Grand Central Station by Emery Roth & Sons with help from architects Pietro Belluschi and Walter Gropius. The 59-story structure has 2.4 million square feet of office space and is the world's largest commercial office building, but its precast concrete curtain wall raises protests because it blocks the vista of Park Avenue which the 43-year-old New York Central building (now the New York General building) had merely interrupted.

Twelve new Manhattan office buildings give the city a total of 6.2 million more square feet of floor space.

Houston's Tenneco building is completed by Skidmore, Owings & Merrill.

U.S. motels have a 70 percent occupancy rate versus 64 percent for conventional hotels. Motel rooms top the million mark, up from 600,000 in 1958.

Holiday Inn motels increase in number to 423 with 76 of them company owned. Seven additional Holiday Inns are in Puerto Rico, the Bahamas, and Can-

1963 (cont.) ada, 65 more are under construction, and 114 new franchises have been sold (*see* 1954).

The New York Hilton goes up on the Avenue of the Americas between 53rd and 54th Streets with 2,200 rooms.

The Athens Hilton opens with 480 rooms.

The London Hilton opens in Park Lane with 510 rooms. The new hotel rises 30 stories high across from Hyde Park.

 Soviet crops fail both in Kazakhstan and in the Ukraine (*see* 1953). Crops fail in the People's Republic of China and both China and the U.S.S.R. are forced to seek grain from the west.

Canada makes a major sale of wheat to the P.R.C. in August and follows it with large sales to the U.S.S.R.

"Comrade Khrushchev has performed a miracle," Muscovites joke: "He has sown wheat in Kazakhstan and has harvested it in Moscow."

Khrushchev declares the Kazakhstan virgin lands experiment a failure and seeks nearly 2 million tons of U.S. wheat. President Kennedy approves the sale, it is opposed by most Republicans including Richard Nixon, but it goes through at year's end with support from President Johnson.

Typhoons destroy nearly half of Japan's standing crops. The resulting food shortages boost Japanese demand for imported foodstuffs.

High-yielding semidwarf wheat developed by Rockefeller Foundation scientists in Mexico is introduced on a commercial basis to Mexican farmers (*see* 1945; Borlaug, 1944).

The U.S. corn crop tops 5 billion bushels for the first time, up from 4 billion in 1906.

The average U.S. farm worker produces enough food and fiber for 31 people, up from 15.5 in 1950 (*see* 1973).

The number of man-hours employed in U.S. agriculture falls below 9 million, down from 20 million in 1940. The number of farmers falls to 13.7 million— 7.1 percent of the population.

Thermal pollution kills an estimated 2 billion striped bass at the new Consolidated Edison nuclear generating plant on the Hudson River (above) before a mesh screen is erected to fence out the anadromous fish and permit them to swim upriver to spawn.

Two U.S. botulism fatalities are traced to some canned tuna fish. They are the first botulism fatalities produced by commercially packed food in the United States since 1941 (*see* 1971).

Weight Watchers is founded by Queens, N.Y., housewife Jean Neditch, 39, who has reduced her own weight from 213 pounds to 142 with help from a high-protein diet developed by Norman Jolliffe, 62, of the New York City Department of Health. Using a form of group therapy, completely proscribing some foods while permitting others without restriction, Weight Watchers will grow into a worldwide operation with average weekly attendance of half a million.

Vitamin E is shown to be useful in treating severe kwashiorkor, macrycitic anemia, and creatinuria (*see* 1938; Williams, 1931).

"Recommended Dietary Allowances" of nutrients are revised by the U.S. National Research Council (*see* 1943), and the USDA revises its Handbook No. 8 to give data on 2,483 food items with vitamin and mineral content plus other information (*see* 1950).

Average U.S. per capita meat consumption reaches 170.6 pounds, but veal consumption drops to 5 pounds, down from 9.7 in 1949. Chicken consumption is 37.8 pounds, up from 23.5 in 1945 when chicken was more costly than beef.

Average U.S. per capita butter consumption falls to 6.7 pounds, down from 18.3 in 1934 and 7.5 in 1960. Margarine consumption averages 9.3 pounds, up from 8.6 in 1957. Cheese consumption reaches 9.4 pounds, up from 7 in 1949.

Tab is introduced by Coca-Cola Company. The new cyclamate-sweetened cola drink competes with Royal Crown's Diet-Rite (*see* 1962; Diet Pepsi, 1965).

Procter & Gamble acquires Folger Coffee Company (*see* 1908).

Julia Child prepares Boeuf Bourguignonne on television in February as she begins a series of cooking demonstrations on Boston's educational TV station.

1964 The Tonkin Gulf Resolution approved by Congress August 7 authorizes President Johnson to "take all necessary measures to repel any armed attack against forces of the United States and to prevent further aggression." Three North Vietnamese PT boats have allegedly fired torpedoes August 2 at a U.S. destroyer in the international waters of Tonkin Gulf 30 miles off the coast of North Vietnam, President Johnson has ordered retaliatory action after a second such alleged attack, U.S. aircraft have bombed North Vietnamese bases August 5, and the resolution has been approved 88 to 2 in the Senate and 416 to 0 in the House of Representatives.

The U.S. objective in Vietnam is not "to save a friend" but "to avoid humiliation," writes Assistant Secretary of Defense John T. McNaughton in a secret memorandum.

Brazil's President Goulart has been overthrown April 1 and has fled to Uruguay after a military coup that followed a presidential order distributing federal lands to landless peasants, doubling the minimum wage, and expropriating lands adjacent to federal highways. A U.S. naval force is assembled in the Caribbean and heads south as President Johnson prepares to intervene to prevent a leftist takeover.

An anti-Communist purge follows the military coup in Brazil (above), U.S. ambassador to Brazil Lincoln

Gordon requests the recall of U.S. naval forces before they reach Brazilian waters, and army chief of staff General Humberto Castelo Branco is elected April 11 by the Brazilian congress to serve out the balance of President Goulart's term.

Greece's Paul I has died March 6 at age 62 after nearly 17 years on the throne and 2 weeks after George Papandreou became premier. Paul is succeeded by his 23-year-old son who assumes the throne as Constantine II, fighting has broken out between Greeks and Turks in Cyprus in February, a 1960 treaty between Greece, Turkey, and Cyprus is abrogated April 4 by Archbishop Makarios, heavy fighting follows in northwestern Cyprus, Greece rejects direct talks with Turkey on the Cyprus question June 11, Turkish planes attack Greek positions in Cyprus August 8, the UN orders a cease-fire August 9, Greece withdraws her units from NATO August 17, and the UN extends its mandate for force in Cyprus December 18.

India's Jawaharlal Nehru dies suddenly May 27 at age 74, after nearly 17 years as prime minister. The "Lion of Kashmir" Sheikh Mohammed Abdullah has been released from prison April 8 after 6 years' confinement and has denounced Indian policy toward Kashmir which is claimed by Pakistan, but New Delhi's policy continues under Nehru's successor Lal Bahadur Shastri, 60 (see 1966).

Malawi is created July 6 out of Nyasaland which has dissolved her federation with Rhodesia and which becomes a new African nation within the British Commonwealth.

Zambia is created October 24 out of Northern Rhodesia and Barotseland with Kenneth Kaunda as president of the new independent state. The British South African Company has released mineral rights in the area on the promise of compensation from London and from the new Zambian government.

The United Republic of Tanzania takes that name October 29 with Julius K. Nyerere as president. African nationalists in Zanzibar overthrew the predominantly Arab government January 12 and set up a People's Republic with Abeid A. Karume as president and with three Communist-trained cabinet members, Zanzibar merged with Tanganyika April 26 at the suggestion of President Nyerere, and the new republic is Communist-oriented.

Rhodesian finance minister Ian D. Smith, 45, has succeeded white supremacy extremist Winston J. Field as prime minister April 13 following dissolution of the Federation of Rhodesia and Nyasaland.

A Soviet coup d'etat September 13 strips Nikita Khrushchev, now 70, of all power. He is succeeded October 14 by Leonid Brezhnev as party leader and by Aleksei Kosygin as premier.

The Warren Commission Report issued September 27 finds that Lee Harvey Oswald alone was responsi-ble for last year's assassination of President Kennedy and that no conspiracy was involved. The report by the presidential commission headed by Chief Justice Earl Warren meets with skepticism in many quarters as various lawyers and publicists come out with books that seek to discredit the Warren Commission.

Britain's Labour party wins the general elections in October, Prime Minister Douglas-Home resigns, and (James) Harold Wilson, 48, begins a ministry that will continue until 1970.

Saudi Arabia's Saud ibn Abdel Aziz is deposed after a 12-year reign. His brother Faisal is proclaimed king November 2 and will reign until 1975.

President Johnson wins reelection with the largest popular vote plurality in U.S. history, receiving 61 percent of the popular vote and 486 electoral votes in a landslide victory over the conservative Republican Senator Barry M. Goldwater, 55, of Arizona. Goldwater has narrowly defeated the more liberal New York governor Nelson A. Rockefeller in the California primary and has been chosen to lead the Republican ticket, he attacks the Democrats for their interference in the life of the individual and for their "big government" competition with private industry, but his suggestions of escalation in the Vietnam war raise wide fears and he receives only 38 percent of the popular vote with 52 electoral votes.

A vast increase in U.S. aid to South Vietnam "to restrain the mounting infiltration of men and equipment by the Hanoi regime in support of the Vietcong" is announced December 11 and a military coup December 19 overthrows South Vietnam's High National Council.

 The Twenty-Fourth Amendment that takes effect February 24 makes U.S. poll taxes unconstitutional.

A 75-day filibuster by southern senators opposed to a civil rights bill ends June 10 when the Senate invokes cloture. The bill wins approval June 19 by a vote of 73 to 27 and goes back to the House; President Johnson signs it into law July 2.

Racial discrimination by a labor union constitutes an unfair labor practice, the National Labor Relations Board rules by a 3 to 2 vote July 2.

Harlem has a race riot July 18; Philadelphia has race riots beginning August 28.

South Africa expands her apartheid racial segregation laws May 6 with a Bantu Laws amendment bill that empowers her minister of Bantu administration to declare "prescribed" areas in which the number of Bantus (Africans) to be employed can be specified. Eight native leaders including Nelson Mandela are sentenced to life imprisonment June 12 for sabotage and subversion and in July the police make massive arrests under the General Laws Amendment Act which permits them to hold suspects for up to 6 months without making their arrests known.

1964 (cont.) Atlanta restaurateur Lester G. Maddox, 48, closes his Pickrick Restaurant rather than submit to federal government orders that he serve blacks as well as whites. His opposition to integration will propel Maddox into the governorship of Georgia in 1967, and when he is unable to succeed himself he will continue as lieutenant governor (Maddox has passed out pickax handles on the street in front of his restaurant to partisans who will cudgel any blacks who try to enter).

A Free Speech Movement begins among University of California students at Berkeley under the leadership of Bettina Aptheker, Mario Savio, and Jack Weinberg, the movement climaxes in the occupation of Sproul Hall, the occupation is ended December 3 by police acting on orders from Governor Edmund G. "Pat" Brown, more than 800 people are hauled out of Sproul Hall and some 732 sit-in demonstrators are arrested in the largest U.S. mass-arrest thus far in history. Suppression of the California demonstration begins a long period of U.S. campus unrest that will develop into an antiwar movement.

$ President Johnson calls for "total victory" in a "national war on poverty" March 16. He signs an Economic Opportunity Act August 20 and appoints R. Sargent Shriver, 48, to head the new Office of Economic Opportunity (OEO). Brother-in-law of the late President Kennedy, Shriver will coordinate such agencies as the Job Corps, the Neighborhood Youth Corps, Volunteers in Service to America (VISTA), Community Action Programs, and a Head Start program designed to help preschool children achieve higher levels of health, nutrition, and preparedness for school.

A Kennedy half-dollar issued by the U.S. Mint replaces the Franklin half-dollar in circulation since 1948. Souvenir collectors hoard the new coins as mementos of the late president.

Negotiations begin at Geneva November 16 to reduce world trade tariffs in the so-called first Kennedy Round of discussions (*see* 1963).

The largest iron ore contract in world history is signed to supply Japan's major steel firms with 65.5 million tons of ore in the next 16 years from Hamersley Range deposits discovered by Lang Hancock in Australia in 1952. The deposits have been acquired by Australia's Conzinc Rio Tinto owned jointly by Kaiser Industries of the United States with backing from French financier Baron Guy de Rothschild, Joseph Hirschhorn's Rio Tinto Mining Company of Canada, and Consolidated Zinc, Ltd. Nearly 6 million tons of the ore will have been shipped to Japan by the end of 1967, and the iron will permit a major expansion of the Japanese steel industry that will help make Japan an industrial superpower.

 Jimmy Hoffa achieves his goal of bringing all U.S. truckers under a single Teamsters Union contract and raises fears that he may paralyze the country with a nationwide strike (*see* 1957). Hoffa has made the Teamsters perhaps the most powerful union in America, he has heightened his power potential by pursuing efforts to unite railway, airline, canal boat, and merchant marine workers with his Teamsters, he has been the chief target since 1962 of Attorney General Robert F. Kennedy and has been resisting investigations by a Senate investigating committee, and he is found guilty of having tampered with the jury in a 1962 trial.

A report on what the U.S. government should do about auto safety is submitted by U.S. lawyer Ralph Nader, 30, who has come to Washington to work as a consultant to the Department of Labor (*see* 1965).

Seat belts are made standard equipment by Studebaker-Packard Corporation which breaks with the majors to become the first U.S. automaker to offer seat belts without charge. However, this smallest of the full-line automakers quits the industry by year's end leaving it to General Motors, Ford, Chrysler, and American Motors (*see* 1954).

The Mustang is introduced by Ford Motor Company whose new sporty compact is essentially a Falcon with different exterior sheet metal (*see* 1959).

The Dodge Coronet and Plymouth Belvedere are introduced by Chrysler Corporation which has had no entries in the intermediate price car market.

Washington's Capital Beltway opens April 11 with 66 miles of six-lane highway designed to handle 49,000 vehicles per day. Traffic on the Beltway through Maryland and Virginia suburban areas will surpass the projected average after 1 year.

Scotland's Forth Road Bridge opens to traffic at Queensferry September 4. The bridge is 1,006 meters in length.

New York's Verrazano Narrows Bridge opens across the harbor to link Brooklyn with Staten Island (*see* Brooklyn Bridge, 1883; George Washington Bridge, 1931). Designed by Swiss-American engineer Othmar A. Ammans, now 85, the 1,298-meter (4,260-foot) bridge is the world's largest single span suspension bridge.

The Volga-Baltic Ship Canal opens to connect the Caspian Sea with Leningrad on the Baltic 224 miles away.

Japan's Tokaido Shin Kansu (New Tokaido Line) begins service October 1 with "bullet" trains that average 102 miles per hour and cut the 309-mile trip between Tokyo and Osaka from 390 minutes to 190 minutes. The new train will bring a sharp decrease in air travel between the two cities, a second line will open in March of 1972 between Osaka and Okayama, and the line will be extended 3 years later to Hakata on the island of Kyushu 668 miles from Tokyo.

The 68-year-old Norfolk and Western Railway absorbs the New York, St. Louis and Chicago (Nickel Plate) Railroad, leases the Wabash Railroad and the Pittsburgh & West Virginia Lines, buys the Pennsylvania Railroad's Akron, Canton & Youngstown line and Sandusky line, and effects a consolidation that creates a network of more than 7,400 miles.

The U.S. Federal Power Commission relaxes its rule that natural gas pipeline companies must have 12 years' reserve before accepting new customers. The FPC acts in response to huge surpluses that have resulted from newly discovered sources and its action produces wide-scale promotion by utility companies of natural gas for heating and appliances.

U.S. gasoline prices in October are 30.3 cents per gallon, up from 29 cents in 1954.

U.S. cigarette consumption reaches 524 billion— more than 4,300 smokes for every American over age 18. The tobacco industry halts advertising in college newspapers, magazines, sports programs, and on college radio stations, in response to public pressure (see Banzhaf, 1966).

Carlton cigarettes are introduced by the American Tobacco Company but low-tar cigarettes will not begin to gain popularity until 1970.

The Surgeon General's Report issued January 11 by Luther L. Terry, 52, links cigarette smoking to lung cancer and other diseases (see Hammond and Horn, 1952). The lung cancer rate among U.S. men is 30 per 100,000 but will increase to 50 per 100,000 in the next decade, the rate among women is below 5 per 100,000 but will more than double in the next decade as young people increase their cigarette smoking despite warnings, 40 percent of U.S. men and 30 percent of U.S. women will still be smoking by 1974, and while increased use of filters will reduce tobacco consumption 18 percent by lowering the tobacco content of each cigarette, and while tar and nicotine content of cigarettes will decline by 32 percent, deaths related to smoking will soar to 250,000 per year (see FTC, 1968).

Methadone helps rehabilitate heroin addicts (see Bayer, 1898). Rockefeller University researcher Vincent P. Dole, 51, and psychiatrist Marie Nyswander use the synthetic opiate invented by German chemists during World War II, some 1,000 addicts will be enrolled in methadone maintenance programs by 1968, nearly 10,000 will be on methadone by 1970, but heroin addiction will remain a source of crime in U.S. cities where addicts are driven to burglary, robbery, and prostitution in order to support their costly habit.

The Kitty Genovese case raises alarms about America's growing isolation, callousness, and inhumanity (see Jacobs book, 1961). An attacker stalks Queens, N.Y., bar manager Catherine Genovese early in the morning of March 13; 38 of her Kew Gardens neighbors hear her wild calls for help; nobody interferes for fear of "getting involved," the neighbors watch from windows while Genovese is stabbed to death; nobody phones the police until half an hour later.

The "Boston Strangler" who has broken into a dozen apartments since mid-1962 to rob, violate, and kill women (not always by strangling them) makes final attack in January. Cambridge police take Albert Henry DeSalvo, 32, into custody November 4 but do not say he is the "strangler." DeSalvo was sentenced to prison on robbery counts in 1961, he was paroled after 11 months, he claims to have raped at least 1,000 women, and he will boast to inmates at Bridgewater State Hospital that he has killed 13 women.

The Roman Catholic liturgy in the United States is changed November 29 to include the use of English in some prayers. Some traditional priests will defy the Vatican by sticking to Latin.

The United Christian Evangelistic Association, Inc., has its beginnings in the Boston Miracle Temple founded by former South Carolina Pentecostal Church pastor Frederick J. Eikeronkoetter, 31, who calls himself the Reverend Ike and who preaches a "Now Religion" of "Green Power." "I have always loved the Lord," says the Reverend Ike, "but it's a lot easier to love the Lord when I have money to pay the bills and meet my needs, when I have a nice car and nice clothes to wear." The "Blessing Plan" offered by the Reverend Ike will soon bring him enough "Green Power" to afford a dozen Rolls-Royces.

U.S. Catholic parochial school enrollment reaches an all-time high of 5.6 million pupils. The figure will fall to below 3.5 million within 10 years.

Zip codes adopted by the U.S. Post Office speed sorting of mail whose volume has increased to 70 billion pieces per year.

BBC-2 begins broadcasting April 30. The second British Broadcasting Corporation television channel transmits on 625 lines to provide high-definition pictures for sets equipped to pick up 625-line signals.

Radio Manx begins broadcasting November 23 to give Britain her first commercial television.

Nonfiction *Understanding Media* by Marshall McLuhan; *Anti-Intellectualism in American Life* by Columbia University history professor Richard Hofstadter, 48; *One-Dimensional Man* by German-American Brandeis University philosophy professor Herbert Marcuse, 66, tries to explain the repressive nature of American society and its potential for totalitarianism (many students will use the Marcuse book to justify abandoning democratic processes in order to achieve radical goals; *Games People Play* by Canadian-American psychiatrist Eric Berne (ne Eric Lennard Bernstein), 54, who pioneers non-Freudian "transactional analysis."

Fiction *Herzog* by Saul Bellow; *Last Exit to Brooklyn* by U.S. novelist Hubert Selby, 38 (a London court convicts Selby of obscenity, but he wins reversal on appeal); *Nothing Like the Sun* by Anthony Burgess; *The Snow Ball* by Irish novelist Brigid Brophy, 33; *The Spire* by William Golding; *The Children at the Gate* by the late Edward Lewis Wallant; *Little Big Man* by Thomas Berger; *Julian* by Gore Vidal; *The Wapshot Scandal* by John Cheever; *Corridors of Power* by C. P. Snow; *The Palace* (*La Palace*) by

Indo-China's rice fields became battlefields in a surrogate war between communists and non-communists.

Claude Simon; *The Makepiece Experiment* (*Lyubimov*) by Andrei Sinyavsky.

Juvenile *Harriet the Spy* by U.S. author Louise Fitzhugh.

Poetry *For the Union Dead* by Robert Lowell; *The Bourgeois Poet* by Karl Shapiro; *The Whitsun Weddings* by Philip Larkin; *Rediscoveries* by Elizabeth Jennings.

Painting *Retroactive I* by Robert Rauschenberg; *The Man in the Bowler Hat, The Great War,* and *The Sin of Man* by René Magritte; *According to What* by Jasper Johns; *Fez* by Frank Stella; *Prime Course* by Kenneth Noland; *Rising Moon* by Hans Hofmann; *Double Red Self-Portrait* (*The Green Line*) by Jim Dine; *Brillo Boxes* by Andy Warhol.

Sculpture *Classic Figure* by Jean Arp, now 77; *Cubi* by David Smith.

Sotheby Parke Bernet is created as London's 220-year-old Sotheby auction house acquires New York's 27-year-old Parke Bernet house.

Agfa Gevaert is created by a merger of Belgium's Gevaert Photo-Production with the Agfa film subsidiary of Germany's Farbenfabriken Bayer.

Theater *The Persecution and Assassination of Marat as Performed by the Inmates of the Asylum of Charenton under the Direction of the Marquis de Sade* (*Die Verfolgung und Ermordung Jean-Paul Marats, dargestellt durch die Schauspielgruppe des Hospizes a Charenton unter Auleitung der Herrn de Sade*) by German playwright-novelist-painter Peter Weiss, 48; *After the Fall* by Arthur Miller 1/23 at New York's ANTA Theater-Washington Square, with Jason Robards, Jr., Barbara Loden, David Wayne, Hal Holbrook, Salome Jens, Ruth Attaway, Faye Dunaway, Zohra Lampert, Ralph Meeker, 208 perfs.; *Any Wednesday* by U.S. playwright Muriel Resnik 2/18

at New York's Music Box Theater, with Sandy Dennis, Gene Hackman, Rosemary Murphy, 982 perfs.; *But for Whom Charlie* by S. N. Behrman 3/12 at New York's ANTA Theater-Washington Square, with Salome Jens, Jason Robards, Jr., Barbara Loden, Ralph Meeker, David Wayne, 39 perfs.; *Benito Cereno* by Robert Lowell 4/1 at New York's American Place Theater in St. Clements Church; *Blues for Mr. Charlie* by James Baldwin 4/23 at New York's ANTA Theater, with Pat Hingle, Rip Torn, Diana Sands, 148 perfs.; *The Entertaining Mr. Sloan* by English playwright Joe Orton, 31, 5/6 at London's New Arts Theatre; *The Subject Was Roses* by U.S. playwright Frank D. Gilroy, 39, 5/25 at New York's Royale Theater, with Martin Sheen, Jack Albertson, Irene Dailey, 832 perfs., Pulitzer prize; *Inadmissable Evidence* by John Osborne 9/9 at London's Royal Court Theatre, with Nicol Williamson; *The Black Swan* (*Der Schwarze Schwan*) by Martin Walser 10/14 at Stuttgart's Staatstheater; *The Sign in Sidney Brustein's Window* by Lorraine Hansberry 10/15 at New York's Longacre Theater, 101 perfs. (Hansberry is ill with cancer and will die early next year at age 36); *Slow Dance on the Killing Ground* by U.S. playwright William Hanley, 33, 11/3 at New York's Plymouth Theater, 88 perfs.; *Luv* by U.S. playwright Murray Schisgal, 37, 11/11 at New York's Booth Theater, with Alan Arkin, Eli Wallach, Anne Jackson, 901 perfs.; *The Royal Hunt of the Sun* by Peter Shaffer 12/8 at London's Old Vic Theatre, with Christopher Plummer as Francisco Pizarro; *Hunger and Thirst* (*La soif et La faim*) by Eugène Ionesco 12/30 at Düsseldorf's Schauspielhaus; *Tiny Alice* by Edward Albee 12/30 at New York's Billy Rose Theater, with John Gielgud, Irene Worth, 167 perfs.

New York State Theater opens in New York's Lincoln Center April 23 with 2,729 seats. Philip Johnson has designed the house.

Films Stanley Kubrick's *Dr. Strangelove, or How I Learned to Stop Worrying and Love the Bomb* with Peter Sellers, George C. Scott, Sterling Hayden, Keenan Wynn; Vittorio De Sica's *Yesterday, Today, and Tomorrow* with Sophia Loren, Marcello Mastroianni; Michael Cocoyannis's *Zorba the Greek* with Anthony Quinn, Alan Bates; Clive Donner's *Nothing but the Best* with Alan Bates, Denholm Elliott; Vittorio De Sica's *Marriage Italian-Style* with Sophia Loren, Marcello Mastroianni; Bryan Forbes's *Seance on a Wet Afternoon* with Kim Stanley, Richard Attenborough; Peter Glenville's *Becket* with Richard Burton, Peter O'Toole, John Gielgud, Franklin Shaffner's *The Best Man* with Henry Fonda, Lee Tracy; Philippe de Broca's *That Man from Rio* with Jean-Paul Belmondo; John Frankenheimer's *Seven Days in May* with Burt Lancaster, Kirk Douglas, Fredric March, Ava Gardner; Jacques Demy's *Umbrellas of Cherbourg* with Catherine Deneuve; Jean-Luc Goddard's *Contempt* with Brigitte Bardot, Fritz Lang, Michel Piccoli; John Guillermin's *Guns at Batasi* with Richard Attenborough, Jack Hawkins, Flora Robson; Jules Dassin's *Topkapi* with Melina Mercouri, Robert Morley, Peter Ustinov; Ronald Neame's *The Chalk Garden* with Deborah Kerr, Hayley Mills, John Mills; George Pollock's *Murder Most Foul* with Margaret Rutherford (as Miss Marple); John Huston's *Night of the Iguana* with Deborah Kerr, Ava Gardner, Richard Burton, Grayson Hall, Sue Lyon; Satayajit Ray's *Charulata;* Hiroshi Teshigahara's *Woman in the Dunes.*

Hollywood musicals   George Cukor's *My Fair Lady* with Audrey Hepburn, Rex Harrison; Richard Lester's *A Hard Day's Night* with the Beatles; Charles Walters's *The Unsinkable Molly Brown* with Debbie Reynolds.

Broadway musicals   *Hello, Dolly!* 1/16 at the St. James Theater with Carol Channing, music and lyrics by Jerry Herman, 2,844 perfs.; *Funny Girl* 3/26 at the Winter Garden Theater, with Barbra Streisand as the late Fanny Brice, music and lyrics by Jule Styne and Bob Merrill, songs that include "People," "Don't Rain on My Parade," 1,348 perfs.; *Fiddler on the Roof* 9/22 at the Imperial Theater, with Zero Mostel, music by Jerry Bock, lyrics by Sheldon Harnick, songs that include "If I Were a Rich Man," "Tradition," "Matchmaker, Matchmaker," "Sunrise, Sunset," 3,242 perfs.

Opera   *Montezuma* 4/19 in West Berlin, with music by Roger Sessions.

First performances   Symphony No. 5 by Roger Sessions 2/7 at the Philadelphia Academy of Music; *Curlew River* (church parable) by Benjamin Britten in July in Aldeburgh, with text by William Plower inspired by a 15th century Japanese Nō drama.

Popular songs   "I Feel Fine" by John Lennon and Paul McCartney of the Beatles; "Love Me, Do" by Lennon and McCartney; "Please, Please Me" by Lennon and McCartney; "She Loves You" by Lennon and McCartney; "I Get Around" by Brian Wilson of the Beach Boys; "My Kind of Town" by James Van Heusen, lyrics by Sammy Cahn (for the film *Robin and the Seven Hoods*); "It Ain't Me, Babe" by Bob Dylan; "Mr. Tambourine Man" by Bob Dylan; "Look of Love" by Jeff Barry and Ellie Greenwich; "King of the Road" by Roger Miller; "I Will Wait for You" by French composer Michel Legrand, lyrics by Jacques Demy (English lyrics by Norman Gimbel) for the film *The Umbrellas of Cherbourg;* "Pass Me By" by Cy Coleman, lyrics by Carolyn Leigh (for the film *Father Goose*).

Cassius Marcellus Clay, 22, knocks out world heavyweight champion Sonny Liston February 25 at Miami to win the title he will hold until 1967.

Kelso wins the Washington, D.C., International at age 7 to cap a 5-year racing career in which the big gelding has won 39 victories in 83 starts to earn an all-time record of nearly $2 million.

A football stadium riot at Lima, Peru, May 24 ends with 300 dead after a soccer match between Peru and Argentina.

New York's Shea Stadium opens at Flushing, Queens, to replace the Polo Grounds and Ebbets Field. The 53,000-seat stadium for the Mets and the Jets is named for New York lawyer William Shea, 56, who has obtained a new National League baseball franchise for New York by threatening to start a rival league and by getting political allies in Washington to threaten other team owners with restraint-of-trade hearings (Shea's cronies receive food, beer, and parking franchises).

The Olympic Games at Tokyo attract 5,541 contestants from 94 nations. Soviet athletes collect 41 gold medals, U.S. athletes, 37.

The U.S. America's Cup defender *Constellation* defeats Britain's *Sovereign* 4 to 0 in the 16th British effort to regain the cup.

The St. Louis Cardinals win the World Series by defeating the New York Yankees 4 games to 3.

The topless bathing suit introduced by California designer Rudi Gernreich will lead to a general abandonment of brassieres by young women.

A San Francisco bar introduces topless dancers June 19. The dancers will be bottomless beginning September 3, 1969.

Dynel is introduced by Union Carbide Corporation whose new synthetic fiber will be used in textiles, fake furs, and hairpieces.

Levi Strauss removes the rivets from the hip pockets of its blue jeans (*see* 1937).

Klear floor wax is introduced by S. C. Johnson Company (*see* 1956; Glo-Coat, 1932; Bravo, 1965).

U.S. sales through retail vending machines total $3.5 billion as Americans drop 83 million coins into vending machines every 24 hours.

Federated Department Stores acquires Bullock's and its subsidiary I. Magnin (*see* 1929).

Boston's Prudential Tower is completed for the Newark-based Prudential Insurance Company and is twice the height of the John Hancock building completed in 1949. The 52-story Prudential Tower spurs John Hancock management to proceed with plans for an even taller structure (*see* 1968).

The Washington Cathedral in the nation's capital gets a new tower that makes it visible from 30 miles away (*see* 1907). Soaring 301 feet above the ground, the Gothic tower has spires that make it taller than the Washington Monument completed in 1888.

Chicago's Marina City apartment houses and offices are completed on the Chicago River. The 60-story round twin towers designed by Bertrand Goldberg are of concrete construction with weight loads carried chiefly by cylindrical cores, the pie-shaped rooms extend into rings of semicircular balconies, and the first 18 floors are taken up by parking space.

New York's curved-facade 200 Central Park South apartment house is completed at Seventh Avenue by Wechsler & Schimenti.

1964 (cont.) The Dorothy Chandler Pavilion with 3,250 seats gives Los Angeles the beginnings of a new cultural center that will be augmented in the next 5 years by the 2,100-seat Ahmanson Theater and the 750-seat Mark Taper Forum.

Hawaii's Mauna Kea Beach Hotel opens on a tract leased from the 117-year-old Parker Ranch at the foot of 13,796-foot Mauna Kea on the island of Hawaii. The $15 million, 154-room resort hotel has been built by Laurance Rockefeller.

Tokyo's New Otani Hotel is completed with 2,000 rooms on the city's highest hilltop where it is surrounded by gardens and an ancient moat.

More than $1 billion in U.S. federal aid for housing and urban renewal is authorized through September 30 of next year by a bill signed into law by President Johnson September 2.

 The worst earthquake felt anywhere in the world since 1960 rocks Alaska March 28. The quake measures 8.4 on the Richter scale (which will be revised in 1977 to give the quake a rating of 9.2), it creates a seismic "tidal" wave (*tsunami*) in the southwest part of the state, and the 220-foot high wave is the largest such wave ever recorded.

High waters in the Adriatic Sea in November cause the Venetian Lagoon to rise 6 feet above normal levels. Disastrous floods wash out the foundations of many buildings, ruin ground-floor frescoes, cause some structures to collapse, and hasten the deterioration of the once powerful city of Venice.

Congress passes a Wilderness Act to protect the country's last remaining wild lands from development (*see* California Wildland Research Center, 1961). The congressmen have been exhorted to act by Wilderness Society executive director Howard Zahniser, 58, and their act provides for immediate protection of 9.1 million acres classified as wilderness by the U.S. Forest Service. The act establishes a procedure to review every 10 years some 5.4 million acres in the national forests that are classed as "primitive" and it gives Congress sole power to designate a national wilderness or to declassify a wilderness once established.

Canyonlands National Park is created by act of Congress. The park embraces 257,640 acres of Utah mesas and rock spires.

 High-yielding dwarf strains of *indica* rice are introduced on experimental basis under the names IR5 and IR8 by the International Rice Research Institute at Los Banos in the Philippines. The new "miracle" rice for tropical cultivation has been developed by crossing ordinary *indica* rice with Japan's high-yielding *japonica* variety (*see* 1962; 1965).

Danish fishermen discover the major feeding grounds of the Atlantic salmon off the southwest coast of Greenland. They begin to take large catches of the fish which average only 7 pounds each, sharply reducing spawning runs up the rivers of Canada, England, France, Iceland, Ireland, Norway, Russia, Scotland, Wales, and the U.S. state of Maine (*see* 1950; 1969).

The U.S. food stamp program conducted at Rochester, N.Y., from 1939 to 1943 is reactivated on a broad scale by the U.S. Department of Agriculture to help feed needy Americans (*see* 1959; 1967).

U.S. October food prices: round steak $1.07 per pound, up from 92 cents in 1954; sugar 59 cents for a 5-pound bag, up from 52 cents; coffee 82 cents per pound, down from $1.10; bread 21 cents per 1-pound loaf, up from 17 cents; eggs 57 cents per dozen, down from 60 cents; milk 48 cents per half gallon, up from 45 cents; butter 76 cents per pound, up from 72 cents; lettuce 25 cents per head, up from 19 cents.

Awake is introduced by General Foods which promotes the synthetic orange juice with a budget of $5 million is—more than is spent to promote pure orange juice, whether frozen, chilled, or fresh.

Maxim is introduced by General Foods which has spent huge sums to develop the freeze-dried instant coffee (*see* 1940; Instant Maxwell House, 1942; Taster's Choice, 1966).

Pop-Tarts toaster pastries are introduced by the Kellogg Company (*see* 1963; 1965).

Lucky Charms breakfast food—50.4 percent sugar—is introduced by General Mills (*see* 1961; 1966).

Curtiss Candy Company is acquired by Standard Brands (*see* 1920; 1923; Planters, 1961).

Standard Fruit and Steamship Company is acquired in large part by Honolulu's 113-year-old firm Castle & Cooke which takes over the Vaccaro family's majority interest and which will operate Standard Fruit as a wholly owned subsidiary (*see* bananas, 1966).

Dole Corporation is acquired by Castle & Cooke (above) which makes Dole a division of its conglomerate and for the first time markets fresh pineapple under the Dole Royal Hawaiian label, using jet planes to rush the fruit to East Coast markets, although most goes by ship to West Coast ports.

Colonel Sanders has more than 600 licensees offering his "finger-lickin' good" Kentucky Fried Chicken (*see* 1955). Now 74, Sanders sells the franchise business for $2 million plus a salary of $40,000 per year for life to act as a goodwill ambassador.

Benihana opens in New York's West 56th Street. The hibachi steak-shrimp-mushroom-beansprout restaurant operated by Japanese-American Hiroaki "Rocky" Aoki, 25, enjoys immediate success and will be followed by Benihana (Red Flower) restaurants in other U.S. cities.

 The Time Has Come by Boston Catholic physician John Rock, now 74, rejects the Church's position against artificial contraceptive methods. Rock helped develop the progesterone contraceptive pill.

The Meaning of the 20th Century by English-American economist Kenneth Ewart Boulding, 54, of the

University of Michigan proposes marketable licenses for producing children.

A dozen U.S. states have tax-supported birth control programs, most of them in the South where Catholic influence is weak and where whites try to hold down black birth rates. There are 450 public birth-control clinics in the nation (*see* 1965).

1965 U.S. bombers pound North Vietnamese targets February 7 and 8 in retaliation for a National Liberation Front (NLF) attack on U.S. ground forces in South Vietnam. Washington announces a general policy of bombing North Vietnam February 11 and President Johnson says, "The people of South Vietnam have chosen to resist [North Vietnamese aggression]. At their request the United States has taken its place beside them in this struggle."

Some 160 U.S. planes bomb North Vietnam March 2, and 3,500 U.S. Marines land at Da Nang March 8 to 9 in the first deployment of U.S. combat troops in Vietnam. A bomb explodes in the U.S. embassy at Saigon March 30.

North Vietnamese MIG fighter planes shoot down U.S. jets April 4, a student demonstration in Washington, D.C., April 17 protests the U.S. bombing of North Vietnam, but a large-scale U.S. raid over North Vietnam comes 6 days after the demonstration.

Australia decides April 29 to send troops to the aid of South Vietnam.

A "teach-in" broadcast May 15 to more than 100 U.S. colleges opposes the war in Vietnam, but Congress authorizes use of U.S. ground troops in direct combat June 8 if the South Vietnamese army so requests. The first full-scale combat offensive by U.S. troops begins June 28.

Some 125,000 U.S. troops are in Vietnam by July 28 and President Johnson announces a doubling of draft calls. He asks the UN to help negotiate a peace, but U.S. troops take part in their first major battle as an independent force in mid-August and they destroy a Viet Cong stronghold near Van Tuong August 19.

The Indonesian army defeats a Communist takeover attempt in late September. Indonesia has withdrawn from the United Nations January 2 (the first nation to do so). The Jakarta government has seized the properties of U.S. oil companies and of Goodyear Tire & Rubber Company March 19, it seizes all remaining foreign-owned properties April 24. Communists kidnap the army chief of staff and five generals at the end of September, but other generals escape capture and thwart the attempted coup. A general massacre of Communists begins October 8, estimates of the dead range up to 400,000, but many of those killed are ethnic Chinese who dominate the Indonesian economy and who are slain because they are landlords or creditors.

"The Vietcong are going to collapse within weeks," says President Johnson's National Security Adviser Walt Whitman Rostow, 48: "Not months, but weeks."

Antiwar rallies October 15 attract crowds in four U.S. cities. Poet Allen Ginsberg at Berkeley, Calif., introduces the term "flower power" to describe a strategy of friendly cooperation. Oakland police have blocked the Berkeley peace marchers from entering the city and the Hell's Angels motorcycle gang has attacked the marchers, calling them "un-American."

Secret peace talks with North Vietnam arranged in September of last year by UN Secretary General U Thant were rejected by Washington, reports *Look* magazine in November.

The AFL-CIO pledges "unstinting support" for the Vietnamese war effort December 15.

U.S. Marines have landed in the Dominican Republic April 28 to protect U.S. citizens and to prevent an allegedly imminent Communist takeover of the Santo Domingo government. An Inter-American Peace Force from the Organization of American States (OAS) takes over peacekeeping operations beginning May 23, but 20,000 U.S. Marines remain for several months.

Romania's Premier Gheorghe Gheorghiu-Dej has died in March after nearly 13 years and has been succeeded as head of state by Nicolae Ceausescu.

The Gambia on the West African Coast has become a fully independent constitutional monarchy under the British Crown February 18. Gambia will become a republic in 1970.

Rhodesia's Prime Minister Ian Smith visits London in early October and demands immediate independence, the British refuse unless the Salisbury government first agrees to expand representation of native Africans in the government with a view to eventual majority rule, Ian Smith declares Rhodesian independence unilaterally November 11 while reaffirming loyalty to the queen, the British governor at Salisbury declares Smith and his government deposed, London calls the declaration illegal and treasonable and proclaims economic sanctions against Rhodesia.

The UN Security Council calls on all nations November 12 to withhold recognition of the new Rhodesian regime and to refuse it aid.

Guinea severs diplomatic relations with France November 15 after discovering a plot to assassinate Sekou Touré and overthrow his regime. The plot is said to involve France and several neighboring African states.

The Independent Congo Republic has a bloodless coup November 24 to 25, 6 weeks after President Kasavubu has dismissed Moise Tshombe as premier. President Kasavubu is deposed by General Joseph D. Mobutu who makes himself president and proceeds to rule by decree (*see* 1966).

Ghana severs relations with the British government on the Rhodesian issue December 3 and threatens to leave the Commonwealth.

1965 (cont.) The Organization of African Unity threatens to break relations with Britain December 5 unless London applies force to suppress Ian Smith's rebellion (above) by December 15.

 Selma, Ala., is the focus of civil rights demonstrations throughout February and March. Martin Luther King, Jr., and 770 others are arrested February 1 at Selma during demonstrations against state regulations relating to voter registration, black marchers leave Selma March 7 for the state capital at Montgomery after 2,000 prospective voters have been arrested in registration lines or in demonstrations, the marchers are attacked by 200 Alabama state police using tear gas, whips, and nightsticks, Governor Wallace refuses to provide protection for a second march and accuses a federal judge who has approved the second march of "prostituting our law in favor of mob rule," President Johnson sends in 3,000 federalized National Guardsmen and military police, the marchers leave Selma March 21 and arrive at Montgomery March 25, white civil rights leader Viola Liuzzo, 38, is shot dead March 25 by four Ku Klux Klansmen outside Montgomery while driving a car with a black passenger, 25,000 attend the rally at Montgomery that day, but the Voting Rights Act becomes law August 10 and federal examiners begin registering black voters in Alabama, Louisiana, and Mississippi.

Malcolm X is shot dead February 21 as the leader of the Organization of Afro-American Unity prepares to address a Sunday afternoon audience at Harlem's Audubon Ballroom on the need for blacks and whites to coexist peacefully. Three alleged assassins will be convicted next year of having shot Malcolm X with a sawed-off shotgun and other weapons, but it will never be established whether or not they were members of the Black Muslim sect with which Malcolm X broke last year.

Chicago police arrest 526 anti-segregation demonstrators from June 11 to 15 after the rehiring of a school superintendent. The demonstrations continue nevertheless and Martin Luther King, Jr., leads a march of 20,000 to City Hall July 26.

The Watts section of Los Angeles has violent race riots beginning August 12 as upwards of 10,000 blacks burn and loot an area of 500 square blocks and destroy an estimated $40 million worth of property. Some 15,000 police and National Guardsmen are called in, 34 persons are killed (28 of them blacks), nearly 4,000 are arrested, and more than 200 business establishments are totally destroyed.

Busing of schoolchildren to achieve racial desegration as required by the 1954 Supreme Court decision is ordered by North Carolina Judge James B. McMillan. The order for crosstown busing in the Charlotte-Mecklenburg County school system starts a pattern of busing that will be followed in much of the country, but although the Supreme Court will uphold McMillan's ruling in 1971 the use of busing creates a storm of controversy and antibusing protests will continue for years.

Amos 'n Andy is withdrawn from syndication following protests against its stereotyped images of blacks. Started as a radio show in 1928, *Amos 'n Andy* has been a leading television program since 1949 with blacks playing the roles originally created by whites.

$ President Johnson outlines programs for a "Great Society" that will eliminate poverty in America January 4 in his State of the Union message and he signs a $1.4 billion program of federal-state economic aid to Appalachia into law March 9, but U.S. military involvement in Southeast Asia escalates, draining the U.S. economy (above).

New York City's welfare roll grows to 480,000. The number of welfare recipients will grow to 1.2 million in the next 10 years and by 1974 the city's welfare agency will account for $3.4 billion of the city's $12 billion budget with half the welfare aid reimbursed by the federal government.

The United States Mint switches to "clad" coins in a move to conserve silver by eliminating dollars, half-dollars, quarters, and dimes that contained 90 percent silver.

The United States contributes roughly 1 percent of her Gross National Product (GNP) to foreign aid as proposed by Adlai Stevenson in 1961, but the percentage will decline sharply (*see* 1967).

Britain freezes wages, salaries, and prices in an effort to check inflation and to improve the nation's worsening trade deficit (*see* 1961; 1967).

The Diners Club of America founded in 1950 reaches a membership of 1.3 million, American Express has 1.2 million cardholders after just 7 years, and major U.S. banks prepare to issue credit cards of their own (*see* BankAmericard, 1958; 1966; Master Charge, 1966). Not only restaurants but also hotels, motels, airlines, travel agencies, car rental agencies, and many retail stores honor the credit cards.

 The Medicare Act that becomes law July 30 sets up the first U.S. government-operated health insurance program for the elderly despite objections from the American Medical Association. Enacted by Congress as an amendment to the Social Security Act of 1935, Medicare is supported by payroll taxes and federal subsidies and covers 20 million elderly Americans.

The U.S. death rate falls to 943.2 per 100,000, down from 1,719 in 1900.

Americans buy $60 million worth of prescription drugs designed to help them lose weight, up from $30 million worth in 1960.

Congress establishes a National Clearinghouse for Smoking and Health and orders that cigarette packages be labeled "Caution: cigarette smoking may be hazardous to your health."

The $2 million appropriated by Congress for the National Clearinghouse (above) is less than 1 percent of the amount spent on TV advertising by the tobacco industry, and the legislation frees the industry from Federal Trade Commission regulations for the next 4 years. The major tobacco companies continue to diversify by acquiring food companies (*see* 1967).

Britain bans cigarette advertising from commercial television beginning August 1.

Alice Crimmins tells New York police that she gave her daughter Alice (Missy), 5, and her son Edmund, Jr., 4, a supper of manicotti and green beans at 7:30 on the evening of July 13, put them to bed at 9, found them well when she checked at midnight, but found them missing when she went to wake them in the morning. The 26-year-old cocktail waitress, whose estranged husband is a mechanic at Kennedy International Airport, occupies a garden apartment at 150-22 72nd Drive in Kew Gardens Hills, Queens. Her little boy's body, strangled by a pajama top, is discovered July 15 in Flushing. The decomposed body of the little girl is found July 19 on an embankment overlooking the Van Wyck Expressway. New York City Medical Examiner Milton Helpern, 63, finds on autopsy that Missy died 2 hours after eating her manicotti and beans, his evidence raises doubts about the mother's testimony, and a court will eventually convict her of murder.

The S.S. *Michelangelo* and the S.S. *Raffaello* go into service for the Italian line. The 45,911-ton sister ships are each 904 feet in length overall.

The Zeeland Bridge opened by Queen Juliana of the Netherlands is the longest bridge in Europe; it connects North Beveland with Schouwen-Duiveland more than a mile away and cuts the Rotterdam-Flushing run from 90 miles to 70 miles.

Germany's Emmerich Bridge opens to span the Rhine. It is 500 meters in length.

The Soviet Antonov AN-22 makes a flight carrying 720 passengers.

Brazil produces her one millionth automobile. Willys-Overland do Brasil, S.A., is Brazil's largest automaker; more than 50 percent owned by Brazilians, it also makes trucks and jeeps (*see* 1945).

A court order requires General Motors Corporation to make its bus patents freely available to other bus makers and to sell parts, engines, and designs to other busmakers in settlement of the suit brought by the Justice Department in 1956, but GM's grip on the bus market will remain virtually undiminished.

U.S. production of soft-top convertibles peaks at 507,000 for the model year 1965. The figure will drop to 28,000 by 1974 as air-pollution, vandalism in the form of top-slashing, higher driving speeds, body rattles, and factory-installed air-conditioning discourage sales of convertibles. By the end of 1975 only the Cadillac Eldorado will be available in soft-top convertible form, and production of Cadillac convertibles will end in 1976.

Unsafe at Any Speed by consumer advocate Ralph Nader notes that more than 51,000 Americans are killed each year by automobiles, a figure the Department of Commerce had projected for 1975. Nader has quit his job with the Department of Labor to crusade for consumer protection and he writes, "For more than half a century, the automobile has brought death, injury and the most inestimable sorrow and deprivation to millions of people."

Avis Rent-A-Car is acquired by International Telephone and Telegraph (ITT) which will promote the 9-year-old Avis firm in competition with Hertz and other car rental companies.

The greatest power failure in history blacks out most of seven states and Ontario November 9 and affects 30 million people in an 80,000 square mile area. New York's power fails at 5:27 in the afternoon, Brooklyn regains power at 2 the next morning, Queens at 4:20 in the morning, Manhattan at 6:58. Telephone companies maintain service and New York has a record 62 million phone calls in one day, nearly double the city's weekly average. Con Edison assures the public that no blackouts will recur, but New York will have a worse one in the summer of 1977.

The International Society for Krishna Consciousness is founded at New York by Calcutta chemist and Sanskrit scholar A. C. Bhaktivedanta, 59, whose followers call him Swami Prabhupada and regard him as the successor to an unbroken chain of Hindu spiritual teachers dating back 5,000 years. The swami has arrived in New York with $50 in rupees and a pair of cymbals, determined to spread the teachings of Lord Krishna, a supreme deity in Hindu mythology. He sits on a sidewalk in the East Village, begins the "Hare Krishna" chant that will soon become familiar throughout the world, offers young people a relatively ascetic life of devotion and proselytizing, an alternative to conventional society and drugs, and is soon holding religious classes in an empty storefront on Second Avenue, attracting youths who shave their heads, wear saffron-colored dhatis, and chant, "Hare Krishna. . . ."

U.S. university enrollments swell as young Americans take advantage of draft deferrals for college students to escape the expanding war in Vietnam, but campuses are tense with unrest.

Congress approves appropriations of $1.3 billion for federal aid to elementary and secondary schools.

Fall, 1967, is set as the target date for complete racial desegration of U.S. public schools (*see* 1954; 1966).

Britain's Universities of Kent and Warwick are founded.

University College is founded at Britain's Cambridge University.

"Early Bird" is put into orbit by the 3-year-old Communications Satellite Corporation (COMSAT) and relays telephone messages and television programs between Europe and the United States. The world's first commercial satellite, "Early Bird" is the first link in a global network of space communications planned by COMSAT.

New York's first all-news radio programming begins April 19 on Westinghouse Broadcasting's WINS whose lead will be followed by WCBS in New York and by other stations across the country as radio stations become more specialized.

Nonfiction *The Psychedelic Reader* by Harvard psychology professor Timothy Leary, 44, who has experimented with marijuana and other behavior-changing drugs. Leary advises readers to "drop out, turn on, tune in"; *The Autobiography of Malcolm X* by the late Afro-American Unity leader (above) and writer Alex Haley, 43, whose book has sales of 6 million. A cook in the U.S. Coast Guard from 1939 to 1959, Haley begins research in the National Archives at Washington to learn the history of his own family which will be published in 1976 under the title *Roots*.

Fiction *Everything That Rises Must Converge* by the late Flannery O'Connor who died last year at age 39 of a rare disease; *The Keeper of the House* by U.S. novelist Shirley Ann Grau, 36; *The Painted Bird* by Polish-American novelist Jerzy Kosinski, 32; *The House of Assignation (La Maison de rendezvous)* by Alain Robbe-Grillet; *The Last of the Pleasure Gardens* by Francis King; *God Bless You, Mr. Rosewater* by Kurt Vonnegut, Jr.; *The Magus* by John Fowles; *Thunderball* by Ian Fleming; *Manchild in the Promised Land* by U.S. reform school veteran Claude Brown.

Poetry *The Old Glory* (three verse dramas based on stories by Herman Melville and Nathaniel Hawthorne) by Robert Lowell; *The Lost World* by Randall Jarrell, who walks in front of an oncoming car at Chapel Hill, N.C., October 14 and dies at age 51.

Painting An oversize Campbell's Tomato Soup can by Andy Warhol; "Op" art that creates optical illusions by using color, form, and perspective in bizarre ways becomes fashionable; *Self-portrait* by Pablo Picasso; *Mystagogie d'espace* by Japanese abstractionist Josaku Maeda. Sculptor David Smith dies at Albany, N.Y., May 24 at age 59 following an automobile accident.

The Nikkormat camera introduced by Japan's Nippon Kogaku K.K. gives the company an entry in the medium-priced 35 mm. single-lens reflex market while its Nikon F of 1959 continues to dominate the high-priced field.

Theater *Loot* by Joe Orton 2/2 at Brighton, England; *The Odd Couple* by Neil Simon 3/10 at New York's Plymouth Theater, with Walter Matthau as Oscar Madison, Art Carney as Felix Ungar, 964 perfs.; *The Amen Corner* by James Baldwin 4/15 at New York's Ethel Barrymore Theater, with Bea Richards, Juanita Hall, Frank Silvera, 84 perfs.; *The Homecoming* by Harold Pinter 6/3 at London's Aldwych Theatre; *Generation* by U.S. playwright William Goodhart 10/6 at New York's Morosco Theater,

with Henry Fonda, 299 perfs.; *The Impossible Years* by U.S. playwrights Bob Fisher and Arthur Marx 10/13 at The Playhouse, New York, with Alan King, 670 perfs.; *Hogan's Goat* by U.S. playwright William Alfred, 43, 11/11 at New York's American Place Theater in St. Clements Church, with Ralph Waite, Cliff Gorman, Faye Dunaway, 607 perfs.; *Cactus Flower* by Abe Burrows 12/8 at New York's Royale Theater, with Lauren Bacall, Barry Nelson, Brenda Vaccaro, 1,234 perfs.

New York's Vivian Beaumont Theater opens in Lincoln Center October 21. Designed by Eero Saarinen, the theater has 1,140 seats.

Films Federico Fellini's *Juliet of the Spirits* with Giuletta Massini; Michelangelo Antonioni's *Red Desert;* David Lean's *Doctor Zhivago* with Omar Sharif, Rod Steiger, Julie Christie, Tom Courtenay, Alec Guinness; Gillo Pontecorvo's *The Battle of Algiers;* Frederic Rossif's *To Die in Madrid;* Sidney Lumet's *The Pawnbroker* with Rod Steiger; John Schlesinger's *Darling* with Julie Christie, Dirk Bogarde, Laurence Harvey; Ivan Passer's *Intimate Lighting;* Elliott Silverstein's *Cat Ballou* with Jane Fonda, Lee Marvin (as Kid Shelleen), Nat King Cole, Stubby Kaye; Blake Edwards's *The Great Race* with Tony Curtis, Jack Lemmon, Peter Falk, Natalie Wood; Alexander Mackendrick's *A High Wind in Jamaica* with Anthony Quinn, James Coburn, Deborah Baxter; Fred Coe's *A Thousand Clowns* with Jason Robards, Jr., Barbara Harris, Barry Gordon, Martin Balsam, Gene Saks; George Stevens's *The Greatest Story Ever Told* with Max von Sydow as Jesus; Ken Annakin's *Those Magnificent Men in Their Flying Machines* with Stuart Whitman, Robert Morley, Sarah Miles, Terry-Thomas, Red Skelton; Mark Robson's *Von Ryan's Express* with Frank Sinatra, Trevor Howard, Edward Mulhare; Luis Buñuel's *Diary of a Chambermaid* with Jeanne Moreau.

Stage musicals *Baker Street* 2/16 at New York's Broadway Theater, with Fritz Weaver as Sherlock Holmes, music and lyrics by Marian Grudeff and Raymond Jessel, 313 perfs.; *The Roar of the Greasepaint—The Smell of the Crowd* 5/16 at New York's Sam S. Shubert Theater, with Anthony Newley, Cyril Ritchard, Sally Smith, book, music, and lyrics by Leslie Bricusse and Newley, 231 perfs.; *Pickwick* 10/4 at New York's 46th Street Theater, with Charlotte Rae, music by Cyril Ornadel, lyrics by Leslie Bricusse, songs that include "If I Ruled the World," 55 perfs.; *Drat! The Cat!* 10/10 at New York's Martin Beck Theater, with Lesley Ann Warren, Elliott Gould, music by Milton Schafer, book and lyrics by Ira Levin, songs that include "She (He) Touched Me," 8 perfs.; *On a Clear Day You Can See Forever* 10/17 at New York's Mark Hellinger Theater, with Barbara Harris, music by Burton Lane, lyrics by Alan Jay Lerner, songs that include the title song, 272 perfs.; *Man of La Mancha* 11/22 at New York's ANTA-Washington Square Theater, with Richard Kiley, Joan Diener, Irving Jacobson, Robert Rounseville, book based on the Cervantes novel *Don Quijote de la Mancha* of 1615, music by Mitch Leigh, 37, lyrics by Joe Darian, 48, songs that include "The Impossible Dream," "Dulcinea," and the title song, 2,329 perfs.; *Charlie Girl* 12/15 at London's Adelphi Theatre, with Christine Holmes, Anna Neagle, music and lyrics by David Heneker and John Taylor, 2,202 perfs.

First performances   Symphony No. 8 by Walter Piston 3/5 at Boston's Symphony Hall; *Gemini Variations* on an Epigram of Kodaly for Flute, Violin, and Piano Duet by Benjamin Britten in June at Aldeburgh's Jubilee Hall; *From the Steeples and Mountains* by the late Charles Ives (who wrote it in 1901) 7/30 at New York's Philharmonic Hall; *The Golden Brown and the Green Apple* by Duke Ellington 7/30 at New York's Philharmonic Hall; *Voices for Today* by Benjamin Britten 10/24 (20th anniversary of the United Nations) at New York, London, and Paris.

The Rolling Stones gain huge success with a recording of "(I Can't Get No) Satisfaction." The 2-year-old English rock group has taken its name from the Muddy Waters song "Rolling Stone Blues," leader Michael Philip "Mick" Jagger, 22, is backed by drummer Charlie Watts and bass guitarist Bill Wyman, and the Rolling Stones invoke a moody, frankly sexual tone derivative of Chuck Berry that makes the Beatles sound like choirboys by comparison.

The Grateful Dead has its beginnings in a San Francisco acid-rock group started at 710 Ashbury Street by local electric guitarist Jerry Garcia, 24, with drummer Mickey Hart (whose father will vanish with the group's profits), Ron "Pigpen" McKernan, and others. Garcia has dropped acid with Ken Kesey, he has taken the name Grateful Dead from an Oxford dictionary notation on the burial of Egyptian pharaohs, he is called Captain Trips by his admirers, but McKernan will die of alcohol and drugs and Garcia will receive a year's probation in New Jersey in 1973 for possession of LSD, marijuana, and cocaine.

Big Brother and the Holding Company is founded by San Francisco rock musicians Peter Albin, 20, Sam Andrew, 23, James Martin Gurley, 23, and Brooklyn-born drummer David Getz, 26, who will add singer Janis Joplin, 22, to their group next year.

Popular songs   "Yesterday" and "Michelle" by John Lennon and Paul McCartney; "Sounds of Silence" by U.S. songwriters Paul Simon, 24, and Art Garfunkel, 25; "I Got You Babe" by U.S. singer-songwriter Sonny Bono, 30, who has married singer Cher Sirkisian, 21; "What the World Needs Now Is Love" by Bert Bachrach, lyrics by Hal David; "It's Not Unusual" by Gordon Mills; "Crying in the Chapel" by Artie Glenn; "Like a Rolling Stone" by Bob Dylan; "The Shadow of Your Smile" by Johnny Mandel, lyrics by Paul Francis Webster (for Vincente Minelli's film *The Sandpiper*); "Lara's Theme (Somewhere My Love)" by Maurice Jarre, lyrics by Paul Francis Webster (for the film *Dr. Zhivago*).

 A British Court convicts 10 professional soccer players of fixing matches.

The Los Angeles Dodgers win the World Series by defeating the Minnesota Twins 4 games to 3.

Bravo floor wax is introduced by S. C. Johnson Company (*see* Glo-Coat, 1932).

The miniskirt appears in December in "swinging" London. Designed by Mary Quant, the provocative new skirt comes to 6 inches above the knee, it will help Quant's 10-year-old Bazaar on King's Road, Chelsea, become an international conglomerate of fashion, cosmetics, fabrics, bed linens, children's books, dolls, and wine (Mary Quant Limited), and the skirt eventually will dwindle to micro-mini lengths.

A U.S. Department of Housing and Urban Affairs (HUD) is inaugurated September 9.

St. Louis's Gateway Arch is completed by Finnish-American architect Eero Saarinen. The 630-foot high memorial on the city's waterfront commemorates the Louisiana Purchase of 1803.

New York's CBS building is completed by Eero Saarinen & Associates on the Avenue of the Americas (Sixth Avenue) at 52nd Street. The building's 38 floors are mainly supported from a central core.

New York's J. C. Penney building designed by Shreve, Lamb & Harmon Associates goes up on the Avenue of the Americas between 52nd and 53rd Streets.

The Washington Hilton opens at the corner of Connecticut and Florida Avenues. The new 1,250-room hotel is the largest in the nation's capital.

The Tel Aviv Hilton opens in Israel. The 16-story hotel has been designed by Israeli architect Jacov Rechter.

London's Royal Garden Hotel opens with 500 rooms. The new 14-story hotel is a deep-balconied, T-shaped steel and glass structure.

Dr. Martin Luther King, Jr., gave the U.S. civil rights movement effective leadership that produced results.

1965 (cont.) Congress appropriates funds to remove U.S. highway billboards at the urging of "Lady Bird" Johnson, wife of the president. All billboards on sections of interstate and primary highways not zoned "commercial or industrial" are to be razed by July 1, 1970, and states are to pass conforming laws and prepare regulations to carry out the intent of the federal law, but billboard company lobbyists, officials, legislators, and bureaucrats collaborate to block billboard removal. The "Lady Bird Bill" will not begin to take effect until 1970 when the Senate will vote unanimously to apply $100 million of the $5.5 billion per year highway trust fund to compensate billboard companies for removal of their signs.

A major drought in the northeastern United States forces New York City to turn off air-conditioning in sealed skyscrapers in order to conserve water. City fountains are turned off, lawn-watering is forbidden, and signs appear reading "Save water: shower with a friend."

 Congress enacts a 5-year, $25-million anadromous fish program to conserve alewives, river sturgeon, salmon, shad, and striped bass which swim upriver to spawn (see Maine, 1948).

 Pakistan and much of India suffer widespread starvation as monsoon rains fail and crops wither in a drought of unprecedented proportions.

"There is a global food catastrophe now building up on the horizon which threatens to engulf the free world and the Communist world alike," says Thomas Ware of the Freedom from Hunger Foundation.

 Soviet Russia suffers another crop failure as it did in 1963 and is forced to pay gold for wheat from Australia and Canada. Moscow is discouraged from buying U.S. wheat by a presidential requirement that half of all shipments be made in U.S. vessels (at high cost) and by a longshoremen's threat not to load any grain for shipment to Communist Russia.

Dwarf Indica rice with higher per-acre yields is introduced in India, the Philippines, and other Asian nations (see Taiwan, 1955).

U.S. farms fall in number to 3.5 million, down from 6.84 million in 1935, 3.7 million in 1959.

 Dry milk sent abroad by the U.S. Department of Agriculture in overseas aid programs is enriched with vitamins A and D at the insistence of the U.S. Public Health Service, but milk for domestic poverty programs (as in Appalachia, above) is not enriched.

Half of all Americans enjoy "good" diets, up from less than one quarter in 1943, according to a new study.

 Greenwich Village, New York, food faddist Beth Ann Simon dies at age 24 after having dwindled away to 70 pounds on a "macrobiotic" diet consisting chiefly of brown rice sprinkled with Gomashio (four parts sesame seeds to one part sea salt) eaten slowly with green tea. Disclaimed by Zen Buddhists, the diet is promoted by writer George Ohsawa whose foundation is raided by Food and Drug Administration agents. They seize literature and illegally labeled foods but cultists in the youth underground extoll Ohsawa's diets and open "macrobiotic" restaurants.

 Cranapple fruit juice is introduced by Ocean Spray Cranberries, Inc. (see 1959).

Diet Pepsi is introduced by Pepsi-Cola Company (see Tab, 1963). Pepsi president Donald M. Kendall, 44, engineers a merger with Frito-Lay, Inc., to create Pepsico, Inc. (see 1950; 1961).

R. J. Reynolds Company acquires Penick and Ford as it continues to diversify (see 1961). The company's products include Brer Rabbit Molasses, Vermont Maid Syrup, My*T*Fine puddings and pie fillings, College Inn chicken a la king, and other College Inn prepared foods (see Chun King, 1966).

Consolidated Food Corporation acquires Popsicle Industries, Inc. (see Epperson, 1924). A court order forces Consolidated to divest itself of 100 supermarkets and 26 drugstores with combined sales of more than $200 million. Consolidated begins to diversify, acquiring the Electrolux Company (see 1921).

Apple Jacks breakfast food—55 percent sugar—is introduced by the Kellogg Company (see 1964; 1966).

Cavenham Foods is founded by British entrepreneur James Goldsmith, 32, who will soon acquire Bovril and who will build his candy and diet foods producer into Europe's third largest food processor after Unilever and Nestlé Alimentana S.A.

Home-delivered milk accounts for 25 percent of U.S. milk sales, down from more than 50 percent before World War II. The figure will be 15 percent by 1975.

 The World Health Organization finds that family planning advice is welcome where such advice was protested in 1962.

Oxfam decides to support family planning projects as well as the programs for famine relief and food production it has supported since its founding in 1942.

Connecticut's 1879 law prohibiting sale of birth control devices is ruled unconstitutional by the Supreme Court.

The United States has 700 public birth control clinics with 33 states giving, or about to give, tax support to birth control (see 1964).

U.S. live births total some 300,000 less than in the peak year of 1957 and in some months are at a rate lower than in 1939.

A new U.S. immigration bill that abolishes the national origins quota system of 1952 is signed into law by President Johnson October 3 at the Statue of Liberty in New York Harbor. The new law permits entry by any alien who meets qualifications of education and skill provided such entry will not jeopardize the job of an American.

The new U.S. immigration act (above) imposes an overall limit of 120,000 visas per year for Western Hemisphere countries and 170,000 per year for the rest of the world, but immediate relatives of U.S. citizens may enter without regard to these limits.

The population of the world reaches 3.3 billion.

1966 An encyclical issued by Pope Paul VI January 1 during a 37-day truce in Vietnam asks for an end to hostilities in Southeast Asia, Japanese prime minister Eisaku Sato announces an international peace mission for Vietnam January 25, the Senate Foreign Relations Committee's chairman J. W. Fulbright challenges the legality of U.S. military intervention in Vietnam January 28, Senator Fulbright questions Secretary of State Dean Rusk, but U.S. bombing of North Vietnam begins by the end of the month.

International Days of Protest in many world cities protest U.S. policy in Vietnam.

India's Prime Minister Lal Bahadur Shastri dies of a heart attack January 11 at age 61. Mrs. Indira Gandhi, daughter of the late Jawaharlal Nehru, is elected to succeed Shastri January 19.

France's President de Gaulle proposes a "Europeanized Europe" free of U.S. and Soviet domination, he announces March 11 that France will withdraw her troops from the integrated NATO command, and he requests that NATO remove all its bases and headquarters from French territory by April 1 of next year (*see* 1949). President de Gaulle's foreign minister visits the capitals of Eastern Europe and de Gaulle himself visits the U.S.S.R. from June 20 to July 1 on which date Supreme Headquarters Allied Powers Europe (SHAPE) moves from Paris to Casteau, Belgium.

Romania's Premier Nicolae Ceausescu proposes dissolution of both the North Atlantic Treaty Organization and the Warsaw Pact alliance in a meeting of Warsaw Pact powers at Bucharest July 4 to 6. Ceausescu also asks that all nations withdraw their troops from the territories of all other nations.

Ghana's army and police officers stage a coup February 24 and oust President Nkrumah who is away on a visit to Peking. Given refuge and named co-president by Guinea's President Sekou Toure, Nkrumah threatens military action to regain the power he held for 15 years.

Uganda's Prime Minister Milton Obote assumes full powers February 22 and deposes Sir Edward Mutesa II from the presidency March 2 (*see* 1962; 1971).

President Mobutu of the Democratic Republic of Congo takes over all legislative powers from Parliament in March and renames the nation's cities July 1. Leopoldville becomes Kinshasa, Stanleyville becomes Kisingani, Elisabethville becomes Lubumbashi (*see* Zaire, 1971).

South Africa's Prime Minister Henrik F. Verwoerd is assassinated September 6 after 8 years in power. He is succeeded a week later by Balthazar J. Vorster who will continue the Verwoerd policies of apartheid and support for the white regime in Rhodesia.

The UN General Assembly terminates South Africa's mandate in Southwest Africa (Namibia), but South Africa calls the action illegal, ignores it, and refuses a UN administrative commission entry into the mandate territory.

Botswana becomes an independent republic within the British Commonwealth September 30 and elects Sir Seretse Khama first president of the bleak territory known heretofore as British Bechuanaland.

Lesotho becomes an independent kingdom within the British Commonwealth October 4. Formerly British Basutoland, the new state ruled by King Moshoeshoe runs into difficulties when the king tries to establish more effective control. He is imprisoned, and he is released only after promising to abide by the constitution.

Rhodesia's President Ian Smith meets with British Prime Minister Wilson on a warship off Gibraltar in early December, they make a tentative agreement that Rhodesia will have majority rule within 10 or 15 years, the Salisbury government rejects the agreement December 5, London appeals December 6 for UN sanctions against the Smith government, the UN Security Council imposes mandatory sanctions, but South Africa and Portugal refuse to participate.

Guyana in South America becomes an independent state within the British Commonwealth May 26. Black leader Forbes Burnham becomes first prime minister of the country once called British Guiana.

The Dominican Republic elects moderate Joaquin Balaguer president over Juan Bosch after more than a year of occupation by an inter-American peace-keeping force. Balaguer has U.S. support and embarks on a program of economic and social reform as the OAS withdraws its peacekeeping force in October.

Jordan suspends relations with the Palestine Liberation Organization in July but is unable to stop PLO raids across the Jordan into Israel. The Jordanian village of Sammu is attacked November 13 by Israeli tanks and aircraft in reprisal for the PLO raids and the undeclared war brings agitation by Palestinians for the overthrow of Jordan's Hussein who is supported by Saudi Arabia and by the United States (*see* Six-Day war, 1967).

President Johnson visits New Zealand, Australia, the Philippines, South Vietnam, Thailand, Malaysia, and South Korea from October 19 to November 2, leaders of the allied nations pledge support for the war in Vietnam in a conference at Manila October 24 to 25, targets around Hanoi are bombed intensively in early December, and by year's end 389,000 U.S. troops are in South Vietnam.

The People's Republic of China fires her first nuclear bomb from a guided missile October 27.

Mao Tse-tung's wife Chiang Chin gets her first political job December 5. Now 52, she is made cultural consultant to the General Political Department of the Chinese Army as Mao acts to end the insolence of Red Guard youths, but Mme. Mao will become increasingly sympathetic toward the youths.

1966 (cont.) Complete decipherment of the genetic code is announced by MIT biochemist Har Gobind Khorana, 44, who synthesized vitamin A in 1959. He has built on the work of National Institutes of Health biochemist Marshall Warren Nirenberg, 39, and of Cornell University biochemist Robert William Holley, 44 (*see* Watson and Crick, 1961).

The Medicare program of health care for the U.S. elderly goes into effect July 1 (*see* 1965). The program is financed through Social Security payments.

The U.S. infant mortality rate falls to 24.3 per thousand live births, down from 29 in 1951 but the British rate falls to 20, down from 30, and the Swedish rate to 15. Inadequate health care delivery systems and poor nutrition among expectant mothers in low income groups are held responsible for the relatively poor U.S. showing.

Economic sanctions against Ian Smith's Rhodesia are ordered March 18 by the U.S. Department of Commerce which prohibits export of anything that may be useful to Rhodesia (*see* 1965).

University of Wisconsin students protest draft deferment examinations. They occupy administration buildings May 16 to begin a sit-in demonstration (*see* 1965; Columbia, 1968).

The National Organization of Women (NOW) is founded to help U.S. women gain equal rights. Founder and president of the new civil rights organization is Betty Friedan.

Federal funds are ordered withheld from 12 Alabama, Louisiana, and Mississippi school districts that are in violation of 1964 Civil Rights Act guidelines, but the May 13 order by Secretary of Health, Education and Welfare John W. Gardner ignores Northern school districts that have done nothing about desegregating schools.

The University of Mississippi's first black graduate James Meredith is shot from ambush and wounded June 6 while walking from Memphis to Jackson, Miss., in a voting rights demonstration (*see* 1962). The march continues until June 26 when 15,000 demonstrators rally before the state capitol.

U.S. police officers must warn anyone taken into custody that he or she has a right to counsel and to remain silent and the courts must provide lawyers for those too poor to pay, the Supreme Court rules June 13 in the case of *Miranda v. Arizona*. The 5-to-4 decision handed down by Chief Justice Earl Warren declares that the privilege against self-incrimination under the Fifth Amendment rules out confessions by persons in police custody unless careful steps are taken to protect the rights of suspects. "No statement obtained [in the atmosphere of the police station] can truly be the product of [the defendant's] free choice," says the majority decision, but Justice Harlan denounces the decision as "dangerous experimentation" at a time of a "high crime rate that is a matter of growing concern" (*see* 1971).

A month of racial riots and looting begins June 23 at Cleveland and blacks in Chicago's West Side riot for three nights in mid-July.

Atlanta has race riots in its black Summerhill section after having been the first city in the South to integrate its public schools without disturbance.

Alabama Governor George C. Wallace signs a bill September 2 forbidding public schools to comply with the Office of Education's desegregation guidelines.

The U.S. Senate votes 49 to 37 September 21 to prohibit voluntary prayers in U.S. public schools (*see* Supreme Court decision, 1963).

Massachusetts voters elect the first black U.S. senator. They send Edward Brooke to Washington to join Edward M. Kennedy.

The largest year-to-year rise in the U.S. cost of living since 1958 is announced April 21 by the Department of Labor's Bureau of Labor Statistics which reports that the March, 1966, figure was 2.8 percent above the figure for the preceding March. The Bureau reports August 22 that the fiscal year ended June 30 was the most inflationary year since 1957.

The United States has 2,377 corporate mergers, up from 844 in 1960 (*see* 1967).

TWA boss Howard Hughes loses his control of the airline, he sells his TWA stock at $86 per share (the price will soon drop to a small fraction of that amount), and he moves to Las Vegas with the $546 million in proceeds. Now 60 and long a recluse, Hughes quickly uses $200 million to buy four hotels, seven gambling casinos, the municipal airport, a regional airline, and mining properties throughout the state of Nevada, including part of the old Comstock Lode of 1859 that with new technology will yield more gold.

BankAmerica Service Corporation is created by California's Bank of America to license other banks to issue the BankAmericard and to participate in the system (*see* 1958). By year's end there are 2 million BankAmericard holders and 64,000 merchant outlets (*see* 1968; Master Charge, below).

Interbank Card Association has its beginnings in Interbank Card, Inc., which is created by a group of U.S. banks that will purchase the Master Charge name and symbol early in 1969 from Western States Bankcard Association and will license other banks to issue the Master Charge card and to participate in the system. Master Charge transactions will total more than $7.87 billion by 1973 as use of the card (which is issued without charge like the BankAmericard to bank customers) expands and is accepted by hotels, restaurants, auto rental agencies, airlines, and the like, as well as by retail merchants.

Pan American World Airways orders 25 Boeing 747 jumbo jets, setting a lead that other carriers will be forced to follow. Depending on seat configuration, the new planes will carry from 342 to 490 passengers, numbers that will tax the capacities of existing terminal facilities. Few airlines will be able to keep their 747 jets filled and many, including Pan Am, will suffer financial reverses as a result of adopting the unprofitable jumbo jets (*see* 1970).

Laker Airways is founded by English aviation executive Freddie Laker, 44, who made his first fortune ferrying cargo to Berlin during the Berlin Blockade of 1948 to 1949. Laker had bought 12 obsolete bombers with a $100,000 loan from a friend, converted them to cargo carriers, and used his profits to help start Britain's largest independent airline (British United), but he has quarreled with BU's chairman and has left to start his own charter airline, carrying passengers but no cargo.

British Motor Holdings is created by a merger of British Motor Corporation with Jaguar Cars, Ltd. (*see* 1952; British Leyland, 1968).

Britain's Rover Group is merged into Leyland Motor Corporation (*see* 1961; British Leyland, 1968).

FIAT chief Vittorio Valletta, 82, signs an agreement to build a $1 billion automobile plant in the Soviet Union. The plant is to be constructed at Togliatti-grad, named for Italian Communist leader Palmiro Togliatti (*see* 1967).

New York makes Fifth Avenue one-way southbound and Madison Avenue one-way northbound beginning January 14 to ease congestion caused by a transit strike (*see* Third and Lexington Avenues, 1960); Tiffany & Co. president Walter Hoving has led opposition to the one-way traffic scheme and says Fifth Avenue is now a "superhighway."

New York City subway fares rise to 20 cents July 5, up from 15 cents in 1953 (*see* 1970).

The Tennessee Valley Authority orders construction of a 1 million kilowatt nuclear power plant at Decatur, Ala., in the heart of the coal country. By late 1972 there will be 30 nuclear plants in the United States with 51 more under construction and 72 on order.

The *Times* of London changes its format after 178 years to run news on its front page rather than classified advertisements. Lord Thompson of Fleet Street, now 72, has gained control and has ordered the change (*see* 1953).

The *New York Herald-Tribune, Journal-American,* and *World-Telegram & Sun* announce a merger March 21 after 2 months of fighting an American Newspaper Guild charge of unfair labor practices by all three. The *Herald-Tribune* is to continue daily morning publication, the *World-Journal* is to appear afternoons, and the *World-Journal & Tribune* is to be a combined Sunday paper. The ANG strikes April 23 and all three papers cease publication. The *World-Journal & Tribune* appears for the first time September 12 and quickly sells out its 930,000 press run, but the Department of Justice forces the new company to offer its syndicated 19 columns and features to other papers (*see* 1967).

The Supreme Court rules that material with redeeming social value is uncensorable. The court modifies its antiobscenity stand of 1957, but still defines obscene material as any matter in which "to the average person applying contemporary standards, the dominant theme taken as a whole appeals to a prurient interest" (*see* 1967).

Wells, Rich, Greene, Inc., advertising is founded by New York advertising copywriter Mary Berg Wells, 37, with her former associates at Jack Tinker & Partners Dick Rich and Stewart Greene. Braniff Airways soon leaves Tinker for WRG, Braniff president Harding Lawrence, 45, will divorce his wife next year to marry Wells, but the agency will subsequently drop the Braniff account to take the larger TWA account.

Radio Corporation of America (RCA) acquires Random House publishers for $40 million.

Nonfiction *Quotations of Chairman Mao* is published at Peking; *On Aggression* by Konrad Lorenz.

Fiction *In Cold Blood* by Truman Capote; *The Fixer* by Bernard Malamud; *The Comedians* by Graham Greene; *The Group* by Mary McCarthy; *Giles Goat-Boy* by John Barth; *The Crying of Lot 49* by Thomas Pynchon; *Black Light* by Galway Kinnell; *The Solid Mandala* by Patrick White; *The Birds Fall Down* by Rebecca West; *Collected Short Stories* by Katherine Ann Porter; *Paradiso* by Cuban novelist-poet José Lezama Lima, 56; *The Valley of the Dolls* by U.S. novelist Jacqueline Susann.

Painting *Le triomph de la musique* by Marc Chagall for New York's new Metropolitan Opera House (below); *Yellow and Red Brushstrokes* by Roy Lichtenstein. Alberto Giacometti dies at Chur, Switzerland, January 11 at age 64; Hans Hofmann dies at New York February 17 at age 85; Maxfield Parrish dies in New Hampshire March 30 at age 95; Jean Arp dies at Basel June 17 at age 78.

Theater *Die Plebem proben den Aufstrand* by Günter Grass; *Black Comedy* by Peter Shaffer; *The Lion in Winter* by U.S. playwright James Goldman, 38, 3/3 at New York's Ambassador Theater, with Robert Preston as Henry II, Rosemary Harris as Eleanor of Aquitaine, 92 perfs.; *A Delicate Balance* by Edward Albee 9/22 at New York's Martin Beck Theater, with Jessica Tandy, Hume Cronyn, 132 perfs., Pulitzer prize 1967; *America Hurrah* by Belgian-American playwright Jean-Claude van Itallie, 31, 11/7 at New York's off-Broadway Pocket Theater, consisting of three one-act plays (*Interview, TV,* and *Motel*)—a savage attack on American life.

U.S. nightclub comedian Lenny Bruce (Leonard Alfred Schneider) is found dead in his Hollywood, Calif., house August 3 at age 39. Bruce was imprisoned for obscenity in 1961, a Los Angeles jury found him guilty of possessing narcotics in 1963, but he had become a cult hero among alienated U.S. youths.

Television drama *Star Trek* in September on NBC stations with Bill Shatner as Captain James T. Kirk,

1966 (cont.) Leonard Nimoy as Mr. Spock in a science-fiction series that will continue for 78 episodes.

Films Mike Nichols's *Who's Afraid of Virginia Woolf?* with Richard Burton, Elizabeth Taylor; Michelangelo Antonioni's *Blow-Up* with Vanessa Redgrave, David Hemmings; Fred Zinneman's *A Man For All Seasons* with Paul Scofield, Robert Shaw; Lewis Gilbert's *Alfie* with Michael Caine, Shelley Winters; Alain Resnais's *La Guerre Est Finie;* Jan Nemec's *A Report on the Party and the Guests;* Silvio Narizzano's *Georgy Girl* with Lynn Redgrave, James Mason, Alan Bates, Charlotte Rampling; Basil Dearden's *Khartoum* with Charleton Heston, Laurence Olivier, Ralph Richardson; Cornel Wilde's *The Naked Prey* with Cornel Wilde; Bryan Forbes's *The Wrong Box* with Ralph Richardson, John Mills, Peter Cook, Dudley Moore, Peter Sellers, Michael Caine; Richard Brooks's *The Professionals* with Burt Lancaster, Lee Marvin, Robert Ryan, Jack Palance, Claudia Cardinale; Karel Reisz's *Morgan!* with Vanessa Redgrave; Billy Wilder's *The Fortune Cookie* with Walter Matthau, Jack Lemmon; Frances Ford Coppola's *You're a Big Boy Now* with Peter Kastner, Elizabeth Hartman; James Hill's *Born Free* with Virginia McKenna, Bill Travers; Norman Jewison's *The Russians Are Coming! The Russians Are Coming!* with Alan Arkin, Carl Reiner, Jonathan Winters, Eva Marie Sainte, Paul Ford, Theodore Bikel; Hiroshi Inagaki's *Chushingura* with Toshiro Mifune.

New York's Metropolitan Opera House opens September 16 to replace the 83-year-old Met that will be razed next year. Designed by Abby Rockefeller's brother-in-law Wallace K. Harrison, the new $45.7 million Met has 2,729 seats and is the largest building in Lincoln Center, and the focal point of the Center's plaza, but its premiere of the opera *Antony and Cleopatra* with Leontyne Price, music by Samuel Barber, is a disaster.

Broadway musicals *Sweet Charity* 1/29 at the Palace Theater, with Gwen Verdon, book by Neil Simon based on the 1957 Federico Fellini film *The Nights of Cabiria,* music by Cy Coleman, lyrics by Dorothy Fields, songs that include "Big Spender," "If My Friends Could See Me Now," 608 perfs.; *It's A Bird! It's A Plane! It's Superman!* 3/29 at the Alvin Theater, with Bob Holliday, music by Charles Strouse, lyrics by Lee Adams, songs that include "You've Got Possibilities," "We Don't Matter at All," 75 perfs.; *Mame* 5/24 at the Winter Garden Theater, with Angela Lansbury, music and lyrics by Jerry Herman, songs that include "If He Walks into My Life," "Open a New Window," "We Need a Little Christmas," 1,508 perfs.; *The Apple Tree* 10/18 at the Shubert Theater, with Barbara Harris, Larry Blyden, Alan Alda, music by Jerry Bock, lyrics by Sheldon Harnick, 463 perfs.; *Cabaret* 11/20 at the Broadhurst Theater, with Jill Haworth as Sally Bowles, Jack Guilford, Lotte Lenya, Joel Grey, book based on Christopher Isherwood's *Berlin Stories,* music by John Kander, 39, lyrics by Fred Ebb, 31, songs that include "Money, Money," "Wilkommen," and the title song, 1,165 perfs.; *I Do! I Do!* 12/5 at the 46th Street Theater, with Mary Martin, Robert Preston, music by Harvey Schmidt, lyrics by Tom Jones, songs that include "My Cup Runneth Over," 584 perfs.

First performances Concerto for Violincello and Orchestra No. 2 by Dmitri Shostakovich 9/25 at Moscow with Mstislav Rostropovich as soloist; Symphony No. 6 by Roger Sessions 11/19 at Newark, N.J.

Popular songs "Yellow Submarine," "Nowhere Man," and "Eleanor Rigby" by John Lennon and Paul McCartney of the Beatles; "Sunshine Superman" and "Mellow Yellow" by Scottish rock singer Donovan Leitch; "If I Were a Carpenter" by Tim Hardin; "Scarborough Fair—Canticle" by Paul Simon and Art Garfunkel; "Monday, Monday" and "California Dreamin'" by John E. A. Phillips, 30, of The Mamas and The Papas (Phillips, Cass Elliott, 22, Dennis Doherty, 24, Holly Michelle Gilliam, 22); *Jefferson Airplane Takes Off* (album) by the Jefferson Airplane (Grace Slick, 22, guitarist-banjoist Paul Kantner, 24, bass guitarist Jack Casady, 22, guitarist Jorma Kankonen, 25, drummer Spencer Dryden, 23), a rock group that has been playing at San Francisco's Fillmore Auditorium; "Summer in the City" by John B. Sebastian, Mark Sebastian, Joe Butler; "These Boots Are Made for Walking" by U.S. singer Lee Hazlewood; "Guantanamero" by Pete Seeger and Hector Angulo, lyrics from a poem by the 19th century Cuban patriot José Marti; "Winchester Cathedral" by English songwriter Geoffrey Stephen; "What Now My Love" ("El Manthout") by French singer-composer Gilbert Becaud, lyrics by P. De-Lanoe, English lyrics by Carl Sigman; "Alfie" by Burt F. Bacharach, lyrics by Hal David (title song for film); "Georgy Girl" by Tom Springfield, lyrics by Jim Dale (title song for film); "Born Free" by John Barry, lyrics by Don Black (title song for film); "Strangers in the Night" by Bert Kaempfort, lyrics by Eddie Snyder (for the film *A Man Could Get Killed*); "Happy Together" by Alan Lee Gordon and Garry Bonner; "Good Vibrations" by Brian Wilson of the Beach Boys.

The electric guitar gains prominence in England where U.S. rock musician Jimi Hendrix, 23, begins to exploit the full potential of the relatively new instrument. Hendrix uses imagination, virtuosity, invention, and sexual pantomime in his stage appearances.

U.S. college athlete Jim Ryun runs the mile in 3 minutes, 51.3 seconds.

Houston's $31 million Astrodome opens to provide the Astros and the Oilers with a 44,500-seat air-conditioned stadium. Louisiana voters approve a constitutional amendment that would permit construction of a New Orleans stadium estimated to cost $35 million, but by the time the 72,675-seat New Orleans Superdome opens in 1975 it will have cost upwards of $175 million.

The Milwaukee Braves become the Atlanta Braves but retain Hank Aaron (*see* 1954; Brewers, 1970).

The Baltimore Orioles win the World Series by defeating the Los Angeles Dodgers 4 games to 0.

England wins her first World Cup in football (soccer) by defeating West Germany 4 to 2 at Wembley Stadium. It is the first victory for a home team since World Cup play began in 1930, Geoff Hurst scores three of the English goals to achieve the first hat trick in World Cup finals, and the game goes into overtime for the first time since 1934.

TV commercials for cigarettes are criticized by Washington, D.C., law clerk John Banzhaf III, 26, of the U.S. District Court who writes a letter to WCBS-TV, New York, citing commercials that present smoking as "socially acceptable and desirable, manly, and a necessary part of a rich full life." Banzhaf requests free time roughly equal to the time spent promoting "the virtues and values of smoking" to "present contrasting views on the issue of the benefits and advisability of smoking" (*see* 1967).

Some 13 million Americans will give up smoking in the next 4 years. The percentage of male smokers will drop from 52 percent to 42 percent, the percentage of female smokers from 34 percent to 31 percent.

Congress approves a plan to send millions of pounds of tobacco to famine-stricken India under terms of the 1954 law P.L. 480 at the recommendation of North Carolina Democrat Harold S. Cooley. Chairman of the House Agriculture Committee, Cooley says the tobacco will ease the tension of starving people and will enable them to eat and assimilate their food better (his remark will be stricken from the *Congressional Record*).

Eight student nurses in a Chicago dormitory in East 100th Street die July 13 at the hands of 24-year-old murderer Richard F. Speck who has served time in Texas for theft, forgery, and parole violations that included threatening a woman with a knife. Speck will go on trial early next year at Peoria, he will be found guilty on all eight counts of murder, and the jury will recommend that he be sent to the electric chair. A psychiatrist who examined Speck for 100 hours will tell newsmen that the man told him he had taken six goofballs (barbiturates), an injection of some other narcotic, and numerous alcoholic drinks on July 13, and that brain damage in conjunction with drugs had left him irresponsible for his acts, the Supreme Court will overrule the death sentence in 1971, and in 1972 a judge will impose eight sentences of from 50 to 150 years each.

New York's Pennsylvania Station of 1910 is demolished to make way for a graceless new rail terminal designed by Charles Luckman Associates plus a 29-story office building, a new 20,000-seat Madison Square Garden sports arena to replace the Garden of 1925, a 1,000-seat Felt Forum, a 500-seat movie theater, and a 48-lane bowling alley.

New York's Pavilion apartment house is completed overlooking the East River at 500 East 77th Street.

The 35-story building has 852 units and is the city's largest single apartment building.

New York's United Nations Plaza is completed by Harrison, Abramovitz & Harris on First Avenue between 48th and 49th Streets. The twin 32-story luxury apartment towers rise above an office block.

Chicago's Civic Center is completed by Jacques Brownson of C. F. Murphy Associates.

Atlanta's Hyatt Regency Hotel opens in Peachtree Center with a dramatic 22-story atrium of rough poured concrete filled with hanging plants and fountains in which lighted glass-walled elevators fly up and down. Local architect John Portman, 42, has designed the 23-story 1,000-room hotel which sets a new pattern of hotel construction that will be followed by Portman-designed hotels at Chicago's O'Hare Airport, at San Francisco, at Detroit, New Orleans, Memphis, Phoenix, and elsewhere with backing from Chicago financier Jay Pritzker and Pritzker's brother-in-law Hugo Friend who will obtain major financing from such firms as Prudential Insurance, Ford Motor Company, and Tenneco, Inc.

The 1924 Oil Pollution Act is emasculated by a revision requiring that government prosecutors prove gross and willful negligence.

California legislators respond to complaints about smog in the air and impose limitations on the amounts of carbon monoxide and hydrocarbons that may be emitted from automobile exhausts. The new standards are to take effect on 1969 model cars and are to raise prices no more than $45 per vehicle.

The first rare and endangered species list issued by the U.S. Department of the Interior contains 78 species. The number will increase in 3 years to 89—14 mammals, 46 birds, 8 reptiles and amphibians, 21 fish.

Guadelupe Mountains National Park is authorized by act of Congress but is not opened to the public. The park embraces 77,518 acres of Permian limestone mountain rising from the Texas desert.

A Welsh landslide October 21 at Landsfford Aberfan kills 116 children and 28 adults as water-soaked coalmine wastes plow into the Pantglas Junior School and 16 homes. Slurry from the Merthyr Vale mine has been "tipped" onto Aberfan's hillsides since 1870 and a subterranean spring under coal tip No. 7 has soaked the waste rock, precipitating the slide.

India suffers her worst famine in more than 20 years and imports more than 8 million tons of U.S. wheat and other foodstuffs, but rice-eaters in Karala State riot in protest against eating wheat flour (*see* 1944).

The world food crisis reaches new intensity as total food production falls 2 percent below last year's output. Food production in Africa, Latin America, and the Far East falls well below prewar levels.

"Human beings will ultimately have to kill and eat one another if the world's population growth continues at its present rate," predicts vitamin pioneer Albert Szent-Györgyi, now 73 (*see* 1928).

President Johnson escalated U.S. involvement in the war between South Vietnam and Communist North Vietnam.

Drought begins in the Sahel, the 2,600-mile semi-desert strip south of Africa's Sahara Desert. The Sahel embraces Mauritania, Senegal, Mali, Upper Volta, Niger, Chad, northern Nigeria, Cameroon, and parts of Ethiopia, the drought will kill thousands of head of cattle by 1975, and it will bring famine.

Washington yields to pressure from commercial fishermen and extends jurisdiction over territorial waters to 12 miles (see Declaration of Santiago, 1952). The United States has been the last major nation to maintain the 3-mile limit.

The Vatican rescinds the rule forbidding U.S. Catholics to eat meat on Friday, but fish sales drop only briefly.

The Hudson River shad catch falls to 116,000 pounds; the Bureau of Commercial Fisheries in the Department of the Interior stops keeping records of Hudson River shad which are in any case generally tainted with oil and other pollutants.

An 8-year-old North Miami schoolboy introduces the giant African snail *Achatina fulica* from Hawaii into Florida. The snail reaches a length of 8 inches and a weight of 1 pound, it has 80,000 teeth, it can devour a head of lettuce overnight, and it will begin to menace Florida crops by 1969.

Castle & Cooke begins developing banana properties on the Philippine Island of Mindinao for shipment to Japanese markets (see Standard Fruit, 1964). Standard Fruit will drop its Cabana brand banana in the U.S. market beginning in 1970 and will sell its bananas under the Dole label.

Kazakhstan in the Soviet Union harvests a record 25.5 million tons of grain (see 1963).

The Rockefeller Foundation and the Mexican government establish the International Maize and Wheat Improvement Center (CIMMYT) under the direction of Norman Borlaug (see 1944).

A Fair Packaging and Labeling Act is passed by Congress (see Kennedy, 1962). The new "Truth in Packaging" law calls for clear labeling of the net weight of every package, it bans phony "cents off" labels and phony "economy size" packages, it imposes controls over the confusing proliferation of package sizes, but food will continue to be sold in packages that make it hard for supermarket customers to know how much they are paying per pound.

Cola drink bottlers and canners receive Food and Drug Administration dispensation not to list caffeine as an ingredient. Cola drinks generally have 4 milligrams of caffeine per fluid ounce, coffee has 12 to 16.

Food prices are higher in poor neighborhoods of U.S. cities than in better neighborhoods according to a study. Ghetto food merchants charge more to compensate for "shrinkage."

Consumers boycott supermarkets at Denver and other cities, protesting high prices. Grand Union in New York puts up store window signs claiming that "Grand Union Earns Less Than 1½ Pennies on Each Dollar of Sales . . . Not Much Is It?" but the National Commission of Food Marketing concludes that store profits are generally higher than for other comparable industries and that in 20 years the grocery chains' returns on investment have averaged 12.5 percent and never been lower than for other industries.

The President's Commission on Food Marketing estimates that consumers pay up to 20 percent more buying nationally advertised food brands rather than high quality local brands.

Bac*Os are introduced by General Mills. The bits of soy protein isolate are flavored to taste like bacon (see 1957; Boyer, 1949).

U.S. per capita consumption of processed potatoes reaches 44.2 pounds per year, up from 6.3 pounds in 1950 (see French's Instant Potato, 1946).

Product 19 breakfast food is introduced by the Kellogg Company (see 1965; 1969).

Taster's Choice freeze-dried instant coffee is introduced by Nestlé Alimentana to compete with the Maxim coffee introduced by General Foods in 1964. Taster's Choice will soon overtake Maxim in sales.

Jeno Paulucci's Chun King Corporation is acquired after 19 years of independent operation by R. J. Reynolds Company which pays $63 million and makes Paulucci chairman of the board of R. J. Reynolds Foods, Inc. (see Penick and Ford, 1965).

Keebler Company is created by a renaming of United Biscuit Co. which is now second only to Nabisco as a U.S. cookie and cracker producer (see 1927).

Maxwell's Plum on New York's 1st Avenue at 64th Street is opened by restaurateur Warner LeRoy, 31, son of Hollywood director Mervyn LeRoy.

A bill calling for reform of New York State's 19th century abortion law is introduced at Albany by assemblymen responding to an appeal by Manhattan borough president Percy Sutton who has seen the costs of illegal abortions in lives and maimings in the New York ghettos (*see* 1970; Colorado, 1967).

The Food and Drug Administration studies "the Pill" and reports having found "no adequate scientific data at this time proving these compounds unsafe for human use." But most U.S. women are reluctant to use "the Pill" (*see* 1960; 1970).

Yale University medical school scientists tell the American Fertility Society that they have found a contraceptive pill that can be taken a week after sexual relations and still prevent implantation of a fertilized egg in the uterine wall.

A Papal Study Commission reports to Pope Paul VI on the birth control issue.

Japan's birth rate falls to 14 per thousand, down from 34 per thousand in the late 1940s (*see* 1948).

China's widespread birth control campaign has been interrupted by Mao Tse-tung's Great Proletarian Cultural Revolution and the birth rate is estimated at between 38 and 43 per thousand.

1967 U.S. popular sentiment turns increasingly against the war in Vietnam as more troops are shipped overseas and as casualties mount. Martin Luther King, Jr., speaks out against the war in February, 5,000 scientists petition for a bombing halt, Dow Chemical Company recruiters are pushed off the University of Wisconsin campus by students who protest Dow's production of napalm, a Women's Strike for Peace demonstrates outside the Pentagon, and Senator Robert F. Kennedy proposes that bombing of North Vietnam be halted so that troop withdrawal may be negotiated.

National Security Adviser Walt W. Rostow says of U.S. involvement in South Vietnam, "It looks very good. The other side is near collapse. In my opinion, victory is near. . . . I'll show you the charts. The charts are very good."

President Ho Chi Minh responds March 15 to President Johnson's proposal for direct U.S.-North Vietnam peace talks by demanding that bombing be halted and U.S. troops withdrawn from South Vietnam before the start of any peace talks.

U.S. officials announce March 22 that Thailand has given permission to use Thai bases for B-52 bombers formerly based on Guam.

The U.S. Government is "the greatest purveyor of violence in the world," says Martin Luther King, Jr., April 4. He encourages draft evasion and proposes a merger between the civil rights movement and the antiwar movement.

Antiwar demonstrations April 15 at New York and San Francisco bring out upwards of 100,000 at New York, 50,000 at San Francisco.

Greece has a right-wing coup April 21 as colonels led by George Papadopoulos and Brigadier General Styliano Patakos begin a 7-year military dictatorship. They arrest leftist leaders including George Papandreou and his son Andreas, they release the elder Papandreou October 7. Constantine II fails to overthrow the junta and restore Greece's democratic institutions, the king and his family flee to Rome December 14. A Christmas amnesty frees Andreas Papandreou, and he calls on the world's democracies to help overthrow Premier Papadopoulos.

A Six-Day Arab-Israeli War begins June 5 following months of conflict between Israel and Syria in which Israeli tanks have crossed into Syria and Israeli Mirage fighters have shot down six Syrian MIG-21 fighters. An Arab invasion of Israel is aborted by Israeli jets and armor, Egyptian and Syrian air forces whose equipment has been supplied largely by Moscow are wiped out, the Israelis take Arab Jerusalem June 7 and incorporate it with the rest of the city June 27, freedom of access to the Holy Places for people of all faiths is guaranteed but the UN asks July 4 that the action be rescinded, the Soviet Union severs diplomatic relations with Israel June 10, the Israeli government rejects the UN request July 14 and retains the strategic Golan Heights in Syria and the West Bank of the Jordan which along with Arab Jerusalem contains half the population of Jordan and half her economic resources.

Egypt's President Nasser is persuaded not to resign, he begins a purge of the Egyptian army and air force, he is visited by Soviet President Podgorny who promises military and economic assistance to help rebuild Egyptian power, but Egypt's Suez Canal is closed (below).

Resolution 242, approved unanimously by the UN Security Council November 22, calls for "withdrawal of Israeli armed forces from territories occupied" and for an end to belligerency and recognition that every state in the area has a "right to live in peace within secure and recognized boundaries" (but *see* 1970).

"Vive le Quebec libre," says France's President de Gaulle July 25 on a state visit to Canada which is celebrating her centennial as a dominion with a great world exposition (Expo 67) at Montreal. De Gaulle openly promises French support for an independent Quebec, he is rebuked by Premier Pearson, he cancels a projected visit to Ottawa and returns to France, but de Gaulle's remarks encourage separatist leader René Levesque in the province of Quebec.

Use of force to end South Africa's mandate over southwest Africa and to topple Rhodesia's Ian Smith regime has been urged by the council of the Organization of African Unity (OAU) meeting from February 27 to March 4. OAU ministers meet in September at Kinshasa and demand the departure of white mercenaries from the Congo.

The Republic of Biafra is proclaimed May 30 by Nigerian General Odumegwu Ojukwu who leads the

1967 (cont.) Ibo tribespeople out of the 13-year-old Nigerian Federation. The Lagos government calls the secession a rebellion, Lagos is supported by all other African states and buys arms from Britain, the Ibos buy arms and supplies from France, Nigerian troops take the Biafran capital Enugu October 4, but the war will continue until 1970 between the Ibos and the Moslem Hansa-Fulani conservatives to the north and the Yorubas to the west.

Former Congo premier Moise Tshombe is sentenced to death March 13 by a military court which has convicted him in absentia of inciting to rebellion, Tshombe's plane is hijacked June 30 over the Mediterranean, he is flown to Algeria and held captive, pro-Tshombe European mercenaries revolt in July at Kisangani, the rebels are driven across the Rwanda border in early November with support from U.S. transport planes.

Rwanda and Burundi have effected a reconciliation March 20 and disarmed Tutsi refugees return to Rwanda after nearly 4 years of attacks on Rwanda from Burundi.

Che Guevara is killed October 9 at age 39 by Bolivian troops. Born in Argentina, Ernesto Guevara helped Fidel and Raul Castro oust Cuba's Batista regime in the late 1950s but resigned his Cuban cabinet post 2 years ago to lead Bolivian guerilla revolutionists.

North Vietnamese forces are vastly outnumbered by more than 1 million South Vietnamese, U.S., and allied troops as U.S. bombers pound targets around Hanoi and attempt to break the Ho Chi Minh supply route that maintains North Vietnam's guerilla forces to the South. Some 50,000 Chinese coolies work to repair the damage done by the U.S. air attacks.

Protests against the Vietnam war and the draft continue in the United States. Among the 260 demonstrators arrested December 5 at New York are physician Benjamin Spock and poet Allen Ginsburg.

The Saigon government threatens December 26 to pursue Communist troops into Cambodia if that country is used as a base for infiltration into South Vietnam. The Peking government replies 3 days later by promising Cambodia Chinese support if U.S. operations are extended to Cambodia.

The People's Republic of China has exploded her first hydrogen bomb June 17 and has increased Soviet fears of a nuclear confrontation with Peking.

The CIA initiates Operation Chaos, exceeding its statutory authority in response to a presidential request that the agency unearth any ties between U.S. antiwar groups and foreign interests. Operation Chaos will index 300,000 names, will keep 13,000 subject files, and will intercept large numbers of letters and cables to compile information on the domestic activities of U.S. citizens.

Heavyweight champion Muhammad Ali is denied conscientious objector status, refuses induction into the U.S. Army, and is arrested April 28.

Race riots rock 127 U.S. cities, killing at least 77 and injuring at least 4,000. Atlanta, Boston, Buffalo, Cincinnati, and Tampa have riots in June, riots in July disrupt Birmingham, Chicago, Detroit, New York, Milwaukee, Minneapolis, New Britain, Conn., Plainfield, N.J., and Rochester, N.Y., but the worst are in Newark and Detroit.

The Newark riots follow the beating of a black man after a traffic arrest July 12, it continues for 5 days over an area of 10 square miles, police and National Guardsmen shoot indiscriminately at blacks, 24 of the 26 killed are blacks, more than 1,500 are injured, 1,397 are arrested, property damage amounts to some $10 million.

The Detroit riots July 23 to 30 follow a police raid on an after-hours club at which they make 73 arrests, enraging the black community. Whites as well as blacks loot 1,700 stores, rioters set 1,142 fires that leave 5,000 homeless, 36 of the 43 killed are black, more than 2,000 are injured, police arrest 5,000, and the disturbances end only after Detroit summons federal troops to quell a civil disturbance since 1942.

A Black Power Conference at Newark July 23 adopts antiwhite, anti-Christian, and antidraft resolutions.

"Burn this town down," cries black militant H. "Rap" Brown (Hubert Gerold Brown) of the Student National Coordinating Committee (SNCC) July 25 at Cambridge, Md. Police arrest Brown for inciting to riot.

A black ghetto section in Washington, D.C., has an episode of arson and rock-throwing August 1.

Martin Luther King, Jr., calls August 15 for a campaign of massive disobedience to bring pressure on Washington to meet black demands (*see* 1968).

SNCC militant leader Stokely Carmichael urges blacks August 17 to arm for "total revolution." Martin Luther King, Jr., (above) has rejected Carmichael's "Black Power" separatist movement.

President Johnson names Thurgood Marshall, 59, to the Supreme Court seat resigned by Justice Thomas C. Clark following the appointment of Clark's son Ramsay to the post of U.S. Attorney General. The first black Supreme Court justice is sworn in October 2.

Antiwar demonstrators march on the Pentagon October 21. Police arrest 647 of the 50,000 to 150,000 involved, and similar demonstrations occur at Chicago, Philadelphia, Los Angeles, and Oakland (where police arrest 125 including singer Joan Baez at the Oakland Draft Induction Center).

College students arrested in antiwar demonstrations will lose their draft deferments, Selective Service director Lewis B. Hershey announces November 7.

Urban Coalitions are organized in 48 U.S. metropolitan areas late in the year following an appeal by former Health, Education and Welfare Secretary John W. Gardner. He has resigned to become head of the National Urban Coalition that will mobilize the private sector to join in social-action projects with representatives of the cities' dispossessed minorities.

"If we don't give the Negro of this country some measure of hope," says Mobil Oil vice-president Christian A. Herter, Jr., "the people at the extreme left of the Negro community will ultimately gain control and we won't have a chance ever to do this job again." Herter has helped found the New York Urban Coalition.

France's largest and most profitable shipyard is struck by workers squeezed by inflation. The strikers at Saint-Azaire in Brittany win support from other workers and from students (*see* 1968).

Mining of the Athabasca tar sands begins in northern Alberta. The field contains some 300 billion barrels of recoverable petroleum, but development of the oil-extraction project will be slow and costly.

Atlantic Richfield Corporation is created by a merger.

Consolidation Coal Co. is acquired by Continental Oil Co. (*see* 1929; 1954).

Soviet engineers complete the world's largest hydroelectric power project on the Yenisei River in Siberia. The Krasnoyarsk Dam will begin generating 6,096 megawatts next year as compared with 2,161 for the Grand Coulee Dam completed in 1941.

Egypt's Suez Canal is closed by scuttled ships and by mines in the Six-Day War (above) and the nation is deprived of some $250 million per year in revenues. Roughly 70 percent of the world's tankers have been able to use the Suez fully laden and all but 1 percent of tankers have been able to go through the canal in ballast but shipbuilders in the next 7 years will concentrate on building supertankers and by the mid-1970s only 35 percent of the world tanker fleet will be able to go through the Suez fully laden (*see* 1968).

McDonnell-Douglas Corporation is created April 28 in a takeover of Douglas Aircraft by the 39-year-old McDonnell Aircraft Corporation which produces military aircraft. Douglas lost $27.6 million last year on sales of more than $1 billion and its working capital has shrunk to $34 million from $187 million in 1958 when the Boeing 707 was introduced.

Montreal gets a new subway system with rubber-tired, air-conditioned cars.

U.S. mass transit rides fall to 8 billion, down from 23 billion in 1945, as prosperous Americans rely at an ever-growing rate on private automobiles to reach suburban homes and shopping centers.

New York State's Adirondack Northway opens from Albany north to the Canadian border.

The Pennsylvania Railroad sends a $1 million experimental train down its tracks May 24 at 156 miles per hour in a public test but the New York Central discontinues its crack *Twentieth Century Limited* December 2 after 65 years on the Chicago run. Both

railroads are in deep financial trouble and have received authorization to merge (*see* 1968).

Canada's 335-meter steel arch bridge across the St. Lawrence opens at Trois Rivierès, Quebec.

Venezuela's 712-meter Angostura Bridge opens at Ciudad Bolivar.

Czechoslovakia's 330-meter steel arch Zdakov Bridge opens to span the Vitava River.

FIAT auto production surpasses that of Volkswagen. The great Italian industrial colossus has been managed for the past year by Giovanni "Gianni" Agnelli, 46, grandson and namesake of FIAT's founder (*see* 1899; Citröen, 1968).

Sweden switches from driving on the left side of the road to driving on the right, but British and Japanese drivers continue to drive on the left.

A new Chevrolet sells for less than $2,500 in the United States.

The Hertz Corp. is acquired by RCA (*see* 1953).

The United Auto Workers union with 1.6 million members quits the AFL-CIO April 22 charging a lack of democratic leadership and a lack of organizing effort.

The United States contributes one-seventh of 1 percent of her Gross National Product (GNP) to foreign aid, down from a full 1 percent in 1965 (*see* 1961).

Master Charge cardholders reach 5.7 million in number and charge $312 million worth of purchases (*see* 1966). By 1976 there will be 40 million Master Charge cardholders and they will run up bills of $13.5 billion.

The United States has 2,975 corporate mergers, up from 2,377 last year.

Champion Papers, Inc., merges with U.S. Plywood.

Glidden Company is acquired by SCM, Inc.

Shetland-Lewyt, Inc., is acquired by SCM, Inc.

Ruberoid Corp. is acquired by GAF Corp.

Britain devalues the pound November 18 from $2.80 to $2.40 in an effort to check inflation and improve the nation's trade deficit (*see* 1965).

A Census Bureau report in December shows that 41 percent of nonwhite families in the United States make less than $3,300 per year versus 12 percent of white families, that 7.3 percent of nonwhites are unemployed versus 3.4 percent of whites, and that 29 percent of blacks live in substandard housing versus 8 percent of whites.

U.S. wage rates will rise by 92 percent in the next 10 years but buying power will rise by only 8 percent.

The Federal Communications Commission notifies CBS that its programs dealing with the effects of smoking on health are not sufficient to offset the influence of the 5 to 10 minutes of cigarette commercials the network's New York television station is broadcasting each day. The FCC acts in response to

1967 (cont.) a formal complaint against WCBS-TV filed by John Banzhaf. While the FCC does not agree with Banzhaf's request for equal time, it does order that all radio and TV cigarette commercials carry a notice of possible danger in cigarette smoking, and it asks WCBS-TV to provide free each week "a significant amount of time for the other viewpoint.... This requirement will not preclude or curtail presentation by stations of cigarette advertising which they choose to carry.... We hold that the fairness doctrine is applicable to such advertisements."

John Banzhaf (above) quits a New York law firm he has joined and organizes Action on Smoking and Health (ASH) with support from prominent physicians. Smoking-withdrawal clinics proliferate across the country but Americans buy 572.6 billion cigarettes—210 packs per adult (*see* 1966; 1969).

Tetrahydrocannabinol (THC) is synthesized by Israeli chemist Raphael Mechouiam who isolated the active ingredient that makes marijuana slightly hallucinogenic 3 years ago from dried leaves of the hemp *Cannabis sativa* now widely smoked by Americans despite severe laws against sale and possession of marijuana.

New York's Phoenix House is started on the fifth floor of a West 85th Street tenement by five detoxified former drug addicts who are all former patients of the Morris Bernstein Institute, one of the few city hospitals that admit addicts. The rehabilitation center for addicts is joined in July by psychiatrist Mitchell S. Rosenthal who has come from California full of enthusiasm for the 9-year-old Syanon program. By 1970 Phoenix House will have returned 150 graduates to society and will have established seminar rap session techniques that other rehabilitation centers will follow.

The Health Consequences of Smoking is published by the U.S. Public Health Service whose study reinforces the conclusions of earlier studies (*see* 1964).

The structure of the enzyme ribonuclease is described for the first time by David Harker, 60, and other biochemists at Buffalo's Roswell Park Memorial Institute.

Parkinson's disease victims get relief from cryogenic surgery developed by U.S. physician Irving S. Cooper, and from L-dopa therapy developed by Greek-American neurologist George C. Cotzias, 49, whose drug counters the deficiency of dopamine in the brain and will be introduced into medical practice in 1970 (*see* 1817). Asked by the World Health Organization to help investigate chronic manganese poisoning among miners in Chile, Cotzias has found their neurological symptoms—rigid facial expression, clenched hands, speech and balance difficulties —similar to those seen in Parkinson's disease. He succeeds in treating patients with L-dopa where others have failed because he uses much larger doses for longer periods of time.

The world's first heart transplant is performed December 3 by Capetown, South Africa, surgeon Christiaan Barnard, 45, whose patient lives for 18 days. The first U.S. heart transplant is performed 4 days later by New York surgeon Adrian Kantrowitz, 49, whose patient survives for only a few hours. Surgeons will attempt some 260 operations on more than 250 patients in the next 7 years, some heart recipients will live for more than 6 years with hearts obtained from donors killed in accidents, but only 20 percent of the recipients will survive for more than 1 year.

The *New York World-Journal & Tribune* closes May 5 after less than 8 months during which the company has had 18 work stoppages (management says the unions have forced it to employ 500 more people than necessary). The combined circulation has been 700,000 daily, 900,000 Sundays, and although the *New York Times* and the *Washington Post* will continue the Paris edition of the *Herald-Tribune*, the end of the *World-Journal & Tribune* leaves New York with only three regular dailies—the *Times*, the *News*, and the *Post*.

S. I. Newhouse buys the *Cleveland Plain-Dealer* for a record $54.3 million.

Rolling Stone magazine begins publication in November. San Francisco entrepreneur Jann Wenner, 21, has started the rock and roll record publication with an initial investment of $7,500, most of it borrowed, his first edition sells 6,000 copies, and circulation will grow to 400,000 in 8 years as *Rolling Stone's* volunteer staff grows to a paid staff of 80 and as the magazine becomes a journal of the counterculture.

Britain's first color TV broadcasting begins July 1 as BBC-2 transmits 7 hours of programming, most of it coverage of lawn tennis from Wimbledon.

A Public Broadcasting Act passed by Congress moves to broaden the scope of noncommercial television in the United States beyond its role of instructional education. Within 3 years there will be more than 200 public TV stations with a Public Broadcasting Service headquartered at Washington to create a network that will rival NBC, CBS, and ABC. PBS will be funded by grants from Washington, from private foundations, from business corporations, and by contributions from the public.

Congress creates a Commission on Obscenity and Pornography. The commission will conclude that pornography does not contribute to crime or sexual deviation and will recommend repeal of all federal, state, and local laws that "interfere with the right of adults who wish to do so to read, obtain, or view explicit sexual materials," but President Nixon will call the commission "morally bankrupt" and will say that "so long as I am in the White House, there will be no relaxation of the national effort to control and eliminate smut from our national life" (*see* 1969).

 Holt, Rinehart and Winston is acquired August 1 by CBS (*see* 1960).

Nonfiction *Children of Crisis* by Harvard psychiatrist-humanist Robert Coles, 37, who begins a decade in which he will write 25 books and nearly 400 articles observing socio-ethical problems affecting U.S. life, destroying one-dimensional stereotypes about blacks, white Southerners, police officers, farm workers, and American youth; The *Naked Ape* by London zoologist Desmond Morris; *Division Street* by "Studs" Terkel; *Our Crowd* by former New York advertising copywriter Stephen Birmingham who has traced the histories of some prominent U.S. Jewish families; *Nicholas and Alexandra* by Robert K. Massie is a history of the last Russian czar and czarina; *Twenty Letters to a Friend* by Svetlana Alliluyeva, daughter of the late Josef Stalin.

Fiction *The Confessions of Nat Turner* by William Styron (*see* 1831); *Up Above the World* by Paul Bowles; *Washington, D.C.* by Gore Vidal; *The Diary of a Mad Housewife* by New York novelist Sue Kauffman, 40; *Rosemary's Baby* by New York author Ira Levin; *Histoire* by Claude Simon; *Ausgefragt* by Günter Grass; *The Eighth Day* by Thornton Wilder, now 70; *Topaz* by Leon Uris.

Poetry *The Light Around the Body* by Robert Bly; *The Lice* by W. S. Merwin.

Painting *Wild Indigo* by Kenneth Noland; *The Art of Loving* by René Magritte; *Guiding Red* by Helen Frankenthaler. Edward Hopper dies at New York May 15 at age 84.

Sculpture *Borne au logos VII* (cast urethane) by Jean Dubuffet.

Theater *MacBird* by U.S. playwright Barbara Garson 2/22 at New York's off-Broadway Village Gate Theater, with Stacy Keach, 386 perfs.; *Fortune and Men's Eyes* by U.S. playwright John Herbert 2/23 at New York's off-Broadway Actor's Playhouse, 382 perfs.; *A Day in the Death of Joe Egg* by English playwright Peter Nichols, 39, at London, 148 perfs.; *You Know I Can't Hear You When the Water's Running* by Robert Anderson 3/13 at New York's Ambassador Theater, with George Grizzard, Eileen Heckhart, Martin Balsam, 755 perfs.; *Rosencrantz and Guildenstern Are Dead* by Czech-born British playwright Tom Stoppard, 29, 4/11 at London's Old Vic Theatre; *Little Murders* by U.S. cartoonist-playwright Jules Feiffer, 38, 4/25 at New York's Broadhurst Theater, with Elliott Gould, Heywood Hale Broun, Barbara Cook; *Soldaten* by Rolf Hochhuth 10/7 at West Berlin's Freie Volksbuhre; *Borstal Boy* by Brendan Behan 10/10 at Dublin's Abbey Theatre, a drama based on Behan's 1958 autobiography.

Television drama *The Forsyte Saga* with Eric Porter as Soames Forsyte, Kenneth More as his cousin, Susan Hampshire as his daughter Fleur in a serialized dramatization of the John Galsworthy novels on BBC and U.S. Public Broadcasting stations.

Films Arthur Penn's *Bonnie and Clyde* with Warren Beatty, Faye Dunaway; Norman Jewison's *In the Heat of the Night* with Rod Steiger, Sidney Poitier; Ingmar Bergman's *Persona;* Mike Nichols's *The Graduate* with Dustin Hoffman, Katherine Ross, Ann Bancroft; Philippe de Broca's *King of Hearts* with Alan Bates; Sergei Bondarchuk's *War and Peace;* John Schlesinger's *Far from the Madding Crowd* with Julie Christie, Peter Finch, Alan Bates, Terence Stamp; Louis Malle's *The Thief of Paris* with Jean-Paul Belmondo; Luis Buñuel's *Belle de Jour* with Catherine Deneuve; Jean-Luc Goddard's *La Chinoise;* Jack Clayton's *Our Mother's House* with Dirk Bogarde, Mark Lester, Pamela Franklin; James Clavell's *To Sir with Love* with Sidney Poitier, Judy Gleeson; Stanley Donen's *Two for the Road* with Audrey Hepburn, Albert Finney; Michael Winner's *The Jokers* with Michael Crawford, Oliver Reed; Ralph Nelson's *Charly* with Cliff Robertson, Claire Bloom; Richard Brooks's *In Cold Blood;* Fred Wiseman's documentary *The Titicut Follies;* Stuart Rosenberg's *Cool Hand Luke* with Paul Newman, Jo Van Fleet, George Kennedy; Robert Aldrich's *The Dirty Dozen* with John Cassavetes, Lee Marvin, Ernest Borgnine, Donald Sutherland, Jim Brown; Irvin Kershner's *The Flim-Flam Man* with George C. Scott, Michael Sarrazin, Sue Lyon; Joseph Losey's *Accident* with Dirk Bogarde; Bo Wilderberg's *Elvira Madigan* with Thommy Berggren, Pia Degermark; Peter Brooks's *Marat/Sade* with the Royal Shakespeare Company; Theodore J. Flicker's *The President's Analyst* with James Coburn, Godfrey Cambridge; Stanley Kramer's *Guess Who's Coming to Dinner* with Spencer Tracy, Katharine Hepburn, Sidney Poitier, Katharine Houghton.

Broadway and off-Broadway musicals *You're a Good Man, Charlie Brown* 3/7 at the Theater 80 St. Marks, with Gary Burghoff, Reva Rose, book based on Charles Schultz's 17-year-old comic strip *Peanuts,* music and lyrics by Clark Gesner, 1,579 perfs.; *Hair* 10/29 at the off-Broadway Public Theater, with Gerome Ragni as Bezar, music by Galt MacDermot, lyrics by Ragni and James Rado, songs that include "Hare Krishna" and "Aquarius," 94 perfs. (plus 1,742 beginning 4/29/68 when *Hair* will open on Broadway at the Biltmore Theater with some nudity.

The Monterey Pop Festival held at Monterey, Cal., is the first large rock gathering. Participating rock stars include the Grateful Dead and Janis Joplin's Big Brother and the Holding Company.

Popular songs "Ode to Billy Joe" by U.S. country singer-songwriter Bobbie Gentry, 23; "Up, Up and Away" by Oklahoma songwriter Jimmy Webb, 21; "Gentle on My Mind" by John Hartford; "Can't Take My Eyes Off of You" by Bob Crewe and Bob Gandio; "Somebody to Love" by the Jefferson Airplane makes the San Francisco rock group the first to gain wide acclaim; "Ruby Tuesday" by Mick Jagger and Keith Richard of The Rolling Stones; "All You Need is Love" and "Penny Lane" by John Lennon and Paul McCartney of the Beatles; *Sergeant Pepper's Lonely Hearts Club Band* (album) by the Beatles reflects the growing drug culture in the song "Lucy

1967 (cont.) in the *Sky* with *Diamonds*"; *Magical Mystery Tour* (album) by the Beatles is similarly drug-oriented (positive references to drugs or drug use occur in 16 of the top 40 U.S. phonograph records); "Light My Fire" by Robert Krieger, James Morrison, Raymond Manzarek, and John Densmore; "Release Me" by Eddie Miller and W. S. Stevenson; "Respect" by Otis Redding who dies December 10 at age 28 along with four younger members of his troupe when his private plane crashes into an icy Wisconsin lake; *Surrealistic Pillow* (album) by the Jefferson Airplane; *Between the Buttons* (album) by the Rolling Stones; *Happy Jack* (album) by the Who (Peter Townshend, 22; John Entwhistle, 21; Roger Daltrey, 22; and Keith Moon, 20), a new English rock group whose members smash up their instruments on stage; "New York Mining Disaster" by the Bee Gees—English rock composer Barry Gibb, 20, and his (unidentical) twin brothers Robin and Maurice, 17; "This Is My Song" by Charlie Chaplin, now 78 (for his film *A Countess from Hong Kong);* "A Man and a Woman" by French composer Francis Lai, lyrics by Jerry Keck (title song for film); "The Beat Goes On" by Sonny Bono.

 The World Boxing Association strips Muhammad Ali (above) of his world heavyweight title (*see* 1968).

The Green Bay Packers of the National Football League defeat the Kansas City Chiefs of the American League in January at Los Angeles in the first Super Bowl Game, an event that will grow to have even more TV viewers than baseball's World Series.

Australian tennis star John Newcombe, 23, wins the Wimbledon and U.S. singles titles. U.S. tennis star Mrs. Billie Jean King, 25, dominates international women's tennis.

Mickey Mantle of the New York Yankees hits his 500th home run in league competition.

The St. Louis Cardinals win the World Series by defeating the Boston Red Sox 4 games to 3 after Boston has won its first pennant since 1946.

Australia's *Dame Pattie* is defeated 4 to 0 by the U.S. defender *Intrepid* in the America's Cup yacht races.

British yachtsman Francis Chichester completes a one-man voyage round the world in 226 days.

 Montreal's Bonaventure complex is completed beside Place Ville Marie by Boston-born planner Vincent Ponte, 48, who has pushed for a multilayer plan to avoid congestion by having cars on one level, pedestrians on a level below (where they are protected from the elements), trains and trucks on a lower level still (*see* 1963).

Habitat is completed for Montreal's Expo 67 by 28-year-old Israeli-born architect Moshe Safde whose idea of an apartment house runs counter to the regimentation of modern apartment blocks. Safde creates what he calls a "sense of house" with private outdoor space for each family in an arrangement that represents a radical departure from prevailing apartment house design.

Chicago's John Hancock Center goes up. Rising 1,107 feet, the skyscraper will be second in height only to New York's Empire State Building of 1931 (*see* 1969).

New York's Ford Foundation building is completed by Kevin Roche, John Dinkeloo Associates in East 42nd Street with offices in an L-shape round a 130-foot high glassed-in atrium garden.

New York's Westvaco building is completed by Emery Roth and Sons on Park Avenue between 48th and 49th Streets.

London's Royal Lancaster Hotel opens with 433 rooms. The 18-story hotel overlooks Hyde Park.

Hilton Hotels International is acquired by Trans World Airlines (TWA) to compete with Pan American's Intercontinental Hotels chain.

 The *Torrey Canyon* is wrecked at Easter in the English Channel off the coast of Cornwall in southern England and creates the biggest oil spill thus far. The 118,000 ton tanker of Liberian registry is owned by Dillon, Read banking house executives who have set up the firm Barracuda Tankers Corporation at Hamilton, Bermuda, to build three tankers for exclusive charter to Union Oil Company of California, the ship has been subleased to British Petroleum Trading, Ltd., it strikes a submerged reef March 18, and its 119,000 tons of crude oil take a heavy toll of marine life, especially of seafowl, but 80 to 90 percent of the damage to beaches and coves is cleaned up in 6 weeks through massive and costly deployment of troops, residents, and fishermen using 2 tons of detergents for every 3 tons of oil that hit the coast and by the end of the season all trace of the spill is gone.

Congress passes an Endangered Species Act, and the Department of the Interior classifies various U.S. fish and game species based on estimated population.

New York's Samuel Paley Plaza opens in East 53rd Street on the site formerly occupied by the Stork Club. The vest-pocket park whose back wall is a thunderous waterfall that muffles the sound of city traffic has been built with a gift of $1 million from CBS chairman William S. Paley who has given the park to memorialize his late cigarmaker father.

A Fisherman's Protective Act passed by Congress appropriates funds to reimburse U.S. commercial fishermen for fines, lost time, and fish spoilage incurred through apprehension by foreign powers in waters the United States considers international (*see* Declaration of Santiago, 1952).

Iran, South Africa, and Turkey have record grain crops but hunger remains widespread in India.

More than 6 million tons of U.S. wheat are shipped to India under terms of the P.L. 480 of 1954. Reserves of wheat stored in U.S. grain elevators fall sharply as more than one-fourth the export crop goes to India.

The World Food Problem is issued by the President's Science Advisory Committee. The three-volume, 1,231-page report appears in a watershed year with respect to food supply relative to pressures of world population and world affluence.

Famine—1975! by U.S. agronomist William Paddock and his brother Paul (a retired Foreign Service career officer) observes that today's infants and young children will be adolescents and young adults by 1975 and will have appetites too great for world food production to satisfy. Famine is inevitable, say the Paddocks, and the United States must decide which countries can be saved and which cannot.

Widespread hunger and malnutrition in the Mississippi Delta is reported to a Senate subcommittee by a medical team that has surveyed the region.

The Department of Agriculture returns $200 million of unused food aid funds to the Treasury.

Some 2.7 million Americans receive food stamp assistance as of Thanksgiving (*see* 1964; 1969).

Mao Tse-tung brings Chinese agriculture into the Great Proletarian Cultural Revolution, but the country is wracked by virtual civil war. Peasants abandon collective grain fields to cultivate private gardens and to sell in the black market, China continues to import from 4 to 7 million tons of wheat, mostly from Australia and Canada, as she has done since 1962.

European fruit and vegetable surpluses are destroyed to maintain prices.

U.S. farm prices fall as huge crops are harvested and Agriculture Secretary Orville H. Freeman comes under attack from farmers. He had urged heavy planting in case India and Pakistan need more U.S. grain.

Nearly 10,000 U.S. farmers receive more than $20,000 each in subsidies, more than 6,500 receive more than $25,000 each, 15 receive between $500,000 and $1 million each, five receive more than $1 million each, one receives more than $4 million.

A U.S. Federal Meat Inspection Act takes effect after a campaign by consumer advocate Ralph Nader has persuaded Congress to strengthen the law of 1906.

Herman Taller is convicted in federal court of conspiracy, mail fraud, and food and drug law violations in connection with his 1961 book *Calories Don't Count* which claimed that polyunsaturated fats as contained in safflower oil would "soften your body fat and help get it out of your system."

The Doctor's Quick Weight Loss Diet by Brooklyn, N.Y., physician Irwin Maxwell Stillman recommends low carbohydrate intake as did the Taller book (above). Stillman urges readers to drink eight 10-ounce glasses of water per day, he claims his program will remove from 7 to 15 pounds per week.

Annual U.S. beef consumption reaches 105.6 pounds per capita, up from 99 pounds in 1960, and the average American eats 71 pounds of other red meat.

Wilson & Co. is acquired by Ling-Temco-Vought which will sell Wilson Sporting Goods to another company and will expand its third largest U.S. meatpacker.

John Morrell & Co. is merged into AMK Corporation, a small company organized by former rabbi Eli M. Black, 46, who has built up American Seal-Kap Corporation from a producer of paper cups for milk bottles into a diversified company that makes lock washers, has an iron foundry, and controls a leading producer of manufacturing equipment for the rubber and plastics industry. Morrell is the fourth largest U.S. meatpacker and its acquisition makes AMK a major conglomerate (*see* United Brands, 1968).

Burger King Corporation is acquired by the Pillsbury Company which moves into the fast food business (*see* 1962).

Sale of yellow margarine is permitted in Wisconsin which becomes the last state to repeal laws against yellow margarine but which like some other states continues to impose special taxes on margarine at the behest of dairy interests (*see* New York, 1952).

U.S. bread sells at 22 to 25 cents per 1-pound loaf.

Imitation milk appears in Arizona supermarkets. Made from corn-syrup solids, vegetable fat, sugar, salt, artificial thickeners, colors, and flavors, sodium caseinate, and water, the "milk" will be sold under such brand names as Moo, Farmer's Daughter, and Country Cousin.

Del Monte Corporation is created by a reorganization of California Packing Corporation (*see* 1917). Del Monte has grown to become an integrated international company that controls vast acreages of U.S. farmland and directly or indirectly employs thousands of U.S. farm workers.

The *Super-Marche de Poche* that opens in Paris is an automated supermarket in which shelves are automatically restocked.

Prospects of global famine spurred efforts to curb the population explosion and to increase food production.

1967 (cont.) The first compact microwave oven for U.S. home use is introduced by Amana Refrigeration, Inc., a subsidiary of Raytheon with facilities at Amana, Iowa, which applies its consumer marketing experience to Raytheon's microwave technology (*see* 1947).

Japanese microwave oven production reaches 50,000 up from 15,000 last year. Many Japanese households move directly from hibachi grills to microwave ovens.

Japan's birth rate climbs to 19.3 per 1,000 after its fall to 14 last year in the Year of the Fiery Horse.

France legalizes birth control, but diaphragms, intrauterine devices, and spermicidal creams and jellies remain generally unavailable.

Israel's population tops 3.5 million with some 2.4 million Jews and more than 1 million Arabs as the Six-Day War (above) expands her territory (*see* 1948).

The U.S. population passes 200 million November 20 after having doubled in just 50 years. Demographers predict a population of 300 million by the year 2000 if present growth rates continue.

Colorado leads the United States in liberalizing abortion laws.

1968 A great Tet offensive begins January 30 as Vietcong and North Vietnamese forces attack some 30 South Vietnamese cities including Hue and Saigon in an effort to topple the regime of Generals Nguyen Cao Ky and Nguyen Van Thieu who are supported by the United States. The Communists besiege Khesanh, a base that commands a major road junction and infiltration route, and while South Vietnamese forces recapture the ancient palace grounds at Hue February 24 and the troops manning Khesanh are successfully evacuated June 27, the power of North Vietnam has impressed the world.

The Tet offensive (above) comes one week after the seizure by North Korea of the spy ship U.S.S. *Pueblo* whose 83-man crew sustains one casualty in the capture of the ship off the port of Wonsan by a torpedo boat and subchaser. North Korea had broadcast warnings that she would not tolerate spy ships, but *Pueblo* commander Lloyd M. Bucher will deny that his ship came within 12 miles of the Korean coast and he will be released with his surviving men after 11 months of captivity. A U.S. intelligence plane is shot down April 15 some 90 miles off the Korean coast.

The United States loses her 10,000th plane over Vietnam January 5.

My Lai village in South Vietnam is the scene of a massacre March 16. U.S. troops of C Company, First Battalion, Twentieth Infantry, Eleventh Brigade, Americal Division enter the village, gather hundreds of men, women, and children into groups, and "waste" them with automatic weapons fire. The soldiers will later say that they acted on orders from Lieutenant William L. Calley, Jr., but news of the My Lai massacre will be suppressed for 20 months.

Opposition to the Vietnam War enables U.S. Senator Eugene McCarthy, 52, to make a strong showing in the New Hampshire primary and his success persuades President Johnson to announce March 31 that he will not be a candidate for reelection.

Cessation of U.S. air and naval bombardment north of the 20th parallel in Vietnam is announced by President Johnson March 31 as he bows out of the race for reelection, but the statement by U.S. General William C. Westmoreland that "the enemy has been defeated at every turn" has a hollow ring.

Nine Roman Catholic priests enter Selective Service offices at Catonsville, Md., in May, they dump hundreds of 1-A classification records into trash baskets, they take the records outside, they burn them, and they await arrest for their "symbolic act" protesting the Vietnam War. Jesuit priest-poet Daniel Berrigan, 47, his brother Philip, 45, and their fellow-priests will be sentenced to prison terms of from 2 to 3.5 years but Daniel Berrigan will avoid apprehension by the authorities after his conviction and exhaustion of appeals and will continue speaking out against the war until arrested in August of 1970.

U.S. Senator Robert F. Kennedy makes a bid for the presidency after seeing the success of Eugene McCarthy in New Hampshire (above). The junior senator from New York captures 174 delegate votes (he wins the Indiana, Nebraska, and California primaries but loses in Oregon), but he is assassinated June 5 in a Los Angeles hotel kitchen pantry after leaving a victory celebration. Jordanian-American Sirhan Bishara Sirhan, 24, is seized as he empties his .22 caliber, 8-shot Ivor Johnson pistol wounding five others in the Ambassador Hotel pantry, but suspicions will be raised that Kennedy was killed by a bullet fired from behind him by local security guard Thane Cesar or by someone else.

Cambodia's Prince Norodam Sihanouk warns American ships to stay out of his part of the Mekong River. His forces seize a U.S. patrol boat July 17.

Czech Communist party secretary Alexander Dubcek declines invitations to attend conferences at Warsaw or Moscow, he receives support from President Tito of Yugoslavia and President Ceausescu, but the "Prague Spring" that has seen a relaxation of oppression ends in August. Some 200,000 Soviet and satellite troops invade Czechoslovakia August 20 on orders from Moscow, but Romanian troops do not participate.

Popular demonstrations in Czechoslovakia raise a threat of revolution like the one in Hungary 12 years ago. Moscow increases the army of occupation to 650,000 and summons Czech leaders to the Kremlin. The leaders return to Prague August 27 and announce the annulment of several important reforms. Soviet foreign minister Kuznetsov arrives at Prague, Party Secretary Dubcek bans political clubs September 6, Czech authorities introduce a censorship system September 13, and the Czech foreign minister who had presented the Czech case at the UN resigns under pressure September 19.

Australia's Prime Minister Harold Holt has drowned January 10 while swimming and is succeeded by the Liberal party leader John Gorton.

The Republic of Nauru is established in the South Pacific. Once a German colony, the island with its rich phosphate deposits has been a British mandate and a United Nations Trust territory.

Communist guerilla activity in northern Malaysia resumes in June.

Saba on the island of Borneo is claimed by Manila which passes a law incorporating the territory into the Philippine Republic September 18 after talks at Bangkok with the Malaysian government have broken down. Malaysia breaks relations with Manila.

The Democratic party convention at Chicago in August is marked by bloody police confrontations with demonstrators protesting U.S. military involvement in Southeast Asia and many domestic policies. Some 10,000 militants protest the rising death toll in Vietnam with a "Festival of Life" in Grant Park and Lincoln Park that includes rock concerts, marijuana smoking, public lovemaking, beach nude-ins, and draft card burnings.

A mobilization of 500,000 at Chicago has been asked by self-styled revolutionists who include Abbot H. "Abbie" Hoffman, 30, and Jerry C. Rubin, 29, of the "Yippies" (Youth International Party), Rennie Davis, 27, and Thomas E. Hayden, 27, of the Students for a Democratic Society (SDS), Black Panther leader Bobby Seale, 31, and civil rights advocate David Dellinger, 52, whose forces are far outnumbered by 16,000 Chicago police officers, 4,000 state police officers, and 4,000 National Guardsmen who are armed with tear gas grenades, nightsticks, and firearms and who brutally crack heads to prevent demonstrators from remaining overnight in city parks, acting on orders from Chicago's Mayor Richard Daley.

Democrats at Chicago nominate Vice President Hubert H. Humphrey to succeed President Johnson.

Former Vice President Richard M. Nixon wins the Republican presidential nomination on the first ballot at Miami Beach, defeating a bid for the nomination by New York's Governor Nelson A. Rockefeller. Nixon actively campaigned for Republican congressional candidates 2 years ago and has regained favor in the party, he campaigns for the presidency with claims that he has a "secret plan" to end the war in Vietnam, and he wins the election by the narrowest margin since his defeat by John F. Kennedy in 1960, receiving 43.4 percent of the popular vote to Humphrey's 43 percent but gaining 302 electoral votes to Humphrey's 191.

Former Alabama governor George C. Wallace, whose wife (and successor) Lurleen died in May, runs for the presidency as the candidate of the American Independent Party. Wallace carries five Southern states with a combined electoral vote of 45.

Complete cessation of U.S. aerial, artillery, and naval bombardment of Vietnam north of the 20th parallel has been announced October 31 in a move to further the peace talks at Paris and to help Vice President Humphrey in his bid for the presidency, but the talks produce no results.

The African continent that was completely white-controlled 10 years ago is controlled south of the Sahara by black regimes in every country except Angola, Mozambique, Rhodesia, South Africa, South-West Africa, and Equatorial Guinea. Within 6 years only Rhodesia, South Africa, and South-West Africa will remain white-controlled.

The gap between rich nations and underdeveloped nations must be narrowed or "men and women will be impelled to revolt," warns India's prime minister Indhira Gandhi in New Delhi.

The Kerner Report February 29 says, "Our nation is moving toward two societies, one black, one white—separate and unequal." The National Advisory Commission on Civil Disorders headed by Illinois Governor Otto Kerner, Jr., 59, was appointed by President Johnson last July, it has included only two blacks, and it charges white society with condoning the black ghetto it has created.

Martin Luther King, Jr., is killed by an assassin April 4 as he steps out on the balcony of his Memphis motel room. The civil rights leader has for 6 years been under surveillance by the FBI whose director J. Edgar Hoover has used wiretaps, electronic bugs, and paid informants to gain information on King's private life that the bureau has circulated in an effort to discredit him. Still only 39, King has been picked off with one shot from a 30.06 Remington rifle fired by a sniper who is not immediately found. Fingerprints indicate that the assassin was ex-convict James Earl Ray, 39, who was serving a 20-year sentence for armed robbery when he escaped last year from Missouri State Penitentiary, Ray is indicted for the murder and is arrested June 8 by Scotland Yard detectives at London Airport. He is extradited to the United States to stand trial, he will plead guilty and will be sentenced next year to 99 years in prison, but doubts will remain as to whether he acted alone.

Race riots erupt at Baltimore, Boston, Chicago, Detroit, Kansas City, Newark, Washington, D.C., and scores of other cities following the assassination of Martin Luther King, Jr. (above). Chicago's mayor Richard J. Daley gives police "shoot to kill" orders to put down the rioting, 46 deaths result across the country, 55,000 federal troops and National Guardsmen are called out to suppress the riots, 21,270 arrests are made.

FBI goals in a "Counter-Intelligence Program" against "Black Nationalist Hate-Groups" have been spelled out March 3 in a memo by J. Edgar Hoover: "1. Prevent the coalition of militant black nationalist groups . . . [which] might be the first step toward a

1968 (cont.) real 'Mau Mau' in America, the beginning of a true black revolution. 2. Prevent the rise of a 'messiah' who could unify and electrify the militant black nationalist movement . . . King could be a very real contender for this position should he abandon his supposed 'obedience' to 'white, liberal doctrines' (nonviolence) and embrace black nationalism . . . ."

A U.S. Civil Rights bill that stresses open housing is signed into law by President Johnson April 11.

A Poor People's March on Washington that had been planned by Martin Luther King, Jr., gets under way May 3 (below).

Columbia University is shut down by demonstrators who protest the building of a university gymnasium in an area needed for low-cost housing. The protestors include members of the radical Students for a Democratic Society (SDS) and black militants H. Rap Brown and Stokely Carmichael. Construction of the gymnasium is halted April 25, students take over five university buildings in a week-long sit-in that is accompanied by wanton destruction, the sit-in is broken April 30 by the New York police who storm the buildings and make 628 arrests, but formal classes are suspended May 5.

French universities close down in May after widespread street fighting that began with violent student demonstrations at the University of Nanterre and spread quickly to the Sorbonne and other schools. Strikes in various industries produce a crisis, President de Gaulle asks for restoration of order in a radio appeal broadcast May 24, French-born German student Daniel Cohn-Bendit ("Danny the Red"), 23, is exiled May 24 as a threat to public order, Parlement is dissolved May 30, but the Communists and other radical parties lose seats in the June elections and the Gaullist party wins a clear majority.

San Francisco State College students strike November 6 demanding open admission and a Third World Studies Department, and the college is closed November 19 following daily confrontations between students and police. Semanticist S. I. Hayakawa of 1939 *Language in Action* fame is named president of the college and reopens it December 2, but then closes it early for the Christmas vacation to avoid having high school students join the protest. The strike continues for 5 months.

National Turn in Your Draft Card Day November 14 features burning of draft cards and war protest rallies at many campuses as the U.S. Vietnam death toll approaches 30,000 and as U.S. troops in Vietnam reach their peak of 550,000.

Data General Corporation is founded in April by former Digital Equipment Corporation Systems designer Edson D. deCastro, 29, who has helped develop the first commercially successful minicomputer, the PDP-8. Digital Equipment has been unwilling to rush into production with deCastro's improvement on the PDP-8, a 16-bit machine that is more powerful, more precise, and is compatible with the magnetic tape drives and terminals of IBM equipment. Digital Equipment engineers Henry Burkhardt III, 25, and Roland G. Sogge, 29, join deCastro in starting the new firm.

Japan's Gross National Product (GNP) climbs 12 percent to $140 billion and passes that of West Germany by $10 billion to make Japan the free world's second strongest economic power after the United States (whose GNP is $860 billion), but Japan's per capita income is $921, little more than that of Ireland.

Production by multinational corporations is exceeded only by the Gross National Products of the United States and the Soviet Union, says French economist Jean-Jacques Servan-Schreiber who edits the 16-year-old newsweekly *L'Express*. Servan-Schreiber's book *The American Challenge* says that American-owned multinationals have been the chief beneficiaries of the European Common Market founded in 1957.

The U.S. Federal Reserve Board updates its 46-year-old bankwire system for reducing physical handling of Treasury certificates in moving them from one Federal Reserve Bank to another. Beginning January 1 the Fed introduces a book-entry system that dispenses completely with certificates (which are subject to theft and other forms of loss) and substitutes a system that uses computers to record transfer of ownership, to pay interest on interest-bearing securities, and to pay principal at maturity (*see* 1922; 1970).

Depository Trust Company (DTC) is founded at New York to create a central depository for security certificates that will eliminate much of the physical transfer of paper and will apply to equities and to non-Treasury bonds the same principle employed by the Fed (above) in its book-entry system. The volume of trade on Wall Street has forced the exchanges to close early in order to catch up with backoffice paperwork, trades fail increasingly because of late delivery of certificates, and brokers act to reduce the need for physical delivery by installing computers that interface with DTC computers to record transfer of ownership simply by debiting and crediting accounts.

Britain's first 5 pence and 10 pence coins are issued April 23 as the nation shifts to the decimal system.

U.S. conglomerates such as ITT, Tenneco, and Ling-Temco-Vought grow by acquisition (below).

Marcor is created by a merger of Montgomery Ward with Container Corporation of America. Mobil Oil Corporation will acquire the new conglomerate in 1974 and 1975.

ITT (International Telephone and Telegraph) pays $112 million to acquire Pennsylvania Glass Sand Corporation, the leading U.S. producer of silica and clay for glass and ceramics.

ITT pays $200 million to acquire Sheraton Hotel Corporation (below).

ITT pays $293 million to acquire Rayonier Corporation, a major producer of chemical cellulose which owns more than a million acres of U.S. and Canadian forestlands.

Tenneco Corporation acquires the Kern County Land Company founded in 1890 whose management has rejected offers by Armand Hammer's Occidental Petroleum (*see* 1957). Tenneco is a giant U.S. complex of natural gas, packing, and chemical interests with more than $3 billion in assets.

Ling-Temco-Vought acquires a controlling interest in Jones & Laughlin Steel (*see* Wilson & Co., 1967).

Ling-Temco-Vought acquires Greatamerica Corporation, a conglomerate that includes insurance companies, a bank, National Car Rental System, and Braniff Airways.

The United States has 4,462 corporate business mergers, up from 2,975 last year (*see* 1969).

The Williams Act passed by Congress gives anyone victimized by fraud in a business takeover the implied right to sue. Congress has acted in response to the growing use of cash tender offers in takeovers.

Economic inflation continues to mount in much of the world. The United States and six West European nations agree March 18 to supply no more gold to private buyers.

President Johnson signs a bill June 28 adding a 10 percent surcharge to income taxes and reducing government spending but the war in Indochina is costing the United States millions of dollars per day.

The Pentagon announces August 1 that it will buy steel only from firms that have not raised prices, but wholesale steel prices beginning at the end of this year will climb in 15 of the next 18 months as American steelmakers negotiate agreements with European and Japanese steelmakers to reduce shipments to the United States and as U.S. industry raises prices in anticipation of possible price controls.

Congress enacts a Consumer Credit Protection Law. The "Truth in Lending" Act requires banks and other lending institutions to disclose clearly the true annual rate of interest and other financing costs on most types of loans.

BankAmericard holders number 14 million by year's end, up from 2 million at the end of 1966, and 316,000 U.S. merchants accept the card, up from 64,000 at the end of 1966. By 1974 there will be more than 26 million BankAmericard holders and at least 33 million Master Charge cardholders, bank credit cards will be used to finance $13 billion worth of business per year in the United States (roughly 2.6 percent of all retail sales), 970,000 U.S. merchants will honor BankAmericard and more thousands will honor Master Charge, thousands of merchants in other countries will honor the cards, and approximately 3.8 percent of U.S. consumer debt will be in loans outstanding on bank credit cards, much of it at interest rates as high as 18 percent per year.

A Delta Airlines jet carrying 169 passengers is hijacked February 21 over southern Florida, the hijacker holds a gun on the pilot and forces him to land in Cuba, similar episodes follow, and the hijackings will lead to airport searches of passengers and luggage.

Pan American World Airways and Aeroflot begin direct service between New York and the Soviet Union July 15. Aeroflot uses the four-jet Il-62 designed by Sergei V. Ilyushin, now 73.

The Tu-144 demonstrated by Aeroflot December 31 is the first supersonic airliner.

The S.S. *QE 2* launched by the Cunard Line replaces the 83,673-ton *Queen Elizabeth* launched in 1940. The new 66,850-ton passenger liner is 963 feet in length overall, carries nearly 3,000 people including crew, and has four swimming pools, 13 decks, 24 elevators, and a 531-seat theater (*see* 1971).

A 326,000-ton supertanker goes into service on charter to Gulf Oil Corporation. She will be followed by five sister ships (*see* 1971).

Penn Central Company is created February 14 by a merger of the 122-year-old Pennsylvania Railroad with the 115-year-old New York Central. Both are in financial trouble as a result of competition from trucks and automobiles that use publicly financed highways and from airlines that use publicly financed airports. The new $5 billion corporation will be bankrupt within 2 years.

U.S. automobile production reaches 8.8 million, truck and bus production approaches 2 million.

Volkswagen captures 57 percent of the U.S. import market, selling 569,292 vehicles in the United States, up from 120,000 in 1959. Seventy percent of the VWs sold are Beetle models priced at less than $1,800 and VWs outsell many U.S. makes including the Pontiac, the Chevrolet Chevelle, the Ford Fairlane, the Plymouth Fury, the Buick, the Tempest, the Ford Mustang, the Oldsmobile, and the Chrysler.

West Germany produces 2.5 million cars and nearly 600,000 trucks; Japan produces 2.1 million cars, 2 million trucks; Britain produces 1.7 million cars, 400,000 trucks and buses; France produces 1.8 million cars, 243,000 trucks; Italy produces 1.5 million cars, 115,000 trucks.

British-Leyland Motor Corporation is created by a merger of British Motor Holdings and the 72-year-old Leyland Motors. The new automotive giant produces Austin, Jaguar, MG, Rover, and Triumph automobiles, it employs 160,000 workers, but in 6 years it will be in such straitened financial circumstances that only a huge government-guaranteed loan will save it from bankruptcy.

The German NSU Ro 80 introduced in Britain is the first Wankel-engine automobile (*see* Wankel, 1957). Japan's Toyo Kgoyo uses the Wankel engine for its new Mazda cars.

FIAT's Gianni Agnelli moves to acquire control of France's 59-year-old Citröen which has been 55 percent owned by the Michelin tire company. In order

1968 (cont.) to overcome objections by President de Gaulle, Agnelli sets up a company owned 51 percent by Michelin and 49 percent by FIAT S.p.a. (*see* 1967).

U.S. natural gas consumption begins to exceed new gas discoveries and reserves for U.S. interstate pipelines begin falling (*see* 1964). Artificially low prices established by the Federal Power Commission are blamed by the industry and by some independent economists for having discouraged exploration for new reserves at a time when demand for natural gas has been increased by FPC actions.

Oil is discovered on Alaska's North Slope, the new reserve is found to be the largest north of the Mexican border, and petroleum companies join forces to establish the Alyeska Pipeline Service Company that will bring the oil south to the ice-free port of Valdez. The port has been rebuilt since the earthquake of 1964 and is favored as a port for shipment by tanker to world markets, but a debate begins as to the environmental impact of the pipeline (*see* 1969).

Peabody Coal Company is acquired by Kennecott Corporation whose takeover of the largest U.S. coal producer will be disallowed by the courts in 1975.

Christiaan N. Barnard performs the most successful heart transplant to date January 2, giving retired Capetown dentist Philip Blaiberg, 58, a heart that will continue to function for 19 months.

Houston cardiovascular surgeon Denton Arthur Cooley, 47, performs the first successful U.S. heart transplant May 2, removing the damaged heart of a 47-year-old male patient and replacing it with the heart of a 15-year-old female who has died of a brain injury. Cooley performs four similar transplants within 4 weeks (two patients die subsequently of other causes), and in July he moderates a Conference on Cardiac Transplants at Capetown.

The United States has only 22,231 reported cases of measles, down from 400,000 in 1962, as a result of the Enders vaccine (*see* 1962).

U.S. cigarette sales decline slightly to 571.1 billion as adults smoke an average of 205 packs, down from 210 last year. FTC studies show that while filter-tipped cigarettes dominate the market most cigarettes yield more tars and nicotine in their smoke because tobacco companies are using tobacco leaf higher in tars and nicotine.

World television set ownership nears 200 million with 78 million sets in the United States, 25 million in the Soviet Union, 20.5 million in Japan, 19 in Britain, 13.5 in West Germany, 10 in France.

The U.S. television industry has advertising revenues of $2 billion, roughly twice the total of radio advertising revenues. Both industries derive heavy support from cigarette advertising (*see* 1969).

U.S. first class postal rates climb to 6 cents, up from 5 cents per ounce in 1963 (*see* 1971).

New York magazine begins publication in the spring under the direction of former *Herald-Tribune* editor Clay S. Felker, 42, who was with *Esquire* until hired by the *Trib* to edit its Sunday magazine in 1963.

Screw begins publication at New York in October. The pornographic weekly has been started by former insurance salesman Al Goldstein, 33, with his friend James Buckley who will sell his interest to Goldstein for $500,000 as the tabloid gains wide readership with explicit photographs.

The medical textbook firm Williams & Wilkins wins a copyright infringement suit against the U.S. government in a case arising from a charge of photocopying articles from the firm's medical journals. The decision is reversed in a 4 to 3 ruling by the United States Court of Claims, but the majority decision calls on Congress to enact new legislation on photocopying that will protect publishers and authors against multiple copying without payment of royalties.

The 911 emergency telephone number instituted in New York to summon emergency police, fire, or ambulance assistance is the first such system in the United States (*see* Britain, 1937). By 1977 some 600 U.S. localities with a total population of 38 million will have 911 systems.

Little, Brown, Inc., publishers is acquired by Time, Inc., after 121 years of independence.

Nonfiction *Soul on Ice* by Black Panther leader Eldridge Cleaver who flees to Cuba in November to avoid going to prison for parole violations. Cleaver begins a 7-year exile; *The Teachings of Don Juan: A Yaqui Way of Knowledge* by California anthropologist Carlos Castaneda, 29, who has explored the jimson weed and peyote drug culture of Sonora, Mexico, where belief in the supernatural is widespread; *The Whole Earth Catalog* by Menlo Park, Calif., Truck Store operator Stewart Brand, 29.

Fiction *A Hundred Years of Solitude* (*Cien anos de soledad*) by Colombian novelist Gabriel Garcia Marquez; *Myra Breckenridge* by Gore Vidal; *The Electric Kool-Aid Acid Test* by Tom Wolfe; *Welcome to the Monkey House* (stories) by Kurt Vonnegut, Jr.; *Couples* by John Updike.

Poetry *White Haired Lover* by Karl Shapiro.

Painting *Untitled* by Frank Stella. Marcel Duchamp dies at Neuilly outside Paris October 1 at age 81.

Theater *The Prime of Miss Jean Brodie* by Jay Allen (who has adapted the novel by Muriel Spark) 1/16 at New York's Helen Hayes Theater, with Zoe Caldwell, 378 perfs.; *I Never Sang for my Father* by Robert Anderson 1/25 at New York's Longacre Theater, with Hal Holbrook, Lillian Gish, Matt Crowley, Teresa Wright, 124 perfs.; *The Price* by Arthur Miller 2/7 at New York's Morosco Theater, with Pat Hingle, Kate Reid, Arthur Kennedy, 429 perfs.; *The Boys in the Band* by Mart Crowley 4/18 at New York's off-Broadway Theater Four, with Cliff Gorman, 1,000 perfs.; *Indians* by Arthur Kopit 7/4 at London's Aldwych Theatre, with Barrie Ingham as "Buffalo Bill"

Cody; *The Great White Hope* by Howard Jackler 10/3 at New York's Alvin Theater, with James Earl Jones, Jane Alexander, 276 perfs.; *Forty Carats* by Jay Allen (who has adapted a French play) 12/26 at New York's Morosco Theater, with Julie Harris, Glenda Farrell, 780 perfs.

Britain's Theatres Act effectively abolishes the Lord Chamberlain's powers of censorship (*see* 1737).

Films Stanley Kubrick's *2001: A Space Odyssey;* Jean-Luc Goddard's *Weekend* with Mireille Darc; Jacques Rivette's *L'Amour Fin;* Ingmar Bergman's *Shame;* Barry Shear's *Wild in the Streets* with Christopher Jones, Shelley Winters, Diane Varsi, Hal Holbrook; Roman Polanski's *Rosemary's Baby* with Mia Farrow, John Cassavetes; Noel Black's *Pretty Poison* with Anthony Perkins, Tuesday Weld; Richard Lester's *Petulia* with Julie Christie, George C. Scott, Richard Chamberlain; Frank and Eleanor Perry's *The Swimmer* with Burt Lancaster, Janice Rule, Kim Hunter; Paul Newman's *Rachel, Rachel* with Joanne Woodward; Jacques Tati's *Playtime;* Jules Dassin's *Uptight* with Raymond St. Jacques, Ruby Dee in a remake of the 1935 John Ford classic *The Informer* set in a black ghetto; Mel Brooks's *The Producers* with Zero Mostel, Gene Wilder; Gene Saks's *The Odd Couple* with Walter Matthau, Jack Lemmon; Jack Smight's *No Way to Treat a Lady* with Rod Steiger, George Segal, Lee Remick; Donald Siegel's *Madigan* with Richard Widmark, Henry Fonda, Harry Giardino, James Whitmore.

Film musicals George Dunning's *Yellow Submarine* with animated drawings that show the Beatles trying to save Pepperland from the Blue Meanies, music and lyrics by John Lennon and Paul McCartney; William Wyler's *Funny Girl* with Barbra Streisand as Fanny Brice.

Stage musicals *Your Own Thing* 1/18 at New York's off-Broadway Orpheum Theater, with music and lyrics by Hal Hester and Danny Appolinar, 933 perfs.; *Canterbury Tales* 3/21 at London's Phoenix Theatre, with music by Richard Hill and John Hawkins, lyrics by Noell Coghill, 2,082 perfs.; *Zorba* 11/17 at New York's Imperial Theater, with Herschel Bernardi, music by John Kander, lyrics by Fred Ebb, 224 perfs.; *Promises, Promises* 12/1 at New York's Shubert Theater, with Jerry Orbach, Jill O'Hara, music and lyrics by Burt Bachrach and Hal David, songs that include "Wherever You Are," "I'll Never Fall in Love Again," 1,281 perfs.

First performances Symphony No. 6 by Howard Hanson 2/29 at New York's Philharmonic Hall; Symphony No. 8 by Roger Sessions 5/2 at New York's Philharmonic Hall; *The Prodigal Son* (church parable) by Benjamin Britten 6/10 at Orford, Suffolk.

U.S. guitar sales reach $130 million, up from $35 million in 1960.

Popular songs "Both Sides Now" by Canadian-born singer-guitarist-songwriter Joni Mitchell (*née* Roberta Joan Anderson), 25; "Mrs. Robinson" by Paul Simon (for the film *The Graduate*); "Galveston" by Jimmy Webb; "Spinning Wheel" by David Clayton Thomas; "Over You" by Jerry Filler; "Do Your Own Thing" by Jerry Leiber and Mike Stoller: "Blond on Blond" by Bob Dylan who becomes a country singer after coming close to death in a motorcycle accident; "Hey, Jude" and "Lady Madonna" by John Lennon and Paul McCartney; "Jumpin' Jack Flash" by Mick Jagger and Keith Richard; *Led Zeppelin No. 1* (album) by the Led Zeppelin, a new English rock group (Jimmy Page, 23, John Paul Jones, 22, John Bonham, 21, and Robert Plant, 21); *Papas and the Mamas—Mamas and the Papas* (album); *Cheap Thrills* (album) by Big Brother and The Holding Company; "Hurdy Gurdy Man" by Donovan Leitch; "Little Green Apples" by Bobby Russell; "The Windmills of Your Mind" by Michel Legrand, lyrics by Alan and Marilyn Bergman (for the film *The Thomas Crown Affair*); "Gotta Get a Message to You" and "I Started a Joke" by the Bee Gees. "Those Were the Days" by Gene Reskin.

Joe Frazier wins the world heavyweight boxing crown March 24 at age 24 by knocking out Buster Mathis in the 11th round of a title bout at New York nearly 10 months after the World Boxing Association took the title away from Muhammad Ali for refusing to accept induction into the U.S. Army (*see* Cassius Clay, 1964). An eight-man title tournament staged by the WBA is won by Jimmy Ellis, 28, who defeats Jerry Quarry, 22, in a 15-round decision April 27 at Oakland but Frazier will gain undisputed right to the title early in 1970.

The Olympic Games at Mexico City attract 6,082 contestants from 109 countries. Unofficial winner is the United States after three consecutive Olympics at which Soviet athletes have triumphed.

The Detroit Tigers win the World Series by defeating the St. Louis Cardinals 4 games to 3.

Harvard ties Yale 29 to 29 November 23 at Harvard Stadium after having trailed Yale 0-22 in the second quarter. The two football teams have met unbeaten and untied for the first time since 1909, Yale has led 29 to 13 in the final quarter with 42 seconds left on the clock, but Harvard substitute quarterback Vic Champi passes to Vic Gatto for a touchdown that is followed by a two-point conversion to make the score 29 to 21, Harvard recovers an on-side kick, Champi passes to Pete Varney for a final touchdown as the clock runs out, and a two-point conversion ties the score with Yale whose backfield includes Calvin Hill.

A Uniform Monday Holiday Law is enacted by Congress to give Americans 3-day holidays. Scheduled to take effect beginning in 1971, the new law follows centuries-old European laws and orders that Washington's Birthday, Memorial Day, Independence Day, Columbus Day, and Veterans Day be observed on Mondays regardless of what day February 22, May 30, July 4, October 30, or November 11 may be.

A Tokyo bank van robbery December 10 nets the equivalent of $1 million for a motorcycle gang that

Man Walks on Moon

Astronauts Begin Exploration Early

"One small step for a man, one giant leap for mankind" was what astronaut Neil Armstrong intended to say.

intercepts an armored truck carrying cash. The perpetrators will not be caught but Japan's crime rate is low by U.S. and European standards and is declining thanks in part to family social structure, low availability of narcotics, effective gun control laws, and a police force that apprehends 96 percent of suspects in murder cases and 92 percent of suspects in other criminal assaults (Japan has as many murders per year as New York City—which has one-tenth the population of Japan).

Construction begins in Boston's Copley Square of a 60-story John Hancock building that will dwarf the Prudential Tower of 1964. Designed by Henry Cox of New York's I. M. Pei & Partners, the Hancock Building will run into problems of falling glass panels and will not open until 1974.

Sheraton Hotel Corporation is acquired for $200 million by International Telephone and Telegraph (above). ITT will build Sheraton hotels in 38 countries to challenge Hilton and Intercontinental.

North Cascades National Park is established by act of Congress which sets aside 505,000 acres of Washington State glaciers, jagged peaks, and mountain lakes.

Redwood National Park is established by act of Congress. The 58,000-acre park extends along 40 miles of California's Pacific Coast and contains coastal redwood forests with virgin groves that include a 369.2-foot redwood—the world's tallest tree.

Enzyme detergents are introduced by Procter & Gamble, Lever Brothers, and Colgate-Palmolive Company. The new laundry products create problems in U.S. water and sewage systems.

Improved IR-8 rice strains from the IRRI in the Philippines produce record yields in Asia (see 1962; 1964). The "miracle" rice, however, requires more

fertilizer and water than do such traditional strains as Bengawan, Intam, Peta, and Sigadio, IR-8 has little innate resistance to a virus carried by green leaf hoppers, and Filipinos do not like the cooking and eating qualities of the sticky new rice milled from IR-8.

India's wheat production is 50 percent above last year's level as a result of intensive aid by Ford Foundation workers who have introduced new Pitic 62 and Penjamo 62 wheat strains from Mexico.

Desert locusts devastate crops in Saudi Arabia and other countries along the Red Sea in the first major locust plague since 1944.

Some 6,000 Utah sheep die when VX nerve gas from the U.S. Army's Dugway Proving Ground blows across the range.

Tenneco Corporation (above) will be a major U.S. producer of lettuce and other field crops.

The average U.S. farm acre can produce 70 bushels of corn, up from 25 in 1916, and some farmers get 200 bushels (see 1973).

U.S. crop acreage produces yields 80 percent above those in 1920 and the output per breeding animal has roughly doubled since 1920.

U.S. farms have 5 million tractors, 900,000 grain combines, 780,000 hay balers, 660,000 corn pickers and shellers. Major crops are all harvested by machine.

Farm labor represents only 7 percent of the U.S. work force, down from 10 percent in 1960, although another 32 percent of the work force is engaged in supplying the farmer or handling his produce.

The average U.S. farm subsidy is nearly $1,000, up from $175 in 1960, as the number of U.S. farms continues to drop off substantially. Many farmers receive far in excess of the average subsidy (see 1967).

A nationwide boycott of table grapes organized by Cesar Chavez of the United Farm Workers Organizing Committee gains support from much of the public (see 1962). Chavez dramatizes "La Causa" ("The Cause") with long fasts.

Thousands die of starvation in Biafra whose Ibo tribespeople have seceded from Nigeria.

Hunger in America, telecast by CBS, documents conditions of kwashiorkor and other deficiency diseases in the world's most affluent nation (see 1951).

A Poor People's March on Washington focuses its protest on U.S. hunger conditions. Originally planned by Martin Luther King (above), the demonstration proceeds from May 3 to June 23 under the leadership of Ralph D. Abernathy, Jr.

The Citizens Board of Inquiry into Hunger and Malnutrition in the United States observes that federal food-aid programs reach only 18 percent of the nation's poor.

The U.S. food stamp program is liberalized (see 1967). The Department of Agriculture expands from two to 42 the number of counties where federal authorities will handle the program which in some areas is resisted by local authorities (see 1969).

Malnutrition is related to brain damage, says Indian Food Minister Chidambara Subramaniam. "On the basis of studies in my own state of Madras, where I was Minister of Education, it has been estimated that between 35 and 40 percent of the children of India have suffered permanent brain damage by the time they reach school age because of protein deficiency. This means that we are, in effect, producing subhuman beings at the rate of 35 million per year. By the time they reach school age they are unable to concentrate sufficiently to absorb and retain knowledge."

Malnutrition in some parts of the United States is as grim as any he has seen in India or any other country, reports U.S. nutrition investigator Arnold E. Schaefer, 51, who at one school has found vitamin A deficiencies worse than those in children who have gone blind from keratomalacia. These Head Start Program children could go blind at any time, "five minutes from now or a year from now," says Schaefer.

The average U.S. diet is estimated to provide 3,200 calories per day with 98 grams of protein but millions of U.S. diets do not approach the average.

The Society for Nutrition Education is founded at San Francisco.

Gorton's of Gloucester is acquired by General Mills for $30 million (see 1755; 1955).

Wakefield Seafoods, Inc., is acquired by Hunt-Wesson Foods (see 1945; 1960; Norton Simon, Inc., 1969).

15 million fish are killed by pollution in the United States by the estimate of the U.S. Department of the Interior. Two-thirds are commercial varieties.

The U.S. Coast Guard reports that 714 major oil spills have occurred during the year, up from 371 in 1966.

Fifty-eight percent of U.S. fish is imported, up from 41.4 percent in 1966.

The average American eats 11 pounds of fish per year, the highest since the mid-1950s.

"Chinese Restaurant Syndrome" (Kwok's disease) is studied by U.S. physicians who trace it to an overuse of monosodium glutamate (MSG) by Chinese chefs (see Ikeda, 1908; Ac'cent, 1947). Symptoms are burning sensations, chest pain, dizziness, facial pressure, headache, and numbness.

Continental Baking is acquired by International Telephone and Telegraph (ITT, above) for $280 million in securities (see Wonder Bread, 1927; Morton Packing, 1955). ITT-Continental has 40 bread bakeries, 22 bakeries that produce both bread and cake, six or seven cake bakeries, and more than a dozen plants that pack Morton Frozen Foods, snack items, and other foods.

United Brands, Inc., is created by Eli Black who takes over the giant United Fruit Company and adds it to the John Morrell and American Seal-Kap interests he merged into AMK Corporation last year (see

Chiquita Banana, 1944). United Brands begins to acquire California growers in an ill-fated move to establish the Chiquita brand trademark for fresh lettuce.

The nickel Hershey bar sold since 1894 is discontinued by Hershey Foods which has shrunk the bar from 1 1/8 ounces in 1947 down to 3/4 and announces that further size reductions are impractical. The 10-cent Hershey bar weighs 1.5 ounces.

London's Brooke Bond Tea, Ltd., merges with Liebig's Extract of Meat Co., Ltd., to create the world's largest tea company with nearly 40,000 acres of tea plantations in India, Sri Lanka (Ceylon), and East Africa, with ranches in Argentina, Paraguay, and Rhodesia that cover more than 2.6 million acres, and with more than 80,000 employees.

The Population Bomb by California biologist Paul Ralph Ehrlich, 36, warns of the horrors in store for a world that does not curb its population growth.

Zero Population Growth, Inc., is founded by Paul Ehrlich (above) with headquarters at Washington, D.C. The organization sets as its goal the "stabilization of U.S. population size, followed by reduction to a more reasonable level; stabilization of energy and resource consumption; land use planning...."

Britain legalizes abortion April 27 as the Abortion Act that received Royal Assent in late November of last year overturns an 1861 law that made abortion a crime under all circumstances. The new law makes an abortion legal if two registered physicians find that "continuance of pregnancy would involve risks to the life or injury to the physical or mental health of the pregnant woman or the future well-being of herself or of the child or her children." Opponents of the new law predict that 400,000 abortions will be performed each year (but see 1969).

1969 Man walks on the moon for the first time July 21 as U.S. astronaut Neil A. Armstrong steps out of the lunar module from Apollo 11 and is joined by his companion Edwin E. "Buzz" Aldrin, Jr. Now 39, Armstrong is watched on television by much of the world but millions of Americans believe the moon walk was staged in a studio to divert attention from the Vietnam War and many millions more demand that money and technology be applied to more socially productive purposes.

U.S. troop strength in South Vietnam is announced at 541,000 March 6 and additional allied forces in the country number 72,000.

President Nixon meets with South Vietnam's President Thieu at Midway June 8 and announces the start of U.S. troop withdrawal and a new "Vietnamization" policy that will help the Indochinese nation deal with her own problems.

North Vietnamese leader Ho Chi Minh dies September 3 at age 79 after 15 years as president.

Soviet Premier Kosygin meets at Peking Airport with Chou En-Lai en route home from the funeral of Ho Chi Minh at Hanoi and the two Communist lead-

1969 (cont.) ers discuss the Chinese-Soviet border clashes that have occurred earlier in the year in East and Central Asia. Formal Soviet-Chinese border conferences begin at Peking October 19 amid signs of deepening divisions in the Communist world.

U.S. Senator from Massachusetts Edward M. Kennedy has defeated the 20-year veteran Russell Long of Louisiana for the post of assistant majority leader January 4, having defied tradition by challenging Long after only 6 years' tenure. But Kennedy's credibility as a political leader is blighted in July, when the body of a 28-year-old campaign worker for the late Robert Kennedy is retrieved on the morning of July 19 from a black 1967 Oldsmobile sedan that plunged into Poucha Pond on Chappaquiddick Island off Martha's Vineyard some hours earlier and is upside down in 8 feet of water. Mary Jo Kopechne left a party at midnight of July 18 with Senator Kennedy who drove off Dike Bridge, allegedly tried to save the young woman, but has failed unaccountably to report the accident to police for 10 hours and has thus raised questions as to his judgment.

"I will say confidently that looking ahead just three years the war will be over," says President Nixon October 12. "It will be over on a lasting basis that will promote lasting peace in the Pacific."

The New Mobilization Committee to End the War in Vietnam demands a moratorium on the war October 15 and masses hundreds of thousands of demonstrators in Washington, D.C., November 15. Police surround the White House with D.C. Transit buses parked bumper to bumper to protect the executive mansion where President Nixon watches a football game on television. The police use tear gas to disperse demonstrators gathered in front of the Justice Department, and the antiwar left charges the FBI and the CIA with spying on them and with breaking into their offices to gather information.

Chicago judge Julius Hoffman, 74, hears testimony in the case of *U.S. v. Dellinger and others* that opened September 24 (*see* 1968). Attorney William Moses Kunstler defends David Dellinger, Rennie Davis, Tom Hayden, Abbie Hoffman, Black Panther leader Bobby Seale, Jerry Rubin, university lecturer Lee Weiner, 32, and chemistry professor John R. Froins. Justice Hoffman has Seale gagged and manacled to his chair in the courtroom and sentences him in November to 4 years in prison for contempt of court.

Chicago police raid an apartment at 4:45 o'clock the morning of December 4 pursuant to a court order. The 14 officers are armed with a Thompson submachine gun, five shotguns, a .357 pistol, and 19 or 20 .38 caliber pistols, Black Panther leader Fred Hampton or Mark Clark fires one shot at the police, the police fire at least 82 shots killing both Hampton and Clark, and they recover illegal weapons.

U.S. radicals who have broken with the Students for a Democratic Society and have called themselves the Weathermen change their name to the Weather Underground. The original name came from the Bob Dylan song "Subterranean Homesick Blues" which contains the words, "You don't need a weatherman to know which way the wind blows." The Weather Underground will plant bombs to register its protest against the continuing war in Vietnam.

Israel's Premier Levi Eshkol has died in February and has been succeeded by Russian-born Milwaukee-raised Palestine pioneer Golda Mabovitch Meir, 70, who will hold office for 5 embattled years.

 Italy's "economic miracle" postwar recovery grinds to a stop after a boom that pulled the country out of a recession early in the decade. Splintered until now by fights between Communists and non-Communists, Italy's trade union movement achieves some unity and employs strikes and violence to win major pay raises but productivity does not increase, agriculture declines, Italy is forced to increase imports to meet the demand fueled by rising living standards, and a slide toward bankruptcy begins.

An antitrust suit against IBM is filed by the U.S. Department of Justice in its last official act under the outgoing Johnson administration (*see* 1956). Largest antitrust action every taken, the case will not come to trial until 1975 by which time International Business Machines will be the world's largest company in terms of the value of its stock (which will be worth more than the combined value of all the stock of all companies listed on the American Stock Exchange).

Washington announces December 19 that it will relax restrictions on U.S. trade with Peking.

A booming U.S. economy employs a record number of workers, unemployment falls to its lowest level in 15 years, the prime interest rate is 7 percent, the dollar is strong in the world money markets, and Wall Street's Dow Jones Industrial Average rises above 1,000 for the first time in history.

Blue Cross health insurance programs cover some 68 million Americans, up from 37 million in 1950, and Blue Shield surgical insurance covers roughly 60 million. Hospital insurance policies issued by private, profitmaking companies (often as part of a package that includes life insurance) cover another 100 million, some 7 million are covered by nonprofit programs other than Blue Cross, and more than 90 percent of most U.S. city hospital bills are paid by third party groups.

The cost of medical care in the United States escalates and a crisis in health care delivery looms in large part because patients can in many cases receive insurance benefits only if hospitalized, because they often are hospitalized unnecessarily by sympathetic physicians, because Blue Cross pays hospitals on a cost-plus basis without scrutinizing costs too carefully, because physicians order countless tests to protect themselves from malpractice suits, because hospital administrators install costly equipment and facilities that are under-utilized, and because hospital workers receive higher wages.

President Nixon bans production of chemical and biological warfare agents in November. Included are bacteria that produce anthrax, tick-borne encephalitis, bubonic plague, psittacosis (parrot fever), Q-fever, brucellosis, tularemia, Rocky Mountain spotted fever, and botulism along with the chemical agents mustard gas, phosgene, and the VX nerve gas that killed 6,000 sheep last year, but riot control agents such as tear gas remain in production.

The United States Lines retires its passenger ship S.S. *United States* after 17 years as competition from transatlantic air carriers and foreign flag liners makes U.S. passenger vessels unprofitable.

The Concorde supersonic jet makes its first flight March 2 from Toulouse and makes its first supersonic flight October 1 (*see* 1962; 1970).

A Venezuelan DC-9 crashes after takeoff from Maracaibo March 16 killing all 84 aboard plus 71 on the ground. A United Arab Ilyushin-18 crashes at Aswan Airport March 20 killing 87; a Mexican Boeing 727 flies into a mountain near Monterrey June 4 killing 79; an Allegheny Airlines DC-9 collides with a student plane at Shelbyville, Ind., September 9 killing 83; a Nigerian VC-10 crashes near Iju November 20 killing 87; an Olympic Airways DC-6B crashes in a storm near Athens December 8 killing 93.

Philadelphia's Lindenwold Line begins service February 15 to serve commuters with a 14.4-mile railroad to Lindenwold, N.J., and nine stations en route. Daily passenger volume, initially 17,000, will more than double by late next year and will average over 41,000 by 1973.

The Trans-Australian Railway marks completion of a track standardization program with a golden spike ceremony November 29 at Broken Hill in New South Wales. The road includes a 29-mile stretch of continuously welded track—the largest such stretch of track in the world (*see* Indian-Pacific Express, 1970).

The Ford Maverick introduced April 17 is a compact car designed to compete with Volkswagen and other foreign makes. General Motors prepares to introduce its Chevrolet Camaro compact.

The average U.S. automobile wholesales at $2,280, up from $1,880 in 1959.

The oil depletion allowance granted to U.S. petroleum producers since 1926 as a tax incentive to encourage exploration for new reserves is reduced from 27.5 percent to 22 percent by act of Congress despite President Nixon's campaign promise last year to maintain the allowance. The new tax allowance is like the old one in that it is based on the selling price of oil rather than on the capital invested in establishing the oil well that is being depleted.

Phillips Petroleum drillers discover a giant oilfield off the coast of Norway. The North Sea basin will prove to be the largest reservoir of oil outside the Middle East and will be found to lie 60 percent in British waters, 40 percent in Norwegian waters.

Exploitation of the Alaskan North Slope petroleum reserve remains the subject of hot debate as storage tanks are built at Prudhoe Bay on the Beaufort Sea. Delays in building pipelines to carry the oil up over the Brooks Range and south to Prince Charles Sound will result in a better designed pipeline with fewer potential danger spots for leakage.

Amerada Hess Corporation is created by a merger of Hess Oil & Chemical with Amerada Petroleum.

Sesame Street begins in November on U.S. Public Service television stations and starts to revolutionize children's attitudes toward learning and adults' attitudes about what children are capable of learning. Designed by the Children's Television Workshop and funded by the Ford Foundation, the Carnegie Corporation, and the U.S. Office of Education, *Sesame Street* teaches preschool children letters and numbers with the same techniques used in commercial television programs such as the 14-year-old *Captain Kangaroo* show. *Sesame Street* introduces characters such as Oscar the Grouch, Big Bird, the Cookie Monster, Ernie, and Grover.

U.S. newspapers and television commentators assail President Nixon's position on Vietnam, his appointment of Clement F. Haynsworth, Jr., to the Supreme Court, and his November 3 appeal to "the great Silent Majority of my fellow Americans." White House speechwriter Patrick Buchanan writes an address for Vice President Agnew to deliver at Des Moines, President Nixon goes over the speech, and Vice President Agnew stands up November 13 to attack the "dozen anchormen, commentators, and executive producers [who] ... decide what 40 to 50 million Americans will learn of the day's events in the nation and in the world ... read the same newspapers ... draw their political and social views from the same sources ... talk constantly to one another, thereby providing artificial reinforcement to their shared viewpoint." President Nixon begins a campaign of intimidation against the press and electronic media.

Doonesbury by U.S. cartoonist Garry Trudeau, 20, comments on U.S. military involvement in Vietnam. Trudeau began the comic strip about one Michael J. Doonesbury under the title *Bull Tales* in the *Yale Daily News* last year, he syndicates it to 25 newspapers through the newly-formed Universal Press Syndicate, nearly 300 newspapers will pick it up, and Doonesbury will win a 1975 Pulitzer prize, the first comic strip to be thus honored.

The Supreme Court declares a Georgia antipornography law unconstitutional and says, "If the First Amendment means anything it means that a state has no business telling a man, sitting alone in his own house, what books he may read or what films he may watch."

Penthouse magazine begins publication at New York in September. U.S. publisher Robert Guccione, 38, started the magazine at London in March 1965. He

1969 (cont.) does not use an airbrush to eliminate pubic hair from nude photographs, and he challenges Hugh Hefner's *Playboy* whose newsstand sales he will overtake by 1975 (*see* 1953).

The Saturday Evening Post ceases publication after 148 years.

Nonfiction *So Human an Animal* by bacteriologist René Dubos.

Fiction *Ada* by Vladimir Nabokov; *Portnoy's Complaint* by Philip Roth; *Slaughterhouse Five, or The Children's Crusade* by Kurt Vonnegut, Jr.; *Bullet Park* by John Cheever; *The Godfather* by U.S. novelist Mario Puzo who writes about the Mafia; *Between Life and Death* (*Entre la vie et la mort*) by Nathalie Sarraute; *La vita e gioco* by Alberto Moravia.

The Soviet Writers Union expels novelist Aleksandr Solzhenitsyn.

Painting *The Finn* by Andrew Wyeth; *Orange Yellow Orange* by Mark Rothko. Ben Shahn dies at New York March 14 at age 70.

Theater *To Be Young, Gifted and Black* by the late Lorraine Hansberry (adapted by Robert Nemiroff) 1/2 at New York's off-Broadway Cherry Lane Theater, with Barbara Baxley, Cicely Tyson, 380 perfs.; *Ceremonies in Dark Old Men* by U.S. playwright Lonnie Elder III 2/4 at New York's St. Marks Playhouse; *No Place to Be Somebody* by U.S. playwright Charles Gordone 5/4 at New York's off-Broadway Public Theater; *Butterflies Are Free* by U.S. playwright Leonard Gersh 10/21 at New York's Booth Theater, with Keir Dullea, Blythe Danner, Eileen Heckart, 1,128 perfs.; *Last of the Red Hot Lovers* by Neil Simon 12/28 at New York's Eugene O'Neill Theater, with James Coco, Linda Lavin, 706 perfs.

Films Dennis Hopper's *Easy Rider* with Hopper, Peter Fonda, Jack Nicholson dramatizes the alienation between the hippie generation and established rural American social values; John Schlesinger's *Midnight Cowboy* with Dustin Hoffman, Jon Voight; Sam Peckinpah's *The Wild Bunch* with William Holden, Robert Ryan, Ernest Borgnine; George Roy Hill's *Butch Cassidy and the Sundance Kid* with Paul Newman, Robert Redford, Katharine Ross, Cloris Leachman, Jeff Corey; Ronald Neame's *The Prime of Miss Jean Brodie* with Maggie Smith; Charles Jarrott's *Anne of the Thousand Days* with Richard Burton as Henry VIII, Genevieve Bujold as Anne Boleyn; Rainer Werner Fassbinder's *Love is Colder than Death, Katzelmacher,* and *Gods of the Plague;* Costa-Gavras's *Z* with Yves Montand, Irene Papas, Jean-Louis Trintignant is based on an actual political assassination; Henri-Georges Clouzot's *La Prisonniere;* Lindsay Anderson's *If* with Malcolm McDowall, David Wood; Karel Reisz's *The Loves of Isadora* with Vanessa Redgrave as Isadora Duncan, Jason Robards, James Fox; Sidney Pollack's *They Shoot Horses, Don't They?* with Jane Fonda, Michael Sarrazin, Susannah York, Red Buttons, Gig Young; Henry Hathaway's *True Grit* with John Wayne, Glen Campbell; Masahiro Shinoda's *Double Suicide* with Kachienon Nakamura, Shira Iwashita; Woody Allen's *Take the Money and Run* with Allen.

Broadway and off-Broadway musicals *Dear World* 2/6 at the Mark Hellinger Theater, with Angela Lansbury, Milo O'Shea in an adaptation of the 1945 Jean Giraudoux play *The Madwoman of Chaillot,* music and lyrics by Jerry Herman, 132 perfs.; *1776* 3/16 at the 46th Street Theater, with book by Peter Stone, music and lyrics by Sherman Edwards, 1,217 perfs.; *Oh! Calcutta!* 6/17 at the off-Broadway Eden Theater, a revue devised by English critic Kenneth Peacock Tynan, 42, with contributions by Samuel Beckett, Jules Feiffer, Dan Greenberg, John Lennon, and others, music and lyrics by the Open Door, scenes that include frontal nudity and simulated sex acts, 704 perfs. (plus 610 more at the Belasco Theater beginning late in February, 1971); *Coco* 12/18 at the Mark Hellinger Theater, with Katharine Hepburn as the late Coco Chanel, music by André Previn, book and lyrics by Alan Jay Lerner, 332 perfs.

Avery Fisher sells his 32-year-old hi-fi business for $31 million.

First performances Symphony No. 14 by Dmitri Shostakovich in September at Leningrad.

The Woodstock Music and Art Fair in the Catskill Mountains at Bethel, N.Y., draws 300,000 youths from all over America for 4 days in August to hear Jimi Hendrix, Joan Baez, Ritchie Havens, the Jefferson Airplane, the Who, the Grateful Dead, Carlos Santana, and other rock stars. Despite traffic jams, thunderstorms, and shortages of food, water, and medical facilities the gathering is orderly with a sense of loving and sharing, but thousands in the audience are stoned or tripping on marijuana ("grass," "pot," "mary jane"), hashish ("hash"), lysergic acid diethylamide (LSD), barbiturates ("downs"), amphetamines ("uppers"), mescaline, cocaine, and other drugs.

The Altamont Music Festival outside San Francisco December 6 draws more than 300,000 to a free Rolling Stones concert. Members of the Hells Angels motorcycle gang, hired to provide security, administer several beatings and stab a boy to death when he tries to reach the stage.

Popular songs "Hot Fun in the Summertime" by Sylvester Stewart; "Get Back" by John Lennon and Paul McCartney; "Honky Tonk Women" by Mick Jagger and Keith Richard; "Lay Lady Lay" by Bob Dylan; "It's Your Thing" by Rudolph, Ronald, and O'Kelley Isley; "Games People Play" by Joe South; "Oh Happy Days" by Edwin R. Hawkins; "Come Saturday Morning" by Dory Previn, lyrics by Fred Kurlin (for the film *The Sterile Cuckoo*); "Raindrops Keep Falling on My Head" by Burt Bachrach (for the film *Butch Cassidy and the Sundance Kid*).

Australia's Rod Laver wins the Grand Slam of tennis for the second time at age 31.

UCLA basketball star Lew Alcindor attracts wide attention with his prowess.

Wilt "the Stilt" Chamberlain of the Los Angeles Lakers leads the National Basketball Association in rebound recoveries for the fourth consecutive year (and for the eighth year in the past 10) at age 35.

Baseball's two major leagues split into eastern and western divisions with two new expansion teams each. The National League adds the Montreal Expos and the San Diego Padres, the American League adds the Kansas City Royals and the Seattle Pilots.

The New York Mets win their first World Series by defeating the Baltimore Orioles 4 games to 1.

World chess champion Tigran Petrosian is defeated by Soviet grandmaster Boris Spassky who will hold the title until 1972.

U.S. pantyhose production reaches 624 million pair, up from 200 million last year, as American women switch from nylon hosiery to nylon pantyhose that require no garters, no garter-belts, no corsets.

The National Association of Broadcasters announces a plan July 8 to phase out cigarette advertising on radio and television over a 3-year period beginning January 1, 1970 (see 1967).

The New Jersey Chapter of the American Civil Liberties Union files suit in federal court charging that marijuana should not be classed with heroin and other dangerous drugs. Marijuana, says the CLU, is harmless both to the user and to society.

Heroin sales to New York schoolchildren have jumped as a result of the federal government's Operation Intercept program to restrict the flow of marijuana from Mexico, says an expert testifying before a joint legislative committee at Washington. The price of marijuana, he says, has climbed so high that heroin sells at a competitive price.

The Tate-LaBianca murders make headlines in August. Screen actress Sharon Tate Polanski, 26, is murdered at her Bel-Air home early in the morning of August 10 along with Folger Coffee heiress Abigail Folger, 25, her common-law husband Wojiciech "Voytek" Frykowski, 32, Hollywood hair stylist Jay Sebring, 35, and delivery boy Steven Earl Parent. Supermarket chain president Leno LaBianca, 44, and his 38-year-old wife Rosemary are murdered later in the day at Los Angeles. The Los Angeles police say the LaBianca murders have no connection with those at the Polanski house in Benedict Canyon, but a jury late next year will find ex-convict Charles M. Manson, 32, and his hippie cult family guilty of all seven murders. (Manson has allegedly mesmerized his followers with drugs, sex, and religion.)

The National Commission on Urban Growth recommends development of 10 new U.S. communities of 100,000 each to accommodate an expected 20 million or more in additional population but no government action is taken.

Boston's new city hall is completed by Kallman, McKinnell, and Knowles.

Chicago's John Hancock Center with 100 floors is completed by Skidmore, Owings & Merrill.

New York's Burlington House with 50 floors goes up on the Avenue of the Americas at 54th Street on the site formerly occupied by a large apartment house and by the Ziegfeld Theater of 1927.

An offshore oil well blowout in California's Santa Barbara Channel covers a 30-mile stretch of shoreline with 235,000 gallons of crude oil beginning January 28. The offshore drilling platforms of Union Oil Company kill fish and wildlife, and while the blowout is contained after 11 days, the platforms will continue to leak oil for years.

Thor Heyerdahl of 1947 *Kon Tiki* fame crosses much of the Atlantic in a papyrus raft he calls *Ra* and observes pollution not seen in the Pacific. Empty bottles, cans, plastic containers, nylon, and—most conspicuously—clots of solidified black petroleum.

Hurricane Camille hits the Mississippi Gulf Coast August 17 with winds 190 miles per hour. Strongest hurricane since 1935, the storm strikes even harder in Virginia and West Virginia, leaves 248 dead, 200,000 homeless, and property damage of $1.5 billion.

California has heavy rains that produce mud slides which destroy or damage 10,000 homes; 100 die.

Europe's Rhine River has a massive fish kill in June 2 years after the disappearance of two 50-pound canisters containing the insecticide Thiodan. The canisters evidently fell overboard in transit from Frankfurt to the Netherlands and experts theorize that the poison has finally leaked into the water to cause the death of millions of fish.

The Northeast Atlantic Fisheries Commission urges a ban on salmon fishing outside national fishing boundaries as the salmon catch declines in rivers of Canada, Britain, Europe, and the United States.

The average U.S. farm worker produces enough food and fiber for 47 people, up from 40 last year, as agricultural productivity continues to climb.

The average Wisconsin dairy cow yields 10 quarts of milk per day, up from 6 in 1940, as a result of breed improvements.

Britain's Ministry of Agriculture forbids use of penicillin and tetracycline in livestock feed lest drug-resistant strains of bacteria pass on their resistant "R-factor" to other bacteria.

The U.S. Food and Drug Administration forbids injections of most antibiotics in U.S. livestock and gives a trade group of veterinary drug producers up to 2 years to prove that a residue of 2 parts per million in meat poses no human health hazard. U.S. feed producers use $72.5 million worth of antibiotics per year, but FDA rules forbid use of such feeds within 3 to 5 days of slaughter.

Use of any antibiotics in feed and use of DDT and herbicides should be banned, says Britain's Swann

1969 (cont.) Committee, a group set up to study the hazards of such substances.

The Ernest Lee Huckleby family at Alamagordo, Tex., just north of El Paso, consumes pork from hogs fed millet seed treated with mercury fungicide. Some of the Huckleby children go blind and suffer brain damage from mercury poisoning (*see* Minamata Bay, 1953).

Japanese lathe operator Takako Nakamura, 28, throws herself off a speeding train after discovering that she has been poisoned by inhaling cadmium fumes while working for the Toho Zinc Company. The incident moves Prime Minister Eisaku Sato to tears and he announces that he is determined to secure passage of strong antipollution laws.

Arizona orders a 1 year moratorium on use of DDT after milk in the state proves to have high levels of the pesticide.

Mother's milk contains four times the amount of DDT permitted in cows' milk, says Sierra Club executive vice president David Brower in testimony before the House Merchant Marine and Fisheries Committee. "Some wit suggested that if [mother's milk] were packaged in some other container we wouldn't allow it across state lines," says Brower.

Coho salmon in Michigan lakes and streams prove to have DDT concentrations of 20 parts per million. The Food and Drug Administration seizes 28,000 pounds of fish and Michigan restricts spraying of crops with DDT.

The FDA (above) notes that 90 percent of fish sold in the United States contains less than 1 part per million of DDT. Some critics demand a zero level but commercial fishermen in some areas demand a higher level and even critics cannot demonstrate any real evidence that DDT is harmful to humans.

U.S. frankfurters have an average fat content of 33 percent, up from 19 percent in the early 1940s, and some franks are more than half fat. The U.S. Department of Agriculture proposes a 33 percent maximum, but a 25 percent maximum is favored by the Consumer Federation of America, the National Consumers League, and New York City Commissioner of Consumer Affairs Bess Myerson, whose pressure on President Nixon's Special Assistant for Consumer Affairs Virginia H. Knauer leads her to endorse a 30 percent maximum, is announced in December.

Use of monosodium glutamate (MSG) in infant foods is halted by Gerber, Heinz, and Beech-Nut pending further study after tests at the Washington University School of Medicine in St. Louis show that mice fed large amounts of MSG suffer damage to the hypothalamus area of their brains (*see* "Chinese Restaurant Syndrome," 1968).

Cyclamates are removed from the Food and Drug Administration's GRAS (generally recognized as safe) list in October and the FDA reveals plans to remove cyclamate-sweetened products from stores. The agency cites bladder cancers in test rats fed excessive

amounts of cyclamates, but serious doubts will be raised as to the validity of the tests (*see* Delaney clause, 1958).

 A White House Conference on Food, Nutrition and Health opens in December under the chairmanship of Harvard's French-American nutritionist Jean Mayer and considers problems of hunger, malnutrition, food safety, food quality, deception and misinformation, nutrition education, food production, and food availability in America. Few of the conference's recommendations will result in legislation, but funding for food stamp programs will increase in the next 5 years from $400 million to more than $3 billion.

Some 21 million U.S. children participate in the National School Lunch Program. About 3.8 million receive lunch free or at substantially reduced prices and the figure soon will rise to 8 million.

 Paris tears down its Les Halles market and moves it 9 miles south of the city to Runges near Orly Airport. Les Halles had been "the belly of France" (in novelist Emile Zola's phrase) since 1137.

Cyclamates (above) are employed in U.S. foods to the tune of 20 million pounds per year as compared with 20 billion pounds of sugar: 70 percent of the cyclamates are used in sugar-free soft drinks.

Kaboom breakfast food is introduced by General Mills. The new cereal is 43.8 percent sugar.

Frosted Mini-Wheats breakfast food is introduced by the Kellogg Company. It is 28 percent sugar.

Norton Simon, Inc., is created by a reorganization of Hunt-Wesson Foods which has just acquired Redi-Whip (*see* 1947; Wakefield, 1968). Simon has acquired distribution rights to some brands of liquor and has acquired some magazines, he puts them all into the new corporation, and he yields control of it in order to devote himself to other interests.

 Some 43 percent of U.S. women over age 16 and 41 percent of all married women are in the labor force, up from 34 percent of women over age 14 and 31 percent of married women in 1960, but only 4 percent are farmhands or domestic servants.

Abortions in Britain number 28,859 for the 10 months ending February 25 and exceed 1,000 per week in England and Wales by late July. The National Health Service pays for 60 percent of the abortions (*see* 1968).

A California antiabortion law is unconstitutional, the state's supreme court rules in September. The law infringes on a woman's right to decide whether to risk childbirth and bear children, says the court.

1970 Paris peace talks to end the Vietnam conflict continue for a second year without progress but Washington reduces U.S. troop strength in Vietnam below 400,000 in response to mounting public pressure as casualties increase.

North Vietnamese troops and tanks in Laos seize a key stronghold in the Plaine des Jarres in mid-February. U.S. military activity in Laos clearly "violates the spirit" of congressional measures seeking to bar use of American ground forces in Laos, says U.S. Senator Charles McC. Mathias of Maryland February 25. Mathias cites a report that the CIA has hired hundreds of former Green Beret troops to serve in Laos.

U.S. authorities at Saigon charge five U.S. Marines with having murdered 11 South Vietnamese women and five children while on patrol south of Danang February 19.

U.S. authorities at Saigon charge Captain Ernest L. Medina and five other U.S. soldiers with having committed premeditated murder and rape at the South Vietnamese village of My Lai (Songmy) in 1968 and with having maimed a suspect during questioning.

General Samuel W. Koster who commanded the Americal Division whose First Battalion C Company men were involved in the My Lai incident resigns as superintendent of the U.S. Military Academy at West Point following accusations that he and 13 other officers suppressed information relevant to the alleged massacre in which 47 civilians were "wasted." A secret army investigation has reportedly found that the number of victims was reduced as information moved up the chain of command but that U.S. troops did indeed commit acts of murder, rape, sodomy, and maiming against "non-combatants."

"The Senate must not remain silent now while the President uses the armed forces of the United States to fight an undeclared and undisclosed war in Laos," says U.S. Senator J. William Fulbright March 11. He proposes a resolution challenging President Nixon's authority to commit U.S. forces to combat in or over Laos.

Cambodians stage peaceful protest demonstrations at Pnompenh over the presence of North Vietnamese forces in the country as the Cambodian government holds secret discussions on the issue with the Vietcong and the North Vietnamese.

Cambodia's chief of state Prince Norodom Sihanouk is overthrown March 18 while away on a visit to Moscow. The premier and defense minister Lon Nol seizes power and begins a reign of terror against Cambodia's 400,000 Vietnamese residents, he appeals for U.S. aid to stop the North Vietnamese from taking over, and a massive South Vietnamese move into Cambodia begins April 29 with support from U.S. planes and advisers.

President Nixon makes a television address April 30 saying that he has ordered U.S. combat troops into part of Cambodia to destroy North Vietnamese "headquarters" and "sanctuaries." The action is intended to save U.S. lives, says the president, and is essential to his plan for "Vietnamizing" the war.

College campus radicals who oppose his policies in Vietnam are "bums," says President Nixon May 1.

Kent State University students in Ohio rally at noon May 4 to protest the widening of the war in Southeast Asia. National Guardsmen open fire on the 1,000 students, four students fall dead including two young women, eight others are wounded.

U.S. colleges close down in antiwar demonstrations and some will remain closed for the balance of the spring term as students coordinate plans for strikes and demonstrations. Secretary of the Interior Walter J. Hickel sends a letter to President Nixon warning that the administration is contributing to anarchy and revolt by turning its back on American youth and that further attacks on the motives of young people by Vice President Agnew will solidify hostility and make communication impossible.

New York construction workers break up an antiwar rally in the Wall Street area May 8, they force City Hall officials to raise the American flag to full staff (it had been lowered to half staff in memory of the Kent State dead), and they invade Pace College. But President Nixon holds his first press conference in 3 months and announces that U.S. troops will be out of Cambodia by mid-June.

An anti-war rally May 9 brings 75,000 to 100,000 peaceful demonstrators to Washington, D.C. President Nixon is unable to sleep and drives to the Lincoln Memorial before dawn to talk for an hour with students protesting the war.

Portuguese dictator Antonio Salazar dies July 27 at age 81, not knowing that he has been replaced as premier by Marcello Caetano after nearly 40 years in power.

Nigeria's civil war ends January 12 with the capitulation of the Biafran chief of staff Brigadier Philip Effiong after more than 30 months of conflict in which some 2 million people have died (see 1967). Brigadier Effiong has assumed leadership following the flight of General Odumegwu Ojukwu to the Ivory Coast.

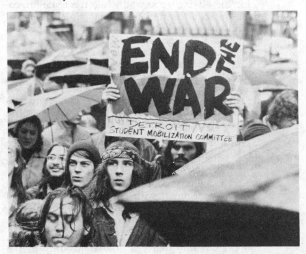

Widespread protests against U.S. involvement in Southeast Asia inspired demonstrations in many cities.

1970 (cont.) Libyan military leader Colonel Mu'ammar el-Qadhafi, 27, assumes power as premier January 16, 4 1/2 months after seizing control of the country. French defense minister Michel Debre announces 5 days later that France will provide Libya with 100 military aircraft—twice the number originally announced—following Libya's promise to end her support of rebels in neighboring Chad.

Israeli jets raid Cairo suburbs in January, Israeli commandos strike within 37 miles of Cairo January 16 and destroy power and telephone pylons on the main road between Cairo and Port Suez.

Representatives of five Arab nations meet at Cairo and vow to continue fighting to recover territory occupied by Israel since the 1967 conflict. They blame the United States for Israel's refusal to give up the territory, they allude to profitable U.S. oil investments, and they warn that the Arabs will not permit their "resources and wealth" to be exploited to help Israel.

The Soviet press agency Tass issues a statement February 16 pledging "necessary support" to the Arab nations but reaffirming Soviet hopes for a diplomatic settlement in the Middle East.

Egypt's President Nasser accepts a U.S. peace formula for the Middle East July 24, Jordan announces her acceptance 2 days later, Syria makes a show of rejecting the formula, Israel announces her acceptance of the formula July 31 as Palestine liberationists meet 25,000 strong at Amman and cheer a guerilla leader's call for rejection of the formula and "liberation" of all Palestine.

Arab and Israeli forces clash on three fronts August 2 as diplomats in world capitals work to end hostilities, a cease-fire goes into effect August 7, guerilla spokesmen at Amman say they will work to undermine the 90-day truce, and while the cease-fire remains intact along the Suez Canal Israeli jets attack guerilla bases in Lebanon August 9, Israeli forces fight infiltrators from Syria in the Golan heights, Israeli intelligence reports installation of new Soviet antiaircraft missiles on the Egyptian side of the Suez Canal 4 hours after the ceasefire went into effect, Israeli planes bomb and strafe Jordanian army posts that are said to make guerilla raids possible, and concerted efforts begin at the UN in New York to settle the disputes in the Middle East.

Egypt's President Nasser dies September 28 at age 52. His friend Anwar el-Sadat, 51, is elected president October 14 by an overwhelming vote.

A Syrian military coup November 13 replaces the civilian government with a rightist regime headed by Defense Minister Lieutenant General Hafez-el-Assad, 40, who is made premier November 19.

The British general elections January 18 have given the Conservative party a 30-seat majority in the House of Commons, Prime Minister Harold Wilson is turned out after more than 5 years of Labour Party government, and a new cabinet takes office with Conservative Edward Heath as prime minister.

An explosion in New York's Greenwich Village March 6 has completely obliterated a townhouse at 18 West 12th Street that has been allegedly used by members of the Weather Underground to produce bombs. Three people were killed.

University of Wisconsin students protesting the university's participation in government war research blow up a university laboratory August 24 killing a research graduate student, injuring four others, and destroying a $1.5 million computer.

Chilean president Salvador Allende Gossens takes office November 3 at age 62. Allende is the first Marxist to be elected head of a government in the Western Hemisphere by a democratic majority, the CIA has made unsuccessful efforts to block his election, he restates his campaign promise to nationalize much of Chile's economy, and he extends recognition to Cuba's Castro government.

France's former president Charles de Gaulle dies November 9 at age 79 at Colombey-les-Deux-Eglises.

Japanese novelist Yukio Mishima harangues 1,000 troops November 25 on the "disgrace" of having lost the Pacific war in 1945, he urges them to support him and his private army in a coup d'etat, he arouses no interest, and he dies by his own hand in a ceremonial act of *seppuku* at age 45.

Poland has riots beginning December 14 at Gdansk (formerly Danzig) 1 week after the signing of a treaty with the German Federal Republic which gives provisional recognition to the Oder-Neisse line as Poland's western frontier. Warsaw has given assent to the repatriation of Germans living east of the Oder-Neisse line but the riots have arisen from food shortages and from higher prices of food and other commodities. The riots spread to other cities, police and troops put down the uprising with heavy loss of life, Wladyslaw Gomulka and other members of the Polish politburo are forced to resign December 20, and Edward Gierek, the party chief in Upper Silesia, succeeds to Gomulka's offices.

The Commission on Civil Rights calls a recent presidential policy statement on school integration inadequate, overcautious, and possibly the signal for a major retreat.

Yale president Kingman Brewster, Jr., says April 24 that he is "skeptical" as to whether black revolutionaries can get "a fair trial anywhere in the United States." A special coroner's jury at Chicago has ruled January 21 that last year's killing of Fred Hampton and another Black Panther in a predawn police raid was "justifiable," Brewster says he is "appalled and ashamed" that such a situation can exist, he blames it on police action against the Black Panthers, but he notes that he is speaking only for himself.

A student dormitory at Jackson State College in Mississippi is riddled with police bullets May 14 killing a student and a local high school senior, both blacks.

NAACP board chairman Bishop Stephen G. Spottswood delivers a keynote address June 29 charging that the Nixon administration has a calculated antiblack policy, but National Urban League executive director Whitney M. Young, Jr., speaks out July 19 denying that the Nixon administration is antiblack.

Former Alabama governor George C. Wallace urges Southern governors to defy federal integration orders. Addressing a noisy Birmingham rally February 8, Wallace says he will run for the presidency again in 1972 "if Nixon doesn't do something about the mess our schools are in."

Northern liberals should drop their "monumental hypocrisy" and concede that de facto segregation exists in the North, says U.S. Senator Abraham A. Ribicoff of Connecticut, February 9.

Congress approves education appropriation bills containing amendments designed to halt busing of children to achieve racial balance (see 1971).

A group of civil rights leaders attacks the policy of "benign neglect" toward blacks advocated by presidential adviser Daniel Patrick Moynihan. They call the policy "a calculated, aggressive, and systematic" effort by the administration to "wipe out" gains made by the civil rights movement.

The Gray Panthers founded by Philadelphia spinster Margaret "Maggie" Kuhn, 65, begins fighting for the rights of retired Americans. Forced to retire from her job with the Presbyterian Church missions because of a mandatory retirement age policy, Kuhn feels "wounded and angry at having been sent out to pasture to get lost."

Boeing 747 jumbo jets go into transatlantic service for Pan American World Airways beginning January 21 (see 1966).

Two armed men hijack a Pan Am Boeing 747 September 6 en route from Amsterdam to New York, reroute the plane to Beirut, take dynamite aboard, fly on to Cairo, evacuate all passengers via emergency exits, and blow up the aircraft 2 minutes later.

An armed man and woman commandeer an Israeli El Al flight September 6 en route from Tel Aviv to London, but security guards on the plane mortally wound the man and passengers subdue the woman. Jailed at London, she turns out to be 24-year-old Leila Khaled, a former student at Beirut's American University who took part in a hijacking last year.

Palestinian militants hijack a TWA 707 and a Swissair DC-8 September 6 and force them to land outside Amman, Jordan. Militants hijack a BOAC VC-10 a few days later and force it to land on the same strip, where the militants blow up all three planes after removing the passengers. They hold the passengers hostage for several weeks until British, West German, Swiss, and Israeli authorities release Leila Khaled (above) and other Arabs.

A Dominican DC-9 crashes into the sea February 15 on takeoff from Santo Domingo killing 102; a British charter jet crashes near Barcelona July 3 killing 112; an Air Canada DC-8 crashes near Toronto July 5 killing 108; a Peruvian turbojet crashes after takeoff from Cuzco August 9 killing 101, including some on the ground.

The Concorde supersonic jet exceeds twice the speed of sound for the first time November 4.

A survey reports that rail travel is 2.5 times as safe as air travel, 1.5 times as safe as bus travel, 23 times as safe as automobile travel.

Burlington Northern, Inc., is created in March by a merger of the Great Northern, the Northern Pacific, and the Chicago, Burlington & Quincy Railroads with the Spokane, Portland, and Seattle Railway. The BN has 25,000 miles of track, it is the longest privately owned railway system in the world, and its 6-mile long Flathead Tunnel opens in November.

The Rail Passenger Service Act passed by Congress creates the National Rail Passenger Corporation (Amtrak) to improve U.S. rail travel.

The *Indian-Pacific Express* between Sydney and Perth begins service in March on the Trans-Australian Railway (see 1969). The twice-a-week transcontinental train runs 2,460 miles through forest, desert, mountains, and wheatlands and is so popular that passengers must book space well in advance.

Mexico City's Metro subway line opens with 537 bright orange cars that carry 1 million passengers per day on a 22.5-mile route with 47 stations, 10 of them above ground. Built with the help of a substantial French loan, the $400 million subway employs rubber-tired, French-built trains, the standard fare is 8 cents, but while the handsome new subway eases congestion, some 40 percent of the city's commuters continue to use private vehicles, going home at noon for lunch and a siesta, returning to work in mid-afternoon, and creating enormous traffic problems.

New York City subway fares have gone to 30 cents January 4, up from 20 cents in 1966.

A rupture in Syria's Tapline May 3 stops the flow of Saudi Arabian crude oil that has been coming through the pipeline at the rate of 500,000 barrels per day. A bulldozer has cut the pipeline by accident, says Damascus, but the Syrians refuse to permit Tapline technicians to come into the country to repair the break. Libya's Mu'ammar el-Qadhafi orders cutbacks in Libyan oil production to conserve petroleum and push up prices.

OPEC nation delegates meeting at Caracas, Venezuela, in December agree to raise the posted prices of Persian Gulf oil and to increase taxes on the oil.

The U.S. Gross National Product (GNP) reaches $977 billion, up from $503 billion in 1960. Government spending accounts for 32 percent, up from 27 percent in 1960.

Bernard Cornfeld loses control of his 14-year-old Investors Overseas Services, Ltd., partly as a result of mismanagement and partly because of a slump in the

1970 (cont.) New York stock market. An interim board takes over IOS, U.S. entrepreneur Robert L. Vesco, 34, arranges a loan to "rescue" IOS and gains control, he will make himself chairman early next year while continuing as president of his New Jersey firm International Controls, and the Securities and Exchange Commission will later charge him with draining $224 million from the crumbling offshore mutual funds syndicate (Vesco will flee to Costa Rica).

Wall Street's Dow Jones Industrial Average bottoms out at 631 and jumps 32.04 points May 27 to close at 663.20—the largest 1-day advance ever recorded.

Daily volume on the New York Stock Exchange averages 11.6 million shares, up from 2.6 million in 1955, 3 million in 1960. Brokerage houses struggle to automate their back rooms to keep up with mounting paperwork (*see* DTC, 1968).

Gold prices in the world market at London fall below the official U.S. price of $35 per ounce.

The Federal Reserve Board's Open Market Committee which buys and sells Treasury securities as a means of controlling the nation's money supply moves its securities into the Fed's book-entry system introduced in 1968. By early 1976 less than $80 billion of the $385 billion outstanding in marketable Treasury securities will still be in physical form.

A U.S. Office of Management and Budget, proposed by President Nixon, is created by Congress in May. The president appoints Secretary of Labor Charles Schultz first OMB director.

The Department of Labor reports June 5 that 5 percent of the U.S. work force is unemployed, the highest rate since 1965. Skilled workers in the aircraft, aerospace, weapons, and automobile industries have been hit hardest by the nation's industrial slowdown.

President Nixon goes on television June 17 to ask that business and labor end inflation by voluntarily resisting wage and profit increases. The president says he will not impose direct wage and price controls but he creates a new national commission and asks it to suggest ways for increasing output per worker.

Some 25.5 million Americans live below the poverty line—$3,908 per year for a family of four—and another 10.2 million live only slightly above the line. Nearly half the 35.7 million total are in the South.

United Automobile Workers strike General Motors plants November 2 and begin a 67-day walkout.

U.S. public schools are for the most part "grim," "joyless," and "oppressive," says a study commissioned by the Carnegie Corporation, and they fail to educate children adequately.

No U.S. scholar specializing in Vietnamese studies has a tenured professorship, no U.S. scholar is devoting most of his time to studying current affairs in North Vietnam, and fewer than 30 Americans are studying the Vietnamese language, a survey reveals.

U.S. colleges close down in antiwar protests (above).

British university students demonstrate against the practice of keeping files on students' political activities.

Paris students protest the banning of a Maoist splinter group and riot in the Latin Quarter to protest prison sentences handed down against two Maoist student leaders.

The Postal Reorganization Act passed by Congress converts the U.S. Post Office Department into the U.S. Postal Service with a postmaster general appointed by a board of governors rather than by the president.

Cleveland's Harris Corporation introduces the first electronic editing terminal for newspapers and installs such terminals in newsrooms of the Gannett group's papers.

Nonfiction *The Making of a Counter Culture* by California State University professor Theodore Roszak, 37; *The Greening of America* by Yale professor Charles Reich, 34; *Up the Organization* by former Avis Rent-a-Car president Robert Townsend, 50; *Future Shock* by U.S. sociologist Alvin Toffler, 41; *Hard Times* by Studs Terkel; *Sexual Politics* by U.S. feminist Kate (Katherine Murray) Millett, 35; *Everything You Always Wanted to Know About Sex* (*but didn't dare to ask*) by U.S. physician David Reuben.

Fiction *Mr. Sammler's Planet* by Saul Bellow; *Vital Parts* by Thomas Berger; *Losing Battles* by Eudora Welty; *Play It As It Lays* by Joan Didion; *Deliverance* by James Dickey; *Islands in the Stream* by the late Ernest Hemingway; *Travels With My Aunt* by Graham Greene; *The French Lieutenant's Woman* by John Fowles; *Love Story* by Yale classics professor Erich Segal, 33 ("Love means never having to say you're sorry"); *Jonathan Livingston Seagull* by former U.S. Navy jet pilot Richard Bach, 33.

Juvenile *The Trumpet of the Swan* by E. B. White.

Poetry *Eye-Beaters, Blood, Victory, Madness, Buckhead and Mercy* by James Dickey.

Painting Mark Rothko dies by his own hand February 25 in New York in a fit of depression at age 66.

Theater *Child's Play* by New York playwright Robert Marasco, 32, 2/17 at New York's Royale Theater, with Pat Hingle, Fritz Weaver, Michael McGuire, 342 perfs.; *The Effect of Gamma Rays on Man-in-the-Moon Marigolds* by U.S. playwright Paul Zindel, 33, 4/7 at New York's off-Broadway Mercer O'Casey Theater, 819 perfs.

Television comedy *All in the Family* debuts in January on CBS stations with Carroll O'Connor as Archie Bunker in a half-hour comedy show by Norman Lear featuring Jean Stapleton as Bunker's "dingbat" wife Edith, Sally Struthers as his daughter Gloria, Rob Reiner as his "meathead" son-in-law. The show violates sacrosanct taboos against ethnic humor and bathroom humor and sets new audience records.

Films Franklin Shaffner's *Patton* with George C. Scott, Karl Malden; Bob Rafelson's *Five Easy Pieces* with Jack Nicholson, Karen Black, Susan Anspach, Billy Green Bush; Robert Altman's *M*A*S*H* with Elliott Gould, Donald Sutherland, Sally Kellerman; Arthur Penn's *Little Big Man* with Dustin Hoffman, Faye Dunaway; Bernardo Bertolucci's *The Garden of the Finzi-Continis;* Max Ophuls's *The Sorrow and the Pity;* Rainer Maria Fassbinder's *The American Soldier;* Michelangelo Antonioni's *Zabriskie Point;* Eric Rohmer's *My Night at Maud's* with Jean-Louis Trintignant; Luis Buñuel's *The Milky Way* with Paul Frankens, Laret Terzieff; François Truffaut's *The Wild Child;* Claude Chabrol's *This Man Must Die* with Jean Yanne, Michael Duchaussoy, Caroline Cellier; Elio Petri's *Investigation of a Citizen Above Suspicion* with Gian Maria Volente; Ken Russell's *Women in Love* with Alan Bates, Oliver Reed, Glenda Jackson, Eleanor Brown; Otto Preminger's *Tell Me That You Love Me, Junie Moon* with Liza Minelli, Ken Howard, Robert Moore; Ossie Davis's *Cotton Comes to Harlem* with Godfrey Cambridge, Raymond St. Jacques, Redd Foxx; Martin Ritt's *The Great White Hope* with James Earl Jones; John Avildsen's *Joe* with Peter Boyle; Arthur Hiller's *Love Story* with Ali MacGraw, Ryan O'Neal.

Film musicals   Michael Wadleigh's *Woodstock* with Joan Baez, Richie Havens, Crosby, Stills and Nash, the Jefferson Airplane, Joe Cocker, Sly and the Family Stone, The Who, and others (a documentary account of last year's bash at Bethel, N.Y.); David Maysles, Albert Maysles, and Charlotte Swerin's *Gimme Shelter* with the Rolling Stones (a documentary account of last year's Altamont rock concert); Gene Kelly's *Hello, Dolly* with Barbra Streisand.

Broadway and off-Broadway musicals   *The Last Sweet Days of Isaac* 1/26 at the Eastside Playhouse with Austin Pendleton, music by Nancy Ford, lyrics by Gretchen Cryer, 465 perfs.; *Purlie* 3/15 at the Broadway Theater with Melba Moore, music by Gary Geld, lyrics by Peter Udell, songs that include "I Got Love," 688 perfs.; *Applause* 3/30 at the Palace with Lauren Bacall, music by Charles Strouse, lyrics by Lee Adams, book by Betty Comden and Adolph Green, 896 perfs.; *Company* 4/26 at the Alvin Theater with Elaine Stritch, music and lyrics by Stephen Sondheim, 706 perfs.; *The Me Nobody Knows* 5/18 at the Orpheum Theater, with music by Gary William Friedman, lyrics by Will Holt, 587 perfs.; *The Rothschilds* 10/19 at the Lunt-Fontanne Theater, with music by Jerry Bock, lyrics by Sheldon Harnick, 507 perfs.; *Two by Two* 11/10 at the Imperial Theater, with Danny Kaye, music by Richard Rodgers, lyrics by Martin Charnin, 352 perfs.

First performances   *The Yale-Princeton Football Game* Orchestral Suite by the late Charles Ives (completed by Gunther Schuller) 11/29 at New York's Carnegie Hall.

Popular songs   "Bridge Over Troubled Water" by Simon and Garfunkel (who will break up their partnership next year); "Your Song" by English singer-pianist-songwriter Elton John (Reginald Kenneth Dwight), 23; "I'll Never Fall in Love Again" by Bobbie Gentry; *Deja Vu* (album) by Crosby, Stills, Nash & Young (Canadian artist Neil Young, 24, has joined the group); *Self Portrait* (album) by Bob Dylan; *Cosmos Factory* (album) by John Fogerty of the Creedence Clearwater Revival; *Blood, Sweat and Tears III* (album) by the Blood, Sweat and Tears; *Led Zeppelin III* (album) by the Led Zeppelin; *Let It Be* (album) by John Lennon and Paul McCartney of the Beatles; *Abraxas* (album) by Santana; *Black Sabbath* and *Paranoid* (albums) by Birmingham (England) rock group the Black Sabbath (John Osbourne, Tony Iommi, Geezer Butler, and Bill Ward). Jimi Hendrix dazzles audiences at a rock festival on the Isle of Wight in August but dies of drugs or alcohol in his London apartment in mid-September at age 27; Janis Joplin dies of a drug overdose at Hollywood, Calif., October 3 at age 27.

Joe Frazier regains the world heavyweight boxing title February 16 by knocking out Jimmy Ellis in the fifth round of a championship bout at New York.

Brazil wins the World Cup football (soccer) championship by defeating Italy 4 to 1 at Mexico City.

British golfer Tony Jacklin becomes the first Briton to win the U.S. Open in 50 years.

The Australian ocean yacht *Gretel II* loses her bid for the America's Cup. The U.S. defender *Intrepid* wins 4 races to the *Gretel's* 1.

The Seattle Pilots become the Milwaukee Brewers and Milwaukee becomes a major league city once again (*see* 1966).

The Baltimore Orioles win the World Series by defeating the Cincinnati Reds 4 games to 1.

Man-made fabrics raise their share of the U.S. textile market to 56 percent, up from 28 percent in 1960, with polyesters enjoying a 41 percent share of the market and cotton only 40 percent, down from 65 percent in 1960. E. I. du Pont's patent on polyester has run out, other companies have entered the market, and some big chemical companies have helped mills that use polyester-cotton blends with massive consumer advertising to proclaim the virtues of durable press fabrics.

Adult Americans give up cigarettes in growing numbers but smoking among teenagers increases: 36.3 percent of Americans aged 21 and over smoke cigarettes, down from 42.5 percent in 1964, 42.3 percent of adult males smoke cigarettes, down from 52.5 percent in 1964, 30.5 percent of adult females smoke cigarettes, down from 31.5 percent, but while only 33.5 percent of adults (39.3 percent of males, 28.9 percent of females) will still be smoking by 1976, total cigarette consumption will increase as a result of growth in the adult population and increased smoking among teenagers, especially teenaged girls.

"Arcosanti" begins to rise from a remote mesa at Cordes Junction 70 miles north of Phoenix, Ariz., where Italian architect Paolo Soleri, 46, envisions an ecologically sound city that will concentrate its popu-

1970 (cont.) lation in 25-story buildings that occupy only a few square miles instead of spreading them over 300 square miles in buildings three or four stories high. Soleri has studied under Frank Lloyd Wright, his book *Arcology: The City in the Image of Man* was published last year, he has acquired an 860-acre tract along the Agua Fria River, and his first segment designed for 3,000 people will occupy only 10 acres of the tract on which he works with dedicated student disciples to incorporate "the natural and man-made world in a mutually respective relationship" free of the problems of transportation, pollution, and waste associated with horizontally spreading cities.

1 New York Plaza, 50 stories high, is completed by Kahn and Jacobs.

 U.S. conservationists win a battle to prevent construction of a giant international jetport near Florida's Everglades.

President Nixon signs an executive order February 4 calling for elimination of all air and water pollution caused by federal agencies. He authorizes expenditure of $359 million to carry out the order with a 3-year deadline to meet state pollution standards.

U.S. Army engineers sink an obsolete Liberty ship carrying 12,540 cannisters of nerve gas in 16,000 feet of water off the Bahamas. Legal action has been taken to prevent the action but initial tests show that no gas has escaped from the ship (critics observe that the cannisters will eventually rust).

Earth Day April 21 sees the first mass demonstrations against pollution and other desecrations of the planet's ecology. Environmentalists block off streets and employ other means to raise U.S. awareness of threats to the environment of spaceship Earth (in the phrase of the late Adlai Stevenson).

The most destructive earthquake in the history of the Western Hemisphere rocks Peru May 31 from an epicenter 15 miles west of Chimbote. Part of the west face of Peru's highest mountain Mt. Huascaran is jarred loose, an estimated 50 million cubic yards of ice and rock tumble down on the town of Yungay at 200 miles per hour and bury the town 20 feet deep, upwards of 15,000 are killed, and Peru's total death toll reaches 70,000 with 50,000 injured and 186,000 buildings destroyed—80 percent of all structures in the region.

Los Angeles buildings sway August 12 as a series of sharp rolling earthquakes make California shudder as far south as San Diego, breaking windows, blocking some highways, and increasing anxieties.

Hurricane Celia strikes Corpus Christi, Tex., August 3 with winds of up to 145 miles per hour. Ninety percent of downtown Corpus Christi is damaged or destroyed.

Southern California has her worst brush fires in history. Thousands in San Diego County are driven from their homes, Los Angeles suburbs are threat-

ened, and the fires in late September strike Sequoia National Forest north of Bakersfield.

A cyclone devastates East Pakistan November 13. Great waves engulf the coast and sweep over islands in the Bay of Bengal, 300,000 are feared dead, and the death toll mounts in the weeks following as poor transportation slows distribution of food to survivors.

The Environmental Protection Agency created by Congress December 2 will be the largest U.S. regulatory agency within 5 years with 9,000 employees and a budget of $2 million per day.

 World cotton production tops 50 million 50-pound bales, up from 21 million in 1920, but U.S. planters account for only 10 million, down from 13 in 1920.

The U.S. corn harvest falls off as a result of a new strain of the fungus *Helminthosporum maydis.* Since most U.S. corn is now genetically similar in its lack of resistance to the blight, much of the crop is lost, raising the prices of meat and poultry.

The Chicago Board of Trade suspends trading in rye futures after 112 years for lack of interest. World rye production comprises less than 10 percent of world wheat production and nearly half the world's rye grows in the Soviet Union where much of the land has a growing season too short for wheat.

 High food prices in Poland have triggered the riot of shipyard and factory workers (above) that brought down the government.

The National Research Council warns expectant mothers in the United States not to restrict weight gain too severely. A Committee on Maternal Nutrition of the NRC says that at least half of infant mortalities are preventable through use of prenatal care, adequately trained personnel at delivery, correction of dietary deficiencies, proper hygiene, and health education and it says that a weight gain of 20 to 25 pounds in pregnancy is permissible.

U.S. breakfast foods come under fire July 23 from former Nixon administration hunger consultant Robert Burnett Choate, Jr., 46, who testifies before a Senate subcommittee that 40 of the top 60 dry cereals have little nutritional content. "The worst cereals are hucksterered to children" on television, says Choate, but Kellogg, General Mills, General Foods, Quaker Oats, and Ralston Purina refute his charges.

 High levels of mercury are found in livers of Alaskan fur seals in the Pribiloff Islands. Liver tissue samples show a mercury content of 58 parts per million and iron supplement pills made from freeze-dried seal liver are withdrawn from the market.

The FDA orders the recall of all lots of canned tunafish in which mercury levels above 0.5 parts per million have been discovered. The December recall order is said to affect nearly one quarter of all canned tuna in U.S. markets but by spring of next year it will turn out that only 3 percent of the canned tuna pack (nearly 200,000 cases) exceeds the 0.5 ppm FDA guideline.

A U.S. Occupational Safety and Health Act signed by President Nixon December 29 compromises differences between labor and management and establishes an office that will work to minimize hazards in industry.

The Poison Prevention Packaging Act passed by Congress December 30 requires that manufacturers of drugs, sulfuric acid, turpentine, and other potentially dangerous products put safety tops on their containers so that children will not be able to open them. The act will take effect in 1972 and fatalities from aspirin and other potential poisons will drop.

Birth control pills may produce blood clots, warns the Food and Drug Administration. The FDA sends letters to more than 300,000 physicians urging them to pay close attention to the risks involved in taking "The Pill" and to inform their patients.

The most liberal abortion law in the United States goes into effect July 1 in New York State. At least 147 women undergo abortions, more than 200 register at municipal hospitals for abortions bringing the application total to more than 1,200, but "Right to Life" groups continue to protest the new law.

The Italian Senate votes October 9 to legalize divorce for the first time in Italy's history.

The world's population reaches 3.63 billion with 1.13 billion in South Asia, 929.9 million in East Asia (including Japan), 462.1 million in Europe, 344.4 million in Africa, 283.3 million in Latin America, 227.6 million in North America, 19.4 million in Oceania.

The U.S.S.R. has only 9 urban centers with populations of 1 million or more versus 35 such urban centers in the United States. Only 8.5 percent of the Soviet population is in these large urban centers versus 41.5 percent of the U.S. population.

Soviet census figures show that Moslem populations in the Uzbek S.S.R., the Tadjik S.S.R., and other Moslem republics have increased by roughly 50 percent since the 1959 census but that the number of Great Russians in these republics has declined. Ethnic Russians remain the largest single national group within the U.S.S.R., they are roughly three times as numerous as the Ukrainians, but they will become a minority by 1976.

Population in the Soviet Union reaches 242.6 million, in the People's Republic of China 760 million, in India 550 million, in the United States 205 million. The United States has 85 people per square mile, the P.R.C. 305, India 655, Japan 1,083.

Note: In terms of using natural and irreplaceable resources and of contaminating air and water with chemical waste, one American is comparable to at least 25 Chinese or Indians. In that light the U.S. population is by some measures effectively more than 4 billion.

1971 A "New Economic Policy" announced by President Nixon August 15 imposes a 90-day freeze on U.S. wages and prices, temporarily suspends conversion of dollars into gold, and asks Congress to impose a 10 percent import surcharge in an effort to strengthen the dollar at home and abroad as the Vietnam War increases inflationary pressures.

West Germany, Austria, Switzerland, and the Netherlands have either revalued their currencies upward or have floated their currencies against the fixed value of the dollar, but while the European move paves the way for more flexible exchange rates the U.S. action unlinking the dollar from any gold value begins the breakdown of the international monetary system in effect since the Bretton Woods Conference of 1944.

Wall Street responds to President Nixon's economic message (above) with enthusiasm. The Dow Jones Industrial Average makes a record 1-day leap of 32.93 points on a record volume of 31.7 million shares, but the AFL-CIO says it has "absolutely no faith in the ability of President Nixon to successfully manage the economy of this nation" and refuses to cooperate in the president's wage freeze.

The average U.S. taxpayer gives the government $400 for defense, $125 to fight the war in Indochina, $40 to build highways, $30 to explore outer space, $315 for health activities ($7 for medical research).

Uganda's President Obote is ousted from office January 25 while returning from a conference at Singapore. A military government headed by Major General Idi Amin, 44, seizes power and begins liquidating political opponents.

Haiti's President Duvalier dies April 22 after a dictatorship of more than 13 years during which "Papa Doc's" Ton Ton Macoute have terrorized the populace. Duvalier is succeeded by his 19-year-old son Jean-Claude who is sworn in as "President for life."

East German Communist party leader Walter Ulbricht resigns in May at age 78 after having headed the party for 25 years. He is succeeded as first secretary of the Central Committee of the Socialist Unity party by Erich Honecker, 58.

East Pakistan has widespread riots and strikes following the announcement March 1 of a delay in convening the new national assembly elected last year. The Awani League whose strength is concentrated in Bengal won 167 out of the 313 seats to be filled in the election, the League's leader protests the delay, a strike cripples the key port of Chittagong, Bengali extremists murder many non-Bengalis, Pakistan's president Yahya Khan flies to East Pakistan to negotiate with the Awami League's leader Sheik Mujib, he denounces Sheik Mujib as a traitor and orders an invasion of Bengal March 25, the East Bengal Regiment defects to the sheik's cause, Bengali separatists blow up major bridges, railroads, and communications lines, the separatists are subdued, but guerrillas resist the Pakistani army of occupation.

India concludes a 20-year friendship pact with the Soviet Union in August to deter any Pakistani attack,

Busing black children to white schools and vice versa helped achieve racial balance but raised cries of protest.

Indian troops invade Bengal December 4, Pakistani forces in Bengal surrender December 16 (*see* Bangladesh, 1972).

Chinese defense minister Lin Pao, 65, leads an abortive coup against Chairman Mao Tse-tung with support from members of the armed forces. Officially designated to succeed Mao, Lin is a veteran of the Long March that began in 1934, he has been a member of the Chinese Politburo since 1955, but he dies September 13 when his plane crashes in Mongolia as he flees the retribution of Chairman Mao.

The Republic of Zaire is created October 27 as President Mobutu Sese Seko (formerly Joseph D. Mobutu) renames the Democratic Republic of Congo and has the Congo River renamed the Zaire (*see* 1966).

 Wilmington, N.C., has racial violence beginning in late January with incidents of arson, dynamitings, and shootings. Black activists headed by United Church of Christ field director for racial justice Ben Chavis, 22, barricade themselves inside Mike's Grocery February 6, saying the police do not protect them from roving whites, a policeman shoots a black teenager that night and unknown assailants kill an armed middle-aged white man near the grocery store. A court early next year will convict Chavis and nine others of firebombing the store, and they will draw sentences of from 29 to 34 years despite international clamor for their release.

The Supreme Court weakens its *Miranda* decision of 1966 in a 5 to 4 decision handed down February 24. The court rules that although a suspect's statement is inadmissible as evidence if the arresting police officers have not advised the suspect of his or her rights, the prosecution may still use the statement to contradict the defendant's testimony in a trial.

Conscientious objectors who seek draft exemption must show that they are opposed to all wars, not just to the Vietnam War, the Supreme Court rules March 8 in an 8 to 1 decision.

So-called "objective" criteria for hiring employees are actually discriminatory, the Supreme Court rules in a case involving a written examination for employment. The criteria are illegal, the court rules, since they result in a relative disadvantage to minorities without "compelling business interest," and future rulings will extend the concept to recruitment practices, job placement, transfers, and promotions. The 8–0 decision handed down March 8 in *Griggs v. Duke Power Co.* is the first major interpretation of the job bias provisions (Title VII) of the Civil Rights Act of 1964.

The Supreme Court upholds busing of schoolchildren to achieve racial balance where segregation has official sanction and where school authorities have offered no acceptable alternative to busing. The court hands down the unanimous decision April 20 in the case of *Swann v. Charlotte-Mecklenburg Board of Education* (*see* 1965). In addition, federal authorities impose a strict busing plan on the Austin, Tex., school system in May, a federal judge for the district rejects the plan in late July. Alabama governor George Wallace charges the Nixon administration with having done more than any preceding administration to desegregate public schools, and President Nixon publicly repudiates the Austin plan August 3 although his attorney general and his secretary of health, education, and welfare have approved the plan. "I have consistently opposed busing of our nation's schoolchildren simply for the sake of busing," says the president, and he orders that busing be limited "to the minimum required by law" (the busing ordered in Charlotte, N.C., is actually less than the busing used to preserve segregation).

Attica Correctional Facility at Attica, N.Y., is the scene of the bloodiest one-day encounter between Americans since the Indian massacres of the late 19th century. Inmates of the overcrowded prison discover inexplicable differences in sentences and parole decisions that appear to have a racial bias, outraged prisoners take over cell blocks beginning September 9, they kill several trusty guards. The state police move in September 13 on orders from Governor Rockefeller, 39 are killed and more than 80 wounded in the 15 minutes it takes for the police to retake the prison, and the total death toll is 43.

The human growth hormone somatropin produced by the pituitary glands is synthesized by Chinese-born biochemist-endocrinologist Choh Hao Li at the University of California in January. The synthetic hormone has roughly 10 percent of the growth-producing properties of the natural hormone but it has great potential for treating pituitary dwarf children who have required hormone extract obtained from the pituitary glands of 650 cadavers (for each child treated). Researchers at Boston's Beth Israel Hospital report that lactogen in the human placenta contains

86 percent of the component amino acids in somatropin and has them in exactly the same order as in the human growth hormone.

The cold sore virus is isolated by researchers at the Anderson Tumor Institute in Texas who isolate the herpes virus from the lymph cell cancer known as Burkitts lymphoma. One form of herpes virus has been associated with the earliest stage of cervical cancer in women (*see* 1960).

Cigarette smoking has become a cause of death comparable to the great epidemic diseases typhoid and cholera in the 19th century, says Britain's Royal College of Physicians in a sharply worded report.

The National Cancer Act signed into law by President Nixon December 24 authorizes appropriations of $1.5 billion per year by the National Cancer Institute to combat the second leading cause of death in America, but the massive effort will yield few practical results in the next 7 years.

U.S. physicians receive a warning in November from the Food and Drug Administration against administering DES (diethylstilbestrol) or related hormones to pregnant women. Massachusetts General Hospital researchers have concluded that daughters of women who took the synthetic hormone to prevent miscarriage have an increased risk of clear-cell adenocarcinoma of the vagina.

Rolls-Royce, Ltd., declares bankruptcy February 4 after having lost huge sums of money developing a jet engine for a new Lockheed Aircraft plane but the British government will bail out Rolls-Royce to maintain national prestige and avoid loss of jobs.

The U.S. Senate votes 51 to 46 to stop all further federal funding of SST (supersonic transport) development. The March 24 vote comes 1 week after a similar vote in the House, the Boeing Company says it will mean the loss of 7,000 jobs at Seattle, environmentalists hail the Senate action, and Britain and France are left to develop their Concorde SST without U.S. competition.

Amtrak (The National Railroad Passenger Corporation) takes over virtually all U.S. passenger railroad traffic in a federally funded effort to halt the decline in rail passenger service. The takeover effectively ends rail passenger service to many cities.

The Brotherhood of Locomotive Engineers agrees May 13 to let U.S. railroads scrap the age-old "divisional rule" that has called 100 miles a day's work and has required freight trains to stop every 100 miles and change crews. The rule has enabled diesel locomotive engineers to earn a day's pay in 150 minutes.

The Cunard Line and its luxury liner S.S. *QE2* are acquired by British entrepreneur Nigel Broackes, 36, who pays £25 million for the failing 131-year-old company. Broackes will make the Cunard Line profitable once again, he will buy the London Ritz for $43 million in 1976, and he will buy the Beaverbrook newspapers the *Daily Express,* the *Sunday Express,* and the *Evening Standard* for $23.5 million in 1977 as he makes his Trafalgar House Investments, Ltd., a great conglomerate.

The *North Central Power Study* produced by a group of U.S. utility companies with help from the Department of the Interior proposes strip-mining of coal in the northern Great Plains, construction of huge mine-mouth generating plants (21 in Montana alone), and a web of transmission lines to serve the Midwest and the Pacific Coast, but environmentalists fight plans to exploit the Fort Union Coal Formation that contains an estimated 1.3 trillion tons of soft coal, most of it low-sulfur coal.

The "Pentagon Papers" excerpted in the *New York Times* beginning June 13 give details of U.S. involvement in Vietnam from the end of World War II to 1968. The highly classified 3,000-page study was written at the order of former Secretary of Defense Robert S. McNamara, the *Times* has received a copy from former Defense Department official Daniel Ellsberg, 39. Attorney General John Mitchell asks the *Times* to cease further publication on grounds that the information revealed will cause "irreparable injury to the defense interests of the United States," the *Times* refuses to halt publication voluntarily, a federal judge orders the *Times* to stop publication of the material pending a hearing, a federal appeals court at Washington issues a temporary order restraining the *Washington Post* from publishing material based on the Pentagon Papers, Ellsberg admits he gave the study to the press, he surrenders to federal authorities at Boston, a federal grand jury at Los Angeles indicts him on charges of having stolen the secret 47-volume study, the information published shows that the U.S. government has consistently lied to the American people about Vietnam, Ellsberg says he has leaked the papers because he has become convinced that the Vietnam War is immoral, Ellsberg and a co-worker at the Rand Institute (Anthony Russo) are indicted December 29 for espionage and conspiracy.

A British postal strike halts mail deliveries for 47 days.

The U.S. Postal Service replaces the Post Office Department July 1 and optimistic speeches hail the semi-independent corporation. Postal rates rise to 8 cents per ounce, up from 6 cents in 1968, and they will rise to 10 cents in 1974, to 13 late in 1975.

Look magazine ceases publication after 34 years and other magazines reduce their format to save postage in accordance with new postal regulations.

Family Circle magazine and other Cowles Communications, Inc., properties are acquired by the *New York Times.*

Nonfiction *Bury My Heart at Wounded Knee, An Indian History of the American West* by Illinois historian Dee Brown.

Fiction *Rabbit Redux* by John Updike; *Maurice* by the late E. M. Forster; *The Tenants* by Bernard

1971 (cont.) Malamud; *The Book of Daniel* by Sarah Lawrence College teacher E. L. (Edgar Lawrence) Doctorow, 39, is based on the 1951 Rosenberg trial. *Another Roadside Attraction* by U.S. novelist Tom Robbins, 35; *Winds of War* by Herman Wouk.

Theater *Butley* by English playwright Simon Gray, 35, 7/5 at London's Criterion Theatre, with Alan Bates; *Where Has Tommy Flowers Gone?* by U.S. playwright Terrence McNally 10/7 at New York's off-Broadway Eastside Playhouse, 78 perfs.,; *The Changing Room* by English playwright David Storey 11/9 at London's Royal Court Theatre; *The Prisoner of Second Avenue* by Neil Simon 11/11 at New York's Eugene O'Neill Theater, with Peter Falk, Lee Grant, Vincent Gardenia, 780 perfs.

Films William Friedkin's *The French Connection* with Gene Hackman, Fernando Rey; Stanley Kubrick's *A Clockwork Orange* with Malcolm McDowell, Patrick Magee; Peter Bogdanovich's *The Last Picture Show* with Timothy Bottoms, Jeff Bridges, Ben Johnson, Cloris Leachman, Ellen Burstyn, Cybill Shepherd, Eileen Brennan; John Schlesinger's *Sunday, Bloody Sunday* with Glenda Jackson, Peter Finch; Alan J. Pakula's *Klute* with Jane Fonda in the role of a call girl, Donald Sutherland; Arthur Hiller's *The Hospital* with George C. Scott, Diana Rigg; Mike Nichols's *Carnal Knowledge* with Jack Nicholson, Candice Bergen, Ann-Margaret, Arthur Garfunkel; Caspar Wrede's *One Day in the Life of Ivan Denisovich* with Tom Courtenay; Charles Jarrott's *Mary, Queen of Scots* with Vanessa Redgrave, Glenda Jackson, Patrick McGoohan; Bernardo Bertolucci's *The Conformist* with Jean-Louis Trintignant, Stefania Sandrelli, Domique Sanda; Federico Fellini's *The Clowns;* Roman Polanski's *Macbeth* with Jon Finch, Francesca Annis; Eric Rohmer's *Claire's Knee* with Jean-Claude Brialy, Aurora Cornu; Louis Malle's *Murmur of the Heart;* Jan Troell's *The Emigrants* with Max von Sydow, Liv Ullmann; Woody Allen's *Bananas* with Allen.

Hollywood musical Norman Jewison's *Fiddler on the Roof* with Chaim Topol as Tevye, violin on sound track by Isaac Stern.

Broadway and off-Broadway musicals *Follies* 4/4 at the Winter Garden Theater, with Gene Nelson, Yvonne De Carlo, Alexis Smith, Dorothy Collins, music and lyrics by Stephen Sondheim, 521 perfs.; *Godspell* 5/17 at the Cherry Lane Theater, with music and lyrics by Stephen Schwartz, songs that include "Day by Day," 2,605 perfs. counting Promenade and Broadhurst Theaters; *Jesus Christ Superstar* 10/10 at the Mark Hellinger Theater, with Jeff Fenholt, music by Andrew Lloyd Webber, lyrics by Tim Rice, book by Tom O'Horgan, 711 perfs.; *Ain't Supposed to Die a Natural Death* 10/20 at the Ethel Barrymore Theater, with music and lyrics by Melvin Van Peebles, 325 perfs.; *Two Gentlemen of Verona* 12/1 at the St. James Theater (after 14 performances at the off-Broadway Public Theater), with Raul Julia, Clifton Davis, Diana Davila, music by Galt MacDermot, lyrics by John Guare, 627 perfs. (total).

Opera *Owen Wingrave* 5/16 at Aldwych, with music by Benjamin Britten, libretto from an 1892 pacifist short story by Henry James.

Washington's John F. Kennedy Center for the Performing Arts opens September 8 with a performance of Leonard Bernstein's new *Mass.* When complete, the center will seat 6,100 in three halls.

Popular songs *Tapestry* (album) by U.S. singer-songwriter Carole King, 29, includes her songs "It's Too Late" and "You've Got a Friend"; "Friends with You," "Take Me Home, Country Roads," and "Poems, Prayers, and Promises" by John Denver; *Blue* (album) by Joni Mitchell; "If Not for You" by Australian vocalist Olivia Newton-John, 21, a granddaughter of Nobel physicist Max Born; *Sticky Fingers* (album) by the Rolling Stones; *Imagine* (album) by John Lennon; *Runes* (album) by the Led Zeppelin; *Who's Next* (album) by the Who; "Shaft" theme for Gordon Parks's film by Isaac Hayes; *Tumbleweed Connection* (album) by Elton John; "Lonely Days" by the Bee Gees.

New York's Off-Track Betting Corporation (OTB) is created April 8 as legislation takes effect legalizing off-track betting in an effort to take business away from organized crime and produce revenues for the city and state. OTB bettors will give New York City $145.8 million in the next 5 years while giving New York State $58.1 million and the racing industry $79.7 million but the "numbers game" based on smaller bets will continue to flourish, fattening the profits of underworld syndicates.

Washington, D.C., loses its major league baseball team at year's end. The Senators become the Texas Rangers.

The Pittsburgh Pirates win the World Series by defeating the Baltimore Orioles 4 games to 3.

U.S. cigarette sales reach 547.2 billion despite the new ban on radio and television advertising.

New York hoodlum Joseph Gallo recruits blacks to replace the depleted ranks of the Mafia. Gallo has rebelled from the leadership of Joseph Colombo who has attracted attention by public protests against insinuations in the book *The Godfather* that there is such a thing as the Mafia and who has organized pickets to demonstrate outside Manhattan FBI headquarters.

Joseph Colombo helps organize an Italian-American Unity Day parade June 28 at New York's Columbus Circle, a black gunman shoots Colombo three times, leaving him crippled, an unidentified gunman immediately kills Colombo's black assailant, but there is disagreement as to whether the assailant was in the pay of Joseph Gallo (above), reputed Mafia leader Carlo Gambino, or someone else.

J. C. Penney dies at New York February 12 at age 95 leaving an empire of 1,660 stores with annual sales of more than $4 billion, the largest nonfood retail enterprise after Sears, Roebuck and Company.

Chicago's Standard Oil of Indiana building is completed. The 1,107-foot structure is higher than the 4-year-old John Hancock Center but will be dwarfed in 3 years by the 1,450-foot Sears Tower.

New York's Standard Oil of New Jersey (Exxon) building opens in September at 1251 Avenue of the Americas. Harrison Abramovitz and Harris have designed the new 54-story tower.

New York's Park Lane Hotel opens on Central Park South.

Acapulco's Princess Hotel opens to give Mexico its largest resort hotel. U.S. shipping magnate Daniel K. Ludwig has built the $64 million hotel.

The U.S. Geological Survey reports that cadmium levels in drinking water are "dangerous" at Birmingham and Huntsville and are above acceptable limits at Hot Springs, Little Rock, East St. Louis, Shreveport, Cape Girardeau, St. Joseph, Wilkes-Barre, Scranton, and Pottsville.

The Food and Drug Administration advises Americans to stop eating swordfish. The advisory issued in early May follows an FDA study of more than 853 swordfish samples of which 811 had an average mercury content of 1 part per million and 8 percent had levels above 1.5 parts per million. Swordfish caught between 1878 and 1909 turn out to have about the same mercury content, and few people can afford to eat enough swordfish to make the mercury content a real danger (average per capita consumption is 2 ounces per year).

Botulism kills New York banker Samuel Cochran, Jr., 61, who enjoys Bon Vivant brand Vichyssoise soup the evening of June 29 at his Bedford Village home and dies late the following evening at Mount Kisco's Northern Westchester Hospital. The FDA shuts down the Bon Vivant plant at Newark, N.J., and the company is forced into bankruptcy after 108 years in business. Campbell Soup Company's Paris, Tex., plant recalls its chicken vegetable soup in mid-July after finding botulinum contamination.

The Chicago Union Stock Yards that opened Christmas Day 1865 close July 30 as meatpackers continue to move their slaughterhouses closer to their source of supply. Operations at the Stock Yards peaked in 1924 and have been declining ever since.

Annual U.S. beef consumption reaches 113 pounds per capita, up from 85.1 pounds in 1960. Consumption will peak at 128.5 pounds in 1976 as Americans eat more than 50 billion hamburgers and pay more than $25 billion for beef in various forms.

1972 President Nixon arrives at Peking February 20 and confers with Chairman Mao Tse-tung and Premier Chou En-lai, ending the U.S. hostility toward the People's Republic of China that has persisted since 1949. The president has 6 days earlier ordered that U.S. trade with Peking be on the same basis as trade with Moscow and with Soviet bloc nations.

Peking's UN ambassador lays claim March 3 to Hong Kong and Macao, he reasserts claims to the uninhab-

ited Senkalu Islands claimed also by Japan, and a PRC UN delegate charges Japan with expansionism.

Premier Chou En-lai meets with North Vietnam's Premier Pham Van Dong to assure him that China has made no secret commitments to President Nixon with regard to Indochina where hostilities continue.

U.S. planes bomb Haiphong and Hanoi April 16. The B-52 raids are the first on the big North Vietnamese cities since 1968 and heated debate on the resumption of bombing begins in the U.S. Senate April 19 as North Vietnamese MIG fighters attack U.S. destroyers which are shelling coastal positions.

The provincial capital of Quang Tri falls to the North Vietnamese May 1, 80 U.S. advisers are evacuated, South Vietnam's Third Division flees to the South, Saigon relieves the commander of the division who later claims to have resigned, more than 150,000 flee the imperial capital of Hue as deserters loot the city, engage in gunfights among themselves, and set fire to the marketplace, President Thieu visits Hue and gives military police authority to shoot looters and arsonists, Communist forces surround Kontum and Pleiku, Saigon fails in efforts to reopen the supply route between the two beleaguered cities, and U.S. planes mine the approaches to Haiphong while intensifying raids on Communist transport lines.

Chinese, Soviet, North Vietnamese, and Mongolian representatives meet at Peking May 19 to speed aid to North Vietnam following the U.S. action in mining Haiphong and other North Vietnamese ports.

President Nixon arrives at Moscow May 22 and confers with Party Secretary Leonid Brezhnev in the first visit of a U.S. president to the Soviet Union. Nixon also visits Iran and Warsaw.

Okinawa is returned to Japan after 27 years of U.S. occupation.

Philippine president Ferdinand Marcos assumes near-dictatorial powers and declares martial law in response to an alleged "Communist rebellion."

Ceylon becomes a republic and changes her name to Sri Lanka.

Bangladesh (formerly East Pakistan) becomes a sovereign state with Sheik Mujibur Rahman as prime minister (see 1971).

Denmark's Frederick IX dies January 14 at age 72 after a 25-year reign. He is succeeded by his daughter who will reign as Margrethe II.

Britain imposes direct rule over Northern Ireland March 30 after years of violence between Catholics and Protestants: 467 Northern Irish are killed in the course of the year (see Bloody Sunday, below).

Gunmen hired by Palestinian guerrillas shoot up Lod Airport near Tel Aviv May 30 killing 24 and wounding 76. Two of the gunmen are Japanese, two are killed by security guards, an Israeli court convicts Kozo Okamoto and sentences him July 17 to life imprisonment.

1972 (cont.) A U.S. Federal Election Campaign Act signed by President Nixon February 7 limits campaign spending in the media to 10 cents per person of voting age in the candidate's constituency and requires that all campaign contributions be reported. Both parties but especially the Republicans receive millions of dollars in contributions before the new law takes effect April 7.

A "confidential" memorandum from ITT lobbyist Mrs. Dita Beard to an ITT vice-president is released to newspapers February 29 by columnist Jack Anderson. The memorandum links a Justice Department settlement favoring ITT in pending antitrust suits to an ITT commitment to supply funds for the Republican National Convention to be held at San Diego.

Alabama governor George C. Wallace campaigns for the Democratic presidential nomination but is shot May 15 by would-be assassin Arthur H. Bremer, 22, at Laurel, Md., while addressing a crowd before a forthcoming primary election. Wallace is paralyzed from the waist down and will be a paraplegic for life.

The Watergate affair that will grow into the greatest constitutional crisis in U.S. history has its beginnings at approximately 2 o'clock in the morning of June 17 when District of Columbia police alerted by security guard Frank Wills, 24, arrest five men inside Democratic party national headquarters in Washington's new Watergate apartment complex. Bernard L. Barker, 55, James W. McCord, 42, Eugenio R. Martinez, 48, Frank A. Sturgis (Fiorini), 47, and Virgilio R. Gonzalez, 46, are seized with their cameras and electronic surveillance equipment, President Nixon's campaign manager John Mitchell states June 18 that the men were not "operating either on our behalf or with our consent," President Nixon's office confirms June 19 that Bernard L. Barker met earlier in June with CIA official E. Howard Hunt, 53, who until March 29 had been acting as consultant to presidential counsel Charles W. Colson, 38, President Nixon tells Colson June 20 that he is involved in a "dangerous job." Hunt has earlier directed CIA activities against Cuban prime minister Fidel Castro and three of the men arrested are Cubans but the motive for their break-in and the source of their support remains a mystery.

U.S. Senator George S. McGovern, 49, of South Dakota receives the Democratic nomination for the presidency at Miami Beach after Republican operatives have aborted the campaign of U.S. Senator Edmund S. Muskie, 58, of Maine who had led President Nixon in the opinion polls. McGovern selects U.S. Senator Thomas Eagleton of Missouri as his running mate but switches to former Peace Corps director Sargent Shriver when Eagleton turns out to have been treated for manic depression, Henry Kissinger says on the eve of election that "Peace is at hand" in Vietnam, and President Nixon wins reelection despite gossip about the Watergate break-in (above). McGovern carries only Massachusetts with its 17 electoral votes, Nixon receives 521 electoral votes,

and the Democrats suffer their worst defeat in the most one-sided presidential election since 1936.

"Bloody Sunday" January 30 in Northern Ireland sees 13 Roman Catholics shot dead by British troops at Londonderry where riots have followed a civil rights march conducted in defiance of a government ban. The Irish Republican Army calls a general strike January 31 to protest the shootings, and the British Embassy at Dublin is destroyed February 2 as an estimated 25,000 demonstrators rally in protest and set fire to the building (*see* direct rule, above).

The death penalty as now administered in the United States constitutes "cruel and unusual punishment" and is therefore unconstitutional, the Supreme Court rules June 29 in a 5 to 4 decision.

An international uranium cartel is organized in the spring under the sponsorship of the Canadian, Australian, and South African governments with tacit support from France. The minutes of the Canadian cartel members at a meeting in Ottawa in the fall contain the statement, "The consensus finally reached was that if the club was to survive as a viable entity, it would be necessary to delineate where the competition was and the nature of its strength, as a prelude to eliminating it once and for all." The price of raw uranium ("yellowcake") will jump from $6 a pound to $41 in the next few years but rising oil prices imposed by the Organization of Petroleum Exporting Companies (OPEC) will be largely responsible for the sudden boom in demand for nuclear fuels and for the steep climb in uranium prices.

Mexican oil prospectors strike petroleum outside Villahermosa in May. The new Chiapas-Tabasco field will prove to be the largest in the Western Hemisphere. Mexico's proven reserves will total 16.8 billion barrels by 1978, and the potential will be estimated at 120 billion.

Baghdad nationalizes the Iraq Petroleum Company's Kirkuk field June 1 (*see* 1927). The field produces 1.1 million barrels of crude oil per day, it is the first key field to be seized by an Arab Persian Gulf nation, Iraq Petroleum threatens action against anyone who buys the oil, and by year's end Iraq is producing only 660,000 barrels per day (Baghdad leaves Basrah Petroleum untouched), down from 1.9 million at the beginning of the year (*see* 1973).

Nearly 30 percent of U.S. petroleum is imported, up from 20 percent in 1967.

The European Economic Community (Common Market) created in 1957 by the Treaty of Rome accepts Britain, Ireland, Denmark, and Norway to membership with the Treaty of Brussels signed January 22. The House of Commons acts July 14 to permit British participation and the Common Market expands to embrace 20 nations with 257 million people in the world's most powerful trading block but Belgian premier Paul Henri Spaak who helped to found the EEC dies July 31 at age 73 and Norway votes to remain outside the EEC.

British coal miners walk out in January for the first time in nearly 50 years demanding an 11 percent raise in their basic wage which remains below $50 per week. The strike continues for 7 weeks before the 280,000 miners accept a settlement.

London area railworkers strike in April in an effort to bring their wages to an average of $78 per week, the strike spreads a week later to stop rail traffic throughout the country, the workers agree to a 14-day cooling off period after 4 days but wildcat strikes continue to slow service.

The strike of London dockworkers and others (above) idles 500 to 600 ships and prevents export goods from leaving the country.

U.S. wages, prices, and profits remain controlled by Phase II economic measures.

Chile's president Salvador Allende Gossens continues to nationalize the country's large industrial firms.

The Star of Sierra Leone discovered February 14 weights 969.8 carats and is the third largest gem-quality diamond ever found.

The United States enters the international money market July 19 and sells German marks at decreasing prices in the first move since August of last year to shore up the dollar.

Wall Street's Dow Jones Industrial Average closes at 1003.16 November 14, up 6.00 to close above the 1,000 mark for the first time in history.

A human skull found in northern Kenya by Richard Leakey and Glynn Isaac allegedly dates the first humans to 2.5 million B.C. and opens a new controversy on the age of man. Leakey's father Louis S. B. Leakey dies October 1 at age 69 (see 1959).

President Nixon signs a bill January 5 authorizing a $5.5 billion 6-year program to develop a space-shuttle craft that will lift off as a rocket and return to earth as an airplane.

The unmanned U.S. spacecraft Pioneer 10 lifts off from Cape Kennedy March 2 on a 639-day, 620 million-mile journey past the planet Jupiter.

The Soviet space craft Venus 8 makes a soft landing on the planet Venus in March.

U.S. Apollo 16 astronauts Charles M. Duke, Jr., Thomas K. Mattingly, and John W. Young blast off April 16 from Cape Kennedy on a flight of nearly 255 hours. Young and Duke spend a record 71 hours, 2 minutes on the surface of the moon beginning April 20, and they return with 214 pounds of lunar soil and rock.

Japan's San-Yo Shin Kansen (New San-Yo Line) railroad opens in April to link Osaka with Okayama 103 miles to the south. Built to even higher standards than the 8-year-old Tokaido line, the new line can handle speeds of 155 miles per hour and is the first stage of a new expansion that will extend the wide-track railroad to Kyushu.

Amtrak increases the number of Metroliner trains between New York and Washington to 14 daily round trips, up from 6 in 1969. (Eastern Airlines operates 16 daily shuttle flights between the two cities.)

The San Francisco Bay Area Rapid Transit System (BART) that goes into service in September is the first new U.S. regional transit system in more than 50 years, but mechanical problems plague the sleek aluminum-bodied trains from the start. The project has been completed 3 years behind schedule, and it has cost $1.6 billion instead of the projected $120 million. Its 71 miles of track link San Francisco, Oakland, and Berkeley with subway and elevated lines that extend to a score of smaller cities to the south and east, but some trains stall beneath the bay and accidents occur on the automated system.

New Jersey voters reject a $650 million transportation bond issue in November. Environmentalists have objected that too much of the money was earmarked for highways, too little for mass transit.

Washington's Metro subway line opens its first station to begin a system that will have 75 miles of track by 1977. Fares vary according to distance traveled.

The Globtik Tokyo launched in Japan is a $56 million 476,025-ton supertanker that dwarfs the 366,813-ton Nisseki Maru launched last year and raises possibilities of a "megaton tanker" with a capacity of a million tons. Indian entrepreneur Ravi Tikkoo, 40, founded Globtik Tankers with $2,500 in 1967 after 3 years of working at London as a middleman between shipowners and bankers. The Japanese trading company Mitsui has loaned 80 percent of the ship's cost at 6 percent interest, a consortium of London banks has loaned the remaining 20 percent, and Globtik charters the new tanker for 20 years to Tokyo Tankers, owned jointly by Nippon Oil and Caltex.

British Airways (formerly BOAC) orders five Concorde supersonic jets July 18 and Air France orders four (see 1970).

Washington Post reporters Bob Woodward, 29, and Carl Bernstein, 28, begin to crack open the Watergate affair (above), working 12 to 18 hours per day 7 days a week. Their story August 1 reports a financial link between the Watergate break-in and the Committee for the Re-Election of the President (CREEP), on September 16 they report that campaign finance chairman Maurice H. Stans and CREEP aides control a "secret fund," on September 17 they report withdrawals from the fund by CREEP executive Jeb Stuart Magruder and his aide Herbert L. Porter, on September 29 they report that former Attorney General John N. Mitchell actually controls the fund, and their story October 10 begins, "F.B.I. agents have established that the Watergate bugging incident stemmed from a massive campaign of political spying and sabotage conducted on behalf of President Nixon's reelection and directed by officials of the White House and the Committee for the Re-Election of the President." White House spokesmen de-

1972 (cont.) nounce the *Post* stories as "shabby journalism," "mud-slinging," "unfounded and unsubstantiated allegations," and "a political effort by the *Washington Post,* well conceived and coordinated, to discredit this administration and individuals in it." President Nixon tells his legal counsel John Dean September 15, "The *Post* is going to have damnable, damnable problems out of this one. They have a television station." The Federal Communications Commission receives three license challenges in the next 3 months against Florida TV stations owned by the *Post.*

Most other newspapers, magazines, and television networks give short shrift to the Watergate break-in story, they dismiss it as a "caper," the White House continues the intimidation of the press that has continued since 1969, and when Carl Bernstein calls John Mitchell September 28 to tell him what the *Washington Post* is about to publish Mitchell says, "All that crap, you're putting it in the paper? It's all been denied. Katie Graham's gonna get her tit caught in a big fat wringer if that's published."

President Nixon has the support of 753 U.S. dailies in his bid for reelection; only 56 endorse McGovern.

Ms. magazine begins publication in July with former *Look* editor Patricia Carbine as publisher, feminist Gloria Steinem as editor.

LIFE magazine suspends weekly publication in December after 36 years, and more magazines reduce their format to conform with new postal regulations.

Billionaire recluse Howard Hughes holds a telephone news conference January 9 from the Bahamas to Hollywood and disclaims a purported "autobiography" that McGraw-Hill has bought from U.S. émigré writer Clifford Irving, 35. The publisher has paid Irving $750,000 (he has said that Hughes demanded the money for his cooperation). Irving is indicted March 9 along with his wife and his researcher on charges of forgery, mail fraud, conspiracy, and grand larceny, and Irving pleads guilty March 13.

Nonfiction *The Foxfire Book* by Georgia schoolteacher Eliot Wigginston, 28, who has enlisted the help of his students at the Raburn Gap-Nachoche School to record with camera and tape recorder the traditions, crafts, and folklore of Appalachia. *The Limits to Growth, A Report for The Club of Rome's Project on the Predicament of Mankind* by a team of MIT scientists using computer techniques developed by MIT systems engineer Jay Forrester.

Fiction *August 1914* by Aleksandr Solzhenitsyn; *The Terminal Man* by Michael Crichton; *The Exorcist* by William P. Blatty; *The Day of the Jackal* by English novelist Frederick Forsyth.

Painting *Turn of the Century Joplin* by Thomas Hart Benton, now 83.

The Polaroid SX-70 system unveiled in April produces a color print that develops outside the camera while the photographer watches.

Theater *Jumpers* by Tom Stoppard 2/2 at London's National Theatre (Old Vic), with Michael Hordern, Diana Riggs; *Sticks and Bones* by U.S. playwright David Rabe, 31, 3/1 at New York's John Golden Theater (after 121 perfs. at the off-Broadway Public Theater), with Tom Aldridge, Elizabeth Wilson, 366 perfs. (total); *Small Craft Warnings* by Tennessee Williams 4/2 at New York's off-Broadway Truck and Warehouse Theater, 200 perfs.; *That Championship Season* by U.S. playwright Jason Miller, 33, 9/14 at New York's Booth Theater (after 144 perfs. at the off-Broadway Public Theater), with Michael McGuire, Walter McGinn, Richard Dysart, 844 perfs. (total); *6 Rooms Riv Vu* by U.S. playwright Bob Randall (Stanley B. Goldstein), 35, 10/17 at New York's Helen Hayes Theater, with Jerry Orbach, Jane Alexander, 247 perfs.; *The River Niger* by U.S. playwright Joseph A. Walker, 37, 12/5 at New York's St. Marks Playhouse (the play will move to the Brooks Atkinson Theater in late March of next year after 120 perfs. and will have 400 perfs. total); *The Sunshine Boys* by Neil Simon 12/20 at New York's Broadhurst Theater, with Jack Albertson, Sam Levene, Lewis J. Stadlen, 538 perfs.

Films John Boorman's *Deliverance* with Jon Voight, Burt Reynolds, Ned Beatty, author James Dickey; Martin Ritt's *Sounder* with Cicely Tyson, Paul Winfield, Kevin Hooks; Francis Ford Coppola's *The Godfather* with Marlon Brando, Al Pacino, James Caan, Diane Keaton; Joseph L. Mankiewicz's *Sleuth* with Laurence Olivier, Michael Caine; Peter Medak's *The Ruling Class* with Peter O'Toole, Alastair Sim; Ingmar Bergman's *Cries and Whispers* with Liv Ullmann, Ingrid Thulin; Luis Buñuel's *The Discreet Charm of the Bourgeoisie* with Fernando Rey, Delphine Seyrig, Stephane Audran, Bulle Ogler; Herbert Ross's *Play It Again, Sam* with Woody Allen, Diane Keaton; Alfred Hitchcock's *Frenzy* with Jon Finch, Barry Foster, Barbara Leigh-Hunt; Lina Wertmuller's *The Seduction of Mimi;* Sam Peckinpah's *Straw Dogs* with Dustin Hoffman.

Hollywood musicals Bob Fosse's *Cabaret* with Liza Minnelli, Michael York, Joel Grey, Helmut Griem.

Broadway musicals *Sugar* 4/9 at the Majestic Theater, with Robert Morse, Cyril Ritchard, music by Jule Styne, lyrics by Bob Merrill, book from the 1959 film *Some Like It Hot,* 505 perfs.; *Don't Bother Me, I Can't Cope* 4/19 at the Playhouse, with Micki Grant, music and lyrics based on ballads, calypso songs, Gospel music, 1,065 perfs.; *Grease* 6/7 at the Broadhurst Theater (after 128 perfs. at the off-Broadway Martin Eden Theater), with music and lyrics by Jim Jacobs, book by Warren Casey, songs that include "Look at Me, I'm Sandra Dee," "We Go Together," "Alone at a Drive-In Movie," "Shakin' at the High School Hop," 2,000+ perfs.; *Pippin* 10/23 at the Imperial Theater, with John Rubinstein, Ben Vereen, music and lyrics by Stephen Schwartz, 1,944 perfs.

Popular songs "American Pie" by U.S. singer-songwriter-guitarist Don McLean, 26; *You Don't Mess*

Around with Jim (album) by U.S. singer-songwriter-guitarist Jim Croce, 30; "Operator" by Jim Croce; *Honky Chateau* (album) by Elton John.

The Olympic Games at Sapporo, Japan, and at Munich attract a record 8,512 athletes from a record 121 countries. Soviet athletes win the most gold medals, U.S. swimmer Mark Spitz wins a record seven gold medals, but the games at Munich are marred by the murder of 11 Israeli athletes at the hands of Palestine Liberation Organization terrorists organized by Mohammed Daoud Mohammed Auda, 35.

Bobby Fischer becomes the first American to win the world chess title. He defeats Soviet grandmaster Boris Spassky 12½ games to 8½ at Reykjavik, Iceland, he wins a record purse of $250,000, and the event focuses unprecedented world attention on chess.

The Oakland Athletics win the World Series by defeating the Cincinnati Reds 3 games to 2.

A new Surgeon General's Report on smoking issued January 10 warns that nonsmokers exposed to cigarette smoke may suffer health hazards (*see* 1964). Later evidence will show that carbon monoxide and other toxins in "sidestream" smoke actually present greater perils to nonsmokers than to smokers, bringing new pressure to protect airline passengers, office workers, and others from the minority whose cigarette smoke threatens their health and comfort.

Reputed Mafia leader Joseph "Crazy Joe" Gallo is gunned down April 7 during a birthday party at Umberto's Clam House in New York's "Little Italy." Six other men with alleged gangland connections meet with violent deaths in 11 days.

Reputed Mafia leader Thomas "Tommy Ryan" Eboli is found dead July 10 on a Brooklyn, N.Y. sidewalk. He has been shot five times in the head.

New York's World Trade Center opens its first offices in one of two 110-story towers designed by Chinese-American architect I. M. (Ieoh Ming) Pei, 56. Soaring 100 feet higher than the 1,250-foot Empire State Building of 1931, the Trade Center will remain the world's tallest building until 1974.

New York's McGraw-Hill building opens in March at 1221 Avenue of the Americas. Designed by Harrison, Abramovitz and Harris, the new 51-story tower replaces the 41-year-old building on West 42nd Street, now a depressed area rife with derelicts.

The IDS Center completed at Minneapolis for Investors Diversified Services, Inc., is a combination 51-story office tower, hotel, and retail center designed by Philip Johnson and John Burgee of New York in association with Edward F. Baker Associates of Minneapolis. The elongated octagon has a glass-covered Crystal Court 12 stories high at its peak.

The Water Pollution Control Act passed by Congress sets a 1977 deadline for the installation of the "best practicable" pollution control equipment for treating fluid waste discharges and sets a 1983 deadline for the installation of the "best available" equipment.

Congress appropriates $18 billion for assistance grants to help municipalities build sewage treatment facilities but the massive correction action has the handicap of statutory ambiguities that must be resolved in the courts.

An earthquake rocks Iran April 10 leveling 45 villages within a 250-mile radius and killing 5,000.

Tropical storm Agnes strikes the eastern United States from June 10 to June 20 and creates what the U.S. Army Corps of Engineers calls the worst natural disaster in U.S. history. Parts of Florida, Virginia, Maryland, Pennsylvania, and New York are declared disaster areas as rivers overflow their banks crippling transportation, destroying crops, buildings, bridges, and roads, isolating communities, forcing thousands to flee their homes, and killing 134. The Susquehanna River breaks through its dikes June 23 and floods the Wyoming Valley, creating havoc in the Wilkes-Barre area.

A Nicaragua earthquake December 22 shatters the city of Managua killing thousands. The government cuts off food supplies to Managua December 25 in an effort to force survivors to leave the city before decaying bodies beneath the rubble can produce an epidemic.

The worst drought since 1963 withers Soviet and Chinese grain crops, forcing Moscow to buy American grain to avoid having to reduce livestock herds and thus risk the political consequences of reduced meat supplies (*see* Poland, 1970). U.S. Secretary of Agriculture Earl L. Butz has visited the Crimea in April and has suggested to the Soviet minister of agriculture Vladimir V. Matskevich that the Ukraine's rich black soil be irrigated but the Soviet budget has allocated few rubles for agricultural progress.

Detente eased tensions between East and West, facilitating increased trade between communist and capitalist countries.

1972 (cont.) Soviet grain buyers arrive in the United States in late June, they find U.S. wheat for July delivery selling at roughly $1.40 per bushel, Continental Grain Company receives assurance from Assistant U.S. Secretary of Agriculture Carroll G. Brunthaver that the USDA will pay export subsidies to maintain the export price of U.S. wheat at $1.63 per bushel ($60 per metric ton), Moscow's buyers contract for 4 million tons of milling wheat July 4 along with at least 500,000 tons of durum wheat and 4.5 million tons of feed grains, they proceed to place additional orders with Continental, Cargill, Cook Industries, Louis Dreyfus Company, Bunge Corporation, and Garnac Grain Company, and in 6 weeks they buy a million tons of soybeans, several million tons of corn, and 20 million tons of wheat—more than half of it U.S. wheat, one quarter of the entire U.S. wheat crop.

Heartland Natural Cereal is introduced by Pet, Inc. (formerly Pet Milk Co.), Quaker Oats introduces Quaker 100% Natural cereal, Kellogg prepares to introduce Country Morning, and General Mills will follow suit with its own heavily sugared version of Granola, made by Lassen Foods of Chico, Calif. Seventh Day Adventist Wayne Schlottauer, 34, sells out his Lassen Foods to a New York conglomerate.

A Massachusetts law prohibiting sale or dispensing of contraceptives to single persons is ruled unconstitutional by the Supreme Court in a decision handed down March 22.

The National Center for Health Statistics reports May 23 that the U.S. birth rate has fallen to 15.8 per 1,000—the lowest since the survey began 1917.

1973 A ceasefire in Vietnam January 28 ends direct involvement of U.S. ground troops in Indochinese hostilities after the U.S. combat death toll has reached 45,958. The last U.S. troops leave South Vietnam March 29, but U.S. bombing of Cambodia continues as prisoners of war are repatriated.

James W. McCord, Jr., implicates Republican party officials in last year's Watergate break-in and pleads guilty with four other defendants before Justice John W. Sirica. President Nixon announces "major developments" in the Watergate case April 17, his aides H. R. Haldeman and John Ehrlichman resign under pressure, former White House legal aid John R. Dean implicates other Nixon intimates in testimony before a Senate investigating committee chaired by U.S. Senator Sam J. Ervin, Jr., of North Carolina.

President Nixon appoints Harvard law professor Archibald Cox as special Watergate prosecutor (but *see* below).

Vice President Agnew resigns under pressure October 10 and pleads no contest to charges of income tax evasion in connection with money received during his tenure as governor of Maryland. President Nixon names House Republican leader Gerald R. Ford Vice President and Ford takes office December 3.

Special Watergate prosecutor Archibald Cox is discharged the night of October 20 when he insists that the president turn over tape recordings of conversations with his aides relevant to the Watergate break-in. Attorney General Elliot L. Richardson who has succeeded John Mitchell in that post resigns in protest, President Nixon names Leon Jaworski to succeed Cox as Watergate prosecutor. The White House releases tapes of the president's conversations in response to a subpoena, but some of the key tapes contain gaps and the White House claims that some missing tapes do not exist.

The Bahamas gain full independence from Britain.

Argentina has a rash of assassinations and kidnappings early in the year, Peronist Hector J. Campora wins election to the presidency in March and takes office May 25, former dictator Juan Peron, now 77, returns June 20 after nearly 18 years in exile.

Chile has a wave of strikes that shut down shops and transportation in nine provinces, a violent coup September 11 overthrows Chile's Marxist president Salvador Allende Gossens who reportedly takes his own life. A military junta names General Augusto Pinochet Ugarte, 57, president, he breaks off relations with Cuba, he vows to "exterminate Marxism" from Chile, he lifts the military curfew in Santiago for 6 hours so that those trapped in buildings may go home, but troops continue to battle snipers in the capital and the military junta warns workers occupying factories that they face execution if they are found to be armed when captured.

Spain's dictator Francisco Franco, now 80, names Admiral Luis Carrero Blanco, 70, premier but remains Chief of State. Assassins kill Premier Carrero Blanco.

Sweden's Gustavus VI dies September 15 at age 90 after a 23-year reign. He is succeeded by his 27-year-old son who ascends the throne as Carl XVI Gustavus but who will reign simply as king of Sweden rather than as king of the Swedes, Goths, and Wends.

The Yom Kippur War that begins in the Middle East October 6 on the Jewish Holy Day of Atonement is the fourth and fiercest Arab-Israeli war since 1948. Hostilities have persisted since January when Israeli fighter planes shot down 13 Syrian MIG-21 jets, both sides accuse the enemy of having begun the new fighting which erupts along the 103-mile-long Suez Canal and on the Golan Heights, UN observers report that Egyptian forces crossed the canal at five points and that Syrian forces attacked at two points on the Golan Heights, Israeli troops push the Syrians back to the 1967 cease-fire line by October 10 despite the arrival of Iraqui troops to support the Syrians, the Israelis push to within 18 miles of Damascus October 12, and Jordan's best troops arrive October 13 to help defend Damascus. Egyptian troops meanwhile force the Israelis to give up the Bar Lev defense line on the East Bank of the Suez Canal, Egyptian SAM-6 missiles stymie Israel's air attacks, Soviet planes airlift equipment to help Arab forces on both fronts, Moscow announces October 15 that it will "assist in every way" the Arab effort to regain the territory taken by Israel in 1967.

Washington announces that it has begun supplying military equipment to Israel to counter the Soviet airlift of arms to the Arabs, Israel sends a task force across the Suez Canal to attack Egyptian tanks, missile sites, and artillery on the West Bank, heavy tank battles begin in the Sinai October 17, Moscow tries to persuade Egypt and Syria to resolve the Middle East conflict through diplomacy, four Arab foreign ministers meet with President Nixon at Washington and urge U.S. mediation of the Arab-Israeli dispute, Soviet premier Aleksei Kosygin meets at Cairo with President Sadat, U.S. Secretary of State Henry A. Kissinger confers at Moscow October 20 with Soviet party leader Leonid A. Brezhnev, a resolution sponsored jointly by the United States and the U.S.S.R. calling for a cease-fire in place receives a 14-0 vote of approval in the UN Security Council early in the morning of October 22, heavy fighting resumes 12 hours after the cease-fire takes effect, Israel and Egypt agree to a new cease-fire October 24, U.S. forces are put on "precautionary alert" October 25, Secretary Kissinger justifies the action by asserting that "ambiguous" signs from Moscow have suggested possible Soviet intervention in the Middle East, the crisis passes, the cease-fire holds, but Israel has lost 4,100 men killed or wounded in 18 days of fighting, Egypt has lost 7,500, Syria, 7,300.

An energy crisis grips the world and an oil embargo by Arab nations in the fall exacerbates the problem.

Saudi Arabia acquires a 25 percent interest in the 40-year-old Aramco petroleum colossus January 1 and moves to enlarge its equity in the company to 51 percent by 1982 (see 1948).

Iraqi Oil Minister Sadoon Hammadi negotiates a settlement with Iraq Petroleum Company (see 1972). IPC recognizes Baghdad's nationalization of the fields and agrees to pay $345 million in back taxes and claims, IPC promises to help boost Iraqi oil output to 3 million barrels per day by 1975, Baghdad agrees to give IPC 15 million tons of oil in compensation, France's Compagnie Française des Petroles agrees to buy 23.75 percent of Iraq's annual oil production.

President Nixon tells Congress April 19 that "in years immediately ahead, we must face up to the possibility of occasional energy shortages and some increases in energy prices." On May 1 Nixon ends the oil import quota system imposed in 1959, he urges additional tax credits to subsidize the oil industry's efforts to find new oil sources, and he urges Congress to end federal regulation of natural gas prices to provide incentive for exploration to find new reserves of natural gas (see 1954).

President Nixon urges the states to encourage use of coal even if it means delaying imposition of secondary air pollution controls and he urges Americans to conserve energy by turning out lights, using less air-conditioning and heating, and tuning up their cars.

"America faces a serious energy problem," President Nixon tells Congress June 29: "While we have 6 percent of the world's population, we consume one-third of the world's energy output. The supply of domestic energy resources available to us is not keeping pace with our ever-growing demand." U.S. demand for oil runs at about 17 million barrels per day, domestic output is little more than 11 million barrels per day, Venezuela and Canada supply most of the imported oil, and at present rates of increase demand will reach 24 million barrels per day by 1980 with domestic sources supplying only half that much.

Oil industry critics charge that there is no real shortage of petroleum but that major oil companies are engaged in a conspiracy to force up prices and drive out competition.

Iran's Shah Pahlevi takes over all properties of the multinational Iranian Consortium including the huge Abadan Refinery, he guarantees the participating companies a 20-year supply of oil in proportion to their interests in the consortium (British Petroleum has the lion's share), and the Majlis ratifies the shah's action August 3.

Saudi Arabia's Faisal announces September 4 that his country will not increase oil production so long as U.S. policy favors Israel at the expense of the Arab countries (above). Saudi Arabia's crude oil production is 6.5 million barrels per day versus 9.5 million by the United States, 5 million by Iran, 3 million by Kuwait, 2.2 million by Libya, 1.2 million by Abu Dhabi, 1.1 million by Iraq, 550,000 by Qatar, 300,000 by Oman.

Other Arab nations cut back oil production in part for political reasons, in part to conserve resources, in part to force up prices in a sellers' market. The Arab oil-producing nations have enough money in reserve to shut down petroleum production completely for 18 months while maintaining normal imports of food and other necessities but Arab oil cutbacks force Europe and Japan to reduce airline service, cut down heating in offices, limit driving, and in other ways conserve dwindling supplies of fuel.

The energy crisis (above) and soaring grain prices precipitate a world monetary crisis and then a worldwide economic recession that is the worst since the Great Depression of the 1930s.

Speculative selling of U.S. dollars on foreign exchanges forces the second devaluation of the dollar in 14 months. Secretary of the Treasury George P. Schultz announces February 12 that the dollar is to be devalued by 10 percent against nearly all other major world currencies in a move to make U.S. goods cheaper—and thus more competitive—in foreign trade, the devaluation makes last year's Soviet grain purchase a bigger bargain than ever for the U.S.S.R. (which has thus far paid only $330 to $400 million), it brings the price of the wheat bought by Moscow down to $1.48 per bushel, fast-rising gold prices in the London market enable the Russians to sell their

1973 **(cont.)** bullion at much more favorable rates than they had expected, but the devaluation in the dollar produces consternation in Japan and boosts the price of imported goods (and imported oil) to U.S. consumers and businessmen.

Bache Halsey Stuart is created by a merger of Bache & Company with Halsey Stuart & Company.

Esmark is created in May—a new conglomerate based on the Swift meatpacking colossus and the Vickers petroleum company. The group will grow to include a chemical fertilizer company, International Playtex, STP Corp., and other firms.

Moscow agrees to abide by the terms of the Universal Copyright Convention and to cease publishing pirated editions of Western works.

Nonfiction *The Best and the Brightest* by U.S. journalist David Halberstam probes U.S. involvement in Vietnam; *Fire in the Lake: The Vietnamese and the Americans in Vietnam* by U.S. journalist Frances Fitzgerald.

Fiction *Gravity's Rainbow* by Thomas Pynchon; *Breakfast of Champions* by Kurt Vonnegut, Jr.; *The Billion Dollar Sure Thing* by U.S. banker-novelist Paul Erdman, who wrote the book while imprisoned at Basel for using $40 million in his depositors' funds to speculate in commodity futures.

Pablo Picasso dies at Mongins, France, April 8 at age 91 leaving works whose value is estimated at more than $1 billion. Active almost to the end, Picasso is hailed as the greatest artist of the 20th Century; Jacques Lipschitz dies at Capril May 26 at age 81.

Theater *Finishing Touches* by Jean Kerr 2/8 at New York's Plymouth Theater, with Barbara Bel Geddes, Robert Lansing, 164 perfs.; *The Hot L Baltimore* by U.S. playwright Lanford Wilson, 35, 3/22 at New York's Circle in the Square Theater; *Equus* by Peter Shaffer 7/26 at London's National Theater (Old Vic), with Alex McCowen; *Cromwell* by David Storey 8/15 at London's Royal Court Theatre, with Albert Finney; *The Good Doctor* by Neil Simon 11/27 at New York's Eugene O'Neill Theater, with Christopher Plummer, Marsha Mason, 208 perfs.

Films Bernardo Bertolucci's *Last Tango in Paris* with Marlon Brando, Maria Schneider; George Roy Hill's *The Sting* with Paul Newman, Robert Redford; George Lucas's *American Graffiti* with Richard Dreyfuss, Candy Clark; Peter Bogdanovich's *Paper Moon* with Ryan O'Neal, Tatum O'Neal, Madeline Kahn; James Bridges's *The Paper Chase* with Timothy Bottoms, Lindsay Wagner, John Houseman; Sydney Pollack's *The Way We Were* with Barbra Streisand, Robert Redford; Lina Wertmuller's *Love and Anarchy* with Giancarlo Giannini; John Hancock's *Bang the Drum Slowly* with Michael Moriarty, Robert De Niro; Jan Troell's *The New Land* with Max von Sydow, Liv Ullmann.

Broadway and off-Broadway musicals *El Grande de Coca-Cola* 2/13 at the Mercer Arts Center, with Ron

House, Diz White, music and lyrics by the cast, 1,114 perfs.; *A Little Night Music* 2/25 at the Shubert Theater, with Len Cariou, Hermione Gingold, Glynis Johns, music and lyrics by Stephen Sondheim, book from the 1955 Ingmar Bergman film *Smiles of a Summer Night*, 600 perfs.; *Seesaw* 3/18 at the Uris Theater, with Michele Lee, music by Cy Coleman, lyrics by Dorothy Fields, book from the 1958 William Gibson play *Two for the Seesaw*, 296 perfs.; *Raisin* 10/18 at the 46th Street Theater, with Joe Morton, Ernestine Jackson, music by Judd Woldon, lyrics by Robert Brittan, book from the 1959 Lorraine Hansberry play *Raisin in the Sun*, 847 perfs.

Popular songs *Goodbye Yellow Brick Road* and *Don't Shoot Me I'm Only the Piano Player* (albums) by Elton John; *Goat's Head Soup* (album) by the Rolling Stones; *The Material World* (album) and "Give Me Love (Give Me Peace)" by former Beatles singer-instrumentalist George Harrison; *Life and Times* (album) and "Bad, Bad Leroy Brown" by Jim Croce; "You Are the Sunshine of My Life" and "Superstition" by Stevie Wonder.

George Foreman gains the world heavyweight boxing championship January 22 by knocking out Joe Frazier in the second round of a title bout at Kingston, Jamaica.

Secretariat wins U.S. horseracing's Triple Crown.

U.S. baseball's American League permits teams to field a tenth player—a "designated hitter" to bat in place of the pitcher.

The Oakland A's win the World Series by defeating the New York Mets 4 games to 3.

A tennis match promoted as the "battle of the sexes" ends in defeat for former Wimbledon champion Bobby Riggs, now 55, who loses 6-4, 6-3, 6-3 to Mrs. Billie Jean King September 20 at the Houston Astrodome.

U.S. textile mills produce 482 million square yards of cotton denim, up from 437 million in 1971. The figure will soar to 820 million by 1976 as demand booms for blue jeans and denim jackets.

The U.S. median sales price of an existing single-family house reaches $28,900, up from $20,000 in 1968. By 1976 the price will be $38,100.

New York's Celanese building opens in the spring at 1211 Avenue of the Americas. Harrison, Abramovitz & Harris have built the 45-story tower.

U.S. farmers plant 322 million acres to wheat, up from 293 million acres last year, in response to higher prices. Wheat production hits a record 1.71 billion bushels—nearly 50 million metric tons.

President Nixon announces a temporary embargo June 27 on exports of soybeans and cottonseeds, shocking Japan, Korea, and other traditional customers for U.S. oilseeds. At least 92 percent of the soybeans Japan uses for *tofu* (bean curd), soy sauce, and cooking oil comes from the United States, soybean prices jump by 40 percent in less than a week in

Japan, the White House lifts the embargo after 5 days in response to State Department pressure, the Department of Commerce approves shipment of all orders received prior to June 13 but announces that special licenses will be required for all subsequent orders and says contracted amounts will be cut in half (by 40 percent for soybean oil, cake, and meal).

Foreign buyers redouble their purchases of U.S. grain lest further controls be applied, more than 30 million tons of U.S. wheat are sold for export by the end of July, U.S. farmers hold back their crops as buyers bid up prices, other farmers and ranchers cull flocks and herds as poultry raising and cattle production become unprofitable.

U.S. corn yields average 96.9 bushels per acre, up from 70 in 1968.

The average U.S. farm worker produces enough food and fiber for 50 people, up from 31 in 1963.

Farm labor represents 5 percent of the U.S. work force, down from 7 percent in 1968.

Nutrition labeling regulations promulgated by the Food and Drug Administration standardize the type of information to be presented on U.S. food packages. Responding to demands by consumer coalitions for more information about the foods in the marketplace, the FDA selects package labels as the vehicle for educating consumers on the nutritive values of foods and suggests a format that provides information per serving on the calories, the grams of protein, carbohydrate, and fat, and the percentage of U.S. Recommended Daily Allowances (RDA) of protein, nine vitamins, and five minerals.

A Universal Product Code (U.P.C.) design for all supermarket items is recommended in April by a committee formed in 1970 by U.S. grocers and manufacturers intent on improving productivity. The committee has retained the management consultant firm McKinsey and Company to suggest ways to speed up the check-out process at supermarkets, to eliminate checker error, to facilitate inventory control, and to reduce noise at checkout counters, the U.P.C. label is designed to permit electronic scanners at checkout counters to "read" the price of each item and trigger a computer that will record the price automatically, but while McKinsey estimates that 7,000 to 8,000 of the nation's 32,000 supermarkets will find scanning systems economically feasible, retailers delay installing the necessary equipment in hopes that they will become less costly and consumers protest the elimination of individually marked prices.

Food prices soar in the United States, Japan, and Europe in the wake of last year's Soviet wheat and soybean purchases which have forced up the price of feedgrains and consequently of meat, poultry, eggs, and dairy products as well as of baked goods. U.S. consumer groups organize boycotts to protest rising prices but prices will continue to rise even without the excuse of a "Russian wheat deal."

President Nixon orders a freeze on all retail food prices June 13 saying he will "not let foreign sales price meat and eggs off the American table."

Cadbury Schweppes chairman Lord Wilkinson has said early in the year, "The era of cheap food is over."

"The era of cheap food is over," echoes U.S. Secretary of Agriculture Earl Butz.

Vodka outsells whiskey for the first time in the United States (see 1965).

Abortion should be a decision between a woman and her physician, the Supreme Court rules January 22. Individual states may not prohibit abortion during the first 6 months of pregnancy, the court rules, but "right to life" groups work to undermine the decision.

Index

Carling's Beer, 903
Carlisle School for Indians, 578
Carlsbad Caverns Natl. Park, 878
Carlsbad Decrees, 393
Carlsberg Brewery, 595
Carlyle, Thomas, 423, 432, 442
Carmelite order, 92
Carmichael, Hoagy, 868, 877, 900, 926, 934, 941, 995, 1002, 1029, 1094
Carmichael, Stokely, 1120, 1128
Carnation evaporated milk, 670, 671, 715
Carnegie, Andrew, 487, 520, 527, 586, 614, 619, 621, 629, 666, 679, 681, 682, 685, 705, 741, 792
Carnegie, Dale, 924
Carnegie Corp. of New York, 740
Carnegie Foundation, 705, 1027
Carnegie Hall, 629, 638, 782, 860, 941, 956, 962, 964, 969, 980, 995, 1001, 1022, 1029, 1060, 1066, 1083, 1143
Carnegie Inst. of Technology, 674
Carnegie Institution, 685, 708
Carnegie Steel Co., 666, 679
Carnot, Nicholas L.S., 403
Caroline, English queen, 395
Caroline Matilda, 317
Carolingians, 71, 75
carotene, 1042
Carpaccio, Vittore, 159, 164
Carpentier, Georges, 808
"carpetbaggers," 518
Carr, John Dickson, 874
Carracci, Annibale, 204, 207, 212, 214
Carrère & Hastings, 599, 689, 743, 757
Carrero Blanco, Admiral Luis, 1154
Carrier, Willis H., 689, 743, 769
Carrier Corp., 769
Carroll, Charles, 411
Carroll, Lewis, 521, 541, 548
Carr's of Carlisle, 419
Carson, Johnny, 1093
Carson, Kit, 443, 452, 510, 515
Carson, Rachel, 1095
Carson, Pirie Scott, 529, 625
Cartagena, 175, 176, 198, 188, 268, 293, 393
Carte, Richard D'Oyly, 585, 621
Carter, Barbara, 814
Carter, Howard, 813
Carter, Nick, 606
Carter v. Carter Coal Co., 924
Carteret, Sir George, 246
Carter's Grove, Virginia, 286
Carter's Little Pills, 978
Carthage, 10, 14, 21, 24, 25, 26, 28, 29, 42, 44, 61, 112
Cartier, Jacques, 176, 177, 234
Cartier's, 459, 665, 688, 783
Caruso, Enrico, 687, 695, 711, 713
Carver, George Washington, 655, 764, 809
Cary, Joyce, 947, 986
Casablanca Conference, 971
Casanova, Giovanni, 303, 434

Case, J.I., 448, 727
Case School, 585
Casement, Roger, 693, 771
Cash, Johnny, 1060
cash register, 578, 597
Caspian Sea, 282, 804
Cassander, 23, 24
Cassatt, Alexander J., 710, 734
Cassatt, Mary, 556, 578, 606, 629, 638, 643, 844
Cassiodorus, 53, 54, 55
Castagno, Andrea del, 144, 145, 148
Castel Sant'angelo, 41, 56
Castelgondolfo, 210
Castiglione, Baldassare, 173
Castile, 73, 78, 79, 81, 82, 84, 93, 102, 103, 106, 109, 114, 116, 127, 130-133, 150-153, 156, 157, 161, 162, 165-167, 207
Castle, Irene, 742, 756, 762
Castle, Vernon B., 731, 742, 756, 762
Castle & Cooke Co., 474, 1106, 1118
Castlereagh, Viscount, 397, 398
Castro, Fidel, 1074, 1079, 1085, 1090
Cateau Cambresis, Treaty of, 187
Caterpillar Tractor Co., 702, 839
Catharine the Great, 308, 309, 312, 316, 324, 332, 334, 339, 341, 343, 356, 358, 359, 361, 363, 550
Cather, Willa, 754, 787, 835, 851, 946
Catherine I, of Russia, 284, 285
Catherine of Aragon, 172
cathode-ray tube, 645
Catholic Emancipation Bill, Britain, 412
Catholic Univ., 610
Catholic Worker, The, 898
Catiline Conspiracy, 31
Catlin, George, 453
Cato, Marcus Porcius, 28
Cato Conspiracy, 291
Cato Street Conspiracy, 395
cattle, 2, 89, 287, 288, 310, 315, 391, 440, 469, 553
Catton, Bruce, 1040
Catulus, Q.L., 29, 30
Caudine Forks, Battle of, 22
Caulaincourt, Marquis de, 382
Cavaignac, Louis E., 460
Cavalcanti, Guido, 117
Cavaliers, 234-236
Cavalli, Francesco, 239, 240
Cavallini, Pietro, 112, 115, 121
Cavell, Edith, 766, 948
Cavendish, Henry, 312, 336
Cavendish, Thomas, 199
Cavenham Foods, 1112
Cavour, Count C.B. di, 483, 496, 503
Cawley, Thomas, 334
Caxton, William, 152, 153, 155
Celanese Corp. of America, 786
celiac disease, 954
Celine, Louis-Ferdinand, 891
Celler-Kefauver Amendment, 1019
Cellini, Benvenuto, 285

cellophane, 745, 842
celluloid, 484, 547, 620
Celsus, Aulus Cornelius, 36
Celts, 16, 21
Census, Bureau of the, U.S., 691, 1120
Central African Republic (Ubangi Shari), 1069, 1079
Central Pacific Railroad, 504, 535, 597, 679
Central Park, New York, 450, 479, 492, 495, 513, 566, 582, 587, 615
Centre College, Danville, Ky., 394, 808
Century Company, The, 581
Century Magazine, 581, 700
Ceresota Flour, 630
Cerf, Bennett, 835, 898, 1022
cerium, 357, 367
Cernuda, Luis, 925
Cerro, Luis Sanchez, 871
Cerro de Pasco mine, 227
certificates of deposit, 1087
Cervantes, 218, 255, 306, 1111
Cesaire, Aime, 947
Cesium-137, 1095
Cessna, Clyde, 890
Ceylon, 52, 54, 76, 138, 162, 243, 354, 356, 365, 386, 405, 538, 599, 621, 1074 (see Sri Lanka)
Cezanne, Paul, 528, 556, 582, 590, 598, 624, 674, 699, 700, 706, 712, 754, 866, 1088
Chabas, Paul E., 747, 755
Chabrier, Emmanuel, 594, 610
Chabrol, Claude, 1142
ChaChaCha, The, 1048
Chaco War, 856
Chad, 1079, 1118
Chadwick, Edwin, 443
Chadwick, Florence, 1030
Chadwick, James, 888
Chaeronea, Battle of, 21
Chagall, Marc, 725, 821, 828, 836, 858, 866, 883, 973, 993, 1016, 1021, 1034, 1040, 1047, 1076, 1115
Chain, Ernest, 954
Chaldeans, 11
Challe, General Maurice, 1086
Chamberlain, Joseph, 604, 674
Chamberlain, Neville, 929, 936, 951
Chamberlain, Wilt, 1137
Chambers Cyclopaedia, 285
Chambers, Robert, 449, 450
Chambers, Sir William, 339
Chambers, Whittaker, 828, 1005, 1034
Chambord, château, 176
Chamfort, Sebastien Roch Nicolas, 310
Champion, Albert, 723
Champion Spark Plug Co., 723
Champlain, Samuel de, 210-212, 214, 220
Champollion, Jean François, 399
Chancellor, Richard, 184, 185
Chancellorsville, Battle of, 510
Chandler, Norman, 1098
Chandler, Otis, 1098
Chandler, Raymond, 947
Chanel, Coco, 756, 802, 1136
Chaney, Lon, 836
Chanin Bldg., New York, 869

Channing, William Ellery, 394, 454
Chanson de Roland, 65
Chantilly, Château de, 172
Chantilly race track, 426
Chaplin, Charlie, 755, 762, 782, 787, 795, 807, 822, 836, 859, 884, 925, 962, 1001, 1019, 1028, 1035, 1038, 1042
Chapman, George, 216, 218
Chapman, John ("Johnny Appleseed"), 365
Chapultepec, Battle of, 457
Char, René, 908
Chardin, J.B.S., 285, 288, 291, 322, 329
Charlemagne, 65-68, 70, 75, 88, 368, 372
Charles, Jacques, 340
Charles I, of England, 223, 224, 226, 229, 231-238, 240, 241; II, 238-240, 245-247, 249, 251, 252, 255, 257, 258
Charles IV, of France, 121; V, 130; VI, 132; VII, 141-143, 145, 146, 149; VII, 154, 156-159; IX, 188, 193; X, 402, 414
Charles the Bald, 68-70
Charles the Bold, 150-152
Charles's law, 340
Charleston, S.C., 252, 256, 268, 276, 278, 291, 292, 307, 315, 318, 319, 324, 329, 331, 333, 339, 380, 412, 415, 430, 479, 482, 502, 518
Charlie McCarthy Show, 933
Charpentier, Gustave, 675
Charter Oak, 263
Chartist Land Assn., 446
Chartres, 55, 203; Cathedral, 110, 166, 254
Chase, Ilka, 891, 925
Chase, Salmon P., 515
Chase, Stuart, 835
Chase and Sanborn's Coffee, 514, 870
Chase-Manhattan Bank, 1052, 1089
Chase National Bank, 567, 857, 871, 1052
Chasen's, Dave, 928
chassepot musket, 523
Chasseriau, Théodore, 437, 439, 442, 462, 478
Château d'Anet, 186
Château Frontenac Hotel, 639, 831
Château-Thierry, 785
Chatelier, Henri L. Le, 612
Chattanooga, Battle of, 510
Chaucer, Geoffrey, 133, 136
Chaumette, Pierre G., 351
Chauncy, Charles, 293, 295
Chautauqua movement, 555, 731
Chavez, Cesar E., 1091, 1132
Chayefsky, Paddy, 1047, 1053, 1077
Checker, Chubby, 1083
Checkers Motors Corp., 812
cheese, 32, 82, 283, 348, 390, 404, 408, 440, 571, 575, 583, 635, 677, 732, 764, 770, 776, 789, 796, 810, 832, 847, 862, 870, 903, 950, 976, 1100
Chekhov, Anton, 610, 653, 664, 669, 681, 700
Chelsea Bridge, London, 494

Geoffrey Plantagenet of Anjou, 90-92
geometry, 7, 24, 202, 220
George, Henry, 577, 919
George I, of England, 277, 278, 283, 285; II, 285, 287, 288, 297, 299, 300, 306; III, of Britain, 306-310, 313, 314, 322, 323; IV, 395, 396, 410, 414, 429; V, 732, 739, 921; VI, 921, 1031
George Washington Bridge, New York, 882
George Washington Univ., 398
Georgetown, 300, 344; Univ., 343
Georgia, 287-289, 291, 294, 303, 319, 328, 331, 341, 348, 358, 388, 390, 394, 405, 417, 423, 434, 444, 446, 449, 451, 497, 502, 510, 514, 519, 528, 529, 542, 602, 627, 685, 709, 733, 766, 809, 897, 910, 982, 1058, 1135; Tech, 602; Univ. of, 337
Georgia (Asia), 96, 108, 220, 339
Georgia Warm Springs Foundation, 850
Georgia-Pacific Corp., 855
Gerard, François P.S., 355, 359
Gerard, John, 205
Gerber Baby Foods Co., 855, 862, 871, 964, 1011, 1031, 1138
Géricault, Théodore, 382, 385, 394, 403
German Democratic Republic (East Germany), 1012
German Federal Republic (West Germany), 1012
German language, 59
Germanic Confederation, 386
Germantown, Pa., 259, 263; Battle of, 326, 330; Cricket Club, 830
Germany, 370, 410, 419, 422, 425, 462, 474, 478, 542, 544-547, 551, 559, 563, 576, 577, 589, 591-593, 596, 597, 600, 608, 612, 613, 622, 623, 627, 641, 646, 651, 656, 671, 672, 709, 733, 752, 758, 759, 764, 766, 770, 772, 776, 778-780, 784-786, 790, 792, 793, 798, 811, 812, 818, 826, 827, 832, 835, 836, 840, 851, 872, 880, 887-889, 894, 895, 904, 906, 911-914, 918, 921-923, 927-930, 935-938, 943, 944, 946, 950-952, 954, 957-960, 963-968, 971, 972, 976-978, 982-984, 989, 993, 998, 1005, 1012, 1014, 1023, 1031, 1050, 1062, 1069, 1081, 1086, 1087, 1090, 1093, 1096, 1109, 1129, 1140, 1145
Germi, Pietro, 1094
Geronimo, 563, 604
Gerry, Elbridge, 357, 381
"Gerrymander," 381
Gershwin, George, 795, 801, 808, 815, 822, 829, 830, 837, 845, 852, 859, 860, 867, 876, 885, 900, 918, 926, 933, 940, 1002, 1028
Gershwin, Ira, 807, 815, 830, 837, 845, 852, 860, 867, 876,

885, 900, 909, 918, 926, 933, 940
Gesell, Arnold L., 972
Gestapo, 922, 966, 978
Getty, John Paul, 1014, 1026
Getty Oil Co., 1058
Gettysburg, Battle of, 510
Gettysburg Address, 510
Gettysburg State College, 421
Ghana, 1062, 1079, 1086, 1107, 1113; Kingdom of, 81, 83
Ghent, 124, 152, 272, 273; Treaty of, 385, 386
Gherig, Lou, 837, 949
Ghiardelli, Domingo, 466
Ghibelline, 90-92, 110, 113, 115
Ghiberti, Lorenzo, 141, 147
Ghirlandajo, 158
Giacometti, Alberto, 899, 1000, 1022, 1115
Giannini, A.P., 709, 857, 871
Gibbon, Edward, 325, 332, 348, 393
Gibbons v. Ogden, 401
Gibbs, Josiah Willard, 563, 685
G.I. Bill, 979, 982, 992
Gibraltar, 49, 51, 127, 196, 271, 277, 285, 328, 333, 334, 370, 442, 1113
Gibran, Kahlil, 821
Gibson, Althea, 1067, 1072
Gibson, William, 1071, 1077
Gide, André, 658, 724, 741, 781, 843
Gideon v. Wainwright, 1096
Gielgud, John, 1001, 1011, 1059, 1104
Gilbert, Cass, 720, 749, 894, 919
Gilbert, Sir Humphrey, 195, 197
Gilbert, William S., 545, 559, 570, 574, 578, 586, 590, 598, 602, 610, 615, 620, 653
Gilgamesh, 4, 5, 547
Gillette, King C., 648, 682, 696, 701
Gillette, William H., 653
Gilmore, Patrick S., 509, 512, 556
Gimbels, 445, 611, 634, 644, 737, 831, 832, 838, 869, 928
gin, 290, 292, 301, 315, 397, 416, 542
ginger, 40, 74, 135, 158, 189, 198, 305
Ginn & Co., 524, 564
Gino's fast food stands, 1068
Ginsberg, Allen, 1053, 1107, 1120
Giordano, Umberto, 653, 768
Giorgione, 164
Giotto di Bondone, 118, 119, 123, 124
Girard, Stephen, 370, 381
Giraudoux, Jean, 866, 917, 986, 1136
Girl Guides, The, 737
Girl Scouts of America, 749
Giroud, Françoise, 1040
Gish, Lillian, 748, 829, 844, 908
Gissing, George, 629
Gitlow v. New York, 834
Glacier Natl. Park, 603, 738
Glackens, William, 725, 916, 940

Gladstone, William E., 530, 562, 580, 600, 604, 631, 641
Glamour, 946
Glasgow, Ellen, 754, 835
Glasgow, 118, 231, 761, 880, 1003; Univ., 146, 311, 323, 470
Glaspell, Susan, 875
Glassboro State College, 820
Glass-Owen Currency Act, 751
Glauber, Johann R., 224, 238
Glauber's salt, 224
Glazunov, Aleksandr, 625
Gleem toothpaste, 1036
Glencoe, Massacre of, 264
Glendower, Owen, 135, 137, 139
Glenlivet, The, 403
Glenn, John H., 1065, 1092
Glidden, Joseph F., 553
Glidden Co., 574, 704
Glinka, Mikhail I., 429, 445
Globe, Boston, 548, 787
Globe-Democrat, St. Louis, 747
Globe Theatre, 207, 217
Glorious Revolution, England, 261, 263
Gloucester, Mass., 223, 277, 293, 303, 1055, 1133
Gluck, Christoph Willibald von, 308, 313, 320, 329, 340, 429, 482, 926
Goddard, Henry H., 747
Goddard, Jean-Luc, 1077, 1104, 1123, 1131
Goddard, Robert H., 792, 806, 841
Godden, Rumer, 947
Godey's Lady's Book, 415, 455, 502, 514
Godfrey, Arthur, 985
Godfrey of Bouillon, 85
Godiva, Lady, 79
Godkin, Edwin L., 520
Godolphin, Sidney, 275
Godunov, Boris, 298, 205, 211, 217
Godwin, William, 351, 359
Goering, Hermann, 895, 913, 922, 989
Goethe, Johann Wolfgang von, 316, 319, 320, 325, 329, 355, 357, 358, 363, 376, 413, 421, 491
Goetz, E. Ray, 782, 815, 822, 860
Gogol, Nikolai, 427, 429, 444, 475, 877
goiter, 75, 224, 708, 767, 777
Golconda, 165
Gold, Harry, 1018
Gold Coast, 150, 920, 1057, 1062
Gold Dust Soap, 599
Gold Medal Flour, 583
gold rush, 462, 474, 490
Goldberg, Rube, 718
Golden, Harry, 1071
Golden Gate Bridge, 930
Golden Gloves, 853
Golden Horde, 106, 107
Golden Pavilion, 135
Golding, William, 1046, 1103
Goldman, Emma, 710, 791
Goldman, Sachs, 536, 713, 864, 870, 972
Goldmark, Peter Carl, 955, 1010

Goldoni, Carlo, 292, 300, 306-308, 314, 317
Goldsmith, Oliver, 295, 310, 312, 314, 316, 319, 335
Goldwater, Barry M., 1101
Goldwyn, Samuel, 755, 829
golf, 148, 184, 302, 339, 462, 501, 634, 638, 643, 648, 654, 669, 748, 776, 790, 802, 816, 823, 845, 853, 877, 885, 910, 918, 1042, 1072, 1094, 1143
Golf Club, Royal and Ancient, St. Andrews, 302
Gompers, Samuel, 604, 722, 766, 791, 804
Goncalves, Lopo, 151
Goncharov, Ivan A., 498
Goncourt, Prix, 694
gondola, Venice, 115, 585
gonorrhea, 577, 596, 624, 686, 717
Gonzaga Univ., 610
Good Housekeeping, 602, 647, 683, 709
Good Humor, The, 803, 847, 870
Gooderham & Worts, 421
Goodhue, Bertram, 764, 789, 823, 846, 894
Goodman, Benny, 876, 918, 941, 1023
Goodman, Paul, 1082
Goodman's matzos, 522, 595
Goodnight, Charles, 566
Goodrich, B.F., Co., 547, 667, 767, 820, 842, 954, 999
Goodspeed Opera House, 565
Goodyear, Charles, 436, 449
Goodyear Tire and Rubber, 663, 767, 806, 954, 1107
Gordon, Charles G., 515, 596, 600
Gordon "No Popery" Riots, 330, 442
Gordon's Gin, 315
Gordy, Berry, Jr., 1067, 1089
Gorée, 309, 334
Goren, Charles H., 927
Gorgas, William C., 680
Gorges, Sir Ferdinando, 222, 226, 256
Gorham silver, 419
Gorki, Maksim, 687, 809
Gorky, Arshile, 1008
Gothic architecture, 87, 90, 96, 104, 110, 112, 120, 143, 152, 162, 166, 183
Gottlieb, Adolf, 1028
Gould, Jay, 536, 546, 586, 735, 774
Gould, Morton, 902, 987, 995, 1001, 1010, 1035, 1066
Goulding, Edmund, 948, 974, 994, 1001
Gounod, Charles, 498, 528
Gourmet, 958
gout, 149, 185, 198, 243, 252, 337, 498
Goya, Francisco de, 336, 370, 374, 377, 385, 411
Gracchus, T.S., 29
Grace, William Russell, 468, 520, 622
Grace Episcopal Church, 456
Gracie Mansion, 361
Grady, Henry W., 578
Graflex camera, 664
Graham, Benjamin, 905
Graham, Billy, 1015

Wells, H.G., 647, 658, 674, 694, 705, 725, 730, 736, 858, 939, 1099
Wells, Horace, 449
Welsbach mantle, 601
Welsers, 173, 178, 181
Welt, Die, 993
Welty, Eudora, 961, 1046
Wembley Stadium, 830, 1117
Wenner-Gren, Axel, 808
Werfel, Franz, 898, 961
Wertmuller, Lina, 1152, 1156
Wesley, Charles, 286, 289, 291, 336, 426
Wesley, John, 286, 289, 291, 296, 336
Wesleyan Univ., 418, 561
Wessel, Horst, 876
Wesson Oil and Snowdrift Co., 611, 671, 840, 1084
West, Benjamin, 317, 329, 353, 396
West, Mae, 892, 899, 956
West, Nathanael, 883, 899
West, Rebecca, 961, 1015, 1065
West Coast Hotel v. Parrish, 929
West Georgia College, 897
West Indies, 1069
West Point, 413, 417, 437
West Side Highway, 930
West Virginia, 510, 568, 591, 614, 711, 757, 833, 972, 1019, 1137; Univ., 528
Westchester Community College, 992
Western Auto Supply Co., 729, 849, 931
Western Electric Co., 548, 562, 590, 666, 754, 767, 793, 835, 844, 868, 934, 1015
Western Health Reform Inst., 524, 564, 640
Western Illinois Univ., 668
Western Kentucky Univ., 711
Western Michigan Univ., 694
Western Montana College, 637
Western New Mexico Univ., 637
Western Pacific Railroad, 692, 1014
Western Union Co., 487, 505, 507, 520, 524, 562, 569, 586, 560, 606, 735, 742, 747, 754
Westinghouse, George, 532, 589, 592, 601, 846
Westminster, Treaty of, 253
Westminster Abbey, 81
Westminster Bank, Ltd., 425
Westminster Bridge, 299
Westminster Cathedral, 696
Westminster Hospital, 281
Westminster Kennel Club, 570
Westmoreland, William C., 1126
Westphalia, Peace of, 237
Westvaco, 614
Wethered, Joyce, 802
Weyden, Roger van der, 143, 144, 147, 149
Weyerhaeuser, Frederick, 541, 630
Weygand, Maxime, 797, 951
whaling, 10, 137, 179, 187, 204, 216, 217, 224-226, 241, 263, 276, 301, 313, 323, 337, 394, 453, 472, 487, 490, 513, 1073

Wharton, Edith, 705, 741, 800, 925
Wharton, Thomas, 243
Wharton School, 584, 586, 963
wheat, 2, 5, 21, 22, 35, 38, 40, 46, 47, 76, 100, 116, 120, 123, 127, 143, 163, 180, 222, 342, 369, 419, 426, 440, 448, 469, 473, 485, 502, 505, 517, 522, 534, 542, 545, 553, 554, 561, 579, 582, 599, 607, 611, 635, 649, 654, 660, 665, 670, 676, 683, 694, 743, 769, 777, 783, 796, 805, 809, 823, 887, 894, 901, 911, 920, 957, 964, 975, 987, 988, 997, 1018, 1049, 1073, 1084, 1100, 1112, 1118, 1124, 1132, 1144, 1154, 1155
Wheatena cereal, 580
Wheaties, 831, 899
Wheaton College, 426
wheel, invention of, 2
Wheeler, Burton K., 943
Wheeler-Lea Act, 942
Whig party, U.S., 449, 460, 474
Whirlpool Corp., 1052
Whiskey Rebellion, U.S., 352
Whistler, James A.M., 498, 512, 548
Whitby, Synod of, 60
White, E.B., 835, 862, 866, 986
White, George, 795, 801, 808, 815, 822, 829, 845, 860, 867, 885, 918, 948
White, Patrick, 1008, 1088, 1115
White, Stanford, 579, 586, 634, 649, 665, 688, 713, 714
White, William Allen, 652, 843
White Camelia, Knights of, 527
White House, D.C., 361, 386, 470, 619, 680, 713, 720, 745, 779, 823, 895, 1019, 1092, 1134, 1138, 1154
White motorcar, 673, 752
White Mountain, Battle of, 221
White Plains, Battle of, 324
White Rock Spring water, 535, 611, 640, 649, 650
White Rose brand, 608, 683, 1043
White Sulphur Springs, 327, 757, 906
White, Weld & Co., 735
Whitehall, Palm Beach, 689
Whitely, William, 513
Whiteman, Paul, 815, 822, 829, 852, 877
Whiting, Richard A., 788, 795, 801, 808, 837, 876, 892, 893, 933
Whitman, Marcus, 428, 446, 457
Whitman, Walt, 484, 521, 590, 610, 860, 995
Whitney, Eli, 348, 352, 359, 364, 367, 381
Whitney, John Hay, 1004
Whitney, William C., 605, 666
Whitney Museum of American Art, 883
Whittier, John Greenleaf, 418, 455, 487, 517, 525
Whittier College, 681
Whittington, Richard, 135, 138

Who, The, 1124, 1136, 1148
Whyte, William H., Jr., 1059
Wichita Mountains Refuge, 708
Wickersham, George, 754, 883
Widehall mansion, 251
Widener, Peter A.B., 506, 625
Widener Library, 767
Wiener, Norbert, 1005
Wiggin, Kate Douglas, 694
Wigglesworth, Michael, 246
Wightman Cup, 822
Wilberforce, William, 340, 346, 372, 400, 422
Wilcox, Ella Wheeler, 594
Wilde, Oscar, 590, 615, 629, 633, 638, 648, 653, 664, 706
Wilder, Billy, 974, 980, 986, 1009, 1022, 1041, 1053, 1066, 1077, 1116
Wilder, Laura Ingalls, 891
Wilder, Thornton, 843, 858, 968, 1059, 1123
Wilderberg, Bo, 1123
Wilderness, Battle of the, 514
Wilderness Act, U.S., 1106
Wilderness Society, 809, 919
Wiley, Harvey W., 595, 689, 721
Wilhelm I, 503, 539, 542, 612; II, 612, 622
Wilhelmina I, 623, 642
Wilkie, Wendell L., 952
Wilkins, Robert W., 1033
Willard Patent Timepiece, 365
Willem I, 435; II, 438; III, 623
Willem of Orange, 191, 198; III, 352
William and Mary, College of, 265, 303, 325
William I, of England, 81-84; II Rufus, 84-86; IV, 414, 419, 428, 430, 432
William of Ockham, 125
Williams, Emlyn, 917
Williams, Oscar, 955
Williams, Roger, 230, 323
Williams, Roger, civil libertarian, 799
Williams, Spencer, 775, 900
Williams, Ted, 949
Williams, Tennessee, 986, 1001, 1009, 1028, 1041, 1053, 1066, 1071, 1077, 1082, 1088, 1099, 1152
Williams, William Carlos, 754, 821, 835, 1046
Williams College, 351, 405, 499
Williams & Wilkins, 1130
Williamsburg, Va., 265, 268, 286, 320, 325, 329, 919
Williamsburg Bridge, 692
Williamsburg Savings Bank, Brooklyn, 471, 869
Willis, Thomas, 244, 253
Willoughby, Sir Hugh, 172
Willson, Meredith, 1066, 1083
Willys, John North, 680, 692, 716, 734, 767
Willys-Overland Motors, 716, 767, 820
Wilmington, Del., 231, 365
Wilshire Boulevard, 646
Wilson, Angus, 1059, 1071
Wilson, Charles E., 1007
Wilson, Edmund, 866, 955, 993
Wilson, Ethel, 1000, 1088

Wilson, Richard, 333
Wilson, Sandy, 1047
Wilson, Woodrow, 711, 716, 745, 751, 759, 763, 765, 767, 771, 772, 773, 774, 778, 779, 784, 790, 799, 962
Wilson & Co., 777, 1125
Wilson-Gorman Tariff Act, 641
Wimbledon tennis, 570, 796, 801, 853, 934, 1067, 1124, 1156
Winchell, Walter, 890
Winchester, 103, 104; Battle of, 515; Cathedral, 152; College, 132
Winchester, Oliver F., 468
Winchester Repeating Arms Co., 500, 524, 601, 643, 979
Wind Cave Natl. Park, 696
Windex, 901
windmill, 6, 915, 991
window tax, England, 266
Windsor Locks Canal, 406
wine, 3, 8, 24, 37, 40, 43, 59, 92, 134, 198, 209, 244, 278, 299, 305, 357, 473, 492, 506, 522, 903, 912
Winged Victory of Samothrace, 512
Winner, Joseph E., 529
Winner, Septimus, 485, 517, 529
Winnipeg, 555, 569, 585
Winsor, Kathleen, 986
Winston, John C., Co., 598, 1082
Winter Palace, St. Petersburg, 293, 302, 779, 783
Winthrop, John, 228
Winton, Alexander, 657, 692
Wisconsin, 229, 420, 429, 441, 448, 454, 455, 458, 460, 461, 462, 471, 480, 484, 490, 526, 530, 545, 548, 571, 579, 586, 594, 600, 611, 614, 629, 663, 670, 717, 745, 773, 784, 788, 790, 796, 838, 843, 911, 1019, 1046, 1125, 1137; Univ. of, 429, 461, 636, 824, 855, 997, 1003, 1024, 1064, 1114, 1140
Wise, Isaac, 525
Wise, Robert, 1089, 1099
Wise, Stephen, 728
Wise Potato Chips, 810
Wiseman, Joseph, 1016, 1123
Wister, Owen, 686
witches, 154, 156, 189, 228, 229, 246, 264, 269, 290
Witte, Sergei Y., 656
Wittenberg, 167, 181, 227; Univ. of, 161
Wittgenstein, Paul, 782
Witz, Konrad, 143, 145
Wodehouse, P.G., 686, 782, 788, 794, 835, 859, 909, 940
Wöhler, Friedrich, 409, 410
Wolesley motorcar, 646
Wolf, Hugo, 653
Wolf-Ferrari, Ermanno, 712
Wolfe, James, 305, 313
Wolfe, Thomas, 866, 916, 947, 955, 1066
Wolfe, Tom, 1130
Wolfenden Report, 1063
Wolff, Kaspar Friedrich, 306
Wollaston, William H., 369, 370, 376, 378, 382